1898 — In *Animal Intelligence*, Edward L. Thorndike, Columbia University, describes his learning experiments with cats in "puzzle boxes." In **1905**, he proposes the "law of effect."

1900 — Sigmund Freud publishes *The Interpretation of Dreams*, his major theoretical work on psychoanalysis.

1901 — Ten founders establish the British Psychological Society.

1904 — Ivan Pavlov is awarded the Nobel Prize for Physiology or Medicine for his studies on the physiology of digestion.

1905 — Mary Whiton Calkins becomes the first woman president of the APA.

— Ivan Petrovich Pavlov begins publishing studies of conditioning in animals.

— Alfred Binet and Théodore Simon produce the first intelligence test for assessing the abilities and academic progress of Parisian schoolchildren.

1909 — Sigmund Freud makes his only trip to America to deliver a series of lectures at Clark University.

1913 — John B. Watson outlines the tenets of behaviorism in a *Psychological Review* article, "Psychology as the Behaviorist Views It."

1914 — During World War I, Robert Yerkes and his staff develop a group intelligence test for evaluating U.S. military personnel, which increases the U.S. public's acceptance of psychological testing.

1920 — Leta Stetter Hollingworth publishes *The Psychology of Subnormal Children*, an early classic. In **1921** she is cited in *American Men of Science* for her research on the psychology of women.

— Francis Cecil Sumner receives a Ph.D. degree in psychology from Clark University, becoming the first African-American to earn a psychology doctorate.

— John B. Watson and Rosalie Rayner report conditioning a fear reaction in a child called "Little Albert."

1921 — Hermann Rorschach, a Swiss psychiatrist, introduces the Rorschach Inkblot Test.

1923 — Developmental psychologist Jean Piaget publishes *The Language and Thought of the Child*.

1924 — Mary Cover Jones reports reconditioning a fear reaction in a child (Peter), a forerunner of systematic desensitization developed by Joseph Wolpe.

1927 — In *Introduction to the Technique of Child Analysis*, Anna Freud discusses psychoanalysis in the treatment of children.

1929 — Wolfgang Köhler publishes *Gestalt Psychology*, which criticizes behaviorism and outlines essential elements of the gestalt position and approach.

1931 — Margaret Floy Washburn becomes the first female psychologist (and the second female scientist in any discipline) elected to the U.S. National Academy of Sciences.

1932 — In *The Wisdom of the Body*, Walter B. Cannon coins the term *homeostasis*, discusses the fight-or-flight response, and identifies hormonal changes associated with stress.

1933 — Inez Beverly Prosser becomes the first African-American woman to receive a doctoral degree in psychology from a U.S. institution (Ph.D., University of Cincinnati).

1935 — Christiana Morgan and Henry Murray introduce the Thematic Apperception Test to elicit fantasies from people undergoing psychoanalysis.

1936 — Egas Moniz, a Portuguese physician, publishes work on the first frontal lobotomies performed on humans.

1938 — B. F. Skinner publishes *The Behavior of Organisms*, which describes operant conditioning of animals.

— In *Primary Mental Abilities*, Louis L. Thurstone proposes seven such abilities.

— Ugo Cerletti and Lucio Bini use electroshock treatment with a human patient.

1939 — David Wechsler publishes the Wechsler–Bellevue intelligence test, forerunner of the Wechsler Intelligence Scale for Children (WISC) and the Wechsler Adult Intelligence Scale (WAIS).

— Mamie Phipps Clark receives a master's degree from Howard University. In collaboration with Kenneth B. Clark, she later extends her thesis, "The Development of Consciousness of Self in Negro Preschool Children," providing joint research cited in the U.S. Supreme Court's **1954** decision to end racial segregation in public schools.

— Edward Alexander Bott helps found the Canadian Psychological Association. He becomes its first president in **1940**.

— World War II provides many opportunities for psychologists to enhance the popularity and influence of psychology, especially in applied areas.

1943 — Psychologist Starke Hathaway and physician J. Charnley McKinley publish the Minnesota Multiphasic Personality Inventory (MMPI).

1945 — Karen Horney, who criticized Freud's theory of female sexual development, publishes *Our Inner Conflicts*.

1946 — Benjamin Spock's first edition of *The Commonsense Book of Baby and Child Care* appears; the book will influence child raising in North America for several decades.

1948 — Alfred Kinsey and his colleagues publish *Sexual Behavior in the Human Male*, and they publish *Sexual Behavior in the Human Female* in **1953**.

— B. F. Skinner's novel, *Walden Two*, describes a Utopian community based on positive reinforcement, which becomes a clarion call for applying psychological principles in everyday living, especially communal living.

— Ernest R. Hilgard publishes *Theories of Learning*, which was required reading for several generations of psychology students in North America.

1949 — Raymond B. Cattell publishes the Sixteen Personality Factor Questionnaire (16PF).

— The scientist-practitioner model of training is approved at The Boulder Conference on Graduate Education in Clinical Psychology.

continued at end of book

Exploring Psychology

Eleventh Edition

DAVID G. MYERS

HOPE COLLEGE
HOLLAND, MICHIGAN

C. NATHAN DEWALL

UNIVERSITY OF KENTUCKY
LEXINGTON, KENTUCKY

worth publishers
Macmillan Learning

New York

Senior Vice President, Content Strategy: Charles Linsmeier
Program Director, Social Sciences: Shani Fisher
Executive Program Manager: Carlise Stembridge
Development Manager, Social Sciences: Christine Brune
Development Editors: Nancy Fleming, Trish Morgan, Danielle Slevens
Associate Editor: Katie Pachnos
Editorial Assistant: Anna Munroe
Executive Marketing Manager: Katherine Nurre
Marketing Assistant: Chelsea Simens
Director of Media Editorial & Assessment, Social Sciences: Noel Hohnstine
Executive Media Editor, Psychology: Laura Burden
Media Editorial Assistant: Stephanie Matamoros
Supplements Editor: Betty Probert
Director, Content Management Enhancement: Tracey Kuehn
Senior Managing Editor: Lisa Kinne
Senior Content Project Manager: Won McIntosh
Director of Digital Production: Keri deManigold
Senior Media Project Manager: Chris Efstratiou
Media Project Manager: Eve Conte
Senior Workflow Supervisor: Susan Wein
Senior Photo Editor: Robin Fadool
Photo Researcher: Donna Ranieri
Director of Design, Content Management: Diana Blume
Design Services Manager: Natasha Wolfe
Design Manager, Cover: John Callahan
Interior Design: Charles Yuen
Art Manager: Matthew McAdams
Interior Illustrations: Evelyn Pence
Composition: Lumina Datamatics, Inc.
Printing and Binding: LSC Communications
Cover Photo: PeopleImages/E+/Getty Images

Library of Congress Control Number: 2018948746

ISBN-13: 978-1-319-10419-1

ISBN-10: 1-319-10419-3

Printed in the United States of America

1   2   3   4   5   6   23   22   21   20   19   18

First printing

David Myers' royalties from the sale of this book are assigned to the David and Carol Myers Foundation, which exists to receive and distribute funds to other charitable organizations.

Worth Publishers
One New York Plaza
Suite 4500
New York, NY 10004-1562
www.macmillanlearning.com

[DM] For Carlise Stembridge, once my marketing manager, now my executive program manager, and always my supportive and encouraging friend.

[ND] For Roy Baumeister, who showed me the joy of writing, the value of hard work, and the gift of curiosity.

About the Authors

David Myers received his B.A. in chemistry from Whitworth University, and his psychology Ph.D. from the University of Iowa. He has spent his career at Hope College in Michigan, where he has taught dozens of introductory psychology sections. Hope College students have invited him to be their commencement speaker and voted him "outstanding professor."

His research and writings have been recognized by the Gordon Allport Intergroup Relations Prize, an Honored Scientist award from the Federation of Associations in Behavioral & Brain Sciences, an Award for Service on Behalf of Personality and Social Psychology, a Presidential Citation from APA Division 2, election as an American Association for the Advancement of Science Fellow, and three honorary doctorates.

With support from National Science Foundation grants, Myers' scientific articles have appeared in three dozen scientific periodicals, including *Science, American Scientist, Psychological Science,* and the *American Psychologist.* In addition to his scholarly and textbook writing, he digests psychological science for the general public. His writings have appeared in four dozen magazines, from *Today's Education* to *Scientific American.* He also has authored five general audience books, including *The Pursuit of Happiness* and *Intuition: Its Powers and Perils.*

David Myers has chaired his city's Human Relations Commission, helped found a thriving assistance center for families in poverty, and spoken to hundreds of college, community, and professional groups worldwide.

Drawing on his experience, he also has written articles and a book (*A Quiet World*) about hearing loss, and he is advocating a transformation in American assistive listening technology (see HearingLoop.org). For his leadership, he has received awards from the American Academy of Audiology, the hearing industry, and the Hearing Loss Association of America.

David and Carol Myers met and married while undergraduates, and have raised sons Peter and Andrew, and a daughter, Laura. They have one grandchild, Allie (seen on page 128).

Nathan DeWall is professor of psychology and director of the Social Psychology Lab at the University of Kentucky. He received his bachelor's degree from St. Olaf College, a master's degree in social science from the University of Chicago, and a master's degree and Ph.D. in social psychology from Florida State University. DeWall received the College of Arts and Sciences Outstanding Teaching Award, which recognizes excellence in undergraduate and graduate teaching. The Association for Psychological Science identified DeWall as a "Rising Star" early in his career for "making significant contributions to the field of psychological science." He is in the top 1 percent of all cited scientists in psychology and psychiatry on the Institute for Scientific Information list, according to the Web of Science.

DeWall conducts research on close relationships, self-control, and aggression. With funding from the National Institutes of Health, the National Science Foundation, and the John Templeton Foundation, he has published over 200 scientific articles and chapters. DeWall's research awards include the SAGE Young Scholars Award from the Foundation for Personality and Social Psychology, the Young Investigator Award from the International Society for Research on Aggression, and the Early Career Award from the International Society for Self and Identity. His research has been covered by numerous media outlets, including Good Morning America, *The Wall Street Journal, Newsweek, The Atlantic Monthly, The New York Times, The Los Angeles Times, Harvard Business Review, USA Today,* National Public Radio, the BBC, and *The Guardian.* He has lectured nationally and internationally, including in Hong Kong, China, the Netherlands, England, Greece, Hungary, Sweden, Australia, and France.

Nathan is happily married to Alice DeWall and is the proud father of Beverly "Bevy" and Ellis. He enjoys playing with his two golden retrievers, Finnegan and Atticus. In his spare time, he writes novels, watches sports, tends his chickens, and runs and runs and runs. He has braved all climates—from the snowy trails of Michigan to the scorching sands of the Sahara Desert—to complete over 1000 miles' worth of ultramarathons—including the Badwater 135 in 2017 (dubbed "the World's toughest foot race").

Brief Contents

Contents

Instructor Preface:
Engage Your Students So They Retain Psychology

FIGURE 1

ENGAGE AND RETAIN You will see these icons flagging instances in the text where students can try out the concepts they are learning about, in an active learning, hands-on way (*Engage*), and where students will find helpful tools for testing their learning (*Retain*).

Psychology is fascinating, and so relevant to our everyday lives. Psychology's insights enable students to be more successful in their courses, more tuned-in as friends and partners, more effective as co-workers, and wiser as parents. And helping students to think more like psychological scientists will arm them with the critical thinking skills they need to challenge our post-truth world. As teachers, we want both to *engage* students and to help them *retain* what they learn. In this new edition, we've inserted "Engage" icons to flag the instances throughout the text where we've offered hands-on opportunities for students to try out the concepts (**FIGURE 1**). We've also inserted "Retain" icons to indicate places where students can connect concepts and test their understanding.

This new edition and its resources will be particularly useful in helping you employ *active learning* in your classes. The text is newly available in an engaging, professionally-produced *Audiobook* version. *LaunchPad* offers engaging and effective Concept Practice exercises, videos, and tutorials. LaunchPad's *Immersive Learning activities* include "How Would You Know?" research activities and "Assess Your Strengths" research-based self-assessments. Students love *LearningCurve* adaptive quizzing in LaunchPad because of its game-like format and the way it boosts their course performance. You will appreciate the way LearningCurve helps students come to class better prepared. We also offer numerous *active learning classroom activities* in our *Instructor's Resources*, and a robust collection of *iClicker questions* to help you engage your class. And our simplest and most affordable new student solution is *Achieve Read & Practice*, which contains the eBook and adaptive quizzing only.

Just as introductory psychology *teachers* differ, introductory psychology *resources* differ. They vary in quality, effectiveness, and ease of use. With help from Worth Publishers, we've heard from hundreds of psychology instructors like you who have told us about their needs and concerns, and about the challenges faced by their students. Here are nine frequently mentioned issues, and how we've responded with this *Exploring Psychology*, Eleventh Edition text and resources.

① "It's very important that I teach my students to think critically, and help them understand that psychology is a science."

Teaching Critical Thinking Is the Foundation of These Resources

We love to write in a way that gets students thinking and keeps their minds active. Students will see how psychological science can help them evaluate competing ideas and highly publicized claims ranging from intuition, subliminal persuasion, and ESP to using only 10 percent of our brain, alternative therapies, and repressed and recovered memories. We help students build the scientific literacy skills they will need to separate intuitive fiction from empirical fact.

In *Exploring Psychology*, Eleventh Edition and its resources, students have many opportunities to learn and practice their critical thinking skills:

- *"To teach critical thinking"* has been the first of the "Eight Guiding Principles" that have guided our work on this text from its inception. (See p. xxiv.)

- *Chapter 1 takes a critical thinking approach to introducing students to psychology's research methods.* Understanding the weak points of our everyday thinking and common sense helps students see the need for psychological science. Critical thinking is introduced as a key term on page 3.

- NEW *"Thinking Critically About . . ." infographics* appear in each chapter. In class testing, students have applauded this visual tool for thinking critically about key psychological concepts (parenting styles, gender bias, sexual aggression, group polarization, introversion, lifestyle changes, and more). See **FIGURE 2** for an example. I [DM] created new *"Thinking Critically About . . ." Infographic Activities* for LaunchPad—with assessment questions targeting higher Bloom's taxonomy levels to teach and reinforce critical thinking.

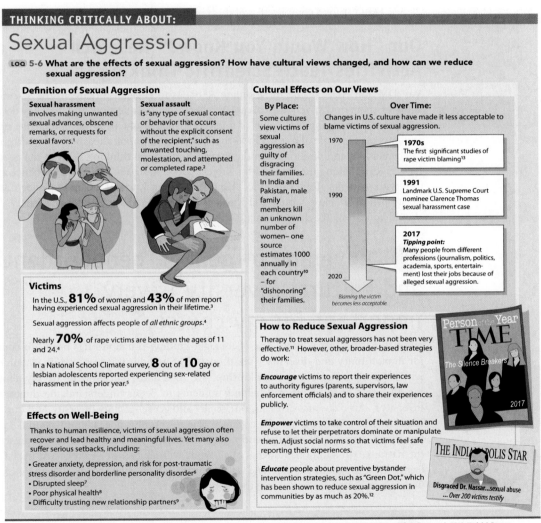

THINKING CRITICALLY ABOUT:

Sexual Aggression

LOQ 5-6 What are the effects of sexual aggression? How have cultural views changed, and how can we reduce sexual aggression?

Definition of Sexual Aggression

Sexual harassment involves making unwanted sexual advances, obscene remarks, or requests for sexual favors.[1]

Sexual assault is "any type of sexual contact or behavior that occurs without the explicit consent of the recipient," such as unwanted touching, molestation, and attempted or completed rape.[2]

Victims

In the U.S., **81%** of women and **43%** of men report having experienced sexual aggression in their lifetime.[3]

Sexual aggression affects people of *all ethnic groups*.[4]

Nearly **70%** of rape victims are between the ages of 11 and 24.[4]

In a National School Climate survey, **8** out of **10** gay or lesbian adolescents reported experiencing sex-related harassment in the prior year.[5]

Effects on Well-Being

Thanks to human resilience, victims of sexual aggression often recover and lead healthy and meaningful lives. Yet many also suffer serious setbacks, including:

- Greater anxiety, depression, and risk for post-traumatic stress disorder and borderline personality disorder[6]
- Disrupted sleep[7]
- Poor physical health[8]
- Difficulty trusting new relationship partners[9]

Cultural Effects on Our Views

By Place:
Some cultures view victims of sexual aggression as guilty of disgracing their families. In India and Pakistan, male family members kill an unknown number of women– one source estimates 1000 annually in each country[10] – for "dishonoring" their families.

Over Time:
Changes in U.S. culture have made it less acceptable to blame victims of sexual aggression.

1970
1970s
The first significant studies of rape victim blaming[13]

1990
1991
Landmark U.S. Supreme Court nominee Clarence Thomas sexual harassment case

2017
Tipping point:
Many people from different professions (journalism, politics, academia, sports, entertainment) lost their jobs because of alleged sexual aggression.

2020
Blaming the victim becomes less acceptable.

How to Reduce Sexual Aggression

Therapy to treat sexual aggressors has not been very effective.[11] However, other, broader-based strategies do work:

Encourage victims to report their experiences to authority figures (parents, supervisors, law enforcement officials) and to share their experiences publicly.

Empower victims to take control of their situation and refuse to let their perpetrators dominate or manipulate them. Adjust social norms so that victims feel safe reporting their experiences.

Educate people about preventive bystander intervention strategies, such as "Green Dot," which has been shown to reduce sexual aggression in communities by as much as 20%.[12]

Person of the Year
TIME
The Silence Breakers
2017

THE INDIANAPOLIS STAR
Disgraced Dr. Nassar...sexual abuse
... Over 200 victims testify

1. McDonald, 2012; U.S.E.E.O.C., 2018. 2. U.S.D.O.J., 2018. 3. Stop Street Harassment, 2018. 4. Black et al., 2011. 5. GLSEN, 2012. 6. Choudhary et al., 2012; Krahé & Berger, 2017; Snipes et al., 2017; Zanarini et al., 1997. 7. Krakow et al., 2001, 2002. 8. Schuyler et al., 2017; Zinzow et al., 2011. 9. Muldoon et al., 2016; Starzynski et al., 2017. 10. HBVA, 2018. 11. Grønnerød et al., 2015. 12. Coker et al., 2017. 13. Burt, 1980.

FIGURE 2

SAMPLE "THINKING CRITICALLY ABOUT" INFOGRAPHIC FROM CHAPTER 5

- *Psychological Science in a Post-Truth World* is a new section in Chapter 1 that will help your students understand why we are so vulnerable to believing untruths and how we can use critical thinking and a scientific mindset to build a real-truth world. This message is supported by my [DM's] new tutorial animation, **"Thinking Critically in Our Post-Truth World"** in LaunchPad.

- *Detective-style stories* throughout the text get students thinking critically about psychology's key research questions. In Chapter 9, for example, we present as a puzzle the history of discoveries about where and how language happens in the brain. We guide students through the puzzle, showing them how researchers put all the pieces together.

- *Critical examinations of pop psychology* spark interest and provide lessons in thinking critically about everyday topics. For example, Chapter 6 scrutinizes ESP, and Chapter 8 explores the controversy over the alleged repression of painful memories.

See **TABLE 1** for a complete list of this text's coverage of critical thinking topics.

Our "How Would You Know?" Research Activities Teach Scientific Thinking

We [DM and ND] created these online activities to engage students in the scientific process, showing them how psychological research begins with a question, and how key decision points can alter the meaning and value of a psychological study. In a fun, interactive environment, students play the role of researcher as they learn about important aspects of research design and interpretation, and develop scientific literacy and critical thinking skills in the process. I [ND] have enjoyed taking the lead on this project and sharing my research experience and enthusiasm with students. Topics include: "How Would You Know If a Cup of Coffee Can Warm Up Relationships?," "How Would You Know If People Can Learn to Reduce Anxiety?," and "How Would You Know If Schizophrenia Is Inherited?"

❷ "Coverage of gender, gender-identity, and cultural diversity is very important for my course."

Since this text's first edition, one of its eight guiding principles has been *"To convey respect for human unity and diversity"* (see p. xxv). Throughout this text and its resources, students will see evidence of our human kinship. We [DM and ND] also care deeply about celebrating all forms of diversity, and helping students to better understand the dimensions of our diversity—our *individual* diversity, our *gender* and *gender-identity* diversity, and our *cultural* and *ethnic* diversity. **TABLE 2** lists the coverage of gender and gender identity. **TABLE 3** provides the integrated coverage of cultural and ethnic diversity. Significant coverage is presented within the narrative. In addition, students of all kinds will see themselves reflected in the photos and examples throughout the text and its resources, which showcase the diversity of individuals within North America and across the globe.

❸ "We need to minimize cost to the student."

Students deserve the highest quality educational resources at an affordable cost. Macmillan Learning has made a big effort to reduce production costs for our texts, which has allowed them to significantly reduce costs to students—especially for loose-leaf and digital options,

TABLE 1

Critical Thinking and Scientific Inquiry Critical thinking coverage and in-depth stories of psychology's process of scientific inquiry can be found on the following pages:

***Thinking Critically About . . .
infographics:***

The Scientific Attitude, p. 4

Correlation and Causation, p. 26

Using More Than 10 Percent of Our Brain, p. 62

Tolerance and Addiction, p. 102

Parenting Styles—Too Hard, Too Soft, Too Uncaring, and Just Right?, p. 139

Gender Bias in the Workplace, p. 164

Sexual Aggression, p. 170

Subliminal Sensation and Subliminal Persuasion, p. 193

The Effects of Viewing Media Violence, p. 263

Can Memories of Childhood Sexual Abuse Be Repressed and Then Recovered?, p. 293

The Fear Factor, p. 302

Cross-Sectional and Longitudinal Studies, p. 332

The Challenges of Obesity and Weight Control, p. 365

Lie Detection, p. 374

Stress and Health, p. 393

The Internet as Social Amplifier, p. 432

The Stigma of Introversion, p. 476

ADHD—Normal High Energy or Disordered Behavior?, p. 498

Therapeutic Lifestyle Change, p. 559

***Critical Examinations of Pop
Psychology:***

The need for psychological science, pp. 15–17

Perceiving order in random events, p. 16

Do we use only 10 percent of our brain?, p. 62

Has the concept of "addiction" been stretched too far?, p. 102

Near-death experiences, p. 108

How much credit or blame do parents deserve?, p. 139

Critiquing the evolutionary perspective, pp. 185–186

Sensory restriction, p. 213

Can hypnosis be therapeutic? Alleviate pain?, p. 224

Is there extrasensory perception?, p. 229–230

Do other species have language?, pp. 317–318

Do violent video games teach social scripts for violence?, pp. 444–445

How valid is the Rorschach test?, pp. 467–468

Is Freud credible?, pp. 468–470

Is repression a myth?, p. 469

Is psychotherapy effective?, pp. 550–552

Evaluating alternative therapies, pp. 552–555

***Thinking Critically With
Psychological Science:***

"Critical thinking" introduced as a key term, p. 3

The limits of intuition and common sense, p. 15

Psychological science in a post-truth world, pp. 18–19

The scientific method, pp. 19–30

Correlation and causation, p. 26

Exploring cause and effect, pp. 24–29

Random assignment, p. 29

Independent and dependent variables, pp. 28–29

Choosing the right research design, p. 29–30

The evolutionary perspective on human sexuality, pp. 192–195

Statistical reasoning, pp. A-1–A-9

Describing data, pp. A-1–A-6

Regression toward the mean, pp. A-5–A-6

Making inferences, pp. A-6–A-8

Scientific Detective Stories:

Is breast milk better than formula?, pp. 27–28

Our divided brain, pp. 65–67

Twin and adoption studies, pp. 70–73

Why do we sleep?, pp. 91–92

Why we dream, pp. 97–99

How a child's mind develops, pp. 125–126

What determines sexual orientation?, pp. 179–182

How do we see in color?, pp. 203–205

Parallel processing, p. 206

How can hypnosis provide pain relief?, p. 224

How are memories constructed?, pp. 269–274

How do we store memories in our brain?, pp. 275–279

Do other species exhibit language?, pp. 317–318

Aging and intelligence, pp. 373–374

Why do we feel hunger?, pp. 361–363

Why—and in whom—does stress contribute to heart disease?, pp. 391–392

How and why is social support linked with health?, pp. 399–401

The pursuit of happiness: Who is happy, and why?, pp. 407–412

Why do people fail to help in emergencies?, pp. 418–419

Self-esteem versus self-serving bias, pp. 487–489

What causes major depressive disorder and bipolar disorder?, pp. 518–519

Do prenatal viral infections increase the risk of schizophrenia?, pp. 525–526

Is psychotherapy effective?, pp. 550–552

including the new, simplified ***Achieve Read & Practice*** with eBook and adaptive quizzing only. See MacmillanLearning.com/Catalog/page/affordable-solutions.

In my [ND's] recent course, ***I required only the LaunchPad key—giving students access to the eBook and full online resources.*** Students had the option of also purchasing a loose-leaf version of the text. The result? In addition to loving the text and online resources, ***9 in 10 students said they felt that the price was fair.***

You may be interested in customizing print or digital resources as a way to save costs for your students, to provide materials for your course that match your syllabus more closely, or to add your own or other Macmillan resources to your course. We were pleased to learn that our custom options are now available for even the smallest of courses via a new "Worth Select" program, which is part of Macmillan's broad Curriculum Solutions program.

TABLE 2

The Psychology of Gender, Gender Identity, and Sexuality Coverage of the psychology of gender, gender identity, and sexuality can be found on the following pages:

TABLE 3

The Psychology of Culture, Ethnicity, and Race Coverage of culture, ethnicity, and race may be found on the following pages:

4 "My administrators are eager to see results—better learning outcomes and improved retention of students."

Our Online Resources May Improve Retention of Students

Students love LaunchPad, and especially the LearningCurve adaptive quizzing engine. When Macmillan Learning asked the thousands of psychology students using LearningCurve in the spring of 2017, 86 percent rated it either "Good" or "Excellent."

When I [ND] taught introductory psychology recently, I asked my students at the end of the course what they liked best about the class. Most answered "LaunchPad!" I've enjoyed using these resources in my classes, because they allow me to engage my students so successfully. In fact, at my institution (University of Kentucky), I've been involved in efforts to improve retention of students. In my own class, I have found that assigning something in LaunchPad on the first day of class, and heavily relying on LaunchPad throughout the term, seems to improve retention in my large (~350-student) classes.

Researchers have begun to do efficacy studies with our online materials, and initial results have been promising. Our Learning Science Team, led by Dr. Adam Black (an award-winning researcher and digital innovation specialist), has several exciting projects underway. (See MacmillanLearning.com/Catalog/page/LearningScience for more information.) Stay tuned as we continue to learn more (and let us know if you'd like to participate).

Our Resources Help Address APA Learning Goals and Outcomes

In 2011, the American Psychological Association (APA) approved the **Principles for Quality Undergraduate Education in Psychology.** These broad-based principles and their associated recommendations are a guide to producing "psychologically literate citizens who apply the principles of psychological science at work and at home." (See apa.org/education/undergrad/principles.aspx.)

APA's more specific **2013 Learning Goals and Outcomes**, from their *Guidelines for the Undergraduate Psychology Major,* Version 2.0, were designed to gauge progress in students graduating with psychology majors. (See apa.org/ed/precollege/about/psymajor-guidelines.pdf.) Many psychology departments use these goals and outcomes to help establish their own benchmarks for departmental assessment purposes. **TABLE 4** outlines the way *Exploring Psychology*, Eleventh Edition can help you and your department address the APA's Learning Goals and Outcomes. In addition, all of the Test Bank items for this text are coded for the APA Outcomes.

5 "Active learning is essential—I need materials that will help me engage students."

Our Materials Engage Students With Active Learning

We've found that engaged students who are learning actively tend to be successful students. They do better in the course and are more likely to stay in school.

NEW Ask Yourself Questions

For this new edition, we've added *Ask Yourself* questions periodically in the text margins to help students relate the material to their own lives. When students make the material meaningful, it also becomes more enjoyable and memorable (**FIGURE 3**).

Scattered throughout this book, students will also find interesting and informative notes and quotes from researchers and others that will encourage them to be active learners and to apply their new knowledge to everyday life.

 (ASK YOURSELF)

Were you surprised to learn that psychology is a science? How would you explain that if someone else now asked you about this?

FIGURE 3

SAMPLE "ASK YOURSELF" QUESTION

TABLE 4

Exploring Psychology, Eleventh Edition Corresponds to 2013 APA Learning Goals

Relevant Feature from *Exploring Psychology,* Eleventh Edition	Knowledge Base in Psychology	Scientific Inquiry and Critical Thinking	Ethical and Social Responsibility in a Diverse World	Communication	Professional Development
Text content	•	•	•	•	•
"Thinking Critically About" infographic features	•	•	•		•
Learning Objective Questions previewing text sections	•	•		•	
Retrieve It self-tests throughout text	•	•		•	
Experience the Testing Effect tests in the text, and Chapter Quizzes online	•	•		•	
"Try this"-style activities integrated throughout	•	•		•	•
Video Activities online	•	•	•		•
Psychology at Work appendix	•	•	•		•
Career Fields in Psychology appendix in the text, with Pursuing a Psychology Career online	•		•		•
Learning Curve formative quizzing online, with personalized study plan	•	•	•	•	•
"How Would You Know?" research activities online	•	•	•	•	•
Assess Your Strengths self-assessment feature online	•	•	•	•	•
PsychSim6 online tutorials	•	•	•		•
Concept Practice activities online	•	•			

Engage

Engage icons mark the many active learning opportunities throughout the text. We often encourage students to imagine themselves as participants in experiments. In Chapter 12, for example, students take the perspective of participants in a Solomon Asch conformity experiment and, later, in one of Stanley Milgram's obedience experiments. We've also asked students to join the fun by taking part in activities they can try along the way. For example, in Chapter 6, students try out a quick sensory adaptation activity. In Chapter 10, they try matching expressions to faces and test the effects of different facial expressions on themselves.

LaunchPad

It has been a joy for me [ND] to teach introductory psychology with this book and its resources. The online materials make it easy to engage students effectively starting on Day 1 of the class when I make a LaunchPad assignment. With immediate engagement, and active learning throughout the course, most students become hooked on psychology and stay in my class. This book and its resources help me not only to *engage* students, but also to *retain* them.

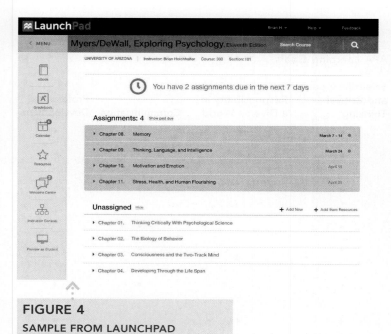

FIGURE 4

SAMPLE FROM LAUNCHPAD

LaunchPad (LaunchPadWorks.com) facilitates active learning as it solves key challenges (see **FIGURE 4**). In combination with the meticulously created text, these online resources give students everything they need to prepare for class and exams, while giving you, the instructor, everything *you* need to quickly set up a course, shape the content to your syllabus, craft presentations and lectures, assign and assess homework, and guide the progress of individual students and the class as a whole.

- Our **NEW eBook** can now go with any student, anywhere. It is fully mobile-compatible and meets accessibility standards.

- Our **NEW Audiobook** has been professionally produced (a real voice—the first of its kind for introductory psychology!) and personalized with an opening and closing message from us [DM and ND]. As an avid audiobook listener, I [ND] know the value of being able to listen to a book as I walk across campus, while I exercise, or as I am on my way to pick up my kids from the babysitter. Students can fit reading assignments into their busy lives or catch up while they're on the go. And some students just prefer to learn this way, with a professional voice bringing the text's narrative to life.

- **LearningCurve's game-like quizzing** motivates students and adapts to their needs based on their performance. It is the perfect tool to get students to engage before class, and review after. Additional reporting tools and metrics will help you assess the progress of individual students and the class as a whole.

- **iClicker offers active learning simplified, and now includes the REEF mobile app (iClicker.com).** iClicker's simple, flexible tools in LaunchPad help you give students a voice and facilitate active learning in the classroom. Students can use iClicker remotes, or the REEF mobile app on their phone, tablet, or laptop to participate more meaningfully. LaunchPad includes a robust collection of iClicker questions for each chapter—readily available for use in your class.

- **The NEW Concept Practice collection** offers 120 dynamic, interactive mini-tutorials that teach and reinforce the course's foundational ideas. Each brief activity (only five minutes to complete) addresses one or two concepts, in a consistent format—review, practice, quiz, and conclusion.

- The **Topic Tutorials: PsychSim6,** Thomas Ludwig's (Hope College) award-winning interactive psychology simulations, were designed for the mobile web. PsychSim immerses students in the world of psychological research, placing them in the role of scientist or participant in activities that highlight important concepts, processes, and experimental approaches.

- In the significantly revised **Assess Your Strengths** activities, students apply what they are learning from the text to their own lives and experiences by considering key "strengths." Each activity starts with a personalized video introduction from us [DM and ND], explaining how that strength ties in to the content of the chapter. Next, students assess themselves on the strength (critical thinking, quality of sleep, self-control, relationship strength, belonging, hope, and more) using scales developed by researchers across psychological science. After showing students their results, we offer tips for nurturing that strength in their own lives. Finally, students take a quiz to help solidify their learning.

- I [DM] have created at least one new **"Thinking Critically About…" Infographic Activity** for each chapter—designed to teach and reinforce critical thinking skills.

- **LMS integration** into your school's system is readily available. Check with your local sales representative for details.

- **The Video Assignment Tool** makes it easy to assign and assess video-based activities and projects, and provides a convenient way for students to submit video coursework.

- The **Gradebook** gives a clear window on performance for the whole class, for individual students, and for individual assignments.

- A **streamlined interface** helps students manage their schedule of assignments, while *social commenting tools* let them connect with classmates, and learn from one another. 24/7 help is a click away, accessible from a link in the upper right corner in LaunchPad.

- We [DM and ND] curated **optional pre-built chapter units**, which can be used as is or customized. Or choose not to use them and build your course from scratch.

- Our **Instructor's Resources** have long been considered the "gold standard" in the field. They include lecture and classroom activity suggestions—with a new grid identifying the *Active Learning Instructor's Resources* (those that work well for think-pair-share, small group, and large group activities), *Lecture Guides* (summarizing key text discussions and connecting instructor's resources with text learning objectives), the best *Test Banks* in the industry (carefully authored, and professionally edited and tightly coordinated with the text by the same fabulous supplements editor since the first edition), and nice starter PowerPoint sets with textbook graphics. For this new edition, you will see that we've offered callouts from the text pages to especially pertinent, helpful online resources. (See **FIGURE 5** for a sample.)

LaunchPad For an interactive, animated explanation of this process, engage online with **Concept Practice: Action Potentials.**

FIGURE 5

SAMPLE CALLOUT TO LAUNCHPAD ONLINE RESOURCES FROM CHAPTER 2

Achieve Read & Practice

Achieve Read & Practice is the marriage of our LearningCurve adaptive quizzing and our mobile, accessible eBook in one, easy-to-use and affordable product **(FIGURE 6)**. New, built-in analytics make it easier than ever for instructors to track student progress and intervene to help students succeed. Instructors who class-tested Achieve Read & Practice were surprised by its truly easy interface, and pleased with their course results. In a study of 227 students at 6 institutions, instructors found a significant improvement in the proportion of students who stayed on track with the assigned reading, and they found that students who retook quizzes (a helpful feature of Achieve Read & Practice) earned higher grades in the course. (Access the full report at MacmillanLearning .com/Catalog/Page/LearningScience.)

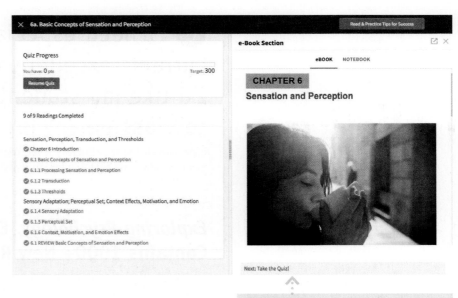

FIGURE 6

SAMPLE FROM ACHIEVE READ & PRACTICE

The Macmillan Community Will Engage You, Too!

The *Macmillan Community* (Community.Macmillan.com) was created *by* instructors *for* instructors. This is an ideal forum for interacting with fellow educators—including Macmillan authors **(FIGURE 7)**. Join ongoing conversations about everything from course prep and presentations to assignments and assessments, to teaching with media, keeping pace with—and influencing—new directions in your field. The Community offers exclusive access to classroom resources, blogs (including my [DM's] TalkPsych.com), webinars, and professional

FIGURE 7

SAMPLE FROM MACMILLAN COMMUNITY (COMMUNITY .MACMILLAN.COM)

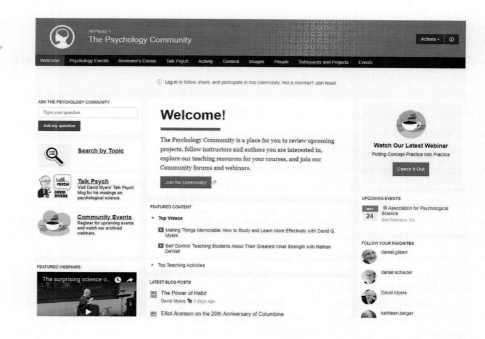

development opportunities. Our mission is to provide the highest quality educational resources to instructors and students. By participating in the Macmillan Community, you will join a group of enthusiastic educators who have unmatched access to high-quality resources and a forum to further your understanding of how to implement them.

6 "I need especially reliable, current, excellent materials, and I'd like my students to come to class better prepared."

Especially at the introductory level, high quality, cohesive, connected materials—text, assessment, review—are essential for students' success.

Exploring Psychology, Eleventh Edition Contains 1000+ New Research Citations

The work of creating our text and online resources begins as we stay current with new psychological research. We scrutinize dozens of scientific periodicals and science news sources. Worth Publishers commissions numerous reviews, and we receive countless emails from instructors and students. These sources feed our reporting on psychology's most important, thought-provoking, and student-relevant new discoveries. Part of the pleasure that sustains this work is learning something new every day! Each new edition is an adventure down the ever-changing road of psychological science. Every topic is inspected closely and painstakingly updated. This time around, it's been particularly fun to watch all of the developments in neuroscience (**TABLE 5**) and in behavior genetics (**TABLE 6**). The end result is more than 1000 new citations for this edition. See MacmillanLearning.com for our lengthy, chapter-by-chapter list of significant *Content Changes*.

TABLE 5

Neuroscience In addition to the coverage found in Chapter 2, **neuroscience** can be found on the following pages:

Aggression, pp. 441–442

Aging: brain training, pp. 154–155

Animal cognition, pp. 309–310

Animal language, pp. 317–318

Antisocial personality disorder, pp. 530–531

Arousal, pp. 176–177

Attention-deficit hyperactivity disorder (ADHD) and the brain, p. 498

Autism spectrum disorder, pp. 130–132

Biofeedback, p. 403

Biopsychosocial approach, pp. 10–11

   aggression, pp. 441–442

   aging, pp. 158–159

   Alzheimer's, p. 279

   dreams, pp. 97–99

   drug use, pp. 110–111

   emotion, pp. 277–278, 373–374

   learning, pp. 254–256

   pain, p. 222

   personality, pp. 482–483

   psychological disorders, pp. 495–496

   sleep, pp. 86–88

   therapeutic lifestyle change, p. 559

Brain development:

   adolescence, p. 142

   experience and, pp. 123–124

   infancy and childhood, pp. 124–125

   sexual differentiation in utero, p. 166

Brain stimulation therapies, pp. 563–564

Cognitive neuroscience, pp. 8–9, 10–12, 80–81

Drug use, pp. 110–111

Dual processing, pp. 84–85

Electroconvulsive therapy, p. 563

Emotion and cognition, pp. 367–368

Fear-learning, p. 241

Fetal alcohol syndrome and brain abnormalities, p. 120

Football and frequent head trauma, pp. 56–57

Hallucinations, p. 88

   and hallucinogens, pp. 61, 108–109

   and near-death experiences, p. 108

   and schizophrenia, p. 523

   and sleep, p. 88

Hormones and:

   abuse, p. 137

   appetite, pp. 362–363

   autism spectrum disorder, treatment of, p. 132

   development, pp. 167–168

   in adolescents, pp. 141–142, 169–170

   of sexual characteristics, pp. 141–142, 169–170

   emotion, pp. 369–370, 373–374

   gender, pp. 165–167

   sex, pp. 165–167, 173–174

   sexual behavior, pp. 173–174

   stress, pp. 123, 133, 388–389, 391, 392, 396–397

   weight control, pp. 362–363

Hunger, pp. 360–363

Insight, pp. 305–306

Intelligence, pp. 324–326

   creativity, pp. 306–307

   twins, pp. 336–337

Language, pp. 316–317, 340

   and deafness, p. 316

   and thinking in images, pp. 321–322

Light-exposure therapy: brain scans, pp. 554–555

Meditation, pp. 403–404

Memory:

   emotional memories, pp. 277–278

   explicit memories, pp. 269–270

   implicit memories, pp. 269–270

   physical storage of, pp. 275–278

   and sleep, p. 91

   and synaptic changes, pp. 278–279

Mirror neurons, pp. 259–260

Neuroscience perspective, defined, p. 12

Neurotransmitters and:

   anxiety-related disorders, p. 512

   biomedical therapy:

   depression, pp. 518–519

   ECT, p. 563

   schizophrenia, p. 524

   child abuse, p. 134

   cognitive-behavioral therapy: obsessive-compulsive disorder, p. 546

   depression, pp. 518–519, 561–562

   drugs, pp. 103, 105–109, 560–562

   exercise, pp. 401–402

   schizophrenia, pp. 526–527

   temperament, pp. 134–135

Observational learning and brain imaging, p. 259

Optimum arousal: brain mechanisms for rewards, pp. 349–350, 351

Orgasm, p. 174

Pain, pp. 221–222

   experienced and imagined pain, p. 261

phantom limb pain, p. 222

virtual reality, p. 224

Parallel processing, p. 268

Perception:

   brain damage and, p. 206

   color vision, pp. 203–205

   feature detection, p. 205

   transduction, p. 191

   visual information processing, pp. 201–203

Perceptual organization, pp. 207–214

Personality

   Big Five and, pp. 477–479

   brain imaging and, p. 476

Posttraumatic stress disorder (PTSD) and the limbic system, pp. 509–510

Priming, p. 193

Psychosurgery: lobotomy, pp. 564–565

Schizophrenia and brain abnormalities, pp. 524–525

Sensation:

   body position and movement, pp. 227–228

   deafness, pp. 218–219

   hearing, pp. 216–220

   sensory adaptation, pp. 194–195

   smell, pp. 225–227

   taste, p. 225

   touch, pp. 220–221

   vision, pp. 199–214

Sexual orientation, pp. 180–181

Sleep:

   cognitive development and, p. 99

   memory and, pp. 91–92

   recuperation during, p. 91

Smell and emotion, p. 227

Unconscious mind, pp. 468–470

TABLE 6

Behavior Genetics and Evolutionary Psychology In addition to the coverage found in Chapter 2, **behavior genetics** is covered on the following pages:

Abuse, intergenerational transmission of, p. 262

Adaptability, pp. 58–59

Aggression, pp. 441–445
  intergenerational transmission of, p. 262

Autism spectrum disorder, pp. 130–132

Behavior genetics perspective, pp. 8-9, 12

Biological perspective, p. 38

Brain plasticity, p. 39

Continuity and stages, p. 117

Deprivation of attachment, pp. 136–138

Depth perception, pp. 208–210

Development, pp. 116–117

Drives and incentives, p. 349

Drug use, pp. 110–113

Eating disorders, pp. 531–533

Epigenetics, pp. 120, 138, 496, 511–512, 519, 527

Happiness, pp. 411–412

Hunger and taste preference, pp. 363–364

Intelligence:
  Down syndrome, p. 331
  genetic and environmental influences, pp. 336–339

Learning, pp. 254–257

Motor development, p. 124

Nature-nurture, p. 8
  twins, p. 9

Obesity and weight control, pp. 365–366

Optimism, pp. 398–399

Pain, pp. 221–223

Parenting styles, pp. 138–140

Perception, pp. 213–214

Personality traits, pp. 475–479

Psychological disorders and:
  ADHD, pp. 497–498
  anxiety-related disorders, pp. 510–512
  biopsychosocial approach, pp. 495–496
  bipolar disorder and major depressive disorder, pp. 518–521
  depressed thinking, p. 521
  obsessive-compulsive disorder, pp. 510–512
  personality disorders, pp. 530–531
  posttraumatic stress disorder, pp. 509–512

schizophrenia, pp. 524–527

suicide, pp. 500–501

violent behavior, pp. 502–503

Reward deficiency syndrome, p. 56

Romantic love, pp. 156–157

Sexual dysfunctions, p. 175

Sexual orientation, pp. 179–182

Sexuality, pp. 172–174

Sleep patterns, pp. 90–91

Smell, pp. 225–227

Stress, personality, and illness, pp. 388–393
  benefits of exercise, pp. 401–402

Traits, gay-straight differences, pp. 182–183

In addition to the coverage found in Chapter 2, the **evolutionary perspective** is covered on the following pages:

Aging, pp. 161–162

Anger, pp. 393–394

Anxiety-related disorders, pp. 511–512

Biological predispositions:
  in learning, pp. 254–255
  in operant conditioning, p. 256

Brainstem, pp. 53–54

Classical conditioning, pp. 254–255

Consciousness, p. 80

Darwin, Charles, pp. 5, 9

Depression and light exposure therapy, pp. 554–555

Emotion, effects of facial expressions and, pp. 380–382

Emotional expression, pp. 378–380

Evolutionary perspective, defined, pp. 11, 12

Fear, p. 302

Feature detection, p. 205

Fight or flight, p. 386

Gene-environment interaction, pp. 73–75

Hearing, p. 216

Hunger and taste preference, pp. 363–364

Instincts, pp. 348–349

Intelligence, pp. 327–328, 340–343

Language, pp. 312–317

Love, pp. 156–157

Math and spatial ability, p. 340

Mating preferences, pp. 184–185

Menopause, p. 151

Need to belong, pp. 352–353

Obesity, p. 365

Overconfidence, pp. 303–304

Perceptual adaptation, pp. 213–214

Sensation, p. 190

Sensory adaptation, pp. 194–195

Sexual orientation, pp. 179–182

Sexuality, pp. 173–174, 179–180, 183–186

Sleep, pp. 86, 91–92

Smell, p. 226

Taste, pp. 225–227

Eight Principles Have Always Guided This Text's Creation

We follow eight guiding principles that have animated all of my [DM's] texts since their first editions.

Facilitating the Learning Experience

1. *To teach critical thinking* By presenting research as intellectual detective work, we illustrate an inquiring, analytical mindset. Whether students are studying development, cognition, or social behavior, they will be drawn into critical reasoning. They will discover how an empirical approach can help them evaluate competing ideas and claims for highly publicized

phenomena—ranging from extrasensory perception and alternative therapies to group differences in intelligence and repressed and recovered memories. (See pp. xii–xiv for more information about critical thinking in this text.)

2. *To integrate principles and applications* Throughout, we relate the findings of basic research to their applications and implications. Knowledge is power when we harness it to bring about positive change in the world. Where psychology can illuminate pressing human issues—overcoming prejudice, pursuing happiness, moving past conflict to peace—we have not hesitated to shine its light. The new "Ask Yourself" questions integrated throughout each chapter of the text help students continue to make personally meaningful what they are learning. And our online "Assess Your Strengths" activities invite students to apply important concepts to their own lives, and to learn ways to develop personal strengths. As the author of an early book devoted to the scientific study of happiness, *The Pursuit of Happiness* (Myers, 1992), I [DM] have a special place in my heart for understanding and cultivating human strengths. Throughout the text we integrate coverage of *positive psychology* (see **TABLE 7**).

3. *To reinforce learning at every step* Everyday examples and thought-provoking questions encourage students to process the material actively. Concepts presented earlier are frequently applied, and reinforced, in later chapters. For instance, in Chapter 1, students learn that much of our information processing occurs outside of our conscious awareness. Subsequent chapters drive home this concept. Self-testing opportunities throughout the text and online resources help students learn and retain important concepts and terminology.

Demonstrating the Science of Psychology

4. *To teach the process of inquiry* We strive to show students not just the outcome of research, but how the research process works. Throughout, the narrative excites the reader's curiosity. It invites students to imagine themselves as participants in classic experiments. Several chapters introduce research stories as mysteries that progressively unravel as one clue after another falls into place. Our online "Immersive Learning: How Would You Know?" activities allow students to play the role of the researcher in thinking about research questions and how psychological scientists attempt to answer them.

5. *To be as up-to-date as possible* Few things dampen students' interest as quickly as the sense that they are reading stale news. While keeping psychology's classic studies and concepts, we also present the discipline's most important recent developments. In this edition, 1173 references are dated 2015–2018. Likewise, new photos and new everyday examples are drawn from today's world.

6. *To put facts in the service of concepts* Our intention is not to overwhelm students with facts, but to reveal psychology's major concepts—to teach students how to think, and to offer psychological ideas worth thinking about. While writing, we keep in mind a simple question: *What does an educated person need to know?* Learning Objective Questions and Retrieve It questions throughout each chapter help students focus on the most important concepts. Online Concept Practice and TopicTutorial activities help ensure student understanding of key points.

Promoting Big Ideas and Broadened Horizons

7. *To enhance comprehension by providing continuity* Many chapters have a significant issue or theme that links subtopics, forming a thread that ties the chapter together. The Learning chapter conveys the idea that bold thinkers can serve as intellectual pioneers. The Thinking, Language, and Intelligence chapter raises the issue of human rationality and irrationality. The Psychological Disorders chapter conveys empathy for, and understanding of, troubled lives. Other threads, such as cognitive neuroscience, dual processing, and cultural, gender, and gender-identity diversity weave throughout the whole book. Although we [DM and ND] occupy separate bodies, we write with a unified voice. (We also have a similar sense of humor.) Our singleness of purpose and our editing of each other give students a familiar companion who will help guide them through psychology's interconnected roads.

8. *To convey respect for human unity and diversity* Throughout the book, readers will see evidence of our human kinship—our shared biological heritage, our common mechanisms

TABLE 7

Examples of Positive Psychology

Coverage of positive psychology topics can be found in the following chapters:	
Topic	**Chapter**
Altruism/ compassion	9, 11, 12, 15
Coping	11
Courage	12
Creativity	5, 9, 13
Emotional Intelligence	9, 12
Empathy	4, 7, 10, 12, 13, 15
Flow	Appendix B
Gratitude	11
Happiness/Life Satisfaction	1, 2, 4, 5, 9, 10, 11
Humility	1
Humor	11, 12
Justice	12
Leadership	5, 13, Appendix B
Love	4, 5, 10, 12, 13, 15
Morality	4
Optimism	11, 13
Personal control	11
Resilience	4, 11, 15
Self-discipline	4, 10, 13
Self-efficacy	13
Self-esteem	10, 13
Spirituality	11
Toughness (grit)	9, 10
Wisdom	9, 11, 12, 13

of seeing and learning, hungering and feeling, loving and hating. They will also better understand the dimensions of our diversity—our individual diversity in development and aptitudes, temperament and personality, and disorder and health; and our cultural diversity in attitudes and expressive styles, child raising and care for the elderly, and life priorities.

Our Resources Are Carefully Designed to Help Students Learn, and Care About Their Learning

We and our team work hard to create top-quality resource materials. To encourage students to read, we communicate psychology's story with crisp writing, vivid storytelling, and occasional humor. We get help from our editors, who work with us line by line. Similar care is devoted to the Instructor's Resources and assessment materials. Our text chapters for this new edition went through eight drafts, and all other resources also went through multiple drafts. This creative process requires our daily focus, as we collect and create new information that will expand students' minds and enlarge their hearts. Working through what is often over *one thousand* edits and comments in a given chapter can be daunting! But in the end it gives students the best chance at success in this life-relevant course. With the support of Worth Publishers, our author and editorial team has no rival in its investment of time and energy.

Students Love This Book

Students seem to appreciate the effort. They read the book! We get a stream of wonderfully encouraging, and sometimes funny, letters from appreciative students. Here are two examples:

> "Mr. Myers: I have been reading . . . your Psychology textbook. . . . The way you write and explain makes me feel like we're buddies."
>
> —From an anonymous student

> "Your text goes above and beyond; your command of language, the . . . witty remarks and puns, the frequent inclusion of concrete psychological experiments pertaining to the . . . subject. I often found myself nodding my head while reading along, as I felt like the information I was taking in was substantiated with real life applications."
>
> —From a student at Santa Monica College

Students also love the online learning resources. We hear repeatedly that students benefit from the LearningCurve formative quizzing system and use it both to explore new concepts and to test their understanding.

7 "My students need truly effective learning tools they will use."

Our Pedagogy Follows Best Practices From Learning and Memory Research

Students want to do well in this course, and we all want to give them the best possible chance of doing so. How can we best enhance student success? We can use findings from psychological science to teach psychological science. Researchers have found that "Achievement is . . . strongly associated with the stimulation of meaningful learning by presenting information in a clear way, relating it to the students, and using conceptually demanding learning tasks" (Schneider & Preckel, 2017). So, for starters, we write and rewrite our materials under scrutiny from each other and our team of editors—ensuring that each sentence is clear and compelling, and that our student readers will readily relate psychology's concepts to their lives.

Our learning system also harnesses the *testing effect*, which documents the benefits of actively retrieving information through regular testing with *immediate feedback* (**FIGURE 8**). Thus, our LearningCurve system, which has been *very* popular with students, offers an adaptive quizzing program that provides a personalized study plan. In the text, each chapter offers 12 to 15

FIGURE 8

HOW TO LEARN AND REMEMBER
For a 5-minute animated guide to more effective studying, visit tinyurl.com/HowToRemember.

🔒 RETRIEVE IT • • • *ANSWERS IN APPENDIX E*

RI-2 Using sound as your example, explain how these concepts differ: *absolute threshold, subliminal stimulation,* and *difference threshold.*

FIGURE 9

SAMPLE OF RETRIEVE IT FEATURE

Retrieve It questions interspersed throughout (**FIGURE 9**). Creating these *desirable difficulties* for students along the way optimizes the testing effect, as does immediate feedback via answers that are available for checking.

Each main section of text begins with a numbered question that establishes a *learning objective* and directs student reading. The Review found at the end of each main section repeats these questions as a further self-testing opportunity (with answers in the Complete Chapter Reviews appendix). The Review section also offers a page-referenced list of **Terms and Concepts to Remember**, and **Experience the Testing Effect** questions in multiple formats to promote optimal retention.

These features enhance the Survey-Question-Read-Retrieve-Review (SQ3R) format. Chapter Overviews allow students to *survey* what's to come. Main sections begin with a learning objective *question* that encourages students to *read* actively. Periodic Retrieve It sections and the section Review (with repeated Learning Objective Questions, Key Terms list, and Experience the Testing Effect questions) encourage students to test themselves by *retrieving* what they know and *reviewing* what they don't. (See Figure 9 for a Retrieve It sample.)

key terms Students will also find complete definitions of each important term in a page corner near the term's introduction in the narrative.

8 "I have a lot of nursing and premed students. I need a book that maps well onto the new MCAT's psychology section."

Since 2015, the Medical College Admission Test (MCAT) has devoted 25 percent of its questions to the "Psychological, Social, and Biological Foundations of Behavior," with most of those questions coming from the psychological science taught in introductory psychology courses. From 1977 to 2014, the MCAT focused on biology, chemistry, and physics. Thereafter, reported the *Preview Guide for MCAT 2015*, the exam also recognizes "the importance of socio-cultural and behavioral determinants of health and health outcomes." The exam's new psychology section beautifully matches this text's topics. For example, see **TABLE 8**, which outlines the precise correlation between this text's coverage of Emotion and Stress, and the corresponding portion of the MCAT exam. In addition, our Test Bank questions are keyed to MCAT topics. To improve their MCAT preparation, I [ND] regularly teach premedical students an intensive course covering the topics that appear in this text. For a complete pairing of the new MCAT psychology topics with this book's contents, see MacmillanLearning.com.

9 "I am eager to use more digital resources but uncertain how to proceed, and in need of assistance in this process."

With up to 350 students in my [ND's] classes, I, too, worried about switching to LaunchPad a few years ago. I spent some extra time the first semester learning about all of the available resources, but it was worth it. LaunchPad has saved me time and allowed me to do things that I thought were impossible with so many students. For example, I now offer a first-day-of-class, gradable assignment in LaunchPad to get students immediately engaged. I also use frequent quizzes throughout the course, which helps my students and me to track their learning progress. LaunchPad has helped make my course a success. *Assigning* materials shows that I value these resources, and I've been delighted to see a significant improvement in student retention rates since I started using LaunchPad.

The best way to get started is to visit LaunchPadWorks.com and consult with your Macmillan Learning representative.

TABLE 8

Sample MCAT Correlation With *Exploring Psychology*, Eleventh Edition

MCAT 2015 Content Category 6C: Responding to the world	*Exploring Psychology*, Eleventh Edition Correlations	Page Numbers
Emotion	Emotion: Introduction to Emotion, Expressing Emotion, Experiencing Emotion	367–382
Three components of emotion (i.e., cognitive, physiological, behavioral)	Emotion: Arousal, Behavior, and Cognition	367–368
Universal emotions (e.g., fear, anger, happiness, surprise, joy, disgust, and sadness)	Culture and Emotional Expression—including the universal emotions	378–380
	The Basic Emotions	372
Adaptive role of emotion	Emotion as the body's adaptive response	367–368
Theories of emotion	*Emotions and the Autonomic Nervous System*	372–373
James-Lange theory	James-Lange Theory: Arousal Comes Before Emotion	368
Cannon-Bard theory	Cannon-Bard Theory: Arousal and Emotion Occur Simultaneously	368–369
Schachter-Singer theory	Schachter and Singer Two-Factor Theory: Arousal + Label = Emotion	369
The role of biological processes in perceiving emotion	Emotions and the Autonomic Nervous System; The Physiology of Emotions	372–374
Brain regions involved in the generation and experience of emotions	Emotions and the Autonomic Nervous System; The Physiology of Emotions	372–374
The role of the limbic system in emotion	The Physiology of Emotions—including the brain's pathways for emotions	373–374
	Emotions and the Autonomic Nervous System	372–373
	The Physiology of Emotions	372–374
Emotion and the autonomic nervous system	*Emotions and the Autonomic Nervous System*	372–373
Physiological markers of emotion (signatures of emotion)	The Physiology of Emotions	373–374
Stress	Stress and Illness	383–394
The nature of stress	Stress: Some Basic Concepts	383–388
Appraisal	*Stress appraisal*	384
Different types of stressors (i.e., cataclysmic events, personal)	*Stressors—Things That Push Our Buttons*	385–386
Effects of stress on psychological functions	*The Stress Response System*	386–388
Stress outcomes/response to stressors	The Stress Response System	386–388
Physiological	The Stress Response System	386–388
Emotional	Stress and Vulnerability to Disease	388–394
Behavioral	*Stress and Heart Disease—Type A/B, anger management*	391–392
	Coping With Stress	395–401
	Posttraumatic Stress Disorder (PTSD)	509–510
	The Stress Response System	386–388
	Coping With Stress	395–401
Managing stress (e.g., exercise, relaxation techniques, spirituality)	Reducing Stress—aerobic exercise, relaxation/meditation, faith communities	401–406

In Appreciation

"Nothing we ever do, however virtuous, can be accomplished alone."

~ Reinhold Niebuhr, 1952

Our authoring is a collective enterprise. Aided by input from thousands of instructors and students over the years, this has become a better, more effective, more accurate book than two authors alone (these authors at least) could write. Our indebtedness continues to the innumerable researchers who have been so willing to share their time and talent to help us accurately report their research, and to the hundreds of instructors who have taken the time to offer feedback. We empathize with long-time *Atlantic* writer James Fallows' observation that "In this business you spend most of your time talking with people who *know more* about a given subject than you do. That is in hopes of eventually being able to explain it to people who know less."

Our gratitude extends to the colleagues who contributed criticism, corrections, and creative ideas related to the content and effectiveness of this new edition and its resources. For their expertise and encouragement, and the gift of their time to the teaching of psychology, we thank the reviewers and consultants listed here.

Christopher Adalio
University of California, Berkeley

Stephanie Afful
Lindenwood University

Lauren Bates
Colorado State University

Barbara Beaver
University of Wisconsin–Whitewater

Michael Brislawn
Olympic College

Amy Buckingham
Red Rocks Community College

Candace Cresap-Blomquist
Bay de Noc Community College

Jennifer Dale
Community College of Aurora

Myra Darty
North Idaho College

Scott Debb
Norfolk State University

Kyle De Young
University of Wyoming

Christyn Dolbier
East Carolina University

Angela Dortch
Ivy Tech Community College

Charles Dufour
University of Maine

Rebecca Ewing
Western New Mexico University

Rebecca Foushee
Lindenwood University

Matt Gray
University of Wyoming

Christine Henderson
SUNY Orange/Orange County Community College

Katie Hodgin
Colorado State University

Kathy Howard
Harding University

Regina Hughes
Collin College

Amy Kausler
Jefferson College

Joanna Key
Gwinnett Technical College

Kimberly Knesting-Lund
University of Wisconsin–Whitewater

Ken Luke
Tyler Junior College

Pamela Lundeberg
Colorado State University

Sharmin Maswood
Elizabethtown College

Nicole McCray
University of Montana

Corinne McNamara
Kennesaw State University

Kelly O'Dell
Community College of Aurora

Maeve O'Donnell
Colorado State University

Lawrence Patihis
University of Southern Mississippi

Michael Rader
Johnson County Community College

Julia Ramey
University of Arkansas–Pulaski Technical College

Edie Sample
Metropolitan Community College

Christopher Stanzione
Georgia Institute of Technology

Kim Stark
University of Central Missouri

Brianna Stinebaugh
Towson University

Daniel Storage
University of Denver

Rose Suggett
Southeast Community College

William Travis Suits
Seminole State College of Florida

Russell Warne
Utah Valley University

Brandon Whittington
Jefferson College

Chrysalis Wright
University of Central Florida

Kevin Zabel
Western New England University

We appreciate the guidance offered by the following teaching psychologists, who reviewed and offered helpful feedback on the development of our significantly revised "Assess Your Strengths" online activities.

Malinde Althaus
Inver Hills Community College

TaMetryce Collins
Hillsborough Community College, Brandon

Lisa Fosbender
Gulf Coast State College

Kelly Henry
Missouri Western State University

Brooke Hindman
Greenville Technical College

Natalie Kemp
University of Mount Olive

David Payne
Wallace Community College

Tanya Renner
Kapi'olani Community College

Lillian Russell
Alabama State University, Montgomery

Amy Williamson
Moraine Valley Community College

And we'd like to offer special thanks to the reviewers and consultants who helped us shape the new Thinking Critically About: Sexual Aggression infographic feature in Chapter 5:

Christia Brown
University of Kentucky

Ann Coker
University of Kentucky

Jane Dickie
Hope College

Sara Dorer
Hope College

Claire Renzetti
University of Kentucky

At Worth Publishers a host of people played key roles in creating this eleventh edition.

Executive Program Manager Carlise Stembridge has been a valued team leader, thanks to her dedication, creativity, and sensitivity. Carlise oversees, encourages, and guides our author-editor team, and she serves as an important liaison with our colleagues in the field.

Noel Hohnstine and Laura Burden expertly coordinated creation of the media resources. Betty Probert efficiently edited and produced the Test Bank questions (working with Chrysalis Wright, University of Central Florida), Instructor's Resources, and Lecture Guides and, in the process, helped fine-tune the whole book. Katie Pachnos and Anna Munroe provided terrific support in commissioning and organizing the multitude of reviews, coordinating our development and production schedules, and providing editorial guidance. Lee McKevitt did a splendid job of laying out each page. Robin Fadool and Donna Ranieri worked together to locate the myriad photos. Art Manager Matt McAdams managed the updating of our art program, and worked with artist Evelyn Pence to create the wonderful new "Thinking Critically About" infographics.

Senior Content Project Manager Won McIntosh and Senior Workflow Supervisor Susan Wein masterfully kept the book to its tight schedule, and Design Services Manager Natasha Wolfe skillfully directed creation of the beautiful new design.

Christine Brune, chief editor for the last three decades, is a wonder worker. She offers just the right mix of encouragement, gentle admonition, attention to detail, and passion for excellence. An author could not ask for more. Development editors Nancy Fleming, Trish Morgan, and Danielle Slevens amazed us with their meticulous focus, impressive knowledge, and helpful editing—and with kindred spirits to our own. And Deborah Heimann did an excellent job with the copyediting. After their several thousand hours of world-class skill invested in guiding and shaping this book, we fully appreciate Helen Keller's comment that "Alone we can do so little. Together we can do so much."

To achieve our goal of supporting the teaching of psychology, these resources not only must be authored, reviewed, edited, and produced, but also made available to teachers of psychology. For their exceptional success in doing that, our author team is grateful to Macmillan Learning's professional sales and marketing team. We are especially grateful to Executive Marketing Manager Kate Nurre, Marketing Manager Clay Bolton, and Learning Solutions Specialists Robyn Burnett and Elizabeth Chaffin Woosley for tirelessly working to inform our teaching colleagues of our efforts to assist their teaching, and for the joy of working with them.

At Hope College, the supporting team members for this edition included Kathryn Brownson, who researched countless bits of information and edited and proofed hundreds of pages. Kathryn is a knowledgeable and sensitive adviser on many matters. Sara Neevel, our longtime manuscript developer and friend, did advance work before we were saddened by her untimely death, leaving us so grateful for her life and her gifts. At the University of Kentucky, Lorie Hailey has showcased a variety of indispensable qualities, including a sharp eye and a strong work ethic.

Again, I [DM] gratefully acknowledge the editing assistance and mentoring of my writing coach, poet Jack Ridl, whose influence resides in the voice you will be hearing in the pages that follow. He, more than anyone, cultivated my delight in dancing with the language, and taught me to approach writing as a craft that shades into art. Likewise, I [ND] am grateful to my intellectual hero and mentor, Roy Baumeister, who taught me how to hone my writing and embrace the writing life. I'm also indebted to John Tierney, who has offered unending support and served as a role model of how to communicate to a general audience.

And we have enjoyed our ongoing work with each other. It has been a joy for me [DM] to continue working with Nathan on this project. This is our sixth book together. Nathan's fresh insights and contributions continue to enrich this book as we work together on each chapter—every day, every month, every year. With support from our wonderful editors, this is a team project. In addition to our work together on the textbook, Nathan and I contribute to the monthly "Teaching Current Directions in Psychological Science" column in the *APS Observer* (tinyurl.com/MyersDeWall). I [DM] also blog at TalkPsych.com, where I share exciting new findings, everyday applications, and observations on all things psychology.

Finally, our gratitude extends to the many students and instructors who have written to offer suggestions, or just an encouraging word. It is for them, and those about to begin their study of psychology, that we have done our best to introduce the field we love.

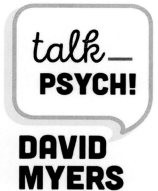

*   *   *

The day this book went to press was the day we started gathering information and ideas for the next edition. Your input will influence how this book continues to evolve. So, please, do share your thoughts.

David Myers

@DavidGMyers
Hope College
Holland, Michigan 49422-9000 USA
DavidMyers.org

Nathan DeWall

@cndewall
University of Kentucky
Lexington, Kentucky 40506-0044 USA
NathanDeWall.com

Student Preface:

Time Management—How to Be a Great Student and Still Have a Life

Richard O. Straub, University of Michigan, Dearborn

We all face challenges in our schedules. This might be your first time living outside of your parents' home, leaving you unsure how to juggle your school and social commitments. Some of you may be taking night classes, others squeezing in an online course between jobs or after putting children to bed at night. Some of you may be veterans using military benefits to jump-start a new life. Whatever your situation, the transition from your previous life situation to this one presents some challenges.

How can you balance all of your life's demands and be successful? Time management. Manage the time you have so that you can find the time you need.

In this section, I will outline a simple, four-step process for improving the way you make use of your time.

1. Keep a time-use diary to understand how you are using your time. You may be surprised at how much time you're wasting.

2. Design a new schedule for using your time more effectively.

3. Make the most of your study time so that your new schedule will work for you.

4. If necessary, refine your new schedule, based on what you've learned.

How Are You Using Your Time Now?

Although everyone gets 24 hours in the day and seven days in the week, we fill those hours and days with different obligations and interests. If you are like most people, you probably use your time wisely in some ways, and not so wisely in others. Answering the questions in

Desislava Draganova/Alamy

TABLE 1

Study Habits Survey

Answer the following questions, writing *Yes* or *No* for each line.

1. Do you usually set up a schedule to budget your time for studying, work, recreation, and other activities? _____

2. Do you often put off studying until time pressures force you to cram? _____

3. Do other students seem to study less than you do, but get better grades? _____

4. Do you usually spend hours at a time studying one subject, rather than dividing that time among several subjects? _____

5. Do you often have trouble remembering what you have just read in a textbook? _____

6. Before reading a chapter in a textbook, do you skim through it and read the section headings? _____

7. Do you try to predict test questions from your class notes and reading? _____

8. Do you usually try to summarize in your own words what you have just finished reading? _____

9. Do you find it difficult to concentrate for very long when you study? _____

10. Do you often feel that you studied the wrong material for a test? _____

Thousands of students have participated in similar surveys. Students who are fully realizing their academic potential usually respond as follows:
(1) yes, (2) no, (3) no, (4) no, (5) no, (6) yes, (7) yes, (8) yes, (9) no, (10) no.
Do your responses fit that pattern? If not, you could benefit from improving your time management and study habits.

TABLE 1 can help you find trouble spots—and hopefully more time for the things that matter most to you.

The next thing you need to know is how you *actually* spend your time. To find out, record your activities in a *time-use diary* for one week. Be realistic. Take notes on how much time you spend attending class, studying, working, commuting, meeting personal and family needs, preparing and eating meals, socializing (don't forget texting, social networking, and gaming), exercising, and anything else that occupies your time, including life's small practical tasks, which can take up plenty of your time. As you record your activities, take notes on how you are feeling at various times of the day. When does your energy slump, and when do you feel most energetic?

Design a Better Schedule

Take a good look at your time-use diary. Where do you think you may be wasting time? Do you spend a lot of time commuting, for example? If so, could you use that time more productively? If you take public transportation, commuting is a great time to read and test yourself for review. You can access the eBook anywhere, anytime! Or you may want to take advantage of the **new Audiobook**.

Did you remember to include time for meals, personal care, work schedules, family commitments, and other fixed activities?

How much time do you sleep? In the battle to meet all of life's daily commitments and interests, we tend to treat sleep as optional. Do your best to manage your life so that you can get enough sleep to feel rested. It's hard to achieve your goals if you don't have the energy to complete them. You will feel better and be healthier, and you will also do better academically and in relationships with your family and friends. (You will read more about this in Chapter 3.)

Are you dedicating enough time for focused study? Take a last look at your notes to see if any other patterns pop out. Now it's time to create a new and more efficient schedule.

LWA/The Image Bank/Getty Images

Plan the Term

Before you draw up your new schedule, think ahead. If your course is not already online—complete with a schedule of assignments, activities, quizzes, and exams for the term—use your phone's calendar feature, or buy a portable calendar. Enter the dates of all exams and assignments. Also be sure to track your own long-range personal plans, including work and family commitments. Keep your personal calendar up-to-date, refer to it often, and change it as needed. Through this process, you will develop a regular schedule that will help you achieve success.

Plan Your Week

To pass those exams, meet those deadlines, and keep up with your life outside of class, you will need to convert your long-term goals into a daily schedule. Be realistic—you will be living with this routine for the entire school term. Here are some more things to add to your personal calendar.

1. Enter your class times, work hours, and any other fixed obligations. Be thorough. Allow plenty of time for such things as commuting, meals, and laundry.

2. Set up a study schedule for each course. Remember what you learned about yourself in the study habits survey (Table 1) and your time-use diary.

3. After you have budgeted time for studying, fill in slots for other obligations, exercise, fun, and relaxation.

More Tips for Effective Scheduling

There are a few other things you will want to keep in mind when you set up your schedule.

Spaced study is more effective than massed study. If you need 3 hours to study one subject, for example, it's best to divide that into shorter periods spaced over several days.

Alternate subjects, but avoid interference. Alternating the subjects you study in any given session will keep you fresh and will, surprisingly, increase your ability to remember what you're learning in each different area. Studying similar topics back-to-back, however, such as two different foreign languages, could lead to interference in your learning. (You will hear more about this in Chapter 8.)

Determine the amount of study time you need to do well in each course. The time you need depends on the difficulty of your courses and the effectiveness of your study methods. Ideally, you would spend at least 1 to 2 hours studying for each hour spent in class. Increase your study time slowly by setting weekly goals that will gradually bring you up to the desired level.

Create a schedule that makes sense. Tailor your schedule to meet the demands of each course. For the course that emphasizes lecture notes, plan a daily review of your notes soon after each class. If you are evaluated for class participation (for example, in a language course), allow time for a review just before the class meets. Schedule study time for your most difficult (or least motivating) courses during hours when you are the most alert and distractions are fewest.

Schedule open study time. Life can be unpredictable. Emergencies and new obligations can throw off your schedule. Or you may simply need some extra time for a project or for review in one of your courses. Try to allow for some flexibility in your schedule each week.

The Importance of Playing Offense

We can't control everything. Car troubles, family problems, and work challenges happen. Sometimes it seems as if we have to play "defense" against the demands and problems that can pile up, leaving us stressed out and unable to achieve our goals. There is a solution: Play "offense" against your environment. Set out with a plan for each day, rather than just letting the day happen to you. You will then have a lot more control over how you spend your time. Establishing routines and making decisions in advance actually conserves energy, as it spares us from some of our daily decision making. If we know we are going to study two hours in the morning before class, we won't waste time and energy weighing the pros and the cons of that choice over breakfast each day.

Earlier, I recommended that in your time-use diary you track the times you feel most energetic. Keep that in mind as you plan your days. Try to match your high-energy times with your most challenging schoolwork and projects. And don't forget to replenish your energy along the way with meals, rest, and social time.

Following these guidelines will help you find a schedule that works for you!

Make Every Minute of Your Study Time Count

Gary S Chapman/The Image Bank/Getty Images

You will hear more about SQ3R in Chapter 1.

How do you study from a textbook? We've learned a lot about effective study techniques from cognitive psychologists. To get the most out of your text, avoid simply reading and rereading in a passive manner. That method may cause you to remember the wrong things—the catchy stories but not the main points that show up later in test questions. And it's clearer than ever that taking effective class notes is essential. Here are some tips that will help you get the most from your text resources and your class.

Use SQ3R to Help You Master This Text

David Myers and Nathan DeWall organized this text by using a system called SQ3R (Survey, Question, Read, Retrieve, Review). Using SQ3R can help you to understand what you read, and to retain that information longer.

Applying SQ3R may feel at first as though it's taking more time and effort to "read" a chapter, but with practice, these steps will become automatic.

Survey

Before you read a chapter, survey its key parts. Scan the chapter outline. Note that main sections have numbered Learning Objective Questions to help you focus. Pay attention to headings, which indicate important subtopics, and to words set in bold type.

Surveying gives you the big picture of a chapter's content and organization. Understanding the chapter's logical sections will help you break your work into manageable pieces in your study sessions.

Question

To show you care about your education, continually ask questions. Doing so signals that you're engaged, curious, and motivated to work hard. Questioning starts while you're reading. As you survey, don't limit yourself to the numbered Learning Objective Questions that appear throughout the chapter. Jotting down additional questions of your own will cause you to look at the material in a new way. (You might, for example, scan this section's headings and ask "What does 'SQ3R' mean?") Information becomes easier to remember when you make it personally meaningful. Trying to answer your questions while reading will keep you in an active learning mode.

Read

As you read, keep your questions in mind and actively search for the answers. If you come to material that seems to answer an important question that you haven't jotted down, stop and write down that new question.

Be sure to read everything. Don't skip photo or art captions, graphs, tables, or quotes. An idea that seems vague when you read about it may become clear when you see it in a graph or table. Keep in mind that instructors sometimes base their test questions on figures and tables. And take advantage of the "Thinking Critically About" infographic features that will help you learn about key concepts.

Retrieve

When you have found the answer to one of your questions, look away and mentally recite the question and its answer. Then write the answer next to the question in your own words. Trying to explain something in your own words will help you figure out where there are gaps in your understanding. These kinds of opportunities to practice *retrieving* develop the skills you will need when you are taking exams. If you study without ever putting your book and notes aside, you may develop false confidence about what you know. With the material available, you may be able to recognize the correct answer to your questions. But will you be able to recall it later, when you take an exam without having your mental props in sight?

Test your understanding as often as you can. Testing yourself is part of successful learning, because the act of testing forces your brain to work at remembering, thus establishing the memory more permanently (so you can find it later for the exam!). Use the self-testing opportunities throughout each chapter, including the periodic Retrieve It items. Also take advantage of the self-testing that is available in the online resources (LaunchPadWorks.com).

Review

After working your way through the chapter, read over your questions and your written answers. Take an extra few minutes to create a brief written summary covering all of your questions and answers. At the end of each main section, you should take advantage of three important opportunities for self-testing and review—a list of that section's Learning Objective Questions for you to try answering before checking Appendix D (Complete Chapter Reviews), a list of that section's key terms for you to try to define before checking the referenced page, and a set of Experience the Testing Effect test questions that cover all of that section's key concepts (with answers in Appendix E).

Take Useful Class Notes

Good notes will boost your understanding and retention. Are yours thorough? Do they form a sensible outline of what you learned in each class? If not, you may need to make some changes.

Keep Each Course's Notes Separate and Organized

Keeping all your notes for a course in one location will allow you to easily find answers to questions. Three options are (1) separate notebooks for each course, (2) clearly marked sections in a shared ring binder, or (3) carefully organized folders if you opt to take notes electronically. For the print options, removable pages will allow you to add new information and weed out past mistakes. Choosing notebook pages with lots of space, or using mark-up options in electronic files, will allow you to add comments when you review and revise your notes after class.

Use an Outline Format

Use roman numerals for major points, letters for supporting arguments, and so on. (See **FIGURE 1** for a sample.) Creating an outline from what you've learned in class will help you to put the information in context and to see the key takeaway points.

Clean Up Your Notes After Class

Try to reorganize your notes soon after class. Expand or clarify your comments and clean up any unclear phrases while the material is fresh in your mind. Write important questions in the margin, or by using an

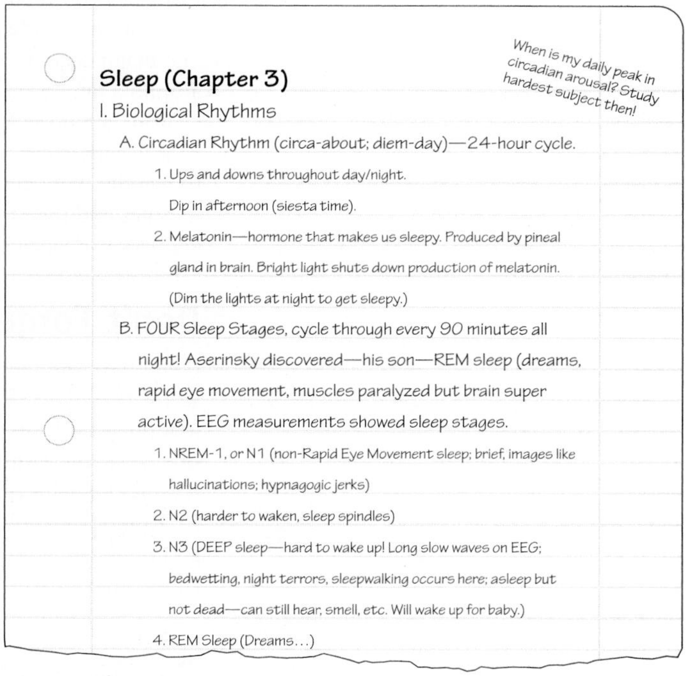

Sleep (Chapter 3)

When is my daily peak in circadian arousal? Study hardest subject then!

I. Biological Rhythms

  A. Circadian Rhythm (*circa*-about; *diem*-day)—24-hour cycle.

    1. Ups and downs throughout day/night.

      Dip in afternoon (siesta time).

    2. Melatonin—hormone that makes us sleepy. Produced by pineal gland in brain. Bright light shuts down production of melatonin. (Dim the lights at night to get sleepy.)

  B. FOUR Sleep Stages, cycle through every 90 minutes all night! Aserinsky discovered—his son—REM sleep (dreams, rapid eye movement, muscles paralyzed but brain super active). EEG measurements showed sleep stages.

    1. NREM-1, or N1 (non-Rapid Eye Movement sleep; brief, images like hallucinations; hypnagogic jerks)

    2. N2 (harder to waken, sleep spindles)

    3. N3 (DEEP sleep—hard to wake up! Long slow waves on EEG; bedwetting, night terrors, sleepwalking occurs here; asleep but not dead—can still hear, smell, etc. Will wake up for baby.)

    4. REM Sleep (Dreams…)

FIGURE 1

SAMPLE CLASS NOTES IN OUTLINE FORM Here is a sample from a student's notes taken in outline form from a class that was focused on sleep.

electronic markup feature, next to notes that answer them. (For example: "What are the sleep stages?") This will help you when you review your notes before a test.

Create a Study Space That Helps You Learn

It's easier to study effectively if your work area is well designed.

Organize Your Space

Work at a desk or table, not on your bed or a comfy chair that will tempt you to nap.

Minimize Distractions

Turn the TV off, turn off your phone and its notifications, and close distracting windows on your computer. If you must listen to music to mask outside noise, play soft instrumentals, not vocal selections that will draw your mind to the lyrics.

Ask Others to Honor Your Quiet Time

Tell roommates, family, and friends about your new schedule. Try to find a study place where you are least likely to be disturbed. Quiet places do exist. Sometimes you just need to do a little detective work to find them.

Set Specific, Realistic Daily Goals

The simple note "7–8 p.m.: Study Psychology" is too broad to be useful. Instead, break your studying into manageable tasks. For example, you will want to subdivide large reading assignments. If you aren't used to studying for long periods, start with relatively short periods of concentrated study, with breaks in between. In this text, for example, you might decide to read one major section before each break. Limit your breaks to 5 or 10 minutes to stretch or move around a bit.

Your attention span is a good indicator of whether you are pacing yourself successfully. At this early stage, it's important to remember that you're in training. If your attention begins to wander, get up immediately and take a short break. It is better to study effectively for 15 minutes and then take a break than to fritter away 45 minutes out of your study hour. As your endurance develops, you can increase the length of study periods.

Don't Forget About Rewards!

If you have trouble studying regularly, giving yourself a reward may help. What kind of reward works best? That depends on what you enjoy. You might start by making a list of 5 or 10 things that put a smile on your face. Spending time with a loved one, taking a walk or going for a bike ride, relaxing with a magazine or novel, or watching a favorite show can provide immediate rewards for achieving short-term study goals.

To motivate yourself when you're having trouble sticking to your schedule, allow yourself an immediate reward for completing a specific task. If running makes you smile, change your shoes, grab a friend, and head out the door! You deserve a reward for a job well done.

Do You Need to Revise Your New Schedule?

What if you've lived with your schedule for a few weeks, but you aren't making progress toward your academic and personal goals? What if your studying hasn't paid off in better grades? Don't despair and abandon your program, but do take a little time to figure out what's gone wrong.

Are You Doing Well in Some Courses But Not in Others?

Perhaps you need to shift your priorities a bit. You may need to allow more study time for chemistry, for example, and less time for some other course.

Have You Received a Poor Grade on a Test?

Did your grade fail to reflect the effort you spent preparing for the test? This can happen to even the hardest-working student, often on a first test with a new instructor. This common experience can be upsetting. "What do I have to do to get an A?" "The test was unfair!" "I studied the wrong material!"

Try to figure out what went wrong. Analyze the questions you missed, dividing them into two categories: class-based questions and text resource-based questions. How many questions did you miss in each category? If you find far more errors in one category than in the other, you'll have some clues to help you revise your schedule. Depending on the pattern you've found, you can add extra study time to the review of class notes, or to studying the text resources.

Are You Trying to Study Regularly for the First Time and Feeling Overwhelmed?

Perhaps you've set your initial goals too high. Remember, the point of time management is to identify a regular schedule that will help you achieve success. Like any skill, time management takes practice. Accept your limitations and revise your schedule to work slowly up to where you know you need to be—perhaps adding 15 minutes of study time per day.

* * *

I hope that these suggestions help make you more successful academically, and that they enhance the quality of your life in general. Having the necessary skills makes any job a lot easier and more pleasant. Let me repeat my warning not to attempt to make too drastic a change in your lifestyle immediately. Good habits require time and self-discipline to develop. Once established, they can last a lifetime.

🔒 REVIEW — STUDENT PREFACE: TIME MANAGEMENT—HOW TO BE A GREAT STUDENT AND STILL HAVE A LIFE

1. **How Are You Using Your Time Now?**
   - Identify your areas of weakness.
   - Keep a time-use diary.
   - Record the time you actually spend on activities.
   - Record your energy levels to find your most productive times.

2. **Design a Better Schedule**
   - Decide on your goals for the term and for each week.
   - Enter class times, work times, social times (for family and friends), and time needed for other obligations and for practical activities.
   - Tailor study times to avoid interference and to meet each course's needs.
   - Play offense with your schedule, so that you take control and use your energy efficiently.

3. **Make Every Minute of Your Study Time Count**
   - Use the SQ3R system (survey, question, read, retrieve, review) to master material covered in your text.
   - Take careful notes (in outline form) that will help you recall and rehearse what you learned in class.
   - Try to eliminate distractions to your study time, and ask friends and family to help you focus on your work.
   - Set specific, realistic daily goals to help you focus on each day's tasks.
   - When you achieve your daily goals, reward yourself with something that you value.

4. **Do You Need to Revise Your New Schedule?**
   - Allocate extra study time for courses that are more difficult, and a little less time for courses that are easy for you.
   - Analyze your test results to help determine a more effective balance in how you spend your study time.
   - Make sure your schedule is not too ambitious. Gradually establish a schedule that will be effective for the long term.

Thinking Critically With Psychological Science

From news and media portrayals, you might think that psychologists analyze personality, offer counseling, dispense child-raising advice, examine crime scenes, and testify in court. Do they? *Yes*—and much more. Consider some of psychology's questions that you may wonder about:

- Have you ever found yourself reacting to something as one of your biological parents would—perhaps in a way you vowed you *never* would—and then wondered how much of your personality you inherited? *To what extent do genes predispose our individual personality differences? To what extent do home and community environments shape us?*

- Have you ever worried about how to act among people of a different culture, race, gender identity, or sexual orientation? *How are we alike as members of the human family? How do we differ?*

- Have you ever awakened from a nightmare and wondered why you had such a crazy dream? *Why do we dream?*

- Have you ever played peekaboo with a 6-month-old and wondered why the baby finds your disappearing/reappearing act so delightful? *What do babies actually perceive and think?*

- Have you ever wondered what fosters school and work success? *Does inborn intelligence explain why some people get richer, think more creatively, or relate more sensitively? Or does gritty effort, and a belief that we can grow smarter, matter more?*

Klaus Vedfelt/Getty Images

- Have you ever become depressed or anxious and wondered whether you'll ever feel "normal"? *What triggers our bad moods—and our good ones? What's the line between a normal mood swing and a psychological disorder?*

Psychology is a science that seeks to answer such questions about us all—how and why we think, feel, and act as we do. ▶

A SMILE IS A SMILE THE WORLD AROUND Throughout this book, you will see examples not only of our cultural and gender diversity but also of the similarities that define our shared human nature. People in different cultures vary in when and how often they smile, but a naturally happy smile *means* the same thing anywhere in the world.

To assist your learning, numbered Learning Objective Questions appear at the beginning of major sections. You can test your understanding by trying to answer the question before, and then again after, you read the section.

Throughout the text, important concepts are **boldfaced.** As you study, you can find these terms with their definitions nearby and in the Glossary at the end of the book.

empirical approach an evidence-based method that draws on observation and experimentation.

critical thinking thinking that does not blindly accept arguments and conclusions. Rather, it examines assumptions, appraises the source, discerns hidden biases, evaluates evidence, and assesses conclusions.

⟶ The History and Scope of Psychology

PSYCHOLOGY IS A SCIENCE

LEARNING OBJECTIVE QUESTION (LOQ)

1-1   How is psychology a science?

Underlying all science is, first, a passion to explore and understand without misleading or being misled. Some questions (*Is there life after death?*) are beyond science. Answering them in any way requires a leap of faith. With many other ideas (*Can some people demonstrate ESP?*), the proof is in the pudding. Let the facts speak for themselves.

Magician James Randi has used this **empirical approach** when testing those claiming to see glowing auras around people's bodies:

Randi: Do you see an aura around my head?

Aura seer: Yes, indeed.

Randi: Can you still see the aura if I put this magazine in front of my face?

Aura seer: Of course.

Randi: Then if I were to step behind a wall barely taller than I am, you could determine my location from the aura visible above my head, right?

Randi once told me [DM] that no aura seer had yet agreed to take this simple test.

No matter how sensible-seeming or how wild an idea, the smart thinker asks: *Does it work?* When put to the test, do the data support its predictions? Subjected to such scrutiny, crazy-sounding ideas sometimes find support. More often, science becomes society's garbage disposal, sending crazy-sounding ideas to the waste heap, atop previous claims of perpetual motion machines, miracle cancer cures, and out-of-body travels into centuries past. To sift reality from fantasy and fact from fiction therefore requires a scientific attitude: being skeptical but not cynical, open-minded but not gullible.

Putting a scientific attitude into practice requires not only curiosity and skepticism but also *humility*—awareness of our own vulnerability to error and openness to surprises and new perspectives. What matters is not my opinion or yours, but the truths revealed by our questioning and testing. If people or other animals don't behave as our ideas predict, then so much the worse for our ideas. This humble attitude was expressed in one of psychology's early mottos: "The rat is always right." (See Thinking Critically About: The Scientific Attitude.)

CRITICAL THINKING

LOQ 1-3   How does critical thinking feed a scientific attitude, and smarter thinking for everyday life?

The scientific attitude—curiosity + skepticism + humility—prepares us to think harder and smarter. This thinking style, called **critical thinking,** examines assumptions, appraises the source, discerns hidden biases, evaluates evidence, and assesses conclusions. Whether reading a research report or an online opinion, or listening to news or a talk show, critical thinkers ask questions: *How do they know that? What is this person's agenda? Is the conclusion based on an anecdote, or on evidence? Does the evidence justify a cause-effect conclusion? What alternative explanations are possible?* By thinking hard, critical thinkers arrive at the smart conclusion.

Critical thinkers wince when people make factual claims based on gut intuition: "I *feel like* climate change is [or isn't] happening." "I *feel like* self-driving cars are more [or less] dangerous." "I *feel like* my candidate is more honest." Such beliefs (commonly mislabeled as feelings) may or may not be true. Critical thinkers are open to the possibility that they (or you) might be wrong. Sometimes, they know, the best evidence confirms our intuitions. Sometimes it challenges them and beckons us to a different way of thinking.

Historians of science tell us that these three attitudes—curiosity, skepticism, and humility—helped make modern science possible. Some deeply religious people may view critical thinking and scientific inquiry, including psychology's, as a threat. Yet many of the leaders of the scientific revolution, including Copernicus and Newton, were deeply religious people acting on the idea that "in order to love and honor God, it is necessary to fully appreciate the wonders of his handiwork" (Stark, 2003a,b).

Critical inquiry can lead us to surprising findings. Some examples from psychological science: Massive losses of brain tissue early in life may have minimal long-term effects (see Chapter 2). Within days, newborns can recognize their mother's odor (see Chapter 4). After brain damage, a person may be able to learn new skills yet be unaware of such learning (see Chapter 8). Diverse groups—men and women, old and young, rich and middle class, those with and without disabilities—report roughly comparable levels of personal happiness (see Chapter 11). The more people use critical thinking, the better they separate intuitive fiction from empirical fact (Bensley et al., 2014).

You will learn how psychological scientists use critical inquiry to sometimes debunk popular presumptions. For example, evidence indicates that sleepwalkers are *not* acting out their dreams (see Chapter 3). Our past experiences are *not* all recorded verbatim in our brains; with brain stimulation or hypnosis, one *cannot* simply replay and relive long-buried or repressed memories (see Chapter 8). Opposites tend *not* to attract (see Chapter 12). Most people do *not* suffer from unrealistically low self-esteem, and high self-esteem is *not* all good (see Chapter 13). In these instances and many others, what psychological scientists have learned is not what is widely believed.

ASK YOURSELF

Were you surprised to learn that psychology is a science? How would you explain that if someone else now asked you about this?

From a tongue-in-cheek Twitter feed: "The problem with quotes on the internet is that you never know if they're true." —Abraham Lincoln

"My deeply held belief is that if a god anything like the traditional sort exists, our curiosity and intelligence are provided by such a god. We would be unappreciative of those gifts . . . if we suppressed our passion to explore the universe and ourselves." —Carl Sagan, *Broca's Brain,* 1979

THINKING CRITICALLY ABOUT:

The Scientific Attitude

Three basic attitudes helped make modern science possible.

LOQ 1-2   What are the three key elements of the scientific attitude, and how do they support scientific inquiry?

1 CURIOSITY:

Does it work?

When put to the test, can its predictions be confirmed?

Can some people read minds?

Are stress levels related to health and well-being? ○

○ *No one has yet been able to demonstrate extrasensory mind-reading.*

○ *Many studies have found that higher stress relates to poorer health.*

2 SKEPTICISM:

What do you mean?

How do you know?

Sifting reality from fantasy requires a healthy skepticism—an attitude that is not cynical (doubting everything), but also not gullible (believing everything).

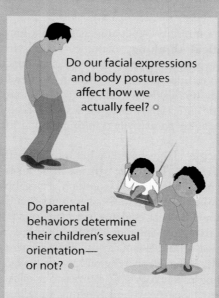

Do our facial expressions and body postures affect how we actually feel? ○

Do parental behaviors determine their children's sexual orientation— or not? ○

○ *Our facial expressions and body postures can affect how we feel.*

○ *As you will see in Chapter 5, there is not a relationship between parental behaviors and their children's sexual orientation.*

3 HUMILITY:

Researchers must be willing to be surprised and follow new ideas. People and other animals don't always behave as our ideas and beliefs would predict.

The rat is always right.

RETAIN 🔒 Study Tip: Memory research reveals a *testing effect:* We retain information much better if we actively retrieve it by self-testing and rehearsing. (More on this at the end of this chapter.) To bolster your learning and memory, take advantage of the *Retrieve It* self-tests you'll find throughout this text.

Psychology's critical inquiry can also identify effective policies. To deter crime, should we invest money in lengthening prison sentences or increase the likelihood of arrest? To help people recover from a trauma, should counselors help them relive it, or not? To increase voting, should we tell people about the low turnout problem, or emphasize that their peers are voting? When put to critical thinking's test—and contrary to common practice—the second option in each case wins (Shafir, 2013). Thinking critically can—and sometimes does—change the world.

LIFE AFTER STUDYING PSYCHOLOGY
The study of psychology, and its critical thinking strategies, have helped prepare people for varied occupations, as illustrated by Facebook founder Mark Zuckerberg (who studied psychology and computer science while in college) and actress and film producer Natalie Portman (who majored in psychology and co-authored a scientific article in college—and on one of her summer breaks was filmed for *Star Wars: Episode I*).

🔒 **RETRIEVE IT • • •**   *ANSWERS IN APPENDIX E*

RI-1 Describe what's involved in critical thinking.

PSYCHOLOGICAL SCIENCE IS BORN

LOQ 1-4   What were some important milestones in psychology's early development?

To be human is to be curious about ourselves and the world around us. Before 300 B.C.E., the Greek naturalist and philosopher Aristotle theorized about learning and memory, motivation and emotion, perception and personality. Today we chuckle at some of his guesses, like his suggestion that a meal makes us sleepy by causing gas and heat to collect around the source of our personality, the heart. But credit Aristotle with asking the right questions.

PSYCHOLOGY'S FIRST LABORATORY Philosophers' thinking about thinking continued until the birth of psychology, as we know it, on a December day in 1879, in a small, third-floor room at Germany's University of Leipzig. There, two young men were helping an austere, middle-aged professor, Wilhelm Wundt, create an experimental apparatus. Their machine measured the time it took for people to press a telegraph key after hearing a ball hit a platform (Hunt, 1993). Curiously, people responded in about one-tenth of a second when asked to press the key as soon as the sound occurred—and in about two-tenths of a second when asked to press the key as soon as they were consciously aware of perceiving the sound. (To be aware of one's awareness takes a little longer.) Wundt was seeking to measure "atoms of the mind"—the fastest and simplest mental processes. So began the first psychological laboratory, staffed by Wundt and by psychology's first graduate students.

PSYCHOLOGY'S FIRST SCHOOLS OF THOUGHT Before long, this new science of psychology became organized into different branches, or schools of thought, each promoted by pioneering thinkers. Two early schools were **structuralism** and **functionalism**. Much as chemists developed the periodic table to classify chemical elements, so psychologist Edward Bradford Titchener aimed to classify and understand elements of the mind's structure. He engaged people in self-reflective *introspection* (looking inward), training them to report elements of their experience as they looked at a rose, listened to a metronome, smelled a scent, or tasted a substance. What were their immediate sensations, their images, their feelings? And how did these relate to one another? Alas, structuralism's technique of introspection proved somewhat unreliable. It required smart, verbal people, and its results varied from person to person and experience to experience. As introspection waned, so did structuralism. Hoping to assemble the mind's structure from simple elements was rather like trying to understand a car by examining its disconnected parts.

Philosopher-psychologist William James thought it would be more fruitful to go beyond labeling our inward thoughts and feelings by considering their evolved *functions*. Smelling is what the nose does; thinking is what the brain does. But *why* do the nose and brain do these things? Under the influence of evolutionary theorist Charles Darwin, James assumed that thinking, like smelling, developed because it was *adaptive*—it helped our ancestors survive and reproduce. Consciousness serves a function. It enables us to

WILHELM WUNDT (1832–1920) Wundt established the first psychology laboratory at the University of Leipzig, Germany.

Throughout the book, information sources are cited in parentheses, with researchers' names and the date the research was published. Every citation can be found in the end-of-book References section, with complete documentation that follows American Psychological Association (APA) style.

structuralism an early school of thought promoted by Wundt and Titchener; used introspection to reveal the structure of the human mind.

functionalism an early school of thought promoted by James and influenced by Darwin; explored how mental and behavioral processes function—how they enable the organism to adapt, survive, and flourish.

EDWARD BRADFORD TITCHENER (1867–1927) Titchener used introspection to search for the mind's structural elements.

WILLIAM JAMES (1842–1910) AND MARY WHITON CALKINS (1863–1930) James was a legendary teacher-writer who authored an important 1890 psychology text. He mentored Calkins, who became a pioneering memory researcher and the first woman to be president of the American Psychological Association.

MARGARET FLOY WASHBURN (1871–1939) The first woman to receive a psychology Ph.D., Washburn synthesized animal behavior research in *The Animal Mind* (1908).

ADDRESSING DIVERSITY DEFICIENCIES At this 1964 meeting of the Society of Experimental Psychologists, Eleanor Gibson was easy to spot among the many male members, all in a sea of white faces. By contrast, women now are 55 percent of Association for Psychological Science members and 75 percent of psychology graduate students. People of color have made enormous contributions to the field (see, for example, coverage of Kenneth Clark and Mamie Phipps Clark later in this chapter), and psychology's diversity continues to grow. (For more on the history of these changes, see the Historical Timeline at the very beginning of this book).

consider our past, adjust to our present, and plan our future. To explore the mind's adaptive functions, James studied down-to-earth emotions, memories, willpower, habits, and moment-to-moment streams of consciousness. James' writings included a textbook of the new science of psychology. More than a century later, people still read his *Principles of Psychology* (1890) and marvel at the brilliance and elegance with which he introduced psychology to the educated public.

PSYCHOLOGY'S FIRST WOMEN James' legacy stems from his Harvard mentoring as well as from his writing. In 1890—thirty years before American women had the right to vote—he admitted Mary Whiton Calkins into his graduate seminar over the objections of Harvard's president (Scarborough & Furumoto, 1987). When Calkins joined, the other students (all men) dropped out. So James tutored her alone. Later, she finished all of Harvard's Ph.D. requirements, outscoring all the male students on the qualifying exams. Alas, Harvard denied her the degree she had earned, offering her instead a degree from Radcliffe College, its undergraduate "sister" school for women. Calkins resisted the unequal treatment and refused the degree. She nevertheless went on to become a distinguished memory researcher and, in 1905, the first female president of the American Psychological Association (APA).

The honor of being the first official female psychology Ph.D. later fell to Margaret Floy Washburn, who also wrote an influential book, *The Animal Mind*, and became the second female APA president in 1921. But Washburn's gender barred doors for her, too. Although her thesis was the first foreign study Wundt published in his psychology journal, she could not join the all-male organization of experimental psychologists founded

1964 meeting of the Society of Experimental Psychologists in Berkeley, California. Reprinted by permission of the Society of Experimental Psychologists. http://www.sepsych.org/1964.php

by Titchener, her own graduate adviser (Johnson, 1997). What a different world from the recent past—1997 to 2017—when women were 10 of the 20 elected presidents of the science-oriented Association for Psychological Science. In the United States, Canada, and Europe, women now earn most psychology doctorates.

🔒 **RETRIEVE IT • • •**   *ANSWERS IN APPENDIX E*

RI-2 What event defined the start of scientific psychology?

RI-3 Why did introspection fail as a method for understanding how the mind works?

RI-4 The school of _____ used introspection to define the mind's makeup; _____ focused on how mental processes enable us to adapt, survive, and flourish.

PSYCHOLOGICAL SCIENCE MATURES

LOQ 1-5 How did behaviorism, Freudian psychology, and humanistic psychology further the development of psychological science?

In psychology's early days, many psychologists shared with English essayist C. S. Lewis the view that "there is one thing, and only one in the whole universe which we know more about than we could learn from external observation." That one thing, Lewis said, is ourselves: "We have, so to speak, inside information" (1960, pp. 18–19). Wundt and Titchener focused on inner sensations, images, and feelings. James also engaged in introspective examination of the stream of consciousness and emotion, hoping to understand their adaptive functions. For these and other early pioneers, *psychology* was defined as "the science of mental life."

BEHAVIORISM That definition endured until the 1920s, when the first of two provocative American psychologists challenged it. John B. Watson, and later B. F. Skinner, dismissed introspection and redefined *psychology* as "the scientific study of observable behavior." After all, they said, science is rooted in observation: What you cannot observe and measure, you cannot scientifically study. You cannot observe a sensation, a feeling, or a thought, but you *can* observe and record people's *behavior* as they are *conditioned*—as they respond to and learn in different situations. Many agreed, and **behaviorism** was one of psychology's two major forces well into the 1960s.

FREUDIAN (PSYCHOANALYTIC) PSYCHOLOGY The second major force was Sigmund Freud's *psychoanalytic psychology,* which emphasized the ways our unconscious mind and childhood experiences affect our behavior. (In chapters to come, we'll look more closely at Freud's ideas.)

behaviorism the view that psychology (1) should be an objective science that (2) studies behavior without reference to mental processes. Most psychologists today agree with (1) but not with (2).

B. F. SKINNER (1904–1990) This leading behaviorist rejected introspection and studied how consequences shape behavior.

JOHN B. WATSON (1878–1958) AND ROSALIE RAYNER (1898–1935) Working with Rayner, Watson championed psychology as the scientific study of behavior. In a controversial study on a baby who became famous as "Little Albert," he and Rayner showed that fear could be learned. (More about this in Chapter 7.)

SIGMUND FREUD (1856–1939) The controversial ideas of this famed personality theorist and therapist have influenced humanity's self-understanding.

humanistic psychology a historically significant perspective that emphasized human growth potential.

cognitive psychology the study of mental processes, such as occur when we perceive, learn, remember, think, communicate, and solve problems.

cognitive neuroscience the interdisciplinary study of the brain activity linked with cognition (including perception, thinking, memory, and language).

psychology the science of behavior and mental processes.

nature–nurture issue the longstanding controversy over the relative contributions that genes and experience make to the development of psychological traits and behaviors. Today's science sees traits and behaviors arising from the interaction of nature and nurture.

ASK YOURSELF

How would you have defined *psychology* before taking this class?

natural selection the principle that inherited traits that better enable an organism to survive and reproduce in a particular environment will (in competition with other trait variations) most likely be passed on to succeeding generations.

evolutionary psychology the study of the evolution of behavior and the mind, using principles of natural selection.

behavior genetics the study of the relative power and limits of genetic and environmental influences on behavior.

culture the enduring behaviors, ideas, attitudes, values, and traditions shared by a group of people and transmitted from one generation to the next.

HUMANISTIC PSYCHOLOGY As the behaviorists had rejected the early 1900's definition of *psychology*, other groups rejected the behaviorists' definition. In the 1960s, **humanistic psychologists,** led by Carl Rogers and Abraham Maslow, found both behaviorism and Freudian psychology too limiting. Rather than focusing on conditioned responses or childhood memories, the humanistic psychologists focused on our needs for love and acceptance and on environments that nurture or limit personal growth.

🔒 **RETRIEVE IT • • •**   *ANSWERS IN APPENDIX E*

RI-5 From the 1920s through the 1960s, the two major forces in psychology were _____ and _____ psychology.

CONTEMPORARY PSYCHOLOGY

LOQ 1-6 How has contemporary psychology focused on cognition, on biology and experience, on culture and gender, and on human flourishing?

Simultaneous with humanistic psychology's emergence, psychologists in the 1960s pioneered a *cognitive revolution*. This led the field back to its early interest in how our mind processes and retains information. **Cognitive psychology** today continues its scientific exploration of how we perceive, process, and remember information, and of how thinking and emotion interact in anxiety, depression, and other disorders. The marriage of cognitive psychology (the science of mind) and neuroscience (the science of brain) gave birth to **cognitive neuroscience.** This specialty, with researchers in many disciplines, studies the brain activity underlying mental activity.

Today's psychology builds on the work of many earlier scientists and schools of thought. To encompass psychology's concern with observable behavior *and* with inner thoughts and feelings, we now define **psychology** as the *science of behavior and mental processes*. Let's unpack this definition. *Behavior* is anything an organism *does*—any action we can observe and record. Yelling, smiling, blinking, sweating, talking, tweeting, and questionnaire marking are all observable behaviors. *Mental processes* are our internal, subjective experiences—our sensations, perceptions, dreams, thoughts, beliefs, and feelings.

The key word in psychology's definition is *science*. Psychology is less a set of findings than a way of asking and answering questions. Our aim, then, is not merely to report results but also to show you how psychologists play their game. You will see how researchers evaluate conflicting opinions and ideas. And you will learn how all of us, whether scientists or simply curious people, can think harder and smarter when experiencing and explaining the events of our lives.

Psychology—the science of behavior and mental processes—has roots in many disciplines and countries. The young science of psychology developed from the more established fields of philosophy and biology. Wundt was both a philosopher and a physiologist. James was an American philosopher. Freud was an Austrian physician. Ivan Pavlov, who pioneered the study of learning, was a Russian physiologist. Jean Piaget, the last century's most influential observer of children, was a Swiss biologist. These "Magellans of the mind," as psychology historian Morton Hunt (1993) called them—illustrate the diversity of psychology's origins.

Like those pioneers, today's estimated 1+ million psychologists are citizens of many lands (Zoma & Gielen, 2015). The International Union of Psychological Science has 82 member nations, from Albania to Zimbabwe. Psychology is *growing* and it is *globalizing*. The story of psychology is being written in many places, with interests ranging from the study of nerve cell activity to the study of international conflicts. Contemporary psychology, shaped by many forces, is particularly influenced by our understanding of biology and experience, culture and gender, and human flourishing.

Evolutionary Psychology and Behavior Genetics

Are our human traits present at birth, or do they develop through experience? The debate over this huge **nature–nurture issue** is ancient. Greek philosopher Plato (428–348 B.C.E.) assumed that we inherit character and intelligence and that certain ideas are inborn. Aristotle (384–322 B.C.E.) countered that there is nothing in the mind that does not first come in from the external world through the senses.

A NATURE-MADE NATURE–NURTURE EXPERIMENT Identical twins have the same genes. This makes them ideal participants in studies designed to shed light on hereditary and environmental influences on personality, intelligence, and other traits. Fraternal twins have different genes but often share a similar environment. Twin studies provide a wealth of findings—described in later chapters—showing the importance of both nature and nurture.

More insight into nature's influence on behavior arose after a 22-year-old seafaring voyager, Charles Darwin, pondered the incredible species variation he encountered, including tortoises on one island that differed from those on nearby islands. Darwin's 1859 *On the Origin of Species* explained this diversity by proposing the evolutionary process of **natural selection:** From among chance variations, nature selects traits that best enable an organism to survive and reproduce in a particular environment. Darwin's principle of natural selection is still with us 150+ years later as biology's organizing principle. Evolution also has become an important principle for twenty-first-century psychology. This would surely have pleased Darwin, who believed his theory explained not only animal structures (such as a polar bear's white coat) but also animal behaviors (such as the emotional expressions associated with human lust and rage).

The nature–nurture issue recurs throughout this text as today's psychologists explore the relative contributions of biology and experience. They ask, for example, how are we humans *alike* because of our common biology and evolutionary history? That's the focus of **evolutionary psychology.** And how do we individually *differ* because of our differing genes and environments? That's the focus of **behavior genetics.**

We can, for example, ask: Are gender differences biologically predisposed or socially constructed? Is children's grammar mostly innate or formed by experience? How are intelligence and personality differences influenced by heredity, and by environment? Are sexual behaviors more "pushed" by inner biology or "pulled" by external incentives? Should we treat psychological disorders—depression, for example—as disorders of the brain, disorders of thought, or both?

Over and over again we will see that in contemporary science, the nature–nurture tension dissolves: *Nurture works on what nature provides.* Our species is biologically endowed with an enormous capacity to learn and adapt. Moreover, every psychological event (every thought, every emotion) is simultaneously a biological event. Thus, depression can be both a brain disorder *and* a thought disorder.

CHARLES DARWIN (1809–1882) Darwin argued that natural selection shapes behaviors as well as bodies.

 **ASK YOURSELF**

Think of one of your own unique traits. How do you think that trait was influenced by nature and nurture?

🔒 **RETRIEVE IT** • • •   *ANSWERS IN APPENDIX E.*

RI-6 How did the cognitive revolution affect the field of psychology?

RI-7 What is natural selection?

RI-8 What is contemporary psychology's position on the nature–nurture issue?

Cross-Cultural and Gender Psychology

What can we learn about people in general from psychological studies done in one time and place—often with participants from what some psychologists have called the WEIRD cultures (Western, Educated, Industrialized, Rich, and Democratic [Henrich et al., 2010])? As we will see time and again, **culture**—shared ideas and behaviors that one generation passes on to the next—matters. Our culture shapes our behavior. It influences our standards of promptness and frankness, our attitudes toward premarital sex and varying body shapes, our tendency to be casual or formal, our willingness to make eye contact, our conversational distance, and much, much more. Being aware of such differences, we can restrain our assumptions that others will think and act as we do.

"All people are the same; only their habits differ." —Confucius, 551–479 B.C.E.

ENGAGE **CULTURE AND KISSING** Kissing crosses cultures. Yet how we do it varies. Imagine yourself kissing someone on the lips. Do you tilt your head right or left? In Western cultures, in which people read from left to right, about two-thirds of couples kiss right, as in William and Kate's famous kiss, and in Auguste Rodin's sculpture, *The Kiss*. In one study, 77 percent of Hebrew- and Arabic-language right-to-left readers kissed tilting left (Shaki, 2013).

Mark Cuthbert/Getty Images

Hemis/Alamy

ENGAGE
 (ASK YOURSELF)

How have your cultural experiences influenced your development?

ENGAGE 📖 **LaunchPad** Our online learning tools will help you excel in this course. Take advantage of adaptive quizzing, interactive simulations, "How Would You Know?" research activities, and "Assess Your Strengths" personal self-assessments. For more information, see LaunchPadWorks.com.

📖 **LaunchPad** For an excellent tour of psychology's roots, view the 9.5-minute **Video: The History of Psychology**.

It is also true, however, that our shared biological heritage unites us as a universal human family. The same underlying processes guide people everywhere. Some examples:

- People diagnosed with specific learning disorder (formerly called dyslexia) exhibit the same brain malfunction whether they are Italian, French, or British (Paulesu et al., 2001).

- Variation in languages may impede communication across cultures. Yet all languages share deep principles of grammar, and people from different corners of the world can communicate with a smile or a frown.

- People in different cultures vary in feelings of loneliness (Lykes & Kemmelmeier, 2014). But across cultures, loneliness is magnified by shyness, low self-esteem, and being unmarried (Jones et al., 1985; Rokach et al., 2002).

We are each in certain respects like all others, like some others, and like no other. Studying people of all races and cultures helps us discern our similarities and our differences, our human kinship and our diversity.

You will see throughout this book that one's socially defined *gender* (as well as one's biologically defined *sex*) matters, too. Researchers report gender differences in what we dream, in how we express and detect emotions, and in our risk for alcohol use disorder, depression, and eating disorders. Gender differences fascinate us, and studying them is potentially beneficial. For example, many researchers have observed that women carry on conversations more readily to build relationships, while men talk more to give information and advice (Tannen, 2001). Understanding these differences can help us prevent conflicts and misunderstandings in everyday interactions.

But again, psychologically as well as biologically, women and men are overwhelmingly similar. Whether female or male, we learn to walk at about the same age. We experience the same sensations of light and sound. We remember vivid emotional events and forget mundane details. We feel the same pangs of hunger, desire, and fear. We exhibit similar overall intelligence and well-being.

The point to remember: Even when specific attitudes and behaviors vary by gender or across cultures, as they often do, the underlying processes are much the same.

Positive Psychology

Psychology's first hundred years focused on understanding and treating troubles, such as abuse and anxiety, depression and disease, prejudice and poverty. Much of today's psychology continues the exploration of such challenges. Without slighting the need to repair damage and cure disease, Martin Seligman and others (2002, 2005, 2011) have called for more research on *human flourishing*. These psychologists call their approach **positive psychology**. They believe that happiness is a by-product of a pleasant, engaged, and meaningful life. Thus, positive psychology uses scientific methods to explore the building of a "good life" that engages our skills, and a "meaningful life" that points beyond ourselves.

Psychology's Three Main Levels of Analysis

LOQ 1-7   What are psychology's levels of analysis and related perspectives?

Each of us is a complex system that is part of a larger social system. But each of us is also composed of smaller systems, such as our nervous system and body organs, which are composed of still smaller systems—cells, molecules, and atoms.

These tiered systems suggest different **levels of analysis,** which offer complementary outlooks. Consider horrific school shootings. Have they occurred because the shooters have brain disorders or genetic tendencies that cause them to be violent? Because they have observed brutality and mayhem in the media or played violent video games? Because they live in a gun-toting society? Such perspectives are complementary because "everything is related to everything else" (Brewer, 1996). Together, different levels of analysis form a

Biological influences:
- genetic *predispositions* (genetically influenced traits)
- genetic *mutations* (random errors in gene replication)
- natural selection of adaptive traits and behaviors passed down through generations
- genes responding to the environment

Psychological influences:
- learned fears and other learned expectations
- emotional responses
- cognitive processing and perceptual interpretations

Behavior or mental process

Social-cultural influences:
- presence of others
- cultural, societal, and family expectations
- peer and other group influences
- compelling models (such as in the media)

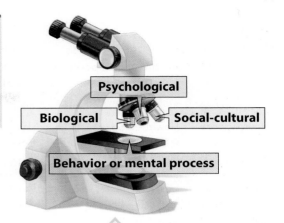

FIGURE 1.1

BIOPSYCHOSOCIAL APPROACH This integrated viewpoint incorporates various levels of analysis and offers a more complete picture of any given behavior or mental process.

biopsychosocial approach, which considers the influences of biological, psychological, and social-cultural factors (**FIGURE 1.1**).

Each level of analysis offers a perspective for looking at a behavior or mental process, yet each by itself is incomplete. Each perspective described in **TABLE 1.1** asks different questions and has its limits, but together they complement one another. Consider, for example, how they shed light on anger:

- Someone working from a *neuroscience perspective* might study brain circuits that cause us to be red in the face and "hot under the collar."

- Someone working from an *evolutionary perspective* might analyze how anger facilitated the survival of our ancestors' genes.

- Someone working from a *behavior genetics perspective* might study how heredity and experience influence our individual differences in temperament.

- Someone working from a *psychodynamic perspective* might view an outburst as an outlet for unconscious hostility.

- Someone working from a *behavioral perspective* might attempt to determine what triggers aggressive acts.

- Someone working from a *cognitive perspective* might study how our interpretation of a situation affects our anger and how our anger affects our thinking.

- Someone working from a *social-cultural perspective* might explore how expressions of anger vary across cultural contexts.

The point to remember: Like two-dimensional views of a three-dimensional object, each of psychology's perspectives is helpful. But each by itself fails to reveal the whole picture.

JUERGEN SCHWARZ/AFP/Getty Images

positive psychology the scientific study of human flourishing, with the goals of discovering and promoting strengths and virtues that help individuals and communities to thrive.

levels of analysis the differing complementary views, from biological to psychological to social-cultural, for analyzing any given phenomenon.

biopsychosocial approach an integrated approach that incorporates biological, psychological, and social-cultural levels of analysis.

ENGAGE

Which of psychology's theoretical perspectives do you find most interesting? Why?

🔒 **RETRIEVE IT** • • •   *ANSWERS IN APPENDIX E*

RI-9 What advantage do we gain by using the biopsychosocial approach in studying psychological events?

RI-10 The _____-_____ perspective in psychology focuses on how behavior and thought differ from situation to situation and from culture to culture, while the _____ perspective emphasizes observation of how we respond to and learn in different situations.

RETAIN 🔒 **TABLE 1.1**

Psychology's Theoretical Perspectives

Perspective	Focus	Sample Questions	Examples of Subfields Using This Perspective
Neuroscience	How the body and brain enable emotions, memories, and sensory experiences	How do pain messages travel from the hand to the brain? How is blood chemistry linked with moods and motives?	Biological; cognitive; clinical
Evolutionary	How the natural selection of traits has promoted the survival of genes	How does evolution influence behavior tendencies?	Biological; developmental; social
Behavior genetics	How our genes and our environment influence our individual differences	To what extent are psychological traits such as intelligence, personality, sexual orientation, and vulnerability to depression products of our genes? Of our environment?	Personality; developmental; legal/forensic
Psychodynamic	How behavior springs from unconscious drives and conflicts	How can someone's personality traits and disorders be explained by unfulfilled wishes and childhood traumas?	Clinical; counseling; personality
Behavioral	How we learn observable responses	How do we learn to fear particular objects or situations? What is the most effective way to alter our behavior, say, to lose weight or stop smoking?	Clinical; counseling; industrial-organizational
Cognitive	How we encode, process, store, and retrieve information	How do we use information in remembering? Reasoning? Solving problems?	Cognitive neuroscience; clinical; counseling; industrial-organizational
Social-cultural	How behavior and thinking vary across situations and cultures	How are we affected by the people around us, and by our surrounding culture?	Developmental; social; clinical; counseling

Psychology's Subfields

LOQ 1-8   What are psychology's main subfields?

Picturing a chemist at work, you may envision a laboratory scientist surrounded by test tubes and high-tech equipment. Picture a psychologist at work and you would be right to envision

- a white-coated scientist probing a rat's brain.

- an intelligence researcher measuring how quickly an infant shows boredom by looking away from a familiar picture.

- an executive evaluating a new "healthy lifestyles" training program for employees.

- a researcher at a computer analyzing "big data" from social media status updates or Google searches.

- a therapist actively listening to a depressed client's thoughts.

- a traveling academic visiting another culture and collecting data on variations in human values and behaviors.

- a teacher or writer sharing the joy of psychology with others.

"I'm a social scientist, Michael. That means I can't explain electricity or anything like that, but if you ever want to know about people I'm your man."

The cluster of subfields we call psychology is a meeting ground for different disciplines. Thus, it's a perfect home for those with wide-ranging interests. In its diverse activities, from biological experimentation to cultural comparisons, psychology is united by a common quest: *describing and explaining behavior and the mind underlying it.*

Some psychologists conduct **basic research** that builds psychology's knowledge base. We will meet a wide variety of such researchers, including *biological psychologists* exploring the links between brain and mind; *developmental psychologists* studying our changing abilities from womb to tomb; *cognitive psychologists* experimenting with how we perceive, think, and solve problems; *personality psychologists* investigating our persistent traits; and *social psychologists* exploring how we view and affect one another.

Ted Fitzgerald/AP Images

These and other psychologists also may conduct **applied research,** tackling practical problems. *Industrial-organizational psychologists,* for example, use psychology's concepts and methods in the workplace to help organizations and companies select and train employees, boost morale and productivity, design products, and implement systems.

Psychology is a science, but it is also a profession that helps people have healthier relationships, overcome anxiety or depression, and raise thriving children. **Counseling psychologists** help people to cope with challenges and crises (including academic, vocational, and relationship issues) and to improve their personal and social functioning. **Clinical psychologists** assess and treat people with mental, emotional, and behavior disorders. Both counseling and clinical psychologists administer and interpret tests, provide counseling and therapy, and sometimes conduct basic and applied research. By contrast, **psychiatrists,** who also may provide psychotherapy, are medical doctors licensed to prescribe drugs and otherwise treat physical causes of psychological disorders.

Rather than seeking to change people to fit their environment, **community psychologists** work to create social and physical environments that are healthy for all (Bradshaw et al., 2009; Trickett, 2009). To prevent bullying, for example, they might consider ways to improve the culture of the school and neighborhood, and how to increase bystander intervention (Polanin et al., 2012).

With perspectives ranging from the biological to the social, and with settings ranging from the laboratory to the clinic to the office, psychology relates to many fields. Psychologists teach in medical schools, business schools, law schools, and theological seminaries, and they work in hospitals, factories, and corporate offices. They engage in interdisciplinary studies, such as psychobiography (the study of the lives and personalities of public figures), psycholinguistics (the study of language and thinking), and psychoceramics (the study of crackpots).[1]

Psychology also influences culture. And psychology deepens our appreciation for how we humans perceive, think, feel, and act. By so doing it can enrich our lives and enlarge

---

1. Confession: I [DM] wrote the last part of this sentence on April Fool's Day.

PSYCHOLOGY IN COURT
Forensic psychologists apply psychology's principles and methods in the criminal justice system. They may assess witness credibility or testify in court on a defendant's state of mind and future risk.

basic research pure science that aims to increase the scientific knowledge base.

applied research a scientific study that aims to solve practical problems.

counseling psychology a branch of psychology that assists people with problems in living (often related to school, work, or marriage) and in achieving greater well-being.

clinical psychology a branch of psychology that studies, assesses, and treats people with psychological disorders.

psychiatry a branch of medicine dealing with psychological disorders; practiced by physicians who sometimes provide medical (for example, drug) treatments as well as psychological therapy.

community psychology a branch of psychology that studies how people interact with their social environments and how social institutions affect individuals and groups.

LAURENT/GLUCK/AGE Fotostock

Hope College Public Relations

Scott J. Ferrell/Getty Images

PSYCHOLOGY: A SCIENCE AND A PROFESSION
Psychologists experiment with, observe, test, and help modify behavior. Here we see psychologists testing a child, measuring emotion-related physiology, and doing face-to-face therapy.

LaunchPad Want to learn more? See Appendix C, Career Fields in Psychology, at the end of this book, and go to our online **Pursuing a Psychology Career** resource to learn about the many interesting options available to those with bachelor's, master's, and doctoral degrees in psychology. To review and test your understanding of psychology's perspectives and subfields, engage online with **Concept Practice: Psychology's Current Perspectives** and **Concept Practice: Psychology's Subfields.**

our vision. Through this book we hope to help guide you toward that end. As educator Charles Eliot said a century ago: "Books are the quietest and most constant of friends, and the most patient of teachers."

RETRIEVE IT • • •   *ANSWERS IN APPENDIX E*

RI-11 Match the specialty (I through III) with the description (a through c).

I. Clinical psychology

II. Psychiatry

III. Community psychology

a. works to create social and physical environments that are healthy for all.

b. studies, assesses, and treats people with psychological disorders but usually does not provide medical therapy.

c. is a branch of medicine dealing with psychological disorders.

REVIEW THE HISTORY AND SCOPE OF PSYCHOLOGY

Learning Objectives

TEST YOURSELF Answer these repeated Learning Objective Questions on your own (before checking the answers in Appendix D) to improve your retention of the concepts (McDaniel et al., 2009, 2015).

1-1 How is psychology a science?

1-2 What are the three key elements of the scientific attitude, and how do they support scientific inquiry?

1-3 How does critical thinking feed a scientific attitude, and smarter thinking for everyday life?

1-4 What were some important milestones in psychology's early development?

1-5 How did behaviorism, Freudian psychology, and humanistic psychology further the development of psychological science?

1-6 How has contemporary psychology focused on cognition, on biology and experience, on culture and gender, and on human flourishing?

1-7 What are psychology's levels of analysis and related perspectives?

1-8 What are psychology's main subfields?

Terms and Concepts To Remember

TEST YOURSELF Write down the definition yourself, then check your answer on the referenced page.

empirical approach, **p. 2**
critical thinking, **p. 2**
structuralism, **p. 5**
functionalism, **p. 5**
behaviorism, **p. 7**
humanistic psychology, **p. 8**
cognitive psychology, **p. 8**
cognitive neuroscience, **p. 8**

psychology, **p. 8**
nature–nurture issue, **p. 8**
natural selection, **p. 8**
evolutionary psychology, **p. 8**
behavior genetics, **p. 8**
culture, **p. 8**
positive psychology, **p. 11**
levels of analysis, **p. 11**

biopsychosocial approach, **p. 11**
basic research, **p. 13**
applied research, **p. 13**
counseling psychology, **p. 13**
clinical psychology, **p. 13**
psychiatry, **p. 13**
community psychology, **p. 13**

Experience the Testing Effect

TEST YOURSELF Answer the following questions on your own first, then check your answers in Appendix E.

1. As scientists, psychologists
   a. keep their methods private so others will not repeat their research.
   b. assume the truth of articles published in leading scientific journals.
   c. reject evidence that competes with traditional findings.
   d. are willing to ask questions and to reject claims that cannot be verified by research.

2. How can critical thinking help you evaluate claims in the media, even if you're not a scientific expert on the issue?

3. In 1879, in psychology's first experiment, _____ and his students measured the time lag between hearing a ball hit a platform and pressing a key.

4. William James would be considered a(n) _____. Wilhelm Wundt and Edward Titchener would be considered _____.
   a. functionalist; structuralists
   b. structuralist; functionalists
   c. evolutionary theorist; structuralists
   d. functionalist; evolutionary theorists

5. In the early twentieth century, _____ redefined psychology as "the science of observable behavior."
   a. John B. Watson   c. William James
   b. Abraham Maslow   d. Sigmund Freud

6. Nature is to nurture as
   a. personality is to intelligence.
   b. biology is to experience.
   c. intelligence is to biology.
   d. psychological traits are to behaviors.

7. "Nurture works on what nature provides." Describe what this means, using your own words.

8. Which of the following is true regarding gender differences and similarities?
   a. Differences between the genders outweigh any similarities.
   b. Despite some gender differences, the underlying processes of human behavior are the same.

c. Both similarities and differences between the genders depend more on biology than on environment.
d. Gender differences are so numerous that it is difficult to make meaningful comparisons.

9. Martin Seligman and other researchers who explore various aspects of human flourishing refer to their field of study as _____ _____.

10. A psychologist treating emotionally troubled adolescents at a local mental health agency is most likely to be a(n)
    a. research psychologist.
    b. psychiatrist.
    c. industrial-organizational psychologist.
    d. clinical psychologist.

11. A mental health professional with a medical degree who can prescribe medication is a _____.

12. A psychologist conducting basic research to expand psychology's knowledge base may
    a. design a computer screen with limited glare and assess the effect on computer operators' eyes after a day's work.
    b. treat older people who are overcome by depression.
    c. observe 3- and 6-year-olds solving puzzles and analyze differences in their abilities.
    d. interview children with behavioral problems and suggest treatments.

Continue testing yourself with 📖 **LearningCurve** or 📖 **Achieve Read & Practice** to learn and remember most effectively.

⤳ Research Strategies: How Psychologists Ask and Answer Questions

THE NEED FOR PSYCHOLOGICAL SCIENCE

LOQ 1-9 How does our everyday thinking sometimes lead us to a wrong conclusion?

Some people suppose that psychology is mere common sense—documenting and dressing in jargon what people already know: "You get paid for using fancy methods to prove what my grandmother knows?" Indeed, Grandma's intuition is often right. As the baseball great Yogi Berra (1925–2015) once said, "You can observe a lot by watching." (We have Berra to thank for other gems, such as "Nobody ever goes there any more—it's too crowded," and "If the people don't want to come out to the ballpark, nobody's gonna stop 'em.") Because we're all behavior watchers, it would be surprising if many of psychology's

hindsight bias the tendency to believe, after learning an outcome, that one would have foreseen it. (Also known as the *I-knew-it-all-along phenomenon*.)

"Those who trust in their own wits are fools." —Proverbs 28:26

"Life is lived forwards, but understood backwards." —Philosopher Søren Kierkegaard, 1813–1855

"Anything seems commonplace, once explained." —Dr. Watson to Sherlock Holmes

findings had *not* been foreseen. Many people believe that love breeds happiness, for example, and they are right (we have what Chapter 10 calls a deep "need to belong").

But sometimes Grandma's common sense, informed by countless casual observations, is wrong. In later chapters, we will see how research has overturned popular ideas—that familiarity breeds contempt, that dreams predict the future, and that most of us use only 10 percent of our brain. We will also see how research has surprised us with discoveries about how the brain's chemical messengers control our moods and memories, about other animals' abilities, and about the effects of stress on our capacity to fight disease.

Other things seem like commonsense truth only because we so often hear them repeated. Mere repetition of statements—whether true or false—makes them easier to process and remember, and thus more true-seeming (Dechêne at al., 2010; Fazio et al., 2015). Easy-to-remember misconceptions ("Zinc prevents the common cold") can therefore overwhelm hard truths. This power of familiar, hard-to-erase falsehoods is a lesson well known to political manipulators, and kept in mind by critical thinkers.

Three roadblocks to critical thinking—*hindsight bias, overconfidence,* and *perceiving patterns in random events*—help illustrate why we cannot rely solely on common sense.

Did We Know It All Along? Hindsight Bias

Consider how easy it is to draw the bull's-eye *after* the arrow strikes. After the stock market drops, people say it was "due for a correction." After the athletic match, we credit the coach if a "gutsy play" wins the game, and fault the coach for the "stupid play" if it doesn't. After a war or an election, its outcome usually seems obvious. Although history may therefore seem like a series of inevitable events, the actual future is seldom foreseen. No one's diary recorded, "Today the Hundred Years War began."

This **hindsight bias** (also known as the *I-knew-it-all-along phenomenon*) is easy to demonstrate by giving half the members of a group some purported psychological finding and giving the other half an opposite result. Tell the first group, for example, "Psychologists have found that separation weakens romantic attraction. As the saying goes, 'Out of sight, out of mind.'" Ask them to imagine why this might be true. Most people can, and after hearing an explanation, nearly all will then view this true finding as unsurprising.

Tell the second group the opposite: "Psychologists have found that separation strengthens romantic attraction. As the saying goes, 'Absence makes the heart grow fonder.'" People given this untrue result can also easily imagine it, and most will also see it as unsurprising. When opposite findings both seem like common sense, there is a problem.

Such errors in people's recollections and explanations show why we need psychological research. It's not that common sense is usually wrong. Rather, common sense describes, after the fact, what *has* happened better than it predicts what *will* happen.

More than 800 scholarly papers have shown hindsight bias in people young and old from across the world (Roese & Vohs, 2012). As physicist Niels Bohr reportedly jested, "Prediction is very difficult, especially about the future."

HINDSIGHT BIAS When drilling its Deepwater Horizon oil well in 2010, BP employees took shortcuts and ignored warning signs, without intending to harm any people, the environment, or their company's reputation. *After* the resulting Gulf oil spill and the death of 11 employees, with the benefit of 20/20 hindsight, the foolishness of those judgments became obvious.

Everett Collection/Newscom

Overconfidence

We humans tend to think we know more than we do. Asked how sure we are of our answers to factual questions (*Is Boston north or south of Paris?*), we tend to be more confident than correct.[2] Or consider these three anagram solutions (from Goranson, 1978):

WREAT   ⟶   WATER
ETRYN   ⟶   ENTRY
GRABE   ⟶   BARGE

About how many seconds do you think it would have taken you to unscramble each of these? Knowing the answer tends to make us overconfident. (Surely the solution would take only 10 seconds or so?) In reality, the average problem solver spends 3 minutes, as you also might, given a similar anagram without the solution: OCHSA.[3]

Are we any better at predicting social behavior? Psychologist Philip Tetlock (1998, 2005) collected more than 27,000 expert predictions of world events, such as the future of South Africa or whether Quebec would separate from Canada. His repeated finding: These predictions, which experts made with 80 percent confidence on average, were right less than 40 percent of the time. Only about 2 percent of people do an excellent job predicting social behavior. Tetlock and science writer Dan Gardner (2016) call them "superforecasters." What is a superforecaster's defining feature? A lack of overconfidence. Faced with a difficult prediction, a superforecaster "gathers facts, balances clashing arguments, and settles on an answer."

🔒 RETRIEVE IT • • •   *ANSWERS IN APPENDIX E*

RI-1 Why, after friends start dating, do we often feel that we *knew* they were meant to be together?

Perceiving Order in Random Events

We're born with an eagerness to make sense of our world. People see a face on the Moon, hear Satanic messages in music, or perceive the Virgin Mary's images on a grilled cheese sandwich. Even in random data, we often find patterns, because—here's a curious fact of life—*random sequences often don't look random* (Falk et al., 2009; Nickerson, 2002, 2005). Flip a coin 50 times and you may be surprised at the streaks of heads and tails—much like supposed "hot" and "cold" streaks in basketball shooting and baseball hitting. In actual random sequences, patterns and streaks (such as repeating digits) occur more often than people expect (Oskarsson et al., 2009). That also makes it hard for people to generate random-like sequences. When embezzlers try to simulate random digits when deciding how much to steal, their nonrandom patterns can alert fraud experts (Poundstone, 2014).

Why do we search for order in random events? For most people, a random, unpredictable world is unsettling (Tullett et al., 2015). To relieve stress, people often make connections between random events (Ma et al., 2017). Making sense of our world helps us stay calm and get on with daily living.

Some happenings, such as winning the lottery twice, seem so extraordinary that we find it difficult to conceive an ordinary, chance-related explanation. "But with a large enough sample," said statisticians Persi Diaconis and Frederick Mosteller (1989), "any outrageous thing is likely to happen." An event that happens to but 1 in 1 billion people every day occurs about 7 times a day, more than 2500 times a year.

The point to remember: Hindsight bias, overconfidence, and our tendency to perceive patterns in random events tempt us to overestimate our intuition. But scientific inquiry can help us sift reality from illusion.

📱 **LaunchPad** Play the role of a researcher using scientific inquiry to think smarter about random hot streaks in sports. Engage online with **Immersive Learning: How Would You Know If There Is a "Hot Hand" in Basketball?**

---

2. Boston is south of Paris.

3. The anagram solution: CHAOS.

BIZARRE-LOOKING, PERHAPS. But actually no more unlikely than any other number sequence.

PSYCHOLOGICAL SCIENCE IN A POST-TRUTH WORLD

LOQ 1-10 Why are we so vulnerable to believing untruths?

In 2017, the Oxford English Dictionary's word of the year was *post-truth*—describing a modern culture where people's emotions and personal beliefs often override their acceptance of objective facts. "Never," says psychology and law professor Dan Kahan (2015), "have human societies *known so much* . . . but *agreed so little* about what they collectively know." Consider two examples of widely shared misinformation:

Belief: U.S. crime rate is rising. Every recent year, 7 in 10 Americans have told Gallup that there is more crime "than there was a year ago" (Swift, 2016).

Fact: For several decades, both violent and property crime rates have been *falling.* In 2015, the violent crime rate was less than half the 1990 rate (BJS, 2017; Statista, 2017).

Belief: Many immigrants are criminals. Memorable incidents feed this narrative. Stories of an immigrant murdering, burglarizing, or lying spread through social networks and news outlets.

Fact: Most immigrants are not criminals. Compared with native-born Americans, immigrants are 44 percent *less* likely to be imprisoned (CATO, 2017).

Political party bias has distorted Americans' thinking.

- **Was unemployment up, and the stock market down under U.S. Democratic President Barack Obama?** At the end of 2016, 67 percent of Republican voters believed that unemployment increased during the Obama years, and only 41 percent said the stock market had risen (PPP, 2016). In reality, the U.S. unemployment rate during the Obama years dropped nearly in half, and the stock market more than doubled (BLS, 2017; Vardi, 2017).

- **Did inflation rise under U.S. Republican President Ronald Reagan?** At the end of the Reagan presidency, more than half of strong Democrats believed inflation had worsened under Reagan. In actuality, it had plummeted—from 13 to 4 percent (Gelman, 2009).

Indeed, psychologist Peter Ditto and his colleagues (2015) report that researchers have found "partisan bias in both liberals and conservatives, and at virtually identical levels." American Democrats discriminate against Republican candidates for college scholarships as much as Republicans discriminate against identically qualified Democratic candidates (Iyengar & Westwood, 2015). So, no Americans can smugly think, "Yes but that doesn't apply to *me*."

U.S. Democrats and Republicans share concern about failures to separate fact from fiction. In his farewell address, President Obama (2017) warned that without a "common baseline of facts," democracy is threatened: "We become so secure in our bubbles that we start accepting only information, whether it's true or not, that fits our opinions instead of basing our opinions on the evidence that is out there." Republican Senator John McCain (2017) similarly expressed alarm about "the growing inability, and even unwillingness, to separate truth from lies."

So why do post-truth era people so often, in the words of psychologist Tom Gilovich (1991), "know what isn't so?"

False news Some misinformation gets fed to us intentionally. It's "lies in the guise of news" (Kristof, 2017). And false news persists. In one analysis of 126,000 stories tweeted by 3 million people, falsehoods—especially false political news—"diffused significantly farther, faster, deeper, and more broadly than the truth" (Vosoughi et al., 2018).

Repetition In experiments, statements become more believable when they are repeated (Dechêne et al., 2010). What we hear over and over—perhaps a made-up smear of a political opponent—gets remembered and comes to seem true (Fazio et al., 2015).

Availability of powerful examples In the media, "if it bleeds it leads." Gruesome violence—a horrific murder, a mass killing, a plane crash—gets reported, with vivid images that implant in our memory and color our judgments. No wonder Americans grossly overestimate their risk of been victimized by crime, terror, and plane crashes.

"I'm sorry, Jeannie, your answer was correct, but Kevin shouted his incorrect answer over yours, so he gets the points."

"Falsehood flies, and truth comes limping after it." —Jonathan Swift, 1710

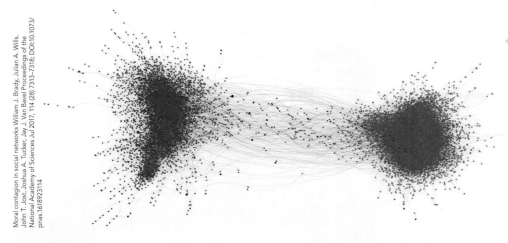

Moral contagion in social networks William J. Brady, Julian A. Wills, John T. Jost, Joshua A. Tucker, Jay J. Van Bavel Proceedings of the National Academy of Sciences Jul 2017, 114 (28) 7313–7318; DOI:10.1073/pnas.1618923114

FIGURE 1.2

THE MEETING OF LIKE MINDS On social media, most people discuss contentious issues, such as gun control, same-sex marriage, and climate change, only with like-minded others. In one Twitter analysis, users overwhelmingly sent messages to, and retweeted messages from, those who shared their liberal (blue) or conservative (red) ideology (Brady et al., 2017).

Group identity and the echo chamber of the like-minded Our social identities matter. Feeling good about our groups helps us feel good about ourselves. On social media we tend to friend people who think as we do (see **FIGURE 1.2**). We often read news sources that affirm our views and demonize news sources that do not.

The good news is that we can build a real-truth world by embracing critical thinking and a scientific mindset. By seeking information with curiosity, skepticism, and humility, we can usually know what really is so.

LaunchPad To experience my [DM's] animated walk through some important, scientific thinking strategies, view the 3.5 minute **Video: Thinking Critically in a "Post-Truth" World.**

THE SCIENTIFIC METHOD

At the foundation of all science is a scientific attitude that combines *curiosity, skepticism,* and *humility*. Psychologists arm their scientific attitude with the *scientific method*—a self-correcting process for evaluating ideas with observation and analysis. Psychological science welcomes hunches and plausible-sounding theories. And it puts them to the test. If a theory works—if the data support its predictions—so much the better for that theory. If the predictions fail, psychological scientists revise or reject the theory.

Constructing Theories

LOQ 1-11   How do theories advance psychological science?

In everyday conversation, we often use *theory* to mean "mere hunch." Someone might, for example, discount evolution as "only a theory"—as if it were mere speculation. In science, a **theory** *explains* behaviors or events by offering ideas that *organize* observations. By using deeper principles to organize isolated facts, a theory summarizes and simplifies. As we connect the observed dots, a coherent picture emerges.

A theory of how sleep affects memory, for example, helps us organize countless sleep-related observations into a short list of principles. Imagine that we observe over and over that people with good sleep habits tend to answer questions correctly in class and do well at test time. We might therefore theorize that sleep improves memory. So far so good: Our principle neatly summarizes a list of observations about the effects of a good night's sleep.

Yet no matter how reasonable a theory may sound—and it does seem reasonable to suggest that sleep boosts memory—we must put it to the test. A good theory produces testable *predictions*, called **hypotheses.** Such predictions specify what results would support the theory and what results would disconfirm it. To test our theory about sleep effects on memory, we might hypothesize that when sleep deprived, people will remember less from the day before. To test that hypothesis, we might assess how well people remember course materials they studied either before a good night's sleep or before a shortened night's sleep (**FIGURE 1.3**). The results will either support our theory or lead us to revise or reject it.

Our theories can bias our observations. Having theorized that better memory springs from more sleep, we may see what we expect: We may perceive sleepy people's comments as less accurate. The urge to see what we expect is ever-present, both inside and outside the laboratory, as when people's views of climate change influence their interpretation of local weather events.

theory an explanation using an integrated set of principles that organizes observations and predicts behaviors or events.

hypothesis a testable prediction, often implied by a theory.

FIGURE 1.3

THE SCIENTIFIC METHOD A self-correcting process for asking questions and observing nature's answers.

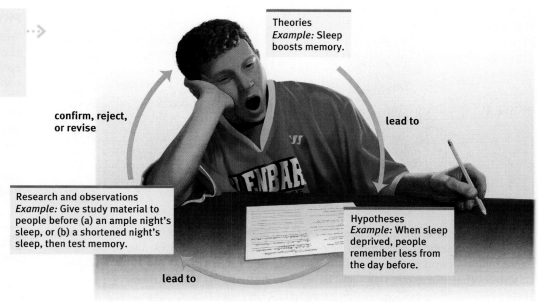

Theories
Example: Sleep boosts memory.

confirm, reject, or revise

lead to

Research and observations
Example: Give study material to people before (a) an ample night's sleep, or (b) a shortened night's sleep, then test memory.

Hypotheses
Example: When sleep deprived, people remember less from the day before.

lead to

operational definition a carefully worded statement of the exact procedures (operations) used in a research study. For example, *human intelligence* may be operationally defined as what an intelligence test measures.

replication repeating the essence of a research study, usually with different participants in different situations, to see whether the basic finding can be reproduced.

meta-analysis a statistical procedure for analyzing the results of multiple studies to reach an overall conclusion.

case study a descriptive technique in which one individual or group is studied in depth in the hope of revealing universal principles.

"Failure to replicate is not a bug; it is a feature. It is what leads us along the path—the wonderfully twisty path—of scientific discovery." —Lisa Feldman Barrett, "Psychology Is Not in Crisis," 2015

For more information about statistical methods that psychological scientists use in their work, see Appendix A, Statistical Reasoning in Everyday Life.

As a check on their own biases, psychologists report their research with precise, measureable **operational definitions** of procedures and concepts. *Sleep deprived,* for example, might be defined as "X hours less" than the person's natural sleep. Using these carefully worded statements, others can **replicate** (repeat) the original observations with different participants, materials, and circumstances. If they get similar results, confidence in the finding's reliability grows. The first study of hindsight bias aroused psychologists' curiosity. Now, after many successful replications with different people and questions, we feel sure of the phenomenon's power. Replication is confirmation.

Replication is an essential part of good science. In psychology, replication efforts have produced mixed results. One cluster of replications brought encouraging news: Only 2 of 13 experiments failed to replicate (Klein et al., 2014). But then when 270 psychologists together redid 100 psychological studies, the results were disheartening: Only 36 percent of the results were replicated (Open Science Collaboration, 2015). (None of the nonreproducible findings appears in this text.) However, another team of scientists found that most of the failed replications did not accurately recreate the original study. "The reproducibility of psychological science" is actually "quite high," they concluded (Gilbert et al., 2016). Still others argue that certain research topics and amount of researcher experience can affect replication success (Bench et al., 2017; Van Bavel et al., 2016). Despite the differing findings, most researchers agree that psychological science benefits from more replications and from greater transparency as researchers increasingly disclose their detailed methods and data (Gilmore & Adolph, 2017; Nosek et al., 2015; Open Science Collaboration, 2017).

Other fields, including genetics, behavioral neuroscience, and brain imaging, also have nonreplicated findings (Baxter & Burwell, 2017; Carter et al., 2017; Eklund et al., 2016). Especially when based on a small sample, a single failure to replicate itself needs replication (Maxwell et al., 2015). In all scientific fields, replication either confirms findings, or enables us to revise our understanding.

Psychological and medical science also harness the power of **meta-analysis.** Meta-analysis is a procedure for statistically synthesizing a body of scientific evidence. By combining the results of many studies, researchers avoid the problem of small samples and arrive at a bottom-line result.

In the end, our theory will be useful if it (1) *organizes* observations and (2) implies *predictions* that anyone can use to check the theory or to derive practical applications. (Does people's sleep predict their retention?) Eventually, our research may (3) stimulate further research that leads to a revised theory that better organizes and predicts.

As we will see next, we can test our hypotheses and refine our theories using *descriptive* methods (which describe behaviors, often through case studies, surveys, or naturalistic observations), *correlational* methods (which associate different factors), and *experimental* methods (which manipulate factors to discover their effects). To think critically about popular psychology claims, we need to understand these methods and know what conclusions they allow.

🔒 **RETRIEVE IT • • •**   *ANSWERS IN APPENDIX E*

RI-2 What does a good theory do?

RI-3 Why is replication important?

Description

LOQ 1-12 How do psychologists use case studies, naturalistic observations, and surveys to observe and describe behavior, and why is random sampling important?

The starting point of any science is description. In everyday life, we all observe and describe people, often drawing conclusions about why they think, feel, and act as they do. Professional psychologists do much the same, though more objectively and systematically, through

- *case studies* (in-depth analyses of individuals or groups).

- *naturalistic observations* (recording the natural behavior of many individuals).

- *surveys* and interviews (asking people questions).

THE CASE STUDY Among the oldest research methods, the **case study** examines one individual or group in depth in the hope of revealing things true of us all. Some examples:

- *Brain damage.* Much of our early knowledge about the brain came from case studies of individuals who suffered a particular impairment after damage to a certain brain region.

- *Children's minds.* Jean Piaget taught us about children's thinking after carefully observing and questioning only a few children.

- *Animal intelligence.* Studies of various animals, including only a few chimpanzees, have revealed their capacity for understanding and language.

Intensive case studies are sometimes very revealing, and they often suggest directions for further study.

But atypical individual cases may mislead us. Both in our everyday lives and in science, unrepresentative information can lead to mistaken conclusions. Indeed, anytime a researcher mentions a finding (*Smokers die younger: 95 percent of men over 85 are nonsmokers*) someone is sure to offer a contradictory anecdote (*Well, I have an uncle who smoked two packs a day and lived to be 89*). Dramatic stories and personal experiences (even psychological case examples) command our attention and are easily remembered. Journalists understand that and often begin their articles with compelling stories. Stories move us. But stories can mislead. Which of the following do you find more memorable? (1) "In one study of 1300 dream reports concerning a kidnapped child, only 5 percent correctly envisioned the child as dead" (Murray & Wheeler, 1937). (2) "I know a man who dreamed his sister was in a car accident, and two days later she died in a head-on collision!" Numbers can be numbing, but *the plural of anecdote is not evidence.* A single story of someone who supposedly changed from gay to straight is not evidence that sexual orientation is a choice. As psychologist Gordon Allport (1954, p. 9) said, "Given a thimbleful of [dramatic] facts we rush to make generalizations as large as as a tub."

The point to remember: Individual cases can suggest fruitful ideas. What's true of all of us can be glimpsed in any one of us. But to find those general truths, we must employ other research methods.

📺 **LaunchPad** See the **Video: Case Studies** for an animated tutorial.

Skye Hohmann/Alamy

FREUD AND LITTLE HANS Sigmund Freud's case study of 5-year-old Hans' extreme fear of horses led Freud to his theory of childhood sexuality. He conjectured that Hans felt unconscious desire for his mother, feared castration by his rival father, and then transferred this fear into his phobia about being bitten by a horse. As Chapter 13 will explain, today's psychological science discounts Freud's theory of childhood sexuality but does agree that much of the human mind operates outside our conscious awareness.

RI-4 We cannot assume that case studies always reveal general principles that apply to all of us. Why not?

"'Well my dear,' said Miss Marple, 'human nature is very much the same everywhere, and of course, one has opportunities of observing it at closer quarters in a village'." –Agatha Christie, *The Tuesday Club Murders*, 1933

NATURALISTIC OBSERVATION A second descriptive method records responses in natural environments. These **naturalistic observations** range from watching chimpanzee societies in the jungle, to videotaping and analyzing parent-child interactions in different cultures, to recording racial differences in students' self-seating patterns in a school lunchroom.

Naturalistic observation has mostly been "small science"—science that can be done with pen and paper rather than fancy equipment and a big budget (Provine, 2012). But new technologies, such as smart-phone apps, body-worn sensors, and social media, are enabling "big data" observations. Using such tools, researchers can track people's location, activities, and opinions—without interference. Want to keep track of how often people go to the gym, a cafe, or the library? All you need is access to their phone's global positioning system (GPS) (Harari et al., 2016). The billions of people on Facebook, Twitter, and Google have also created a huge new opportunity for big-data naturalistic observation. One research team studied the ups and downs of human moods by counting positive and negative words in 504 million Twitter messages from 84 countries (Golder & Macy, 2011). As **FIGURE 1.4** shows, people seem happier on weekends, shortly after waking, and in the evenings. (Are late Saturday evenings often a happy time for you, too?) Another study found that negative emotion (especially anger-related) words in 148 million tweets from 1347 U.S. counties predicted the counties' heart disease rates better than other predictors such as smoking and obesity rates (Eichstaedt et al., 2015). Google data—on the words people search and the questions they ask—can pinpoint a geographical area's level of racism and depression (Stephens-Davidowitz, 2017).

Like the case study, naturalistic observation does not *explain* behavior. It *describes* it. Nevertheless, descriptions can be revealing. We once thought, for example, that only humans use tools. Then naturalistic observation revealed that chimpanzees sometimes insert a stick in a termite mound and withdraw it, eating the stick's load of termites. Such unobtrusive naturalistic observations paved the way for later studies of animal thinking, language, and emotion, which further expanded our understanding of our fellow animals. Thanks to researchers' observations, we know that chimpanzees and baboons use deception: Psychologists repeatedly saw one young baboon pretending to have been attacked by another as a tactic to get its mother to drive the other baboon away from its food (Byrne & Whiten, 1988; Whiten & Byrne, 1988).

Naturalistic observations also illuminate human behavior. Here are two findings you might enjoy:

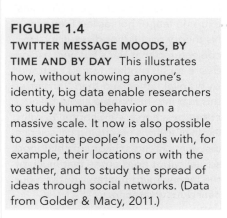

FIGURE 1.4

TWITTER MESSAGE MOODS, BY TIME AND BY DAY This illustrates how, without knowing anyone's identity, big data enable researchers to study human behavior on a massive scale. It now is also possible to associate people's moods with, for example, their locations or with the weather, and to study the spread of ideas through social networks. (Data from Golder & Macy, 2011.)

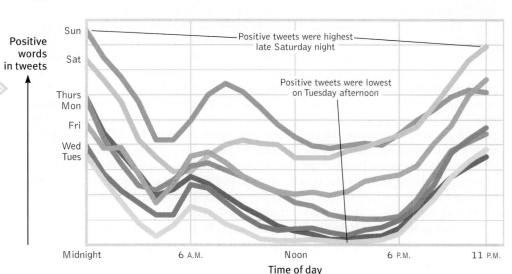

- *A funny finding* We humans laugh 30 times more often in social situations than in solitary situations (Provine, 2001). (Have you noticed how seldom you laugh when alone?)

- *Culture and the pace of life* Naturalistic observation also enabled Robert Levine and Ara Norenzayan (1999) to compare the pace of life—walking speed, accuracy of public clocks, and so forth—in 31 countries. Their conclusion: Life is fastest paced in Japan and Western Europe and slower paced in economically less-developed countries.

Naturalistic observation offers interesting snapshots of everyday life, but it does so without controlling for all the factors that may influence behavior. It's one thing to observe the pace of life in various places, but another to understand what makes some people walk faster than others. Nevertheless, descriptions can be revealing: The starting point of any science is description.

THE SURVEY A **survey** looks at many cases in less depth, asking people to report their behavior or opinions. Questions about everything from sexual practices to political opinions are put to the public. In recent surveys:

- Compared with those born in the 1960s and 1970s, twice as many millennials born in the 1990s reported having no sexual partners since age 18 (Twenge et al., 2017).

- 1 in 5 people across 22 countries report believing that alien beings have come to Earth and now walk among us disguised as humans (Ipsos, 2010).

- 68 percent of all humans—some 4.6 billion people—say that religion is important in their daily lives (Diener et al., 2011).

But asking questions is tricky, and the answers often depend on how questions are worded and how respondents are chosen.

MICHAEL NICHOLS/National Geographic Creative

A NATURAL OBSERVER
"Observations, made in the natural habitat," noted chimpanzee observer Jane Goodall (1998), "helped to show that the societies and behavior of animals are far more complex than previously supposed."

LaunchPad See the **Video: Naturalistic Observation** for a helpful tutorial animation.

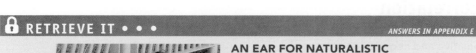

RETRIEVE IT • • •   *ANSWERS IN APPENDIX E*

Courtesy of Matthias Mehl

AN EAR FOR NATURALISTIC OBSERVATION Psychologists Matthias Mehl and James Pennebaker have used electronically activated recorders (EARs) to sample naturally occurring slices of daily life.

RI-5 What are the advantages and disadvantages of naturalistic observation, such as Mehl and his colleagues used in this study?

naturalistic observation a descriptive technique of observing and recording behavior in naturally occurring situations without trying to manipulate and control the situation.

survey a descriptive technique for obtaining the self-reported attitudes or behaviors of a particular group, usually by questioning a representative, *random sample* of the group.

WORDING EFFECTS Even subtle changes in the order or wording of questions can have major effects. People are much more approving of "aid to the needy" than of "welfare," of "affirmative action" than of "preferential treatment," of "not allowing" televised pornography than of "censoring" it, of "gun safety" laws than of "gun control" laws, and of "revenue enhancers" than of "taxes." Because wording is such a delicate matter, critical thinkers will reflect on how the phrasing of a question might affect people's expressed opinions.

RANDOM SAMPLING In everyday thinking, we tend to generalize from samples we observe, especially vivid cases. An administrator who reads (a) a statistical summary of a professor's student evaluations and (b) the vivid comments of two irate students may be influenced as much by the biased sample of two unhappy students as by the many favorable evaluations in the statistical summary. The temptation to succumb to the *sampling bias*—to generalize from a few vivid but unrepresentative cases—is nearly irresistible.

So how do you obtain a *representative sample?* Say you want to learn how students at your college or university feel about a proposed tuition increase. It's often not possible to survey the whole group. How then could you choose a group that would represent the total student body? Typically, you would seek a **random sample,** in which every person in the entire **population** has an equal chance of being included in the sample group. You might number the names in the general student listing and then use a random number generator to pick your survey participants. (Sending each student a questionnaire wouldn't work because the conscientious people who returned it would not be a random sample.) Large representative samples are better than small ones, but a smaller representative sample of 100 is better than a larger unrepresentative sample of 500.

Political pollsters sample voters in national election surveys just this way. Using some 1500 randomly sampled people, drawn from all areas of a country, they can provide a remarkably accurate snapshot of the nation's opinions. Without random sampling, large samples—including unrepresentative call-in phone samples and TV or website polls—often give misleading results.

The point to remember: Before accepting survey findings, think critically. Consider the sample. The best basis for generalizing is from a representative sample. You cannot compensate for an unrepresentative sample by simply adding more people.

> 🔒 **RETRIEVE IT** • • •   *ANSWERS IN APPENDIX E*
>
> **RI-6** What is an unrepresentative sample, and how do researchers avoid it?

With very large samples, estimates become quite reliable. *E* is estimated to represent 12.7 percent of the letters in written English. *E*, in fact, is 12.3 percent of the 925,141 letters in Melville's *Moby-Dick*, 12.4 percent of the 586,747 letters in Dickens' *A Tale of Two Cities*, and 12.1 percent of the 3,901,021 letters in 12 of Mark Twain's works (*Chance News*, 1997).

random sample a sample that fairly represents a population because each member has an equal chance of inclusion.

population all those in a group being studied, from which samples may be drawn. (*Note:* Except for national studies, this does not refer to a country's whole population.)

correlation a measure of the extent to which two factors vary together, and thus of how well either factor predicts the other.

correlation coefficient a statistical index of the relationship between two things (from –1.00 to +1.00).

Correlation

LOQ 1-13 What does it mean when we say two things are correlated, and what are positive and negative correlations?

Describing behavior is a first step toward predicting it. Naturalistic observations and surveys often show us that one trait or behavior tends to coincide with another. In such cases, we say the two **correlate.** A statistical measure (the **correlation coefficient**) helps us figure how closely two things vary together, and thus how well either one *predicts* the other. Knowing how much aptitude test scores *correlate* with school success tells us how well the scores *predict* school success.

A *positive correlation* (above 0 to +1.00) indicates a *direct* relationship, meaning that two things increase together or decrease together. For example, height and weight are positively correlated.

A *negative correlation* (below 0 to –1.00) indicates an *inverse* relationship: As one thing increases, the other decreases. The weekly number of hours spent in TV watching and video gaming correlates negatively with grades. Negative correlations could go as low as –1.00, which means that, like people on opposite ends of a teeter-totter, one set of scores goes down precisely as the other goes up.

Though informative, psychology's correlations usually explain only part of the variation among individuals. As we will see, there is a positive correlation between parents' abusiveness and their children's later abusiveness when they become parents. But this does not mean that most abused children become abusive. The correlation simply indicates a statistical relationship: Most abused children do not grow into abusers, but nonabused children are even less likely to become abusive. Correlations point us toward predictions, but usually imperfect ones.

Other times correlations can lead us astray. Just because two things vary together doesn't mean they cause each other. Consider the strong positive correlation ($r = +0.79$) between chocolate consumption in 23 countries and their number of Nobel laureates (Messerli, 2012). Eating more chocolate will not cause a country to have more Nobel laureates. But for whatever reason, chocolate-loving countries have knowledge-loving Nobel laureates.

The point to remember: A correlation coefficient helps us see the world more clearly by revealing the extent to which two things relate. But correlational research, although it helpfully reveals relationships, cannot explain them. See Thinking Critically About: Correlation and Causation.

LaunchPad For an animated tutorial on correlations, engage online with **Concept Practice: Positive and Negative Correlations.** See also the **Video: Correlational Studies** for another helpful tutorial animation.

🔒 RETRIEVE IT • • •

ANSWERS IN APPENDIX E

RI-7 Indicate whether each association is a positive correlation or a negative correlation.

a. The more husbands viewed internet pornography, the worse their marital relationships (Muusses et al., 2015). _____

b. The less sexual content teens saw on TV, the less likely they were to have sex (Collins et al., 2004). _____

c. The longer children were breast-fed, the greater their later academic achievement (Horwood & Fergusson, 1998). _____

d. The more income rose among a sample of poor families, the fewer psychiatric symptoms their children experienced (Costello et al., 2003). _____

Experimentation

LOQ 1-15 What are the characteristics of experimentation that make it possible to isolate cause and effect?

Happy are they, remarked the Roman poet Virgil, "who have been able to perceive the causes of things." How might psychologists sleuth out the causes in correlational studies, such as the correlation between breast feeding and intelligence?

EXPERIMENTAL MANIPULATION Some researchers (not all) have found that breast-fed infants develop higher childhood intelligence scores than do bottle-fed babies—an average 3 test-point difference in a review of 17 studies (Horta et al., 2015; von Stumm & Plomin, 2015; Walfisch et al., 2014). Moreover, the longer infants breast-feed, the higher their later intelligence test scores (Jedrychowski et al., 2012; Victora et al., 2015).

What do such findings mean? Do the nutrients of mother's milk contribute to brain development? Or do smarter mothers have smarter children? (Breast-fed children tend to be healthier and higher achieving than other children. But their bottle-fed siblings, born and raised in the same families, tend to be similarly healthy and high achieving [Colen & Ramey, 2014].) Even big data from a million or a billion mothers and their offspring couldn't tell us. To find answers to such questions—to isolate cause and effect—researchers must **experiment.** Experiments enable researchers to isolate the effects of one or more factors by (1) *manipulating the factors of interest* and (2) *holding constant (controlling) other factors.* To do so, they often create an **experimental group,** in which people receive the treatment, and a contrasting **control group** that does not receive the treatment. To minimize any preexisting differences between the two groups, researchers **randomly assign** people to the two conditions. Random assignment—whether with a random numbers table or flip of the coin—effectively equalizes the two groups. If one-third of the volunteers for

experiment a research method in which an investigator manipulates one or more factors (independent variables) to observe the effect on some behavior or mental process (the dependent variable). By *random assignment* of participants, the experimenter aims to control other relevant factors.

experimental group in an experiment, the group exposed to the treatment, that is, to one version of the independent variable.

control group in an experiment, the group *not* exposed to the treatment; contrasts with the experimental group and serves as a comparison for evaluating the effect of the treatment.

random assignment assigning participants to experimental and control groups by chance, thus minimizing preexisting differences between the different groups.

THINKING CRITICALLY ABOUT:

Correlation and Causation

LOQ 1-14   Why do correlations enable prediction but not cause-effect explanation?

Mental illness *correlates* with smoking—meaning that those who experience mental illness are also more likely to be smokers.[1] Does this tell us anything about what *causes* mental illness or smoking? **NO.**

There may be something about smoking that leads to mental illness.

Those with mental illness may be more likely to smoke.

OR

There may be some *third variable*, such as a stressful home life, for example, that triggers *both* smoking and mental illness.

So, then, how would you interpret these recent findings:
  a) sexual hook-ups correlate with college women's experiencing depression, and
  b) *delaying* sexual intimacy
correlates with positive outcomes such as greater relationship satisfaction and stability?[2]

Possible explanations:

1. Sexual restraint	→ Better mental health and stronger relationships
2. Depression	→ People being more likely to hook up
3. Some third factor, such as lower impulsivity	→ Sexual restraint, psychological well-being, and better relationships

Correlations do help us predict. Consider: Self-esteem correlates negatively with (and therefore predicts) depression. The lower people's self-esteem, the greater their risk for depression.

Possible interpretations:

1. Low self-esteem	→ Depression
2. Depression	→ Low self-esteem
3. Some third factor, such as distressing events or biological predisposition	→ Both low self-esteem and depression

You try it!
A survey of over 12,000 adolescents found that the more teens feel loved by their parents, the less likely they are to behave in unhealthy ways—having early sex, smoking, abusing alcohol and drugs, exhibiting violence.[3] What are three possible ways we could interpret that finding?[4]

The point to remember: **Correlation does not prove causation.**
Correlation suggests a possible cause-effect relationship but does not prove it. Remember this principle and you will be wiser as you read and hear news of scientific studies.

1. Belluck, 2013. 2. Fielder et al., 2013; Willoughby et al., 2014. 3. Resnick et al., 1997. 4. *ANSWERS:* a. Parental love may produce healthy teens. b. Well-behaved teens may feel more parental love and approval. c. Some third factor, such as income or neighborhood, may influence both parental love AND teen behaviors.

Nancy Brown/Getty Images

🔒 **RETRIEVE IT • • •**   ANSWERS IN APPENDIX E

RI-8 Length of marriage positively correlates with hair loss in men. Does this mean that marriage causes men to lose their hair (or that balding men make better husbands)?

an experiment can wiggle their ears, then about one-third of the people in each group will be ear wigglers. So, too, with ages, attitudes, and other characteristics, which will be similar in the experimental and control groups. Thus, if the groups differ at the experiment's end, we can surmise that the treatment had an effect. (Note the difference between random *sampling*—which creates a representative survey sample—and random *assignment,* which equalizes the experimental and control groups.)

To experiment with breast feeding, one research team randomly assigned some 17,000 Belarus newborns and their mothers either to a control group given normal pediatric care, or to an experimental group that promoted breast feeding, thus increasing expectant mothers' breast intentions (Kramer et al., 2008). At 3 months of age, 43 percent of the experimental group infants were being exclusively breast-fed, as were 6 percent in the control group. At age 6, when nearly 14,000 of the children were restudied, those who had been in the breast-feeding-promotion group had intelligence test scores averaging 6 points higher than their control condition counterparts.

With parental permission, one British research team directly experimented with breast milk. They randomly assigned 424 hospitalized premature infants either to formula feedings or to breast-milk feedings (Lucas et al., 1992). Their finding: On intelligence tests taken at age 8, those nourished with breast milk scored significantly higher than those who were formula-fed. Breast was best.

No single experiment is conclusive, of course. But randomly assigning participants to one feeding group or the other effectively eliminated all factors except nutrition. If test performance changes when we vary infant nutrition, then we infer that nutrition matters.

Lane Oatey/Getty Images

The point to remember: Unlike correlational studies, which uncover naturally occurring relationships, an experiment manipulates a factor to determine its effect.

PROCEDURES AND THE PLACEBO EFFECT Consider, then, how we might assess therapeutic interventions. Our tendency to seek new remedies when we are ill or emotionally down can produce misleading testimonies. If three days into a cold we start taking zinc tablets and find our cold symptoms lessening, we may credit the pills rather than the cold naturally subsiding. In the 1700s, bloodletting *seemed* effective. People sometimes improved after the treatment; when they didn't, the practitioner inferred the disease was too advanced to be reversed. So, whether or not a remedy is truly effective, enthusiastic users will probably endorse it. To determine its effect, we must control for other factors.

And that is precisely how new drugs and new methods of psychological therapy are evaluated (Chapter 15). Investigators randomly assign participants in these studies to research groups. One group receives a treatment (such as an antidepressant medication). The other group receives a pseudotreatment—an inert *placebo* (perhaps a pill with no drug in it). The participants are often *blind* (uninformed) about what treatment, if any, they are receiving. If the study is using a **double-blind procedure,** neither the participants nor those who administer the drug and collect the data will know which group is receiving the treatment.

In double-blind studies, researchers check a treatment's actual effects apart from the participants' and the staff's belief in its healing powers. Just *thinking* you are getting a treatment can boost your spirits, relax your body, and relieve your symptoms. This **placebo effect** is well documented in reducing pain, depression, anxiety, and auditory hallucinations in schizophrenia (Dollfus et al., 2016; Kirsch, 2010). Athletes have run faster when given a supposed performance-enhancing drug (McClung & Collins, 2007). Decaf-coffee drinkers have reported increased vigor and alertness—when they thought their brew had caffeine in it (Dawkins et al., 2011). People have felt better after receiving a phony mood-enhancing drug (Michael et al., 2012). And the more expensive the placebo, the more "real" it seems to us—a fake pill that costs $2.50 works better than one costing 10 cents (Waber et al., 2008). To know how effective a therapy really is, researchers must control for a possible placebo effect.

RETAIN 🔒 Recall that in a well-done survey, *random sampling* is important. In an experiment, *random assignment* is equally important.

📖 **LaunchPad** See the **Video: Random Assignment** for a tutorial animation.

double-blind procedure an experimental procedure in which both the research participants and the research staff are ignorant (blind) about whether the research participants have received the treatment or a placebo. Commonly used in drug-evaluation studies.

placebo [pluh-SEE-bo; Latin for "I shall please"] **effect** experimental results caused by expectations alone; any effect on behavior caused by the administration of an inert substance or condition, which the recipient assumes is an active agent.

"If I don't think it's going to work, will it still work?"

independent variable in an experiment, the factor that is manipulated; the variable whose effect is being studied.

confounding variable in an experiment, a factor other than the factor being studied that might influence a study's results.

dependent variable in an experiment, the outcome that is measured; the variable that may change when the independent variable is manipulated.

A similar experiment on a drug approved to increase women's sexual arousal produced a result described as, um, anticlimactic—an additional "half of one satisfying sexual encounter a month" (Ness, 2016; Tavernise, 2016).

"[We must guard] against not just racial slurs, but . . . against the subtle impulse to call Johnny back for a job interview, but not Jamal."
—U.S. President Barack Obama, Eulogy for Clementa Pinckney, June 26, 2015

🔒 RETRIEVE IT • • •

ANSWERS IN APPENDIX E

RI-9 What measures do researchers use to prevent the *placebo effect* from confusing their results?

INDEPENDENT AND DEPENDENT VARIABLES Here is an even more potent example: The drug Viagra was approved for use after 21 clinical trials. One trial was an experiment in which researchers randomly assigned 329 men with erectile disorder to either an experimental group (Viagra takers) or a control group (placebo takers given an identical-looking pill). The procedure was double-blind—neither the men nor the person giving them the pills knew what they were receiving. The result: At peak doses, 69 percent of Viagra-assisted attempts at intercourse were successful, compared with 22 percent for men receiving the placebo (Goldstein et al., 1998). Viagra performed.

This simple experiment manipulated just one factor: the drug (Viagra versus no Viagra). We call this experimental factor the **independent variable** because we can vary it *independently* of other factors, such as the men's age, weight, and personality. Other factors that can potentially influence a study's results are called **confounding variables.** Random assignment controls for possible confounding variables.

Experiments examine the effect of one or more independent variables on some measurable behavior, called the **dependent variable** because it can vary *depending* on what takes place during the experiment. Both variables are given precise *operational definitions,* which specify the procedures that manipulate the independent variable (the exact drug dosage and timing in this study) or measure the dependent variable (the men's responses to questions about their sexual performance). These definitions answer the "What do you mean?" question with a level of precision that enables others to replicate the study. (See **FIGURE 1.5** for the British breast milk experiment's design.)

🔒 Let's pause to check your understanding using a simple psychology experiment: To test the effect of perceived ethnicity on the availability of rental housing, Adrian Carpusor and William Loges (2006) sent identically worded email inquiries to 1115 Los Angeles-area landlords. The researchers varied the ethnic connotation of the sender's name and tracked the percentage of positive replies (invitations to view the apartment in person). "Patrick McDougall," "Said Al-Rahman," and "Tyrell Jackson" received, respectively, 89 percent, 66 percent, and 56 percent invitations. In this experiment, what was the independent variable? What was the dependent variable?[4]

Experiments can also help us evaluate social programs. Do early childhood education programs boost impoverished children's chances for success? What are the effects of different antismoking campaigns? Do school sex-education programs reduce teen pregnancies? To answer such questions, we can experiment: If an intervention is welcomed but resources are scarce, we could use a lottery to randomly assign some people (or regions) to experience the new program and others to a control condition. If later the two groups differ, the intervention's effect will be supported (Passell, 1993).

---

4. The independent variable, which the researchers manipulated, was the implied ethnicity of the applicants' names. The dependent variable, which the researchers measured, was the rate of positive responses from the landlords.

FIGURE 1.5

EXPERIMENTATION To discern causation, psychologists control for confounding variables by randomly assigning some participants to an experimental group, others to a control group. Measuring the dependent variable (later intelligence test score) will determine the effect of the independent variable (type of milk).

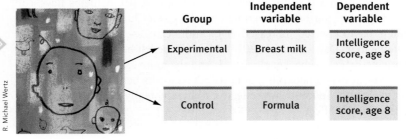

Random assignment (controlling for other confounding variables such as parental intelligence and environment)

Group	Independent variable	Dependent variable
Experimental	Breast milk	Intelligence score, age 8
Control	Formula	Intelligence score, age 8

R. Michael Wertz

Let's recap. A *variable* is anything that can vary (infant nutrition, intelligence, TV exposure—anything within the bounds of what is feasible and ethical). Experiments aim to *manipulate* an *independent* variable, *measure* a *dependent* variable, and control *confounding* variables. An experiment has at least two different conditions: an *experimental condition* and a *comparison* or *control condition*. *Random assignment* works to minimize preexisting differences between the groups before any treatment effects occur. In this way, an experiment tests the effect of at least one independent variable (what we manipulate) on at least one dependent variable (the outcome we measure).

LaunchPad See the **Videos: Experiments** and **Confounding Variables** for helpful tutorial animations.

🔒 **RETRIEVE IT • • •**   *ANSWERS IN APPENDIX E*

RI-10 By using *random assignment*, researchers are able to control for _____ _____, which are other factors besides the independent variable(s) that may influence research results.

RI-11 Match the term (I through III) with the description (a through c).

I.	Double-blind procedure	a. helps researchers generalize from a small set of survey responses to a larger population.
II.	Random sampling	b. helps minimize preexisting differences between experimental and control groups.
III.	Random assignment	c. controls for the placebo effect; neither researchers nor participants know who receives the real treatment.

RI-12 Why, when testing a new drug to control blood pressure, would we learn more about its effectiveness from giving it to half the participants in a group of 1000 than to all 1000 participants?

Research Design

LOQ 1-16   How would you know which research design to use?

Throughout this book, you will read about amazing psychological science discoveries. But how do we know fact from fiction? How do psychological scientists choose research methods and design their studies in ways that provide meaningful results? Understanding how research is done—how testable questions are developed and studied—is key to appreciating all of psychology. **TABLE 1.2** compares the features of psychology's main research methods. In later chapters, you will read about other research designs, including *twin studies* (Chapter 2) and *cross-sectional* and *longitudinal research* (Chapter 9).

In psychological research, no questions are off limits, except untestable (or unethical) ones: Does free will exist? Are people born evil? Is there an afterlife? Psychologists can't test those questions. But they *can* test whether free will beliefs, aggressive personalities, and a belief in life after death influence how people think, feel, and act (Dechesne et al., 2003; Shariff et al., 2014; Webster et al., 2014).

🔒 **TABLE 1.2**

Comparing Research Methods

Research Method	Basic Purpose	How Conducted	What Is Manipulated	Weaknesses
Descriptive	To observe and record behavior	Do case studies, naturalistic observations, or surveys	Nothing	No control of variables; single cases may be misleading
Correlational	To detect naturally occurring relationships; to assess how well one variable predicts another	Collect data on two or more variables; no manipulation	Nothing	Cannot specify cause and effect
Experimental	To explore cause and effect	Manipulate one or more factors; use random assignment	The independent variable(s)	Sometimes not feasible; results may not generalize to other contexts; not ethical to manipulate certain variables

ASK YOURSELF

If you could conduct a study on any psychological question, which would you choose? How would you do it?

To help you build your understanding, your critical thinking, and your *scientific literacy skills,* we created online Immersive Learning research activities. In these "How Would You Know?" activities, you get to play the role of the researcher, making choices about the best ways to test interesting questions. Some examples: How Would You Know If Having Children Relates to Being Happier?, How Would You Know If a Cup of Coffee Can Warm Up Relationships?, and How Would You Know If People Can Learn to Reduce Anxiety?

☒ LaunchPad To review and test your understanding of research methods, engage online with **Concept Practice: Psychology's Research Methods** and **The Language of Experiments,** and the interactive **Topic Tutorial: PsychSim6, Understanding Psychological Research.** For a 9.5-minute video synopsis of psychology's scientific research strategies, see the **Video: Research Methods.**

☒ LaunchPad See the **Video: Research Ethics** for a helpful tutorial animation.

Having chosen their question, psychologists then select the most appropriate research design—*experimental, correlational, case study, naturalistic observation, twin study, longitudinal,* or *cross-sectional*—and determine how to set it up most effectively. They consider how much money and time are available, ethical issues, and other limitations. For example, it wouldn't be ethical for a researcher studying child development to use the experimental method and randomly assign children to loving versus punishing homes.

Next, psychological scientists decide how to measure the behavior or mental process being studied. For example, researchers could measure aggressive behavior by measuring participants' willingness to blast a stranger with supposed intense noise.

Researchers want to have confidence in their findings, so they carefully consider confounding variables—factors other than those being studied that may affect their interpretation of results.

Psychological research is a creative adventure. Researchers *design* each study, *measure* target behaviors, *interpret* results, and learn more about the fascinating world of behavior and mental processes along the way.

Predicting Everyday Behavior

LOQ 1-17   How can simplified laboratory conditions illuminate everyday life?

When you see or hear about psychological research, do you ever wonder whether people's behavior in the lab will predict their behavior in real life? Does detecting the blink of a faint red light in a dark room say anything useful about flying a plane at night? After viewing a violent, sexually explicit film, does an aroused man's increased willingness to push buttons that he thinks will deliver a noise blast to a woman really say anything about whether viewing violent pornography makes a man more likely to abuse a woman?

Before you answer, consider: The experimenter *intends* the laboratory environment to be a simplified reality—one that simulates and controls important features of everyday life. Just as a wind tunnel lets airplane designers re-create airflow forces under controlled conditions, a laboratory experiment lets psychologists re-create psychological forces under controlled conditions.

An experiment's purpose is not to re-create the exact behaviors of everyday life, but to test *theoretical principles* (Mook, 1983). In aggression studies, deciding whether to push a button that delivers a noise blast may not be the same as slapping someone in the face, but the principle is the same. It is the *resulting principles—not the specific findings—that help explain everyday behaviors.*

When psychologists apply laboratory research on aggression to actual violence, they are applying theoretical principles of aggressive behavior, principles refined through many experiments. Similarly, it is the principles of the visual system, developed from experiments in artificial settings (such as looking at red lights in the dark), that researchers apply to more complex behaviors such as night flying. And many investigations show that principles derived in the laboratory typically generalize to the everyday world (Mitchell, 2012).

The point to remember: Psychological science focuses less on specific behaviors than on revealing general principles that help explain many behaviors.

PSYCHOLOGY'S RESEARCH ETHICS

LOQ 1-18   Why do psychologists study animals, and what ethical guidelines safeguard human and animal research participants? How do psychologists' values influence psychology?

We have reflected on how a scientific approach can restrain biases. We have seen how case studies, naturalistic observations, and surveys help us describe behavior. We have also noted that correlational studies assess the association between two factors, showing how well one predicts another. We have examined the logic that underlies experiments, which use control conditions and random assignment of participants to isolate the causal effects of an independent variable on a dependent variable.

Yet, even knowing this much, you may still be approaching psychology with a mixture of curiosity and apprehension. So before we plunge in, let's entertain some common questions about psychology's ethics and values.

Protecting Research Participants

STUDYING AND PROTECTING ANIMALS Many psychologists study nonhuman animals because they find them fascinating. They want to understand how different species learn, think, and behave. Psychologists also study animals to learn about people. We humans are not *like* animals; we *are* animals, sharing a common biology. Animal experiments have therefore led to treatments for human diseases—insulin for diabetes, vaccines to prevent polio and rabies, transplants to replace defective organs.

Humans are complex. But some of the same processes by which we learn are present in rats, monkeys, and even sea slugs. The simplicity of the sea slug's nervous system is precisely what makes it so revealing of the neural mechanisms of learning. Ditto for the honeybee, which resembles us humans in how it learns to cope with stress (Dinges et al., 2017).

Sharing such similarities, should we not respect our animal relatives? The animal protection movement protests the use of animals in psychological, biological, and medical research.

Out of this heated debate, two issues emerge. The basic one is whether it is right to place the well-being of humans above that of other animals. In experiments on stress and cancer, is it right that mice get tumors in the hope that people might not? Should some monkeys be exposed to an HIV-like virus in the search for an AIDS vaccine? Humans raise and slaughter 56 billion animals a year—a rate expected to double by 2050 (Worldwatch Institute, 2017). Is our use and consumption of other animals as natural as the behavior of carnivorous hawks, cats, and whales?

For those who give human life top priority, a second question emerges: What safeguards should protect the well-being of animals in research? One survey of animal researchers gave an answer. Some 98 percent supported government regulations protecting primates, dogs, and cats, and 74 percent also supported regulations providing for the humane care of rats and mice (Plous & Herzog, 2000). Many professional associations and funding agencies already have such guidelines. British Psychological Society (BPS) guidelines call for housing animals under reasonably natural living conditions, with companions for social animals (Lea, 2000). American Psychological Association (APA) guidelines state that researchers must provide "humane care and healthful conditions" and that testing should "minimize discomfort" (APA, 2012). The European Parliament also mandates standards for animal care and housing (Vogel, 2010). Most universities screen research proposals, often through an animal care ethics committee, and laboratories are regulated and inspected.

Animals have themselves benefited from animal research. One Ohio team of research psychologists measured stress hormone levels in samples of millions of dogs brought each year to animal shelters. They devised handling and stroking methods to reduce stress and ease the dogs' transition to adoptive homes (Tuber et al., 1999). Other studies have helped improve care and management in animals' natural habitats. By revealing our behavioral kinship with animals and the remarkable intelligence of chimpanzees, gorillas, and other animals, experiments have also led to increased empathy and protection for them. At its best, a psychology concerned for humans and sensitive to animals serves the welfare of both.

STUDYING AND PROTECTING HUMANS What about human participants? Does the image of white-coated scientists seeming to deliver electric shocks trouble you? Actually, most psychological studies are free of such stress. Blinking lights, flashing words, and pleasant social interactions are more common. Moreover, psychology's experiments are mild compared with the stress and humiliation often inflicted in reality TV "experiments." In two episodes of *The Bachelor*, a man dumped his new fiancee—on camera—for a woman who earlier had been runner-up (Collins, 2009; Bonos, 2018).

Occasionally, though, researchers do temporarily stress or deceive people, but only when they believe it is essential to a justifiable end, such as understanding and controlling violent behavior or studying mood swings. Some experiments won't work if participants know everything beforehand. (Wanting to be helpful, the participants might try to confirm the researcher's predictions.)

The ethics codes of the APA and Britain's BPS urge researchers to (1) obtain potential participants' **informed consent** to take part, (2) protect participants from greater-than-usual harm and discomfort, (3) keep information about individual participants confidential, and (4) fully **debrief** people (explain the research afterward, including any temporary deception). As with nonhuman animals, most university ethics committees have guidelines that screen research proposals and safeguard participants' well-being.

informed consent giving potential participants enough information about a study to enable them to choose whether they wish to participate.

debriefing the postexperimental explanation of a study, including its purpose and any deceptions, to its participants.

"Rats are very similar to humans except that they are not stupid enough to purchase lottery tickets." —Dave Barry, July 2, 2002

"Please do not forget those of us who suffer from incurable diseases or disabilities who hope for a cure through research that requires the use of animals." —Psychologist Dennis Feeney (1987)

"The greatness of a nation can be judged by the way its animals are treated." —Mahatma Gandhi, 1869–1948

ANIMAL RESEARCH BENEFITING ANIMALS Psychologists have helped zoos enrich animal environments, such as by reducing the "learned helplessness" of captivity by giving animals more choices (Kurtycz, 2015; Weir, 2013). Thanks partly to research on the benefits of novelty, control, and stimulation, these gorillas are enjoying an improved quality of life in New York's Bronx Zoo.

MARY ALTAFFER/AP Images

🔒 **RETRIEVE IT** • • •

ANSWERS IN APPENDIX E

RI-13 How are animal subjects and human research participants protected?

FIGURE 1.6

WHAT DO YOU SEE? Our expectations influence what we perceive. Did you see a duck or a rabbit? Show some friends this image with the rabbit photo covered up and see if they are more likely to perceive a duck instead. (Inspired by Shepard, 1990.)

Rubberball/Mike Kemp/Getty Images

"There can be no peace until they renounce their Rabbit God and accept our Duck God."

 (ASK YOURSELF)

What other questions or concerns do you have about psychology?

Values in Psychology

Values affect what we study, how we study it, and how we interpret results. Researchers' values influence their choice of topics. Should we study worker productivity or worker morale? Sex discrimination or gender differences? Conformity or independence? Values can also color "the facts"—our observations and interpretations; sometimes we see what we want or expect to see (**FIGURE 1.6**).

Even the words we use to describe traits and tendencies can reflect our values. In psychology and in everyday speech, labels describe and labels evaluate: One person's *rigidity* is another's *consistency*. One person's *undocumented worker* is another's *illegal alien*. One person's *faith* is another's *fanaticism*. One country's *enhanced interrogation techniques* become *torture* when practiced by its enemies. Our labeling someone as *firm* or *stubborn*, *careful* or *picky*, *discreet* or *secretive* reveals our own attitudes.

Popular applications of psychology also contain hidden values. If you defer to "professional" guidance about how to live—how to raise children, how to achieve self-fulfillment, how to respond to sexual feelings, how to get ahead at work—you are accepting value-laden advice. A science of behavior and mental processes can help us reach our goals. But it cannot decide what those goals should be.

If some people see psychology as merely common sense, others have a different concern—that it is becoming dangerously powerful. Might psychology be used to manipulate people?

Knowledge, like all power, can be used for good or evil. Nuclear power has been used to light up cities—and to demolish them. Persuasive power has been used to educate people—and to deceive them. Although psychology does have the power to deceive, its purpose is to enlighten. Every day, psychologists explore ways to enhance learning, creativity, and compassion. Psychology speaks to many of our world's great problems—war, overpopulation, inequality, prejudice, family crises, crime—all of which involve attitudes and behaviors. Psychology also speaks to our deepest longings—for nourishment, for love, for happiness. Psychology cannot address all of life's great questions, but it speaks to some mighty important ones.

PSYCHOLOGY SPEAKS In making its historic 1954 school desegregation decision, the U.S. Supreme Court cited the expert testimony and research of psychologists Kenneth Clark and Mamie Phipps Clark (1947). The Clarks reported that, when given a choice between Black and White dolls, most African-American children chose the White doll, which seemingly indicated internalized anti-Black prejudice.

USE PSYCHOLOGY TO BECOME A STRONGER PERSON—AND A BETTER STUDENT

LOQ 1-19   How can psychological principles help you learn, remember, and thrive?

Throughout this text, we will offer evidence-based suggestions that you can use to live a happy, effective, flourishing life, including the following:

- *Get a full night's sleep.* Unlike sleep-deprived people, who live with fatigue and gloomy moods, well-rested people live with greater energy, alertness, and productivity.

- *Make space for exercise.* Aerobic activity not only increases health and energy, it also is an effective remedy for mild to moderate depression and anxiety.

- *Set long-term goals, with daily aims.* Successful people take time each day to work toward their goals, such as exercising or sleeping more, or eating more healthfully. Over time, they often find that their daily practice becomes a habit.

- *Have a growth mindset.* Rather than seeing their abilities as fixed, successful people view their mental abilities as like a muscle—something that grows stronger with effortful use.

- *Prioritize relationships.* We humans are social animals. We flourish when connected in close relationships. We are both happier and healthier when supported by (and supporting) caring friends.

Psychology's research also shows how we can learn and retain information. Many students assume that the way to cement new learning is to reread. What helps even more—and what this book therefore encourages—is repeated self-testing and rehearsal of previously studied material. Memory researchers Henry Roediger and Jeffrey Karpicke (2006) call this phenomenon the **testing effect.** (It is also sometimes called the *retrieval practice effect* or *test-enhanced learning*.) They note that "testing is a powerful means of improving learning, not just assessing it." In one study, English-speaking students recalled the meaning of 20 previously learned Lithuanian words better if tested repeatedly than if they spent the same time restudying the words (Ariel & Karpicke, 2017). Repetitive testing's rewards also make it reinforcing: Students who used repetitive testing once more often used it later when learning new material. Many other studies, including in college classrooms, confirm that *frequent quizzing and self-testing boosts students' retention* (Cho et al., 2017; Foss & Pirozzolo, 2017; Trumbo et al., 2016).

As you will see in Chapter 8, to master information you must *actively process it*. In one digest of 225 studies, students engaged in active learning showed the highest examination performance in science, technology, engineering, and mathematics (STEM) (Freeman et al., 2014). So don't treat your mind like your stomach, something to be filled passively. Treat it more like a muscle that grows stronger with exercise. Countless experiments reveal that people learn and remember best when they put material in their own words, rehearse it, and then retrieve and review it again.

The **SQ3R** study method incorporates these principles (McDaniel et al., 2009; Robinson, 1970). SQ3R is an acronym for its five steps: *Survey, Question, Read, Retrieve,*[5] *Review.*

To study a chapter, first *survey*, taking a bird's-eye view. Scan the table of contents on the chapter's first page, and notice the organization.

Before you read each main section, try to answer its numbered Learning Objective *Question* (for this section: "How can psychological principles help you learn, remember, and thrive?"). Roediger and Bridgid Finn (2010) have found that "trying and failing to retrieve the answer is actually helpful to learning." Those who test their understanding *before* reading, and discover what they don't yet know, will learn and remember better.

testing effect enhanced memory after retrieving, rather than simply rereading, information. Also referred to as a *retrieval practice effect* or *test-enhanced learning*.

SQ3R a study method incorporating five steps: *Survey, Question, Read, Retrieve, Review.*

"If you read a piece of text through twenty times, you will not learn it by heart so easily as if you read it ten times while attempting to recite it from time to time and consulting the text when your memory fails." —Francis Bacon, *Novum Organum,* 1620

---

5. Also sometimes called "Recite."

Then *read*, actively searching for the answer to the question. At each sitting, read only as much of the chapter (usually a single main section) as you can absorb without tiring. Read actively and critically. Ask questions. Take notes. Make the ideas your own: How does what you've read relate to your own life? Does it support or challenge your assumptions? How convincing is the evidence? Write out what you know. "Writing is often a tool for learning," said one group of researchers (Arnold et al., 2017).

Having read a section, *retrieve* its main ideas. "Active retrieval promotes meaningful learning," says Karpicke (2012). So *test yourself*. This will not only help you figure out what you know, the testing itself will help you learn and retain the information more effectively. Even better, test yourself repeatedly. To facilitate this, we offer periodic *Retrieve It* self-tests throughout each chapter (see, for example, the questions at the end of this section). After answering these questions for yourself, you can check your answers, and then reread as needed.

Finally, *review:* Read over any notes you have taken, again with an eye on the chapter's organization, and quickly review the whole chapter. Write or say what a concept is before rereading to check your understanding.

Survey, question, read, retrieve, review. We have organized this book's chapters to facilitate your use of the SQ3R study system. Each chapter begins with an outline that aids your *survey*. Headings and Learning Objective *Questions* suggest issues and concepts you should consider as you *read*. The material is organized into sections of readable length. The Retrieve It questions will challenge you to retrieve what you have learned, and thus *retain* it better. The end-of-section *Review* is set up as a self-test, with the collected Learning Objective Questions and key terms listed, along with Experience the Testing Effect questions in a variety of formats. In the eBook, answer-checking is a click away. In the printed text, answers may be found in Appendix D and Appendix E.

Four additional study tips may further boost your learning:

Distribute your study time. One of psychology's oldest findings is that *spaced practice* promotes better retention than does massed practice. You'll remember material better if you space your time over several study periods—perhaps one hour a day, six days a week—rather than cram it into one week-long or all-night study blitz. For example, rather than trying to read an entire chapter in a single sitting, read just one main section and then turn to something else. *Interleaving* your study of psychology with your study of other subjects boosts long-term retention and protects against overconfidence (Kornell & Bjork, 2008; Taylor & Rohrer, 2010).

Spacing your study sessions requires a disciplined approach to managing your time. At the beginning of this text, Richard O. Straub explains time management in a helpful preface.

Learn to think critically. Whether you are reading or in class, note people's assumptions and values. What perspective or bias underlies an argument? Evaluate evidence. Is it anecdotal? Or is it based on informative experiments? Assess conclusions. Are there alternative explanations?

Process class information actively. Listen for a lecture's main ideas and sub-ideas. *Write them down.* Ask questions during and after class. In class, as in your private study, process the information actively and you will understand and retain it better. As psychologist William James urged a century ago, *"No reception without reaction, no impression without . . . expression."* Make the information your own. Engage with the Ask Yourself questions found periodically throughout each chapter to relate what you read to your own life. Tell someone else about it. (As any teacher will confirm, to teach is to remember.)

Also, take notes *by hand.* Handwritten notes, in your own words, typically engage more active processing, with better retention, than does verbatim note-taking on laptops (Mueller & Oppenheimer, 2014).

Overlearn. Psychology tells us that overlearning improves retention. We are prone to overestimating how much we know. You may understand a chapter as you read it, but that feeling of familiarity can be deceptively comforting. By using the Retrieve It and Experience the Testing Effect questions as well as our online learning opportunities, you can test your knowledge and *overlearn* in the process.

Worth Publishers

MORE LEARNING TIPS To learn more about the testing effect and the SQ3R method, view the 5-minute animation, "Make Things Memorable," at tinyurl.com/HowToRemember.

Memory experts Elizabeth Bjork and Robert Bjork (2011, p. 63) offer simple, scientifically supported advice for how to improve your retention and your grades:

> Spend less time on the input side and more time on the output side, such as summarizing what you have read from memory or getting together with friends and asking each other questions. Any activities that involve testing yourself—that is, activities that require you to retrieve or generate information, rather than just representing information to yourself—will make your learning both more durable and flexible. (p. 63)

ENGAGE **ASK YOURSELF**

Of all of these helpful principles, which ones seem most relevant and important for improving your own life and studies?

🔒 RETRIEVE IT • • •
ANSWERS IN APPENDIX E

RI-14 The _____ _____ describes the enhanced memory that results from repeated retrieval (as in self-testing) rather than from simple rereading of new information.

RI-15 What does the acronym SQ3R stand for?

🔒 REVIEW   RESEARCH STRATEGIES: HOW PSYCHOLOGISTS ASK AND ANSWER QUESTIONS

⟶ Learning Objectives

TEST YOURSELF Answer these repeated Learning Objective Questions on your own (before checking the answers in Appendix D) to improve your retention of the concepts (McDaniel et al., 2009, 2015).

1-9 How does our everyday thinking sometimes lead us to a wrong conclusion?

1-10 Why are we so vulnerable to believing untruths?

1-11 How do theories advance psychological science?

1-12 How do psychologists use case studies, naturalistic observations, and surveys to observe and describe behavior, and why is random sampling important?

1-13 What does it mean when we say two things are correlated, and what are positive and negative correlations?

1-14 Why do correlations enable prediction but not cause-effect explanation?

1-15 What are the characteristics of experimentation that make it possible to isolate cause and effect?

1-16 How would you know which research design to use?

1-17 How can simplified laboratory conditions illuminate everyday life?

1-18 Why do psychologists study animals, and what ethical guidelines safeguard human and animal research participants? How do psychologists' values influence psychology?

1-19 How can psychological principles help you learn, remember, and thrive?

⟶ Terms and Concepts to Remember

TEST YOURSELF Write down the definition yourself, then check your answer on the referenced page.

placebo [pluh-SEE-bo] effect, **p. 27**   dependent variable, **p. 28**   testing effect, **p. 33**
independent variable, **p. 28**   informed consent, **p. 31**   SQ3R, **p. 33**
confounding variable, **p. 28**   debriefing, **p. 31**

⟫ Experience the Testing Effect

TEST YOURSELF Answer the following questions on your own first, then check your answers in Appendix E.

1. _____ _____ refers to our tendency to perceive events as obvious or inevitable after the fact.

2. Theory-based predictions are called _____.

3. Which of the following is NOT one of the *descriptive* methods psychologists use to observe and describe behavior?
   a. A case study
   b. Naturalistic observation
   c. Correlational research
   d. A phone survey

4. For your survey, you need to establish a group of people who represent the country's entire adult population. To do this, you will need to question a _____ sample of the population.

5. A study finds that the more childbirth training classes women attend, the less pain medication they require during childbirth. This finding can be stated as a _____ (positive/negative) correlation.

6. Knowing that two events are correlated provides
   a. a basis for prediction.
   b. an explanation of why the events are related.
   c. proof that as one increases, the other also increases.
   d. an indication that an underlying third factor is at work.

7. Here are some recently reported correlations, with interpretations drawn by journalists. Knowing just these correlations, can you come up with other possible explanations for each of these?
   a. Alcohol use is associated with violence. (One interpretation: Drinking triggers or unleashes aggressive behavior.)
   b. Educated people live longer, on average, than less-educated people. (One interpretation: Education lengthens life and enhances health.)
   c. Teens engaged in team sports are less likely to use drugs, smoke, have sex, carry weapons, and eat junk food than are teens who do not engage in team sports. (One interpretation: Team sports encourage healthy living.)
   d. Adolescents who frequently see smoking in movies are more likely to smoke. (One interpretation: Movie stars' behavior influences impressionable teens.)

8. To explain behaviors and clarify cause and effect, psychologists use _____.

9. To test the effect of a new drug on depression, we randomly assign people to control and experimental groups. Those in the control group take a pill that contains no medication. This pill is a _____.

10. In a double-blind procedure,
    a. only the participants know whether they are in the control group or the experimental group.
    b. experimental and control group members will be carefully matched for age, sex, income, and education level.
    c. neither the participants nor the researchers know who is in the experimental group or control group.
    d. someone separate from the researcher will ask people to volunteer for the experimental group or the control group.

11. A researcher wants to determine whether noise level affects workers' blood pressure. In one group, she varies the level of noise in the environment and records participants' blood pressure. In this experiment, the level of noise is the _____ _____.

12. The laboratory environment is designed to
    a. exactly re-create the events of everyday life.
    b. re-create psychological forces under *controlled* conditions.
    c. re-create psychological forces under *random* conditions.
    d. minimize the use of animals and humans in psychological research.

13. In defending their experimental research with animals, psychologists have noted that
    a. animals' physiology and behavior can tell us much about our own.
    b. animal experimentation sometimes helps animals as well as humans.
    c. animals are fascinating creatures and worthy of study.
    d. all of these statements are correct.

Continue testing yourself with 📖 **LearningCurve** or 📖 **Achieve Read &
Practice** to learn and remember most effectively.

The Biology of Behavior

Peoplelmages/Getty Images

A Chinese transplant surgeon, Xiaoping Ren, is building an international team that hopes to undertake a really, really bold medical venture—a full-body transplant (Kean, 2016; Tatlow, 2016). Wang Huanming, who is paralyzed from the neck down, volunteered to become one of ten volunteers for this mind-boggling experiment. What would Wang have to do? Have his fully-functioning head transferred to a brain-dead person's still-functioning body.

Ignore for the moment the experiment's serious ethical issues, including the near-certainty that the surgery will end Wang's life (Kean, 2016). And ignore the seeming impossibility of precisely connecting the head-to-spinal-cord nerves. Imagine, just imagine, that the procedure could work. With the same brain and a new body, would Wang still be Wang? After recovering, to whose home should he return? If the old Wang was once a skilled musician, would the new Wang conceivably retain that skill—or would that depend on the muscle memories stored in the new body? And if he (assuming the new body was male) later had a child, whom should the birth certificate list as the father?

Most of us twenty-first-century people (you, too?) presume that, even with a new body, Wang would still be Wang. We presume that our brain, designed by our genes and sculpted by our experience, provides our identity and enables our mind. No brain, no mind.

We are, indeed, living brains, but more. We are bodies alive. No principle is more central to today's psychology, or to this book, than this: *Everything psychological is simultaneously biological.* Your every idea, every mood, every urge is a biological happening.

37

"You're certainly a lot less fun since the operation."

You love, laugh, and cry with your body. To think, feel, or act without a body would be like running without legs. Without your body—your genes, your nervous system, your hormones, your appearance—you truly would be nobody. Moreover, your body and your brain influence and are influenced by your experience.

In this chapter, we explore the mind's biology. We start small and build from the bottom up—from nerve cells up to the brain. But we'll also discuss how our behavior and environment can influence our biology from the top down. Life changes us. You've heard it before and you'll hear it again: *Nurture works on what nature provides.* ▶

(⋯⟶) Neural and Hormonal Systems

BIOLOGY, BEHAVIOR, AND MIND

LEARNING OBJECTIVE QUESTION (LOQ)

2-1   Why are psychologists concerned with human biology?

Our understanding of how the brain gives birth to the mind has come a long way. The ancient Greek physician, Hippocrates, correctly located the mind in the brain. His contemporary, the philosopher Aristotle, believed the mind was in the heart, which pumps warmth and vitality to the body. The heart remains our symbol for love, but science has long since overtaken philosophy on this issue: It's your brain, not your heart, that falls in love.

In the early 1800s, German physician Franz Gall proposed that *phrenology,* studying bumps on the skull, could reveal a person's mental abilities and character traits. At one point, Britain had 29 phrenological societies, and phrenologists traveled North America giving skull readings (Dean, 2012; Hunt, 1993). Using a false name, humorist Mark Twain put one famous phrenologist to the test. "He found a cavity [and] startled me by saying that that cavity represented the total absence of the sense of humor!" Three months later, Twain sat for a second reading, this time identifying himself. Now "the cavity was gone, and in its place was . . . the loftiest bump of humor he had ever encountered in his life-long experience!" (Lopez, 2002). The "science" of phrenology remains known today as a reminder of our need for critical thinking and scientific analysis. Phrenology did at least succeed in focusing attention on the *localization of function*—the idea that various brain regions have particular functions.

Today, we are living in a time Gall could only dream about. **Biological psychologists** use advanced technologies to study the links between biological (genetic, neural, hormonal) processes and psychological processes. They and other researchers working from a biological perspective are announcing discoveries about the interplay of our biology and our behavior and mind at an exhilarating pace. Within little more than the past century, researchers seeking to understand the biology of the mind have discovered that

- our adaptive brain is wired by our experiences.
- among the body's cells are nerve cells that conduct electricity and "talk" to one another by sending chemical messages across a tiny gap that separates them.
- specific brain systems serve specific functions (though not the functions Gall supposed).
- we integrate information processed in these different brain systems to construct our experience of sights and sounds, meanings and memories, pain and passion.

We have also realized that we are each a system composed of subsystems that are in turn composed of even smaller subsystems. Tiny cells organize to form body organs.

These organs form larger systems for digestion, circulation, and information processing. And those systems are part of an even larger system—the individual, who in turn is a part of a family, culture, and community. Thus, we are *biopsychosocial* systems. To understand our behavior, we need to study how these biological, psychological, and social-cultural systems work and interact. Let's begin with the brain's ability to rewire itself as it adapts to experience.

🔒 **RETRIEVE IT • • •**   *ANSWERS IN APPENDIX E*

RI-1 What do phrenology and biological psychology have in common?

THE POWER OF PLASTICITY

LOQ 2-2   How do biology and experience interact in neural plasticity?

Your brain is sculpted not only by your genes but also by your life. Under the surface of your awareness, your brain is constantly changing, building new pathways as it adjusts to little mishaps and new experiences. This neural change is called **plasticity.** Although plasticity is strongest in childhood, it continues throughout life (Gutchess, 2014).

To see plasticity at work, consider London's taxi driver trainees, who spend years learning and remembering the city's 25,000 street locations and connections. For the half who pass the difficult final test, big rewards are in store: not only a better income but also an enlarged hippocampus, one of the brain's memory centers that processes spatial memories. London's bus drivers, who navigate a smaller set of roads, gain no similar neural rewards (Maguire et al., 2000, 2006).

We also see plasticity in well-practiced pianists, who have a larger-than-usual auditory cortex area (a sound-processing region) that encodes piano sounds (Bavelier et al., 2000; Pantev et al., 1998). After years of practice, the brains of ballerinas and jugglers reflect other changes related to improved performance (Draganski et al., 2004; Hänggi et al., 2010; Herholz & Zatorre, 2012). Your brain, too, is a work in progress. It changes with the focus and practice you're devoting to the ideas, skills, and people you care about the most. The brain you were born with is not the brain you will die with.

Plasticity is part of what makes the human brain unique (Gómez-Robles et al., 2015). More than for any other species, our brain is designed to change, and thus to adapt to our changing world.

NEURAL COMMUNICATION

For scientists, it is a happy fact of nature that the information systems of humans and other animals operate similarly. This similarity allows researchers to study relatively simple animals to discover how our neural systems operate. Cars differ, but all have engines, accelerators, steering wheels, and brakes. A space alien could study any one of them and grasp the operating principles. Likewise, animals differ, yet their nervous systems operate similarly.

Neurons

LOQ 2-3   What are *neurons*, and how do they transmit information?

Our body's neural information system is complexity built from simplicity. Its building blocks are **neurons,** or nerve cells. Throughout life, new neurons are born and unused neurons wither away (O'Leary et al., 2014; Shors, 2014). To fathom our thoughts and actions, our memories and moods, we must first understand how neurons work and communicate.

Neurons differ, but all are variations on the same theme (**FIGURE 2.1**). Each consists of a **cell body** and its branching fibers. The often bushy **dendrite** fibers receive and integrate information, conducting it toward the cell body (Stuart & Spruston, 2015). From there, the cell's single lengthy **axon** fiber passes the message through its terminal branches to other neurons or to muscles or glands (see **FIGURE 2.2**). Dendrites listen. Axons speak.

Volker Corell Photography

THE MIND'S EYE Daniel Kish, who is completely blind, enjoys going for walks in the woods. To stay safe, he uses echolocation—the same navigation method used by bats and dolphins. Blind echolocation experts such as Kish engage the brain's visual centers to navigate their surroundings (Thaler et al., 2011, 2014). Although Kish is blind, his flexible brain helps him to "see."

biological psychology the scientific study of the links between biological (genetic, neural, hormonal) and psychological processes. Some biological psychologists call themselves *behavioral neuroscientists, neuropsychologists, behavior geneticists, physiological psychologists,* or *biopsychologists.*

plasticity the brain's ability to change, especially during childhood, by reorganizing after damage or by building new pathways based on experience.

neuron a nerve cell; the basic building block of the nervous system.

cell body the part of a neuron that contains the nucleus; the cell's life-support center.

dendrites a neuron's often bushy, branching extensions that receive and integrate messages, conducting impulses toward the cell body.

axon the neuron extension that passes messages through its branches to other neurons or to muscles or glands.

myelin [MY-uh-lin] **sheath** a fatty tissue layer segmentally encasing the axons of some neurons; enables vastly greater transmission speed as neural impulses hop from one node to the next.

glial cells (glia) cells in the nervous system that support, nourish, and protect neurons; they may also play a role in learning, thinking, and memory.

action potential a neural impulse; a brief electrical charge that travels down an axon.

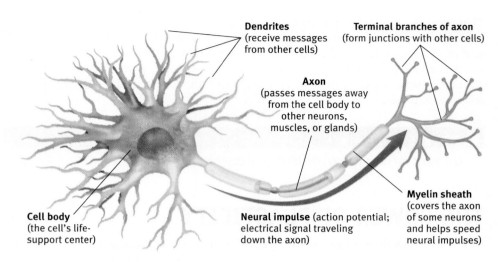

Dendrites
(receive messages
from other cells)

Terminal branches of axon
(form junctions with other cells)

Axon
(passes messages away
from the cell body to
other neurons,
muscles, or glands)

Cell body
(the cell's life-
support center)

Neural impulse (action potential;
electrical signal traveling
down the axon)

Myelin sheath
(covers the axon
of some neurons
and helps speed
neural impulses)

FIGURE 2.1
A MOTOR NEURON

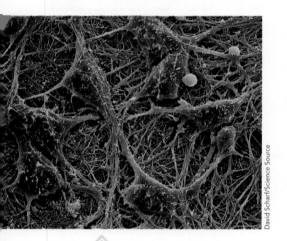

David Scharf/Science Source

FIGURE 2.2

NEURONS COMMUNICATING

When we learn about neurons, we often see them one at a time to learn their parts. But our billions of neurons exist in a vast and densely interconnected web. One neuron's terminal branches send messages to neighboring dendrites. Read on to learn more about this complex and fascinating electrochemical communication process.

 (ASK YOURSELF)

Does it surprise you to learn that despite your brain's complexity, your reaction time is slower than a computer's? What does this suggest regarding which tasks might be more readily performed by computers rather than humans?

Unlike the short dendrites, axons may be very long, projecting several feet through the body. A human neuron carrying orders to a leg muscle, for example, has a cell body and axon roughly on the scale of a basketball attached to a 4-mile-long rope. Much as home electrical wire is insulated, some axons are encased in a **myelin sheath,** a layer of fatty tissue that insulates them and speeds their impulses. As myelin is laid down up to about age 25, neural efficiency, judgment, and self-control grow (Fields, 2008). If the myelin sheath degenerates, *multiple sclerosis* results: Communication to muscles slows, with eventual loss of muscle control.

Supporting our billions of nerve cells are spidery **glial cells** ("glue cells"). Neurons are like queen bees; on their own they cannot feed or sheathe themselves. Glial cells are worker bees. They provide nutrients and insulating myelin, guide neural connections, and clean up after neurons send messages to one another. Glia also play a role in learning, thinking, and memory. By "chatting" with neurons they participate in information transmission and memory (Fields, 2011, 2013; Martín et al., 2015).

In more complex animal brains, the proportion of glia to neurons increases. A postmortem analysis of Albert Einstein's brain did not find more or larger-than-usual neurons, but it did reveal a much greater concentration of glial cells than found in an average Albert's head (Fields, 2004). Einstein's glial cells likely kept his brain abuzz with activity.

The Neural Impulse

Neurons transmit messages when stimulated by our senses or by neighboring neurons. A neuron sends a message by firing an impulse, called the **action potential**—a brief electrical charge that travels down its axon.

Depending on the type of fiber, a neural impulse travels at speeds ranging from a sluggish 2 miles (3 kilometers) per hour to more than 200 miles (320 kilometers) per hour. But even its top speed is 3 million times slower than that of electricity through a wire. We measure brain activity in milliseconds (thousandths of a second) and computer activity in nanoseconds (billionths of a second). Thus, unlike the nearly instantaneous reactions of a computer, your reaction to a sudden event, such as a child darting in front of your car, may take a quarter-second or more. Your brain is vastly more complex than a computer but slower at executing simple responses. And if you were an elephant— whose round-trip message travel time from a yank on the tail to the brain and back to the tail is 100 times longer than that of a tiny shrew—your reflexes would be slower yet (More et al., 2010).

Like batteries, neurons generate electricity from chemical events. In the neuron's chemistry-to-electricity process, *ions* (electrically charged atoms) are exchanged. The fluid outside an axon's membrane has mostly positively charged sodium ions. A resting axon's fluid interior (which includes both large, negatively charged protein ions and smaller, positively charged potassium ions) has a mostly negative charge. Like a tightly guarded facility, the axon's surface is selective about what it allows through its gates.

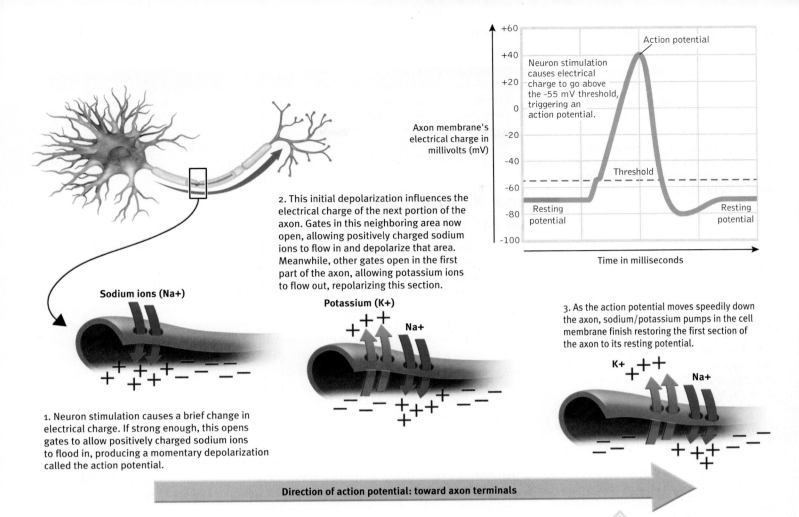

2. This initial depolarization influences the electrical charge of the next portion of the axon. Gates in this neighboring area now open, allowing positively charged sodium ions to flow in and depolarize that area. Meanwhile, other gates open in the first part of the axon, allowing potassium ions to flow out, repolarizing this section.

Sodium ions (Na+)

Potassium (K+)

3. As the action potential moves speedily down the axon, sodium/potassium pumps in the cell membrane finish restoring the first section of the axon to its resting potential.

1. Neuron stimulation causes a brief change in electrical charge. If strong enough, this opens gates to allow positively charged sodium ions to flood in, producing a momentary depolarization called the action potential.

Direction of action potential: toward axon terminals

We say the axon's surface is *selectively permeable.* This positive-outside/negative-inside state is called the *resting potential.*

When a neuron fires, the first section of the axon opens its gates, rather like a storm sewer cover flipping open, and positively charged sodium ions (attracted to the negative interior) flood in through the now-open channels. The loss of the inside/outside charge difference, called *depolarization,* causes the next section of axon channels to open, and then the next, like a line of falling dominos. This temporary inflow of positive ions is the neural impulse—the action potential. Each neuron is itself a miniature decision-making device performing complex calculations as it receives signals from hundreds, even thousands, of other neurons. The mind boggles when imagining this electrochemical process repeating up to 100 or even 1000 times a second. But this is just the first of many astonishments.

Most neural signals are *excitatory,* somewhat like pushing a neuron's gas pedal. Some are *inhibitory,* more like pushing its brake. If excitatory signals exceed the inhibitory signals by a minimum intensity, or **threshold** (**FIGURE 2.3**), the combined signals trigger an action potential. (Think of it this way: If the excitatory party animals outvote the inhibitory party poopers, the party's on.) The action potential then travels down the axon, which branches into junctions with hundreds or thousands of other neurons or with the body's muscles and glands.

Neurons need short breaks (a tiny fraction of an eyeblink). During a resting pause called the **refractory period,** subsequent action potentials cannot occur until the axon returns to its resting state. Then the neuron can fire again.

Increasing the level of stimulation above the threshold will not increase the neural impulse's intensity. The neuron's reaction is an **all-or-none response:** Like guns, neurons either fire or they don't. How, then, do we detect the intensity of a stimulus? How do we distinguish a gentle touch from a big hug? A strong stimulus can trigger *more* neurons to fire, and to fire more often. But it does not affect the action potential's strength or speed. Squeezing a trigger harder won't make a bullet go faster.

FIGURE 2.3

ACTION POTENTIAL Bodily sensations and actions—detecting a hug or kicking a soccer ball—happen when our neurons are stimulated enough that their membrane's electrical charge reaches a threshold (–55 mV in this example—see graph). This prompts each of those neurons to "fire" an impulse—an action potential—which travels down its axon (see numbered drawings) and transmits a message to other neurons, muscles, or glands.

threshold the level of stimulation required to trigger a neural impulse.

refractory period in neural processing, a brief resting pause that occurs after a neuron has fired; subsequent action potentials cannot occur until the axon returns to its resting state.

all-or-none response a neuron's reaction of either firing (with a full-strength response) or not firing.

"What one neuron tells another neuron is simply how much it is excited."
—Francis Crick, *The Astonishing Hypothesis*, 1994

 **LaunchPad** For an interactive, animated explanation of this process, engage online with **Concept Practice: Action Potentials.**

"All information processing in the brain involves neurons 'talking to' each other at synapses." —Neuroscientist Solomon H. Snyder, 1984

ENGAGE

(ASK YOURSELF)

Why was the discovery of neurons' communication mechanism so important?

synapse [SIN-aps] the junction between the axon tip of the sending neuron and the dendrite or cell body of the receiving neuron. The tiny gap at this junction is called the *synaptic gap* or *synaptic cleft*.

neurotransmitters chemical messengers that cross the synaptic gap between neurons. When released by the sending neuron, neurotransmitters travel across the synapse and bind to receptor sites on the receiving neuron, thereby influencing whether that neuron will generate a neural impulse.

reuptake a neurotransmitter's reabsorption by the sending neuron.

🔒 RETRIEVE IT • • • ANSWERS IN APPENDIX E

RI-2 When a neuron fires an action potential, the information travels through the axon, the dendrites, and the cell body, but not in that order. Place these three structures in the correct order.

RI-3 How does our nervous system allow us to experience the difference between a slap and a tap on the back?

How Neurons Communicate

LOQ 2-4 How do nerve cells communicate with other nerve cells?

Neurons interweave so intricately that even with a microscope, you would struggle to see where one neuron ends and another begins. Scientists once believed that the axon of one cell fused with the dendrites of another in an uninterrupted fabric. Then British physiologist Sir Charles Sherrington (1857–1952) noticed that neural impulses were taking an unexpectedly long time to travel a neural pathway. Inferring that there must be a brief interruption in the transmission, Sherrington called the meeting point between neurons a **synapse.**

We now know that the axon terminal of one neuron is in fact separated from the receiving neuron by a tiny *synaptic gap* (or *synaptic cleft*). Spanish anatomist Santiago Ramón y Cajal (1852–1934) marveled at these near-unions of neurons, calling them "protoplasmic kisses." "Like elegant ladies air-kissing so as not to muss their makeup, dendrites and axons don't quite touch," noted poet Diane Ackerman (2004, p. 37). How do the neurons execute this protoplasmic kiss, sending information across the synaptic gap? The answer is one of the important scientific discoveries of our age.

When an action potential reaches the knob-like terminals at an axon's end, it triggers the release of chemical messengers, called **neurotransmitters** (FIGURE 2.4). Within 1/10,000th of a second, the neurotransmitter molecules cross the synaptic gap and bind to receptor sites on the receiving neuron—as precisely as a key fits a lock. For an instant, the neurotransmitter unlocks tiny channels at the receiving site, and electrically charged atoms flow in, exciting or inhibiting the receiving neuron's readiness to fire. The excess neurotransmitters finally drift away, are broken down by enzymes, or are reabsorbed by the sending neuron—a process called **reuptake.** Some antidepressant medications partially block the reuptake of mood-enhancing neurotransmitters.

🔒 RETRIEVE IT • • • ANSWERS IN APPENDIX E

RI-4 What happens in the *synaptic gap*?

RI-5 What is *reuptake*? What two other things can happen to excess neurotransmitters after a neuron reacts?

How Neurotransmitters Influence Us

LOQ 2-5 How do neurotransmitters influence behavior, and how do drugs and other chemicals affect neurotransmission?

In their quest to understand neural communication, researchers have discovered several dozen neurotransmitters and almost as many new questions: Are certain neurotransmitters found only in specific places? How do neurotransmitters affect our moods, memories, and mental abilities? Can we boost or diminish these effects through drugs or diet?

Later chapters explore neurotransmitter influences on hunger and thinking, depression and euphoria, addictions and therapy. For now, let's glimpse how neurotransmitters influence our motions and emotions.

One of the best-understood neurotransmitters, *acetylcholine (ACh),* plays a role in learning and memory. It is also the messenger at every junction between motor neurons (which carry information from the brain and spinal cord to the body's tissues) and skeletal muscles. When ACh is released to our muscle cell receptors, the muscle contracts. If ACh transmission is blocked, as happens during some kinds of anesthesia and with some poisons, the muscles cannot contract and we are paralyzed.

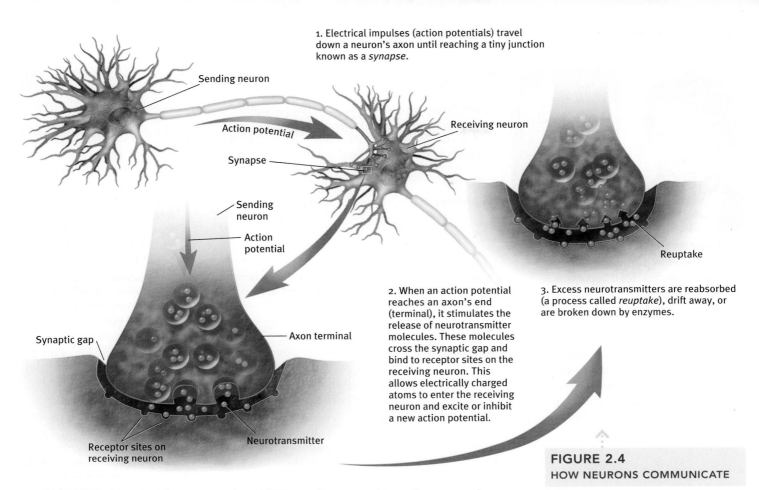

1. Electrical impulses (action potentials) travel down a neuron's axon until reaching a tiny junction known as a *synapse*.

Sending neuron

Action potential

Receiving neuron

Synapse

Sending neuron

Action potential

Synaptic gap

Axon terminal

Reuptake

2. When an action potential reaches an axon's end (terminal), it stimulates the release of neurotransmitter molecules. These molecules cross the synaptic gap and bind to receptor sites on the receiving neuron. This allows electrically charged atoms to enter the receiving neuron and excite or inhibit a new action potential.

3. Excess neurotransmitters are reabsorbed (a process called *reuptake*), drift away, or are broken down by enzymes.

Receptor sites on receiving neuron

Neurotransmitter

FIGURE 2.4
HOW NEURONS COMMUNICATE

Candace Pert and Solomon Snyder (1973) made an exciting discovery about neurotransmitters when they attached a harmless radioactive tracer to morphine, an opiate drug that elevates mood and eases pain. As the researchers tracked the morphine in an animal's brain, they noticed it was binding to receptors in areas linked with mood and pain sensations. But why would the brain have these "opiate receptors"? Why would it have a chemical lock, unless it also had a key—a natural painkiller—to open it?

Researchers soon confirmed that the brain does indeed produce its own naturally occurring opiates. Our body releases several types of neurotransmitter molecules similar to morphine in response to pain and vigorous exercise. These **endorphins** (short for *end*ogenous [produced within] m*orphine*) help explain good feelings such as the "runner's high," the painkilling effects of acupuncture, and the indifference to pain in some severely injured people (Boecker et al., 2008; Fuss et al., 2015). But once again, new knowledge led to new questions.

HOW DRUGS AND OTHER CHEMICALS ALTER NEUROTRANSMISSION If natural endorphins lessen pain and boost mood, why not increase this effect by flooding the brain with artificial opiates, thereby intensifying the brain's own "feel-good" chemistry? Because it would disrupt the brain's chemical balancing act. When flooded with opiate drugs such as heroin and morphine, the brain, to maintain its chemical balance, may stop producing its own natural opiates. When the drug is withdrawn, the brain may then be deprived of any form of opiate, causing intense discomfort. For suppressing the body's own neurotransmitter production, nature charges a price.

Drugs and other chemicals affect brain chemistry, often by either exciting or inhibiting neurons' firing. **Agonist** molecules increase a neurotransmitter's action. Some agonists may increase the production or release of neurotransmitters, or block reuptake in the synapse. Other agonists may be similar enough to a neurotransmitter to bind to its receptor and mimic its excitatory or inhibitory effects. Some opiate drugs are agonists and produce a temporary "high" by amplifying normal sensations of arousal or pleasure.

Antagonists decrease a neurotransmitter's action by blocking production or release. Botulin, a poison that can form in improperly canned food, causes paralysis by blocking ACh release. (Small injections of botulin—Botox—smooth wrinkles by paralyzing the

Physician Lewis Thomas, on the endorphins: "There it is, a biologically universal act of mercy. I cannot explain it, except to say that I would have put it in had I been around at the very beginning, sitting as a member of a planning committee." —*The Youngest Science*, 1983

 **ASK YOURSELF**

Can you recall a time, perhaps after a workout, when you felt the effects of endorphins? How would you describe these feelings?

endorphins [en-DOR-fins] "morphine within"—natural, opiate-like neurotransmitters linked to pain control and to pleasure.

agonist a molecule that increases a neurotransmitter's action.

antagonist a molecule that inhibits or blocks a neurotransmitter's action.

DEPENDENT UPON DOPAMINE The neurotransmitter dopamine helps us move, think, and feel. Too much increases the odds of developing schizophrenia; too little may produce the tremors and loss of motor control of Parkinson's disease (NIH, 2016). More than 10 million people worldwide have Parkinson's disease (Parkinson's Foundation, 2018). Well-known people diagnosed with the disease include actor Michael J. Fox and the late boxing legend Muhammad Ali.

RETAIN 🔒 TABLE 2.1

Some Neurotransmitters and Their Functions

Neurotransmitter	Function	Examples of Malfunctions
Acetylcholine (ACh)	Enables muscle action, learning, and memory	With Alzheimer's disease, ACh-producing neurons deteriorate.
Dopamine	Influences movement, learning, attention, and emotion	Oversupply linked to schizophrenia. Undersupply linked to tremors and decreased mobility in Parkinson's disease.
Serotonin	Affects mood, hunger, sleep, and arousal	Undersupply linked to depression. Some drugs that raise serotonin levels are used to treat depression.
Norepinephrine	Helps control alertness and arousal	Undersupply can depress mood.
GABA (gamma-aminobutyric acid)	A major inhibitory neurotransmitter	Undersupply linked to seizures, tremors, and insomnia.
Glutamate	A major excitatory neurotransmitter; involved in memory	Oversupply can overstimulate the brain, producing migraines or seizures (which is why some people avoid MSG, monosodium glutamate, in food).
Endorphins	Neurotransmitters that influence the perception of pain or pleasure	Oversupply with opiate drugs can suppress the body's natural endorphin supply.

"When it comes to the brain, if you want to see the action, follow the neurotransmitters." —Neuroscientist Floyd Bloom, 1993

RETAIN 🔒 ≋ **LaunchPad** For an illustrated review of neural communication, visit **Topic Tutorial: PsychSim6, Neural Messages.**

underlying facial muscles.) These antagonists are enough like the natural neurotransmitter to occupy its receptor site and block its effect, but are not similar enough to stimulate the receptor (rather like foreign coins that fit into, but won't operate, a vending machine). Curare, a poison some South American Indians have applied to hunting-dart tips, occupies and blocks ACh receptor sites on muscles, producing paralysis in their prey.

See **TABLE 2.1** for an overview of key neurotransmitters and the specific behaviors and emotions they affect.

🔒 **RETRIEVE IT • • •**   *ANSWERS IN APPENDIX E*

RI-6 Curare poisoning paralyzes its victims by blocking ACh receptors involved in muscle movements. Morphine mimics endorphin actions. Which is an agonist, and which is an antagonist?

RI-7 Serotonin, dopamine, and endorphins are all chemical messengers called _____

THE NERVOUS SYSTEM

LOQ 2-6 What are the functions of the nervous system's main divisions, and what are the three main types of neurons?

Neurons communicating with neurotransmitters make up our body's **nervous system,** a communication network that takes in information from the world and the body's tissues, makes decisions, and sends back information and orders to the body's tissues (**FIGURE 2.5**).

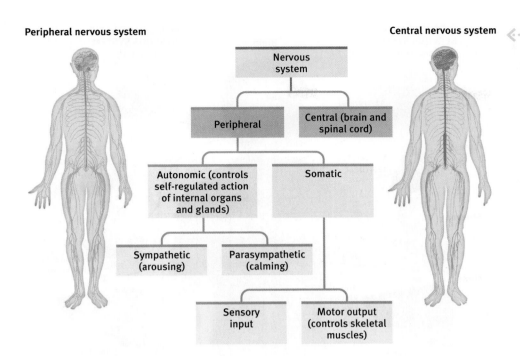

Peripheral nervous system

Central nervous system

FIGURE 2.5

THE FUNCTIONAL DIVISIONS OF THE HUMAN NERVOUS SYSTEM

A quick overview: The brain and spinal cord form the **central nervous system (CNS),** the body's decision maker. The **peripheral nervous system (PNS)** is responsible for gathering information and for transmitting CNS decisions to other body parts. **Nerves,** electrical cables formed from bundles of axons, link the CNS with the body's sensory receptors, muscles, and glands. The optic nerve, for example, bundles a million axons into a single cable carrying the messages from the eye to the brain (Mason & Kandel, 1991).

Information travels in the nervous system through three types of neurons. **Sensory neurons** carry messages from the body's tissues and sensory receptors inward (thus, they are *afferent*) to the brain and spinal cord for processing. **Motor neurons** (which are *efferent*) carry instructions from the central nervous system outward to the body's muscles and glands. Between the sensory input and motor output, information is processed via **interneurons.** Our complexity resides mostly in these interneurons. Our nervous system has a few million sensory neurons, a few million motor neurons, and billions and billions of interneurons.

RETRIEVE IT • • •

ANSWERS IN APPENDIX E

RI-8 Match the type of neuron (I–III) to its description (a–c).

Type:	Description:
I. Motor neurons	a. Carry incoming messages from sensory receptors to the CNS.
II. Sensory neurons	b. Communicate within the CNS and process information between incoming and outgoing messages.
III. Interneurons	c. Carry outgoing messages from the CNS to muscles and glands.

The Peripheral Nervous System

Our peripheral nervous system has two components—somatic and autonomic. Our **somatic nervous system** enables voluntary control of our skeletal muscles. As you reach the end of this page, your somatic nervous system will report to your brain the current state of your skeletal muscles and carry instructions back, triggering a response from your hand so you can read on.

Our **autonomic nervous system (ANS)** controls our glands and our internal organ muscles. The ANS influences functions such as glandular activity, heartbeat, and

nervous system the body's speedy, electrochemical communication network, consisting of all the nerve cells of the peripheral and central nervous systems.

central nervous system (CNS) the brain and spinal cord.

peripheral nervous system (PNS) the sensory and motor neurons that connect the central nervous system (CNS) to the rest of the body.

nerves bundled axons that form neural cables connecting the central nervous system with muscles, glands, and sense organs.

sensory (afferent) neurons neurons that carry incoming information from the body's tissues and sensory receptors to the brain and spinal cord.

motor (efferent) neurons neurons that carry outgoing information from the brain and spinal cord to the muscles and glands.

interneurons neurons within the brain and spinal cord; they communicate internally and process information between the sensory inputs and motor outputs.

somatic nervous system the division of the peripheral nervous system that controls the body's skeletal muscles. Also called the *skeletal nervous system.*

autonomic [aw-tuh-NAHM-ik] **nervous system (ANS)** the part of the peripheral nervous system that controls the glands and the muscles of the internal organs (such as the heart). Its sympathetic division arouses; its parasympathetic division calms.

FIGURE 2.6

THE DUAL FUNCTIONS OF THE AUTONOMIC NERVOUS SYSTEM
The autonomic nervous system controls the more autonomous (or self-regulating) internal functions. Its sympathetic division arouses and expends energy. Its parasympathetic division calms and conserves energy, allowing routine maintenance activity. For example, sympathetic stimulation accelerates heartbeat, whereas parasympathetic stimulation slows it.

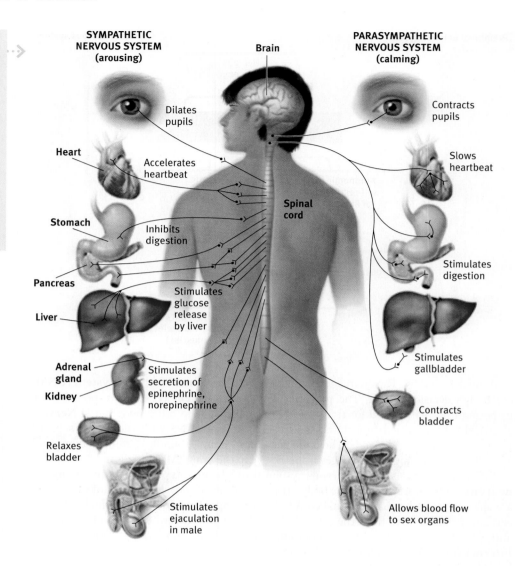

SYMPATHETIC NERVOUS SYSTEM (arousing)

Brain

PARASYMPATHETIC NERVOUS SYSTEM (calming)

Dilates pupils

Contracts pupils

Heart

Accelerates heartbeat

Slows heartbeat

Spinal cord

Stomach

Inhibits digestion

Stimulates digestion

Pancreas

Liver

Stimulates glucose release by liver

Stimulates gallbladder

Adrenal gland

Kidney

Stimulates secretion of epinephrine, norepinephrine

Contracts bladder

Relaxes bladder

Stimulates ejaculation in male

Allows blood flow to sex organs

sympathetic nervous system the division of the autonomic nervous system that arouses the body, mobilizing its energy.

parasympathetic nervous system the division of the autonomic nervous system that calms the body, conserving its energy.

ASK YOURSELF

Think back to a time when you felt your sympathetic nervous system kick in at a stressful moment. What was your body preparing you for? Were you able to sense your parasympathetic nervous system's response when the challenge had passed?

digestion. (*Autonomic* means "self-regulating.") Like an automatic pilot, this system may be consciously overridden, but usually it operates on its own (autonomously).

The autonomic nervous system's subdivisions serve two important functions (**FIGURE 2.6**). The **sympathetic nervous system** arouses and expends energy. If something alarms or challenges you (such as a longed-for job interview), your sympathetic nervous system will accelerate your heartbeat, raise your blood pressure, slow your digestion, raise your blood sugar, and cool you with perspiration, making you alert and ready for action. When the stress subsides (the interview is over), your **parasympathetic nervous system** will produce the opposite effects, conserving energy as it calms you. The sympathetic and parasympathetic nervous systems work together to keep us in a steady internal state called *homeostasis* (more on this in Chapter 10).

I [DM] recently experienced my ANS in action. Before sending me into an MRI machine for a shoulder scan, the technician asked if I had issues with claustrophobia. "No, I'm fine," I assured her, with perhaps a hint of macho swagger. Moments later, as I found myself on my back, stuck deep inside a coffin-sized box and unable to move, my sympathetic nervous system had a different idea. Claustrophobia overtook me. My heart began pounding, and I felt a desperate urge to escape. Just as I was about to cry out for release, I felt my calming parasympathetic nervous system kick in. My heart rate slowed and my body relaxed, though my arousal surged again before the 20-minute confinement ended. "You did well!" the technician said, unaware of my ANS roller-coaster ride.

⚠ EMERGENCY ALERTS now

Emergency Alert
BALLISTIC MISSILE THREAT INBOUND TO HAWAII. SEEK IMMEDIATE SHELTER. THIS IS NOT A DRILL.
Slide for more

BALLISTIC STRESS In 2018, Hawaiians received this terrifying alert, amid concerns about North Korean nuclear warheads. "We fully felt we were about to die," reported one panicked mother (Nagourney et al., 2018). Thirty-eight minutes later, the alert was declared a false alarm.

RI-9 How was the ANS involved in Hawaiians' terrified responses, and in calming their bodies once they realized it was a false alarm?

The Central Nervous System

From neurons "talking" to other neurons arises the complexity of the central nervous system's brain and spinal cord.

It is the brain that enables our humanity—our thinking, feeling, and acting. Tens of billions of neurons, each communicating with thousands of other neurons, yield an ever-changing wiring diagram. By one estimate—projecting from neuron counts in small brain samples—our brain has some 86 billion neurons (Azevedo et al., 2009; Herculano-Houzel, 2012).

Rather like individual pixels combining to form a picture, the brain's individual neurons cluster into work groups called *neural networks*. To understand why, Stephen Kosslyn and Olivier Koenig (1992, p. 12) have invited us to "think about why cities exist; why don't people distribute themselves more evenly across the countryside?" Like people networking with people, neurons network with nearby neurons with which they can have short, fast connections.

The other part of the CNS, the *spinal cord*, is a two-way information highway connecting the peripheral nervous system and the brain. Ascending neural fibers send up sensory information, and descending fibers send back motor-control information. The neural pathways governing our **reflexes**, our automatic responses to stimuli, illustrate the spinal cord's work. A simple spinal reflex pathway is composed of a single sensory neuron and a single motor neuron. These often communicate through an interneuron. The knee-jerk response, for example, involves one such simple pathway. A headless warm body could do it.

Another neural circuit enables the pain reflex (**FIGURE 2.7**). When your finger touches a flame, neural activity (excited by the heat) travels via sensory neurons to interneurons in your spinal cord. These interneurons respond by activating motor neurons leading to the muscles in your arm. Because the simple pain-reflex pathway runs through the spinal cord and right back out, your hand jerks away from the candle's flame *before* your brain receives and responds to the information that causes you to feel pain. That's why it feels as if your hand jerks away not by your choice, but on its own.

Information travels to and from the brain by way of the spinal cord. Were the top of your spinal cord severed, you would not feel pain from your paralyzed body below. Nor would you feel pleasure. With your brain literally out of touch with your body, you would lose all sensation and voluntary movement in body regions with sensory and motor connections to the spinal cord below its point of injury. You would exhibit the knee-jerk response without feeling the tap. To produce bodily pain or pleasure, the sensory information must reach the brain.

"The body is made up of millions and millions of crumbs."

reflex a simple, automatic response to a sensory stimulus, such as the knee-jerk response.

FIGURE 2.7
A SIMPLE REFLEX

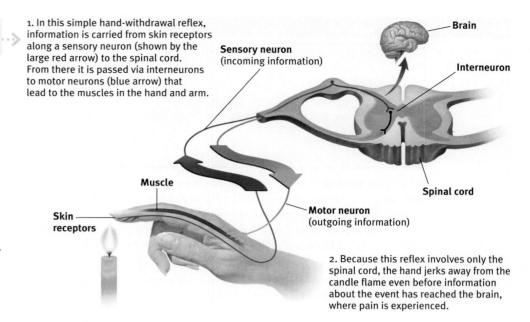

1. In this simple hand-withdrawal reflex, information is carried from skin receptors along a sensory neuron (shown by the large red arrow) to the spinal cord. From there it is passed via interneurons to motor neurons (blue arrow) that lead to the muscles in the hand and arm.

Brain

Sensory neuron (incoming information)

Interneuron

Spinal cord

Muscle

Skin receptors

Motor neuron (outgoing information)

2. Because this reflex involves only the spinal cord, the hand jerks away from the candle flame even before information about the event has reached the brain, where pain is experienced.

endocrine [EN-duh-krin] **system** the body's "slow" chemical communication system; a set of glands that secrete hormones into the bloodstream.

hormones chemical messengers that are manufactured by the endocrine glands, travel through the bloodstream, and affect other tissues.

adrenal [ah-DREEN-el] **glands** a pair of endocrine glands that sit just above the kidneys and secrete hormones (epinephrine and norepinephrine) that help arouse the body in times of stress.

pituitary gland the endocrine system's most influential gland. Under the influence of the hypothalamus, the pituitary regulates growth and controls other endocrine glands.

THE ENDOCRINE SYSTEM

LOQ 2-7 How does the endocrine system transmit information and interact with the nervous system?

So far, we have focused on the body's speedy electrochemical information system. Interconnected with your nervous system is a second communication system, the **endocrine system** (FIGURE 2.8). The endocrine system's glands secrete another form of chemical messengers, **hormones,** which travel through the bloodstream and affect other tissues, including the brain. When hormones act on the brain, they influence our interest in sex, food, and aggression.

Some hormones are chemically identical to neurotransmitters (the chemical messengers that diffuse across a synapse and excite or inhibit an adjacent neuron). The endocrine system and nervous system are therefore close relatives: Both produce molecules that act on receptors elsewhere. Like many relatives, they also differ. The speedier nervous system zips messages from eyes to brain to hand in a fraction of a second. Endocrine messages trudge along in the bloodstream, taking several seconds or more to travel from the gland to the target tissue. If the nervous system transmits information with text-message speed, the endocrine system delivers an old-fashioned letter. But slow and steady sometimes wins the race. Endocrine messages tend to outlast the effects of neural messages. Have you ever felt angry long after the cause of your angry feelings was resolved (say, your friend apologized for her rudeness)? You may have experienced an "endocrine hangover" from lingering emotion-related hormones.

In a moment of danger, the ANS orders the **adrenal glands** on top of the kidneys to release *epinephrine* and *norepinephrine* (also called *adrenaline* and *noradrenaline*). These hormones increase heart rate, blood pressure, and blood sugar, providing a surge of energy. When the emergency passes, the hormones—and the feelings—linger a while.

The most influential endocrine gland is the **pituitary gland,** a pea-sized structure located in the core of the brain, where it is controlled by an adjacent brain area, the *hypothalamus* (more on that shortly). Among the hormones released by the pituitary is a growth hormone that stimulates physical

FIGURE 2.8
THE ENDOCRINE SYSTEM

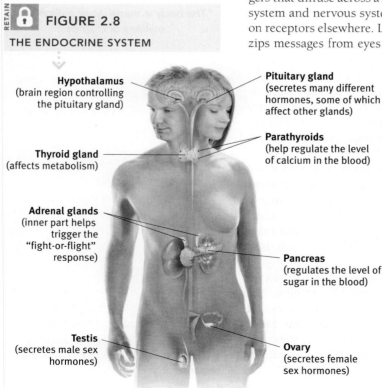

Hypothalamus (brain region controlling the pituitary gland)

Pituitary gland (secretes many different hormones, some of which affect other glands)

Thyroid gland (affects metabolism)

Parathyroids (help regulate the level of calcium in the blood)

Adrenal glands (inner part helps trigger the "fight-or-flight" response)

Pancreas (regulates the level of sugar in the blood)

Testis (secretes male sex hormones)

Ovary (secretes female sex hormones)

development. Another is *oxytocin*, which enables social bonding (De Dreu et al., 2010; Marsh et al., 2017; Pfundmair et al., 2017).

Pituitary secretions also direct other endocrine glands to release their hormones. The pituitary, then, is a *master gland* (whose own master is the hypothalamus). For example, under the brain's influence, the pituitary triggers your sex glands to release sex hormones. These in turn influence your brain and behavior (Goetz et al., 2014).

This feedback system (brain ⟶ pituitary ⟶ other glands ⟶ hormones ⟶ body and brain) reveals the intimate connection of the nervous and endocrine systems. The nervous system directs endocrine secretions, which then affect the nervous system. Conducting and coordinating this whole electrochemical orchestra is that flexible maestro we call the brain.

ENGAGE

ASK YOURSELF

Do you remember feeling the lingering effects of a hormonal response, such as anger, after some particularly aggravating event? How did it feel? How long did it last?

🔒 **RETRIEVE IT • • •**   *ANSWERS IN APPENDIX E*

> **RI-10** Why is the pituitary gland called the "master gland"?
>
> **RI-11** How are the nervous and endocrine systems alike, and how do they differ?

🔒 REVIEW NEURAL AND HORMONAL SYSTEMS

⟩⟩ Learning Objectives

TEST YOURSELF Answer these repeated Learning Objective Questions on your own (before checking the answers in Appendix D) to improve your retention of the concepts (McDaniel et al., 2009, 2015).

2-1 Why are psychologists concerned with human biology?

2-2 How do biology and experience interact in neural plasticity?

2-3 What are *neurons,* and how do they transmit information?

2-4 How do nerve cells communicate with other nerve cells?

2-5 How do neurotransmitters influence behavior, and how do drugs and other chemicals affect neurotransmission?

2-6 What are the functions of the nervous system's main divisions, and what are the three main types of neurons?

2-7 How does the endocrine system transmit information and interact with the nervous system?

⟩⟩ Terms and Concepts to Remember

TEST YOURSELF Write down the definition yourself, then check your answer on the referenced page.

biological psychology, **p. 39**

plasticity, **p. 39**

neuron, **p. 39**

cell body, **p. 39**

dendrites, **p. 39**

axon, **p. 39**

myelin [MY-uh-lin] sheath, **p. 40**

glial cells (glia), **p. 40**

action potential, **p. 40**

threshold, **p. 41**

refractory period, **p. 41**

all-or-none response, **p. 41**

synapse [SIN-aps], **p. 42**

neurotransmitters, **p. 42**

reuptake, **p. 42**

endorphins [en-DOR-fins], **p. 43**

agonist, **p. 43**

antagonist, **p. 43**

nervous system, **p. 45**

central nervous system (CNS), **p. 45**

peripheral nervous system (PNS), **p. 45**

nerves, **p. 45**

sensory (afferent) neurons, **p. 45**

motor (efferent) neurons, **p. 45**

interneurons, **p. 45**

somatic nervous system, **p. 45**

autonomic [aw-tuh-NAHM-ik] nervous system (ANS), **p. 45**

sympathetic nervous system, **p. 46**

parasympathetic nervous system, **p. 46**

reflex, **p. 47**

endocrine [EN-duh-krin] system, **p. 48**

hormones, **p. 48**

adrenal [ah-DREEN-el] glands, **p. 48**

pituitary gland, **p. 48**

⟩⟩ Experience the Testing Effect

TEST YOURSELF Answer the following questions on your own first, then check your answers in Appendix E.

1. What do psychologists mean when they say the brain is "plastic"?

2. The neuron fiber that passes messages through its branches to other neurons or to muscles and glands is the _____.

3. The tiny space between the axon of one neuron and the dendrite or cell body of another is called the
   a. axon terminal.
   c. synaptic gap.
   b. branching fiber.
   d. threshold.

4. Regarding a neuron's response to stimulation, the intensity of the stimulus determines
   a. whether or not an impulse is generated.
   b. how fast an impulse is transmitted.
   c. how intense an impulse will be.
   d. whether reuptake will occur.

5. In a sending neuron, when an action potential reaches an axon terminal, the impulse triggers the release of chemical messengers called _____.

6. Endorphins are released in the brain in response to
   a. morphine or heroin.
   b. pain or vigorous exercise.
   c. the all-or-none response.
   d. all of the above.

7. The autonomic nervous system controls internal functions, such as heart rate and glandular activity. The word *autonomic* means
   a. calming.
   c. self-regulating.
   b. voluntary.
   d. arousing.

8. The sympathetic nervous system arouses us for action and the parasympathetic nervous system calms us down. Together, the two systems make up the _____ nervous system.

9. The neurons of the spinal cord are part of the _____ nervous system.

10. The most influential endocrine gland, known as the "master gland," is the
    a. pituitary.
    c. thyroid.
    b. hypothalamus.
    d. pancreas.

11. The _____ _____ secrete(s) epinephrine and norepinephrine, helping to arouse the body during times of stress.

Continue testing yourself with 📖 **LearningCurve** or 📖 **Achieve Read & Practice** to learn and remember most effectively.

⟶ Tools of Discovery, Older Brain Structures, and the Limbic System

The mind seeking to understand the brain—that is among the ultimate scientific challenges. And so it will always be. To paraphrase cosmologist John Barrow, a brain simple enough to be fully understood is too simple to produce a mind able to understand it.

When you think *about* your brain, you're thinking *with* your brain—by releasing billions of neurotransmitter molecules across trillions of synapses. Indeed, say neuroscientists, *the mind is what the brain does.*

"I am a brain, Watson. The rest of me is a mere appendix." —Sherlock Holmes, in Arthur Conan Doyle's "The Adventure of the Mazarin Stone," 1921

THE TOOLS OF DISCOVERY: HAVING OUR HEAD EXAMINED

LOQ 2-8   How do neuroscientists study the brain's connections to behavior and mind?

For most of human history, scientists had no tools high powered yet gentle enough to reveal a living brain's activity. Early case studies helped localize some brain functions. Damage to one side of the brain often caused numbness or paralysis on the opposite side, suggesting that the body's right side is wired to the brain's left side, and vice versa.

Damage to the back of the brain disrupted vision, and damage to the left-front part of the brain produced speech difficulties. Gradually, these early explorers were mapping the brain.

Now, within a lifetime, a new generation of neural mapmakers is charting the known universe's most amazing organ. Scientists can selectively **lesion** (destroy) tiny clusters of normal or defective brain cells, observing any effect on brain function. Today's neuroscientists can also stimulate various brain parts—electrically, chemically, or magnetically—and note the effect. Depending on the stimulated brain part, people may—to name a few examples—giggle, hear voices, turn their head, feel themselves falling, or have an out-of-body experience (Selimbeyoglu & Parvizi, 2010).

Scientists can even snoop on the messages of individual neurons. With tips small enough to detect the electrical pulse in a single neuron, modern electrodes can, for example, now detect exactly where the information goes in a rat's brain when someone tickles its belly (Ishiyama & Brecht, 2017). They can also eavesdrop on the chatter of billions of neurons and see color representations of the brain's energy-consuming activity.

Right now, your mental activity is emitting telltale electrical, metabolic, and magnetic signals that would enable neuroscientists to observe your brain at work. Electrical activity in your brain's billions of neurons sweeps in regular waves across its surface. An **EEG (electroencephalogram)** is an amplified readout of such waves. Researchers record the brain waves through a shower-cap-like hat that is filled with electrodes covered with a conductive gel.

A related technique, **MEG (magnetoencephalography)**, measures magnetic fields from the brain's natural electrical activity. Participants sit underneath a head coil that resembles a hair salon hairdryer. While participants complete activities, tens of thousands of neurons create electrical pulses, which in turn create magnetic fields. The speed and strength of the magnetic fields enable researchers to understand how certain tasks influence brain activity.

"You must look into people, as well as at them," advised Lord Chesterfield in a 1746 letter to his son. Newer neuroimaging techniques give us that Superman-like ability to see inside the living brain. One such tool, the **PET (positron emission tomography) scan** (FIGURE 2.9), depicts brain activity by showing each brain area's consumption of its chemical fuel, the sugar glucose. Active neurons gobble glucose. Our brain, though only about 2 percent of our body weight, consumes 20 percent of our calorie intake. After a person receives temporarily radioactive glucose, the PET scan can track the gamma rays released by this "food for thought" as a task is performed. Rather like weather radar showing rain activity, PET-scan "hot spots" show the most active brain areas as the person does mathematical calculations, looks at images of faces, or daydreams.

In **MRI (magnetic resonance imaging)** brain scans, the person's head is put in a strong magnetic field, which aligns the spinning atoms of brain molecules. Then, a radiowave pulse momentarily disorients the atoms. When the atoms return to their normal spin, they emit signals that provide a detailed picture of soft tissues, including the brain.

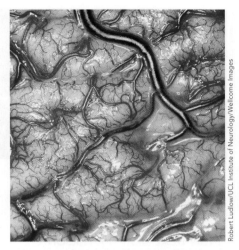

A LIVING HUMAN BRAIN EXPOSED
Today's neuroscience tools enable us to "look under the hood" and glimpse the brain at work, enabling the mind.

lesion [LEE-zhuhn] tissue destruction. A brain lesion is a naturally or experimentally caused destruction of brain tissue.

EEG (electroencephalogram) an amplified recording of the waves of electrical activity sweeping across the brain's surface. These waves are measured by electrodes placed on the scalp.

MEG (magnetoencephalography) a brain-imaging technique that measures magnetic fields from the brain's natural electrical activity.

PET (positron emission tomography) scan a visual display of brain activity that detects where a radioactive form of glucose goes while the brain performs a given task.

MRI (magnetic resonance imaging) a technique that uses magnetic fields and radio waves to produce computer-generated images of soft tissue. MRI scans show brain anatomy.

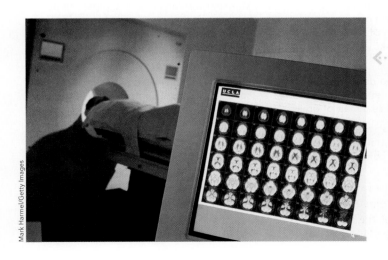

FIGURE 2.9

THE PET SCAN To obtain a PET scan, researchers inject volunteers with a low and harmless dose of a short-lived radioactive sugar. Detectors around the person's head pick up the release of gamma rays from the sugar, which has concentrated in active brain areas. A computer then processes and translates these signals into a map of the brain at work.

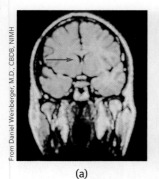 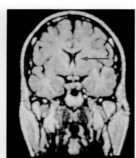

(a)   (b)

FIGURE 2.10

MRI SCAN OF A HEALTHY INDIVIDUAL (a) AND A PERSON WITH SCHIZOPHRENIA (b) Note the enlarged ventricle, the fluid-filled brain region at the tip of the arrow in the brain of the person with schizophrenia (b).

MRI scans have revealed a larger-than-average neural area in the left hemisphere of musicians who display perfect pitch (Schlaug et al., 1995). They have also revealed enlarged *ventricles*—fluid-filled brain areas (marked by the red arrows in **FIGURE 2.10**)—in some patients who have schizophrenia, a disabling psychological disorder.

A special application of MRI—**fMRI (functional MRI)**—can reveal the brain's functioning as well as its structure. Where the brain is especially active, blood goes. By comparing successive MRI scans, researchers can watch as specific brain areas activate, showing increased oxygen-laden blood flow. As a person looks at a scene, for example, the fMRI machine detects blood rushing to the back of the brain, which processes visual information. See **TABLE 2.2** to compare these imaging techniques.

Such snapshots of the brain's activity provide new insights into how the brain divides its labor. A mountain of recent fMRI studies suggests which brain areas are most active when people feel pain or rejection, listen to angry voices, think about scary things, feel happy, or become sexually excited. The technology enables a very crude sort of mind reading. One neuroscience team scanned 129 people's brains as they did eight different mental tasks (such as reading, gambling, or rhyming). Later, they were able, with 80 percent accuracy, to identify which of these mental activities their participants had been doing (Poldrack et al., 2009).

You've seen the pictures—of colorful brains with accompanying headlines, such as "your brain on music." Hot brains make hot news (Bowers, 2016; Fine, 2010). In one study, students rated scientific explanations as more believable and interesting when they contained neuroscience (Fernandez-Duque et al., 2015). But "neuroskeptics" caution against overblown claims about any ability to predict customer preferences, detect lies, and foretell crime (Rose & Rose, 2016; Satel & Lilienfeld, 2013; Schwartz et al., 2016).

RETAIN 🔒 **TABLE 2.2**

Types of Neural Measures

Name	How Does It Work?	Sample Finding
EEG (Electroencephalogram)	Electrodes placed on the scalp measure electrical activity in neurons.	Symptoms of depression and anxiety correlate with increased activity in the right frontal lobe, a brain area associated with behavioral withdrawal and negative emotion (Thibodeau et al., 2006).
MEG (Magnetoencephalography)	A head coil records magnetic fields from the brain's natural electrical currents.	Soldiers with posttraumatic stress disorder (PTSD), compared with those who do not have PTSD, show stronger magnetic fields in the visual cortex when they view trauma-related images (Todd et al., 2015).
PET (Positron emission tomography)	Tracks where a temporarily radioactive form of glucose goes while the brain of the person given it performs a task.	Monkeys with an anxious temperament have brains that use more glucose in regions related to fear, memory, and expectations of reward and punishment (Fox et al., 2015).
MRI (Magnetic resonance imaging)	People sit or lie down in a chamber that uses magnetic fields and radio waves to provide a map of brain structure.	People with a history of violence tend to have smaller frontal lobes, especially in regions that aid moral judgment and self-control (Glenn & Raine, 2014).
fMRI (Functional magnetic resonance imaging)	Measures blood flow to brain regions by comparing continuous MRI scans.	Years after surviving a near plane crash, passengers who viewed material related to their trauma showed greater activation in the brain's fear, memory, and visual centers than when they watched footage related to the 9/11 terrorist attacks (Palombo et al., 2015).

Neuromarketing, neurolaw, neuropolitics, and neurotheology are often neurohype. Imaging techniques illuminate brain structure and activity, and sometimes help us test different theories of behavior (Mather et al., 2013). But given that all human experience is brain-based, it's no surprise that different brain areas become active when one listens to a lecture or lusts for a lover.

Today's techniques for peering into the thinking, feeling brain are doing for psychology what the microscope did for biology and the telescope did for astronomy. Europe's Human Brain Project promises $1 billion for brain computer modeling. The PsychENCODE project enables researchers to examine differences between the brains of healthy people and those with various disorders, such as autism spectrum disorder, bipolar disorder, and schizophrenia (Akbarian et al., 2015). The $40 million Human Connectome Project seeks "neural pathways [that] will reveal much about what makes us uniquely human and what makes every person different from all others" (2013; Gorman, 2014; Smith et al., 2015). It harnesses the power of *diffusion spectrum imaging,* a type of MRI technology that maps long-distance brain fiber connections (Jarbo & Verstynen, 2015) (**FIGURE 2.11**). Such efforts have led to the creation of a new brain map with 100 neural centers not previously described (Glasser et al., 2016). This truly is the golden age of brain science.

FIGURE 2.11

BEAUTIFUL BRAIN CONNECTIONS The Human Connectome Project is using cutting-edge methods to map the brain's interconnected network of neurons. Scientists created this multicolored "symphony" of neural fibers transporting water through different brain regions.

RETAIN 🔒 **LaunchPad** To check your understanding of brain scans and their functions, engage online with **Concept Practice: Scanning the Brain.**

🔒 **RETRIEVE IT • • •**   *ANSWERS IN APPENDIX E*

RI-1 Match the scanning technique (I–III) with the correct description (a–c).

Technique:	Description:
I. fMRI scan	a. tracks radioactive glucose to reveal brain *activity.*
II. PET scan	b. tracks successive images of brain tissue to show brain *function.*
III. MRI scan	c. uses magnetic fields and radio waves to show brain *anatomy.*

OLDER BRAIN STRUCTURES

LOQ 2-9 What structures make up the brainstem, and what are the functions of the brainstem, thalamus, reticular formation, and cerebellum?

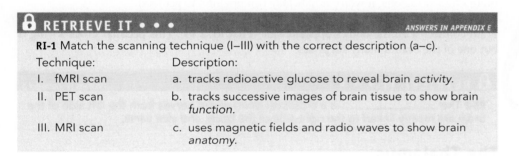

An animal's capacities come from its brain structures. In primitive animals, such as sharks, a not-so-complex brain primarily regulates basic survival functions: breathing, resting, and feeding. In lower mammals, such as rodents, a more complex brain enables emotion and greater memory. In advanced mammals, such as humans, a brain that processes more information enables increased foresight as well.

The brain's increasing complexity arises from new brain systems built on top of the old, much as Earth's landscape covers the old with the new. Digging down, one discovers the fossil remnants of the past—brainstem components performing for us much as they did for our distant ancestors. Let's start with the brain's base and work up to the newer systems.

imageBROKER/Alamy

The Brainstem

The **brainstem** is the brain's oldest and innermost region. Its base is the **medulla,** the slight swelling in the spinal cord just after it enters the skull (**FIGURE 2.12**). Here lie the controls for your heartbeat and breathing. As some brain-damaged patients in a vegetative state illustrate, we need no higher brain or conscious mind to orchestrate our heart's pumping and lungs' breathing. The brainstem handles those tasks. Just above the medulla sits the *pons,* which helps coordinate movements and control sleep.

📺 **LaunchPad** For an introductory 12.5-minute overview of the brain, see the **Video: The Central Nervous System—Spotlight on the Brain.**

---

fMRI (functional MRI) a technique for revealing blood flow and, therefore, brain activity by comparing successive MRI scans. fMRI scans show brain function as well as structure.

brainstem the oldest part and central core of the brain, beginning where the spinal cord swells as it enters the skull; the brainstem is responsible for automatic survival functions.

medulla [muh-DUL-uh] the base of the brainstem; controls heartbeat and breathing.

FIGURE 2.12

THE BRAINSTEM AND THALAMUS The brainstem, including the pons and medulla, is an extension of the spinal cord. The thalamus is attached to the top of the brainstem. The reticular formation passes through both structures.

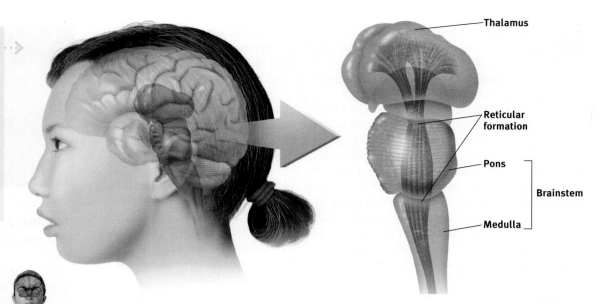

FIGURE 2.13
THE BODY'S WIRING

thalamus [THAL-uh-muss] the brain's sensory control center, located on top of the brainstem; it directs messages to the sensory receiving areas in the cortex and transmits replies to the cerebellum and medulla.

reticular formation a nerve network that travels through the brainstem into the thalamus and plays an important role in controlling arousal.

cerebellum [sehr-uh-BELL-um] the "little brain" at the rear of the brainstem; functions include processing sensory input, coordinating movement output and balance, and enabling nonverbal learning and memory.

If a cat's brainstem is severed from the rest of the brain above it, the animal will still breathe and live—and even run, climb, and groom (Klemm, 1990). But cut off from the brain's higher regions, it won't *purposefully* run or climb to get food.

The brainstem is a crossover point, where most nerves to and from each side of the brain connect with the body's opposite side (**FIGURE 2.13**). This peculiar cross-wiring is but one of the brain's many surprises.

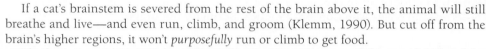

🔒 RETRIEVE IT • • •　　　　　　　　　　　　　ANSWERS IN APPENDIX E

RI-2 The _____ is a crossover point where nerves from the left side of the brain are mostly linked to the right side of the body, and vice versa.

The Thalamus

Sitting atop the brainstem is the **thalamus,** a pair of egg-shaped structures that act as the brain's sensory control center (see Figure 2.12). The thalamus receives information from all the senses except smell, and routes that information to higher brain regions that deal with seeing, hearing, tasting, and touching. The thalamus also receives some of the higher brain's replies, which it then directs to the medulla and to the cerebellum. Think of the thalamus as being to sensory information what London is to England's trains: a hub through which traffic passes en route to various destinations.

The Reticular Formation

Inside the brainstem, between your ears, lies the **reticular** ("netlike") **formation,** a neuron network extending from the spinal cord right up through the thalamus. As the spinal cord's sensory input flows up to the thalamus, some of it travels through the reticular formation, which filters incoming stimuli and relays important information to other brain areas. Have you multitasked today? You can thank your reticular formation (Wimmer et al., 2015).

The reticular formation also controls arousal, as Giuseppe Moruzzi and Horace Magoun discovered in 1949. Electrically stimulating a sleeping cat's reticular formation almost instantly produced an awake, alert animal. When Magoun *severed* a cat's reticular formation without damaging nearby sensory pathways, the effect was equally dramatic: The cat lapsed into a coma from which it never awakened.

The Cerebellum

Extending from the rear of the brainstem is the baseball-sized **cerebellum,** meaning "little brain," which is what its two wrinkled halves resemble (**FIGURE 2.14**). The cerebellum enables nonverbal learning and skill memory. It also helps us judge time, modulate our emotions, and discriminate sounds and textures (Bower & Parsons, 2003). And (with assistance from the pons) it coordinates voluntary movement. When a soccer player masterfully controls the ball, give the player's cerebellum some credit. Under alcohol's influence, coordination suffers. And if you injured your cerebellum, you would have difficulty walking, keeping your balance, or shaking hands. Your movements would be jerky and exaggerated. Gone would be any dreams of being a dancer or guitarist.

* * *

Note: These older brain functions all occur without any conscious effort. This illustrates another of our recurring themes: *Our brain processes most information outside of our awareness.* We are aware of the *results* of our brain's labor—say, our current visual experience—but not *how* we construct the visual image. Likewise, whether we are asleep or awake, our brainstem manages its life-sustaining functions, freeing our newer brain regions to think, talk, dream, or savor a memory.

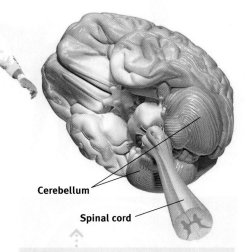

Cerebellum

Spinal cord

FIGURE 2.14

THE BRAIN'S ORGAN OF AGILITY Hanging at the back of the brain, the cerebellum coordinates our voluntary movements, as when soccer star Cristiano Ronaldo controls the ball.

> 🔒 **RETRIEVE IT • • •**   *ANSWERS IN APPENDIX E*
>
> **RI-3** In what brain region would damage be most likely to (a) disrupt your ability to jump rope? (b) disrupt your ability to hear? (c) leave you in a coma? (d) cut off the very breath and heartbeat of life?

THE LIMBIC SYSTEM

LOQ 2-10 What are the limbic system's structures and functions?

We've considered the brain's oldest parts, but we've not yet reached its newest and highest regions, the *cerebral hemispheres* (the two halves of the brain). Between the oldest and newest brain areas lies the **limbic system** (*limbus* means "border"). This system contains the *amygdala,* the *hypothalamus,* and the *hippocampus* (**FIGURE 2.15**).

The Amygdala

Research has linked the **amygdala,** two lima-bean-sized neural clusters, to aggression and fear. In 1939, psychologist Heinrich Klüver and neurosurgeon Paul Bucy surgically removed a rhesus monkey's amygdala, turning the normally ill-tempered animal into the most mellow of creatures. So, too, with human patients. Those with amygdala lesions often display reduced arousal to fear- and anger-arousing stimuli (Berntson et al., 2011). One such woman, patient S. M., has been called "the woman with no fear," even if being threatened with a gun (Feinstein et al., 2013).

What then might happen if we electrically stimulated the amygdala of a normally placid domestic animal, such as a cat? Do so in one spot and the cat prepares to attack, hissing with its back arched, its pupils dilated, its hair on end. Move the electrode only slightly within the amygdala, cage the cat with a small mouse, and now it cowers in terror.

These and other experiments have confirmed the amygdala's role in fear and rage. Monkeys and humans with amygdala damage become less fearful of strangers (Harrison et al., 2015). Other studies link criminal behavior with amygdala dysfunction (Boccardi et al., 2011; da Cunha-Bang et al., 2017; Ermer et al., 2012a). But we must be careful. The brain is not neatly organized into structures that correspond to our behavior categories. The amygdala is engaged with other mental phenomena as well. And when we feel afraid or act aggressively, there is neural activity in many areas of our brain—not just the amygdala. If you destroy a car's battery, it's true that you won't be able to start the engine. Yet the battery is merely one link in an integrated system.

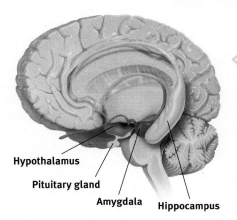

Hypothalamus

Pituitary gland

Amygdala   Hippocampus

FIGURE 2.15

THE LIMBIC SYSTEM This neural system sits between the brain's older parts and its cerebral hemispheres. The limbic system's hypothalamus controls the nearby pituitary gland.

limbic system neural system (including the *amygdala, hypothalamus,* and *hippocampus*) located below the cerebral hemispheres; associated with emotions and drives.

amygdala [uh-MIG-duh-la] two lima-bean-sized neural clusters in the limbic system; linked to emotion.

GK Hart/Vikki Hart/Getty Images

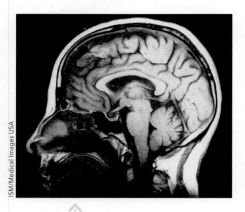

ISM/Medical Images USA

FIGURE 2.16

THE HYPOTHALAMUS This small but important structure, colored yellow/orange in this MRI scan, helps keep the body's internal environment in a steady state.

"If you were designing a robot vehicle to walk into the future and survive, . . . you'd wire it up so that behavior that ensured the survival of the self or the species—like sex and eating—would be naturally reinforcing." —Candace Pert (1986)

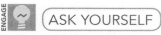

ENGAGE

ASK YOURSELF

Why do you think our brain evolved into so many interconnected structures with varying functions?

🔒 **RETRIEVE IT** • • • ANSWERS IN APPENDIX E

RI-4 Electrical stimulation of a cat's amygdala provokes angry reactions. Which *autonomic nervous system* division is activated by such stimulation?

The Hypothalamus

Just below (*hypo*) the thalamus is the **hypothalamus** (FIGURE 2.16), an important link in the command chain governing bodily maintenance. Some neural clusters in the hypothalamus influence hunger; others regulate thirst, body temperature, and sexual behavior. Together, they help maintain a steady (*homeostatic*) internal state.

To monitor your body state, the hypothalamus tunes into your blood chemistry and any incoming orders from other brain parts. For example, picking up signals from your brain's cerebral cortex that you are thinking about sex, your hypothalamus will secrete hormones. These hormones will in turn trigger the adjacent "master gland" of the endocrine system, your pituitary (see Figure 2.15), to influence your sex glands to release *their* hormones. These hormones will intensify the thoughts of sex in your cerebral cortex. (Note the interplay between the nervous and endocrine systems: The brain influences the endocrine system, which in turn influences the brain.)

A remarkable discovery about the hypothalamus illustrates how progress in science often occurs—when curious, open-minded investigators make an unexpected observation. Two young McGill University neuropsychologists, James Olds and Peter Milner (1954), were trying to implant an electrode in a rat's reticular formation when they made a magnificent mistake: They placed the electrode incorrectly (Olds, 1975). Curiously, as if seeking more stimulation, the rat kept returning to the location where it had been stimulated by this misplaced electrode. On discovering that they had actually placed the device in a region of the hypothalamus, Olds and Milner realized they had stumbled upon a brain center that provides pleasurable rewards (Olds, 1975).

Later experiments located other such regions. Just how rewarding are these reward centers? Enough to cause rats to self-stimulate these brain regions more than 1000 times per hour. In other species, including dolphins and monkeys, researchers later discovered other limbic system reward centers, such as the *nucleus accumbens* in front of the hypothalamus (Hamid et al., 2016). Animal research has also revealed both a general dopamine-related reward system and specific centers associated with the pleasures of eating, drinking, and sex. Animals, it seems, come equipped with built-in systems that reward activities essential to survival.

Do humans have limbic centers for pleasure? To calm violent patients, one neurosurgeon implanted electrodes in such areas. Stimulated patients reported mild pleasure; unlike Olds' rats, however, they were not driven to a frenzy (Deutsch, 1972; Hooper & Teresi, 1986). Moreover, newer research reveals that stimulating the brain's "hedonic hotspots" (its reward circuits) produces more *desire* than pure enjoyment (Kringelbach & Berridge, 2012).

Some researchers believe that substance use disorders may stem from malfunctions in natural brain systems for pleasure and well-being (Balodis & Potenza, 2015). People genetically predisposed to this *reward deficiency syndrome* may crave whatever provides that missing pleasure or relieves negative feelings (Blum et al., 1996).

The Hippocampus

The **hippocampus**—a seahorse-shaped brain structure—processes conscious, explicit memories and decreases in size and function as we grow older. Humans who lose their hippocampus to surgery or injury also lose their ability to form new memories of facts and events (Clark & Maguire, 2016). Those who survive a hippocampal brain tumor in childhood struggle to remember new information in adulthood (Jayakar et al., 2015). National Football League players who experience one or more loss-of-consciousness concussions may later have a shrunken hippocampus and poor memory (Strain et al., 2015). Hippocampus size and function decrease as we grow older, which furthers cognitive decline. Chapter 8 explains how our two-track mind uses the hippocampus to process our memories.

Elise Amendola/AP Images

HAS PROFESSIONAL FOOTBALL DAMAGED PLAYERS' BRAINS?

When researchers analyzed the brains of 111 deceased National Football League players, 99 percent showed signs of degeneration related to frequent head trauma (Mez et al., 2017). In 2017, NFL player Aaron Hernandez (#81) committed suicide while imprisoned for murder. An autopsy demonstrated that his brain, at age 27, was already showing advanced degeneration (Kilgore, 2017). Will today's more protective gear and rules protect players' brains?

hypothalamus [hi-po-THAL-uh-muss] a neural structure lying below *(hypo)* the thalamus; it directs several maintenance activities (eating, drinking, body temperature), helps govern the endocrine system via the pituitary gland, and is linked to emotion and reward.

hippocampus a neural center located in the limbic system; helps process explicit (conscious) memories—of facts and events—for storage.

* * *

FIGURE 2.17 locates the brain areas we've discussed, as well as the *cerebral cortex*—the body's ultimate control and information-processing center.

LaunchPad To review and assess your understanding, engage online with **Concept Practice: The Limbic System.**

🔒 RETRIEVE IT • • •
ANSWERS IN APPENDIX E

RI-5 What are the three key structures of the limbic system, and what functions do they serve?

🔒 FIGURE 2.17

BRAIN STRUCTURES AND THEIR FUNCTIONS

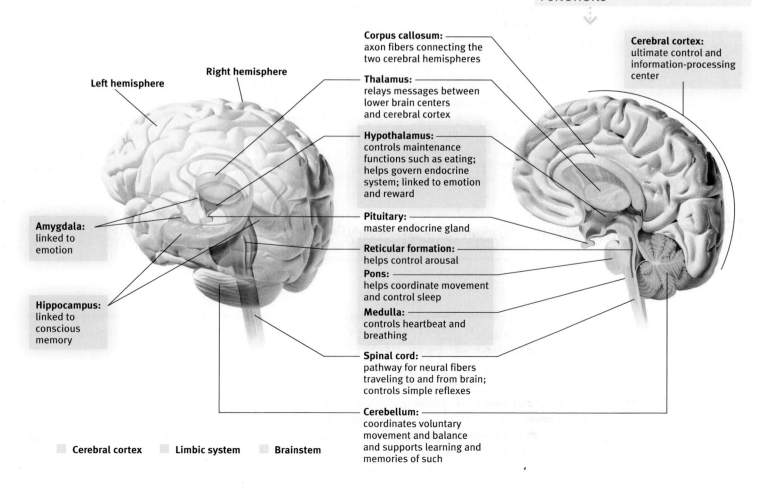

Corpus callosum: axon fibers connecting the two cerebral hemispheres

Cerebral cortex: ultimate control and information-processing center

Right hemisphere

Left hemisphere

Thalamus: relays messages between lower brain centers and cerebral cortex

Hypothalamus: controls maintenance functions such as eating; helps govern endocrine system; linked to emotion and reward

Amygdala: linked to emotion

Pituitary: master endocrine gland

Reticular formation: helps control arousal

Pons: helps coordinate movement and control sleep

Hippocampus: linked to conscious memory

Medulla: controls heartbeat and breathing

Spinal cord: pathway for neural fibers traveling to and from brain; controls simple reflexes

Cerebellum: coordinates voluntary movement and balance and supports learning and memories of such

Cerebral cortex   Limbic system   Brainstem

🔒 REVIEW TOOLS OF DISCOVERY, OLDER BRAIN STRUCTURES, AND THE LIMBIC SYSTEM

⟶ Learning Objectives

TEST YOURSELF Answer these repeated Learning Objective Questions on your own (before checking the answers in Appendix D) to improve your retention of the concepts (McDaniel et al., 2009, 2015).

2-8 How do neuroscientists study the brain's connections to behavior and mind?

2-9 What structures make up the brainstem, and what are the functions of the brainstem, thalamus, reticular formation, and cerebellum?

2-10 What are the limbic system's structures and functions?

⟶ Terms and Concepts to Remember

TEST YOURSELF Write down the definition yourself, then check your answer on the referenced page.

lesion [LEE-zhuhn], **p. 51**

EEG (electroencephalogram), **p. 51**

MEG (magnetoencephalography), **p. 51**

PET (positron emission tomography) scan, **p. 51**

MRI (magnetic resonance imaging), **p. 51**

fMRI (functional MRI), **p. 53**

brainstem, **p. 53**

medulla [muh-DUL-uh], **p. 53**

thalamus [THAL-uh-muss], **p. 54**

reticular formation, **p. 54**

cerebellum [sehr-uh-BELL-um], **p. 54**

limbic system, **p. 55**

amygdala [uh-MIG-duh-la], **p. 55**

hypothalamus [hi-po-THAL-uh-muss], **p. 57**

hippocampus, **p. 57**

⟶ Experience the Testing Effect

TEST YOURSELF Answer the following questions on your own first, then check your answers in Appendix E.

1. The part of the brainstem that controls heartbeat and breathing is the
   a. cerebellum.
   b. medulla.
   c. cortex.
   d. thalamus.

2. The thalamus functions as a
   a. memory bank.
   b. balance center.
   c. breathing regulator.
   d. sensory control center.

3. The lower brain structure that governs arousal is the
   a. spinal cord.
   b. cerebellum.
   c. reticular formation.
   d. medulla.

4. The part of the brain that coordinates voluntary movement and enables nonverbal learning and memory is the _____.

5. Two parts of the limbic system are the amygdala and the
   a. cerebral hemispheres.
   b. hippocampus.
   c. thalamus.
   d. pituitary.

6. A cat's ferocious response to electrical brain stimulation would lead you to suppose the electrode had touched the _____.

7. The neural structure that most directly regulates eating, drinking, and body temperature is the
   a. endocrine system.
   b. hypothalamus.
   c. hippocampus.
   d. amygdala.

8. The initial reward center discovered by Olds and Milner was located in the _____.

Continue testing yourself with 📚 **LearningCurve** or ≋ **Achieve Read & Practice** to learn and remember most effectively.

⟶ The Cerebral Cortex

LOQ 2-11 What four lobes make up the cerebral cortex, and what are the functions of the motor cortex, somatosensory cortex, and association areas?

Older brain networks sustain basic life functions and enable memory, emotions, and basic drives. Newer neural networks within the *cerebrum*—the two cerebral hemispheres contributing 85 percent of the brain's weight—form specialized work teams that enable our perceiving, thinking, and speaking. Like other structures above the brainstem (including the thalamus, hippocampus, and amygdala), the cerebral hemispheres come as a pair. Covering those hemispheres, like bark on a tree, is the **cerebral cortex,** a thin surface layer of interconnected neural cells. In our brain's evolutionary history, the cerebral cortex—our brain's thinking crown—is a relative newcomer.

As we move up the ladder of animal life, the cerebral cortex expands, tight genetic controls relax, and the organism's adaptability increases. Frogs and other small-cortex amphibians operate extensively on preprogrammed genetic instructions. The larger cortex of mammals offers increased capacities for learning and thinking, enabling them to adapt to ever-changing environments. What makes us distinctively human mostly arises from the complex functions of our cerebral cortex.

RETAIN The people who first dissected and labeled the brain used the language of scholars—Latin and Greek. Their words are actually attempts at graphic description: For example, *cortex* means "bark," *cerebellum* is "little brain," and *thalamus* is "inner chamber."

RETRIEVE IT • • • *ANSWERS IN APPENDIX E*

RI-1 Which area of the human brain is most similar to that of less complex animals? Which part of the human brain distinguishes us most from less complex animals?

STRUCTURE OF THE CORTEX

If you opened a human skull, exposing the brain, you would see a wrinkled organ, shaped somewhat like an oversized walnut. Without these wrinkles, a flattened cerebral cortex would require triple the area—roughly that of a large pizza. The brain's left and right hemispheres are filled mainly with axons connecting the cortex to the brain's other regions. The cerebral cortex—that thin surface layer—contains some 20 to 23 billion of the brain's nerve cells and 300 trillion synaptic connections (de Courten-Myers, 2005). Being human takes a lot of nerve.

ENGAGE Each hemisphere's cortex is subdivided into four *lobes,* separated by prominent *fissures,* or folds (**FIGURE 2.18**). Starting at the front of your brain and moving over the top, there are the **frontal lobes** (behind your forehead), the **parietal lobes** (at the top and to the rear), and the **occipital lobes** (at the back of your head). Reversing direction and moving forward, just above your ears, you find the **temporal lobes.** Each of the four lobes carries out many functions, and many functions require the interplay of several lobes.

cerebral [seh-REE-bruhl] **cortex** the intricate fabric of interconnected neural cells covering the cerebral hemispheres; the body's ultimate control and information-processing center.

frontal lobes the portion of the cerebral cortex lying just behind the forehead; involved in speaking and muscle movements and in making plans and judgments.

parietal [puh-RYE-uh-tuhl] **lobes** the portion of the cerebral cortex lying at the top of the head and toward the rear; receives sensory input for touch and body position.

occipital [ahk-SIP-uh-tuhl] **lobes** the portion of the cerebral cortex lying at the back of the head; includes areas that receive information from the visual fields.

temporal lobes the portion of the cerebral cortex lying roughly above the ears; includes the auditory areas, each receiving information primarily from the opposite ear.

FUNCTIONS OF THE CORTEX

More than a century ago, surgeons found damaged cortical areas during autopsies of people who had been partially paralyzed or speechless. This rather crude evidence did not prove that specific parts of the cortex control complex functions like movement or speech. A laptop with a broken power cord might go dead, but we would be fooling ourselves if we thought we had "localized" the internet in the cord.

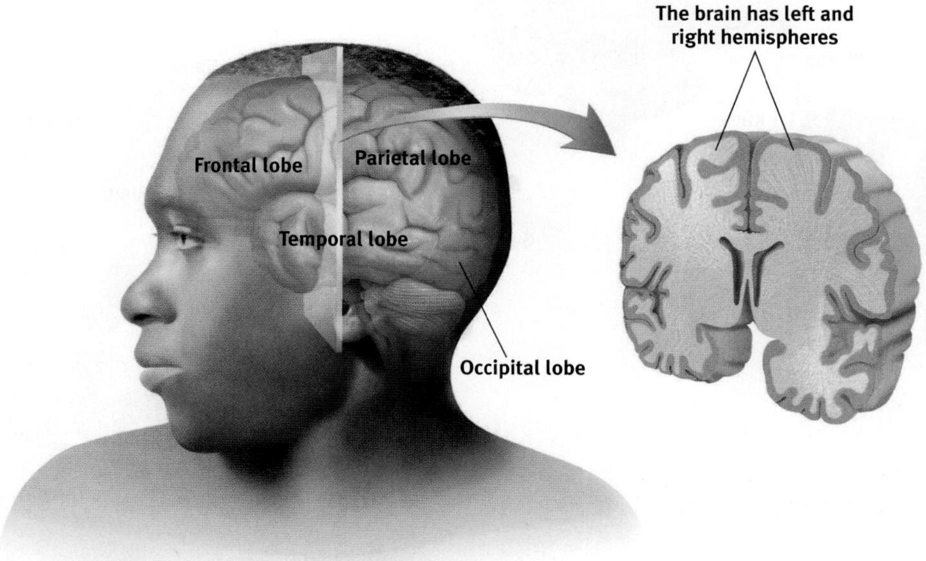

FIGURE 2.18
THE CORTEX AND ITS BASIC SUBDIVISIONS

Motor Functions

Scientists had better luck in localizing simpler brain functions. For example, in 1870, German physicians Gustav Fritsch and Eduard Hitzig made an important discovery: Mild electrical stimulation to parts of an animal's cortex made parts of its body move. The effects were selective: Stimulation caused movement only when applied to an arch-shaped region at the back of the frontal lobe, running roughly ear-to-ear across the top of the brain. Moreover, stimulating parts of this region in the left or right hemisphere caused movements of specific body parts on the *opposite* side of the body. Fritsch and Hitzig had discovered what is now called the **motor cortex.**

MAPPING THE MOTOR CORTEX Lucky for brain surgeons and their patients, the brain has no sensory receptors. Knowing this, in the 1930s, Otfrid Foerster and Wilder Penfield were able to map the motor cortex in hundreds of wide-awake patients by stimulating different cortical areas and observing the body's responses. They discovered that body areas requiring precise control, such as the fingers and mouth, occupy the greatest amount of cortical space (**FIGURE 2.19**). In one of his many demonstrations of motor behavior mechanics, Spanish neuroscientist José Delgado stimulated a spot on a patient's left motor cortex, triggering the right hand to make a fist. Asked to keep the fingers open during the next stimulation, the patient, whose fingers closed despite his best efforts, remarked, "I guess, Doctor, that your electricity is stronger than my will" (Delgado, 1969, p. 114).

More recently, scientists were able to predict a monkey's arm motion a tenth of a second *before* it moved—by repeatedly measuring motor cortex activity preceding specific arm movements (Gibbs, 1996). Such findings have opened the door to research on brain-controlled computer technology.

FIGURE 2.19

MOTOR CORTEX AND SOMATOSENSORY CORTEX TISSUE DEVOTED TO EACH BODY PART As you can see from this classic though inexact representation, the amount of cortex devoted to a body part in the motor cortex (in the frontal lobes) or in the somatosensory cortex (in the parietal lobes) is not proportional to that body part's size. Rather, the brain devotes more tissue to sensitive areas and to areas requiring precise control. Thus, the fingers have a greater representation in the cortex than does the upper arm.

🔒 **RETRIEVE IT • • •**   *ANSWERS IN APPENDIX E*

RI-2 Try moving your right hand in a circular motion, as if cleaning a table. Then start your right foot doing the same motion, synchronized with your hand. Now reverse the right foot's motion, but not the hand's. Finally, try moving the *left* foot opposite to the right hand.

a. Why is reversing the right foot's motion so hard?

b. Why is it easier to move the left foot opposite to the right hand?

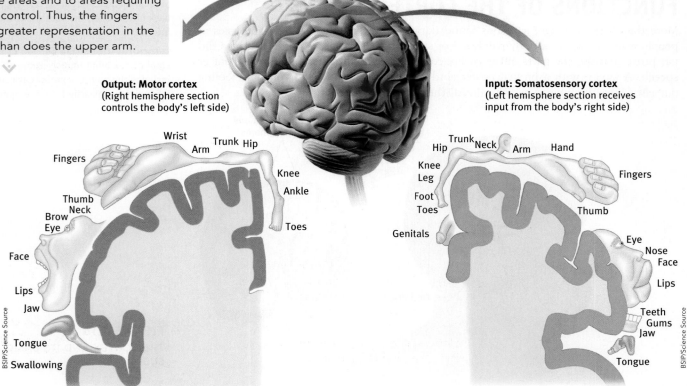

Output: Motor cortex
(Right hemisphere section controls the body's left side)

Input: Somatosensory cortex
(Left hemisphere section receives input from the body's right side)

BRAIN-MACHINE INTERFACES What might happen if researchers implant a device to detect motor cortex activity in humans? Could such devices help people with paralysis learn to command a cursor to write email or work online? Clinical trials are now under way with people who have severe paralysis or have lost a limb (Andersen et al., 2010; Nurmikko et al., 2010). The first patient, a 25-year-old man with paralysis, was able to mentally control a TV, draw shapes on a computer screen, and play video games—all thanks to an aspirin-sized chip with 100 microelectrodes recording activity in his motor cortex (Hochberg et al., 2006). Since then, others with paralysis who have received implants have learned to direct robotic arms with their thoughts (Clausen et al., 2017).

Sensory Functions

If the motor cortex sends messages out to the body, where does the cortex receive incoming messages? Penfield identified a cortical area—at the front of the parietal lobes, parallel to and just behind the motor cortex—that specializes in receiving information from the skin senses, such as touch and temperature, and from the movement of body parts. We now call this area the **somatosensory cortex.** Stimulate a point on the top of this band of tissue and a person may report being touched on the shoulder; stimulate some point on the side and the person may feel something on the face.

The more sensitive the body region, the larger the somatosensory cortex area devoted to it (see Figure 2.19). Your supersensitive lips project to a larger brain area than do your toes, which is one reason we kiss rather than touch toes. Rats have a large area of the brain devoted to their whisker sensations, and owls to their hearing sensations.

Scientists have identified additional areas where the cortex receives input from senses other than touch. Any visual information you are receiving now is going to the visual cortex in your occipital lobes, at the back of your brain (**FIGURES 2.20** and **2.21**). If you have normal vision, you might see flashes of light or dashes of color if stimulated in your occipital lobes. (In a sense, we *do* have eyes in the back of our head!) Having lost much of his right occipital lobe to a tumor removal, a friend of mine [DM's] was blind to the left half of his field of vision. Visual information travels from the occipital lobes to other areas that specialize in tasks such as identifying words, detecting emotions, and recognizing faces.

Any sound you now hear is processed by your auditory cortex in your temporal lobes (just above your ears; see Figure 2.21). Most of this auditory information travels a circuitous route from one ear to the auditory receiving area above your opposite ear. If stimulated in your auditory cortex, you might hear a sound. Researchers studying fMRI scans of people with schizophrenia have found active auditory areas in the temporal lobes during the false sensory experience of auditory *hallucinations* (Lennox et al., 1999). Even the phantom ringing sound experienced by people with hearing loss is—if heard in one ear—associated with activity in the temporal lobe on the brain's opposite side (Muhlnickel, 1998).

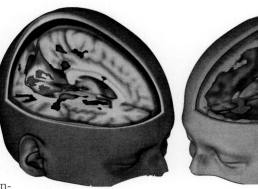
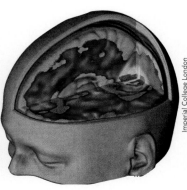

(a)   (b)

Imperial College London

FIGURE 2.20

SEEING WITHOUT EYES The psychoactive drug LSD often produces vivid *hallucinations.* Why? It dramatically increases communication between the visual cortex (in the occipital lobe) and other brain regions. (a) This fMRI (functional MRI) scan shows a research participant with closed eyes who has been given a placebo. (b) In this fMRI, the same person is under the influence of LSD (color represents increased blood flow) (Carhart-Harris et al., 2016; Cormier, 2016).

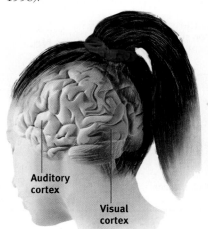

Auditory cortex

Visual cortex

FIGURE 2.21

THE VISUAL CORTEX AND AUDITORY CORTEX The visual cortex in the occipital lobes at the rear of your brain receives input from your eyes. The auditory cortex in your temporal lobes—above your ears—receives information from your ears.

motor cortex an area at the rear of the frontal lobes that controls voluntary movements.

somatosensory cortex an area at the front of the parietal lobes that registers and processes body touch and movement sensations.

association areas areas of the cerebral cortex that are not involved in primary motor or sensory functions; rather, they are involved in higher mental functions such as learning, remembering, thinking, and speaking.

RI-3 Our brain's _____ cortex registers and processes body touch and movement sensations. The _____ cortex controls our voluntary movements.

Association Areas

So far, we have pointed out small cortical areas that either receive sensory input or direct muscular output. Together, these occupy about one-fourth of the human brain's thin, wrinkled cover. What, then, goes on in the remaining vast regions of the cortex? In these **association areas,** neurons are busy with higher mental functions—many of the tasks that make us human.

Electrically probing an association area won't trigger any observable response. So, unlike the somatosensory and motor areas, association area functions cannot be neatly mapped. Does this mean we don't use them? See Thinking Critically About: Using More Than 10 Percent of Our Brain.

Association areas are found in all four lobes. The *prefrontal cortex* in the forward part of the frontal lobes enables judgment, planning, social interactions, and processing of new memories (de la Vega et al., 2016; Silwa & Frehwald, 2017). People with damaged frontal lobes may have high intelligence test scores and great cake-baking skills. Yet they would not be able to plan ahead to *begin* baking a cake for a birthday party (Huey et al., 2006). And if they did begin to bake, they might forget the recipe (MacPherson et al., 2016).

Frontal lobe damage also can alter personality and remove a person's inhibitions. Consider the classic case of railroad worker Phineas Gage. One afternoon in 1848, Gage, then 25 years old, was using a tamping iron to pack gunpowder into a rock. A spark ignited the gunpowder, shooting the rod up through his left cheek and out the top of his skull, leaving his frontal lobes damaged (**FIGURE 2.22**). To everyone's amazement, Gage was immediately able to sit up and speak, and after the wound healed, he returned to work. But having lost some of the neural tracts that enabled his frontal lobes to control

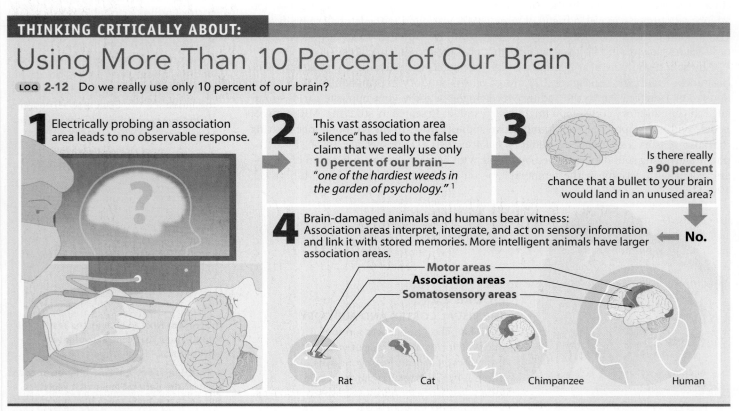

THINKING CRITICALLY ABOUT:

Using More Than 10 Percent of Our Brain

LOQ 2-12   Do we really use only 10 percent of our brain?

1 Electrically probing an association area leads to no observable response.

2 This vast association area "silence" has led to the false claim that we really use only **10 percent of our brain**— *"one of the hardiest weeds in the garden of psychology."* [1]

3 Is there really a **90 percent** chance that a bullet to your brain would land in an unused area?

No.

4 Brain-damaged animals and humans bear witness: Association areas interpret, integrate, and act on sensory information and link it with stored memories. More intelligent animals have larger association areas.

Motor areas
Association areas
Somatosensory areas

Rat   Cat   Chimpanzee   Human

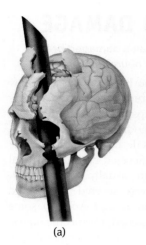
(a)

(b)

FIGURE 2.22

A BLAST FROM THE PAST (a) Phineas Gage's skull was kept as a medical record. Using measurements and modern neuroimaging techniques, researchers have reconstructed the probable path of the rod through Gage's brain (Van Horn et al., 2012). (b) This photo shows Gage after his accident. (The image has been reversed to show the features correctly. Early photos, including this one, were actually mirror images.)

his emotions, the affable, soft-spoken man was now irritable, profane, and dishonest (Van Horn et al., 2012). This person, said his friends, was "no longer Gage." His mental abilities and memories were intact, but for the next few years his personality was not. (Gage later lost his railroad job, but over time, he adapted to his injury and found work as a stage-coach driver [Macmillan & Lena, 2010].)

Studies of others with damaged frontal lobes have revealed similar impairments. Not only do they become less inhibited (without the frontal lobe brakes on their impulses), but their moral judgments also seem unrestrained. Cecil Clayton lost 20 percent of his left frontal lobe in a 1972 sawmill accident. Thereafter, his intelligence test score dropped to an elementary school level and he displayed increased impulsivity. In 1996, he fatally shot a deputy sheriff. In 2015, when he was 74, the State of Missouri executed him (Williams, 2015).

Would you advocate pushing one person in front of a runaway trolley to save five others? Most people would not, but those with damage to the frontal lobe are often untroubled by such ethical dilemmas (Koenigs et al., 2007). The frontal lobes help steer us away from violent actions (Molenberghs et al., 2015; Yang & Raine, 2009). With their frontal lobes ruptured, people's moral compass seems to disconnect from their behavior.

Association areas also perform other mental functions. The parietal lobes, parts of which were large and unusually shaped in Einstein's normal-weight brain, enable mathematical and spatial reasoning (Burrell, 2015; Ibos & Freedman, 2014). On the underside of the right temporal lobe, another association area enables us to recognize faces. If a stroke or head injury destroyed this area of your brain, you would still be able to describe facial features and to recognize someone's gender and approximate age, yet be strangely unable to identify the person as, say, Miley Cyrus, or even your grandmother.

Nevertheless, complex mental functions don't reside in any one place. During a complex task, a brain scan shows many islands of brain activity working together—some running automatically in the background, and others under conscious control (Chein & Schneider, 2012). Your memory, language, and attention result from *functional connectivity*—communication among distinct brain areas and neural networks (Knight, 2007). Ditto for religious experience. More than 40 distinct brain regions become active in different religious states, such as prayer and meditation, indicating that there is no simple "God spot" (Fingelkurts & Fingelkurts, 2009). *The point to remember:* Our mental experiences arise from coordinated brain activity.

LaunchPad See the **Video: Case Studies** for a helpful tutorial animation.

MISSING FRONTAL LOBE BRAKES With part of his left frontal lobe (in this downward-facing brain scan) lost to injury, Cecil Clayton became more impulsive and killed a deputy sheriff. Nineteen years later, his state executed him for this crime.

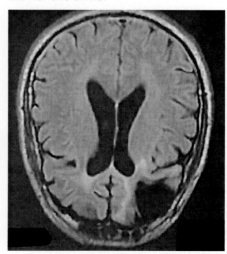

🔒 **RETRIEVE IT • • •**   *ANSWERS IN APPENDIX E*

RI-4 Why are association areas important?

LaunchPad Check your understanding of the parts of the brain by engaging online with **Concept Practice: Brain Areas Within the Head.**

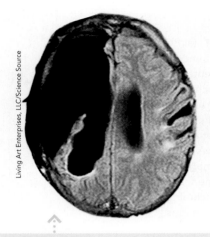

FIGURE 2.23

BRAIN WORK IS CHILD'S PLAY
This 6-year-old had surgery to end her life-threatening seizures. Although most of an entire hemisphere was removed (see MRI of hemispherectomy), her remaining hemisphere compensated by putting other areas to work. One Johns Hopkins medical team reflected on the child hemispherectomies they had performed. Although use of the opposite arm was compromised, the team reported being "awed" by how well the children had retained their memory, personality, and humor (Vining et al., 1997). The younger the child, the greater the chance that the remaining hemisphere can take over the functions of the one that was surgically removed (Choi, 2008; Danelli et al., 2013).

neurogenesis the formation of new neurons.

corpus callosum [KOR-pus kah-LOW-sum] the large band of neural fibers connecting the two brain hemispheres and carrying messages between them.

split brain a condition resulting from surgery that isolates the brain's two hemispheres by cutting the fibers (mainly those of the corpus callosum) connecting them.

RESPONSES TO DAMAGE

LOQ 2-13 To what extent can a damaged brain reorganize itself, and what is *neurogenesis*?

Earlier, we learned about the brain's *plasticity*—how our brain adapts to new situations. What happens when we experience mishaps, big and little? Let's explore the brain's ability to modify itself after damage.

Most brain-damage effects described earlier can be traced to two hard facts: (1) Severed brain and spinal cord neurons, unlike cut skin, usually do not regenerate. (If your spinal cord were severed, you would probably be permanently paralyzed.) And (2) some brain functions seem preassigned to specific areas. One newborn who suffered damage to temporal lobe facial recognition areas was never able to recognize faces (Farah et al., 2000). But there is good news: Some neural tissue can *reorganize* in response to damage.

Plasticity may also occur after serious damage, especially in young children (Kolb, 1989; see also **FIGURE 2.23**). The brain's plasticity is good news for those with vision or hearing loss. Blindness or deafness makes unused brain areas available for other uses (Amedi et al., 2005). If a blind person uses one finger to read Braille, the brain area dedicated to that finger expands as the sense of touch invades the visual cortex that normally helps people see (Barinaga, 1992; Sadato et al., 1996).

Plasticity also helps explain why some studies have found that deaf people who learned sign language before another language have enhanced peripheral and motion-detection vision (Bosworth & Dobkins, 1999; Shiell et al., 2014). In deaf people whose native language is sign, the temporal lobe area normally dedicated to hearing waits in vain for stimulation. Finally, it looks for other signals to process, such as those from the visual system used to see and interpret signs.

Similar reassignment may occur when disease or damage frees up other brain areas normally dedicated to specific functions. If a slow-growing left hemisphere tumor disrupts language (which resides mostly in the left hemisphere), the right hemisphere may compensate (Thiel et al., 2006). If a finger is amputated, the somatosensory cortex that received its input will begin to receive input from the adjacent fingers, which then become more sensitive (Oelschläger et al., 2014). So what do you suppose was the sexual intercourse experience of one patient whose lower leg had been amputated? "I actually experience my orgasm in my [phantom] foot. [Note that in Figure 2.19, the toes region is adjacent to the genitals.] And there it's much bigger than it used to be because it's no longer just confined to my genitals" (Ramachandran & Blakeslee, 1998, p. 36).

Although the brain often attempts self-repair by reorganizing existing tissue, it sometimes attempts to mend itself through **neurogenesis**—producing new neurons. Researchers have found baby neurons deep in the brains of adult mice, birds, monkeys, and humans (He & Jin, 2016; Jessberger et al., 2008). These neurons may then migrate elsewhere and form connections with neighboring neurons (Aimone et al., 2010; Egeland et al., 2015; Gould, 2007).

Master stem cells that can develop into any type of brain cell have also been discovered in the human embryo. If mass-produced in a lab and injected into a damaged brain, might neural stem cells turn themselves into replacements for lost brain cells? Researchers at universities and biotech companies continue to break new ground on how to produce stem cells that resemble functioning human neurons (Lu et al., 2016; Paşca et al., 2015). Such stem cell research not only helps treat the diseased or damaged brain, but also aids understanding of brain development, memory, and other basic psychological processes (Mariani et al., 2012; Sun et al, 2015; Zhang et al., 2016). Might surgeons someday be able to rebuild damaged brains, much as we reseed damaged lawns? Stay tuned. In the meantime, we can all benefit from natural promoters of neurogenesis, such as exercise, sleep, and nonstressful but stimulating environments (Iso et al., 2007; Pereira et al., 2007; Sexton et al., 2016).

THE DIVIDED BRAIN

LOQ 2-14 What do split brains reveal about the functions of our two brain hemispheres?

Our brain's look-alike left and right hemispheres serve differing functions. This *lateralization* is apparent after brain damage. Research spanning more than a century has shown that left hemisphere accidents, strokes, and tumors can impair reading, writing, speaking, arithmetic reasoning, and understanding. Similar right hemisphere damage has less visibly dramatic effects. Does this mean that the right hemisphere is just along for the ride? Many believed this was the case until the 1960s, when a fascinating chapter in psychology's history began to unfold: Researchers found that the "minor" right hemisphere was not so limited after all.

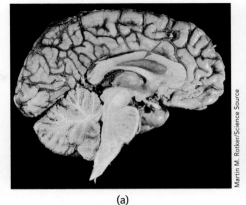
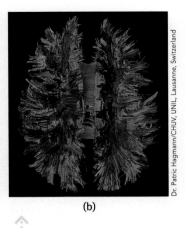

(a)   (b)

Martin M. Rotker/Science Source

Dr. Patric Hagmann/CHUV, UNIL, Lausanne, Switzerland

Splitting the Brain

In 1961, Los Angeles neurosurgeons Philip Vogel and Joseph Bogen speculated that major epileptic seizures were caused by an amplification of abnormal brain activity bouncing back and forth between the two cerebral hemispheres, which work together as a whole system. If so, they wondered, could they end this biological tennis match by severing the **corpus callosum,** the wide band of axon fibers connecting the two hemispheres and carrying messages between them (**FIGURE 2.24**)? Vogel and Bogen knew that psychologists Roger Sperry, Ronald Myers, and Michael Gazzaniga had divided cats' and monkeys' brains in this manner, with no serious ill effects.

So the surgeons operated. The result? The seizures all but disappeared. The patients with these **split brains** were surprisingly normal, their personality and intellect hardly affected. Waking from surgery, one even joked that he had a "splitting headache" (Gazzaniga, 1967). By sharing their experiences, these patients have greatly expanded our understanding of interactions between the intact brain's two hemispheres.

To appreciate these findings, we need to focus for a minute on the peculiar nature of our visual wiring, illustrated in **FIGURE 2.25**. Note that each eye receives sensory information from the entire visual field. But in each eye, information from the left half of your field of vision goes to your right hemisphere, and information from the right half of your visual field goes to your left hemisphere, which usually controls speech. Information received by either hemisphere is quickly transmitted to the other across the corpus callosum. In a person with a severed corpus callosum, this information-sharing does not take place.

Knowing these facts, Sperry and Gazzaniga could send information to a patient's left or right hemisphere. As the person stared at a spot, they flashed a stimulus to its right or left. They could do this with you, too, but in your intact brain, the hemisphere receiving the information would instantly pass the news to the other side. Because the split-brain surgery had cut the communication lines between the hemispheres, the researchers could, with these patients, quiz each hemisphere separately.

In an early experiment, Gazzaniga (1967) asked split-brain patients to stare at a dot as he flashed

FIGURE 2.24

THE CORPUS CALLOSUM This large band of neural fibers connects the two brain hemispheres. (a) To photograph this half brain, a surgeon separated the hemispheres by cutting through the corpus callosum (see blue arrow) and lower brain regions. (b) This high-resolution diffusion spectrum image, showing a top-facing brain from above, reveals brain neural networks within the two hemispheres, and the corpus callosum neural bridge between them.

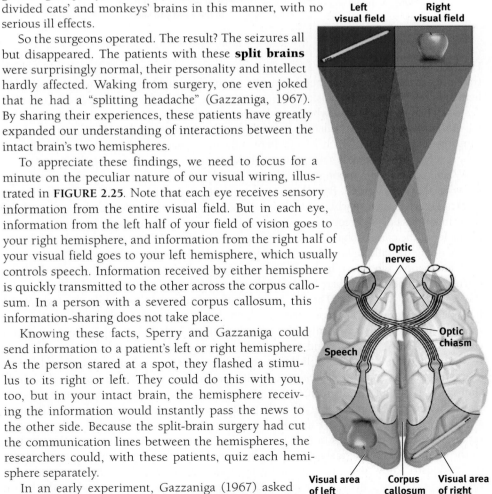

Left visual field   **Right visual field**

Optic nerves

Optic chiasm

Speech

Visual area of left hemisphere   Corpus callosum   Visual area of right hemisphere

FIGURE 2.25

THE INFORMATION HIGHWAY FROM EYE TO BRAIN

FIGURE 2.26

ONE SKULL, TWO MINDS When an experimenter flashes the word HEART across the visual field, a woman with a split brain verbally reports seeing the portion of the word transmitted to her left hemisphere. However, if asked to indicate with her left hand what she saw, she points to the portion of the word transmitted to her right hemisphere (Gazzaniga, 1983).

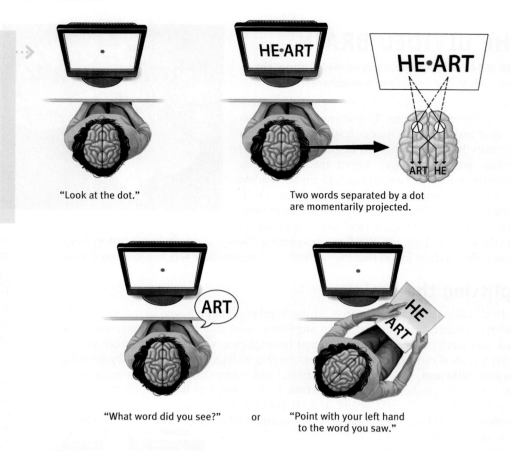

"Look at the dot."

Two words separated by a dot are momentarily projected.

"What word did you see?"   or   "Point with your left hand to the word you saw."

HE·ART on a screen (**FIGURE 2.26**). Thus, HE appeared in their left visual field (which transmits to the right hemisphere) and ART in the right field (which transmits to the left hemisphere). When he then asked them to *say* what they had seen, the patients reported that they had seen ART. But when asked to *point* to what they had seen, they were startled when their left hand (controlled by the right hemisphere) pointed to HE. Given an opportunity to express itself, each hemisphere indicated what it had seen. The right hemisphere (controlling the left hand) intuitively knew what it could not verbally report.

When a picture of a spoon was flashed to their right hemisphere, the patients could not *say* what they had viewed. But when asked to *identify* what they had viewed by feeling an assortment of hidden objects with their left hand, they readily selected the spoon. If the experimenter said, "Correct!" the patient might reply, "What? Correct? How could I possibly pick out the correct object when I don't know what I saw?" It is, of course, the left hemisphere doing the talking here, bewildered by what the nonverbal right hemisphere knows.

A few people who have had split-brain surgery have been for a time bothered by the unruly independence of their left hand. It seemed the left hand truly didn't know what the right hand was doing. The left hand might unbutton a shirt while the right hand buttoned it, or put grocery store items back on the shelf after the right hand put them in the cart. It was as if each hemisphere was thinking "I've half a mind to wear my green (blue) shirt today." Indeed, said Sperry (1964), split-brain surgery leaves people "with two separate minds." With a split brain, both hemispheres can comprehend and follow an instruction to copy—*simultaneously*—different figures with the left and right hands (Franz et al., 2000; see also **FIGURE 2.27**). (Reading these reports, can you imagine a patient enjoying a solitary game of "rock, paper, scissors"—left versus right hand?)

When the "two minds" are at odds, the left hemisphere does mental gymnastics to rationalize reactions it does not understand. If a patient follows an order ("Walk") sent to the right hemisphere, a strange thing happens. The left hemisphere, unaware of the order, doesn't know why the patient begins walking. But if asked, the patient doesn't reply, "I don't know." Instead, the left hemisphere improvises—"I'm going into the house to get a Coke." Gazzaniga (2006), who described these patients as "the most fascinating

"Do not let your left hand know what your right hand is doing." —Matthew 6:3

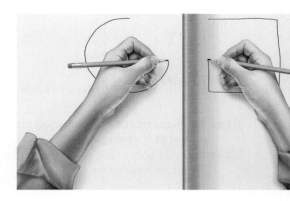

FIGURE 2.27

TRY THIS! People who have had split-brain surgery can simultaneously draw two different shapes.

people on earth," realized that the conscious left hemisphere resembles an "interpreter" that instantly constructs explanations. The brain, he concluded, often runs on autopilot; it acts first and then explains itself.

> **🔒 RETRIEVE IT • • •**   *ANSWERS IN APPENDIX E*
>
> **RI-5** (1) If we flash a red light to the right hemisphere of a person with a split brain, and flash a green light to the left hemisphere, will each observe its own color? (2) Will the person be aware that the colors differ? (3) What will the person verbally report seeing?

Right-Left Differences in the Intact Brain

So, what about the 99.99+ percent of us with undivided brains? Does each of *our* hemispheres also perform distinct functions? The short answer is *Yes*. When a person performs a *perceptual* task, a brain scan often reveals increased activity (brain waves, blood flow, and glucose consumption) in the *right* hemisphere. When the person speaks or does a math calculation, activity usually increases in the *left* hemisphere.

A dramatic demonstration of hemispheric specialization happens before some types of brain surgery. To locate the patient's language centers, the surgeon injects a sedative into the neck artery feeding blood to the left hemisphere, which usually controls speech. Before the injection, the patient is lying down, arms in the air, chatting with the doctor. Can you predict what happens when the drug puts the left hemisphere to sleep? Within seconds, the person's right arm falls limp. If the left hemisphere is controlling language, the patient will be speechless until the drug wears off. If the drug is injected into the artery to the right hemisphere, the *left* arm will fall limp, but the person will still be able to speak.

To the brain, language is language, whether spoken or signed. Just as hearing people usually use the left hemisphere to process spoken language, deaf people use the left hemisphere to process sign language (Corina et al., 1992; Hickok et al., 2001). Thus, a left hemisphere stroke disrupts a deaf person's signing, much as it would disrupt a hearing person's speaking (Corina, 1998).

Although the left hemisphere is skilled at making quick, literal interpretations of language, the right hemisphere excels at *making inferences* (Beeman & Chiarello, 1998; Bowden & Beeman, 1998; Mason & Just, 2004). It also *helps us modulate our speech* to make meaning clear—as when we say "Let's eat, Grandpa" instead of "Let's eat Grandpa" (Heller, 1990). The right hemisphere also *helps orchestrate our self-awareness.* People who suffer partial paralysis will sometimes stubbornly deny their impairment—mysteriously claiming they can move a paralyzed limb—if the damage is to the right hemisphere (Berti et al., 2005).

Simply looking at the two hemispheres, so alike to the naked eye, who would suppose they each contribute uniquely to the harmony of the whole? Yet a variety of observations—of people with split brains, of people with normal brains, and even of other species' brains—converge beautifully, leaving little doubt that we have unified brains with specialized parts (Hopkins & Cantalupo, 2008; MacNeilage et al., 2009).

How does the brain's intricate networking emerge? How does our *heredity*—the legacy of our ancestral history—conspire with our experiences to organize and "wire" the brain? To that we turn next.

LaunchPad Have you ever been asked if you are "left-brained" or "right-brained"? Consider this popular misconception by engaging online with **Immersive Learning: How Would You Know If People Can Be "Left-Brained" or "Right-Brained"?**

Brain scans show that, like humans, dogs usually process words with their left hemisphere and intonation with a right hemisphere region. One study demonstrated that giving praise was ineffective if what the dogs heard didn't match *how* it was spoken (Andics et al., 2016).

LaunchPad For a helpful animated review of this research, see **Topic Tutorial: PsychSim6, Hemispheric Specialization.**

🔒 REVIEW THE CEREBRAL CORTEX

⊙ Learning Objectives

TEST YOURSELF Answer these repeated Learning Objective Questions on your own (before checking the answers in Appendix D) to improve your retention of the concepts (McDaniel et al., 2009, 2015).

2-11 What four lobes make up the cerebral cortex, and what are the functions of the motor cortex, somatosensory cortex, and association areas?

2-12 Do we really use only 10 percent of our brain?

2-13 To what extent can a damaged brain reorganize itself, and what is *neurogenesis*?

2-14 What do split brains reveal about the functions of our two brain hemispheres?

⊙ Terms and Concepts to Remember

TEST YOURSELF Write down the definition yourself, then check your answer on the referenced page.

cerebral [seh-REE-bruhl] cortex, **p. 59**

frontal lobes, **p. 59**

parietal [puh-RYE-uh-tuhl] lobes, **p. 59**

occipital [ahk-SIP-uh-tuhl] lobes, **p. 59**

temporal lobes, **p. 59**

motor cortex, **p. 61**

somatosensory cortex, **p. 61**

association areas, **p. 62**

neurogenesis, **p. 64**

corpus callosum [KOR-pus kah-LOW-sum], **p. 64**

split brain, **p. 64**

⊙ Experience the Testing Effect

TEST YOURSELF Answer the following questions on your own first, then check your answers in Appendix E.

1. If a neurosurgeon stimulated your right motor cortex, you would most likely
   a. see light.
   b. hear a sound.
   c. feel a touch on the right arm.
   d. move your left leg.

2. How do different neural networks communicate with one another to let you respond when a friend greets you at a party?

3. Which of the following body regions has the greatest representation in the somatosensory cortex?
   a. Upper arm
   b. Toes
   c. Lips
   d. All regions are equally represented.

4. Judging and planning are enabled by the _____ lobes.

5. The "uncommitted" areas that make up about three-fourths of the cerebral cortex are called _____ _____.

6. The flexible brain's ability to respond to damage is especially evident in the brains of
   a. split-brain patients.
   b. young adults.
   c. young children.
   d. right-handed people.

7. An experimenter flashes the word HERON across the visual field of a man whose corpus callosum has been severed. HER is transmitted to his right hemisphere and ON to his left hemisphere. When asked to indicate what he saw, the man says he saw _____ but his left hand points to _____.

8. Studies of people with split brains and brain scans of those with undivided brains indicate that the left hemisphere excels in
   a. processing language.   c. making inferences.
   b. visual perceptions.   d. neurogenesis.

9. Damage to the brain's right hemisphere is most likely to reduce a person's ability to
   a. recite the alphabet rapidly.
   b. make inferences.
   c. understand verbal instructions.
   d. solve arithmetic problems.

Continue testing yourself with 📖 **LearningCurve** or 📖 **Achieve Read & Practice** to learn and remember most effectively.

⟶ Genetics, Evolutionary Psychology, and Behavior

BEHAVIOR GENETICS: PREDICTING INDIVIDUAL DIFFERENCES

LOQ 2-15 What are *chromosomes, DNA, genes,* and the human *genome*? How do behavior geneticists explain our individual differences?

Our shared brain architecture predisposes some common behavioral tendencies. Whether we live in the Arctic or the tropics, we sense the world, develop language, and feel hunger through identical mechanisms. We prefer sweet tastes to sour. We divide the color spectrum into similar colors. And we feel drawn to behaviors that produce and protect offspring.

Our human family shares not only a common biological heritage—cut us and we bleed—but also common social behaviors. Whether named Gonzales, Nkomo, Smith, or Wong, we start fearing strangers at about eight months, and as adults we prefer the company of those with attitudes and attributes similar to our own. As members of one species, we affiliate, conform, return favors, punish offenses, organize hierarchies of status, and grieve a child's death. A visitor from outer space could drop in anywhere and find humans dancing and feasting, singing and worshiping, playing sports and games, laughing and crying, living in families and forming groups. We are the leaves of one tree.

But in important ways, we also are each unique. We are each a one-of-a-kind package of looks, language, personality, interests, and cultural background. What causes our striking diversity? How much of it is shaped by our differing genes, and how much by our **environment**—by every external influence, from maternal nutrition while in the womb to social support while nearing the tomb? How does our **heredity** interact with our experiences to create both our universal human nature and our individual and social diversity? Such questions intrigue **behavior geneticists.**

Genes: Our Codes for Life

Barely more than a century ago, few would have guessed that every cell nucleus in your body contains the genetic master code for your entire body. It's as if every room in Dubai's Burj Khalifa (the world's tallest building) contained a book detailing the architect's plans for the entire structure. The plans for your own book of life run to 46 chapters—23 donated by your mother's egg and 23 by your father's sperm. Each of these 46 chapters, called a **chromosome,** is composed of a coiled chain of the molecule **DNA (deoxyribonucleic acid). Genes,** small segments of the giant DNA molecules, form the words of those chapters (**FIGURE 2.28**). Altogether, you have some 20,000 genes, which are either active (*expressed*) or inactive. Environmental events "turn on" genes, rather like hot water enabling a tea bag to express its flavor. When turned on, genes provide the code for creating *protein molecules,* our body's building blocks.

Genetically speaking, every other human is nearly your identical twin. Human **genome** researchers have discovered the common sequence within human DNA. This shared genetic profile is what makes us humans, rather than tulips, bananas, or chimpanzees.

The occasional variations found at particular gene sites in human DNA fascinate geneticists and psychologists. Slight person-to-person variations from the common pattern give clues to our uniqueness—why one person has a disease that another does not, why one person is tall and another short, why one is anxious and another calm.

Most of our traits have complex genetic roots. How tall you are, for example, reflects the size of your face, vertebrae, leg bones, and so forth—each of which may be influenced

environment every nongenetic influence, from prenatal nutrition to the people and things around us.

heredity the genetic transfer of characteristics from parents to offspring.

behavior genetics the study of the relative power and limits of genetic and environmental influences on behavior.

chromosomes threadlike structures made of DNA molecules that contain the genes.

DNA (deoxyribonucleic acid) a complex molecule containing the genetic information that makes up the chromosomes.

genes the biochemical units of heredity that make up the chromosomes; segments of DNA capable of synthesizing proteins.

genome the complete instructions for making an organism, consisting of all the genetic material in that organism's chromosomes.

A Thousand Words Photography by Erica Corner

THE NURTURE OF NATURE Parents everywhere wonder: Will my baby grow up to be peaceful or aggressive? Plain or attractive? Successful or struggling at every step? What comes built in, and what is nurtured—and how? Research reveals that nature and nurture together shape our development— every step of the way.

"Your DNA and mine are 99.9 percent the same. . . . At the DNA level, we are clearly all part of one big worldwide family." —Francis Collins, Human Genome Project director, 2007

"We share half our genes with the banana." —Evolutionary biologist Robert May, president of Britain's Royal Society, 2001

FIGURE 2.28

THE LIFE CODE The nucleus of every human cell contains chromosomes, each of which is made up of two strands of DNA connected in a double helix. Genes are DNA segments that, when expressed (turned on), direct the development of proteins that influence a person's individual development.

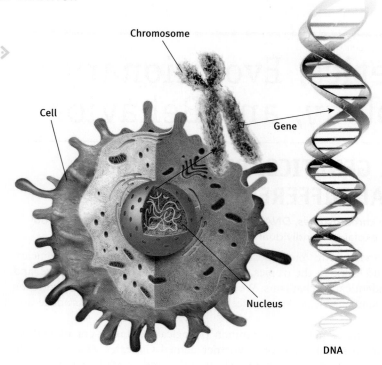

Chromosome

Cell

Gene

Nucleus

DNA

"Thanks for almost everything, Dad."

📺 **LaunchPad** See the **Video: Twin Studies** for a helpful tutorial animation.

identical (monozygotic) twins individuals that develop from a single fertilized egg that splits in two, creating two genetically identical organisms.

fraternal (dizygotic) twins individuals that develop from separate fertilized eggs. They are genetically no closer than ordinary siblings, but they share a prenatal environment.

by different genes interacting with your specific environment. Traits such as intelligence, happiness, and aggressiveness are similarly influenced by many genes. Indeed, one of the big take-home findings of today's behavior genetics is that there is no single smart gene, gay (or straight) gene, or schizophrenia gene. Rather, our differing traits are influenced by "many genes of small effect" (Okbay et al., 2016; Plomin et al., 2016).

So, our many genes help explain both our shared human nature and our human diversity. But—another take-home finding—knowing our heredity tells only part of our story. To form us, environmental influences interact with our genetic predispositions.

🔒 **RETRIEVE IT • • •**   *ANSWERS IN APPENDIX E*

RI-1 Put the following cell structures in order from smallest to largest: nucleus, gene, chromosome.

Twin and Adoption Studies

LOQ 2-16 How do twin and adoption studies help us understand the effects and interactions of nature and nurture?

To scientifically tease apart the influences of environment and heredity, behavior geneticists could wish for two types of experiments. The first would control heredity while varying the home environment. The second would control the home environment while varying heredity. Although such experiments with human infants would be unethical, nature has done this work for us.

IDENTICAL VERSUS FRATERNAL TWINS **Identical (monozygotic) twins** develop from a single fertilized egg that splits. Thus they are *genetically* identical—nature's own human clones (**FIGURE 2.29**). Indeed, they are clones who share not only the same genes but the same conception and uterus, and usually the same birth date and cultural history.

Fraternal (dizygotic) twins develop from two separate fertilized eggs. Although they share a prenatal environment, they are genetically no more similar than ordinary siblings.

Shared genes can translate into shared experiences. A person whose identical twin has *autism spectrum disorder,* for example, has about a 3 in 4 risk of being similarly diagnosed. If the affected twin is fraternal, the co-twin has about a 1 in 3 risk (Ronald & Hoekstra, 2011). To study the effects of genes and environments, several thousand medical and psychological researchers have studied nearly 15 million identical and fraternal twin pairs (Polderman et al., 2015).

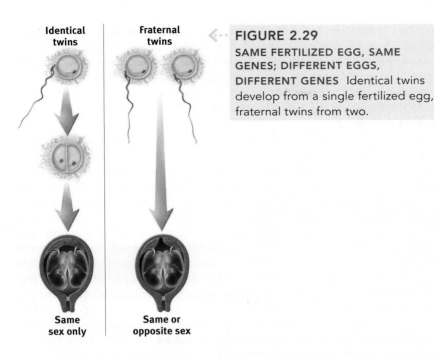

Identical twins

Fraternal twins

Same sex only

Same or opposite sex

FIGURE 2.29

SAME FERTILIZED EGG, SAME GENES; DIFFERENT EGGS, DIFFERENT GENES Identical twins develop from a single fertilized egg, fraternal twins from two.

Are genetically identical twins also *behaviorally* more similar than fraternal twins? Studies of thousands of twin pairs have found that identical twins are much more alike in *extraversion* (outgoingness) and *neuroticism* (emotional instability) than are fraternal twins (Kandler et al., 2011; Laceulle et al., 2011; Loehlin, 2012).

Identical twins, more than fraternal twins, look alike. So, do people's responses to their looks account for their similarities? *No.* In a clever approach, researcher (and twin) Nancy Segal (2013; Segal et al., 2013) compared personality similarity between identical twins and unrelated look-alike pairs. Only the identical twins reported similar personalities. Other studies have shown that identical twins whose parents treated them alike (for example, dressing them identically) were not psychologically more alike than other identical twins (Kendler et al., 1994; Loehlin & Nichols, 1976). In explaining individual differences, genes matter.

SEPARATED TWINS Imagine the following science fiction experiment: A mad scientist decides to separate identical twins at birth, then raise them in differing environments. Better yet, consider a *true* story:

In 1979, some time after divorcing, Jim Lewis awoke next to his second wife. Determined to make this marriage work, Jim made a habit of leaving love notes around the house. As he lay in bed he thought about others he had loved, including his son, James Alan, and his faithful dog, Toy.

Jim enjoyed spending part of the day in his basement woodworking shop building furniture, picture frames, and other items, including a white bench now circling a tree in his front yard. Jim also liked to drive his Chevy, watch stock-car racing, and drink Miller Lite beer.

What was extraordinary about Jim Lewis, however, was that at that same moment (we are not making this up) there existed another man—also named Jim—for whom all these things (right down to the dog's name) were also true.[1] This other Jim—Jim Springer—just happened, 38 years earlier, to have been his womb-mate. Thirty-seven days after their birth, these genetically identical twins were separated, adopted, and raised with no contact or knowledge of each other's whereabouts until the day Jim Lewis received a call from his genetic clone (who, having been told he had a twin, set out to find him).

One month later, the brothers became the first of many separated twin pairs tested by University of Minnesota psychologist Thomas Bouchard and his colleagues (Miller, P., 2012).

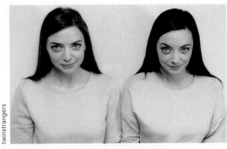

DO LOOK-ALIKES ACT ALIKE? Genetically unrelated look-alikes, such as these doppelgangers, tend not to have notably similar personalities (Segal, 2013).

Twins Lorraine and Levinia Christmas, driving to deliver Christmas presents to each other near Flitcham, England, collided (Shepherd, 1997).

---

1. Actually, this description of the two Jims errs in one respect: Jim Lewis named his son James Alan. Jim Springer named his James Allan.

Bouchard's famous twin research was, appropriately enough, conducted in Minneapolis, the "Twin City" (with St. Paul) and home to the Minnesota Twins baseball team.

The brothers' voice intonations and inflections were so similar that, hearing a playback of an earlier interview, Jim Springer guessed, "That's me." Wrong—it was Jim Lewis. Given tests measuring their personality, intelligence, heart rate, and brain waves, the Jim twins—despite 38 years of separation—were virtually as alike as the same person tested twice. Both married women named Dorothy Jane Scheckelburger. Okay, the last item is a joke. But as Judith Rich Harris (2006) has noted, it would hardly be weirder than some other reported similarities.

Aided by media publicity, Bouchard (2009) and his colleagues located and studied 74 pairs of identical twins raised apart. They continued to find similarities not only of tastes and physical attributes but also of personality, abilities, attitudes, interests, and fears.

Stories of startling twin similarities have not impressed critics, who remind us that "the plural of *anecdote* is not *data*." They note that if any two strangers were to spend hours comparing their behaviors and life histories, they would probably discover many coincidental similarities. If researchers created a control group of biologically unrelated pairs of the same age, sex, and ethnicity, who had not grown up together but who were as similar to one another in economic and cultural background as are many of the separated twin pairs, wouldn't these pairs also exhibit striking similarities (Joseph, 2001)? Twin researchers have replied that separated fraternal twins do not exhibit similarities comparable with those of separated identical twins.

The impressive data from personality assessments are clouded by the reunion of many of the separated twins some years before they were tested. Adoption agencies also tend to place separated twins in similar homes. Despite these criticisms, the striking twin-study results helped shift scientific thinking toward a greater appreciation of genetic influences.

If genetic influences help explain individual differences, can the same be said of trait differences *between* groups? Not necessarily. Individual differences in height and weight, for example, are highly heritable; yet nutrition (an environmental factor) rather than genetic influences explains why, as a group, today's adults are taller and heavier than those of a century ago. The two groups differ, but not because human genes have changed in a mere century's eyeblink of time. Ditto aggressiveness, a genetically influenced trait. Today's peaceful Scandinavians differ from their more aggressive Viking ancestors, despite carrying many of the same genes.

BIOLOGICAL VERSUS ADOPTIVE RELATIVES For behavior geneticists, nature's second real-life experiment—adoption—creates two groups: *genetic relatives* (biological parents and siblings) and *environmental relatives* (adoptive parents and siblings). For personality or any other given trait, we can therefore ask whether adopted children are more like their biological parents, who contributed their genes, or their adoptive parents, who contribute a home environment. And while sharing that home environment, do adopted siblings come to share traits?

The stunning finding from studies of hundreds of adoptive families is that, apart from identical twins, people who grow up together—whether biologically related or not—do not much resemble one another in personality (McGue & Bouchard, 1998; Plomin, 2011; Rowe, 1990). In personality traits such as extraversion and agreeableness, for example, people who have been adopted are more similar to their *biological* parents than their caregiving adoptive parents.

The finding is important enough to bear repeating: The normal range of environments shared by a family's children has little discernible impact on their personalities. Two adopted children raised in the same home are no more likely to share personality traits with each other than with the child down the block.

Heredity shapes other primates' personalities, too. Macaque monkeys raised by foster mothers exhibited social behaviors that resembled their biological, rather than foster, mothers (Maestripieri, 2003).

The genetic leash may limit the family environment's influence on personality, but it does not mean that adoptive parenting is a fruitless venture. As an adoptive parent, I [ND] especially find it heartening to know that parents do influence their children's attitudes, values, manners, politics, and faith (Kandler & Riemann, 2013). This was dramatically illustrated by separated identical twins Jack Yufe, a Jew, and Oskar Stöhr, a member

ASK YOURSELF

Do you know of any biological siblings who, despite having been raised in the same home, have very different personalities? (Are *you* one of these siblings, perhaps?) Knowing what you do of their lives and upbringing, what do you think contributed to these differences?

ADOPTION MATTERS Country music singer Faith Hill and late Apple founder Steve Jobs both benefited from one of the biggest gifts of love: adoption.

of Germany's Hitler Youth. After later reuniting, Oskar mused to Jack: "If we had been switched, I would have been the Jew, and you would have been the Nazi" (Segal, 2005, p. 70). Parenting—and the cultural environments in which parents place children—matters!

Moreover, child neglect and abuse and even parental divorce are rare in adoptive homes. (Adoptive parents are carefully screened; biological parents are not.) So it is not surprising that studies have shown that, despite a slightly greater risk of psychological disorder, most adopted children thrive, especially when adopted as infants (Loehlin et al., 2007; van IJzendoorn & Juffer, 2006; Wierzbicki, 1993). Seven in eight adopted children have reported feeling strongly attached to one or both adoptive parents. As children of self-giving parents, they have grown up to be more self-giving and altruistic than average (Sharma et al., 1998). Many scored higher than their biological parents and raised-apart biological siblings on intelligence tests, and most grew into happier and more stable adults (Kendler et al., 2015b; van IJzendoorn et al., 2005). In one Swedish study, children adopted as infants grew up with fewer problems than were experienced by children whose biological mothers initially registered them for adoption but then decided to raise the children themselves (Bohman & Sigvardsson, 1990). *The bottom line:* Regardless of personality differences between adoptive family members, most adopted children benefit from adoption.

Siblings so different: Hermann Goering was outgoing, loved crowds, and became Hitler's right-hand man and founder of the Nazi Gestapo. His younger brother Albert Goering was quiet and reclusive, and worked to save Jews that brother Hermann's regime was killing (Brennan, 2010).

 **RETRIEVE IT • • •** ANSWERS IN APPENDIX E

RI-2 How do researchers use twin and adoption studies to learn about psychological principles?

Gene-Environment Interaction

LOQ 2-17 How do heredity and environment work together?

Among our similarities, the most important—the behavioral hallmark of our species—is our enormous adaptive capacity. Some human traits, such as having two eyes, develop the same way in virtually every environment. But other traits are expressed only in particular environments. Go barefoot for a summer and you will develop toughened, callused feet—a biological adaptation to friction. Meanwhile, your shod neighbor will remain a tenderfoot. The difference between the two of you is an effect of environment. But it is the product of a biological mechanism—adaptation.

Genes and environment—nature and nurture—work together, like two hands clapping. Genes are *self-regulating.* Rather than acting as blueprints that lead to the same result no matter the context, genes react. An African butterfly that is green in summer turns brown in fall, thanks to a temperature-controlled genetic switch. The same genes that produce green in one situation produce brown in another.

GENETIC SPACE EXPLORATION In 2015, Scott Kelly (on the left) and Mark Kelly (on the right) embarked on a twin study that was literally out of this world. Scott spent 340 days orbiting the planet in the International Space Station. His identical twin, Mark, remained on Earth. Both twins underwent the same physical and psychological testing. The study results will help scientists understand how genes and environment—in outer space and on Earth—interact.

FIGURE 2.30

EPIGENETICS INFLUENCES GENE EXPRESSION Beginning in the womb, life experiences lay down epigenetic marks—often organic methyl molecules—that can influence the expression of any gene in the DNA segment they affect. (Research from Champagne, 2010.)

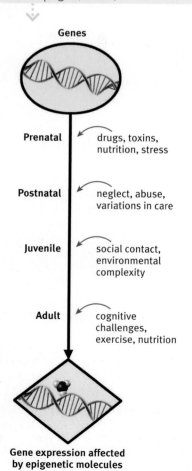

Genes

Prenatal — drugs, toxins, nutrition, stress

Postnatal — neglect, abuse, variations in care

Juvenile — social contact, environmental complexity

Adult — cognitive challenges, exercise, nutrition

Gene expression affected by epigenetic molecules

To say that genes and experience are *both* important is true. But more precisely, they **interact.** Imagine two babies, one genetically predisposed to be attractive, sociable, and easygoing, the other less so. Assume further that the first baby attracts more affectionate and stimulating care and so develops into a warmer and more outgoing person. As the two children grow older, the more naturally outgoing child may seek more activities and friends that encourage further social confidence.

What has caused their resulting personality differences? Neither heredity nor experience act alone. Environments trigger gene activity. And our genetically influenced traits *evoke* significant responses in others. Thus, a child's impulsivity and aggression may evoke an angry response from a parent or teacher, who reacts warmly to well-behaved children in the family or classroom. In such cases, the child's nature and the adult's nurture interact. Gene and scene dance together.

Identical twins not only share the same genetic predispositions, they also seek and create similar experiences that express their shared genes (Kandler et al., 2012). This helps explain why identical twins raised in different families have recalled their parents' warmth as remarkably similar—almost as similar as if they had been raised by the same parents (Plomin et al., 1988, 1991, 1994). Fraternal twins have more differing recollections of their early family life—even if raised in the same family. "Children experience us as different parents, depending on their own qualities," noted Sandra Scarr (1990).

Recall that genes can be either active (expressed, as the hot water activates the tea bag) or inactive. **Epigenetics** (meaning "in addition to" or "above and beyond" genetics) studies the molecular mechanisms by which environments can trigger or block genetic expression. Our experiences create *epigenetic marks,* which are often organic methyl molecules attached to part of a DNA strand (**FIGURE 2.30**). If a mark instructs the cell to ignore any gene present in that DNA segment, those genes will be "turned off"—they will prevent the DNA from producing the proteins coded by that gene. As one geneticist explained, "Things written in pen you can't change. That's DNA. But things written in pencil you can. That's epigenetics" (Reed, 2011).

Environmental factors such as diet, drugs, and stress can affect the epigenetic molecules that regulate gene expression. Mother rats normally lick their infants. Deprived of this licking in experiments, infant rats had more epigenetic molecules blocking access to their brain's "on" switch for developing stress hormone receptors. When stressed, those animals had above-average levels of free-floating stress hormones and were more stressed (Champagne et al., 2003; Champagne & Mashoodh, 2009).

Epigenetics provides a mechanism by which the effects of childhood trauma, poverty, or malnutrition may last a lifetime (Nugent et al., 2016; Peter et al., 2016; Swartz et al., 2016). Child abuse may leave its fingerprints in a person's genome. Moreover, it now appears that some epigenetic changes are passed down to future generations. In one study, Holocaust trauma survivors shared epigenetic alterations with their offspring (Yehuda et al., 2016).

Epigenetics research may solve some scientific mysteries, such as why only one member of an identical twin pair may develop a genetically influenced mental disorder (Spector, 2012). Epigenetics can also help explain why identical twins may look slightly different. Researchers studying mice have found that in utero exposure to certain chemicals can cause genetically identical twins to have different-colored fur (Dolinoy et al., 2007).

So, if Beyoncé and Jay Z's daughter, Blue Ivy, grows up to be a popular recording artist, should we attribute her musical talent to her "superstar genes"? To her growing up in a musically rich environment? To high expectations? The best answer seems to be "All of the above." From conception onward, we are the product of a cascade of interactions between our genetic predispositions and our surrounding environments (McGue, 2010). Our genes affect how people react to and influence us. Forget nature *versus* nurture; think nature *via* nurture.

LaunchPad For a 7-minute explanation of genes and environment, watch the **Video: Behavior Genetics.**

🔒 **RETRIEVE IT • • •**   *ANSWERS IN APPENDIX E*

RI-3 Match the following terms (I–II) to the correct explanation (a–b).

Term:	Explanation:
I. Epigenetics	a. Study of the relative effects of our genes and our environment on our behavior.
II. Behavior genetics	b. Study of environmental factors that affect how our genes are *expressed*.

EVOLUTIONARY PSYCHOLOGY: UNDERSTANDING HUMAN NATURE

LOQ 2-18 How do evolutionary psychologists use natural selection to explain behavior tendencies?

Behavior geneticists explore the genetic and environmental roots of human differences. **Evolutionary psychologists** instead focus mostly on what makes us so much alike as humans. They use Charles Darwin's principle of **natural selection** to understand the roots of behavior and mental processes. The idea, simplified, is this:

- Organisms' varied offspring compete for survival.

- Certain biological and behavioral variations increase organisms' reproductive and survival chances in their particular environment.

- Offspring that survive are more likely to pass their genes to ensuing generations.

- Thus, over time, population characteristics may change.

To see these principles at work, let's consider a straightforward example in foxes.

Natural Selection and Adaptation

A fox is a wild and wary animal. If you capture a fox and try to befriend it, be careful: If the timid fox cannot flee, it may snack on your fingers. Russian scientist Dmitry Belyaev wondered how our human ancestors had domesticated dogs from their equally wild wolf forebears. Might he, within a comparatively short stretch of time, accomplish a similar feat by transforming the fearful fox into a friendly fox?

To find out, Belyaev set to work with 30 male and 100 female foxes. From their offspring he selected and mated the tamest 5 percent of males and 20 percent of females. (He measured tameness by the foxes' responses to attempts to feed, handle, and stroke them.) Over more than 30 generations of foxes, Belyaev and his successor, Lyudmila Trut, repeated that simple procedure. Forty years and 45,000 foxes later, they had a new breed of foxes that, in Trut's (1999) words, were "docile, eager to please, and unmistakably domesticated. . . . Before our eyes, 'the Beast' has turned into 'beauty,' as the aggressive behavior of our herd's wild [ancestors] entirely disappeared." So friendly and eager for human contact were these animals, so inclined to whimper to attract attention and to lick people like affectionate dogs, that the cash-strapped institute seized on a way to raise funds—marketing its friendly foxes as house pets.

Eric Isselée/Shutterstock

Adrian Wyld/The Canadian Press via AP

LASTING EFFECTS Canadian Senator Murray Sinclair, seen here with Prime Minister Justin Trudeau, was honored for an in-depth report on the devastating effects of Canada's long running residential school program that removed Aboriginal Canadian children from their families. As psychologist Susan Pinker (2015) observed, the epigenetic effects of forced family separation "can play out, not only in the survivors of residential schools but in subsequent generations."

---

interaction the interplay that occurs when the effect of one factor (such as environment) depends on another factor (such as heredity).

epigenetics "above" or "in addition to" *(epi)* genetics; the study of the molecular mechanisms by which environments can influence genetic expression (without a DNA change).

evolutionary psychology the study of the evolution of behavior and the mind, using principles of natural selection.

natural selection the principle that inherited traits that better enable an organism to survive and reproduce in a particular environment will (in competition with other trait variations) most likely be passed on to subsequent generations.

mutation a random error in gene replication that leads to a change.

Does the same process work with naturally occurring selection? Does natural selection explain our human tendencies? Nature has indeed selected advantageous variations from the new gene combinations produced at each human conception plus the **mutations** (random errors in gene replication) that sometimes result. But the tight genetic leash that predisposes a dog's retrieving, a cat's pouncing, or a bird's nesting is looser on humans. The genes selected during our ancestral history provide more than a long leash; they give us a great capacity to learn and therefore to *adapt* to life in varied environments, from the tundra to the jungle. Genes and experience together wire the brain. Our adaptive flexibility in responding to different environments contributes to our *fitness*—our ability to survive and reproduce.

> 🔒 **RETRIEVE IT • • •**   *ANSWERS IN APPENDIX E*
>
> **RI-4** How are Belyaev and Trut's breeding practices similar to, and how do they differ from, the way natural selection normally occurs?

Evolutionary Success Helps Explain Similarities

Our similarities arise from our shared human genome, our common genetic profile. How did we develop our genetic kinship?

OUR GENETIC LEGACY At the dawn of human history, our ancestors faced certain questions: Who is my ally, who is my foe? With whom should I mate? What food should I eat? Some individuals answered those questions more successfully than others. For example, women who experienced nausea in the critical first three months of pregnancy were genetically predisposed to avoid certain bitter, strongly flavored, and novel foods. Avoiding such foods had survival value, since they are the very foods most often toxic to prenatal development (Profet, 1992; Schmitt & Pilcher, 2004). Early humans disposed to eat nourishing rather than poisonous foods survived to contribute their genes to later generations. Those who deemed leopards "nice to pet" often did not.

Similarly successful were those whose mating helped them produce and nurture offspring. Over generations, the genes of individuals not disposed to mate or nurture tended to be lost from the human gene pool. As success-enhancing genes continued to be selected, behavioral tendencies and learning capacities emerged that prepared our Stone Age ancestors to survive, reproduce, and send their genes into the future, and into you.

As heirs to this prehistoric legacy, we are genetically predisposed to behave in ways that promoted our ancestors' surviving and reproducing. But in some ways, we are biologically prepared for a world that no longer exists. We love the taste of sweets and fats, nutrients that prepared our physically active ancestors to survive food shortages. But few of us now hunt and gather our food; instead, we find sweets and fats in fast-food outlets and vending machines. Our natural dispositions, rooted deep in history, are mismatched with today's junk-food and often inactive lifestyle.

EVOLUTIONARY PSYCHOLOGY TODAY Darwin's theory of evolution has become one of biology's fundamental organizing principles and lives on in the *second Darwinian revolution:* the application of evolutionary principles to psychology. In concluding *On the Origin of Species,* Darwin (1859, p. 346) anticipated this, foreseeing "open fields for far more important researches. Psychology will be based on a new foundation."

Elsewhere in this text, we address questions that intrigue evolutionary psychologists: Why do infants start to fear strangers about the time they become mobile? Why do so many more people have phobias about spiders, snakes, and heights than about more dangerous threats, such as guns and electricity? And why do we fear safe air travel so much more than dangerous driving?

* * *

We know from our correspondence and from surveys that some readers are troubled by the naturalism and evolutionism of contemporary science. (A note to readers from other nations: In the United States there is a wide gulf between scientific and lay thinking about evolution.) "The idea that human minds are the product of evolution is . . .

Count yourself fortunate: Despite high infant mortality and rampant disease in past millennia, not one of your countless ancestors died childless.

Those who are troubled by an apparent conflict between scientific and religious accounts of human origins may find it helpful to consider that different perspectives on life can be complementary. For example, the scientific account attempts to tell us *when* and *how;* religious creation stories usually aim to tell about an ultimate *who* and *why.* As Galileo explained to the Grand Duchess Christina, "The Bible teaches how to go to heaven, not how the heavens go."

unassailable fact," declared a 2007 editorial in *Nature,* a leading science journal. In *The Language of God,* Human Genome Project director Francis Collins (2006, pp. 141, 146), a self-described evangelical Christian, compiled the "utterly compelling" evidence that led him to conclude that Darwin's big idea is "unquestionably correct." Yet Gallup pollsters report that 42 percent of U.S. adults believe that humans were created "pretty much in their present form" within the last 10,000 years (Newport, 2014). Many people who dispute the scientific story worry that a science of behavior (and evolutionary science in particular) will destroy our sense of the beauty, mystery, and spiritual significance of the human creature. For those concerned, we offer some reassuring thoughts.

When Isaac Newton explained the rainbow in terms of light of differing wavelengths, the British poet John Keats feared that Newton had destroyed the rainbow's mysterious beauty. Yet, as evolutionary biologist Richard Dawkins (1998) noted in *Unweaving the Rainbow,* Newton's analysis led to an even deeper mystery—Einstein's theory of special relativity. Nothing about Newton's optics need diminish our appreciation for the dramatic elegance of a rainbow arching across a brightening sky.

When Galileo assembled evidence that Earth revolved around the Sun, not vice versa, he did not offer irrefutable proof for his theory. Rather, he offered a coherent explanation for a variety of observations, such as the changing shadows cast by the Moon's mountains. His explanation eventually won the day because it described and explained things in a way that made sense, that hung together. Darwin's theory of evolution likewise is a coherent view of natural history. It offers an organizing principle that unifies various observations.

Many people of faith find the scientific idea of human origins congenial with their spirituality. In the fifth century, St. Augustine (quoted by Wilford, 1999) wrote, "The universe was brought into being in a less than fully formed state, but was gifted with the capacity to transform itself from unformed matter into a truly marvelous array of structures and life forms." Some 1600 years later, Pope Francis in 2015 welcomed a science-religion dialogue, saying, "Evolution in nature is not inconsistent with the notion of creation, because evolution requires the creation of beings that evolve."

Meanwhile, many people of science are awestruck at the emerging understanding of the universe and the human creature. It boggles the mind—the entire universe popping out of a point some 14 billion years ago, and instantly inflating to cosmological size. Had the energy of this Big Bang been the tiniest bit less, the universe would have collapsed back on itself. Had it been the tiniest bit more, the result would have been a soup too thin to support life. Astronomer Sir Martin Rees has described *Just Six Numbers* (1999), any one of which, if changed ever so slightly, would produce a cosmos in which life could not exist. Had gravity been a tad stronger or weaker, or had the weight of a carbon proton been a wee bit different, our universe just wouldn't have worked.

What caused this almost-too-good-to-be-true, finely tuned universe? Why is there something rather than nothing? How did it come to be, in the words of Harvard-Smithsonian astrophysicist Owen Gingerich (1999), "so extraordinarily right, that it seemed the universe had been expressly designed to produce intelligent, sentient beings"? On such matters, a humble, awed, scientific silence is appropriate, suggested philosopher Ludwig Wittgenstein: "Whereof one cannot speak, thereof one must be silent" (1922, p. 189).

Rather than fearing science, we can welcome its enlarging our understanding and awakening our sense of awe. In *The Fragile Species,* Lewis Thomas (1992) described his utter amazement that Earth in time gave rise to bacteria and eventually to Bach's Mass in B Minor. In a short 4 billion years, life on Earth has come from nothing to structures as complex as a 6-billion-unit strand of DNA and the incomprehensible intricacy of the human brain. Atoms no different from those in a rock somehow formed dynamic entities that produce extraordinary, self-replicating, information-processing systems—us (Davies, 2007). Although we appear to have been created from dust, over eons of time, the end result is a priceless creature, one rich with potential beyond our imagining.

🔒 REVIEW GENETICS, EVOLUTIONARY PSYCHOLOGY, AND BEHAVIOR

⟶ Learning Objectives

TEST YOURSELF Answer these repeated Learning Objective Questions on your own (before checking the answers in Appendix D) to improve your retention of the concepts (McDaniel et al., 2009, 2015).

2-15 What are *chromosomes, DNA, genes,* and the human *genome*? How do behavior geneticists explain our individual differences?

2-16 How do twin and adoption studies help us understand the effects and interactions of nature and nurture?

2-17 How do heredity and environment work together?

2-18 How do evolutionary psychologists use natural selection to explain behavior tendencies?

⟶ Terms and Concepts to Remember

TEST YOURSELF Write down the definition yourself, then check your answer on the referenced page.

environment, **p. 69**

heredity, **p. 69**

behavior genetics, **p. 69**

chromosomes, **p. 69**

DNA (deoxyribonucleic acid), **p. 69**

genes, **p. 69**

genome, **p. 69**

identical (monozygotic) twins, **p. 70**

fraternal (dizygotic) twins, **p. 70**

interaction, **p. 75**

epigenetics, **p. 75**

evolutionary psychology, **p. 75**

natural selection, **p. 75**

mutation, **p. 76**

⟶ Experience the Testing Effect

TEST YOURSELF Answer the following questions on your own first, then check your answers in Appendix E.

1. The threadlike structures made largely of DNA molecules are called _____.

2. A small segment of DNA that codes for particular proteins is referred to as a _____.

3. When the mother's egg and the father's sperm unite, each contributes
   a. one chromosome pair.
   b. 23 chromosomes.
   c. 23 chromosome pairs.
   d. 25,000 chromosomes.

4. Fraternal twins result when
   a. a single egg is fertilized by a single sperm and then splits.
   b. a single egg is fertilized by two sperm and then splits.
   c. two eggs are fertilized by two sperm.
   d. two eggs are fertilized by a single sperm.

5. _____twins share the same DNA.

6. Adoption studies seek to understand genetic influences on personality. They do this mainly by
   a. comparing adopted children with nonadopted children.
   b. evaluating whether adopted children's personalities more closely resemble those of their adoptive parents or their biological parents.
   c. studying the effect of prior neglect on adopted children.
   d. studying the effect of children's age at adoption.

7. Epigenetics is the study of the molecular mechanisms by which _____ trigger or block genetic expression.

8. Behavior geneticists are most interested in exploring _____ (commonalities/differences) in our behaviors. Evolutionary psychologists are most interested in exploring _____ (commonalities/differences).

9. Evolutionary psychologists are most likely to focus on
   a. how individuals differ from one another.
   b. the social consequences of learned behaviors.
   c. the natural selection of traits that helped our ancestors survive and reproduce.
   d. twin and adoption studies.

Continue testing yourself with 📚 **LearningCurve** or ≈ **Achieve Read & Practice** to learn and remember most effectively.

Consciousness and the Two-Track Mind

Consciousness can be a funny thing. It offers us weird experiences, as when entering sleep or leaving a dream. And sometimes it leaves us wondering who is really in control. After zoning me [DM] out with nitrous oxide, my dentist tells me to turn my head to the left. My conscious mind resists: "No way," I silently say. "You can't boss me around!" Whereupon my robotic head, ignoring my conscious mind, turns obligingly under the dentist's control.

Then there are those times when consciousness seems to split. Sometimes, my [ND's] mind wanders while singing portions of the *Moana* soundtrack daily with my toddler daughter. When reading *Green Eggs and Ham* to one of my [DM's] preschoolers for the umpteenth time, my obliging mouth could say the words while my mind flitted in and out of the story. And if a friend interrupts you mid-text to ask what you're doing for lunch, it's not a problem. Your thumbs complete their keyboard dance as you suggest getting tacos.

What do such experiences tell us? Does the mind's wandering while singing, reading, or texting reveal a split in consciousness? And what exactly is *consciousness*? How do our states of consciousness play out in our sleep and dreams? And was that drug-induced dental episode akin to people's experiences with other mood- and perception-altering *psychoactive drugs*? ▶

THE MIND-BODY PROBLEM

Get up.

No.

Roz Chast The New Yorker Collection/The Cartoon Bank

"Psychology must discard all reference to consciousness." —Behaviorist John B. Watson (1913)

⊙→ Consciousness: Some Basic Concepts

Every science has concepts so fundamental they are nearly impossible to define. Biologists agree on what is alive but not on precisely what *life* is. In physics, *matter* and *energy* elude simple definition. To psychologists, *consciousness* is similarly a fundamental yet slippery concept.

DEFINING CONSCIOUSNESS

LEARNING OBJECTIVE QUESTION (LOQ)

3-1   What is the place of consciousness in psychology's history?

At its beginning, *psychology* was "the description and explanation of states of consciousness" (Ladd, 1887). But during the first half of the twentieth century, the difficulty of scientifically studying consciousness led many psychologists—including those in the emerging school of *behaviorism*—to turn to direct observations of behavior. By the 1960s, psychology had nearly lost consciousness and was defining itself as "the science of behavior." Consciousness was likened to a car's speedometer: "It doesn't make the car go, it just reflects what's happening" (Seligman, 1991, p. 24).

After 1960, psychology began regaining consciousness. Neuroscience advances linked brain activity to sleeping, dreaming, and other mental states. Researchers began studying consciousness altered by drugs, hypnosis, and meditation. (More on hypnosis in Chapter 6 and meditation in Chapter 11.) Psychologists of all persuasions were affirming the importance of *cognition,* or mental processes.

Most psychologists today define **consciousness** as our subjective awareness of ourselves and our environment (Feinberg & Mallatt, 2016):

- This awareness allows us to assemble information from many sources as we reflect on our past, adapt to our present, and plan for our future. First-year college and university students may think back to their high school years, adjust to the ups and downs of academic life, and look ahead to their life beyond graduation.

- Conscious awareness focuses our attention when we learn a complex concept or behavior. When learning to drive, we focus on the car and the traffic. With practice, driving becomes semi-automatic, freeing us to focus our attention elsewhere.

- Over time, we flit between different *states of consciousness,* including normal waking awareness and various altered states (**FIGURE 3.1**).

INSADCO Photography/Alamy

FIGURE 3.1
ALTERED STATES OF CONSCIOUSNESS In addition to normal, waking awareness, consciousness comes to us in altered states, including daydreaming, drug-induced hallucinating, and meditating.

Some states occur spontaneously	Daydreaming	Drowsiness	Dreaming
Some are physio-logically induced	Hallucinations	Orgasm	Food or oxygen starvation
Some are psycho-logically induced	Sensory deprivation	Hypnosis	Meditation

COGNITIVE NEUROSCIENCE

Today's science explores the biology of consciousness. Scientists now assume, in the words of neuroscientist Marvin Minsky (1986, p. 287), that "the mind is what the brain does."

Evolutionary psychologists presume that consciousness offers a reproductive advantage (Barash, 2006; Murdik et al., 2011). By considering consequences and reading others' intentions, consciousness helps us to cope with novel situations, act in ways that further our long-term goals, and foster relationships through sacrificing our self-interest (Mrkva, 2017). Even so, that leaves us with what researchers call the "hard problem": How do brain cells jabbering to one another create our awareness of the taste of toast, the idea of infinity, the feeling of fright? The question of how consciousness arises from the material brain is one of life's deepest mysteries. Such questions are at the heart of **cognitive neuroscience**— the interdisciplinary study of the brain activity linked with our mental processes.

A stunning demonstration of consciousness appeared in brain scans of a noncommunicative patient—a 23-year-old woman who had been in a car accident and showed no outward signs of conscious awareness (Owen, 2014; Owen et al., 2006). When researchers asked her to *imagine* playing tennis, fMRI scans revealed activity in a brain area that normally controls arm and leg movements (**FIGURE 3.2**). Even in a motionless body, the researchers concluded, the brain—and the mind—may still be active. A follow-up analysis of 42 behaviorally unresponsive patients revealed 13 more who also showed meaningful, though diminished, brain responses to questions (Stender et al., 2014).

Conscious experience arises from synchronized activity across the brain (Chennu et al., 2014). If a stimulus activates enough brain-wide coordinated neural activity—as strong signals in one brain area trigger activity elsewhere—it crosses a threshold for consciousness. A weaker stimulus—perhaps a word flashed too briefly to be consciously perceived—may trigger localized visual cortex activity that quickly fades. A stronger stimulus will engage other brain areas, such as those involved with language, attention, and memory. Such reverberating activity (detected by brain scans) is a telltale sign of conscious awareness (Boly et al., 2011; Silverstein et al., 2015). For example, awareness of your body involves communication between several brain areas (Blanke, 2012; Olivé et al., 2015). How the synchronized activity produces awareness—how matter makes mind—remains a mystery.

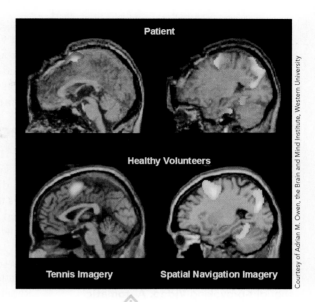

Patient

Healthy Volunteers

Tennis Imagery   Spatial Navigation Imagery

Courtesy of Adrian M. Owen, the Brain and Mind Institute, Western University

FIGURE 3.2

EVIDENCE OF AWARENESS?
When asked to imagine playing tennis or navigating her home, a noncommunicative patient's brain (top) exhibited activity similar to a healthy person's brain (bottom). Researchers wonder if such fMRI scans might enable a "conversation" with some unresponsive patients, by instructing them, for example, to answer yes to a question by imagining playing tennis (top and bottom left), and no by imagining walking around their home (top and bottom right).

🔒 **RETRIEVE IT • • •**   *ANSWERS IN APPENDIX E*

RI-1 Those working in the interdisciplinary field called _____ _____ study the brain activity associated with the mental processes of perception, thinking, memory, and language.

SELECTIVE ATTENTION

LOQ 3-2   How does selective attention direct our perceptions?

Through **selective attention,** our awareness focuses, like a flashlight beam, on a minute aspect of all that we experience. We may think we can fully attend to a conversation or a class lecture while checking and returning text messages. Actually, our consciousness focuses on but one thing at a time.

By one estimate, our five senses take in 11,000,000 bits of information per second, of which we consciously process about 40 (Wilson, 2002). Yet our mind's unconscious track intuitively makes great use of the other 10,999,960 bits.

What captures our limited attention? Things we deem important. A classic example of selective attention is the *cocktail party effect*—your ability to attend to only one voice within a sea of many. But what happens when another voice speaks your name?

consciousness our subjective awareness of ourselves and our environment.

cognitive neuroscience the interdisciplinary study of the brain activity linked with cognition (including perception, thinking, memory, and language).

selective attention the focusing of conscious awareness on a particular stimulus.

"Has a generation of texters, surfers, and twitterers evolved the enviable ability to process multiple streams of novel information in parallel? Most cognitive psychologists doubt it."
—Steven Pinker, "Not at All," 2010

"I wasn't texting. I was building this ship in a bottle."

🎬 **LaunchPad** Watch the thought-provoking **Video: Automatic Skills—Disrupting a Pilot's Performance.**

inattentional blindness failing to see visible objects when our attention is directed elsewhere.

change blindness failing to notice changes in the environment; a form of *inattentional blindness.*

Your cognitive radar, operating on your mind's other track, instantly brings that unattended voice into consciousness. This effect might have prevented an embarrassing and dangerous situation in 2009, when two Northwest Airlines pilots "lost track of time." Focused on their laptops and in conversation, they ignored alarmed air traffic controllers' attempts to reach them and overflew their Minneapolis destination by 150 miles. If only the controllers had known and spoken the pilots' names.

Selective Attention and Accidents

Have you, like 60 percent of American drivers, read or sent a text message or viewed a phone map while driving in the last month (Gliklich et al., 2016)? Such digital distraction can have tragic consequences (Stavrinos et al., 2017). Why do digital devices make us dangerous drivers? Our selective attention shifts back and forth between the road and its digital competition. Indeed, our attention shifts more often than we realize. One study left people in a room for 28 minutes with full internet and television access. On average, participants guessed their attention switched 15 times during the 28-minute session. But they were not even close. Eye-tracking revealed eight times that many attentional switches—120 on average (Brasel & Gips, 2011).

Rapid toggling between activities is today's great enemy of sustained, focused attention. When we switch attentional gears, especially when we shift to complex tasks like noticing and avoiding cars around us, we pay a toll—a slight and sometimes fatal delay in coping (Rubenstein et al., 2001). When a driver attends to a conversation, activity in brain areas vital to driving decreases an average of 37 percent (Just et al., 2008). To stay safe, drivers should limit external distractions and keep their eyes on the road (Mackenzie & Harris, 2017).

Texting or phone chatting accompanies about 28 percent of traffic accidents (NSC, 2010; Pew, 2011). One video cam study of teen drivers found that driver distraction from passengers or phones occurred right before 58 percent of their crashes (AAA, 2015). Talking with passengers makes the risk of an accident 1.6 times higher than normal. Talking on a cell phone (even with a hands-free set) makes the risk 4 times higher than normal—equal to the risk of drunk driving (McEvoy et al., 2005, 2007). And while talking is distracting, texting wins the danger game. One 18-month video cam study tracked the driving habits of long-haul truckers. When they were texting, their risk of a collision increased 23 times (Olson et al., 2009)! Many European countries and most American states and Canadian provinces now ban texting while driving (CBC News, 2014; Rosenthal, 2009). So the next time you're behind the wheel, put the brakes on your texts. Your passengers and fellow drivers will thank you.

Inattentional Blindness

At the level of conscious awareness, we are "blind" to all but a tiny sliver of visual stimuli. Ulric Neisser (1979) and Robert Becklen and Daniel Cervone (1983) demonstrated this **inattentional blindness** dramatically by showing people a 1-minute video of basketball players, three in black shirts and three in white shirts, tossing a ball. Researchers told the viewers to press a key every time they saw a black-shirted player pass the ball. Most viewers were so intent on their task that they failed to notice a young woman carrying an umbrella saunter across the screen midway through the video (**FIGURE 3.3**). Watching a later replay, viewers were astonished to see her (Mack & Rock, 2000). This inattentional blindness is a by-product of what we are really good at: focusing attention on some part of our environment.

In a repeat of the experiment, smart-aleck researchers sent a gorilla-suited assistant through a swirl of players (Simons & Chabris, 1999). During its 5- to 9-second cameo appearance, the gorilla paused and thumped its chest. But the gorilla did not steal the show: Half the conscientious pass-counting viewers failed to see it. Psychologists like to have fun, and have continued to do so with the help of invisible gorillas. When 24 radiologists were looking for cancer nodules in lung scans, 20 of them missed the gorilla superimposed in the upper right (**FIGURE 3.4**)—though, to their credit, their focus enabled them to discover the much tinier cancer tissue (Drew et al., 2013). The point of these purposeful pranks: Attention is powerfully selective. Your conscious mind is in one place at a time.

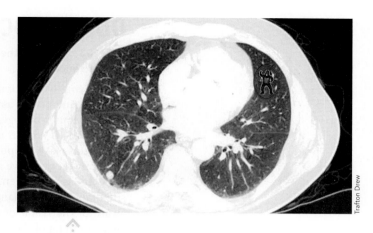

FIGURE 3.3

INATTENTIONAL BLINDNESS Viewers who were attending to basketball tosses among the black-shirted players usually failed to notice the umbrella-toting woman sauntering across the screen (Neisser, 1979).

FIGURE 3.4

THE INVISIBLE GORILLA STRIKES AGAIN When repeatedly exposed to the gorilla in the upper right (which we've circled in red) while searching for much tinier cancer nodules, radiologists usually failed to see it (Drew et al., 2013).

🖿 **LaunchPad** For more on the limits of our attention, engage online with **Concept Practice: Selective Attention and Multitasking**.

Given that most people miss someone in a gorilla suit while their attention is riveted elsewhere, imagine the fun that others can have by manipulating our selective attention. Misdirect people's attention and they will miss the hand slipping into the pocket. "Every time you perform a magic trick, you're engaging in experimental psychology," says magician Teller (2009), a master of mind-messing methods. Clever thieves know this, too. One Swedish psychologist was surprised in Stockholm by a woman suddenly exposing herself; only later did he realize that he had been pickpocketed, outwitted by thieves who understood the limits of our selective attention (Gallace, 2012).

In other experiments, people exhibited a form of inattentional blindness called **change blindness.** Participants in laboratory experiments failed to notice that, after a brief visual interruption, a big Coke bottle had disappeared, a railing had risen, clothing had changed color—and construction workers had changed places (**FIGURE 3.5**) (Chabris & Simons, 2010; Resnick et al., 1997). Out of sight, out of mind.

🔒 **RETRIEVE IT • • •**
ANSWERS IN APPENDIX E

RI-2 Explain two attentional principles that magicians may use to fool us.

ENGAGE 💡 (ASK YOURSELF)

Can you recall a recent time when, as your attention focused on one thing, you were oblivious to something else (perhaps to pain, to someone's approach, or to background music)?

FIGURE 3.5

CHANGE BLINDNESS While a man (in red) provides directions to another (a), two experimenters rudely pass between them carrying a door (b). During this interruption, the original worker switches places with another person wearing different-colored clothing (c). Most people, focused on their direction giving, do not notice the switch (Simons & Levin, 1998).

(a)   (b)   (c)

DUAL PROCESSING: THE TWO-TRACK MIND

LOQ 3-3   What is the *dual processing* being revealed by today's cognitive neuroscience?

Discovering which brain regions become active with a particular conscious experience strikes many people as interesting, but not mind blowing. If everything psychological is simultaneously biological, then our ideas, emotions, and spirituality must all, somehow, be embodied. What *is* mind blowing to many of us is evidence that we have, so to speak, two minds, each supported by its own neural equipment.

At any moment, we are aware of little more than what's on the screen of our consciousness. But as we've seen, beneath the surface, unconscious information processing occurs simultaneously on many parallel tracks. When we look at a bird flying, we are consciously aware of the result of our cognitive processing ("It's a hummingbird!") but not of our subprocessing of the bird's color, form, movement, and distance. One of the grand ideas of recent cognitive neuroscience is that much of our brain work occurs off stage, out of sight. Perception, memory, thinking, language, and attitudes all operate on two independent levels—a conscious, deliberate "high road," and an unconscious, automatic "low road" (Wang, Y., et al., 2017). The high road is reflective, the low road intuitive (Evans & Stanovich, 2013; Kahneman, 2011). Today's researchers call this **dual processing.** We know more than we know we know.

If you are a driver, consider how you move into the right lane. Drivers know this unconsciously but cannot accurately explain it (Eagleman, 2011). Most say they would bank to the right, then straighten out—a procedure that would actually steer them off the road. In reality, an experienced driver, after moving right, automatically reverses the steering wheel just as far to the left of center, and only then returns to the center position. The lesson: The human brain is a device for converting conscious into unconscious knowledge.

Or consider this story, which illustrates how science can be stranger than science fiction. During my sojourns at Scotland's University of St Andrews, I [DM] came to know cognitive neuroscientists David Milner and Melvyn Goodale (2008). They studied a local woman, D. F., who suffered brain damage when overcome by carbon monoxide, leaving her unable to recognize and discriminate objects visually. Consciously, D. F. could see nothing. Yet she exhibited **blindsight**—she acted *as though* she could see. Asked to slip a postcard into a vertical or horizontal mail slot, she could do so without error. Asked the width of a block in front of her, she was at a loss, but she could grasp it with just the right finger-thumb distance.

How could this be? Don't we have one visual system? Goodale and Milner knew from animal research that the eye sends information simultaneously to different brain areas, which support different tasks (Weiskrantz, 2009, 2010). Sure enough, a scan of D. F.'s brain activity revealed normal activity in the area concerned with reaching for, grasping, and navigating objects, but damage in the area concerned with consciously recognizing objects. (See another example in **FIGURE 3.6**.)

How strangely intricate is this thing we call vision, conclude Goodale and Milner in their aptly titled book, *Sight Unseen* (2004). We may think of our vision as a single system that controls our visually guided actions. Actually, it is a dual-processing system (Foley et al., 2015). A *visual perception track* enables us "to think about the world"—to recognize things and to plan future actions. A *visual action track* guides our moment-to-moment movements.

The dual-track mind also appeared in a patient who lost all of his left visual cortex, leaving him blind to objects and faces presented on the right side of his field of vision. He nevertheless could sense the emotion expressed in faces that he did not consciously perceive (de Gelder, 2010). The same is true of normally sighted people whose visual cortex has been disabled with magnetic stimulation. Such findings suggest that brain areas below the cortex process emotion-related information.

People often have trouble accepting that much of our everyday thinking, feeling, and acting operates outside our conscious awareness (Bargh & Chartrand, 1999). Some "80 to 90 percent of what we do is unconscious," says Nobel laureate and memory expert Eric Kandel (2008). We are understandably inclined to believe that our intentions and deliberate choices rule our lives. But they don't. Consciousness, though enabling us to exert

FIGURE 3.6

WHEN THE BLIND CAN "SEE" In this compelling demonstration of blindsight and the two-track mind, researcher Lawrence Weiskrantz trailed a blindsight patient down a cluttered hallway. Although told the hallway was empty, the patient meandered around all the obstacles without any awareness of them.

voluntary control and to communicate our mental states to others, is but the tip of the information-processing iceberg. Just ask the volunteers who chose a card after watching a magician shuffle through the deck (Olson et al., 2015). In nearly every case, the magician swayed participants' decisions by subtly allowing one card to show for longer—but 91 percent of participants believed they had made the choice on their own. Being intensely focused on an activity (such as reading this chapter, we hope) increases your total brain activity no more than 5 percent above its baseline rate. Even when you rest, activity whirls inside your head (Raichle, 2010).

Unconscious parallel processing is faster than conscious sequential processing, but both are essential. **Parallel processing** enables your mind to take care of routine business. **Sequential processing** is best for solving new problems, which requires your focused attention on one thing at a time. Try this: If you are right-handed, move your right foot in a smooth counterclockwise circle and write the number 3 repeatedly with your right hand—at the same time. Try something equally difficult: Tap a steady beat three times with your left hand while tapping four times with your right hand. Both tasks require conscious attention, which can be in only one place at a time. If time is nature's way of keeping everything from happening at once, then consciousness is nature's way of keeping us from thinking and doing everything at once.

dual processing the principle that information is often simultaneously processed on separate conscious and unconscious tracks.

blindsight a condition in which a person can respond to a visual stimulus without consciously experiencing it.

parallel processing processing many aspects of a stimulus or problem at once.

sequential processing processing one aspect of a stimulus or problem at a time; generally used to process new information or to solve difficult problems.

🔒 **RETRIEVE IT • • •**   ANSWERS IN APPENDIX E

RI-3 What are the mind's two tracks, and what is *dual processing*?

📖 **LaunchPad** To think further about conscious awareness and decision making, engage online with **Topic Tutorial: PsychSim6, Who's in Charge?**

🔒 **REVIEW** CONSCIOUSNESS: SOME BASIC CONCEPTS

⟶ Learning Objectives

TEST YOURSELF Answer these repeated Learning Objective Questions on your own (before checking the answers in Appendix D) to improve your retention of the concepts (McDaniel et al., 2009, 2015).

3-1 What is the place of consciousness in psychology's history?

3-2 How does selective attention direct our perceptions?

3-3 What is the *dual processing* being revealed by today's cognitive neuroscience?

⟶ Terms and Concepts to Remember

TEST YOURSELF Write down the definition yourself, then check your answer on the referenced page.

consciousness, **p. 81**

cognitive neuroscience, **p. 81**

selective attention, **p. 81**

inattentional blindness, **p. 82**

change blindness, **p. 82**

dual processing, **p. 85**

blindsight, **p. 85**

parallel processing, **p. 85**

sequential processing, **p. 85**

⟶ Experience the Testing Effect

TEST YOURSELF Answer the following questions on your own first, then check your answers in Appendix E.

1. Failure to see visible objects because our attention is occupied elsewhere is called _____ _____.

2. We register and react to stimuli outside of our awareness by means of _____ processing. When we devote

deliberate attention to stimuli, we use _____ processing.

3. Inattentional blindness is a product of our _____ attention.

Continue testing yourself with 📖 **LearningCurve** or 📖 **Achieve Read & Practice** to learn and remember most effectively.

sleep a periodic, natural loss of consciousness—as distinct from unconsciousness resulting from a coma, general anesthesia, or hibernation. (Adapted from Dement, 1999.)

circadian [ser-KAY-dee-an] **rhythm** our biological clock; regular bodily rhythms (for example, of temperature and wakefulness) that occur on a 24-hour cycle.

REM (R) sleep rapid eye movement sleep; a recurring sleep stage during which vivid dreams commonly occur. Also known as *paradoxical sleep,* because the muscles are relaxed (except for minor twitches) but other body systems are active.

alpha waves the relatively slow brain waves of a relaxed, awake state.

"I love to sleep. Do you? Isn't it great? It really is the best of both worlds. You get to be alive and unconscious." —Comedian Rita Rudner, 1993

Some students sleep like the fellow who stayed up all night to see where the Sun went. (Then it dawned on him.)

⤳ Sleep and Dreams

LOQ 3-4   What is *sleep*?

Sleep—the irresistible tempter to whom we inevitably succumb. Sleep—the equalizer of presidents and peasants. Sleep—sweet, renewing, mysterious sleep. While sleeping, we may feel "dead to the world," but we are not. Although the roar of my [ND's] neighborhood garbage truck leaves me undisturbed, my baby's cry will shatter my sleep. Even when you are deeply asleep, your perceptual window is open a crack. You move around on your bed, but you manage not to fall out. The sound of your name can also cause your unconscious body to perk up. EEG recordings confirm that the brain's auditory cortex responds to sound stimuli even during sleep (Kutas, 1990). And when you sleep, as when awake, you process most information outside your conscious awareness.

By recording the brain waves and muscle movements of sleeping participants, and by observing and occasionally waking them, researchers are solving some of sleep's deepest mysteries. Perhaps you can anticipate some of their discoveries. Are the following statements true or false?

1. When people dream of performing some activity, their limbs often move in concert with the dream.

2. Older adults sleep more than young adults.

3. Sleepwalkers are acting out their dreams.

4. Sleep experts recommend treating insomnia with an occasional sleeping pill.

5. Some people dream every night; others seldom dream.

All these statements (adapted from Palladino & Carducci, 1983) are *false.* To see why, read on.

BIOLOGICAL RHYTHMS AND SLEEP

Like the ocean, life has its rhythmic tides. Over varying time periods, our bodies fluctuate, and with them, our minds. Let's look more closely at two of those biological rhythms—our 24-hour biological clock and our 90-minute sleep cycle.

Circadian Rhythm

LOQ 3-5   How do our biological rhythms influence our daily functioning?

The rhythm of the day parallels the rhythm of life—from our waking at a new day's birth to our nightly return to what Shakespeare called "death's counterfeit." Our bodies roughly synchronize with the 24-hour cycle of day and night thanks to an internal biological clock called the **circadian rhythm** (from the Latin *circa,* "about," and *diem,* "day"). As morning nears, body temperature rises; it then peaks during the day, dips for a time in early afternoon (when many people take siestas), and begins to drop again in the evening. Thinking is sharpest and memory most accurate as we approach our daily peak in circadian arousal. Have you ever pulled an all-nighter? Perhaps you recall feeling groggiest in the middle of the night but with a sense of new alertness with the arrival of your normal wake-up time.

Age and experience can alter our circadian rhythm. Most 20-year-olds are evening-energized "owls," with performance improving across the day (May & Hasher, 1998). Most older adults experience more fragile sleep and are morning-loving "larks." For our ancestors (and for today's hunter-gatherers), a grandparent who awakened easily and early helped protect the family from predators (Samson et al., 2017).

Eric Isselée/Shutterstock

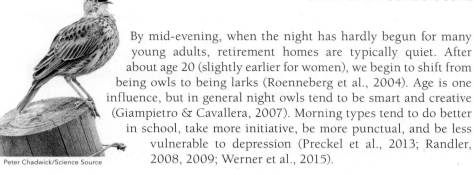

By mid-evening, when the night has hardly begun for many young adults, retirement homes are typically quiet. After about age 20 (slightly earlier for women), we begin to shift from being owls to being larks (Roenneberg et al., 2004). Age is one influence, but in general night owls tend to be smart and creative (Giampietro & Cavallera, 2007). Morning types tend to do better in school, take more initiative, be more punctual, and be less vulnerable to depression (Preckel et al., 2013; Randler, 2008, 2009; Werner et al., 2015).

Peter Chadwick/Science Source

Sleep Stages

LOQ 3-6   What is the biological rhythm of our sleeping and dreaming stages?

Sooner or later, sleep overtakes us all, and consciousness fades as different parts of our brain's cortex stop communicating (Massimini et al., 2005). Yet the sleeping brain remains active and has its own biological rhythm.

About every 90 minutes, you cycle through distinct sleep stages. This fact came to light when 8-year-old Armond Aserinsky went to bed one night in 1952. His father, Eugene, a University of Chicago graduate student, needed to test an electroencephalograph he had repaired that day (Aserinsky, 1988; Seligman & Yellen, 1987). Placing electrodes near Armond's eyes to record the rolling eye movements then believed to occur during sleep, Aserinsky watched the machine go wild, tracing deep zigzags on the graph paper. Could the machine still be broken? As the night proceeded and the activity recurred, Aserinsky realized that the periods of fast, jerky eye movements were accompanied by energetic brain activity. Awakened during one such episode, Armond reported having a dream. Aserinsky had discovered what we now know as **REM sleep** (*r*apid *e*ye *m*ovement sleep; also called *R sleep*). Similar procedures used with thousands of volunteers showed the cycles were a normal part of sleep (Kleitman, 1960). To appreciate these studies, imagine yourself as a participant. As the hour grows late, you feel sleepy and yawn in response to reduced brain metabolism. (Yawning, which is also socially contagious, stretches your neck muscles and increases your heart rate, which increases your alertness [Moorcroft, 2003].) When you are ready for bed, a researcher comes in and tapes electrodes to your scalp (to detect your brain waves), your chin (to detect muscle tension), and just outside the corners of your eyes (to detect eye movements) (**FIGURE 3.7**). Other devices may record your heart rate, respiration rate, and genital arousal.

When you are in bed with your eyes closed, the researcher in the next room sees on the EEG the relatively slow **alpha waves** of your awake but relaxed state (**FIGURE 3.8**). As you adapt to all this equipment, you grow tired and, in an unremembered moment, slip into sleep (**FIGURE 3.9**). This transition is marked by the slowed breathing and the irregular brain waves of what the American Academy of Sleep Medicine classifies as *NREM-1* (or *N1*) sleep (Silber et al., 2007).

ASK YOURSELF

Would you consider yourself a night owl or a morning lark? When do you usually feel most energetic? What time of day works best for you to study?

Dolphins, porpoises, and whales sleep with one side of their brain at a time (Miller et al., 2008).

Hank Morgan/Science Source

Left eye movements

Right eye movements

EMG (muscle tension)

EEG (brain waves)

FIGURE 3.7

MEASURING SLEEP ACTIVITY Sleep researchers measure brain-wave activity, eye movements, and muscle tension with electrodes that pick up weak electrical signals from the brain, eyes, and facial muscles (Dement, 1978).

hallucinations false sensory experiences, such as seeing something in the absence of an external visual stimulus.

delta waves the large, slow brain waves associated with deep sleep.

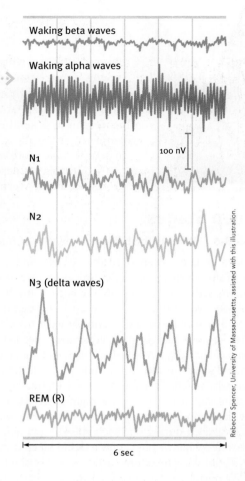

FIGURE 3.8

BRAIN WAVES AND SLEEP STAGES The beta waves of an alert, waking state and the regular alpha waves of an awake, relaxed state differ from the slower, larger delta waves of deep N3 sleep. Although the rapid REM (R) sleep waves resemble the near-waking N1 sleep waves, the body is more internally aroused during REM sleep than during NREM sleep (the N1, N2, and N3 stages).

Rebecca Spencer, University of Massachusetts, assisted with this illustration.

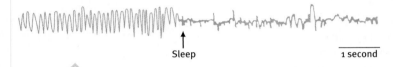

Sleep

1 second

FIGURE 3.9

THE MOMENT OF SLEEP We seem unaware of the moment we fall into sleep, but someone watching our brain waves could tell (Dement, 1999).

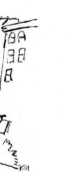

Sidney Harris/Science Cartoons Plus

"My problem has always been an overabundance of alpha waves."

ENGAGE To catch your own hypnagogic experiences, you might use your alarm's snooze function.

LaunchPad To better understand EEG readings and their relationship to consciousness, sleep, and dreams, experience the tutorial and simulation of **Topic Tutorial: PsychSim6, EEG and Sleep Stages.**

In one of his 15,000 research participants, William Dement (1999) observed the moment the brain's perceptual window to the outside world slammed shut. Dement asked this sleep-deprived young man with eyelids taped open to press a button every time a strobe light flashed in his eyes (about every 6 seconds). After a few minutes, the young man missed one. Asked why, he said, "Because there was no flash." But there was a flash. He missed it because (as his brain activity revealed) he had fallen asleep for 2 seconds, missing not only the flash 6 inches from his nose but also the awareness of the abrupt moment of entry into sleep.

During this brief N1 sleep you may experience fantastic images resembling **hallucinations**—sensory experiences that occur without a sensory stimulus. You may have a sensation of falling (when your body may suddenly jerk) or of floating weightlessly. These *hypnagogic* (also called *hypnic*) sensations may later be incorporated into your memories. People who claim they were abducted by aliens—often shortly after getting into bed—commonly recall being floated off (or pinned down on) their beds (Clancy, 2005; McNally, 2012).

You then relax more deeply and begin about 20 minutes of *NREM-2 (N2)* sleep, with its periodic *sleep spindles*—bursts of rapid, rhythmic brain-wave activity that aid memory processing (Studte et al., 2017). Although you could still be awakened without too much difficulty, you are now clearly asleep.

Then you transition to the deep sleep of *NREM-3 (N3)*. During this slow-wave sleep, which lasts for about 30 minutes, your brain emits large, slow **delta waves** and you are hard to awaken. Have you ever said, "That thunder was so loud last night!" only to have a friend respond, "What thunder?" Those who missed the storm may have been in delta sleep. (It is at the end of this stage that children may wet the bed.)

REM (R) Sleep

About an hour after you first fall asleep, a strange thing happens. Rather than continuing in deep slumber, you ascend from your initial sleep dive. Returning through N2 (where you'll ultimately spend about half your night), you enter the most intriguing sleep phase—REM (R) sleep (**FIGURE 3.10**). For about 10 minutes, your brain waves become rapid and saw-toothed, more like those of the nearly awake N1 sleep. But unlike N1, during REM sleep your heart

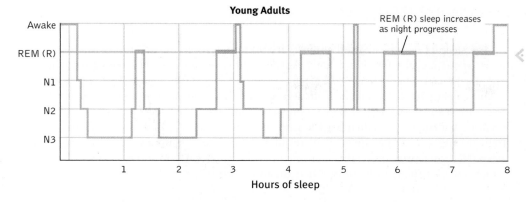

Young Adults

REM (R) sleep increases as night progresses

Hours of sleep

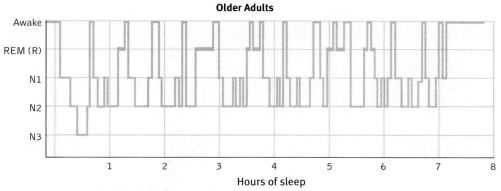

Older Adults

Hours of sleep

FIGURE 3.10

THE STAGES IN A TYPICAL NIGHT'S SLEEP People pass through a multistage sleep cycle several times each night, with the periods of deep sleep diminishing and REM (R) sleep periods increasing in duration. As people age, sleep becomes more fragile, with awakenings common among older adults (Kamel & Gammack, 2006; Neubauer, 1999).

rate rises, your breathing becomes rapid and irregular, and every half-minute or so your eyes dart around in momentary bursts of activity behind closed lids. These eye movements announce the beginning of a dream—often emotional, usually story-like, and richly hallucinatory. Dreams aren't real, but REM sleep tricks your brain into responding as if they were (Andrillon et al., 2015). Because anyone watching a sleeper's eyes can notice these REM bursts, it is amazing that science was ignorant of REM sleep until 1952.

Except during very scary dreams, your genitals become aroused during REM sleep. You may have an erection or increased vaginal lubrication and clitoral engorgement, regardless of whether the dream's content is sexual (Karacan et al., 1966). Men's common "morning erection" stems from the night's last REM period, often just before waking. In young men, sleep-related erections outlast REM periods, lasting 30 to 45 minutes on average (Karacan et al., 1983; Schiavi & Schreiner-Engel, 1988). A typical 25-year-old man therefore has an erection during nearly half his night's sleep, a 65-year-old man for one-quarter. Many men troubled by occasional erectile difficulties have sleep-related erections, suggesting the problem is not between their legs.

During REM sleep, your brain's motor cortex is active, but your brainstem blocks its messages. This leaves your muscles relaxed, so much so that, except for an occasional finger, toe, or facial twitch, you are essentially paralyzed. Moreover, you cannot easily be awakened. REM sleep is thus sometimes called *paradoxical sleep:* The body is internally aroused, with waking-like brain activity, yet asleep and externally calm. We spend about 600 hours a year experiencing some 1500 dreams, or more than 100,000 dreams over a typical lifetime—dreams swallowed by the night but not acted out, thanks to REM's protective paralysis.

People rarely snore during dreams. When REM starts, snoring stops.

Horses, which spend 92 percent of each day standing and can sleep standing, must lie down for REM sleep (Morrison, 2003).

🔒 **RETRIEVE IT • • •** ANSWERS IN APPENDIX E

RI-1 Why would communal sleeping provide added protection for those whose safety depends upon vigilance, such as these soldiers?

The sleep cycle repeats itself about every 90 minutes for younger adults (with shorter, more frequent cycles for older adults). As the night wears on, deep N3 sleep grows shorter and disappears. The REM and N2 sleep periods get longer (see Figure 3.10). By morning, we have spent 20 to 25 percent of an average night's sleep—some 100 minutes—in REM sleep. In sleep lab studies, 37 percent of participants have reported rarely or never having dreams that they "can remember the next morning" (Moore, 2004). Yet even they, more than 80 percent of the time, could recall a dream after being awakened during REM sleep. Neuroscientists have also identified brain regions that are active during dreaming, which enables them to identify when dreaming occurs, whether during or outside of REM sleep (Sicarli et al., 2017).

🔒 RETRIEVE IT • • •   *ANSWERS IN APPENDIX E*

RI-2 What are the four sleep stages, and in what order do we normally travel through those stages?

RI-3 Can you match the cognitive experience (a–c) with the sleep stage (I–III)?

Sleep Stage:	Cognitive experience:
I. N1	a. story-like dream
II. N3	b. fleeting images
III. REM (R)	c. minimal awareness

What Affects Our Sleep Patterns?

LOQ 3-7   How do biology and environment interact in our sleep patterns?

True or false? "Everyone needs 8 hours of sleep." *False.* Newborns often sleep two-thirds of their day, most adults no more than one-third (with some thriving on fewer than 6 hours nightly, others racking up 9 or more). But there is more to our sleep differences than age. Some are awake between nightly sleep periods—sometimes called "first sleep" and "second sleep" (Randall, 2012). And some find that a 15-minute midday nap is as effective as another hour of nighttime sleep (Horne, 2011).

Sleep patterns are genetically influenced, and researchers are tracking the sleep-regulating genes in humans and animals (Hayashi et al., 2015; Mackenzie et al., 2015). Sleep patterns are also culturally influenced. Canadian, American, British, German, and Japanese adults average 7 hours of sleep on workdays and 7 to 8 hours on other days (NSF, 2013). Earlier school start times, more extracurricular activities, and fewer parent-set bedtimes lead American adolescents to get less sleep than their Australian counterparts (Short et al., 2013). Thanks to modern lighting, shift work, and social media diversions, many who might have gone to bed at 9:00 P.M. in days past are now up until 11:00 P.M. or later. With sleep, as with waking behavior, biology and environment interact.

Being bathed in (or deprived of) light disrupts our 24-hour biological clock (Czeisler et al., 1999; Dement, 1999). Whether for work or play, bright light affects our sleepiness by activating light-sensitive retinal proteins. This signals the brain's **suprachiasmatic nucleus (SCN)** to decrease production of *melatonin*, a sleep-inducing hormone (Chang et al., 2015; Gandhi et al., 2015) (**FIGURE 3.11**). (A 2017 Nobel Prize was awarded for research on the molecular biology that runs our biological clock.)

Night-shift workers may experience a chronic state of *desynchronization*. As a result, they become more likely to develop fatigue, stomach problems, heart disease, and, for women, breast cancer (Knutsson & Bøggild, 2010; Lin et al., 2015; Puttonen et al., 2009). Curiously—given that our ancestors' body clocks were attuned to the rising and setting Sun of the 24-hour day—many of today's young adults adopt something closer to a 25-hour day, by staying up too late to get 8 hours of sleep. Approximately 90 percent of Americans report using a light-emitting electronic device one hour before going to sleep (Chang et al., 2015). Such artificial light delays sleep.

Sleep often eludes those who stay up late and sleep in on weekends, and then go to bed earlier on Sunday to prepare for the week ahead (Oren & Terman, 1998). Like New

suprachiasmatic nucleus (SCN) a pair of cell clusters in the hypothalamus that controls circadian rhythm. In response to light, the SCN causes the pineal gland to adjust melatonin production, thus modifying our feelings of sleepiness.

ASK YOURSELF

How does your need for sleep compare with that of others you know? Do you see age-related differences among your friends and family?

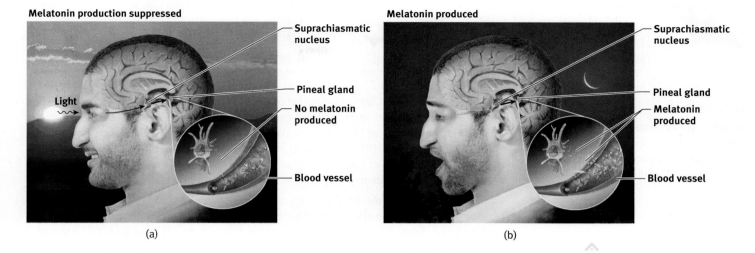

Melatonin production suppressed

- Suprachiasmatic nucleus
- Pineal gland
- No melatonin produced
- Light
- Blood vessel

(a)

Melatonin produced

- Suprachiasmatic nucleus
- Pineal gland
- Melatonin produced
- Blood vessel

(b)

FIGURE 3.11

THE BIOLOGICAL CLOCK (a) Light striking the retina signals the suprachiasmatic nucleus (SCN) to suppress the pineal gland's production of the sleep hormone melatonin. (b) At night, the SCN quiets down, allowing the pineal gland to release melatonin into the bloodstream.

Yorkers readjusting after a trip to California, they experience "social jet lag." For North Americans who fly to Europe and need to be up when their circadian rhythm cries "*SLEEP*," bright light (spending the next day outdoors) helps reset the biological clock (Czeisler et al., 1986, 1989; Eastman et al., 1995).

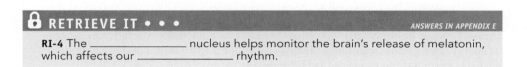

🔒 RETRIEVE IT • • •   *ANSWERS IN APPENDIX E*

RI-4 The _____ nucleus helps monitor the brain's release of melatonin, which affects our _____ rhythm.

WHY DO WE SLEEP?

LOQ 3-8   What are sleep's functions?

So, our sleep patterns differ from person to person and from culture to culture. But why do we have this need for sleep? Psychologists offer five possible reasons:

1. ***Sleep protects.*** When darkness shut down the day's hunting, gathering, and travel, our distant ancestors were better off asleep in a cave, out of harm's way. Those who didn't wander around dark cliffs were more likely to leave descendants. This fits a broader principle: A species' sleep pattern tends to suit its ecological niche (Siegel, 2009). Animals with the greatest need to graze and the least ability to hide tend to sleep less. Animals also sleep less, with no ill effects, during times of mating and migration (Siegel, 2012). (For a sampling of animal sleep times, see **FIGURE 3.12**.)

2. ***Sleep helps us recuperate.*** Sleep helps restore the immune system and repair brain tissue. Sleep gives resting neurons time to repair themselves, while pruning or weakening unused connections (Ascády & Harris, 2017; Ding et al., 2016; Li et al., 2017). Bats and other animals with high waking metabolism burn a lot of calories, producing *free radicals,* molecules that are toxic to neurons. Sleep sweeps away this toxic waste (Xie et al., 2013). Think of it this way: When consciousness leaves your house, workers come in to clean, saying "Good night. Sleep tidy."

3. ***Sleep helps restore and rebuild our fading memories of the day's experiences.*** To sleep is to strengthen. Sleep *consolidates* our memories by replaying recent learning and strengthening neural connections (Pace-Schott et al., 2015; Yang et al., 2014). It reactivates recent experiences stored in the hippocampus and shifts them for permanent storage elsewhere in the cortex (Racsmány et al., 2010; Urbain et al., 2016). Adults, children, and infants trained to perform tasks therefore recall them better after a night's sleep, or even after a short nap, than after several hours awake (Friedrich et al.,

A circadian disadvantage: One study of more than 24,000 Major League Baseball games found that teams who had crossed three time zones before playing a series had a nearly 60 percent chance of losing their first game (Winter et al., 2009). A follow-up study replicated this effect in the National Basketball Association and National Hockey League (Roy & Forest, 2017).

"Sleep faster, we need the pillows."
—Yiddish proverb

"Corduroy pillows make headlines."
—Anonymous

20 hours
Kruglov Orda/Shutterstock

16 hours
Andrew D. Myers

12 hours
Utekhina Anna/Shutterstock

10 hours
Steffen Foerster/Shutterstock

8 hours
Rubberball Productions/Getty Images

4 hours
Eric Isselée/Shutterstock

2 hours
pandapa/Shutterstock

FIGURE 3.12

ANIMAL SLEEP TIME Would you rather be a brown bat and sleep 20 hours a day or a giraffe and sleep 2 hours a day? (Data from NIH, 2010.)

2015; Horváth et al., 2017; Sandoval et al., 2017; Seehagen et al., 2015). Even bad experiences linger more in memory when people sleep on them (Liu et al., 2016).

Older adults' more frequently disrupted sleep also disrupts their memory consolidation (Boyce et al., 2016; Pace-Schott & Spencer, 2011). After sleeping well, older people remember more of recently learned material (Drummond, 2010). Sleep, it seems, strengthens memories in a way that being awake does not.

4. **Sleep feeds creative thinking.** Dreams can inspire noteworthy artistic and scientific achievements, such as the dreams that clued chemist August Kekulé to the structure of benzene (Ross, 2006) and inspired medical researcher Carl Alving (2011) to invent the vaccine patch. More commonplace is the boost that a complete night's sleep gives to our thinking and learning. After working on a task, then sleeping on it, people solve difficult problems more insightfully than do those who stay awake (Barrett, 2011; Sio et al., 2013). They also are better at spotting connections among novel pieces of information (Ellenbogen et al., 2007; Whitehurst et al., 2016). To think smart and see connections, it often pays to ponder a problem just before bed and then sleep on it.

5. **Sleep supports growth.** During slow-wave sleep, the pituitary gland releases a human growth hormone that is necessary for muscle development. A regular full night's sleep can also "*dramatically* improve your athletic ability," report James Maas and Rebecca Robbins (2010). Well-rested athletes have faster reaction times, more energy, and greater endurance. Teams that build 8 to 10 hours of daily sleep into their training show improved performance.

Given all the benefits of sleep, it's no wonder that sleep loss hits us so hard.

🔒 **RETRIEVE IT • • •**   *ANSWERS IN APPENDIX E*

RI-5 What are five proposed reasons for our need for sleep?

SLEEP DEPRIVATION AND SLEEP DISORDERS

LOQ 3-9   How does sleep loss affect us, and what are the major sleep disorders?

When our body yearns for sleep but does not get it, we begin to feel terrible. Trying to stay awake, we will eventually lose. In the tiredness battle, sleep always wins.

Effects of Sleep Loss

Modern sleep patterns leave us not only sleepy but drained of energy and our sense of well-being. Some researchers see today's tiredness as a "Great Sleep Recession" (Keyes et al., 2015). After several 5-hour nights, we accumulate a sleep debt that cannot be satisfied by one long sleep. "The brain keeps an accurate count of sleep debt for at least two weeks," reported sleep researcher William Dement (1999, p. 64).

Obviously, then, we need sleep. Sleep commands roughly one-third of our lives—some 25 years, on average. Allowed to sleep unhindered, most adults will sleep at least 9 hours a night (Coren, 1996). With that much sleep, we awaken refreshed, sustain better moods, and perform more efficiently and accurately. The U.S. Navy and the National Institutes of Health have demonstrated the benefits of unrestricted sleep in experiments in which volunteers spent 14 hours daily in bed for at least a week. For the first few days, the volunteers averaged 12 hours of sleep or more per day, apparently paying off a sleep debt that averaged 25 to 30 hours. That accomplished, they then settled back to 7.5 to 9 hours nightly and felt energized and happier (Dement, 1999). In one Gallup survey, 63 percent of

In 1989, Michael Doucette was named America's Safest Driving Teen. In 1990, while driving home from college, he fell asleep at the wheel and collided with an oncoming car, killing both himself and the other driver. Michael's driving instructor later acknowledged never having mentioned sleep deprivation and drowsy driving (Dement, 1999).

adults who reported getting the sleep they needed also reported being "very satisfied" with their personal life (as did only 36 percent of those needing more sleep) (Mason, 2005).

College and university students are especially sleep deprived; 69 percent in one national survey reported "feeling tired" or "having little energy" on at least several days during the last two weeks (AP, 2009). Less sleep also predicts more conflicts in friend-ships and romantic relationships (Gordon & Chen, 2014; Tavernier & Willoughby, 2014). Tiredness triggers testiness. In another survey, 28 percent of high school students acknowledged falling asleep in class at least once a week (NSF, 2006). The going needn't get boring before students start snoring.

Sleep loss is also a predictor of depression (Baglioni et al., 2016). Researchers who stud-ied 15,500 12- to 18-year-olds found that those who slept 5 or fewer hours a night had a 71 percent higher risk of depression than their peers who slept 8 hours or more (Gangwisch et al., 2010). This link does not appear to reflect an effect of depression on sleep. When chil-dren and youth are followed through time, sleep loss predicts depression rather than vice versa (Gregory et al., 2009). Moreover, REM sleep's processing of emotional experiences helps protect against depression (Walker & van der Helm, 2009). After a good night's sleep, we often do feel better the next day. And that may help to explain why parentally enforced bedtimes predict less depression, and why pushing back school start time leads to improved adolescent sleep, alertness, and mood (Morgenthaler et al., 2016; Winsler et al., 2015). Thus, the American Academy of Pediatrics (2014) advocates delaying adolescents' school start times to "allow students the opportunity to achieve optimal levels of sleep (8.5–9.5 hours)."

Sleep-deprived students often function below their peak. And they know it: Four in five teens and three in five 18- to 29-year-olds wish they could get more sleep on week-days (Mason, 2003, 2005). "Sleep deprivation has consequences—difficulty studying, diminished productivity, tendency to make mistakes, irritability, fatigue," noted Dement (1999, p. 231). Yet teens who stagger glumly out of bed in response to an unwelcome alarm, yawn through morning classes, and feel half-depressed much of the day may feel energized at 11:00 P.M., heedless of the next day's looming sleepiness (Carskadon, 2002).

Lack of sleep can also make you gain weight. Sleep deprivation

- increases *ghrelin,* a hunger-arousing hormone, and decreases its hunger-suppressing partner, *leptin* (Shilsky et al., 2012).

- decreases metabolic (energy use) rate (Buxton et al., 2012).

- increases *cortisol,* a stress hormone that stimulates the body to make fat.

- enhances limbic brain responses to the mere sight of food and decreases cortical responses that help us resist temptation (Benedict et al., 2012; Greer et al., 2013; St-Onge et al., 2012).

Thus, children and adults who sleep less are heavier than average, and in recent decades people have been sleeping less and weighing more (Shiromani et al., 2012; Suglia et al., 2014). Moreover, experimental sleep deprivation increases appetite and eating; our tired brain finds fatty foods more enticing (Fang et al., 2015; Hanlon et al., 2016). So, sleep loss helps explain the weight gain common among sleep-deprived students (Hull et al., 2007).

Sleep also affects our physical health. When infections do set in, we typically sleep more, boosting our immune cells. Sleep deprivation can suppress the immune cells that battle viral infections and cancer (Möller-Levet et al., 2013; Motivala & Irwin, 2007; Opp & Krueger, 2015). In one experiment, when researchers exposed volunteers to a cold virus, those who had averaged less than 5 hours sleep a night were 4.5 times more likely to develop a cold than those who slept more than 7 hours a night (Prather et al., 2015). Sleep's protective effect may help explain why people who sleep 7 to 8 hours a night tend to outlive those who are chronically sleep deprived, and why older adults who have no difficulty falling or staying asleep tend to live longer than their sleep-deprived agemates (Dew et al., 2003; Parthasarathy et al., 2015; Scullin & Bliwise, 2015).

Sleep deprivation slows reactions and increases errors on visual attention tasks similar to those involved in screening airport baggage, performing surgery, and reading X-rays (Caldwell, 2012; Lim & Dinges, 2010). Slow responses can also spell disaster for those operating equipment, piloting, or driving. After 2017 U.S. Navy warship collisions, one prescribed remedy was "more sleep" for the captains (Schmitt, 2017). Drowsy driving

"Maybe 'Bring Your Pillow To Work Day' wasn't such a good idea."

LaunchPad To see whether you are one of the many sleep-deprived students, engage online with the **Immersive Learning** self-assessment activity **Assess Your Strengths: Are You Sleep Deprived? How Can You Improve Your Sleep?**

"Remember to sleep because you have to sleep to remember." —James B. Maas and Rebecca S. Robbins, *Sleep for Success,* 2010

Sleep stealers "You wake up in the middle of the night and grab your smartphone to check the time—it's 3 A.M.—and see an alert. Before you know it, you fall down a rabbit hole of email and Twitter. Sleep? Forget it." —Nick Bilton, "Disruptions: For a Restful Night, Make Your Smartphone Sleep on the Couch," 2014

94

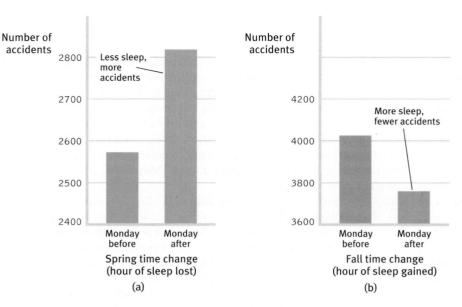

FIGURE 3.13

LESS SLEEP = MORE ACCIDENTS
(a) On the Monday after the spring time change, when people lose one hour of sleep, accidents increased, as compared with the Monday before. (b) In the fall, traffic accidents normally increase because of greater snow, ice, and darkness, but they diminished after the time change. (Data from Coren, 1996.)

"So shut your eyes
Kiss me goodbye
And sleep
Just sleep."
—My Chemical Romance, "Sleep"

ENGAGE **⚡ 📖 LaunchPad** Consider how researchers have addressed these issues by engaging online with **Immersive Learning: How Would You Know If Sleep Deprivation Affects Academic Performance?**

has also contributed to an estimated 1 in 6 American traffic accidents (AAA, 2010) and to some 30 percent of Australian highway deaths (Maas, 1999). One 2-year study examined the driving accidents of more than 20,000 Virginia 16- to 18-year-olds in two major cities. In one city, the high schools started 75 to 80 minutes later than in the other. The late starters had about 25 percent fewer crashes (Vorona et al., 2011). When sleepy frontal lobes confront an unexpected situation, misfortune often results.

Stanley Coren capitalized on what is, for many North Americans, a semi-annual sleep-manipulation experiment—the "spring forward" to daylight saving time and "fall back" to standard time. Searching millions of Canadian and American records, Coren found that accidents increased immediately after the spring-forward time change, which shortens sleep (**FIGURE 3.13**).

FIGURE 3.14 summarizes the effects of sleep deprivation. But there is good news! Psychologists have discovered a treatment that strengthens memory, increases concentration, boosts mood, moderates hunger, reduces obesity, fortifies the immune system, and lessens the risk of fatal accidents. Even better news: The treatment feels good, it can be self-administered, and it's free! If you are a typical university-age student, often going to bed near 2:00 A.M. and dragged out of bed 6 hours later by the dreaded alarm, the

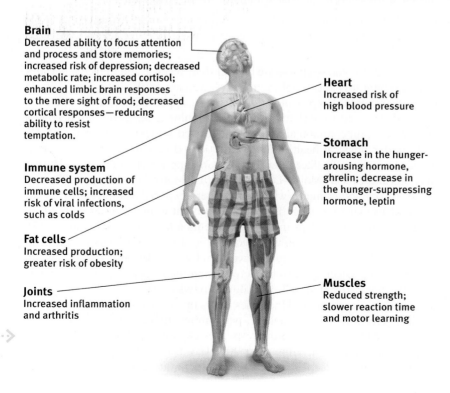

RETAIN **🔒 FIGURE 3.14**

HOW SLEEP DEPRIVATION AFFECTS US

TABLE 3.1

Get a Better Night's Sleep: Natural Sleep Aids

- Exercise regularly but not in the late evening. (Late afternoon is best.)

- Avoid caffeine after early afternoon, and avoid food and drink near bedtime. The exception would be a glass of milk, which provides raw materials for the manufacture of serotonin, a neurotransmitter that facilitates sleep.

- Relax before bedtime, using dimmer light.

- Sleep on a regular schedule (rise at the same time even after a restless night) and avoid long naps.

- Hide time displays so you aren't tempted to check repeatedly.

- Reassure yourself that temporary sleep loss causes no great harm.

- Focus your mind on nonarousing, engaging thoughts, such as song lyrics or vacation travel (Gellis et al., 2013).

- Manage stress. Realize that for any stressed organism, being vigilant is natural and adaptive. Less stress = better sleep.

insomnia recurring problems in falling or staying asleep.

narcolepsy a sleep disorder characterized by uncontrollable sleep attacks. The sufferer may lapse directly into REM sleep, often at inopportune times.

sleep apnea a sleep disorder characterized by temporary cessations of breathing during sleep and repeated momentary awakenings.

night terrors a sleep disorder characterized by high arousal and an appearance of being terrified; unlike nightmares, night terrors occur during N3 sleep, within two or three hours of falling asleep, and are seldom remembered.

ENGAGE (ASK YOURSELF)

What have you learned about sleep that you could apply to yourself?

treatment is simple. Each night, try to add 15 minutes to your sleep until you feel more like a rested and energized student than a zombie. For some additional tips on getting better quality sleep, see **TABLE 3.1.**

Major Sleep Disorders

Do you have trouble sleeping when anxious or excited? Most of us do. An occasional loss of sleep is nothing to worry about. But for those who have a major sleep disorder—**insomnia, narcolepsy, sleep apnea,** sleepwalking (*somnambulism*), sleeptalking, or **night terrors**— trying to sleep can be a nightmare. (See **TABLE 3.2** for a summary of these disorders).

DID BRAHMS NEED HIS OWN LULLABIES? Cranky, overweight, and nap-prone, classical composer Johannes Brahms exhibited common symptoms of sleep apnea (Margolis, 2000).

RETAIN 🔒

TABLE 3.2

Sleep Disorders

Disorder	Rate	Description	Effects
Insomnia	1 in 10 adults; 1 in 4 older adults	Ongoing difficulty falling or staying asleep.	Chronic tiredness. Reliance on sleeping pills and alcohol, which reduce REM sleep and lead to tolerance—a state in which increasing doses are needed to produce an effect.
Narcolepsy	1 in 2000 adults	Sudden attacks of overwhelming sleepiness.	Risk of falling asleep at a dangerous moment. Narcolepsy attacks usually last less than 5 minutes, but they can happen at the worst and most emotional times. Everyday activities, such as driving, require extra caution.
Sleep apnea	1 in 20 adults	Stopping breathing repeatedly while sleeping.	Fatigue and depression (as a result of slow-wave sleep deprivation). Associated with obesity (especially among men).
Sleepwalking and sleeptalking	1–15 in 100 in the general population for sleepwalking (NSF, 2016); about half of young children for sleeptalking (Reimão & Lefévre, 1980)	Doing normal waking activities (sitting up, walking, speaking) while asleep. Sleeptalking can occur during any sleep stage. Sleepwalking happens in N3 sleep.	Few serious concerns. Sleepwalkers return to their beds on their own or with the help of a family member, rarely remembering their trip the next morning.
Night terrors	1 in 100 adults; 1 in 30 children	Appearing terrified, talking nonsense, sitting up, or walking around during N3 sleep; different from nightmares.	Doubling of a child's heart and breathing rates during the attack. Luckily, children remember little or nothing of the fearful event the next day. As people age, night terrors become more and more rare.

off the mark.com   by Mark Parisi

LET ME GET THIS STRAIGHT, IT'S BEEN TWO CONSECUTIVE HOURS SINCE YOU'VE SLEPT?

WHEN CATS EXPERIENCE INSOMNIA

About 1 in 10 adults, and 1 in 4 older adults, complain of insomnia—persistent problems in either falling or staying asleep (Irwin et al., 2006). The result is tiredness and increased risk of depression (Baglioni et al., 2016). From middle age on, awakening occasionally during the night becomes the norm, not something to fret over or treat with medication (Vitiello, 2009). Ironically, insomnia becomes worse when we fret about it. In laboratory studies, people with insomnia do sleep less than others. But they typically overestimate how long it takes them to fall asleep and underestimate how long they actually have slept (Harvey & Tang, 2012). Even if we have been awake only an hour or two, we may *think* we have had very little sleep because it's the waking part we remember.

The most common quick fixes for true insomnia—sleeping pills and alcohol—typically aggravate the problem, reducing REM sleep and leaving the person with next-day blahs. Such aids can also lead to *tolerance*—a state in which increasing doses are needed to produce an effect.

🔒 **RETRIEVE IT • • •**   *ANSWERS IN APPENDIX E*

RI-6 A well-rested person would be more likely to have _____ (trouble concentrating/quick reaction times) and a sleep-deprived person would be more likely to _____ (gain weight/fight off a cold).

DREAMS

LOQ 3-10   What do we dream, and what functions have theorists proposed for dreams?

Now playing at an inner theater near you: the premiere of a sleeping person's vivid dream. This never-before-seen mental movie features captivating characters wrapped in a plot so original and unlikely, yet so intricate and so seemingly real, that the viewer later marvels at its creation.

Unlike daydreams, REM **dreams** are vivid, emotional, and often bizarre (Loftus & Ketchum, 1994). Waking from one, we may wonder how our brain can so creatively, colorfully, and completely construct this alternative world. In the shadowland between our dreaming and waking consciousness, we may even wonder for a moment which is real. Awakening from a nightmare, a 4-year-old may be sure there is a bear in the house.

Discovering the link between REM sleep and dreaming ushered in a new era in dream research. Instead of relying on someone's hazy recall hours later, researchers could catch dreams as they happened, awakening people during or within 3 minutes of a REM sleep period to hear a vivid account.

What We Dream

We spend 6 years of our life in dreams, many of which are anything but sweet. For both women and men, 8 in 10 dreams are marked by at least one negative event or emotion (Domhoff, 2007). Common themes include repeatedly failing in an attempt to do something; being attacked, pursued, or rejected; or experiencing misfortune (Hall et al., 1982). Dreams with sexual imagery occur less often than you might think. In one study, only 1 in 10 dreams among young men and 1 in 30 among young women had sexual content (Domhoff, 1996).

More commonly, a dream's story line incorporates traces of previous days' nonsexual experiences and preoccupations (Nikles et al., 2017):

- *Trauma and dreams* After suffering a trauma, people commonly report nightmares, which help extinguish daytime fears (Levin & Nielsen, 2007, 2009). One sample of Americans recording their dreams during September, 2001 reported an increase in threatening dreams following the 9/11 terrorist attacks (Propper et al., 2007). Compared with Palestinian children living in a peaceful town in Galilee, those living in the conflict-ridden Gaza Strip more often dreamed of aggression (Punamäki & Joustie, 1998).

- *Musicians' dreams* Compared with nonmusicians, musicians report twice as many dreams of music (Uga et al., 2006).

- *Blind people's dreams* Studies in four countries have found blind people mostly dreaming of using their nonvisual senses (Buquet, 1988; Taha, 1972; Vekassy, 1977). But even natively blind people sometimes "see" in their dreams (Bértolo, 2005). Likewise, people born paralyzed below the waist sometimes dream of walking, standing, running, or cycling (Saurat et al., 2011; Voss et al., 2011).

- *Media experiences and dreams* In a study of 1287 Turkish people, "participants who consumed violent media tended to have violent dreams, and participants who consumed sexual media tended to have sexual dreams" (Van den Bulck et al., 2016).

Our two-track mind continues to monitor our environment while we sleep. Sensory stimuli—a particular odor or a phone's ringing—may be instantly and ingeniously woven into the dream story. In a classic experiment, researchers lightly sprayed cold water on dreamers' faces (Dement & Wolpert, 1958). Compared with sleepers who did not get the cold-water treatment, these people were more likely to dream about a waterfall, a leaky roof, or even about being sprayed by someone.

So, could we learn a foreign language by hearing it played while we sleep? If only. While sleeping, we can learn to associate a sound with a mild electric shock (and to react to the sound accordingly). We can also learn to associate a particular sound with a pleasant or unpleasant odor (Arzi et al., 2012). But we do not remember recorded information played while we are soundly asleep (Eich, 1990; Wyatt & Bootzin, 1994). In fact, anything that happens during the 5 minutes just before we fall asleep is typically lost from memory (Roth et al., 1988). This explains why sleep apnea patients, who repeatedly awaken with a gasp and then immediately fall back to sleep, do not recall the episodes. Ditto someone who awakens momentarily, sends a text message, and the next day can't remember doing so. It also explains why dreams that momentarily awaken us are mostly forgotten by morning. To remember a dream, get up and stay awake for a few minutes.

Why We Dream

Dream theorists have proposed several explanations of why we dream, including these five:

To satisfy our own wishes. In 1900, in his landmark book *The Interpretation of Dreams,* Sigmund Freud offered what he thought was "the most valuable of all the discoveries it has been my good fortune to make." He proposed that dreams provide a psychic safety valve that discharges otherwise unacceptable feelings. He viewed a dream's **manifest content** (the apparent and remembered story line) as a censored, symbolic version of its **latent content,** the unconscious drives and wishes (often erotic) that would be threatening if expressed directly. Thus, a gun might be a disguised representation of a penis.

Freud considered dreams the key to understanding our inner conflicts. However, his critics say it is time to wake up from Freud's dream theory, which they regard as a scientific nightmare. Seth Stephens-Davidowitz (2017) analyzed whether phallic-shaped foods "sneak into our dreams with unexpected frequency." His answer: They do not. In dreams, bananas are the second most common fruit. They also are the second most consumed fruit. Cucumbers are the seventh most dreamt vegetable, and the seventh most consumed vegetable. Thus, "there is no reason to believe any of Freud's specific claims about dreams and their purposes," observed dream researcher William Domhoff (2003).

Some contend that even if dreams are symbolic, they could be interpreted any way one wished. Others maintain that dreams hide nothing: A dream about a gun is a dream about a gun. Legend has it that even Freud, who loved to smoke cigars, acknowledged that "sometimes, a cigar is just a cigar." Freud's wish-fulfillment theory of dreams has in large part given way to other theories.

To file away memories. The *information-processing* perspective proposes that dreams may help sift, sort, and fix the day's experiences in our memory. Some studies support this view. When tested the day after learning a task, those who had been deprived of both slow-wave and REM sleep did not do as well as those who had slept undisturbed (Stickgold, 2012). Other studies showed similar memory lapses for new material among people who were awakened every time they began REM sleep (Empson & Clarke, 1970; Karni & Sagi, 1994).

dream a sequence of images, emotions, and thoughts passing through a sleeping person's mind.

manifest content according to Freud, the symbolic, remembered story line of a dream (as distinct from its latent, or hidden, content).

latent content according to Freud, the underlying meaning of a dream (as distinct from its manifest content).

A popular sleep myth: If you dream you are falling and hit the ground (or if you dream of dying), you die. Unfortunately, those who could confirm these ideas are not around to do so. Many people, however, have had such dreams and are alive to report them.

"Follow your dreams, except for that one where you're naked at work." —Attributed to comedian Henny Youngman

"When people interpret [a dream] as if it were meaningful and then sell those interpretations, it's quackery." —Sleep researcher J. Allan Hobson (1995)

(a) Learning.

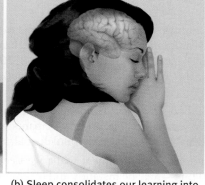

(b) Sleep consolidates our learning into long-term memory.

(c) Learning is retained.

Brain scans confirm the link between REM sleep and memory. The brain regions that were active as rats learned to navigate a maze, or as people learned to perform a visual-discrimination task, became active again later during REM sleep (Louie & Wilson, 2001; Maquet, 2001). So precise were these activity patterns that scientists could tell where in the maze the rat would be if awake. To sleep, perchance to remember.

This is important news for students, many of whom, observed researcher Robert Stickgold (2000), suffer from a kind of sleep bulimia—sleep deprived on weekdays and binge sleeping on the weekend. "If you don't get good sleep and enough sleep after you learn new stuff, you won't integrate it effectively into your memories," he warned. That helps explain why high school students with high grades slept about 25 minutes longer each night than their lower-achieving classmates (Wolfson & Carskadon, 1998; see **FIGURE 3.15**). Sacrificing sleep time to study actually *worsens* academic performance, by making it harder the next day to understand class material or do well on a test (Gillen-O'Neel et al., 2013).

> ***To develop and preserve neural pathways.*** Perhaps dreams, or the brain activity associated with REM sleep, serve a *physiological* function, providing the sleeping brain with periodic stimulation. This theory makes developmental sense. Stimulating experiences preserve and expand the brain's neural pathways. Infants, whose neural networks are fast developing, spend much of their abundant sleep time in REM sleep (**FIGURE 3.16**).

Rapid eye movements also stir the liquid behind the cornea; this delivers fresh oxygen to corneal cells, preventing their suffocation.

> ***To make sense of neural static.*** Other theories propose that dreams erupt from *neural activation* spreading upward from the brainstem (Antrobus, 1991; Hobson, 2003, 2004, 2009). According to the *activation-synthesis theory,* dreams are the brain's attempt to synthesize random neural activity. Much as a neurosurgeon can produce hallucinations by stimulating different parts of a patient's cortex, so can stimulation originating within the brain. As Freud might have expected, PET scans of sleeping people also reveal increased activity in the emotion-related limbic system (in the amygdala) during emotional dreams (Schwartz, 2012). In contrast, frontal lobe regions responsible for inhibition and logical

swissmacky/Shutterstock

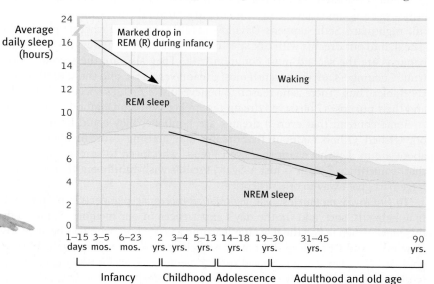

thinking seem to idle, which may explain why our dreams are less inhibited than we are when awake (Maquet et al., 1996). Add the limbic system's emotional tone to the brain's visual bursts and—Voila!—we dream. Damage either the limbic system or the visual centers active during dreaming, and dreaming itself may be impaired (Domhoff, 2003).

To reflect cognitive development. Some dream researchers prefer to see dreams as part of brain maturation and cognitive development (Domhoff, 2010, 2011; Foulkes, 1999). For example, prior to age 9, children's dreams seem more like a slide show and less like an active story in which the dreamer is an actor. Dreams overlap with waking cognition and feature coherent speech. They *simulate reality* by drawing on our concepts and knowledge. They engage brain networks that also are active during daydreaming—and so may be viewed as intensified mind-wandering, enhanced by visual imagery (Fox et al., 2013). Unlike the idea that dreams arise from bottom-up brain activation, the cognitive perspective emphasizes our mind's top-down control of our dream content (Nir & Tononi, 2010).

TABLE 3.3 compares these major dream theories. Although today's sleep researchers debate dreams' functions—and some are skeptical that dreams serve any function—there is one thing they agree on: We need REM sleep. Deprived of it by repeated awakenings, people return more and more quickly to the REM stage after falling back to sleep. When finally allowed to sleep undisturbed, they literally sleep like babies—with increased REM sleep, a phenomenon called **REM rebound.** Most other mammals also experience REM rebound, suggesting that the causes and functions of REM sleep are deeply biological. (That REM sleep occurs in mammals—and not in animals such as fish, whose behavior is less influenced by learning—fits the information-processing theory of dreams.)

So does this mean that because dreams serve physiological functions and extend normal cognition, they are psychologically meaningless? Not necessarily. Every psychologically meaningful experience involves an active brain. We are once again reminded of a basic principle: *Biological and psychological explanations of behavior are partners, not competitors.*

Dreams are a fascinating altered state of consciousness. But they are not the only altered state. As we will see next, drugs also alter conscious awareness.

REM rebound the tendency for REM sleep to increase following REM sleep deprivation.

Question: Does eating spicy foods cause us to dream more?
Answer: A spicy food that causes you to awaken more increases your chance of recalling a dream (Moorcroft, 2003).

ASK YOURSELF

Which explanation for why we dream makes the most sense to you? How well does it explain your own dreams?

TABLE 3.3

Dream Theories

Theory	Explanation	Critical Considerations
Freud's wish-fulfillment	Dreams provide a "psychic safety valve"—expressing otherwise unacceptable feelings; dreams contain manifest (remembered) content and a deeper layer of latent content (a hidden meaning).	Lacks any scientific support; dreams may be interpreted in many different ways.
Information-processing	Dreams help us sort out the day's events and consolidate our memories.	But why do we sometimes dream about things we have not experienced and about past events?
Physiological function	Regular brain stimulation from REM sleep may help develop and preserve neural pathways.	This does not explain why we experience *meaningful* dreams.
Activation-synthesis	REM sleep triggers neural activity that evokes random visual memories, which our sleeping brain weaves into stories.	The individual's brain is weaving the stories, which still tells us something about the dreamer.
Cognitive development	Dream content reflects dreamers' level of cognitive development—their knowledge and understanding. Dreams simulate our lives, including worst-case scenarios.	Does not propose an adaptive function of dreams.

RETRIEVE IT • • •   *ANSWERS IN APPENDIX E*

RI-7 What five theories propose explanations for why we dream?

🔒 REVIEW SLEEP AND DREAMS

⤳ Learning Objectives

TEST YOURSELF Answer these repeated Learning Objective Questions on your own (before checking the answers in Appendix D) to improve your retention of the concepts (McDaniel et al., 2009, 2015).

3-4 What is *sleep*?

3-5 How do our biological rhythms influence our daily functioning?

3-6 What is the biological rhythm of our sleeping and dreaming stages?

3-7 How do biology and environment interact in our sleep patterns?

3-8 What are sleep's functions?

3-9 How does sleep loss affect us, and what are the major sleep disorders?

3-10 What do we dream, and what functions have theorists proposed for dreams?

⤳ Terms and Concepts to Remember

TEST YOURSELF Write down the definition yourself, then check your answer on the referenced page.

sleep, **p. 86**

circadian [ser-KAY-dee-an] rhythm, **p. 86**

REM (R) sleep, **p. 86**

alpha waves, **p. 86**

hallucinations, **p. 88**

delta waves, **p. 88**

suprachiasmatic nucleus (SCN), **p. 90**

insomnia, **p. 95**

narcolepsy, **p. 95**

sleep apnea, **p. 95**

night terrors, **p. 95**

dream, **p. 97**

manifest content, **p. 97**

latent content, **p. 97**

REM rebound, **p. 99**

⤳ Experience the Testing Effect

TEST YOURSELF Answer the following questions on your own first, then check your answers in Appendix E.

1. Our body temperature tends to rise and fall in sync with a biological clock, which is referred to as _____ _____.

2. During the NREM-1 (N1) sleep stage, a person is most likely to experience
   a. sleep spindles.
   b. hallucinations.
   c. night terrors or nightmares.
   d. rapid eye movements.

3. The brain emits large, slow delta waves during _____ sleep.

4. As the night progresses, what happens to the REM (R) stage of sleep?

5. Which of the following is NOT one of the reasons that have been proposed to explain why we need sleep?
   a. Sleep has survival value.
   b. Sleep helps us recuperate.
   c. Sleep rests the eyes.
   d. Sleep plays a role in the growth process.

6. What is the difference between narcolepsy and sleep apnea?

7. In interpreting dreams, Freud was most interested in their
   a. information-processing function.
   b. physiological function.
   c. manifest content, or story line.
   d. latent content, or hidden meaning.

8. How has *activation-synthesis* been used to explain why we dream?

9. "For what one has dwelt on by day, these things are seen in visions of the night" (Menander of Athens [342–292 B.C.E.], *Fragments*). How might we use the information-processing perspective on dreaming to interpret this ancient Greek quote?

10. The tendency for REM sleep to increase following REM sleep deprivation is referred to as _____ _____.

Continue testing yourself with 📖 **LearningCurve** or 📖 **Achieve Read & Practice** to learn and remember most effectively.

⟶ Drugs and Consciousness

TOLERANCE AND ADDICTION IN SUBSTANCE USE DISORDERS

LOQ 3-11 What are *substance use disorders?*

Let's imagine a day in the life of a legal-drug user. It begins with a wake-up energy drink. By midday, several cigarettes have calmed frazzled nerves before an appointment at the plastic surgeon's office for wrinkle-smoothing Botox injections. An afternoon latté provides a needed boost to get through the day, with a beer at home for relaxation. A diet pill before dinner helps curb the appetite. Later, two Advil PMs help offset those stimulating effects. And if performance needs enhancing, there are beta blockers for onstage performers, Viagra for middle-aged and older men, and Adderall for students hoping to focus their concentration.

Such substances are **psychoactive drugs**—chemicals that change perceptions and moods. Most of us manage to use some psychoactive drugs in moderation and without disrupting our lives. But sometimes, drug use crosses the line between moderation and **substance use disorder (TABLE 3.4).** A drug's overall effect depends not only on its biological effects but also on the user's expectations, which vary with social and cultural contexts (Gu et al., 2015; Ward, 1994). If one culture assumes that a particular drug produces euphoria (or aggression or sexual arousal) and another does not, each culture

---

TABLE 3.4

When Is Drug Use a Disorder? According to the American Psychiatric Association, a person may be diagnosed with *substance use disorder* when drug use continues despite significant life disruption. Resulting brain changes may persist after quitting use of the substance (thus leading to strong cravings when exposed to people and situations that trigger memories of drug use). The severity of substance use disorder varies from *mild* (two to three of the indicators listed below) to *moderate* (four to five indicators) to *severe* (six or more indicators). (*Source:* American Psychiatric Association, 2013.)

Diminished Control

1. Uses more substance, or for longer, than intended.

2. Tries unsuccessfully to regulate use of substance.

3. Spends much time acquiring, using, or recovering from effects of substance.

4. Craves the substance.

Diminished Social Functioning

5. Use disrupts commitments at work, school, or home.

6. Continues use despite social problems.

7. Causes reduced social, recreational, and work activities.

Hazardous Use

8. Continues use despite hazards.

9. Continues use despite worsening physical or psychological problems.

Drug Action

10. Experiences tolerance (needing more substance for the desired effect).

11. Experiences withdrawal when attempting to end use.

---

psychoactive drug a chemical substance that alters perceptions and moods.

substance use disorder a disorder characterized by continued substance craving and use despite significant life disruption and/or physical risk.

Tolerance and Addiction

LOQ 3-12 What roles do tolerance and addiction play in substance use disorders, and how has the concept of *addiction* changed?

Tolerance

With continued use of alcohol and some other drugs (but not marijuana), users develop **tolerance** as their brain chemistry adapts to offset the drug effect (*neuroadaptation*). To experience the same effect, users require larger and larger doses, which increase the risk of becoming *addicted* and developing a *substance use disorder*.

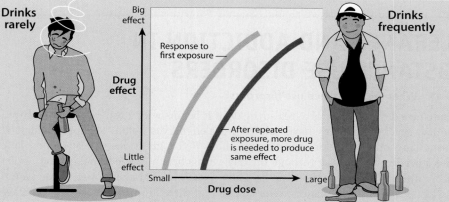

Drinks rarely

Drinks frequently

Big effect

Response to first exposure —

Drug effect

After repeated exposure, more drug is needed to produce same effect

Little effect

Small — Large

Drug dose

Addiction

Caused by ever-increasing doses of most psychoactive drugs (including prescription painkillers). Prompts user to crave the drug, to continue use despite adverse consequences, and to struggle when attempting to **withdraw** from it. These behaviors suggest a *substance use disorder*. Once in the grip of addiction, people *want* the drug more than they *like* the drug.[1]

4% of the world's people have an alcohol use disorder.[2]

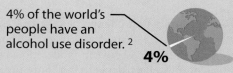

4%

The lifetime odds of getting hooked after using various drugs:

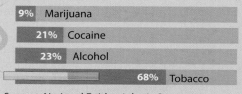

9%	Marijuana
21%	Cocaine
23%	Alcohol
68%	Tobacco

Source: National Epidemiologic Survey on Alcohol and Related Conditions[3]

Therapy or group support, such as from Alcoholics Anonymous, may help. It also helps to believe that addictions are controllable and that people can change. Many people do voluntarily stop using addictive drugs, without any treatment. Most ex-smokers have kicked the habit on their own.[4]

Behavior Addictions

Psychologists try to avoid using "addiction" to label driven, excessive behaviors such as eating, work, sex, and accumulating wealth.

I'm ADDICTED to cheeseburgers!

Yet some behaviors can become compulsive and dysfunctional—similar to problematic alcohol and drug use.[5]

• Behavior addictions include *gambling disorder*.
• *Internet gaming disorder* has been proposed "for further study."[6] Some internet users display an apparent inability to resist logging on and staying on, even when this excessive use impairs their work and relationships.[7]

Psychological and drug therapies may be "highly effective" for problematic internet use.[8]

1. Berridge et al., 2009; Robinson & Berridge, 2003. 2. WHO, 2014b. 3. Lopez-Quintero et al., 2011. 4. Newport, 2013b. 5. Gentile, 2009; Griffiths, 2001; Hoeft et al., 2008. 6. American Psychiatric Association, 2013.; Wittek et al., 2016; Wu et al., 2016. 7. Cheng & Li, 2014; Ko et al., 2005. 8. Winkler et al., 2013.

may find its expectations fulfilled. We'll take a closer look at these interacting forces in the use and potential abuse of particular psychoactive drugs. But first, to consider what contributes to the disordered use of various substances, see Thinking Critically About: Tolerance and Addiction.

tolerance the diminishing effect with regular use of the same dose of a drug, requiring the user to take larger and larger doses before experiencing the drug's effect.

withdrawal the discomfort and distress that follow discontinuing an addictive drug or behavior.

RI-1 What is the process that leads to drug tolerance?

RI-2 Can someone become "addicted" to shopping?

TYPES OF PSYCHOACTIVE DRUGS

The three major categories of psychoactive drugs are *depressants, stimulants,* and *hallucinogens.* All do their work at the brain's synapses, stimulating, inhibiting, or mimicking the activity of the brain's own chemical messengers, the neurotransmitters.

Depressants

LOQ 3-13 What are *depressants,* and what are their effects?

Depressants are drugs such as alcohol, barbiturates (tranquilizers), and opiates that calm neural activity and slow body functions.

ALCOHOL True or false? Alcohol is a depressant in large amounts but a stimulant in small amounts. *False.* In any amount, alcohol is a depressant. Low doses of alcohol may, indeed, enliven a drinker, but they do so by acting as a *disinhibitor*—they slow brain activity that controls judgment and inhibitions. Alcohol is an equal-opportunity drug: It increases (disinhibits) helpful tendencies, as when tipsy restaurant patrons leave extravagant tips and social drinkers bond in groups (Fairbairn & Sayette, 2014; Lynn, 1988). And it increases harmful tendencies, as when sexually aroused men become more disposed to sexual aggression. When drinking, both men and women are more disposed to casual sex (Claxton et al., 2015; Johnson & Chen, 2015). *The bottom line:* The urges you would feel if sober are the ones you will more likely act upon when intoxicated. And that helps us understand why, among 18- to 24-year old Americans, there are each year more than 1800 alcohol-related deaths and nearly 700,000 alcohol-related assaults, including some 97,000 sexual assaults (NIH, 2015).

The prolonged and excessive drinking that characterizes **alcohol use disorder** can shrink the brain and contribute to premature death (Kendler et al., 2016; **FIGURE 3.17**). Girls and young women (who have less of a stomach enzyme that digests alcohol) can become addicted to alcohol more quickly than boys and young men do, and they are at risk for lung, brain, and liver damage at lower consumption levels (CASA, 2003).

SLOWED NEURAL PROCESSING Alcohol slows sympathetic nervous system activity. Larger doses cause reactions to slow, speech to slur, and skilled performance to deteriorate. Paired with sleep deprivation, alcohol is a potent sedative. Add these physical effects to lowered inhibitions, and the result can be deadly. Worldwide, several hundred thousand lives are lost each year in alcohol-related accidents and violent crime. As blood-alcohol levels rise and judgment falters, people's qualms about drinking and driving lessen. When drunk, people aren't aware of how drunk they are (Moore et al., 2016). In experiments, virtually all drinkers who had insisted when sober that they would not drive under the influence later decided to drive home from a bar, even when given a Breathalyzer test and told they were intoxicated (Denton & Krebs, 1990; MacDonald et al., 1995). Alcohol can also be life threatening when heavy drinking follows an earlier period of moderate drinking, which depresses the vomiting response. People may poison themselves with an overdose that their bodies would normally throw up.

MEMORY DISRUPTION Alcohol can disrupt memory formation, and heavy drinking can have long-term effects on the brain and cognition. In rats, at a developmental period corresponding to human adolescence, binge drinking contributes to nerve cell death and reduces the birth of new nerve cells. It also impairs the growth of synaptic connections (Crews et al., 2006, 2007). In humans, heavy drinking may lead to blackouts, in which drinkers are unable to recall people they met the night before or what they said or did while intoxicated. These blackouts result partly from the way alcohol suppresses REM sleep, which helps fix the day's experiences into permanent memories.

REDUCED SELF-AWARENESS In one experiment, those who consumed alcohol (rather than a placebo beverage) were doubly likely to be caught mind-wandering during a reading task, yet were *less*

depressants drugs (such as alcohol, barbiturates, and opiates) that reduce neural activity and slow body functions.

alcohol use disorder (popularly known as *alcoholism*) alcohol use marked by tolerance, withdrawal, and a drive to continue problematic use.

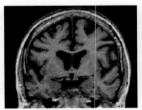
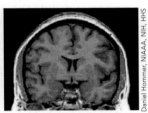

Scan of woman with alcohol use disorder
(a)

Scan of woman without alcohol use disorder
(b)

FIGURE 3.17

DISORDERED DRINKING SHRINKS THE BRAIN MRI scans show brain shrinkage in women with alcohol use disorder (a) compared with women in a control group (b).

DRINKING DISASTER DEMO

Firefighters reenacted the trauma of an alcohol-related car accident, providing a memorable demonstration for these high school students. Alcohol consumption leads to feelings of invincibility, which become especially dangerous behind the wheel of a car.

barbiturates drugs that depress central nervous system activity, reducing anxiety but impairing memory and judgment.

opiates opium and its derivatives, such as morphine and heroin; depress neural activity, temporarily lessening pain and anxiety.

stimulants drugs (such as caffeine, nicotine, and the more powerful cocaine, amphetamines, methamphetamine, and Ecstasy) that excite neural activity and speed up body functions.

amphetamines drugs (such as methamphetamine) that stimulate neural activity, causing accelerated body functions and associated energy and mood changes.

nicotine a stimulating and highly addictive psychoactive drug in tobacco.

likely to notice that they zoned out (Sayette et al., 2009). Sometimes we mind-wander to give our brains a break, but unintentional zoning out—while driving, for example—can cause later regret, especially if we've endangered ourselves or others (Seli et al., 2016). Alcohol not only reduces self-awareness, it also produces a sort of "myopia" by focusing attention on an arousing situation (say, a provocation) and distracting it from normal inhibitions and future consequences (Giancola et al., 2010; Hull & Bond, 1986; Steele & Josephs, 1990).

Reduced self-awareness may help explain why people who want to suppress their awareness of failures or shortcomings are more likely to drink than are those who feel good about themselves. Losing a business deal, a game, or a romantic partner sometimes elicits a drinking binge.

EXPECTANCY EFFECTS As with other drugs, expectations influence behavior. Expectations help explain why adolescents—presuming that alcohol will lift their spirits—sometimes drink when they're upset and alone. Solitary drinking actually does not boost mood, but it does increase the likelihood of developing a substance use disorder (Creswell et al., 2014; Fairbairn & Sayette, 2014).

Simply *believing* we're consuming alcohol can cause us to act out alcohol's presumed influence (Christiansen et al., 2016; Moss & Albery, 2009). In a classic experiment, researchers gave Rutgers University men (who had volunteered for a study on "alcohol and sexual stimulation") either an alcoholic or a nonalcoholic drink (Abrams & Wilson, 1983). (Both had strong tastes that masked any alcohol.) After watching an erotic movie clip, the men who *thought* they had consumed alcohol were more likely to report having strong sexual fantasies and feeling guilt free. Being able to *attribute* their sexual responses to alcohol released their inhibitions—whether or not they had actually consumed any alcohol.

So, alcohol's effect lies partly in that powerful sex organ, the mind. Fourteen "intervention studies" have educated college drinkers about that very point (Scott-Sheldon et al., 2014). Most participants have come away with lower positive expectations of alcohol and reduced their drinking the ensuing month.

BARBITURATES Like alcohol, the **barbiturate** drugs, which are *tranquilizers,* depress nervous system activity. Barbiturates such as Nembutal, Seconal, and Amytal are sometimes prescribed to induce sleep or reduce anxiety. In larger doses, they can impair memory and judgment. If combined with alcohol—as sometimes happens when people take a sleeping pill after an evening of heavy drinking—the total depressive effect on body functions can be lethal.

OPIATES The **opiates**—opium and its derivatives—also depress neural functioning. Opiates include *heroin* and its medically prescribed substitute, *methadone.* They also include pain-relief *narcotics* such as codeine, OxyContin, and morphine (and its much more powerful synthetic counterpart, fentanyl). As blissful pleasure replaces pain and anxiety, the user's pupils constrict, breathing slows, and lethargy sets in. Those who become addicted to this short-term pleasure may pay a long-term price: a gnawing craving for another fix, a need for progressively larger doses (as tolerance develops), and the extreme discomfort of withdrawal. When repeatedly flooded with an artificial opiate, the brain eventually stops producing *endorphins,* its own opiates. If the artificial opiate is then withdrawn, the brain will lack the normal level of these painkilling neurotransmitters. An alarming number of Americans have become unable or unwilling to tolerate this state and have paid an ultimate price—death by overdose. Between 2013 and 2016, the U.S. rate of overdose deaths from synthetic opioids more than quadrupled to 20,000 per year, with another 44,000 annual deaths due to other opioids (CDC, 2017). The opioid crisis is "a major problem," declared U.S. President Trump (2017) in announcing a government initiative to stop opioid abuse.

🔒 RETRIEVE IT • • •   *ANSWERS IN APPENDIX E*

RI-3 Alcohol, barbiturates, and opiates are all in a class of drugs called
_____.

Stimulants

LOQ 3-14 What are *stimulants*, and what are their effects?

A **stimulant** excites neural activity and speeds up body functions. Pupils dilate, heart and breathing rates increase, and blood sugar levels rise, causing a drop in appetite. Energy and self-confidence also rise.

Stimulants include caffeine, nicotine, and the more powerful cocaine, **amphetamines,** methamphetamine ("speed"), and Ecstasy. People use stimulants to feel alert, lose weight, or boost mood or athletic performance. Some students resort to stimulants in hopes of boosting their academic performance, despite the fact that they may offer only small benefit (Ilieva et al., 2015). Stimulants can also be addictive, as you may know if you are one of the many who use caffeine daily in your coffee, tea, soda, or energy drinks. Cut off from your usual dose, you may crash into fatigue, headaches, irritability, and depression (Silverman et al., 1992). A mild dose of caffeine typically lasts three or four hours, which—if taken in the evening—may impair sleep.

NICOTINE Tobacco products deliver highly addictive **nicotine.** Imagine that cigarettes were harmless—except, once in every 25,000 packs, an occasional innocent-looking one was filled with dynamite instead of tobacco. Not such a bad risk of having your head blown off. But with 250 million packs a day consumed worldwide, we could expect more than 10,000 gruesome daily deaths (more than three times the 9/11 terrorist fatalities each and every day)—surely enough to have cigarettes banned everywhere.[1]

The lost lives from these dynamite-loaded cigarettes approximate those from today's actual cigarettes. A teen-to-the-grave smoker has a 50 percent chance of dying from the habit, and each year, tobacco kills nearly 5.4 million of its 1.3 billion customers worldwide. (Imagine the outrage if 25 loaded jumbo jets crashed today, let alone tomorrow and every day thereafter.) By 2030, annual tobacco deaths are expected to increase to 8 million. That means that *1 billion* twenty-first-century people may be killed by tobacco (WHO, 2012).

Tobacco products include cigarettes, cigars, chewing tobacco, pipe tobacco, snuff, and—most recently—e-cigarettes. Inhaling e-cigarette vapor ("vaping") gives users a jolt of nicotine without cancer-causing tar. As a result, their sale has boomed: Between 2013 and 2014, youth e-cigarette use tripled (Das et al., 2016). But there is a downside: E-cigarettes deliver toxic chemicals and can increase one's chances of using conventional cigarettes (Barrington-Trimis et al., 2016; Farsalinos et al., 2014).

Smoke a cigarette and nature will charge you 12 minutes—ironically, just about the length of time you spend smoking it (*Discover,* 1996). (Researchers don't yet know how e-cigarette smoking affects life expectancy.) Smokers die, on average, at least a decade before nonsmokers (Jha et al., 2013). Eliminating smoking would increase life expectancy more than any other preventive measure.

Tobacco products are as powerfully and quickly addictive as heroin and cocaine. Attempts to quit even within the first weeks of smoking often fail (DiFranza, 2008). As with other addictions, smokers develop *tolerance,* and quitting causes withdrawal symptoms, including craving, insomnia, anxiety, irritability, and distractibility. Nicotine-deprived smokers trying to focus on a task experience a tripled rate of mind-wandering (Sayette et al., 2010). When not craving a cigarette, they tend to underestimate the power of such cravings (Sayette et al., 2008).

All it takes to relieve this aversive state is a single puff on a cigarette. Within 7 seconds, a rush of nicotine will signal the central nervous system to release a flood of neurotransmitters (**FIGURE 3.18**). Epinephrine and norepinephrine will diminish appetite and boost alertness and mental efficiency. Dopamine and opioids will temporarily calm anxiety and reduce sensitivity to pain (Ditre et al., 2011; Gavin, 2004). No wonder ex-smokers will sometimes, under stress, return to smoking—as did some 1 million Americans after the 9/11 terrorist attacks (Pesko, 2014). Ditto for people with major depressive disorder, who are more likely than others to see their efforts to quit go up in smoke (Zvolensky et al., 2015).

Vasca/Shutterstock

ENGAGE   **ASK YOURSELF**

Have you ever relied on caffeinated drinks to stay awake for a late-night study session, and then struggled to fall asleep afterward? How do you think this pattern affects next-day performance in class or at work? How might you plan your study sessions to avoid this?

"Smoking cures weight problems . . . eventually." —Comedian writer Steven Wright

For HIV patients who smoke, the virus is now much less lethal than the smoking (Helleberg et al., 2013).

---

1. This analogy, adapted here with world-based numbers, was suggested by mathematician Sam Saunders, as reported by K. C. Cole (1998).

FIGURE 3.18

WHERE THERE'S SMOKE . . . : THE PHYSIOLOGICAL EFFECTS OF NICOTINE Nicotine reaches the brain within 7 seconds, twice as fast as intravenous heroin. Within minutes, the amount in the blood soars.

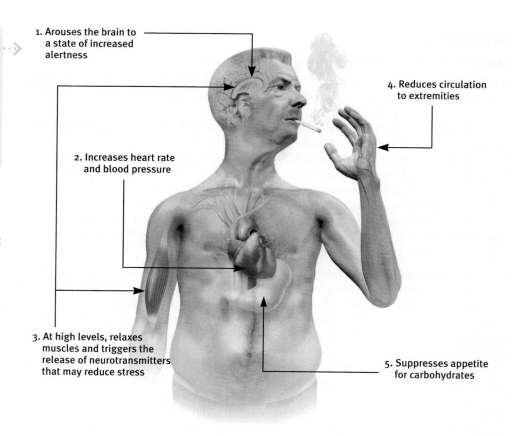

1. Arouses the brain to a state of increased alertness
2. Increases heart rate and blood pressure
3. At high levels, relaxes muscles and triggers the release of neurotransmitters that may reduce stress
4. Reduces circulation to extremities
5. Suppresses appetite for carbohydrates

cocaine a powerful and addictive stimulant derived from the coca plant; produces temporarily increased alertness and euphoria.

methamphetamine a powerfully addictive drug that stimulates the central nervous system, with accelerated body functions and associated energy and mood changes; over time, appears to reduce baseline dopamine levels.

Ecstasy (MDMA) a synthetic stimulant and mild hallucinogen. Produces euphoria and social intimacy, but with short-term health risks and longer-term harm to serotonin-producing neurons and to mood and cognition.

Humorist Dave Barry (1995) recalling why he smoked his first cigarette the summer he turned 15: "Arguments against smoking: 'It's a repulsive addiction that slowly but surely turns you into a gasping, gray-skinned, tumor-ridden invalid, hacking up brownish gobs of toxic waste from your one remaining lung.' Arguments for smoking: 'Other teenagers are doing it.' Case closed! Let's light up!"

ASK YOURSELF

Think of a friend or family member who is addicted to nicotine. What do you think would be most effective to say to that person to convince them to try to quit?

These rewards keep people smoking, even among the 3 in 4 smokers who wish they could stop (Newport, 2013b). Each year, fewer than 1 in 7 who want to quit will be able to resist. Even those who know they are committing slow-motion suicide may be unable to stop (Saad, 2002).

Nevertheless, repeated attempts seem to pay off. The worldwide smoking rate—25 percent among men and 5 percent among women—is down about 30 percent since 1990 (GBD, 2017). Half of all Americans who have ever smoked have quit, sometimes aided by a nicotine replacement drug and with encouragement from a counselor or support group. Some researchers argue that it is best to quit abruptly—to go "cold turkey" (Lindson-Hawley et al., 2016). Others suggest that success is equally likely whether smokers quit abruptly or gradually (Fiore et al., 2008; Lichtenstein et al., 2010). For those who endure, the acute craving and withdrawal symptoms gradually dissipate over the ensuing 6 months (Ward et al., 1997). After a year's abstinence, only 10 percent will relapse in the next year (Hughes, 2010). These nonsmokers may live not only healthier but also happier lives. Smoking correlates with higher rates of depression, chronic disabilities, and divorce (Doherty & Doherty, 1998; Edwards & Kendler, 2012; Vita et al., 1998). Healthy living seems to add both years to life and life to years. Awareness of nonsmokers' better health and happiness has contributed to U.S. high school seniors' increasing disapproval (87 percent) of smoking a pack or more a day, and also to a plunge in their smoking rate, from 37 percent in 1997 to 10 percent in 2017 (Johnston et al., 2018).

RETRIEVE IT • • •

ANSWERS IN APPENDIX E

RI-4 What withdrawal symptoms should your friend expect when she finally decides to quit smoking?

COCAINE **Cocaine** is a powerfully addictive stimulant derived from the coca plant. The recipe for Coca-Cola originally included a coca extract, creating a cocaine tonic for tired elderly people. Between 1896 and 1905, Coke was indeed "the real thing." But no longer. Cocaine is now snorted, injected, or smoked (sometimes as *crack cocaine*, a

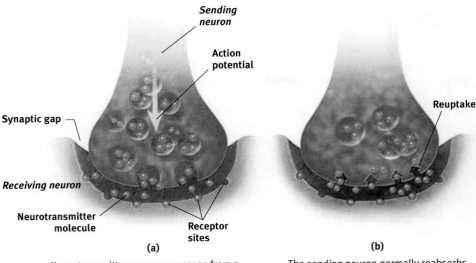

(a)

Neurotransmitters carry a message from a sending neuron across a synapse to receptor sites on a receiving neuron.

(b)

The sending neuron normally reabsorbs excess neurotransmitter molecules, a process called *reuptake*.

(c)

By binding to the sites that normally reabsorb neurotransmitter molecules, cocaine blocks reuptake of dopamine, norepinephrine, and serotonin (Ray & Ksir, 1990). The extra neurotransmitter molecules therefore remain in the synapse, intensifying their normal mood-altering effects and producing a euphoric rush. When the cocaine level drops, the absence of these neurotransmitters produces a crash.

FIGURE 3.19
COCAINE EUPHORIA AND CRASH

"Cocaine makes you a new man. And the first thing that new man wants is more cocaine." —Comedian George Carlin (1937–2008)

faster-working crystallized form that produces a briefer but more intense high, followed by a more intense crash). Cocaine enters the bloodstream quickly, producing a rush of euphoria that depletes the brain's supply of the neurotransmitters dopamine, serotonin, and norepinephrine (**FIGURE 3.19**). Within the hour, a crash of agitated depression follows as the drug's effect wears off. After several hours, the craving for more wanes, only to return several days later (Gawin, 1991).

In situations that trigger aggression, ingesting cocaine may heighten reactions. Caged rats fight when given foot shocks, and they fight even more when given cocaine *and* foot shocks. Likewise, humans who voluntarily ingest high doses of cocaine in laboratory experiments impose higher shock levels on a presumed opponent than do those receiving a placebo (Licata et al., 1993). Cocaine use may also lead to emotional disturbances, suspiciousness, convulsions, cardiac arrest, or respiratory failure.

Cocaine use is powerfully rewarding (Keramati et al., 2017). Its psychological effects vary with the dosage and form consumed, but the situation and the user's expectations and personality also play a role. Given a placebo, cocaine users who *thought* they were taking cocaine often had a cocaine-like experience (Byck & Van Dyke, 1982).

In national surveys, 2.7 percent of American twelfth graders and 6 percent of British 18- to 24-year-olds reported having tried cocaine during the past year (ACMD, 2009; Johnston et al., 2018).

METHAMPHETAMINE Amphetamines stimulate neural activity. As body functions speed up, the user's energy rises and mood soars. Amphetamines are the parent drug for the highly addictive **methamphetamine**, which is chemically similar but has greater effects (NIDA, 2002, 2005). Methamphetamine triggers the release of the neurotransmitter dopamine, which stimulates brain cells that enhance energy and mood, leading to 8 hours or so of heightened energy and euphoria. Its aftereffects may include irritability, insomnia, hypertension, seizures, social isolation, depression, and occasional violent outbursts (Homer et al., 2008). Over time, methamphetamine may reduce baseline dopamine levels, leaving the user with depressed functioning.

ECSTASY **Ecstasy,** a street name for **MDMA** (methylenedioxymethamphetamine, also known in its powder form as *Molly*), is both a stimulant and a mild hallucinogen. As an amphetamine derivative, Ecstasy triggers dopamine release, but its major effect is releasing stored serotonin and blocking its reuptake, thus prolonging serotonin's feel-good flood (Braun, 2001). Users feel the effect about a half-hour after taking an Ecstasy pill. For 3 or 4 hours, they experience high energy, emotional elevation, and (given a social context) connectedness with those around them ("I love everyone").

DRAMATIC DRUG-INDUCED DECLINE
In the 18 months between these two mug shots, this woman's methamphetamine addiction led to obvious physical changes.

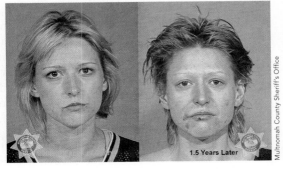

1.5 Years Later

Multnomah County Sheriff's Office

THE HUG DRUG MDMA, known as Ecstasy and often taken at clubs, produces a euphoric high and feelings of intimacy. But repeated use can destroy serotonin-producing neurons, impair memory, and permanently deflate mood.

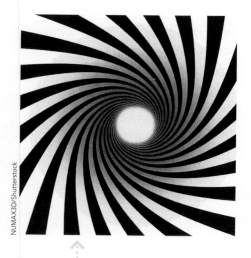

FIGURE 3.20

NEAR-DEATH VISION OR HALLUCINATION? Psychologist Ronald Siegel (1977) reported that people under the influence of hallucinogenic drugs often see "a bright light in the center of the field of vision. . . . The location of this point of light create[s] a tunnel-like perspective." This is very similar to others' near-death experiences.

Synthetic marijuana (*K2*, also called *Spice*) mimics THC. Its harmful side effects can include agitation and hallucinations (Fattore, 2016; Sherif et al., 2016).

During the 1990s, Ecstasy's popularity soared as a "club drug" taken at nightclubs and all-night dance parties (Landry, 2002). The drug's popularity crosses national borders, with an estimated 60 million tablets consumed annually in Britain (ACMD, 2009). There are, however, reasons not to be ecstatic about Ecstasy. One is its dehydrating effect, which—when combined with prolonged dancing—can lead to severe overheating, increased blood pressure, and death. Another is that long-term, repeated leaching of brain serotonin can damage serotonin-producing neurons, leading to decreased output and increased risk of permanently depressed mood (Croft et al., 2001; McCann et al., 2000; Roiser et al., 2005). Ecstasy also suppresses the disease-fighting immune system, impairs memory, slows thought, and disrupts sleep by interfering with serotonin's control of the circadian clock (Laws & Kokkalis, 2007; Schilt et al., 2007; Wagner et al., 2012). Ecstasy delights for the night but dispirits the morrow.

Hallucinogens

LOQ 3-15   What are *hallucinogens*, and what are their effects?

Hallucinogens distort perceptions and evoke sensory images in the absence of sensory input (which is why these drugs are also called *psychedelics*, meaning "mind-manifesting"). Some, such as LSD and MDMA (Ecstasy), are synthetic. Others, including psilocybin and the mild hallucinogen marijuana, are natural substances.

Whether provoked to hallucinate by drugs, loss of oxygen, or extreme sensory deprivation, the brain hallucinates in basically the same way (Siegel, 1982). The experience typically begins with simple geometric forms, such as a lattice, cobweb, or spiral. The next phase consists of more meaningful images; some may be superimposed on a tunnel or funnel, others may be replays of past emotional experiences. Brain scans of people on an LSD trip reveal that their visual cortex becomes hypersensitive and strongly connected to their brain's emotion centers (Carhart-Harris et al., 2016). As the hallucination peaks, people frequently feel separated from their body and experience dreamlike scenes. Their sense of self dissolves, which also dissolves the border between themselves and the external world (Lebedev et al., 2015).

These sensations are strikingly similar to the **near-death experience,** an altered state of consciousness reported by about 10 to 15 percent of those revived from cardiac arrest (Agrillo, 2011; Greyson, 2010; Parnia et al., 2014). Many describe visions of tunnels (**FIGURE 3.20**), bright lights, a replay of old memories, and out-of-body sensations (Siegel, 1980). These experiences can later enhance spirituality and promote feelings of personal growth (Khanna & Greyson, 2014, 2015). Given that oxygen deprivation and other insults to the brain are known to produce hallucinations, it is difficult to resist wondering whether a brain under stress manufactures the near-death experience. During epileptic seizures and migraines, people may experience similar hallucinations of geometric patterns (Billock & Tsou, 2012). So have solitary sailors and polar explorers while enduring monotony, isolation, and cold (Suedfeld & Mocellin, 1987). The philosopher-neuroscientist Patricia Churchland (2013, p. 70) surmises that such experiences represent "neural funny business."

LSD Chemist Albert Hofmann created—and on one Friday afternoon in April 1943 accidentally ingested—**LSD** (lysergic acid diethylamide). The result—"an uninterrupted stream of fantastic pictures, extraordinary shapes with intense, kaleidoscopic play of colors"—reminded him of a childhood mystical experience that had left him longing for another glimpse of "a miraculous, powerful, unfathomable reality" (Siegel, 1984; Smith, 2006).

The emotions of an LSD (or *acid*) trip range from euphoria to detachment to panic. Users' current mood and expectations (their "high hopes") color the emotional experience, but the perceptual distortions and hallucinations have some commonalities.

MARIJUANA The straight dope on marijuana: Marijuana leaves and flowers contain **THC** (delta-9-tetrahydrocannabinol). Whether smoked (getting to the brain in about 7 seconds) or eaten (traveling at a slower, unpredictable rate), THC produces a mix of effects.

It is usually classified as a mild hallucinogen because it amplifies sensitivity to colors, sounds, tastes, and smells. But like the depressant alcohol, marijuana relaxes, disinhibits, and may produce a euphoric high. Both alcohol and marijuana impair the motor coordination, perceptual skills, and reaction time necessary for safely operating an automobile or other machine. "THC causes animals to misjudge events," reported Ronald Siegel (1990, p. 163). "Pigeons wait too long to respond to buzzers or lights that tell them food is available for brief periods; and rats turn the wrong way in mazes."

Marijuana and alcohol also differ. The body eliminates alcohol within hours. THC and its by-products linger in the body for more than a week, which means that regular users experience less abrupt withdrawal and may achieve a high with smaller-than-usual drug amounts. This is the opposite of typical tolerance, in which repeat users need larger doses to feel the same effect.

After considering more than 10,000 scientific reports, the U.S. National Academies of Sciences, Engineering, and Medicine (2017) concluded that marijuana use

- alleviates chronic pain and chemotherapy-related nausea,

- is not associated with tobacco-related cancers, such as lung cancer,

- is predictive of increased risk of traffic accidents, chronic bronchitis, psychosis, social anxiety disorder, and suicidal thoughts, and

- likely contributes to impaired attention, learning, and memory, and possibly to academic underachievement.

A marijuana user's experience can vary with the situation. If the person feels anxious or depressed, marijuana may intensify the feelings. The more often the person uses marijuana, especially during adolescence, the greater the risk of anxiety, depression, or addiction (Bambico et al., 2010; Hurd et al., 2013; Volkow et al., 2016).

Some countries and U.S. states have passed laws legalizing marijuana possession. Greater legal acceptance helps explain why Americans' marijuana use nearly doubled between 2013 and 2016, from 7 to 13 percent (McCarthy, 2016).

* * *

Despite their differences, the psychoactive drugs summarized in **TABLE 3.5** (with the exception of marijuana) share a common feature: They trigger negative aftereffects that offset their immediate positive effects and grow stronger with repetition. This helps explain both tolerance and withdrawal.

hallucinogens psychedelic ("mind-manifesting") drugs, such as LSD, that distort perceptions and evoke sensory images in the absence of sensory input.

near-death experience an altered state of consciousness reported after a close brush with death (such as cardiac arrest); often similar to drug-induced hallucinations.

LSD *(lysergic acid diethylamide)* a powerful hallucinogenic drug; also known as *acid.*

THC the major active ingredient in marijuana; triggers a variety of effects, including mild hallucinations.

LaunchPad To review the basic psychoactive drugs and their actions, and to play the role of experimenter as you administer drugs and observe their effects, visit **Topic Tutorial: PsychSim6, Your Mind on Drugs.**

TABLE 3.5

A Guide to Selected Psychoactive Drugs

Drug	Type	Pleasurable Effects	Negative Aftereffects
Alcohol	Depressant	Initial high followed by relaxation and disinhibition	Depression, memory loss, organ damage, impaired reactions
Heroin	Depressant	Rush of euphoria, relief from pain	Depressed physiology, agonizing withdrawal
Caffeine	Stimulant	Increased alertness and wakefulness	Anxiety, restlessness, and insomnia in high doses; uncomfortable withdrawal
Nicotine	Stimulant	Arousal and relaxation, sense of well-being	Heart disease, cancer
Cocaine	Stimulant	Rush of euphoria, confidence, energy	Cardiovascular stress, suspiciousness, depressive crash
Methamphetamine	Stimulant	Euphoria, alertness, energy	Irritability, insomnia, hypertension, seizures
Ecstasy (MDMA)	Stimulant; mild hallucinogen	Emotional elevation, disinhibition	Dehydration, overheating, depressed mood, impaired cognitive and immune functioning
LSD	Hallucinogen	Visual "trip"	Risk of panic
Marijuana (THC)	Mild hallucinogen	Enhanced sensation, relief of pain, distortion of time, relaxation	Impaired learning and memory, increased risk of psychological disorders

INFLUENCES ON DRUG USE

LOQ 3-16   Why do some people become regular users of consciousness-altering drugs?

Drug use by North American youth increased during the 1970s. Then, with increased drug education and a more realistic and deglamorized media depiction of taking drugs, drug use declined sharply (except for a small rise in the mid-1980s). After the early 1990s, the cultural antidrug voice softened, and some drugs for a time were again glamorized in music and films. Consider these historical trends in the use of marijuana:

- In the University of Michigan's annual survey of 15,000 U.S. high school seniors, the proportion who said there is "great risk" in regular marijuana use rose from 35 percent in 1978 to 79 percent in 1991, then retreated to 29 percent in 2017 (Johnston et al., 2018).

- After peaking in 1978, marijuana use by U.S. high school seniors declined through 1992, then rose and held steady until beginning to trend back up in 2017 (see **FIGURE 3.21**). Canadian use among 15- to 24-year-olds has been similarly trending upward since 2012 (CCSA, 2017). European teen drug use is lower, but with trends mirroring those in North America: rising marijuana and declining cigarette and alcohol use (Wadley & Lee, 2016).

For some adolescents, occasional drug use represents thrill seeking. Yet why do some teens, but not others, become regular drug users? In search of answers, researchers have engaged biological, psychological, and social-cultural levels of analysis.

FIGURE 3.21

TRENDS IN DRUG USE The percentage of U.S. high school seniors who said they had used alcohol, marijuana, or cocaine during the past 30 days largely declined from the late 1970s to 1992, when it partially rebounded for a few years. (Data from Johnston et al., 2018; Miech et al., 2016.)

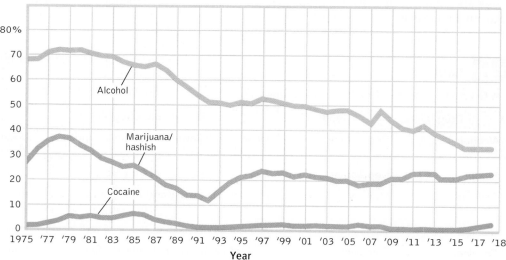

U.S. high school seniors reporting drug use

Year

Biological Influences

Some people may be biologically vulnerable to particular drugs. For example, heredity influences some aspects of substance use problems, especially those appearing by early adulthood (Crabbe, 2002):

- If an identical rather than fraternal twin is diagnosed with alcohol use disorder, the other twin is at increased risk for alcohol problems (Kendler et al., 2002). In marijuana use, too, identical twins more closely resemble each other than do fraternal twins.

 LaunchPad See the **Video: Twin Studies** for a helpful tutorial animation about this type of research design.

- Researchers have identified genes associated with alcohol use disorder, and they are seeking genes that contribute to tobacco addiction (Stacey et al., 2012). These culprit genes seemingly produce deficiencies in the brain's natural dopamine reward system: While triggering temporary dopamine-produced pleasure, the addictive drugs disrupt normal dopamine balance. Studies of how drugs reprogram the brain's reward systems raise hopes for anti-addiction drugs that might block or blunt the effects of alcohol and other drugs (Miller, 2008; Wilson & Kuhn, 2005).

- Biological influences on drug use extend to other drugs as well. One study tracked 18,115 Swedish adoptees. Those with drug-abusing biological parents were at doubled risk of drug abuse, indicating a genetic influence—a finding confirmed in another Swedish study of 14,000+ twins and 1.3 million other siblings. But then those with drug-abusing adoptive siblings also had a doubled risk of drug abuse, indicating an environmental influence (Kendler et al., 2012; Maes et al., 2016). So, what might those environmental influences be?

Warning signs of alcohol use disorder:
- Drinking binges (five drinks for men and four for women over two hours)
- Craving alcohol
- Use results in unfulfilled work, school, or home tasks
- Failing to honor a resolve to drink less
- Continued use despite health risk
- Avoiding family or friends when drinking

Psychological and Social-Cultural Influences

Throughout this text, we see that biological, psychological, and social-cultural factors interact to produce behavior. So, too, with problematic drug use (**FIGURE 3.22**). One psychological factor that has appeared in studies of youth and young adults is the feeling that life is meaningless and directionless (Newcomb & Harlow, 1986). This feeling is common among school dropouts who subsist without job skills, without privilege, and with little hope.

Sometimes the psychological influence is obvious. Many heavy users of alcohol, marijuana, and cocaine have experienced significant stress or failure and are depressed. Girls with a history of depression, eating disorders, or sexual or physical abuse are at increased risk for substance addiction. So are youth undergoing school or neighborhood transitions (CASA, 2003; Logan et al., 2002). Undergraduates who have not yet achieved a clear identity are also at greater risk (Bishop et al., 2005). By temporarily dulling the pain of self-awareness, psychoactive drugs may offer a way to avoid coping with depression, anger, anxiety, or insomnia. The relief may be temporary, but behavior is often controlled more by its immediate consequences than by its later ones.

Smoking and vaping usually begin during early adolescence. (If you are in college or university, and the cigarette manufacturers haven't yet made you their devoted customer, they almost surely never will.) Adolescents, self-conscious and often thinking the world is watching their every move, are vulnerable to smoking's allure. They may first light up to imitate glamorous celebrities, to project a mature image, to handle stress, or to get the social reward of acceptance by other smokers (Cin et al., 2007; DeWall & Pond, 2011; Tickle et al., 2006). Mindful of these tendencies, cigarette companies have effectively modeled smoking with themes that appeal to youths:

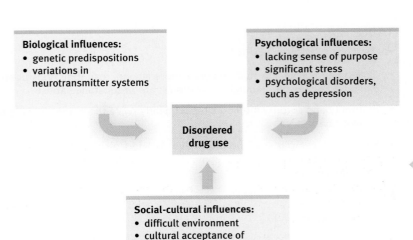

Biological influences:
- genetic predispositions
- variations in neurotransmitter systems

Psychological influences:
- lacking sense of purpose
- significant stress
- psychological disorders, such as depression

Disordered drug use

Social-cultural influences:
- difficult environment
- cultural acceptance of drug use
- negative peer influences

FIGURE 3.22
LEVELS OF ANALYSIS FOR DISORDERED DRUG USE The biopsychosocial approach enables researchers to investigate disordered drug use from complementary perspectives.

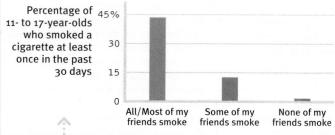

Percentage of 11- to 17-year-olds who smoked a cigarette at least once in the past 30 days

All/Most of my friends smoke	Some of my friends smoke	None of my friends smoke

FIGURE 3.23

PEER INFLUENCE Kids don't smoke if their friends don't (Philip Morris, 2003). A correlation-causation question: Does the close link between teen smoking and friends' smoking reflect peer influence? Teens seeking similar friends? Or both?

NIC-A-TEEN Virtually nobody starts smoking past the vulnerable teen years. Eager to hook customers whose addiction will give them business for years to come, cigarette companies target teens. Portrayals of smoking by popular actors—such as Scarlett Johansson in *Hail, Caesar!*—tempt teens to imitate.

attractiveness, independence, adventure-seeking, social approval (Surgeon General, 2012).

Rates of drug use vary across cultural and ethnic groups. One survey of European teens found that lifetime marijuana use ranged from 5 percent in Norway to more than eight times that in the Czech Republic (Romelsjö et al., 2014). Independent U.S. government studies of drug use in households and among high schoolers nationwide reveal that African-American teens have sharply lower rates of drinking, smoking, and cocaine use (Johnston et al., 2007). Alcohol and other drug addiction rates have also been low among actively religious people, with extremely low rates among Orthodox Jews, Mormons, Mennonites, and the Amish (DeWall et al., 2014; Salas-Wright et al., 2012).

Typically, teens who start smoking also have friends who smoke, who suggest its pleasures and offer them cigarettes (Rose et al., 1999). Among teens whose parents and best friends are nonsmokers, the smoking rate is close to zero (Moss et al., 1992; also see **FIGURE 3.23**). Similarly, if an adolescent's friends use drugs, the odds are that he or she will, too. If the friends do not, the opportunity may not even arise. Whether in cities or rural areas, peers throw the parties and provide (or don't provide) the drugs. Teens who come from happy families, who do not begin drinking before age 15, and who do well in school tend not to use drugs, largely because they rarely associate with those who do (Bachman et al., 2007; Hingson et al., 2006; Odgers et al., 2008).

Adolescents' expectations—what they *believe* friends are doing and favoring—also influence their behavior (Vitória et al., 2009). One study surveyed sixth graders in 22 U.S. states. How many believed their friends had smoked marijuana? About 14 percent. How many of those friends acknowledged doing so? Only 4 percent (Wren, 1999). University students are not immune to such misperceptions: Drinking dominates social occasions partly because students overestimate their peers' enthusiasm for alcohol and underestimate their views of its risks (Prentice & Miller, 1993; Self, 1994) (**TABLE 3.6**). When students' overestimates of peer drinking are corrected, alcohol use often subsides (Moreira et al., 2009).

TABLE 3.6

Facts About "Higher" Education

- College and university students drink more alcohol than their nonstudent peers and exhibit 2.5 times the general population's rate of substance abuse.

- Fraternity and sorority members report nearly twice the binge-drinking rate of nonmembers.

- Since 1993, campus smoking rates have declined, alcohol use has been steady, and abuse of prescription opioids, stimulants, tranquilizers, and sedatives has increased, as has marijuana use.

Source: NCASA, 2007.

People whose beginning use of drugs was influenced by their peers are more likely to stop using when friends stop or their social network changes (Chassin & MacKinnon, 2015; Kandel & Raveis, 1989). One study that followed 12,000 adults over 32 years found that smokers tend to quit in clusters (Christakis & Fowler, 2008). Within a social network, the odds of a person quitting increased when a spouse, friend, or co-worker stopped smoking. Similarly, most soldiers who engaged in problematic drug use while in Vietnam ceased after returning home (Robins et al., 1974).

As always with correlations, the traffic between friends' drug use and our own may be two-way: Our friends influence us. Social networks matter. But we also select as friends those who share our likes and dislikes.

What do the findings on drug use suggest for drug prevention and treatment programs? Three channels of influence seem possible:

- Educate young people about the long-term costs of a drug's temporary pleasures.

- Help young people find other ways to boost their self-esteem and discover their purpose in life.

- Attempt to modify peer associations or to "inoculate" youth against peer pressures by training them in refusal skills.

People rarely abuse drugs if they understand the physical and psychological costs, feel good about themselves and the direction their lives are taking, and are in a peer group that disapproves of using drugs. These educational, psychological, and social-cultural factors may help explain why 26 percent of U.S. high school dropouts, but only 6 percent of those with a postgraduate education, report smoking (CDC, 2011).

"Substance use disorders don't discriminate; they affect the rich and the poor; they affect all ethnic groups. This is a public health crisis, but we do have solutions." —U.S. Surgeon General Vivek Murthy, November 2016

🔒 **RETRIEVE IT • • •**   *ANSWERS IN APPENDIX E*

RI-6 Why do tobacco companies try so hard to get customers hooked as teens?

RI-7 Studies have found that people who begin drinking in their early teens are much more likely to develop alcohol use disorder than those who begin at age 21 or after. What possible explanations might there be for this correlation?

🔒 REVIEW DRUGS AND CONSCIOUSNESS

⟶ Learning Objectives

TEST YOURSELF Answer these repeated Learning Objective Questions on your own (before checking the answers in Appendix D) to improve your retention of the concepts (McDaniel et al., 2009, 2015).

3-11 What are *substance use disorders*?

3-12 What roles do tolerance and addiction play in substance use disorders, and how has the concept of *addiction* changed?

3-13 What are *depressants*, and what are their effects?

3-14 What are *stimulants*, and what are their effects?

3-15 What are *hallucinogens*, and what are their effects?

3-16 Why do some people become regular users of consciousness-altering drugs?

⟶ Terms and Concepts to Remember

TEST YOURSELF Write down the definition yourself, then check your answer on the referenced page.

psychoactive drug, **p. 101**

substance use disorder, **p. 101**

tolerance, **p. 102**

withdrawal, **p. 102**

depressants, **p. 103**

alcohol use disorder, **p. 103**

barbiturates, **p. 104**

opiates, **p. 104**

stimulants, **p. 104**

amphetamines, **p. 104**

nicotine, **p. 104**

cocaine, **p. 106**

methamphetamine, **p. 106**

Ecstasy (MDMA), **p. 106**

hallucinogens, **p. 109**

near-death experience, **p. 109**

LSD, **p. 109**

THC, **p. 109**

⟶ Experience the Testing Effect

TEST YOURSELF Answer the following questions on your own first, then check your answers in Appendix E.

1. After continued use of a psychoactive drug, the drug user needs to take larger doses to get the desired effect. This is referred to as _____.

2. The depressants include alcohol, barbiturates,
   a. and opiates.
   b. cocaine, and morphine.
   c. caffeine, nicotine, and marijuana.
   d. and amphetamines.

3. Why might alcohol make a person more helpful *or* more aggressive?

4. Long-term use of Ecstasy can
   a. depress sympathetic nervous system activity.
   b. deplete the brain's supply of epinephrine.
   c. deplete the brain's supply of dopamine.
   d. damage serotonin-producing neurons.

5. Near-death experiences are strikingly similar to the experiences evoked by _____ drugs.

6. Use of marijuana
   a. impairs motor coordination, perception, reaction time, and memory.
   b. inhibits people's emotions.
   c. leads to dehydration and overheating.
   d. stimulates brain cell development.

7. An important psychological contributor to drug use is
   a. inflated self-esteem.
   b. the feeling that life is meaningless and directionless.
   c. genetic predispositions.
   d. overprotective parents.

Continue testing yourself with 📘 **LearningCurve** or 📘 **Achieve Read & Practice** to learn and remember most effectively.

Developing Through the Life Span

Life is a journey, from womb to tomb. So it is for me [DM], and so it will be for you. My story, and yours, began when a man and a woman together contributed 20,000+ genes to an egg that became a unique person. Those genes coded the protein building blocks that, with astonishing precision, formed our bodies and predisposed our traits. My grandmother handed down to my mother a rare hearing-loss pattern, which she, in turn, gave to me (the least of her gifts). My father was an amiable extravert, and sometimes I forget to stop talking (although as a child, my talking was impeded by embarrassing stuttering, for which Seattle Public Schools provided speech therapy).

Along with my parents' nature, I also received their nurture. Like you, I was born into a particular family and culture, with its own way of viewing the world. My values have been shaped by a family culture filled with talking and laughter, by a religious culture that speaks of love and justice, and by an academic culture that encourages critical thinking (asking, *What do you mean? How do you know?*).

We are formed by our genes and by our contexts, so our stories will differ. But in many ways we are each like nearly everyone else on Earth. Being human, you and I have a need to belong. My mental video library, which began after age 4, is filled with scenes of social attachment. Over time, my attachments to parents loosened as peer friendships grew. After lacking confidence to date in high school, I fell in love with a college classmate and married at age 20. Natural selection predisposes us to survive and perpetuate our genes. Sure enough, two years later a child entered our lives and I experienced a new form of love that surprised me with its intensity.

developmental psychology a branch of psychology that studies physical, cognitive, and social change throughout the life span.

But life is marked by change. That child and his brother now live 2000 miles away, and their sister has found her calling in South Africa. The tight rubber bands linking parent and child have loosened, as yours likely have as well.

Change also marks most vocational lives, which for me transitioned from a teen working in the family insurance agency, to a premed chemistry major and hospital aide, to (after discarding my half-completed medical school applications) a psychology professor and author. I predict that in 10 years you, too, will be doing things you do not currently anticipate.

Stability also marks our development: Our life situations change, but we experience a continuous self. When I look in the mirror I do not see the person I once was, but I feel like the person I have always been. I am the same person who, as a late teen, played basketball and discovered love. A half-century later, I still play basketball and still love (with less passion but more security) the life partner with whom I have shared life's griefs and joys.

We experience a continuous self, but that self morphs through stages—for me, growing up, raising children, enjoying a career, and, eventually, life's final stage, which will demand my presence. As I wend my way through this cycle of life and death, I am mindful that life's journey is a continuing process of development, seeded by nature and shaped by nurture, animated by love and focused by work, begun with wide-eyed curiosity and completed, for those blessed to live to a good old age, with peace and never-ending hope.

Across the life span, we grow from newborn to toddler, from toddler to teenager, and from teenager to mature adult. At each stage of life there are physical, cognitive, and social milestones. We begin with prenatal development and the newborn. Then we'll turn our attention to infancy and childhood, adolescence, and adulthood. ▶

⟶ Developmental Issues, Prenatal Development, and the Newborn

---

DEVELOPMENTAL PSYCHOLOGY'S MAJOR ISSUES

LEARNING OBJECTIVE QUESTION (LOQ)

4-1 What three issues have engaged developmental psychologists?

Researchers find human development interesting for the same reasons most of the rest of us do—they want to understand more about how we've become our current selves, and how we may change in the years ahead. **Developmental psychology** examines our physical, cognitive, and social development across the life span, with a focus on three major issues:

1. **Nature and nurture:** How does our genetic inheritance (our *nature*) interact with our experiences (our *nurture*) to influence our development? How have your nature and your nurture influenced *your* life story?

2. **Continuity and stages:** What parts of development are gradual and continuous, like riding an escalator? What parts change abruptly in separate stages, like climbing rungs on a ladder?

3. **Stability and change:** Which of our traits persist through life? How do we change as we age?

"Nature is all that a man brings with him into the world; nurture is every influence that affects him after his birth." —Francis Galton, *English Men of Science*, 1874

Nature and Nurture

The unique gene combination created when our mother's egg engulfed our father's sperm helped form us, as individuals. Genes predispose both our shared humanity and our individual differences.

But our experiences also shape us. Our families and peer relationships teach us how to think and act. Even differences initiated by our nature may be amplified by our nurture. We are not formed by either nature or nurture, but by the interaction between them. Biological, psychological, and social-cultural forces interact.

Mindful of how others differ from us, however, we often fail to notice the similarities stemming from our shared biology. Regardless of our culture, we humans share the same life cycle. We speak to our infants in similar ways and respond similarly to their coos and cries (Bornstein et al., 1992a,b). Although ethnic groups have differed in some ways, including average school achievement, the differences are "no more than skin deep." To the extent that family structure, peer influences, and parental education predict behavior in one of these ethnic groups, they do so for the others as well. Compared with the person-to-person differences within groups, between-group differences are small.

Continuity and Stages

Do adults differ from infants as a giant redwood differs from its seedling—a difference created by gradual, cumulative growth? Or do they differ as a butterfly differs from a caterpillar—a difference of distinct stages?

Researchers who emphasize experience and learning typically see development as a slow, continuous shaping process. Those who emphasize biological maturation tend to see development as a sequence of genetically predisposed stages or steps: Although progress through the various stages may be quick or slow, everyone passes through the stages in the same order.

Are there clear-cut stages of psychological development, as there are physical stages such as walking before running? The *stage theories* we will consider—of Jean Piaget on cognitive development, Lawrence Kohlberg on moral development, and Erik Erikson on psychosocial development—propose developmental stages (summarized in **FIGURE 4.1**). But as we will also see, some research casts doubt on the idea that life proceeds through neatly defined age-linked stages.

Although many modern developmental psychologists do not identify as stage theorists, the stage concept remains useful. The human brain does experience growth spurts during childhood and puberty that correspond roughly to Piaget's stages (Thatcher et al., 1987). And stage theories contribute a developmental perspective on the whole life span by suggesting how people of one age think and act differently when they arrive at a later age.

Stages of the life cycle.

FIGURE 4.1

COMPARING THE STAGE THEORIES[1]

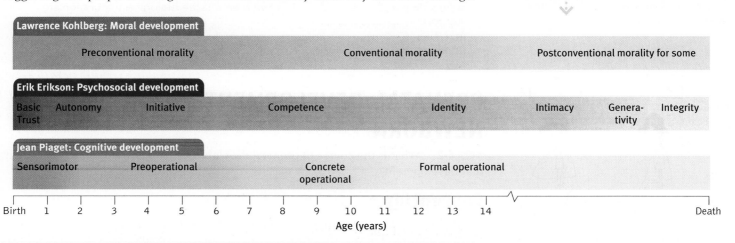

1. With thanks to Dr. Sandra Gibbs, Muskegon Community College, for inspiring this illustration.

(a)

(b)

SMILES PREDICT MARITAL STABILITY
In one study of 306 U.S. college alums, 1 in 4 with yearbook expressions like the one in photo (a) later divorced, as did only 1 in 20 with smiles like the one in photo (b) (Hertenstein et al., 2009).

"At 70, I would say the advantage is that you take life more calmly. You know that 'this, too, shall pass'!" —Eleanor Roosevelt, 1954

"When I look at myself in the first grade and I look at myself now, I'm basically the same. The temperament is not that different." —Donald J. Trump to his biographer in *Never Enough*, 2015

"As at 7, so at 70." —Jewish proverb

ASK YOURSELF

Are you the same person you were as a preschooler? As an 8-year-old? As a 12-year-old? How do you differ? How are you the same?

BEFORE   AFTER

As adults grow older, there is continuity of self.

Stability and Change

As we follow lives through time, do we find more evidence for stability or change? If reunited with a long-lost grade-school friend, do we instantly realize that "it's the same old Andy"? Or do long-ago friends now seem like strangers? (At least one acquaintance of mine [DM's] would choose the second option. At his 40-year college reunion, he failed to recognize a former classmate. The understandably appalled classmate was his first wife!)

We experience both stability and change. Some of our characteristics, such as *temperament,* are very stable. One research team that studied 1000 people from ages 3 to 38 was struck by the consistency of temperament and emotionality across time (Moffitt et al., 2013; Slutske et al., 2012). Out-of-control 3-year-olds were the most likely to engage in teen smoking, adult criminal behavior, or out-of-control gambling. Researchers have also confirmed stability of moods when following 174 Scots across 63 years—from age 14 to 77 (Harris et al., 2016). Other studies report that the children who are repeatedly cruel to animals often become violent adults, and, on a happier note, that the widest smilers in childhood and college photos are, years later, the ones most likely to enjoy enduring marriages (Hensley et al., 2017; Hertenstein et al., 2009).

We cannot, however, predict all aspects of our future selves based on our early life. Our social attitudes, for example, are much less stable than our temperament, especially during the impressionable late adolescent years (Krosnick & Alwin, 1989; Rekker et al., 2015). Older children and adolescents learn new ways of coping. Although delinquent children have elevated rates of later problems, many confused and troubled children blossom into mature, successful adults (Moffitt et al., 2002; Roberts et al., 2013; Thomas & Chess, 1986). Life is a process of becoming. Our present struggles may lay the foundation for a happier tomorrow.

In some ways, we *all* change with age. Most shy, fearful toddlers begin opening up by age 4, and most people become more conscientious, stable, agreeable, and self-confident in the years after adolescence (Lucas & Donnellan, 2009; Shaw et al., 2010; Van den Akker et al., 2014). Risk-prone adolescents tend to become more cautious adults (Mata et al., 2016). Indeed, many irresponsible 18-year-olds have matured into 40-year-old business or cultural leaders. (If you are the former, you aren't done yet.)

Life requires *both* stability and change. Stability provides our identity. Change gives us our hope for a brighter future, allowing us to adapt and grow with experience.

> **🔒 RETRIEVE IT • • •**   *ANSWERS IN APPENDIX E*
>
> **RI-1** Developmental researchers who consider how biological, psychological, and social-cultural forces interact are focusing on _____ and _____.
>
> **RI-2** Developmental researchers who emphasize learning and experience are supporting _____; those who emphasize biological maturation are supporting _____.
>
> **RI-3** What findings in psychology support (1) the stage theory of development and (2) the idea of stability in personality across the life span?

PRENATAL DEVELOPMENT AND THE NEWBORN

LOQ 4-2   What is the course of prenatal development, and how do *teratogens* affect that development?

Conception

Nothing is more natural than a species reproducing itself. And nothing is more wondrous. For you, the process started inside your *grandmother*—as an egg formed inside a developing female inside of her. (Your mother was born with all the immature

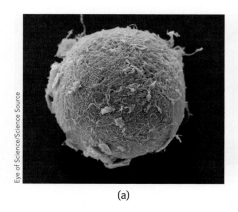
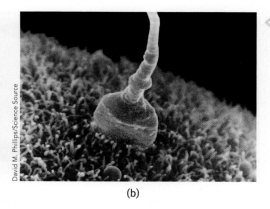

(a)   (b)

Eye of Science/Science Source

David M. Phillips/Science Source

FIGURE 4.2

LIFE IS SEXUALLY TRANSMITTED
(a) Sperm cells surround an egg.
(b) As one sperm penetrates the egg's jellylike outer coating, a series of chemical events begins that will cause sperm and egg to fuse into a single cell. If all goes well, that cell will subdivide again and again to emerge 9 months later as a 37-trillion-cell human being.

eggs she would ever have.) Your father, in contrast, began producing sperm cells nonstop at *puberty*—in the beginning at a rate of more than 1000 sperm during the second it takes to read this phrase.

Some time after puberty, your mother's ovary released a mature egg—a cell roughly the size of the period that ends this sentence. Like space voyagers approaching a huge planet, some 250 million deposited sperm began their frantic race upstream, approaching a cell 85,000 times their own size. The small number reaching the egg released digestive enzymes that ate away the egg's protective coating (**FIGURE 4.2a**). The one winning sperm penetrated the coating and was welcomed in (Figure 4.2b), the egg's surface blocking out the others. Before half a day elapsed, the egg nucleus and the sperm nucleus fused: The two became one.

Consider it your most fortunate of moments. Among 250 million sperm, the one needed to make you, in combination with that one particular egg, won the race. And so it was for innumerable generations before us. If any one of our ancestors had been conceived with a different sperm or egg, or died before conceiving, or not chanced to meet their partner or. . . . The mind boggles at the improbable, unbroken chain of events that produced us.

Prenatal Development

How many fertilized eggs, called **zygotes,** survive beyond the first 2 weeks? Fewer than half (Grobstein, 1979; Hall, 2004). But for us, good fortune prevailed. One cell became 2, then 4—each just like the first—until this cell division had produced some 100 identical cells within the first week. Then the cells began to differentiate—to specialize in structure and function ("I'll become a brain, you become intestines!").

About 10 days after conception, the zygote attaches to the mother's uterine wall, beginning approximately 37 weeks of the closest human relationship. The zygote's inner cells become the **embryo** (**FIGURE 4.3a**). Many of its outer cells become the *placenta,* the lifelink that transfers nutrients and oxygen from mother to embryo. Over the next 6 weeks, the embryo's organs begin to form and function. The heart begins to beat.

By 9 weeks after conception, an embryo looks unmistakably human (Figure 4.3b). It is now a **fetus** (Latin for "offspring" or "young one"). During the sixth month, organs such as the stomach have developed enough to give the fetus a good chance of surviving and thriving if born prematurely.

At each prenatal stage, genetic and environmental factors affect our development. By the sixth month, the fetus is responsive to sound. Microphone readings taken inside the uterus reveal that the fetus is exposed to the sound of its mother's muffled voice (Ecklund-Flores, 1992; Hepper, 2005). Immediately after emerging from their underwater world, newborns prefer their mother's voice to another woman's, or to their father's (DeCasper et al., 1986, 1994; Lee & Kisilevsky, 2014).

They also prefer hearing their mother's language. In one study, day-old American and Swedish newborns paused more in their pacifier sucking when listening to familiar vowels from their mother's language (Moon et al., 2013). After repeatedly hearing a fake word (*tatata*) in the womb, Finnish newborns' brain waves displayed recognition when hearing the word after birth (Partanen et al., 2013). If their mother spoke two languages during

zygote the fertilized egg; it enters a 2-week period of rapid cell division and develops into an embryo.

embryo the developing human organism from about 2 weeks after fertilization through the second month.

fetus the developing human organism from 9 weeks after conception to birth.

 Care to guess your body's total number of cells?[2]

ENGAGE

---
2. ANSWER: By one careful estimate, the average human has 37.2 trillion cells (Bianconi et al., 2013).

FIGURE 4.3

PRENATAL DEVELOPMENT (a) The embryo grows and develops rapidly. At 40 days, the spine is visible and the arms and legs are beginning to grow. (b) By the start of the ninth week, when the fetal period begins, facial features, hands, and feet have formed. (c) As the fetus enters the sixteenth week, its 3 ounces could fit in the palm of your hand.

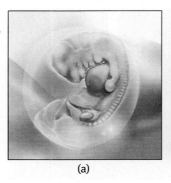 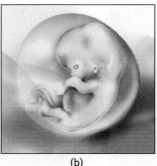 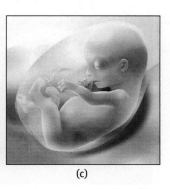

(a)   (b)   (c)

teratogens (literally, "monster makers") agents, such as chemicals and viruses, that can reach the embryo or fetus during prenatal development and cause harm.

fetal alcohol syndrome (FAS) physical and cognitive abnormalities in children caused by a pregnant woman's heavy drinking. In severe cases, signs include a small, out-of-proportion head and abnormal facial features.

🔒 Prenatal development

Zygote: Conception to 2 weeks
Embryo: 2 to 9 weeks
Fetus: 9 weeks to birth

"You shall conceive and bear a son. So then drink no wine or strong drink."
—Judges 13:7

🔒 📖 LaunchPad For an interactive review of prenatal development, see **Topic Tutorial: PsychSim6, Conception to Birth.** See also the 8-minute **Video: Prenatal Development.**

pregnancy, newborns displayed interest in both (Byers-Heinlein et al., 2010). And just after birth, the melodic ups and downs of newborns' cries bear the tuneful signature of their mother's native tongue (Mampe et al., 2009). Babies born to French-speaking mothers tended to cry with the rising intonation of French; babies born to German-speaking mothers cried with the falling tones of German. Would you have guessed? The learning of language begins in the womb.

In the two months before birth, fetuses demonstrate learning in other ways, as when they adapt to a vibrating, honking device placed on their mother's abdomen (Dirix et al., 2009). Like people who adapt to the sound of trains in their neighborhood, fetuses get used to the honking. Moreover, four weeks later, they recall the sound (as evidenced by their blasé response, compared with the reactions of those fetuses not previously exposed).

Sounds are not the only environmental factors that impact fetal development. In addition to transferring nutrients and oxygen from mother to fetus, the placenta screens out many harmful substances. But some slip by. **Teratogens,** agents such as viruses and drugs, can damage an embryo or fetus. This is one reason pregnant women are advised not to drink alcoholic beverages or smoke cigarettes or marijuana (Saint Louis, 2017). A pregnant woman never drinks or smokes alone. When alcohol enters her bloodstream and that of her fetus, it reduces activity in both their central nervous systems. Alcohol use during pregnancy may prime the woman's offspring to like alcohol and may put them at risk for heavy drinking and alcohol use disorder during their teen years. In experiments, when pregnant rats drank alcohol, their young offspring later displayed a liking for alcohol's taste and odor (Youngentob & Glendinning, 2009; Youngentob et al. 2007).

Even light drinking or occasional binge drinking can affect the fetal brain (Braun, 1996; Marjonen et al., 2015). Persistent heavy drinking puts the fetus at risk for a dangerously low birth weight, birth defects, future behavior problems, and lower intelligence. For 1 in about 700 children, the effects are visible as **fetal alcohol syndrome (FAS),** the most serious of all fetal alcohol spectrum disorders, marked by lifelong physical and mental abnormalities (May et al., 2014). The fetal damage may occur because alcohol has an *epigenetic effect:* It leaves chemical marks on DNA that switch genes abnormally on or off (Liu et al., 2009). Smoking during pregnancy also leaves epigenetic scars that weaken infants' ability to handle stress (Stroud et al., 2014).

If a pregnant woman experiences extreme stress, the stress hormones flooding her body may indicate a survival threat to the fetus and produce an earlier delivery (Glynn & Sandman, 2011). Some stress in early life prepares us to cope with later adversity. But substantial prenatal stress exposure, including famine or malnourishment, puts a child at increased risk for health problems such as hypertension, heart disease, obesity, and psychiatric disorders (Barker, 2012).

🔒 RETRIEVE IT • • •   *ANSWERS IN APPENDIX E*

RI-4 The first two weeks of prenatal development is the period of the _____. The period of the _____ lasts from 9 weeks after conception until birth. The time between those two prenatal periods is considered the period of the _____.

The Competent Newborn

LOQ 4-3 What are some newborn abilities, and how do researchers explore infants' mental abilities?

Babies come with apps preloaded. Having survived prenatal hazards, we as newborns came equipped with automatic reflex responses ideally suited for our survival. We withdrew our limbs to escape pain. If a cloth over our face interfered with our breathing, we turned our head from side to side and swiped at it.

New parents are often in awe of the coordinated sequence of reflexes by which their baby gets food. When something touches their cheek, babies turn toward that touch, open their mouth, and vigorously *root* for a nipple. Finding one, they automatically close on it and begin *sucking*. (Failing to find satisfaction, the hungry baby may cry—a behavior parents find highly unpleasant, and very rewarding to relieve.) Other adaptive reflexes include the *startle* reflex (when arms and legs spring out, quickly followed by fist clenching and loud crying) and the surprisingly strong *grasping* reflex, both of which may have helped infants stay close to their caregivers.

The pioneering American psychologist William James presumed that newborns experience a "blooming, buzzing confusion," an assumption few people challenged until the 1960s. Then scientists discovered that babies can tell you a lot—if you know how to ask. To ask, you must capitalize on what babies can do—gaze, suck, and turn their heads. So, equipped with eye-tracking machines and pacifiers wired to electronic gear, researchers set out to answer parents' age-old questions: What can my baby see, hear, smell, and think?

Consider how researchers exploit **habituation**—decreased responding with repeated stimulation. We saw this earlier when fetuses adapted to a vibrating, honking device placed on their mother's abdomen. The novel stimulus gets attention when first presented. With repetition, the response weakens. This seeming boredom with familiar stimuli gives us a way to ask infants what they see and remember.

As newborns, we prefer sights and sounds that facilitate social responsiveness. We turn our heads in the direction of human voices. We gaze longer at a drawing of a face-like image (**FIGURE 4.4**). Even late-stage fetuses look more at face-like patterns in red lights shined through the womb (Reid et al., 2017). As young infants, we also prefer to look at objects 8 to 12 inches away, which—wonder of wonders—just happens to be about the distance between a nursing infant's eyes and its mother's (Maurer & Maurer, 1988). Our brain's default settings help us connect socially.

Within days after birth, our brain's neural networks were stamped with the smell of our mother's body. Week-old nursing babies, placed between a gauze pad from their mother's bra and one from another nursing mother, have usually turned toward the smell of their own mother's pad (MacFarlane, 1978). What's more, that smell preference lasts. One experiment capitalized on the fact that some nursing mothers in a French maternity ward used a chamomile-scented balm to prevent nipple soreness (Delaunay-El Allam et al., 2010). Twenty-one months later, their toddlers preferred playing with chamomile-scented toys! Their peers who had not sniffed the scent while breast-feeding showed no such preference. (This makes us wonder: Will these children grow up to become devoted chamomile tea drinkers?) Such studies reveal the remarkable abilities with which we enter our world.

"I felt like a man trapped in a woman's body. Then I was born." —Comedian Chris Bliss

habituation decreasing responsiveness with repeated stimulation. As infants gain familiarity with repeated exposure to a stimulus, their interest wanes and they look away sooner.

FIGURE 4.4

NEWBORNS' PREFERENCE FOR FACES When shown these two stimuli with the same elements, Italian newborns spent nearly twice as many seconds looking at the face-like image (Johnson & Morton, 1991). Canadian newborns—average age 53 minutes in one study—displayed the same apparently inborn preference to look toward faces (Mondloch et al., 1999).

PREPARED TO FEED AND EAT Humans and other animals are predisposed to respond to their offspring's cries for nourishment, even if they are in the middle of a 314-mile ultramarathon, as I [ND] was when my 18-month-old Bevy decided that only Daddy could feed her.

🔒 **RETRIEVE IT** • • •   *ANSWERS IN APPENDIX E*

RI-5 Infants' _____ to repeated stimulation helps developmental psychologists study what infants can learn and remember.

🔒 **REVIEW** DEVELOPMENTAL ISSUES, PRENATAL DEVELOPMENT, AND THE NEWBORN

⟶ Learning Objectives

TEST YOURSELF Answer these repeated Learning Objective Questions on your own (before checking the answers in Appendix D) to improve your retention of the concepts (McDaniel et al., 2009, 2015).

4-1 What three issues have engaged developmental psychologists?

4-2 What is the course of prenatal development, and how do *teratogens* affect that development?

4-3 What are some newborn abilities, and how do researchers explore infants' mental abilities?

⟶ Terms and Concepts to Remember

TEST YOURSELF Write down the definition yourself, then check your answer on the referenced page.

developmental psychology, **p. 116**

zygote, **p. 119**

embryo, **p. 119**

fetus, **p. 119**

teratogens, **p. 120**

fetal alcohol syndrome (FAS), **p. 120**

habituation, **p. 121**

⟶ Experience the Testing Effect

TEST YOURSELF Answer the following questions on your own first, then check your answers in Appendix E.

1. The three major issues that interest developmental psychologists are nature/nurture, stability/change, and _____/_____.

2. Although development is lifelong, there is stability of personality over time. For example,

   a. most personality traits emerge in infancy and persist throughout life.

   b. temperament tends to remain stable throughout life.

   c. few people change significantly after adolescence.

   d. people tend to undergo greater personality changes as they age.

3. Body organs first begin to form and function during the period of the _____; within 6 months, during the period of the _____, organs are sufficiently functional to provide a good chance of surviving and thriving.

   a. zygote; embryo

   b. zygote; fetus

   c. embryo; fetus

   d. placenta; fetus

4. Chemicals that the placenta isn't able to screen out that may harm an embryo or fetus are called _____.

Continue testing yourself with 📚 **LearningCurve** or 🌊 **Achieve Read & Practice** to learn and remember most effectively.

⟶ Infancy and Childhood

maturation biological growth processes that enable orderly changes in behavior, relatively uninfluenced by experience.

"It is a rare privilege to watch the birth, growth, and first feeble struggles of a living human mind." —Annie Sullivan, in Helen Keller's *The Story of My Life*, 1903

As a flower unfolds in accord with its genetic instructions, so do we. **Maturation**—the orderly sequence of biological growth—decrees many of our commonalities. Babies first stand, then walk. Toddlers first use nouns, then adjectives. Severe deprivation or abuse can slow development, but genetic growth patterns are inborn. Maturation (nature) sets the basic course of development; experience (nurture) adjusts it. Genes and scenes interact.

PHYSICAL DEVELOPMENT

LOQ 4-4 During infancy and childhood, how do the brain and motor skills develop?

Brain Development

Our formative nurture began at conception, with the prenatal environment in the womb. Nurture continued outside the womb, where our early experiences fostered brain development.

In your mother's womb, your developing brain formed nerve cells at the explosive rate of nearly one-quarter million per minute. On the day you were born, you had most of the brain cells you would ever have. However, the wiring among these cells—your nervous system—was immature: After birth, these neural networks had a wild growth spurt branching and linking in patterns that would eventually enable you to walk, talk, and remember (**FIGURE 4.5**). This rapid development helps explain why infant brain size increases rapidly in the early days after birth (Holland et al., 2014).

From ages 3 to 6, the most rapid brain growth was in your frontal lobes, which enable rational planning. During those years, your brain required vast amounts of energy (Kuzawa et al., 2014). This energy-intensive process caused rapid progress in your ability to control your attention and behavior (Garon et al., 2008; Thompson-Schill et al., 2009). Frontal lobe development continues into adolescence and beyond.

The brain's association areas—those linked with thinking, memory, and language— were the last cortical areas to develop. As they did, your mental abilities surged (Chugani & Phelps, 1986; Thatcher et al., 1987). Fiber pathways supporting agility, language, and self-control proliferated into puberty. Under the influence of adrenal hormones, tens of billions of synapses formed and organized, while a use-it-or-lose-it *pruning* process shut down unused links (Paus et al., 1999; Thompson et al., 2000).

Your genes dictate your overall brain architecture, rather like the lines of a coloring book, but experience fills in the details (Kenrick et al., 2009). So how do early experiences leave their "fingerprints" in the brain? Mark Rosenzweig, David Krech, and their colleagues (1962) opened a window on that process when they raised some young rats in solitary confinement, and others in a communal playground that simulated a natural environment. When the researchers later analyzed the rats' brains, those living in the enriched environment had usually developed a heavier and thicker brain cortex (**FIGURE 4.6**). So great are the effects that, shown brief video clips of the rats, you could tell from their activity and curiosity whether their environment had been impoverished or enriched (Renner & Renner, 1993). After 60 days in the enriched environment, the rats' brain weights increased 7 to 10 percent and the number of synapses mushroomed by about 20 percent (Kolb & Whishaw, 1998).

Such results have motivated improvements in environments for laboratory, farm, and zoo animals—and for children in institutions. Stimulation by touch or massage also benefits infant rats and premature babies (Field et al., 2007; Sarro et al., 2014). "Handled" infants of both species develop faster neurologically and gain weight more rapidly. Preemies who have had skin-to-skin contact with their mothers sleep better, experience less stress, and show better cognitive development 10 years later (Feldman et al., 2014).

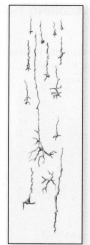

Newborn   3 months   15 months

FIGURE 4.5

INFANT BRAIN DEVELOPMENT In humans, the brain is immature at birth. As the child matures, the neural networks grow increasingly complex.

PA Archive/The Image Works

THE BABY EXPERIMENT This "electrode cap" allows researchers to detect changes in brain activity triggered by different stimuli.

FIGURE 4.6

EXPERIENCE AFFECTS BRAIN DEVELOPMENT Mark Rosenzweig, David Krech, and their colleagues (1962) raised rats either alone in an environment without playthings, or with other rats in an environment enriched with playthings changed daily. In 14 of 16 repetitions of this basic experiment, rats in the enriched environment developed significantly more cerebral cortex (relative to the rest of the brain's tissue) than did those in the impoverished environment.

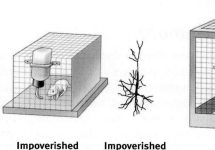
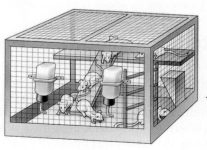

Impoverished   Impoverished   Enriched   Enriched
environment   rat brain cell   environment   rat brain cell

critical period an optimal period early in the life of an organism when exposure to certain stimuli or experiences produces normal development.

"Genes and experiences are just two ways of doing the same thing—wiring synapses." —Joseph LeDoux, *The Synaptic Self* (2002)

PHYSICAL DEVELOPMENT Sit, crawl, walk, run—the sequence of these motor development milestones is the same around the world, though babies reach them at varying ages.

Juice Images/JupiterImages/Getty Images

In the eight years following the 1994 launch of a U.S. Back to Sleep educational campaign, the number of infants sleeping on their stomach dropped from 70 to 11 percent—and sudden unexpected infant deaths fell significantly (Braiker, 2005).

"Someday we'll look back at this time in our lives and be unable to remember it."

Nature and nurture interact to sculpt our synapses. Brain maturation provides us with an abundance of neural connections. Experiences—sights and smells, touches and tastes, music and movement—activate and strengthen some neural pathways while others weaken from disuse. Like forest pathways, popular tracks are broadened and less-traveled ones gradually disappear. The result by puberty is a massive loss of unemployed connections.

Here at the juncture of nurture and nature is the biological reality of early childhood learning. During early childhood—while excess connections are still on call—youngsters can most easily master such skills as the grammar and accent of another language. We seem to have a **critical period** for some skills. Lacking any exposure to spoken, written, or signed language before adolescence, a person will never master any language. Likewise, lacking visual experience during the early years, a person whose vision is restored by cataract removal will never achieve normal perceptions (Gregory, 1978; Wiesel, 1982). Without that early visual stimulation, the brain cells normally assigned to vision will die during the pruning process or be diverted to other uses. The maturing brain's rule: Use it or lose it.

Although normal stimulation during the early years is critical, the brain's development does not end with childhood. Thanks to the brain's amazing *plasticity,* our neural tissue is ever changing and reorganizing in response to new experiences. New neurons also are born. If a monkey pushes a lever with the same finger many times a day, brain tissue controlling that finger changes to reflect the experience. Human brains work similarly. Whether learning to keyboard, skateboard, or navigate London's streets, we perform with increasing skill as our brain incorporates the learning (Ambrose, 2010; Maguire et al., 2000).

Motor Development

The developing brain enables physical coordination. Skills emerge as infants exercise their maturing muscles and nervous system. With occasional exceptions, the motor development sequence is universal. Babies roll over before they sit unsupported, and they usually crawl before they walk. These behaviors reflect not imitation but a maturing nervous system; blind children, too, crawl before they walk.

Genes guide motor development. In the United States, 25 percent of all babies walk by 11 months of age, 50 percent within a week after their first birthday, and 90 percent by age 15 months (Frankenburg et al., 1992). Identical twins typically begin walking on nearly the same day (Wilson, 1979). Maturation—including the rapid development of the cerebellum at the back of the brain—creates our readiness to learn walking at about age 1. The same is true for other physical skills, including bowel and bladder control. Before necessary muscular and neural maturation, neither pleading nor punishment will produce successful toilet training. You can't rush a child's first flush.

Still, nurture may amend what nature intends. In some regions of Africa, the Caribbean, and India, caregivers frequently massage and exercise babies, which can accelerate the process of learning to walk (Karasik et al., 2010). The recommended infant *back to sleep position* (putting babies to sleep on their backs to reduce crib-death risk) has been associated with somewhat later crawling but not with later walking (Davis et al., 1998; Lipsitt, 2003).

🔒 **RETRIEVE IT** • • •   *ANSWERS IN APPENDIX E*

RI-1 The biological growth process called _____ explains why most children begin walking by about 12 to 15 months.

Brain Maturation and Infant Memory

ENGAGE Can you recall your first day of preschool or your third birthday party? Most of us *consciously* recall little from before age 4. Mice and monkeys also forget their early life, as rapid neuron growth disrupts the circuits that stored old memories (Akers et al., 2014). But as children mature, this *infantile amnesia* wanes, and they become increasingly capable of remembering experiences, even for a year or more (Bauer & Larkina, 2014; Morris et al., 2010). The brain areas underlying memory, such as the hippocampus and frontal lobes, continue to mature during and after adolescence (Luby et al., 2016; Murty et al., 2016).

Despite consciously recalling little from our early years, our brain was processing and storing information. While finishing her doctoral work in psychology, Carolyn Rovee-Collier observed nonverbal infant memory in action. Her colicky 2-month-old, Benjamin, could be calmed by moving a crib mobile. Weary of hitting the mobile, she strung a cloth ribbon connecting the mobile to Benjamin's foot. Soon, he was kicking his foot to move the mobile. Thinking about her unintended home experiment, Rovee-Collier realized that, contrary to popular opinion in the 1960s, babies can learn. To know for sure that her son wasn't just a whiz kid, she repeated the experiment with other infants (Rovee-Collier, 1989, 1999). Sure enough, they, too, soon kicked more when hitched to a mobile, both on the day of the experiment and the day after. If, however, she hitched them to a different mobile the next day, the infants showed no learning, indicating that they remembered the original mobile and recognized the difference. Moreover, when tethered to the familiar mobile a month later, they remembered the association and again began kicking (**FIGURE 4.7**).

Traces of forgotten childhood languages may also persist. One study tested English-speaking British adults who had no conscious memory of the Hindi or Zulu they had spoken as children. Yet, up to age 40, they could relearn subtle sound contrasts in these languages that other English speakers could *not* learn (Bowers et al., 2009). Chinese adoptees living in Canada since age 1 process Chinese sounds as do native speakers, even if they have no conscious recollection of Chinese words (Pierce et al., 2014). Again, our two-track mind is at work: What the conscious mind does not know and cannot express in words, the nervous system and unconscious mind somehow remember.

COGNITIVE DEVELOPMENT

LOQ 4-5   From the perspectives of Piaget, Vygotsky, and today's researchers, how does a child's mind develop?

Somewhere on your life journey, you became conscious. When was that? And once conscious, how did your mind grow? Jean Piaget [pee-ah-ZHAY] was a pioneering developmental psychologist who spent his life searching for the answers to such questions. He studied children's developing **cognition**—all the mental activities associated with thinking, knowing, remembering, and communicating. His interest in children's cognitive development began in 1920, when he was in Paris developing questions for children's intelligence tests. While administering the tests, Piaget became intrigued by children's wrong answers, which were often strikingly similar among same-age children. Where others saw childish mistakes, Piaget saw intelligence at work. Such accidental discoveries are among the fruits of psychological science.

A half-century spent with children convinced Piaget that a child's mind is not a miniature model of an adult's. Thanks partly to his careful observations, we now understand that children reason differently than adults, in "wildly illogical ways" (Brainerd, 1996).

Piaget's studies led him to believe that a child's mind develops through a series of stages, in an upward march from the newborn's simple reflexes to the adult's abstract reasoning power. Thus, an 8-year-old can comprehend things a toddler cannot, such as the analogy that "getting an idea is like having a light turn on in your head."

Piaget's core idea was that our intellectual progression reflects an unceasing struggle to make sense of our experiences. To this end, the maturing brain builds **schemas**—concepts or mental molds into which we pour our experiences.

To explain how we use and adjust our schemas, Piaget proposed two more concepts. First, we **assimilate** new experiences—we interpret them in terms of our current understandings (schemas). Having a simple schema for *dog,* for example, a toddler may call all four-legged animals *dogs.* But as we interact with the world, we also adjust, or **accommodate,** our schemas to incorporate information provided by new experiences.

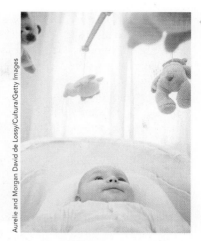

FIGURE 4.7

INFANT AT WORK Babies only 3 months old learned that kicking moves a mobile, and they retained that learning for a month (Rovee-Collier, 1989, 1997).

ENGAGE (ASK YOURSELF)

What do you regard as your earliest memory? Now that you know about infantile amnesia, has your opinion changed about the accuracy of that memory?

cognition all the mental activities associated with thinking, knowing, remembering, and communicating.

schema a concept or framework that organizes and interprets information.

assimilation interpreting our new experiences in terms of our existing schemas.

accommodation adapting our current understandings (schemas) to incorporate new information.

JEAN PIAGET (1896–1980) "If we examine the intellectual development of the individual or of the whole of humanity, we shall find that the human spirit goes through a certain number of stages, each different from the other" (1930).

FIGURE 4.8

A CHANGING MARRIAGE SCHEMA
A generation ago, most people had a schema of marriage as a union between a man and a woman. The Netherlands was the first country to change its marriage laws to accommodate same-sex marriage (in 2001). Today, more than 20 other countries have also legalized same-sex marriage.

ENGAGE 💡 (ASK YOURSELF)

Can you recall a time when you misheard some song lyrics because you assimilated them into your own schema? (For hundreds of examples of this phenomenon, visit kissthisguy.com.)

sensorimotor stage in Piaget's theory, the stage (from birth to nearly 2 years of age) during which infants know the world mostly in terms of their sensory impressions and motor activities.

object permanence the awareness that things continue to exist even when not perceived.

FIGURE 4.9

OBJECT PERMANENCE Infants younger than 6 months seldom understand that things continue to exist when they are out of sight. But for this older infant, out of sight is definitely not out of mind.

Thus, the child soon learns that the original *dog* schema is too broad and accommodates by refining the category. By adulthood we have built countless schemas, ranging from *cats* and *dogs* to our concept of *love* (**FIGURE 4.8**).

Piaget's Theory and Current Thinking

Piaget believed that children construct their understanding of the world while interacting with it. Their minds experience spurts of change, followed by greater stability as they move from one cognitive plateau to the next, each with distinctive characteristics that permit specific kinds of thinking. In Piaget's view, cognitive development consisted of four major stages—*sensorimotor, preoperational, concrete operational,* and *formal operational.*

SENSORIMOTOR STAGE In the **sensorimotor stage,** from birth to nearly age 2, babies take in the world through their senses and actions—through looking, hearing, touching, mouthing, and grasping. As their hands and limbs begin to move, they learn to make things happen.

Very young babies seem to live in the present: Out of sight is out of mind. In one test, Piaget showed an infant an appealing toy and then flopped his beret over it. Before the age of 6 months, the infant acted as if the toy ceased to exist. Young infants lack **object permanence**—the awareness that objects continue to exist when not perceived. By 8 months, infants begin exhibiting memory for things no longer seen. If you hide a toy, the infant will momentarily look for it (**FIGURE 4.9**). Within another month or two, the infant will look for it even after being restrained for several seconds.

So does object permanence in fact blossom suddenly at 8 months, much as tulips blossom in spring? Today's researchers believe object permanence unfolds gradually, and they see development as more continuous than Piaget did. Even young infants will at least momentarily look for a toy where they saw it hidden a second before (Wang et al., 2004).

Researchers also believe Piaget and his followers underestimated young children's competence. Young children think like little scientists. They test ideas, make causal inferences, and learn from statistical patterns (Gopnik et al., 2015). Consider these simple experiments:

- **Baby physics:** Like adults staring in disbelief at a magic trick (the *"Whoa!"* look), infants look longer at and explore an unexpected, impossible, or unfamiliar scene—a car seeming to pass through a solid object, a ball stopping in midair, or an object violating object permanence by magically disappearing (Baillargeon, 2008; Shuwairi & Johnson, 2013; Stahl & Feigenson, 2015). Why do infants show this visual bias? Because impossible events violate infants' expectations (Baillargeon et al., 2016).

- **Baby math:** Karen Wynn (1992, 2000, 2008) showed 5-month-olds one or two objects (**FIGURE 4.10a**). Then she hid the objects behind a screen, and visibly removed or added one (Figure 4.10d). When she lifted the screen, the infants sometimes did a double take, staring longer when shown a wrong number of objects (Figure 4.10f). But were they just responding to a greater or smaller *mass* of objects, rather than a change in *number* (Feigenson et al., 2002)? Later experiments showed that babies' number sense extends to larger numbers, to ratios, and to such things as drumbeats and motions (Libertus & Brannon, 2009; McCrink & Wynn, 2004; Spelke et al., 2013). If accustomed to a Daffy Duck puppet jumping three times on stage, they showed surprise if it jumped only twice.

Clearly, infants are smarter than Piaget appreciated. Even as babies, we had a lot on our minds.

  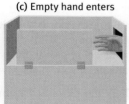 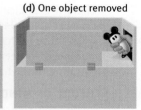

(a) Objects placed in case   **(b)** Screen comes up   **(c)** Empty hand enters   **(d)** One object removed

PREOPERATIONAL STAGE Piaget believed that until about age 6 or 7, children are in a **preoperational stage**—able to represent things with words and images but too young to perform *mental operations* (such as imagining an action and mentally reversing it). For a 5-year-old, the milk that seems "too much" in a tall, narrow glass may become just right if poured into a short, wide glass. Focusing only on the height dimension, this child cannot perform the operation of mentally pouring the milk back. Before about age 6, said Piaget, children lack the concept of **conservation**—the principle that quantity remains the same despite changes in shape (**FIGURE 4.11**).

📲 **LaunchPad** For quick video examples of children being tested for conservation, visit **Concept Practice: Piaget and Conservation.**

PRETEND PLAY Symbolic thinking and *pretend play* appear at an earlier age than Piaget supposed. Judy DeLoache (1987) showed children a model of a room and hid a miniature stuffed dog behind its miniature couch. The 2½-year-olds easily remembered where to find the miniature toy, but they could not use the model to locate an actual stuffed dog

preoperational stage in Piaget's theory, the stage (from about 2 to 6 or 7 years of age) during which a child learns to use language but does not yet comprehend the mental operations of concrete logic.

conservation the principle (which Piaget believed to be a part of concrete operational reasoning) that properties such as mass, volume, and number remain the same despite changes in the forms of objects.

FIGURE 4.10

BABY MATH Shown a numerically impossible outcome, 5-month-old infants stare longer (Wynn, 1992).

Then either: possible outcome
(e) Screen drops revealing 1 object

or: impossible outcome
(f) Screen drops revealing 2 objects

FIGURE 4.11

PIAGET'S TEST OF CONSERVATION This visually focused preoperational child does not yet understand the principle of conservation. When the milk is poured into a tall, narrow glass, it suddenly seems like "more" than when it was in the shorter, wider glass. In another year or so, she will understand that the amount stays the same.

EGOCENTRISM IN ACTION "Look, Granddaddy, a match!" So said my [DM's] granddaughter, Allie, at age 4, when showing me two memory game cards with matching pictures—that faced her.

"The curse of knowledge is the single best explanation I know of why good people write bad prose. It simply doesn't occur to the writer that her readers don't know what she knows." —Psychologist Steven Pinker, *The Sense of Style*, 2014

Use your finger to trace a capital E on your forehead. When Adam Galinsky and his colleagues (2006) invited people to do that (as you can, with a friend), they were more egocentric—less likely to draw it from the perspective of someone looking at them—if they were first made to feel powerful. Other studies confirm that feeling powerful reduces people's sensitivity to how others see, think, and feel.

egocentrism in Piaget's theory, the pre-operational child's difficulty taking another's point of view.

theory of mind people's ideas about their own and others' mental states—about their feelings, perceptions, and thoughts, and the behaviors these might predict.

concrete operational stage in Piaget's theory, the stage of cognitive development (from about 7 to 11 years of age) during which children gain the mental operations that enable them to think logically about concrete events.

behind a couch in a real room. Three-year-olds—only 6 months older—usually went right to the actual stuffed animal in the real room, showing they *could* think of the model as a symbol for the room. Although Piaget did not view the stage transitions as abrupt, he probably would have been surprised to see symbolic thinking at such an early age.

EGOCENTRISM Piaget taught us that preschool children are **egocentric:** They have difficulty perceiving things from another's point of view. They are like the person who, when asked by someone across a river, "How do I get to the other side?" answered "You're *on* the other side." Asked to "show Mommy your picture," 2-year-old Gabriella holds the picture up facing her own eyes. Three-year-old Gray makes himself "invisible" by putting his hands over his eyes, assuming that if he can't see his grandparents, they can't see him. Children's conversations also reveal their egocentrism, as one young boy demonstrated (Phillips, 1969, p. 61):

"Do you have a brother?"
"Yes."
"What's his name?"
"Jim."
"Does Jim have a brother?"
"No."

Like Gabriella, TV-watching preschoolers who block your view of the TV assume that you see what they see. They simply have not yet developed the ability to take another's viewpoint. Even adolescents egocentrically overestimate how much others are noticing them (Lin, 2016). And adults may overestimate the extent to which others share our opinions, knowledge, and perspectives. We assume that something will be clear to others if it is clear to us, or that email recipients will "hear" our "just kidding" intent (Epley et al., 2004; Kruger et al., 2005). Perhaps you can recall asking someone to guess a simple tune such as "Happy Birthday" as you clapped or tapped it out. With the tune in your head, it seemed so obvious! But you suffered the egocentric *curse of knowledge,* assuming that what was in your head was also in someone else's.

THEORY OF MIND When Little Red Riding Hood realized her "grandmother" was really a wolf, she swiftly revised her ideas about the creature's intentions and raced away. Preschoolers, although still egocentric, develop this ability to infer others' mental states when they begin forming a **theory of mind** (Premack & Woodruff, 1978). The theory of mind concept was first used to describe chimpanzees' seeming ability to read others' intentions. Later, psychologists aimed to identify when humans develop a theory of mind.

As the ability to take another's perspective gradually develops, preschoolers come to understand what made a playmate angry, when a sibling will share, and what might make a parent buy a toy. They begin to tease, empathize, and persuade. And when making decisions, they use their understanding of how their actions will make others feel (Repacholi et al., 2016). Children who have an advanced ability to understand others' minds tend to be helpful and well-liked (Imuta et al., 2016; Slaughter et al., 2015).

Between about ages 3 and 4½, children worldwide come to realize that others may hold false beliefs (Callaghan et al., 2005; Rubio-Fernández & Geurts, 2013; Sabbagh et al., 2006). Jennifer Jenkins and Janet Astington (1996) showed Canadian children a Band-Aid box and asked them what was inside. Expecting Band-Aids, the children were surprised to discover that the box actually contained pencils. Asked what a child who had never seen the box would think was inside, 3-year-olds typically answered "pencils." By age 4 to 5, the children's theory of mind had leapt forward, and they anticipated their friends' false belief that the box would hold Band-Aids. Children with *autism spectrum disorder* have difficulty understanding that another's state of mind differs from their own.

CONCRETE OPERATIONAL STAGE By about age 7, said Piaget, children enter the **concrete operational stage.** Given concrete (physical) materials, they begin to grasp operations such as conservation. Understanding that change in form does not mean change in quantity, they can mentally pour milk back and forth between glasses of different shapes. They also enjoy jokes that use this new understanding:

Mr. Jones went into a restaurant and ordered a whole pizza for his dinner. When the waiter asked if he wanted it cut into 6 or 8 pieces, Mr. Jones said, "Oh, you'd better make it 6, I could never eat 8 pieces!" (McGhee, 1976)

RETAIN 🔒 **TABLE 4.1**

Piaget's Stages of Cognitive Development

Typical Age Range	Stage and Description	Key Milestones
Birth to nearly 2 years	*Sensorimotor* Experiencing the world through senses and actions (looking, hearing, touching, mouthing, and grasping)	• Object permanence • Stranger anxiety
About 2 to 6 or 7 years	*Preoperational* Representing things with words and images; using intuitive rather than logical reasoning	• Pretend play • Egocentrism
About 7 to 11 years	*Concrete operational* Thinking logically about concrete events; grasping concrete analogies and performing arithmetical operations	• Conservation • Mathematical transformations
About 12 through adulthood	*Formal operational* Reasoning abstractly	• Abstract logic • Potential for mature moral reasoning

PRETEND PLAY

Image Source/Getty Images

Piaget believed that during the concrete operational stage, children become able to comprehend mathematical transformations and conservation. When my [DM's] daughter, Laura, was 6, I was astonished at her inability to reverse simple arithmetic. Asked, "What is 8 plus 4?" she required 5 seconds to compute "12," and another 5 seconds to then compute 12 minus 4. By age 8, she could answer a reversed question instantly.

FORMAL OPERATIONAL STAGE By about age 12, our reasoning expands from the purely concrete (involving actual experience) to encompass abstract thinking (involving imagined realities and symbols). As children approach adolescence, said Piaget, they can ponder hypothetical propositions and deduce consequences: *If* this, *then* that. Systematic reasoning, what Piaget called **formal operational** thinking, is now within their grasp.

ENGAGE 💡 Although full-blown logic and reasoning await adolescence, the rudiments of formal operational thinking begin earlier than Piaget realized. Consider this simple problem:

If John is in school, then Mary is in school. John is in school. What can you say about Mary?

Formal operational thinkers have no trouble answering correctly. But neither do most 7-year-olds (Suppes, 1982). **TABLE 4.1** summarizes the four stages in Piaget's theory.

An Alternative Viewpoint: Lev Vygotsky and the Social Child

As Piaget was forming his theory of cognitive development, Russian psychologist Lev Vygotsky was also studying how children think and learn. Where Piaget emphasized how the child's mind grows through interaction with the physical environment, Vygotsky emphasized how the child's mind grows through interaction with the *social* environment. If Piaget's child was a young scientist, Vygotsky's was a young apprentice. By giving children new words and mentoring them, parents, teachers, and other children provide what we now call a temporary **scaffold** from which children can step to higher levels of thinking (Renninger & Granott, 2005; Wood et al., 1976). Children learn best when their social environment presents them with something in the sweet spot between too easy and too difficult.

Language, an important ingredient of social mentoring, provides the building blocks for thinking, noted Vygotsky (who was born the same year as Piaget, but died prematurely of tuberculosis). By age 7, children increasingly think in words and use words to solve problems. They do this, Vygotsky said, by internalizing their culture's language and relying on inner speech (Fernyhough, 2008). Parents who say *"No, no, Bevy!"* when pulling their child's hand away from a cup of hot coffee are giving her a self-control tool. When Bevy later needs to resist temptation, she may likewise think, *"No, no, Bevy!"*

formal operational stage in Piaget's theory, the stage of cognitive development (normally beginning about age 12) during which people begin to think logically about abstract concepts.

scaffold a framework that offers children temporary support as they develop higher levels of thinking.

LEV VYGOTSKY (1896–1934)
Vygotsky, pictured here with his daughter, was a Russian developmental psychologist. He studied how a child's mind feeds on the language of social interaction.

James V. Wertsch/Washington University

Second graders who muttered to themselves while doing math problems grasped third-grade math better the following year (Berk, 1994). Whether out loud or inaudibly, talking to themselves helps children control their behavior and emotions and master new skills. (It helps adults, too. Adults who motivate themselves using self-talk—"You can do it!"—experience better performance [Kross et al., 2014].)

"It's too late, Roger—they've seen us." Roger has not outgrown his early childhood egocentrism.

🔒 **RETRIEVE IT • • •**   *ANSWERS IN APPENDIX E*

RI-2 Object permanence, pretend play, conservation, and abstract logic are developmental milestones for which of Piaget's stages, respectively?

RI-3 Label each of the following developmental phenomena (I–VI) with the correct cognitive developmental stage: (a) sensorimotor, (b) preoperational, (c) concrete operational, or (d) formal operational.

   I. Thinking about abstract concepts, such as "freedom."
   II. Enjoying imaginary play (such as dress-up).
   III. Understanding that physical properties stay the same even when objects change form.
   IV. Having the ability to reverse math operations.
   V. Understanding that something is not gone for good when it disappears from sight, as when Mom "disappears" behind the shower curtain.
   VI. Having difficulty taking another's point of view (as when blocking someone's view of the TV).

Reflecting on Piaget's Theory

What remains of Piaget's ideas about the child's mind? Plenty—enough to merit his being singled out by *Time* magazine as one of the twentieth century's 20 most influential scientists and thinkers, and his being rated in a survey of British psychologists as the last century's greatest psychologist (*Psychologist,* 2003). Piaget identified significant cognitive milestones and stimulated worldwide interest in how the mind develops. His emphasis was less on the ages at which children typically reach specific milestones than on their sequence. Studies around the globe, from aboriginal Australia to Algeria to North America, have confirmed that human cognition unfolds basically in the sequence Piaget described (Lourenco & Machado, 1996; Segall et al., 1990).

However, today's researchers see development as more continuous than did Piaget. By detecting the beginnings of each type of thinking at earlier ages, they have revealed conceptual abilities Piaget missed. Moreover, they see formal logic as a smaller part of cognition than he did. Today, as part of our own cognitive development, we are adapting Piaget's ideas to accommodate new findings.

IMPLICATIONS FOR PARENTS AND TEACHERS Future parents and teachers, remember this: Young children are incapable of adult logic. Preschoolers who block one's view of the TV simply have not learned to take another's viewpoint. What seems simple and obvious to us—getting off a seesaw will cause a friend on the other end to crash—may be incomprehensible to a 3-year-old. Also remember that children are not passive receptacles waiting to be filled with knowledge. Better to build on what they already know, engaging them in concrete demonstrations and stimulating them to think for themselves. Finally, accept children's cognitive immaturity as adaptive. It is nature's strategy for keeping children close to protective adults and providing time for learning and socialization (Bjorklund & Green, 1992).

Autism Spectrum Disorder

LOQ 4-6   What is *autism spectrum disorder*?

Autism spectrum disorder (ASD) is a cognitive and social-emotional disorder that is marked by social deficiencies and repetitive behaviors. Once believed to affect 1 in 2500 children (and referred to simply as *autism*), ASD is now diagnosed in 1 in 68 American

---

"Assessing the impact of Piaget on developmental psychology is like assessing the impact of Shakespeare on English literature." —Developmental psychologist Harry Beilin (1992)

"Childhood has its own way of seeing, thinking, and feeling, and there is nothing more foolish than the attempt to put ours in its place." —Philosopher Jean-Jacques Rousseau, 1798

▶ **LaunchPad** For a 7-minute synopsis of Piaget's concepts, see the **Video: Cognitive Development.**

autism spectrum disorder (ASD) a disorder that appears in childhood and is marked by significant deficiencies in communication and social interaction, and by rigidly fixated interests and repetitive behaviors.

children by age 8. Rates range from 1 in 34 in the studied area of New Jersey to only 1 in 77 in Arkansas. Outside the U.S., rates also vary, from 1 in 38 in South Korea to 1 in 100 in Britain (CDC, 2014c; Kim et al., 2011; NAS, 2011). The increase in ASD diagnoses has been offset by a decrease in the number of children with a "cognitive disability" or "learning disability," which suggests a relabeling of children's disorders (Gernsbacher et al., 2005; Grinker, 2007; Shattuck, 2006).

The underlying source of ASD's symptoms seems to be poor communication among brain regions that normally work together to let us take another's viewpoint. From age 2 months on, children normally spend more and more time looking into others' eyes; those who later develop ASD do so less and less (Baron-Cohen, 2017; Moriuchi et al., 2017). People with ASD are said to have an *impaired theory of mind* (Rajendran & Mitchell, 2007; Senju et al., 2009). Mind reading that most of us find intuitive (*Is that face conveying a smirk or a sneer?*) is difficult for those with ASD. They have difficulty inferring and remembering others' thoughts and feelings, appreciating that playmates and parents might view things differently, and understanding that their teachers know more than they do (Boucher et al., 2012; Frith & Frith, 2001; Knutsen et al., 2015). Partly for such reasons, a national survey of parents and school staff reported that 46 percent of adolescents with ASD had suffered the taunts and torments of bullying—about four times the 11 percent rate for other children (Sterzing et al., 2012). Children with ASD do make friends, but their peers often find such relationships emotionally unsatisfying (Mendelson et al., 2016).

ASD has differing levels of severity. Some (those diagnosed with what used to be called *Asperger syndrome*) generally function at a high level. They have normal intelligence, often accompanied by exceptional skill or talent in a specific area, but deficient social and communication skills and a tendency to become distracted by irrelevant stimuli (Remington et al., 2009). Those at the spectrum's more severe end struggle to use language.

Biological factors, including genetic influences and abnormal brain development, contribute to ASD (Colvert et al., 2015; Makin, 2015; Tick et al., 2015). Studies suggest that the prenatal environment matters, especially when altered by maternal infection and inflammation, psychiatric drug use, or stress hormones (NIH, 2013; Wang, 2014). Childhood vaccinations do *not* contribute to ASD (Taylor et al., 2014). Based on a fraudulent 1998 study—"the most damaging medical hoax of the last 100 years" (Flaherty, 2011)—some parents were misled into thinking that the childhood MMR vaccine increased risk of ASD. The unfortunate result was a drop in vaccination rates and an increase in cases of measles and mumps. Some unvaccinated children suffered long-term harm or even death. Unvaccinated children also place at risk other children who are too young to be fully vaccinated.

ASD afflicts about three boys for every girl (Loomes et al., 2017). Psychologist Simon Baron-Cohen (2010) believes this is because boys more often than girls are "systemizers." They tend to understand things according to rules or laws, as in mathematical and mechanical systems. Girls, he contends, are more often predisposed to be "empathizers." They tend to excel at reading facial expressions and gestures (van Honk et al., 2011). Whether male or female, those with ASD are systemizers who have more difficulty reading facial expressions (Baron-Cohen at al., 2015).

Numerous studies verify biology's influence. If one identical twin is diagnosed with ASD, the chances are 50 to 70 percent that the co-twin will be as well (Tick et al., 2015). A younger genetic sibling of a child with ASD also is at a heightened risk (Sutcliffe, 2008). No one "autism gene" accounts for the disorder. Rather, many genes—with more than 400 identified so far—appear to contribute (Krishnan et al., 2016; Yuen et al., 2016). Random genetic mutations in sperm cells may also play a role. As men age, these mutations become more frequent, which may help explain why an over-40 man has a much higher risk of fathering a child with ASD than does a man under 30 (Wu et al., 2017).

Researchers are also sleuthing ASD's telltale signs in the brain's structure. Several studies have revealed "underconnectivity"—fewer-than-normal fiber tracts connecting the front of the brain to the back (Picci et al., 2016). With underconnectivity, there is less of the whole-brain synchrony that, for example, integrates visual and emotional information.

AUTISM SPECTRUM DISORDER This speech-language pathologist is helping a boy with ASD learn to form sounds and words. ASD is marked by deficient social communication and difficulty grasping others' states of mind.

"AUTISM" CASE NUMBER 1 In 1943, Donald Gray Triplett, an "odd" child with unusual gifts and social deficits, was the first person to receive the diagnosis of "autism." (After a 2013 change in the diagnosis manual, his condition is now called *autism spectrum disorder.*) In 2016, at age 82, Triplett was still living in his family home and Mississippi town, where he often played golf (Atlas, 2016).

(a)

(b)

FIGURE 4.12

TRANSPORTED INTO A WORLD OF EMOTION A research team at Cambridge University's Autism Research Centre introduced children with ASD to emotions experienced and displayed by (a) toy vehicles and (b) human faces. Children matched the correct face with the story ("The neighbor's dog has bitten people before. He is barking at Louise. Point to the face that shows how Louise is feeling"). (The graph shows data for two trials.)

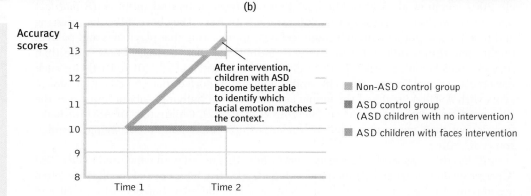

Accuracy scores

After intervention, children with ASD become better able to identify which facial emotion matches the context.

Non-ASD control group

ASD control group (ASD children with no intervention)

ASD children with faces intervention

Time 1   Time 2

Biology's role in ASD also appears in the brain's functioning. People without ASD often yawn after seeing others yawn. And as they view and imitate another's smiling or frowning, they feel something of what the other is feeling. Not so among those with ASD, who are less imitative and show less activity in brain areas involved in mirroring others' actions (Edwards, 2014; Yang & Hoffman, 2015). When people with ASD watch another person's hand movements, for example, their brain displays less-than-normal mirroring activity (Oberman & Ramachandran, 2007; Théoret et al., 2005). Scientists are exploring and debating this idea that the brains of people with ASD have "broken mirrors" (Gallese et al., 2011). And they are exploring whether treatment with oxytocin, the hormone that promotes social bonding, might improve social understanding in those with ASD (Gordon et al., 2013; Lange & McDougle, 2013).

Seeking to "systemize empathy," Baron-Cohen and his Cambridge University colleagues (2007; Golan et al., 2010) collaborated with Britain's National Autistic Society and a film production company. Knowing that television shows with vehicles have been popular among kids with ASD, they created animations with toy vehicle characters in a pretend boy's bedroom, grafting emotion-conveying faces onto toy trams, trains, and tractors (**FIGURE 4.12**). After the boy leaves for school, the characters come to life and have experiences that lead them to display various emotions (see TheTransporters.com). The children were surprisingly able to generalize what they had learned to a new, real-life context. By the intervention's end, their previously deficient ability to recognize emotions on real faces now equaled that of children without ASD.

🔒 **RETRIEVE IT • • •**   *ANSWERS IN APPENDIX E*

RI-4 What does *theory of mind* have to do with autism spectrum disorder?

SOCIAL DEVELOPMENT

LOQ 4-7   How do parent-infant attachment bonds form?

From birth, most babies are social creatures, developing an intense attachment to their caregivers. Infants come to prefer familiar faces and voices, then to coo and gurgle when given a parent's attention. After about 8 months, soon after object permanence emerges and children become mobile, a curious thing happens: They develop **stranger anxiety.**

They may greet strangers by crying and reaching for familiar caregivers: "No! Don't leave me!" Children this age have schemas for familiar faces; when they cannot assimilate the new face into these remembered schemas, they become distressed (Kagan, 1984). Once again, we see an important principle: *The brain, mind, and social-emotional behavior develop together.*

Origins of Attachment

One-year-olds typically cling tightly to a parent when they are frightened or expect separation. Reunited after being apart, they often shower the parent with smiles and hugs. This striking parent-infant **attachment** bond is a powerful survival impulse that keeps infants close to their caregivers. Infants normally become attached to those—typically their parents—who are comfortable and familiar. For many years, psychologists reasoned that infants became attached to those who satisfied their need for nourishment. But an accidental finding overturned this explanation.

BODY CONTACT During the 1950s, University of Wisconsin psychologists Harry Harlow and Margaret Harlow bred monkeys for their learning studies. To equalize experiences and to isolate any disease, they separated the infant monkeys from their mothers shortly after birth and raised them in individual cages, each including a cheesecloth baby blanket (Harlow et al., 1971). Then came a surprise: When their soft blankets were taken to be washed, the monkeys became distressed.

The Harlows recognized that this intense attachment to the blanket contradicted the idea that attachment derives from an association with nourishment. But how could they show this more convincingly? To pit the drawing power of a food source against the contact comfort of the blanket, they created two artificial mothers. One was a bare wire cylinder with a wooden head and an attached feeding bottle, the other a cylinder wrapped with terry cloth.

When raised with both, the monkeys overwhelmingly preferred the comfy cloth mother (**FIGURE 4.13**). Like other infants clinging to their live mothers, the monkey babies would cling to their cloth mothers when anxious. When exploring their environment, they used her as a *secure base,* as if attached to her by an invisible elastic band that stretched only far before pulling them back. Researchers soon learned that other qualities—rocking, warmth, and feeding—made the cloth mother even more appealing.

Science Source

Human infants, too, become attached to parents who are soft and warm and who rock, feed, and pat. Much parent-infant emotional communication occurs via touch, which can be either soothing (snuggles) or arousing (tickles) (Hertenstein et al., 2006). Indeed, when asked to describe the ideal mother, people across the globe agreed that she "shows affection by touching" (Mesman et al., 2015). Such parental affection not only feels good, it aids brain development and later cognitive performance (Davis et al., 2017).

Human attachment also consists of one person providing another with a secure base from which to explore and a safe haven when distressed. As we mature, our secure base and safe haven shift—from parents to peers and partners (Cassidy & Shaver, 1999). But at all ages we are social creatures. We gain strength when someone offers, by words and actions, a safe haven: "I will be here. I am interested in you. Come what may, I will support you" (Crowell & Waters, 1994).

FAMILIARITY Contact is one key to attachment. Another is familiarity. In many animals, attachments based on familiarity form during a *critical period*—an optimal period when certain events must take place to facilitate proper development (Bornstein, 1989).

stranger anxiety the fear of strangers that infants commonly display, beginning by about 8 months of age.

attachment an emotional tie with another person; shown in young children by their seeking closeness to their caregiver and showing distress on separation.

FIGURE 4.13

THE HARLOWS' MONKEY MOTHERS Psychologists Harry Harlow and Margaret Harlow raised monkeys with two artificial mothers—one a bare wire cylinder with a wooden head and an attached feeding bottle, the other a cylinder with no bottle but covered with foam rubber and wrapped with terry cloth. The Harlows' discovery surprised many psychologists: The infants much preferred contact with the comfortable cloth mother, even while feeding from the wire nourishing mother.

Nina Leen/Getty Images

IMPRINTING Konrad Lorenz (1937) explored this rigid attachment process. He wondered: What would ducklings do if he was the first moving creature they observed? What they did was follow him around: Everywhere that Konrad went, the ducks were sure to go. Although baby birds imprint best to their own species, they also will imprint on a variety of moving objects—an animal of another species, a box on wheels, or a bouncing ball (Colombo, 1982; Johnson, 1992). Once formed, this attachment is difficult to reverse.

Humans seem to have a critical period for language. Goslings, ducklings, and chicks have a critical period for attachment, called **imprinting,** which falls in the hours shortly after hatching, when the first moving object they see is normally their mother. From then on, the young fowl follow her, and her alone.

Children—unlike ducklings—do not imprint. However, they do become attached to what they've known. *Mere exposure* to people and things fosters fondness. Children like to reread the same books, rewatch the same movies, reenact family traditions. They prefer to eat familiar foods, live in the same familiar neighborhood, attend school with the same old friends. Familiarity is a safety signal. Familiarity breeds content.

🔒 **RETRIEVE IT • • •**   ANSWERS IN APPENDIX E

RI-5 What distinguishes imprinting from attachment?

Attachment Differences

LOQ 4-8   How have psychologists studied attachment differences, and what have they learned?

What accounts for children's attachment differences? To answer this question, Mary Ainsworth (1979) designed the *strange situation* experiment. She observed mother-infant pairs at home during their first six months. Later she observed the 1-year-old infants in a strange situation (usually a laboratory playroom) with and without their mothers. Such research has shown that about 60 percent of infants and young children display *secure attachment* (Moulin et al., 2014). In their mother's presence they play comfortably, happily exploring their new environment. When she leaves, they become distressed; when she returns, they seek contact with her.

Other infants show *insecure attachment,* marked either by anxiety or avoidance of trusting relationships. These infants are less likely to explore their surroundings; they may even cling to their mother. When she leaves, they either cry loudly and remain upset or seem indifferent to her departure and return (Ainsworth, 1973, 1989; Kagan, 1995; van IJzendoorn & Kroonenberg, 1988).

Ainsworth and others found that sensitive, responsive mothers—those who noticed what their babies were doing and responded appropriately—had infants who exhibited secure attachment (De Wolff & van IJzendoorn, 1997). Insensitive, unresponsive mothers—mothers who attended to their babies when they felt like doing so but ignored them at other times—often had infants who were insecurely attached. The Harlows' monkey studies, with unresponsive artificial mothers, produced even more striking effects. When put in strange situations without their artificial mothers, the deprived infants were terrified (**FIGURE 4.14**).

Although remembered by some as the researcher who tortured helpless monkeys, Harry Harlow defended his methods: "Remember, for every mistreated monkey there exist a million mistreated children," he said, expressing the hope that his research would sensitize people to child abuse and neglect. "No one who knows Harry's work could ever argue that babies do fine without companionship, that a caring mother doesn't matter," noted Harlow biographer Deborah Blum (2011, pp. 292, 307). "And since we . . . didn't fully believe that before Harry Harlow came along, then perhaps we needed—just once— to be smacked really hard with that truth so that we could never again doubt."

So, caring parents matter. But is attachment style the *result* of parenting? Or are other factors also at work?

FIGURE 4.14

SOCIAL DEPRIVATION AND FEAR In the Harlows' experiments, monkeys raised with inanimate surrogate mothers were overwhelmed when placed in strange situations without that source of emotional security. (Today there is greater oversight and concern for animal welfare, which would regulate this type of study.)

TEMPERAMENT AND ATTACHMENT How does **temperament**—a person's characteristic emotional reactivity and intensity—affect attachment style? Twin and developmental studies reveal that heredity affects temperament, and temperament affects attachment style (Picardi et al., 2011; Raby et al., 2012).

As most parents will tell you after having their second child, babies differ even before gulping their first breath. Some babies are noticeably *difficult*—irritable, intense, and

Science Source

unpredictable. Others are *easy*—cheerful, relaxed, and predictably feeding and sleeping (Chess & Thomas, 1987). Identical twins, more than fraternal twins, often have similar temperaments (Fraley & Tancredy, 2012; Kandler et al., 2013). And differences in temperament appear in physiological differences. Anxious, inhibited infants have high and variable heart rates and a reactive nervous system. When facing new or strange situations, they become more physiologically aroused (Kagan & Snidman, 2004; Roque et al., 2012).

Temperament differences typically persist. The most emotionally reactive newborns tend also to be the most reactive 9-month-olds (Wilson & Matheny, 1986; Worobey & Blajda, 1989). Emotionally intense preschoolers tend to become relatively intense young adults (Larsen & Diener, 1987). In one study of more than 900 New Zealanders, emotionally reactive and impulsive 3-year-olds developed into somewhat more impulsive, aggressive, and crime-prone adults (Caspi et al., 2016).

Parenting studies that neglect such inborn differences, noted Judith Harris (1998), do the equivalent of "comparing foxhounds reared in kennels with poodles reared in apartments." To separate the effects of nature and nurture on attachment, we would need to vary parenting while controlling temperament. (Pause and think: If you were the researcher, how might you do this?)

Dutch researcher Dymphna van den Boom's solution was to randomly assign 100 temperamentally difficult 6- to 9-month-olds to either an experimental group, in which mothers received personal training in sensitive responding, or to a control group, in which they did not. At 12 months of age, 68 percent of the experimental group were securely attached, as were only 28 percent of the control group infants. Other studies confirm that intervention programs can increase parental sensitivity and, to a lesser extent, infant attachment security (Bakermans-Kranenburg et al., 2003; Van Zeijl et al., 2006). Such "positive parenting" interventions seem to be especially beneficial for children with difficult temperaments (Slagt et al., 2016).

As many of these examples indicate, researchers have more often studied mother care than father care, but fathers are more than just mobile sperm banks. Despite the widespread attitude that "fathering a child" means impregnating, and "mothering" means nurturing, nearly 100 studies worldwide have shown that a father's love and acceptance are comparable with a mother's love in predicting an offspring's health and well-being (Rohner & Veneziano, 2001; see also **TABLE 4.2**). Fathers matter.

In one large British study following 7259 children from birth to adulthood, those whose fathers were most involved in parenting (through outings, reading to them, and taking an interest in their education) tended to achieve more in school, even after controlling for other factors such as parental education and family wealth (Flouri & Buchanan, 2004). Girls with involved fathers are also less likely to engage in risky sexual behavior or to befriend those who do (DelPriore et al., 2017). Increasing nonmarital births and the greater instability of cohabiting versus married partnerships has, however, meant more father-absent families (Hymowitz et al., 2013). In Europe and the United States,

imprinting the process by which certain animals form strong attachments during early life.

temperament a person's characteristic emotional reactivity and intensity.

LaunchPad Play the role of a researcher studying temperament and personality by engaging online with **Immersive Learning: How Would You Know If Personality Runs in Our Genes?**

TABLE 4.2
Dual Parenting Positives

- *Active dads are caregiving more.* Today's co-parenting fathers are more engaged, with a doubling in the weekly hours spent with their children, compared with fathers in 1965 (Livingston & Parker, 2011).

- *Couples that share housework and child care are happier in their relationships and less divorce prone* (Wilcox & Marquardt, 2011).

- *Dual parenting supports children.* After controlling for other factors, children average better life outcomes "if raised by both parents" (Taylor, 2014).

- *Parents' gender and sexual orientation do not affect children's well-being.* The American Academy of Pediatrics (2013) reports that what matters is competent, secure, nurturing parents. The American Sociological Association (2013) concurs: Parental stability and resources matter, but "whether a child is raised by same-sex or opposite-sex parents has no bearing on a child's well-being."

FIGURE 4.15

INFANTS' DISTRESS OVER SEPARATION FROM PARENTS In an experiment, infants were left by their mothers in an unfamiliar room. Regardless of whether the infant had experienced day care, the percentage who cried when the mother left peaked at about 13 months of age (Kagan, 1976).

Jouke van Keulen/Shutterstock

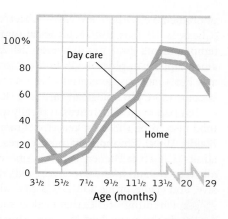

Percentage of infants who cried when their mothers left

for example, children born to married parents are (compared to cohabiting parents) about half as likely to experience their parents' separation, which often entails diminished father care (Brown et al., 2016; Wilcox & DeRose, 2017). Even after controlling for parents' income, education, and race, children co-parented by two married parents experience a lower rate of school problems (Zill & Wilcox, 2017).

Children's anxiety over separation from parents peaks at around 13 months, then gradually declines (**FIGURE 4.15**). This happens whether they live with one parent or two, are cared for at home or in day care, live in North America, Guatemala, or the Kalahari Desert. Does this mean our need for and love of others also fades away? Hardly. Our capacity for love grows, and our pleasure in touching and holding those we love never ceases.

ATTACHMENT STYLES AND LATER RELATIONSHIPS Developmental theorist Erik Erikson (1902–1994), working with his wife, Joan Erikson (1902–1997), believed that securely attached children approach life with a sense of **basic trust**—a sense that the world is predictable and reliable. He attributed basic trust not to environment or inborn temperament, but to early parenting. He theorized that infants blessed with sensitive, loving caregivers form a lifelong attitude of trust rather than fear.

Many researchers now believe that our early attachments form the foundation for our adult relationships (Birnbaum et al., 2006; Fraley et al., 2013). People who report secure relationships with their parents tend to enjoy secure friendships (Gorrese & Ruggieri, 2012). Students leaving home to attend college or university—another kind of "strange situation"— tend to adjust well if securely attached to parents (Mattanah et al., 2011). Children with sensitive, responsive mothers tend to flourish socially and academically (Raby et al., 2014).

Feeling insecurely attached to others may take one of two main forms (Fraley et al., 2011). One is *anxious attachment,* in which people constantly crave acceptance but remain alert to signs of possible rejection. The other is *avoidant attachment,* in which people experience discomfort getting close to others and use avoidant strategies to maintain distance from others. In romantic relationships, an anxious attachment style creates constant concern over rejection, leading people to cling to their partners. An avoidant style decreases commitment and increases conflict (DeWall et al., 2011; Overall et al., 2015).

Adult attachment styles can also affect relationships with one's own children. But say this for those (nearly half of all people) who exhibit wary, insecure attachments: Anxious or avoidant tendencies have helped our groups detect or escape dangers (Ein-Dor et al., 2010).

Deprivation of Attachment

LOQ 4-9 How does childhood neglect or abuse affect children's attachments?

If secure attachment fosters social trust, what happens when circumstances prevent a child's forming any attachments? In all of psychology, there is no sadder research literature. Babies locked away at home under conditions of abuse or extreme neglect are often withdrawn, frightened, even speechless. The same is true of those raised in institutions without the stimulation and attention of a regular caregiver, as was tragically illustrated

For some people, a perceived relationship with God functions as do other attachments, by providing a secure base for exploration and a safe haven when threatened (Granqvist et al., 2010; Kirkpatrick, 1999).

ENGAGE

(ASK YOURSELF)

How would you describe the style of your parents or primary caregivers? How do you think this has affected your attachment style or your other traits and behaviors?

ENGAGE

LaunchPad To consider how your own attachment style may be affecting your current relationships, engage online with **Immersive Learning: Assess Your Strengths— What Is Your Attachment Style?**

during the 1970s and 1980s in Romania. Having decided that economic growth for his impoverished country required more human capital, Nicolae Ceauşescu, Romania's Communist dictator, outlawed contraception, forbade abortion, and taxed families with fewer than five children. The birthrate skyrocketed. But unable to afford the children they had been coerced into having, many families had to leave them at government-run orphanages with untrained and overworked staff. Child-to-caregiver ratios often were 15 to 1, so the children were deprived of healthy attachments with at least one adult. When tested after Ceauşescu's 1989 execution, these socially deprived children had lower intelligence scores, reduced brain development, abnormal stress responses, and quadruple the rate of attention-deficit/hyperactivity disorder (ADHD) found in children assigned to quality foster care settings (Bick et al., 2015; Kennedy et al., 2016; McLaughlin et al., 2015; Nelson et al., 2014). Dozens of other studies across 19 countries have shown that orphaned children tend to fare better on later intelligence tests if raised in family homes. This is especially so for those placed at an early age (van IJzendoorn et al., 2008, 2017).

Most children growing up under adversity (such as the surviving children of the Holocaust and victims of childhood sexual abuse) are *resilient;* they withstand the trauma and become well-adjusted adults (Clancy, 2010; Helmreich, 1992; Masten, 2001). And hardship short of trauma often boosts mental toughness (Seery, 2011). Moreover, although enduring the hardship of growing up poor puts children at risk for some social pathologies, growing up rich puts them at risk for other problems. Affluent children are at elevated risk for substance abuse, eating disorders, anxiety, and depression (Lund & Dearing, 2012; Luthar et al., 2013). So when you face adversity, consider the possible silver lining. Your coping may strengthen your resilience—your tendency to bounce back and go on to lead a better life.

But many who experience enduring abuse don't bounce back so readily. The Harlows' monkeys raised in total isolation, without even an artificial mother, bore lifelong scars. As adults, when placed with other monkeys their age, they either cowered in fright or lashed out in aggression. When they reached sexual maturity, most were incapable of mating. If artificially impregnated, females often were neglectful, abusive, even murderous toward their first-born. Another primate experiment confirmed the abuse-breeds-abuse phenomenon in rhesus monkeys: 9 of 16 females who had been abused by their mothers became abusive parents, as did *none* of the females raised by a nonabusive mother (Maestripieri, 2005).

In humans, too, the unloved may become the unloving. Most abusive parents—and many condemned murderers—have reported being neglected or battered as children (Kempe & Kempe, 1978; Lewis et al., 1988). Some 30 percent of people who have been abused later abuse their children—a rate lower than that found in the primate study, but four times the U.S. national rate of child abuse (Dumont et al., 2007; Kaufman & Zigler, 1987).

Although most abused children do *not* later become violent criminals or abusive parents, extreme early trauma may nevertheless leave footprints on the brain (Teicher and Samson, 2016). Like battle-stressed soldiers, abused children's brains respond to angry faces with heightened activity in threat-detecting areas (McCrory et al., 2011). In conflict-plagued homes, even sleeping infants' brains show heightened reactivity to hearing angry speech (Graham et al., 2013). As adults, these children exhibit stronger startle responses (Jovanovic et al., 2009). If repeatedly threatened and attacked while young, normally placid golden hamsters grow up to be cowards when caged with same-sized hamsters, or bullies when caged with weaker ones (Ferris, 1996). Such animals show changes in the brain chemical serotonin, which calms aggressive impulses. A similarly sluggish serotonin response has been found in abused children who become aggressive teens and adults. By sensitizing the stress response system, early stress can permanently heighten reactions to later stress and increase stress-related disease (Fagundes & Way, 2014; van Zuiden et al., 2012; Wei et al., 2012). Child abuse can also leave *epigenetic* marks—chemical tags—that can alter normal gene expression (Lutz et al., 2017; Romens et al., 2015).

basic trust according to Erik Erikson, a sense that the world is predictable and trustworthy; said to be formed during infancy by appropriate experiences with responsive caregivers.

"Out of the conflict between trust and mistrust, the infant develops hope, which is the earliest form of what gradually becomes faith in adults."
—Erik Erikson (1983)

THE DEPRIVATION OF ATTACHMENT In this 1980s Romanian orphanage, the 250 children between ages one and five outnumbered caregivers 15 to 1.

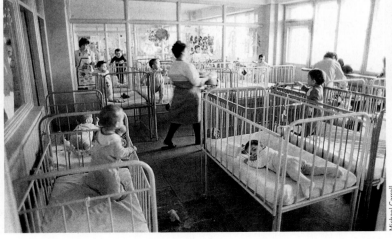

Michael Carroll

"What is learned in the cradle, lasts to the grave." —French proverb

Such findings help explain why young children who have survived severe or prolonged physical abuse, childhood sexual abuse, bullying, or wartime atrocities are at increased risk for health problems, psychological disorders, substance abuse, criminality, and, for women, earlier death (Chen et al., 2016; Lereya et al., 2015; Whitelock et al., 2013; Wolke et al., 2013). In one national study of 43,093 adults, 8 percent reported experiencing physical abuse at least fairly often before age 18 (Sugaya et al., 2012). Among these, 84 percent had experienced at least one psychiatric disorder. Moreover, the greater the abuse, the greater the odds of anxiety, depression, substance use disorder, and attempted suicide. Abuse victims are at especially heightened risk for depression if they carry a gene variation that spurs stress-hormone production (Bradley et al., 2008). As we will see again and again, behavior and emotion arise from a particular environment interacting with particular genes. Nature *and* nurture matter.

We adults also suffer when our attachment bonds are severed. Whether through death or separation, a break produces a predictable sequence. Agitated preoccupation with the lost partner is followed by deep sadness and, eventually, the beginnings of emotional detachment and a return to normal living (Hazan & Shaver, 1994). Newly separated couples who have long ago ceased feeling affection are sometimes surprised at their desire to be near the former partner. Detaching is a process, not an event.

Parenting Styles

LOQ 4-10 What are the four main parenting styles?

Some parents spank; others reason. Some are strict; others are lax. Some show little affection; others liberally hug and kiss. How do parenting-style differences affect children?

The most heavily researched aspect of parenting has been how, and to what extent, parents seek to control their children. Parenting styles can be described as a combination of two traits: how responsive and how demanding parents are (Kakinami et al., 2015). Investigators have identified four parenting styles (Baumrind, 1966, 1967; Steinberg, 2001):

1. *Authoritarian* parents are *coercive*. They impose rules and expect obedience: "Don't interrupt." "Keep your room clean." "Don't stay out late or you'll be grounded." "Why? Because I said so."

2. *Permissive* parents are *unrestraining*. They make few demands, set few limits, and use little punishment.

3. *Negligent* parents are *uninvolved*. They are neither demanding nor responsive. They are careless, inattentive, and do not seek a close relationship with their children.

4. *Authoritative* parents are *confrontive*. They are both demanding and responsive. They exert control by setting rules, but, especially with older children, they encourage open discussion and allow exceptions.

For more on parenting styles and their associated outcomes, see Thinking Critically About: Parenting Styles.

Parents who struggle with conflicting advice should also remember that *all advice reflects the advice-giver's values*. For parents who prize unquestioning obedience or whose children live in dangerous environments, an authoritarian style may have the desired effect. For those who value children's sociability and self-reliance, authoritative firm-but-open parenting is advisable.

CULTURE AND CHILD RAISING Child-raising practices reflect not only individual values, but also cultural values that vary across time and place. Should children be independent or obedient? If you live in a Westernized culture, you likely prefer independence. "You are responsible for yourself," families and schools tell their children. "Follow your conscience. Be true to yourself. Discover your gifts." Some Western parents go further, telling their children, "You are more special than other children" (Brummelman et al., 2015). (Not surprisingly, these children tend to have inflated self-views years later.) In the past, Western cultural values placed greater priority on obedience, respect, and sensitivity to others (Alwin, 1990; Remley, 1988). "Be true to your traditions," parents then taught their children. "Be loyal to your heritage and country. Show respect toward your parents and other superiors." Cultures change.

Stephen H. Reehl

CULTURES VARY Parents everywhere care about their children, but raise and protect them differently depending on the surrounding culture. In big cities, parents keep their children close. In smaller, close-knit communities, such as Scotland's Orkney Islands' town of Stromness, social trust has enabled parents to park their toddlers outside shops.

Parenting Styles—
Too Hard, Too Soft, Too Uncaring, and Just Right?

LOQ 4-11 What outcomes are associated with each parenting style?

Researchers have identified four parenting styles,[1] which have been associated with varying outcomes.

1 Authoritarian parents

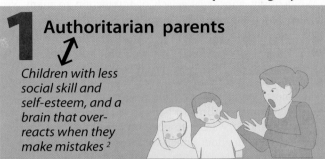

Children with less social skill and self-esteem, and a brain that over-reacts when they make mistakes [2]

2 Permissive parents

Children who are more aggressive and immature [3]

HOWEVER, Correlation ≠ Causation!

What other factors might explain this parenting-competence link?

• **Children's traits may influence parenting.** Parental warmth and control vary somewhat from child to child, even in the same family.[6] Maybe socially mature, agreeable, easygoing children evoke greater trust and warmth from their parents? Twin studies have supported this possibility.[7]

• **Some underlying third factor may be at work.** Perhaps, for example, competent parents and their competent children share genes that predispose social competence. Twin studies have also supported this possibility. [8]

3 Negligent parents

Children with poor academic and social outcomes [4]

4 Authoritative parents

Children with the highest self-esteem, self-reliance, self-regulation, and social competence [5]

1. Kakinami et al., 2015. 2. Meyer et al., 2015. 3. Luyckx et al., 2011. 4. Pinquart, 2015; Steinberg et al., 1994. 5. Baumrind, 1996, 2013; Buri et al.,1988; Coopersmith, 1967; Sulik et al., 2015. 6. Holden & Miller, 1999; Klahr & Burt, 2014. 7. Kendler, 1996. 8. South et al., 2008.

Children across time and place have thrived under various child-raising systems. Many North Americans now give children their own bedrooms and entrust them to day care. Upper-class British parents traditionally handed off routine caregiving to nannies, then sent their 10-year-olds away to boarding school. These children generally grew up to be pillars of British society.

Asians and Africans more often live in cultures that value emotional closeness. Infants and toddlers may sleep with their mothers and spend their days close to a family member (Morelli et al., 1992; Whiting & Edwards, 1988). These cultures encourage a strong sense of *family self*—a feeling that what shames the child shames the family, and what brings honor to the family brings honor to the self.

LaunchPad See the **Video: Correlational Studies** for a helpful tutorial animation about correlational research design.

In traditional African Gusii society, babies nursed freely but spent most of the day on their mother's or siblings' back—with lots of body contact but little face-to-face and language interaction. Ditto for members of some rural villages in Senegal, whose cultural traditions discourage caregivers' talking with young children. Encouraging Senegalese caregivers to talk with children improved the children's language development one year later (Weber et al., 2017). But are the language improvements worth the cost of disrupting cultural traditions? What might appear as a lack of interaction to many Westerners might, to these Gusii and Senegalese parents, seem far preferable to the lesser body contact experienced by babies pushed in strollers and left in playpens (Small, 1997).

Such diversity in child raising cautions us against presuming that our culture's way is the only way to raise children successfully. One thing is certain, however: Whatever our culture, the investment in raising a child buys many years of joy and love, but also of worry and irritation. Yet for most people who become parents, a child is one's legacy—one's personal investment in the human future. To paraphrase psychiatrist Carl Jung, we reach backward into our parents and forward into our children, and through their children into a future we will never see, but about which we must therefore care.

"You are the bows from which your children as living arrows are sent forth." —Kahlil Gibran, *The Prophet*, 1923

🔒 RETRIEVE IT • • •

ANSWERS IN APPENDIX E

RI-6 The four parenting styles may be described as "too hard, too soft, too uncaring, and just right." Which parenting style goes with each of these descriptions, and how do children benefit from the "just right" style?

🔒 REVIEW   INFANCY AND CHILDHOOD

⟫ Learning Objectives

TEST YOURSELF Answer these repeated Learning Objective Questions on your own (before checking the answers in Appendix D) to improve your retention of the concepts (McDaniel et al., 2009, 2015).

4-4 During infancy and childhood, how do the brain and motor skills develop?

4-5 From the perspectives of Piaget, Vygotsky, and today's researchers, how does a child's mind develop?

4-6 What is *autism spectrum disorder*?

4-7 How do parent-infant attachment bonds form?

4-8 How have psychologists studied attachment differences, and what have they learned?

4-9 How does childhood neglect or abuse affect children's attachments?

4-10 What are the four main parenting styles?

4-11 What outcomes are associated with each parenting style?

⟫ Terms and Concepts to Remember

TEST YOURSELF Write down the definition yourself, then check your answer on the referenced page.

maturation, **p. 122**

critical period, **p. 124**

cognition, **p. 125**

schema, **p. 125**

assimilation, **p. 125**

accommodation, **p. 125**

sensorimotor stage, **p. 126**

object permanence, **p. 126**

preoperational stage, **p. 127**

conservation, **p. 127**

egocentrism, **p. 128**

theory of mind, **p. 128**

concrete operational stage, **p. 128**

formal operational stage, **p. 129**

scaffold, **p. 129**

autism spectrum disorder (ASD), **p. 130**

stranger anxiety, **p. 133**

attachment, **p. 133**

imprinting, **p. 135**

temperament, **p. 135**

basic trust, **p. 137**

⟫ Experience the Testing Effect

TEST YOURSELF Answer the following questions on your own first, then check your answers in Appendix E.

1. Stroke a newborn's cheek and the infant will root for a nipple. This illustrates
   a. a reflex.
   b. nurture.
   c. a preference.
   d. continuity.

2. Between ages 3 and 6, the human brain experiences the greatest growth in the _____ lobes, which enable rational planning and aid memory.

3. Which of the following is true of motor-skill development?
   a. It is determined solely by genetic factors.
   b. The sequence, but not the timing, is universal.
   c. The timing, but not the sequence, is universal.
   d. It is determined solely by environmental factors.

4. Why can't we consciously recall learning to walk?

5. Use Piaget's first three stages of cognitive development to explain why young children are not just miniature adults in the way they think.

6. Although Piaget's stage theory continues to inform our understanding of children's thinking, many researchers believe that

   a. Piaget's stages begin earlier and development is more continuous than he realized.

   b. children do not progress as rapidly as Piaget predicted.

   c. few children progress to the concrete operational stage.

   d. there is no way of testing much of Piaget's theoretical work.

7. An 8-month-old infant who reacts to a new babysitter by crying and clinging to his father's shoulder is showing _____ _____.

8. In a series of experiments, the Harlows found that monkeys raised with artificial mothers tended, when afraid, to cling to their cloth mother, rather than to a wire mother holding the feeding bottle. Why was this finding important?

Continue testing yourself with **LearningCurve** or **Achieve Read & Practice** to learn and remember most effectively.

⟨⋯→⟩ Adolescence

adolescence the transition period from childhood to adulthood, extending from puberty to independence.

puberty the period of sexual maturation, during which a person becomes capable of reproducing.

LOQ 4-12 How is *adolescence* defined, and how do physical changes affect developing teens?

Many psychologists once believed that childhood sets our traits. Today's developmental psychologists see development as lifelong. As this *life-span perspective* emerged, psychologists began to look at how maturation and experience shape us not only in infancy and childhood, but also in adolescence and beyond. **Adolescence**—the years spent morphing from child to adult—starts with the physical beginnings of sexual maturity and ends with the social achievement of independent adult status. In some cultures, where teens are self-supporting, this means that adolescence hardly exists.

G. Stanley Hall (1904), one of the first psychologists to describe adolescence, believed that the tension between biological maturity and social dependence creates a period of "storm and stress." It's a time when teens crave social acceptance, but often feel socially disconnected. Three in four U.S. friendships started in seventh grade dissolve by the time adolescents complete eighth grade (Hartl et al., 2015). Indeed, after age 30, many who grow up in independence-fostering Western cultures look back on their teenage years as a time they would not want to relive—a time when their peers' social approval was imperative, their sense of direction in life was in flux, and their feeling of alienation from their parents was deepest (Arnett, 1999; Macfarlane, 1964). But for others, adolescence is a time of vitality without the cares of adulthood, a time of rewarding friendships, heightened idealism, and a growing sense of life's exciting possibilities.

PHYSICAL DEVELOPMENT

Adolescence begins with **puberty,** the time when we mature sexually. Puberty follows a surge of hormones, which may intensify moods and which trigger a series of bodily changes outlined in Chapter 5.

The Timing of Puberty

Just as in the earlier life stages, the *sequence* of physical changes in puberty (for example, breast buds and visible pubic hair before *menarche*—the first menstrual period) is far more predictable than their *timing*. Some girls start their growth spurt at 9, some boys as late as age 16. How do girls and boys experience early maturation?

For boys, early maturation has mixed effects. Boys who are stronger and more athletic during their early teen years tend to be more popular, self-assured, and independent,

At a five-year high school reunion, former best friends may be surprised at their divergence; a decade or more later, they may have trouble sustaining a conversation.

though also more at risk for alcohol use, delinquency, and premature sexual activity (Conley & Rudolph, 2009; Copeland et al., 2010; Lynne et al., 2007). For girls, early maturation can be a challenge (Mendle et al., 2007). If a young girl's body and hormone-fed feelings are out of sync with her emotional maturity and her friends' physical development and experiences, she may begin associating with older adolescents, suffer teasing or sexual harassment, and experience increased *rumination* with anxiety or depression (Alloy et al., 2016; Ge & Natsuaki, 2009; Weingarden & Renshaw, 2012).

The Teenage Brain

An adolescent's brain is a work in progress. Until puberty, brain cells increase their connections, like trees growing more roots and branches. Then, during adolescence, comes a selective *pruning* of unused neurons and connections (Blakemore, 2008). What we don't use, we lose.

As teens mature, their frontal lobes also continue to develop. The continuing growth of *myelin,* the fatty tissue that forms around axons and speeds neurotransmission, enables better communication with other brain regions (Whitaker et al., 2016). These developments bring improved judgment, impulse control, and long-term planning.

Maturation of the frontal lobes nevertheless lags behind that of the emotional limbic system. Puberty's hormonal surge and limbic system development help explain teens' occasional impulsiveness, risky behaviors, and emotional storms—slamming doors and turning up the music (Casey and Caudle, 2013; Casey et al., 2008; Fuhrmann et al., 2015). No wonder younger teens (whose unfinished frontal lobes aren't yet fully equipped for making long-term plans and curbing impulses) may succumb to the tobacco corporations. Teens actually don't underestimate the risks of smoking—or fast driving or unprotected sex. They just, when reasoning from their gut, weigh the immediate benefits more heavily (Reyna & Farley, 2006; Steinberg, 2007, 2010). Teens find rewards more exciting than adults do. They are like a car with a forceful accelerator but an incompletely developed brake pedal (**FIGURE 4.16**).

So, when Junior drives recklessly and struggles academically, should his parents reassure themselves that "he can't help it; his frontal cortex isn't yet fully grown"? They can take hope: Brain changes underlie teens' new self-consciousness about what others are thinking as well as their valuing of risky rewards (Barkley-Levenson & Galván, 2014; Somerville et al., 2013). And the brain with which Junior begins his teens differs from the brain with which he will end his teens. Unless he slows his brain development with heavy drinking—leaving him prone to impulsivity and addiction—his frontal lobes will continue maturing until about age 25 (Crews et al., 2007; Giedd, 2015). They will also become better connected with the limbic system, enabling better emotion regulation (Cohen et al., 2016; Steinberg, 2012).

In 2004, the American Psychological Association (APA) joined seven other medical and mental health associations in filing U.S. Supreme Court briefs arguing against the death penalty for 16- and 17-year-olds. The briefs documented the teen brain's immaturity "in areas that bear upon adolescent decision making." Brain scans of young teens reveal that frontal lobe immaturity is most evident among juvenile offenders and drug users (Shannon et al., 2011; Whelan et al., 2012). Thus, teens are "less guilty by reason of adolescence," suggested psychologist Laurence Steinberg and law professor Elizabeth Scott (2003; Steinberg et al., 2009). In 2005, by a 5-to-4 margin, the Court concurred, declaring juvenile death penalties unconstitutional. In 2012, the APA offered similar arguments against sentencing juveniles to life without parole (Banville, 2012; Steinberg, 2013). Once again, the Court, by a narrow 5-to-4 vote, concurred.

"Young man, go to your room and stay there until your cerebral cortex matures."

"Be afraid to try new things!"

ENGAGE How will you look back on your life 10 years from now? Are you making choices that someday you will recollect with satisfaction?

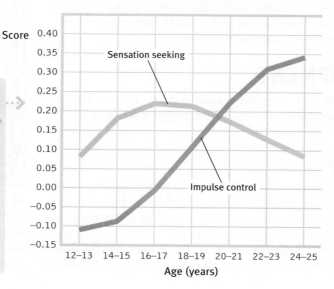

FIGURE 4.16

IMPULSE CONTROL LAGS REWARD SEEKING Surveys of more than 7000 American 12- to 24-year-olds reveal that sensation seeking peaks in the mid-teens, with impulse control developing more slowly as frontal lobes mature. (National Longitudinal Study of Youth and Children and Young Adults survey data presented by Steinberg, 2013.)

COGNITIVE DEVELOPMENT

LOQ 4-13 How did Piaget, Kohlberg, and later researchers describe adolescent cognitive and moral development?

During the early teen years, reasoning is often self-focused. Adolescents may think their private experiences are unique, something parents just could not understand: "But, Mom, *you* don't really know how it feels to be in love" (Elkind, 1978). Capable of thinking about their own thinking, and about other people's thinking, they also begin imagining what others are thinking about *them*. (They might worry less if they understood their peers' similar self-absorption.) Gradually, though, most begin to reason more abstractly.

Developing Reasoning Power

When adolescents achieve the intellectual summit that Jean Piaget called *formal operations,* they apply their new abstract reasoning tools to the world around them. They may think about what is ideally possible and compare that with the imperfect reality of their society, their parents, and themselves. They may debate human nature, good and evil, truth and justice. Their sense of what's fair changes from simple equality to equity—to what's proportional to merit (Almås et al., 2010). Having left behind the concrete images of early childhood, they may search for spirituality and a deeper meaning of life (Boyatzis, 2012; Elkind, 1970). Reasoning hypothetically and deducing consequences also enables adolescents to detect inconsistencies and spot hypocrisy in others' reasoning, sometimes leading to heated debates with parents and silent vows never to lose sight of their own ideals (Peterson et al., 1986).

> "When the pilot told us to brace and grab our ankles, the first thing that went through my mind was that we must all look pretty stupid." —Jeremiah Rawlings, age 12, after surviving a 1989 plane crash in Sioux City, Iowa

FED UP WITH FIREARMS After a 2018 mass shooting at a Parkland, Florida high school, student survivors started the #NeverAgain movement to demand U.S. gun law reform. Hundreds of thousands of teens have since participated in school walkouts (shown here), and marches, demonstrating their ability to think logically about abstract topics and to voice their ideals. According to Piaget, these teens are in the final cognitive stage, formal operations.

Samuel Corum/Anadolu Agency/Getty Images

Developing Morality

Two crucial tasks of childhood and adolescence are discerning right from wrong and developing character—the psychological muscles for controlling impulses. Children learn to empathize with others, an ability that continues to develop in adolescence. To be a moral person is to *think* morally and *act* accordingly. Jean Piaget and Lawrence Kohlberg proposed that moral reasoning guides moral actions. A more recent view builds on psychology's game-changing new recognition that much of our functioning occurs not on the "high road" of deliberate, conscious thinking but on the "low road," unconscious and automatic.

MORAL REASONING Piaget (1932) believed that children's moral judgments build on their cognitive development. Agreeing with Piaget, Lawrence Kohlberg (1981, 1984) sought to describe the development of *moral reasoning,* the thinking that occurs as we consider right and wrong. Kohlberg posed moral dilemmas (for example, whether a person should

> "I helped a so-called friend commit armed robbery and murder. . . . I was just 17 years old. . . . Been in prison for over 20 years . . . longer than I was ever free. . . . I am among the 300 plus "Juvenile Lifers" in Michigan prisons. I learned and matured a lot since my time incarcerated. I experience great remorse and regret over the tragedy that I ashamedly participated in. But I salvage this experience by learning and growing from it." —M. H., Michigan prison inmate, personal correspondence, 2015

Kohlberg's Levels of Moral Thinking Kohlberg posed moral dilemmas, such as: "Is it okay to steal medicine to save a loved one?"

Level (approximate age)	Focus	Example of Moral Reasoning
Preconventional morality (before age 9)	Self-interest; obey rules to avoid punishment or gain concrete rewards.	"If you save your loved one, you'll be a hero."
Conventional morality (early adolescence)	Uphold laws and rules to gain social approval or maintain social order.	"If you steal the medicine, everyone will think you're a criminal."
Postconventional morality (adolescence and beyond)	Actions reflect belief in basic rights and self-defined ethical principles.	"People have a right to live."

MORAL REASONING Some Houston, Texas residents faced a moral dilemma in 2017 when Hurricane Harvey caused disastrous flooding. Should they risk their lives to try to rescue family, friends, and neighbors in dangerously flooded areas? Their reasoning likely reflected different levels of moral thinking, even if they behaved similarly.

Luke Sharrett/Bloomberg via Getty Images

steal medicine to save a loved one's life) and asked children, adolescents, and adults whether the action was right or wrong. His analysis of their answers led him to propose three basic levels of moral thinking: *preconventional, conventional,* and *postconventional* (**TABLE 4.3**). Kohlberg claimed these levels form a moral ladder. As with all stage theories, the sequence is unvarying. We begin on the bottom rung and rise to varying heights; at the post-conventional level, we may place others' comfort above our own (Crockett et al., 2014). Infants recognize right and wrong, preferring moral over immoral action (Cowell & Decety, 2015). Preschoolers, typically identifying with their cultural group, conform to and enforce its moral norms (Haun et al., 2014; Schmidt & Tomasello, 2012). When those norms reward kind actions, preschoolers help others (Carragan & Dweck, 2014). Kohlberg's critics have noted that his postconventional stage is culturally limited, appearing mostly among people from large societies that prize individualism (Barrett et al., 2016; Eckensberger, 1994; Miller & Bersoff, 1995).

RI-1 According to Kohlberg, _____ morality focuses on self-interest, _____ morality focuses on self-defined ethical principles, and _____ morality focuses on upholding laws and social rules.

RI-2 How has Kohlberg's theory of moral reasoning been criticized?

MORAL INTUITION Psychologist Jonathan Haidt [pronounced HITE] (2002, 2012) believes that much of our morality is rooted in *moral intuitions*—"quick gut feelings, or affectively laden intuitions." According to this intuitionist view, the mind makes moral judgments in much the same way that it makes aesthetic judgments—quickly and automatically. Feelings of disgust or of elation trigger moral reasoning, says Haidt.

One woman recalled traveling through her snowy neighborhood with three young men as they passed "an elderly woman with a shovel in her driveway. . . . [O]ne of the guys . . . asked the driver to let him off there. . . . [M]y mouth dropped in shock as I realized that he was offering to shovel her walk for her." Witnessing this unexpected goodness triggered elevation: "I felt like jumping out of the car and hugging this guy. I felt like singing and running, or skipping and laughing. I felt like saying nice things about people" (Haidt, 2000).

"Could human morality really be run by the moral emotions," Haidt wonders, "while moral reasoning struts about pretending to be in control?" Consider the desire to punish. Laboratory games reveal that the desire to punish wrongdoing is mostly driven not by reason (such as an objective calculation that punishment deters crime) but rather by emotional reactions, such as moral outrage and the pleasure of revenge (Chester & DeWall, 2016; Darley, 2009). After the emotional fact, moral reasoning—our mind's press secretary—aims to convince us and others of the logic of what we have intuitively felt.

ENGAGE This intuitionist perspective on morality finds support in a study of moral paradoxes. Imagine seeing a runaway trolley headed for five people. All will certainly be killed unless you throw a switch that diverts the trolley onto another track, where it will kill one person. Should you throw the switch? Most say *Yes.* Kill one, save five.

Now imagine the same dilemma, except that your opportunity to save the five requires you to push a large stranger onto the tracks, where he will die as his body stops the trolley. The logic is the same—kill one, save five?—but most say *No.* Seeking to understand why, researchers used brain imaging to spy on people's neural responses as they contemplated such dilemmas. Only the body-pushing type of moral dilemma activated the brain's emotion areas (Greene et al., 2001). Thus, our moral judgments provide another example of the two-track mind—of dual processing (Feinberg et al., 2012). Moral reasoning, centered in one brain area, says throw the switch. Our intuitive moral emotions, rooted in other brain areas, override reason when saying *don't* push the man. We may liken our moral cognition to our phone's camera settings. Usually, we rely on the default settings. Yet sometimes we use reason to manually override those settings and make adjustments (Greene, 2010).

MORAL ACTION Our moral thinking and feeling surely affect our moral talk. But sometimes talk is cheap and emotions are fleeting. Morality involves *doing* the right thing, and what we do also depends on social influences. As political theorist Hannah Arendt (1963) observed, many Nazi concentration camp guards during World War II were ordinary "moral" people who were corrupted by a powerfully evil situation.

Today's character education programs tend to focus on the whole moral package—thinking, feeling, and *doing* the right thing. In service-learning programs, teens have tutored, cleaned up their neighborhoods, and assisted older adults. The result? The teens' sense of competence and desire to serve has increased, their school absenteeism and dropout rates have dropped, and their violent behavior has diminished (Andersen, 1998; Heller, 2014; Piliavin, 2003). Moral action feeds moral attitudes.

A big part of moral development is the self-discipline needed to restrain one's own impulses—to delay small gratifications now to enable bigger rewards later. In one of psychology's best-known experiments, Walter Mischel (2014) gave 4-year-olds a choice between one marshmallow now, or two marshmallows when he returned a few minutes later. The children who delayed gratification went on to have higher college completion rates and incomes, and less often suffered addiction.

A newer and larger study found that a 4-year-old's single act of willpower only modestly predicted the child's long-term academic success, especially after controlling for other factors (Watts et al., 2018). The larger point remains: Our capacity to *delay gratification*—to decline small rewards now for bigger rewards later—is basic to our future academic, vocational, and social success (Daly et al., 2015; Funder & Block, 1989; Sawyer et al., 2015). A preference for large-later rather than small-now rewards minimizes one's risk of problem gambling, smoking, and delinquency (Callan et al., 2011; Ert et al., 2013; Lee et al., 2017).

What enables our ability to delay gratification? Brain scans reveal a larger prefrontal cortex among adolescents who excel at delaying gratification, which may also help explain their better academic performance (Wang, Y., et al., 2017). An analysis of 36 species yielded similar results: Animals with larger brains showed a better ability to delay gratification (MacLean et al., 2014). But a bigger brain is not the only factor that enhances this ability. Our beliefs about willpower, our motivation, and our cultural views also play a role (Berkman et al., 2017; Job et al., 2010; Lamm et al., 2017). *The bottom line:* This is an ability worth cultivating. Delaying gratification—living with one eye on the future—fosters flourishing.

"This might not be ethical. Is that a problem for anybody?"

"It is a delightful harmony when doing and saying go together." —Michel Eyquem de Montaigne (1533–1592)

"The best time to plant a tree was 20 years ago. The second best time is now." —Chinese proverb

SOCIAL DEVELOPMENT

LOQ 4-14 What are the social tasks and challenges of adolescence?

Theorist Erik Erikson (1963) contended that each stage of life has its own *psychosocial task*, a crisis that needs resolution. Young children wrestle with issues of *trust,* then *autonomy* (independence), then *initiative.* School-age children strive for *competence,* feeling able and productive. The adolescent's task is to synthesize past, present, and future possibilities into a clearer sense of self (**TABLE 4.4**). Adolescents wonder, "Who am I as an individual? What do I want to do with my life? What values should I live by? What do I believe in?" Erikson called this quest the adolescent's *search for identity.*

Competence vs. inferiority

Intimacy vs. isolation

RETAIN 🔒 **TABLE 4.4**

Erikson's Stages of Psychosocial Development

Stage (approximate age)	Issue	Description of Task
Infancy (to 1 year)	Trust vs. mistrust	If needs are dependably met, infants develop a sense of basic trust.
Toddlerhood (1 to 3 years)	Autonomy vs. shame and doubt	Toddlers learn to exercise their will and do things for themselves, or they doubt their abilities.
Preschool (3 to 6 years)	Initiative vs. guilt	Preschoolers learn to initiate tasks and carry out plans, or they feel guilty about their efforts to be independent.
Elementary school (6 years to puberty)	Competence vs. inferiority	Children learn the pleasure of applying themselves to tasks, or they feel inferior.
Adolescence (teen years into 20s)	Identity vs. role confusion	Teenagers work at refining a sense of self by testing roles and then integrating them to form a single identity, or they become confused about who they are.
Young adulthood (20s to early 40s)	Intimacy vs. isolation	Young adults struggle to form close relationships and to gain the capacity for intimate love, or they feel socially isolated.
Middle adulthood (40s to 60s)	Generativity vs. stagnation	Middle-aged people discover a sense of contributing to the world, usually through family and work, or they may feel a lack of purpose.
Late adulthood (late 60s and up)	Integrity vs. despair	Reflecting on their lives, older adults may feel a sense of satisfaction or failure.

Forming an Identity

To refine their sense of identity, adolescents in individualist cultures usually try out different "selves" in different situations. They may act out one self at home, another with friends, and still another at school or online. If two situations overlap—as when a teenager brings new friends home—the discomfort can be considerable (Klimstra et al., 2015). The teen often wonders, "Which self should I be? Which is the real me?" The eventual resolution is a self-definition that unifies the various selves into a consistent and comfortable sense of who one is—an **identity.**

For both adolescents and adults, group identities are often formed by how we differ from those around us. When living in Britain, I [DM] become conscious of my Americanness. When spending time in Hong Kong, I [ND] become conscious of my minority White race. For international students, for those of a minority ethnic or religious group, for gay and transgender people, or for people with a disability, a **social identity** often forms around their distinctiveness.

"Somewhere between the ages of 10 and 13 (depending on how hormone-enhanced their beef was), children entered adolescence, a.k.a. 'the de-cutening.'" —Jon Stewart et al., *Earth (The Book),* 2010

Erikson noticed that some adolescents forge their identity early, simply by adopting their parents' values and expectations. Other adolescents may adopt the identity of a particular peer group—jocks, preps, geeks, band kids, debaters. Traditional, collectivist cultures teach adolescents who they are, rather than encouraging them to decide on their own. Bicultural adolescents form complex identities as they integrate multiple group memberships and their feelings about them (Marks et al., 2011).

ENGAGE 💡 Most young people do develop a sense of contentment with their lives. A question: Which statement best describes you? "I would choose my life the way it is right now" or "I wish I were somebody else"? When American teens answered, 81 percent picked the first, and 19 percent the second (Lyons, 2004). Reflecting on their existence, 75 percent of American collegians say they "discuss religion/spirituality" with friends, "pray," and agree that "we are all spiritual beings" and "search for meaning/purpose in life" (Astin et al., 2004; Bryant & Astin, 2008). This would not surprise Stanford

Nine times out of ten, it's all about peer pressure.

psychologist William Damon and his colleagues (2003), who have contended that a key task of adolescence is to achieve a purpose—a desire to accomplish something personally meaningful that makes a difference to the world beyond oneself.

Several studies indicate that self-esteem typically falls during the early to mid-teen years, and, for girls, depression scores often increase. But then self-image rebounds during the late teens and twenties, and self-esteem gender differences become small (Zuckerman et al., 2016). Late adolescence is also a time when agreeableness and emotional stability scores increase (Klimstra et al., 2009).

 LaunchPad For an interactive self-assessment of your own identity, see **Topic Tutorial: PsychSim6, Who Am I?**

These are the years when many people in industrialized countries begin exploring new opportunities by attending college or working full time. Many college seniors have achieved a clearer identity and a more positive self-concept than they had as first-year students (Waterman, 1988). Those who have achieved a clear sense of identity are less prone to alcohol misuse (Bishop et al., 2005).

Erikson contended that adolescent identity formation (which continues into adulthood) is followed in young adulthood by a developing capacity for **intimacy,** the ability to form emotionally close relationships. When Mihaly Csikszentmihalyi [chick-SENT-me-hi] and Jeremy Hunter (2003) used a beeper to sample the daily experiences of American teens, they found them unhappiest when alone and happiest when with friends. Romantic relationships, which tend to be emotionally intense, are reported by some two in three North American 17-year-olds, but by fewer in collectivist countries such as China (Collins et al., 2009; Li et al., 2010). Those who enjoy high-quality (intimate, supportive) relationships with family and friends tend also to enjoy similarly high-quality romantic relationships in adolescence, which set the stage for healthy adult relationships. Such relationships are, for most of us, a source of great pleasure.

Parent and Peer Relationships

LOQ 4-15 How do parents and peers influence adolescents?

As adolescents in Western cultures seek to form their own identities, they begin to pull away from their parents (Shanahan et al., 2007). The preschooler who can't be close enough to her mother, who loves to touch and cling to her, becomes the 14-year-old who wouldn't be caught dead holding hands with Mom. The transition occurs gradually, but this period is typically a time of diminishing parental influence and growing peer influence. As children, we more readily recognize adult than other children's faces; by adolescence, we display superior recognition for our peers' faces (Picci & Scherf, 2016). Puberty alters attachments and primes perceptions.

As Aristotle long ago recognized, we humans are "the social animal." At all ages, but especially during childhood and adolescence, we seek to fit in with our groups (Harris, 1998, 2002). Teens who start smoking typically have friends who model smoking, suggest its pleasures, and offer cigarettes (Rose et al., 1999, 2003). Part of this peer similarity may result from a *selection effect,* as kids seek out peers with similar attitudes and interests. Those who smoke (or don't) may select as friends those who also smoke (or don't). Put two teens together and their brains become hypersensitive to reward (Albert et al., 2013). This increased activation helps explain why teens take more driving risks when with friends than they do alone (Chein et al., 2011).

By adolescence, parent-child arguments occur more often, usually over mundane things—household chores, bedtime, homework (Tesser et al., 1989). Conflict during the transition to adolescence tends to be greater with first-born than with second-born children, and greater with mothers than with fathers (Burk et al., 2009; Shanahan et al., 2007).

For a minority of parents and their adolescents, differences lead to real splits and great stress (Steinberg & Morris, 2001). But most disagreements are at the level of harmless bickering. With sons, the issues often are behavior problems, such as acting out or

WHO SHALL I BE TODAY? By varying the way they look, adolescents try out different "selves." Although we eventually form a consistent and stable sense of identity, the self we present may change with the situation.

"Self-consciousness, the recognition of a creature by itself as a 'self,' [cannot] exist except in contrast with an 'other,' a something which is not the self."
—C. S. Lewis, *The Problem of Pain,* 1940

"She says she's someone from your past who gave birth to you, and raised you, and sacrificed everything so you could have whatever you wanted."

identity our sense of self; according to Erikson, the adolescent's task is to solidify a sense of self by testing and integrating various roles.

social identity the "we" aspect of our self-concept; the part of our answer to "Who am I?" that comes from our group memberships.

intimacy in Erikson's theory, the ability to form close, loving relationships; a primary developmental task in young adulthood.

"I love u guys." —Emily Keyes' final text message to her parents before dying in a Colorado school shooting, 2006

hygiene; for daughters, the issues commonly involve relationships, such as dating and friendships (Schlomer et al., 2011). In a survey of nearly 6000 adolescents in 10 countries—from Australia to Bangladesh to Turkey—most said they like their parents (Offer et al., 1988). "We usually get along but . . . ," adolescents often report (Galambos, 1992; Steinberg, 1987).

Positive parent-teen relations and positive peer relations often go hand in hand. High school girls who had the most affectionate relationships with their mothers tended also to enjoy the most intimate friendships with girlfriends (Gold & Yanof, 1985). And teens who felt close to their parents have tended to be healthy and happy and to do well in school (Resnick et al., 1997). Of course, we can state this correlation the other way: Misbehaving teens are more likely to have tense relationships with parents and other adults.

Although heredity does much of the heavy lifting in forming individual temperament and personality differences, parents and peers influence teen's behaviors and attitudes. When with peers, teens discount the future and focus more on immediate rewards (O'Brien et al., 2011). Most teens are herd animals, talking, dressing, and acting more like their peers than their parents. What their friends are, they often become, and what "everybody's doing," they often do. Teens' social media use illustrates the power of peer influence. Compared to photos with few likes, teens prefer photos with many other likes. Moreover, when viewing many-liked photos, teens' brains become more active in areas associated with reward processing and imitation (Sherman et al., 2016). Liking and doing what everybody else likes and does feels good.

Part of what everybody's doing is networking—a lot. Teens rapidly adopt social media. U.S. teens typically send 30 text messages daily and average 145 Facebook friends (Lenhart, 2015b). They tweet, post videos to Snapchat, and share pictures on Instagram. Online communication stimulates intimate self-disclosure—both for better (support groups) and for worse (online predators and extremist groups) (Subrahmanyam & Greenfield, 2008; Valkenburg & Peter, 2009; Wilson et al., 2012).

Both online and face-to-face, for those who feel excluded and bullied by their peers, the pain is acute. Most excluded "students suffer in silence. . . . A small number act out in violent ways against their classmates" (Aronson, 2001). The pain of exclusion also persists. In one large study, those who were bullied as children showed poorer physical health and greater psychological distress 40 years later (Takizawa et al., 2014). Peer approval matters.

HOW MUCH CREDIT OR BLAME DO PARENTS DESERVE? In procreation, a woman and a man shuffle their gene decks and deal a life-forming hand to their child-to-be, who is then subjected to countless influences beyond their control. Parents, nonetheless, feel enormous satisfaction in their children's successes or guilt and shame over their failures. They beam over the child who wins trophies and titles. They wonder where they went wrong with the child who is repeatedly in trouble.

Freudian psychiatry and psychology encouraged such ideas by blaming problems from asthma to schizophrenia on "bad mothering." Believing that parents shape their offspring as a potter molds clay, many people praise parents for their children's virtues and blame them for their children's vices, and for the psychological harm that toxic parents presumably inflict on their fragile children. No wonder having and raising children can seem so risky.

"I'm fourteen, Mom, I don't do hugs."

ENGAGE

(ASK YOURSELF)

What are the most positive and the most negative things you remember about your own adolescence? Who do you credit or blame more—your parents or your peers?

But do parents really produce wounded future adults by being (take your pick from the toxic-parenting lists) overbearing—or uninvolved? Pushy—or indecisive? Overprotective—or distant? Should we then blame our parents for our failings, and ourselves for our children's failings? Or does talk of wounding fragile children through normal parental mistakes trivialize the brutality of real abuse?

Parents do matter. But parenting wields its largest effects at the extremes: the abused children who become abusive, the deeply loved but firmly handled who become self-confident and socially competent. The power of the family environment also appears in the remarkable academic and vocational successes of many children of people who leave their home countries, such as those of refugees who fled war-torn Vietnam and Cambodia—successes attributed to close-knit, supportive, even demanding families (Caplan et al., 1992). Asian-Americans and European-Americans often differ in their parenting expectations. An Asian-American

"First, I did things for my parents' approval, then I did things for my parents' disapproval, and now I don't know why I do things."

mother may push her children to do well, but usually not in a way that strains their relationship (Fu & Markus, 2014). Having a supportive "Tiger Mother"—one who pushes her children and works alongside them—tends to motivate children (whose culture prepares them to expect such pushing) to work harder. European-Americans, however, might see this as going overboard and undermining children's motivation (Deal, 2011).

Yet in personality measures, shared environmental influences from the womb onward typically account for less than 10 percent of children's differences. In the words of behavior geneticists Robert Plomin and Denise Daniels (1987; Plomin, 2011), "Two children in the same family are [apart from their shared genes] as different from one another as are pairs of children selected randomly from the population." To developmental psychologist Sandra Scarr (1993), this implied that "parents should be given less credit for kids who turn out great and blamed less for kids who don't." So, knowing that children's personalities are not easily sculpted by parental nurture, perhaps parents can relax and love their children for who they are.

> ## 🔒 RETRIEVE IT • • •   ANSWERS IN APPENDIX E
>
> **RI-3** What is the *selection effect,* and how might it affect a teen's decision to join sports teams at school?

EMERGING ADULTHOOD

LOQ 4-16 What is *emerging adulthood?*

In the Western world, adolescence now roughly corresponds to the teen years. At earlier times, and in other parts of the world today, this slice of life has been much smaller (Baumeister & Tice, 1986). Shortly after sexual maturity, young people would assume adult responsibilities and status. The event might be celebrated with an elaborate initiation—a public rite of passage. The new adult would then work, marry, and have children.

When schooling became compulsory in many Western countries, independence was put on hold until after graduation. Adolescents are now taking more time to establish themselves as adults. In the United States, for example, the average age at first marriage has increased more than 5 years since 1960 (to 29 for men, 27 for women). In 1960, three in four women and two in three men had, by age 30, finished school, left home, become financially independent, married, and had a child. In the early twenty-first century, fewer than half of 30-year-old women and one-third of men were meeting these five milestones (Henig, 2010). In 2016, 15 percent of 25- to 35-year-old Americans—double the 1981 proportion—were living in their parents' home (Fry, 2017).

Together, later independence and earlier sexual maturity have widened the once-brief interlude between biological maturity and social independence (**FIGURE 4.17**). In prosperous communities, the time from 18 to the mid-twenties is an increasingly not-yet-settled phase of life, now often called **emerging adulthood** (Arnett, 2006, 2007; Reitzle, 2006).

emerging adulthood a period from about age 18 to the mid-twenties, when many in Western cultures are no longer adolescents but have not yet achieved full independence as adults.

"Men resemble the times more than they resemble their fathers." —Ancient Arab proverb

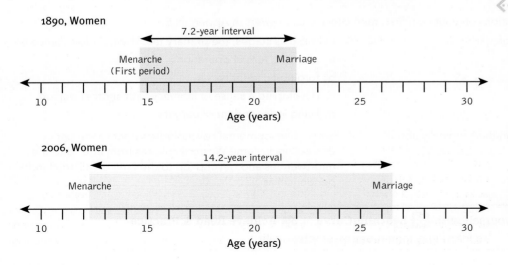

FIGURE 4.17

THE TRANSITION TO ADULTHOOD IS BEING STRETCHED FROM BOTH ENDS In the 1890s, the average interval between a woman's first menstrual period and marriage, which typically marked a transition to adulthood, was about 7 years. By 2006 in industrialized countries, that gap had widened to about 14 years (Finer & Philbin, 2014; Guttmacher Institute, 1994). Although many adults are unmarried, later marriage combines with prolonged education and earlier menarche to help stretch out the transition to adulthood.

ENGAGE

(ASK YOURSELF)

What do you think makes a person an adult? Do you feel like an adult? Why or why not?

"I just don't know what to do with myself in that long stretch after college but before social security."

No longer adolescents, these emerging adults, having not yet assumed full adult responsibilities and independence, feel "in between." After high school, those who enter the job market or go to college may be managing their own time and priorities. Yet they may be doing so from their parents' home, unable to afford their own place and perhaps still emotionally dependent as well. Recognizing today's more gradually emerging adulthood, the U.S. government now allows dependent children up to age 26 to remain on their parents' health insurance (Cohen, 2010).

🔒 RETRIEVE IT • • •

ANSWERS IN APPENDIX E

RI-4 Match the psychosocial development stage (I–VIII) with the issue that Erikson believed we wrestle with at that stage (a–h).

I.	Infancy	a.	Generativity vs. stagnation
II.	Toddlerhood	b.	Integrity vs. despair
III.	Preschool	c.	Initiative vs. guilt
IV.	Elementary school	d.	Intimacy vs. isolation
V.	Adolescence	e.	Identity vs. role confusion
VI.	Young adulthood	f.	Competence vs. inferiority
VII.	Middle adulthood	g.	Trust vs. mistrust
VIII.	Late adulthood	h.	Autonomy vs. shame and doubt

🔒 REVIEW ADOLESCENCE

⤚⤳ Learning Objectives

TEST YOURSELF Answer these repeated Learning Objective Questions on your own (before checking the answers in Appendix D) to improve your retention of the concepts (McDaniel et al., 2009, 2015).

4-12 How is *adolescence* defined, and how do physical changes affect developing teens?

4-13 How did Piaget, Kohlberg, and later researchers describe adolescent cognitive and moral development?

4-14 What are the social tasks and challenges of adolescence?

4-15 How do parents and peers influence adolescents?

4-16 What is *emerging adulthood*?

⤚⤳ Terms and Concepts to Remember

TEST YOURSELF Write down the definition yourself, then check your answer on the referenced page.

adolescence, **p. 141**

puberty, **p. 141**

identity, **p. 147**

social identity, **p. 147**

intimacy, **p. 147**

emerging adulthood, **p. 149**

⤚⤳ Master the Material

TEST YOURSELF Answer the following questions on your own first, then check your answers in Appendix E.

1. Adolescence is marked by the onset of
   a. an identity crisis.
   b. puberty.
   c. moral reasoning.
   d. parent-child conflict.

2. According to Piaget, a person who can think logically about abstractions is in the _____ _____ stage.

3. In Erikson's stages, the primary task during adolescence is
   a. attaining formal operations.
   b. forging an identity.
   c. developing a sense of intimacy with another person.
   d. living independent of parents.

4. Some developmental psychologists refer to the period that occurs in some Western cultures from age 18 to the mid-twenties and beyond (up to the time of full adult independence) as _____ _____.

Continue testing yourself with 📚 **LearningCurve** or 📖 **Achieve Read & Practice** to learn and remember most effectively.

Adulthood

The unfolding of our lives continues across the life span. It is, however, more difficult to generalize about adulthood stages than about life's early years. If you know that James is a 1-year-old and Jamal is a 10-year-old, you could say a great deal about each child. Not so with adults who differ by a similar number of years. The boss may be 30 or 60; the marathon runner may be 20 or 50; the 19-year-old may be a parent who supports a child or a child who receives an allowance. Yet our life courses are in some ways similar. Physically, cognitively, and especially socially, we differ at age 50 from our 25-year-old selves. In the discussion that follows, we recognize these differences and use three terms: *early adulthood* (roughly twenties and thirties), *middle adulthood* (to age 65), and *late adulthood* (the years after 65). Within each of these stages, people will vary widely in physical, psychological, and social development.

PHYSICAL DEVELOPMENT

LOQ 4-17 What physical changes occur during middle and late adulthood?

Like the declining daylight after the summer solstice, our physical abilities—muscular strength, reaction time, sensory keenness, and cardiac output—all begin an almost imperceptible decline in our mid-twenties. Athletes are often the first to notice. Baseball players peak at about age 27—with 60 percent of Most Valuable Player awardees since 1985 coming within 2 years of that age (Silver, 2012). But most of us—especially those of us whose daily lives do not require top physical performance—hardly perceive the early signs of decline.

Physical Changes in Middle Adulthood

Athletes over 40 know all too well that physical decline gradually accelerates. During early and middle adulthood, physical vigor has less to do with age than with a person's health and exercise habits. Many physically fit 50-year-olds run 4 miles with ease, while sedentary 25-year-olds find themselves huffing and puffing up two flights of stairs.

Aging also brings a gradual decline in fertility, especially for women. For a 35- to 39-year-old woman, the chance of getting pregnant after a single act of intercourse is half that of a woman 19 to 26 (Dunson et al., 2002). Men experience a gradual decline in sperm count, testosterone level, and speed of erection and ejaculation. Women experience **menopause** as menstrual cycles end, usually within a few years of age 50. Some may experience distress, as do some men who experience declining virility and physical capacities. But most people age without such problems.

With age, sexual activity lessens. Nevertheless, most men and women remain capable of satisfying sexual activity, and most express satisfaction with their sex life. This was true of 70 percent of Canadians surveyed (ages 40 to 64) and 75 percent of Finns (ages 65 to 74) (Kontula & Haavio-Mannila, 2009; Wright, 2006). In other surveys, 75 percent of respondents reported being sexually active into their eighties. It seems that, for most older people, life's "sexual wisdom" sustains sexual satisfaction even as sexual frequency subsides (Schick et al., 2010). In an American Association of Retired Persons sexuality survey, it was not until age 75 or older that most women and nearly half of men reported little sexual desire (DeLamater, 2012; DeLamater & Sill, 2005). As Alex Comfort (2002, p. 226) jested, "The things that stop you having sex with age are exactly the same as those that stop you riding a bicycle (bad health, thinking it looks silly, no bicycle)."

Physical Changes in Late Adulthood

Is old age "more to be feared than death" (Juvenal, *The Satires*)? Or is life "most delightful when it is on the downward slope" (Seneca, *Epistulae ad Lucilium*)? What is it like to grow old?

menopause the time of natural cessation of menstruation; also refers to the biological changes a woman experiences as her ability to reproduce declines.

ENGAGE (ASK YOURSELF)

Imagining the future, how do you think you might change? How might you stay the same?

ENGAGE How old does a person have to be before you think of him or her as old? Depends on who you ask. For 18- to 29-year-olds, 67 was old. For those 60 and over, old was 76 (Yankelovich Partners, 1995).

ADULT ABILITIES VARY WIDELY
George Blair was, at age 92, the world's oldest barefoot water skier. He is shown here in 2002 when he first set the record, at age 87. (He died in 2013 at age 98.)

Rick Doyle/Corbis Documentary/Getty Images

The New Yorker Collection, 1999 Tom Cheney from cartoonbank.com

"Happy fortieth. I'll take the muscle tone in your upper arms, the girlish timbre of your voice, your amazing tolerance for caffeine, and your ability to digest french fries. The rest of you can stay."

"For some reason, possibly to save ink, the restaurants had started printing their menus in letters the height of bacteria." —Dave Barry, *Dave Barry Turns Fifty,* 1998

SUITING UP FOR OLD AGE A long life is a gift. To reach old age, it takes good genes, a nurturing environment, and a little luck. New technology allows you to put yourself in your elders' shoes. In these special suits, younger people can hear, see, and move as if they were 85 years old.

Nicole Bengiveno/The New York Times/Redux Pictures

SENSORY ABILITIES, STRENGTH, AND STAMINA Although physical decline begins in early adulthood, we are not usually acutely aware of it until later in life, when the stairs get steeper, the print gets smaller, and other people seem to mumble more. Muscle strength, reaction time, and stamina diminish in late adulthood. As a lifelong basketball player, I [DM] find myself increasingly not racing for that loose ball. But even diminished vigor is sufficient for normal activities.

With age, visual sharpness diminishes, as does distance perception and adaptation to light-level changes. The eye's pupil shrinks and its lens becomes less transparent, reducing the amount of light reaching the retina: A 65-year-old retina receives only about one-third as much light as its 20-year-old counterpart (Kline & Schieber, 1985). Thus, to see as well as a 20-year-old when reading or driving, a 65-year-old needs three times as much light—a reason for buying cars with untinted windshields. This also explains why older people sometimes ask younger people, "Don't you need better light for reading?"

The senses of smell, hearing, and touch also diminish. In Wales, teens' loitering around a convenience store has been discouraged by a device that emits an aversive high-pitched sound almost no one over 30 can hear (Lyall, 2005).

HEALTH As people age, they care less about what their bodies look like and more about how their bodies function. For those growing older, there is both bad and good news about health. The bad news: The body's disease-fighting immune system weakens, making older adults more susceptible to life-threatening ailments such as cancer and pneumonia. The good news: Thanks partly to a lifetime's accumulation of antibodies, people over 65 suffer fewer short-term ailments, such as common flu and cold viruses. One study found they were half as likely as 20-year-olds and one-fifth as likely as preschoolers to suffer upper respiratory flu each year (National Center for Health Statistics, 1990).

THE AGING BRAIN Up to the teen years, we process information with greater and greater speed (Fry & Hale, 1996; Kail, 1991). But compared with teens and young adults, older people take a bit more time to react, to solve perceptual puzzles, even to remember names (Bashore et al., 1997; Verhaeghen & Salthouse, 1997). At video games, most 70-year-olds are no match for a 20-year-old. This processing lag can also have deadly consequences (Aichele et al., 2016). As **FIGURE 4.18** indicates, fatal accident rates per mile driven increase sharply after age 75. By age 85, they exceed the 16-year-old level. Older drivers appear to focus well on the road ahead, but attend less to vehicles approaching from the side (Pollatsek et al., 2012). Nevertheless, because older people drive less, they account for fewer than 10 percent of crashes (Coughlin et al., 2004).

Brain regions important to memory begin to atrophy during aging (Fraser et al., 2015; Ritchie et al., 2015). The blood-brain barrier also breaks down beginning in the hippocampus, which furthers cognitive decline (Montagne et al., 2015). No wonder older adults feel even older after taking a memory test: It's like "aging 5 years in 5 minutes," joked one research team (Hughes et al., 2013). In early adulthood, a small, gradual net loss of brain cells begins, contributing by age 80 to a brain-weight reduction of 5 percent or so. Earlier, we noted that late-maturing frontal lobes, which help us override our undesirable urges,

FIGURE 4.18

AGE AND DRIVER FATALITIES Slowing reactions contribute to increased accident risks among those 75 and older, and older adults' greater fragility increases their risk of death when accidents happen (NHTSA, 2000). Would you favor driver exams based on performance, not age, to screen out those whose slow reactions or sensory impairments indicate accident risk?

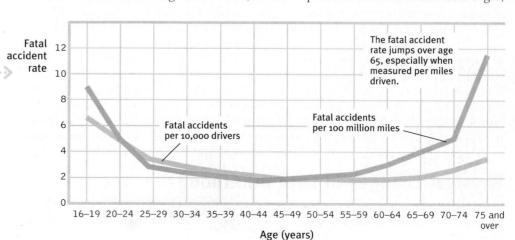

help account for teen impulsivity. Late in life, some of that impulsiveness often returns as those same frontal lobes begin to atrophy, seemingly explaining older people's occasional blunt questions ("Have you put on weight?") or inappropriate comments (von Hippel, 2007, 2015). But good news: There is still some plasticity in the aging brain, which partly compensates for what it loses by recruiting and reorganizing neural networks (Park & McDonough, 2013). During memory tasks, for example, the left frontal lobes are especially active in young adult brains, while older adult brains use both left and right frontal lobes.

EXERCISE AND AGING And more good news: Exercise slows aging, as shown in studies of identical twin pairs in which only one twin exercised (Iso-Markku et al., 2016; Rottensteiner et al., 2015). Midlife and older adults who do more exercising and less TV watching tend to be mentally quick older adults (Hoang et al., 2016). Physical exercise not only enhances muscles, bones, and energy and helps prevent obesity and heart disease, it maintains the *telomeres* that protect the chromosome ends and even appears to slow the progression of Alzheimer's disease (Kivipelto & Håkansson, 2017; Loprinzi et al., 2015; Smith et al., 2014).

Exercise also stimulates brain cell development and neural connections, thanks perhaps to increased oxygen and nutrient flow (Erickson et al., 2013; Fleischman et al., 2015; Pereira et al., 2007).

Sedentary older adults randomly assigned to aerobic exercise programs exhibit enhanced memory, sharpened judgment, and reduced risk of severe cognitive decline (Raji et al., 2016; Smith, 2016). In aging brains, exercise reduces brain shrinkage (Gow et al., 2012). It promotes neurogenesis (the birth of new nerve cells) in the hippocampus, a brain region important for memory (Erickson, 2009; Pereira et al., 2007). And it increases the cellular mitochondria that help power both muscles and brain cells (Steiner et al., 2011). We are more likely to rust from disuse than to wear out from overuse. Fit bodies support fit minds.

COGNITIVE DEVELOPMENT
Aging and Memory

LOQ 4-18 How does memory change with age?

Among the most intriguing developmental psychology questions is whether adult cognitive abilities, such as memory, intelligence, and creativity, parallel the gradually accelerating decline of physical abilities.

As we age, we remember some things well. Looking back in later life, adults asked to recall the one or two most important events over the last half-century tend to name events from their teens or twenties (Conway et al., 2005; Rubin et al., 1998). They also display this "reminiscence bump" when asked to name their all-time favorite music, movies, and athletes (Janssen et al., 2012). Whatever people experience around this time of life—the Vietnam war, the 9/11 terrorist attacks, the election of the first Black U.S. president—becomes pivotal (Pillemer, 1998; Schuman & Scott, 1989). Our teens and twenties hold so many memorable "firsts"—first kiss, first job, first day at college or university, first meeting our romantic partner.

Early adulthood is indeed a peak time for some types of learning and remembering. In one test of recall, people watched video clips as 14 strangers said their names, using a common format: "Hi, I'm Larry" (Crook & West, 1990). Then those strangers reappeared and gave additional details. For example, they said, "I'm from Philadelphia," providing more visual *and* voice cues for remembering the person's name. As **FIGURE 4.19** shows, after a second and third replay of the introductions, everyone remembered more names, but younger adults consistently surpassed older adults. How well older people remember depends in part on the task. In another experiment, when asked to *recognize* 24 words they had earlier tried to memorize, older adults showed no memory decline. When asked to *recall* that information without clues, however, the decline was greater (**FIGURE 4.20**).

In our capacity to learn and remember, as in other areas of development, we show individual differences. Younger adults vary in their abilities to learn and remember, but 70-year-olds vary much more. "Differences between the most and least able 70-year-olds

Most stairway falls taken by older people occur on the top step, precisely where the person typically descends from a window-lit hallway into the darker stairwell (Fozard & Popkin, 1978). Our knowledge of aging could be used to design environments that would reduce such accidents (National Research Council, 1990).

"I've been working out for six months, but all my gains have been in cognitive function."

"I am still learning." —Michelangelo, 1560, at age 85

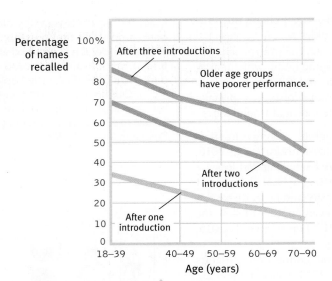

FIGURE 4.19

TESTS OF RECALL Recalling new names introduced once, twice, or three times is easier for younger adults than for older ones. (Data from Crook & West, 1990.)

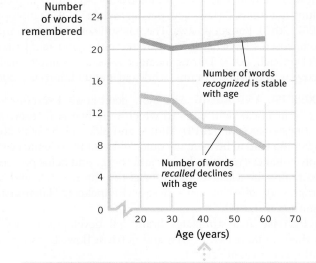

FIGURE 4.20

RECALL AND RECOGNITION IN ADULTHOOD In this experiment, the ability to *recall* new information declined during early and middle adulthood, but the ability to *recognize* new information did not. (Data from Schonfield & Robertson, 1966.)

become much greater than between the most and least able 50-year-olds," reports Oxford researcher Patrick Rabbitt (2006). Some 70-year-olds perform below nearly all 20-year-olds; other 70-year-olds match or outdo the average 20-year-old.

No matter how quick or slow we are, remembering seems also to depend on the type of information we are trying to retrieve. If the information is meaningless—nonsense syllables or unimportant events—then the older we are, the more errors we are likely to make. If the information is *meaningful,* older people's rich web of existing knowledge will help them to hold it. But they may take longer than younger adults to *produce* the words and things they know. Older adults also more often experience tip-of-the-tongue forgetting (Ossher et al., 2012). Quick-thinking game show winners are usually young or middle-aged adults (Burke & Shafto, 2004).

Maintaining Mental Abilities

Psychologists who study the aging mind debate whether "brain fitness" computer-based training programs can build mental muscles and stave off cognitive decline. Our brains remain plastic throughout life (Gutchess, 2014). So, can exercising our brains on a "cognitive treadmill"—with memory, visual tracking, and problem-solving exercises—avert losing our minds? "At every point in life, the brain's natural plasticity gives us the ability to improve . . . function," said one neuroscientist-entrepreneur (Merzenich, 2007). One analysis of cognitive training programs showed that they consistently improved scores on tests related to their training (Simons et al., 2016).

Based on such findings, some computer game makers have been marketing daily brain-exercise programs for older adults. But other researchers, after reviewing all the available studies, advise caution (Melby-Lervåg et al., 2016). One team of experts reported "extensive evidence that brain-training interventions improve performance on the trained tasks, less evidence that such interventions improve performance on closely related tasks, and little evidence that training enhances performance on distantly related tasks or that training improves everyday cognitive performance" (Simons et al., 2016, p. 103). As researcher Zach Hambrick (2014) explains, "Play a video game and you'll get better at that video game, and maybe at very similar video games"—but not at driving a car or filling out your tax return.

cross-sectional study research that compares people of different ages at the same point in time.

longitudinal study research that follows and retests the same people over time.

social clock the culturally preferred timing of social events such as marriage, parenthood, and retirement.

In 2016, the maker of one prominent brain-training program, Lumosity, was fined $2 million for deceiving customers about the program's supposed benefits. "Lumosity preyed on consumers' fears about age-related cognitive decline," said the Federal Trade Commission's Jessica Rich (FTC, 2016). "But Lumosity simply did not have the science to back up its ads."

Chapter 9 explores another dimension of cognitive development: intelligence. As we will see, **cross-sectional studies** and **longitudinal studies** have identified mental abilities that do and do not change as people age. Age is less a predictor of memory and intelligence than is proximity to death. Knowing whether someone is 8 months or 8 years from a natural death, regardless of age, gives a clue to that person's mental ability. In the last three or four years of life and especially as death approaches, negative feelings and cognitive decline typically increase (Vogel et al., 2013; Wilson et al., 2007). Researchers call this near-death drop *terminal decline* (Backman & MacDonald, 2006). Our goals also shift: We're driven less to learn and more to connect socially (Carstensen, 2011).

SOCIAL DEVELOPMENT

LOQ 4-19 What themes and influences mark our social journey from early adulthood to death?

Many differences between younger and older adults are created by significant life events. A new job means new relationships, new expectations, and new demands. Marriage brings the joy of intimacy and the stress of merging two lives. The three years surrounding the birth of a child bring increased life satisfaction for most parents (Dyrdal & Lucas, 2011). The death of a loved one creates an irreplaceable loss. Do these adult life events shape a sequence of life changes?

Adulthood's Ages and Stages

As people enter their forties, they undergo a transition to middle adulthood, a time when they realize that life will soon be mostly behind instead of ahead of them. Some psychologists have argued that for many the *midlife transition* is a crisis, a time of great struggle, regret, or even feeling struck down by life. The popular image of the midlife crisis—an early-forties man who forsakes his family for a younger romantic partner and a hot sports car—is more a myth than reality. Unhappiness, job dissatisfaction, marital dissatisfaction, divorce, anxiety, and suicide do *not* surge during the early forties (Hunter & Sundel, 1989; Mroczek & Kolarz, 1998). Divorce, for example, is most common among those in their twenties, suicide among those in their seventies and eighties. One study of emotional instability in nearly 10,000 men and women found "not the slightest evidence" that distress peaks anywhere in the midlife age range (McCrae & Costa, 1990).

For the 1 in 4 adults who report experiencing a life crisis, the trigger is not age but a major event, such as illness, divorce, or job loss (Lachman, 2004). Some middle-aged adults describe themselves as a "sandwich generation," simultaneously supporting their aging parents and their emerging adult children or grandchildren (Riley & Bowen, 2005).

Life events trigger transitions to new life stages at varying ages. The **social clock**—the definition of "the right time" to leave home, get a job, marry, have children, or retire— varies from era to era and culture to culture. The once-rigid sequence has loosened; the social clock still ticks, but people feel freer about being out of sync with it.

Even *chance events* can have lasting significance, by deflecting us down one road rather than another. Albert Bandura (1982, 2005) recalls the ironic true story of a book editor who came to one of Bandura's lectures on the "Psychology of Chance Encounters and Life Paths"—and ended up marrying the woman who happened to sit next to him. The sequence that led to my [DM's] authoring this book (which was not my idea) began with my being seated near, and getting to know, a distinguished colleague at an international conference. The road to my [ND's] co-authoring this book began in a similarly unplanned manner: After stumbling on an article about my professional life, DM invited me to visit his college. There, we began a conversation that resulted in our collaboration. Chance events can change our lives.

LaunchPad See the **Video: Longitudinal and Cross-Sectional Studies** for a helpful tutorial animation.

"The sudden knowledge of the fragility of his life narrowed his focus and altered his desires. . . . It made him visit with his grandchildren more often, put in an extra trip to see his family in India, and tamp down new ventures." —Atul Gawande, *Being Mortal: Medicine and What Matters in the End*, 2014, describing his father's terminal condition and the way it changed his perspective

"The important events of a person's life are the products of chains of highly improbable occurrences." —Joseph Traub, "Traub's Law," 2003

Adulthood's Commitments

Two basic aspects of our lives dominate adulthood. Erik Erikson called them *intimacy* (forming close relationships) and *generativity* (being productive and supporting future generations). Sigmund Freud (1935/1960) put this more simply: The healthy adult, he said, is one who can *love* and *work*.

LOVE We typically flirt, fall in love, and commit—one person at a time. "Pair-bonding is a trademark of the human animal," observed anthropologist Helen Fisher (1993). From an evolutionary perspective, relatively monogamous pairing makes sense: Parents who cooperated to nurture their children to maturity were more likely to have their genes passed along to posterity than were parents who didn't.

Adult bonds of love are most satisfying and enduring when marked by a similarity of interests and values, a sharing of emotional and material support, and intimate self-disclosure. And for better or for worse, our standards have risen over the years: We now hope not only for an enduring bond, but also for a mate who is a wage earner, caregiver, intimate friend, and warm and responsive lover (Finkel, 2017). There also appears to be "vow power." Straight and gay relationships sealed with commitment more often endure (Balsam et al., 2008; Rosenfeld, 2014). Such bonds are especially likely to last when couples marry after age 20 and are well educated. Compared with their counterparts of 30 years ago, people in Western countries *are* better educated and marrying later (Wolfinger, 2015). These trends may help explain why the American divorce rate, which surged from 1960 to 1980, has since slightly declined. Canadian divorce rates since the 1980s have followed a similar pattern (Statistics Canada, 2011).

Historically, couples have met at school, on the job, or through friends and family. Thanks to the internet, many couples now meet online—as have nearly a quarter of heterosexual couples and some two-thirds of same-sex couples in one recent national survey (**FIGURE 4.21**).

Might test-driving life together minimize divorce risk? In Europe, Canada, and the United States, those who live together before marriage (and especially before engagement) have had *higher* rates of divorce and marital dysfunction than those who did not (Goodwin et al., 2010; Jose et al., 2010; Manning & Cohen, 2012; Stanley et al., 2010). Three factors contribute. First, those who live together tend to be initially less committed to the ideal of enduring marriage. Second, they may become even less marriage-supporting while living together. Third, it's more awkward to break up with a cohabiting partner than with a dating partner, leading some cohabiters to marry someone "they otherwise would have left behind" (Stanley & Rhoades, 2016a,b).

Although there is more variety in relationships today, the institution of marriage endures. Ninety-five percent of Americans have either married or want to (Newport & Wilke, 2013). In Western countries, what counts as a "very important" reason to marry? Among Americans, 31 percent say financial stability, and 93 percent say love (Cohn, 2013). And marriage is a predictor of happiness, sexual satisfaction, income, and physical and mental health (Scott et al., 2010). National Opinion Research Center surveys of more than

LOVE Intimacy, attachment, commitment—love by whatever name—is central to healthy and happy adulthood.

Blend Images/Alamy

FIGURE 4.21

THE CHANGING WAY AMERICANS MEET THEIR PARTNERS A national survey of 2452 straight couples and 462 gay and lesbian couples reveals the increasing role of the internet. (Data from Rosenfeld, 2013; Rosenfeld & Thomas, 2012.)

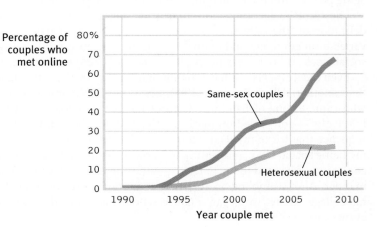

50,000 heterosexual Americans between 1972 and 2014 reveal that 40 percent of married adults, and only 23 percent of unmarried adults, have reported being "very happy." Lesbian couples, too, report greater well-being than those who are single (Peplau & Fingerhut, 2007; Wayment & Peplau, 1995). Moreover, neighborhoods with high marriage rates typically have low rates of social pathologies such as crime, delinquency, and emotional disorders among children (Myers & Scanzoni, 2005).

Relationships that last are not always devoid of conflict. Some couples fight but also shower each other with affection. Other couples never raise their voices yet also seldom praise each other or nuzzle. Both styles can last. After observing the interactions of 2000 couples, John Gottman (1994) reported one indicator of marital success: at least a five-to-one ratio of positive to negative interactions. Stable marriages provide five times more instances of smiling, touching, complimenting, and laughing than of sarcasm, criticism, and insults. So, if you want to predict which couples will stay together, don't pay attention to how passionately they are in love. The pairs who make it are more often those who refrain from putting down their partners. To prevent a cancerous negativity, successful couples learn to fight fair (to state feelings without insulting) and to steer conflict away from chaos with comments like "I know it's not your fault" or "I'll just be quiet for a moment and listen."

Often, love bears children. For most people, this most enduring of life changes is a happy event—one that adds meaning, joy, and occasional stress (Nelson et al., 2013; Witters, 2014). "I feel an overwhelming love for my children unlike anything I feel for anyone else," said 93 percent of American mothers in a national survey (Erickson & Aird, 2005). Many fathers feel the same. A few weeks after the birth of my first child I [DM] was suddenly struck by a realization: "So *this* is how my parents felt about me!"

When children begin to absorb time, money, and emotional energy, satisfaction with the marriage itself may decline (Doss et al., 2009). This is especially likely among employed women who, more than they expected, may also carry the burden of doing more chores at home. Putting effort into creating an equitable relationship can thus pay double dividends: greater satisfaction, which breeds better parent-child relations (Erel & Burman, 1995).

Eventually, children leave home. This departure is a significant and sometimes difficult event. But for most people, an empty nest is a happy place (Adelmann et al., 1989; Gorchoff et al., 2008). Many parents experience a "postlaunch honeymoon," especially if they maintain close relationships with their children (White & Edwards, 1990). As Daniel Gilbert (2006) said, "The only known symptom of 'empty nest syndrome' is increased smiling."

WORK For many adults, the answer to "Who are you?" depends a great deal on the answer to "What do you do?" For women and men, choosing a career path is difficult, especially during bad economic times. Even in the best of times, few students in their first two years of college or university can predict their later careers.

In the end, happiness is about having work that fits your interests and provides you with a sense of competence and accomplishment. It is having a close, supportive companion, or family and friends, who notice and cheer your accomplishments (Gable et al., 2006). And for some, it includes having children who love you and whom you love and feel proud of.

What do you think? Does marriage correlate with happiness because marital support and intimacy breed happiness, because happy people more often marry and stay married, or both?

"Our love for children is so unlike any other human emotion. I fell in love with my babies so quickly and profoundly, almost completely independently of their particular qualities. And yet 20 years later I was (more or less) happy to see them go—I had to be happy to see them go. We are totally devoted to them when they are little and yet the most we can expect in return when they grow up is that they regard us with bemused and tolerant affection." —Developmental psychologist Alison Gopnik, "The Supreme Infant," 2010

"To understand your parents' love, bear your own children." —Chinese proverb

LaunchPad Play the role of a researcher exploring the connection between parenting and happiness by engaging online with **Immersive Learning: How Would You Know If Having Children Relates to Being Happier?**

JOB SATISFACTION AND LIFE SATISFACTION Work can provide us with a sense of identity and competence, and opportunities for accomplishment. Perhaps this is why challenging and interesting occupations enhance people's happiness. For more on work, including discovering your own strengths, see Appendix B: Psychology at Work.

Well-Being Across the Life Span

LOQ 4-20 How does our well-being change across the life span?

To live is to grow older. This moment marks the oldest you have ever been and the young-est you will henceforth be. That means we all can look back with satisfaction or regret, and forward with hope or dread. When asked what they would have done differently if they could relive their lives, people's most common answer has been "taken my education more seriously and worked harder at it" (Kinnier & Metha, 1989; Roese & Summerville, 2005). Other regrets—"I should have told my father I loved him," "I regret that I never went to Europe"—have also focused less on mistakes made than on the things one *failed* to do (Gilovich & Medvec, 1995).

But prior to the very end, the over-65 years are not notably unhappy. Self-esteem remains stable (Wagner et al., 2013). The Gallup Organization asked 658,038 people worldwide to rate their lives on a ladder from 0 ("the worst possible life") to 10 ("the best possible life"). Age—from 15 to over 90 years—gave no clue to life satisfaction (Morrison et al., 2014). Positive feelings, supported by enhanced emotional control, tend to grow after midlife, and negative feelings subside (Stone et al., 2010; Urry & Gross, 2010). Compared with younger Chinese and American adults, for example, older adults are *more* attentive to positive news (Isaacowitz, 2012; Wang et al., 2015a).

Compared with teens and young adults, older adults do, however, tend to have a smaller social network, with fewer friendships and greater loneliness (Luhmann & Hawkley, 2016; Wagner et al., 2016). Like people of all ages, older adults are happiest when not alone (**FIGURE 4.22**). Older adults experience fewer problems in their relationships—less attachment anxiety, stress, and anger (Chopik et al., 2013; Fingerman & Charles, 2010; Stone et al., 2010). With age, we become more stable and more accepting (Carstensen et al., 2011; Shallcross et al., 2013).

The aging brain may help nurture these positive feelings. Brain scans of older adults show that the amygdala, a neural processing center for emotions, responds less actively to negative events (but not to positive events) (Mather et al., 2004). Brain-wave reactions to negative images also diminish with age (Kisley et al., 2007). As we reach the later chapters of our lives, our brain enables a contented culmination (Mather, 2016).

Moreover, at all ages, the bad feelings we associate with negative events fade faster than do the good feelings we associate with positive events (Walker et al., 2003). This

"When you were born, you cried and the world rejoiced. Live your life in a manner so that when you die the world cries and you rejoice." —Native American proverb

"Still married after all these years?
No mystery.
We are each other's habit,
And each other's history."

—Judith Viorst, "The Secret of Staying Married," 2007

"At 20 we worry about what others think of us. At 40 we don't care what others think of us. At 60 we discover they haven't been thinking about us at all." —Anonymous

FIGURE 4.22

HUMANS ARE SOCIAL CREATURES
Both younger and older adults report greater happiness when spending time with others. (Note this correlation could also reflect happier people being more social.) (Gallup survey data reported by Crabtree, 2011.)

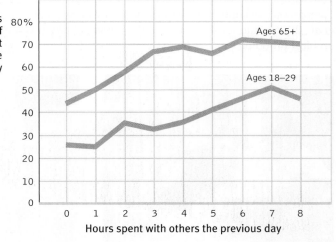

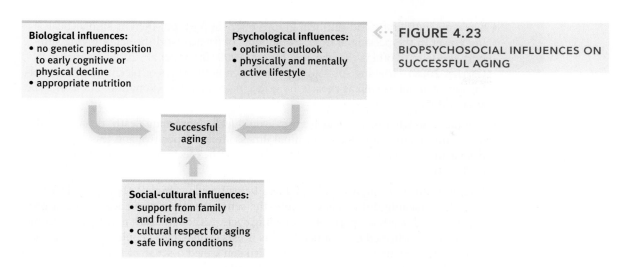

FIGURE 4.23
BIOPSYCHOSOCIAL INFLUENCES ON SUCCESSFUL AGING

Biological influences:
• no genetic predisposition to early cognitive or physical decline
• appropriate nutrition

Psychological influences:
• optimistic outlook
• physically and mentally active lifestyle

Successful aging

Social-cultural influences:
• support from family and friends
• cultural respect for aging
• safe living conditions

leaves most older people with the comforting feeling that life, on balance, has been mostly good. Thanks to biological, psychological, and social-cultural influences, more and more people flourish into later life (**FIGURE 4.23**).

"The best thing about being 100 is *no peer pressure.*" —Lewis W. Kuester, 2005, on turning 100

🔒 **RETRIEVE IT • • •**   *ANSWERS IN APPENDIX E*

RI-2 What are some of the most significant challenges and rewards of growing old?

Death and Dying

LOQ 4-21 A loved one's death triggers what range of reactions?

Warning: If you begin reading the next paragraph, you will die.

But of course, if you hadn't read this, you would still die in due time. "Time is a great teacher," noted the nineteenth-century composer Hector Berlioz, "but unfortunately it kills all its pupils." Death is our inevitable end. We enter the world with a wail, and usually leave it in silence.

Most of us will also cope with the deaths of relatives and friends. For most people, the most difficult separation they will experience is the death of a partner—a loss suffered by four times more women than men. Maintaining everyday engagements and relationships increases resilience in the face of such a loss (Infurna & Luthar, 2016a). But for some, grief is severe, especially when a loved one's death comes suddenly and before its expected time on the social clock. I [ND] experienced this firsthand when a tragic accident claimed the life of my 60-year-old mother. Such tragedies may trigger a year or more of memory-laden mourning that eventually subsides to a mild depression (Lehman et al., 1987).

For some, the loss is unbearable. One Danish long-term study of more than 1 million people found that about 17,000 of them had suffered the death of a child under 18. In the 5 years following that death, 3 percent of them had a first psychiatric hospitalization, a 67 percent higher rate than among other parents (Li et al., 2005).

Reactions to a loved one's death range more widely than most suppose. Some cultures encourage public weeping and wailing; others hide grief. Within any culture, individuals differ. Given similar losses, some people grieve hard and long, others less so (Ott et al., 2007). Contrary to popular misconceptions, however:

"Love—why, I'll tell you what love is: It's you at 75 and her at 71, each of you listening for the other's step in the next room, each afraid that a sudden silence, a sudden cry, could mean a lifetime's talk is over." —Brian Moore, *The Luck of Ginger Coffey*, 1960

• Terminally ill and bereaved people do not go through identical predictable stages, such as denial before anger (Friedman & James, 2008; Nolen-Hoeksema & Larson, 1999).

• Those who express the strongest grief immediately do not purge their grief more quickly (Bonanno & Kaltman, 1999; Wortman & Silver, 1989). But grieving parents who try to protect their partner by "staying strong" and not discussing their child's death may actually prolong the grieving (Stroebe et al., 2013).

• Bereavement therapy and self-help groups offer support, but there is similar healing power in the passing of time, the support of friends, and the act of giving support and help to others (Baddeley & Singer, 2009; Brown et al., 2008; Neimeyer & Carrier, 2009). Grieving spouses who talk often with others or receive grief counseling adjust about as well as those who grieve more privately (Bonanno, 2004; Stroebe et al., 2005).

• Compared to what people *imagine* they would feel when facing death, those actually facing imminent death due to terminal illness are more positive and less sad and despairing. In the researchers' words, "Dying is unexpectedly positive" (Goranson et al., 2017).

Facing death with dignity and openness helps people complete the life cycle with a sense of life's meaningfulness and unity—the sense that their existence has been good and that life and death are parts of an ongoing cycle. Although death may be unwelcome, life itself can be affirmed even at death. This is especially so for people who review their lives not with despair but with what Erik Erikson called a sense of *integrity*—a feeling that one's life has been meaningful and worthwhile.

🔒 REVIEW ADULTHOOD

⟩⟩ Learning Objectives

TEST YOURSELF Answer these repeated Learning Objective Questions on your own (before checking the answers in Appendix D) to improve your retention of the concepts (McDaniel et al., 2009, 2015).

4-17 What physical changes occur during middle and late adulthood?

4-18 How does memory change with age?

4-19 What themes and influences mark our social journey from early adulthood to death?

4-20 How does our well-being change across the life span?

4-21 A loved one's death triggers what range of reactions?

⟩⟩ Terms and Concepts to Remember

TEST YOURSELF Write down the definition yourself, then check your answer on the referenced page.

menopause, **p. 151**

cross-sectional study, **p. 154**

longitudinal study, **p. 154**

social clock, **p. 154**

⟩⟩ Experience the Testing Effect

TEST YOURSELF Answer the following questions on your own first, then check your answers in Appendix E.

1. By age 65, a person would be most likely to experience a cognitive decline in the ability to
   a. recall and list all the important terms and concepts in a chapter.
   b. select the correct definition in a multiple-choice question.
   c. recall their own birth date.
   d. practice a well-learned skill, such as knitting.

2. How do cross-sectional and longitudinal studies differ?

3. Freud defined the healthy adult as one who is able to love and work. Erikson agreed, observing that the adult struggles to attain intimacy and _____.

4. Contrary to what many people assume,
   a. older people are significantly less happy than adolescents are.
   b. we become less happy as we move from our teen years into midlife.
   c. positive feelings tend to grow after midlife.
   d. those whose children have recently left home—the empty nesters—have the lowest level of happiness of all groups.

Continue testing yourself with 📖 **LearningCurve** or 📖 **Achieve Read & Practice** to learn and remember most effectively.

Sex, Gender, and Sexuality

CHAPTER
5

Cultures change, and their ideas about gender change, too. Several decades apart, this text's two authors had similar experiences with different outcomes. In 1972, as the young chair of our psychology department, I [DM] was proud to make the announcement: We had concluded our search for a new colleague. We had found just who we were looking for—a bright, warm, enthusiastic woman about to receive her Ph.D. in developmental psychology. The vote was unanimous. Alas, our elderly chancellor rejected our recommendation. "As a mother of a preschooler," he said, "she should be home with her child, *not* working full time." No amount of pleading or arguing (for example, that it might be possible to parent a child while employed) could change his mind. So, with a heavy heart, I drove to her city to explain, face to face, my embarrassment in being able to offer her only a temporary position.

This case ended well. She accepted the temporary position and quickly became a beloved, tenured colleague who went on to found our college's women's studies program. Today, she and I marvel at the swift transformation in our culture's thinking about gender.

In 2011, I [ND] experienced something quite different. We, too, were concluding our search for a new colleague. Our department faculty had assessed several candidates, and the top two vote-getters were a man and a woman. Our faculty hiring committee would make the final choice. Before they announced their decision, a senior committee member spoke out. "Look around the table. We're all men. We need to consider that." The accomplished woman was offered the position.

Image Source/Alamy Stock Photo

Clearly, social and cultural factors influence our gender expectations. But how do nature and nurture interact to form our unique gender identities? How are we alike as males and females, and how and why do we differ? This chapter explores these issues. We'll also gain insight about the psychology and biology of sexual attraction and intimacy. And as part of the journey, we'll see how evolutionary psychologists explain our sexuality.

Let's start at the beginning. What is gender and how does it develop? ▶

⊙→ Gender Development

LEARNING OBJECTIVE QUESTION (LOQ)

5-1   How does the meaning of *gender* differ from the meaning of *sex*?

We humans share an irresistible urge to organize our worlds into simple categories. Among the ways we classify people—as tall or short, dull or smart, cheerful or churlish—one stands out. Immediately after your birth (or before), everyone wanted to know, "Boy or girl?" Your parents may have offered clues with pink or blue clothing. Their answer described your **sex,** your biological status, defined by your chromosomes and anatomy. For most people, those biological traits help define their assigned **gender,** their culture's expectations about what it means to be a man or a woman.

Simply said, your body defines your sex; your mind defines your gender. But your mind's understanding of gender arises from the interplay between your biology and your experiences (Eagly & Wood, 2013). Before we consider that interplay in more detail, let's take a closer look at some ways that males and females are both similar and different.

HOW ARE WE ALIKE? HOW DO WE DIFFER?

LOQ 5-2   What are some ways in which males and females tend to be alike and to differ?

Whether male or female, each of us receives 23 chromosomes from our mother and 23 from our father. Of those 46 chromosomes, 45 are *unisex*—the same for males and females. Both men and women needed to survive, reproduce, and avoid predators, and so today we are in most ways alike. Survival for both men and women involved traveling long distances, and in today's ultramarathons men and women often have similar finishing times. Identify yourself as male or female and you give no clues to your vocabulary, happiness, or ability to see, learn, and remember. Males and females, on average, have comparable creativity and intelligence and feel the same emotions and longings (Hyde, 2014). Our "opposite" sex is, in reality, our very similar sex.

But in some areas, males and females do differ, and differences command attention. Some oft-noted differences (like the difference in self-esteem shown in **FIGURE 5.1**) are actually quite modest (Zell et al., 2015). Others are more striking. The average girl enters puberty about a year earlier than the average boy, and her life expectancy is 5 years longer. She expresses emotions more freely, smiling and crying more, and, in Facebook updates, more often expresses "love" and being "sooo excited!!!" (Fischer & LaFrance, 2015; Schwartz et al., 2013). She can detect fainter odors, receives offers of help more often, and can become sexually re-aroused sooner after orgasm. She also has twice the risk of developing depression and anxiety, and 10 times the risk of developing an eating disorder. Yet the average man is 4 times more likely to die by suicide or to develop an alcohol use disorder. His "more likely" list also includes autism spectrum disorder, color-deficient vision, and attention-deficit/hyperactivity disorder (ADHD). And as an adult, he is more at risk for antisocial personality disorder. Male or female, each has its own heightened risks.

Gender similarities and differences appear throughout this book, but for now let's take a closer look at three gender differences. Although individuals vary widely, the *average* male and female differ in aggression, social power, and social connectedness.

Pink and blue baby outfits illustrate how cultural norms vary and change. "The generally accepted rule is pink for the boy and blue for the girl," declared the *Earnshaw's Infants' Department* in 1918 (Frassanito & Pettorini, 2008). "Pink being a more decided and stronger color is more suitable for the boy, while blue, which is more delicate and dainty, is prettier for the girls."

sex in psychology, the biologically influenced characteristics by which people define *male* and *female*.

gender in psychology, the socially influenced characteristics by which people define *boy, girl, man,* and *woman*.

aggression any physical or verbal behavior intended to harm someone physically or emotionally.

relational aggression an act of aggression (physical or verbal) intended to harm a person's relationship or social standing.

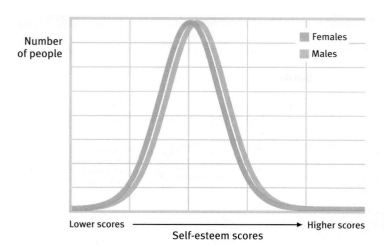

FIGURE 5.1

MUCH ADO ABOUT A SMALL DIFFERENCE IN SELF-ESTEEM These two normal distributions differ by the approximate magnitude (0.21 standard deviation) of the sex difference in self-esteem, averaged over all available samples (Hyde, 2005). Moreover, such comparisons illustrate differences between the *average* female and male. The variation *among* individual females or *among* individual males greatly exceeds this difference.

Aggression

To a psychologist, **aggression** is any physical or verbal behavior intended to hurt someone physically or emotionally (Bushman & Huesmann, 2010). Think of examples of aggressive people. Are most of them men? Likely yes. Men generally admit to more aggression, especially extreme physical violence (Wölfer & Hewstone, 2015; Yount et al., 2017). In romantic relationships between men and women, minor acts of physical aggression, such as slaps, are roughly equal, but the most violent acts are mostly committed by men (Archer, 2000; Johnson, 2008).

Laboratory experiments confirm a gender difference in aggression. Men have been more willing to blast people with what they believed was intense and prolonged noise (Bushman et al., 2007). And outside the laboratory, men—worldwide—commit more violent crime (Antonaccio et al., 2011; Caddick & Porter, 2012; Frisell et al., 2012). They also take the lead in hunting, fighting, warring, and supporting war (Liddle et al., 2012; Wood & Eagly, 2002, 2007).

Here's another question: Think of examples of people harming others by passing along hurtful gossip, or by shutting someone out of a social group or situation. Were most of those people men? Perhaps not. Those behaviors are acts of **relational aggression,** and women are slightly more likely than men to commit them (Archer, 2004, 2007, 2009).

DEADLY RELATIONAL AGGRESSION Sladjana Vidovic was a high school student who died by suicide after suffering constant relational aggression by bullies.

Social Power

Imagine you've walked into a job interview and are taking your first look at the two interviewers. The unsmiling person on the left oozes self-confidence and independence, maintaining steady eye contact. The person on the right gives you a warm, welcoming smile but makes less eye contact and seems to expect the other interviewer to take the lead.

Which interviewer is male?

If you said the person on the left, you're not alone. Around the world, from Nigeria to New Zealand, people have perceived gender differences in power (Williams & Best, 1990). For more on this topic, see Thinking Critically About: Gender Bias in the Workplace.

Social Connectedness

Whether male or female, we all have a need to belong, though we may satisfy this need in different ways (Baumeister, 2010). Males tend to be *independent*. Even as children, males typically form large play groups that brim with activity and competition, with little intimate discussion (Rose & Rudolph, 2006). As adults, men enjoy side-by-side activities, and their conversations often focus on problem solving (Tannen, 1990; Wright, 1989). When asked a difficult question—"Do you have any idea why the sky is blue?"—men are more likely than women to hazard answers than to admit they don't know, a phenomenon researchers have called the *male answer syndrome* (Giuliano et al., 1998).

"I said, 'I wonder what it means,' not 'Tell me what it means.'"

THINKING CRITICALLY ABOUT:

Gender Bias in the Workplace

LOQ 5-3   What factors contribute to gender bias in the workplace?

Differences in PERCEPTION

"She's so aggressive!"

"He's so take-charge!"

Among politicians who seem power-hungry, women are less successful than men.[1]

Most political leaders are men:

Men held 77% of seats in the world's governing parliaments in 2018.[2]

men

Political leaders

women

People around the world tend to see men as more powerful.[3]

When groups form, whether as juries or companies, leadership tends to go to males.[4]

Differences in COMPENSATION

Women in traditionally male occupations have received less than their male colleagues.[5]

Medicine U.S. salary disparity between male and female physicians:[6]

$150,053 **women**

$211,526 **men**

Academia Female research grant applicants have received lower "quality of researcher" ratings and have been less likely to be funded.[7] (But as we will see, gender attitudes and roles are changing.)

Differences in FAMILY-CARE RESPONSIBILITY

U.S. mothers still do nearly **twice** as much child care as **fathers**.[8] In the workplace, women are less often driven by money and status, compromise more, and more often opt for reduced work hours.[9]

What else contributes to WORKPLACE GENDER BIAS?

Social norms

In most societies, men place more importance on power and achievement, and are socially dominant.[10]

Leadership styles

Men are more *directive*, telling people what to do and how to do it.

Women are more *democratic*, welcoming others' input in decision making.[11]

Interaction styles

Men are more likely to offer opinions.[12]

Women are more likely to express support.[12]

Everyday behavior

Men are more likely to talk assertively, interrupt, initiate touches, and stare.[13]

Women smile and apologize more than men.[13]

Yet GENDER ROLES VARY WIDELY across place and time.

Women are increasingly represented in leadership (now 50% of Canada's cabinet ministers) and in the workforce. In 1963, the Harvard Business School admitted its first women students. Among its Class of 2016, 41% were women.[14] In 1960, women were 6% of U.S. medical students. Today they are about half.[15]

1. Okimoto & Brescoll, 2010. 2. IPU, 2018. 3. Williams & Best, 1990. 4. Colarelli et al., 2006. 5. Willett et al., 2015. 6. Census Bureau, 2014. 7. van der Lee & Ellemers, 2015. 8. CEA, 2014; Parker & Wang, 2013; Pew, 2015. 9. Nikolova & Lamberton, 2016; Pinker, 2008. 10. Gino et al., 2015; Schwartz & Rubel-Lifschitz, 2009. 11. Eagly & Carli, 2007; van Engen & Willemsen, 2004. 12. Aries, 1987; Wood, 1987. 13. Leaper & Ayres, 2007; Major et al., 1990; Schumann & Ross, 2010. 14. Peck, 2015. 15. AAMC, 2014.

Scans of more than 1400 brains show no striking sex differences: "Human brains cannot be categorized into two distinct classes—male brain/female brain" (Joel et al., 2015). Brain scans do, however, suggest that a woman's brain, more than a man's, is wired in a way that enables social relationships (Ingalhalikar et al., 2013). This helps explain why females tend to be more *interdependent*. In childhood, girls usually play in small groups, often with one friend. They compete less and imitate social relationships more (Maccoby, 1990; Roberts, 1991). Teen girls spend more time with friends and less time alone (Wong & Csikszentmihalyi, 1991). In late adolescence, they spend more time on social networking sites, and average twice as many text messages per day as boys

EVERY MAN FOR HIMSELF, OR "TEND AND BEFRIEND"? Sex differences in the way we interact with others begin to appear at a very young age.

(Lenhart, 2015a; Pryor et al., 2007, 2011). Girls' and women's friendships are more intimate, with more conversation that explores relationships (Maccoby, 2002). In one analysis of 10 million Facebook posts, women's status updates were as assertive as men's, but used warmer words, while men more often swore or expressed anger (Park et al., 2016). An analysis of over 700 million Facebook words found women also used more family-related words, whereas men used more work-related words (Schwartz et al., 2013).

When searching for understanding from someone who will share their worries and hurts, people usually turn to women. Both men and women have reported that their friendships with women are more intimate, enjoyable, and nurturing (Kuttler et al., 1999; Rubin, 1985; Sapadin, 1988). And how do women cope with stress? Compared with men, women are more likely to turn to others for support. They are said to *tend and befriend* (Tamres et al., 2002; Taylor, 2002).

Gender differences in both social connectedness and power are greatest in late adolescence and early adulthood—the prime years for dating and mating. By their teen years, girls become less assertive and more flirtatious, and boys appear more dominant and less expressive (Chaplin, 2015). In adulthood, after the birth of a first child, attitude and behavior differences often peak. Mothers especially may express more traditionally female attitudes and behaviors (Ferriman et al., 2009; Katz-Wise et al., 2010). By age 50, most parenting-related gender differences subside. Men become less domineering and more empathic, and women—especially those with paid employment—become more assertive and self-confident (Kasen et al., 2006; Maccoby, 1998). Worldwide, fewer women than men work full-time for an employer (19 percent versus 33 percent). But, similar to men, women are more satisfied with their lives when employed rather than unemployed (Ryan, 2016).

So, although women and men are more alike than different, there are some behavior differences between the average woman and man. Are such differences dictated by our biology? Shaped by our cultures and other experiences? Do we vary in the extent to which we are male or female? Read on.

Question: Why does it take 200 million sperm to fertilize one egg?
Answer: Because they won't stop for directions.

"In the long years liker must they grow; The man be more of woman, she of man." —Alfred Lord Tennyson, *The Princess*, 1847

🔒 **RETRIEVE IT • • •**   *ANSWERS IN APPENDIX E*

RI-1 _____ (Men/Women) are more likely to commit relational aggression, and _____ (men/women) are more likely to commit physical aggression.

THE NATURE OF GENDER: OUR BIOLOGICAL SEX

LOQ 5-4   How do sex hormones influence prenatal and adolescent sexual development, and what is an *intersex* condition?

In most physical ways—regulating heat with sweat, preferring energy-rich foods, growing calluses where the skin meets friction—men and women are similar. When looking for a mate, men and women also prize many of the same traits—someone who is kind, honest, and intelligent. But in some mating-related domains, say evolutionary psychologists, guys

X chromosome the sex chromosome found in both males and females. Females typically have two X chromosomes; males typically have one. An X chromosome from each parent produces a female child.

Y chromosome the sex chromosome typically found only in males. When paired with an X chromosome from the mother, it produces a male child.

testosterone the most important male sex hormone. Both males and females have it, but the additional testosterone in males stimulates the growth of the male sex organs during the fetal period, and the development of the male sex characteristics during puberty.

puberty the period of sexual maturation, when a person becomes capable of reproducing.

primary sex characteristics the body structures (ovaries, testes, and external genitalia) that make sexual reproduction possible.

secondary sex characteristics nonreproductive sexual traits, such as female breasts and hips, male voice quality, and body hair.

spermarche [sper-MAR-key] the first ejaculation.

menarche [meh-NAR-key] the first menstrual period.

act like guys whether they're chimpanzees or elephants, rural peasants or corporate presidents (Geary, 2010).

Biology does not *dictate* gender. But in two ways, biology influences our gender psychology:

• *Genetically*—males and females have differing *sex chromosomes*.

• *Physiologically*—males and females have differing concentrations of *sex hormones,* which trigger other anatomical differences.

These two influences began to form you long before you were born.

Prenatal Sexual Development

Six weeks after you were conceived, you and someone of the other sex looked much the same. Then, as your genes kicked in, your biological sex—determined by your twenty-third pair of chromosomes (the two sex chromosomes)—became more apparent. Whether you are male or female, your mother's contribution to that chromosome pair was an **X chromosome.** From your father, you received the 1 chromosome out of 46 that is not unisex—either another X chromosome, making you female, or a **Y chromosome,** making you male.

About seven weeks after conception, a single gene on the Y chromosome throws a master switch, which triggers the testes to develop and to produce **testosterone,** the main *androgen* (male hormone) that promotes male sex organ development. (Females also have testosterone, but less of it.)

Later, during the fourth and fifth prenatal months, sex hormones bathe the fetal brain and influence its wiring. Different patterns for males and females develop under the influence of the male's greater testosterone and the female's ovarian hormones (Hines, 2004; Udry, 2000). If, however, females are prenatally exposed to unusually high levels of male hormones, they tend to grow up with more male-typical activity interests (Endendijk et al., 2016). Prenatal hormones help sculpt what we love to do.

Adolescent Sexual Development

A flood of hormones triggers another period of dramatic physical change during adolescence, when boys and girls enter **puberty.** In this two-year period of rapid sexual maturation, pronounced male-female differences emerge. A variety of changes begin at about age 11 in girls and at about age 12 in boys, though the subtle beginnings of puberty, such as enlarging testes, appear earlier (Herman-Giddens et al., 2012). A year or two before the physical changes are visible, boys and girls often feel the first stirrings of sexual attraction (McClintock & Herdt, 1996).

Girls' slightly earlier entry into puberty can at first propel them to greater height than boys of the same age (**FIGURE 5.2**). But boys catch up when they begin puberty, and by age 14, they are usually taller than girls. During these growth spurts, the

Pubertal boys may not at first like their sparse beard. (But then it grows on them.)

FIGURE 5.2

HEIGHT DIFFERENCES
Throughout childhood, boys and girls are similar in height. At puberty, girls surge ahead briefly, but then boys typically overtake them at about age 14. (Data from Tanner, 1978.)

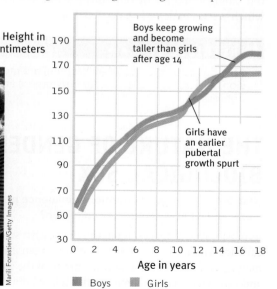

Marili Forastieri/Getty Images

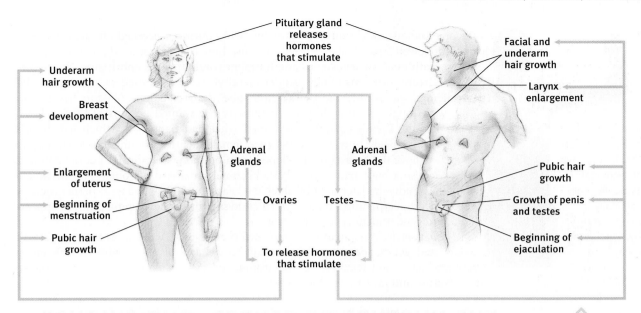

FIGURE 5.3

BODY CHANGES AT PUBERTY At about age 11 in girls and age 12 in boys, a surge of hormones triggers a variety of visible physical changes.

primary sex characteristics—the reproductive organs and external genitalia—develop dramatically. So do the nonreproductive **secondary sex characteristics.** Girls develop breasts and larger hips. Boys' facial hair begins growing and their voices deepen. Pubic and underarm hair emerges in both girls and boys (**FIGURE 5.3**).

For boys, puberty's landmark is the first ejaculation, which often occurs first during sleep (as a "wet dream"). This event, called **spermarche,** usually happens by about age 14.

In girls, the landmark is the first menstrual period, **menarche,** usually within a year of age 12½ (Anderson et al., 2003). Scientists have identified nearly 250 genes that predict when girls experience menarche (Day et al., 2017). But environment matters, too. Early menarche is more likely following stresses related to father absence, sexual abuse, insecure attachments, or a history of a mother's smoking during pregnancy (Rickard et al., 2014; Shrestha et al., 2011; Sung et al., 2016). Girls in various countries are developing breasts and reaching puberty earlier today than in the past, a phenomenon variously attributed to increased body fat, increased hormone-mimicking chemicals in the diet, and increased stress related to family disruption (Biro et al., 2010, 2012; Ellis et al., 2012; Herman-Giddens, 2013). But the good news is that a secure child-mother attachment can provide a buffer against childhood stresses, including those related to early puberty (Sung et al., 2016). Remember: *Nature and nurture interact.*

Girls prepared for menarche usually view it as a positive life transition (Chang et al., 2009). Males report mostly positive emotional reactions to spermarche (Fuller & Downs, 1990).

LaunchPad For a 7-minute discussion of sexual development, see the **Video: Gender Development.**

🔒 **RETRIEVE IT • • •**   *ANSWERS IN APPENDIX E*

RI-2 Prenatal sexual development begins about _____ weeks after conception. Adolescence is marked by the onset of _____.

Sexual Development Variations

Nature may blur the biological line between males and females. People with **intersex** conditions may be born with unusual combinations of male and female chromosomes, hormones, and anatomy. For example, a genetic male may be born with two or more X chromosomes as well as a Y chromosome (*Klinefelter syndrome*), often resulting in sterility and small testes. Genetic females born with only one X chromosome (*Turner syndrome*) may not have menstrual periods, develop breasts, or be able to have children without reproductive assistance. Such individuals may struggle with their gender identity.

In the past, medical professionals often recommended *sex-reassignment surgery* to create an unambiguous sex identity for some children with these conditions. One study reviewed 14 cases of genetic boys who had undergone early surgery and been raised as girls. Of those cases, 6 had later identified as male, 5 were living as females, and 3 reported an unclear male or female identity (Reiner & Gearhart, 2004).

intersex a condition present at birth due to unusual combinations of male and female chromosomes, hormones, and anatomy; possessing biological sexual characteristics of both sexes.

"I AM WHO I AM." Dramatic improvements in South African track star Caster Semenya's race times prompted the International Association of Athletics Federations to undertake sex testing in 2009. Semenya was reported to have physical characteristics not typically male or female. She was officially cleared to continue competing as a woman. Semenya declared, "God made me the way I am and I accept myself. I am who I am" (*YOU*, 2009). In 2016, she won an Olympic gold medal.

Michael Dalder/SEMENYA Reuters/Newscom

"Sex brought us together, but gender drove us apart."

New Yorker Collection, 2001. Barbara Smaller from cartoonbank.com

THE GENDERED TSUNAMI In Sri Lanka, Indonesia, and India, the gendered division of labor helps explain the excess of female deaths from the 2004 tsunami. In some villages, 80 percent of those killed were women, who were mostly at home while the men were more likely to be at sea fishing or doing outdoor chores (Oxfam, 2005).

Dinodia/The Image Works

In one famous case, a little boy lost his penis during a botched circumcision. His parents followed a psychiatrist's advice to raise him as a girl rather than as a damaged boy. So, with male chromosomes and hormones and a female upbringing, did nature or nurture form this child's gender identity? Although raised as a girl, "Brenda" Reimer was not like most other girls. "She" didn't like dolls. She tore her dresses with rough-and-tumble play. At puberty she wanted no part of kissing boys. Finally, Brenda's parents explained what had happened, which led Brenda immediately to reject the assigned female identity. He underwent surgery to remove the breasts he developed from hormone therapy. He cut his hair and chose a male name, David. He eventually married a woman and became a stepfather. Sadly, he later died by suicide (Colapinto, 2000). Today, experts generally recommend postponing surgery until a child's naturally developing physical appearance and gender identity become clear.

The bottom line: "Sex matters," concluded the National Academy of Sciences (2001). Sex-related genes and physiology "result in behavioral and cognitive differences between males and females." Yet environmental factors matter, too, as we will see next. Nature and nurture work together.

THE NURTURE OF GENDER: OUR CULTURE AND EXPERIENCES

LOQ 5-5   How do gender roles and gender identity differ?

For many people, biological sex and gender coexist in harmony. Biology draws the outline, and culture paints the details. The physical traits that define a newborn as male or female are the same worldwide. But the gender traits that define how men (or boys) and women (or girls) *should* act, interact, or feel about themselves differ across time and place (Zentner & Eagly, 2015).

Gender Roles

Cultures shape our behaviors by defining how we ought to behave in a particular social position, or **role.** We can see this shaping power in **gender roles**—the social expectations that guide our behavior as men or women.

In just a thin slice of history, gender roles worldwide have undergone an extreme makeover. At the beginning of the twentieth century, only one country in the world—New Zealand—granted women the right to vote (Briscoe, 1997). By 2015, all countries granted that right. A century ago, American women could not vote in national elections, serve in the military, or divorce a husband without cause. And if a woman worked for pay, she would more likely have been a seamstress than a surgeon. Now, nearly half the workforce is female (DOL, 2015). In the STEM fields (science, technology, engineering, and mathematics), men still hold most faculty positions and receive greater financial research support (Ceci et al., 2014; Sege et al., 2015; Sheltzer & Smith, 2014). But signs point to increases in supply and demand for women in the STEM fields. For example, U.S. women, compared with men, earn more college degrees and higher college grades, and show equal competence at STEM-related activities, such as writing computer code (Keiser et al., 2016; Terrell et al., 2017). When researchers invited U.S. professors to recommend candidates for STEM positions, most said they preferred hiring the highly talented women over the equally talented men (Williams & Ceci, 2015). This is good news for budding female scientists and engineers, who benefit from having capable and motivated female mentors (Dennehy & Dasgupta, 2017).

Gender roles also vary from one place to another. Nomadic societies of food-gathering people have had little division of labor by sex. Boys and girls receive much the same upbringing. In agricultural societies, where women typically work in the nearby fields and men roam while herding livestock, cultures have shaped children to assume more distinct gender roles (Segall et al., 1990; Van Leeuwen, 1978).

ENGAGE Take a minute to check your own gender expectations. Would you agree that "When jobs are scarce, men should have more rights to a job?" In the United States, Britain, and Spain, barely over 12 percent of adults agree. In Nigeria, Pakistan, and India, about 80 percent of adults agree (Pew, 2010). We're all human, but my, how our views differ. Northern European countries offer the greatest gender equity, Middle Eastern and North African countries the least (UN, 2015a).

Expectations about gender roles also factor into cultural attitudes about **sexual aggression.** In the United States, 2017 marked the beginning of a massive cultural shift in such attitudes, as a number of famous and powerful men—in politics, movie-making, broadcasting, sports, academia—faced credible accusations. (See Thinking Critically About: Sexual Aggression.)

How Do We Learn Gender?

A *gender role* describes how others expect us to think, feel, and act. Our **gender identity** is our personal sense of being male, female, or, occasionally, some combination of the two. How do we develop that personal viewpoint?

Social learning theory assumes that we acquire our identity in childhood, by observing and imitating others' gender-linked behaviors and by being rewarded or punished for acting in certain ways. ("Tatiana, you're such a good mommy to your dolls"; "Big boys don't cry, Armand.") But some critics think there's more to gender identity than imitating parents and being repeatedly rewarded for certain responses. They point out that **gender typing**—taking on a traditional male or female role—varies from child to child (Tobin et al., 2010).

Parents do help to transmit their culture's views on gender. In one analysis of 43 studies, parents with traditional gender views were more likely to have gender-typed children who shared their culture's expectations about how males and females should act (Tenenbaum & Leaper, 2002). When fathers share equally in housework, their daughters develop higher aspirations for work outside the home (Croft et al., 2014).

But no matter how much parents encourage or discourage traditional gender behavior, children may drift toward what feels right to them. Some organize themselves into "boy worlds" and "girl worlds," each guided by their understanding of the rules. Others conform to these rules more flexibly. Still others seem to prefer **androgyny:** a blend of male and female roles feels right to them. Androgyny has benefits. As adults, androgynous people are more adaptable. They are more flexible in their actions and in their career choices (Bem, 1993). From childhood onward, they tend to be more resilient and self-accepting, and they experience less depression (Lam & McBride-Chang, 2007; Mosher & Danoff-Burg, 2008; Pauletti et al., 2017).

Feelings matter, but so does how we think. Early in life, we all form *schemas,* or concepts that help us make sense of our world. Our *gender schemas* organize our experiences of male-female characteristics and help us think about our gender identity, about who we are (Bem, 1987, 1993; Martin et al., 2002).

As young children, we were "gender detectives" (Martin & Ruble, 2004). Before our first birthday, we knew the difference between a male and female voice or face (Martin et al., 2002). After we turned 2, language forced us to label the world in terms of gender. English classifies people as *he* and *she.* Other languages classify objects as masculine ("*le* train") or feminine ("*la* table").

Once children grasp that two sorts of people exist—and that they are of one of these two sorts—they search for clues about gender. In every culture, people communicate their gender in many ways. Their *gender expression* drops hints not only in their language but also in their clothing, interests, and possessions. Having picked up such clues, 3-year-olds may divide the human world in half. They will then like their own kind better and seek them out for play. "Girls," they may decide, are the ones who watch *My Little Pony* and have long hair. "Boys" watch *Transformers* and don't wear dresses. Armed with their newly collected "proof," they then adjust their behaviors to fit their concept of gender. These stereotypes are most rigid at about age 5 or 6. If the new neighbor is a girl, a 6-year-old boy may assume he cannot share her interests. For young children, gender looms large.

In 2018, women were 23.4 percent of legislators in the world's national parliaments (IPU, 2018).

"You cannot put women and men on an equal footing. It is against nature." —Turkish President Recept Tayyip Erdoğan

role a set of expectations (norms) about a social position, defining how those in the position ought to behave.

gender role a set of expected behaviors, attitudes, and traits for males or for females.

sexual aggression any physical or verbal behavior of a sexual nature that is intended to harm someone physically or emotionally. Can be expressed as either *sexual harassment* or *sexual assault.*

gender identity our sense of being male, female, or some combination of the two.

social learning theory the theory that we learn social behavior by observing and imitating and by being rewarded or punished.

gender typing the acquisition of a traditional masculine or feminine role.

androgyny displaying both traditional masculine and feminine psychological characteristics.

"We need to keep changing the attitude that raises our girls to be demure and our boys to be assertive, that criticizes our daughters for speaking out and our sons for shedding a tear." —U.S. President Barack Obama, 2016

THE SOCIAL LEARNING OF GENDER Children observe and imitate parental models.

Courtesy of David Myers

THINKING CRITICALLY ABOUT:

Sexual Aggression

LOQ 5-6 **What are the effects of sexual aggression? How have cultural views changed, and how can we reduce sexual aggression?**

Definition of Sexual Aggression

Sexual harassment involves making unwanted sexual advances, obscene remarks, or requests for sexual favors.[1]

Sexual assault is "any type of sexual contact or behavior that occurs without the explicit consent of the recipient," such as unwanted touching, molestation, and attempted or completed rape.[2]

Victims

In the U.S., **81%** of women and **43%** of men report having experienced sexual aggression in their lifetime.[3]

Sexual aggression affects people of *all ethnic groups*.[4]

Nearly **70%** of rape victims are between the ages of 11 and 24.[4]

In a National School Climate survey, **8** out of **10** gay or lesbian adolescents reported experiencing sex-related harassment in the prior year.[5]

Effects on Well-Being

Thanks to human resilience, victims of sexual aggression often recover and lead healthy and meaningful lives. Yet many also suffer serious setbacks, including:

• Greater anxiety, depression, and risk for post-traumatic stress disorder and borderline personality disorder[6]
• Disrupted sleep[7]
• Poor physical health[8]
• Difficulty trusting new relationship partners[9]

Cultural Effects on Our Views

By Place:

Some cultures view victims of sexual aggression as guilty of disgracing their families. In India and Pakistan, male family members kill an unknown number of women— one source estimates 1000 annually in each country[10] – for "dishonoring" their families.

Over Time:

Changes in U.S. culture have made it less acceptable to blame victims of sexual aggression.

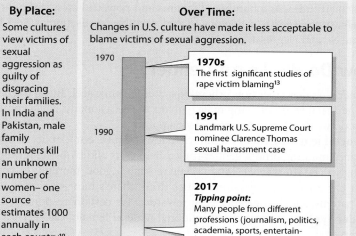

1970

1990

2020

1970s
The first significant studies of rape victim blaming[13]

1991
Landmark U.S. Supreme Court nominee Clarence Thomas sexual harassment case

2017
Tipping point:
Many people from different professions (journalism, politics, academia, sports, entertainment) lost their jobs because of alleged sexual aggression.

Blaming the victim becomes less acceptable.

How to Reduce Sexual Aggression

Therapy to treat sexual aggressors has not been very effective.[11] However, other, broader-based strategies do work:

Encourage victims to report their experiences to authority figures (parents, supervisors, law enforcement officials) and to share their experiences publicly.

Empower victims to take control of their situation and refuse to let their perpetrators dominate or manipulate them. Adjust social norms so that victims feel safe reporting their experiences.

Educate people about preventive bystander intervention strategies, such as "Green Dot," which has been shown to reduce sexual aggression in communities by as much as 20%.[12]

Disgraced Dr. Nassar...sexual abuse ... *Over 200 victims testify*

1. McDonald, 2012; U.S.E.E.O.C., 2018. 2. U.S.D.O.J., 2018. 3. Stop Street Harassment, 2018. 4. Black et al., 2011. 5. GLSEN, 2012. 6. Choudhary et al., 2012; Krahé & Berger, 2017; Snipes et al., 2017; Zanarini et al., 1997. 7. Krakow et al., 2001, 2002. 8. Schuyler et al., 2017; Zinzow et al., 2011. 9. Muldoon et al., 2016; Starzynski et al., 2017. 10. HBVA, 2018. 11. Grønnerød et al., 2015. 12. Coker et al., 2017. 13. Burt, 1980.

transgender an umbrella term describing people whose gender identity or expression differs from that associated with their birth-designated sex.

For someone who identifies as **transgender**, gender identity differs from what's typical for that person's birth-designated sex (APA, 2010; Bockting, 2014). Even as 5- to 12-year-olds, transgender children typically view themselves in terms of their expressed gender rather than their birth-designated sex (Olson et al., 2015). From childhood onward, a person may feel like a male in a female body, or a female in a male body. Brain scans reveal that those who seek medical sex-reassignment have some neural tracts that differ from those whose gender identity matches their birth-designated sex (Kranz et al., 2014;

Van Kesteren et al., 1997). Biologist Robert Sapolsky (2015) explains: "It's not that [these] individuals think they are a different gender than they actually are. It's that they [are] stuck with bodies that are a different gender from who they actually are."

In most countries, it's not easy being transgender. In a national survey of lesbian, gay, bisexual, and transgender Americans, 71 percent saw "some" or "a lot" of social acceptance for gay men, and 85 percent said the same for lesbians. But only 18 percent saw similar acceptance for transgender people, who number about 1.4 million in the United States (Flores et al., 2016; Sandstrom, 2015). And that is the experience of transgender people—46 percent of whom, in a survey of 27,175 transgender Americans, reported being verbally harassed in the last year (James et al., 2016). The psychiatric profession no longer considers gender nonconformity as a mental disorder, and thus no longer labels transgender people as having a "gender identity disorder." But some transgender people (not surprisingly, given the social disapproval) may experience profound distress and be diagnosed with *gender dysphoria*.

Transgender people may attempt to align their outward appearance and everyday lives with their internal gender identity. Such affirming of one's internal gender identity can help transgender people avoid depression and low self-esteem (Glynn et al., 2017). Note that *gender identity* is distinct from *sexual orientation* (the direction of one's sexual attraction). Transgender people may be sexually attracted to people of the other gender, the same gender, or both genders, or to no one at all. Your sexual orientation, as some say, is who you fantasize going to bed *with*; your gender identity is who you go to bed *as*.

Axelle/Bauer-Griffin/Getty Images

BOYS WILL BE BOYS Chaz Bono, writer, musician, advocate, and actor, is the transgender son of famous singer and actress Cher and author of the book *Family Outing*.

Colin McPherson/Getty Images

"MY FATHER . . . IS . . . A WOMAN." So said Mark Morris (2015) of his famous parent, the transgender Welsh writer Jan Morris. After gender reassignment surgery in 1973, Jan Morris was forced by law to divorce Mark's mother. "They continued to live together in a remarkably strong marital bond," until remarrying when same-sex marriages became legal in Britain.

LaunchPad For a 6.5-minute exploration of one pioneering transgender person's journey, see the **Video: Renée Richards—A Long Journey.**

ENGAGE (ASK YOURSELF)

How gender-typed are you? What has influenced your feelings of masculinity, femininity, or some combination of the two?

🔒 **RETRIEVE IT • • •**   *ANSWERS IN APPENDIX E*

RI-3 What are gender roles, and what do their variations tell us about our human capacity for learning and adaptation?

🔒 **REVIEW** GENDER DEVELOPMENT

⤵ Learning Objectives

TEST YOURSELF Answer these repeated Learning Objective Questions on your own (before checking the answers in Appendix D) to improve your retention of the concepts (McDaniel et al., 2009, 2015).

5-1 How does the meaning of *gender* differ from the meaning of *sex*?

5-2 What are some ways in which males and females tend to be alike and to differ?

5-3 What factors contribute to gender bias in the workplace?

5-4 How do sex hormones influence prenatal and adolescent sexual development, and what is an *intersex* condition?

5-5 How do gender roles and gender identity differ?

5-6 What are the effects of sexual aggression? How have cultural views changed, and how can we reduce sexual aggression?

(···>) Terms and Concepts to Remember

TEST YOURSELF Write down the definition yourself, then check your answer on the referenced page.

sex, **p. 162**

gender, **p. 162**

aggression, **p. 162**

relational aggression, **p. 162**

X chromosome, **p. 166**

Y chromosome, **p. 166**

testosterone, **p. 166**

puberty, **p. 166**

primary sex characteristics, **p. 166**

secondary sex characteristics, **p. 166**

spermarche [sper-MAR-key], **p. 166**

menarche [meh-NAR-key], **p. 166**

intersex, **p. 167**

role, **p. 169**

gender role, **p. 169**

sexual aggression, **p. 169**

gender identity, **p. 169**

social learning theory, **p. 169**

gender typing, **p. 169**

androgyny, **p. 169**

transgender, **p. 170**

(···>) Experience the Testing Effect

TEST YOURSELF Answer the following questions on your own first, then check your answers in Appendix E.

1. In psychology, _____ is the biologically influenced characteristics by which people define male and female. The socially influenced characteristics by which people define boy, girl, man and woman is _____.

2. Females and males are very similar, but one way they differ is that
   a. females are more physically aggressive than males.
   b. males are more democratic than females in their leadership roles.
   c. as children, females tend to play in small groups, while males tend to play in large groups.
   d. females are more likely to die by suicide.

3. A fertilized egg will develop into a male if it receives a/n _____ chromosome from its father.

4. Primary sex characteristics relate to _____; secondary sex characteristics refer to _____.
   a. spermarche; menarche
   b. breasts and facial hair; ovaries and testes

   c. emotional maturity; hormone surges
   d. reproductive organs; nonreproductive traits

5. On average, girls begin puberty at about the age of _____, boys at about the age of _____.

6. A person born with sexual anatomy that differs from typical male or female anatomy may be considered to have a(n) _____ condition.

7. *Gender role* refers to our
   a. personal sense of being male or female.
   b. culture's expectations about the "right" way for males and females to behave.
   c. assigned birth sex—our chromosomes and anatomy.
   d. unisex characteristics.

8. Our sense of being male, female, or some combination of the two is known as our _____ _____.

Continue testing yourself with 📖 **LearningCurve** or 📖 **Achieve Read & Practice** to learn and remember most effectively.

In one British survey of 18,876 people, and in other surveys since, about 1 percent acknowledge being asexual, having "never felt sexually attracted to anyone at all" (Bogaert, 2004, 2015). People identifying as asexual are, however, nearly as likely as others to report masturbating, noting that it feels good, reduces anxiety, or "cleans out the plumbing."

(···>) Human Sexuality

As you've probably noticed, we can hardly talk about gender without talking about our sexuality. For all but the tiny fraction of us considered **asexual**, dating and mating become a high priority from puberty on. Biologist Alfred Kinsey (1894–1956) pioneered the study of human sexuality (Kinsey et al., 1948, 1953). Kinsey and his colleagues' findings ignited debate and controversy, but they also motivated future scientific research devoted to understanding male and female sexual behavior. Our sexual feelings and behaviors reflect both physiological and psychological influences.

THE PHYSIOLOGY OF SEX

Sex is not like hunger, because it is not an actual *need*. (Without it, we may feel like dying, but we will not.) Yet sex is a part of life. Had this not been so for all of your biological ancestors, you would not be alive and reading these words. Sexual motivation is nature's clever way of making people procreate, thus enabling our species' survival. Life is sexually transmitted.

Hormones and Sexual Behavior

LOQ 5-7   How do hormones influence human sexual motivation?

Among the forces driving sexual behavior are the *sex hormones*. The main male sex hormone, as we saw earlier, is *testosterone*. The main female sex hormones are the **estrogens,** such as *estradiol*. Sex hormones influence us at several points in the life span:

- During the prenatal period, they direct our development as males or females.

- During puberty, a sex hormone surge ushers us into adolescence.

- After puberty and well into the late adult years, sex hormones facilitate sexual behavior.

In most mammals, nature neatly synchronizes sex with fertility. Females become sexually receptive (in nonhumans, "in heat") when their estrogens peak at ovulation, and researchers can cause female animals to become receptive by injecting them with estrogens. Male hormone levels are more constant, and hormone injection does not so easily affect the sexual behavior of male animals. Nevertheless, male hamsters that have had their testosterone-making testes surgically removed will gradually lose much of their interest in receptive females. They gradually regain it if injected with testosterone (Piekarski et al., 2009).

Hormones do influence human sexual behavior, but more loosely. Researchers are exploring and debating whether women's mate preferences change across the menstrual cycle, especially at ovulation, when both estrogens and testosterone rise (Gildersleeve et al., 2014; Haselton & Gildersleeve, 2011, 2016; Wood et al., 2014a). Some evidence suggests that, among women with mates, sexual desire rises slightly at ovulation—a change that men can sometimes detect in women's behaviors and voices (Haselton & Gildersleeve, 2011, 2016).

Women have much less testosterone than men do. But more than other mammalian females, women are responsive to their testosterone level (Davison & Davis, 2011; van Anders, 2012). If a woman's natural testosterone level drops, as happens with removal of the ovaries or adrenal glands, her sexual interest may wane. And as experiments with surgically or naturally menopausal women have demonstrated, testosterone-replacement therapy can often restore diminished sexual activity, arousal, and desire (Braunstein et al., 2005; Buster et al., 2005; Petersen & Hyde, 2011).

In human males with abnormally low testosterone levels, testosterone-replacement therapy often increases sexual desire and also energy and vitality (Khera et al., 2011). But normal fluctuations in testosterone levels, from man to man and hour to hour, have little effect on sexual drive (Byrne, 1982). Indeed, male hormones sometimes vary in *response* to sexual stimulation (Escasa et al., 2011). In one study, Australian skateboarders' testosterone surged in the presence of an attractive female, contributing to riskier moves and more crash landings (Ronay & von Hippel, 2010). Thus, sexual arousal can be a *cause* as well as a consequence of increased testosterone levels.

Large hormonal surges or declines affect sexual desire in shifts that tend to occur at two predictable points in the life span, and sometimes at an unpredictable third point:

1. ***The pubertal surge in sex hormones triggers the development of sex characteristics and sexual interest.*** If puberty's hormonal surge is precluded—as it was during the 1600s and 1700s for prepubertal boys who were castrated to preserve their soprano voices for Italian opera—sex characteristics and sexual desire do not develop normally (Peschel & Peschel, 1987).

"It is a near-universal experience, the invisible clause on one's birth certificate stipulating that one will, upon reaching maturity, feel the urge to engage in activities often associated with the issuance of more birth certificates." —Science writer Natalie Angier, 2007

asexual having no sexual attraction toward others.

estrogens sex hormones, such as estradiol, that contribute to female sex characteristics and are secreted in greater amounts by females than by males. Estrogen levels peak during ovulation. In nonhuman mammals, this promotes sexual receptivity.

2. *In later life, sex hormone levels fall.* Women experience menopause as their estrogen levels decrease; males experience a more gradual change (Chapter 4). Sex remains a part of life, but as hormone levels decline, sexual fantasies and intercourse decline as well (Leitenberg & Henning, 1995).

3. *For some, surgery or drugs may cause hormonal shifts.* When adult men were castrated, their sex drive typically fell as testosterone levels declined sharply (Hucker & Bain, 1990). Male sex offenders who took Depo-Provera, a drug that reduces their testosterone level to that of a prepubertal boy, similarly lost much of their sexual urge (Bilefsky, 2009; Money et al., 1983).

To summarize: We might compare human sex hormones, especially testosterone, to the fuel in a car. Without fuel, a car will not run. But if the fuel level is minimally adequate, adding more fuel to the gas tank won't change how the car runs. The analogy is imperfect, because hormones and sexual motivation interact. However, it correctly suggests that biology is a necessary but incomplete explanation of human sexual behavior. The hormonal fuel is essential, but so are the psychological stimuli that turn on the engine, keep it running, and shift it into high gear.

> **🔒 RETRIEVE IT • • •**   *ANSWERS IN APPENDIX E*
>
> **RI-1** The primary male sex hormone is _____. The primary female sex hormones are the _____.

The Sexual Response Cycle

LOQ 5-8   What is the human *sexual response cycle,* and how do sexual dysfunctions and paraphilias differ?

The scientific process often begins with careful observations of complex behaviors. When gynecologist-obstetrician William Masters and his collaborator Virginia Johnson (1966) applied this process to human sexual intercourse in the 1960s, they made headlines. They recorded the physiological responses of volunteers who came to their lab to masturbate or have intercourse. (The volunteers, 382 women and 312 men, were a somewhat atypical sample, consisting only of people able and willing to display arousal and orgasm while scientists observed.) Masters and Johnson reported observing more than 10,000 sexual "cycles." Their description of the **sexual response cycle** identified four stages:

1. *Excitement* The genital areas become engorged with blood, causing a woman's clitoris and a man's penis to swell. A woman's vagina expands and secretes lubricant; her breasts and nipples may enlarge.

2. *Plateau* Excitement peaks as breathing, pulse, and blood pressure rates continue to increase. A man's penis becomes fully engorged—to an average length of 5.6 inches among 1661 men who measured themselves for condom fitting (Herbenick et al., 2014). Some fluid—frequently containing enough live sperm to enable conception—may appear at its tip. A woman's vaginal secretion continues to increase, and her clitoris retracts. Orgasm feels imminent.

3. *Orgasm* Muscle contractions appear all over the body and are accompanied by further increases in breathing, pulse, and blood pressure rates. The pleasurable feeling of sexual release is much the same for both sexes. One panel of experts could not reliably distinguish between descriptions of orgasm written by men and those written by women (Vance & Wagner, 1976). In another study, PET scans showed that the same subcortical brain regions were active in men and women during orgasm (Holstege et al., 2003a,b).

4. *Resolution* The body gradually returns to its unaroused state as the genital blood vessels release their accumulated blood. This happens relatively quickly if orgasm has occurred, relatively slowly otherwise. (It's like the nasal tickle that goes away rapidly if you have sneezed, slowly otherwise.) Men then enter a **refractory period** that lasts from a few minutes to a day or more, during which they are incapable of another orgasm. A woman's much shorter refractory period may enable her, if restimulated during or soon after resolution, to have more orgasms.

A nonsmoking 50-year-old male has about a 1-in-a-million chance of a heart attack during any hour. This increases to merely 2-in-a-million in the two hours during and following sex (with no increase for those who exercise regularly). Compared with risks associated with heavy exertion or anger, this risk seems not worth losing sleep (or sex) over (Jackson, 2009; Muller et al., 1996).

🔒 As you learned in Chapter 2, there is also a *refractory period* in neural processing—the brief resting pause that occurs after a neuron has fired.

Sexual Dysfunctions and Paraphilias

Masters and Johnson sought not only to describe the human sexual response cycle but also to understand and treat the inability to complete it. **Sexual dysfunctions** are problems that consistently impair sexual arousal or functioning at any point in this cycle. Some involve sexual motivation, especially lack of sexual energy and arousability. For men, others include **erectile disorder** (inability to have or maintain an erection) and *premature ejaculation*. For women, the problem may be pain or **female orgasmic disorder** (distress over infrequently or never experiencing orgasm). In separate surveys of some 3000 Boston women and 32,000 other American women, about 4 in 10 reported a sexual problem, such as orgasmic disorder or low desire, but only about 1 in 8 reported that this caused personal distress (Lutfey et al., 2009; Shifren et al., 2008). Most women who have experienced sexual distress have related it to their emotional relationship with their partner during sex (Bancroft et al., 2003).

Psychological and medical therapies can help men and women with sexual dysfunctions (Frühauf et al., 2013). In behaviorally oriented therapy, for example, men learn ways to control their urge to ejaculate, and women are trained to bring themselves to orgasm. Starting with the introduction of Viagra in 1998, erectile disorder has been routinely treated by taking a pill. Researchers have struggled to develop reliable drug treatments for *female sexual interest/arousal disorder.*

Sexual dysfunction involves problems with arousal or sexual functioning. People with **paraphilias** (mostly men) do experience sexual desire, but they direct it in unusual ways (Baur et al., 2016). The American Psychiatric Association (2013) only classifies such behavior as disordered if

- a person experiences distress from an unusual sexual interest *or*
- it entails harm or risk of harm to others.

The serial killer Jeffrey Dahmer had *necrophilia,* a sexual attraction to corpses. Those with *exhibitionism* derive pleasure from exposing themselves sexually to others, without consent. People with the paraphilic disorder *pedophilia* experience sexual arousal toward children who haven't entered puberty.

Sexually Transmitted Infections

LOQ 5-9   How can sexually transmitted infections be prevented?

Every day, more than 1 million people worldwide acquire a *sexually transmitted infection* (*STI*; also called *STD*, for *sexually transmitted disease*) (WHO, 2013). Common STIs include chlamydia, gonorrhea, herpes simplex virus (HSV), and human papillomavirus (HPV) infection. "Compared with older adults," reports the Centers for Disease Control and Prevention (CDC, 2016b), "sexually active adolescents aged 15–19 years and young adults aged 20–24 years are at higher risk." Teenage girls, for example, are at heightened risk given their not yet fully mature anatomy and lower levels of protective antibodies (Dehne & Riedner, 2005; Guttmacher Institute, 1994).

Condoms offer only limited protection against certain skin-to-skin STIs, such as herpes, but they do reduce other risks (NIH, 2001). The effects were clear when Thailand promoted condom use by commercial sex workers. Over a four-year period, as condom use soared from 14 to 94 percent, the annual number of bacterial STIs plummeted from 410,406 to 27,362 (WHO, 2000). When used by people with an infected partner, condoms also have been 80 percent effective in preventing transmission of *HIV* (*human immunodeficiency virus*—the virus that causes **AIDS**) (Weller & Davis-Beaty, 2002; WHO, 2003). Although HIV can be transmitted by other means, such as needle sharing during drug use, its sexual transmission is most common. Half of all humans with HIV (and one fourth of Americans with HIV) are women. Because the virus is spread more easily from men to women, women's proportion of the worldwide AIDS population is growing.

Just over half of Americans with AIDS are between ages 30 and 49 (CDC, 2013). AIDS' long incubation period means that many were infected in their teens and twenties. In 2012, the death of 1.6 million people with AIDS worldwide left behind countless grief-stricken loved ones, including millions of orphaned children (UNAIDS, 2013).

LaunchPad To explore the stories of participants in a drug therapy program for sexual dysfunctions, see the 6-minute **Video: Sexual Dysfunctions and Their Treatments.**

sexual response cycle the four stages of sexual responding described by Masters and Johnson—excitement, plateau, orgasm, and resolution.

refractory period in human sexuality, a resting period that occurs after orgasm, during which a person cannot achieve another orgasm.

sexual dysfunction a problem that consistently impairs sexual arousal or functioning at any point in the sexual response cycle.

erectile disorder inability to develop or maintain an erection due to insufficient blood flow to the penis.

female orgasmic disorder distress due to infrequently or never experiencing orgasm.

paraphilias sexual arousal from fantasies, behaviors, or urges involving nonhuman objects, the suffering of self or others, and/or nonconsenting persons.

AIDS (acquired immune deficiency syndrome) a life-threatening, sexually transmitted infection caused by the *human immunodeficiency virus (HIV)*. AIDS depletes the immune system, leaving the person vulnerable to infections.

social script a culturally modeled guide for how to act in various situations.

In Sub-Saharan Africa, home to two-thirds of those with HIV, medical treatment to extend life and care for the dying is sapping needed resources.

Having sex with one person means also partnering with that person's past partners—any one of whom might have unknowingly transmitted an STI. Hence, the first step in preventing STIs is knowing one's status, and sharing it with one's sexual partner.

> **🔒 RETRIEVE IT • • •**   *ANSWERS IN APPENDIX E*
>
> **RI-2** Someone who is distressed by impaired sexual arousal may be diagnosed with a _____ _____. Exhibitionism would be considered a _____.

THE PSYCHOLOGY OF SEX

LOQ 5-10   How do external and imagined stimuli contribute to sexual arousal?

Biological factors powerfully influence our sexual motivation and behavior. Yet the wide variations over time, across place, and among individuals document the great influence of psychological factors as well (**FIGURE 5.4**). Thus, despite the shared biology that underlies sexual motivation, the 281 reasons study participants expressed for having sex ranged widely—from "to get closer to God" to "to get my boyfriend to shut up" (Buss, 2008; Meston & Buss, 2007).

External Stimuli

Men and women become aroused when they see, hear, or read erotic material (Heiman, 1975; Stockton & Murnen, 1992). In men more than in women, *feelings* of sexual arousal closely mirror their (more obvious) physical genital responses (Chivers et al., 2010).

People may find sexual arousal either pleasing or disturbing. (Those who wish to control their arousal often limit their exposure to arousing materials, just as those wishing to avoid overeating limit their exposure to tempting food cues.) With repeated exposure to any stimulus, including an erotic stimulus, the emotional response lessens, or *habituates*. During the 1920s, when Western women's hemlines rose to the knee, an exposed leg made hearts flutter. Today, many would barely notice.

Can exposure to sexually explicit material have adverse effects? Research indicates that it can, in three ways.

- *Believing rape is acceptable* Depictions of women being sexually coerced—and appearing to enjoy it—have increased viewers' belief in the false idea that women want to be overpowered, and have increased male viewers' expressed willingness to hurt women and to commit rape after viewing such scenes (Allen et al., 1995, 2000; Foubert et al., 2011; Zillmann, 1989).

- *Reducing satisfaction with a partner's appearance or with a relationship* After viewing images or erotic films of sexually attractive women and men, people have judged an average person, their own partner, or their spouse as less attractive. And they have found their own relationship less satisfying (Kenrick & Gutierres, 1980; Lambert et al., 2012). Perhaps reading or watching erotica's unlikely scenarios creates expectations that few men and women can fulfill.

- *Desensitization* Some studies have found that extensive online pornography exposure desensitizes young men to normal sexuality, thus contributing to erectile problems, lowered sexual desire, and diminished brain activation in response to sexual images. "Porn is messing with your manhood," argue Philip Zimbardo and colleagues (2016). In one brain-imaging study, men who frequently watched pornography had smaller-sized brain regions that aid sexual pleasure (Kühn & Gallinat, 2014).

Digital Vision/Getty Images

FIGURE 5.4

BIOPSYCHOSOCIAL INFLUENCES ON SEXUAL MOTIVATION Compared with our motivation for eating, our sexual motivation is less influenced by biological factors. Psychological and social-cultural factors play a bigger role.

Biological influences:
- sexual maturity
- sex hormones, especially testosterone

Psychological influences:
- exposure to stimulating conditions
- sexual fantasies

Sexual motivation

Social-cultural influences:
- family and society values
- religious and personal values
- cultural expectations
- media

Imagined Stimuli

The brain, it has been said, is our most significant sex organ. The stimuli inside our heads—our imagination—can influence sexual arousal and desire. Lacking genital sensation because of a spinal-cord injury, people can still feel sexual desire (Willmuth, 1987).

Both men and women (about 95 percent of each) report having sexual fantasies, which for a few women can, by themselves, produce orgasms (Komisaruk & Whipple, 2011). Men, regardless of sexual orientation, tend to have more frequent, more physical, and less romantic fantasies (Schmitt et al., 2012). They also prefer less personal and faster-paced sexual content in books and videos (Leitenberg & Henning, 1995). Fantasizing about sex does *not* indicate a sexual problem or dissatisfaction. If anything, sexually active people have more sexual fantasies.

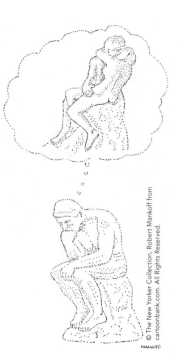

© The New Yorker Collection, Robert Mankoff from cartoonbank.com. All Rights Reserved.

🔒 RETRIEVE IT • • • ANSWERS IN APPENDIX E

RI-3 What factors influence our sexual motivation and behavior?

Sexual Risk Taking and Teen Pregnancy

LOQ 5-11 What factors influence teenagers' sexual behaviors and use of contraceptives?

Sexual attitudes and behaviors vary dramatically across cultures and eras. "Sex between unmarried adults" is "morally unacceptable," agree 97 percent of Indonesians and 6 percent of Germans (Pew, 2014b). And thanks to decreased sexual activity and increased protection, American teen pregnancy rates are declining (CDC, 2016b; Twenge et al., 2016b). What environmental factors contribute to teen pregnancy?

COMMUNICATION ABOUT BIRTH CONTROL Many teenagers are uncomfortable discussing contraception with parents, partners, and peers. But teens who talk freely and openly with their parents and with their partner in an exclusive relationship are more likely to use contraceptives (Aspy et al., 2007; Milan & Kilmann, 1987).

IMPULSIVITY Among sexually active 12- to 17-year-old American girls, 72 percent said they regretted having had sex (Reuters, 2000). If passion overwhelms intentions (either to use contraceptives or to delay having sex), unplanned sexual activity may result in pregnancy (Ariely & Loewenstein, 2006; MacDonald & Hynie, 2008).

ALCOHOL USE Among late teens and young adults, most sexual hook-ups (casual encounters outside of a relationship) occur after alcohol use, often without knowing consent (Fielder et al., 2013; Garcia et al., 2013; Johnson & Chen, 2015). Those who use alcohol prior to sex are less likely to use condoms (Kotchick et al., 2001). By depressing the brain centers that control judgment, inhibition, and self-awareness, alcohol disarms normal restraints—a phenomenon well known to sexually coercive people.

MASS MEDIA Perceived peer norms influence teens' sexual behavior (Lyons et al., 2015; van de Bongardt et al., 2015). Teens attend to other teens, who, in turn, are influenced by popular media. Media help write the **social scripts** that affect our perceptions and actions. The more sexual content adolescents and young adults view or read (even when controlling for other predictors of early sexual activity), the more likely they are to perceive their peers as sexually active, to develop sexually permissive attitudes, and to experience early intercourse (Escobar-Chaves et al., 2005; Kim & Ward, 2012; Parkes et al., 2013). One study asked more than a thousand 12- to 14-year-olds what movies they had seen, and then after age 18 asked them about their sexual experiences (O'Hara et al., 2012). After controlling for various adolescent and family characteristics, the more the adolescents viewed movies with high sexual content, the greater was their sexual risk taking—with earlier first sex, more partners, and inconsistent condom use.

KEEPING ABREAST OF HYPERSEXUALITY An analysis of the 60 top-selling video games found 489 characters, 86 percent of whom were males (like most of the game players). The female characters were much more likely than the male characters to be "hypersexualized"—partially nude or revealingly clothed, with large breasts and tiny waists (Downs & Smith, 2010). Such depictions can lead to unrealistic expectations about sexuality and contribute to the early sexualization of girls. The American Psychological Association suggests countering this by teaching girls to "value themselves for who they are rather than how they look" (APA, 2007).

dpa/picture-alliance/Newscom

"Condoms should be used on every conceivable occasion." –Anonymous

FATHER PRESENCE

ASK YOURSELF

What strategies might be effective for reducing teen pregnancy?

Several factors predict sexual restraint:

- *High intelligence* Teens with high rather than average intelligence test scores more often delayed sex, partly because they considered possible negative consequences and were more focused on future achievement than on here-and-now pleasures (Harden & Mendle, 2011).

- *Religious engagement* Actively religious teens more often reserve sexual activity for adulthood or long-term relationships (Hull et al., 2011; Schmitt & Fuller, 2015; Štulhofer et al., 2011).

- *Father presence* In studies that followed hundreds of New Zealand and U.S. girls from age 5 to 18, having Dad around has reduced the risk of teen pregnancy and of sexual activity before age 16 (Ellis et al., 2003). These associations held even after adjusting for other influences, such as poverty. Close family attachments—as in families that eat together and where parents know their teens' activities and friends—also predict later sexual initiation (Coley et al., 2008).

- *Service learning participation* Several experiments have found that American teens volunteering as tutors or teachers' aides, or participating in community projects, had lower pregnancy rates than did comparable teens randomly assigned to control conditions (Kirby, 2002; O'Donnell et al., 2002). Researchers are unsure why. Does service learning promote a sense of personal competence, control, and responsibility? Does it encourage more future-oriented thinking? Or does it simply reduce opportunities for unprotected sex? (After-school activities and later school start times also reduced unplanned pregnancies [Bryan et al., 2016; Steinberg, 2015].)

> **🔒 RETRIEVE IT • • •**   *ANSWERS IN APPENDIX E*
>
> **RI-4** Which THREE of the following five factors contribute to unplanned teen pregnancies?
> a. Alcohol use
> b. Higher intelligence level
> c. Father absence
> d. Mass media models
> e. Participating in service learning programs

SEXUAL ORIENTATION

LOQ 5-12   What has research taught us about sexual orientation?

We express the *direction* of our sexual interest in our **sexual orientation**—which usually is our enduring sexual attraction toward members of our own sex (*homosexual orientation*) or the other sex (*heterosexual orientation*). Other variations include an attraction to both sexes (*bisexual orientation*). Cultures vary in their attitudes toward same-sex attractions. "Should society accept homosexuality?" *Yes*, say 88 percent of Spaniards and 1 percent of Nigerians, with women everywhere being more accepting than men (Pew, 2013a). Yet whether a culture condemns or accepts same-sex unions, heterosexuality is most common and homosexuality and bisexuality exist. In most African countries, same-sex relationships are illegal. Yet the ratio of lesbian, gay, or bisexual people "is no different from other countries in the rest of the world," reports the Academy of Science of South Africa (2015). What is more, same-sex activity spans human history.

Sexual Orientation: The Numbers

How many people are exclusively homosexual? According to more than a dozen national surveys in Europe and the United States, about 3 or 4 percent of men and 2 percent of women (Chandra et al., 2011; Herbenick et al., 2010; Savin-Williams et al., 2012). When the U.S. National Center for Health Statistics asked 34,557 Americans about their sexual identity, they found that all but 3.4 percent answered "straight," with 1.6 percent answering "gay" or "lesbian" and 0.7 percent saying "bisexual" (Ward et al., 2014). In a follow-up

sexual orientation an enduring sexual attraction toward members of one's own sex (*homosexual* orientation), the other sex (*heterosexual* orientation), or both sexes (*bisexual* orientation).

survey, 1.6 percent of women and 2.3 percent of men anonymously reported feeling "mostly" or "only" same-sex attraction (Copen et al., 2016). A larger number of adults—13 percent of women and 5 percent of men—report some same-sex sexual contact during their lives (Chandra et al., 2011).

In less tolerant places, people are more likely to hide their sexual orientation. About 3 percent of California men express a same-sex preference on Facebook, for example, as do only about 1 percent in Mississippi. Yet about 5 percent of Google pornography searches in both states are for gay porn. And Craigslist ads for males seeking "casual encounters" with other men tend to be at least as common in less tolerant states, where there are also more Google searches for "gay sex" and "Is my husband gay?" (MacInnis & Hodson, 2015; Stephens-Davidowitz, 2013).

ENGAGE What does it feel like to have same-sex attractions in a majority heterosexual culture? If you are heterosexual, imagine how you would feel if you were socially isolated for openly admitting or displaying your feelings. How would you react if you overheard people making crude jokes about heterosexual people, or if most movies, TV shows, and advertisements portrayed (or implied) homosexuality? And how would you answer if your family members were pleading with you to change your heterosexual "life-style" and to enter into a homosexual marriage?

Facing such reactions, some individuals struggle with their sexual attractions, especially during adolescence and if feeling rejected by parents or harassed by peers. If lacking social support, nonheterosexual teens express greater anxiety and depression, and an increased risk of contemplating and attempting suicide (Becker et al., 2014; Lyons, 2015; Wang et al., 2012, 2015b). They may at first try to ignore or deny their desires, hoping they will go away. But they don't. They may try to change their orientation through psychotherapy, willpower, or prayer. But the feelings typically persist, as do those of heterosexual people—who are similarly incapable of change (Haldeman, 1994, 2002; Myers & Scanzoni, 2005).

Today's psychologists view sexual orientation as neither willfully chosen nor willfully changed. Sexual orientation in some ways is like handedness: Most people are one way, some the other. A very few are truly ambidextrous. Regardless, the way one is endures. "Efforts to change sexual orientation are unlikely to be successful and involve some risk of harm," declared a 2009 American Psychological Association report. Recognizing this, in 2016, Malta became the first European country to outlaw the controversial practice of "conversion therapy," which aims to change people's gender identities or sexual orientations. Several U.S. states have likewise banned conversion therapy with minors.

Sexual orientation is especially persistent for men. Women's sexual orientation tends to be less strongly felt and, for some women, is more fluid and changing (Dickson et al., 2013; Norris et al., 2015). In general, men are sexually simpler. Men's lesser sexual variability is apparent in many ways (Baumeister, 2000). Across time, across cultures, across situations, and across differing levels of education, religious observance, and peer influence, men's sexual drive and interests are less flexible and varying than are women's. Women, for example, more often prefer to alternate periods of high sexual activity with periods of almost none (Mosher et al., 2005). Baumeister calls this flexibility *erotic plasticity.*

Origins of Sexual Orientation

ENGAGE So, our sexual orientation seems to be something we do not choose and (especially for males) cannot change. Where, then, do these preferences come from? See if you can anticipate the conclusions that have emerged from hundreds of research studies by responding *Yes* or *No* to the following questions:

1. Is homosexuality linked with a child's problematic relationships with parents, such as with a domineering mother and an ineffectual father, or a possessive mother and a hostile father?

2. Does homosexuality involve a fear or hatred of people of the other sex, leading individuals to direct their desires toward members of their own sex?

3. Is sexual orientation linked with sex hormone levels?

4. As children, were most homosexuals molested, seduced, or otherwise sexually victimized by an adult homosexual?

In tribal cultures in which homosexual behavior is expected of all boys before marriage, most men are heterosexual (Hammack, 2005; Money, 1987). As this illustrates, homosexual *behavior* does not always indicate a homosexual *orientation.*

DRIVEN TO SUICIDE In 2010, Rutgers University student Tyler Clementi jumped off this bridge after his room-mate secretly filmed, shared, and tweet-ed about Clementi's intimate encounter with another man. Reports then surfaced of other gay teens who had reacted in a similarly tragic fashion after being taunted. Since 2010, Americans—especially those under 30—have been increasingly supportive of those with same-sex orientations.

STAN HONDA/Getty Images

The answer to all these questions has been *No* (Storms, 1983). In a search for possible environmental influences on sexual orientation, Kinsey Institute investigators interviewed nearly 1000 homosexuals and 500 heterosexuals. They assessed nearly every imaginable psychological cause of homosexuality—parental relationships, childhood sexual experiences, peer relationships, dating experiences (Bell et al., 1981; Hammersmith, 1982). Their findings: Homosexuals are no more likely than heterosexuals to have been smothered by maternal love or neglected by their father. In one national survey of nearly 35,000 adults, those with a same-sex attraction were somewhat more likely to report having experienced child sexual abuse. But 86 percent of the men and 75 percent of the women with same-sex attraction reported no such abuse (Roberts et al., 2013).

And consider this: If "distant fathers" were more likely to produce homosexual sons, then shouldn't boys growing up in father-absent homes more often be gay? (They are not.) And shouldn't the rising number of such homes have led to a noticeable increase in the gay population? (It has not.) Most children raised by gay or lesbian parents grow up straight (Gartrell & Bos, 2010). And they grow up with health and emotional well-being similar to (and sometimes better than) children with straight parents (Bos et al., 2016; Farr, 2017; Miller et al., 2017).

The bottom line from a half-century's theory and research: If there are environmental factors that influence sexual orientation after we're born, we do not yet know what they are. The lack of evidence for environmental causes of homosexuality has motivated researchers to explore possible biological influences. They have considered these possibilities:

- Same-sex behaviors in other species,
- Gay-straight brain differences,
- Genetic influences, and
- Prenatal influences.

SAME-SEX ATTRACTION IN OTHER SPECIES In Boston's Public Gardens, caretakers solved the mystery of why a much-loved swan couple's eggs never hatched. Both swans were female. In New York City's Central Park Zoo, penguins Silo and Roy spent several years as devoted same-sex partners. Same-sex sexual behaviors have also been observed in several hundred other species, including grizzlies, gorillas, monkeys, flamingos, and owls (Bagemihl, 1999). Among rams, for example, some 7 to 10 percent display same-sex attraction by shunning ewes and seeking to mount other males (Perkins & Fitzgerald, 1997). Homosexual behavior seems a natural part of the animal world.

GAY-STRAIGHT BRAIN DIFFERENCES Researcher Simon LeVay (1991) studied sections of the hypothalamus (a brain structure linked to emotion) taken from deceased heterosexual and homosexual people. As a gay scientist, LeVay wanted to do "something connected with my gay identity." To avoid biasing the results, he did a *blind study,* not knowing which donors were gay. For nine months he peered through his microscope at a cell cluster that varied in size among donors. Then, one morning, he broke the code: One cell cluster was reliably larger in heterosexual men than in women and homosexual men. "I was almost in a state of shock," LeVay said (1994). "I took a walk by myself on the cliffs over the ocean. I sat for half an hour just thinking what this might mean."

It should not surprise us that brains differ with sexual orientation. Remember, *everything psychological is simultaneously biological.* But when did the brain difference begin? At conception? During childhood or adolescence? Did experience produce the difference? Or was it genes or prenatal hormones (or genes activating prenatal hormones)?

LeVay does not view this cell cluster as an "on-off button" for sexual orientation. Rather, he believes it is an important part of a brain pathway that is active during sexual behavior. He agrees that sexual behavior patterns could influence the brain's anatomy. (Neural pathways in our brain do grow stronger with use.) In fish, birds, rats, and humans, brain structures vary with experience—including sexual experience (Breedlove, 1997). But LeVay believes it more likely that brain anatomy influences sexual orientation. His hunch seems confirmed by the discovery of a similar difference between

"There is no sound scientific evidence that sexual orientation can be changed." —UK Royal College of Psychiatrists, 2009

LaunchPad See the **Video: Naturalistic Observation** for a helpful tutorial animation.

JULIET AND JULIET Boston's beloved swan couple, "Romeo and Juliet," were discovered actually to be, as are many other animal partners, a same-sex pair.

The Boston Globe/Getty Images

male sheep that do and don't display same-sex attraction (Larkin et al., 2002; Roselli et al., 2002, 2004). Moreover, such differences seem to develop soon after birth, and perhaps even before birth (Rahman & Wilson, 2003).

Since LeVay's discovery, other researchers have reported additional gay-straight brain activity differences. One is an area of the hypothalamus that governs sexual arousal (Savic et al., 2005). When straight women were given a whiff of a scent derived from men's sweat (which contains traces of male hormones), this area became active. Gay men's brains responded similarly to the men's scent. Straight men's brains did not. They showed the arousal response only to a female hormone sample. In a similar study, lesbians' responses differed from those of straight women (Kranz & Ishai, 2006; Martins et al., 2005). Researcher Qazi Rahman (2015) sums it up: Compared with heterosexuals, "gay men appear, on average, more 'female typical' in brain pattern responses and lesbian women are somewhat more 'male typical.'"

GENETIC INFLUENCES Evidence indicates that "about a third of variation in sexual orientation is attributable to genetic influences" (Bailey et al., 2016). A same-sex orientation does tend to run in families. And identical twins are somewhat more likely than fraternal twins to share a homosexual orientation (Alanko et al., 2010; Långström et al., 2010). But because sexual orientations differ in many identical twin pairs, especially female twins, we know that other factors besides genes are also at work—including, it appears, epigenetic marks that help distinguish gay and straight identical twins (Balter, 2015).

By altering a single gene in fruit flies, experimenters have created female fruit flies that pursued other females during courtship, and males that pursued other males (Demir & Dickson, 2005; Dickson, 2005). With humans, it's likely that multiple genes, possibly in interaction with other influences, shape sexual orientation. A genome-wide study of 409 pairs of gay brothers identified sexual orientation links with areas of two chromosomes, one maternally transmitted (Sanders et al., 2015).

Researchers have speculated about possible reasons why "gay genes" might exist in the human gene pool, given that same-sex couples cannot naturally reproduce. One possible answer is kin selection. Recall from Chapter 2 the evolutionary psychology reminder that many of our genes also reside in our biological relatives. Perhaps, then, gay people's genes live on through their supporting the survival and reproductive success of their relatives.

A *fertile females theory* suggests that maternal genetics may also be at work (Bocklandt et al., 2006). Homosexual men tend to have more homosexual relatives on their mother's side than on their father's (Camperio-Ciani et al., 2004, 2009, 2012; VanderLaan et al., 2012; VanderLaan & Vasey, 2011). And the relatives on the mother's side also produce more offspring than do the maternal relatives of heterosexual men. Perhaps the genes that dispose some women to conceive more children with men also dispose some men to be attracted to men (LeVay, 2011). Thus, the decreased reproduction by gay men appears to be offset by the increased reproduction by their maternal extended family.

PRENATAL INFLUENCES Twins share not only genes, but also a prenatal environment. Recall that in the womb, sex hormones direct our development as male or female. Two sets of findings indicate that the prenatal environment matters.

First, in humans, a critical period for fetal brain development seems to be the second trimester (Ellis & Ames, 1987; Garcia-Falgueras & Swaab, 2010; Meyer-Bahlburg, 1995). Exposure to the hormone levels typically experienced by female fetuses during this period may predispose a person (female or male) later to become attracted to males. When pregnant sheep were injected with testosterone during a similar critical period, their female offspring later showed homosexual behavior (Money, 1987).

Second, the mother's immune system may play a role in the development of sexual orientation. Men with older brothers are somewhat more likely to be gay—about one-third more likely for each additional older brother (Blanchard, 2004, 2008a,b, 2014; Bogaert, 2003). If the odds of homosexuality are roughly 2 percent among first sons, they would rise to about 2.6 percent among second sons, 3.5 percent for third sons, and so on for each additional older brother (Bailey et al., 2016). This is called the *older-brother* or *fraternal birth-order effect* (see **FIGURE 5.5**).

"Gay men simply don't have the brain cells to be attracted to women." –Simon LeVay, *The Sexual Brain*, 1993

📕 **LaunchPad** See the **Video: Twin Studies** for a helpful tutorial animation.

FIGURE 5.5

THE OLDER BROTHER EFFECT Researcher Ray Blanchard (2008a) offers these approximate curves depicting a man's likelihood of homosexuality as a function of the number of biological (not adopted) older brothers he has. This correlation has been found in several studies, but only among right-handed men (as about 9 in 10 men are).

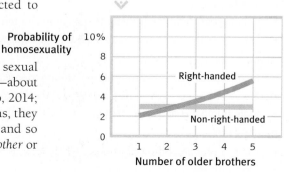

"Modern scientific research indicates that sexual orientation is . . . partly determined by genetics, but more specifically by hormonal activity in the womb." —Glenn Wilson and Qazi Rahman, *Born Gay: The Psychobiology of Sex Orientation*, 2005

 (ASK YOURSELF)

Has learning more about what contributes to sexual orientation influenced your views? If so, in what ways?

LaunchPad For an 8-minute overview of the biology of sexual orientation, see the **Video: Homosexuality and the Nature–Nurture Debate.**

Note that the scientific question is not "What causes homosexuality?" (or "What causes heterosexuality?") but "What causes differing sexual orientations?" In pursuit of answers, psychological science compares the backgrounds and physiology of people whose sexual orientations *differ*.

The reason for this curious effect is unclear. But the explanation does seem biological. The effect does not occur among adopted brothers (Bogaert, 2006). Researchers suspect the mother's immune system may have a defensive response to substances produced by male fetuses. After each pregnancy with a male fetus, the maternal antibodies may become stronger and may prevent the fetal brain from developing in a typical male pattern.

Gay-Straight Trait Differences

Comparing the traits of gay and straight people is akin to comparing the heights of men and women. The average man is taller than most women, but many women are taller than most men. And just as knowing someone's height doesn't specify their sex, neither does knowing someone's traits tell you their sexual orientation. Yet on several traits, the average homosexual female or male is intermediate between straight females and males (**TABLE 5.1**; see also LeVay, 2011; Rahman & Koerting, 2008; Rieger et al., 2016).

Gay-straight spatial abilities also differ. On mental rotation tasks such as the one illustrated in **FIGURE 5.6**, straight men tend to outscore straight women (Boone & Hegarty, 2017). Scores of gays and lesbians tend to fall between those of straight men and women (Rahman & Koerting, 2008; Rahman et al., 2004). But straight women and gays have both outperformed straight men at remembering objects' spatial locations in memory game tasks (Hassan & Rahman, 2007).

* * *

Taken together, the brain, genetic, and prenatal findings offer strong support for a biological explanation of sexual orientation (LeVay, 2011; Rahman & Koerting, 2008). If you see sexual orientation as inborn—as shaped by biological and prenatal influences—then you likely favor "equal rights for homosexual and bisexual people" (Bailey et al., 2016). People who see same-sex attraction as a lifestyle choice often oppose equal rights for nonheterosexual people. To justify his signing a 2014 bill that made some homosexual acts punishable by life in prison, the president of Uganda, Yoweri Museveni, declared that homosexuality is not inborn but rather is a matter of "choice" (Balter, 2014; Landau et al., 2014). Stay tuned for whether the new biological research can encourage care and compassion for people of all sexual orientations.

TABLE 5.1

Biological Correlates of Sexual Orientation

Gay-straight trait differences

Sexual orientation is part of a package of traits. Studies—some in need of replication—indicate that homosexuals and heterosexuals differ in the following biological and behavioral traits:

- spatial abilities
- fingerprint ridge counts
- auditory system development
- handedness
- occupational preferences
- relative finger lengths
- gender nonconformity
- age of onset of puberty in males
- face structure and birth size/weight
- sleep length
- physical aggression
- walking style

On average (the evidence is strongest for males), results for gays and lesbians fall between those of straight men and straight women. Three biological influences—brain, genetic, and prenatal—may contribute to these differences.

Brain differences

- One hypothalamic cell cluster is smaller in women and gay men than in straight men.
- Gay men's hypothalamus reacts as does straight women's to the smell of men's sex-related hormones.

Genetic influences

- Shared sexual orientation is higher among identical twins than among fraternal twins.
- Sexual attraction in fruit flies can be genetically manipulated.
- Male homosexuality often appears to be transmitted from the mother's side of the family.

Prenatal influences

- Altered prenatal hormone exposure may lead to homosexuality in humans and other animals.
- Men with several older biological brothers are more likely to be gay, possibly due to a maternal immune-system reaction.

Which one of the options below matches the Original?

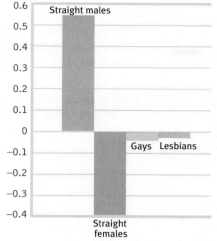

Original

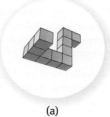

(a)

(b)

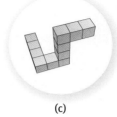

(c)

RI-5 Which THREE of the following five factors have researchers found to have an effect on sexual orientation?

a. A domineering mother

b. The size of a certain cell cluster in the hypothalamus

c. Prenatal hormone exposure

d. A distant or ineffectual father

e. For right-handed men, having multiple older biological brothers

ENGAGE **FIGURE 5.6**

SPATIAL ABILITIES AND SEXUAL ORIENTATION Which of the three figures can be rotated to match the Original figure?[1] Straight males tend to find this type of mental rotation task easier than do straight females, with gays and lesbians falling in between (see graph) (Rahman et al., 2004).

AN EVOLUTIONARY EXPLANATION OF HUMAN SEXUALITY

LOQ 5-13 How might an evolutionary psychologist explain male-female differences in sexuality and mating preferences?

Having faced many similar challenges throughout history, males and females have adapted in similar ways: We eat the same foods, avoid the same dangers, and perceive, learn, and remember similarly. It is only in those domains where we have faced differing adaptive challenges—most obviously in behaviors related to reproduction—that we differ, say evolutionary psychologists.

Male-Female Differences in Sexuality

And differ we do. Consider sex drives. Both men and women are sexually motivated, some women more so than many men. Yet, on average, who thinks more about sex? Hooks up more often? Masturbates more often? Views more pornography? The answers worldwide: *men, men, men,* and *men* (Baumeister et al., 2001; Hall et al., 2017; Lippa, 2009; Petersen & Hyde, 2010). No surprise, then, that in one BBC survey of more than 200,000 people in 53 nations, men everywhere more strongly agreed that "I have a strong sex drive" and "It doesn't take much to get me sexually excited" (Lippa, 2008).

And there are other sexuality differences between males and females (Hyde, 2005; Petersen & Hyde, 2010; Regan & Atkins, 2007). To see if you can predict some of these differences in Americans, take the quiz in **TABLE 5.2**.

Many gender similarities and differences transcend sexual orientation. Compared with lesbians, gay men (like straight men) report more responsiveness to visual sexual stimuli, and more concern with their partner's physical attractiveness (Bailey et al., 1994; Doyle, 2005; Schmitt, 2007; Sprecher et al., 2013). Gay male couples also report having sex more often than do lesbian couples (Peplau & Fingerhut, 2007). And (also like straight men) gay men report more interest in uncommitted sex (Schmitt, 2003).

📺 **LaunchPad** To listen to experts discuss evolutionary psychology and sex differences, see the 4-minute **Video: Evolutionary Psychology and Sex Differences.**

"It's not that gay men are oversexed; they are simply men whose male desires bounce off other male desires rather than off female desires." —Steven Pinker, *How the Mind Works,* 1997

1. Answer: Figure (c).

TABLE 5.2

Predict the Responses

Researchers asked samples of U.S. adults whether they agreed or disagreed with the following statements. For each item, give your best guess about the percentage who agreed with the statement.[2]

Statement	Percentage of males who agreed	Percentage of females who agreed
1. If two people really like each other, it's all right for them to have sex even if they've known each other for a very short time.	_____	_____
2. I can imagine myself being comfortable and enjoying "casual" sex with different partners.	_____	_____
3. Affection was the reason I first had intercourse.	_____	_____
4. I think about sex every day, or several times a day.	_____	_____
5. Pornography is "morally acceptable."	_____	_____

Information from Bailey et al., 2000; Dugan, 2015; Laumann et al., 1994; Pryor et al., 2005.

Natural Selection and Mating Preferences

Natural selection is nature selecting traits and appetites that contribute to survival and reproduction. Evolutionary psychologists use this principle to explain how men and women differ more in the bedroom than in the boardroom. Our natural yearnings, they say, are our genes' way of reproducing themselves. "Humans are living fossils—collections of mechanisms produced by prior selection pressures" (Buss, 1995).

Why do women tend to be choosier than men when selecting sexual partners? Women have more at stake. To send her genes into the future, a woman must—at a minimum—conceive and protect a fetus growing inside her body for up to nine months, and may often nurse for an extended period following birth. No surprise then, that heterosexual women prefer partners who will offer their joint offspring support and protection—stick-around dads over likely cads. Heterosexual women are attracted to tall men with slim waists and broad shoulders—all signs of reproductive success (Mautz et al., 2013). And they prefer men who seem mature, dominant, bold, and affluent (Conroy-Beam et al., 2015; Fales et al., 2016; Lukaszewski et al., 2016). One study of hundreds of Welsh pedestrians asked people to rate a driver pictured at the wheel of a humble Ford Fiesta or a swanky Bentley. Men said a female driver was equally attractive in both cars. Women, however, found a male driver more attractive if he was in the luxury car (Dunn & Searle, 2010).

The data are in, say evolutionists: Men pair widely; women pair wisely. And what traits do straight men find desirable? Some, such as a woman's smooth skin and youthful shape, cross place and time, and they convey health and fertility (Buss, 1994). Mating with such women might increase a man's chances of sending his genes into the future. And sure enough, men feel most attracted to women whose waist is roughly a third narrower than their hips—a sign of future fertility (Lewis et al., 2015; Perilloux et al., 2010). Even blind men show this preference for women with a low waist-to-hip ratio (Karremans et al., 2010). Men are most attracted to women whose ages in the ancestral past (when ovulation began later than today) would be associated with peak fertility (Kenrick et al., 2009). Thus, teen boys are most excited by a woman several years older

2. ANSWERS: (1) males, 58 percent; females, 34 percent. (2) males, 48 percent; females, 12 percent. (3) males, 25 percent; females, 48 percent. (4) males, 54 percent; females, 19 percent. (5) males, 43 percent; females, 25 percent.

than themselves, mid-twenties men prefer women around their own age, and older men prefer younger women. This pattern consistently appears across European singles ads, Indian marital ads, and marriage records from North and South America, Africa, and the Philippines (Singh, 1993; Singh & Randall, 2007).

There is a principle at work here, say evolutionary psychologists: Nature selects behaviors that increase genetic success. As mobile gene machines, we are designed to prefer whatever worked for our ancestors in their environments. They were genetically predisposed to act in ways that produce children, grandchildren, and beyond. Had they not been, we wouldn't be here. As carriers of their genetic legacy, we are similarly predisposed.

THE MATING GAME Evolutionary psychologists are not surprised that older men, and not just George Clooney (pictured with his wife, Amal Clooney, who is 16 years younger), often prefer younger women whose features suggest fertility.

Critiquing the Evolutionary Perspective

LOQ 5-14 What are the key criticisms of evolutionary explanations of human sexuality, and how do evolutionary psychologists respond?

Most psychologists agree that natural selection prepares us for survival and reproduction. But critics say there is a weakness in evolutionary psychology's explanation of our mating preferences. Let's consider how an evolutionary psychologist might explain the findings in a startling study (Clark & Hatfield, 1989), and how a critic might object.

In this experiment, someone posing as a stranger approached people of the other sex and remarked, "I have been noticing you around campus. I find you to be very attractive." The "stranger" then asked a question, which was sometimes "Would you go to bed with me tonight?" What percentage of men and women do you think agreed? An evolutionary explanation of sexuality would predict that women would be choosier than men in selecting their sexual partners. In fact, not a single woman agreed—but 70 percent of the men did. A repeat of this study in France produced a similar result (Guéguen, 2011). The research seemed to support an evolutionary explanation.

Or did it? Critics note that evolutionary psychologists start with an effect—in this case, the survey result showing that men were more likely to accept casual sex offers—and work backward to explain what happened. What if research showed the opposite effect? If men refused an offer for casual sex, might we not reason that men who partner with one woman for life make better fathers, whose children more often survive?

Other critics ask why we should try to explain today's behavior based on decisions our distant ancestors made thousands of years ago. Don't cultural expectations also bend the genders? Alice Eagly and Wendy Wood (1999; Eagly, 2009) point to the smaller behavioral differences between men and women in cultures with greater gender equality. Such critics believe that *social learning theory* offers a better, more immediate explanation for these results. We all learn *social scripts*—our culture's guide to how people should act in certain situations. By watching and imitating others in their culture, women may learn that sexual encounters with strangers can be dangerous, and that casual sex may not offer much sexual pleasure (Conley, 2011). This alternative explanation of the study's effects proposes that women react to sexual encounters in ways that their modern culture teaches them. And men's reactions may reflect their learned social scripts: "Real men" take advantage of every opportunity to have sex.

A third criticism focuses on the social consequences of accepting an evolutionary explanation. Are heterosexual men truly hardwired to have sex with any woman who approaches them? If so, does it mean that men have no moral responsibility to remain faithful to their partners? Does this explanation excuse men's sexual aggression—"boys will be boys"—because of our evolutionary history?

Evolutionary psychologists agree that much of who we are is *not* hardwired. "Evolution forcefully rejects a genetic determinism," insisted one research team (Confer et al., 2010). Genes are not destiny. And evolutionary psychologists remind us that men and women, having faced similar adaptive problems, are far more alike than different. Natural selection has prepared us to be flexible. We humans have a great capacity for learning and social progress. We adjust and respond to varied environments. We adapt and survive, whether we live in the Arctic or the desert.

LaunchPad To observe an experiment showing men's and women's attitudes toward casual sex, see the **Video: Openness to Casual Sex—A Study of Men Versus Women.**

LaunchPad For an interactive demonstration of evolutionary psychology and mating preferences, visit **Topic Tutorial: PsychSim6, Dating and Mating.**

MGP/Getty Images

Evolutionary psychologists also agree with their critics that some traits and behaviors, such as suicide, are hard to explain in terms of natural selection (Barash, 2012; Confer et al., 2010). But they ask us to remember evolutionary psychology's scientific goal: to explain behaviors and mental traits by offering testable predictions using principles of natural selection (Lewis et al., 2017). We may, for example, predict that people are more likely to perform favors for those who share their genes or can later return those favors. Is this true? (The answer is *Yes*.) And evolutionary psychologists remind us that studying how we *came to be* need not dictate how we *ought to be*. Understanding our tendencies can help us overcome them.

> 🔒 **RETRIEVE IT • • •**   *ANSWERS IN APPENDIX E*
>
> **RI-6** How do evolutionary psychologists explain male-female differences in sexuality?
>
> **RI-7** What are the three main criticisms of the evolutionary explanation of human sexuality?

SEX AND HUMAN RELATIONSHIPS

LOQ 5-15   What role do social factors play in our sexuality?

Human sexuality research does not aim to define the personal meaning of sex in our own lives. We could know every available fact about sex—that the initial spasms of male and female orgasm come at 0.8-second intervals, that female nipples expand 10 millimeters at the peak of sexual arousal, that systolic blood pressure rises some 60 points and respiration rate reaches 40 breaths per minute—but fail to understand the human significance of sexual intimacy.

Surely one significance of such intimacy is its expression of our profoundly social nature. In one national study that followed participants to age 30, later first sex predicted greater satisfaction in one's marriage or partnership (Harden, 2012). Another study asked 2035 married people when they started having sex (while controlling for education, religious engagement, and relationship length). Those whose relationship first developed to a deep commitment, and then included sex, not only reported greater relationship satisfaction and stability but also better sex than those who had sex very early in their relationship (Busby et al., 2010; Galinsky & Sonenstein, 2013). For both men and women, but especially for women, sex is more satisfying (with less regret and more orgasms) for those in a committed relationship, rather than a brief sexual hook-up (Armstrong et al., 2012; Garcia et al., 2012, 2013). Partners who share regular meals are more likely than one-time dinner companions to understand what seasoning touches suit each other's food tastes; so, too, with the touches of loyal partners who share a bed.

Sex is a socially significant act. Men and women can achieve orgasm alone, yet most people find greater satisfaction—and experience a much greater surge in *prolactin*, the hormone associated with sexual satisfaction and satiety—after intercourse and orgasm with their loved one (Brody & Tillmann, 2006). Thanks to their overlapping brain reward areas, sexual desire and love feed each other (Cacioppo et al., 2012). Sex at its human best is life uniting and love renewing.

Increased sex ≠ more happiness Among married couples, more frequent sex correlates with happiness. So, would systematically increasing sexual frequency *cause* people to be happier? Alas, heterosexual married couples randomly assigned to double their intercourse frequency over three months became slightly *less* happy (Loewenstein et al., 2015).

REFLECTIONS ON THE NATURE AND NURTURE OF SEX, GENDER, AND SEXUALITY

LOQ 5-16   How do nature, nurture, and our own choices influence gender roles?

Our ancestral history helped form us as a species. Where there is variation, natural selection, and heredity, there will be evolution. Our genes form us. This is a great truth about human nature.

But our culture and experiences also form us. If their genes and hormones predispose males to be more physically aggressive than females, culture can amplify this gender difference through norms that reward macho men and gentle women. If men are encouraged toward roles that demand physical power, and women toward more nurturing roles, each may act accordingly. By exhibiting the actions expected of those who fill such roles, men and women shape their own traits. Presidents in time typically become more presidential, servants more servile. Gender roles similarly shape us.

In many modern cultures, gender roles are merging. Brute strength has become less important for power and status (think "philanthrocapitalists" Priscilla Chan and Mark Zuckerberg). From 1965 to 2016, women soared from 9 percent to 47 percent of U.S. medical students (AAMC, 2014, 2016). In 1965, U.S. married women devoted eight times as many hours to housework as did their husbands; by 2012, this gap had shrunk to less than twice as many (Parker & Wang, 2013; Sayer, 2016). Such swift changes signal that biology does not fix gender roles.

If nature and nurture jointly form us, are we "nothing but" the product of nature and nurture? Are we rigidly determined?

We *are* the product of nature and nurture, but we are also an open system. Genes are all-pervasive but not all-powerful. People may reject their evolutionary role as transmitters of genes and choose not to reproduce. Culture, too, is all-pervasive but not all-powerful. People may defy peer pressures and resist social expectations.

Moreover, we cannot excuse our failings by blaming them solely on bad genes or bad influences. In reality, we are both creatures and creators of our worlds. So many things about us—including our gender roles—are the products of our genes and environments. Yet the stream that runs into the future flows through our present choices. Our decisions today design our environments tomorrow. We are its architects. Our hopes, goals, and expectations influence our destiny. And that is what enables cultures to vary and to change. Mind matters.

CULTURE MATTERS As this exhibit at San Diego's Museum of Man illustrates, children learn their culture. A baby's foot can step into any culture.

San Diego Museum of Man, photograph by Rose Tyson

ENGAGE **ASK YOURSELF**

Based on what you've learned so far, how would you say that genes, the brain, hormones, and environment work together to influence sexual development and sexual behavior?

🔒 REVIEW HUMAN SEXUALITY

⟶ Learning Objectives

TEST YOURSELF Answer these repeated Learning Objective Questions on your own (before checking the answers in Appendix D) to improve your retention of the concepts (McDaniel et al., 2009, 2015).

5-7 How do hormones influence human sexual motivation?

5-8 What is the human *sexual response cycle,* and how do sexual dysfunctions and paraphilias differ?

5-9 How can sexually transmitted infections be prevented?

5-10 How do external and imagined stimuli contribute to sexual arousal?

5-11 What factors influence teenagers' sexual behaviors and use of contraceptives?

5-12 What has research taught us about sexual orientation?

5-13 How might an evolutionary psychologist explain male-female differences in sexuality and mating preferences?

5-14 What are the key criticisms of evolutionary explanations of human sexuality, and how do evolutionary psychologists respond?

5-15 What role do social factors play in our sexuality?

5-16 How do nature, nurture, and our own choices influence gender roles?

⟶ Terms and Concepts to Remember

TEST YOURSELF Write down the definition yourself, then check your answer on the referenced page.

asexual, **p. 173**

estrogens, **p. 173**

sexual response cycle, **p. 175**

refractory period, **p. 175**

sexual dysfunction, **p. 175**

erectile disorder, **p. 175**

female orgasmic disorder, **p. 175**

paraphilias, **p. 175**

AIDS (acquired immune deficiency syndrome), **p. 175**

social script, **p. 176**

sexual orientation, **p. 178**

⟶ Experience the Testing Effect

TEST YOURSELF Answer the following questions on your own first, then check your answers in Appendix E.

1. A striking effect of hormonal changes on human sexual behavior is the
   a. end of sexual desire in men over 60.
   b. sharp rise in sexual interest at puberty.
   c. decrease in women's sexual desire at the time of ovulation.
   d. increase in testosterone levels in castrated males.

2. In describing the sexual response cycle, Masters and Johnson noted that
   a. a plateau phase follows orgasm.
   b. people experience a refractory period during which they cannot experience orgasm.
   c. the feeling that accompanies orgasm is stronger in men than in women.
   d. testosterone is released equally in women and men.

3. What is the difference between sexual dysfunctions and paraphilias?

4. Using condoms during sex _____ (does/doesn't) reduce the risk of getting HIV and _____ (does/doesn't) fully protect against skin-to-skin STIs.

5. An example of an external stimulus that might influence sexual behavior is
   a. the level of testosterone in the bloodstream.
   b. the onset of puberty.
   c. a sexually explicit film.
   d. an erotic fantasy or dream.

6. Which factors have researchers thus far found to be *unrelated* to the development of our sexual orientation?

7. How do evolutionary psychologists use the principle of *natural selection* to explain differences in mating preferences in men and women?

Continue testing yourself with 🔊 **LearningCurve** or 🔊 **Achieve Read & Practice**
to learn and remember most effectively.

Sensation and Perception

Superstudio/Getty Images

"I have perfect vision," explains writer and teacher Heather Sellers. Her vision may be perfect, but her perception is not. In her memoir, *You Don't Look Like Anyone I Know,* she tells of awkward moments resulting from her lifelong *prosopagnosia*—face blindness (Sellers, 2010).

In college, on a date at the Spaghetti Station, I returned from the bathroom and plunked myself down in the wrong booth, facing the wrong man. I remained unaware he was not my date even as my date (a stranger to me) accosted Wrong Booth Guy, and then stormed out. . . . I do not recognize myself in photos or videos. I can't recognize my stepsons in the soccer pick-up line; I failed to determine which husband was mine at a party, in the mall, at the market.

To avoid being perceived as snobby or aloof, Sellers sometimes fakes recognition. She often smiles at people she passes, in case she knows them. Or she pretends to know the person with whom she is talking. (Similarly, those of us with hearing loss often fake hearing.) But, Sellers points out, there is an upside: When encountering someone who previously irritated her, she typically feels no ill will—she doesn't recognize the person.

Unlike Sellers, most of us have a functioning area on the underside of our brain's right hemisphere that helps us recognize a familiar human face as soon as we detect it—in only one-seventh of a second (Jacques & Rossion, 2006; Rossion & Boremanse, 2011).

sensation the process by which our sensory receptors and nervous system receive and represent stimulus energies from our environment.

sensory receptors sensory nerve endings that respond to stimuli.

perception the process of organizing and interpreting sensory information, enabling us to recognize meaningful objects and events.

bottom-up processing analysis that begins with the sensory receptors and works up to the brain's integration of sensory information.

top-down processing information processing guided by higher-level mental processes, as when we construct perceptions drawing on our experience and expectations.

This remarkable ability illustrates a broader principle. *Nature's sensory gifts enable each animal to obtain essential information.* Other examples:

- Human ears are most sensitive to sound frequencies that include human voices, especially a baby's cry.
- Frogs, which feed on flying insects, have cells in their eyes that fire only in response to small, dark, moving objects. A frog could starve to death knee-deep in motionless flies. But let one zoom by and the frog's "bug detector" cells snap awake. (As Kermit the Frog said, "Time's fun when you're having flies.")
- Male silkworm moths' odor receptors can detect one-billionth of an ounce of chemical sex attractant per second, released by a female one mile away (Sagan, 1977). That is why there continue to be silkworms.

In this chapter, we'll look more closely at what psychologists have learned about how we sense and perceive our world. We begin by considering some basic principles that apply to all our senses. ▶

⟶ Basic Concepts of Sensation and Perception

How do we create meaning from the blizzard of sensory stimuli that bombards our body 24 hours a day? Meanwhile, in a silent, cushioned, inner world, our brain floats in utter darkness. By itself, it sees nothing. It hears nothing. It feels nothing. *So, how does the world out there get in?* To phrase the question scientifically: How do we construct our representations of the external world? How do a campfire's flicker, crackle, and smoky scent activate neural connections? And how, from this living neurochemistry, do we create our conscious experience of the fire's motion and temperature, its aroma and beauty? In search of answers, let's examine the basics of sensation and perception.

PROCESSING SENSATIONS AND PERCEPTIONS

LEARNING OBJECTIVE QUESTION (LOQ)

6-1 What are *sensation* and *perception*? What do we mean by *bottom-up processing* and *top-down processing*?

Heather Sellers' curious mix of "perfect vision" and face blindness illustrates the distinction between *sensation* and *perception*. When she looks at a friend, her **sensation** is normal: Her **sensory receptors** detect the same information yours would, and her nervous system transmits that information to her brain. Her **perception**—the processes by which her brain organizes and interprets sensory input—is *almost* normal. Thus, she may recognize people from their hair, gait, voice, or particular physique, just not from their face. Her experience is much like the struggle any human would have trying to recognize a specific penguin.

Under normal circumstances, sensation and perception blend into one continuous process.

- **Bottom-up processing** starts at your sensory receptors and works up to higher levels of processing.
- **Top-down processing** constructs perceptions from this sensory input by drawing on your experience and expectations.

As your brain absorbs the information in **FIGURE 6.1**, bottom-up processing enables your sensory systems to detect the lines, angles, and colors that form the flower and leaves. Using top-down processing, you interpret what your senses detect.

FIGURE 6.1

WHAT'S GOING ON HERE? Our sensory and perceptual processes work together to help us sort out complex images, including the hidden couple in Sandro Del-Prete's drawing, *The Flowering of Love.*

© Sandro Del-Prete/www.sandrodelprete.com

TRANSDUCTION

LOQ 6-2 What three steps are basic to all our sensory systems?

Every second of every day, our sensory systems perform an amazing feat: They convert one form of energy into another. Vision processes light energy. Hearing processes sound waves. All our senses

- *receive* sensory stimulation, often using specialized receptor cells.
- *transform* that stimulation into neural impulses.
- *deliver* the neural information to our brain.

The process of converting one form of energy into another that our brain can use is called **transduction.** Transduction is rather like translation—of a physical energy such as light waves into the brain's electrochemical language. Later in this chapter, we'll focus on individual sensory systems. How do we see? Hear? Feel pain? Taste? Smell? Keep our balance? In each case, one of our sensory systems receives, transforms, and delivers the information to our brain.

Let's explore some strengths and weaknesses in our ability to detect and interpret stimuli in the vast sea of energy around us.

🔒 RETRIEVE IT • • •   *ANSWERS IN APPENDIX E*

RI-1 What is the rough distinction between *sensation* and *perception*?

THRESHOLDS

LOQ 6-3 How do *absolute thresholds* and *difference thresholds* differ?

At this moment, we are being struck by X-rays and radio waves, ultraviolet and infrared light, and sound waves of very high and very low frequencies. To all of these we are blind and deaf. Other animals with differing needs detect a world that lies beyond our experience. Migrating birds stay on course aided by an internal magnetic compass. Bats and dolphins locate prey using sonar, bouncing echoing sound off objects. Bees navigate on cloudy days by detecting invisible (to us) polarized light.

Our senses open the shades just a crack, allowing us a restricted awareness of this vast sea of energy. But for our needs, this is enough.

Absolute Thresholds

To some kinds of stimuli we are exquisitely sensitive. Standing atop a mountain on an utterly dark, clear night, most of us could see a candle flame atop another mountain 30 miles away. We could feel the wing of a bee falling on our cheek. We could smell a single drop of perfume in a three-room apartment (Galanter, 1962).

German scientist and philosopher Gustav Fechner (1801–1887) studied the edge of our awareness of these faint stimuli, which he called an **absolute threshold**—the minimum stimulation necessary to detect a particular light, sound, pressure, taste, or odor 50 percent of the time. To test your absolute threshold for sounds, a hearing specialist would send tones, at varying levels, into each of your ears and record whether you could hear each tone (**FIGURE 6.2**). The test results would show the point where, for any sound frequency, half the time you could detect the sound and half the time you could not. That 50-50 point would define your absolute threshold.

Detecting a weak stimulus, or signal (such as a hearing-test tone), depends not only on its strength but also on our psychological state— our experience, expectations, motivation, and alertness. **Signal detection theory** predicts when we will detect weak signals (measured

transduction conversion of one form of energy into another. In sensation, the transforming of stimulus energies, such as sights, sounds, and smells, into neural impulses our brain can interpret.

absolute threshold the minimum stimulus energy needed to detect a particular stimulus 50 percent of the time.

signal detection theory a theory predicting how and when we detect the presence of a faint stimulus *(signal)* amid background stimulation *(noise)*. Assumes there is no single absolute threshold and that detection depends partly on a person's experience, expectations, motivation, and alertness.

FIGURE 6.2

ABSOLUTE THRESHOLD Can I detect this sound? An *absolute threshold* is the intensity at which a person can detect a stimulus half the time. Hearing tests locate these thresholds for various frequencies.

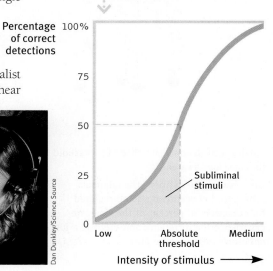

SIGNAL DETECTION When reading mammograms, health professionals seek to detect the presence of a faint cancer stimulus (*signal*) amid background stimulation (*noise*), and without raising false alarms. New 3D ultrasound breast imaging technologies aim to clarify the signal and reduce the rate of false alarms.

Tamara Collins/Delphinus Medical Technologies, Inc.

as our ratio of "hits" to "false alarms"). Signal detection theorists seek to understand why people respond differently to the same stimuli, and why the same person's reactions vary as circumstances change.

Stimuli you cannot consciously detect 50 percent of the time are **subliminal**—below your absolute threshold (Figure 6.2). One experiment using subliminal stimuli illustrated the deep reality of sexual orientation. As people gazed at the center of a screen, a photo of a nude person was flashed on one side and a scrambled version of the photo on the other side (Jiang et al., 2006). Because the nude images were immediately masked by a colored checkerboard, viewers consciously perceived nothing but flashes of color and so were unable to state on which side the nude had appeared. To test whether this unseen image had unconsciously attracted their attention, the experimenters then flashed a geometric figure on one side or the other. This, too, was quickly followed by a masking stimulus that interrupts the brain's processing before conscious perception (Herring et al., 2013; Van den Bussche et al., 2009). When asked to give the figure's angle, straight men guessed more accurately when it appeared where a nude *woman* had been a moment earlier (**FIGURE 6.3**). Gay men (and straight women) guessed more accurately when the geometric figure replaced a nude *man*. As other experiments confirm, we can evaluate a stimulus even when we are not consciously aware of it—and even when we are unaware of our evaluation (Ferguson & Zayas, 2009). So can we be *controlled* by subliminal messages? For more on that question, see Thinking Critically About: Subliminal Sensation and Subliminal Persuasion.

FIGURE 6.3

THE HIDDEN MIND After an image of a nude man or woman was flashed on a screen, then masked before it could be consciously perceived, people's attention was unconsciously drawn to images in a way that reflected their sexual orientation (Jiang et al., 2006).

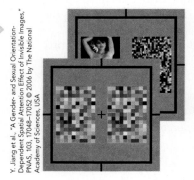

Y. Jiang et al., "A Gender- and Sexual Orientation-Dependent Spatial Attention Effect of Invisible Images," PNAS, 103, 17048–17052 © 2006 by The National Academy of Sciences, USA

LaunchPad For a helpful tutorial animation about this type of research method, see the **Video: Experiments.**

Difference Thresholds

To function effectively, we need absolute thresholds low enough to allow us to detect important sights, sounds, textures, tastes, and smells. We also need to detect small differences among stimuli. A musician must detect minute discrepancies when tuning an instrument. Parents must detect the sound of their own child's voice amid other children's voices. Even after I [DM] had spent two years in Scotland, all sheep *baa*s sounded alike to my ears. But not to their mother's, as I observed. After shearing, each ewe would streak directly to the *baa* of *her* lamb amid the chorus of other distressed lambs.

The **difference threshold** (or the *just noticeable difference [jnd]*) is the minimum stimulus difference a person can detect half the time. That detectable difference increases with the size of the stimulus. If we listen to our music at 40 decibels, we might barely detect an added 5 decibels (the jnd). But if we increase the volume to 110 decibels, we probably won't detect an additional 5-decibel change.

In the late 1800s, Ernst Weber described this with a principle so simple and so widely applicable that

Eric Isselée/Shutterstock

subliminal below one's absolute threshold for conscious awareness.

difference threshold the minimum difference between two stimuli required for detection 50 percent of the time. We experience the difference threshold as a *just noticeable difference* (or *jnd*).

ENGAGE 💡 **THE DIFFERENCE THRESHOLD** In this computer-generated copy of the Twenty-third Psalm, each line of the typeface increases slightly. How many lines are required for you to experience a just noticeable difference?

The LORD is my shepherd;
    I shall not want.
He maketh me to lie down
        in green pastures:
    he leadeth me
        beside the still waters.
He restoreth my soul:
    he leadeth me
        in the paths of righteousness
        for his name's sake.
Yea, though I walk through the valley
        of the shadow of death,
    I will fear no evil:
    for thou art with me;
        thy rod and thy staff
        they comfort me.
Thou preparest a table before me
        in the presence of mine enemies:
    thou anointest my head with oil,
        my cup runneth over.
Surely goodness and mercy
        shall follow me
        all the days of my life:
    and I will dwell
        in the house of the LORD
        for ever.

THINKING CRITICALLY ABOUT:

Subliminal Sensation and Subliminal Persuasion

LOQ 6-4   How are we affected by subliminal stimuli?

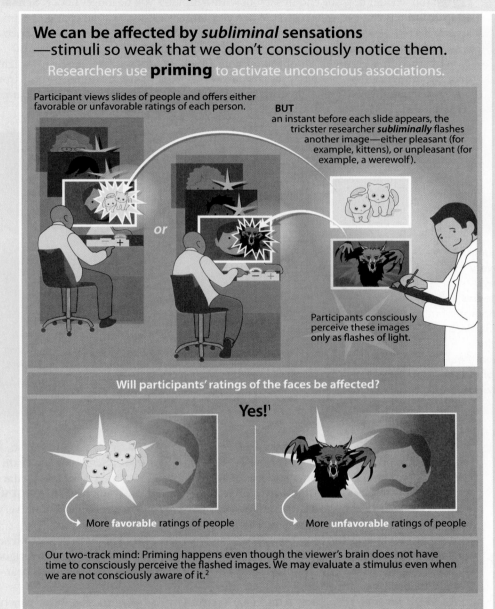

We can be affected by *subliminal* sensations
—stimuli so weak that we don't consciously notice them.
Researchers use **priming** to activate unconscious associations.

Participant views slides of people and offers either favorable or unfavorable ratings of each person.

BUT
an instant before each slide appears, the trickster researcher *subliminally* flashes another image—either pleasant (for example, kittens), or unpleasant (for example, a werewolf).

or

Participants consciously perceive these images only as flashes of light.

Will participants' ratings of the faces be affected?

Yes![1]

More **favorable** ratings of people

More **unfavorable** ratings of people

Our two-track mind: Priming happens even though the viewer's brain does not have time to consciously perceive the flashed images. We may evaluate a stimulus even when we are not consciously aware of it.[2]

So, we can be *primed*, but **can we be *persuaded* by subliminal stimuli,** for example to lose weight, stop smoking, or improve our memory?

Quiz 100%

Audio and video messages subliminally (without recipients' conscious awareness) announce:

"I am thin,"
"Cigarette smoke tastes bad,"
and
"I do well on tests. I have total recall of information."

Results from 16 experiments[3] showed no powerful, enduring influence on behavior. Not one of the recordings helped more than a placebo, which works only because we believe it will.

1. Krosnick et al., 1992.   2. Ferguson & Zayas, 2009.   3. Greenwald et al., 1991, 1992.

we still refer to it as **Weber's law:** For an average person to perceive a difference, two stimuli must differ by a constant minimum *percentage* (not a constant *amount*). The exact percentage varies, depending on the stimulus. Two lights, for example, must differ in intensity by 8 percent. Two objects must differ in weight by 2 percent. And two tones must differ in frequency by only 0.3 percent (Teghtsoonian, 1971).

🔒 RETRIEVE IT • • •   *ANSWERS IN APPENDIX E*

RI-2 Using sound as your example, explain how these concepts differ: *absolute threshold, subliminal stimulation,* and *difference threshold.*

priming the activation, often unconsciously, of certain associations, thus predisposing one's perception, memory, or response.

Weber's law the principle that, to be perceived as different, two stimuli must differ by a constant minimum percentage (rather than a constant amount).

sensory adaptation diminished sensitivity as a consequence of constant stimulation.

perceptual set a mental predisposition to perceive one thing and not another.

SENSORY ADAPTATION

LOQ 6-5   What is the function of sensory adaptation?

Sitting down on the bus, you are overwhelmed by your seatmate's heavy perfume. You wonder how she endures it, but within minutes you no longer notice. **Sensory adaptation** has come to your rescue. When constantly exposed to an unchanging stimulus, we become less aware of it because our nerve cells fire less frequently. (To experience sensory adaptation, roll up your sleeve. You will feel it—but only for a few moments.)

Why, then, if we stare at an object without flinching, does it *not* vanish from sight? Because, unnoticed by us, our eyes are always moving. This continual flitting from one spot to another ensures that stimulation on the eyes' receptors continually changes (**FIGURE 6.4**).

FIGURE 6.4

THE JUMPY EYE Our gaze jumps from one spot to another every third of a second or so, as eye-tracking equipment illustrated as a person looked at this photograph of Edinburgh's Princes Street Gardens (Henderson, 2007). The circles represent visual fixations, and the numbers indicate the time of fixation in milliseconds (300 milliseconds = 3/10ths of a second).

"We need above all to know about changes; no one wants or needs to be reminded 16 hours a day that his shoes are on." —Neuroscientist David Hubel (1979)

What if we actually could stop our eyes from moving? Would sights seem to vanish, as odors do? To find out, psychologists have devised ingenious instruments that maintain a constant image on the eye's inner surface. Imagine that we have fitted a volunteer, Mary, with such an instrument—a miniature projector mounted on a contact lens (**FIGURE 6.5a**). When Mary's eye moves, the image from the projector moves as well. So everywhere that Mary looks, the scene is sure to go.

If we project images through this instrument, what will Mary see? At first, she will see the complete image. But within a few seconds, as her sensory system begins to fatigue, things get weird. Bit by bit, the image vanishes, only to reappear and then disappear—often in fragments (Figure 6.5b).

Although sensory adaptation reduces our sensitivity, it offers an important benefit: freedom to focus on informative changes in our environment. Technology companies

FIGURE 6.5

SENSORY ADAPTATION: NOW YOU SEE IT, NOW YOU DON'T! (a) A projector mounted on a contact lens makes the projected image move with the eye. (b) Initially, the person sees the stabilized image. But thanks to sensory adaptation, her eye soon becomes accustomed to the unchanging stimulus. Rather than the full image, she begins to see fragments fading and reappearing.

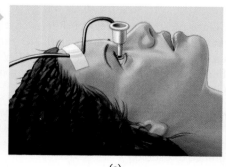

(a)

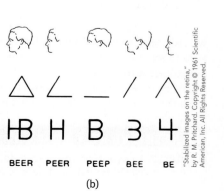

(b)

understand the attention-grabbing power of changing stimulation: New tweets, likes, snapchats, breaking news stories, and other background chatter popping up on our phones are hard to ignore. "There's always another hashtag to click on," one of Instagram's founding engineers told psychologist Adam Alter (2017). "Then it takes on its own life, like an organism, and people can become obsessive." If we're performing other tasks, these intrusions can harm our performance (Stothart et al., 2015).

Sensory adaptation even influences our perception of emotions. By creating a 50-50 morphed blend of an angry face and a scared face (**FIGURE 6.6b**), researchers showed that our visual system adapts to a static facial expression (as in Figure 6.6a or Figure 6.6c) by becoming less responsive to it (Butler et al., 2008). The effect is created by our brain, not our retinas. We know this because the illusion also works when we view either image (a) or (c) with one eye, and image (b) with the other eye.

The point to remember: Our sensory system is alert to novelty; bore it with repetition and it frees our attention for more important things. We see this principle again and again: *We perceive the world not exactly as it is, but as it is useful for us to perceive it.*

 (ASK YOURSELF)

What types of sensory adaptation have you experienced in the last 24 hours?

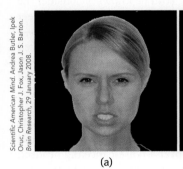 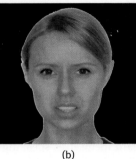 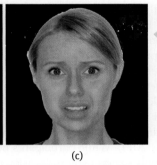

Scientific American Mind, Andrea Butler, Ipek Oruc, Christopher J. Fox, Jason J. S. Barton. *Brain Research,* 29 January 2008.

(a)   (b)   (c)

 **FIGURE 6.6**

EMOTION ADAPTATION Gaze at the angry face in image (a) for 20 to 30 seconds, then look at the face in image (b)—looks scared, yes? Then gaze at the scared face in image (c) for 20 to 30 seconds, before returning to the image (b) face—now looks angry, yes? (From Butler et al., 2008.)

🔒 **RETRIEVE IT** • • •   *ANSWERS IN APPENDIX E*

RI-3 Why is it that after wearing shoes for a while, you cease to notice them (until questions like this draw your attention back to them)?

PERCEPTUAL SET

LOQ 6-6 How do our expectations, contexts, motivation, and emotions influence our perceptions?

To see is to believe. As we less fully appreciate, to believe is to see. Through experience, we come to expect certain results. Those expectations may give us a **perceptual set**—a set of mental tendencies and assumptions that affects, top-down, what we hear, taste, feel, and see.

Consider **FIGURE 6.7**: Is image (b) an old or young woman? What we see in such a drawing can be influenced by first looking at either image (a) or image (b), which are both unambiguous versions (Boring, 1930). Likewise, in **FIGURE 6.8**, our expectations affect our perception.

IT'S AMAZING HOW PEOPLE SLOW DOWN WHEN YOU POINT A HAIR DRYER AT THEM.

The New Yorker Collection, 2002, Leo Cullum from cartoonbank.com

W. E. Hill, 1915.

(a)   (b)   (c)

 FIGURE 6.7

PERCEPTUAL SET Show a friend either image (a) or image (c). Then show image (b) and ask, "What do you see?" Whether your friend reports seeing an old woman's face or young woman's profile may depend on which of the other two drawings was viewed first. In each of those images, the meaning is clear, and it will establish perceptual expectations.

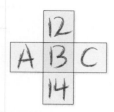

Do you perceive a number or a letter in the middle? If you read from left to right, you likely perceive a letter. But if you read from top to bottom, you may perceive the same center image as a number.

There
Are Two
Errors in The
The Title Of
This Book

—Title of a book by Robert M. Martin, 2011

In the note above, did you perceive what you expected in this title—and miss the errors? If you are still puzzled, see explanation below.[1]

"We hear and apprehend only what we already half know." —Henry David Thoreau, *Journal*, 1860

FIGURE 6.8

BELIEVING IS SEEING
What do you perceive? Is this Nessie, the Loch Ness monster, or a log?

Keystone/Getty Images

Everyday examples abound of perceptual set—of "mind over mind." In 1972, a British newspaper published unretouched photographs of a "monster" in Scotland's Loch Ness— "the most amazing pictures ever taken," stated the paper. If this information creates in you the same expectations it did in most of the paper's readers, you, too, will see the monster in a similar photo in Figure 6.8. But when a skeptical researcher approached the original photos with different expectations, he saw a curved tree limb—as had others the day that photo was shot (Campbell, 1986). What a difference a new perceptual set makes.

Perceptual set also affects what we hear—"stuffy nose" or "stuff he knows"? Consider the kindly airline pilot who, on a takeoff run, looked over at his sad co-pilot and said, "Cheer up." Expecting to hear the usual "Gear up," the co-pilot promptly raised the wheels— before they left the ground (Reason & Mycielska, 1982). Or ask the little boy who loved the prelude to U.S. baseball games when people rose to sing to him: "Jose, can you see?" Or tell people about a couple who suffered from their experience with some bad sects and (depending on what's on their mind) they may hear something quite different (bad sex).

Now consider this odd question: If you said one thing but heard yourself saying another, what would you think you said? To find out, a clever Swedish research team invited people to name a font color, such as saying "gray" when the word *green* appeared in a gray font (Lind et al., 2014). While participants heard themselves speaking over a noise-canceling headset, the wily experimenters occasionally substituted the participant's own previously recorded voice, such as saying "green" instead of "gray." Surprisingly, people usually missed the switch—and experienced the inserted word as self-produced. Again, hearing was believing.

Our expectations can also influence our taste perceptions. In one experiment, preschool children, by a 6-to-1 margin, thought french fries tasted better when served in a McDonald's bag rather than a plain white bag (Robinson et al., 2007). Another experiment invited campus bar patrons at the Massachusetts Institute of Technology to sample free beer (Lee et al., 2006). When researchers added a few drops of vinegar to a brand-name beer and called it "MIT brew," the tasters preferred it—unless they had been told they were drinking vinegar-laced beer. In that case, they expected, and usually experienced, a worse taste.

What determines our perceptual set? Through experience we form concepts, or *schemas,* that organize and interpret unfamiliar information. Our preexisting schemas for monsters and tree trunks influence how we apply top-down processing to interpret ambiguous sensations.

In everyday life, stereotypes about gender (another instance of perceptual set) can color perception. Without the obvious cues of pink or blue, people will struggle over whether to call the new baby "he" or "she." But told an infant is "David," people (especially children) have perceived "him" as bigger and stronger than when the same infant was called "Diana" (Stern & Karraker, 1989). Some differences, it seems, exist merely in the eyes of their beholders.

🔒 **RETRIEVE IT • • •**   *ANSWERS IN APPENDIX E*

RI-4 Does *perceptual set* involve bottom-up or top-down processing? Why?

CONTEXT, MOTIVATION, AND EMOTION

Perceptual set influences how we interpret stimuli. But our immediate context, and the motivation and emotion we bring to a situation, also affect our interpretations.

CONTEXT Social psychologist Lee Ross invited us to recall our own perceptions in different contexts: "Ever notice that when you're driving you hate pedestrians,

 **ASK YOURSELF**

Can you recall a time when your expectations influenced how you perceived a person or group? What happened?

---
1. The title's first error is its repeated "The." Its ironic second error is its misstatement that there are two errors, when there is only one.

 FIGURE 6.9

CULTURE AND CONTEXT EFFECTS What is above the woman's head? In one classic study, most rural East Africans questioned said the woman was balancing a metal box or can on her head (a typical way to carry water at that time). They also perceived the family as sitting under a tree. Westerners, used to running water and box-like houses with corners, were more likely to perceive the family as being indoors, with the woman sitting under a window (Gregory & Gombrich, 1973).

the way they saunter through the crosswalk, almost daring you to hit them, but when you're walking you hate drivers?" (Jaffe, 2004).

Some other examples of the power of context:

- When holding a gun, people become more likely to perceive another person as gun-toting—a phenomenon that has led to the shooting of some unarmed people who were actually holding their phone or wallet (Witt & Brockmole, 2012).

- Imagine hearing a noise interrupted by the words "eel is on the wagon." Likely, you would actually perceive the first word as *wheel*. Given "eel is on the orange," you would more likely hear *peel*. In each case, the context creates an expectation that, top-down, influences our perception (Grossberg, 1995).

- Cultural context helps inform our perceptions, so it's not surprising that people from different cultures view things differently, as in **FIGURE 6.9**.

- How is the woman in **FIGURE 6.10** feeling? The context provided in **FIGURE 6.11** will leave no doubt.

MOTIVATION Motives give us energy as we work toward a goal. Like context, they can bias our interpretations of neutral stimuli:

- Desirable objects, such as a water bottle viewed by a thirsty person, seem closer than they really are (Balcetis & Dunning, 2010). This perceptual bias energizes our going for it.

- A to-be-climbed hill can seem steeper when we are carrying a heavy backpack, and a walking destination further away when we are feeling tired (Burrow et al., 2016; Philbeck & Witt, 2015; Proffitt, 2006a,b). Going on a diet can lighten our biological "backpack" (Taylor-Covill & Eves, 2016). When heavy people lose weight, hills and stairs no longer seem so steep.

- A softball appears bigger when you are hitting well, as researchers observed after asking players to choose a circle the size of the ball they had just hit well or poorly (Witt & Proffitt, 2005). There's also a reciprocal phenomenon: Seeing a target as bigger—as happens when athletes focus directly on a target—improves performance (Witt et al., 2012).

EMOTION Other clever experiments have demonstrated that emotions can shove our perceptions in one direction or another:

- Hearing sad music can predispose people to perceive a sad meaning in spoken homophonic words—*mourning* rather than *morning*, *die* rather than *dye*, *pain* rather than *pane* (Halberstadt et al., 1995).

- A hill seems less steep to people who feel others understand them (Oishi et al., 2013).

Craig Klomparens/Hope College

 FIGURE 6.10

WHAT EMOTION IS THIS? (See Figure 6.11.)

"When you're hitting the ball, it comes at you looking like a grapefruit. When you're not, it looks like a black-eyed pea." —Former Major League Baseball player George Scott

HEARING HYPE Why do people pay millions of dollars for old Italian violins? They believe the sound quality is unmatched. Unfortunately, a recent study showed that, under blind conditions, listeners generally preferred the sound of inexpensive, modern violins over expensive, old Italian violins (Fritz et al., 2017).

Inti St. Clair/Getty Images

- When angry, people more often perceive neutral objects as guns (Baumann & DeSteno, 2010).

- When made to feel mildly upset by subliminal exposure to a scowling face, people perceive a neutral face as less attractive and less likeable (Anderson et al., 2012).

Emotions and motives color our *social* perceptions, too. People more often perceive solitary confinement, sleep deprivation, and cold temperatures as "torture" when experiencing a small dose of such themselves (Nordgren et al., 2011). Spouses who feel loved and appreciated perceive less threat in stressful marital events—"He's just having a bad day" (Murray et al., 2003).

The point to remember: Much of what we perceive comes not just from what's "out there," but also from what's behind our eyes and between our ears. Through top-down processing, our experiences, assumptions, expectations—and even our context, motivation, and emotions—can shape and color our views of reality.

FIGURE 6.11
CONTEXT MAKES CLEARER The Hope College volleyball team celebrates its national championship winning moment.

Craig Klomparens/Hope College

🔒 REVIEW BASIC CONCEPTS OF SENSATION AND PERCEPTION

⟫ Learning Objectives

TEST YOURSELF Answer these repeated Learning Objective Questions on your own (before checking the answers in Appendix D) to improve your retention of the concepts (McDaniel et al., 2009, 2015).

6-1 What are *sensation* and *perception*? What do we mean by *bottom-up processing* and *top-down processing*?

6-2 What three steps are basic to all our sensory systems?

6-3 How do *absolute thresholds* and *difference thresholds* differ?

6-4 How are we affected by subliminal stimuli?

6-5 What is the function of sensory adaptation?

6-6 How do our expectations, contexts, motivation, and emotions influence our perceptions?

⟫ Terms and Concepts to Remember

TEST YOURSELF Write down the definition yourself, then check your answer on the referenced page.

sensation, **p. 190**

sensory receptors, **p. 190**

perception, **p. 190**

bottom-up processing, **p. 190**

top-down processing, **p. 190**

transduction, **p. 191**

absolute threshold, **p. 191**

signal detection theory, **p. 191**

subliminal, **p. 192**

difference threshold, **p. 192**

priming, **p. 193**

Weber's law, **p. 193**

sensory adaptation, **p. 194**

perceptual set, **p. 194**

⟫ Experience the Testing Effect

TEST YOURSELF Answer the following questions on your own first, then check your answers in Appendix E.

1. Sensation is to _____ as perception is to
_____.

   a. absolute threshold; difference threshold

   b. bottom-up processing; top-down processing

   c. interpretation; detection

   d. grouping; priming

2. The process by which we organize and interpret sensory information is called _____.

3. Subliminal stimuli are
   a. too weak to be processed by the brain.
   b. consciously perceived more than 50 percent of the time.
   c. strong enough to affect our behavior at least 75 percent of the time.
   d. below our absolute threshold for conscious awareness.

4. Another term for *difference threshold* is the

   _____ _____ _____.

5. Weber's law states that for a difference to be perceived, two stimuli must differ by
   a. a fixed or constant energy amount.
   b. a constant minimum percentage.

   c. a constantly changing amount.
   d. more than 7 percent.

6. Sensory adaptation helps us focus on
   a. visual stimuli.
   b. auditory stimuli.
   c. constant features of the environment.
   d. important changes in the environment.

7. Our perceptual set influences what we perceive. This mental tendency reflects our
   a. experiences, assumptions, and expectations.
   b. sensory adaptation.
   c. priming ability.
   d. difference thresholds.

Continue testing yourself with 📖 **LearningCurve** or 📖 **Achieve Read & Practice** to learn and remember most effectively.

⟶ Vision: Sensory and Perceptual Processing

LIGHT ENERGY AND EYE STRUCTURES

LOQ 6-7   What are the characteristics of the energy that we see as visible light? What structures in the eye help focus that energy?

Our eyes receive light energy and *transduce* (transform) it into neural messages. From this neural input, our brain—in one of life's greatest wonders—then creates what we consciously see. How does such a taken-for-granted yet extraordinary thing happen?

The Stimulus Input: Light Energy

When you look at a bright red tulip, the stimuli striking your eyes are not particles of the color red but pulses of electromagnetic energy that your visual system *perceives* as red. What we see as visible light is but a thin slice of the wide spectrum of electromagnetic energy, ranging from imperceptibly short gamma waves to the long waves of radio transmission (**FIGURE 6.12**). Other portions are visible to other animals. Bees, for instance, cannot see what we perceive as red but can see ultraviolet light.

Light travels in waves, and the shape of those waves influences what we see. Light's **wavelength** is the distance from one wave peak to the next (**FIGURE 6.13a**). Wavelength determines **hue,** the color we experience, such as a tulip's red petals or green leaves. A light wave's *amplitude,* or height, determines its **intensity**—the amount of energy the wave contains. Intensity influences brightness (Figure 6.13b).

To understand *how* we transform physical energy into color and meaning, we need to know more about vision's window—the eye.

The Eye

Light enters the eye through the *cornea,* which bends light to help provide focus (**FIGURE 6.14**). The light then passes through the *pupil,* a small adjustable opening. Surrounding the pupil and controlling its size is the *iris,* a colored muscle that dilates or constricts in response to light intensity. Each iris is so distinctive that an iris-scanning machine can confirm your identity.

wavelength the distance from the peak of one light wave or sound wave to the peak of the next. Electromagnetic wavelengths vary from the short gamma waves to the long pulses of radio transmission.

hue the dimension of color that is determined by the wavelength of light; what we know as the color names *blue, green,* and so forth.

intensity the amount of energy in a light wave or sound wave, which influences what we perceive as brightness or loudness. Intensity is determined by the wave's amplitude (height).

FIGURE 6.12

THE WAVELENGTHS WE SEE What we see as light is only a tiny slice of a wide spectrum of electromagnetic energy, which ranges from gamma rays as short as the diameter of an atom to radio waves over a mile long. The wavelengths visible to the human eye (shown enlarged) extend from the shorter waves of blue-violet light to the longer waves of red light.

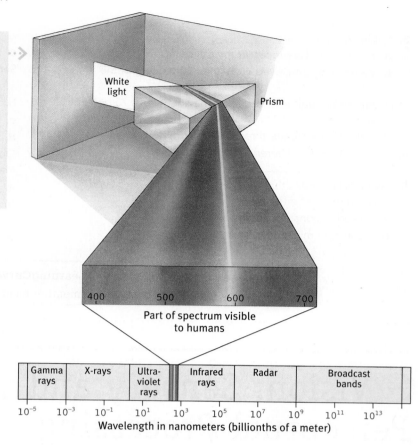

Part of spectrum visible to humans

Wavelength in nanometers (billionths of a meter)

FIGURE 6.13

THE PHYSICAL PROPERTIES OF WAVES (a) Waves vary in *wavelength* (the distance between successive peaks). *Frequency*, the number of complete wavelengths that can pass a point in a given time, depends on the wavelength. The shorter the wavelength, the higher the frequency. Wavelength determines the perceived *color* of light. (b) Waves also vary in amplitude (the height from peak to trough). Wave *amplitude* influences the perceived *brightness* of colors.

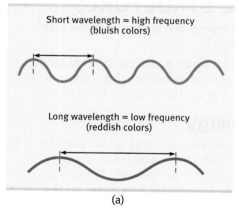

(a)

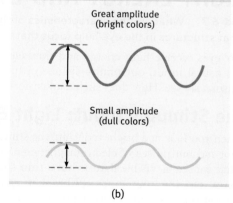

(b)

FIGURE 6.14

THE EYE Light rays reflected from a candle pass through the cornea, pupil, and lens. The curvature and thickness of the lens change to bring nearby or distant objects into focus on the retina. Rays from the top of the candle strike the bottom of the retina, and those from the left side of the candle strike the right side of the retina. The candle's image on the retina thus appears upside down and reversed.

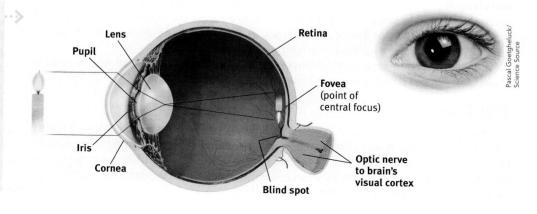

Pascal Goetgheluck/ Science Source

The iris responds to your cognitive and emotional states. Imagine a sunny sky and your iris will constrict, making your pupil smaller; imagine a dark room and it will dilate (Laeng & Sulutvedt, 2014). The iris also constricts when you feel disgust or you are about to answer *No* to a question (de Gee et al., 2014; Goldinger & Papesh, 2012). And when you're feeling amorous, your telltale dilated pupils and resulting dark eyes subtly signal your interest.

After passing through your pupil, light hits the transparent *lens* in your eye. The lens then focuses the light rays into an image on your **retina,** a multilayered tissue on the eyeball's sensitive inner surface. To focus the rays, the lens changes its curvature and thickness, in a process called **accommodation.** If the lens focuses the image on a point in front of the retina, you see near objects clearly but not distant objects. This nearsightedness—*myopia*—can be remedied with glasses, contact lenses, or surgery.

For centuries, scientists knew that an image of a candle passing through a small opening will cast an inverted mirror image on a dark wall behind. If the image passing through the pupil casts this sort of upside-down image on the retina, as in Figure 6.14, how can we see the world right side up? Eventually, the answer became clear: The retina doesn't "see" a whole image. Rather, its millions of receptor cells convert particles of light energy into neural impulses and forward those to the brain. *There,* the impulses are reassembled into a perceived, upright-seeming image. And along the way, visual information processing percolates through progressively more abstract levels, all at astonishing speed. Consider: As a baseball pitcher's fastball approaches home plate, the light signals work their way from the batter's retina to the visual cortex, which then informs the motor cortex, which then sends out orders to contract the muscles—all within the 4/10ths of a second that the ball is in flight.

retina the light-sensitive inner surface of the eye, containing the receptor rods and cones plus layers of neurons that begin the processing of visual information.

accommodation the process by which the eye's lens changes shape to focus near or far objects on the retina.

rods retinal receptors that detect black, white, and gray, and are sensitive to movement; necessary for peripheral and twilight vision, when cones don't respond.

cones retinal receptors that are concentrated near the center of the retina and that function in daylight or in well-lit conditions. Cones detect fine detail and give rise to color sensations.

optic nerve the nerve that carries neural impulses from the eye to the brain.

blind spot the point at which the optic nerve leaves the eye, creating a "blind" spot because no receptor cells are located there.

INFORMATION PROCESSING IN THE EYE AND BRAIN

The Eye-to-Brain Pathway

LOQ 6-8   How do the rods and cones process information, and what is the path information travels from the eye to the brain?

Imagine that you could follow behind a single light-energy particle after it entered your eye. First, you would thread your way through the retina's sparse outer layer of cells. Then, reaching the back of your eye, you would encounter its buried receptor cells, the **rods** and **cones** (**FIGURE 6.15**). There, you would see the light energy trigger chemical changes. That chemical reaction would spark neural signals in nearby *bipolar cells.* You could then watch the bipolar cells activate neighboring *ganglion cells,* whose axons twine together like the strands of a rope to form the **optic nerve.** After a momentary stopover at the thalamus, the information would fly on to the final destination, your visual cortex, in the occipital lobe at the back of your brain.

The optic nerve is an information highway from the eye to the brain. This nerve can send nearly 1 million messages at once through its nearly 1 million ganglion fibers. (The auditory nerve, which enables hearing, carries much less information through its mere 30,000 fibers.) We pay a small price for this high-speed connection, however. Your eye has a **blind spot,** with no receptor cells, where the optic nerve leaves the eye (**FIGURE 6.16**). Close one eye and you won't see a black hole, however. Without seeking your approval, your brain fills in the hole.

FIGURE 6.15
THE RETINA'S REACTION TO LIGHT

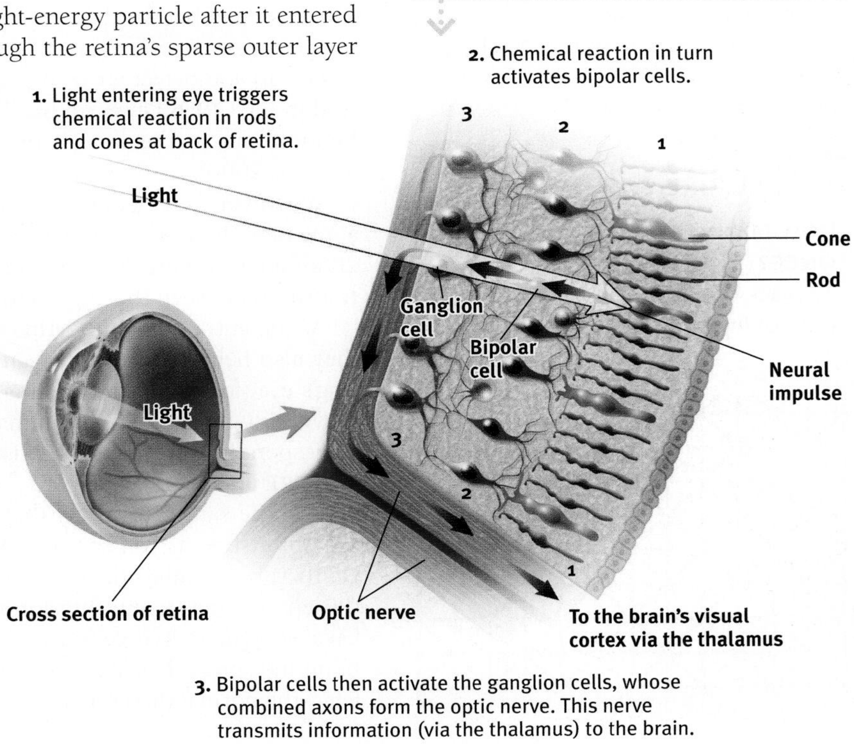

1. Light entering eye triggers chemical reaction in rods and cones at back of retina.

2. Chemical reaction in turn activates bipolar cells.

Cone
Rod
Ganglion cell
Bipolar cell
Neural impulse
Light
Cross section of retina
Optic nerve
To the brain's visual cortex via the thalamus

3. Bipolar cells then activate the ganglion cells, whose combined axons form the optic nerve. This nerve transmits information (via the thalamus) to the brain.

ENGAGE

FIGURE 6.16

THE BLIND SPOT

🔒 **RETRIEVE IT • • •**

ANSWERS IN APPENDIX E

RI-1 There are no receptor cells where the optic nerve leaves the eye. This creates a blind spot in your vision. To demonstrate, close your left eye, look at the spot above, and move your face away until one of the cars disappears. (Which one do you predict it will be?) Repeat with your right eye closed—and note that now the other car disappears. Can you explain why?

RETAIN

🔒 **TABLE 6.1**

Receptors in the Human Eye: Rod-Shaped Rods and Cone-Shaped Cones

Omikron/Science Source

	Cones	Rods
Number	6 million	120 million
Location in retina	Center	Periphery
Sensitivity in dim light	Low	High
Color sensitivity	High	Low
Detail sensitivity	High	Low

Rods and cones are our eyes' light-sensitive *photoreceptors*. They differ in where they're found and what they do (**TABLE 6.1**). *Cones* cluster in and around the **fovea,** the retina's area of central focus (Figure 6.14). Many cones have their own hotline to the brain: One cone transmits its message to a single bipolar cell, which relays the message to the visual cortex (where a large area receives input from the fovea). These direct connections preserve the cones' precise information, making them better able to detect fine detail. Although cones can detect white, they also enable you to perceive color (Sabesan et al., 2016). But in dim light, they become unresponsive, so you see no colors.

ENGAGE

Unlike cones, which cluster in the center of your retina, *rods* are located around the retina's outer regions. Rods remain sensitive in dim light, and they enable black-and-white vision. Rods have no hotline to the brain. If cones are soloists, rods perform as a chorus. Several rods pool their faint energy output and funnel it onto a single bipolar cell, which sends the combined message to your brain. Cones and rods each provide a special sensitivity—cones to detail and color, and rods to faint light and peripheral motion. Stop for a minute and experience this rod-cone difference. Pick a word in this sentence and stare directly at it, focusing its image on the cones in your fovea. Notice that words a few inches off to the side appear blurred? Their image is striking your retina's outer regions, where rods predominate. Thus, when you drive or bike, rods help you detect a car in your peripheral vision well before you perceive its details. And in **FIGURE 6.17**, which has 12 black dots, you can see barely two at a time, with your brain filling in the less distinct peripheral input (Kitaoka, 2016, adapting Ninio & Stevens, 2000).

When you enter a darkened theater or turn off the light at night, your pupils dilate to allow more light to reach your retina. Your eyes adapt, but fully adapting typically takes 20 minutes or more. This period of dark adaptation matches the average natural twilight transition between the Sun's setting and darkness. How wonderfully made we are.

At the entry level, the retina's neural layers don't just pass along electrical impulses; they also help to encode and analyze sensory information. (The third neural layer in a frog's eye, for example, contains those "bug detector" cells that fire only in response to moving fly-like stimuli.) In human eyes, any given retinal area relays its information to a corresponding location in the visual cortex, in the occipital lobe at the back of your brain (**FIGURE 6.18**).

ENGAGE

The same sensitivity that enables retinal cells to fire messages can lead them to misfire, as you can demonstrate. Turn your eyes to the left, close them, and then gently rub the right side of your right eyelid with your fingertip. Note the patch of light to the left, moving as your finger moves. Why do you see light? Why at the left? This happens because your retinal cells are so responsive that even pressure triggers them. But your brain interprets their firing as light. Moreover, it interprets the light as coming from the left—the normal direction of light that activates the right side of the retina.

ENGAGE

FIGURE 6.17

HOW MANY DOTS CAN YOU SEE AT ONCE? Look at or near any of the 12 black dots and you can see them, but not in your peripheral vision.

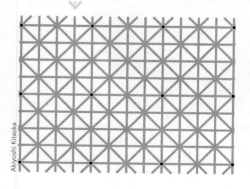

Akiyoshi Kitaoka

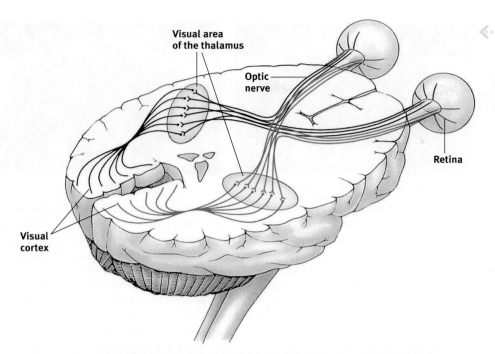

Visual area of the thalamus

Optic nerve

Retina

Visual cortex

⟵ **FIGURE 6.18**

PATHWAY FROM THE EYES TO THE VISUAL CORTEX Ganglion axons forming the optic nerve run to the thalamus, where they synapse with neurons that run to the visual cortex.

🔒 **RETRIEVE IT • • •**   *ANSWERS IN APPENDIX E*

RI-2 Some nocturnal animals, such as toads, mice, rats, and bats, have impressive night vision thanks to having many more _____ (rods/cones) than _____ (rods/cones) in their retinas. These creatures probably have very poor _____ (color/black-and-white) vision.

RI-3 Cats are able to open their _____ much wider than we can, which allows more light into their eyes so they can see better at night.

Kruglov_Orda/Shutterstock

ENGAGE   (ASK YOURSELF)

Consider your activities in the last hour. Which of them relied on your rods? Which relied on your cones? How would these activities be different—or impossible—without these cells' different abilities?

Color Processing

LOQ 6-9 How do we perceive color in the world around us?

We talk as though objects possess color: "A tomato is red." Recall the old question, "If a tree falls in the forest and no one hears it, does it make a sound?" We can ask the same of color: If no one sees the tomato, is it red?

The answer is *No.* First, the tomato is everything *but* red, because it *rejects* (reflects) the long wavelengths of red. Second, the tomato's color is our mental construction. As Sir Isaac Newton (1704) noted, "The [light] rays are not colored." Like all aspects of vision, our perception of color resides not in the object itself but in the theater of our brain, as evidenced by our dreaming in color.

One of vision's most basic and intriguing mysteries is how we see the world in color. How, from the light energy striking the retina, does our brain construct our experience of such a multitude of colors?

Modern detective work on the mystery of color vision began in the nineteenth century, when Hermann von Helmholtz built on the insights of an English physicist, Thomas Young. They knew that any color can be created by combining the light waves of three primary colors—red, green, and blue. So Young and von Helmholtz formed a hypothesis: The eye must therefore have three corresponding types of color receptors.

Years later, researchers confirmed the **Young-Helmholtz trichromatic (three-color) theory.** By measuring the response of various cones to different color stimuli, they confirmed that the retina does indeed have three types of color receptors, each especially sensitive to the wavelengths of red, green, and blue. When light stimulates combinations of these cones, we see other colors. For example, the retina has no separate receptors especially sensitive to yellow. But when red and green wavelengths stimulate both red-sensitive and green-sensitive cones, we see yellow.

"Only mind has sight and hearing; all things else are deaf and blind."
—Epicharmus, *Fragments*, 550 B.C.E.

fovea the central focal point in the retina, around which the eye's cones cluster.

Young-Helmholtz trichromatic (three-color) theory the theory that the retina contains three different types of color receptors—one most sensitive to red, one to green, one to blue—which, when stimulated in combination, can produce the perception of any color.

FIGURE 6.19

COLOR-DEFICIENT VISION The photo in image (a) shows how people with red-green deficiency perceived a 2015 Buffalo Bills versus New York Jets football game. "For the 8 percent of Americans like me that are red-green colorblind, this game is a nightmare to watch," tweeted one fan. "Everyone looks like they're on the same team," said another. The photo in image (b) shows how the game looked for those with normal color vision.

(a)   (b)

BEN SOLOMON/The New York Times/Redux Pictures

opponent-process theory the theory that opposing retinal processes (red-green, blue-yellow, white-black) enable color vision. For example, some cells are stimulated by green and inhibited by red; others are stimulated by red and inhibited by green.

feature detectors nerve cells in the brain's visual cortex that respond to specific features of the stimulus, such as shape, angle, or movement.

By one estimate, we can see differences among more than 1 million color variations (Neitz et al., 2001). Some lucky (mostly female) souls can see up to 100 million colors thanks to a genetic condition known as *tetrachromatic color vision* (Jordan et al., 2010). Asked to look at a leaf, a woman with tetrachromatic color vision said, "You might see dark green but I'll see violet, turquoise, blue. It's like a mosaic of color" (Ossola, 2014). Some other unlucky (mostly male) people—about 1 in 50—are "colorblind." Most people with color-deficient vision are not actually blind to all colors. They simply lack functioning red- or green-sensitive cones, or sometimes both. Their vision—perhaps unknown to them, because their lifelong vision *seems* normal—is monochromatic (one-color) or dichromatic (two-color) instead of trichromatic, making it impossible to distinguish the red and green in **FIGURE 6.19** (Boynton, 1979). Dogs, too, lack receptors for the wavelengths of red, giving them only limited, dichromatic color vision (Neitz et al., 1989).

But why do people blind to red and green often still see yellow? And why does yellow appear to be a pure color and not a mixture of red and green, the way purple is of red and blue? As physiologist Ewald Hering—a contemporary of von Helmholtz—noted, trichromatic theory leaves some parts of the color vision mystery unsolved.

Hering found a clue in *afterimages*. Stare at a green square for a while and then look at a white sheet of paper, and you will see red, green's *opponent color*. Stare at a yellow square and its opponent color, blue, will appear on the white paper. (To experience this, try the flag demonstration in **FIGURE 6.20**.) Hering formed another hypothesis: Color vision must involve two *additional* color processes, one responsible for red-versus-green perception, and one for blue-versus-yellow perception.

Indeed, a century later, researchers also confirmed Hering's hypothesis, now called the **opponent-process theory.** This concept is tricky, but here's the gist: Color vision depends on three sets of opposing retinal processes—*red-green, blue-yellow,* and *white-black.* As impulses travel to the visual cortex, some neurons in both the retina and the thalamus are turned "on" by red but turned "off" by green. Others are turned on by green but off by red (DeValois & DeValois, 1975). Like red and green marbles sent down a narrow tube, "red" and "green" messages cannot both travel at once. Red and green are thus opponents, so we see either red or green, not a reddish-green mixture. But red and blue travel in separate channels, so we *can* see a reddish-blue magenta.

So how does opponent-process theory help us understand negative afterimages, as in the flag demonstration? Here's the answer (for the green changing to red): First, you stared at green bars, which tired your green response. Then you stared at a white area. White contains all colors, including red. Because you had tired your green response, only the red part of the green-red pairing fired normally.

FIGURE 6.20

AFTERIMAGE EFFECT Stare at the center of the flag for a minute and then shift your eyes to the dot in the white space beside it. What do you see? (After tiring your neural response to black, green, and yellow, you should see their opponent colors.) Stare at a white wall and note how the size of the flag grows with the projection distance.

RETAIN The present solution to the mystery of color vision is therefore roughly this: *Color processing occurs in two stages.*

1. The retina's red, green, and blue cones respond in varying degrees to different color stimuli, as the Young-Helmholtz trichromatic theory suggested.

2. The cones' responses are then processed by opponent-process cells, as Hering's theory proposed.

🔒 RETRIEVE IT • • •   *ANSWERS IN APPENDIX E*

RI-4 What are two key theories of color vision? Are they contradictory or complementary? Explain.

Feature Detection

LOQ 6-10 Where are feature detectors located, and what do they do?

Scientists once likened the brain to a movie screen on which the eye projected images. Then along came David Hubel and Torsten Wiesel (1979), who showed that our visual processing deconstructs visual images and then reassembles them. Hubel and Wiesel received a Nobel Prize for their work on **feature detectors,** nerve cells in the occipital lobe's visual cortex that respond to a scene's specific visual features—to particular edges, lines, angles, and movements.

Using microelectrodes, they had discovered that some neurons fired actively when cats were shown lines at one angle, while other neurons responded to lines at a different angle. They surmised that these specialized neurons, now known as feature detectors, receive information from individual ganglion cells in the retina. Feature detectors pass this specific information to other cortical areas, where teams of cells (*supercell clusters*) respond to more complex patterns.

For biologically important objects and events, monkey brains (and surely ours as well) have a "vast visual encyclopedia" distributed as specialized cells (Perrett et al., 1990, 1992, 1994). These cells respond to one type of stimulus, such as a specific gaze, head angle, posture, or body movement. Other supercell clusters integrate this information and fire only when the cues collectively indicate the direction of someone's attention and approach. This instant analysis, which aided our ancestors' survival, also helps a soccer player anticipate where to strike the ball, and a driver to anticipate a pedestrian's next movement.

One temporal lobe area by your right ear (**FIGURE 6.21**) enables you to perceive faces and, thanks to a specialized neural network, to recognize them from varied viewpoints (Connor, 2010). If stimulated in this *fusiform face area,* you might spontaneously see faces—as did the participant who reported to an experimenter that "You just turned into someone else. Your face metamorphosed" (Koch, 2015). If this face recognition region were damaged, you might recognize other forms and objects, but not familiar faces.

When researchers temporarily disrupt the brain's face-processing areas with magnetic pulses, people are unable to recognize faces. But they can still recognize other objects, such as houses, because the brain's face perception occurs separately from its object perception (McKone et al., 2007; Pitcher et al., 2007). Thus, functional MRI (fMRI) scans have shown different brain areas activating when people viewed varied objects (Downing et al., 2001). Brain activity is so specific that, with the help of brain scans, researchers can tell whether people are "looking at a shoe, a chair, or a face, based on the pattern of their brain activity" (Haxby, 2001).

ENGAGE **💡 (ASK YOURSELF)**

Does it surprise you to learn that colors don't "live" in the objects we perceive—that in fact, these objects are everything *but* the color we experience? If someone had asked you "Is grass green?" before you read this section, how would you have responded?

RETAIN **🔒 📖 LaunchPad** For an interactive review of these color vision principles, visit **Topic Tutorial: PsychSim6, Colorful World.**

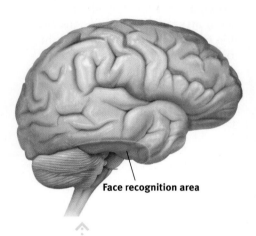

Face recognition area

FIGURE 6.21

FACE RECOGNITION PROCESSING In social animals such as humans, a large right temporal lobe area (shown here in a right-facing brain) is dedicated to the crucial task of face recognition.

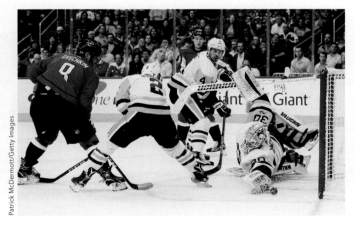

Patrick McDermott/Getty Images

SUPERCELLS SCORE In this 2017 National Hockey League game, Alex Ovechkin (in red) instantly processed visual information about the positions and movements of three opponents. By using his pattern-detecting supercells, Ovechkin somehow managed to get the puck into the net.

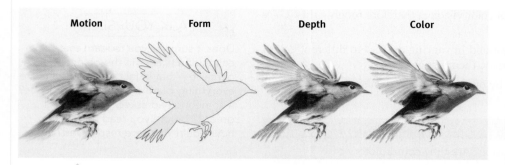

Motion   Form   Depth   Color

FIGURE 6.22

PARALLEL PROCESSING Studies of patients with brain damage suggest that the brain delegates the work of processing motion, form, depth, and color to different areas. After taking a scene apart, the brain integrates these subdimensions into the perceived image. How does the brain do this? The answer to this *binding problem* (how does the brain bind multiple sensory inputs into a single perception?) is the Holy Grail of vision research.

Parallel Processing

LOQ 6-11 How does the brain use parallel processing to construct visual perceptions?

Our brain achieves these and other remarkable feats by **parallel processing:** doing many things at once. To analyze a visual scene, the brain divides it into subdimensions—motion, form, depth, color—and works on each aspect simultaneously (**FIGURE 6.22**). We then construct our perceptions by integrating (*binding*) the separate but parallel work of these different visual teams (Livingstone & Hubel, 1988).

To recognize a face, your brain integrates information projected by your retinas to several visual cortex areas and compares it with stored information, thus enabling your fusiform face area to recognize the face: *Grandmother!* Scientists have debated whether this stored information is contained in a single cell or, more likely, distributed over a network of cells that build a facial image bit by bit. Some supercells—actually nicknamed *"grandmother cells"*—do appear to respond very selectively to 1 or 2 faces in 100 (Bowers, 2009; Quiroga et al., 2013). The whole face recognition process requires tremendous brain power: 30 percent of the cortex (10 times the brain area devoted to hearing).

Destroy or disable a neural workstation for a visual subtask, and something peculiar results, as happened to "Mrs. M." (Hoffman, 1998). After a stroke damaged areas near the rear of both sides of her brain, she could not perceive motion. People in a room seemed "suddenly here or there but I [had] not seen them moving." Pouring tea into a cup was a challenge because the fluid appeared frozen—she could not perceive it rising in the cup.

After stroke or surgery has damaged the brain's visual cortex, others have experienced *blindsight*. Shown a series of sticks, they report seeing nothing. Yet when asked to guess whether the sticks are vertical or horizontal, their visual intuition typically offers the correct response. When told, "You got them all right," they are astounded. There is, it seems, a second "mind"—a parallel processing system—operating unseen. These separate visual systems for perceiving and for acting illustrate once again the astonishing dual processing of our two-track mind.

LaunchPad For a 4-minute depiction of a blindsight patient, see the **Video— Blindsight: Seeing Without Awareness.**

* * *

Think about the wonders of visual processing. As you read these words, the letters reflect light rays onto your retina, which triggers a process that sends formless nerve impulses to several areas of your brain, which integrate the information and decode meaning. The amazing result: We have transferred information across time and space, from our minds to your mind (**FIGURE 6.23**). That all of this happens instantly, effortlessly, and continuously is indeed awesome. As Roger Sperry (1985) observed, the "insights of science give added, not lessened, reasons for awe, respect, and reverence."

"I am . . . wonderfully made." —King David, Psalm 139:14

FIGURE 6.23

A SIMPLIFIED SUMMARY OF VISUAL INFORMATION PROCESSING

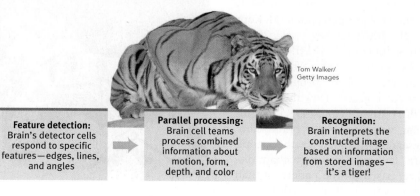

Tom Walker/ Getty Images

| Scene | → | **Retinal processing:** Receptor rods and cones → bipolar cells → ganglion cells | → | **Feature detection:** Brain's detector cells respond to specific features—edges, lines, and angles | → | **Parallel processing:** Brain cell teams process combined information about motion, form, depth, and color | → | **Recognition:** Brain interprets the constructed image based on information from stored images— it's a tiger! |

RI-5 What is the rapid sequence of events that occurs when you see and recognize a friend?

PERCEPTUAL ORGANIZATION

LOQ 6-12 How did the Gestalt psychologists understand perceptual organization, and how do figure-ground and grouping principles contribute to our perceptions?

It's one thing to understand how we see colors and shapes. But how do we organize and interpret those sights so that they become *meaningful* perceptions—a rose in bloom, a familiar face, a sunset?

Early in the twentieth century, a group of German psychologists noticed that people who are given a cluster of sensations tend to organize them into a **gestalt,** a German word meaning a "form" or a "whole." As we look straight ahead, we cannot separate the perceived scene into our left and right fields of view (each as seen with one eye closed). Our conscious perception is, at every moment, a seamless scene—an integrated whole.

Consider **FIGURE 6.24**: The individual elements of this figure, called a *Necker cube,* are really nothing but eight blue circles, each containing three converging white lines. When we view these elements all together, however, we see a cube that sometimes reverses direction. This phenomenon nicely illustrates a favorite saying of Gestalt psychologists: *In perception, the whole may exceed the sum of its parts.*

Over the years, the Gestalt psychologists demonstrated many principles we use to organize our sensations into perceptions (Wagemans et al., 2012a,b). Underlying all of them is a fundamental truth: *Our brain does more than register information about the world.* Perception is not just opening a shutter and letting a picture print itself on the brain. We filter incoming information and *construct* perceptions. Mind matters.

American Journal of Psychology. Copyright 1977 by the Board of Trustees of the University of Illinois. Used with permission of the University of Illinois Press.

parallel processing   processing many aspects of a stimulus or problem at once.

gestalt   an organized whole. Gestalt psychologists emphasized our tendency to integrate pieces of information into meaningful wholes.

figure-ground   the organization of the visual field into objects (the *figures*) that stand out from their surroundings (the *ground*).

FIGURE 6.24

A NECKER CUBE What do you see: circles with white lines, or a cube? If you stare at the cube, you may notice that it reverses location, moving the tiny X in the center from the front edge to the back. At times, the cube may seem to float forward, with circles behind it. At other times, the circles may become holes through which the cube appears, as though it were floating behind them. There is far more to perception than meets the eye. (From Bradley et al., 1976.)

Form Perception

Imagine designing a video-computer system that, like your eye-brain system, could recognize faces at a glance. What abilities would it need?

FIGURE AND GROUND To start with, the system would need to perceive **figure-ground**—to separate faces from their backgrounds. In our eye-brain system, this is our first perceptual task—perceiving any object (the *figure*) as distinct from its surroundings (the *ground*). As you read, the words are the figure; the white space is the ground. This perception applies to our hearing, too. As you hear voices at a party, the one you attend to becomes the figure; all others are part of the ground. Sometimes the same stimulus can trigger more than one perception. In **FIGURE 6.25**, the figure-ground relationship continually reverses. First we see the vase, then the faces, but we always organize the stimulus into a figure seen against a ground.

GROUPING Having discriminated figure from ground, we (and our video-computer system) must also organize the figure into a *meaningful*

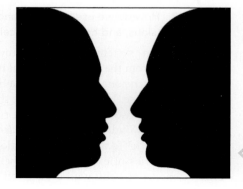

FIGURE 6.25
REVERSIBLE FIGURE AND GROUND

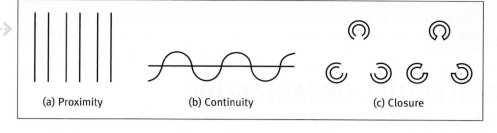

(a) Proximity   (b) Continuity   (c) Closure

FIGURE 6.26

THREE PRINCIPLES OF GROUPING
(a) Thanks to *proximity*, we group nearby figures together. We see not six separate lines, but three sets of two lines. (b) Through *continuity*, we perceive smooth, continuous patterns rather than discontinuous ones. This pattern could be a series of alternating semicircles, but we perceive it as two continuous lines—one wavy, one straight. (c) Using *closure*, we fill in gaps to create a complete, whole object. Thus we assume that the circles on the left are complete but partially blocked by the (illusory) triangle. Add nothing more than little line segments to close off the circles and your brain stops constructing a triangle.

form. Some basic features of a scene—such as color, movement, and light-dark contrast—we process instantly and automatically (Treisman, 1987). Our minds bring order and form to other stimuli by following certain rules for **grouping,** also identified by the Gestalt psychologists. These rules, which we apply even as infants and even in our touch perceptions, illustrate how the perceived whole differs from the sum of its parts (Gallace & Spence, 2011; Quinn et al., 2002; Rock & Palmer, 1990). See **FIGURE 6.26** for three examples. Such principles usually help us construct reality. Sometimes, however, they lead us astray, as when we look at the doghouse in **FIGURE 6.27**.

Photo by Walter Wick. Reprinted by permission from GAMES Magazine © 1983 PCS Games Limited Partnership

 FIGURE 6.27

GREAT GESTALT! What's the secret to this impossible doghouse? You probably perceive this doghouse as a gestalt—a whole (though impossible) structure. Actually, your brain imposes this sense of wholeness on the picture. As Figure 6.31 shows, Gestalt grouping principles such as closure and continuity are at work here.

🔒 **RETRIEVE IT • • •**   *ANSWERS IN APPENDIX E*

RI-6 In terms of perception, a band's lead singer would be considered _____ (figure/ground), and the other musicians would be considered _____ (figure/ground).

RI-7 What do we mean when we say that, in perception, "the whole may exceed the sum of its parts"?

Depth Perception

LOQ 6-13 How do we use binocular and monocular cues to perceive the world in three dimensions, and how do we perceive motion?

Our eye-brain system performs many remarkable feats, among which is **depth perception.** From the two-dimensional images falling on our retinas, we somehow organize three-dimensional perceptions that let us estimate the distance of an oncoming car or a faraway house. How do we acquire this ability? Are we born with it? Do we learn it?

As Eleanor Gibson picnicked on the rim of the Grand Canyon, her scientific curiosity kicked in. She wondered: *Would a toddler peering over the rim perceive the dangerous drop-off and draw back?* To answer that question and others, Gibson and Richard Walk (1960) designed a series of experiments in their Cornell University laboratory using a **visual cliff**—a model of a cliff with a "drop-off" area that was actually covered by sturdy glass.

grouping the perceptual tendency to organize stimuli into coherent groups.

depth perception the ability to see objects in three dimensions although the images that strike the retina are two-dimensional; allows us to judge distance.

visual cliff a laboratory device for testing depth perception in infants and young animals.

binocular cue a depth cue, such as retinal disparity, that depends on the use of two eyes.

retinal disparity a binocular cue for perceiving depth. By comparing retinal images from the two eyes, the brain computes distance—the greater the disparity (difference) between the two images, the closer the object.

They placed 6- to 14-month-old infants on the edge of the "cliff" and had the infants' mothers coax them to crawl out onto the glass (**FIGURE 6.28**). Most infants refused to do so, indicating that they could perceive depth.

Had they *learned* to perceive depth? Learning appears also to be part of the human story, because crawling, no matter when it begins, seems to increase infants' wariness of heights (Adolph et al., 2014; Campos et al., 1992). But depth perception is also partly innate. Mobile newborn animals—even those with no visual experience (including young kittens, a day-old goat, and newly hatched chicks)—also refuse to venture across the visual cliff. Thus, biology prepares us to be wary of heights, and experience amplifies that fear.

If we were to build the ability to perceive depth into our video-computer system, what rules might enable it to convert two-dimensional images into a single three-dimensional perception? A good place to start would be the depth cues our brain receives from information supplied by one or both of our eyes.

BINOCULAR CUES People who see with two eyes perceive depth thanks partly to **binocular cues.** Here's an example: With both eyes open, hold two pens or pencils in front of you and touch their tips together. Now do so with one eye closed. A more difficult task, yes?

We use binocular cues to judge the distance of nearby objects. One such cue is *convergence,* the inward angle of the eyes focusing on a near object. Another is **retinal disparity.** Because your eyes are about 2 inches apart, your retinas receive slightly different images of the world. By comparing these two images, your brain can judge how close an object is to you. The greater the disparity (difference) between the two retinal images, the closer the object. Try it. Hold your two index fingers, with the tips about half an inch apart, directly in front of your nose, and your retinas will receive quite different views. If you close one eye and then the other, you can see the difference. (Bring your fingers close and you can create a finger sausage, as in **FIGURE 6.29**.) At a greater distance—say, when you hold your fingers at arm's length—the disparity is smaller.

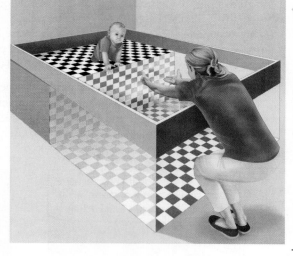

FIGURE 6.28

VISUAL CLIFF Eleanor Gibson and Richard Walk devised this miniature cliff with a glass-covered drop-off to determine whether crawling infants and newborn animals can perceive depth. Even when coaxed, infants are reluctant to venture onto the glass over the cliff.

LaunchPad See the **Video: Experiments** for a helpful tutorial animation about this type of research method.

LaunchPad Check your understanding of these cues by engaging online with **Concept Practice: Depth Cues.**

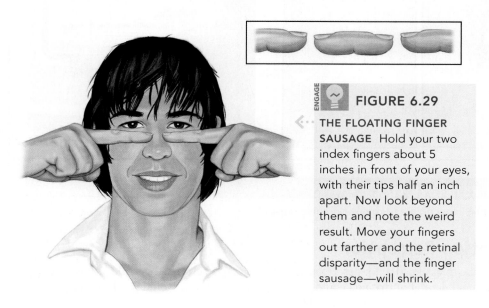

FIGURE 6.29

THE FLOATING FINGER SAUSAGE Hold your two index fingers about 5 inches in front of your eyes, with their tips half an inch apart. Now look beyond them and note the weird result. Move your fingers out farther and the retinal disparity—and the finger sausage—will shrink.

"I can't go on living with such lousy depth perception."

monocular cue a depth cue, such as interposition or linear perspective, available to either eye alone.

We could easily include retinal disparity in our video-computer system. Moviemakers sometimes film a scene with two cameras placed a few inches apart. Viewers then watch the film through glasses that allow the left eye to see only the image from the left camera, and the right eye to see only the image from the right camera. The resulting effect, as 3-D movie fans know, mimics or exaggerates normal retinal disparity giving the perception of depth.

MONOCULAR CUES How do we judge whether a person is 10 or 100 meters away? Retinal disparity won't help us here, because there won't be much difference between the images cast on our right and left retinas. At such distances, we depend on **monocular cues** (depth cues available to each eye separately). See **FIGURE 6.30** for some examples.

FIGURE 6.30

MONOCULAR DEPTH CUES

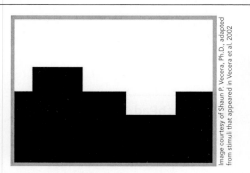

RELATIVE HEIGHT We perceive objects higher in our field of vision as farther away. Because we assume the lower part of a figure-ground illustration is closer, we perceive it as figure (Vecera et al., 2002). Invert this illustration and the black will become ground, like a night sky.

LIGHT AND SHADOW Shading produces a sense of depth consistent with our assumption that light comes from above. If you invert this illustration, the hollow will become a hill.

RELATIVE SIZE If we assume two objects are similar in size, *most* people perceive the one that casts the smaller retinal image as farther away.

LINEAR PERSPECTIVE Parallel lines appear to meet in the distance. The sharper the angle of convergence, the greater the perceived distance.

INTERPOSITION If one object partially blocks our view of another, we perceive it as closer.

RELATIVE MOTION As we move, objects that are actually stable may appear to move. If while riding on a bus you fix your gaze on some point—say, a house—the objects beyond the fixation point will appear to move with you. Objects in front of the point will appear to move backward. The farther an object is from the fixation point, the faster it will seem to move.

DIRECTION OF PASSENGER'S MOTION →

RETRIEVE IT • • •

ANSWERS IN APPENDIX E

RI-8 How do we normally perceive depth?

Motion Perception

Imagine that, like Mrs. M. described earlier, you could perceive the world as having color, form, and depth but that you could not see motion. Not only would you be unable to bike or drive, you would have trouble writing, eating, and walking.

Normally your brain computes motion based partly on its assumption that shrinking objects are retreating (not getting smaller) and enlarging objects are approaching. But sometimes our brain is tricked into believing what it is not seeing. When large and small objects move at the same speed, the large objects appear to move more slowly. Thus, trains seem to move slower than cars, and jumbo jets seem to land more slowly than little jets.

Our brain also perceives a rapid series of slightly varying still images as continuous movement—a phenomenon called *stroboscopic movement*. As film animators know well, a super-fast slide show of 24 still images a second will create an illusion of movement. We construct that motion in our head, just as we construct movement in blinking marquees and holiday lights. We perceive two adjacent stationary lights blinking on and off in quick succession as one single light jumping back and forth. Lighted signs exploit this **phi phenomenon** with a succession of lights that creates the impression of, say, a moving arrow.

Perceptual Constancy

LOQ 6-14 How do perceptual constancies help us construct meaningful perceptions?

So far, we have noted that our video-computer system must perceive objects as we do—as having a distinct form and location. Its next task is to recognize objects without being deceived by changes in their color, brightness, shape, or size—a *top-down* process called **perceptual constancy.** Regardless of the viewing angle, distance, and illumination, we can identify people and things in less time than it takes to draw a breath. This feat, which challenges even advanced computers, would be a monumental challenge for a video-computer system.

COLOR AND BRIGHTNESS CONSTANCIES Our experience of color depends on an object's *context*. This would be clear if you viewed an isolated tomato through a paper tube over the course of a day. As the light—and thus the tomato's reflected wavelengths—changed, the tomato's color would also seem to change. But if you discarded the paper tube and viewed the tomato as one item in a salad bowl, its perceived color would remain essentially constant. This perception of consistent color we call *color constancy.*

Though we take color constancy for granted, this ability is truly remarkable. A blue poker chip under indoor lighting reflects wavelengths that match those reflected by a sunlit gold chip (Jameson, 1985). Yet bring a goldfinch indoors and it won't look like a bluebird. The color is not in the bird's feathers. We see color thanks to our brain's computations of the light reflected by an object *relative to the objects surrounding it.* **FIGURE 6.32** dramatically illustrates the ability of a blue object to appear very different in three different contexts. Yet we have no trouble seeing these disks as blue. Nor does knowing the truth—that these disks are identically colored—diminish our perception that they are quite different. Because we construct our perceptions, we can simultaneously accept alternative objective and subjective realities.

phi phenomenon an illusion of movement created when two or more adjacent lights blink on and off in quick succession.

perceptual constancy perceiving objects as unchanging (having consistent color, brightness, shape, and size) even as illumination and retinal images change.

Photo by Walter Wick. Reprinted from GAMES Magazine ©1983 PCS Games Limited Partnership

FIGURE 6.31

THE SOLUTION Another view of the impossible doghouse in Figure 6.27 reveals the secrets of this illusion. From the photo angle in Figure 6.27, the grouping principles of closure and continuity lead us to perceive the boards as continuous.

"From there to here, from here to there, funny things are everywhere." — Dr. Seuss, *One Fish, Two Fish, Red Fish, Blue Fish*, 1960

R. Beau Lotto/Lottolab

(a)

(b)

FIGURE 6.32

COLOR DEPENDS ON CONTEXT
(a) Believe it or not, these three blue disks are identical in color.
(b) Remove the surrounding context and see what results.

FIGURE 6.33

RELATIVE LUMINANCE Because of its surrounding context, we perceive Square A as lighter than Square B. But believe it or not, they are identical. To channel comedian Richard Pryor, "Who you gonna believe: me, or your lying eyes?" If you believe your lying eyes—actually, your lying brain—you can photocopy (or screen-capture and print) the illustration, then cut out the squares and compare them. (Information from Edward Adelson.)

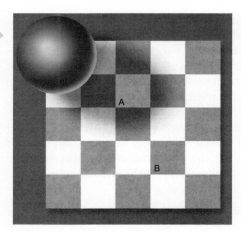

Brightness constancy (also called *lightness constancy*) similarly depends on context. We perceive an object as having a constant brightness even as its illumination varies. This perception of constancy depends on *relative luminance*—the amount of light an object reflects *relative to its surroundings* (**FIGURE 6.33**). White paper reflects 90 percent of the light falling on it; black paper, only 10 percent. Although a black paper viewed in sunlight may reflect 100 times more light than does a white paper viewed indoors, it will still look black (McBurney & Collings, 1984). But try viewing sunlit black paper through a narrow tube so nothing else is visible and it may look gray, because in bright sunshine it reflects a fair amount of light. View it without the tube and it is again black, because it reflects much less light than the objects around it.

This principle—that we perceive objects not in isolation but in their environmental context—matters to artists, interior decorators, and clothing designers. Our perception of the color and brightness of a wall or of a streak of paint on a canvas is determined not just by the paint in the can but by the surrounding colors. The take-home lesson: *Context governs our perceptions.*

SHAPE AND SIZE CONSTANCIES Thanks to *shape constancy,* we perceive the form of familiar objects, such as the door in **FIGURE 6.34**, as constant even while our retinas receive changing images of them. Our brain manages this feat because visual cortex neurons rapidly learn to associate different views of an object (Li & DiCarlo, 2008).

Thanks to *size constancy,* we perceive an object as having an unchanging size, even while our distance from it varies. We assume a car is large enough to carry people, even when we see its tiny image from two blocks away. This assumption also illustrates the close connection between perceived *distance* and perceived *size.* Perceiving an object's distance gives us cues to its size. Likewise, knowing its general size—that the object is a car—provides us with cues to its distance.

"Sometimes I wonder: Why is that Frisbee getting bigger? And then it hits me." —Anonymous

Even in size-distance judgments, however, we consider an object's context. This interplay between perceived size and perceived distance helps explain several well-known illusions, including the *Moon illusion:* The Moon looks up to 50 percent larger when near the horizon than when high in the sky. Can you imagine why?

For at least 22 centuries, scholars have wondered (Hershenson, 1989). One reason is that monocular cues to objects' distances make the horizon Moon appear farther away. If it's farther away, our brain assumes, it must be larger than the Moon high in the night sky (Kaufman & Kaufman, 2000). But again, if you use a paper tube to take away the distance cue, the horizon Moon will immediately seem smaller.

Perceptual illusions reinforce a fundamental lesson: Perception is not merely a projection of the world onto our brain. Rather, our sensations are disassembled into information bits that our brain then reassembles into its own functional model of the external world. During this reassembly process, our assumptions—such as the usual relationship between distance and size—can lead us astray. *Our brain constructs our perceptions.*

📱 **LaunchPad** To experience more visual illusions, and to understand what they reveal about how you perceive the world, visit **Topic Tutorial: PsychSim6, Visual Illusions.**

FIGURE 6.34

SHAPE CONSTANCY A door casts an increasingly trapezoidal image on our retinas as it opens. Yet we still perceive it as rectangular.

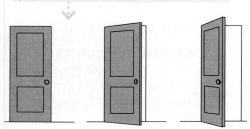

* * *

Form perception, depth perception, motion perception, and perceptual constancies illuminate how we organize our visual experiences. Perceptual organization applies to our other senses, too. Listening to an unfamiliar language, we have trouble hearing where one word stops and the next one begins. Listening to our own language, we automatically hear distinct words. This, too, reflects perceptual organization. But it is more, for we even organize a string of letters—THEDOGATEMEAT—into words that make an intelligible phrase, more likely "The dog ate meat" than "The do gate me at" (McBurney & Collings, 1984). This process involves not only the organization we've been discussing, but also interpretation—discerning meaning in what we perceive.

PERCEPTUAL INTERPRETATION

Philosophers have debated whether our perceptual abilities should be credited to our nature or our nurture. To what extent do we *learn* to perceive? German philosopher Immanuel Kant (1724–1804) maintained that knowledge comes from our *inborn* ways of organizing sensory experiences. Indeed, we come equipped to process sensory information. But British philosopher John Locke (1632–1704) argued that through our experiences we also *learn* to perceive the world. Indeed, we learn to link an object's distance with its size. So, just how important is experience? How radically does it shape our perceptual interpretations?

Experience and Visual Perception

LOQ 6-15 What does research on restored vision, sensory restriction, and perceptual adaptation reveal about the effects of experience on perception?

RESTORED VISION AND SENSORY RESTRICTION Writing to John Locke, William Molyneux wondered whether "a man *born* blind, and now adult, taught by his *touch* to distinguish between a cube and a sphere" could, if made to see, visually distinguish the two. Locke's answer was *No*, because the man would never have *learned* to see the difference. Molyneux's hypothetical case has since been put to the test with people who, though blind from birth, later gained sight (Gandhi et al., 2017; Gregory, 1978; Huber et al., 2015; von Senden, 1932). Most were born with cataracts—clouded lenses that allowed them to see only diffused light, rather as a sighted person might see a foggy image through a Ping-Pong ball sliced in half. After cataract surgery, the patients could distinguish figure from ground, could differentiate colors, and could distinguish faces from nonfaces—suggesting that these aspects of perception are innate. But much as Locke supposed, they often could not visually recognize objects that were familiar by touch.

Seeking to gain more control than is provided by clinical cases, researchers have outfitted infant kittens and monkeys with goggles through which they could see only diffuse, unpatterned light (Wiesel, 1982). After infancy, when their vision was restored, these animals behaved much like the humans born with cataracts. They could distinguish color and brightness, but not the form of a circle from that of a square. Their eyes had not degenerated; their retinas still relayed signals to their visual cortex. But lacking stimulation, their brain's cortical cells had not developed normal connections. Thus, the animals remained functionally blind to shape. Surgery on children in India reveals that those who are blind from birth can benefit from removal of cataracts, and the younger they are, the more they will benefit. But their visual acuity (sharpness) may never be normal (Chatterjee, 2015; Gandhi et al., 2014). For normal sensory and perceptual development, there is a *critical period*—an optimal period when exposure to certain stimuli or experiences is required.

Once this critical period has passed, sensory restrictions later in life do no permanent harm. When researchers cover an adult animal's eye for several months, its vision will be unaffected after the eye patch is removed. When surgeons remove cataracts that develop during late adulthood, most people are thrilled at the return to normal vision.

PERCEPTUAL ADAPTATION Given a new pair of glasses, we may feel slightly disoriented, even dizzy. Within a day or two, we adjust. Our **perceptual adaptation** to changed visual input makes the world seem normal again. But imagine a far more dramatic new pair of glasses—one that shifts the apparent location of objects 40 degrees to the left. When you first put them on and toss a ball to a friend, it sails off to the left. Walking forward to shake hands with someone, you veer to the left.

Could you adapt to this distorted world? Not if you were a baby chicken. When fitted with such lenses, baby chicks continue to peck where food grains *seem* to be (Hess, 1956; Rossi, 1968). But we humans adapt to distorting lenses quickly. Within a few minutes your throws would again be accurate, your stride on target. Remove the lenses and you would experience an aftereffect: At first your throws would err in the *opposite* direction, sailing off to the right; but again, within minutes you would readapt.

LEARNING TO SEE At age 3, Mike May lost his vision in an explosion. Decades later, after a new cornea restored vision to his right eye, he got his first look at his wife and children. Alas, although signals were now reaching his visual cortex, it lacked the experience to interpret them. May could not recognize expressions, or faces, apart from features such as hair. Yet he can see an object in motion and has learned to navigate his world and to marvel at such things as dust floating in sunlight (Abrams, 2002; Gorlick, 2010; Huber et al., 2015).

Marcio Jose Sanchez/AP Images

perceptual adaptation the ability to adjust to changed sensory input, including an artificially displaced or even inverted visual field.

PERCEPTUAL ADAPTATION "Oops, missed," thought researcher Hubert Dolezal as he attempted a handshake while viewing the world through inverting goggles. Yet, believe it or not, kittens, monkeys, and humans can adapt to an inverted world.

Courtesy of Hubert Dolezal

Indeed, given an even more radical pair of glasses—one that literally turns the world upside down—you could still adapt. Psychologist George Stratton (1896) experienced this. He invented, and for eight days wore, optical headgear that flipped left to right *and* up to down, making him the first person to experience a right-side-up retinal image while standing upright. The ground was up, the sky was down.

At first, when Stratton wanted to walk, he found himself searching for his feet, which were now "up." Eating was nearly impossible. He became nauseated and depressed. But he persisted, and by the eighth day he could comfortably reach for an object and, if his hands were in view, could walk without bumping into things. When Stratton finally removed the headgear, he readapted quickly.

So did research participants who wore such gear in later experiments—while riding a motorcycle, skiing the Alps, or flying an airplane (Dolezal, 1982; Kohler, 1962). By actively moving about in their topsy-turvy world, they adapted to their new context and learned to coordinate their movements.

So, do we learn to perceive the world? In part we do, as we constantly adjust to changed sensory input. Research on critical periods teaches us that early nurture sculpts what nature has provided. In less dramatic ways, nurture continues to do so throughout our lives. Experience guides, sustains, and maintains the brain pathways that enable our perception.

ENGAGE

(ASK YOURSELF)

Consider someone you know who has a visual disability (could be yourself). What sort of disrupted visual process causes that disability?

🔒 REVIEW VISION: SENSORY AND PERCEPTUAL PROCESSING

⟫ Learning Objectives

TEST YOURSELF Answer these repeated Learning Objective Questions on your own (before checking the answers in Appendix D) to improve your retention of the concepts (McDaniel et al., 2009, 2015).

6-7 What are the characteristics of the energy that we see as visible light? What structures in the eye help focus that energy?

6-8 How do the rods and cones process information, and what is the path information travels from the eye to the brain?

6-9 How do we perceive color in the world around us?

6-10 Where are feature detectors located, and what do they do?

6-11 How does the brain use parallel processing to construct visual perceptions?

6-12 How did the Gestalt psychologists understand perceptual organization, and how do figure-ground and grouping principles contribute to our perceptions?

6-13 How do we use binocular and monocular cues to perceive the world in three dimensions, and how do we perceive motion?

6-14 How do perceptual constancies help us construct meaningful perceptions?

6-15 What does research on restored vision, sensory restriction, and perceptual adaptation reveal about the effects of experience on perception?

⟫ Terms and Concepts to Remember

TEST YOURSELF Write down the definition yourself, then check your answer on the referenced page.

wavelength, **p. 199**

hue, **p. 199**

intensity, **p. 199**

retina, **p. 201**

accommodation, **p. 201**

rods, **p. 201**

cones, **p. 201**

optic nerve, **p. 201**

blind spot, **p. 201**

fovea, **p. 203**

Young-Helmholtz trichromatic (three-color) theory, **p. 203**

opponent-process theory, **p. 204**

feature detectors, **p. 204**

parallel processing, **p. 207**

gestalt, **p. 207**

figure-ground, **p. 207**

grouping, **p. 208**

depth perception, **p. 208**

visual cliff, **p. 208**

binocular cue, **p. 208**

retinal disparity, **p. 208**

monocular cue, **p. 210**

phi phenomenon, **p. 211**

perceptual constancy, **p. 211**

perceptual adaptation, **p. 213**

⟶ Experience the Testing Effect

TEST YOURSELF Answer the following questions on your own first, then check your answers in Appendix E.

1. The characteristic of light that determines the color we experience, such as blue or green, is _____.

2. The amplitude of a light wave determines our perception of
   a. brightness.
   b. color.
   c. meaning.
   d. distance.

3. The blind spot in your retina is located where
   a. there are rods but no cones.
   b. there are cones but no rods.
   c. the optic nerve leaves the eye.
   d. the bipolar cells meet the ganglion cells.

4. Cones are the eye's receptor cells that are especially sensitive to _____ light and are responsible for our _____ vision.
   a. bright; black-and-white
   b. dim; color
   c. bright; color
   d. dim; black-and-white

5. Two theories together account for color vision. The Young-Helmholtz trichromatic theory shows that the eye contains _____, and Hering's theory accounts for the nervous system's having _____.
   a. opposing retinal processes; three pairs of color receptors
   b. opponent-process cells; three types of color receptors
   c. three pairs of color receptors; opposing retinal processes
   d. three types of color receptors; opponent-process cells

6. What mental processes allow you to perceive a lemon as yellow?

7. The cells in the visual cortex that respond to certain lines, edges, and angles are called _____ _____.

8. The brain's ability to process many aspects of an object or a problem simultaneously is called _____ _____.

9. In listening to a concert, you attend to the solo instrument and perceive the orchestra as accompaniment. This illustrates the organizing principle of
   a. figure-ground.   c. grouping.
   b. shape constancy.   d. depth perception.

10. Our tendencies to fill in the gaps and to perceive a pattern as continuous are two different examples of the organizing principle called
    a. interposition.
    b. depth perception.
    c. shape constancy.
    d. grouping.

11. The visual cliff experiments suggest that
    a. infants have not yet developed depth perception.
    b. crawling human infants and very young animals perceive depth.
    c. we have no way of knowing whether infants can perceive depth.
    d. unlike other species, humans are able to perceive depth in infancy.

12. Depth perception underlies our ability to
    a. group similar items in a gestalt.
    b. perceive objects as having a constant shape or form.
    c. judge distances.
    d. fill in the gaps in a figure.

13. Two examples of _____ depth cues are interposition and linear perspective.

14. Perceiving a tomato as consistently red, despite lighting shifts, is an example of
    a. shape constancy.
    b. perceptual constancy.
    c. a binocular cue.
    d. continuity.

15. After surgery to restore vision, adults who had been blind from birth had difficulty
    a. recognizing objects by touch.
    b. recognizing objects by sight.
    c. distinguishing figure from ground.
    d. distinguishing between bright and dim light.

16. In experiments, people have worn glasses that turned their visual fields upside down. After a period of adjustment, they learned to function quite well. This ability is called _____ _____.

Continue testing yourself with 📖 **LearningCurve** or 📖 **Achieve Read & Practice**
to learn and remember most effectively.

audition the sense or act of hearing.

frequency the number of complete wavelengths that pass a point in a given time (for example, per second).

pitch a tone's experienced highness or lowness; depends on frequency.

middle ear the chamber between the eardrum and cochlea containing three tiny bones (malleus, incus, and stapes) that concentrate the vibrations of the eardrum on the cochlea's oval window.

cochlea [KOHK-lee-uh] a coiled, bony, fluid-filled tube in the inner ear; sound waves traveling through the cochlear fluid trigger nerve impulses.

inner ear the innermost part of the ear, containing the cochlea, semicircular canals, and vestibular sacs.

⟶ The Nonvisual Senses

HEARING

Like our other senses, our hearing, or **audition,** helps us adapt and survive. Hearing provides information and enables relationships. Hearing humanizes us; people seem more thoughtful, competent, and likable when we hear their words than when we read their words (Schroeder & Epley, 2015, 2016). And hearing is pretty spectacular. It lets us communicate invisibly—shooting unseen air waves across space and receiving the same from others. Hearing loss is therefore an invisible disability. To not catch someone's name, to not grasp what someone is asking, and to miss the hilarious joke is to be deprived of what others know, and sometimes to feel excluded. As a person with hearing loss, I [DM] know the feeling, and can understand why adults with significant hearing loss experience a doubled risk of depression (Li et al., 2014).

Most of us, however, can hear a wide range of sounds, and the ones we hear best are those in the range of the human voice. With normal hearing, we are remarkably sensitive to faint sounds, such as a child's whimper. (If our ears were only slightly more sensitive, we would hear a constant hiss from the movement of air molecules.) Our distant ancestors' survival depended on this keen hearing when hunting or being hunted.

We are also remarkably attuned to sound variations. Among thousands of possible voices, we easily recognize an unseen friend's. Moreover, hearing is fast. "It might take you a full second to notice something out of the corner of your eye, turn your head toward it, recognize it, and respond to it," notes auditory neuroscientist Seth Horowitz (2012). "The same reaction to a new or sudden sound happens at least 10 times as fast." A fraction of a second after such events stimulate your ear's receptors, millions of neurons have simultaneously coordinated in extracting the essential features, comparing them with past experience, and identifying the stimulus (Freeman, 1991). For hearing as for our other senses, we wonder: How do we do it?

The Stimulus Input: Sound Waves

LOQ 6-16 What are the characteristics of air pressure waves that we hear as sound?

Draw a bow across a violin, and you will unleash the energy of sound waves. Air molecules, each bumping into the next, create waves of compressed and expanded air, like the ripples on a pond circling out from a tossed stone. As we swim in our ocean of moving air molecules, our ears detect these brief air pressure changes.

Like light waves, sound waves vary in shape (**FIGURE 6.35**). The height, or *amplitude,* of sound waves determines their perceived *loudness.* Their length, or **frequency,** determines the **pitch** we experience. Long waves have low frequency—and low pitch. Short waves have high frequency—and high pitch. Sound waves produced by a violin are much shorter and faster than those produced by a cello or a bass guitar.

FIGURE 6.35

THE PHYSICAL PROPERTIES OF WAVES (a) Waves vary in *wavelength* (the distance between successive peaks). *Frequency,* the number of complete wavelengths that can pass a point in a given time, depends on the wavelength. The shorter the wavelength, the higher the frequency. Wavelength determines the *pitch* of sound. (b) Waves also vary in *amplitude* (the height from peak to trough). Wave amplitude influences sound *intensity.*

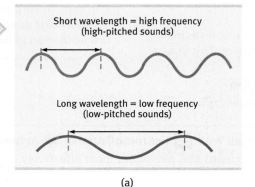

(a)

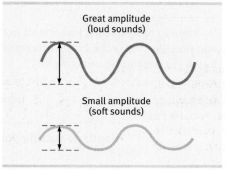

(b)

We measure sounds in *decibels,* with zero decibels representing the absolute threshold for hearing. Every 10 decibels correspond to a tenfold increase in sound intensity. Thus, normal conversation (60 decibels) is 10,000 times more intense than a 20-decibel whisper. And a temporarily tolerable 100-decibel passing subway train is 10 billion times more intense than the faintest detectable sound. If prolonged, exposure to sounds above 85 decibels can produce hearing loss. Tell that to basketball fans at the University of Kentucky who, in 2017, broke the Guinness World Record for the noisiest indoor stadium at 126 decibels (WKYT, 2017). Hear today, gone tomorrow.

Zdorov Kirill Vladimirovich/ Shutterstock

sbarabu/Shutterstock

THE SOUNDS OF MUSIC A violin's short, fast waves create a high pitch. The longer, slower waves of a cello or bass create a lower pitch. Differences in the waves' height, or amplitude, also create differing degrees of loudness.

The Ear

LOQ 6-17 How does the ear transform sound energy into neural messages?

How does vibrating air trigger nerve impulses that your brain can decode as sounds? The process begins when sound waves strike your *eardrum,* causing this tight membrane to vibrate (**FIGURE 6.36**).

In your **middle ear,** a piston made of three tiny bones—the *hammer* (malleus), *anvil* (incus), and *stirrup* (stapes)—picks up the vibrations and transmits them to the **cochlea,** a snail-shaped tube in the **inner ear.**

The incoming vibrations then cause the cochlea's membrane-covered opening (the *oval window*) to vibrate, jostling the fluid inside the cochlea. This motion causes ripples in the *basilar membrane,* bending the *hair cells* lining its surface, rather like wheat stalks bending in the wind.

The hair cell movements in turn trigger impulses in the adjacent nerve cells, whose axons converge to form the *auditory nerve.* The auditory nerve carries the neural messages

FIGURE 6.36

HEAR HERE: HOW WE TRANSFORM SOUND WAVES INTO NERVE IMPULSES THAT OUR BRAIN INTERPRETS (a) The outer ear funnels sound waves to the eardrum. The bones of the middle ear (hammer, anvil, and stirrup) amplify and relay the eardrum's vibrations through the oval window into the fluid-filled cochlea. (b) As shown in this detail of the middle and inner ear, the resulting pressure changes in the cochlear fluid cause the basilar membrane to ripple, bending the hair cells on its surface. Hair cell movements trigger impulses at the base of the nerve cells, whose fibers converge to form the auditory nerve. That nerve sends neural messages to the thalamus and on to the auditory cortex.

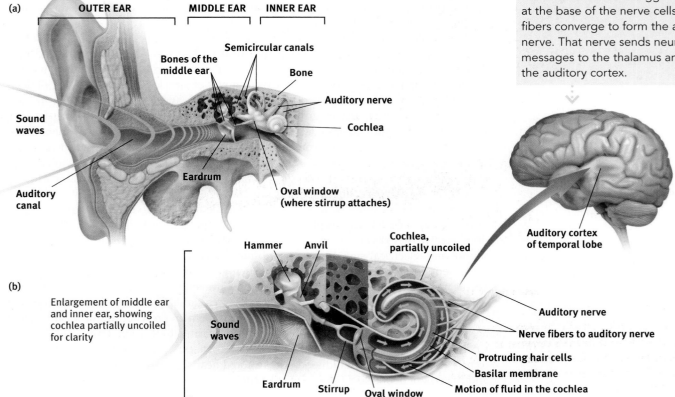

(a)

OUTER EAR   MIDDLE EAR   INNER EAR

Semicircular canals

Bones of the middle ear

Bone

Auditory nerve

Sound waves

Cochlea

Eardrum

Auditory canal

Oval window (where stirrup attaches)

Cochlea, partially uncoiled

Auditory cortex of temporal lobe

(b)

Enlargement of middle ear and inner ear, showing cochlea partially uncoiled for clarity

Hammer   Anvil

Sound waves

Auditory nerve

Nerve fibers to auditory nerve

Protruding hair cells

Basilar membrane

Eardrum   Stirrup   Oval window   Motion of fluid in the cochlea

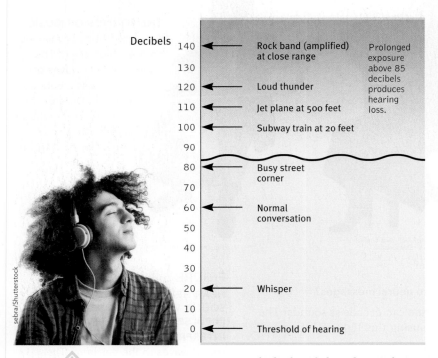

Decibels
- 140 — Rock band (amplified) at close range
- 130
- 120 — Loud thunder
- 110 — Jet plane at 500 feet
- 100 — Subway train at 20 feet
- 90
- 80 — Busy street corner
- 70
- 60 — Normal conversation
- 50
- 40
- 30
- 20 — Whisper
- 10
- 0 — Threshold of hearing

Prolonged exposure above 85 decibels produces hearing loss.

sebra/Shutterstock

FIGURE 6.37

THE INTENSITY OF SOME COMMON SOUNDS One study of 3 million Germans found professional musicians with almost four times the normal rate of noise-induced hearing loss (Schink et al., 2014). Some modern headphones block out environmental noise, reducing the need to blast the music at dangerous volumes.

to the thalamus and then on to the *auditory cortex* in the brain's temporal lobe. From vibrating air, to tiny moving bones, to fluid waves, to electrical impulses to the brain: Voila! You hear.

Perhaps the most intriguing part of the hearing process is the hair cells—"quivering bundles that let us hear" thanks to their "extreme sensitivity and extreme speed" (Goldberg, 2007). A cochlea has 16,000 of them, which sounds like a lot until we compare that with an eye's 130 million or so photoreceptors. But consider a hair cell's responsiveness. Deflect the tiny bundles of *cilia* on its tip by only the width of an atom—imagine—and the alert hair cell, thanks to a special protein at its tip, will trigger a neural response (Corey et al., 2004).

Damage to the cochlea's hair cell receptors or the auditory nerve can cause **sensorineural hearing loss** (or nerve deafness). With auditory nerve damage, people may hear sound but have trouble discerning what someone is saying (Liberman, 2015).

Occasionally, disease damages hair cell receptors, but more often the culprits are biological changes linked with heredity and aging, and prolonged exposure to ear-splitting noise or music. Sensorineural hearing loss is more common than **conduction hearing loss,** which is caused by damage to the mechanical system—the eardrum and middle ear bones—that conducts sound waves to the cochlea.

The cochlea's hair cells have been likened to carpet fibers. Walk around on them and they will spring back. But leave a heavy piece of furniture on them and they may never rebound. As a general rule, any noise we cannot talk over (loud machinery, fans screaming at a sports event, music blasting at maximum volume) may be harmful, especially if prolonged and repeated (Roesser, 1998) (**FIGURE 6.37**). And if our ears ring after exposure to such experiences, we have been bad to our unhappy hair cells. As pain alerts us to possible bodily harm, ringing of the ears alerts us to possible hearing damage. It is hearing's equivalent of bleeding.

Worldwide, 1.23 billion people are challenged by hearing loss (Global Burden of Disease, 2015). Since the early 1990s, teen hearing loss has risen by a third and now affects 1 in 5 teens (Shargorodsky et al., 2010). Exposure to loud music, both live and through headphones, is a culprit: After three hours of a rock concert averaging 99 decibels, 54 percent of teens reported not hearing as well, and 1 in 4 had ringing in their ears. Teen boys more than teen girls or adults blast themselves with loud volumes for long periods (Zogby, 2006). Males' greater noise exposure may help explain why men's hearing tends to be less acute than women's. But regardless of gender, those who spend many hours in a loud nightclub, behind a power mower, or above a jackhammer should wear earplugs, or they risk needing a hearing aid later. "Condoms or, safer yet, abstinence," say sex educators. "Earplugs or walk away," say hearing educators.

Nerve deafness cannot be reversed. For now, the only way to restore hearing is a sort of bionic ear—a **cochlear implant.** Some 50,000 people, including some 30,000 children, receive these electronic devices each year (Hochmair, 2013). The implants translate sounds into electrical signals that, wired into the cochlea's nerves, convey information about sound to the brain (**FIGURE 6.38**). When given to deaf kittens and human infants, cochlear implants have seemed to trigger an "awakening" of the pertinent brain area (Klinke et al., 1999; Sireteanu, 1999). These devices can help children become proficient in oral communication (especially if they receive them as preschoolers or ideally before age 1) (Dettman et al., 2007; Schorr et al., 2005). Hearing, like vision, has a *critical period.* Cochlear implants can help restore hearing for most adults, but only if their brain learned to process sound during childhood. The restored hearing can also reduce social isolation and the risk of depression (Mosnier et al., 2015).

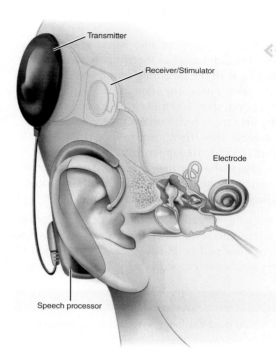

Transmitter

Receiver/Stimulator

Electrode

Speech processor

◄··· FIGURE 6.38

HARDWARE FOR HEARING Cochlear implants work by translating sounds into electrical signals that are transmitted to the cochlea and, via the auditory nerve, relayed to the brain.

🔒 **RETRIEVE IT • • •**

ANSWERS IN APPENDIX E

RI-1 The amplitude of a sound wave determines our perception of _____ (loudness/pitch).

RI-2 The longer the sound waves are, the _____ (lower/higher) their frequency and the _____ (higher/lower) their pitch.

Perceiving Loudness, Pitch, and Location

LOQ 6-18 How do we detect loudness, discriminate pitch, and locate sounds?

RESPONDING TO LOUD AND SOFT SOUNDS How do we detect loudness? If you guessed that it's related to the intensity of a hair cell's response, you'd be wrong. Rather, a soft, pure tone activates only the few hair cells attuned to its frequency. Given louder sounds, neighboring hair cells also respond. Thus, your brain interprets loudness from the *number* of activated hair cells.

If a hair cell loses sensitivity to soft sounds, it may still respond to loud sounds. This helps explain another surprise: Really loud sounds may seem loud to people with or without normal hearing. As a person with hearing loss, I [DM] used to wonder what really loud music must sound like to people with normal hearing. Now I realize it sounds much the same; where we differ is in our perception of soft sounds.

HEARING DIFFERENT PITCHES How do we know whether a sound is the high-frequency, high-pitched chirp of a bird or the low-frequency, low-pitched roar of a truck? Current thinking on how we discriminate pitch combines two theories.

- **Place theory** presumes that we hear different pitches because different sound waves trigger activity at different places along the cochlea's basilar membrane. Thus, the brain determines a sound's pitch by recognizing the specific place (on the membrane) that is generating the neural signal. When Nobel laureate-to-be Georg von Békésy (1957) cut holes in the cochleas of guinea pigs and human cadavers and looked inside with a microscope, he discovered that the cochlea vibrated, rather like a shaken bedsheet, in response to sound. High frequencies produced large vibrations near the beginning of the cochlea's membrane. Low frequencies vibrated more of the membrane and were not so easily localized. So, there is a problem: Place theory can explain how we hear high-pitched sounds but not low-pitched sounds.

sensorineural hearing loss hearing loss caused by damage to the cochlea's receptor cells or to the auditory nerves; the most common form of hearing loss, also called *nerve deafness*.

conduction hearing loss a less common form of hearing loss, caused by damage to the mechanical system that conducts sound waves to the cochlea.

cochlear implant a device for converting sounds into electrical signals and stimulating the auditory nerve through electrodes threaded into the cochlea.

place theory in hearing, the theory that links the pitch we hear with the place where the cochlea's membrane is stimulated.

frequency theory in hearing, the theory that the rate of nerve impulses traveling up the auditory nerve matches the frequency of a tone, thus enabling us to sense its pitch. (Also called *temporal theory*.)

🔒 〽 **LaunchPad** For an interactive review of how we perceive sound, visit **Topic Tutorial: PsychSim6, The Auditory System.** For an animated test of your knowledge, engage online with **Concept Practice: The Auditory Pathway.**

- **Frequency theory** (also called *temporal theory*) suggests an alternative: The brain reads pitch by monitoring the frequency of neural impulses traveling up the auditory nerve. The whole basilar membrane vibrates with the incoming sound wave, triggering neural impulses to the brain at the same rate as the sound wave. If the sound wave has a frequency of 100 waves per second, then 100 pulses per second travel up the auditory nerve. But frequency theory also has a problem: An individual neuron cannot fire faster than 1000 times per second. How, then, can we sense sounds with frequencies above 1000 waves per second (roughly the upper third of a piano keyboard)? Enter the *volley principle:* Like soldiers who alternate firing so that some can shoot while others reload, neural cells can alternate firing. By firing in rapid succession, they can achieve a *combined frequency* above 1000 waves per second.

So, place theory and frequency theory work together to enable our perception of pitch. Place theory best explains how we sense *high pitches*. Frequency theory, extended by the volley principle, also explains how we sense *low pitches*. Finally, some combination of place and frequency theories likely explains how we sense *pitches in the intermediate range*.

🔒 **RETRIEVE IT • • •**   *ANSWERS IN APPENDIX E*

RI-3 Which theory of pitch perception would best explain a symphony audience's enjoyment of a high-pitched piccolo? How about a low-pitched cello?

LOCATING SOUNDS Why don't we have one big ear—perhaps above our one nose? "All the better to hear you with," as the wolf said to Little Red Riding Hood. Thanks to the placement of our two ears, we enjoy stereophonic ("three-dimensional") hearing. Two ears are better than one for at least two reasons (**FIGURE 6.39**). If a car to your right honks, your right ear will receive a more *intense* sound, and it will receive the sound slightly *sooner* than your left ear.

Because sound travels 761 miles per hour and human ears are but 6 inches apart, the intensity difference and the time lag are extremely small. A just noticeable difference in the direction of two sound sources corresponds to a time difference of just 0.000027 second! Lucky for us, our supersensitive auditory system can detect such minute differences—and locate the sound (Brown & Deffenbacher, 1979; Middlebrooks & Green, 1991).

THE OTHER SENSES

Sharks and dogs rely on their outstanding sense of smell, aided by large smell-related brain areas. Our human brain allocates more real estate to seeing and hearing. But extraordinary happenings also occur within our other senses. Without our senses of touch, taste, smell, and body position and movement, we humans would be seriously hampered, and our capacities for enjoying the world would be greatly diminished.

Touch

LOQ 6-19 How do we sense touch?

Touch, our tactile sense, is vital. Right from the start, touch aids our development. Infant rats deprived of their mother's grooming produce less growth hormone and have a lower metabolic rate—a good way to keep alive until the mother returns, but a reaction that stunts growth if prolonged. Infant monkeys that are allowed to see, hear, and smell—but not touch—their mother become desperately unhappy (Suomi et al., 1976). Premature human babies gain weight faster and go home sooner if they are stimulated by hand massage (Field et al., 2006). As adults, we still yearn to touch—to kiss, to stroke, to snuggle.

Humorist Dave Barry was perhaps right to jest that your skin "keeps people from seeing the inside of your body, which is repulsive, and it prevents your organs from falling onto the ground." But skin does much more. Touching various spots on the skin with a soft hair, a warm or cool wire, and the point of a pin reveals that some spots are especially sensitive to *pressure*, others to *warmth*, others to *cold*, still others to *pain*. Our "sense

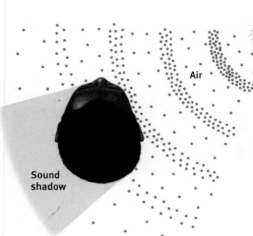

Air

Sound shadow

FIGURE 6.39

HOW WE LOCATE SOUNDS Sound waves strike one ear sooner and more intensely than the other. From this information, our nimble brain can compute the sound's location. As you might therefore expect, people who lose all hearing in one ear often have difficulty locating sounds.

of touch" is actually a mix of these four basic and distinct skin senses, and our other skin sensations are variations of pressure, warmth, cold, and pain. For example, stroking adjacent pressure spots creates a tickle. Repeated gentle stroking of a pain spot creates an itching sensation. Touching adjacent cold and pressure spots triggers a sense of wetness (which you can experience by touching dry, cold metal).

Touch sensations involve more than tactile stimulation, however. A self-administered tickle produces less somatosensory cortex activation than does the same tickle from something or someone else (Blakemore et al., 1998). Likewise, a sensual leg caress evokes a different somatosensory cortex response when a heterosexual man believes it comes from an attractive woman rather than a man (Gazzola et al., 2012). Such responses reveal how quickly cognition influences our brain's sensory response.

THE PRECIOUS SENSE OF TOUCH As William James wrote in his *Principles of Psychology* (1890), "Touch is both the alpha and omega of affection."

Pain

LOQ 6-20 What biological, psychological, and social-cultural influences affect our experience of pain? How do placebos, distraction, and hypnosis help control pain?

Be thankful for occasional pain. Pain is your body's way of telling you something has gone wrong. By drawing your attention to a burn, a break, or a sprain, pain orders you to change your behavior—"Stay off that turned ankle!" The rare people born without the ability to feel pain may experience severe injury or even death before early adulthood. Without the discomfort that makes us occasionally shift position, their joints can fail from excess strain. Without the warnings of pain, infections can run wild and injuries can accumulate (Neese, 1991).

More numerous are those who live with chronic pain, which is rather like an alarm that won't shut off. Persistent backaches, arthritis, headaches, and cancer-related pain prompt two questions: What is pain? How might we control it?

UNDERSTANDING PAIN Our experience of pain reflects both *bottom-up* sensations and *top-down* cognition. Pain is a biopsychosocial phenomenon (Hadjistavropoulos et al., 2011). As such, pain experiences vary widely, from group to group and from person to person. Viewing pain from many perspectives can help us better understand how to cope with it and treat it (**FIGURE 6.40**).

"PAIN IS A GIFT." So said a doctor studying Ashlyn Blocker, who has a rare genetic mutation that prevents her from feeling pain. At birth, she didn't cry. As a child, she ran around for two days on a broken ankle. She has put her hands on a hot machine and burned the flesh off. And she has reached into boiling water to retrieve a dropped spoon. "Everyone in my class asks me about it, and I say, 'I can feel pressure, but I can't feel pain.' *Pain!* I cannot feel it!"

Jeff Riedel/Contour/Getty Images

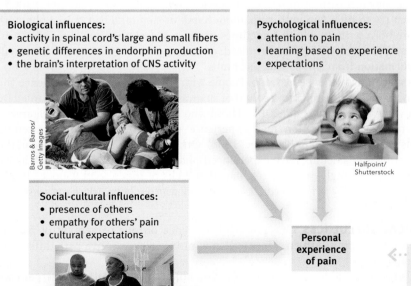

Biological influences:
• activity in spinal cord's large and small fibers
• genetic differences in endorphin production
• the brain's interpretation of CNS activity

Psychological influences:
• attention to pain
• learning based on experience
• expectations

Social-cultural influences:
• presence of others
• empathy for others' pain
• cultural expectations

Personal experience of pain

FIGURE 6.40

BIOPSYCHOSOCIAL APPROACH TO PAIN Our experience of pain is much more than the neural messages sent to our brain.

FIGURE 6.41

THE PAIN CIRCUIT Sensory receptors (*nociceptors*) respond to potentially damaging stimuli by sending an impulse to the spinal cord, which passes the message to the brain, which interprets the signal as pain.

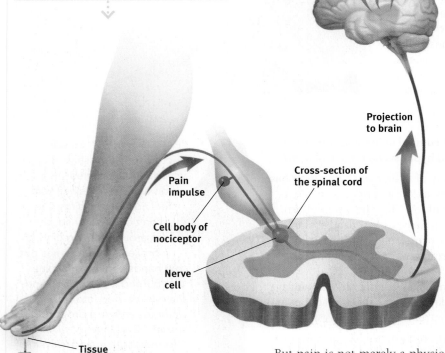

Projection to brain

Cross-section of the spinal cord

Pain impulse

Cell body of nociceptor

Nerve cell

Tissue injury

gate-control theory the theory that the spinal cord contains a neurological "gate" that blocks pain signals or allows them to pass on to the brain. The "gate" is opened by the activity of pain signals traveling up small nerve fibers and is closed by activity in larger fibers or by information coming from the brain.

"I'd know my tinnitus anywhere and this isn't it."

BIOLOGICAL INFLUENCES Pain is a physical event produced by your senses. But pain differs from some of your other sensations. No one type of stimulus triggers pain the way light triggers vision. And no specialized receptors process pain signals, the way your retina receptors react to light rays. Instead, sensory receptors called *nociceptors*—mostly in your skin but also in your muscles and organs—detect hurtful temperatures, pressure, or chemicals (**FIGURE 6.41**).

Your experience of pain depends in part on the genes you inherited and on your physical characteristics (Gatchel et al., 2007; Reimann et al., 2010). Women are more sensitive to pain than men are (their senses of hearing and smell also tend to be more sensitive) (Ruau et al., 2012; Wickelgren, 2009).

No pain theory can explain all available findings. One useful model, **gate-control theory,** was proposed by psychologist Ronald Melzack and biologist Patrick Wall (1965, 1983; Melzack & Katz, 2013, with support from Foster et al., 2015). This theory suggests that the spinal cord contains a neurological "gate" that controls the transmission of pain messages to the brain.

Small spinal cord nerve fibers conduct most pain signals. Melzack and Wall theorized that when tissue is injured, the small fibers activate and open the gate. The pain signals can then travel to your brain, and you feel pain. But large-fiber activity (stimulated by massage, electric stimulation, or acupuncture) can close the gate, blocking pain signals. Brain-to-spinal-cord messages can also close the gate. Thus, chronic pain can be treated both by gate-closing stimulation, such as massage, and by mental activity, such as distraction (Wall, 2000).

But pain is not merely a physical phenomenon of injured nerves sending impulses to a definable brain or spinal cord area—like pulling on a rope to ring a bell. The brain can also create pain, as it does in *phantom limb sensations* after a limb amputation. Without normal sensory input, the brain may misinterpret and amplify spontaneous but irrelevant central nervous system activity. As the dreamer may see with eyes closed, so 7 in 10 such people may feel pain or movement in nonexistent limbs (Melzack, 1992, 2005). Some may even try to lift a cup with a phantom hand, or step off a bed onto a phantom leg. Even those born without a limb sometimes perceive sensations from the absent arm or leg. The brain, Melzack (1998) has surmised, comes prepared to anticipate "that it will be getting information from a body that has limbs."

Phantoms may haunt other senses, too. People with hearing loss often experience the sound of silence: *tinnitus,* the phantom sound of ringing in the ears that's accompanied by auditory brain activity (Sedley et al., 2015). Those who lose vision to glaucoma, cataracts, diabetes, or macular degeneration may experience phantom sights—nonthreatening hallucinations (Ramachandran & Blakeslee, 1998). Others who have nerve damage in the systems for tasting and smelling have experienced phantom tastes or smells, such as ice water that seems sickeningly sweet or fresh air that reeks of rotten food (Goode, 1999). The point to remember: *We feel, see, hear, taste, and smell with our brain, which can sense even without functioning senses.*

PSYCHOLOGICAL INFLUENCES One powerful influence on our perception of pain is the attention we focus on it. Athletes, focused on winning, may perceive pain differently and play through it.

We also seem to edit our *memories* of pain, which often differ from the pain we actually experienced. In experiments, and after painful experiences such as medical procedures or childbirth, people overlook a pain's duration. Their memory snapshots instead record two factors: their pain's *peak* moment (which can lead them to recall variable pain, with peaks, as worse [Chajut et al., 2014; Stone et al., 2005]), and how much pain they felt at the *end*. In one experiment, people immersed one hand in painfully cold water for 60 seconds, and then the other hand in the same painfully cold water for 60 seconds followed by a slightly less painful 30 seconds more (Kahneman et al., 1993). Which experience would you expect they recalled as most painful?

Curiously, when asked which trial they would prefer to repeat, most preferred the 90-second trial, with more net pain—but less pain at the end. Physicians have used this principle with patients undergoing colon exams—lengthening the discomfort by a minute but lessening its intensity at the end (Kahneman, 1999). Patients experiencing this taper-down treatment later recalled the exam as less painful than did those whose pain ended abruptly. (If, as a painful root canal is ending, the oral surgeon asks if you'd rather go home or to have a few more minutes of milder discomfort, there's a case to be made for prolonging your hurt.)

The end of an experience can color our memory of pleasures, too. In one simple experiment, some people, on receiving a fifth and last piece of chocolate, were told it was their "next" one. Others, told it was their "last" piece, liked it better and also rated the whole experiment as being more enjoyable (O'Brien & Ellsworth, 2012). Endings matter.

SOCIAL-CULTURAL INFLUENCES   Pain is a product of our attention, our expectations, and also our culture (Gatchel et al., 2007; Reimann et al., 2010). Not surprisingly, then, our perception of pain varies with our social situation and our cultural traditions. We tend to perceive more pain when others seem to be experiencing pain (Symbaluk et al., 1997). This may help explain the apparent social aspects of pain, as when groups of Australian keyboard operators during the mid-1980s suffered outbreaks of severe pain while typing or performing other repetitive work—without any discernible physical abnormalities (Gawande, 1998). Sometimes the pain in sprain is mainly in the brain—literally. When people felt empathy for another's pain, their own brain activity partly mirrored the activity of the actual brain in pain (Singer et al., 2004).

CONTROLLING PAIN   If pain is where body meets mind—if it is both a physical and a psychological phenomenon—then it should be treatable both physically and psychologically. Depending on the symptoms, pain control therapies may include drugs, surgery, acupuncture, electrical stimulation, massage, exercise, hypnosis, relaxation training, meditation, and thought distraction.

When in pain we also benefit from our own built-in pain controls. Our brain releases a natural painkiller—endorphins—in response to severe pain or even vigorous exercise. Thus, when we are distracted from pain and soothed by endorphin release, the pain we experience may be greatly reduced. Sports injuries may go unnoticed until the after-game shower. People who carry a gene that boosts the availability of endorphins are less bothered by pain, and their brain is less responsive to pain (Zubieta et al., 2003). Others, who carry a mutated gene that disrupts pain circuit neurotransmission, may be unable to experience pain (Cox et al., 2006). Such discoveries point the way toward future pain medications that mimic these genetic effects.

PLACEBOS   Even *placebos* can help, by dampening the central nervous system's attention and responses to painful experiences—mimicking painkilling drugs (Eippert et al., 2009; Wager & Atlas, 2013). After being injected in the jaw with a stinging saltwater solution, men in one experiment received a placebo they had been told would relieve the pain. It did—they immediately felt better. "Nothing" worked. The men's belief in the fake painkiller triggered their brain to respond by dispensing endorphins, as revealed by activity in an area that releases natural painkilling opiates (Scott et al., 2007; Zubieta et al., 2005). "Believing becomes reality," noted one commentator (Thernstrom, 2006), as "the mind unites with the body."

DISTRACTION   Have you ever had a health care professional suggest that you focus on a pleasant image (*"Think of a warm, comfortable environment"*) or perform some task (*"Count backward by 3's"*)? Drawing attention away from the painful stimulation is an effective way to activate brain pathways that inhibit pain and increase pain tolerance (Edwards et al., 2009).

Reinhold Matay/AP Images

NOT PAYING ATTENTION TO PAIN
After a tackle in the first half of a competitive game, Mohammed Ali Khan (here playing for BK Häcken in white) said he "had a bit of pain" but thought it was "just a bruise." With his attention focused on the game, he played on. In the second half he was surprised to learn from an attending doctor that his leg was broken.

ACUPUNCTURE: A JAB WELL DONE
This acupuncturist is attempting to help this woman gain relief from back pain by using needles on points of the patient's hand.

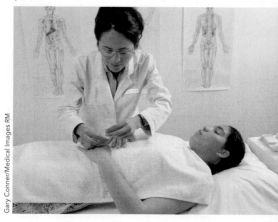

Gary Conner/Medical Images RM

"Pain is increased by attending to it."
—Charles Darwin, *The Expression of Emotions in Man and Animals*, 1872

For burn victims receiving excruciating wound care, an even more effective distraction is escaping into a computer-generated 3-D world. Functional MRI (fMRI) scans have revealed that playing in the virtual reality reduces the brain's pain-related activity (Hoffman, 2004). Because pain is in the brain, diverting the brain's attention may bring relief.

HYPNOSIS Better yet, research suggests, maximize pain relief by combining a placebo with distraction (Buhle et al., 2012) and amplifying their effects with **hypnosis.** Imagine you are about to be hypnotized. The hypnotist invites you to sit back, fix your gaze on a spot high on the wall, and relax. You hear a quiet, low voice suggest, "Your eyes are growing tired. . . . Your eyelids are becoming heavy . . . now heavier and heavier. . . . They are beginning to close. . . . You are becoming more deeply relaxed. . . . Your breathing is now deep and regular. . . . Your muscles are becoming more and more relaxed. . . . Your whole body is beginning to feel like lead." After a few minutes of this *hypnotic induction,* you may experience hypnosis. Words will have changed your brain.

Hypnotists have no magical mind-control power; they merely focus people's attention on certain images or behaviors. To some extent, we are all open to suggestion. But highly hypnotizable people—such as the 20 percent who can carry out a suggestion not to react to an open bottle of smelly ammonia—are especially suggestible and imaginative (Barnier & McConkey, 2004; Silva & Kirsch, 1992). Their brain also displays altered activity when under hypnosis (Jiang et al., 2016).

Can hypnosis relieve pain? *Yes.* When unhypnotized people put their arm in an ice bath, they felt intense pain within 25 seconds (Elkins et al., 2012; Jensen, 2008). When hypnotized people did the same after being given suggestions to feel no pain, they indeed reported feeling little pain. As some dentists know, light hypnosis can reduce fear, thus reducing hypersensitivity to pain. Hypnosis has also lessened some forms of chronic and disability-related pain (Adachi et al., 2014; Bowker & Dorstyn, 2016).

In surgical experiments, hypnotized patients have required less medication, recovered sooner, and left the hospital earlier than unhypnotized control patients (Askay & Patterson, 2007; Hammond, 2008; Spiegel, 2007). Nearly 10 percent of us can become so deeply hypnotized that even major surgery can be performed without anesthesia. Half of us can gain at least some pain relief from hypnosis. The surgical use of hypnosis has flourished in Europe, where one Belgian medical team has performed more than 5000 surgeries with a combination of hypnosis, local anesthesia, and a mild sedative (Song, 2006).

Psychologists have proposed two explanations for how hypnosis works:

- *Social influence theory* contends that hypnosis is a by-product of normal social and mental processes (Lynn et al., 1990, 2015; Spanos & Coe, 1992). In this view, hypnotized people, like actors caught up in a role, begin to feel and behave in ways appropriate for "good hypnotic subjects." They may allow the hypnotist to direct their attention and fantasies away from pain.

- *Dissociation theory* proposes that hypnosis is a special dual-processing state of **dissociation**—a split between different levels of consciousness. Dissociation theory seeks to explain why, when no one is watching, hypnotized people may carry out **posthypnotic suggestions** (which are made during hypnosis but carried out after the person is no longer hypnotized) (Perugini et al., 1998). It also offers an explanation for why people hypnotized for pain relief may show brain activity in areas that receive sensory information, but not in areas that normally process pain-related information (Rainville et al., 1997).

Selective attention may also play a role in hypnotic pain relief. Brain scans show that hypnosis increases activity in frontal lobe attention systems (Oakley & Halligan, 2013). So, while hypnosis does not block sensory input itself, it may block our attention to those stimuli. This helps explain why injured soldiers, caught up in battle, may feel little or no pain until they reach safety.

DISSOCIATION OR SOCIAL INFLUENCE? This hypnotized woman being tested by famous researcher Ernest Hilgard showed no pain when her arm was placed in an ice bath. But asked to press a key if some part of her felt the pain, she did so. To Hilgard (1986, 1992), this was evidence of dissociation, or divided consciousness. The social influence perspective, however, maintains that people responding this way are caught up in playing the role of "good subject."

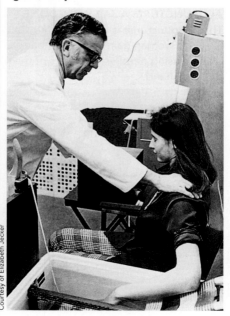

Courtesy of Elizabeth Jecker

Taste

LOQ 6-21 In what ways are our senses of taste and smell similar, and how do they differ?

Like touch, *gustation*—our sense of taste—involves several basic sensations. Taste's sensations were once thought to be *sweet, sour, salty,* and *bitter,* with all others stemming from mixtures of these four (McBurney & Gent, 1979). Then, as investigators searched for specialized nerve fibers for the four taste sensations, they encountered a receptor for what we now know is a fifth—the savory, meaty taste of *umami,* best experienced as the flavor enhancer monosodium glutamate (MSG).

Tastes exist for more than our pleasure (see **TABLE 6.2**). Pleasureful tastes attracted our ancestors to energy- or protein-rich foods that enabled their survival. Aversive tastes deterred them from new foods that might be toxic. We see the inheritance of this biological wisdom in today's 2- to 6-year-olds, who are typically fussy eaters, especially when offered new meats or bitter-tasting vegetables, such as spinach and brussels sprouts (Cooke et al., 2003). Meat and plant toxins were both potentially dangerous sources of food poisoning for our ancestors, especially for children. Given repeated small tastes of disliked new foods, however, most children begin to accept them (Wardle et al., 2003). We come to like what we eat. Compared with breast-fed babies, German babies bottle-fed vanilla-flavored milk grew up to be adults with a striking preference for vanilla flavoring (Haller et al., 1999).

Taste is a chemical sense. Inside each little bump on the top and sides of your tongue are 200 or more taste buds, each containing a pore that catches food chemicals and releases neurotransmitters (Roper & Chaudhari, 2017). In each taste bud pore, 50 to 100 taste receptor cells project antenna-like hairs that sense food molecules. Some receptors respond mostly to sweet-tasting molecules, others to salty-, sour-, umami-, or bitter-tasting ones. Each receptor transmits its message to a matching partner cell in your brain's temporal lobe (Barretto et al., 2015). It doesn't take much to trigger a taste response. If a stream of water is pumped across your tongue, the addition of a concentrated salty or sweet taste for but one-tenth of a second will get your attention (Kelling & Halpern, 1983). When a friend asks for "just a taste" of your soft drink, you can squeeze off the straw after a mere instant.

Taste receptors reproduce themselves every week or two, so if you burn your tongue it hardly matters. However, as you grow older, the number of taste buds decreases, as does taste sensitivity (Cowart, 1981). (No wonder adults enjoy strong-tasting foods that children resist.) Smoking and alcohol use accelerate these declines. Those who have lost their sense of taste have reported that food tastes like "straw" and is hard to swallow (Cowart, 2005).

There's more to taste than meets the tongue. Expectations can influence taste. When told a sausage roll was "vegetarian," nonvegetarian people judged it decidedly inferior to its identical partner labeled "meat" (Allen et al., 2008). In another experiment, hearing that a wine cost $90 rather than its real $10 price made it taste better and triggered more activity in a brain area that responds to pleasant experiences (Plassmann et al., 2008). Contrary to Shakespeare's presumption (in *Romeo and Juliet*) that "a rose by any other name would smell as sweet," labels matter. And speaking of smell . . .

Smell

Inhale, exhale. Between birth's first inhale and death's last exhale, about 500 million breaths of life-sustaining air will bathe your nostrils in a stream of scent-laden molecules. The resulting experience of smell (**olfaction**) is strikingly intimate. With every breath, you inhale something of whatever or whoever it is you smell.

Smell, like taste, is a chemical sense. We smell something when molecules of a substance carried in the air reach a tiny cluster of receptor cells at the top of each nasal cavity (**FIGURE 6.42**). These 20 million olfactory receptors, waving like sea anemones on a reef, respond selectively—to the aroma of a cake baking, to a wisp of smoke, to a friend's fragrance. Instantly, they alert the brain through their axon fibers.

Being part of an old, primitive sense, olfactory neurons bypass the brain's sensory control center, the thalamus. Eons before our cerebral cortex had fully evolved, our

hypnosis a social interaction in which one person (the hypnotist) suggests to another (the subject) that certain perceptions, feelings, thoughts, or behaviors will spontaneously occur.

dissociation a split in consciousness, which allows some thoughts and behaviors to occur simultaneously with others.

posthypnotic suggestion a suggestion, made during a hypnosis session, to be carried out after the subject is no longer hypnotized; used by some clinicians to help control undesired symptoms and behaviors.

olfaction our sense of smell.

Lauren Burke/Getty Images

RETAIN **TABLE 6.2**

The Survival Functions of Basic Tastes

Taste	Indicates
Sweet	Energy source
Salty	Sodium essential to physiological processes
Sour	Potentially toxic acid
Bitter	Potential poisons
Umami	Proteins to grow and repair tissue

Impress your friends with your new word for the day: People unable to see are said to experience blindness. People unable to hear experience deafness. People unable to smell experience *anosmia.* The 1 in 7500 people born with anosmia not only have trouble cooking and eating, but also are somewhat more prone to depression, accidents, and relationship insecurity (Croy et al., 2012, 2013).

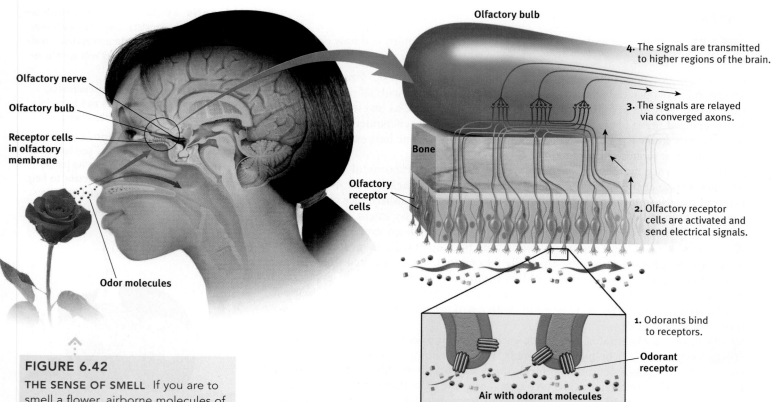

Olfactory bulb

Olfactory nerve

Olfactory bulb

Receptor cells in olfactory membrane

Odor molecules

4. The signals are transmitted to higher regions of the brain.

3. The signals are relayed via converged axons.

Bone

Olfactory receptor cells

2. Olfactory receptor cells are activated and send electrical signals.

1. Odorants bind to receptors.

Odorant receptor

Air with odorant molecules

FIGURE 6.42

THE SENSE OF SMELL If you are to smell a flower, airborne molecules of its fragrance must reach receptors at the top of your nose. Sniffing swirls air up to the receptors, enhancing the aroma. The receptor cells send messages to the brain's olfactory bulb, and then onward to the temporal lobe's primary smell cortex and to the parts of the limbic system involved in memory and emotion.

THE NOSE KNOWS Humans have some 20 million olfactory receptors. A bloodhound has 220 million (Herz, 2007).

mammalian ancestors sniffed for food—and for predators. They also smelled molecules called *pheromones,* secreted by other members of their species. Some pheromones serve as sexual attractants.

Odor molecules come in many shapes and sizes—so many, in fact, that it takes many different receptors to detect them. A large family of genes designs the 350 or so receptor proteins that recognize particular odor molecules (Miller, 2004). Linda Buck and Richard Axel (1991) discovered (in work for which they received a 2004 Nobel Prize) that these receptor proteins are embedded on the surface of nasal cavity neurons. As a key slips into a lock, so odor molecules slip into these receptors. Yet we don't seem to have a distinct receptor for each detectable odor. Odors trigger combinations of receptors, in patterns that are interpreted by the olfactory cortex. As the English alphabet's 26 letters can combine to form many words, so odor molecules bind to different receptor arrays, producing at least 1 trillion odors that we could potentially discriminate (Bushdid et al., 2014). Neuroscientists have identified complex combinations of olfactory receptors that trigger different neural networks, allowing us to distinguish between delightful and disagreeable odors (Zou et al., 2016).

Aided by smell, a mother fur seal returning to a beach crowded with pups will find her own. Human mothers and nursing infants also quickly learn to recognize each other's scents (McCarthy, 1986).

The brain knows what the nose doesn't like (Cook et al., 2017; Zou et al., 2016). When mice sniff a predator's scent, their brain instinctively sends signals to stress-related neurons (Kondoh et al., 2016). But a smell's appeal—or lack of it—also depends on learned associations (Herz, 2001). In the United States, people associate the smell of wintergreen with candy and gum, and they tend to like it. In Great Britain, wintergreen often is associated with medicine, and people find it less appealing. Odors also evoked unpleasant emotions when researchers frustrated Brown University students with a rigged computer game in a scented room (Herz et al., 2004). Later, if exposed to the same odor while working on a verbal task, the students' frustration was rekindled and they gave up sooner than others exposed to a different odor or no odor.

Although important, our sense of smell is less acute than our senses of seeing and hearing. Looking out across a garden, we see its forms and colors in exquisite detail and hear a variety of birds singing, yet we smell little of it without sticking our nose into the blossoms. Compared with how we experience and remember sights and sounds, smells are primitive and harder to describe and recall (Richardson & Zucco, 1989; Zucco, 2003).

We might struggle to recall odors by name, but we have a remarkable capacity to recognize long-forgotten odors and their associated memories (Engen, 1987; Schab, 1991). Our brain's circuitry helps explain why certain odors—the smell of the sea, the scent of a perfume, or an aroma of a favorite relative's kitchen—can bring to mind a happy time. Other odors remind us of traumatic events—childhood physical abuse, tragedy on the battlefield—activating brain regions related to fear (Kadohisa, 2013). Indeed, a hotline runs between the brain area receiving information from the nose and the brain's ancient limbic centers associated with memory and emotion (**FIGURE 6.43**). Thus, when put in a foul-smelling room, people have expressed harsher judgments of immoral acts (such as lying or keeping a found wallet) (Inbar et al., 2011; Schnall et al., 2008). Exposed to a fishy smell, people became more suspicious (Lee et al., 2015). And when riding on a train car with the citrus scent of a cleaning product, people have left behind less trash (de Lange et al., 2012).

Gender, age, and physical condition influence our ability to identify scents. Women tend to have a better sense of smell, but for all of us, the sense of smell peaks in early adulthood and gradually declines thereafter (Doty, 2001; Wickelgren, 2009; Wysocki & Gilbert, 1989).

 RETRIEVE IT • • •   *ANSWERS IN APPENDIX E*

RI-5 How does our system for sensing smell differ from our sensory systems for touch and taste?

Body Position and Movement

LOQ 6-22   How do we sense our body's position and movement?

Millions of position and motion sensors in muscles, tendons, and joints all over your body provide constant feedback to your brain, enabling your sense of **kinesthesia,** which keeps you aware of your body parts' position and movement. Twist your wrist one degree and your brain receives an immediate update.

You can momentarily imagine being without sight or sound. Close your eyes or plug your ears, and experience the dark silence. But what would it be like to live without touch or kinesthesia—without being able to sense the positions of your limbs when you wake during the night? Ian Waterman of Hampshire, England, knows. In 1972, at age 19, Waterman contracted a rare viral infection that destroyed the nerves enabling his sense of light touch and of body position and movement. People with this condition report feeling disembodied, as though their body is dead, not real, not theirs (Sacks, 1985). With prolonged practice, Waterman learned to walk and eat—by visually focusing on his limbs and directing them accordingly. But if the lights went out, he would crumple to the floor (Azar, 1998).

Vision interacts with kinesthesia for you, too. Stand with your right heel in front of your left toes. Easy. Now close your eyes and try again. Did you wobble?

A companion **vestibular sense** monitors your head's (and thus your body's) position and movement. The biological gyroscopes for this sense of equilibrium are two structures in your inner ear. The first, your fluid-filled *semicircular canals,* look like a three-dimensional pretzel (Figure 6.36a). The second structure is the pair of calcium-crystal–filled *vestibular sacs.* When your head rotates or tilts, the movement of these organs stimulates hair-like receptors, which send nerve signals to your cerebellum at the back of your brain, enabling you to sense your body position and maintain your balance.

If you twirl around and then come to an abrupt halt, neither the fluid in your semicircular canals nor your kinesthetic receptors will immediately return to their neutral state.

LaunchPad Test your understanding of how we smell by engaging online with **Concept Practice: Sense of Smell.**

"There could be a stack of truck tires burning in the living room, and I wouldn't necessarily smell it. Whereas my wife can detect a lone spoiled grape two houses away." —Dave Barry, 2005

FIGURE 6.43

TASTE, SMELL, AND MEMORY Information from the taste buds (yellow arrow) travels to an area between the frontal and temporal lobes of the brain. It registers in an area not far from where the brain receives information from our sense of smell, which interacts with taste. The brain's circuitry for smell (red area) also connects with areas involved in memory storage, which helps explain why a smell can trigger a memory.

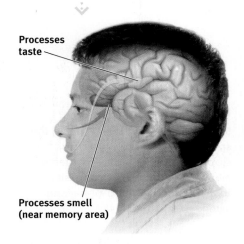

Processes taste

Processes smell (near memory area)

kinesthesia [kin-ehs-THEE-zhuh] our movement sense—our system for sensing the position and movement of individual body parts.

vestibular sense our sense of balance—our sense of body movement and position that enables our sense of balance.

© Robert Kanavel

BODIES IN SPACE Each of these high school competitive cheer team members can thank her inner ears for the information that enables her brain to monitor her body's position so expertly.

sensory interaction the principle that one sense may influence another, as when the smell of food influences its taste.

embodied cognition the influence of bodily sensations, gestures, and other states on cognitive preferences and judgments.

extrasensory perception (ESP) the controversial claim that perception can occur apart from sensory input; includes telepathy, clairvoyance, and precognition.

FIGURE 6.44

SENSORY INTERACTION Seeing the speaker forming the words, which Apple's FaceTime video-chat feature allows, makes those words easier to understand for hard-of-hearing listeners (Knight, 2004).

© Albrecht Weisser/Westend61/Corbis

The dizzy aftereffect fools your brain with the sensation that you're still spinning. This illustrates a principle that underlies perceptual illusions: *Mechanisms that normally give us an accurate experience of the world can, under certain conditions, fool us.* Understanding how we get fooled provides clues to how our perceptual system works.

One little-known fact about your vestibular sense: It is super speedy. If you slip, your vestibular sensors automatically and instantly order your skeletal response, well before you have consciously decided how to right yourself.

ENGAGE Try this: Hold one of your thumbs in front of your face then move it rapidly right to left and back. Notice how your thumb blurs (your vision isn't fast enough to track it). Now hold your thumb still and swivel your head from left to right. Surprise! Your thumb stays clear—because your vestibular system, which is monitoring your head position, speedily moves the eyes. Head moves right, eyes move left. Vision is fast, but the vestibular sense is faster.

> 🔒 **RETRIEVE IT • • •**   *ANSWERS IN APPENDIX E*
>
> **RI-6** Where are the kinesthetic receptors and the vestibular sense receptors located?

SENSORY INTERACTION

LOQ 6-23 How does *sensory interaction* influence our perceptions, and what is *embodied cognition*?

We have seen that vision and kinesthesia interact. Actually, none of our senses acts alone. All of them—seeing, hearing, tasting, smelling, touching—eavesdrop on one another, and our brain blends their inputs to interpret the world (Rosenblum, 2013). This is **sensory interaction** at work. One sense can influence another.

ENGAGE Consider how smell sticks its nose into the business of taste. Hold your nose, close your eyes, and have someone feed you various foods. A slice of apple may be indistinguishable from a chunk of raw potato. A piece of steak may taste like cardboard. Without their smells, a cup of cold coffee may be hard to distinguish from a glass of red wine. A big part of taste is right under your nose.

Thus, to savor a taste, we normally breathe the aroma through our nose. Like smoke rising in a chimney, food molecules rise into your nasal cavity. This is why food tastes bland when you have a bad cold. Smell can also change our perception of taste: A drink's strawberry odor enhances our perception of its sweetness. Even touch can influence taste. Depending on its texture, a potato chip "tastes" fresh or stale (Smith, 2011). Smell + texture + taste = flavor. Yet perhaps you have noticed: Despite smell's contribution, flavor feels located in the mouth, not in the nose (Stevenson, 2014).

Vision and hearing may similarly interact. A weak flicker of light that we have trouble perceiving becomes more visible when accompanied by a short burst of sound (Kayser, 2007). The reverse is also true: We can hear soft sounds more easily if they are paired with a visual cue. If I [DM], as a person with hearing loss, watch a video with on-screen captions, I have no trouble hearing the words I am seeing. But if I then decide I don't need the captions and turn them off, I will quickly realize I do need them. The eyes guide the ears (**FIGURE 6.44**).

So our senses interact. But what happens if they disagree? What if our eyes *see* a speaker form one sound but our ears *hear* another sound? Surprise: Our brain may perceive a third sound that blends both inputs. Seeing the mouth movements for *ga* while hearing *ba* we may perceive *da*. This phenomenon is known as the *McGurk effect,* after Scottish psychologist Harry McGurk, who, with his assistant John MacDonald, discovered the effect (1976). For all of us, lip reading is part of hearing.

We have seen that our perceptions have two main ingredients: Our bottom-up sensations and our top-down cognitions (such as expectations, attitudes, thoughts, and memories). In everyday life, sensation and perception are two points on a continuum. It's not surprising, then, that the brain circuits processing our physical sensations sometimes interact with brain circuits responsible for cognition. The result is **embodied cognition.** We think from within a body. Some examples from playful experiments:

- *Physical warmth may promote social warmth.* After holding a warm drink rather than a cold one, people were more likely to rate someone more warmly, feel closer to them, and behave more generously (IJzerman & Semin, 2009; Williams & Bargh, 2008). Have hot tea with Jose and iced tea with his identical twin Juan, and you may perceive Jose to be a warmer person.

- *Pose your fingers, prime your mind.* After using their fingers to show a number (2, 3, or 4), people more quickly identified that same number when they heard it (Sixtus et al., 2017). Numbers made with fingers make thoughts of numbers linger.

- *Judgments of others may also mimic body sensations.* Sitting at a wobbly desk and chair makes others' relationships, or even one's own romantic relationship, seem less stable (Forest et al., 2015: Kille et al., 2013).

 **ASK YOURSELF**

When have you experienced a feeling that you think could be explained by embodied cognition?

LaunchPad Are you wondering how researchers test these kinds of questions? Play the role of researcher by engaging online with **Immersive Learning: How Would You Know If a Cup of Coffee Can Warm Up Relationships?**

As we attempt to decipher our world, our brain blends inputs from multiple channels. But in a few select individuals, the brain circuits for two or more senses become joined in a phenomenon called *synesthesia,* where the stimulation of one sense (such as hearing sound) triggers an experience of another (such as seeing color). Early in life, "exuberant neural connectivity" produces some arbitrary associations among the senses, which later are normally—but not always—pruned (Wagner & Dobkins, 2011). Thus, hearing music may activate color-sensitive cortex regions and trigger a sensation of color (Brang et al., 2008; Hubbard et al., 2005). Seeing the number 3 may evoke a taste or color sensation (Ward, 2003). People with synesthesia experience such sensory shifts.

* * *

For a summary of our sensory systems, see **TABLE 6.3**.

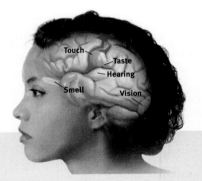

TABLE 6.3

Summarizing the Senses

Sensory System	Source	Receptors	Key Brain Areas
Vision	Light waves striking the eye	Rods and cones in the retina	Occipital lobes
Hearing	Sound waves striking the outer ear	Cochlear hair cells (cilia) in the inner ear	Temporal lobes
Touch	Pressure, warmth, cold, harmful chemicals	Receptors (including pain-sensitive *nociceptors*), mostly in the skin, which detect pressure, warmth, cold, and pain	Somatosensory cortex
Taste	Chemical molecules in the mouth	Basic taste receptors for sweet, sour, salty, bitter, and umami	Frontal temporal lobe border
Smell	Chemical molecules breathed in through the nose	Millions of receptors at top of nasal cavities	Olfactory bulb
Body position—kinesthesia	Any change in position of a body part, interacting with vision	Kinesthetic sensors in joints, tendons, and muscles	Cerebellum
Body movement—vestibular sense	Movement of fluids in the inner ear caused by head/ body movement	Hair-like receptors in the ears' semicircular canals and vestibular sacs	Cerebellum

ESP—PERCEPTION WITHOUT SENSATION?

LOQ 6-24 What are the claims of *ESP,* and what have most research psychologists concluded after putting these claims to the test?

The river of perception is fed by streams of sensation, cognition, and emotion. If perception is the product of these three sources, what can we say about **extrasensory perception (ESP)**, which claims that perception can occur apart from sensory input? Are there indeed people—any people—who can read minds, see through walls, or foretell the future? Nearly half of Americans have agreed there are (AP, 2007; Moore, 2005).

LaunchPad Do you think you might have ESP? Test your skills by engaging online with **Immersive Learning: Assess Your Strengths—ESP and Critical Thinking.**

Will you marry me, live happily for 3 years, become bored, pretend to be taking a pottery class but actually be having an affair, then agree to go to marriage counseling to stay together for the sake of our hyperactive son, Derrick?

WHEN PSYCHICS PROPOSE

A headline you've never seen: "Psychic wins lottery."

If ESP is real, we would need to overturn the scientific understanding that we are creatures whose minds are tied to our physical brains and whose perceptual experiences of the world are built of sensations. The most testable and, for this discussion, most relevant ESP claims are

- *telepathy:* mind-to-mind communication.
- *clairvoyance:* perceiving remote events, such as a house on fire in another state.
- *precognition:* perceiving future events, such as an unexpected death in the next month.

Closely linked is *psychokinesis,* or "mind moving matter," such as levitating a table or influencing the roll of a die. (The claim, also called *telekinesis,* is illustrated by the wry request, "Will all those who believe in psychokinesis please raise my hand?")

Most research psychologists and scientists have been skeptical that paranormal phenomena exist. But in several reputable universities, **parapsychology** researchers perform scientific experiments searching for possible ESP phenomena (Storm et al., 2010a,b; Turpin, 2005). Before seeing how they conduct their research, let's consider some popular beliefs.

Premonitions or Pretensions?

Can psychics see into the future? Although one might wish for a psychic stock forecaster, the tallied forecasts of "leading psychics" reveal meager accuracy. During the 1990s, the tabloid psychics were all wrong in predicting surprising events. (Madonna did not become a gospel singer, the Statue of Liberty did not lose both its arms in a terrorist blast, Queen Elizabeth did not abdicate her throne to enter a convent.) And the psychics have missed big-news events. Where were the psychics on 9/10 when we needed them? Why, despite a $50 million reward, could no psychics help locate Osama bin Laden after 9/11? And why, when the Chilean government consulted four psychics after a mine collapse trapped 33 miners in 2010, did those psychics sorrowfully decide "They're all dead" (Kraul, 2010)? Imagine their surprise when all 33 miners were rescued 69 days later.

After Amanda Berry went missing in Cleveland in 2003, her distraught and desperate mother turned to a famed TV psychic detective for answers. "She's not alive, honey," the psychic told the devastated mom, who died without living to see her daughter rescued in 2013 (Radford, 2013). According to one analysis, this result brought that psychic's record on 116 missing person and death cases to 83 unknown outcomes, 33 incorrect, and zero mostly correct. To researcher Ryan Shaffer (2013), that's the record of a "psychic defective."

The psychic visions offered to police departments have been no more accurate than guesses made by others (Nickell, 1994, 2005; Radford, 2010; Reiser, 1982). But their sheer volume does increase the odds of an occasional correct guess, which psychics can then report to the media. Such visions can sound amazingly correct when later retrofitted to match events. Nostradamus, a sixteenth-century French psychic, explained in an unguarded moment that his ambiguous prophecies "could not possibly be understood till they were interpreted after the event and by it."

Are everyday people's "visions" any more accurate than the psychics' predictions? Do our dreams foretell the future, or do they only seem to do so when we recall or reconstruct them in light of what has already happened? Are our remembered visions merely revisions? After famed aviator Charles Lindbergh's baby son was kidnapped and murdered in 1932, but before the body was discovered, two Harvard psychologists invited people to report their dreams about the child (Murray & Wheeler, 1937). How many visionaries replied? 1300. How many accurately envisioned the child dead? Five percent. How many also correctly anticipated the body's location—buried among trees? Only 4. Although this number was surely no better than chance, to those 4 dreamers, the accuracy of their apparent precognitions must have seemed uncanny.

Given the countless events in the world each day, and given enough days, some stunning coincidences are sure to occur. By one careful estimate, chance alone would predict that more than a thousand times per day, someone on Earth will think of another person and then, within the next five minutes, learn of that person's death (Charpak & Broch, 2004). Thus, when explaining an astonishing event, we should "give chance a chance" (Lilienfeld, 2009). With enough time and people, the improbable becomes inevitable.

parapsychology the study of paranormal phenomena, including ESP and psychokinesis (also called *telekinesis*).

Putting ESP to Experimental Test

When faced with claims of mind reading or out-of-body travel or communication with the dead, how can we separate fiction from strange-but-true fact? Psychological science offers a simple answer: *Test them to see if they work.* If they do, so much the better for the ideas. If they don't, so much the better for our skepticism.

Both believers and skeptics agree that what parapsychology needs is a reproducible phenomenon and a theory to explain it. Parapsychologist Rhea White (1998) spoke for many in saying that "the image of parapsychology that comes to my mind, based on nearly 44 years in the field, is that of a small airplane [that] has been perpetually taxiing down the runway of the Empirical Science Airport since 1882 . . . its movement punctuated occasionally by lifting a few feet off the ground only to bump back down on the tarmac once again. It has never taken off for any sustained flight."

How might we test ESP claims in a controlled, reproducible experiment? An experiment differs from a staged demonstration. In the laboratory, the experimenter controls what the "psychic" sees and hears. On stage, the psychic controls what the audience sees and hears.

Daryl Bem, a respected social psychologist, once quipped that "a psychic is an actor playing the role of a psychic" (1984). Yet this one-time skeptic reignited hopes for replicable evidence of ESP with nine experiments that seemed to show people anticipating future events (2011). In one, when an erotic scene was about to appear on a screen in one of two randomly selected positions, Cornell University participants guessed the right placement 53.1 percent of the time (beating 50 percent by a small but statistically significant margin).

Despite the paper having survived critical reviews by a top-tier journal, critics scoffed. Some found the methods "badly flawed" (Alcock, 2011) or the statistical analyses "biased" (Wagenmakers et al., 2011). Others predicted the results could not be replicated by "independent and skeptical researchers" (Helfand, 2011).

Anticipating such skepticism, Bem has made his research materials available to anyone who wishes to replicate his studies. Multiple attempts have met with minimal success and continuing controversy (Bem et al., 2014; Galak et al., 2012; Ritchie et al., 2012; Wagenmakers, 2014). Regardless, science is doing its work:

- It has been open to a finding that challenges its own assumptions.
- Through follow-up research, it has assessed the reliability and validity of that finding.

And that is how science sifts crazy-sounding ideas, leaving most on the historical waste heap while occasionally surprising us.

For 19 years, one skeptic, magician James Randi, offered $1 million "to anyone who proves a genuine psychic power under proper observing conditions" (Randi, 1999; Thompson, 2010). French, Australian, and Indian groups have made similar offers of up to 200,000 euros (CFI, 2003). Large as these sums are, the scientific seal of approval would be worth far more. To refute those who say there is no ESP, one need only produce a single person who can demonstrate a single, reproducible ESP event. (To refute those who say pigs can't talk would take but one talking pig.) So far, no such person has emerged.

* * *

To feel awe, mystery, and a deep reverence for life, we need look no further than our own perceptual system and its capacity for organizing formless nerve impulses into colorful sights, vivid sounds, and evocative smells. As Shakespeare's Hamlet recognized, "There are more things in Heaven and Earth, Horatio, than are dreamt of in your philosophy." Within our ordinary sensory and perceptual experiences lies much that is truly extraordinary—surely much more than has so far been dreamt of in our psychology.

Courtesy of Claire Cole

TESTING PSYCHIC POWERS IN THE BRITISH POPULATION Psychologists created a "mind machine" to see if people could influence or predict a coin toss (Wiseman & Greening, 2002). Using a touch-sensitive screen, visitors to British festivals were given four attempts to call heads or tails, playing against a computer that kept score. By the time the experiment ended, nearly 28,000 people had predicted 110,959 tosses—with 49.8 percent correct.

"A person who talks a lot is sometimes right." —Spanish proverb

"At the heart of science is an essential tension between two seemingly contradictory attitudes—an openness to new ideas, no matter how bizarre or counterintuitive they may be, and the most ruthless skeptical scrutiny of all ideas, old and new." —Carl Sagan (1987)

RETRIEVE IT • • • ANSWERS IN APPENDIX E

RI-7 If an ESP event occurred under controlled conditions, what would be the next best step to confirm that ESP really exists?

⟶ Learning Objectives

TEST YOURSELF Answer these repeated Learning Objective Questions on your own (before checking the answers in Appendix D) to improve your retention of the concepts (McDaniel et al., 2009, 2015).

6-16 What are the characteristics of air pressure waves that we hear as sound?

6-17 How does the ear transform sound energy into neural messages?

6-18 How do we detect loudness, discriminate pitch, and locate sounds?

6-19 How do we sense touch?

6-20 What biological, psychological, and social-cultural influences affect our experience of pain? How do placebos, distraction, and hypnosis help control pain?

6-21 In what ways are our senses of taste and smell similar, and how do they differ?

6-22 How do we sense our body's position and movement?

6-23 How does *sensory interaction* influence our perceptions, and what is *embodied cognition*?

6-24 What are the claims of *ESP*, and what have most research psychologists concluded after putting these claims to the test?

⟶ Terms and Concepts to Remember

TEST YOURSELF Write down the definition yourself, then check your answer on the referenced page.

audition, **p. 216**

frequency, **p. 216**

pitch, **p. 216**

middle ear, **p. 216**

cochlea [KOHK-lee-uh], **p. 216**

inner ear, **p. 216**

sensorineural hearing loss, **p. 219**

conduction hearing loss, **p. 219**

cochlear implant, **p. 219**

place theory, **p. 219**

frequency theory, **p. 220**

gate-control theory, **p. 222**

hypnosis, **p. 225**

dissociation, **p. 225**

posthypnotic suggestion, **p. 225**

olfaction, **p. 225**

kinesthesia, **p. 227**

vestibular sense, **p. 227**

sensory interaction, **p. 228**

embodied cognition, **p. 228**

extrasensory perception (ESP), **p. 228**

parapsychology, **p. 230**

⟶ Experience the Testing Effect

TEST YOURSELF Answer the following questions on your own first, then check your answers in Appendix E.

1. The snail-shaped tube in the inner ear, where sound waves are converted into neural activity, is called the _____.

2. What are the basic steps in transforming sound waves into perceived sound?

3. _____ theory explains how we hear high-pitched sounds, and _____ theory, extended by the _____ principle, explains how we hear low-pitched sounds.

4. The sensory receptors that are found mostly in the skin and that detect hurtful temperatures, pressure, or chemicals are called _____.

5. The gate-control theory of pain proposes that
   a. special pain receptors send signals directly to the brain.
   b. pain is a property of the senses, not of the brain.
   c. small spinal cord nerve fibers conduct most pain signals, but large-fiber activity can close access to those pain signals.
   d. pain can often be controlled and managed effectively through the use of relaxation techniques.

6. How does the biopsychosocial approach explain our experience of pain? Provide examples.

7. We have specialized nerve receptors for detecting which five tastes? How did this ability aid our ancestors?

8. _____ is your sense of body position and movement. Your _____ _____ specifically monitors your head's movement, with sensors in the inner ear.

9. Why do you feel a little dizzy immediately after a roller-coaster ride?

10. A food's aroma can greatly enhance its taste. This is an example of
    a. olfaction.
    b. synesthesia.
    c. kinesthesia.
    d. sensory interaction.

11. Which of the following ESP phenomena is supported by solid, replicable scientific evidence?
    a. Telepathy
    b. Clairvoyance
    c. Precognition
    d. None of these phenomena

Continue testing yourself with 📖 **LearningCurve** or 📖 **Achieve Read & Practice**
to learn and remember most effectively.

Learning

Imgorthand/Getty Images

In the early 1940s, University of Minnesota graduate students Marian Breland and Keller Breland witnessed the power of a new learning technology. Their mentor, B. F. Skinner, would become famous for *shaping* rat and pigeon behaviors by delivering well-timed rewards as the animals inched closer and closer to a desired behavior. Impressed by Skinner's results, the Brelands began shaping the behavior of cats, chickens, parakeets, turkeys, pigs, ducks, and hamsters (Bailey & Gillaspy, 2005). They eventually formed Animal Behavior Enterprises and spent the next half-century training more than 15,000 animals from 140 species. Their efforts helped pave the way for training animals to help humans, including police officers and people with vision loss or seizure disorders.

Like other animals, humans learn from experience. Indeed, nature's most important gift may be our *adaptability*—our capacity to learn new behaviors that help us cope with our changing world. We can learn how to build grass huts or snow shelters, submarines or space stations, and thereby adapt to almost any environment.

Oprah Winfrey is a living example of adaptability. Growing up in poverty with her grandmother, Winfrey wore dresses made of potato sacks. She was a constant target of racism. Beginning at age nine, she was molested by several family members, leading her to run away from home at age 13. She became pregnant at age 14, but her son died shortly after birth.

To overcome such tremendous adversity, Winfrey learned how to adapt to new situations. She joined her high school speech team and used this talent to win a college

233

scholarship. After graduating, she moved to Chicago and took over as the host of a struggling talk show, transforming it into the most popular show in America. "Education," Winfrey said, "is the key to unlocking the world, a passport to freedom."

Winfrey shows us how learning breeds hope. What is learnable we can potentially teach—a fact that encourages parents, educators, coaches, and animal trainers. What has been learned we can potentially change by new learning—an assumption that underlies counseling, psychotherapy, and rehabilitation programs. No matter how unhappy, unsuccessful, or unloving we are, that need not be the end of our story.

No topic is closer to the heart of psychology than *learning*. In earlier chapters we considered infants' learning, and the learning of visual perceptions, of a drug's expected effect, and of gender roles. In later chapters we will see how learning shapes our thoughts and language, our motivations and emotions, our personalities and attitudes. Here in this chapter we examine the heart of learning: classical conditioning, operant conditioning, the effects of biology and cognition on learning, and learning by observation. ▶

⟳→ Basic Learning Concepts and Classical Conditioning

HOW DO WE LEARN?

LEARNING OBJECTIVE QUESTION (LOQ)

7-1   How do we define *learning*, and what are some basic forms of learning?

By **learning**, we humans adapt to our environments. We learn to expect and prepare for significant events such as food or pain (*classical conditioning*). We learn to repeat acts that bring rewards and to avoid acts that bring unwanted results (*operant conditioning*). We learn new behaviors by observing events and people, and through language, we learn things we have neither experienced nor observed (*cognitive learning*). But *how* do we learn?

One way we learn is by *association*. Our mind naturally connects events that occur in sequence. Suppose you see and smell freshly baked bread, eat some, and find it satisfying. The next time you see and smell fresh bread, you will expect that eating it will again be satisfying. So, too, with sounds. If you associate a sound with a frightening consequence, hearing the sound alone may trigger your fear. As one 4-year-old exclaimed after watching a TV character get mugged, "If I had heard that music, I wouldn't have gone around the corner!" (Wells, 1981).

Learned associations also feed our habitual behaviors (Wood et al., 2014b). Habits can form when we repeat behaviors in a given context—sleeping in a certain posture in bed, biting our nails in class, eating popcorn in a movie theater. As behavior becomes linked with the context, our next experience of the context will evoke our habitual response. Especially when our willpower is depleted, as when we're mentally fatigued, we tend to fall back on our habits (Neal et al., 2013). That's true of both good habits (eating fruit) and bad (overindulging in alcohol) (Graybiel & Smith, 2014). To increase our self-control, and to connect our resolutions with positive outcomes, the key is forming "beneficial habits" (Galla & Duckworth, 2015).

How long does it take to form a beneficial habit? To find out, one British research team asked 96 university students to choose some healthy behavior (such as running before dinner or eating fruit with lunch), to do it daily for 84 days, and to record whether the behavior felt automatic (something they did without thinking and would find it hard not to). On average, behaviors became habitual after about 66 days (Lally et al., 2010). Is there something you'd like to make a routine or essential part of your life?

learning the process of acquiring through experience new and relatively enduring information or behaviors.

associative learning learning that certain events occur together. The events may be two stimuli (as in classical conditioning) or a response and its consequence (as in operant conditioning).

stimulus any event or situation that evokes a response.

respondent behavior behavior that occurs as an automatic response to some stimulus.

operant behavior behavior that operates on the environment, producing a consequence.

Two related events:

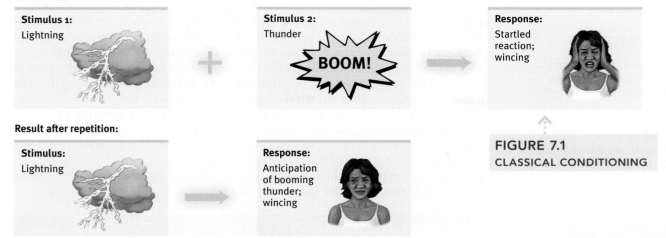

| Stimulus 1:
Lightning | + | Stimulus 2:
Thunder
BOOM! | → | Response:
Startled reaction; wincing |

Result after repetition:

| Stimulus:
Lightning | → | Response:
Anticipation of booming thunder; wincing |

FIGURE 7.1
CLASSICAL CONDITIONING

Just do it every day for two months, or a bit longer for exercise, and you likely will find yourself with a new habit. This happened for both of us—with a midday workout [DM] or late afternoon run [ND] having long ago become an automatic daily routine.

Other animals also learn by association. Disturbed by a squirt of water, the sea slug *Aplysia* protectively withdraws its gill. If the squirts continue, as happens naturally in choppy water, the withdrawal response diminishes. But if the sea slug repeatedly receives an electric shock just after being squirted, its protective response to the squirt instead grows stronger. The animal has associated the squirt with the impending shock.

Complex animals can learn to associate their own behavior with its outcomes. An aquarium seal will repeat behaviors, such as slapping and barking, that prompt people to toss it a herring.

By linking two events that occur close together, both sea slugs and seals are exhibiting **associative learning**. The sea slug associates the squirt with an impending shock; the seal associates slapping and barking with a herring treat. Each animal has learned something important to its survival: anticipating the immediate future.

This process of learning associations is *conditioning*. It takes two main forms:

- In *classical conditioning,* we learn to associate two stimuli and thus to anticipate events. (A **stimulus** is any event or situation that evokes a response.) We learn that a flash of lightning signals an impending crack of thunder; when lightning flashes nearby, we start to brace ourselves (**FIGURE 7.1**). We associate stimuli that we do not control, and we respond automatically (exhibiting **respondent behavior**).

- In *operant conditioning,* we learn to associate a response (our behavior) and its consequence. Thus, we (and other animals) learn to repeat acts followed by good results (**FIGURE 7.2**) and avoid acts followed by bad results. These associations produce **operant behaviors** (which operate on the environment to produce consequences).

"Watch your thoughts, they become words;
watch your words, they become actions;
watch your actions, they become habits;
watch your habits, they become character;
watch your character, for it becomes your destiny."
—Attributed to nineteenth-century fugitive cowboy Frank Outlaw, 1977

ENGAGE Most of us would be unable to name the order of the songs on our favorite album or playlist. Yet, hearing the end of one piece cues (by association) an anticipation of the next. Likewise, when singing your national anthem, you associate the end of each line with the beginning of the next. (Pick a line out of the middle and notice how much harder it is to recall the *previous* line.)

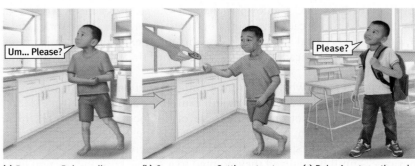

(a) Response: Being polite   (b) Consequence: Getting a treat   (c) Behavior strengthened

FIGURE 7.2
OPERANT CONDITIONING

ASK YOURSELF

Can you remember examples from your childhood of learning through *classical conditioning* (salivating at the sound or smell of some delicious food cooking in the kitchen?), *operant conditioning* (deciding not to repeat a behavior because you disliked its consequence?), and *cognitive learning* (repeating or avoiding what you watched someone else do)?

IVAN PAVLOV "Experimental investigation. . . should lay a solid foundation for a future true science of psychology" (1927).

cognitive learning the acquisition of mental information, whether by observing events, by watching others, or through language.

classical conditioning a type of learning in which we link two or more stimuli; as a result, to illustrate with Pavlov's classic experiment, the first stimulus (a tone) comes to elicit behavior (drooling) in anticipation of the second stimulus (food).

behaviorism the view that psychology (1) should be an objective science that (2) studies behavior without reference to mental processes. Most research psychologists today agree with (1) but not with (2).

neutral stimulus (NS) in classical conditioning, a stimulus that elicits no response before conditioning.

unconditioned response (UR) in classical conditioning, an unlearned, naturally occurring response (such as salivation) to an unconditioned stimulus (US) (such as food in the mouth).

unconditioned stimulus (US) in classical conditioning, a stimulus that unconditionally—naturally and automatically—triggers an unconditioned response (UR).

To simplify, we will explore these two types of associative learning separately. Often, though, they occur together, as on one Japanese cattle ranch, where the clever rancher outfitted his herd with electronic pagers which he called from his cell phone. After a week of training, the animals learned to associate two stimuli—the beep of their pager and the arrival of food (classical conditioning). But they also learned to associate their hustling to the food trough with the pleasure of eating (operant conditioning), which simplified the rancher's work. Classical conditioning + operant conditioning did the trick.

Conditioning is not the only form of learning. Through **cognitive learning** we acquire mental information that guides our behavior. *Observational learning,* one form of cognitive learning, lets us learn from others' experiences. Chimpanzees, for example, sometimes learn behaviors merely by watching other chimpanzees perform them. If one animal sees another solve a puzzle and gain a food reward, the observer may perform the trick more quickly. So, too, in humans: We look and we learn.

🔒 **RETRIEVE IT • • •**   *ANSWERS IN APPENDIX E*

RI-1 Why are habits, such as having something sweet with that cup of coffee, so hard to break?

CLASSICAL CONDITIONING

LOQ 7-2   What is behaviorism's view of learning?

For many people, the name Ivan Pavlov (1849–1936) rings a bell. His early twentieth-century experiments—now psychology's most famous research—are classics, and the phenomenon he explored we justly call **classical conditioning**.

Pavlov's work laid the foundation for many of psychologist John B. Watson's ideas. In searching for laws underlying learning, Watson (1913) urged his colleagues to discard reference to inner thoughts, feelings, and motives. The science of psychology should instead study how organisms respond to stimuli in their environments, said Watson: "Its theoretical goal is the prediction and control of behavior. Introspection forms no essential part of its methods." Simply said, psychology should be an objective science based on observable behavior.

This view, which Watson called **behaviorism**, influenced North American psychology, especially during the first half of the twentieth century. Pavlov and Watson came to share both a disdain for "mentalistic" concepts (such as consciousness) and a belief that the basic laws of learning were the same for all animals—whether dogs or humans. Few researchers today agree that psychology should ignore mental processes, but most do agree that classical conditioning is a basic form of learning by which all organisms adapt to their environment.

Pavlov's Experiments

LOQ 7-3   Who was Pavlov, and what are the basic components of classical conditioning?

Pavlov was driven by a lifelong passion for research. After setting aside his initial plan to follow his father into the Russian Orthodox priesthood, Pavlov earned a medical degree at age 33 and spent the next two decades studying dogs' digestive system. This work earned him, in 1904, Russia's first Nobel Prize. But it was his novel experiments on learning, which consumed the last three decades of his life, that earned this feisty, intense scientist his place in history (Todes, 2014).

Pavlov's new direction came when his creative mind seized on an incidental observation: Without fail, putting food in a dog's mouth caused the animal to salivate. Moreover, the dog began salivating not only to the taste of the food, but also to the mere sight of the food, or the food dish, or the person delivering the food, or even the sound of that person's approaching footsteps. At first, Pavlov considered these "psychic secretions" an annoyance—until he realized they pointed to a simple but fundamental form of learning.

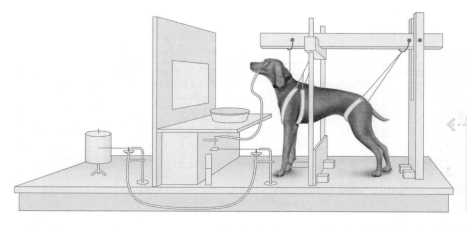

FIGURE 7.3

PAVLOV'S DEVICE FOR RECORDING SALIVATION A tube in the dog's cheek collects saliva, which is measured in a cylinder outside the chamber.

Pavlov and his assistants tried to imagine what the dog was thinking and feeling as it drooled in anticipation of the food. This only led them into fruitless debates. So, to explore the phenomenon more objectively, they experimented. To eliminate other possible influences, they isolated the dog in a small room, secured it in a harness, and attached a device to divert its saliva to a measuring instrument (**FIGURE 7.3**). From the next room, they presented food—first by sliding in a food bowl, later by blowing meat powder into the dog's mouth at a precise moment. They then paired various **neutral stimuli (NS)**—events the dog could see or hear but didn't associate with food—with food in the dog's mouth. If a sight or sound regularly signaled the arrival of food, would the dog learn the link? If so, would it begin salivating in anticipation of the food?

The answers proved to be *Yes* and *Yes*. Just before placing food in the dog's mouth to produce salivation, Pavlov sounded a tone. After several pairings of tone and food, the dog, now anticipating the meat powder, began salivating to the tone alone. In later experiments, a buzzer,[1] a light, a touch on the leg, even the sight of a circle set off the drooling. (This procedure works with people, too. When hungry young Londoners viewed abstract figures before smelling peanut butter or vanilla, their brain soon responded in anticipation to the abstract images alone [Gottfried et al., 2003].)

A dog does not learn to salivate in response to food in its mouth. Rather, food in the mouth automatically, *unconditionally,* triggers a dog's salivary reflex (**FIGURE 7.4**). Thus, Pavlov called this drooling an **unconditioned response (UR)**. And he called the food an **unconditioned stimulus (US)**.

---

1. The "buzzer" (English translation) was perhaps the bell people commonly associate with Pavlov (Tully, 2003). Pavlov used various stimuli, but some have questioned whether he used a bell.

FIGURE 7.4

PAVLOV'S CLASSIC EXPERIMENT Pavlov presented a neutral stimulus (a tone) just before an unconditioned stimulus (food in mouth). The neutral stimulus then became a conditioned stimulus, producing a conditioned response.

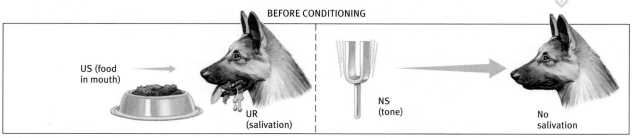

BEFORE CONDITIONING

US (food in mouth) → UR (salivation)

An unconditioned stimulus (US) produces an unconditioned response (UR).

NS (tone) → No salivation

A neutral stimulus (NS) produces no salivation response.

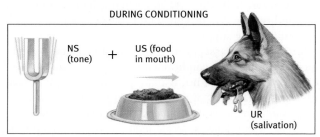

DURING CONDITIONING

NS (tone) + US (food in mouth) → UR (salivation)

The US is repeatedly presented just after the NS. The US continues to produce a UR.

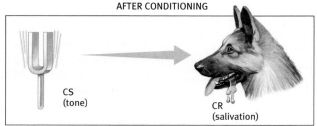

AFTER CONDITIONING

CS (tone) → CR (salivation)

The previously neutral stimulus alone now produces a conditioned response (CR), thereby becoming a conditioned stimulus (CS).

conditioned response (CR) in classical conditioning, a learned response to a previously neutral (but now conditioned) stimulus (CS).

conditioned stimulus (CS) in classical conditioning, an originally neutral stimulus that, after association with an unconditioned stimulus (US), comes to trigger a conditioned response (CR).

acquisition in classical conditioning, the initial stage, when one links a neutral stimulus and an unconditioned stimulus so that the neutral stimulus begins triggering the conditioned response. In operant conditioning, the strengthening of a reinforced response.

extinction the diminishing of a conditioned response; occurs in classical conditioning when an unconditioned stimulus (US) does not follow a conditioned stimulus (CS); occurs in operant conditioning when a response is no longer reinforced.

spontaneous recovery the reappearance, after a pause, of an extinguished conditioned response.

generalization the tendency, once a response has been conditioned, for stimuli similar to the conditioned stimulus to elicit similar responses. (In operant conditioning, generalization occurs when responses learned in one situation occur in other, similar situations.)

PEANUTS

Peanuts reprinted with permission of United Features Syndicate

Salivation in response to a tone, however, is learned. It is *conditional* upon the dog's associating the tone with the food. Thus, we call this response the **conditioned response (CR)**. The stimulus that used to be neutral (in this case, a previously meaningless tone that now triggers salivation) is the **conditioned stimulus (CS)**. Distinguishing these two kinds of stimuli and responses is easy: Conditioned = learned; *unconditioned* = *unlearned*.

If Pavlov's demonstration of associative learning was so simple, what did he do for the next three decades? What discoveries did his research factory publish in his 532 papers on salivary conditioning (Windholz, 1997)? He and his associates explored five major conditioning processes: *acquisition, extinction, spontaneous recovery, generalization,* and *discrimination*.

🔒 **RETRIEVE IT • • •**   *ANSWERS IN APPENDIX E*

RI-2 An experimenter sounds a tone just before delivering an air puff that causes your eye to blink. After several repetitions, you blink to the tone alone. What is the NS? The US? The UR? The CS? The CR?

ACQUISITION

LOQ 7-4 In classical conditioning, what are the processes of *acquisition, extinction, spontaneous recovery, generalization,* and *discrimination*?

Acquisition is the initial learning of an association. Pavlov and his associates wondered: How much time should elapse between presenting the NS (the tone, the light, the touch) and the US (the food)? In most cases, not much—half a second usually works well.

What do you suppose would happen if the food (US) appeared before the tone (NS) rather than after? Would conditioning occur? Not likely. Conditioning usually won't occur when the NS follows the US. Remember: *Classical conditioning is biologically adaptive because it helps humans and other animals prepare for good or bad events.* To Pavlov's dogs, the originally neutral tone became a CS after signaling an important biological event—the arrival of food (US). To deer in the forest, the snapping of a twig (CS) may signal a predator's approach (US).

Research on male Japanese quail shows how a CS can signal another important biological event (Domjan, 1992, 1994, 2005). Just before presenting a sexually approachable female quail, the researchers turned on a red light. Over time, as the red light continued to herald the female's arrival, the light alone caused the male quail to become excited. They developed a preference for their cage's red light district, and when a female appeared, they mated with her more quickly and released more semen and sperm (Matthews et al., 2007). This capacity for classical conditioning supports reproduction.

In humans, too, objects, smells, and sights associated with sexual pleasure—even a geometric figure in one experiment—can become conditioned stimuli for sexual arousal (Byrne, 1982; Hoffman, 2012). Onion breath does not usually produce sexual arousal. But when repeatedly paired with a passionate kiss, it can become a CS and do just that (**FIGURE 7.5**). The larger lesson: *Conditioning helps an animal survive and reproduce—by responding to cues that help it gain food, avoid dangers, locate mates, and produce offspring* (Hollis, 1997). Learning makes for yearning.

ENGAGE

🔆 **ASK YOURSELF**

Psychologist Michael Tirrell recalled coming to associate his girlfriend's onion breath with arousal. Can you remember ever experiencing something that would normally be neutral (or even unpleasant) that came to mean something special?

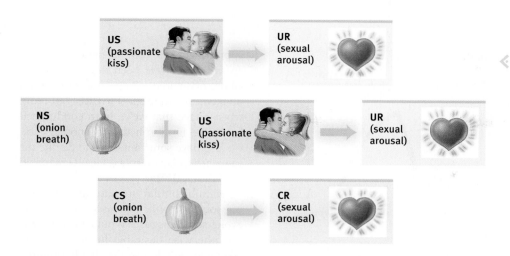

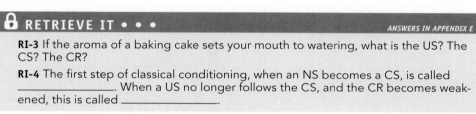

FIGURE 7.5

AN UNEXPECTED CS Psychologist Michael Tirrell (1990) recalled: "My first girlfriend loved onions, so I came to associate onion breath with kissing. Before long, onion breath sent tingles up and down my spine. Oh what a feeling!"

EXTINCTION AND SPONTANEOUS RECOVERY What would happen, Pavlov wondered, if, after conditioning, the CS occurred repeatedly without the US? If the tone sounded again and again, but no food appeared, would the tone still trigger salivation? The answer was mixed. The dogs salivated less and less, a reaction known as **extinction**. Extinction is the diminished responding that occurs when the CS (tone) no longer signals an impending US (food). But a different picture emerged when Pavlov allowed several hours to elapse before sounding the tone again. After the delay, the dogs would again begin salivating to the tone (**FIGURE 7.6**). This **spontaneous recovery**—the reappearance of a (weakened) CR after a pause—suggested to Pavlov that extinction was suppressing the CR rather than eliminating it.

Remember:

NS = **N**eutral **S**timulus
US = **U**nconditioned **S**timulus
UR = **U**nconditioned **R**esponse
CS = **C**onditioned **S**timulus
CR = **C**onditioned **R**esponse

🔒 RETRIEVE IT • • •   *ANSWERS IN APPENDIX E*

RI-3 If the aroma of a baking cake sets your mouth to watering, what is the US? The CS? The CR?

RI-4 The first step of classical conditioning, when an NS becomes a CS, is called _____. When a US no longer follows the CS, and the CR becomes weakened, this is called _____.

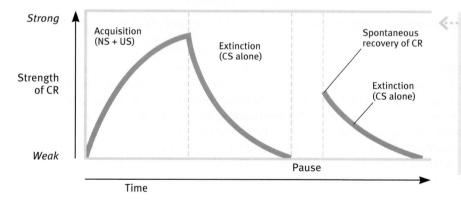

FIGURE 7.6

IDEALIZED CURVE OF ACQUISITION, EXTINCTION, AND SPONTANEOUS RECOVERY The rising curve shows the CR rapidly growing stronger as the NS becomes a CS due to repeated pairing with the US *(acquisition)*. The CR then weakens rapidly as the CS is presented alone *(extinction)*. After a pause, the (weakened) CR reappears *(spontaneous recovery)*.

GENERALIZATION Pavlov and his students noticed that a dog conditioned to the sound of one tone also responded somewhat to the sound of a new and different tone. Likewise, a dog conditioned to salivate when rubbed would also drool a bit when scratched (Windholz, 1989) or when touched on a different body part (**FIGURE 7.7**). This tendency to respond to stimuli similar to the CS is called **generalization** (or *stimulus generalization*).

Generalization can be adaptive, as when toddlers who learn to fear moving cars also become afraid of moving trucks and motorcycles. And generalized fears can linger. For two months after being in a car collision, sensitized young drivers are less vulnerable to repeat collisions (O'Brien et al., 2017). Years after being tortured, one Argentine writer reported still flinching with fear at the sight of black shoes—his first glimpse of his torturers as they

FIGURE 7.7

GENERALIZATION Pavlov demonstrated generalization by attaching miniature vibrators to various parts of a dog's body. After conditioning salivation to stimulation of the thigh, he stimulated other areas. The closer a stimulated spot was to the dog's thigh, the stronger the conditioned response. (Data from Pavlov, 1927.)

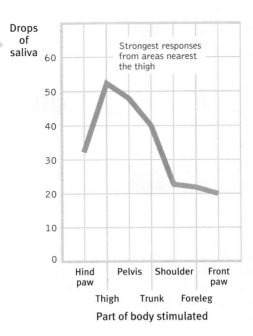

approached his cell. Generalized anxiety reactions have been demonstrated in laboratory studies comparing abused with nonabused children (**FIGURE 7.8**). And when a face that we've been conditioned to dislike is morphed into another face, we also have some tendency to dislike the vaguely similar morphed face (Gawronski & Quinn, 2013).

Stimuli similar to naturally disgusting objects will, by association, also evoke some disgust. Would most people eat otherwise desirable fudge shaped to resemble dog feces? Or drink sanitary, filtered water that had been collected from a toilet? *No* and *No*. Both situations cause people to feel repulsed (Rozin et al., 1986, 2015). These examples show how people's emotional reactions to one stimulus can generalize to similar stimuli.

🔒 **RETRIEVE IT** • • •   *ANSWERS IN APPENDIX E*

"I don't care if she's a tape dispenser. I love her."

RI-5 What conditioning principle is influencing the snail's affections?

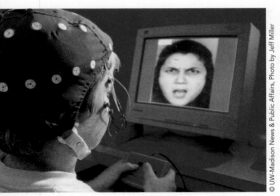

FIGURE 7.8

CHILD ABUSE LEAVES TRACKS IN THE BRAIN Abused children's sensitized brains react more strongly to angry faces (Pollak et al., 1998). This generalized anxiety response may help explain their greater risk of psychological disorder.

DISCRIMINATION Pavlov's dogs also learned to respond to the sound of a particular tone and *not* to other tones. One stimulus (tone) predicted the US, and the others did not. This learned ability to *distinguish* between a conditioned stimulus (which predicts the US) and other, irrelevant stimuli is called **discrimination**. Being able to recognize differences is adaptive. Slightly different stimuli can be followed by vastly different consequences. Kenyan elephants flee the scent of Maasai hunters, whom they have learned to fear, but not the scent of nonthreatening Kamba men (Rhodes, 2017). Facing a guard dog, your heart may race; facing a guide dog, it probably will not.

Pavlov's Legacy

LOQ 7-5   Why does Pavlov's work remain so important?

What remains today of Pavlov's ideas? A great deal. Most psychologists now agree that classical conditioning is a basic form of learning. Modern neuroscience has also supported Pavlov's ideas—by identifying neural circuits that link a conditioned stimulus (warning signal) with an impending unconditioned stimulus (threat) (Harnett et al., 2016). Judged with today's knowledge of the interplay of our biology, psychology, and social-cultural environment, some of Pavlov's ideas were incomplete. But if we see further than Pavlov did, it is because we stand on his shoulders.

Why does Pavlov's work remain so important? If he had merely taught us that old dogs can learn new tricks, his experiments would long ago have been forgotten. Why should we care that dogs can be conditioned to salivate to the sound of a tone? The importance lies first in this finding: *Many other responses to many other stimuli can be classically conditioned in many other organisms*—in fact, in every species tested, from earthworms to fish to dogs to monkeys to people (Schwartz, 1984). Thus, classical conditioning is one way that virtually all organisms learn to adapt to their environment.

Second, *Pavlov showed us how a process such as learning can be studied objectively.* He was proud that his methods involved virtually no subjective judgments or guesses about what went on in a dog's mind. The salivary response is a behavior measurable in cubic centimeters of saliva. Pavlov's success therefore suggested a scientific model for how the young discipline of psychology might proceed—by isolating the basic building blocks of complex behaviors and studying them with objective laboratory procedures.

🔒 RETRIEVE IT • • •   *ANSWERS IN APPENDIX E*

RI-6 In horror movies, sexually arousing images of women are sometimes paired with violence against women. Based on classical conditioning principles, what might be an effect of this pairing?

APPLICATIONS OF CLASSICAL CONDITIONING

LOQ 7-6   What have been some applications of Pavlov's work to human health and well-being? How did Watson apply Pavlov's principles to learned fears?

Other chapters in this text—on consciousness, motivation, emotion, health, psychological disorders, and therapy—show how Pavlov's principles can influence human health and well-being. Three examples:

- *Drug cravings.* Former drug users often feel a craving when they are again in the drug-using context—with people or in places they associate with previous highs. Thus, drug counselors advise their clients to steer clear of people and settings that may trigger these cravings (Siegel, 2005).

- *Food cravings.* Classical conditioning makes dieting difficult. Sugary substances evoke sweet sensations. Researchers have conditioned healthy volunteers to experience cravings after only one instance of eating a sweet food (Blechert et al., 2016). Eating one cookie can create hunger for another. People who struggle with their weight often have eaten unhealthy foods thousands of times, leaving them with strongly conditioned responses to eat the very foods that will keep them in poor health (Hill, 2007).

- *Immune responses.* Classical conditioning even works on the body's disease-fighting immune system. When a particular taste accompanies a drug that influences immune responses, the taste by itself may come to produce an immune response (Ader & Cohen, 1985).

Pavlov's work also provided a basis for Watson's (1913) idea that human emotions and behaviors, though biologically influenced, are mainly a bundle of conditioned responses. Working with an 11-month-old, Watson and his graduate student Rosalie Rayner (1920; Harris, 1979) showed how specific fears might be conditioned. Like most infants, "Little Albert" feared loud noises but not white rats. Watson and Rayner presented a white rat and, as Little Albert reached to touch it, struck a hammer against a steel bar just behind his head. After seven repeats of seeing the rat and hearing the frightening noise, Albert burst into tears at the mere sight of the rat. Five days later, he reportedly generalized this startled fear reaction to the sight of a rabbit, a dog, and even a furry coat. Although a modern reanalysis questions Watson's evidence for Albert's conditioning, the case remains legendary (Powell & Schmaltz, 2017).

For years, people wondered what became of Little Albert. Sleuthing by Russell Powell and his colleagues (2014) found a well-matched child of one of the hospital's wet nurses.

discrimination in classical conditioning, the learned ability to distinguish between a conditioned stimulus and similar stimuli that do not signal an unconditioned stimulus. (In operant conditioning, the ability to distinguish responses that are reinforced from similar responses that are not reinforced.)

🖵 LaunchPad Play the role of experimenter in classical conditioning research by visiting **Topic Tutorial: PsychSim6, Classical Conditioning.** And review Pavlov's classic work by watching a 3-minute re-creation of Pavlov's lab in the **Video: Pavlov's Discovery of Classical Conditioning.**

JOHN B. WATSON Watson (1924) admitted to "going beyond my facts" when offering his famous boast: "Give me a dozen healthy infants, well-formed, and my own specified world to bring them up in and I'll guarantee to take any one at random and train him to become any type of specialist I might select—doctor, lawyer, artist, merchant-chief, and, yes, even beggar-man and thief, regardless of his talents, penchants, tendencies, abilities, vocations, and race of his ancestors."

The child, William Albert Barger, went by Albert B.—precisely the name used by Watson and Rayner. This Albert, who died in 2007, was an easygoing person, though, perhaps coincidentally, he had an aversion to dogs. He died without ever knowing of his early life in a hospital residence or his role in psychology's history.

People also wondered what became of Watson. After losing his Johns Hopkins professorship over an affair with Rayner (whom he later married), he joined an advertising agency as the company's resident psychologist. There, he used his knowledge of associative learning to conceive many successful advertising campaigns, including one for Maxwell House that helped make the "coffee break" an American custom (Hunt, 1993).

The treatment of Little Albert would be unethical by today's standards. Also, some psychologists had difficulty repeating Watson and Rayner's findings with other children. Nevertheless, Little Albert's learned fears led many psychologists to wonder whether each of us might be a walking warehouse of conditioned emotions. If so, might extinction procedures or new conditioning help us change our unwanted responses to emotion-arousing stimuli?

One patient, who for 30 years had feared entering an elevator alone, did just that. Following his therapist's advice, he forced himself to enter 20 elevators a day. Within 10 days, his fear had nearly vanished (Ellis & Becker, 1982). In Chapter 15, we will see more examples of how psychologists use behavioral techniques such as *counterconditioning* to treat emotional disorders and promote personal growth.

LaunchPad See the **Video: Research Ethics** for a helpful tutorial animation.

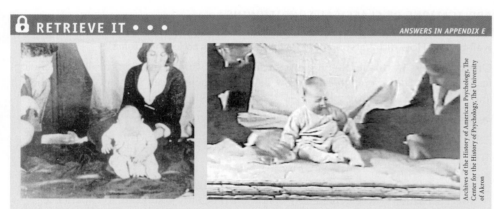

🔒 **RETRIEVE IT • • •**   *ANSWERS IN APPENDIX E*

Archives of the History of American Psychology, The Center for the History of Psychology, The University of Akron

RI-7 In Watson and Rayner's experiments, "Little Albert" learned to fear a white rat after repeatedly experiencing a loud noise as the rat was presented. In these experiments, what was the US? The UR? The NS? The CS? The CR?

🔒 **REVIEW** BASIC LEARNING CONCEPTS AND CLASSICAL CONDITIONING

⟳ Learning Objectives

TEST YOURSELF Answer these repeated Learning Objective Questions on your own (before checking the answers in Appendix D) to improve your retention of the concepts (McDaniel et al., 2009, 2015).

7-1 How do we define *learning*, and what are some basic forms of learning?

7-2 What is behaviorism's view of learning?

7-3 Who was Pavlov, and what are the basic components of classical conditioning?

7-4 In classical conditioning, what are the processes of *acquisition, extinction, spontaneous recovery, generalization,* and *discrimination*?

7-5 Why does Pavlov's work remain so important?

7-6 What have been some applications of Pavlov's work to human health and well-being? How did Watson apply Pavlov's principles to learned fears?

⟳ Terms and Concepts to Remember

TEST YOURSELF Write down the definition yourself, then check your answer on the referenced page.

learning, **p. 234**

associative learning, **p. 234**

stimulus, **p. 234**

respondent behavior, **p. 234**

operant behavior, **p. 234**

cognitive learning, **p. 236**

Experience the Testing Effect

TEST YOURSELF Answer the following questions on your own first, then check your answers in Appendix E.

1. Learning is defined as "the process of acquiring through experience new and relatively enduring _____ or _____."

2. Two forms of associative learning are classical conditioning, in which the organism associates _____, and operant conditioning, in which the organism associates _____.

   a. two or more responses; a response and consequence

   b. two or more stimuli; two or more responses

   c. two or more stimuli; a response and consequence

   d. two or more responses; two or more stimuli

3. In Pavlov's experiments, the tone started as a neutral stimulus, and then became a(n) _____ stimulus.

4. Dogs have been taught to salivate to a circle but not to a square. This process is an example of _____.

5. After Watson and Rayner classically conditioned Little Albert to fear a white rat, the child later showed fear in response to a rabbit, a dog, and a furry coat. This illustrates

   a. extinction.

   b. generalization.

   c. spontaneous recovery.

   d. discrimination between two stimuli.

6. "Sex sells!" is a common saying in advertising. Using classical conditioning terms, explain how sexual images in advertisements can condition your response to a product.

Continue testing yourself with 📚 **LearningCurve** or 🌊 **Achieve Read & Practice** to learn and remember most effectively.

Operant Conditioning

LOQ 7-7   What is *operant conditioning?*

It's one thing to classically condition a dog to salivate to the sound of a tone, or a child to fear moving cars. But to teach an elephant to walk on its hind legs or a child to say *please*, we turn to operant conditioning.

Classical conditioning and operant conditioning are both forms of associative learning, yet their differences are straightforward:

- *Classical conditioning* forms associations between stimuli (a CS and the US it signals). It also involves *respondent behavior*—automatic responses to a stimulus (such as salivating in response to meat powder, and later in response to a tone).

- In **operant conditioning**, organisms associate their own actions with consequences. Actions followed by reinforcers increase; those followed by punishers often decrease. Behavior that *operates* on the environment to *produce* rewarding or punishing stimuli is called *operant behavior*.

🔒 **RETRIEVE IT** • • •   *ANSWERS IN APPENDIX E*

RI-1 With classical conditioning, we learn associations between events we _____ (do/do not) control. With operant conditioning, we learn associations between our behavior and _____ (resulting/random) events.

operant conditioning a type of learning in which a behavior becomes more likely to recur if followed by a reinforcer or less likely to recur if followed by a punisher.

SKINNER'S EXPERIMENTS

LOQ 7-8   Who was Skinner, and how is operant behavior reinforced and shaped?

B. F. Skinner (1904–1990) was a college English major and aspiring writer who, seeking a new direction, enrolled as a graduate student in psychology. He went on to become modern behaviorism's most influential and controversial figure. Skinner's work elaborated on what psychologist Edward L. Thorndike (1874–1949) called the **law of effect:** Rewarded behavior tends to recur (**FIGURE 7.9**). Using Thorndike's law of effect as a starting point, Skinner developed a behavioral technology that revealed principles of *behavior control.* By shaping pigeons' natural walking and pecking behaviors, for example, Skinner was able to teach pigeons such unpigeon-like behaviors as walking in a figure 8, playing Ping-Pong, and keeping a missile on course by pecking at a screen target.

FIGURE 7.9

CAT IN A PUZZLE BOX Thorndike used a fish reward to entice cats to find their way out of a puzzle box through a series of maneuvers. The cats' performance tended to improve with successive trials, illustrating Thorndike's *law of effect.* (Data from Thorndike, 1898.)

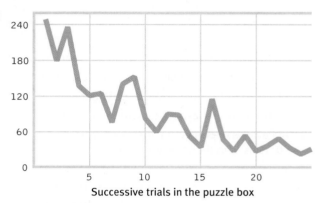

Time required to escape (seconds) / Successive trials in the puzzle box

FIGURE 7.10

A SKINNER BOX Inside the box, the rat presses a bar for a food reward. Outside, measuring devices (not shown here) record the animal's accumulated responses.

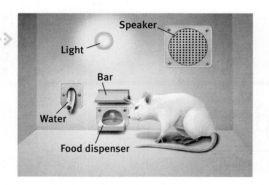

Speaker
Light
Bar
Water
Food dispenser

For his pioneering studies, Skinner designed an **operant chamber,** popularly known as a *Skinner box* (**FIGURE 7.10**). The box has a bar (a lever) that an animal presses—or a key (a disc) the animal pecks—to release a reward of food or water. It also has a device that records these responses. This creates a stage on which rats and other animals act out Skinner's concept of **reinforcement:** any event that strengthens (increases the frequency of) a preceding response. What is reinforcing depends on the animal and the conditions. For people, it may be praise, attention, or a paycheck. For hungry and thirsty rats, food and water work well. Skinner's experiments have done far more than teach us how to pull habits out of a rat. They have explored the precise conditions that foster efficient and enduring learning.

law of effect Thorndike's principle that behaviors followed by favorable consequences become more likely, and that behaviors followed by unfavorable consequences become less likely.

operant chamber in operant conditioning research, a chamber (also known as a *Skinner box*) containing a bar or key that an animal can manipulate to obtain a food or water reinforcer; attached devices record the animal's rate of bar pressing or key pecking.

reinforcement in operant conditioning, any event that *strengthens* the behavior it follows.

shaping an operant conditioning procedure in which reinforcers guide behavior toward closer and closer approximations of the desired behavior.

Shaping Behavior

Imagine that you wanted to condition a hungry rat to press a bar. Like Skinner, you could tease out this action with **shaping,** gradually guiding the rat's actions toward the desired behavior. First, you would watch how the animal naturally behaves, so that you could build on its existing behaviors. You might give the rat a bit of food each time it approaches the bar. Once the rat is approaching regularly, you would give the food only when it moves close to the bar, then closer still. Finally, you would require it to touch the bar to get food. By rewarding *successive approximations,* you reinforce only those responses that are ever-closer to the final desired behavior. By making rewards contingent on desired behaviors, researchers and animal trainers gradually shape complex behaviors. We can also readily shape our own behavior. For example, let's say you want to get in shape to run your first 5K race. You set up a daily running plan and treat yourself to a cookie once you've worked up to running 1 mile without stopping, then again when you can run 1.5 miles, and so on for every additional half mile—rewarding successive approximations of your target behavior.

Shaping can also help us understand what nonverbal organisms can perceive. Can a dog distinguish red and green? Can a baby hear the difference between lower- and higher-pitched tones? If we can shape them to respond to one stimulus and not to another, then we know they can perceive the difference. Such experiments have even shown that some nonhuman animals can form concepts. When experimenters reinforced pigeons for pecking after seeing a human face, but not after seeing other images, the pigeons' behavior showed that they could recognize human faces (Herrnstein & Loveland, 1964). In this experiment, the human face was a *discriminative stimulus*. Like a green traffic light, discriminative stimuli signal that a response will be reinforced. After being trained to discriminate among classes of events or objects—flowers, people, cars, chairs—pigeons were usually able to identify the category in which a new pictured object belonged (Bhatt et al., 1988; Wasserman, 1993). They have even been trained to discriminate between the music of Bach and Stravinsky (Porter & Neuringer, 1984).

Skinner noted that we continually reinforce and shape others' everyday behaviors, though we may not mean to do so. Isaac's nagging annoys his dad, for example, but consider how Dad typically responds:

ISAAC: *Could you take me to the mall?*

DAD: *(Continues reading paper.)*

ISAAC: *Dad, I need to go to the mall.*

DAD: *Uh, yeah, in a few minutes.*

ISAAC: *DAAAAD! The mall!*

DAD: *Show me some manners! Okay, where are my keys . . .*

Isaac's nagging is reinforced, because he gets something desirable—a trip to the mall. Dad's response is reinforced, because it gets rid of something aversive—Isaac's nagging.

Or consider a teacher who sticks gold stars on a wall chart beside the names of children scoring 100 percent on spelling tests. As everyone can then see, some children consistently do perfect work. The others, who may have worked harder than the academic all-stars, get no rewards. The teacher would be better advised to apply the principles of operant conditioning—to reinforce all spellers for gradual improvements (successive approximations toward perfect spelling of words they find challenging).

Types of Reinforcers

LOQ 7-9 How do positive and negative reinforcement differ, and what are the basic types of reinforcers?

Until now, we've mainly been discussing **positive reinforcement**, which strengthens responding by *presenting* a typically *pleasurable* stimulus immediately after a response. But, as the nagging Isaac story illustrates, there are two basic kinds of reinforcement (**TABLE 7.1**). **Negative reinforcement** strengthens a response by *reducing or removing* something negative. Isaac's nagging was *positively* reinforced, because Isaac got something desirable—a trip to the mall. His dad's response (doing what Isaac wanted) was *negatively* reinforced, because it ended an aversive event—Isaac's nagging. Similarly, taking aspirin may relieve your headache, and hitting *snooze* will silence your irritating alarm. These welcome results provide negative reinforcement and increase the odds that you will repeat these behaviors. For those with drug addiction, the negative reinforcement

REINFORCERS VARY WITH CIRCUMSTANCES What is reinforcing (a heat lamp) to one animal (a cold meerkat) may not be to another (an overheated child). What is reinforcing in one situation (a cold snap at the Taronga Zoo in Sydney) may not be in another (a sweltering summer day). Reinforcers also vary among humans. Food that is reinforcing to one person (chocolate) might not be to another person (a vanilla-lover).

Will Burgess/Reuters/Newscom

BIRD BRAINS SPOT TUMORS After being rewarded with food when correctly spotting breast tumors, pigeons became as skilled as humans at discriminating cancerous from healthy tissue (Levenson et al., 2015). Other animals have been shaped to sniff out land mines or locate people amid rubble (La Londe et al., 2015).

Levenson RM, Krupinski EA, Navarro VM, Wasserman EA (2015) Pigeons (Columba livia) as Trainable Observers of Pathology and Radiology Breast Cancer Images. PLoS ONE

ENGAGE **ASK YOURSELF**

Can you recall a time when a teacher, coach, family member, or employer helped you learn something by shaping your behavior in little steps until you achieved your goal?

positive reinforcement increasing behaviors by presenting positive reinforcers. A positive reinforcer is any stimulus that, when *presented* after a response, strengthens the response.

negative reinforcement increasing behaviors by stopping or reducing aversive stimuli. A negative reinforcer is any stimulus that, when *removed* after a response, strengthens the response. (*Note:* Negative reinforcement is not punishment.)

RETAIN 🔒 **TABLE 7.1**

Ways to Increase Behavior

Operant Conditioning Term	Description	Examples
Positive reinforcement	Add a desirable stimulus	Pet a dog that comes when you call it; pay someone for work done.
Negative reinforcement	Remove an aversive stimulus	Take painkillers to end pain; fasten seatbelt to end loud beeping.

of ending withdrawal pangs can be a compelling reason to resume using (Baker et al., 2004). Note that *negative reinforcement is not punishment.* (Some friendly advice: Repeat the italicized words in your mind.) Rather, negative reinforcement—psychology's most misunderstood concept—*removes* a punishing (aversive) event. Think of negative reinforcement as something that provides relief—from that nagging teen, bad headache, or annoying alarm clock.

Sometimes negative and positive reinforcement coincide. Imagine a worried student who, after goofing off and getting a bad exam grade, studies harder for the next exam. This increased effort may be *negatively* reinforced by reduced anxiety, and *positively* reinforced by a better grade. We reap the rewards of escaping the aversive stimulus, which increases the chances that we will repeat our behavior. *The point to remember:* Whether it works by reducing something aversive, or by providing something desirable, *reinforcement is any consequence that strengthens behavior.*

🔒 **RETRIEVE IT • • •**   *ANSWERS IN APPENDIX E*

RI-2 How is operant conditioning at work in this cartoon?

PRIMARY AND CONDITIONED REINFORCERS Getting food when hungry or having a painful headache go away is innately satisfying. These **primary reinforcers** are unlearned. **Conditioned reinforcers**, also called *secondary reinforcers,* get their power through learned association with primary reinforcers. If a rat in a Skinner box learns that a light reliably signals a food delivery, the rat will work to turn on the light. The light has become a conditioned reinforcer. Our lives are filled with conditioned reinforcers—money, good grades, a pleasant tone of voice—each of which has been linked with more basic rewards.

IMMEDIATE AND DELAYED REINFORCERS Let's return to the imaginary shaping experiment in which you were conditioning a rat to press a bar. Before performing this "wanted" behavior, the hungry rat will engage in a sequence of "unwanted" behaviors—scratching, sniffing, and moving around. If you present food immediately after any one of these behaviors, the rat will likely repeat that rewarded behavior. But what if the rat presses the bar while you are distracted, and you delay giving the reinforcer? If the delay lasts longer than about 30 seconds, the rat will not learn to press the bar. It will have moved on to other incidental behaviors, such as scratching, sniffing, and moving, and one of these behaviors will instead get reinforced. Delays also decrease human learning. Students learn class material better when they complete frequent quizzes that provide them with immediate feedback (Healy et al., 2017).

---

primary reinforcer an innately reinforcing stimulus, such as one that satisfies a biological need.

conditioned reinforcer a stimulus that gains its reinforcing power through its association with a primary reinforcer; also known as a *secondary reinforcer.*

reinforcement schedule a pattern that defines how often a desired response will be reinforced.

continuous reinforcement schedule reinforcing the desired response every time it occurs.

partial (intermittent) reinforcement schedule reinforcing a response only part of the time; results in slower acquisition of a response but much greater resistance to extinction than does continuous reinforcement.

fixed-ratio schedule in operant conditioning, a reinforcement schedule that reinforces a response only after a specified number of responses.

variable-ratio schedule in operant conditioning, a reinforcement schedule that reinforces a response after an unpredictable number of responses.

fixed-interval schedule in operant conditioning, a reinforcement schedule that reinforces a response only after a specified time has elapsed.

But unlike rats, humans *can* respond to delayed reinforcers: the paycheck at the end of the week, the good grade at the end of the term, the trophy at the end of the sports season. Indeed, to function effectively we must learn how to master the difficult task of delaying gratification. In one of psychology's most famous studies, some 4-year-olds showed this ability. In choosing a piece of candy or a marshmallow, these impulse-controlled children preferred having a big one tomorrow to munching on a small one right away. Learning to control our impulses in order to achieve more valued rewards is a big step toward maturity and can later protect us from committing an impulsive crime (Åkerlund et al., 2016; Logue, 1998a,b). Children who delay gratification have tended to become socially competent and high-achieving adults (Mischel, 2014).

To our detriment, small but immediate pleasures (the enjoyment of watching late-night TV, for example) are sometimes more alluring than big but delayed rewards (feeling rested for a big exam tomorrow). For many teens, the immediate gratification of risky, unprotected sex in passionate moments prevails over the delayed gratifications of safe sex or saved sex. And for many people, the immediate rewards of today's gas-guzzling vehicles, air travel, and air conditioning prevail over the bigger future consequences of global climate change, rising seas, and extreme weather.

Reinforcement Schedules

LOQ 7-10 How do different reinforcement schedules affect behavior?

In most of our examples, the desired response has been reinforced every time it occurs. But **reinforcement schedules** vary. With **continuous reinforcement**, learning occurs rapidly, which makes it the best choice for mastering a behavior. But extinction also occurs rapidly. When reinforcement stops—when we stop delivering food after the rat presses the bar—the behavior soon stops (is *extinguished*). If a normally dependable candy machine fails to deliver a chocolate bar twice in a row, we stop putting money into it (although a week later we may exhibit *spontaneous recovery* by trying again).

Real life rarely provides continuous reinforcement. Salespeople do not make a sale with every pitch. But they persist because their efforts are occasionally rewarded. This persistence is typical with **partial (intermittent) reinforcement schedules**, in which responses are sometimes reinforced, sometimes not. Learning is slower to appear, but *resistance to extinction* is greater than with continuous reinforcement. Imagine a pigeon that has learned to peck a key to obtain food. If you gradually phase out the food delivery until it occurs only rarely, in no predictable pattern, the pigeon may peck 150,000 times without a reward (Skinner, 1953). Slot machines reward gamblers in much the same way—occasionally and unpredictably. And like pigeons, slot players keep trying, time and time again. With intermittent reinforcement, hope springs eternal.

Lesson for parents: Partial reinforcement also works with children. *Occasionally* giving in to children's tantrums for the sake of peace and quiet intermittently reinforces the tantrums. This is the very best procedure for making a behavior persist.

Skinner (1961) and his collaborators compared four schedules of partial reinforcement and their effects on behavior.

Fixed-ratio schedules reinforce behavior after a set number of responses. Coffee shops may reward us with a free drink after every 10 purchased. Once conditioned, rats may be reinforced on a fixed ratio of, say, one food pellet for every 30 responses. Once conditioned, animals will pause only briefly after a reinforcer before returning to a high rate of responding (**FIGURE 7.11**).

Variable-ratio schedules provide reinforcers after a seemingly unpredictable number of responses. This unpredictable reinforcement is what slot-machine players and fly fishers experience, and it's what makes gambling and fly fishing so hard to extinguish even when they don't produce the desired results. Because reinforcers increase as the number of responses increases, variable-ratio schedules produce high rates of responding.

Fixed-interval schedules reinforce the first response after a fixed time period. Animals on this type of schedule tend to respond more frequently as the anticipated time for reward draws near. People check more frequently for the mail as delivery time approaches. A hungry child jiggles the Jell-O more often to see if it has set. Pigeons peck keys more rapidly as the time for reinforcement draws nearer (see Figure 7.11).

"Oh, not bad. The light comes on, I press the bar, they write me a check. How about you?"

"The charm of fishing is that it is the pursuit of what is elusive but attainable, a perpetual series of occasions for hope." —Scottish author John Buchan (1875–1940)

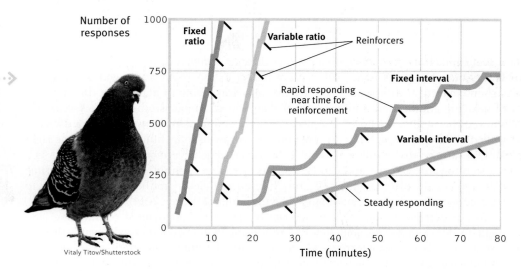

Vitaly Titov/Shutterstock

FIGURE 7.11

INTERMITTENT REINFORCEMENT SCHEDULES Skinner's (1961) laboratory pigeons produced these response patterns to each of four reinforcement schedules. (Reinforcers are indicated by diagonal marks.) For people, as for pigeons, reinforcement linked to number of responses (a *ratio* schedule) produces a higher response rate than reinforcement linked to amount of time elapsed (an *interval* schedule). But the predictability of the reward also matters. An unpredictable *(variable)* schedule produces more consistent responding than does a predictable *(fixed)* schedule. (Data from Skinner, 1961.)

Variable-interval schedules reinforce the first response after *varying* time intervals. At unpredictable times, a food pellet rewarded Skinner's pigeons for persistence in pecking a key. Like the longed-for message that finally rewards persistence in checking our phone, variable-interval schedules tend to produce slow, steady responding. This makes sense, because there is no knowing when the waiting will be over (**TABLE 7.2**).

In general, response rates are higher when reinforcement is linked to the number of responses (a ratio schedule) rather than to time (an interval schedule). But responding is more consistent when reinforcement is unpredictable (a variable schedule) than when it is predictable (a fixed schedule). Animal behaviors differ, yet Skinner (1956) contended that the reinforcement principles of operant conditioning are universal. It matters little, he said, what response, what reinforcer, or what species you use. The effect of a given reinforcement schedule is pretty much the same: "Pigeon, rat, monkey, which is which? It doesn't matter. . . . Behavior shows astonishingly similar properties."

TABLE 7.2

Schedules of Partial Reinforcement

	Fixed	Variable
Ratio	*Every so many:* reinforcement after every *nth* behavior, such as buy 10 coffees, get 1 free, or pay workers per product unit produced	*After an unpredictable number:* reinforcement after a random number of behaviors, as when playing slot machines or fly fishing
Interval	*Every so often:* reinforcement for behavior after a fixed time, such as Tuesday discount prices	*Unpredictably often:* reinforcement for behavior after a random amount of time, as when checking our phone for a message

🔒 RETRIEVE IT • • •   *ANSWERS IN APPENDIX E*

RI-3 People who send spam email are reinforced by which schedule? Home bakers checking the oven to see if the cookies are done are reinforced on which schedule? Donut shops that offer a free donut after every 10 donuts purchased are using which reinforcement schedule?

Punishment

LOQ 7-11 How does punishment differ from negative reinforcement, and how does punishment affect behavior?

Reinforcement increases a behavior; **punishment** does the opposite. A *punisher* is any consequence that *decreases* the frequency of a preceding behavior (**TABLE 7.3**). Swift and sure punishers can powerfully restrain unwanted behavior. The rat that is shocked after touching a forbidden object and the child who is burned by touching a hot stove will learn not to repeat those behaviors.

variable-interval schedule in operant conditioning, a reinforcement schedule that reinforces a response at unpredictable time intervals.

punishment an event that tends to *decrease* the behavior that it follows.

RETAIN 🔒 **TABLE 7.3**

Ways to Decrease Behavior

Type of Punisher	Description	Examples
Positive punishment	Administer an aversive stimulus.	Spray water on a barking dog; give a traffic ticket for speeding.
Negative punishment	Withdraw a rewarding stimulus.	Take away a misbehaving teen's driving privileges; revoke a rude person's chat room access.

Criminal behavior, much of it impulsive, is also influenced more by swift and sure punishers than by the threat of severe sentences (Darley & Alter, 2013). Thus, when Arizona introduced an exceptionally harsh sentence for first-time drunk drivers, the drunk-driving rate changed very little. But when Kansas City police started patrolling a high crime area to increase the swiftness and sureness of punishment, that city's crime rate dropped dramatically.

What do punishment studies imply for parenting? One analysis of over 160,000 children found that physical punishment rarely corrects unwanted behavior (Gershoff & Grogan-Kaylor, 2016). Many psychologists note five major drawbacks of physical punishment (Finkenauer et al., 2015; Gershoff, 2002; Marshall, 2002).

1. **Punished behavior is suppressed, not forgotten. This temporary state may (negatively) reinforce parents' punishing behavior.** The child swears, the parent swats, the child stops swearing in their parents' presence, so the parents believe the punishment successfully stopped the behavior. No wonder spanking is a hit with so many parents—with 68 percent of American adults believing that a child sometimes needs a "good hard spanking" (Smith et al., 2017).

2. **Physical punishment does not replace the unwanted behavior.** Physical punishment may reduce or even eliminate unwanted behavior, but it does not provide direction for appropriate behavior. A child who is spanked for screaming in the car may stop yelling but continue to throw her food or steal her brother's toys.

3. **Punishment teaches discrimination among situations.** In operant conditioning, *discrimination* occurs when an organism learns that certain responses, but not others, will be reinforced. Did the punishment effectively end the child's swearing? Or did the child simply learn that while it's not okay to swear around the house, it's okay elsewhere?

4. **Punishment can teach fear.** In operant conditioning, *generalization* occurs when an organism's response to similar stimuli is also reinforced. A punished child may associate fear not only with the undesirable behavior but also with the person who delivered the punishment or the place it occurred. Thus, children may learn to fear a punishing teacher and try to avoid school, or may become more anxious (Gershoff et al., 2010). For such reasons, most European countries and 31 U.S. states now ban hitting children in schools and child-care institutions (EndCorporalPunishment.org). As of 2017, 51 countries outlaw hitting by parents. A large survey in Finland, the second country to pass such a law, revealed that children born after the law passed were, indeed, less often slapped and beaten (Österman et al., 2014).

5. **Physical punishment may increase aggression by modeling violence as a way to cope with problems.** Studies find that spanked children are at increased risk for aggression (MacKenzie et al., 2013). We know, for example, that many aggressive delinquents and abusive parents come from abusive families (Straus & Gelles, 1980; Straus et al., 1997).

Some researchers question this logic. Physically punished children may be more aggressive, they say, for the same reason that people who have undergone psychotherapy are more likely to suffer depression—because they had preexisting problems that triggered the treatments (Ferguson, 2013a; Larzelere, 2000; Larzelere et al., 2004). So, does spanking cause misbehavior, or does misbehavior trigger spanking? Correlations don't hand us an answer.

📺 **LaunchPad** See the **Video: Correlational Studies** for a helpful tutorial animation.

The debate continues. Some researchers note that frequent spankings predict future aggression—even when studies control for preexisting bad behavior (Taylor et al., 2010). Other researchers believe that lighter spankings pose less of a problem (Baumrind et al., 2002; Larzelere & Kuhn, 2005). That is especially so if physical punishment is used only as a backup for milder disciplinary tactics, and if it is combined with a generous dose of reasoning and reinforcing.

Parents of delinquent youths are often unaware of how to achieve desirable behaviors without screaming, hitting, or threatening their children with punishment (Patterson et al., 1982). Training programs can help transform dire threats ("You clean up your room this minute or no dinner!") into positive incentives ("You're welcome at the dinner table after you get your room cleaned up"). Stop and think about it. Aren't many threats of punishment just as forceful, and perhaps more effective, when rephrased positively? Thus, "If you don't get your homework done, there'll be no car" could be phrased more positively as. . . .

In classrooms, too, teachers can give feedback by saying, "No, but try this . . ." and "Yes, that's it!" Such responses reduce unwanted behavior while reinforcing more desirable alternatives. Remember: *Punishment tells you what not to do; reinforcement tells you what to do.* Thus, punishment trains a particular sort of morality—one focused on prohibition (what *not* to do) rather than positive obligations (Sheikh & Janoff-Bulman, 2013).

What punishment often teaches, said Skinner, is how to avoid it. Most psychologists now favor an emphasis on reinforcement: Notice people doing something right and affirm them for it.

> "A pat on the back, though only a few vertebrae removed from a kick in the pants, is miles ahead in results."
> —Attributed to publisher Bennett Cerf (1898–1971)

🔒 RETRIEVE IT • • •

ANSWERS IN APPENDIX E

RI-4 Fill in the blanks with one of the following terms: positive reinforcement (PR), negative reinforcement (NR), positive punishment (PP), and negative punishment (NP). We have provided the first answer (PR) for you.

Type of Stimulus	Give It	Take It Away
Desired (for example, a teen's use of the car)	1. PR	2.
Undesired/aversive (for example, an insult)	3.	4.

SKINNER'S LEGACY

LOQ 7-12 Why did Skinner's ideas provoke controversy, and how might his operant conditioning principles be applied at school, in sports, at work, in parenting, and for self-improvement?

B. F. Skinner stirred a hornet's nest with his outspoken beliefs. He repeatedly insisted that external influences, not internal thoughts and feelings, shape behavior. He argued that brain science isn't needed for psychological science, saying that "a science of behavior is independent of neurology" (Skinner, 1938/1966, pp. 423–424). And he urged people to use operant conditioning principles to influence others' behavior at school, work, and home. Knowing that behavior is shaped by its results, he argued that we should use rewards to evoke more desirable behavior.

Skinner's critics objected, saying that he dehumanized people by neglecting their personal freedom and by seeking to control their actions. Skinner's reply: External consequences already haphazardly control people's behavior. Why not administer those consequences toward human betterment? Wouldn't reinforcers be more humane than the punishments used in homes, schools, and prisons? And if it is humbling to think that our history has shaped us, doesn't this very idea also give us hope that we can shape our future?

Applications of Operant Conditioning

In later chapters, we will see how psychologists apply operant conditioning principles to help people reduce high blood pressure or gain social skills. Reinforcement techniques have also been used in schools, sports, workplaces, and homes, and these principles can support our self-improvement as well (Flora, 2004).

B. F. SKINNER "I am sometimes asked, 'Do you think of yourself as you think of the organisms you study?' The answer is yes. So far as I know, my behavior at any given moment has been nothing more than the product of my genetic endowment, my personal history, and the current setting" (1983).

📷 **LaunchPad** Simulate operant conditioning and shaping by visiting **Topic Tutorial: PsychSim6, Operant Conditioning** and also **Topic Tutorial: PsychSim6, Shaping.**

AT SCHOOL More than 50 years ago, Skinner and others worked toward a day when "machines and textbooks" would shape learning in small steps, by immediately reinforcing correct responses. Such machines and texts, they said, would revolutionize education and free teachers to focus on each student's special needs. "Good instruction demands two things," said Skinner (1989). "Students must be told immediately whether what they do is right or wrong and, when right, they must be directed to the step to be taken next."

Skinner might be pleased to know that many of his ideals for education are now possible. Teachers used to find it difficult to pace material to each student's rate of learning, and to provide prompt feedback. Online adaptive quizzing, such as the LearningCurve and Achieve Read & Practice systems available with this text, do both. Students move through quizzes at their own pace, according to their own level of understanding. And they get immediate feedback on their efforts, including personalized study plans.

IN SPORTS The key to shaping behavior in athletic performance, as elsewhere, is first reinforcing small successes and then gradually increasing the challenge. Golf students can learn putting by starting with very short putts, and eventually, as they build mastery, stepping back farther and farther. Novice batters can begin with half swings at an oversized ball pitched from 10 feet away, giving them the immediate pleasure of smacking the ball. As the hitters' confidence builds with their success and they achieve mastery at each level, the pitcher gradually moves back and eventually introduces a standard baseball and pitching distance. Compared with children taught by conventional methods, those trained by this behavioral method have shown faster skill improvement (Simek & O'Brien, 1981, 1988).

AT WORK Knowing that reinforcers influence productivity, many organizations have invited employees to share the risks and rewards of company ownership. Others have focused on reinforcing a job well done. Rewards are most likely to increase productivity if the desired performance is both well-defined and achievable. The message for managers? *Reward specific, achievable behaviors, not vaguely defined "merit."*

Operant conditioning also reminds us that reinforcement should be *immediate*. IBM legend Thomas Watson understood. When he observed an achievement, he wrote the employee a check on the spot (Peters & Waterman, 1982). But rewards need not be material, or lavish. An effective manager may simply walk the floor and sincerely affirm people for good work, or write notes of appreciation for a completed project. As Skinner said, "How much richer would the whole world be if the reinforcers in daily life were more effectively contingent on productive work?"

THE VICE-PRESIDENT IN CHARGE OF SINCERITY

IN PARENTING As we have seen, parents can learn from operant conditioning practices. Parent-training researchers remind us that by saying, "Get ready for bed" and then caving in to protests or defiance, parents reinforce such whining and arguing (Wierson & Forehand, 1994). Exasperated, they may then yell or gesture menacingly. When the child, now frightened, obeys, that reinforces the parents' angry behavior. Over time, a destructive parent-child relationship develops.

To disrupt this cycle, parents should remember that basic rule of shaping: *Notice people doing something right and affirm them for it.* Give children attention and other reinforcers when they are behaving *well*. Target a specific behavior, reward it, and watch it increase. When children misbehave or are defiant, don't yell at them or hit them. Simply explain the misbehavior and take away the iPad, remove a misused toy, or give a brief time-out.

TO CHANGE YOUR OWN BEHAVIOR Finally, we can use operant conditioning in our own lives. To reinforce your own desired behaviors (perhaps to improve your study habits) and extinguish the undesired ones (to stop smoking, for example), psychologists suggest taking these steps:

1. *State a realistic goal in measurable terms and announce it.* You might, for example, aim to boost your study time by an hour a day. To increase your commitment and odds of success, share that goal with friends.

2. *Decide how, when, and where you will work toward your goal.* Take time to plan. Those who specify how they will implement goals become more focused on those goals and more often fulfill them (Gollwitzer & Oettingen, 2012).

LaunchPad Operant conditioning principles may be used to help us achieve our goals. What else affects our goal achievement? To find out, engage online with the **Immersive Learning** activity, **Assess Your Strengths: How Might Your Willingness to Think of the Future Affect Your Ability to Achieve Long-Term Goals?**

"I wrote another five hundred words. Can I have another cookie?"

ENGAGE **ASK YOURSELF**

Think of a bad habit of yours or of a friend. How could you or your friend use operant conditioning to break it?

3. ***Monitor how often you engage in your desired behavior.*** You might log your current study time, noting under what conditions you do and don't study. (When we began writing textbooks, we each logged our time and were amazed to discover how much we were wasting.)

4. ***Reinforce the desired behavior.*** People's persistence toward long-term goals, such as New Year's resolutions to study or exercise more, is powered mostly by immediate rewards (Woolley & Fishbach, 2017). So to increase your study time, give yourself a reward (a snack or some activity you enjoy) only after you finish your extra hour of study. Agree with your friends that you will join them for weekend activities only if you have met your realistic weekly studying goal.

5. ***Reduce the rewards gradually.*** As your new behaviors become more habitual, give yourself a mental pat on the back instead of a cookie.

ENGAGE 🖲 **LaunchPad** Conditioning principles may also be applied in clinical settings. Play the role of a researcher exploring these applications by engaging online with **Immersive Learning: How Would You Know If People Can Learn to Reduce Anxiety?**

🔒 **RETRIEVE IT • • •**   *ANSWERS IN APPENDIX E*

RI-5 Ethan constantly misbehaves at preschool even though his teacher scolds him repeatedly. Why does Ethan's misbehavior continue, and what can his teacher do to stop it?

CONTRASTING CLASSICAL AND OPERANT CONDITIONING

LOQ 7-13 How does operant conditioning differ from classical conditioning?

Both classical and operant conditioning are forms of *associative learning.* Both involve *acquisition, extinction, spontaneous recovery, generalization,* and *discrimination.* But these two forms of learning also differ. Through classical (Pavlovian) conditioning, we associate different stimuli we do not control, and we respond automatically *(respondent behaviors)* (**TABLE 7.4**). Through operant conditioning, we associate our own behaviors—which act on our environment to produce rewarding or punishing stimuli *(operant behaviors)*—with their consequences.

As we shall next see, our biology and cognitive processes influence both classical and operant conditioning.

"O! This learning, what a thing it is."
—William Shakespeare, *The Taming of the Shrew,* 1597

RETAIN 🔒 **TABLE 7.4**

Comparison of Classical and Operant Conditioning

	Classical Conditioning	Operant Conditioning
Basic idea	Learning associations between events we do not control.	Learning associations between our behavior and its consequences.
Response	Involuntary, automatic.	Voluntary, operates on environment.
Acquisition	Associating events; NS is paired with US and becomes CS.	Associating a response with a consequence (reinforcer or punisher).
Extinction	CR decreases when CS is repeatedly presented alone.	Responding decreases when reinforcement stops.
Spontaneous recovery	The reappearance, after a rest period, of an extinguished CR.	The reappearance, after a rest period, of an extinguished response.
Generalization	The tendency to respond to stimuli similar to the CS.	Responses learned in one situation occurring in other, similar situations.
Discrimination	Learning to distinguish between a CS and other stimuli that do not signal a US.	Learning that some responses, but not others, will be reinforced.

🔒 RETRIEVE IT • • •

ANSWERS IN APPENDIX E

RI-6 Salivating in response to a tone paired with food is a(n) _____ behavior; pressing a bar to obtain food is a(n) _____ behavior.

🔒 REVIEW   OPERANT CONDITIONING

⟩⟩ Learning Objectives

TEST YOURSELF Answer these repeated Learning Objective Questions on your own (before checking the answers in Appendix D) to improve your retention of the concepts (McDaniel et al., 2009, 2015).

7-7 What is *operant conditioning*?

7-8 Who was Skinner, and how is operant behavior reinforced and shaped?

7-9 How do positive and negative reinforcement differ, and what are the basic types of reinforcers?

7-10 How do different reinforcement schedules affect behavior?

7-11 How does punishment differ from negative reinforcement, and how does punishment affect behavior?

7-12 Why did Skinner's ideas provoke controversy, and how might his operant conditioning principles be applied at school, in sports, at work, in parenting, and for self-improvement?

7-13 How does operant conditioning differ from classical conditioning?

⟩⟩ Terms and Concepts to Remember

TEST YOURSELF Write down the definition yourself, then check your answer on the referenced page.

operant conditioning, **p. 243**
law of effect, **p. 244**
operant chamber, **p. 244**
reinforcement, **p. 244**
shaping, **p. 244**
positive reinforcement, **p. 245**
negative reinforcement, **p. 245**

primary reinforcer, **p. 246**
conditioned reinforcer, **p. 246**
reinforcement schedule, **p. 246**
continuous reinforcement schedule, **p. 246**
partial (intermittent) reinforcement schedule, **p. 246**

fixed-ratio schedule, **p. 246**
variable-ratio schedule, **p. 246**
fixed-interval schedule, **p. 246**
variable-interval schedule, **p. 248**
punishment, **p. 248**

⟩⟩ Experience the Testing Effect

TEST YOURSELF Answer the following questions on your own first, then check your answers in Appendix E.

1. Thorndike's law of effect was the basis for _____'s work on operant conditioning and behavior control.

2. One way to change behavior is to reward natural behaviors in small steps, as the organism gets closer and closer to a desired behavior. This process is called _____.

3. Your dog is barking so loudly that it's making your ears ring. You clap your hands, the dog stops barking, your ears stop ringing, and you think to yourself, "I'll have to do that when he barks again." The end of the barking was for you a
   a. positive reinforcer.
   b. negative reinforcer.
   c. positive punishment.
   d. negative punishment.

4. How could your psychology instructor use negative reinforcement to encourage your attentive behavior during class?

5. Reinforcing a desired response only some of the times it occurs is called _____ reinforcement.

6. A restaurant is running a special deal. After you buy four meals at full price, you will get a free appetizer. This is an example of a _____-_____ schedule of reinforcement.
   a. fixed-ratio
   b. variable-ratio
   c. fixed-interval
   d. variable-interval

7. The partial reinforcement schedule that reinforces a response after unpredictable time periods is a _____-_____ schedule.

8. A medieval proverb notes that "a burnt child dreads the fire." In operant conditioning, the burning would be an example of a
   a. primary reinforcer.
   b. negative reinforcer.
   c. punisher.
   d. positive reinforcer.

Continue testing yourself with 📖 **LearningCurve** or ≈ **Achieve Read & Practice** to learn and remember most effectively.

preparedness a biological predisposition to learn associations, such as between taste and nausea, that have survival value.

⟶ Biology, Cognition, and Learning

From drooling dogs, running rats, and pecking pigeons we have learned much about the basic processes of learning. But conditioning principles don't tell us the whole story. Today's learning theorists recognize that learning is the product of the interaction of biological, psychological, and social-cultural influences (**FIGURE 7.12**).

FIGURE 7.12
BIOPSYCHOSOCIAL INFLUENCES ON LEARNING Our learning results not only from environmental experiences, but also from cognitive and biological influences.

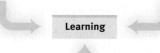

Biological influences:
• genetic predispositions
• unconditioned responses
• adaptive responses
• neural mirroring

Psychological influences:
• previous experiences
• predictability of associations
• generalization
• discrimination
• expectations

Learning

Social-cultural influences:
• culturally learned preferences
• motivation, affected by presence of others
• modeling

BIOLOGICAL CONSTRAINTS ON CONDITIONING

LOQ 7-14   How do biological constraints affect classical and operant conditioning?

Ever since Charles Darwin, scientists have assumed that all animals share a common evolutionary history and thus share commonalities in their makeup and functioning. Pavlov and Watson, for example, believed the basic laws of learning were essentially similar in all animals. So it should make little difference whether one studied pigeons or people. Moreover, it seemed that any natural response could be conditioned to any neutral stimulus.

Biological Limits on Classical Conditioning

In 1956, learning researcher Gregory Kimble proclaimed, "Just about any activity of which the organism is capable can be conditioned and . . . these responses can be conditioned to any stimulus that the organism can perceive" (p. 195). Twenty-five years later, he humbly acknowledged that "half a thousand" scientific reports had proven him wrong (Kimble, 1981). More than the early behaviorists realized, an animal's capacity for conditioning is limited by biological constraints. For example, each species' predispositions *prepare* it to learn the associations that enhance its survival—a phenomenon called **preparedness**. Environments are not the whole story. Biology matters.

John Garcia was among those who challenged the prevailing idea that all associations can be learned equally well. While researching the effects of radiation on laboratory animals, Garcia and Robert Koelling (1966) noticed that rats began to avoid drinking water from the plastic bottles in radiation chambers. Could classical conditioning be the culprit? Might the rats have linked the plastic-tasting water (a CS) to the sickness (UR) triggered by the radiation (US)?

JOHN GARCIA As the laboring son of California farmworkers, Garcia attended school only in the off-season during his early childhood years. After entering junior college in his late twenties, and earning his Ph.D. in his late forties, he received the American Psychological Association's Distinguished Scientific Contribution Award "for his highly original, pioneering research in conditioning and learning." He was also elected to the National Academy of Sciences.

To test their hunch, Garcia and Koelling exposed the rats to a particular taste, sight, or sound (CS) and later also to radiation or drugs (US) that led to nausea and vomiting (UR). Two startling findings emerged: First, even if sickened as late as several hours after tasting a particular novel flavor, the rats thereafter avoided that flavor. This appeared to violate the widely held belief that for conditioning to occur, the US must immediately follow the CS.

Second, the sickened rats developed aversions to tastes but not to sights or sounds. This contradicted the behaviorists' idea that any perceivable stimulus could serve as a CS. But it made adaptive sense. For rats, the easiest way to identify tainted food is to taste it; if sickened after sampling a new food, they thereafter avoid it. This response, called *taste aversion,* makes it difficult to eradicate a population of "bait-shy" rats by poisoning.

Humans, too, seem biologically prepared to learn some associations rather than others. If you become violently ill four hours after eating contaminated oysters, you will probably develop an aversion to the *taste* of oysters more readily than to the sight of the associated restaurant, its plates, the people you were with, or the music you heard there. (In contrast, birds, which hunt by sight, appear biologically primed to develop aversions to the *sight* of tainted food [Nicolaus et al., 1983].)

Garcia and Koelling's taste-aversion research is but one instance in which psychological experiments that began with the discomfort of some laboratory animals ended by enhancing the welfare of many others. In one conditioned taste-aversion study, coyotes and wolves were tempted into eating sheep carcasses laced with a sickening poison. Thereafter, they developed an aversion to sheep meat; two wolves later penned with a live sheep seemed actually to fear it (Gustavson et al., 1974, 1976). These studies not only saved the sheep from their predators, but also saved the sheep-shunning coyotes and wolves from angry ranchers and farmers who had wanted to destroy them. Similar applications have prevented baboons from raiding African gardens, raccoons from attacking chickens, and ravens and crows from feeding on crane eggs. In all these cases, research helped preserve both the prey and their predators, all of which occupy an important ecological niche (Dingfelder, 2010; Garcia & Gustavson, 1997).

Such research supports Darwin's principle that natural selection favors traits that aid survival. Our ancestors who readily learned taste aversions were unlikely to eat the same toxic food again and were more likely to survive and leave descendants. Nausea, like anxiety, pain, and other bad feelings, serves a good purpose. Like a car's low-fuel warning light, each alerts the body to a threat (Davidson & Riley, 2015; Neese, 1991).

Our preparedness to associate a CS with a US that follows predictably and immediately is adaptive. Causes often do immediately precede effects. But as we saw in the taste-aversion findings, our predisposition to associate an effect with a preceding event can trick us. When chemotherapy triggers nausea and vomiting more than an hour following treatment, cancer patients may, over time, develop classically conditioned nausea (and sometimes anxiety) to the sights, sounds, and smells associated with the clinic (**FIGURE 7.13**) (Hall, 1997). Merely returning to the clinic's waiting room or seeing the nurses can provoke these conditioned feelings (Burish & Carey, 1986; Davey, 1992). Under normal circumstances, such revulsion to sickening stimuli would be adaptive.

TASTE AVERSION If you became violently ill after eating oysters, you would probably have a hard time eating them again. Their smell and taste would have become a CS for nausea. This learning occurs readily because our biology prepares us to learn taste aversions to toxic foods.

"Once bitten, twice shy." —G. F. Northall, *Folk-Phrases,* 1894

ANIMAL TASTE AVERSION As an alternative to killing wolves and coyotes that preyed on sheep, some ranchers have sickened the animals with lamb laced with a drug to create a taste aversion.

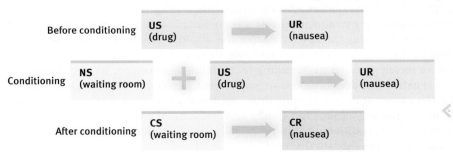

Before conditioning	US (drug)	→	UR (nausea)
Conditioning	NS (waiting room) + US (drug)	→	UR (nausea)
After conditioning	CS (waiting room)	→	CR (nausea)

FIGURE 7.13
NAUSEA CONDITIONING IN CANCER PATIENTS

NATURAL ATHLETES Animals can most easily learn and retain behaviors that draw on their biological predispositions, such as horses' inborn ability to move around obstacles with speed and agility.

For more information on animal behavior, see books by (we are not making this up) Robin Fox and Lionel Tiger.

🔒 **RETRIEVE IT • • •**   *ANSWERS IN APPENDIX E*

RI-1 How did Garcia and Koelling's taste-aversion studies help disprove Gregory Kimble's early claim that "just about any activity of which the organism is capable can be conditioned . . . to any stimulus that the organism can perceive"?

Biological Limits on Operant Conditioning

Nature also constrains each species' capacity for operant conditioning. Science fiction writer Robert Heinlein (1907–1988) said it well: "Never try to teach a pig to sing; it wastes your time and annoys the pig."

We most easily learn and retain behaviors that reflect our biological predispositions. Thus, using food as a reinforcer, you could easily condition a hamster to dig or to rear up, because these are among the animal's natural food-searching behaviors. But you won't be so successful if you use food as a reinforcer to shape face washing and other hamster behaviors that aren't normally associated with food or hunger (Shettleworth, 1973). Similarly, you could easily teach pigeons to flap their wings to avoid being shocked, and to peck to obtain food: Fleeing with their wings and eating with their beaks are natural pigeon behaviors. However, pigeons would have a hard time learning to peck to avoid a shock, or to flap their wings to obtain food (Foree & LoLordo, 1973). The principle: *Biological constraints predispose organisms to learn associations that are naturally adaptive.*

In the early years of their work, animal trainers Marian Breland and Keller Breland presumed that operant principles would work on almost any response an animal could make. But they, too, learned about biological constraints. In one act, pigs trained to pick up large wooden "dollars" and deposit them in a piggy bank began to drift back to their natural ways. They dropped the coin, pushed it with their snouts as pigs are prone to do, picked it up again, and then repeated the sequence—delaying their food reinforcer. This **instinctive drift** occurred as the animals reverted to their biologically predisposed patterns.

📱 **LaunchPad** To learn more about biology's influence on learning, engage online with **Concept Practice: Biologically Adaptive Associations.**

COGNITION'S INFLUENCE ON CONDITIONING

LOQ 7-15 How do cognitive processes affect classical and operant conditioning?

Cognition and Classical Conditioning

In their dismissal of "mentalistic" concepts such as consciousness, Pavlov and Watson underestimated the importance of not only biological constraints such as preparedness and instinctive drift, but also the effects of cognitive processes (thoughts, perceptions, expectations). The early behaviorists believed that rats' and dogs' learned behaviors could be reduced to mindless mechanisms, so there was no need to consider cognition. But Robert Rescorla and Allan Wagner (1972) showed that an animal can learn the *predictability* of an event. If a shock always is preceded by a tone, and then may also be preceded by a light that accompanies the tone, a rat will react with fear to the tone but not to the light. Although the light is always followed by the shock, it adds no new information; the tone is a better predictor. The more predictable the association, the stronger the conditioned response. It's as if the animal learns an *expectancy,* an awareness of how likely it is that the US will occur.

Classical conditioning treatments that ignore cognition often have limited success. For example, people receiving therapy for alcohol use disorder may be given alcohol spiked with a nauseating drug. Will they then associate alcohol with sickness? If classical conditioning were merely a matter of "stamping in" stimulus associations, we might hope so, and to some extent this does occur (as we will see in Chapter 15). However, one's awareness that the nausea is induced by the drug, not the alcohol, often weakens the association between drinking alcohol and feeling sick, reducing the treatment's effectiveness. So, even in classical conditioning, it is—especially with humans—not simply the CS-US association but also the thought that counts.

"All brains are, in essence, anticipation machines." —Daniel C. Dennett, *Consciousness Explained*, 1991

Cognition and Operant Conditioning

B. F. Skinner acknowledged the biological underpinnings of behavior and the existence of private thought processes. Nevertheless, many psychologists criticized him for discounting cognition's importance.

A mere eight days before dying of leukemia in 1990, Skinner stood before the American Psychological Association convention. In this final address, he still resisted the growing belief that cognitive processes have a necessary place in the science of psychology and even in our understanding of conditioning. He viewed "cognitive science" as a throwback to early twentieth-century introspectionism. For Skinner, thoughts and emotions were behaviors that follow the same laws as other behaviors.

Nevertheless, the evidence of cognitive processes cannot be ignored. For example, animals on a *fixed-interval reinforcement schedule* respond more and more frequently as the time approaches when a response will produce a reinforcer. Although a strict behaviorist would object to talk of "expectations," the animals behave as if they expected that repeating the response would soon produce the reward.

Evidence of cognitive processes has also come from studying rats in mazes. Rats exploring a maze, given no obvious rewards, seem to develop a **cognitive map**, a mental representation of the maze. When an experimenter then places food in the maze's goal box, these rats run the maze as quickly as other rats that were previously reinforced with food for this result. Like people sightseeing in a new town, the exploring rats seemingly experienced **latent learning** during their earlier tours. That learning became apparent only when there was some incentive to demonstrate it. Children, too, may learn from watching a parent but demonstrate the learning only much later, as needed. *The point to remember:* There is more to learning than associating a response with a consequence; there is also cognition. In Chapter 9, we will encounter more striking evidence of animals' cognitive abilities in solving problems and in using aspects of language.

TABLE 7.5 compares the biological and cognitive influences on classical and operant conditioning.

"Bathroom? Sure, it's just down the hall to the left, jog right, left, another left, straight past two more lefts, then right, and it's at the end of the third corridor on your right."

LATENT LEARNING Animals, like people, can learn from experience, with or without reinforcement. In a classic experiment, rats in one group repeatedly explored a maze, always with a food reward at the end. Rats in another group explored the maze with no food reward. But once given a food reward at the end, rats in the second group thereafter ran the maze as quickly as (and even faster than) the always-rewarded rats (Tolman & Honzik, 1930).

TABLE 7.5

Biological and Cognitive Influences on Conditioning

	Classical Conditioning	Operant Conditioning
Biological influences	Natural predispositions constrain what stimuli and responses can easily be associated.	Organisms most easily learn behaviors similar to their natural behaviors; unnatural behaviors instinctively drift back toward natural ones.
Cognitive influences	Organisms develop an expectation that a CS signals the arrival of a US.	Organisms develop an expectation that a response will be reinforced or punished; they also exhibit latent learning, without reinforcement.

instinctive drift the tendency of learned behavior to gradually revert to biologically predisposed patterns.

cognitive map a mental representation of the layout of one's environment. For example, after exploring a maze, rats act as if they have learned a cognitive map of it.

latent learning learning that occurs but is not apparent until there is an incentive to demonstrate it.

RETRIEVE IT • • •   *ANSWERS IN APPENDIX E*

RI-2 Instinctive drift and latent learning are examples of what important idea?

LEARNING BY OBSERVATION

LOQ 7-16 What is *observational learning?*

Cognition supports **observational learning** (also called *social learning*), in which higher animals, especially humans, learn without direct experience, by watching and imitating others. A child who sees his sister burn her fingers on a hot stove learns not to touch it. We learn our native languages and various other specific behaviors by observing and imitating others, a process called **modeling**.

ALBERT BANDURA "The Bobo doll follows me wherever I go. The photographs are published in every introductory psychology text and virtually every undergraduate takes introductory psychology. I recently checked into a Washington hotel. The clerk at the desk asked, 'Aren't you the psychologist who did the Bobo doll experiment?' I answered, 'I am afraid that will be my legacy.' He replied, 'That deserves an upgrade. I will put you in a suite in the quiet part of the hotel'" (2005). A recent analysis of citations, awards, and textbook coverage identified Bandura—shown here receiving a 2016 U.S. National Medal of Science from President Obama—as the world's most eminent psychologist (Diener et al., 2014).

Picture this scene from an experiment by Albert Bandura, the pioneering researcher of observational learning (Bandura et al., 1961): A preschool child is working on a drawing, while an adult in another part of the room builds with Tinkertoys. As the child watches, the adult gets up and for nearly 10 minutes pounds, kicks, and throws around the room a large inflated Bobo doll, yelling, "Sock him in the nose. . . . Hit him down. . . . Kick him."

The child is then taken to another room filled with appealing toys. Soon the experimenter returns and tells the child she has decided to save these good toys "for the other children." She takes the now-frustrated child to a third room containing a few toys, including a Bobo doll. Left alone, what does the child do?

Compared with children not exposed to the adult model, those who viewed the model's actions were more likely to lash out at the doll. Observing the aggressive outburst apparently lowered their inhibitions. But *something more* was also at work, for the children imitated the very acts they had observed and used the very words they had heard (**FIGURE 7.14**).

📺 **LaunchPad** For 3 minutes of classic footage, see the **Video: Bandura's Bobo Doll Experiment.**

That "something more," Bandura suggested, was this: By watching models, we experience *vicarious reinforcement* or *vicarious punishment,* and we learn to anticipate a behavior's consequences in situations like those we are observing. We are especially likely to learn from people we perceive as similar to ourselves, or as successful, or as admirable. fMRI scans show that when people observe someone winning a reward (and especially when

FIGURE 7.14
THE FAMOUS BOBO DOLL EXPERIMENT Notice how the children's actions directly imitate the adult's.

it's someone likable and similar to themselves), their own brain reward systems activate, much as if they themselves had won the reward (Mobbs et al., 2009). When we identify with someone, we experience their outcomes vicariously. Even our learned fears may extinguish as we observe another safely navigating the feared situation (Golkar et al., 2013). Lord Chesterfield (1694–1773) had the idea: "We are, in truth, more than half what we are by imitation."

Bandura's work provides an example of how basic research "pursued for its own sake" can have a broader purpose. "The Bobo Doll studies," he reflected (2016), "provided the principles for unforeseen global applications 25 years later." Insights derived from his research have been used not only to restrain televised violence, but also to offer social models that have helped reduce unplanned childbearing, protect against AIDS, and promote environmental conservation.

Mirrors and Imitation in the Brain

LOQ 7-17 How may observational learning be enabled by neural mirroring?

In 1991, on a hot summer day in Parma, Italy, a lab monkey awaited its researchers' return from lunch. The researchers had implanted wires next to its motor cortex, in a frontal lobe brain region that enabled the monkey to plan and enact movements. The monitoring device would alert the researchers to activity in that region of the monkey's brain. When the monkey moved a peanut into its mouth, for example, the device would buzz. That day, as one of the researchers reentered the lab, ice cream cone in hand, the monkey stared at him. As the researcher raised the cone to lick it, the monkey's monitor buzzed—as if the motionless monkey had itself moved (Blakeslee, 2006; Iacoboni, 2008, 2009).

The same buzzing had been heard earlier, when the monkey watched humans or other monkeys move peanuts to their mouths. The flabbergasted researchers had, they believed, stumbled onto a previously unknown type of neuron (Rizzolatti et al., 2002, 2006). These presumed **mirror neurons**, they argued, provide a neural basis for everyday imitation and observational learning. When a monkey grasps, holds, or tears something, these neurons fire. And they likewise fire when the monkey observes another doing so. When one monkey sees, its neurons mirror what another monkey does. (For a debate regarding the importance of mirror neurons, which are sometimes overblown in the popular press, see Gallese et al., 2011; Hickok, 2014.)

Imitation is widespread in other species. Primates observe and imitate all sorts of novel tool use behaviors, such as how to crack nuts using stone hammers (Fragaszy et al., 2017). These types of behaviors are then transmitted from generation to generation within their local culture (Hopper et al., 2008; Whiten et al., 2007). In one study, researchers trained vervet monkeys to prefer either blue or pink corn by soaking one color in a disgusting-tasting solution (van de Waal et al., 2013). Four to six months later, after a new generation of monkeys was born, the adults stuck with whatever color they had learned to prefer—and, on observing them, so did all but one of 27 infant monkeys. Moreover,

observational learning learning by observing others.

modeling the process of observing and imitating a specific behavior.

mirror neurons frontal lobe neurons that some scientists believe fire when we perform certain actions or observe another doing so. The brain's mirroring of another's action may enable imitation and empathy.

MIRROR NEURONS AT WORK?

"Your back is killing me!"

ANIMAL SOCIAL LEARNING (a) Whacking the water, which drives prey fish into a clump and thus boosts feeding, has spread among humpback whales through social learning (Allen et al., 2013). (b) Likewise, monkeys learn to prefer whatever color corn they observe other monkeys eating.

(a)

(b)

Meltzoff, A. N., Kuhl, P. K., Movellan, J. & Sejnowski, T. J. (2009). Foundations for a new science of learning. Science, 325, 284–288.

FIGURE 7.15

IMITATION This 12-month-old infant sees an adult look left, and immediately follows her gaze (Meltzoff et al., 2009).

"This instinct to humiliate, when it's modeled by someone in the public platform, by someone powerful, it filters down into everybody's life, because it . . . gives permission for other people to do the same thing." —Meryl Streep, U.S. Golden Globe Award speech, 2017

"Children need models more than they need critics." —Joseph Joubert, *Pensées*, 1842

when blue- (or pink-) preferring males migrated to the other group, they switched preferences and began eating as the other group did. Monkey see, monkey do.

In humans, imitation is pervasive. Our catchphrases, fashions, ceremonies, foods, traditions, morals, and fads all spread by one person copying another. Children, and even infants, are natural imitators (Marshall & Meltzoff, 2014). By 8 to 16 months, infants imitate various novel gestures (Jones, 2007). By 12 months (**FIGURE 7.15**), they look where an adult is looking (Meltzoff et al., 2009). And by 14 months, children imitate acts modeled on TV (Meltzoff, 1988; Meltzoff & Moore, 1989, 1997). Even as 2½-year-olds, when many of their mental abilities are near those of adult chimpanzees, young humans surpass chimps at social tasks such as imitating another's solution to a problem (Herrmann et al., 2007). Children see, children do.

So strong is the human predisposition to learn from watching adults that 2- to 5-year-old children *overimitate*. Whether living in urban Australia or rural Africa, they copy even irrelevant adult actions. Before reaching for a toy in a plastic jar, they will first stroke the jar with a feather if that's what they have observed (Lyons et al., 2007). Or, imitating an adult, they will wave a stick over a box and then use the stick to push on a knob that opens the box—when all they needed to do to open the box was to push on the knob (Nielsen & Tomaselli, 2010).

Humans, like monkeys, have brains that support empathy and imitation. Researchers cannot insert experimental electrodes in human brains, but they can use fMRI scans to see brain activity associated with performing and with observing actions. So, is the human capacity to simulate another's action and to share in another's experience due to specialized mirror neurons? Or is it due to distributed brain networks? That issue is under debate (Fox et al., 2016; Gallese et al., 2011; Hickok, 2014; Iacoboni, 2008, 2009; Spaulding, 2013). Regardless, children's brains do enable their empathy and their ability to infer another's mental state, an ability known as *theory of mind*.

Our brain's response to observing others makes emotions contagious. Our brain simulates and vicariously experiences what we observe. So real are these mental instant replays that we may misremember an action we have observed as one we have performed (Lindner et al., 2010). But through these reenactments, we grasp others' states of mind. Observing others' postures, faces, voices, and writing styles, we unconsciously synchronize our own to theirs—which helps us feel what they are feeling (Bernieri et al., 1994; Ireland & Pennebaker, 2010). Imitation helps us gain friends, leading us to mimic those we like (Chartrand & Lakin, 2013). We find ourselves yawning when they yawn, smiling when they smile, laughing when they laugh.

Seeing a loved one's pain, our faces mirror the other's emotion. But as **FIGURE 7.16** shows, so do our brains. In this fMRI scan, the pain imagined by an empathic romantic partner triggered some of the same brain activity experienced by the loved one who actually had the pain (Singer et al., 2004). Observing others' pain also releases our body's natural painkillers, thus calming our distress and enabling our helping (Haaker et al., 2017). Even fiction reading may trigger such activity, as we mentally simulate (and vicariously experience) the feelings and actions described (Mar & Oatley, 2008; Speer et al., 2009). Students who read *Harry Potter*—the bestselling kid wizard series that masterfully modeled tolerance—reported less prejudice against immigrants, refugees, and gay people (Vezzali et al., 2015).

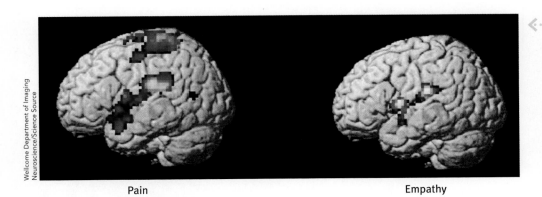

Pain   Empathy

Wellcome Department of Imaging Neuroscience/Science Source

FIGURE 7.16
EXPERIENCED AND IMAGINED PAIN IN THE BRAIN Brain activity related to actual pain is mirrored in the brain of an observing loved one. Empathy in the brain shows up in emotional brain areas, but not in the somatosensory cortex, which receives the physical pain input.

Applications of Observational Learning

LOQ 7-18 What is the impact of prosocial modeling and of antisocial modeling?

The big news from Bandura's studies and the mirror-neuron research is that we look, we mentally imitate, and we learn. Models—in our family, our neighborhood, or the media we consume—may have effects, good and bad.

PROSOCIAL EFFECTS The good news is that people's modeling of **prosocial** (positive, helpful) **behaviors** can have prosocial effects. Many business organizations effectively use *behavior modeling* to help new employees learn communication, sales, and customer service skills (Taylor et al., 2005). Trainees gain these skills faster when they are able to observe the skills being modeled effectively by experienced workers (or actors simulating them).

People who exemplify nonviolent, helpful behavior can also prompt similar behavior in others. After observing someone helping (assisting a woman with dropped books), people become more helpful, such as by assisting someone who dropped a dollar (Burger et al., 2015). India's Mahatma Gandhi and America's Martin Luther King, Jr., both drew on the power of modeling, making nonviolent action a powerful force for social change in both countries (Matsumoto et al., 2015). The media offer models. For example, one research team found that across seven countries, viewing prosocial TV, movies, and video games boosted later helping behavior (Prot et al., 2014).

Parents are also powerful models. European Christians who risked their lives to rescue Jews from the Nazis usually had a close relationship with at least one parent who modeled a strong moral or humanitarian concern; this was also true for U.S. civil rights activists in the 1960s (London, 1970; Oliner & Oliner, 1988). The observational learning of morality begins early. Socially responsive toddlers who readily imitated their parents tended to become preschoolers with a strong internalized conscience (Forman et al., 2004).

Models are most effective when their actions and words are consistent. To encourage children to read, read to them and surround them with books and people who read. To increase the odds that your children will practice your religion, worship and attend religious activities with them. Sometimes, however, models say one thing and do another. Many parents seem to operate according to the principle "Do as I *say*, not as I do."

Zumapress/Newscom

A MODEL CAREGIVER This girl is learning orphan-nursing skills, as well as compassion, by observing her mentor in this Humane Society program. As the sixteenth-century proverb states, "Example is better than precept."

prosocial behavior positive, constructive, helpful behavior. The opposite of antisocial behavior.

CHILDREN SEE, CHILDREN DO? Children who often experience physical punishment tend to display more aggression.

David Strickler/The Image Works

Experiments suggest that children learn to do both (Rice & Grusec, 1975; Rushton, 1975). Exposed to a hypocrite, they tend to imitate the hypocrisy—by doing what the model did and saying what the model said.

🔒 **RETRIEVE IT • • •**   *ANSWERS IN APPENDIX E*

RI-3 Jason's parents and older friends all drive over the speed limit, but they advise him not to. Juan's parents and friends drive within the speed limit, but they say nothing to deter him from speeding. Will Jason or Juan be more likely to speed?

ANTISOCIAL EFFECTS The bad news is that observational learning may also have *antisocial effects*. This helps us understand why abusive parents might have aggressive children, why children who are lied to become more likely to cheat and lie, and why many men who beat their wives had wife-battering fathers (Hays & Carver, 2014; Stith et al., 2000). Critics note that such aggressiveness could be genetic. But with monkeys, we know it can be environmental. In study after study, young monkeys separated from their mothers and subjected to high levels of aggression grew up to be aggressive themselves (Chamove, 1980). The lessons we learn as children are not easily replaced as adults, and they are sometimes visited on future generations.

TV shows, movies, and online videos are sources of observational learning. While watching, children may learn that bullying is an effective way to control others, that free and easy sex brings pleasure without later misery or disease, or that men should be tough and women gentle. And they have ample time to learn such lessons. During their first 18 years, most children in developed countries spend more time watching TV than they spend in school. The average teen watches more than 4 hours a day; the average adult, 3 hours (Robinson & Martin, 2009; Strasburger et al., 2010).

Viewers are learning about life from a peculiar storyteller, one that reflects the culture's mythology rather than its reality. Between 1998 and 2006, prime-time violence on TV reportedly increased 75 percent (PTC, 2007). An analysis of more than 3000 network and cable programs aired during one closely studied year revealed that nearly 6 in 10 featured violence, that 74 percent of the violence went unpunished, that 58 percent did not show the victims' pain, that nearly half the incidents involved "justified" violence, and that nearly half involved an attractive perpetrator. These conditions define the recipe for the *violence-viewing effect* described in many studies and recognized by a near-consensus of media researchers (Bushman et al., 2015; Donnerstein, 1998, 2011).

In 2012, a well-armed man targeted young children and their teachers in a horrifying mass shooting at Connecticut's Sandy Hook Elementary School. Was the American media correct in wondering whether the killer was influenced by the violent video games found stockpiled in his home? (See Thinking Critically About: The Effects of Viewing Media Violence.)

"The problem with television is that the people must sit and keep their eyes glued to a screen: The average American family hasn't time for it. Therefore the showmen are convinced that . . . television will never be a serious competitor of [radio] broadcasting." —*The New York Times, 1939*

 Screen time's greatest effect may stem from what it displaces. Children and adults who spend several hours a day in front of a screen spend that many fewer hours in other pursuits—talking, studying, playing, reading, or socializing face-to-face with friends. What would you have done with your extra time if you had spent even half as many hours in front of a screen? How might you be different as a result?

ASK YOURSELF

Who has been a significant role model for you? What did you learn from observing this person? For whom are you a role model?

THINKING CRITICALLY ABOUT:

The Effects of Viewing Media Violence

LOQ 7-19 What is the violence-viewing effect?

Introduction of TV, 1957–1974 ⟷ Doubling of homicide rate in U.S. and Canada[1]   Introduction of TV for White South Africans in 1975 ⟷ Near-doubling of homicide rate in South Africa[1]   Heavy exposure to media violence for U.S. 9–11-year-olds ⟷ Increased fighting, and more violent behavior later as teens[2]

BUT, CORRELATION ≠ CAUSATION!

Experimental studies have also found that media violence viewing can **cause** aggression:

Viewing violence (compared to entertaining nonviolence) ➡ participants react more cruelly when provoked. (Effect is strongest if the violent person is attractive, the violence seems justified and realistic, the act goes unpunished, and the viewer does not see pain or harm caused.)

What prompts the *violence-viewing effect*?

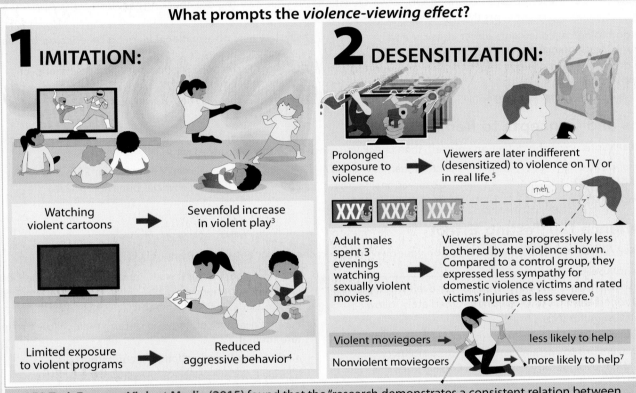

1 IMITATION:

Watching violent cartoons ➡ Sevenfold increase in violent play[3]

Limited exposure to violent programs ➡ Reduced aggressive behavior[4]

2 DESENSITIZATION:

Prolonged exposure to violence ➡ Viewers are later indifferent (desensitized) to violence on TV or in real life.[5]

meh.

Adult males spent 3 evenings watching sexually violent movies. ➡ Viewers became progressively less bothered by the violence shown. Compared to a control group, they expressed less sympathy for domestic violence victims and rated victims' injuries as less severe.[6]

Violent moviegoers ➡ less likely to help

Nonviolent moviegoers ➡ more likely to help[7]

- **APA Task Force on Violent Media (2015)** found that the "research demonstrates a consistent relation between violent video game use and increases in aggressive behavior, aggressive cognitions, and aggressive affect, and decreases in prosocial behavior, empathy, and sensitivity to aggression."

- **American Academy of Pediatrics (2009)** has advised pediatricians that "media violence can contribute to aggressive behavior, desensitization to violence, nightmares, and fear of being harmed."

1. Centerwall, 1989. 2. Boxer at al., 2009; Gentile et al., 2011; Gentile & Bushman, 2012. 3. Boyatzis et al., 1995. 4. Christakis et al., 2013. 5. Fanti et al., 2009; Rule & Ferguson, 1986. 6. Mullin & Linz, 1995. 7. Bushman & Anderson, 2009.

* * *

Bandura's work—like that of Ivan Pavlov, John Watson, B. F. Skinner, and thousands of others who advanced our knowledge of learning principles—illustrates the impact that can result from single-minded devotion to a few well-defined problems and ideas. These researchers defined the issues and impressed on us the importance of learning. As their legacy demonstrates, intellectual history is often made by people who risk going to extremes in pushing ideas to their limits (Simonton, 2000).

RI-4 Match the examples (I–V) to the appropriate underlying learning principle (a–e):

I. Knowing the way from your bed to the bathroom in the dark	a. Classical conditioning
II. Your little brother getting in a fight after watching a violent action movie	b. Operant conditioning
III. Salivating when you smell brownies in the oven	c. Latent learning
IV. Disliking the taste of chili after becoming violently sick a few hours after eating chili	d. Observational learning
V. Your dog racing to greet you on your arrival home	e. Biological predispositions

🔒 REVIEW BIOLOGY, COGNITION, AND LEARNING

⟳ Learning Objectives

TEST YOURSELF Answer these repeated Learning Objective Questions on your own (before checking the answers in Appendix D) to improve your retention of the concepts (McDaniel et al., 2009, 2015).

7-14 How do biological constraints affect classical and operant conditioning?

7-15 How do cognitive processes affect classical and operant conditioning?

7-16 What is *observational learning*?

7-17 How may observational learning be enabled by neural mirroring?

7-18 What is the impact of prosocial modeling and of antisocial modeling?

7-19 What is the violence-viewing effect?

⟳ Terms and Concepts to Remember

TEST YOURSELF Write down the definition yourself, then check your answer on the referenced page.

preparedness, **p. 254**

instinctive drift, **p. 257**

cognitive map, **p. 257**

latent learning, **p. 257**

observational learning, **p. 259**

modeling, **p. 259**

mirror neurons, **p. 259**

prosocial behavior, **p. 261**

⟳ Experience the Testing Effect

TEST YOURSELF Answer the following questions on your own first, then check your answers in Appendix E.

1. Garcia and Koelling's _____-_____ studies showed that conditioning can occur even when the unconditioned stimulus (US) does not immediately follow the neutral stimulus (NS).

2. Taste-aversion research has shown that some animals develop aversions to certain tastes but not to sights or sounds. What evolutionary psychology finding does this support?

3. Evidence that cognitive processes play an important role in learning comes in part from studies in which rats running a maze develop a _____ _____ of the maze.

4. Rats that explored a maze without any reward were later able to run the maze as well as other rats that had received food rewards for running the maze. The rats that had learned without reinforcement demonstrated _____ _____.

5. Children learn many social behaviors by imitating parents and other models. This type of learning is called _____ _____.

6. According to Bandura, we learn by watching models because we experience _____ reinforcement or _____ punishment.

7. Parents are most effective in getting their children to imitate them if
   a. their words and actions are consistent.
   b. they have outgoing personalities.
   c. one parent works and the other stays home to care for the children.
   d. they carefully explain why a behavior is acceptable in adults but not in children.

8. Some scientists believe that the brain has _____ neurons that enable empathy and imitation.

9. Most experts agree that repeated viewing of media violence
   a. makes all viewers significantly more aggressive.
   b. has little effect on viewers.
   c. is a risk factor for viewers' increased aggression.
   d. makes viewers angry and frustrated.

Continue testing yourself with 📖 **LearningCurve** or ≋ **Achieve Read & Practice** to learn and remember most effectively.

Memory

Be thankful for memory. We take it for granted, except when it malfunctions. But it is our memory that accounts for time and defines our life. It is our memory that enables us to recognize family, speak our language, and find our way home. It is our memory that enables us to enjoy an experience and then mentally replay and enjoy it again. It is our memory that enables us to build histories with those we love. And it is our memory that occasionally pits us against those whose offenses we cannot forget. Our shared memories help bind us together as Irish or Icelandic, Syrian or Samoan.

In large part, we are what we remember. Without memory—our storehouse of accumulated learning—there would be no savoring of past joys, no guilt or anger over painful recollections. We would instead live in an enduring present, each moment fresh. Each person would be a stranger, every language foreign, every task—dressing, cooking, biking—a new challenge. You would even be a stranger to yourself, lacking that continuous sense of self that extends from your distant past to your momentary present.

Researchers study memory from many perspectives. We'll begin by looking at the measuring, modeling, and encoding of memories, and we will examine how memories are stored and retrieved. Then we'll explore what happens when our memories fail us, and look at ways to improve memory. ▶

⟶ Studying and Encoding Memories

STUDYING MEMORY

LEARNING OBJECTIVE QUESTION (LOQ)

8-1   What is *memory*, and how is it measured?

Memory is learning that persists over time; it is information that has been acquired and stored and can be retrieved. Research on memory's extremes has helped us understand how memory works. At age 92, my [DM's] father suffered a small stroke that had but one peculiar effect. He was as mobile as before. His genial personality was intact. He knew us and enjoyed poring over family photo albums and reminiscing about his past. But he had lost most of his ability to lay down new memories of conversations and everyday episodes. He could not tell me what day of the week it was, or what he'd had for lunch. Told repeatedly of his brother-in-law's recent death, he was surprised and saddened each time he heard the news.

Some disorders slowly strip away memory. *Alzheimer's disease* begins as difficulty remembering new information, progressing to an inability to do everyday tasks. Complex speech becomes simple sentences; family members and close friends become strangers; the brain's memory centers, once strong, become weak and wither away (Desikan et al., 2009). Over several years, someone with Alzheimer's may become unknowing and unknowable. Lost memory strikes at the core of our humanity, leaving people robbed of a sense of joy, meaning, and companionship.

At the other extreme are people who win gold medals in memory competitions. When two-time World Memory Champion Feng Wang was a 21-year-old college student, he didn't need help from his phone to remember his friends' numbers. The average person can parrot back a string of about 7—maybe even 9—digits. Feng could repeat up to 200, if they were read about 1 second apart in an otherwise silent room (Ericsson et al., 2017). At one competition, he even memorized 300 digits!

Amazing? Yes, but consider your own impressive memory. You remember countless faces, places, and happenings; tastes, smells, and textures; voices, sounds, and songs. In one study, students listened to snippets—a mere four-tenths of a second—from popular songs. How often did they recognize the artist and song? More than 25 percent of the time (Krumhansl, 2010). We often recognize songs as quickly as we recognize a familiar voice.

So, too, with faces and places. Imagine viewing more than 2500 slides of faces and places for 10 seconds each. Later, you see 280 of these slides, paired with others you've never seen. Actual participants recognized 90 percent of the slides they had viewed in the first round (Haber, 1970). In a follow-up experiment, people exposed to 2800 images for only 3 seconds each spotted the repeats with 82 percent accuracy (Konkle et al., 2010). Look for a target face in a sea of faces and you later will recognize other faces from the scene as well (Kaunitz et al., 2016). Some super-recognizers display an extraordinary ability to recognize faces. Eighteen months after viewing a video of an armed robbery, one such police officer spotted and arrested the robber walking on a busy street (Davis et al., 2013). And it's not just humans who have shown remarkable memory for faces. Sheep remember faces, too (**FIGURE 8.1**). And so has at least one fish species—as demonstrated by their spitting at familiar faces to trigger a food reward (Newport et al., 2016).

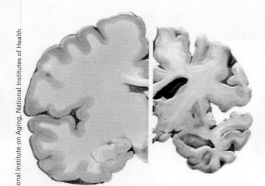

Healthy brain   Severe Alzheimer's disease

EXTREME FORGETTING Alzheimer's disease severely damages the brain, and in the process strips away memory.

ASK YOURSELF

Imagine having an injury or disorder that significantly impaired your memory. Now, imagine having a record-setting ability to remember, like Feng Wang. How would each condition affect your daily routine?

FIGURE 8.1

OTHER ANIMALS ALSO DISPLAY FACE SMARTS After food rewards are repeatedly associated with some sheep faces, but not with others, sheep remember those food-associated faces for two years (Kendrick & Feng, 2011).

Eric Isselee/Shutterstock

ENGAGE How do we humans accomplish such memory feats? How does our brain pluck information from the world around us and tuck it away for later use? How can we remember things we have not thought about for years, yet forget the name of someone we just met? How are memories stored in our brain? Why will you be likely, later in this chapter, to misrecall this sentence: *The angry rioter threw the rock at the window*? In this chapter, we'll consider these fascinating questions and more.

Measuring Retention

To a psychologist, evidence that learning persists includes these three *retention measures*:

- **recall**—*retrieving* information that is not currently in your conscious awareness but that was learned at an earlier time. A fill-in-the-blank question tests your recall.

- **recognition**—*identifying* items previously learned. A multiple-choice question tests your recognition.

- **relearning**—*learning something more quickly* when you learn it a second or later time. When you study for a final exam or engage a language used in early childhood, you will relearn the material more easily than you did initially.

ENGAGE Long after you cannot recall most of the people in your high school graduating class, you may still be able to recognize their yearbook pictures and spot their names in a list of names. In one experiment, people who had graduated 25 years earlier could not recall many of their old classmates. But they could *recognize* 90 percent of their pictures and names (Bahrick et al., 1975). If you are like most students, you, too, could probably recognize more names of Snow White's seven dwarfs than you could recall (Miserandino, 1991).

Our recognition memory is impressively quick and vast. "Is your friend wearing a new or old outfit?" "Old." "Is this five-second movie clip from a film you've ever seen?" "Yes." "Have you ever seen this person before?" "No." Before the mouth can form our answer to any of millions of such questions, the mind knows, and knows that it knows.

Our response speed when recalling or recognizing information indicates memory strength, as does our speed at *relearning*. Pioneering memory researcher Hermann Ebbinghaus (1850–1909) showed this over a century ago, using nonsense syllables. He randomly selected a sample of syllables, practiced them, and tested himself. To get a feel for his experiments, rapidly read aloud, eight times over, the following list (from Baddeley, 1982), then look away and try to recall the items:

JIH, BAZ, FUB, YOX, SUJ, XIR, DAX, LEQ, VUM, PID, KEL, WAV, TUV, ZOF, GEK, HIW.

The day after learning such a list, Ebbinghaus could recall few of the syllables. But they weren't entirely forgotten. As **FIGURE 8.2** portrays, the more frequently he repeated the list aloud on Day 1, the less time he required to relearn the list on Day 2. Additional rehearsal (*overlearning*) of verbal information increases retention—especially when practice is distributed over time. For students, this means that it helps to rehearse course material even after you know it. Better to rehearse and overlearn than relax and remember too little.

The point to remember: Tests of recognition and of time spent relearning demonstrate that we remember more than we can recall.

"If any one faculty of our nature may be called *more* wonderful than the rest, I do think it is memory." —Jane Austen, *Mansfield Park*, 1814

REMEMBERING THINGS PAST Even if Taylor Swift and Bruno Mars had not become famous, their high school classmates would most likely still recognize them in these photos.

memory the persistence of learning over time through the encoding, storage, and retrieval of information.

recall a measure of memory in which the person must retrieve information learned earlier, as on a fill-in-the-blank test.

recognition a measure of memory in which the person identifies items previously learned, as on a multiple-choice test.

relearning a measure of memory that assesses the amount of time saved when learning material again.

encoding the process of getting information into the memory system—for example, by extracting meaning.

storage the process of retaining encoded information over time.

retrieval the process of getting information out of memory storage.

parallel processing processing many aspects of a stimulus or problem at once.

sensory memory the immediate, very brief recording of sensory information in the memory system.

short-term memory activated memory that holds a few items briefly, such as digits of a phone number while calling, before the information is stored or forgotten.

long-term memory the relatively permanent and limitless storehouse of the memory system. Includes knowledge, skills, and experiences.

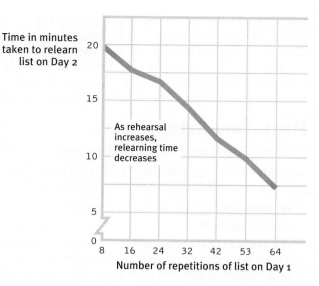

FIGURE 8.2
EBBINGHAUS' RETENTION CURVE
Ebbinghaus found that the more times he practiced a list of nonsense syllables on Day 1, the less time he required to relearn it on Day 2. Speed of relearning is one measure of memory retention. (Data from Baddeley, 1982.)

Time in minutes taken to relearn list on Day 2

As rehearsal increases, relearning time decreases

Number of repetitions of list on Day 1

🔒 **RETRIEVE IT** • • •

ANSWERS IN APPENDIX E

RI-1 Multiple-choice questions test our _____. Fill-in-the-blank questions test our _____.

RI-2 If you want to be sure to remember what you're learning for an upcoming test, would it be better to use *recall* or *recognition* to check your memory? Why?

Memory Models

LOQ 8-2   How do psychologists describe the human memory system?

Architects make virtual house models to help clients imagine their future homes. Similarly, psychologists create memory models that, even if imperfect, are useful. Such models help us think about how our brain forms and retrieves memories. History offers us multiple memory models: Memory is like a wax tablet (Aristotle), a "mystic writing pad" (Freud), a house, a library, or the once-commonplace videotape or telephone switchboard (Roediger, 1980). Today's *information-processing model* likens human memory to computer operations. Thus, to remember any event, we must

- get information into our brain, a process called **encoding.**
- retain that information, a process called **storage.**
- later get the information back out, a process called **retrieval.**

Like all analogies, computer models have their limits. Our memories are less literal and more fragile than a computer's. Most computers also process information sequentially, even while alternating between tasks. Our agile brain processes many things simultaneously (some of them unconsciously) by means of **parallel processing.** To focus on multitrack processing, one information-processing model, *connectionism,* views memories as products of interconnected neural networks. Specific memories arise from particular activation patterns within these networks. Every time you learn something new, your brain's neural connections change, forming and strengthening pathways that allow you to interact with and learn from your constantly changing environment.

To explain our memory-forming process, Richard Atkinson and Richard Shiffrin (1968, 2016) proposed a three-stage model:

1. We first record to-be-remembered information as a fleeting **sensory memory.**

2. From there, we process information into **short-term memory,** where we encode it through *rehearsal.*

3. Finally, information moves into **long-term memory** for later retrieval.

This model has since been updated (**FIGURE 8.3**) with important newer concepts, including *working memory* and *automatic processing.*

ENGAGE
ASK YOURSELF

What has your memory system encoded, stored, and retrieved today?

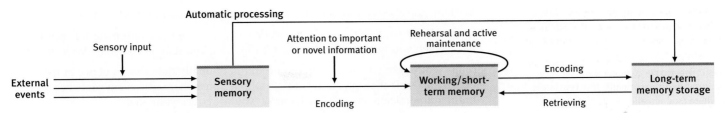

WORKING MEMORY Alan Baddeley and others (Baddeley, 2002; Barrouillet et al., 2011; Engle, 2002) extended Atkinson and Shiffrin's initial view of short-term memory as a space for briefly storing recent thoughts and experiences. This stage is not just a temporary shelf for holding incoming information. It's an active scratchpad where your brain actively processes information by making sense of new input and linking it with long-term memories. It also works in the opposite direction, by processing already stored information. Whether we hear "eye-screem" as *ice cream* or *I scream* depends on how the context and our experience guide our interpreting and encoding of the sounds. To emphasize the active processing that takes place in this middle stage, psychologists use the term **working memory.** Right now, you are using your working memory to link the information you're reading with your previously stored information (Cowan, 2010, 2016; Kail & Hall, 2001).

For most of you, what you are reading enters working memory through vision. You might also repeat the information using auditory rehearsal. As you integrate these memory inputs with your existing long-term memory, your attention is focused. In Baddeley's (2002) model, a *central executive* coordinates this focused processing.

Without focused attention, information often fades. If you think you can look something up later, you attend to it less and forget it more quickly. In one experiment, people read and typed new bits of trivia they would later need, such as "An ostrich's eye is bigger than its brain." If they knew the information would be available online, they invested less energy and remembered it less well (Sparrow et al., 2011; Wegner & Ward, 2013). Online, out of mind.

FIGURE 8.3

A MODIFIED THREE-STAGE PROCESSING MODEL OF MEMORY
Atkinson and Shiffrin's classic three-step model helps us to think about how memories are processed, but today's researchers recognize other ways long-term memories form. For example, some information slips into long-term memory via a "back door," without our consciously attending to it *(automatic processing).* And so much active processing occurs in the short-term memory stage that many now prefer the term *working memory.*

RETRIEVE IT • • •   ANSWERS IN APPENDIX E

RI-3 How does the *working memory* concept update the classic Atkinson-Shiffrin three-stage information-processing model?

RI-4 What are two basic functions of working memory?

LaunchPad For a 14-minute explanation and demonstration of our memory systems, see the **Video: Models of Memory.**

ENCODING MEMORIES

Dual-Track Memory: Effortful Versus Automatic Processing

LOQ 8-3 How do explicit and implicit memories differ?

Atkinson and Shiffrin's model focuses on how we process our **explicit memories**—the facts and experiences we can consciously know and "declare" (thus, also called *declarative memories*). We encode explicit memories through conscious **effortful processing.** But behind the scenes, other information skips the conscious encoding track and barges directly into storage. This **automatic processing,** which happens without our awareness, produces **implicit memories** (also called *nondeclarative memories*).

Our two-track mind, then, helps us encode, retain, and recall information through both effortful and automatic tracks. Let's begin by seeing how automatic processing assists the formation of implicit memories.

Automatic Processing and Implicit Memories

LOQ 8-4 What information do we process automatically?

Our implicit memories include *procedural* memory for automatic skills (such as how to ride a bike) and classically conditioned *associations* among stimuli. If attacked by a dog in childhood, years later you may, without recalling the conditioned association, automatically tense up as a dog approaches.

working memory a newer understanding of short-term memory that adds conscious, active processing of incoming sensory information, and of information retrieved from long-term memory.

explicit memory retention of facts and experiences that we can consciously know and "declare." (Also called *declarative memory.*)

effortful processing encoding that requires attention and conscious effort.

automatic processing unconscious encoding of incidental information, such as space, time, and frequency, and of well-learned information, such as word meanings.

implicit memory retention of learned skills or classically conditioned associations independent of conscious recollection. (Also called *nondeclarative memory.*)

iconic memory a momentary sensory memory of visual stimuli; a photographic or picture-image memory lasting no more than a few tenths of a second.

echoic memory a momentary sensory memory of auditory stimuli; if attention is elsewhere, sounds and words can still be recalled within 3 or 4 seconds.

chunking organizing items into familiar, manageable units; often occurs automatically.

 (ASK YOURSELF)

Does it surprise you to learn how much of your memory processing is automatic? What might life be like if *all* memory processing were effortful?

Without conscious effort you also automatically process information about

- *space.* While studying, you often encode the place where certain material appears; later, when you want to retrieve the information, you may visualize its location.
- *time.* While going about your day, you unintentionally note the sequence of its events. Later, realizing you've left your phone somewhere, the event sequence your brain automatically encoded will enable you to retrace your steps.
- *frequency.* You effortlessly keep track of how many times things happen, as when you realize, "This is the third time I've run into her today!"

Our two-track mind engages in impressively efficient information processing. As one track automatically tucks away routine details, the other track is free to focus on conscious, effortful processing. Mental feats such as vision, thinking, and memory may seem to be single abilities, but they are not. Rather, we split information into different components for separate and simultaneous processing.

Effortful Processing and Explicit Memories

Automatic processing happens effortlessly. When you see words in your native language, perhaps on the side of a delivery truck, you can't help but read them and register their meaning. *Learning* to read wasn't automatic. You may recall working hard to pick out letters and connect them to certain sounds. But with experience and practice, your reading became automatic. Imagine now learning to read sentences in reverse:

.citamotua emoceb nac gnissecorp luftroffE

At first, this requires effort, but after enough practice, you would also perform this task much more automatically. We develop many skills in this way: driving, texting, and speaking a new language.

SENSORY MEMORY

LOQ 8-5   How does sensory memory work?

Sensory memory (recall Figure 8.3) feeds our active working memory. For example, our mind records momentary images, echoes of sounds, and strong scents. How much of this page could you sense and recall with less exposure than a lightning flash? In one experiment, people viewed three rows of three letters each, for only one-twentieth of a second (**FIGURE 8.4**). After the nine letters disappeared, they could recall only about half of them.

Was it because they had insufficient time to glimpse them? *No.* People actually *could* see and recall all the letters, but only momentarily. Rather than ask them to recall all nine letters at once, researcher George Sperling sounded a high, medium, or low tone immediately *after* flashing the nine letters. This tone directed participants to report only the letters of the top, middle, or bottom row, respectively. Now they rarely missed a letter, showing that all nine letters were momentarily available for recall.

Sperling's experiment demonstrated **iconic memory,** a fleeting sensory memory of visual stimuli. For a few tenths of a second, our eyes register a picture-image memory of a scene, and we can recall any part of it in amazing detail. But delaying the tone signal by more than half a second caused the image to fade and memory to suffer. We also have an impeccable, though fleeting, memory for auditory stimuli, called **echoic memory** (Cowan, 1988; Lu et al., 1992). Picture yourself becoming distracted by a text message while you sit in class. If your mildly irked professor tests you by asking, "What did I just say?" you can recover the last few words from your mind's echo chamber. Auditory echoes tend to linger for 3 or 4 seconds.

SHORT-TERM MEMORY CAPACITY

LOQ 8-6   What is our short-term memory capacity?

Recall that short-term memory refers to what we can briefly retain. The related idea of working memory also includes our active processing, as our brain makes sense of incoming information and links it with stored memories. What are the limits of what we can hold in this middle, short-term stage?

FIGURE 8.4

TOTAL RECALL—BRIEFLY When George Sperling (1960) flashed a group of letters similar to this for one-twentieth of a second, people could recall only about half the letters. But when signaled to recall a particular row immediately after the letters had disappeared, they could do so with near-perfect accuracy.

K   Z   R

Q   B   T

S   G   N

George Miller (1956) proposed that we can store about seven pieces of information (give or take two) in short-term memory. Miller's magical number seven is psychology's contribution to the list of magical sevens—the seven wonders of the world, the seven seas, the seven deadly sins, the seven colors of the rainbow, the seven musical scale notes, the seven days of the week—seven magical sevens. Other researchers have confirmed that we can, if nothing distracts us, recall about seven digits. But the number varies by task; we tend to remember about six letters and only about five words (Baddeley et al., 1975; Cowan, 2015). And how quickly do our short-term memories disappear? To find out, Lloyd Peterson and Margaret Peterson (1959) asked people to remember three-consonant groups, such as *CHJ*. To prevent rehearsal, the researchers asked them, for example, to start at 100 and begin counting aloud backward by threes. After 3 seconds, people recalled the letters only about half the time; after 12 seconds, they seldom recalled them at all (**FIGURE 8.5**). Without the active processing that we now understand to be a part of our working memory, short-term memories have a limited life.

Working-memory capacity varies, depending on age and other factors. Young adults tend to have greater working-memory capacity—the ability to juggle multiple items while processing information—than do children and older adults. This helps young adults to better retain information after sleeping and to solve problems creatively (De Dreu et al., 2012; Fenn & Hambrick, 2012; Wiley & Jarosz, 2012). But whatever our age, we do better and more efficient work when focused, without distractions, on one task at a time. *The bottom line:* It's probably a bad idea to try to stream videos, text your friends, and write a psychology paper all at the same time, with your attention switching between them (Willingham, 2010)!

 LaunchPad For a review of memory stages and a test of your own short-term memory capacity, visit **Topic Tutorial: PsychSim6, Short-Term Memory.**

🔒 **RETRIEVE IT • • •**   *ANSWERS IN APPENDIX E*

RI-5 What is the difference between *automatic* and *effortful* processing, and what are some examples of each?

RI-6 At which of Atkinson-Shiffrin's three memory stages would *iconic* and *echoic* memory occur?

 EFFORTFUL PROCESSING STRATEGIES

LOQ 8-7 What are some effortful processing strategies that can help us remember new information?

Several effortful processing strategies boost our ability to form new memories. Later, when we try to retrieve a memory, these strategies can make the difference between success and failure.

CHUNKING Glance for a few seconds at the first set of letters (row 1) in **FIGURE 8.6**, then look away and try to reproduce what you saw. Impossible, yes? But you can easily reproduce set 2, which is no less complex. Similarly, you will probably remember sets 4 and 6 more easily than the same elements in sets 3 and 5. As this demonstrates, **chunking** information—organizing items into familiar, manageable units—enables us to recall it more easily. Try remembering 43 individual numbers and letters. It would be impossible, unless chunked into, say, seven meaningful chunks, such as "Try remembering 43 individual numbers and letters." ☺

Chunking usually occurs so naturally that we take it for granted. If you are a native English speaker, you can reproduce perfectly the 150 or so line segments that make up the words in the three phrases of set 6 in Figure 8.6. It would astonish someone unfamiliar with the language. Similarly amazing is a Chinese reader's ability to glance at **FIGURE 8.7** and reproduce all the strokes, or a varsity basketball player's recall of all the players' positions after a 4-second peek at a basketball play (Allard & Burnett, 1985). We all remember information best when we can organize it into personally meaningful arrangements.

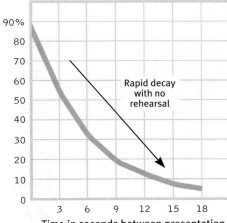

Percentage who recalled consonants

Time in seconds between presentation of consonants and recall request (no rehearsal allowed)

FIGURE 8.5

SHORT-TERM MEMORY DECAY Unless rehearsed, verbal information may be quickly forgotten. (Data from Peterson & Peterson, 1959; see also Brown, 1958.)

After Miller's 2012 death, his daughter recalled his best moment of golf: "He made the one and only hole-in-one of his life at the age of 77, on the seventh green . . . with a seven iron. He loved that" (quoted by Vitello, 2012).

🔒 **FIGURE 8.6**

CHUNKING EFFECTS Organizing information into meaningful units, such as letters, words, and phrases, helps us recall it more easily (Hintzman, 1978).

1. M Ɔ Λ S Я W ⊥

2. W G V S R M T

3. VRESLI UEGBN GSORNW CDOUL LWLE NTOD WTO
4. SILVER BEGUN WRONGS CLOUD WELL DONT TWO

5. SILVER BEGUN WRONGS CLOUD DONT TWO
    HALF MAKE WELL HAS A
    EVERY IS RIGHT A DONE LINING

6. WELL BEGUN IS HALF DONE
    EVERY CLOUD HAS A SILVER LINING
    TWO WRONGS DONT MAKE A RIGHT

春夏
秋冬

FIGURE 8.7

AN EXAMPLE OF CHUNKING—FOR THOSE WHO READ CHINESE After looking at these characters, can you reproduce them exactly? If so, you can read Chinese.

MNEMONICS To help encode lengthy passages and speeches, ancient Greek scholars and orators developed **mnemonics.** Many of these memory aids use vivid imagery, because we are particularly good at remembering mental pictures. We more easily remember concrete, visualizable words than we do abstract words (Akpinar & Berger, 2015). (When we quiz you later, which three of these words—*bicycle, void, cigarette, inherent, fire, process*—will you most likely recall?) If you still recall the rock-throwing rioter sentence, it is probably not only because of the meaning you encoded but also because the sentence painted a mental image.

Memory whizzes understand the power of such systems. Star performers in the World Memory Championships do not usually have exceptional intelligence, but rather are superior at using mnemonic strategies (Maguire et al., 2003b). Frustrated by his ordinary memory, science writer Joshua Foer wanted to see how much he could improve it. After a year of intense practice, he won the U.S. Memory Championship by memorizing a pack of 52 playing cards in under two minutes. How did Foer do it? He added vivid new details to memories of a familiar place—his childhood home. Each card, presented in any order, could then match up with the clear picture in his head. As the test subject of his own wild memory experiment, he learned the power of painting pretty pictures in his mind (Foer, 2011).

When combined, chunking and mnemonic techniques can be great memory aids for unfamiliar material. Want to remember the colors of the rainbow in order of wavelength? Think of the mnemonic ROY G. BIV (*r*ed, *o*range, *y*ellow, *g*reen, *b*lue, *i*ndigo, *v*iolet). Need to recall the names of North America's five Great Lakes? Just remember HOMES (*H*uron, *O*ntario, *M*ichigan, *E*rie, *S*uperior). In each case, we chunk information into a more familiar form by creating a word (called an *acronym*) from the first letters of the to-be-remembered items.

HIERARCHIES When people develop expertise in an area, they often process information in *hierarchies* composed of a few broad concepts divided and subdivided into narrower concepts and facts. (Figure 8.11 ahead provides a hierarchy of our automatic and effortful memory processing systems.)

Organizing knowledge in hierarchies helps us retrieve information efficiently, as Gordon Bower and his colleagues (1969) demonstrated by presenting words either randomly or grouped into categories. When the words were organized into categories, recall was two to three times better. Such results show the benefits of organizing what you study—of giving special attention to chapter headings, and, in this text, to numbered Learning Objective questions. Taking lecture and textbook notes in outline format—a type of hierarchical organization—may also prove helpful.

DISTRIBUTED PRACTICE We retain information better when our encoding is distributed over time. Experiments have consistently revealed the benefits of this **spacing effect** (Cepeda et al., 2006; Soderstrom et al., 2016). *Massed practice* (cramming) can produce speedy short-term learning and a feeling of confidence. But to paraphrase memory researcher Hermann Ebbinghaus (1885), those who learn quickly also forget quickly. *Distributed practice* produces better long-term recall. After you've studied long enough to master the material, further study at that time becomes inefficient. Better to spend that extra reviewing time later—a day later if you need to remember something 10 days hence, or a month later if you need to remember something 6 months hence (Cepeda et al., 2008). The spacing effect is one of psychology's most reliable findings, and it extends to motor skills and online game performance, too (Stafford & Dewar, 2014). Memory researcher Henry Roediger (2013) sums it up: "Hundreds of studies have shown that distributed practice leads to more durable learning."

One effective way to distribute practice is *repeated* self-testing, a phenomenon that Roediger and Jeffrey Karpicke (2006) have called the **testing effect.** Testing does more than assess learning and memory: It improves them (Brown et al., 2014; Pan et al., 2015; Trumbo et al., 2016). Testing also protects our memory from the harmful effects of stress, which usually impairs memory retrieval (Smith et al., 2016). In this textbook, the Retrieve It questions and Review sections, including the Experience the Testing Effect questions, offer opportunities to improve learning and memory. Better to practice retrieval (as any

"The mind is slow in unlearning what it has been long in learning." —Roman philosopher Seneca, 4 B.C.E.–65 C.E.

exam will demand) than to merely reread material (which may lull you into a false sense of mastery). Roediger (2013) explains, "Two techniques that students frequently report using for studying—highlighting (or underlining) text and rereading text—[have been found] ineffective." Happily, "retrieval practice (or testing) is a powerful and general strategy for learning." As another memory expert explained, "What we recall becomes more recallable" (Bjork, 2011). No wonder daily online quizzing improves introductory psychology students' course performance (Batsell et al., 2017; Pennebaker et al., 2013).

The point to remember: Spaced study and self-assessment beat cramming and rereading. Practice may not make perfect, but smart practice—occasional rehearsal with self-testing—makes for lasting memories.

  LEVELS OF PROCESSING

LOQ 8-8 What are the levels of processing, and how do they affect encoding?

Memory researchers have discovered that we process verbal information at different levels, and that depth of processing affects our long-term retention. **Shallow processing** encodes on an elementary level, such as a word's letters or, at a more intermediate level, a word's sound. Thus, we may type *there* when we mean *their, write* when we mean *right,* and *two* when we mean *too.* **Deep processing** encodes *semantically,* based on the meaning of the words. The deeper (more meaningful) the processing, the better our retention.

In one classic experiment, researchers Fergus Craik and Endel Tulving (1975) flashed words at viewers. Then they asked them questions that would elicit different levels of processing. To experience the task yourself, rapidly answer the following sample questions:

Sample Questions to Elicit Different Levels of Processing	Word Flashed	Yes	No
Most shallow: Is the word in capital letters?	CHAIR	_____	_____
Shallow: Does the word rhyme with train?	Brain	_____	_____
Deep: Would the word fit in this sentence? The girl put the _____ on the table.	Doll	_____	_____

Which type of processing would best prepare you to recognize the words at a later time? In Craik and Tulving's experiment, the deeper, semantic processing triggered by the third question yielded a much better memory than did the shallower processing elicited by the second question or the very shallow processing elicited by the first question (which was especially ineffective).

  MAKING MATERIAL PERSONALLY MEANINGFUL If new information is neither meaningful nor related to our experience, we have trouble processing it. Imagine being asked to remember the following recorded passage:

> The procedure is actually quite simple. First you arrange things into different groups. Of course, one pile may be sufficient depending on how much there is to do. . . . After the procedure is completed, one arranges the materials into different groups again. Then they can be put into their appropriate places. Eventually they will be used once more and the whole cycle will then have to be repeated. However, that is part of life.

When some students heard the paragraph you have just read, without a meaningful context, they remembered little of it (Bransford & Johnson, 1972). When others were told the paragraph described washing clothes (something meaningful), they remembered much more of it—as you probably could now after rereading it.

Can you repeat the sentence about the rioter that we gave you at this chapter's beginning ("The angry rioter threw . . .")? Perhaps, like those in an experiment by William

RETAIN **LaunchPad** For suggestions on how to apply the *testing effect* to your own learning, watch my [DM's] 5-minute **Video: Make Things Memorable** in LaunchPad or at: tinyurl.com/HowToRemember.

mnemonics [nih-MON-iks] memory aids, especially those techniques that use vivid imagery and organizational devices.

spacing effect the tendency for distributed study or practice to yield better long-term retention than is achieved through massed study or practice.

testing effect enhanced memory after retrieving, rather than simply rereading, information. Also sometimes referred to as a *retrieval practice effect* or *test-enhanced learning.*

shallow processing encoding on a basic level, based on the structure or appearance of words.

deep processing encoding semantically, based on the meaning of the words; tends to yield the best retention.

Brewer (1977), you recalled the sentence by the meaning you encoded when you read it (for example, "The angry rioter threw the rock *through* the window") and not as it was written ("The angry rioter threw the rock *at* the window"). Referring to such mental mismatches, some researchers have likened our minds to theater directors who, given a raw script, imagine the finished stage production (Bower & Morrow, 1990). Asked later what we heard or read, we recall not the literal text but what we encoded. Thus, studying for an exam, you may remember your lecture notes rather than the lecture itself.

We can avoid some of these mismatches by rephrasing what we see and hear into meaningful terms. From his experiments on himself, Ebbinghaus estimated that, compared with learning nonsense material, learning meaningful material required one-tenth the effort. As memory researcher Wayne Wickelgren (1977, p. 346) noted, "The time you spend thinking about material you are reading and relating it to previously stored material is about the most useful thing you can do in learning any new subject matter."

Psychologist-actor team Helga Noice and Tony Noice (2006) have described how actors inject meaning into the daunting task of learning "all those lines." They do it by first coming to understand the flow of meaning: "One actor divided a half-page of dialogue into three [intentions]: 'to flatter,' 'to draw him out,' and 'to allay his fears.'" With this meaningful sequence in mind, the actor more easily remembered the lines.

Most people excel at remembering personally relevant information. Asked how well certain adjectives describe someone else, we often forget them; asked how well the adjectives describe us, we often remember them. This tendency, called the *self-reference effect*, is especially strong in members of individualist Western cultures (Symons & Johnson, 1997; Wagar & Cohen, 2003). Information deemed "relevant to me" is processed more deeply and remains more accessible. In contrast, members of collectivist Eastern cultures remember self-relevant and family-relevant information equally well (Sparks et al., 2016).

The point to remember: The amount remembered depends both on the time spent learning and on your making it meaningful for deep processing.

ENGAGE In the discussion of mnemonics, we gave you six words and told you we would quiz you about them later. How many of these words can you now recall? Of these, how many are high-imagery words? How many are low-imagery?[1]

🔒 RETRIEVE IT • • •   *ANSWERS IN APPENDIX E*

RI-7 Which strategies are better for long-term retention: cramming and rereading material, or spreading out learning over time and repeatedly testing yourself?

RI-8 If you try to make the material you are learning personally meaningful, are you processing at a shallow or a deep level? Which level leads to greater retention?

---

1. bicycle, void, cigarette, inherent, fire, process.

🔒 REVIEW   STUDYING AND ENCODING MEMORIES

⟶ Learning Objectives

TEST YOURSELF Answer these repeated Learning Objective Questions on your own (before checking the answers in Appendix D) to improve your retention of the concepts (McDaniel et al., 2009, 2015).

8-1 What is *memory,* and how is it measured?

8-2 How do psychologists describe the human memory system?

8-3 How do explicit and implicit memories differ?

8-4 What information do we process automatically?

8-5 How does sensory memory work?

8-6 What is our short-term memory capacity?

8-7 What are some effortful processing strategies that can help us remember new information?

8-8 What are the levels of processing, and how do they affect encoding?

⟶ Terms and Concepts to Remember

TEST YOURSELF Write down the definition yourself, then check your answer on the referenced page.

memory, **p. 267**

recall, **p. 267**

recognition, **p. 267**

relearning, **p. 267**

encoding, **p. 268**

storage, **p. 268**

retrieval, **p. 268**

parallel processing, **p. 268**

sensory memory, **p. 268**

⟶ Experience the Testing Effect

TEST YOURSELF Answer the following questions on your own first, then check your answers in Appendix E.

1. A psychologist who asks you to write down as many objects as you can remember having seen a few minutes earlier is testing your _____.

2. The psychological terms for taking in information, retaining it, and later getting it back out are _____, _____, and _____.

3. The concept of working memory

   a. clarifies the idea of short-term memory by focusing on the active processing that occurs in this stage.

   b. splits short-term memory into two substages—sensory memory and iconic memory.

   c. splits short-term memory into two types—implicit and explicit memory.

   d. clarifies the idea of short-term memory by focusing on space, time, and frequency.

4. Sensory memory may be visual (_____ memory) or auditory (_____ memory).

5. Our short-term memory for new information is limited to about _____ digits.

6. Memory aids that use visual imagery or other organizational devices (such as acronyms) are called _____.

Continue testing yourself with 📖 **LearningCurve** or 📖 **Achieve Read & Practice** to learn and remember most effectively.

⟶ Storing and Retrieving Memories

MEMORY STORAGE

LOQ 8-9 What is the capacity of long-term memory? Are our long-term memories processed and stored in specific locations?

In Arthur Conan Doyle's *A Study in Scarlet,* Sherlock Holmes offers a popular theory of memory capacity:

> I consider that a man's brain originally is like a little empty attic, and you have to stock it with such furniture as you choose. . . . It is a mistake to think that that little room has elastic walls and can distend to any extent. Depend upon it, there comes a time when for every addition of knowledge you forget something that you knew before.

Contrary to Holmes' "memory model," our brain is *not* like an attic, which once filled can store more items only if we discard old ones. Our capacity for storing long-term memories is essentially limitless. One research team, after studying the brain's neural connections, estimated its storage capacity as "in the same ballpark as the World Wide Web" (Sejnowski, 2016).

Retaining Information in the Brain

I [DM] marveled at my aging mother-in-law, a retired pianist and organist. At age 88, her blind eyes could no longer read music. But let her sit at a keyboard and she would flawlessly play any of hundreds of hymns, including ones she had not thought of for 20 years. Where did her brain store those thousands of sequenced notes?

semantic memory explicit memory of facts and general knowledge; one of our two conscious memory systems (the other is *episodic memory*).

episodic memory explicit memory of personally experienced events; one of our two conscious memory systems (the other is *semantic memory*).

hippocampus a neural center located in the limbic system; helps process explicit (conscious) memories—of facts and events—for storage.

memory consolidation the neural storage of a long-term memory.

"Our memories are flexible and superimposable, a panoramic blackboard with an endless supply of chalk and erasers." —Elizabeth Loftus and Katherine Ketcham, *The Myth of Repressed Memory*, 1994

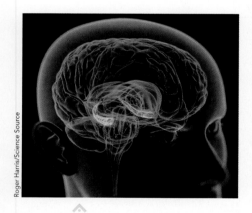

Roger Harris/Science Source

FIGURE 8.8

THE HIPPOCAMPUS Explicit memories for facts and episodes are processed in the hippocampus (orange structures) and fed to other brain regions for storage.

HIPPOCAMPUS HERO Among animals, one contender for champion memorist would be a mere birdbrain—the Clark's Nutcracker—which during winter and spring can locate up to 6000 caches of pine seed it had previously buried (Shettleworth, 1993).

For a time, some surgeons and memory researchers marveled at patients' apparently vivid memories triggered by brain stimulation during surgery. Did this prove that our whole past, not just well-practiced music, is "in there," in complete detail, just waiting to be relived? On closer analysis, the seeming flashbacks appeared to have been invented, not a vivid reliving of long-forgotten experiences (Loftus & Loftus, 1980). In a further demonstration that memories do not reside in single, specific spots, psychologist Karl Lashley (1950) trained rats to find their way out of a maze, then surgically removed pieces of their brain's cortex and retested their memory. No matter which small brain section he removed, the rats retained at least a partial memory of how to navigate the maze. Memories *are* brain-based, but the brain distributes the components of a memory across a network of locations. These specific locations include some of the circuitry involved in the original experience: Some brain cells that fire when we experience something fire again when we recall it (Miller, G., 2012; Miller et al., 2013).

The point to remember: Despite the brain's vast storage capacity, we do not store information as libraries store their books, in single, precise locations. Instead, brain networks encode, store, and retrieve the information that forms our complex memories.

EXPLICIT MEMORY SYSTEM: THE FRONTAL LOBES AND HIPPOCAMPUS

LOQ 8-10 What roles do the frontal lobes and hippocampus play in memory processing?

Explicit, conscious memories are either **semantic** (facts and general knowledge) or **episodic** (experienced events). The network that processes and stores new explicit memories for these facts and episodes includes your frontal lobes and hippocampus. When you summon up a mental encore of a past experience, many brain regions send input to your *prefrontal cortex* (the front part of your frontal lobes) for working memory processing (de Chastelaine et al., 2016; Michalka et al., 2015). The left and right frontal lobes process different types of memories. Recalling a password and holding it in working memory, for example, would activate the left frontal lobe. Calling up a visual party scene would more likely activate the right frontal lobe.

Cognitive neuroscientists have found that the **hippocampus,** a temporal lobe neural center located in the limbic system, can be likened to a "save" button for explicit memories (**FIGURE 8.8**). As children mature, their hippocampus grows, enabling them to construct detailed memories (Keresztes et al., 2017). Brain scans reveal activity in the hippocampus and nearby brain networks as people form explicit memories of names, images, and events (Terada et al., 2017; Wang et al., 2014).

Damage to this structure therefore disrupts the formation and recall of explicit memories. If their hippocampus is severed, chickadees and other birds will continue to cache food in hundreds of places, but later be unable to find them (Kamil & Cheng, 2001; Sherry & Vaccarino, 1989). With left-hippocampus damage, people have trouble remembering verbal information, but they have no trouble recalling visual designs and locations. With right-hippocampus damage, the problem is reversed (Schacter, 1996).

Subregions of the hippocampus also serve different functions. One part is active as people and mice learn social information (Okuyama et al., 2016; Zeineh et al., 2003). Another part is active as memory champions engage in spatial mnemonics (Maguire et al., 2003a). The rear area, which processes spatial memory, grows bigger as London cabbies navigate the city's complicated maze of streets (Woolett & Maguire, 2011).

Memories are not permanently stored in the hippocampus. Instead, the hippocampus acts as a loading dock where the brain registers and temporarily holds the elements of a to-be-remembered episode—its smell, feel, sound, and location. Then, like older files shifted to a basement storeroom, memories migrate to the cortex for storage. This storage process is called **memory consolidation.**

Sleep supports memory consolidation. In one experiment, students who learned material in a study/sleep/restudy condition remembered material better, both a week and six months later, than those who studied in the morning and restudied in the evening without intervening sleep (Mazza et al., 2016). During deep sleep, the hippocampus processes

Tim Zurowski/All Canada Photos/Getty Images

memories for later retrieval. After a training experience, the greater one's hippocampus activity during sleep, the better the next day's memory will be (Peigneux et al., 2004; Whitehurst et al., 2016). Researchers have watched the hippocampus and brain cortex displaying simultaneous activity rhythms during sleep, as if they were having a dialogue (Euston et al., 2007; Mehta, 2007). They suspect that the brain is replaying the day's experiences as it transfers them to the cortex for long-term storage (Squire & Zola-Morgan, 1991). When our learning is distributed over days rather than crammed into a single day, we experience more sleep-induced memory consolidation. And that helps explain the spacing effect.

IMPLICIT MEMORY SYSTEM: THE CEREBELLUM AND BASAL GANGLIA

LOQ 8-11 What roles do the cerebellum and basal ganglia play in memory processing?

Your hippocampus and frontal lobes are processing sites for your *explicit* memories. But you could lose those areas and still, thanks to automatic processing, lay down *implicit* memories for skills and newly conditioned associations. Joseph LeDoux (1996) recounted the story of a brain-damaged patient whose amnesia left her unable to recognize her physician as, each day, he shook her hand and introduced himself. One day, she yanked her hand back, for the physician had pricked her with a tack in his palm. The next time he returned to introduce himself she refused to shake his hand but couldn't explain why. Having been classically conditioned, she just wouldn't do it. Implicitly, she felt what she could not explain.

The *cerebellum* plays a key role in forming and storing the implicit memories created by classical conditioning. With a damaged cerebellum, people cannot develop certain conditioned reflexes, such as associating a tone with an impending puff of air—and thus do not blink in anticipation of the puff (Daum & Schugens, 1996; Green & Woodruff-Pak, 2000). Implicit memory formation needs the cerebellum.

The *basal ganglia*, deep brain structures involved in motor movement, facilitate formation of our procedural memories for skills (Mishkin, 1982; Mishkin et al., 1997). The basal ganglia receive input from the cortex, but do not return the favor of sending information back to the cortex for conscious awareness of procedural learning. If you have learned how to ride a bike, thank your basal ganglia.

Our implicit memory system, enabled partly by these more ancient brain areas, helps explain why the reactions and skills we learned during infancy reach far into our future. Yet as adults, our *conscious* memory of our first four years is largely blank, an experience called *infantile amnesia*. In one study, events children experienced and discussed with their mothers at age 3 were 60 percent remembered at age 7 but only 34 percent remembered at age 9 (Bauer et al., 2007). Two influences contribute to infantile amnesia: First, we index much of our explicit memory with a command of language that young children do not possess. Second, the hippocampus is one of the last brain structures to mature, and as it does, more gets retained (Akers et al., 2014).

🔒 RETRIEVE IT • • •

ANSWERS IN APPENDIX E

RI-1 Which parts of the brain are important for *implicit* memory processing, and which parts play a key role in *explicit* memory processing?

RI-2 Your friend has experienced brain damage in an accident. He can remember how to tie his shoes but has a hard time remembering anything you tell him during a conversation. How can implicit versus explicit information processing explain what's going on here?

THE AMYGDALA, EMOTIONS, AND MEMORY

LOQ 8-12 How do emotions affect our memory processing?

Our emotions trigger stress hormones that influence memory formation. When we are excited or stressed, these hormones make more glucose energy available to fuel brain activity, signaling the brain that something important is happening. Moreover, stress hormones focus memory. Stress provokes the *amygdala* (two limbic system, emotion-processing clusters) to initiate a memory trace that boosts activity in the brain's memory-forming areas (Buchanan, 2007; Kensinger, 2007) (**FIGURE 8.9**). It's as if the amygdala says, "Brain, encode this moment for future reference!" The result? Emotional arousal can sear certain events into the brain, while disrupting memory for irrelevant events that occur around the same time (Brewin et al., 2007; McGaugh, 2015).

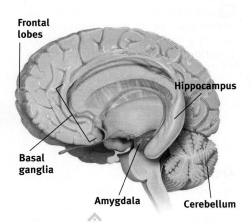

Frontal lobes

Hippocampus

Basal ganglia

Amygdala

Cerebellum

RETAIN 🔒 **FIGURE 8.9**

REVIEW KEY MEMORY STRUCTURES IN THE BRAIN

Frontal lobes and *hippocampus*: explicit memory formation
Cerebellum and *basal ganglia*: implicit memory formation
Amygdala: emotion-related memory formation

flashbulb memory a clear memory of an emotionally significant moment or event.

long-term potentiation (LTP) an increase in a cell's firing potential after brief, rapid stimulation; a neural basis for learning and memory.

Significantly stressful events can form unforgettable memories. After a traumatic experience—a school shooting, a house fire, a rape—vivid recollections of the horrific event may intrude again and again. It is as if they were burned in: "Stronger emotional experiences make for stronger, more reliable memories," noted James McGaugh (1994, 2003). Such experiences even strengthen recall for relevant, immediately preceding events (Dunsmoor et al., 2015). This makes adaptive sense: Memory helps us anticipate the future and alerts us to potential dangers. Emotional events produce tunnel vision memory. They focus our attention and recall on high-priority information, and reduce our recall of irrelevant details (Mather & Sutherland, 2012). Whatever rivets our attention gets well recalled, at the expense of the surrounding context.

ENGAGE Emotion-triggered hormonal changes help explain why we long remember exciting or shocking events, such as our first kiss or our whereabouts when learning of a loved one's death. In a 2006 Pew survey, 95 percent of American adults said they could recall exactly where they were or what they were doing when they first heard the news of the 9/11 terrorist attacks. This perceived clarity of memories of surprising, significant events (where were you when learning that Donald Trump was elected U.S. president?) leads some psychologists to call them **flashbulb memories.**

The people who experienced a 1989 San Francisco earthquake had perfect recall of where they had been and what they were doing (verified by their recorded thoughts within a day or two of the quake). Others' memories for the circumstances under which they merely *heard* about the quake were more prone to errors (Neisser et al., 1991; Palmer et al., 1991).

Our flashbulb memories are noteworthy for their vividness and our confidence in them. But as we relive, rehearse, and discuss them, even these memories may come to err. With time, some errors crept into people's 9/11 recollections (compared with their reports taken right afterward). Mostly, however, people's memories of 9/11 remained consistent over the next two to three years (Conway et al., 2009; Hirst et al., 2009).

ENGAGE Which is more important—your experiences or your memories of them?

Dramatic experiences remain clear in our memory in part because we rehearse them (Hirst & Phelps, 2016). We think about them and describe them to others. Memories of personally important experiences also endure (Storm & Jobe, 2012; Talarico & Moore, 2012). Compared with non-Catholics, devout Catholics recalled better the resignation of Pope Benedict XVI (Curci et al., 2015). Ditto for baseball fans' memories of their team's championship games (Breslin & Safer, 2011). When their team won, fans enjoyed recalling and recounting the victory, leading to longer-lasting memories.

Synaptic Changes

LOQ 8-13 How do changes at the synapse level affect our memory processing?

LaunchPad For an 8-minute examination of emotion's effect on memory, see the **Video: The Role of Emotion.**

As you now think and learn about memory processes, your brain is changing. Given increased activity in particular pathways, neural interconnections are forming and strengthening.

The quest to understand the physical basis of memory—how information becomes embedded in brain matter—has sparked study of the synaptic meeting places where neurons communicate with one another via their neurotransmitter messengers. Eric Kandel and James Schwartz (1982) observed synaptic changes during learning in the neurons of the California sea slug, *Aplysia,* a simple animal with a mere 20,000 or so unusually large and accessible nerve cells. A sea slug can be classically conditioned (with mild electric shock) to reflexively withdraw its gills when squirted with water, much as a soldier traumatized by combat might jump at the sound of a firecracker. When learning occurs, Kandel and Schwartz discovered, the slug releases more of the neurotransmitter *serotonin* into certain neurons. These cells' synapses then become more efficient at transmitting signals. Experience and learning can increase—even double—the number of synapses, even in slugs (Kandel, 2012).

APLYSIA The California sea slug, which neuroscientist Eric Kandel studied for 45 years, has increased our understanding of the neural basis of learning and memory.

In experiments with people, rapidly stimulating certain memory-circuit connections has increased their sensitivity for hours or even weeks to come. The sending neuron now needs less prompting to release its neurotransmitter, and more connections exist between neurons. This increased efficiency of potential neural firing, called **long-term potentiation (LTP),** provides a neural basis for learning and remembering associations (Lynch, 2002; Whitlock et al., 2006) (**FIGURE 8.10**). Several lines of evidence confirm that LTP is a physical basis for memory:

- Drugs that block LTP interfere with learning (Lynch & Staubli, 1991).

- Drugs that mimic what happens during learning increase LTP (Harward et al., 2016).

- Rats given a drug that enhanced LTP learned a maze with half the usual number of mistakes (Service, 1994).

After LTP has occurred, passing an electric current through the brain won't disrupt old memories. But the current will wipe out very recent memories. Such is the experience both of laboratory animals and of severely depressed people given *electroconvulsive therapy* (ECT). A blow to the head can do the same. Football players and boxers momentarily knocked unconscious typically have no memory of events just before the knockout (Yarnell & Lynch, 1970). Their working memory had no time to consolidate the information into long-term memory before the lights went out.

Recently, I [DM] did a little test of memory consolidation. While on an operating table for a basketball-related tendon repair, I was given a face mask and soon could smell the anesthesia gas. "So how much longer will I be with you?" I asked the anesthesiologist. My last moment of memory was her answer: "About 10 seconds." My brain spent that 10 seconds consolidating a memory for her 2-second answer, but could not tuck any further memory away before I was out cold.

Some memory-biology explorers have helped found companies that are competing to develop memory-altering drugs. The target market for memory-boosting drugs includes millions of people with memory-destroying Alzheimer's disease, millions more with *mild cognitive impairment* that often becomes Alzheimer's, and countless millions who would love to turn back the clock on age-related memory decline. Meanwhile, students already have one safe and free memory enhancer: effective study techniques followed by adequate *sleep!*

Some of us may wish for memory-*blocking* drugs that, when taken after a traumatic experience, might blunt intrusive memories (Adler, 2012; Kearns et al., 2012). In one experiment, victims of car accidents, rapes, and other traumas received, for 10 days following their horrific event, either one such drug, propranolol, or a placebo. When tested three months later, half the placebo group but none of the drug-treated group showed signs of stress (Pitman & Delahanty, 2005; Pitman et al., 2002).

FIGURE 8.11 summarizes the brain's two-track memory processing and storage system for implicit (automatic) and explicit (effortful) memories. *The bottom line:* Learn something and you change your brain a little.

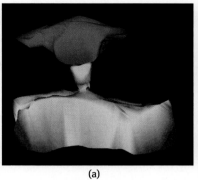
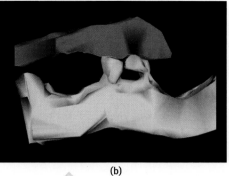

(a)   (b)

FIGURE 8.10

DOUBLED RECEPTOR SITES An electron microscope image (a) shows just one receptor site (gray) reaching toward a sending neuron before long-term potentiation. Image (b) shows that, after LTP, the receptor sites have doubled. This means the receiving neuron has increased sensitivity for detecting the presence of the neurotransmitter molecules that may be released by the sending neuron (Toni et al., 1999).

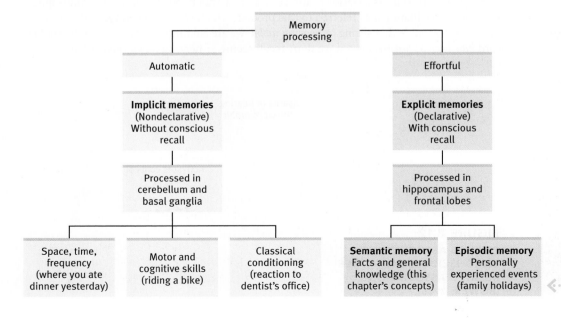
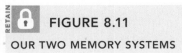

FIGURE 8.11 OUR TWO MEMORY SYSTEMS

priming the activation, often unconsciously, of particular associations in memory.

encoding specificity principle the idea that cues and contexts specific to a particular memory will be most effective in helping us recall it.

mood-congruent memory the tendency to recall experiences that are consistent with one's current good or bad mood.

"Memory is not like a container that gradually fills up; it is more like a tree growing hooks onto which memories are hung." —Peter Russell, *The Brain Book*, 1979

📺 **LaunchPad** For an 8-minute synopsis of how we access what's stored in our brain, see the **Video: Memory Retrieval.**

MEMORY RETRIEVAL

After the magic of brain encoding and storage, we still have the daunting task of retrieving the information. What triggers retrieval?

Retrieval Cues

LOQ 8-14 How do external cues, internal emotions, and order of appearance influence memory retrieval?

Imagine a spider suspended in the middle of her web, held up by the many strands extending outward from her in all directions to different points. If you were to trace a pathway to the spider, you would first need to locate an anchor point and then follow the strand down into the web.

The process of retrieving a memory follows a similar principle, because memories are held in storage by a web of associations, each piece of information interconnected with others. When you encode into memory a target piece of information, such as the name of the person sitting next to you in class, you associate with it other bits of information about your surroundings, mood, seating position, and so on. These bits can serve as *retrieval cues* that you can later use to access the information. The more retrieval cues you have, the better your chances of finding a route to the suspended memory. To remember to do something (say, to write a note tomorrow), one effective strategy is to mentally associate the act with a cue (perhaps a pen left in the middle of your desk) (Rogers & Milkman, 2016).

The best retrieval cues come from associations we form at the time we encode a memory—smells, tastes, and sights that can evoke our memory of the associated person or event. To call up visual cues when trying to recall something, we may mentally place ourselves in the original context. After losing his sight, British scholar John Hull (1990, p. 174) described his difficulty recalling such details:

> I knew I had been somewhere, and had done particular things with certain people, but where? I could not put the conversations . . . into a context. There was no background, no features against which to identify the place. Normally, the memories of people you have spoken to during the day are stored in frames which include the background.

PRIMING Often our associations are activated without our awareness. Philosopher-psychologist William James referred to this process, which we call **priming**, as the "wakening of associations." After seeing or hearing *rabbit,* we are later more likely to spell the spoken word *hair/hare* as *h-a-r-e,* even if we don't recall seeing or hearing *rabbit* (**FIGURE 8.12**).

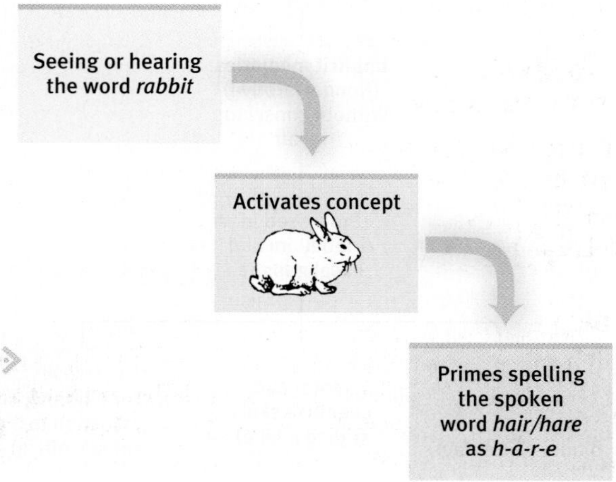

Seeing or hearing the word *rabbit*

Activates concept

Primes spelling the spoken word *hair/hare* as *h-a-r-e*

FIGURE 8.12
PRIMING ASSOCIATIONS UNCONSCIOUSLY ACTIVATES RELATED ASSOCIATIONS (BOWER, 1986).

Priming is often "memoryless memory"—an implicit, invisible memory, without your conscious awareness. If you see a poster of a missing child, you may then unconsciously be primed to interpret an ambiguous adult-child interaction as a possible kidnapping (James, 1986). Although you no longer have the poster in mind, it predisposes your interpretation.

Priming can influence behaviors as well (Herring et al., 2013). Adults and children primed with money-related words and materials were less likely to help another person when asked (Gasiorowska et al., 2016; Vohs et al., 2006). In such cases, money may prime our materialism and self-interest rather than the social norms that encourage us to help (Ariely, 2009).

CONTEXT-DEPENDENT MEMORY Have you noticed? Putting yourself back in the context where you earlier experienced something can prime your memory retrieval. Remembering, in many ways, depends on our environment (Palmer, 1989). When you visit your childhood home or neighborhood, old memories surface. When scuba divers listened to a word list in two different settings (either 10 feet underwater or sitting on the beach), they recalled more words when later tested in the same place where they first heard the list (Godden & Baddeley, 1975).

ENGAGE By contrast, experiencing something outside the usual setting can be confusing. Have you ever run into a former teacher in an unusual place, such as at the store or park? Perhaps you felt a glimmer of recognition, but struggled to realize who it was and how you were acquainted. The **encoding specificity principle** helps us understand how cues *specific* to an event or person will most effectively trigger that memory. In new settings, you may not have the memory cues needed for speedy face recognition. Our memories are *context-dependent,* and are affected by the cues we have associated with that context.

In several experiments, Carolyn Rovee-Collier (1993) found that a familiar context could activate memories even in 3-month-olds. After infants learned that kicking would make a crib mobile move (via a connecting ribbon from their ankle), the infants kicked more when tested again in the same crib than when in a different context.

STATE-DEPENDENT MEMORY Closely related to context-dependent memory is *state-dependent memory.* What we learn in one state—be it drunk or sober—may be more easily recalled when we are again in that state. What people learn when drunk they don't recall well in any state (alcohol disrupts memory storage). But they recall it slightly better when again drunk. Someone who hides money when drunk may forget the location until drunk again.

Our mood states provide an example of memory's state dependence. Emotions that accompany good or bad events become retrieval cues (Gaddy & Ingram, 2014). Thus, our memories are somewhat **mood congruent.** If you've had a bad evening—your plans with friends fell through, your favorite jeans have disappeared, your internet went out 10 minutes before the end of the show—your gloomy mood may facilitate recalling other bad times. Being depressed sours memories by priming negative associations, which we then use to explain our current mood. In many experiments, people put in a buoyant mood—whether under hypnosis or just by the day's events (a World Cup soccer victory for German participants in one study)—recall the world through rose-colored glasses (DeSteno et al., 2000; Forgas et al., 1984; Schwarz et al., 1987). They recall their behaviors as competent and effective, other people benevolent, happy events more frequent.

ENGAGE Have you ever noticed that your mood influences your perceptions of family members? In one study, adolescents' ratings of parental warmth in one week gave little clue to how they would rate their parents six weeks later (Bornstein et al., 1991). When teens were down, their parents seemed cruel; as their mood brightened, their parents morphed from devils into angels. We may nod our heads knowingly. Yet, in a good or bad mood, we persist in attributing to reality our own changing judgments, memories, and interpretations. In a bad mood, we may read someone's look as a glare and feel even worse. In a good mood, we may encode the same look as interest and feel even better. Moods magnify.

Mood effects on retrieval help explain why our moods persist. When happy, we recall happy events and therefore see the world as a happy place, which helps prolong our good mood. When depressed, we recall sad events, which darkens our interpretations of current events. For those of us predisposed to depression, this process can help maintain a vicious, dark cycle.

"I can't remember what we're arguing about, either. Let's keep yelling, and maybe it will come back to us."

"When a feeling was there, they felt as if it would never go; when it was gone, they felt as if it had never been; when it returned, they felt as if it had never gone." —George MacDonald, *What's Mine's Mine,* 1886

ENGAGE

What sort of mood have you been in lately? How has your mood colored your memories, perceptions, and expectations?

FIGURE 8.13

THE SERIAL POSITION EFFECT Immediately after Pope Francis made his way through this receiving line of special guests, he would probably have recalled the names of the last few people best *(recency effect)*. But later he may have been able to recall the first few people best *(primacy effect)*.

Vincenzo Pinto/AFP/Getty Images

Graph: Percentage of words recalled (y-axis, 0 to 90%) vs. Position of word in list (x-axis, 1 to 12)

Immediate recall: last items best (recency effect)

Later recall: only first items recalled well (primacy effect)

serial position effect our tendency to recall best the last *(recency effect)* and first *(primacy effect)* items in a list.

SERIAL POSITION EFFECT Another memory-retrieval quirk, the **serial position effect,** explains why we may have large holes in our memory of a list of recent events. Imagine it's your first day in a new job, and your manager is introducing co-workers. As you meet each person, you silently repeat everyone's name, starting from the beginning. As the last person smiles and turns away, you feel confident you'll be able to greet your new co-workers by name the next day.

Don't count on it. Because you have spent more time rehearsing the earlier names than the later ones, those are the names you'll probably recall more easily the next day. In experiments, when people viewed a list of items (words, names, dates, even experienced odors or tastes) and immediately tried to recall them in any order, they fell prey to the serial position effect (Daniel & Katz, 2017; Reed, 2000). They briefly recalled the last items especially quickly and well (a *recency effect*), perhaps because those last items were still in working memory. But after a delay, when their attention was elsewhere, their recall was best for the first items (a *primacy effect;* see **FIGURE 8.13**).

LaunchPad For a simulated experiment showing the probability of recalling a specific item from a list, engage online with **Concept Practice: The Serial Position Effect.**

🔒 RETRIEVE IT • • •

ANSWERS IN APPENDIX E

RI-5 What is *priming*?

RI-6 When we are tested immediately after viewing a list of words, we tend to recall the first and last items best, which is known as the _____ _____ effect.

🔒 REVIEW   STORING AND RETRIEVING MEMORIES

⟶ Learning Objectives

TEST YOURSELF Answer these repeated Learning Objective Questions on your own (before checking the answers in Appendix D) to improve your retention of the concepts (McDaniel et al., 2009, 2015).

8-9 What is the capacity of long-term memory? Are our long-term memories processed and stored in specific locations?

8-10 What roles do the frontal lobes and hippocampus play in memory processing?

8-11 What roles do the cerebellum and basal ganglia play in memory processing?

8-12 How do emotions affect our memory processing?

8-13 How do changes at the synapse level affect our memory processing?

8-14 How do external cues, internal emotions, and order of appearance influence memory retrieval?

⟿ Terms and Concepts to Remember

TEST YOURSELF Write down the definition yourself, then check your answer on the referenced page.

semantic memory, **p. 276**

episodic memory, **p. 276**

hippocampus, **p. 276**

memory consolidation, **p. 276**

flashbulb memory, **p. 278**

long-term potentiation (LTP), **p. 278**

priming, **p. 280**

encoding specificity principle, **p. 280**

mood-congruent memory, **p. 280**

serial position effect, **p. 282**

⟿ Experience the Testing Effect

TEST YOURSELF Answer the following questions on your own first, then check your answers in Appendix E.

1. The hippocampus seems to function as a
   a. temporary processing site for explicit memories.
   b. temporary processing site for implicit memories.
   c. permanent storage area for emotion-based memories.
   d. permanent storage area for iconic and echoic memories.

2. Hippocampus damage typically leaves people unable to learn new facts or recall recent events. However, they may be able to learn new skills, such as riding a bicycle, which is an _____ (explicit/implicit) memory.

3. Long-term potentiation (LTP) refers to
   a. emotion-triggered hormonal changes.
   b. the role of the hippocampus in processing explicit memories.
   c. an increase in a cell's firing potential.
   d. aging people's potential for learning.

4. Specific odors, visual images, emotions, or other associations that help us access a memory are examples of _____ _____.

5. When you feel sad, why might it help to look at pictures that reawaken some of your best memories?

6. When tested immediately after viewing a list of words, people tend to recall the first and last items more readily than those in the middle. When retested after a delay, they are most likely to recall
   a. the first items on the list.
   b. the first and last items on the list.
   c. a few items at random.
   d. the last items on the list.

Continue testing yourself with 📖 **LearningCurve** or 📖 **Achieve Read & Practice** to learn and remember most effectively.

⟿ Forgetting, Memory Construction, and Improving Memory

FORGETTING

LOQ 8-15   Why do we forget?

Amid all the applause for memory—all the efforts to understand it, all the books on how to improve it—have any voices been heard in praise of forgetting? William James (1890, p. 680) was such a voice: "If we remembered everything, we should on most occasions be as ill off as if we remembered nothing." To discard the clutter of useless or out-of-date information—where we parked the car yesterday, our old phone number, restaurant orders already cooked and served—is surely a blessing (Nørby, 2015). The Russian journalist and memory whiz Solomon Shereshevsky, who had merely to listen while other reporters

"Oh, is that today?"

THE WOMAN WHO CAN'T FORGET
Jill Price remembers every day of her life since age 14 in incredible detail, including both the joys and the hurts. Researchers have identified enlarged brain areas in people with super memory (Ally et al., 2013; LePort et al., 2012).

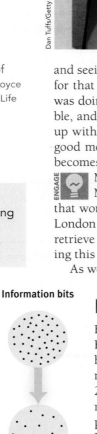

Dan Tuffs/Getty Images

"Amnesia seeps into the crevices of our brains, and amnesia heals." —Joyce Carol Oates, "Words Fail, Memory Blurs, Life Wins," 2001

FIGURE 8.14

WHEN DO WE FORGET? Forgetting can occur at any memory stage. When we process information, we filter, alter, or lose much of it.

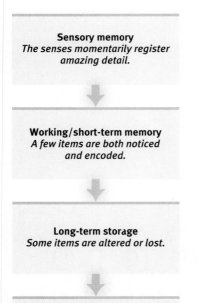

Sensory memory
The senses momentarily register amazing detail.

Working/short-term memory
A few items are both noticed and encoded.

Long-term storage
Some items are altered or lost.

Retrieval from long-term memory
Depending on interference, retrieval cues, moods, and motives, some things get retrieved, some don't.

Information bits

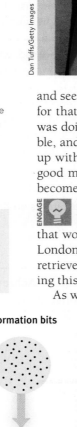

scribbled notes, was haunted by his junk heap of memories (Luria, 1968). They dominated his consciousness. He had difficulty thinking abstractly—generalizing, organizing, evaluating. After reading a story, he could recite it but would struggle to summarize its gist.

A more recent case of a life overtaken by memory is Jill Price, whose experience has been studied by a University of California at Irvine research team, along with several dozen other cases of "highly superior autobiographical memory" (McGaugh & LePort, 2014; Parker et al., 2006). Price compares her memory to "a running movie that never stops. It's like a split screen. I'll be talking to someone and seeing something else. . . . Whenever I see a date flash on the television (or anywhere for that matter) I automatically go back to that day and remember where I was, what I was doing, what day it fell on, and on and on and on and on. It is nonstop, uncontrollable, and totally exhausting." Jill, and others like her, are prone to having their minds fill up with information that, once it enters memory storage, never leaves (Patihis, 2016). A good memory is helpful, but so is the ability to forget. If a memory-enhancing pill ever becomes available, it had better not be *too* effective.

More often, however, our unpredictable memory dismays and frustrates us. Memories are quirky. My [DM's] own memory can easily call up such episodes as that wonderful first kiss with the woman I love, or trivial facts like the air mileage from London to Detroit. Then it abandons me when I discover I have failed to encode, store, or retrieve a student's name, or where I left my sunglasses. See how you do with remembering this sentence when we ask you about it later: *The fish attacked the swimmer.*

As we process information, we sift, change, or lose most of it (**FIGURE 8.14**).

Forgetting and the Two-Track Mind

For some, memory loss is severe and permanent. Consider Henry Molaison (or H. M., as he was known until his 2008 death). Surgeons removed much of his hippocampus in order to stop persistent seizures. This resulted "in severe disconnection of the remaining hippocampus" from the rest of the brain (Annese et al., 2014). For his remaining 55 years, Molaison was unable to form new conscious memories. He was, as before his surgery, intelligent and did daily crossword puzzles. Yet, reported neuroscientist Suzanne Corkin (2005, 2013), "I've known H. M. since 1962, and he still doesn't know who I am." For about 20 seconds during a conversation he could keep something in mind. When distracted, he would lose what was just said or what had just occurred. Without the neural tissue for turning new information into long-term memories, he never could name the current president of the United States (Ogden, 2012).

Molaison suffered from **anterograde amnesia**—he could recall his past, but he could not form new memories. (Those who cannot recall their past—the old information stored in long-term memory—suffer from **retrograde amnesia**.)

Neurologist Oliver Sacks (1985, pp. 26–27) described another patient, Jimmie, who had anterograde amnesia resulting from brain damage. Jimmie had no memories—thus, no sense of elapsed time—beyond his injury in 1945.

When Jimmie gave his age as 19, Sacks set a mirror before him: "Look in the mirror and tell me what you see. Is that a 19-year-old looking out from the mirror?"

Jimmie turned ashen, gripped the chair, cursed, then became frantic: "What's going on? What's happened to me? Is this a nightmare? Am I crazy? Is this a joke?"

When his attention was diverted to some children playing baseball, his panic ended, the dreadful mirror forgotten.

Sacks showed Jimmie a photo from *National Geographic.* "What is this?" he asked.

"It's the Moon," Jimmie replied.

"No, it's not," Sacks answered. "It's a picture of the Earth taken from the Moon."

"Doc, you're kidding! Someone would've had to get a camera up there!"

"Naturally."

"Hell! You're joking—how the hell would you do that?" Jimmie's wonder was that of a bright young man from the 1940s, amazed by his travel back to the future.

Careful testing of these unique people reveals something even stranger: Although incapable of recalling new facts or anything they have done recently, Molaison, Jimmie, and others with similar conditions can learn nonverbal tasks. Shown hard-to-find figures in pictures (in the *Where's Waldo?* series), they can quickly spot them again later. They can find their way to the bathroom, though without being able to tell you where it is. They can learn to read mirror-image writing or do a jigsaw puzzle, and they have even learned complicated *procedural* job skills (Schacter, 1992, 1996; Xu & Corkin, 2001). They can be classically conditioned. However, *they do all these things with no awareness of having learned them.* "Well, this is strange," Molaison said, after demonstrating his nondeclarative memory of skillful mirror tracing. "I thought that would be difficult. But it seems as though I've done it quite well" (Shapin, 2013).

Molaison and Jimmie lost their ability to form new explicit memories, but their automatic processing ability remained intact. Like Alzheimer's patients, whose *explicit* memories for new people and events are lost, they could form new *implicit* memories (Lustig & Buckner, 2004). These patients can learn *how* to do something, but they will have no conscious recall of learning their new skill. Such sad case studies confirm that we have two distinct memory systems, controlled by different parts of the brain.

For most of us, forgetting is a less drastic process. Let's consider some of the reasons we forget.

Encoding Failure

Much of what we sense we never notice, and what we fail to encode, we will never remember (**FIGURE 8.15**). English novelist and critic C. S. Lewis (1967, p. 107) described the enormity of what we never encode:

> [We are] bombarded every second by sensations, emotions, thoughts . . . nine-tenths of which [we] must simply ignore. The past [is] a roaring cataract of billions upon billions of such moments: Any one of them too complex to grasp in its entirety, and the aggregate beyond all imagination. . . . At every tick of the clock, in every inhabited part of the world, an unimaginable richness and variety of "history" falls off the world into total oblivion.

Age can affect encoding efficiency. The brain areas that jump into action when young adults encode new information are less responsive in older adults. This slower encoding helps explain age-related memory decline (Grady et al., 1995).

But no matter how young we are, we selectively attend to few of the myriad sights and sounds continually bombarding us. Consider: You have surely seen the Apple computer logo thousands of times. Can you draw it? In one study, only 1 of 85 UCLA students (including 52 Apple users) could do so accurately (Blake et al., 2015). Without encoding effort, many potential memories never form.

"Waiter, I'd like to order, unless I've eaten, in which case bring me the check."

anterograde amnesia an inability to form new memories.

retrograde amnesia an inability to retrieve information from one's past.

LaunchPad For a helpful tutorial animation about this type of research method, see the **Video: Case Studies.**

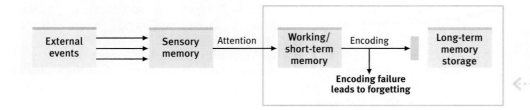

| External events | → | Sensory memory | Attention → | Working/ short-term memory | Encoding → | | Long-term memory storage |

Encoding failure leads to forgetting

FIGURE 8.15

FORGETTING AS ENCODING FAILURE We cannot remember what we have not encoded.

FIGURE 8.16

EBBINGHAUS' FORGETTING CURVE
After learning lists of nonsense syllables, such as *YOX* and *JIH*, Ebbinghaus studied how much he retained up to 30 days later. He found that memory for novel information fades quickly, then levels off. (Data from Ebbinghaus, 1885.)

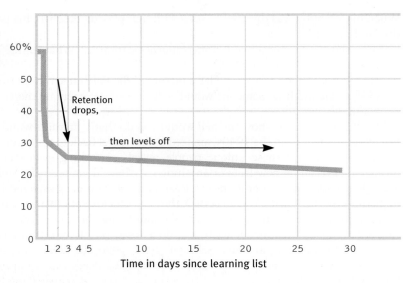

FIGURE 8.17

THE FORGETTING CURVE FOR SPANISH LEARNED IN SCHOOL
Compared with people just completing a Spanish course, those 3 years out of the course remembered much less (on a vocabulary recognition test). Compared with the 3-year group, however, those who studied Spanish even longer ago did not forget much more. (Data from Bahrick, 1984.)

Storage Decay

Even after encoding something well, we sometimes later forget it. To study the durability of stored memories, Ebbinghaus (1885) learned more lists of nonsense syllables and measured how much he retained when relearning each list, from 20 minutes to 30 days later. The result, confirmed by later experiments, was his famous forgetting curve: *The course of forgetting is initially rapid, then levels off with time* (**FIGURE 8.16**; Wixted & Ebbesen, 1991). Harry Bahrick (1984) found a similar forgetting curve for Spanish vocabulary learned in school. Compared with those just completing a high school or college Spanish course, people 3 years out of school had forgotten much of what they had learned (**FIGURE 8.17**). However, what people remembered then, they still remembered 25 and more years later. Their forgetting had leveled off.

One explanation for these forgetting curves is a gradual fading of the physical memory trace. Cognitive neuroscientists are getting closer to solving the mystery of the physical storage of memory and are increasing our understanding of how memory storage could decay. Like books you can't find in your campus library, memories may be inaccessible for many reasons. Some were never acquired (not encoded). Others were discarded (stored memories decay). And others are out of reach because we can't retrieve them.

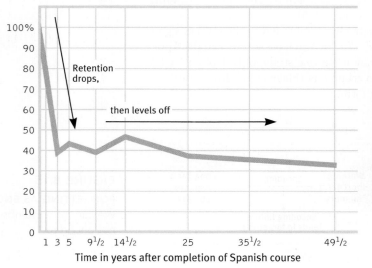

Retrieval Failure

Often, forgetting is not memories faded, but memories unretrieved. We store in long-term memory what's important to us or what we've rehearsed. But sometimes important events defy our attempts to access them (**FIGURE 8.18**). How frustrating when a name lies poised on the tip of our tongue, just beyond reach. Given retrieval cues (*"It begins with an M"*), we may easily retrieve the elusive memory. Retrieval problems contribute to the occasional memory failures of older adults, who more frequently are frustrated by tip-of-the-tongue forgetting (Abrams, 2008; Salthouse & Mandell, 2013).

Deaf persons fluent in sign language experience a parallel "tip of the fingers" phenomenon (Thompson et al., 2005).

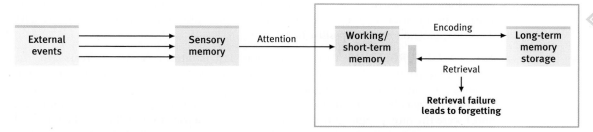

FIGURE 8.18

RETRIEVAL FAILURE Sometimes even stored information cannot be accessed, which leads to forgetting.

Do you recall the gist of the sentence about the attacked swimmer that we asked you to remember? If not, does the word *shark* serve as a retrieval cue? Experiments show that *shark* (likely what you visualized) more readily retrieves the image you stored than does the sentence's actual word, *fish* (Anderson et al., 1976). (The sentence was *The fish attacked the swimmer.*)

Retrieval problems occasionally stem from interference and even from motivated forgetting.

INTERFERENCE As you collect more and more information, your mental attic never fills, but it does get cluttered. Your brain tries to keep things tidy: Using a new password weakens your memory of competing old passwords (Wimber et al., 2015). But sometimes the clutter wins, and new and old learning collide. **Proactive** *(forward-acting)* **interference** occurs when prior learning disrupts your recall of new information. If you buy a new combination lock, your well-rehearsed old combination may interfere with your retrieval of the new one.

Retroactive *(backward-acting)* **interference** occurs when new learning disrupts recall of old information. If someone sings new lyrics to the tune of an old song, you may have trouble remembering the original words. It is rather like a second stone tossed in a pond, disrupting the waves rippling out from the first.

Information presented in the hour before sleep suffers less retroactive interference because the opportunity for interfering events is minimized (Mercer, 2015). Researchers John Jenkins and Karl Dallenbach (1924) first discovered this in a now-classic experiment. Day after day, two people each learned some nonsense syllables, then tried to recall them after up to eight hours of being awake or asleep at night. As **FIGURE 8.19** shows,

proactive interference the forward-acting disruptive effect of older learning on the recall of *new* information.

retroactive interference the backward-acting disruptive effect of newer learning on the recall of *old* information.

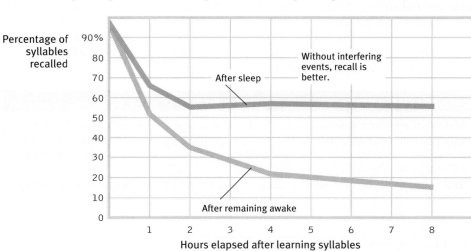

Percentage of syllables recalled

Without interfering events, recall is better.

After sleep

After remaining awake

Hours elapsed after learning syllables

FIGURE 8.19

RETROACTIVE INTERFERENCE More forgetting occurred when a person stayed awake and experienced other new material. (Data from Jenkins & Dallenbach, 1924.)

📖 **LaunchPad** To experience a demonstration and explanation of interference effects on memory, visit **Topic Tutorial: PsychSim6, Forgetting.**

Peter Johansky/Photolibrary/Getty Images

forgetting occurred more rapidly after being awake and involved with other activities. The investigators surmised that "forgetting is not so much a matter of the decay of old impressions and associations as it is a matter of interference, inhibition, or obliteration of the old by the new" (1924, p. 612).

The hour before sleep is a good time to commit information to memory (Scullin & McDaniel, 2010), though information presented in the *seconds* just before sleep is seldom remembered (Wyatt & Bootzin, 1994). If you're considering learning *while* sleeping, forget it. We have little memory for information played aloud in the room during sleep, although the ears do register it (Wood et al., 1992).

Old and new learning do not always compete with each other, of course. Previously learned information (Latin) often facilitates our learning of new information (French). This phenomenon is called *positive transfer.*

MOTIVATED FORGETTING To remember our past is often to revise it. Years ago, the huge cookie jar in my [DM's] kitchen was jammed with freshly baked chocolate chip cookies. Still more were cooling across racks on the counter. Twenty-four hours later, not a crumb was left. Who had taken them? During that time, my wife, three children, and I were the only people in the house. So while memories were still fresh, I conducted a little memory test. Andy admitted wolfing down as many as 20. Peter thought he had eaten 15. Laura guessed she had stuffed her then-6-year-old body with 15 cookies. My wife, Carol, recalled eating 6, and I remembered consuming 15 and taking 18 more to the office. We sheepishly accepted responsibility for 89 cookies. Still, we had not come close; there had been 160.

Why do our memories fail us? This happens in part because memory is an "unreliable, self-serving historian" (Tavris & Aronson, 2007, p. 6). Consider one study, in which researchers told some participants about the benefits of frequent toothbrushing. Those individuals then recalled (more than others did) having frequently brushed their teeth in the preceding two weeks (Ross et al., 1981).

So why were my family and I so far off in our estimates of the cookies we had eaten? Was it an *encoding* problem? (Did we just not notice what we had eaten?) Was it a storage problem? (Might our memories of cookies, like Ebbinghaus' memory of nonsense syllables, have melted away almost as fast as the cookies themselves?) Or was the information still intact but not *retrievable* because it would be embarrassing to remember?[2]

Sigmund Freud might have argued that our memory systems self-censored this information. He proposed that we **repress** painful or unacceptable memories to protect our self-concept and to minimize anxiety. But the repressed memory lingers, he believed, and can be retrieved by some later cue or during therapy. Repression was central to Freud's psychoanalytic theory and remains a popular idea. Indeed, an American study revealed that 81 percent of university students, and 60 to 90 percent of therapists (depending on their perspective), believe "traumatic memories are often repressed" (Patihis et al., 2014a,b). However, most memory researchers think repression rarely, if ever, occurs. People succeed in forgetting unwanted neutral information (yesterday's parking place), but it's harder to forget emotional events (Payne & Corrigan, 2007). Trauma releases stress hormones that cause people to pay attention and remember a threat (Quaedflieg & Schwabe, 2017). Thus, we may have intrusive memories of the very same traumatic experiences we would most like to forget.

🔒 **RETRIEVE IT** • • •　　　　　　　　　　　　*ANSWERS IN APPENDIX E*

RI-1 What are three ways we forget, and how does each of these happen?

RI-2 You will experience less _____ (proactive/retroactive) interference if you learn new material in the hour before sleep than you will if you learn it before turning to another subject.

RI-3 Freud believed that we _____ unacceptable memories to minimize anxiety.

---

2. One of my cookie-scarfing sons, on reading this in his father's textbook years later, confessed he had fibbed "a little."

Stringer/European Pressphoto Agency/Lages/PORTUGAL/Newscom

MEMORY CONSTRUCTION ERRORS

LOQ 8-16 How do misinformation, imagination, and source amnesia influence our memory construction? How do we decide whether a memory is real or false?

Nearly two-thirds of Americans agree: "Human memory works like a video camera, accurately recording the events we see and hear so that we can review and inspect them later" (Simons & Chabris, 2011). Actually, memory is not so precise. Even people with exceptional memories, such as Feng Wang and Jill Price, sometimes make mistakes (Johnson, 2017; Patihis et al., 2013). Like scientists who infer a dinosaur's appearance from its remains, we infer our past from stored information plus what we later imagined, expected, saw, and heard. We don't just retrieve memories, we reweave them. Our memories are like Wikipedia pages, capable of constant revision. When we "replay" a memory, we often replace the original with a slightly modified version, rather like what happens in the telephone game, as a whispered message gets progressively altered when passed from person to person (Hardt et al., 2010). Memory researchers call this **reconsolidation.** So, in a sense, said Joseph LeDoux (2009), "your memory is only as good as your last memory. The fewer times you use it, the more pristine it is." This means that, to some degree, "all memory is false" (Bernstein & Loftus, 2009b).

Despite knowing all this, I [DM] recently rewrote my own past. It happened at an international conference, where memory researcher Elizabeth Loftus (2012) was demonstrating how memory works. Loftus showed us a handful of individual faces that we were to identify later, as if in a police lineup. Then she showed us some pairs of faces, one face we had seen earlier and one we had not, and asked us to identify the one we had seen. But one pair she had slipped in included *two* new faces, one of which was rather *like* a face we had seen earlier. Most of us understandably but wrongly identified this face as one we had previously seen. To climax the demonstration, she showed us the originally seen face and the previously chosen wrong face, and asked us to choose the original face we had seen. Most of us picked the wrong face! As a result of our memory reconsolidation, we—an audience of psychologists who should have known better—had replaced the original memory with a false memory.

Clinical researchers have experimented with memory reconsolidation. People recalled a traumatic or negative experience and then had the reconsolidation of that memory disrupted, with a drug or brief, painless electroconvulsive shock (Kroes et al., 2014; Lonergan et al., 2013; Treanor et al., 2017). Someday it might become possible to erase your memory of a specific traumatic experience—by reactivating your memory and then disrupting its storage in this way. Would you wish for this? If brutally assaulted, would you welcome having your memory of the attack and its associated fears deleted?

DO PEOPLE VIVIDLY REMEMBER—OR REPRESS—TRAUMATIC EXPERIENCES?

Imagine yourself several hours into Flight AT236 From Toronto to Lisbon. A fractured fuel line begins leaking. Soon the engines go silent and primary electrical power is lost. In the eerie silence, the pilots instruct you and the other terrified passengers to don life jackets, and, when hearing the countdown to ocean impact, to assume a brace position. After minutes of descent the pilot declares above the passengers' screams and prayers, "About to go into the water." Death awaits.

But no! "We have a runway! We have a runway! Brace! Brace! Brace!" The plane makes a hard landing at an Azores airbase, averting death for you and the 305 other passengers and crew.

Among the passengers thinking "I'm going to die" was psychologist Margaret Mckinnon. Seizing the opportunity, she tracked down 15 of her fellow passengers to test their trauma memories. Did they repress the experience? To the contrary, all exhibited vivid, detailed memories. With trauma comes not repression, but, far more often, "robust" memory (Mckinnon et al., 2015).

repression in psychoanalytic theory, the basic defense mechanism that banishes from consciousness anxiety-arousing thoughts, feelings, and memories.

reconsolidation a process in which previously stored memories, when retrieved, are potentially altered before being stored again.

Misinformation and Imagination Effects

In more than 200 experiments involving more than 20,000 people, Loftus has shown how eyewitnesses reconstruct their memories after a crime or accident. In one important study, two groups of people watched a film clip of a traffic accident and then answered questions about what they had seen (Loftus & Palmer, 1974). Those asked, "About how fast were the cars going when they *smashed* into each other?" gave higher speed estimates than those asked, "About how fast were the cars going when they *hit* each other?" A week later, when asked whether they recalled seeing any broken glass, people who had heard *smashed* were more than twice as likely to report seeing glass fragments (**FIGURE 8.20**). In fact, the film showed no broken glass.

FIGURE 8.20

MEMORY CONSTRUCTION In this experiment, people viewed a film clip of a car accident. Those who later were asked a leading question recalled a more serious accident than they had witnessed (Loftus & Palmer, 1974).

Leading question:
"About how fast were the cars going when they smashed into each other?"

Image of actual accident   **Memory construction**

"Memory is insubstantial. Things keep replacing it. Your batch of snapshots will both fix and ruin your memory. . . . You can't remember anything from your trip except the wretched collection of snapshots." —Annie Dillard, "To Fashion a Text," 1988

In many follow-up experiments around the world, others have witnessed an event, received or not received misleading information about it, and then taken a memory test. The repeated result is a **misinformation effect:** People may misremember when exposed to subtly misleading information, despite feeling confident (Loftus et al., 1992). Across studies, about half of people show some vulnerability to the misinformation effect (Brewin & Andrews, 2017; Scoboria et al., 2017). A yield sign becomes a stop sign, hammers become screwdrivers, Coke cans become peanut cans, breakfast cereal becomes eggs, and a clean-shaven man morphs into a man with a mustache.

So powerful is the misinformation effect that it can influence later attitudes and behaviors (Bernstein & Loftus, 2009a). One experiment falsely suggested to some Dutch university students that, as children, they became ill after eating spoiled egg salad (Geraerts et al., 2008). After absorbing that suggestion, they were less likely to eat egg-salad sandwiches, both immediately and four months later.

Even repeatedly *imagining* nonexistent actions and events can create false memories. In one study, Canadian university students were asked to recall two events from their past. One event actually happened; the other was a false event that involved committing a crime, such as assaulting someone with a weapon. Initially, none of the lawful students remembered breaking the law. But after repeated interviewing, 70 percent reported a detailed false memory of having committed the crime (Shaw & Porter, 2015). Telling lies can likewise change people's memory for the truth; fibbing feeds false memories (Otgaar & Baker, 2018).

Digitally altered photos have also produced this *imagination inflation*. In experiments, researchers have altered photos from a family album to show some family members

WAS ALEXANDER HAMILTON A U.S. PRESIDENT? Sometimes our mind tricks us into misremembering dates, places, and names. This often happens because we misuse familiar information. In one study, many people mistakenly recalled Alexander Hamilton—the subject of a popular Broadway musical whose face also appears on the U.S. $10 bill—as a U.S. president (Roediger & DeSoto, 2016).

Evan Agostini/Invision/AP Photos

"LYIN' BRIAN"? OR A VICTIM OF FALSE MEMORY? In 2015, *NBC Nightly News* anchor Brian Williams recounted a story about traveling in a military helicopter that was hit with a rocket-propelled grenade. But the event never happened as he described. The public branded him a liar, leading his bosses to fire him. Several memory researchers, including psychologist Christopher Chabris, had a different opinion: "I think a lot of people don't appreciate the extent to which false memories can happen even when we are extremely confident in the memory" (2015).

taking a hot-air balloon ride. After viewing these photos (rather than photos showing just the balloon), children reported more false memories and indicated high confidence in those memories. When interviewed several days later, they reported even richer details of their false memories (Strange et al., 2008; Wade et al., 2002).

In British and Canadian university surveys, nearly one-fourth of students have reported autobiographical memories that they later realized were not accurate (Foley, 2015; Mazzoni et al., 2010). I [DM] empathize. For decades, my cherished earliest memory was of my parents getting off the bus and walking to our house, bringing my baby brother home from the hospital. When, in middle age, I shared that memory with my father, he assured me they did *not* bring their newborn home on the Seattle Transit System. The human mind, it seems, comes with built-in Photoshopping software. The moral: Don't believe everything you remember.

Source Amnesia

What is the frailest part of a memory? Its source. We may recognize someone but have no idea where we have seen the person. We may remember learning something on social media but be uncertain whether it was real or false news. We may dream an event and later be unsure whether it really happened. We may tell a friend some gossip, only to learn we got the news from the friend. Famed child psychologist Jean Piaget was startled as an adult to learn that a vivid, detailed memory from his childhood—a nursemaid's thwarting his kidnapping—was utterly false. He apparently constructed the memory from repeatedly hearing the story (which his nursemaid, after undergoing a religious conversion, later confessed had never happened). In attributing his "memory" to his own experiences, rather than to his nursemaid's stories, Piaget exhibited **source amnesia** (also called *source misattribution*). Misattribution is at the heart of many false memories. Authors, songwriters, and stand-up comedians sometimes suffer from it. They think an idea came from their own creative imagination, when in fact they are unintentionally plagiarizing something they earlier read or heard.

Even preschoolers experience source amnesia. In one study, preschoolers interacted with "Mr. Science," who engaged them in activities such as blowing up a balloon with baking soda and vinegar (Poole & Lindsay, 1995, 2001). Three months later, on three successive days, their parents read them a story describing some things the children had experienced with Mr. Science and some they had not. When a new interviewer asked what Mr. Science had done with them—"Did Mr. Science have a machine with ropes to pull?"—4 in 10 children spontaneously recalled him doing things that had happened only in the story.

Source amnesia also helps explain **déjà vu** (French for "already seen"). Two-thirds of us have experienced this fleeting, eerie sense that "I've been in this exact situation before." The key to déjà vu seems to be familiarity with a stimulus without a clear idea of where we encountered it before (Brown & Marsh, 2009; Cleary, 2008). Normally, we experience a feeling of *familiarity* (thanks to temporal lobe processing) before we consciously remember details (thanks to hippocampus and frontal lobe processing). When these functions

"It isn't so astonishing, the number of things I can remember, as the number of things I can remember that aren't so." —Author Mark Twain, 1835–1910

misinformation effect occurs when misleading information has corrupted one's memory of an event.

source amnesia faulty memory for how, when, or where information was learned or imagined. (Also called *source misattribution*.) Source amnesia, along with the misinformation effect, is at the heart of many false memories.

déjà vu that eerie sense that "I've experienced this before." Cues from the current situation may unconsciously trigger retrieval of an earlier experience.

"Do you ever get that strange feeling of vujà dé? Not déjà vu; vujà dé. It's the distinct sense that, somehow, something just happened that has never happened before. Nothing seems familiar. And then suddenly the feeling is gone. Vujà dé."
—Comedian George Carlin, in *Funny Times*, December 2001

(and brain regions) are out of sync, we may experience a feeling of familiarity without conscious recall. Our amazing brains try to make sense of such an improbable situation, and we get an eerie feeling that we're reliving some earlier part of our life. Our source amnesia forces us to do our best to make sense of an odd moment.

Discerning True and False Memories

Since memory is reconstruction as well as reproduction, we can't be sure whether a memory is real by how real it feels. Much as perceptual illusions may seem like real perceptions, unreal memories *feel* like real memories. Because the misinformation effect and source amnesia happen outside our awareness, it is hard to separate false memories from real ones (Schooler et al., 1986). Perhaps you can recall describing a childhood experience to a friend and filling in memory gaps with reasonable guesses and assumptions. We all do it, and after more retellings, those guessed details—now absorbed into our memories—may feel as real as if you had actually experienced them (Roediger et al., 1993). False memories, like fake diamonds, seem so real.

False memories can be persistent. Imagine that we were to read aloud a list of words such as *candy, sugar, honey,* and *taste*. Later, we ask you to recognize the presented words from a larger list. If you are at all like the people tested by Henry Roediger and Kathleen McDermott (1995), you would err three out of four times—by falsely remembering a nonpresented similar word, such as *sweet*. We more easily remember the gist than the words themselves.

False memories are socially contagious. When we hear others falsely remember events, we tend to make the same memory mistakes (Roediger et al., 2001). Your Facebook friend may misremember a shy classmate acting rude, leading you to also mistakenly remember the classmate negatively. It's easy to see how false news, whether it comes from bloggers, social media, or politicians, can spread and become false memories.

Memory construction also helps explain why some people have been sent to prison for crimes they never committed. Of 351 people who were later proven not guilty by DNA testing, 70 percent had been convicted because of faulty eyewitness identification (Innocence Project, 2015; Smalarz & Wells, 2015). It explains why "hypnotically refreshed" memories of crimes so easily incorporate errors, some of which originate with the hypnotist's leading questions (*Did you hear loud noises?*). It explains why dating partners who fell in love have *over*estimated their first impressions of one another (*It was love at first sight*), while those who broke up *under*estimated their earlier liking (*We never really clicked*) (McFarland & Ross, 1987). And it explains why people asked how they felt 10 years ago about marijuana or gender issues recalled attitudes closer to their current views than to the views they had actually reported a decade earlier (Markus, 1986). People tend to recall having always felt as they feel today (Mazzoni & Vannucci, 2007). As George Vaillant (1977, p. 197) noted after following adult lives through time, "It is all too common for caterpillars to become butterflies and then to maintain that in their youth they had been little butterflies. Maturation makes liars of us all." Memory construction errors also seem to be at work in many "recovered" memories of childhood abuse. See Thinking Critically About: Can Memories of Childhood Sexual Abuse Be Repressed and Then Recovered?

ASK YOURSELF

Think of a memory you frequently recall. How might you have changed it without conscious awareness?

LaunchPad To participate in a simulated experiment on false memory formation, and to review related research, visit **Topic Tutorial: PsychSim6, Can You Trust Your Memory?**

Children's Eyewitness Recall

LOQ 8-18   How reliable are young children's eyewitness descriptions?

If memories can be sincere, yet sincerely wrong, how can jurors decide cases in which children's memories of sexual abuse are the only evidence? "It would be truly awful to ever lose sight of the enormity of child abuse," observed Stephen Ceci (1993). Yet Ceci and Maggie Bruck's (1993, 1995) studies of children's memories have made them aware of how easily children's memories can be molded. For example, they asked 3-year-olds to show on anatomically correct dolls where a pediatrician had touched them. Of the children who had not received genital examinations, 55 percent pointed to either genital or anal areas.

In other experiments, the researchers studied the effect of suggestive interviewing techniques (Bruck & Ceci, 1999, 2004). In one study, children chose a card from a deck of possible happenings, and an adult then read the card to them. For example, "Think real hard, and tell me if this ever happened to you. Can you remember going to the

THINKING CRITICALLY ABOUT:

Can Memories of Childhood Sexual Abuse Be Repressed and Then Recovered?

LOQ 8-17   Why have reports of repressed and recovered memories been so hotly debated?

Two Possible Tragedies:

1. People doubt childhood sexual abuse survivors who tell their secret.

2. Innocent people are falsely accused, as therapists prompt "recovered" memories of childhood sexual abuse:

"Victims of sexual abuse often have your symptoms. So maybe you were abused and *repressed* the memory. Let's see if I can help you recover the memory, by digging back and visualizing your trauma."

Well-intentioned therapist

Misinformation effect and **source amnesia:** Adult client may form image of threatening person.

With *rehearsal* (repeated therapy sessions), the image grows more vivid.

Client is stunned, angry, and ready to confront or sue the remembered abuser.

Accused person is equally stunned and vigorously denies the long-ago accusation.

Professional organizations (including the American Medical, American Psychological, and American Psychiatric Associations) are working to find sensible common ground to resolve psychology's "memory war": [1]

• **Childhood sexual abuse happens** and can leave its victims at risk for problems ranging from sexual dysfunction to depression.[2] But there is no "survivor syndrome"—no group of symptoms that lets us spot victims of sexual abuse.[3]

• **Injustice happens.** Innocent people have been falsely convicted. And guilty people have avoided punishment by casting doubt on their truth-telling accusers.

• **Forgetting happens.** Children abused when very young may not have understood the meaning of their experience or remember it. Forgetting long-ago good and bad events is an ordinary part of everyday life.

• **Recovered memories are common.** Cued by a remark or an experience, we may recover pleasant or unpleasant memories of long-forgotten events. But does the unconscious mind *forcibly*

repress painful experiences, and can these experiences be *recovered* by therapist-aided techniques?[4] Memories that surface naturally are more likely to be true.[5]

• **Memories of events before age 4 are unreliable.** *Infantile amnesia* results from not yet developed brain pathways. Most psychologists therefore doubt "recovered" memories of abuse during infancy.[6] The older a child was when suffering sexual abuse, and the more severe the abuse, the more likely it is to be remembered.[7]

• **Memories "recovered" under hypnosis are especially unreliable.**

• **Memories, whether real or false, can be emotionally upsetting.** What was born of mere suggestion can become, like an actual event, a stinging memory that drives bodily stress.[8]

Psychologists question whether *repression* ever occurs. (See Chapter 13 for more on this concept—the cornerstone of Freud's theory and of so much popular psychology.)

Traumatic experiences (witnessing a loved one's murder, being terrorized by a hijacker or rapist, losing everything in a natural disaster) → **TYPICALLY LEAD TO** → **vivid, persistent, haunting memories**[9]

The Royal College of Psychiatrists Working Group on Reported Recovered Memories of Child Sexual Abuse advised that "when memories are 'recovered' after long periods of amnesia, particularly when extraordinary means were used to secure the recovery of memory, there is a high probability that the memories are false."[10]

1. Patihis et al., 2014a.   2. Freyd et al., 2007.   3. Kendall-Tackett et al., 1993.   4. McNally & Geraerts, 2009.   5. Geraerts et al., 2007.
6. Gore-Felton et al., 2000; Knapp & VandeCreek, 2000.   7. Goodman et al., 2003. 8. McNally, 2003, 2007. 9. Porter & Peace, 2007. 10. Brandon et al., 1998.

Darren Matthews/Alamy

LaunchPad Consider how researchers have studied these issues by engaging online with **Immersive Learning: How Would You Know If People's Memories Are Accurate?**

Like children (whose frontal lobes have not fully matured), older adults—especially those whose frontal lobe functioning has declined—are more susceptible than young adults to false memories. This makes older adults more vulnerable to scams, as when a repair person overcharges by falsely claiming, "I told you it would cost x, and you agreed to pay" (Jacoby et al., 2005; Jacoby & Rhodes, 2006; Roediger & Geraci, 2007; Roediger & McDaniel, 2007).

hospital with a mousetrap on your finger?" In interviews, the same adult repeatedly asked children to think about several real and fictitious events. After 10 weeks of this, a new adult asked the same question. The stunning result: 58 percent of preschoolers produced false (often vivid) stories regarding one or more events they had never experienced (Ceci et al., 1994). Here's one:

> My brother Colin was trying to get Blowtorch [an action figure] from me, and I wouldn't let him take it from me, so he pushed me into the wood pile where the mousetrap was. And then my finger got caught in it. And then we went to the hospital, and my mommy, daddy, and Colin drove me there, to the hospital in our van, because it was far away. And the doctor put a bandage on this finger.

Given such detailed stories, professional psychologists who specialize in interviewing children could not reliably separate the real memories from the false ones. Nor could the children themselves. The above child, reminded that his parents had told him several times that the mousetrap incident never happened—that he had imagined it—protested, "But it really did happen. I remember it!" Unfortunately, this type of error is common. In one analysis of eyewitness data from over 20,000 participants, children regularly identified innocent suspects as guilty (Fitzgerald & Price, 2015). "[The] research," said Ceci (1993), "leads me to worry about the possibility of false allegations. It is not a tribute to one's scientific integrity to walk down the middle of the road if the data are more to one side."

Children can, however, be accurate eyewitnesses. When questioned about their experiences in neutral words they understand, children often accurately recall what happened and who did it (Brewin & Andrews, 2017; Goodman, 2006). When interviewers have used less suggestive, more effective techniques, even 4- to 5-year-old children have produced more accurate recall (Holliday & Albon, 2004; Pipe et al., 2004). Children are especially accurate when they haven't talked with involved adults prior to the interview and when their disclosure was made in a first interview with a neutral person who asked nonleading questions.

🔒 RETRIEVE IT • • •   *ANSWERS IN APPENDIX E*

RI-4 What—given the commonness of source amnesia—might life be like if we remembered all our waking experiences and all our dreams?

RI-5 Imagine being a jury member in a trial for a parent accused of sexual abuse based on a recovered memory. What insights from memory research should you share with the rest of the jury?

IMPROVING MEMORY

LOQ 8-19 How can you use memory research findings to do better in this and other courses?

Biology's findings benefit medicine. Botany's findings benefit agriculture. So, too, can memory researchers' findings benefit education. Here, for easy reference, is a summary of some research-based suggestions that can help you remember information when you need it. The SQ3R—*Survey, Question, Read, Retrieve, Review*—study technique used in this book incorporates several of these strategies:

Rehearse repeatedly. To master material, remember the *spacing effect* and use *distributed (spaced) practice.* To learn a concept, give yourself many separate study sessions. Take advantage of life's little intervals—riding a bus, walking across campus, waiting for class to start. New memories are weak; exercise them and they will strengthen. To memorize specific facts or figures, research has shown that you should "rehearse the name or number you are trying to memorize, wait a few seconds, rehearse again, wait a little longer, rehearse again, then wait longer still and rehearse yet again. The waits should be as long as possible without losing the information" (Landauer, 2001). Reading complex material with minimal rehearsal yields little retention. Producing information—saying, writing, or typing it—beats silently reading it (a phenomenon called the *production effect*) (MacLeod & Bodner, 2017). Rehearsal and critical reflection help even more. As the *testing effect* has shown, it pays to study actively. Taking lecture notes by hand, which requires summarizing material in your own words, leads to better retention than does verbatim laptop note taking. "The pen is mightier than the keyboard," note researchers Pam Mueller and Daniel Oppenheimer (2014).

Make the material meaningful. You can build a network of retrieval cues by taking notes in your own words, and then increase these cues by forming as many associations as possible. Apply the concepts to your own life. Form images. Understand and organize information. Relate the material to what you already know or have experienced. As William James (1890) suggested, "Knit each new thing on to some acquisition already there." Mindlessly repeating someone else's words without taking the time to really understand what they mean won't supply many retrieval cues. On an exam, you may find yourself stuck when a question uses phrasing different from the words you memorized.

Activate retrieval cues. Remember the importance of *context-dependent* and *state-dependent memory*. Mentally re-create the situation and the mood in which your original learning occurred. Jog your memory by allowing one thought to cue the next.

Use mnemonic devices. Make up a story that incorporates *vivid images* of the items. *Chunk* information into acronyms. Create rhythmic rhymes (such as "*i* before *e*, except after *c*").

Minimize proactive and retroactive interference. Study before sleep. Do not schedule back-to-back study times for topics that are likely to interfere with each other, such as Spanish and French.

Sleep more. During sleep, the brain reorganizes and *consolidates* information for long-term memory. Sleep deprivation disrupts this process (Frenda et al., 2014; Lo et al., 2016). Even 10 minutes of waking rest enhances memory of what we have read (Dewar et al., 2012). So, after a period of hard study, you might just sit or lie down for a few minutes before tackling the next subject.

Test your own knowledge, both to rehearse it and to find out what you don't yet know. The testing effect is real, and it is powerful. Don't be lulled into overconfidence by your ability to *recognize* information. Test your *recall* using the periodic Retrieve It items and the numbered Learning Objective and Experience the Testing Effect questions in the Review sections. Outline sections using a blank page. Define the terms and concepts listed at each section's end before turning back to their definitions. Take practice tests; the online resources that accompany many textbooks, including this one, are a good source for such tests.

THINKING AND MEMORY Actively thinking as we read, by rehearsing and relating ideas, and by making the material personally meaningful, yields the best retention.

Laptop distraction? In one study of university introductory psychology students, the average student spent one-third of the class hour browsing online. More time spent online predicted poorer exam performance, even after controlling for aptitude and expressed interest (Ravizza et al., 2017).

ENGAGE (ASK YOURSELF)

Which three of these study and memory strategies will be most important for you to employ to improve your own learning and retention?

ENGAGE 🔗 **LaunchPad** Evaluate your own memory skills by engaging online with **Immersive Learning: Assess Your Strengths—How Might You Improve Your Memory?**

🔒 **RETRIEVE IT • • •**   *ANSWERS IN APPENDIX E*

RI-6 Which memory strategies can help you study smarter and retain more information?

🔒 **REVIEW** FORGETTING, MEMORY CONSTRUCTION, AND IMPROVING MEMORY

Learning Objectives

TEST YOURSELF Answer these repeated Learning Objective Questions on your own (before checking the answers in Appendix D) to improve your retention of the concepts (McDaniel et al., 2009, 2015).

8-15 Why do we forget?

8-16 How do misinformation, imagination, and source amnesia influence our memory construction? How do we decide whether a memory is real or false?

8-17 Why have reports of repressed and recovered memories been so hotly debated?

8-18 How reliable are young children's eyewitness descriptions?

8-19 How can you use memory research findings to do better in this and other courses?

⟨⟩ Terms and Concepts to Remember

TEST YOURSELF Write down the definition yourself, then check your answer on the referenced page.

anterograde amnesia, **p. 285**

retrograde amnesia, **p. 285**

proactive interference, **p. 287**

retroactive interference, **p. 287**

repression, **p. 289**

reconsolidation, **p. 289**

misinformation effect, **p. 291**

source amnesia, **p. 291**

déjà vu, **p. 291**

⟨⟩ Experience the Testing Effect

TEST YOURSELF Answer the following questions on your own first, then check your answers in Appendix E.

1. When forgetting is due to encoding failure, information has not been transferred from
   a. the environment into sensory memory.
   b. sensory memory into long-term memory.
   c. long-term memory into short-term memory.
   d. short-term memory into long-term memory.

2. Ebbinghaus' "forgetting curve" shows that after an initial decline, memory for novel information tends to
   a. increase slightly.
   b. decrease slightly.
   c. decrease greatly.
   d. level off.

3. The hour before sleep is a good time to memorize information, because going to sleep after learning new material minimizes _____ interference.

4. Freud proposed that painful or unacceptable memories are blocked from consciousness through a mechanism called _____.

5. One reason false memories form is our tendency to fill in memory gaps with our reasonable guesses and assumptions, sometimes based on misleading information. This tendency is an example of
   a. proactive interference.
   b. the misinformation effect.
   c. retroactive interference.
   d. the forgetting curve.

6. Eliza's family loves to tell the story of how she "stole the show" as a 2-year-old, dancing at her aunt's wedding reception. Even though she was so young, Eliza says she can recall the event clearly. How is this possible?

7. We may recognize a face at a social gathering but be unable to remember how we know that person. This is an example of _____ _____.

8. When a situation triggers the feeling that "I've been here before," you are experiencing _____ _____.

9. Children can be accurate eyewitnesses if
   a. interviewers give the children hints about what really happened.
   b. a neutral person asks nonleading questions soon after the event.
   c. the children have a chance to talk with involved adults before the interview.
   d. interviewers use precise technical and medical terms.

10. Psychologists involved in the study of memories of abuse tend to *disagree* with each other about which of the following statements?
    a. Memories of events that happened before age 4 are not reliable.
    b. We tend to repress extremely upsetting memories.
    c. Memories can be emotionally upsetting.
    d. Sexual abuse happens.

Continue testing yourself with ⟨⟩ **LearningCurve** or ⟨⟩ **Achieve Read & Practice** to learn and remember most effectively.

Thinking, Language, and Intelligence

Thomas Barwick/Getty Images

Throughout history, we humans have both celebrated our wisdom and bemoaned our foolishness. The poet T. S. Eliot was struck by "the hollow men . . . Headpiece filled with straw." But Shakespeare's Hamlet extolled the human species as "noble in reason! . . . infinite in faculties! . . . in apprehension how like a god!" Throughout this text, we likewise marvel at both our abilities and our errors.

We study the human brain—three pounds of wet tissue the size of a small cabbage, yet containing staggeringly complex circuitry. We appreciate the amazing abilities of newborns. We marvel at our visual system, which converts physical stimuli into nerve impulses, distributes them for parallel processing, and reassembles them into colorful perceptions. We ponder our memory's enormous capacity, and the ease with which our two-track mind processes information, with and without our awareness. Little wonder that our species has had the collective genius to invent the camera, the car, and the computer; to unlock the atom and crack the genetic code; to travel out to space and into our brain's depths.

Yet we also see that in some other ways we are less than noble in reason. Our species is kin to the other animals, influenced by the same principles that produce learning in rats and pigeons. We note that we not-so-wise humans are easily deceived by perceptual illusions, pseudopsychic claims, and false memories.

In this chapter, we encounter further instances of these two aspects of the human condition—the rational and the irrational. We will consider thinking and how we use—and sometimes ignore or misuse—information about the world around us. We will look at our gift for language and why and how it develops. We will consider a century's research on intelligence—what it is and how (and why) we measure it. And we will reflect on how deserving we are of our species name, *Homo sapiens*—wise human. ▶

⟶ Thinking

CONCEPTS

LEARNING OBJECTIVE QUESTION (LOQ)

9-1   What is *cognition*, and what are the functions of concepts?

Psychologists who study **cognition** focus on the mental activities associated with thinking, knowing, remembering, and communicating information. One of these activities is forming **concepts**—mental groupings of similar objects, events, ideas, or people. The concept *chair* includes many items—a baby's high chair, a reclining chair, a dentist's chair—all for sitting. Concepts simplify our thinking. Imagine life without them. We could not ask a child to "throw the ball" because there would be no concept of *throw* or *ball*. Instead of saying, "They were angry," we would have to describe expressions, intensities, and words. Concepts such as *ball* and *anger* give us much information with little cognitive effort.

We often form our concepts by developing a **prototype**—a mental image or best example of a category (Rosch, 1978). People more quickly agree that "a crow is a bird" than that "a penguin is a bird." For most of us, the crow is the birdier bird; it more closely resembles our *bird* prototype. Similarly, for people in modern multiethnic Germany, Caucasian Germans are more prototypically German (Kessler et al., 2010). When something closely matches our prototype of a concept—such as *bird* or *German*—we more readily recognize it as an example of the concept.

When we categorize people, we mentally shift them toward our category prototypes. Such was the experience of Belgian students who viewed ethnically blended faces. When viewing a blended face in which 70 percent of the features were Caucasian and 30 percent were Asian, the students categorized the face as Caucasian (**FIGURE 9.1**). Later, as their memory shifted toward the Caucasian prototype, they were more likely to remember an 80 percent Caucasian face than the 70 percent Caucasian face they had actually seen (Corneille et al., 2004). Likewise, if shown a 70 percent Asian face, they later remembered a more prototypically Asian face. So, too, with gender: People who viewed 70 percent male faces categorized them as male (no surprise there) and then later misremembered them as even more prototypically male (Huart et al., 2005).

Move away from our prototypes, and category boundaries may blur. Is a tomato a fruit? Is a 16-year-old female a girl or a woman? Is a whale a fish or a mammal? Because a whale fails to match our *mammal* prototype, we are slower to recognize it as a mammal. Similarly, when symptoms don't fit one of our disease prototypes, we are slow to perceive an illness (Bishop, 1991). People whose heart attack symptoms (shortness of breath, exhaustion, a dull

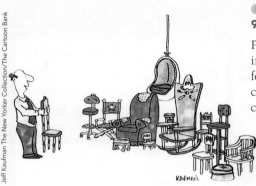

"Attention, everyone! I'd like to introduce the newest member of our family."

FIGURE 9.1

CATEGORIZING FACES INFLUENCES RECOLLECTION
Shown a face that was 70 percent Caucasian, people tended to classify the person as Caucasian and to recollect the face as more Caucasian than it was. (Re-creation of experiment courtesy of Olivier Corneille.)

| 90% CA | 80% CA | 70% CA | 60% CA | 50%/50% | 60% AS | 70% AS | 80% AS | 90% AS |

weight in the chest) don't match their *heart attack* prototype (sharp chest pain) may not seek help. And when behaviors don't fit our *discrimination* prototypes—of White against Black, male against female, young against old—we often fail to notice prejudice. People more easily detect male prejudice against females than female against males or female against females (Cunningham et al., 2009; Inman & Baron, 1996). Although concepts speed and guide our thinking, they don't always make us wise.

PROBLEM SOLVING: STRATEGIES AND OBSTACLES

LOQ 9-2   What cognitive strategies assist our problem solving, and what obstacles hinder it?

One tribute to our rationality is our problem-solving skill. What's the best route around this traffic jam? How should we handle a friend's criticism? How, without our keys, can we get in the house?

Some problems we solve through *trial and error*. Thomas Edison tried thousands of light bulb filaments before stumbling upon one that worked. For other problems, we use **algorithms,** step-by-step procedures that guarantee a solution. But step-by-step algorithms can be laborious and exasperating. To find a word using the 10 letters in *SPLOYOCHYG,* for example, you could try each letter in each of the 10 positions—907,200 permutations in all. Rather than give you a computing brain the size of a beach ball, nature resorts to **heuristics,** simpler thinking strategies. Thus, you might reduce the number of options in the *SPLOYOCHYG* example by grouping letters that often appear together (*CH* and *GY*) and excluding rare letter combinations (such as YY). By using heuristics and then applying trial and error, you may hit on the answer. Have you guessed it?[1]

Sometimes we puzzle over a problem and the pieces suddenly fall together in a flash of **insight**—an abrupt, true-seeming, and often satisfying solution (Topolinski & Reber, 2010). Ten-year-old Johnny Appleton had one of these Aha! moments and solved a problem that had stumped construction workers: how to rescue a young robin from a narrow 30-inch-deep hole in a cement-block wall. Johnny's solution: Slowly pour in sand, giving the bird enough time to keep its feet on top of the constantly rising pile (Ruchlis, 1990).

Brain scans (EEGs or fMRIs) show bursts of activity associated with sudden flashes of insight (Kounios & Beeman, 2014). In one study, researchers asked people to think of a word that forms a compound word or phrase with each of three other words in a set (such as *pine, crab,* and *sauce*) and to press a button to sound a bell when they knew the answer. (Need a hint? The word is a fruit.[2]) A sudden Aha! insight led to about half the solutions. Before the Aha! moment, the problem solvers' frontal lobes (involved in focusing attention) were active. At the instant of discovery, there was a burst of activity in the right temporal lobe, just above the ear (**FIGURE 9.2**).

Insight strikes suddenly, with no prior sense of "getting warmer" or feeling close to a solution (Knoblich & Oellinger, 2006; Metcalfe, 1986). When the answer pops into mind (*apple!*), we feel a happy sense of satisfaction. The joy of a joke may similarly lie in our sudden comprehension of an unexpected ending or a double meaning: "You don't need a parachute to skydive. You only need a parachute to skydive twice." Groucho Marx was a master at this: "I once shot an elephant in my pajamas. How he got in my pajamas I'll never know."

Insightful as we are, other cognitive tendencies may lead us astray. **Confirmation bias,** for example, leads us to seek evidence *for* our ideas more

cognition   all the mental activities associated with thinking, knowing, remembering, and communicating.

concept   a mental grouping of similar objects, events, ideas, or people.

prototype   a mental image or best example of a category. Matching new items to a prototype provides a quick and easy method for sorting items into categories (as when comparing feathered creatures to a prototypical bird, such as a crow).

algorithm   a methodical, logical rule or procedure that guarantees solving a particular problem. Contrasts with the usually speedier—but also more error-prone—use of *heuristics.*

heuristic   a simple thinking strategy that often allows us to make judgments and solve problems efficiently; usually speedier but also more error-prone than an *algorithm.*

insight   a sudden realization of a problem's solution; contrasts with strategy-based solutions.

confirmation bias   a tendency to search for information that supports our preconceptions and to ignore or distort contradictory evidence.

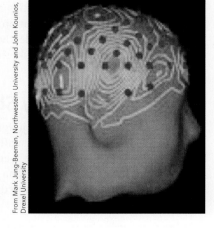

From Mark Jung-Beeman, Northwestern University and John Kounios, Drexel University

← FIGURE 9.2

THE AHA! MOMENT   A burst of right temporal lobe activity accompanied insight solutions to word problems (Jung-Beeman et al., 2004). The red dots designate EEG electrodes. The light gray lines show the distribution of high-frequency activity accompanying insight. The insight-related activity is centered in the right temporal lobe (yellow area).

---

1. Answer to SPLOYOCHYG anagram: PSYCHOLOGY.

2. The word is *apple:* pineapple, crabapple, applesauce.

eagerly than *against* them (Klayman & Ha, 1987; Skov & Sherman, 1986). In a now-classic experiment, Peter Wason (1960) gave British university students a set of three numbers *(2-4-6)* and told them the series was based on a rule. Their task was to guess the rule. (It was simple: any three ascending numbers.) Before submitting answers, students generated their own three-number sets, and Wason told them whether their sets conformed to his rule. Once *certain* they had the rule, they could announce it. The result? Most students formed a wrong idea *("Maybe it's counting by twos")* and then searched only for confirming evidence (by testing *6-8-10, 100-102-104,* and so forth). Seldom right but never in doubt.

"Ordinary people," said Wason (1981), "evade facts, become inconsistent, or systematically defend themselves against the threat of new information relevant to the issue." Thus, having formed a belief—that vaccines cause (or do not cause) autism spectrum disorder, that people can (or cannot) change their sexual orientation, that gun control fails (or does not fail) to save lives—we prefer information that supports our belief. And once we get hung up on an incorrect view of a problem, it's hard to approach it from a different angle. This obstacle to problem solving is called **fixation**, an inability to come to a fresh perspective. See if fixation prevents you from solving the matchstick problem in **FIGURE 9.3**. (For the solution, see **FIGURE 9.4**.)

A prime example of fixation is **mental set,** our tendency to approach a problem with the mindset of what has worked for us previously. Indeed, solutions that worked in the past often do work on new problems. Consider:

Given the sequence *O-T-T-F-?-?-?,* what are the final three letters?

Most people have difficulty recognizing that the three final letters are *F*(ive), *S*(ix), and *S*(even). But solving this problem may make the next one easier:

Given the sequence *J-F-M-A-?-?-?,* what are the final three letters? (If you don't get this one, ask yourself what month it is.)

As a *perceptual set* predisposes what we perceive, a mental set predisposes how we think. Sometimes this can be an obstacle to problem solving, as when our mental set from our past experiences with matchsticks predisposes us to arrange them in two dimensions.

FORMING GOOD (AND BAD) DECISIONS AND JUDGMENTS

LOQ 9-3   What is *intuition,* and how can the representativeness and availability heuristics influence our decisions and judgments?

When making each day's hundreds of judgments and decisions *(Should I take a jacket? Can I trust this person? Should I shoot the basketball or pass to the player who's hot?),* we seldom take the time and effort to reason systematically. We just follow our **intuition,** our fast, automatic, unreasoned feelings and thoughts. After interviewing policy makers in government, business, and education, social psychologist Irving Janis (1986) concluded that they "often do not use a reflective problem-solving approach. How do they usually arrive at their decisions? If you ask, they are likely to tell you . . . they do it mostly *by the seat of their pants.*"

Two Quick But Risky Shortcuts

When we need to make snap judgments, heuristics enable quick thinking without conscious awareness, and they usually serve us well (Gigerenzer, 2015). But as research by cognitive psychologists Amos Tversky and Daniel Kahneman (1974) on the *representativeness* and *availability heuristics* has shown, these intuitive mental shortcuts can lead even the smartest people into dumb decisions.[3]

FIGURE 9.3

THE MATCHSTICK PROBLEM How would you arrange six matches to form four equilateral triangles?

3. Tversky and Kahneman's joint work on decision making received a 2002 Nobel Prize; sadly, only Kahneman was alive to receive the honor. As Kahneman wrote in a vignette for my [DM's] *Social Psychology* text, "Amos and I shared the wonder of together owning a goose that could lay golden eggs—a joint mind that was better than our separate minds."

"In creating these problems, we didn't set out to fool people. All our problems fooled us, too." —Amos Tversky (1985)

"Intuitive thinking [is] fine most of the time. . . . But sometimes that habit of mind gets us in trouble." —Daniel Kahneman (2005b)

fixation in cognition, the inability to see a problem from a new perspective; an obstacle to problem solving.

mental set a tendency to approach a problem in one particular way, often a way that has been successful in the past.

intuition an effortless, immediate, automatic feeling or thought, as contrasted with explicit, conscious reasoning.

representativeness heuristic estimating the likelihood of events in terms of how well they seem to represent, or match, particular prototypes; may lead us to ignore other relevant information.

availability heuristic estimating the likelihood of events based on their availability in memory; if instances come readily to mind (perhaps because of their vividness), we presume such events are common.

THE REPRESENTATIVENESS HEURISTIC To judge the likelihood of something by intuitively comparing it to particular prototypes is to use the **representativeness heuristic**. Imagine someone who is short, slim, and likes to read poetry. Is this person more likely to be an Ivy League university English professor or a truck driver (Nisbett & Ross, 1980)?

Many people guess English professor—because the person better fits their prototype of nerdy professor than of truck driver. In doing so, they fail to consider the base rate number of Ivy League English professors (fewer than 400) and truck drivers (3.5 million in the United States alone). Thus, even if the description is 50 times more typical of English professors than of truck drivers, the fact that there are about 7000 times more truck drivers means that the poetry reader is many times more likely to be a truck driver.

Some prototypes have social consequences. Consider the reaction of some non-Arab travelers soon after 9/11, when a young male of Arab descent boarded their plane. The young man fit (represented) their "terrorist" prototype, and the representativeness heuristic kicked in. His presence evoked anxiety among his fellow passengers—even though nearly 100 percent of those who fit this prototype are peace-loving citizens.

Or consider the questions one mother of two Black and three White teens asked other parents, "Do store personnel follow your children when they are picking out their Gatorade flavors? They didn't follow my White kids. . . . When your kids trick-or-treat dressed as a ninja and a clown, do they get asked who they are with and where they live, door after door? My White kids didn't get asked. Do your kids get pulled out of the TSA line time and again for additional screening? My White kids didn't" (Roper, 2016). If people have a prototype—a stereotype—of delinquent Black teens, they may unconsciously use the representativeness heuristic when judging individuals. The result, even if unintended, is racism.

THE AVAILABILITY HEURISTIC The **availability heuristic** operates when we estimate the commonality of an event *based on its mental availability*. Anything that makes information pop into mind—its vividness, recency, or distinctiveness—can make it seem commonplace. Casinos entice us to gamble by broadcasting wins with noisy bells and flashing lights. The big losses are soundlessly invisible.

The availability heuristic can also distort our judgments of risks. Dramatic air crashes or horrific terrorist attacks capture attention and strike unwarranted fears. If people from a particular ethnic or religious group commit a terrorist act, as seen in pictures of innocent people about to be beheaded, our readily available memory of the dramatic event may shape our impression of the whole group. Terrorists aim to evoke excessive terror. If terrorists were to kill 1000 people in the United States this year, Americans would be

"Kahneman and his colleagues and students have changed the way we think about the way people think." —American Psychological Association President Sharon Brehm, 2007

AVAILABILITY HEURISTIC With scenes from terrorist attacks flooding people's minds, 27 percent of Americans recently identified terrorism as their biggest worry—up from 8 percent just before the 2015 Paris attacks—and 38 percent said terrorist threats made them less likely to attend large events (Reinhart, 2017; Reuters, 2015). This hijacking of our rationality by fears of terrorist guns and trucks (when other risks, such as driving or influenza, kill so many more) illustrates how we often fear the wrong things.

The Fear Factor

LOQ 9-4 What factors exaggerate our fear of unlikely events?

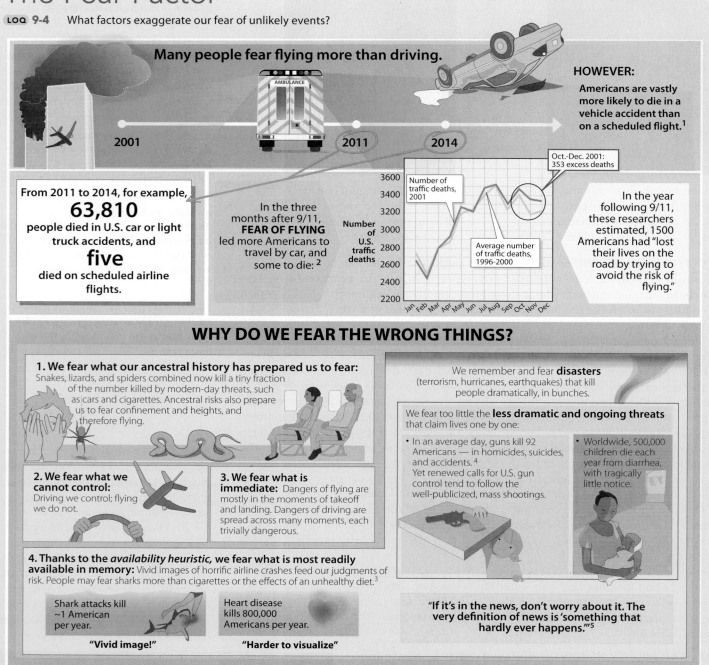

Many people fear flying more than driving.

2001   2011   2014

HOWEVER:

Americans are vastly more likely to die in a vehicle accident than on a scheduled flight.[1]

From 2011 to 2014, for example,

63,810

people died in U.S. car or light truck accidents, and

five

died on scheduled airline flights.

In the three months after 9/11, **FEAR OF FLYING** led more Americans to travel by car, and some to die:[2]

Number of U.S. traffic deaths

Number of traffic deaths, 2001

Oct.-Dec. 2001: 353 excess deaths

Average number of traffic deaths, 1996-2000

Jan Feb Mar Apr May Jun Jul Aug Sep Oct Nov Dec

In the year following 9/11, these researchers estimated, 1500 Americans had "lost their lives on the road by trying to avoid the risk of flying."

WHY DO WE FEAR THE WRONG THINGS?

1. We fear what our ancestral history has prepared us to fear: Snakes, lizards, and spiders combined now kill a tiny fraction of the number killed by modern-day threats, such as cars and cigarettes. Ancestral risks also prepare us to fear confinement and heights, and therefore flying.

2. We fear what we cannot control: Driving we control; flying we do not.

3. We fear what is immediate: Dangers of flying are mostly in the moments of takeoff and landing. Dangers of driving are spread across many moments, each trivially dangerous.

4. Thanks to the *availability heuristic,* we fear what is most readily available in memory: Vivid images of horrific airline crashes feed our judgments of risk. People may fear sharks more than cigarettes or the effects of an unhealthy diet.[3]

Shark attacks kill ~1 American per year.

"Vivid image!"

Heart disease kills 800,000 Americans per year.

"Harder to visualize"

We remember and fear **disasters** (terrorism, hurricanes, earthquakes) that kill people dramatically, in bunches.

We fear too little the **less dramatic and ongoing threats** that claim lives one by one:

- In an average day, guns kill 92 Americans — in homicides, suicides, and accidents.[4] Yet renewed calls for U.S. gun control tend to follow the well-publicized, mass shootings.

- Worldwide, 500,000 children die each year from diarrhea, with tragically little notice.

"If it's in the news, don't worry about it. The very definition of news is 'something that hardly ever happens.'"[5]

1. National Safety Council, 2017. 2. Gaissmater & Gigerenzer, 2012; Gigerenzer, 2004, 2006. 3. Daley, 2011. 4. Xu et al., 2016. 5. Schneier, 2007.

mighty afraid. Yet they would have reason to be 30 times more afraid of homicidal, suicidal, and accidental death by guns, which take more than 30,000 lives annually. In 2015 and again in 2016, feared foreign terrorists shot and killed fewer Americans than did armed toddlers (Ingraham, 2016; LaCapria, 2015). The bottom line: *We often fear the wrong things.* (See Thinking Critically About: The Fear Factor.)

"Don't believe everything you think."
—Bumper sticker

 **RETRIEVE IT** • • •   *ANSWERS IN APPENDIX E*

RI-1 Why can news be described as "something that hardly ever happens"? How does knowing this help us assess our fears?

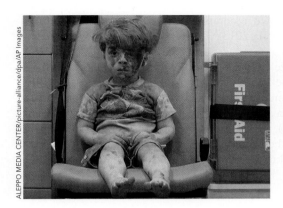

THE POWER OF A VIVID EXAMPLE
The unforgettable (cognitively available) photo of 5-year-old Omran Daqneesh—dazed after being pulled from the rubble of yet another air strike in Aleppo, Syria—did more than an armload of statistics to awaken Western nations to the plight of Syrian migrants fleeing violence.

overconfidence the tendency to be more confident than correct—to overestimate the accuracy of our beliefs and judgments.

Meanwhile, the lack of available images of future climate change disasters—which some scientists regard as "Armageddon in slow motion"—has left most people unconcerned (Pew, 2014a). What's more cognitively available than slow climate change is our recently experienced local weather, which tells us nothing about long-term planetary trends (Egan & Mullin, 2012; Kaufmann et al., 2017; Zaval et al., 2014). Unusually hot local weather increases people's worry about global climate warming, while a recent cold day reduces their concern and overwhelms less memorable scientific data (Li et al., 2011). As Stephen Colbert (November 18, 2014) tweeted, "Global warming isn't real because it was cold today! Also great news: World hunger is over because I just ate."

Over 40 nations have sought to harness the positive power of vivid, memorable images by putting eye-catching warnings and graphic photos on cigarette packages (Riordan, 2013). This campaign has worked because we reason emotionally (Huang et al., 2013). We overfeel and underthink (Slovic, 2007). In one study, Red Cross donations to Syrian refugees were 55 times greater in response to the publication of an iconic photo of a child killed, than in response to statistics describing the hundreds of thousands of other refugee deaths (Slovic et al., 2017). Dramatic outcomes make us gasp; probabilities we hardly grasp.

Overconfidence

LOQ 9-5 How are our decisions and judgments affected by overconfidence, belief perseverance, and framing?

Sometimes our judgments and decisions go awry simply because we are more confident than correct. Across various tasks, people overestimate their performance (Metcalfe, 1998). If 60 percent of people correctly answer a factual question, such as "Is absinthe a liqueur or a precious stone?" they will typically average 75 percent confidence (Fischhoff et al., 1977). (It's a licorice-flavored liqueur.) This tendency to overestimate the accuracy of our knowledge and judgments is **overconfidence.**

It is overconfidence that drives stockbrokers and investment managers to market their ability to outperform stock market averages—which, as a group, they cannot (Malkiel, 2016). A purchase of stock X, recommended by a broker who judges this to be the time to buy, is usually balanced by a sale made by someone who judges this to be the time to sell. Despite their confidence, buyer and seller cannot both be right. And it is overconfidence that so often leads us to succumb to a *planning fallacy*—overestimating our future leisure time and income (Zauberman & Lynch, 2005). Students and others often expect to finish assignments ahead of schedule (Buehler et al., 1994, 2002). In fact, such projects generally take about twice the predicted time. Anticipating how much more time we will have next month, we happily accept invitations. And believing we'll surely have more money next year, we take out loans or buy on credit.

Overconfidence—the bias that Kahneman (2015), if given a magic wand, would most like to eliminate—can also feed extreme political views. One research team tested 743 intelligence analysts' ability to predict future events—predictions that typically are overconfident. Those whose predictions most often failed tended to be inflexible and closed-minded (Mellers et al., 2015). Ordinary citizens with a shallow understanding of complex proposals, such as cap-and-trade or a flat tax, may also express strong views. Sometimes the less we know, the more definite we sound. Asking such people to explain the details

 ASK YOURSELF

What do you fear? Are some of those fears out of proportion to statistical risk? Are there other areas of your life where you need to take more precautions?

To offer a vivid depiction of climate change, Cal Tech scientists created an interactive map of global temperatures over the past 120 years. (See tinyurl. com/TempChange.)

FIGURE 9.4

SOLUTION TO THE MATCHSTICK PROBLEM To solve this problem, you must view it from a new perspective, breaking the fixation of limiting solutions to two dimensions.

Hofstadter's Law: It always takes longer than you expect, even when you take into account Hofstadter's Law.
—Douglas Hofstadter, *Gödel, Escher, Bach: The Eternal Golden Braid*, 1979

"When you know a thing, to hold that you know it; and when you do not know a thing, to allow that you do not know it; this is knowledge." —Confucius, 551–479 B.C.E., *Analects*

PREDICT YOUR OWN BEHAVIOR When will you finish reading this chapter?

belief perseverance clinging to one's initial conceptions after the basis on which they were formed has been discredited.

framing the way an issue is posed; how an issue is worded can significantly affect decisions and judgments.

nudge a framing of choices by which governments and companies can, without coercion or altered incentives, encourage people to make choices that support their health, retirement savings, and well-being.

of these policies exposes them to their own ignorance, which in turn leads them to express more moderate views (Fernbach et al., 2013). To confront one's own ignorance is to become wiser.

Nevertheless, overconfidence can have adaptive value. Believing that their decisions are right and they have time to spare, self-confident people tend to live more happily. They make tough decisions more easily, and they seem competent (Anderson et al., 2012). Given prompt and clear feedback, we can also learn to be more realistic about the accuracy of our judgments (Fischhoff, 1982). That's true of weather forecasters: Extensive feedback has enabled them to estimate their forecast accuracy ("a 60 percent chance of rain"). The wisdom to know when we know a thing and when we do not is born of experience.

Belief Perseverance

Our overconfidence is startling. Equally so is our **belief perseverance**—our tendency to cling to our beliefs in the face of contrary evidence. A classic study of belief perseverance engaged people with opposing views of capital punishment (Lord et al., 1979). After studying two supposedly new research findings, one supporting and the other refuting the claim that the death penalty deters crime, each side was more impressed by the study supporting its own beliefs. And each readily disputed the other study. Thus, showing the pro- and anti-capital-punishment groups the *same* mixed evidence actually *increased* their disagreement. Rather than using evidence to draw conclusions, they used their conclusions to assess evidence—a phenomenon also known as *motivated reasoning*. In other studies and in everyday life, people have similarly welcomed belief-supporting evidence—about climate change, same-sex marriage, or politics—while discounting challenging evidence (Friesen et al., 2015; Sunstein et al., 2016). Often, prejudice persists. Beliefs persevere.

To rein in belief perseverance, a simple remedy exists: *Consider the opposite.* When the same researchers repeated the capital-punishment study, they asked some participants to be "as *objective* and *unbiased* as possible" (Lord et al., 1984). The plea did nothing to reduce biased evaluations of evidence. They also asked another group to consider "whether you would have made the same high or low evaluations had exactly the same study produced results on the *other* side of the issue." Having imagined and pondered *opposite* findings, these people became much less biased.

Once beliefs form and get justified, it takes more compelling evidence to change them than it did to create them. Having explained to ourselves why candidate X or Y will be a better commander-in-chief, we then tend to ignore evidence undermining our belief. As an old Chinese proverb says, "Two-thirds of what we see is behind our eyes."

The Effects of Framing

Framing—the way we present an issue—can be a powerful tool of persuasion, as psychologists and economists have together learned. As a young scholar, behavioral economist Richard Thaler worked closely with cognitive psychologists Amos Tversky and Daniel Kahneman at Stanford University. Thaler and others have shown how the framing of options can influence—or as they say—**nudge** people toward beneficial decisions (Bohannon, 2016; Benartzi et al., 2017; Thaler & Sunstein, 2008).

- *Saving for retirement.* U.S. companies once required employees who wanted to contribute to a retirement plan to choose a lower take-home pay, which few people did. Thanks to a new law, they can now automatically enroll their employees in the plan but allow them to opt out. Either way, the decision to contribute is the employee's. But under the new "opt-out" arrangement, enrollments in one analysis of 3.4 million workers soared from 59 to 86 percent (Rosenberg, 2010). Britain's 2012 change to an opt-out framing similarly led to 5 million more retirement savers (Halpern, 2015).

- *Choosing to live or die.* Imagine two surgeons explaining the risk of an upcoming surgery. One explains that during this type of surgery, 10 percent of people die. The other explains that 90 percent survive. The information is the same. The effect is not. In real-life surveys, patients and physicians overwhelmingly say the risk is greater when they hear that 10 percent *die* (Marteau, 1989; McNeil et al., 1988; Rothman & Salovey, 1997).

- **Becoming an organ donor.** In many European countries as well as in the United States, people renewing their driver's license can decide whether to be organ donors. In some countries, the default option is *Yes,* but people can opt out. Nearly 100 percent of the people in opt-out countries have agreed to be donors. In countries where the default option is *No,* most do *not* agree to be donors (Hajhosseini et al., 2013; Johnson & Goldstein, 2003).

The point to remember: Framing can nudge our attitudes and decisions.

The Perils and Powers of Intuition

LOQ 9-6   How do smart thinkers use intuition?

The perils of intuition can persist even when people are offered extra pay for thinking smart, even when they are asked to justify their answers, and even among expert physicians, clinicians, and U.S. federal intelligence agents (Reyna et al., 2014; Shafir & LeBoeuf, 2002; Stanovich et al., 2013). Very smart people can make not-so-smart judgments.

So, are our heads indeed "filled with straw," as T. S. Eliot suggested? Good news: Cognitive scientists are also revealing intuition's powers:

Throughout this book you will see examples of smart intuition. In brief,

- **Intuition is recognition born of experience.** It is implicit (unconscious) knowledge— what we've recorded in our brains but can't fully explain (Chassy & Gobet, 2011; Gore & Sadler-Smith, 2011). We see this ability to size up a situation and react in an eyeblink in chess masters playing speed chess, as they intuitively know the right move (Burns, 2004). We see it in the smart and quick judgments of experienced nurses, firefighters, art critics, and car mechanics. We see it in skilled athletes who react *without thinking.* Indeed, conscious thinking may disrupt well-practiced movements, leading skilled athletes to choke under pressure, as when shooting free throws (Beilock, 2010). And we would see this instant intuition in you, too, for anything in which you have developed knowledge based on experience.

- **Intuition is usually adaptive, enabling quick reactions.** Our fast and frugal heuristics let us intuitively assume that fuzzy-looking objects are far away—which they usually are, except on foggy mornings. Our learned associations surface as gut feelings, right or wrong. Seeing a stranger who looks like someone who has harmed or threatened us in the past, we may automatically react with distrust. Newlyweds' implicit attitudes toward their new spouses likewise predict their future marital happiness (McNulty et al., 2013).

- **Intuition is huge.** Unconscious, automatic influences are constantly affecting our judgments (Custers & Aarts, 2010). Consider: Most people guess that the more complex the choice, the smarter it is to make decisions rationally rather than intuitively (Inbar et al., 2010). Actually, in making complex decisions, we sometimes benefit by letting our brain work on a problem without consciously thinking about it (Strick et al., 2010, 2011). In one series of experiments, three groups of people read complex information (for example, about apartments or soccer matches). Those in the first group stated their preference immediately after reading information about four possible options. The second group, given several minutes to analyze the information, made slightly smarter decisions. But wisest of all, in several studies, were those in the third group, whose attention was distracted for a time, enabling their minds to engage in automatic, unconscious processing of the complex information. The practical lesson: Letting a problem incubate while we attend to other things can pay dividends (Dijksterhuis & Strick, 2016). Facing a difficult decision involving lots of facts, we're wise to gather all the information we can, and then say, "Give me some time *not* to think about this, even to sleep on it." Thanks to our ever-active brain, nonconscious thinking (reasoning, problem solving, decision making, planning) can be surprisingly astute (Creswell et al., 2013; Hassin, 2013; Lin & Murray, 2015).

"The problem is I can't tell the difference between a deeply wise, intuitive nudge from the Universe and one of my own bone-headed ideas!"

Bradford Veley/CartoonStock

Critics note that some studies have not found the supposed power of unconscious thought, and they remind us that deliberate, conscious thought also furthers smart thinking (Newell, 2015; Nieuwenstein et al., 2015; Phillips et al., 2016). In challenging situations, superior decision makers, including chess players, take time to think (Moxley et al., 2012). And with many sorts of problems, deliberative thinkers are aware of the intuitive option, but know when to override it (Mata et al., 2013).

 Consider:

1. A bat and a ball together cost 110 cents. The bat costs 100 cents more than the ball. How much does the ball cost?

2. Emily's father has three daughters. The first two are named April and May. What is the third daughter's name?

Most people's intuitive responses—10 cents and June—are wrong, and a few moments of deliberate thinking reveals why.[4]

The bottom line: Our two-track mind makes sweet harmony as smart, critical thinking listens to the creative whispers of our vast unseen mind and then evaluates evidence, tests conclusions, and plans for the future.

THINKING CREATIVELY

LOQ 9-7 What is *creativity*, and what fosters it?

Creativity is the ability to produce ideas that are both novel and valuable (Hennessey & Amabile, 2010). Consider Princeton mathematician Andrew Wiles' incredible, creative moment. Pierre de Fermat, a seventeenth-century mischievous genius, had challenged mathematicians of his day to match his solutions to various number theory problems. His most famous challenge—*Fermat's last theorem*—baffled the greatest mathematical minds, even after a $2 million prize (in today's dollars) was offered in 1908 to whoever first created a proof.

Wiles had pondered Fermat's theorem for more than 30 years and had come to the brink of a solution. One morning, out of the blue, the final "incredible revelation" struck him. "It was so indescribably beautiful; it was so simple and so elegant. I couldn't understand how I'd missed it. . . . It was the most important moment of my working life" (Singh, 1997, p. 25).

Creativity like Wiles' is supported by a certain level of *aptitude* (ability to learn). Those who score exceptionally high in quantitative aptitude as 13-year-olds, for example, are later more likely to create published or patented work (Park et al., 2008; Robertson et al., 2010). Yet there is more to creativity than aptitude, or what intelligence tests reveal. Indeed, brain activity associated with intelligence differs from that associated with creativity (Jung & Haier, 2013; Shen et al., 2017) Aptitude tests (such as the SAT) require **convergent thinking**—an ability to provide a single correct answer.

Creativity tests (*How many uses can you think of for a brick?*) require expansive, **divergent thinking**—the ability to consider many different options and to think in novel ways. Injury to certain areas of the frontal lobes can leave reading, writing, and arithmetic skills intact but destroy imagination (Kolb & Whishaw, 2006).

Robert Sternberg and his colleagues believe creativity has five components (Sternberg, 1988, 2003; Sternberg & Lubart, 1991, 1992):

1. *Expertise*—well-developed knowledge—furnishes the ideas, images, and phrases we use as mental building blocks. "Chance favors only the prepared mind," observed Louis Pasteur. The more blocks we have, the more chances we have to combine them in novel ways. Wiles' well-developed knowledge put the needed theorems and methods at his disposal.

ASK YOURSELF

Can you recall a time when contradictory information challenged one of your views? Was it hard for you to consider the opposite view? Did you change your mind?

CREATIVE WOMEN Researcher Sally Reis (2001) found that notably creative women, such as Nobel laureate geneticist Barbara McClintock, were typically "intelligent, hard working, imaginative, and strong willed" as girls. In her acceptance speech for the 2013 Nobel Prize for Literature, author Alice Munro, shown here, described story writing creativity as hard work: "The part that's hardest is when you go over the story and realize how bad it is. You know, the first part, excitement, the second, pretty good, but then you pick it up one morning and you think, 'what nonsense,' and that is when you really have to get to work."

PETER MUHLY/Getty Images

---

4. The first answer is 5 cents. The bat would then cost $1.05, for a $1.10 total. If the ball cost the intuitive answer of 10 cents, the bat would then have to cost $1.10 (for a bat-and-ball total of $1.20, not $1.10). The second answer is Emily. If you answered incorrectly, don't feel bad—so do many other people (Frederick, 2005; Thomson & Oppenheimer, 2016).

2. *Imaginative thinking skills* provide the ability to see things in novel ways, to recognize patterns, and to make connections. Having mastered a problem's basic elements, we can redefine or explore it in a new way. Wiles' imaginative solution combined two partial solutions.

3. *A venturesome personality* seeks new experiences, tolerates ambiguity and risk, and perseveres in overcoming obstacles. Wiles said he labored in near-isolation from the mathematics community partly to stay focused and avoid distraction. Such determination is an enduring trait.

4. *Intrinsic motivation* is the quality of being driven more by interest, satisfaction, and challenge than by external pressures (Amabile & Hennessey, 1992). Creative people focus less on extrinsic motivators—meeting deadlines, impressing people, or making money—than on the pleasure and stimulation of the work itself. As Wiles noted, "I was so obsessed by this problem that . . . I was thinking about it all the time—[from] when I woke up in the morning to when I went to sleep at night" (Singh & Riber, 1997).

5. *A creative environment* sparks, supports, and refines creative ideas. Wiles stood on the shoulders of others and collaborated with a former student. A study of the careers of 2026 prominent scientists and inventors revealed that the most eminent were mentored, challenged, and supported by their colleagues (Simonton, 1992). Creativity-fostering environments support innovation, team building, and communication (Hülsheger et al., 2009). They also minimize anxiety and foster contemplation (Byron & Khazanchi, 2011). While on a retreat in a monastery, Jonas Salk solved a problem that led to the polio vaccine. Later, when he designed the Salk Institute, he provided contemplative spaces where scientists could work without interruption (Sternberg, 2006).

ENGAGE For those seeking to boost the creative process, research offers some ideas:

• *Develop your expertise.* Ask yourself what you care about and most enjoy. Follow your passion by broadening your knowledge base and becoming an expert at something.

• *Allow time for incubation.* Think hard on a problem, but then set it aside and come back to it later. For those with enough knowledge—the needed mental building blocks—a period of inattention to a problem ("sleeping on it") allows for automatic processing to form associations (Zhong et al., 2008).

• *Set aside time for the mind to roam freely.* Creativity springs from "defocused attention" (Simonton, 2012a,b). So detach from attention-grabbing television, social networking, and video gaming. Jog, go for a long walk, or meditate. Serenity seeds spontaneity.

• *Experience other cultures and ways of thinking.* Living abroad sometimes sets the creative juices flowing. Controlled studies show that students who have spent time abroad and embraced their host culture are more adept at working out creative solutions to problems (Lee et al., 2012; Tadmor et al., 2012). Even getting out of your neighborhood and exposing yourself to multicultural experiences fosters flexible thinking (Kim et al., 2013; Ritter et al., 2012).

For a summary of some key ideas from this section, see **TABLE 9.1.**

creativity the ability to produce new and valuable ideas.

convergent thinking narrowing the available problem solutions to determine the single best solution.

divergent thinking expanding the number of possible problem solutions; creative thinking that diverges in different directions.

A CREATIVE ENVIRONMENT

Mick Stevens The New Yorker Collection/The Cartoon Bank

IMAGINATIVE THINKING Cartoonists often display creativity as they see things in new ways or make unusual connections.

WELL, I TOLD YOU TO ADD YEAST TO YOUR SHAMPOO.

© Dave Coverly/speedbump.com

"For the love of God, is there a doctor in the house?"

Christopher Weyant The New Yorker Collection/The Cartoon Bank

TABLE 9.1

Comparing Cognitive Processes and Strategies

Process or Strategy	Description	Powers	Perils
Algorithm	Methodical rule or procedure	Guarantees solution	Requires time and effort
Heuristic	Simple thinking shortcut, such as the availability heuristic (which estimates likelihood based on how easily events come to mind)	Lets us act quickly and efficiently	Puts us at risk for errors
Insight	Sudden Aha! reaction	Provides instant realization of solution	May not happen
Confirmation bias	Tendency to search for support for our own views and ignore contradictory evidence	Lets us quickly recognize supporting evidence	Hinders recognition of contradictory evidence
Fixation	Inability to view problems from a new angle	Focuses thinking	Hinders creative problem solving
Intuition	Fast, automatic feelings and thoughts	Is based on our experience; huge and adaptive	Can lead us to overfeel and underthink
Overconfidence	Overestimating the accuracy of our beliefs and judgments	Allows us to be happy and to make decisions easily	Puts us at risk for errors
Belief perseverance	Ignoring evidence that proves our beliefs are wrong	Supports our enduring beliefs	Closes our mind to new ideas
Framing	Wording a question or statement so that it evokes a desired response	Can influence others' decisions	Can produce a misleading result
Creativity	Ability to innovate valuable ideas	Produces new insights and products	May distract from structured, routine work

RI-2 Match the process or strategy listed below (I–X) with the description (a–j).

I.   Algorithm

II. Intuition

III. Insight

IV. Heuristic

V.   Fixation

VI. Confirmation bias

VII. Overconfidence

VIII. Creativity

IX. Framing

X.   Belief perseverance

a. Inability to view problems from a new angle; focuses thinking but hinders creative problem solving

b. Methodological rule or procedure that guarantees a solution but requires time and effort

c. Your fast, automatic, effortless feelings and thoughts based on your experience; huge and adaptive but can lead you to overfeel and underthink

d. Simple thinking shortcut that enables quick and efficient decisions but puts us at risk for errors

e. Sudden Aha! reaction that instantly reveals the solution

f. Tendency to search for support for your own views and to ignore contradictory evidence

g. Holding on to your beliefs even after they are proven wrong; closing your mind to new ideas

h. Overestimating the accuracy of your beliefs and judgments; allows you to be happier and to make decisions more easily, but puts you at risk for errors

i. Wording a question or statement so that it evokes a desired response; can mislead people and influence their decisions

j. The ability to produce novel and valuable ideas

DO OTHER SPECIES SHARE OUR COGNITIVE SKILLS?

LOQ 9-8   What do we know about thinking in other species?

Other animals are surprisingly smart (de Waal, 2016). In her 1908 book, *The Animal Mind,* pioneering psychologist Margaret Floy Washburn argued that animal consciousness and intelligence can be inferred from their behavior. In 2012, neuroscientists convening at the University of Cambridge added that animal consciousness can also be inferred from their brains: "Nonhuman animals, including all mammals and birds," possess the *neural networks* "that generate consciousness" (Low et al., 2012). Consider, then, what animal brains can do.

USING CONCEPTS AND NUMBERS   By touching screens in quest of a food reward, black bears have learned to sort pictures into animal and nonanimal categories, or concepts (Vonk et al., 2012). The great apes—a group that includes chimpanzees and gorillas— also form concepts, such as *cat* and *dog*. After monkeys have learned these concepts, certain frontal lobe neurons in their brain fire in response to new "cat-like" images, others to new "dog-like" images (Freedman et al., 2001). Even pigeons—mere bird-brains—can sort objects (pictures of cars, cats, chairs, flowers) into categories. Shown a picture of a never-before-seen chair, pigeons will reliably peck a key that represents *chairs* (Wasserman, 1995).

DISPLAYING INSIGHT   Psychologist Wolfgang Köhler (1925) showed that humans are not the only creatures to display insight. He placed a piece of fruit and a long stick outside the cage of a chimpanzee named Sultan, beyond his reach. Inside the cage, Köhler placed a short stick, which Sultan grabbed, using it to try to reach the fruit. After several failed attempts, the chimpanzee dropped the stick and seemed to survey the situation. Then suddenly (as if thinking "Aha!"), Sultan jumped up and seized the short stick again. This time, he used it to pull in the longer stick—which he then used to reach the fruit. Apes have even exhibited foresight by storing a tool they could use to retrieve food the next day (Mulcahy & Call, 2006). (For one example of a chimpanzee's use of foresight, see **FIGURE 9.5a**.) And apes have displayed an ability to read others' minds—by anticipating where a human will look for an object, even if it's no longer there (Krupenye et al., 2016).

Birds, too, have displayed insight. One experiment, by (yes) Christopher Bird and Nathan Emery (2009), brought to life an Aesop fable in which a thirsty crow is unable to reach the water in a partly filled pitcher. See the crow's solution in Figure 9.5b. Other crows have fashioned wire or sticks for extracting food, such as insects in rotting logs (Rutz et al., 2016). Ravens are similarly adept at inventive tool use, and can plan hours ahead for future events (Kabadayi & Osvath, 2017).

TRANSMITTING CULTURE   Like humans, other species invent behaviors and transmit cultural patterns to their observing peers and offspring (Boesch-Achermann & Boesch, 1993). Dolphins form coalitions, cooperatively hunt, and learn tool use from one another

(a)

(b)

ANIMAL COGNITION IN ACTION
Alex, an African Grey parrot, was able to categorize and name objects (Pepperberg, 2009, 2012, 2013). Among his jaw-dropping numerical skills was the ability to comprehend numbers up to 8. He could speak the number of objects. He could add two small clusters of objects and announce the sum. He could indicate which of two numbers was greater. And he gave correct answers when shown various groups of objects. Asked, for example, "What color four?" (meaning "What's the color of the objects of which there are four?"), he could speak the answer.

FIGURE 9.5

ANIMAL TALENTS (a) One male chimpanzee in Sweden's Furuvik Zoo was observed every morning collecting stones into a neat little pile, which later in the day he used as ammunition to pelt visitors (Osvath & Karvonen, 2012). (b) Crows studied by Christopher Bird and Nathan Emery (2009) quickly learned to raise the water level in a tube and nab a floating worm by dropping in stones. Other crows have used twigs to probe for insects, and bent strips of metal to reach food.

(Bearzi & Stanford, 2010). In Shark Bay, Western Australia, one small group of dolphins learned to use marine sponges as protective nose guards when probing the sea floor for fish (Krützen et al, 2005).

Forest-dwelling chimpanzees select different tools for different purposes—a heavy stick for making holes, a light, flexible stick for fishing for termites, or a pointed stick for roasting marshmallows. (Just kidding: They don't roast marshmallows, but they have surprised us with their sophisticated tool use [Sanz et al., 2004]). Researchers have found at least 39 local customs related to chimpanzee tool use, grooming, and courtship (Claidière & Whiten, 2012; Whiten & Boesch, 2001). One group may slurp termites directly from a stick, another group may pluck them off individually. One group may break nuts with a stone hammer, while their neighbors use a wooden hammer. One chimpanzee discovered that tree moss could absorb water for drinking from a waterhole, and within six days seven other observant chimpanzees began doing the same (Hobaiter et al., 2014). These transmitted behaviors, along with differing communication and hunting styles, are the chimpanzee version of cultural diversity.

OTHER COGNITIVE SKILLS A baboon in an 80-member troop can distinguish every other member's voice (Jolly, 2007). Great apes, dolphins, and elephants recognize themselves in a mirror, demonstrating self-awareness. Elephants also display their abilities to learn, remember, discriminate smells, empathize, cooperate, teach, and spontaneously use tools (Byrne et al., 2009). Chimpanzees have shown altruism, cooperation, and group aggression. Like humans, they will purposefully kill their neighbor to gain land, and they grieve over dead relatives (Anderson et al., 2010; Biro et al., 2010; Mitani et al., 2010).

* * *

Thinking about other species' abilities brings us back to our initial question: How deserving are we of the label *Homo sapiens*—wise human? Let's pause to give our species some midterm grades. On decision making and risk assessment, our smart but error-prone species might rate a B-. On problem solving, where humans are inventive yet vulnerable to confirmation bias and fixation, we would probably receive a better mark, perhaps a B+. And on cognitive efficiency and creativity, our quick (though sometimes faulty) heuristics and divergent thinking would surely earn us an A.

🔒 REVIEW THINKING

⤵ Learning Objectives

TEST YOURSELF Answer these repeated Learning Objective Questions on your own (before checking the answers in Appendix D) to improve your retention of the concepts (McDaniel et al., 2009, 2015).

9-1 What is *cognition*, and what are the functions of concepts?

9-2 What cognitive strategies assist our problem solving, and what obstacles hinder it?

9-3 What is *intuition*, and how can the representativeness and availability heuristics influence our decisions and judgments?

9-4 What factors exaggerate our fear of unlikely events?

9-5 How are our decisions and judgments affected by overconfidence, belief perseverance, and framing?

9-6 How do smart thinkers use intuition?

9-7 What is *creativity*, and what fosters it?

9-8 What do we know about thinking in other species?

⤵ Terms and Concepts to Remember

TEST YOURSELF Write down the definition yourself, then check your answer on the referenced page.

cognition, **p. 299**

concept, **p. 299**

prototype, **p. 299**

algorithm, **p. 299**

heuristic, **p. 299**

insight, **p. 299**

confirmation bias, **p. 299**

fixation, **p. 301**

mental set, **p. 301**

intuition, **p. 301**

representativeness heuristic, **p. 301**

availability heuristic, **p. 301**

overconfidence, **p. 303**

belief perseverance, **p. 304**

framing, **p. 304**

nudge, **p. 304**

creativity, **p. 307**

convergent thinking, **p. 307**

divergent thinking, **p. 307**

⟶ Experience the Testing Effect

TEST YOURSELF Answer the following questions on your own first, then check your answers in Appendix E.

1. A mental grouping of similar things is called a _____.

2. The most systematic procedure for solving a problem is a(n) _____.

3. Oscar describes his political beliefs as "strongly liberal," but he is interested in exploring opposing viewpoints. How might he be affected by confirmation bias and belief perseverance?

4. A major obstacle to problem solving is fixation, which is a(n)
   a. tendency to base our judgments on vivid memories.
   b. tendency to wait for insight to occur.
   c. inability to view a problem from a new perspective.
   d. rule of thumb for judging the likelihood of an event in terms of our mental image of it.

5. Terrorist attacks made Americans more fearful of being victimized by terrorism than of other, greater threats. Such exaggerated fear after dramatic events illustrates the _____ heuristic.

6. When consumers respond more positively to ground beef described as "75 percent lean" than to the same product labeled "25 percent fat," they have been influenced by _____.

7. Which of the following is NOT a characteristic of a creative person?
   a. Expertise
   b. Extrinsic motivation
   c. A venturesome personality
   d. Imaginative thinking skills

8. In the early twentieth century, some psychologists noted that animal consciousness can be inferred from their behavior. In the early twenty-first century, other scientists argued that animal consciousness can be inferred from their brain's _____ _____.

Continue testing yourself with 📖 **LearningCurve** or 〰 **Achieve Read & Practice** to learn and remember most effectively.

⟶ Language and Thought

language our spoken, written, or signed words and the ways we combine them to communicate meaning.

Imagine an alien species that could pass thoughts from one head to another merely by pulsating air molecules in the space between them. Perhaps these weird creatures could inhabit a future science fiction movie? Actually, we are those creatures. When we speak, our brain and voice apparatus transmit air-pressure waves that we send banging against another's eardrum—enabling us to transfer thoughts from our brain into theirs. As cognitive psychologist Steven Pinker (1998) noted, we sometimes sit for hours "listening to other people make noise as they exhale, because those hisses and squeaks contain *information*." And thanks to all those funny sounds created from the air pressure waves we send out, we get people's attention. We get them to do things. And we maintain relationships (Guerin, 2003). Depending on how you vibrate the air, you may get a scowl or a kiss.

Language is more than vibrating air—it is our spoken, written, or signed words, and the ways we combine them to communicate meaning. When I [DM] created this paragraph, my fingers on a keyboard generated electronic binary numbers that were translated into the squiggles in front of you. When transmitted by reflected light rays into your retina, these squiggles trigger formless nerve impulses that travel to several areas of your brain, which integrate the information, compare it to stored information, and decode meaning. Thanks to language, information is moving from my mind to yours. Many animals know little more than what they sense. Thanks to language, we comprehend much that we've never seen and that our distant ancestors never knew.

Let's begin our study of language by examining some of its components.

LANGUAGE TRANSMITS KNOWLEDGE Whether spoken, written, or signed, language—the original wireless communication—enables mind-to-mind information transfer, and with it the transmission of civilization's accumulated knowledge across generations.

M. Spencer Green/AP Photo

STEVE INVALIDATES HIS WEDDING VOWS THROUGH THE CLEVER USE OF HOMOPHONES.

J.C. Duffy The New Yorker Collection/
The Cartoon Bank

"Eye dew."

LANGUAGE STRUCTURE

LOQ 9-9   What are the structural components of a language?

Consider how we might go about inventing a language. For a spoken language, we would need three building blocks:

- **Phonemes** are the smallest distinctive sound units in a language. To say *bat,* English speakers utter the phonemes *b, a,* and *t.* (Phonemes aren't the same as letters. *That* also has three phonemes—*th, a,* and *t.*) English uses about 40 phonemes; other languages use anywhere from half to more than twice that many. As a general rule, consonant phonemes carry more information than do vowel phonemes. *The treth ef thes stetement shed be evedent frem thes bref demenstretien.*

- **Morphemes** are the smallest language units that carry meaning. In English, a few morphemes are also phonemes—the article *a,* for instance. But most morphemes combine two or more phonemes. The word *readers,* for example, contains three morphemes: "read," "er" (signaling that we mean "one who reads"), and "s" (signaling that we mean not one, but multiple readers). Every word in a language contains one or more morphemes.

- **Grammar** is a language's set of rules that enable people to communicate. Grammatical rules guide us in deriving meaning from sounds (*semantics*) and ordering words into sentences (*syntax*).

Like life constructed from the genetic code's simple alphabet, language is complexity built of simplicity. In English, for example, 40 or so phonemes can be combined to form more than 100,000 morphemes, which alone or in combination produce the 600,000 variations of past and present words in the *Oxford English Dictionary.* Using those words, we can then create an infinite number of sentences, most of which (like this one) are original.

We humans have an astonishing knack for language. With remarkable efficiency, we sample tens of thousands of words in our memory, effortlessly assemble them with near-perfect syntax, and spew them out, three words a second (Vigliocco & Hartsuiker, 2002). Seldom do we form sentences in our minds before speaking them. Rather, we organize them on the fly as we speak. And while doing all this, we adapt our utterances to our social and cultural context. We also follow norms for speaking (*How far apart should we stand?*) and listening (*Is it OK to interrupt?*). Given how many ways there are to mess up, it's amazing that we master this social dance. How and when does it happen?

phoneme in a language, the smallest distinctive sound unit.

morpheme in a language, the smallest unit that carries meaning; may be a word or a part of a word (such as a prefix).

grammar in a language, a system of rules that enables us to communicate with and understand others. *Semantics* is the language's set of rules for deriving meaning from sounds, and *syntax* is its set of rules for combining words into grammatically sensible sentences.

> 🔒 **RETRIEVE IT • • •**   *ANSWERS IN APPENDIX E*
>
> **RI-1** How many morphemes are in the word *cats*? How many phonemes?

LANGUAGE ACQUISITION AND DEVELOPMENT

To Steven Pinker (1990), language is "the jewel in the crown of cognition." Without sight or hearing, you could still have friends and a job. But without language, could you have these things? If you were able to retain only one cognitive ability, make it language, suggested researcher Lera Boroditsky (2009). "Language is so fundamental to our experience, so deeply a part of being human, that it's hard to imagine life without it."

Language Acquisition: How Do We Learn Language?

LOQ 9-10   How do we acquire language, and what is *universal grammar*?

Linguist Noam Chomsky has argued language is an unlearned human trait, separate from other parts of human cognition. He theorized that a built-in predisposition to learn grammar rules, which he called *universal grammar,* helps explain why preschoolers pick up language so readily and use grammar so well. It happens so naturally—as naturally as birds learn to fly—that training hardly helps.

"The secret to our ancestors' survival was probably our use of language to develop new modes of cooperation."
—David Grinspoon, "Can Humans Outsmart Extinction?," 2016

CREATING A LANGUAGE Brought together as if on a desert island (actually a school), Nicaragua's young deaf children over time drew upon sign gestures from home to create their own Nicaraguan Sign Language, complete with words and intricate grammar. Our biological predisposition for language does not create language in a vacuum. But activated by a social context, nature and nurture work creatively together (Osborne, 1999; Sandler et al., 2005; Senghas & Coppola, 2001).

Other researchers note that children learn grammar as they discern patterns in the language they hear (Ibbotson & Tomasello, 2016). And even Chomsky agrees that we are not born with a built-in *specific* language or *specific* set of grammatical rules. The world's languages are structurally very diverse—more so than the universal grammar idea implies (Bergen, 2014). But all human languages—and there are more than 6000 of them—have nouns, verbs, and adjectives as grammatical building blocks, and order and utter words in some common ways (Blasi et al., 2016; Futrell et al., 2015). Whatever language we experience as children, whether spoken or signed, we will readily learn its specific grammar and vocabulary (Bavelier et al., 2003). And no matter what language we learn, we start speaking it mostly in nouns (*kitty, da-da*) rather than in verbs and adjectives (Bornstein et al., 2004). Biology and experience work together.

Language Development: When Do We Learn Language?

LOQ 9-11 What are the milestones in language development, and when is the critical period for acquiring language?

Make a quick guess: How many words of your native language did you learn between your first birthday and your high school graduation? Although you use only 150 words for about half of what you say, you probably learned about 60,000 words (Bloom, 2000; McMurray, 2007). That averages (after age 2) nearly 3500 words each year, or nearly 10 each day! How you did it—how those 3500 words could so far outnumber the roughly 200 words your schoolteachers consciously taught you each year—is one of the great human wonders.

Could you even now state the rules of syntax (the correct way to string words together to form sentences) for the language(s) you speak fluently? Most of us cannot. Yet before you were able to add 2 + 2, you were creating your own original sentences and applying these rules. As a preschooler, you comprehended and spoke with a facility that would put to shame college students struggling to learn a new language.

RECEPTIVE LANGUAGE Children's language development moves from simplicity to complexity. Infants start without language (*in fantis* means "not speaking"). Yet by 4 months of

A NATURAL TALENT Human infants come with a remarkable capacity to soak up language. But the particular language they learn will reflect their unique interactions with others.

age, babies can recognize differences in speech sounds (Stager & Werker, 1997). They can also read lips: We know this because in experiments, babies have preferred looking at a face that matches a sound—an *"ah"* coming from wide open lips and an *"ee"* from a mouth with corners pulled back (Kuhl & Meltzoff, 1982). Recognizing such differences marks the beginning of the development of babies' *receptive language,* their ability to understand what is said to and about them.

Infants' language comprehension greatly outpaces their language production. Even at 6 months, long before speaking, many infants recognize object names (Bergelson & Swingley, 2012, 2013). At 7 months and beyond, they grow in their power to do what adults find difficult when listening to an unfamiliar language: to segment spoken sounds into individual words.

PRODUCTIVE LANGUAGE Long after the beginnings of receptive language, babies' *productive language,* their ability to produce words, matures. Before nurture molds babies' speech, nature enables a wide range of possible sounds in the **babbling stage,** beginning around 4 months. Many of these spontaneously uttered sounds are consonant-vowel pairs formed by simply bunching the tongue in the front of the mouth (*da-da, na-na, ta-ta*) or by opening and closing the lips (*ma-ma*), both of which babies do naturally for feeding (MacNeilage & Davis, 2000). Babbling does not imitate the adult speech babies hear—it includes sounds from various languages. From this early babbling, a listener could not identify an infant as being, say, French, Korean, or Ethiopian.

By about 10 months old, infants' babbling has changed so that a trained ear can identify the household language (de Boysson-Bardies et al., 1989). Deaf infants who observe their deaf parents signing begin to babble more with their hands (Petitto & Marentette, 1991). Without exposure to other languages, babies lose their ability to do what we (believe it or not) cannot—to discriminate and produce sounds and tones outside our native language (Kuhl et al., 2014; Meltzoff et al., 2009; Pallier et al., 2001). Thus, by adulthood, those who speak only English cannot discriminate certain sounds in Japanese speech. Nor can Japanese adults with no training in English hear the difference between the English *r* and *l*. For a Japanese-speaking adult, *"la-la-ra-ra"* may sound like the same syllable repeated.

Around their first birthday, most children enter the **one-word stage.** They have already learned that sounds carry meanings, and if repeatedly trained to associate, say, *fish* with a picture of a fish, 1-year-olds will look at a fish when a researcher says, "Fish, fish! Look at the fish!" (Schafer, 2005). They begin to use sounds—usually only one barely recognizable syllable, such as *ma* or *da*—to communicate meaning. But family members learn to understand, and gradually the infant's language conforms more to the family's language. Across the world, baby's first words are often nouns that label objects or people (Tardif et al., 2008). At this one-word stage, a single inflected word (*"Doggy!"*) may communicate a sentence (*"Look at the dog out there!"*).

At about 18 months, children's word learning explodes from about a word per week to a word per day. By their second birthday, most have entered the **two-word stage** (TABLE 9.2). They start uttering two-word sentences in **telegraphic speech.** Like yesterday's telegrams that charged by the word (TERMS ACCEPTED. SEND MONEY), a 2-year-old's speech contains mostly nouns and verbs (*"Want juice"*). Also like telegrams, their speech follows rules of syntax, arranging words in a sensible order. English-speaking children typically place adjectives before nouns—*white house* rather than *house white*. Spanish reverses this order, as in *casa blanca*.

Moving out of the two-word stage, children quickly begin uttering longer phrases (Fromkin & Rodman, 1983). By early elementary school, they understand complex sentences and begin to enjoy the humor conveyed by double meanings: "You never starve in the desert because of all the sand-which-is there."

"Got idea. Talk better. Combine words. Make sentences."

DON'T MEANS DON'T—NO MATTER HOW YOU SAY IT! Deaf children of deaf-signing parents and hearing children of hearing parents have much in common. They develop language skills at about the same rate, and they are equally effective at opposing parental wishes and demanding their way.

TABLE 9.2

Summary of Language Development

Month (approximate)	Stage
4	Babbles many speech sounds ("ah-goo")
10	Babbling resembles household language ("ma-ma")
12	One-word speech ("Kitty!")
24	Two-word speech ("Get ball.")
24+	Rapid development into complete sentences

RETRIEVE IT • • •
ANSWERS IN APPENDIX E

RI-3 What is the difference between *receptive* and *productive* language, and when do children normally hit these milestones in language development?

babbling stage beginning around 4 months, the stage of speech development in which an infant spontaneously utters various sounds at first unrelated to the household language.

one-word stage the stage in speech development, from about age 1 to 2, during which a child speaks mostly in single words.

two-word stage beginning about age 2, the stage in speech development during which a child speaks mostly in two-word statements.

telegraphic speech the early speech stage in which a child speaks like a telegram—"go car"—using mostly nouns and verbs.

CRITICAL PERIODS Some children—such as those who received a cochlear implant to enable hearing, or those who are adopted by a family in another country—get a late start on learning a particular language. For these late bloomers, language development follows the same sequence, although usually at a faster pace (Ertmer et al., 2007; Snedeker et al., 2007). But there is a limit on how long language learning can be delayed. Childhood seems to represent a *critical* (or "sensitive") *period* for mastering certain aspects of language before the language-learning window closes (Hernandez & Li, 2007; Lenneberg, 1967). In one study, Korean language exposure in just the first months of life enabled Korean adoptees in the Netherlands to do what others could not—to readily learn the consonant sounds of their forgotten language (Choi et al., 2017). Some of what was forgotten was unconsciously retained.

Later-than-usual exposure—at age 2 or 3—unleashes the idle language capacity of a child's brain, producing a rush of language. But by about age 7, those who have not been exposed to either a spoken or a signed language gradually lose their ability to master *any* language. And children exposed to low-quality language—such as 4-year-olds in classrooms with 3-year-olds, or some children from impoverished homes—often display less language skill (Ansari et al., 2015; Hirsh-Pasek et al., 2015).

Thanks to the shared human ability to learn language, even Europeans and Native Australia–New Zealand populations—groups that have been geographically separated for 50,000 years—can readily learn each other's languages (Chater et al., 2009). But if we learn a new language as adults, we will usually speak it with the accent of our native language, and we will also have difficulty mastering the new grammar. In one experiment, U.S. immigrants from South Korea and China considered 276 English sentences (*"Yesterday the hunter shoots a deer"*) and decided whether they were grammatically correct or incorrect (Johnson & Newport, 1991). All had been in the United States for approximately 10 years: Some had arrived in early childhood, others as adults. As **FIGURE 9.6** reveals, those who learned their second language early learned it best. The older we are when moving to a new country, the harder it is to learn its language and to absorb its culture (Cheung et al., 2011; Hakuta et al., 2003). Cognitive psychologist Stephen Kosslyn (2008) summed it up nicely: "Children can learn multiple languages without an accent and with good grammar, if they are exposed to the language before puberty. But after puberty, it's very difficult to learn a second language so well." Similarly, when I [ND] first went to Japan, I was told not even to bother trying to bow, that there were something like a dozen different bows and I was always going to "bow with an accent."

RETRIEVE IT • • •
ANSWERS IN APPENDIX E

RI-4 Why is it so difficult to learn a new language in adulthood?

FIGURE 9.6

OUR ABILITY TO LEARN A NEW LANGUAGE DIMINISHES WITH AGE
Ten years after coming to the United States, Asian immigrants took an English grammar test. Although there is no sharply defined critical period for second language learning, those who arrived before age 8 understood American English grammar as well as native speakers did. Those who arrived later did not. (Data from Johnson & Newport, 1991.)

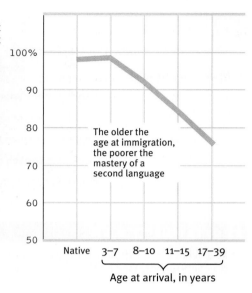

Percentage correct on grammar test

The older the age at immigration, the poorer the mastery of a second language

Native   3–7   8–10   11–15   17–39

Age at arrival, in years

HEARING IMPROVED A boy in Malawi experiences new hearing aids.

Deafness and Language Development

The impact of early experiences is evident in language learning in prelingually (before learning language) deaf children born to hearing-nonsigning parents. These children typically do not experience language during their early years. Natively deaf children who learn sign language after age 9 never learn it as well as those who learned it early in life (Mayberry et al., 2002). Those who learn to sign as teens or adults are like immigrants who learn a second language after childhood: They can master basic words and learn to order them, but they never become as fluent as native signers in producing and comprehending subtle grammatical differences (Newport, 1990). As a flower's growth will be stunted without nourishment, so, too, children will typically become linguistically stunted if isolated from language during the critical period for its acquisition.

THE BRAIN AND LANGUAGE

LOQ 9-12   What brain areas are involved in language processing and speech?

We think of speaking and reading, or writing and reading, or singing and speaking as merely different examples of the same general ability—language. But consider this curious finding: Damage to any of several cortical areas can produce **aphasia,** impairment of language. Even more curious, some people with aphasia can speak fluently but cannot read (despite good vision). Others can comprehend what they read but cannot speak. Still others can write but not read, read but not write, read numbers but not letters, or sing but not speak. These cases suggest that language is complex, and that different brain areas must serve different language functions.

Indeed, in 1865, French physician Paul Broca confirmed a fellow physician's observation that after damage to an area of the left frontal lobe (later called **Broca's area**) a person would struggle to *speak* words, yet could still sing familiar songs and comprehend speech. A decade later, German investigator Carl Wernicke discovered that after damage to a specific area of the left temporal lobe (**Wernicke's area**), people were unable to *understand* others' words and could speak only meaningless words. Asked to describe a picture that showed two boys stealing cookies behind a woman's back, one patient responded: "Mother is away her working her work to get her better, but when she's looking the two boys looking the other part. She's working another time" (Geschwind, 1979).

Today's neuroscience has confirmed brain activity in Broca's and Wernicke's areas during language processing (**FIGURE 9.7**). For people with aphasia, electrical stimulation

aphasia impairment of language, usually caused by left hemisphere damage either to Broca's area (impairing speaking) or to Wernicke's area (impairing understanding).

Broca's area helps control language expression—an area of the frontal lobe, usually in the left hemisphere, that directs the muscle movements involved in speech.

Wernicke's area a brain area involved in language comprehension and expression; usually in the left temporal lobe.

of Broca's area can help restore speaking abilities (Marangolo et al., 2016). But we also now know that the brain's processing of language is complex. Broca's area coordinates the brain's processing of language in other areas as well (Flinker et al., 2015; Tremblay & Dick, 2016). Although you experience language as a single, unified stream, fMRI scans would show that your brain is busily multitasking and networking. Different neural networks are activated by nouns and verbs (or objects and actions); by different vowels; by stories of visual versus motor experiences; by who spoke and what was said; and by many other stimuli (Perrachione et al., 2011; Shapiro et al., 2006; Speer et al., 2009). Moreover, if you're lucky enough to be natively fluent in two languages, your brain processes them in similar areas (Kim et al., 2017). But your brain doesn't use the same areas if you learned a second language after the first or if you sign rather than speak your second language (Berken et al., 2015; Kovelman et al., 2014).

The point to remember: In processing language, as in other forms of information processing, the brain operates by dividing its mental functions—speaking, perceiving, thinking, remembering—into subfunctions. Your conscious experience of reading this page *seems* indivisible, but, thanks to your parallel processing, many different neural networks are pooling their work to give the word strings coherence and meaning (Fedorenko et al., 2016). *E pluribus unum:* Out of many, one.

LaunchPad To review research on left and right hemisphere language processing—and to test your own processing speed—see **Topic Tutorial: PsychSim6, Dueling Hemispheres.**

🔒 RETRIEVE IT • • •

ANSWERS IN APPENDIX E

RI-5 _____ _____ is one part of the brain that, if damaged, might impair your ability to speak words. Damage to _____ _____ might impair your ability to understand language.

DO OTHER SPECIES HAVE LANGUAGE?

LOQ 9-13 What do we know about other species' capacity for language?

Humans have long and proudly proclaimed that language sets us above all other animals. "When we study human language," asserted Chomsky (1972), "we are approaching what some might call the 'human essence,' the qualities of mind that are, so far as we know, unique [to humans]." Is it true that humans, alone, have language?

Some animals display basic language processing. Pigeons can learn the difference between words and nonwords, but they could never read this book (Scarf et al., 2016). Other animals show impressive comprehension and communication. Various monkey species sound different alarm cries for different predators, such as a barking call for a leopard, a cough for an eagle, and a chuttering for a snake. Hearing the leopard alarm, vervets climb the nearest tree. Hearing the eagle alarm, they rush into the bushes. Hearing the snake chutter, they stand up and scan the ground (Byrne, 1991; Clarke et al., 2015; Coye et al., 2015). To indicate such things as a type of threat—an eagle, a leopard, a falling tree, a neighboring group—monkeys will combine 6 different calls into a 25-call sequence (Balter, 2010). But are such communications language?

In the late 1960s, psychologists Allen Gardner and Beatrix Gardner (1969) aroused enormous scientific and public interest with their work with Washoe, a young chimpanzee. Building on chimpanzees' natural tendencies for gestured communication, they taught Washoe sign language. After four years, Washoe could use 132 signs; by her life's end in 2007, she was using 250 signs (Metzler, 2011; Sanz et al., 1998).

During the 1970s, more and more reports came in. Some chimpanzees were stringing signs together to form sentences. Washoe, for example, signed "You me go out, please." Some word combinations seemed creative—saying *water bird* for "swan" or *apple-which-is-orange* for "orange" (Patterson, 1978; Rumbaugh, 1977).

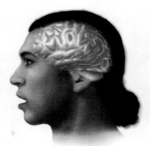
(a)
Speaking words
(Broca's area and
the motor cortex)

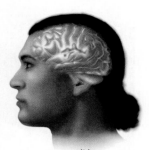
(b)
Hearing words
(Wernicke's area and
the auditory cortex)

FIGURE 9.7
BRAIN ACTIVITY WHEN SPEAKING AND HEARING WORDS

"It is the way systems interact and have a dynamic interdependence that is—unless one has lost all sense of wonder—quite awe-inspiring." —Simon Conway Morris, "The Boyle Lecture," 2005

TALKING HANDS Human language appears to have evolved from gestured communications (Corballis, 2002, 2003; Pollick & de Waal, 2007). Even today, gestures are naturally associated with spontaneous speech, and similarly so for blind and sighted speakers of a given language (Özçaliskan et al., 2016). Both gesture and speech communicate, and when they convey the same rather than different information (as they do in baseball's sign language), we humans understand faster and more accurately (Hostetter, 2011; Kelly et al., 2010). Outfielder William Hoy, the first deaf player to join the major leagues (1892), reportedly helped invent hand signals for "Strike!," "Safe!" (shown here), and "Yerr out!" (Pollard, 1992). Referees in all sports now use invented signs, and fans are fluent in sports sign language.

Jim Cummins/Getty Images

COMPREHENDING CANINE Border collie Rico had a vocabulary of 200 human words. If asked to retrieve a toy with a name he had never heard, Rico would pick out a new toy from a group of familiar items (Kaminski et al., 2004). Hearing that name for the second time four weeks later, Rico more often than not would retrieve the same toy. Another border collie, Chaser, has set an animal record by learning 1000 object names (Pilley, 2013). Like a 3-year-old child, she can also categorize them by function and shape. She can "fetch a ball" or "fetch a doll."

BUT IS THIS LANGUAGE?
Chimpanzees' ability to express themselves in American Sign Language (ASL) raises questions about the very nature of language. Here, the trainer is asking, "What is this?" The sign in response is "Baby." Does the response constitute language?

But by the late 1970s, other psychologists were growing skeptical. Were the chimps language champs or were the researchers chumps? Consider, said the skeptics:

- Ape vocabularies and sentences are simple, rather like those of a 2-year-old child. And unlike speaking or signing children, apes gain their limited vocabularies only with great difficulty (Wynne, 2004, 2008).

- Chimpanzees can make signs or push buttons in a sequence to get a reward. But pigeons, too, can peck a sequence of keys to get grain (Straub et al., 1979). The apes' signing might be nothing more than aping their trainers' signs and learning that certain arm movements produce rewards (Terrace, 1979).

- When information is unclear, we are prone to *perceptual set*—a tendency to see what we want or expect to see. Interpreting chimpanzee signs as language may have been little more than the trainers' wishful thinking (Terrace, 1979). When Washoe signed *water bird*, she may have been separately naming *water* and *bird*.

- "Give orange me give eat orange me eat orange . . ." is a far cry from the exquisite syntax of a 3-year-old (Anderson, 2004; Pinker, 1995). Rules of syntax in human language govern the order of words in sentences. So to a child, "You tickle" and "Tickle you" communicate different ideas. A chimpanzee, lacking these rules of syntax, might use the same sequence of signs for both phrases.

Controversy can stimulate progress, and in this case, it triggered more evidence of other species' abilities to think and communicate. Kanzi, a bonobo with a reported 384-word vocabulary, could understand syntax in spoken English (Savage-Rumbaugh et al., 1993, 2009). Kanzi, who appears to have the receptive language ability of a human 2-year-old, has responded appropriately when asked, "Can you show me the light?" and "Can you bring me the [flash]light?" and "Can you turn the light on?" Given stuffed animals and asked—for the first time—to "make the dog bite the snake," he put the snake to the dog's mouth.

So, how should we interpret such studies? Are humans the only language-using species? If by *language* we mean an ability to communicate through a meaningful sequence of symbols, then apes are indeed capable of language. But if we mean a verbal or signed expression of complex grammar, most psychologists would now agree that humans alone possess language. Moreover, humans, alone, have a version of a gene (*FOXP2*) that helps enable the lip, tongue, and vocal cord movements of human speech (Lieberman, 2013). Humans with a mutated form of this gene have difficulty speaking words.

One thing is certain: Studies of animal language and thinking have moved psychologists toward a greater appreciation of other species' remarkable abilities (Friend, 2004; Rumbaugh & Washburn, 2003; Wilson et al., 2015). In the past, many psychologists doubted that other species could plan, form concepts, count, use tools, or show compassion (Thorpe, 1974). Today, thanks to animal researchers, we know better. Other species exhibit insight, show family loyalty, communicate with and care for one another, and transmit cultural patterns across generations. Working out what this means for the moral rights of other animals is an unfinished task.

LaunchPad For examples of intelligent communication and problem solving among orangutans, elephants, and killer whales, see the 6-minute **Video: How Intelligent Are Animals?** See also **Video: Case Studies** for a helpful tutorial animation on this type of research method.

🔒 RETRIEVE IT • • • ANSWERS IN APPENDIX E

RI-6 If your dog barks at a stranger at the door, does this qualify as language? What if the dog yips in a telltale way to let you know she needs to go out?

THINKING AND LANGUAGE

LOQ 9-14 What is the relationship between thinking and language, and what is the value of thinking in images?

Thinking and language—which comes first? This is one of psychology's great chicken-and-egg questions. Do our ideas come first and then the words to name them? Or are our thoughts conceived in words and therefore unthinkable without them?

Language Influences Thinking

Linguist Benjamin Lee Whorf (1956) contended that "language itself shapes a [person's] basic ideas." The Hopi, who have no past tense for their verbs, could not readily *think* about the past, he said. Today's psychologists believe that a strong form of Whorf's idea—**linguistic determinism**—is too extreme. We all think about things for which we have no words. (Can you think of a shade of blue you cannot name?) And we routinely have *unsymbolized* (wordless, imageless) thoughts, as when someone, watching two men carry a load of bricks, wondered whether the men would drop them (Heavey & Hurlburt, 2008; Hurlburt et al., 2013).

A weaker version of linguistic determinism—**linguistic relativism**—recognizes that our words influence our thinking (Gentner, 2016). To those who speak two dissimilar languages, such as English and Japanese, it seems obvious that a person may think differently in different languages (Brown, 1986). Unlike English, which has a rich vocabulary for self-focused emotions such as anger, Japanese has more words for interpersonal emotions such as sympathy (Markus & Kitayama, 1991). Many bilingual individuals report having different senses of self—that they feel like different people—depending on which language they are using (Matsumoto, 1994; Pavlenko, 2014). In one series of studies with bilingual Israeli Arabs (who spoke both Arabic and Hebrew), participants thought differently about their social world, with differing automatic associations with Arabs and Jews, depending on which language the testing session used (Danziger & Ward, 2010).

Depending on which emotion they want to express, bilingual people will often switch languages. "When my mom gets angry at me, she'll speak in Mandarin," explained one Chinese-American student. "If she's really mad, she'll switch to Cantonese" (Chen et al., 2012). Bilingual individuals may even reveal different personality profiles when taking the same test in two languages, with their differing cultural associations (Chen & Bond, 2010; Dinges & Hull, 1992). When China-born, bilingual University of Waterloo students were asked to describe themselves in English, their responses fit typical Canadian profiles, expressing mostly positive self-statements and moods. When responding in Chinese, the same students gave typically Chinese self-descriptions, reporting more agreement with Chinese values and roughly equal positive and negative self-statements and moods (Ross et al., 2002). Similar attitude and personality changes have been shown when bicultural, bilingual people shift between the cultural frames associated with Spanish and English, or Arabic and English (Ogunnaike et al., 2010; Ramírez-Esparza et al., 2006). "Learn a new language and get a new soul," says a Czech proverb. When responding in their second language, bilingual people's moral judgments also reflect less emotion—they respond with more "head" than "heart" (Costa et al., 2014).

So our words do *influence* our thinking (Boroditsky, 2011). Words define our mental categories. In Brazil, the isolated Piraha people have words for the numbers 1 and 2, but numbers above that are simply "many." Thus, if shown 7 nuts in a row, they find it difficult to lay out the same number from their own pile (Gordon, 2004).

Words also influence our thinking about colors. Whether we live in New Mexico, New South Wales, or New Guinea, we *see* colors much the same, but we use our native language to *classify* and *remember* them (Davidoff, 2004; Roberson et al., 2004, 2005). Imagine viewing three colors and calling two of them "yellow" and one of them "blue." Later you would likely recall the yellows as being more similar. But if you speak the language of Papua New Guinea's Berinmo tribe, which has words for two different shades of yellow, you would more speedily perceive and better recall the variations between the two yellows. And if your language is Russian, which has distinct names for various

linguistic determinism Whorf's hypothesis that language determines the way we think.

linguistic relativism the idea that language has an influence on the way we think.

 ASK YOURSELF

Consider a language you began to learn *after* learning your first language. How did your learning this other language differ from learning your first language? Does speaking it feel different?

CULTURE AND COLOR In Papua New Guinea, Berinmo children have words for different shades of "yellow," which might enable them to spot and recall yellow variations more quickly. Here and everywhere, "the languages we speak profoundly shape the way we think, the way we see the world, the way we live our lives," noted psychologist Lera Boroditsky (2009).

"All words are pegs to hang ideas on." —Henry Ward Beecher, *Proverbs from Plymouth Pulpit*, 1887

ENGAGE 🎧 **LaunchPad** Play the role of a researcher studying the benefits of learning more than one language by engaging online with **Immersive Learning: How Would You Know If There Is a Bilingual Advantage?**

shades of blue, such as *goluboy* and *siniy,* you might recall the yellows as more similar and remember the blue better. Words matter.

Perceived differences grow as we assign different names. On the color spectrum, blue blends into green—until we draw a dividing line between the portions we call "blue" and "green." Although equally different on the color spectrum, two different items that share the same color name (as the two "blues" do in **FIGURE 9.8**, contrast B) are harder to distinguish than two items with different names ("blue" and "green," as in Figure 9.8, contrast A) (Özgen, 2004). Likewise, two places seem closer and more vulnerable to the same natural disaster if labeled as in the same state rather than at an equal distance in adjacent states (Burris & Branscombe, 2005; Mishra & Mishra, 2010). Tornadoes don't know about state lines, but people do.

Given words' subtle influence on thinking, we do well to choose our words carefully. Is "A child learns language as *he* interacts with *his* caregivers" any different from "Children learn language as *they* interact with *their* caregivers"? Many studies have found that it is. When hearing the generic *he* (as in "the artist and his work") people are more likely to picture a male (Henley, 1989; Ng, 1990). If *he* and *his* were truly gender free, we shouldn't skip a beat when hearing that "man, like other mammals, nurses his young."

To expand language is to expand the ability to think. Young children's thinking develops hand in hand with their language (Gopnik & Meltzoff, 1986). Indeed, it is very difficult to think about or conceptualize certain abstract ideas (*commitment, freedom,* or *rhyming*) without language! And what is true for preschoolers is true for everyone: *It pays to increase your word power.* That's why most textbooks, including this one, introduce new words—to teach new ideas and new ways of thinking.

Increased word power helps explain what McGill University researcher Wallace Lambert has called the *bilingual advantage* (1992; Lambert et al., 1993). In some studies (though not all), bilingual people have exhibited skill at inhibiting one language while using the other (Bialystok et al., 2015; de Bruin et al., 2015a,b). And thanks to their well-practiced "executive control" over language, they also more readily inhibit their attention to irrelevant information (Bak et al., 2014; Bialystok, 2017; Kroll et al., 2014). Bilingual children also exhibit enhanced social skill, by being better able to shift to understand another's perspective (Fan et al., 2015). The bilingual advantage even extends to aging by preserving healthy brain functioning later in life (Li et al., 2017).

Bilingual people's switching between different languages does, however, take a moment (Kleinman & Gollan, 2016; Palomar-García et al., 2015). That's a phenomenon I [DM] failed to realize before speaking to bilingual Chinese colleagues in Beijing. While I spoke in English, my accompanying slides were in Chinese. Alas, I later learned, the translated slides required constant "code switching" from my spoken words, thus making it *hard* for my audience to process both.

Lambert helped devise a Canadian program that has, since 1981, immersed millions of English-speaking children in French (Statistics Canada, 2013). Not surprisingly, the children attain a natural French fluency unrivaled by other methods of language teaching. Moreover, compared with similarly capable children in control groups, they do so without detriment to their English fluency, and with increased aptitude scores, creativity, and appreciation for French-Canadian culture (Genesee & Gándara, 1999; Lazaruk, 2007).

Whether we are in the linguistic minority or majority, language links us to one another. Language also connects us to the past and the future. "To destroy a people," goes a saying, "destroy their language."

FIGURE 9.8

LANGUAGE AND PERCEPTION When people view blocks of equally different colors, they perceive those with different names as more different. Thus the "green" and "blue" in contrast A may appear to differ more than the two equally different blues in contrast B (Özgen, 2004).

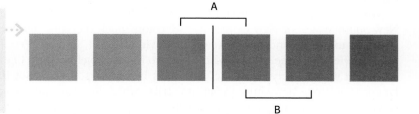

🔒 **RETRIEVE IT** • • •   *ANSWERS IN APPENDIX E*

RI-7 Benjamin Lee Whorf's controversial hypothesis, called _____ _____, suggested that we cannot think about things unless we have words for those concepts or ideas.

Thinking in Images

When you are alone, do you talk to yourself? Is "thinking" simply conversing with yourself? Words do convey ideas. But sometimes ideas precede words. To turn on the cold water in your bathroom, in which direction do you turn the handle? To answer, you probably thought not in words but with *implicit* (nondeclarative, procedural) memory—a mental picture of how you do it.

Indeed, we often think in images. Artists think in images. So do composers, poets, mathematicians, athletes, and scientists. Albert Einstein reported that he achieved some of his greatest insights through visual images and later put them into words. Pianist Liu Chi Kung harnessed the power of thinking in images. One year after placing second in the 1958 Tchaikovsky piano competition, Liu was imprisoned during China's cultural revolution. Soon after his release, after seven years without touching a piano, he was back on tour. Critics judged Liu's musicianship as better than ever. How did he continue to develop without practice? "I did practice," said Liu, "every day. I rehearsed every piece I had ever played, note by note, in my mind" (Garfield, 1986).

For someone who has learned a skill, such as ballet dancing, even *watching* the activity will activate the brain's internal simulation of it (Calvo-Merino et al., 2004). So, too, will *imagining* a physical experience, which activates some of the same neural networks that are active during the actual experience (Grèzes & Decety, 2001). Small wonder, then, that mental practice has become a standard part of training for Olympic athletes (Blumenstein & Orbach, 2012; Ungerleider, 2005).

One experiment on mental practice and basketball free-throw shooting tracked the University of Tennessee women's team over 35 games (Savoy & Beitel, 1996). During that time, the team's free-throw accuracy increased from approximately 52 percent in games following standard physical practice, to some 65 percent after mental practice. Players had repeatedly imagined making free throws under various conditions, including being "trash-talked" by their opposition. In a dramatic conclusion, Tennessee won the national championship game in overtime, thanks in part to their free-throw shooting.

Mental rehearsal can also help you achieve an academic goal, as research- ers demonstrated with two groups of introductory psychology students facing a midterm exam one week later (Taylor et al., 1998). (Students who were not engaged in any mental rehearsal formed a control group.) The first group spent five minutes each day visualizing themselves scanning the posted grade list, seeing their A, beaming with joy, and feeling proud. This daily *outcome simulation* had little effect, adding only 2 points to their exam-score average. The second group spent five minutes each day visualizing themselves effectively studying—reading their text, going over notes, eliminating distractions, declining an offer to go out. This daily *process simulation* paid off: The group began studying sooner, spent more time at it, and beat the others' average score by 8 points.

 The point to remember: It's better to spend your fantasy time planning *how* to reach your goal than to focus on your desired destination.

💡 📚 **LaunchPad** To experience your own thinking as (a) manipulating words and (b) manipulating images, see **Topic Tutorial: PsychSim6, My Head Is Spinning!**

* * *

What, then, should we say about the relationship between thinking and language? As we have seen, language influences our thinking. But if thinking did not also affect language, there would never be any new words. And new words and new combinations of old words express new ideas. The basketball term *slam dunk* was coined after the act itself had

"When we see a person walking down the street talking to himself, we generally assume that he is mentally ill. But we all talk to ourselves continuously—we just have the good sense of keeping our mouths shut. . . . It's as though we are having a conversation with an imaginary friend possessed of infinite patience. Who are we talking to?" —Sam Harris, "We Are Lost in Thought," 2011

💡 **ASK YOURSELF**

How could you use mental practice to improve your performance in some area of your life?

Blend Images/Getty Images

FIGURE 9.9

THE INTERPLAY OF THOUGHT AND LANGUAGE The traffic runs both ways between thinking and language. Thinking affects our language, which affects our thought.

Thinking

Language

Jupiterimages/Getty Images

become fairly common. *Blogs* became part of our language after "web logs" appeared. So, let us say that *thinking affects our language, which then affects our thought* (**FIGURE 9.9**).

Psychological research on thinking and language mirrors the mixed impressions of our species by those in fields such as literature and religion. The human mind is simultaneously capable of striking intellectual failures and of striking intellectual power. Misjudgments are common and can have disastrous consequences. So we do well to appreciate our capacity for error. Yet our ingenuity at problem solving and our extraordinary power of language mark humankind as (in Shakespeare's words), almost "infinite in faculties."

🔒 **RETRIEVE IT • • •**

ANSWERS IN APPENDIX E

RI-8 What is mental practice, and how can it help you to prepare for an upcoming event?

🔒 **REVIEW** **LANGUAGE AND THOUGHT**

🔁 Learning Objectives

TEST YOURSELF Answer these repeated Learning Objective Questions on your own (before checking the answers in Appendix D) to improve your retention of the concepts (McDaniel et al., 2009, 2015).

9-9 What are the structural components of a language?

9-10 How do we acquire language, and what is *universal grammar*?

9-11 What are the milestones in language development, and when is the critical period for acquiring language?

9-12 What brain areas are involved in language processing and speech?

9-13 What do we know about other species' capacity for language?

9-14 What is the relationship between thinking and language, and what is the value of thinking in images?

🔁 Terms and Concepts to Remember

TEST YOURSELF Write down the definition yourself, then check your answer on the referenced page.

language, **p. 311**

phoneme, **p. 312**

morpheme, **p. 312**

grammar, **p. 312**

babbling stage, **p. 315**

one-word stage, **p. 315**

two-word stage, **p. 315**

telegraphic speech, **p. 315**

aphasia, **p. 316**

Broca's area, **p. 316**

Wernicke's area, **p. 316**

linguistic determinism, **p. 319**

linguistic relativism, **p. 319**

🔁 Experience the Testing Effect

TEST YOURSELF Answer the following questions on your own first, then check your answers in Appendix E.

1. Children reach the one-word stage of speech development at about
   a. 4 months.
   b. 6 months.
   c. 1 year.
   d. 2 years.

2. The three basic building blocks of language are
   _____, _____, and _____.

3. When young children speak in short phrases using mostly verbs and nouns, this is referred to as _____ _____.

4. According to Chomsky, humans have a built-in pre-disposition to learn grammar rules; he called this trait _____ _____.

5. Most researchers agree that apes can
   a. communicate through symbols.
   b. reproduce most human speech sounds.
   c. master language in adulthood.
   d. surpass a human 3-year-old in language skills.

Continue testing yourself with **LearningCurve** or **Achieve Read & Practice** to learn and remember most effectively.

Intelligence and Its Assessment

In and beyond psychology, few topics have sparked more debate than the intelligence controversy: Does each of us have an inborn general mental capacity (intelligence)? Can we quantify this capacity as a meaningful number? How much does intelligence vary within and between groups, and why? And can we measure intelligence without bias?

WHAT IS INTELLIGENCE?

LOQ 9-15 How do psychologists define *intelligence*, and what are the arguments for *g*?

In many studies, *intelligence* has been defined as whatever *intelligence tests* measure, which has tended to be school smarts. But intelligence is not a quality like height or weight, which has the same meaning to everyone worldwide. People assign this term to the qualities that enable success in their own time and culture (Sternberg & Kaufman, 1998). In Cameroon's equatorial forest, *intelligence* may reflect understanding the medicinal qualities of local plants. In a North American high school, it may reflect mastering difficult concepts in calculus or chemistry. In both places, **intelligence** is the ability to learn from experience, solve problems, and use knowledge to adapt to new situations.

You probably know some people with talents in science, others who excel in the humanities, and still others gifted in athletics, art, music, or dance. You may also know a talented artist who is stumped by the simplest math problem, or a brilliant math student who struggles when discussing literature. Are all these people intelligent? Could you rate their intelligence on a single scale? Or would you need several different scales?

Is Intelligence One General Ability?

Charles Spearman (1863–1945) believed we have one **general intelligence** (often shortened to **g**) that is at the heart of all of our intelligent behavior, from navigating the sea to excelling in school. He granted that people often have special, outstanding abilities. But he noted that those who score high in one area, such as verbal intelligence, typically score higher than average in other areas, such as spatial or reasoning ability.

Spearman's (1904) belief stemmed in part from his work with *factor analysis*, a statistical procedure that identifies clusters of related items. In this view, mental abilities are much like physical abilities: Athleticism is not one thing, but many. The ability to run fast is distinct from the eye-hand coordination required to throw a ball on target. Yet there remains some tendency for good things to come packaged together—for running speed and throwing accuracy to correlate. So, too, with intelligence. Several distinct

imageBROKER/Alamy

HANDS-ON HEALING The socially constructed concept of intelligence varies from culture to culture. This natural healer in Cameroon displays intelligence in his knowledge about medicinal plants and his understanding of the needs of the people he is helping.

"g is one of the most reliable and valid measures in the behavioral domain . . . and it predicts important social outcomes such as educational and occupational levels far better than any other trait." —Behavior geneticist Robert Plomin (1999)

intelligence the ability to learn from experience, solve problems, and use knowledge to adapt to new situations.

general intelligence (g) according to Spearman and others, underlies all mental abilities and is therefore measured by every task on an intelligence test.

abilities tend to cluster together and to correlate enough to define a general intelligence factor. Distinct brain networks enable distinct abilities, with *g* explained by their coordinated activity (Cole et al., 2015; Hampshire et al., 2012). The result is a chorus of actions orchestrated from distributed mental resources (Carroll & Bright, 2016; Lee et al., 2015).

Theories of Multiple Intelligences

LOQ 9-16 How do Gardner's and Sternberg's theories of multiple intelligences differ, and what criticisms have they faced?

Other psychologists, particularly since the mid-1980s, have sought to extend the definition of *intelligence* beyond the idea of academic smarts. One prominent theory based on the work of Raymond Cattell, John Horn, and John Carroll—the *Cattell-Horn-Carroll (CHC) theory*—affirmed a general intellectual ability factor, but also identified more specific abilities, such as reading and writing ability, memory capacity, and processing speed (Schneider & McGrew, 2012). Other psychologists have also offered theories of varied intelligence domains.

GARDNER'S MULTIPLE INTELLIGENCES Howard Gardner has identified eight *relatively independent intelligences,* including the verbal and mathematical aptitudes assessed by standardized tests (**FIGURE 9.10**). Thus, the computer programmer, the poet, the street-smart adolescent, and the basketball team's play-making point guard exhibit different kinds of intelligence (Gardner, 1998). Gardner (1999a) has also proposed a ninth possible intelligence—*existential intelligence*—the ability "to ponder large questions about life, death, existence."

Gardner (1983, 2006, 2011; Davis et al., 2011) views these intelligence domains as multiple abilities that come in different packages. Brain damage, for example, may destroy one ability but leave others intact. And consider people with **savant syndrome,** who have an island of brilliance but often score low on intelligence tests and may have limited or no language ability (Treffert, 2010). Some can compute complicated calculations

ISLANDS OF GENIUS: SAVANT SYNDROME After a brief helicopter ride over Singapore followed by five days of drawing, British savant artist Stephen Wiltshire accurately reproduced an aerial view of the city from memory.

RETAIN 🔒 **FIGURE 9.10**

GARDNER'S EIGHT INTELLIGENCES Gardner has also proposed existential intelligence (the ability to ponder deep questions about life) as a ninth possible intelligence.

almost instantly, or identify the day of the week of any given historical date, or render incredible works of art or music (Miller, 1999).

About four in five people with savant syndrome are male, and many also have *autism spectrum disorder (ASD)*, a developmental disorder. The late memory whiz Kim Peek (who did not have ASD) inspired the movie *Rain Man*. In 8 to 10 seconds, he could read and remember a page. During his lifetime, he memorized 9000 books, including Shakespeare's works and the Bible. He could provide GPS-like travel directions within any major U.S. city. Yet he could not button his clothes, and he had little capacity for abstract concepts. Asked by his father at a restaurant to lower his voice, he slid down in his chair to lower his voice box. Asked for Lincoln's Gettysburg Address, he responded, "227 North West Front Street. But he only stayed there one night—he gave the speech the next day" (Treffert & Christensen, 2005).

Courtesy of Cameras on Wheels

📺 **LaunchPad** To witness extraordinary savant ability in music, see the **Video: Savant Musical Skills.**

STERNBERG'S THREE INTELLIGENCES Robert Sternberg (1985, 2011) agrees with Gardner that there is more to success than traditional intelligence and that we have multiple intelligences. But Sternberg's *triarchic theory* proposes three, not eight or nine, intelligences:

- *Analytical (academic problem-solving) intelligence* is assessed by intelligence tests, which present well-defined problems having a single right answer. Such tests predict school grades reasonably well and vocational success more modestly.

- *Creative intelligence* is demonstrated in innovative smarts: the ability to adapt to new situations and generate novel ideas.

- *Practical intelligence* is required for everyday tasks that may be poorly defined and may have multiple solutions.

Gardner and Sternberg differ in some areas, but they agree on two important points: Multiple abilities can contribute to life success, and differing varieties of giftedness bring both spice to life and challenges for education. Trained to appreciate such variety, many teachers have applied multiple intelligence theories in their classrooms.

CRITICISMS OF MULTIPLE INTELLIGENCE THEORIES Wouldn't it be nice if the world were so fair that a weakness in one area would be compensated by genius in another? Alas, say critics, the world is not fair (Ferguson, 2009; Scarr, 1989). Research using factor analysis confirms that there *is* a general intelligence factor; g matters (Johnson et al., 2008). It predicts performance on various complex tasks and in various jobs (Gottfredson, 2002a,b, 2003a,b; see also **FIGURE 9.11**). And extremely high cognitive-ability scores predict exceptional achievements, such as doctoral degrees and publications (Kuncel & Hezlett, 2010).

Even so, "success" is not a one-ingredient recipe. It also helps to have the luck of an advantaged home and school, and to have been born in a time and place where your talents matter. And though high intelligence will help you get into a profession (via schools and training programs), it won't make you successful once there. Success is a combination of talent and *grit*: Those who become highly successful tend also to be conscientious, well connected, and doggedly energetic. K. Anders Ericsson and others report a *10-year rule*: A common ingredient of expert performance in chess, dance, sports, computer programming, music, and medicine is "about 10 years of intense, daily practice" (Ericsson, 2002; Ericsson & Pool, 2016; Simon & Chase, 1973). Becoming a

SPATIAL INTELLIGENCE GENIUS In 1998, World Checkers Champion Ron "Suki" King of Barbados set a new record by simultaneously playing 385 players in 3 hours and 44 minutes. Thus, while his opponents often had hours to plot their game moves, King could only devote about 35 seconds to each game. Yet he still managed to win all 385 games!

David R. Frazier Photolibrary, Inc./Alamy

STREET SMARTS This child selling candy on the streets of Manaus, Brazil, is developing practical intelligence at a very young age.

ENGAGE (ASK YOURSELF)

The concept of multiple intelligences assumes that the analytical school smarts measured by traditional intelligence tests are important, but that other abilities are also important. Different people have different gifts. What are yours?

FIGURE 9.11

SMART AND RICH? Jay Zagorsky (2007) tracked 7403 participants in the U.S. National Longitudinal Survey of Youth across 25 years. As shown in this illustrative scatterplot, their intelligence scores correlated +.30, a moderate positive correlation, with their later income.

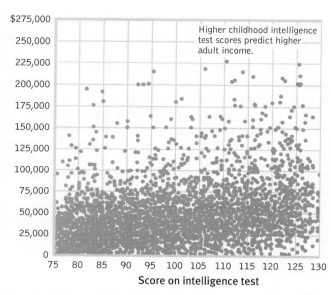

Annual income

Higher childhood intelligence test scores predict higher adult income.

Score on intelligence test

For more on how self-disciplined grit feeds achievement, see Chapter 10.

The procrastinator's motto: "Hard work pays off later; laziness pays off now."

"You have to be careful, if you're good at something, to make sure you don't think you're good at other things that you aren't necessarily so good at. . . . Because I've been very successful at [software development] people come in and expect that I have wisdom about topics that I don't." —Microsoft co-founder Bill Gates (1998)

professional musician or an elite athlete requires, first, native ability (Macnamara et al., 2014, 2016). But it also requires years of practice—about 11,000 hours on average, and a *minimum* of 3000 hours (Campitelli & Gobet, 2011). The recipe for success is a gift of nature plus a whole lot of nurture.

🔒 RETRIEVE IT • • •
ANSWERS IN APPENDIX E

RI-1 How does the existence of savant syndrome support Gardner's theory of multiple intelligences?

Emotional Intelligence

LOQ 9-17 What are the four components of emotional intelligence?

Social intelligence is the know-how involved in understanding social situations and managing yourself successfully (Cantor & Kihlstrom, 1987). Psychologist Edward Thorndike first proposed the concept in 1920, noting that "the best mechanic in a factory may fail as a foreman for lack of social intelligence" (Goleman, 2006, p. 83).

A critical part of social intelligence, **emotional intelligence,** consists of four abilities (Mayer et al., 2002, 2012, 2016):

- *Perceiving* emotions (recognizing them in faces, music, and stories)
- *Understanding* emotions (predicting them and how they may change and blend)
- *Managing* emotions (knowing how to express them in varied situations)
- *Using* emotions to enable adaptive or creative thinking

Emotionally intelligent people are both socially aware and self-aware. They avoid being hijacked by overwhelming depression, anxiety, or anger. They can read others' emotional cues and know what to say to soothe a grieving friend, encourage a workmate, and manage a conflict. They can delay gratification in pursuit of long-range rewards. Thus, emotionally intelligent people more often succeed in relationship, career, and parenting situations where academically smarter but less emotionally intelligent people might fail (Cherniss, 2010a,b; Czarna et al., 2016; Miao et al., 2016). They also tend to be happy and healthy (Sánchez-Álvarez et al., 2016; Schutte et al., 2007, 2016). Aware of these benefits, school-based programs have sought to increase teachers' and students' emotional intelligence (Castillo-Gualda et al., 2017; Nathanson et al., 2016).

"You're wise, but you lack tree smarts."

Some scholars, however, are concerned that emotional intelligence stretches the intelligence concept too far (Visser et al., 2006). Howard Gardner (1999b) includes interpersonal and intrapersonal intelligences as two of his multiple intelligences. But he notes that we should respect emotional sensitivity, creativity, and motivation as important but different. Stretch *intelligence* to include everything we prize and the word will lose its meaning.

* * *

For a summary of these theories of intelligence, see **TABLE 9.3**.

 LaunchPad Engage online with **Concept Practice: Theories of Intelligence** to review these different approaches to intelligence.

TABLE 9.3

Comparing Theories of Intelligence

Theory	Summary	Strengths	Other Considerations
Spearman's general intelligence (g)	A basic intelligence predicts our abilities in varied academic areas.	Different abilities, such as verbal and spatial, do have some tendency to correlate.	Human abilities are too diverse to be encapsulated by a single general intelligence factor.
Gardner's multiple intelligences	Our abilities are best classified into eight or nine independent intelligences, which include a broad range of skills beyond traditional school smarts.	Intelligence is more than just verbal and mathematical skills. Other abilities are equally important to our human adaptability.	Should all our abilities be considered *intelligences*? Shouldn't some be called less vital *talents*?
Sternberg's triarchic theory	Our intelligence is best classified into three areas that predict real-world success: analytical, creative, and practical.	These three domains can be reliably measured.	These three domains may be less independent than Sternberg thought and may actually share an underlying *g* factor.
Emotional intelligence	Social intelligence is an important indicator of life success. Emotional intelligence is a key aspect, consisting of perceiving, understanding, managing, and using emotions.	These four components predict social success and emotional well-being.	Does this stretch the concept of intelligence too far?

ASSESSING INTELLIGENCE

LOQ 9-18   What is an *intelligence test,* and how do achievement and aptitude tests differ?

An **intelligence test** assesses people's mental aptitudes and compares them with those of others, using numerical scores. How do psychologists design such tests, and what makes them credible?

In your lifetime, you've taken dozens of mental ability tests, which can be categorized into two general categories:

- **Achievement tests,** which are intended to *reflect* what you have learned. Your final exam will measure what you learned in this class.

- **Aptitude tests,** which are intended to *predict* your ability to learn some new skill. If you took a college entrance exam, it was designed to predict your ability to do college work.

Let's consider why psychologists created and used such tests of mental abilities.

What Do Intelligence Tests Test?

LOQ 9-19   When and why were intelligence tests created, and how do today's tests differ from early intelligence tests?

Barely more than a century ago, psychologists began designing tests to assess people's mental abilities. Modern intelligence testing traces its birth to early-twentieth-century France.

emotional intelligence the ability to perceive, understand, manage, and use emotions.

intelligence test a method for assessing an individual's mental aptitudes and comparing them with those of others, using numerical scores.

achievement test a test designed to assess what a person has learned.

aptitude test a test designed to predict a person's future performance; *aptitude* is the capacity to learn.

 (ASK YOURSELF)

What achievement or aptitude tests have you taken? In your opinion, how well did these tests assess what you'd learned or predict what you were capable of learning?

ALFRED BINET (1857–1911) "Some recent philosophers have given their moral approval to the deplorable verdict that an individual's intelligence is a fixed quantity, one which cannot be augmented. We must protest and act against this brutal pessimism" (Binet, 1909, p. 141).

"The IQ test was invented to predict academic performance, nothing else. If we wanted something that would predict life success, we'd have to invent another test completely."
—Social psychologist Robert Zajonc (1984b)

ALFRED BINET: PREDICTING SCHOOL ACHIEVEMENT With a new French law that required all children to attend school, officials knew that some children, including many newcomers to Paris, would struggle and need special classes. But how could the schools make fair judgments about children's learning potential? Teachers might assess children who had little prior education as slow learners. Or they might sort children into classes on the basis of their social backgrounds. To minimize such bias, France's minister of public education gave psychologist Alfred Binet the task of designing fair tests.

Binet and his student, Théodore Simon, began by assuming that all children follow the same course of intellectual development but that some develop more rapidly (Nicolas & Levine, 2012). A "dull" child should score much like a typical younger child, and a "bright" child like a typical older child. Thus, their goal became measuring each child's **mental age,** the level of performance typically associated with a certain chronological age. The average 8-year-old, for example, has a mental age of 8. An 8-year-old with a below-average mental age (perhaps performing at the level of a typical 6-year-old) would struggle with schoolwork considered normal for 8-year-olds.

Binet and Simon tested a variety of reasoning and problem-solving questions on Binet's two daughters, and then on "bright" and "backward" Parisian schoolchildren. Items answered correctly could then predict how well other French children would handle their schoolwork. Binet hoped his test would be used to improve children's education, but he also feared it would be used to label children and limit their opportunities (Gould, 1981).

🔒 **RETRIEVE IT • • •**   *ANSWERS IN APPENDIX E*

RI-2 What did Binet hope to achieve by establishing a child's mental age?

LEWIS TERMAN: MEASURING INNATE INTELLIGENCE After Binet's death in 1911, others adapted his tests for use as a numerical measure of intelligence. Stanford University professor Lewis Terman (1877–1956) tried the Paris-developed questions and age norms with California kids. Adapting some of Binet's original items, adding others, and establishing new age norms, Terman extended the upper end of the test's range from age 12 to "superior adults." He also gave his revision the name today's version retains—the **Stanford-Binet.**

From such tests, German psychologist William Stern derived the famous **intelligence quotient,** or **IQ.** The IQ was simply a person's mental age divided by chronological age and multiplied by 100 to get rid of the decimal point. Thus, an average child, whose mental age (8) and chronological age (8) are the same, has an IQ of 100. But an 8-year-old who answers questions at the level of a typical 10-year-old has an IQ of 125:

$$IQ = \frac{\text{mental age of 10}}{\text{chronological age of 8}} \times 100 = 125$$

The original IQ formula worked fairly well for children but not for adults. (Should a 40-year-old who does as well on the test as an average 20-year-old be assigned an IQ of only 50?) Most current intelligence tests, including the Stanford-Binet, no longer compute an IQ in this manner (though the term *IQ* still lingers in everyday vocabulary as shorthand for "intelligence test score"). Instead, they represent the test-taker's performance *relative to the average performance* (which is arbitrarily set at 100) of others the same age. Most people—about 68 percent of those taking an intelligence test)—fall between 85 and 115.

Terman inferred that intelligence tests revealed a mental capacity present from birth. He also assumed that some ethnic groups were naturally more intelligent than others. And he supported the controversial *eugenics* movement—the much-criticized nineteenth-century movement that proposed measuring human traits and using the results to encourage only smart and fit people to reproduce.

With Terman's help, the U.S. government developed new tests to evaluate both newly arriving immigrants and World War I army recruits—the world's first mass administration of an intelligence test. To some psychologists, the results indicated the inferiority of people not sharing their Anglo-Saxon heritage. Such findings were part of the cultural climate that led to a 1924 immigration law that reduced Southern and Eastern immigration quotas to be less than a fifth of those for Northern and Western Europe.

THAT'S MY BOY, MARK... HE'S 39, BUT HE'S ALREADY READING AT A 42-YEAR-OLD LEVEL...

Mrs. Randolph takes mother's pride too far.

Binet probably would have been horrified that his test had been adapted and used to draw such conclusions. Indeed, such sweeping judgments became an embarrassment to most of those who championed testing. Even Terman came to appreciate that test scores reflected not only people's innate mental abilities but also their education, native language, and familiarity with the culture assumed by the test. Abuses of the early intelligence tests serve to remind us that science can be value-laden. Behind a screen of scientific objectivity, ideology sometimes lurks.

DAVID WECHSLER: TESTING SEPARATE STRENGTHS Psychologist David Wechsler created what is now the most widely used individual intelligence test, the **Wechsler Adult Intelligence Scale (WAIS).** There is a version for school-age children (the *Wechsler Intelligence Scale for Children [WISC]*), and another for preschool children (Evers et al., 2012). The 2008 WAIS edition (with a new version anticipated in 2020) consists of 15 subtests, including:

- *Similarities*—reasoning the commonality of two objects or concepts ("In what way are wool and cotton alike?")
- *Vocabulary*—naming pictured objects, or defining words ("What is a guitar?")
- *Block design*—visual abstract processing ("Using the four blocks, make one just like this.")
- *Letter-number sequencing*—on hearing a series of numbers and letters ("R-2-C-1-M-3"), repeating the numbers in ascending order, and then the letters in alphabetical order

The WAIS yields both an overall intelligence score and separate scores for verbal comprehension, perceptual reasoning, working memory, and processing speed. In such ways, this test helps realize Binet's aim: to identify those who could benefit from special educational opportunities for improvement.

MATCHING PATTERNS Block-design puzzles test visual abstract processing ability. Wechsler's individually administered intelligence test comes in forms suited for adults and children.

Richard T. Nowitz/Getty Images

🔒 **RETRIEVE IT • • •**   *ANSWERS IN APPENDIX E*

RI-3 What is the IQ of a 4-year-old with a mental age of 5?

RI-4 An employer with a pool of applicants for a single available position is interested in testing each applicant's potential. To determine that, she should use an _____ (achievement/aptitude) test. That same employer wishing to test the effectiveness of a new, on-the-job training program would be wise to use an _____ (achievement/aptitude) test.

ENGAGE 🔲 **LaunchPad** To learn more about the promise and perils of intelligence testing, watch the **Video: Locking Away the "Feebleminded"— A Shameful History.** And to test your own performance on simulated WAIS subtasks, see **Concept Practice: Wechsler Intelligence Tasks.**

Three Tests of a "Good" Test

LOQ 9-20 What is a *normal curve,* and what does it mean to say that a test has been *standardized* and is *reliable* and *valid*?

To be widely accepted, a psychological test must be *standardized, reliable,* and *valid.* The Stanford-Binet and Wechsler tests meet these requirements.

WAS THE TEST STANDARDIZED? The number of questions you answer correctly on an intelligence test would reveal almost nothing. To know how well you performed, you would need some basis for comparison. That's why test-makers give new tests to a representative sample of people. The scores from this pretested group become the basis for future comparisons. If you then take the test following the same procedures, your score will be meaningful when compared with others. This process is called **standardization.** To keep the average score near 100, the Stanford-Binet and Wechsler scales are periodically restandardized. If you recently took the WAIS, Fourth Edition, your performance was compared with the standardization sample who took the test during 2007, not to David Wechsler's initial 1930s sample.

mental age a measure of intelligence test performance devised by Binet; the level of performance typically associated with children of a certain chronological age. Thus, a child who does as well as an average 8-year-old is said to have a mental age of 8.

Stanford-Binet the widely used American revision (by Terman at Stanford University) of Binet's original intelligence test.

intelligence quotient (IQ) defined originally as the ratio of mental age *(ma)* to chronological age *(ca)* multiplied by 100 (thus, $IQ = ma/ca \times 100$). On contemporary intelligence tests, the average performance for a given age is assigned a score of 100.

Wechsler Adult Intelligence Scale (WAIS) the WAIS and its companion versions for children are the most widely used intelligence tests; they contain verbal and performance (nonverbal) subtests.

standardization defining uniform testing procedures and meaningful scores by comparison with the performance of a pretested group.

FIGURE 9.12

THE NORMAL CURVE Scores on aptitude tests tend to form a normal, or bell-shaped, curve around an average score. For the Wechsler scale, for example, the average score is 100.

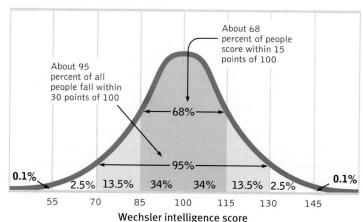

 Number of scores

About 95 percent of all people fall within 30 points of 100

About 68 percent of people score within 15 points of 100

68%

95%

0.1%   2.5% 13.5% 34% 34% 13.5% 2.5%   0.1%

55   70   85   100   115   130   145

Wechsler intelligence score

If we construct a graph of test-takers' scores, the scores typically form a bell-shaped pattern called the *bell curve, or* **normal curve.** For many human attributes—including height, weight, and mental aptitude—the curve's highest point is the average score. On an intelligence test, we give this average score a value of 100 (**FIGURE 9.12**). Moving out from the average, toward either extreme, we find fewer and fewer people. For both the Stanford-Binet and Wechsler tests, a person's score indicates whether that person's performance fell above or below the average. A performance higher than all but 2.5 percent of all scores earns an intelligence score of 130. A performance lower than 97.5 percent of all scores earns an intelligence score of 70.

IS THE TEST RELIABLE? Knowing where you stand in comparison to a standardization group still won't say much about your intelligence unless the test has **reliability.** A reliable test gives consistent scores, no matter who takes the test or when they take it. To check a test's reliability, researchers test people many times. They may split the test in half (*split-half:* agreement of odd-question scores and even-question scores), test with alternative forms of the test, or retest with the same test (*test-retest*). The higher the *correlation* between the two scores, the higher the test's reliability. The tests we have considered—the Stanford-Binet, the WAIS, and the WISC—are very reliable after early childhood (with *correlation coefficients* of about +.9). In retests, sometimes decades later, people's scores generally are similar to the first score (Lyons et al., 2017).

LaunchPad Watch the **Video: Correlational Studies** for a helpful tutorial animation.

IS THE TEST VALID? High reliability does not ensure a test's **validity**—the extent to which the test actually measures or predicts what it promises. Imagine using a tape measure with faulty markings. If you use it to measure people's heights, your results will be very reliable. No matter how many times you measure, people's heights will be the same. But your faulty height results will not be valid.

We expect intelligence tests to have **predictive validity:** They should predict future performance, and to some extent they do. The predictive power of aptitude tests is fairly strong in the early school years (Roth et al., 2015). But later it weakens.

RETRIEVE IT • • •

ANSWERS IN APPENDIX E

RI-5 What are the three criteria that a psychological test must meet in order to be widely accepted? Explain.

RI-6 Correlation coefficients were used in this section. Here's a quick review: Correlations do not indicate cause-effect, but they do tell us whether two things are associated in some way. A correlation of −1.00 represents perfect _____ (agreement/disagreement) between two sets of scores: As one score goes up, the other score goes _____ (up/down). A correlation of _____ represents no association. The highest correlation, +1.00, represents perfect _____ (agreement/disagreement): As the first score goes up, the other score goes _____ (up/down).

Extremes of Intelligence

LOQ 9-21 What are the traits of those at the low and high intelligence extremes?

One way to glimpse the validity and significance of any test is to compare people who score at the two extremes of the normal curve. The two groups should differ noticeably, and on intelligence tests, they do.

THE LOW EXTREME **Intellectual disability** (formerly called *mental retardation*) is a developmental condition that is apparent before age 18, sometimes with a known physical cause. (*Down syndrome,* for example, is a disorder of varying intellectual and physical severity caused by an extra copy of chromosome 21 in the person's genetic makeup.) To be diagnosed with an intellectual disability, a person must meet two criteria:

1. An intelligence test score indicating performance that is in the lowest 3 percent of the general population, or about 70 or below (Schalock et al., 2010).

2. Difficulty adapting to the normal demands of independent living, as expressed in three areas, or skills: *conceptual* (language, reading, and concepts of money, time, and number); *social* (interpersonal skills, being socially responsible, following basic rules and laws, avoiding being victimized); and *practical* (health and personal care, occupational skill, and travel). In mild forms, intellectual disability, like normal intelligence, results from a combination of genetic and environmental factors (Reichenberg et al., 2016).

For some, intelligence test scores can mean life or death. In the United States (one of the only industrialized countries with the death penalty), fewer people are now eligible for execution. Why? Because in 2002, the U.S. Supreme Court ruled that the execution of people with an intellectual disability—defined as a test score below 70—is "cruel and unusual punishment." For Teresa Lewis, that cutoff was high stakes. Lewis, a "dependent personality" with limited intellect (a reported test score of 72), allegedly agreed to a plot in which two men killed her husband and stepson in exchange for a split of a life insurance payout (Eckholm, 2010). The State of Virginia executed Lewis in 2010. If only she had scored 69.

In 2014, the U.S. Supreme Court recognized the imprecision and arbitrariness of a fixed cutoff score of 70. And it required states with death row inmates who have scored just above 70 to consider other evidence. Thus Ted Herring, who had scored 72 and 74 on intelligence tests—but without knowing that summer follows spring or how to transfer between buses—was taken off Florida's death row (Alvarez & Schwartz, 2014).

> 🔒 **RETRIEVE IT • • •**   *ANSWERS IN APPENDIX E*
>
> **RI-7** Why do psychologists NOT diagnose an intellectual disability based solely on a person's intelligence test score?

THE HIGH EXTREME In one famous project begun in 1921, Lewis Terman studied more than 1500 California schoolchildren with IQ scores over 135. Terman's high-scoring children (later called the "Termites") were—like those in later studies—healthy, well adjusted, and unusually successful academically (Friedman & Martin, 2012; Koenen et al., 2009; Lubinski, 2009, 2016). When restudied over the next seven decades, most people in Terman's group had attained high levels of education (Austin et al., 2002; Holahan & Sears, 1995). Many were doctors, lawyers, professors, scientists, and writers, though none were Nobel Prize winners.

Other studies have followed the lives of precocious youths who had aced the math SAT at age 13—by scoring in the top 1 percent of their age group. By their fifties, these 1650 math whizzes had secured 681 patents (Lubinski et al., 2014). Another group of 13-year-old verbal aptitude high scorers were, by age 38, twice as likely as the math aces to have become humanities professors or written a novel (Kell et al., 2013). About 1 percent of Americans earn doctorates. But for the 12- and 13-year-olds who scored in the top 1 in 10,000 among those of their age taking the SAT, about 4 in 10 had done so (Kell et al., 2013; Makel et al., 2016). One of psychology's whiz kids was Jean Piaget, who by age 15 was publishing scientific articles on mollusks and who went on to become

normal curve the bell-shaped curve that describes the distribution of many physical and psychological attributes. Most scores fall near the average, and fewer and fewer scores lie near the extremes.

reliability the extent to which a test yields consistent results, as assessed by the consistency of scores on two halves of the test, on alternative forms of the test, or on retesting.

validity the extent to which a test measures or predicts what it is supposed to. (See also *predictive validity*.)

predictive validity the success with which a test predicts the behavior it is designed to predict; it is assessed by computing the correlation between test scores and the criterion behavior. (Also called *criterion-related validity*.)

intellectual disability a condition of limited mental ability, indicated by an intelligence test score of 70 or below and difficulty adapting to the demands of life. (Formerly referred to as *mental retardation*.)

"Zach is in the gifted-and-talented-and-you're-not class."

Terman did test two future Nobel laureates in physics, but they failed to score above his gifted sample cutoff (Hulbert, 2005).

Among the high-scoring whiz kids in national searches for precocious youth were Google co-founder Sergey Brin, Facebook's Mark Zuckerberg, and musician Stefani Germanotta (Lady Gaga) (Clynes, 2016). Another became a professional poker player with $100,000+ annual earnings (Lubinski, 2016).

the twentieth century's most famous developmental psychologist (Hunt, 1993). Children with extraordinary academic gifts are sometimes more isolated, shy, and in their own worlds (Winner, 2000). But most thrive.

INTELLIGENCE ACROSS THE LIFE SPAN

What happens to our intellectual muscles as we age? Do they gradually decline, as does our body strength? Or do they remain constant? To see how psychologists track intelligence across the lifetime, see Thinking Critically About: Cross-Sectional and Longitudinal Studies. The quest for answers to such questions illustrates psychology's self-correcting process.

Stability or Change?

LOQ 9-23 How stable are intelligence test scores over the life span?

What can we predict from a child's early-life intelligence scores? Will a precocious 2-year-old mature into a talented college student and a brilliant senior citizen? Maybe—or maybe not. For most children, casual observation and intelligence tests before age 3 only modestly predict their future aptitudes (Humphreys & Davey, 1988; Tasbihsazan et al., 2003). Even Albert Einstein was once thought "slow"—as he was in learning to talk (Quasha, 1980).

By age 4, however, children's performance on intelligence tests begins to predict their adolescent and adult scores. The consistency of scores over time increases with the age of the child (Tucker-Drob & Briley, 2014). By age 11, the stability becomes impressive, as Ian Deary and his colleagues (2004, 2009b, 2013) discovered when they retested the same **cohort**—the same group of people—over a period of years. Their amazing longitudinal

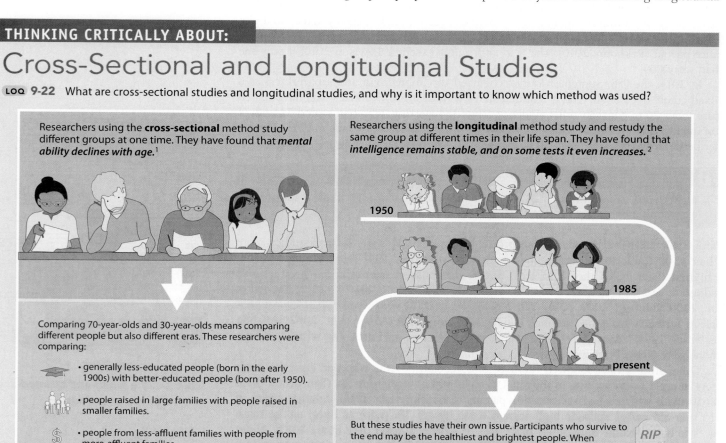

THINKING CRITICALLY ABOUT:

Cross-Sectional and Longitudinal Studies

LOQ 9-22 What are cross-sectional studies and longitudinal studies, and why is it important to know which method was used?

Researchers using the **cross-sectional** method study different groups at one time. They have found that *mental ability declines with age.*[1]

Comparing 70-year-olds and 30-year-olds means comparing different people but also different eras. These researchers were comparing:

- generally less-educated people (born in the early 1900s) with better-educated people (born after 1950).
- people raised in large families with people raised in smaller families.
- people from less-affluent families with people from more-affluent families.

Researchers using the **longitudinal** method study and restudy the same group at different times in their life span. They have found that *intelligence remains stable, and on some tests it even increases.*[2]

1950

1985

present

But these studies have their own issue. Participants who survive to the end may be the healthiest and brightest people. When researchers adjust for loss of participants, they find an intelligence decline, especially after age 85.[3]

RIP

1. Wechsler, 1972. 2. Salthouse, 2010, 2014; Schaie & Geiwitz, 1982. 3. Brayne et al., 1999.

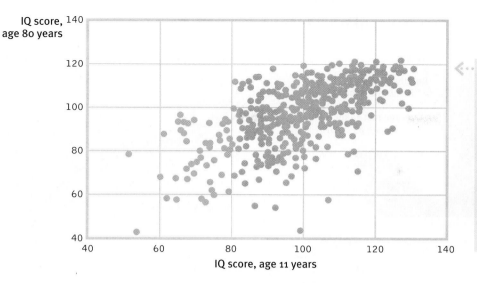

FIGURE 9.13

INTELLIGENCE ENDURES When Ian Deary and his colleagues retested 80-year-old Scots, using an intelligence test they had taken as 11-year-olds, their scores across seven decades correlated +0.66, as shown here. (Data from Deary et al., 2004.) When 106 survivors were again retested at age 90, the correlation with their age 11 scores was +0.54 (Deary et al., 2013).

studies have been enabled by their country, Scotland, doing something no nation has done before or since. On June 1, 1932, essentially every child in the country born in 1921—87,498 children around age 11—took an intelligence test. The aim was to identify working-class children who would benefit from further education. Sixty-five years later to the day, Patricia Whalley, the wife of Deary's co-worker, Lawrence Whalley, discovered the test results on dusty storeroom shelves at the Scottish Council for Research in Education, not far from Deary's Edinburgh University office. "This will change our lives," Deary replied when Whalley told him the news.

And so it has, with dozens of studies of the stability and the predictive capacity of these early test results. One of Deary's studies, for example, retested 542 survivors—now turn-of-the-millennium 80-year-olds—using the same intelligence test they had taken as 11-year-olds in 1932. The result? The correlation between the two sets of scores—after nearly 70 years of varied life experiences—was striking (**FIGURE 9.13**). Ditto when 106 survivors were retested at age 90 (Deary et al., 2013). Another study that followed Scots born in 1936 from ages 11 to 70 confirmed the remarkable stability of intelligence, independent of life circumstance (Johnson et al., 2010).

Children and adults who are more intelligent tend to live healthier and longer lives (Calvin et al., 2017). Why might this be the case? Deary (2008) has proposed four possible explanations:

1. Intelligence facilitates more education, better jobs, and a healthier environment.
2. Intelligence encourages healthy living: less smoking, better diet, more exercise.
3. Prenatal events or early childhood illnesses can influence both intelligence and health.
4. A "well-wired body," as evidenced by fast reaction speeds, perhaps fosters both intelligence and longevity.

LaunchPad Play the role of a researcher studying these issues by engaging online with **Immersive Learning: How Would You Know If Intelligence Changes With Age?**

Aging and Intelligence

LOQ 9-24 How does aging affect crystallized and fluid intelligence?

Does intelligence increase, decrease, or remain constant as we age? The answer depends on the type of intellectual performance we measure:

- **Crystallized intelligence**—our accumulated knowledge as reflected in vocabulary and analogies tests—*increases* up to old age.
- **Fluid intelligence**—our ability to reason speedily and abstractly, as when solving novel logic problems—*decreases* beginning in the twenties and thirties, slowly up to age 75 or so, then more rapidly, especially after age 85 (Cattell, 1963; Deary & Ritchie, 2016; Salthouse, 2009; 2013).

"Whether you live to collect your old-age pension depends in part on your IQ at age 11." —Ian Deary, "Intelligence, Health, and Death," 2005

Women scoring in the highest 25 percent on the Scottish national intelligence test at age 11 tended to live longer than those who scored in the lowest 25 percent. "On average," reports Deary (2016), "a girl with a 30-point disadvantage in IQ on this 45-minute test at age 11 was half as likely to be alive" 65 years later.

cohort a group of people sharing a common characteristic, such as being from a given time period.

cross-sectional study research that compares people of different ages at the same point in time.

longitudinal study research that follows and retests the same people over time.

crystallized intelligence our accumulated knowledge and verbal skills; tends to increase with age.

fluid intelligence our ability to reason speedily and abstractly; tends to decrease with age, especially during late adulthood.

FIGURE 9.14

WITH AGE, WE LOSE AND WE WIN.

Studies reveal that word power grows with age, while fluid intelligence declines. (Data from Salthouse, 2010.)

Ann Baldwin/Shutterstock

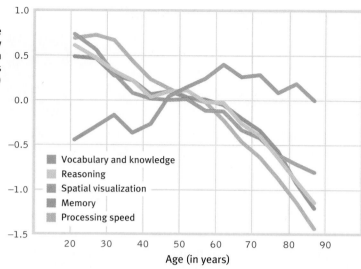

Relative performance above or below average (with average test-taker's score as zero)

Vocabulary and knowledge
Reasoning
Spatial visualization
Memory
Processing speed

Age (in years)

"Knowledge is knowing a tomato is a fruit; wisdom is not putting it in a fruit salad." —Anonymous

"We're looking for someone with the wisdom of a 50-year-old, the experience of a 40-year-old, the drive of a 30-year-old, and the payscale of a 20-year-old."

"In youth we learn, in age we understand." —Marie Von Ebner-Eschenbach, *Aphorisms*, 1883

With age we lose and we win. We lose recall memory and processing speed, but we gain vocabulary and knowledge (**FIGURE 9.14**). Fluid intelligence may decline, but older adults' social-reasoning skills increase, as shown by an ability to take multiple perspectives, to appreciate knowledge limits, and to offer helpful wisdom in times of social conflict (Grossman et al., 2010). Decisions also become less distorted by negative emotions such as anxiety, depression, and anger (Blanchard-Fields, 2007; Carstensen & Mikels, 2005).

Age-related cognitive differences help explain why older adults are less likely to embrace new technologies (Charness & Boot, 2009; Pew, 2017). These cognitive differences also help explain why mathematicians and scientists produce much of their most creative work during their late twenties or early thirties, when fluid intelligence is at its peak (Jones et al., 2014). In contrast, authors, historians, and philosophers tend to produce their best work in their forties, fifties, and beyond—after accumulating more knowledge (Simonton, 1988, 1990). Poets, for example, who depend on fluid intelligence, reach their peak output earlier than prose authors, who need the deeper knowledge reservoir that accumulates with age. This finding holds in every major literary tradition, for both living and dead languages.

🔒 RETRIEVE IT • • •

ANSWERS IN APPENDIX E

RI-8 Researcher A wants to study how intelligence changes over the life span. Researcher B wants to study the intelligence of people who are now at various life stages. Which researcher should use the cross-sectional method, and which the longitudinal method?

LaunchPad Watch the **Video: Longitudinal and Cross-Sectional Studies** for a helpful tutorial animation.

🔒 REVIEW   INTELLIGENCE AND ITS ASSESSMENT

⟩⟩ Learning Objectives

TEST YOURSELF Answer these repeated Learning Objective Questions on your own (before checking the answers in Appendix D) to improve your retention of the concepts (McDaniel et al., 2009, 2015).

9-15 How do psychologists define *intelligence,* and what are the arguments for *g*?

9-16 How do Gardner's and Sternberg's theories of multiple intelligences differ, and what criticisms have they faced?

9-17 What are the four components of emotional intelligence?

9-18 What is an *intelligence test,* and how do achievement and aptitude tests differ?

9-19 When and why were intelligence tests created, and how do today's tests differ from early intelligence tests?

9-20 What is a *normal curve*, and what does it mean to say that a test has been *standardized* and is *reliable* and *valid*?

9-21 What are the traits of those at the low and high intelligence extremes?

9-22 What are cross-sectional studies and longitudinal studies, and why is it important to know which method was used?

9-23 How stable are intelligence test scores over the life span?

9-24 How does aging affect crystallized and fluid intelligence?

⟶ Terms and Concepts to Remember

TEST YOURSELF Write down the definition yourself, then check your answer on the referenced page.

intelligence, **p. 323**
general intelligence *(g)*, **p. 323**
savant syndrome, **p. 324**
emotional intelligence, **p. 327**
intelligence test, **p. 327**
achievement test, **p. 327**
aptitude test, **p. 327**
mental age, **p. 329**

Stanford-Binet, **p. 329**
intelligence quotient (IQ), **p. 329**
Wechsler Adult Intelligence Scale (WAIS), **p. 329**
standardization, **p. 329**
normal curve, **p. 331**
reliability, **p. 331**
validity, **p. 331**

predictive validity, **p. 331**
intellectual disability, **p. 331**
cohort, **p. 333**
cross-sectional study, **p. 333**
longitudinal study, **p. 333**
crystallized intelligence, **p. 333**
fluid intelligence, **p. 333**

⟶ Experience the Testing Effect

TEST YOURSELF Answer the following questions on your own first, then check your answers in Appendix E.

1. Charles Spearman suggested we have one
_____ _____ underlying success across a variety of intellectual abilities.

2. The existence of savant syndrome seems to support
   a. Sternberg's distinction among three types of intelligence.
   b. criticism of multiple intelligence theories.
   c. Gardner's theory of multiple intelligences.
   d. Thorndike's view of social intelligence.

3. Sternberg's three types of intelligence are
_____, _____, and
_____.

4. Emotionally intelligent people tend to
   a. seek immediate gratification.
   b. understand their own emotions but not those of others.
   c. understand others' emotions but not their own.
   d. succeed in their careers.

5. The IQ of a 6-year-old with a measured mental age of 9 would be
   a. 67.
   b. 133.
   c. 86.
   d. 150.

6. The Wechsler Adult Intelligence Scale (WAIS) is best able to tell us
   a. what part of an individual's intelligence is determined by genetic inheritance.
   b. whether the test-taker will succeed in a job.
   c. how the test-taker compares with other adults in vocabulary and arithmetic reasoning.
   d. whether the test-taker has specific skills for music and the performing arts.

7. The Stanford-Binet, the Wechsler Adult Intelligence Scale, and the Wechsler Intelligence Scale for Children yield consistent results, for example on retesting. In other words, these tests have high _____.

8. Use the concepts of crystallized and fluid intelligence to explain why writers tend to produce their most creative work later in life, while scientists often hit their peak much earlier.

9. Which of the following is NOT a possible explanation for the fact that more intelligent people tend to live longer, healthier lives?
   a. Intelligence facilitates more education, better jobs, and a healthier environment.
   b. Intelligence encourages a more health-promoting lifestyle.
   c. Intelligent people have slower reaction times, so are less likely to put themselves at risk.
   d. Prenatal events or early childhood illnesses could influence both intelligence and health.

Continue testing yourself with ≈ **LearningCurve** or ≈ **Achieve Read & Practice** to learn and remember most effectively.

⟶ Genetic and Environmental Influences on Intelligence

"I told my parents that if grades were so important they should have paid for a smarter egg donor."

Intelligence runs in families. But why? Are our intellectual abilities mostly inherited? Or are they molded by our environment? Few issues in psychology arouse so much passion. Let's examine some of the evidence, focusing on these questions:

- What do twin and adoption studies tell us about how heredity and experience influence intelligence?
- Can extreme environmental influences amplify or diminish intelligence?
- What intelligence test score similarities and differences exist among groups, and what accounts for those differences?

HEREDITY AND INTELLIGENCE

LOQ 9-25 What is *heritability*, and what do twin and adoption studies tell us about the nature and nurture of intelligence?

Heritability is the portion of variation among people in a group that we can attribute to genes. Estimates of the heritability of intelligence—the extent to which intelligence test score variation within a group can be attributed to genetic variation—range from 50 to 80 percent (Madison et al., 2016; Plomin et al., 2016). Does this mean that we can assume that 50 percent of *your* intelligence is due to your genes, and the rest to your environment? *No.* Heritability never applies to an individual, only to *why people in a group differ from one another*.

The heritability of intelligence varies from study to study. To see why, consider humorist Mark Twain's fantasy of raising boys in barrels until age 12, feeding them through a hole. Let's take his joke a step further and say we'll give all those boys an intelligence test at age 12. Since their *environments* were all equal, any difference in their test scores could only be due to heredity—thus, heritability would be 100 percent. But what if a mad scientist cloned 100 boys and raised them in drastically different environments (some in barrels and others in mansions)? In this case, *heredity* would be equal, so any test-score differences could only be due to environment. The environmental effect would be 100 percent, and heritability would be zero.

In real life, we can't clone people to study the effects of heredity and environment. But nature has done that work for us. Identical twins share the same genes. Do they also share the same mental abilities? As you can see from **FIGURE 9.15**, which summarizes many studies, the answer is clearly *Yes*. Even when adopted by two different families, their intelligence test scores are very similar. When raised together, their scores are nearly as similar as those of the same person taking the same test twice (Haworth et al., 2009; Lykken, 2006; Plomin et al., 2016). Identical twins also exhibit substantial similarity (and heritability) in specific talents, such as music, math, and sports.

Scans reveal that identical twins' brains have similar gray- and white-matter volume, and the areas associated with verbal and spatial intelligence are virtually the same (Deary et al., 2009a; Thompson et al., 2001). Their brains also show similar activity while doing mental tasks (Koten et al., 2009).

Although genes matter, there is no known "genius" gene. When 200 researchers pooled their data on 126,559 people, all the gene variations analyzed accounted for only about 2 percent of the differences in educational achievement (Rietveld et al., 2013, 2014). Others have replicated this modest effect (Belsky et al., 2016). One follow-up British study, using

heritability the proportion of variation among individuals in a group that we can attribute to genes. The heritability of a trait may vary, depending on the range of populations and environments studied.

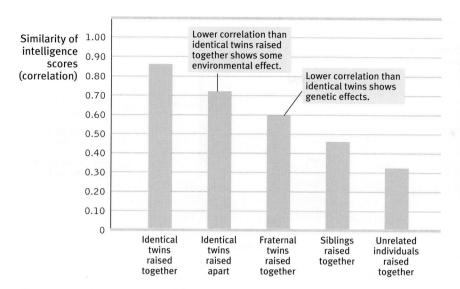

Similarity of intelligence scores (correlation)

Lower correlation than identical twins raised together shows some environmental effect.

Lower correlation than identical twins shows genetic effects.

Identical twins raised together | Identical twins raised apart | Fraternal twins raised together | Siblings raised together | Unrelated individuals raised together

FIGURE 9.15

INTELLIGENCE: NATURE AND NURTURE The most genetically similar people have the most similar intelligence scores. Remember: 1.00 indicates a perfect correlation; zero indicates no correlation at all. (Data from McGue et al., 1993.)

a new genetic method, found genes that together predicted 9 percent of school achievement variation at age 16 (Selzam et al., 2016). This much seems clear: Like height, intelligence is *polygenetic,* involving many genes (Johnson, 2010). More than 50 specific gene variations together account for 5 percent of our individual height differences, leaving the rest yet to be discovered. What matters for intelligence (as for height, personality, sexual orientation, schizophrenia, or just about any human trait) is the combination of many genes—including 52 intelligence-linked genes identified in one pooling of findings from nearly 80,000 people (Sniekers et al., 2017).

ENVIRONMENT AND INTELLIGENCE

Fraternal twins are genetically no more alike than other siblings, but they usually share an environment and are often treated similarly. Their intelligence test scores are also more alike than are the scores of two other siblings (see Figure 9.15). So environment does have some effect. Adoption studies help us assess the influence of environment. Seeking to untangle genes and environment, researchers have compared the intelligence test scores of adopted children with those of their

- *biological parents* (who provided their genes).
- *adoptive parents* (who provided their home environment).
- *adoptive siblings* (who shared that home environment).

Several studies suggest that a shared environment exerts a modest influence on intelligence test scores.

- Adoption from poverty into middle-class homes enhances children's intelligence test scores (Nisbett et al., 2012). One large Swedish study looked at this effect among children adopted into wealthier families with more educated parents. The adopted children's test scores were higher, by an average of 4.4 points, than those of their not-adopted biological siblings (Kendler et al., 2015a).
- Adoption of mistreated or neglected children also enhances their intelligence scores (Almas et al., 2017).
- The intelligence scores of "virtual twins"—same-age, unrelated siblings adopted as infants and raised together—correlate at a level higher than chance: +0.28 (Segal et al., 2012).

So during childhood, adoptive siblings' test scores correlate modestly. What do you think happens as the years go by and adopted children settle in with their adoptive families? Would you expect the family-environment effect to grow stronger and the genetic-legacy effect to shrink?

"Selective breeding has given me an aptitude for the law, but I still love fetching a dead duck out of freezing water."

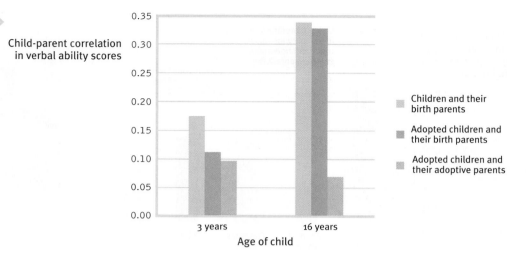

FIGURE 9.16

IN VERBAL ABILITY, WHOM DO ADOPTED CHILDREN RESEMBLE? As the years went by in their adoptive families, children's verbal ability scores became more like their *biological* parents' scores. (Data from Plomin & DeFries, 1998.)

Child-parent correlation in verbal ability scores

Age of child

- Children and their birth parents
- Adopted children and their birth parents
- Adopted children and their adoptive parents

If you said *Yes*, behavior geneticists have a stunning surprise for you. Adopted children's intelligence test scores resemble those of their biological parents much more than their adoptive families (Loehlin, 2016). And over time, adopted children's verbal ability scores become even more like those of their biological parents **(FIGURE 9.16)**. Mental similarities between adopted children and their adoptive families wane with age (McGue et al., 1993). Who would have guessed?

Genetic influences become more apparent as we accumulate life experience. Identical twins' similarities, for example, continue or increase into their eighties. In one massive study of 11,000 twin pairs in four countries, the heritability of general intelligence (g) increased from 41 percent in middle childhood to 55 percent in adolescence to 66 percent in young adulthood (Haworth et al., 2010). Thus, report Ian Deary and his colleagues (2009a, 2012), the heritability of general intelligence increases from "about 30 percent" in early childhood to "well over 50 percent in adulthood."

ENGAGE 🔲 **LaunchPad** For a helpful tutorial animation, watch the **Video: Twin Studies.** Then try to predict the correlation of intelligence scores in **Concept Practice: Studying Twins and Adopted Children.**

🔒 **RETRIEVE IT • • •**   *ANSWERS IN APPENDIX E*

RI-1 A check on your understanding of heritability: If environments become more equal, the heritability of intelligence will

   a. increase.   b. decrease.   c. be unchanged.

GENE-ENVIRONMENT INTERACTIONS

LOQ 9-26 How can environmental influences affect cognitive development?

Genes and experience together weave the fabric of intelligence. *Epigenetics* studies the microbiology of this nature–nurture meeting place. With all our abilities—whether mental or physical—our genes shape the experiences that shape us. If you have a natural aptitude for sports, you will probably play more often than others (getting more practice, coaching, and experience). Or, if you have a natural aptitude for academics, you will more likely stay in school, read books, and ask questions—all of which will increase your brain power. The same would be true for your identical twin—who might, not just for genetic reasons, also become a star performer. In gene-environment interactions, small genetic advantages can trigger social experiences that multiply our original skills.

Sometimes, however, environmental conditions work in reverse, depressing physical or cognitive development. Severe deprivation leaves footprints on the brain, as J. McVicker Hunt (1982) observed in a destitute Iranian orphanage. The typical child Hunt observed there could not sit up unassisted at age 2 or walk at age 4. The little care infants received was not in response to their crying, cooing, or other behaviors, so the children developed little sense of personal control over their environment. They were instead becoming passive "glum lumps." Extreme deprivation was crushing native intelligence—a finding confirmed by other studies of children raised in poorly run orphanages in Romania and elsewhere (Nelson et al., 2009, 2013; van IJzendoorn et al., 2008).

DEVASTATING NEGLECT Some Romanian orphans, such as this child in the Leaganul Pentru Copii orphanage in 1990, had minimal interaction with caregivers, and suffered delayed development.

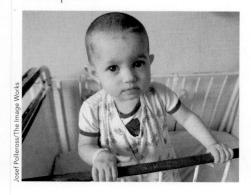

Josef Polleross/The Image Works

Aware of both the dramatic effects of early experiences and the impact of early intervention, Hunt began a training program for Iranian caregivers, teaching them to play language-fostering games with 11 infants. They imitated the babies' babbling. They engaged them in vocal follow-the-leader. And, finally, they taught the infants sounds from the Persian language. The results were dramatic. By 22 months of age, the infants could name more than 50 objects and body parts. They so charmed visitors that most were adopted—an unprecedented success for the orphanage.

Hunt's findings are an extreme case of a more general finding: The poor environmental conditions that accompany poverty can depress cognitive development and produce stresses that impede cognitive performance (Heberle & Carter, 2015; Tuerk, 2005). And this may help explain another finding: Where environments vary widely, as they do among children of less-educated parents, environmental differences are more predictive of intelligence scores (Tucker-Drob & Bates, 2016). Like a computer that slows when running multiple operations, impoverished people's worries and distractions consume cognitive bandwidth and can diminish their thinking capacity. On tests of cognitive functioning, sugar cane farmers in India scored better after being paid for their harvest—when their money worries dropped (Mani et al., 2013).

If extreme conditions—sensory deprivation, social isolation, poverty—can slow normal brain development, could the reverse also be true? Could an "enriched" environment amplify normal development and give children a superior intellect? Most experts are doubtful (Bruer, 1999; DeLoache et al., 2010; Reichert et al., 2010). There is no environmental recipe for fast-forwarding a normal infant into a genius. All babies should have normal exposure to sights, sounds, and speech. Beyond that, Sandra Scarr's (1984) verdict still is widely shared: "Parents who are very concerned about providing special educational lessons for their babies are wasting their time."

More encouraging results come from intensive, post-babyhood preschool programs (Dodge et al., 2017; Garcia et al., 2016; Tucker-Drob, 2012). Across a number of experiments, intelligence scores also rise with nutritional supplements to pregnant mothers and newborns (3.5 points), with quality preschool experiences (4 points), and with interactive reading programs (6 points) (Protzko et al., 2013).

Growth Mindset

Schooling and intelligence interact, and both enhance later income (Ceci & Williams, 1997, 2009). But what we accomplish with our intelligence depends also on our own beliefs and motivation. One analysis of 72,431 undergraduates found that study motivation and study skills rivaled aptitude and previous grades as predictors of academic achievement (Credé & Kuncel, 2008). Motivation can even affect intelligence test performance. Four dozen studies show that, when promised money for doing well, adolescents score higher on such tests (Duckworth et al., 2011).

These observations would not surprise psychologist Carol Dweck (2012a,b, 2015). She reports that believing intelligence is changeable fosters a *growth mindset,* a focus on learning and growing. Dweck teaches young teens to adopt a growth mindset. She and her team explain that the brain is like a muscle, growing stronger with use as neuron connections grow. Receiving praise for *effort* and for tackling challenges, rather than for being smart or accomplished, helps teens understand the link between hard work and success (Gunderson et al., 2013). Although a growth mindset doesn't alter intelligence, it can make children and youth more resilient when others frustrate them (Paunesku et al., 2015; Yeager et al., 2013, 2014, 2016a).

More than 300 studies confirm that ability + opportunity + motivation = success in fields from sports to science to music (Ericsson et al., 2007). High school students' math proficiency and college students' grades reflect their aptitude but also their self-discipline, their belief in the power of effort, and a curious "hungry mind" (Murayama et al., 2013; Richardson et al., 2012;

"It is our choices . . . that show what we truly are, far more than our abilities." —Professor Dumbledore to Harry Potter in J. K. Rowling's *Harry Potter and the Chamber of Secrets*, 1999

A HUNGRY MIND

Dave Nagel/Getty Images

U.S. SPELLING CHAMPS Nihar Janga, 11, and Jairam Hathwar, 13, celebrate their co-winning the 2016 Scripps National Spelling Bee. What were Nihar and Jairam's winning words? "Gesellschaft" and "Feldenkrais."

ENGAGE

(ASK YOURSELF)

Are you working to the potential reflected in your standardized test scores? What, other than your aptitude, is affecting your school performance?

von Stumm et al., 2011). And consider: Between 2008 and 2016, youth of South-Asian heritage won all nine U.S. national spelling bee contests—an incredible achievement likely influenced by a cultural belief that strong effort will bring success (Rattan et al., 2012; Shankar, 2016).

Some researchers caution that applying growth mindset findings in large-scale interventions with at-risk students can have a downside: the social cost of blaming struggling individuals for their circumstances (Ikizer & Blanton, 2016). Sometimes people need more than the power of positive thinking to overcome their harsh conditions.

GROUP DIFFERENCES IN INTELLIGENCE TEST SCORES

If there were no group differences in aptitude scores, psychologists would have less debate over hereditary and environmental influences. But there are group differences. What are they? And what shall we make of them?

Gender Similarities and Differences

LOQ 9-27 How and why do the genders differ in mental ability scores?

In science, as in everyday life, differences, not similarities, excite interest. In worldwide studies, men estimate their own intelligence higher than do women (Furnham, 2016). Yet compared with their anatomical and physiological differences, men and women's intelligence differences are minor. In that 1932 testing of all Scottish 11-year-olds, for example, girls' average intelligence score was 100.6 and boys' was 100.5 (Deary et al., 2003). So far as g is concerned, boys and girls, men and women, are the same.

Yet most people find differences more newsworthy. In cultures where both boys and girls benefit from schooling, girls outpace boys in spelling, verbal fluency, and locating objects (Voyer & Voyer, 2014). They are better emotion detectors and are more sensitive to touch, taste, and color (Halpern et al., 2007). In math computation and overall math performance, girls and boys hardly differ (Else-Quest et al., 2010; Hyde & Mertz, 2009; Lindberg et al., 2010).

On complex math problems, boys outperform girls. But the most reliable male edge appears in spatial ability tests like the one shown in **FIGURE 9.17** (Maeda & Yoon, 2013; Palejwala & Fine, 2015). (To solve the problem, you must quickly rotate three-dimensional objects in your mind.) Males' mental ability scores (and brains) also vary more than females'. Worldwide, boys outnumber girls at both the low and high extremes (Ball et al., 2017; Brunner et al., 2013). Boys, for example, are more often found in special education classes, but also among those scoring very high on the SAT math test.

Psychologist Steven Pinker (2005) has argued the evolutionary perspective—that biology affects gender differences in life priorities (women's somewhat greater interest in people versus men's in money and things), in risk-taking (with men more reckless), and in math reasoning and spatial abilities. Such differences are, he noted, observed across cultures, stable over time, influenced by prenatal hormones, and observed in genetic boys raised as girls.

"That's an excellent suggestion, Miss Triggs. Perhaps one of the men would like to suggest it."

Give females long-term testosterone therapy (for female-to-male sex reassignment) and their brain language-processing areas become, after losing some gray matter, more male-like (Hahn et al., 2016).

Which one of the options below matches the Original?

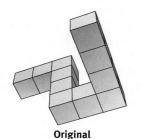

Original

 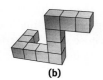

(a)   (b)   (c)

FIGURE 9.17

THE MENTAL ROTATION TEST This illustrates the type of items found on a spatial abilities test. See answer below.[5]

But social expectations and opportunities also construct gender by shaping interests and abilities (Crawford et al., 1995; Eccles et al., 1990). In Asia and Russia, teen girls have outperformed boys in an international science exam; in North America and Britain, boys have scored higher (Fairfield, 2012). More gender-equal cultures, such as Sweden and Iceland, exhibit little of the gender math gap found in gender-unequal cultures, such as Turkey and Korea (Guiso et al., 2008; Kane & Mertz, 2012). And since the 1970s, as gender equity has increased in the United States, the boy-to-girl ratio among 12- to 14-year-olds with very high SAT math scores (above 700) has declined from 13 to 1 to 3 to 1 (Nisbett et al., 2012; Makel et al. 2016).

Maryam Mirzakhani/Getty Images

MINDING THE MATH GAP In 2014, Iranian math professor Maryam Mirzakhani (1977–2017) became the first woman to win math's most admired award, the Fields Medal. What was her advice to people who want to know more about math? Practice patience. "The beauty of mathematics," Mirzakhani said, "only shows itself to more patient followers" (*The Guardian*, 2014).

Racial and Ethnic Similarities and Differences

LOQ 9-28 How and why do racial and ethnic groups differ in mental ability scores?

Fueling the group-differences debate are two other disturbing but scientifically agreed-upon facts:

- Racial and ethnic groups differ in their average intelligence test scores.
- High-scoring people (and groups) are more likely to attain high levels of education and income.

Larry Williams/Getty Images

5. The correct answer is c.

There are many group differences in average intelligence test scores. New Zealanders of European descent outscore native Maori New Zealanders. Israeli Jews outscore Israeli Arabs. Most Japanese outscore most Burakumin, a stigmatized Japanese minority. And White Americans have outscored Black Americans. This Black-White difference appears to have diminished somewhat in recent years, especially among children (Dickens & Flynn, 2006; Nisbett et al., 2012).

One more agreed-upon fact is that *group* differences provide little basis for judging individuals. Worldwide, women outlive men by four years, but knowing that you are male or female won't tell us how long you will live.

We have seen that heredity contributes to *individual* differences in intelligence. But group differences in a heritable trait may be entirely environmental, as in our earlier boys-in-barrels versus boys-in-mansions example. Consider one of nature's experiments: Allow some children to grow up hearing their culture's dominant language, while others, born deaf, do not. Then give both groups an intelligence test rooted in the dominant language. The result? No surprise. Those with expertise in the dominant language will score higher than those who were born deaf (Braden, 1994; Steele, 1990; Zeidner, 1990).

Might the racial and ethnic gaps be similarly environmental? Consider:

Genetics research reveals that under the skin, we humans are remarkably alike. Despite some racial variation, such as in health risks, the average genetic difference between two Icelandic villagers or between two Kenyans greatly exceeds the group difference between Icelanders and Kenyans (Cavalli-Sforza et al., 1994; Rosenberg et al., 2002). Moreover, looks can deceive. Light-skinned Europeans and dark-skinned Africans are genetically closer than are dark-skinned Africans and dark-skinned Aboriginal Australians.

Race is not a neatly defined biological category. Many social scientists see race primarily as a social construction without well-defined physical boundaries, as each race blends seamlessly into the race of its geographical neighbors (Helms et al., 2005; Smedley & Smedley, 2005). In one genetic analysis of more than 160,000 people living in the United States, most with less than 28 percent African ancestry said they were White; those with more than 28 percent mostly said they were African-American (Byrc et al., 2015). Moreover, with increasingly mixed ancestries, more and more people defy neat racial categorization and self-identify as multiracial (Pauker et al., 2009).

Within the same populations, there are generation-to-generation differences in test scores. Test scores of today's better-fed, better-educated, and more test-prepared populations exceed the scores of 1930's populations (Flynn, 2012; Pietschnig & Voracek, 2015; Trahan et al., 2014). The scores of the two generations differ by a greater margin than the intelligence test score of the average U.S. White today exceeding that of the average U.S. Black. One research review noted that the average intelligence test performance of today's sub-Saharan Africans is the same as that of British adults in 1948 (Wicherts et al., 2010). No one credits genetics for such generation-to-generation differences.

Schools and culture matter. Countries whose economies create a large wealth gap between rich and poor tend also to have a large rich-versus-poor intelligence test score gap (Nisbett, 2009). In China and Turkey, people in poorer regions have the lowest scores, and those in wealthier regions have the highest (Lynn et al., 2015, 2016). Moreover, educational policies (such as kindergarten attendance, school discipline, and instructional time per year) predict national differences in intelligence and knowledge tests (Lynn & Vanhanen, 2012; Rindermann & Ceci, 2009). Math achievement, aptitude test differences, and especially grades may reflect conscientiousness more than competence (Poropat, 2014). Asian students, who have outperformed North American students on such tests, have also spent 30 percent more time in school and much more time in and out of school studying math (Geary et al., 1996; Larson & Verma, 1999; Stevenson, 1992). Women in college and university

WORLD SCRABBLE CHAMPS In 2015, Team Nigeria was the top country in the World Scrabble Championship. Five of its six members finished among the top 50 contestants, including Wellington Jighere, center, the individual world Scrabble champion.

similarly outperform equally able men, thanks partly to their greater conscientiousness (Keiser et al., 2016).

*In **different eras, different ethnic groups have experienced golden ages—periods of remarkable achievement.*** Twenty-five hundred years ago, it was the Greeks and the Egyptians, then the Romans. In the eighth and ninth centuries, genius seemed to reside in the Arab world. Five hundred years ago, the Aztec Indians and the peoples of Northern Europe were the superachievers. Today, many people notice Asian technological genius and Jewish cultural success. Cultures rise and fall over centuries; the gene pool changes more slowly.

"Do not obtain your slaves from Britain, because they are so stupid and so utterly incapable of being taught." —Cicero, 106–43 B.C.E.

🔒 **RETRIEVE IT • • •**   *ANSWERS IN APPENDIX E*

RI-2 The heritability of intelligence scores will be greater in a society marked by equal opportunity than in a society of peasants and aristocrats. Why?

THE QUESTION OF BIAS

LOQ 9-29 Are intelligence tests biased or unfair? What is *stereotype threat,* and how does it affect test-takers' performance?

Knowing there are group differences in intelligence test scores leads us to wonder whether those differences are built into the tests. Is intelligence testing a constructive way to guide people toward suitable opportunities? Or is it a potent, discriminatory weapon camouflaged as science? In short, are intelligence tests biased? The answer depends on which of two very different definitions of bias we use.

The *scientific* meaning of *bias* hinges solely on a test's validity—on whether it predicts future behavior for all groups of test-takers, not just for some. For example, if the SAT accurately predicted the college achievement of women but not that of men, then the test would be biased. In this scientific meaning of the term, the near-consensus among psychologists has been that the major U.S. aptitude tests are *not* biased (Berry & Zhao, 2015; Neisser et al., 1996; Wigdor & Garner, 1982). The tests' predictive validity is roughly the same, regardless of gender, race, ethnicity, or socioeconomic level. If an intelligence test score of 95 predicts slightly below-average grades, that rough prediction usually applies equally to all.

But in everyday language we may consider a test "biased" if it is unfair—if test scores will be influenced by the test-taker's cultural experience. This in fact happened to Eastern

stereotype threat a self-confirming concern that one will be evaluated based on a negative stereotype

European immigrants in the early 1900s. Lacking the experience to answer questions about their new culture, many were classified as "feebleminded."

If we use "biased" in this popular sense, then yes, intelligence tests may be considered unfair (even if scientifically unbiased). Why? Because they measure the test-takers' developed abilities, which reflect, in part, their education and experiences. Some researchers therefore recommend creating culture-neutral questions—such as assessing people's ability to learn novel words, sayings, and analogies—to enable *culture-fair* aptitude tests (Fagan & Holland, 2007, 2009).

Other researchers believe that blaming a test for a group's lower scores is like blaming a messenger for bad news. Why blame the tests for exposing unequal experiences and opportunities? If, because of malnutrition, people were to suffer stunted growth, would you blame the measuring stick that reveals it? If unequal past experiences predict unequal future achievements, a valid aptitude test will detect such inequalities.

As you have seen in so many contexts throughout this text, expectations and attitudes influence perceptions and behaviors. For intelligence test makers, expectations can introduce bias. And for intelligence test takers, they can become self-fulfilling prophecies.

🔒 **RETRIEVE IT • • •**   *ANSWERS IN APPENDIX E*

RI-3 What is the difference between a test that is culturally "biased" and a test that is scientifically biased?

Test-Takers' Expectations

"Math class is tough!" — "Teen Talk" talking Barbie doll (introduced July 1992, recalled October 1992)

When Steven Spencer and his colleagues (1997) gave a difficult math test to equally capable men and women, women did not do as well—except when they had been led to expect that women usually do as well as men on the test. Otherwise, something affected their performance. There was a "threat in the air" (Spencer et al., 2016). And with Claude Steele and Joshua Aronson, Spencer (2002) again observed this self-fulfilling **stereotype threat** when Black students performed worse after being reminded of their race just before taking verbal aptitude tests. Follow-up experiments have confirmed that negatively stereotyped minorities and women may have unrealized academic potential (Grand, 2016; Nguyen & Ryan, 2008; Walton & Spencer, 2009). If, when taking an intelligence test or performing a work-related task, you are worried that your group or "type" often doesn't do well, your self-doubts and self-monitoring may hijack your working memory and impair your performance (Hutchison et al., 2013). Such thoughts and worries about what others are thinking about you can be distracting. For such reasons, stereotype threat may impair attention, performance, and learning (Inzlicht & Kang, 2010; Rydell et al., 2010). Remove the threat—by labeling the assessment a "warm-up" exercise rather than a "test"—and stereotyped minorities often perform better (Taylor & Walton, 2011).

Stereotype threat helps explain why Blacks have scored higher when tested by Blacks than when tested by Whites (Danso & Esses, 2001; Inzlicht & Ben-Zeev, 2000). It implies a possible effect of non-Black teachers having lower expectations for Black students than do Black teachers (Gershenson et al., 2016). And it gives us insight into why women have scored higher on math tests with no male test-takers present, and why women's online chess performance drops sharply when they *think* they are playing a male opponent (Maass et al., 2008). From such studies, Steele (1995, 2010) has concluded that telling students they probably won't succeed (as is sometimes implied by remedial "minority support" programs) can function as a stereotype and erode performance.

Other research teams have demonstrated benefits of self-affirmation exercises (Cohen & Sherman, 2014; Goyer et al., 2017; Harackiewicz et al., 2014, 2016). When challenged to believe in their potential, increase their sense of belonging, or focus on intelligence as malleable, disadvantaged university students have earned markedly higher grades and have had lower dropout rates (Tibbetts et al., 2016; Yeager et al., 2016b).

* * *

Perhaps, then, our goals for tests of mental abilities should be threefold. First, we should realize the benefits that intelligence-testing pioneer Alfred Binet foresaw—to enable schools to recognize who might profit most from early intervention. Second, we must remain alert to Binet's wish that intelligence test scores not be misinterpreted as literal measures of a person's worth and potential. Third, we must remember that the competence that general intelligence tests sample is important; it helps enable success in some life paths. Without such tests, those who decide on jobs and admissions would rely more on other considerations, such as personal opinion. But these tests reflect only one important aspect of personal competence (Stanovich et al., 2013, 2014a,b). Our rationality, practical intelligence, and emotional intelligence matter, too, as do other forms of creativity, talent, and character.

The point to remember: There are many ways of being successful: Our differences are variations of human adaptability. Life's great achievements result not only from "can do" abilities (and fair opportunity) but also from "will do" motivation. Competence + Diligence → Accomplishment.

"Almost all the joyful things of life are outside the measure of IQ tests."
—Madeleine L'Engle, *A Circle of Quiet*, 1972

"[Einstein] showed that genius equals brains plus tenacity squared." —Walter Isaacson, "Einstein's Final Quest," 2009

🔒 RETRIEVE IT • • •   *ANSWERS IN APPENDIX E*

RI-4 What psychological principle helps explain why women tend to perform more poorly when they believe their online chess opponent is male?

📖 LaunchPad To explore how you perceive your own intelligence, engage online with **Immersive Learning: Assess Your Strengths—What Is Your Theory of Intelligence, and How Is That Affecting Your Success?**

ENGAGE

💡 What time is it now? When we asked you (in the section on overconfidence) to estimate how quickly you would finish this chapter, did you underestimate or overestimate?

ENGAGE

🔒 REVIEW   GENETIC AND ENVIRONMENTAL INFLUENCES ON INTELLIGENCE

⟩ Learning Objectives

TEST YOURSELF Answer these repeated Learning Objective Questions on your own (before checking the answers in Appendix D) to improve your retention of the concepts (McDaniel et al., 2009, 2015).

9-25 What is *heritability*, and what do twin and adoption studies tell us about the nature and nurture of intelligence?

9-26 How can environmental influences affect cognitive development?

9-27 How and why do the genders differ in mental ability scores?

9-28 How and why do racial and ethnic groups differ in mental ability scores?

9-29 Are intelligence tests biased or unfair? What is *stereotype threat*, and how does it affect test-takers' performance?

⟩ Terms and Concepts to Remember

TEST YOURSELF Write down the definition yourself, then check your answer on the referenced page.

heritability, **p. 336**   stereotype threat, **p. 344**

⟩ Experience the Testing Effect

TEST YOURSELF Answer the following questions on your own first, then check your answers in Appendix E.

1. To say that the heritability of intelligence is about 50 percent means that 50 percent of
   a. an individual's intelligence is due to genetic factors.
   b. the similarities between two groups of people are attributable to genes.
   c. the variation in intelligence within a group of people is attributable to genetic factors.
   d. an individual's intelligence is due to each parent's genes.

2. The strongest support for heredity's influence on intelligence is the finding that
   a. identical twins, but not other siblings, have nearly identical intelligence test scores.
   b. the correlation between intelligence test scores of fraternal twins is not higher than that for other siblings.
   c. mental similarities between adopted siblings increase with age.
   d. children in impoverished families have similar intelligence scores.

3. The environmental influence that has the clearest, most profound effect on intellectual development is
   a. exposing normal infants to enrichment programs before age 1.
   b. growing up in an economically disadvantaged home or neighborhood.
   c. being raised in conditions of extreme deprivation.
   d. being an identical twin.

4. _____ _____ can lead to poor performance on tests by undermining test-takers' belief that they can do well on the test.

Continue testing yourself with ▨ **LearningCurve** or ≋ **Achieve Read &
Practice** to learn and remember most effectively.

Motivation and Emotion

Flashpop/Getty Images

How well I [DM] remember asking my first discussion question in a new introductory psychology class. Several hands rose, along with one left foot. The foot belonged to Chris Klein, who was the unlikeliest person to have made it to that class. At birth, Chris suffered oxygen deprivation that required 40 minutes of CPR. "One doctor wanted to let him go," recalled his mother.

The result was severe cerebral palsy. With damage to the brain area that controls muscle movement, Chris is unable to control his constantly moving hands. He cannot feed, dress, or care for himself. And he cannot speak. But what Chris can control are his keen mind and left foot. With that blessed foot, he operates the joystick on his motorized wheelchair. Using his left big toe, he can type sentences, which his communication system can store, send, or speak. And Chris is motivated, very motivated.

When Chris was a high school student in suburban Chicago, three teachers doubted he would be able to leave home for college. Yet he persisted, and, with much support, attended my school, Hope College. Five years later, as his left foot drove him across the stage to receive his diploma, his admiring classmates honored his achievement with a spontaneous standing ovation.

Today, Chris is an inspirational speaker for schools, churches, and community events, giving "a voice to those that have none, and a helping hand to those with disabilities." He is writing a book, *Lessons from the Big Toe*. And he has found love and married.

Few of us face Chris Klein's challenges. But we all seek to direct our energy in ways that will produce satisfaction and success. We are moved by our feelings along the way,

A MOTIVATED MAN: CHRIS KLEIN To see and hear Chris presenting his story, visit tinyurl.com/ChrisPsychStudent.

and we inspire them in others. We are pushed by social motives, such as affiliation and achievement, and biological ones, such as hunger. We feel hope and happiness, sadness and pain, tenderness and triumph. Chris Klein's fierce will to live, learn, and love highlights the close ties between our own *motivations* and *emotions,* which energize, direct, and enrich our lives.

⟶ Basic Motivational Concepts, Affiliation, and Achievement

MOTIVATIONAL CONCEPTS

LEARNING OBJECTIVE QUESTION (LOQ)

10-1 How do psychologists define *motivation?* From what perspectives do they view motivated behavior?

Our **motivations** arise from the interplay between nature (the bodily "push") and nurture (the "pulls" from our personal experiences, thoughts, and culture). That is usually, but not always, for the better. When our bodies tell us we're hungry, we respond by eating foods we have learned to trust and enjoy. But when our motivations get hijacked, our lives go awry. Those with *substance use disorder,* for example, may find their cravings for an addictive substance override their longings for sustenance, safety, and social support.

In their attempts to understand motivated behavior, psychologists have viewed it from four perspectives:

- *Instinct theory* (now replaced by the *evolutionary perspective*) focuses on genetically predisposed behaviors.
- *Drive-reduction theory* focuses on how we respond to inner pushes and outer pulls.
- *Arousal theory* focuses on finding the right level of stimulation.
- *Abraham Maslow's hierarchy of needs* focuses on the priority of some needs over others.

Instincts and Evolutionary Theory

To qualify as an **instinct**, a complex behavior must have a fixed pattern throughout a species and be unlearned (Tinbergen, 1951). Such unlearned behaviors include *imprinting* in birds and the return of salmon to their birthplace. A few human behaviors, such as infants' innate reflexes to root for a nipple and suck, exhibit unlearned fixed patterns. But many more are directed by both physiological needs and psychological wants.

SAME MOTIVE, DIFFERENT WIRING The more complex the nervous system, the more adaptable the organism. Both humans and weaverbirds satisfy their need for shelter in ways that reflect their inherited capacities. Human behavior is flexible; we can learn whatever skills we need to build a house. The bird's behavior pattern is fixed; it can build only this kind of nest.

Although instincts cannot explain most human motives, the underlying assumption endures in *evolutionary psychology:* Genes do predispose some species-typical behavior. Chapter 7 discussed the limits that biological predispositions place on conditioning. Later in this chapter, we'll see how our taste preferences aid our survival. And we will see in later discussions how evolution might influence our helping behaviors and our romantic attractions.

Drives and Incentives

In addition to our predispositions, we have *drives.* **Physiological needs** (such as for food or water) create an aroused, motivated state—a drive (such as hunger or thirst)—that pushes us to reduce the need. **Drive-reduction theory** explains that, with few exceptions, when a physiological need increases, so does our psychological drive to reduce it.

Drive reduction is one way our bodies strive for **homeostasis** (literally "staying the same")—the maintenance of a steady internal state. For example, our body regulates its temperature in a way similar to a room's thermostat. Both systems operate through feedback loops: Sensors feed room temperature to a control device. If the room's temperature cools, the control device switches on the furnace. Likewise, if our body's temperature cools, our blood vessels constrict (to conserve warmth) and we feel driven to put on more clothes or seek a warmer environment (**FIGURE 10.1**).

Not only are we *pushed* by our need to reduce drives, we also are *pulled* by **incentives**—positive or negative environmental stimuli that lure or repel us. Such stimuli increase our dopamine levels, causing our underlying drives (such as for food or sex) to become active impulses (Hamid et al., 2016). And the more those impulses are satisfied and reinforced, the stronger the drive may become: As Roy Baumeister (2015) noted, "Getting begets wanting." Thus, our learning influences our motives. Depending on our learning, the aroma of good food, whether roasted peanuts or toasted ants, can motivate our behavior. So can the sight of those we find attractive or threatening.

When there is both a need and an incentive, we feel strongly driven. The food-deprived person who smells pizza baking may feel a strong hunger drive, and the baking pizza may become a compelling incentive. For each motive, we can therefore ask, "How is it pushed by our inborn physiological needs and pulled by learned incentives in the environment?"

FIGURE 10.1

DRIVE-REDUCTION THEORY Drive-reduction motivation arises from *homeostasis*—an organism's natural tendency to maintain a steady internal state. Thus, if we are water deprived, our thirst drives us to drink to restore the body's normal state.

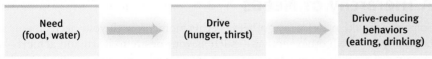

Need (food, water) → Drive (hunger, thirst) → Drive-reducing behaviors (eating, drinking)

Arousal Theory

We are much more than calm homeostatic systems, however. Some motivated behaviors actually *increase* rather than decrease arousal. Well-fed animals will leave their shelter to explore and gain information, seemingly in the absence of any need-based drive. Curiosity drives monkeys to monkey around trying to figure out how to unlock a latch that opens nothing, or how to open a window that allows them to see outside their room (Butler, 1954). It drives newly mobile infants to investigate every accessible corner of the house. It drove students, in one experiment, to click on pens to see whether they did or didn't deliver an electric shock (Hsee & Ruan, 2016). It drives the scientists whose work this text discusses. And it drives explorers and adventurers such as mountaineer George Mallory. Asked why he wanted to climb Mount Everest, Mallory famously answered, "Because it's there." Sometimes uncertainty brings excitement, which amplifies motivation (Shen et al., 2015). Those who, like Mallory, enjoy high arousal are most likely to seek out intense music, novel foods, and risky behaviors and careers (Roberti et al., 2004; Zuckerman, 1979, 2009). Although they have been called *sensation-seekers,* risk takers may also be motivated to master their emotions and actions (Barlow et al., 2013).

So, human motivation aims not to eliminate arousal but to seek optimum levels of arousal. Having all our biological needs satisfied, we feel driven to experience stimulation and we hunger for information. Lacking stimulation, we feel bored and look for a way to increase arousal. If left alone, most people prefer to do something—even, when given no other option, to self-administer mild electric shocks (Wilson et al., 2014). Why might

motivation a need or desire that energizes and directs behavior.

instinct a complex behavior that is rigidly patterned throughout a species and is unlearned.

physiological need a basic bodily requirement.

drive-reduction theory the idea that a physiological need creates an aroused state (a drive) that motivates an organism to satisfy the need.

homeostasis a tendency to maintain a balanced or constant internal state; the regulation of any aspect of body chemistry, such as blood glucose, around a particular level.

incentive a positive or negative environmental stimulus that motivates behavior.

DRIVEN BY CURIOSITY Young monkeys and children are fascinated by the unfamiliar. Their drive to explore maintains an optimum level of arousal and is one of several motives that do not fill any immediate physiological need.

ASK YOURSELF

Does boredom ever motivate you to do things just to figure out something new? When was the last time that happened, and what did you find?

people seek to increase their arousal? Moderate arousal and even anxiety can be motivating—leading to higher levels of math achievement, for example (Wang et al., 2015c). However, given too much stimulation or stress, we look for ways to decrease arousal. In one experiment, people felt less stress when they cut back checking email to three times a day rather than being continually accessible (Kushlev & Dunn, 2015).

Two early twentieth-century psychologists studied the relationship of arousal to performance and identified the **Yerkes-Dodson law:** *moderate arousal leads to optimal performance* (Yerkes & Dodson, 1908). When taking an exam, it pays to be moderately aroused—alert but not trembling with nervousness. (If already anxious, it's better not to become further aroused with caffeine.) Between bored low arousal and anxious hyperarousal lies a flourishing life. But optimal arousal levels depend on the task, with more difficult tasks requiring lower arousal for best performance (Hembree, 1988).

> ## 🔒 RETRIEVE IT • • •   *ANSWERS IN APPENDIX E*
>
> **RI-1** Performance peaks at lower levels of arousal for difficult tasks, and at higher levels for easy or well-learned tasks. (1) How might this phenomenon affect marathon runners? (2) How might this phenomenon affect anxious test-takers facing a difficult exam?

A Hierarchy of Needs

Some needs take priority over others. At this moment, with your needs for air and water hopefully satisfied, other motives—such as your desire to learn and achieve—are energizing and directing your behavior. Let your need for water go unsatisfied, however, and your thirst will preoccupy you. Deprived of air, you'd instantly find your thirst disappear.

Abraham Maslow (1970) described these priorities as a **hierarchy of needs** (**FIGURE 10.2**). At the base of this pyramid are our physiological needs, such as for food and water. Only if these needs are met are we prompted to meet our need for safety, and then to satisfy our needs to give and receive love and to enjoy self-esteem. Beyond this, said Maslow (1971), lies the need for *self-actualization*—to realize our full potential.

Near the end of his life, Maslow proposed that some of us also reach a level of *self-transcendence*. At the self-actualization level, we seek to realize our own potential. At the self-transcendence level, we strive for meaning, purpose, and communion in a way that is transpersonal—beyond the self (Koltko-Rivera, 2006). Maslow's contemporary, psychiatrist Viktor Frankl (1962), a Nazi concentration camp survivor, concurred that the search for meaning is an important human motive: "Life is never made unbearable by circumstances, but only by lack of meaning and purpose."

"Do you feel your life has an important purpose or meaning?" When Gallup asked this of people in 132 countries, 91 percent answered *Yes* (Oishi & Diener, 2014). People sense meaning when they experience their life as having *purpose* (goals), *significance* (value), and *coherence* (sense)—sentiments that may be nourished by strong social connections, a religious faith, an orderly world, and social status (King et al., 2016; Martela & Steger, 2016). Moreover, meaning matters: People's sense of life's meaning predicts their psychological and physical well-being, and their capacity to delay gratification (Heine et al., 2006; Van Tongeren et al., 2018).

📖 LaunchPad To test your understanding of the hierarchy of needs, engage online with **Concept Practice: Building Maslow's Hierarchy**

ASK YOURSELF

Consider your own experiences in relation to Maslow's hierarchy of needs. Have you ever experienced hunger or thirst that displaced your concern for other, higher-level needs? Do you usually feel safe? Loved? Confident? How often do you feel you are able to address what Maslow called "self-actualization" needs? What about "self-transcendence" needs?

Self-transcendence needs
Need to find meaning and identity beyond the self

Self-actualization needs
Need to live up to our fullest and unique potential

Esteem needs
Need for self-esteem, achievement, competence, and independence; need for recognition and respect from others

Belongingness and love needs
Need to love and be loved, to belong and be accepted; need to avoid loneliness and separation

Safety needs
Need to feel that the world is organized and predictable; need to feel safe, secure, and stable

Physiological needs
Need to satisfy hunger and thirst

FIGURE 10.2

MASLOW'S HIERARCHY OF NEEDS
Reduced to semistarvation by their rulers, inhabitants of Suzanne Collins' fictional nation, Panem, hunger for food and survival. *Hunger Games* heroine Katniss Everdeen (played in the movie by Jennifer Lawrence, shown here) expresses higher-level needs for actualization and transcendence, and in the process inspires the nation.

The order of Maslow's hierarchy is not universally fixed: People have starved themselves, for example, to make a political statement. Culture also influences our priorities: Self-esteem matters most in individualist nations, whose citizens tend to focus more on personal achievements than on family and community identity (Oishi et al., 1999). And, while agreeing with Maslow's basic levels of need, today's psychologists add that gaining and retaining mates, parenting offspring, and desiring social status are also universal human motives (Anderson et al., 2015; Kenrick et al., 2010).

Nevertheless, the simple idea that some motives are more compelling than others provides a framework for thinking about motivation. Worldwide life-satisfaction surveys support this basic idea (Oishi et al., 1999; Tay & Diener, 2011). In poorer nations that lack easy access to money and the food and shelter it buys, financial satisfaction more strongly predicts feelings of well-being. In wealthy nations, where most are able to meet their basic needs, social connections better predict well-being.

With these classic motivation theories in mind (**TABLE 10.1**), let's now take a closer look at two specific, higher-level motives: the *need to belong* and the *need to achieve*. As you read about these motives, watch for ways that incentives (the psychological "pull") interact with physiological needs (the biological "push").

"Hunger is the most urgent form of poverty." —Alliance to End Hunger, 2002

TABLE 10.1

Classic Motivation Theories

Theory	Its Big Idea
Instincts and evolutionary theory	There is a genetic basis for unlearned, species-typical behavior (such as birds building nests or infants rooting for a nipple).
Drive-reduction theory	Physiological needs (such as hunger and thirst) create an aroused state that drives us to reduce the need (for example, by eating or drinking).
Arousal theory	Our need to maintain an optimal level of arousal motivates behaviors that meet no physiological need (such as our yearning for stimulation and our hunger for information).
Maslow's hierarchy of needs	We prioritize survival-based needs and then social needs more than the needs for esteem and meaning.

Yerkes-Dodson law the principle that performance increases with arousal only up to a point, beyond which performance decreases.

hierarchy of needs Maslow's pyramid of human needs, beginning at the base with physiological needs that must first be satisfied before people can fulfill their higher-level safety needs and then psychological needs.

THE NEED TO BELONG

LOQ 10-2   What evidence points to our human affiliation need—our need to belong?

We are what the ancient Greek philosopher Aristotle called the *social animal.* Cut off from friends or family—alone in prison or at a new school or in a foreign land—most people feel keenly their lost connections with important others. This deep *need to belong*—our **affiliation need**—seems a central human motivation (Baumeister & Leary, 1995). Mark Zuckerberg (2012) understands this, noting that he founded Facebook "to accomplish a social mission—to make the world more open and connected." Although people vary in their wish for privacy and solitude, most of us seek to affiliate—to become strongly attached to certain others in enduring, close relationships. Human beings, contended personality theorist Alfred Adler, have an "urge to community" (Ferguson, 1989, 2001, 2010).

The Benefits of Belonging

Social bonds boosted our early ancestors' chances of survival. Adults who formed attachments were more likely to survive and reproduce, and to co-nurture their offspring to maturity. Attachment bonds motivated caregivers to keep children close, calming them and protecting them from threats (Esposito et al., 2013). Indeed, to be "wretched" literally means, in its Middle English origin *(wrecched),* to be without kin nearby.

Cooperating with friends and acquaintances also enhanced survival. In solo combat, our ancestors were not the toughest predators. But as hunters, they learned that six hands were better than two. As food gatherers, they gained protection from two-footed and four-footed enemies by traveling in groups. Those who felt a need to belong survived and reproduced most successfully, and their genes now predominate. Our innate need to belong drives us to befriend people who cooperate and to avoid those who exploit (Feinberg et al., 2014). People in every society on Earth belong to groups and prefer and favor "us" over "them." Having a social identity—feeling part of a group—boosts people's health and well-being (Allen et al., 2015; Greenaway et al., 2015, 2016).

Do you have close friends—people with whom you freely disclose your ups and downs? Having someone who rejoices with us over good news helps us feel better about both the news and the friendship (Reis et al., 2010). Such companionship creates connection and cooperation (Canavello & Crocker, 2017). A stranger's grateful thank-you can warm our heart (Williams & Bartlett, 2015). And close friends can literally make us feel warm, as if we are holding a soothing cup of warm tea (Inagaki & Eisenberger, 2013). The need to belong runs deeper, it seems, than any need to be rich. One study found that very happy university students were distinguished not by their money but by their "rich and satisfying close relationships" (Diener & Seligman, 2002).

The need to belong colors our thoughts and emotions. We spend a great deal of time thinking about actual and hoped-for relationships. Falling in mutual love, people have been known to feel their cheeks ache from their irrepressible grins. Asked, "What is necessary for your happiness?" or "What is it that makes your life meaningful?" most people have mentioned—before anything else—close, satisfying relationships with family, friends, or romantic partners (Berscheid, 1985). Happiness hits close to home.

💡 **ENGAGE** Consider: What was your most satisfying moment in the past week? Researchers asked that question of American and South Korean university students, then asked them to rate how much that moment had satisfied various needs (Sheldon et al., 2001). In both countries, the peak moment had satisfied self-esteem and relatedness-belonging needs. According to **self-determination theory,** we strive to satisfy three needs: *competence, autonomy* (a sense of personal control), and *relatedness* (Deci & Ryan, 2012; Ryan &

Photodisc/Getty Images

"We must love one another or die."
—W. H. Auden, "September 1, 1939"

Deci, 2000). Fulfilling these motives increases our health, improves our performance, and boosts our self-esteem (Cerasoli et al., 2016; Deci & Ryan, 2009; Guertin et al., 2017). Indeed, self-esteem is a gauge of how valued and accepted we feel (Leary, 2012).

Small wonder, then, that our social behavior so often aims to increase our feelings of belonging. To gain acceptance, we generally conform to group standards. We monitor our behavior, hoping to make a good impression. We spend billions on clothes, cosmetics, and diet and fitness aids—all motivated by our search for love and acceptance.

Thrown together in groups at school, at work, or at camp, we behave like magnets, moving closer, forming bonds. Parting, we feel distress. We promise to call, to write, to return for reunions. By drawing a sharp circle around "us," the need to belong feeds both deep attachments to those inside the circle (loving families, faithful friendships, and team loyalty) and hostilities toward those outside (teen gangs, ethnic rivalries, and fanatic nationalism). Feelings of love activate brain reward and safety systems. In one experiment, deeply in love university students exposed to heat felt less pain when looking at their beloved's picture (Younger et al., 2010). Pictures of our loved ones activate a brain region—the prefrontal cortex—that dampens feelings of physical pain (Eisenberger et al., 2011). Love is a natural painkiller.

Even when bad relationships end, people suffer. In one 16-nation survey, and in repeated U.S. surveys, separated and divorced people have been half as likely as married people to say they are "very happy" (Inglehart, 1990; NORC, 2016a). Is that simply because happy people more often marry and stay married? A national study following British lives through time revealed that, even after controlling for premarital life satisfaction, "the married are still more satisfied, suggesting a causal effect" of marriage (Grover & Helliwell, 2014). Divorce also predicts earlier mortality. Data from more than 600 million (!) people in 24 countries reveal that, compared with married people, separated and divorced people are at greater risk for early death (Shor et al., 2012). "If you're in a happy marriage, you will tend to live longer," says data scientist Lyle Ungar (2014). "[A happy marriage] is perhaps as important as not smoking, which is to say: huge."

Children who move through a series of foster homes or through repeated family relocations know the fear of being alone. After repeated disruption of budding relationships, they may have difficulty forming deep attachments (Oishi & Schimmack, 2010b). The evidence is clearest at the extremes. Children who grow up in institutions without a sense of belonging to anyone, or who are locked away at home and severely neglected often become withdrawn, frightened, even speechless.

No matter how secure our early years were, we all experience anxiety, loneliness, jealousy, or guilt when something threatens or dissolves our social ties. Much as life's best moments occur when close relationships begin—making a new friend, falling in love, having a baby—life's worst moments happen when close relationships end (Beam et al., 2016). Bereaved, we may feel life is empty or pointless, and we may overeat to fill that emptiness (Yang et al., 2016). Even the first months of living on campus can be distressing (English et al., 2017). But our need to belong usually pushes us to form new social connections (Oishi et al., 2013).

For immigrants and refugees moving alone to new places, the stress and loneliness can be depressing. After years of placing individual families in isolated communities, U.S. immigration policies began to encourage *chain migration* (Pipher, 2002). The second Syrian refugee family settling in a town generally has an easier adjustment than the first.

Social isolation can put us at risk for mental decline and ill health (Cacioppo et al., 2015). Lonely older adults, for example, make more doctor visits and are at greater risk of dementia (Gerst-Emerson & Jayawardhana, 2015; Holwerda et al., 2014). Social isolation can hurt our health as much as physical inactivity and diabetes do (Yang et al., 2016). But if feelings of acceptance and connection increase sufficiently, so will self-esteem, positive feelings, and physical health (Blackhart et al., 2009; Holt-Lunstad et al., 2010; Li & Kanazawa, 2016). The World Health Organization (2017b) lists social connection to family, friends, and community as a "determinant of health." A socially connected life is often a happy and healthy life.

affiliation need the need to build relationships and to feel part of a group.

self-determination theory the theory that we feel motivated to satisfy our needs for competence, autonomy, and relatedness.

ENGAGE **LaunchPad** To improve your own relationships, try the online **Immersive Learning: Assess Your Strengths—How Strong Is Your Relationship, and How Might You Increase Its Strength?**

THE NEED TO CONNECT Six days a week, women from the Philippines work as domestic helpers in thousands of Hong Kong households. On Sundays, they throng to the central business district to picnic, dance, sing, talk, and laugh. "Humanity could stage no greater display of happiness," reported one observer (*Economist*, 2001).

VINCENT YU/AP Images

ENDURING THE PAIN OF OSTRACISM
White cadets at the United States Military Academy at West Point ostracized Henry Flipper for years, hoping he would drop out. He persevered in spite of their cruelty and in 1877 became the first African-American West Point graduate.

"How can we subject prisoners to unnecessary solitary confinement, knowing its effects, and then expect them to return to our communities as whole people? It doesn't make us safer. It's an affront to our common humanity." —U.S. President Barack Obama, 2016

LaunchPad To consider your own need to belong, try the online **Immersive Learning: Assess Your Strengths—How Strong Is Your Need to Belong, and How Can You Strengthen Your Feelings of Belonging?**

ENGAGE

The Pain of Being Shut Out

Can you recall feeling excluded, ignored, or shunned? Perhaps your texts went unanswered, or you were unfriended or ignored online. Perhaps others gave you the silent treatment, avoided you, looked away, mocked you, or shut you out in some other way. Or perhaps you have felt excluded when among people speaking an unfamiliar language (Dotan-Eliaz et al., 2009). All these experiences are instances of **ostracism**—of social exclusion (Williams, 2007, 2009). Worldwide, humans use many forms of ostracism— exile, imprisonment, solitary confinement—to punish, and therefore control, social behavior. For children, even a brief time-out in isolation can be punishing. Asked to describe personal episodes that made them feel especially *bad* about themselves, people will—about four times in five—describe a broken or painful social relationship (Pillemer et al., 2007).

Being shunned threatens one's need to belong (Vanhalst et al., 2015; Wirth et al., 2010). "It's the meanest thing you can do to someone, especially if you know they can't fight back. I never should have been born," said Lea, a lifelong victim of the silent treatment by her mother and grandmother. Like Lea, people often respond to ostracism with initial efforts to restore their acceptance, with depressed moods, and finally with withdrawal. Prisoner William Blake (2013) has spent more than a quarter-century in solitary confinement. "I cannot fathom how dying any death could be harder and more terrible than living through all that I have been forced to endure," he observed. To many, social exclusion is a sentence worse than death.

To experience ostracism is to experience real pain, as social psychologists Kipling Williams and his colleagues were surprised to discover in their studies of exclusion on social media (Gonsalkorale & Williams, 2006). Such ostracism, they discovered, takes a toll: It elicits increased activity in brain areas, such as the *anterior cingulate cortex,* that also respond to physical pain (Lieberman & Eisenberger et al., 2015; Rotge et al., 2015).

When people view pictures of romantic partners who caused their heart to break, their brain and body begin to ache (Kross et al., 2011). That helps explain another surprising finding: The pain reliever acetaminophen (as in Tylenol) lessens *social* as well as physical pain (DeWall et al., 2010). Across cultures, people use the same words (for example, *hurt, crushed*) for social pain and physical pain (MacDonald & Leary, 2005). Psychologically, we seem to experience social pain with the same emotional unpleasantness that marks physical pain.

Pain, whatever its source, focuses our attention and motivates corrective action. Rejected and unable to remedy the situation, people may relieve stress by seeking new friends, eating calorie-laden comfort foods, or strengthening their religious faith (Aydin et al., 2010; Maner et al., 2007; Sproesser et al., 2014). Or they may turn hostile. Ostracism breeds disagreeableness, which leads to further ostracism (Hales et al., 2016).

SOCIAL ACCEPTANCE AND REJECTION Successful participants on the reality TV show *Survivor* form alliances and gain acceptance among their peers. The rest receive the ultimate social punishment as they are "voted off the island."

In one series of experiments, researchers told some students (who had taken a personality test) that they were "the type likely to end up alone later in life," or that people they had met didn't want them in a group that was forming (Gaertner et al., 2008; Twenge et al., 2001).[1] They told other students that they would have "rewarding relationships throughout life," or that "everyone chose you as someone they'd like to work with." Those who were excluded became much more likely to engage in self-defeating behaviors and to act in disparaging or aggressive ways against those who had excluded them (blasting them with noise, for example). "If intelligent, well-adjusted, successful . . . students can turn aggressive in response to a small laboratory experience of social exclusion," noted the research team, "it is disturbing to imagine the aggressive tendencies that might arise from . . . chronic exclusion from desired groups in actual social life." Indeed, as Williams (2007) has observed, ostracism "weaves through case after case of school violence."

> 🔒 **RETRIEVE IT • • •**　　　　　　　　　*ANSWERS IN APPENDIX E*
>
> **RI-3** How have students reacted in studies where they were made to feel rejected and unwanted? What helps explain these results?

Connecting and Social Networking

LOQ 10-3 How does social networking influence us?

As social creatures, we live for connection. Researcher George Vaillant (2013) was asked what he had learned from studying 238 Harvard University men from the 1930s to the end of their lives. He replied, "Happiness is love." A South African Zulu saying captures the idea: *Umuntu ngumuntu ngabantu*—"a person is a person through other persons."

 MOBILE NETWORKS AND SOCIAL MEDIA Look around and see humans connecting: talking, tweeting, texting, posting, chatting, social gaming, emailing. Walking across campus, you may see students glued to their phones, making little eye contact with passersby (or perhaps that's you?). Today have you observed more students engaging with each other face-to-face, or silently checking their phones, as one research team's phone app counted students doing 56 times a day (Elias et al., 2016)? The changes in how we connect have been fast and vast:

- *Mobile phones:* At the end of 2016, 95 percent of the world's 7.5 billion people lived in an area covered by a mobile-cellular network (ITU, 2016).

- *Texts:* The typical U.S. teen sends 30 texts a day (Lenhart, 2015b). Half of 18- to 29-year-olds check their phone multiple times per hour, and "can't imagine . . . life without [it]" (Newport, 2015; Saad, 2015).

- *The internet:* Worldwide in 2015, 68 percent of adults have used the internet (Poushter, 2016).

- *Social networking:* Among 2014's entering American college students, 94 percent were using social networking sites (Eagan et al., 2014). With one's friends online, it's hard not to be: Check in or miss out.

THE NET RESULT: SOCIAL EFFECTS OF SOCIAL NETWORKING By connecting like-minded people, the internet serves as a social amplifier. In times of social crisis or personal stress, it provides information and supportive connections. But it also enables people to compare their lives with others, which can create envy and be depressing (Verduyn et al., 2017). Gaining a large number of likes does activate the brain's reward centers (Blease, 2015; Sherman et al., 2016). And the internet can function as a match-maker (as I [ND] can attest: I met my wife online). Dating websites aren't for everyone, and their algorithms might have limitations (Joel et al., 2017). But dating websites can widen the pool of potential matches, making it easier to find a desirable partner.

"If no one turned around when we entered, answered when we spoke, or minded what we did, but if every person we met 'cut us dead,' and acted as if we were non-existing things, a kind of rage and impotent despair would ere long well up in us."
—William James, *Principles of Psychology*, 1890/1950, pp. 293–294

⚡ **ENGAGE** （ ASK YOURSELF ）

Have there been times when you felt out of the loop with family and friends, or even ostracized by them? How did you respond?

---

1. The researchers later *debriefed* and reassured the participants.

ostracism deliberate social exclusion of individuals or groups.

"Look, until there's a Tinder for Pandas, we have to meet the old-fashioned way: being locked in a room together by scientists."

"The women on these dating sites don't seem to believe I'm a prince."

Online networking is double-edged: Nature has designed us for face-to-face relationships, and those who spend hours online are *less* likely to know and draw help from their real-world neighbors. But it does help us connect with friends, stay in touch with extended family, and find support when facing challenges (Pew, 2009; Pinker, 2014; Rainie et al., 2011). When used in moderation, social networking predicts longer life (Hobbs et al., 2016).

DOES ELECTRONIC COMMUNICATION STIMULATE HEALTHY SELF-DISCLOSURE? *Self-disclosure* is sharing ourselves—our joys, worries, and weaknesses—with others. Confiding can be a healthy way of coping with day-to-day challenges. When communicating electronically, rather than face-to-face, we often are less focused on others' reactions. We are less self-conscious, and thus less inhibited. Sometimes this is taken to an extreme, as when bullies hound a victim, hate groups post messages promoting bigotry, or people send photos of themselves they later regret. More often, however, the increased self-disclosure serves to deepen friendships (Valkenburg & Peter, 2009).

DOES SOCIAL NETWORKING PROMOTE NARCISSISM?   **Narcissism** is self-esteem gone wild. Narcissistic people are self-important, self-focused, and self-promoting. To measure your narcissistic tendencies, you might rate your agreement with personality test items such as "I like to be the center of attention" and "If I ruled the world it would be a better place." People who agree with these statements tend to have high narcissism scores—and they are especially active on social networking sites (Liu & Baumeister, 2016). They collect more superficial "friends." They offer more staged, glamorous photos. They retaliate more against negative comments. And, not surprisingly, they *seem* more narcissistic to strangers (Buffardi & Campbell, 2008; Weiser, 2015).

For narcissists, social networking sites are more than a gathering place; they are a feeding trough. In one study, college students were *randomly assigned* either to edit and explain their online profiles for 15 minutes, or to use that time to study and explain a Google Maps routing (Freeman & Twenge, 2010). After completing their tasks, all were tested. Who then scored higher on a narcissism measure? Those who had spent the time focused on themselves.

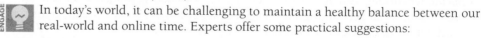

LaunchPad See the **Video: Random Assignment** for a helpful tutorial animation.

MAINTAINING BALANCE AND FOCUS   It will come as no surprise that excessive online socializing and gaming have correlated with lower grades and with increased anxiety and depression (Brooks, 2015; Lepp et al., 2014; Walsh et al., 2013). In one U.S. survey, 47 percent of the heaviest users of the internet and other media were receiving mostly C grades or lower, as were just 23 percent of the lightest users (Kaiser Family Foundation, 2010). In another national survey, young adults who used seven or more social media platforms were three times more likely to be depressed or anxious than those who used two or fewer (Primack et al., 2016).

In today's world, it can be challenging to maintain a healthy balance between our real-world and online time. Experts offer some practical suggestions:

- *Monitor your time.* Keep a log of how you use your time. Then ask yourself, "Does my time use reflect my priorities? Am I spending more time online than I intended? Is my time online interfering with my school or work performance or my relationships?"

- *Monitor your feelings.* Ask yourself, "Am I emotionally distracted by my online interests? When I disconnect and move to another activity, how do I feel? Have family or friends commented on this?"

- *Hide from your incessantly posting online friends when necessary.* And in your own postings, practice the golden rule. Ask yourself, "Is this something I'd care about if someone else posted it?"

- *When studying, get in the practice of checking your phone and email less often.* Selective attention—the flashlight of your mind—can be in only one place at a time. When we try to do two things at once, we don't do either one of them very

narcissism excessive self-love and self-absorption.

well (Willingham, 2010). If you want to study or work productively, resist the temptation to be always available. Disable sound alerts, vibration, and pop-ups. (To reduce internet distraction, I [DM] am working on this chapter in a coffee shop without Wi-Fi.)

- *Refocus by taking a nature walk.* People learn better after a peaceful walk in a park, which—unlike a walk on a busy street—refreshes our capacity for focused attention (Berman et al., 2008). Connecting with nature boosts our spirits and sharpens our minds (Zelenski & Nisbet, 2014).

As psychologist Steven Pinker (2010) said, "The solution is not to bemoan technology but to develop strategies of self-control, as we do with every other temptation in life."

"It keeps me from looking at my phone every two seconds."

🔒 RETRIEVE IT • • •

ANSWERS IN APPENDIX E

RI-4 Social networking tends to _____ (strengthen/weaken) your relationships with people you already know and _____ (increase/decrease) your self-disclosure.

ACHIEVEMENT MOTIVATION

LOQ 10-4 What is *achievement motivation,* and what are some ways to encourage achievement?

Some motives seem to have little obvious survival value. Billionaires may be motivated to make ever more money, reality TV stars to attract ever more social media followers, politicians to achieve ever more power, daredevils to seek ever greater thrills. Motives vary across cultures. In an individualist culture, employees may work to receive an "employee of the month" award; in a collectivist culture, they may strive to join a company's hardest-working team. Such motives seem not to diminish when they are fed. The more we achieve, the more we may need to achieve. Psychologist Henry Murray (1938) defined **achievement motivation** as a desire for significant accomplishment, for mastering skills or ideas, for control, and for attaining a high standard.

Thanks to their persistence and eagerness for challenge, people with high achievement motivation do accomplish more. They tend to have greater financial success, healthy social relationships, good physical health, and emotional well-being (Steptoe & Wardle, 2017). One famous study followed the lives of 1528 California children whose intelligence test scores were in the top 1 percent. Forty years later, researchers compared those who were most and least successful professionally. What did the researchers discover? A motivational difference. The most successful were more ambitious, energetic, and persistent. As children, they had more active hobbies. As adults, they participated in more groups and sports (Goleman, 1980). Gifted children are able learners. Accomplished adults are tenacious doers. Most of us are energetic doers when starting and when finishing a project. It's easiest—have you noticed?—to get stuck in the middle. That's when high achievers keep going (Bonezzi et al., 2011).

In some studies of both secondary school and university students, self-discipline has surpassed intelligence test scores in predicting school performance, attendance, and graduation honors. For school performance, "discipline outdoes talent," concluded researchers Angela Duckworth and Martin Seligman (2005, 2006).

Discipline focuses and refines talent. By their early twenties, top violinists have accumulated thousands of lifetime practice hours—in fact, double the practice time of other violin students aiming to be teachers (Ericsson 2001, 2006, 2007). A study of outstanding scholars, athletes, and artists found that all were highly motivated and self-disciplined, willing to dedicate hours every day to the pursuit of their goals (Bloom, 1985). But as young Mozart composing at age 8 illustrates, native talent matters, too (Hambrick & Meinz, 2011; Ruthsatz & Urbach, 2012). In sports, music, and chess, people's practice-time differences, while significant, account for a third or less of their performance differences (Hambrick et al., 2014a,b; Macnamara et al., 2014, 2016; Ullén et al., 2016). High achievers benefit from passion and perseverance, but the superstars among them are also distinguished by their extraordinary natural talent.

ENGAGE 💡 (ASK YOURSELF)

Do your connections on social media increase your sense of belonging, or do they make you feel lonelier? At busy times, what strategies do you use to maintain balance and focus?

"Genius is 1% inspiration and 99% perspiration." —Thomas Edison (1847–1931)

achievement motivation a desire for significant accomplishment, for mastery of skills or ideas, for control, and for attaining a high standard.

CALUM'S ROAD: WHAT GRIT CAN ACCOMPLISH Having spent his life on the Scottish island of Raasay, farming a small patch of land, tending its lighthouse, and fishing, Malcolm ("Calum") MacLeod (1911–1988) felt anguished. His local government repeatedly refused to build a road that would enable vehicles to reach his north end of the island. With the once-flourishing population there having dwindled to two—MacLeod and his wife—he responded with heroic determination. One spring morning in 1964, MacLeod, then in his fifties, gathered an ax, a chopper, a shovel, and a wheelbarrow. By hand, he began to transform the existing footpath into a 1.75-mile road (Miers, 2009).

"With a road," a former neighbor explained, "he hoped new generations of people would return to the north end of Raasay," restoring its culture (Hutchinson, 2006). Day after day he worked through rough hillsides, along hazardous cliff faces, and over peat bogs. Finally, 10 years later, he completed his supreme achievement. The road, which the government has since surfaced, remains a visible example of what vision plus determined grit can accomplish. It bids us each to ponder: What "roads"—what achievements— might we, with sustained effort, build in the years before us?

From Calum's Road by Roger Hutchinson, reproduced courtesy of Birlinn Ltd.

Duckworth (2016) has a name for passionate dedication to an ambitious, long-term goal: **grit**. When combined with self-control (regulating one's attention and actions in the face of temptation), gritty goal-striving can produce great achievements. Researchers have begun to sleuth the neural and genetic markers of grit (Nemmi et al., 2016; Rimfeld et al., 2016). As the saying goes, "If you want to look good in front of thousands, you have to outwork thousands in front of nobody."

Although intelligence is distributed like a bell curve, achievements are not. This tells us that achievement involves much more than raw ability. That is why it pays to know how best to engage people's motivations to achieve. Promising people a reward for an enjoyable task can backfire. Excessive rewards can destroy **intrinsic motivation**—the desire to perform a behavior effectively for its own sake. In experiments, children have been promised a payoff for playing with an interesting puzzle or toy. Later, they played with the toy *less* than did unpaid children (Deci et al., 1999; Tang & Hall, 1995). Likewise, rewarding children with toys or candy for reading diminishes the time they spend reading (Marinak & Gambrell, 2008). It is as if they think, "If I have to be bribed into doing this, it must not be worth doing!"

To sense the difference between intrinsic motivation and **extrinsic motivation** (behaving in certain ways that gain external rewards or avoid threatened punishment), think about your experience in this course. Like most students, you probably want to earn a high grade. But what motivates your actions to achieve your goal? Do you feel pressured to finish this reading before a deadline? Are you worried about your grade? Eager for the credits that will count toward graduation? If *Yes*, then you are extrinsically motivated (as, to some extent, all students must be). Do you also find the material interesting? Does learning it make you feel more competent? If there were no grade at stake, might you be curious enough to want to learn the material for its own sake? If *Yes*, intrinsic motivation also fuels your efforts.

Students who focus on learning (intrinsic reward) often get good grades and graduate (extrinsic rewards). Doctors who focus on healing (intrinsic reward) generally make a good living (extrinsic reward). Indeed, research suggests that people who focus on their work's meaning and significance not only do better work but ultimately earn more extrinsic rewards (Wrzesniewski et al., 2014).

Extrinsic rewards work well when people perform tasks that don't naturally inspire complex, creative thinking (Hewett & Conway, 2015). They're also effective when used to signal a job well done (rather than to bribe or control someone) (Boggiano et al., 1985). "Most improved player" awards, for example, can boost feelings of competence and increase enjoyment of a sport. Rightly administered, rewards can improve performance and spark creativity (Eisenberger & Aselage, 2009; Henderlong & Lepper, 2002). And the rewards that often follow academic achievement, such as access to scholarships and a variety of jobs, can have long-lasting benefits.

Organizational psychologists seek ways to engage and motivate ordinary people doing ordinary jobs (see Appendix B: Psychology at Work). Indeed, each of us can adopt some research-based strategies for achieving our goals:

1. *Do make that resolution.* Challenging goals motivate achievement (Harkin et al., 2016). Concrete goals—"finish that psychology paper by Tuesday"—direct attention and motivate persistence.

2. *Announce the goals to friends or family.* We're more likely to follow through after making a public commitment.

grit in psychology, passion and perseverance in the pursuit of long-term goals.

intrinsic motivation the desire to perform a behavior effectively for its own sake.

extrinsic motivation the desire to perform a behavior to receive promised rewards or avoid threatened punishment.

3. ***Develop an implementation plan.*** An action strategy should specify when, where, and how we will progress toward our goal. People who flesh out goals with detailed plans become more focused and more likely to succeed (Gollwitzer & Oettingen, 2012). Better to center on small steps—the day's running goal, say—than to fantasize about the marathon.

4. ***Create short-term rewards that support long-term goals.*** Although delayed rewards motivate us to set goals, immediate rewards best predict our persistence toward them (Woolley & Fishbach, 2017).

5. ***Monitor and record progress.*** If striving for more exercise, use a wearable fitness tracker such as Fitbit. It's even more motivating when progress is shared rather than kept secret (Harkin et al., 2016).

6. ***Create a supportive environment.*** When trying to eat healthily, keep junk food out of the cupboards. Decrease portion sizes. When focusing on a project, hole up in the library. When sleeping, stash the phone. Such "situational self-control strategies" prevent tempting impulses (Duckworth et al., 2016).

7. ***Transform the hard-to-do behavior into a must-do habit.*** Habits form when we repeat behaviors in a given context (Chapter 7). As our behavior becomes linked with the context, our next experience of that context evokes our habitual response. To increase our self-control, to connect our resolutions with positive outcomes, the key is forming "beneficial habits" (Galla & Duckworth, 2015). Do something every day for about two months and it will become an ingrained habit.

To achieve important life goals, we often know what to do. We *know* that a full night's sleep boosts our alertness, energy, and mood. We *know* that exercise lessens depression and anxiety, sculpts our body, and strengthens our heart and mind. We *know* that what we put into our body—junk food or balanced nutrition, addictive substances or clean air—affects our health and longevity. Alas, as T. S. Eliot foresaw, "Between the idea/And the reality . . . Falls the Shadow." Nevertheless, by taking these seven steps—resolving, announcing, planning, rewarding, monitoring, controlling, and persistently acting—we can create a bridge between the idea and the reality.

ENGAGE

ASK YOURSELF

What goal would you like to achieve? How might you use the seven strategies offered in this section to meet that goal?

🔒 **RETRIEVE IT** • • •   *ANSWERS IN APPENDIX E*

RI-5 What have researchers found to be an even better predictor of school performance than intelligence test scores?

🔒 **REVIEW** BASIC MOTIVATIONAL CONCEPTS, AFFILIATION, AND ACHIEVEMENT

⟫ Learning Objectives

TEST YOURSELF Answer these repeated Learning Objective Questions on your own (before checking the answers in Appendix D) to improve your retention of the concepts (McDaniel et al., 2009, 2015).

10-1 How do psychologists define *motivation*? From what perspectives do they view motivated behavior?

10-2 What evidence points to our human affiliation need—our need to belong?

10-3 How does social networking influence us?

10-4 What is *achievement motivation*, and what are some ways to encourage achievement?

⟫ Terms and Concepts to Remember

TEST YOURSELF Write down the definition yourself, then check your answer on the referenced page.

motivation, **p. 349**

instinct, **p. 349**

physiological need, **p. 349**

drive-reduction theory, **p. 349**

homeostasis, **p. 349**

incentive, **p. 349**

Yerkes-Dodson law, **p. 351**

hierarchy of needs, **p. 351**

affiliation need, **p. 353**

self-determination theory, **p. 353**

ostracism, **p. 355**

narcissism, **p. 356**

achievement motivation, **p. 357**

grit, **p. 358**

intrinsic motivation, **p. 358**

extrinsic motivation, **p. 358**

⟶ Experience the Testing Effect

TEST YOURSELF Answer the following questions on your own first, then check your answers in Appendix E.

1. Today's evolutionary psychology shares an idea that was an underlying assumption of instinct theory. This idea is that
   a. physiological needs arouse psychological states.
   b. genes predispose species-typical behavior.
   c. physiological needs increase arousal.
   d. external needs energize and direct behavior.

2. An example of a physiological need is _____.
   An example of a psychological drive is _____.
   a. hunger; a "push" to find food
   b. a "push" to find food; hunger
   c. curiosity; a "push" to reduce arousal
   d. a "push" to reduce arousal; curiosity

3. Danielle walks into a friend's kitchen, smells cookies baking, and begins to feel very hungry. The smell of baking cookies is a(n) _____ (incentive/drive).

4. _____ theory attempts to explain behaviors that do NOT reduce physiological needs.

5. With a challenging task, such as taking a difficult exam, performance is likely to peak when arousal is
   a. very high.
   b. moderate.
   c. very low.
   d. absent.

6. According to Maslow's hierarchy of needs, our most basic needs are physiological, including the need for food and water; just above these are _____ needs.
   a. safety
   b. self-esteem
   c. belongingness
   d. self-transcendence

7. Which of the following is NOT evidence supporting the view that humans are strongly motivated by a need to belong?
   a. Students who rated themselves as "very happy" also tended to have satisfying close relationships.
   b. Social exclusion—such as exile or solitary confinement—is considered a severe form of punishment.
   c. As adults, adopted children tend to resemble their biological parents.
   d. Children who are extremely neglected become withdrawn, frightened, and speechless.

8. What are some ways to manage our social networking time successfully?

9. If we want to increase our chance of success in achieving a new goal, such as stopping smoking, we _____ (should/should not) announce the goal publicly, and we _____ (should/should not) share with others our progress toward achieving that goal.

Continue testing yourself with 📖 **LearningCurve** or ≈ **Achieve Read & Practice** to learn and remember most effectively.

⟶ Hunger

> "Nobody wants to kiss when they are hungry." —Journalist Dorothy Dix (1861–1951)

> "Nature often equips life's essentials—sex, eating, nursing—with built-in gratification." —Frans de Waal, "Morals Without God?" 2010

Those who have tried to restrict their eating know that physiological influences are powerful. This was vividly demonstrated when Ancel Keys and his research team (1950) studied semistarvation among volunteers, who participated as an alternative to military service. After feeding 200 men normally for three months, researchers halved the food intake for 36 of them. These semistarved men became listless and apathetic as their bodies conserved energy. Eventually, their body weights stabilized about 25 percent below their starting weights.

Consistent with Abraham Maslow's idea of a needs hierarchy, the men became food obsessed. They talked food. They daydreamed food. They collected recipes, read cookbooks, and feasted their eyes on delectable forbidden food. Preoccupied with their unmet basic need, they lost interest in sex and social activities. As one man reported, "If we see a show, the most interesting part of it is contained in scenes where people are eating. I couldn't laugh at the funniest picture in the world, and love scenes are completely dull." The semistarved men's preoccupations illustrate how powerful motives can hijack our consciousness.

When you are hungry, thirsty, fatigued, or sexually aroused, little else may seem to matter. In studies, people in a motivational "hot" state (from fatigue, hunger, or sexual arousal) have easily recalled such feelings in their own past and have perceived them

HUNGER HIJACKS THE MIND World War II survivor Louis Zamperini (protagonist of the book and movie *Unbroken*, shown here) went down with his plane over the Pacific Ocean. He and two other crew members drifted for 47 days, subsisting on an occasional bird or a fish. To help pass time, the hunger-driven men recited recipes or recalled their mothers' home cooking.

as driving forces in others' behavior (Nordgren et al., 2006, 2007). (You may recall from Chapter 8 a parallel effect of our current good or bad mood on our memories of good or bad moods.) In another experiment, people were given money to bid for foods. When hungry, people *over*bid for snacks they were told they could eat later when they would be full. When full, people *under*bid for snacks they were told they could eat later when they would be hungry (Fisher & Rangel, 2014). It's hard to imagine what we're not feeling! Grocery shop with an empty stomach and you are more likely to see those jelly-filled doughnuts as just what you've always loved and will be wanting tomorrow. *Motives matter mightily.*

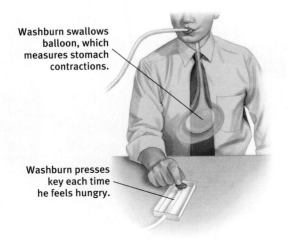

"Never hunt when you're hungry."

THE PHYSIOLOGY OF HUNGER

LOQ 10-5 What physiological factors produce hunger?

Deprived of a normal food supply, Keys' semistarved volunteers were clearly hungry. But what precisely triggers hunger? Is it the pangs of an empty stomach? So it seemed to A. L. Washburn. Working with Walter Cannon, Washburn agreed to swallow a balloon attached to a recording device (Cannon & Washburn, 1912) **(FIGURE 10.3)**. When inflated to fill his stomach, the balloon transmitted his stomach contractions. Washburn supplied information about his *feelings* of hunger by pressing a key each time he felt a hunger pang. The discovery: Whenever Washburn felt hungry, he was indeed having stomach contractions.

Can hunger exist without stomach pangs? To answer that question, researchers removed some rats' stomachs and created a direct path to their small intestines (Tsang, 1938). Did the rats continue to eat? Indeed they did. Some hunger similarly persists in humans whose ulcerated or cancerous stomachs have been removed. So the pangs of an empty stomach are not the *only* source of hunger. What else might trigger hunger?

"The full person does not understand the needs of the hungry." —Irish proverb

Washburn swallows balloon, which measures stomach contractions.

Washburn presses key each time he feels hungry.

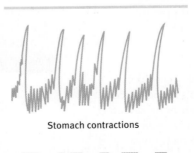

Stomach contractions

Hunger pangs

0 1 2 3 4 5 6 7 8 9 10
Time in minutes

FIGURE 10.3

MONITORING STOMACH CONTRACTIONS (Information from Cannon, 1929.)

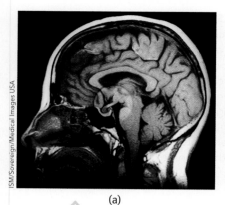

(a)   (b)

FIGURE 10.4

THE HYPOTHALAMUS (a) The hypothalamus (colored orange) performs various body maintenance functions, including control of hunger. Blood vessels supply the hypothalamus, enabling it to respond to our current blood chemistry as well as to incoming neural information about the body's state. (b) The fat mouse on the left has nonfunctioning receptors in the appetite-suppressing part of the hypothalamus.

LaunchPad For an interactive and visual tutorial on the brain and eating, visit **Topic Tutorial: PsychSim6, Hunger and the Fat Rat.**

Body Chemistry and the Brain

Somehow, somewhere, your body is keeping tabs on the energy it takes in and the energy it uses. If this weren't true, you would be unable to maintain a stable body weight. A major source of energy in your body is the blood sugar **glucose.** If your blood glucose level drops, you won't consciously feel the lower blood sugar, but your stomach, intestines, and liver will signal your brain to motivate eating. Your brain, which is automatically monitoring your blood chemistry and your body's internal state, will then trigger hunger.

How does the brain integrate these messages and sound the alarm? The work is done by several neural areas, some housed deep in the brain within the hypothalamus, a neural traffic intersection (**FIGURE 10.4**). For example, one neural network (called the *arcuate nucleus*) has a center that secretes appetite-stimulating hormones. When stimulated electrically, well-fed animals begin to eat. If the area is destroyed, even starving animals have no interest in food. Another neural center secretes appetite-suppressing hormones. When electrically stimulated, animals will stop eating. Destroy this area and animals can't stop eating and will become obese (see Figure 10.4b) (Duggan & Booth, 1986; Hoebel & Teitelbaum, 1966).

Blood vessels connect the hypothalamus to the rest of the body, so it can respond to our current blood chemistry and other incoming information. One of its tasks is monitoring levels of appetite hormones, such as *ghrelin,* a hunger-arousing hormone secreted by an empty stomach. During bypass surgery for severe *obesity,* surgeons seal off or remove part of the stomach. The remaining stomach then produces much less ghrelin, reducing the person's appetite and making food less enticing (Ammori, 2013; Lemonick, 2002; Scholtz et al., 2013). Other appetite hormones include *orexin, insulin, leptin,* and *PYY;* **FIGURE 10.5** describes how they influence your feelings of hunger.

You can also blame your brain for weight regain (Cornier, 2011). The interaction of appetite hormones and brain activity suggests that the body has some sort of "weight thermostat." When semistarved rats fall below their normal weight, this system signals

FIGURE 10.5

THE APPETITE HORMONES

Increases appetite
- *Ghrelin:* Hormone secreted by empty stomach; sends "I'm hungry" signals to the brain.
- *Orexin:* Hunger-triggering hormone secreted by hypothalamus.

Decreases appetite
- *Insulin:* Hormone secreted by pancreas; controls blood glucose.
- *Leptin:* Protein hormone secreted by fat cells; when abundant, causes brain to increase metabolism and decrease hunger.
- *PYY:* Digestive tract hormone; sends "I'm *not* hungry" signals to the brain.

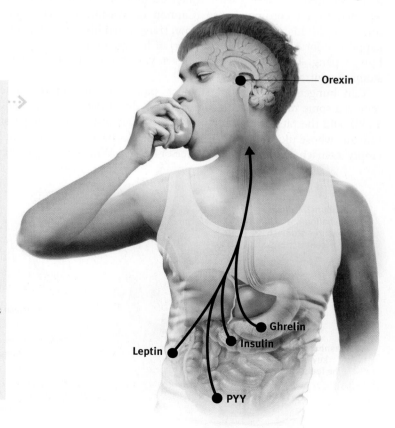

the body to restore the lost weight. It's as though fat cells cry out "Feed me!" and grab glucose from the bloodstream (Ludwig & Friedman, 2014). Hunger increases and energy output decreases. In this way, rats (and humans) tend to hover around a stable weight, or **set point,** influenced in part by heredity (Keesey & Corbett, 1984).

We humans (and other species, too) vary in our **basal metabolic rate,** the resting rate of energy expenditure for maintaining basic body functions. But we share a common response to decreased food intake: Our basal metabolic rate drops, as it did for participants in Keys' experiment. After 24 weeks of semistarvation they stabilized at three-quarters of their normal weight, even though they were taking in only *half* their previous calories. How did they achieve this dieter's nightmare? They reduced their energy expenditure, partly because they were less active, but partly because their basal metabolic rate dropped by 29 percent.

Some researchers have suggested that the idea of a biologically *fixed* set point is too rigid to explain some things. One thing it doesn't address is that slow, sustained changes in body weight can alter a person's set point (Assanand et al., 1998). Another is that when we have unlimited access to a wide variety of tasty foods, we tend to overeat and gain weight (Raynor & Epstein, 2001). And set points don't explain why psychological factors influence hunger. For all these reasons, some prefer the looser term *settling point* to indicate the level at which a person's weight settles in response to caloric intake and energy use. As we will see next, these factors are influenced by environment as well as biology.

🔒 RETRIEVE IT • • •

ANSWERS IN APPENDIX E

RI-1 Hunger occurs in response to _____ (low/high) blood glucose and _____ (low/high) levels of ghrelin.

THE PSYCHOLOGY OF HUNGER

LOQ 10-6 What cultural and situational factors influence hunger?

Our internal hunger is pushed by our physiology—our body chemistry and brain activity. Yet there is more to hunger than meets the stomach. This was strikingly apparent when researchers tested two patients who had no memory for events occurring more than a minute ago (Rozin et al., 1998). If offered a second lunch 20 minutes after eating a normal lunch, both patients readily consumed it . . . and usually a third meal offered 20 minutes after they finished the second. This suggests that one part of our decision to eat is our memory of the time of our last meal. As time passes, we think about eating again, and those thoughts trigger feelings of hunger.

Taste Preferences: Biology and Culture

Body cues and environmental factors together influence not only the *when* of hunger, but also the *what*—our taste preferences. When feeling tense or depressed, do you tend to take solace in high-calorie foods, as has been found in ardent football fans after a big loss (Cornil & Chandon, 2013)? The carbohydrates in pizza, chips, and sweets help boost levels of the neurotransmitter serotonin, which has calming effects. When stressed, both rats and many humans find it extra rewarding to scarf chocolate cookies (Artiga et al., 2007; Sproesser et al., 2014).

Our preferences for sweet and salty tastes are genetic and universal, but conditioning can intensify or alter those preferences. People given highly salted foods may develop a liking for excess salt (Beauchamp, 1987). People sickened by a food may develop an aversion to it. (The frequency of children's illnesses provides many chances for them to learn to avoid certain foods.)

Our culture teaches us that some foods are delicious but others are not. Many Japanese people enjoy *nattō*, a fermented soybean dish, which smell expert Rachel Herz (2012) reports "smells like the marriage of ammonia and a tire fire." Asians, she adds, are often repulsed by what many Westerners love—"the rotted bodily fluid of an ungulate" (a.k.a. cheese, some varieties of which have the same bacteria and odor as stinky feet).

"Never get a tattoo when you're drunk and hungry."

glucose the form of sugar that circulates in the blood and provides the major source of energy for body tissues. When its level is low, we feel hunger.

set point the point at which your "weight thermostat" may be set. When your body falls below this weight, increased hunger and a lowered metabolic rate may combine to restore lost weight.

basal metabolic rate the body's resting rate of energy output.

AN ACQUIRED TASTE People everywhere learn to enjoy the fatty, bitter, or spicy foods common in their culture. For these Alaska Natives, but not for most other North Americans, whale blubber is a tasty treat. For Peruvians, roasted guinea pig is similarly delicious.

FIGURE 10.6

HOT CULTURES LIKE HOT SPICES Countries with hot climates, in which food historically spoiled more quickly, feature recipes with more bacteria-inhibiting spices (Sherman & Flaxman, 2001). India averages nearly 10 spices per meat recipe; Finland, 2 spices.

(Graph: Spices per recipe vs. Mean annual temperature (degrees Celsius). Caption in graph: "The hotter the climate, the more spices used." X-axis 0–30, Y-axis 0–10.)

ASK YOURSELF

Do you usually eat only when your body sends hunger signals? How much does the sight or smell of delicious food tempt you even when you're full?

But there is biological wisdom to many of our taste preferences. For example, in hot climates (where foods spoil more quickly) recipes often include spices that inhibit bacteria growth (**FIGURE 10.6**). Pregnancy-related food dislikes—and the nausea associated with them—peak about the tenth week, when the developing embryo is most vulnerable to toxins.

Rats tend to avoid unfamiliar foods (Sclafani, 1995). So do we, especially those that are animal-based. This *neophobia* (dislike of unfamiliar things) surely was adaptive for our ancestors by protecting them from potentially toxic substances. We can overcome harmless food dislikes by repeatedly trying small samples of an unfamiliar food or drink. In experiments, this tends to increase people's appreciation for the new taste (Pliner, 1982; Pliner et al., 1993).

Situational Influences on Eating

To a surprising extent, situations also control our eating—a phenomenon psychologists have called the *ecology of eating*. Here are four situational influences you may have noticed but underestimated:

- *Friends and food* Do you eat more when eating with others? Most of us do (Herman et al., 2003; Hetherington et al., 2006). After a party, you may realize you've overeaten. This happens because the presence of others tends to amplify our natural behavior tendencies. (More about this *social facilitation* in Chapter 12.)

- *Serving size is significant* Investigators studied the effects of portion size by offering people varieties of free snacks (Geier et al., 2006). For example, in an apartment building's lobby, they laid out full or half pretzels, big or little Tootsie Rolls, or a small or large serving scoop with a bowl of M&M'S. Their consistent result: Offered a supersized portion, people put away more calories. Larger portions induce bigger bites, which may increase intake by decreasing oral exposure time (Herman et al., 2015). Children also eat more when using adult-sized (rather than child-sized) dishware (DiSantis et al., 2013). Portion size matters.

- *Selections stimulate* Food variety also stimulates eating. Offered a dessert buffet, people eat more than they do when choosing a portion from one favorite dessert. For our early ancestors, variety was healthy. When foods were abundant and varied, eating more provided a wide range of vitamins and minerals and produced protective fat for winter cold or famine. When a bounty of varied foods was unavailable, eating less extended the food supply until winter or famine ended (Polivy et al., 2008; Remick et al., 2009).

- *Nudging nutrition* One research team quadrupled carrots taken by offering schoolchildren carrots before they picked up other foods in a lunch line (Redden et al., 2015). Such "nudges" support U.S. President Barack Obama's 2015 executive order to use "behavioral science insights to serve the American people."

* * *

To consider how hunger and other factors affect our risks for **obesity**, see Thinking Critically About: The Challenges of Obesity and Weight Control. And for tips on shedding unwanted weight, see **TABLE 10.2**.

obesity defined as a body mass index (BMI) measurement of 30 or higher, which is calculated from our weight-to-height ratio. (Overweight individuals have a BMI of 25 or higher.)

🔒 **RETRIEVE IT • • •**   *ANSWERS IN APPENDIX E*

RI-2 After an 8-hour hike without food, your long-awaited favorite dish is placed in front of you, and your mouth waters in anticipation. Why?

THINKING CRITICALLY ABOUT:

The Challenges of Obesity and Weight Control

LOQ 10-7 How does obesity affect physical and psychological health, and what factors are involved in weight management?

A Growing Problem

Obesity is associated with:
- **physical health risks**, including diabetes, high blood pressure, heart disease, gallstones, arthritis, and certain types of cancer. [1]

- **increased depression**, especially among women.[2]
- **bullying,** outranking race and sexual orientation as the biggest reason for youth bullying in Western cultures. [3]

Percentage Overweight in 195 Countries Studied [4]

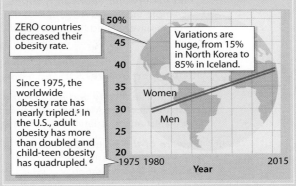

ZERO countries decreased their obesity rate.

Variations are huge, from 15% in North Korea to 85% in Iceland.

Since 1975, the worldwide obesity rate has nearly tripled.[5] In the U.S., adult obesity has more than doubled and child-teen obesity has quadrupled. [6]

Women
Men

50% 45 40 35 30 25 20
1975 1980   Year   2015

Body Mass Index (BMI)

Overweight   *Obese*

25+ 30+

See how your BMI compares to others in your country and in the world.

tinyurl.com/GiveMyBMI

How Did We Get Here?

Does obesity reflect a simple lack of willpower, as some people presume? [7]
No. Many factors contribute to obesity.

PHYSIOLOGY FACTORS

Storing fat was adaptive.
- This ideal form of stored energy carried our ancestors through periods of famine. People in impoverished places still find heavier bodies attractive, as plumpness signals affluence and status. [8]
- In food-rich countries, the drive for fat has become dysfunctional. [9]

fat cell

Set point and metabolism matter.
- Fat (lower metabolic rate than muscle) requires less food intake to maintain than it did to gain.
- If weight drops below *set point/settling point*, the brain triggers ⬆ hunger and ⬇ metabolism.
- Body perceives STARVATION; adapts by burning fewer calories. Most dieters in the long run regain what they lose on weight-loss programs.[10]
- 30 weeks of competition on *The Biggest Loser* ➡ 6 years later ➡ Only 1 of 14 contestants kept the weight off. On average they regained 70% of what they lost and were still struggling with lessened caloric burn from their slowed metabolism. [11]

Genes influence us.
- Lean people seem naturally disposed to move about, burning more calories than energy-conserving overweight people, who tend to sit still longer. [12]
- Adoptive siblings' body weights are uncorrelated with one another or with their adoptive parents, instead resembling their biological parents' weight. [13]
- Identical twins have closely similar weights, even if raised apart. [14] Much lower *fraternal* twin weight correlation suggests genes explain 2/3 of our varying body mass. [15]
- More than 100 genes have been identified as each affecting weight in some small way. [16]

ENVIRONMENTAL FACTORS

- **Sleep loss** makes us more vulnerable to obesity. [17]

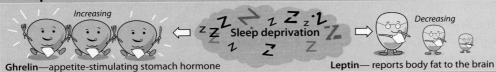

Increasing   *Decreasing*

z z z Sleep deprivation z z z

Ghrelin—appetite-stimulating stomach hormone   **Leptin**— reports body fat to the brain

NOTE: With weight, as with intelligence and other characteristics, there can be high levels of *heritability* (genetic influence on individual differences) without heredity explaining *group* differences. Genes mostly determine why one person today is heavier than another. Environment mostly determines why people today are heavier than their counterparts 50 years ago.

- **Social influences:** Our own odds of becoming obese triple if a close friend becomes obese. [18]
- **Food and activity levels:** Worldwide, we eat more and move less, with 31% of adults (including 43% of Americans and 25% of Europeans) now sedentary—averaging <20 minutes per day of moderate activity such as walking. [19]

1. Kitahara et al., 2014. 2. de Wit et al., 2010; Luppino et al., 2010. 3. Puhl et al., 2015. 4. GBD, 2017. 5. NCD, 2016. 6. Flegal et al., 2010, 2012, 2016. 7. NORC, 2016b. 8. Furnham & Baguma, 1994; Nettle et al., 2017; Swami, 2015. 9. Hall, 2016. 10. Mann et al., 2015. 11. Fothergill et al., 2016. 12. Levine et al., 2005. 13. Grilo & Pogue-Geile, 1991. 14. Hjelmborg et al., 2008; Plomin et al., 1997. 15. Maes et al., 1997. 16. Akiyama et al., 2017. 17. Keith et al., 2006; Nedeltcheva et al., 2010; Taheri, 2004; Taheri et al., 2004. 18. Christakis & Fowler, 2007. 19. Hallal et al., 2012.

"Remember when we used to have to fatten the kids up first?"

TABLE 10.2

Waist Management

People struggling with obesity should seek medical evaluation and guidance. For others who wish to lose weight, researchers have offered these tips:

- ***Begin only if you feel motivated and self-disciplined.*** Permanent weight loss usually requires a lifelong change in eating habits combined with increased exercise.

- ***Exercise and get enough sleep.*** Especially when supported by 7 to 8 hours of sleep a night, exercise empties fat cells, builds muscle, speeds up metabolism, helps lower your settling point, and reduces stress and stress-induced craving for carbohydrate-rich comfort foods (Bennett, 1995; Ruotsalainen et al., 2015; Thompson et al., 1982). Among *Biggest Loser* competitors, exercise predicted less weight regain (Kerns et al., 2017).

- ***Minimize exposure to tempting food cues.*** Food shop on a full stomach. Keep tempting foods out of the house, and tuck away special-occasion foods.

- ***Limit variety and eat healthy foods.*** Given more variety, people consume more. So eat simple meals with vegetables, fruits, and whole grains. Healthy fats, such as those found in olive oil and fish, help regulate appetite (Taubes, 2001, 2002). Water- and vitamin-rich veggies can fill the stomach with few calories. Better crispy greens than Krispy Kremes.

- ***Reduce portion sizes.*** Offered more, people consume more.

- ***Don't starve all day and eat one big meal at night.*** This common eating pattern slows metabolism. Moreover, those who eat a balanced breakfast are, by late morning, more alert and less fatigued (Spring et al., 1992).

- ***Beware of the binge.*** Drinking alcohol or feeling anxious or depressed can unleash the urge to eat (Herman & Polivy, 1980). And men especially should note that eating slowly can lead to eating less (Martin et al., 2007).

- ***Before eating with others, decide how much you want to eat.*** Eating with friends can distract us from monitoring our own eating (Ward & Mann, 2000).

- ***Remember, most people occasionally lapse.*** A lapse need not become a collapse.

- ***Chart your progress online.*** Those who record and disclose their progress toward a goal more often achieve it (Harkin et al., 2016).

- ***Connect to a support group.*** Join with others, either face-to-face or online, to share goals and progress updates (Freedman, 2011).

LaunchPad For a 7-minute review of hunger, see the **Video: Hunger and Eating.**

RETRIEVE IT • • •

ANSWERS IN APPENDIX E

RI-3 Why can two people of the same height, age, and activity level maintain the same weight, even if one of them eats much less than the other does?

REVIEW HUNGER

Learning Objectives

TEST YOURSELF Answer these repeated Learning Objective Questions on your own (before checking the answers in Appendix D) to improve your retention of the concepts (McDaniel et al., 2009, 2015).

10-5 What physiological factors produce hunger?

10-6 What cultural and situational factors influence hunger?

10-7 How does obesity affect physical and psychological health, and what factors are involved in weight management?

Terms and Concepts to Remember

TEST YOURSELF Write down the definition yourself, then check your answer on the referenced page.

glucose, p. 363

set point, p. 363

basal metabolic rate, p. 363

obesity, p. 365

⟶ Experience the Testing Effect

TEST YOURSELF Answer the following questions on your own first, then check your answers in Appendix E.

1. Journalist Dorothy Dix once remarked, "Nobody wants to kiss when they are hungry." How does Maslow's hierarchy of needs support her statement?

2. According to the concept of _____ _____, our body maintains itself at a particular weight level.

3. Which of the following is a genetically predisposed response to food?
   a. An aversion to eating cats and dogs
   b. An interest in novel foods
   c. A preference for sweet and salty foods
   d. An aversion to carbohydrates

4. Blood sugar provides the body with energy. When it is _____ (low/high), we feel hungry.

5. The rate at which your body expends energy while at rest is referred to as the _____ _____ rate.

6. Obese people find it very difficult to lose weight permanently. This is due to several factors, including the fact that
   a. dieting triggers neophobia.
   b. the set point of obese people is lower than average.
   c. with dieting, metabolism increases.
   d. there is a genetic influence on body weight.

7. Sanjay recently adopted the typical college diet, increasing his intake of processed foods and sugar. He knows he may gain weight, but he figures it's no big deal because he can simply lose it in the future. How would you evaluate Sanjay's plan?

Continue testing yourself with 📖 **LearningCurve** or ✷ **Achieve Read & Practice** to learn and remember most effectively.

⟶ Theories and Physiology of Emotion

EMOTION: AROUSAL, BEHAVIOR, AND COGNITION

LOQ 10-8 How do arousal, expressive behavior, and cognition interact in emotion?

Motivated behavior is often connected to powerful emotions. My [DM's] own need to belong was unforgettably disrupted one day. I went to a huge store and brought along Peter, my toddler first-born child. As I set Peter down on his feet for a moment so I could do some paperwork, a passerby warned, "You'd better be careful or you'll lose that boy!" Not more than a few breaths later, I turned and found no Peter beside me.

With mild anxiety, I looked around one end of the store aisle. No Peter in sight. With slightly more anxiety, I peered around the other side. No Peter there, either. Now, with my heart accelerating, I circled the neighboring counters. Still no Peter anywhere. As anxiety turned to panic, I began racing up and down the store aisles. He was nowhere to be found. The alerted store manager used the public-address system to ask customers to assist in looking for a missing child. Soon after, I passed the customer who had warned me. "I told you that you were going to lose him!" he now scolded. With visions of kidnapping (strangers routinely adored that beautiful child), I braced for the unthinkable possibility that my negligence had caused me to lose what I loved above all else, and that I might have to return home and face my wife after losing our only child.

But then, as I passed the customer service counter yet again, there he was, having been found and returned by some obliging customer. In an instant, the arousal of terror spilled into ecstasy. Clutching my son, with tears suddenly flowing, I found myself unable to speak my thanks and stumbled out of the store awash in grateful joy.

Courtesy of David Myers

Emotions are subjective. But they are real, says researcher Lisa Feldman Barrett (2012, 2013): "My experience of anger is not an illusion. When I'm angry, I feel angry. That's real." Where do our emotions come from? Why do we have them? What are they made of?

Emotions are our body's adaptive response. They support our survival. When we face challenges, emotions focus our attention and energize our actions (Cyders & Smith, 2008). Our heart races. Our pace quickens. All our senses go on high alert. Receiving unexpected good news, we may find our eyes tearing up. We raise our hands triumphantly. We feel exuberance and a newfound confidence. Yet negative and prolonged emotions can harm our health.

As my panicked search for Peter illustrates, **emotions** are a mix of:

- *bodily arousal* (heart pounding).
- *expressive behaviors* (quickened pace).
- *conscious experience* (*Is this a kidnapping?*) *and feelings* (panic, fear, joy).

The puzzle for psychologists is figuring out how these three pieces fit together. To do that, the first researchers of emotion considered two big questions:

1. A chicken-and-egg debate: Does your bodily arousal come *before* or *after* your emotional feelings? (Did I first notice my racing heart and faster step, and then feel terror about losing Peter? Or did my sense of fear come first, stirring my heart and legs to respond?)

2. How do *thinking* (cognition) and *feeling* interact? Does cognition always come before emotion? (Did I think about a kidnapping threat before I reacted emotionally?)

The psychological study of emotion began with the first question: How do bodily responses relate to emotions? Two of the earliest emotion theories offered different answers.

James-Lange Theory: Arousal Comes Before Emotion

Common sense tells most of us that we cry because we are sad, lash out because we are angry, tremble because we are afraid. But to pioneering psychologist William James, this commonsense view of emotion had things backward. Rather, "We feel sorry because we cry, angry because we strike, afraid because we tremble" (1890, p. 1066). To James, emotions result from attention to our bodily activity. James' idea was also proposed by Danish physiologist Carl Lange, and so is called the **James-Lange theory.** James and Lange would have guessed that I noticed my racing heart and then, shaking with fright, felt the whoosh of emotion—that my feeling of fear *followed* my body's response.

Cannon-Bard Theory: Arousal and Emotion Occur Simultaneously

Physiologist Walter Cannon (1871–1945) disagreed with the James-Lange theory. Does a racing heart signal fear or anger or love? The body's responses—heart rate, perspiration, and body temperature—are too similar, and they change too slowly, to *cause* the different emotions, said Cannon. He, and later another physiologist, Philip Bard, concluded that our bodily responses and experienced emotions occur separately but simultaneously. So, according to the **Cannon-Bard theory,** my heart began pounding *as* I experienced fear. The emotion-triggering stimulus traveled to my sympathetic nervous system, causing my body's arousal. *At the same time,* it traveled to my brain's cortex, causing my awareness of my emotion. My pounding heart did not cause my feeling of fear, nor did my feeling of fear cause my pounding heart.

But are they really independent of each other? The Cannon-Bard theory has been challenged by studies of people with severed spinal cords, including a survey of 25 World War II soldiers (Hohmann, 1966). Those with *lower-spine injuries,* who had lost sensation only in their legs, reported little change in their emotions' intensity. Those with *high spinal cord injury,* who could feel nothing below the neck, did report changes. Some reactions were much less intense than before the injuries. Anger, one man with a high spinal cord injury confessed, "just doesn't have the heat to it that it used to. It's a mental kind

RETAIN Not only emotion, but most psychological phenomena (vision, sleep, memory, sex, and so forth) can be approached these three ways—physiologically, behaviorally, and cognitively.

JOY EXPRESSED According to the James-Lange theory, we don't just smile because we share our teammates' joy. We also share the joy because we are smiling with them.

MATT SULLIVAN/REUTERS/Newscom

of anger." Other emotions, those expressed mostly in body areas above the neck, were felt *more* intensely. These men reported increases in weeping, lumps in the throat, and getting choked up when saying good-bye, worshiping, or watching a touching movie. Such evidence has led some researchers to view feelings as "mostly shadows" of our bodily responses and behaviors (Damasio, 2003). Brain activity underlies our emotions and our emotion-fed actions (Davidson & Begley, 2012).

But our emotions also involve cognition (Averill, 1993; Barrett, 2006). Here we arrive at psychology's second big emotion question: How do thinking and feeling interact? Whether we fear the man behind us on a dark street depends entirely on whether or not we interpret his actions as threatening.

> ## 🔒 RETRIEVE IT • • •
> *ANSWERS IN APPENDIX E*
>
> **RI-1** According to the Cannon-Bard theory, (a) our *physiological response* to a stimulus (for example, a pounding heart), and (b) the *emotion we experience* (for example, fear) occur _____ (simultaneously/sequentially). According to the James-Lange theory, (a) and (b) occur _____ (simultaneously/sequentially).

Schachter-Singer Two-Factor Theory: Arousal + Label = Emotion

LOQ 10-9 To experience emotions, must we consciously interpret and label them?

Stanley Schachter and Jerome Singer (1962) demonstrated that how we *appraise* (interpret) our experiences also matters. Our physical reactions *and our thoughts* (perceptions, memories, and interpretations) together create emotion. In their **two-factor theory,** emotions have two ingredients: physical arousal and cognitive appraisal. An emotional experience, they argued, requires a conscious interpretation of arousal.

Consider how arousal spills over from one event to the next. Imagine arriving home after an invigorating run and finding a message that you got a longed-for job. With arousal lingering from the run, would you feel more elated than if you heard this news after staying awake all night studying?

To explore this *spillover effect,* Schachter and Singer injected college men with the hormone epinephrine, which triggers feelings of arousal. But the trickster researchers told one group of men that the drug would just help test their eyesight. Picture yourself as a participant: After receiving the injection, you go to a waiting room, where you find yourself with another person (actually an accomplice of the experimenters) who is acting either euphoric or irritated. As you observe this person, you begin to feel your heart race, your body flush, and your breathing become more rapid. If you had been in the group who were told to expect these effects from the injection, what would you feel? In the actual experiment, these volunteers felt little emotion—because they correctly attributed their arousal to the drug. But if you had been told the injection would help assess your eyesight, what would you feel? Perhaps you would react as this group of participants did. They "caught" the apparent emotion of the other person in the waiting room. They became happy if the accomplice was acting euphoric, and testy if the accomplice was acting irritated.

This discovery—that a stirred-up state can be experienced as one emotion or another, depending on how we interpret and label it—has been replicated in dozens of experiments and continues to influence modern emotion research (MacCormack & Lindquist, 2016; Reisenzein, 1983; Sinclair et al., 1994). As Daniel Gilbert (2006) noted, "Feelings that one interprets as fear in the presence of a sheer drop may be interpreted as lust in the presence of a sheer blouse."

The point to remember: Arousal fuels emotion; cognition channels it.

emotion a response of the whole organism, involving (1) physiological arousal, (2) expressive behaviors, and (3) conscious experience.

James-Lange theory the theory that our experience of emotion is our awareness of our physiological responses to an emotion-arousing stimulus.

Cannon-Bard theory the theory that an emotion-arousing stimulus simultaneously triggers (1) physiological responses and (2) the subjective experience of emotion.

two-factor theory the Schachter-Singer theory that to experience emotion one must (1) be physically aroused and (2) cognitively label the arousal.

THE SPILLOVER EFFECT Arousal from a soccer match can fuel anger, which can descend into rioting or other violent confrontations.

OLEG POPOV/REUTERS/Newscom

📡 **LaunchPad** For a 4-minute demonstration of the relationship between arousal and cognition, see the **Video: Emotion = Arousal Plus Interpretation.**

🔒 **RETRIEVE IT** • • •   *ANSWERS IN APPENDIX E*

RI-2 According to Schachter and Singer, two factors lead to our experience of an emotion: (1) physiological arousal and (2) _____ appraisal.

Zajonc, LeDoux, and Lazarus: Does Cognition Always Precede Emotion?

But is the heart always subject to the mind? Must we *always* interpret our arousal before we can experience an emotion? Robert Zajonc [ZI-yence] (1923–2008) didn't think so. He contended that we actually have many emotional reactions apart from, or even before, our conscious interpretation of a situation (1980, 1984a). Perhaps you can recall liking something or someone immediately, without knowing why.

Even when people repeatedly view stimuli flashed too briefly for them to interpret, they come to prefer those stimuli (Kunst-Wilson & Zajonc, 1980). Unaware of having previously seen them, they nevertheless like them. We also have an acutely sensitive automatic radar for emotionally significant information; even a subliminally flashed stimulus can prime us to feel better or worse about a follow-up stimulus (Murphy et al., 1995; Zeelenberg et al., 2006).

Neuroscientists are charting the neural pathways of emotions (Ochsner et al., 2009). Our emotional responses can follow two different brain pathways. Some emotions (especially more complex feelings such as hatred and love) travel a "high road." A stimulus following this path would travel (by way of the thalamus) to the brain's cortex (**FIGURE 10.7a**). There, it would be analyzed and labeled before the response command is sent out, via the amygdala (an emotion-control center).

But sometimes our emotions (especially simple likes, dislikes, and fears) take what Joseph LeDoux (2002, 2015) has called the more direct "low road," a neural shortcut that bypasses the cortex. Following the low road, a fear-provoking stimulus would travel from the eye or ear (again via the thalamus) directly to the amygdala (Figure 10.7b). This shortcut enables our greased-lightning emotional response before our intellect intervenes. Like speedy reflexes (that also operate separately from the brain's thinking cortex), the amygdala's reactions are so fast that we may be unaware of what's transpired (Dimberg et al., 2000). A cortex-produced conscious fear experience then occurs as we become aware that our brain has detected danger (LeDoux & Brown, 2017).

The amygdala sends more neural projections up to the cortex than it receives back, which makes it easier for our feelings to hijack our thinking than for our thinking to rule our feelings (LeDoux & Armony, 1999). Thus, in the forest, we can jump at the sound

FIGURE 10.7

THE BRAIN'S PATHWAYS FOR EMOTIONS In the two-track brain, sensory input may be routed (a) to the cortex (via the thalamus) for analysis and then transmission to the amygdala; or (b) directly to the amygdala (via the thalamus) for an instant emotional reaction.

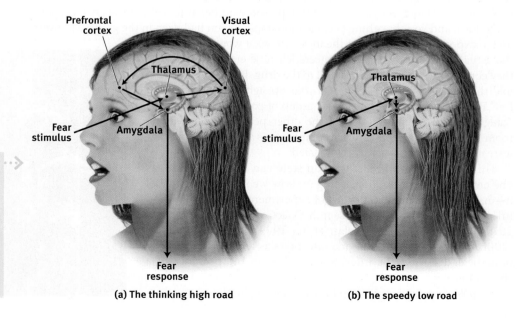

(a) The thinking high road   (b) The speedy low road

TABLE 10.3

Summary of Emotion Theories

Theory	Explanation of Emotions	Example
James-Lange	Emotions arise from our awareness of our specific bodily responses to emotion-arousing stimuli.	We observe our heart racing after a threat and then feel afraid.
Cannon-Bard	Emotion-arousing stimuli trigger our bodily responses and simultaneous subjective experience.	Our heart races at the same time that we feel afraid.
Schachter-Singer two-factor	Our experience of emotion depends on two factors: general arousal and a conscious cognitive label.	We may interpret our arousal as fear or excitement, depending on the context.
Zajonc's; LeDoux's	Some embodied responses happen instantly, without conscious appraisal.	We automatically feel startled by a sound in the forest before labeling it as a threat.
Lazarus'	Cognitive appraisal ("Is it dangerous or not?")—sometimes without our awareness—defines emotion.	The sound is "just the wind."

of rustling bushes nearby, leaving it to our cortex to decide later whether the sound was made by a snake or by the wind. Such experiences support Zajonc's and LeDoux's belief that *some* of our emotional reactions involve no deliberate thinking.

Emotion researcher Richard Lazarus (1991, 1998) conceded that our brain processes vast amounts of information without our conscious awareness, and that some emotional responses do not require *conscious* thinking. Much of our emotional life operates via the automatic, speedy low road. But he wondered: How would we *know* what we are reacting to if we did not in some way appraise the situation? The appraisal may be effortless and we may not be conscious of it, but it is still a mental function. To know whether a stimulus is good or bad, the brain must have some idea of what it is (Storbeck et al., 2006). Thus, said Lazarus, emotions arise when we *appraise* an event as harmless or dangerous. We appraise the sound of the rustling bushes as the presence of a threat. Later, we realize that it was "just the wind."

So, let's sum up (see also **TABLE 10.3**). As Zajonc and LeDoux have demonstrated, some simple emotional responses involve no conscious thinking (**FIGURE 10.8**). When I [ND] see a big spider trapped behind glass, I experience fear, even though I *know* the spider can't hurt me. Such responses are difficult to alter by changing our thinking. Within a fraction of a second, we may automatically perceive one person as more likable or trustworthy than another (Willis & Todorov, 2006). This instant appeal can even influence our political decisions, if we vote (as many people do) for the candidate we *like* over the candidate who expresses positions closer to our own (Westen, 2007).

But other emotions—including depressive moods and complex feelings such as hatred and love—are greatly affected by our conscious and unconscious information processing: our memories, expectations, and interpretations. For these emotions, we have more conscious control. When we feel emotionally overwhelmed, we can change our interpretations (Gross, 2013). Such *reappraisal* often reduces distress and the corresponding amygdala response (Buhle et al., 2014; Denny et al., 2015). Reappraisal not only reduces stress, it also helps students achieve higher exam scores (Jamieson et al., 2016). Don't stress about your stress. Embrace it, and approach your next exam with this mindset: "Stress evolved to help maintain my focus and solve problems." Although the emotional low road functions automatically, the thinking high road allows us to retake some control over our emotional life. *The bottom line:* Together, automatic emotion and conscious thinking weave the fabric of our emotional lives.

FIGURE 10.8

TWO PATHWAYS FOR EMOTIONS
Zajonc and LeDoux emphasized that some emotional responses are immediate, before any conscious appraisal. Lazarus, Schachter, and Singer emphasized that our appraisal and labeling of events also determine our emotional responses.

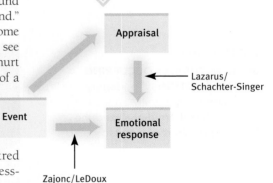

RETRIEVE IT • • •

ANSWERS IN APPENDIX E

RI-3 Emotion researchers have disagreed about whether emotional responses occur in the absence of cognitive processing. How would you characterize the approach of each of the following researchers: Zajonc, LeDoux, Lazarus, Schachter, and Singer?

EMBODIED EMOTION

Whether you are falling in love or grieving a death, you need little convincing that emotions involve the body. Feeling without a body is like breathing without lungs. Some physical responses are easy to notice. Other emotional responses we experience without awareness. Before examining our physical responses to specific emotions, consider another big question: How many distinct emotions are there?

The Basic Emotions

LOQ 10-10 What are some of the basic emotions?

When surveyed, most emotion scientists agreed that anger, fear, disgust, sadness, and happiness are basic human emotions (Ekman, 2016). Carroll Izard (1977) isolated 10 basic emotions (joy, interest-excitement, surprise, sadness, anger, disgust, contempt, fear, shame, and guilt), most present in infancy (**FIGURE 10.9**). Others believe that pride and love are also basic emotions (Shaver et al., 1996; Tracy & Robins, 2004). Izard has argued that other emotions are combinations of these 10, with love, for example, being a mixture of joy and interest-excitement. But are these emotions biologically distinct? Does our body know the difference between fear and anger?

Emotions and the Autonomic Nervous System

LOQ 10-11 What is the link between emotional arousal and the autonomic nervous system?

In a crisis, the *sympathetic division* of your *autonomic nervous system (ANS)* mobilizes your body for action (**FIGURE 10.10**). It triggers your adrenal glands to release the stress hormones epinephrine (adrenaline) and norepinephrine (noradrenaline). To provide energy, your liver pours extra sugar into your bloodstream. To help burn the sugar, your respiration increases to supply needed oxygen. Your heart rate and blood pressure increase. Your digestion slows, diverting blood from your internal organs to your muscles. With blood sugar driven into the large muscles, running becomes easier. Your pupils

FIGURE 10.9
SOME NATURALLY OCCURRING INFANT EMOTIONS To identify the emotions generally present in infancy, Carroll Izard analyzed the facial expressions of infants.

(a) Joy (mouth forming smile, cheeks lifted, twinkle in eye)

(b) Anger (brows drawn together and downward, eyes fixed, mouth squarish)

(c) Interest (brows raised or knitted, mouth softly rounded, lips may be pursed)

(d) Disgust (nose wrinkled, upper lip raised, tongue pushed outward)

(e) Surprise (brows raised, eyes widened, mouth rounded in oval shape)

(f) Sadness (brow's inner corners raised, mouth corners drawn down)

(g) Fear (brows level, drawn in and up, eyelids lifted, mouth corners retracted)

Sympathetic division (arousing)		Parasympathetic division (calming)
Pupils dilate	EYES	Pupils contract
Decreases	SALIVATION	Increases
Perspires	SKIN	Dries
Increases	RESPIRATION	Decreases
Accelerates	HEART	Slows
Inhibits	DIGESTION	Activates
Secrete stress hormones	ADRENAL GLANDS	Decrease secretion of stress hormones
Reduced	IMMUNE SYSTEM FUNCTIONING	Enhanced

dilate, letting in more light. To cool your stirred-up body, you perspire. If wounded, your blood would clot more quickly.

When the crisis passes, the *parasympathetic division* of your ANS gradually calms your body, as stress hormones slowly leave your bloodstream. After your next crisis, think of this: Without any conscious effort, your body's response to danger is wonderfully coordinated and adaptive—preparing you to *fight* or *flee*. So, do the different emotions have distinct arousal fingerprints?

 LaunchPad To review and then check your understanding of the ANS in action, engage online with **Concept Practice: The Autonomic Nervous System.**

The Physiology of Emotions

LOQ 10-12 Do different emotions activate different physiological and brain-pattern responses?

 Imagine conducting an experiment measuring the physiological responses of emotion. In each of four rooms, you have someone watch a movie: In the first, the person views a horror film; in the second, an anger-provoking film; in the third, a sexually arousing film; in the fourth, a boring film. From the control center, you monitor each person's perspiration, pupil size, breathing, and heart rate. Could you tell who is frightened? Who is angry? Who is sexually aroused? Who is bored?

With training, you could probably pick out the bored viewer. But discerning physiological differences among fear, anger, and sexual arousal is much more difficult (Barrett, 2006). Different emotions can share common biological signatures.

A single brain region can also serve as the seat of seemingly different emotions. Consider the broad emotional portfolio of the *insula,* a neural center deep inside the brain. The insula is activated when we experience various negative social emotions, such as lust, pridefulness, and disgust. In brain scans, it becomes active when people bite into some disgusting food, smell disgusting food, think about biting into a disgusting cockroach, or feel moral disgust over a sleazy business exploiting a saintly widow (Sapolsky, 2010). Similar multitasking regions are found in other brain areas.

Yet our varying emotions *feel* different to us, and they often *look* different to others. We may appear "paralyzed with fear" or "ready to explode." Fear and joy prompt a similar increased heart rate, but they stimulate different facial muscles. During fear, your brow muscles tense.

 FIGURE 10.10

EMOTIONAL AROUSAL Like a crisis control center, the autonomic nervous system arouses the body in a crisis and calms it when danger passes.

"Fear lends wings to his feet." —Virgil, *Aeneid*, 19 B.C.E.

ENGAGE (ASK YOURSELF)

Can you think of a recent time when you noticed your body's reactions to an emotionally charged situation, such as a difficult social setting, or perhaps a test or game you had been worrying about in advance? How would you describe your sympathetic nervous system's responses?

Gary Dobner/Alamy

SCARY THRILLS Elated excitement and panicky fear involve similar physiological arousal, which allows us to flip rapidly between the two emotions.

polygraph a machine used in attempts to detect lies that measures emotion-linked changes in perspiration, heart rate, and breathing.

"No one ever told me that grief felt so much like fear. I am not afraid, but the sensation is like being afraid. The same fluttering in the stomach, the same restlessness, the yawning. I keep on swallowing." —C. S. Lewis, *A Grief Observed*, 1961

ENGAGE 🔆 📚 **LaunchPad** To see how skilled you are at lie detection, visit **Topic Tutorial: PsychSim6, Catching Liars.**

During joy, muscles in your cheeks and under your eyes pull into a smile (Witvliet & Vrana, 1995).

Some of our emotions also have distinct brain circuits (Panksepp, 2007). Observers watching fearful faces showed more amygdala activity than did other observers who watched angry faces (Whalen et al., 2001). Brain scans and EEG recordings show that emotions also activate different areas of the brain's cortex. When you experience negative emotions such as disgust, your right prefrontal cortex tends to be more active than the left. Depression-prone people, and those with generally negative perspectives, have also shown more right frontal lobe activity (Harmon-Jones et al., 2002).

Positive moods tend to trigger more left frontal lobe activity. People with positive personalities—exuberant infants and alert, energized, and persistently goal-directed adults—have also shown more activity in the left frontal lobe than in the right (David-son, 2000; Urry et al., 2004).

To sum up, we can't easily see differences in emotions from tracking heart rate, breathing, and perspiration. But facial expressions and brain activity can vary from one emotion to another. So, do we, like Pinocchio, give off telltale signs when we lie? For more on that question, see Thinking Critically About: Lie Detection.

🔒 **RETRIEVE IT • • •**   *ANSWERS IN APPENDIX E*

RI-4 How do the two divisions of the autonomic nervous system affect our emotional responses?

THINKING CRITICALLY ABOUT:

Lie Detection

LOQ 10-13   How effective are polygraphs in using body states to detect lies?

Polygraphs measure emotion-linked autonomic arousal, as reflected in changed breathing, heart rate, and perspiration. Can we use these results to detect lies?

In the last 20 years, have you ever taken something that didn't belong to you?

Did you ever steal anything from your previous employer?

No!

Uh, no.

Many people tell a little white lie in response to this *control question*, prompting elevated arousal readings that give the examiner a baseline for comparing responses to other questions.

This person shows greater arousal in response to the *critical question* than she did to the control question, so the examiner may infer she is lying.

But is it true that *only a thief becomes nervous when denying a theft?*

1. We have similar bodily arousal in response to anxiety, irritation, and guilt. So, is she really guilty, or just anxious?

2. Many innocent people *do* get tense and nervous when accused of a bad act. (Many rape victims, for example, have "failed" these tests because they had strong emotional reactions while telling the truth about the rapist.[1])

About one-third of the time, polygraph test results are *just wrong*.[2]

Innocent people

Guilty people

○ Judged innocent by polygraph   ● Judged guilty by polygraph

If these polygraph experts had been the judges, more than one-third of the innocent would have been declared guilty, and nearly one-fourth of the guilty would have gone free.

The CIA and other U.S. agencies have spent millions of dollars testing tens of thousands of employees. Yet the U.S. National Academy of Sciences (2002) has reported that "no spy has ever been caught [by] using the polygraph."

The Concealed Information Test is more effective. Innocent people are seldom wrongly judged to be lying.

Questions focus on specific crime-scene details known only to the police and the guilty person.[3] (If a camera and computer had been stolen, for example, only a guilty person should react strongly to the brand names of the stolen items.)

---

1. Lykken, 1991. 2. Kleinmuntz & Szucko, 1984. 3. Ben-Shakhar & Elaad, 2003; Verschuere & Meijer, 2014; Vrij & Fisher, 2016.

⟶ Learning Objectives

TEST YOURSELF Answer these repeated Learning Objective Questions on your own (before checking the answers in Appendix D) to improve your retention of the concepts (McDaniel et al., 2009, 2015).

10-8 How do arousal, expressive behavior, and cognition interact in emotion?

10-9 To experience emotions, must we consciously interpret and label them?

10-10 What are some of the basic emotions?

10-11 What is the link between emotional arousal and the autonomic nervous system?

10-12 Do different emotions activate different physiological and brain-pattern responses?

10-13 How effective are polygraphs in using body states to detect lies?

⟶ Terms and Concepts to Remember

TEST YOURSELF Write down the definition yourself, then check your answer on the referenced page.

emotion, **p. 369**

James-Lange theory, **p. 369**

Cannon-Bard theory, **p. 369**

two-factor theory, **p. 369**

polygraph, **p. 374**

⟶ Experience the Testing Effect

TEST YOURSELF Answer the following questions on your own first, then check your answers in Appendix E.

1. The _____-_____ theory of emotion maintains that a physiological response happens BEFORE we know what we are feeling.

2. Assume that after spending an hour on a treadmill, you receive a letter saying that your scholarship application has been approved. The two-factor theory of emotion would predict that your physical arousal will

   a. weaken your happiness.

   b. intensify your happiness.

   c. transform your happiness into relief.

   d. have no particular effect on your happiness.

3. Zajonc and LeDoux have maintained that some emotional reactions occur before we have had the chance to consciously label or interpret them. Lazarus noted the importance of how we appraise events. These psychologists differ in the emphasis they place on _____ in emotional responses.

   a. physical arousal

   b. the hormone epinephrine

   c. cognitive processing

   d. learning

4. What does a polygraph measure, and why are its results questionable?

Continue testing yourself with 📖 **LearningCurve** or 📖 **Achieve Read & Practice** to learn and remember most effectively.

⟶ Expressing and Experiencing Emotion

Expressive behavior implies emotion. Dolphins, with smiles seemingly plastered on their faces, appear happy. To decipher people's emotions we read their bodies, listen to their voice tones, and study their faces. Does nonverbal language vary with culture—or is it universal? And do our expressions influence our experienced emotions?

"Your face, my thane, is a book where men may read strange matters." —Lady Macbeth to her husband, in William Shakespeare's *Macbeth*

DETECTING EMOTION IN OTHERS

LOQ 10-14 How do we communicate nonverbally?

To Westerners, a firm handshake conveys an outgoing, expressive personality (Chaplin et al., 2000). A gaze communicates intimacy, while darting eyes may signal anxiety (Kleinke, 1986; Perkins et al., 2012). When two people are passionately in love, they typically spend

A SILENT LANGUAGE OF EMOTION
Hindu classic dance uses the face and body to effectively convey 10 different emotions (Hejmadi et al., 2000).

time—quite a bit of time—gazing into each other's eyes (Bolmont et al., 2014; Rubin, 1970). Would such gazes stir these feelings between strangers? To find out, researchers have asked unacquainted (and presumed heterosexual) male-female pairs to gaze intently for 2 minutes either at each other's hands or into each other's eyes. After separating, the eye gazers reported feeling a tingle of attraction and affection (Kellerman et al., 1989).

Our brain is an amazing detector of subtle expressions, helping most of us read nonverbal cues well. We are adept at detecting a hint of a smile (Maher et al., 2014). Shown 10 seconds of video from the end of a speed-dating interaction, people can often tell whether one person is attracted to the other (Place et al., 2009). Signs of status are also easy to spot. When shown someone with arms raised, chest expanded, and a slight smile, people—from Canadian undergraduates to Fijian villagers—perceive that person as experiencing pride and having high status (Tracy et al., 2013). Even glimpsing a face for one-tenth of a second has enabled viewers to judge people's attractiveness or trust-worthiness, or to rate politicians' competence and predict their voter support (Willis & Todorov, 2006). "First impressions . . . occur with astonishing speed," note Christopher Olivola and Alexander Todorov (2010).

We also excel at detecting nonverbal threats. We readily sense subliminally presented negative words, such as *snake* or *bomb* (Dijksterhuis & Aarts, 2003). A single, angry face will "pop out" of a crowd (Pinkham et al., 2010). Experience can sensitize us to particular emotions, as shown by experiments using a series of faces (like those in **FIGURE 10.11**) that morph from anger to fear (or sadness). Viewing such faces, physically abused children are much quicker than other children to spot the signals of anger. Shown a face that is 50 percent fear and 50 percent anger, those with a history of being abused are more likely to perceive anger than fear. Their perceptions become sensitively attuned to glim-mers of danger that nonabused children miss.

Hard-to-control facial muscles can reveal signs of emotions, even ones you are trying to conceal. Lifting just the inner part of your eyebrows, which few people do consciously, reveals distress or worry. Eyebrows raised and pulled together signal fear. Raised cheeks and activated muscles under the eyes suggest a natural smile. A feigned smile, such as one we make for a photographer, is often frozen in place for several seconds, then suddenly switched off (**FIGURE 10.12**). Genuine happy smiles tend to be briefer but to fade less abruptly (Bugental, 1986). If you have the urge to hide your happiness, remember that genuine smiles cause others to perceive us as trust-worthy, authentic, and attractive (Gunnery & Ruben, 2016). Let your smile shine.

Despite our brain's emotion-detecting skill, we find it difficult to discern deceit. The behavioral differences between liars and truth tellers are too minute for most people to detect (Hartwig & Bond, 2011). In one digest of many studies, people were just 54 percent accurate in discerning truth from lies—barely better than a coin toss (Bond & DePaulo, 2006). Moreover, virtually no one—save perhaps police professionals in high-stakes situ-ations—beats chance by much, not even when detecting children's lies (Gongola et al., 2017; O'Sullivan et al., 2009; ten Brinke et al., 2016).

Some of us more than others are sensitive to the physical cues of various emotions. In one study, people named the emotion displayed in brief film clips. The clips showed portions of a person's emotionally expressive face or body, sometimes accompanied by a garbled voice (Rosenthal et al., 1979). For example, after a 2-second scene revealing only the face of an upset woman, the researchers asked whether the woman was criticizing someone for being late or was talking about her divorce. Given such "thin slices," some people were much better emotion detectors than others. Introverts tend to excel at read-ing others' emotions, while extraverts are generally easier to read (Ambady et al., 1995).

FIGURE 10.11

EXPERIENCE INFLUENCES HOW WE PERCEIVE EMOTIONS Viewing the morphed middle face, evenly mixing anger with fear, physically abused children were more likely than nonabused children to perceive the face as angry (Pollak & Kistler, 2002; Pollak & Tolley-Schell, 2003).

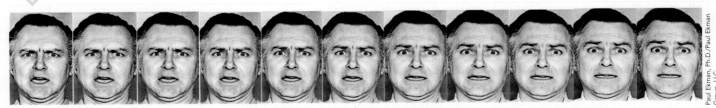

Gestures, facial expressions, and voice tones, which are absent in written communication, convey important information. The difference was clear when study participants in one group heard 30-second recordings of people describing their marital separations. Participants in the other group read a script of the recording. Those who heard the recording were better able to predict people's current and future adjustment (Mason et al., 2010). Just hearing a stranger say "hello" is enough to give listeners some clue to the speaker's personality. Researcher Phil McAleer and his colleagues (2014) call this "the Jerry Maguire effect," after the movie in which Renée Zellweger says to Tom Cruise, "You had me at hello."

The absence of expressive emotion can make for ambiguous emotion in electronic communications. To partly remedy that, we often embed cues to emotion 😊 in our messages. Without the vocal nuances that signal whether our statement is serious, kidding, or sarcastic, we are in danger of what developmental psychologist Jean Piaget called *egocentrism*, by failing to perceive how others interpret our "just kidding" message (Kruger et al., 2005).

(a)   (b)

FIGURE 10.12

WHICH OF RESEARCHER PAUL EKMAN'S SMILES IS FEIGNED, WHICH NATURAL? Smile (b) engages the facial muscles of a natural smile.

GENDER, EMOTION, AND NONVERBAL BEHAVIOR

LOQ 10-15 How do the genders differ in their ability to communicate nonverbally?

Do women have greater sensitivity than men to nonverbal cues, as so many believe? After analyzing 176 studies, Judith Hall and her colleagues (2016) concluded that, when given thin slices of behavior, women generally do surpass men at reading people's emotional cues. The female advantage emerges early in development. Female infants, children, and adolescents have outperformed males in many studies (McClure, 2000).

Women's nonverbal sensitivity helps explain their greater emotional literacy. When invited to describe how they would feel in certain situations, men tend to describe simpler emotional reactions (Barrett et al., 2000). You might like to try this yourself: Ask some people how they might feel when saying good-bye to friends after graduation. Research suggests men are more likely to say, simply, "I'll feel bad," and women to express more complex emotions: "It will be bittersweet; I'll feel both happy and sad."

Women's skill at decoding others' emotions may also contribute to their greater emotional responsiveness and expressiveness, especially for positive emotions (Fischer & LaFrance, 2015; McDuff et al., 2017). In studies of 23,000 people from 26 cultures, women more than men reported themselves open to feelings (Costa et al., 2001). Girls also express stronger emotions than boys do, hence the extremely strong perception that emotionality is "more true of women"—a perception expressed by nearly 100 percent of 18- to 29-year-old Americans (Chaplin & Aldao, 2013; Newport, 2001).

One exception: Quickly—imagine an angry face. What gender is the person? If you are like 3 in 4 Arizona State University students, you imagined a male (Becker et al., 2007). And when a gender-neutral face was made to look angry, most people perceived it as male. If the face was smiling, they were more likely to perceive it as female (**FIGURE 10.13**). Anger strikes most people as a more masculine emotion.

"Now, that wasn't so hard, was it?"

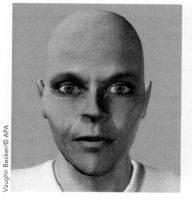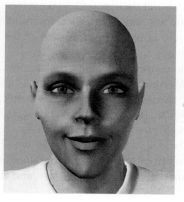

FIGURE 10.13

MALE OR FEMALE? Researchers manipulated a gender-neutral face. People were more likely to see it as male when it wore an angry expression and female when it wore a smile (Becker et al., 2007).

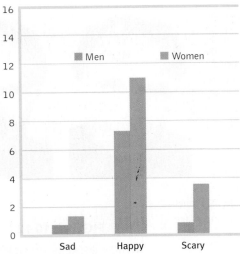

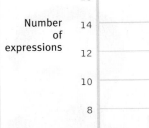

FIGURE 10.14

GENDER AND EXPRESSIVENESS
Male and female film viewers did not differ dramatically in self-reported emotions or physiological responses. But the women's faces showed much more emotion. (Data from Kring & Gordon, 1998.)

UNIVERSAL EMOTIONS No matter where on Earth you live, you have no trouble recognizing the joy experienced by Chicago Cubs fans over their 2016 World Series victory following a 108-year wait.

The perception of women's emotionality also feeds—and is fed by—people's attributing women's emotionality to their disposition and men's to their circumstances: "She's emotional" versus "He's having a bad day" (Barrett & Bliss-Moreau, 2009). Many factors influence our attributions, including cultural norms (Mason & Morris, 2010). Nevertheless, there are some gender differences in descriptions of emotional experiences. When surveyed, women are far more likely than men to describe themselves as empathic. If you have *empathy,* you identify with others. You consider things from their point of view. You imagine being in their skin. You appraise a situation as they do, rejoicing with those who rejoice and weeping with those who weep (Wondra & Ellsworth, 2015). Fiction readers, who immerse themselves in the lives of their favorite characters, report higher empathy levels and indeed are more often women (Mar et al., 2009; Tepper, 2000). But physiological measures, such as heart rate while seeing another's distress, reveal a much smaller gender gap (Eisenberg & Lennon, 1983; Rueckert et al., 2010).

Females are also more likely to *express* empathy—to display more emotion when observing others' emotions. As **FIGURE 10.14** shows, this gender difference was clear when male and female students watched film clips that were sad (children with a dying parent), happy (slapstick comedy), or frightening (a man nearly falling off the ledge of a tall building) (Kring & Gordon, 1998). Women also tend to experience emotional events, such as viewing pictures of mutilation, more deeply and with more brain activation in areas sensitive to emotion. And they remember the scenes better three weeks later (Canli et al., 2002).

🔒 RETRIEVE IT • • •   *ANSWERS IN APPENDIX E*

RI-1 _____ (Women/Men) report experiencing emotions more deeply, and they tend to be more adept at reading nonverbal behavior.

CULTURE AND EMOTION

LOQ 10-16 How are gestures and facial expressions understood within and across cultures?

The meaning of *gestures* varies from culture to culture. U.S. President Richard Nixon learned this after making the North American "A-OK" sign before a welcoming crowd of Brazilians, not realizing it was a crude insult in that country. The importance of cultural definitions of gestures was again demonstrated in 1968, when North Korea publicized photos of supposedly happy officers from a captured U.S. Navy spy ship. In the photo, three men had raised their middle finger, telling their captors it was a "Hawaiian good luck sign" (Fleming & Scott, 1991).

Do *facial expressions* also have different meanings in different cultures? To find out, two investigative teams showed photographs of various facial expressions to people in different parts of the world and asked them to guess the emotion (Ekman, 1994, 2016; Izard, 1977, 1994). You can try this matching task yourself by pairing the six emotions with the six faces in **FIGURE 10.15**.

Regardless of your cultural background, you probably did pretty well. A smile's a smile the world around. Ditto for sadness. Other emotional expressions are less universally recognized (Crivelli et al., 2016a; Jack et al., 2012). But there is no culture where people frown when they are happy.

Facial expressions do convey some nonverbal accents that provide clues to one's culture (Crivelli et al., 2016b; Marsh et al., 2003). Thus, data from 182 studies have shown slightly enhanced accuracy when people judged emotions from their own culture (Elfenbein & Ambady, 2002; Laukka et al., 2016). Still, the telltale signs of emotion generally cross cultures. The world over, children cry when distressed, shake their heads when defiant, and smile when they are happy. So, too, with blind children who have never seen a face (Eibl-Eibesfeldt, 1971). People blind from birth spontaneously exhibit the common facial expressions associated with such emotions as joy, sadness, fear, and anger (Galati et al., 1997).

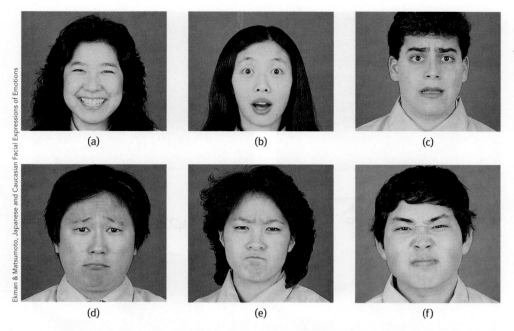

Ekman & Matsumoto, Japanese and Caucasian Facial Expressions of Emotions

(a)   (b)   (c)

(d)   (e)   (f)

FIGURE 10.15

CULTURE-SPECIFIC OR CULTURALLY UNIVERSAL EXPRESSIONS? As people of differing cultures, do our faces speak differing languages? Which face expresses disgust? Anger? Fear? Happiness? Sadness? Surprise? (From Matsumoto & Ekman, 1989.)[2]

Do these shared emotional categories reflect shared *cultural* experiences, such as movies and TV shows seen around the world? Apparently not. Paul Ekman and Wallace Friesen (1971) asked isolated people in New Guinea to respond to such statements as, "Pretend your child has died." When North American undergraduates viewed the recorded responses, they easily read the New Guineans' facial reactions.

So we can say that facial muscles speak a universal language. This discovery would not have surprised Charles Darwin (1809–1882), who argued that in prehistoric times, before our ancestors communicated in words, they communicated threats, greetings, and submission with facial expressions. Their shared expressions helped them survive (Hess & Thibault, 2009). In confrontations, for example, a human sneer retains elements of an animal baring its teeth in a snarl. Emotional expressions may enhance our survival in other ways, too. Surprise raises the eyebrows and widens the eyes, enabling us to take in more information. Disgust wrinkles the nose, closing it from foul odors.

Smiles are social as well as emotional events. Euphoric Olympic gold-medal winners typically don't smile when they are awaiting their award ceremony. But they wear broad grins when interacting with officials and when facing the crowd and cameras (Fernández-Dols & Ruiz-Belda, 1995).

Although we share a universal facial language for some emotions, it has been adaptive for us to interpret faces in particular contexts (**FIGURE 10.16**). People judge an angry face set in a frightening situation as afraid. They judge a fearful face set in a painful situation as pained (Carroll & Russell, 1996). Movie directors harness this phenomenon by creating scenes and soundtracks that amplify our perceptions of particular emotions.

Cultures share a facial language, but they differ in how *much* emotion they express. Those that encourage individuality, as in Western Europe, Australia, New Zealand, and North America, display visible emotions (van Hemert et al., 2007). Those that encourage people to adjust to others, as in Japan and China, often have less visible emotional displays (Matsumoto et al., 2009; Tsai et al., 2007). In Japan, people infer emotion more from the surrounding context. Moreover, the mouth, often so expressive in North Americans, conveys less emotion than do the telltale eyes (Masuda et al., 2008; Yuki et al., 2007). Compared with their counterparts in China, where calmness is emphasized, European-American leaders express excited smiles six times more frequently in their official photos (**FIGURE 10.17**) (Tsai et al., 2006, 2016). If we're happy and we know it, our culture will surely teach us how to show it.

"For news of the heart, ask the face."
—Guinean proverb

LaunchPad For a 4-minute demonstration of our universal facial language, see the **Video: Emotions and Facial Expression.**

While weightless, astronauts' internal bodily fluids move toward their upper body and their faces become puffy. This makes nonverbal communication more difficult, especially among multinational crews (Gelman, 1989).

2. (a) happiness, (b) surprise, (c) fear, (d) sadness, (e) anger, (f) disgust.

FIGURE 10.16

WE READ FACES IN CONTEXT
Whether we perceive the man as
(a) disgusted or (b) angry depends
on which body his face appears
on (Aviezer et al., 2008). Tears on
a woman's face in (c) make her
expression seem sadder than in (d)
(Provine et al., 2009).

(a)   (b)

AM I SAD?   AM I SAD?

(c)   (d)

[a, b] Paul Ekman, Ph.D./Paul Ekman Group, LLC.

[c, d] R. R. Provine. Emotional tears and NGF: A biographical appreciation and research beginning. *Archives Italiennes de Biologie, 149,* 271–276.

Peter Probst/Alamy

AP Photo

FIGURE 10.17

CULTURE AND SMILING Former
U.S. Vice President Joe Biden's
broad smile and Chinese President
Xi Jinping's more reserved one
illustrate a cultural difference in facial
expressiveness.

"Whenever I feel afraid
I hold my head erect
And whistle a happy tune."
—Richard Rodgers and Oscar Hammerstein,
The King and I, 1958

Cultural differences also exist *within* nations. The Irish and their Irish-American descendants have tended to be more expressive than the Scandinavians and their Scandinavian-American descendants (Tsai & Chentsova-Dutton, 2003). And that reminds us of a familiar lesson: Like most psychological events, emotion is best understood not only as a biological and cognitive phenomenon, but also as a social-cultural phenomenon.

🔒 **RETRIEVE IT • • •**   *ANSWERS IN APPENDIX E*

RI-2 Are people more likely to differ culturally in their interpretations of facial expressions, or of gestures?

THE EFFECTS OF FACIAL EXPRESSIONS

LOQ 10-17 How do our facial expressions influence our feelings?

As William James (1890) struggled with feelings of depression and grief, he came to believe that we can control emotions by going "through the outward movements" of any emotion we want to experience. "To feel cheerful," he advised, "sit up cheerfully, look around cheerfully, and act as if cheerfulness were already there."

Studies of emotional effects of facial expressions support what James predicted. Expressions not only communicate emotion, they also amplify and regulate it. In *The Expression of the Emotions in Man and Animals,* Charles Darwin (1872) contended that "the free expression by outward signs of an emotion intensifies it. . . . He who gives way to violent gestures will increase his rage."

Want to test Darwin's hypothesis? Try this: Fake a big grin. Now scowl. Can you feel the "smile therapy" difference? Participants in dozens of experiments have felt a difference. Researchers subtly induced students to make a frowning expression by asking them to "contract these muscles" and "pull your brows together" (supposedly to help the researchers attach facial electrodes) (Laird, 1974, 1984; Laird & Lacasse, 2014).

The results? The students reported feeling a little angry, as do people who are naturally frowning (by squinting) when facing the Sun (Marzoli et al., 2013). So, too, for other basic emotions. For example, people reported feeling more fear than anger, disgust, or sadness when made to construct a fearful expression: "Raise your eyebrows. And open your eyes wide. Move your whole head back, so that your chin is tucked in a little bit, and let your mouth relax and hang open a little" (Duclos et al., 1989).

This **facial feedback effect** has been found many times, in many places, for many basic emotions (**FIGURE 10.18**). Just activating one of the smiling muscles by holding a pen in the teeth (rather than gently between the lips, which produces a neutral expression) makes stressful situations less upsetting (Kraft & Pressman, 2012). A hearty smile—made not just with the mouth but with raised cheeks that crinkle the eyes—enhances positive feelings even more when you are reacting to something pleasant or funny (Soussignan, 2001). When happy we smile, and when smiling we become happier. Although some researchers question the reliability of the facial feedback effect (Wagenmakers et al., 2016), many others have replicated it (Strack, 2016).

So, your face is more than a billboard that displays your feelings; it also feeds your feelings. Scowl and the whole world scowls back. No wonder some depressed patients reportedly felt better after Botox injections paralyzed their frowning muscles (Parsaik et al., 2016). Four months after treatment, they continued to report lower depression levels. Botox paralysis of the frowning muscles slows people's reading of sadness- or anger-related sentences, and it slows activity in emotion-related brain circuits (Havas et al., 2010; Hennenlotter et al., 2008).

Other researchers have observed a broader **behavior feedback effect** (Carney et al., 2015; Flack, 2006). You can duplicate the participants' experience: Walk for a few minutes with short, shuffling steps, keeping your eyes downcast. Now walk around taking long strides, with your arms swinging and your eyes looking straight ahead. Can you feel your mood shift? Going through the motions awakens the emotions.

You can use your understanding of feedback effects to become more empathic: Let your own face mimic another person's expression. Acting as another acts helps us feel what another feels (Vaughn & Lanzetta, 1981). Losing this ability to mimic others can leave us struggling to make emotional connections, as one social worker with Moebius

A request from your authors: Smile often as you read this book.

🔒 RETRIEVE IT • • •

ANSWERS IN APPENDIX E

FIGURE 10.18

HOW TO MAKE PEOPLE SMILE WITHOUT TELLING THEM TO SMILE Do as Kazuo Mori and Hideko Mori (2009) did with students in Japan: Attach rubber bands to the sides of the face with adhesive bandages, and then run them either over the head or under the chin.

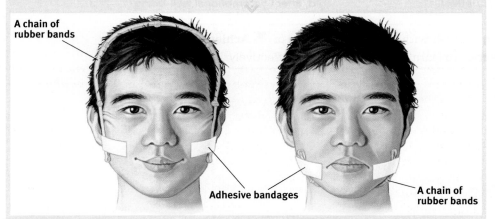

A chain of rubber bands

Adhesive bandages

A chain of rubber bands

RI-3 (1) Based on the *facial feedback effect*, how might students report feeling when the rubber bands raise their cheeks as though in a smile? (2) How might students report feeling when the rubber bands pull their cheeks downward?

facial feedback effect the tendency of facial muscle states to trigger corresponding feelings such as fear, anger, or happiness.

behavior feedback effect the tendency of behavior to influence our own and others' thoughts, feelings, and actions.

syndrome, a rare facial paralysis disorder, discovered while working with Hurricane Katrina refugees: When people made a sad expression, "I wasn't able to return it. I tried to do so with words and tone of voice, but it was no use. Stripped of the facial expression, the emotion just dies there, unshared" (Carey, 2010).

Our natural mimicry of others' emotions helps explain why emotions are contagious (Dimberg et al., 2000; Neumann & Strack, 2000; Peters & Kashima, 2015). Positive, upbeat Facebook posts create a ripple effect, leading Facebook friends to also express more positive emotions (Kramer, 2012).

* * *

We have seen how our motivated behaviors, triggered by the forces of nature and nurture, frequently go hand in hand with significant emotional responses. Our often-adaptive psychological emotions likewise come equipped with physical reactions. Nervous about an important encounter, we feel stomach butterflies. Anxious over public speaking, we frequent the bathroom. Smoldering over a family conflict, we get a splitting headache. As this text's discussion of stress and health next shows, negative emotions and the prolonged high arousal that may accompany them can tax the body and harm our health.

ENGAGE

ASK YOURSELF

Imagine one situation in which you would like to change the way you feel. How could you do so by altering your facial expressions or the way you carry yourself?

🔒 REVIEW　EXPRESSING AND EXPERIENCING EMOTION

⟩⟩ Learning Objectives

TEST YOURSELF Answer these repeated Learning Objective Questions on your own (before checking the answers in Appendix D) to improve your retention of the concepts (McDaniel et al., 2009, 2015).

10-14 How do we communicate nonverbally?

10-15 How do the genders differ in their ability to communicate nonverbally?

10-16 How are gestures and facial expressions understood within and across cultures?

10-17 How do our facial expressions influence our feelings?

⟩⟩ Terms and Concepts to Remember

TEST YOURSELF Write down the definition yourself, then check your answer on the referenced page.

facial feedback effect, **p. 381**　　　　behavior feedback effect, **p. 381**

⟩⟩ Experience the Testing Effect

TEST YOURSELF Answer the following questions on your own first, then check your answers in Appendix E.

1. When people are induced to assume fearful expressions, they often report feeling a little fear. This response is known as the ＿＿＿＿＿＿＿ ＿＿＿＿＿＿＿ effect.

2. Aiden has a bad cold and finds himself shuffling to class with his head down. How might his posture, as well as his cold, affect his emotional well-being?

Continue testing yourself with 📖 **LearningCurve** or 📖 **Achieve Read & Practice** to learn and remember most effectively.

Stress, Health, and Human Flourishing

Sir Ranulph Fiennes, called "the world's greatest living explorer" by Guinness World Records, has experienced significant stress—much of it self-imposed. He has persevered through what should have been impossible Arctic expeditions and grueling long-distance athletic endeavors. Yet he has thrived.

Just before Fiennes' birth, his father died in WWII, which was a particularly difficult time to grow up fatherless. As an adult adventurer, Fiennes tried to walk solo to the North Pole, but his sleds fell through the ice. He pulled them out by hand and later sawed off his own frostbitten fingertips. Years later, as he was preparing to run seven marathons on seven continents in seven days, he experienced a heart attack and had double bypass surgery. Then his beloved wife of 33 years died of cancer. And when he tried to become the oldest Briton to climb Mount Everest, he had to quit near the summit when having another heart attack.

Despite those setbacks, Fiennes chose to press on with his relentless, can-do spirit. With his upbeat nature, Fiennes' presence could light up a room. He did finally achieve his goal of running seven marathons on seven continents in seven days, and of becoming the oldest Briton to summit Mount Everest. He remarried and has enjoyed parenting his daughter. And in 2015, at age 71, he finished a 6-day, 156-mile running race across the Sahara desert. After the race, he described his exhausting ordeal as "more hellish than hell" (Silverman, 2015). (After completing the same race in 2017, I [ND] know what he means.) And yet Fiennes is already planning for his next big challenge.

CHAPTER OVERVIEW

⊙ **Stress and Illness**
Stress: Some Basic Concepts
Stress and Vulnerability to Disease
THINKING CRITICALLY ABOUT:
Stress and Health

⊙ **Health and Happiness**
Coping With Stress
Reducing Stress
Happiness

How often do you experience *stress* in your daily life? Do you feel differently about stressors that seem imposed on you (deadlines, assignments, tragic events) than about the stress you impose on yourself (adventures, challenges, happy changes)? As we will see, our interpretation of events affects our experience of those events and whether we even consider them "stressful."

Fiennes' life, and yours, embodies what this chapter explores: the difficulty of unwanted stress, the important ways we are affected by our interpretation of events, how we cope with stress and setbacks, and the possibilities for a happy, flourishing life. ▶

EXTREME STRESS From the audio recording of a 911 caller reporting Ben Carpenter's distress: "You are not going to believe this. There is a semitruck pushing a guy in a wheelchair on Red Arrow highway!"

⟶ Stress and Illness

Stress often strikes without warning. Imagine being 21-year-old Ben Carpenter, who experienced the world's wildest and fastest wheelchair ride. As he crossed a street, the light changed and a semitruck moved into the intersection. When they bumped, Ben's wheelchair handles got stuck in the truck's grille. The driver, who hadn't seen Ben and couldn't hear his cries for help, took off down the highway, pushing the wheelchair at 50 miles per hour until reaching his destination two miles away. "It was very scary," said Ben.

In this section, we take a closer look at stress—what it is and how it affects our health and well-being. Let's begin with some basic terms.

STRESS: SOME BASIC CONCEPTS

LEARNING OBJECTIVE QUESTION (LOQ)

11-1 How does our appraisal of an event affect our stress reaction, and what are the three main types of stressors?

Stress is the process of appraising and responding to a threatening or challenging event (**FIGURE 11.1**). But stress is a slippery concept. We sometimes use the word informally to describe threats or challenges ("Ben was under a lot of stress"), and at other times our responses ("Ben experienced acute stress"). To a psychologist, the terrifying truck ride was a *stressor*. Ben's physical and emotional responses were a *stress reaction*. And the process by which he related to the threat was *stress*. Stress arises less from events themselves than from how we appraise them (Lazarus, 1998). One person, alone in a house, ignores its creaking sounds and experiences no stress; someone else suspects an intruder and becomes alarmed. One person regards a new job as a welcome challenge; someone else appraises it as risking failure.

When short-lived, or when perceived as challenges, stressors can have positive effects. A momentary stress can mobilize the immune system for fending off infections and healing wounds (Segerstrom, 2007). Stress also arouses and motivates us to conquer problems.

FIGURE 11.1

STRESS APPRAISAL The events of our lives flow through a psychological filter. How we appraise an event influences how much stress we experience and how effectively we respond.

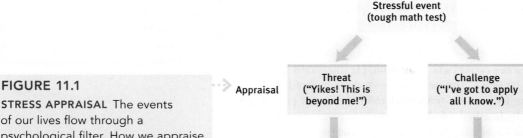

Championship athletes, successful entertainers, motivated students, and great teachers and leaders all thrive and excel when aroused by a challenge (Blascovich & Mendes, 2010; Wang et al., 2015a). In games and athletic contests, the stress of not knowing who will win makes the competition enjoyable (Abuhamdeh et al., 2015). Having conquered cancer or rebounded from a lost job, some people emerge with stronger self-esteem and a deepened spirituality and sense of purpose. Indeed, experiencing some stress early in life builds *resilience* (Seery, 2011). Adversity can produce growth.

But extreme or prolonged stress can harm us. Stress can trigger risky decisions and unhealthy behaviors (Cohen et al., 2016; Starcke & Brand, 2016). When facing stress, people may smoke or drink. And stress can affect health directly, making us more vulnerable to disease. Pregnant women with overactive stress systems tend to have shorter pregnancies, which pose health risks for their infants (Guardino et al., 2016).

So there is an interplay between our head and our health. Psychological states are physiological events that influence other parts of our physiological system. Just pausing to *think* about biting into an orange wedge—the sweet, tangy juice from the pulpy fruit flooding across your tongue—can trigger salivation. We'll explore that interplay shortly, but first, let's look more closely at stressors and stress reactions.

Stressors—Things That Push Our Buttons

Stressors fall into three main types: catastrophes, significant life changes, and daily hassles (including social stress). All can be toxic.

CATASTROPHES Catastrophes are large-scale disasters such as earthquakes, floods, wildfires, and storms. After such events, damage to emotional and physical health can be significant. In the four months after Hurricane Katrina, New Orleans' suicide rate reportedly tripled (Saulny, 2006). And in surveys taken in the three weeks after the 9/11 terrorist attacks, 58 percent of Americans said they were experiencing greater-than-average arousal and anxiety (Silver et al., 2002). In the New York City area, people were especially likely to report such symptoms, and sleeping pill prescriptions rose by a reported 28 percent (HMHL, 2002; NSF, 2001). Extensively watching 9/11 television footage predicted worse health outcomes two to three years later (Silver et al., 2013). A similar uptick in health issues, from heart problems to suicides, immediately followed the 2011 terrorist attacks in Norway (Strand et al., 2016).

For those who respond to catastrophes by relocating to another country, the stress may be twofold. The trauma of uprooting and family separation may combine with the challenges of adjusting to a new culture's language, ethnicity, climate, and social norms (Pipher, 2002; Williams & Berry, 1991). In the first half-year, before their morale begins to rebound, newcomers often experience culture shock and deteriorating well-being (Markovizky & Samid, 2008). This *acculturative stress* declines over time, especially when people engage in meaningful activities and connect socially (Bostean & Gillespie, 2017; Kim et al., 2012). In years to come, such relocations may become increasingly common due to climate change.

SIGNIFICANT LIFE CHANGES Life transitions—leaving home, having a loved one die, taking on student debt, losing a job, getting divorced—are often keenly felt. Even happy events, such as graduating or getting married, can be stressful life transitions. Many of these changes happen during young adulthood. One survey asked 15,000 Canadian adults whether they were "trying to take on too many things at once." It found the highest stress levels among young adults (Statistics Canada, 1999). When 650,000 Americans were asked if they had experienced a lot of stress "yesterday," young adults likewise reported the most stress (Newport & Pelham, 2009).

Some psychologists study the health effects of life changes by following people over time. Others compare the life challenges experienced by those who have (or have not) suffered a health problem, such as a heart attack. In such studies, those recently widowed, fired, or divorced have been more vulnerable to disease (Dohrenwend et al., 1982; Sbarra et al., 2015; Strully, 2009). One Finnish study of 96,000 widowed people found that the survivor's risk of death doubled in the week following a partner's death (Kaprio et al., 1987). A cluster of crises—losing a job, home, and partner—puts one even more at risk.

stress the process by which we perceive and respond to certain events, called *stressors*, that we appraise as threatening or challenging.

"Too many parents make life hard for their children by trying, too zealously, to make it easy for them." —German author Johann Wolfgang von Goethe (1749–1832)

© Julien Tack

SEISMIC STRESS Unpredictable large-scale events, such as the catastrophic earthquake that devastated Haiti in 2010 (aftermath shown here), trigger significant levels of stress-related ills. When an earthquake struck Los Angeles in 1994, sudden-death heart attacks increased fivefold. Most occurred in the first two hours after the quake and near its center and were unrelated to physical exertion (Muller & Verrier, 1996).

general adaptation syndrome (GAS) Selye's concept of the body's adaptive response to stress in three phases—alarm, resistance, exhaustion.

DAILY HASSLES AND SOCIAL STRESS Events don't have to remake our lives to cause stress. Stress also comes from *daily hassles*—dead cell phones, aggravating housemates, and too many things to do (Lazarus, 1990; Pascoe & Richman, 2009; Ruffin, 1993). We might have to give a public speech or do difficult math problems (Balodis et al., 2010; Dickerson & Kemeny, 2004) (**FIGURE 11.2**). Some people shrug off such hassles; others cannot. This is especially the case for those who wake up each day facing housing problems, unreliable child care, budgets that won't stretch to the next payday, and poor health. Such stressors add up and take a toll on health and well-being (DeLongis et al., 1982, 1988; Piazza et al., 2013; Sin et al., 2015).

Daily pressures may be compounded by prejudice against our gender identity, sexual orientation, or ethnicity, which—like other stressors—can have both psychological and physical consequences (Lick et al., 2013; Pascoe & Richman, 2009; Schetter et al., 2013). Thinking that some of the people you encounter each day will dislike, distrust, or doubt you makes daily life stressful. When prolonged, such stress takes a toll on our health. For many African-Americans, for example, the stress of racial discrimination can lead to unhealthy blood pressure levels and sleep deprivation, which can reduce academic achievement (Levy et al., 2016). In the aftermath of the 2016 U.S. presidential election, 7 in 10 African-Americans and nearly 6 in 10 Asian- and Hispanic-Americans said the outcome was a source of stress for them (APA, 2017).

The Stress Response System

LOQ 11-2   How do we respond and adapt to stress?

Medical interest in stress dates back to Hippocrates (460–377 B.C.E.). Centuries later, Walter Cannon (1929) confirmed that the stress response is part of a unified mind-body system. He observed that extreme cold, lack of oxygen, and emotion-arousing events all trigger an outpouring of the adrenal stress hormones epinephrine (adrenaline) and norepinephrine (noradrenaline) from the core of the adrenal glands. When alerted by any of a number of brain pathways, the sympathetic nervous system arouses us, preparing the body for the wonderfully adaptive response that Cannon called *fight or flight*. It increases heart rate and respiration, diverts blood from digestion to the skeletal muscles, dulls feelings of pain, and releases sugar and fat from the body's stores. By fighting or fleeing, we increase our chances of survival.

Canadian scientist Hans Selye's (1936, 1976) 40 years of research on stress extended Cannon's findings. His studies of animals' reactions to various stressors, such as electric shock and surgery, helped make stress a major concept in both psychology and medicine. Selye proposed that the body's adaptive response to stress is so general that, like a single burglar alarm, it sounds, no matter what intrudes. He named this response the **general adaptation syndrome (GAS),** and he saw it as a three-phase process.

Let's say you suffer a physical or an emotional trauma:

- In **Phase 1,** you have an **alarm reaction,** as your sympathetic nervous system is suddenly activated. Your heart rate zooms. Blood is diverted to your skeletal muscles. You feel the faintness of shock. With your resources mobilized, you are now ready to fight back.

- During **Phase 2, resistance,** your temperature, blood pressure, and respiration remain high. Your adrenal glands pump hormones into your bloodstream. You are fully engaged, summoning all your resources to meet the challenge. As time passes, with no relief from stress, your body's reserves dwindle.

- You have reached **Phase 3, exhaustion.** With exhaustion, you become more vulnerable to illness or even, in extreme cases, collapse and death.

Selye's basic point: Although the human body copes well with temporary stress, prolonged stress can damage it. Severe childhood stress gets under the skin, leading to greater adult stress. Three examples: In one two-decade study, severely stressed Welsh children were three times more likely to develop heart disease as adults (Ashton

Participants chew gum so that collecting saliva is easy.

Researcher takes a saliva sample from each participant at the beginning of the experiment to measure levels of the stress hormone, cortisol.

Participant gives simulated job interview speech to a critical panel.

What is 1223 minus 17?

Next, the participant is asked to compute difficult math problems out loud.

Cortisol (stress hormone) levels

High
Medium
Low

Beginning of experiment | After social stress

(Balodis et al., 2010; Dickerson & Kemeny, 2004)

Measuring cortisol in participants' saliva before and after tells us that although they enter the lab experiencing some stress, that level goes up 40 percent after they experience social stress.

Research team thanks and *debriefs* the participant—explaining the purpose of the experiment and the role she played.

FIGURE 11.2

STUDYING STRESS Most people experience stress when giving a public speech. To study stress, researchers re-create this type of situation. At the end, they *debrief* and reassure each participant.

FIGURE 11.3

SELYE'S GENERAL ADAPTATION SYNDROME Due to the ongoing conflict, Syria's White Helmets (volunteer rescuers) are perpetually in "alarm reaction" mode, rushing to pull victims from the rubble after each fresh attack. As their resistance depletes, they risk exhaustion.

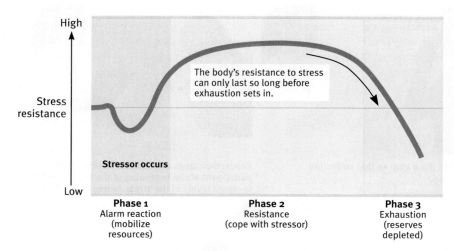

The body's resistance to stress can only last so long before exhaustion sets in.

High

Stress resistance

Stressor occurs

Low

| Phase 1 | Phase 2 | Phase 3 |
| Alarm reaction (mobilize resources) | Resistance (cope with stressor) | Exhaustion (reserves depleted) |

Sultan Kitaz/Reuters/REUTERS/Newscom

Sebastiano Tomada/Getty Images Reportage

"We sleep afraid, we wake up afraid, and leave our homes afraid." —15-year-old girl's Facebook post, describing her family's daily life in war-torn Yemen (al-Asaadi, 2016)

Matthew Diffee The New Yorker Collection/The Cartoon Bank

"You may be suffering from what's known as full-nest syndrome."

et al., 2016). Syria's civil war has taken a toll on the health of its refugees (Al Ibraheem et al., 2017). And former prisoners of war, who experienced constant stress and suffering, develop shorter *telomeres* protecting the chromosome ends. That may explain why, compared with noncaptive soldiers, former war prisoners tend to die sooner (Solomon et al., 2014, 2017). (See **FIGURE 11.3**.)

We respond to stress in other ways, too. One response is common after a loved one's death: Withdraw. Pull back. Conserve energy. Faced with an extreme disaster, such as a ship sinking, some people become paralyzed by fear. Another response, found often among women, is to give and receive support—what's called the **tend-and-befriend response** (Lim & DeSteno, 2016; Taylor, 2006; Taylor et al., 2000).

Facing stress, men more often than women tend to withdraw socially, turn to alcohol, or become emotionally insensitive (Bodenmann et al., 2015). Women more often respond to stress by nurturing and banding together.

🔒 **RETRIEVE IT** • • •   *ANSWERS IN APPENDIX E*

RI-1 The stress response system: When alerted to a negative, uncontrollable event, our _____ nervous system arouses us. Heart rate and respiration _____ (increase/decrease). Blood is diverted from digestion to the skeletal _____. The body releases sugar and fat. All this prepares the body for the _____-_____-_____ response.

STRESS AND VULNERABILITY TO DISEASE

LOQ 11-3   How does stress make us more vulnerable to disease?

It often pays to spend our resources in fighting or fleeing an external threat. But we do so at a cost. When stress is momentary, the cost is small. When stress persists, the cost may be greater, in the form of lowered resistance to infections and other threats to mental and physical well-being.

To study how stress—and healthy and unhealthy behaviors—influence health and illness, psychologists and physicians created the interdisciplinary field of *behavioral medicine,* integrating behavioral and medical knowledge. **Health psychology** provides psychology's contribution to behavioral medicine. A branch of health psychology called **psychoneuroimmunology** focuses on mind-body interactions (Kiecolt-Glaser, 2009). This awkward name makes sense when said slowly: Your thoughts and feelings (*psycho*) influence your brain (*neuro),* which influences the endocrine hormones that affect your disease-fighting *immune* system. And this subfield is the study (*ology*) of those interactions. If you've ever had a stress headache, or felt your blood pressure rise with anger, you don't need to be convinced that our psychological states have physiological effects. Stress can even leave you less able to fight off disease because your nervous and endocrine systems influence your immune system (Sternberg, 2009). You can think of your immune system as a complex surveillance system. When it functions properly, it keeps you healthy by isolating and destroying bacteria, viruses, and other invaders. Four types of cells are active in these search-and-destroy missions (**FIGURE 11.4**).

Your age, nutrition, genetics, body temperature, and stress all influence your immune system's activity. If it doesn't function properly, your immune system can err in two directions:

1. Responding too strongly, the immune system may attack the body's own tissues, causing an allergic reaction or a self-attacking disease such as lupus, multiple sclerosis, or some forms of arthritis. Women, who are immunologically stronger than men, are more susceptible to self-attacking diseases (Nussinovitch & Schoenfeld, 2012; Schwartzman-Morris & Putterman, 2012).

2. Underreacting, the immune system may allow a bacterial infection to flare, a dormant virus to erupt, or cancer cells to multiply. To protect transplanted organs, which the recipient's body treats as foreign invaders, surgeons may deliberately suppress the patient's immune system.

Stress can also trigger immune suppression by reducing the release of disease-fighting lymphocytes. This has been observed when animals were stressed by physical restraints, unavoidable electric shocks, noise, crowding, cold water, social defeat, or separation from their mothers (Maier et al., 1994). One study monitored immune responses in 43 monkeys over six months (Cohen et al., 1992). Half were left in stable groups. The rest were stressed by being housed with new roommates—3 or 4 new monkeys each month. By the end of the experiment, the socially disrupted monkeys had weaker immune systems.

Human immune systems react similarly. Three examples:

- ***Surgical wounds heal more slowly in stressed people.*** In one experiment, dental students received punch wounds (precise small holes punched in the skin). Compared with wounds placed during summer vacation, those placed three days before a major exam healed 40 percent more slowly (Kiecolt-Glaser et al., 1998). In other studies, marriage conflict has also slowed punch-wound healing (Kiecolt-Glaser et al., 2005).

tend-and-befriend response under stress, people (especially women) often provide support to others (tend) and bond with and seek support from others (befriend).

health psychology a subfield of psychology that provides psychology's contribution to behavioral medicine.

psychoneuroimmunology the study of how psychological, neural, and endocrine processes together affect the immune system and resulting health.

Possible Responses:

Intruders!

Is it a bacterial infection?

Is it a cancer cell, virus, or other "foreign substance"?

Is it some other harmful intruder, or perhaps a worn-out cell needing to be cleaned up?

Are there diseased cells (such as those infected by viruses or cancer) that need to be cleared out?

Send in: *B lymphocytes,* which fight bacterial infections. (This one is shown in front of a macrophage.)

Send in: *T lymphocytes,* which attack cancer cells, viruses, and foreign substances

Send in: *macrophage cells* ("big eaters"), which attack harmful invaders and worn-out cells. (This one is engulfing tuberculosis bacteria.)

Send in: *natural killer cells* (NK cells), which attack diseased cells. (These two are attacking a cancer cell.)

FIGURE 11.4

A SIMPLIFIED VIEW OF IMMUNE RESPONSES Four types of cells carry out the work of our immune system:

- *B lymphocytes* (white blood cells) release antibodies that fight bacterial infections.

- *T lymphocytes* (white blood cells) attack cancer cells, viruses, and foreign substances.

- *Macrophage cells* ("big eaters") identify, pursue, and ingest harmful invaders and worn-out cells.

- *Natural killer cells (NK cells)* attack diseased cells (such as those infected by viruses or cancer).

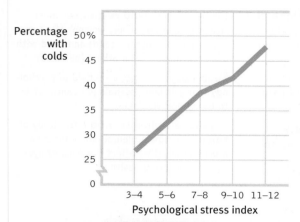

FIGURE 11.5

STRESS AND COLDS People with the highest life stress scores were also most vulnerable when exposed to an experimentally delivered cold virus (Cohen et al., 1991).

"I didn't give myself cancer." —Mayor Barbara Boggs Sigmund (1939–1990), Princeton, New Jersey

When organic causes of illness are unknown, it is tempting to invent psychological explanations. Before the germ that causes tuberculosis was discovered, personality explanations of TB were popular (Sontag, 1978).

- *Stressed people are more vulnerable to colds.* Major life stress increases the risk of a respiratory infection (Pedersen et al., 2010). When researchers dropped a cold virus into people's noses, 47 percent of those living stress-filled lives developed colds (**FIGURE 11.5**). Among those living relatively free of stress, only 27 percent did. In follow-up research, the happiest and most relaxed people were likewise markedly less vulnerable to an experimentally delivered cold virus (Cohen et al., 2003, 2006; Cohen & Pressman, 2006).

- *Stress can hasten the course of disease.* As its name tells us, *AIDS (acquired immune deficiency syndrome)* is an immune disorder, caused by the *human immunodeficiency virus (HIV)*. Stress cannot give people AIDS. But an analysis of 33,252 participants from around the world found that stress and negative emotions sped the transition from HIV infection to AIDS. And stress predicted a faster decline in those with AIDS (Chida & Vedhara, 2009). The greater the stress that HIV-infected people experienced, the faster their disease progressed.

The stress effect on immunity makes physiological sense. It takes energy to track down invaders, produce swelling, and maintain fevers. Thus, when diseased, your body reduces its muscular energy output by decreasing activity (and increasing sleep). Stress does the opposite. It creates a competing energy need. During an aroused fight-or-flight reaction, your stress responses divert energy from your disease-fighting immune system and send it to your muscles and brain. This increases your vulnerability to illness. *The point to remember:* Stress does not make us sick, but it does alter our immune functioning, which leaves us less able to resist infection.

🔒 RETRIEVE IT • • •   ANSWERS IN APPENDIX E

RI-2 The field of _____ studies mind-body interactions, including the effects of psychological, neural, and endocrine functioning on the immune system and overall health.

RI-3 What general effect does stress have on our health?

Stress and Cancer

Stress does not create cancer cells. But in a healthy, functioning immune system, lymphocytes, macrophages, and NK cells search out and destroy cancer cells and cancer-damaged cells. If stress weakens the immune system, might this weaken a person's ability to fight off cancer? To explore a possible stress-cancer connection, experimenters have implanted tumor cells in rodents or given them *carcinogens* (cancer-producing substances). They then exposed some rodents to uncontrollable stress, such as inescapable shocks, that weakened their immune systems (Sklar & Anisman, 1981). Stressed rodents, compared with their unstressed counterparts, developed cancer more often, experienced tumor growth sooner, and grew larger tumors.

Does this stress-cancer link also hold with humans? The results are generally the same (Lutgendorf & Andersen, 2015). Some studies find that people are at increased risk for cancer within a year after experiencing significant stress or bereavement (Chida et al., 2008; Steptoe et al., 2010). In one large Swedish study, the risk of colon cancer was 5.5 times greater among people with a history of workplace stress than among those who reported no such problems. This difference was not due to group differences in age, smoking, drinking, or physical characteristics (Courtney et al., 1993). Not all studies, however, have found a link between stress and human cancer (Coyne et al., 2010; Petticrew et al., 1999, 2002). Concentration camp survivors and former prisoners of war, for example, do not have elevated cancer rates. One danger in overstating the link between emotions and cancer is that some patients may then blame themselves for their illness.

It's important enough to repeat: *Stress does not create cancer cells.* At worst, it may affect their growth by weakening the body's natural defenses against multiplying malignant cells (Lutgendorf et al., 2008; Nausheen et al., 2010; Sood et al., 2010). Although a relaxed, hopeful state may enhance these defenses, we should be aware of the thin line that divides science from wishful thinking. The powerful biological processes at work in advanced cancer are not likely to be completely derailed by avoiding stress or maintaining a relaxed but determined spirit (Anderson, 2002). And that explains why research consistently indicates that psychotherapy does not extend cancer patients' survival (Coyne et al., 2007, 2009; Coyne & Tennen, 2010).

Stress and Heart Disease

LOQ 11-4 Why are some of us more prone than others to coronary heart disease?

Imagine a world where you wake up each day, eat your breakfast, and check the news. Among the headlines, you see that four 747 jumbo jet airplanes crashed again yesterday, killing another 1642 passengers. You finish your breakfast, grab your bag, and head to class. It's just an average day.

Replace airline crashes with **coronary heart disease,** the United States' leading cause of death, and you have reentered reality. About 610,000 Americans die annually from heart disease (CDC, 2016a). High blood pressure and a family history of the disease increase the risk. So do smoking, obesity, an unhealthy diet, physical inactivity, and a high cholesterol level.

Stress and personality also play a big role in heart disease. The more psychological trauma people experience, the more their bodies generate *inflammation*, which is associated with heart and other health problems, including depression (Haapakoski et al., 2015; O'Donovan et al., 2012). Plucking a hair and measuring its level of cortisol (a stress hormone) can help indicate whether a child has experienced prolonged stress or predict whether an adult will have a future heart attack (Karlén et al., 2015; Pereg et al., 2011; Vliegenthart et al., 2016). Even cortisol in a fingernail clipping can indicate people's prior stress exposure (Izawa et al., 2017).

THE EFFECTS OF PERSONALITY, PESSIMISM, AND DEPRESSION In a classic study, Meyer Friedman, Ray Rosenman, and their colleagues tested the idea that stress increases vulnerability to heart disease by measuring the blood cholesterol level and clotting speed of 40 U.S. male tax accountants at different times of year (Friedman & Ulmer, 1984). From January through March, the test results were completely normal. But as the accountants began scrambling to finish their clients' tax returns before the April 15 filing deadline, their cholesterol and clotting measures rose to dangerous levels. In May and June, with the deadline past, the measures returned to normal. For these men, stress predicted heart attack risk.

So, are some of us at high risk of stress-related coronary heart disease? To answer this question, the researchers launched a *longitudinal study* of more than 3000 healthy men, aged 35 to 59. The researchers first interviewed each man for 15 minutes, noting his work and eating habits, manner of talking, and other behavior patterns. Those who seemed the most reactive, competitive, hard-driving, impatient, time-conscious, super-motivated, verbally aggressive, and easily angered they called **Type A.** The roughly equal number who were more easygoing they called **Type B.**

Nine years later, 257 men had suffered heart attacks, and 69 percent of them were Type A. Moreover, not one of the "pure" Type Bs—the most mellow and laid-back of their group—had suffered a heart attack.

As often happens in science, this exciting discovery provoked enormous public interest. After that initial honeymoon period, researchers wanted to know more. Was the finding reliable? If so, what was the toxic component of the Type A profile: Time-consciousness? Competitiveness? Anger?

More than 700 studies have explored possible psychological correlates or predictors of cardiovascular health (Chida & Hamer, 2008; Chida & Steptoe, 2009). These reveal that Type A's toxic core is negative emotions—especially the anger associated with an aggressively reactive temperament. When challenged, our active sympathetic nervous system redistributes blood flow to our muscles, pulling it away from our internal organs. The liver, which normally removes cholesterol and fat from the blood, can't do its job. Thus, excess cholesterol and fat may continue to circulate in the blood and later get deposited around the heart. Hostility also correlates with other risk factors, such as smoking, drinking, and obesity (Bunde & Suls, 2006). Our mind and heart interact.

LaunchPad For a 7-minute demonstration of the links between stress, cancer, and the immune system, see the **Video: Fighting Cancer— Mobilizing the Immune System.**

coronary heart disease the clogging of the vessels that nourish the heart muscle; the leading cause of death in many developed countries.

Type A Friedman and Rosenman's term for competitive, hard-driving, impatient, verbally aggressive, and anger-prone people.

Type B Friedman and Rosenman's term for easygoing, relaxed people.

LaunchPad See the **Video: Longitudinal and Cross-Sectional Studies** for a helpful tutorial animation about these types of research studies.

In both India and the United States, Type A bus drivers are literally hard-driving: They brake, pass, and honk their horns more often than their more easygoing Type B colleagues (Evans et al., 1987).

ASK YOURSELF

Do you think you are Type A, Type B, or somewhere in between? In what ways has this been helpful to you, and in what ways has this been a challenge?

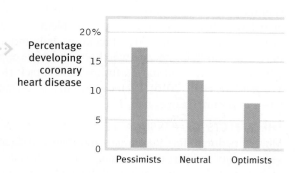

Hundreds of other studies of young and middle-aged men and women confirm that people who react with anger over little things are the most coronary-prone. In Western cultures, suppressing negative emotions only heightens the risk (Kitayama et al., 2015; Kupper & Denollet, 2007). Rage "seems to lash back and strike us in the heart muscle" (Spielberger & London, 1982).

"The fire you kindle for your enemy often burns you more than him." —Chinese proverb

Pessimism seems to be similarly toxic (Pänkäläinen et al., 2016). One longitudinal study followed 1306 initially healthy men who a decade earlier had scored as optimists, pessimists, or neither (Kubzansky et al., 2001). Even after adjusting for other risk factors such as smoking, pessimists were more than twice as likely as optimists to develop heart disease (**FIGURE 11.6**). Happy and consistently satisfied people tend to be healthy and to outlive their unhappy peers (Diener et al., 2017; Gana et al., 2016; Martín-María et al., 2017). People with big smiles tend to have extensive social networks, which predict longer life (Hertenstein, 2009). Having a happy spouse also predicts better health. Happy you, healthy me (Chopik & O'Brien, 2017).

© PhotoSpin, Inc/Alamy

FIGURE 11.6

PESSIMISM AND HEART DISEASE A Harvard School of Public Health team found pessimistic men at doubled risk of developing heart disease over a 10-year period. (Data from Kubzansky et al., 2001.)

Percentage developing coronary heart disease

20%

15

10

5

0

Pessimists   Neutral   Optimists

"A cheerful heart is a good medicine, but a downcast spirit dries up the bones." —Proverbs 17:22

Many studies show that depression can likewise be lethal (Wulsin et al., 1999). In one study, nearly 4000 English adults (ages 52 to 79) provided mood reports from a single day. Compared with those in a good mood, those in a depressed mood were twice as likely to be dead five years later (Steptoe & Wardle, 2011). In a U.S. survey of 164,102 adults, those who had experienced a heart attack were twice as likely to report also having been depressed at some point in their lives (Witters & Wood, 2015). And in the years following a heart attack, people with high scores for depression were four times more likely than their low-scoring counterparts to develop further heart problems (Frasure-Smith & Lesperance, 2005). Depression is disheartening.

A BROKEN HEART? The day after the death of her beloved daughter, Carrie Fisher (right), actress Debbie Reynolds (left) also died. People wondered: Might grief-related depression and stress hormones have contributed to Reynolds' stroke (Carey, 2016)?

LaunchPad To play the role of a researcher studying these issues, engage online with **Immersive Learning: How Would You Know If Stress Increases Risk of Disease?**

Jason LaVeris/Getty Images

STRESS AND INFLAMMATION Depressed people tend to smoke more and exercise less (Whooley et al., 2008). But stress itself is also disheartening: Work stress, involuntary job loss, and trauma-related stress symptoms increase heart disease risk (Allesøe et al., 2010; Gallo et al., 2006; Kubzansky et al., 2009; Slopen et al., 2010).

Both heart disease and depression may result when chronic stress triggers blood vessel inflammation (Miller & Blackwell, 2006; Mommersteeg et al., 2016). As the body focuses its energies on fleeing or fighting a threat, stress hormones boost the production of proteins that contribute to inflammation. Persistent inflammation can lead to asthma or clogged arteries and can worsen depression.

In many ways stress can affect our health. (See Thinking Critically About: Stress and Health.) The stress-illness connection is a price we pay for the benefits of stress. Stress invigorates our lives by arousing and motivating us. An unstressed life would hardly be challenging, productive, or even safe.

Stress and Health

LOQ 11-5 So, does stress *cause* illness?

Unhealthy behaviors (smoking, drinking, poor nutrition, sleep loss), which contribute to illness and disease

Anger, pessimism, or depression

½ empty

Persistent stressors

Past due

pay immediately

You're Fired

Release of stress hormones

Autonomic nervous system effects (headaches, high blood pressure, inflammation)

Immune suppression

102.0

Heart disease

Stress may not directly cause illness, but it does make us more vulnerable, by influencing our behaviors and our physiology.

Anger Management

LOQ 11-6 What are the causes and consequences of anger?

When we face a threat or challenge, fear triggers flight but anger triggers fight—each at times an adaptive behavior. Yet chronic hostility, as in the Type A personality, is linked to heart disease. How, then, can we manage our anger?

Individualist cultures encourage people to vent their rage. Such advice is seldom heard in cultures where people's identity is centered more on the group. People who keenly sense their *inter*dependence see anger as a threat to group harmony (Markus & Kitayama, 1991). In Tahiti, for instance, people learn to be considerate and gentle. In Japan, from infancy on, angry expressions are less common than in Western cultures, where in recent politics and on social media anger seems all the rage.

The Western vent-your-anger advice presumes that aggressive action or fantasy enables emotional release, or **catharsis.** Expressing anger can indeed be *temporarily* calming if it does not leave us feeling guilty or anxious (Geen & Quanty, 1977; Hokanson & Edelman, 1966).

However, catharsis usually fails to cleanse our rage. More often, expressing anger breeds more anger. For one thing, it may provoke further retaliation, causing a minor conflict to escalate into a major confrontation. For another, expressing anger can magnify anger. As *behavior feedback* research demonstrates, *acting* angry can make us *feel* angrier (Flack, 2006; Snodgrass et al., 1986). Anger's backfire potential appeared in a study of people who were asked to wallop a punching bag while ruminating about a person who had recently angered them (Bushman, 2002). Later, when given a chance for revenge, those who vented their anger became even more aggressive.

Angry outbursts that temporarily calm us may also become reinforcing and therefore habit forming. If stressed managers find they can temporarily drain off some of their tension by berating an employee, then the next time they feel irritated and tense they may be more likely to explode again.

ENGAGE What are some better ways to manage anger? Experts offer three suggestions:

• **Wait.** Doing so will reduce your physiological arousal. "What goes up must come down," noted Carol Tavris (1982). "Any emotional arousal will simmer down if you just wait long enough."

"Venting to reduce anger is like using gasoline to put out a fire." —Psychologist Brad Bushman, 2002

catharsis in psychology, the idea that "releasing" aggressive energy (through action or fantasy) relieves aggressive urges.

BLOWING OFF STEAM Fans seem to experience a *temporary* release while cheering at World Cup soccer match-es, such as this one in South Africa. My [DM's] daughter, a resident, noted, "Every time I got angry at Uruguay, blow-ing that vuvuzela and joining the chorus of dissent released something in me."

"Anger will never disappear so long as thoughts of resentment are cherished in the mind." —The Buddha, 500 B.C.E.

• *Find a healthy distraction or support.* Calm yourself by exercising, playing an instrument, or talking it through with a friend. Brain scans show that ruminating inwardly about why you are angry serves only to increase amygdala blood flow (Fabiansson et al., 2012).

• *Distance yourself.* Try to move away from the situation mentally, as if you are watching it unfold from a distance or the future. Self-distancing reduces rumination, anger, and aggression (Kross & Ayduk, 2011; Mischkowski et al., 2012; White et al., 2015).

Anger is not always wrong. Used wisely, it communicates strength and competence (Tiedens, 2001). Anger also motivates people to act courageously and achieve goals (Aarts & Custers, 2012; Halmburger et al., 2015). Controlled expressions of anger are more adaptive than either hostile outbursts or pent-up angry feelings. Civility means not only keeping silent about trivial irritations but also communicating important ones clearly and assertively. A nonaccusing statement of feeling—perhaps letting one's housemate know that "I get irritated when I have to clean up your dirty dishes"—can help resolve conflicts. Anger that expresses a grievance in ways that promote reconciliation rather than retaliation can benefit a relationship.

What if someone's behavior really hurts you, and you cannot resolve the conflict? Research commends the age-old response of forgiveness. Without letting the offender off the hook or inviting further harm—sometimes we need to distance ourselves from an abusive person—forgiveness may release anger and calm the body. In a study of the neural effects of forgiveness, German students had their brain scanned while some-one thwarted their opportunity to earn money (Strang et al., 2014). Next, the students were asked whether or not they forgave the wrongdoer. Forgiveness increased blood flow to brain regions that help people understand their own emotions and make socially appropriate decisions.

🔒 **RETRIEVE IT • • •**   *ANSWERS IN APPENDIX E*

RI-4 Which component of the Type A personality has been linked most closely to coronary heart disease?

RI-5 Which one of the following is an effective strategy for reducing angry feelings?

a. Retaliate verbally or physically.

b. Wait or "simmer down."

c. Express anger in action or fantasy.

d. Review the grievance silently.

* * *

Traditionally, people have thought about their health only when something goes wrong and they visit a physician for diagnosis and treatment. That, say health psychologists, is like ignoring a car's maintenance and going to a mechanic only when the car breaks down. Health maintenance begins with implementing strategies that prevent illness by alleviating stress, managing anger, and enhancing well-being.

🔒 **REVIEW** **STRESS AND ILLNESS**

⟶ Learning Objectives

TEST YOURSELF Answer these repeated Learning Objective Questions on your own (before checking the answers in Appendix D) to improve your retention of the concepts (McDaniel et al., 2009, 2015).

11-1 How does our appraisal of an event affect our stress reaction, and what are the three main types of stressors?

11-2 How do we respond and adapt to stress?

11-3 How does stress make us more vulnerable to disease?

11-4 Why are some of us more prone than others to coronary heart disease?

11-5 So, does stress *cause* illness?

11-6 What are the causes and consequences of anger?

⟶ Terms and Concepts to Remember

TEST YOURSELF Write down the definition yourself, then check your answer on the referenced page.

stress, **p. 385**

general adaptation syndrome (GAS), **p. 386**

tend-and-befriend response, **p. 389**

health psychology, **p. 389**

psychoneuroimmunology, **p. 389**

coronary heart disease, **p. 391**

Type A, **p. 391**

Type B, **p. 391**

catharsis, **p. 393**

⟶ Experience the Testing Effect

TEST YOURSELF Answer the following questions on your own first, then check your answers in Appendix E.

1. Selye's general adaptation syndrome (GAS) consists of an alarm reaction followed by _____, then _____.

2. When faced with stress, women are more likely than men to show a _____-and-_____ response.

3. The number of short-term illnesses and stress-related psychological disorders was higher than usual in the months following an earthquake. Such findings suggest that
   a. daily hassles have adverse health consequences.
   b. experiencing a very stressful event increases a person's vulnerability to illness.
   c. the amount of stress a person feels is directly related to the number of stressors experienced.
   d. daily hassles don't cause stress, but catastrophes can be toxic.

4. Which of the following is NOT one of the three main types of stressors?
   a. Catastrophes
   b. Significant life changes
   c. Daily hassles
   d. Pessimism

5. Stress can suppress the immune system by prompting a decrease in the release of _____, the immune cells that ordinarily attack bacteria, viruses, cancer cells, and other foreign substances.

6. Research has shown that people are at increased risk for cancer a year or so after experiencing depression, helplessness, or bereavement. In describing this link, researchers are quick to point out that
   a. accumulated stress causes cancer.
   b. anger is the negative emotion most closely linked to cancer.
   c. stress does not create cancer cells, but it weakens the body's natural defenses against them.
   d. feeling optimistic about chances of survival increases the likelihood of a cancer patient's recovery.

7. A Chinese proverb warns, "The fire you kindle for your enemy often burns you more than him." How is this true of Type A individuals?

Continue testing yourself with 📖 **LearningCurve** or 📖 **Achieve Read & Practice** to learn and remember most effectively.

⟶ Health and Happiness

COPING WITH STRESS

LOQ 11-7   In what two ways do people try to alleviate stress?

Stressors are unavoidable. This fact, coupled with the fact that persistent stress correlates with heart disease, depression, and lowered immunity, gives us a clear message: We need to learn to **cope** with the stress in our lives, alleviating it with emotional, cognitive, or behavioral methods.

Some stressors we address directly, with **problem-focused coping.** If our impatience leads to a family fight, we may go directly to that family member to work things out. We tend to use problem-focused strategies when we feel a sense of control over a situation and think we can change the circumstances, or at least change ourselves to deal with the circumstances more capably. We turn to **emotion-focused coping** when we believe

coping alleviating stress using emotional, cognitive, or behavioral methods.

problem-focused coping attempting to alleviate stress directly—by changing the stressor or the way we interact with that stressor.

emotion-focused coping attempting to alleviate stress by avoiding or ignoring a stressor and attending to emotional needs related to our stress reaction.

personal control our sense of controlling our environment rather than feeling helpless.

learned helplessness the hopelessness and passive resignation an animal or person learns when unable to avoid repeated aversive events.

external locus of control the perception that chance or outside forces beyond our personal control determine our fate.

internal locus of control the perception that we control our own fate.

we cannot change a situation. If, despite our best efforts, we cannot get along with that family member, we may relieve stress by reaching out to friends for support and comfort. Sometimes our emotion-focused coping can harm our health, such as when we respond by eating comforting but fattening foods. When challenged, some of us tend to respond with cool problem-focused coping, others with emotion-focused coping (Connor-Smith & Flachsbart, 2007). Our feelings of personal control, our explanatory style, and our supportive connections all influence our ability to cope successfully.

Perceived Loss of Control

LOQ 11-8 How does a perceived lack of control affect health?

Picture the scene: Two rats receive simultaneous shocks. Only one of them can turn a wheel to stop the shocks. The helpless rat, but not the wheel turner, becomes more susceptible to ulcers and lowered immunity to disease (Laudenslager & Reite, 1984). In humans, too, uncontrollable threats trigger the strongest stress responses (Dickerson & Kemeny, 2004).

Any of us may feel helpless, hopeless, and depressed after experiencing a series of bad events beyond our **personal control.** Martin Seligman and his colleagues have shown that for some animals and people, a series of uncontrollable events creates a state of **learned helplessness,** with feelings of passive resignation (**FIGURE 11.7**). In one series of experiments, dogs were strapped in a harness and given repeated shocks, with no opportunity to avoid them (Seligman & Maier, 1967). Later, when placed in another situation where they *could* escape the punishment by simply leaping a hurdle, the dogs displayed learned helplessness; they cowered as if without hope. Other dogs that had been able to escape the first shocks reacted differently. They had learned they were in control and easily escaped the shocks in the new situation (Seligman & Maier, 1967). People have shown similar patterns of learned helplessness (Abramson et al., 1978, 1989; Seligman, 1975).

Perceiving a loss of control, we become more vulnerable to ill health. This is a special problem for the elderly, who are particularly susceptible to health problems and also perceive the greatest loss of control (Drewelies et al., 2017). In a famous study of elderly nursing home residents, those who perceived the least amount of control over their activities declined faster and died sooner than those given more control (Rodin, 1986). Workers able to adjust office furnishings and control interruptions and distractions in their work environment have experienced less stress (O'Neill, 1993). Such findings help explain why British executives have tended to outlive those in clerical or laboring positions, and why Finnish workers with low job stress have been less than half as likely to die of stroke or heart disease as those with a demanding job and little control. The more control workers have, the longer they live (Bosma et al., 1997, 1998; Kivimaki et al., 2002; Marmot et al., 1997).

Increasing control—allowing prisoners to move chairs and to control room lights and the TV, having workers participate in decision making, allowing people to personalize their work space—has noticeably improved health and morale (Humphrey et al., 2007; Ng et al., 2012; Ruback et al., 1986). In the case of nursing home residents, 93 percent of those who were encouraged to exert more control became more alert, active, and happy (Rodin, 1986). As researcher Ellen Langer concluded, "Perceived control is basic to human functioning" (1983, p. 291).

Control also helps explain a link between economic status and longevity (Jokela et al., 2009). In one study of 843 grave markers in an old cemetery in Glasgow, Scotland, those with the costliest, highest pillars (indicating the most affluence) tended to have lived the longest (Carroll et al., 1994). Likewise, American presidents, who are generally wealthy and well-educated, have had above-average life spans (Olshansky, 2011). Across cultures, high economic status predicts a lower risk of heart and respiratory diseases (Sapolsky,

FIGURE 11.7

LEARNED HELPLESSNESS When animals and people experience no control over repeated bad events, they often learn helplessness.

| Uncontrollable bad events | → | Perceived lack of control | → | Generalized helpless behavior |

2005). Wealthy parents also tend to have wealthy, healthy children (Savelieva et al., 2016). With higher economic status come reduced risks of low birth weight, infant mortality, smoking, and violence. Even among other primates, individuals at the bottom of the social pecking order have been more likely than their higher-status counterparts to become sick when exposed to a cold-like virus (Cohen et al., 1997).

Why does perceived loss of control predict health problems? Because losing control provokes an outpouring of stress hormones. When rats cannot control shock or when humans or other primates feel unable to control their environment, stress hormone levels rise, blood pressure increases, and immune responses drop (Rodin, 1986; Sapolsky, 2005). Captive animals experience more stress and are more vulnerable to disease than their wild counterparts (Roberts, 1988). Human studies confirm that stress increases when we lack control. The greater nurses' workload, the higher their cortisol level and blood pressure—but only among nurses who reported little control over their environment (Fox et al., 1993). The crowding in high-density neighborhoods, prisons, and college and university dorms is another source of diminished feelings of control—and of elevated levels of stress hormones and blood pressure (Fleming et al., 1987; Ostfeld et al., 1987).

HAPPY TO HAVE CONTROL Working alongside Habitat for Humanity volunteers, this family helped build their own new home.

INTERNAL VERSUS EXTERNAL LOCUS OF CONTROL If experiencing a loss of control can be stressful and unhealthy, do people who generally *perceive* they have control of their lives enjoy better health? Consider your own perceptions of control. Do you believe that your life is beyond your control? That getting a good job depends mainly on being in the right place at the right time? Or do you more strongly believe that you control your own fate? That being a success is a matter of hard work? Did your parents influence your feelings of control? Did your culture?

Hundreds of studies have compared people who differ in their perceptions of control. On one side are those who have what psychologist Julian Rotter called an **external locus of control**—the perception that chance or outside forces control their fate. In one study of more than 1200 Israeli individuals exposed to missile attacks, those with an external locus of control experienced the most *posttraumatic stress* symptoms (Hoffman et al., 2016). On the other side are those who perceive an **internal locus of control,** who believe they control their own destiny. In study after study, the "internals" have achieved more in school and work, acted more independently, enjoyed better health, and felt less depressed than did the "externals" (Lefcourt, 1982; Ng et al., 2006). In longitudinal research on more than 7500 people, those who had expressed a more internal locus of control at age 10 exhibited less obesity, lower blood pressure, and less distress at age 30 (Gale et al., 2008). Compared with nonleaders, military and business leaders have lower-than-average levels of stress hormones and report less anxiety, thanks to their greater sense of control (Sherman et al., 2012).

Compared with their parents' generation, today's young Americans more often express an external locus of control (Twenge et al., 2004). This shift may help explain an associated increase in rates of depression and other psychological disorders in young people (Twenge et al., 2010b).

Another way to say that we believe we are in control of our own life is to say we have *free will.* Studies show that people who believe they have free will learn better, perform better at work, and behave more helpfully (Job et al., 2010; Stillman et al., 2010). They tend to enjoy making decisions, oppose behavior-restricting government regulations, and favor punishing rule breakers (Clark et al., 2014; Feldman et al., 2014; Hannikainen et al., 2016). Belief in free will also predicts another type of control known as *willpower* or *self-control*—an important related topic we turn to next.

 ASK YOURSELF

How much control do you have over your life? What changes could you make to increase your sense of control?

🔒 RETRIEVE IT • • •   *ANSWERS IN APPENDIX E*

RI-1 To cope with stress when we feel in control of our world, we tend to use _____ (emotion/problem) -focused strategies. To cope with stress when we believe we cannot change a situation, we tend to use _____ (emotion/problem) -focused strategies.

EXTREME SELF-CONTROL Our ability to exert self-control increases with practice, and some of us have practiced more than others! A number of performing artists make their living as very convincing human statues, as does this actress performing on The Royal Mile in Edinburgh, Scotland.

BUILDING SELF-CONTROL

LOQ 11-9 Why is self-control important, and can our self-control be depleted?

When we have a sense of personal control over our lives, we are more likely to develop **self-control**—the ability to control impulses and delay short-term gratification for longer-term rewards. Self-control predicts good health, higher income, and better school performance (Bub et al., 2016; Keller et al., 2016; Moffitt et al., 2011). In studies of American, Asian, and New Zealander children, self-control outdid intelligence test scores in predicting future academic and life success (Duckworth & Seligman, 2005; Poulton et al., 2015; Wu et al., 2016).

Strengthening self-control is an important key to coping effectively with stress. Doing so requires attention and energy—similar to strengthening a muscle. It's easy to form bad habits, but it takes hard work to break them. With frequent practice in overcoming unwanted urges, people have strengthened their self-control, as seen in their improved self-management of anger, dishonesty, smoking, and impulsive spending (Beames et al., 2017; Wang, J., et al., 2017a).

Researchers disagree about the factors that deplete self-control. Self-control varies over time. Like a muscle, it tends to weaken after use, recover after rest, and grow stronger with exercise (Baumeister & Vohs, 2016). Does exercising willpower temporarily deplete the mental energy we need for self-control on other tasks (see Grillon et al., 2015; Luethi et al., 2016; Vohs et al., 2012 versus Hagger et al., 2016)? In one famous experiment, hungry people who had spent some of their willpower resisting the temptation to eat chocolate chip cookies then abandoned a tedious task sooner than did others (Baumeister et al., 1998a). While some researchers debate the reliability of this "depletion effect," the big lesson of self-control remains: Develop self-discipline, and your self-control can help you lead a healthier, happier, and more successful life (Tuk et al., 2015). The next time you face the temptation of studying versus partying, remember that delaying a little fun now can lead to bigger future rewards.

LaunchPad Test your own self-control with **Immersive Learning: Assess Your Strengths—How Much Self-Control Do You Have, and Why Is This Worth Working to Increase?**

Explanatory Style: Optimism Versus Pessimism

LOQ 11-10 How does an optimistic outlook affect health and longevity?

In *The How of Happiness* (2008), social psychologist Sonja Lyubomirsky tells the true story of Randy. By any measure, Randy has lived a hard life. His dad and best friend both died by suicide. Growing up, his mother's boyfriend treated him poorly. Randy's first wife was unfaithful, and they divorced. Despite these misfortunes, Randy has a sunny disposition. He remarried and enjoys being the stepfather to three boys. His work is rewarding. Randy says he survived his life challenges by seeing the "silver lining in the cloud."

Randy's story illustrates how our outlook—what we expect from the world—influences how we cope with stress. Pessimists expect things to go badly (Aspinwall & Tedeschi, 2010; Carver et al., 2010; Rasmussen et al., 2009). When bad things happen, pessimists knew it all along. They attribute their poor performance to a basic lack of ability ("I can't do this") or to situations enduringly beyond their control ("There is nothing I can do about it"). Optimists, such as Randy, expect to have more control, to cope better with stressful events, and to enjoy better health (Aspinwall & Tedeschi, 2010; Boehm & Kubzansky, 2012; Hernandez et al., 2015). During a semester's final month, students previously identified as optimistic reported less fatigue and fewer coughs, aches, and pains than did their more pessimistic counterparts. And during the stressful first few weeks of law school, those who were optimistic ("It's unlikely that I will fail") enjoyed better moods and stronger immune systems (Segerstrom et al., 1998). Optimists also respond to stress with smaller increases in blood pressure, and they recover more quickly from heart bypass surgery.

Optimistic students have also tended to get better grades because they often respond to setbacks with the hopeful attitude that effort, good study habits, and self-discipline make a difference (Noel et al., 1987; Peterson & Barrett, 1987). When dating couples wrestle

self-control the ability to control impulses and delay short-term gratification for greater long-term rewards.

LatitudeStock - Brian Fairbrother/Getty Images

with conflicts, optimists and their partners see each other as engaging constructively, and they then tend to feel more supported and satisfied with the resolution and with their relationship (Srivastava et al., 2006). Optimism relates to well-being and success in many places, including China and Japan (Qin & Piao, 2011). Realistic positive expectations fuel motivation and success (Oettingen & Mayer, 2002).

Consider the consistency and startling magnitude of the optimism and positive emotions factor in several other studies:

- When one research team followed 70,021 nurses over time, they discovered that those scoring in the top quarter on optimism were nearly 30 percent less likely to have died than those scoring in the bottom quarter (Kim et al., 2017). Even greater optimism-longevity differences have been found in studies of Finnish men and American Vietnam War veterans (Everson et al., 1996; Phillips et al., 2009).

- A famous study followed up on 180 Catholic nuns who had written brief autobiographies at about 22 years of age and had thereafter lived similar lifestyles. Those who had expressed happiness, love, and other positive feelings in their autobiographies lived an average 7 years longer than their more dour counterparts (Danner et al., 2001). By age 80, some 54 percent of those expressing few positive emotions had died, as had only 24 percent of the most positive-spirited.

- Optimists not only live long lives, but they maintain a positive view as they approach the end of their lives. One study followed more than 68,000 American women, ages 50 to 79 years, for nearly two decades (Zaslavsky et al., 2015). As death grew nearer, the optimistic women tended to feel more life satisfaction than did the pessimistic women.

Optimism runs in families, so some people truly are born with a sunny, hopeful outlook. If one identical twin is optimistic, the other often will be as well (Bates, 2015; Mosing et al., 2009). One genetic marker of optimism is a gene that enhances the social-bonding hormone *oxytocin,* which in humans is released, for example, by cuddling, massage, and breast feeding (Campbell, 2010; Saphire-Bernstein et al., 2011).

The good news is that all of us, even the most pessimistic, can learn to become more optimistic. Compared with a control group of pessimists who simply kept diaries of their daily activities, pessimists in a skill-building group—who learned ways of seeing the bright side of difficult situations and of viewing their goals as achievable—reported lower levels of depression (Sergeant & Mongrain, 2014). Optimism is the light bulb that can brighten anyone's mood.

Social Support

LOQ 11-11 How does social support promote good health?

Social support—feeling liked and encouraged by intimate friends and family—promotes both happiness and health. In massive investigations, some following thousands of people for several years, close relationships have predicted happiness and health in both individualist and collectivist cultures (Brannan et al., 2013; Gable et al., 2012; Rueger et al., 2016). People are less likely to die early if supported by close relationships (Shor et al., 2013). When Brigham Young University researchers combined data from 70 studies of 3.4 million people worldwide, they confirmed a striking effect of social support (Holt-Lunstad et al., 2015, 2017). Compared with those who had ample social connections, those who were socially isolated or felt lonely had a 30 percent greater death rate during the 7-year study period. Social isolation's association with risk of death is equivalent to that of smoking (Holt-Lunstad et al., 2010).

To combat social isolation, we need to do more than collect lots of acquaintances. We need people who genuinely care about us (Cacioppo et al., 2014; Hawkley et al., 2008). Some fill this need by connecting with friends, family, co-workers, members of a faith community, or other support groups. Others connect in positive, happy, supportive marriages. One seven-decade-long study found that at age 50, healthy

POSITIVE EXPECTATIONS OFTEN MOTIVATE EVENTUAL SUCCESS:

Sam Gross The New Yorker Collection/The Cartoon Bank

"We just haven't been flapping them hard enough."

"The optimist proclaims we live in the best of all possible worlds; and the pessimist fears this is true." —James Branch Cabell, *The Silver Stallion*, 1926

LAUGHTER AMONG FRIENDS IS GOOD MEDICINE Laughter arouses us, massages muscles, and then leaves us feeling relaxed (Robinson, 1983). Humor (though not hostile sarcasm) may defuse stress, ease pain, and strengthen immune activity (Ayan, 2009; Berk et al., 2001; Dunbar et al., 2011; Kimata, 2001). People who laugh a lot have also tended to have lower rates of heart disease (Clark et al., 2001).

Rubberball/Mark Andersen/Getty Images

aging was better predicted by a good marriage than by a low cholesterol level (Vaillant, 2002). On the flip side, divorce predicts poor health. In one analysis of 600 million people in 24 countries, separated and divorced people were more likely to die early (Shor et al., 2012). But it's less marital status than marital *quality* that predicts health—to about the same extent as a healthy diet and physical activity do (Robles, 2015; Smith & Baucom, 2017).

What explains the link between social support and health? Are middle-aged and older adults who live alone more likely to smoke, be obese, and have high cholesterol—and therefore to have a doubled risk of heart attacks (Nielsen et al., 2006)? Or are healthy people simply more sociable? Possibly. But research suggests that social support does have health benefits.

Social support calms us and reduces blood pressure and stress hormones (Baron et al., 2016; Hostinar et al., 2014; Uchino et al., 1996, 2017). To see if social support might calm people's response to threats, one research team subjected happily married women, while lying in an fMRI machine, to the threat of electric shock to an ankle (Coan et al., 2006). During the experiment, some women held their husband's hand. Others held the hand of an unknown person or no hand at all. While awaiting the occasional shocks, women holding their husband's hand showed less activity in threat-responsive areas. This soothing benefit was greatest for those reporting the highest-quality marriages. People with supportive marriages also had below-average stress hormone levels 10 years later (Slatcher et al., 2015). Even animal support, such as a companionable pet, helps buffer stress (Siegel, 1990).

Social support fosters stronger immune functioning. Volunteers in studies of resistance to cold viruses showed this effect (Cohen, 2004; Cohen et al., 1997). Healthy volunteers inhaled nasal drops laden with a cold virus and were quarantined and observed for five days. (In these experiments, the more than 600 participants were well-paid volunteers.) Age, race, sex, and health habits being equal, those with close social ties were least likely to catch a cold. People whose daily life included frequent hugs likewise experienced fewer cold symptoms and less symptom severity (Cohen et al., 2015). The cold fact: The effect of social ties is nothing to sneeze at!

Close relationships give us an opportunity for "open heart therapy"—a chance to confide painful feelings (Frattaroli, 2006). Talking about a long-ago stressful event can temporarily arouse us, but in the long run it calms us (Lieberman et al., 2007; Mendolia & Kleck, 1993; Niles et al., 2015). In one study, 33 Holocaust survivors spent two hours recalling their experiences, many in intimate detail never before disclosed (Pennebaker et al., 1989). In the weeks following, most watched a video of their recollections and showed it to family and friends. Those who were most self-disclosing had the most improved health 14 months later. In another study, of surviving spouses of people who had committed suicide or died in car accidents, those who bore their grief alone had more health problems than those who could share it with others (Pennebaker & O'Heeron, 1984). Confiding is good for the body and the soul.

Suppressing emotions can be detrimental to physical health. When psychologist James Pennebaker (1985) surveyed more than 700 undergraduate women, those who had experienced a traumatic sexual experience in childhood reported more headaches and stomach ailments than those who had experienced other traumas—possibly because

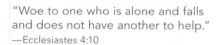

"Woe to one who is alone and falls and does not have another to help."
—Ecclesiastes 4:10

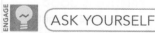

ENGAGE   (ASK YOURSELF)

Can you remember a time when you felt better after discussing a problem with a loved one, or even after playing with your pet? How did doing so help you to cope?

survivors of sexual abuse are less likely to confide in others. Another study, of 437 Australian ambulance drivers, supported the ill effects of suppressing one's emotions after witnessing traumas (Wastell, 2002).

Even writing about personal traumas in a diary can help (Burton & King, 2008; Kállay, 2015; Lyubomirsky et al., 2006). In an analysis of 633 trauma victims, writing therapy was as effective as psychotherapy in reducing psychological trauma (van Emmerik et al., 2013). In another experiment, volunteers who wrote trauma diaries had fewer health problems during the ensuing 4 to 6 months (Pennebaker, 1990). As one participant explained, "Although I have not talked with anyone about what I wrote, I was finally able to deal with it, work through the pain instead of trying to block it out. Now it doesn't hurt to think about it."

ENGAGE 💡 If we are aiming to exercise more, drink less, quit smoking, or attain a healthy weight, our social ties can tug us away from or toward our goal. If you are trying to achieve some goal, think about whether your social network will help or hinder you.

PETS ARE FRIENDS, TOO Pets can provide social support. Having a pet may increase the odds of survival after a heart attack, relieve depression among people with AIDS, and lower blood pressure and other coronary risk factors (Allen, 2003; McConnell et al., 2011; Wells, 2009). To lower blood pressure, pets are no substitute for effective drugs and exercise. But for people who enjoy animals, and especially for those who live alone, pets are a healthy pleasure (Reis et al., 2017).

Photos.com/Getty Images

REDUCING STRESS

Having a sense of control, developing more optimistic thinking, and building social support can help us *experience* less stress and thus improve our health. Moreover, these factors interrelate: People who are upbeat about themselves and their future have tended also to enjoy health-promoting social ties (Stinson et al., 2008). But sometimes we cannot alleviate stress and simply need to *manage* our stress. Aerobic exercise, relaxation, meditation, and active spiritual engagement may help us gather inner strength and lessen stress effects.

Aerobic Exercise

LOQ 11-12 How effective is aerobic exercise as a way to manage stress and improve well-being?

Aerobic exercise is sustained, oxygen-consuming exertion—such as jogging, swimming, or biking—that increases heart and lung fitness. It's hard to find bad things to say about exercise. Estimates vary, but moderate exercise adds to your quantity of life— about seven hours longer life for every exercise hour (Lee et al., 2017; Zahrt & Crum, 2017)—*and* your quality of life, with more energy, better mood, and stronger relationships (Flueckiger et al., 2016; Hogan et al., 2015).

Exercise helps fight heart disease by strengthening the heart, increasing blood flow, keeping blood vessels open, and lowering both blood pressure and the blood pressure reaction to stress (Ford, 2002; Manson, 2002). Compared with inactive adults, people who exercise suffer about half as many heart attacks (Evenson et al., 2016; Visich & Fletcher, 2009). Dietary fat contributes to clogged arteries, but exercise makes our muscles hungry for those fats and helps clean them out of our arteries (Barinaga, 1997). In one study of over 650,000 American adults, walking 150 minutes per week predicted living seven years longer than nonexercisers (Moore et al., 2012). A follow-up study of 1.44 million Americans and Europeans found that exercise predicted "lower risks of many cancer types" (Moore et al., 2016). Scottish mail carriers, who spend their days walking, have lower heart disease risk than Scottish mail office workers (Tigbe et al., 2017). Regular exercise in later life also predicts better cognitive functioning and reduced risk of neurocognitive disorder and Alzheimer's disease (Kramer & Erickson, 2007).

Does exercise also boost the spirit? In a 21-country survey of university students, physical exercise was a strong and consistent predictor of life satisfaction (Grant et al., 2009). Americans, Canadians, and Britons who do aerobic exercise at least three times a week manage stress better, exhibit more self-confidence, have more vigor, and feel less depressed and fatigued than their inactive peers (Rebar et al., 2015; Smits et al., 2011).

off the mark.com by Mark Parisi

PHARMACY

ASK ABOUT OUR ANTI-DEPRESSANTS

offthemark.com ©2007 MARK PARISI DIST. BY UFS INC.

Mark Parisi/Off the Mark/Atlantic Feature Syndicate

aerobic exercise sustained exercise that increases heart and lung fitness; also helps alleviate depression and anxiety.

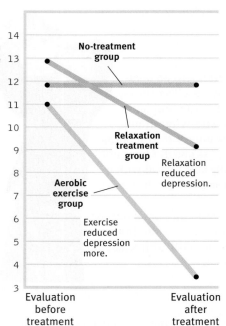

FIGURE 11.8

AEROBIC EXERCISE REDUCES MILD DEPRESSION (Data from McCann & Holmes, 1984.)

THE MOOD BOOST When energy or spirits are sagging, few things reboot the day better than exercising, as I [DM] can confirm from my noontime biking and basketball, and as I [ND] can confirm from my running.

Going from active exerciser to couch potato can increase the likelihood of depression—by 51 percent in two years for the women in one study (Wang et al., 2011). Among people with depression, getting off the couch and into a more physically active life reduces depressive symptoms (Kvam et al., 2016; Snippe et al., 2016). "Exercise has a large and significant antidepressant effect," concluded one digest of 25 controlled studies (Schuch et al., 2016a).

But we could state this observation another way: Stressed and depressed people exercise less. These findings are correlations, and cause and effect are unclear. To sort out cause and effect, researchers experiment. They *randomly assign* stressed, depressed, or anxious people either to an aerobic exercise group or to a control group. Next, they measure whether aerobic exercise (compared with a control activity not involving exercise) produces a change in stress, depression, anxiety, or some other health-related outcome. One classic experiment randomly assigned mildly depressed female college students to three groups. One-third participated in a program of aerobic exercise. Another third took part in a program of relaxation exercises. The remaining third (the control group) formed a no-treatment group (McCann & Holmes, 1984). As **FIGURE 11.8** shows, 10 weeks later, the women in the aerobic exercise program reported the greatest decrease in depression. Many had, quite literally, run away from their troubles.

Dozens of other experiments and longitudinal studies confirm that exercise prevents or reduces depression and anxiety (Catalan-Matamoros et al., 2016; Harvey et al., 2018; Stubbs et al., 2017). When experimenters randomly assigned depressed people to an exercise group, an antidepressant group, or a placebo pill group, exercise diminished depression as effectively as antidepressants—and with longer-lasting effects (Hoffman et al., 2011).

LaunchPad See the **Video: Random Assignment** for a helpful tutorial animation about this important part of effective research design.

Vigorous exercise provides a substantial and immediate mood boost (Watson, 2000). Even a 10-minute walk stimulates 2 hours of increased well-being by raising energy levels and lowering tension (Thayer, 1987, 1993). Exercise works its magic in several ways. It increases arousal, thus counteracting depression's low arousal state. It produces toned muscles, which filter a depression-causing toxin (Agudelo et al., 2014). It enables muscle relaxation and sounder sleep. Like an antidepressant drug, it orders up mood-boosting chemicals from our body's internal pharmacy—neurotransmitters such as norepinephrine, serotonin, and the endorphins (Jacobs, 1994; Salmon, 2001). Exercise also fosters *neurogenesis*. In mice, exercise causes the brain to produce a molecule that stimulates the production of new, stress-resistant neurons (Hunsberger et al., 2007; Reynolds, 2009; van Praag, 2009).

On a simpler level, the sense of accomplishment and improved physique and body image that often accompany a successful exercise routine may enhance one's self-image, leading to a better emotional state. Frequent exercise is like a drug that prevents and treats disease, increases energy, calms anxiety, and boosts mood—a drug we would all take, if available. Yet few people (only 1 in 4 in the United States) do it (Mendes, 2010).

Relaxation and Meditation

LOQ **11-13** In what ways might relaxation and meditation influence stress and health?

Knowing the damaging effects of stress, could we learn to counteract our stress responses by altering our thinking and lifestyle? In the late 1960s, psychologists began experimenting with *biofeedback,* a system of recording, amplifying, and feeding back information about subtle physiological responses, many controlled by the autonomic nervous system. Biofeedback instruments mirror the results of a person's own efforts, enabling the person to learn which techniques do (or do not) control a particular physiological response. After a decade of study, however, the initial claims for biofeedback seemed overblown and oversold (Miller, 1985). In 1995, a National Institutes of Health panel declared that biofeedback works best on tension headaches.

Simple methods of relaxation, which require no expensive equipment, produce many of the results biofeedback once promised. Figure 11.8 pointed out that aerobic exercise reduces depression. But did you notice in that figure that depression also decreased among women in the relaxation treatment group? More than 60 studies have found that relaxation procedures can also help alleviate headaches, hypertension, anxiety, and insomnia (Nestoriuc et al., 2008; Stetter & Kupper, 2002).

Such findings would not surprise Meyer Friedman, Ray Rosenman, and their colleagues. They tested relaxation in a program designed to help *Type A* heart attack survivors (hard-driving people who are more prone to heart attacks than their relaxed *Type B* peers) reduce their risk of future attacks. They randomly assigned hundreds of middle-aged men to one of two groups. The first group received standard advice from cardiologists about medications, diet, and exercise habits. The second group received similar advice, but they also were taught ways of modifying their lifestyles. They learned to slow down and relax by walking, talking, and eating more slowly. They learned to smile at others and laugh at themselves. They learned to admit their mistakes, to take time to enjoy life, and to renew their religious faith. The training paid off (**FIGURE 11.9**). During the next three years, the lifestyle modification group had half as many repeat heart attacks as did the first group. This, wrote the exuberant Friedman, was an unprecedented, spectacular reduction in heart attack recurrence. A smaller-scale British study spanning 13 years similarly showed a halved death rate among high-risk people trained to alter their thinking and lifestyle (Eysenck & Grossarth-Maticek, 1991). After suffering a heart attack at age 55, Friedman started taking his own behavioral medicine—and lived to age 90 (Wargo, 2007).

Time may heal all wounds, but relaxation can help speed that process. In one study, surgery patients were randomly assigned to two groups. Both groups received standard treatment, but the second group also experienced a 45-minute relaxation exercise and

FURRY FRIENDS FOR FINALS WEEK
Some schools bring cuddly critters on campus for finals week as a way to help students relax and bring disruptive stress levels down. This student at Emory University is relaxing with dogs and puppies. Other schools offer petting zoos or encourage instructors to bring in their own pets that week.

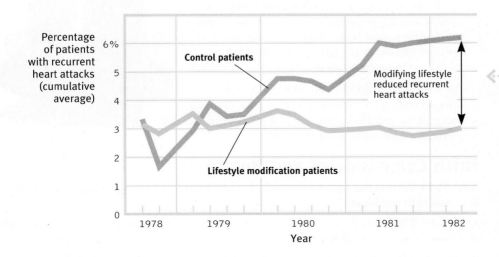

FIGURE 11.9
RECURRENT HEART ATTACKS AND LIFESTYLE MODIFICATION The San Francisco Recurrent Coronary Prevention Project offered counseling from a cardiologist to survivors of heart attacks. Those who were also guided in modifying their Type A lifestyle suffered fewer repeat heart attacks. (Data from Friedman & Ulmer, 1984.)

mindfulness meditation a reflective practice in which people attend to current experiences in a nonjudgmental and accepting manner.

"Sit down alone and in silence. Lower your head, shut your eyes, breathe out gently, and imagine yourself looking into your own heart. . . . As you breathe out, say 'Lord Jesus Christ, have mercy on me.' . . . Try to put all other thoughts aside. Be calm, be patient, and repeat the process very frequently." —Gregory of Sinai, died 1346

And then there are the mystics who seek to use the mind's power to enable novocaine-free cavity repair. Their aim: transcend dental medication.

received relaxation recordings to use before and after surgery. A week after surgery, patients in the relaxation group reported lower stress and showed better wound healing (Broadbent et al., 2012).

Meditation is a modern practice with a long history. In many world religions, meditation has been used to reduce suffering and improve awareness, insight, and compassion. Numerous studies have confirmed the psychological benefits of different types of meditation (Goyal et al., 2014; Rosenberg et al., 2015; Sedlmeier et al., 2012). One type, **mindfulness meditation**, has found a new home in stress management programs. If you were taught this practice, you would relax and silently attend to your inner state, without judging it (Brown et al., 2016; Kabat-Zinn, 2001). You would sit down, close your eyes, and mentally scan your body from head to toe. Zooming in on certain body parts and responses, you would remain aware and accepting. You would also pay attention to your breathing, attending to each breath as if it were a material object.

Practicing mindfulness may lessen anxiety and depression (Goyal et al., 2014). In one study of 1140 people, some received mindfulness-based therapy for several weeks. Others did not. Levels of anxiety and depression were lower among those who received the therapy (Hofmann et al., 2010). Mindfulness practices have also been linked with improved sleep, interpersonal relationships, and immune system functioning (Gong et al., 2016; Rosenkranz et al., 2013; Sedlmeier et al., 2012; Tang et al., 2007). Just a few minutes of daily mindfulness meditation is enough to improve concentration and decision making (Hafenbrack et al., 2014; Rahl et al., 2016).

Some researchers caution that mindfulness may be over-hyped (Coronado-Montoya et al., 2016; Van Dam et al., 2018). But the positive results make us wonder: What's going on in the brain as we practice mindfulness? Correlational and experimental studies offer three explanations. Mindfulness

- *strengthens connections among regions in our brain.* The affected regions are those associated with focusing our attention, processing what we see and hear, and being reflective and aware (Berkovich-Ohana et al., 2014; Ives-Deliperi et al., 2011; Kilpatrick et al., 2011).

- *activates brain regions associated with more reflective awareness* (Davidson et al., 2003; Way et al., 2010). When labeling emotions, mindful people show less activation in the amygdala, a brain region associated with fear, and more activation in the prefrontal cortex, which aids emotion regulation (Creswell et al., 2007; Gotink et al., 2016).

- *calms brain activation in emotional situations.* This lower activation was clear in one study in which participants watched two movies—one sad, one neutral. Those in the control group, who were not trained in mindfulness, showed strong differences in brain activation when watching the two movies. Those who had received mindfulness training showed little change in brain response to the two movies (Farb et al., 2010). Emotionally unpleasant images also trigger weaker electrical brain responses in mindful people than in their less mindful counterparts (Brown et al., 2013). A mindful brain is strong, reflective, and calm.

Djomas/Shutterstock

Exercise and meditation are not the only routes to healthy relaxation. Massage helps relax both premature infants and those suffering pain, and it relaxes muscles and helps reduce depression (Hou et al., 2010).

Faith Communities and Health

LOQ 11-14 What is the *faith factor,* and what are some possible explanations for the link between faith and health?

A wealth of studies—some 1800 of them in the twenty-first century's first decade alone—has revealed another curious correlation: the *faith factor* (Koenig et al., 2012). Religiously active people tend to live longer than those who are not religiously active. One

AlisaNata/Shutterstock   Getty Images/Fuse   Sura Nualpradid/Shutterstock   casejustin/Shutterstock

Georgios Kollidas/Alamy   Georgios Kollidas/Shutterstock   ppart/Shutterstock

such study compared the death rates for 3900 people living in two Israeli communities. The first community contained 11 religiously orthodox collective settlements; the second contained 11 matched, nonreligious collective settlements (Kark et al., 1996). Over a 16-year period, "belonging to a religious collective was associated with a strong protective effect" not explained by age or economic differences. In every age group, religious community members were about half as likely to have died as were their nonreligious counterparts. This difference is roughly comparable to the gender difference in mortality. A more recent study followed 74,534 nurses over 20 years. When controlling for various health risk factors, those who attended religious services more than weekly were a third less likely to have died than were nonattenders (Li et al., 2016).

How should we interpret such findings, given that we cannot experiment by randomly assigning people to be religiously engaged or not? Correlations are not cause-effect statements, and they leave many factors uncontrolled (Sloan, 2005; Sloan et al., 1999, 2000, 2002). Here is another possible interpretation: Women are more religiously active than men, and women outlive men. Might religious involvement merely reflect this gender-longevity link? Apparently not. One 8-year National Institutes of Health study followed 92,395 women, ages 50 to 79. After controlling for many factors, researchers found that women attending religious services at least weekly experienced an approximately 20 percent reduced risk of death during the study period (Schnall et al., 2010). Moreover, the association between religious involvement and life expectancy is also found among men (Benjamins et al., 2010; McCullough et al., 2000; McCullough & Laurenceau, 2005). A 28-year study that followed 5286 Californians found that, after controlling for age, gender, ethnicity, and education, frequent religious attenders were 36 percent less likely to have died in any year (**FIGURE 11.10**). In another 8-year controlled study of more than 20,000 people (Hummer et al., 1999), this effect translated into a life expectancy of 83 years for those frequently attending religious services and only 75 years for nonattenders.

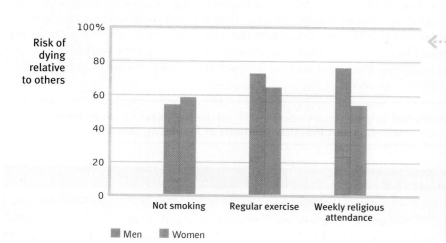

Risk of dying relative to others

Men   Women

FIGURE 11.10

PREDICTORS OF LONGER LIFE: NOT SMOKING, FREQUENT EXERCISE, AND REGULAR RELIGIOUS ATTENDANCE One 28-year study followed 5286 Alameda, California, adults (Oman et al., 2002; Strawbridge, 1999; Strawbridge et al., 1997). Controlling for age and education, the researchers found that not smoking, regular exercise, and religious attendance all predicted a lowered risk of death in any given year. Women attending weekly religious services, for example, were only 54 percent as likely to die in a typical study year as were nonattenders.

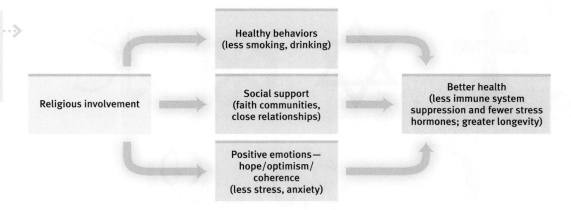

FIGURE 11.11

POSSIBLE EXPLANATIONS FOR THE CORRELATION BETWEEN RELIGIOUS INVOLVEMENT AND HEALTH/ LONGEVITY

These correlational findings do not indicate that nonattenders can suddenly add 8 years of life if they start attending services and change nothing else. Nevertheless, the findings do indicate that religious involvement, like nonsmoking and exercise, is a *predictor* of health and longevity. Research points to three possible explanations for the religiosity-longevity correlation (**FIGURE 11.11**):

- *Healthy behaviors* Religion promotes self-control (DeWall et al., 2014; McCullough & Willoughby, 2009). And that helps explain why religiously active people tend to smoke and drink much less and to have healthier lifestyles (Islam & Johnson, 2003; Koenig & Vaillant, 2009; Masters & Hooker, 2013; Park, 2007). In one Gallup survey of 550,000 Americans, 15 percent of the very religious were smokers, as were 28 percent of the nonreligious (Newport et al., 2010). But such lifestyle differences are not great enough to explain the dramatically reduced mortality in the Israeli religious settlements. In American studies, too, about 75 percent of the longevity difference remained when researchers controlled for unhealthy behaviors, such as inactivity and smoking (Musick et al., 1999).

- *Social support* Could social support explain the faith factor (Ai et al., 2007; Kim-Yeary et al., 2012)? Faith is often a communal experience. To belong to a faith community is to participate in a support network. Religiously active people are there for one another when misfortune strikes. In the 20-year nurses study, social support was the biggest contributor to the religiosity factor—explaining a fourth of its effect. Moreover, religion encourages marriage, another predictor of health and longevity. In the Israeli religious settlements, for example, divorce was almost nonexistent.

- *Positive emotions* Even after controlling for social support, gender, unhealthy behaviors, and preexisting health problems, the mortality studies have found that religiously engaged people tend to live longer (Chida et al., 2009). Researchers speculate that religiously active people may benefit from a stable, coherent worldview, a sense of hope for the long-term future, feelings of ultimate acceptance, and the relaxed meditation of prayer or other religious observances. These intervening variables may also help to explain why the religiously active seem to have healthier immune functioning, fewer hospital admissions, and, for people with AIDS, fewer stress hormones and longer survival (Ironson et al., 2002; Koenig & Larson, 1998; Lutgendorf et al., 2004).

ENGAGE

ASK YOURSELF

What strategies have you used to cope with stress in your life? How well have they worked? What other strategies could you try?

 **LaunchPad** To check your understanding of the best ways to handle stress, engage online with **Concept Practice: Methods of Managing Stress.**

🔒 **RETRIEVE IT • • •**   *ANSWERS IN APPENDIX E*

RI-2 What are some of the tactics we can use to successfully manage the stress we cannot avoid?

HAPPINESS

LOQ 11-15 What is the *feel-good, do-good phenomenon,* and what is the focus of positive psychology research?

People aspire to, and wish one another, health and happiness. And for good reason. Our state of happiness or unhappiness colors everything. Happy people perceive the world as safer. Their eyes are drawn toward emotionally positive information (Raila et al., 2015). They are more confident and decisive, and they cooperate more easily. They rate job applicants more favorably, savor their positive past experiences without dwelling on the negative, and are more socially connected. They live healthier and more energized and satisfied lives (Boehm et al., 2015; De Neve et al., 2013; Stellar et al., 2015). And they are more generous (Boenigk & Mayr, 2016). The simple conclusion: *Moods matter.* When your mood is gloomy, life as a whole seems depressing and meaningless—and you think more skeptically and attend more critically to your surroundings. Let your mood brighten and your thinking broadens, becoming more playful and creative (Baas et al., 2008; Forgas, 2008; Fredrickson, 2013).

Young adults' happiness helps predict their future life course. One study showed that the happiest 20-year-olds were later more likely to marry and less likely to divorce (Stutzer & Frey, 2006). In another study, which surveyed thousands of U.S. college students in 1976 and restudied them at age 37, happy students had gone on to earn significantly more money than their less-happy-than-average peers (Diener et al., 2002). When we are happy, our relationships, self-image, and hopes for the future also seem more promising.

Moreover—and this is one of psychology's most consistent findings—happiness doesn't just feel good, it *does* good. In study after study, a mood-boosting experience such as recalling a happy event has made people more likely to give money, pick up someone's dropped papers, volunteer time, and do other good deeds. Psychologists call it the **feel-good, do-good phenomenon** (Salovey, 1990).

The reverse is also true: Doing good also promotes good feeling. One survey of more than 200,000 people in 136 countries found that, nearly everywhere, people report feeling happier after spending money on others rather than on themselves (Aknin et al., 2013; Dunn et al., 2014). Kidney donation leaves donors feeling good (Brethel-Haurwitz & Marsh, 2014). Young children also show more positive emotion when they give, rather than receive, gifts (Aknin et al., 2015). Why does doing good feel so good? One reason is that it strengthens our social relationships (Aknin & Human, 2015; Yamaguchi et al., 2015). Some happiness coaches harness this *do-good, feel-good phenomenon* as they assign people to perform a daily "random act of kindness" and to record the results.

Positive Psychology

William James was writing about the importance of happiness ("the secret motive for all [we] do") as early as 1902. By the 1960s, the *humanistic psychologists* were interested in advancing human fulfillment. In the twenty-first century, under the leadership of American Psychological Association past-president Martin Seligman, **positive psychology** is using scientific methods to study human flourishing. This young subfield includes studies of **subjective well-being**—our feelings of happiness (sometimes defined as a high ratio of positive to negative feelings) or our sense of satisfaction with life.

Taken together, satisfaction with the past, happiness with the present, and optimism about the future define the positive psychology movement's first pillar: *positive well-being.*

Positive psychology is about building not just a pleasant life, says Seligman, but also a good life that engages one's skills, and a meaningful life that points beyond oneself. Thus, the second pillar, *positive traits,* focuses on exploring and enhancing creativity, courage, compassion, integrity, self-control, leadership, wisdom, and spirituality. Seligman views happiness as a by-product of a pleasant, engaged, and meaningful life.

ENGAGE **LaunchPad** To assess your own well-being and consider ways to improve it, engage online with **Immersive Learning: Assess Your Strengths—How Satisfied Are You With Your Life, and How Could You Be More Satisfied?**

feel-good, do-good phenomenon people's tendency to be helpful when in a good mood.

positive psychology the scientific study of human flourishing, with the goals of discovering and promoting strengths and virtues that help individuals and communities to thrive.

subjective well-being self-perceived happiness or satisfaction with life. Used along with measures of objective well-being (for example, physical and economic indicators) to evaluate people's quality of life.

MARTIN E. P. SELIGMAN "The main purpose of a positive psychology is to measure, understand, and then build the human strengths and the civic virtues."

The third pillar, *positive groups, communities, and cultures,* seeks to foster a positive social ecology. This includes healthy families, communal neighborhoods, effective schools, socially responsible media, and civil dialogue.

"Positive psychology," Seligman and colleagues have said (2005), "is an umbrella term for the study of positive emotions, positive character traits, and enabling institutions." Its focus differs from psychology's traditional interests in understanding and alleviating negative states—abuse and anxiety, depression and disease, prejudice and poverty. Indeed, psychology articles published since 1887 on depression have outnumbered those related to happiness by 15 to 1.

In ages past, times of relative peace and prosperity have enabled cultures to turn their attention from repairing weakness and damage to promoting what Seligman (2002) has called "the highest qualities of life." Prosperous fifth-century Athens nurtured philosophy and democracy. Flourishing fifteenth-century Florence nurtured great art. Victorian England, flush with the bounty of the British Empire, nurtured honor, discipline, and duty. In this millennium, Seligman believes, thriving Western cultures have a parallel opportunity to create, as a "humane, scientific monument," a more positive psychology, concerned not only with weakness and damage but also with strength and virtue. Thanks to his leadership, and to more than $200 million in funding, the movement has gained strength, with supporters in 77 countries (IPPA, 2017; Seligman, 2016).

What Affects Our Well-Being?

LOQ 11-16 How do time, wealth, adaptation, and comparison affect our happiness levels?

THE SHORT LIFE OF EMOTIONAL UPS AND DOWNS Are some days of the week happier than others? In what may be psychology's biggest-ever data sample, social psychologist Adam Kramer (at my [DM's] request and in cooperation with Facebook) did a naturalistic observation of emotion words in *billions* of status updates. After eliminating exceptional days, such as holidays, he tracked the frequency of positive and negative emotion words by day of the week. The days with the most positive moods? Friday and Saturday (**FIGURE 11.12**). Similar analyses of questionnaire responses and 59 million Twitter messages found Friday to Sunday the week's happiest days (Golder & Macy, 2011; Helliwell & Wang, 2015; Young & Lim, 2014). For you, too?

📺 **LaunchPad** See the **Video: Naturalistic Observation** for a helpful tutorial animation about this type of research design.

FIGURE 11.12

USING WEB SCIENCE TO TRACK HAPPY DAYS Adam Kramer (2010) tracked positive and negative emotion words in many "billions" (the exact number is proprietary information) of status updates of U.S. Facebook users between September 7, 2007, and November 17, 2010.

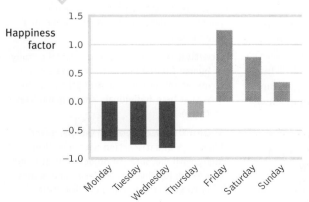

Over the long run, our emotional ups and downs tend to balance out, even over the course of the day. Positive emotion rises over the early to middle part of most days and then drops off (Kahneman et al., 2004; Watson, 2000). A stressful event—an argument, a sick child, a car problem—can trigger a bad mood. No surprise there. But by the next day, the gloom nearly always lifts (Affleck et al., 1994; Bolger et al., 1989; Stone & Neale, 1984). Our overall judgments of our lives often show lingering effects of good or bad events, but our daily moods typically rebound (Luhmann et al., 2012). If anything, people tend to bounce back from a bad day to a *better*-than-usual good mood the following day.

Worse events—the loss of a spouse or a job—can drag us down for longer periods (Infurna & Luthar, 2016a). But eventually, our bad mood usually ends. A romantic breakup feels devastating, but in time the wound heals. In one study, faculty members up for tenure expected their lives would be deflated by a negative decision. Actually, 5 to 10 years later, their happiness level was about the same as for those who received tenure (Gilbert et al., 1998).

Grief over the loss of a loved one or anxiety after a severe trauma (such as child abuse, rape, or the terrors of war) can linger. But usually, even tragedy is not permanently depressing. People who become blind or paralyzed may not completely recover their previous well-being, but those with an agreeable personality usually recover near-normal levels of day-to-day happiness (Boyce & Wood, 2011; Hall et al., 1999). So do those who count their blessings and remain optimistic in the wake of a school shooting or terrorist bombing (Birkeland et al., 2016; Vieselmeyer et al., 2017). Even if you lose the use of all four limbs, explained Daniel Kahneman (2005a), "you will gradually start thinking of other things, and the more time you spend thinking of other things the less miserable you are going to be." Contrary to what many people believe, even most patients "locked-in" a motionless body report a mostly positive outlook and no wish to die (Bruno et al., 2008, 2011; Chaudhary et al., 2017; Nizzi et al., 2012).

The surprising reality: *We overestimate the duration of our emotions and underestimate our resiliency.*

WEALTH AND WELL-BEING Would you be happier if you made more money? In a 2006 Gallup poll, 73 percent of Americans thought they would be. How important is "being very well off financially"? "Very important" or "essential," say 82 percent of entering U.S. college students (Eagen et al., 2016).

Money does buy happiness, up to a point, especially for people during their midlife working years (Cheung & Lucas, 2015). Moreover, people in rich countries are happier than those in poor countries (Diener & Tay, 2015). Having enough money to buy your way out of hunger, to have a sense of control over your life, and to treat yourself to something special predicts greater happiness (Fischer & Boer, 2011; Ruberton et al., 2016). As Australian data confirm, the power of more money to increase happiness is strongest at low incomes (Cummins, 2006). A 10 percent wage increase does a lot more for someone making $10,000 per year than for someone making $100,000. Raising low incomes will increase happiness more than will raising high incomes.

Once we have enough money for comfort and security, piling up more and more matters less and less. Experiencing luxury diminishes our savoring of life's simpler pleasures (Cooney et al., 2014; Quoidbach et al., 2010). If you ski the Alps once, your neighborhood sledding hill pales. If you ski the Alps every winter, it becomes an ordinary part of life rather than an experience to treasure (Quoidbach et al., 2015).

And consider this: During the last half-century, the average U.S. citizen's buying power almost tripled—enabling larger homes and twice as many cars per person, not to mention tablets and smart phones. Did it also buy more happiness? As **FIGURE 11.13** shows, Americans have become no happier. In 1957, some 35 percent said they were "very happy," as did slightly fewer—33 percent—in 2014. Much the same has been true of

> "Weeping may tarry for the night, but joy comes with the morning."
> —Psalm 30:5

"But on the positive side, money can't buy happiness—so who cares?"

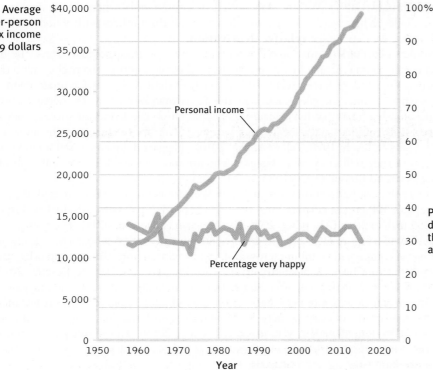

FIGURE 11.13

DOES MONEY BUY HAPPINESS? It surely helps us to avoid certain types of pain. Yet, though average buying power has nearly tripled since the 1950s, Americans' reported happiness has remained almost unchanged. (Happiness data from National Opinion Research Center surveys; income data from *Historical Statistics of the United States* and *Economic Indicators*.)

"Researchers say I'm not happier for being richer, but do you know how much researchers make?"

"Continued pleasures wear off. . . . Pleasure is always contingent upon change and disappears with continuous satisfaction." —Dutch psychologist Nico Frijda (1988)

"I have a 'fortune cookie maxim' that I'm very proud of: Nothing in life is quite as important as you think it is while you are thinking about it. So, nothing will ever make you as happy as you think it will." —Nobel laureate psychologist Daniel Kahneman, Gallup interview, "What Were They Thinking?" 2005

The effect of comparison with others helps explain why students tend to have a higher academic self-concept if they attend a school where most other students are not exceptionally able (Marsh & Parker, 1984; Rogers & Feller, 2016; Salchegger, 2016). If you were near the top of your graduating class, you might feel inferior or discouraged upon entering a college or university where all students were near the top of their class.

Europe, Canada, Australia, and Japan, where increasing real incomes have *not* produced increasing happiness (Australian Unity, 2008; Diener & Biswas-Diener, 2008; Di Tella & MacCulloch, 2010; Zuzanek, 2013). Ditto China, where living standards have risen but life satisfaction has not (Davey & Rato, 2012; Easterlin et al., 2012). These findings lob a bombshell at modern materialism: *Economic growth in affluent countries has provided no apparent boost to people's morale or social well-being.*

HAPPINESS IS RELATIVE: ADAPTATION AND COMPARISON Two psychological principles explain why, for those who are not poor, more money buys little more than temporary happiness and why our emotions seem attached to elastic bands that pull us back from highs or lows. In its own way, each principle suggests that happiness is relative.

HAPPINESS IS RELATIVE TO OUR OWN EXPERIENCE The **adaptation-level phenomenon** describes our tendency to judge various stimuli in comparison with our past experiences. As psychologist Harry Helson (1898–1977) explained, we adjust our *neutral* levels—the points at which sounds seem neither loud nor soft, temperatures neither hot nor cold, events neither pleasant nor unpleasant—based on our experience. We then notice and react to variations up or down from these levels. Thus, after an initial surge of pleasure, improvements become our "new normal," and we then require something even better to give us a boost of happiness.

So, could we ever create a permanent social paradise? Probably not (Campbell, 1975; Di Tella et al., 2010). People who have experienced a recent windfall—from a lottery, an inheritance, or a surging economy—typically feel elated (Diener & Oishi, 2000; Gardner & Oswald, 2007). So would you, if you woke up tomorrow to your utopia—perhaps a world with no bills, no ills, and perfect exam scores. But eventually, your utopia would become your new normal. Before long, you would again sometimes feel gratified (when events exceed your expectations) and sometimes feel deprived (when they fall below). *The point to remember:* Feelings of satisfaction and dissatisfaction, success and failure are judgments we make based partly on expectations formed by our recent experience (Rutledge et al., 2014). Satisfaction, as Richard Ryan (1999) said, "has a short half-life." Ditto disappointment, which means that you may bounce back from a setback or from your team's defeat sooner than you expect.

HAPPINESS IS RELATIVE TO OTHERS' SUCCESS We are always comparing ourselves with others. And whether we feel good or bad depends on who those others are (Lyubomirsky, 2001). We are slow-witted or clumsy only when others are smarter or more agile. When we sense that we are worse off than others with whom we compare ourselves, we experience **relative deprivation.**

When expectations soar above attainments, we feel disappointed. Thus, the middle- and upper-income people in a given country, who can compare themselves with the relatively poor, tend to have greater life satisfaction than their less-fortunate compatriots. Nevertheless, once people reach a moderate income level, further increases buy little additional happiness. Why? Because as people climb the ladder of success they mostly compare themselves with local peers who are at or above their current level (Gruder, 1977; Suls & Tesch, 1978; Zell & Alicke, 2010). "Beggars do not envy millionaires, though of course they will envy other beggars who are more successful," noted British philosopher Bertrand Russell (1930/1985, p. 90).

Over the last half-century, inequality in Western countries has increased. For CEOs at America's 500 largest corporations, the CEO-to-worker pay ratio—20 to 1 in 1965—rose to 335 to 1 in 2015 (AFL-CIO, 2016; Kiatpongsan & Norton, 2014). The rising economic tide shown in Figure 11.13 has lifted the yachts more than the rowboats. Increasing inequality has accompanied economic growth. Does it matter? Does this explain why economic growth has not been associated with increased happiness (Oishi & Kesebir, 2015)? *Yes.* Brain scans reveal that experiencing economic inequality activates the amygdala, leading to greater depression a year later (Tanaka et al., 2017). Places with greater inequality have more crime, obesity, anxiety, and drug use, and lower life expectancy (Burkhauser et al., 2016; Ratcliff, 2013; Wilkinson & Pickett, 2009). Times and places with greater income inequality also tend to be less happy—a result that people's social comparisons help explain (Cheung & Lucas, 2016; Helliwell et al., 2013; Roth et al., 2016).

Just as comparing ourselves with those who are better off creates envy, so counting our blessings as we compare ourselves with those worse off boosts our contentment. In one study, university women considered others' deprivation and suffering (Dermer et al., 1979). They viewed vivid depictions of how grim city life could be in 1900. They imagined and then wrote about various personal tragedies, such as being burned and disfigured. Later, the women expressed greater satisfaction with their own lives. Similarly, when mildly depressed people have read about someone who was even more depressed, they felt somewhat better (Gibbons, 1986). "I cried because I had no shoes," states a Persian saying, "until I met a man who had no feet."

What Predicts Our Happiness Levels?

LOQ 11-17 What predicts happiness, and how can we be happier?

Happy people share many characteristics (**TABLE 11.1**). But why are some people normally so joyful and others so somber? Here, as in so many other areas, the answer is found in the interplay between nature and nurture.

Genes matter. In one analysis of over 55,000 identical and fraternal twins, 36 percent of the differences among people's happiness ratings was heritable—attributable to genes (Bartels, 2015). Even identical twins raised apart are often similarly happy. Moreover, researchers are now drilling down to identify how specific genes influence our happiness (De Neve et al., 2012; Fredrickson et al., 2013).

But our personal history and our culture matter, too. On the personal level, as we have seen, our emotions tend to balance around a level defined by our experience. On the cultural level, groups vary in the traits they value. Self-esteem and achievement matter more in Western cultures, which value individualism. Social acceptance and harmony matter more in communal cultures such as Japan, which stress family and community (Diener et al., 2003; Fulmer et al., 2010; Uchida & Kitayama, 2009).

Depending on our genes, our outlook, and our recent experiences, our happiness seems to fluctuate around a "happiness set point," which disposes some people to be ever upbeat and others more negative. Even so, after following thousands of lives over two decades, researchers have determined that our satisfaction with life can change (Lucas & Donnellan, 2007). Happiness rises and falls, and can be influenced by factors that are under our control (Layous & Lyubomirsky, 2014; Nes et al., 2010). See **TABLE 11.2** for research-based suggestions for improving your mood and increasing your satisfaction with life.

> "Comparison is the thief of joy."
> —Attributed to Theodore Roosevelt

LaunchPad For a 6.5-minute examination of historical and modern views of happiness, see the **Video: The Search for Happiness.**

"I could cry when I think of the years I wasted accumulating money, only to learn that my cheerful disposition is genetic."

TABLE 11.1
Happiness Is . . .

Researchers Have Found That Happy People Tend to	However, Happiness Seems Not Much Related to Other Factors, Such as
Have high self-esteem (in individualist countries).	Age.
Be optimistic, outgoing, and agreeable.	Gender (women are more often depressed, but also more often joyful).
Have close, positive, and lasting relationships.	Physical attractiveness.
Have work and leisure that engage their skills.	
Have an active religious faith (especially in more religious cultures).	
Sleep well and exercise.	

Information from De Neve & Cooper (1998); Diener et al. (2003, 2011); Headey et al. (2010); Lucas et al. (2004); Myers (1993, 2000); Myers & Diener (1995, 1996); Steel et al. (2008). Veenhoven (2014, 2015) offers a database of 13,000+ correlates of happiness at WorldDatabaseofHappiness.eur.nl.

adaptation-level phenomenon our tendency to form judgments (of sounds, of lights, of income) relative to a neutral level defined by our prior experience.

relative deprivation the perception that one is worse off relative to those with whom one compares oneself.

RubberBall Selects/Alamy

 TABLE 11.2

Evidence-Based Suggestions for a Happier Life

- **Take control of your time.** Happy people feel in control of their lives: Set goals and divide them into daily aims. We all tend to overestimate how much we will accomplish in any given day, but the good news is that we generally *underestimate* how much we can accomplish in a year, given just a little daily progress.

- **Act happy.** Research shows that people who are manipulated into a smiling expression feel better. So put on a happy face. Talk *as if* you feel positive self-esteem, are optimistic, and are outgoing. We can often act our way into a happier state of mind.

- **Seek work and leisure that engage your skills.** Happy people often are in a zone called *flow*—absorbed in tasks that challenge but don't overwhelm them. Passive forms of leisure (watching TV) often provide less flow experience than exercising, socializing, or expressing artistic interests.

- **Buy shared experiences rather than things.** Money buys more happiness when spent on experiences, especially socially shared experiences, that you look forward to, enjoy, remember, and talk about (Caprariello & Reis, 2013; Carter & Gilovich, 2010; Kumar & Gilovich, 2013, 2015). As pundit Art Buchwald said, "The best things in life aren't things."

- **Join the "movement" movement.** Aerobic exercise can relieve mild depression and anxiety as it promotes health and energy. Sound minds reside in sound bodies.

- **Give your body the sleep it wants.** Happy people live active lives yet reserve time for renewing sleep. Sleep debt results in fatigue, diminished alertness, and gloomy moods. If you sleep now, you'll smile later.

- **Give priority to close relationships.** Compared with unhappy people, happy people engage in less superficial small talk and more meaningful conversations (Mehl et al., 2010). Resolve to nurture your closest relationships by *not* taking your loved ones for granted: Give them the sort of kindness and affirmation you give others. Relationships matter.

- **Focus and find meaning beyond self.** Reach out to those in need. Perform acts of kindness. Happiness increases helpfulness, but doing good also makes us feel good. We feel happier when our life has meaning and purpose.

- **Challenge your negative thinking.** Reframe "I failed" to "I can learn from this." Remind yourself that stuff happens, and that in a month or a year, this bad experience may not seem like that big a deal.

- **Count your blessings and record your gratitude.** Keeping a gratitude journal heightens well-being (Davis et al., 2016). Take time to savor positive experiences and achievements, and to appreciate why they occurred (Sheldon & Lyubomirsky, 2012). Express your gratitude to others.

- **Nurture your spiritual self.** Meditation helps us stay steady, emotionally. And for many people, faith provides a support community, a reason to focus beyond self, and a sense of purpose and hope. That helps explain why people active in faith communities report greater-than-average happiness and often cope well with crises.

If we can enhance our happiness on an *individual* level, could we use happiness research to refocus our *national* priorities more on the pursuit of happiness? Many psychologists believe we could. Ed Diener (2006, 2009, 2013), supported by 52 colleagues, has proposed ways in which nations might measure national well-being. Happiness research offers new ways to assess the impacts of various public policies, argue Diener and his colleagues (Diener et al., 2015). Happy societies are not only prosperous, but also places where people trust one another, feel free, and enjoy close relationships (Helliwell et al., 2013; Oishi & Schimmack, 2010a). Thus, in debates about the minimum wage, economic inequality, tax rates, divorce laws, health care, and city planning, people's psychological well-being can be a consideration. Many political leaders agree: 43 nations have begun measuring their citizens' well-being (Diener et al., 2015). Britain's Annual Population Survey, for example, asks its citizens how satisfied they are with their lives, how worthwhile they judge their lives, and how happy and how anxious they felt yesterday (ONS, 2015).

ASK YOURSELF

Were you surprised by any of the findings related to happiness? What things might you change in your life to increase your happiness?

🔒 RETRIEVE IT • • •
ANSWERS IN APPENDIX E

RI-3 Which of the following factors does NOT predict self-reported happiness?
a. Age
b. Personality traits
c. Sleep and exercise
d. Active religious faith

🔒 REVIEW HEALTH AND HAPPINESS

Learning Objectives

TEST YOURSELF Answer these repeated Learning Objective Questions on your own (before checking the answers in Appendix D) to improve your retention of the concepts (McDaniel et al., 2009, 2015).

11-7 In what two ways do people try to alleviate stress?

11-8 How does a perceived lack of control affect health?

11-9 Why is self-control important, and can our self-control be depleted?

11-10 How does an optimistic outlook affect health and longevity?

11-11 How does social support promote good health?

11-12 How effective is aerobic exercise as a way to manage stress and improve well-being?

11-13 In what ways might relaxation and meditation influence stress and health?

11-14 What is the *faith factor,* and what are some possible explanations for the link between faith and health?

11-15 What is the *feel-good, do-good phenomenon,* and what is the focus of positive psychology research?

11-16 How do time, wealth, adaptation, and comparison affect our happiness levels?

11-17 What predicts happiness, and how can we be happier?

Terms and Concepts to Remember

TEST YOURSELF Write down the definition yourself, then check your answer on the referenced page.

coping, **p. 395**
problem-focused coping, **p. 395**
emotion-focused coping, **p. 395**
personal control, **p. 396**
learned helplessness, **p. 396**

external locus of control, **p. 396**
internal locus of control, **p. 396**
self-control, **p. 398**
aerobic exercise, **p. 401**
mindfulness meditation, **p. 404**

feel-good, do-good phenomenon, **p. 407**
positive psychology, **p. 407**
subjective well-being, **p. 407**
adaptation-level phenomenon, **p. 411**
relative deprivation, **p. 411**

Experience the Testing Effect

TEST YOURSELF Answer the following questions on your own first, then check your answers in Appendix E.

1. When faced with a situation over which you feel you have little control, you are more likely to turn to _____ (emotion/problem)-focused coping.

2. Seligman's research showed that a dog will respond with learned helplessness if it has received repeated shocks and has had
   a. the opportunity to escape.
   b. no control over the shocks.
   c. pain or discomfort.
   d. no food or water prior to the shocks.

3. When elderly patients take an active part in managing their own care and surroundings, their morale and health tend to improve. Such findings indicate that people do better when they experience an _____ (internal/external) locus of control.

4. People who have close relationships are less likely to die prematurely than those who do not, supporting the idea that
   a. social ties can be a source of stress.
   b. gender influences longevity.
   c. Type A behavior is responsible for many premature deaths.
   d. social support has a beneficial effect on health.

5. Because it triggers the release of mood-boosting neurotransmitters such as norepinephrine, serotonin, and the endorphins, _____ exercise raises energy levels and helps alleviate depression and anxiety.

6. Research on the faith factor has found that
   a. pessimists tend to be healthier than optimists.
   b. our expectations influence our feelings of stress.
   c. religiously active people tend to outlive those who are not religiously active.
   d. religious engagement promotes social isolation and repression.

7. One of the most consistent findings of psychological research is that happy people are also
   a. more likely to express anger.
   b. generally luckier than others.
   c. concentrated in the wealthier nations.
   d. more likely to help others.

8. _____ psychology is a scientific field of study focused on how humans thrive and flourish.

9. After moving to a new apartment, you find the street noise irritatingly loud, but after a while it no longer bothers you. This reaction illustrates the
   a. relative deprivation principle.
   b. adaptation-level phenomenon.
   c. feel-good, do-good phenomenon.
   d. catharsis principle.

10. A philosopher observed that we cannot escape envy, because there will always be someone more successful, more accomplished, or richer with whom to compare ourselves. In psychology, this observation is embodied in the _____ _____ principle.

Continue testing yourself with 📖 **LearningCurve** or 〰 **Achieve Read & Practice** to learn and remember most effectively.

Social Psychology

Dirk Willems faced a moment of decision in 1569. Threatened with torture and death as a member of a persecuted religious minority, he escaped from his Asperen, Holland, prison and fled across an ice-covered pond. His stronger and heavier jailer pursued him but fell through the ice and, unable to climb out, pleaded for help.

With his freedom in front of him, Willems acted with ultimate selflessness. He turned back and rescued his pursuer, who, under orders, took him back to captivity. A few weeks later Willems was condemned to be "executed with fire, until death ensues." For his martyrdom, present-day Asperen has named a street in honor of its folk hero (Toews, 2004).

What drives people to feel contempt for minority-group members, such as Dirk Willems, and to act so spitefully? What motivates people, such as his jailer, to carry out unfair orders? And what inspired the selflessness of Willems' response, and of so many who have died trying to save others? Indeed, what motivates any of us who volunteer kindness and generosity?

As such examples demonstrate, we are social animals. We cannot live for ourselves alone. Your life is connected by "a thousand fibres" through which "run your actions as causes, and return to you as effects" (Melvill, 1855). *Social psychologists* explore these connections by scientifically studying how we *think about, influence*, and *relate to* one another. ▶

> **CHAPTER OVERVIEW**
>
> ⊙ **Social Thinking and Social Influence**
> Social Thinking
> Social Influence
> **THINKING CRITICALLY ABOUT: The Internet as Social Amplifier**
>
> ⊙ **Antisocial Relations**
> Prejudice
> Aggression
>
> ⊙ **Prosocial Relations**
> Attraction
> Altruism
> From Conflict to Peace

415

Dirk Willemſz. 1569.

AN ETCHING OF DIRK WILLEMS BY DUTCH ARTIST JAN LUYKEN (from *The Martyrs Mirror*, 1685)

Unlike sociology, which studies societies and social groupings, social psychologists focus more on how *individuals* view and affect one another.

Social Thinking and Social Influence

LEARNING OBJECTIVE QUESTION (LOQ)

12-1 What do social psychologists study? How do we tend to explain others' behavior and our own?

SOCIAL THINKING

Personality psychologists focus on the person. They study the personal traits and dynamics that explain why, in a given situation, *different people* may act differently. (Would you have acted as Willems did, helping his jailer out of the icy water?) **Social psychologists** focus on the situation. They study the social influences that explain why *the same person* acts differently in *different situations*. (Might the jailer have acted differently—opting not to march Willems back to jail—under other circumstances?)

The Fundamental Attribution Error

Our social behavior arises from our social thinking. Especially when the unexpected occurs, we want to understand and explain why people act as they do. After studying how people explain others' behavior, Fritz Heider (1958) proposed an **attribution theory:** We can attribute the behavior to the person's stable, enduring traits (a *dispositional attribution*), or we can attribute it to the situation (a *situational attribution*).

For example, in class, we notice that Juliette seldom talks. Over coffee, Jack talks nonstop. That must be the sort of people they are, we decide. Juliette must be shy and Jack outgoing. Such attributions—to their dispositions—can be valid. People do have enduring personality traits. But sometimes we fall prey to the **fundamental attribution error** (Ross, 1977): We overestimate the influence of personality and underestimate the influence of situations. In class, Jack may be as quiet as Juliette. Catch Juliette at a party and you may hardly recognize your quiet classmate.

The fundamental attribution error was demonstrated in an experiment with Williams College students (Napolitan & Goethals, 1979). Students talked, one at a time, with a woman who acted either cold and critical or warm and friendly. Before the conversations, the researchers told half the students that the woman's behavior would be spontaneous. They told the other half the truth—that they had instructed her to *act* friendly or unfriendly.

Did hearing the truth affect students' impressions of the woman? Not at all! If the woman acted friendly, both groups decided she really was a warm person. If she acted unfriendly, both decided she really was a cold person. They attributed her behavior to her personal disposition *even when told that her behavior was situational*—that she was merely acting that way for the purposes of the experiment.

We all commit the fundamental attribution error. Outside their assigned roles, professors seem less professorial, presidents less presidential, managers less managerial.

WHAT FACTORS AFFECT OUR ATTRIBUTIONS? One factor is culture. Westerners more often attribute behavior to people's personal traits. People in East Asian cultures are somewhat more sensitive to the power of the situation (Kitayama et al., 2009; Riemer et al., 2014). In experiments that asked people to view scenes, such as a big fish swimming, Americans focused more on the attributes of the individual fish. Japanese viewers focused more on the scene—the situation (Chua et al., 2005; Nisbett, 2003).

Another factor is *whose* behavior. When we explain *our own* behavior, we are sensitive to how behavior changes with the situation (Idson & Mischel, 2001). We also are

social psychology the scientific study of how we think about, influence, and relate to one another.

attribution theory the theory that we explain someone's behavior by crediting either the situation or the person's disposition.

fundamental attribution error the tendency for observers, when analyzing others' behavior, to underestimate the impact of the situation and to overestimate the impact of personal disposition.

sensitive to the power of the situation when we explain the behavior of people we have seen in many different contexts. We more often commit the fundamental attribution error when a stranger acts badly. Having only seen that enraged fan screaming at the referee in the heat of competition, we may assume he is an angry person. But outside the stadium he may be a good neighbor and a great parent.

Would taking an observer's viewpoint make us more aware of our own personal style? Researchers tested this idea by using separate cameras to film two people interacting. When they showed each person a replay of the interaction—filmed from the other person's perspective—participants credited their own behavior more to their disposition, much as an observer typically would (Lassiter & Irvine, 1986; Storms, 1973).

Two important exceptions to our usual view of our own actions: Our deliberate and *admirable* actions we often attribute to our own good reasons, not to the situation (Malle, 2006; Malle et al., 2007). And as we age, we tend to attribute our younger selves' behavior mostly to our traits (Pronin & Ross, 2006). In five or ten years, your current self may seem like another person.

HOW DO OUR ATTRIBUTIONS MATTER? The way we explain others' actions, attributing them to the person or the situation, can have important real-life effects (Fincham & Bradbury, 1993; Fletcher et al., 1990). Does a warm greeting reflect romantic interest or social courtesy? Does a manager's tart-tongued remark reflect a job threat or a bad day? Was a shooting malicious or an act of self-defense? In one study, 181 U.S. state judges gave lighter sentences to a violent offender who a scientist testified had a gene that altered brain areas related to aggressiveness (Aspinwall et al., 2012). Attributions matter.

Do you attribute poverty or unemployment to social circumstances, or to personal traits and bad choices? In Britain, India, Australia, and the United States, political conservatives have tended to attribute responsibility to the personal dispositions of the poor and unemployed (Furnham, 1982; Pandey et al., 1982; Wagstaff, 1982; Zucker & Weiner, 1993). "People generally get what they deserve. Those who take initiative can choose to get ahead." In experiments, those who reflect on the power of choice—either by recalling their own choices or taking note of another's choices—become more likely to think that people get what they deserve (Savani & Rattan, 2012). Political liberals, and those not primed to consider the power of choice, are more likely to blame past and present situations: "If you or I had to live with the same poor education, lack of opportunity, and discrimination, would we be any better off?"

The point to remember: Our attributions—to a person's disposition or to the situation—have real consequences.

Some 7 in 10 college women report having experienced a man misattributing her friendliness as a sexual come-on (Jacques-Tiura et al., 2007).

"If the King destroys a man, that's proof to the King it must have been a bad man." —Thomas Cromwell, in Robert Bolt's *A Man for All Seasons*, 1960

LaunchPad For a quick interactive tutorial, engage online with **Concept Practice: Making Attributions.**

Richard Ellis/Alamy

DISPOSITIONAL VERSUS SITUATIONAL ATTRIBUTIONS Should the 2015 slaughter of nine African-Americans attending a church Bible study in Charleston, West Virginia, be attributed to the shooter's disposition? (Nikki Haley, then South Carolina governor: "There is one person to blame here. A person filled with hate.") To America's gun culture? (U.S. President Barack Obama: "At some point, we as a country will have to reckon with the fact that this type of mass violence does not happen in other advanced countries . . . with this kind of frequency.") Or to both?

attitude feelings, often influenced by our beliefs, that predispose us to respond in a particular way to objects, people, and events.

peripheral route persuasion occurs when people are influenced by incidental cues, such as a speaker's attractiveness.

central route persuasion occurs when interested people focus on the arguments and respond with favorable thoughts.

foot-in-the-door phenomenon the tendency for people who have first agreed to a small request to comply later with a larger request.

role a set of expectations (*norms*) about a social position, defining how those in the position ought to behave.

Attitudes and Actions

LOQ 12-2 How do attitudes and actions interact?

Attitudes are feelings, often influenced by our beliefs, that predispose our reactions to objects, people, and events. If we *believe* someone is threatening us, we may *feel* fear and anger toward the person and *act* defensively. The traffic between our attitudes and our actions is two-way. Our attitudes affect our actions. And our actions affect our attitudes (much as our emotional expressions can affect our emotions).

ATTITUDES AFFECT ACTIONS In any debate, people on both sides aim to persuade. These efforts to *persuade* generally take two forms:

- **Peripheral route persuasion** uses attention-getting cues to trigger emotion-based snap judgments. One experiment gave some people information that debunked the vaccines-cause-autism myth; others were shown photos of children suffering mumps, measles, or rubella, along with a parent's description of measles. Only those given the vivid disease depictions became more supportive of vaccines (Horne et al., 2015). Endorsements by beautiful or famous people also can influence people's attitudes, whether the judgment is about choosing a political candidate or buying the latest tech gadget. When environmental activist and actor Leonardo DiCaprio urges action to counter climate change, or when Pope Francis (2015) states that "Climate change is a global problem with grave implications," they hope to harness their appeal for peripheral route persuasion. The same is true of heart-tugging ads for greeting cards, pet adoption, or support for the starving.

- **Central route persuasion** offers evidence and arguments that aim to trigger careful thinking. To persuade buyers to purchase a new gadget, an ad might itemize all the latest features. To marshal support for climate change intervention, effective arguments have focused on the accumulating greenhouse gases, melting Arctic ice, rising world temperatures and seas, and increasing extreme weather (van der Linden et al., 2015). Central route persuasion works well for people who are naturally analytical or involved in an issue. And because it is more thoughtful and less superficial, it is more durable.

Persuaders try to influence our behavior by changing our attitudes. But situational factors, such as strong social pressures, can override the attitude-behavior connection (Wallace et al., 2005). Politicians may vote as their supporters demand, despite privately disagreeing (Nagourney, 2002).

Attitudes are especially likely to affect behavior when external influences are minimal, and when the attitude is stable, specific to the behavior, and easily recalled (Glasman & Albarracín, 2006). One experiment used vivid, easily recalled information to persuade White sun-tanning college students that repetitive tanning put them at risk for future skin cancer. One month later, 72 percent of the participants, and only 16 percent of those in a waitlist control group, had lighter skin (McClendon & Prentice-Dunn, 2001). Persuasion changed attitudes (about skin cancer risk), which changed behavior (less tanning).

ACTIONS AFFECT ATTITUDES Now consider a more surprising principle: Not only will we stand up for what we believe, but we also will more strongly believe in what we have stood up for. Many streams of evidence confirm that *attitudes follow behavior* (**FIGURE 12.1**).

THE FOOT-IN-THE-DOOR PHENOMENON How do you think you would react if someone induced you to act against your beliefs? In many cases, people adjust their attitudes. During the Korean war, many U.S. prisoners were held in Chinese communist war camps. The captors secured prisoners' collaboration in various activities, ranging from simple tasks (running errands to gain privileges) to more serious actions (false confessions, informing on other prisoners, and divulging military information). After doing so, the prisoners sometimes adjusted their beliefs to be more consistent with their public acts (Lifton, 1961). When the war ended, 21 prisoners chose to stay with the communists. Some others returned home convinced that communism was a good thing for Asia (though not literally "brainwashed," as has often been said).

FIGURE 12.1

ATTITUDES FOLLOW BEHAVIOR Cooperative actions, such as those performed by people on sports teams (including Germany, shown here celebrating a World Cup victory), feed mutual liking. Such attitudes, in turn, promote positive behavior.

Actions

Attitudes

Matthias Hangst/Getty Images

The Chinese captors succeeded in part thanks to the **foot-in-the-door phenomenon:** They knew that people who agree to a small request will find it easier to comply later with a larger one. The captors began with harmless requests, such as copying a trivial statement, but gradually escalated their demands (Schein, 1956). The next statement to be copied might list flaws of capitalism. Then, to gain privileges, the prisoners would move up to participating in group discussions, writing self-criticisms, and finally uttering public confessions. The point is simple: To get people to agree to something big, start small and build (Cialdini, 1993). A trivial act makes the next act easier. Telling a small lie paves the way to telling a bigger lie. Succumb to a temptation and the next temptation becomes harder to resist.

In dozens of experiments, researchers have coaxed people into acting against their attitudes or violating their moral standards, with the same result: Doing becomes believing. After giving in to an order to harm an innocent victim—by making nasty comments or delivering presumed electric shocks—people begin to look down on their victim. After speaking or writing on behalf of a position they have qualms about, they begin to believe their own words.

Fortunately, the attitudes-follow-behavior principle works with good deeds as well. In one classic experiment, researchers sought permission to place a large "Drive Carefully" sign in people's front yards (Freedman & Fraser, 1966). The 17 percent rate of agreement soared to 76 percent among those who first did a small favor—placing a 3-inch-high "Be a Safe Driver" sign in their window.

The foot-in-the-door tactic has helped boost charitable contributions, blood donations, and U.S. school desegregation. With the passage of the Civil Rights Act of 1964, school desegregation became law. In the years that followed, White Americans expressed diminishing racial prejudice. And as Americans in different regions came to act more alike—thanks to more uniform national standards against discrimination—they began to think more alike.

ROLE PLAYING AFFECTS ATTITUDES When you adopt a new **role**—when you become a college student, marry, or begin a new job—you strive to follow the social prescriptions. At first, your behaviors may feel phony, because you are *acting* a role. Soldiers may at first feel they are playing war games. Newlyweds may feel they are "playing house." Before long, however, what began as playacting in the theater of life becomes *you*. As *Mad Men*'s Bobbie Barrett advised, "Pick a job and then become the person [who] does it."

Role playing was dramatized in one famous, controversial study in which male college students volunteered to spend time in a simulated prison. Stanford psychologist Philip Zimbardo (1972) randomly assigned some volunteers to be guards. He gave them uniforms, clubs, and whistles and instructed them to enforce rules. Others became prisoners, locked in barren cells and forced to wear humiliating outfits. For a day or two, the volunteers self-consciously played their roles. But then, reports Zimbardo, most guards developed disparaging attitudes and "became tyrannical," devising cruel and degrading routines. One by one, the prisoners broke down, rebelled, or became passively resigned. After only six days, Zimbardo called off the study.

Critics question the reliability of Zimbardo's results (Griggs, 2014; Reicher & Haslam, 2006). Others argue that Zimbardo stage-managed the experiment to get his predicted results, and that volunteers for a "prison experiment" would have had above-average levels of aggressiveness and authoritarianism (Bartels et al., 2016; McFarland & Carnahan, 2009). But this much seems true: There is power in the situation. In the real world, role playing has even been used to train people to become torturers (Staub, 1989). In the early 1970s, the Greek military government eased men into their roles. First, a trainee stood guard outside an interrogation cell. After this foot-in-the-door step, he stood guard inside. Only then was he ready to become actively involved in the questioning and torture. In one study of German men, military training toughened their personalities, leaving them less agreeable even five years later, after leaving the military (Jackson et al., 2012). Every time we act like the people around us, we slightly change ourselves to be more like them, and less like who we used to be.

Yet people differ. In real-life atrocity-producing situations, some people have succumbed to the situation and others have not (Haslam & Reicher, 2007, 2012; Mastroianni & Reed, 2006; Zimbardo, 2007). Person and situation interact.

ENGAGE · Experiments also reveal a *door-in-the-face* effect: Approach someone with an unreasonable request ("Could you volunteer every day for the next two weeks?"). After you get turned down (the door in the face), a follow-up moderate request becomes more acceptable ("Could you volunteer for the next 30 minutes?").

ENGAGE · (ASK YOURSELF)

Do you have an attitude or tendency you would like to change? Using the attitudes-follow-behavior principle, how might you go about changing that attitude?

"Fake it until you make it." —Alcoholics Anonymous saying

NEW NURSE Pulling on scrubs for the first time can feel like playing dress-up. But over time that role defines the player, as she jumps in to the day-to-day work and follows the social cues in her new environment.

Paul Burns/Blend Images/Alamy

COGNITIVE DISSONANCE: RELIEF FROM TENSION So far, we have seen that actions can affect attitudes, sometimes turning prisoners into collaborators, and doubters into believers. But why? One explanation is that when we become aware that our attitudes and actions don't coincide, we experience tension, or *cognitive dissonance*. Indeed, the brain regions that become active when people experience other forms of mental tension and negative arousal also become active when people experience cognitive dissonance (Harmon-Jones et al., 2015; Kitayama et al., 2013). To relieve this mental tension, according to Leon Festinger's (1957) **cognitive dissonance theory,** we often bring our attitudes into line with our actions.

RETAIN 🔒 ≋ **LaunchPad** To check your understanding of cognitive dissonance, engage online with **Concept Practice: Cognitive Dissonance.**

ENGAGE 💡 Dozens of experiments have tested the cognitive dissonance theory. Many have made people feel responsible for behavior that clashed with their attitudes and had foreseeable consequences. As a participant in one of these experiments, you might agree for a measly $2 to help a researcher by writing an essay supporting something you don't believe in (perhaps a tuition increase). Feeling responsible for the statements (which are inconsistent with your attitudes), you would probably feel dissonance, especially if you thought your essay might influence an administrator. To reduce the uncomfortable tension, you might start believing your phony words. It's as if we rationalize, "If I chose to do it (or say it), I must believe in it." The less coerced and more responsible we feel for a troubling act, the more dissonance we feel. The more dissonance we feel, the more motivated we are to find and project consistency, such as changing our attitudes to help justify the act.

The attitudes-follow-behavior principle has a heartening implication: We cannot directly control all our feelings, but we can influence them by altering our behavior. If we are depressed, we can alter our attributions and explain events in more positive terms, with more self-acceptance and fewer self-put-downs (Rubenstein et al., 2016). If we are unloving, we can become more loving by behaving *as if* we were—by doing thoughtful things, expressing affection, giving affirmation. "Each time you ask yourself, 'How should I act?'" observes Robert Levine (2016), "you are also asking, 'Who is the person I want to become?'" That helps explain why teens' doing volunteer work promotes a compassionate identity. Pretense can become reality. Conduct sculpts character. What we do we become.

The point to remember: We can act ourselves into a way of thinking about as easily as we can think ourselves into a way of acting.

"Sit all day in a moping posture, sigh, and reply to everything with a dismal voice, and your melancholy lingers. . . . If we wish to conquer undesirable emotional tendencies in ourselves, we must . . . go through the outward movements of those contrary dispositions which we prefer to cultivate." —William James, *Principles of Psychology* (1890)

🔒 RETRIEVE IT • • •   *ANSWERS IN APPENDIX E*

RI-1 Driving to school one snowy day, Marco narrowly misses a car that slides through a red light. "Slow down! What a terrible driver," he thinks to himself. Moments later, Marco himself slips through an intersection and yelps, "Wow! These roads are awful. The city plows need to get out here." What social psychology principle has Marco just demonstrated? Explain.

RI-2 How do our attitudes and our actions affect each other?

RI-3 When people act in a way that is not in keeping with their attitudes, and then change their attitudes to match those actions, _____ _____ theory attempts to explain why.

SOCIAL INFLUENCE

Social psychology's great lesson is the enormous power of social influence. This influence stems in part from social **norms**—rules for expected and accepted behavior. On campus, jeans are the norm; on New York's Wall Street or London's Bond Street, business attire is expected. When we know how to act, how to groom, how to talk, life functions smoothly.

But sometimes social pressure moves people in dreadful directions. Isolated with others who share their grievances, dissenters may gradually become rebels, and rebels may become terrorists. Shootings, suicides, bomb threats, and airplane hijackings all have a curious tendency to come in clusters. After a mass killing (of four or more people), the probability of another such attack increases for the ensuing 13 days (Towers et al., 2015). Let's start by considering the nature of our cultural influences. Then we will examine the pull of our social strings. How strong are they? How do they operate? When do we break them?

Cultural Influences

LOQ 12-3 How does culture affect our behavior?

Compared with the narrow path taken by flies, fish, and foxes, the road along which environment drives us is wider. The mark of our species—nature's great gift to us—is our ability to learn and adapt. We come equipped with a huge cerebral hard drive ready to receive cultural software.

Culture is the behaviors, ideas, attitudes, values, and traditions shared by a group of people and transmitted from one generation to the next (Brislin, 1988; Cohen, 2009). Human nature, noted Roy Baumeister (2005), seems designed for culture. We are social animals, but more. Wolves are social animals; they live and hunt in packs. Ants are incessantly social, never alone. But "culture is a better way of being social," observed Baumeister. Wolves function pretty much as they did 10,000 years ago. We enjoy electricity, indoor plumbing, antibiotics, and the internet—things unknown to most of our ancestors.

We can thank our culture's mastery of language for this *preservation of innovation*. The *division of labor* also helps. Although two lucky people get their names on this book (which transmits accumulated cultural wisdom), the product actually results from the coordination and commitment of a team of gifted people, no one of whom could produce it alone.

Across cultures, we differ in our language, money, sports, religion, and customs. But beneath these differences lies our great similarity—our capacity for culture. Culture works. It transmits the customs and beliefs that enable us to communicate, to exchange money for things, to play, to eat, and to drive with agreed-upon rules and without crashing into one another.

VARIATION ACROSS CULTURES We see our adaptability in cultural variations among our beliefs and our values, in how we nurture our children and bury our dead, and in what we wear (or whether we wear anything at all). We are ever mindful that the worldwide readers of this book are culturally diverse. You and your ancestors reach from Australia to Africa and from Singapore to Sweden.

"Have you ever noticed how one example—good or bad—can prompt others to follow? How one illegally parked car can give permission for others to do likewise? How one racial joke can fuel another?" —Marian Wright Edelman, *The Measure of Our Success*, 1992

cognitive dissonance theory the theory that we act to reduce the discomfort (dissonance) we feel when two of our thoughts (cognitions) are inconsistent. For example, when we become aware that our attitudes and our actions clash, we can reduce the resulting dissonance by changing our attitudes.

norms understood rules for accepted and expected behavior. Norms prescribe "proper" behavior.

culture the enduring behaviors, ideas, attitudes, values, and traditions shared by a group of people and transmitted from one generation to the next.

Riding along with a unified culture is like biking with the wind: As it carries us along, we hardly notice it. When we try biking *against* the wind, we feel its force. Face-to-face with a different culture, we become aware of the cultural winds. Stationed in Iraq, Afghanistan, and Kuwait, American and European soldiers were reminded how liberal their home cultures were. Each cultural group evolves its own norms. The British have a norm for orderly waiting in line. Many South Asians use only the right hand for eating. Sometimes social expectations seem oppressive: "Why should it matter what I wear?" Yet, norms—how to greet, how to eat—grease the social machinery.

When cultures collide, their differing norms often befuddle. Should we greet people by shaking hands, bowing, or kissing one or both cheeks? Knowing what sorts of gestures and compliments are culturally appropriate helps us avoid accidental insults and embarrassment.

VARIATION OVER TIME Like biological creatures, cultures vary and compete for resources, and thus evolve over time (Mesoudi, 2009). Consider how rapidly cultures may change. English poet Geoffrey Chaucer (1342–1400) is separated from a modern Briton by only 25 generations, but the two would have difficulty communicating. At the beginning of the last century, your ancestors lived in a world without cars, radio broadcasting, or electric lighting. And in the thin slice of history since 1960, most Western cultures have changed with astonishing speed. People enjoy expanded human rights. Middle-class people enjoy the convenience of air-conditioned housing, online shopping, anywhere-anytime electronic communication, and—enriched by doubled per-person real income—eating out more than twice as often as did their grandparents.

But some changes seem not so wonderfully positive. Had you fallen asleep in the United States in 1960 and awakened today, you would open your eyes to a culture with more depression and more economic inequality. You would also find North Americans—like their counterparts in Britain, Australia, and New Zealand—spending more hours at work, fewer hours with friends and family, and fewer hours asleep (BLS, 2011; Putnam, 2000).

Whether we love or loathe these changes, we cannot fail to be impressed by their breathtaking speed. And we cannot explain them by changes in the human gene pool, which evolves far too slowly to account for high-speed cultural transformations. Cultures vary. Cultures change. And cultures shape our lives.

Conformity: Complying With Social Pressures

LOQ 12-4 How is social contagion a form of conformity, and how do conformity experiments reveal the power of social influence?

"Most people are other people. Their thoughts are someone else's opinions, their lives a mimicry." —Irish dramatist Oscar Wilde "The Soul of Man Under Socialism," 1895

SOCIAL CONTAGION Fish swim in schools. Birds fly in flocks. And humans, too, tend to go with their group, to do what it does and think what it thinks. Behavior is contagious. If one of us yawns, laughs, coughs, scratches, stares at the sky, or checks our phone, others in our group will often do the same (Holle et al., 2012). Even just reading about yawning increases people's yawning (Provine, 2012), as perhaps you have noticed? Yawn mimicry also occurs in other species—among chimpanzees, for example (Anderson et al., 2004)—and even across species: Dogs more often yawn after observing their owners' yawn (Silva et al., 2012).

Tanya Chartrand and John Bargh (1999) call this social contagion the *chameleon effect*, likening it to chameleon lizards' ability to take on the color of their surroundings. They captured it by having students work in a room alongside another person (actually a "confederate" working for the experimenters). Sometimes the confederates rubbed their own face. Sometimes they shook their foot. Sure enough, students tended to rub their face with the face-rubbing person and shake their foot with the foot-shaking person.

Social contagion is not confined to behavior. We human chameleons also take on the emotional tones of those around us—their expressions, postures, and voice tones—and even their grammar (Ireland & Pennebaker, 2010). Just hearing someone reading a neutral text in either a happy- or sad-sounding voice creates *mood contagion* in listeners (Neumann & Strack, 2000).

This natural mimicry enables us to *empathize*—to feel what others are feeling. This helps explain why we feel happier around happy people than around depressed people. It also helps explain why studies of groups of British workers have revealed *mood linkage*—or the sharing of moods (Totterdell et al., 1998). Empathic mimicking fosters fondness (Chartrand & van Baaren, 2009; Lakin et al., 2008). Perhaps you've noticed that when someone nods their head as you do and echoes your words, you feel a certain rapport and liking?

Suggestibility and mimicry sometimes lead to tragedy. In the eight days following the 1999 shooting rampage at Colorado's Columbine High School, every U.S. state except Vermont experienced threats of copycat violence. Pennsylvania alone recorded 60 such threats (Cooper, 1999). Spikes in suicide rates sometimes follow a highly publicized suicide (Phillips et al., 1985, 1989).

What causes behavior clusters? Do people act similarly because of their influence on one another? Or because they are simultaneously exposed to the same events and conditions? Seeking answers to such questions, social psychologists have conducted experiments on conformity.

THAT CONTAGIOUS LAUGH
Laughter, like yawns, is infectious. That's what "Chewbacca Mom's" (Candace Payne's) viewers discovered after her spontaneous hilarity became, with 164 million views, Facebook Live's most watched 2016 video (tinyurl.com/ThatLaugh).

"When I see synchrony and mimicry—whether it concerns yawning, laughing, dancing, or aping—I see social connection and bonding."
—Primatologist Frans de Waal "The Empathy Instinct," 2009

NON SEQUITUR   by WILEY

BANKING on the YOUTH MARKET...

TATTOO & PIERCING

BE LIKE ALL YOUR FRIENDS AND EXPRESS YOUR INDIVIDUALITY
OPEN

CONFORMITY AND SOCIAL NORMS Suggestibility and mimicry are subtle types of **conformity**—adjusting our behavior or thinking toward some group standard. To study conformity, Solomon Asch (1955) devised a simple test. Imagine yourself a participant in a supposed study of visual perception. You arrive in time to take a seat at a table with five other people. The experimenter asks the group to state, one by one, which of three comparison lines is identical to a standard line. You see clearly that the answer is Line 2, and you wait your turn to say so. Your boredom begins to show when the next set of lines proves equally easy.

Now comes the third trial, and the correct answer seems just as clear-cut (**FIGURE 12.2**). But the first person gives what strikes you as a wrong answer: "Line 3." When the second person and then the third and fourth give the same wrong answer, you sit up straight and squint. When the fifth person agrees with the first four, you feel your heart begin to pound. The experimenter then looks to you for your answer. Torn between the unanimity voiced by the five others and the evidence of your own eyes, you feel tense and suddenly unsure. You hesitate before answering, wondering whether you should suffer the discomfort of being the oddball. What answer do you give?

In Asch's experiments, college students, answering questions alone, erred less than 1 percent of the time. But what happened when several others—confederates—answered incorrectly? Although most people told the truth even when others did not, Asch was disturbed by his result: More than one-third of the time, these "intelligent and well-meaning" college students were "willing to call white black" by going along with the group.

"I love the little ways you're identical to everyone else."

conformity adjusting our behavior or thinking to coincide with a group standard.

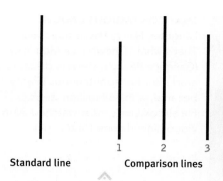

Standard line   Comparison lines

William Vendivert/Scientific American

 ENGAGE

FIGURE 12.2

ASCH'S CONFORMITY EXPERIMENTS
Which of the three comparison lines is equal to the standard line? What do you suppose most people would say after hearing five others say, "Line 3"? In this photo from one of Asch's experiments, the student in the center shows the severe discomfort that comes from disagreeing with the responses of other group members (in this case, accomplices of the experimenter).

TATTOOS: YESTERDAY'S NONCON-FORMITY, TODAY'S CONFORMITY?
As tattoos become perceived as fashion conformity, their popularity may wane.

normative social influence influence resulting from a person's desire to gain approval or avoid disapproval.

informational social influence influence resulting from a person's willingness to accept others' opinions about reality.

SanneBerg/Getty Images

Later investigations have not always found as much conformity as Asch found, but they have revealed that we are more likely to conform when we

- are made to feel incompetent or insecure.
- are in a group with at least three people.
- are in a group in which everyone else agrees. (If just one other person disagrees, the odds of our disagreeing greatly increase.)
- admire the group's status and attractiveness.
- have not made a prior commitment to any response.
- know that others in the group will observe our behavior.
- are from a culture that strongly encourages respect for social standards.

Why do we so often do as others do and think as they think? Why, when asked controversial questions, are students' answers more similar when they raise their hands and more diverse when they use anonymous electronic clickers (Stowell et al., 2010)? Why do we clap when others clap, eat as others eat, believe what others believe, say what others say, even see what others see?

Frequently, we conform to avoid rejection or to gain social approval (Williams & Sommer, 1997). In such cases, we are responding to **normative social influence.** We are sensitive to social norms because the price we pay for being different can be severe. We need to belong. At other times, we conform because we want to be accurate. Groups provide information, and only an uncommonly stubborn person will never listen to others. When we accept others' opinions about reality, as when reading online movie and restaurant reviews, we are responding to **informational social influence.** Sometimes it pays to assume others are right and to follow their lead. One Welsh driver set a record for the longest distance driven on the wrong side of a British divided highway—30 miles, with only one minor sideswipe, before the motorway ran out and police were able to puncture her tires. The driver, who was intoxicated, later explained that she thought the hundreds of other drivers coming at her were all on the wrong side of the road (Woolcock, 2004).

Is conformity good or bad? Conformity can be bad—leading people to agree with falsehoods or go along with bullying. Or it can be good—leading people to give more generously after observing others' generosity (Nook et al., 2016). The answer also depends partly on our culturally influenced values. People in many Asian, African, and Latin American countries place a higher value on *collectivism* (emphasizing group standards). Western Europeans and people in most English-speaking countries tend to prize *individualism* (emphasizing an independent self). Experiments across 17 countries have found lower conformity rates in individualist cultures (Bond & Smith, 1996).

 **LaunchPad** To review the classic conformity studies and experience a simulated experiment, visit **Topic Tutorial: PsychSim6, Everybody's Doing It!**

🔒 RETRIEVE IT • • •   ANSWERS IN APPENDIX E

RI-4 What is *culture,* and how does its transmission distinguish us from other social animals?

RI-5 Which of the following strengthens conformity to a group?

a. Finding the group attractive

b. Feeling secure

c. Coming from an individualist culture

d. Having made a prior commitment

RI-6 Despite her mother's pleas to use a more ergonomic backpack, Antonia insists on trying to carry all of her books to school in an oversized purse the way her fashionable friends all seem to do. Antonia is affected by what type of social influence?

> "Those who never retract their opinions love themselves more than they love truth." —French essayist Joseph Joubert (1754–1824)

Like humans, migrating and herding animals conform for both informational and normative reasons (Claidière & Whiten, 2012). Following others is informative; compared with solo geese, a flock of geese migrate more accurately. (There is wisdom in the crowd.) And staying with the herd also sustains group membership.

 **ASK YOURSELF**

How have you found yourself conforming, or perhaps "conforming to nonconformity"? In what ways have you seen others identifying themselves with those of the same culture or subculture?

Obedience: Following Orders

LOQ 12-5 What did Milgram's obedience experiments teach us about the power of social influence?

Social psychologist Stanley Milgram (1963, 1974), a high school classmate of Philip Zimbardo and later a student of Solomon Asch, knew that people often give in to social pressures. But what about outright commands? Would they respond as did those who carried out Holocaust atrocities? (Some of Milgram's family members had survived Nazi concentration camps.) To find out, he undertook what have become social psychology's most famous and controversial experiments (Benjamin & Simpson, 2009).

Imagine yourself as one of the nearly 1000 people who took part in Milgram's 20 experiments. You respond to an ad for participants in a Yale University psychology study of the effect of punishment on learning. Professor Milgram's assistant asks you and another person to draw slips from a hat to see who will be the "teacher" and who will be the "learner." You draw a "teacher" slip (unknown to you, both slips say "teacher"). The supposed learner, a mild and submissive-seeming man, is led to an adjoining room and strapped into a chair. From the chair, wires run through the wall to a shock machine. You sit down in front of the machine and are given your task: Teach and then test the learner on a list of word pairs. If the learner gives a wrong answer, you are to flip a switch to deliver a brief electric shock. For the first wrong answer, you will flip the switch labeled "15 Volts—Slight Shock." With each succeeding error, you will move to the next higher voltage. With each flip of a switch, lights flash and electronic switches buzz.

LaunchPad See the **Video: Research Ethics** for a helpful tutorial animation.

The experiment begins, and you deliver the shocks after the first and second wrong answers. If you continue, you hear the learner grunt when you flick the third, fourth, and fifth switches. After you activate the eighth switch ("120 Volts—Moderate Shock"), the learner cries out that the shocks are painful. After the tenth switch ("150 Volts—Strong Shock"), he begins shouting: "Get me out of here! I won't be in the experiment anymore! I refuse to go on!" You draw back, but the stern experimenter prods you: "Please continue—the experiment requires that you continue." You resist, but the experimenter insists, "It is absolutely essential that you continue," or "You have no other choice, you *must* go on."

If you obey, you hear the learner shriek in apparent agony as you continue to raise the shock level after each new error. After the 330-volt level, the learner refuses to answer and falls silent. Still, the experimenter pushes you toward the final, 450-volt switch. "Ask the question," he says, "and if no correct answer is given, administer the next shock level."

Would you follow the experimenter's commands to shock someone? At what level would you refuse to obey? Before undertaking the experiments, Milgram asked nonparticipants what they would do. Most were sure they would stop soon after the learner first indicated pain, certainly before he shrieked in agony. Forty psychiatrists agreed with that prediction. Were the predictions accurate? Not even close. When Milgram conducted the experiment with other men aged 20 to 50, he was astonished. More than 60 percent complied fully—right up to the last switch. When he ran a new study, with 40 new "teachers" and a learner who complained of a "slight heart condition," the results were similar. A full 65 percent of the new teachers obeyed the experimenter right up to 450 volts (**FIGURE 12.3**). In 10 later studies, women obeyed at rates similar to men's (Blass, 1999).

Were Milgram's results a product of the 1960s American mindset? *No.* In a more recent replication, 70 percent of the participants complied up to the 150-volt point (only a modest reduction from Milgram's 83 percent at that level) (Burger, 2009). A Polish research team found 90 percent compliance to the same level (Doliński et al., 2017). And in a French reality TV show replication, 81 percent of teachers, egged on by a cheering audience, obeyed and tortured a screaming victim (Beauvois et al., 2012).

Did Milgram's teachers figure out the hoax—that no real shock was being delivered and the learner was in fact a confederate pretending to feel pain? Did they realize the experiment was really testing their willingness to comply with commands to inflict punishment? *No.* The teachers typically displayed genuine distress: They perspired, trembled, laughed nervously, and bit their lips.

Milgram's use of deception and stress triggered a debate over his research ethics. In his own defense, Milgram pointed out that, after the participants learned of the deception and actual research purposes, virtually none regretted taking part (though perhaps by then the participants had reduced their cognitive dissonance—the discomfort they

FIGURE 12.3

MILGRAM'S FOLLOW-UP OBEDIENCE EXPERIMENT In a repeat of the earlier experiment, 65 percent of the adult male "teachers" fully obeyed the experimenter's commands to continue. They did so despite the "learner's" earlier mention of a heart condition and despite hearing cries of protest after they administered what they thought were 150 volts and agonized protests after 330 volts. (Data from Milgram, 1974.)

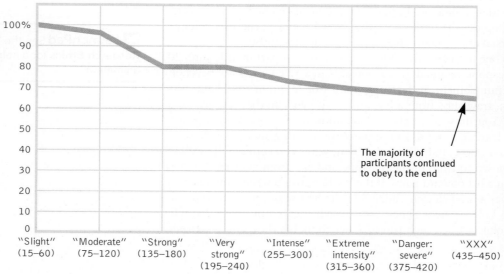

The majority of participants continued to obey to the end

Percentage of participants who obeyed experimenter

Shock levels in volts
"Slight" (15–60)
"Moderate" (75–120)
"Strong" (135–180)
"Very strong" (195–240)
"Intense" (255–300)
"Extreme intensity" (315–360)
"Danger: severe" (375–420)
"XXX" (435–450)

felt when their actions conflicted with their attitudes). When 40 of the teachers who had agonized most were later interviewed by a psychiatrist, none appeared to be suffering emotional aftereffects. All in all, said Milgram, the experiments provoked less enduring stress than university students experience when facing and failing big exams (Blass, 1996). Other scholars, however, after delving into Milgram's archives, report that his debriefing was less extensive and his participants' distress greater than he had suggested (Nicholson, 2011; Perry, 2013). Critics have also speculated that participants may have been identifying with the researcher and his scientific goals rather than simply being blindly obedient (Haslam et al., 2014, 2016).

In later experiments, Milgram discovered some conditions that influence people's behavior. When he varied the situation, full obedience ranged from 0 to 93 percent. Obedience was highest when

- *the person giving the orders was close at hand and was perceived to be a legitimate authority figure.* This was the case in 2005 when Temple University's basketball coach sent a 250-pound bench player, Nehemiah Ingram, into a game with instructions to commit "hard fouls." Following orders, Ingram fouled out in four minutes after breaking an opposing player's right arm.

- *the authority figure was supported by a powerful or prestigious institution.* Compliance was somewhat lower when Milgram dissociated his experiments from Yale University. People have wondered: Why, during the 1994 Rwandan Genocide, did so many Hutu citizens slaughter their Tutsi neighbors? It was partly because they were part of "a culture in which orders from above, even if evil," were understood as having the force of law (Kamatali, 2014).

- *the victim was depersonalized or at a distance, even in another room.* Similarly, many soldiers in combat either have not fired their rifles at an enemy they could see, or have not aimed them properly. Such refusals to kill are rarer among soldiers operating long-distance artillery or aircraft weapons (Padgett, 1989). Those who kill from a distance—by operating remotely piloted drones—also suffer stress, though much less posttraumatic stress than do veterans of on-the-ground conflict in Afghanistan and Iraq (Miller, 2012).

- *there were no role models for defiance.* "Teachers" did not see any other participant disobey the experimenter.

The power of legitimate, close-at-hand authorities was apparent among those who followed orders to carry out the Nazis' Holocaust atrocities. Obedience alone does not explain the Holocaust—anti-Semitic ideology produced eager killers as well (Fenigstein, 2015; Mastroianni, 2015). But obedience was a factor. In the summer of 1942, nearly 500 middle-aged German reserve police officers were dispatched to German-occupied Jozefow, Poland. On July 13, the group's visibly upset commander informed his recruits, mostly family men, of their orders. They were to round up the village's Jews, who were said to be aiding the enemy. Able-bodied men would be sent to work camps, and the rest would be shot on the spot.

The commander gave the recruits a chance to refuse to participate in the executions. Only about a dozen immediately refused. Within 17 hours, the remaining 485 officers killed 1500 helpless citizens, including women, children, and the elderly, shooting them in the back of the head as they lay face down. Hearing the victims' pleas, and seeing the gruesome results, some 20 percent of the officers did eventually dissent, managing either to miss their victims or to slip away and hide until the slaughter was over (Browning, 1992). In real life, as in Milgram's experiments, those who resisted were the minority.

A different story played out in the French village of Le Chambon. There, villagers openly defied orders to cooperate with the "New Order": They sheltered French Jews destined for deportation to Germany, and they sometimes helped them escape across the Swiss border. The villagers' Protestant ancestors had themselves been persecuted, and their pastors taught them to "resist whenever our adversaries will demand of us obedience contrary

STANDING UP FOR DEMOCRACY
Some individuals—roughly one in three in Milgram's experiments—resist social coercion, as did this unarmed man in Beijing, by single-handedly challenging an advancing line of tanks the day after the 1989 Tiananmen Square student uprising was suppressed.

Jeff Widener/AP Photo

to the orders of the Gospel" (Rochat, 1993). Ordered by police to give a list of sheltered Jews, the head pastor modeled defiance: "I don't know of Jews, I only know of human beings." At great personal risk, the people of Le Chambon made an initial commitment to resist. Throughout the long, terrible war, they suffered poverty and were punished for their disobedience. Still, supported by their beliefs, their role models, their interactions with one another, and their own initial acts, they remained defiant to the war's end.

LESSONS FROM THE CONFORMITY AND OBEDIENCE STUDIES

LOQ 12-6 What do the social influence studies teach us about ourselves? How much power do we have as individuals?

How do the laboratory experiments on social influence relate to real life? How does judging the length of a line or flicking a shock switch relate to everyday social behavior? Psychological experiments aim not to re-create the actual, complex behaviors of everyday life but to capture and explore the underlying processes that shape those behaviors. Solomon Asch and Stanley Milgram devised experiments that forced a familiar choice: Do I adhere to my own standards, even when they conflict with the expectations of others?

In Milgram's experiments and their modern replications, participants were torn. Should they respond to the pleas of the victim or the orders of the experimenter? Their moral sense warned them not to harm another, yet it also prompted them to obey the experimenter and to be a good research participant. With kindness and obedience on a collision course, obedience usually won.

These experiments demonstrated that strong social influences induce many people to conform to falsehoods or capitulate to cruelty. Milgram saw this as the fundamental lesson of this work: "Ordinary people, simply doing their jobs, and without any particular hostility on their part, can become agents in a terrible destructive process" (1974, p. 6).

Focusing on the end point—450 volts, or someone's real-life violence—we can hardly comprehend the inhumanity. But Milgram did not entrap his teachers by asking them first to zap learners with enough electricity to make their hair stand on end. Using the foot-in-the-door technique, he instead began with a little tickle of electricity and escalated step by step. In the minds of those throwing the switches, the small action became justified, making the next act tolerable. So it happens when people succumb, gradually, to evil.

In any society, great evils often grow out of people's compliance with lesser evils. The Nazi leaders suspected that most German civil servants would resist shooting or gassing Jews directly, but they found them willing to handle the paperwork of the Holocaust (Silver & Geller, 1978). Milgram found a similar reaction in his experiments. When he asked 40 men to administer the learning test while someone else did the shocking, 93 percent complied. Cruelty does not require devilish villains. All it takes is ordinary people corrupted by an evil situation. Ordinary students may follow orders to haze initiates into their group. Ordinary employees may follow orders to produce and market harmful products. Ordinary soldiers may follow orders to punish and torture prisoners (Lankford, 2009).

In Jozefow and Le Chambon, as in Milgram's experiments, those who resisted usually did so early. After the first acts of compliance or resistance, attitudes began to follow and justify behavior.

What have social psychologists learned about the power of the individual? *Social control* (the power of the situation) and *personal control* (the power of the individual) interact. Much as water dissolves salt but not sand, so rotten situations turn some people into bad apples while others resist (Johnson, 2007).

When feeling pressured, some people react by doing the opposite of what is expected (Brehm & Brehm, 1981). The power of one or two individuals to sway majorities is *minority influence* (Moscovici, 1985). One research finding repeatedly stands out. When you are the minority, you are far more likely to sway the majority if you hold firmly to your position and don't waffle. This tactic won't make you popular, but it may make you influential, especially if your self-confidence stimulates others to consider why you react as you do. Even when a minority's influence is not yet visible, people may privately develop sympathy for the minority position and rethink their views (Wood et al., 1994).

"I was only following orders." —Adolf Eichmann, director of Nazi deportation of Jews to concentration camps

"All evil begins with 15 volts." —Philip Zimbardo, Stanford lecture, 2010

The powers of social influence are enormous, but so are the powers of the committed individual. Were this not so, communism would have remained an obscure theory, Christianity would be a small Middle Eastern sect, and Rosa Parks' refusal to sit at the back of the bus would not have ignited the U.S. civil rights movement. Social forces matter. But individuals matter, too.

🔒 **RETRIEVE IT • • •**

ANSWERS IN APPENDIX E

RI-7 Psychology's most famous obedience experiments, in which most participants obeyed an authority figure's demands to inflict presumed painful, dangerous shocks on an innocent participant, were conducted by social psychologist
_____ _____.

RI-8 Which situations have researchers found to be most likely to encourage obedience in participants?

Group Behavior

LOQ 12-7 How does the presence of others influence our actions, via social facilitation, social loafing, and deindividuation?

ENGAGE 💡 Imagine standing in a room holding a fishing pole. Your task is to wind the reel as fast as you can. On some occasions you wind in the presence of another participant, who is also winding as fast as possible. Will the other's presence affect your own performance?

In one of social psychology's first experiments, Norman Triplett (1898) reported that adolescents would wind a fishing reel faster in the presence of someone doing the same thing. Although a modern reanalysis revealed that the difference was modest (Stroebe, 2012), Triplett inspired later social psychologists to study how others' presence affects our behavior. Group influences operate both in simple groups—one person in the presence of another—and in more complex groups.

SOCIAL FACILITATION Triplett's claim—of strengthened performance in others' presence—is called **social facilitation.** But studies revealed that the truth is more complicated: The presence of others strengthens our most *likely* response—the correct one on an easy task, an incorrect one on a difficult task (Guerin, 1986; Zajonc, 1965). Why? Because when others observe us, we become aroused, and this arousal amplifies our reactions. Thus, expert pool players who made 71 percent of their shots when alone made 80 percent when four people came to watch them (Michaels et al., 1982). Poor shooters, who made 36 percent of their shots when alone, made only 25 percent when watched.

The energizing effect of an enthusiastic audience probably contributes to the home advantage that has shown up in studies of more than a quarter-million college and professional athletic events in various countries (Allen & Jones, 2014; Jamieson, 2010). Home teams win about 6 in 10 games for most sports.

A MINORITY OF ONE To be August Landmesser, standing defiantly with arms folded as everyone else salutes their allegiance to the Nazi Party and Adolph Hitler, requires extraordinary courage. But sometimes such individuals have inspired others, demonstrating the power of minority influence.

THE POWER OF ONE After former gymnast Rachel Denhollander went public with her report of childhood sexual molestation by U.S. Gymnastics doctor Lawrence Nassar, she suffered six months of public shaming, later noting, "I was left alone and isolated . . . My sexual assault was wielded like a weapon against me . . . I was subjected to lies and attacks on my character." But eventually more than 300 other women stepped forward to publicly testify to similar abuse, and Nassar was jailed for life (Correa & Louttit, 2018). After Denhollander concluded the testimonies given at one of Nassar's criminal sentence hearings, Judge Rosemarie Aquilina said, "You made this happen. You are the bravest person I've ever had in my courtroom" (Macur, 2018).

social facilitation improved performance on simple or well-learned tasks in the presence of others.

Hope College

SOCIAL FACILITATION Skilled athletes often find they are "on" before an audience. What they do well, they do even better when people are watching.

ENGAGE (**ASK YOURSELF**)

What could you do to discourage social loafing in a group project assigned for a class?

Jessica Kourkounis/Reuters/Newscom

DEINDIVIDUATION In the excitement that followed the Philadelphia Eagles winning their first NFL Super Bowl (2018), some fans, disinhibited by social arousal and the anonymity provided by their "underdog" masks, became destructive.

The point to remember: What you do well, you are likely to do even better in front of an audience, especially a friendly audience. What you normally find difficult may seem all but impossible when you are being watched.

Social facilitation also helps explain a funny effect of crowding. Comedians know that a "good house" is a full one. What they may not know is that crowding triggers arousal. Comedy routines that are mildly amusing in an uncrowded room seem funnier in a densely packed room (Aiello et al., 1983; Freedman & Perlick, 1979). When seated close to one another, people like a friendly person even more and an unfriendly person even less (Schiffenbauer & Schiavo, 1976; Storms & Thomas, 1977). So, to increase the chances of lively interaction at your next event, choose a room or set up seating that will just barely accommodate everyone.

SOCIAL LOAFING Social facilitation experiments test the effect of others' presence on the performance of an individual task, such as shooting pool. But what happens when people perform as a group—say, in a team tug-of-war? Would you exert more, less, or the same effort as you would exert in a one-on-one match?

To find out, a University of Massachusetts research team asked blindfolded students "to pull as hard as [they] can" on a rope. When they fooled the students into believing three others were also pulling behind them, students exerted only 82 percent as much effort as when they knew they were pulling alone (Ingham et al., 1974). And consider what happened when blindfolded people seated in a group clapped or shouted as loudly as they could while hearing (through headphones) other people clapping or shouting loudly (Latané, 1981). When they thought they were part of a group effort, the participants produced about one-third less noise than when clapping or shouting "alone."

This diminished effort is called **social loafing** (Jackson & Williams, 1988; Latané, 1981). Experiments in the United States, India, Thailand, Japan, China, and Taiwan have found social loafing on various tasks, though it was especially common among men in individualist cultures (Karau & Williams, 1993). What causes social loafing? When people act as part of a group, they may

- *feel less accountable* and therefore worry less about what others think.
- *view individual contributions as dispensable* (Harkins & Szymanski, 1989; Kerr & Bruun, 1983).
- *overestimate their own contributions,* downplaying others' efforts (Schroeder et al., 2016).
- *free ride on others' efforts.* Unless highly motivated and strongly identified with the group, people may slack off (as you perhaps have observed on group assignments), especially when they share equally in the benefits, regardless of how much they contribute.

DEINDIVIDUATION We've seen that the presence of others can arouse people (social facilitation), or it can diminish their feelings of responsibility (social loafing). But sometimes the presence of others does both. The uninhibited behavior that results can range from a food fight to vandalism or rioting. This process of losing self-awareness and self-restraint, called **deindividuation,** often occurs when group participation makes people both *aroused* and *anonymous.* Compared with identifiable women in a control group, New York University women dressed in depersonalizing Ku Klux Klan–style hoods delivered twice as much presumed electric shock to a victim (Zimbardo, 1970).

Deindividuation thrives, for better or for worse, in many settings. Online anonymity can unleash mocking or cruel words; cyber-trolls report enjoyment from verbally abusing others (Buckels et al., 2014; Sest & March, 2017). They might never say "you're disgusting" to someone's face, but can hide behind their anonymity online. Tribal warriors who depersonalize themselves with face paints or masks are more likely than those with exposed faces to kill, torture, or mutilate captured enemies (Watson, 1973). When we shed self-awareness and self-restraint—whether in a mob, at a concert, at a ball game, or at worship—we become more responsive to the group experience, bad or good. For a comparison of social facilitation, social loafing, and deindividuation, see **TABLE 12.1.**

* * *

RETAIN 🔒 **TABLE 12.1**

Behavior in the Presence of Others: Three Phenomena

Phenomenon	Social context	Psychological effect of others' presence	Behavioral effect
Social facilitation	Individual being observed	Increased arousal	Amplified dominant behavior, such as doing better what one does well (or doing worse what is difficult)
Social loafing	Group projects	Diminished feelings of responsibility when not individually accountable	Decreased effort
Deindividuation	Group setting that fosters arousal and anonymity	Reduced self-awareness	Lowered self-restraint

social loafing the tendency for people in a group to exert less effort when pooling their efforts toward attaining a common goal than when individually accountable.

deindividuation the loss of self-awareness and self-restraint occurring in group situations that foster arousal and anonymity.

group polarization the enhancement of a group's prevailing inclinations through discussion within the group.

We have examined the conditions under which the *presence* of others can motivate people to exert themselves or tempt them to free ride on the efforts of others, make easy tasks easier or difficult tasks harder, and enhance humor or fuel mob violence. Research also shows that *interacting* with others can similarly have both bad and good effects.

Group Polarization

LOQ 12-8 How can group interaction enable group polarization?

We live in an increasingly polarized world. The Middle East is torn by warring factions. The European Union is struggling with nationalist divisions. In 1990, a one-minute speech in the U.S. Congress would enable you to guess the speaker's party just 55 percent of the time; by 2009, partisanship was evident 83 percent of the time (Gentzkow et al., 2016). In 2016, for the first time in survey history, most U.S. Republicans and Democrats reported having "*very*" unfavorable views of the other party (Doherty & Kiley, 2016). And a record 77 percent of Americans perceived their nation as divided (Jones, 2016).

A powerful principle helps us understand this increasing polarization: The beliefs and attitudes we bring to a group grow stronger as we discuss them with like-minded others. This process, called **group polarization,** can have beneficial results, as when low-prejudice students become even more accepting while discussing racial issues. As George Bishop and I [DM] discovered, it can also be socially toxic, as when high-prejudice students who discuss racial issues together become *more* prejudiced (Myers & Bishop, 1970) (**FIGURE 12.4**). Our repeated finding: Like minds polarize.

Analyses of terrorist organizations around the world reveal that the terrorist mentality emerges slowly among those who share a grievance (McCauley, 2002; McCauley & Segal, 1987; Merari, 2002). As susceptible individuals interact in isolation (sometimes with other "brothers" and "sisters" in camps or in prisons), their views grow more and more extreme. Increasingly, they categorize the world as "us" against "them" (Chulov, 2014; Moghaddam, 2005). Knowing that group polarization occurs when like-minded people segregate, a 2006 U.S. National Intelligence estimate speculated "that the operational threat from self-radicalized cells will grow."

The internet offers us a connected global world, yet also provides an easily accessible medium for group polarization. When I [DM] got my start in social psychology with experiments on group polarization, I never imagined the potential power of polarization in *virtual* groups. Progressives friend progressives and share links

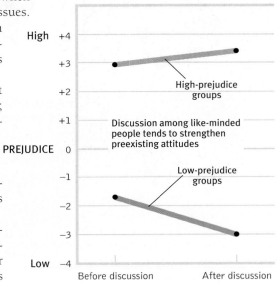

FIGURE 12.4

GROUP POLARIZATION If a group is like-minded, discussion strengthens its prevailing opinions. Talking over racial issues increased prejudice in a high-prejudice group of high school students and decreased it in a low-prejudice group. (Data from Myers & Bishop, 1970.)

"Dear Satan, thank you for having my Internet news feeds tailored especially for ME!" —Comedian Steve Martin, 2016 tweet

to sites that affirm their shared views. Conservatives connect with conservatives and likewise share conservative perspectives. With news feeds and retweets, we fuel one another with information—and misinformation—and click on content we agree with (Bakshy et al., 2015; Barberá et al., 2015). Thus, within the internet's echo chamber of the like-minded, views become more extreme. Suspicion becomes conviction. Disagreements with the other tribe can escalate to demonization. Mindful of the viral false news phenomenon, Facebook and Google are working on ways to promote media literacy. For more on the internet's role in group polarization—toward ends that are good as well as bad—see Thinking Critically About: The Internet as Social Amplifier.

THINKING CRITICALLY ABOUT:

The Internet as Social Amplifier

LOQ 12-9 What role does the internet play in group polarization?

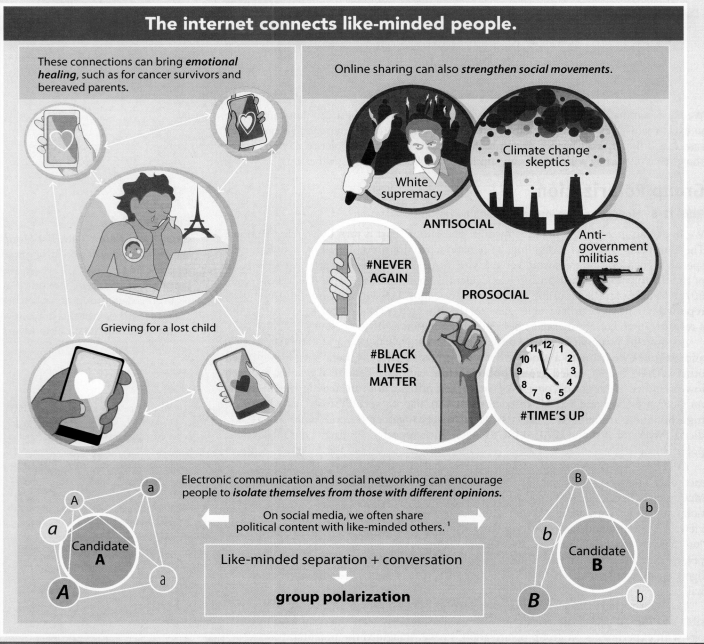

The internet connects like-minded people.

These connections can bring *emotional healing*, such as for cancer survivors and bereaved parents.

Grieving for a lost child

Online sharing can also *strengthen social movements*.

White supremacy

Climate change skeptics

ANTISOCIAL

Anti-government militias

#NEVER AGAIN

PROSOCIAL

#BLACK LIVES MATTER

#TIME'S UP

Electronic communication and social networking can encourage people to *isolate themselves from those with different opinions.*

On social media, we often share political content with like-minded others. [1]

Candidate **A**

Candidate **B**

Like-minded separation + conversation

group polarization

1. Bakshy et al., 2015; Barberá et al., 2015.

Groupthink

LOQ 12-10 How can group interaction enable groupthink?

Does group influence ever distort important national decisions? Consider the Bay of Pigs fiasco. In 1961, U.S. President John F. Kennedy and his advisers decided to invade Cuba with 1400 CIA-trained Cuban exiles. When the invaders were easily captured and quickly linked to the U.S. government, Kennedy wondered aloud, "How could I have been so stupid?"

Social psychologist Irving Janis (1982) studied the decision-making process leading to the ill-fated invasion. He discovered that the soaring morale of the recently elected president and his advisers fostered undue confidence. To preserve the good feeling, group members suppressed or self-censored their dissenting views, especially after President Kennedy voiced his enthusiasm for the scheme. Since no one spoke strongly against the idea, everyone assumed the support was unanimous. To describe this harmonious but unrealistic group thinking, Janis coined the term **groupthink.**

Later studies showed that groupthink—fed by overconfidence, conformity, self-justification, and group polarization—contributed to other fiascos as well. Among them were the failure to anticipate the 1941 Japanese attack on Pearl Harbor; the escalation of the Vietnam war; the U.S. Watergate cover-up; the Chernobyl nuclear reactor accident (Reason, 1987); the U.S. space shuttle *Challenger* explosion (Esser & Lindoerfer, 1989); and the Iraq war, launched on the false idea that Iraq had weapons of mass destruction (U.S. Senate Intelligence Committee, 2004).

Despite the dangers of groupthink, two heads are often better than one. Knowing this, Janis also studied instances in which U.S. presidents and their advisers collectively made good decisions, such as when the Truman administration formulated the Marshall Plan, which offered assistance to Europe after World War II, and when the Kennedy administration successfully prevented the Soviets from installing missiles in Cuba. His conclusion? Groupthink is prevented when a leader—whether in government or in business—welcomes various opinions, invites experts' critiques of developing plans, and assigns people to identify possible problems. Just as the suppression of dissent bends a group toward bad decisions, open debate often shapes good ones. This is especially the case with diverse groups, whose varied perspectives often enable creative or superior outcomes (Nemeth & Ormiston, 2007; Page, 2007). None of us is as smart as all of us.

groupthink the mode of thinking that occurs when the desire for harmony in a decision-making group overrides a realistic appraisal of alternatives.

"One of the dangers in the White House, based on my reading of history, is that you get wrapped up in groupthink and everybody agrees with everything, and there's no discussion and there are no dissenting views." —Barack Obama, December 1, 2008, press conference

"If you have an apple and I have an apple and we exchange apples then you and I will still each have one apple. But if you have an idea and I have an idea and we exchange these ideas, then each of us will have two ideas." —Attributed to dramatist George Bernard Shaw (1856–1950)

"If evil is contagious, so is goodness." —Pope Francis tweet, 2017

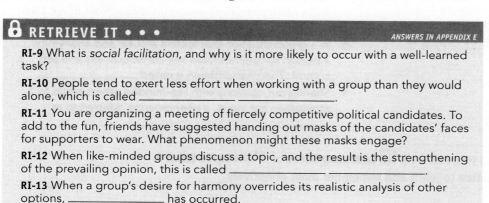

🔒 RETRIEVE IT • • •

ANSWERS IN APPENDIX E

RI-9 What is *social facilitation*, and why is it more likely to occur with a well-learned task?

RI-10 People tend to exert less effort when working with a group than they would alone, which is called _____ _____.

RI-11 You are organizing a meeting of fiercely competitive political candidates. To add to the fun, friends have suggested handing out masks of the candidates' faces for supporters to wear. What phenomenon might these masks engage?

RI-12 When like-minded groups discuss a topic, and the result is the strengthening of the prevailing opinion, this is called _____ _____.

RI-13 When a group's desire for harmony overrides its realistic analysis of other options, _____ has occurred.

 **ASK YOURSELF**

How have you been influenced by group polarization in your online activities?

🔒 REVIEW   SOCIAL THINKING AND SOCIAL INFLUENCE

⇨ Learning Objectives

TEST YOURSELF Answer these repeated Learning Objective Questions on your own (before checking the answers in Appendix D) to improve your retention of the concepts (McDaniel et al., 2009, 2015).

12-1 What do social psychologists study? How do we tend to explain others' behavior and our own?

12-2 How do attitudes and actions interact?

12-3 How does culture affect our behavior?

12-4 How is social contagion a form of conformity, and how do conformity experiments reveal the power of social influence?

12-5 What did Milgram's obedience experiments teach us about the power of social influence?

12-6 What do the social influence studies teach us about ourselves? How much power do we have as individuals?

12-7 How does the presence of others influence our actions, via social facilitation, social loafing, and deindividuation?

12-8 How can group interaction enable group polarization?

12-9 What role does the internet play in group polarization?

12-10 How can group interaction enable groupthink?

⟶ Terms and Concepts to Remember

TEST YOURSELF Write down the definition yourself, then check your answer on the referenced page.

social psychology, **p. 416**

attribution theory, **p. 416**

fundamental attribution error, **p. 416**

attitude, **p. 418**

peripheral route persuasion, **p. 418**

central route persuasion, **p. 418**

foot-in-the-door phenomenon, **p. 418**

role, **p. 418**

cognitive dissonance theory, **p. 421**

norms, **p. 421**

culture, **p. 421**

conformity, **p. 423**

normative social influence, **p. 424**

informational social influence, **p. 424**

social facilitation, **p. 429**

social loafing, **p. 431**

deindividuation, **p. 431**

group polarization, **p. 431**

groupthink, **p. 433**

⟶ Experience the Testing Effect

TEST YOURSELF Answer the following questions on your own first, then check your answers in Appendix E.

1. If we encounter a person who appears to be high on drugs, and we make the fundamental attribution error, we will probably attribute the person's behavior to
   a. moral weakness or an addictive personality.
   b. peer pressure.
   c. the easy availability of drugs on city streets.
   d. society's acceptance of drug use.

2. Celebrity endorsements in advertising often lead consumers to purchase products through _____ (central/peripheral) route persuasion.

3. We tend to agree to a larger request more readily if we have already agreed to a small request. This tendency is called the _____-_____-_____-_____ phenomenon.

4. Jamal's therapist has suggested that Jamal should "act as if" he is confident, even though he feels insecure and shy. Which social psychological theory would best support this suggestion, and what might the therapist be hoping to achieve?

5. Researchers have found that a person is most likely to conform to a group if
   a. the group members have diverse opinions.
   b. the person feels competent and secure.
   c. the person admires the group's status.
   d. no one else will observe the person's behavior.

6. In Milgram's experiments, the rate of compliance was highest when
   a. the "learner" was at a distance from the "teacher."
   b. the "learner" was close at hand.
   c. other "teachers" refused to go along with the experimenter.
   d. the "teacher" disliked the "learner."

7. Dr. Huang, a popular music professor, delivers fascinating lectures on music history but gets nervous and makes mistakes when describing exam statistics in front of the class. Why does his performance vary by task?

8. In a group situation that fosters arousal and anonymity, a person sometimes loses self-consciousness and self-control. This phenomenon is called _____.

9. Sharing our opinions with like-minded others tends to strengthen our views, a phenomenon referred to as _____ _____.

Continue testing yourself with 📖 **LearningCurve** or ≈ **Achieve Read & Practice** to learn and remember most effectively.

⟶ Antisocial Relations

Social psychology studies how we think about and influence one another, and also how we *relate* to one another. What are the roots of prejudice? What causes people sometimes to hate and harm, and other times to love and help? And when destructive conflicts arise, how can we move toward a just peace? In this section we ponder insights into *antisocial* relations gleaned by researchers who have studied prejudice and aggression.

PREJUDICE

LOQ 12-11 What is *prejudice*? How do explicit and implicit prejudice differ?

Prejudice means "prejudgment." It is an unjustifiable and usually negative *attitude* toward a group and its members—who often are people of a particular racial or ethnic group, gender, sexual orientation, or belief system. You may recall that attitudes are feelings, influenced by beliefs, that predispose us to act in certain ways. The ingredients in prejudice's three-part mixture are

- *negative emotions,* such as hostility or fear.

- **stereotypes**, which are generalized beliefs about a group of people. Our stereotypes sometimes reflect reality. If you presume that young men tend to drive faster than elderly women, you may be right. But stereotypes often overgeneralize or exaggerate—as when liberals and conservatives overestimate the extremity of each other's views, or Christians and atheists misperceive each other's values (Graham et al., 2012; Simpson & Rios, 2016).

- a predisposition to **discriminate**—to act in negative and unjustifiable ways toward members of the group. Sometimes prejudice is blatant. Other times it is more subtle, taking the form of *microaggressions,* such as race-related traffic stops, a reluctance to choose a train seat next to someone of a different race, or longer Uber wait times and less Airbnb acceptance for people with African-American names (Edelman et al., 2017; Ge et al., 2016; Wang et al., 2011).

To believe that obese people are gluttonous, and to feel dislike for an obese person, is to be prejudiced. To pass over obese people on a dating site, or to reject an obese job candidate, is to discriminate.

Explicit and Implicit Prejudice

Again and again, we have seen that our brain processes thoughts, memories, and attitudes on two different tracks. Sometimes that processing is *explicit*—on the radar screen of our awareness. More often, it is *implicit*—an unthinking knee-jerk response operating below the radar, leaving us unaware of how our attitudes are influencing our behavior. In 2015, the U.S. Supreme Court, in upholding the Fair Housing Act, recognized implicit bias research, noting that "unconscious prejudices" can cause discrimination even when people do not consciously intend to discriminate.

 Psychologists study implicit prejudice by

- *testing for unconscious group associations.* Tests in which people quickly pair a person's image with a trait demonstrate that even people who deny any racial prejudice may harbor negative associations (Banaji & Greenwald, 2013). Millions of people have taken the Implicit Association Test (as you can, too, at Implicit.Harvard.edu). Critics question the test's reliability and caution against using it to assess or label individuals (Oswald et al., 2013, 2015). But defenders counter that implicit biases predict behaviors ranging from simple acts of friendliness to the evaluation of work quality (Greenwald et al., 2015).

- *considering unconscious patronization.* In one experiment, White university women assessed flawed student essays they believed had been written by either a White or a Black student. The women gave low evaluations, often with harsh comments, to the essays supposedly written by a White student. When the same essay was attributed to a Black student, their assessment was more positive (Harber, 1998). In real-world evaluations, such low expectations and the resulting "inflated praise and insufficient criticism" could hinder minority student achievement, the researcher noted, which is one reason why many teachers read essays while "blind" to their authors' race.

- *monitoring reflexive bodily responses.* Even people who consciously express little prejudice may give off telltale signals as their body responds selectively to an image of a person from another ethnic group. Neuroscientists can detect signals of implicit prejudice in the viewer's facial-muscle responses and in the activation of the emotion-processing amygdala (Cunningham et al., 2004; Eberhardt, 2005; Stanley et al., 2008).

"But who can detect their errors? Clear me from hidden faults."
—Psalm 19:12

prejudice an unjustifiable and usually negative attitude toward a group and its members. Prejudice generally involves negative emotions, stereotyped beliefs, and a predisposition to discriminatory action.

stereotype a generalized (sometimes accurate but often overgeneralized) belief about a group of people.

discrimination unjustifiable negative behavior toward a group or its members.

RESPONDING TO AN AMERICAN TRAGEDY Does implicit bias research—now being integrated into police and corporate diversity training programs in the United States and beyond—help us understand the 2013 death of Trayvon Martin (shown here 7 months before he was killed)? As he walked alone to his father's fiancée's house in a gated Florida neighborhood, a suspicious resident started following him. A confrontation led to the unarmed Martin being shot. Martin's death sparked public outrage related to racism, gun control, and social justice. Commentators wondered: Had Martin been an unarmed White teen, would he have been perceived and treated the same way?

"If we can't help our latent biases, we can help our behavior in response to those instinctive reactions, which is why we work to design systems and processes that overcome that very human part of us all." —U.S. FBI Director James B. Comey, "Hard Truths: Law Enforcement and Race," 2015

Targets of Prejudice

LOQ 12-12 What groups are frequent targets of prejudice?

RACIAL AND ETHNIC PREJUDICE Americans' expressed racial attitudes have changed dramatically in the last half-century. "Marriage between Blacks and Whites" was approved by 4 percent of Americans in 1958 and 87 percent in 2013 (Newport, 2013a). Six in ten Americans—double the number in most European countries—now agree that "an increasing number of people of many different races, ethnic groups, and nationalities in our country makes it a better place to live" (Drake & Poushter, 2016).

Yet as overt interracial prejudice wanes, *subtle* prejudice lingers. People with darker skin tones experience greater criticism and accusations of immoral behavior (Alter et al., 2016). And although many people *say* they would feel upset with someone making racist (or homophobic) slurs, they respond indifferently when they actually hear prejudice-laden language (Kawakami et al., 2009).

As noted, prejudice is not just subtle, but often unconscious (implicit). An Implicit Association Test found 9 in 10 White respondents taking longer to identify pleasant words (such as *peace* and *paradise*) as "good" when presented with Black-sounding names (such as *Latisha* and *Darnell*) than they did with White-sounding names (such as *Katie* and *Ian*). Moreover, people who more quickly associate good things with White names or faces also are the quickest to perceive anger and apparent threat in Black faces (Hugenberg & Bodenhausen, 2003). A greater association of pleasant words with European-American than African-American names has also been observed in more than 800 billion internet words (Caliskan et al., 2017). In the 2008 U.S. presidential election, those demonstrating explicit *or* implicit prejudice were less likely to vote for candidate Barack Obama. His election, however, reduced implicit prejudice (Bernstein et al., 2010; Payne et al., 2010; Stephens-Davidowitz, 2014).

Our perceptions can also reflect implicit bias. In 1999, Amadou Diallo was accosted as he approached his doorway by police officers looking for a rapist. When he pulled out his wallet, the officers, perceiving a gun, riddled his body with 19 bullets from 41 shots. In one analysis of 59 unarmed suspect shootings in Philadelphia over seven years, 49 involved the misidentification of an object (such as a phone) or movement (such as pants tugging). Black suspects were more than twice as likely to be misperceived as threatening, even by Black officers (Blow, 2015). Across the United States, nearly 40 percent of the unarmed people shot and killed by police during 2015 and 2016 were Black (*Washington Post*, 2017). One research team, drawing on responses from more than 2 million Americans, found that a region's implicit bias toward African-Americans predicted its number of African-Americans killed by police, even after accounting for other factors such as income and population density (Hehman et al., 2018).

To better understand such tragic shootings, researchers have also simulated the situation (Correll et al., 2007, 2015; Plant & Peruche, 2005; Sadler et al., 2012b). They asked viewers to press buttons quickly to "shoot" or not shoot men who suddenly appeared on screen. Some of the on-screen men held a gun. Others held a harmless object, such as a flashlight or bottle. People (both Blacks and Whites, including police officers) more often shot Black men holding the harmless object. Priming people with a flashed Black face rather than a White face also made them more likely to misperceive a flashed tool as a gun (**FIGURE 12.5**). Fatigue, which diminishes one's conscious control and increases automatic reactions, amplifies racial bias in decisions to shoot (Ma et al., 2013).

FIGURE 12.5

RACE PRIMES PERCEPTIONS In experiments by Keith Payne (2006), people viewed (a) a White or Black face, instantly followed by (b) a flashed gun or hand tool, which was then followed by (c) a masking screen. Participants were more likely to misperceive a tool as a gun when it was preceded by a Black rather than White face.

(a)

(b)

(c)

GENDER PREJUDICE Overt gender prejudice has also declined sharply. The one-third of Americans who in 1937 told Gallup pollsters that they would vote for a qualified woman whom their party nominated for president soared to 95 percent in 2012 (Jones, 2012; Newport, 1999). Although women worldwide still represent nearly two-thirds of illiterate adults, and 30 percent have experienced intimate partner violence, 65 percent of all people now say it is very important that women have the same rights as men (UN, 2015b; WHO, 2016b; Zainulbhai, 2016).

Nevertheless, both implicit and explicit gender prejudice and discrimination persist. In Western countries, we pay more to those (usually men) who care for our streets than to those (usually women) who care for our children. From 2007 through 2016, male directors of 1000 popular films (the top 100 for each year) outnumbered female directors by 24 to 1 (Smith et al., 2017). Gender bias even applies to beliefs about intelligence: Despite equality between the sexes in intelligence test scores, people tend to perceive their fathers as more intelligent than their mothers and their sons as brighter than their daughters (Furnham, 2016).

Unwanted female infants are no longer left out on a hillside to die of exposure, as was the practice in ancient Greece. Yet the normal male-to-female newborn ratio (105-to-100) doesn't explain the world's estimated 163 million (say that number slowly) "missing women" (Hvistendahl, 2011). In many places, sons are valued more than daughters. In India, there are 3.5 times more Google searches asking how to conceive a boy than how to conceive a girl (Stephens-Davidowitz, 2014). With scientific testing that enables sex-selective abortions, some countries are experiencing a shortfall in female births. India's newborn sex ratio was recently 112 boys for every 100 girls. China's has been 111 to 100, despite China's declaring sex-selective abortions—gender genocide—a criminal offense (CIA, 2014). With under-age-20 males exceeding females by 32 million, many Chinese bachelors will be unable to find mates (Zhu et al., 2009). A shortage of women also contributes to increased crime, violence, prostitution, and trafficking of women (Brooks, 2012).

LGBTQ PREJUDICE In most of the world, gay, lesbian, and transgender people cannot openly and comfortably disclose who they are and whom they love (Katz-Wise & Hyde, 2012; UN, 2011). Although by 2018 two dozen countries had allowed same-sex marriage, dozens more had laws criminalizing same-sex relationships. Cultural variation is enormous—ranging from the 98 percent in Ghana to the 6 percent in Spain for whom "homosexuality is morally unacceptable" (Pew, 2014b). Worldwide, anti-gay attitudes are most common among men, older adults, and those who are unhappy, unemployed, and less educated (Haney, 2016; Jäckle & Wenzelburger, 2015).

Explicit anti-LGBTQ prejudice persists, even in countries with legal protections in place. When U.S. and U.K. experimenters sent thousands of responses to employment ads, those whose resumes included "Treasurer, Progressive and Socialist Alliance" received more replies than did those for resumes that specified "Treasurer, Gay and Lesbian Alliance" (Agerström et al., 2012; Bertrand & Mullainathan, 2003; Drydakis, 2009, 2015). Other evidence has appeared in national surveys of LGBTQ Americans:

- 39 percent reported having been "rejected by a friend or family member" because of their sexual orientation or gender identity (Pew, 2013b).

- 58 percent reported being "subject to slurs or jokes" (Pew, 2013b).

- 54 percent reported having been harassed at school and at work (Grant et al., 2011; James et al., 2016).

Do attitudes and practices that label, disparage, and discriminate against gay, lesbian, and transgender people increase their risk of psychological disorder and ill health? In U.S. states without protections against LGBTQ hate crime and discrimination, gay and lesbian people experience substantially higher rates of depression and related disorders, even after controlling for income and education differences. In communities where anti-gay prejudice is high, so are gay and lesbian suicide and cardiovascular deaths. In 16 states that banned same-sex marriage between 2001 and 2005, gays and lesbians (but not heterosexuals) experienced a 37 percent increase in depressive disorder rates, a 42 percent increase in alcohol use disorder, and a 248 percent increase in generalized anxiety disorder. Meanwhile, gays and lesbians in other states did not experience increased psychiatric disorders (Hatzenbuehler, 2014).

"Until I was a man, I had no idea how good men had it at work. . . . The first time I spoke up in a meeting in my newly low, quiet voice and noticed that sudden, focused attention, I was so uncomfortable that I found myself unable to finish my sentence." —Thomas Page McBee, 2016, after transitioning from female to male

just-world phenomenon the tendency for people to believe the world is just and that people therefore get what they deserve and deserve what they get.

ingroup "us"—people with whom we share a common identity.

outgroup "them"—those perceived as different or apart from our ingroup.

ingroup bias the tendency to favor our own group.

scapegoat theory the theory that prejudice offers an outlet for anger by providing someone to blame.

other-race effect the tendency to recall faces of one's own race more accurately than faces of other races. (Also called the *cross-race effect* and the *own-race bias*.)

BELIEF SYSTEMS PREJUDICE In the aftermath of the 9/11 terrorist attacks, the Iraq and Afghanistan wars, and the brutal scare tactics of violent extremist groups, many Americans have developed irrational fear and anger toward *all* Muslims (and those they *think* might be Muslim). (The reality since 2001: U.S. attacks by homegrown White supremacists and other non-Muslim extremists were nearly twice as likely [Shane, 2015].) As a result, nearly half of Muslim Americans have reported personally experiencing discrimination in the last year—more than double the average among U.S. Jews, Catholics, and Protestants (Gallup, 2017).

Roots of Prejudice

LOQ 12-13 What are some social, emotional, and cognitive roots of prejudice, and what are some ways to eliminate prejudice?

Prejudice springs from a culture's divisions, the heart's passions, and the mind's natural workings.

SOCIAL INEQUALITIES AND DIVISIONS When some people have money, power, and prestige and others do not, the "haves" usually develop attitudes that justify things as they are. The **just-world phenomenon** reflects an idea we commonly teach our children—that good is rewarded and evil is punished. From this it is but a short and sometimes automatic leap to assume that those who succeed must be good and those who suffer must be bad. Such reasoning enables the rich to see both their own wealth and the poor's misfortune as justly deserved. When slavery existed in the United States, slaveholders perceived slaves as innately lazy, ignorant, and irresponsible—as having the very traits that justified enslaving them. Stereotypes rationalize inequalities.

Victims of discrimination may react with either self-blame or anger (Allport, 1954). Either reaction can feed others' prejudice through the classic *blame-the-victim* dynamic. Do the circumstances of poverty breed a higher crime rate? If so, that higher crime rate can be used to justify discrimination against those who live in poverty.

Dividing the world into "us" and "them" can entail conflict, racism, and war, but it also provides the benefits of communal solidarity. Thus, we cheer for our groups, kill for them, die for them. Indeed, we define who we are—our *social identity*—partly in terms of our groups (Greenaway et al., 2016; Hogg, 1996, 2006; Turner, 1987, 2007). When Ian identifies himself as a man, an Aussie, a University of Sydney student, a Catholic, and a MacGregor, he knows who he is, and so do we. Mentally drawing a circle defines "us," the **ingroup.** But the social definition of who we are also states who we are not. People outside that circle are "them," the **outgroup.** An **ingroup bias**—a favoring of our own group—soon follows. In experiments, people have favored their own group (arbitrarily created by a simple coin toss) when dividing rewards (Tajfel, 1982; Wilder, 1981). Across 17 countries, ingroup bias appears more as ingroup favoritism than as harm to the outgroup (Romano et al., 2017). Discrimination is triggered less by outgroup hostility than by ingroup networking and mutual support—such as hiring a friend's child at the expense of other candidates (Greenwald & Pettigrew, 2014).

We have inherited our Stone Age ancestors' need to belong, to live and love in groups. There was safety in solidarity: Whether hunting, defending, or attacking, 10 hands were better than 2. Evolution prepared us, when encountering strangers, to make instant judgments: friend or foe? This urge to distinguish enemies from friends, and to "otherize" as different those not like us, predisposes prejudice against strangers (Whitley, 1999). To Greeks of the classical era, all non-Greeks were "barbarians." In our own era, most children believe their school is better than all other schools in town. Many high school students form cliques—jocks, preps, nerds—and disparage those outside their own

ASK YOURSELF

What are some examples of ingroup bias in your community?

Mike Hewitt/Getty Images

THE INGROUP Scotland's famed "Tartan Army" soccer fans, shown here during a match against archrival England, share a social identity that defines "us" (the Scottish ingroup) and "them" (the English outgroup).

group. Even chimpanzees have been seen to wipe clean the spot where they were touched by a chimpanzee from another group (Goodall, 1986). They also display ingroup empathy by yawning more after seeing ingroup (rather than outgroup) members yawn (Campbell & de Waal, 2011). Although an ideal world might prioritize justice and love for all, in our real world, ingroup love often outranks universal justice.

NEGATIVE EMOTIONS Negative emotions nourish prejudice. When facing death, fearing threats, or experiencing frustration, people cling more tightly to their ingroup. As fears of terrorism heighten patriotism, they also produce loathing and aggression toward those who appear to threaten our world (Pyszczynski et al., 2002, 2008). **Scapegoat theory** notes that when things go wrong, finding someone to blame can provide a target for our negative emotions. After anti-immigrant sentiments flared in 2016 during the Brexit referendum in Britain and the contentious presidential election in the United States, reports of harassment, bullying, and hate crime rose (Crandall & White, 2016; Hassan, 2016; Kenyon, 2016; North, 2016). "Fear and anger create aggression, and aggression against citizens of different ethnicity or race creates racism and, in turn, new forms of terrorism," noted Philip Zimbardo (2001).

Evidence for the scapegoat theory of prejudice comes in two forms: (1) Economically frustrated people tend to express heightened prejudice. (2) Experiments that create temporary frustration intensify prejudice. Students who experience failure or are made to feel insecure often restore their self-esteem by disparaging a rival school or another person (Cialdini & Richardson, 1980; Crocker et al., 1987). Denigrating others may boost our own sense of status, which explains why a rival's misfortune sometimes provides a twinge of pleasure. (The German language has a word—*Schadenfreude*—for this secret joy that we sometimes take in another's failure.) By contrast, those made to feel loved and supported become more open to and accepting of others who differ (Mikulincer & Shaver, 2001).

COGNITIVE SHORTCUTS Stereotyped beliefs are in part a by-product of how we cognitively simplify the world. To help understand the world around us, we sometimes form categories. Chemists categorize molecules as organic and inorganic. Therapists categorize psychological disorders. We all categorize people by gender, ethnicity, race, age, and many other characteristics. But when we categorize people into groups, we often stereotype. We recognize how greatly *we* differ from other individuals in *our* groups. But we overestimate the extent to which members of other groups are alike (Bothwell et al., 1989). We perceive *outgroup homogeneity*—uniformity of attitudes, personality, and appearance. Our greater recognition for individual own-race faces—called the **other-race effect** (or *cross-race effect* or *own-race bias*)—emerges during infancy, between 3 and 9 months of age (Anzures et al., 2013; Telzer et al., 2013). (We also have an *own-age bias*—better recognition memory for faces of our own age group [Rhodes & Anastasi, 2012]).

Sometimes, however, people don't fit easily into our racial categories. If so, they are often assigned to their minority identity. Researchers believe this happens because,

"If the Tiber reaches the walls, if the Nile does not rise to the fields, if the sky doesn't move or the Earth does, if there is famine, if there is plague, the cry is at once: 'The Christians to the lion!'" —Tertullian, *Apologeticus*, 197 C.E.

"The misfortunes of others are the taste of honey." —Japanese saying

| 100% Chinese | 80% Chinese 20% Caucasian | 60% Chinese 40% Caucasian | 40% Chinese 60% Caucasian | 20% Chinese 80% Caucasian | 100% Caucasian |

Dr. Jamin Halberstadt

FIGURE 12.6

CATEGORIZING MIXED-RACE PEOPLE When New Zealanders quickly classified 104 photos by race, those of European descent more often than those of Chinese descent classified the ambiguous middle two as Chinese (Halberstadt et al., 2011).

FIGURE 12.7

VIVID CASES FEED STEREOTYPES Global terrorism has created, in many minds, an exaggerated stereotype of Muslims as terrorism-prone. Actually, reported a U.S. National Research Council panel on terrorism, when offering this inexact illustration, most terrorists are not Muslim and "the vast majority of Islamic people have no connection with and do not sympathize with terrorism" (Smelser & Mitchell, 2002).

after learning the features of a familiar racial group, the observer's *selective attention* is drawn to the distinctive features of the less-familiar minority. Jamin Halberstadt and his colleagues (2011) illustrated this learned-association effect by showing New Zealanders blended Chinese-Caucasian faces. Compared with participants of Chinese descent, European-descent New Zealanders more readily classified ambiguous faces as Chinese (see **FIGURE 12.6**). With effort and with experience, people get better at recognizing individual faces from another group (Hugenberg et al., 2010; Young et al., 2012).

REMEMBERING VIVID CASES We also simplify our world by employing *heuristics*—mental shortcuts that enable snap judgments. The *availability heuristic* is the tendency to estimate the frequency of an event by how readily it comes to mind. Vivid cases are memorable and they come to mind easily, so it's no surprise that they feed our stereotypes. In a classic experiment, researchers showed two groups of University of Oregon students lists containing information about 50 men (Rothbart et al., 1978). The first group's list included 10 men arrested for *nonviolent* crimes, such as forgery. The second group's list included 10 men arrested for *violent* crimes, such as assault. Later, both groups were asked how many men on their list had committed *any* sort of crime. The second group overestimated the number. Violent crimes form vivid memories (**FIGURE 12.7**).

Muslims   Terrorism

🔒 📖 **LaunchPad** To review attribution research and experience a simulation of how stereotypes form, visit **Topic Tutorial: PsychSim6, Not My Type**. And for a 6.5-minute synopsis of the cognitive and social psychology of prejudice, see the **Video: Prejudice**.

VICTIM BLAMING As we noted earlier, people often justify their prejudices by blaming victims. If the world is just, they assume, people must get what they deserve. As one German civilian is said to have remarked when visiting the Bergen-Belsen concentration camp shortly after World War II, "What terrible criminals these prisoners must have been to receive such treatment."

Hindsight bias amplifies victim blaming (Carli & Leonard, 1989). Have you ever heard people say that rape victims, abused spouses, or people with AIDS got what they deserved? In some countries, such as Pakistan, rape victims have been sentenced to severe punishment for violating adultery prohibitions (Mydans, 2002). In one experiment, two groups were given a detailed account of a date (Janoff-Bulman et al., 1985). The first group's account reported that the date ended with the woman being raped. Members of that group perceived the woman's behavior as at least partly to blame, and in hindsight, they thought, "She should have known better." The second group, given the same account with the rape ending deleted, did not perceive the woman's behavior as inviting rape. Hindsight bias promoted a blame-the-victim mentality among members of the first group. Blaming the victim also serves to reassure people that it couldn't happen to them.

People also have a basic tendency to justify their culture's social systems (Jost et al., 2009; Kay et al., 2009). We're inclined to see the way things are as the way they ought to be and deserve to be: If people are rich, they must be smart (Hussak & Cimpian, 2015). This natural conservatism makes it difficult to legislate major social changes, such as health care improvements or climate change policies. Once such policies are in place, our "system justification" tends to preserve them.

aggression any physical or verbal behavior intended to harm someone physically or emotionally.

🔒 **RETRIEVE IT • • •**   *ANSWERS IN APPENDIX E*

RI-1 When prejudiced judgment causes us to blame an undeserving person for a problem, that person is called a _____.

* * *

If your own gut-check reveals you sometimes have feelings you would rather not have about other people, remember this: It is what we *do* with our feelings that matters. By monitoring our feelings and actions, and by replacing old habits with new ones based on new friendships, we can work to free ourselves from prejudice.

AGGRESSION

LOQ 12-14 How does psychology's definition of *aggression* differ from everyday usage? What biological factors make us more prone to hurt one another?

Prejudice hurts, but aggression sometimes hurts more. In psychology, **aggression** is any physical or verbal behavior intended to harm someone, whether done out of hostility or as a calculated means to an end. The assertive, persistent salesperson is not aggressive. Nor is the dentist who makes you wince with pain. But the gossip who passes along a vicious rumor about you, the bully who torments you in person or online, and the attacker who robs you are aggressive.

Aggressive behavior emerges from the interaction of biology and experience. For a gun to fire, the trigger must be pulled; with some people, as with hair-trigger guns, it doesn't take much to trip an explosion. Let's look first at some biological factors that influence our thresholds for aggressive behavior, then at the psychological factors that pull the trigger.

DO GUNS IN THE HOME SAVE OR TAKE MORE LIVES? "Personal safety/protection" is the number one reason U.S. gun owners give for firearm ownership (Swift, 2013). Yet in the last 40 years, well over one million Americans have suffered nonwar firearm deaths—more than all American war deaths. Compared with people of the same sex, race, age, and neighborhood, those who keep a gun in the home have been twice as likely to be murdered and three times as likely to die by suicide (Anglemyer et al., 2014; Stroebe, 2013). States and countries with high gun ownership rates also tend to have high gun death rates (VPC, 2016).

The Biology of Aggression

Aggression varies too widely from culture to culture, era to era, and person to person to be considered an unlearned instinct. But biology does *influence* aggression. We can look for biological influences at three levels—genetic, neural, and biochemical.

GENETIC INFLUENCES Genes influence aggression. Animals have been bred for aggressiveness—sometimes for sport, sometimes for research. The effect of genes also appears in human *twin studies* (Miles & Carey, 1997; Rowe et al., 1999). If one identical twin admits to "having a violent temper," the other twin will often independently admit the same. Fraternal twins are much less likely to respond similarly.

Researchers continue to search for genetic markers in those who commit violent acts. One is already well known and is carried by half the human race: the Y chromosome. Another such marker is the *monoamine oxidase A (MAOA) gene,* which helps break down neurotransmitters such as dopamine and serotonin. Sometimes called the "warrior gene," people who have low *MAOA* gene expression tend to behave aggressively when provoked. In one experiment, low (compared with high) *MAOA* gene carriers gave more unpleasant hot sauce to someone who provoked them (McDermott et al., 2009; Tiihonen et al., 2015).

"It's a guy thing."

NEURAL INFLUENCES There is no one spot in the brain that controls aggression. Aggression is a complex behavior, and it occurs in particular contexts. But animal and human brains have neural systems that, given provocation, will either inhibit or facilitate aggression (Falkner et al., 2016; Moyer, 1983; Wilkowski et al., 2011). Consider:

- Researchers implanted a radio-controlled electrode in the brain of the domineering leader of a caged monkey colony. The electrode was in an area that, when stimulated, inhibits aggression. When researchers placed the control button for the electrode in the colony's cage, one small monkey learned to push it every time the boss became threatening.

- A neurosurgeon, seeking to diagnose a disorder, implanted an electrode in the amygdala of a mild-mannered woman. Because the brain has no sensory receptors, she was unable to feel the stimulation. But at the flick of a switch she snarled, "Take my blood pressure. Take it now," then stood up and began to strike the doctor.

- Studies of violent criminals have revealed diminished activity in the frontal lobes, which play an important role in controlling impulses. If the frontal lobes are damaged, inactive, disconnected, or not yet fully mature, aggression may be more likely (Amen et al., 1996; Davidson et al., 2000; Raine, 2013).

BIOCHEMICAL INFLUENCES Our genes engineer our individual nervous systems, which operate electrochemically. The hormone testosterone, for example, circulates in the bloodstream and influences the neural systems that control aggression. A raging bull becomes a gentle giant when castration reduces its testosterone level. Conversely, when injected with testosterone, gentle, castrated mice once again become aggressive.

Humans are less sensitive to hormonal changes. But as men's testosterone levels diminish with age, hormonally charged, aggressive 17-year-olds mature into quieter and gentler 70-year-olds. Drugs that sharply reduce testosterone levels also subdue men's aggressive tendencies.

Another drug that sometimes circulates in the bloodstream—alcohol—*unleashes* aggressive responses to frustration. Across police data, prison surveys, and experiments, aggression-prone people are more likely to drink, and to become violent when intoxicated (White et al., 1993). Alcohol is a disinhibitor—it slows the brain activity that controls judgment and inhibitions. Under its influence, people may interpret ambiguous acts (such as being bumped in a crowd) as provocations and react aggressively (Bègue et al., 2010; Giancola & Gorman, 2007). Alcohol has been a factor in 73 percent of homicides in Russia and 57 percent in the United States (Landberg & Norström, 2011).

Just *thinking* you've imbibed alcohol can increase aggression (Bègue et al., 2009). But so, too, does unknowingly ingesting alcohol slipped into a drink. Thus, alcohol affects aggression both biologically and psychologically (Bushman, 1993; Ito et al., 1996; Taylor & Chermack, 1993).

"We could avoid two-thirds of all crime simply by putting all able-bodied young men in cryogenic sleep from the age of 12 through 28." —David T. Lykken, *The Antisocial Personalities*, 1995

Chris Courteau/AGE Fotostock

A LEAN, MEAN FIGHTING MACHINE— THE TESTOSTERONE-LADEN FEMALE HYENA The hyena's unusual embryology pumps testosterone into female fetuses. The result is revved-up young female hyenas who seem born to fight.

Psychological and Social-Cultural Factors in Aggression

LOQ 12-15 What psychological and social-cultural factors may trigger aggressive behavior?

Biological factors influence how easily aggression is triggered. But what psychological and social-cultural factors pull the trigger?

AVERSIVE EVENTS Suffering sometimes builds character. In laboratory experiments, however, those made miserable have often made others miserable (Berkowitz, 1983, 1989). Aversive stimuli—hot temperatures, physical pain, personal insults, foul odors, cigarette smoke, crowding, and a host of others—can evoke hostility. Even hunger can feed anger—making people "hangry" (Bushman et al., 2014). A prime example of this phenomenon is the **frustration-aggression principle:** Frustration creates anger, which can spark aggression.

The frustration-aggression link was illustrated in an analysis of 27,667 hit-by-pitch Major League Baseball incidents between 1960 and 2004 (Timmerman, 2007). Pitchers were most likely to hit batters when they had been frustrated by one of three events: the previous batter had hit a home run, the current batter had hit a home run the last time at bat, or the pitcher's teammate had been hit by a pitch in the previous half-inning. A separate study found a similar link between rising temperatures and the number of hit batters (Reifman et al., 1991; see **FIGURE 12.8**).

In the wider world, violent crime and spousal abuse rates have been higher during hotter years, seasons, months, and days (Anderson et al., 1997). Studies from other social science fields converge in finding that throughout history, higher temperatures have predicted increased individual violence, wars, and revolutions (Hsiang et al., 2013). Craig Anderson and his colleagues (2000, 2011) have projected that, other things being equal, global warming of 4 degrees Fahrenheit (about 2 degrees Celsius) could induce tens of thousands of additional assaults and murders—and that's before the added violence inducement from climate change–related drought, poverty, food insecurity, and migration. When overheated, we think, feel, and act more aggressively.

> **LaunchPad** How have researchers studied these concepts? Play the role of a researcher by designing one of these studies in **Immersive Learning: How Would You Know If Hot Temperatures Cause Aggression?**

REINFORCEMENT AND MODELING Aggression may naturally follow aversive events, but learning can alter natural reactions. We learn when our behavior is reinforced, and we learn by watching others.

In situations where experience has taught us that aggression pays, we are likely to act aggressively again. Children whose aggression has successfully intimidated other children may become bullies. Animals that have successfully fought to get food or mates become increasingly ferocious. To foster a kinder, gentler world we had best model and reward sensitivity and cooperation from an early age, perhaps by training parents to discipline without modeling violence. Parent-training programs often advise parents to avoid modeling violence by not screaming and hitting. Instead, parents should reinforce desirable behaviors and frame statements positively. ("When you finish loading the dishwasher you can go play," rather than "If you don't load the dishwasher, you'd better watch out.").

Different cultures model, reinforce, and evoke different tendencies toward violence. For example, crime rates have been higher and average happiness lower in times and places marked by a great disparity between rich and poor (Messias et al., 2011; Oishi et al., 2011; Wilkinson & Pickett, 2009). And fathers matter (Triandis, 1994). Even after controlling for parental education, race, income, and teen motherhood, American male youths from father-absent homes are incarcerated at twice the rate of their peers (Harper & McLanahan, 2004).

Violence can vary by culture within a country. Richard Nisbett and Dov Cohen (1996) analyzed violence among White Americans in southern towns settled by Scots-Irish herders whose tradition emphasized "manly honor," the use of arms to protect one's flock, and a history of coercive slavery. Compared with their White counterparts in New England towns settled by the more traditionally peaceful Puritan, Quaker, and Dutch farmer-artisans, the cultural descendants of those herders had triple the homicide rates and were more supportive of physically punishing children, of warfare initiatives, and of uncontrolled gun ownership. "Culture of honor" states also have had higher rates of students bringing weapons to school and of school shootings (Brown et al., 2009).

MEDIA MODELS FOR VIOLENCE Parents are hardly the only aggression models. Television, films, video games, and the internet offer supersized portions of violence. An adolescent boy faced with a real-life challenge may "act like a man"—at least an action-film man—by

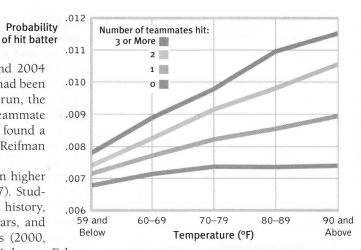

FIGURE 12.8

TEMPERATURE AND RETALIATION Researchers looked for occurrences of batters hit by pitches during 4,566,468 pitcher-batter matchups across 57,293 Major League Baseball games since 1952 (Larrick et al., 2011). The probability of a hit batter increased if one or more of the pitcher's teammates had been hit, and also with temperature.

frustration-aggression principle the principle that frustration—the blocking of an attempt to achieve some goal—creates anger, which can generate aggression.

social script a culturally modeled guide for how to act in various situations.

intimidating or eliminating the threat. Violent video game playing tends to make us less sensitive to cruelty (Arriaga et al., 2015). It also primes us to respond aggressively when provoked. And media violence teaches us **social scripts**—culturally provided mental files for how to act in certain situations. As more than 100 studies confirm, we sometimes imitate what we've viewed. Watching risk-glorifying behaviors (dangerous driving, extreme sports, unprotected sex) increases real-life risk taking (Fischer et al., 2011). Watching violent behaviors (murder, robbery) can increase real-life aggressiveness (Anderson et al., 2017).

Music lyrics also write social scripts. German university men who listened to woman-hating song lyrics administered the most hot chili sauce to a woman. Listening to man-hating song lyrics had a similar effect upon women (Fischer & Greitemeyer, 2006).

How does repeatedly watching pornographic films affect viewers? As pornography has become readily available, rates of reported sexual violence have decreased in the United States (though not in Canada, Australia, and Europe). Nevertheless, just as repeated viewing of on-screen violence helps immunize us to aggression, repeated viewing of pornography—even nonviolent pornography—makes sexual aggression seem less serious (Harris, 1994). In one experiment, undergraduates viewed six brief films each week for six weeks (Zillmann & Bryant, 1984). Some viewed sexually explicit films; others viewed films with no sexual content. Three weeks later, both groups, after reading a newspaper report about a man convicted of raping a female hitchhiker, suggested an appropriate prison term. Compared with sentences recommended by the control group, the sex film viewers recommended terms that were half as long. In other studies that explored pornography's effects on aggression toward relationship partners, pornography consumption predicted both self-reported aggression and participants' willingness to administer laboratory noise blasts to their partner (Lambert et al., 2011; Peter & Valkenburg, 2016).

Pornography with violent sexual content can increase men's readiness to behave aggressively toward women. A statement by 21 social scientists noted, "Pornography that portrays sexual aggression as pleasurable for the victim increases the acceptance of the use of coercion in sexual relations" (Surgeon General, 1986). Contrary to much popular opinion, viewing such depictions does not provide an outlet for bottled-up impulses. Rather, "in laboratory studies measuring short-term effects, exposure to violent pornography increases punitive behavior toward women."

DO VIOLENT VIDEO GAMES TEACH SOCIAL SCRIPTS FOR VIOLENCE? Experiments worldwide indicate that playing positive games produces positive effects (Greitemeyer & Mügge, 2014; Prot et al., 2014). For example, playing the classic video game *Lemmings*, where a goal was to help others, increased real-life helping. So, might a parallel effect occur after playing games that enact violence? Violent video games became an issue for public debate after teenagers in more than a dozen places seemed to mimic the carnage in the shooter games they had so often played (Anderson, 2004, 2013).

In 2002, three young men in Michigan spent part of a night drinking beer and playing *Grand Theft Auto III*. Using simulated cars, they ran down pedestrians, then beat them with fists, leaving a bloody body behind (Kolker, 2002). These same young men then went out for a real drive. Spotting a 38-year-old man on a bicycle, they ran him down with their car, got out, stomped and punched him, and returned home to play the game some more. (The victim, a father of three, died six days later.)

This is but one anecdote, and, as we social scientists say, "The plural of anecdote is not evidence." Yet such incidents of violent mimicry make us wonder: What are the effects of actively role-playing aggression? Does it cause people to become less sensitive to violence and more open to violent acts? Nearly 400 studies of 130,000 people offer some answers (Anderson et al., 2010; Calvert et al., 2017). Video games can prime aggressive thoughts, decrease empathy, and increase aggression. University men who spent the most hours playing violent video games have also tended to be the most physically aggressive (Anderson & Dill, 2000). For example, they more often acknowledged having hit or attacked someone else. And people randomly assigned to play a game involving bloody murders with groaning victims (rather than to play nonviolent *Myst*) became more hostile. On a follow-up task, they were more likely to blast intense noise at a fellow student.

COINCIDENCE OR CAUSE? In 2011, Norwegian Anders Behring Breivik bombed government buildings in Oslo, and then went to a youth camp where he shot and killed 69 people, mostly teens. As a player of first-person shooter games, Breivik stirred debate when he commented that "I see MW2 [*Modern Warfare 2*] more as a part of my training-simulation than anything else." Did his violent game playing—and that of the 2012 mass murderer of Newtown, Connecticut's first-grade children—contribute to the violence, or was it a merely coincidental association? To explore such questions, psychologists experiment.

AFP/Getty Images

Studies of young adolescents reveal that those who play a lot of violent video games become more aggressive and see the world as more hostile (Bushman, 2016; Exelmans et al., 2015; Gentile, 2009). Compared with nongaming kids, they get into more arguments and fights and earn poorer grades.

Ah, but is this merely because naturally hostile kids are drawn to such games? Apparently not. Comparisons of gamers and nongamers who scored low on hostility measures revealed a difference in the number of fights reported. Almost 4 in 10 violent-game players had been in fights, compared with only 4 in 100 of the nongaming kids (Anderson, 2004). Some researchers believe that, due partly to the more active participation and rewarded violence of game play, violent video games have even greater effects on aggressive behavior and cognition than do violent TV shows and movies (Anderson & Warburton, 2012).

Other researchers are unimpressed by such findings (Ferguson, 2013b, 2014, 2015). They note that from 1996 to 2006, video game sales increased yet youth violence declined. They argue that other factors—depression, family violence, peer influence—better predict aggression. The focused fun of game playing can also satisfy basic needs for a sense of competence, control, and social connection (Granic et al., 2014).

* * *

To sum up, research reveals biological, psychological, and social-cultural influences on aggressive behavior. Complex behaviors, including violence, have many causes, making any single explanation an oversimplification. Asking what causes violence is therefore like asking what causes cancer. Those who study the effects of asbestos exposure on cancer rates may remind us that asbestos is indeed a cancer cause, but it is only one among many. Like so much else, aggression is a biopsychosocial phenomenon (**FIGURE 12.9**).

A happy concluding note: Historical trends suggest that the world is becoming less violent over time (Pinker, 2011). That people vary across time and place reminds us that environments differ. Yesterday's plundering Vikings have become today's peace-promoting Scandinavians. Like all behavior, aggression arises from the interaction of persons and situations.

"Study finds exposure to violent children causes increased aggression in video game characters." —The [satirical] Onion, March 6, 2017

"Research demonstrates a consistent relation between violent video game use and increases in aggressive behavior, aggressive cognitions and aggressive affect, and decreases in prosocial behavior, empathy and sensitivity to aggression." —American Psychological Association Task Force on Violent Media, 2015

ENGAGE **ASK YOURSELF**

In what ways have you been affected by social scripts for aggression? How have shows, movies, and video games contributed such scripts?

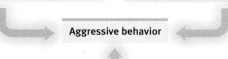

Biological influences:
• heredity
• biochemical factors, such as testosterone and alcohol
• neural factors, such as a severe head injury

Psychological influences:
• dominating behavior (which boosts testosterone levels in the blood)
• believing that alcohol has been ingested (whether it has or not)
• frustration
• aggressive role models
• rewards for aggressive behavior
• low self-control

Aggressive behavior

Social-cultural influences:
• *deindividuation*, or a loss of self-awareness and self-restraint
• challenging environmental factors, such as crowding, heat, and direct provocations
• parental models of aggression
• minimal father involvement
• rejection from a group
• exposure to violent media

 FIGURE 12.9

BIOPSYCHOSOCIAL UNDERSTANDING OF AGGRESSION Because many factors contribute to aggressive behavior, there are many ways to change such behavior, including learning anger management and communication skills, and avoiding violent media and video games.

RETRIEVE IT • • •   *ANSWERS IN APPENDIX E*

RI-2 What biological, psychological, and social-cultural influences interact to produce aggressive behaviors?

🔒 REVIEW ANTISOCIAL RELATIONS

⤵ Learning Objectives

TEST YOURSELF Answer these repeated Learning Objective Questions on your own (before checking the answers in Appendix D) to improve your retention of the concepts (McDaniel et al., 2009, 2015).

12-11 What is *prejudice*? How do explicit and implicit prejudice differ?

12-12 What groups are frequent targets of prejudice?

12-13 What are some social, emotional, and cognitive roots of prejudice, and what are some ways to eliminate prejudice?

12-14 How does psychology's definition of *aggression* differ from everyday usage? What biological factors make us more prone to hurt one another?

12-15 What psychological and social-cultural factors may trigger aggressive behavior?

⤵ Terms and Concepts to Remember

TEST YOURSELF Write down the definition yourself, then check your answer on the referenced page.

prejudice, **p. 435**

stereotype, **p. 435**

discrimination, **p. 435**

just-world phenomenon, **p. 438**

ingroup, **p. 438**

outgroup, **p. 438**

ingroup bias, **p. 438**

scapegoat theory, **p. 438**

other-race effect, **p. 438**

aggression, **p. 441**

frustration-aggression principle, **p. 443**

social script, **p. 444**

⤵ Experience the Testing Effect

TEST YOURSELF Answer the following questions on your own first, then check your answers in Appendix E.

1. Prejudice toward a group involves negative feelings, a tendency to discriminate, and overly generalized beliefs referred to as _____.

2. If several well-publicized murders are committed by members of a particular group, we may tend to react with fear and suspicion toward all members of that group. What psychological principle can help explain this reaction?

3. The other-race effect occurs when we assume that other groups are _____ (more/less) homogeneous than our own group.

4. Evidence of a biochemical influence on aggression is the finding that
   a. aggressive behavior varies widely from culture to culture.
   b. animals can be bred for aggressiveness.
   c. stimulation of an area of the brain's limbic system produces aggressive behavior.
   d. a higher-than-average level of the hormone testosterone is associated with violent behavior in males.

5. When those who feel frustrated become angry and aggressive, this is referred to as the _____- _____ _____.

6. Studies show that parents of delinquent young people tend to use physical force to enforce discipline. This suggests that aggression can be
   a. learned through direct rewards.
   b. triggered by exposure to violent media.
   c. learned through observation of aggressive models.
   d. caused by hormone changes at puberty.

7. A conference of social scientists studying the effects of pornography unanimously agreed that violent pornography
   a. has little effect on most viewers.
   b. is the primary cause of reported and unreported rapes.
   c. leads viewers to be more accepting of coercion in sexual relations.
   d. has no effect, other than short-term arousal and entertainment.

8. The aspect of pornographic films that most directly influences men's aggression toward women seems to be the
   a. length of the film.
   b. eroticism portrayed.
   c. depictions of sexual violence.
   d. attractiveness of the actors.

Continue testing yourself with 📖 **LearningCurve** or 📖 **Achieve Read & Practice** to learn and remember most effectively.

⟿ Prosocial Relations

mere exposure effect the phenomenon that repeated exposure to novel stimuli increases liking of them.

As social animals—as people who need people—we often approach others not with closed fists, but with open arms. Social psychologists focus not only on the dark side of social relationships, but also on the bright side, by studying *prosocial* behavior—behavior that intends to help or benefit someone. Our positive behaviors toward others are evident from explorations of attraction, altruism, and peacemaking.

ATTRACTION

ENGAGE Pause a moment and think about your relationships with two people—a close friend and someone who has stirred your romantic feelings. What psychological chemistry binds us together in friendship or love? Social psychology suggests some answers.

The Psychology of Attraction

LOQ 12-16 Why do we befriend or fall in love with some people but not others?

We endlessly wonder how we can win others' affection and what makes our own affections flourish or fade. Does familiarity breed contempt, or does it amplify affection? Do birds of a feather flock together, or do opposites attract? Is it what's inside that counts, or does physical attractiveness matter, too? To explore these questions, let's consider three ingredients of our liking for one another: proximity, attractiveness, and similarity.

PROXIMITY Before friendships become close, they must begin. *Proximity*—geographic nearness—is friendship's most powerful predictor. Proximity can provide opportunities for aggression. But much more often it breeds liking (and sometimes even marriage) among those who live in the same neighborhood, sit nearby in class, work in the same office, share the same parking lot, or eat in the same dining hall. Look around. Mating starts with meeting.

Proximity breeds liking partly because of the **mere exposure effect.** Repeated exposure to novel visual stimuli increases our liking for them. By age 3 months, infants prefer photos of the race they most often see—usually their own race (Kelly et al., 2007). Familiarity with a face also makes it look happier (Carr et al., 2017). Mere exposure increases our liking not only for familiar faces, but also for familiar nonsense syllables, geometric figures, and Chinese characters, and for the letters of our own name (Moreland & Zajonc, 1982; Nuttin, 1987; Zajonc, 2001). So, within certain limits (after which the effect wears off), familiarity feeds fondness (Bornstein, 1989, 1999; Montoya et al., 2017). This would come as no surprise to the young Taiwanese man who wrote more than 700 letters to his girlfriend, urging her to marry him. She did marry—the mail carrier (Steinberg, 1993).

No face is more familiar than your own. And that helps explain an interesting finding by Lisa DeBruine (2002, 2004): We like other people when their faces incorporate some

Jeffrey Mayer/Getty Images

(a)   (b)

ENGAGE **WHICH IS THE REAL SOFÍA VERGARA?** The mere exposure effect applies even to ourselves. Because the human face is not perfectly symmetrical, the face we see in the mirror is not the same face our friends see. Most of us prefer the familiar mirror image, while our friends like the reverse (Mita et al., 1977). The person actress Sofía Vergara sees in the mirror each morning is shown in (b), and that's the photo she would probably prefer.

morphed features of our own. When McMaster University students played a game with a supposed other player, they were more trusting and cooperative when the other person's image had some of their own facial features morphed into it. In me I trust.

MODERN MATCHMAKING Those who have not found a romantic partner in their immediate proximity may cast a wider net by joining an online dating service. Millions search for love on one of 8000 dating sites (Hatfield, 2016). In 2015, 27 percent of 18- to 24-year-old Americans tried an online dating service or mobile dating app (Smith, 2016).

Online matchmaking definitely expands the pool of potential mates (Finkel et al., 2012a,b). But how effective is the matchmaking? Compared with those formed in person, internet-formed friendships and romantic relationships are, on average, slightly more likely to last and be satisfying (Bargh & McKenna, 2004; Bargh et al., 2002; Cacioppo et al., 2013). In one study, people disclosed more, with less posturing, to those whom they met online (McKenna et al., 2002). When conversing online with someone for 20 minutes, they felt more liking for that person than they did for someone they had met and talked with face-to-face. This was true even when (unknown to them) it was the same person! Internet friendships often feel as real and important as in-person relationships.

Small wonder that a survey found a leading online matchmaker enabling more than 500 U.S. marriages a day (Harris Interactive, 2010). By one estimate, online dating is now responsible for about a fifth of U.S. marriages (Crosier et al., 2012). And in a national survey of straight and gay/lesbian couples, nearly a quarter of heterosexual couples and some two-thirds of same-sex couples met online (Rosenfeld & Thomas, 2012; see **FIGURE 12.10**).

Speed dating pushes the search for romance into high gear. In a process pioneered by a matchmaking Jewish rabbi, people meet a succession of prospective partners, either in person or via webcam (Bower, 2009). After a 3- to 8-minute conversation, people move on to the next prospect. (In an in-person heterosexual meeting, one group—usually the women—remains seated while the other group circulates.) Those who want to meet again can arrange for future contact. For many participants, 4 minutes is enough time to form a feeling about a conversational partner and to register whether the partner likes them (Eastwick & Finkel, 2008a,b).

For researchers, speed dating offers a unique opportunity for studying influences on our first impressions of potential romantic partners. Some recent findings:

- *People who fear rejection often elicit it.* After a 3-minute speed date, those who most feared rejection were least often selected for a follow-up date (McClure & Lydon, 2014).

- *Given more options, people make more superficial choices.* When people meet lots of potential partners, they focus on more easily assessed characteristics, such as height and weight (Lenton & Francesconi, 2010).

- *Men wish for future contact with more of their speed dates; women tend to be choosier.* But this difference disappears if the conventional roles are reversed, so that men stay seated while women circulate (Finkel & Eastwick, 2009).

PHYSICAL ATTRACTIVENESS Once proximity affords us contact, what most affects our first impressions? The person's sincerity? Intelligence? Personality? Hundreds of experiments (all in a heterosexual context) reveal that it is something more superficial: physical appearance. This finding is unnerving for those of us taught that "beauty is only skin deep" and "appearances can be deceiving."

In one early study, researchers randomly matched new University of Minnesota students for a Welcome Week dance (Walster et al., 1966). Before the dance, the researchers gave each student a battery of personality and aptitude tests, and they rated each student's physical attractiveness. During the blind date, the couples danced and talked for more than two hours and then took a brief intermission to rate their dates.

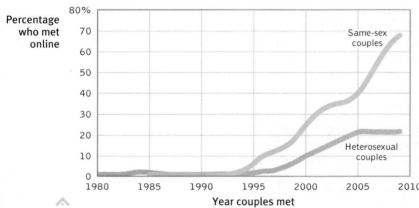

FIGURE 12.10
PERCENTAGE OF HETEROSEXUAL AND SAME-SEX COUPLES WHO MET ONLINE (Data from Rosenfeld & Thomas, 2012.)

"I'd like to meet the algorithm that thought we'd be a good match."

What predicted whether they liked each other? Only one thing: appearance. Both the men and the women liked good-looking dates best. Women are more likely than men to say that another's looks don't affect them (Lippa, 2007). But studies show that a man's looks do affect women's behavior (Eastwick et al., 2014a,b). In speed-dating experiments, as in Tinder swipes, attractiveness influences first impressions for both sexes (Belot & Francesconi, 2006; Finkel & Eastwick, 2008).

Physical attractiveness also predicts how often people date and how popular they feel. And it affects initial impressions of people's personalities. We don't assume that attractive people are more compassionate, but we do perceive them as healthier, happier, more sensitive, more successful, and more socially skilled (Eagly et al., 1991; Feingold, 1992; Hatfield & Sprecher, 1986).

For those who find the importance of looks unfair and unenlightened, three other findings may be reassuring.

- People's attractiveness is surprisingly unrelated to their self-esteem and happiness (Diener et al., 1995; Major et al., 1984). Unless we have just compared ourselves with superattractive people, few of us (thanks, perhaps, to the mere exposure effect) view ourselves as unattractive (Thornton & Moore, 1993).

- Strikingly attractive people are sometimes suspicious that praise for their work may simply be a reaction to their looks. Less attractive people have been more likely to accept praise as sincere (Berscheid, 1981).

- For couples who were friends before lovers—who became romantically involved long after first meeting—looks matter less (Hunt et al., 2015). With slow-cooked love, shared values and interests matter more.

Beauty is also in the eye of the culture. Hoping to look attractive, people across the globe have pierced and tattooed their bodies, lengthened their necks, bound their feet, dyed their hair, and artificially lightened or darkened their skin and hair. They have gorged themselves to achieve a full figure or liposuctioned fat to achieve a slim one, applied chemicals hoping to rid themselves of unwanted hair or to regrow wanted hair, strapped on leather garments to make their breasts seem smaller or relied on push-up bras and surgery to make them look bigger. Cultural ideals change over time. For women in North America, the ultrathin ideal of the Roaring Twenties gave way to the soft, voluptuous Marilyn Monroe ideal of the 1950s, only to be replaced by today's lean yet busty ideal.

Some aspects of heterosexual attractiveness, however, do cross place and time (Cunningham et al., 2005; Langlois et al., 2000). By providing reproductive clues, bodies influence sexual attraction. As evolutionary psychologists explain, men in many cultures, from Australia to Zambia, judge women as more attractive if they have a youthful, fertile appearance, suggested by a low waist-to-hip ratio (Karremans et al., 2010; Perilloux et al., 2010; Platek & Singh, 2010). Women feel attracted to healthy-looking men, but especially to those who seem mature, dominant, masculine, and affluent (Gallup & Frederick, 2010; Gangestad et al., 2010). But faces matter, too. When people rate opposite-sex faces and bodies separately, the face tends to be the better predictor of overall physical attractiveness (Currie & Little, 2009; Peters et al., 2007).

"Personal beauty is a greater recommendation than any letter of introduction." —Aristotle, *Apothegms*, 330 B.C.E.

Sean Caffrey/Getty Images

Blend Images/Alamy

svetikd/Getty Images

IN THE EYE OF THE BEHOLDER
Conceptions of attractiveness vary by culture and over time. Yet some adult physical features, such as a healthy appearance and a relatively symmetrical face, seem attractive everywhere.

EXTREME MAKEOVER In affluent, beauty-conscious cultures, increasing numbers of people, such as reality TV star Kylie Jenner, have turned to cosmetic procedures to change their looks.

Our feelings also influence our attractiveness judgments. Imagine two people: One is honest, humorous, and polite. The other is rude, unfair, and abusive. Which one is more attractive? Most people perceive the person with the appealing traits as more physically attractive (Lewandowski et al., 2007). Or imagine being paired with a stranger of the sex you find attractive, who listens intently to your self-disclosures. Might you feel a twinge of sexual attraction toward that empathic person? Student volunteers did, in several experiments (Birnbaum & Reis, 2012). Our feelings influence our perceptions. Those we like we find attractive.

In a Rodgers and Hammerstein musical of the fairy tale, Prince Charming asks Cinderella, "Do I love you because you're beautiful, or are you beautiful because I love you?" Chances are it's both. As we see our loved ones again and again, their physical imperfections grow less noticeable and their attractiveness grows more apparent (Beaman & Klentz, 1983; Gross & Crofton, 1977). Shakespeare said it in *A Midsummer Night's Dream:* "Love looks not with the eyes, but with the mind." Come to love someone and watch beauty grow. Love sees loveliness.

SIMILARITY So proximity has brought you into contact with someone, and your appearance has made an acceptable first impression. What influences whether you will become friends? As you get to know each other, will the chemistry be better if you are opposites or if you are alike?

It makes a good story—extremely different types liking or loving each other: Rat, Mole, and Badger in *The Wind in the Willows,* the Beauty and the Beast, Frog and Toad in Arnold Lobel's books. These stories delight us by expressing what we seldom experience. In real life, opposites retract (Rosenbaum, 1986; Montoya & Horton, 2013). Compared with randomly paired people, friends and couples are far more likely to share common attitudes, beliefs, and interests (and, for that matter, age, religion, race, education, intelligence, smoking behavior, and economic status). Moreover, the more alike people are, the more their liking endures (Byrne, 1971). Journalist Walter Lippmann was right to suppose that love lasts "when the lovers love many things together, and not merely each other." Similarity breeds content.

Proximity, attractiveness, and similarity are not the only determinants of attraction. We also like those who like us. This is especially true when our self-image is low. When we believe someone likes us, we feel good and respond to them warmly, which leads them to like us even more (Curtis & Miller, 1986). To be liked is powerfully rewarding.

Indeed, all the findings we have considered so far can be explained by a simple *reward theory of attraction:* We will like those whose behavior is rewarding to us, including those who are both able and willing to help us achieve our goals (Montoya & Horton, 2014). When people live or work in close proximity to us, it requires less time and effort to develop the friendship and enjoy its benefits. When people are attractive, they are aesthetically pleasing, and associating with them can be socially rewarding. When people share our views, they reward us by validating our beliefs.

YOU'RE WHITE WITH BLACK STRIPES, I'M BLACK WITH WHITE STRIPES. MAYBE WE'RE JUST TOO DIFFERENT FOR THIS TO WORK.

Similarity attracts; perceived dissimilarity does not.

"I like the Pope unless the Pope doesn't like me. Then I don't like the Pope." —Donald Trump, February 18, 2016

ASK YOURSELF

To what extent have your closest relationships been affected by proximity, physical attractiveness, and similarity?

LaunchPad Test your own ability to improve your relationships by engaging online with **Immersive Learning: Assess Your Strengths—Are You a "Skilled Opener," and How Does This Affect Your Relationships?**

Romantic Love

LOQ 12-17 How does romantic love typically change as time passes?

Sometimes people move quickly from initial impressions to friendship to the more intense, complex, and mysterious state of romantic love. If love endures, temporary *passionate love* will mellow into a lingering *companionate love* (Hatfield, 1988).

PASSIONATE LOVE **Passionate love** mixes something new with something positive (Aron et al., 2000; Coulter & Malouff, 2013). We intensely desire to be with our partner, and seeing our partner stimulates blood flow to a brain region linked to craving and obsession (Acevedo et al., 2012; Hatfield et al., 2015).

The *two-factor theory of emotion* (Chapter 10) explains the intense positive absorption of passionate love (Hatfield, 1988). That theory assumes that

- emotions have two ingredients—*physical arousal* plus *cognitive appraisal*.
- arousal from any source can enhance one emotion or another, depending on how we interpret and label the arousal.

In one classic experiment, researchers studied men crossing two bridges above British Columbia's rocky Capilano River (Dutton & Aron, 1974, 1989). One, a swaying footbridge, was 230 feet (70 meters) above the rocks; the other was low and solid. As the men came off each bridge, an attractive young woman working for the researchers intercepted them and asked them to fill out a short questionnaire. She then offered her phone number in case they wanted to hear more about her project. Far more of the men who had just crossed the high bridge—which left their hearts pounding—accepted the number and later called the woman.

To be revved up and to associate some of that arousal with a desirable person is to feel the pull of passion. Adrenaline makes the heart grow fonder. Sexual desire + a growing attachment = passionate love (Berscheid, 2010).

COMPANIONATE LOVE Although the desire and attachment of romantic love often endure, the intense absorption in the other, the thrill of the romance, the giddy "floating on a cloud" feelings typically fade. Does this mean the French are correct in saying that "love makes the time pass and time makes love pass"? Or can friendship and commitment keep a relationship going after the passion cools?

As love matures, it typically becomes a steadier **companionate love**—a deep, affectionate attachment (Hatfield, 1988). Like a passing storm, the flood of passion-facilitating hormones (testosterone, dopamine, adrenaline) subsides. But another hormone, *oxytocin*, remains, supporting feelings of trust, calmness, and bonding with the mate. This shift from passion to attachment may have adaptive value (Reis & Aron, 2008). Passionate love often produces children, whose survival is aided by the parents' waning obsession with each another.

In the most satisfying of marriages, attraction and sexual desire endure, minus the obsession of early stage romance (Acevedo & Aron, 2009). Indeed, failure to appreciate passionate love's limited half-life can doom a relationship (Berscheid et al., 1984). Recognizing the short duration of obsessive passionate love, some societies deem such feelings an irrational reason for marrying. Better, they say, to search for (or have someone search for you) a partner with a compatible background and interests. Non-Western cultures, where people often rate love as less important for marriage, do have lower divorce rates (Levine et al., 1995).

passionate love an aroused state of intense positive absorption in another, usually present at the beginning of a romantic relationship.

companionate love the deep affectionate attachment we feel for those with whom our lives are intertwined.

Snapshots at jasonlove.com

Bill looked at Susan, Susan at Bill. Suddenly death didn't seem like an option. This was love at first sight.

HI & LOIS

"When two people are under the influence of the most violent, most insane, most delusive, and most transient of passions, they are required to swear that they will remain in that excited, abnormal, and exhausting condition continuously until death do them part." —George Bernard Shaw, "Getting Married," 1908

One key to a gratifying and enduring relationship is **equity.** When equity exists—when both partners receive in proportion to what they give—the chances for sustained and satisfying companionate love have been good (Gray-Little & Burks, 1983; Van Yperen & Buunk, 1990). In one national survey, "sharing household chores" ranked third, after "faithfulness" and a "happy sexual relationship," on a list of nine things people associated with successful marriages. As the Pew Research Center (2007) summarized, "I like hugs. I like kisses. But what I really love is help with the dishes."

Equity's importance extends beyond marriage. Mutually sharing one's self and possessions, making decisions together, giving and getting emotional support, promoting and caring about each other's welfare—all of these acts are at the core of every type of loving relationship (Sternberg & Grajek, 1984). It's true for lovers, for parent and child, and for close friends.

Sharing includes **self-disclosure,** revealing intimate details about ourselves—our likes and dislikes, our dreams and worries, our proud and shameful moments. "When I am with my friend," noted the Roman statesman Seneca, "methinks I am alone, and as much at liberty to speak anything as to think it." Self-disclosure breeds liking, and liking breeds self-disclosure (Collins & Miller, 1994). As one person reveals a little, the other reciprocates, the first then reveals more, and on and on, as friends or lovers move to deeper intimacy (Baumeister & Bratslavsky, 1999).

One experiment marched some student pairs through 45 minutes of increasingly self-disclosing conversation—from "What is the greatest accomplishment of your life?" to "When did you last cry in front of another person? By yourself?" Other pairs spent the time with small-talk questions, such as "What was your high school like?" (Aron et al., 1997). By the experiment's end, those experiencing the escalating intimacy felt much closer to their conversation partner than did the small-talkers. Likewise, after dating couples spent 45 minutes answering such questions, they felt increased love (Welker et al., 2014).

In addition to equity and self-disclosure, a third key to enduring love is *positive support.* Relationship conflicts are inevitable, but hurtful communications are not. Do we more often express sarcasm or support, scorn or sympathy, sneers or smiles? For unhappy couples, disagreements, criticisms, and put-downs are routine. For happy couples in enduring relationships, positive interactions (compliments, touches, laughing) outnumber negative interactions (sarcasm, disapproval, insults) by at least 5 to 1 (Gottman, 2007; see also Sullivan et al., 2010).

In the mathematics of love, self-disclosing intimacy + mutually supportive equity = enduring companionate love.

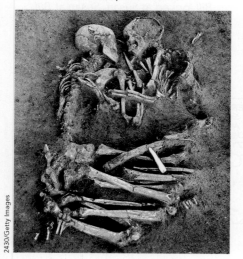

LOVE IS AN ANCIENT THING This 5000- to 6000-year-old "Romeo and Juliet" young couple was unearthed locked in embrace, near Rome.

2430/Getty Images

🔒 **RETRIEVE IT • • •**   *ANSWERS IN APPENDIX E*

RI-3 How does the two-factor theory of emotion help explain *passionate love?*

RI-4 Two vital components for maintaining *companionate love* are
_____ and _____-_____.

ALTRUISM

LOQ 12-18 What is *altruism?* When are people most—and least—likely to help?

Altruism is an unselfish concern for the welfare of others. In rescuing his jailer, Dirk Willems exemplified altruism. Willems fits the definition of a *hero*—moral, courageous, and protective of those in need (Kinsella et al., 2015). Carl Wilkens and Paul Rusesabagina displayed another heroic example of altruism in Kigali, Rwanda. Wilkens, a Seventh-day Adventist missionary, was living there in 1994 with his family when militia from the Hutu ethnic group began to slaughter members of a minority ethnic group, the Tutsis. The U.S. government, church leaders, and friends all implored Wilkens to leave. He refused. After evacuating his family, and even after every other American had left Kigali, he alone stayed and contested the 800,000-person genocide. When the militia came to kill him and his Tutsi servants, Wilkens' Hutu neighbors deterred them. Despite repeated death threats, he spent his days running roadblocks to take food and water to orphanages and to negotiate, plead, and bully his way through the bloodshed, saving lives time and again. "It just seemed the right thing to do," he later explained (Kristof, 2004).

Elsewhere in Kigali, Rusesabagina, a Hutu married to a Tutsi and the acting manager of a luxury hotel, was sheltering more than 1200 terrified Tutsis and moderate Hutus. When most international peacekeepers abandoned the city and hostile militia threatened his guests in the "Hotel Rwanda" (as it came to be called in a 2004 movie), the courageous Rusesabagina began cashing in past favors. He bribed the militia and telephoned influential people abroad to exert pressure on local authorities, thereby sparing the lives of the hotel's occupants, despite the surrounding chaos. Both Wilkens and Rusesabagina were displaying altruism.

Altruism became a major concern of social psychologists after an especially vile act. On March 13, 1964, a stalker repeatedly stabbed Kitty Genovese, then raped her as she lay dying outside her Queens, New York, apartment at 3:30 A.M. "Oh, my God, he stabbed me!" Genovese screamed into the early morning stillness. "Please help me!" Windows opened and lights went on as some neighbors heard her screams. Her attacker fled and then returned to stab and rape her again. Until it was too late, no one called police or came to her aid.

Bystander Intervention

Reflecting on initial reports of the Genovese murder and other such tragedies, most commentators were outraged by the bystanders' apparent "apathy" and "indifference." Rather than blaming the onlookers, social psychologists John Darley and Bibb Latané (1968b) attributed their inaction to an important situational factor—the presence of others. Given certain circumstances, they suspected, most of us might behave similarly. To paraphrase the French writer Voltaire, we all are guilty of the good we did not do.

After staging emergencies under various conditions, Darley and Latané assembled their findings into a decision scheme: We will help only if the situation enables us first to *notice* the incident, then to *interpret* it as an emergency, and finally to *assume responsibility* for helping (**FIGURE 12.11**). At each step, the presence of others can turn us away from the path that leads to helping.

One of Darley and Latané's experiments staged a fake emergency as students in separate laboratory rooms took turns talking over an intercom. Only the person whose microphone was switched on could be heard. When his turn came, one student (an accomplice of the experimenters) pretended to have an epileptic seizure, and he called for help (Darley & Latané, 1968a).

How did the others react? As **FIGURE 12.12** shows, those who believed only they could hear the victim—and therefore thought they alone were responsible for helping him—usually went to his aid. Students who thought others could also hear the victim's cries were more likely to do nothing. When more people shared responsibility for helping—when there was a *diffusion of responsibility*—any single listener was less likely to help. Indeed, inattention and diffused responsibility contribute to the "global bystander nonintervention" as millions of far-away people die of hunger, disease, and genocide (Pittinsky & Diamante, 2015).

equity a condition in which people receive from a relationship in proportion to what they give to it.

self-disclosure the act of revealing intimate aspects of ourselves to others.

altruism unselfish regard for the welfare of others.

 FIGURE 12.11

THE DECISION-MAKING PROCESS FOR BYSTANDER INTERVENTION Before helping, one must first notice an emergency, then correctly interpret it, and then feel responsible. (Data from Darley & Latané, 1968b.)

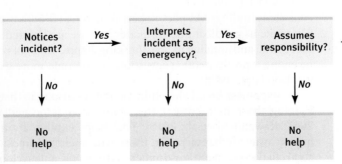

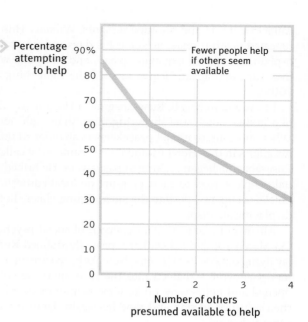

FIGURE 12.12

RESPONSES TO A SIMULATED EMERGENCY When people thought they alone heard the calls for help from a person they believed to be having an epileptic seizure, they usually helped. But when they thought four others were also hearing the calls, fewer than one-third responded. (Data from Darley & Latané, 1968a.)

Percentage attempting to help

Fewer people help if others seem available

Number of others presumed available to help

🔒 📖 LaunchPad To test your understanding of emergency helping, engage online with **Concept Practice: When Will People Help Others?**

© 2006 Nick Downes

ASK YOURSELF

Imagine being a newcomer needing directions at a busy bus terminal. What could you do to increase the odds that someone would assist you, and what sort of person would be most likely to help?

Hundreds of additional experiments have confirmed this **bystander effect.** For example, researchers and their assistants took 1497 elevator rides in three cities and "accidentally" dropped coins or pencils in front of 4813 fellow passengers (Latané & Dabbs, 1975). When alone with the person in need, 40 percent helped; in the presence of 5 other bystanders, only 20 percent helped. Ironically, Kitty Genovese's killer, Winston Moseley, was captured thanks to the intervention of a single bystander who confronted him as he later burgled a home. Disbelieving Moseley's explanation that he was helping the owners move, the bystander called another neighbor, who called police, and then pulled wires to disable Moseley's car (Kassin, 2017).

Observations of behavior in thousands of these situations—relaying an emergency phone call, aiding a stranded motorist, donating blood, picking up dropped books, contributing money, giving time—show that the odds of our helping someone depend on the characteristics of the person, the situation, and our own internal state. The odds of helping are highest when

- the person appears to need and deserve help.
- the person is in some way similar to us.
- the person is a woman.
- we have just observed someone else being helpful.
- we are not in a hurry.
- we are in a small town or rural area.
- we are feeling guilty.
- we are focused on others and not preoccupied.
- we are in a good mood.

This last result, that happy people are helpful people, is one of psychology's most consistent findings. As poet Robert Browning (1868) observed, "Oh, make us happy and you make us good!" It doesn't matter how we are cheered. Whether by being made to feel successful and intelligent, by thinking happy thoughts, by finding money, or even by receiving a posthypnotic suggestion, we become more generous and more eager to help (Carlson et al., 1988).

So happiness breeds helpfulness. But it's also true that helpfulness breeds happiness. Helping those in need activates brain areas associated with reward (Harbaugh et al., 2007; Kawamichi et al., 2015). That helps explain a curious finding: People who give money away are happier than those who spend it almost entirely on themselves. In one controlled experiment, researchers gave people an envelope with cash and instructed one group to spend it on themselves and another to spend it on others (Dunn et al., 2008;

Dunn & Norton, 2013). Which group was happiest at the day's end? It was, indeed, those assigned to the spend-it-on-others condition. And in a survey of more than 200,000 people worldwide, people in both rich and poor countries were happier with their lives if they had donated to a charity in the last month. Just reflecting on an instance of spending money on others provides most people with a mood boost (Aknin et al., 2013).

> 🔒 **RETRIEVE IT • • •** *ANSWERS IN APPENDIX E*
>
> **RI-5** Why didn't anybody help Kitty Genovese? What social psychology principle did this incident illustrate?

Helping: Self-Interest or Socialization?

LOQ 12-19 How do social exchange theory and social norms explain helping behavior?

Why do we help? One widely held view is that self-interest underlies all human interactions, that our constant goal is to maximize rewards and minimize costs. Accountants call it *cost-benefit analysis*. Philosophers call it *utilitarianism*. Social psychologists call it **social exchange theory.** If you are considering donating blood, you may weigh the costs of doing so (time, discomfort, anxiety) against the benefits (reduced guilt, social approval, good feelings). If the rewards exceed the costs, you will help.

Others believe we help because we have been socialized to do so, through norms that prescribe how we *ought* to behave. (Everett et al., 2015). Two such norms are the *reciprocity norm* and the *social-responsibility norm*.

The **reciprocity norm** is the expectation that we should return help, not harm, to those who have helped us. In our relations with others of similar status, this norm compels us to give (in favors, gifts, or social invitations) about as much as we receive. Sometimes this means "paying it forward," as happened in one experiment, when people who were treated generously became more likely to be generous to a stranger (Tsvetkova & Macy, 2014). Returning favors feels good, making the norm of reciprocity a pleasant strategy to help others (Hein et al., 2016).

The reciprocity norm kicked in after Dave Tally, a Tempe, Arizona, homeless man, found $3300 in a backpack that an Arizona State University student had misplaced on his way to buy a used car (Lacey, 2010). Instead of using the cash for much-needed bike repairs, food, and shelter, Tally turned the backpack in to the social service agency where he volunteered. To reciprocate Tally's help, the backpack's owner thanked him with a monetary reward. Hearing about Tally's self-giving deeds, dozens of others also sent him money and job offers.

The **social-responsibility norm** is the expectation that we should help those who need our help—young children and others who cannot give as much as they receive—even if the costs outweigh the benefits. Europeans are most welcoming of asylum seekers who are most vulnerable—those, for example, who have been tortured or have no surviving family (Bansak et al., 2016). Many world religions encourage their followers to practice the social-responsibility norm, and sometimes this leads to prosocial behavior. Between 2006 and 2008, Gallup polls sampled more than 300,000 people across 140 countries, comparing the "highly religious" (who said religion was important to them and who had attended a religious service in the prior week) to the less religious. The highly religious, despite being poorer, were about 50 percent more likely to report having "donated money to a charity in the last month" and to have volunteered time to an organization (Pelham & Crabtree, 2008).

FROM CONFLICT TO PEACE

Positive social norms encourage generosity and enable group living. But conflicts often divide us. One response to recent conflict- and scarcity-driven mass migrations has been increasing nationalism and nativism. Moreover, *every day* the world continues to spend almost $5 billion for arms and armies—money that could be used for needed housing, nutrition, education, and health care. Knowing that wars begin in human minds, psychologists have wondered: What in the human mind causes destructive conflict? How might the perceived threats of social diversity be replaced by a spirit of cooperation?

bystander effect the tendency for any given bystander to be less likely to give aid if other bystanders are present.

social exchange theory the theory that our social behavior is an exchange process, the aim of which is to maximize benefits and minimize costs.

reciprocity norm an expectation that people will help, not hurt, those who have helped them.

social-responsibility norm an expectation that people will help those needing their help.

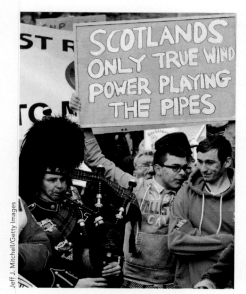

NOT IN MY OCEAN! Many people support alternative energy sources, including wind turbines. But proposals to construct wind farms in real-world places elicit less support. Wind turbines in the Highlands and off the coast of Scotland have produced heated debate over the benefits of clean energy versus the costs of altering treasured scenic views.

Elements of Conflict

LOQ **12-20** How do social traps and mirror-image perceptions fuel social conflict?

To a social psychologist, a **conflict** is a perceived incompatibility of actions, goals, or ideas. The elements of conflict are much the same, whether partners sparring, political groups feuding, or nations at war. In each situation, conflict may seed positive change, or be a destructive process that can produce unwanted results. Among the destructive processes are *social traps* and *distorted perceptions*.

SOCIAL TRAPS In some situations, pursuing our personal interests also supports our collective well-being. As capitalist Adam Smith wrote in *The Wealth of Nations* (1776), "It is not from the benevolence of the butcher, the brewer, or the baker that we expect our dinner, but from their regard to their own interest." In other situations, we *harm* our collective well-being by pursuing our personal interests. Such situations are **social traps.**

Researchers have created mini social traps in laboratory games that require two participants to choose between pursuing their immediate self-interest, at others' expense, versus cooperating for mutual benefit. Many real-life situations similarly pit our individual interests against our communal well-being. Individual car owners reason, "Electric cars are more expensive. Besides, the fuel that I burn in my one car doesn't noticeably add to the greenhouse gases." When enough people reason similarly, the collective result risks disaster—climate change with rising seas and more extreme weather. In 2018, as Cape Town faced the prospect of "Day Zero"—when their water reservoir was predicted to be depleted after three years of drought—the city pleaded for voluntary water conservation. Alas, with nearly 4 million residents, it was easy for any individual to think that "my washing my hair or flushing the toilet won't noticeably affect the remaining water." The result: Businesses and residents conserved less than hoped for, hastening the reservoir depletion (Maxmen, 2018).

Social traps challenge us to reconcile our right to pursue our personal well-being with our responsibility for the well-being of all. Psychologists have therefore explored ways to convince people to cooperate for their mutual betterment—through agreed-upon *regulations,* through better *communication,* and through promoting *awareness* of our responsibilities toward community, nation, and the whole of humanity (Dawes, 1980; Linder, 1982; Sato, 1987). Given effective regulations, communication, and awareness, people more often cooperate, whether playing a laboratory game or the real game of life.

ENEMY PERCEPTIONS Psychologists have noted that those in conflict have a curious tendency to form diabolical images of one another. These distorted images are, ironically, so similar that we call them **mirror-image perceptions:** As we see "them"—as untrustworthy, with evil intentions—so "they" see us. Each demonizes the other. My political party has benevolent motives; the other party is malevolent (Waytz et al., 2014).

Mirror-image perceptions can often feed a vicious cycle of hostility. If Juan believes Maria is annoyed with him, he may snub her, causing her to act in ways that justify his perception. As with individuals, so with countries. Perceptions can become **self-fulfilling prophecies**—beliefs that confirm themselves by influencing the other country to react in ways that seem to justify them.

Individuals and nations alike tend to see their own actions as responses to provocation, not as the causes of what happens next. Perceiving themselves as returning tit for tat, they often hit back harder, as University College London volunteers did in one experiment (Shergill et al., 2003). After feeling pressure on their own finger, they were to use a mechanical device to press on another volunteer's finger. Although told to reciprocate with the same amount of pressure, they typically responded with about 40 percent more force than they had just experienced. Despite seeking only to respond in kind, their touches soon escalated to hard presses, much as when each child after a fight claims that "I just poked him, but he hit me harder."

Mirror-image perceptions feed similar cycles of hostility on the world stage. To most people, torture seems more justified when done by "us" rather than "them" (Tarrant et al., 2012). In some American media reports, Muslims who kill have been portrayed as fanatical, hateful terrorists, while an American who allegedly killed 16 Afghans was portrayed as stressed out from marriage problems, four tours of duty, and a friend's having had his leg blown off (Greenwald, 2012).

conflict a perceived incompatibility of actions, goals, or ideas.

social trap a situation in which the conflicting parties, by each pursuing their self-interest rather than the good of the group, become caught in mutually destructive behavior.

mirror-image perceptions mutual views often held by conflicting people, as when each side sees itself as ethical and peaceful and views the other side as evil and aggressive.

self-fulfilling prophecy a belief that leads to its own fulfillment.

The point is not that truth must lie midway between two such views (one may be more accurate). The point is that enemy perceptions often form mirror images. Moreover, as enemies change, so do perceptions. In American minds and media, the "bloodthirsty, cruel, treacherous" Japanese of World War II later became our "intelligent, hardworking, self-disciplined, resourceful allies" (Gallup, 1972).

> 🔒 **RETRIEVE IT • • •**   *ANSWERS IN APPENDIX E*
>
> **RI-6** Why do sports fans tend to feel a sense of satisfaction when their archrival team loses? Do such feelings, in other settings, make conflict resolution more challenging?

Promoting Peace

LOQ 12-21 What can we do to promote peace?

How can we make peace? Can contact, cooperation, communication, and conciliation transform the antagonisms fed by prejudice and conflict into attitudes that promote peace? Research indicates that, in some cases, they can.

CONTACT Does it help to put two conflicting parties into close contact? It depends. Negative contact increases *dis*liking (Graf et al., 2014; Paolini et al., 2014). But positive contact—especially noncompetitive contact between parties of equal status, such as fellow store clerks—typically helps. Initially prejudiced co-workers of different races have, in such circumstances, usually come to accept one another. This finding is confirmed by a statistical digest of more than 500 studies of face-to-face contact between majority people and outgroups (such as ethnic minorities, older and LGBTQ people, and those with disabilities). Among the quarter-million people studied across 38 nations, contact has correlated with (and in experiments has led to) more positive attitudes (Al Ramiah & Hewstone, 2013; Lemmer & Wagner, 2015; Pettigrew & Tropp, 2011). Some examples:

- With cross-racial contact, South Africans' interracial attitudes have moved "into closer alignment" (Dixon et al., 2007; Finchilescu & Tredoux, 2010; Swart et al., 2011).

- Heterosexuals' attitudes toward gay people are influenced not only by *what* they know but also by *whom* they know (Collier et al., 2012; Smith et al., 2009). In surveys, the reason people most often give for becoming more supportive of same-sex marriage is "having friends, family, or acquaintances who are gay or lesbian" (Pew, 2013a). And in the United States, where attitudes toward gays have become more positive, 87 percent of people now say they know someone who is gay (Pew, 2016).

- Friendly interracial contact, say between Blacks and Whites as roommates, improves attitudes toward others of the different race, and even toward other racial groups (Gaither & Sommers, 2013; Tausch et al., 2010).

However, contact is not always enough. In many schools, ethnic groups segregate themselves in lunchrooms, in classrooms, and elsewhere on school grounds (Alexander & Tredoux, 2010; Clack et al., 2005; Schofield, 1986). People in each group often think that they would welcome more contact with the other group, but they assume the other group does not reciprocate the wish (Richeson & Shelton, 2007). "I don't reach out to them, because I don't want to be rebuffed; they don't reach out to me, because they're just not interested." When such mirror-image misperceptions are corrected, friendships may form and prejudices melt.

COOPERATION To see if enemies could overcome their differences, researcher Muzafer Sherif (1966) set a conflict in motion at a boys' summer camp. He separated 22 Oklahoma City boys into two separate camp areas. Then he had the two groups compete for prizes in a series of activities. Before long, each group became intensely proud of itself and hostile to the other group's "sneaky," "smart-alecky stinkers." Food wars broke out. Cabins were ransacked. Fistfights had to be broken up by camp counselors. Brought together, the two groups avoided each other, except to taunt and threaten. Little did they know that within a few days, they would be friends.

Rosiland Beckton

STRANGERS COMING TOGETHER
When a family got stuck in a Florida rip current, no less than 80 of their fellow beachgoers formed a human chain, rescuing them. Said one of the witnesses, Rosalind Beckton: "All races & ages join[ed] together to save lives" (AP, 2017).

"Me against my brother, my brothers and me against my cousins, then my cousins and me against strangers."
—Bedouin proverb

"Most of us have overlapping identities which unite us with very different groups. We *can* love what we are, without hating what—and who—we are *not*. We can thrive in our own tradition, even as we learn from others." —Nobel Peace Prize lecture, UN Secretary-General Kofi Annan, 2001

SUPERORDINATE GOALS OVERRIDE DIFFERENCES Cooperative efforts to achieve shared goals are an effective way to break down social barriers.

Grant Hindsley/AP Photo

Sherif accomplished this by giving them **superordinate goals**—shared goals that could be achieved only through cooperation. When he arranged for the camp water supply to "fail," all 22 boys had to work together to restore the water. To rent a movie in those pre-Netflix days, they all had to pool their resources. To move a stalled truck, the boys needed to combine their strength, pulling and pushing together. Having used isolation and competition to make strangers into enemies, Sherif used shared predicaments and goals to turn enemies into friends. What reduced conflict was not mere contact, but *cooperative* contact.

Critics suggest that Sherif's research team encouraged the conflict, in hopes the study would illustrate their expectations about socially toxic competition and socially beneficial cooperation (Perry, 2018). Yet shared predicaments have had powerfully unifying effects on other groups as well. Minority-group members facing rejection or discrimination develop strong ingroup identification (Bauer et al., 2014; Ramos et al., 2012). Children and youth exposed to war or conflict also develop strong social identities. Israeli children growing up in conflict areas often develop conflict-supportive perceptions, beliefs, and emotions regarding their shared adversary (Nasie et al., 2016). Such interpretations build ingroup solidarity but also insensitivity to the pain experienced by those in the outgroup (Levy et al., 2016).

In the aftermath of a divisive U.S. primary election, party members will usually eventually reunify when facing their shared threat—the opposition party candidate. At such times, cooperation can lead people to define a new, inclusive group that dissolves their former subgroups (Dovidio & Gaertner, 1999). If this were a social psychology experiment, you might seat members of two groups not on opposite sides, but alternately around a table. Give them a new, shared name. Have them work together. Then watch "us" and "them" become "we." After the 9/11 terrorist attacks, one 18-year-old New Jersey man described this shift in his own social identity: "I just thought of myself as Black. But now I feel like I'm an American, more than ever" (Sengupta, 2001). In an actual experiment, White Americans who read a newspaper article about a terrorist threat against all Americans subsequently expressed reduced prejudice against Black Americans (Dovidio et al., 2004).

If cooperative contact between rival group members encourages positive attitudes, might this principle bring diverse students together? Could cooperative learning in classrooms create interracial friendships, while also enhancing student achievement? Experiments with adolescents from 11 countries confirm that, in each case, the answer is *Yes* (Roseth et al., 2008). In the classroom as in the sports arena, members of multi-ethnic groups who work together on projects typically come to feel friendly toward one another. Knowing this, thousands of teachers have made multiethnic cooperative learning part of their classroom experience.

The power of cooperative activity to make friends of former enemies has led psychologists to urge increased international exchange and cooperation. Some experiments have found that just imagining the shared threat of global climate change reduces international hostilities (Pyszczynski et al., 2012). From adjacent Brazilian tribes to European countries, formerly conflicting groups have managed to build interconnections, interdependence, and a shared social identity as they seek common goals (Fry, 2012). As we engage in mutually beneficial trade, as we work to protect our common destiny on this fragile planet, and as we become more aware that our hopes and fears are shared, we can transform misperceptions that feed conflict into feelings of solidarity based on common interests.

COMMUNICATION When real-life conflicts become intense, a third-party mediator—a marriage counselor, labor mediator, diplomat, community volunteer—may facilitate much-needed communication (Rubin et al., 1994). Mediators help each party voice its viewpoint and understand the other's needs and goals. If successful, mediators can replace a competitive *win-lose* orientation with a cooperative *win-win* orientation that leads to a mutually beneficial resolution. A classic example: Two friends, after quarreling over an orange, agreed to split it. One squeezed his half for juice. The other used the peel from her half to flavor a cake. If only the two had communicated their motives to one another, they could have hit on the win-win solution of one having all the juice, the other all the peel.

CONCILIATION Understanding and cooperative resolution are most needed, yet least likely, in times of anger or crisis (Bodenhausen et al., 1994; Tetlock, 1988). When conflicts intensify, images become more stereotyped, judgments more rigid, and communication more difficult, or even impossible. Each party is likely to threaten, coerce, or retaliate. In the weeks before the 1990 Gulf War, U.S. President George H. W. Bush threatened, in the full glare of publicity, to "kick Saddam's ass." Iraqi President Saddam Hussein communicated in kind, threatening to make Americans "swim in their own blood." In 2017, U.S. President Donald Trump insulted North Korean leader Kim Jong-un as "Little Rocket Man" and threatened North Korea with "fire and fury like the world has never seen," to which Kim replied, "I will surely and definitely tame the mentally deranged U.S. dotard with fire (Glasser, 2017)."

Under such conditions, is there an alternative to war or surrender? Social psychologist Charles Osgood (1962, 1980) advocated a strategy of *Graduated and Reciprocated Initiatives in Tension-Reduction,* nicknamed **GRIT.** In applying GRIT, one side first announces its recognition of mutual interests and its intent to reduce tensions. It then initiates one or more small, conciliatory acts. Without weakening one's retaliatory capability, this modest beginning opens the door for reciprocity by the other party. Should the enemy respond with hostility, one reciprocates in kind. But so, too, with any conciliatory response.

In laboratory experiments, small conciliatory gestures—a smile, a touch, a word of apology—have allowed both parties to begin edging down the tension ladder to a safer rung where communication and mutual understanding can begin (Lindskold, 1978; Lindskold & Han, 1988). In a real-world international conflict, U.S. President John F. Kennedy's gesture of stopping atmospheric nuclear tests began a series of reciprocated conciliatory acts that culminated in the 1963 atmospheric test-ban treaty. (At the time of this writing, even Trump and Kim were negotiating.)

As working toward shared goals reminds us, we are more alike than different. Civilization advances not by conflict and cultural isolation, but by tapping the knowledge, the skills, and the arts that are each culture's legacy to the whole human race. Open societies are enriched by cultural sharing (Sowell, 1991). We have China to thank for paper and printing and for the magnetic compass that enabled the great explorations. We have Egypt to thank for trigonometry. We have the Islamic world and India's Hindus to thank for our Arabic numerals. While celebrating and claiming these diverse cultural legacies, we can also welcome the continuing enrichment of today's cultural diversity. We can view ourselves as instruments in a human orchestra. And we can therefore affirm our own culture's heritage while building bridges of communication, understanding, and cooperation across our cultural traditions.

POLARIZED AMERICANS FINDING COMMON GROUND In local communities across the United States, mediators are helping "red" (conservative) and "blue" (liberal) citizens discover their common ground and form friendships (see Better-Angels.org).

 ASK YOURSELF

ENGAGE

Do you regret not getting along with some friend or family member? How might you resolve the conflict using concepts you have just learned?

superordinate goals shared goals that override differences among people and require their cooperation.

GRIT Graduated and Reciprocated Initiatives in Tension-Reduction—a strategy designed to decrease international tensions.

 **RETRIEVE IT** • • •   *ANSWERS IN APPENDIX E*

RI-7 What are some ways to reconcile conflicts and promote peace?

🔒 REVIEW PROSOCIAL RELATIONS

⟩ Learning Objectives

TEST YOURSELF Answer these repeated Learning Objective Questions on your own (before checking the answers in Appendix D) to improve your retention of the concepts (McDaniel et al., 2009, 2015).

12-16 Why do we befriend or fall in love with some people but not others?

12-17 How does romantic love typically change as time passes?

12-18 What is *altruism*? When are people most—and least—likely to help?

12-19 How do social exchange theory and social norms explain helping behavior?

12-20 How do social traps and mirror-image perceptions fuel social conflict?

12-21 What can we do to promote peace?

⟩ Terms and Concepts to Remember

TEST YOURSELF Write down the definition yourself, then check your answer on the referenced page.

mere exposure effect, **p. 447**

passionate love, **p. 451**

companionate love, **p. 451**

equity, **p. 453**

self-disclosure, **p. 453**

altruism, **p. 453**

bystander effect, **p. 455**

social exchange theory, **p. 455**

reciprocity norm, **p. 455**

social-responsibility norm, **p. 455**

conflict, **p. 456**

social trap, **p. 456**

mirror-image perceptions, **p. 456**

self-fulfilling prophecy, **p. 456**

superordinate goals, **p. 459**

GRIT, **p. 459**

⟩ Experience the Testing Effect

TEST YOURSELF Answer the following questions on your own first, then check your answers in Appendix E.

1. The more familiar a stimulus becomes, the more we tend to like it. This exemplifies the _____ _____ effect.

2. A happy couple celebrating their fiftieth wedding anniversary is likely to experience deep _____ love, even though their _____ love has probably decreased over the years.

3. After vigorous exercise, you meet an attractive person, and you are suddenly seized by romantic feelings for that person. This response supports the two-factor theory of emotion, which assumes that emotions, such as passionate love, consist of physical arousal plus
   a. a reward.
   b. proximity.
   c. companionate love.
   d. our interpretation of that arousal.

4. The bystander effect states that a particular bystander is less likely to give aid if
   a. the victim is similar to the bystander in appearance.
   b. no one else is present.
   c. other people are present.
   d. the incident occurs in a deserted or rural area.

5. Our enemies often have many of the same negative impressions of us as we have of them. This exemplifies the concept of _____-_____ perceptions.

6. One way of resolving conflicts and fostering cooperation is by giving rival groups shared goals that help them override their differences. These are called _____ goals.

Continue testing yourself with 📚 **LearningCurve** or ≋ **Achieve Read & Practice** to learn and remember most effectively.

Personality

CHAPTER 13

People Images/Getty Images

Lady Gaga dazzles millions with her unique musical arrangements, tantalizing outfits, and provocative performances. In shows worldwide, Lady Gaga's most predictable feature is her unpredictability. She has worn a meat dress to an award show, sported 16-inch heels to meet with U.S. President Barack Obama (who later described the interaction as "a little intimidating"), and inspired Super Bowl viewers with her halftime musical performance.

Yet even unpredictable Lady Gaga exhibits distinctive and enduring ways of thinking, feeling, and behaving. Her fans and critics alike can depend on her openness to new experiences and the energy she gets from the spotlight. And they can also rely on her painstaking dedication to her music and performances. She describes her high school self as "very dedicated, very studious, and very disciplined." Now, in adulthood, she shows similar self-discipline: "I'm very detailed—every minute of the show has got to be perfect." This chapter focuses on the ways we all demonstrate unique and persistent patterns of thinking, feeling, and behaving—our *personality*.

Much of this book deals with personality. Earlier chapters considered biological influences on personality; personality development across the life span; how personality relates to learning, motivation, emotion, and health; and social influences on personality. The next chapter will study disorders of personality. This chapter focuses on personality itself—what it is and how researchers study it.

We begin with two historically important theories of personality that have become part of Western culture: Sigmund Freud's *psychoanalytic theory* and the *humanistic theories*.

personality an individual's characteristic pattern of thinking, feeling, and acting.

psychodynamic theories theories that view personality with a focus on the unconscious and the importance of childhood experiences.

psychoanalysis Freud's theory of personality that attributes thoughts and actions to unconscious motives and conflicts; the techniques used in treating psychological disorders by seeking to expose and interpret unconscious tensions.

These sweeping perspectives on human nature laid the foundation for later personality theorists and for what this chapter presents next: newer scientific explorations of personality.

Today's personality researchers study the basic dimensions of personality, and the interaction of persons and environments. They also study self-esteem, self-serving bias, and cultural influences on our concept of self—that sense of "Who I am." And they study the unconscious mind—with findings that probably would have surprised even Freud. ▶

Classic Perspectives on Personality

WHAT IS PERSONALITY?

LEARNING OBJECTIVE QUESTION (LOQ)

13-1 What is *personality,* and what theories inform our understanding of personality?

Psychologists have varied ways to view and study **personality**—our characteristic pattern of thinking, feeling, and acting. Sigmund Freud's *psychoanalytic theory* proposed that childhood sexuality and unconscious motivations influence personality. The *humanistic theories* focused on our inner capacities for growth and self-fulfillment. Later theorists built upon these two broad perspectives. *Trait theories* examine characteristic patterns of behavior *(traits).* *Social-cognitive theories* explore the interaction between people's traits (including their thinking) and their social context. Let's begin with Freud's work, and its modern-day descendant, *psychodynamic theories.*

PSYCHODYNAMIC THEORIES

Psychodynamic theories of personality view human behavior as a dynamic interaction between the conscious mind and unconscious mind, including associated motives and conflicts. These theories are descended from Freud's **psychoanalysis**—his theory of personality and the associated treatment techniques. Freud was the first to focus clinical attention on our unconscious mind.

Freud's Psychoanalytic Perspective: Exploring the Unconscious

LOQ 13-2 How did Sigmund Freud's treatment of psychological disorders lead to his view of the unconscious mind?

Ask 100 people on the street to name a notable deceased psychologist, suggested Keith Stanovich (1996, p. 1), and "Freud would be the winner hands down." In the popular mind, he is to psychology what Elvis Presley is to rock music. Freud's influence lingers not only in psychiatry and clinical psychology, but also in literary and film interpretation. Almost 9 in 10 American college courses that reference psychoanalysis have been outside of psychology departments (Cohen, 2007). Freud's early twentieth-century concepts penetrate our twenty-first-century language. Without realizing their source, we may speak of *ego, repression, projection, sibling rivalry, Freudian slips,* and *fixation.* So, who was Freud, and what did he teach?

Like all of us, Sigmund Freud was a product of his times. His late 1800s Victorian era was a time of tremendous discovery and scientific advancement, but also of sexual suppression and male dominance. Men's and women's roles were clearly defined, with male superiority assumed and only male sexuality generally acknowledged (discreetly).

SIGMUND FREUD (1856–1939) "I was the only worker in a new field."

These assumptions influenced Freud's thinking about personality. He believed that psychological troubles resulted from men's and women's unresolved conflicts with their expected roles.

Long before entering the University of Vienna in 1873, young Freud showed signs of independence and brilliance. He so loved reading plays, poetry, and philosophy that he once ran up a bookstore debt beyond his means. As a teen he often took his evening meal in his tiny bedroom in order to lose no time from his studies. After medical school he set up a private practice specializing in nervous disorders. Before long, however, he faced patients whose disorders made no neurological sense. A patient might have lost all feeling in a hand—yet there is no sensory nerve that, if damaged, would numb the entire hand and nothing else. Freud's search for a cause for such disorders set his mind running in a direction destined to change human self-understanding.

Do some neurological disorders have psychological causes? Observing patients led Freud to his "discovery" of the **unconscious.** He speculated that lost feeling in one's hand might be caused by a fear of touching one's genitals; that unexplained blindness or deafness might be caused by not wanting to see or hear something that aroused intense anxiety. How might such disorders be treated? After some early unsuccessful trials with hypnosis, Freud turned to **free association,** in which he told the patient to relax and say whatever came to mind, no matter how embarrassing or trivial. He assumed that a line of mental dominoes had fallen from his patients' distant past to their troubled present, and that the chain of thought revealed by free association would allow him to retrace that line into his patients' unconscious. There, painful memories, often from childhood, could then be retrieved, reviewed, and released.

Basic to Freud's theory was his belief that the mind is mostly hidden (**FIGURE 13.1**). Our *conscious* awareness is like the part of an iceberg that floats above the surface. Beneath this awareness is the larger *unconscious* mind, with its thoughts, wishes, feelings, and memories. Some of these thoughts we store temporarily in a *preconscious* area, from which we can retrieve them into conscious awareness. Of greater interest to Freud was the mass of unacceptable passions and thoughts that he believed we *repress,* or forcibly block from our consciousness because they would be too unsettling to acknowledge. Freud believed that without our awareness, these troublesome feelings and ideas powerfully influence us. Such feelings, he said, sometimes surface in disguised forms—the work we choose, the beliefs we hold, our daily habits, our upsetting symptoms.

"The female . . . acknowledges the fact of her castration, and with it, too, the superiority of the male and her own inferiority; but she rebels against this unwelcome state of affairs." —Sigmund Freud, *Female Sexuality,* 1931

FIGURE 13.1

FREUD'S IDEA OF THE MIND'S STRUCTURE Psychologists have used an iceberg image to illustrate Freud's idea that the mind is mostly hidden beneath the conscious surface. Note that the *id* is totally unconscious, but *ego* and *superego* operate both consciously and unconsciously. Unlike the parts of a frozen iceberg, however, the id, ego, and superego interact.

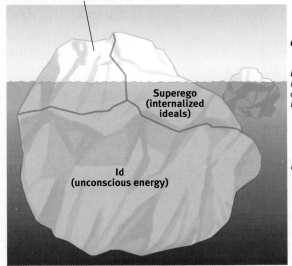

Ego (mostly conscious; makes peace between the id and the superego)

Superego (internalized ideals)

Id (unconscious energy)

Conscious mind

Preconscious (outside awareness but accessible)

Unconscious mind

PERSONALITY STRUCTURE

LOQ 13-3 What was Freud's view of personality?

Freud believed that human personality, including its emotions and strivings, arises from a conflict between impulse and restraint—between our aggressive, pleasure-seeking biological urges and our internalized social controls over these urges. Freud believed personality arises from our efforts to resolve this basic conflict—to express these impulses in ways that bring satisfaction without also bringing guilt or punishment. To understand the mind's dynamics during this conflict, Freud proposed three interacting systems: the *id, ego,* and *superego* (Figure 13.1).

The **id's** unconscious psychic energy constantly strives to satisfy basic drives to survive, reproduce, and aggress. The id operates on the *pleasure principle:* It seeks immediate gratification. To understand the id's power, think of a newborn infant crying out for satisfaction, caring nothing for the outside world's conditions and demands. Or think of people with a present rather than future time perspective—those who abuse tobacco, alcohol, and other drugs, and would sooner party now than sacrifice today's temporary pleasure for future success and happiness (Fernie et al., 2013; Friedel et al., 2014; Keough et al., 1999).

unconscious according to Freud, a reservoir of mostly unacceptable thoughts, wishes, feelings, and memories. According to contemporary psychologists, information processing of which we are unaware.

free association in psychoanalysis, a method of exploring the unconscious in which the person relaxes and says whatever comes to mind, no matter how trivial or embarrassing.

id a reservoir of unconscious psychic energy that, according to Freud, strives to satisfy basic sexual and aggressive drives. The id operates on the *pleasure principle,* demanding immediate gratification.

"Fifty is plenty."   "Hundred and fifty."

THE EGO STRUGGLES TO RECONCILE THE DEMANDS OF SUPEREGO AND ID, SAID FREUD.

"I heard that as soon as we become aware of our sexual impulses, whatever they are, we'll have to hide them."

"Oh, for goodness' sake! Smoke!"

As the **ego** develops, the young child responds to the real world. The ego, operating on the *reality principle,* seeks to gratify the id's impulses in realistic ways that will bring long-term pleasure. (Imagine what would happen if, lacking an ego, we acted on our unrestrained sexual or aggressive impulses.) The ego contains our partly conscious perceptions, thoughts, judgments, and memories.

Around age 4 or 5, Freud theorized, a child's ego recognizes the demands of the newly emerging **superego,** the voice of our moral compass (conscience) that forces the ego to consider not only the real but also the *ideal.* The superego focuses on how we *ought* to behave. It strives for perfection, judging actions and producing positive feelings of pride or negative feelings of guilt. Someone with an exceptionally strong superego may be virtuous yet guilt ridden; another with a weak superego may be outrageously self-indulgent and remorseless.

Because the superego's demands often oppose the id's, the ego struggles to reconcile the two. The ego is the personality "executive," mediating among the impulsive demands of the id, the restraining demands of the superego, and the real-life demands of the external world. If chaste Conner feels sexually attracted to Tatiana, his ego may satisfy both his id and superego by joining a volunteer organization that Tatiana attends regularly.

 LaunchPad To review Freud's components of personality, take advantage of the online **Concept Practice: Freud's Personality Structure.**

PERSONALITY DEVELOPMENT

LOQ 13-4 What developmental stages did Freud propose?

Analysis of his patients' histories convinced Freud that personality forms during life's first few years. He concluded that children pass through a series of **psychosexual stages,** during which the id's pleasure-seeking energies focus on distinct pleasure-sensitive areas of the body called *erogenous zones* (**TABLE 13.1**). Each stage offers its own challenges, which Freud saw as conflicting tendencies.

Freud believed that during the *phallic stage,* for example, boys develop both unconscious sexual desires for their mother and jealousy and hatred for their father, whom they consider a rival. These feelings, he thought, lead boys to feel guilty and to fear punishment, perhaps by castration, from their father. Such was Freud's (1897) own experience: "I have found, in my own case too, [the phenomenon of] being in love with my mother and jealous of my father, and I now consider it a universal event in early childhood." He called this collection of feelings the **Oedipus complex** after the Greek legend of Oedipus, who unknowingly killed his father and married his mother. Some psychoanalysts in Freud's era believed that girls experience a parallel *Electra complex* (named after a mythological plotting daughter).

Children eventually cope with the threatening feelings, said Freud, by repressing them and by trying to become like the rival parent. It's as though something inside the

TABLE 13.1

Freud's Psychosexual Stages

Stage	Focus
Oral (0–18 months)	Pleasure centers on the mouth—sucking, biting, chewing
Anal (18–36 months)	Pleasure focuses on bowel and bladder elimination; coping with demands for control
Phallic (3–6 years)	Pleasure zone is the genitals; coping with incestuous sexual feelings
Latency (6 years to puberty)	A phase of dormant sexual feelings
Genital (puberty on)	Maturation of sexual interests

child decides, "If you can't beat 'em [the same-sex parent], join 'em." Through this **iden-tification** process, children's superegos gain strength as they incorporate many of their parents' values. Freud believed that identification with the same-sex parent provides what psychologists now call our *gender identity*—our sense of being male, female, or some combination of the two. Freud presumed that our early childhood relations—especially with our parents and other caregivers—influence our developing identity, personality, and frailties.

In Freud's view, conflicts unresolved during earlier psychosexual stages could surface as maladaptive behavior in the adult years. At any point in the oral, anal, or phallic stages, strong conflict could lock, or **fixate,** the person's pleasure-seeking energies in that stage. A person who had been either orally overindulged or deprived (perhaps by abrupt, early weaning) might fixate at the oral stage. This orally fixated adult could exhibit either passive dependence (like that of a nursing infant) or an exaggerated denial of this depen-dence (by acting tough or uttering biting sarcasm). Or the person might continue to seek oral gratification by smoking or excessive eating. In such ways, Freud suggested, the twig of personality is bent at an early age.

DEFENSE MECHANISMS

LOQ 13-5 How did Freud think people defended themselves against anxiety?

Anxiety, said Freud, is the price we pay for civilization. As members of social groups, we must control our sexual and aggressive impulses, not act them out. But sometimes the ego fears losing control of this inner id-superego war. The presumed result is a dark cloud of unfocused anxiety that leaves us feeling unsettled but unsure why.

Freud proposed that the ego protects itself with **defense mechanisms**—tactics that reduce or redirect anxiety by distorting reality (**TABLE 13.2**). For Freud, *all defense mechanisms function indirectly and unconsciously.* Just as the body unconsciously defends itself against disease, so also does the ego unconsciously defend itself against anxiety. For example, **repression** banishes anxiety-arous-ing wishes and feelings from consciousness. According to Freud, *repression underlies all the other defense mechanisms.* However, because repression is often incomplete, repressed urges may appear as symbols in dreams or as slips of the tongue in casual conversation.

> "I remember your name perfectly but I just can't think of your face." —Oxford professor W. A. Spooner (1844–1930) famous for his linguistic flip-flops (spoonerisms). Spooner rebuked one student for "fighting a liar in the quadrangle" and another who "hissed my mystery lecture," adding "You have tasted two worms."

ego the largely conscious, "executive" part of personality that, according to Freud, mediates among the demands of the id, the superego, and reality. The ego operates on the *reality principle,* satisfying the id's desires in ways that will realistically bring pleasure rather than pain.

superego the part of personality that, according to Freud, represents internalized ideals and provides standards for judgment (the conscience) and for future aspirations.

psychosexual stages the childhood stages of development (oral, anal, phallic, latency, genital) during which, according to Freud, the id's pleasure-seeking energies focus on distinct erogenous zones.

Oedipus [ED-uh-puss] complex according to Freud, a boy's sexual desires toward his mother and feelings of jealousy and hatred for the rival father.

identification the process by which, according to Freud, children incorporate their parents' values into their developing superegos.

fixation in personality theory, according to Freud, a lingering focus of pleasure-seek-ing energies at an earlier psychosexual stage, in which conflicts were unresolved.

defense mechanisms in psychoanalytic theory, the ego's protective methods of reducing anxiety by unconsciously distorting reality.

repression in psychoanalytic theory, the basic defense mechanism that banishes from consciousness anxiety-arousing thoughts, feelings, and memories.

 TABLE 13.2

Six Defense Mechanisms

Freud believed that *repression,* the basic mechanism that banishes anxiety-arousing impulses, enables other defense mechanisms, six of which are listed here.

Defense mechanism	Unconscious Process Employed to Avoid Anxiety-Arousing Thoughts or Feelings	Example
Regression	Retreating to an earlier psychosexual stage, where some psychic energy remains fixated	A little boy reverts to the oral comfort of thumb sucking in the car on the way to his first day of school.
Reaction formation	Switching unacceptable impulses into their opposites	Repressing angry feelings, a person displays exaggerated friendliness.
Projection	Disguising one's own threatening impulses by attributing them to others	"The thief thinks everyone else is a thief" (an El Salvadoran saying).
Rationalization	Offering self-justifying explanations in place of the real, more threatening unconscious reasons for one's actions	A habitual drinker says she drinks with her friends "just to be sociable."
Displacement	Shifting sexual or aggressive impulses toward a more acceptable or less threatening object or person	A little girl kicks the family dog after her mother puts her in a time-out.
Denial	Refusing to believe or even perceive painful realities	A partner denies evidence of his loved one's affair.

"Good morning, beheaded—uh, I mean beloved."

REGRESSION Faced with a mild stressor, children and young orangutans seek protection and comfort from their caregivers. Freud might have interpreted these behaviors as regression, a retreat to an earlier developmental stage.

collective unconscious Carl Jung's concept of a shared, inherited reservoir of memory traces from our species' history.

Thematic Apperception Test (TAT) a projective test in which people express their inner feelings and interests through the stories they make up about ambiguous scenes.

projective test a personality test, such as the Rorschach or TAT, that provides ambiguous images designed to trigger projection of one's inner dynamics.

Rorschach inkblot test the most widely used projective test; a set of 10 inkblots, designed by Hermann Rorschach; seeks to identify people's inner feelings by analyzing their interpretations of the blots.

Freud believed he could glimpse the unconscious seeping through when a financially stressed patient, not wanting any large pills, said, "Please do not give me any bills, because I cannot swallow them." (Today we call these "Freudian slips.") Freud also viewed jokes as expressions of repressed sexual and aggressive tendencies, and dreams as the "royal road to the unconscious." The remembered content of dreams (their *manifest content*) he believed to be a censored expression of the dreamer's unconscious wishes (the dream's *latent content*). In his dream analyses, Freud searched for patients' inner conflicts.

🔒 **RETRIEVE IT • • •**   *ANSWERS IN APPENDIX E*

RI-1 According to Freud's ideas about the three-part personality structure, the _____ operates on the *reality principle* and tries to balance demands in a way that produces long-term pleasure rather than pain; the _____ operates on the *pleasure principle* and seeks immediate gratification; and the _____ represents the voice of our internalized ideals (our *conscience*).

RI-2 In the psychoanalytic view, conflicts unresolved during one of the psychosexual stages may lead to _____ at that stage.

RI-3 Freud believed that our defense mechanisms operate _____ (consciously/unconsciously) and defend us against _____.

The Neo-Freudian and Later Psychodynamic Theorists

LOQ 13-6 Which of Freud's ideas did his followers accept or reject?

In a historical period when people rarely talked about sex, and certainly not unconscious desires for sex with one's parent, Freud's writings sparked intense debate. "In the Middle Ages, they would have burned me," observed Freud to a friend. "Now they are content with burning my books" (Jones, 1957). Despite the controversy, Freud attracted followers. Several young, ambitious physicians formed an inner circle around their strong-minded leader. These pioneering psychoanalysts, whom we often call *neo-Freudians,* adopted Freud's interviewing techniques and accepted his basic ideas: the personality structures of id, ego, and superego; the importance of the unconscious; the childhood roots of personality; and the dynamics of anxiety and the defense mechanisms. But they broke away from Freud in two important ways. First, they placed more emphasis on the conscious mind's role in interpreting experience and in coping with the environment. And second, they doubted that sex and aggression were all-consuming motivations. Instead, they tended to emphasize loftier motives and social interactions.

Alfred Adler and Karen Horney [HORN-eye], for example, agreed with Freud that childhood is important. But they believed that childhood *social*, not sexual, tensions are crucial for personality formation (Ferguson, 2003, 2015). Adler (who gave us the still popular *inferiority complex* idea) had struggled to overcome childhood illnesses and accidents. He believed that much of our behavior is driven by efforts to conquer childhood inferiority feelings that trigger our strivings for superiority and power. Horney said childhood anxiety triggers our desire for love and security. She also opposed Freud's assumptions that women have weak superegos and suffer "penis envy," and she attempted to balance his masculine bias.

Carl Jung [Yoong], Freud's disciple-turned-dissenter, placed less emphasis on social factors and agreed with Freud that the unconscious exerts a powerful influence. But to Jung, the unconscious contains more than our repressed thoughts and feelings. He believed we also have a **collective unconscious,** a common reservoir of images, or *archetypes,* derived from our species' universal experiences. Jung said that the collective unconscious explains why, for many people, spiritual concerns are deeply rooted and why people in different cultures share certain myths and images. Most of today's psychologists discount the idea of inherited experiences. But they do believe that our shared evolutionary history shaped some universal dispositions, and that experience can leave *epigenetic* marks affecting gene expression (see Chapter 2).

Freud died in 1939. Since then, some of his ideas have been incorporated into the diverse perspectives that make up modern psychodynamic theory. "Most contemporary

ALFRED ADLER (1870–1937) "The individual feels at home in life and feels his existence to be worthwhile just so far as he is useful to others and is overcoming feelings of inferiority" (*Problems of Neurosis*, 1964).

KAREN HORNEY (1885–1952) "The view that women are infantile and emotional creatures, and as such, incapable of responsibility and independence is the work of the masculine tendency to lower women's self-respect" (*Feminine Psychology*, 1932).

CARL JUNG (1875–1961) "From the living fountain of instinct flows everything that is creative; hence the unconscious is the very source of the creative impulse" (*The Structure and Dynamics of the Psyche*, 1960).

[psychodynamic] theorists and therapists are not wedded to the idea that sex is the basis of personality," noted Drew Westen (1996). They "do not talk about ids and egos, and do not go around classifying their patients as oral, anal, or phallic characters." What they do assume, with Freud and with much support from today's psychological science, is that much of our mental life is unconscious. With Freud, they also assume that we often struggle with inner conflicts among our wishes, fears, and values, and that childhood shapes our personality and ways of becoming attached to others.

Assessing Unconscious Processes

LOQ 13-7   What are *projective tests*, how are they used, and what are some criticisms of them?

Personality tests reflect the basic ideas of particular personality theories. So, what might be the assessment tool of choice for someone working in the Freudian tradition? It would need to provide some sort of road into the unconscious—to unearth the residue of early childhood experiences, move beneath surface thoughts, and reveal hidden conflicts and impulses. Objective assessment tools, such as agree-disagree or true-false questionnaires, would be inadequate because they would merely tap the conscious surface.

Henry Murray (1933) demonstrated a possible basis for such a test at a party hosted by his 11-year-old daughter. Murray engaged the children in a frightening game called "Murder." When shown some photographs after the game, the children perceived the photos as more malicious than they had before the game. These children, it seemed to Murray, had *projected* their inner feelings into the pictures.

A few years later, Murray introduced the **Thematic Apperception Test (TAT)**—a **projective test** in which people view ambiguous pictures and make up stories about them. Shown a daydreaming boy, those who imagine he is fantasizing about an achievement are presumed to be projecting their own goals. "As a rule," said Murray, "the subject leaves the test happily unaware that he has presented the psychologist with what amounts to an X-ray of his inner self" (quoted by Talbot, 1999).

Numerous studies suggest that Murray was right: The TAT provides a valid and reliable map of people's implicit motives (Jenkins, 2017). For example, such storytelling has been used to assess *achievement* and *affiliation motivation* (Drescher & Schultheiss, 2016; Schultheiss et al., 2014). TAT responses also show consistency over time (Lundy, 1985; Schultheiss & Pang, 2007). Show people a picture today, and they'll imagine a story similar to one they will tell when, a month later, they see the same picture.

Swiss psychiatrist Hermann Rorschach [ROAR-shock; 1884–1922] created the most widely used projective test. He based his famous **Rorschach inkblot test,** in which people describe what they see in a series of inkblots (**FIGURE 13.2**), on a childhood game.

LaunchPad For a helpful 9-minute overview, view the **Video: Psychodynamic Theories of Personality.**

FIGURE 13.2

THE RORSCHACH TEST In this projective test, people tell what they see in a series of symmetrical inkblots. Some who use this test are confident that the interpretation of ambiguous images will reveal unconscious aspects of the test-taker's personality.

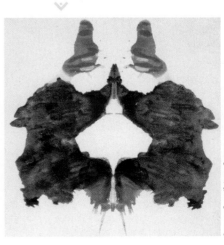

Spencer Grant/Science Source

"We don't see things as they are; we see things as we are." —The Talmud

"The Rorschach [inkblot test] has the dubious distinction of being, simultaneously, the most cherished and the most reviled of all psychological assessment tools." —John Hunsley and J. Michael Bailey (1999)

"Many aspects of Freudian theory are indeed out of date, and they should be: Freud died in 1939, and he has been slow to undertake further revisions." —Psychologist Drew Westen (1998)

He and his friends would drip ink on a paper, fold it, and then say what they saw in the resulting blot (Sdorow, 2005). Do you see predatory animals or weapons? Perhaps you have aggressive tendencies. But is this a reasonable assumption? The answer varies.

Some clinicians cherish the Rorschach test, even offering Rorschach-based assessments of criminals' violence potential. Others view the test as a source of suggestive leads, an icebreaker, or a revealing interview technique.

Critics of the Rorschach insist the test is no emotional MRI. They argue that only a few of the many Rorschach-derived scores, such as those for cognitive impairment and thought disorder, have demonstrated reliability and validity (Mihura et al., 2013, 2015; Wood et al., 2015). And inkblot assessments have inaccurately diagnosed many healthy adults as pathological (Wood, 2003; Wood et al., 2006).

Evaluating Freud's Psychoanalytic Perspective and Modern Views of the Unconscious

LOQ 13-8 How do contemporary psychologists view Freud's psychoanalysis?

MODERN RESEARCH CONTRADICTS MANY OF FREUD'S IDEAS We critique Freud from a twenty-first-century perspective. Freud did not have access to neurotransmitter or DNA studies, or to all that we have since learned about human development, thinking, and emotion. To criticize his theory by comparing it with today's thinking is like criticizing Henry Ford's Model T by comparing it with Elon Musk's Tesla Model S. How tempting it always is to judge the past from the perspective of our present.

Nevertheless, both Freud's devotees and his detractors agree that recent research contradicts many of his specific ideas. Today's developmental psychologists see our development as lifelong, not fixed in childhood. They doubt that infants' neural networks are mature enough to sustain as much emotional trauma as Freud assumed. Some think Freud overestimated parental influence and underestimated peer influence. They also doubt that conscience and gender identity form as the child resolves the Oedipus complex at age 5 or 6. We gain our gender identity earlier, and those who become strongly masculine or feminine do so even without a same-sex parent present. And they note that Freud's ideas about childhood sexuality arose from stories of childhood sexual abuse told by his female patients—stories that some scholars believe Freud doubted, and attributed to his patients' own childhood sexual wishes and conflicts (Esterson, 2001; Powell & Boer, 1994). Today, we know that *childhood sexual abuse happens,* and we also understand how Freud's questioning might have created false memories of abuse.

Modern dream research disputes Freud's belief that dreams disguise and fulfill wishes. And slips of the tongue can be explained as competition between similar verbal choices in our memory network. Someone who says "I don't want to do that—it's a lot of brothel" may simply be blending *bother* and *trouble* (Foss & Hakes, 1978). Searching the more than 250,000 emails I [DM] have received since 2000, I see that (among other such hilarities) friends have written me about their experience on "Wisconsin Pubic Radio," about accessibility in "pubic venues," and about their work as an organization's "Director of Pubic Policy." Such mistakes are likely mere random typos, concludes one big data analysis of typing errors (Stephens-Davidowitz, 2017).

Researchers find little support for Freud's idea that defense mechanisms disguise sexual and aggressive impulses (though our cognitive gymnastics do indeed work to protect our self-esteem). History also has failed to support another of Freud's ideas—that suppressed sexuality causes psychological disorders. From Freud's time to ours, sexual inhibition has diminished; psychological disorders have not.

Psychologists further criticize Freud's theory for its scientific shortcomings. Recall from Chapter 1 that good scientific theories explain observations and offer testable hypotheses. Freud's theory rests on few objective observations, and parts of it offer few testable hypotheses. For Freud, his own recollections and interpretations of patients' free associations, dreams, and slips—sometimes selected to support his theory—were evidence enough.

What is the most serious problem with Freud's theory? It offers after-the-fact explanations of any characteristic (of one person's smoking, another's fear of horses, another's sexual orientation), yet fails to *predict* such behaviors and traits. If you feel angry at your mother's death, you illustrate Freud's theory because "your unresolved childhood dependency needs are threatened." If you do not feel angry, you again illustrate his theory because "you are repressing your anger." That "is like betting on a horse after the race has been run" (Hall & Lindzey, 1978, p. 68). A good theory makes testable predictions.

So, should psychology post an "Allow Natural Death" order on this old theory? Freud's supporters object. To criticize Freudian theory for not making testable predictions is, they say, like criticizing baseball for not being an aerobic exercise—something it was never intended to be. Freud never claimed that psychoanalysis was predictive science. He merely claimed that, looking back, psychoanalysts could find meaning in our state of mind (Rieff, 1979).

Freud's supporters also note that some of his ideas *are* enduring. It was Freud who drew our attention to the unconscious and the irrational, at a time when such ideas were not popular. Today, many researchers study our irrationality (Ariely, 2010; Thaler, 2015). Psychologist Daniel Kahneman (in 2002) and behavioral economist Richard Thaler (in 2017) each won Nobel Prizes for their studies of our faulty decision making. Freud also drew our attention to the importance of human sexuality, and to the tension between our biological impulses and our social well-being. It was Freud who challenged our self-righteousness, exposed our self-protective defenses, and reminded us of our potential for evil.

MODERN RESEARCH CHALLENGES THE IDEA OF REPRESSION Psychoanalytic theory hinges on the assumption that our mind often *represses* offending wishes, banishing them into the unconscious until they resurface, like long-lost books in a dusty attic. Recover and resolve childhood's conflicted wishes, and emotional healing should follow. Repression became a widely accepted concept, used to explain hypnotic phenomena and psychological disorders. Some psychodynamic followers extended repression to explain apparently lost and recovered memories of childhood traumas (Boag, 2006; Cheit, 1998; Erdelyi, 2006). In one survey, 88 percent of university students believed that painful experiences commonly get pushed out of awareness and into the unconscious (Garry et al., 1994).

Today's researchers agree that we sometimes preserve our self-esteem by neglecting threatening information (Green et al., 2008). Yet many contend that repression, if it ever occurs, is a rare mental response to terrible trauma. Even those who have witnessed a parent's murder or survived Nazi death camps have retained their unrepressed memories of the horror (Helmreich, 1992, 1994; Malmquist, 1986; Pennebaker, 1990). "Dozens of formal studies have yielded not a single convincing case of repression in the entire literature on trauma," concluded personality researcher John Kihlstrom (2006).

Some researchers do believe that extreme, prolonged stress, such as the stress some severely abused children experience, might disrupt memory by damaging the hippocampus, which is important for processing conscious memories (Schacter, 1996). But the far more common reality is that high stress and associated stress hormones *enhance* memory. Indeed, rape, torture, and other traumatic events haunt survivors, who experience unwanted flashbacks. They are seared onto the soul. "You see the babies," said Holocaust survivor Sally H. (1979). "You see the screaming mothers. You see hanging people. You sit and you see that face there. It's something you don't forget."

LaunchPad For a helpful 13-minute exploration, see the **Video: Repression—Reality or Myth?**

THE MODERN UNCONSCIOUS MIND

LOQ 13-9 How has modern research developed our understanding of the unconscious?

Freud was right about a big idea that underlies today's psychodynamic thinking: We have limited access to all that goes on in our mind (Erdelyi, 1985, 1988, 2006; Norman, 2010). Our two-track mind has a vast out-of-sight realm. Some researchers even argue that "most of a person's everyday life is determined by unconscious thought processes" (Bargh & Chartrand, 1999). (Perhaps, for example, you can recall being sad or mad without consciously knowing why.)

"We are arguing like a man who should say, 'If there were an invisible cat in that chair, the chair would look empty; but the chair does look empty; therefore there is an invisible cat in it'." —C. S . Lewis, *Four Loves*, 1958

"Although [Freud] clearly made a number of mistakes in the formulation of his ideas, his understanding of unconscious mental processes was pretty much on target. In fact, it is very consistent with modern neuroscientists' belief that most mental processes are unconscious." —Nobel Prize–winning neuroscientist Eric Kandel (2012)

"During the Holocaust, many children . . . were forced to endure the unendurable. For those who continue to suffer [the] pain is still present, many years later, as real as it was on the day it occurred." —Eric Zillmer, Molly Harrower, Barry Ritzler, and Robert Archer, *The Quest for the Nazi Personality*, 1995

humanistic theories theories that view personality with a focus on the potential for healthy personal growth.

hierarchy of needs Maslow's pyramid of human needs, beginning at the base with physiological needs that must first be satisfied before people can fulfill their higher-level safety needs and then psychological needs.

self-actualization according to Maslow, one of the ultimate psychological needs that arises after basic physical and psychological needs are met and self-esteem is achieved; the motivation to fulfill one's potential.

self-transcendence according to Maslow, the striving for identity, meaning, and purpose beyond the self.

unconditional positive regard a caring, accepting, nonjudgmental attitude, which Carl Rogers believed would help people develop self-awareness and self-acceptance.

Yet many research psychologists now think of the unconscious not as seething passions and repressive censoring but as cooler information processing that occurs without our awareness. To these researchers, the unconscious also involves (as we see elsewhere in this text)

* the *schemas* that automatically control our perceptions and interpretations (Chapter 6).
* the *priming* by stimuli to which we have not consciously attended (Chapters 6 and 8).
* the right-hemisphere activity that enables the *split-brain* patient's left hand to carry out an instruction the patient cannot verbalize (Chapter 2).
* the *implicit memories* that operate without conscious recall, even among those with amnesia (Chapter 8).
* the *emotions* that activate instantly, before conscious analysis (Chapter 10).
* the *stereotypes* and *implicit prejudice* that automatically and unconsciously influence how we process information about others (Chapter 12).

More than we realize, we fly on autopilot. Our lives are guided by off-screen, out-of-sight, unconscious information processing. The unconscious mind is huge. However, our current understanding of unconscious information processing is more like the pre-Freudian view of an underground, unattended stream of thought from which spontaneous behavior and creative ideas surface (Bargh & Morsella, 2008).

Research also supports two of Freud's defense mechanisms. One study demonstrated *reaction formation* (trading unacceptable impulses for their opposite) in men who reported strong anti-gay attitudes. Compared with those who did not report such attitudes, these anti-gay men experienced greater physiological arousal (assessed with a device that measured blood flow to the penis) when watching videos of homosexual men having sex, even though they said the films did not make them sexually aroused (Adams et al., 1996). Likewise, some evidence suggests that people who unconsciously identify as homosexual—but who consciously identify as straight—report more negative attitudes toward gays (Weinstein et al., 2012).

Freud's *projection* (attributing our own threatening impulses to others) has also been confirmed. People do tend to see their traits, attitudes, and goals in others (Baumeister et al., 1998b; Maner et al., 2005). Today's researchers call this the *false consensus effect*—the tendency to overestimate the extent to which others share our beliefs and behaviors. People who binge-drink or break speed limits tend to think many others do the same. However, neuroscience research shows that projection seems motivated less by suppressing our sexual and aggressive undercurrents, as Freud imagined, than by our need to maintain a positive self-image (Welborn et al., 2017).

ENGAGE

(ASK YOURSELF)

What understandings and impressions of Freud did you bring to this course? Are you surprised to find that some of his ideas (especially the big idea of our unconscious mind) had merit?

🔒 **RETRIEVE IT • • •**   *ANSWERS IN APPENDIX E*

RI-4 What are three big ideas that have survived from Freud's psychoanalytic theory? What are three ways in which Freud's theory has been criticized?

RI-5 Which elements of traditional psychoanalysis have modern-day *psychodynamic* theorists and therapists retained, and which elements have they mostly left behind?

HUMANISTIC THEORIES

LOQ 13-10 How did humanistic psychologists view personality, and what was their goal in studying personality?

By the 1960s, some personality psychologists had become discontented with the sometimes bleak focus on drives and conflicts in psychodynamic theory, and the mechanistic psychology of B. F. Skinner's *behaviorism* (see Chapter 7). Two pioneering theorists—Abraham Maslow (1908–1970) and Carl Rogers (1902–1987)—offered a *third-force perspective* that emphasized our potential for healthy personal growth. In contrast to Freud's emphasis on disorders born out of dark conflicts, these **humanistic theorists** emphasized the ways people strive for self-determination and self-realization. In contrast to behaviorism's scientific objectivity, they studied people through their own self-reported experiences and feelings.

Abraham Maslow's Self-Actualizing Person

Maslow proposed that we are motivated by a **hierarchy of needs** (Chapter 10). If our physiological needs are met, we become concerned with personal safety. If we achieve a sense of security, we then seek to love, to be loved, and to love ourselves. With our love needs satisfied, we seek self-esteem. Having achieved self-esteem, we ultimately seek **self-actualization** (the process of fulfilling our potential) and **self-transcendence** (meaning, purpose, and identity beyond the self).

Maslow (1970) developed his ideas by studying healthy, creative people rather than troubled clinical cases. He based his description of self-actualization on a study of people, such as Abraham Lincoln, who seemed notable for their meaningful and productive lives. Maslow reported that such people shared certain characteristics: They were self-aware and self-accepting, open and spontaneous, loving and caring, and not paralyzed by others' opinions. Secure in their sense of who they were, their interests were problem-centered rather than self-centered. They focused their energies on a particular task, one they often regarded as their mission in life. Most enjoyed a few deep relationships rather than many superficial ones. Many had been moved by spiritual or personal *peak experiences* that surpassed ordinary consciousness.

These, said Maslow, are mature adult qualities found in those who have learned enough about life to be compassionate, to have outgrown their mixed feelings toward their parents, to have found their calling, to have "acquired enough courage to be unpopular, to be unashamed about being openly virtuous."

Carl Rogers' Person-Centered Perspective

Fellow humanistic psychologist Carl Rogers agreed with much of Maslow's thinking. Rogers' *person-centered perspective* held that people are basically good and are, as Maslow said, endowed with self-actualizing tendencies. Unless thwarted by a growth-inhibiting environment, each of us is like an acorn, primed for growth and fulfillment. Rogers (1980) believed that a growth-promoting social climate provides:

- *Acceptance.* When people are *accepting,* they offer **unconditional positive regard,** an attitude of grace that values us even knowing our failings. It is a profound relief to drop our pretenses, confess our worst feelings, and discover that we are still accepted. In a good marriage, a close family, or an intimate friendship, we are free to be spontaneous without fearing the loss of others' esteem.

- *Genuineness.* When people are *genuine,* they are open with their own feelings, drop their facades, and are transparent and self-disclosing.

- *Empathy.* When people are *empathic,* they share and mirror other's feelings and reflect their meanings. "Rarely do we listen with real understanding, true empathy," said Rogers. "Yet listening, of this very special kind, is one of the most potent forces for change that I know."

ABRAHAM MASLOW (1908–1970) "Any theory of motivation that is worthy of attention must deal with the highest capacities of the healthy and strong person as well as with the defensive maneuvers of crippled spirits" (*Motivation and Personality,* 1970, p. 33).

A FATHER *NOT* OFFERING UNCONDITIONAL POSITIVE REGARD:

Pat Byrnes The New Yorker Collection/The Cartoon Bank

"Just remember, son, it doesn't matter whether you win or lose—unless you want Daddy's love."

ENGAGE 💡 (ASK YOURSELF)

Think back to a conversation you had when you knew someone was just waiting for their turn to speak instead of listening to you. Now consider the last time someone heard you with empathy. How did those two experiences differ?

THE PICTURE OF EMPATHY Being open and sharing confidences is easier when the listener shows real understanding. Within such relationships we can relax and fully express our true selves.

CARL ROGERS (1902–1987) "The curious paradox is that when I accept myself just as I am, then I can change." (*On Becoming a Person*, 1961).

ENGAGE   **LaunchPad** To consider how this theory applies to your own life, try the online **Immersive Learning: Assess Your Strengths —What Is Your Self-Concept?**

So, some things get better with *age:* acceptance, genuineness, and empathy. These are, Rogers believed, the water, sun, and nutrients that enable people to grow like vigorous oak trees. For "as persons are accepted and prized, they tend to develop a more caring attitude toward themselves" (Rogers, 1980, p. 116). As persons are empathically heard, "it becomes possible for them to listen more accurately to the flow of inner experiencings."

Writer Calvin Trillin (2006) recalled an example of parental acceptance and genuineness at a camp for children with severe disorders, where his wife, Alice, worked. L., a "magical child," had genetic diseases that meant she had to be tube-fed and could walk only with difficulty. Alice wondered "what this child's parents could have done . . . to make her the most optimistic, most enthusiastic, most hopeful human being I had ever encountered." One day Alice spotted a note that L. received from her mom, which read, "If God had given us all of the children in the world to choose from, L., we would only have chosen you." Inspired, Alice approached a co-worker. "Quick. Read this," she whispered. "It's the secret of life."

Maslow and Rogers would have smiled knowingly. For them, a central feature of personality is one's **self-concept**—all the thoughts and feelings we have in response to the question, "Who am I?" If our self-concept is positive, we tend to act and perceive the world positively. If it is negative—if in our own eyes we fall far short of our *ideal self*—said Rogers, we feel dissatisfied and unhappy. A worthwhile goal for therapists, parents, teachers, and friends is therefore, he said, to help others know, accept, and be true to themselves.

Assessing the Self

LOQ 13-11   How did humanistic psychologists assess a person's sense of self?

Humanistic psychologists sometimes assessed personality by asking people to fill out questionnaires that would evaluate their self-concept. One questionnaire, inspired by Carl Rogers, asked people to describe themselves both as they would *ideally* like to be and as they *actually* are. When the ideal and the actual self are nearly alike, said Rogers, the self-concept is positive. Assessing his clients' personal growth during therapy, he looked for successively closer ratings of actual and ideal selves.

Some humanistic psychologists believed that any standardized assessment of personality, even a questionnaire, is depersonalizing. Rather than forcing the person to respond to narrow categories, these humanistic psychologists presumed that interviews and intimate conversation would provide a better understanding of each person's unique experiences. Some researchers believe our identity may be revealed using the *life story approach*—collecting a rich narrative detailing each person's unique life history (Adler et al., 2016; McAdams & Guo, 2015). A lifetime of stories can show more of a person's complete identity than can the responses to a few questions.

Evaluating Humanistic Theories

LOQ 13-12   How have humanistic theories influenced psychology? What criticisms have they faced?

One thing said of Freud can also be said of the humanistic psychologists: Their impact has been pervasive. Maslow's and Rogers' ideas have influenced counseling, education, child raising, and management. And they laid the groundwork for today's scientific *positive psychology* subfield (Chapter 11).

These theorists have also influenced—sometimes in unintended ways—much of today's popular psychology. Is a positive self-concept the key to happiness and success? Do acceptance and empathy nurture positive feelings about ourselves? Are people basically good and capable of self-improvement? Many people answer *Yes, Yes,* and *Yes.* In 2006, U.S. high school students reported notably higher self-esteem and greater expectations of future career success than did students living in 1975 (Twenge & Campbell, 2008). Given a choice, today's North American college students mostly say they'd rather get a self-esteem boost, such as a compliment or good grade on a paper, than enjoy a favorite food or sexual activity (Bushman et al., 2011). Humanistic psychology's message has been heard.

self-concept   all our thoughts and feelings about ourselves, in answer to the question, "Who am I?"

But the prominence of the humanistic perspective set off a backlash of criticism. First, said the critics, its concepts are vague and subjective. Consider Maslow's description of self-actualizing people as open, spontaneous, loving, self-accepting, and productive. Is this a scientific description? Or is it merely a description of the theorist's own values and ideals? Maslow, noted M. Brewster Smith (1978), offered impressions of his own personal heroes. Imagine another theorist who began with a different set of heroes—perhaps Napoleon, John D. Rockefeller, Sr., and U.S. President Donald Trump. This theorist might describe self-actualizing people as "undeterred by others' opinions," "motivated to achieve," and "comfortable with power."

Critics also objected to the idea that, as Rogers (1985) put it, "The only question which matters is, 'Am I living in a way which is deeply satisfying to me, and which truly expresses me?'" This emphasis on *individualism*—trusting and acting on one's feelings, being true to oneself, fulfilling oneself—could lead to self-indulgence, selfishness, and an erosion of moral restraint (Campbell & Specht, 1985; Wallach & Wallach, 1983). Imagine working on a group project with people who refuse to complete any task that is not deeply satisfying or does not truly express their identity.

Humanistic psychologists have replied that a secure, nondefensive self-acceptance is actually the first step toward loving others. Indeed, people who feel intrinsically liked and accepted—for who they are, not just for their achievements—exhibit less defensive attitudes (Schimel et al., 2001). Those feeling liked and accepted by a romantic partner report being happier in their relationships and acting more kindly toward their partner (Gordon & Chen, 2010).

A final critique has been that humanistic psychology is naive—that it fails to appreciate the reality of our human capacity for evil (May, 1982). Faced with climate change, overpopulation, terrorism, and the spread of nuclear weapons, we may become apathetic from either of two rationalizations. One is a starry-eyed optimism that denies the threat ("People are basically good; everything will work out"). The other is a dark despair ("It's hopeless; why try?"). Action requires enough realism to fuel concern and enough optimism to provide hope.

"We do pretty well when you stop to think that people are basically good."

🔒 RETRIEVE IT • • •

ANSWERS IN APPENDIX E

RI-6 How did the *humanistic theories* provide a fresh perspective?

RI-7 What does it mean to be *empathic?* How about *self-actualized?* Which humanistic psychologists used these terms?

🔒 REVIEW CLASSIC PERSPECTIVES ON PERSONALITY

⏩ Learning Objectives

TEST YOURSELF Answer these repeated Learning Objective Questions on your own (before checking the answers in Appendix D) to improve your retention of the concepts (McDaniel et al., 2009, 2015).

13-1 What is *personality,* and what theories inform our understanding of personality?

13-2 How did Sigmund Freud's treatment of psychological disorders lead to his view of the unconscious mind?

13-3 What was Freud's view of personality?

13-4 What developmental stages did Freud propose?

13-5 How did Freud think people defended themselves against anxiety?

13-6 Which of Freud's ideas did his followers accept or reject?

13-7 What are *projective tests,* how are they used, and what are some criticisms of them?

13-8 How do contemporary psychologists view Freud's psychoanalysis?

13-9 How has modern research developed our understanding of the unconscious?

13-10 How did humanistic psychologists view personality, and what was their goal in studying personality?

13-11 How did humanistic psychologists assess a person's sense of self?

13-12 How have humanistic theories influenced psychology? What criticisms have they faced?

⟩⟩ Terms and Concepts to Remember

TEST YOURSELF Write down the definition yourself, then check your answer on the referenced page.

personality, **p. 462**

psychodynamic theories, **p. 462**

psychoanalysis, **p. 462**

unconscious, **p. 463**

free association, **p. 463**

id, **p. 463**

ego, **p. 465**

superego, **p. 465**

psychosexual stages, **p. 465**

Oedipus [ED-uh-puss] complex, **p. 465**

identification, **p. 465**

fixation, **p. 465**

defense mechanisms, **p. 465**

repression, **p. 465**

collective unconscious, **p. 466**

Thematic Apperception Test (TAT), **p. 466**

projective test, **p. 466**

Rorschach inkblot test, **p. 466**

humanistic theories, **p. 470**

hierarchy of needs, **p. 470**

self-actualization, **p. 470**

self-transcendence, **p. 470**

unconditional positive regard, **p. 470**

self-concept, **p. 472**

⟩⟩ Experience the Testing Effect

TEST YOURSELF Answer the following questions on your own first, then check your answers in Appendix E.

1. Freud believed that we may block painful or unacceptable thoughts, wishes, feelings, or memories from consciousness through an unconscious process called _____.

2. According to Freud's view of personality structure, the "executive" system, the _____, seeks to gratify the impulses of the _____ in more acceptable ways.
   a. id; ego
   b. ego; superego
   c. ego; id
   d. id; superego

3. Freud proposed that the development of the "voice of our moral compass" is related to the _____, which internalizes ideals and provides standards for judgments.

4. According to the psychoanalytic view of development, we all pass through a series of psychosexual stages, including the oral, anal, and phallic stages. Conflicts unresolved at any of these stages may lead to
   a. dormant sexual feelings.
   b. fixation at that stage.
   c. preconscious blocking of impulses.
   d. a distorted gender identity.

5. Freud believed that defense mechanisms are unconscious attempts to distort or disguise reality, all in an effort to reduce our _____.

6. _____ tests ask test-takers to respond to an ambiguous image by describing it or telling a story about it.

7. In general, neo-Freudians such as Adler and Horney accepted many of Freud's views but placed more emphasis than he did on
   a. development throughout the life span.
   b. the collective unconscious.
   c. the role of the id.
   d. social interactions.

8. Modern-day psychodynamic theorists and therapists agree with Freud about
   a. the existence of unconscious mental processes.
   b. the Oedipus complex.
   c. the predictive value of Freudian theory.
   d. the superego's role as the executive part of personality.

9. Which of the following is NOT part of the contemporary view of the unconscious?
   a. Repressed memories of anxiety-provoking events
   b. Schemas that influence our perceptions and interpretations
   c. Stereotypes that affect our information processing
   d. Instantly activated emotions and implicit memories of learned skills

10. Maslow's hierarchy of needs proposes that we must satisfy basic physiological and safety needs before we seek ultimate psychological needs, such as self-actualization. Maslow based his ideas on
    a. Freudian theory.
    b. his experiences with patients.
    c. a series of laboratory experiments.
    d. his study of healthy, creative people.

11. How might Rogers explain how environment influences the development of a criminal?

12. The total acceptance Rogers advocated as part of a growth-promoting environment is called _____ _____ _____.

Continue testing yourself with 📖 **LearningCurve** or 📖 **Achieve Read & Practice** to learn and remember most effectively.

trait a characteristic pattern of behavior or a disposition to feel and act in certain ways, as assessed by self-report inventories and peer reports.

⟶ Contemporary Perspectives on Personality

TRAIT THEORIES

LOQ 13-13 How do psychologists use traits to describe personality?

Rather than focusing on unconscious forces and thwarted growth opportunities, some researchers attempt to define personality in terms of stable and enduring behavior patterns, such as Lady Gaga's self-discipline and openness to new experiences. This perspective can be traced in part to a remarkable meeting in 1919, when Gordon Allport, a curious 22-year-old psychology student, interviewed Sigmund Freud in Vienna. Allport soon discovered just how preoccupied the founder of psychoanalysis was with finding hidden motives, even in Allport's own behavior during the interview. That experience ultimately led Allport to do what Freud did not do: to describe personality in terms of fundamental **traits**, or people's characteristic behaviors and conscious motives (such as the curiosity that actually motivated Allport to see Freud). Meeting Freud, said Allport, "taught me that [psychoanalysis], for all its merits, may plunge too deep, and that psychologists would do well to give full recognition to manifest motives before probing the unconscious." Allport came to define personality in terms of identifiable behavior patterns. He was concerned less with *explaining* individual traits than with *describing* them.

Exploring Traits

We are each a unique complex of multiple traits. So how can we describe our personalities in a way that captures our individuality? We might describe an apple by placing it along several trait dimensions—relatively large or small, red or green, sweet or tart. By placing people on several trait dimensions simultaneously, psychologists can describe countless individual personality variations. (Remember from Chapter 6 that variations on just three color dimensions—*hue, saturation,* and *brightness*—create many thousands of colors.)

ENGAGE What trait dimensions describe personality? If you were looking at profiles on a dating site or app, what personality traits would give you the best sense for each person? Allport and his associate H. S. Odbert (1936) counted all the words in an unabridged dictionary with which one could describe people. There were almost 18,000! How, then, could psychologists condense the list to a manageable number of basic traits?

FACTOR ANALYSIS One technique is *factor analysis,* a statistical procedure that identifies clusters (factors) of test items that tap basic components of a trait (McCabe & Fleeson, 2016). Imagine that people who describe themselves as outgoing also tend to say that they like excitement and practical jokes and dislike quiet reading. Such a statistically correlated cluster of behaviors reflects a basic factor, or trait—in this case, *extraversion.*

British psychologists Hans Eysenck and Sybil Eysenck [EYE-zink] believed that we can reduce many of our normal individual variations to two dimensions: *extraversion–introversion* and *emotional stability–instability* (**FIGURE 13.3**). People in 35 countries around the world, from China to Uganda to Russia, have taken the *Eysenck Personality Questionnaire.* When their answers were analyzed, the extraversion and emotionality factors inevitably emerged as basic personality dimensions (Eysenck, 1990, 1992). The Eysencks believed, and research confirms, that these factors are genetically influenced.

BIOLOGY AND PERSONALITY Brain-activity scans of extraverts add to the growing list of traits and mental states now being explored with brain-imaging procedures. Such studies indicate that extraverts seek stimulation because their normal *brain arousal* is

"Russ is the sort of person who never wants to be alone with his thoughts."

UNSTABLE

Moody · Touchy
Anxious · Restless
Rigid · Aggressive
Sober · Excitable
Pessimistic · Changeable
Reserved · Impulsive
Unsociable · Optimistic
Quiet · Active

INTROVERTED ———————— **EXTRAVERTED**

Passive · Sociable
Careful · Outgoing
Thoughtful · Talkative
Peaceful · Responsive
Controlled · Easygoing
Reliable · Lively
Even-tempered · Carefree
Calm · Dominant

STABLE

FIGURE 13.3

TWO PERSONALITY DIMENSIONS
Mapmakers can tell us a lot by using two axes (north–south and east–west). Two primary personality factors (extraversion–introversion and stability–instability) are similarly useful as axes for describing personality variation. Varying combinations define other, more specific traits (Eysenck & Eysenck, 1963). Successful comedians, including Stephen Colbert, are often natural extraverts who love constant social engagement and spontaneity. However, many accomplished actors, such as Emma Watson, are introverts—particularly capable of solitary study to become each character they portray.

relatively low. For example, PET scans have shown that a frontal lobe area involved in behavior inhibition is less active in extraverts than in introverts (Johnson et al., 1999). Dopamine and dopamine-related neural activity tend to be higher in extraverts (Kim et al., 2008; Wacker et al., 2006).

Our biology influences our personality in other ways as well. Recall from the twin and adoption studies in Chapter 2 that our genes have much to say about the *temperament* and behavioral style that shape our personality. Jerome Kagan (2010), for example, has explained differences in children's shyness and inhibition as a function of their autonomic nervous system reactivity (see Thinking Critically About: The Stigma of Introversion). Those with a reactive autonomic nervous system respond to stress with greater anxiety and inhibition. The fearless, curious child may become the rock-climbing or fast-driving adult.

THINKING CRITICALLY ABOUT:

The Stigma of Introversion

LOQ 13-14 What are some common misunderstandings about introversion?

Western cultures are hard on introverts:

Superheroes tend to be extraverted. Black Panther unites five tribes of people with his engaging strength of character. Take-charge Elastigirl saves the day in *The Incredibles*.

What do job interviewers want in their employees? Extraversion outranks most other personality traits.[1]

87% of Westerners want to be more extraverted.[2]

Being introverted seems to imply that we don't have the "right stuff."[3]

Attractive, successful people are presumed to be extraverts.

What is introversion?

Introverts tend to gain energy from time alone, and may find social interactions exhausting. Extraverts, by contrast, tend to draw energy from time spent with others.

Introverts are not "shy." (Shy people remain quiet because they fear others will evaluate them negatively.)

Introverted people seek low levels of stimulation from their environment because they're *sensitive*. For example, when given lemon juice, introverted people salivated more than extraverted people.[4]

Introversion has many benefits:

• Introverted leaders outperform extraverted leaders in some contexts, such as when their employees voice new ideas and challenge existing norms.[5]

• Introverts handle conflict well. In response, they seek solitude rather than revenge.[6]

• Many introverts flourish, including Bill Gates, Mother Teresa, and Jeff Bezos. Faced with the decision to start Amazon, Bezos spent days alone thinking about it. "I went away," he said.[7]

---

1. Kluemper et al., 2015; Salgado & Moscoso, 2002. 2. Hudson & Roberts, 2014. 3. Cain, 2012. 4. Corcoran, 1964. 5. Grant et al., 2011. 6. Ren et al., 2016. 7. Mejia, 2017.

Personality differences among dogs (in energy, affection, reactivity, and curious intelligence) are as evident, and as consistently judged, as personality differences among humans (Gosling et al., 2003; Jones & Gosling, 2005). Monkeys, bonobos, chimpanzees, orangutans, sea lions, and even birds and fish also have distinct and stable personalities (Ciardelli et al., 2017; Latzman et al., 2015; Pennisi, 2016; Weiss et al., 2017). Among the Great tit (a European relative of the American chickadee), bold birds more quickly inspect new objects and explore trees (Groothuis & Carere, 2005; Verbeek et al., 1994). Through selective breeding, researchers can produce bold or shy birds. Both have their place in natural history: In lean years, bold birds are more likely to find food; in abundant years, shy birds feed with less risk.

PUPS HAVE PERSONALITY

> ## 🔒 RETRIEVE IT • • •
> *ANSWERS IN APPENDIX E*
>
> **RI-1** Which two primary dimensions did Hans Eysenck and Sybil Eysenck propose for describing personality variation?

Assessing Traits

LOQ 13-15 What are *personality inventories,* and what are their strengths and weaknesses as trait-assessment tools?

If stable and enduring traits guide our actions, can we devise valid and reliable tests of them? Several trait-assessment techniques exist—some more valid than others. Some provide quick assessments of a single trait, such as extraversion, anxiety, or self-esteem. **Personality inventories**—longer questionnaires covering a wide range of feelings and behaviors—assess several traits at once.

The classic personality inventory is the **Minnesota Multiphasic Personality Inventory (MMPI).** Although the MMPI was originally developed to identify emotional disorders, it also assesses people's personality traits. One of its creators, Starke Hathaway (1960), compared his effort with that of Alfred Binet (who, as you may recall from Chapter 9, developed the first intelligence test by selecting items that identified children who would probably have trouble progressing normally in French schools). Like Binet's items, the MMPI items were **empirically derived:** From a large pool of items, Hathaway and his colleagues selected those on which particular diagnostic groups differed. "My hands and feet are usually warm enough" may seem superficial, but it just so happened that anxious people were more likely to answer *False.* The researchers grouped the questions into 10 clinical scales, including scales that assess depressive tendencies, masculinity–femininity, and introversion–extraversion. Today's MMPI-2 has additional scales that assess work attitudes, family problems, and anger.

Whereas most projective tests (such as the Rorschach) are scored subjectively, personality inventories are scored objectively. (Software can administer and score these tests, and can also provide descriptions of people who previously responded similarly.) Objectivity does not, however, guarantee validity. Individuals taking the MMPI for employment purposes can give socially desirable answers to create a good impression. But in so doing they may also score high on a *lie scale* that assesses faking (as when people respond *False* to a universally true statement, such as "I get angry sometimes"). In other cases, the MMPI can be used to identify people pretending to have a disorder in order to avoid their work or other responsibilities (Chmielewski et al., 2017). The objectivity of the MMPI has contributed to its popularity and its translation into more than 100 languages.

The Big Five Factors

LOQ 13-16 Which traits seem to provide the most useful information about personality variation?

Today's trait researchers believe that simple trait factors, such as the Eysencks' introversion–extraversion and stability–instability dimensions, are important, but they do not tell the whole story. A slightly expanded set of factors—dubbed the *Big Five*—does a better job (Costa & McCrae, 2011; Soto & John, 2017). If a test specifies where you are on the five

LaunchPad Might astrology hold the secret to our personality traits? Play the role of a researcher testing this question by engaging online with **Immersive Learning: How Would You Know If Astrologers Can Describe People's Personality?**

People have had fun spoofing the MMPI with their own mock items: "Weeping brings tears to my eyes," "Frantic screams make me nervous," and "I stay in the bathtub until I look like a raisin" (Frankel et al., 1983).

personality inventory a questionnaire (often with *true-false* or *agree-disagree* items) on which people respond to items designed to gauge a wide range of feelings and behaviors; used to assess selected personality traits.

Minnesota Multiphasic Personality Inventory (MMPI) the most widely researched and clinically used of all personality tests. Originally developed to identify emotional disorders (still considered its most appropriate use), this test is now used for many other screening purposes.

empirically derived test a test (such as the MMPI) created by selecting from a pool of items those that discriminate between groups.

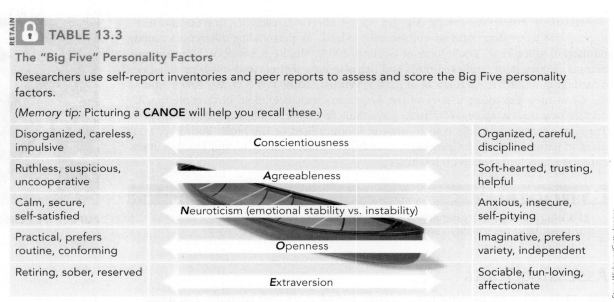

RETAIN

🔒 TABLE 13.3

The "Big Five" Personality Factors

Researchers use self-report inventories and peer reports to assess and score the Big Five personality factors.

(*Memory tip:* Picturing a **CANOE** will help you recall these.)

Disorganized, careless, impulsive	**C**onscientiousness	Organized, careful, disciplined
Ruthless, suspicious, uncooperative	**A**greeableness	Soft-hearted, trusting, helpful
Calm, secure, self-satisfied	**N**euroticism (emotional stability vs. instability)	Anxious, insecure, self-pitying
Practical, prefers routine, conforming	**O**penness	Imaginative, prefers variety, independent
Retiring, sober, reserved	**E**xtraversion	Sociable, fun-loving, affectionate

Information from McCrae & Costa (1986, 2008).

Steve Wisbauer/Getty Images

dimensions (conscientiousness, agreeableness, neuroticism, openness, and extraversion; see **TABLE 13.3**), it has said much of what there is to say about your personality. Some clinical psychologists have begun to use the Big Five to understand personality disorders, schizophrenia, and other types of dysfunction (Ohi et al., 2016; Widiger et al., 2016).

Around the world—across 56 nations and 29 languages in one study (Schmitt et al., 2007)—people describe others in terms roughly consistent with this list. The Big Five—today's "common currency for personality psychology" (Funder, 2001)—has been the most active personality research topic since the early 1990s and is currently our best approximation of the basic trait dimensions.

Big Five research has explored various questions:

- *How stable are these traits?* One research team analyzed 1.25 million participants ages 10 to 65. They learned that personality continues to develop and change through late childhood and adolescence. Up to age 40, we show signs of a *maturity principle:* We become more conscientious and agreeable and less neurotic (emotionally unstable) (Milojev & Sibley, 2017; Rohrer et al., 2018). Great apes show similar personality maturation (Weiss & King, 2015). After age 40, our traits further stabilize.

- *How heritable are these traits?* Heritability (the extent to which individual differences are attributable to genes) generally runs about 40 percent for each dimension (Vukasović & Bratko, 2015). Many genes, each having small effects, combine to influence our traits (McCrae et al., 2010; van den Berg et al., 2016).

- *Do these traits reflect differing brain structure?* The size and thickness of brain tissue correlates with several Big Five traits (DeYoung et al., 2010; Grodin & White, 2015; Riccelli et al., 2017). For example, those who score high on conscientiousness tend to have a larger frontal lobe area that aids in planning and controlling behavior. Brain connections also influence the Big Five traits (Adelstein et al., 2011). People high in neuroticism have brains that are wired to experience stress intensely (Shackman et al., 2016; Xu & Potenza, 2012).

- *Do these traits reflect birth order?* After controlling for other variables such as family size, are first-born children, for example, more conscientious and agreeable? Contrary to popular opinion, several massive studies failed to find any association between birth order and personality (Damian & Roberts, 2015; Harris, 2009; Rohrer et al., 2015).

- *How well do these traits apply to various cultures?* The Big Five dimensions describe personality in various cultures reasonably well (Fetvadjiev et al., 2017; Schmitt et al., 2007; Vazsonyi et al., 2015). After studying people from 50 cultures, Robert McCrae and 79 co-researchers concluded that "features of personality traits are common to all human groups" (2005).

HOW DO YOU VOTE? LET ME COUNT THE LIKES Researchers can use your Facebook likes to predict your Big Five traits, your opinions, and your political attitudes (Youyou et al., 2015). Companies gather these "big data" for advertisers (who then personalize the ads you see). They do the same for political candidates, who can target you with persuasive messages (Matz et al., 2017). In the 2016 U.S. presidential campaign, "both sides were certainly using big data . . . to win over voters," says researcher Michal Kosinski (Zakaria, 2017).

- *Do the Big Five traits predict our actual behaviors?* *Yes.* Conscientiousness and agreeableness predict workplace success (Sackett & Walmsley, 2014). Agreeable people tend to help others, whereas people high in neuroticism are often unhelpful (Habashi et al., 2016; McCann, 2017). Traits also characterize certain career paths. For example, U.S. politicians tend to have "big" personalities, outscoring the general public on extraversion, agreeableness, conscientiousness, and emotional stability (low neuroticism) (Hanania, 2017). Our traits also appear in our language patterns. In text messaging, extraversion predicts use of personal pronouns. Neuroticism predicts negative-emotion words (Holtgraves, 2011).

By exploring such questions, Big Five research has sustained trait psychology and renewed appreciation for the importance of personality. (To describe your personality, try the brief self-assessment in **FIGURE 13.4**.) Traits matter. In the next section, we will see that situations matter, too.

ENGAGE (ASK YOURSELF)

Before trying the self-assessment in Figure 13.4, where would you have placed yourself on the Big Five personality dimensions? Where might your family and friends place you? Did the actual results surprise you, and do you think these results would surprise them?

ENGAGE **FIGURE 13.4**

THE BIG FIVE SELF-ASSESSMENT

How Do You Describe Yourself?

Describe yourself as you generally are now, not as you wish to be in the future. Describe yourself as you honestly see yourself, in relation to other people you know of the same sex and roughly the same age. Use the scale below to enter a number for each statement. Then, use the scoring guide at the bottom to see where you fall on the spectrum for each of the Big Five traits.

1	2	3	4	5
Very Inaccurate	Moderately Inaccurate	Neither Accurate Nor Inaccurate	Moderately Accurate	Very Accurate

1. ____ Am the life of the party
2. ____ Sympathize with others' feelings
3. ____ Get stressed out easily
4. ____ Am always prepared
5. ____ Am full of ideas
6. ____ Start conversations
7. ____ Take time out for others
8. ____ Follow a schedule
9. ____ Worry about things
10. ____ Have a vivid imagination

SCORING GUIDE SORTED BY BIG FIVE PERSONALITY TRAITS

Conscientiousness: statements 4, 8

Agreeableness: statements 2, 7

Neuroticism: statements 3, 9

Openness: statements 5, 10

Extraversion: statements 1, 6

How to score:
Separate your responses by each Big Five personality trait, as noted at left, and divide by two to obtain your score for each trait. So, for example, for the "Agreeableness" trait let's say you scored 3 for statement 2 ("Sympathize with others' feelings") and 4 for statement 7 ("Take time out for others"). That means on a scale from 1 to 5, your overall score for the "Agreeableness" trait is 3 + 4 = 7 ÷ 2 = 3.5.

Scale data from Goldberg, L. R. (1992). The development of markers for the Big-Five factor structure. *Psychological Assessment, 4*, 26–42.

"I'm going to France—I'm a different person in France."

"There is as much difference between us and ourselves, as between us and others." —Michel de Montaigne, *Essays*, 1588

RETAIN

Roughly speaking, the temporary, external influences on behavior are the focus of *social psychology,* (Chapter 12), and the enduring, inner influences are the focus of *personality psychology.* In actuality, behavior always depends on the interaction of persons with situations.

Evaluating Trait Theories

LOQ 13-17   Does research support the consistency of personality traits over time and across situations?

Are our personality traits stable and enduring? Or does our behavior depend on where and with whom we find ourselves? In some ways, our personality seems stable. Cheerful, friendly children tend to become cheerful, friendly adults. At a college reunion, I [DM] was amazed to find that my jovial former classmates were still jovial, the shy ones still shy, the happy-seeming people still smiling and laughing *50 years later.* But it's also true that a fun-loving jokester can suddenly turn serious and respectful at a job interview. New situations and major life events can shift the personality traits we express. Becoming unemployed, for example, may make us less agreeable and open-minded (Boyce et al., 2015).

THE PERSON-SITUATION CONTROVERSY   Our behavior is influenced by the interaction of our inner disposition with our environment. Still, the question lingers: Which is more important? When we explore this *person-situation controversy,* we look for genuine personality traits that persist over time *and* across situations. Are some people dependably conscientious and others unreliable? Some cheerful and others dour? Some friendly and outgoing and others shy? If we are to consider friendliness a trait, friendly people must act friendly at different times and places. Do they?

In considering research that has followed lives through time, some scholars (especially those who study infants) are impressed with personality change; others are struck by personality stability during adulthood. As **FIGURE 13.5** illustrates, data from 152 long-term *(longitudinal)* studies reveal that personality trait scores are positively correlated with scores obtained seven years later, and that as people grow older, their personality stabilizes. Interests may change—the avid tropical-fish collector may become an avid gardener. Careers may change—the determined salesperson may become a determined social worker. Relationships may change—the hostile spouse may start over and antagonize a new partner. But most people recognize just who they are, as Robert McCrae and Paul Costa noted (1994), "and it is well that they do. A person's recognition of the inevitability of his or her one and only personality is . . . the culminating wisdom of a lifetime."

So most people—including most psychologists—would probably presume the stability of personality traits. Moreover, our traits are socially significant. They influence our health, our thinking, and our job choices and performance (Hogan, 1998; Jackson et al., 2012; Sutin et al., 2011). Studies that follow thousands of people through time show that personality traits rival socioeconomic status and cognitive ability as predictors of mortality, divorce, and occupational attainment (Graham et al., 2017; Roberts et al., 2007).

FIGURE 13.5

PERSONALITY STABILITY With age, personality traits become more stable, as reflected in the stronger correlation of trait scores with follow-up scores 7 years later. (Data from Roberts & DelVecchio, 2000.)

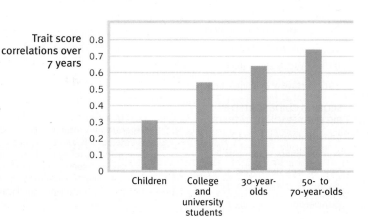

Although our personality *traits* may be both stable and potent, the consistency of our specific *behaviors* from one situation to the next is another matter. What relationship would you expect to find between being conscientious in one situation (say, showing up for class on time) and being conscientious in another (say, avoiding unhealthy foods)? If you've noticed how outgoing you are in some situations and how reserved you are in others, perhaps you said, "Very little." That's what researchers have found—only a small correlation (Mischel, 1968; Sherman et al., 2015). This inconsistency in behaviors also makes personality test scores weak predictors of behaviors. People's scores on an extraversion test, for example, do not neatly predict how sociable they actually will be on any given occasion.

If we remember such results, we will be more cautious about labeling and pigeonholing individuals (Mischel, 1968). Years in advance, science can tell us the phase of the Moon for any given date. A day in advance, meteorologists can often predict the weather. But we are much further from being able to predict how *you* will feel and act tomorrow. However, people's *average* outgoingness, happiness, or carelessness over many situations is predictable (Epstein, 1983a,b). This tendency toward trait-consistent actions occurs across cultures, from the United States to Venezuela to Japan (Locke et al., 2017). People who know someone well, therefore, generally agree when rating that person's shyness or agreeableness (Jackson et al., 2015; Kenrick & Funder, 1988). By collecting snippets of people's daily experience via body-worn recording devices, researchers confirmed that extraverts really do talk more (Mehl et al., 2006). (I [DM] have repeatedly vowed to cut back on my jabbering and joking during my noontime pickup basketball games with friends. Alas, moments later, the irrepressible chatterbox inevitably reoccupies my body. And I [ND] have a similar experience whenever I buy groceries. Somehow, I always end up chatting with the cashier!) As our best friends can verify, we do have persistent, genetically influenced personality traits. And our personality traits get expressed in our

- **music preferences.** Your playlist reveals something of your personality. Classical, jazz, blues, and folk music lovers tend to be open to experience and verbally intelligent. Extraverts tend to prefer upbeat and energetic music. Country, pop, and religious music lovers tend to be cheerful, outgoing, and conscientious (Langmeyer et al., 2012; Rentfrow & Gosling, 2003, 2006).

- **written communications.** If you have ever felt you could detect someone's personality from their writing voice, you are right!! What a cool finding!!! ☺ People's writings—even their brief tweets and Facebook posts—often express their extraversion, self-esteem, and agreeableness (Orehek & Human, 2017; Park et al., 2015; Pennebaker, 2011). "Off to meet a friend. Woohoo!!!" posted one Facebook user who had scored high on extraversion (Kern et al., 2014). Extraverts also use more adjectives.

- **online and personal spaces.** Are online profiles, websites, and avatars also a canvas for self-expression? Or are they an opportunity for people to present themselves in false or misleading ways? It's more the former (Back et al., 2010; Gosling et al., 2007; Marcus et al., 2006). People who seemed most likable on their Facebook or Twitter pages also seemed most likable in person (Qiu et al., 2012; Weisbuch et al., 2009). Even mere photos, with their associated clothes, expressions, and postures, can give clues to personality and how people act in person (Gunyadin et al., 2017; Naumann et al., 2009). Our living and working spaces also help us express our identity. They all offer clues to our extraversion, agreeableness, conscientiousness, and openness (Back et al., 2010; Fong & Mar, 2015; Gosling, 2008).

In unfamiliar, formal situations—perhaps as a guest in the home of a person from another culture—our traits remain hidden as we carefully attend to social cues. In familiar, informal situations—just hanging out with friends—we feel less constrained, allowing our traits to emerge (Buss, 1989). In these informal situations, our expressive styles—our animation, manner of speaking, and gestures—are impressively consistent. Viewing "thin slices" of someone's behavior—such as seeing a photo for a mere fraction of a second, or seeing several 2-second clips of a teacher in action—can tell us a lot about the person's basic personality traits (Ambady, 2010; Tackett et al., 2016).

my hair over time

childhood

teens and twenties - experimentation

thirties and up   *Mitra Farmand*

IT'S NOT JUST PERSONALITY THAT STABILIZES WITH AGE.

Change and consistency can coexist. If all people were to become somewhat less shy with age, there would be personality change, but also relative stability and predictability.

 ASK YOURSELF

How do you think your own personality traits shine through in your music preferences, communication style, and online and personal spaces?

ROOM WITH A CUE Even at "zero acquaintance," people can catch a glimpse of others' personality from looking at their online and personal spaces. So, what's your read on this person?

Gary Houlder/Getty Images

To sum up, we can say that at any moment the immediate situation powerfully influences a person's behavior. Social psychologists have learned that this is especially so when a "strong situation" makes clear demands (Cooper & Withey, 2009). We can better predict drivers' behavior at traffic lights from knowing the color of the lights than from knowing the drivers' personalities. Averaging our behavior across many occasions does, however, reveal distinct personality traits. Traits exist. We differ. And our differences matter.

📺 **LaunchPad** For a demonstration of trait research, view the 8-minute **Video: Trait Theories of Personality.**

🔒 **RETRIEVE IT ● ● ●**   *ANSWERS IN APPENDIX E*

RI-3 How well do personality test scores predict our behavior? Explain.

SOCIAL-COGNITIVE THEORIES

LOQ 13-18 How do social-cognitive theorists view personality development, and how do they explore behavior?

The **social-cognitive perspective** on personality, proposed by Albert Bandura (1986, 2006, 2008), emphasizes the interaction of our traits with our situations. Much as nature and nurture always work together, so do individuals and their situations.

Social-cognitive theorists believe we learn many of our behaviors either through conditioning or by observing and imitating others. (That's the "social" part.) They also emphasize the importance of mental processes: What we *think* about a situation affects our behavior in that situation. (That's the "cognitive" part.) Instead of focusing solely on how our environment *controls* us (behaviorism), social-cognitive theorists focus on how we and our environment *interact:* How do we interpret and respond to external events? How do our schemas, our memories, and our expectations influence our behavior patterns?

Reciprocal Influences

Bandura (1986, 2006) views the person-environment interaction as **reciprocal determinism.** "Behavior, internal personal factors, and environmental influences," he said, "all operate as interlocking determinants of each other" (**FIGURE 13.6**). We can see this interaction in people's relationships. For example, Rosa's past romantic experiences (her behaviors) influence her romantic attitudes (internal factor), which affect how she now responds to Ryan (environmental factor).

Consider three specific ways in which individuals and environments interact:

1. ***Different people choose different environments.*** The schools we attend, the reading we do, the careers we pursue, the music we listen to, the social media we use, the friends we associate with—all are part of an environment we have chosen, based

social-cognitive perspective a view of behavior as influenced by the interaction between people's traits (including their thinking) and their social context.

reciprocal determinism the interacting influences of behavior, internal cognition, and environment.

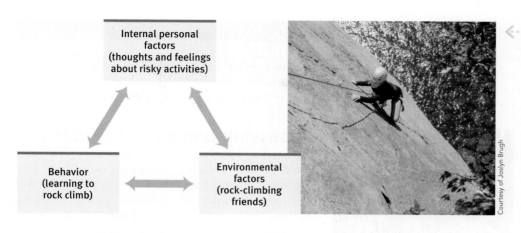

Internal personal factors (thoughts and feelings about risky activities)

Behavior (learning to rock climb)

Environmental factors (rock-climbing friends)

Courtesy of Joslyn Brugh

← FIGURE 13.6
RECIPROCAL DETERMINISM

partly on our dispositions (Denissen et al., 2018; Funder, 2009). And the environments we choose then shape us. People with inflated self-esteem post frequent selfies in online environments, for example, where they can receive the public attention and praise they crave. This leads to even greater self-love (Halpern et al., 2016).

2. *Our personalities shape how we interpret and react to events.* Anxious people tend to attend and react strongly to relationship threats (Campbell & Marshall, 2011). If we perceive the world as threatening, we will watch for threats and be prepared to defend ourselves.

3. *Our personalities help create situations to which we react.* How we view and treat people influences how they then treat us. If we expect that others will not like us, our bragging and other efforts to seek their approval might actually cause them to reject us (Scopelliti et al., 2015).

In addition to the interaction of internal personal factors, the environment, and our behaviors, we also experience *gene-environment interaction.* Our genetically influenced traits evoke certain responses from others, which may nudge us in one direction or another. In one well-replicated classic study, those with the interacting factors of (1) having a specific gene associated with aggression, and (2) being raised in a difficult environment were most likely to demonstrate adult antisocial behavior (Byrd & Manuck, 2014; Caspi et al., 2002).

In such ways, we are both the products and the architects of our environments: *Behavior emerges from the interplay of external and internal influences.* Boiling water turns an egg hard and a potato soft. A threatening environment turns one person into a hero, another into a scoundrel. Extraverts enjoy greater well-being in an extraverted culture than in an introverted one (Fulmer et al., 2010). *At every moment,* our behavior is influenced by our biology, our social and cultural experiences, and our cognition and dispositions (**FIGURE 13.7**).

ENGAGE

(ASK YOURSELF)

How have your experiences shaped your personality? How has your personality helped shape your environment?

LaunchPad To explore the influence of the person-environment interaction on behavior, engage online with **Concept Practice: Reciprocal Determinism.**

Biological influences:
• genetically determined temperament
• autonomic nervous system reactivity
• brain activity

Psychological influences:
• learned responses
• unconscious thought processes
• expectations and interpretations

Personality

Social-cultural influences:
• childhood experiences
• situational factors
• cultural expectations
• social support

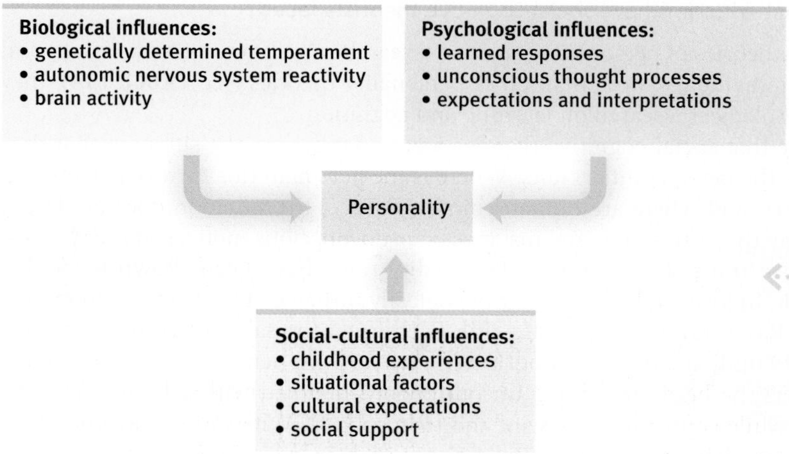

RETAIN

← FIGURE 13.7

THE BIOPSYCHOSOCIAL APPROACH TO THE STUDY OF PERSONALITY As with other psychological phenomena, personality is fruitfully studied at multiple levels.

IF YOU CAN'T STAND THE HEAT . . .
On the Food Network's *Chopped*, contestants are pitted against one another in stressful situations. The entertaining episodes illustrate a valid point: A chef's behavior in such job-relevant situations can help predict job performance.

Gustavo Caballero/Getty Images

Assessing Behavior in Situations

To predict behavior, social-cognitive psychologists often observe behavior in realistic situations. One ambitious example was the U.S. Army's World War II strategy for assessing candidates for spy missions. Rather than using paper-and-pencil tests, Army psychologists subjected the candidates to simulated undercover conditions. They tested their ability to handle stress, solve problems, maintain leadership, and withstand intense interrogation without blowing their cover. Although time-consuming and expensive, this assessment of behavior in a realistic situation helped predict later success on actual spy missions (OSS Assessment Staff, 1948).

Military and educational organizations and many Fortune 500 companies have adopted similar strategies, known as the *assessment center* approach (Bray & Byham, 1991, 1997; Eurich et al., 2009). AT&T has observed prospective managers doing simulated managerial work. Many colleges assess nursing students' potential by observing their clinical work, and they assess potential faculty members' teaching abilities by observing them teach. Most American cities with populations of 50,000 or more have used assessment centers in evaluating police officers and firefighters (Lowry, 1997).

These procedures exploit the principle that the best means of predicting future behavior is neither a personality test nor an interviewer's intuition; rather, it is *the person's past behavior patterns in similar situations* (Lyons et al., 2011; Mischel, 1981; Schmidt & Hunter, 1998). As long as the situation and the person remain much the same, the best predictor of future job performance is past job performance; the best predictor of future grades is past grades; the best predictor of future aggressiveness is past aggressiveness. If you can't check the person's past behavior, the next best thing is to create an assessment situation that simulates the task so you can see how the person handles it (Lievens et al., 2009; Meriac et al., 2008).

"What's past is prologue." —William Shakespeare, *The Tempest*, 1611

Evaluating Social-Cognitive Theories

LOQ 13-19 What criticisms have social-cognitive theorists faced?

Social-cognitive theories of personality sensitize researchers to how situations affect, and are affected by, individuals. More than other personality theories (see **TABLE 13.4**), they build from psychological research on learning and cognition.

Critics charge that social-cognitive theories focus so much on the situation that they fail to appreciate the person's inner traits. Where is the person in this view of personality, ask the dissenters, and where are human emotions? True, the situation does guide our behavior. But, say the critics, in many instances our unconscious motives, our emotions, and our pervasive traits shine through. Personality traits have been shown to predict behavior at work, in love, and at play. Our biologically influenced traits really do matter. Consider Percy Ray Pridgen and Charles Gill. Each faced the same situation: They had jointly won a $90 million lottery jackpot (Harriston, 1993). When Pridgen learned of the winning numbers, he began trembling uncontrollably, huddled with a friend behind a bathroom door while confirming the win, and then sobbed. When Gill heard the news, he told his wife and then went to sleep.

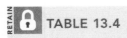

TABLE 13.4

Comparing the Major Personality Theories

Personality Theory	Key Proponents	Assumptions	View of Personality	Personality Assessment Methods
Psychoanalytic	Freud	Emotional disorders spring from unconscious dynamics, such as unresolved sexual and other childhood conflicts, and fixation at various developmental stages. Defense mechanisms fend off anxiety.	Personality consists of pleasure-seeking impulses (the id), a reality-oriented executive (the ego), and an internalized set of ideals (the superego).	Free association, projective tests, dream analysis
Psychodynamic	Adler, Horney, Jung	The unconscious and conscious minds interact. Childhood experiences and defense mechanisms are important.	The dynamic interplay of conscious and unconscious motives and conflicts shapes our personality.	Projective tests, therapy sessions
Humanistic	Rogers, Maslow	Rather than examining the struggles of sick people, it's better to focus on the ways healthy people may strive for self-realization.	If our basic human needs are met, we will strive toward self-actualization. In a climate of unconditional positive regard, we can develop self-awareness and a more realistic and positive self-concept.	Questionnaires, therapy sessions
Trait	Allport, H. Eysenck, S. Eysenck, McCrae, Costa	We have certain stable and enduring characteristics, influenced by genetic predispositions.	Scientific study of traits has isolated important dimensions of personality, such as the Big Five traits (conscientiousness, agreeableness, neuroticism, openness, and extraversion).	Personality inventories
Social-Cognitive	Bandura	Our traits interact with the social context to produce our behaviors.	Conditioning and observational learning interact with cognition to create behavior patterns. Our behavior in one situation is best predicted by considering our past behavior in similar situations.	Observing behavior in realistic situations

---

RETRIEVE IT • • •   *ANSWERS IN APPENDIX E*

RI-5 What is the best way to predict a person's future behavior?

LaunchPad To review the perspectives and methods discussed in this chapter, engage online with **Concept Practice: Comparing Personality Theories.**

EXPLORING THE SELF

LOQ 13-20 Why has psychology generated so much research on the self? How important is self-esteem to our well-being?

Our personality feeds our sense of self. Asked to consider "Who I am," people draw on their distinctive and enduring ways of thinking, feeling, and acting. Psychology's concern with our sense of self dates back at least to William James, who devoted more than 100 pages of his 1890 *Principles of Psychology* to the topic. By 1943, Gordon Allport lamented that the self had become "lost to view." Although humanistic psychology's later emphasis on the self did not instigate much scientific research, it did help renew the concept of self and keep it alive. Now, more than a century after James, the self is one of Western psychology's most vigorously researched topics. Every year, new studies galore appear on self-esteem, self-disclosure, self-awareness, self-schemas, self-monitoring, and more. Even neuroscientists have searched for the self, by identifying a central frontal lobe region that activates when people respond to self-reflective questions about their traits and dispositions (Damasio, 2010; Mitchell, 2009; Pauly et al., 2013). The **self,** as organizer of our thoughts, feelings, and actions, occupies the center of personality.

One example of thinking about self is the concept of *possible selves* (Markus & Nurius, 1986; Rathbone et al., 2016). Your possible selves include your visions of the self you dream of becoming—the rich self, the successful self, the loved and admired self. Your possible selves also include the self you fear becoming—the unemployed self, the academically failed self, the lonely and unpopular self. Possible selves motivate us to lay out specific goals that direct our energy effectively and efficiently (Landau et al., 2014). Middle school students whose families struggle financially are more likely to earn high grades if they have a clear vision of themselves succeeding in school (Duckworth et al., 2013). Dreams do often give birth to achievements.

Our self-focused perspective may motivate us, but it can also lead us to presume too readily that others are noticing and evaluating us. Most of them aren't. Thomas Gilovich (1996) has demonstrated this **spotlight effect** by having students don T-shirts featuring 1970s soft-rock icon Barry Manilow before entering a room with other students. Feeling self-conscious, the T-shirt wearers guessed that nearly half their peers would take note of the shirt as they walked in. How many actually noticed? Only 23 percent. The point to remember: *We stand out less than we imagine,* even with dorky clothes, bad hair, nervousness, or irritation (Gilovich & Savitsky, 1999). Even after a blunder (setting off a library alarm, showing up in the wrong clothes), we stick out like a sore thumb less than we imagine (Savitsky et al., 2001).

To turn down the spotlight's brightness, we can use two strategies. The first is simply to know and remember the spotlight effect. Public speakers perform better if they understand that their natural nervousness is hardly noticeable (Savitsky & Gilovich, 2003). The second is to take the audience's perspective. When we imagine audience members empathizing with our situation, we tend to expect we will not be judged as harshly (Epley et al., 2002).

Trinity Mirror/Mirrorpix/Alamy;
Tim Large/Shutterstock

The Benefits of Self-Esteem

Self-esteem—our feelings of high or low self-worth—matters. So does **self-efficacy,** our sense of competence on a task (Bandura, 1977). (A student might feel high self-efficacy in a math course yet low overall self-esteem.) People who feel good about themselves (who strongly agree with self-affirming questionnaire statements, such as "I am fun to be with") have fewer sleepless nights. They succumb less to pressures to conform. They make more positive Facebook posts, causing others to like them more (Forest & Wood, 2012). They are more persistent at difficult tasks. They feel less shy, anxious, and lonely, and are just plain happier (Greenberg, 2008; Orth & Robins, 2014; Swann et al., 2007). Our self-esteem grows from venturesome experiences and achievement, and therefore changes as we age (Hutteman et al., 2015). In one study of nearly 1 million people across 48 nations, self-esteem increased from adolescence to middle adulthood (Bleidorn et al., 2016).

But is high self-esteem the horse or the cart? Is it really "the armor that protects kids" from life's problems (McKay, 2000)? Some psychologists have their doubts (Baumeister, 2006; Dawes, 1994; Leary, 1999; Seligman, 1994, 2002). Children's academic self-efficacy—their confidence that they can do well in a subject—predicts school achievement. But general self-image does not (Marsh & Craven, 2006; Swann et al., 2007; Trautwein et al., 2006). Maybe self-esteem simply reflects reality. Maybe it's a side effect of meeting challenges and surmounting difficulties. Maybe self-esteem is a gauge that reports the state of our relationships with others (Reitz et al., 2016). If so, isn't pushing the gauge artificially

---

"The first step to better times is to imagine them." —Chinese fortune cookie

(ASK YOURSELF)

What possible selves do you dream of—or fear—becoming? To what extent do these imagined selves motivate you now?

---

self in contemporary psychology, assumed to be the center of personality, the organizer of our thoughts, feelings, and actions.

spotlight effect overestimating others' noticing and evaluating our appearance, performance, and blunders (as if we presume a spotlight shines on us).

self-esteem one's feelings of high or low self-worth.

self-efficacy one's sense of competence and effectiveness.

self-serving bias a readiness to perceive oneself favorably.

higher with empty compliments much like forcing a car's low fuel gauge to display "full"?

If feeling good *follows* doing well, then giving praise in the absence of good performance may actually harm people. After receiving weekly self-esteem-boosting messages, struggling students earned *lower*-than-expected grades (Forsyth et al., 2007). Other research showed that giving people random rewards hurt their productivity. Martin Seligman (2012) reported that "when good things occurred that weren't earned, like nickels coming out of slot machines, it did not increase people's well-being. It produced helplessness. People gave up and became passive."

There is, however, an important *effect* of low self-esteem. When researchers temporarily deflated participants' self-image (by telling them they did poorly on an aptitude test or by disparaging their personality), those participants became more likely to disparage others or to express heightened racial prejudice (vanDellen et al., 2011; van Dijk et al., 2011; Ybarra, 1999). Self-image threat even increases unconscious racial bias (Allen & Sherman, 2011). Those who are negative about themselves have also tended to be oversensitive and judgmental (Baumgardner et al., 1989; Pelham, 1993). Self-esteem threats also lead people to spend more time with their online profiles—safe havens in which to rebuild their self-worth (Toma & Hancock, 2013). Such findings are consistent with humanistic psychology's ideas about the benefits of a healthy self-image. Accept yourself and you'll find it easier to accept others. Disparage yourself and you will be prone to the floccinaucinihilipilification[1] of others. Said more simply, some "love their neighbors as themselves"; others loathe their neighbors as themselves. People who are down on themselves tend to be down on others.

Self-Serving Bias

LOQ 13-21 What evidence reveals self-serving bias, and how do defensive and secure self-esteem differ?

ENGAGE Imagine dashing to class, hoping not to miss the first few minutes. But you arrive five minutes late, huffing and puffing. As you sink into your seat, what sorts of thoughts go through your mind? Do you go through a negative door, thinking "I'm so stupid" and "I always ruin things"? Or do you go through a positive door, telling yourself, "At least I made it to class" and "I really tried to get here on time"?

Personality psychologists have found that most people choose the second door, which leads to positive self-thoughts. We have a good reputation with ourselves. We show a **self-serving bias**—a readiness to perceive ourselves favorably (Myers, 2010). Consider:

People accept more responsibility for good deeds than for bad, and for successes than for failures. Athletes often privately credit their victories to their own prowess, and their losses to bad breaks, lousy officiating, or the other team's exceptional performance. Most students who receive poor exam grades criticize the exam or the instructor, not themselves. Drivers filling out insurance forms explain their accidents in such words as "As I reached an intersection, a hedge sprang up, obscuring my vision, and I did not see the other car" and "A pedestrian hit me and went under my car." The question "What have I done to deserve this?" is one we usually ask of our troubles, not our successes. Although a self-serving bias can lead us to avoid uncomfortable truths, it can also motivate us to approach difficult tasks with confidence instead of despair (Tomaka et al., 1992; von Hippel & Trivers, 2011).

ENGAGE *Most people see themselves as better than average.* Compared with most other people, how moral are you? How easy to get along with? Where would you rank yourself, from the 1st to the 99th percentile? Most people put themselves well above the 50th percentile. This better-than-average effect appears for nearly any subjectively assessed and socially desirable behavior. Some examples:

- In U.S. surveys, most business executives say they are more ethical than their average counterpart. In several studies, 90 percent of business managers and more than 90 percent of college professors also rated their performance as superior to that of their average peer.

---

1. We couldn't resist throwing that in. But don't worry, you won't be tested on floccinaucinihilipilification, which is the act of estimating something as worthless (and was the longest nontechnical word in the first edition of the *Oxford English Dictionary*).

"When kids increase in self-control, their grades go up later. But when kids increase their self-esteem, there is no effect on their grades." —Angela Duckworth, *In Character* interview, 2009

"The enthusiastic claims of the self-esteem movement mostly range from fantasy to hogwash. The effects of self-esteem are small, limited, and not all good." —Roy Baumeister (1996)

Mike Twohy The New Yorker Collection/ The Cartoon Bank

"I never blame myself when I'm not hitting. I just blame the bat and if it keeps up, I change bats." —Baseball great Yogi Berra (1925–2015)

"If you are like most people, then like most people, you don't know you're like most people. Science has given us a lot of facts about the average person, and one of the most reliable of these facts is the average person doesn't see herself as average." —Daniel Gilbert, *Stumbling on Happiness*, 2006

BLINDNESS TO ONE'S OWN INCOMPETENCE Ironically, people often are most overconfident when most incompetent. That, say Justin Kruger and David Dunning (1999), is because it often takes competence to recognize competence. Our ignorance of what we don't know sustains our self-confidence, leading us to make the same mistakes (Williams et al., 2013).

"The [self-]portraits that we actually believe, when we are given freedom to voice them, are dramatically more positive than reality can sustain."
—Shelley Taylor, *Positive Illusions*, 1989

- In Australia, 86 percent of people rate their job performance as above average, and only 1 percent as below average.

- In the U.S. National Survey of Families and Households, 49 percent of men said they provided half or more of the child care, though only 31 percent of their wives or partners saw things that way (Galinsky et al., 2008).

Self-serving bias reflects both an overestimation of the self and a desire to maintain a positive self-view (Brown, 2012; Epley & Dunning, 2000). This motivation to see ourselves positively is weaker in Asia, where people tend to value modesty (Church et al., 2014; Falk et al., 2009). Yet self-serving biases have been observed worldwide: In every one of 53 countries surveyed, people expressed self-esteem above the midpoint of the most widely used scale (Schmitt & Allik, 2005).

Finding their self-esteem threatened, people with large egos may react violently. Researchers Brad Bushman and Roy Baumeister (1998; Bushman et al., 2009) had undergraduate volunteers write a brief essay, in response to which another supposed student gave them either praise ("Great essay!") or stinging criticism ("One of the worst essays I have read!"). The essay writers were then allowed to lash out at their evaluators by blasting them with unpleasant noise. Can you anticipate the result? After criticism, those with inflated self-esteem were "exceptionally aggressive." They delivered three times the auditory torture than did those with normal self-esteem. Over 80 studies have replicated the dangerous effect of **narcissism** (excessive self-love and self-focus) on aggression (Rasmussen, 2016). Researchers have concluded that "conceited, self-important individuals turn nasty toward those who puncture their bubbles of self-love" (Baumeister, 2001).

After tracking self-importance across several decades, psychologist Jean Twenge (2006; Twenge & Foster, 2010) reported that what she called *Generation Me*—born in the 1980s and early 1990s—expressed more narcissism (by agreeing more often with statements such as, "If I ruled the world, it would be a better place," or "I think I am a special person"). Why does a rise in narcissism matter? Narcissists tend to be materialistic, desire fame, have inflated expectations, hook up more often without commitment, and gamble and cheat more—all of which have been increasing as narcissism has increased.

Narcissistic people (more often men) forgive others less, take a game-playing approach to their romantic relationships, and engage in sexually forceful behavior (Blinkhorn et al., 2015; Bushman et al., 2003; Grijalva et al., 2015). They crave adulation, are active on social media, and often become enraged when criticized (Geukes et al., 2016; Krizan

PEANUTS

narcissism excessive self-love and self-absorption.

& Johar, 2015; McCain & Campbell, 2016). Many had parents who told them they were superior to others (Brummelman et al., 2015). They typically make good first impressions, which wane over time as their arrogance and bragging gets old (Czarna et al., 2016; Leckelt et al., 2015). Reality TV stars are often narcissistic (Rubinstein, 2016; Young & Pinsky, 2006).

Some critics of the concept of self-serving bias claim that it overlooks those who feel worthless and unlovable: If self-serving bias prevails, why do so many people disparage themselves? For four reasons: (1) Self-directed put-downs can be *subtly strategic*—they elicit reassuring strokes. Saying "No one likes me" may at least elicit "But not everyone has met you!" (2) Before an important event, such as a game or an exam, self-disparaging comments *prepare us for possible failure*. The coach who extols the superior strength of the upcoming opponent makes a loss understandable, a victory noteworthy. (3) A self-disparaging "How could I have been so stupid!" can help us *learn from our mistakes*. (4) Self-disparagement frequently *pertains to one's old self*. Asked to remember their really bad behaviors, people recall things from long ago; good behaviors more easily come to mind from their recent past (Escobedo & Adolphs, 2010). Even when they have not changed, people are much more critical of their distant past selves than of their current selves (Wilson & Ross, 2001). "At 18, I was a jerk; today I'm more sensitive." In their own eyes, chumps yesterday, champs today.

Even so, all of us some of the time (and some of us much of the time) do feel inferior. This is especially true when we compare ourselves with those who are a step or two higher on the ladder of status, looks, income, or ability. Olympians who win silver medals, barely missing gold, show greater sadness on the awards podium compared with the bronze medal winners (Medvec et al., 1995). The deeper and more frequently we have such feelings, the more unhappy or even depressed we become. But for most people, thinking has a naturally positive bias.

While recognizing the dark side of self-serving bias and self-esteem, some researchers identify two types of self-esteem—defensive and secure (Kernis, 2003; Lambird & Mann, 2006; Ryan & Deci, 2004). *Defensive self-esteem* is fragile. It focuses on sustaining itself, which makes failure and criticism feel threatening. Defensive people may respond to such perceived threats with anger or aggression (Crocker & Park, 2004; Donnellan et al., 2005).

Secure self-esteem is less fragile, because it is less contingent on external evaluations. Feeling accepted for who we are, and not for our looks, wealth, or acclaim, relieves pressures to succeed and enables us to focus beyond ourselves. By losing ourselves in relationships and purposes larger than ourselves, we may achieve a more secure self-esteem, satisfying relationships, and greater quality of life (Crocker & Park, 2004). Authentic pride, rooted in actual achievement, supports self-confidence and leadership (Tracy et al., 2009; Weidman et al., 2016; Williams & DeSteno, 2009).

> "If you compare yourself with others, you may become vain and bitter; for always there will be greater and lesser persons than yourself." —Max Ehrmann, "Desiderata," 1927

> "True humility is not thinking less of yourself; it is thinking of yourself less." —C. S. Lewis, *Mere Christianity*, 1952

🔒 **RETRIEVE IT** • • •   *ANSWERS IN APPENDIX E*

RI-6 What are the positive and negative effects of high self-esteem?

RI-7 The tendency to accept responsibility for success and blame circumstances or bad luck for failure is called _____ - _____ _____.

RI-8 _____ (Secure/Defensive) self-esteem is linked to angry and aggressive behavior. _____ (Secure/Defensive) self-esteem is a healthier self-image that allows us to focus beyond ourselves and enjoy a higher quality of life.

Culture and the Self

LOQ 13-22 How do individualist and collectivist cultures differ in their values and goals?

ENGAGE 💡 Our consideration of personality—of people's characteristic ways of thinking, feeling, and acting—concludes with a look at cultural variations. Imagine that someone ripped away your social connections, making you a solitary refugee in a foreign land. How much of your identity would remain intact?

CONSIDERATE COLLECTIVISTS
Japan's collectivist values, including duty to others and social harmony, were on display after the devastating 2011 earthquake and tsunami. Virtually no looting was reported, and residents remained calm and orderly, as shown here while waiting for drinking water.

COLLECTIVIST CULTURE Although the United States is largely individualist, many cultural subgroups remain collectivist. This is true for Alaska Natives, who demonstrate respect for tribal elders, and whose identity springs largely from their group affiliations.

"One needs to cultivate the spirit of sacrificing the *little me* to achieve the benefits of the *big me*." —Chinese saying

The tolerance of a Starbucks barista is severely tested.

If you are an **individualist,** a great deal. You would have an independent sense of "me," and an awareness of your unique personal convictions and values. Individualists prioritize personal goals. They define their identity mostly in terms of personal traits. They strive for personal control and individual achievement.

Individualists do share the human need to belong. They join groups. But they are less focused on group harmony and doing their duty to the group (Brewer & Chen, 2007). Being more self-contained, individualists move in and out of social groups more easily. They feel relatively free to switch places of worship, change jobs, or even leave their extended families and migrate to a new place. Marriage is often for as long as they both shall love.

If set adrift in a foreign land as a **collectivist,** you might experience a greater loss of identity. Cut off from family, groups, and loyal friends, you would lose the connections that have defined who you are. *Group identifications* provide a sense of belonging, a set of values, and an assurance of security. Collectivists have deep attachments to their groups—their family, clan, company, or country. Elders receive respect. For example, Chinese law states that parents aged 60 or above can sue their sons and daughters if they fail to provide "for the elderly, taking care of them and comforting them, and cater[ing] to their special needs."

Collectivists are like athletes who take more pleasure in their team's victory than in their own performance. They find satisfaction in advancing their groups' interests, even at the expense of personal needs. They preserve group spirit by avoiding direct confrontation, blunt honesty, and uncomfortable topics. They value humility, not self-importance (Bond et al., 2012). Instead of dominating conversations, collectivists hold back and display shyness when meeting strangers (Cheek & Melchior, 1990). Given the priority on "we," not "me," that super-customized latte that feels so soothing to a North American might sound selfishly demanding in Seoul (Kim & Markus, 1999).

A question: What do you think of people who willingly change their behavior to suit different people and situations? People in individualist countries (the United States and Brazil) typically describe them as "dishonest," "untrustworthy," and "insincere" (Levine, 2016). In traditionally collectivist countries (China, India, and Nepal), people more often describe them as "mature," "honest," "trustworthy," and "sincere."

Within many countries, there are also distinct subcultures related to one's religion, economic status, and region (Cohen, 2009). In China, greater collectivist thinking occurs in provinces that have produced rice, a difficult-to-grow crop that involves cooperation to sustain irrigation (Talhelm et al., 2014). In collectivist Japan, a spirit of individualism marks the "northern frontier" island of Hokkaido (Kitayama et al., 2006). And even in the most individualist countries, people have some collectivist values. But in general, people (especially men) in competitive, individualist cultures have more personal freedom, are less geographically bound to their families, enjoy more privacy, and take more pride in personal achievements (**TABLE 13.5**).

Individualists even prefer unusual names, as Jean Twenge noticed while seeking a name for her first child. When she and her colleagues (2010a, 2016a) analyzed the first names of 358 million American babies born between 1880 and 2015, they discovered

TABLE 13.5

Value Contrasts Between Individualism and Collectivism

Concept	Individualism	Collectivism
Self	Independent (identity from individual traits)	Interdependent (identity from belonging to groups)
Life task	Discover and express one's uniqueness	Maintain connections, fit in, perform role
What matters	Me—personal achievement and fulfillment; rights and liberties; self-esteem	Us—group goals and solidarity; social responsibilities and relationships; family duty
Coping method	Change reality	Accommodate to reality
Morality	Defined by the individual (self-based)	Defined by social networks (duty-based)
Relationships	Many, often temporary or casual; confrontation acceptable	Few, close, and enduring; harmony is valued
Attributing behavior	Behavior reflects the individual's personality and attitudes	Behavior reflects social norms and roles

Information from Thomas Schoeneman (1994) and Harry Triandis (1994).

individualism giving priority to one's own goals over group goals and defining one's identity in terms of personal attributes rather than group identifications.

collectivism giving priority to the goals of one's group (often one's extended family or work group) and defining one's identity accordingly.

that the most common baby names had become less common. As **FIGURE 13.8** illustrates, the percentage of boys and girls given one of the 10 most common names for their birth year has plunged. Collectivist Japan provides a contrast: Half of Japanese baby names are among the country's 10 most common names (Ogihara et al., 2015).

Individualists demand romance and personal fulfillment in marriage (Dion & Dion, 1993). In one survey, "keeping romance alive" was rated as important to a good marriage by 78 percent of U.S. women but only 29 percent of Japanese women (*American Enterprise*, 1992). In China, love songs have often expressed enduring commitment and friendship (Rothbaum & Tsang, 1998): "We will be together from now on . . . I will never change from now to forever."

What predicts change in one culture over time, or differences between cultures? Social history matters. Individualism and independence have been fostered by voluntary emigration, a capitalist economy, and a sparsely populated, challenging environment (Kitayama et al., 2009, 2010; Varnum et al., 2010). In Western cultures over the last century and now in all but the poorest countries, individualism has increased, following closely on the heels of increasing affluence (Grossmann & Varnum, 2015; Santos et al., 2017). Might biology also play a role? One study comparing collectivists' and individualists' brain activity suggested that collectivists experienced greater emotional pain when they viewed others in distress (Cheon et al., 2013). As we have seen in personality and beyond, we are biopsychosocial creatures.

ASK YOURSELF

Do you consider yourself to be more of a collectivist or an individualist? How do you think this sense of self has influenced your behavior, emotions, and thoughts?

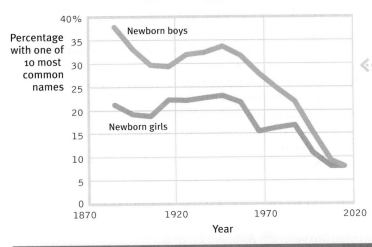

FIGURE 13.8

A CHILD LIKE NO OTHER Americans' individualist tendencies are reflected in their choices of names for their babies. In recent years, the percentage of American babies receiving one of that year's 10 most common names has plunged. (Data from Twenge et al., 2010a, 2016a.)

RETRIEVE IT • • •

ANSWERS IN APPENDIX E

RI-9 How do people in individualist and collectivist cultures differ?

⤷ Learning Objectives

TEST YOURSELF Answer these repeated Learning Objective Questions on your own (before checking the answers in Appendix D) to improve your retention of the concepts (McDaniel et al., 2009, 2015).

13-13 How do psychologists use traits to describe personality?

13-14 What are some common misunderstandings about introversion?

13-15 What are *personality inventories,* and what are their strengths and weaknesses as trait-assessment tools?

13-16 Which traits seem to provide the most useful information about personality variation?

13-17 Does research support the consistency of personality traits over time and across situations?

13-18 How do social-cognitive theorists view personality development, and how do they explore behavior?

13-19 What criticisms have social-cognitive theorists faced?

13-20 Why has psychology generated so much research on the self? How important is self-esteem to our well-being?

13-21 What evidence reveals self-serving bias, and how do defensive and secure self-esteem differ?

13-22 How do individualist and collectivist cultures differ in their values and goals?

⤷ Terms and Concepts to Remember

TEST YOURSELF Write down the definition yourself, then check your answer on the referenced page.

trait, **p. 475**

personality inventory, **p. 477**

Minnesota Multiphasic Personality Inventory (MMPI), **p. 477**

empirically derived test, **p. 477**

social-cognitive perspective, **p. 482**

reciprocal determinism, **p. 482**

self, **p. 486**

spotlight effect, **p. 486**

self-esteem, **p. 486**

self-efficacy, **p. 486**

self-serving bias, **p. 486**

narcissism, **p. 488**

individualism, **p. 491**

collectivism, **p. 491**

⤷ Experience the Testing Effect

TEST YOURSELF Answer the following questions on your own first, then check your answers in Appendix E.

1. _____ theories of personality focus on describing characteristic behavior patterns, such as agreeableness or extraversion.

2. The most widely used personality inventory is the
   a. Extraversion–Introversion Scale.
   b. Person–Situation Inventory.
   c. MMPI.
   d. Rorschach.

3. Which of the following is NOT one of the Big Five personality factors?
   a. Conscientiousness   c. Extraversion
   b. Anxiety   d. Agreeableness

4. Our scores on personality tests best predict
   a. our behavior on a specific occasion.
   b. our average behavior across many situations.
   c. behavior involving a single trait, such as conscientiousness.
   d. behavior that depends on the situation or context.

5. The social-cognitive perspective proposes that our personality is shaped by a process called reciprocal determinism, as internal factors, environmental factors, and behaviors interact. An example of an environmental factor is
   a. the presence of books in a home.
   b. a preference for outdoor play.
   c. the ability to read at a fourth-grade level.
   d. the fear of violent action on television.

6. Critics say that _____-_____ personality theory is very sensitive to an individual's interactions with particular situations, but that it gives too little attention to the person's enduring traits.

7. The tendency to overestimate others' attention to and evaluation of our appearance, performance, and blunders is called the _____ _____.

8. Researchers have found that low self-esteem tends to be linked with life problems. How should this link be interpreted?
   a. Life problems cause low self-esteem.
   b. The answer isn't clear because the link is correlational and does not indicate cause and effect.
   c. Low self-esteem leads to life problems.
   d. Because of the self-serving bias, we must assume that external factors cause low self-esteem.

9. A fortune cookie advises, "Love yourself and happiness will follow." Is this good advice?

10. Individualist cultures tend to value _____; collectivist cultures tend to value _____.
    a. interdependence; independence
    b. independence; interdependence
    c. solidarity; uniqueness
    d. duty; fulfillment

Continue testing yourself with 📖 **LearningCurve** or 📖 **Achieve Read & Practice** to learn and remember most effectively.

Psychological Disorders

I felt the need to clean my room . . . and would spend four to five hours at it. I would take every book out of the bookcase, dust and put it back . . . I couldn't stop.

Marc, diagnosed with obsessive-compulsive disorder (from Summers, 1996)

Whenever I get depressed it's because I've lost a sense of self. I can't find reasons to like myself. I think I'm ugly. I think no one likes me.

Greta, diagnosed with depression (from Thorne, 1993, p. 21)

Voices, like the roar of a crowd, came. I felt like Jesus; I was being crucified.

Stuart, diagnosed with schizophrenia (from Emmons et al., 1997)

Now and then, all of us feel, think, or act in ways that may resemble a psychological disorder. We feel anxious, depressed, withdrawn, or suspicious. So it's no wonder that we sometimes see ourselves in the mental illnesses we study. Personally or through friends or family, many of us will know the confusion and pain of unexplained physical symptoms, irrational fears, or a feeling that life is not worth living. Among American college students, 1 in 3 report an apparent mental health problem (Eisenberg et al., 2011).

Worldwide, more than half a billion people live with mental or behavioral disorders (WHO, 2017c). This chapter examines these disorders, and the next chapter considers their *treatment*. ▶

psychological disorder a syndrome marked by a clinically significant disturbance in an individual's cognition, emotion regulation, or behavior.

"Who in the rainbow can draw the line where the violet tint ends and the orange tint begins? Distinctly we see the difference of the colors, but where exactly does the one first blendingly enter into the other? So with sanity and insanity." —Herman Melville, *Billy Budd, Sailor*, 1924

Basic Concepts of Psychological Disorders

LEARNING OBJECTIVE QUESTION (LOQ)

14-1 How should we draw the line between normality and disorder?

Most of us would agree that someone who is depressed and stays mostly in bed for three months has a psychological disorder. But what about a grieving father who can't resume his usual social activities three months after his child has died? Where do we draw the line between understandable grief and clinical depression? Between fear and a phobia? Between normality and abnormality? In their search for answers, theorists and clinicians ask:

- How should we define psychological disorders?

- How should we understand disorders? How do underlying biological factors contribute to disorder? How do troubling environments influence our well-being? And how do these effects of nature and nurture interact?

- How should we classify psychological disorders? And can we do so in a way that allows us to help people without stigmatizing or labeling them?

- Are those with psychological disorders at risk of doing harm to themselves or others?

- What do we know about rates of psychological disorders? How many people have them? Who is vulnerable, and when?

A **psychological disorder** is a syndrome (a symptom collection) marked by a "clinically significant disturbance in an individual's cognition, emotion regulation, or behavior" (American Psychiatric Association, 2013). Such thoughts, emotions, or behaviors are *dysfunctional* or *maladaptive*—they interfere with normal day-to-day life. Believing your home must be thoroughly cleaned every weekend is not a disorder. But if cleaning rituals interfere with work and leisure, as Marc's uncontrollable rituals did, they may be signs of a disorder. Occasional sad moods that persist and become disabling may likewise signal a psychological disorder.

Distress often accompanies such dysfunction. Marc, Greta, and Stuart were all distressed by their thoughts, emotions, or behaviors.

Over time, definitions of what makes for a "significant disturbance" have varied. In 1973, the American Psychiatric Association dropped homosexuality as a disorder after mental health workers came to consider same-sex attraction as not inherently dysfunctional or distressing. In the twenty-first century, controversies swirl over other new or altered diagnoses in the most recent edition of a common classification tool for describing disorders.

CULTURE AND NORMALITY Young American men may plan elaborate invitations for big events, as did this student (a) who appealed (successfully) to his date for prom. Young men of the West African Wodaabe tribe (b) traditionally put on decorative makeup and costumes to attract women. Each culture may view the other's behavior as abnormal.

(a)

(b)

UNDERSTANDING PSYCHOLOGICAL DISORDERS

LOQ 14-2 How do the medical model and the biopsychosocial approach influence our understanding of psychological disorders?

The way we view a problem influences how we try to solve it. In earlier times, people often thought that strange behaviors were evidence of strange forces—the movements of the stars, godlike powers, or evil spirits—at work. Had you lived during the Middle Ages, you might have said, "The devil made him do it." To drive out demons, people considered "mad" were sometimes caged or given "therapies" such as genital mutilation, beatings, removal of teeth or lengths of intestines, or transfusions of animal blood (Farina, 1982).

Reformers, such as Philippe Pinel (1745–1826) in France, opposed such brutal treatments. Madness is not demonic possession, he insisted, but a sickness of the mind caused by severe stress and inhumane conditions. Curing the illness, he said, requires *moral treatment,* including boosting patients' spirits by unchaining them and talking with them. He and others worked to replace brutality with gentleness, isolation with activity, and filth with clean air and sunshine.

In some places, cruel treatments for mental illness—including chaining people to beds or confining them in spaces with wild animals—linger even today. The World Health Organization has launched a reform that aims to transform hospitals "into patient-friendly and humane places with minimum restraints" (WHO, 2014a).

The Medical Model

A medical breakthrough around 1900 prompted further reforms. Researchers discovered that syphilis, a sexually transmitted infection, invades the brain and distorts the mind. This discovery triggered an eager search for physical causes of other mental disorders, and for treatments that would cure them. Hospitals replaced asylums, and the **medical model** of mental disorders was born. This model is reflected in words we still use today. We speak of the mental *health* movement. A mental *illness* (also called a psycho*pathology*) needs to be *diagnosed* on the basis of its *symptoms*. It needs to be *treated* through *therapy*, which may include treatment in a psychiatric *hospital*. The medical perspective has been energized by more recent discoveries that genetically influenced abnormalities in brain structure and biochemistry contribute to many disorders (Insel & Cuthbert, 2015). A growing number of clinical psychologists now work in medical hospitals, where they collaborate with physicians to determine how the mind and body operate together.

The Biopsychosocial Approach

To call psychological disorders "sicknesses" tilts research heavily toward the influence of biology and away from the influence of our personal histories and social and cultural surroundings. But as we have seen throughout this text, biological, psychological, and social-cultural influences together weave the fabric of our thoughts, feelings, and behaviors. As individuals, we differ in the amount of stress we experience and in the ways we cope with stressors. Cultures also differ in the sources of stress they produce and in their traditional ways of coping. We are physically embodied and socially embedded.

Two disorders—major depressive disorder and schizophrenia—occur worldwide. From Asia to Africa and across the Americas, schizophrenia's symptoms often include irrational and incoherent speech. Other disorders tend to be associated with specific cultures.

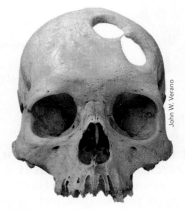

John W. Verano

YESTERDAY'S "THERAPY" Through the ages, psychologically disordered people have received brutal treatments, including the trephination evident in this Stone Age patient's skull. Drilling skull holes like these may have been an attempt to release evil spirits and cure those with mental disorders. Did this patient survive the "cure"?

medical model the concept that diseases, in this case psychological disorders, have physical causes that can be *diagnosed, treated,* and, in most cases, *cured,* often through treatment in a *hospital.*

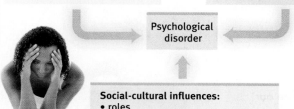

Biological influences:	Psychological influences:
• evolution	• stress
• individual genes	• trauma
• brain structure and chemistry	• learned helplessness
	• mood-related perceptions and memories

Psychological disorder

Wavebreakmedia Ltd/
Getty Images

Social-cultural influences:
• roles
• expectations
• definitions of *normality* and *disorder*

RETAIN 🔒 **FIGURE 14.1**

THE BIOPSYCHOSOCIAL APPROACH TO PSYCHOLOGICAL DISORDERS
Today's psychology studies how biological, psychological, and social-cultural factors interact to produce specific psychological disorders.

Latin America lays claim to *susto,* a condition marked by severe anxiety, restlessness, and a fear of black magic. In Japanese culture, people may experience *taijin kyofusho*—social anxiety about physical appearance, combined with a readiness to blush and a fear of eye contact. The eating disorders *anorexia nervosa* and *bulimia nervosa* occur mostly in food-abundant Western cultures. Such disorders may share an underlying dynamic (such as anxiety) while differing in the symptoms (an eating problem or a type of fear) manifested in a particular culture. Even disordered aggression may have varying explanations in different cultures. In Malaysia, *amok* describes a sudden outburst of violent behavior (as in the English phrase "run amok").

Disorders reflect genetic predispositions and physiological states, inner psychological dynamics, and social and cultural circumstances. The biopsychosocial approach emphasizes that mind and body are inseparable (**FIGURE 14.1**). Negative emotions can contribute to physical illness, and physical abnormalities can likewise contribute to negative emotions. The biopsychosocial approach gave rise to the *vulnerability-stress model,* which argues that individual characteristics combine with environmental stressors to increase or decrease the likelihood of developing a psychological disorder (Monroe & Simons, 1991; Zuckerman, 1999). Research on **epigenetics** (literally, "in addition to genetics") supports the vulnerability-stress model by showing how our DNA and our environment interact. In one environment, a gene will be *expressed,* but in another it may lie dormant. For some, that will be the difference between developing a disorder or not developing it.

🔒 **RETRIEVE IT • • •**   *ANSWERS IN APPENDIX E*

RI-2 Are psychological disorders universal or culture-specific? Explain with examples.

RI-3 What is the biopsychosocial approach, and why is it important in our understanding of psychological disorders?

CLASSIFYING DISORDERS—AND LABELING PEOPLE

LOQ 14-3 How and why do clinicians classify psychological disorders, and why do some psychologists criticize the use of diagnostic labels?

In biology, classification creates order. To classify an animal as a "mammal" says a great deal—that it is likely to be warm-blooded, have hair or fur, and produce milk to feed its young. In psychiatry and psychology, too, classification aims to order and describe symptoms. To classify a person's disorder as "schizophrenia" suggests that the person talks incoherently, has bizarre beliefs, shows either little emotion or inappropriate emotion, or is socially withdrawn. "Schizophrenia" is a quick way of describing a complex disorder.

But diagnostic classification gives more than a thumbnail sketch of a person's disordered behavior, thoughts, or feelings. In psychiatry and psychology, classification also aims to *predict* a disorder's future course, *suggest* appropriate treatment, and *prompt* research into its causes. To study a disorder, we must first name and describe it.

In the United States and many other countries, the most common tool for describing disorders and estimating how often they occur is the American Psychiatric Association's *Diagnostic and Statistical Manual of Mental Disorders,* now in its fifth edition (**DSM-5**). Physicians and mental health workers use the detailed "diagnostic criteria and codes" in the DSM-5 to guide medical diagnoses and treatment. For example, a person may be diagnosed with and treated for *insomnia disorder* if he or she meets *all* of the criteria in **TABLE 14.1**. The DSM-5's diagnostic criteria and codes closely resemble those in the World Health Organization's *International Classification of Diseases* (ICD), making it easy to track worldwide trends in psychological disorders.

Sidney Harris

"I'm always like this, and my family was wondering if you could prescribe a mild depressant."

J. Harris

TABLE 14.1
Insomnia Disorder

- Feeling unsatisfied with amount or quality of sleep (trouble falling asleep, staying asleep, or returning to sleep)

- Sleep disruption causes distress or diminished everyday functioning

- Happens three or more nights each week

- Occurs during at least three consecutive months

- Happens even with sufficient sleep opportunities

- Independent from other sleep disorders (such as narcolepsy)

- Independent from substance use or abuse

- Independent from other mental disorders or medical conditions

Information from: American Psychiatric Association, 2013.

In the DSM-5, some diagnostic labels changed. The conditions formerly called "autism" and "Asperger's syndrome" were combined under the label *autism spectrum disorder* (see Chapter 4). "Mental retardation" became *intellectual disability.* New disorders, such as *hoarding disorder* and *binge-eating disorder,* were added.

In real-world tests (*field trials*) assessing the reliability of the new DSM-5 categories, some diagnoses have fared well and others have fared poorly (Freedman et al., 2013). Clinician agreement on adult *posttraumatic stress disorder* and childhood autism spectrum disorder, for example, was near 70 percent. (If one psychiatrist or psychologist diagnosed someone with one of these disorders, there was a 70 percent chance that another mental health worker would independently give the same diagnosis.) But for *antisocial personality disorder* and *generalized anxiety disorder,* agreement was closer to 20 percent.

Critics have long faulted the DSM for casting too wide a net, and for bringing "almost any kind of behavior within the compass of psychiatry" (Eysenck et al., 1983). Some now worry that the DSM-5's even wider net will extend the pathologizing of everyday life. For example, the DSM has broadened the diagnostic criteria for **attention-deficit/hyper-activity disorder (ADHD).** For those who experience these challenging symptoms, diagnosis and treatment can be a relief and bring improved functioning (Kupfer, 2012; Maciejewski et al., 2016). However, critics suggest that the criteria are now too broad and may turn normal, childish rambunctiousness into a disorder (Frances, 2013, 2014). (See Thinking Critically About: ADHD—Normal High Energy or Disordered Behavior?) The DSM also now classifies severe grief following the death of a loved one as a possible *depressive disorder.* Critics suggest that such grief could instead simply be considered a normal reaction to tragic life events.

Seeking a new but complementary approach to classification, the U.S. National Institute of Mental Health has established the Research Domain Criteria (RDoC) project (Insel et al., 2010; NIMH, 2017). The RDoC aims to bring "the power of modern research approaches in genetics, neuroscience, and behavioral science" to the study of psychological disorders (Insel & Lieberman, 2013). This framework helps organize disorders according to behaviors and brain activity.

Other critics of classification register a more basic complaint—that diagnostic labels can be subjective, or even value judgments masquerading as science. Once we label a person, we view that person differently (Bathje & Pryor, 2011; Farina, 1982; Sadler et al., 2012a). Labels can change reality by putting us on alert for evidence that confirms our view. If we hear that a new co-worker is mean-spirited, we may treat her suspiciously. She may in turn react to us as a mean-spirited person would. Teachers who were told certain students were "gifted" then acted in ways that brought out the creative behaviors they expected (Snyder, 1984). Labels can be self-fulfilling, and, if negative, can be stigmatizing.

The biasing power of labels was clear in a classic, controversial study. David Rosenhan (1973) and seven others went to hospital admissions offices, complaining

A book of case illustrations accompanying a previous DSM edition provided several examples for this chapter.

epigenetics "above" or "in addition to" *(epi)* genetics; the study of the molecular mechanisms by which environments can influence genetic expression (without a DNA change).

DSM-5 the American Psychiatric Association's *Diagnostic and Statistical Manual of Mental Disorders,* Fifth Edition; a widely used system for classifying psychological disorders.

attention-deficit/hyperactivity disorder (ADHD) a psychological disorder marked by extreme inattention and/or hyperactivity and impulsivity.

THINKING CRITICALLY ABOUT:

ADHD—Normal High Energy or Disordered Behavior?

LOQ 14-4   Why is there controversy over attention-deficit/hyperactivity disorder?

Diagnosis in the U.S.

Twice as often in BOYS as in girls

11%[1] **4- to 17-year-olds**   **2.5%**[2] **adults**

Symptoms

- inattention and distractibility [3]
- hyperactivity [4]
- impulsivity

SKEPTICS note:

Energetic child + boring school = ADHD overdiagnosis
- Children are not designed to sit for hours in chairs inside.
- The youngest children in a class tend to be more fidgety—and more often diagnosed. [5]
- Older students may seek out stimulant ADHD prescription drugs–"good-grade pills." [6]
- What are the long-term effects of drug treatment?
- Why the increased diagnoses worldwide? [7]

SUPPORTERS note:
- More diagnoses reflect increased awareness.
- "ADHD is a real neurobiological disorder whose existence should no longer be debated." [8]
- ADHD is associated with abnormal brain structure, abnormal brain activity patterns, and future risky or antisocial behavior. [9]

Causes?
- May co-exist with a learning disorder or with defiant and temper-prone behavior.
- May be genetic. [10]

Treatment

- Stimulant drugs (Ritalin and Adderall) calm hyperactivity, and increase ability to sit and focus.[11] So do behavior therapy and aerobic exercise. [12]
- Psychological therapies help with the distress of ADHD. [13]

The bottom line:

Extreme inattention, hyperactivity, and impulsivity can derail social, academic, and work achievements. These symptoms can be treated with medication and other therapies. But the debate continues over whether normal high energy is too often diagnosed as a psychiatric disorder, and whether there is a cost to the long-term use of stimulant drugs in treating ADHD.

1. Schwarz & Cohen, 2013. 2. Simon et al., 2009. 3. Martel et al., 2016. 4. Kofler et al., 2016. 5. Chen et al., 2016. 6. Schwarz, 2012. 7. Ellison, 2015. 8. World Federation for Mental Health, 2005. 9. Barkley et al., 2002; Hoogman et al., 2017. 10. Nikolas & Burt, 2010; Poelmans et al., 2011; Volkow et al., 2009; Williams et al., 2010. 11. Barbaresi et al., 2007. 12. Cerrillo-Urbina et al., 2015; Pelham et al., 2016. 13. Fabiano et al., 2008.

(falsely) of "hearing voices" saying *empty, hollow,* and *thud.* Apart from this complaint and giving false names and occupations, they answered questions truthfully. All eight healthy people were misdiagnosed with disorders.

Should we be surprised? Surely not. As one psychiatrist noted, if someone swallowed blood, went to an emergency room, and spat it up, we wouldn't blame a doctor for diagnosing a bleeding ulcer. But what followed the diagnoses was startling. Until being released an average of 19 days later, these eight "patients" showed no other symptoms. Yet after analyzing their (quite normal) life histories, clinicians were able to "discover" the causes of their disorders, such as having mixed emotions about a parent.

Labels matter. In another study, people watched recorded interviews. If told the interviewees were job applicants, the viewers perceived them as normal (Langer & Abelson, 1974; Langer & Imber, 1980). Other viewers who were told they were watching cancer or psychiatric patients perceived the same interviewees as "different from most people." Therapists who thought they were watching an interview of a psychiatric patient perceived him as "frightened of his own aggressive impulses," a "passive, dependent type," and so forth. Labels also have power outside the laboratory. Getting a job or finding a place to rent can be a challenge for people recently released from a psychiatric hospital. Label someone as "mentally ill" and people may fear them as potentially violent. That reaction is fading as people come to better understand that psychological disorders are not failures of character. The more contact we have with people with disorders, the more accepting our attitudes become (Corrigan et al., 2014). Public figures have helped foster this understanding by speaking openly about their own struggles with disorders such as depression and substance abuse—and how beneficial it was to seek help, receive diagnosis, and get better through treatment.

Despite their risks, diagnostic labels have benefits. They help mental health professionals communicate about their cases and study the causes and treatments of disorders. Clients are often relieved to learn that their suffering has a name, and that they are not alone in experiencing their symptoms.

 LaunchPad To test your own ability to form diagnoses, try **Topic Tutorial: PsychSim6, Classifying Disorders.**

STRUGGLES AND RECOVERY During his campaign, Boston Mayor Martin Walsh spoke openly about his past struggles with alcohol. His story of recovery helped him win in 2014—the closest Boston mayoral election in decades—and again in 2017.

"What's the use of their having names," the Gnat said, "if they won't answer to them?"
"No use to *them*," said Alice; "but it's useful to the people that name them, I suppose." —Lewis Carroll, *Through the Looking-Glass,* 1871

 ASK YOURSELF

Do you know someone (could be you) who has been diagnosed with a psychological disorder? How do you think a diagnostic label might help or hurt this person?

BETTER PORTRAYALS Old stereotypes are slowly being replaced in media portrayals of psychological disorders. Modern films offer fairly realistic depictions. *Iron Man 3* (2013) portrayed a main character, shown here, with posttraumatic stress disorder. *Black Swan* (2010) dramatized a lead character suffering a delusional disorder. *A Single Man* (2009) depicted depression.

🔒 **RETRIEVE IT • • •**   *ANSWERS IN APPENDIX E*

RI-4 What is the value, and what are the dangers, of labeling individuals with disorders?

RISK OF HARM TO SELF AND OTHERS

People with psychological disorders are more likely to harm themselves. Are they also more likely to harm others?

Understanding Suicide

LOQ 14-5 What factors increase the risk of suicide, and what do we know about non-suicidal self-injury?

Each year over 800,000 despairing people worldwide will elect a permanent solution to what might have been a temporary problem (WHO, 2014c). A death by suicide will likely occur in the 40 seconds or so that it takes you to read this paragraph. For those who have been anxious, the risk of suicide is tripled, and for those who have been depressed, the risk is quintupled (Bostwick & Pankratz, 2000; Kanwar et al., 2013). People seldom die by suicide while in the depths of depression, when energy and initiative are lacking. The risk increases when they begin to rebound and become capable of following through (Chu et al., 2016).

Comparing the suicide rates of different groups, researchers have found

- **national differences:** In Britain, Italy, and Spain, suicide rates have been little more than half those of Canada, Australia, and the United States. Austria's and Finland's are about double (WHO, 2011). Within Europe, people in the most suicide-prone country (Belarus) have been 16 times more likely to die by suicide than those in the least suicide-prone country (Georgia).

- **racial differences:** Within the United States, Whites and Native Americans die by suicide twice as often as Blacks, Hispanics, and Asians (CDC, 2012).

- **gender differences:** Women are much more likely than men to attempt suicide (WHO, 2011). But men are two to four times more likely (depending on the country) to actually end their lives. Men use more lethal methods, such as firing a bullet into the head, the method of choice in 6 of 10 U.S. suicides.

- **trait differences:** Among Swedes, those with obsessive-compulsive disorder are at higher risk of depression, thereby increasing their risk of suicide (de la Cruz et al., 2017). So, too, are self-critical, perfectionist people, especially when feeling like they have failed to meet others' expectations (Smith et al., 2018).

- **age differences and trends:** In late adulthood, rates increase, with the highest rate among 45- to 64-year-olds and the second-highest among those 85 and older (AFSP, 2015). In the last half of the twentieth century, the global rate of annual suicide deaths nearly doubled (WHO, 2008). In the U.S., teen depression and suicide rates have jumped about a third since 2010, in tandem with increased cell phone use and decreased time spent face-to-face with friends (Twenge et al., 2018). Studies indicate that, over time, increasing social media use predicts increased unhappiness, while unhappiness does not lead to more social media use.

- **other group differences:** Suicide rates have been much higher among the rich, the nonreligious, and those single, widowed, or divorced (Hoyer & Lund, 1993; Norko et al., 2017; Okada & Samreth, 2013; VanderWeele et al., 2016, 2017). Witnessing physical pain and trauma can increase the risk of suicide, which may help explain veterans' and physicians' elevated suicide rates (Bender et al., 2012; Cornette et al., 2009). Gay, transgender, and gender-nonconforming youth facing an unsupportive environment, including family or peer rejection, are also at increased risk of attempting suicide (Goldfried, 2001; Haas et al., 2011; Hatzenbuehler, 2011; Testa et al., 2017). Among people with alcohol use disorder, 3 percent die by suicide. This rate is roughly 37 times greater for those who have just been heavily drinking (Borges et al., 2017).

- **day-of-the-week and seasonal differences:** Negative emotion tends to go up midweek, which can have tragic consequences (Watson, 2000). A surprising 25 percent of U.S. suicides occur on Wednesdays (Kposowa & D'Auria, 2009). Suicide rates are highest in April and May, and not (as commonly believed) over the winter holidays (Nock, 2016).

Social suggestion may trigger suicide. Following highly publicized suicides and TV programs featuring suicide, known suicides sometimes increase. So do fatal auto and private airplane "accidents." One six-year study tracked suicide cases among all 1.2 million people who lived in metropolitan Stockholm at any time during the 1990s

"But life, being weary of these worldly bars,
Never lacks power to dismiss itself."
—William Shakespeare, *Julius Caesar*, 1599

(Hedström et al., 2008). Men exposed to a family suicide were 8 times more likely to die by suicide than were nonexposed men. That phenomenon may be partly attributable to family genes. But shared genetic predispositions cannot explain why men exposed to a co-worker's suicide were 3.5 times more likely to also take their own lives, compared with nonexposed men.

Suicide is not generally an act of hostility or revenge. People—especially older adults—may choose death as an alternative to current or future suffering, a way to switch off unendurable pain and relieve a perceived burden on family members. Suicidal urges typically arise when people feel disconnected from others and a burden to them, or when they feel defeated and trapped by an inescapable situation (Joiner, 2010; Taylor et al., 2011). Thus, suicide rates increase with unemployment during economic recessions (DeFina & Hannon, 2015; Reeves et al., 2014). Suicidal thoughts also may increase when people are driven to reach a goal or standard—to become thin or straight or rich—and find it unattainable (Chatard & Selimbegović, 2011).

In hindsight, families and friends may recall signs they believe should have forewarned them—verbal hints, giving possessions away, a sudden mood change, or withdrawal and preoccupation with death (Bagge et al., 2017). To judge from surveys of 84,850 people across 17 nations, about 9 percent of people at some point in their lives have thought seriously of suicide. About 3 in 10 of those who think about it will actually attempt suicide (Nock et al., 2008). Only 3 percent of Americans die in that attempt (Han et al., 2016). In one study that followed people for up to 25 years after a first suicide attempt, some 5 percent died by suicide (Bostwick et al., 2016). One group of clinical psychologists summarized 50 years of research on suicide's unpredictability: "The vast majority of people who possess a specific risk factor [for suicide] will never engage in suicidal behavior" (Franklin et al., 2017, p. 217). But researchers continue to try to solve the suicide puzzle. Although most suicide attempts fail, the risk of eventual death by suicide is seven times greater among those who have previously attempted suicide (Al-Sayegh et al., 2015).

Each year, about 40,000 Americans will die by suicide—about two-thirds using guns. (Drug overdoses account for about 80 percent of suicide attempts, but only 14 percent of suicide fatalities.) States with high gun ownership are states with high suicide rates, even after controlling for poverty and urbanization (Miller et al., 2002, 2016; Tavernise, 2013). After Missouri repealed its tough handgun law, its suicide rate went up 15 percent; when Connecticut enacted such a law, its suicide rate dropped 16 percent (Crifasi et al., 2015). Thus, although U.S. gun owners often keep a gun to feel safer, having a gun in the home makes one less safe, because it substantially increases the odds of a family member dying by suicide or homicide (Kposowa et al., 2016; VPC, 2015; Vyse, 2016).

ENGAGE How can we be helpful to someone who is talking suicide—who says, for example, "I wish I could just end it all" or "I hate my life; I can't go on"? If people write such things online, you can anonymously contact various social media safety teams (including on Facebook, Twitter, Instagram, YouTube, and Tumblr). If a friend or family member talks suicide, you can

1. *listen* and empathize;

2. *connect* the person with your campus counseling center; with (in the United States) the National Suicide Prevention Lifeline (1-800-273-8255[TALK]) or Crisis Text Line (by texting HOME to 74174); or with their counterparts in other countries (such as the LifeLine App in Canada); and

3. *protect* someone who appears at immediate risk by seeking help from a doctor, the nearest hospital emergency room, or 911. Better to share a secret than to attend a funeral.

> "People desire death when two fundamental needs are frustrated to the point of extinction: The need to belong with or connect to others, and the need to feel effective with or to influence others."
> —Thomas Joiner (2006, p. 47)

Nonsuicidal Self-Injury

Self-harm takes many forms. Some people may engage in *nonsuicidal self-injury (NSSI)*, which is more common in adolescence and among females (CDC, 2009) (**FIGURE 14.2**). Such behavior, though painful, is not fatal. Those who engage in NSSI may cut or burn their skin, hit themselves, insert objects under their nails or skin, or self-administer tattoos. People who engage in NSSI tend to experience bullying, harassment, and other life

FIGURE 14.2

RATES OF NONFATAL SELF-INJURY IN THE UNITED STATES Self-injury rates peak higher for females than for males. (Data from CDC, 2009.)

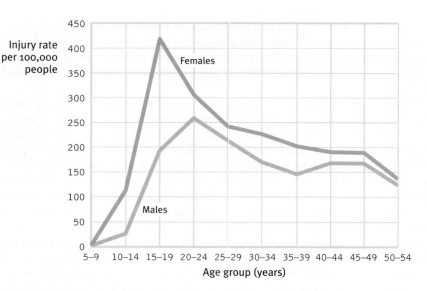

stress (Liu et al., 2016; van Geel et al., 2015). They are generally less able to tolerate and regulate emotional distress (Hamza et al., 2015). They are often extremely self-critical, and struggle to communicate, solve problems, and perform academically (Kiekens et al., 2016; Nock, 2010; You et al., 2015). Why do they hurt themselves? Reinforcement processes are at work (Bentley et al., 2014). Through NSSI they may

- find relief from intense negative thoughts through the distraction of pain.
- attract attention and possibly get help.
- relieve guilt by punishing themselves.
- get others to change their negative behavior (bullying, criticism).
- fit in with a peer group.

Does NSSI lead to suicide? Usually not. Those who engage in NSSI are typically suicide gesturers, not suicide attempters (Nock & Kessler, 2006). Nevertheless, NSSI is a risk factor for suicidal thoughts and future suicide attempts, especially when coexisting with bipolar disorder (Runeson et al., 2016; Willoughby et al., 2015). If people do not find help, their nonsuicidal behavior may escalate to suicidal thoughts and, finally, to suicide attempts.

Does Disorder Equal Danger?

LOQ 14-6 Do psychological disorders predict violent behavior?

September 16, 2013, started like any other Monday at the Navy Yard in Washington, DC, with people arriving early to begin work. Then government contractor Aaron Alexis entered the building and began shooting. An hour later, 13 people were dead, including the shooter. Reports later confirmed that Alexis had a history of mental illness, and had stated that an "ultra low frequency attack is what I've been subject to for the last three months. And to be perfectly honest, that is what has driven me to this." This devastating mass shooting, like the one in a Connecticut elementary school in 2012 and many others since then, reinforced public perceptions that people with psychological disorders pose a threat (Barry et al., 2013; Jorm et al., 2012). "People with mental illness are getting guns and committing these mass shootings," said U.S. Speaker of the House Paul Ryan (2015). In one survey, 84 percent of Americans agreed that "increased government spending on mental health screening and treatment" would be a "somewhat" or "very" effective "approach to preventing mass shootings at schools" (Newport, 2012). That was U.S. President Donald Trump's assumption, in the aftermath of a 2018 Florida school massacre. He proposed opening more mental hospitals that could house would-be mass murderers: "When you have some person like this, you can bring them into a mental institution."

Do disorders actually increase risk of violence? And can clinicians predict who is likely to do harm? *No* and *no*. Most violent criminals are not mentally ill, and most mentally ill people are not violent (Fazel & Grann, 2006; Skeem et al., 2016). Moreover, clinical prediction of violence is unreliable. The few people with disorders who commit violent acts tend to be either those, like the Navy Yard shooter, who experience threatening delusions and hallucinated voices that command them to act, who have suffered a financial crisis or lost relationship, or who abuse substances (Douglas et al., 2009; Elbogen et al., 2016; Fazel et al., 2009, 2010). In seeking some form of explanation for terrible acts, we may look for mental disorders to be involved. Yet the offenders are often "ordinary" people with no obvious mental disorder, such as the California couple arrested in 2018 who had imprisoned, starved, and assaulted their children for decades.

People with disorders are more likely to be *victims* than perpetrators of violence (Marley & Bulia, 2001). According to the U.S. Surgeon General's Office (1999, p. 7), "there is very little risk of violence or harm to a stranger from casual contact with an individual who has a mental disorder." *The bottom line:* Psychological disorders only rarely lead to violent acts, and focusing gun restrictions only on mentally ill people will likely not reduce gun violence (Friedman, 2012). Better predictors of violence are use of alcohol or drugs, previous violence, gun availability, and—as in the case of the repeatedly head-injured and ultimately homicidal National Football League player Aaron Hernandez—brain damage (Belson, 2017). The mass-killing shooters have one more thing in common: They tend to be young males.

Whether people with mental disorders who turn violent should be held responsible for their behavior remains controversial. U.S. President Ronald Reagan's near-assassin, John Hinckley, was sent to a hospital rather than to prison. The public was outraged. They were outraged again in 2011, when Jared Lee Loughner killed six people and injured several others, including U.S. Representative Gabrielle Giffords. Loughner was diagnosed with schizophrenia but nevertheless sentenced to life in prison without parole.

Which decision—hospital or prison—was correct? As we come to better understand the biological and environmental bases for human behavior, from generosity to murder, we may better determine when and how to hold people accountable for their actions.

MENTAL HEALTH AND MASS SHOOTINGS Following the 2012 Newtown, Connecticut, slaughter of 26 schoolchildren and adults, and again following the 2018 Parkland, Florida, massacre of 17 youth and adults, people wondered if such tragedies couldn't be prevented through mental health screenings. Could people with psychological disorders who are violence-prone (a tiny percentage) be identified in advance by mental health workers and prevented from gun ownership? Even if this kind of prediction could be done with complete accuracy (it can't), it turns out that in 85 percent of U.S. mass killings between 1982 and 2017, the killer had no known prior contact with mental health professionals. Most homicide "is committed by healthy people in the grip of everyday emotions using guns" (Friedman, 2017).

RATES OF PSYCHOLOGICAL DISORDERS

LOQ 14-7 How many people have, or have had, a psychological disorder? What are some of the risk factors?

Who is most vulnerable to psychological disorders? At what times of life? To answer such questions, many countries have conducted lengthy, structured interviews with representative samples of thousands of their citizens. After asking hundreds of questions that probe for symptoms—"Has there ever been a period of two weeks or more when you felt like you wanted to die?"—the researchers have estimated the current, prior-year, and lifetime prevalence of various disorders.

How many people have, or have had, a psychological disorder? More than most of us suppose.

- A World Health Organization study—based on 90-minute interviews with thousands of people who were representative of their country's population—estimated the number of prior-year mental disorders in 28 countries (Kessler et al., 2009). Cultures vary, and as **FIGURE 14.3** illustrates, the lowest rate of reported mental disorders was in Nigeria, the highest rate in the United States. Moreover, immigrants to the United States from Mexico, Africa, and Asia averaged better mental health than their U.S.-born counterparts with the same ethnic heritage (Breslau et al., 2007; Maldonado-Molina et al., 2011). For example, compared with Mexican-Americans born in the United States, Mexican-Americans who have recently immigrated are less at risk of mental disorder—a phenomenon known as the *immigrant paradox* (Schwartz et al., 2010).

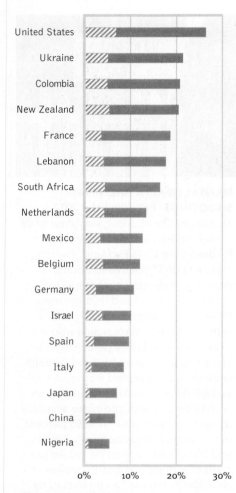

■ Percentage with any mental disorder

▨ Proportion of those disorders considered "serious"

FIGURE 14.3

PRIOR-YEAR PREVALENCE OF DISORDERS IN SELECTED AREAS
From interviews in 28 countries. (Data from Kessler et al., 2009).

TABLE 14.2

Percentage of Americans Reporting Selected Psychological Disorders in the Past Year

Psychological Disorder	Percentage
Depressive disorders or bipolar disorder	9.3
Phobia of specific object or situation	8.7
Social anxiety disorder	6.8
Attention-deficit/hyperactivity disorder (ADHD)	4.1
Posttraumatic stress disorder (PTSD)	3.5
Generalized anxiety disorder	3.1
Schizophrenia	1.1
Obsessive-compulsive disorder	1.0

Data from: National Institute of Mental Health, 2015.

- The U.S. National Institute of Mental Health (2015) has estimated that just under 1 in 5 adult Americans currently have a "mental, behavioral, or emotional disorder (excluding developmental and substance use disorders)" or have had one within the past year (**TABLE 14.2**).

What increases vulnerability to mental disorders? As **TABLE 14.3** indicates, there is a wide range of risk and protective factors for mental disorders. But one predictor of mental disorders—poverty—crosses ethnic and gender lines. The incidence of serious psychological disorders is 2.5 times higher among those below the poverty line (CDC, 2014a).

TABLE 14.3

Risk and Protective Factors for Mental Disorders

Risk Factors	Protective Factors
Academic failure	Aerobic exercise
Birth complications	Community offering empowerment, opportunity, and security
Caring for those who are chronically ill or who have a neurocognitive disorder	Economic independence
Child abuse and neglect	Effective parenting
Chronic insomnia	Feelings of mastery and control
Chronic pain	Feelings of security
Family disorganization or conflict	High self-esteem
Low birth weight	Literacy
Low socioeconomic status	Positive attachment and early bonding
Medical illness	Positive parent-child relationships
Neurochemical imbalance	Problem-solving skills
Parental mental illness	Resilient coping with stress and adversity
Parental substance abuse	Social and work skills
Personal loss and bereavement	Social support from family and friends
Poor work skills and habits	
Reading disabilities	
Sensory disabilities	
Social incompetence	
Stressful life events	
Substance abuse	
Trauma experiences	

Research from: World Health Organization (WHO, 2004a, b).

This *correlation*, like so many others, raises further questions: Does poverty cause disorders? Or do disorders cause poverty? It is both, though the answer varies with the disorder. Schizophrenia understandably leads to poverty. Yet the stresses and demoralization of poverty can also breed disorders, especially depression in women and substance abuse in men (Dohrenwend et al., 1992). In one natural experiment investigating the poverty-pathology link, researchers tracked rates of behavior problems in North Carolina Native American children as economic development enabled a dramatic reduction in their community's poverty rate. As the study began, children of poverty exhibited more deviant and aggressive behaviors. After four years, children whose families had moved above the poverty line exhibited a 40 percent decrease in behavior problems. Those who maintained their previous positions below or above the poverty line exhibited no change (Costello et al., 2003).

At what times of life do disorders strike? Usually by early adulthood. "Over 75 percent of our sample with any disorder had experienced [their] first symptoms by age 24," reported Lee Robins and Darrel Regier (1991, p. 331). Among the earliest to appear are the symptoms of antisocial personality disorder (median age 8) and of phobias (median age 10). Alcohol use disorder, obsessive-compulsive disorder, bipolar disorder, and schizophrenia symptoms appear at a median age near 20. Major depressive disorder often hits somewhat later, at a median age of 25.

> **LaunchPad** See the **Video: Correlational Studies** for a helpful tutorial about this research design. For a summary of disorder rates, engage online with **Concept Practice: Risks and Rates of Disorders.**

🔒 RETRIEVE IT • • •
ANSWERS IN APPENDIX E

RI-5 What is the relationship between poverty and psychological disorders?

🔒 REVIEW BASIC CONCEPTS OF PSYCHOLOGICAL DISORDERS

⟩ Learning Objectives

TEST YOURSELF Answer these repeated Learning Objective Questions on your own (before checking the answers in Appendix D) to improve your retention of the concepts (McDaniel et al., 2009, 2015).

14-1 How should we draw the line between normality and disorder?

14-2 How do the medical model and the biopsychosocial approach influence our understanding of psychological disorders?

14-3 How and why do clinicians classify psychological disorders, and why do some psychologists criticize the use of diagnostic labels?

14-4 Why is there controversy over attention-deficit/hyperactivity disorder?

14-5 What factors increase the risk of suicide, and what do we know about nonsuicidal self-injury?

14-6 Do psychological disorders predict violent behavior?

14-7 How many people have, or have had, a psychological disorder? What are some of the risk factors?

⟩ Terms and Concepts to Remember

TEST YOURSELF Write down the definition yourself, then check your answer on the referenced page.

psychological disorder, **p. 494**

medical model, **p. 495**

epigenetics, **p. 497**

DSM-5, **p. 497**

attention-deficit/hyperactivity disorder (ADHD), **p. 497**

⟩ Experience the Testing Effect

TEST YOURSELF Answer the following questions on your own first, then check your answers in Appendix E.

1. Two major disorders that are found worldwide are schizophrenia and _____ _____ _____.

2. Anna is embarrassed that it takes her several minutes to parallel park her car. She usually gets out of the car once or twice to inspect her distance both from the curb and from the nearby cars. Should she worry about having a psychological disorder?

3. What is *susto*, and is this a culture-specific or universal psychological disorder?

4. A therapist says that psychological disorders are sicknesses, and people with these disorders should be treated as patients in a hospital. This therapist's belief reflects the _____ model.

5. Many psychologists reject the disorders-as-illness view and instead contend that other factors may also be involved—for example, the person's level of stress and ways of coping with it. This view represents the _____ approach.
   a. medical
   b. epigenetics
   c. biopsychosocial
   d. diagnostic

6. Why is the DSM, and the DSM-5 in particular, considered controversial?

7. One predictor of psychiatric disorders that crosses ethnic and gender lines is _____.

8. The symptoms of _____ appear around age 10; _____ tend[s] to appear later, around age 25.
   a. schizophrenia; bipolar disorder
   b. bipolar disorder; schizophrenia
   c. major depressive disorder; phobias
   d. phobias; major depressive disorder

Continue testing yourself with 📖 **LearningCurve** or 📖 **Achieve Read & Practice** to learn and remember most effectively.

⊙→ Anxiety Disorders, OCD, and PTSD

Anxiety is part of life. Speaking in front of a class, peering down from a ladder, or waiting to learn the results of a final exam might make any one of us feel nervous. Anxiety may even cause us to avoid talking or making eye contact—"shyness," we call it. Fortunately for most of us, our uneasiness is not intense and persistent. Some, however, are more prone to fear the unknown and to notice and remember perceived threats (Gorka et al., 2017; Mitte, 2008). When the brain's danger-detection system becomes hyperactive, we are at greater risk for an *anxiety disorder,* and for two other disorders that involve anxiety: *obsessive-compulsive disorder (OCD)* and *posttraumatic stress disorder (PTSD)*.[1]

ANXIETY DISORDERS

LOQ 14-8 How do generalized anxiety disorder, panic disorder, and phobias differ?

The **anxiety disorders** are marked by distressing, persistent anxiety or by dysfunctional anxiety-reducing behaviors. For example, people with *social anxiety disorder* become extremely anxious in social settings where others might judge them, such as parties, class presentations, or even eating in public. One university student experienced palpitations, tremors, blushing, and sweating when giving a presentation, taking an exam, or meeting an authority figure, and also feared that he would embarrass himself. He therefore avoided parties, phone calls, and other social contacts. By staying home he avoided the anxious feelings, but it was maladaptive: This prevented him from learning to cope with the world and left him feeling lonely (Leichsenring & Leweke, 2017).

Let's take a closer look at three other anxiety disorders:

- *generalized anxiety disorder,* in which a person is, for no obvious reason, continually tense and uneasy;
- *panic disorder,* in which a person experiences *panic attacks*—sudden episodes of intense dread—and fears the next episode's unpredictable onset; and
- *phobias,* in which a person is intensely and irrationally afraid of something.

anxiety disorders psychological disorders characterized by distressing, persistent anxiety or maladaptive behaviors that reduce anxiety.

---

1. OCD and PTSD were formerly classified as anxiety disorders, but the DSM-5 now classifies them separately.

Generalized Anxiety Disorder

For two years, Tom, a 27-year-old electrician, was bothered by dizziness, sweating palms, and irregular heartbeat. He felt on edge and sometimes found himself shaking. Tom was fairly successful in hiding his symptoms from his family and co-workers. But he allowed himself few other social contacts, and occasionally he had to leave work. Neither his family doctor nor a neurologist was able to find any physical problem.

Tom's unfocused, out-of-control, agitated feelings suggest **generalized anxiety disorder,** which is marked by excessive and uncontrollable worry that persists for six months or more. People with this condition (two-thirds women) worry continually, and they are often jittery, on edge, and sleep-deprived (McLean & Anderson, 2009). They become fixated on potential threats (Pergamin-Hight et al., 2015). Concentration suffers as everyday worries demand continual attention. Their *autonomic nervous system* arousal may leak out through furrowed brows, twitching eyelids, trembling, perspiration, or fidgeting.

Those affected usually cannot identify, relieve, or avoid their anxiety; to use Sigmund Freud's term, the anxiety is *free-floating* (not linked to a specific stressor or threat). Generalized anxiety disorder and depression often go hand in hand, but even without depression, this disorder tends to be disabling (Hunt et al., 2004; Moffitt et al., 2007). Moreover, it may lead to physical problems, such as high blood pressure.

Panic Disorder

Many people can experience an intense anxiety that escalates into a terrifying panic attack—a minutes-long episode of intense fear that something horrible is about to happen. Irregular heartbeat, chest pains, shortness of breath, choking, trembling, or dizziness may accompany the panic. One woman recalled suddenly feeling

> hot and as though I couldn't breathe. My heart was racing and I started to sweat and tremble and I was sure I was going to faint. Then my fingers started to feel numb and tingly and things seemed unreal. It was so bad I wondered if I was dying and asked my husband to take me to the emergency room. By the time we got there (about 10 minutes) the worst of the attack was over and I just felt washed out (Greist et al., 1986).

For the 3 percent of people with **panic disorder,** panic attacks are recurrent. These anxiety tornados strike suddenly, wreak havoc, and disappear, but are not forgotten. Ironically, worries about anxiety—perhaps fearing another panic attack, or fearing anxiety-related symptoms in public—can amplify anxiety symptoms (Olatunji & Wolitzky-Taylor, 2009). After several panic attacks, people may come to fear the fear itself. This may trigger *agoraphobia*—fear or avoidance of public situations from which escape might be difficult. People with agoraphobia may avoid being outside the home, in a crowd, or in an elevator. Smokers have at least a doubled risk of panic disorder and greater symptoms when they do have an attack (Knuts et al., 2010; Zvolensky & Bernstein, 2005). Because nicotine is a stimulant, lighting up doesn't lighten us up.

generalized anxiety disorder an anxiety disorder in which a person is continually tense, apprehensive, and in a state of autonomic nervous system arousal.

panic disorder an anxiety disorder marked by unpredictable, minutes-long episodes of intense dread in which a person may experience terror and accompanying chest pain, choking, or other frightening sensations; often followed by worry over a possible next attack.

PANIC ON THE COURSE Golfer Charlie Beljan experienced what he later learned were panic attacks during an important tournament. His thumping heartbeat and shortness of breath led him to think he was having a heart attack. But hospital tests revealed that his symptoms were not related to a physical illness. He recovered, went on to win $846,000, and has become an inspiration to others.

phobia an anxiety disorder marked by a persistent, irrational fear and avoidance of a specific object, activity, or situation.

Charles Darwin began suffering from panic disorder at age 28, after spending five years sailing the world. He moved to the country, avoided social gatherings, and traveled only in his wife's company. But the relative seclusion did free him to further develop his evolutionary theory. "Even ill health," he reflected, "has saved me from the distraction of society and its amusements" (quoted in Ma, 1997).

Phobias

We all live with some fears. But people with **phobias** are consumed by a persistent, irrational fear and avoidance of some object, activity, or situation. *Specific phobias* may focus on particular animals, insects, heights, blood, or closed spaces (**FIGURE 14.4**). Many people avoid the triggers, such as high places, that arouse their fear. Marilyn, an otherwise healthy and happy 28-year-old, so feared thunderstorms that she felt anxious as soon as a weather forecaster mentioned possible storms later in the week. If her husband was away and a storm was forecast, she often stayed with a close relative. During a storm, she hid from windows and buried her head to avoid seeing the lightning.

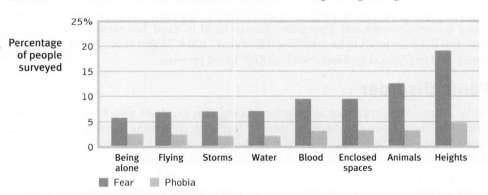

Martin Harvey/Getty Images

FIGURE 14.4

SOME COMMON SPECIFIC FEARS
Researchers surveyed Dutch people to identify the most common events or objects they feared. A strong fear becomes a phobia if it provokes a compelling but irrational desire to avoid the dreaded object or situation. (Data from Depla et al., 2008.)

> 🔒 **RETRIEVE IT • • •**   *ANSWERS IN APPENDIX E*
>
> **RI-1** Unfocused tension, apprehension, and arousal are symptoms of _____ _____ disorder.
>
> **RI-2** Those who experience unpredictable periods of terror and intense dread, accompanied by frightening physical sensations, may be diagnosed with a _____ disorder.
>
> **RI-3** If a person is focusing anxiety on specific feared objects or situations, that person may have a _____.

THRIVING WITH OCD Music star Justin Timberlake says support from his family and a sense of humor have helped him cope with the challenges of obsessive-compulsive disorder.

Michael Campanella/WireImage/Getty Images

OBSESSIVE-COMPULSIVE DISORDER (OCD)

LOQ 14-9 What is *OCD*?

As with the anxiety disorders, we can see aspects of our own behavior in **obsessive-compulsive disorder (OCD).** *Obsessive thoughts* are unwanted and seemingly unending. *Compulsive behaviors* are responses to those thoughts.

We all are at times obsessed with thoughts and we may behave compulsively. Have you ever felt a bit anxious about how your place will appear to others and found yourself compulsively cleaning one last time before your guests arrived? Or, perhaps worried about an upcoming exam, you caught yourself lining up your study materials "just so" before studying? Our lives are full of little rehearsals and fussy behaviors. They cross the fine line between normality and disorder when they *persistently interfere* with everyday life and cause us distress. Checking that you locked the door is normal; checking 10 times is not. Washing your hands is normal; washing so often that your skin becomes raw is not. (**TABLE 14.4** offers more examples.) At some time during their lives, often during their late teens or early adulthood, about 2 percent of people cross that line from normal preoccupations and fussy behaviors to debilitating disorder (Kessler et al., 2012). Although people know their anxiety-fueled obsessive thoughts are irrational, the

TABLE 14.4

Common Obsessions and Compulsions Among Children and Adolescents With Obsessive-Compulsive Disorder

Thought or Behavior	Percentage Reporting Symptom
Obsessions (repetitive *thoughts*)	
Concern with dirt, germs, or toxins	40
Something terrible happening (fire, death, illness)	24
Symmetry, order, or exactness	17
Compulsions (repetitive *behaviors*)	
Excessive hand washing, bathing, toothbrushing, or grooming	85
Repeating rituals (in/out of a door, up/down from a chair)	51
Checking doors, locks, appliances, car brakes, homework	46

Data from: Rapoport, 1989.

obsessive-compulsive disorder (OCD) a disorder characterized by unwanted repetitive thoughts (obsessions), actions (compulsions), or both.

posttraumatic stress disorder (PTSD) a disorder characterized by haunting memories, nightmares, hypervigilance, avoidance of trauma-related stimuli, social withdrawal, jumpy anxiety, numbness of feeling, and/or insomnia that lingers for four weeks or more after a traumatic experience.

thoughts can become so haunting, and the compulsive rituals so senselessly time consuming, that effective functioning becomes impossible.

OCD is more common among teens and young adults than among older people (Nestadt & Samuels, 1997). A 40-year follow-up study of 144 Swedes diagnosed with the disorder found that, for most, the obsessions and compulsions had gradually lessened, though only 1 in 5 had completely recovered (Skoog & Skoog, 1999).

Some people experience other OCD-related disorders, such as *hoarding disorder* (cluttering one's space with acquired possessions one can't let go), *body dysmorphic disorder* (preoccupation with perceived body defects), or—new words to impress your friends—*trichotillomania* (hair pulling) or *excoriation disorder* (excessive skin-picking).

ENGAGE 📱 **LaunchPad** For an eye-opening, 7-minute snapshot of one person's challenges with compulsive rituals, see the **Video: Obsessive-Compulsive Disorder—A Young Mother's Struggle.**

POSTTRAUMATIC STRESS DISORDER (PTSD)

LOQ 14-10 What is *PTSD*?

While serving overseas, one soldier, Jesse, observed the killing "of children and women. It was just horrible for anyone to experience." Back home, he suffered "real bad flashbacks" (Welch, 2005).

Jesse is not alone. In one study of 103,788 veterans returning from Iraq and Afghanistan, 25 percent were diagnosed with a psychological disorder (Seal et al., 2007). Some had *traumatic brain injuries (TBI)*, but the most frequent diagnosis was **posttraumatic stress disorder (PTSD).** Survivors of accidents, disasters, war-related refugee displacement, and violent and sexual assaults (including an estimated two-thirds of prostitutes) have also experienced PTSD symptoms (Brewin et al., 1999; Guo et al., 2017; Reebs et al., 2017). Typical symptoms include recurring haunting memories and nightmares, laser-focused attention to and avoidance of possible threats, social withdrawal, jumpy anxiety, and trouble sleeping (Germain, 2013; Hoge et al., 2007; Yuval et al., 2017).

The greater one's emotional distress during a trauma, the higher the risk for posttraumatic symptoms (Ozer et al., 2003).

Many of us will experience a traumatic event. And many people will display *survivor resiliency*—by recovering after severe stress (Bonanno, 2004, 2005; Infurna & Luthar, 2016b). Although philosopher Friedrich Nietzsche's (1889) idea that "what does not kill me makes me stronger" is not true for all, some will even experience *posttraumatic growth* (see Chapter 15). Why do some 5 to 10 percent of people develop PTSD after a traumatic event while others do not (Bonanno et al., 2011)? One factor seems to be the amount of trauma-related emotional distress: The higher the distress (such as the level of physical torture suffered by prisoners of war), the greater the risk for posttraumatic symptoms (King et al., 2015; Ozer et al., 2003). Among American military personnel in Afghanistan, 7.6 percent of

PTSD FROM PARKLAND In the 2018 Parkland, FL school shooting, Samantha Fuentes (at right) witnessed friends dying. Shrapnel struck her face and legs. She later reported PTSD symptoms, including a fear of returning to the school and jumping at the sound of a slammed door.

Chip Somodevilla/Getty Images

combatants and 1.4 percent of noncombatants developed PTSD (McNally, 2012). Among survivors of the 9/11 terrorist attack on New York's World Trade Center, the rates of subsequent PTSD diagnoses for those who had been inside were double the rates of those who had been outside (Bonanno et al., 2006).

What else can influence PTSD development? Some people may have a more sensitive emotion-processing limbic system that floods their bodies with stress hormones, which explains why PTSD may coexist with another disorder (Duncan et al., 2017; Kosslyn, 2005; Ozer & Weiss, 2004). The odds of experiencing PTSD after a traumatic event are also higher for women than for men (Olff et al., 2007; Ozer & Weiss, 2004).

Some psychologists believe that PTSD has been overdiagnosed (Dobbs, 2009; McNally, 2003). Too often, say critics, PTSD gets stretched to include normal stress-related bad memories and dreams. And some well-intentioned procedures—such as "debriefing" people by asking them to revisit the experience and vent their emotions—may worsen normal stress reactions (Bonanno et al., 2010; Wakefield & Spitzer, 2002). Other research shows that reliving traumas (such as the 2013 Boston Marathon bombing) through media coverage sustains the stress response (Holman et al., 2014). Nevertheless, people diagnosed with PTSD can benefit from other therapies (see Chapter 15).

🔒 RETRIEVE IT • • •   ANSWERS IN APPENDIX E

RI-4 Those who express anxiety through unwanted repetitive thoughts or actions may have a(n) _____-_____ disorder.

RI-5 Those with symptoms of recurring memories and nightmares, hypervigilance, avoidance, social withdrawal, jumpy anxiety, numbness of feeling, and/or insomnia for weeks after a traumatic event may be diagnosed with _____ _____ disorder.

UNDERSTANDING ANXIETY DISORDERS, OCD, AND PTSD

LOQ 14-11 How do conditioning, cognition, and biology contribute to the feelings and thoughts that mark anxiety disorders, OCD, and PTSD?

Anxiety is both a feeling and a cognition—a doubt-laden self-appraisal. How do these anxious feelings and cognitions arise? Few psychologists now interpret anxiety the way Sigmund Freud did. His psychoanalytic theory proposed that, beginning in childhood, people *repress* intolerable impulses, ideas, and feelings. Freud believed that this submerged mental energy sometimes leaks out in odd symptoms, such as anxious hand washing. Most of today's psychologists believe that three modern perspectives—conditioning, cognition, and biology—are more helpful.

Conditioning

Through *classical conditioning*, our fear responses can become linked with formerly neutral objects and events. Researchers have created anxious animals by giving rats unpredictable electric shocks (Schwartz, 1984). The rats, like assault victims who report feeling anxious when returning to the scene of the crime, learned to become uneasy in their lab environment. The lab became a cue for fear.

Such research helps explain how anxious or traumatized people learn to associate their anxiety with certain cues, and why anxious people are hyperattentive to possible threats (Bar-Haim et al., 2007; Duits et al., 2015). In one survey, 58 percent of those with social anxiety disorder said their disorder began after a traumatic event (Ost & Hugdahl, 1981). Anxiety or an anxiety-related disorder is more likely to develop when bad events happen unpredictably and uncontrollably (Field, 2006; Mineka & Oehlberg, 2008). Even a single painful and frightening event may trigger a full-blown phobia, thanks to two conditioning processes: classical conditioning's *stimulus generalization* and operant conditioning's *reinforcement*.

Stimulus generalization occurs when a person experiences a fearful event and later develops a fear of similar events. My [DM's] car was once struck by another whose driver missed a stop sign. For months afterward, I felt a twinge of unease when any car approached from a side street. Likewise, I [ND] was watching a terrifying movie about spiders, *Arachnophobia,* when a severe thunderstorm struck and the theater lost power. For months, I experienced anxiety at the sight of spiders or cobwebs. Those fears eventually disappeared, but sometimes fears linger and grow. Marilyn's thunderstorm phobia may have similarly generalized after a terrifying or painful experience during a thunderstorm.

Reinforcement helps maintain learned fears and anxieties. Anything that enables us to avoid or escape a feared situation can reinforce maladaptive behaviors. Fearing a panic attack, we may decide not to leave the house. Reinforced by feeling calmer, we are likely to repeat that behavior in the future (Antony et al., 1992). So, too, with compulsive behaviors. If washing our hands relieves our feelings of anxiety, we may wash our hands again when those feelings return.

Cognition

Conditioning influences our feelings of anxiety, but so does cognition—our thoughts, memories, interpretations, and expectations. We learn some fears by observing others. Nearly all monkeys raised in the wild fear snakes, yet lab-raised monkeys do not. Surely, most wild monkeys do not actually suffer snake bites. Do they learn their fear through observation? To find out, Susan Mineka (1985, 2002) experimented with six monkeys raised in the wild (all strongly fearful of snakes) and their lab-raised offspring (virtually none of which feared snakes). After repeatedly observing their parents or peers refusing to reach for food in the presence of a snake, the younger monkeys developed a similar strong fear of snakes. When the monkeys were retested three months later, their learned fear persisted. We humans similarly learn many of our own fears by observing others (Helsen et al., 2011; Olsson et al., 2007).

Hemera Technologies/
PhotoObjects.net/360/Getty

Our interpretations and expectations also shape our reactions. Whether we interpret the creaky sound simply as the wind or as a possible knife-wielding attacker determines whether we panic. People with anxiety disorders tend to be *hypervigilant.* They *attend* more to threatening stimuli. They more often *interpret* stimuli as threatening: A pounding heart signals a heart attack, a lone spider near the bed indicates an infestation, and an everyday disagreement with a friend or a boss spells doom for the relationship. And they more readily *remember* threatening events (Van Bockstaele et al., 2014). Anxiety is especially common when people cannot switch off such intrusive thoughts and perceive a loss of control and a sense of helplessness (Franklin & Foa, 2011).

Biology

Some aspects of anxiety disorders, OCD, and PTSD are not easily understandable in terms of conditioning and cognitive processes alone. Why do some of us develop lasting phobias after suffering traumas, but others do not? Why do we all learn some fears more readily than others? The answers lie in part in our biology.

GENES Among monkeys, fearfulness runs in families. A monkey reacts more strongly to stress if its close biological relatives have sensitive, high-strung temperaments (Suomi, 1986). So, too, with people. Although twins in general are not at higher risk for any disorder, if one identical twin has an anxiety disorder, the other is also at risk (Polderman et al., 2015). Even when raised separately, identical twins may develop similar phobias (Carey, 1990; Eckert et al., 1981). One pair of separated identical twins independently became so afraid of water that each would wade into the ocean backward and only up to her knees.

Given the genetic contribution to anxiety disorders, researchers are now sleuthing the culprit genes. Among their findings are 17 gene variations associated with typical anxiety disorder symptoms (Hovatta et al., 2005), and others that are associated specifically with OCD (Mattheisen et al., 2015; Taylor, 2013).

ENGAGE | ASK YOURSELF

Can you recall a fear that you have learned? How were conditioning or cognition involved?

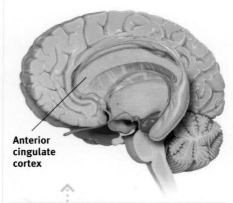

FIGURE 14.5

AN OBSESSIVE-COMPULSIVE BRAIN When people engaged in a challenging cognitive task, those with OCD showed the most activity in the anterior cingulate cortex in the brain's frontal area (Maltby et al., 2005).

Anterior cingulate cortex

Some genes can influence anxiety disorders by regulating brain levels of neurotransmitters. These include *serotonin,* which influences sleep, mood, and attending to threats (Canli, 2008; Pergamin-Hight et al., 2012), and *glutamate,* which heightens activity in the brain's alarm centers (Lafleur et al., 2006; Welch et al., 2007).

So genes matter. Some of us have genes that make us like orchids—fragile, yet capable of beauty under favorable circumstances. Others of us are like dandelions—hardy, and able to thrive in varied circumstances (Ellis & Boyce, 2008; Pluess & Belsky, 2013).

But experience affects gene expression. Among those with PTSD, a history of child abuse leaves long-term *epigenetic marks,* which are often organic molecules. These molecular tags attach to our chromosomes and turn certain genes on or off. Thus, experiences such as abuse can increase the likelihood that a genetic vulnerability to a disorder will be expressed (Mehta et al., 2013; Zannas et al., 2015). People who die by suicide show a similar epigenetic effect (Lockwood et al., 2015; McGowan et al., 2009).

THE BRAIN Our experiences change our brain, paving new pathways. Traumatic fear-learning experiences can leave tracks in the brain, creating fear circuits within the amygdala (Etkin & Wager, 2007; Herringa et al., 2013; Kolassa & Elbert, 2007). These fear pathways create easy inroads for more fear experiences (Armony et al., 1998). Some antidepressant drugs dampen this fear-circuit activity and associated obsessive-compulsive behaviors.

Generalized anxiety disorder, panic attacks, phobias, OCD, and PTSD express themselves biologically as overarousal of brain areas involved in impulse control and habitual behaviors. These disorders reflect a brain danger-detection system gone hyperactive—producing anxiety when no danger exists. In OCD, for example, when the brain detects that something is amiss, it seems to generate a mental hiccup of repeating thoughts (obsessions) or actions (compulsions) (Gehring et al., 2000). Brain scans reveal elevated activity in specific brain areas during behaviors such as compulsive hand washing, checking, ordering, or hoarding (Insel, 2010; Mataix-Cols et al., 2004, 2005). The *anterior cingulate cortex,* a brain region that monitors our actions and checks for errors, is often especially hyperactive (Maltby et al., 2005) **(FIGURE 14.5).**

NATURAL SELECTION We seem biologically prepared to fear the threats our ancestors faced—spiders and snakes, enclosed spaces and heights, storms and darkness. Those who did not fear these threats were less likely to survive and leave descendants. Even in Britain, which has only one poisonous snake species, people often fear snakes. Nine-month-old infants attend more to sounds signaling ancient threats (hisses, thunder) than they do to sounds representing modern dangers (a bomb exploding, breaking glass) (Erlich et al., 2013). It is easy to condition and hard to extinguish fears of such "evolutionarily relevant" stimuli (Coelho & Purkis, 2009; Davey, 1995; Öhman, 2009). Some of our modern fears may also have an evolutionary explanation. A fear of flying may be rooted in our biological predisposition to fear confinement and heights.

FEARLESS The biological perspective helps us understand why most people are more fearful of heights than Alex Honnold, shown here in 2017 becoming the first person to free-solo climb (no safety ropes) Yosemite National Park's massive El Capitan granite wall.

Compare our easy-to-learn fears with those we *do not* easily learn. World War II air raids, for example, produced remarkably few lasting phobias. As the air strikes continued, the British, Japanese, and German populations did not become more and more panicked. Rather, they grew increasingly indifferent to planes outside their immediate neighborhoods (Mineka & Zinbarg, 1996). Evolution has not prepared us to fear bombs dropping from the sky.

Our phobias focus on dangers our ancestors faced. Our compulsive acts typically exaggerate behaviors that helped them survive. Grooming had survival value. Gone wild, it becomes compulsive hair pulling. So, too, with washing up, which becomes ritual hand washing. And checking territorial boundaries becomes checking and rechecking already locked doors (Rapoport, 1989). Although natural selection shaped our behaviors, when taken to an extreme, these behaviors can interfere with daily life.

Peter Bohler/Redux

RI-6 Researchers believe that conditioning and cognitive processes are aspects of learning that contribute to anxiety-related disorders. What *biological* factors also contribute to these disorders?

🔒 REVIEW   ANXIETY DISORDERS, OCD, AND PTSD

⟫ Learning Objectives

TEST YOURSELF Answer these repeated Learning Objective Questions on your own (before checking the answers in Appendix D) to improve your retention of the concepts (McDaniel et al., 2009, 2015).

14-8 How do generalized anxiety disorder, panic disorder, and phobias differ?

14-9 What is *OCD*?

14-10 What is *PTSD*?

14-11 How do conditioning, cognition, and biology contribute to the feelings and thoughts that mark anxiety disorders, OCD, and PTSD?

⟫ Terms and Concepts to Remember

TEST YOURSELF Write down the definition yourself, then check your answer on the referenced page.

anxiety disorders, **p. 506**

generalized anxiety disorder, **p. 507**

panic disorder, **p. 507**

phobia, **p. 508**

obsessive-compulsive disorder (OCD), **p. 509**

posttraumatic stress disorder (PTSD), **p. 509**

⟫ Experience the Testing Effect

TEST YOURSELF Answer the following questions on your own first, then check your answers in Appendix E.

1. An episode of intense dread that can be accompanied by chest pains, choking, or other frightening sensations is called

   a. an obsession.   **c.** a panic attack.

   b. a compulsion.   **d.** a specific phobia.

2. Anxiety that takes the form of an irrational and maladaptive fear of a specific object, activity, or situation is called a _____.

3. Marina became consumed with the need to clean the entire house and refused to participate in any other activities. Her family consulted a therapist, who diagnosed her as having _____-_____ disorder.

4. When a person with an anxiety disorder eases anxiety by avoiding or escaping a situation that inspires fear, this is called

   a. free-floating anxiety.   **c.** an epigenetic mark.

   b. reinforcement.   **d.** hypervigilance.

5. The learning perspective proposes that phobias are

   a. the result of individual genetic makeup.

   b. a way of repressing unacceptable impulses.

   c. conditioned fears.

   d. a symptom of having been abused as a child.

Continue testing yourself with 📖 **LearningCurve** or ✎ **Achieve Read & Practice** to learn and remember most effectively.

⟫ Major Depressive Disorder and Bipolar Disorder

LOQ 14-12 How do major depressive disorder and bipolar disorder differ?

ENGAGE 💡 In the past year, have you at some time "felt so depressed that it was difficult to function"? If so, you were not alone. In one national survey, 31 percent of American college students answered *Yes* (ACHA, 2009). You may feel deeply discouraged about

"My life had come to a sudden stop. I was able to breathe, to eat, to drink, to sleep. I could not, indeed, help doing so; but there was no real life in me."
—Leo Tolstoy, *My Confession*, 1887

MINDING THE GUT Digestive system bacteria produce neurotransmitters that influence human emotions and social interactions. Healthy, diverse gut microbes can reduce the risk of anxiety, depression, and PTSD (Hemmings et al., 2017; Nowakowski et al., 2016).

"If someone offered you a pill that would make you permanently happy, you would be well advised to run fast and run far. Emotion is a compass that tells us what to do, and a compass that is perpetually stuck on NORTH is worthless." —Daniel Gilbert, "The Science of Happiness," 2006

ASK YOURSELF

Can you think of a time when feeling temporarily depressed actually helped you in some way? Did your rumination enable you to re-evaluate your situation or make new plans?

"Depression is a silent, slow motion tsunami of dark breaking over me. I can't swim away from it." —Effy Redman, "Waiting for Depression to Lift," 2017

Brad Wenner/Getty Images

the future, dissatisfied with your life, or socially isolated. You may lack the energy to get things done, to see people, or even to force yourself out of bed. You may be unable to concentrate, eat, or sleep normally. You might even wonder if you would be better off dead. Perhaps academic success came easily to you before, but now you find that disappointing grades jeopardize your goals. Perhaps social stresses, such as loneliness, feeling you are the target of prejudice, or experiencing a romantic breakup, have plunged you into despair. And perhaps low self-esteem increases your brooding, worsening your self-torment (Orth et al., 2016). Likely you think you are more alone in having such negative feelings than you really are (Jordan et al., 2011). Most of us will have some direct or indirect experience with depression. Misery has more company than most suppose.

Anxiety is a response to the threat of future loss. Depression is often a response to past and current loss. To feel bad in reaction to profoundly sad events (such as the death of a loved one) is to be in touch with reality. In such times, depression is like a car's low-fuel light—a signal that warns us to stop and take appropriate measures. People with *major depressive disorder* experience hopelessness and lethargy lasting several weeks or months. Those with *bipolar disorder* (formerly called *manic-depressive disorder*) alternate between depression and overexcited hyperactivity.

Biologically speaking, life's purpose is survival and reproduction, not happiness. Coughing, vomiting, and various sorts of pain protect our body from dangerous toxins and stimuli. Depression similarly protects us, sending us into a sort of psychic hibernation. It slows us down, prompting us, when losing a relationship or blocked from a goal, to conserve energy (Beck & Bredemeier, 2016; Gershon et al., 2016). When we grind temporarily to a halt and reassess our life, as depressed people do, we can redirect our energy in more promising ways (Watkins, 2008). There is sense to suffering. Even mild sadness helps people process and recall faces more accurately (Hills et al., 2011). They also tend to pay more attention to details, think more critically (with less gullibility), and make better decisions (Forgas, 2009, 2013, 2017). Bad moods can serve good purposes. But sometimes depression becomes seriously maladaptive. How do we recognize the fine line between a blue mood and disabling depression?

MAJOR DEPRESSIVE DISORDER

Joy, contentment, sadness, and despair exist at different points on a continuum, points at which any of us may find ourselves at any given moment. The difference between a blue mood after bad news and **major depressive disorder** is like the difference between breathing heavily after a hard run and being chronically exhausted. Major depressive disorder occurs when at least five signs of depression (including either depressed mood or loss of interest or pleasure) last two or more weeks (**TABLE 14.5**). To sense what major depressive disorder feels like, imagine combining the anguish of grief with the exhaustion you would feel after pulling an all-nighter.

Depression is the number-one reason people seek mental health services. Indeed, the World Health Organization declared depression "the leading cause of disability worldwide" (WHO, 2017a). In one survey conducted in 21 countries, 4.6 percent of people interviewed were experiencing moderate or severe depression (Thornicroft et al., 2017).

For some people, depressive symptoms may have a *seasonal pattern,* returning each winter. When asked, "Have you cried today?" Americans in one survey answered *Yes* doubly often in the winter (*Time*/CNN, 1994). But some researchers report that people in

RETAIN 🔒 **TABLE 14.5**

Diagnosing Major Depressive Disorder

The DSM-5 classifies major depressive disorder as the presence of at least five of the following symptoms over a 2-week period of time (minimally including depressed mood or reduced interest) (American Psychiatric Association, 2013).

- Depressed mood most of the time
- Dramatically reduced interest or enjoyment in most activities most of the time
- Significant challenges regulating appetite and weight
- Significant challenges regulating sleep
- Physical agitation or lethargy
- Feeling listless or with much less energy
- Feeling worthless, or feeling unwarranted guilt
- Problems in thinking, concentrating, or making decisions
- Thinking repetitively of death and suicide

major depressive disorder a disorder in which a person experiences, in the absence of drugs or another medical condition, two or more weeks with five or more symptoms, at least one of which must be either (1) depressed mood or (2) loss of interest or pleasure.

bipolar disorder a disorder in which a person alternates between the hopelessness and lethargy of depression and the overexcited state of mania. (Formerly called *manic-depressive disorder*.)

mania a hyperactive, wildly optimistic state in which dangerously poor judgment is common.

northerly or cloudier places do *not* experience more wintertime depression. Thus, they now question how often seasonal depression occurs (LoBello, 2017; Traffanstedt et al., 2016). So, stay tuned.

BIPOLAR DISORDER

Our genes dispose some of us, more than others, to respond emotionally to good and bad events (Whisman et al., 2014). In **bipolar disorder,** people bounce from one emotional extreme to the other (week to week, rather than day to day or moment to moment). When a depressive episode ends, a euphoric, overly talkative, and excessively optimistic state called **mania** follows. But before long, the elated mood either returns to normal or plunges again into depression.

If depression is living in slow motion, mania is fast forward. During the manic phase, people with bipolar disorder typically have little need for sleep. They show fewer sexual inhibitions. Their positive emotions persist abnormally (Gruber, 2011; Gruber et al., 2013). Their speech is loud, flighty, and hard to interrupt. They find advice irritating. Yet they need protection from their own poor judgment, which may lead to reckless spending or unsafe sex. Thinking fast feels good, but it also increases risk taking (Chandler & Pronin, 2012; Pronin, 2013).

Clusters of genes associated with creativity increase the likelihood of having bipolar disorder, and risk factors for developing bipolar disorder predict greater creativity (Baas et al., 2016; Power et al., 2015; Taylor, 2017). George Frideric Handel (1685–1759), who

Life as a Two-Headed Beast: Bipolar, Abigail Southworth

BIPOLAR DISORDER Artist Abigail Southworth illustrated her experience of bipolar disorder.

CREATIVITY AND BIPOLAR DISORDER There have been many creative artists, composers, writers, and musical performers with bipolar disorder. Some, like Russell Brand, developed a substance abuse disorder as well. Others, like Virginia Woolf, turned to suicide.

Actor Russell Brand   Writer Virginia Woolf

many believe suffered from a mild form of bipolar disorder, composed his nearly four-hour-long *Messiah* during three weeks of intense, creative energy in 1742 (Keynes, 1980). Bipolar disorder strikes more often among those who rely on emotional expression and vivid imagery, such as poets and artists, and less often among those who rely on precision and logic, such as architects, designers, and journalists (Jamison, 1993, 1995; Kaufman & Baer, 2002; Ludwig, 1995). Indeed, one analysis of over a million individuals showed that the only psychiatric condition linked to working in a creative profession was bipolar disorder (Kyaga et al., 2013).

Bipolar disorder is much less common than major depressive disorder, but it is often more dysfunctional. It is also a potent predictor of suicide (Schaffer et al., 2015). Unlike major depressive disorder, for which women are at highest risk, bipolar disorder afflicts as many men as women. The diagnosis has risen among adolescents, whose mood swings, sometimes prolonged, may vary from raging to bubbly. In the decade between 1994 and 2003, bipolar diagnoses in under-20 Americans showed an astonishing 40-fold increase—from an estimated 20,000 to 800,000 (Carey, 2007; Flora & Bobby, 2008; Moreno et al., 2007). Americans are twice as likely as people elsewhere to have ever had a bipolar disorder diagnosis (Merikangas et al., 2011). The new DSM-5 classifications have, however, begun to reduce the number of child and adolescent bipolar diagnoses: Some of those who are persistently irritable and who have frequent and recurring behavior outbursts are now instead diagnosed with *disruptive mood dysregulation disorder* (Faheem et al., 2017).

UNDERSTANDING MAJOR DEPRESSIVE DISORDER AND BIPOLAR DISORDER

LOQ 14-13 How can the biological and social-cognitive perspectives help us understand major depressive disorder and bipolar disorder?

From thousands of studies of the causes, treatment, and prevention of major depressive disorder and bipolar disorder, researchers have pulled out some common threads. Here, we focus primarily on major depressive disorder. Any theory of depression must explain at least the following (Lewinsohn et al., 1985, 1998, 2003):

LIFE AFTER DEPRESSION Author J. K. Rowling reported suffering acute depression—a "dark time," with suicidal thoughts—between ages 25 and 28. It was a "terrible place," she said, but it formed a foundation that allowed her "to come back stronger" (McLaughlin, 2010).

- **Behaviors and thoughts change with depression.** People trapped in a depressed mood become inactive and feel alone, empty, and without a bright or meaningful future (Bullock & Murray, 2014; Khazanoy & Ruscio, 2016; Smith & Rhodes, 2014). They avoid positive information and attend selectively to negative events (Peckham et al., 2010; Winer & Salem, 2016). They more often recall negative information. And they expect negative outcomes (my team will lose, my grades will fall, my love will fail). When the depression lifts, these behaviors and thoughts disappear. Nearly half the time, people with depression also have symptoms of another disorder, such as anxiety or substance abuse.

- **Depression is widespread.** Worldwide, 350 million people have major depressive disorder and 60 million people have bipolar disorder (WHO, 2017c). At some point during their lifetime, depression has plagued 11 percent of Canadian 15- to 24-year-olds (Findlay, 2017). Depression's commonality suggests that its causes must also be common.

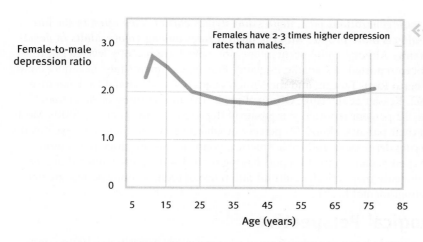

Female-to-male depression ratio

Females have 2-3 times higher depression rates than males.

Age (years)

FIGURE 14.6

FEMALE-TO-MALE DEPRESSION RATIO, WORLDWIDE Researchers Rachel Salk, Janet Hyde, and Lyn Abramson (2017) found that, compared with males, females have twice the risk of depression, and a nearly tripled rate during early adolescence. For many girls, being 13 to 15 years old is a tough time of life.

- **Women's risk of major depressive disorder is roughly double men's.** In 2009, when Gallup pollsters asked more than a quarter-million Americans if they had ever been diagnosed with depression, 13 percent of men and 22 percent of women said *Yes* (Pelham, 2009). When Gallup asked Americans if they had experienced sadness "during a lot of the day yesterday," 17 percent of men and 28 percent of women answered *Yes* (Mendes & McGeeney, 2012). A recent analysis of nearly 2 million people in 90 countries found that the depression gender gap is worldwide, and that it begins at puberty and peaks in early adolescence (Kuehner, 2017; see also **FIGURE 14.6**).

  The depression gender gap fits a bigger pattern: Women are generally more vulnerable to disorders involving internalized states, such as depression, anxiety, and inhibited sexual desire. Women experience more situations that increase their risk for depression, such as receiving less pay for equal work, juggling multiple roles, and caring for children and elderly family members (Freeman & Freeman, 2013). Men's disorders tend to be more external—alcohol use disorder, and disorders related to antisocial conduct and lack of impulse control. When women get sad, they often get sadder than men do. When men get mad, they often get madder than women do.

- **Most major depressive episodes end on their own.** Therapy often helps and tends to speed recovery. But even without professional help, most people recover from depression and return to normal. The black cloud of depression comes and, after sustained struggle, it often goes. For about half of those people, however, the dark cloud eventually returns (Curry et al., 2011; Klein & Kotov, 2016). The condition will be chronic for about 20 percent (Klein, 2010). On average, a person with major depressive disorder today will spend about three-fourths of the next decade in a normal, nondepressed state (Furukawa et al., 2009). In one study of over 20,000 Canadians, an enduring recovery was more likely if the first episode struck later in life, there was no prior history of depression, people experienced minimal physical or psychological stress, and they had ample social support (Fuller-Thomson et al., 2016).

- **Work, marriage, and relationship stresses often precede depression.** Experiencing childhood abuse doubles a person's risk of adult depression (Nelson et al., 2017). About 1 person in 4 diagnosed with depression has been brought down by a significant loss or trauma, such as a loved one's death, a ruptured marriage, a physical assault, or a lost job (Kendler et al., 2008; Monroe & Reid, 2009; Orth et al., 2009; Wakefield et al., 2007). Moving to a new culture also increases risk for depression, especially among younger people who have not yet formed their identities (Zhang et al., 2013). One long-term study tracked rates of depression in 2000 people (Kendler, 1998). Among those who had experienced no stressful life event in the preceding month, the risk of depression was less than 1 percent. Among those who had experienced three such events in that month, the risk was 24 percent. For some, grappling with life's minor daily stressors can also negatively affect mental health. People who overreacted to minor stressors, such as a broken appliance, were more often depressed 10 years later (Charles et al., 2013).

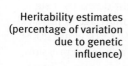

LaunchPad For a 9-minute story about one young man's struggle with depression, see the **Video: Depression.**

• *Compared with generations past, depression strikes earlier (now often in the late teens) and affects more people, with the highest rates among young adults in developed countries.* Although adolescent depression rates have recently leveled off, this trend has been reported in Canada, England, France, Germany, Italy, Lebanon, New Zealand, Puerto Rico, Taiwan, and the United States (Cross-National Collaborative Group, 1992; Kessler et al., 2010; Olfson et al., 2015). In one study of Australian adolescents, 12 percent reported symptoms of depression (Sawyer et al., 2000). Most hid it from their parents, almost 90 percent of whom perceived their depressed teen as *not* suffering depression. In North America, young adults are three times more likely than their grandparents to report having recently—or ever—suffered depression. This increase may reflect a cultural difference of today's young adults' greater openness about mental health.

The Biological Perspective

Depression is a whole-body disorder. It involves genetic predispositions, brain connectivity issues, and biochemical imbalances, as well as negative thoughts and a gloomy mood.

GENES AND DEPRESSION Major depressive disorder and bipolar disorder run in families. The risk of being diagnosed with one of these disorders increases if your parent or sibling has the disorder (Sullivan et al., 2000; Weissman et al., 2016). If one identical twin is diagnosed with major depressive disorder, the chances are about 1 in 2 that at some time the other twin will be, too. If one identical twin has bipolar disorder, the chances of a similar diagnosis for the co-twin are even higher—7 in 10—even for twins raised apart (DiLalla et al., 1996). Summarizing the major twin studies, one research team estimated the heritability of major depressive disorder—the extent to which individual differences are attributable to genes—at 40 percent (Polderman et al., 2015; see also **FIGURE 14.7** for another study's heritability findings for this and other disorders).

Emotions are "postcards from our genes" (Plotkin, 1994). To tease out the genes that put people at risk for depression, researchers may use *linkage analysis*. First, geneticists find families in which the disorder appears across several generations. Next, the researchers look for differences in DNA from affected and unaffected family members. Linkage analysis points them to a chromosome neighborhood; "A house-to-house search is then needed to find the culprit gene" (Plomin & McGuffin, 2003). But depression is a complex condition. Many genes work together, producing a mosaic of small effects that interact with other factors to put some people at greater risk. Researchers continue to identify culprit gene variations that may open the door to more effective drug therapy (Hyde et al., 2016; Power et al., 2017; Ripke et al., 2013).

THE DEPRESSED BRAIN Scanning devices let us eavesdrop on the brain's activity during depressed and manic states. During depression, brain activity slows; during mania, it increases (**FIGURE 14.8**). The left frontal lobe and an adjacent brain reward center become more active during positive emotions (Davidson et al., 2002; Heller et al., 2009; Robinson et al., 2012).

FIGURE 14.7

THE HERITABILITY OF VARIOUS PSYCHOLOGICAL DISORDERS Using aggregated data from studies of identical and fraternal twins, researchers estimated the heritability of bipolar disorder, schizophrenia, anorexia nervosa, major depressive disorder, and generalized anxiety disorder (Bienvenu et al., 2011). (Heritability was calculated by a formula that compares the extent of similarity among identical versus fraternal twins.)

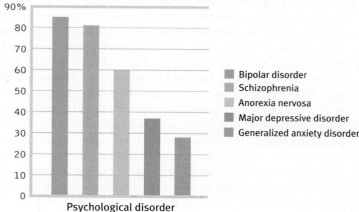

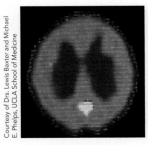
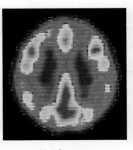
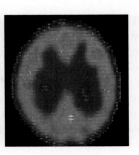

Depressed state
(May 17)

Manic state
(May 18)

Depressed state
(May 27)

FIGURE 14.8

THE UPS AND DOWNS OF BIPOLAR DISORDER These top-facing PET scans show that brain energy consumption rises and falls with the patient's emotional switches. Red areas are where the brain rapidly consumes *glucose*, an important energy source.

Analyses of *functional connectivity* help scientists understand how different brain regions work together, and can underlie psychological disorders. People with major depressive disorder tend to show low connectivity between brain regions involved in experiencing (a) emotion and (b) emotion regulation; these two types of brain regions don't "talk" to each other well (Kaiser et al., 2015). This poor neural communication may help explain why people with depression often struggle to regulate their emotions (Etkin et al., 2015; Miller et al., 2015).

At least two neurotransmitter systems are at work during the periods of brain inactivity and hyperactivity that accompany major depressive disorder and bipolar disorder. *Norepinephrine,* which increases arousal and boosts mood, is scarce during depression and over-abundant during mania. Drugs that decrease mania reduce norepinephrine.

Serotonin is also scarce or inactive during depression (Carver et al., 2008). Drugs that relieve depression tend to increase serotonin or norepinephrine supplies by blocking either their reuptake (as Prozac, Zoloft, and Paxil do with serotonin) or their chemical breakdown. Repetitive physical exercise, such as jogging, reduces depression in part because it increases serotonin (Airan et al., 2007; Harvey et al., 2018; Ilardi, 2009). In one study, running for two hours increased brain activation in regions associated with euphoria (Boecker et al., 2008). To get away from a bad mood, some people have used their own two feet.

NUTRITIONAL EFFECTS What's good for the heart is also good for the brain and mind. People who eat a heart-healthy "Mediterranean diet" (heavy on vegetables, fish, and olive oil) have a comparatively low risk of developing heart disease, stroke, late-life cognitive decline, and depression—all of which are associated with inflammation in the body (Kaplan et al., 2015; Psaltopoulou et al., 2013; Rechenberg, 2016). Excessive alcohol use also correlates with depression, partly because depression can increase alcohol use but mostly because alcohol misuse *leads to* depression (Fergusson et al., 2009).

The Social-Cognitive Perspective

Biological influences contribute to depression, but in the nature–nurture dance, our life experiences also play a part. Diet, drugs, stress, and other environmental influences lay down *epigenetic marks,* molecular genetic tags that can turn certain genes on or off. Animal studies suggested that long-lasting epigenetic influences may play a role in depression (Nestler, 2011).

Thinking matters, too. The *social-cognitive perspective* explores how people's assumptions and expectations influence what they perceive. Many depressed people see life through the dark glasses of low self-esteem (Orth et al., 2016). They have intensely negative views of themselves, their situation, and their future. Listen to Norman, a Canadian university professor, recalling his depression:

> I [despaired] of ever being human again. I honestly felt subhuman, lower than the lowest vermin. Furthermore, I . . . could not understand why anyone would want to associate with me, let alone love me. . . . I was positive that I was a fraud and a phony and that I didn't deserve my Ph.D. . . . I didn't deserve the research grants I had been awarded; I couldn't understand how I had written books and journal articles. . . . I must have conned a lot of people. (Endler, 1982, pp. 45–49)

Expecting the worst, depressed people magnify bad experiences and minimize good ones (Wenze et al., 2012). Their *self-defeating beliefs* and *negative explanatory style* feed their depression.

"I think I, like a lot of people, have that type of brain where I find it interesting or fulfilling to worry about something."
—Comedian Maria Bamford

RUMINATION RUNS WILD It's normal to think about our flaws. But dwelling constantly on negative thoughts—particularly negative thoughts about ourselves—makes it difficult to believe in ourselves and solve problems. People sometimes seek therapy to reduce their rumination.

NEGATIVE THOUGHTS, NEGATIVE MOODS, AND GENDER   Why are women nearly twice as vulnerable as men to depression, and twice as likely to take antidepressant drugs (Pratt et al., 2017)? Women may respond more strongly to stress (Hankin & Abramson, 2001; Mazure et al., 2002; Nolen-Hoeksema, 2001, 2003). Do you agree or disagree that you "at least occasionally feel overwhelmed by all I have to do"? In a survey of women and men, 38 percent of women, but only 17 percent of men, agreed (Pryor et al., 2006). Relationship stresses also affect teen girls more than boys (Hamilton et al., 2015).

Susan Nolen-Hoeksema (2003) related women's higher risk of depression to what she described as their tendency to ruminate or *overthink*. Staying focused on a problem—thanks to the continuous activation of an attention-sustaining frontal lobe area—can be adaptive (Altamirano et al., 2010; Andrews & Thomson, 2009a,b). But relentless, self-focused **rumination** can distract us, increase negative emotions, and disrupt daily activities (Johnson et al., 2016; Leary, 2018; Yang et al., 2017). Comparisons can also feed misery. While Josh is happily playing video games, lonely Lauren scrolls through her social media feed and sees Maria having a blast at a party, Angelique enjoying a family vacation, and Tyra looking super in a swimsuit. In response, Lauren broods: "My life is terrible."

Even so, why do life's unavoidable failures lead only some people to become depressed? The answer lies partly in their *explanatory style*—who or what they blame for their failures. Think of how you might feel if you failed a test. If you can blame someone else ("What an unfair test!"), you are more likely to feel angry. If you blame yourself, you probably will feel stupid and depressed.

Depression-prone people respond to bad events in an especially self-focused, self-blaming way (Huang, 2015; Mor & Winquist, 2002; Wood et al., 1990a,b). As **FIGURE 14.9** illustrates, they explain bad events in terms that are *stable* ("I'll never get over this"), *global* ("I can't do anything right"), and *internal* ("It's all my fault").

Self-defeating beliefs may arise from *learned helplessness,* the hopelessness and passive resignation humans and other animals learn when they experience uncontrollable painful events (Maier & Seligman, 2016). Pessimistic, overgeneralized, self-blaming attributions may create a depressing sense of hopelessness (Abramson et al., 1989; Groß et al., 2017). As Martin Seligman has noted, "A recipe for severe depression is preexisting pessimism encountering failure" (1991, p. 78). What, then, might we expect of new college students who exhibit a pessimistic explanatory style? Lauren Alloy and her colleagues (1999) monitored several hundred students every 6 weeks for 2.5 years. Among those identified as having a pessimistic thinking style, 17 percent had a first episode of major depression, as did only 1 percent of those who began college with an optimistic thinking style.

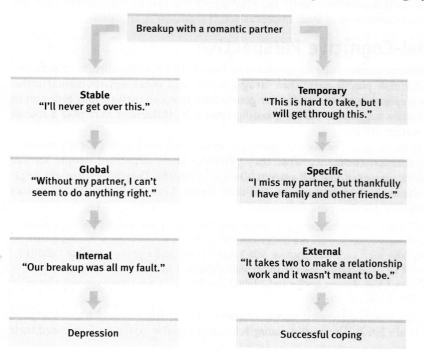

FIGURE 14.9
EXPLANATORY STYLE AND DEPRESSION   After a negative experience, a depression-prone person may respond with a negative explanatory style.

rumination compulsive fretting; *over-thinking* our problems and their causes.

LaunchPad To explore your own thinking style, engage online with **Immersive Learning: Assess Your Strengths—How Hopeful Are You? Why Is This Important?**

Critics note a chicken-and-egg problem nesting in the social-cognitive explanation of depression. Which comes first? The pessimistic explanatory style, or the depressed mood? The negative explanations *coincide* with a depressed mood, and they are *indicators* of depression. (Before or after being depressed, people's thoughts are less negative.) But do negative thoughts *cause* depression, any more than a speedometer's reading causes a car's speed? Perhaps a depressed mood triggers negative thoughts. If you temporarily put people in a bad or sad mood, their memories, judgments, and expectations suddenly become more pessimistic—a phenomenon that memory researchers call *state-dependent memory*.

Cultural forces may also nudge people toward or away from depression. Why is depression so common among young Westerners? Seligman (1991, 1995) has pointed to the rise of individualism and the decline of commitment to religion and family. In non-Western cultures, where close-knit relationships and cooperation are the norm, major depressive disorder is less common and less tied to self-blame over personal failure (Ferrari et al., 2013). In Japan, for example, depressed people instead tend to report feeling shame over letting others down (Draguns, 1990).

DEPRESSION'S VICIOUS CYCLE No matter which comes first, rejection and depression feed each other. Depression is both a cause and an effect of stressful experiences that disrupt our sense of who we are and why we are worthy. Such disruptions can lead to brooding, which is rich soil for growing negative feelings. And that negativity—being withdrawn, self-focused, and complaining—can by itself cause others to reject us (Furr & Funder, 1998; Gotlib & Hammen, 1992). Indeed, people deep in depression are at high risk for divorce, job loss, and other stressful life events. Weary of the person's fatigue, hopeless attitude, and negativity, a spouse may threaten to leave, or a boss may begin to question the person's competence. New losses and stress then plunge the already-depressed person into even deeper misery. Misery may love another's company, but company does not love another's misery.

We can now assemble pieces of the depression puzzle (**FIGURE 14.10**): (1) Stressful experiences interpreted through (2) a brooding, negative explanatory style create (3) a hopeless, depressed state that (4) hampers the way the person thinks and acts. These thoughts and actions, in turn, fuel (1) further stressful experiences such as rejection. Depression is a snake that bites its own tail.

It is a cycle we can all recognize. When we feel down, we think negatively and remember bad experiences. Britain's Prime Minister Winston Churchill called depression a "black dog" that periodically hounded him. Abraham Lincoln was so withdrawn and brooding as a young man that his friends feared he might take his own life (Kline, 1974). Olympic swimming gold medalists Michael Phelps and Grant Hackett have both battled anxiety and depression (Crouse, 2017). As their lives remind us, people can and do struggle through depression. Most regain their capacity to love, to work, and even to succeed at the highest levels.

"You should never engage in unsupervised introspection."

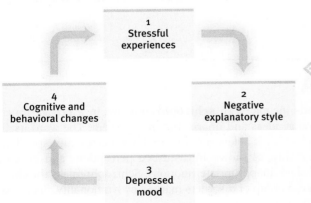

FIGURE 14.10

THE VICIOUS CYCLE OF DEPRESSED THINKING Therapists recognize this cycle, and they work to help depressed people break out of it by changing their negative thinking, turning their attention outward, and engaging them in more pleasant and competent behavior.

🔒 RETRIEVE IT •••   *ANSWERS IN APPENDIX E*

RI-1 What does it mean to say that "depression is a whole-body disorder"?

🔒 REVIEW MAJOR DEPRESSIVE DISORDER AND BIPOLAR DISORDER

⟶ Learning Objectives

TEST YOURSELF Answer these repeated Learning Objective Questions on your own (before checking the answers in Appendix D) to improve your retention of the concepts (McDaniel et al., 2009, 2015).

14-12 How do major depressive disorder and bipolar disorder differ?

14-13 How can the biological and social-cognitive perspectives help us understand major depressive disorder and bipolar disorder?

⟶ Terms and Concepts to Remember

TEST YOURSELF Write down the definition yourself, then check your answer on the referenced page.

major depressive disorder, **p. 515**   mania, **p. 515**

bipolar disorder, **p. 515**   rumination, **p. 521**

⟶ Experience the Testing Effect

TEST YOURSELF Answer the following questions on your own first, then check your answers in Appendix E.

1. The gender gap in depression refers to the finding that _____ (men's/women's) risk of depression is roughly double that of _____ (men's/women's).

2. Rates of bipolar disorder in the United States rose dramatically in the decade between 1994 and 2003, especially among
   a. middle-aged women.
   b. middle-aged men.
   c. people 20 and over.
   d. people 20 and under.

3. Treatment for depression often includes drugs that increase supplies of the neurotransmitters _____ and _____.

4. Psychologists who emphasize the importance of negative perceptions, beliefs, and thoughts in depression are working within the _____-_____ perspective.

Continue testing yourself with 📚 **LearningCurve** or 📚 **Achieve Read & Practice** to learn and remember most effectively.

⟶ Schizophrenia and Other Disorders

SCHIZOPHRENIA

schizophrenia a disorder characterized by delusions, hallucinations, disorganized speech, and/or diminished, inappropriate emotional expression.

psychotic disorders a group of disorders marked by irrational ideas, distorted perceptions, and a loss of contact with reality.

During their most severe periods, people with **schizophrenia** live in a private inner world, preoccupied with the strange ideas and images that haunt them. The word itself means "split" (*schizo*) "mind" (*phrenia*). It refers *not* to a multiple personality split but rather to the mind's split from reality, as shown in disturbed perceptions and beliefs, disorganized speech, and diminished, inappropriate emotions. Schizophrenia is the chief example of a **psychotic disorder**, a group of disorders marked by irrationality, distorted perceptions, and lost contact with reality.

As you can imagine, these characteristics profoundly disrupt relationships and work. Given a supportive environment and medication, over 40 percent of people with schizophrenia will have periods of a year or more of normal life experience (Jobe & Harrow, 2010). But only 1 in 7 experience a full and enduring recovery (Jääskeläinen et al., 2013).

Symptoms of Schizophrenia

LOQ 14-14 What patterns of perceiving, thinking, and feeling characterize schizophrenia?

Schizophrenia comes in varied forms. People with schizophrenia display symptoms that are *positive* (*inappropriate* behaviors are *present*) or negative (*appropriate* behaviors are *absent*). Those with positive symptoms may experience disturbed perceptions, talk in disorganized and deluded ways, or exhibit inappropriate laughter, tears, or rage. Those with negative symptoms may exhibit an absence of emotion in their voices, expressionless faces, or unmoving—mute and rigid—bodies.

DISTURBED PERCEPTIONS AND BELIEFS People with schizophrenia sometimes *hallucinate*—they see, hear, feel, taste, or smell things that exist only in their minds. Most often, the hallucinations are voices, which sometimes make insulting remarks or give orders. The voices may tell the person that she is bad or that she must burn herself with a cigarette lighter. Imagine your own reaction if a dream broke into your waking consciousness, making it hard to separate your experience from your imagination. When the unreal seems real, the resulting perceptions are at best bizarre, at worst terrifying.

Hallucinations are false *perceptions*. People with schizophrenia also have disorganized, fragmented thinking, often distorted by false *beliefs* called **delusions.** If they have *paranoid* tendencies, they may believe they are being threatened or pursued.

One cause of disorganized thinking may be a breakdown in *selective attention*. Normally, we have a remarkable capacity for giving our undivided attention to one set of sensory stimuli while filtering out others. People with schizophrenia are easily distracted by tiny unrelated stimuli, such as the grooves on a brick or the tones in a voice. This selective-attention difficulty is but one of dozens of cognitive differences associated with schizophrenia (Reichenberg & Harvey, 2007).

DISORGANIZED SPEECH Maxine, a young woman with schizophrenia, believed she was Mary Poppins. Communicating with Maxine was difficult because her thoughts spilled out in no logical order. Her biographer, Susan Sheehan (1982, p. 25), observed her saying aloud to no one in particular, "This morning, when I was at Hillside [Hospital], I was making a movie. I was surrounded by movie stars. . . . I'm Mary Poppins. Is this room painted blue to get me upset? My grandmother died four weeks after my eighteenth birthday."

Jumbled ideas may make no sense even within sentences, forming what is known as *word salad*. One young man begged for "a little more allegro in the treatment," and suggested that "liberationary movement with a view to the widening of the horizon" will "ergo extort some wit in lectures."

DIMINISHED AND INAPPROPRIATE EMOTIONS The expressed emotions of schizophrenia are often utterly inappropriate, split off from reality (Kring & Caponigro, 2010). Maxine laughed after recalling her grandmother's death. On other occasions, she cried when others laughed, or became angry for no apparent reason. Others with schizophrenia lapse into an emotionless *flat affect* state of no apparent feeling. For example, monetary perks fail to provide the normal brain reward center activation (Radua et al., 2015). Most also have an *impaired theory of mind*—they have difficulty reading other people's facial expressions and state of mind (Green & Horan, 2010; Kohler et al., 2010). Unable to understand others' mental states, those with schizophrenia struggle to feel sympathy and compassion (Bonfils et al., 2016). These emotional deficiencies occur early in the illness and have a genetic basis (Bora & Pantelis, 2013). *Motor behavior* may also be inappropriate and disruptive. Those with schizophrenia may experience *catatonia*, characterized by motor behaviors ranging from a physical stupor—remaining motionless for hours—to senseless, compulsive actions, such as continually rocking or rubbing an arm, to severe and dangerous agitation.

CRAIG 克雷格   2006   催淋 © Craig Geiser

ART BY SOMEONE DIAGNOSED WITH SCHIZOPHRENIA Commenting on the kind of artwork shown here (from Craig Geiser's 2010 art exhibit in Michigan), poet and art critic John Ashbery (1927–2017) wrote: "The lure of the work is strong, but so is the terror of the unanswerable riddles it proposes."

"Now consider this: The regulator that funnels certain information to you and filters out other information suddenly shuts off. Immediately, every sight, every sound, every smell coming at you carries equal weight; every thought, feeling, memory, and idea presents itself to you with an equally strong and demanding intensity." —Elyn R. Saks, *The Center Cannot Hold*, 2007

delusion a false belief, often of persecution or grandeur, that may accompany psychotic disorders.

chronic schizophrenia (also called *process schizophrenia*) a form of schizophrenia in which symptoms usually appear by late adolescence or early adulthood. As people age, psychotic episodes last longer and recovery periods shorten.

acute schizophrenia (also called *reactive schizophrenia*) a form of schizophrenia that can begin at any age, frequently occurs in response to a traumatic event, and from which recovery is much more likely.

Most people with schizophrenia smoke, which stimulates brain activity that helps focus their attention. But their smoking contributes to people with schizophrenia having a 14.5 year shorter-than-average life expectancy (Hjorthøj et al., 2017; Zhuo et al., 2017).

Onset and Development of Schizophrenia

LOQ 14-15 How do *chronic schizophrenia* and *acute schizophrenia* differ?

This year, 1 in 100 people will join an estimated 21 million others worldwide who have schizophrenia (WHO, 2017c). This disorder knows no national boundaries and typically strikes as young people are maturing into adulthood. Men tend to be struck earlier, more severely, and more often (Aleman et al., 2003; Eranti et al., 2013; Picchioni & Murray, 2007).

When schizophrenia is a slow-developing process, called **chronic schizophrenia,** recovery is doubtful (Harrison et al., 2001; Jääskeläinen et al., 2013). This was the case with Maxine, whose schizophrenia took a slow course, emerging from a long history of social inadequacy and poor school performance (MacCabe et al., 2008). Social withdrawal, a negative symptom, is often found among those with chronic schizophrenia (Kirkpatrick et al., 2006). Men, whose schizophrenia develops on average four years earlier than women's, more often exhibit negative symptoms and chronic schizophrenia (Räsänen et al., 2000).

When previously well-adjusted people develop schizophrenia rapidly following particular life stresses, this is called **acute schizophrenia,** and recovery is much more likely. They more often have positive symptoms that respond to drug therapy (Fenton & McGlashan, 1991, 1994; Fowles, 1992).

Understanding Schizophrenia

Schizophrenia is one of the most heavily researched psychological disorders. Most studies now link it with abnormal brain tissue and genetic predispositions. Schizophrenia is a disease of the brain manifested in symptoms of the mind.

BRAIN ABNORMALITIES

LOQ 14-16 What brain abnormalities are associated with schizophrenia?

Might chemical imbalances in the brain explain schizophrenia? Scientists have long known that strange behavior can have strange chemical causes. Have you ever heard the saying "as mad as a hatter"? That phrase is often thought to refer to the psychological deterioration of British hat makers whose brains, it was later discovered, were slowly poisoned by the mercury-laden felt material (Smith, 1983). Could schizophrenia symptoms have a similar biochemical key? Scientists are searching for blood proteins that might predict schizophrenia onset (Chan et al., 2015). And they are tracking the mechanisms by which chemicals produce hallucinations and other symptoms.

DOPAMINE OVERACTIVITY One possible answer emerged when researchers examined schizophrenia patients' brains after death. They found an excess number of *dopamine* receptors, including a sixfold excess for the dopamine receptor D4 (Seeman et al., 1993; Wong et al., 1986). The resulting hyper-responsive dopamine system could intensify brain signals, creating positive symptoms such as hallucinations and paranoia (Maia & Frank, 2017). Drugs that block dopamine receptors often lessen these symptoms. Drugs that increase dopamine levels, such as nicotine, amphetamines, and cocaine, sometimes intensify them (Basu & Basu, 2015; Farnia et al., 2014).

ABNORMAL BRAIN ACTIVITY AND ANATOMY Abnormal brain activity and brain structures accompany schizophrenia. Some people diagnosed with schizophrenia have abnormally low brain activity in the brain's frontal lobes, which help us reason, plan, and solve problems (Morey et al., 2005; Pettegrew et al., 1993; Resnick, 1992). The brain waves that reflect synchronized neural firing in the frontal lobes decline noticeably (Spencer et al., 2004; Symond et al., 2005).

One study took PET scans of brain activity while people with schizophrenia were hallucinating (Silbersweig et al., 1995). When participants heard a voice or saw something, their brain became vigorously active in several core regions. One was the thalamus, the structure that filters incoming sensory signals and transmits them to the brain's cortex. Another PET scan study of people with paranoia found increased activity in the amygdala, a fear-processing center (Epstein et al., 1998).

Many studies have also found enlarged, fluid-filled ventricles and a corresponding shrinkage and thinning of cerebral tissue (Goldman et al., 2009; van Haren et al., 2016). People often inherit these brain differences. If one affected identical twin shows brain abnormalities, the odds are at least 1 in 2 that the other twin's brain will have them (van Haren et al., 2012). Some studies have even found these abnormalities in people who *later* developed the disorder (Karlsgodt et al., 2010). The greater the brain shrinkage, the more severe the thought disorder (Collinson et al., 2003; Nelson et al., 1998; Shenton, 1992).

Smaller-than-normal areas may include the cortex, the hippocampus, and the corpus callosum connecting the brain's two hemispheres (Arnone et al., 2008; Bois et al., 2016). Often, the thalamus is also smaller than normal, which may explain why filtering sensory input and focusing attention can be difficult for people with schizophrenia (Andreasen et al., 1994; Ellison-Wright et al., 2008). Schizophrenia also tends to involve a loss of neural connections across the brain network (Bohlken et al., 2016; Kambeitz et al., 2016). *The bottom line:* Schizophrenia involves not one isolated brain abnormality but problems with several brain regions and their interconnections (Andreasen, 1997, 2001; Arnedo et al., 2015).

PRENATAL ENVIRONMENT AND RISK

LOQ 14-17 What prenatal events are associated with increased risk of developing schizophrenia?

What causes these brain abnormalities seen in people with schizophrenia? Some scientists point to mishaps during prenatal development or delivery (Fatemi & Folsom, 2009; Walker et al., 2010). Risk factors include low birth weight, maternal diabetes, older paternal age, and oxygen deprivation during delivery (King et al., 2010). Famine may also increase risks. People conceived during the peak of World War II's Dutch famine later developed schizophrenia at twice the normal rate. Those conceived during the famine of 1959 to 1961 in eastern China also displayed this doubled rate (St. Clair et al., 2005; Susser et al., 1996).

Let's consider another possible culprit. Might a midpregnancy viral infection impair fetal brain development (Brown & Patterson, 2011)? To test this fetal-virus idea, scientists have asked these questions:

- *Are people at increased risk of schizophrenia if, during the middle of their fetal development, their country experienced a flu epidemic?* The repeated answer has been *Yes* (Mednick et al., 1994; Murray et al., 1992; Wright et al., 1995).

- *Are people born in densely populated areas, where viral diseases spread more readily, at greater risk for schizophrenia?* The answer, confirmed in a study of 1.75 million Danes, has again been *Yes* (Jablensky, 1999; Mortensen, 1999).

- *Are people born during the winter and spring months—those who were in utero during the fall-winter flu season—also at increased risk?* The answer is again *Yes* (Fox, 2010; Schwartz, 2011; Torrey & Miller, 2002; Torrey et al., 1997).

- *In the Southern Hemisphere, where the seasons are the reverse of the Northern Hemisphere, are the months of above-average pre-schizophrenia births similarly reversed?* Again, the answer has been *Yes*. In Australia, people born between August and October are at greater risk. But people born in the Northern Hemisphere who later moved to Australia still have a greater risk if they were born between January and March (McGrath et al., 1995; McGrath & Welham, 1999).

- *Are mothers who report being sick with influenza during pregnancy more likely to bear children who develop schizophrenia?* In one study of nearly 8000 women, the answer was *Yes*. The schizophrenia risk increased from the customary 1 percent to about 2 percent—but only when infections occurred during the second trimester (Brown et al., 2000). Maternal influenza infection during pregnancy affects brain development in monkeys as well (Short et al., 2010).

- *Does blood drawn from pregnant women whose offspring develop schizophrenia show higher-than-normal levels of antibodies that suggest a viral infection?* In several studies, the answer has again been *Yes* (Brown et al., 2004; Buka et al., 2001; Canetta et al., 2014).

STUDYING THE NEUROPHYSIOLOGY OF SCHIZOPHRENIA Psychiatrist E. Fuller Torrey has collected the brains of hundreds of people who died as young adults and suffered disorders such as schizophrenia and bipolar disorder.

© Chris Mueller/Redux Pictures

These converging lines of evidence suggest that fetal-virus infections contribute to the development of schizophrenia. This finding strengthens the U.S. government recommendation that "pregnant women need a flu shot" (CDC, 2014b).

GENETIC INFLUENCES

LOQ 14-18 How do genes influence schizophrenia?

Fetal-virus infections may increase the odds that a child will develop schizophrenia. But many women get the flu during their second trimester of pregnancy, and only 2 percent of them bear children who develop schizophrenia. Why does prenatal exposure to the flu virus put some children at risk but not others? Might some people be more genetically vulnerable to schizophrenia? *Yes.* The 1-in-100 odds of any one person being diagnosed with schizophrenia become about 1 in 10 among those who have a sibling or parent with the disorder. If the affected sibling is an identical twin, the odds increase to nearly 1 in 2 (**FIGURE 14.11**). Those odds are unchanged even when the twins are reared apart (Plomin et al., 1997). (Only about a dozen such cases are on record.)

Remember, though, that identical twins share more than their genes. They also share a prenatal environment. About two-thirds also share a placenta and the blood it supplies; the other third have separate placentas. Shared placentas matter. If the co-twin of an identical twin with schizophrenia shared the placenta, the chances of developing the disorder are 6 in 10. If the identical twins had separate placentas, the co-twin's chances of developing schizophrenia drop to 1 in 10 (Davis et al., 1995; Davis & Phelps, 1995; Phelps et al., 1997). Twins who share a placenta are more likely to share the same prenatal viruses. So perhaps shared germs as well as shared genes produce identical twin similarities.

Adoption studies help untangle genetic and environmental influences. Children adopted by someone who develops schizophrenia do not "catch" the disorder. Rather, adopted children have a higher risk if a *biological* parent has schizophrenia (Gottesman, 1991). Genes matter.

The search is on for specific genes that, in some combination, predispose schizophrenia-inducing brain abnormalities (**FIGURE 14.12**). (It is not our genes but our brains that directly control our behavior.) In the biggest-ever study of the genetics of psychiatric disorder, scientists from 35 countries pooled data from the genomes of 37,000 people with schizophrenia and 113,000 people without (Balter, 2017; Schizophrenia Working Group, 2014). They found 103 genome locations linked with the disorder. Some of these genes influence the activity of dopamine and other brain neurotransmitters. Others affect the production of *myelin,* a fatty substance that coats the axons of nerve cells and lets impulses travel at high speed through neural networks.

Although genes matter, the genetic formula is not as straightforward as the inheritance of eye color. Schizophrenia is a group of disorders influenced by many genes, each with very small effects (Arnedo et al., 2015; Darby et al., 2016; International Schizophrenia Consortium, 2009). As we have seen in so many different contexts, nature and nurture interact. Recall that *epigenetic* factors influence whether genes will be expressed. Like hot water activating a tea bag, environmental factors such as viral infections, nutritional deprivation, and maternal stress can "turn on" the genes that put some of us at higher risk for this disorder. Identical twins' differing histories in the womb and beyond explain why they may show differing gene expressions (Dempster et al., 2013; Walker et al., 2010). Our heredity and our life experiences work together. Neither hand claps alone.

LaunchPad See the **Video: Twin Studies** for a helpful tutorial animation about this type of research design.

FIGURE 14.11

RISK OF DEVELOPING SCHIZOPHRENIA The lifetime risk of developing schizophrenia varies with one's genetic relatedness to someone having this disorder. Across countries, barely more than 1 in 10 fraternal twins, but some 5 in 10 identical twins, share a schizophrenia diagnosis. (Data from Gottesman, 2001.)

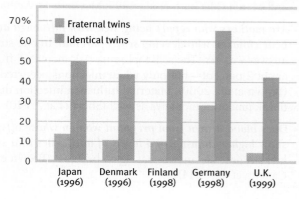
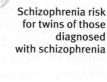

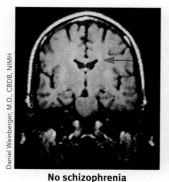
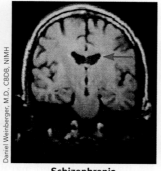

No schizophrenia
(a)

Schizophrenia
(b)

FIGURE 14.12

SCHIZOPHRENIA IN IDENTICAL TWINS When twins differ, only the one afflicted with schizophrenia typically has enlarged, fluid-filled cranial cavities (b) (Suddath et al., 1990). The difference between the twins implies some nongenetic factor, such as a virus, is also at work.

Thanks to our expanding understanding of genetic and brain influences on maladies such as schizophrenia, the general public increasingly recognizes the potency of biological factors in psychiatric disorders (Pescosolido et al., 2010).

ENGAGE 🔆 🎞 **LaunchPad** Take the role of a researcher studying these issues by engaging online with **Immersive Learning: How Would You Know If Schizophrenia Is Inherited?**

* * *

Few of us can relate to the strange thoughts, perceptions, and behaviors of schizophrenia. Sometimes our thoughts jump around, but we rarely talk nonsensically. Occasionally we feel unjustly suspicious of someone, but we do not believe the world is plotting against us. Often our perceptions err, but rarely do we see or hear things that are not there. We feel regret after laughing at someone's misfortune, but we rarely giggle in response to our own bad news. At times we just want to be alone, but we do not retreat into fantasy worlds. However, millions of people around the world do talk strangely, suffer delusions, hear nonexistent voices, see things that are not there, laugh or cry at inappropriate times, or withdraw into private imaginary worlds. The quest to solve the cruel puzzle of schizophrenia continues, more vigorously than ever.

🎞 **LaunchPad** For an 8-minute description of how clinicians define and treat schizophrenia, see the **Video: Schizophrenia—New Definitions, New Therapies.**

🔒 **RETRIEVE IT • • •**   *ANSWERS IN APPENDIX E*

RI-1 A person with schizophrenia who has _____ (positive/negative) symptoms may have an expressionless face and toneless voice. These symptoms are most common with _____ (chronic/acute) schizophrenia and are not likely to respond to drug therapy. Those with _____ (positive/negative) symptoms are likely to experience delusions and to be diagnosed with _____ (chronic/acute) schizophrenia, which is much more likely to respond to drug therapy.

RI-2 What factors contribute to the onset and development of schizophrenia?

ENGAGE 🔆 (**ASK YOURSELF**)

Can you recall a time when you heard something or someone casually described as "schizophrenic"? Now that you know more about this disorder, how might you correct such descriptions?

OTHER DISORDERS
Dissociative Disorders

LOQ 14-19 What are *dissociative disorders*, and why are they controversial?

Among the most bewildering disorders are the rare **dissociative disorders,** in which a person's conscious awareness *dissociates* (separates) from painful memories, thoughts, and feelings. The result may be a *fugue state*, a sudden loss of memory or change in identity, often in response to an overwhelmingly stressful situation (Harrison et al., 2017). Such was the case for one Vietnam veteran who was haunted by his comrades' deaths, and who had left his World Trade Center office shortly before the 9/11 terrorist attack. Later, he disappeared. Six months later, when he was discovered in a Chicago homeless shelter, he reported no memory of his identity or family (Stone, 2006).

dissociative disorders controversial, rare disorders in which conscious awareness becomes separated (dissociated) from previous memories, thoughts, and feelings.

MULTIPLE IDENTITIES IN THE MOVIES Chris Sizemore's story, told in the book and movie *The Three Faces of Eve*, gave early visibility to what is now called dissociative identity disorder. This controversial disorder continues to influence modern media, as in the 2017 movie *Split*, where "Kevin" (James McAvoy), pictured here, displays 24 different personalities.

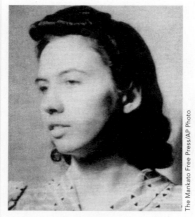

WIDESPREAD DISSOCIATION Shirley Mason was a psychiatric patient diagnosed with dissociative identity disorder. Her life formed the basis of the bestselling book, *Sybil* (Schreiber, 1973), and of two movies. The book and movies' popularity likely fueled the dramatic rise in diagnoses of DID in North America. A 2011 book complicated matters by revealing Mason's claim, in 1958, that she did not have the disorder (Nathan, 2011).

"Pretense may become reality."
—Chinese proverb

DISSOCIATIVE IDENTITY DISORDER Dissociation itself is not so rare. Any one of us may have a fleeting sense of being unreal, of being separated from our body, of watching ourselves as if in a movie. A massive dissociation of self from ordinary consciousness is said to occur in **dissociative identity disorder** (**DID**—formerly called *multiple personality disorder*), in which two or more distinct identities—each with its own voice and mannerisms—seem to control the person's behavior. Thus, the person may be prim and proper one moment, loud and flirtatious the next. Typically, the original identity denies any awareness of the other(s).

People diagnosed with DID are rarely violent. But cases have been reported of dissociations into a "good" and a "bad" (or aggressive) identity—a modest version of the Dr. Jekyll–Mr. Hyde split immortalized in Robert Louis Stevenson's story. One unusual case involved Kenneth Bianchi, accused in the "Hillside Strangler" rapes and murders of 10 California women. During a hypnosis session, Bianchi's psychologist "called forth" a hidden identity: "I've talked a bit to Ken, but I think that perhaps there might be another part of Ken that . . . maybe feels somewhat differently from the part that I've talked to. . . . Would you talk with me, Part, by saying, 'I'm here'?" Bianchi answered "Yes" and then claimed to be "Steve" (Watkins, 1984).

Speaking as Steve, Bianchi stated that he hated Ken because Ken was nice and that he (Steve), aided by a cousin, had murdered women. He also claimed Ken knew nothing about Steve's existence and was innocent of the murders. Was Bianchi's second identity a trick, simply a way of disavowing responsibility for his actions? Indeed, Bianchi—a practiced liar who had read about this disorder in psychology books—was later convicted.

UNDERSTANDING DISSOCIATIVE IDENTITY DISORDER Skeptics question DID. They find it suspicious that the disorder has such a short and localized history. Between 1930 and 1960, the number of North American DID diagnoses averaged 2 per decade. By the 1980s, when the American Psychiatric Association's *Diagnostic and Statistical Manual of Mental Disorders* (DSM) contained the first formal code for this disorder, the number had exploded to more than 20,000 (McHugh, 1995). The average number of displayed identities also mushroomed—from 3 to 12 per patient (Goff & Simms, 1993). And although diagnoses have been increasing in countries where DID has been publicized, the disorder is much less prevalent outside North America (Lilienfeld, 2017).

Skeptics have also asked if DID could be an extension of our normal capacity for identity shifts. Nicholas Spanos (1986, 1994, 1996) asked college students to pretend they were accused murderers being examined by a psychiatrist. Given the same hypnotic treatment Bianchi received, most spontaneously expressed a second identity. This discovery made Spanos wonder: Perhaps dissociative identities are simply a more extreme version of the varied "selves" we normally present—to our friends, say, versus our grandparents. Are clinicians who discover multiple identities merely triggering role playing by fantasy-prone people in a particular social context (Giesbrecht et al., 2008, 2010; Lynn et al., 2014; Merskey, 1992)? After all, clients do not enter therapy saying, "Allow me to introduce myselves." Rather, charge the critics, some therapists go fishing for multiple identities: *"Have you ever felt like another part of you does things you can't control?" "Does this part of you have a name?" "Can I talk to the angry part of you?"* Once clients permit a therapist to talk, by name, "to the part of you that says those angry things," they begin acting out the fantasy. Like actors who lose themselves in their roles, vulnerable patients may "become" the parts they are acting out. The result may be the experience of another self.

Other researchers and clinicians believe DID is a real disorder. They cite findings of distinct body and brain states associated with differing identities (Putnam, 1991). Abnormal brain anatomy and activity can also accompany DID. Brain scans show shrinkage in areas that aid memory and detection of threat (Vermetten et al., 2006). Heightened activity appears in brain areas linked with the control and inhibition of traumatic memories

(Elzinga et al., 2007). Both the psychodynamic and learning perspectives have interpreted DID symptoms as ways of coping with anxiety. Some psychodynamic theorists see them as defenses against the anxiety caused by unacceptable impulses. In this view, a second identity could allow the discharge of forbidden impulses. Learning theorists see dissociative disorders as behaviors reinforced by anxiety reduction.

Some clinicians include dissociative disorders under the umbrella of posttraumatic stress disorder—a natural, protective response to traumatic experiences during childhood (Brand et al., 2016; Spiegel, 2008). Many people being treated for DID recall being physically, sexually, or emotionally abused as children (Gleaves, 1996; Lilienfeld et al., 1999). In one study of 12 murderers diagnosed with DID, 11 had suffered severe abuse, even torture, in childhood (Lewis et al., 1997). One had been set afire by his parents. Another had been used in child pornography and was scarred from being made to sit on a stove burner. Critics wonder, however, whether vivid imagination or therapist suggestion contributed to such recollections (Kihlstrom, 2005). So the scientific debate continues. Stay tuned.

> 🔓 **RETRIEVE IT** • • •   *ANSWERS IN APPENDIX E*
>
> **RI-3** The psychodynamic and learning perspectives agree that dissociative identity disorder symptoms are ways of dealing with anxiety. How do their explanations differ?

Personality Disorders

LOQ 14-20 What are the three clusters of personality disorders? What behaviors and brain activity characterize the antisocial personality?

The inflexible and enduring behavior patterns of **personality disorders** interfere with social functioning. These ten disorders in DSM-5 tend to form three clusters, characterized by

- *anxiety,* such as a fearful sensitivity to rejection that predisposes the withdrawn *avoidant personality disorder.*

- *eccentric or odd behaviors,* such as actions prompted by the magical thinking of *schizotypal personality disorder.*

- *dramatic or impulsive behaviors,* such as the unstable, attention-getting *borderline personality disorder,* the self-focused and self-inflating *narcissistic personality disorder,* and—what we next discuss as an in-depth example—the callous, and often dangerous, *antisocial personality disorder.*

ANTISOCIAL PERSONALITY DISORDER People with **antisocial personality disorder,** usually male, can display symptoms by age 8. Their lack of conscience becomes plain before age 15, as they begin to lie, steal, fight, or display unrestrained sexual behavior (Cale & Lilienfeld, 2002). Not all children with these traits become antisocial adults. (Note that *antisocial* means disruptive, not merely unsociable.) Those who do—about half—will generally act in violent or otherwise criminal ways, be unable to keep a job, and behave irresponsibly toward family members (Farrington, 1991). But criminality is not an essential component of antisocial behavior (Skeem & Cooke, 2010). Moreover, many criminals do not fit the description of antisocial personality disorder. Why? Because they are not impulsively antisocial (Geurts et al., 2016). Rather, they show responsible concern for their friends and family members. People with antisocial personality disorder (sometimes called *sociopaths* or *psychopaths*) may show lower *emotional intelligence*—the ability to understand, manage, and perceive emotions (Ermer et al., 2012b).

Antisocial personalities behave impulsively, and then feel and fear little (Fowles & Dindo, 2009). Their impulsivity can have horrific consequences (Camp et al., 2013). Consider the case of Henry Lee Lucas. He killed his first victim when he was 13. He felt little regret then or later. During his years of crime, he brutally murdered 157 women, men, and children. For the last six years of his reign of terror, Lucas teamed with Ottis Elwood Toole, who reportedly slaughtered people he "didn't think was worth living anyhow" (Darrach & Norris, 1984).

"Though this be madness, yet there is method in 't." —William Shakespeare, *Hamlet,* 1600

 ENGAGE (ASK YOURSELF)

Do you ever flip between displays of different aspects of your personality, depending on your surroundings? How is your experience similar to and different from the described symptoms of dissociative identity disorder?

"Would it be possible to speak with the personality that pays the bills?"

dissociative identity disorder (DID) a rare dissociative disorder in which a person exhibits two or more distinct and alternating identities. (Formerly called *multiple personality disorder.*)

personality disorders inflexible and enduring behavior patterns that impair social functioning.

antisocial personality disorder a personality disorder in which a person (usually a man) exhibits a lack of conscience for wrongdoing, even toward friends and family members; may be aggressive and ruthless or a clever con artist.

NO REMORSE Dennis Rader, known as the "BTK killer" in Kansas, was convicted in 2005 of killing 10 people over a 30-year span. Rader exhibited the extreme lack of conscience that marks antisocial personality disorder.

"Thursday is out. I have jury duty."

Many criminals, like this one, display a sense of conscience and responsibility in other areas of their life, and thus do not exhibit antisocial personality disorder.

Does a full Moon trigger "madness" in some people? Researchers examined data from 37 studies that related lunar phase to crime (including homicides specifically), crisis calls, and psychiatric hospital admissions (Rotton & Kelley, 1985). Their conclusion: There is virtually no evidence of "Moon madness." Nor does lunar phase correlate with suicides, assaults, emergency room visits, or traffic disasters (Martin et al., 1992; Raison et al., 1999).

UNDERSTANDING ANTISOCIAL PERSONALITY DISORDER Antisocial personality disorder is woven of both biological and psychological strands. Twin and adoption studies reveal that biological relatives of people with antisocial and unemotional tendencies are at increased risk for antisocial behavior (Frisell et al., 2012; Kendler et al., 2015b). No single gene codes for a complex behavior such as crime. Molecular geneticists have identified some specific genes that are more common in those with antisocial personality disorder (Gunter et al., 2010; Tielbeek et al., 2017). There may be a genetic predisposition toward a fearless and uninhibited life. The genes that put people at risk for antisocial behavior also increase the risk for substance use disorder, which helps explain why these disorders often appear together (Dick, 2007).

Genetic influences, often in combination with negative environmental factors such as childhood abuse, family instability, or poverty, help wire the brain (Dodge, 2009). This is true even in chimpanzees, which, like humans, vary in antisocial tendencies (Latzman et al., 2017). In people with antisocial criminal tendencies, the emotion-controlling amygdala is smaller (Pardini et al., 2014). The genetic vulnerability of people with antisocial and unemotional tendencies appears as low arousal in response to threats. Awaiting events that most people would find unnerving, such as electric shocks or loud noises, they show little autonomic nervous system arousal (Hare, 1975; Hoppenbrouwers et al., 2016). Long-term studies show that their stress hormone levels were lower than average as teens, before committing any crime (**FIGURE 14.13**). And those who were slow to develop conditioned fears at age 3 were also more likely to commit a crime later in life (Gao et al., 2010). Other studies have found that preschool boys who later became aggressive or antisocial adolescents tended to be impulsive, uninhibited, unconcerned with social rewards, and low in anxiety (Caspi et al., 1996; Tremblay et al., 1994).

Traits such as fearlessness and dominance can be adaptive. If channeled in more productive directions, fearlessness may lead to athletic stardom, adventurism, or courageous heroism (Smith et al., 2013). Indeed, 42 American presidents scored higher than the general population on such traits as fearlessness and dominance (Lilienfeld et al., 2012, 2016). Patient S. M., a 49-year-old woman with amygdala damage, showed fearlessness and impulsivity but also heroism: She gave a man in need her only coat and scarf, and donated her hair to the Locks of Love charity after befriending a child with cancer (Lilienfeld et al., 2017). Lacking a sense of social responsibility, the same disposition may produce a cool con artist or killer (Lykken, 1995).

With antisocial behavior, as with so much else, nature and nurture interact: The biopsychosocial perspective helps us understand the whole story. To further explore the neural basis of antisocial personality disorder, scientists are trying to identify brain

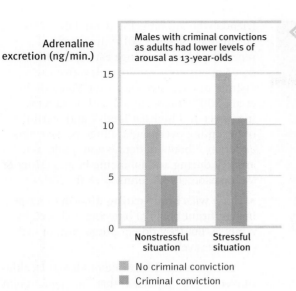

FIGURE 14.13

COLD-BLOODED AROUSABILITY AND RISK OF CRIME Levels of the stress hormone adrenaline were measured in two groups of 13-year-old Swedish boys. In both stressful and nonstressful situations, those who would later be convicted of a crime as 18- to 26-year-olds showed relatively low arousal. (Data from Magnusson, 1990.)

activity differences in antisocial criminals. Shown emotionally evocative photographs, such as a man holding a knife to a woman's throat, criminals with antisocial personality disorder display blunted heart rate and perspiration responses, and less activity in brain areas that typically respond to emotional stimuli (Harenski et al., 2010; Kiehl & Buckholtz, 2010). They also have a larger and hyper-reactive dopamine reward system, which predisposes their impulsive drive to do something rewarding despite the consequences (Buckholtz et al., 2010; Glenn et al., 2010). One study compared PET scans of 41 murderers' brains with those from people of similar age and sex. The murderers' frontal lobes, an area that helps control impulses, displayed reduced activity (Raine, 1999, 2005; **FIGURE 14.14**). The reduced activation was especially apparent in those who murdered impulsively. In a follow-up study, researchers found that violent repeat offenders had 11 percent less frontal lobe tissue than normal (Raine et al., 2000). This helps explain another finding: People with antisocial personality disorder fall far below normal in aspects of thinking such as planning, organization, and inhibition, which are all frontal lobe functions (Morgan & Lilienfeld, 2000). Such data remind us: Everything psychological is also biological.

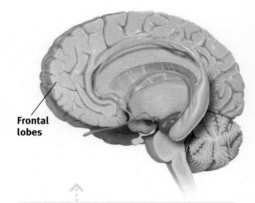

FIGURE 14.14

MURDEROUS MINDS Researchers have found reduced activation in a murderer's frontal lobes. This brain area (shown in a left-facing brain) helps brake impulsive, aggressive behavior (Raine, 1999).

RETRIEVE IT • • •   *ANSWERS IN APPENDIX E*

RI-4 How do biological and psychological factors contribute to antisocial personality disorder?

Eating Disorders

LOQ 14-21 What are the three main eating disorders, and how do biological, psychological, and social-cultural influences make people more vulnerable to them?

Our bodies are naturally disposed to maintain a steady weight, including storing energy for times when food becomes unavailable. But sometimes psychological influences overwhelm biological wisdom. This becomes painfully clear in three eating disorders:

- **Anorexia nervosa** typically begins as a weight-loss diet. People with anorexia—usually female adolescents, but some women, men, and boys as well—drop significantly below normal weight. Yet they feel fat, fear being fat, diet obsessively, and sometimes exercise excessively.

- **Bulimia nervosa,** unlike anorexia, is marked by weight fluctuations within or above normal ranges, making the condition easier to hide. Bulimia may also be triggered by a weight-loss diet that is broken by gorging on forbidden foods. People with this disorder—mostly women in their late teens or early twenties (but also some men)—eat in spurts, sometimes influenced by negative emotion or by

anorexia nervosa an eating disorder in which a person (usually an adolescent female) maintains a starvation diet despite being significantly underweight; sometimes accompanied by excessive exercise.

bulimia nervosa an eating disorder in which a person's binge eating (usually of high-calorie foods) is followed by inappropriate weight-loss promoting behavior, such as vomiting, laxative use, fasting, or excessive exercise.

SIBLING RIVALRY GONE AWRY Twins Maria and Katy Campbell have anorexia nervosa. As children they competed to see who could be thinner. Now, says Maria, her anorexia nervosa is "like a ball and chain around my ankle that I can't throw off" (Foster, 2011).

friends who are bingeing (Crandall, 1988; Haedt-Matt & Keel, 2011). In a cycle of repeating episodes, binge eating is followed by compensatory vomiting, laxative use, fasting, or excessive exercise (Wonderlich et al., 2007). Preoccupied with food (craving sweet and high-fat foods), and fearful of becoming overweight, binge-purge eaters experience bouts of depression, guilt, and anxiety during and following binges (Hinz & Williamson, 1987; Johnson et al., 2002).

• Those with **binge-eating disorder** engage in significant bouts of bingeing, followed by remorse. But they do not purge, fast, or exercise excessively.

A U.S. National Institute of Mental Health–funded study reported that, at some point during their lifetime, 0.6 percent of Americans met the criteria for anorexia, 1 percent for bulimia, and 2.8 percent for binge-eating disorder (Hudson et al., 2007). Anorexia and bulimia can be deadly. They harm the body and mind, resulting in shorter life expectancy and greater risk of suicide and nonsuicidal self-injury (Cucchi et al., 2016; Fichter & Quadflieg, 2016; Smith et al., 2016).

UNDERSTANDING EATING DISORDERS Eating disorders are *not* (as some have speculated) a telltale sign of childhood sexual abuse (Smolak & Murnen, 2002; Stice, 2002). The family environment may influence eating disorders in other ways, however. For example, families of those with anorexia tend to be competitive, high achieving, and protective (Ahrén et al., 2013; Berg et al., 2014; Yates, 1989, 1990). Those with eating disorders often have low self-evaluations, set perfectionist standards, fret about falling short of expectations, and are intensely concerned with how others perceive them (Culbert et al., 2015; Farstad et al., 2016; Yiend et al., 2014). Some of these factors also predict teen boys' pursuit of unrealistic muscularity (Karazsia et al., 2017; Ricciardelli & McCabe, 2004).

A DISTORTED BODY IMAGE UNDERLIES ANOREXIA NERVOSA.

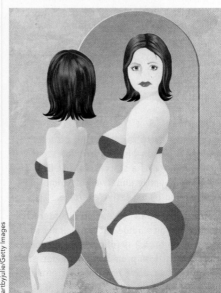

📺 **LaunchPad** For an inside look at one man's experience with eating disorders, see the **Video: Overcoming Anorexia Nervosa.**

Heredity also matters. Identical twins share these disorders more often than fraternal twins do (Culbert et al., 2009; Klump et al., 2009; Root et al., 2010). Scientists are now searching for culprit genes. Data from 15 studies indicate that having a gene that reduces available serotonin adds 30 percent to a person's risk of anorexia or bulimia (Calati et al., 2011). A comparison of the genomes of nearly 3500 anorexia patients with 11,000 others identified a gene difference on chromosome 12 (Duncan et al., 2017).

But eating disorders also have cultural and gender components. Ideal shapes vary across culture and time. Plump may mean prosperity and thin may signal poverty or illness in countries with high poverty rates (Knickmeyer, 2001; Swami et al., 2010). Bigger less often seems better in wealthy Western cultures. In one analysis of 222 studies, the rise in eating disorders in the last half of the twentieth century coincided with a dramatic increase in Western women having a poor body image (Feingold & Mazzella, 1998).

Those most vulnerable to eating disorders are also those (usually women or gay men) who most idealize thinness and have the greatest body dissatisfaction (Feldman & Meyer, 2010; Kane, 2010; Stice et al., 2010). Should it surprise us, then, that women who view real and doctored images of unnaturally thin models and celebrities often feel ashamed, depressed, and dissatisfied with their own bodies—the very attitudes that predispose eating disorders (Grabe et al., 2008; Myers & Crowther, 2009; Tiggeman & Miller, 2010)?

Eric Stice and his colleagues (2001) tested this modeling idea by giving some adolescent girls (but not others) a 15-month subscription to an American teen-fashion magazine. Compared with those who had not received the magazine, vulnerable girls—defined as those who were already dissatisfied, idealizing thinness, and lacking social support—exhibited increased body dissatisfaction and eating disorder tendencies. Even ultra-thin models do not reflect the impossible standard of the original Barbie doll, who had, when adjusted to a height of 5 feet 7 inches, a 32–16–29 figure (in centimeters, 82–41–73) (Norton et al., 1996).

There is, however, more to body dissatisfaction and anorexia than media effects (Ferguson et al., 2011). Peer influences, such as teasing and harassment, also matter. Nevertheless, the sickness of today's eating disorders stems in part from today's weight-obsessed culture—a culture that says "fat is bad" in countless ways, that motivates millions of women to diet constantly, and that invites eating binges by pressuring women to live in a constant state of semistarvation. One former model recalled walking into a meeting with her agent, starving and with her organs failing due to anorexia (Caroll, 2013). Her agent's greeting: "Whatever you are doing, keep doing it."

Most people diagnosed with an eating disorder do improve. In one 22-year study, 2 in 3 women with anorexia nervosa or bulimia nervosa had recovered (Eddy et al., 2017). Prevention is also possible. Interactive programs that teach people (especially girls over age 15) to accept their bodies reduce the likelihood of an eating disorder (Beintner et al., 2012; Melioli et al., 2016; Vocks et al., 2010). By combating cultural learning, those at risk may instead live long and healthy lives.

"Up until that point, Bernice had never once had a problem with low self-esteem."

binge-eating disorder significant binge-eating episodes, followed by distress, disgust, or guilt, but without the compensatory behavior that marks bulimia nervosa.

"Why do women have such low self-esteem? There are many complex psychological and societal reasons, by which I mean Barbie." —Humorist Dave Barry, 1999

TOO THIN Many worry that superthin models make self-starvation seem fashionable. Concerned about promoting an unhealthy body image, British advertising regulators banned this advertisement because the female model appeared "unhealthily thin."

* * *

The bewilderment, fear, and sorrow caused by psychological disorders are real. But as our next topic—therapy—shows, hope, too, is real.

RI-5 People with _____ _____ (anorexia nervosa/bulimia nervosa) continue to want to lose weight even when they are underweight. Those with _____ _____ (anorexia nervosa/bulimia nervosa) tend to have weight that fluctuates within or above normal ranges.

🔒 REVIEW SCHIZOPHRENIA AND OTHER DISORDERS

⤳ Learning Objectives

TEST YOURSELF Answer these repeated Learning Objective Questions on your own (before checking the answers in Appendix D) to improve your retention of the concepts (McDaniel et al., 2009, 2015).

14-14 What patterns of perceiving, thinking, and feeling characterize schizophrenia?

14-15 How do *chronic schizophrenia* and *acute schizophrenia* differ?

14-16 What brain abnormalities are associated with schizophrenia?

14-17 What prenatal events are associated with increased risk of developing schizophrenia?

14-18 How do genes influence schizophrenia?

14-19 What are *dissociative disorders*, and why are they controversial?

14-20 What are the three clusters of personality disorders? What behaviors and brain activity characterize the antisocial personality?

14-21 What are the three main eating disorders, and how do biological, psychological, and social-cultural influences make people more vulnerable to them?

⤳ Terms and Concepts to Remember

TEST YOURSELF Write down the definition yourself, then check your answer on the referenced page.

schizophrenia, **p. 522**

psychotic disorders, **p. 522**

delusion, **p. 523**

chronic schizophrenia, **p. 524**

acute schizophrenia, **p. 524**

dissociative disorders, **p. 527**

dissociative identity disorder (DID), **p. 529**

personality disorders, **p. 529**

antisocial personality disorder, **p. 529**

anorexia nervosa, **p. 531**

bulimia nervosa, **p. 531**

binge-eating disorder, **p. 533**

⤳ Experience the Testing Effect

TEST YOURSELF Answer the following questions on your own first, then check your answers in Appendix E.

1. Victor exclaimed, "The weather has been so schizophrenic lately: It's hot one day and freezing the next!" In addition to being insensitive to those with schizophrenia, this comparison is inaccurate. Explain.

2. A person with positive symptoms of schizophrenia is most likely to experience
   a. catatonia.
   b. delusions.
   c. withdrawal.
   d. flat emotion.

3. People with schizophrenia may hear voices urging self-destruction, an example of a(n) _____.

4. Chances for recovery from schizophrenia are best when
   a. onset is sudden, in response to stress.
   b. deterioration occurs gradually, during childhood.
   c. no environmental causes can be identified.
   d. there is a detectable brain abnormality.

5. Dissociative identity disorder is controversial because
   a. dissociation is quite rare.
   b. it was reported frequently in the 1920s but rarely today.
   c. it is almost never reported outside North America.
   d. its symptoms are nearly identical to those of obsessive-compulsive disorder.

6. A personality disorder, such as antisocial personality, is characterized by
   a. depression.
   b. hallucinations.
   c. inflexible and enduring behavior patterns that impair social functioning.
   d. an elevated level of autonomic nervous system arousal.

7. PET scans of murderers' brains have revealed
   a. higher-than-normal activation in the frontal lobes.
   b. lower-than-normal activation in the frontal lobes.
   c. more frontal lobe tissue than normal.
   d. no differences in brain structures or activity.

8. Which of the following statements is true of bulimia nervosa?
   a. People with bulimia continue to want to lose weight even when they are underweight.
   b. Bulimia is marked by weight fluctuations within or above normal ranges.
   c. Those with bulimia are equally likely to be male or female.
   d. If one twin is diagnosed with bulimia, the chances of the other twin's sharing the disorder are greater if they are fraternal rather than identical twins.

Continue testing yourself with 📖 **LearningCurve** or 📖 **Achieve Read & Practice** to learn and remember most effectively.

Therapy

K ay Redfield Jamison is both an award-winning clinical psychologist and a world expert on the emotional extremes of bipolar disorder. She knows her subject firsthand: "For as long as I can remember," she recalled in her memoir *An Unquiet Mind,* "I was frighteningly, although often wonderfully, beholden to moods. Intensely emotional as a child, mercurial as a young girl, first severely depressed as an adolescent, and then unrelentingly caught up in the cycles of manic-depressive illness [now known as bipolar disorder] by the time I began my professional life, I became, both by necessity and intellectual inclination, a student of moods" (1995, pp. 4–5). Jamison's life was blessed with times of intense sensitivity and passionate energy. But like her father's, it was also sometimes plagued by reckless spending, racing conversation, and sleeplessness, alternating with swings into "the blackest caves of the mind."

Then, "in the midst of utter confusion," she made a life-changing decision. Risking professional embarrassment, she made an appointment with a therapist, a psychiatrist she would visit weekly for years to come:

> He kept me alive a thousand times over. He saw me through madness, despair, wonderful and terrible love affairs, disillusionments and triumphs, recurrences of illness, an almost fatal suicide attempt, the death of a man I greatly loved, and the enormous pleasures and aggravations of my professional life. . . . He was very tough, as well as very kind, and even though he understood more than anyone how much I felt I was losing—in energy, vivacity, and originality—by taking medication, he never [lost] sight of the overall perspective of how costly, damaging, and life threatening my illness was. . . . Although I went to him to be treated for an illness, he taught me . . . the total beholdenness of brain to mind and mind to brain (pp. 87–88).

DOROTHEA DIX "I . . . call your attention to the state of the Insane Persons confined within this Commonwealth, in cages." (*Memorial to the Legislature of Massachusetts*, 1843)

THE HISTORY OF TREATMENT Visitors to eighteenth-century mental hospitals paid to gawk at patients, as though they were viewing zoo animals. William Hogarth's (1697–1764) painting captured one of these visits to London's St. Mary of Bethlehem hospital (commonly called Bedlam).

"Psychotherapy heals," Jamison reports. "It makes some sense of the confusion, reins in the terrifying thoughts and feelings, returns some control and hope and possibility from it all."

This chapter explores some of the healing options available to therapists and the people who seek their help. We begin by exploring and evaluating *psychotherapies,* and then focus on *biomedical therapies* and preventing disorders. ▶

⟶ Introduction to Therapy and the Psychological Therapies

The long history of efforts to treat psychological disorders has included a bewildering mix of harsh and gentle methods. Would-be healers have cut holes in people's heads and restrained, bled, or "beat the devil" out of them. But they also have given warm baths and massages and placed people in sunny, serene environments. They have given them drugs. And they have talked with them about childhood experiences, current feelings, and maladaptive thoughts and behaviors.

Reformers Philippe Pinel (1745–1826) and Dorothea Dix (1802–1887) pushed for gentler, more humane treatments and for constructing mental hospitals. Their efforts largely paid off. Since the 1950s, the introduction of effective drug therapies and community-based treatment programs has emptied most of those hospitals.

TREATING PSYCHOLOGICAL DISORDERS

LEARNING OBJECTIVE QUESTION (LOQ)

15-1   How do *psychotherapy* and the *biomedical therapies* differ?

Modern Western therapies can be classified into two main categories.

- In **psychotherapy,** a trained therapist uses psychological techniques to assist someone seeking to overcome difficulties and achieve personal growth. The therapist may explore a client's early relationships, encourage the client to adopt new ways of thinking, or coach the client in replacing old behaviors with new ones.

- **Biomedical therapy** offers medication or other biological treatments. For example, a person with severe depression may receive antidepressants, electroconvulsive shock therapy (ECT), or deep brain stimulation.

The care provider's training and expertise, as well as the disorder itself, influence the choice of treatment. Psychotherapy and medication are often combined. Kay Redfield Jamison received psychotherapy in her meetings with her psychiatrist, and she took medications to control her wild mood swings.

Let's look first at some influential psychotherapy options for those treated with "talk therapies." Each is built on one or more of psychology's major theories: psychodynamic, humanistic, behavioral, and cognitive. Most of these techniques can be used one-on-one or in groups. Some therapists combine techniques. Indeed, many psychotherapists describe their approach as **eclectic,** using a blend of therapies.

PSYCHOANALYSIS AND PSYCHODYNAMIC THERAPIES

LOQ 15-2 What are the goals and techniques of psychoanalysis, and how have they been adapted in psychodynamic therapy?

The first major psychological therapy was Sigmund Freud's **psychoanalysis**. Although few clinicians today practice therapy as Freud did, his work deserves discussion. It helped form the foundation for treating psychological disorders, and it continues to influence modern therapists working from the *psychodynamic* perspective.

The Goals of Psychoanalysis

Freud believed that in therapy, people could achieve healthier, less anxious living by releasing the energy they had previously devoted to id-ego-superego conflicts (Chapter 13). Freud assumed that we do not fully know ourselves. He believed that there are threatening things we *repress*—things we do not want to know, so we disavow or deny them. Psychoanalysis was Freud's method of helping people to bring these repressed feelings into conscious awareness. By helping them reclaim their unconscious thoughts and feelings, and by giving them *insight* into the origins of their disorders, the therapist (*analyst*) could help them reduce growth-impeding inner conflicts.

The Techniques of Psychoanalysis

Psychoanalytic theory emphasizes the power of childhood experiences to mold the adult. Thus, psychoanalysis is historical reconstruction. It aims to unearth the past in the hope of loosening its bonds on the present. After discarding hypnosis as an unreliable excavator, Freud turned to *free association*.

Imagine yourself as a patient using free association. You begin by relaxing, perhaps by lying on a couch. The psychoanalyst, who sits out of your line of vision, asks you to say aloud whatever comes to mind. At one moment, you're relating a childhood memory. At another, you're describing a dream or recent experience. It sounds easy, but soon you notice how often you edit your thoughts as you speak. You pause for a second before uttering an embarrassing thought. You omit what seems trivial, irrelevant, or shameful. Sometimes your mind goes blank or you clutch up, unable to remember important details. You may joke or change the subject to something less threatening.

To the analyst, these mental blocks indicate **resistance.** They hint that anxiety lurks and you are defending against sensitive material. The analyst will note your resistance and then provide insight into its meaning. If offered at the right moment, this **interpretation**—of, say, your not wanting to discuss, text, or message your mother—may illuminate the underlying wishes, feelings, and conflicts you are avoiding. The analyst may also offer an explanation of how this resistance fits with other pieces of your psychological puzzle, including those based on analysis of your dream content.

Over many such sessions, your relationship patterns surface in your interaction with your therapist. You may find yourself experiencing strong positive or negative feelings for your analyst. The analyst may suggest you are **transferring** feelings, such as dependency or mingled love and anger, that you experienced in earlier relationships with family members or other important people. By exposing such feelings, you may gain insight into your current relationships.

Relatively few North American therapists now offer traditional psychoanalysis. Much of its underlying theory is not supported by scientific research (Chapter 13). Analysts' interpretations cannot be proven or disproven. And psychoanalysis takes considerable time and money, often years of several expensive sessions per week. Some of these problems have been addressed in the modern *psychodynamic perspective* that has evolved from psychoanalysis.

psychotherapy treatment involving psychological techniques; consists of interactions between a trained therapist and someone seeking to overcome psychological difficulties or achieve personal growth.

biomedical therapy prescribed medications or procedures that act directly on the person's physiology.

eclectic approach an approach to psychotherapy that uses techniques from various forms of therapy.

psychoanalysis Sigmund Freud's therapeutic technique. Freud believed the patient's free associations, resistances, dreams, and transferences—and the analyst's interpretations of them—released previously repressed feelings, allowing the patient to gain self-insight.

resistance in psychoanalysis, the blocking from consciousness of anxiety-laden material.

interpretation in psychoanalysis, the analyst's noting of supposed dream meanings, resistances, and other significant behaviors and events in order to promote insight.

transference in psychoanalysis, the patient's transfer to the analyst of emotions linked with other relationships (such as love or hatred for a parent).

"I'm more interested in hearing about the eggs you're hiding from yourself."

Psychodynamic Therapy

Although influenced by Freud's ideas, **psychodynamic therapists** don't talk much about id-ego-superego conflicts. Instead, they try to help people understand their current symptoms by focusing on important relationships, including childhood experiences and the therapist-client relationship. "We can have loving feelings and hateful feelings toward the same person," observed psychodynamic therapist Jonathan Shedler (2009), and "we can desire something and also fear it." Client-therapist meetings take place once or twice a week (rather than several times weekly), and often for only a few weeks or months. Rather than lying on a couch, out of the therapist's line of vision, clients meet with their therapist face-to-face and gain perspective by exploring defended-against thoughts and feelings.

Therapist David Shapiro (1999, p. 8) illustrated this with the case of a young man who had told women that he loved them, when he knew that he didn't. The client's explanation: They expected it, so he said it. But later, with his wife, who wished he would say that he loved her, he found he *couldn't* do that—"I don't know why, but I can't."

Therapist: Do you mean, then, that if you could, you would like to?

Patient: Well, I don't know. . . . Maybe I can't say it because I'm not sure it's true. Maybe I don't love her.

Further interactions revealed that the client could not express real love because it would feel "mushy" and "soft" and therefore unmanly. He was "in conflict with himself, and . . . cut off from the nature of that conflict." Shapiro noted that with such patients, who are estranged from themselves, therapists using psychodynamic techniques "are in a position to introduce them to themselves. We can restore their awareness of their own wishes and feelings, and their awareness, as well, of their reactions against those wishes and feelings."

Exploring past relationship troubles may help clients understand the origin of their current difficulties. Shedler (2010a) recalled "Jeffrey's" complaints of difficulty getting along with his colleagues and wife, who saw him as hypercritical. Jeffrey then "began responding to me as if I were an unpredictable, angry adversary." Shedler seized this opportunity to help Jeffrey recognize the relationship pattern and its roots in the attacks and humiliation he had experienced from his alcohol-abusing father. Jeffrey was then able to work through and let go of this defensive style of responding to people. Thus, without embracing all of Freud's theory, psychodynamic therapists aim to help people gain insight into unconscious dynamics that arise from their life experience.

HUMANISTIC THERAPIES

LOQ 15-3 What are the basic themes of humanistic therapy? What are the specific goals and techniques of Rogers' client-centered approach?

The *humanistic* perspective (Chapter 13) emphasizes people's innate potential for self-fulfillment. Not surprisingly, humanistic therapies attempt to reduce the inner conflicts that interfere with natural development and growth. To achieve this goal, humanistic therapists try to give clients new insights. Indeed, because they share this goal, the psychodynamic and humanistic therapies are often referred to as **insight therapies.** But humanistic therapies differ from psychodynamic therapies in many other ways:

- Humanistic therapists aim to boost people's self-fulfillment by helping them grow in self-awareness and self-acceptance.

- Promoting this growth, not curing illness, is the therapy focus. Thus, those in therapy have become "clients" or just "persons" rather than "patients" (a change many other therapists have adopted).

psychodynamic therapy therapy deriving from the psychoanalytic tradition; views individuals as responding to unconscious forces and childhood experiences, and seeks to enhance self-insight.

insight therapies therapies that aim to improve psychological functioning by increasing a person's awareness of underlying motives and defenses.

- The path to growth is taking immediate responsibility for one's feelings and actions, rather than uncovering hidden causes.

- Conscious thoughts are more important than the unconscious.

- The present and future are more important than the past. Therapy thus focuses on exploring feelings as they occur, rather than on achieving insight into the childhood origins of those feelings.

All these themes are present in the widely used humanistic technique that Carl Rogers (1902–1987) developed and called **client-centered therapy.** In this *nondirective therapy,* the client leads the discussion. The therapist listens, without judging or interpreting, and refrains from directing the client toward certain insights.

Believing that most people possess the resources for growth, Rogers (1961, 1980) encouraged therapists to foster that growth by exhibiting *acceptance, genuineness,* and *empathy.* By being *accepting,* therapists may help clients feel freer and more open to change. By being *genuine,* therapists hope to encourage clients to likewise express their true feelings. By being *empathic,* therapists try to sense and reflect their clients' feelings, helping clients experience a deeper self-understanding and self-acceptance (Hill & Nakayama, 2000). As Rogers (1980, p. 10) explained:

> Hearing has consequences. When I truly hear a person and the meanings that are important to him at that moment, hearing not simply his words, but him, and when I let him know that I have heard his own private personal meanings, many things happen. There is first of all a grateful look. He feels released. He wants to tell me more about his world. He surges forth in a new sense of freedom. He becomes more open to the process of change.
>
> I have often noticed that the more deeply I hear the meanings of the person, the more there is that happens. Almost always, when a person realizes he has been deeply heard, his eyes moisten. I think in some real sense he is weeping for joy. It is as though he were saying, "Thank God, somebody heard me. Someone knows what it's like to be me."

To Rogers, "hearing" was **active listening.** The therapist echoes, restates, and seeks clarification of what the client expresses (verbally or nonverbally). The therapist also acknowledges those expressed feelings. Active listening is now an accepted part of counseling practices in many schools, colleges, and clinics. Counselors listen attentively. They interrupt only to restate and confirm feelings, to accept what was said, or to check their understanding of something. In the following brief excerpt, note how Rogers tried to provide a psychological mirror that would help the client see himself more clearly (Meador & Rogers, 1984, p. 167):

Rogers: Feeling that now, hm? That you're just no good to yourself, no good to anybody. Never will be any good to anybody. Just that you're completely worthless, huh?—Those really are lousy feelings. Just feel that you're no good at all, hm?

Client: Yeah. (Muttering in low, discouraged voice) *That's what this guy I went to town with just the other day told me.*

Rogers: This guy that you went to town with really told you that you were no good? Is that what you're saying? Did I get that right?

Client: M-hm.

Rogers: I guess the meaning of that if I get it right is that here's somebody that meant something to you and what does he think of you? Why, he's told you that he thinks you're no good at all. And that just really knocks the props out from under you. (Client weeps quietly.) *It just brings the tears.* (Silence of 20 seconds)

Client: (Rather defiantly) *I don't care though.*

Rogers: You tell yourself you don't care at all, but somehow I guess some part of you cares because some part of you weeps over it.

Can a therapist be a perfect mirror, without selecting and interpreting what is reflected? Rogers conceded that no one can be *totally* nondirective. Nevertheless, he

client-centered therapy a humanistic therapy, developed by Carl Rogers, in which the therapist uses techniques such as *active listening* within an accepting, genuine, empathic environment to facilitate clients' growth. (Also called *person-centered therapy.*)

active listening empathic listening in which the listener echoes, restates, and clarifies. A feature of Rogers' client-centered therapy.

"We have two ears and one mouth that we may listen the more and talk the less." —Zeno, 335–263 B.C.E., *Diogenes Laertius*

ACTIVE LISTENING Carl Rogers (right) empathized with a client during this group therapy session.

said, the therapist's most important contribution is to accept and understand the client. Given a nonjudgmental, grace-filled environment that provides **unconditional positive regard,** people may accept even their worst traits and feel valued and whole.

How can we improve communication in our own relationships by listening more actively? Three Rogers-inspired hints may help:

1. *Paraphrase.* Check your understanding by summarizing the person's words out loud, in your own words.

2. *Invite clarification.* "What might be an example of that?" may encourage the person to say more.

3. *Reflect feelings.* "It sounds frustrating" might mirror what you're sensing from the person's body language and intensity.

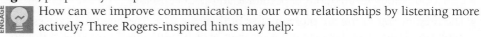 **LaunchPad** To learn more about how therapists may use these approaches, see the **Video: Psychodynamic and Humanistic Therapies.**

BEHAVIOR THERAPIES

LOQ 15-4 How does the basic assumption of behavior therapy differ from the assumptions of psychodynamic and humanistic therapies? What techniques are used in exposure therapies and aversive conditioning?

The insight therapies assume that self-awareness and psychological well-being go hand in hand. Psychodynamic therapists expect people's problems to diminish as they gain insight into their unresolved and unconscious tensions. Humanistic therapists expect problems to diminish as people get in touch with their feelings. **Behavior therapists,** however, doubt the healing power of self-awareness. Rather than delving deeply below the surface looking for inner causes, behavior therapists assume that problem behaviors *are* the problems. (You can become aware of why you are highly anxious during exams and still be anxious.) If phobias, sexual dysfunctions, or other maladaptive symptoms are learned behaviors, why not replace them with new, constructive behaviors?

Classical Conditioning Techniques

One cluster of behavior therapies derives from principles developed in Ivan Pavlov's early twentieth-century conditioning experiments (Chapter 7). As Pavlov and others showed, we learn various behaviors and emotions through classical conditioning. If we're attacked by a dog, we may thereafter have a conditioned fear response when other dogs approach. (Our fear generalizes, and all dogs become conditioned stimuli.)

Could maladaptive symptoms be examples of conditioned responses? If so, might reconditioning be a solution? Learning theorist O. H. Mowrer thought so. He developed a successful conditioning therapy for chronic bed-wetters, using a liquid-sensitive pad connected to an alarm. If the sleeping child wets the bed pad, moisture triggers the alarm, waking the child. After a number of trials, the child associates bladder relaxation with waking. In three out of four cases, the treatment has been effective and the success boosted the child's self-image (Christophersen & Edwards, 1992; Houts et al., 1994).

Can we unlearn fear responses, such as to public speaking or flying, through new conditioning? Many people have. An example: The fear of riding in an elevator is often a learned aversion to being in a confined space. **Counterconditioning,** such as with *exposure therapy,* pairs the trigger stimulus (in this case, the enclosed space of the elevator) with a new response (relaxation) that is incompatible with fear.

ASK YOURSELF

Think of your closest friends. Do they tend to express more empathy than those you don't feel as close to? How have your own active-listening skills changed as you've gotten older?

unconditional positive regard a caring, accepting, nonjudgmental attitude, which Carl Rogers believed would help clients develop self-awareness and self-acceptance.

behavior therapy therapy that applies learning principles to the elimination of unwanted behaviors.

counterconditioning behavior therapy procedures that use classical conditioning to evoke new responses to stimuli that are triggering unwanted behaviors; include *exposure therapies* and *aversive conditioning.*

exposure therapies behavioral techniques, such as *systematic desensitization* and *virtual reality exposure therapy,* that treat anxieties by exposing people (in imaginary or actual situations) to the things they fear and avoid.

🔒 **RETRIEVE IT • • •**   *ANSWERS IN APPENDIX E*

RI-2 What might a psychodynamic therapist say about Mowrer's therapy for bed-wetting? How might a behavior therapist defend it?

EXPOSURE THERAPIES Picture this scene: Behavioral psychologist Mary Cover Jones is working with 3-year-old Peter, who is petrified of rabbits and other furry objects. To rid Peter of his fear, Jones plans to associate the fear-evoking rabbit with the pleasurable, relaxed response associated with eating. As Peter begins his midafternoon snack, she introduces a caged rabbit on the other side of the huge room. Peter, eagerly munching away on his crackers and drinking his milk, hardly notices. On succeeding days, she gradually moves the rabbit closer and closer. Within two months, Peter is holding the rabbit in his lap, even stroking it while he eats. Moreover, his fear of other furry objects subsides as well, having been *countered*, or replaced, by a relaxed state that cannot coexist with fear (Fisher, 1984; Jones, 1924).

Unfortunately for many who might have been helped by Jones' counterconditioning procedures, her story of Peter and the rabbit did not enter psychology's lore when it was reported in 1924. It was more than 30 years before psychiatrist Joseph Wolpe (1958; Wolpe & Plaud, 1997) refined Jones' counterconditioning technique into the **exposure therapies** used today. These therapies, in a variety of ways, try to change people's reactions by repeatedly exposing them to stimuli that trigger unwanted reactions. With repeated exposure to what they normally avoid or escape, people adapt. We all experience this process in everyday life. A person moving to a new apartment may be annoyed by nearby loud traffic noise, but only for a while. The person adapts. So, too, with people who have fear reactions to specific events. Exposed repeatedly to the situation that once petrified them, they can learn to react less anxiously (Barrera et al., 2013; Foa & McLean, 2016; Langkaas et al., 2017).

One exposure therapy widely used to treat phobias is **systematic desensitization.** You cannot simultaneously be anxious and relaxed. Therefore, if you can repeatedly relax when facing anxiety-provoking stimuli, you can gradually eliminate your anxiety. The trick is to proceed gradually. If you fear public speaking, a behavior therapist might first help you construct a hierarchy of anxiety-triggering speaking situations. Yours might range from mildly anxiety-provoking situations (perhaps speaking up in a small group of friends) to panic-provoking situations (having to address a large audience).

Next, the therapist would train you in *progressive relaxation.* You would learn to release tension in one muscle group after another, until you achieve a comfortable, complete relaxation. Then the therapist might ask you to imagine, with your eyes closed, a mildly anxiety-arousing situation: You are having coffee with a group of friends and are trying to decide whether to speak up. If imagining the scene causes you to feel any anxiety, you will signal by raising your finger. Seeing the signal, the therapist will instruct you to switch off the mental image and go back to deep relaxation. This imagined scene is repeatedly paired with relaxation until you feel no trace of anxiety.

The therapist will then move to the next item in your anxiety hierarchy, again using relaxation techniques to desensitize you to each imagined situation. After several sessions, you move to actual situations and practice what you had only *imagined* before, beginning with relatively easy tasks and gradually moving to more anxiety-filled ones. Conquering your anxiety in an actual situation, not just in your imagination, will increase your self-confidence (Foa & Kozak, 1986; Williams, 1987). Eventually, you may even become a confident public speaker. Often people fear not just a situation, such as public speaking, but also being incapacitated by their own fear response. As their fear subsides, so also does their fear of the fear.

Some anxiety-arousing situations (such as fears of flying, heights, particular animals, and public performances) may be too expensive, difficult, or embarrassing to re-create. In such cases, the therapist may recommend **virtual reality exposure therapy,** in which you don a head-mounted display unit that projects a lifelike three-dimensional virtual world tailored to your particular fear. If you fear flying, for example, you could peer out a virtual window of a simulated plane, feel the engine's vibrations, and hear it roar as the plane taxis down the runway and takes off. If you fear social interactions, you could experience simulated stressful situations, such as entering a roomful of people. In controlled studies, people participating in virtual reality exposure therapy have experienced significant relief from real-life fear and social anxiety (Anderson et al., 2017; Parsons & Rizzo, 2008; Turner & Casey, 2014).

systematic desensitization a type of exposure therapy that associates a pleasant relaxed state with gradually increasing anxiety-triggering stimuli. Commonly used to treat phobias.

virtual reality exposure therapy a counterconditioning technique that treats anxiety through creative electronic simulations in which people can safely face their greatest fears, such as airplane flying, spiders, or public speaking.

VIRTUAL REALITY EXPOSURE THERAPY Within the confines of a room, virtual reality technology exposes people to vivid simulations of feared stimuli, such as walking across a rickety bridge high off the ground.

"The only thing we have to fear is fear itself." —U.S. President Franklin D. Roosevelt, First Inaugural Address, 1933

FIGURE 15.1

AVERSION THERAPY FOR ALCOHOL USE DISORDER After repeatedly imbibing an alcoholic drink mixed with a drug that produces severe nausea, some people with a history of alcohol use disorder develop at least a temporary conditioned aversion to alcohol. (Remember: US is unconditioned stimulus, UR is unconditioned response, NS is neutral stimulus, CS is conditioned stimulus, and CR is conditioned response.)

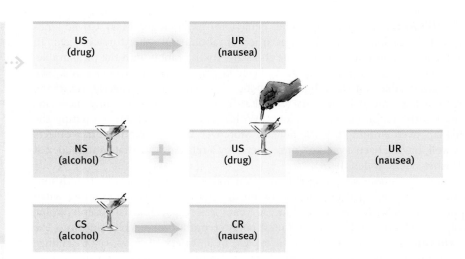

AVERSIVE CONDITIONING An exposure therapy enables a more relaxed, positive response to an upsetting *harmless* stimulus. It helps you accept what you *should* do. **Aversive conditioning** creates a negative (aversive) response to a *harmful* stimulus (such as alcohol). It helps you to learn what you *should not* do. The aversive conditioning procedure is simple: It associates the unwanted behavior with unpleasant feelings. To treat nail biting, the therapist may suggest painting the fingernails with a nasty-tasting nail polish (Baskind, 1997). To treat alcohol use disorder, the therapist may offer the client appealing drinks laced with a drug that produces severe nausea. If that therapy links alcohol with violent nausea, the person's reaction to alcohol may change from positive to negative (**FIGURE 15.1**).

Taste aversion learning has been a successful alternative to killing predators in some animal protection programs (Dingfelder, 2010; Garcia & Gustavson, 1997). After being sickened by eating a tainted sheep, wolves may avoid sheep. Does aversive conditioning also transform humans' reactions to alcohol? In the short run it may. In one classic study, 685 hospital patients with alcohol use disorder completed an aversion therapy program (Wiens & Menustik, 1983). Over the next year, they returned for several booster treatments that paired alcohol with sickness. At the end of that year, 63 percent were not drinking alcohol. But after three years, only 33 percent were alcohol free.

In therapy, as in research, cognition influences conditioning. People know that outside the therapist's office they can drink without fear of nausea. This ability to discriminate between the therapy situation and all others can limit aversive conditioning's effectiveness. Thus, therapists often combine aversive conditioning with other treatments.

Operant Conditioning Techniques

LOQ 15-5 What is the main premise of therapy based on operant conditioning principles, and what are the views of its proponents and critics?

ENGAGE

If you have learned to swim, you learned how to put your head under water without suffocating, how to pull your body through the water, and perhaps even how to dive safely. Operant conditioning shaped your swimming. You were reinforced for safe, effective behaviors. And you were naturally punished, as when you swallowed water, for improper swimming behaviors.

Consequences strongly influence our voluntary behaviors. Knowing this basic principle of operant conditioning, behavior therapists can practice *behavior modification*. They reinforce behaviors they consider desirable, and they fail to reinforce—or sometimes punish—behaviors they consider undesirable.

Using operant conditioning to solve specific behavior problems has raised hopes for some seemingly hopeless cases. Children with intellectual disabilities have been taught to care for themselves. Socially withdrawn children with autism spectrum disorder (ASD) have learned to interact. People with schizophrenia have been helped to behave more rationally in their hospital ward. In such cases, therapists used positive reinforcers to *shape* behavior. In a step-by-step manner, they rewarded closer and closer approximations of the desired behavior.

In extreme cases, treatment must be intensive. One study worked with 19 withdrawn, uncommunicative 3-year-olds with ASD. For two years, 40 hours each week, the children's parents attempted to shape their behavior (Lovaas, 1987). They positively reinforced desired behaviors and ignored or punished aggressive and self-abusive behaviors. The combination worked wonders for some children. By first grade, 9 of the 19 were functioning successfully in school and exhibiting normal intelligence. In a group of 40 comparable children not undergoing this effortful treatment, only one showed similar improvement. Later studies focused on positive reinforcement—the effective aspect of this early intensive behavioral intervention (Reichow, 2012).

Rewards used to modify behavior vary. For some people, the reinforcing power of attention or praise is sufficient. Others require concrete rewards, such as food. In institutional settings, therapists may create a **token economy.** When people display a desired behavior, such as getting out of bed, washing, dressing, eating, talking meaningfully, cleaning their rooms, or playing cooperatively, they receive a token or plastic coin. Later, they can exchange a number of these tokens for rewards, such as candy, TV time, day trips, or better living quarters. Token economies have been used successfully in homes, classrooms, and correctional institutions, and among people with various disabilities (Matson & Boisjoli, 2009).

Behavior modification critics express two concerns.

- *How durable are the behaviors?* Will people become so dependent on extrinsic rewards that the desired behaviors will stop when the reinforcers stop? Behavior modification advocates believe the behaviors will endure if therapists wean people from the tokens by shifting them toward other, real-life rewards, such as social approval. As people become more socially competent, the intrinsic satisfactions of social interaction may sustain the behaviors.

- *Is it right for one human to control another's behavior?* Those who set up token economies deprive people of something they desire and decide which behaviors to reinforce. To critics, this whole process feels too authoritarian. Advocates reply that control already exists: People's destructive behavior patterns are being maintained and perpetuated by natural reinforcers and punishers in their environments. Isn't using positive rewards to reinforce adaptive behavior more humane than institutionalizing or punishing people? Advocates also argue that the right to effective treatment and an improved life justifies temporary deprivation.

> **🔒 RETRIEVE IT • • •**   *ANSWERS IN APPENDIX E*
>
> **RI-3** What are the *insight therapies,* and how do they differ from *behavior therapies?*
>
> **RI-4** Some maladaptive behaviors are learned. What hope does this fact provide?
>
> **RI-5** Exposure therapies and aversive conditioning are applications of _____ conditioning. Token economies are an application of _____ conditioning.

COGNITIVE THERAPIES

LOQ 15-6 What are the goals and techniques of the cognitive therapies and of cognitive-behavioral therapy?

People with specific fears and problem behaviors may respond to behavior therapy. But how might behavior therapists modify the wide assortment of behaviors that accompany depressive disorders? Or treat people with generalized anxiety disorder, where unfocused anxiety doesn't lend itself to a neat list of anxiety-triggering situations? The *cognitive revolution* that has profoundly changed other areas of psychology during the last half-century has influenced therapy as well.

aversive conditioning associates an unpleasant state (such as nausea) with an unwanted behavior (such as drinking alcohol).

token economy an operant conditioning procedure in which people earn a token for exhibiting a desired behavior and can later exchange the tokens for privileges or treats.

 **ENGAGE** 💡 **ASK YOURSELF**

What is your judgment of behavior modification techniques, such as those used in token economies? Do you agree or disagree with this approach?

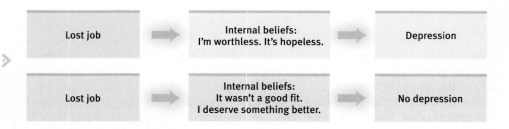

FIGURE 15.2

A COGNITIVE PERSPECTIVE ON PSYCHOLOGICAL DISORDERS The person's emotional reactions are produced not directly by the event, but by the person's thoughts in response to the event.

"Life does not consist mainly, or even largely, of facts and happenings. It consists mainly of the storm of thoughts that are forever blowing through one's mind." —Mark Twain, 1835–1910

The **cognitive therapies** assume that our thinking colors our feelings (**FIGURE 15.2**). Between an event and our response lies the mind. Anxiety, for example, can arise from an "attention bias to threat" (MacLeod & Clarke, 2015). Self-blaming and overgeneralized explanations of bad events feed depression. If depressed, we may interpret a suggestion as criticism, disagreement as dislike, praise as flattery, friendliness as pity. Dwelling on such thoughts sustains negative thinking. Cognitive therapies aim to help people change their mind with new, more constructive ways of perceiving and interpreting events (Kazdin, 2015). Let's look more closely at classic cognitive therapy, which is based on the premise that changing people's thinking can change the way they function.

Beck's Therapy for Depression

In the late 1960s, a woman left a party early. Things had not gone well. She felt disconnected from the other party-goers and assumed no one cared for her. A few days later, she visited therapist Aaron Beck. Rather than go down the traditional path to her childhood, Beck challenged her thinking. After she then listed a dozen people who *did* care for her, Beck realized that challenging people's automatic negative thoughts could be therapeutic. And thus was born his cognitive therapy (Spiegel, 2015).

Depressed people, Beck found, often reported dreams with negative themes of loss, rejection, and abandonment. These thoughts extended into their waking thoughts, and even into therapy, as clients recalled and rehearsed their failings and worst impulses (Kelly, 2000). With cognitive therapy, Beck and his colleagues (1979) sought to reverse clients' negativity about themselves, their situations, and their futures. With this technique, gentle questioning seeks to reveal irrational thinking, and then to persuade people to remove the dark glasses through which they view life (Beck et al., 1979, pp. 145–146):

Client: I agree with the descriptions of me but I guess I don't agree that the way I think makes me depressed.

Beck: How do you understand it?

Client: I get depressed when things go wrong. Like when I fail a test.

Beck: How can failing a test make you depressed?

Client: Well, if I fail I'll never get into law school.

Beck: So failing the test means a lot to you. But if failing a test could drive people into clinical depression, wouldn't you expect everyone who failed the test to have a depression? . . . Did everyone who failed get depressed enough to require treatment?

Client: No, but it depends on how important the test was to the person.

Beck: Right, and who decides the importance?

Client: I do.

Beck: And so, what we have to examine is your way of viewing the test (or the way that you think about the test) and how it affects your chances of getting into law school. Do you agree?

Client: Right.

Beck: Do you agree that the way you interpret the results of the test will affect you? You might feel depressed, you might have trouble sleeping, not feel like eating, and you might even wonder if you should drop out of the course.

Client: I have been thinking that I wasn't going to make it. Yes, I agree.

Beck: Now what did failing mean?

Client: (tearful) That I couldn't get into law school.

Beck: And what does that mean to you?

cognitive therapy therapy that teaches people new, more adaptive ways of thinking; based on the assumption that thoughts intervene between events and our emotional reactions.

Client: That I'm just not smart enough.

Beck: Anything else?

Client: That I can never be happy.

Beck: And how do these thoughts make you feel?

Client: Very unhappy.

Beck: So it is the meaning of failing a test that makes you very unhappy. In fact, believing that you can never be happy is a powerful factor in producing unhappiness. So, you get yourself into a trap—by definition, failure to get into law school equals "I can never be happy."

We often think in words. Therefore, getting people to change what they say to themselves is an effective way to change their thinking. Perhaps you can identify with the anxious students who, before an exam, make matters worse with self-defeating thoughts: "This exam's probably going to be impossible. All these other students seem so relaxed and confident. I wish I were better prepared. I'm so nervous I'll forget everything." Psychologists call this sort of relentless, overgeneralized, self-blaming behavior *catastrophizing.*

To change such negative self-talk, therapists have offered *stress inoculation training:* teaching people to restructure their thinking in stressful situations (Meichenbaum, 1977, 1985). Sometimes it may be enough simply to say more positive things to yourself: "Relax. The exam may be hard, but it will be hard for everyone else, too. I studied harder than most people. Besides, I don't need a perfect score to get a good grade." After learning to "talk back" to negative thoughts, depression-prone children, teens, and college students have shown a greatly reduced rate of future depression (Reivich et al., 2013; Seligman et al., 2009). To a large extent, it *is* the thought that counts. For a sampling of commonly used cognitive therapy techniques, see **TABLE 15.1.**)

PEANUTS

TABLE 15.1

Selected Cognitive Therapy Techniques

Aim of Technique	Technique	Therapists' Directives
Reveal beliefs	Question your interpretations	Explore your beliefs, revealing faulty assumptions such as "I need to be liked by everyone."
	Rank thoughts and emotions	Gain perspective by ranking your thoughts and emotions from mildly to extremely upsetting.
Test beliefs	Examine consequences	Explore difficult situations, assessing possible consequences and challenging faulty reasoning.
	Decatastrophize thinking	Work through the actual worst-case consequences of the situation you face (it is often not as bad as imagined). Then determine how to cope with the real situation you face.
Change beliefs	Take appropriate responsibility	Challenge total self-blame and negative thinking, noting aspects for which you may be truly responsible, as well as aspects that aren't your responsibility.
	Resist extremes	Develop new ways of thinking and feeling to replace maladaptive habits. For example, change from thinking "I am a total failure" to "I got a failing grade on that paper, and I can make these changes to succeed next time."

cognitive-behavioral therapy (CBT)
a popular integrative therapy that combines cognitive therapy (changing self-defeating thinking) with behavior therapy (changing behavior).

ASK YOURSELF

Have you ever struggled to reach a goal at school or work because of your own self-defeating thoughts? How could you challenge those thoughts?

LaunchPad To learn more about how cognitive therapy can be used to help those with anxiety, see the **Video: Cognitive Therapies.**

COGNITIVE-BEHAVIORAL THERAPY FOR EATING DISORDERS AIDED BY JOURNALING Cognitive-behavioral therapists guide people with eating disorders toward new ways of explaining their good and bad food-related experiences (Linardon et al., 2017). By recording positive events and how she has enabled them, this woman may become more mindful of her self-control and more optimistic.

It's not just depressed people who can benefit from positive self-talk. We all talk to ourselves (thinking "I wish I hadn't said that" can protect us from repeating the blunder). The findings of nearly three dozen sport psychology studies show that self-talk interventions can enhance the learning of athletic skills (Hatzigeorgiadis et al., 2011). For example, novice basketball players may be trained to think "focus" and "follow through," swimmers to think "high elbow," and tennis players to think "look at the ball." People anxious about public speaking have grown in confidence if asked to recall a speaking success, and then to "Explain WHY you were able to achieve such a successful performance" (Zunick et al., 2015).

Cognitive-Behavioral Therapy

"The trouble with most therapy," said therapist Albert Ellis (1913–2007), "is that it helps you to feel better. But you don't get better. You have to back it up with action, action, action." **Cognitive-behavioral therapy (CBT)** takes a combined approach to depression and other disorders. This widely practiced *integrative* therapy aims to alter not only the way people *think* but also the way they *act*. Like other cognitive therapies, CBT seeks to make people aware of their irrational negative thinking and to replace it with new ways of thinking. And like other behavior therapies, it trains people to *practice* the more positive approach in everyday settings.

Anxiety, depressive disorders, and bipolar disorder share a common problem: emotion regulation (Aldao & Nolen-Hoeksema, 2010; Szkodny et al., 2014). An effective CBT program for these emotional disorders trains people both to replace their catastrophizing thinking with more realistic appraisals and, as homework, to practice behaviors that are incompatible with their problem (Kazantzis & Dattilio, 2010; Kazantzis et al., 2010; Moses & Barlow, 2006). A person might keep a log of daily situations associated with negative and positive emotions and engage more in activities that lead to feeling good. Those who fear social situations might learn to restrain the negative thoughts surrounding their social anxiety and practice approaching people.

CBT effectively treats people with obsessive-compulsive disorder (Öst et al., 2015). In one classic study, people learned to prevent their compulsive behaviors by relabeling their obsessive thoughts (Schwartz et al., 1996). Feeling the urge to wash their hands again, they would tell themselves, "I'm having a compulsive urge." They would explain to themselves that the hand-washing urge was a result of their brain's abnormal activity, which they had previously viewed in PET scans. Then, instead of giving in, they would spend 15 minutes in an enjoyable, alternative behavior—practicing an instrument, taking a walk, gardening. This helped "unstick" the brain by shifting attention and engaging other brain areas. For two or three months, the weekly therapy sessions continued, with relabeling and refocusing practice at home. By the study's end, most participants' symptoms had diminished, and their PET scans revealed normalized brain activity. Many other studies confirm CBT's effectiveness for treating anxiety, depression, eating disorders, and ADHD (Cristea et al., 2015; Knouse et al., 2017; Linardon et al., 2017; Milrod et al., 2015). Even online or app-guided CBT quizzes and exercises—therapy without a face-to-face therapist—have helped alleviate insomnia, depression, and anxiety (Andersson, 2016; Christensen et al., 2016; Kampmann et al., 2016; Vigerland et al., 2016). By offering flexible, affordable, and effective treatments, online CBT can reach members of disadvantaged groups who may struggle to attend face-to-face therapy sessions (Sheeber et al., 2017).

A newer CBT variation, *dialectical behavior therapy (DBT),* helps change harmful and even suicidal behavior patterns (Linehan et al., 2015; Mehlum et al., 2016; Valentine et al., 2015). *Dialectical* means "opposing," and this therapy attempts to make peace between two opposing forces—acceptance and change. Therapists create an accepting and encouraging environment, helping clients

Lara Jo Regan

feel they have an ally who will offer them constructive feedback and guidance. In individual sessions, clients learn new ways of thinking that help them tolerate distress and regulate their emotions. They also receive training in social skills and in mindfulness meditation, which helps alleviate depression (Gu et al., 2015; Kuyken et al., 2016). Group training sessions offer additional opportunities to practice new skills in a social context, with further practice as homework.

> 🔒 **RETRIEVE IT • • •**   *ANSWERS IN APPENDIX E*
>
> **RI-6** How do the humanistic and cognitive therapies differ?
>
> **RI-7** A critical attribute of the _____ _____ developed by Aaron Beck focuses on the belief that changing people's thinking can change their functioning.
>
> **RI-8** What is cognitive-behavioral therapy, and what sorts of problems does this therapy best address?

GROUP AND FAMILY THERAPIES

LOQ 15-7 What are the aims and benefits of group and family therapies?

Group Therapy

Except for traditional psychoanalysis, most therapies may also occur in small groups. **Group therapy** does not provide the same degree of therapist involvement with each client. However, it offers other benefits:

- *It saves therapists' time and clients' money* and often is no less effective than individual therapy (Burlingame et al., 2016).

- *It offers a social laboratory for exploring social behaviors and developing social skills.* Therapists frequently suggest group therapy for people experiencing frequent conflicts or whose behavior distresses others. The therapist guides people's interactions as they discuss issues and try out new behaviors.

- *It enables people to see that others share their problems.* It can be a relief to discover that others, despite their composure, experience some of the same troublesome feelings and behaviors (Ooi et al., 2016).

- *It provides feedback as clients try out new ways of behaving.* Hearing that you look poised, even though you feel anxious and self-conscious, can be very reassuring.

group therapy therapy conducted with groups rather than individuals, providing benefits from group interaction.

family therapy therapy that treats people in the context of their family system. Views an individual's unwanted behaviors as influenced by, or directed at, other family members.

Family Therapy

One special type of group interaction, **family therapy,** assumes that no person is an island. We live and grow in relation to others, especially our families. We struggle to differentiate ourselves from our families, but we also need to connect with them emotionally. These two opposing tendencies can create stress for both the individual and the family.

Family therapists tend to view families as systems, in which each person's actions trigger reactions from others. A child's rebellion, for example, affects and is affected by other family tensions. Therapists are often successful in helping family members identify their roles within the family's social system, improve communication, and discover new ways of preventing or resolving conflicts (Hazelrigg et al., 1987; Shadish et al., 1993).

FAMILY THERAPY This type of therapy often acts as a preventive mental health strategy and may include marriage therapy, as shown here at a retreat for U.S. military families. The therapist helps family members understand how their ways of relating to one another create problems. The treatment's emphasis is not on changing the individuals, but on changing their relationships and interactions.

Self-Help Groups

More than 100 million Americans have belonged to small religious, interest, or support groups that meet regularly—with 9 in 10 reporting that group members "support each other emotionally" (Gallup, 1994). One analysis of more than 14,000 self-help groups reported that most focus on stigmatized or hard-to-discuss illnesses (Davison et al., 2000). AIDS patients were 250 times more likely than hypertension patients to be in support groups. People with anorexia and alcohol use disorder often join groups; those with migraines and ulcers usually do not.

The grandparent of support groups, Alcoholics Anonymous (AA), reports having 2.1 million members in 118,000 groups worldwide. Its famous 12-step program, emulated by many other self-help groups, asks members to admit their powerlessness, to seek help from a higher power and from one another, and (the twelfth step) to take the message to others in need of it (Galanter, 2016). Studies of 12-step programs such as AA have found that they help reduce alcohol use disorder at rates comparable to other treatment interventions (Ferri et al., 2006; Moos & Moos, 2005). An eight-year, $27 million investigation found that AA participants reduced their drinking sharply, as did those assigned to CBT or an alternative therapy (Project Match, 1997). Another study of 2300 veterans who sought treatment for alcohol use disorder found that a high level of AA involvement was followed by diminished alcohol problems (McKellar et al., 2003). The more meetings AA members attend, the greater their alcohol abstinence (Moos & Moos, 2006). Those whose personal stories include a "redemptive narrative"—who see something good as having come from their struggles—more often sustain sobriety (Dunlop & Tracy, 2013).

In an individualist age, with more and more people living alone or feeling isolated, the popularity of support groups—for the addicted, the bereaved, the divorced, or simply those seeking fellowship and growth—may reflect a longing for community and connectedness.

With more than 2 million members worldwide, AA is said to be "the largest organization on Earth that nobody wanted to join" (Finlay, 2000).

* * *

For a synopsis of these modern psychotherapies, see **TABLE 15.2**.

RETAIN 🔒 ≋ **LaunchPad** To study and remember the aims and techniques of different psychotherapies, review **Concept Practice: Types of Therapies and Therapists**. Assess your ability to recognize excerpts from each type with **Topic Tutorial: PsychSim6, Mystery Therapist**.

RETAIN 🔒 **TABLE 15.2**

Comparing Modern Psychotherapies

Therapy	Presumed Problem	Therapy Aim	Therapy Technique
Psychodynamic	Unconscious conflicts from childhood experiences	Reduce anxiety through self-insight.	Interpret clients' memories and feelings.
Client-centered	Barriers to self-understanding and self-acceptance	Enable growth via unconditional positive regard, acceptance, genuineness, and empathy.	Listen actively and reflect clients' feelings.
Behavior	Dysfunctional behaviors	Learn adaptive behaviors; extinguish problem ones.	Use classical conditioning (via exposure or aversion therapy) or operant conditioning (as in token economies).
Cognitive	Negative, self-defeating thinking	Promote healthier thinking and self-talk.	Train people to dispute negative thoughts and attributions.
Cognitive-behavioral	Self-harmful thoughts and behaviors	Promote healthier thinking and adaptive behaviors.	Train people to counter self-harmful thoughts and to act out their new ways of thinking.
Group and family	Stressful relationships	Heal relationships.	Develop an understanding of family and other social systems, explore roles, and improve communication.

🔒 REVIEW INTRODUCTION TO THERAPY AND THE PSYCHOLOGICAL THERAPIES

⟶ Learning Objectives

TEST YOURSELF Answer these repeated Learning Objective Questions on your own (before checking the answers in Appendix D) to improve your retention of the concepts (McDaniel et al., 2009, 2015).

15-1 How do *psychotherapy* and the *biomedical therapies* differ?

15-2 What are the goals and techniques of psychoanalysis, and how have they been adapted in psychodynamic therapy?

15-3 What are the basic themes of humanistic therapy? What are the specific goals and techniques of Rogers' client-centered approach?

15-4 How does the basic assumption of behavior therapy differ from the assumptions of psychodynamic and humanistic therapies? What techniques are used in exposure therapies and aversive conditioning?

15-5 What is the main premise of therapy based on operant conditioning principles, and what are the views of its proponents and critics?

15-6 What are the goals and techniques of the cognitive therapies and of cognitive-behavioral therapy?

15-7 What are the aims and benefits of group and family therapies?

⟶ Terms and Concepts to Remember

TEST YOURSELF Write down the definition yourself, then check your answer on the referenced page.

psychotherapy, **p. 537**

biomedical therapy, **p. 537**

eclectic approach, **p. 537**

psychoanalysis, **p. 537**

resistance, **p. 537**

interpretation, **p. 537**

transference, **p. 537**

psychodynamic therapy, **p. 538**

insight therapies, **p. 538**

client-centered therapy, **p. 539**

active listening, **p. 539**

unconditional positive regard, **p. 540**

behavior therapy, **p. 540**

counterconditioning, **p. 540**

exposure therapies, **p. 540**

systematic desensitization, **p. 541**

virtual reality exposure therapy, **p. 541**

aversive conditioning, **p. 543**

token economy, **p. 543**

cognitive therapy, **p. 544**

cognitive-behavioral therapy (CBT), **p. 546**

group therapy, **p. 547**

family therapy, **p. 547**

⟶ Experience the Testing Effect

TEST YOURSELF Answer the following questions on your own first, then check your answers in Appendix E.

1. A therapist who helps patients search for the unconscious roots of their problem and offers interpretations of their behaviors, feelings, and dreams is drawing from
   a. psychoanalysis.
   b. humanistic therapies.
   c. client-centered therapy.
   d. behavior therapy.

2. _____ therapies are designed to help individuals discover the thoughts and feelings that guide their motivation and behavior.

3. Compared with psychoanalysts, humanistic therapists are more likely to emphasize
   a. hidden or repressed feelings.
   b. childhood experiences.
   c. psychological disorders.
   d. self-fulfillment and growth.

4. A therapist who restates and clarifies the client's statements is practicing the technique of _____.

5. The goal of behavior therapy is to
   a. identify and treat the underlying causes of the problem.
   b. improve learning and insight.
   c. eliminate the unwanted behavior.
   d. improve communication and social sensitivity.

6. Behavior therapies often use _____ techniques, such as systematic desensitization and aversive conditioning to encourage clients to produce new responses to old stimuli.

7. The technique of _____ _____ teaches people to relax in the presence of progressively more anxiety-provoking stimuli.

8. After a near-fatal car accident, Rico developed such an intense fear of driving on the freeway that he takes lengthy alternative routes to work each day. Which psychological therapy might best help Rico overcome his phobia, and why?

9. At a treatment center, people who display a desired behavior receive coins that they can later exchange for other rewards. This is an example of a(n) _____.

10. Cognitive therapy has been especially effective in treating
    a. nail biting.
    b. phobias.
    c. alcohol use disorder.
    d. depression.

11. _____-_____ therapy helps people to change their self-defeating ways of thinking and to act out those changes in their daily behavior.

12. In family therapy, the therapist assumes that
    a. only one family member needs to change.
    b. each person's actions trigger reactions from other family members.
    c. dysfunctional family behaviors are based largely on genetic factors.
    d. therapy is most effective when clients are treated apart from the family unit.

Continue testing yourself with 📖 **LearningCurve** or ≈ **Achieve Read & Practice** to learn and remember most effectively.

ED WAS IN THERAPY FOR BELIEVING HE WAS A THERAPIST.

Jon Carter/Cartoonstock

⊙⟩⟩ Evaluating Psychotherapies

Many Americans have great confidence in psychotherapy's effectiveness. "Seek counseling" or "Ask your mate to find a therapist," advice columnists often urge. Before 1950, psychiatrists were the primary providers of mental health care. Today's providers include clinical and counseling psychologists; clinical social workers; pastoral, marital, abuse, and school counselors; and psychiatric nurses. With such an enormous outlay of time as well as money and effort, it is important to ask: Are the millions of people worldwide justified in placing their hopes in psychotherapy?

IS PSYCHOTHERAPY EFFECTIVE?

LOQ 15-8   Does psychotherapy work? How can we know?

The question, though simply put, is not simply answered. If an infection quickly clears, we may assume an antibiotic has been effective. But how can we assess psychotherapy's effectiveness? By how we feel about our progress? By how our therapist feels about it? By how our friends and family feel about it? By how our behavior has changed?

Clients' Perceptions

If clients' testimonials were the only measuring stick, we could strongly affirm psychotherapy's effectiveness. Consider the 2900 *Consumer Reports* readers who related their experiences with mental health professionals (1995; Kotkin et al., 1996; Seligman, 1995). How many were at least "fairly well satisfied"? Almost 90 percent (as was Kay Redfield Jamison, as we saw at this chapter's beginning). Among those who recalled feeling *fair* or *very poor* when beginning therapy, 9 in 10 now were feeling *very good, good,* or at least *so-so*. We have their word for it—and who should know better?

We should not dismiss these testimonials. But critics note reasons for skepticism:

- **People often enter therapy in crisis.** When, with the normal ebb and flow of events, the crisis passes, people may attribute their improvement to the therapy. Depressed people often get better no matter what they do.

- **Clients believe that treatment will be effective.** The *placebo effect* is the healing power of positive expectations.

- *Clients generally speak kindly of their therapists.* Even if the problems remain, clients "work hard to find something positive to say. The therapist had been very understanding, the client had gained a new perspective, he learned to communicate better, his mind was eased, anything at all so as not to have to say treatment was a failure" (Zilbergeld, 1983, p. 117).

- *Clients want to believe the therapy was worth the effort.* To admit investing time and money in something ineffective is like admitting to repeatedly hiring a mechanic who never fixes your car.

Clinicians' Perceptions

If clinicians' perceptions were proof of therapy's effectiveness, we would have even more reason to celebrate. Case studies of successful treatment abound. The problem is that clients justify entering psychotherapy by emphasizing their unhappiness, and justify leaving by emphasizing their well-being. Therapists treasure compliments from clients as they say good-bye or later express their gratitude. But they hear little from clients who experience only temporary relief and seek out new therapists for their recurring problems. Thus, therapists are most aware of the failures of *other* therapists. The same person, with the same recurring anxieties, depression, or marital difficulty, may be a "success" story in several therapists' files. Moreover, therapists, like the rest of us, are vulnerable to cognitive errors, such as *confirmation bias* and *illusory correlation* (Lilienfeld et al., 2015).

Outcome Research

How, then, can we objectively measure the effectiveness of psychotherapy? What *outcomes* can we expect—what types of people and problems are helped, and by what type of psychotherapy?

In search of answers, psychologists have turned to the well-traveled path of controlled research. Similar research in the 1800s transformed the field of medicine when skeptical physicians began to realize that many patients were dying despite receiving fashionable treatments (bleeding, purging), and many others were getting better on their own. Sorting fact from superstition required observing patients and recording outcomes with and without a particular treatment. Typhoid fever patients, for example, often improved after being bled, convincing most physicians that the treatment worked. Then came the shock. A control group was given mere bed rest, and after five weeks of fever, 70 percent improved, showing that the bleeding was worthless (Thomas, 1992).

A similar shock—and a spirited debate—followed in the twentieth century, when British psychologist Hans Eysenck (1952) summarized 24 studies of psychotherapy outcomes. He found that two-thirds of those receiving psychotherapy for disorders not involving hallucinations or delusions improved markedly. To this day, no one disputes that optimistic estimate. But there was a catch: Eysenck also reported similar improvement among people who were *untreated,* such as those on treatment waiting lists. With or without psychotherapy, he said, roughly two-thirds improved noticeably. Time was a great healer.

Later research revealed shortcomings in Eysenck's analyses. His sample was small—only 24 outcome studies in 1952, compared with hundreds available today. The best of these are *randomized clinical trials*, in which researchers randomly assign people on a waiting list to therapy or to no therapy. Later, they evaluate everyone and compare outcomes, with tests and assessments by others who don't know whether therapy was given.

A glimpse of psychotherapy's overall effectiveness can then be provided by means of a **meta-analysis**, a statistical procedure that combines the conclusions of a large number of different studies. Simply said, a meta-analysis summarizes the bottom-line results of lots of studies. Therapists welcomed the first meta-analysis of some 475 psychotherapy outcome studies (Smith et al., 1980). It showed that the average therapy client ends up better off than 80 percent of the untreated individuals on waiting lists (**FIGURE 15.3**). The claim is modest—by definition, about 50 percent of untreated people also are better off than the average untreated person. Nevertheless, Mary Lee Smith and her colleagues exulted that "psychotherapy benefits people of all ages as reliably as schooling educates them, medicine cures them, or business turns a profit" (p. 183).

LaunchPad To consider the impact of clients' belief in the treatment, see **Video: Therapeutic Effectiveness—The Placebo Effect.**

meta-analysis a statistical procedure for analyzing the results of multiple studies to reach an overall conclusion.

FIGURE 15.3

TREATMENT VERSUS NO TREATMENT These two normal distribution curves based on data from 475 studies show the improvement of untreated people and psychotherapy clients. The outcome for the average therapy client surpassed the outcome for 80 percent of the untreated people. (Data from Smith et al., 1980.)

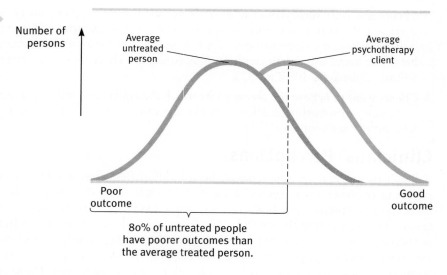

Number of persons

Average untreated person

Average psychotherapy client

Poor outcome

Good outcome

80% of untreated people have poorer outcomes than the average treated person.

TRAUMA These women were mourning the tragic loss of lives and homes in the 2010 earthquake in China. Those who suffer through such trauma may benefit from counseling, though many people recover on their own or with the help of supportive relationships with family and friends. "Life itself still remains a very effective therapist," noted psychodynamic therapist Karen Horney (*Our Inner Conflicts*, 1945).

Feng Li/Getty Images

Dozens of subsequent summaries have now examined psychotherapy's effectiveness. Their verdict echoes earlier results: *Those not undergoing therapy often improve, but those undergoing therapy are more likely to improve—and to improve more quickly and with less risk of relapse* (Kolovos et al., 2017; Weisz et al., 2017). (One qualification: Compared with studies that find no therapy benefit, those that do find a positive therapy effect are more likely to get published [Driessen et al., 2015].) Even so, many people exhibit a more stable, patient, and outgoing personality after therapy (Roberts et al., 2017). And some people experience sudden symptom reductions between their treatment sessions for depression or anxiety. Those "sudden gains" bode well for long-term improvement (Aderka et al., 2012; Wucherpfennig et al., 2017).

Psychotherapy also can be cost-effective. Studies show that when people seek psychological treatment, their search for other medical treatment drops—by 16 percent in one digest of 91 studies (Chiles et al., 1999). Psychological disorders and substance abuse exert a staggering cost on society, including crime, accidents, lost work, and treatment. By one estimate, the U.S. opioid epidemic cost the nation $95 billion in 2016 (Center for Value in Health Care, 2017). Given these enormous costs, psychotherapy is a good investment, much like money spent on prenatal and well-baby care (Chisholm et al., 2016; Ising et al., 2015). Both *reduce* long-term costs. Boosting employees' psychological well-being can lower medical costs, improve work efficiency, and diminish absenteeism.

But note that the claim—that psychotherapy, *on average,* is somewhat effective—refers to no one therapy in particular. It is like reassuring lung-cancer patients that "on average," medical treatment of health problems is effective. What people want to know is whether a *particular* treatment is effective for their specific problem.

🔒 **RETRIEVE IT • • •**   ANSWERS IN APPENDIX E

RI-1 How might the *placebo effect* bias clients' and clinicians' appraisals of the effectiveness of psychotherapies?

WHICH PSYCHOTHERAPIES WORK BEST?

LOQ 15-9 Are some psychotherapies more effective than others for specific disorders?

The early statistical summaries and surveys did not find that any one type of psychotherapy is generally better than others (Smith & Glass, 1977; Smith et al., 1980). Later studies have similarly found that clients can benefit from psychotherapy regardless of their clinicians' experience, training, supervision, and licensing (Cuijpers, 2017; Kivlighan et al., 2015; Wampold et al., 2017). A *Consumer Reports* survey confirmed this result (Seligman, 1995). Were clients treated by a psychiatrist, psychologist, or social worker? Were they seen in a group or individual context? Did the therapist have extensive or relatively limited training and experience? It didn't matter. Clients seemed equally satisfied.

So, was the dodo bird in *Alice in Wonderland* right: "Everyone has won and all must have prizes"? Not quite. One general finding emerges from the studies: The more specific the problem, the greater the hope that psychotherapy might solve it (Singer, 1981; Westen & Morrison, 2001). Those who experience phobias or panic, who are unassertive, or who are frustrated by sexual performance problems can hope for improvement. Those with less-focused problems, such as depression and anxiety, usually benefit in the short term but often relapse later. There often is also an overlapping or *comorbidity* of disorders.

Nevertheless, some forms of therapy do get prizes for effectively treating *particular* problems:

- *Cognitive and cognitive-behavioral therapies*—anxiety, posttraumatic stress disorder, insomnia, and depression (Qaseem et al., 2016; Scaini et al., 2016; Tolin, 2010).

- *Behavioral conditioning therapies*—specific behavior problems, such as bed-wetting, phobias, compulsions, marital problems, and sexual dysfunctions (Baker et al., 2008; Hunsley & DiGiulio, 2002; Shadish & Baldwin, 2005).

- *Psychodynamic therapy*—depression and anxiety (Driessen et al., 2010; Leichsenring & Rabung, 2008; Shedler, 2010b). Indeed, some analyses suggest that psychodynamic therapy is as effective as cognitive-behavioral therapy in reducing depression (Driessen et al., 2017; Steinert et al., 2017).

- *Nondirective (client-centered) counseling*—mild to moderate depression (Cuijpers et al., 2012).

The evaluation question—which therapies get prizes and which do not?—lies at the heart of what some call psychology's civil war. To what extent should science guide both clinical practice and the willingness of health care providers and insurers to pay for psychotherapy? On one side are research psychologists using scientific methods to extend the list of well-defined and validated therapies for various disorders. They decry clinicians who "give more weight to their personal experience than to science" (Baker et al., 2008). On the other side are nonscientist therapists who view their practice as more art than science: People are too complex and psychotherapy is too intuitive to describe in a manual or test in an experiment. Between these two factions stand the science-oriented clinicians calling for **evidence-based practice,** which has been endorsed by the American Psychological Association (APA) and others (2006; Lilienfeld et al., 2013). Therapists using this approach integrate the best available research with clinical expertise and with patient preferences and characteristics (**FIGURE 15.4**). After rigorous evaluation, clinicians apply therapies suited to their own skills and their patients' unique situations. Increasingly, insurer and government support for mental health services requires evidence-based practice.

"Different sores have different salves."
—English proverb

FIGURE 15.4
EVIDENCE-BASED CLINICAL DECISION MAKING The ideal clinical decision making can be visualized as a three-legged stool, upheld by research evidence, clinical expertise, and knowledge of the client.

Clinical decision making

Patient's values, characteristics, preferences, circumstances

Clinical expertise

Best available research evidence

🔒 RETRIEVE IT • • •   *ANSWERS IN APPENDIX E*

RI-2 Therapy is most likely to be helpful for those with problems that _____ (are/are not) well-defined.

RI-3 What is evidence-based clinical decision making?

EVALUATING ALTERNATIVE THERAPIES

LOQ 15-10 How do alternative therapies fare under scientific scrutiny?

The tendency of many abnormal states of mind to return to normal, combined with the placebo effect (the healing power of mere belief in a treatment), creates fertile soil for pseudotherapies. Bolstered by anecdotes, boosted by the media, and broadcast on the internet, alternative therapies—newer, nontraditional therapies, which often claim healing powers for various ailments—can spread like wildfire. In one national survey, 57 percent of those with a history of anxiety attacks and 54 percent of those with a history of depression had used alternative treatments, such as herbal medicine and spiritual healing (Kessler et al., 2001).

Proponents of alternative therapies often feel that their personal testimonials are evidence enough. But how well do these therapies stand up to scientific scrutiny? There

evidence-based practice clinical decision making that integrates the best available research with clinical expertise and patient characteristics and preferences.

is little evidence for or against most of them. Some, however, have been the subject of controlled research. No prizes—and no scientific support—go to certain alternative therapies (Arkowitz & Lilienfeld, 2006; Lilienfeld et al., 2015). We would all be wise to avoid *energy therapies* that propose to manipulate the client's invisible "energy fields"; *recovered-memory therapies* that aim to unearth "repressed memories" of early child abuse; and *rebirthing therapies* that reenact the supposed trauma of a client's birth.

As with some medical treatments, some psychological treatments are not only ineffective but also harmful (Barlow, 2010; Castonguay et al., 2010; Dimidjian & Hollon, 2010). The National Science and Technology Council has cited the Scared Straight program (seeking to deter children and youth from crime by having them visit with adult inmates) as an example of one such well-intentioned but ineffective program. The American Psychiatric Association and British Psychological Society have warned against "conversion therapy" for those with same-sex attractions. Conversion therapies, including "reparative therapy," aim to "repair" "something that is not a mental illness and therefore does not require therapy," declared APA president Barry Anton (2015). "There is insufficient scientific evidence that they work, and they have the potential to harm the client."

Let's look more closely at two other alternative therapies. As we do, remember that sifting sense from nonsense requires the scientific attitude: being skeptical but not cynical, open to surprises but not gullible.

Eye Movement Desensitization and Reprocessing (EMDR)

EMDR (eye movement desensitization and reprocessing) is a therapy adored by thousands and dismissed by thousands more as a sham. Psychologist Francine Shapiro (1989, 2007, 2012) developed EMDR while walking in a park and observing that anxious thoughts vanished as her eyes spontaneously darted about. Back in the clinic, she had people imagine traumatic scenes while she triggered eye movements by waving her finger in front of their eyes, supposedly enabling them to unlock and reprocess previously frozen memories. Thousands of mental health professionals from more than 75 countries have since undergone training (EMDR, 2011).

Does EMDR work? Shapiro (1999, 2002) believes it does, and she cites four studies in which it worked for 84 to 100 percent of single-trauma victims. Other studies have confirmed its benefits with trauma survivors and people with major depressive disorder (Chen et al., 2015; Littel et al., 2017; Wood et al., 2018). Why, wonder skeptics, would rapidly moving one's eyes while recalling traumas be therapeutic? Some argue that the eye movements relax or distract patients, thus allowing memory-associated emotions to extinguish (Gunter & Bodner, 2008). (Part of therapeutic change is calling up old memories and associating them with new emotions [Lane et al., 2015].) Others believe the eye movements themselves are *not* the therapeutic ingredient (nor is watching high-speed Ping-Pong therapeutic). Trials in which people imagined traumatic scenes and tapped a finger, or just stared straight ahead while the therapist's finger wagged, have also produced therapeutic results (Devilly, 2003).

Skeptics acknowledge that EMDR does work better than doing nothing (Lilienfeld & Arkowitz, 2007). But they suspect that what is therapeutic is the combination of exposure therapy—repeatedly calling up traumatic memories and reconsolidating them in a safe and reassuring context—and perhaps some placebo effect.

Light Exposure Therapy

Have you ever found yourself oversleeping, gaining weight, and feeling lethargic, perhaps during the dark mornings and overcast days of winter? Slowing down and conserving energy during the cold, barren winters likely gave our distant ancestors a survival advantage. To counteract lethargy, National Institute of Mental Health researchers in the early 1980s had an idea: Give people a timed daily dose of intense light. Sure enough, people reported feeling better.

Was light exposure a bright idea, or another dim-witted example of the placebo effect? Research illuminates the issue. One study exposed some people with a seasonal pattern in

"Studies indicate that EMDR is just as effective with fixed eyes. If that conclusion is right, what's useful in the therapy (chiefly behavioral desensitization) is not new, and what's new is superfluous." —Harvard Mental Health Letter, 2002

SEASONAL FUND-RAISING FOR THE YOUNG ENTREPRENEUR

GOT WINTER BLUES? LIGHT Therapy 5¢

© Katheryn LeMieux, distributed by King Features Syndicate

their depression symptoms to 90 minutes of bright light and others to a sham placebo treatment—a hissing "negative ion generator" about which the staff expressed similar enthusiasm (but which was actually just producing white noise). After four weeks, 61 percent of those exposed to morning light had greatly improved, as had 50 percent of those exposed to evening light and 32 percent of those exposed to the placebo (Eastman et al., 1998).

Some studies have cast a shadow on light therapy. Nevertheless, others have found that 30 minutes of morning exposure of up to 10,000-lux white fluorescent light produces relief for most people with major depressive disorder and bipolar disorder. Moreover, it does so as effectively as taking antidepressant drugs or undergoing cognitive-behavioral therapy (Lam et al., 2006, 2016; Rohan et al., 2007, 2015; Sit et al., 2018). Brain scans help explain the benefit: Light therapy sparks activity in a brain region that influences the body's arousal and hormone levels (Ishida et al., 2005).

Christine Brune

LIGHT THERAPY To counteract winter depression, some people spend time each morning exposed to intense light that mimics natural outdoor light. Light boxes are available from health supply and lighting stores.

🔒 **RETRIEVE IT • • •**   *ANSWERS IN APPENDIX E*

RI-4 What does the evidence suggest about the effectiveness of EMDR and light therapy?

HOW DO PSYCHOTHERAPIES HELP PEOPLE?

LOQ 15-11 What three elements are shared by all forms of psychotherapy?

Why have studies found little correlation between therapists' training and experience and clients' outcomes? The answer seems to be that all psychotherapies offer three basic benefits (Frank, 1982; Wampold, 2007).

- *Hope for demoralized people* People seeking therapy typically feel anxious, depressed, self-disapproving, and incapable of turning things around. What any psychotherapy offers is the expectation that, with commitment from the therapy seeker, things can and will get better. This belief, apart from any therapy technique, may improve morale, create feelings of self-efficacy, and diminish symptoms (Corrigan, 2014; Meyerhoff & Rohan, 2016).

- *A new perspective* Every psychotherapy offers people a plausible explanation of their symptoms. Armed with a believable fresh perspective, they may approach life with a new attitude, open to making changes in their behaviors and their views of themselves.

- *An empathic, trusting, caring relationship* To say that psychotherapy outcome is unrelated to training and experience is not to say that all *therapists* are equally effective. No matter what technique they use, effective therapists are empathic. They seek to understand the client's experience. They communicate care and concern, and they earn trust through respectful listening, reassurance, and guidance. These qualities were clear in recorded therapy sessions from 36 recognized master therapists (Goldfried et al., 1998). Some took a cognitive-behavioral approach. Others used psychodynamic principles. Although the master therapists used different approaches, they showed some striking behavioral *similarities*. At key moments, the empathic therapists of both persuasions would help clients evaluate themselves, link one aspect of their life with another, and gain insight into their interactions with others. The emotional bond between therapist and client—the **therapeutic alliance**—helps explain why empathic, caring therapists are especially effective (Klein et al., 2003; Wampold, 2001). A therapeutic alliance may even save lives. In one analysis of a dozen studies, a strong therapeutic alliance predicted less frequent suicidal thoughts, self-harming behaviors, and suicide attempts (Dunster-Page et al., 2017).

therapeutic alliance a bond of trust and mutual understanding between a therapist and client, who work together constructively to overcome the client's problem.

"The thing is, you have to really want to change."

ENGAGE (ASK YOURSELF)

Based on what you've read, would you seek therapy if you were experiencing a problem? Why or why not? If you've already undergone therapy, how does what you've learned alter your feelings about the experience?

These three common elements—hope, a fresh perspective, and an empathic, caring relationship—help us understand why *paraprofessionals* (briefly trained caregivers) can assist many troubled people so effectively (Bryan & Arkowitz, 2015; Christensen & Jacobson, 1994). They also are part of what the growing numbers of self-help and support groups offer their members. And they are part of what traditional healers have offered (Jackson, 1992). Healers everywhere—special people to whom others disclose their suffering, whether psychiatrists or shamans—have listened in order to understand and to empathize, reassure, advise, console, interpret, or explain (Torrey, 1986). Such qualities may explain why people who feel supported by close relationships—who enjoy the fellowship and friendship of caring people—have been less likely to seek therapy (Frank, 1982; O'Connor & Brown, 1984).

* * *

To recap, people who seek help usually improve. So do many of those who do not undergo psychotherapy, and that is a tribute to our human resourcefulness and our capacity to care for one another. Nevertheless, though the therapist's orientation and experience appear not to matter much, people who receive some psychotherapy usually improve more than those who do not. People with clear-cut, specific problems tend to improve the most.

🔒 **RETRIEVE IT • • •**   *ANSWERS IN APPENDIX E*

RI-5 Those who undergo psychotherapy are _____ (more/less) likely to show improvement than those who do not undergo psychotherapy.

CULTURE AND VALUES IN PSYCHOTHERAPY

LOQ 15-12 How do culture and values influence the therapist-client relationship?

All psychotherapies offer hope. Nearly all psychotherapists attempt to enhance their clients' sensitivity, openness, personal responsibility, and sense of purpose (Jensen & Bergin, 1988). But in matters of culture and values, psychotherapists also differ from one another and may differ from their clients (Delaney et al., 2007; Kelly, 1990).

These differences can create a mismatch when a therapist from one culture interacts with a client from another. In North America, Europe, and Australia, for example, most psychotherapists reflect their culture's *individualism,* which often gives priority to personal desires and identity. Clients with a *collectivist* perspective, as with many from Asian cultures, may assume people will be more mindful of social and family responsibilities, harmony, and group goals. These clients may have trouble relating to therapies that require them to think only of their own well-being (Markus & Kitayama, 1991).

Cultural differences help explain some groups' reluctance to use mental health services. People living in "cultures of honor" prize being strong and tough. They may feel that seeking mental health care is an admission of weakness rather than an opportunity for growth (Brown et al., 2014). And some minority groups tend to be both reluctant to seek therapy and quick to leave it (Chen et al., 2009; Sue et al., 2009). In one experiment, Asian-American clients matched with counselors who shared their cultural values (rather than mismatched with those who did not) perceived more counselor empathy and felt a stronger alliance with the counselor (Kim et al., 2005).

Client-therapist mismatches may also stem from religious values. Highly religious people may prefer and benefit from religiously similar therapists and may have trouble forming an emotional bond with one who does not share their values (Masters, 2010; Pearce et al., 2015).

ENGAGE
FINDING A MENTAL HEALTH PROFESSIONAL

LOQ 15-13 What should a person look for when selecting a therapist?

Life for everyone is marked by a mix of serenity and stress, blessing and bereavement, good moods and bad. So, when should we seek a mental health professional's help?

The APA offers these common trouble signals:

- Feelings of hopelessness
- Deep and lasting depression
- Self-destructive behavior, such as substance abuse
- Disruptive fears
- Sudden mood shifts
- Thoughts of suicide
- Compulsive rituals, such as hand washing
- Sexual difficulties
- Hearing voices or seeing things that others don't experience

In looking for a therapist, you may want to have a preliminary consultation with two or three. College health centers are generally good starting points, and may offer some free services. You can describe your problem and learn each therapist's treatment approach. You can ask questions about the therapist's values, credentials (**TABLE 15.3**), and fees. And you can assess your own feelings about each of them. The emotional bond between therapist and client is perhaps the most important factor in effective therapy.

The APA recognizes the importance of a strong therapeutic alliance and it welcomes diverse therapists who can relate well to diverse clients. It accredits programs that provide training in cultural sensitivity (for example, differing values, communication styles, and language) and that recruit underrepresented cultural groups.

TABLE 15.3

Therapists and Their Training

Type	Therapy Description
Clinical psychologists	Most are psychologists with a Ph.D. (includes research training) or Psy.D. (focuses on therapy) supplemented by a supervised internship and, often, post-doctoral training. About half work in agencies and institutions, half in private practice.
Psychiatrists	Psychiatrists are physicians who specialize in the treatment of psychological disorders. Not all psychiatrists have had extensive training in psychotherapy, but as M.D.s or D.O.s they can prescribe medications. Thus, they tend to see those with the most serious problems. Many have their own private practice.
Clinical or psychiatric social workers	A two-year master of social work graduate program plus postgraduate supervision prepares some social workers to offer psychotherapy, mostly to people with everyday personal and family problems. About half have earned the National Association of Social Workers' designation of clinical social worker.
Counselors	Marriage and family counselors specialize in problems arising from family relations. Clergy provide counseling to countless people. Abuse counselors work with substance abusers and with spouse and child abusers and their victims. Mental health and other counselors may be required to have a two-year master's degree.

🔒 REVIEW EVALUATING PSYCHOTHERAPIES

⟩ Learning Objectives

TEST YOURSELF Answer these repeated Learning Objective Questions on your own (before checking the answers in Appendix D) to improve your retention of the concepts (McDaniel et al., 2009, 2015).

15-8 Does psychotherapy work? How can we know?

15-9 Are some psychotherapies more effective than others for specific disorders?

15-10 How do alternative therapies fare under scientific scrutiny?

15-11 What three elements are shared by all forms of psychotherapy?

15-12 How do culture and values influence the therapist-client relationship?

15-13 What should a person look for when selecting a therapist?

⤳ Terms and Concepts to Remember

TEST YOURSELF Write down the definition yourself, then check your answer on the referenced page.

meta-analysis, **p. 551**   evidence-based practice, **p. 553**   therapeutic alliance, **p. 555**

⤳ Experience the Testing Effect

TEST YOURSELF Answer the following questions on your own first, then check your answers in Appendix E.

1. The most enthusiastic or optimistic view of the effectiveness of psychotherapy comes from
   a. outcome research.
   b. randomized clinical trials.
   c. reports of clinicians and clients.
   d. a government study of treatment for depression.

2. Studies show that _____ therapy is the most effective treatment for most psychological disorders.
   a. behavior
   b. humanistic
   c. psychodynamic
   d. no one type of

3. What are the three components of evidence-based practice?

4. How does the placebo effect bias patients' attitudes about the effectiveness of various therapies?

Continue testing yourself with 📘 **LearningCurve** or 📘 **Achieve Read & Practice** to learn and remember most effectively.

⤳ The Biomedical Therapies and Preventing Psychological Disorders

Psychotherapy is one way to treat psychological disorders. The other is *biomedical therapy.* Biomedical treatments can change the brain's chemistry with drugs; affect its circuitry with electrical stimulation, magnetic impulses, or psychosurgery; or influence its responses with lifestyle changes.

Are you surprised to find *lifestyle changes* in this list? We find it convenient to talk of separate psychological and biological influences, but everything psychological is also biological. Thus, our lifestyle—our exercise, nutrition, relationships, recreation, service to others, relaxation, and religious or spiritual engagement—affects our mental health (Schuch et al., 2016b; Walsh, 2011). (See Thinking Critically About: Therapeutic Lifestyle Change.)

Every thought and feeling depends on the functioning brain. Every creative idea, every moment of joy or anger, every period of depression emerges from the electrochemical activity of the living brain. Anxiety disorders, obsessive-compulsive disorder, posttraumatic stress disorder, major depressive disorder, bipolar disorder, and schizophrenia are all biological events. Some psychologists consider even psychotherapy to be a biological treatment, because changing the way we think and behave is a brain-changing experience (Kandel, 2013). When psychotherapy relieves behaviors associated with obsessive-compulsive disorder or schizophrenia, PET scans reveal a calmer brain (Habel et al., 2010; Schwartz et al., 1996). As we have seen over and over, *a human being is an integrated biopsychosocial system.*

"No twisted thought without a twisted molecule." —Attributed to psychologist Ralph Gerard

THINKING CRITICALLY ABOUT:

Therapeutic Lifestyle Change

LOQ 15-14 Why is therapeutic lifestyle change considered an effective biomedical therapy, and how does it work?

LIFESTYLE
(exercise, nutrition, relationships, recreation, service to others, relaxation, and religious or spiritual engagement)

→ **influences our BRAIN AND BODY**

→ **affects our MENTAL HEALTH** [1]

Our shared history has prepared us to be physically active and socially engaged.

Our ancestors hunted, gathered, and built in groups.

Modern researchers have found that outdoor activity in a natural environment reduces stress and promotes health. [2]

APPLICATION TO THERAPY

Training seminars promote therapeutic lifestyle change. [3] Small groups of people with depression undergo a 12-week training program with the following goals:

Aerobic exercise, 30 minutes a day, at least three times weekly (increases fitness and vitality, stimulates endorphins)

Regular aerobic exercise rivals the healing power of antidepressant drugs. [4]

Adequate sleep, with a goal of 7 to 8 hours per night.

A complete night's sleep boosts immunity and increases energy, alertness, and mood. [5]

zzzzzzzzzzzzzzzzzzzzzzzzzz

Light exposure, 15 to 30 minutes each morning with a light box (amplifies arousal, influences hormones)

Social connection, with less alone time and at least two meaningful social engagements weekly (helps satisfy the human need to belong)

Reducing rumination, by identifying and redirecting negative thoughts (enhances positive thinking)

Nutritional supplements, including a daily fish oil supplement with omega-3 fatty acids (aids in healthy brain functioning)

Initial small study (74 participants)[6]

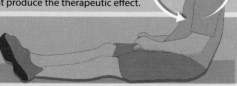

77% of those who completed the program experienced relief from depressive symptoms.

Only 19% of those assigned to a treatment-as-usual control group showed similar results.

Future research will try to identify which parts of the treatment produce the therapeutic effect.

The biomedical therapies assume that mind and body are a unit: Affect one and you will affect the other.

1. Sánchez-Villegas et al., 2015; Walsh, 2011. 2. MacKerron & Mourato, 2013; NEEF, 2015; Phillips, 2011. 3. Ilardi, 2009. 4. Babyak et al., 2000; Salmon, 2001; Schuch et al., 2016b. 5. Gregory et al., 2009; Walker & van der Helm, 2009. 6. Ilardi, 2009, 2016.

🔒 **RETRIEVE IT • • •**

ANSWERS IN APPENDIX E

RI-1 What are some examples of lifestyle changes people can make to enhance their mental health?

ENGAGE

💡 (ASK YOURSELF)

Which lifestyle changes are most important for *you* to make to improve your mental health?

DRUG THERAPIES

LOQ 15-15 What are the drug therapies? How do double-blind studies help researchers evaluate a drug's effectiveness?

By far the most widely used biomedical treatments today are the drug therapies. Most drugs for anxiety and depression are prescribed by primary care providers, followed by psychiatrists and, in some states, psychologists.

"Our psychopharmacologist is a genius."

Since the 1950s, discoveries in **psychopharmacology** (the study of drug effects on mind and behavior) have revolutionized the treatment of people with severe disorders, liberating hundreds of thousands from hospital confinement. Thanks to drug therapy and local community mental health programs, the resident population of U.S. state and county mental hospitals is now a small fraction of what it was in the mid-twentieth century. For some who are unable to care for themselves, however, release from hospitals has meant homelessness, not liberation.

Almost any new treatment, including drug therapy, is greeted by an initial wave of enthusiasm as many people apparently improve. But that enthusiasm often diminishes on closer examination. To evaluate the effectiveness of any new drug, researchers also need to know normal recovery rates.

- How many people recover without treatment, and how quickly?

- Is recovery due to the drug or to the placebo effect? When patients or mental health workers expect positive results, they may see what they expect, not what really happened. Even mere exposure to advertising about a drug's supposed effectiveness can increase its effect (Kamenica et al., 2013).

To control for these influences, drug researchers give half the patients the drug, and the other half a similar-appearing placebo. Because neither the staff nor the patients know who gets which, this is called a *double-blind procedure*. The good news: In double-blind studies, several types of drugs effectively treat psychological disorders.

Antipsychotic Drugs

An accidental discovery launched a treatment revolution for people with *psychosis*. The discovery: Certain drugs, used for other medical purposes, calmed the hallucinations or delusions that are part of these patients' split from reality. First-generation **antipsychotic drugs,** such as chlorpromazine (sold as Thorazine), dampened responsiveness to irrelevant stimuli. Thus, they provided the most help to patients experiencing positive (actively inappropriate) symptoms of schizophrenia, such as auditory hallucinations and paranoia (Leucht et al., 2017). (Antipsychotic drugs are less effective in changing negative symptoms such as apathy and withdrawal.)

The molecules of most conventional antipsychotic drugs are similar enough to molecules of the neurotransmitter dopamine to occupy its receptor sites and block its activity. This finding reinforces the idea that an overactive dopamine system contributes to schizophrenia.

Perhaps you can guess an occasional side effect of L-dopa, a drug that raises dopamine levels for Parkinson's patients: hallucinations.

Antipsychotics also have powerful side effects. Some produce sluggishness, tremors, and twitches similar to those of Parkinson's disease (Kaplan & Saddock, 1989). Long-term use of antipsychotics can produce *tardive dyskinesia,* with involuntary movements of the facial muscles (such as grimacing), tongue, and limbs. Although not more effective in controlling schizophrenia symptoms, many of the newer-generation antipsychotics, such as risperidone (Risperdal) and olanzapine (Zyprexa), work best for those with severe symptoms and have fewer of these effects (Furukawa et al., 2015). These drugs may, however, increase the risk of obesity and diabetes (Buchanan et al., 2010; Tiihonen et al., 2009).

psychopharmacology the study of the effects of drugs on mind and behavior.

antipsychotic drugs drugs used to treat schizophrenia and other forms of severe thought disorder.

Antipsychotics, combined with life-skills programs and family support, have given new hope to many people with schizophrenia (Goff et al., 2017; Guo, 2010). Hundreds of thousands of patients have left the wards of mental hospitals and returned to work and to near-normal lives (Leucht et al., 2003). Elyn Saks (2007), a University of Southern California law professor, knows what it means to live with schizophrenia. Thanks to her treatment, which combines an antipsychotic drug and psychotherapy, she noted, "Now I'm mostly well. I'm mostly thinking clearly. I do have episodes, but it's not like I'm struggling all of the time to stay on the right side of the line."

Antianxiety Drugs

Like alcohol, **antianxiety drugs,** such as Xanax or Ativan, depress central nervous system activity (and so should not be used in combination with alcohol). Some antianxiety drugs have been successfully used in combination with psychological therapy to enhance exposure therapy's extinction of learned fears and to help relieve the symptoms of posttraumatic stress disorder and obsessive-compulsive disorder (Davis, 2005; Kushner et al., 2007).

Some critics fear that antianxiety drugs may reduce symptoms without resolving underlying problems, especially when used as an ongoing treatment. "Popping a Xanax" at the first sign of tension can create a learned response: The immediate relief reinforces a person's tendency to take drugs when anxious. Antianxiety drugs can also be addictive. Regular users who stop taking these drugs may experience increased anxiety, insomnia, and other withdrawal symptoms.

Antidepressant Drugs

The **antidepressant drugs** were named for their ability to lift people up from a state of depression, and this was their main use until recently. The label is a bit of a misnomer now that these drugs are increasingly used to treat anxiety disorders, obsessive-compulsive disorder, and posttraumatic stress disorder (Wetherell et al., 2013). Many work by increasing the availability of neurotransmitters, such as norepinephrine or serotonin, which elevate arousal and mood and are scarce when a person experiences feelings of depression or anxiety. The most commonly prescribed drugs in this group, including Prozac and its cousins Zoloft and Paxil, work by blocking the normal reuptake process (**FIGURE 15.5**). Given their use in treating disorders other than depression—from anxiety to strokes—these drugs are most often called *SSRIs—selective serotonin reuptake inhibitors* (rather than antidepressants) (Kramer, 2011).

Some of the older antidepressant drugs work by blocking the reabsorption or breakdown of both norepinephrine and serotonin. Though effective, these dual-action drugs have more potential side effects, such as dry mouth, weight gain, hypertension, or dizzy spells (Anderson, 2000; Mulrow, 1999). Administering them by means of a patch, which bypasses the intestines and liver, helps reduce such side effects (Bodkin & Amsterdam, 2002). Some professionals prefer the SSRIs over other antidepressants (Jakubovski et al., 2015; Kramer, 2011).

antianxiety drugs drugs used to control anxiety and agitation.

antidepressant drugs drugs used to treat depression, anxiety disorders, obsessive-compulsive disorder, and posttraumatic stress disorder. (Several widely used antidepressant drugs are *selective serotonin reuptake inhibitors—SSRIs.*)

FIGURE 15.5
BIOLOGY OF ANTIDEPRESSANTS Shown here is the action of Prozac, which partially blocks the reuptake of serotonin.

Message is sent across synaptic gap.

Message is received; excess serotonin molecules are reabsorbed by sending neuron.

Prozac partially blocks normal reuptake of the neurotransmitter serotonin; excess serotonin in synapse enhances its mood-lifting effect.

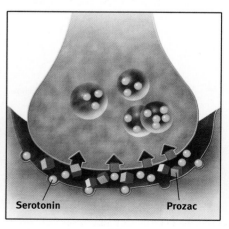

Sending neuron

Action potential

Synaptic gap

Receiving neuron

Serotonin molecule

Receptor

Reuptake

Serotonin

Prozac

(a)

(b)

(c)

But be advised: Patients with depression who begin taking antidepressants do not wake up the next morning singing "It's a beautiful day!" SSRIs begin to influence neurotransmission within hours, but their full psychological effect may take four weeks (and may involve a side effect of diminished sexual desire). One possible reason for the delay is that increased serotonin promotes new synapses plus *neurogenesis*—the birth of new brain cells, perhaps reversing stress-induced loss of neurons (Launay et al., 2011). Researchers are also exploring the possibility of quicker-acting antidepressants. One, ketamine, which is also an anesthetic and a risky, psychedelic party drug, blocks hyperactive receptors for glutamate, a neurotransmitter, and causes a burst of new synapses. It can provide relief from depression within hours of an infusion, often after transient hallucinations (Sanacora et al., 2017). Some drug companies are hoping to develop a ketamine-like, fast-acting drug without its side effects (Kirby, 2015).

Antidepressant drugs are not the only way to give the body a lift. Aerobic exercise can calm people who feel anxious, energize those who feel depressed, and offer other positive side effects. Cognitive therapy, by helping people reverse their habitual negative thinking style, can boost drug-aided relief from depression and reduce posttreatment relapses (Amick et al., 2015). Some clinicians attack depression (and anxiety) from both below and above (Cuijpers et al., 2010; Hollon et al., 2014; Kennard et al., 2014). They use antidepressant drugs (which work, bottom-up, on the emotion-forming limbic system) in conjunction with cognitive-behavioral therapy (which works, top-down, to alter frontal lobe activity and change thought processes).

Researchers generally agree that people with depression often improve after a month on antidepressant drugs. But after allowing for natural recovery and the placebo effect, how big is the drug effect? Not big, report some researchers (Kirsch et al., 1998, 2014, 2016). In double-blind clinical trials, placebos produced improvement comparable to about 75 percent of the active drug's effect. For those with severe depression, the placebo effect is less and the added drug benefit somewhat greater (Fournier et al., 2010; Kirsch et al., 2008; Olfson & Marcus, 2009). Given that antidepressants often have unwanted side effects, and that aerobic exercise and cognitive-behavioral therapy are also effective antidotes to mild or moderate depression, Irving Kirsch (2016) recommends more limited antidepressant use: "If they are to be used at all, it should be as a last resort." *The bottom line:* If you're concerned about your mental health, consult with a mental health professional to determine the best treatment for you.

"If this doesn't help you don't worry, it's a placebo."

ENGAGE **LaunchPad** To play the role of a clinical researcher exploring these questions, engage online with **Immersive Learning: How Would You Know How Well Antidepressants Work?**

Mood-Stabilizing Medications

In addition to antipsychotic, antianxiety, and antidepressant drugs, psychiatrists have *mood-stabilizing drugs* in their arsenal. One of them, Depakote, was originally used to treat epilepsy. It was also found effective in controlling the manic episodes associated with bipolar disorder. Another, the simple salt *lithium*, effectively levels the emotional highs and lows of this disorder.

Australian physician John Cade discovered the benefits of lithium in the 1940s when he administered it to a patient with severe mania and the patient became well in less than a week (Snyder, 1986). About 7 in 10 people with bipolar disorder benefit from a long-term daily dose of this cheap salt, which helps prevent or ease manic episodes and, to a lesser extent, lifts depression (Solomon et al., 1995). Kay Redfield Jamison (1995, pp. 88–89) described the effect:

> Lithium prevents my seductive but disastrous highs, diminishes my depressions, clears out the wool and webbing from my disordered thinking, slows me down, gentles me out, keeps me from ruining my career and relationships, keeps me out of a hospital, alive, and makes psychotherapy possible.

Taking lithium also correlates with a lower risk of suicide among people with bipolar disorder—about one-sixth the risk of those not taking lithium (Oquendo et al., 2011). Naturally occurring lithium in drinking water has also correlated with lower suicide rates (across 18 Japanese cities and towns) and lower crime rates (across 27 Texas counties) (Ohgami et al., 2009; Schrauzer & Shrestha, 1990, 2010; Terao et al., 2010). Lithium works.

"First of all I think you should know that last quarter's sales figures are interfering with my mood-stabilizing drugs."

BRAIN STIMULATION

LOQ 15-16 How are brain stimulation and psychosurgery used in treating specific disorders?

Electroconvulsive Therapy

Another biomedical treatment, **electroconvulsive therapy (ECT),** manipulates the brain by shocking it. When ECT was first introduced in 1938, the wide-awake patient was strapped to a table and jolted with electricity to the brain. The procedure, which produced convulsions and brief unconsciousness, gained a barbaric image. Although that image lingers, today's ECT is much kinder and gentler, and no longer "convulsive." The patient receives a general anesthetic and a muscle relaxant (to prevent bodily convulsions). A psychiatrist then delivers a brief pulse of electrical current, sometimes only to the brain's right side, which triggers a 30- to 60-second seizure. Within 30 minutes, the patient awakens and remembers nothing of the treatment or of the preceding hours.

Study after study confirms that ECT can effectively treat severe depression in "treatment-resistant" patients who have not responded to drug therapy (Bailine et al., 2010; Fink, 2009; Lima et al., 2013; Medda et al., 2015). After three such sessions each week for two to four weeks, 70 percent or more of those receiving today's ECT improve markedly, without discernible brain damage and with less memory loss than with earlier versions of ECT (HMHL, 2007). ECT also reduces suicidal thoughts and has been credited with saving many from suicide (Kellner et al., 2006). A *Journal of the American Medical Association* editorial concluded that "the results of ECT in treating severe depression are among the most positive treatment effects in all of medicine" (Glass, 2001).

How does ECT relieve severe depression? After more than 70 years, no one knows for sure. One patient likened ECT to the smallpox vaccine, which was saving lives before we knew how it worked. Perhaps the brief electric current calms neural centers where overactivity produces depression. Some research indicates that ECT stimulates neurogenesis (new neurons) and new synaptic connections (Joshi et al., 2016; Rotheneichner et al., 2014; Wang et al., 2017b).

No matter how impressive the results, the idea of electrically shocking a person's brain still strikes many as barbaric, especially given our ignorance about why ECT works. Moreover, the mood boost may not last long. Many ECT-treated patients eventually relapse back into depression, although relapses are somewhat fewer for those who also receive antidepressant drugs or who do aerobic exercise (Rosenquist et al., 2016; Salehi et al., 2016). *The bottom line:* In the minds of many psychiatrists and patients, ECT is a lesser evil than severe depression's misery, anguish, and risk of suicide. As research psychologist Norman Endler (1982) reported after ECT alleviated his deep depression, "A miracle had happened in two weeks."

Alternative Neurostimulation Therapies

Three other neural stimulation techniques—mild cranial electrical stimulation, magnetic stimulation, and deep brain stimulation—also aim to treat the depressed brain (**FIGURE 15.6**).

TRANSCRANIAL ELECTRICAL STIMULATION In contrast to ECT, which produces a brain seizure with about 800 milliamps of electricity, *transcranial direct current stimulation (tDCS)* administers a weak 1- to 2-milliamp current to the scalp. The current is so mild that some people have attempted to use the tDCS machines to stimulate their own cognitive abilities, though skeptics argue that such a current is too weak to penetrate to the brain and that studies do not confirm cognitive benefits (Horvath et al., 2015; Underwood, 2016). After reviewing recent studies, two European expert panels did, however, report "probable efficacy" of tDCS as a depression treatment (Brunoni et al., 2016; Lefaucheur et al., 2017).

The medical use of electricity is an ancient practice. Physicians treated the Roman Emperor Claudius (10 B.C.E.–54 C.E.) for headaches by pressing electric eels to his temples. Today, about 17 people per 100,000—people whose depression has not responded to other treatments—have received ECT (Lesage et al., 2016).

"I used to . . . be unable to shake the dread even when I was feeling good, because I knew the bad feelings would return. ECT has wiped away that foreboding. It has given me a sense of control, of hope." —Kitty Dukakis, 2006

 LaunchPad To witness the powerful effects of ECT, see the **Video: Electroconvulsive Therapy.**

electroconvulsive therapy (ECT) a biomedical therapy for severely depressed patients in which a brief electric current is sent through the brain of an anesthetized patient.

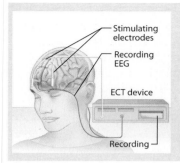

Stimulating
electrodes

Recording
EEG

ECT device

Recording

Electroconvulsive therapy (ECT)
Psychiatrist administers a strong
current, which triggers a seizure
in the anesthetized patient.

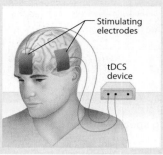

Stimulating
electrodes

tDCS
device

**Transcranial direct current
stimulation (tDCS)**
Psychiatrist applies a weak
current to the scalp.

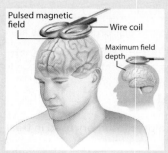

Pulsed magnetic
field

Wire coil

Maximum field
depth

**Repetitive transcranial magnetic
stimulation (rTMS)**
Psychiatrist sends a painless
magnetic field through the skull
to the surface of the cortex to
alter brain activity.

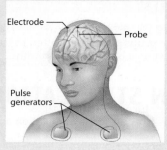

Electrode

Probe

Pulse
generators

Deep brain stimulation (DBS)
Psychiatrist stimulates electrodes
implanted in "sadness centers" to
calm those areas.

FIGURE 15.6

A STIMULATING EXPERIENCE

Today's neurostimulation therapies
apply strong or mild electricity, or
magnetic energy, either to the skull's
surface or directly to brain neurons.

A meta-analysis of 17 clinical
experiments found that one other
stimulation procedure alleviates
depression: massage therapy (Hou
et al., 2010).

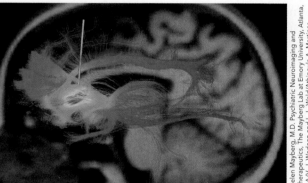

Helen Mayberg, M.D. Psychiatric Neuroimaging and
Therapeutics, The Mayberg Lab at Emory University, Atlanta,
GA/V. J. Wedeen and L. L. Wald/Athinoula A. Martinos
Center For Biomedical Imaging and The Human Connectome
Project, Boston, MA

A DEPRESSION SWITCH? By comparing the brains of patients with and
without depression, researcher Helen
Mayberg identified a brain area (high-
lighted in red) that appears active in
people who are depressed or sad, and
whose activity may be calmed by deep
brain stimulation.

MAGNETIC STIMULATION Depressed moods also sometimes improve when a painless
procedure—called **repetitive transcranial magnetic stimulation (rTMS)**—is performed on wide-awake patients over several weeks. Repeated pulses surging through a
magnetic coil held close to the skull can stimulate or suppress activity in areas of the
cortex. Like tDCS (and unlike ECT), the rTMS procedure produces no memory loss or
other serious side effects, aside from possible headaches.

Some studies have found that, for 30 to 40 percent of people with depression, rTMS
works (Becker et al., 2016; Brunoni et al., 2017; Taylor et al., 2017). How it works is
unclear. One possible explanation is that the stimulation energizes the brain's left frontal
lobe, which is relatively inactive during depression (Helmuth, 2001). Repeated stimulation may cause nerve cells to form new functioning circuits through the process of *long-
term potentiation*.

DEEP BRAIN STIMULATION Other patients whose depression has resisted both drugs and
ECT have benefited from an experimental treatment pinpointing a neural hub that bridges
the thinking frontal lobes to the limbic system (Becker et al., 2016; Brunoni et al., 2017;
Ryder & Holtzheimer, 2016). This area, which is overactive in the
brain of a depressed or temporarily sad person, calms when treated
by ECT or antidepressants. To experimentally activate neurons that
inhibit this negative activity, neuroscientist Helen Mayberg drew
upon the *deep brain stimulation* (DBS) technology, sometimes used
to treat Parkinson's tremors. Since 2003, she and her colleagues
have used DBS to treat some 200 depressed patients with implanted
electrodes in a brain area that functions as the neural "sadness center" (Lozano & Mayberg, 2015). About one-third reportedly have
responded "extremely well" and another 30 percent have modestly
improved (Underwood, 2013). Some felt suddenly more aware and
became more talkative and engaged; others improved only slightly,
if at all. Other studies have found little benefit when DBS is compared with "sham" (placebo) electrode treatments (Witter & Ward,
2016). With 15 new National Institutes of Health–funded studies of DBS under way in
2017, we will soon have a better understanding of its efficacy (Underwood, 2017).

PSYCHOSURGERY

Because its effects are irreversible, **psychosurgery**—surgery that removes or destroys
brain tissue—is the most drastic and least-used biomedical intervention for changing
behavior. In the 1930s, Portuguese physician Egas Moniz developed what would become
the best-known psychosurgical operation: the **lobotomy.** Moniz found that cutting the
nerves connecting the frontal lobes with the emotion-controlling centers of the inner
brain calmed uncontrollably emotional and violent patients. In what would later become,

in others' hands, a crude but quick and easy procedure, a neurosurgeon would shock the patient into a coma, hammer an icepick-like instrument through each eye socket into the brain, and then wiggle it to sever connections running up to the frontal lobes. Between 1936 and 1954, tens of thousands of severely disturbed people were "lobotomized" (Valenstein, 1986).

Although the intention was simply to disconnect emotion from thought, the effect was often more drastic. A lobotomy usually decreased the person's misery or tension, but it also produced a permanently lethargic, immature, uncreative person. During the 1950s, after some 35,000 people had been lobotomized in the United States alone, calming drugs became available and psychosurgery became scorned—as in the saying sometimes attributed to W. C. Fields that "I'd rather have a bottle in front of me than a frontal lobotomy."

Today, lobotomies are history. More precise, microscale psychosurgery is sometimes used in extreme cases. For example, if a patient suffers uncontrollable seizures, surgeons can deactivate the specific nerve clusters that cause or transmit the convulsions. MRI-guided precision surgery is also occasionally done to cut the circuits involved in severe major depressive disorder and obsessive-compulsive disorder (Carey, 2009, 2011; Kim et al., 2018; Sachdev & Sachdev, 1997). Because these procedures are irreversible, neurosurgeons perform them only as a last resort.

* * *

TABLE 15.4 summarizes some aspects of the biomedical therapies we've discussed.

FAILED LOBOTOMY This 1940 photo shows Rosemary Kennedy (center) at age 22 with brother (and future U.S. president) John and sister Jean. A year later her father, on medical advice, approved a lobotomy that was promised to control her reportedly violent mood swings. The procedure left her confined to a hospital with an infantile mentality until her death in 2005 at age 86.

New York Times Co./Getty Images

ENGAGE

ASK YOURSELF

What were your impressions of biomedical therapies before reading this section? Are any of your views different now? Why or why not?

TABLE 15.4

Comparing Biomedical Therapies

Therapy	Presumed Problem	Therapy Aim	Therapy Technique
Therapeutic lifestyle change	Stress and unhealthy lifestyle	Restore healthy biological state.	Alter lifestyle through adequate exercise, sleep, nutrition, and other changes.
Drug therapies	Neurotransmitter malfunction	Control symptoms of psychological disorders.	Alter brain chemistry through drugs.
Brain stimulation	Depression (ECT is used only for severe, treatment-resistant depression.)	Alleviate depression, especially when it is unresponsive to drugs or other forms of therapy.	Stimulate brain through electroconvulsive shock, mild electrical stimulation, magnetic impulses, or deep brain stimulation.
Psychosurgery	Brain malfunction	Relieve severe disorders.	Remove or destroy brain tissue.

repetitive transcranial magnetic stimulation (rTMS) the application of repeated pulses of magnetic energy to the brain; used to stimulate or suppress brain activity.

psychosurgery surgery that removes or destroys brain tissue in an effort to change behavior.

lobotomy a psychosurgical procedure once used to calm uncontrollably emotional or violent patients. The procedure cut the nerves connecting the frontal lobes to the emotion-controlling centers of the inner brain.

🔒 RETRIEVE IT • • •

ANSWERS IN APPENDIX E

RI-4 Severe depression that has not responded to other therapy may be treated with _____ _____, which can cause brain seizures and memory loss. More moderate neural stimulation techniques designed to help alleviate depression include _____ direct current stimulation, _____ _____ magnetic stimulation, and _____ _____ stimulation.

PREVENTING PSYCHOLOGICAL DISORDERS AND BUILDING RESILIENCE

LOQ 15-17 What is the rationale for preventive mental health programs, and why is it important to develop resilience?

Psychotherapies and biomedical therapies tend to locate the cause of psychological disorders within the person. We infer that people who act cruelly must be cruel and that people who act "crazy" must be "sick." We attach labels to such people, thereby distinguishing them from "normal" folks. It follows, then, that we try to treat "abnormal" people by giving them insight into their problems, by changing their thinking, by helping them gain control with drugs.

There is an alternative viewpoint: We could interpret many psychological disorders as understandable responses to a disturbing and stressful society. According to this view, it is not just the person who needs treatment, but also the person's social context. Better to prevent a problem by reforming an unhealthy situation and by developing people's coping competencies than to wait for and treat problems.

Preventive Mental Health

A story about the rescue of a drowning person from a rushing river illustrates this viewpoint: Having successfully administered first aid to the first victim, the rescuer spots another struggling person and pulls her out, too. After a half-dozen repetitions, the rescuer suddenly turns and starts running away while the river sweeps yet another floundering person into view. "Aren't you going to rescue that fellow?" asks a bystander. "Heck no," the rescuer replies. "I'm going upstream to find out what's pushing all these people in."

Preventive mental health is upstream work. It seeks to prevent psychological casualties by identifying and alleviating the conditions that cause them. As George Albee (1986, 2006) pointed out, there is abundant evidence that poverty, meaningless work, constant criticism, unemployment, racism, and sexism undermine people's sense of competence, personal control, and self-esteem. Such stresses increase their risk of depression, alcohol use disorder, and suicide.

To prevent psychological casualties we should, Albee contended, support programs that alleviate these demoralizing situations. We eliminated smallpox not by treating the afflicted but by inoculating the unafflicted. We conquered yellow fever by controlling mosquitoes. Better to drain the swamps than swat the mosquitoes.

Preventing psychological problems means empowering those who have learned an attitude of helplessness and changing environments that breed loneliness. It means renewing fragile family ties and boosting parents' and teachers' skills at nurturing children's competence and belief in their abilities. It means harnessing positive psychology interventions to enhance human flourishing. One intervention taught adolescents that personality isn't fixed—people can change—and reduced their incidence of future depression by 40 percent (Miu & Yeager, 2015). In short, "everything aimed at improving the human condition, at making life more fulfilling and meaningful, may be considered part of primary prevention of mental or emotional disturbance" (Kessler & Albee, 1975, p. 557). Prevention can sometimes provide a double payoff. People with a strong sense of life's meaning are more engaging socially (Stillman et al., 2011). If we can strengthen people's sense of meaning in life, we may also lessen their loneliness as they grow into more engaging companions.

Among the upstream prevention workers are *community psychologists*. Mindful of how people interact with their environment, they focus on creating environments that support psychological health. Through their research and social action, community psychologists aim to empower people and to enhance their competence, health, and well-being.

Building Resilience

Preventive mental health includes efforts to build individuals' **resilience**—the ability to cope with stress and recover from adversity.

"It is better to prevent than to cure." —Peruvian folk wisdom

"Mental disorders arise from physical ones, and likewise physical disorders arise from mental ones." —The Mahabharata, 200 B.C.E.

Horst Faas/AP Images

Nancy Kaszerman/ZUMA Press/Newscom

RESILIENT GROWTH FROM PRISONER TO POLITICIAN Before becoming a U.S. senator, John McCain (1936–2018) spent more than five years as a Vietnam War prisoner. He was regularly beaten and tortured, which left him permanently unable to lift his arms above his head. Yet he found strength in reflecting positively on his experience. "I put the war behind me when I left," he said. "The memories I have are of the wonderful people I had the privilege of serving with" (Myre, 2000). When diagnosed with brain cancer in 2017, his daughter Meghan tweeted that "The one of us who is most confident and calm is my father."

Faced with unforeseen trauma, most adults exhibit resilience. This was true of New Yorkers in the aftermath of the September 11 terror attacks, especially for those who enjoyed supportive close relationships and who had not recently experienced other stressful events (Bonanno et al., 2007). More than 9 in 10 New Yorkers, although stunned and grief-stricken by 9/11, did *not* have a dysfunctional stress reaction. Among those who did, the stress symptoms were mostly gone by the following January (Person et al., 2006). Even most combat-stressed veterans, most political rebels who have survived torture, and most people with spinal cord injuries do not later exhibit posttraumatic stress disorder (Bonanno et al., 2012; Mineka & Zinbarg, 1996).

Struggling with challenging crises can even lead to **posttraumatic growth.** Many cancer survivors have reported a greater appreciation for life, more meaningful relationships, increased personal strength, changed priorities, and a richer spiritual life (Tedeschi & Calhoun, 2004). Out of even our worst experiences, some good can come, especially when we can imagine new possibilities (Roepke, 2015; Roepke & Seligman, 2015). Suffering can beget new sensitivity and strength.

🔒 RETRIEVE IT • • •

ANSWERS IN APPENDIX E

RI-5 What is the difference between preventive mental health and the psychological and biomedical therapies?

ENGAGE 📱 **LaunchPad** Consider ways to build your own resilience by engaging with **Immersive Learning: Assess Your Strengths—How Resilient Are You, and Why Should You Build More Resilience?**

* * *

ENGAGE 📱 If you just finished reading this book, your introduction to psychological science is completed. Our tour of psychological science has taught us much—and you, too?—about our moods and memories, about the reach of our unconscious, about how we flourish and struggle, about how we perceive our physical and social worlds, and about how our biology and culture shape us. Our hope, as your guides on this tour, is that you have shared some of our fascination, grown in your understanding and compassion, and sharpened your critical thinking. And we hope you enjoyed the ride.

With every good wish in your future endeavors,

David G. Myers
DavidMyers.org

Nathan DeWall
NathanDeWall.com

resilience the personal strength that helps most people cope with stress and recover from adversity and even trauma.

posttraumatic growth positive psychological changes as a result of struggling with extremely challenging circumstances and life crises.

🔒 REVIEW THE BIOMEDICAL THERAPIES AND PREVENTING PSYCHOLOGICAL DISORDERS

⤳ Learning Objectives

TEST YOURSELF Answer these repeated Learning Objective Questions on your own (before checking the answers in Appendix D) to improve your retention of the concepts (McDaniel et al., 2009, 2015).

15-14 Why is therapeutic lifestyle change considered an effective biomedical therapy, and how does it work?

15-15 What are the drug therapies? How do double-blind studies help researchers evaluate a drug's effectiveness?

15-16 How are brain stimulation and psychosurgery used in treating specific disorders?

15-17 What is the rationale for preventive mental health programs, and why is it important to develop resilience?

⤳ Terms and Concepts to Remember

TEST YOURSELF Write down the definition yourself, then check your answer on the referenced page.

psychopharmacology, **p. 560**

antipsychotic drugs, **p. 560**

antianxiety drugs, **p. 561**

antidepressant drugs, **p. 561**

electroconvulsive therapy (ECT), **p. 563**

repetitive transcranial magnetic stimulation (rTMS), **p. 565**

psychosurgery, **p. 565**

lobotomy, **p. 565**

resilience, **p. 567**

posttraumatic growth, **p. 567**

⤳ Experience the Testing Effect

TEST YOURSELF Answer the following questions on your own first, then check your answers in Appendix E.

1. Some antipsychotic drugs, used to calm people with schizophrenia, can have unpleasant side effects, most notably
   a. hyperactivity.
   b. convulsions and momentary memory loss.
   c. sluggishness, tremors, and twitches.
   d. paranoia.

2. Drugs such as Xanax and Ativan, which depress central nervous system activity, can become addictive when used as ongoing treatment. These drugs are referred to as _____ drugs.

3. A simple salt that often brings relief to patients suffering the highs and lows of bipolar disorder is _____.

4. When drug therapies have not been effective, electroconvulsive therapy (ECT) may be used as treatment, largely for people with
   a. severe obsessive-compulsive disorder.
   b. severe depression.
   c. schizophrenia.
   d. anxiety disorders.

5. An approach that seeks to identify and alleviate conditions that put people at high risk for developing psychological disorders is called
   a. deep brain stimulation.
   b. the mood-stabilizing perspective.
   c. spontaneous recovery.
   d. preventive mental health.

Continue testing yourself with 📖 **LearningCurve** or 📖 **Achieve Read & Practice** to learn and remember most effectively.

Statistical Reasoning in Everyday Life

Statistics are important tools in psychological research. But statistics also benefit us all, by helping us see what the unaided eye might miss. To be an educated person today is to be able to apply simple statistical principles to everyday reasoning. We needn't memorize complicated formulas to think more clearly and critically about data.

Off-the-top-of-the-head estimates often misread reality and mislead the public. Someone throws out a big, round number. Others echo it, and before long the big, round number becomes public misinformation. Two examples:

- ***Ten percent of people are gay or lesbian.*** Or is it 2 to 4 percent, as suggested by various national surveys (Chapter 5)?

- ***We ordinarily use only 10 percent of our brain.*** Or is it closer to 100 percent (Chapter 2)?

 If you see an attention-grabbing headline presented without evidence—that nationally there are one million teen pregnancies, two million homeless seniors, or three million alcohol-related car accidents—you can be pretty sure that someone is guessing. If they want to emphasize the problem, they will be motivated to guess big. If they want to minimize the problem, they will guess small. *The point to remember:* Use critical thinking when presented with big, round, undocumented numbers.

Statistical illiteracy also feeds needless health scares (Gigerenzer, 2010). In the 1990s, the British press reported a study showing that women taking a particular contraceptive pill had a 100 percent increased risk of blood clots that could produce strokes. The story went viral, causing thousands of women to stop taking the pill. What happened as a result? A wave of unwanted pregnancies and an estimated 13,000 additional abortions (which also are associated with increased blood clot risk). Distracted by big, round numbers, few people focused on the study's actual findings: A 100 percent increased risk, indeed—but only from 1 in 7000 to 2 in 7000. Such false alarms underscore the need to think critically, to teach statistical reasoning, and to present statistical information more transparently.

> ### ⇢ Describing Data
> **Measures of Central Tendency**
>
> **Measures of Variation**
>
> **Correlation: A Measure of Relationships**
>
> ### ⇢ Significant Differences
> **When Is an Observed Difference Reliable?**
>
> **When Is an Observed Difference Significant?**

When setting goals, we love big, round numbers. We're far more likely to want to lose 20 pounds than 19 or 21 pounds (or an even 10 kilograms rather than 9.07 kilograms). And by modifying their behavior, batters are nearly four times more likely to finish the season with a .300 average than with a .299 average (Pope & Simonsohn, 2011).

"Figures can be misleading—so I've written a song which I think expresses the real story of the firm's performance this quarter."

⇢ Describing Data

LEARNING OBJECTIVE QUESTION (LOQ)

A-1 How do we describe data using three measures of central tendency, and what is the relative usefulness of the two measures of variation?

Once researchers have gathered their data, they may organize that data using *descriptive statistics*. One way to do this is to show the data in a simple *bar graph*, as in **FIGURE A.1**, which displays a distribution of different brands of trucks still on the road after a decade. When reading statistical graphs such as this one, take care. It's easy to design a graph to make a

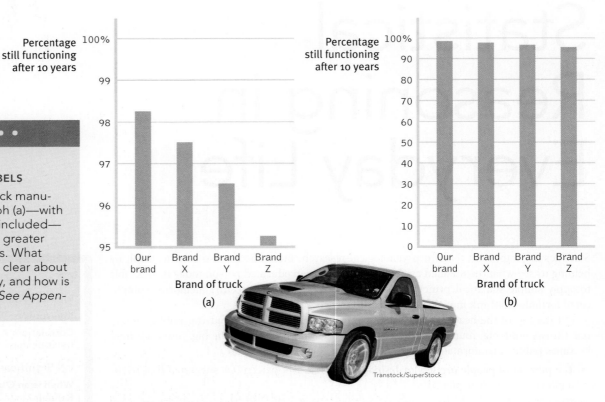

Percentage still functioning after 10 years

(a)   Brand of truck

(b)   Brand of truck

Transtock/SuperStock

ENGAGE

💡 (ASK YOURSELF)

Find a graph in your social media news feed. How does the article's author use (or abuse) statistics to make a point?

The average person has one ovary and one testicle.

mode the most frequently occurring score(s) in a distribution.

mean the arithmetic average of a distribution, obtained by adding the scores and then dividing by the number of scores.

median the middle score in a distribution; half the scores are above it and half are below it.

difference look big (Figure A.1a) or small (Figure A.1b). The secret lies in how you label the vertical scale (the *y-axis*).

The point to remember: Think smart. When viewing graphs, read the scale labels and note their *range*.

Measures of Central Tendency

The next step is to summarize the data using some *measure of central tendency,* a single score that represents a whole set of scores. The simplest measure is the **mode,** the most frequently occurring score or scores. The most familiar is the **mean,** or arithmetic average—the total sum of all the scores divided by the number of scores. The midpoint—the 50th percentile—is the **median.** On a divided highway, the median is the middle. So, too, with data: If you arrange all the scores in order from the highest to the lowest, half will be above the median and half will be below it.

Measures of central tendency neatly summarize data. But consider what happens to the mean when a distribution is lopsided, when it's *skewed* by a few way-out scores. With income data, for example, the mode, median, and mean often tell very different stories (**FIGURE A.2**). This happens because the mean is biased by a few extreme incomes. When Amazon founder Jeff Bezos sits down in a small café, its average (mean) customer instantly becomes a billionaire. But median customer wealth remains unchanged. Understanding this, you can see why, according to the 2010 U.S. Census, nearly 65 percent of U.S. households have "below average" income. The bottom half of earners receive much less than half of the total national income. So, most Americans make less than the mean. Mean and median tell different true stories.

The point to remember: Always note which measure of central tendency is reported. If it is a mean, consider whether a few atypical scores could be distorting it.

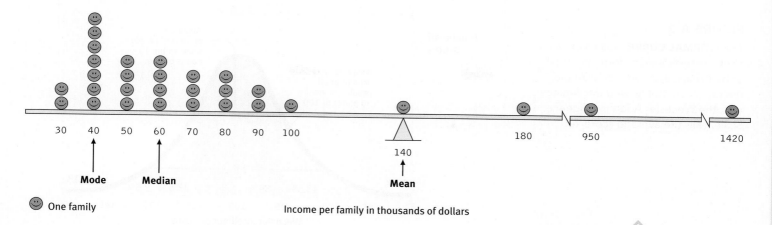

Mode   **Median**   **Mean**

😐 One family

Income per family in thousands of dollars

Measures of Variation

Knowing the value of an appropriate measure of central tendency can tell us a great deal. But the single number omits other information. It helps to know something about the amount of *variation* in the data—how similar or diverse the scores are. Averages derived from scores with low variability are more reliable than averages based on scores with high variability. Consider a basketball player who scored between 13 and 17 points in each of the season's first 10 games. Knowing this, we would be more confident that she would score near 15 points in her next game than if her scores had varied from 5 to 25 points.

The **range** of scores—the gap between the lowest and highest—provides only a crude estimate of variation. In an otherwise similar group, a couple of extreme scores, such as the $950,000 and $1,420,000 incomes in Figure A.2, will create a deceptively large range.

The more useful standard for measuring how much scores deviate from one another is the **standard deviation.** It better gauges whether scores are packed together or dispersed, because it uses information from each score. The computation[1] assembles information about how much individual scores differ from the mean, which can be very telling. Let's say test scores from Class A and Class B both have the same mean (75 percent correct) but very different standard deviations (5.0 for Class A and 15.0 for Class B). Have you ever had test experiences like that—where two-thirds of your classmates in one course score in the 70 to 80 percent range, with scores in another course more spread out (two-thirds between 60 and 90 percent)? The standard deviation, as well as the mean score, tell us about how each class is faring.

You can grasp the meaning of the standard deviation if you consider how scores naturally tend to be distributed. Large numbers of data—heights, intelligence scores, life expectancy (though not incomes)—often form a symmetrical, *bell-shaped* distribution. Most cases fall near the mean, and fewer cases fall near either extreme. This *bell-shaped* distribution is so typical that we call the curve it forms the **normal curve.**

As **FIGURE A.3** shows, a useful property of the normal curve is that roughly 68 percent of the cases fall within one standard deviation on either side of the mean. About 95 percent of cases fall within two standard deviations. Thus, as Chapter 9 notes, about 68 percent of people taking an intelligence test will score within ±15 points of 100. About 95 percent will score within ±30 points.

FIGURE A.2

A SKEWED DISTRIBUTION This graphic representation of the distribution of a village's incomes illustrates the three measures of central tendency—mode, median, and mean. Note how just a few high incomes make the mean— the fulcrum point that balances the incomes above and below— deceptively high.

range the difference between the highest and lowest scores in a distribution.

standard deviation a computed measure of how much scores vary around the mean score.

normal curve a symmetrical, bell-shaped curve that describes the distribution of many types of data; most scores fall near the mean (about 68 percent fall within one standard deviation of it) and fewer and fewer near the extremes. (Also called a *normal distribution*.)

📚 **LaunchPad** For an interactive review of these statistical concepts, visit **Topic Tutorial: PsychSim6, Descriptive Statistics.**

1. The actual standard deviation formula is: $\sqrt{\dfrac{Sum\ of\ (deviations\ from\ mean)^2}{Number\ of\ scores - 1}}$

FIGURE A.3

THE NORMAL CURVE Scores on aptitude tests tend to form a normal, or bell-shaped, curve. For example, the most commonly used intelligence test, the Wechsler Adult Intelligence Scale, calls the average score 100.

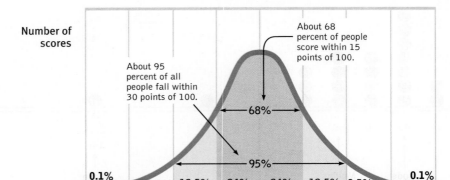

Number of scores

About 95 percent of all people fall within 30 points of 100.

About 68 percent of people score within 15 points of 100.

68%

95%

0.1%   2.5% 13.5% 34% 34% 13.5% 2.5% 0.1%

55   70   85   100   115   130   145

Wechsler intelligence score

🔒 **RETRIEVE IT • • •**   *SEE APPENDIX E FOR ANSWERS*

RI-2 The average of a distribution of scores is the _____. The score that shows up most often is the _____. The score right in the middle of a distribution (half the scores above it; half below) is the _____. We determine how much scores vary around the average in a way that includes information about the _____ of scores (difference between highest and lowest) by using the _____ _____ formula.

variable anything that can vary and is feasible and ethical to measure.

correlation coefficient a statistical index of the relationship between two things (from −1.00 to +1.00).

scatterplot a graphed cluster of dots, each of which represents the values of two variables. The slope of the points suggests the direction of the relationship between the two variables. The amount of scatter suggests the strength of the correlation (little scatter indicates high correlation).

RETAIN 🔒 FIGURE A.4

SCATTERPLOTS, SHOWING PATTERNS OF CORRELATION Correlations—abbreviated *r*—can range from +1.00 (scores for one variable increase in direct proportion to scores for another), to 0.00 (no relationship), to −1.00 (scores for one variable decrease precisely as scores rise for the other).

Correlation: A Measure of Relationships

LOQ A-2   How do correlations measure relationships between variables?

Throughout this book, we often ask how strongly two **variables** are related: For example, how closely related are the personality test scores of identical twins? How well do intelligence test scores predict career achievement? How closely is stress related to disease?

As we saw in Chapter 1, describing behavior is a first step toward predicting it. When naturalistic observation and surveys reveal that one trait or behavior accompanies another, we say the two *correlate*. A **correlation coefficient** is a statistical measure of relationship. In such cases, **scatterplots** can be very revealing.

Each dot in a scatterplot represents the values of two variables. The three scatterplots in **FIGURE A.4** illustrate the range of possible correlations from a perfect positive to a perfect negative. (Perfect correlations rarely occur in the real world.) A correlation is positive if two sets of scores, such as for height and weight, tend to rise or fall together.

Saying that a correlation is "negative" says nothing about its strength. A correlation is negative if two sets of scores relate inversely, one set going up as the other goes down. The correlation between people's height and the distance from their head to the ceiling is strongly (perfectly, in fact) negative.

Statistics can help us see what the naked eye sometimes misses. To demonstrate this for yourself, try an imaginary project. You wonder if tall men are more or less easygoing, so you collect two sets of scores: men's heights and men's anxiety. You measure the

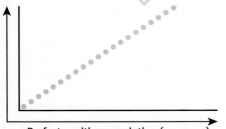

Perfect positive correlation (*r* = +1.00)

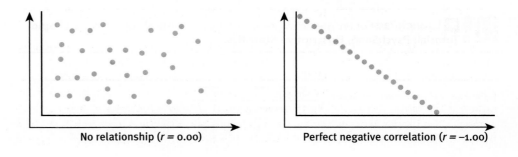

No relationship (*r* = 0.00)   Perfect negative correlation (*r* = −1.00)

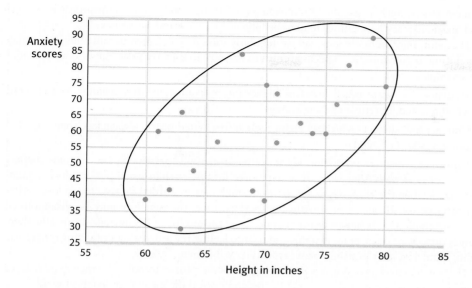

FIGURE A.5

SCATTERPLOT FOR HEIGHT AND ANXIETY This display of data from 20 imagined people (each represented by a data point) reveals an upward slope, indicating a positive correlation. The considerable scatter of the data indicates the correlation is much lower than +1.00.

TABLE A.1
Height and Anxiety Scores of 20 Men

Person	Height in Inches	Anxiety Score
1	80	75
2	63	66
3	61	60
4	79	90
5	74	60
6	69	42
7	62	42
8	75	60
9	77	81
10	60	39
11	64	48
12	76	69
13	71	72
14	66	57
15	73	63
16	70	75
17	63	30
18	71	57
19	68	84
20	70	39

heights of 20 men, and you have them complete an anxiety test, with scores ranging from 0 (*extremely calm*) to 100 (*highly anxious*).

With all the relevant data right in front of you (**TABLE A.1**), can you tell whether the correlation between height and anxiety is positive, negative, or close to zero?

Comparing the columns in Table A.1, most people detect very little relationship between height and anxiety. In fact, the correlation in this imaginary example is positive ($r = +0.63$), as we can see if we display the data as a scatterplot (**FIGURE A.5**).

If we fail to see a relationship when data are presented as systematically as in Table A.1, how much less likely are we to notice them in everyday life? To see what is right in front of us, we sometimes need statistical illumination. We can easily see evidence of gender discrimination when given statistically summarized information about job level, seniority, performance, gender, and salary. But we often see no discrimination when the same information dribbles in, case by case (Twiss et al., 1989).

The point to remember: Correlation coefficients tell us nothing about cause and effect, but they can help us see the world more clearly by revealing the extent to which two things relate.

📕 **LaunchPad** For an animated tutorial on correlations, engage online with **Concept Practice: Positive and Negative Correlations.** See also the **Video: Correlational Studies** for another helpful tutorial animation.

Illusory Correlations and Regression Toward the Mean

LOQ A-3 What are *illusory correlations,* and what is *regression toward the mean?*

Correlations not only make visible the relationships we might otherwise miss, they also restrain our "seeing" nonexistent relationships. When we believe there is a relationship between two things, we are likely to notice and recall instances that confirm our belief. If we believe that dreams forecast actual events, we may notice and recall confirming instances more than disconfirming instances. The result is an **illusory correlation.**

Illusory correlations can feed an illusion of control—that chance events are subject to our personal control. Gamblers, remembering their lucky rolls, may come to believe they can influence the roll of the dice by again throwing gently for low numbers and hard for high numbers. The illusion that uncontrollable events correlate with our actions is also fed by a statistical phenomenon called **regression toward the mean.** Average results are more typical

illusory correlation perceiving a relationship where none exists, or perceiving a stronger-than-actual relationship.

regression toward the mean the tendency for extreme or unusual scores or events to fall back (regress) toward the average.

than extreme results. Thus, after an unusual event, things tend to return toward their average level; extraordinary happenings tend to be followed by more ordinary ones.

The point may seem obvious, yet we regularly miss it: We sometimes attribute what may be a normal regression (the expected return to normal) to something we have done. Consider two examples:

- Students who score much lower or higher on an exam than they usually do are likely, when retested, to return to their average.

- Unusual ESP subjects who defy chance when first tested nearly always lose their "psychic powers" when retested.

Failure to recognize regression is the source of many superstitions and of some ineffective practices as well. After berating an employee for poorer-than-usual performance, a manager may—when the employee regresses to normal—feel rewarded for the "tough love." After lavishing praise for an exceptionally fine performance, the manager may be disappointed when the employee's behavior again migrates back toward his or her average. Ironically, then, regression toward the average can mislead us into feeling rewarded after criticizing others and feeling punished after praising them (Tversky & Kahneman, 1974).

The point to remember: When a fluctuating behavior returns to normal, fancy explanations for why it does so are probably wrong. Regression toward the mean is probably at work.

"Once you become sensitized to it, you see regression everywhere."
—Psychologist Daniel Kahneman (1985)

🔒 **RETRIEVE IT • • •**   *SEE APPENDIX E FOR ANSWERS*

RI-3 You hear the school basketball coach telling her friend that she rescued her team's winning streak by yelling at the players after an unusually bad first half. What is another explanation of why the team's performance improved?

⊕ Significant Differences

LOQ A-4   How do we know whether an observed difference can be generalized to other populations?

Data are "noisy." The average score in one group could conceivably differ from the average score in another group not because of any real difference but merely because of chance fluctuations in the people sampled. How confidently, then, can we *infer* that an observed difference is not just a fluke—a chance result from the research sample? For guidance, we can ask whether the observed difference between the two groups is reliable and statistically significant. These *inferential statistics* help us determine if results describe a larger population (all those in a group being studied).

When Is an Observed Difference Reliable?

In deciding when it is safe to generalize from a sample, we should keep three principles in mind:

1. *Representative samples are better than biased (unrepresentative) samples.* The best basis for generalizing is from a representative sample of cases, not from the exceptional and memorable cases one finds at the extremes. Research never randomly samples the whole human population. Thus, it pays to keep in mind what population a study has sampled.

2. *Less-variable observations are more reliable than those that are more variable.* As we noted earlier in the example of the basketball player whose game-to-game points were consistent, an average is more reliable when it comes from scores with low variability.

3. **More cases are better than fewer cases.** An eager prospective student visits two universities campuses, each for a day. At the first, the student randomly attends two classes and discovers both instructors to be witty and engaging. At the next campus, the two sampled instructors seem dull and uninspiring. Returning home, the student (discounting the small sample size of only two teachers at each institution) tells friends about the "great teachers" at the first school and the "bores" at the second. Again, we know it but we ignore it: *Averages based on many cases are more reliable* (less variable) than averages based on only a few cases. After noticing that small schools were overrepresented among the most successful schools, several foundations invested in splitting larger schools into smaller ones—without realizing that small schools were also overrepresented among the *least* successful, because schools with fewer students have more variable outcomes (Nisbett, 2015). Again, more cases make for a more reliable average.

The point to remember: Smart thinkers are not overly impressed by a few anecdotes. Generalizations based on a few unrepresentative cases are unreliable.

"The poor are getting poorer, but with the rich getting richer it all averages out in the long run."

When Is an Observed Difference Significant?

 Let's say you compared men's and women's scores on a laboratory test of aggression and found a gender difference. But individuals differ. How likely is it that the difference you observed was just a fluke? Statistical testing can estimate the probability of the result occurring by chance.

Here is the underlying logic: When averages from two samples are each reliable measures of their respective populations (as when each is based on many observations that have small variability), then their *difference* is probably reliable as well. (Example: The less the variability in women's and in men's aggression scores, the more confidence we would have that any observed gender difference is reliable.) And when the difference between the sample averages is *large,* we have even more confidence that the difference between them reflects a real difference in their populations.

In short, when sample averages are reliable, and when the difference between them is relatively large, we say the difference has **statistical significance.** This means that the observed difference is probably not due to chance variation between the samples.

In judging statistical significance, psychologists are conservative. They are like juries who must presume innocence until guilt is proven. For most psychologists, proof beyond a reasonable doubt means not making much of a finding unless the probability (p) of it occurring by chance, if no real effect exists, is less than 5 percent ($p < .05$). Some researchers, wanting to make sure that only the most reliable findings are published, suggest that psychologists might consider making more conservative statistical significance judgments (Benjamin et al., 2018). For now, psychologists will continue to use $p < .05$, but stay tuned.

When reading about research, you should remember that, given large enough or homogeneous enough samples, a difference between them may be "statistically significant" yet have little *practical* significance. In one controversial study of nearly 700,000 Facebook users, researchers exposed people to status updates with more or with less positive words. Given

statistical significance a statistical statement of how likely it is that an obtained result occurred by chance.

ENGAGE (ASK YOURSELF)

Can you think of a situation where you were fooled by a writer or speaker's attempts to persuade you with statistics? What have you learned in this appendix that will be most helpful in the future to avoid being misled?

PEANUTS

LaunchPad For a 9.5-minute synopsis of psychology's scientific research strategies, see the **Video: Research Methods.**

the supersized sample's "statistical power," the tweaking produced a "statistically significant" but trivial effect. For example, those who received fewer posts with positive words responded with 0.1 percent fewer positive words themselves—a "statistically significant" effect (it was not due to chance), though one too tiny to have real-world meaning (Morin, 2014). Comparisons of intelligence test scores among hundreds of thousands of first-born and later-born individuals indicate a highly significant tendency for first-born individuals to have higher average scores than their later-born siblings (Rohrer et al., 2015; Zajonc & Markus, 1975). But because the scores differ only slightly, the "significant" difference has little practical importance.

The point to remember: Statistical significance indicates the *likelihood* that a result could have happened by chance. But this does not say anything about the *importance* of the result.

🔒 RETRIEVE IT • • •   *SEE APPENDIX E FOR ANSWERS*

RI-4 Can you solve this puzzle?

The registrar's office at the University of Michigan has found that usually about 100 students in Arts and Sciences have perfect marks at the end of their first term at the university. However, only about 10 to 15 students graduate with perfect marks. What do you think is the most likely explanation for the fact that there are more perfect marks after one term than at graduation (Jepson et al., 1983)?

RI-5 _____ statistics summarize data, while _____ statistics determine if data can be generalized to other populations.

🔒 REVIEW   STATISTICAL REASONING IN EVERYDAY LIFE

⟫ Learning Objectives

TEST YOURSELF Answer these repeated Learning Objective Questions on your own (before checking the answers in Appendix D) to improve your retention of the concepts (McDaniel et al., 2009, 2015).

A-1 How do we describe data using three measures of central tendency, and what is the relative usefulness of the two measures of variation?

A-2 How do correlations measure relationships between variables?

A-3 What are *illusory correlations*, and what is *regression toward the mean*?

A-4 How do we know whether an observed difference can be generalized to other populations?

⟫ Terms and Concepts to Remember

TEST YOURSELF Write down the definition yourself, then check your answer on the referenced page.

mode, p. A-2	standard deviation, p. A-3	scatterplot, p. A-4
mean, p. A-2	normal curve, p. A-3	illusory correlation, p. A-5
median, p. A-2	variable, p. A-4	regression toward the mean, p. A-5
range, p. A-3	correlation coefficient, p. A-4	statistical significance, p. A-7

⟫ Experience the Testing Effect

TEST YOURSELF Answer the following questions on your own first, then check your answers in Appendix E.

1. Which of the three measures of central tendency is most easily distorted by a few very large or very small scores?

    a. The mode

    b. The mean

    c. The median

    d. They are all equally vulnerable to distortion from atypical scores.

2. The standard deviation is the most useful measure of variation in a set of data because it tells us

    a. the difference between the highest and lowest scores in the set.

    b. the extent to which the sample being used deviates from the bigger population it represents.

    c. how much individual scores differ from the mode.

    d. how much individual scores differ from the mean.

3. Another name for a bell-shaped distribution, in which most scores fall near the middle and fewer scores fall at each extreme, is a _____ _____.

4. In a _____ correlation, the scores rise and fall together; in a(n) _____ correlation, one score falls as the other rises.

   a. positive; negative
   b. positive; illusory
   c. negative; weak
   d. strong; weak

5. If a study revealed that tall people were less anxious than short people, this would suggest that the correlation between height and anxiety is _____ (positive/ negative).

6. A _____ provides a visual representation of the direction and the strength of a relationship between two variables.

7. What is regression toward the mean, and how can it influence our interpretation of events?

8. When sample averages are _____ and the difference between them is _____, we can say the difference has statistical significance.

   a. reliable; large
   b. reliable; small
   c. due to chance; large
   d. due to chance; small

Find answers to these questions in Appendix E.

Continue testing yourself with 〰 **LearningCurve** or 〰 **Achieve Read & Practice** to learn and remember most effectively.

Psychology at Work

For most people, to live is to work. Work is life's biggest waking activity. Work helps satisfy multiple needs. Work supports us, enabling food, water, and shelter. Work connects us, meeting our social needs. Work helps define us. Meeting someone for the first time and wondering about their identity, we may ask, "So, what do you do?"

We vary in our job satisfaction. On the day we leave the workforce, some of us will sadly bid our former employer farewell; others will bid our former employer good riddance. What factors influence our perceptions of work as an activity marked by frustration versus *flow,* as a necessary chore versus a meaningful calling, or as an opportunity to do the bare minimum versus maximize our potential?

⊙ Work and Life Satisfaction

Flow at Work

LEARNING OBJECTIVE QUESTION (LOQ)

B-1 What is *flow?*

Individuals across various occupations vary in their attitudes toward their work. Some view their work as a *job,* an unfulfilling but necessary way to make money. Others view their work as a *career,* an opportunity to advance from one position to a better position. The rest—those who view their work as a *calling,* a fulfilling and socially useful activity—report the highest satisfaction with their work and with their lives (Dik & Duffy, 2012; Wrzesniewski & Dutton, 2001). For example, physicians who find meaning in their work tend to avoid burnout and enjoy their careers (Levin et al., 2017).

This finding would not surprise Mihaly Csikszentmihalyi [chick-SENT-me-hi] (1990, 1999). He observed that our quality of life increases when we are purposefully engaged. Between the anxiety of being overwhelmed and stressed, and the apathy of being underwhelmed and bored, lies a zone in which we experience **flow.** When was the last time you experienced flow? Perhaps you can recall being in a zoned-out flow state while texting or playing a video game. If so, then perhaps you can sympathize with the two Northwest Airlines pilots who in 2009 were so focused on their laptops that they missed their control tower's messages. The pilots flew 150 miles past their Minneapolis destination—and lost their jobs.

Csikszentmihalyi formulated the flow concept after studying artists who spent hour after hour painting or sculpting with focused concentration. Immersed in a project, they worked as if nothing else mattered, and then, when finished, they promptly moved on. The artists seemed driven less by external rewards—money, praise, promotion—than by the intrinsic rewards of creating their art. Nearly 200 other studies confirm that *intrinsic motivation* enhances performance (Cerasoli et al., 2014).

The jobs people do: Columnist Gene Weingarten (2002) noted that sometimes a humorist knows "when to just get out of the way." Here are some sample job titles from the U.S. Department of Labor *Dictionary of Occupational Titles:* animal impersonator, human projectile, banana ripening-room supervisor, impregnator, impregnator helper, dope sprayer, finger waver, rug scratcher, egg smeller, bottom buffer, cookie breaker, brain picker, hand pouncer, bosom presser, and mother repairer.

Have you ever noticed that when you are immersed in an activity, time flies? And that when you are watching the clock, it seems to move more slowly? French researchers have confirmed that the more we attend to an event's duration, the longer it seems to last (Coull et al., 2004).

flow a completely involved, focused state, with diminished awareness of self and time; results from full engagement of our skills.

LIFE DISRUPTED Playing and socializing online are ever-present sources of distraction. It takes energy to resist checking our phones, and time to refocus mental concentration after each disruption. Such frequent interruptions disrupt flow, so it's a good idea to instead schedule regular breaks for checking our devices.

Jacob Ammentorp Lund/Getty Images

Csikszentmihalyi studied dancers, chess players, surgeons, writers, parents, mountain climbers, sailors, and farmers. His research included Australians, North Americans, Koreans, Japanese, and Italians. Participants ranged in age from the teen years to the golden years. A clear principle emerged: It's exhilarating to flow with an activity that fully engages our skills (Fong et al., 2015). Flow experiences boost our sense of self-esteem, competence, and well-being. Idleness may sound like bliss, but purposeful work enriches our lives. Busy people are happier (Hsee et al., 2010; Robinson & Martin, 2008). One research team interrupted people on about a quarter-million occasions (using a phone app), and found people's minds wandering 47 percent of the time. They were, on average, happier when their mind was *not* wandering (Killingsworth & Gilbert, 2010). A focused mind is a happy mind.

ENGAGE 💡 Finding Your Own Flow, and Matching Interests to Work

"Find a job you love, and you'll never work another day of your life."
—Facebook hiring video, 2016

Want to identify your own path to flow? You can start by pinpointing your strengths and the types of work that may prove satisfying and successful. Marcus Buckingham and Donald Clifton (2001) suggested asking yourself four questions.

- What activities give me pleasure? Bringing order out of chaos? Playing host? Helping others? Challenging sloppy thinking?
- What activities leave me wondering, "When can I do this again?" rather than, "When will this be over?"
- What sorts of challenges do I relish? And which do I dread?
- What sorts of tasks do I learn easily? And which do I struggle with?

You may find your skills engaged and time flying when teaching or selling or writing or cleaning or consoling or creating or repairing. If an activity feels good, if it comes easily, if you look forward to it, then look deeper. You'll see your strengths at work (Buckingham, 2007). For a free (requires registration) assessment of your own strengths, take the "Brief Strengths Test" at www.AuthenticHappiness.sas.upenn.edu.

The U.S. Department of Labor also offers a career interest questionnaire through its Occupational Information Network (O*NET). At MyNextMove.org/explore/ip you will need about 10 minutes to respond to 60 items, indicating how much you would like or dislike activities ranging from building kitchen cabinets to playing a musical instrument. You will then receive feedback on how strongly your responses reflect six interest types (Holland, 1996):

- **Realistic** (hands-on doers)
- **Investigative** (thinkers)
- **Artistic** (creators)
- **Social** (helpers, teachers)
- **Enterprising** (persuaders, deciders)
- **Conventional** (organizers)

Finally, depending on how much training you are willing to complete, you will be shown occupations that fit your interest pattern (selected from a national database of 900+ occupations).

Do what you love and you will love what you do. A career counseling science aims, first, to assess people's differing values, personalities, and, especially, *interests,* which are remarkably stable and predictive of future life choices and outcomes (Dik & Rottinghaus, 2013; Stoll et al., 2017). (Your job may change, but your interests today will likely still be your interests in 10 years.) Second, it aims to alert people to well-matched vocations—vocations with a good *person-environment fit.* It pays to have a personality that fits your job. People high in openness earn more if they hold jobs that demand openness (actors), whereas people high in conscientiousness earn more if they work in jobs that require conscientiousness (financial managers) (Denissen et al., 2017).

Another study assessed 400,000 high school students' interests and then followed them over time. The take-home finding: "Interests uniquely predict academic and career success over and above cognitive ability and personality" (Rounds & Su, 2014). Sixty other studies confirm the point both for students in school and workers on the job: Interests predict both performance and persistence (Nye et al., 2012). Lack of job fit can fuel frustration, resulting in unproductive and even hostile work behavior (Harold et al., 2016). One fee-based online service, jobzology.com, was developed by industrial-organizational psychologists to implement career counseling science. First, it assesses people's interests, values, personalities, and workplace culture preferences. It then suggests occupations and connects them to job listings.

ENGAGE

ASK YOURSELF

What have you learned about your own strengths and about the kind of career you might see yourself pursuing?

Industrial-Organizational Psychology

LOQ B-2 What are three key areas of study related to industrial-organizational psychology?

In developed nations work has expanded, from farming to manufacturing to *knowledge work.* More and more work is *outsourced* to temporary employees and consultants, or to workers telecommuting from off-site workplaces (Allen, T. D., et al., 2015). (This book and its teaching package are developed and produced by a team of women and men in a dozen cities, from Alberta to Florida.) As work has changed, have our attitudes toward our work also changed? Has our satisfaction with work increased or decreased? Has the *psychological contract*—the sense of mutual obligations between workers and employers—become more or less trusting and secure? These are among the questions that fascinate **industrial-organizational (I/O) psychologists** as they apply psychology's principles to the workplace (**TABLE B.1**).

industrial-organizational (I/O) psychology the application of psychological concepts and methods to optimizing human behavior in workplaces.

TABLE B.1

I/O Psychology and Human Factors Psychology at Work

As scientists, consultants, and management professionals, industrial-organizational (I/O) psychologists may be found helping organizations to resolve work-family conflicts, build employee retention, address organizational climate, or promote teamwork. Human factors psychologists contribute to human safety and improved designs.

Personnel Psychology: Maximizing Human Potential	Organizational Psychology: Building Better Organizations
Developing training programs to increase job seekers' success	**Developing organizations**
	• Analyzing organizational structures
Selecting and placing employees	• Maximizing worker satisfaction and productivity
• Developing and testing assessment tools for selecting, placing, and promoting workers	• Facilitating organizational change
• Analyzing job content	**Enhancing quality of work life**
• Optimizing worker placement	• Expanding individual productivity
Training and developing employees	• Identifying elements of satisfaction
• Identifying needs	• Redesigning jobs
• Designing training programs	• Balancing work and nonwork life in an era of social media, smartphones, and other technologies
• Evaluating training programs	
Appraising performance	**Human Factors Psychology**
• Developing guidelines	• Designing optimum work environments
• Measuring individual performance	• Optimizing person-machine interactions
• Measuring organizational performance	• Developing systems technologies

Information from the Society of Industrial and Organizational Psychology. For more information about I/O psychology and related job opportunities, visit siop.org.

THE MODERN WORKFORCE The editorial team that guides, edits, and assesses this text and its resources works both in-house and from far-flung places. In column 1: Nancy Fleming in Massachusetts, Kathryn Brownson in Michigan, and Anna Munroe in New York. In column 2: Lorie Hailey in Kentucky, Trish Morgan in Alberta, Carlise Stembridge in Minnesota, and Laura Burden in New York. In column 3: Danielle Slevens in Massachusetts, Betty Probert in Florida, and Christine Brune in Washington, DC.

• The I/O psychology subfield of **personnel psychology** applies psychology's methods and principles to selecting, placing, training, and evaluating workers. Personnel psychologists match people with jobs by identifying and placing well-suited candidates. The **organizational psychology** subfield considers how work environments and management styles influence worker motivation, satisfaction, and productivity. It focuses on modifying jobs and supervision in ways that boost morale and productivity.

• **Human factors psychology,** now a distinct field allied with I/O psychology, explores how machines and environments can be optimally designed to fit human abilities. Human factors psychologists study people's natural perceptions and inclinations, using this research to create user-friendly machines and work settings.

RETRIEVE IT • • •   ANSWERS IN APPENDIX E

RI-1 What is the value of finding flow in our work?

⟳ Personnel Psychology

LOQ B-3 How do personnel psychologists facilitate job seeking, employee selection, work placement, and performance appraisal?

Psychologists assist organizations at various stages of selecting and assessing employees. They may help identify needed job skills, develop effective selection methods, recruit and evaluate diverse applicants, introduce and train new employees, appraise performance, and facilitate team building among people with differing cultural backgrounds. They also help job seekers. Across four dozen studies, training programs (which teach job-search skills, improve self-presentation, boost self-confidence, promote goal setting, and enlist support) have nearly tripled job-seekers' success (Liu et al., 2014).

Using Strengths for Successful Selection

As a new AT&T human resources executive, psychologist Mary Tenopyr (1997) was assigned to solve a problem: Customer-service representatives were failing at a high rate. After concluding that many of the hires were ill-matched to the demands of their new job, Tenopyr developed a new selection instrument:

1. She asked new applicants to respond to various test questions (without as yet making any use of their responses).

2. She followed up later to assess which of the applicants excelled on the job.

3. She identified the earlier test questions that best predicted success.

The happy result of her data-driven work was a new test that enabled AT&T to identify likely-to-succeed representatives. Personnel selection techniques such as this one aim to recruit people with the kind of strengths that will enable them and their organization to flourish. Marry the strengths of people with the tasks of organizations and the result is often prosperity and profit.

Do Interviews Predict Performance?

Employee selection usually includes an interview. And many interviewers feel confident of their ability to predict long-term job performance from a get-acquainted (*unstructured*) interview. What's therefore shocking is how error-prone interviewers' predictions may be when predicting job or graduate school success. Informal interviews are less informative than aptitude tests, work samples, job knowledge tests, and past job performance. After studying thousands of informal interviews and later job success, Google found "zero relationship. It's a complete random mess" (Bock, 2013). *Structured interviews,* however, can produce more accurate predictions.

Unstructured Interviews and the Interviewer Illusion

Traditional, *unstructured interviews* can provide a sense of someone's personality—their expressiveness, warmth, and verbal ability, for example. But these informal interviews also give interviewees considerable power to control the impression they are making in the interview situation (Barrick et al., 2009). Why, then, do many interviewers have such faith in their ability to discern interviewees' fitness for a job? "I have excellent interviewing skills," I/O psychology consultants often hear, "so I don't need reference checking as much as someone who doesn't have my ability to read people." Overrating one's ability to predict people's futures is called the *interviewer illusion* (Dana et al., 2013; Nisbett, 1987). Five factors explain interviewers' overconfidence:

- *Interviewers presume that people are what they seem to be in the interview situation.* An unstructured interview may create a false impression of a person's behavior toward others in different situations. Some interviewees may feign desired attitudes; others may be nervous. As personality psychologists explain, when meeting others, we discount the enormous influence of varying situations and mistakenly presume that what we see is what we will get. But research on everything from chattiness to conscientiousness reveals that how we behave reflects not only our enduring traits, but also the details of the particular situation (such as wanting to impress in a job interview).

- *Interviewers' preconceptions and moods color how they perceive interviewees' responses* (Cable & Gilovich, 1998; Macan & Dipboye, 1994). If interviewers instantly like a person who is similar to themselves (opening the door to unintended racial bias), they may interpret the person's assertiveness as indicating "confidence" rather than "arrogance." If told certain applicants have been prescreened, interviewers are disposed to judge them more favorably. Such interviewers are showing *confirmation bias* (see Chapter 9): They search for

personnel psychology an I/O psychology subfield that helps with job seeking, and with employee recruitment, selection, placement, training, appraisal, and development.

organizational psychology an I/O psychology subfield that examines organizational influences on worker satisfaction and productivity and facilitates organizational change.

human factors psychology a field of psychology allied with I/O psychology that explores how people and machines interact and how machines and physical environments can be made safe and easy to use.

information that supports their preconceptions about a job candidate and ignore or distort contradictory evidence (Skov & Sherman, 1986).

- *Interviewers judge people relative to those interviewed just before and after them* (Simonsohn & Gino, 2013). If you are being interviewed for a job or graduate program, hope for a day when the other interviewees have been weak.

- *Interviewers more often follow the successful careers of those they have hired than the successful careers of those they have rejected.* This missing feedback prevents interviewers from getting a reality check on their hiring ability.

- *Interviews disclose the interviewee's good intentions, which are less revealing than habitual behaviors* (Ouellette & Wood, 1998). Intentions matter. People can change. But the best predictor of the person we will be is the person we have been. Educational attainments predict job performance partly because people who make a habit of showing up for school each day and staying on task also tend to show up for work and stay on task (Ng & Feldman, 2009). Wherever we go, we take ourselves along.

Hoping to improve prediction and selection, personnel psychologists have put people in simulated work situations, sought information on past performance, aggregated evaluations from multiple interviews, administered tests, and developed job-specific interviews.

Structured Interviews

Unlike casual conversation aimed at getting a feel for someone, **structured interviews** offer a disciplined method of collecting information. A personnel psychologist may analyze a job, script questions, and train interviewers. The interviewers then ask all applicants the same questions, in the same order, and rate each applicant on established scales.

In an unstructured interview, someone might ask, "How organized are you?" "How well do you get along with people?" or "How do you handle stress?" Street-smart applicants know how to score high: "Although I sometimes drive myself too hard, I handle stress by prioritizing and delegating, and leaving time for sleep and exercise."

By contrast, structured interviews pinpoint strengths (attitudes, behaviors, knowledge, and skills) that distinguish high performers in a particular line of work. The process includes outlining job-specific situations and asking candidates to explain how they would handle them, and how they handled similar situations in their prior employment. "Tell me about a time when you were caught between conflicting demands, without time to accomplish both. How did you handle that?" In its interviews, Google has asked, "Give me an example of a time when you solved an analytically difficult problem."

To reduce memory distortions and bias, the interviewer takes notes and makes ratings as the interview proceeds and avoids irrelevant and follow-up questions. The structured interview therefore feels less warm, but that can be explained to the applicant: "This conversation won't typify how we relate to each other in this organization."

A review of 150 findings revealed that structured interviews had double the predictive accuracy of unstructured interviews (Schmidt & Hunter, 1998; Wiesner & Cronshaw, 1988). Structured interviews also reduce bias, such as against overweight applicants (Kutcher & Bragger, 2004).

If, instead, we let our intuitions bias the hiring process, noted writer Malcolm Gladwell (2000, p. 86), then "all we will have done is replace the old-boy network, where you hired your nephew, with the new-boy network, where you hire whoever impressed you most when you shook his hand. Social progress, unless we're careful, can merely be the means by which we replace the obviously arbitrary with the not so obviously arbitrary."

To recap, personnel psychologists help train job seekers, and they assist organizations in analyzing jobs, recruiting well-suited applicants, and selecting and placing employees. They also appraise employees' performance (**FIGURE B.1**)—our next topic.

Appraising Performance

Performance appraisal serves organizational purposes: It helps decide who to keep on staff, how to appropriately reward and pay people, and how to better harness employee strengths, sometimes with job shifts or promotions. Performance appraisal also serves individual purposes: Feedback affirms workers' strengths and helps motivate needed improvement.

"Between the idea / And the reality . . . / Falls the Shadow." —T. S. Eliot, *The Hollow Men*, 1925

structured interview an interview process that asks the same job-relevant questions of all applicants, each of whom is rated on established scales.

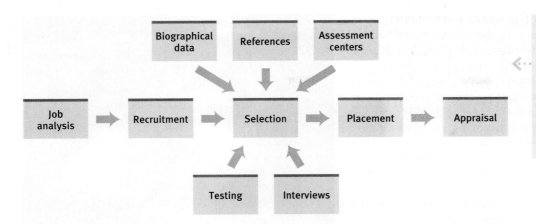

FIGURE B.1

PERSONNEL PSYCHOLOGISTS AT WORK Personnel psychologists consult in human resources activities, from job definition to recruitment to employee appraisal. The assessment center approach (see Chapter 9) may be used to evaluate potential and existing employees.

Performance appraisal methods include

- *checklists* on which supervisors simply check specific behaviors that describe the worker ("always attends to customers' needs"; "takes long breaks").
- *graphic rating scales* on which a supervisor checks, perhaps on a five-point scale, how often a worker is dependable, productive, and so forth.
- *behavior rating scales* on which a supervisor checks scaled behaviors that describe a worker's performance. If rating the extent to which a worker "follows procedures," the supervisor might mark the employee somewhere between "often takes shortcuts" and "always follows established procedures" (Levy, 2003).

In some organizations, performance feedback comes not only from supervisors but also from all organizational levels. If you join an organization that practices *360-degree feedback* (**FIGURE B.2**), you will rate yourself, your manager, and your other colleagues, and you will be rated by your manager, other colleagues, and customers (Green, 2002). The net result is often more open communication and more complete appraisal.

Performance appraisal, like other social judgments, is vulnerable to bias (Murphy & Cleveland, 1995). *Halo errors* occur when one's overall evaluation of an employee, or of a personal trait such as their friendliness, biases ratings of their specific work-related behaviors, such as their reliability. *Leniency* and *severity errors* reflect evaluators' tendencies to be either too easy or too harsh on everyone. *Recency errors* occur when raters focus only on easily remembered recent behavior. By using multiple raters and developing objective, job-relevant performance measures, personnel psychologists seek to support their organizations while also helping employees perceive the appraisal process as fair.

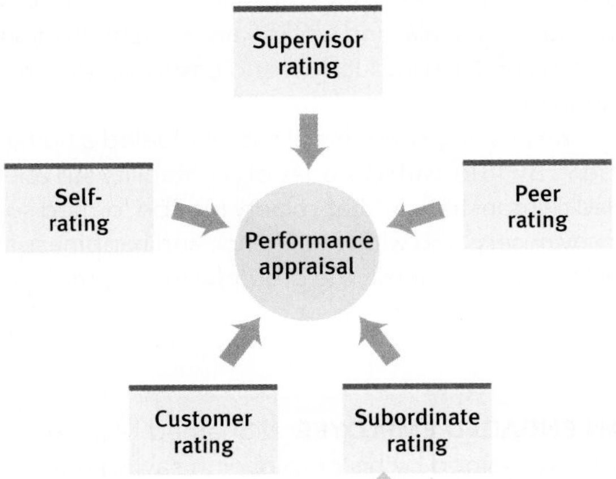

FIGURE B.2

360-DEGREE FEEDBACK With multisource 360-degree feedback, our knowledge, skills, and behaviors are rated by ourselves and surrounding others. Professors, for example, may be rated by their department chairs, their students, and their colleagues. After receiving all these ratings, professors discuss the 360-degree feedback with their department chair.

🔒 **RETRIEVE IT • • •**   *ANSWERS IN APPENDIX E*

RI-2 A human resources director explains to you that "I don't bother with tests or references. It's all about the interview." Based on I/O psychology research, what concerns does this raise?

⤳ Organizational Psychology

LOQ B-4 What is the role of organizational psychologists?

Recruiting, hiring, training, and appraising capable and diverse workers matters, but so does employee motivation and morale. Organizational psychologists assist with efforts to motivate and engage employees.

DOING WELL WHILE DOING GOOD—"THE GREAT EXPERIMENT"

At the end of the 1700s, the New Lanark, Scotland, cotton mill had more than 1000 workers. Many were children drawn from Glasgow's poorhouses. They worked 13-hour days and lived in grim conditions.

On a visit to Glasgow, Welsh-born Robert Owen—an idealistic young cotton-mill manager—chanced to meet and marry the mill owner's daughter. Owen and some partners purchased the mill and on the first day of the 1800s began what he called "the most important experiment for the happiness of the human race that had yet been instituted at any time in any part of the world" (Owen, 1814). The exploitation of child and adult labor was, he observed, producing unhappy and inefficient workers. Owen showed *transformational leadership* when he undertook numerous innovations: a nursery for preschool children, education for older children (with encouragement rather than corporal punishment), Sundays off, health care, paid sick days, unemployment pay for days when the mill could not operate, and a company store selling goods at reduced prices. He also innovated a goals- and worker-assessment program that included detailed records of daily productivity and costs but with "no beating, no abusive language."

The ensuing commercial success fueled a humanitarian reform movement. By 1816, with decades of profitability still ahead, Owen believed he had demonstrated "that society may be formed so as to exist without crime, without poverty, with health greatly improved, with little if any misery, and with intelligence and happiness increased a hundredfold." Although his utopian vision has not been fulfilled, Owen's great experiment laid the groundwork for employment practices that have today become accepted in much of the world.

Courtesy of New Lanark Trust

AN ENGAGED EMPLOYEE Mohamed Mamow, left, was joined by his employer in saying the Pledge of Allegiance as he became a U.S. citizen. Mamow and his wife met in a Somali refugee camp and have five children, whom he has supported by working as a machine operator. Mindful of his responsibility—"I don't like to lose my job. I have a responsibility for my children and my family"—he would arrive for work a half hour early and tend to every detail on his shift. "He is an extremely hard-working employee," noted his employer, and "a reminder to all of us that we are really blessed" (Roelofs, 2010).

MLive/Advance/Barcroft Media

Satisfaction and Engagement at Work

I/O psychologists have found that satisfaction with work, and with work-life balance, feeds overall satisfaction with life (Bowling et al., 2010). Married people with supportive spouses often enjoy a healthy balance between work and home life, with success in both arenas (Solomon & Jackson, 2014). Moreover, as health psychologists tell us, lower job stress, sometimes supported by telecommuting, feeds better health (Allen, T. D., et al., 2015).

Satisfied employees also contribute to successful organizations. Positive moods at work enhance creativity, persistence, and helpfulness (Ford et al., 2011; Jeffrey et al., 2014; Shockley et al., 2012). Are engaged, happy workers also less often absent? Less likely to quit? Less prone to theft? More punctual? More productive? Statistical digests of prior research have found a modest positive correlation between individual job satisfaction and performance (Judge et al., 2001; Ng et al., 2009; Parker et al., 2003). In one analysis of 4500 employees at 42 British manufacturing companies, the most productive workers were those who found their work environment satisfying (Patterson et al., 2004).

Some organizations seem to have a knack for cultivating more engaged and productive employees. In the United States, *Fortune's* "100 Best Companies to Work For" have also produced markedly higher-than-average returns for their investors (Fulmer et al., 2003). And consider a study of more than 198,000 employees in nearly 8000 business units of 36 large companies (including some 1100 bank branches, 1200 stores, and 4200 teams or departments). James Harter, Frank Schmidt, and Theodore Hayes (2002) explored correlations between various measures of organizational success and *employee engagement*—the extent of workers' involvement, enthusiasm, and identification with their organizations (**TABLE B.2**). They found that engaged workers (compared with disengaged workers who are just putting in their time) knew what was expected of them, had what they needed to do their work, felt fulfilled in their work, had regular opportunities to do what they do best, perceived that they were part of something significant, and had opportunities to learn and develop. They also found that business units with engaged employees had more loyal customers, lower turnover rates, higher productivity, and greater profits.

TASK SIGNIFICANCE People find their work meaningful and engaging when it has "task significance"—when they view their work as benefiting others (Allan, 2017).

TABLE B.2
Three Types of Employees

Engaged: working with passion and feeling a profound connection to their company or organization.

Not engaged: putting in the time but investing little passion or energy in their work.

Actively disengaged: unhappy workers undermining what their colleagues accomplish.

Information from Gallup via Crabtree, 2005.

But what causal arrows explain this correlation between business success and employee morale and engagement? Does success boost morale, or does high morale boost success? In a follow-up longitudinal study of 142,000 workers, researchers found that, over time, employee attitudes predicted *future* business success (more than the other way around) (Harter et al., 2010). Many other studies confirm that happy workers tend to be good workers (Ford et al., 2011; Seibert et al., 2011; Shockley et al., 2012). One analysis compared companies with top-quartile versus below-average employee engagement levels. Over a three-year period, earnings grew 2.6 times faster for the companies with highly engaged workers (Ott, 2007). It pays to have employees engaged.

Effective Leadership

LOQ B-5 How can leaders be most effective?

Great managers support employees' well-being, articulate goals clearly, and lead in ways that suit the situation and consider the cultural context.

Setting Specific, Challenging Goals

Measurable objectives, such as "finish gathering the history paper information by Friday," focus our attention and stimulate us to persist and to be creative. Goals motivate achievement, especially when combined with progress reports (Harkin et al., 2016). For many people, a landmark in time—a special birthday, the new year or new school term, graduation, a new job—spurs personal goal setting (Dai et al., 2014). Action plans that break large goals into smaller steps (*subgoals*) and that specify *implementation intentions*—when, where, and how to achieve those steps—increase the chances of completing a project on time (Fishbach et al., 2006; Gollwitzer & Sheeran, 2006). Through a task's ups and downs, we best sustain our mood and motivation when we focus on immediate goals (such as daily study) rather than distant goals (such as a course grade). Better to have our nose to the grindstone than our eye on the ultimate prize (Houser-Marko & Sheldon, 2008).

THE POWER OF POSITIVE COACHING Football coach Pete Carroll, who led the University of Southern California to two national championships and the Seattle Seahawks to a Super Bowl championship, combined positive enthusiasm and fun workouts with "a commitment to a nurturing environment that allows people to be themselves while still being accountable to the team" (Trotter, 2014). "It shows you can win with positivity," noted Seahawks star defensive player Richard Sherman. "It's literally all positive reinforcement," said teammate Jimmy Graham (Belson, 2015).

leadership an individual's ability to motivate and influence others to contribute to their group's success.

task leadership goal-oriented leadership that sets standards, organizes work, and focuses attention on goals.

social leadership group-oriented leadership that builds teamwork, mediates conflict, and offers support.

"Good leaders don't ask more than their constituents can give, but they often ask—and get—more than their constituents intended to give or thought it was possible to give."
—John W. Gardner, *Excellence*, 1984

Thus, before beginning each new edition of this book, our author-editor-staff team *manages by objectives*—we agree on target dates for the completion and editing of each chapter draft. If we focus on achieving each of these short-term goals, then the prize—an on-time book—takes care of itself. So, to motivate high productivity, effective leaders work with people to define explicit goals, subgoals, and implementation plans, and then provide feedback on progress.

Choosing an Appropriate Leadership Style

Effective leaders of laboratory groups, work teams, and large corporations often exude *charisma* (Goethals & Allison, 2014; House & Singh, 1987; Shamir et al., 1993). People with charisma have the capacity to inspire others' loyalty and to focus their enthusiasm (Grabo & van Vugt, 2016).

Charismatic leaders' ability to inspire can bolster **leadership**—the ability to motivate and influence people to enable their group's success. Leadership styles vary, depending both on the leader and the situation. In some situations (think of a commander leading troops into battle), a *directive* style may be needed (Fiedler, 1981). In other situations—developing a comedy show, for example—a leader might get better results using a *democratic* style that welcomes team member creativity.

Leaders differ in the personal qualities they bring to the job. Some excel at **task leadership**—by setting standards, organizing work, and focusing attention on goals. To keep the group centered on its mission, task leaders typically use a directive style, which can work well if the leader gives good directions (Fiedler, 1987).

Other managers excel at **social leadership**. They explain decisions, help group members solve their conflicts, and build teams that work well together (Evans & Dion, 1991; Pfaff et al., 2013). Social leaders, many of whom are women, often have a democratic style. They share authority and welcome team members' opinions. Social leadership and team-building increases morale and productivity (Shuffler et al., 2011, 2013). We usually feel more satisfied and motivated, and perform better, when we can participate in decision making (Cawley et al., 1998; Pereira & Osburn, 2007). Moreover, when members are sensitive to one another and participate equally, groups solve problems with greater "collective intelligence" (Woolley et al., 2010).

In one study of 50 Dutch companies, the firms with the highest morale had chief executives who most inspired their colleagues "to transcend their own self-interests for the sake of the collective" (de Hoogh et al., 2004). *Transformational leadership* of this kind motivates others to identify with and commit themselves to the group's mission. Transformational leaders, many of whom are natural extraverts, articulate high standards, inspire people to share their vision, and offer personal attention (Bono & Judge, 2004). The frequent result is more engaged, trusting, and effective workers (Turner et al., 2002). Women more than men tend to exhibit transformational leadership qualities. Alice Eagly (2007, 2013) believes this helps explain why companies with female top managers have tended to enjoy superior financial results, even after controlling for such variables as company size.

Studies in India, Taiwan, and Iran suggest that effective managers—whether in coal mines, banks, or government offices—often exhibit a high degree of *both* task and social leadership

(Smith & Tayeb, 1989). As achievement-minded people, effective managers certainly care about how well work is done, yet they are sensitive to their subordinates' needs. Workers in family-friendly organizations that offer flexible hours report feeling greater job satisfaction and loyalty to their employers (Butts et al., 2013; Roehling et al., 2001). Over time, U.S. senators who practice common virtues (humility, wisdom, courage) become more influential in leadership roles than do those who practice manipulation and intimidation (ten Brinke et al., 2016). Social virtues work.

POSITIVE REINFORCEMENT Effective leadership often builds on a basic principle of *operant conditioning:* To teach a behavior, catch a person doing something right and reinforce it. It sounds simple, but many managers are like parents who, when a child brings home a near-perfect school report card, focus on the one low grade in a troublesome biology class and ignore the rest. "Sixty-five percent of Americans received NO praise or recognition in the workplace last year," reported the Gallup organization (2004).

FULFILLING THE NEED TO BELONG A work environment that satisfies employees' need to belong is energizing. Employees who enjoy high-quality colleague relationships engage their work with more vigor (Carmeli et al., 2009). Gallup researchers have asked more than 15 million employees worldwide if they have a "best friend at work." The 30 percent who do "are *seven times* as likely to be engaged in their jobs" as those who don't, researchers report (Rath & Harter, 2010). And, as we noted earlier, positive, engaged employees are a mark of thriving organizations.

PARTICIPATIVE MANAGEMENT Employee participation in decision making is common in Sweden, Japan, the United States, and elsewhere (Cawley et al., 1998; Sundstrom et al., 1990). Workers given a chance to voice their opinion and be part of the decision-making process have responded more positively to the final decision (van den Bos & Spruijt, 2002). They also feel more empowered, and are likely, therefore, to be more creative and committed (Hennessey & Amabile, 2010; Seibert et al., 2011).

The ultimate in employee participation is the employee-owned company. One such company in my [DM's] town is the Fleetwood Group—a thriving 165-employee manufacturer of educational furniture and wireless electronic clickers. Every employee owns part of the company, and as a group they own 100 percent. The more years employees work, the more they own, yet no one owns more than 5 percent. Like every corporate president, Fleetwood's president works for his stockholders—who also just happen to be his employees.

As a company that endorses faith-inspired "respect and care for each team member-owner," Fleetwood is free to place people above profits. Thus, when orders lagged during a recession, the employee-owners decided that job security meant more to them than profits. So the company paid otherwise idle workers to do community service, such as answering phones at nonprofit agencies and building Habitat for Humanity houses. Employee ownership attracts and retains talented people, which for Fleetwood has meant company success.

Cultural Influences on Leadership Styles

LOQ B-6 What cultural influences need to be considered when choosing an effective leadership style?

I/O psychology sprang from North American roots. So, how well do its leadership principles apply to cultures worldwide?

Investigators worldwide have undertaken Project GLOBE (Global Leadership and Organizational Behavior Effectiveness) to study cultural variations in leadership expectations (House et al., 2001). Some cultures, for example, encourage collective sharing of resources and rewards; others are more individualist. Some cultures minimize and others accentuate traditional gender roles. Some cultures prioritize being friendly, caring, and kind, and others encourage aggressiveness. The program's first research phase studied 17,300 leaders of 950 organizations in 61 countries (Brodbeck et al., 2008; Dorfman et al., 2012). One finding: Leaders who fulfill expectations, such as by being directive in some cultures or participative in others, tend to be successful. Cultures shape leadership and what makes for leadership success.

Nevertheless, some leader behaviors are universally effective. From its massive study of nearly 50,000 business units in 45 countries, the Gallup Organization observed that thriving companies tend to focus on identifying and enhancing employee *strengths* (rather than punishing their deficiencies). Doing so predicts increased employee engagement, customer satisfaction, and profitability (Rigoni & Asplund, 2016a,b). "Strengths-based" leadership pays dividends, supporting happier, more creative, more productive workers with less absenteeism and turnover (Amabile & Kramer, 2011; De Neve et al., 2013). Moreover, the same principles affect student satisfaction, retention, and future success (Larkin et al., 2013; Ray & Kafka, 2014). Students who feel supported by caring friends and mentors, and engaged in their campus life, tend to persist and ultimately succeed during school and after graduation.

* * *

We have considered *personnel psychology* (the I/O psychology subfield that focuses on training job seekers and assisting with employee selection, placement, appraisal, and development). And we have considered *organizational psychology* (the I/O psychology subfield that focuses on worker satisfaction and productivity, and on organizational change). Finally, we turn to *human factors psychology,* which explores the human-machine interface.

🔒 RETRIEVE IT • • •
ANSWERS IN APPENDIX E

RI-3 What characteristics are important for *transformational leaders*?

⤳ Human Factors Psychology

LOQ B-7   How do human factors psychologists work to create user-friendly machines and work settings?

Designs sometimes neglect the human factor. Cognitive scientist Donald Norman (2001) bemoaned the complexity of assembling his new HDTV, related components, and seven remotes into a usable home theater system: "I was VP of Advanced Technology at Apple. I can program dozens of computers in dozens of languages. I understand television, really, I do. . . . It doesn't matter: I am overwhelmed."

Human factors psychologists work with designers and engineers to tailor appliances, machines, and work settings to our natural perceptions and inclinations. Bank ATM machines are internally more complex than remote controls ever were, yet thanks to human factors engineering, ATMs are easier to operate. Digital recorders have solved the TV recording problem with a simple select-and-click menu system ("record that one"). Apple similarly engineered easy usability with the iPhone and iPad. Handheld and wearable technologies are increasingly making use of *haptic* (touch-based) feedback—opening a phone with a thumbprint, sharing your heartbeat via a smartwatch, or having GPS directional instructions ("turn left" arrow) "drawn" on your skin with other wrist-worn devices.

Norman hosts a website (jnd.org) that illustrates good designs that fit people (**FIGURE B.3**). Human factors psychologists also help design efficient environments. An ideal kitchen layout, researchers have found, puts needed items close to their usage point and near eye level. It locates work areas to enable doing tasks in order, such as placing the refrigerator, stove, and sink in a triangle. It creates counters that enable hands to work at or slightly below elbow height (Boehm-Davis, 2005).

Understanding human factors can help prevent accidents. By studying the human factor in driving accidents, psychologists seek to devise ways to reduce the distractions, fatigue, and inattention that contribute to 1.25 million annual worldwide traffic fatalities (WHO, 2016a). At least two-thirds of commercial air accidents have been caused by human error (Shappell et al., 2007). After beginning commercial flights in the 1960s, the Boeing 727 was involved in several landing accidents caused by pilot error. Psychologist Conrad Kraft (1978) noted a common context for these

ASK YOURSELF

In what type of leadership role do you think you would most excel? How could you grow to become a more effective leader?

FIGURE B.3

DESIGNING PRODUCTS THAT FIT PEOPLE Human factors expert Donald Norman offers these and other examples of effectively designed products. The Ride On Carry On foldable chair attachment, "designed by a flight attendant mom," enables a small suitcase to double as a stroller. The OXO measuring cup allows the user to see the quantity from above.

Ride On Carry On

OXO Good Grips

accidents: All took place at night, and all involved landing short of the runway after crossing a dark stretch of water or unilluminated ground. Kraft reasoned that, on rising terrain, city lights beyond the runway would project a larger retinal image, making the ground seem farther away than it was. By re-creating these conditions in flight simulations, Kraft discovered that pilots were deceived into thinking they were flying higher than their actual altitudes (**FIGURE B.4**). Aided by Kraft's finding, airlines began requiring the co-pilot to monitor the altimeter—calling out altitudes during the descent—and the accidents diminished.

Human factors psychologists can also help us to function in other settings. Consider the available *assistive listening* technologies in various theaters, auditoriums, and places of worship. One technology, commonly available in the United States, requires a headset attached to a pocket-sized receiver. The well-meaning people who provide these systems correctly understand that the technology puts sound directly into the user's ears. Alas, few people with hearing loss elect the hassle and embarrassment of locating, requesting, wearing, and returning a conspicuous headset. Most such units therefore sit in closets. Britain, the Scandinavian countries, Australia, and now many parts of the United States have instead installed *loop systems* (see HearingLoop.org) that broadcast customized sound directly through a person's own hearing aid. When suitably equipped, a hearing aid can be transformed by a discreet touch of a switch into a customized in-the-ear speaker. When offered convenient, inconspicuous, personalized sound, many more people elect to use assistive listening.

Designs that enable safe, easy, and effective interactions between people and technology often seem obvious after the fact. Why, then, aren't they more common? Technology developers, like all of us, sometimes mistakenly assume that others share their expertise—that what's clear to them will similarly be clear to others (Camerer et al., 1989; Nickerson, 1999). When people rap their knuckles on a table to convey a familiar tune (try this with a friend), they often expect their listener to recognize it. But for the listener, this is a near-impossible task (Newton, 1991). When you know a thing, it's hard to mentally simulate what it's like not to know, and that is called the *curse of knowledge*.

The point to remember: Everyone benefits when designers and engineers tailor machines, technologies, and environments to fit human abilities and behaviors, when they user-test their work before production and distribution, and when they remain mindful of the curse of knowledge.

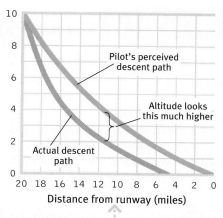

FIGURE B.4

THE HUMAN FACTOR IN ACCIDENTS Lacking distance cues when approaching a runway from over a dark surface, pilots simulating a night landing tended to fly too low. (Data from Kraft, 1978.)

"The better you know something, the less you remember about how hard it was to learn." —Psychologist Steven Pinker, *The Sense of Style*, 2014

ASK YOURSELF

What situations have you experienced (using new technology, visiting buildings, using transportation) in which the design did not work well? What situations have you experienced in which planners did a particularly good job matching machines and physical environments to our abilities and expectations?

THE HUMAN FACTOR IN SAFE LANDINGS Advanced cockpit design and rehearsed emergency procedures aided pilot Chesley "Sully" Sullenberger, a U.S. Air Force Academy graduate who earned a Master's degree in industrial psychology. In 2009, Sullenberger's instantaneous decisions safely guided his disabled airplane onto New York City's Hudson River, where all 155 of the passengers and crew were safely evacuated.

🔒 RETRIEVE IT • • •

ANSWERS IN APPENDIX E

RI-4 What is the *curse of knowledge*, and what does it have to do with the work of human factors psychologists?

🔒 REVIEW REVIEW PSYCHOLOGY AT WORK

⟫ Learning Objectives

TEST YOURSELF Answer these repeated Learning Objective Questions on your own (before checking the answers in Appendix D) to improve your retention of the concepts (McDaniel et al., 2009, 2015).

B-1 What is *flow*?

B-2 What are three key areas of study related to industrial-organizational psychology?

B-3 How do personnel psychologists facilitate job seeking, employee selection, work placement, and performance appraisal?

B-4 What is the role of organizational psychologists?

B-5 How can leaders be most effective?

B-6 What cultural influences need to be considered when choosing an effective leadership style?

B-7 How do human factors psychologists work to create user-friendly machines and work settings?

⟫ Terms and Concepts to Remember

TEST YOURSELF Write down the definition yourself, then check your answer on the referenced page.

flow, **p. B-1**

industrial-organizational (I/O) psychology, **p. B-3**

personnel psychology, **p. B-5**

organizational psychology, **p. B-5**

human factors psychology, **p. B-5**

structured interview, **p. B-6**

leadership, **p. B-10**

task leadership, **p. B-10**

social leadership, **p. B-10**

⟫ Experience the Testing Effect

TEST YOURSELF Answer the following questions on your own first, then check your answers in Appendix E.

1. People who view their work as a calling often experience _____, a focused state of consciousness, with diminished awareness of themselves and of time.

2. _____ psychologists assist with job seeking, and the recruitment, selection, placement, training, appraisal, and development of employees; _____ _____ psychologists focus on how people and machines interact, and on optimizing devices and work environments.

3. A personnel psychologist scripted a set of questions to ask all applicants for a job opening. She then trained the firm's interviewers to ask only those questions, to take notes, and to rate applicants' responses. This technique is known as a(n)

   a. structured interview.

   b. unstructured interview.

   c. performance appraisal checklist.

   d. behavior rating scale.

4. In your job, you rate your own performance, your manager's, and your peers'. Your manager, your peers, and your customers also rate your performance. Your organization is using a form of performance appraisal called

   a. flow procedure.   c. structured interviews.

   b. graphic feedback.   d. 360-degree feedback

5. What type of goals will best help you stay focused and motivated to do your finest work in this class?

6. Research indicates that women are often social leaders. They are also more likely than men to have a _____ leadership style.

7. Effective managers often exhibit

   a. only task leadership.

   b. only social leadership.

   c. both task and social leadership, depending on the situation and the person.

   d. task leadership for building teams and social leadership for setting standards.

8. Human factors psychologists focus primarily on

   a. training and developing employees.

   b. appraising employee performance.

   c. maximizing worker satisfaction.

   d. improving the design of machines and environments.

Continue testing yourself with 📚 **LearningCurve** or ≈ **Achieve Read &**
Practice to learn and remember most effectively.

Career Fields in Psychology

APPENDIX C

Jennifer Zwolinski
University of San Diego

What can you do with a degree in psychology? Lots!

As a psychology major, you will graduate with a scientific mindset and an awareness of basic principles of human behavior (biological mechanisms, nature–nurture interactions, life-span development, cognition, psychological disorders, social interaction). This background will prepare you for success in many areas, including business, the helping professions, health services, marketing, law, sales, and teaching. You may even go on to graduate school for specialized training to become a psychology professional. This appendix provides an overview of some of psychology's key career fields.[1] For more detailed information, see *Pursuing a Psychology Career* in LaunchPad (LaunchPadWorks.com), where you can learn more about the many interesting options available to those with bachelor's, master's, and doctoral degrees in psychology.

If you are like most psychology students, you may be unaware of the wide variety of specialties and work settings available in psychology (Terre & Stoddart, 2000). To date, the American Psychological Association (APA) has 54 divisions (**TABLE C.1**) that represent the popular subfields and interest groups of APA members. APA Division 2 (Society for the Teaching of Psychology) offers an excellent career exploration resource for those interested in learning about the hundreds of career options available for students with an undergraduate degree in psychology.

The following paragraphs (arranged alphabetically) describe some of psychology's main career fields, most of which require a graduate degree in psychology.

CLINICAL PSYCHOLOGISTS promote psychological health in individuals, groups, and organizations. Some clinical psychologists specialize in specific psychological disorders. Others treat a range of disorders, from adjustment difficulties to severe psychopathology. Clinical psychologists often provide therapy but may also engage in research, teaching, assessment, and consultation. Clinical psychologists work in a variety of settings, including private practice, mental health service organizations, schools, universities, industries, legal systems, medical systems, counseling centers, government agencies, correctional facilities, nonprofit organizations, and military services.

To become a clinical psychologist, you will need to earn a doctorate from a clinical psychology program. The APA sets the standards for clinical psychology graduate programs, offering accreditation (official recognition) to those who meet their standards. In all U.S. states, clinical psychologists working in independent practice must obtain a license to offer services such as therapy and testing.

COGNITIVE PSYCHOLOGISTS study thought processes and focus on such topics as perception, language, attention, problem solving, memory, judgment and decision making, forgetting, and intelligence. Research interests include designing computer-based models of thought processes and identifying biological correlates of cognition. As a cognitive psychologist, you might work as a professor, industrial consultant, or human factors specialist in an educational or business setting.

COMMUNITY PSYCHOLOGISTS move beyond focusing on specific individuals or families and deal with broad problems of mental health in community settings. These psychologists believe that human behavior is powerfully influenced by the interaction between people and their physical, social, political, and economic environments.

Karen Moskowitz/The Image Bank/Getty Images

COGNITIVE CONSULTING Cognitive psychologists may advise businesses on how to operate more effectively by understanding the human factors involved.

---

1. Although this text covers the world of psychology for students in many countries, this appendix draws primarily from available U.S. data. Its descriptions of psychology's career fields are, however, also applicable in many other countries.

C-1

TABLE C.1

APA Divisions by Number and Name

1. Society for General Psychology	29. Society for the Advancement of Psychotherapy
2. Society for the Teaching of Psychology	30. Society of Psychological Hypnosis
3. Society for Experimental Psychology and Cognitive Science	31. State, Provincial, and Territorial Psychological Association Affairs
4. *There is no active Division 4.*	32. Society for Humanistic Psychology
5. Quantitative and Qualitative Methods	33. Intellectual and Developmental Disabilities/Autism Spectrum Disorder
6. Society for Behavioral Neuroscience and Comparative Psychology	34. Society for Environmental, Population, and Conservation Psychology
7. Developmental Psychology	35. Society for the Psychology of Women
8. Society for Personality and Social Psychology	36. Society for the Psychology of Religion and Spirituality
9. Society for the Psychological Study of Social Issues (SPSSI)	37. Society for Child and Family Policy and Practice
10. Society for the Psychology of Aesthetics, Creativity, and the Arts	38. Society for Health Psychology
11. *There is no active Division 11.*	39. Psychoanalysis
12. Society of Clinical Psychology	40. Society for Clinical Neuropsychology
13. Society of Consulting Psychology	41. American Psychology-Law Society
14. Society for Industrial and Organizational Psychology	42. Psychologists in Independent Practice
15. Educational Psychology	43. Society for Couple and Family Psychology
16. School Psychology	44. Society for the Psychology of Sexual Orientation and Gender Diversity
17. Society of Counseling Psychology	45. Society for the Psychological Study of Culture, Ethnicity, and Race
18. Psychologists in Public Service	46. Society for Media Psychology and Technology
19. Society for Military Psychology	47. Society for Sport, Exercise, and Performance Psychology
20. Adult Development and Aging	48. Society for the Study of Peace, Conflict, and Violence: Peace Psychology Division
21. Applied Experimental and Engineering Psychology	49. Society of Group Psychology and Group Psychotherapy
22. Rehabilitation Psychology	50. Society of Addiction Psychology
23. Society for Consumer Psychology	51. Society for the Psychological Study of Men and Masculinity
24. Society for Theoretical and Philosophical Psychology	52. International Psychology
25. Behavior Analysis	53. Society of Clinical Child and Adolescent Psychology
26. Society for the History of Psychology	54. Society of Pediatric Psychology
27. Society for Community Research and Action: Division of Community Psychology	55. American Society for the Advancement of Pharmacotherapy
28. Psychopharmacology and Substance Abuse	56. Trauma Psychology

Source: American Psychological Association

They seek to promote psychological health by enhancing environmental settings—focusing on preventive measures and crisis intervention, with special attention to the problems of underserved groups and ethnic minorities. Some community psychologists collaborate with professionals in other areas, such as public health, with a shared emphasis on prevention. As a community psychologist, your work settings could include federal, state, and local departments of mental health, corrections, and welfare. You might conduct research or help evaluate research in health service settings, serve as an independent consultant for a private or government agency, or teach and consult as a college or university faculty member.

COUNSELING PSYCHOLOGISTS help people adjust to life transitions or make lifestyle changes. Although similar to clinical psychologists, counseling psychologists typically help people with adjustment problems rather than severe psychopathology. Like clinical psychologists, counseling psychologists conduct therapy and provide assessments to individuals and groups. As a counseling psychologist, you would likely emphasize your clients' strengths, helping them to use their own skills, interests, and abilities to cope during transitions. You might find yourself working in an academic setting as a faculty member or administrator or in a university counseling center, community mental health center, business, or

COMMUNITY CARE Community psychologists in Haiti have helped residents work through the ongoing emotional challenges that followed the devastating 2010 earthquake and the widely destructive 2016 hurricane.

private practice. As with clinical psychology, if you plan to work in independent practice you will need to obtain a state license to provide counseling services to the public.

DEVELOPMENTAL PSYCHOLOGISTS conduct research on age-related behavioral changes and apply their scientific knowledge to educational, child-care, policy, and related settings. As a developmental psychologist, you would investigate change across a broad range of topics, including the biological, psychological, cognitive, and social aspects of development. Developmental psychology informs a number of applied fields, including educational psychology, school psychology, child psychopathology, and gerontology. The field also informs public policy in areas such as education and child-care reform, maternal and child health, and attachment and adoption. You would probably specialize in a specific stage of the life span, such as infancy, childhood, adolescence, or middle or late adulthood. Your work setting could be an educational institution, day-care center, youth group program, or senior center.

EDUCATIONAL PSYCHOLOGISTS are interested in the psychological processes involved in learning. They study the relationship between learning and the physical and social environments, and they develop strategies for enhancing the learning process. As an educational psychologist, working in a university psychology department or school of education, you might conduct basic research on topics related to learning, or develop innovative methods of teaching to enhance the learning process. You might design effective tests, including measures of aptitude and achievement. You might be employed by a school or government agency or charged with designing and implementing effective employee-training programs in a business setting.

ENVIRONMENTAL PSYCHOLOGISTS study the interaction of individuals with their natural and built (urban) environments. They are interested in how we influence and are affected by these environments. As an environmental psychologist, you might study wildlife conservation, the impact of urbanization on health, or cognitive factors involved in sustainable lifestyle choices. Environmental psychologists tend to address these kinds of questions by working with other professionals as part of an interdisciplinary team. As an environmental psychologist, you might work in a consulting firm, an academic setting, the nonprofit sector, or the government.

EXPERIMENTAL PSYCHOLOGISTS are a diverse group of scientists who investigate a variety of basic behavioral processes in humans and other animals. Prominent areas of experimental research include comparative methods of science, motivation, learning, thought, attention, memory, perception, and language. Most experimental psychologists identify with a particular subfield, such as cognitive psychology, depending on their interests and training. Experimental research methods are not limited to the field of experimental psychology; many other subfields rely on experimental methodology to conduct studies. As an experimental psychologist, you would most likely work in an academic setting, teaching courses and supervising students' research in addition to conducting your own research. Or you might be employed by a research institution, zoo, business, or government agency.

FORENSIC PSYCHOLOGISTS apply psychological principles to legal issues. They conduct research on the interface of law and psychology, help to create public policies related to mental health, help law-enforcement agencies in criminal investigations, or consult on jury selection and deliberation processes. They also provide assessment to assist the legal community. Although most forensic psychologists are clinical psychologists, many have expertise in other areas of psychology, such as social or cognitive psychology. Some also hold law degrees. As a forensic psychologist, you might

CRIMINAL INVESTIGATION Forensic psychologists may be called on to assist police officers who are investigating a crime scene, as seen here after a shooting in Florida. Most forensic work, however, occurs in the lab and for the judicial system.

work in a university psychology department, law school, research organization, community mental health agency, law-enforcement agency, court, or correctional setting.

HEALTH PSYCHOLOGISTS are researchers and practitioners concerned with psychology's contribution to promoting health and preventing disease. As applied psychologists or clinicians, they may help individuals lead healthier lives by designing, conducting, and evaluating programs to stop smoking, lose weight, improve sleep, manage pain, prevent the spread of sexually transmitted infections, or treat psychosocial problems associated with chronic and terminal illnesses. As researchers and clinicians, they identify conditions and practices associated with health and illness to help create effective interventions. In public service, health psychologists study and work to improve government policies and health care systems. As a health psychologist, you could be employed in a hospital, medical school, rehabilitation center, public health agency, college or university, or, if you are also a clinical psychologist, in private practice.

INDUSTRIAL-ORGANIZATIONAL (I/O) PSYCHOLOGISTS study the relationship between people and their working environments. They may develop new ways to increase productivity, improve personnel selection, or promote job satisfaction in an organizational setting. Their interests include organizational structure and change, consumer behavior, and personnel selection and training. As an I/O psychologist, you might conduct workplace training or provide organizational analysis and development. You may find yourself working in business, industry, the government, or a college or university. Or you may be self-employed as a consultant or work for a management consulting firm. (For more on I/O psychology, see Appendix B, Psychology at Work.)

NEUROPSYCHOLOGISTS investigate the relationship between neurological processes (structure and function of the brain) and behavior. As a neuropsychologist you might assess, diagnose, or treat central nervous system disorders, such as Alzheimer's disease or stroke. You might also evaluate individuals for evidence of head injuries; learning and developmental disabilities, such as autism spectrum disorder; and other psychiatric disorders, such as attention-deficit hyperactivity disorder (ADHD). If you are a *clinical neuropsychologist,* you might work in a hospital's neurology, neurosurgery, or psychiatric unit. Neuropsychologists also work in academic settings, where they conduct research and teach.

PSYCHOMETRIC AND QUANTITATIVE PSYCHOLOGISTS study the methods and techniques used to acquire psychological knowledge. A psychometric psychologist may update existing neurocognitive or personality tests or devise new tests for use in clinical and school settings or in business and industry. These psychologists also administer, score, and interpret such tests. Quantitative psychologists collaborate with researchers to design, analyze, and interpret the results of research programs. As a psychometric or quantitative psychologist, you will need to be well trained in research methods, statistics, and computer technology. You will most likely be employed by a university or college, a testing company, a private research firm, or a government agency.

REHABILITATION PSYCHOLOGISTS are researchers and practitioners who work with people who have lost optimal functioning

ASSESSING AND SUPPORTING CHILDREN School psychologists may find themselves working with children individually or in groups. They receive interdisciplinary training in mental health assessment and behavior analysis, research methods and design, and special needs education. They work primarily in schools, but also in a range of other settings, including pediatric hospitals, mental health centers, and correctional facilities.

after an accident, illness, or other event. As a rehabilitation psychologist, you would probably work in a medical rehabilitation institution or hospital. You might also work in a medical school, university, state or federal vocational rehabilitation agency, or in private practice serving people with physical disabilities.

SCHOOL PSYCHOLOGISTS are involved in the assessment of and intervention for children in educational settings. They diagnose and treat cognitive, social, and emotional problems that may negatively influence children's learning or overall functioning at school. As a school psychologist, you would collaborate with teachers, parents, and administrators, making recommendations to improve student learning. You would work in an academic setting, a federal or state government agency, a child guidance center, or a behavioral research laboratory.

SOCIAL PSYCHOLOGISTS are interested in our interactions with others. Social psychologists study how our beliefs, feelings, and behaviors are affected by and influence other people. They study topics such as attitudes, aggression, prejudice, interpersonal attraction, group behavior, and leadership. As a social psychologist, you would probably be a college or university faculty member. You might also work in organizational consultation, market research, or an applied psychology field, such as social neuroscience. Some social psychologists work for hospitals, federal agencies, social networking sites, or businesses performing applied research.

SPORT PSYCHOLOGISTS study the psychological factors that influence, and are influenced by, participation in sports and other physical activities. Their professional activities include coach

Phil Walter/Getty Images

CRICKET CURES Sport psychologists often work directly with athletes to help them improve their performance. Here a sport psychologist consults with Brendon McCullum, a record-breaking athlete who played international cricket for New Zealand.

education and athlete preparation, as well as research and teaching. Sport psychologists who also have a clinical or counseling degree can apply those skills to working with individuals with psychological problems, such as anxiety or substance abuse, that might interfere with optimal performance. As a sport psychologist, if you were not working in an academic or research setting, you would most likely work as part of a team or an organization or in a private capacity.

* * *

So, the next time someone asks you what you will do with your psychology degree, tell them you have a lot of options. You might use your acquired skills and understanding to get a job and succeed in any number of fields, or you might pursue graduate school and then career opportunities in associated professions. In any case, what you have learned about behavior and mental processes will surely enrich your life (Hammer, 2003).

Complete Chapter Reviews

Thinking Critically With Psychological Science

 The History and Scope of Psychology

1-1   How is psychology a science?

Psychology's findings, based on an *empirical approach,* are the result of careful observation and testing. Sifting sense from nonsense requires a scientific attitude.

1-2   What are the three key elements of the scientific attitude, and how do they support scientific inquiry?

The scientific attitude equips us to be curious, skeptical, and humble in scrutinizing competing ideas or our own observations. Curiosity triggers new ideas, skepticism encourages attention to the facts, and humility helps us discard predictions that can't be verified by research. Together, these three key elements make modern science possible.

1-3   How does critical thinking feed a scientific attitude, and smarter thinking for everyday life?

Critical thinking puts ideas to the test by examining assumptions, appraising the source, discerning hidden biases, evaluating evidence, and assessing conclusions.

1-4   What were some important milestones in psychology's early development?

Wilhelm Wundt established the first psychological laboratory in 1879 in Germany. Two early schools of thought in psychology were *structuralism* and *functionalism.* Mary Whiton Calkins and Margaret Floy Washburn were two of the first women in the field.

1-5   How did behaviorism, Freudian psychology, and humanistic psychology further the development of psychological science?

Early researchers defined *psychology* as "the science of mental life." In the 1920s, under the influence of John B. Watson and the behaviorists, the field's focus changed to the "scientific study of observable behavior." *Behaviorism* became one of psychology's two major forces well into the 1960s. However, the second major force of Freudian psychology, along with the influence of *humanistic psychology,* revived interest in the study of mental processes.

1-6   How has contemporary psychology focused on cognition, on biology and experience, on culture and gender, and on human flourishing?

The *cognitive* revolution in the 1960s led psychology back to its early interest in the mind, and to its current definition as the science of behavior and mental processes. The field of *cognitive neuroscience* now examines the brain activity underlying mental activity. Our growing understanding of biology and experience has fed psychology's most enduring debate. The *nature–nurture issue* centers on the relative contributions of genes and experience, and their interaction in specific environments. Charles Darwin's view that *natural selection* shapes behaviors as well as bodies led to *evolutionary psychology's* study of our similarities because of our common biology and evolutionary history, and *behavior genetics'* focus on the relative power and limits of genetic and environmental influences on behavior. Cross-cultural and gender studies have diversified psychology's assumptions while also reminding us of our similarities. Attitudes and behaviors may vary somewhat by gender or across *cultures,* but because of our shared human kinship, the underlying processes and principles are more similar than different. Psychology's traditional focus on understanding and treating troubles has expanded with *positive psychology's* call for more research on human flourishing and its attempt to discover and promote traits that help people to thrive.

1-7   What are psychology's levels of analysis and related perspectives?

The *biopsychosocial approach* integrates information from three differing but complementary *levels of analysis:* biological, psychological, and social-cultural. This approach offers a more complete understanding than could usually be reached by relying on only one of psychology's current theoretical perspectives (neuroscience, evolutionary, behavior genetics, psychodynamic, behavioral, cognitive, and social-cultural).

1-8   What are psychology's main subfields?

Within the science of psychology, researchers may conduct *basic research* to increase the field's knowledge base (often in biological, developmental, cognitive, personality, and social psychology) or *applied research* to solve practical problems (in industrial-organizational psychology and other areas). Those who engage in psychology as a helping profession may assist people as *counseling psychologists,* helping people with challenges and crises (including academic, vocational, and relationship issues) and to improve their personal and social functioning, or as *clinical psychologists,* assessing and treating people with mental, emotional, and behavior disorders. (*Psychiatrists* also assess and treat people with disorders, but as medical doctors, they may prescribe drugs in addition to psychotherapy.) *Community psychologists* work to create healthy social and physical environments (in schools, for example).

⟢ Research Strategies: How Psychologists Ask and Answer Questions

1-9 How does our everyday thinking sometimes lead us to a wrong conclusion?

Our everyday thinking can lead us astray because of three phenomena. *Hindsight bias* (the "I-knew-it-all-along phenomenon") is the tendency to believe, after learning an outcome, that we would have foreseen it. Overconfidence is often the result of our readiness to be more confident than correct. These tendencies, along with our eagerness to perceive patterns in random events, lead us to overestimate the weight of commonsense thinking. Although limited by the testable questions it can address, scientific inquiry can help us overcome such biases and shortcomings.

1-10 Why are we so vulnerable to believing untruths?

In our modern "post-truth" culture, our emotions, beliefs, and group affiliations may color our judgments, prevent our acknowledgement of objective facts, and prompt us to accept only the information that confirms our views. Misinformation may spread as a result of repetition and memorable examples, contributing to the post-truth culture. Critical evaluation of information and a scientific mindset can help to combat our biases and distorted thinking.

1-11 How do theories advance psychological science?

Psychological *theories* apply an integrated set of principles to organize observations and to generate *hypotheses.* By testing their hypotheses, researchers can confirm, reject, or revise their theories. To enable other researchers to *replicate* the studies, researchers report them using precise *operational definitions* of their procedures and concepts. If others achieve similar results, confidence in the conclusion will be greater. By combining the results of many studies, *meta-analysis* helps increase researchers' confidence in their results by avoiding the problem of small sample sizes.

1-12 How do psychologists use case studies, naturalistic observations, and surveys to observe and describe behavior, and why is random sampling important?

Descriptive methods, which include *case studies* (in-depth analyses of individuals or groups), *naturalistic observations* (recording many individuals' natural behavior), and *surveys* (asking people questions), show us what can happen, and they may offer ideas for further study. The best basis for generalizing about a *population* is a representative sample; in a *random sample,* every person in the entire population being studied has an equal chance of participating. Descriptive methods describe but do not *explain* behavior; they cannot show cause and effect because researchers cannot control variables.

1-13 What does it mean when we say two things are correlated, and what are positive and negative correlations?

Correlation is the degree to which two variables are related, and how well one predicts the other. In a positive correlation, two *variables* increase or decrease together; in a negative correlation, one variable increases as the other decreases. The strength and direction of their relationship is expressed as a *correlation coefficient,* which ranges from +1.00 (a perfect positive correlation) through 0 (no correlation) to −1.00 (a perfect negative correlation).

1-14 Why do correlations enable prediction but not cause-effect explanation?

Correlations enable prediction because they show how two factors are related—either positively or negatively. A correlation can indicate the possibility of a cause-effect relationship, but it does not prove the direction of the influence, or whether an underlying third factor may explain the correlation.

1-15 What are the characteristics of experimentation that make it possible to isolate cause and effect?

To discover cause-effect relationships, psychologists conduct *experiments,* manipulating one or more variables of interest and controlling other variables. Using *random assignment,* they can minimize *confounding variables,* such as preexisting differences between the *experimental group* (exposed to the treatment) and the *control group* (not given the treatment). The *independent variable* is the factor the experimenter manipulates to study its effect; the *dependent variable* is the factor the experimenter measures to discover any changes occurring in response to the manipulation of the independent variable. Studies may use a *double-blind procedure* to avoid the *placebo effect* and researcher bias.

1-16 How would you know which research design to use?

Psychological scientists design studies and choose research methods that will best provide meaningful results. Researchers generate testable questions, and then carefully consider the best design to use in studying those questions (experimental, correlational, case study, naturalistic observation, twin study, longitudinal, or cross-sectional). Next, psychologists measure the variables they are studying, and finally they interpret their results, keeping possible confounding variables in mind. (The online Immersive Learning "How Would You Know?" research activities allow you to play the role of the researcher, making choices about the best ways to test interesting questions.)

1-17 How can simplified laboratory conditions illuminate everyday life?

Researchers intentionally create a controlled, artificial environment in the laboratory to test general theoretical principles. It is the general principles—not the specific findings—that help explain everyday behaviors.

1-18   Why do psychologists study animals, and what ethical guidelines safeguard human and animal research participants? How do psychologists' values influence psychology?

Some psychologists are primarily interested in animal behavior; others want to better understand the physiological and psychological processes shared by humans and other species. Government agencies have established standards for animal care and housing. Professional associations and funding agencies also have guidelines for protecting animals' well-being. The ethics codes of the American Psychological Association (APA) and the British Psychological Society (BPS) outline standards for safeguarding human participants' well-being, including obtaining their *informed consent* and *debriefing* them later. Psychologists' values influence their choice of research topics, their theories and observations, their labels for behavior, and their professional advice. Applications of psychology's principles have been used mainly in the service of humanity.

1-19   How can psychological principles help you learn, remember, and thrive?

The *testing effect* shows that learning and memory are enhanced by actively retrieving, rather than simply rereading, previously studied material. The *SQ3R* study method—survey, question, read, retrieve, and review—applies principles derived from memory research and can help you learn and remember material. Four additional tips are (1) distribute your study time; (2) learn to think critically; (3) process class information actively; and (4) overlearn. Psychological research has shown that people who live happy, thriving lives manage their time to get a full night's sleep; make space for exercise; set long-term goals, with daily aims; have a growth mindset; and prioritize relationships.

CHAPTER 2

The Biology of Behavior

(>>) Neural and Hormonal Systems

2-1   Why are psychologists concerned with human biology?

Psychologists working from a *biological* perspective study the links between biological processes and psychological processes. We are biopsychosocial systems, in which biological, psychological, and social-cultural factors interact to influence behavior.

2-2   How do biology and experience interact in neural plasticity?

Plasticity enables our brain to adjust to new experiences, thereby being sculpted by both genes and life. While this is a lifelong ability, plasticity is greatest in childhood. With practice, our brain develops unique patterns that reflect our life experiences.

2-3   What are *neurons*, and how do they transmit information?

Neurons are the elementary components of the nervous system, the body's speedy electrochemical information system. A neuron (a *cell body* and its branching fibers) receives signals through its often bushy, branching *dendrites* and sends signals through its *axons.* Some axons are encased in a *myelin sheath,* which enables faster transmission. *Glial cells* support, nourish, and protect neurons and also play a role in learning, thinking, and memory. If the combined signals received by a neuron exceed a minimum *threshold,* the neuron fires, transmitting an electrical impulse (the *action potential*) down its axon by means of a chemistry-to-electricity process. Neurons need a short rest called the *refractory period,* after which they can fire again. The neuron's reaction is an *all-or-none response.*

2-4   How do nerve cells communicate with other nerve cells?

When action potentials reach the end of an axon (the axon terminals), they stimulate the release of *neurotransmitters.* These chemical messengers carry a message from the sending neuron across a *synapse* to receptor sites on a receiving neuron. The sending neuron, in a process called *reuptake,* then normally reabsorbs the excess neurotransmitter molecules in the synaptic gap. If incoming signals are strong enough, the receiving neuron generates its own action potential and relays the message to other cells.

2-5   How do neurotransmitters influence behavior, and how do drugs and other chemicals affect neurotransmission?

Neurotransmitters travel designated pathways in the brain and may influence specific behaviors and emotions. Acetylcholine (ACh) enables muscle action, learning, and memory. *Endorphins* are natural opiates released in response to pain and exercise. Drugs and other chemicals affect brain chemistry at synapses. *Agonists* increase a neurotransmitter's action, and may do so in various ways. *Antagonists* decrease a neurotransmitter's action by blocking production or release.

2-6   What are the functions of the nervous system's main divisions, and what are the three main types of neurons?

The *central nervous system (CNS)*—the brain and the spinal cord—is the *nervous system's* decision maker. The *peripheral nervous system (PNS),* which connects the CNS to the rest of the body by means of *nerves,* gathers information and transmits CNS decisions to the rest of the body. The two main PNS divisions are the *somatic nervous system* (which enables voluntary control of the skeletal muscles) and the *autonomic nervous system* (which controls involuntary muscles and glands by means of its *sympathetic* and *parasympathetic* divisions). The three types of neurons cluster into working networks: (1) *Sensory (afferent) neurons* carry incoming information from the body's tissues and sensory receptors to the brain and spinal cord. (2) *Motor (efferent) neurons* carry outgoing information from the brain and spinal cord to the muscles and glands. (3) *Interneurons* communicate within the brain and spinal cord and process information between the sensory inputs and motor outputs.

2-7   How does the endocrine system transmit information and interact with the nervous system?

The *endocrine system* secretes *hormones* into the bloodstream, where they travel through the body and affect other tissues, including the brain. The endocrine system's master gland, the *pituitary,* influences hormone release by other glands, including the *adrenal glands.*

In an intricate feedback system, the brain's hypothalamus influences the pituitary gland, which influences other glands, which release hormones, which in turn influence the brain.

(⟶) Tools of Discovery, Older Brain Structures, and the Limbic System

2-8   How do neuroscientists study the brain's connections to behavior and mind?

Clinical observations and *lesioning* reveal the general effects of brain damage. Electrical, chemical, or magnetic stimulation can also reveal aspects of information processing in the brain. *MRI* scans show anatomy. *EEG, MEG, PET,* and *fMRI (functional MRI)* recordings reveal brain function.

2-9   What structures make up the brainstem, and what are the functions of the brainstem, thalamus, reticular formation, and cerebellum?

The *brainstem,* the oldest part of the brain, is responsible for automatic survival functions. It includes the *medulla* (which controls heartbeat and breathing), the pons (which helps coordinate movements and control sleep), and the *reticular formation* (which filters incoming stimuli, relays information to other brain areas, and affects arousal). The *thalamus,* sitting above the brainstem, acts as the brain's sensory control center. The *cerebellum,* attached to the rear of the brainstem, coordinates muscle movement and balance and enables nonverbal learning and memory.

2-10   What are the limbic system's structures and functions?

The *limbic system* is linked to emotions, memory, and drives. Its neural centers include the *amygdala* (involved in responses of aggression and fear); the *hypothalamus* (directs various bodily maintenance functions, helps govern the endocrine system, and is linked to emotion and reward); and the *hippocampus* (helps process explicit, conscious memories). The hypothalamus controls the pituitary (the "master gland") by stimulating it to trigger the release of hormones.

(⟶) The Cerebral Cortex

2-11   What four lobes make up the cerebral cortex, and what are the functions of the motor cortex, somatosensory cortex, and association areas?

The *cerebral cortex* has two hemispheres, and each hemisphere has four lobes: the *frontal, parietal, occipital,* and *temporal.* Each lobe performs many functions and interacts with other areas of the cortex. The *motor cortex,* at the rear of the frontal lobes, controls voluntary movements. The *somatosensory cortex,* at the front of the parietal lobes, registers and processes body touch and movement sensations. Body parts requiring precise control (in the motor cortex) or those that are especially sensitive (in the somatosensory cortex) occupy the greatest amount of space. Most of the brain's cortex—the major portion of each of the four lobes—is devoted to uncommitted *association areas,* which integrate information involved in higher mental functions such as learning, remembering, thinking, and speaking. Our mental experiences arise from coordinated brain activity.

2-12   Do we really use only 10 percent of our brain?

The unresponsiveness of our association areas to electrical probing led to the false claim that we only use 10 percent of our brain. But these vast areas of the brain are responsible for interpreting, integrating, and acting on sensory information and linking it with stored memories. Evidence from brain damage shows that the neurons in association areas are busy with higher mental functions; a bullet would not land in an "unused" area.

2-13   To what extent can a damaged brain reorganize itself, and what is neurogenesis?

While brain and spinal cord neurons usually do not regenerate, some neural tissue can reorganize in response to damage. The damaged brain may demonstrate plasticity, especially in young children, as new pathways are built and functions migrate to other brain regions. Reassignment of functions to different areas of the brain may also occur in blindness and deafness, or as a result of damage and disease. The brain sometimes mends itself by forming new neurons, a process known as *neurogenesis.*

2-14   What do split brains reveal about the functions of our two brain hemispheres?

Split-brain research (experiments on people with a severed *corpus callosum*) has confirmed that in most people, the left hemisphere is the more verbal. The right hemisphere excels in visual perception and making inferences, and helps us modulate our speech and orchestrate our self-awareness. Studies of healthy people with intact brains confirm that each hemisphere makes unique contributions to the integrated functioning of the whole brain.

(⟶) Genetics, Evolutionary Psychology, and Behavior

2-15   What are *chromosomes, DNA, genes,* and the human *genome?* How do behavior geneticists explain our individual differences?

Genes are the biochemical units of heredity that make up *chromosomes,* the threadlike coils of *DNA.* When genes are expressed, they provide the code for creating the proteins that form our body's building blocks. Most human traits are influenced by many genes acting together. The human *genome* is the shared genetic profile that distinguishes humans from other species, consisting at an individual level of all the genetic material in an organism's chromosomes. *Behavior geneticists* study the relative power and limits of genetic and *environmental* influences on behavior. Most of our differing traits are influenced by many genes, and by the interaction of our individual environments with these genetic predispositions.

2-16   How do twin and adoption studies help us understand the effects and interactions of nature and nurture?

Studies of *identical (monozygotic) twins* versus *fraternal (dizygotic) twins,* separated twins, and biological versus adoptive relatives allow researchers to consider the effects of shared environment and shared genes, which sheds light on how nature and nurture influence our traits. Shared family environments have surprisingly little effect on personality, though parenting does influence other factors.

2-17   How do heredity and environment work together?

Our genetic predispositions and our specific environments *interact*. Environments can trigger or block genetic expression, and genetically influenced traits can influence the experiences we seek and the responses we evoke from others. The field of *epigenetics* studies the influences on gene expression that occur without changes in DNA.

2-18   How do evolutionary psychologists use natural selection to explain behavior tendencies?

Evolutionary psychologists seek to understand how our traits and behavior tendencies are shaped by *natural selection*. Genetic variations that increase the odds of reproducing and surviving in a particular environment are most likely to be passed on to future generations. Some variations arise from *mutations*, others from new gene combinations at conception. Humans share a genetic legacy and are predisposed to behaviors that promoted our ancestors' survival and reproduction. Charles Darwin's theory of evolution is one of biology's fundamental organizing principles. He anticipated today's application of evolutionary principles in psychology.

CHAPTER 3

Consciousness and the Two-Track Mind

Consciousness: Some Basic Concepts

3-1   What is the place of consciousness in psychology's history?

After initially claiming consciousness as their area of study in the nineteenth century, psychologists abandoned it in the first half of the twentieth century, turning instead to the study of observable behavior because they believed consciousness was too difficult to study scientifically. Since 1960, under the influence of cognitive psychology, neuroscience, and *cognitive neuroscience,* our awareness of ourselves and our environment—our *consciousness*—has reclaimed its place as an important area of research.

3-2   How does selective attention direct our perceptions?

We *selectively attend* to, and process, a very limited portion of incoming information, blocking out much and often shifting the spotlight of our attention from one thing to another. Focused intently on one task, we often display *inattentional blindness* to other events, including *change blindness* to changes around us.

3-3   What is the *dual processing* being revealed by today's cognitive neuroscience?

Scientists studying the brain mechanisms underlying consciousness and cognition have discovered that the mind processes information on two separate tracks, one operating at a conscious level (*sequential processing*) and the other at an unconscious level (*parallel processing*). Parallel processing takes care of the routine business, while sequential processing is best for solving new problems that require our attention. Together, this *dual processing*—conscious and unconscious—affects our perception, memory, attitudes, and other cognitions.

Sleep and Dreams

3-4   What is *sleep*?

Sleep is the periodic, natural loss of normal consciousness—as distinct from unconsciousness resulting from a coma, general anesthesia, or hibernation.

3-5   How do our biological rhythms influence our daily functioning?

Our bodies have an internal biological clock, roughly synchronized with the 24-hour cycle of night and day. This *circadian rhythm* appears in our daily patterns of body temperature, arousal, sleeping, and waking. Age and experience can alter these patterns, resetting our biological clock.

3-6   What is the biological rhythm of our sleeping and dreaming stages?

Younger adults cycle through four distinct sleep stages about every 90 minutes. (The sleep cycle repeats more frequently for older adults.) Leaving the *alpha waves* of the awake, relaxed stage, we descend into the irregular brain waves of non-REM stage 1 (NREM-1 or N1) sleep, often with *hallucinations*. NREM-2 (N2) sleep (in which we spend about half our sleep time) follows, lasting about 20 minutes, with its characteristic sleep spindles. We then enter NREM-3 (N3) sleep, lasting about 30 minutes, with large, slow *delta waves*. About an hour after falling asleep, we ascend from our initial sleep dive and begin periods of *REM* (rapid eye movement or R) *sleep*. REM sleep is described as a paradoxical sleep stage because of internal arousal but external calm (near paralysis). It includes most dreaming, and lengthens as the night goes on. During a normal night's sleep, N3 sleep shortens and REM and N2 sleep lengthens.

3-7   How do biology and environment interact in our sleep patterns?

Our biology—our circadian rhythm as well as our age and our body's production of melatonin (influenced by the brain's *suprachiasmatic nucleus*)—interacts with cultural expectations and individual behaviors to determine our sleeping and waking patterns. Being bathed in (or deprived of) light disrupts our 24-hour biological clock; night-shift workers may experience chronic desynchronization.

3-8   What are sleep's functions?

Sleep may have played a protective role in human evolution by keeping people safe during potentially dangerous periods. Sleep also helps restore and repair damaged neurons. Sleep consolidates our memories by replaying recent learning and strengthening neural connections. Sleep promotes creative problem solving the next day. During slow-wave sleep, the pituitary gland secretes a growth hormone necessary for muscle development.

3-9   How does sleep loss affect us, and what are the major sleep disorders?

Sleep deprivation causes fatigue and irritability, and it impairs concentration, productivity, and memory consolidation. It can also lead to depression, obesity, joint inflammation, a suppressed immune system, and slowed performance (with greater vulnerability to accidents). Sleep disorders include *insomnia* (recurring problems in falling or staying asleep); *narcolepsy* (sudden uncontrollable sleepiness, sometimes lapsing directly into REM sleep); *sleep apnea* (the repeated stopping of breathing while asleep; associated with obesity, especially in men); *night terrors* (high arousal and the appearance of being terrified; NREM-3 disorder found mainly in children); sleepwalking; and sleeptalking.

3-10   What do we dream, and what functions have theorists proposed for dreams?

We usually *dream* of ordinary events and everyday experiences, most involving some anxiety or misfortune. Fewer than 10 percent of dreams among men (and fewer still among women) have any sexual content. Most dreams occur during REM sleep; those that happen during NREM sleep tend to be vague fleeting images. There are five major views of the function of dreams. (1) Freud's wish-fulfillment: Dreams provide a psychic "safety valve," with *manifest content* (story line) acting as a censored version of *latent content* (underlying meaning that gratifies our unconscious wishes). (2) Information-processing: Dreams help us sort out the day's events and consolidate them in memory. (3) Physiological function: Regular brain stimulation may help develop and preserve neural pathways in the brain. (4) Neural activation: The brain attempts to make sense of neural static by weaving it into a story line. (5) Cognitive development: Dreams reflect the dreamers' level of development—their knowledge and understanding. Most sleep theorists agree that REM sleep and its associated dreams serve an important function, as shown by the *REM rebound* that occurs following REM deprivation in humans and other species.

 Drugs and Consciousness

3-11   What are *substance use disorders*?

Those with a *substance use disorder* experience continued substance craving and use despite significant life disruption and/or physical risk. *Psychoactive drugs* alter perceptions and moods.

3-12   What roles do tolerance and addiction play in substance use disorders, and how has the concept of *addiction* changed?

Psychoactive drugs may produce *tolerance*—requiring larger doses to achieve the desired effect—and *withdrawal*—significant discomfort, due to strong addictive cravings, accompanying attempts to quit. Addiction prompts users to crave the drug and to continue use despite known adverse consequences. Therapy or group support may help; it helps to believe that addictions are controllable and that people can change. Although psychologists try to avoid overuse of the term "addiction" to label driven, excessive behaviors, there are some behavior addictions (such as gambling disorder) in which behaviors become compulsive and dysfunctional.

3-13   What are *depressants*, and what are their effects?

Depressants, such as alcohol, *barbiturates,* and the *opiates,* reduce neural activity and slow body functions. Alcohol disinhibits, increasing the likelihood that we will act on our impulses, whether harmful or helpful. It also impairs judgment by slowing neural processing, disrupts memory processes by suppressing REM sleep, and reduces self-awareness and self-control. User expectations strongly influence alcohol's behavioral effects. Alcohol can shrink the brain in those with *alcohol use disorder* (marked by tolerance, withdrawal if use is suspended, and a drive to continue problematic use).

3-14   What are *stimulants*, and what are their effects?

Stimulants—including caffeine, nicotine, cocaine, the amphetamines, methamphetamine, and Ecstasy—excite neural activity and speed up body functions, triggering energy and mood changes. All are highly addictive. *Nicotine's* effects make tobacco product use a difficult habit to kick, yet repeated attempts to quit seem to pay off. *Cocaine* gives users a fast high, followed shortly by a crash. Its risks include cardiac arrest, respiratory failure, and emotional disturbances. *Amphetamines* stimulate neural activity, leading to heightened energy and mood. *Methamphetamine* use may permanently reduce dopamine production. *Ecstasy (MDMA)* is a combined stimulant and mild hallucinogen that produces euphoria and feelings of intimacy. Its users risk immune system suppression, permanent damage to mood and memory, and (if taken during physical activity) dehydration and escalating body temperatures.

3-15   What are *hallucinogens*, and what are their effects?

Hallucinogens, such as *LSD* and marijuana, distort perceptions and evoke hallucinations. The user's mood and expectations influence the effects of LSD, but common experiences are hallucinations and emotions varying from euphoria to panic. Marijuana's main ingredient, *THC,* may trigger feelings of disinhibition, euphoria, relaxation, relief from pain, and intense sensitivity to sensory stimuli, but may increase the risk of psychological disorders and lead to impaired learning and memory.

3-16   Why do some people become regular users of consciousness-altering drugs?

Some people may be biologically vulnerable to particular drugs. Psychological factors (such as stress, depression, and hopelessness) and social factors (such as peer pressure) combine to lead many people to experiment with—and sometimes become addicted to—drugs. Cultural and ethnic groups have differing rates of drug use. Each type of influence—biological, psychological, and social-cultural—offers a possible path for drug misuse prevention and treatment programs.

CHAPTER 4

Developing Through the Life Span

Developmental Issues, Prenatal Development, and the Newborn

4-1   What three issues have engaged developmental psychologists?

Developmental psychologists study physical, cognitive, and social changes throughout the life span. They focus on three issues: nature and nurture (the interaction between our genetic inheritance and our experiences); continuity and stages (which aspects of development are gradual and continuous and which change relatively abruptly); and stability and change (whether our traits endure or change as we age).

4-2   What is the course of prenatal development, and how do *teratogens* affect that development?

The life cycle begins at conception, when one sperm cell unites with an egg to form a *zygote*. The zygote's inner cells become the *embryo,* and the outer cells become the placenta. In the next 6 weeks, body organs begin to form and function, and by 9 weeks, the *fetus* is recognizably human. *Teratogens* are potentially harmful agents that can pass through the placenta and harm the developing embryo or fetus, as happens with *fetal alcohol syndrome.*

4-3   What are some newborn abilities, and how do researchers explore infants' mental abilities?

Babies are born with sensory equipment and reflexes that facilitate their survival and their social interactions with adults. For example, they quickly learn to discriminate their mother's smell, and they prefer the sound of human voices. Researchers use techniques that test *habituation,* such as the novelty-preference procedure, to explore infants' abilities.

⟫ Infancy and Childhood

4-4   During infancy and childhood, how do the brain and motor skills develop?

The brain's nerve cells are sculpted by heredity and experience. As a child's brain develops, neural connections grow more numerous and complex. Experiences then trigger a pruning process, in which unused connections weaken and heavily used ones strengthen. Early childhood is an important period for shaping the brain, but thanks to its plasticity, our brain modifies itself in response to our learning throughout life. In childhood, complex motor skills—sitting, standing, walking—develop in a predictable sequence, though the timing of that sequence is a function of individual *maturation* and culture. For some skills, we seem to have a *critical period.* We have few or no conscious memories of events occurring before about age 4. This infantile amnesia occurs in part because major brain areas have not yet matured.

4-5   From the perspectives of Piaget, Vygotsky, and today's researchers, how does a child's mind develop?

In his theory of *cognitive* development, Jean Piaget proposed that children actively construct and modify their understanding of the world through the processes of *assimilation* and *accommodation.* They form *schemas* that help them organize their experiences. Progressing from the simplicity of the *sensorimotor stage* of the first two years, in which they develop *object permanence,* children move to more complex ways of thinking. In the *preoperational stage* (about age 2 to about 6 or 7), they develop a *theory of mind.* In the preoperational stage, children are *egocentric* and unable to perform simple logical operations. By about age 7, they enter the *concrete operational stage* and are able to comprehend the principle of *conservation.* By age 12, children enter the *formal operational stage* and can reason systematically. Research supports the sequence Piaget proposed, but it also shows that young children are more capable, and their

development more continuous, than he believed. Lev Vygotsky's studies of child development focused on the ways a child's mind grows by interacting with the social environment. In his view, parents and caretakers provide temporary *scaffolds* enabling children to step to higher levels of thinking.

4-6   What is *autism spectrum disorder?*

Autism spectrum disorder (ASD) is a disorder marked by social deficiencies and repetitive behaviors, with differing levels of severity. Children with ASD have an impaired theory of mind. By age eight, 1 in 68 U.S. children now gets diagnosed with ASD (though the reported rates vary by place). The increase in diagnoses has been offset by a decrease in the number of children with a "cognitive disability" or "learning disability." Genetic influences, abnormal brain development, and the prenatal environment—especially when altered by infection, drugs, or hormones—likely contribute to ASD.

4-7   How do parent-infant attachment bonds form?

At about 8 months, soon after object permanence develops, children separated from their caregivers display *stranger anxiety.* Infants form *attachments* with caregivers who gratify biological needs but, more importantly, who are comfortable, familiar, and responsive. Many birds and other animals have a more rigid attachment process, called *imprinting,* that occurs during a critical period.

4-8   How have psychologists studied attachment differences, and what have they learned?

Attachment has been studied in strange situation experiments, which show that some children are securely attached and others are insecurely (anxiously or avoidantly) attached. Infants' differing attachment styles reflect both their individual *temperament* and the responsiveness of their parents and child-care providers. Adult relationships seem to reflect the attachment styles of early childhood, lending support to Erik Erikson's idea that *basic trust* is formed in infancy by our experiences with responsive caregivers.

4-9   How does childhood neglect or abuse affect children's attachments?

Most children are resilient, but those who are abused or severely neglected by their caregivers, or otherwise prevented from forming attachments at an early age, may be at risk for attachment problems. Extreme trauma in childhood may alter the brain, affecting our stress responses or leaving epigenetic marks.

4-10   What are the four main parenting styles?

The main parenting styles are authoritarian (coercive), permissive (unrestraining), negligent (uninvolved), and authoritative (confrontive).

4-11   What outcomes are associated with each parenting style?

Authoritative parenting is associated with greater self-esteem, self-reliance, self-regulation, and social competence; authoritarian parenting with lower self-esteem, less social skill, and a brain that overreacts to mistakes; permissive parenting with greater aggression and immaturity; and negligent parenting with poor academic and social outcomes. However, correlation does not equal causation (it's possible that children with positive characteristics are more likely to bring out positive parenting methods).

Adolescence

4-12   How is *adolescence* defined, and how do physical changes affect developing teens?

Adolescence is the transition period from childhood to adulthood, extending from *puberty* to social independence. Boys seem to benefit (though with risks) from "early" maturation, whereas girls tend to experience greater risk from early maturation. The brain's frontal lobes mature and myelin growth increases during adolescence and the early twenties, enabling improved judgment, impulse control, and long-term planning.

4-13   How did Piaget, Kohlberg, and later researchers describe adolescent cognitive and moral development?

Piaget theorized that adolescents develop a capacity for formal operations and that this development is the foundation for moral judgment. Lawrence Kohlberg proposed a stage theory of moral reasoning, from a preconventional morality of self-interest, to a conventional morality concerned with upholding laws and social rules, to (in some people) a postconventional morality of universal ethical principles. Other researchers believe that morality lies in moral intuition and moral action as well as thinking. Kohlberg's critics note that the postconventional level is culturally limited, representing morality only from the perspective of an individualist society.

4-14   What are the social tasks and challenges of adolescence?

Erik Erikson proposed eight stages of psychosocial development across the life span. He believed we need to achieve: trust, autonomy, initiative, competency, *identity* (in adolescence), *intimacy* (in young adulthood), generativity, and integrity. Each life stage has its own psychosocial task. Solidifying one's sense of self in adolescence means trying out a number of different roles. *Social identity* is the part of the self-concept that comes from a person's group memberships.

4-15   How do parents and peers influence adolescents?

During adolescence, parental influence diminishes and peer influence increases, in part because of the selection effect—the tendency to choose similar others. Adolescents adopt their peers' ways of dressing, acting, and communicating. Parents do have an influence on teens' behaviors and attitudes, but personalities and temperaments are shaped more by nature than by parental nurture.

4-16   What is emerging adulthood?

Due to earlier sexual maturity and later independence, the transition from adolescence to adulthood is taking longer than it once did. *Emerging adulthood* is the period from age 18 to the mid-twenties, when many young people are not yet fully independent. This stage is found mostly in today's Western cultures.

Adulthood

4-17   What physical changes occur during middle and late adulthood?

Muscular strength, reaction time, sensory abilities, and cardiac output begin to almost imperceptibly decline in the mid-twenties; this downward trajectory accelerates through middle and late adulthood. Women's period of fertility ends with *menopause* around age 50; men experience a more gradual decline. In late adulthood, the immune system weakens, increasing susceptibility to life-threatening illnesses. But longevity-supporting genes, low stress, and healthful habits may enable good health even in late life.

4-18   How does memory change with age?

Recall begins to decline, especially for meaningless information, but recognition memory remains strong. Developmental researchers study age-related changes such as in memory with *cross-sectional studies* (comparing people of different ages at one point in time) and *longitudinal studies* (retesting the same people over a period of years). "Terminal decline" describes the cognitive decline in the final few years of life.

4-19   What themes and influences mark our social journey from early adulthood to death?

Adults do not progress through an orderly sequence of age-related social stages. Chance events can determine life choices. The *social clock* is a culture's preferred timing for events such as marriage, parenthood, and retirement. Adulthood's dominant themes are love and work (Erikson's intimacy and generativity).

4-20   How does our well-being change across the life span?

Surveys show that life satisfaction is unrelated to age until the terminal decline phase. Positive emotions increase after midlife and negative ones decrease; with age come fewer extremes of emotion and mood.

4-21   A loved one's death triggers what range of reactions?

People do not grieve in predictable stages, as was once supposed, and bereavement therapy is not significantly more effective than grieving without such aid. Life can be affirmed even at death, especially for those who experience what Erikson called a sense of integrity—a feeling that one's life has been meaningful.

CHAPTER 5

Sex, Gender, and Sexuality

Gender Development

5-1   How does the meaning of *gender* differ from the meaning of *sex*?

In psychology, *gender* refers to the socially and culturally constructed expectations about what it means to be a boy, girl, man, or woman. *Sex* refers to our biological status as male or female, defined by our chromosomes and anatomy. We might say that our body defines our sex, while our mind defines our gender.

5-2   What are some ways in which males and females tend to be alike and to differ?

We are more alike than different, thanks to our similar genetic makeup—we see, learn, and remember similarly, with comparable creativity, intelligence, and emotions. Males and females do differ in age of onset of puberty, life expectancy, and vulnerability to certain disorders. Men admit to more *aggression* than women do, and they are more likely to be physically (rather than *relationally*) aggressive. Women focus more on social connectedness; they are more interdependent, and they "tend and befriend."

5-3   What factors contribute to gender bias in the workplace?

Differences in male-female perceptions, compensation, and family responsibility both influence and reflect workplace gender bias. In most societies, men have more social power, and their leadership style tends to be directive, whereas women's tends to be more democratic. In their everyday behaviors and interactions, men tend to act more assertive and opinionated; women tend to act more supportive and apologetic.

5-4   How do sex hormones influence prenatal and adolescent sexual development, and what is an *intersex* condition?

Both sex chromosomes and sex hormones influence development. About seven weeks after conception, a gene on the *Y chromosome* from the father—who can contribute either this or an *X chromosome* (the mother always contributes the latter)—triggers the production of *testosterone*. This promotes male sex organ development. During the fourth and fifth prenatal months, sex hormones bathe the fetal brain, with different patterns developing due to the male's greater testosterone and the female's ovarian hormones. Prenatal exposure of females to unusually high levels of male hormones can later dispose them to more male-typical interests. Another flood of hormones occurs in *puberty*, triggering a growth spurt, the development of *primary* and *secondary sex characteristics*, and the landmark events of *menarche* and *spermarche*. Individuals with *intersex* conditions are born with unusual combinations of male and female chromosomes, hormones, and anatomy.

5-5   How do gender roles and gender identity differ?

Gender roles, the behaviors a culture expects from its men and women, vary across place and time. *Social learning theory* proposes that we learn *gender identity*—our personal sense of being male, female, or some combination of the two—as we learn other things: through reinforcement, punishment, and observation. Critics argue that cognition also plays a role, as *gender typing* varies among children. We seem to conform in ways that feel comfortable to us, whether that means taking on a male role, female role, or blend of the two (*androgyny*). *Transgender* people's gender identity or expression differs from the behaviors or traits considered typical for their birth-designated sex. Their sexual orientation may be heterosexual, homosexual, bisexual, or asexual.

5-6   What are the effects of sexual aggression? How have cultural views changed, and how can we reduce sexual aggression?

Sexual aggression, which includes sexual harassment and sexual assault, can cause anxiety and depression, increase victims' risk for posttraumatic stress disorder and borderline personality disorder, disrupt sleep and health, and make it difficult to trust new relationship partners. Cultural views of sexual aggression differ across time and place, with some cultures continuing to blame victims, but changes in the U.S. over the last half-century have made victim-blaming less acceptable. Therapy for sexual aggressors has not proven effective, but we may reduce sexual aggression by empowering victims, encouraging people to report and share their experiences, and educating communities about preventive bystander intervention strategies.

Human Sexuality

5-7   How do hormones influence human sexual motivation?

For all but those few of us considered *asexual*, dating and mating become a high priority from puberty on. The female *estrogen* and male *testosterone* hormones influence human sexual behavior less directly than they influence sexual behavior in other species. Women's sexuality is more responsive to testosterone level than to estrogen level. Short-term shifts in testosterone level are normal in men, partly in response to stimulation.

5-8   What is the human *sexual response cycle*, and how do sexual dysfunctions and paraphilias differ?

William Masters and Virginia Johnson described four stages in the human *sexual response cycle*: excitement, plateau, orgasm, and resolution. During resolution there is a *refractory period* in which renewed arousal and orgasm are impossible. *Sexual dysfunctions* are problems that consistently impair sexual arousal or functioning. They include *erectile disorder* and *female orgasmic disorder,* and can often be successfully treated by behaviorally oriented therapy or drug therapy. *Paraphilias* are considered disordered if a person experiences distress from an unusual sexual interest or if it entails harm or risk of harm to others.

5-9   How can sexually transmitted infections be prevented?

Safe-sex practices help prevent sexually transmitted infections (STIs). Condoms are especially effective in preventing transmission of HIV, the virus that causes *AIDS*. Knowing one's STI status, and sharing it with one's sexual partner, is an important first step in STI prevention.

5-10   How do external and imagined stimuli contribute to sexual arousal?

External stimuli can trigger sexual arousal in both men and women. Sexually explicit material may lead people to perceive their partners as comparatively less appealing and to devalue their relationships. Viewing sexually coercive material can lead to increased acceptance of violence toward women. Extensive online pornography exposure may desensitize young men to normal sexuality, leading to erectile problems and lowered sexual desire in real life. Imagined stimuli (dreams and fantasies) also influence sexual arousal.

5-11   What factors influence teenagers' sexual behaviors and use of contraceptives?

Teen sexuality varies from culture to culture and era to era. Factors contributing to these variations include communication about birth control; impulsivity; alcohol use; and mass media. High intelligence, religious engagement, father presence, and service learning participation predict teen sexual restraint.

5-12   What has research taught us about sexual orientation?

Sexual orientation is an enduring sexual attraction toward members of one's own sex, the other sex, or both sexes. About 3 or 4 percent of men and 2 percent of women in Europe and the United States identify as exclusively homosexual. There is no evidence that environmental influences determine sexual orientation. Evidence for biological influences includes same-sex attraction in other species;

gay-straight trait and brain differences; genetic influences; and pre-natal influences.

5-13   How might an evolutionary psychologist explain male-female differences in sexuality and mating preferences?

Women tend to be more selective than men when choosing sexual partners. Evolutionary psychologists reason that men's attraction to multiple healthy, fertile-appearing partners increases their chances of spreading their genes widely. Because women incubate and nurse babies, they increase their own and their children's chances of survival by searching for mates with the potential for long-term investment in their joint offspring.

5-14   What are the key criticisms of evolutionary explanations of human sexuality, and how do evolutionary psychologists respond?

Critics argue that evolutionary psychologists start with an effect and work backward to an explanation, minimize contemporary social and cultural influences (including learned *social scripts*), and relieve people from taking responsibility for their sexual behavior. Evolutionary psychologists respond that they recognize the impor-tance of social and cultural influences, but note the value in test-able predictions based on evolutionary principles: Understanding our predispositions can help us overcome them.

5-15   What role do social factors play in our sexuality?

Scientific research on sexual motivation does not attempt to define the personal meaning of sex in our lives, which is influenced by many social factors. Sex is a socially significant act and is an expression of our profoundly social nature. Sex at its human best is life uniting and love renewing.

5-16   How do nature, nurture, and our own choices influence gender roles?

Individual development results from the interaction of biological, psychological, and social-cultural influences. Biological influences include our shared human genome; individual variations; prena-tal environment; and sex-related genes, hormones, and physiology. Psychological influences include gene-environment interactions; the effect of early experiences on neural networks; responses evoked by our own characteristics, such as gender and tempera-ment; and personal beliefs, feelings, and expectations. Social-cultural influences include parental and peer influences; cultural traditions and values; and cultural gender norms. And our individ-ual choices affect the way all of these influences interact.

`CHAPTER 6`

Sensation and Perception

 Basic Concepts of Sensation and Perception

6-1   What are *sensation* and *perception*? What do we mean by *bottom-up processing* and *top-down processing*?

Sensation is the process by which our *sensory receptors* and ner-vous system receive and represent stimulus energies from our environment. *Perception* is the process of organizing and interpret-ing this information, enabling recognition of meaningful events. Sensation and perception are one continuous process. *Bottom-up processing* is sensory analysis that begins at the entry level, with information flowing from the sensory receptors to the brain. *Top-down processing* is information processing guided by high-level mental processes, as when we construct perceptions by filtering information through our experience and expectations.

6-2   What three steps are basic to all our sensory systems?

Our senses (1) receive sensory stimulation (often using specialized receptor cells); (2) transform that stimulation into neural impulses; and (3) deliver the neural information to the brain. *Transduction* is the process of converting one form of energy into another.

6-3   How do *absolute thresholds* and *difference thresholds* differ?

Our *absolute threshold* for any stimulus is the minimum stimulation necessary for us to be consciously aware of it 50 percent of the time. *Signal detection theory* predicts how and when we will detect a faint stimulus amid background noise. Individual absolute thresholds vary, depending on the strength of the signal and also on our expe-rience, expectations, motivation, and alertness. Our *difference thresh-old* (also called the *just noticeable difference,* or *jnd*) is the difference we can discern between two stimuli 50 percent of the time. *Weber's law* states that two stimuli must differ by a constant minimum per-centage (not a constant amount) to be perceived as different.

6-4   How are we affected by subliminal stimuli?

We do sense some stimuli *subliminally*—less than 50 percent of the time—and can be affected by these sensations. But although we can be *primed,* subliminal sensations have no powerful, enduring influence.

6-5   What is the function of sensory adaptation?

Sensory adaptation (our diminished sensitivity to constant or rou-tine odors, sounds, and touches) focuses our attention on informa-tive changes in our environment.

6-6   How do our expectations, contexts, motivation, and emotions influence our perceptions?

Perceptual set is a mental predisposition that functions as a lens through which we perceive the world. Our learned concepts (sche-mas) prime us to organize and interpret ambiguous stimuli in cer-tain ways. Our motivation, as well as our physical and emotional context, can create expectations and color our interpretation of events and behaviors.

 Vision: Sensory and Perceptual Processing

6-7   What are the characteristics of the energy that we see as visible light? What structures in the eye help focus that energy?

What we see as light is only a thin slice of the broad spectrum of electromagnetic energy. The portion visible to humans extends from the blue-violet to the red light wavelengths. After entering the eye through the cornea, passing through the pupil and iris, and being focused by a *lens,* light energy particles strike the eye's inner surface, the *retina.* The *hue* we perceive in a light depends on its *wavelength,* and its brightness depends on its *intensity.*

6-8   How do the rods and cones process information, and what is the path information travels from the eye to the brain?

Light entering the eye triggers chemical changes that convert light energy into neural impulses. *Cones* and *rods* at the back of the retina each provide a special sensitivity—cones to detail and color, rods to faint light and peripheral motion. After processing by bipolar and ganglion cells, neural impulses travel from the retina through the *optic nerve* to the thalamus, and on to the visual cortex.

6-9   How do we perceive color in the world around us?

According to the *Young-Helmholtz trichromatic (three-color) theory,* the retina contains three types of color receptors. Contemporary research has found three types of cones, each most sensitive to the wavelengths of one of the three primary colors of light (red, green, or blue). According to Hering's *opponent-process theory,* there are three additional color processes (red-versus-green, blue-versus-yellow, black-versus-white). Research has confirmed that, en route to the brain, neurons in the retina and the thalamus code the color-related information from the cones into pairs of opponent colors. These two theories, and the research supporting them, show that color processing occurs in two stages.

6-10   Where are feature detectors located, and what do they do?

Feature detectors, specialized nerve cells in the visual cortex, respond to specific features of the visual stimulus, such as shape, angle, or movement. Feature detectors pass information on to other cortical areas, where supercell clusters respond to more complex patterns.

6-11   How does the brain use parallel processing to construct visual perceptions?

Through *parallel processing,* the brain handles many aspects of vision (color, movement, form, and depth) simultaneously. Other neural teams integrate the results, comparing them with stored information and enabling perceptions.

6-12   How did the Gestalt psychologists understand perceptual organization, and how do figure-ground and grouping principles contribute to our perceptions?

Gestalt psychologists searched for rules by which the brain organizes fragments of sensory data into *gestalts,* or meaningful forms. In pointing out that the whole may exceed the sum of its parts, they noted that we filter sensory information and construct our perceptions. To recognize an object, we must first perceive it (see it as a *figure*) as distinct from its surroundings (the *ground*). We bring order and form to stimuli by organizing them into meaningful *groups,* following such rules as proximity, continuity, and closure.

6-13   How do we use binocular and monocular cues to see the world in three dimensions?

Depth perception is our ability to see objects in three dimensions and judge distance. The *visual cliff* and other research demonstrate that many species perceive the world in three dimensions at, or very soon after, birth. *Binocular cues,* such as *retinal disparity,* are depth cues that rely on information from both eyes. *Monocular cues* (such as relative height, relative size, interposition, relative motion, linear perspective, and light and shadow) let us judge depth using information transmitted by only one eye. As objects move, we assume that shrinking objects are retreating and enlarging objects are approaching. The brain computes motion imperfectly, with young children especially at risk of incorrectly perceiving approaching hazards such as vehicles. A quick succession of images on the retina can create an illusion of movement, as in stroboscopic movement or the *phi phenomenon.*

6-14   How do perceptual constancies help us construct meaningful perceptions?

Perceptual constancies, such as in color, brightness (or lightness), shape, or size, enable us to perceive objects as stable despite the changing image they cast on our retinas. Our brain constructs our experience of an object's color or brightness through comparisons with other surrounding objects. Knowing an object's size gives us clues to its distance; knowing its distance gives clues about its size, but we sometimes misread monocular distance cues and reach the wrong conclusions, as in the Moon illusion.

6-15   What does research on restored vision, sensory restriction, and perceptual adaptation reveal about the effects of experience on perception?

Experience guides our perceptual interpretations. People blind from birth who gained sight after surgery lack the experience to visually recognize shapes and forms. Sensory restriction research indicates that there is a critical period for some aspects of sensory and perceptual development. Without early stimulation, the brain's neural organization does not develop normally. People given glasses that shift the world slightly to the left or right, or even upside down, experience *perceptual adaptation.* They are initially disoriented, but they manage to adapt to their new context.

⬎ The Nonvisual Senses

6-16   What are the characteristics of air pressure waves that we hear as sound?

Sound waves are bands of compressed and expanded air. Our ears detect these changes in air pressure and transform them into neural impulses, which the brain decodes as sound. Sound waves vary in amplitude, which we perceive as differing loudness, and in *frequency,* which we experience as differing *pitch.*

6-17   How does the ear transform sound energy into neural messages?

The *middle ear* is the chamber between the eardrum and *cochlea;* the *inner ear* consists of the cochlea, semicircular canals, and vestibular sacs. Sound waves traveling through the auditory canal cause tiny vibrations in the eardrum. The bones of the middle ear amplify the vibrations and relay them to the fluid-filled cochlea. Rippling of the basilar membrane, caused by pressure changes in the cochlear fluid, causes movement of the tiny hair cells, triggering neural messages to be sent (via the thalamus) to the auditory cortex in the brain. *Sensorineural hearing loss* (or nerve deafness) results from damage to the cochlea's hair cells or their associated nerves. *Conduction hearing loss* results from damage to the mechanical system that transmits sound waves to the cochlea. *Cochlear implants* can restore hearing for some people.

6-18   How do we detect loudness, discriminate pitch, and locate sounds?

Loudness is not related to the intensity of a hair cell's response, but rather to the number of activated hair cells. *Place theory* explains how we hear high-pitched sounds, and *frequency theory* explains how we hear low-pitched sounds. A combination of the two theories explains how we hear pitches in the middle range. Sound waves strike one ear sooner and more intensely than the other. To locate sounds, the brain analyzes the minute differences in the sounds received by the two ears and computes the sound's source.

6-19   How do we sense touch?

Our sense of touch is actually several senses—pressure, warmth, cold, and pain—that combine to produce other sensations, such as "itchy" or "wet."

6-20   What biological, psychological, and social-cultural influences affect our experience of pain? How do placebos, distraction, and hypnosis help control pain?

The biopsychosocial perspective views our perception of pain as the sum of biological, psychological, and social-cultural influences. Pain reflects bottom-up sensations and top-down processes. One theory of pain is that a *"gate"* in the spinal cord either opens to permit pain signals traveling up small nerve fibers to reach the brain, or closes to prevent their passage. Pain treatments often combine physical and psychological elements. Combining a placebo with distraction, and amplifying the effect with *hypnosis* (which increases our response to suggestions), can help relieve pain. *Post-hypnotic suggestion* is used by some clinicians to control undesired symptoms and behavior.

6-21   In what ways are our senses of taste and smell similar, and how do they differ?

Taste and smell are both chemical senses. Taste is a composite of five basic sensations—sweet, sour, salty, bitter, and umami—and of the aromas that interact with information from the taste receptor cells of the taste buds. There are no basic sensations for smell (*olfaction*). We smell something when airborne molecules reach a tiny cluster of 20 million receptor cells at the top of each nasal cavity. Odor molecules trigger combinations of receptors, in patterns that the olfactory cortex interprets. The receptor cells send messages to the brain's olfactory bulb, then to the temporal lobe, and to parts of the limbic system.

6-22   How do we sense our body's position and movement?

Through *kinesthesia*, we sense the position and movement of our body parts. We monitor our head's (and thus our body's) position and movement, and maintain our balance, with our *vestibular sense,* which relies on the semicircular canals and vestibular sacs to sense the tilt or rotation of our head.

6-23   How does *sensory interaction* influence our perceptions, and what is *embodied cognition*?

Our senses influence one another. This *sensory interaction* occurs, for example, when the smell of a favorite food amplifies its taste. *Embodied cognition* is the influence of bodily sensations, gestures, and other states on cognitive preferences and judgments.

6-24   What are the claims of *ESP*, and what have most research psychologists concluded after putting these claims to the test?

Parapsychology is the study of paranormal phenomena, including *extrasensory perception* (ESP) and psychokinesis. The three most testable forms of ESP are telepathy (mind-to-mind communication), clairvoyance (perceiving remote events), and precognition (perceiving future events). To believe in ESP is to believe the brain is capable of perceiving without sensory input; researchers have been unable to replicate ESP phenomena under controlled conditions.

CHAPTER 7

Learning

Basic Learning Concepts and Classical Conditioning

7-1   How do we define *learning*, and what are some basic forms of learning?

Learning is the process of acquiring through experience new information or behaviors. In *associative learning*, we learn that certain events occur together. In classical conditioning, we learn to associate two or more *stimuli*. Automatically responding to stimuli we do not control is called *respondent behavior*. In operant conditioning, we learn to associate a response and its consequence. These associations produce *operant behaviors*. Through *cognitive learning*, we acquire mental information that guides our behavior. For example, in observational learning, we learn new behaviors by observing events and watching others.

7-2   What is behaviorism's view of learning?

Ivan Pavlov's work on classical conditioning laid the foundation for *behaviorism*, the view that psychology should be an objective science that studies behavior without reference to mental processes. The behaviorists believed that the basic laws of learning are the same for all species, including humans.

7-3   Who was Pavlov, and what are the basic components of classical conditioning?

Ivan Pavlov, a Russian physiologist, created novel experiments on learning. His early twentieth-century research over the last three decades of his life demonstrated that classical conditioning is a basic form of learning. *Classical conditioning* is a type of learning in which an organism comes to associate stimuli and anticipate events. A *UR* is an event that occurs naturally (such as salivation), in response to some stimulus. A *US* is something that naturally and automatically (without learning) triggers the unlearned response (as food in the mouth triggers salivation). A *CS* is originally an *NS* (neutral stimulus, such as a tone) that, after association with a US (such as food) comes to trigger a CR. A *CR* is the learned response (salivating) to the originally neutral (but now conditioned) stimulus.

7-4 In classical conditioning, what are the processes of *acquisition, extinction, spontaneous recovery, generalization,* and *discrimination?*

In classical conditioning, the first stage is *acquisition,* associating an NS with the US so that the NS begins triggering the CR. Acquisition occurs most readily when the NS is presented just before (ideally, about a half-second before) a US, preparing the organism for the upcoming event. This finding supports the view that classical conditioning is biologically adaptive. *Extinction* is diminished responding, which occurs if the CS appears repeatedly by itself without the US. *Spontaneous recovery* is the appearance of a formerly extinguished conditioned response, following a rest period. *Generalization* is the tendency to respond to stimuli that are similar to a CS. *Discrimination* is the learned ability to distinguish between a CS and other irrelevant stimuli.

7-5 Why does Pavlov's work remain so important?

Pavlov taught us that significant psychological phenomena can be studied objectively, and that classical conditioning is a basic form of learning that applies to all species.

7-6 What have been some applications of Pavlov's work to human health and well-being? How did Watson apply Pavlov's principles to learned fears?

Classical conditioning techniques are used to improve human health and well-being in many areas, including behavioral therapy for some types of psychological disorders. The body's immune system may also respond to classical conditioning. Pavlov's work also provided a basis for Watson's idea that human emotions and behaviors, though biologically influenced, are mainly a bundle of conditioned responses. Watson applied classical conditioning principles in his studies of "Little Albert" to demonstrate how specific fears might be conditioned.

⟶ Operant Conditioning

7-7 What is *operant conditioning?*

Operant conditioning is a type of learning in which behavior is strengthened if followed by a reinforcer or diminished if followed by a punisher.

7-8 Who was Skinner, and how is operant behavior reinforced and shaped?

B. F. Skinner was a college English major and aspiring writer who later entered psychology graduate school. He became modern behaviorism's most influential and controversial figure. Expanding on Edward Thorndike's *law of effect,* Skinner and others found that the behavior of rats or pigeons placed in an *operant chamber* (Skinner box) can be *shaped* by using reinforcers to guide successive approximations of the desired behavior.

7-9 How do positive and negative reinforcement differ, and what are the basic types of reinforcers?

Reinforcement is any consequence that strengthens behavior. *Positive reinforcement* adds a desirable stimulus to increase the frequency of a behavior. *Negative reinforcement* reduces or removes an aversive stimulus to increase the frequency of a behavior. *Primary reinforcers* (such as receiving food when hungry or having nausea end during an illness) are innately satisfying—no learning is required. *Conditioned* (or secondary) *reinforcers* (such as cash) are satisfying because we have learned to associate them with more basic rewards (such as the food or medicine we buy with them). Immediate reinforcers (such as a purchased treat) offer immediate payback; delayed reinforcers (such as a paycheck) require the ability to delay gratification.

7-10 How do different reinforcement schedules affect behavior?

A *reinforcement schedule* defines how often a response will be reinforced. In *continuous reinforcement* (reinforcing desired responses every time they occur), learning is rapid, but so is extinction if rewards cease. In *partial (intermittent) reinforcement* (reinforcing responses only sometimes), initial learning is slower, but the behavior is much more resistant to extinction. *Fixed-ratio schedules* reinforce behaviors after a set number of responses; *variable-ratio schedules,* after an unpredictable number. *Fixed-interval schedules* reinforce behaviors after set time periods; *variable-interval schedules,* after unpredictable time periods.

7-11 How does punishment differ from negative reinforcement, and how does punishment affect behavior?

Punishment administers an undesirable consequence (such as spanking) or withdraws something desirable (such as taking away a favorite toy) to decrease the frequency of a behavior (a child's disobedience). Negative reinforcement (taking an aspirin) removes an aversive stimulus (a headache). This desired consequence (freedom from pain) increases the likelihood that the behavior (taking aspirin to end pain) will be repeated. Punishment can have undesirable side effects, such as suppressing rather than changing unwanted behaviors, encouraging discrimination (so that the undesirable behavior appears when the punisher is not present), creating fear, and teaching aggression.

7-12 Why did Skinner's ideas provoke controversy, and how might his operant conditioning principles be applied at school, in sports, at work, in parenting, and for self-improvement?

Critics of Skinner's principles believed the approach dehumanized people by neglecting their personal freedom and seeking to control their actions. Skinner replied that people's actions are already controlled by external consequences, and that reinforcement is more humane than punishment as a means for controlling behavior. Teachers can use shaping techniques to guide students' behaviors, and use interactive media such as online adaptive quizzing to provide immediate feedback. (The LaunchPad LearningCurve and

Achieve Read & Practice systems available with this text provide such feedback, and allow students to direct the pace of their own learning.) Coaches can build players' skills and self-confidence by rewarding small improvements. Managers can boost productivity and morale by rewarding well-defined and achievable behaviors. Parents can reward desired behaviors but not undesirable ones. We can shape our own behaviors by stating realistic goals, planning how to work toward those goals, monitoring the frequency of desired behaviors, reinforcing desired behaviors, and gradually reducing rewards as behaviors become habitual.

7-13   How does operant conditioning differ from classical conditioning?

In operant conditioning, an organism learns associations between its own behavior and resulting events; this form of conditioning involves operant behavior (behavior that operates on the environment, producing rewarding or punishing consequences). In classical conditioning, the organism forms associations between stimuli—events it does not control; this form of conditioning involves respondent behavior (automatic responses to some stimulus).

Biology, Cognition, and Learning

7-14   How do biological constraints affect classical and operant conditioning?

An animal's capacity for conditioning is limited by biological constraints, so some associations are easier to learn. Each species learns behaviors that aid its survival—a phenomenon called *preparedness.* Those who readily learned taste aversions were unlikely to eat the same toxic food again and were more likely to survive and leave descendants. Nature constrains each species' capacity for both classical conditioning and operant conditioning. Our preparedness to associate a CS with a US that follows predictably and immediately is often (but not always) adaptive. During operant training, animals may display *instinctive drift* by reverting to biologically predisposed patterns.

7-15   How do cognitive processes affect classical and operant conditioning?

In classical conditioning, animals may learn when to expect a US and may be aware of the link between stimuli and responses. In operant conditioning, *cognitive mapping* and *latent learning* research demonstrate the importance of cognitive processes in learning.

7-16   What is *observational learning*?

Observational learning (also called social learning) involves learning by watching and imitating, rather than through direct experience.

7-17   How may observational learning be enabled by neural mirroring?

Our brain's frontal lobes have a demonstrated ability to mirror the activity of another's brain, which may enable imitation and observational learning. Some scientists argue that *mirror neurons* are responsible for this ability, while others attribute it to distributed brain networks.

7-18   What is the impact of prosocial modeling and of antisocial modeling?

Children tend to imitate what a model does and says, whether the behavior being *modeled* is *prosocial* (positive, constructive, and helpful) or antisocial. If a model's actions and words are inconsistent, children may imitate the hypocrisy they observe.

7-19   What is the violence-viewing effect?

Media violence can contribute to aggression. This violence-viewing effect may be prompted by imitation and desensitization. Correlation does not equal causation, but study participants have reacted more cruelly when they have viewed violence (instead of entertaining nonviolence).

CHAPTER 8

Memory

Studying and Encoding Memories

8-1   What is *memory*, and how is it measured?

Memory is learning that has persisted over time, through the encoding, storage, and retrieval of information. Evidence of memory may be seen in an ability to *recall* information, *recognize* it, or *relearn* it more easily on a later attempt.

8-2   How do psychologists describe the human memory system?

Psychologists use memory models to think and communicate about memory. Information-processing models involve three processes: *encoding, storage,* and *retrieval.* Our agile brain processes many things simultaneously by means of *parallel processing.* The connectionism information-processing model focuses on this multitrack processing, viewing memories as products of interconnected neural networks. The three processing stages in the Atkinson-Shiffrin model are *sensory memory, short-term memory,* and *long-term memory.* This model has since been updated to include two important concepts: (1) *working memory,* to stress the active processing occurring in the second memory stage; and (2) automatic processing, to address the processing of information outside of conscious awareness.

8-3   How do explicit and implicit memories differ?

The human brain processes information on dual tracks, consciously and unconsciously. *Explicit* (declarative) *memories*—our conscious memories of facts and experiences—form through *effortful processing,* which requires conscious effort and attention. *Implicit* (nondeclarative) *memories*—of skills and classically conditioned associations—happen without our awareness, through *automatic processing.*

8-4   What information do we process automatically?

In addition to skills and classically conditioned associations, we automatically process incidental information about space, time, and frequency.

8-5   How does sensory memory work?

Sensory memory feeds some information into working memory for active processing there. An *iconic memory* is a very brief (a few tenths of a second) sensory memory of visual stimuli; an *echoic memory* is a three- or four-second sensory memory of auditory stimuli.

8-6   What is our short-term memory capacity?

Short-term memory capacity is about seven items, plus or minus two, but this information disappears from memory quickly without rehearsal. Our working memory capacity for active processing varies, depending on age and other factors.

8-7   What are some effortful processing strategies that can help us remember new information?

Effective effortful processing strategies include *chunking, mnemonics*, hierarchies, and distributed practice sessions (the *spacing effect*). The *testing effect* is the finding that consciously retrieving, rather than simply rereading, information enhances memory.

8-8   What are the levels of processing, and how do they affect encoding?

Depth of processing affects long-term retention. In *shallow processing*, we encode words based on their structure or appearance. Retention is best when we use *deep processing*, encoding words based on their meaning. We also more easily remember material that is personally meaningful—the self-reference effect.

⟫ Storing and Retrieving Memories

8-9   What is the capacity of long-term memory? Are our long-term memories processed and stored in specific locations?

Our long-term memory capacity is essentially unlimited. Memories are not stored intact in the brain in single spots. Many parts of the brain interact as we encode, store, and retrieve memories.

8-10   What roles do the frontal lobes and hippocampus play in memory processing?

The frontal lobes and *hippocampus* are parts of the brain network dedicated to explicit memory formation. Many brain regions send information to the frontal lobes for processing. The hippocampus, with the help of surrounding areas of cortex, registers and temporarily holds elements of explicit memories (which are either *semantic* or *episodic*) before moving them to other brain regions for long-term storage. The neural storage of long-term memories is called *memory consolidation*.

8-11   What roles do the cerebellum and basal ganglia play in memory processing?

The cerebellum and basal ganglia are parts of the brain network dedicated to implicit memory formation. The cerebellum is important for storing classically conditioned memories. The basal ganglia are involved in motor movement and help form procedural memories for skills. Many reactions and skills learned during our first four years continue into our adult lives, though we cannot consciously remember learning these associations and skills (infantile amnesia).

8-12   How do emotions affect our memory processing?

Emotional arousal causes an outpouring of stress hormones, which lead to activity in the brain's memory-forming areas. Significantly stressful events can trigger very clear *flashbulb memories*.

8-13   How do changes at the synapse level affect our memory processing?

Long-term potentiation (LTP) is the neural basis of learning. In LTP, neurons become more efficient at releasing and sensing the presence of neurotransmitters, and more connections develop between neurons.

8-14   How do external cues, internal emotions, and order of appearance influence memory retrieval?

External cues activate associations that help us retrieve memories; this process may occur without our awareness, as it does in *priming*. The *encoding specificity principle* is the idea that cues and contexts specific to a particular memory will be most effective in helping us recall it. Returning to the same physical context or emotional state (*mood congruency*) in which we formed a memory can help us retrieve it. The *serial position effect* accounts for our tendency to recall best the last items (which may still be in working memory) and the first items (which we've spent more time rehearsing) in a list.

⟫ Forgetting, Memory Construction, and Improving Memory

8-15   Why do we forget?

Anterograde amnesia is an inability to form new memories. *Retrograde amnesia* is an inability to retrieve old memories. Normal forgetting can happen because we have never encoded information (encoding failure); because the physical trace has decayed (storage decay); or because we cannot retrieve what we have encoded and stored (retrieval failure). Retrieval problems may result from *proactive* (forward-acting) *interference*, as prior learning interferes with recall of new information, or from *retroactive* (backward-acting) *interference*, as new learning disrupts recall of old information. Motivated forgetting occurs, but researchers have found little evidence of *repression*.

8-16   How do misinformation, imagination, and source amnesia influence our memory construction? How do we decide whether a memory is real or false?

Memories can be continually revised when retrieved, a process memory researchers call *reconsolidation*. In experiments demonstrating the *misinformation effect,* people have formed false memories, incorporating misleading details, after receiving wrong information after an event, or after repeatedly imagining and rehearsing something that never happened. When we reassemble a memory during retrieval, we may attribute it to the wrong source (*source amnesia*). Source amnesia may help explain *déjà vu*. False memories feel like real memories and can be persistent but are usually limited to the gist of the event.

8-17   Why have reports of repressed and recovered memories been so hotly debated?

The debate focuses on whether memories of early childhood abuse are repressed and can be recovered during therapy. Unless the victim was a child too young to remember, such traumas are usually remembered vividly, not repressed. Psychologists agree that childhood sexual abuse happens; injustice happens; forgetting happens; recovered memories are common; memories of events that happened before age 4 are unreliable; memories "recovered" under hypnosis are especially unreliable; and memories, whether real or false, can be emotionally upsetting.

8-18 How reliable are young children's eyewitness descriptions?

Children's eyewitness descriptions are subject to the same memory influences that distort adult reports. If questioned soon after an event in neutral words they understand, children can accurately recall events and people involved in them.

8-19 How can you use memory research findings to do better in this and other courses?

Memory research findings suggest the following strategies for improving memory: Rehearse repeatedly, make the material meaningful, activate retrieval cues, use mnemonic devices, minimize proactive and retroactive interference, sleep more, and test yourself to be sure you can retrieve, as well as recognize, material.

CHAPTER 9

Thinking, Language, and Intelligence

Thinking

9-1 What is *cognition*, and what are the functions of concepts?

Cognition refers to all the mental activities associated with thinking, knowing, remembering, and communicating. We use *concepts,* mental groupings of similar objects, events, ideas, or people, to simplify and order the world around us. We form most concepts around *prototypes,* or best examples of a category.

9-2 What cognitive strategies assist our problem solving, and what obstacles hinder it?

An *algorithm* is a methodical, logical rule or procedure (such as a step-by-step description for evacuating a building during a fire) that guarantees a solution to a problem. A *heuristic* is a simpler strategy (such as running for an exit if you smell smoke) that is usually speedier than an algorithm but is also more error prone. *Insight* is not a strategy-based solution, but rather a sudden flash of inspiration that solves a problem. Obstacles to problem solving include *confirmation bias,* which predisposes us to verify rather than challenge our hypotheses, and *fixation,* such as *mental set,* which may prevent us from taking the fresh perspective that would lead to a solution.

9-3 What is *intuition*, and how can the availability and representativeness heuristics influence our decisions and judgments?

Intuition is the effortless, immediate, automatic feelings or thoughts we often use instead of systematic reasoning. Heuristics, such as the *representativeness heuristic,* enable snap judgments. Using the *availability heuristic,* we judge the likelihood of things based on how readily they come to mind.

9-4 What factors exaggerate our fear of unlikely events?

We tend to be afraid of what our ancestral history has prepared us to fear, what we cannot control, what is immediate, and what is most readily available. We fear too little the ongoing threats that claim lives one by one, such as traffic accidents and diseases.

9-5 How are our decisions and judgments affected by overconfidence, belief perseverance, and framing?

Overconfidence can lead us to overestimate the accuracy of our beliefs. When a belief we have formed and explained has been discredited, *belief perseverance* may cause us to cling to that belief. A remedy for belief perseverance is to consider how we might have explained an opposite result. *Framing* is the way a question or statement is presented. Subtle differences in presentation can dramatically alter our responses.

9-6 How do smart thinkers use intuition?

Smart thinkers welcome their intuitions (which are usually adaptive), but also know when to override them. When making complex decisions we may benefit from gathering as much information as possible and then taking time to let our two-track mind process it.

9-7 What is *creativity*, and what fosters it?

Creativity, the ability to produce novel and valuable ideas, correlates somewhat with aptitude, but is more than school smarts. Aptitude tests require *convergent thinking,* but creativity requires *divergent thinking.* Robert Sternberg has proposed that creativity involves expertise; imaginative thinking skills; a venturesome personality; intrinsic motivation; and a creative environment that sparks, supports, and refines creative ideas.

9-8 What do we know about thinking in other species?

Researchers make inferences about other species' consciousness and intelligence based on behavior. Evidence from studies of various species shows that many other animals use concepts, numbers, and tools and that they transmit learning from one generation to the next (cultural transmission). And, like humans, some other species show insight, self-awareness, altruism, cooperation, and grief.

Language and Thought

9-9 What are the structural components of a language?

Phonemes are a *language's* basic units of sound. *Morphemes* are the elementary units of meaning. *Grammar*—the system of rules that enables us to communicate—includes semantics (rules for deriving meaning) and syntax (rules for ordering words into sentences).

9-10 How do we acquire language, and what is *universal grammar?*

As our biology and experience interact, we readily learn the specific grammar and vocabulary of the language we experience as children. Linguist Noam Chomsky has proposed that all human languages share a universal grammar—the basic building blocks of language—and that humans are born with a predisposition to learn language. Human languages do share some commonalities, but other researchers note that children learn grammar as they discern language patterns.

9-11 What are the milestones in language development, and when is the critical period for acquiring language?

Language development's timing varies, but all children follow the same sequence. Receptive language (the ability to understand what is said to or about you) develops before productive language (the ability to produce words). At about 4 months of age, infants *babble,* making sounds found in languages from all over the world, which by about 10 months includes only the sounds found in their household language. Around 12 months of age, children begin to speak in single words. This *one-word stage* evolves into *two-word (telegraphic)* utterances before their second birthday, after which they begin speaking in full sentences. Childhood is a critical period for learning language. A delay in exposure until age 2 or 3 produces a rush of language. But children not exposed to either a spoken or a signed language until age 7 will never master any language. The importance of early language experiences is often evident in deaf children born to hearing-nonsigning parents.

9-12 What brain areas are involved in language processing and speech?

Aphasia is an impairment of language, usually caused by left-hemisphere damage. Two important language- and speech-processing areas are *Broca's area,* a region of the left frontal lobe that controls language expression, and *Wernicke's area,* a region in the left temporal lobe that controls language reception. Language processing is spread across other brain areas as well, with different neural networks handling specific linguistic subtasks.

9-13 What do we know about other species' capacity for language?

Chimpanzees and bonobos have learned to communicate with humans by signing or by pushing buttons. Some have developed vocabularies of nearly 400 words, communicated by stringing these words together, and have demonstrated some understanding of syntax. While only humans communicate in complex sentences, other animals' impressive abilities to think and communicate challenge humans to consider what this means about the moral rights of other species.

9-14 What is the relationship between thinking and language, and what is the value of thinking in images?

Although Benjamin Lee Whorf's *linguistic determinism* hypothesis suggested that language determines thought, it is more accurate to say that language influences thought (*linguistic relativism*). Different languages embody different ways of thinking, and immersion in bilingual education can enhance thinking. We often think in images when we use implicit (nondeclarative, procedural) memory—our automatic memory system for motor and cognitive skills and classically conditioned associations. Thinking in images can increase our skills when we mentally practice upcoming events. Process simulation (focusing on the steps needed to reach a goal) is effective, but outcome simulation (fantasizing about having achieved the goal) does little.

Intelligence and Its Assessment

9-15 How do psychologists define *intelligence*, and what are the arguments for *g*?

Intelligence is the ability to learn from experience, solve problems, and use knowledge to adapt to new situations. Charles Spearman proposed that we have one *general intelligence* (*g*) underlying all mental abilities. Through his work with factor analysis, a statistical procedure that identifies clusters of related abilities, he noted that those who score high in one area typically score higher than average in other areas.

9-16 How do Gardner's and Sternberg's theories of multiple intelligences differ, and what criticisms have they faced?

Howard Gardner proposed eight independent intelligences (linguistic, logical-mathematical, musical, spatial, bodily-kinesthetic, intrapersonal, interpersonal, and naturalist), as well as a possible ninth (existential intelligence). The different intelligences of people with *savant syndrome,* autism spectrum disorder (ASD), and certain kinds of brain damage seem to support his view. Robert Sternberg's triarchic theory proposes three intelligence areas that predict real-world skills: analytical (academic problem solving), creative (innovative smarts), and practical (street smarts). Critics note research that has confirmed a general intelligence factor, which widely predicts performance. But highly successful people also tend to be conscientious, well-connected, and doggedly energetic; their achievements arise from both ability *and* motivation.

9-17 What are the four components of emotional intelligence?

Emotional intelligence, which is an aspect of social intelligence, includes the abilities to perceive, understand, manage, and use emotions. Emotionally intelligent people tend to be happy, healthy, and more successful personally and professionally. Some critics question whether calling these abilities "intelligence" stretches that concept too far.

9-18 What is an *intelligence test,* and how do achievement and aptitude tests differ?

An *intelligence test* assesses an individual's mental aptitudes and compares them with those of others, using numerical scores. *Aptitude tests* measure the ability to learn, while *achievement tests* measure what we have already learned.

9-19 When and why were intelligence tests created, and how do today's tests differ from early intelligence tests?

Alfred Binet, who tended toward an environmental explanation of intelligence differences, started the modern intelligence-testing movement in France in the early 1900s, when he developed questions to help predict children's future progress in the Paris school system. Binet hoped his test would improve children's education but feared it might be used to label them. During the early twentieth century, Lewis Terman of Stanford University revised Binet's work for use in the United States. Terman thought his *Stanford-Binet* could help guide people toward appropriate opportunities, but his belief in an intelligence that was fixed at birth and differed among ethnic groups realized Binet's fear that intelligence tests would be used to limit children's opportunities. William Stern contributed the concept of the *IQ (intelligence quotient)*. The most widely used intelligence tests today are the *Wechsler Adult Intelligence Scale (WAIS)* and Wechsler's tests for children. These tests differ from their predecessors in the way they offer an overall intelligence score as well as scores for verbal comprehension, perceptual organization, working memory, and processing speed.

9-20   What is a *normal curve*, and what does it mean to say that a test has been standardized and is reliable and valid?

The distribution of test scores often forms a *normal* (bell-shaped) *curve* around the central average score, with fewer and fewer scores at the extremes. *Standardization* establishes a basis for meaningful score comparisons by giving a test to a representative sample of future test-takers. *Reliability* is the extent to which a test yields consistent results (on two halves of the test, on alternative forms of the test, or upon retesting). *Validity* is the extent to which a test measures or predicts what it is supposed to. A test has *predictive validity* if it predicts a behavior it was designed to predict. (Aptitude tests have predictive validity if they can predict future achievements; their predictive power is best for the early school years.)

9-21   What are the traits of those at the low and high intelligence extremes?

An intelligence test score of or below 70 is one diagnostic criterion for the diagnosis of *intellectual disability;* other criteria are limited conceptual, social, and practical skills. People at the high intelligence extreme tend to be healthy and well-adjusted, as well as unusually successful academically.

9-22   What are cross-sectional studies and longitudinal studies, and why is it important to know which method was used?

The differing intelligence findings of cross-sectional and longitudinal studies—that mental ability declines with age or that it remains stable (or even increases)—illustrate the fact that *cross-sectional studies* compare people of different eras and life circumstances. This can provide an excellent snapshot of a particular point in time, but *longitudinal studies* are superior for tracing the evolution of traits over a longer period.

9-23   How stable are intelligence test scores over the life span?

The stability of intelligence test scores increases with age. At age 4, scores begin to predict adolescent and adult scores. By age 11, scores are very stable and predictive.

9-24   How does aging affect crystallized and fluid intelligence?

Cross-sectional and longitudinal studies have shown that *fluid intelligence* declines in older adults, in part because neural processing slows. However, *crystallized intelligence* tends to increase.

Genetic and Environmental Influences on Intelligence

9-25   What is *heritability*, and what do twin and adoption studies tell us about the nature and nurture of intelligence?

Studies of twins, family members, and adoptive parents and siblings indicate a significant hereditary contribution to intelligence scores. Intelligence is polygenetic. *Heritability* is the proportion of variation among individuals in a group that can be attributed to genes.

9-26   How can environmental influences affect cognitive development?

Studies of children raised in impoverished environments with minimal social interaction indicate that life experiences significantly influence cognitive development. No evidence supports the idea that normal, healthy children can be molded into geniuses by growing up in an exceptionally enriched environment.

9-27   How and why do the genders differ in mental ability scores?

Males and females have the same average intelligence test scores, but they tend to differ in some specific abilities. Girls, on average, are better spellers, more verbally fluent, better at locating objects, better at detecting emotions, and more sensitive to touch, taste, and color. Boys outperform girls at spatial ability and complex mathematics, though boys and girls hardly differ in math computation and overall math performance. Boys also outnumber girls at the low and high extremes of mental abilities. Evolutionary and cultural explanations have been proposed for these gender differences.

9-28   How and why do racial and ethnic groups differ in mental ability scores?

Racial and ethnic groups differ in their average intelligence test scores. Evidence suggests that environmental differences are responsible for these group differences.

9-29   Are intelligence tests biased or unfair? What is *stereotype threat*, and how does it affect test-takers' performance?

The scientific meaning of bias hinges on a test's ability to predict future behavior for all test-takers, not just for some. In this sense, most experts consider the major aptitude tests unbiased. However, if we consider bias to mean that a test may be influenced by the test-taker's cultural experience, then intelligence tests, by that definition, may be considered unfair. *Stereotype threat,* a self-confirming concern that one will be evaluated based on a negative stereotype, affects performance on all kinds of tests.

CHAPTER 10

Motivation and Emotion

Basic Motivational Concepts, Affiliation, and Achievement

10-1   How do psychologists define *motivation*? From what perspectives do they view motivated behavior?

Motivation is a need or desire that energizes and directs behavior. The *instinct*/evolutionary perspective explores genetic influences on complex behaviors. *Drive-reduction theory* explores how *physiological needs* create aroused tension states (drives) that direct us to satisfy those needs. Environmental *incentives* can intensify drives. Drive-reduction's goal is *homeostasis*, maintaining a steady internal state. Arousal theory proposes that some behaviors (such as those driven by curiosity) do not reduce physiological needs but rather are prompted by a search for an optimum level of arousal. The *Yerkes-Dodson law* describes the relationship between arousal and performance. Abraham Maslow's *hierarchy of needs* proposes a pyramid of human needs, from basic needs up to higher-level needs.

10-2   What evidence points to our human affiliation need—our need to belong?

Our *affiliation need*—to feel connected and identified with others—had survival value for our ancestors, which may explain why humans in every society live in groups. According to *self-determination theory,* we strive to satisfy our needs for competence, autonomy, and relatedness. Social bonds help us to be healthier and happier, and feeling loved activates brain regions associated with reward and safety systems. *Ostracism* is the deliberate exclusion of individuals or groups. Social isolation can put us at risk mentally and physically.

10-3   How does social networking influence us?

We connect with others through social networking, strengthening our relationships with those we already know and meeting new friends or romantic partners. When networking, people tend toward increased self-disclosure. People with high *narcissism* are especially active on social networking sites. Working out strategies for self-control and disciplined usage can help people maintain a healthy balance between their real-world and online time.

10-4   What is *achievement motivation*, and what are some ways to encourage achievement?

Achievement motivation is a desire for significant accomplishment, for mastery of skills or ideas, for control, and for attaining a high standard. High achievement motivation leads to greater success, especially when combined with determined, persistent *grit.* Research shows that excessive rewards (driving *extrinsic motivation*) can undermine *intrinsic motivation.*

Hunger

10-5   What physiological factors produce hunger?

Hunger pangs correspond to stomach contractions, but hunger also has other causes. Neural areas in the brain, some within the hypothalamus, monitor blood chemistry (including level of *glucose*) and incoming information about the body's state. Appetite hormones include ghrelin (secreted by an empty stomach); insulin (controls blood glucose); leptin (secreted by fat cells); orexin (secreted by the hypothalamus); and PYY (secreted by the digestive tract). *Basal metabolic rate* is the body's resting rate of energy expenditure. The body may have a *set point* (a biologically fixed tendency to maintain an optimum weight) or a looser settling point (also influenced by the environment).

10-6   What cultural and situational factors influence hunger?

Hunger reflects our memory of when we last ate and our expectation of when we should eat again. Humans as a species prefer certain tastes (such as sweet and salty), but our individual preferences are also influenced by conditioning, culture, and situation. Some taste preferences have survival value. Situations, such as the presence of others, serving size, and the variety of foods offered, can also influence what and how much we eat.

10-7   How does obesity affect physical and psychological health, and what factors are involved in weight management?

Obesity, defined by a body mass index (BMI) of 30 or above, is associated with increased depression (especially among women) and bullying, and with many physical health risks. Genes and environment interact to produce obesity. Storing fat was adaptive to our ancestors, and fat requires less food intake to maintain than it did to gain. Set point and metabolism matter. Twin and adoption studies indicate that body weight is also genetically influenced. Environmental influences include sleep loss, social influence, and food and activity levels. Those wishing to lose weight are advised to make a lifelong change in habits: Begin only if you feel motivated and self-disciplined; exercise and get enough sleep; minimize exposure to tempting food cues; limit variety and eat healthy foods; reduce portion sizes; space meals throughout the day; beware of the binge; plan ahead to control eating during social events; forgive the occasional lapse; publicly chart your progress; and connect to a support group.

Theories and Physiology of Emotion

10-8   How do arousal, expressive behavior, and cognition interact in emotion?

Emotions are responses of the whole organism, involving physiological arousal, expressive behaviors, and conscious experience. Theories of emotion generally address two major questions: (1) Does physiological arousal come before or after emotional feelings? and (2) how do feeling and cognition interact? The *James-Lange theory* maintains that emotional feelings follow our body's response to emotion-inducing stimuli (we observe our heart pounding and feel fear). The *Cannon-Bard theory* proposes that our physiological response to an emotion-inducing stimulus occurs at the same time as our subjective feeling of the emotion (one does not cause the other).

10-9 To experience emotions, must we consciously interpret and label them?

The Schachter-Singer *two-factor theory* holds that our emotions have two ingredients, physical arousal and a cognitive label; the cognitive labels we put on our states of arousal are an essential ingredient of emotion. Lazarus agreed that many important emotions arise from our interpretations or inferences. But Zajonc and LeDoux have contended that some simple emotional responses occur instantly, not only outside our conscious awareness, but before any cognitive processing occurs. This interplay between emotion and cognition illustrates our two-track mind.

10-10 What are some of the basic emotions?

Carroll Izard's 10 basic emotions are joy, interest-excitement, surprise, sadness, anger, disgust, contempt, fear, shame, and guilt.

10-11 What is the link between emotional arousal and the autonomic nervous system?

The arousal component of emotion is regulated by the autonomic nervous system's sympathetic (arousing) and parasympathetic (calming) divisions. In a crisis, the fight-or-flight response automatically mobilizes your body for action.

10-12 Do different emotions activate different physiological and brain-pattern responses?

The large-scale body changes that accompany fear, anger, and sexual arousal are very similar (increased perspiration, breathing, and heart rate), though they feel different. Emotions may be similarly arousing, but some subtle physiological responses, such as facial muscle movements, distinguish them. More meaningful differences have been found in activity in some brain pathways and cortical areas.

10-13 How effective are polygraphs in using body states to detect lies?

Polygraphs (lie detectors) attempt to measure several physiological indicators of emotion, but are not accurate enough to justify widespread use in business and law enforcement. Using the Concealed Information Test may produce better indications of lying.

Expressing and Experiencing Emotion

10-14 How do we communicate nonverbally?

Much of our communication is through body movements, facial expressions, and voice tones. Even seconds-long filmed slices of behavior can reveal feelings.

10-15 How do the genders differ in their ability to communicate nonverbally?

Women tend to read emotional cues more easily and to be more empathic. They also express more emotion.

10-16 How are gestures and facial expressions understood within and across cultures?

The meaning of gestures varies with culture, but facial expressions, such as those of happiness and sadness, are common the world over. Cultures also differ in the amount of emotion they express.

10-17 How do our facial expressions influence our feelings?

Research on the *facial feedback effect* shows that our facial expressions can trigger emotional feelings and signal our body to respond accordingly. We also mimic others' expressions, which helps us empathize. A similar *behavior feedback effect* is the tendency of behavior to influence our own and others' thoughts, feelings, and actions.

CHAPTER 11

Stress, Health, and Human Flourishing

Stress and Illness

11-1 How does our appraisal of an event affect our stress reaction, and what are the three main types of stressors?

Stress is the process by which we appraise and respond to stressors that challenge or threaten us. If we appraise an event as challenging, we will be aroused and focused in preparation for success; if we appraise it as a threat, we will experience a stress reaction, and our health may suffer. The three main types of stressors are catastrophes, significant life changes, and daily hassles and social stress.

11-2 How do we respond and adapt to stress?

Walter Cannon viewed the stress response as a fight-or-flight system. Hans Selye proposed a general three-phase (alarm, resistance, exhaustion) *general adaptation syndrome (GAS)*. Facing stress, women may have a *tend-and-befriend* response; men may withdraw socially, turn to alcohol, or become emotionally insensitive.

11-3 How does stress make us more vulnerable to disease?

Psychoneuroimmunology is the study of how psychological, neural, and endocrine processes together affect the immune system and resulting health. Stress diverts energy from the immune system, inhibiting the activities of its B and T lymphocytes, macrophages, and NK cells. Stress does not cause illness, but by altering our immune functioning it may make us more vulnerable to diseases and influence their progression.

11-4 Why are some of us more prone than others to coronary heart disease?

Coronary heart disease has been linked with the reactive, anger-prone *Type A* personality. Compared with relaxed, easygoing *Type B* personalities, who are less likely to experience heart disease, Type A people secrete more stress hormones. Chronic stress also contributes to persistent inflammation, which is associated with heart and other health problems, including depression.

11-5 So, does stress *cause* illness?

Stress may not directly cause illness, but it does make us more vulnerable, by influencing our behaviors and our physiology.

11-6 What are the causes and consequences of anger?

Facing a threat or a challenge may trigger anger, and our culture can influence how we express that anger. Chronic hostility is a key negative emotion linked to heart disease. Emotional *catharsis* may be temporarily calming, but it does not reduce anger; expressing anger can make us angrier. Experts suggest reducing the level of physiological arousal of anger by waiting, finding a healthy distraction or support, and trying to move away from the situation mentally. Controlled assertions of feelings may resolve conflicts, and forgiveness may rid us of angry feelings.

Health and Happiness

11-7 In what two ways do people try to alleviate stress?

We use *problem-focused coping* to change the stressor or the way we interact with it. We use *emotion-focused coping* to avoid or ignore stressors and attend to emotional needs related to stress reactions.

11-8 How does a perceived lack of control affect health?

A perceived lack of *personal control* provokes an outpouring of hormones that put people's health at risk. Being unable to avoid repeated aversive events can lead to *learned helplessness*. People who perceive an *internal locus of control* achieve more, enjoy better health, and are happier than those who perceive an *external locus of control*.

11-9 Why is self-control important, and can our self-control be depleted?

Self-control requires attention and energy, but predicts good health, higher income, and better school performance; it does better than an intelligence test score in predicting future academic and life success. Self-control varies over time. Researchers disagree about the factors influencing self-control, but strengthening it can lead to a healthier, happier, and more successful life.

11-10 How does an optimistic outlook affect health and longevity?

Studies of people with an optimistic outlook show that their immune system is stronger, their blood pressure does not increase as sharply in response to stress, their recovery from heart bypass surgery is faster, and their life expectancy is longer, compared with their pessimistic counterparts.

11-11 How does social support promote good health?

Social support promotes health by calming us, by reducing blood pressure and stress hormones, and by fostering stronger immune functioning. We can significantly reduce our stress and increase our health by building and maintaining relationships, and by confiding rather than suppressing painful feelings.

11-12 How effective is aerobic exercise as a way to manage stress and improve well-being?

Aerobic exercise is sustained, oxygen-consuming activity that increases heart and lung fitness. It increases arousal, leads to muscle relaxation and sounder sleep, triggers the production of neurotransmitters, and enhances self-image. It can relieve depression and, in later life, is associated with better cognitive functioning and longer life.

11-13 In what ways might relaxation and meditation influence stress and health?

Relaxation and meditation have been shown to lower stress, improve immune functioning, and lessen anxiety and depression. *Mindfulness meditation* is a reflective practice of attending to current experiences in a nonjudgmental and accepting manner. Massage therapy also relaxes muscles and reduces depression.

11-14 What is the *faith factor,* and what are some possible explanations for the link between faith and health?

The faith factor is the finding that religiously active people tend to live longer than those who are not religiously active. Possible explanations may include intervening variables such as the healthy behaviors, social support, or positive emotions often found among people who regularly attend religious services.

11-15 What is the *feel-good, do-good phenomenon,* and what is the focus of positive psychology research?

Happy people tend to be healthy, energized, and satisfied with life, making them more willing to help others (the *feel-good, do-good phenomenon*). *Positive psychologists* use scientific methods to study human flourishing, aiming to discover and promote strengths and virtues that help individuals and communities to thrive.

11-16 How do time, wealth, adaptation, and comparison affect our happiness levels?

The moods triggered by good or bad events seldom last beyond that day. Even significant good events, such as sudden wealth, seldom increase happiness for long. Happiness is relative to our own experiences (the *adaptation-level phenomenon*) and to others' success (the *relative deprivation* principle).

11-17 What predicts happiness, and how can we be happier?

Some individuals, because of their genetic predispositions and personal histories, are happier than others. Cultures, which vary in the traits they value and the behaviors they expect and reward, also influence personal levels of happiness. Tips for increasing happiness levels: take charge of your schedule, act happy, seek meaningful work and leisure, buy shared experiences rather than things, exercise, sleep enough, foster friendships, focus beyond the self, challenge negative thinking, and nurture gratitude and spirituality.

CHAPTER 12

Social Psychology

Social Thinking and Social Influence

12-1 What do social psychologists study? How do we tend to explain others' behavior and our own?

Social psychologists use scientific methods to study how people think about, influence, and relate to one another. They study the social influences that explain why the same person will act differently in different situations. When explaining others' behavior, we may—especially if we come from an individualist Western culture—commit the *fundamental attribution error*, by underestimating the influence of the situation and overestimating the effects of stable, enduring traits. When explaining our own behavior, we more readily attribute it to the influence of the situation.

12-2 How do attitudes and actions interact?

Peripheral route persuasion uses incidental cues (such as celebrity endorsement) to try to produce fast but relatively thoughtless changes in attitudes. *Central route persuasion* offers evidence and arguments to trigger thoughtful responses. When other influences are minimal, attitudes that are stable, specific, and easily recalled can affect our actions. Actions can modify attitudes, as in the *foot-in-the-door phenomenon* and *role* playing. When our attitudes don't fit with our actions, *cognitive dissonance theory* suggests that we will reduce tension by changing our attitudes to match our actions.

12-3 How does culture affect our behavior?

A *culture* is an enduring set of behaviors, ideas, attitudes, values, and traditions shared by a group and transmitted from one generation to the next. Cultural *norms* are understood rules that inform members of a culture about accepted and expected behaviors. Cultures differ across time and space.

12-4 How is social contagion a form of conformity, and how do conformity experiments reveal the power of social influence?

Social contagion (the chameleon effect)—our tendency to unconsciously imitate others' behavior, expressions, postures, voice tones, and moods—is a form of *conformity*. Solomon Asch and others found that we are most likely to adjust our behavior or thinking to coincide with a group standard when we feel incompetent or insecure, our group has at least three people, everyone else agrees, we admire the group's status and attractiveness, we have not already committed to another response, we know we are being observed, and our culture encourages respect for social standards. We may conform to gain approval (*normative social influence*) or because we are willing to accept others' opinions as new information (*informational social influence*).

12-5 What did Milgram's obedience experiments teach us about the power of social influence?

Stanley Milgram's experiments—in which people obeyed orders even when they thought they were harming another person—demonstrated that strong social influences can make ordinary people conform to falsehoods or capitulate to cruelty. Obedience was highest when the person giving orders was nearby and was perceived as a legitimate authority figure, the research was supported by a prestigious institution, the victim was depersonalized or at a distance, and there were no role models for defiance.

12-6 What do the social influence studies teach us about ourselves? How much power do we have as individuals?

These experiments have demonstrated that strong social influences can influence behavior. The power of the individual (personal control) and the power of the situation (social control) interact. A small minority that consistently expresses its views may sway the majority, as may even a single committed individual.

12-7 How does the presence of others influence our actions, via social facilitation, social loafing, and deindividuation?

In *social facilitation,* the mere presence of others arouses us, improving our performance on easy or well-learned tasks but decreasing it on difficult ones. In *social loafing,* group work makes us feel less responsible, and we may free ride on others' efforts. When the presence of others both arouses us and makes us feel anonymous, we may experience *deindividuation*—loss of self-awareness and self-restraint.

12-8 How can group interaction enable group polarization?

In *group polarization,* group discussions with like-minded others strengthen members' prevailing beliefs and attitudes.

12-9 What role does the internet play in group polarization?

Internet communication magnifies the effect of connecting like-minded people, for better and for worse. People find support, which strengthens their ideas, but also often isolation from those with different opinions. Separation plus conversation may thus lead to group polarization.

12-10 How can group interaction enable groupthink?

Groupthink is driven by a desire for harmony within a decision-making group, overriding realistic appraisal of alternatives. Group leaders can harness the benefits of group interaction by assigning people to identify possible problems, and by welcoming various opinions and expert critique.

⤵ Antisocial Relations

12-11 What is *prejudice*? How do explicit and implicit prejudice differ?

Prejudice is an unjustifiable, usually negative attitude toward a group and its members. Prejudice's three components are beliefs (often *stereotypes*), emotions, and predispositions to action (*discrimination*). Prejudice may be explicit (overt), or it may be implicit—an unthinking knee-jerk response operating below conscious awareness. Implicit prejudice can cause discrimination even when people do not consciously intend to discriminate.

12-12 What groups are frequent targets of prejudice?

Prejudice involves explicit and implicit negative attitudes toward people of a particular racial or ethnic group, gender identity, sexual orientation, or belief system. In the United States, frequently targeted groups include Black Americans, women, Muslim Americans, and gay, lesbian, and transgender people.

12-13 What are some social, emotional, and cognitive roots of prejudice, and what are some ways to eliminate prejudice?

The social roots of prejudice include social inequalities and divisions. Higher-status groups often justify their privileged position with the *just-world phenomenon*. We tend to favor our own group (ingroup bias) as we divide ourselves into "us" (the ingroup) and "them" (the outgroup). Prejudice can also be a tool for protecting our emotional well-being, as when we focus our anger by blaming events on a *scapegoat*. The cognitive roots of prejudice grow from our natural ways of processing information: forming categories, remembering vivid cases, and believing that the world is just (and that our own and our group's ways of doing things are the right ways). Monitoring our feelings and actions, as well as developing new friendships, can help us free ourselves from prejudice.

12-14 How does psychology's definition of *aggression* differ from everyday usage? What biological factors make us more prone to hurt one another?

In psychology's more specific meaning, *aggression* is any act intended to harm someone physically or emotionally. Biology influences our threshold for aggressive behaviors at three levels: genetic (inherited traits), neural (activity in key brain areas), and biochemical (such as alcohol or excess testosterone in the bloodstream). Aggression is a complex behavior resulting from the interaction of biology and experience.

12-15 What psychological and social-cultural factors may trigger aggressive behavior?

Frustration (the *frustration-aggression principle*), previous reinforcement for aggressive behavior, observing aggressive role models, and poor self-control all contribute to aggression. Media violence provides *social scripts* that children learn to follow. Viewing sexual violence contributes to greater aggression toward women. Playing violent video games can increase aggressive thoughts, emotions, and behaviors.

⟫ Prosocial Relations

12-16 Why do we befriend or fall in love with some people but not others?

Proximity (geographical nearness) increases liking, in part because of the *mere exposure effect*—exposure to novel stimuli increases liking of those stimuli. Physical attractiveness increases social opportunities and improves the way we are perceived. Similarity of attitudes and interests greatly increases liking, especially as relationships develop. We also like those who like us.

12-17 How does romantic love typically change as time passes?

Intimate love relationships start with *passionate love*—an intensely aroused state. Over time, the strong affection of *companionate love* may develop, especially if enhanced by an *equitable* relationship, intimate *self-disclosure,* and positive support.

12-18 What is *altruism*? When are people most—and least—likely to help?

Altruism is unselfish regard for the well-being of others. We are most likely to help when we notice an incident, interpret it as an emergency, and assume responsibility for helping. Other factors, including our mood and our similarity to the victim, also affect our willingness to help. We are least likely to help if other bystanders are present (the *bystander effect*).

12-19 How do social exchange theory and social norms explain helping behavior?

Social exchange theory is the view that we help others because it is in our own self-interest; in this view, the goal of social behavior is maximizing personal benefits and minimizing costs. Others believe that helping results from socialization, in which we are taught guidelines for expected behaviors in social situations, such as the *reciprocity norm* and the *social-responsibility norm.*

12-20 How do social traps and mirror-image perceptions fuel social conflict?

Social traps are situations in which people in conflict pursue their own individual self-interest, harming the collective well-being. Individuals and cultures in conflict also tend to form *mirror-image perceptions:* Each party views the opponent as untrustworthy and evil-intentioned, and itself as an ethical, peaceful victim. Perceptions can become *self-fulfilling prophecies.*

12-21 What can we do to promote peace?

Peace can result when individuals or groups work together to achieve *superordinate* (shared) *goals*. Research indicates that contact, cooperation, communication, and conciliation—such as the Graduated and Reciprocated Initiatives in Tension-Reduction (GRIT) strategy—help promote peace.

CHAPTER 13

Personality

⟫ Classic Perspectives on Personality

13-1 What is *personality*, and what theories inform our understanding of personality?

Personality is an individual's characteristic pattern of thinking, feeling, and acting. Psychoanalytic (and later psychodynamic) theory and humanistic theory have become part of our cultural legacy. They also laid the foundation for later theories, such as trait and social-cognitive theories of personality.

13-2 How did Sigmund Freud's treatment of psychological disorders lead to his view of the unconscious mind?

Psychodynamic theories view personality from the perspective that behavior is a dynamic interaction between the conscious and unconscious mind. These theories trace their origin to Sigmund Freud's theory of *psychoanalysis*. In treating patients whose disorders had no clear physical explanation, Freud concluded that these problems reflected unacceptable thoughts and feelings, hidden away in the *unconscious* mind. To explore this hidden part of a patient's mind, Freud used *free association* and dream analysis.

13-3 What was Freud's view of personality?

Freud believed that personality results from conflict arising from the interaction among the mind's three systems: the *id* (pleasure-seeking impulses), *ego* (reality-oriented executive), and *superego* (internalized set of ideals, or conscience).

13-4   What developmental stages did Freud propose?

He believed children pass through five *psychosexual stages* (oral, anal, phallic, latency, and genital). According to this view, unresolved conflicts at any stage can leave a person's pleasure-seeking impulses *fixated* (stalled) at that stage.

13-5   How did Freud think people defended themselves against anxiety?

For Freud, anxiety was the product of tensions between the demands of the id and superego. The ego copes by using unconscious *defense mechanisms,* such as *repression,* which he viewed as the basic mechanism underlying and enabling all the others.

13-6   Which of Freud's ideas did his followers accept or reject?

Freud's early followers, the neo-Freudians, accepted many of his ideas. They differed in placing more emphasis on the conscious mind and in stressing social motives more than sex or aggression. Most contemporary psychodynamic theorists and therapists reject Freud's emphasis on sexual motivation. They stress, with support from modern research findings, the view that much of our mental life is unconscious, and they believe that our childhood experiences influence our adult personality and attachment patterns. Many also believe that our species' shared evolutionary history shaped some universal predispositions.

13-7   What are *projective tests,* how are they used, and what are some criticisms of them?

Projective tests attempt to assess personality by showing people stimuli open to many possible interpretations and treating their answers as revelations of unconscious motives. The *Thematic Apperception Test (TAT)* and the *Rorschach inkblot test* are two such tests. The TAT provides a valid and reliable map of people's implicit motives that is consistent over time. The Rorschach has low reliability and validity, but some clinicians value it as a source of suggestive leads, an icebreaker, or a revealing interview technique.

13-8   How do contemporary psychologists view Freud's psychoanalysis?

They give Freud credit for drawing attention to the vast unconscious, to the struggle to cope with anxiety and sexuality, to the conflict between biological impulses and social restraints, and for some forms of defense mechanisms. But his concept of repression, and his view of the unconscious as a collection of repressed and unacceptable thoughts, wishes, feelings, and memories, cannot survive scientific scrutiny. Freud offered after-the-fact explanations, which are hard to test scientifically. Research does not support many of Freud's specific ideas, such as the view that development is fixed in childhood. (We now know it is lifelong.)

13-9   How has modern research developed our understanding of the unconscious?

Research confirms that we do not have full access to all that goes on in our mind, though today's science views the unconscious as a separate and parallel track of information processing that occurs outside our awareness. This processing includes schemas that control our perceptions, priming, implicit memories of learned skills, instantly activated emotions, and stereotypes that filter our information processing of others' traits and characteristics. Research also supports reaction formation and projection (the false consensus effect).

13-10 How did humanistic psychologists view personality, and what was their goal in studying personality?

The *humanistic* psychologists' view of personality focused on the potential for healthy personal growth and people's striving for self-determination and self-realization. Abraham Maslow proposed that human motivations form a *hierarchy of needs;* if basic needs are fulfilled, people will strive toward *self-actualization* and *self-transcendence.* Carl Rogers believed that the ingredients of a growth-promoting environment are acceptance (including *unconditional positive regard*), genuineness, and empathy. *Self-concept* was a central feature of personality for both Maslow and Rogers.

13-11 How did humanistic psychologists assess a person's sense of self?

Some rejected any standardized assessments and relied on interviews and conversations. Rogers sometimes used questionnaires in which people described their ideal and actual selves, which he later used to judge progress during therapy.

13-12 How have humanistic theories influenced psychology? What criticisms have they faced?

Humanistic psychology helped renew interest in the concept of self, and also laid the groundwork for today's scientific subfield of positive psychology. Critics have said that humanistic psychology's concepts are vague and subjective, its values self-centered, and its assumptions naively optimistic.

⟩ Contemporary Perspectives on Personality

13-13 How do psychologists use traits to describe personality?

Trait theorists see personality as a stable and enduring pattern of behavior. They have been more interested in trying to describe our differences than in explaining them. Using factor analysis, they identify clusters of behavior tendencies that occur together. Genetic predispositions influence many traits.

13-14 What are some common misunderstandings about introversion?

Western cultures prize extraversion, but introverts have different, equally important skills. Introversion does not equal shyness, and extraverts don't always outperform introverts as leaders or in sales success. Introverts often experience great achievement; many introverts prosper.

13-15 What are *personality inventories,* and what are their strengths and weaknesses as trait-assessment tools?

Personality inventories (such as the *MMPI*) are questionnaires on which people respond to items designed to gauge a wide range of feelings and behaviors. Test items are *empirically derived,* and the tests are objectively scored. Objectivity does not guarantee validity; people can fake their answers to create a good impression (but may then score high on a lie scale that assesses faking).

13-16 Which traits seem to provide the most useful information about personality variation?

The Big Five personality factors—conscientiousness, agreeableness, neuroticism, openness, and extraversion (CANOE)—currently offer our best approximation of the basic trait dimensions. These factors are quite stable and appear to be found in all cultures. Many genes, each having small effects, combine to influence our traits, and heritability generally runs about 40 percent for each dimension.

13-17 Does research support the consistency of personality traits over time and across situations?

A person's average traits persist over time and are predictable over many different situations. But traits cannot predict behavior in any one situation.

13-18 How do social-cognitive theorists view personality development, and how do they explore behavior?

Albert Bandura first proposed the *social-cognitive perspective,* which emphasizes the interaction of our traits with our situations. Social-cognitive researchers apply principles of learning, cognition, and social behavior to personality. *Reciprocal determinism* describes the interaction and mutual influence of behavior, internal cognition, and environment. Assessment situations involving simulated conditions exploit the principle that the best predictor of future behavior is a person's actions in similar situations.

13-19 What criticisms have social-cognitive theorists faced?

Social-cognitive theorists build on well-established concepts of learning and cognition, sensitizing researchers to the ways situations affect, and are affected by, individuals. They have been faulted for underemphasizing the importance of unconscious motives, emotions, and biologically influenced traits.

13-20 Why has psychology generated so much research on the self? How important is self-esteem to our well-being?

The *self* is the center of personality, organizing our thoughts, feelings, and actions. Considering possible selves helps motivate us toward positive development, but focusing too intensely on ourselves can lead to the *spotlight effect.* High *self-esteem* correlates with less pressure to conform, with persistence at difficult tasks, and with happiness. But the direction of the correlation is unclear. Rather than unrealistically promoting self-worth, it's better to reward children's achievements, thus promoting feelings of competence.

13-21 What evidence reveals self-serving bias, and how do defensive and secure self-esteem differ?

Self-serving bias is our tendency to perceive ourselves favorably, as when viewing ourselves as better than average or when accepting credit for our successes but not blame for our failures. Defensive self-esteem is fragile, focuses on sustaining itself, and views failure or criticism as a threat. Secure self-esteem enables us to feel accepted for who we are.

13-22 How do individualist and collectivist cultures differ in their values and goals?

Although individuals vary, different cultures tend to emphasize either individualism or collectivism. Cultures based on self-reliant *individualism* tend to value personal independence and individual achievement. They define identity in terms of self-esteem, personal goals and attributes, and personal rights and liberties. Cultures based on socially connected *collectivism* tend to value group goals, social identity, and commitments. They define identity in terms of interdependence, tradition, and harmony.

CHAPTER 14

Psychological Disorders

 Basic Concepts of Psychological Disorders

14-1 How should we draw the line between normality and disorder?

According to psychologists and psychiatrists, *psychological disorders* are marked by a clinically significant disturbance in an individual's cognition, emotion regulation, or behavior. Such dysfunctional or maladaptive thoughts, emotions, or behaviors interfere with daily life, and thus are disordered.

14-2 How do the medical model and the biopsychosocial approach influence our understanding of psychological disorders?

The *medical model* assumes that psychological disorders have physical causes that can be diagnosed, treated, and often cured through therapy, sometimes in a hospital. The biopsychosocial perspective assumes that disordered behavior comes from the interaction of biological characteristics, psychological dynamics, and social-cultural circumstances. This approach has given rise to the vulnerability-stress model, in which individual characteristics and environmental stressors combine to increase or decrease the likelihood of developing a psychological disorder, a model supported by *epigenetics* research.

14-3 How and why do clinicians classify psychological disorders, and why do some psychologists criticize the use of diagnostic labels?

The American Psychiatric Association's *DSM-5* (*Diagnostic and Statistical Manual of Mental Disorders,* Fifth Edition) contains diagnostic labels and descriptions that provide a common language and shared concepts for communication and research. Critics of the DSM say it casts too wide a net, pathologizing normal behaviors. A complementary approach to classification is the U.S. National Institute of Mental Health's Research Domain Criteria (RDoC) project, a framework that organizes disorders according to behaviors and brain activity along several dimensions. Any classification attempt produces diagnostic labels that may create preconceptions, which bias perceptions of the labeled person's past and present behavior.

14-4 Why is there controversy over attention-deficit/hyperactivity disorder?

A child (or, less commonly, an adult) who displays extreme inattention and/or hyperactivity and impulsivity may be diagnosed with *attention-deficit/hyperactivity disorder (ADHD).* Controversies center on whether the growing number of ADHD cases reflect overdiagnosis or increased awareness of the disorder, and on the long-term effects of stimulant-drug treatment.

14-5   What factors increase the risk of suicide, and what do we know about nonsuicidal self-injury?

Suicide rates differ by nation, race, gender, age group, income, religious involvement, marital status, and other factors. Those lacking social support, such as many gay, transgender, and gender nonconforming youth, are at increased risk, as are people who have been anxious or depressed. Forewarnings of suicide may include verbal hints, giving away possessions, withdrawal, and preoccupation with death. People who talk about suicide should be taken seriously: listen and empathize, connect them to help, and protect those who appear at immediate risk. Nonsuicidal self-injury (NSSI) does not usually lead to suicide but may escalate to suicidal thoughts and acts if untreated. People who engage in NSSI do not tolerate stress well and tend to be self-critical, with poor communication and problem-solving skills.

14-6   Do psychological disorders predict violent behavior?

Mental disorders seldom lead to violence, but when they do, they raise moral and ethical questions about whether society should hold people with disorders responsible for their violent actions. Most people with disorders are nonviolent and are more likely to be victims than attackers.

14-7   How many people have, or have had, a psychological disorder? What are some of the risk factors?

Psychological disorder rates vary, depending on the time and place of the survey. In one multinational survey, the lowest rate of reported mental disorders was in Nigeria (6 percent), the highest rate in the United States (27 percent). Poverty is a risk factor. But some disorders, such as schizophrenia, can also drive people into poverty. Immigrants to the United States may average better mental health than their U.S. counterparts with the same ethnic heritage (a phenomenon known as the *immigrant paradox*).

Anxiety Disorders, OCD, and PTSD

14-8   How do generalized anxiety disorder, panic disorder, and phobias differ?

Anxiety disorders are psychological disorders characterized by distressing, persistent anxiety or maladaptive behaviors that reduce anxiety. People with *generalized anxiety disorder* feel persistently and uncontrollably tense and apprehensive, for no apparent reason. In the more extreme *panic disorder,* anxiety escalates into periodic episodes of intense dread. Those with a *phobia* may be irrationally afraid of a specific object, activity, or situation.

14-9   What is OCD?

Persistent and repetitive thoughts (obsessions), actions (compulsions), or both characterize *obsessive-compulsive disorder (OCD).*

14-10 What is PTSD?

Symptoms of *posttraumatic stress disorder (PTSD)* include four or more weeks of haunting memories, nightmares, hypervigilance, avoidance of trauma-related stimuli, social withdrawal, jumpy anxiety, numbness of feeling, and/or sleep problems following some traumatic experience.

14-11 How do conditioning, cognition, and biology contribute to the feelings and thoughts that mark anxiety disorders, OCD, and PTSD?

The learning perspective views anxiety disorders, OCD, and PTSD as products of fear conditioning, stimulus generalization, fearful-behavior reinforcement, and observational learning of others' fears and cognitions. The biological perspective considers genetic predispositions for high levels of emotional reactivity and neurotransmitter production; abnormal responses in the brain's fear circuits; and the role that fears of life-threatening dangers played in natural selection and evolution.

Major Depressive Disorder and Bipolar Disorder

14-12 How do major depressive disorder and bipolar disorder differ?

A person with *major depressive disorder* experiences at least five symptoms of depression (including either depressed mood or loss of interest or pleasure) for two or more weeks. A person with the less common condition of *bipolar disorder* experiences not only depression but also *mania*—episodes of hyperactive and wildly optimistic, impulsive behavior.

14-13 How can the biological and social-cognitive perspectives help us understand major depressive disorder and bipolar disorder?

The biological perspective on depressive disorders and bipolar disorder focuses on genetic predispositions, abnormalities in brain structures and function (including those found in neurotransmitter systems), and nutritional (and drug) effects. The social-cognitive perspective views depression as an ongoing cycle of stressful experiences (interpreted through negative beliefs, attributions, and memories, often with relentless *rumination*) leading to negative moods, thoughts, and actions, thereby fueling new stressful experiences.

Schizophrenia and Other Disorders

14-14 What patterns of perceiving, thinking, and feeling characterize schizophrenia?

Schizophrenia is a *psychotic disorder* characterized by delusions, hallucinations, disorganized speech, and/or diminished, inappropriate emotional expression. Hallucinations are sensory experiences without sensory stimulation; *delusions* are false beliefs. Schizophrenia symptoms may be positive (the presence of inappropriate behaviors) or negative (the absence of appropriate behaviors).

14-15 How do chronic schizophrenia and acute schizophrenia differ?

Schizophrenia typically strikes during late adolescence, affects males slightly more often, and occurs in all cultures. In *chronic* (or process) *schizophrenia,* development is gradual and recovery is doubtful. In *acute* (or reactive) *schizophrenia,* onset is sudden—in reaction to stress—and prospects for recovery are brighter.

14-16 What brain abnormalities are associated with schizophrenia?

People with schizophrenia have an excess number of dopamine receptors, which may intensify brain signals, creating positive symptoms such as hallucinations and paranoia. Brain scans have revealed abnormal activity in the frontal lobes, thalamus, and amygdala, as well as a loss of neural connections across the brain network. Brain abnormalities associated with schizophrenia include enlarged, fluid-filled areas and corresponding shrinkage and thinning of cerebral tissue.

14-17 What prenatal events are associated with increased risk of developing schizophrenia?

Possible contributing factors include maternal diabetes, older paternal age, viral infections or famine conditions during the mother's pregnancy, and low weight or oxygen deprivation at birth.

14-18 How do genes influence schizophrenia?

Twin and adoption studies indicate that the predisposition to schizophrenia is inherited. Multiple genes interact to produce schizophrenia. No environmental causes invariably produce schizophrenia, but environmental events (such as prenatal viruses or maternal stress) may "turn on" genes in those who are predisposed to this disorder.

14-19 What are *dissociative disorders*, and why are they controversial?

Dissociative disorders are controversial, rare conditions in which conscious awareness seems to become separated from previous memories, thoughts, and feelings. Skeptics note that *dissociative identity disorder (DID)* increased dramatically in the late twentieth century; is rarely found outside North America; and may reflect role playing by people vulnerable to therapists' suggestions. Others view DID as a manifestation of feelings of anxiety, or as a response learned when behaviors are reinforced by anxiety-reduction.

14-20 What are the three clusters of personality disorders? What behaviors and brain activity characterize the antisocial personality?

Personality disorders are inflexible and enduring behavior patterns that impair social functioning. The ten DSM-5 disorders tend to form three clusters, characterized by (1) anxiety, (2) eccentric or odd behaviors, and (3) dramatic or impulsive behaviors. *Antisocial personality disorder* (one of those in the third cluster) is characterized by a lack of conscience and, sometimes, by aggressive and fearless behavior. The amygdala is smaller and the frontal lobes less active in people with this disorder, leading to impaired frontal lobe cognitive functions and decreased responsiveness to others' distress. Genetic predispositions may interact with the environment to produce these characteristics.

14-21 What are the three main eating disorders, and how do biological, psychological, and social-cultural influences make people more vulnerable to them?

In those with eating disorders (most often women or gay men), psychological factors overwhelm the body's tendency to maintain a normal weight. Despite being significantly underweight, people with *anorexia nervosa* (usually adolescent females) continue to diet and sometimes exercise excessively because they view themselves as fat. Those with *bulimia nervosa* (usually women in their late teens and early twenties) secretly binge and then compensate by purging, fasting, or excessively exercising. Those with *binge-eating disorder* binge but do not follow with purging, fasting, and exercising. Cultural pressures, low self-esteem, and negative emotions interact with stressful life experiences and genetics to produce eating disorders.

CHAPTER 15

Therapy

⟶ Introduction to Therapy and the Psychological Therapies

15-1 How do *psychotherapy* and the *biomedical therapies* differ?

Psychotherapy is treatment involving psychological techniques that consists of interactions between a trained therapist and someone seeking to overcome psychological difficulties or achieve personal growth. The major psychotherapies derive from psychology's psychodynamic, humanistic, behavioral, and cognitive perspectives. *Biomedical therapy* treats psychological disorders with medications or procedures that act directly on a patient's physiology. An *eclectic approach* combines techniques from various forms of therapy.

15-2 What are the goals and techniques of psychoanalysis, and how have they been adapted in psychodynamic therapy?

Through *psychoanalysis,* Sigmund Freud tried to give people self-insight and relief from their disorders by bringing anxiety-laden feelings and thoughts into conscious awareness. Psychoanalytic techniques included using free association and *interpretation* of instances of *resistance* and *transference. Psychodynamic therapy* has been influenced by traditional psychoanalysis but differs from it in many ways, including the lack of belief in id, ego, and superego. This contemporary therapy is briefer, less expensive, and more focused on helping the client find relief from current symptoms. Psychodynamic therapists help clients understand how past relationships create themes that may be acted out in present relationships.

15-3 What are the basic themes of humanistic therapy? What are the specific goals and techniques of Rogers' client-centered approach?

Both psychodynamic and humanistic therapies are *insight therapies*—they attempt to improve functioning by increasing clients' awareness of motives and defenses. Humanistic therapy's goals include helping clients grow in self-awareness and self-acceptance; promoting personal growth rather than curing illness; helping clients take responsibility for their own growth; focusing on conscious thoughts rather than unconscious motivations; and seeing the present and future as more important than the past. Carl Rogers' *client-centered therapy* proposed that therapists' most important contributions are to function as a psychological mirror through *active listening* and to provide a growth-fostering environment of *unconditional positive regard.*

15-4 How does the basic assumption of behavior therapy differ from the assumptions of psychodynamic and humanistic therapies? What techniques are used in exposure therapies and aversive conditioning?

Behavior therapies are not insight therapies, and instead assume that problem behaviors *are* the problem. Their goal is to apply learning principles to modify these problem behaviors. Classical conditioning techniques, including *exposure therapies* (such as *systematic desensitization* or *virtual reality exposure therapy*) and *aversive conditioning,* attempt to change behaviors through *counterconditioning*—evoking new responses to old stimuli that trigger unwanted behaviors.

15-5 What is the main premise of therapy based on operant conditioning principles, and what are the views of its proponents and critics?

Operant conditioning operates under the premise that voluntary behaviors are strongly influenced by their consequences. Therapy based on operant conditioning principles therefore uses behavior modification techniques to change unwanted behaviors by positively reinforcing desired behaviors and ignoring or punishing undesirable behaviors. Critics maintain that (1) techniques such as those used in *token economies* may produce behavior changes that disappear when rewards end, and (2) deciding which behaviors should change is authoritarian and unethical. Proponents argue that treatment with positive rewards is more humane than punishing people or institutionalizing them for undesired behaviors.

15-6 What are the goals and techniques of the cognitive therapies and of cognitive-behavioral therapy?

The *cognitive therapies,* such as Aaron Beck's cognitive therapy for depression, assume that our thinking influences our feelings, and that the therapist's role is to change clients' self-defeating thinking by training them to perceive and interpret events in more constructive ways. The widely researched and practiced *cognitive-behavioral therapy (CBT)* combines cognitive therapy and behavior therapy by helping clients regularly try out their new ways of thinking and behaving in their everyday life. A newer CBT variation, dialectical behavior therapy (DBT), teaches clients cognitive tactics for tolerating distress and regulating emotions, and trains them in social skills and mindfulness meditation.

15-7 What are the aims and benefits of group and family therapies?

Group therapy sessions can help more people with less cost than individual therapy. Clients may benefit from exploring feelings and developing social skills in a group situation, from learning that others have similar problems, and from getting feedback on new ways of behaving. *Family therapy* views a family as an interactive system. It attempts to help members discover the roles they play and learn to communicate more openly and directly.

Evaluating Psychotherapies

15-8 Does psychotherapy work? How can we know?

Clients' and therapists' positive testimonials cannot prove that psychotherapy is effective, and the placebo effect makes it difficult to judge whether improvement occurred because of the treatment. Using *meta-analyses* to statistically combine the results of hundreds of randomized psychotherapy outcome studies, researchers have found that those not undergoing treatment often improve, but those undergoing psychotherapy are more likely to improve—and to improve more quickly and with less risk of relapse.

15-9 Are some psychotherapies more effective than others for specific disorders?

No one type of psychotherapy is generally superior to all others. Therapy is most effective for those with clear-cut, specific problems. Some therapies—such as behavior conditioning for treating phobias and compulsions—are more effective for specific disorders. Cognitive and cognitive-behavioral therapies have been effective in coping with anxiety, posttraumatic stress disorder, insomnia, and depression; behavioral conditioning therapies with specific behavior problems; psychodynamic therapy for depression and anxiety; and nondirective (client-centered) counseling for mild to moderate depression. *Evidence-based practice* integrates the best available research with clinicians' expertise and patients' characteristics and preferences.

15-10 How do alternative therapies fare under scientific scrutiny?

Abnormal states tend to return to normal on their own, and the placebo effect can create the impression that a treatment has been effective. These two tendencies complicate assessments of nontraditional therapies that claim to cure certain ailments. Eye movement desensitization and reprocessing (EMDR) has shown some effectiveness—but not from the eye movement (rather from the exposure therapy nature of the treatments). Light exposure therapy does seem to help those with a seasonal pattern in depression symptoms by activating a brain region that influences arousal and hormones.

15-11 What three elements are shared by all forms of psychotherapy?

All psychotherapies offer new hope for demoralized people; a fresh perspective; and (if the therapist is effective) an empathic, trusting, and caring relationship. The emotional bond of trust and understanding between therapist and client—the *therapeutic alliance*—is an important element in effective therapy.

15-12 How do culture and values influence the client-therapist relationship?

Therapists differ in the values that influence their goals in therapy and their views of progress. These differences may create problems if therapists and clients differ in their cultural or religious perspectives.

15-13 What should a person look for when selecting a therapist?

Campus health centers are generally good starting points for counseling options, and they may offer some free services. A person seeking therapy may want to ask about the therapist's treatment approach, values, credentials, and fees. An important consideration is whether the therapy seeker feels comfortable and able to establish a bond with the therapist. Recognizing the importance of a strong therapeutic alliance, the American Psychological Association accredits programs that provide training in cultural sensitivity and that recruit underrepresented cultural groups.

⟶ The Biomedical Therapies and Preventing Psychological Disorders

15-14 Why is therapeutic lifestyle change considered an effective biomedical therapy, and how does it work?

Therapeutic lifestyle change is considered a biomedical therapy because it influences the way the brain responds. Mind and body are a unit; affect one and you will affect the other. Our exercise, nutrition, relationships, recreation, relaxation, and religious or spiritual engagement affect our mental health. People who undergo a program of aerobic exercise, adequate sleep, light exposure, social engagement, rumination reduction, and better nutrition have gained relief from depressive symptoms.

15-15 What are the drug therapies? How do double-blind studies help researchers evaluate a drug's effectiveness?

Psychopharmacology has helped make drug therapy the most widely used biomedical therapy. *Antipsychotic drugs* are used in treating schizophrenia; some block dopamine activity. Side effects may include tardive dyskinesia (involuntary movements of facial muscles, tongue, and limbs) or increased risk of obesity and diabetes. *Antianxiety drugs,* which depress central nervous system activity, are used to treat anxiety disorders, obsessive-compulsive disorder, and posttraumatic stress disorder, and can be addictive. *Antidepressant drugs,* which often increase the availability of serotonin and norepinephrine, are used to treat depression, anxiety disorders, obsessive-compulsive disorder, and posttraumatic stress disorder with modest effectiveness. Given their widening use (from depression to anxiety to strokes), some professionals prefer the term SSRIs (selective serotonin reuptake inhibitors) rather than antidepressants. Lithium and Depakote are mood stabilizers prescribed for those with bipolar disorder. Studies may use a double-blind procedure to avoid the placebo effect and researcher bias.

15-16 How are brain stimulation and psychosurgery used in treating specific disorders?

Electroconvulsive therapy (ECT), in which a brief electric current is sent through the brain of an anesthetized patient, is an effective, last-resort treatment for people with severe depression who have not responded to other therapy. Newer alternative treatments for depression include transcranial direct current stimulation (tDCS; also used for scientifically unproven cognitive benefits), *repetitive transcranial magnetic stimulation (rTMS),* and deep-brain stimulation (DBS; said to work by calming an overactive brain region linked with negative emotions, and has shown benefit in some patients). *Psychosurgery* removes or destroys brain tissue in hopes of modifying behavior. Radical psychosurgical procedures such as *lobotomy* are no longer performed. Today's microscale psychosurgery and MRI-guided precision brain surgery are rare, last-resort treatments because the effects are irreversible.

15-17 What is the rationale for preventive mental health programs, and why is it important to develop resilience?

Preventive mental health programs are based on the idea that many psychological disorders could be prevented by changing oppressive, esteem-destroying environments into more benevolent, nurturing environments that foster growth, self-confidence, and *resilience.* Struggling with challenges can lead to *posttraumatic growth.* Community psychologists work to prevent psychological disorders by turning destructive environments into more nurturing places that foster competence, health, and well-being.

APPENDIX A

Statistical Reasoning in Everyday Life

A-1   How do we describe data using three measures of central tendency, and what is the relative usefulness of the two measures of variation?

Researchers use descriptive statistics to measure and describe characteristics of groups under study. A measure of central tendency is a single score that represents a whole set of scores. Three such measures that we use to describe data are the *mode* (the most frequently occurring score), the *mean* (the arithmetic average), and the *median* (the middle score in a group of data). Measures of central tendency neatly summarize data; measures of variation tell us how diverse data are. Two measures of variation are the *range* (which describes the gap between the highest and lowest scores) and the *standard deviation* (which states how much scores vary around the mean, or average, score). Scores often form a *normal* (or bell-shaped) *curve.*

A-2   How do correlations measure relationships between variables?

Correlation is the degree to which two variables are related, and how well one predicts the other. In a positive correlation, two *variables* increase or decrease together; in a negative correlation, one variable increases as the other decreases. The strength and direction of their relationship is expressed as a *correlation coefficient,* which ranges from +1.00 (a perfect positive correlation) through 0 (no correlation) to −1.00 (a perfect negative correlation). The relationship may be displayed in a *scatterplot,* in which each dot represents a value for the two variables.

A-3   What are *illusory correlations,* and what is *regression toward the mean?*

Illusory correlations are random events that we notice and falsely assume are related. *Regression toward the mean* is the tendency for extreme or unusual scores to fall back (regress) toward their average.

A-4   How do we know whether an observed difference can be generalized to other populations?

Researchers use inferential statistics (which include ways of determining the reliability and significance of an observed difference between the results for different groups) to determine if results can be generalized to a larger population. Reliable differences are based on samples that are representative of the larger population being studied; that demonstrate low variability, on average; and that consist of many cases. We can say that an observed difference has *statistical significance* if the sample averages are reliable, and when the difference between them is large.

Psychology at Work

B-1   What is *flow*?

Flow is a completely involved, focused state of consciousness with diminished awareness of self and time. It results from fully engaging one's skills. Interests predict both performance and persistence, so people should find vocations with a strong person-environment fit.

B-2   What are three key areas of study related to industrial-organizational psychology?

Three key areas of study related to *industrial-organizational (I/O) psychology* are *personnel, organizational,* and *human factors psychology.* Each uses psychological principles to study and benefit the wide range of today's workers, workplaces, and work activities.

B-3   How do personnel psychologists facilitate job seeking, employee selection, work placement, and performance appraisal?

Personnel psychologists work to provide training programs for job seekers; devise selection methods for new employees; recruit and evaluate diverse applicants; design and evaluate training programs; identify people's interests and strengths; analyze job content; and appraise individual and organizational performance. Unstructured, subjective interviews foster the interviewer illusion; *structured interviews* pinpoint job-relevant strengths and are better predictors of performance. Checklists, graphic rating scales, and behavior rating scales are useful performance appraisal methods.

B-4   What is the role of organizational psychologists?

Organizational psychologists examine influences on worker satisfaction and productivity and facilitate organizational change. Employee satisfaction and engagement tend to correlate with organizational success; in fact, employee attitudes predict future business success.

B-5   How can leaders be most effective?

Effective leaders set specific, challenging goals and choose an appropriate *leadership* style. Leadership style may be goal-oriented (*task leadership*), group-oriented (*social leadership*), or some combination of the two. Effective management often involves positive reinforcement, fulfilling the need to belong, and participative management.

B-6   What cultural influences need to be considered when choosing an effective leadership style?

Project GLOBE studies cultural variations in leadership expectations. Leaders who fulfill expectations (being directive in some cultures or participative in others) tend to be successful. But thriving companies worldwide tend to focus on identifying and enhancing employee strengths; strengths-based leadership pays dividends everywhere.

B-7   How do human factors psychologists work to create user-friendly machines and work settings?

Human factors psychologists contribute to human safety and improved design by encouraging developers and designers to consider human abilities and behaviors, to user-test their work before production and distribution, and to remain mindful of the curse of knowledge.

Answers to the Retrieve It and Experience the Testing Effect Questions

---

Thinking Critically With Psychological Science

 **The History and Scope of Psychology**

Retrieve It Answers

RI-1 Evaluating evidence, appraising the source, assessing conclusions, and examining our own assumptions are essential parts of critical thinking. **RI-2** Scientific psychology began in Germany in 1879 when Wilhelm Wundt opened the first psychology laboratory. **RI-3** People's self-reports varied, depending on the experience and the person's intelligence and verbal ability. **RI-4** structuralism; functionalism. **RI-5** behaviorism; Freudian. **RI-6** It recaptured the field's early interest in mental processes and made them legitimate topics for scientific study. **RI-7** This is the process by which nature selects from chance variations the traits that best enable an organism to survive and reproduce in a particular environment. **RI-8** Psychological events often stem from the interaction of nature and nurture, rather than from either of them acting alone. **RI-9** By incorporating three different levels of analysis, the biopsychosocial approach can provide a more complete view than any one perspective could offer. **RI-10** social-cultural; behavioral. **RI-11** I. b, II. c, III. a.

Experience the Testing Effect Answers

1. d. **2.** Critical thinking is smart thinking. When evaluating media claims (even about topics you might not know much about), look for empirical evidence. Ask the following questions in your analysis: Are the claims based on scientific findings? Have several studies replicated the findings and confirmed them? Are any experts cited? If so, are they affiliated with a credible institution? Have they conducted or written about scientific research? What agenda might they have? What alternative explanations are possible? **3.** Wilhelm Wundt. **4.** a. **5.** a. **6.** b. **7.** The environment (nurture) has an influence on us, but that influence is constrained by our biology (nature). Nature and nurture interact. People predisposed to be very tall (nature), for example, are unlikely to become Olympic gymnasts, no matter how hard they work (nurture). **8.** b **9.** positive psychology. **10.** d. **11.** psychiatrist. **12.** c.

Research Strategies: How Psychologists Ask and Answer Questions

Retrieve It Answers

RI-1 We often suffer from hindsight bias—after we've learned a situation's outcome, that outcome seems familiar and therefore obvious. **RI-2** A good theory *organizes* observed facts and implies hypotheses that offer testable *predictions* and, sometimes, practical applications. It also often stimulates further research. **RI-3** When other investigators are able to replicate an experiment with the same (or stronger) results, scientists can confirm the result and become more confident of its reliability. **RI-4** Case studies involve only one individual or group, so we can't know for sure whether the principles observed would apply to a larger population. **RI-5** These researchers were able to carefully observe and record naturally occurring behaviors outside the artificiality of a laboratory. However, outside the lab they were not able to control for all the factors that may have influenced the everyday interactions they were recording. **RI-6** An unrepresentative sample is a group that does not represent the population being studied. *Random sampling* helps researchers form a representative sample, because each member of the population has an equal chance of being included. **RI-7** a. negative, b. positive, c. positive, d. negative. **RI-8** In this case, as in many others, a third factor can explain the correlation: Golden anniversaries and baldness both accompany aging. **RI-9** Research designed to prevent the placebo effect randomly assigns participants to an *experimental group* (which receives the real treatment) or to a *control group* (which receives a placebo). A double-blind procedure prevents people's beliefs and hopes from affecting the results, because neither the participants nor those collecting the data know who receives the placebo. A comparison of the results will demonstrate whether the real treatment produces better results than *belief* in that treatment. **RI-10** confounding variables. **RI-11** I. c, II. a, III. b. **RI-12** We learn more about the drug's effectiveness when we can compare the results of those who took the drug (the experimental group) with the results of those who did not (the control group). If we gave the drug to all 1000 participants, we would have no way of knowing whether the drug is serving as a placebo or is actually medically effective. **RI-13** Animal protection legislation, laboratory regulation and inspection, and local and university ethics committees (which screen research proposals) attempt to safeguard animal welfare. International psychological organizations urge researchers involving human participants to obtain *informed consent*, protect them from greater-than-usual harm and discomfort, treat their personal information confidentially, and *debrief* them fully at the end of the experiment. **RI-14** testing effect. **RI-15** Survey, Question, Read, Retrieve, Review.

Experience the Testing Effect Answers

1. Hindsight bias. **2.** hypotheses. **3.** c. **4.** representative. **5.** negative. **6.** a. **7.** (a) *Alcohol use is associated with violence. (One interpretation: Drinking triggers or unleashes aggressive behavior.)* Perhaps anger triggers drinking, or perhaps the same genes or child-raising practices are predisposing both drinking and aggression. (Here researchers have learned that drinking does indeed trigger aggressive behavior.) (b) *Educated people live longer, on average, than less-educated people. (One interpretation: Education lengthens life and enhances health.)* Perhaps richer people can afford more education and better health care. (Research supports this conclusion.) (c) *Teens engaged in team sports are less likely to use drugs, smoke, have sex, carry weapons, and eat junk food than are teens who do not engage in team sports. (One interpretation: Team sports encourage healthy living.)* Perhaps some third factor explains this correlation—teens who use drugs, smoke, have sex, carry weapons, and eat junk food may be "loners" who do not enjoy playing on any team. (d) *Adolescents who frequently see smoking in movies are more likely to smoke. (One interpretation: Movie stars' behavior influences impressionable teens.)* Perhaps adolescents who smoke and attend movies frequently have less parental supervision and more access to spending money than other adolescents. **8.** experiments. **9.** placebo. **10.** c. **11.** independent variable. **12.** b. **13.** d.

CHAPTER 2

The Biology of Behavior

Neural and Hormonal Systems

Retrieve It Answers

RI-1 They share a focus on the links between the brain and behavior. Phrenology faded because it had no scientific basis—skull bumps don't reveal mental traits and abilities. **RI-2** dendrites, cell body, axon. **RI-3** Stronger stimuli (the slap) cause more neurons to fire and to fire more frequently than happens with weaker stimuli (the tap). **RI-4** Neurons send neurotransmitters (chemical messengers) across this tiny space between one neuron's terminal branch and the next neuron's dendrite or cell body. **RI-5** Reuptake occurs when excess neurotransmitters are reabsorbed by the sending neuron. Neurotransmitters can also drift away or be broken down

by enzymes. **RI-6** Morphine is an agonist; curare is an antagonist. **RI-7** neurotransmitters. **RI-8** I. c, II. a, III. b. **RI-9** The sympathetic division of the autonomic nervous system would have directed arousal (accelerated heartbeat, inhibited digestion, etc.), and the parasympathetic division would have directed calming. **RI-10** Responding to signals from the hypothalamus, the pituitary releases hormones that trigger other endocrine glands to secrete hormones, which in turn influence brain and behavior. **RI-11** Both of these communication systems produce chemical molecules that act on the body's receptors to influence our behavior and emotions. The endocrine system, which secretes hormones into the bloodstream, delivers its messages much more slowly than the speedy nervous system, and the effects of the endocrine system's messages tend to linger much longer than those of the nervous system.

Experience the Testing Effect Answers

1. The human brain is uniquely designed to be flexible; it can reorganize after damage and it can build new pathways based on experience. This plasticity enables us to adapt to our changing world. **2.** axon. **3.** c. **4.** a. **5.** neurotransmitters. **6.** b. **7.** c. **8.** autonomic. **9.** central. **10.** a. **11.** adrenal glands.

 Tools of Discovery, Older Brain Structures, and the Limbic System

Retrieve It Answers

RI-1 I. b, II. a, III. c. **RI-2** brainstem. **RI-3** (a) cerebellum, (b) thalamus, (c) reticular formation, (d) medulla. **RI-4** The sympathetic nervous system. **RI-5** (1) The *amygdala* is involved in aggression and fear responses. (2) The *hypothalamus* is involved in bodily maintenance, pleasurable rewards, and control of the hormonal systems. (3) The *hippocampus* processes memories of facts and events.

Experience the Testing Effect Answers

1. b. **2.** d. **3.** c. **4.** cerebellum. **5.** b. **6.** amygdala. **7.** b. **8.** hypothalamus.

The Cerebral Cortex

Retrieve It Answers

RI-1 the brainstem; the cerebral cortex. **RI-2** a. The right limbs' opposed activities interfere with each other because both are controlled by the same (left) side of your brain. b. Opposite sides of your brain control your left and right limbs, so the reversed motion causes less interference. **RI-3** somatosensory; motor. **RI-4** Association areas are involved in higher mental functions—interpreting, integrating, and acting on information processed in other areas. **RI-5** (1) yes, (2) no, (3) green.

Experience the Testing Effect Answers

1. d. **2.** The visual cortex is a neural network of sensory neurons connected via interneurons to other neural networks, including auditory networks. This allows you to integrate visual and auditory information to respond when a friend you recognize greets you at a party. **3.** c. **4.** frontal. **5.** association areas. **6.** c. **7.** ON; HER. **8.** a. **9.** b.

Genetics, Evolutionary Psychology, and Behavior

Retrieve It Answers

RI-1 gene, chromosome, nucleus. **RI-2** Researchers use twin and adoption studies to understand how much variation among individuals is due to genetic makeup and how much is due to environmental factors. Some studies compare the traits and behaviors of identical twins (same genes) and fraternal twins (different genes, as in any two siblings). They also compare adopted children with their adoptive and biological parents. Some studies compare traits and behaviors of twins raised together or separately. **RI-3** I. b, II. a. **RI-4** Over multiple generations, Belyaev and Trut selected and bred foxes that exhibited a trait they desired: tameness. This process is similar to naturally occurring selection, but it differs in that natural selection is much slower, and normally favors traits (including those arising from mutations) that contribute to reproduction and survival.

Experience the Testing Effect Answers

1. chromosomes. **2.** gene. **3.** b. **4.** c. **5.** Identical. **6.** b. **7.** environments. **8.** differences; commonalities. **9.** c.

Consciousness and the Two-Track Mind

 ## Consciousness: Some Basic Concepts

Retrieve It Answers

RI-1 cognitive neuroscience. **RI-2** Our *selective attention* allows us to focus on only a limited portion of our surroundings. *Inattentional blindness* explains why we don't perceive some things when we are distracted. *Change blindness,* for example, happens when we fail to notice a relatively unimportant change in our environment. These principles help magicians fool us, as they direct our attention elsewhere to perform their tricks. **RI-3** Our mind simultaneously processes information on a conscious track and an unconscious track (dual processing) as we organize and interpret information.

Experience the Testing Effect Answers

1. inattentional blindness. **2.** unconscious; conscious. **3.** selective.

Sleep and Dreams

Retrieve It Answers

RI-1 With each soldier cycling through the sleep stages independently, at any given time at least one likely will be in an easily awakened stage. **RI-2** REM (R), NREM-1 (N1), NREM-2 (N2), NREM-3 (N3); normally we move through N1, then N2, then N3, then back up through N2 before we experience REM sleep. **RI-3** I. b, II. c, III. a. **RI-4** suprachiasmatic; circadian. **RI-5** (1) Sleep has survival value. (2) Sleep helps us restore the immune system and repair brain tissue. (3) During sleep we consolidate memories. (4) Sleep fuels creativity. (5) Sleep plays a role in the growth

process. **RI-6** quick reaction times; gain weight. **RI-7** (1) Freud's wish-fulfillment (dreams as a psychic safety valve), (2) information-processing (dreams sort the day's events and consolidate memories), (3) physiological function (dreams pave neural pathways), (4) activation-synthesis (REM sleep triggers random neural activity that the mind weaves into stories), and (5) cognitive development (dreams reflect the dreamer's developmental stage).

Experience the Testing Effect Answers

1. circadian rhythm. **2.** b. **3.** N3. **4.** It increases in duration. **5.** c. **6.** With narcolepsy, the person periodically falls directly into REM sleep, with no warning; with sleep apnea, the person repeatedly awakens during the night. **7.** d. **8.** The activation-synthesis theory suggests that dreams are the brain's attempt to synthesize random neural activity. **9.** The information-processing explanation of dreaming proposes that brain activity during REM sleep enables us to sift through the daily events and activities we have been thinking about (*what one has dwelt on by day*). **10.** REM rebound.

 ### Drugs and Consciousness

Retrieve It Answers

RI-1 With repeated exposure to a psychoactive drug, the user's brain chemistry adapts and the drug's effect lessens. Thus, it takes bigger doses to get the desired effect. **RI-2** Unless it becomes compulsive or dysfunctional, simply having a strong interest in shopping is not the same as having a physical addiction to a drug. It typically does not involve obsessive craving in spite of known negative consequences. **RI-3** depressants. **RI-4** Nicotine-withdrawal symptoms include strong cravings, insomnia, anxiety, irritability, distractibility, and difficulty concentrating. However, if your friend sticks with it, the craving and withdrawal symptoms will gradually dissipate over about 6 months. **RI-5** Psychoactive drugs create pleasure by altering brain chemistry. With repeated use of the drug, the user develops tolerance and needs more of the drug to achieve the desired effect. (Marijuana is an exception.) Discontinuing use of the substance then produces painful or psychologically unpleasant withdrawal symptoms. **RI-6** Nicotine is powerfully addictive, and those who start paving the neural pathways when young may find it very hard to stop using it. As a result, tobacco companies may have lifelong customers. Moreover, evidence suggests that if cigarette manufacturers haven't hooked customers by early adulthood, they most likely won't. **RI-7** Possible explanations include (a) biological factors (a person could have a biological predisposition to both early use and later abuse, or alcohol use could modify a person's neural pathways); (b) psychological factors (early use could establish taste preferences for alcohol); and (c) social-cultural factors (early use could influence enduring habits, attitudes, activities, or peer relationships that could foster alcohol use disorder).

Experience the Testing Effect Answers

1. tolerance. **2.** a. **3.** Alcohol is a disinhibitor—it makes us more likely to do what we would have done when sober, whether that is being helpful or being aggressive. **4.** d. **5.** hallucinogenic. **6.** a. **7.** b.

CHAPTER 4

Developing Through the Life Span

⟶ Developmental Issues, Prenatal Development, and the Newborn

Retrieve It Answers

RI-1 nature; nurture. **RI-2** continuity; stages. **RI-3** (1) Stage theory is supported by the work of Piaget (cognitive development), Kohlberg (moral development), and Erikson (psychosocial development). (2) Some traits, such as temperament, exhibit remarkable stability across many years. **RI-4** zygote; fetus; embryo. **RI-5** habituation.

Experience the Testing Effect Answers

1. continuity/stages. **2.** b. **3.** c. **4.** teratogens.

⟶ Infancy and Childhood

Retrieve It Answers

RI-1 maturation. **RI-2** Object permanence for the sensorimotor stage, pretend play for the preoperational stage, conservation for the concrete operational stage, and abstract logic for the formal operational stage. **RI-3** I. d, II. b, III. c, IV. c, V. a, VI. b. **RI-4** Theory of mind focuses on our ability to understand our own and others' mental states. Those with autism spectrum disorder struggle with this ability. **RI-5** Attachment is the normal process by which we form emotional ties with important others. Imprinting occurs only in certain animals that have a critical period very early in their development during which they must form their attachments, and they do so in an inflexible manner. **RI-6** The authoritarian style would be described as too hard, the permissive style too soft, the negligent style too uncaring, and the authoritative style just right. Parents using the authoritative style tend to have children with high self-esteem, self-reliance, self-regulation, and social competence.

Experience the Testing Effect Answers

1. a. **2.** frontal. **3.** b. **4.** We consciously recall little from before age 4, in part because major brain areas have not yet matured. **5.** Infants in Piaget's *sensorimotor stage* tend to be focused only on their own perceptions of the world and may, for example, be unaware that objects continue to exist when unseen. A child in the *preoperational stage* is still egocentric and incapable of appreciating simple logic, such as the reversibility of operations. A preteen in the *concrete operational stage* is beginning to think logically about concrete events but not about abstract concepts. **6.** a. **7.** stranger anxiety. **8.** Before these studies, many psychologists believed that infants simply became attached to those who nourished them.

⟶ Adolescence

Retrieve It Answers

RI-1 preconventional; postconventional; conventional. **RI-2** Kohlberg's work reflected an individualist worldview, so his theory is less culturally universal than he supposed. **RI-3** Adolescents tend to *select* similar others and to sort themselves into like-minded groups. For an athletic teen, this could lead to finding other athletic teens and joining school teams together. **RI-4** I. g, II. h, III. c, IV. f, V. e, VI. d, VII. a, VIII. b.

Experience the Testing Effect Answers

1. b. **2.** formal operational. **3.** b. **4.** emerging adulthood.

⟶ Adulthood

Retrieve It Answers

RI-1 love; work. **RI-2** Challenges: decline of muscular strength, reaction times, stamina, sensory keenness, cardiac output, and immune system functioning. Risk of cognitive decline increases. Rewards: positive feelings tend to grow; negative emotions subside; and anger, stress, worry, and social-relationship problems decrease.

Experience the Testing Effect Answers

1. a. **2.** Cross-sectional studies compare people of different ages at one point in time. Longitudinal studies restudy and retest the same people over a long period of time. **3.** generativity. **4.** c.

CHAPTER 5

Sex, Gender, and Sexuality

⟶ Gender Development

Retrieve It Answers

RI-1 Women; men. **RI-2** seven; puberty. **RI-3** *Gender roles* are social rules or norms for accepted and expected behavior for females and males. The norms associated with various roles, including gender roles, vary widely in different cultural contexts, which is proof that we are able to learn and adapt to the social demands of different environments.

Experience the Testing Effect Answers

1. sex; gender. **2.** c. **3.** Y. **4.** d. **5.** 11; 12. **6.** intersex. **7.** b. **8.** gender identity.

⟶ Human Sexuality

Retrieve It Answers

RI-1 testosterone; estrogens. **RI-2** sexual dysfunction; paraphilia. **RI-3** Influences include biological factors such as sexual maturity and sex hormones, psychological factors such as environmental stimuli and fantasies, and social-cultural factors such as the values and expectations absorbed from family and the surrounding culture. **RI-4** a, c, d. **RI-5** b, c, e. **RI-6** Evolutionary psychologists theorize that females have inherited their ancestors' tendencies to be more cautious sexually because of the challenges associated with incubating and nurturing offspring. Males have inherited a tendency to be more casual about sex, because their act of fathering requires a smaller investment. **RI-7** (1) It starts with an effect and works backward to propose an explanation. (2) This explanation may overlook the effects of cultural expectations and socialization. (3) Men could use such explanations to rationalize irresponsible behavior toward women.

Experience the Testing Effect Answers

1. b. **2.** b. **3.** Sexual dysfunctions are problems that consistently impair sexual arousal or sexual function. Paraphilias are conditions,

which may be classified as psychological disorders, in which sexual arousal is associated with nonhuman objects, the suffering of self or others, and/or nonconsenting persons. **4.** does; doesn't. **5.** c. **6.** Researchers have found no evidence that any environmental factor (parental relationships, childhood experiences, peer relationships, or dating experiences) influences the development of our sexual orientation. **7.** Natural selection favors traits and behaviors that enable survival and reproduction. Evolutionary psychologists argue that women are choosier about their mates because of the investment required to conceive, protect, birth, and nurse children. Heterosexual women tend to prefer men who seem capable of supporting and protecting their joint offspring. Men, who have less at stake, tend to be more casual about sex, and heterosexual men tend to prefer women whose traits convey health and fertility.

CHAPTER 6

Sensation and Perception

⤵ Basic Concepts of Sensation and Perception

Retrieve It Answers

RI-1 *Sensation* is the bottom-up process by which your sensory receptors and your nervous system receive and represent stimuli. *Perception* is the top-down process by which your brain creates meaning by organizing and interpreting what your senses detect. **RI-2** *Absolute threshold* is the minimum stimulation needed to detect a particular sound (such as an approaching bike on the sidewalk behind you) 50 percent of the time. *Subliminal stimulation* happens when, without your awareness, your sensory system processes a sound that is below your absolute threshold. A *difference threshold* is the minimum difference needed to distinguish between two stimuli (such as between the sound of a bike and the sound of a runner coming up behind you) 50 percent of the time. **RI-3** The shoes provide constant stimulation. Thanks to *sensory adaptation,* we tend to focus primarily on changing stimuli. **RI-4** It involves top-down processing, because it draws on your experiences, assumptions, and expectations when interpreting stimuli.

Experience the Testing Effect Answers

1. b. **2.** perception. **3.** d. **4.** just noticeable difference. **5.** b. **6.** d. **7.** a.

⤵ Vision: Sensory and Perceptual Processing

Retrieve It Answers

RI-1 Your blind spot is on the nose side of each retina, which means that objects to your right may fall onto the right eye's blind spot. Objects to your left may fall on the left eye's blind spot. The blind spot does not normally impair your vision, because your eyes are moving and because one eye catches what the other misses. Moreover, even with only one eye open, your brain gives you a perception without a hole in it. **RI-2** rods; cones; color. **RI-3** pupils. **RI-4** The *Young-Helmholtz trichromatic theory* shows that the retina contains color receptors for red, green, and blue. The *opponent-process theory* shows that we have opponent-process cells in the retina and thalamus for red-green, blue-yellow, and white-black. These theories are complementary and

outline the two stages of color vision: (1) The retina's receptors for red, green, and blue respond to different color stimuli. (2) The receptors' signals are then processed by the opponent-process cells on their way to the visual cortex in the brain. **RI-5** Light waves reflect off the person and travel into your eyes. Receptor cells in your retina convert the light waves' energy into neural impulses sent to your brain. Your brain detector cells and work teams process the subdimensions of this visual input—including color, movement, form, and depth—separately but simultaneously. Your brain interprets this information, based on previously stored information and your expectations, and forms a conscious perception of your friend. **RI-6** figure; ground. **RI-7** Gestalt psychologists used this saying to describe our perceptual tendency to organize clusters of sensations into meaningful forms or coherent groups. **RI-8** We are normally able to perceive depth thanks to (1) binocular cues (such as retinal disparity), and (2) monocular cues (which include relative height, relative size, interposition, linear perspective, light and shadow, and relative motion).

Experience the Testing Effect Answers

1. wavelength. **2.** a. **3.** c. **4.** c. **5.** d. **6.** Your brain constructs this perception of color in two stages. In the first stage, the lemon reflects light energy into your eyes, where it is transformed into neural messages. Three sets of cones, each sensitive to a different light frequency (red, blue, and green) process color. In this case, the light energy stimulates both red-sensitive and green-sensitive cones. In the second stage, opponent-process cells sensitive to paired opposites of color (red/green, yellow/blue, and black/white) evaluate the incoming neural messages as they pass through your optic nerve to the thalamus and visual cortex. When the yellow-sensitive opponent-process cells are stimulated, you identify the lemon as yellow. **7.** feature detectors. **8.** parallel processing. **9.** a. **10.** d. **11.** b. **12.** c. **13.** monocular. **14.** b. **15.** b. **16.** perceptual adaptation.

⤵ The Nonvisual Senses

Retrieve It Answers

RI-1 loudness. **RI-2** lower; lower. **RI-3** place theory; frequency theory. **RI-4** c. **RI-5** We have four basic touch senses and five basic taste sensations. But we have no specific smell receptors. Instead, different combinations of odor receptors send messages to the brain, enabling us to recognize some 1 trillion different smells. **RI-6** Kinesthetic receptors are located in our joints, tendons, and muscles. Vestibular sense receptors are located in our inner ear. **RI-7** The ESP event would need to be reproduced in other scientific studies.

Experience the Testing Effect Answers

1. cochlea. **2.** The outer ear collects sound waves, which are translated into mechanical waves by the *middle ear* and turned into fluid waves in the *inner ear*. The *auditory nerve* then translates the energy into electrical waves and sends them to the brain, which perceives and interprets the sound. **3.** Place; frequency; volley. **4.** nociceptors. **5.** c. **6.** Our experience of pain is influenced by biological factors (such as genetic differences in endorphin production), psychological factors (such as our attention), and social-cultural factors (such as the presence of others). **7.** We have specialized receptors for detecting sweet, salty, sour, bitter, and umami tastes. Being able to detect pleasurable tastes enabled our ancestors to seek out energy- or protein-rich foods. Detecting aversive tastes deterred them from eating toxic substances, increasing their chances of survival. **8.** Kinesthesia; vestibular sense. **9.** Your vestibular sense regulates balance and body positioning through kinesthetic receptors triggered by fluid in your inner ear. Wobbly legs and a spinning world are signs that these receptors are still responding to the ride's turbulence. As your vestibular sense adjusts to solid ground, your balance will be restored. **10.** d. **11.** d.

CHAPTER 7

Learning

⟶ Basic Learning Concepts and Classical Conditioning

Retrieve It Answers

RI-1 Habits form when we repeat behaviors in a given context and, as a result, learn associations—often without our awareness. For example, we may have eaten a sweet pastry with a cup of coffee often enough to associate the flavor of the coffee with the treat, so that the cup of coffee alone just doesn't seem right anymore! **RI-2** NS = tone before conditioning; US = air puff; UR = blink to air puff; CS = tone after conditioning; CR = blink to tone. **RI-3** The cake (including its taste) is the US. The associated aroma is the CS. Salivation to the aroma is the CR. **RI-4** acquisition; extinction. **RI-5** generalization. **RI-6** If viewing an attractive nude or seminude woman (a US) elicits sexual arousal (a UR), then pairing the US with a new NS (violence) could turn the violence into a conditioned stimulus (CS) that also becomes sexually arousing, a conditioned response (CR). **RI-7** The US was the loud noise; the UR was the fear response to the noise; the NS was the rat before it was paired with the noise; the CS was the rat after pairing; the CR was fear of the rat.

Experience the Testing Effect Answers

1. information; behaviors. **2.** c. **3.** conditioned. **4.** discrimination. **5.** b. **6.** A sexual image is a US that triggers a UR of interest or arousal. Before the ad pairs a product with a sexual image, the product is an NS. Over time the product can become a CS that triggers the CR of interest or arousal.

⟶ Operant Conditioning

Retrieve It Answers

RI-1 do not; resulting. **RI-2** The baby negatively reinforces her parents' behavior when she stops crying once they grant her wish. Her parents positively reinforce her cries by letting her sleep with them. **RI-3** Spammers are reinforced on a variable-ratio schedule (after sending a varying number of emails). Cookie checkers are reinforced on a fixed-interval schedule. Donut rewards programs use a fixed-ratio schedule. **RI-4** 1. PR (positive reinforcement); 2. NP (negative punishment); 3. PP (positive punishment); 4. NR

(negative reinforcement). **RI-5** If Ethan is seeking attention, the teacher's scolding may be reinforcing rather than punishing. To change Ethan's behavior, his teacher could offer reinforcement (such as praise) each time he behaves well. The teacher might encourage Ethan toward increasingly appropriate behavior through shaping, or by rephrasing rules as rewards instead of punishments. ("You can use the blocks if you play nicely with the other children" [reward] rather than "You may not use the blocks if you misbehave!" [punishment].) **RI-6** respondent; operant.

Experience the Testing Effect Answers

1. Skinner. **2.** shaping. **3.** b. **4.** Your instructor could reinforce your attentive behavior by taking away something you dislike. For example, your instructor could offer to shorten the length of an assigned paper or replace standard lecture time with an interesting in-class activity. In both cases, the instructor would remove something aversive in order to negatively reinforce your focused attention. **5.** partial (intermittent). **6.** a. **7.** variable-interval. **8.** c.

⟶ Biology, Cognition, and Learning

Retrieve It Answers

RI-1 Garcia and Koelling demonstrated that rats may learn an aversion to tastes, on which their survival depends, but not to sights or sounds. **RI-2** The success of operant conditioning is affected not just by environmental cues, but also by biological and cognitive factors. **RI-3** Jason may be more likely to speed. Observational learning studies suggest that children tend to do as others do and say what they say. **RI-4** I. c, II. d, III. a, IV. e, V. b.

Experience the Testing Effect Answers

1. taste-aversion. **2.** This finding supports Darwin's principle that natural selection favors traits that aid survival. **3.** cognitive map. **4.** latent learning. **5.** observational learning. **6.** vicarious; vicarious. **7.** a. **8.** mirror. **9.** c.

CHAPTER 8

Memory

⟶ Studying and Encoding Memories

Retrieve It Answers

RI-1 recognition; recall. **RI-2** It would be better to test your memory with *recall* (such as with short-answer or fill-in-the-blank self-test questions) rather than *recognition* (such as with multiple-choice questions). Recalling information is harder than recognizing it. So if you can recall it, that means your retention of the material is better than if you could only recognize it. Your chances of test success are therefore greater. **RI-3** The newer idea of a *working memory* emphasizes the active processing that we now know takes place in Atkinson-Shiffrin's short-term memory stage. While the Atkinson-Shiffrin model viewed short-term memory as a temporary holding space, working memory plays a key role in processing new information and connecting it to previously stored information.

RI-4 (1) Active processing of incoming visual and auditory information, and (2) focusing our spotlight of attention. **RI-5** *Automatic* processing occurs unconsciously (automatically) for such things as the sequence and frequency of a day's events, and reading and comprehending words in our own language(s). *Effortful* processing requires attentive awareness and happens, for example, when we work hard to learn new material in class, or new lines for a play. **RI-6** sensory memory. **RI-7** Although cramming and rereading may lead to short-term gains in knowledge, distributed practice and repeated self-testing will result in the greatest long-term retention. **RI-8** Making material personally meaningful involves processing at a deep level, because you are processing *semantically*—based on the meaning of the words. Deep processing leads to greater retention.

Experience the Testing Effect Answers

1. recall. **2.** encoding; storage; retrieval. **3.** a. **4.** iconic; echoic. **5.** seven. **6.** mnemonics.

Storing and Retrieving Memories

Retrieve It Answers

RI-1 The cerebellum and basal ganglia are important for *implicit* memory processing, and the frontal lobes and hippocampus are key to *explicit* memory formation. **RI-2** Our *explicit* conscious memories of facts and episodes differ from our *implicit* memories of skills (such as tying shoelaces) and classically conditioned responses. The parts of the brain involved in explicit memory processing (the frontal lobes and hippocampus) may have sustained damage in the accident, while the parts involved in implicit memory processing (the cerebellum and basal ganglia) appear to have escaped harm. **RI-3** the amygdala. **RI-4** long-term potentiation. **RI-5** *Priming* is the activation (often without our awareness) of associations. Seeing a gun, for example, might temporarily predispose someone to interpret an ambiguous face as threatening or to recall a boss as nasty. **RI-6** serial position.

Experience the Testing Effect Answers

1. a. **2.** implicit. **3.** c. **4.** retrieval cues. **5.** Memories are stored within a web of many associations, one of which is mood. When you recall happy moments from your past, you activate these positive links. You may then experience mood-congruent memory and recall other happy moments, which could improve your mood and brighten your interpretation of current events. **6.** a.

Forgetting, Memory Construction, and Improving Memory

Retrieve It Answers

RI-1 (1) *Encoding failure:* Unattended information never entered our memory system. (2) *Storage decay:* Information fades from our memory. (3) *Retrieval failure:* We cannot access stored information accurately, sometimes due to interference or motivated forgetting. **RI-2** retroactive. **RI-3** repress. **RI-4** Real experiences would be confused with those we dreamed. When seeing someone we know, we might therefore be unsure whether we were reacting to something

they previously did or to something we dreamed they did. **RI-5** It will be important to remember the key points agreed upon by most researchers and professional associations: Sexual abuse, injustice, forgetting, and memory construction all happen; recovered memories are common; memories from before age 4 are unreliable; memories claimed to be recovered through hypnosis are especially unreliable; and memories, whether real or false, can be emotionally upsetting. **RI-6** Spend more time rehearsing or actively thinking about the material to boost long-term recall. Schedule spaced (not crammed) study times. Make the material personally meaningful, with well-organized and vivid associations. Refresh your memory by returning to contexts and moods to activate retrieval cues. Use mnemonic devices. Minimize proactive and retroactive interference. Plan ahead to ensure a complete night's sleep. Test yourself repeatedly—retrieval practice is a proven retention strategy.

Experience the Testing Effect Answers

1. d. **2.** d. **3.** retroactive. **4.** repression. **5.** b. **6.** Eliza's immature hippocampus and minimal verbal skills would have prevented her from encoding an explicit memory of the wedding reception at the age of two. It's more likely that Eliza learned information (from hearing the story repeatedly) that she eventually constructed into a memory that feels very real. **7.** source amnesia. **8.** déjà vu. **9.** b. **10.** b.

CHAPTER 9

Thinking, Language, and Intelligence

Thinking

Retrieve It Answers

RI-1 If a tragic event such as a plane crash makes the news, it is noteworthy and unusual, unlike much more common bad events, such as traffic accidents. Knowing this, we can worry less about unlikely events and think more about improving the safety of our everyday activities. (For example, we can wear a seat belt when in a vehicle and use the crosswalk when walking.) **RI-2** I. b, II. c, III. e, IV. d, V. a, VI. f, VII. h, VIII. j, IX. i, X. g.

Experience the Testing Effect Answers

1. concept. **2.** algorithm. **3.** Oscar will need to guard against *confirmation bias* (searching for support for his own views and ignoring contradictory evidence) as he seeks out opposing viewpoints. Even if Oscar encounters new information that disproves his beliefs, *belief perseverance* may lead him to cling to these views anyway. It will take more compelling evidence to change his political beliefs than it took to create them. **4.** c. **5.** availability. **6.** framing. **7.** b. **8.** neural networks.

Language and Thought

Retrieve It Answers

RI-1 Two morphemes—*cat* and *s,* and four phonemes—*c, a, t,* and *s.* **RI-2** Chomsky maintained that humans are biologically predisposed to learn the grammar rules of language. **RI-3** Infants normally start developing receptive language skills (ability to understand what is said to and about them) around 4 months of age. Then, starting with babbling at 4 months and beyond, infants normally start building productive language skills (ability to produce sounds and eventually words). **RI-4** Our brain's *critical period* for language learning is in childhood, when we can absorb language structure almost effortlessly. As we move past that stage in our brain's development, our ability to learn a new language diminishes dramatically. **RI-5** Broca's area; Wernicke's area. **RI-6** These are definitely communications. But if language consists of words and the grammatical rules we use to combine them to communicate meaning, few scientists would label a dog's barking and yipping as language. **RI-7** linguistic determinism. **RI-8** Mental practice uses visual imagery to mentally rehearse future behaviors, activating some of the same brain areas used during the actual behaviors. Visualizing the details of the process is more effective than visualizing only your end goal.

Experience the Testing Effect Answers

1. c. 2. phonemes; morphemes; grammar. 3. telegraphic speech. 4. universal grammar. 5. a.

Intelligence and Its Assessment

Retrieve It Answers

RI-1 People with savant syndrome have limited mental ability overall but possess one or more exceptional skills. According to Howard Gardner, this suggests that our abilities come in separate packages rather than being fully expressed by one general intelligence that encompasses all of our talents. **RI-2** Binet hoped that determining the child's mental age (the age that typically corresponds to a certain level of performance) would help identify appropriate school placements. **RI-3** 125 (5 ÷ 4 × 100 = 125). **RI-4** aptitude; achievement. **RI-5** A psychological test must be *standardized* (pretested on a representative sample of people), *reliable* (yielding consistent results), and *valid* (measuring and predicting what it is supposed to). **RI-6** disagreement; down; zero; agreement; up. **RI-7** An intelligence test score is only one measure of a person's ability to function. Other important factors to consider in an overall assessment include conceptual skills, social skills, and practical skills. **RI-8** Researcher A should develop a *longitudinal study* to examine how intelligence changes in the same people over the life span. Researcher B should develop a *cross-sectional study* to examine the intelligence of people now at various life stages.

Experience the Testing Effect Answers

1. general intelligence (*g*). 2. c. 3. analytical; creative; practical. 4. d. 5. d. 6. c. 7. reliability. 8. Writers' work relies more on crystallized intelligence, or accumulated knowledge, which increases with age. For top performance, scientists doing research may need more fluid intelligence (speedy and abstract reasoning), which tends to decrease with age. 9. c.

Genetic and Environmental Influences on Intelligence

Retrieve It Answers

RI-1 a. (Heritability—variation explained by genetic influences—will increase as environmental variation decreases.) **RI-2** Perfectly equal opportunity would create 100 percent heritability, because genes alone would account for any human differences. **RI-3** A test may be *culturally* "biased" (unfair) if higher scores are achieved by those with certain cultural experiences. That same test is not scientifically biased as long as it has *predictive validity*—if it predicts what it is supposed to predict. For example, the SAT may favor those with experience in the U.S. school system, but it does still accurately predict U.S. college success. **RI-4** stereotype threat.

Experience the Testing Effect Answers

1. c. 2. a. 3. c. 4. Stereotype threat.

CHAPTER 10

Motivation and Emotion

Basic Motivational Concepts, Affiliation, and Achievement

Retrieve It Answers

RI-1 (1) Well-practiced runners tend to excel when aroused by competition. (2) High anxiety about a difficult exam may disrupt test-takers' performance. **RI-2** According to Maslow, our drive to meet the physiological needs of hunger and thirst takes priority over our safety needs, prompting us to take risks at times. **RI-3** They engaged in more self-defeating behaviors and displayed more disparaging and aggressive behavior. These students' basic *need to belong* seems to have been disrupted. **RI-4** strengthen; increase. **RI-5** self-discipline (*grit*).

Experience the Testing Effect Answers

1. b. 2. a. 3. incentive. 4. Arousal. 5. b. 6. a. 7. c. 8. Monitor our time spent online, as well as our feelings about that time. Hide distracting online friends when necessary. Check your phone and email less often. Get outside and away from technology regularly. 9. should; should

Hunger

Retrieve It Answers

RI-1 low; high. **RI-2** You have learned to respond to the sight and aroma that signal the food about to enter your mouth. Both *physiological* cues (low blood sugar) and *psychological* cues (anticipation of the tasty meal) heighten your experienced hunger. **RI-3** Genetically influenced set/settling points, metabolism, and other factors (such as adequate sleep) influence the way our bodies burn calories.

Experience the Testing Effect Answers

1. Maslow's hierarchy of needs supports this statement because it addresses the primacy of some motives over others. Once our basic physiological needs are met, safety concerns are addressed next, followed by belongingness and love needs (such as the desire to kiss). 2. set point. 3. c. 4. low. 5. basal metabolic. 6. d. 7. Sanjay's plan is problematic. After he gains weight, the extra fat will require less energy to maintain than it did to gain in the first place. Sanjay may have a hard time getting rid of it later, when his metabolism slows down in an effort to retain his body weight.

 **Theories and Physiology of Emotion**

Retrieve It Answers

RI-1 simultaneously; sequentially (first the physiological response, and then the experienced emotion). **RI-2** cognitive. **RI-3** Zajonc and LeDoux suggested that we experience some emotions without any conscious, cognitive appraisal. Lazarus, Schachter, and Singer emphasized the importance of appraisal and cognitive labeling in our experience of emotion. **RI-4** The *sympathetic division* of the ANS arouses us for more intense experiences of emotion, pumping out the stress hormones epinephrine and norepinephrine to prepare our body for fight or flight. The *parasympathetic division* of the ANS takes over when a crisis passes, restoring our body to a calm physiological and emotional state.

Experience the Testing Effect Answers

1. James-Lange. **2.** b. **3.** c. **4.** A polygraph measures emotion-linked physiological changes, such as in perspiration, heart rate, and breathing. But the measure cannot distinguish between emotions with similar physiology (such as anxiety and guilt).

 **Expressing and Experiencing Emotion**

Retrieve It Answers

RI-1 Women. **RI-2** gestures. **RI-3** (1) Most students report feeling more happy than sad when their cheeks are raised upward. (2) Most students report feeling more sad than happy when their cheeks are pulled downward.

Experience the Testing Effect Answers

1. facial feedback. **2.** Aiden's droopy posture could negatively affect his mood thanks to the behavior feedback effect, which tends to make us feel the way we act.

CHAPTER 11

Stress, Health, and Human Flourishing

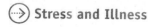 **Stress and Illness**

Retrieve It Answers

RI-1 sympathetic; increase; muscles; fight-or-flight. **RI-2** psychoneuroimmunology. **RI-3** Stress tends to reduce our immune system's ability to function properly, so that higher stress generally leads to greater risk of physical illness. **RI-4** Feeling angry and negative much of the time. **RI-5** b.

Experience the Testing Effect Answers

1. resistance; exhaustion. **2.** tend; befriend. **3.** b. **4.** d. **5.** lymphocytes. **6.** c. **7.** Type A individuals frequently experience negative emotions (anger, impatience), during which the sympathetic nervous system diverts blood away from the liver. This leaves fat and cholesterol circulating in the bloodstream for deposit near the heart and other organs, increasing the risk of heart disease and other health problems. Thus, Type A individuals actually harm themselves by directing anger at others.

Health and Happiness

Retrieve It Answers

RI-1 problem; emotion. **RI-2** Aerobic exercise, relaxation procedures, mindfulness meditation, and religious engagement. **RI-3** a. Age does NOT effectively predict happiness levels. Better predictors are personality traits, sleep and exercise, and religious faith.

Experience the Testing Effect Answers

1. emotion. **2.** b. **3.** internal. **4.** d. **5.** aerobic. **6.** c. **7.** d. **8.** Positive. **9.** b. **10.** relative deprivation.

CHAPTER 12

Social Psychology

Social Thinking and Social Influence

Retrieve It Answers

RI-1 By attributing the other person's behavior to the person ("What a terrible driver") and his own to the situation ("These roads are awful"), Marco has exhibited the fundamental attribution error. **RI-2** Our attitudes often influence our actions as we behave in ways consistent with our beliefs. However, our actions also influence our attitudes; we come to believe in what we have done. **RI-3** cognitive dissonance. **RI-4** Culture represents our shared behaviors, ideas, attitudes, values, and traditions, which we transmit across generations by way of our language ability. Culture, with its language and efficient division of labor, allows us to preserve innovation. **RI-5** a. **RI-6** normative social influence. **RI-7** Stanley Milgram. **RI-8** The Milgram studies showed that people were most likely to follow orders when the experimenter was nearby and was perceived to be a legitimate authority figure, the authority figure was supported by a powerful or prestigious institution, the victim was depersonalized or at a distance, and there were no models for defiance. **RI-9** This improved performance in the presence of others is most likely to occur with a well-learned task, because the added arousal caused by an audience tends to strengthen the most likely response. This also predicts poorer performance on a difficult task in others' presence. **RI-10** social loafing. **RI-11** The anonymity provided by the masks, combined with the arousal of the contentious setting, might create deindividuation (lessened self-awareness and self-restraint). **RI-12** group polarization. **RI-13** groupthink.

Experience the Testing Effect Answers

1. a. **2.** peripheral. **3.** foot-in-the-door. **4.** Cognitive dissonance theory best supports this suggestion. If Jamal acts confident, his behavior will contradict his negative self-thoughts, creating cognitive dissonance. To relieve the tension, Jamal may realign his attitudes with his actions by viewing himself as more outgoing and confident. **5.** c. **6.** a. **7.** The presence of a large audience generates arousal and strengthens Dr. Huang's most likely response: enhanced performance on a task he has mastered (teaching music history) and impaired performance on a task he finds difficult (statistics). **8.** deindividuation. **9.** group polarization.

Antisocial Relations

Retrieve It Answers

RI-1 scapegoat. **RI-2** Our biology (our genes, neural systems, and bio-chemistry—including testosterone and alcohol levels) influences our aggressive tendencies. Psychological factors (such as frustration, previous rewards for aggressive acts, and observation of others' aggression) can trigger any aggressive tendencies we may have. Social influences, such as exposure to violent media or being personally insulted, and cultural influences, such as whether we've grown up in a "culture of honor" or a father-absent home, can also affect our aggressive responses.

Experience the Testing Effect Answers

1. stereotypes.   **2.** This reaction could occur because we tend to overgeneralize from vivid, memorable cases.   **3.** more.   **4.** d.   **5.** frustration-aggression principle.   **6.** c.   **7.** c.   **8.** c.

Prosocial Relations

Retrieve It Answers

RI-1 mere exposure effect.   **RI-2** Being physically attractive tends to elicit positive first impressions. People tend to assume that attractive people are healthier, happier, more sensitive, more successful, and more socially skilled than others are.   **RI-3** Emotions consist of (1) physical arousal and (2) our interpretation of that arousal. Researchers have found that any source of arousal may be interpreted as passion in the presence of a desirable person.   **RI-4** equity; self-disclosure. **RI-5** In the presence of others, an individual is less likely to notice a situation, correctly interpret it as an emergency, and take responsibility for offering help. The Kitty Genovese case demonstrated this bystander effect, as each witness assumed many others were also aware of the event.   **RI-6** Sports fans may feel they are a part of an ingroup that sets itself apart from an outgroup (fans of the archrival team). Ingroup bias tends to develop, leading to prejudice and the view that the outgroup "deserves" misfortune. So, the archrival team's loss may seem justified. In conflicts, this kind of thinking is problematic, especially when each side in the conflict develops mirror-image perceptions of the other (distorted, negative images that are ironically similar).   **RI-7** Peacemakers should encourage equal-status contact, cooperation to achieve superordinate goals (shared goals that override differences), understanding through communication, and reciprocated conciliatory gestures (each side gives a little).

Experience the Testing Effect Answers

1. mere exposure.   **2.** companionate; passionate.   **3.** d.   **4.** c.   **5.** mirror-image.   **6.** superordinate.

Personality

Classic Perspectives on Personality

Retrieve It Answers

RI-1 ego; id; superego.   **RI-2** fixation.   **RI-3** unconsciously; anxiety.   **RI-4** Freud is credited with first drawing attention to

(1) the importance of childhood experiences, (2) the existence of the unconscious mind, and (3) our self-protective defense mechanisms. Freud's theory has been criticized as (1) not scientifically testable and offering after-the-fact explanations, (2) focusing too much on sexual conflicts in childhood, and (3) being based on the idea of repression, which has not been supported by modern research. **RI-5** Today's psychodynamic theorists and therapists still rely on the interviewing techniques that Freud used, and they still tend to focus on childhood experiences and attachments, unresolved conflicts, and unconscious influences. However, they are not likely to dwell on fixation at any psychosexual stage, or the idea that sexual issues are the basis of our personality.   **RI-6** The humanistic theories sought to turn psychology's attention away from drives and conflicts and toward our growth potential. This movement's focus on the way people strive for self-determination and self-realization was in contrast to Freudian theory and strict behaviorism. **RI-7** To be *empathic* is to share and mirror another person's feelings. Carl Rogers believed that people nurture growth in others by being empathic. Abraham Maslow proposed that *self-actualization* is the motivation to fulfill one's potential, and one of the ultimate psychological needs (the other is self-transcendence).

Experience the Testing Effect Answers

1. repression.   **2.** c.   **3.** superego.   **4.** b.   **5.** anxiety.   **6.** Projective.   **7.** d.   **8.** a.   **9.** a.   **10.** d.   **11.** Rogers might assert that the criminal was raised in an environment lacking genuineness, acceptance (unconditional positive regard), and empathy, which inhibited psychological growth and led to a negative self-concept.   **12.** unconditional positive regard.

Contemporary Perspectives on Personality

Retrieve It Answers

RI-1 extraversion–introversion and emotional stability–instability. **RI-2** The Big Five personality factors are *c*onscientiousness, *a*greeableness, *n*euroticism (emotional stability vs. instability), *o*penness, and *e*xtraversion: CANOE. These factors may be objectively measured, they are relatively stable over the life span, and they apply to all cultures in which they have been studied.   **RI-3** Our scores on personality tests predict our *average* behavior across many situations much better than they predict our specific behavior in any given situation.   **RI-4** social-cognitive; reciprocal determinism. **RI-5** Examine the person's past behavior patterns in similar situations.   **RI-6** People who feel confident in their abilities are often happier, have greater motivation, and are less susceptible to depression. Inflated self-esteem can lead to self-serving bias, greater aggression, and narcissism.   **RI-7** self-serving bias.   **RI-8** Defensive; Secure.   **RI-9** Individualists give priority to personal goals over group goals and tend to define their identity in terms of their own personal attributes. Collectivists give priority to group goals over individual goals and tend to define their identity in terms of group identifications.

Experience the Testing Effect Answers

1. Trait.   **2.** c.   **3.** b.   **4.** b.   **5.** a.   **6.** social-cognitive.   **7.** spotlight effect.   **8.** b.   **9.** Yes, if that self-love is of the *secure* type. Secure self-esteem promotes a focus beyond the self and a higher quality of life. Excessive self-love may promote artificially high or defensive self-esteem, which is fragile; perceived threats may be met with anger or aggression. **10.** b.

CHAPTER 14

Psychological Disorders

 Basic Concepts of Psychological Disorders

Retrieve It Answers

RI-1 dysfunctional or maladaptive. **RI-2** Some psychological disorders are culture-specific. For example, anorexia nervosa occurs mostly in Western cultures, and *taijin kyofusho* appears largely in Japan. Other disorders, such as major depressive disorder and schizophrenia, are universal—they occur in all cultures. **RI-3** Biological, psychological, and social-cultural influences combine to produce psychological disorders. This approach helps us understand that our well-being is affected by our genes, brain functioning, inner thoughts and feelings, and the influences of our social and cultural environment. **RI-4** Therapists and others apply disorder labels to communicate with one another using a common language, and to share concepts during research. Clients may benefit from knowing that they are not the only ones with these symptoms. The dangers of labeling people are that (1) overly broad classifications may pathologize normal behavior, and (2) the labels can trigger assumptions that will change people's behavior toward those labeled. **RI-5** Poverty-related stresses can help trigger disorders, but disabling disorders can also contribute to poverty. Thus, poverty and disorder are often a chicken-and-egg situation; it's hard to know which came first.

Experience the Testing Effect Answers

1. depression. **2.** No. Anna's behavior is unusual, causes her distress, and may make her a few minutes late on occasion, but it does not appear to significantly disrupt her ability to function. Like most of us, Anna demonstrates some unusual behaviors. Since they are not disabling or dysfunctional, they do not suggest a psychological disorder. **3.** *Susto* is a condition marked by severe anxiety, restlessness, and a fear of black magic. It is culture-specific to Latin America. **4.** medical. **5.** c. **6.** Critics have expressed concerns about the negative effects of labeling by the DSM and other classification systems. Labels have the potential to be both subjective and stigmatizing. Further, critics suggest that the DSM-5 casts too wide a net on disorders, pathologizing normal behavior. **7.** poverty. **8.** d.

 Anxiety Disorders, OCD, and PTSD

Retrieve It Answers

RI-1 generalized anxiety. **RI-2** panic. **RI-3** phobia. **RI-4** obsessive-compulsive. **RI-5** posttraumatic stress. **RI-6** Biological factors include inherited temperament differences and other gene variations; experience-altered brain pathways; and outdated, inherited responses that had survival value for our distant ancestors.

Experience the Testing Effect Answers

1. phobia. **2.** c. **3.** obsessive-compulsive. **4.** b. **5.** c.

 Major Depressive Disorder and Bipolar Disorder

Retrieve It Answers

RI-1 Many factors contribute to depression, including the biological influences of genetics and brain function. Social-cognitive factors also matter, including the interaction of explanatory style, mood, our responses to stressful experiences, changes in our patterns of thinking and behaving, and cultural influences. Depression involves the whole body and may disrupt sleep, energy levels, and concentration.

Experience the Testing Effect Answers

1. women's; men's. **2.** d. **3.** norepinephrine; serotonin. **4.** social-cognitive.

 Schizophrenia and Other Disorders

Retrieve It Answers

RI-1 negative; chronic; positive; acute. **RI-2** Biological factors include abnormalities in brain structure and function and a genetic predisposition to the disorder. Environmental factors such as nutritional deprivation, exposure to virus, and maternal stress contribute to activating the genes that increase risk. **RI-3** The psychodynamic explanation of DID symptoms is that they are defenses against anxiety generated by unacceptable urges. The learning perspective attempts to explain these symptoms as behaviors that have been reinforced by relieving anxiety. **RI-4** Twin and adoption studies show that biological relatives of people with this disorder are at increased risk for antisocial behavior. Researchers have also observed differences in the brain activity and structure of antisocial criminals. Negative environmental factors, such as poverty or childhood abuse, may channel genetic traits such as fearlessness in more dangerous directions—toward aggression and away from social responsibility. **RI-5** anorexia nervosa; bulimia nervosa.

Experience the Testing Effect Answers

1. Schizophrenia involves the altered perceptions, emotions, and behaviors of a mind split from reality. It does not involve the rapid changes in mood or identity suggested by this comparison. **2.** b. **3.** hallucination. **4.** a. **5.** c. **6.** c. **7.** b. **8.** b.

CHAPTER 15

Therapy

 Introduction to Therapy and the Psychological Therapies

Retrieve It Answers

RI-1 transference; resistance; interpretation. **RI-2** A psychodynamic therapist might be more interested in helping the child develop insight about the underlying problems that have caused the bed-wetting response. A behavior therapist would be more likely to agree with Mowrer that the bed-wetting symptom *is* the problem, and that counterconditioning the unwanted behavior would indeed bring emotional relief. **RI-3** The *insight therapies*—psychodynamic and humanistic therapies—seek to relieve problems by providing an understanding of their origins. *Behavior therapies* assume the problem behavior *is* the problem and treat it directly, paying less attention to its origins. **RI-4** If a behavior can be learned, it can be *unlearned* and replaced by other more adaptive responses. **RI-5** classical; operant. **RI-6** By reflecting clients' feelings in a non-directive setting, the *humanistic therapies* attempt to foster personal growth by helping clients become more self-aware and self-accepting. By making clients aware of self-defeating patterns of thinking, *cognitive therapies* guide people toward more adaptive ways of thinking about themselves and their world. **RI-7** cognitive therapy. **RI-8** This integrative therapy helps people change self-defeating thinking and behavior. It has been shown to be effective for those with anxiety disorders, obsessive-compulsive disorder, depressive disorders, bipolar disorder, and eating disorders.

Experience the Testing Effect Answers

1. a.   **2.** Insight.   **3.** d.   **4.** active listening.   **5.** c.   **6.** counterconditioning.   **7.** systematic desensitization.   **8.** Behavior therapies are often the best choice for treating phobias. Viewing Rico's fear of the freeway as a learned response, a behavior therapist might help Rico learn to replace his anxious response to freeway driving with a relaxation response.   **9.** token economy.   **10.** d.   **11.** Cognitive-behavioral.   **12.** b.

Evaluating Psychotherapies

Retrieve It Answers

RI-1 The *placebo effect* is the healing power of *belief* in a treatment. Patients and therapists who expect a treatment to be effective may believe it was.   **RI-2** are.   **RI-3** Using this approach, therapists make decisions about treatment based on research evidence, clinical expertise, and knowledge of the client.   **RI-4** EMDR has shown some effectiveness with trauma survivors and people with major depressive disorder. Skeptics acknowledge that EMDR works better than doing nothing, though they believe exposure therapy and the placebo effect, and not eye movements, are responsible for the treatment's successes. Light exposure therapy, while still somewhat controversial, has been shown to benefit those with a seasonal pattern in depression symptoms, as well as those with major depressive disorder and bipolar disorder.   **RI-5** more.

Experience the Testing Effect Answers

1. c.   **2.** d.   **3.** research evidence, clinical expertise, and knowledge of the patient.   **4.** The placebo effect is the healing power of belief in a treatment. When patients expect a treatment to be effective, they may believe it was.

The Biomedical Therapies and Preventing Psychological Disorders

Retrieve It Answers

RI-1 Exercise regularly, get enough sleep, get more exposure to light (get outside or use a light box), nurture important relationships, redirect negative thinking, and eat a diet rich in omega-3 fatty acids.   **RI-2** Researchers assign people to treatment and no-treatment conditions to see if those who receive the drug therapy improve more than those who don't. Double-blind controlled studies are most effective. If neither the therapist nor the client knows which participants have received the drug treatment, then any difference between the treated and untreated groups will reflect the drug treatment's actual effect.   **RI-3** antidepressants; antipsychotic.   **RI-4** electroconvulsive therapy; transcranial; repetitive transcranial; deep brain.   **RI-5** Psychological and biomedical therapies attempt to relieve people's suffering from psychological disorders. Preventive mental health attempts to prevent suffering by identifying and eliminating the conditions that cause disorders, as well as by building resilience.

Experience the Testing Effect Answers

1. c.   **2.** antianxiety.   **3.** lithium.   **4.** b.   **5.** d.

Statistical Reasoning in Everyday Life

Retrieve It Answers

RI-1 Note how the *y*-axis of each graph is labeled. The range for the *y*-axis label in graph (a) is only from 95 to 100. The range for graph (b) is from 0 to 100. All the trucks rank as 95 percent and up, so almost all are still functioning after 10 years, which graph (b) makes clear.   **RI-2** mean; mode; median; range; standard deviation.   **RI-3** The team's poor performance was not their typical behavior. The return to their normal—their winning streak—may just have been a case of regression toward the mean.   **RI-4** Averages based on fewer courses are more variable, which guarantees a greater number of extremely low and high marks at the end of the first term.   **RI-5** Descriptive; inferential.

Experience the Testing Effect Answers

1. b.   **2.** d.   **3.** normal curve.   **4.** a.   **5.** negative.   **6.** scatterplot.   **7.** Regression toward the mean is a statistical phenomenon describing the tendency of extreme scores or outcomes to return to normal after an unusual event. Without knowing this, we may inaccurately decide the return to normal was a result of our own behavior.   **8.** a.

Psychology at Work

Retrieve It Answers

RI-1 We become more likely to view our work as fulfilling and socially useful, and we experience higher self-esteem, feelings of competence, and overall well-being.   **RI-2** (1) Interviewers may presume people are what they seem to be in interviews. (2) Interviewers' preconceptions and moods color how they perceive interviewees' responses. (3) Interviewers judge people relative to other recent interviewees. (4) Interviewers tend to track the successful careers of those they hire, not the successful careers of those they reject. (5) Interviews tend to disclose prospective workers' good intentions, not their habitual behaviors. **RI-3** *Transformational leaders* are able to inspire others to share a vision and commit themselves to a group's mission. They tend to be naturally extraverted and set high standards. **RI-4** To develop safer machines and work environments, human factors psychologists stay mindful of the curse of knowledge—the tendency for experts to mistakenly assume that others share their knowledge.

Experience the Testing Effect Answers

1. flow.　**2.** Personnel; human factors.　**3.** a.　**4.** d.　**5.** Focusing on specific, short-term goals, such as maintaining a regular study schedule, will be more helpful than focusing on more distant general goals, such as earning a good grade in this class.　**6.** transformational.　**7.** c.　**8.** d.

Glossary

absolute threshold the minimum stimulus energy needed to detect a particular stimulus 50 percent of the time. (p. 191)

accommodation (1) in developmental psychology, adapting our current understandings (schemas) to incorporate new information. (2) in sensation and perception, the process by which the eye's lens changes shape to focus near or far objects on the retina. (pp. 125, 201)

achievement motivation a desire for significant accomplishment, for mastery of skills or ideas, for control, and for attaining a high standard. (p. 357)

achievement test a test designed to assess what a person has learned. (p. 327)

acquisition in classical conditioning, the initial stage, when one links a neutral stimulus and an unconditioned stimulus so that the neutral stimulus begins triggering the conditioned response. In operant conditioning, the strengthening of a reinforced response. (p. 238)

action potential a neural impulse; a brief electrical charge that travels down an axon. (p. 40)

active listening empathic listening in which the listener echoes, restates, and clarifies. A feature of Rogers' client-centered therapy. (p. 539)

acute schizophrenia (also called *reactive schizophrenia*) a form of schizophrenia that can begin at any age, frequently occurs in response to a traumatic event, and from which recovery is much more likely. (p. 524)

adaptation-level phenomenon our tendency to form judgments (of sounds, of lights, of income) relative to a neutral level defined by our prior experience. (p. 411)

adolescence the transition period from childhood to adulthood, extending from puberty to independence. (p. 141)

adrenal [ah-DREEN-el] **glands** a pair of endocrine glands that sit just above the kidneys and secrete hormones (epinephrine and norepinephrine) that help arouse the body in times of stress. (p. 48)

aerobic exercise sustained exercise that increases heart and lung fitness; also helps alleviate depression and anxiety. (p. 401)

affiliation need the need to build relationships and to feel part of a group. (p. 353)

aggression any physical or verbal behavior intended to harm someone physically or emotionally. (pp. 162, 441)

agonist a molecule that increases a neurotransmitter's action. (p. 43)

AIDS (acquired immune deficiency syndrome) a life-threatening, sexually transmitted infection caused by the *human immunodeficiency virus (HIV)*. AIDS depletes the immune system, leaving the person vulnerable to infections. (p. 175)

alcohol use disorder (popularly known as *alcoholism*) alcohol use marked by tolerance, withdrawal, and a drive to continue problematic use. (p. 103)

algorithm a methodical, logical rule or procedure that guarantees solving a particular problem. Contrasts with the usually speedier—but also more error-prone—use of *heuristics*. (p. 299)

all-or-none response a neuron's reaction of either firing (with a full-strength response) or not firing. (p. 41)

alpha waves the relatively slow brain waves of a relaxed, awake state. (p. 86)

altruism unselfish regard for the welfare of others. (p. 453)

amphetamines drugs (such as methamphetamine) that stimulate neural activity, causing accelerated body functions and associated energy and mood changes. (p. 104)

amygdala [uh-MIG-duh-la] two lima-bean-sized neural clusters in the limbic system; linked to emotion. (p. 55)

androgyny displaying both traditional masculine and feminine psychological characteristics. (p. 169)

anorexia nervosa an eating disorder in which a person (usually an adolescent female) maintains a starvation diet despite being significantly underweight; sometimes accompanied by excessive exercise. (p. 531)

antagonist a molecule that inhibits or blocks a neurotransmitter's action. (p. 43)

anterograde amnesia an inability to form new memories. (p. 285)

antianxiety drugs drugs used to control anxiety and agitation. (p. 561)

antidepressant drugs drugs used to treat depression, anxiety disorders, obsessive- compulsive disorder, and posttraumatic stress disorder. (Several widely used antidepressant drugs are *selective serotonin reuptake inhibitors—SSRIs*.) (p. 561)

antipsychotic drugs drugs used to treat schizophrenia and other forms of severe thought disorder. (p. 560)

antisocial personality disorder a personality disorder in which a person (usually a man) exhibits a lack of conscience for wrongdoing, even toward friends and family members; may be aggressive and ruthless or a clever con artist. (p. 529)

anxiety disorders psychological disorders characterized by distressing, persistent anxiety or maladaptive behaviors that reduce anxiety. (p. 506)

aphasia impairment of language, usually caused by left hemisphere damage either to Broca's area (impairing speaking) or to Wernicke's area (impairing understanding). (p. 316)

applied research a scientific study that aims to solve practical problems. (p. 13)

aptitude test a test designed to predict a person's future performance; *aptitude* is the capacity to learn. (p. 327)

asexual having no sexual attraction toward others. (p. 173)

assimilation interpreting our new experiences in terms of our existing schemas. (p. 125)

association areas areas of the cerebral cortex that are not involved in primary motor or sensory functions; rather, they are involved in higher mental functions such as learning, remembering, thinking, and speaking. (p. 62)

associative learning learning that certain events occur together. The events may be two stimuli (as in classical conditioning) or a response and its consequence (as in operant conditioning). (p. 234)

attachment an emotional tie with another person; shown in young children by their seeking closeness to their caregiver and showing distress on separation. (p. 133)

attention-deficit/hyperactivity disorder (ADHD) a psychological disorder marked by extreme inattention and/or hyperactivity and impulsivity. (p. 497)

attitude feelings, often influenced by our beliefs, that predispose us to respond in a particular way to objects, people, and events. (p. 418)

attribution theory the theory that we explain someone's behavior by crediting either the situation or the person's disposition. (p. 416)

audition the sense or act of hearing. (p. 216)

autism spectrum disorder (ASD) a disorder that appears in childhood and is marked by significant deficiencies in communication and social interaction, and by rigidly fixated interests and repetitive behaviors. (p. 130)

automatic processing unconscious encoding of incidental information, such as space, time, and frequency, and of well-earned information, such as word meanings. (p. 269)

autonomic [aw-tuh-NAHM-ik] **nervous system (ANS)** the part of the peripheral nervous system that controls the glands and the muscles of the internal organs (such as the heart). Its sympathetic division arouses; its parasympathetic division calms. (p. 45)

availability heuristic estimating the likelihood of events based on their availability in memory; if instances come readily to mind (perhaps because of their vividness), we presume such events are common. (p. 301)

aversive conditioning associates an unpleasant state (such as nausea) with an unwanted behavior (such as drinking alcohol). (p. 543)

axon the neuron extension that passes messages through its branches to other neurons or to muscles or glands. (p. 39)

babbling stage beginning around 4 months, the stage of speech development in which an infant spontaneously utters various sounds at first unrelated to the household language. (p. 315)

barbiturates drugs that depress central nervous system activity, reducing anxiety but impairing memory and judgment. (p. 104)

basal metabolic rate the body's resting rate of energy output. (p. 363)

basic research pure science that aims to increase the scientific knowledge base. (p. 13)

basic trust according to Erik Erikson, a sense that the world is predictable and trustworthy; said to be formed during infancy by appropriate experiences with responsive caregivers. (p. 137)

behavior feedback effect the tendency of behavior to influence our own and others' thoughts, feelings, and actions. (p. 381)

behavior genetics the study of the relative power and limits of genetic and environmental influences on behavior. (pp. 8, 69)

behavior therapy therapy that applies learning principles to the elimination of unwanted behaviors. (p. 540)

behaviorism the view that psychology (1) should be an objective science that (2) studies behavior without reference to mental processes. Most psychologists today agree with (1) but not with (2). (pp. 7, 236)

belief perseverance clinging to one's initial conceptions after the basis on which they were formed has been discredited. (p. 304)

binge-eating disorder significant binge-eating episodes, followed by distress, disgust, or guilt, but without the compensatory behavior that marks bulimia nervosa. (p. 533)

binocular cue a depth cue, such as retinal disparity, that depends on the use of two eyes. (p. 208)

biological psychology the scientific study of the links between biological (genetic, neural, hormonal) and psychological processes. Some biological psychologists call themselves *behavioral neuroscientists, neuropsychologists, behavior geneticists, physiological psychologists,* or *biopsychologists.* (p. 39)

biomedical therapy prescribed medications or procedures that act directly on the person's physiology. (p. 537)

biopsychosocial approach an integrated approach that incorporates biological, psychological, and social-cultural levels of analysis. (p. 11)

bipolar disorder a disorder in which a person alternates between the hopelessness and lethargy of depression and the overexcited state of mania. (Formerly called *manic-depressive disorder.*) (p. 515)

blind spot the point at which the optic nerve leaves the eye, creating a "blind" spot because no receptor cells are located there. (p. 201)

blindsight a condition in which a person can respond to a visual stimulus without consciously experiencing it. (p. 85)

bottom-up processing analysis that begins with the sensory receptors and works up to the brain's integration of sensory information. (p. 190)

brainstem the oldest part and central core of the brain, beginning where the spinal cord swells as it enters the skull; the brainstem is responsible for automatic survival functions. (p. 53)

Broca's area helps control language expression—an area of the frontal lobe, usually in the left hemisphere, that directs the muscle movements involved in speech. (p. 316)

bulimia nervosa an eating disorder in which a person's binge eating (usually of high-calorie foods) is followed by inappropriate weight-loss promoting behavior, such as vomiting, laxative use, fasting, or excessive exercise. (p. 531)

bystander effect the tendency for any given bystander to be less likely to give aid if other bystanders are present. (p. 455)

Cannon-Bard theory the theory that an emotion-arousing stimulus simultaneously triggers (1) physiological responses and (2) the subjective experience of emotion. (p. 369)

case study a descriptive technique in which one individual or group is studied in depth in the hope of revealing universal principles. (p. 20)

catharsis in psychology, the idea that "releasing" aggressive energy (through action or fantasy) relieves aggressive urges. (p. 393)

cell body the part of a neuron that contains the nucleus; the cell's life-support center. (p. 39)

central nervous system (CNS) the brain and spinal cord. (p. 45)

central route persuasion occurs when interested people focus on the arguments and respond with favorable thoughts. (p. 418)

cerebellum [sehr-uh-BELL-um] the "little brain" at the rear of the brainstem; functions include processing sensory input, coordinating movement output and balance, and enabling nonverbal learning and memory. (p. 54)

cerebral [seh-REE-bruhl] **cortex** the intricate fabric of interconnected neural cells covering the cerebral hemispheres; the body's ultimate control and information-processing center. (p. 59)

change blindness failing to notice changes in the environment; a form of *inattentional blindness.* (p. 82)

chromosomes threadlike structures made of DNA molecules that contain the genes. (p. 69)

chronic schizophrenia (also called *process schizophrenia*) a form of schizophrenia in which symptoms usually appear by late adolescence or early adulthood. As people age, psychotic episodes last longer and recovery periods shorten. (p. 524)

chunking organizing items into familiar, manageable units; often occurs automatically. (p. 270)

circadian [ser-KAY-dee-an] **rhythm** our biological clock; regular bodily rhythms (for example, of temperature and wakefulness) that occur on a 24-hour cycle. (p. 86)

classical conditioning a type of learning in which we link two or more stimuli; as a result, to illustrate with Pavlov's classic experiment, the first stimulus (a tone) comes to elicit behavior (drooling) in anticipation of the second stimulus (food). (p. 236)

client-centered therapy a humanistic therapy, developed by Carl Rogers, in which the therapist uses techniques such as *active listening* within an accepting, genuine, empathic environment to facilitate clients' growth. (Also called *person-centered therapy*.) (p. 539)

clinical psychology a branch of psychology that studies, assesses, and treats people with psychological disorders. (p. 13)

cocaine a powerful and addictive stimulant derived from the coca plant; produces temporarily increased alertness and euphoria. (p. 106)

cochlea [KOHK-lee-uh] a coiled, bony, fluid- filled tube in the inner ear; sound waves traveling through the cochlear fluid trigger nerve impulses. (p. 216)

cochlear implant a device for converting sounds into electrical signals and stimulating the auditory nerve through electrodes threaded into the cochlea. (p. 219)

cognition all the mental activities associated with thinking, knowing, remembering, and communicating. (pp. 125, 299)

cognitive dissonance theory the theory that we act to reduce the discomfort (dissonance) we feel when two of our thoughts (cognitions) are inconsistent. For example, when we become aware that our attitudes and our actions clash, we can reduce the resulting dissonance by changing our attitudes. (p. 421)

cognitive learning the acquisition of mental information, whether by observing events, by watching others, or through language. (p. 236)

cognitive map a mental representation of the layout of one's environment. For example, after exploring a maze, rats act as if they have learned a cognitive map of it. (p. 257)

cognitive neuroscience the interdisciplinary study of the brain activity linked with cognition (including perception, thinking, memory, and language). (pp. 8, 81)

cognitive psychology the study of mental processes, such as occur when we perceive, learn, remember, think, communicate, and solve problems. (p. 8)

cognitive therapy therapy that teaches people new, more adaptive ways of thinking; based on the assumption that thoughts intervene between events and our emotional reactions. (p. 544)

cognitive-behavioral therapy (CBT) a popular integrative therapy that combines cognitive therapy (changing self-defeating thinking) with behavior therapy (changing behavior). (p. 546)

cohort a group of people sharing a common characteristic, such as being from a given time period. (p. 333)

collective unconscious Carl Jung's concept of a shared, inherited reservoir of memory traces from our species' history. (p. 466)

collectivism giving priority to the goals of one's group (often one's extended family or work group) and defining one's identity accordingly. (p. 491)

community psychology a branch of psychology that studies how people interact with their social environments and how social institutions affect individuals and groups. (p. 13)

companionate love the deep affectionate attachment we feel for those with whom our lives are intertwined. (p. 451)

concept a mental grouping of similar objects, events, ideas, or people. (p. 299)

concrete operational stage in Piaget's theory, the stage of cognitive development (from about 7 to 11 years of age) during which children gain the mental operations that enable them to think logically about concrete events. (p. 128)

conditioned reinforcer a stimulus that gains its reinforcing power through its association with a primary reinforcer; also known as a *secondary reinforcer*. (p. 246)

conditioned response (CR) in classical conditioning, a learned response to a previously neutral (but now conditioned) stimulus (CS). (p. 238)

conditioned stimulus (CS) in classical conditioning, an originally neutral stimulus that, after association with an unconditioned stimulus (US), comes to trigger a conditioned response (CR). (p. 238)

conduction hearing loss a less common form of hearing loss, caused by damage to the mechanical system that conducts sound waves to the cochlea. (p. 219)

cones retinal receptors that are concentrated near the center of the retina and that function in daylight or in well-lit conditions. Cones detect fine detail and give rise to color sensations. (p. 201)

confirmation bias a tendency to search for information that supports our preconceptions and to ignore or distort contradictory evidence. (p. 299)

conflict a perceived incompatibility of actions, goals, or ideas. (p. 456)

conformity adjusting our behavior or thinking to coincide with a group standard. (p. 423)

confounding variable in an experiment, a factor other than the factor being studied that might influence a study's results. (p. 28)

consciousness our subjective awareness of ourselves and our environment. (p. 81)

conservation the principle (which Piaget believed to be a part of concrete operational reasoning) that properties such as mass, volume, and number remain the same despite changes in the forms of objects. (p. 127)

continuous reinforcement schedule reinforcing the desired response every time it occurs. (p. 246)

control group in an experiment, the group *not* exposed to the treatment; contrasts with the experimental group and serves as a comparison for evaluating the effect of the treatment. (p. 25)

convergent thinking narrowing the available problem solutions to determine the single best solution. (p. 307)

coping alleviating stress using emotional, cognitive, or behavioral methods. (p. 395)

coronary heart disease the clogging of the vessels that nourish the heart muscle; the leading cause of death in many developed countries. (p. 391)

corpus callosum [KOR-pus kah-LOW-sum] the large band of neural fibers connecting the two brain hemispheres and carrying messages between them. (p. 64)

correlation a measure of the extent to which two factors vary together, and thus of how well either factor predicts the other. (p. 24)

correlation coefficient a statistical index of the relationship between two things (from −1.00 to +1.00). (pp. 24, A-4)

counseling psychology a branch of psychology that assists people with problems in living (often related to school, work, or marriage) and in achieving greater well-being. (p. 13)

counterconditioning behavior therapy procedures that use classical conditioning to evoke new responses to stimuli that are triggering unwanted behaviors; include *exposure therapies* and *aversive conditioning*. (p. 540)

creativity the ability to produce new and valuable ideas. (p. 307)

critical period an optimal period early in the life of an organism when exposure to certain stimuli or experiences produces normal development. (p. 122)

critical thinking thinking that does not blindly accept arguments and conclusions. Rather, it examines assumptions, appraises the source, discerns hidden biases, evaluates evidence, and assesses conclusions. (p. 2)

cross-sectional study research that compares people of different ages at the same point in time. (pp. 154, 333)

crystallized intelligence our accumulated knowledge and verbal skills; tends to increase with age. (p. 333)

culture the enduring behaviors, ideas, attitudes, values, and traditions shared by a group of people and transmitted from one generation to the next. (pp. 8, 421)

debriefing the postexperimental explanation of a study, including its purpose and any deceptions, to its participants. (p. 31)

deep processing encoding semantically, based on the meaning of the words; tends to yield the best retention. (p. 273)

defense mechanisms in psychoanalytic theory, the ego's protective methods of reducing anxiety by unconsciously distorting reality. (p. 465)

deindividuation the loss of self-awareness and self-restraint occurring in group situations that foster arousal and anonymity. (p. 431)

déjà vu that eerie sense that "I've experienced this before." Cues from the current situation may unconsciously trigger retrieval of an earlier experience. (p. 291)

delta waves the large, slow brain waves associated with deep sleep. (p. 88)

delusion a false belief, often of persecution or grandeur, that may accompany psychotic disorders. (p. 523)

dendrites a neuron's often bushy, branching extensions that receive and integrate messages, conducting impulses toward the cell body. (p. 39)

dependent variable in an experiment, the outcome that is measured; the variable that may change when the independent variable is manipulated. (p. 28)

depressants drugs (such as alcohol, barbiturates, and opiates) that reduce neural activity and slow body functions. (p. 103)

depth perception the ability to see objects in three dimensions although the images that strike the retina are two-dimensional; allows us to judge distance. (p. 208)

developmental psychology a branch of psychology that studies physical, cognitive, and social change throughout the life span. (p. 116)

difference threshold the minimum difference between two stimuli required for detection 50 percent of the time. We experience the difference threshold as a *just noticeable difference* (or *jnd*). (p. 192)

discrimination (1) in classical conditioning, the learned ability to distinguish between a conditioned stimulus and similar stimuli that do not signal an unconditioned stimulus; in operant conditioning, the ability to distinguish responses that are reinforced from similar responses that are not reinforced. (2) in social psychology, unjustifiable negative behavior toward a group or its members. (pp. 241, 435)

dissociation a split in consciousness, which allows some thoughts and behaviors to occur simultaneously with others. (p. 225)

dissociative disorders controversial, rare disorders in which conscious awareness becomes separated (dissociated) from previous memories, thoughts, and feelings. (p. 527)

dissociative identity disorder (DID) a rare dissociative disorder in which a person exhibits two or more distinct and alternating identities. (Formerly called *multiple personality disorder*.) (p. 529)

divergent thinking expanding the number of possible problem solutions; creative thinking that diverges in different directions. (p. 307)

DNA (deoxyribonucleic acid) a complex molecule containing the genetic information that makes up the chromosomes. (p. 69)

double-blind procedure an experimental procedure in which both the research participants and the research staff are ignorant (blind) about whether the research participants have received the treatment or a placebo. Commonly used in drug-evaluation studies. (p. 27)

dream a sequence of images, emotions, and thoughts passing through a sleeping person's mind. (p. 97)

drive-reduction theory the idea that a physiological need creates an aroused state (a drive) that motivates an organism to satisfy the need. (p. 349)

DSM-5 the American Psychiatric Association's *Diagnostic and Statistical Manual of Mental Disorders*, Fifth Edition; a widely used system for classifying psychological disorders. (p. 497)

dual processing the principle that information is often simultaneously processed on separate conscious and unconscious tracks. (p. 85)

echoic memory a momentary sensory memory of auditory stimuli; if attention is elsewhere, sounds and words can still be recalled within 3 or 4 seconds. (p. 270)

eclectic approach an approach to psychotherapy that uses techniques from various forms of therapy. (p. 537)

Ecstasy (MDMA) a synthetic stimulant and mild hallucinogen. Produces euphoria and social intimacy, but with short-term health risks and longer-term harm to serotonin- producing neurons and to mood and cognition. (p. 106)

EEG (electroencephalogram) an amplified recording of the waves of electrical activity sweeping across the brain's surface. These waves are measured by electrodes placed on the scalp. (p. 51)

effortful processing encoding that requires attention and conscious effort. (p. 269)

ego the largely conscious, "executive" part of personality that, according to Freud, mediates among the demands of the id, the superego, and reality. The ego operates on the *reality principle*, satisfying the id's desires in ways that will realistically bring pleasure rather than pain. (p. 465)

egocentrism in Piaget's theory, the preoperational child's difficulty taking another's point of view. (p. 128)

electroconvulsive therapy (ECT) a biomedical therapy for severely depressed patients in which a brief electric current is sent through the brain of an anesthetized patient. (p. 563)

embodied cognition the influence of bodily sensations, gestures, and other states on cognitive preferences and judgments. (p. 228)

embryo the developing human organism from about 2 weeks after fertilization through the second month. (p. 119)

emerging adulthood a period from about age 18 to the mid-twenties, when many in Western cultures are no longer adolescents but have not yet achieved full independence as adults. (p. 149)

emotion a response of the whole organism, involving (1) physiological arousal, (2) expressive behaviors, and (3) conscious experience. (p. 369)

emotional intelligence the ability to perceive, understand, manage, and use emotions. (p. 327)

emotion-focused coping attempting to alleviate stress by avoiding or ignoring a stressor and attending to emotional needs related to our stress reaction. (p. 395)

empirical approach an evidence-based method that draws on observation and experimentation. (p. 2)

empirically derived test a test (such as the MMPI) created by selecting from a pool of items those that discriminate between groups. (p. 477)

encoding the process of getting information into the memory system—for example, by extracting meaning. (p. 268)

encoding specificity principle the idea that cues and contexts specific to a particular memory will be most effective in helping us recall it. (p. 280)

endocrine [EN-duh-krin] **system** the body's "slow" chemical communication system; a set of glands that secrete hormones into the bloodstream. (p. 48)

endorphins [en-DOR-fins] "morphine within"— natural, opiate-like neurotransmitters linked to pain control and to pleasure. (p. 43)

environment every nongenetic influence, from prenatal nutrition to the people and things around us. (p. 69)

epigenetics "above" or "in addition to" (*epi*) genetics; the study of the molecular mechanisms by which environments can influence genetic expression (without a DNA change). (pp. 75, 497)

episodic memory explicit memory of personally experienced events; one of our two conscious memory systems (the other is *semantic memory*). (p. 276)

equity a condition in which people receive from a relationship in proportion to what they give to it. (p. 453)

erectile disorder inability to develop or maintain an erection due to insufficient blood flow to the penis. (p. 175)

estrogens sex hormones, such as estradiol, that contribute to female sex characteristics and are secreted in greater amounts by females than by males. Estrogen levels peak during ovulation. In nonhuman mammals, this promotes sexual receptivity. (p. 173)

evidence-based practice clinical decision making that integrates the best available research with clinical expertise and patient characteristics and preferences. (p. 553)

evolutionary psychology the study of the evolution of behavior and the mind, using principles of natural selection. (pp. 8, 75)

experiment a research method in which an investigator manipulates one or more factors (independent variables) to observe the effect on some behavior or mental process (the dependent variable). By *random assignment* of participants, the experimenter aims to control other relevant factors. (p. 25)

experimental group in an experiment, the group exposed to the treatment, that is, to one version of the independent variable. (p. 25)

explicit memory retention of facts and experiences that we can consciously know and "declare." (Also called *declarative memory*.) (p. 269)

exposure therapies behavioral techniques, such as *systematic desensitization* and *virtual reality exposure therapy,* that treat anxieties by exposing people (in imaginary or actual situations) to the things they fear and avoid. (p. 540)

external locus of control the perception that chance or outside forces beyond our personal control determine our fate. (p. 396)

extinction the diminishing of a conditioned response; occurs in classical conditioning when an unconditioned stimulus (US) does not follow a conditioned stimulus (CS); occurs in operant conditioning when a response is no longer reinforced. (p. 238)

extrasensory perception (ESP) the controversial claim that perception can occur apart from sensory input; includes telepathy, clairvoyance, and precognition. (p. 228)

extrinsic motivation the desire to perform a behavior to receive promised rewards or avoid threatened punishment. (p. 358)

facial feedback effect the tendency of facial muscle states to trigger corresponding feelings such as fear, anger, or happiness. (p. 381)

family therapy therapy that treats people in the context of their family system. Views an individual's unwanted behaviors as influenced by, or directed at, other family members. (p. 547)

feature detectors nerve cells in the brain's visual cortex that respond to specific features of the stimulus, such as shape, angle, or movement. (p. 204)

feel-good, do-good phenomenon people's tendency to be helpful when in a good mood. (p. 407)

female orgasmic disorder distress due to infrequently or never experiencing orgasm. (p. 175)

fetal alcohol syndrome (FAS) physical and cognitive abnormalities in children caused by a pregnant woman's heavy drinking. In severe cases, signs include a small, out-of-proportion head and abnormal facial features. (p. 120)

fetus the developing human organism from 9 weeks after conception to birth. (p. 119)

figure-ground the organization of the visual field into objects (the *figures*) that stand out from their surroundings (the *ground*). (p. 207)

fixation (1) in thinking, the inability to see a problem from a new perspective; an obstacle to problem solving. (2) in personality theory, according to Freud, a lingering focus of pleasure-seeking energies at an earlier psychosexual stage, in which conflicts were unresolved. (pp. 301, 465)

fixed-interval schedule in operant conditioning, a reinforcement schedule that reinforces a response only after a specified time has elapsed. (p. 246)

fixed-ratio schedule in operant conditioning, a reinforcement schedule that reinforces a response only after a specified number of responses. (p. 246)

flashbulb memory a clear memory of an emotionally significant moment or event. (p. 278)

flow a completely involved, focused state, with diminished awareness of self and time; results from full engagement of our skills. (p. B-1)

fluid intelligence our ability to reason speedily and abstractly; tends to decrease with age, especially during late adulthood. (p. 333)

fMRI (functional MRI) a technique for revealing blood flow and, therefore, brain activity by comparing successive MRI scans. fMRI scans show brain function as well as structure. (p. 53)

foot-in-the-door phenomenon the tendency for people who have first agreed to a small request to comply later with a larger request. (p. 418)

formal operational stage in Piaget's theory, the stage of cognitive development (normally beginning about age 12) during which people begin to think logically about abstract concepts. (p. 129)

fovea the central focal point in the retina, around which the eye's cones cluster. (p. 203)

framing the way an issue is posed; how an issue is worded can significantly affect decisions and judgments. (p. 304)

fraternal (dizygotic) twins individuals that develop from separate fertilized eggs. They are genetically no closer than ordinary siblings, but they share a prenatal environment. (p. 70)

free association in psychoanalysis, a method of exploring the unconscious in which the person relaxes and says whatever comes to mind, no matter how trivial or embarrassing. (p. 463)

frequency the number of complete wavelengths that pass a point in a given time (for example, per second). (p. 216)

frequency theory in hearing, the theory that the rate of nerve impulses traveling up the auditory nerve matches the frequency of a tone, thus enabling us to sense its pitch. (Also called *temporal theory*.) (p. 220)

frontal lobes the portion of the cerebral cortex lying just behind the forehead; involved in speaking and muscle movements and in making plans and judgments. (p. 59)

frustration-aggression principle the principle that frustration—the blocking of an attempt to achieve some goal—creates anger, which can generate aggression. (p. 443)

functionalism an early school of thought promoted by James and influenced by Darwin; explored how mental and behavioral processes function—how they enable the organism to adapt, survive, and flourish. (p. 5)

fundamental attribution error the tendency for observers, when analyzing others' behavior, to underestimate the impact of the situation and to overestimate the impact of personal disposition. (p. 416)

gate-control theory the theory that the spinal cord contains a neurological "gate" that blocks pain signals or allows them to pass on to the brain. The "gate" is opened by the activity of pain signals traveling up small nerve fibers and is closed by activity in larger fibers or by information coming from the brain. (p. 222)

gender identity our sense of being male, female, or some combination of the two. (p. 169)

gender in psychology, the socially influenced characteristics by which people define *boy, girl, man,* and *woman.* (p. 162)

gender role a set of expected behaviors, attitudes, and traits for males or for females. (p. 169)

gender typing the acquisition of a traditional masculine or feminine role. (p. 169)

general adaptation syndrome (GAS) Selye's concept of the body's adaptive response to stress in three phases—alarm, resistance, exhaustion. (p. 386)

general intelligence (*g*) according to Spearman and others, underlies all mental abilities and is therefore measured by every task on an intelligence test. (p. 323)

generalization the tendency, once a response has been conditioned, for stimuli similar to the conditioned stimulus to elicit similar responses. (In operant conditioning, generalization occurs when responses learned in one situation occur in other, similar situations.) (p. 238)

generalized anxiety disorder an anxiety disorder in which a person is continually tense, apprehensive, and in a state of autonomic nervous system arousal. (p. 507)

genes the biochemical units of heredity that make up the chromosomes; segments of DNA capable of synthesizing proteins. (p. 69)

genome the complete instructions for making an organism, consisting of all the genetic material in that organism's chromosomes. (p. 69)

gestalt an organized whole. Gestalt psychologists emphasized our tendency to integrate pieces of information into meaningful wholes. (p. 207)

glial cells (glia) cells in the nervous system that support, nourish, and protect neurons; they may also play a role in learning, thinking, and memory. (p. 40)

glucose the form of sugar that circulates in the blood and provides the major source of energy for body tissues. When its level is low, we feel hunger. (p. 363)

grammar in a language, a system of rules that enables us to communicate with and understand others. *Semantics* is the language's set of rules for deriving meaning from sounds, and *syntax* is its set of rules for combining words into grammatically sensible sentences. (p. 312)

GRIT Graduated and Reciprocated Initiatives in Tension-Reduction—a strategy designed to decrease international tensions. (p. 459)

grit in psychology, passion and perseverance in the pursuit of long-term goals. (p. 358)

group polarization the enhancement of a group's prevailing inclinations through discussion within the group. (p. 431)

group therapy therapy conducted with groups rather than individuals, providing benefits from group interaction. (p. 547)

grouping the perceptual tendency to organize stimuli into coherent groups. (p. 208)

groupthink the mode of thinking that occurs when the desire for harmony in a decision-making group overrides a realistic appraisal of alternatives. (p. 433)

habituation decreasing responsiveness with repeated stimulation. As infants gain familiarity with repeated exposure to a stimulus, their interest wanes and they look away sooner. (p. 121)

hallucinations false sensory experiences, such as seeing something in the absence of an external visual stimulus. (p. 88)

hallucinogens psychedelic ("mind-manifesting") drugs, such as LSD, that distort perceptions and evoke sensory images in the absence of sensory input. (p. 109)

health psychology a subfield of psychology that provides psychology's contribution to behavioral medicine. (p. 389)

heredity the genetic transfer of characteristics from parents to offspring. (p. 69)

heritability the proportion of variation among individuals in a group that we can attribute to genes. The heritability of a trait may vary, depending on the range of populations and environments studied. (p. 336)

heuristic a simple thinking strategy that often allows us to make judgments and solve problems efficiently; usually speedier but also more error-prone than an *algorithm*. (p. 299)

hierarchy of needs Maslow's pyramid of human needs, beginning at the base with physiological needs that must first be satisfied before people can fulfill their higher- level safety needs and then psychological needs. (pp. 351, 470)

hindsight bias the tendency to believe, after learning an outcome, that one would have foreseen it. (Also known as the *I-knew-it- all-along phenomenon.*) (p. 16)

hippocampus a neural center located in the limbic system; helps process explicit (conscious) memories—of facts and events—for storage. (pp. 57, 276)

homeostasis a tendency to maintain a balanced or constant internal state; the regulation of any aspect of body chemistry, such as blood glucose, around a particular level. (p. 349)

hormones chemical messengers that are manufactured by the endocrine glands, travel through the bloodstream, and affect other tissues. (p. 48)

hue the dimension of color that is determined by the wavelength of light; what we know as the color names *blue, green,* and so forth. (p. 199)

human factors psychology a field of psychology allied with I/O psychology that explores how people and machines interact and how machines and physical environments can be made safe and easy to use. (p. B-5)

humanistic psychology a historically significant perspective that emphasized human growth potential. (p. 8)

humanistic theories theories that view personality with a focus on the potential for healthy personal growth. (p. 470)

hypnosis a social interaction in which one person (the hypnotist) suggests to another (the subject) that certain perceptions, feelings, thoughts, or behaviors will spontaneously occur. (p. 225)

hypothalamus [hi-po-THAL-uh-muss] a neural structure lying below (*hypo*) the thalamus; it directs several maintenance activities (eating, drinking, body temperature), helps govern the endocrine system via the pituitary gland, and is linked to emotion and reward. (p. 57)

hypothesis a testable prediction, often implied by a theory. (p. 19)

iconic memory a momentary sensory memory of visual stimuli; a photographic or picture-image memory lasting no more than a few tenths of a second. (p. 270)

id a reservoir of unconscious psychic energy that, according to Freud, strives to satisfy basic sexual and aggressive drives. The id operates on the *pleasure principle*, demanding immediate gratification. (p. 463)

identical (monozygotic) twins individuals that develop from a single fertilized egg that splits in two, creating two genetically identical organisms. (p. 70)

identification the process by which, according to Freud, children incorporate their parents' values into their developing superegos. (p. 465)

identity our sense of self; according to Erikson, the adolescent's task is to solidify a sense of self by testing and integrating various roles. (p. 147)

illusory correlation perceiving a relationship where none exists, or perceiving a stronger- than-actual relationship. (p. A-5)

implicit memory retention of learned skills or classically conditioned associations independent of conscious recollection. (Also called *nondeclarative memory*.) (p. 269)

imprinting the process by which certain animals form strong attachments during early life. (p. 135)

inattentional blindness failing to see visible objects when our attention is directed elsewhere. (p. 82)

incentive a positive or negative environmental stimulus that motivates behavior. (p. 349)

independent variable in an experiment, the factor that is manipulated; the variable whose effect is being studied. (p. 28)

individualism giving priority to one's own goals over group goals and defining one's identity in terms of personal attributes rather than group identifications. (p. 491)

industrial-organizational (I/O) psychology the application of psychological concepts and methods to optimizing human behavior in workplaces. (p. B-3)

informational social influence influence resulting from a person's willingness to accept others' opinions about reality. (p. 424)

informed consent giving potential participants enough information about a study to enable them to choose whether they wish to participate. (p. 31)

ingroup "us"—people with whom we share a common identity. (p. 438)

ingroup bias the tendency to favor our own group. (p. 438)

inner ear the innermost part of the ear, containing the cochlea, semicircular canals, and vestibular sacs. (p. 216)

insight a sudden realization of a problem's solution; contrasts with strategy-based solutions. (p. 299)

insight therapies therapies that aim to improve psychological functioning by increasing a person's awareness of underlying motives and defenses. (p. 538)

insomnia recurring problems in falling or staying asleep. (p. 95)

instinct a complex behavior that is rigidly patterned throughout a species and is unlearned. (p. 349)

instinctive drift the tendency of learned behavior to gradually revert to biologically predisposed patterns. (p. 257)

intellectual disability a condition of limited mental ability, indicated by an intelligence test score of 70 or below and difficulty adapting to the demands of life. (Formerly referred to as *mental retardation*.) (p. 331)

intelligence the ability to learn from experience, solve problems, and use knowledge to adapt to new situations. (p. 323)

intelligence quotient (IQ) defined originally as the ratio of mental age (*ma*) to chronological age (*ca*) multiplied by 100 (thus, IQ = *ma/ca* × 100). On contemporary intelligence tests, the average performance for a given age is assigned a score of 100. (p. 329)

intelligence test a method for assessing an individual's mental aptitudes and comparing them with those of others, using numerical scores. (p. 327)

intensity the amount of energy in a light wave or sound wave, which influences what we perceive as brightness or loudness. Intensity is determined by the wave's amplitude (height). (p. 199)

interaction the interplay that occurs when the effect of one factor (such as environment) depends on another factor (such as heredity). (p. 75)

internal locus of control the perception that we control our own fate. (p. 396)

interneurons neurons within the brain and spinal cord; they communicate internally and process information between the sensory inputs and motor outputs. (p. 45)

interpretation in psychoanalysis, the analyst's noting of supposed dream meanings, resistances, and other significant behaviors and events in order to promote insight. (p. 537)

intersex a condition present at birth due to unusual combinations of male and female chromosomes, hormones, and anatomy; possessing biological sexual characteristics of both sexes. (p. 167)

intimacy in Erikson's theory, the ability to form close, loving relationships; a primary developmental task in young adulthood. (p. 147)

intrinsic motivation the desire to perform a behavior effectively for its own sake. (p. 358)

intuition an effortless, immediate, automatic feeling or thought, as contrasted with explicit, conscious reasoning. (p. 301)

James-Lange theory the theory that our experience of emotion is our awareness of our physiological responses to an emotion- arousing stimulus. (p. 369)

just-world phenomenon the tendency for people to believe the world is just and that people therefore get what they deserve and deserve what they get. (p. 438)

kinesthesia [kin-ehs-THEE-zhuh] our movement sense—our system for sensing the position and movement of individual body parts. (p. 227)

language our spoken, written, or signed words and the ways we combine them to communicate meaning. (p. 311)

latent content according to Freud, the underlying meaning of a dream (as distinct from its manifest content). (p. 97)

latent learning learning that occurs but is not apparent until there is an incentive to demonstrate it. (p. 257)

law of effect Thorndike's principle that behaviors followed by favorable consequences become more likely, and that behaviors followed by unfavorable consequences become less likely. (p. 244)

leadership an individual's ability to motivate and influence others to contribute to their group's success. (p. B-10)

learned helplessness the hopelessness and passive resignation an animal or person learns when unable to avoid repeated aversive events. (p. 396)

learning the process of acquiring through experience new and relatively enduring information or behaviors. (p. 234)

lesion [LEE-zhuhn] tissue destruction. A brain lesion is a naturally or experimentally caused destruction of brain tissue. (p. 51)

levels of analysis the differing complementary views, from biological to psychological to social-cultural, for analyzing any given phenomenon. (p. 11)

limbic system neural system (including the *amygdala, hypothalamus,* and *hippocampus*) located below the cerebral hemispheres; associated with emotions and drives. (p. 55)

linguistic determinism Whorf's hypothesis that language determines the way we think. (p. 319)

linguistic relativism the idea that language has an influence on the way we think. (p. 319)

lobotomy a psychosurgical procedure once used to calm uncontrollably emotional or violent patients. The procedure cut the nerves connecting the frontal lobes to the emotion-controlling centers of the inner brain. (p. 565)

longitudinal study research that follows and retests the same people over time. (pp. 154, 333)

long-term memory the relatively permanent and limitless storehouse of the memory system. Includes knowledge, skills, and experiences. (p. 268)

long-term potentiation (LTP) an increase in a cell's firing potential after brief, rapid stimulation; a neural basis for learning and memory. (p. 278)

LSD (*lysergic acid diethylamide*) a powerful hallucinogenic drug; also known as *acid.* (p. 109)

major depressive disorder a disorder in which a person experiences, in the absence of drugs or another medical condition, two or more weeks with five or more symptoms, at least one of which must be either (1) depressed mood or (2) loss of interest or pleasure. (p. 515)

mania a hyperactive, wildly optimistic state in which dangerously poor judgment is common. (p. 515)

manifest content according to Freud, the symbolic, remembered story line of a dream (as distinct from its latent, or hidden, content). (p. 97)

maturation biological growth processes that enable orderly changes in behavior, relatively uninfluenced by experience. (p. 122)

mean the arithmetic average of a distribution, obtained by adding the scores and then dividing by the number of scores. (p. A-2)

median the middle score in a distribution; half the scores are above it and half are below it. (p. A-2)

medical model the concept that diseases, in this case psychological *disorders,* have physical causes that can be diagnosed, treated, and, in most cases, *cured,* often through treatment in a *hospital.* (p. 495)

medulla [muh-DUL-uh] the base of the brainstem; controls heartbeat and breathing. (p. 53)

MEG (magnetoencephalography) a brain-imaging technique that measures magnetic fields from the brain's natural electrical activity. (p. 51)

memory the persistence of learning over time through the encoding, storage, and retrieval of information. (p. 267)

memory consolidation the neural storage of a long-term memory. (p. 276)

menarche [meh-NAR-key] the first menstrual period. (p. 166)

menopause the time of natural cessation of menstruation; also refers to the biological changes a woman experiences as her ability to reproduce declines. (p. 151)

mental age a measure of intelligence test performance devised by Binet; the level of performance typically associated with children of a certain chronological age. Thus, a child who does as well as an average 8-yearold is said to have a mental age of 8. (p. 329)

mental set a tendency to approach a problem in one particular way, often a way that has been successful in the past. (p. 301)

mere exposure effect the phenomenon that repeated exposure to novel stimuli increases liking of them. (p. 447)

meta-analysis a statistical procedure for analyzing the results of multiple studies to reach an overall conclusion. (pp. 20, 551)

methamphetamine a powerfully addictive drug that stimulates the central nervous system, with accelerated body functions and associated energy and mood changes; over time, appears to reduce baseline dopamine levels. (p. 106)

middle ear the chamber between the eardrum and cochlea containing three tiny bones (malleus, incus, and stapes) that concentrate the vibrations of the eardrum on the cochlea's oval window. (p. 216)

mindfulness meditation a reflective practice in which people attend to current experiences in a nonjudgmental and accepting manner. (p. 404)

Minnesota Multiphasic Personality Inventory (MMPI) the most widely researched and clinically used of all personality tests. Originally developed to identify emotional disorders (still considered its most appropriate use), this test is now used for many other screening purposes. (p. 477)

mirror neurons frontal lobe neurons that some scientists believe fire when we perform certain actions or observe another doing so. The brain's mirroring of another's action may enable imitation and empathy. (p. 259)

mirror-image perceptions mutual views often held by conflicting people, as when each side sees itself as ethical and peaceful and views the other side as evil and aggressive. (p. 456)

misinformation effect occurs when misleading information has corrupted one's memory of an event. (p. 291)

mnemonics [nih-MON-iks] memory aids, especially those techniques that use vivid imagery and organizational devices. (p. 273)

mode the most frequently occurring score(s) in a distribution. (p. A-2)

modeling the process of observing and imitating a specific behavior. (p. 259)

monocular cue a depth cue, such as interposition or linear perspective, available to either eye alone. (p. 210)

mood-congruent memory the tendency to recall experiences that are consistent with one's current good or bad mood. (p. 280)

morpheme in a language, the smallest unit that carries meaning; may be a word or a part of a word (such as a prefix). (p. 312)

motivation a need or desire that energizes and directs behavior. (p. 349)

motor (efferent) neurons neurons that carry outgoing information from the brain and spinal cord to the muscles and glands. (p. 45)

motor cortex an area at the rear of the frontal lobes that controls voluntary movements. (p. 61)

MRI (magnetic resonance imaging) a technique that uses magnetic fields and radio waves to produce computer-generated images of soft tissue. MRI scans show brain anatomy. (p. 51)

mutation a random error in gene replication that leads to a change. (p. 76)

myelin [MY-uh-lin] **sheath** a fatty tissue layer segmentally encasing the axons of some neurons; enables vastly greater transmission speed as neural impulses hop from one node to the next. (p. 40)

narcissism excessive self-love and self-absorption. (pp. 356, 488)

narcolepsy a sleep disorder characterized by uncontrollable sleep attacks. The sufferer may lapse directly into REM sleep, often at inopportune times. (p. 95)

natural selection the principle that inherited traits that better enable an organism to survive and reproduce in a particular environment will (in competition with other trait variations) most likely be passed on to succeeding generations. (pp. 8, 75)

naturalistic observation a descriptive technique of observing and recording behavior in naturally occurring situations without trying to manipulate and control the situation. (p. 23)

nature–nurture issue the longstanding controversy over the relative contributions that genes and experience make to the development of psychological traits and behaviors. Today's science sees traits and behaviors arising from the interaction of nature and nurture. (p. 8)

near-death experience an altered state of consciousness reported after a close brush with death (such as cardiac arrest); often similar to drug-induced hallucinations. (p. 109)

negative reinforcement increasing behaviors by stopping or reducing aversive stimuli. A negative reinforcer is any stimulus that, when *removed* after a response, strengthens the response. (*Note:* Negative reinforcement is not punishment.) (p. 245)

nerves bundled axons that form neural cables connecting the central nervous system with muscles, glands, and sense organs. (p. 45)

nervous system the body's speedy, electrochemical communication network, consisting of all the nerve cells of the peripheral and central nervous systems. (p. 45)

neurogenesis the formation of new neurons. (p. 64)

neuron a nerve cell; the basic building block of the nervous system. (p. 39)

neurotransmitters chemical messengers that cross the synaptic gap between neurons. When released by the sending neuron, neurotransmitters travel across the synapse and bind to receptor sites on the receiving neuron, thereby influencing whether that neuron will generate a neural impulse. (p. 42)

neutral stimulus (NS) in classical conditioning, a stimulus that elicits no response before conditioning. (p. 236)

nicotine a stimulating and highly addictive psychoactive drug in tobacco. (p. 104)

night terrors a sleep disorder characterized by high arousal and an appearance of being terrified; unlike nightmares, night terrors occur during N3 sleep, within two or three hours of falling asleep, and are seldom remembered. (p. 95)

normal curve a symmetrical, bell-shaped curve that describes the distribution of many types of data; most scores fall near the mean (about 68 percent fall within one standard deviation of it) and fewer and fewer near the extremes. (Also called a *normal distribution*.) (pp. 331, A-3)

normative social influence influence resulting from a person's desire to gain approval or avoid disapproval. (p. 424)

norms understood rules for accepted and expected behavior. Norms prescribe "proper" behavior. (p. 421)

nudge a framing of choices by which governments and companies can, without coercion or altered incentives, encourage people to make choices that support their health, retirement savings, and well-being. (p. 304)

obesity defined as a body mass index (BMI) measurement of 30 or higher, which is calculated from our weight-to-height ratio. (Overweight individuals have a BMI of 25 or higher.) (p. 365)

object permanence the awareness that things continue to exist even when not perceived. (p. 126)

observational learning learning by observing others. (p. 259)

obsessive-compulsive disorder (OCD) a disorder characterized by unwanted repetitive thoughts (obsessions), actions (compulsions), or both. (p. 509)

occipital [ahk-SIP-uh-tuhl] **lobes** the portion of the cerebral cortex lying at the back of the head; includes areas that receive information from the visual fields. (p. 59)

Oedipus [ED-uh-puss] **complex** according to Freud, a boy's sexual desires toward his mother and feelings of jealousy and hatred for the rival father. (p. 465)

olfaction our sense of smell. (p. 225)

one-word stage the stage in speech development, from about age 1 to 2, during which a child speaks mostly in single words. (p. 315)

operant behavior behavior that operates on the environment, producing a consequence. (p. 234)

operant chamber in operant conditioning research, a chamber (also known as a *Skinner box*) containing a bar or key that an animal can manipulate to obtain a food or water reinforcer; attached devices record the animal's rate of bar pressing or key pecking. (p. 244)

operant conditioning a type of learning in which a behavior becomes more likely to recur if followed by a reinforcer or less likely to recur if followed by a punisher. (p. 243)

operational definition a carefully worded statement of the exact procedures (operations) used in a research study. For example, *human intelligence* may be operationally defined as what an intelligence test measures. (p. 20)

opiates opium and its derivatives, such as morphine and heroin; depress neural activity, temporarily lessening pain and anxiety. (p. 104)

opponent-process theory the theory that opposing retinal processes (red-green, blue-yellow, white-black) enable color vision. For example, some cells are stimulated by green and inhibited by red; others are stimulated by red and inhibited by green. (p. 204)

optic nerve the nerve that carries neural impulses from the eye to the brain. (p. 201)

organizational psychology an I/O psychology subfield that examines organizational influences on worker satisfaction and productivity and facilitates organizational change. (p. B-5)

ostracism deliberate social exclusion of individuals or groups. (p. 355)

other-race effect the tendency to recall faces of one's own race more accurately than faces of other races. (Also called the *crossrace effect* and the *own-race bias*.) (p. 438)

outgroup "them"—those perceived as different or apart from our ingroup. (p. 438)

overconfidence the tendency to be more confident than correct—to overestimate the accuracy of our beliefs and judgments. (p. 303)

panic disorder an anxiety disorder marked by unpredictable, minutes-long episodes of intense dread in which a person may experience terror and accompanying chest pain, choking, or other frightening sensations; often followed by worry over a possible next attack. (p. 507)

parallel processing processing many aspects of a stimulus or problem at once. (pp. 85, 207, 268)

paraphilias sexual arousal from fantasies, behaviors, or urges involving nonhuman objects, the suffering of self or others, and/ or nonconsenting persons. (p. 175)

parapsychology the study of paranormal phenomena, including ESP and psychokinesis (also called *telekinesis*). (p. 230)

parasympathetic nervous system the division of the autonomic nervous system that calms the body, conserving its energy. (p. 46)

parietal [puh-RYE-uh-tuhl] **lobes** the portion of the cerebral cortex lying at the top of the head and toward the rear; receives sensory input for touch and body position. (p. 59)

partial (intermittent) reinforcement schedule reinforcing a response only part of the time; results in slower acquisition of a response but much greater resistance to extinction than does continuous reinforcement. (p. 246)

passionate love an aroused state of intense positive absorption in another, usually present at the beginning of a romantic relationship. (p. 451)

perception the process of organizing and interpreting sensory information, enabling us to recognize meaningful objects and events. (p. 190)

perceptual adaptation the ability to adjust to changed sensory input, including an artificially displaced or even inverted visual field. (p. 213)

perceptual constancy perceiving objects as unchanging (having consistent color, brightness, shape, and size) even as illumination and retinal images change. (p. 211)

perceptual set a mental predisposition to perceive one thing and not another. (p. 194)

peripheral nervous system (PNS) the sensory and motor neurons that connect the central nervous system (CNS) to the rest of the body. (p. 45)

peripheral route persuasion occurs when people are influenced by incidental cues, such as a speaker's attractiveness. (p. 418)

personal control our sense of controlling our environment rather than feeling helpless. (p. 396)

personality an individual's characteristic pattern of thinking, feeling, and acting. (p. 462)

personality disorders inflexible and enduring behavior patterns that impair social functioning. (p. 529)

personality inventory a questionnaire (often with *true-false* or *agree-disagree* items) on which people respond to items designed to gauge a wide range of feelings and behaviors; used to assess selected personality traits. (p. 477)

personnel psychology an I/O psychology subfield that helps with job seeking, and with employee recruitment, selection, placement, training, appraisal, and development. (p. B-5)

PET (positron emission tomography) scan a visual display of brain activity that detects where a radioactive form of glucose goes while the brain performs a given task. (p. 51)

phi phenomenon an illusion of movement created when two or more adjacent lights blink on and off in quick succession. (p. 211)

phobia an anxiety disorder marked by a persistent, irrational fear and avoidance of a specific object, activity, or situation. (p. 508)

phoneme in a language, the smallest distinctive sound unit. (p. 312)

physiological need a basic bodily requirement. (p. 349)

pitch a tone's experienced highness or lowness; depends on frequency. (p. 216)

pituitary gland the endocrine system's most influential gland. Under the influence of the hypothalamus, the pituitary regulates growth and controls other endocrine glands. (p. 48)

place theory in hearing, the theory that links the pitch we hear with the place where the cochlea's membrane is stimulated. (p. 219)

placebo [pluh-SEE-bo; Latin for "I shall please"] **effect** experimental results caused by expectations alone; any effect on behavior caused by the administration of an inert substance or condition, which the recipient assumes is an active agent. (p. 27)

plasticity the brain's ability to change, especially during childhood, by reorganizing after damage or by building new pathways based on experience. (pp. 39, 64)

polygraph a machine used in attempts to detect lies that measures emotion-linked changes in perspiration, heart rate, and breathing. (p. 374)

population all those in a group being studied, from which samples may be drawn. (*Note:* Except for national studies, this does not refer to a country's whole population.) (p. 24)

positive psychology the scientific study of human flourishing, with the goals of discovering and promoting strengths and virtues that help individuals and communities to thrive. (pp. 11, 407)

positive reinforcement increasing behaviors by presenting positive reinforcers. A positive reinforcer is any stimulus that, when *presented* after a response, strengthens the response. (p. 245)

posthypnotic suggestion a suggestion, made during a hypnosis session, to be carried out after the subject is no longer hypnotized; used by some clinicians to help control undesired symptoms and behaviors. (p. 225)

posttraumatic growth positive psychological changes as a result of struggling with extremely challenging circumstances and life crises. (p. 567)

posttraumatic stress disorder (PTSD) a disorder characterized by haunting memories, nightmares, hypervigilance, avoidance of trauma-related stimuli, social withdrawal, jumpy anxiety, numbness of feeling, and/or insomnia that lingers for four weeks or more after a traumatic experience. (p. 509)

predictive validity the success with which a test predicts the behavior it is designed to predict; it is assessed by computing the correlation between test scores and the criterion behavior. (Also called *criterion- related validity*.) (p. 331)

prejudice an unjustifiable and usually negative attitude toward a group and its members. Prejudice generally involves negative emotions, stereotyped beliefs, and a predisposition to discriminatory action. (p. 435)

preoperational stage in Piaget's theory, the stage (from about 2 to 6 or 7 years of age) during which a child learns to use language but does not yet comprehend the mental operations of concrete logic. (p. 127)

preparedness a biological predisposition to learn associations, such as between taste and nausea, that have survival value. (p. 254)

primary reinforcer an innately reinforcing stimulus, such as one that satisfies a biological need. (p. 246)

primary sex characteristics the body structures (ovaries, testes, and external genitalia) that make sexual reproduction possible. (p. 166)

priming the activation, often unconsciously, of certain associations, thus predisposing one's perception, memory, or response. (pp. 193, 280)

proactive interference the forwardacting disruptive effect of older learning on the recall of *new* information. (p. 287)

problem-focused coping attempting to alleviate stress directly—by changing the stressor or the way we interact with that stressor. (p. 395)

projective test a personality test, such as the Rorschach or TAT, that provides ambiguous images designed to trigger projection of one's inner dynamics. (p. 466)

prosocial behavior positive, constructive, helpful behavior. The opposite of antisocial behavior. (p. 261)

prototype a mental image or best example of a category. Matching new items to a prototype provides a quick and easy method for sorting items into categories (as when comparing feathered creatures to a prototypical bird, such as a crow). (p. 299)

psychiatry a branch of medicine dealing with psychological disorders; practiced by physicians who sometimes provide medical (for example, drug) treatments as well as psychological therapy. (p. 13)

psychoactive drug a chemical substance that alters perceptions and moods. (p. 101)

psychoanalysis (1) Freud's theory of personality that attributes thoughts and actions to unconscious motives and conflicts. (2) Freud's therapeutic technique used in treating psychological disorders. Freud believed the patient's free associations, resistances, dreams, and transferences—and the analyst's interpretations of them—released previously repressed feelings, allowing the patient to gain self-insight. (pp. 462, 537)

psychodynamic theories theories that view personality with a focus on the unconscious and the importance of childhood experiences. (p. 462)

psychodynamic therapy therapy deriving from the psychoanalytic tradition; views individuals as responding to unconscious forces and childhood experiences, and seeks to enhance self-insight. (p. 538)

psychological disorder a syndrome marked by a clinically significant disturbance in an individual's cognition, emotion regulation, or behavior. (p. 494)

psychology the science of behavior and mental processes. (p. 8)

psychoneuroimmunology the study of how psychological, neural, and endocrine processes together affect the immune system and resulting health. (p. 389)

psychopharmacology the study of the effects of drugs on mind and behavior. (p. 560)

psychosexual stages the childhood stages of development (oral, anal, phallic, latency, genital) during which, according to Freud, the id's pleasure-seeking energies focus on distinct erogenous zones. (p. 465)

psychosurgery surgery that removes or destroys brain tissue in an effort to change behavior. (p. 565)

psychotherapy treatment involving psychological techniques; consists of interactions between a trained therapist and someone seeking to overcome psychological difficulties or achieve personal growth. (p. 537)

psychotic disorders a group of disorders marked by irrational ideas, distorted perceptions, and a loss of contact with reality. (p. 522)

puberty the period of sexual maturation, during which a person becomes capable of reproducing. (pp. 141, 166)

punishment an event that tends to *decrease* the behavior that it follows. (p. 248)

random assignment assigning participants to experimental and control groups by chance, thus minimizing preexisting differences between the different groups. (p. 25)

random sample a sample that fairly represents a population because each member has an equal chance of inclusion. (p. 24)

range the difference between the highest and lowest scores in a distribution. (p. A-3)

recall a measure of memory in which the person must retrieve information learned earlier, as on a fill-in-the-blank test. (p. 267)

reciprocal determinism the interacting influences of behavior, internal cognition, and environment. (p. 482)

reciprocity norm an expectation that people will help, not hurt, those who have helped them. (p. 455)

recognition a measure of memory in which the person identifies items previously learned, as on a multiple-choice test. (p. 267)

reconsolidation a process in which previously stored memories, when retrieved, are potentially altered before being stored again. (p. 289)

reflex a simple, automatic response to a sensory stimulus, such as the knee-jerk response. (p. 47)

refractory period (1) in neural processing, a brief resting pause that occurs after a neuron has fired; subsequent action potentials cannot occur until the axon returns to its resting state. (2) in human sexuality, a resting period that occurs after orgasm, during which a person cannot achieve another orgasm. (pp. 41, 175)

regression toward the mean the tendency for extreme or unusual scores or events to fall back (regress) toward the average. (p. A-5)

reinforcement in operant conditioning, any event that *strengthens* the behavior it follows. (p. 244)

reinforcement schedule a pattern that defines how often a desired response will be reinforced. (p. 246)

relational aggression an act of aggression (physical or verbal) intended to harm a person's relationship or social standing. (p. 162)

relative deprivation the perception that one is worse off relative to those with whom one compares oneself. (p. 411)

relearning a measure of memory that assesses the amount of time saved when learning material again. (p. 267)

reliability the extent to which a test yields consistent results, as assessed by the consistency of scores on two halves of the test, on alternative forms of the test, or on retesting. (p. 331)

REM (R) sleep rapid eye movement sleep; a recurring sleep stage during which vivid dreams commonly occur. Also known as *paradoxical sleep*, because the muscles are relaxed (except for minor twitches) but other body systems are active. (p. 86)

REM rebound the tendency for REM sleep to increase following REM sleep deprivation. (p. 99)

repetitive transcranial magnetic stimulation (rTMS) the application of repeated pulses of magnetic energy to the brain; used to stimulate or suppress brain activity. (p. 565)

replication repeating the essence of a research study, usually with different participants in different situations, to see whether the basic finding can be reproduced. (p. 20)

representativeness heuristic estimating the likelihood of events in terms of how well they seem to represent, or match, particular prototypes; may lead us to ignore other relevant information. (p. 301)

repression in psychoanalytic theory, the basic defense mechanism that banishes from consciousness anxiety-arousing thoughts, feelings, and memories. (pp. 289, 465)

resilience the personal strength that helps most people cope with stress and recover from adversity and even trauma. (p. 567)

resistance in psychoanalysis, the blocking from consciousness of anxiety-laden material. (p. 537)

respondent behavior behavior that occurs as an automatic response to some stimulus. (p. 234)

reticular formation a nerve network that travels through the brainstem into the thalamus and plays an important role in controlling arousal. (p. 54)

retina the light-sensitive inner surface of the eye, containing the receptor rods and cones plus layers of neurons that begin the processing of visual information. (p. 201)

retinal disparity a binocular cue for perceiving depth. By comparing retinal images from the two eyes, the brain computes distance— the greater the disparity (difference) between the two images, the closer the object. (p. 208)

retrieval the process of getting information out of memory storage. (p. 268)

retroactive interference the backward-acting disruptive effect of newer learning on the recall of *old* information. (p. 287)

retrograde amnesia an inability to retrieve information from one's past. (p. 285)

reuptake a neurotransmitter's reabsorption by the sending neuron. (p. 42)

rods retinal receptors that detect black, white, and gray, and are sensitive to movement; necessary for peripheral and twilight vision, when cones don't respond. (p. 201)

role a set of expectations (norms) about a social position, defining how those in the position ought to behave. (pp. 169, 418)

Rorschach inkblot test the most widely used projective test; a set of 10 inkblots, designed by Hermann Rorschach; seeks to identify people's inner feelings by analyzing their interpretations of the blots. (p. 466)

rumination compulsive fretting; *overthinking* our problems and their causes. (p. 521)

savant syndrome a condition in which a person otherwise limited in mental ability has an exceptional specific skill, such as in computation or drawing. (p. 324)

scaffold a framework that offers children temporary support as they develop higher levels of thinking. (p. 129)

scapegoat theory the theory that prejudice offers an outlet for anger by providing someone to blame. (p. 438)

scatterplot a graphed cluster of dots, each of which represents the values of two variables. The slope of the points suggests the direction of the relationship between the two variables. The amount of scatter suggests the strength of the correlation (little scatter indicates high correlation). (p. A-4)

schema a concept or framework that organizes and interprets information. (p. 125)

schizophrenia a disorder characterized by delusions, hallucinations, disorganized speech, and/or diminished, inappropriate emotional expression. (p. 522)

secondary sex characteristics nonreproductive sexual traits, such as female breasts and hips, male voice quality, and body hair. (p. 166)

selective attention the focusing of conscious awareness on a particular stimulus. (p. 81)

self in contemporary psychology, assumed to be the center of personality, the organizer of our thoughts, feelings, and actions. (p. 486)

self-actualization according to Maslow, one of the ultimate psychological needs that arises after basic physical and psychological needs are met and self-esteem is achieved; the motivation to fulfill one's potential. (p. 470)

self-concept all our thoughts and feelings about ourselves, in answer to the question, "Who am I?" (p. 472)

self-control the ability to control impulses and delay short-term gratification for greater long-term rewards. (p. 398)

self-determination theory the theory that we feel motivated to satisfy our needs for competence, autonomy, and relatedness. (p. 353)

self-disclosure the act of revealing intimate aspects of ourselves to others. (p. 453)

self-efficacy one's sense of competence and effectiveness. (p. 486)

self-esteem one's feelings of high or low self-worth. (p. 486)

self-fulfilling prophecy a belief that leads to its own fulfillment. (p. 456)

self-serving bias a readiness to perceive oneself favorably. (p. 486)

self-transcendence according to Maslow, the striving for identity, meaning, and purpose beyond the self. (p. 470)

semantic memory explicit memory of facts and general knowledge; one of our two conscious memory systems (the other is *episodic memory*). (p. 276)

sensation the process by which our sensory receptors and nervous system receive and represent stimulus energies from our environment. (p. 190)

sensorimotor stage in Piaget's theory, the stage (from birth to nearly 2 years of age) during which infants know the world mostly in terms of their sensory impressions and motor activities. (p. 126)

sensorineural hearing loss hearing loss caused by damage to the cochlea's receptor cells or to the auditory nerves; the most common form of hearing loss, also called *nerve deafness*. (p. 219)

sensory adaptation diminished sensitivity as a consequence of constant stimulation. (p. 194)

sensory interaction the principle that one sense may influence another, as when the smell of food influences its taste. (p. 228)

sensory memory the immediate, very brief recording of sensory information in the memory system. (p. 268)

sensory (afferent) neurons neurons that carry incoming information from the body's tissues and sensory receptors to the brain and spinal cord. (p. 45)

sensory receptors sensory nerve endings that respond to stimuli. (p. 190)

sequential processing processing one aspect of a stimulus or problem at a time; generally used to process new information or to solve difficult problems. (p. 85)

serial position effect our tendency to recall best the last (*recency effect*) and first (*primacy effect*) items in a list. (p. 282)

set point the point at which your "weight thermostat" may be set. When your body falls below this weight, increased hunger and a lowered metabolic rate may combine to restore lost weight. (p. 363)

sex in psychology, the biologically influenced characteristics by which people define *male* and *female*. (p. 162)

sexual aggression any physical or verbal behavior of a sexual nature that is intended to harm someone physically or emotionally. Can be expressed as either *sexual harassment* or *sexual assault*. (p. 169)

sexual dysfunction a problem that consistently impairs sexual arousal or functioning at any point in the sexual response cycle. (p. 175)

sexual orientation an enduring sexual attraction toward members of one's own sex (*homosexual* orientation), the other sex (*heterosexual* orientation), or both sexes (*bisexual* orientation). (p. 178)

sexual response cycle the four stages of sexual responding described by Masters and Johnson—excitement, plateau, orgasm, and resolution. (p. 175)

shallow processing encoding on a basic level, based on the structure or appearance of words. (p. 273)

shaping an operant conditioning procedure in which reinforcers guide behavior toward closer and closer approximations of the desired behavior. (p. 244)

short-term memory activated memory that holds a few items briefly, such as digits of a phone number while calling, before the information is stored or forgotten. (p. 268)

signal detection theory a theory predicting how and when we detect the presence of a faint stimulus (*signal*) amid background stimulation (*noise*). Assumes there is no single absolute threshold and that detection depends partly on a person's experience, expectations, motivation, and alertness. (p. 191)

sleep a periodic, natural loss of consciousness— as distinct from unconsciousness resulting from a coma, general anesthesia, or hibernation. (Adapted from Dement, 1999.) (p. 86)

sleep apnea a sleep disorder characterized by temporary cessations of breathing during sleep and repeated momentary awakenings. (p. 95)

social clock the culturally preferred timing of social events such as marriage, parenthood, and retirement. (p. 154)

social exchange theory the theory that our social behavior is an exchange process, the aim of which is to maximize benefits and minimize costs. (p. 455)

social facilitation improved performance on simple or well-learned tasks in the presence of others. (p. 429)

social identity the "we" aspect of our self-concept; the part of our answer to "Who am I?" that comes from our group memberships. (p. 147)

social leadership group-oriented leadership that builds teamwork, mediates conflict, and offers support. (p. B-10)

social learning theory the theory that we learn social behavior by observing and imitating and by being rewarded or punished. (p. 169)

social loafing the tendency for people in a group to exert less effort when pooling their efforts toward attaining a common goal than when individually accountable. (p. 431)

social psychology the scientific study of how we think about, influence, and relate to one another. (p. 416)

social script a culturally modeled guide for how to act in various situations. (pp. 176, 444)

social trap a situation in which the conflicting parties, by each pursuing their self-interest rather than the good of the group, become caught in mutually destructive behavior. (p. 456)

social-cognitive perspective a view of behavior as influenced by the interaction between people's traits (including their thinking) and their social context. (p. 482)

social-responsibility norm an expectation that people will help those needing their help. (p. 455)

somatic nervous system the division of the peripheral nervous system that controls the body's skeletal muscles. Also called the *skeletal nervous system*. (p. 45)

somatosensory cortex an area at the front of the parietal lobes that registers and processes body touch and movement sensations. (p. 61)

source amnesia faulty memory for how, when, or where information was learned or imagined. (Also called *source misattribution*.) Source amnesia, along with the misinformation effect, is at the heart of many false memories. (p. 291)

spacing effect the tendency for distributed study or practice to yield better long-term retention than is achieved through massed study or practice. (p. 273)

spermarche [sper-MAR-key] the first ejaculation. (p. 166)

split brain a condition resulting from surgery that isolates the brain's two hemispheres by cutting the fibers (mainly those of the corpus callosum) connecting them. (p. 64)

spontaneous recovery the reappearance, after a pause, of an extinguished conditioned response. (p. 238)

spotlight effect overestimating others' noticing and evaluating our appearance, performance, and blunders (as if we presume a spotlight shines on us). (p. 486)

SQ3R a study method incorporating five steps: Survey, Question, Read, Retrieve, Review. (p. 33)

standard deviation a computed measure of how much scores vary around the mean score. (p. A-3)

standardization defining uniform testing procedures and meaningful scores by comparison with the performance of a pretested group. (p. 329)

Stanford-Binet the widely used American revision (by Terman at Stanford University) of Binet's original intelligence test. (p. 329)

statistical significance a statistical statement of how likely it is that an obtained result occurred by chance. (p. A-7)

stereotype a generalized (sometimes accurate but often overgeneralized) belief about a group of people. (p. 435)

stereotype threat a self-confirming concern that one will be evaluated based on a negative stereotype (p. 344)

stimulants drugs (such as caffeine, nicotine, and the more powerful cocaine, amphetamines, methamphetamine, and Ecstasy) that excite neural activity and speed up body functions. (p. 104)

stimulus any event or situation that evokes a response. (p. 234)

storage the process of retaining encoded information over time. (p. 268)

stranger anxiety the fear of strangers that infants commonly display, beginning by about 8 months of age. (p. 133)

stress the process by which we perceive and respond to certain events, called *stressors*, that we appraise as threatening or challenging. (p. 385)

structuralism an early school of thought promoted by Wundt and Titchener; used introspection to reveal the structure of the human mind. (p. 5)

structured interview an interview process that asks the same job-relevant questions of all applicants, each of whom is rated on established scales. (p. B-6)

subjective well-being self-perceived happiness or satisfaction with life. Used along with measures of objective well-being (for example, physical and economic indicators) to evaluate people's quality of life. (p. 407)

subliminal below one's absolute threshold for conscious awareness. (p. 192)

substance use disorder a disorder characterized by continued substance craving and use despite significant life disruption and/or physical risk. (p. 101)

superego the part of personality that, according to Freud, represents internalized ideals and provides standards for judgment (the conscience) and for future aspirations. (p. 465)

superordinate goals shared goals that override differences among people and require their cooperation. (p. 459)

suprachiasmatic nucleus (SCN) a pair of cell clusters in the hypothalamus that controls circadian rhythm. In response to light, the SCN causes the pineal gland to adjust melatonin production, thus modifying our feelings of sleepiness. (p. 90)

survey a descriptive technique for obtaining the self-reported attitudes or behaviors of a particular group, usually by questioning a representative, *random sample* of the group. (p. 23)

sympathetic nervous system the division of the autonomic nervous system that arouses the body, mobilizing its energy. (p. 46)

synapse [SIN-aps] the junction between the axon tip of the sending neuron and the dendrite or cell body of the receiving neuron. The tiny gap at this junction is called the *synaptic gap* or *synaptic cleft*. (p. 42)

systematic desensitization a type of exposure therapy that associates a pleasant relaxed state with gradually increasing anxiety- triggering stimuli. Commonly used to treat phobias. (p. 541)

task leadership goal-oriented leadership that sets standards, organizes work, and focuses attention on goals. (p. B-10)

telegraphic speech the early speech stage in which a child speaks like a telegram—" go car"—using mostly nouns and verbs. (p. 315)

temperament a person's characteristic emotional reactivity and intensity. (p. 135)

temporal lobes the portion of the cerebral cortex lying roughly above the ears; includes the auditory areas, each receiving information primarily from the opposite ear. (p. 59)

tend-and-befriend response under stress, people (especially women) often provide support to others (tend) and bond with and seek support from others (befriend). (p. 389)

teratogens (literally, "monster makers") agents, such as chemicals and viruses, that can reach the embryo or fetus during prenatal development and cause harm. (p. 120)

testing effect enhanced memory after retrieving, rather than simply rereading, information. Also referred to as a *retrieval practice effect* or *test-enhanced learning*. (pp. 33, 273)

testosterone the most important male sex hormone. Both males and females have it, but the additional testosterone in males stimulates the growth of the male sex organs during the fetal period, and the development of the male sex characteristics during puberty. (p. 166)

thalamus [THAL-uh-muss] the brain's sensory control center, located on top of the brainstem; it directs messages to the sensory receiving areas in the cortex and transmits replies to the cerebellum and medulla. (p. 54)

THC the major active ingredient in marijuana; triggers a variety of effects, including mild hallucinations. (p. 109)

Thematic Apperception Test (TAT) a projective test in which people express their inner feelings and interests through the stories they make up about ambiguous scenes. (p. 466)

theory an explanation using an integrated set of principles that organizes observations and predicts behaviors or events. (p. 19)

theory of mind people's ideas about their own and others' mental states—about their feelings, perceptions, and thoughts, and the behaviors these might predict. (p. 128)

therapeutic alliance a bond of trust and mutual understanding between a therapist and client, who work together constructively to overcome the client's problem. (p. 555)

threshold the level of stimulation required to trigger a neural impulse. (p. 41)

token economy an operant conditioning procedure in which people earn a token for exhibiting a desired behavior and can later exchange the tokens for privileges or treats. (p. 543)

tolerance the diminishing effect with regular use of the same dose of a drug, requiring the user to take larger and larger doses before experiencing the drug's effect. (p. 102)

top-down processing information processing guided by higher-level mental processes, as when we construct perceptions drawing on our experience and expectations. (p. 190)

trait a characteristic pattern of behavior or a disposition to feel and act in certain ways, as assessed by self-report inventories and peer reports. (p. 475)

transduction conversion of one form of energy into another. In sensation, the transforming of stimulus energies, such as sights, sounds, and smells, into neural impulses our brain can interpret. (p. 191)

transference in psychoanalysis, the patient's transfer to the analyst of emotions linked with other relationships (such as love or hatred for a parent). (p. 537)

transgender an umbrella term describing people whose gender identity or expression differs from that associated with their birth-designated sex. (p. 170)

two-factor theory the Schachter-Singer theory that to experience emotion one must (1) be physically aroused and (2) cognitively label the arousal. (p. 369)

two-word stage beginning about age 2, the stage in speech development during which a child speaks mostly in two-word statements. (p. 315)

Type A Friedman and Rosenman's term for competitive, hard-driving, impatient, verbally aggressive, and anger-prone people. (p. 391)

Type B Friedman and Rosenman's term for easygoing, relaxed people. (p. 391)

unconditional positive regard a caring, accepting, nonjudgmental attitude, which Carl Rogers believed would help people develop self-awareness and self-acceptance. (pp. 470, 540)

unconditioned response (UR) in classical conditioning, an unlearned, naturally occurring response (such as salivation) to an unconditioned stimulus (US) (such as food in the mouth). (p. 236)

unconditioned stimulus (US) in classical conditioning, a stimulus that unconditionally— naturally and automatically— triggers an unconditioned response (UR). (p. 236)

unconscious according to Freud, a reservoir of mostly unacceptable thoughts, wishes, feelings, and memories. According to contemporary psychologists, information processing of which we are unaware. (p. 463)

validity the extent to which a test measures or predicts what it is supposed to. (See also *predictive validity*.) (p. 331)

variable anything that can vary and is feasible and ethical to measure. (p. A-4)

variable-interval schedule in operant conditioning, a reinforcement schedule that reinforces a response at unpredictable time intervals. (p. 248)

variable-ratio schedule in operant conditioning, a reinforcement schedule that reinforces a response after an unpredictable number of responses. (p. 246)

vestibular sense our sense of balance— our sense of body movement and position that enables our sense of balance. (p. 227)

virtual reality exposure therapy a counterconditioning technique that treats anxiety through creative electronic simulations in which people can safely face their greatest fears, such as airplane flying, spiders, or public speaking. (p. 541)

visual cliff a laboratory device for testing depth perception in infants and young animals. (p. 208)

wavelength the distance from the peak of one light wave or sound wave to the peak of the next. Electromagnetic wavelengths vary from the short gamma waves to the long pulses of radio transmission. (p. 199)

Weber's law the principle that, to be perceived as different, two stimuli must differ by a constant minimum percentage (rather than a constant amount). (p. 193)

Wechsler Adult Intelligence Scale (WAIS) the WAIS and its companion versions for children are the most widely used intelligence tests; they contain verbal and performance (nonverbal) subtests. (p. 329)

Wernicke's area a brain area involved in language comprehension and expression; usually in the left temporal lobe. (p. 316)

withdrawal the discomfort and distress that follow discontinuing an addictive drug or behavior. (p. 102)

working memory a newer understanding of short-term memory that adds conscious, active processing of incoming sensory information, and of information retrieved from long-term memory. (p. 269)

X chromosome the sex chromosome found in both males and females. Females typically have two X chromosomes; males typically have one. An X chromosome from each parent produces a female child. (p. 166)

Y chromosome the sex chromosome typically found only in males. When paired with an X chromosome from the mother, it produces a male child. (p. 166)

Yerkes-Dodson law the principle that performance increases with arousal only up to a point, beyond which performance decreases. (p. 351)

Young-Helmholtz trichromatic (three-color) theory the theory that the retina contains three different types of color receptors—one most sensitive to red, one to green, one to blue—which, when stimulated in combination, can produce the perception of any color. (p. 203)

zygote the fertilized egg; it enters a 2-week period of rapid cell division and develops into an embryo. (p. 119)

References

AAA. (2010). *Asleep at the wheel: The prevalence and impact of drowsy driving.* AAA Foundation for Traffic Safety (aaafoundation.org/pdf/2010DrowsyDrivingReport.pdf). (p. 94)

AAA. (2015). *Teen driver safety: Environmental factors and driver behaviors in teen driver crashes.* AAA Foundation for Traffic Safety (aaafoundation.org/sites/default/files/2015TeenCrashCausationFS.pdf). (p. 82)

AAMC. (2014). *Medical students, selected years, 1965–2013.* Association of American Medical Colleges (aamc.org). (pp. 164, 187)

AAMC. (2016). *Total enrollment by U.S. medical school and sex, 2011–2012 through 2015–2016.* Association of American Medical Colleges (aamc.org). (p. 187)

Aarts, H., & Custers, R. (2012). Unconscious goal pursuit: Nonconscious goal regulation and motivation. In R. M. Ryan (Ed.), *The Oxford handbook of human motivation* (pp. 232–247). New York: Oxford University Press. (p. 394)

Abrams, D. B., & Wilson, G. T. (1983). Alcohol, sexual arousal, and self-control. *Journal of Personality and Social Psychology, 45,* 188–198. (p. 104)

Abrams, L. (2008). Tip-of-the-tongue states yield language insights. *American Scientist, 96,* 234–239. (p. 287)

Abrams, M. (2002, June). Sight unseen—Restoring a blind man's vision is now a real possibility through stem-cell surgery. But even perfect eyes cannot see unless the brain has been taught to use them. *Discover, 23,* 54–60. (p. 213)

Abramson, L. Y., Metalsky, G. I., & Alloy, L. B. (1989). Hopelessness depression: A theory-based subtype. *Psychological Review, 96,* 358–372. (p. 396, 520)

Abramson, L. Y., Seligman, M. E. P., & Teasdale, J. D. (1978). Learned helplessness in humans: Critique and reformulation. *Journal of Abnormal Psychology, 87,* 49–74. (p. 396)

Abuhamdeh, S., Csikszentmihalyi, M., & Jalal, B. (2015). Enjoying the possibility of defeat: Outcome uncertainty, suspense, and intrinsic motivation. *Motivation and Emotion, 39,* 1–10. (p. 385)

Academy of Science of South Africa. (2015). *Diversity in human sexuality: Implications for policy in Africa.* Retrieved from assaf.co.za/wp-content/uploads/2015/06/8-June-Diversity-in-human-sexuality1.pdf (p. 178)

Acevedo, B. P., & Aron, A. (2009). Does a long-term relationship kill romantic love? *Review of General Psychology, 13,* 59–65. (p. 451)

Acevedo, B. P., Aron, A., Fisher, H. E., & Brown, L. L. (2012). Neural correlates of long-term intense romantic love. *Social Cognitive and Affective Neuroscience, 7,* 145–159. (p. 451)

ACHA. (2009). *American College Health Association-National College Health Assessment II: Reference group executive summary Fall 2008.* Baltimore: American College Health Association. (p. 513)

Ackerman, D. (2004). *An alchemy of mind: The marvel and mystery of the brain.* New York: Scribner. (p. 42)

ACMD. (2009). *MDMA ('Ecstasy'): A review of its harms and classification under the Misuse of Drugs Act 1971.* London: Home Office & Advisory Council on the Misuse of Drugs. (pp. 107, 108)

Adachi, T., Fujino, H., Nakae, A., Mashimo, T., & Sasaki, J. (2014). A meta-analysis of hypnosis for chronic pain problems: A comparison between hypnosis, standard care, and other psychological interventions. *International Journal of Clinical and Experimental Hypnosis, 62,* 1–28. (p. 224)

Adams, H. E., Wright, L. W., Jr., & Lohr, B. A. (1996). Is homophobia associated with homosexual arousal? *Journal of Abnormal Psychology, 105,* 440–446. (p. 470)

Adelmann, P. K., Antonucci, T. C., Crohan, S. F., & Coleman, L. M. (1989). Empty nest, cohort, and employment in the well-being of midlife women. *Sex Roles, 20,* 173–189. (p. 157)

Adelstein, J. S., Shehzad, Z., Mennes, M., DeYoung, C. G., Zuo, X.-N., Kelly, C., . . . Milham, M. P. (2011). Personality is reflected in the brain's intrinsic functional architecture. *PLoS ONE, 6,* e27633. (p. 478)

Ader, R., & Cohen, N. (1985). CNS-immune system interactions: Conditioning phenomena. *Behavioral and Brain Sciences, 8,* 379–394. (p. 241)

Aderka, I. M., Nickerson, A., Bøe, H. J., & Hofmann, S. G. (2012). Sudden gains during psychological treatments of anxiety and depression: A meta-analysis. *Journal of Consulting and Clinical Psychology, 80,* 93–101. (p. 552)

Adler, J. (2012). Erasing painful memories. *Scientific American, 306,* 56–61. (p. 279)

Adler, J. M., Lodi-Smith, J., Philippe, F. L., & Houle, I. (2016). The incremental validity of narrative identity in predicting well-being: A review of the field and recommendations for the future. *Personality and Social Psychology Review, 20,* 142–175. (p. 472)

Adolph, K. E., Kretch, K. S., & LoBue, V. (2014). Fear of heights in infants? *Current Directions in Psychological Science, 23,* 60–66. (p. 209)

Affleck, G., Tennen, H., Urrows, S., & Higgins, P. (1994). Person and contextual features of daily stress reactivity: Individual differences in relations of undesirable daily events with mood disturbance and chronic pain intensity. *Journal of Personality and Social Psychology, 66,* 329–340. (p. 408)

AFL-CIO. (2016). Executive pay. American Federation of Labor and Congress of Industrial Organizations (aflcio.org/Corporate-Watch/Paywatch-2016). (p. 410)

AFSP. (2015). *Facts and figures.* American Foundation for Suicide Prevention (afsp.org/understanding-suicide/facts-and-figures). (p. 500)

Agerström, J., Björklund, F., Carlsson, R., & Rooth, D.-O. (2012). Warm and competent Hassan = cold and incompetent Eric: A harsh equation of real-life hiring discrimination. *Basic and Applied Social Psychology, 34,* 359–366. (p. 437)

Agrillo, C. (2011). Near-death experience: Out-of-body and out-of-brain? *Review of General Psychology, 15,* 1–10. (p. 108)

Agudelo, L. Z., Femenía, T., Orhan, F., Porsmyr-Palmertz, M., Goiny, M., Martinez-Redondo, V., . . . Ruas, J. L. (2014). Skeletal muscle PGC-1α1 modulates kynurenine metabolism and mediates resilience to stress-induced depression. *Cell, 159,* 33–45. (p. 402)

Ahrén, J. C., Chiesa, F., Koupil, I., Magnusson, C., Dalman, C., & Goodman, A. (2013). We are family—parents, siblings, and eating disorders in a prospective total-population study of 250,000 Swedish males and females. *International Journal of Eating Disorders, 46,* 693–700. (p. 532)

Ai, A. L., Park, C. L., Huang, B., Rodgers, W., & Tice, T. N. (2007). Psychosocial mediation of religious coping styles: A study of short-term psychological distress following cardiac surgery. *Personality and Social Psychology Bulletin, 33,* 867–882. (p. 406)

Aichele, S., Rabbitt, P., & Ghisletta, P. (2016). Think fast, feel fine, live long: A 29-year study of cognition, health, and survival in middle-aged and older adults. *Psychological Science, 27,* 518–529. (p. 152)

Aiello, J. R., Thompson, D. D., & Brodzinsky, D. M. (1983). How funny is crowding anyway? Effects of room size, group size, and the introduction of humor. *Basic and Applied Social Psychology, 4,* 193–207. (p. 430)

Aimone, J. B., Jessberger, S., & Gage, F. H. (2010). Adult neurogenesis. *Scholarpedia, 2*(2), 2100. Retrieved from http://www.scholarpedia.org/article/Adult_neurogenesis (p. 64)

Ainsworth, M. D. S. (1973). The development of infant-mother attachment. In B. Caldwell & H. Ricciuti (Eds.), *Review of child development research* (Vol. 3). Chicago: University of Chicago Press. (p. 134)

Ainsworth, M. D. S. (1979). Infant-mother attachment. *American Psychologist, 34,* 932–937. (p. 134)

Ainsworth, M. D. S. (1989). Attachments beyond infancy. *American Psychologist, 44,* 709–716. (p. 134)

Airan, R. D., Meltzer, L. A., Roy, M., Gong, Y., Chen, H., & Deisseroth, K. (2007). High-speed imaging reveals neurophysiological links to behavior in an animal model of depression. *Science, 317,* 819–823. (p. 519)

Akbarian, S., Liu, C., Knowles, J. A., Vaccarino, F. M., Farnham, P. J., Crawford, G. E., . . . Mill, J. (2015). The PsychENCODE project. *Nature Neuroscience, 18,* 1707–1712. (p. 53)

Åkerlund, D., Golsteyn, B. H., Grönqvist, H., & Lindahl, L. (2016). Time discounting and criminal behavior. *PNAS, 113,* 6160–6165. (p. 247)

Akers, K. G., Martinez-Canabal, A., Restivo, L., Yiu, A. P., De Cristofara, A., Hsiang, H.-L., . . . Frankland, P. W. (2014). Hippocampal neurogenesis regulates forgetting during adulthood and infancy. *Science, 344,* 598–602. (p. 124, 277)

Akiyama, M., Okada, Y., Kanai, M., Takahashi, A., Momozawa, Y., Ikeda, M., . . . Iwasaki, M. (2017). Genome-wide association study identifies 112 new loci for body mass index in the Japanese population. *Nature Genetics, 49,* 1458–1467. (p. 365)

Aknin, L. B., Barrington-Leigh, C., Dunn, E. W., Helliwell, J. F., Burns, J., Biswas-Diener, R., . . . Norton, M. I. (2013). Prosocial spending and well-being: Cross-cultural evidence for a psychological universal. *Journal of Personality and Social Psychology, 104,* 635–652. (pp. 407, 455)

Aknin, L. B., Broesch, T., Kiley Hamlin, J., & Van de Vondervoort, J. W. (2015). Pro-social behavior leads to happiness in a small-scale rural society. *Journal of Experimental Psychology: General, 144,* 788–795. (p. 407)

Aknin, L. B., & Human, L. J. (2015). Give a piece of you: Gifts that reflect givers promote closeness. *Journal of Experimental Social Psychology, 60,* 8–16. (p. 407)

Akpinar, E., & Berger, J. (2015). Drivers of cultural success: The case of sensory metaphors. *Journal of Personality and Social Psychology, 109,* 20–34. (p. 272)

Alanko, K., Santtila, P., Harlaar, N., Witting, K., Varjonen, M., Jern, P., . . . Sandnabba, N. K. (2010). Common genetic effects of gender atypical behavior in childhood and sexual orientation in adulthood: A study of Finnish twins. *Archives of Sexual Behavior, 39,* 81–92. (p. 181)

al-Asaadi, M. (2016). "We sleep afraid, we wake up afraid": A child's life in Yemen. *The New York Times* (nytimes.com). (p. 388)

Albee, G. W. (1986). Toward a just society: Lessons from observations on the primary prevention of psychopathology. *American Psychologist, 41,* 891–898. (p. 566)

Albee, G. W. (2006). Historical overview of primary prevention of psychopathology: Address to the 3rd world conference on the promotion of mental health and prevention of mental and behavioral disorders. September 15–17, 2004, Auckland, New Zealand. *The Journal of Primary Prevention, 27,* 449–456. (p. 566)

Albert, D., Chein, J., & Steinberg, L. (2013). Peer influences on adolescent decision making. *Current Directions in Psychological Science, 22,* 80–86. (p. 147)

Alcock, J. E. (2011, March/April). Back from the future: Parapsychology and the Bem affair. *Skeptical Inquirer,* pp. 31–39. (p. 231)

Aldao, A., & Nolen-Hoeksema, S. (2010). Emotion-regulation strategies across psychopathology: A meta-analytic review. *Clinical Psychology Review, 30,* 217–237. (p. 546)

Aleman, A., Kahn, R. S., & Selten, J.-P. (2003). Sex differences in the risk of schizophrenia: Evidence from meta-analysis. *Archives of General Psychiatry, 60,* 565–571. (p. 524)

Alexander, L., & Tredoux, C. (2010). The spaces between us: A spatial analysis of informal segregation. *Journal of Social Issues, 66,* 367–386. (p. 457)

Al Ibraheem, B., Kira, I. A., Aljakoub, J., & Al Ibraheem, A. (2017). The health effect of the Syrian conflict on IDPs and refugees. *Peace and Conflict: Journal of Peace Psychology, 23,* 140–152. (p. 388)

Allan, B. A. (2017). Task significance and meaningful work: A longitudinal study. *Journal of Vocational Behavior, 102,* 174–182. (p. B-9)

Allard, F., & Burnett, N. (1985). Skill in sport. *Canadian Journal of Psychology, 39,* 294–312. (p. 271)

Allen, J. P., Uchino, B. N., & Hafen, C. A. (2015). Running with the pack: Teen peer-relationship qualities as predictors of adult physical health. *Psychological Science, 26,* 1574–1583. (p. 352)

Allen, J., Weinrich, M., Hoppitt, W., & Rendell, L. (2013). Network-based diffusion analysis reveals cultural transmission of lobtail feeding in humpback whales. *Science, 340,* 485–488. (p. 259)

Allen, K. (2003). Are pets a healthy pleasure? The influence of pets on blood pressure. *Current Directions in Psychological Science, 12,* 236–239. (p. 401)

Allen, M. S., & Jones, M. V. (2014). The "home advantage" in athletic competitions. *Current Directions in Psychological Science, 23,* 48–53. (p. 429)

Allen, M., D'Alessio, D., & Emmers-Sommer, T. M. (2000). Reactions of criminal sexual offenders to pornography: A meta-analytic summary. In M. Roloff (Ed.), *Communication Yearbook 22* (pp. 139–169). Thousand Oaks, CA: Sage. (p. 176)

Allen, M., Emmers, T. M., Gebhardt, L., & Giery, M. (1995). Pornography and rape myth acceptance. *Journal of Communication, 45,* 5–26. (p. 176)

Allen, M. W., Gupta, R., & Monnier, A. (2008). The interactive effect of cultural symbols and human values on taste evaluation. *Journal of Consumer Research, 35,* 294–308. (p. 225)

Allen, T., & Sherman, J. (2011). Ego threat and intergroup bias: A test of motivated-activation versus self-regulatory accounts. *Psychological Science, 22,* 331–333. (p. 487)

Allen, T. D., Golden, T. D., & Shockley, K. M. (2015). How effective is telecommuting? Assessing the status of our scientific findings. *Psychological Science in the Public Interest, 16,* 40–68. (pp. B-3, B-8)

Allesøe, K., Hundrup, V. A., Thomsen, J. F., & Osler, M. (2010). Psychosocial work environment and risk of ischaemic heart disease in women: The Danish Nurse Cohort Study. *Occupational and Environmental Medicine, 67,* 318–322. (p. 392)

Alloy, L. B., Abramson, L. Y., Whitehouse, W. G., Hogan, M. E., Tashman, N. A., Steinberg, D. L., . . . Donovan, P. (1999). Depressogenic cognitive styles: Predictive validity, information processing and personality characteristics, and developmental origins. *Behaviour Research and Therapy, 37,* 503–531. (p. 520)

Alloy, L. B., Hamilton, J. L., Hamlat, E. J., & Abramson, L. Y. (2016). Pubertal development, emotion regulatory styles, and the emergence of sex differences in internalizing disorders and symptoms in adolescence. *Clinical Psychological Science, 4,* 867–881. (p. 142)

Allport, G. W. (1954). *The nature of prejudice.* New York: Addison-Wesley. (pp. 21, 438)

Allport, G. W., & Odbert, H. S. (1936). Trait-names: A psycho-lexical study. *Psychological Monographs, 47.* (p. 475)

Ally, B. A., Hussey, E. P., & Donahue, M. J. (2013). A case of hyperthymesia: Rethinking the role of the amygdala in autobiographical memory. *Neurocase, 19,* 166–181. (p. 284)

Almas, A. N., Degnan, K. A., Nelson, C. A., Zeanah, C. H., & Fox, N. A. (2017). IQ at age 12 following a history of institutional care: Findings from the Bucharest Early Intervention Project. *Developmental Psychology, 52,* 1858–1866. (p. 337)

Almås, I., Cappelen, A. W., Sørensen, E. Ø., & Tungodden, B. (2010). Fairness and the development of inequality acceptance. *Science, 328,* 1176–1178. (p. 143)

Al Ramiah, A., & Hewstone, M. (2013). Intergroup contact as a tool for reducing, resolving, and preventing intergroup conflict: Evidence, limitations, and potential. *American Psychologist, 68,* 527–542. (p. 457)

Al-Sayegh, H., Lowry, J., Polur, R. N., Hines, R. B., Liu, F., & Zhang, J. (2015). Suicide history and mortality: A follow-up of a national cohort in the United States. *Archives of Suicide Research, 19,* 35–47. (p. 501)

Altamirano, L. J., Miyake, A., & Whitmer, A. J. (2010). When mental inflexibility facilitates executive control: Beneficial side effects of ruminative tendencies on goal maintenance. *Psychological Science, 21,* 1377–1382. (p. 520)

Alter, A. (2017). *Irresistible: The rise of addictive technology and the business of keeping us hooked.* New York: Penguin. (p. 195)

Alter, A. L., Stern, C., Granot, Y., & Balcetis, E. (2016). The "bad is black" effect: Why people believe evildoers have darker skin than do-gooders. *Personality & Social Psychology Bulletin, 42,* 1653–1665. (p. 436)

Alvarez, L., & Schwartz, J. (2014, May 30). On death row with low I.Q., and new hope for a reprieve. *The New York Times* (nytimes.com). (p. 331)

Alving, C. R. (2011, March 2). "I was swimming in a pool of liposomes." Podcast, *Science* (membercentral.aas.org). (p. 92)

Alwin, D. F. (1990). Historical changes in parental orientations to children. In N. Mandell (Ed.), *Sociological studies of child development* (Vol. 3, pp. 65–86). Greenwich, CT: JAI Press. (p. 138)

Amabile, T. M., & Hennessey, B. A. (1992). The motivation for creativity in children. In A. K. Boggiano & T. S. Pittman (Eds.), *Achievement and motivation: A social-developmental perspective.* New York: Cambridge University Press. (p. 307)

Amabile, T. M., & Kramer, S. J. (2011). *The progress principle: Using small wins to ignite joy, engagement, and creativity at work.* Cambridge, MA: Harvard Business Review Press. (p. B-12)

Ambady, N. (2010). The perils of pondering: Intuition and thin slice judgments. *Psychological Inquiry, 21,* 271–278. (p. 481)

Ambady, N., Hallahan, M., & Rosenthal, R. (1995). On judging and being judged accurately in zero-acquaintance situations. *Journal of Personality and Social Psychology, 69,* 518–529. (p. 376)

Ambrose, C. T. (2010). The widening gyrus. *American Scientist, 98,* 270–274. (p. 124)

Amedi, A., Merabet, L. B., Bermpohl, F., & Pascual-Leone, A. (2005). The occipital cortex in the blind: Lessons about plasticity and vision. *Current Directions in Psychological Science, 14,* 306–311. (p. 64)

Amen, D. G., Stubblefield, M., Carmichael, B., & Thisted, R. (1996). Brain SPECT findings and aggressiveness. *Annals of Clinical Psychiatry, 8,* 129–137. (p. 442)

American Academy of Pediatrics. (2009). Policy statement—media violence. *Pediatrics, 124,* 1495–1503. (p. 263)

American Academy of Pediatrics. (2013). *Promoting the well-being of children whose parents are gay or lesbian.* Retrieved from pediatrics.aapublications.org (p. 135)

American Academy of Pediatrics. (2014). Policy statement: School start times for adolescents. *Pediatrics, 134,* 642–649. (p. 93)

American Enterprise. (1992, January/February). Women, men, marriages and ministers. *The American Enterprise,* p. 106. (p. 491)

American Psychiatric Association. (2013). *Diagnostic and statistical manual of mental disorders* (Fifth ed.). Arlington, VA: American Psychiatric Publishing. (pp. 101, 102, 175, 494, 497, 515)

American Sociological Association. (2013, February 28). Brief of *Amicus Curiae* American Sociological Association in support of respondent Kristin M. Perry and Respondent Edith Schlain Windsor. Supreme Court of the United States, Nos. 12–144, 12–307. (p. 135)

Amick, H. R., Gartlehner, G., Gaynes, B. N., Forneris, C., Asher, G. N., Morgan, L. C., . . . Lohr, K. N. (2015). Comparative benefits and harms of second generation antidepressants and cognitive behavioral therapies in initial treatment of major depressive disorder: Systematic review and meta-analysis. *BMJ, 351,* h6019. (p. 562)

Ammori, B. (2013, January 4). Viewpoint: Benefits of bariatric surgery. *GP* (gponline.com). (p. 362)

Andersen, R. A., Hwang, E. J., & Mulliken, G. H. (2010). Cognitive neural prosthetics. *Annual Review of Psychology, 61*, 169–190. (p. 61)

Andersen, S. M. (1998, September). *Service learning: A national strategy for youth development.* Washington, DC: Institute for Communitarian Policy Studies, George Washington University. (p. 145)

Anderson, B. L. (2002). Biobehavioral outcomes following psychological interventions for cancer patients. *Journal of Consulting and Clinical Psychology, 70*, 590–610. (p. 391)

Anderson, C., Hildreth, J. A. D., & Howland, L. (2015). Is the desire for status a fundamental human motive? A review of the empirical literature. *Psychological Bulletin, 141*, 574–601. (p. 351)

Anderson, C. A. (2004). An update on the effects of playing violent video games. *Journal of Adolescence, 27*, 113–122. (pp. 318, 444, 445)

Anderson, C. A. (2013, June). Guns, games, and mass shootings in the U.S. *Bulletin of the International Society for Research on Aggression*, pp. 14–19. (p. 444)

Anderson, C. A., Anderson, K. B., Dorr, N., DeNeve, K. M., & Flanagan, M. (2000). Temperature and aggression. In M. P. Zanna (Ed.), *Advances in experimental social psychology*. San Diego: Academic Press. (p. 443)

Anderson, C. A., Brion, S., Moore, D. A., & Kennedy, J. A. (2012). A status-enhancement account of overconfidence. *Journal of Personality and Social Psychology, 103*, 718–735. (pp. 198, 304)

Anderson, C. A., Bushman, B. J., & Groom, R. W. (1997). Hot years and serious and deadly assault: Empirical tests of the heat hypothesis. *Journal of Personality and Social Psychology, 73*, 1213–1223. (p. 443)

Anderson, C. A., & Delisi, M. (2011). Implications of global climate change for violence in developed and developing countries. In J. Forgas, A. Kruglanski, & K. Williams (Eds.), *The psychology of social conflict and aggression* (pp. 249–265). New York: Psychology Press. (p. 443)

Anderson, C. A., & Dill, K. E. (2000). Video games and aggressive thoughts, feelings, and behavior in the laboratory and in life. *Journal of Personality and Social Psychology, 78*, 772–790. (p. 444)

Anderson, C. A., Shibuya, A., Ihori, N., Swing, E. L., Bushman, B. J., Sakamoto, A., . . . Saleem, M. (2010). Violent video game effects on aggression, empathy, and prosocial behavior in Eastern and Western countries: A meta-analytic review. *Psychological Bulletin, 136*, 151–173. (p. 310, 444)

Anderson, C. A., Suzuki, K., Swing, E. L., Groves, C. L., Gentile, D. A., Prot, S., . . . Jelic, M. (2017). Media violence and other aggression risk factors in seven nations. *Personality and Social Psychology Bulletin, 43*, 986–998. (p. 444)

Anderson, C. A., & Warburton, W. A. (2012). The impact of violent video games: An overview. In W. Warburton & D. Braunstein (Eds.), *Growing up fast and furious*. Annandale, NSW, Australia: The Federation Press. (p. 445)

Anderson, I. M. (2000). Selective serotonin reuptake inhibitors versus tricyclic antidepressants: A meta-analysis of efficacy and tolerability. *Journal of Affective Disorders, 58*, 19–36. (p. 561)

Anderson, J. R., Myowa-Yamakoshi, M., & Matsuzawa, T. (2004). Contagious yawning in chimpanzees. *Biology Letters, 271*, S468–S470. (p. 422)

Anderson, P. L., Edwards, S. M., & Goodnight, J. R. (2017). Virtual reality and exposure group therapy for social anxiety disorder: Results from a 4-6 year follow-up. *Cognitive Therapy and Research, 41*, 230–236. (p. 541)

Anderson, R. C., Pichert, J. W., Goetz, E. T., Schallert, D. L., Stevens, K. V., & Trollip, S. R. (1976). Instantiation of general terms. *Journal of Verbal Learning and Verbal Behavior, 15*, 667–679. (p. 287)

Anderson, S. E., Dallal, G. E., & Must, A. (2003). Relative weight and race influence average age at menarche: Results from two nationally representative surveys of U.S. girls studied 25 years apart. *Pediatrics, 111*, 844–850. (p. 167)

Andersson, G. (2016). Internet-delivered psychological treatments. *Annual Review of Clinical Psychology, 12*, 157–179. (p. 546)

Andics, A., Gábor, A., Gácsi, M., Faragó, T., Szabó, D., & Miklósi, Á. (2016). Neural mechanisms for lexical processing in dogs. *Science, 353*, 1030–1032. (p. 67)

Andreasen, N. C. (1997). Linking mind and brain in the study of mental illnesses: A project for a scientific psychopathology. *Science, 275*, 1586–1593. (p. 525)

Andreasen, N. C. (2001). *Brave new brain: Conquering mental illness in the era of the genome.* New York: Oxford University Press. (p. 525)

Andreasen, N. C., Arndt, S., Swayze, V., II, Cizadlo, T., & Flaum, M. (1994). Thalamic abnormalities in schizophrenia visualized through magnetic resonance image averaging. *Science, 266*, 294–298. (p. 525)

Andrews, P. W., & Thomson, J. A., Jr. (2009a). The bright side of being blue: Depression as an adaptation for analyzing complex problems. *Psychological Review, 116*, 620–654. (p. 520)

Andrews, P. W., & Thomson, J. A., Jr. (2009b). Depression's evolutionary roots. *Scientific American Mind, 20*, 56–61. (p. 520)

Andrillon, T., Nir, Y., Cirelli, C., Tononi, G., & Fried, I. (2015). Single-neuron activity and eye movements during human REM sleep and awake vision. *Nature Communications, 6*, Article 7884. doi:10.1038/ncomms8884 (p. 89)

Anglemyer, A., Horvath, T., & Rutherford, G. (2014). The accessibility of firearms and risk for suicide and homicide victimization among household members. *Annals of Internal Medicine, 160*, 101–112. (p. 441)

Annese, J., Schenker-Ahmed, N. M., Bartsch, H., Maechler, P., Sheh, C., Thomas, N., . . . Corkin, S. (2014). Postmortem examination of patient H. M.'s brain based on histological sectioning and digital 3D reconstruction. *Nature Communications, 5*, Article 3122. doi:10.1038/ncomms4122 (p. 284)

Ansari, A., Purtell, K., & Gershoff, E. (2015). Classroom age composition and the school readiness of 3- and 4-year-olds in the Head Start program. *Psychological Science, 27*, 53–63. (p. 315)

Anton, B. S. (2015, June). Quoted in, "APA applauds President Obama's call to end use of therapies intended to change sexual orientation." *Monitor, 46*, p. 10. (p. 554)

Antonaccio, O., Botchkovar, E. V., & Tittle, C. R. (2011). Attracted to crime: Exploration of criminal motivation among respondents in three European cities. *Criminal Justice and Behavior, 38*, 1200–1221. (p. 163)

Antony, M. M., Brown, T. A., & Barlow, D. H. (1992). Current perspectives on panic and panic disorder. *Current Directions in Psychological Science, 1*, 79–82. (p. 511)

Antrobus, J. (1991). Dreaming: Cognitive processes during cortical activation and high afferent thresholds. *Psychological Review, 98*, 96–121. (p. 98)

Anzures, G., Quinn, P. C., Pascalis, O., Slater, A. M., Tanaka, J. W., & Lee, K. (2013). Developmental origins of the other-race effect. *Current Directions in Psychological Science, 22*, 173–178. (p. 439)

AP. (2007). AP-Ipsos poll of 1,013 U.S. adults taken October 16–18, 2007 and distributed via Associated Press. (p. 229)

AP. (2009, May 9). *AP-mtvU AP 2009 Economy, College Stress and Mental Health Poll.* Associated Press (surveys.ap.org). (p. 93)

AP. (2017). Strangers on beach form 80-link human chain, rescue family from rip current. CBC. Retrieved from cbc.ca/news/world/human-chain-saves-family-in-water-1.4199181 (p. 458)

APA. (2006). Evidence-based practice in psychology (from APA Presidential Task Force on Evidence-Based Practice). *American Psychologist, 61*, 271–285. (p. 553)

APA. (2007). *Report of the task force on the sexualization of girls.* Washington, DC: American Psychological Association (apa.org). (p. 177)

APA. (2009). *Report of the APA task force on appropriate therapeutic responses to sexual orientation.* American Psychological Association (apa.org). (p. 179)

APA. (2010). *Answers to your questions about transgender individuals and gender identity.* American Psychological Association (apa.org). (p. 170)

APA. (2012). *Guidelines for ethical conduct in the care and use of nonhuman animals in research.* Washington, DC: American Psychological Association. (p. 31)

APA. (2017). Stress in America: Coping with change. Washington, DC: American Psychological Association. (p. 386)

APA Task Force on Violent Media. (2015). *Technical report on the review of the violent video game literature.* American Psychological Association (apa.org/pi/families/review-video-games.pdf). (p. 263)

Archer, J. (2000). Sex differences in aggression between heterosexual partners: A meta-analytic review. *Psychological Bulletin, 126*, 651–680. (p. 163)

Archer, J. (2004). Sex differences in aggression in real-world settings: A meta-analytic review. *Review of General Psychology, 8*, 291–322. (p. 163)

Archer, J. (2007). A cross-cultural perspective on physical aggression between partners. *Issues in Forensic Psychology, 6*, 125–131. (p. 163)

Archer, J. (2009). Does sexual selection explain human sex differences in aggression? *Behavioral and Brain Sciences, 32*, 249–311. (p. 163)

Arendt, H. (1963). *Eichmann in Jerusalem: A report on the banality of evil.* New York: Viking. (p. 145)

Ariel, R., & Karpicke, J. D. (2017). Improved self-regulated learning with a retrieval practice intervention. *Journal of Experimental Psychology: Applied.* Advance online publication. doi:10.1037/xap0000133 (p. 33)

Ariely, D. (2009). *Predictably irrational: The hidden forces that shape our decisions.* New York: HarperCollins. (p. 281)

Ariely, D. (2010). *Predictably irrational, revised and expanded edition: The hidden forces that shape our decisions.* New York: Harper Perennial. (p. 469)

Ariely, D., & Loewenstein, G. (2006). The heat of the moment: The effect of sexual arousal on sexual decision making. *Journal of Behavioral Decision Making, 19*, 87–98. (p. 177)

Aries, E. (1987). Gender and communication. In P. Shaver & C. Henrick (Eds.), *Review of Personality and Social Psychology, 7*, 149–176. (p. 164)

Arkowitz, H., & Lilienfeld, S. O. (2006, April/May). Psychotherapy on trial. *Scientific American: Mind*, pp. 42–49. (p. 554)

Armony, J. L., Quirk, G. J., & LeDoux, J. E. (1998). Differential effects of amygdala lesions on early and late plastic components of auditory cortex spike trains during fear conditioning. *Journal of Neuroscience, 18,* 2592–2601. (p. 512)

Armstrong, E. A., England, P., & Fogarty, A. C. K. (2012). Accounting for women's orgasm and sexual enjoyment in college hookups and relationships. *American Sociological Review, 77,* 435–462. (p. 186)

Arnedo, J., Mamah, D., Baranger, D. A., Harms, M. P., Barch, D. M., Svrakic, D. M., . . . Zwir, I. (2015). Decomposition of brain diffusion imaging data uncovers latent schizophrenias with distinct patterns of white matter anisotropy. *NeuroImage, 120,* 43–54. (pp. 525, 526)

Arnett, J. J. (1999). Adolescent storm and stress, reconsidered. *American Psychologist, 54,* 317–326. (p. 141)

Arnett, J. J. (2006). Emerging adulthood: Understanding the new way of coming of age. In J. J. Arnett & J. L. Tanner (Eds.), *Emerging adults in America: Coming of age in the 21st century* (pp. 3–19). Washington, DC: American Psychological Association. (p. 149)

Arnett, J. J. (2007). Socialization in emerging adulthood: From the family to the wider world, from socialization to self-socialization. In J. E. Grusec & P. D. Hastings (Eds.), *Handbook of socialization: Theory and research* (pp. 208–230). New York: Guilford Press. (p. 149)

Arnold, K. M., Umanath, S., Thio, K., Reilly, W. B., McDaniel, M. A., & Marsh, E. J. (2017). Understanding the cognitive processes involved in writing to learn. *Journal of Experimental Psychology: Applied, 23,* 115–127. (p. 34)

Arnone, D., McIntosh, A. M., Tan, G. M. Y., & Ebmeier, K. P. (2008). Meta-analysis of magnetic resonance imaging studies of the corpus callosum in schizophrenia. *Schizophrenia Research, 101,* 124–132. (p. 525)

Aron, A. P., Melinat, E., Aron, E. N., Vallone, R. D., & Bator, R. J. (1997). The experimental generation of interpersonal closeness: A procedure and some preliminary findings. *Personality and Social Psychology Bulletin, 23,* 363–377. (p. 452)

Aron, A., Norman, C. C., Aron, E. N., McKenna, C., & Heyman, R. E. (2000). Couples' shared participation in novel and arousing activities and experienced relationship quality. *Journal of Personality and Social Psychology, 78,* 273–284. (p. 451)

Aronson, E. (2001, April 13). Newsworthy violence. [E-mail to Society for Personality and Social Psychology discussion list, drawing from *Nobody left to hate: Teaching compassion after Columbine.* (2000). New York: Freeman]. (p. 148)

Arriaga, P., Adrião, J., Madeira, F., Cavaleiro, I., Maia e Silva, A., Barahona, I., & Esteves, F. (2015). A "dry eye" for victims of violence: Effects of playing a violent video game on pupillary dilation to victims and on aggressive behavior. *Psychology of Violence, 5,* 199–208. (p. 444)

Artiga, A. I., Viana, J. B., Maldonado, C. R., Chandler-Laney, P. C., Oswald, K. D., & Boggiano, M. M. (2007). Body composition and endocrine status of long-term stress-induced binge-eating rats. *Physiology and Behavior, 91,* 424–431. (p. 363)

Arzi, A., Shedlesky, L., Ben-Shaul, M., Nasser, K., Oksenberg, A., Hairston, I. S., & Sobel, N. (2012). Humans can learn new information during sleep. *Nature Neuroscience, 15,* 1460–1465. (p. 97)

Ascády, L., & Harris, K. D. (2017). Synaptic scaling in sleep. *Science, 355,* 457. (p. 91)

Asch, S. E. (1955). Opinions and social pressure. *Scientific American, 193,* 31–35. (p. 423)

Aserinsky, E. (1988, January 17). Personal communication. (p. 87)

Ashton, K., Bellis, M., Davies, A., Hardcastle, K., & Hughes, K. (2016). *Adverse childhood experiences and their association with chronic disease and health service use in the Welsh adult population.* Welsh Adverse Childhood Experiences (ACE) Study, NHS Wales Public Trust. Retrieved from wales.nhs.uk/ (p. 386)

Askay, S. W., & Patterson, D. R. (2007). Hypnotic analgesia. *Expert Review of Neurotherapeutics, 7,* 1675–1683. (p. 224)

Aspinwall, L. G., Brown, T. R., & Tabery, J. (2012). The double-edged sword: Does biomechanism increase or decrease judges' sentencing of psychopaths? *Science, 337,* 846–849. (p. 417)

Aspinwall, L. G., & Tedeschi, R. G. (2010). The value of positive psychology for health psychology: Progress and pitfalls in examining the relation of positive phenomena to health. *Annals of Behavioral Medicine, 39,* 4–15. (p. 398)

Aspy, C. B., Vesely, S. K., Oman, R. F., Rodine, S., Marshall, L., & McLeroy, K. (2007). Parental communication and youth sexual behaviour. *Journal of Adolescence, 30,* 449–466. (p. 177)

Assanand, S., Pinel, J. P. J., & Lehman, D. R. (1998). Personal theories of hunger and eating. *Journal of Applied Social Psychology, 28,* 998–1015. (p. 363)

Astin, A. W., Astin, H. S., & Lindholm, J. A. (2004). *Spirituality in higher education: A national study of college students' search for meaning and purpose.* Los Angeles: Higher Education Research Institute, University of California, Los Angeles. (p. 146)

Atkinson, R. C., & Shiffrin, R. M. (1968). Human memory: A control system and its control processes. In K. Spence (Ed.), *The psychology of learning and motivation* (Vol. 2). New York: Academic Press. (p. 268)

Atkinson, R. C., & Shiffrin, R. M. (2016). Human memory: A proposed system and its control processes. In R. J. Sternberg, S. T. Fiske, & D. J. Foss (Eds.), *Scientists making a difference: One hundred eminent behavioral and brain scientists talk about their most important contributions.* New York: Cambridge University Press. (p. 268)

Atlas, D. (2016, January 29). Autism's first-ever patient, now 82, "has continued to grow his whole life." *People* (people.com/article/donald-triplett-first-ever-autism-case). (p. 131)

Austin, E. J., Deary, I. J., Whiteman, M. C., Fowkes, F. G. R., Pedersen, N. L., Rabbitt, P., . . . McInnes, L. (2002). Relationships between ability and personality: Does intelligence contribute positively to personal and social adjustment? *Personality and Individual Differences, 32,* 1391–1411. (p. 331)

Australian Unity. (2008). *What makes us happy? The Australian Unity Wellbeing Index.* South Melbourne: Australian Unity. (p. 410)

Averill, J. R. (1993). William James's other theory of emotion. In M. E. Donnelly (Ed.), *Reinterpreting the legacy of William James.* Washington, DC: American Psychological Association. (p. 369)

Aviezer, H., Hassin, R. R., Ryan, J., Grady, C., Susskind, J., Anderson, A., . . . Bentin, S. (2008). Angry, disgusted, or afraid? Studies on the malleability of emotion perception. *Psychological Science, 19,* 724–732. (p. 380)

Ayan, S. (2009). Laughing matters. *Scientific American Mind, 20,* 24–31. (p. 399)

Aydin, N., Fischer, P., & Frey, D. (2010). Turning to God in the face of ostracism: Effects of social exclusion on religiousness. *Personality and Social Psychology Bulletin, 36,* 742–753. (p. 354)

Azar, B. (1998, June). Why can't this man feel whether or not he's standing up? *APA Monitor* (apa.org/monitor/jun98/touch.html). (p. 227)

Azevedo, F. A., Carvalho, L. R., Grinberg, L. T., Farfel, J. M., Ferretti, R. E., Leite, R. E., . . . Herculano-Houzel, S. (2009). Equal numbers of neuronal and nonneuronal cells make the human brain an isometrically scaled-up primate brain. *Journal of Comparative Neurology, 513,* 532–541. (p. 47)

Baas, M., De Dreu, C. K. W., & Nijstad, B. A. (2008). A meta-analysis of 25 years of mood-creativity research: Hedonic tone, activation, or regulatory focus? *Psychological Bulletin, 134,* 779–806. (p. 407)

Baas, M., Nijstad, B. A., Boot, N. C., & De Dreu, C. K. (2016). Mad genius revisited: Vulnerability to psychopathology, biobehavioral approach-avoidance, and creativity. *Psychological Bulletin, 142,* 668–692. (p. 515)

Babyak, M., Blumenthal, J. A., Herman, S., Khatri, P., Doraiswamy, M., Moore, K., . . . Krishnan, K. R. (2000). Exercise treatment for major depression: Maintenance of therapeutic benefit at ten months. *Psychosomatic Medicine, 62,* 633–638. (p. 559)

Bachman, J., O'Malley, P. M., Schulenberg, J. E., Johnston, L. D., Freedman-Doan, P., & Messersmith, E. E. (2007). *The education–drug use connection: How successes and failures in school relate to adolescent smoking, drinking, drug use, and delinquency.* Mahwah, NJ: Erlbaum. (p. 112)

Back, M. D., Stopfer, J. M., Vazire, S., Gaddis, S., Schmukle, S. C., Egloff, B., & Gosling, S. D. (2010). Facebook profiles reflect actual personality, not self-idealization. *Psychological Science, 21,* 372–374. (p. 481)

Backman, L., & MacDonald, S. W. S. (2006). Death and cognition: Synthesis and outlook. *European Psychologist, 11,* 224–235. (p. 155)

Baddeley, A. D. (1982). *Your memory: A user's guide.* New York: Macmillan. (pp. 267, 268)

Baddeley, A. D. (2002, June). Is working memory still working? *European Psychologist, 7,* 85–97. (p. 269)

Baddeley, A. D., Thomson, N., & Buchanan, M. (1975). Word length and the structure of short-term memory. *Journal of Verbal Learning and Verbal Behavior, 14,* 575–589. (p. 271)

Baddeley, J. L., & Singer, J. A. (2009). A social interactional model of bereavement narrative disclosure. *Review of General Psychology, 13,* 202–218. (p. 160)

Bagemihl, B. (1999). *Biological exuberance: Animal homosexuality and natural diversity.* New York: St. Martin's Press. (p. 180)

Bagge, C. L., Littlefield, A. K., & Glenn, C. R. (2017). Trajectories of affective response as warning signs for suicide attempts: An examination of the 48 hours prior to a recent suicide attempt. *Clinical Psychological Science, 5,* 259–271. (p. 501)

Baglioni, C., Nanovska, S., Regen, W., Spiegelhalder, K., Feige, B., Nissen, C., . . . Riemann, D. (2016). Sleep and mental disorders: A meta-analysis of polysomnographic research. *Psychological Bulletin, 142,* 969–990. (pp. 93, 96)

Bahrick, H. P. (1984). Semantic memory content in permastore: Fifty years of memory for Spanish learned in school. *Journal of Experimental Psychology: General, 111,* 1–29. (p. 286)

Bahrick, H. P., Bahrick, P. O., & Wittlinger, R. P. (1975). Fifty years of memory for names and faces: A cross-sectional approach. *Journal of Experimental Psychology: General, 104,* 54–75. (p. 267)

Bailey, J. M., Gaulin, S., Agyei, Y., & Gladue, B. A. (1994). Effects of gender and sexual orientation on evolutionary relevant aspects of human mating psychology. *Journal of Personality and Social Psychology, 66,* 1081–1093. (p. 183)

Bailey, J. M., Kirk, K. M., Zhu, G., Dunne, M. P., & Martin, N. G. (2000). Do individual differences in sociosexuality represent genetic or environmentally contingent strategies? Evidence from the Australian twin registry. *Journal of Personality and Social Psychology, 78*, 537–545. (p. 184)

Bailey, J. M., Vasey, P. L., Diamond, L. M., Breedlove, S. M., Vilain, E., & Epprecht, M. (2016). Sexual orientation, controversy, and science. *Psychological Science in the Public Interest, 17*, 45–101. (pp. 181, 182)

Bailey, R. E., & Gillaspy, J. A., Jr. (2005). Operant psychology goes to the fair: Marian and Keller Breland in the popular press, 1947–1966. *The Behavior Analyst, 28*, 143–159. (p. 233)

Bailine, S., Fink, M., Knapp, R., Petrides, G., Husain, M. M., Rasmussen, K., . . . Kellner, C. H. (2010). Electroconvulsive therapy is equally effective in unipolar and bipolar depression. *Acta Psychiatrica Scandinavica, 121*, 431–436. (p. 563)

Baillargeon, R. (2008). Innate ideas revisited: For a principle of persistence in infants' physical reasoning. *Perspectives in Psychological Science, 3*, 2–13. (p. 127)

Baillargeon, R., Scott, R. M., & Bian, L. (2016). Psychological reasoning in infancy. *Annual Review of Psychology, 67*, 159–186. (p. 127)

Bak, T. H., Nissan, J. J., Allerhand, M. M., & Deary, I. J. (2014, June). Does bilingualism influence cognitive aging? *Annals of Neurology, 75*, 959–963. (p. 320)

Baker, T. B., McFall, R. M., & Shoham, V. (2008). Current status and future prospects of clinical psychology: Toward a scientifically principled approach to mental and behavioral health care. *Psychological Science in the Public Interest, 9*, 67–103. (p. 553)

Baker, T. B., Piper, M. E., McCarthy, D. E., Majeskie, M. R., & Fiore, M. C. (2004). Addiction motivation reformulated: An affective processing model of negative reinforcement. *Psychological Review, 111*, 33–51. (p. 246)

Bakermans-Kranenburg, M. J., van IJzendoorn, M. H., & Juffer, F. (2003). Less is more: Meta-analyses of sensitivity and attachment interventions in early childhood. *Psychological Bulletin, 129*, 195–215. (p. 135)

Bakshy, E., Messing, S., & Adamic, L. A. (2015). Exposure to ideologically diverse news and opinion on Facebook. *Science, 348*, 1130–1132. (p. 432)

Balcetis, E., & Dunning, D. (2010). Wishful seeing: More desire objects are seen as closer. *Psychological Science, 21*, 147–152. (p. 197)

Ball, G., Adamson, C., Beare, R., & Seal, M. L. (2017). Modelling neuroanatomical variation due to age and sex during childhood and adolescence. Unpublished manuscript: biorxiv.org/content/early/2017/07/16/126441 (p. 340)

Balodis, I. M., & Potenza, M. N. (2015). Anticipatory reward processing in addicted populations: A focus on the monetary incentive delay task. *Biological Psychiatry, 77*, 434–444. (p. 56)

Balodis, I. M., Wynne-Edwards, K. E., & Olmstead, M. C. (2010). The other side of the curve: Examining the relationship between pre-stressor physiological responses and stress reactivity. *Psychoneuroendocrinology, 35*, 1363–1373. (p. 386)

Balsam, K. F., Beauchaine, T. P., Rothblum, E. S., & Solomon, S. E. (2008). Three-year follow-up of same-sex couples who had civil unions in Vermont, same-sex couples not in civil unions, and heterosexual married couples. *Developmental Psychology, 44*, 102–116. (p. 156)

Balter, M. (2010). Animal communication helps reveal roots of language. *Science, 328*, 969–970. (p. 317)

Balter, M. (2014). Science misused to justify Ugandan antigay law. *Science, 343*, 956. (p. 182)

Balter, M. (2015). Can epigenetics explain homosexuality puzzle? *Science, 350*, 148. (p. 181)

Balter, M. (2017, May). Schizophrenia's unyielding mysteries. *Scientific American*, pp. 55–61. (p. 526)

Bambico, F. R., Nguyen N.-T., Katz, N., & Gobbi, G. (2010). Chronic exposure to cannabinoids during adolescence but not during adulthood impairs emotional behaviour and monoaminergic neurotransmission. *Neurobiology of Disease, 37*, 641–655. (p. 109)

Banaji, M. R., & Greenwald, A. G. (2013). *Blindspot: Hidden biases of good people*. New York: Delacorte Press. (p. 435)

Bancroft, J., Loftus, J., & Long, J. S. (2003). Distress about sex: A national survey of women in heterosexual relationships. *Archives of Sexual Behavior, 32*, 193–208. (p. 175)

Bandura, A. (1977). Self-efficacy: Toward a unifying theory of behavior. *Psychological Review, 84*, 191–215. (p. 486)

Bandura, A. (1982). The psychology of chance encounters and life paths. *American Psychologist, 37*, 747–755. (p. 155)

Bandura, A. (1986). *Social foundations of thought and action: A social-cognitive theory*. Englewood Cliffs, NJ: Prentice-Hall. (p. 482)

Bandura, A. (2005). The evolution of social cognitive theory. In K. G. Smith & M. A. Hitt (Eds.), *Great minds in management: The process of theory development* (pp. 9–35). Oxford: Oxford University Press. (pp. 155, 258)

Bandura, A. (2006). Toward a psychology of human agency. *Perspectives on Psychological Science, 1*, 164–180. (p. 482)

Bandura, A. (2008). An agentic perspective on positive psychology. In S. J. Lopez (Ed.), *The science of human flourishing*. Westport, CT: Praeger. (p. 482)

Bandura, A. (2016). The power of observational learning through social modeling. In R. J. Sternberg, S. T. Fiske, & D. J. Foss (Eds.), *Scientists making a difference: One hundred eminent behavioral and brain scientists talk about their most important contributions*. New York: Cambridge University Press, pp. 235–239. (p. 259)

Bandura, A., Ross, D., & Ross, S. A. (1961). Transmission of aggression through imitation of aggressive models. *Journal of Abnormal and Social Psychology, 63*, 575–582. (p. 258)

Bansak, K., Hainmueller, J., & Hangartner, D. (2016). How economic, humanitarian, and religious concerns shape European attitudes toward asylum seekers. *Science, 354*, 217–222. (p. 455)

Banville, J. (2012, April). APA weighs in on the constitutionality of life without parole for juvenile offenders. *Monitor on Psychology*, p. 12. (p. 142)

Barash, D. P. (2006, July 14). I am, therefore I think. *The Chronicle of Higher Education*, pp. B9, B10. (p. 81)

Barash, D. P. (2012). *Homo mysterius: Evolutionary puzzles of human nature*. New York: Oxford University Press. (p. 186)

Barbaresi, W. J., Katusic, S. K., Colligan, R. C., Weaver, A. L., & Jacobsen, S. J. (2007). Modifiers of long-term school outcomes for children with attention deficit/hyperactivity disorder: Does treatment with stimulant medication make a difference? Results from a population-based study. *Journal of Developmental and Behavioral Pediatrics, 28*, 274–287. (p 498)

Barberá, P., Jost, J. T., Nagler, J., Tucker, J. A., & Bonneau, R. (2015). Tweeting from left to right: Is online political communication more than an echo chamber? *Psychological Science, 26*, 1531–1542. (p. 432)

Bargh, J. A., & Chartrand, T. L. (1999). The unbearable automaticity of being. *American Psychologist, 54*, 462–479. (pp. 84, 469)

Bargh, J. A., & McKenna, K. Y. A. (2004). The internet and social life. *Annual Review of Psychology, 55*, 573–590. (p. 448)

Bargh, J. A., McKenna, K. Y. A., & Fitzsimons, G. M. (2002). Can you see the real me? Activation and expression of the "true self" on the internet. *Journal of Social Issues, 58*, 33–48. (p. 448)

Bargh, J. A., & Morsella, E. (2008). The unconscious mind. *Perspectives on Psychological Science, 3*, 73–79. (p. 470)

Bar-Haim, Y., Lamy, D., Pergamin, L., Bakermans-Kranenburg, M. J., & van IJzendoorn, M. H. (2007). Threat-related attentional bias in anxious and nonanxious individuals: A meta-analytic study. *Psychological Bulletin, 133*, 1–24. (p. 510)

Barinaga, M. B. (1992). The brain remaps its own contours. *Science, 258*, 216–218. (p. 64)

Barinaga, M. B. (1997). How exercise works its magic. *Science, 276*, 1325. (p. 401)

Barker, D. J. P. (2012). Developmental origins of chronic disease. *Public Health, 126*, 185–189. (p. 120)

Barkley, R. A., et al. (2002). International consensus statement (January 2002). *Clinical Child and Family Psychology Review, 5*(2), 89–111. (p. 498)

Barkley-Levenson, E., & Galván, A. (2014). Neural representation of expected value in the adolescent brain. *PNAS, 111*, 1646–1651. (p. 142)

Barlow, D. H. (2010). Negative effects from psychological treatments: A perspective. *American Psychologist, 65*, 13–20. (p. 554)

Barlow, M., Woodman, T., & Hardy, L. (2013). Great expectations: Different high-risk activities satisfy different motives. *Journal of Personality and Social Psychology, 105*, 458–475. (p. 349)

Barnier, A. J., & McConkey, K. M. (2004). Defining and identifying the highly hypnotizable person. In M. Heap, R. J. Brown, & D. A. Oakley (Eds.), *The highly hypnotizable person: Theoretical, experimental and clinical issues* (pp. 30–60). London: Brunner-Routledge. (p. 224)

Baron, C. E., Smith, T. W., Uchino, B. N., Baucom, B. R., & Birmingham, W. C. (2016). Getting along and getting ahead: Affiliation and dominance predict ambulatory blood pressure. *Health Psychology, 35*, 253–261. (p. 400)

Baron-Cohen, S. (2010). Autism and the empathizing-systemizing (E-S) theory. In P. D. Zelazo, M. Chandler & E. Crone (Eds.), *Developmental social cognitive neuroscience*. New York: Psychology Press, pp. 125–138. (p. 131)

Baron-Cohen, S. (2017). The eyes as window to the mind. *American Journal of Psychiatry, 174*, 1–2. (p. 131)

Baron-Cohen, S., Bowen, D. C., Rosemary, J. H., Allison, C., Auyeung, B., Lombardo, M. V., & Lai, M.-C. (2015). The "reading the mind in the eyes" test: Complete absence of typical difference in ~400 men and women with autism. *PLoS ONE, 10*, e0136521. (p. 131)

Baron-Cohen, S., Golan, O., Chapman, E., & Granader, Y. (2007). Transported to a world of emotion. *The Psychologist, 20*, 76–77. (p. 132)

Barrera, T. L., Mott, J. M., Hofstein, R. F., & Teng, E. J. (2013). A meta-analytic review of exposure in group cognitive behavioral therapy for posttraumatic stress disorder. *Clinical Psychology Review, 33*, 24–32. (p. 541)

Barrett, D. (2011). Answers in your dreams. *Scientific American Mind, 22*, 26–33. (p. 92)

Barrett, H. C., Bolyanatz, A., Crittenden, A. N., Fessler, D. M., Fitzpatrick, S., Gurven, M., . . . Scelza, B. A. (2016). Small-scale societies exhibit fundamental variation in the role of intentions in moral judgment. *PNAS, 113*, 4688–4693. (p. 144)

Barrett, L. F. (2006). Are emotions natural kinds? *Perspectives on Psychological Science, 1*, 28–58. (pp. 369, 373)

Barrett, L. F. (2012). Emotions are real. *Emotion, 12*, 413–429. (p. 368)

Barrett, L. F. (2013). Quoted by Fischer, S. About face: Emotional and facial expressions may not be directly related. *Boston Magazine.* (p. 368)

Barrett, L. F., & Bliss-Moreau, E. (2009). She's emotional. He's having a bad day: Attributional explanations for emotion stereotypes. *Emotion, 9*, 649–658. (p. 378)

Barrett, L. F., Lane, R. D., Sechrest, L., & Schwartz, G. E. (2000). Sex differences in emotional awareness. *Personality and Social Psychology Bulletin, 26*, 1027–1035. (p. 377)

Barretto, R. P., Gillis-Smith, S., Chandrashekar, J., Yarmolinsky, D. A., Schnitzer, M. J., Ryba, N. J., & Zuker, C. S. (2015). The neural representation of taste quality at the periphery. *Nature, 517*, 373–376. (p. 225)

Barrick, M. R., Shaffer, J. A., & DeGrassi, S. W. (2009). What you see may not be what you get: Relationships among self-presentation tactics and ratings of interview and job performance. *Journal of Applied Psychology, 94*, 1304–1411. (p. B-5)

Barrington-Trimis, J. L., Berhane, K., Unger, J. B., Cruz, T. B., Urman, R., Chou, C. P., . . . Huh, J. (2016). The e-cigarette social environment, e-cigarette use, and susceptibility to cigarette smoking. *Journal of Adolescent Health, 59*, 75–80. (p. 105)

Barrouillet, P., Portrat, S., & Camos, V. (2011). On the law relating processing to storage in working memory. *Psychological Review, 118*, 175–192. (p. 269)

Barry, C. L., McGinty, E. E., Vernick, J. S., & Webster, D. W. (2013). After Newtown—Public opinion on gun policy and mental illness. *New England Journal of Medicine, 368*, 1077–1081. (p. 502)

Barry, D. (1995, September 17). Teen smokers, too, get cool, toxic, waste-blackened lungs. *The Asbury Park Press*, p. D3. (p. 106)

Bartels, J. M., Milovich, M. M., & Moussier, S. (2016). Coverage of the Stanford prison experiment in introductory psychology courses: A survey of introductory psychology instructors. *Teaching of Psychology, 43*, 136–141. (p. 419)

Bartels, M. (2015). Genetics of wellbeing and its components with life, happiness, and quality of life: A review of meta-analysis of heritability studies. *Behavior Genetics, 45*, 137–156. (p. 411)

Bashore, T. R., Ridderinkhof, K. R., & van der Molen, M. W. (1997). The decline of cognitive processing speed in old age. *Current Directions in Psychological Science, 6*, 163–169. (p. 152)

Baskind, D. E. (1997, December 14). Personal communication, from Delta College. (p. 542)

Basu, S., & Basu, D. (2015). The relationship between psychoactive drugs, the brain and psychosis. *International Archives of Addiction Research and Medicine, 1*(003). (p. 524)

Bates, T. C. (2015). The glass is half full and half empty: A population-representative twin study testing if optimism and pessimism are distinct systems. *Journal of Positive Psychology, 10*, 533–542. (p. 399)

Bathje, G. J., & Pryor, J. B. (2011). The relationships of public and self-stigma to seeking mental health services. *Journal of Mental Health Counseling, 33*, 161–177. (p. 497)

Batsell, W. R., Perry, J. L., Hanley, E., & Hostetter, A. B. (2017). Ecological validity of the testing effect: The use of daily quizzes in introductory psychology. *Teaching of Psychology, 44*, 18–23. (p. 273)

Bauer, M., Cassar, A., Chytilová, J., & Henrich, J. (2014). War's enduring effects on the development of egalitarian motivations and in-group biases. *Psychological Science, 25*, 47–57. (p. 458)

Bauer, P. J., Burch, M. M., Scholin, S. E., & Güler, O. E. (2007). Using cue words to investigate the distribution of autobiographical memories in childhood. *Psychological Science, 18*, 910–916. (p. 277)

Bauer, P. J., & Larkina, M. (2014). The onset of childhood amnesia in childhood: A prospective investigation of the course and determinants of forgetting of early-life events. *Memory, 22*, 907–924. (p. 124)

Baumann, J., & DeSteno, D. (2010). Emotion guided threat detection: Expecting guns where there are none. *Journal of Personality and Social Psychology, 99*, 595–610. (p. 198)

Baumeister, R. F. (1996). Should schools try to boost self-esteem? Beware the dark side. *American Educator, 20*, 43. (p. 489)

Baumeister, R. F. (2000). Gender differences in erotic plasticity: The female sex drive as socially flexible and responsive. *Psychological Bulletin, 126*, 347–374. (p. 179)

Baumeister, R. F. (2001). Violent pride: Do people turn violent because of self-hate, or self-love? *Scientific American, 17*, 96–101. (p. 488)

Baumeister, R. F. (2005). *The cultural animal: Human nature, meaning, and social life.* New York: Oxford University Press. (p. 421)

Baumeister, R. F. (2006). Violent pride. *Scientific American Mind, 17*, 54–59. (p. 486)

Baumeister, R. F. (2010). *Is there anything good about men?: How cultures flourish by exploiting men.* New York: Oxford University Press. (p. 163)

Baumeister, R. F. (2015). Toward a general theory of motivation: Problems, challenges, opportunities, and the big picture. *Motivation and Emotion, 40*, 1–10. (p. 349)

Baumeister, R. F., & Bratslavsky, E. (1999). Passion, intimacy, and time: Passionate love as a function of change in intimacy. *Personality and Social Psychology Review, 3*, 49–67. (p. 452)

Baumeister, R. F., Bratslavsky, E., Muraven, M., & Tice, D. M. (1998a). Ego depletion: Is the active self a limited resource? *Journal of Personality and Social Psychology, 74*, 1252–1265. (p. 398)

Baumeister, R. F., Catanese, K. R., & Vohs, K. D. (2001). Is there a gender difference in strength of sex drive? Theoretical views, conceptual distinctions, and a review of relevant evidence. *Personality and Social Psychology Review, 5*, 242–273. (p. 183)

Baumeister, R. F., Dale, K., & Sommer, K. L. (1998b). Freudian defense mechanisms and empirical findings in modern personality and social psychology: Reaction formation, projection, displacement, undoing, isolation, sublimation, and denial. *Journal of Personality, 66*, 1081–1125. (p. 470)

Baumeister, R. F., & Leary, M. R. (1995). The need to belong: Desire for interpersonal attachments as a fundamental human motivation. *Psychological Bulletin, 117*, 497–529. (p. 352)

Baumeister, R. F., & Tice, D. M. (1986). How adolescence became the struggle for self: A historical transformation of psychological development. In J. Suls & A. G. Greenwald (Eds.), *Psychological perspectives on the self* (Vol. 3, pp. 183–201). Hillsdale, NJ: Erlbaum. (p. 149)

Baumeister, R. F., & Vohs, K. D. (2016). Strength model of self-regulation as limited resource: Assessment, controversies, update. *Advances in Experimental Social Psychology, 54*, 67–127. (p. 398)

Baumgardner, A. H., Kaufman, C. M., & Levy, P. E. (1989). Regulating affect interpersonally: When low esteem leads to greater enhancement. *Journal of Personality and Social Psychology, 56*, 907–921. (p. 487)

Baumrind, D. (1966). Effects of authoritative parental control on child behavior. *Child Development*, 887–907. (pp. 138, 139)

Baumrind, D. (1967). Child care practices anteceding three patterns of preschool behavior. *Genetic Psychology Monographs, 75*, 43–88. (p. 138)

Baumrind, D. (1996). The discipline controversy revisited. *Family Relations, 45*, 405–414.

Baumrind, D. (2013). Is a pejorative view of power assertion in the socialization process justified? *Review of General Psychology, 17*, 420–427. (p. 139)

Baumrind, D., Larzelere, R. E., & Cowan, P. A. (2002). Ordinary physical punishment: Is it harmful? Comment on Gershoff (2002). *Psychological Bulletin, 128*, 602–611. (p. 250)

Baur, E., Forsman, M., Santtila, P., Johansson, A., Sandnabba, K., & Långström, N. (2016). Paraphilic sexual interests and sexually coercive behavior: A population-based twin study. *Archives of Sexual Behavior, 45*, 1163–1172. (p. 175)

Bavelier, D., Newport, E. L., & Supalla, T. (2003). Children need natural languages, signed or spoken. *Cerebrum, 5*, 19–32. (p. 313)

Bavelier, D., Tomann, A., Hutton, C., Mitchell, T., Corina, D., Liu, G., & Neville, H. (2000). Visual attention to the periphery is enhanced in congenitally deaf individuals. *Journal of Neuroscience, 20*, 1–6. (p. 39)

Baxter, M. G., & Burwell, R. D. (2017). Promoting transparency and reproducibility in *Behavioral Neuroscience:* Publishing replications, registered reports, and null results. *Behavioral Neuroscience, 131*, 275–276. (p. 20)

Beam, C. R., Emery, R. E., Reynolds, C. A., Gatz, M., Turkheimer, R., & Pedersen, N. L. (2016). Widowhood and the stability of late life depressive symptomatology in the Swedish Adoption Twin Study of Aging. *Behavior Genetics, 46*, 100–113. (p. 353)

Beaman, A. L., & Klentz, B. (1983). The supposed physical attractiveness bias against supporters of the women's movement: A meta-analysis. *Personality and Social Psychology Bulletin, 9*, 544–550. (p. 450)

Beames, J. R., Schofield, T. P., & Denson, T. F. (2017). A meta-analysis of improving self-control with practice. In D. T. D. de Ridder, M. A. Adriaanse, & K. Fujita (Eds.), *Handbook of self-control in health and well-being.* New York: Routledge. (p. 398)

Bearzi, M., & Stanford, C. (2010). A bigger, better brain. *American Scientist, 98*, 402–409. (p. 310)

Beauchamp, G. K. (1987). The human preference for excess salt. *American Scientist, 75*, 27–33. (p. 363)

Beauvois, J.-L., Courbet, D., & Oberlé, D. (2012). The prescriptive power of the television host: A transposition of Milgram's obedience paradigm to the context of TV game show. *European Review of Applied Psychology/Revue Européenne De Psychologie Appliquée, 62*, 111–119. (p. 426)

Beck, A. T., & Bredemeier, K. (2016). A unified model of depression: Integrating clinical, cognitive, biological, and evolutionary perspectives. *Clinical Psychological Science, 4,* 596–619. (p. 514)

Beck, A. T., Rush, A. J., Shaw, B. F., & Emery, G. (1979). *Cognitive therapy of depression.* New York: Guilford Press. (p. 544)

Becker, D. V., Kenrick, D. T., Neuberg, S. L., Blackwell, K. C., & Smith, D. M. (2007). The confounded nature of angry men and happy women. *Journal of Personality and Social Psychology, 92,* 179–190. (p. 377)

Becker, J. E., Maley, C., Shultz, E., & Taylor, W. D. (2016). Update on transcranial magnetic stimulation for depression and other neuropsychiatric illnesses. *Psychiatric Annals, 46,* 637–641. (p. 564)

Becker, M., Cortina, K. S., Tsai, Y., & Eccles, J. S. (2014). Sexual orientation, psychological well-being, and mental health: A longitudinal analysis from adolescence to young adulthood. *Psychology of Sexual Orientation and Gender Diversity, 1,* 132–145. (p. 179)

Becklen, R., & Cervone, D. (1983). Selective looking and the noticing of unexpected events. *Memory and Cognition, 11,* 601–608. (p. 82)

Beeman, M. J., & Chiarello, C. (1998). Complementary right- and left-hemisphere language comprehension. *Current Directions in Psychological Science, 7,* 2–8. (p. 67)

Bègue, L., Bushman, B. J., Giancola, P. R., Subra, B., & Rosset, E. (2010). "There is no such thing as an accident," especially when people are drunk. *Personality and Social Psychology Bulletin, 36,* 1301–1304. (p. 442)

Bègue, L., Subra, B., Arvers, P., Muller, D., Bricout, V., & Zorman, M. (2009). A message in a bottle: Extrapharmacological effects of alcohol on aggression. *Journal of Experimental Social Psychology, 45,* 137–142. (p. 442)

Beilin, H. (1992). Piaget's enduring contribution to developmental psychology. *Developmental Psychology, 28,* 191–204. (p. 130)

Beilock, S. (2010). *Choke: What the secrets of the brain reveal about getting it right when you have to.* New York: Free Press. (p. 305)

Beintner, I., Jacobi, C., & Taylor, C. B. (2012). Effects of an internet-based prevention programme for eating disorders in the USA and Germany: A meta-analytic review. *European Eating Disorders Review, 20,* 1–8. (p. 533)

Bell, A. P., Weinberg, M. S., & Hammersmith, S. K. (1981). *Sexual preference: Its development in men and women.* Bloomington: Indiana University Press. (p. 180)

Belluck, P. (2013, February 5). People with mental illness more likely to be smokers, study finds. *The New York Times* (nytimes.com). (p. 26)

Belot, M., & Francesconi, M. (2006, November). *Can anyone be "the one"? Evidence on mate selection from speed dating.* London: Centre for Economic Policy Research (cepr.org). (p. 449)

Belsky, D. W., Moffitt, T. E., Corcoran, D. L., Domingue, B., Harrington, H., Hogan, S., . . . Poulton, R. (2016). The genetics of success: How single-nucleotide polymorphisms associated with educational attainment relate to life-course development. *Psychological Science, 27,* 957–972. (p. 336)

Belson, K. (2015, September 6). No foul mouths on this field: Football with a New Age twist. *The New York Times* (nytimes.com). (p. B-9)

Belson, K. (2017, September 21). Aaron Hernandez had severe C.T.E. when he died at age 27. *The New York Times* (nytimes.com). (p. 503)

Bem, D., Tressoldi, P. E., Rabeyron, T., & Duggan, M. (2014, April 11). *Feeling the future: A meta-analysis of 90 experiments on the anomalous anticipation of random future events.* Retrieved from papers.ssrn.com/sol3/papers.cfm?abstract_id=2423692 (p. 231)

Bem, D. J. (1984). Quoted in *The Skeptical Inquirer, 8,* 194. (p. 231)

Bem, D. J. (2011). Feeling the future: Experimental evidence for anomalous retroactive influences on cognition and affect. *Journal of Personality and Social Psychology, 100,* 407–425. (p. 231)

Bem, S. L. (1987). Masculinity and femininity exist only in the mind of the perceiver. In J. M. Reinisch, L. A. Rosenblum, & S. A. Sanders (Eds.), *Masculinity/femininity: Basic perspectives* (pp. 304–311). New York: Oxford University Press. (p. 169)

Bem, S. L. (1993). *The lenses of gender: Transforming the debate on sexual inequality.* New Haven, CT: Yale University Press. (p. 169)

Benartzi, S., Beshears, J., Milkman, K. L., Sunstein, C. R., Thaler, R. H., Shankar, M., . . . Galing, S. (2017). Should governments invest more in nudging? *Psychological Science, 28,* 1041–1055. (p. 304)

Bench, S. W., Rivera, G. N., Schlegel, R. J., Hicks, J. A., & Lench, H. C. (2017). Does expertise matter in replication? An examination of the reproducibility project. *Journal of Experimental Social Psychology, 68,* 181–184. (p. 20)

Bender, T. W., Anestis, M. D., Anestis, J. C., Gordon, K. H., & Joiner, T. E. (2012). Affective and behavioral paths toward the acquired capacity for suicide. *Journal of Social and Clinical Psychology, 31,* 81–100. (p. 500)

Benedict, C., Brooks, S. J., O'Daly, O. G., Almen, M. S., Morell, A., Aberg, K., . . . Schiöth, H. B. (2012). Acute sleep deprivation enhances the brain's response to hedonic food stimuli: An fMRI study. *Journal of Clinical Endocrinology and Metabolism, 97,* 2011–2759. (p. 93)

Benjamin, D. J., Bergerg, J. O., Johannesson, M., Nosek, B. A., Wagenmakers, E.-J., Berk, R., . . . Johnson, V. E. (2018). Redefine statistical significance. *Nature Human Behaviour, 2,* 6–10. (p. A-7)

Benjamin, L. T., Jr., & Simpson, J. A. (2009). The power of the situation: The impact of Milgram's obedience studies on personality and social psychology. *American Psychologist, 64,* 12–19. (p. 425)

Benjamins, M. R., Ellison, C. G., & Rogers, R. G. (2010). Religious involvement and mortality risk among pre-retirement aged U.S. adults. In C. E. Ellison & R. A. Hummer (Eds.), *Religion, families, and health: Population-based research in the United States.* New Brunswick, NJ: Rutgers University Press. (p. 405)

Bennett, W. I. (1995). Beyond overeating. *New England Journal of Medicine, 332,* 673–674. (p. 366)

Ben-Shakhar, G., & Elaad, E. (2003). The validity of psychophysiological detection of information with the guilty knowledge test: A meta-analytic review. *Journal of Applied Psychology, 88,* 131–151. (p. 374)

Bensley, D. A., Lilienfeld, S. O., & Powell, L. A. (2014). A new measure of psychological misconceptions: Relations with academic background, critical thinking, and acceptance of paranormal and pseudoscientific claims. *Learning and Individual Differences, 36,* 9–18. (p. 3)

Bentley, K. H., Nock, M. K., & Barlow, D. H. (2014). The four-function model of nonsuicidal self-injury: Key directions for future research. *Clinical Psychological Science, 2,* 638–656. (p. 502)

Berg, J. M., Wall, M., Larson, N., Eisenberg, M. E., Loth, K. A., & Neumark-Sztainer, D. (2014). The unique and additive associations of family functioning and parenting practices with disordered eating behaviors in diverse adolescents. *Journal of Behavioral Medicine, 37,* 205–217. (p. 532)

Bergelson, E., & Swingley, D. (2012). At 6–9 months, human infants know the meanings of many common nouns. *PNAS, 109,* 3253–3258. (p. 314)

Bergelson, E., & Swingley, D. (2013). The acquisition of abstract words by young infants. *Cognition, 127,* 391–397. (p. 314)

Bergen, B. K. (2014). Universal grammar. Response to 2014 Edge question: What scientific idea is ready for retirement? *The Edge* (edge.org). (p. 313)

Berk, L. E. (1994, November). Why children talk to themselves. *Scientific American,* pp. 78–83. (p. 130)

Berk, L. S., Felten, D. L., Tan, S. A., Bittman, B. B., & Westengard, J. (2001). Modulation of neuroimmune parameters during the eustress of humor-associated mirthful laughter. *Alternative Therapies, 7,* 62–76. (p. 399)

Berken, J. A., Gracco, V. L., Chen, J., Soles, J., Watkins, K. E., Baum, S., . . . Klein, D. (2015). Neural activation in speech production and reading aloud in native and non-native languages. *NeuroImage, 112,* 208–217. (p. 317)

Berkman, E. T., Hutcherson, C. A., Livingston, J. L., Kahn, L. E., & Inzlicht, M. (2017). Self-control as a value-based choice. *Current Directions in Psychological Science.* Advance online publication. doi:10.17605/OSF.IO/N4YY2 (p. 145)

Berkovich-Ohana, A., Glickson, J., & Goldstein, A. (2014). Studying the default mode and its mindfulness-induced changes using EEF functional connectivity. *Social Cognitive and Affective Neuroscience, 9,* 1616–1624. (p. 404)

Berkowitz, L. (1983). Aversively stimulated aggression: Some parallels and differences in research with animals and humans. *American Psychologist, 38,* 1135–1144. (p. 442)

Berkowitz, L. (1989). Frustration-aggression hypothesis: Examination and reformulation. *Psychological Bulletin, 106,* 59–73. (p. 442)

Berman, M. G., Jonides, J., & Kaplan, S. (2008). The cognitive benefits of interacting with nature. *Psychological Science, 19,* 1207–1212. (p. 357)

Bernieri, F., Davis, J., Rosenthal, R., & Knee, C. (1994). Interactional synchrony and rapport: Measuring synchrony in displays devoid of sound and facial affect. *Personality and Social Psychology Bulletin, 20,* 303–311. (p. 260)

Bernstein, D. M., & Loftus, E. F. (2009a). The consequences of false memories for food preferences and choices. *Perspectives on Psychological Science, 4,* 135–139. (p. 290)

Bernstein, D. M., & Loftus, E. F. (2009b). How to tell if a particular memory is true or false. *Perspectives on Psychological Science, 4,* 370–374. (p. 289)

Bernstein, M. J., Young, S. G., & Claypool, H. M. (2010). Is Obama's win a gain for Blacks? Changes in implicit racial prejudice following the 2008 election. *Social Psychology, 41,* 147–151. (p. 436)

Berntson, G. G., Norman, G. J., Bechara, A., Bruss, J., Tranel, D., & Cacioppo, J. T. (2011). The insula and evaluative processes. *Psychological Science, 22,* 80–86. (p. 55)

Berridge, K. C., Robinson, T. E., & Aldridge, J. W. (2009). Dissecting components of reward: "liking", "wanting", and learning. *Current Opinion in Pharmacology, 9,* 65–73. (p. 102)

Berry, C. M., & Zhao, P. (2015). Addressing criticisms of existing predictive bias research: Cognitive ability test scores still overpredict African Americans' job performance. *Journal of Applied Psychology, 100,* 162–179. (p. 343)

Berscheid, E. (1981). An overview of the psychological effects of physical attractiveness and some comments upon the psychological effects of knowledge of the effects of physical attractiveness. In G. W. Lucker, K. Ribbens, & J. A. McNamara (Eds.), *Psychological aspects of facial form* (Craniofacial Facial Growth Series). Ann Arbor: Center for Human Growth and Development, University of Michigan. (p. 449)

Berscheid, E. (1985). Interpersonal attraction. In G. Lindzey & E. Aronson (Eds.), *The handbook of social psychology.* New York: Random House. (p. 352)

Berscheid, E. (2010). Love in the fourth dimension. *Annual Review of Psychology, 61,* 1–25. (p. 451)

Berscheid, E., Gangestad, S. W., & Kulakowski, D. (1984). Emotion in close relationships: Implications for relationship counseling. In S. D. Brown & R. W. Lent (Eds.), *Handbook of counseling psychology.* New York: Wiley. (p. 451)

Berti, A., Cottini, G., Gandola, M., Pia, L., Smania, N., Stracciari, A., . . . Paulesu, E. (2005). Shared cortical anatomy for motor awareness and motor control. *Science, 309,* 488–491. (p. 67)

Bértolo, H. (2005). Visual imagery without visual perception? *Psicológica, 26,* 173–188. (p. 97)

Bertrand, M., & Mullainathan, S. (2003). *Are Emily and Greg more employable than Lakisha and Jamal? A field experiment on labor market discrimination.* Massachusetts Institute of Technology, Department of Economics, Working Paper 03–22. (p. 437)

Bhatt, R. S., Wasserman, E. A., Reynolds, W. F., Jr., & Knauss, K. S. (1988). Conceptual behavior in pigeons: Categorization of both familiar and novel examples from four classes of natural and artificial stimuli. *Journal of Experimental Psychology: Animal Behavior Processes, 14,* 219–234. (p. 245)

Bialystok, E. (2017). The bilingual adaptation: How minds accommodate experience. *Psychological Bulletin, 143,* 233–262. (p. 320)

Bialystok, E., Kroll, J. F., Green, D. W., MacWhinney, B., & Craik, F. I. M. (2015). Publication bias and the validity of evidence: What's the connection? *Psychological Science, 26,* 944–946. (p. 320)

Bianconi, E., Piovesan, A., Facchin, F., Beraudi, A., Casadei, R., Frabetti, F., . . . Canaider, S. (2013). An estimation of the number of cells in the human body. *Annals of Human Biology, 40,* 463–471. (p. 119)

Bick, J., Fox, N., Zeanah, C., & Nelson, C. A. (2015). Early deprivation, atypical brain development, and internalizing symptoms in late childhood. *Neuroscience.* Advance online publication. doi:10.1016/j.neuroscience.2015.09.026 (p. 137)

Bienvenu, O. J., Davydow, D. S., & Kendler, K. S. (2011). Psychiatric "diseases" versus behavioral disorders and degree of genetic influence. *Psychological Medicine, 41,* 33–40. (p. 518)

Bilefsky, D. (2009, March 10). Europeans debate castration of sex offenders. *The New York Times* (nytimes.com). (p. 174)

Billock, V. A., & Tsou, B. H. (2012). Elementary visual hallucinations and their relationships to neural pattern-forming mechanisms. *Psychological Bulletin, 138,* 744–774. (p. 108)

Binet, A. (1909). Les idées modernes sur les enfants [Modern ideas about children]. Paris: Flammarion. Quoted in A. Clarke & A. Clarke (2006), Born to be bright. *The Psychologist, 19,* 409. (p. 328)

Bird, C. D., & Emery, N. J. (2009). Rooks use stones to raise the water level to reach a floating worm. *Current Biology, 19,* 1410–1414. (p. 309)

Birkeland, M. S., Blix, I., Solberg, Ø., & Heir, T. (2016). Does optimism act as a buffer against posttraumatic stress over time? A longitudinal study of the protective role of optimism after the 2011 Oslo bombing. *Psychological Trauma.* Advance online publication. dx.doi.org/10.1037/tra0000188 (p. 409)

Birnbaum, G. E., & Reis, H. T. (2012). When does responsiveness pique sexual interest? Attachment and sexual desire in initial acquaintanceships. *Personality and Social Psychology Bulletin, 38,* 946–958. (p. 450)

Birnbaum, G. E., Reis, H. T., Mikulincer, M., Gillath, O., & Orpaz, A. (2006). When sex is more than just sex: Attachment orientations, sexual experience, and relationship quality. *Journal of Personality and Social Psychology, 91,* 929–943. (p. 136)

Biro, D., Humle, T., Koops, K., Sousa, C., Hayashi, M., & Matsuzawa, T. (2010). Chimpanzee mothers at Bossou, Guinea carry the mummified remains of their dead infants. *Current Biology, 20,* R351–R352. (p. 310)

Biro, F. M., Galvez, M. P., Greenspan, L. C., Succop, P. A., Vangeepuram, N., Pinney, S. M., . . . Wolff, M. S. (2010). Pubertal assessment method and baseline characteristics in a mixed longitudinal study of girls. *Pediatrics, 126,* e583–e590. doi:10.1542/peds.2009-3079. (p. 167)

Biro, F. M., Greenspan, L. C., & Galvez, M. P. (2012). Puberty in girls of the 21st century. *Journal of Pediatric and Adolescent Gynecology, 25,* 289–294. (p. 167)

Bishop, D. I., Weisgram, E. S., Holleque, K. M., Lund, K. E., & Wheeler, J. R. (2005). Identity development and alcohol consumption: Current and retrospective self-reports by college students. *Journal of Adolescence, 28,* 523–533. (p. 147)

Bishop, G. D. (1991). Understanding the understanding of illness: Lay disease representations. In J. A. Skelton & R. T. Croyle (Eds.), *Mental representation in health and illness.* New York: Springer-Verlag. (p. 298)

Bjork, E. L., & Bjork, R. (2011). Making things hard on yourself, but in a good way: Creating desirable difficulties to enhance learning. In M. A. Gernsbacher, M. A. Pew, L. M. Hough, & J. R. Pomerantz (Eds.), *Psychology and the real world* (pp. 55–64). New York: Worth. (p. 35)

Bjork, R. (2011, January 20). Quoted by P. Belluck, To really learn, quit studying and take a test. *The New York Times* (nytimes.com). (p. 273)

Bjorklund, D. F., & Green, B. L. (1992). The adaptive nature of cognitive immaturity. *American Psychologist, 47,* 46–54. (p. 130)

BJS. (2017). *Data collection: National Crime Victimization Survey (NCVS).* Retrieved from Bureau of Justice Statistics (bjs.gov/index.cfm?ty=dcdetail&iid=245). (p. 18)

Black, M. C., Basile, K. C., Breiding, M. J., Smith, S. G., Walters, M. L., Merrick, M. T., . . . Stevens, M. R. (2011). *The National Intimate Partner and Sexual Violence Survey (NISVS): 2010 summary report.* Atlanta, GA: National Center for Injury Prevention and Control, Centers for Disease Control and Prevention. (p. 170)

Blackhart, G. C., Nelson, B. C., Knowles, M. L., & Baumeister, R. F. (2009). Rejection elicits emotional reactions but neither causes immediate distress nor lowers self-esteem: A meta-analytic review of 192 studies on social exclusion. *Personality and Social Psychology Bulletin, 13,* 269–309. (p. 353)

Blake, A., Nazarian, M., & Castel, A. (2015). The Apple of the mind's eye: Everyday attention, metamemory, and reconstructive memory for the Apple logo. *Quarterly Journal of Experimental Psychology, 68,* 858–865. (p. 285)

Blake, W. (2013, March). Voices from solitary: A sentence worse than death. Essay published at *Solitary Watch, News from a Nation in Lockdown* (solitarywatch.com). (p. 354)

Blakemore, S.-J. (2008). Development of the social brain during adolescence. *Quarterly Journal of Experimental Psychology, 61,* 40–49. (p. 142)

Blakemore, S.-J., Wolpert, D. M., & Frith, C. D. (1998). Central cancellation of self-produced tickle sensation. *Nature Neuroscience, 1,* 635–640. (. 221)

Blakeslee, S. (2006, January 10). Cells that read minds. *The New York Times* (nytimes.com). (p. 259)

Blanchard, R. (2004). Quantitative and theoretical analyses of the relation between older brothers and homosexuality in men. *Journal of Theoretical Biology, 230,* 173–187. (p. 181)

Blanchard, R. (2008a). Review and theory of handedness, birth order, and homosexuality in men. *Laterality, 13,* 51–70. (p. 181)

Blanchard, R. (2008b). Sex ratio of older siblings in heterosexual and homosexual, right-handed and non-right-handed men. *Archives of Sexual Behavior, 37,* 977–981. (p. 181)

Blanchard, R. (2014). Detecting and correcting for family size differences in the study of sexual orientation and fraternal birth order. *Archives of Sexual Behavior, 43,* 845–852. (p. 181)

Blanchard-Fields, F. (2007). Everyday problem solving and emotion: An adult developmental perspective. *Current Directions in Psychological Science, 16,* 26–31. (p. 334)

Blanke, O. (2012). Multisensory brain mechanisms of bodily self-consciousness. *Nature Reviews Neuroscience, 13,* 556–571. (p. 81)

Blascovich, J., & Mendes, W. B. (2010). Social psychophysiology and embodiment. In S. T. Fiske, D. T. Gilbert, & G. Lindzey (Eds.), *The handbook of social psychology,* 5th ed. (pp. 194–227). New York: Wiley. (p. 385)

Blasi, D. E., Wichmann, S., Hammarström, H., Stadler, P. F., & Christiansen, M. H. (2016). Sound-meaning association biases evidenced across thousands of languages. *PNAS, 113,* 10818–10823. (p. 313)

Blass, T. (1996). Stanley Milgram: A life of inventiveness and controversy. In G. A. Kimble, C. A. Boneau, & M. Wertheimer (Eds.), *Portraits of pioneers in psychology* (Vol. II). Washington, DC, and Mahwah, NJ: American Psychological Association and Lawrence Erlbaum. (p. 427)

Blass, T. (1999). The Milgram paradigm after 35 years: Some things we now know about obedience to authority. *Journal of Applied Social Psychology, 29,* 955–978. (p. 426)

Blease, C. R. (2015). Too many "friends," too few "likes"? Evolutionary psychology and "Facebook depression." *Review of General Psychology, 19,* 1–13. (p. 355)

Blechert, J., Testa, G., Georgii, C., Klimesch, W., & Wilhelm, F. H. (2016). The Pavlovian craver: Neural and experiential correlates of single trial naturalistic food conditioning in humans. *Physiology & Behavior, 158,* 18–25. (p. 241)

Bleidorn, W., Arslan, R. C., Denissen, J. J. A., Rentfrow, P. J., Gebauer, J. E., Potter, J., & Gosling, S. D. (2016). Age and gender differences in self-esteem—a cross-cultural window. *Journal of Personality and Social Psychology, 111,* 396–410. (p. 486)

Blinkhorn, V., Lyons, M., & Almond, L. (2015). The ultimate femme fatale: Narcissism predicts serious and aggressive sexually coercive behavior in females. *Personality and Individual Differences, 87,* 219–223. (p. 488)

Bloom, B. C. (Ed.). (1985). *Developing talent in young people.* New York: Ballantine. (p. 357)

Bloom, P. (2000). *How children learn the meanings of words.* Cambridge, MA: MIT Press. (p. 313)

Blow, C. M. (2015, March 26). Officers' race matters less than you think. *The New York Times* (nytimes.com). (p. 436)

BLS. (2011, June 22). *American time use survey summary.* Bureau of Labor Statistics (bls.gov). (p. 422)

BLS. (2017). *Labor force statistics from the Current Population Survey.* Retrieved from Bureau of Labor Statistics (data.bls.gov/timeseries/LNS14000000). (p. 18)

Blum, D. (2011). Love at Goon Park: Harry Harlow and the science of affection (2nd edition). New York: Perseus. (p. 134)

Blum, K., Cull, J. G., Braverman, E. R., & Comings, D. E. (1996). Reward deficiency syndrome. *American Scientist, 84,* 132–145. (p. 56)

Blumenstein, B., & Orbach, I. (2012). *Mental practice in sport: Twenty case studies.* New York: Novinka/Nova Science. (p. 321)

Boag, S. (2006). Freudian repression, the common view, and pathological science. *Review of General Psychology, 10,* 74–86. (p. 469)

Boccardi, M., Frisoni, G. B., Hare, R. D., Cavedo, E., Najt, P., Pievani, M., . . . Tiihonen, J. (2011). Cortex and amygdala morphology in psychopathy. *Psychiatry Research: Neuroimaging, 193,* 85–92. (p. 55)

Bock, L. (2013, June 19). Interview by Adam Bryant, "In head-hunting, big data may not be such a big deal." *The New York Times* (nytimes.com). (p. B-5)

Bocklandt, S., Horvath, S., Vilain, E., & Hamer, D. H. (2006). Extreme skewing of X chromosome inactivation in mothers of homosexual men. *Human Genetics, 118,* 691–694. (p. 181)

Bockting, W. O. (2014). Transgender identity development. In D. L. Tolman & L. M. Diamond (Eds.), *APA handbook of sexuality and psychology: Vol. 1. Person-based approaches* (pp. 739–758). Washington, DC: American Psychological Association. (p. 170)

Bodenhausen, G. V., Sheppard, L. A., & Kramer, G. P. (1994). Negative affect and social judgment: The differential impact of anger and sadness. *European Journal of Social Psychology, 24,* 45–62. (p. 459)

Bodenmann, G., Meuwly, N., Germann, J., Nussbeck, F. W., Heinrichs, M., & Bradbury, T. N. (2015). Effects of stress on the social support provided by men and women in intimate relationships. *Psychological Science, 26,* 1584–1594. (p. 388)

Bodkin, J. A., & Amsterdam, J. D. (2002). Transdermal selegiline in major depression: A double-blind, placebo-controlled, parallel-group study in outpatients. *American Journal of Psychiatry, 159,* 1869–1875. (p. 561)

Boecker, H., Sprenger, T., Spilker, M. E., Henriksen, G., Koppenhoefer, M., Wagner, K. J., . . . Tolle, T. R. (2008). The runner's high: Opioidergic mechanisms in the human brain. *Cerebral Cortex, 18,* 2523–2531. (pp. 43, 519)

Boehm, J. K., & Kubzansky, L. D. (2012). The heart's content: The association between positive psychological well-being and cardiovascular health. *Psychological Bulletin, 138,* 655–691. (p. 398)

Boehm, J. K., Trudel-Fitzgerald, C., Kivimaki, M., & Kubzansky, L. D. (2015). The prospective association between positive psychological well-being and diabetes. *Health Psychology, 34,* 1013–1021. (p. 407)

Boehm-Davis, D. A. (2005). Improving product safety and effectiveness in the home. In R. S. Nickerson (Ed.), *Reviews of human factors and ergonomics.* Volume 1. Santa Monica, CA: Human Factors and Ergonomics Society, pp. 219–253. (p. B-12)

Boenigk, S., & Mayr, M. L. (2016). The happiness of giving: Evidence from the German socioeconomic panel that happier people are more generous. *Journal of Happiness Studies, 17,* 1825–1846. (p. 407)

Boesch-Achermann, H., & Boesch, C. (1993). Tool use in wild chimpanzees: New light from dark forests. *Current Directions in Psychological Science, 2,* 18–21. (p. 309)

Bogaert, A. F. (2003). Number of older brothers and sexual orientation: New texts and the attraction/behavior distinction in two national probability samples. *Journal of Personality and Social Psychology, 84,* 644–652. (p. 181)

Bogaert, A. F. (2004). Asexuality: Prevalence and associated factors in a national probability sample. *Journal of Sex Research, 41,* 279–287. (p. 172)

Bogaert, A. F. (2006). Biological versus nonbiological older brothers and men's sexual orientation. *PNAS, 103,* 10771–10774. (p. 182)

Bogaert, A. F. (2015). Asexuality: What it is and why it matters. *Journal of Sex Research, 52,* 362–379. (p. 172)

Boggiano, A. K., Harackiewicz, J. M., Bessette, M. M., & Main, D. S. (1985). Increasing children's interest through performance-contingent reward. *Social Cognition, 3,* 400–411. (p. 358)

Bohannon, J. (2016). Government "nudges" prove their worth. *Science, 352,* 1042. (p. 304)

Bohlken, M. M., Brouwer, R. M., Mandl, R. C. W., Van, d. H., Hedman, A. M., De Hert, M., . . . Hulshoff Pol, H. E. (2016). Structural brain connectivity as a genetic marker for schizophrenia. *JAMA Psychiatry, 73,* 11–19. (p. 525)

Bohman, M., & Sigvardsson, S. (1990). Outcome in adoption: Lessons from longitudinal studies. In D. Brodzinsky & M. Schechter (Eds.), *The psychology of adoption* (pp. 93–106). New York: Oxford University Press. (p. 73)

Bois, C., Levita, L., Ripp, I., Owens, D. C. G., Johnstone, E. C., Whalley, H. C., & Lawrie, S. M. (2016). Longitudinal changes in hippocampal volume in the Edinburgh High Risk Study of Schizophrenia. *Schizophrenia Research, 173,* 146–151. (p. 525)

Bolger, N., DeLongis, A., Kessler, R. C., & Schilling, E. A. (1989). Effects of daily stress on negative mood. *Journal of Personality and Social Psychology, 57,* 808–818. (p. 408)

Bolmont, M., Cacioppo, J. T., & Cacioppo, S. (2014). Love is in the gaze: An eyetracking study of love and sexual desire. *Psychological Science, 25,* 1748–1756. (p. 375)

Boly, M., Garrido, M. I., Gosseries, O., Bruno, M.-A., Boveroux, P., Schnakers, C., . . . Friston, K. (2011). Preserved feed-forward but impaired top-down processes in the vegetative state. *Science, 332,* 858–862. (p. 81)

Bonanno, G. A. (2004). Loss, trauma, and human resilience: Have we underestimated the human capacity to thrive after extremely aversive events? *American Psychologist, 59,* 20–28. (pp. 160, 509)

Bonanno, G. A. (2005). Adult resilience to potential trauma. *Current Directions in Psychological Science, 14,* 135–137. (p. 509)

Bonanno, G. A., Brewin, C. R., Kaniasty, K., & La Greca, A. M. (2010). Weighing the costs of disaster: Consequences, risks, and resilience in individuals, families, and communities. *Psychological Science in the Public Interest, 11,* 1–49. (p. 510)

Bonanno, G. A., Galea, S., Bucciarelli, A., & Vlahov, D. (2006). Psychological resilience after disaster. *Psychological Science, 17,* 181–186. (p. 510)

Bonanno, G. A., Galea, S., Bucciarelli, A., & Vlahov, D. (2007). What predicts psychological resilience after disaster? The role of demographics, resources, and life stress. *Journal of Consulting and Clinical Psychology, 75,* 671–682. (p. 567)

Bonanno, G. A., & Kaltman, S. (1999). Toward an integrative perspective on bereavement. *Psychological Bulletin, 125,* 760–777. (p. 159)

Bonanno, G. A., Kennedy, P., Galatzer-Levy, I. R., Lude, P., & Elfström, M. L. (2012). Trajectories of resilience, depression, and anxiety following spinal cord injury. *Rehabilitation Psychology, 57,* 236–247. (p. 567)

Bonanno, G. A., Westphal, M., & Mancini, A. D. (2011). Resilience to loss and potential trauma. *Annual Review of Clinical Psychology, 11,* 511–535. (p. 509)

Bond, C. F., Jr., & DePaulo, B. M. (2006). Accuracy of deception judgments. *Personality and Social Psychology Review, 10,* 214–234. (p. 376)

Bond, M. H., Lun, V. M.-C., Chan, J., Chan, W. W.-Y., & Wong, D. (2012). Enacting modesty in Chinese culture: The joint contribution of personal characteristics and contextual features. *Asian Journal of Social Psychology, 15,* 14–25. (p. 490)

Bond, R., & Smith, P. B. (1996). Culture and conformity: A meta-analysis of studies using Asch's (1952b, 1956) line judgment task. *Psychological Bulletin, 119,* 111–137. (p. 425)

Bonezzi, A., Brendl, C. M., & DeAngelis, M. (2011). Stuck in the middle: The psychophysics of goal pursuit. *Psychological Science, 22,* 607–612. (p. 357)

Bonfils, K. A., Lysaker, P. H., Minor, K. S., & Salyers, M. P. (2016). Affective empathy in schizophrenia: A meta-analysis. *Schizophrenia Research, 175,* 109–117. (p. 523)

Bono, J. E., & Judge, T. A. (2004). Personality and transformational and transactional leadership: A meta-analysis. *Journal of Applied Psychology, 89,* 901–910. (p. B-10)

Bonos, L. (2018, March 8). A legislator has a bill to ban *The Bachelor's* Arie Luyendyk Jr. from Minnesota. *The Washington Post* (washingtonpost.com). (p. 31)

Boone, A. P., & Hegarty, M. (2017). Sex differences in mental rotation tasks: Not just in the mental rotation process! *Journal of Experimental Psychology: Learning, Memory, and Cognition, 43,* 1005–1019. (p. 182)

Bora, E., & Pantelis, C. (2013). Theory of mind impairments in first-episode psychosis, individuals at ultra-high risk for psychosis and in first-degree relatives of schizophrenia: Systematic review and meta-analysis. *Schizophrenia Research, 144,* 31–36. (p. 523)

Borges, G., Bagge, C. L., Cherpitel, C. J., Conner, K. R., Orozco, R., & Rossow, I. (2017). A meta-analysis of acute use of alcohol and the risk of suicide attempt. *Psychological Medicine, 47,* 949–957. (p. 500)

Boring, E. G. (1930). A new ambiguous figure. *American Journal of Psychology, 42,* 444–445. (p. 195)

Bornstein, M. H., Cote, L. R., Maital, S., Painter, K., Park, S.-Y., Pascual, L., . . . Vyt, A. (2004). Cross-linguistic analysis of vocabulary in young children: Spanish, Dutch, French, Hebrew, Italian, Korean, and American English. *Child Development, 75,* 1115–1139. (p. 313)

Bornstein, M. H., Tal, J., Rahn, C., Galperin, C. Z., Pecheux, M.-G., Lamour, M., . . . Tamis-LeMonda, C. S. (1992a). Functional analysis of the contents of maternal speech to infants of 5 and 13 months in four cultures: Argentina, France, Japan, and the United States. *Developmental Psychology, 28,* 593–603. (p. 117)

Bornstein, M. H., Tamis-LeMonda, C. S., Tal, J., Ludemann, P., Toda, S., Rahn, C. W., . . . Vardi, D. (1992b). Maternal responsiveness to infants in three societies: The United States, France, and Japan. *Child Development, 63,* 808–821. (p. 117)

Bornstein, R. F. (1989). Exposure and affect: Overview and meta-analysis of research, 1968–1987. *Psychological Bulletin, 106,* 265–289. (pp. 133, 447)

Bornstein, R. F. (1999). Source amnesia, misattribution, and the power of unconscious perceptions and memories. *Psychoanalytic Psychology, 16,* 155–178. (p. 447)

Bornstein, R. F., Galley, D. J., Leone, D. R., & Kale, A. R. (1991). The temporal stability of ratings of parents: Test-retest reliability and influence of parental contact. *Journal of Social Behavior and Personality, 6,* 641–649. (p. 281)

Boroditsky, L. (2009, June 12). How does our language shape the way we think? *The Edge* (edge.org). (pp. 312, 320)

Boroditsky, L. (2011, February). How language shapes thought. *Scientific American,* pp. 63–65. (p. 319)

Bos, H. M. W., Knox, J. R., van Rijn-van Gelderen, L., & Gartrell, N. K. (2016). Same-sex and different-sex parent households and child health outcomes: Findings from the national survey of children's health. *Journal of Developmental and Behavioral Pediatrics, 37,* 179–187. (p. 180)

Bosma, H., Marmot, M. G., Hemingway, H., Nicolson, A. C., Brunner, E., & Stansfeld, S. A. (1997). Low job control and risk of coronary heart disease in Whitehall II (prospective cohort) study. *British Medical Journal, 314,* 558–565. (p. 396)

Bosma, H., Peter, R., Siegrist, J., & Marmot, M. (1998). Two alternative job stress models and the risk of coronary heart disease. *American Journal of Public Health, 88,* 68–74. (p. 396)

Bostean, G., & Gillespie, B. J. (2017). Acculturation, acculturative stressors, and family relationships among Latina/o immigrants. *Cultural Diversity and Ethnic Minority Psychology.* Advance online publication. http://dx.doi.org/10.1037/cdp0000169 (p. 385)

Bostwick, J. M., Pabbati, C., Geske, J. R., & McKean, A. J. (2016). Suicide attempt as a risk factor for completed suicide: Even more lethal than we knew. *The American Journal of Psychiatry, 173,* 1094–1100. (p. 501)

Bostwick, J. M., & Pankratz, V. S. (2000). Affective disorders and suicide risk: A re-examination. *American Journal of Psychiatry, 157,* 1925–1932. (p. 500)

Bosworth, R. G., & Dobkins, K. R. (1999). Left-hemisphere dominance for motion processing in deaf signers. *Psychological Science, 10,* 256–262. (p. 64)

Bothwell, R. K., Brigham, J. C., & Malpass, R. S. (1989). Cross-racial identification. *Personality and Social Psychology Bulletin, 15,* 19–25. (p. 439)

Bouchard, T. J., Jr. (2009). Genetic influences on human intelligence (Spearman's *g*): How much? *Annals of Human Biology, 36,* 527–544. (p. 72)

Boucher, J., Mayes, A., & Bigham, S. (2012). Memory in autistic spectrum disorder. *Psychological Bulletin, 138,* 458–496. (p. 131)

Bowden, E. M., & Beeman, M. J. (1998). Getting the right idea: Semantic activation in the right hemisphere may help solve insight problems. *Psychological Science, 9,* 435–440. (p. 67)

Bower, B. (2009, February 14). The dating go round. *Science News,* pp. 22–25. (p. 448)

Bower, G. H. (1986). Prime time in cognitive psychology. In P. Eelen (Ed.), *Cognitive research and behavior therapy: Beyond the conditioning paradigm.* Amsterdam: North Holland Publishers. (p. 280)

Bower, G. H., Clark, M. C., Lesgold, A. M., & Winzenz, D. (1969). Hierarchical retrieval schemes in recall of categorized word lists. *Journal of Verbal Learning and Verbal Behavior, 8,* 323–343. (p. 272)

Bower, G. H., & Morrow, D. G. (1990). Mental models in narrative comprehension. *Science, 247,* 44–48. (p. 274)

Bower, J. M., & Parsons, L. M. (2003, August). Rethinking the "lesser brain." *Scientific American,* pp. 50–57. (p. 55)

Bowers, J. S. (2009). On the biological plausibility of grandmother cells: Implications for neural network theories in psychology and neuroscience. *Psychological Review, 116,* 220–251. (p. 206)

Bowers, J. S. (2016). The practical and principled problems with educational neuroscience. *Psychological Review.* Advance online publication. dx.doi.org/10.1037/rev0000025. (p. 52)

Bowers, J. S., Mattys, S. L., & Gage, S. H. (2009). Preserved implicit knowledge of a forgotten childhood language. *Psychological Science, 20,* 1064–1069. (p. 125)

Bowker, E., & Dorstyn, D. (2016). Hypnotherapy for disability-related pain: A meta-analysis. *Journal of Health Psychology, 21,* 526–539. (p. 224)

Bowling, N. A., Eschleman, K. J., & Wang, Q. (2010). A meta-analytic examination of the relationship between job satisfaction and subjective well-being. *Journal of Occupational and Organizational Psychology, 83,* 915–934. (p. B-8)

Boxer, P., Huesmann, L. R., Bushman, B. J., O'Brien, M., & Moceri, D. (2009). The role of violent media preference in cumulative developmental risk for violence and general aggression. *Journal of Youth and Adolescence, 38,* 417–428. (p. 263)

Boyatzis, C. J. (2012). Spiritual development during childhood and adolescence. In L. J. Miller (Ed.), *The Oxford handbook of psychology and spirituality* (pp. 151–164). New York: Oxford University Press. (p. 143)

Boyatzis, C. J., Matillo, G. M., & Nesbitt, K. M. (1995). Effects of the "Mighty Morphin Power Rangers" on children's aggression with peers. *Child Study Journal, 25,* 45–55. (p. 263)

Boyce, C. J., & Wood, A. M. (2011). Personality prior to disability determines adaptation: Agreeable individuals recover lost life satisfaction faster and more completely. *Psychological Science, 22,* 1397–1402. (p. 408)

Boyce, C. J., Wood, A. M., Daly, M., & Sedikides, C. (2015). Personality change following unemployment. *Journal of Applied Psychology, 100,* 991–1011. (p. 480)

Boyce, R., Glasgow, S. D., Williams, S., & Adamantidis, A. (2016). Causal evidence for the role of REM sleep theta rhythm in contextual memory consolidation. *Science, 352,* 812–816. (p. 92)

Boynton, R. M. (1979). *Human color vision.* New York: Holt, Rinehart & Winston. (p. 204)

Braden, J. P. (1994). *Deafness, deprivation, and IQ.* New York: Plenum. (p. 342)

Bradley, D. R., Dumais, S. T., & Petry, H. M. (1976). Reply to Cavonius. *Nature, 261,* 78. (p. 207)

Bradley, R. B., Binder, E. B., Epstein, M. P., Tang, Y., Nair, H. P., Liu, W., . . . Ressler, K. J. (2008). Influence of child abuse on adult depression: Moderation by the corticotropin-releasing hormone receptor gene. *Archives of General Psychiatry, 65,* 190–200. (p. 138)

Bradshaw, C., Sawyer, A., & O'Brennan, L. (2009). A social disorganization perspective on bullying-related attitudes and behaviors: The influence of school context. *American Journal of Community Psychology, 43,* 204–220. (p. 13)

Brady, W. J., Wills, J. A., Jost, J. T., Tucker, J. A., & Van Bavel, J. J. (2017). Emotion shapes the diffusion of moralized content in social networks. *PNAS, 114,* 7313–7318. (p. 19)

Braiker, B. (2005, October 18). A quiet revolt against the rules on SIDS. *The New York Times* (nytimes.com). (p. 124)

Brainerd, C. J. (1996). Piaget: A centennial celebration. *Psychological Science, 7,* 191–195. (p. 125)

Brand, B. L., Sar, V., Stavropoulos, P., Krüger, C., Korzekwa, M., Martínez-Taboas, A., & Middleton, W. (2016). Separating fact from fiction: An empirical examination of six myths about dissociative identity disorder. *Harvard Review of Psychiatry, 24,* 257–270. (p. 529)

Brandon, S., Boakes, J., Glaser, D., & Green, R. (1998). Recovered memories of childhood sexual abuse: Implications for clinical practice. *British Journal of Psychiatry, 172,* 294–307. (p. 293)

Brang, D., Edwards, L., Ramachandran, V. S., & Coulson, S. (2008). Is the sky 2? Contextual priming in grapheme-color synaesthesia. *Psychological Science, 19,* 421–428. (p. 229)

Brannan, D., Biswas-Diener, R., Mohr, C., Mortazavi, S., & Stein, N. (2013). Friends and family: A cross-cultural investigation of social support and subjective well-being among college students. *Journal of Positive Psychology, 8,* 65–75. (p. 399)

Bransford, J. D., & Johnson, M. K. (1972). Contextual prerequisites for understanding: Some investigations of comprehension and recall. *Journal of Verbal Learning and Verbal Behavior, 11,* 717–726. (p. 273)

Brasel, S. A., & Gips, J. (2011). Media multitasking behavior: Concurrent television and computer usage. *Cyberpsychology, Behavior, and Social Networking, 14,* 527–534. (p. 82)

Braun, S. (1996). New experiments underscore warnings on maternal drinking. *Science, 273,* 738–739. (p. 120)

Braun, S. (2001, April). Seeking insight by prescription. *Cerebrum,* pp. 10–21. (p. 107)

Braunstein, G. D., Sundwall, D. A., Katz, M., Shifren, J. L., Buster, J. E., Simon, J. A., . . . Watts, N. B. (2005). Safety and efficacy of a testosterone patch for the treatment of hypoactive sexual desire disorder in surgically menopausal women: A randomized, placebo-controlled trial. *Archives of Internal Medicine, 165,* 1582–1589. (p. 173)

Bray, D. W., & Byham, W. C. (1991, Winter). Assessment centers and their derivatives. *Journal of Continuing Higher Education,* pp. 8–11. (p. 484)

Bray, D. W., & Byham, W. C., interviewed by Mayes, B. T. (1997). Insights into the history and future of assessment centers: An interview with Dr. Douglas W. Bray and Dr. William Byham. *Journal of Social Behavior and Personality, 12,* 3–12. (p. 484)

Brayne, C., Spiegelhalter, D. J., Dufouil, C., Chi, L.-Y., Dening, T. R., Paykel, E. S., . . . Huppert, F. A. (1999). Estimating the true extent of cognitive decline in the old old. *Journal of the American Geriatrics Society, 47,* 1283–1288. (p. 332)

Breedlove, S. M. (1997). Sex on the brain. *Nature, 389,* 801. (p. 180)

Brehm, S., & Brehm, J. W. (1981). *Psychological reactance: A theory of freedom and control.* New York: Academic Press. (p. 428)

Brennan, Z. (2010, April 8). The Goering who saved Jews: While Hermann masterminded the Final Solution his brother Albert rescued Gestapo victims. *Daily Mail* (dailymail.co.uk). (p. 73)

Breslau, J., Aguilar-Gaxiola, S., Borges, G., Kendler, K. S., Su, M., & Kessler, R. C. (2007). Risk for psychiatric disorder among immigrants and their US-born descendants. *Journal of Nervous and Mental Disease, 195,* 189–195. (p. 503)

Breslin, C. W., & Safer, M. A. (2011). Effects of event valence on long-term memory for two baseball championship games. *Psychological Science, 22,* 1408–1412. (p. 278)

Brethel-Haurwitz, K. M., & Marsh, A. A. (2014, March). Geographical differences in subjective well-being predict extraordinary altruism. *Psychological Science, 25,* 762–771. (p. 407)

Brewer, C. L. (1996). Personal communication. (p. 10)

Brewer, M. B., & Chen, Y.-R. (2007). Where (who) are collectives in collectivism? Toward conceptual clarification of individualism and collectivism. *Psychological Review, 114,* 133–151. (p. 490)

Brewer, W. F. (1977). Memory for the pragmatic implications of sentences. *Memory & Cognition, 5,* 673–678. (p. 274)

Brewin, C. R., & Andrews, B. (2017). Creating memories for false autobiographical events in childhood: A systematic review. *Applied Cognitive Psychology, 31,* 2–23. (pp. 290, 294)

Brewin, C. R., Andrews, B., Rose, S., & Kirk, M. (1999). Acute stress disorder and posttraumatic stress disorder in victims of violent crime. *American Journal of Psychiatry, 156,* 360–366. (p. 509)

Brewin, C. R., Kleiner, J. S., Vasterling, J. J., & Field, A. P. (2007). Memory for emotionally neutral information in posttraumatic stress disorder: A meta-analytic investigation. *Journal of Abnormal Psychology, 116,* 448–463. (p. 277)

Briscoe, D. (1997, February 16). Women lawmakers still not in charge. *The Grand Rapids Press,* p. A23. (p. 168)

Brislin, R. W. (1988). Increasing awareness of class, ethnicity, culture, and race by expanding on students' own experiences. In I. Cohen (Ed.), *The G. Stanley Hall lecture series.* Washington, DC: American Psychological Association. (p. 421)

Broadbent, E., Kakokehr, A., Booth, R. J., Thomas, J., Windsor, J. A., Buchanan, C. M., . . . Hill, A. G. (2012). A brief relaxation intervention reduces stress and improves surgical wound healing response: A randomized trial. *Brain, Behavior, and Immunity, 26,* 212–217. (p. 404)

Brodbeck, F. C., Chhokar, J. S., & House, R. J. (2008). Culture and leadership in 25 societies: Integration, conclusions, and future directions. In J. S. Chhokar, F. C. Brodbeck & R. J. House (Eds.), *Culture and leadership across the world: The GLOBE book of in-depth studies of 25 societies,* pp. 1023–1099. Mahwah, NJ: Lawrence Erlbaum, Mahwah, NJ. (p. B-12)

Brody, S., & Tillmann, H. C. (2006). The post-orgasmic prolactin increase following intercourse is greater than following masturbation and suggests greater satiety. *Biological Psychology, 71,* 312–315. (p. 185)

Brooks, R. (2012). "Asia's missing women" as a problem in applied evolutionary psychology? *Evolutionary Psychology, 12,* 910–925. (p. 437)

Brooks, S. (2015). Does personal social media usage affect efficiency and well-being? *Computers in Human Behavior, 46,* 26–37. (p. 356)

Brown, A. S., Begg, M. D., Gravenstein, S., Schaefer, C. A., Wyatt, R. J., Bresnahan, M., . . . Susser, E. S. (2004). Serologic evidence of prenatal influenza in the etiology of schizophrenia. *Archives of General Psychiatry, 61,* 774–780. (p. 525)

Brown, A. S., & Marsh, E. (2009). Creating illusions of past encounter through brief exposure. *Psychological Science, 20,* 534–538. (p. 291)

Brown, A. S., & Patterson, P. H. (2011). Maternal infection and schizophrenia: Implications for prevention. *Schizophrenia Bulletin, 37,* 284–290. (p. 525)

Brown, A. S., Schaefer, C. A., Wyatt, R. J., Goetz, R., Begg, M. D., Gorman, J. M., & Susser, E. S. (2000). Maternal exposure to respiratory infections and adult schizophrenia spectrum disorders: A prospective birth cohort study. *Schizophrenia Bulletin, 26,* 287–295. (p. 525)

Brown, E. L., & Deffenbacher, K. (1979). *Perception and the senses.* New York: Oxford University Press. (p. 220)

Brown, J. A. (1958). Some tests of the decay theory of immediate memory. *Quarterly Journal of Experimental Psychology, 10,* 12–21. (p. 271)

Brown, J. D. (2012). Understanding the better than average effect: Motives (still) matter. *Personality and Social Psychology Bulletin, 38,* 209–219. (p. 488)

Brown, K. W., Goodman, R. J., & Inzlicht, M. (2013). Dispositional mindfulness and the attenuation of neural responses to emotional stimuli. *Social Cognitive and Affective Neuroscience, 8,* 93–99. (p. 404)

Brown, P. C., Roediger, H. L., III, & McDaniel, M. A. (2014). *Make it stick: The science of successful learning.* Cambridge, MA: Harvard University Press. (pp. 272, 556)

Brown, R. (1986). Linguistic relativity. In S. H. Hulse & B. F. Green, Jr. (Eds.), *One hundred years of psychological research in America.* Baltimore: Johns Hopkins University Press. (p. 319)

Brown, R. P., Osterman, L. L., & Barnes, C. D. (2009). School violence and the culture of honor. *Psychological Science, 20,* 1400–1405. (p. 443)

Brown, S. L., Brown, R. M., House, J. S., & Smith, D. M. (2008). Coping with spousal loss: Potential buffering effects of self-reported helping behavior. *Personality and Social Psychology Bulletin, 34,* 849–861. (p. 160)

Brown, S. L., Stykes, J. B., & Manning, W. D. (2016). Trends in children's family instability, 1995–2010. *Journal of Marriage and Family, 78,* 1173–1183. (pp. 136, 404)

Browning, C. (1992). *Ordinary men: Reserve Police Battalion 101 and the final solution in Poland.* New York: HarperCollins. (p. 427)

Browning, R. (1868). *The ring and the book. IV—Tertium quid.* New York: Thomas Y. Crowell. (p. 454)

Bruck, M., & Ceci, S. J. (1999). The suggestibility of children's memory. *Annual Review of Psychology, 50,* 419–439. (p. 292)

Bruck, M., & Ceci, S. J. (2004). Forensic developmental psychology: Unveiling four common misconceptions. *Current Directions in Psychological Science, 15,* 229–232. (p. 292)

Bruer, J. T. (1999). *The myth of the first three years: A new understanding of early brain development and lifelong learning.* New York: Free Press. (p. 339)

Brummelman, E., Thomaes, S., Nelemans, S. A., Orobio de Castro, B., Overbeek, G., & Bushman, B. J. (2015). Origins of narcissism in children. *PNAS, 112,* 3659–3662. (pp. 138, 489)

Brunner, M., Gogol, K. M., Sonnleitner, P., Keller, U., Krauss, S., & Preckel, F. (2013). Gender differences in the mean level, variability, and profile shape of student achievement: Results from 41 countries. *Intelligence, 41,* 378–395. (p. 340)

Bruno, M.-A., Bernheim, J. L., Ledoux, D., Pellas, F., Demertzi, A., & Laureys, S. (2011). A survey on self-assessed well-being in a cohort of chronic locked-in syndrome patients: Happy majority, miserable minority. *BMJ Open, 1,* e000039. (p. 409)

Bruno, M.-A., Pellas, F., & Laureys, S. (2008). Quality of life in locked-in syndrome survivors. In J. L. Vincent (Ed.), *2008 yearbook of intensive care and emergency medicine.* New York: Springer. (p. 409)

Brunoni, A. R., Chaimani, A., Moffa, A. H., Razza, L. B., Gattaz, W. F., Daskalakis, Z. J., & Carvalho, A. F. (2017). Repetitive transcranial magnetic stimulation for the acute treatment of major depressive episodes: A systematic review with network meta-analysis. *JAMA Psychiatry, 74,* 143–152. (p. 564)

Brunoni, A. R., Moffa, A. H., Fregni, F., Palm, U., Padberg, F., Blumberger, D. M., . . . Loo, C. K. (2016). Transcranial direct current stimulation for acute major depressive episodes: Meta-analysis of individual patient data. *The British Journal of Psychiatry, 208,* 522–531. (p. 563)

Bryan, A. D., Gillman, A. S., & Hansen, N. S. (2016). Changing the context is important and necessary, but not sufficient, for reducing adolescent risky sexual behavior: A reply to Steinberg (2015). *Perspectives on Psychological Science, 11,* 535–538. (p. 178)

Bryan, A. E. B., & Arkowitz, H. (2015). Meta-analysis of the effects of peer-administered psychosocial interventions on symptoms of depression. *American Journal of Community Psychology, 55,* 455–471. (p. 556)

Bryant, A. N., & Astin, H. A. (2008). The correlates of spiritual struggle during the college years. *Journal of Higher Education, 79,* 1–27. (p. 146)

Bub, K. L., Robinson, L. E., & Curtis, D. S. (2016). Longitudinal associations between self-regulation and health across childhood and adolescence. *Health Psychology, 35,* 1235–1245. (p. 398)

Buchanan, R. W., Kreyenbuhl, J., Kelly, D. L., Noel, J. M., Boggs, D. L., Fischer, B. A., . . . Keller, W. (2010). The 2009 schizophrenia PORT psychopharmacological treatment recommendations and summary statements. *Schizophrenia Bulletin, 36,* 71–93. (p. 560)

Buchanan, T. W. (2007). Retrieval of emotional memories. *Psychological Bulletin, 133,* 761–779. (p. 277)

Buck, L. B., & Axel, R. (1991). A novel multigene family may encode odorant receptors: A molecular basis for odor recognition. *Cell, 65,* 175–187. (p. 226)

Buckels, E. E., Trapnell, P. D., & Paulhus, D. L. (2014). Trolls just want to have fun. *Personality and Individual Differences, 67,* 97–102. (p. 430)

Buckholtz, J. W., Treadway, M. T., Cowan, R. L., Woodward, N. D., Benning, S. D., Li, R., . . . Zald, D. H. (2010). Mesolimbic dopamine reward system hypersensitivity in individuals with psychopathic traits. *Nature Neuroscience, 13,* 419–421. (p. 531)

Buckingham, M. (2007). *Go put your strengths to work: 6 powerful steps to achieve outstanding performance.* New York: Free Press. (p. B-2)

Buckingham, M., & Clifton, D. O. (2001). *Now, discover your strengths.* New York: Free Press. (p. B-2)

Buehler, R., Griffin, D., & Ross, M. (1994). Exploring the "planning fallacy": Why people underestimate their task completion times. *Journal of Personality and Social Psychology, 67,* 366–381. (p. 303)

Buehler, R., Griffin, D., & Ross, M. (2002). Inside the planning fallacy: The causes and consequences of optimistic time predictions. In T. Gilovich, D. Griffin, & D. Kahneman (Eds.), *Heuristics and biases: The psychology of intuitive judgment.* Cambridge: Cambridge University Press. (p. 303)

Buffardi, L. E., & Campbell, W. K. (2008). Narcissism and social networking web sites. *Personality and Social Psychology Bulletin, 34,* 1303–1314. (p. 356)

Bugental, D. B. (1986). Unmasking the "polite smile": Situational and personal determinants of managed affect in adult-child interaction. *Personality and Social Psychology Bulletin, 12,* 7–16. (p. 376)

Buhle, J. T., Silvers, J. A., Wager, T. D., Lopez, R., Onyemekwu, C., Kober, H., . . . Ochsner, K. N. (2014). Cognitive reappraisal of emotion: A meta-analysis of human neuroimaging studies. *Cerebral Cortex, 24,* 2981–2990. (p. 371)

Buhle, J. T., Stevens, B. L., Friedman, J. J., & Wager, T. D. (2012). Distraction and placebo: Two separate routes to pain control. *Psychological Science, 23,* 246–253. (p. 224)

Buka, S. L., Tsuang, M. T., Torrey, E. F., Klebanoff, M. A., Wagner, R. L., & Yolken, R. H. (2001). Maternal infections and subsequent psychosis among offspring. *Archives of General Psychiatry, 58,* 1032–1037. (p. 525)

Bullock, B., & Murray, G. (2014). Reduced amplitude of the 24-hour activity rhythm: A biomarker of vulnerability to bipolar disorder? *Clinical Psychological Science, 2,* 86–96. (p. 516)

Bunde, J., & Suls, J. (2006). A quantitative analysis of the relationship between the Cook-Medley Hostility Scale and traditional coronary artery disease risk factors. *Health Psychology, 25,* 493–500. (p. 391)

Buquet, R. (1988). Le rêve et les déficients visuels [Dreams and the visually impaired]. *Psychanalyse-a-l'Universite, 13,* 319–327. (p. 97)

Burger, J. M. (2009). Replicating Milgram: Would people still obey today? *American Psychologist, 64,* 1–11. (p. 426)

Burger, J. M., Bender, T. J., Day, L., DeBolt, J. A., Guthridge, L., How, H. W., . . . Taylor, S. (2015). The power of one: The relative influence of helpful and selfish models. *Social Influence, 10,* 77–84. (p. 261)

Buri, J. R., Louiselle, P. A., Misukanis, T. M., & Mueller, R. A. (1988). Effects of parental authoritarianism and authoritativeness on self-esteem. *Personality and Social Psychology Bulletin, 14,* 271–282. (p. 139)

Burish, T. G., & Carey, M. P. (1986). Conditioned aversive responses in cancer chemotherapy patients: Theoretical and developmental analysis. *Journal of Counseling and Clinical Psychology, 54,* 593–600. (p. 255)

Burk, W. J., Denissen, J., Van Doorn, M. D., Branje, S. J. T., & Laursen, B. (2009). The vicissitudes of conflict measurement: Stability and reliability in the frequency of disagreements. *European Psychologist, 14,* 153–159. (p. 147)

Burke, D. M., & Shafto, M. A. (2004). Aging and language production. *Current Directions in Psychological Science, 13,* 21–24. (p. 154)

Burkhauser, R. V., De Neve, J.-E., & Powdthavee, N. (2016, January). *Top incomes and human well-being around the world.* London School of Economic and Political Science: Centre for Economic Performance, CEP Discussion Paper No. 1400. (p. 410)

Burlingame, G. M., Seebeck, J. D., Janis, R. A., Whitcomb, K. E., Barkowski, S., Rosendahl, J., & Strauss, B. (2016). Outcome differences between individual and group formats when identical and nonidentical treatments, patients, and doses are compared: A 25-year meta-analytic perspective. *Psychotherapy, 53,* 446–461. (p. 547)

Burns, B. C. (2004). The effects of speed on skilled chess performance. *Psychological Science, 15,* 442–447. (p. 305)

Burrell, B. D. (2015). Genius in a jar: The bizarre journey of Einstein's brain illustrates the pitfalls in science's search for the origins of brilliance. *Scientific American, 313,* 82–87. (p. 63)

Burris, C. T., & Branscombe, N. R. (2005). Distorted distance estimation induced by a self-relevant national boundary. *Journal of Experimental Social Psychology, 41,* 305–312. (p. 320)

Burrow, A. L., Hill, P. L., & Sumner, R. (2016). Leveling mountains: Purpose attenuates links between perceptions of effort and steepness. *Personality and Social Psychology Bulletin, 42,* 94–103. (p. 197)

Burt, M. R. (1980). Cultural myths and supports for rape. *Journal of Personality and Social Psychology, 38,* 217–230. (p. 170)

Burton, C. M., & King, L. A. (2008). Effects of (very) brief writing on health: The two-minute miracle. *British Journal of Health Psychology, 13,* 9–14. (p. 401)

Busby, D. M., Carroll, J. S., & Willoughby, B. J. (2010). Compatibility or restraint? The effects of sexual timing on marriage relationships. *Journal of Family Psychology, 24,* 766–774. (p. 186)

Bushdid, C., Magnasco, M. O., Vosshall, L. B., & Keller, A. (2014). Humans can discriminate more than 1 trillion olfactory stimuli. *Science, 343,* 1370–1372. (p. 226)

Bushman, B. J. (1993). Human aggression while under the influence of alcohol and other drugs: An integrative research review. *Current Directions in Psychological Science, 2,* 148–152. (p. 442)

Bushman, B. J. (2002). Does venting anger feed or extinguish the flame? Catharsis, rumination, distraction, anger, and aggressive responding. *Personality and Social Psychology Bulletin, 28,* 724–731. (p. 393)

Bushman, B. J. (2016). Violent media and hostile appraisals: A meta-analytic review. *Aggressive Behavior, 42,* 605–613. (p. 445)

Bushman, B. J., & Anderson, C. A. (2009). Comfortably numb: Desensitizing effects of violent media on helping others. *Psychological Science, 20,* 273–277. (p. 263)

Bushman, B. J., & Baumeister, R. F. (1998). Threatened egotism, narcissism, self-esteem, and direct and displaced aggression: Does self-love or self-hate lead to violence? *Journal of Personality and Social Psychology, 75,* 219–229. (p. 488)

Bushman, B. J., Baumeister, R. F., Thomaes, S., Ryu, E., Begeer, S., & West, S. G. (2009). Looking again, and harder, for a link between low self-esteem and aggression. *Journal of Personality, 77,* 427–446. (p. 488)

Bushman, B. J., Bonacci, A. M., van Dijk, M., & Baumeister, R. F. (2003). Narcissism, sexual refusal, and aggression: Testing a narcissistic reactance model of sexual coercion. *Journal of Personality and Social Psychology, 84,* 1027–1040. (p. 488)

Bushman, B. J., DeWall, C. N., Pond, R. S., Jr., & Hanus, M. D. (2014). Low glucose relates to greater aggression in married couples. *PNAS, 111,* 6254–6257. (p. 442)

Bushman, B. J., Gollwitzer, M., & Cruz, C. (2015). There is broad consensus: Media researchers agree that violent media increase aggression in children, and pediatricians and parents concur. *Psychology of Popular Media Culture, 4,* 200–214. (p. 262)

Bushman, B. J., & Huesmann, L. R. (2010). Aggression. In S. T. Fiske, D. T. Gilbert, & G. Lindzey (Eds.), *Handbook of social psychology* (5th ed., pp. 833–863). New York: Wiley. (p. 163)

Bushman, B. J., Moeller, S. J., & Crocker, J. (2011). Sweets, sex, or self-esteem? Comparing the value of self-esteem boosts with other pleasant rewards. *Journal of Personality, 79,* 993–1012. (p. 472)

Bushman, B. J., Ridge, R. D., Das, E., Key, C. W., & Busath, G. L. (2007). When God sanctions killing: Effects of scriptural violence on aggression. *Psychological Science, 18,* 204–207. (p. 163)

Buss, A. H. (1989). Personality as traits. *American Psychologist, 44,* 1378–1388. (p. 481)

Buss, D. M. (1994). The strategies of human mating: People worldwide are attracted to the same qualities in the opposite sex. *American Scientist, 82,* 238–249. (p. 184)

Buss, D. M. (1995). Evolutionary psychology: A new paradigm for psychological science. *Psychological Inquiry, 6,* 1–30. (p. 184)

Buss, D. M. (2008). *Female sexual psychology.* Retrieved from edge.org/q2008/q08_12. html#buss (p. 176)

Buster, J. E., Kingsberg, S. A., Aguirre, O., Brown, C., Breaux, J. G., Buch, A., . . . Casson, P. (2005). Testosterone patch for low sexual desire in surgically menopausal women: A randomized trial. *Obstetrics and Gynecology, 105,* 944–952. (p. 173)

Butler, A., Oruc, I., Fox, C. J., & Barton, J. J. S. (2008). Factors contributing to the adaptation aftereffects of facial expression. *Brain Research, 1191,* 116–126. (p. 195)

Butler, R. A. (1954, February). Curiosity in monkeys. *Scientific American,* pp. 70–75. (p. 349)

Butts, M. M., Casper, W. J., & Yang, T. S. (2013). How important are work-family support policies? A meta-analytic investigation of their effects on employee outcomes. *Journal of Applied Psychology, 98,* 1–25. (p. B-11)

Buxton, O. M., Cain, S. W., O'Connor, S. P., Porter, J. H., Duffy, J. F., Wang, W., . . . Shea, S. A. (2012). Adverse metabolic consequences in humans of prolonged sleep restriction combined with circadian disruption. *Science Translational Medicine, 4,* 129–143. (p. 93)

Byck, R., & Van Dyke, C. (1982, March). Cocaine. *Scientific American,* pp. 128–141. (p. 107)

Byers-Heinlein, K., Burns, T. C., & Werker, J. F. (2010). The roots of bilingualism in newborns. *Psychological Science, 21,* 343–348. (p. 120)

Byrc, K., Durand, E. Y., Macpherson, J. M., Reich, D., & Mountain, J. L. (2015). The genetic ancestry of African Americans, Latinos, and European Americans across the United States. *American Journal of Human Genetics 96,* 37–53. (p. 342)

Byrd, A. L., & Manuck, S. B. (2014). MAOA, childhood maltreatment, and antisocial behavior: Meta-analysis of a gene-environment interaction. *Biological Psychiatry, 75,* 9–17. (p. 483)

Byrne, D. (1971). *The attraction paradigm.* New York: Academic Press. (p. 450)

Byrne, D. (1982). Predicting human sexual behavior. In A. G. Kraut (Ed.), *The G. Stanley Hall Lecture Series* (Vol. 2, pp. 211–254). Washington, DC: American Psychological Association. (pp. 173, 238)

Byrne, R. W. (1991, May/June). Brute intellect. *The Sciences,* pp. 42–47. (p. 317)

Byrne, R. W., Bates, L. A., & Moss, C. J. (2009). Elephant cognition in primate perspective. *Comparative Cognition & Behavior Reviews, 4,* 1–15. (p. 310)

Byrne, R. W., & Whiten, A. (1988). Toward the next generation in data quality: A new survey of primate tactical deception. *Behavioral and Brain Sciences, 11,* 267–273. (p. 22)

Byron, K., & Khazanchi, S. (2011). A meta-analytic investigation of the relationship of state and trait anxiety to performance on figural and verbal creative tasks. *Personality and Social Psychology Bulletin, 37,* 269–283. (p. 307)

Cable, D. M., & Gilovich, T. (1998). Looked over or overlooked? Prescreening decisions and post-interview evaluations. *Journal of Personality and Social Psychology, 83,* 501–508. (p. B-5)

Cacioppo, J. T., Cacioppo, S., Capitanio, J. P., & Cole, S. W. (2015). The neuroendocrinology of social isolation. *Annual Review of Psychology, 66,* 733–767. (p. 353)

Cacioppo, J. T., Cacioppo, S., Gonzaga, G. C., Ogburn, E. L., & VanderWeele, T. J. (2013). Marital satisfaction and break-ups differ across on-line and off-line meeting venues. *PNAS, 110,* 10135–10140. (p. 448)

Cacioppo, S., Bianchi-Demicheli, F., Frum, C., Pfaus, J. G., & Lewis, J.W. (2012). The common neural bases between sexual desire and love: A multilevel kernel density fMRI analysis. *Journal of Sexual Medicine, 12,* 1048–1054. (p. 186)

Cacioppo, S., Capitanio, J. P., & Cacioppo, J. T. (2014). Toward a neurology of loneliness. *Psychological Bulletin, 140,* 1464–1504. (p. 399)

Caddick, A., & Porter, L. E. (2012). Exploring a model of professionalism in multiple perpetrator violent crime in the UK. *Criminological and Criminal Justice, 12,* 61–82. (p. 163)

Cain, S. (2012). *Quiet: The power of introverts in a world that can't stop talking.* New York: Crown. (p. 476)

Calati, R., De Ronchi, D., Bellini, M., & Serretti, A. (2011). The 5-HTTLPR polymorphism and eating disorders: A meta-analysis. *International Journal of Eating Disorders, 44,* 191–199. (p. 532)

Caldwell, J. A. (2012). Crew schedules, sleep deprivation, and aviation performance. *Current Directions in Psychological Science, 21,* 85–89. (p. 93)

Cale, E. M., & Lilienfeld, S. O. (2002). Sex differences in psychopathy and antisocial personality disorder: A review and integration. *Clinical Psychology Review, 22,* 1179–1207. (p. 530)

Caliskan, A., Bryson, J. J., & Narayanan, A. (2017). Semantics derived automatically from language corpora contain human-like biases. *Science, 356,* 183–186. (p. 436)

Callaghan, T., Rochat, P., Lillard, A., Claux, M. L., Odden, H., Itakura, S., . . . Singh, S. (2005). Synchrony in the onset of mental-state reasoning. *Psychological Science, 16,* 378–384. (p. 128)

Callan, M. J., Shead, N. W., & Olson, J. M. (2011). Personal relative deprivation, delay discounting, and gambling. *Journal of Personality and Social Psychology, 101,* 955–973. (p. 145)

Calvert, S. L., Appelbaum, M., Dodge, K. A., Graham, S., Nagayama Hall, G. C., Hamby, S., . . . Hedges, L. V. (2017). The American Psychological Association Task Force assessment of violent video games: Science in the service of public interest. *American Psychologist, 72,* 126–143. (p. 444)

Calvin, C. M., Batty, G. D., Der, G., Brett, C. E., Taylor, A., Pattie, A., . . . Deary, I. J. (2017). Childhood intelligence in relation to major causes of death in 68 year follow-up: Prospective population study. *BMJ: British Medical Journal, 357,* 13 (j2708). (p. 333)

Calvo-Merino, B., Glaser, D. E., Grèzes, J., Passingham, R. E., & Haggard, P. (2004). Action observation and acquired motor skills: An fMRI study with expert dancers. *Cerebral Cortex, 15,* 1243–1249. (p. 321)

Camerer, C. F., Loewenstein, G., & Weber, M. (1989). The curse of knowledge in economic settings: An experimental analysis. *Journal of Political Economy, 97,* 1232–1254. (p. B-13)

Camp, J. P., Skeem, J. L., Barchard, K., Lilienfeld, S. O., & Poythress, N. G. (2013). Psychopathic predators? Getting specific about the relation between psychopathy and violence. *Journal of Consulting and Clinical Psychology, 81,* 467–480. (p. 530)

Campbell, A. (2010). Oxytocin and human social behavior. *Personality and Social Psychology Review, 14,* 281–205. (p. 399)

Campbell, D. T. (1975). On the conflicts between biological and social evolution and between psychology and moral tradition. *American Psychologist, 30,* 1103–1126. (p. 410)

Campbell, D. T., & Specht, J. C. (1985). Altruism: Biology, culture, and religion. *Journal of Social and Clinical Psychology, 3,* 33–42. (p. 473)

Campbell, L., & Marshall, T. (2011). Anxious attachment and relationship processes: An interactionist perspective. *Journal of Personality, 79,* 1219–1249. (p. 483)

Campbell, M. W., & de Waal, F. B. M. (2011). Ingroup-outgroup bias in contagious yawning by chimpanzees supports link to empathy. *PLoS ONE, 6,* e18283. (p. 438)

Campbell, S. (1986). *The Loch Ness Monster: The evidence.* Wellingborough, England: Aquarian Press. (p. 196)

Camperio-Ciani, A., Corna, F., & Capiluppi, C. (2004). Evidence for maternally inherited factors favouring male homosexuality and promoting female fecundity. *Proceedings of the Royal Society of London B, 271,* 2217–2221. (p. 181)

Camperio-Ciani, A., Lemmola, F., & Blecher, S. R. (2009). Genetic factors increase fecundity in female maternal relatives of bisexual men as in homosexuals. *Journal of Sexual Medicine, 6,* 449–455. (p. 181)

Camperio-Ciani, A., & Pellizzari, E. (2012). Fecundity of paternal and maternal non-parental female relatives of homosexual and heterosexual men. *PLoS ONE, 7,* e51088. (p. 181)

Campitelli, G., & Gobet, F. (2011). Deliberate practice: Necessary but not sufficient. *Current Directions in Psychological Science, 20,* 280–285. (p. 326)

Campos, J. J., Bertenthal, B. I., & Kermoian, R. (1992). Early experience and emotional development: The emergence of wariness and heights. *Psychological Science, 3,* 61–64. (p. 209)

Canavello, A., & Crocker, J. (2017). Compassionate goals and affect in social situations. *Motivation and Emotion, 41,* 158–179. (p. 352)

Canetta, S., Sourander, A., Surcel, H., Hinkka-Yli-Salomäki, S., Leiviskä, J., Kellendonk, C., . . . Brown, A. S. (2014). Elevated maternal C-reactive protein and increased risk of schizophrenia in a national birth cohort. *American Journal of Psychiatry, 171,* 960–968. (p. 525)

Canli, T. (2008). The character code. *Scientific American Mind, 19,* 52–57. (p. 512)

Canli, T., Desmond, J. E., Zhao, Z., & Gabrieli, J. D. E. (2002). Sex differences in the neural basis of emotional memories. *PNAS, 99,* 10789–10794. (p. 378)

Cannon, W. B. (1929). *Bodily changes in pain, hunger, fear, and rage.* New York: Branford. (pp. 361, 386)

Cannon, W. B., & Washburn, A. L. (1912). An explanation of hunger. *American Journal of Physiology, 29,* 441–454. (p. 361)

Cantor, N., & Kihlstrom, J. F. (1987). *Personality and social intelligence.* Englewood Cliffs, NJ: Prentice-Hall. (p. 326)

Caplan, N., Choy, M. H., & Whitmore, J. K. (1992, February). Indochinese refugee families and academic achievement. *Scientific American,* pp. 36–42. (p. 148)

Caprariello, P. A., & Reis, H. T. (2013). To do, to have, or to share? Valuing experiences over material possessions depends on the involvement of others. *Journal of Personality and Social Psychology, 104,* 199–215. (p. 412)

Carey, B. (2007, September 4). Bipolar illness soars as a diagnosis for the young. *The New York Times* (nytimes.com). (p. 516)

Carey, B. (2009, November 27). Surgery for mental ills offers both hope and risk. *The New York Times* (nytimes.com). (p. 565)

Carey, B. (2010). Seeking emotional clues without facial cues. *The New York Times* (nytimes.com). (p. 382)

Carey, B. (2011, February 14). Wariness on surgery of the mind. *The New York Times* (nytimes.com).

Carey, B. (2016, December 29). Did Debbie Reynolds die of a broken heart? *The New York Times* (nytimes.com). (p. 392)

Carey, G. (1990). Genes, fears, phobias, and phobic disorders. *Journal of Counseling and Development, 68,* 628–632. (p. 511)

Carhart-Harris, R. L., Muthukumaraswamy, S., Roseman, L., Kaelen, M., Droog, W., Murphy, K., . . . Leech, R. (2016). Neural correlates of the LSD experience revealed by multimodal neuroimaging. *PNAS, 113,* 4853–4858. (p. 108)

Carli, L. L., & Leonard, J. B. (1989). The effect of hindsight on victim derogation. *Journal of Social and Clinical Psychology, 8,* 331–343. (p. 440)

Carlson, M., Charlin, V., & Miller, N. (1988). Positive mood and helping behavior: A test of six hypotheses. *Journal of Personality and Social Psychology, 55,* 211–229. (p. 454)

Carmeli, A., Ben-Hador, B., Waldman, D. A., & Rupp, D. E. (2009). How leaders cultivate social capital and nurture employee vigor: Implications for job performance. *Journal of Applied Psychology, 94,* 1553–1561. (p. B-11)

Carney, D. R., Cuddy, A. J. C., & Yap, A. J. (2015). Review and summary of research on the embodied effects of expansive (vs. contractive) nonverbal displays. *Psychological Science, 26,* 657–663. (p. 381)

Caroll, H. (2013, October). Teen fashion model Georgina got so thin her organs were failing. But fashion designers still queued up to book her. Now she's telling her story to shame the whole industry. *The Daily Mail* (dailymail.co.uk). (p. 533)

Carpusor, A., & Loges, W. E. (2006). Rental discrimination and ethnicity in names. *Journal of Applied Social Psychology, 36,* 934–952. (p. 28)

Carr, E. W., Brady, T. F., & Winkielman, P. (2017). Are you smiling, or have I seen you before? Familiarity makes faces look happier. *Psychological Science, 28,* 1087–1102. (p. 447)

Carragan, R. C., & Dweck, C. S. (2014). Rethinking natural altruism: Simple reciprocal interactions trigger children's benevolence. *PNAS, 111,* 17071–17074. (p. 144)

Carroll, D., Davey Smith, G., & Bennett, P. (1994, March). Health and socioeconomic status. *The Psychologist,* pp. 122–125. (p. 396)

Carroll, E. L., & Bright, P. (2016). Involvement of Spearman's g in conceptualization versus execution of complex tasks. *Acta Psychologica, 170,* 112–126. (p. 324)

Carroll, J. M., & Russell, J. A. (1996). Do facial expressions signal specific emotions? Judging emotion from the face in context. *Journal of Personality and Social Psychology, 70,* 205–218. (p. 379)

Carskadon, M. (2002). *Adolescent sleep patterns: Biological, social, and psychological influences.* New York: Cambridge University Press. (p. 93)

Carstensen, L. L. (2011). *A long bright future: Happiness, health and financial security in an age of increased longevity.* New York: PublicAffairs. (p. 155)

Carstensen, L. L., & Mikels, J. A. (2005). At the intersection of emotion and cognition: Aging and the positivity effect. *Current Directions in Psychological Science, 14,* 117–121. (p. 334)

Carstensen, L. L., Turan, B., Scheibe, S., Ram, N., Ersner-Hershfield, H., Samanez-Larkin, G. R., . . . Nesselroade, J. R. (2011). Emotional experience improves with age: Evidence based on over 10 years of experience sampling. *Psychology and Aging, 26,* 21–33. (p. 158)

Carter, C. S., Bearden, C. E., Bullmore, E. T., Geschwind, D. H., Glahn, D. C., Gur, R. E., . . . Weinberger, D. R. (2017). Enhancing the informativeness and replicability of imaging genomics studies. *Biological Psychiatry, 82,* 157–164. (p. 20)

Carter, T. J., & Gilovich, T. (2010). The relative relativity of material and experiential purchases. *Journal of Personality and Social Psychology, 98,* 146–159. (p. 412)

Carver, C. S., Johnson, S. L., & Joormann, J. (2008). Serotonergic function, two-mode models of self-regulation, and vulnerability to depression: What depression has in common with impulsive aggression. *Psychological Bulletin, 134,* 912–943. (p. 519)

Carver, C. S., Scheier, M. F., & Segerstrom, S. C. (2010). Optimism. *Clinical Psychology Review, 30,* 879–889. (p. 398)

CASA. (2003). *The formative years: Pathways to substance abuse among girls and young women ages 8–22.* National Center on Addiction and Substance Use at Columbia University (casacolumbia.org/addiction-research/reports/formative-years-pathways-substance-abuse-among-girls-and-young-women-ages). (pp. 103, 111)

Casey, B. J., & Caudle, K. (2013). The teenage brain: Self-control. *Current Directions in Psychological Science, 22,* 82–87. (p. 142)

Casey, B. J., Getz, S., & Galvan, A. (2008). The adolescent brain. *Developmental Review, 28,* 62–77. (p. 142)

Casey, B. J., Somerville, L. H., Gotlib, I. H., Ayduk, O., Franklin, N. T., Askren, M. K., . . . Shoda, Y. (2011). Behavioral and neural correlates of delay of gratification 40 years later. *PNAS, 108,* 14998–15003. (p. 145)

Caspi, A., Houts, R. M., Belsky, D. W., Harrington, H., Hogan, S., Ramrakha, S., . . . Moffitt, T. E. (2016). Childhood forecasting of a small segment of the population with large economic burden. *Nature Human Behavior, 1,* article 0005. (p. 135)

Caspi, A., McClay, J., Moffitt, T., Mill, J., Martin, J., Craig, I. W., . . . Poulton, R. (2002). Role of genotype in the cycle of violence in maltreated children. *Science, 297,* 851–854. (p. 483)

Caspi, A., Moffitt, T. E., Newman, D. L., & Silva, P. A. (1996). Behavioral observations at age 3 years predict adult psychiatric disorders: Longitudinal evidence from a birth cohort. *Archives of General Psychiatry, 53,* 1033–1039. (p. 530)

Cassidy, J., & Shaver, P. R. (1999). *Handbook of attachment: Theory, research, and clinical applications.* New York: Guilford Press. (p. 133)

Castillo-Gualda, R., Cabello, R., Herrero, M., Rodríguez-Carvajal, R., & Fernández-Berrocal, P. (2017). A three-year emotional intelligence intervention to reduce adolescent aggression: The mediating role of unpleasant affectivity. *Journal of Research on Adolescence.* Advance online publication. doi:10.1111/jora.12325 (p. 326)

Castonguay, L. G., Boswell, J. F., Constantino, M. J., Goldfried, M. R., & Hill, C. E. (2010). Training implications of harmful effects of psychological treatments. *American Psychologist, 65,* 34–49. (p. 554)

Catalan-Matamoros, D., Gomez-Conesa, A., Stubbs, B., & Vancampfort, D. (2016). Exercise improves depressive symptoms in older adults: An umbrella review of systematic reviews and meta-analyses. *Psychiatry Research, 244,* 202–209. (p. 402)

CATO Institute. (2017). Criminal immigrants: Their numbers, demographics, and countries of origin. Retrieved from object.cato.org/sites/cato.org/files/pubs/pdf/immigration_brief-1.pdf (p. 18)

Cattell, R. B. (1963). Theory of fluid and crystallized intelligence: A critical experiment. *Journal of Educational Psychology, 54,* 1–22. (p. 333)

Cavalli-Sforza, L., Menozzi, P., & Piazza, A. (1994). *The history and geography of human genes.* Princeton, NJ: Princeton University Press. (p. 342)

Cawley, B. D., Keeping, L. M., & Levy, P. E. (1998). Participation in the performance appraisal process and employee reactions: A meta-analytic review of field investigations. *Journal of Applied Psychology, 83,* 615–633. (pp. B-10, B-11)

CBC News. (2014, March 19). *Distracted driving laws across Canada.* CBC News (cbc.ca). (p. 82)

CCSA. (2017, August). Canadian drug use summary: Cannabis. Canadian Centre on Substance Use and Addiction (ccsa.ca). (p. 110)

CDC. (2009). *Self-harm, all injury causes, nonfatal injuries and rates per 100,000.* National Center for Injury Prevention and Control. Retrieved from webappa.cdc.gov/cgi-bin/broker.exe (pp. 501, 502)

CDC. (2011, February). *HIV surveillance report: Vol. 21. Diagnoses of HIV infection and AIDS in the United States and dependent areas, 2009.* Centers for Disease Control and Prevention (cdc.gov/hiv/pdf/statistics_2009_hiv_surveillance_report_vol_21.pdf). (p. 113)

CDC. (2012, May 11). *Suicide rates among persons ages 10 years and older, by race/ethnicity and sex, United States, 2005–2009.* National Suicide Statistics at a Glance, Centers for Disease Control and Prevention (cdc.gov). (p. 500)

CDC. (2013). *Diagnoses of HIV infection in the United States and dependent areas, 2013.* HIV Surveillance Report, Volume 25. Washington, DC: Centers for Disease Control and Prevention. (p. 175)

CDC. (2014a, December). *Depression in the U.S. household population, 2009–2012* (NCHS Data Brief No. 172). Centers for Disease Control and Prevention (cdc.gov). (p. 504)

CDC. (2014b). *Pregnant women need a flu shot.* Centers for Disease Control and Prevention. Retrieved from cdc.gov/flu/pdf/freeresources/pregnant/flushot_pregnant_factsheet.pdf (p. 526)

CDC. (2014c, March 28). Prevalence of autism spectrum disorder among children aged 8 years—Autism and developmental disabilities monitoring network, 11 sites. United States, 2010. *Morbidity and Mortality Weekly Report (MMWR), 63*(SS02), 1–21. (p. 131)

CDC. (2016a). Heart disease facts. Centers for Disease Control and Prevention. Retrieved from cdc.gov/heartdisease/facts.htm (p. 391)

CDC. (2016b, accessed January 21). *Reproductive health: Teen pregnancy.* Centers for Disease Control and Prevention. Retrieved from cdc.gov/teenpregnancy (pp. 175, 177)

CDC. (2017). Drugs involved in U.S. overdose deaths, 2000 to 2016. Centers for Disease Control and Prevention. Retrieved from https://www.drugabuse.gov/related-topics/trends-statistics/overdose-death-rates. (p. 104)

CEA. (2014). *Nine facts about American families and work.* Office of the President of the United States: Council of Economic Advisers. (p. 164)

Ceci, S. J. (1993). *Cognitive and social factors in children's testimony.* Master lecture presented at the Annual Convention of the American Psychological Association. (pp. 292, 294)

Ceci, S. J., & Bruck, M. (1993). Child witnesses: Translating research into policy. *Social Policy Report (Society for Research in Child Development), 7,* 1–30. (p. 292)

Ceci, S. J., & Bruck, M. (1995). *Jeopardy in the courtroom: A scientific analysis of children's testimony.* Washington, DC: American Psychological Association. (p. 292)

Ceci, S. J., Ginther, D. K., Kahn, S., & Williams, W. M. (2014). Women in academic science: A changing landscape. *Psychological Science in the Public Interest, 15,* 75–141. (p. 168)

Ceci, S. J., Huffman, M. L. C., Smith, E., & Loftus, E. F. (1994). Repeatedly thinking about a non-event: Source misattributions among preschoolers. *Consciousness and Cognition, 3,* 388–407. (p. 294)

Ceci, S. J., & Williams, W. M. (1997). Schooling, intelligence, and income. *American Psychologist, 52,* 1051–1058. (p. 339)

Ceci, S. J., & Williams, W. M. (2009). *The mathematics of sex: How biology and society conspire to limit talented women and girls.* New York: Oxford University Press. (p. 339)

Census Bureau. (2014). Industry and occupation. Table 1: Full-time, year-round workers and median earnings in the past 12 months by sex and detailed occupation. Washington, DC: Bureau of the Census. (p. 164)

Center for Value in Health Care. (2017). The potential societal benefit of eliminating opioid overdoses, deaths, and substance use disorders exceeds $95 billion per year. Retrieved from https://altarum.org/about/news-and-events/burden-of-opioid-crisis-reached-95-billion-in-2016-private-sector-hit-hardest (p. 552)

Centerwall, B. S. (1989). Exposure to television as a risk factor for violence. *American Journal of Epidemiology, 129,* 643–652. (p. 263)

Cepeda, N. J., Pashler, H., Vul, E., Wixted, J. T., & Rohrer, D. (2006). Distributed practice in verbal recall tasks: A review and quantitative synthesis. *Psychological Bulletin, 132,* 354–380. (p. 272)

Cepeda, N. J., Vul, E., Rohrer, D., Wixed, J. T., & Pashler, H. (2008). Spacing effects in learning: A temporal ridgeline of optimal retention. *Psychological Science, 19,* 1095–1102. (p. 272)

Cerasoli, C. P., Nicklin, J. M., & Ford, M. T. (2014). Intrinsic motivation and extrinsic incentives jointly predict performance: A 40-year meta-analysis. *Psychological Bulletin, 140,* 980–1008. (p. B-1)

Cerasoli, C. P., Nicklin, J. M., & Nassrelgrgawi, A. S. (2016). Performance, incentives, and needs for autonomy, competence, and relatedness: A meta-analysis. *Motivation and Emotion, 40,* 781–813. (p. 353)

Cerrillo-Urbina, A. J., García-Hermoso, A., Sánchez-López, M., Pardo-Guijarro, M. J., Santos Gómez, J. L., & Martínez-Vizcaíno, V. (2015). The effects of physical exercise in children with attention deficit hyperactivity disorder: A systematic review and meta-analysis of randomized control trials. *Child: Care, Health and Development, 41,* 779–788. (p. 498)

CFI. (2003, July). *International developments. Report.* Amherst, NY: Center for Inquiry International. (p. 231)

Chabris, C. (2015, February 9). Quoted by Parker-Pope, T. Was Brian Williams a victim of false memory? *The New York Times* (nytimes.com). (p. 291)

Chabris, C. F., & Simons, D. (2010). *The invisible gorilla: And other ways our intuitions deceive us.* New York: Crown. (p. 83)

Chajut, E., Caspi, A., Chen, R., Hod, M., & Ariely, D. (2014). In pain thou shalt bring forth children: The peak-and-end rule in recall of labor pain. *Psychological Science, 25,* 2266–2271. (p. 223)

Chamove, A. S. (1980). Nongenetic induction of acquired levels of aggression. *Journal of Abnormal Psychology, 89,* 469–488. (p. 262)

Champagne, F. A. (2010). Early adversity and developmental outcomes: Interaction between genetics, epigenetics, and social experiences across the life span. *Perspectives on Psychological Science, 5,* 564–574. (p. 74)

Champagne, F. A., Francis, D. D., Mar, A, & Meaney, M. J. (2003). Variations in maternal care in the rat as a mediating influence for the effects of environment on development. *Physiology & Behavior, 79,* 359–371. (p. 74)

Champagne, F. A., & Mashoodh, R. (2009). Genes in context: Gene–environment interplay and the origins of individual differences in behavior. *Current Directions in Psychological Science, 18,* 127–131. (p. 74)

Chan, M. K., Krebs, M. O., Cox, D., Guest, P. C., Yolken, R. H., Rahmoune, H., . . . Bahn, S. (2015, July 14). Development of a blood-based molecular biomarker test for identification of schizophrenia before disease onset. *Translational Psychiatry, 5,* e601. (p. 524)

Chance News. (1997, 25 November). More on the frequency of letters in texts. Dart. Chance@Dartmouth.edu. (p. 24)

Chandler, J. J., & Pronin, E. (2012). Fast thought speed induces risk taking. *Psychological Science, 23,* 370–374. (p. 515)

Chandra, A., Mosher, W. D., & Copen, C. (2011, March 3). *Sexual behavior, sexual attraction, and sexual identity in the United States: Data from the 2006–2008 National Survey of Family Growth* (National Health Statistics Report No. 36). Retrieved from cdc.gov/nchs/data/nhsr/nhsr036.pdf (pp. 178, 179)

Chang, A.-M., Aeschbach, D., Duggy, J. F., & Czeisler, C. A. (2015). Evening use of light-emitting eReaders negatively affects sleep, circadian timing, and next-morning alertness. *PNAS, 112,* 1232–1237. (p. 90)

Chang, Y.-T., Chen, Y.-C., Hayter, M., & Lin, M.-L. (2009). Menstrual and menarche experience among pubescent female students in Taiwan: Implications for health education and promotion service. *Journal of Clinical Nursing, 18,* 2040–2048. (p. 167)

Chaplin, T. M. (2015). Gender and emotion expression: A developmental contextual perspective. *Emotion Review, 7,* 14–21. (p. 165)

Chaplin, T. M., & Aldao, A. (2013). Gender differences in emotion expression in children: A meta-analytic review. *Psychological Bulletin, 139,* 735–765. (p. 377)

Chaplin, W. F., Phillips, J. B., Brown, J. D., Clanton, N. R., & Stein, J. L. (2000). Handshaking, gender, personality, and first impressions. *Journal of Personality and Social Psychology, 79,* 110–117. (p. 375)

Charles, S. T., Piazza, J. R., Mogle, J., Sliwinski, M. J., & Almeida, D. M. (2013). The wear and tear of daily stressors on mental health. *Psychological Science, 24,* 733–741. (p. 517)

Charness, N., & Boot, W. R. (2009). Aging and information technology use. *Current Directions in Psychological Science, 18,* 253–258. (p. 334)

Charpak, G., & Broch, H. (2004). *Debunked! ESP, telekinesis, and other pseudoscience.* Baltimore, MD: Johns Hopkins University Press. (p. 230)

Chartrand, T. L., & Bargh, J. A. (1999). The chameleon effect: The perception-behavior link and social interaction. *Journal of Personality and Social Psychology, 76,* 893–910. (p. 422)

Chartrand, T. L., & Lakin, J. (2013). The antecedents and consequences of human behavioral mimicry. *Annual Review of Psychology, 64,* 285–308. (p. 260)

Chartrand, T. L., & van Baaren, R. (2009). Human mimicry. In M. P. Zanna (Ed.), *Advances in experimental social psychology* (pp. 219–274). San Diego, CA: Elsevier Academic Press. (p. 423)

Chassin, M. R. L., & MacKinnon, D. P. (2015). Role transitions and young adult maturing out of heavy drinking: Evidence for larger effects of marriage among more severe premarriage problem drinkers. *Alcoholism: Clinical and Experimental Research, 39,* 1064–1074. (p. 113)

Chassy, P., & Gobet, F. (2011). A hypothesis about the biological basis of expert intuition. *Review of General Psychology, 15,* 198–212. (p. 305)

Chatard, A., & Selimbegović, L. (2011). When self-destructive thoughts flash through the mind: Failure to meet standards affects the accessibility of suicide-related thoughts. *Journal of Personality and Social Psychology, 100,* 587–605. (p. 501)

Chater, N., Reali, F., & Christiansen, M. H. (2009). Restrictions on biological adaptation in language evolution. *PNAS, 106,* 1015–1020. (p. 315)

Chatterjee, R. (2015, October 3). Out of the darkness. *Science, 350,* 372–375. (p. 213)

Chaudhary, U., Xia, B., Silvoni, S., Cohen, L. G., & Birbaumer, N. (2017). Brain–computer interface–based communication in the completely locked-in state. *PLoS Biology, 15,* 25. (p. 409)

Cheek, J. M., & Melchior, L. A. (1990). Shyness, self-esteem, and self-consciousness. In H. Leitenberg (Ed.), *Handbook of social and evaluation anxiety* (pp. 47–82). New York: Plenum Press. (p. 490)

Chein, J., Albert, D., O'Brien, L., Uckert, K., & Steinberg, L. (2011). Peers increase adolescent risk taking by enhancing activity in the brain's reward circuitry. *Developmental Science, 14,* F1–F10. (p. 147)

Chein, J. M., & Schneider, W. (2012). The brain's learning and control architecture. *Current Directions in Psychological Science, 21,* 78–84. (p. 63)

Cheit, R. E. (1998). Consider this, skeptics of recovered memory. *Ethics & Behavior, 8,* 141–160. (p. 469)

Chen, A. W., Kazanjian, A., & Wong, H. (2009). Why do Chinese Canadians not consult mental health services: Health status, language or culture? *Transcultural Psychiatry, 46,* 623–640. (p. 556)

Chen, E., Turiano, N. A., Mroczek, D. K., & Miller, G. E. (2016). Association of reports of childhood abuse and all-cause mortality rates in women. *JAMA Psychiatry, 73,* 920–927. (p. 138)

Chen, L., Zhang, G., Hu, M., & Liang, X. (2015). Eye movement desensitization and reprocessing versus cognitive-behavioral therapy for adult posttraumatic stress disorder: Systematic review and meta-analysis. *Journal of Nervous and Mental Disease, 203,* 443–451. (p. 554)

Chen, M.-H., Lan, W.-H., Bai, Y.-M., Huang, K.-L., Su, T.-P., Tsai, S.-J., . . . Hsu, J.-W. (2016). Influence of relative age on diagnosis and treatment of attention-deficit hyperactivity disorder in Taiwanese children. *Journal of Pediatrics, 172,* 162–167. (p. 498)

Chen, S. H., Kennedy, M., & Zhou, Q. (2012). Parents' expression and discussion of emotion in the multilingual family: Does language matter? *Perspectives on Psychological Science, 7,* 365–383. (p. 319)

Chen, S. X., & Bond, M. H. (2010). Two languages, two personalities? Examining language effects on the expression of personality in a bilingual context. *Personality and Social Psychology Bulletin, 36,* 1514–1528. (p. 319)

Cheng, C., & Li, A. Y.-I. (2014). Internet addiction prevalence and quality of (real) life: A meta-analysis of 31 nations across seven world regions. *Cyberpsychology, Behavior, and Social Networking, 17,* 755–760. (p. 102)

Chennu, S., Pinoia, P., Kamau, E. Allanson, J., Williams, G. B., Monti, M. M., . . . Bekinschtein, T. A. (2014). Spectral signatures of reorganised brain network in disorders of consciousness. *PLoS Computational Biology, 10:*e1003887. (p. 81)

Cheon, B. K., Im, D.-M., Harada, T., Kim, J.-S., Mathur, V. A., Scimeca, J. M., . . . Chiao, J. Y. (2013). Cultural modulation of the neural correlates of emotional pain perception: The role of other-focusedness. *Neuropsychologia, 51,* 1177–1186. (p. 491)

Cherniss, C. (2010a). Emotional intelligence: New insights and further clarifications. *Industrial and Organizational Psychology, 3,* 183–191. (p. 326)

Cherniss, C. (2010b). Emotional intelligence: Toward clarification of a concept. *Industrial and Organizational Psychology, 3,* 110–126. (p. 326)

Chess, S., & Thomas, A. (1987). *Know your child: An authoritative guide for today's parents.* New York: Basic Books. (p. 135)

Chester, D. S., & DeWall, C. N. (2016). The pleasure of revenge: Retaliatory aggression arises from a neural imbalance toward reward. *Social Cognitive and Affective Neuroscience, 11,* 1173–1182. (p. 144)

Cheung, B. Y., Chudek, M., & Heine, S. J. (2011). Evidence for a sensitive period for acculturation: Younger immigrants report acculturating at a faster rate. *Psychological Science, 22,* 147–152. (p. 315)

Cheung, F., & Lucas, R. E. (2015). When does money matter most? Examining the association between income and life satisfaction over the life course. *Psychology and Aging, 30,* 120–135. (p. 409)

Cheung, F., & Lucas, R. E. (2016). Income inequality is associated with stronger social comparison effects: The effect of relative income on life satisfaction. *Journal of Personality and Social Psychology, 110,* 332–341. (p. 410)

Chida, Y., & Hamer, M. (2008). Chronic psychosocial factors and acute physiological responses to laboratory-induced stress in healthy populations: A quantitative review of 30 years of investigations. *Psychological Bulletin, 134,* 829–885. (p. 391)

Chida, Y., Hamer, M., Wardle, J., & Steptoe, A. (2008). Do stress-related psychosocial factors contribute to cancer incidence and survival? *Nature Reviews: Clinical Oncology, 5,* 466–475. (p. 390)

Chida, Y., & Steptoe, A. (2009). The association of anger and hostility with future coronary heart disease: A meta-analytic review of prospective evidence. *Journal of the American College of Cardiology, 17,* 936–946. (p. 391)

Chida, Y., Steptoe, A., & Powell, L. H. (2009). Religiosity/spirituality and mortality. *Psychotherapy and Psychosomatics, 78,* 81–90. (p. 406)

Chida, Y., & Vedhara, K. (2009). Adverse psychosocial factors predict poorer prognosis in HIV disease: A meta-analytic review of prospective investigations. *Brain, Behavior, and Immunity, 23,* 434–445. (p. 390)

Chiles, J. A., Lambert, M. J., & Hatch, A. L. (1999). The impact of psychological interventions on medical cost offset: A meta-analytic review. *Clinical Psychology: Science and Practice, 6,* 204–220. (p. 552)

Chisholm, D., Sweeny, K., Sheehan, P., Rasmussen, B., Smit, F., Cuijpers, P., & Saxena, S. (2016). Scaling-up treatment of depression and anxiety: A global return on investment analysis. *The Lancet Psychiatry, 3,* 415–424. (p. 552)

Chivers, M. L., Seto, M. C., Lalumière, M. L., Laan, E., & Grimbos, T. (2010). Agreement of self-reported and genital measures of sexual arousal in men and women: A meta-analysis. *Archives of Sexual Behavior, 39,* 5–56. (p. 176)

Chmielewski, M., Zhu, J., Burchett, D., Bury, A. S., & Bagby, R. M. (2017). The comparative capacity of the Minnesota Multiphasic Personality Inventory–2 (MMPI–2) and MMPI-2 Restructured Form (MMPI-2-RF) validity scales to detect suspected malingering in a disability claimant sample. *Psychological Assessment, 29,* 199–208. (p. 477)

Cho, K. W., Neely, J. H., Crocco, S., & Vitrano, D. (2017). Testing enhances both encoding and retrieval for both tested and untested items. *The Quarterly Journal of Experimental Psychology, 70,* 1211–1235. (p. 33)

Choi, C. Q. (2008, March). Do you need only half your brain? *Scientific American.* Retrieved from scientificamerican.com/article/do-you-need-only-half-your-brain/ (p. 64)

Choi, J., Broersma, M., & Cutler, A. (2017). Early phonology revealed by international adoptees' birth language retention. *PNAS, 114,* 7307–7312. (p. 315)

Chomsky, N. (1972). *Language and mind.* New York: Harcourt Brace. (p. 317)

Chopik, W., & O'Brien, E. (2017). Happy you, healthy me? Having a happy partner is independently associated with better health in oneself. *Health Psychology, 36,* 21–30. (p. 392)

Chopik, W. J., Edelstein, R. S., & Fraley, R. C. (2013). From the cradle to the grave: Age differences in attachment from early adulthood to old age. *Journal of Personality, 81,* 171–183. (p. 158)

Choudhary, E., Smith, M., & Bossarte, R. M. (2012). Depression, anxiety, and symptom profiles among female and male victims of sexual violence. *American Journal of Men's Health, 6,* 28–36. (p. 170)

Christakis, D. A., Garrison, M. M., Herrenkohl, T., Haggerty, K., Rivara, K. P., Zhou, C., & Liekweg, K. (2013). Modifying media content for preschool children: A randomized control trial. *Pediatrics, 131,* 431–438. (p. 263)

Christakis, N. A., & Fowler, J. H. (2007). The spread of obesity in a large social network over 32 years. *New England Journal of Medicine, 357,* 370–379. (p. 365)

Christakis, N. A., & Fowler, J. H. (2008). The collective dynamics of smoking in a large social network. *New England Journal of Medicine, 358,* 2249–2258. (p. 113)

Christensen, A., & Jacobson, N. S. (1994). Who (or what) can do psychotherapy: The status and challenge of nonprofessional therapies. *Psychological Science, 5,* 8–14. (p. 556)

Christensen, H., Batterham, P. J., Gosling, J. A., Ritterband, L. M., Griffiths, K. M., Thorndike, F. P., . . . Mackinnon, A. J. (2016). Effectiveness of an online insomnia program (SHUTi) for prevention of depressive episodes (the GoodNight study): A randomised controlled trial: Correction. *The Lancet Psychiatry, 3,* 331–341. (p. 546)

Christiansen, P., Jennings, E., & Rose, A. K. (2016). Anticipated effects of alcohol stimulate craving and impair inhibitory control. *Psychology of Addictive Behaviors, 30,* 383–388. (p. 104)

Christophersen, E. R., & Edwards, K. J. (1992). Treatment of elimination disorders: State of the art 1991. *Applied & Preventive Psychology, 1,* 15–22. (p. 540)

Chu, C., Podlogar, M. C., Hagan, C. R., Buchman-Schmitt, J. M., Silva, C., Chiurliza, B., . . . Joiner, T. E. (2016). The interactive effects of the capability for suicide and major depressive episodes on suicidal behavior in a military sample. *Cognitive Therapy and Research, 40,* 22–30. (p. 500)

Chua, H. F., Boland, J. E., & Nisbett, R. E. (2005). Cultural variation in eye movements during scene perception. *PNAS, 102,* 12629–12633. (p. 416)

Chugani, H. T., & Phelps, M. E. (1986). Maturational changes in cerebral function in infants determined by 18FDG positron emission tomography. *Science, 231,* 840–843. (p. 123)

Chulov, M. (2014, December 11). ISIS: The inside story. *The Guardian* (theguardian.com). (p. 431)

Church, A. T., Katigbak, M. S., Mazuera Arias, R., Rincon, B. C., Vargas-Flores, J., Ibáñez-Reyes, J., . . . Ortiz, F. A. (2014). A four-culture study of self-enhancement and adjustment using the social relations model: Do alternative conceptualizations and indices make a difference? *Journal of Personality and Social Psychology, 106,* 997–1014. (p. 488)

Churchland, P. S. (2013). *Touching a nerve: The self as brain.* New York: Norton. (p. 108)

CIA. (2014, accessed April 23). Sex ratio. *The world fact book* (cia.gov). (p. 437)

Cialdini, R. B. (1993). *Influence: Science and practice* (3rd ed.). New York: HarperCollins. (p. 419)

Cialdini, R. B., & Richardson, K. D. (1980). Two indirect tactics of image management: Basking and blasting. *Journal of Personality and Social Psychology, 39,* 406–415. (p. 439)

Ciardelli, L. E., Weiss, A., Powell, D. M., & Reiss, D. (2017). Personality dimensions of the captive California sea lion (*Zalophus californianus*). *Journal of Comparative Psychology, 131,* 50–58. (p. 477)

Cin, S. D., Gibson, B., Zanna, M. P., Shumate, R., & Fong, G. T. (2007). Smoking in movies, implicit associations of smoking with the self, and intentions to smoke. *Psychological Science, 18,* 559–563. (p. 111)

Clack, B., Dixon, J., & Tredoux, C. (2005). Eating together apart: Patterns of segregation in a multi-ethnic cafeteria. *Journal of Community and Applied Social Psychology, 15,* 1–16. (p. 457)

Claidière, N., & Whiten, A. (2012). Integrating the study of conformity and culture in humans and nonhuman animals. *Psychological Bulletin, 138,* 126–145. (pp. 310, 425)

Clancy, S. A. (2005). *Abducted: How people come to believe they were kidnapped by aliens.* Cambridge, MA: Harvard University Press. (p. 88)

Clancy, S. A. (2010). *The trauma myth: The truth about the sexual abuse of children—and its aftermath.* New York: Basic Books. (p. 137)

Clark, A., Seidler, A., & Miller, M. (2001). Inverse association between sense of humor and coronary heart disease. *International Journal of Cardiology, 80,* 87–88. (p. 399)

Clark, C. J., Luguri, J. B., Ditto, P. H., Knobe, J., Shariff, A. F., & Baumeister, R. F. (2014). Free to punish: A motivated account of free will belief. *Journal of Personality and Social Psychology, 106,* 501–513. (p. 397)

Clark, I. A., & Maguire, E. A. (2016). Remembering preservation in hippocampal amnesia. *Annual Review of Psychology, 67,* 51–82. (p. 56)

Clark, K. B., & Clark, M. P. (1947). Racial identification and preference in Negro children. In T. M. Newcomb & E. L. Hartley (Eds.), *Readings in social psychology.* New York: Holt. (p. 32)

Clark, R. D., III, & Hatfield, E. (1989). Gender differences in willingness to engage in casual sex. *Journal of Psychology and Human Sexuality, 2,* 39–55. (p. 185)

Clarke, E., Reichard, U. H., & Zuberbuehler, K. (2015). Context-specific close-range "hoo" calls in wild gibbons (Hylobates lar). *BMC Evolutionary Biology, 15,* 56. (p. 317)

Clausen, J., Fetz, E., Donoghue, J., Ushiba, J., Spöhase, J., Birbaummer, N., & Soekadar, S. R. (2017). Help, hope, and hype: Ethical dimensions of neuroprosthetics. *Science, 356,* 1338–1339. (p. 61)

Claxton, S. E., DeLuca, H. K., & van Dulmen, M. H. (2015). The association between alcohol use and engagement in casual sexual relationships and experiences: A meta-analytic review of non-experimental studies. *Archives of Sexual Behavior, 44,* 837–856. (p. 103)

Cleary, A. M. (2008). Recognition memory, familiarity, and déjà vu experiences. *Current Directions in Psychological Science, 17,* 353–357. (p. 291)

Clynes, T. (2016). How to raise a genius. *Nature, 537,* 152–155. (p. 332)

Coan, J. A., Schaefer, H. S., & Davidson, R. J. (2006). Lending a hand: Social regulation of the neural response to threat. *Psychological Science, 17,* 1032–1039. (p. 400)

Coelho, C. M., & Purkis, H. (2009). The origins of specific phobias: Influential theories and current perspectives. *Review of General Psychology, 13,* 335–348. (p. 512)

Cohen, A. B. (2009). Many forms of culture. *American Psychologist, 64,* 194–204. (pp. 421, 490)

Cohen, A. O., Breiner, K., Steinberg, L., Bonnie, R. J., Scott, E. S., Taylor-Thompson, K. A., . . . Silverman, M. R. (2016). When is an adolescent an adult? Assessing cognitive control in emotional and nonemotional contexts. *Psychological Science, 27,* 549–562. (pp. 142, 385)

Cohen, G. L., & Sherman, D. K. (2014). The psychology of change: Self-affirmation and social psychological intervention. *Annual Review of Psychology, 65,* 333–371. (p. 344)

Cohen, P. (2007, November 15). Freud is widely taught at universities, except in the psychology department. *The New York Times* (nytimes.com). (p. 462)

Cohen, P. (2010, June 11). Long road to adulthood is growing even longer. *The New York Times* (nytimes.com). (p. 150)

Cohen, S. (2004). Social relationships and health. *American Psychologist, 59,* 676–684. (p. 400)

Cohen, S., Alper, C. M., Doyle, W. J., Treanor, J. J., & Turner, R. B. (2006). Positive emotional style predicts resistance to illness after experimental exposure to rhinovirus or influenza A virus. *Psychosomatic Medicine, 68,* 809–815. (p. 390)

Cohen, S., Doyle, W. J., Skoner, D. P., Rabin, B. S., & Gwaltney, J. M., Jr. (1997). Social ties and susceptibility to the common cold. *Journal of the American Medical Association, 277,* 1940–1944. (pp. 397, 400)

Cohen, S., Doyle, W. J., Turner, R., Alper, C. M., & Skoner, D. P. (2003). Sociability and susceptibility to the common cold. *Psychological Science, 14,* 389–395. (p. 390)

Cohen, S., Janicki-Deverts, D., Turner, R. B., & Doyle, W. J. (2015). Does hugging provide stress-buffering social support? A study of susceptibility to upper respiratory infection and illness. *Psychological Science, 26,* 135–147. (p. 400)

Cohen, S., Kaplan, J. R., Cunnick, J. E., Manuck, S. B., & Rabin, B. S. (1992). Chronic social stress, affiliation, and cellular immune response in nonhuman primates. *Psychological Science, 3,* 301–304. (p. 389)

Cohen, S., & Pressman, S. D. (2006). Positive affect and health. *Current Directions in Psychological Science, 15,* 122–125. (p. 390)

Cohen, S., Tyrrell, D. A. J., & Smith, A. P. (1991). Psychological stress and susceptibility to the common cold. *New England Journal of Medicine, 325,* 606–612. (p. 390)

Cohn, D. (2013, February 13). *Love and marriage.* Retrieved from pewsocialtrends.org/2013/02/13/love-and-marriage/ (p. 156)

Coker, A. L., Bush, H. M., Cook-Craig, P. G., DeGue, S. A., Clear, E. R., Brancato, C. J., . . . Recktenwald, E. A. (2017). RCT testing bystander effectiveness to reduce violence. *American Journal of Preventative Medicine, 52,* 566–578. (p. 170)

Colapinto, J. (2000). *As nature made him: The boy who was raised as a girl.* New York: HarperCollins. (p. 168)

Colarelli, S. M., Spranger, J. L., & Hechanova, M. R. (2006). Women, power, and sex composition in small groups: An evolutionary perspective. *Journal of Organizational Behavior, 27,* 163–184. (p. 154)

Cole, K. C. (1998). *The universe and the teacup: The mathematics of truth and beauty.* New York: Harcourt Brace. (p. 105)

Cole, M. W., Ito, T., & Braver, T. S. (2015). Lateral prefrontal cortex contributes to fluid intelligence through multinetwork connectivity. *Brain Connectivity, 5,* 497–504. (p. 324)

Colen, C. G., & Ramey, D. M. (2014). Is breast truly best? Estimating the effects of breastfeeding on long-term child health and well-being in the United States using sibling comparisons. *Social Science & Medicine, 109,* 55–65. (p. 25)

Coley, R. L., Medeiros, B. L., & Schindler, H. (2008). Using sibling differences to estimate effects of parenting on adolescent sexual risk behaviors. *Journal of Adolescent Health, 43,* 133–140. (p. 178)

Collier, K. L., Bos, H. M. W., & Sandfort, T. G. M. (2012). Intergroup contact, attitudes toward homosexuality, and the role of acceptance of gender non-conformity in young adolescents. *Journal of Adolescence, 35,* 899–907. (p. 457)

Collins, F. (2006). *The language of God.* New York: Free Press. (p. 77)

Collins, G. (2009, March 4). The rant list. *The New York Times* (nytimes.com). (p. 31)

Collins, N. L., & Miller, L. C. (1994). Self-disclosure and liking: A meta-analytic review. *Psychological Bulletin, 116,* 457–475. (p. 452)

Collins, R. L., Elliott, M. N., Berry, S. H., Danouse, D. E., Kunkel, D., Hunter, S. B., & Miu, A. (2004). Watching sex on television predicts adolescent initiation of sexual behavior. *Pediatrics, 114,* 280–289. (p. 25)

Collins, W. A., Welsh, D. P., & Furman, W. (2009). Adolescent romantic relationships. *Annual Review of Psychology, 60,* 631–652. (p. 147)

Collinson, S. L., MacKay, C. E., James, A. C., Quested, D. J., Phillips, T., Roberts, N., & Crow, T. J. (2003). Brain volume, asymmetry and intellectual impairment in relation to sex in early-onset schizophrenia. *British Journal of Psychiatry, 183,* 114–120. (p. 525)

Colombo, J. (1982). The critical period concept: Research, methodology, and theoretical issues. *Psychological Bulletin, 91,* 260–275. (p. 134)

Colvert, E., Beata, T., McEwen, F., Stewart, C., Curran, S. R., Woodhouse, E., . . . Bolton, P. (2015). Heritability of autism spectrum disorder in a UK population-based twin sample. *JAMA Psychiatry, 72,* 415–423. (p. 131)

Comfort, A. (2002). *The joy of sex: Fully revised & completely updated for the 21st century.* New York: Crown. (p. 151)

Confer, J. C., Easton, J. A., Fleischman, D. S., Goetz, C. D., Lewis, D. M. G., Perilloux, C., & Buss, D. M. (2010). Evolutionary psychology: Controversies, questions, prospects, and limitations. *American Psychologist, 65,* 110–126. (pp. 185, 186)

Conley, C. S., & Rudolph, K. D. (2009). The emerging sex difference in adolescent depression: Interacting contributions of puberty and peer stress. *Development and Psychopathology, 21,* 593–620. (p. 142)

Conley, T. D. (2011). Perceived proposer personality characteristics and gender differences in acceptance of casual sex offers. *Journal of Personality and Social Psychology, 100,* 309–329. (p. 185)

Connor, C. E. (2010). A new viewpoint on faces. *Science, 330,* 764–765. (p. 205)

Connor-Smith, J. K., & Flachsbart, C. (2007). Relations between personality and coping: A meta-analysis. *Journal of Personality and Social Psychology, 93,* 1080–1107. (p. 396)

Conroy-Beam, D., Buss, D. M., Pham, M. N., & Shackelford, T. K. (2015). How sexually dimorphic are human mate preferences? *Personality and Social Psychology Bulletin, 41,* 1082–1093. (p. 184)

Consumer Reports. (1995, November). Does therapy help? pp. 734–739. (p. 550)

Conway, A. R. A., Skitka, L. J., Hemmerich, J. A., & Kershaw, T. C. (2009). Flashbulb memory for 11 September 2001. *Applied Cognitive Psychology, 23,* 605–623. (p. 278)

Conway, M. A., Wang, Q., Hanyu, K., & Haque, S. (2005). A cross-cultural investigation of autobiographical memory. On the universality and cultural variation of the reminiscence bump. *Journal of Cross-Cultural Psychology, 36,* 739–749. (p. 153)

Cook, S., Kokmotou, K., Soto, V., Fallon, N., Tyson-Carr, J., Thomas, A., . . . Stancak, A. (2017). Pleasant and unpleasant odour-face combinations influence face and odour perception: An event-related potential study. *Behavioural Brain Research, 333,* 304–313. (p. 226)

Cooke, L. J., Wardle, J., & Gibson, E. L. (2003). Relationship between parental report of food neophobia and everyday food consumption in 2–6-year-old children. *Appetite, 41,* 205–206. (p. 225)

Cooney, G., Gilbert, D. T., & Wilson, T. D. (2014). The unforeseen costs of extraordinary experience. *Psychological Science, 25,* 2259–2265. (p. 409)

Cooper, K. J. (1999, May 1). This time, copycat wave is broader. *The Washington Post.* Retrieved from washingtonpost.com/wp-srv/national/longterm/juvmurders/stories/copycat050199.htm (p. 423)

Cooper, W. H., & Withey, M. J. (2009). The strong situation hypothesis. *Personality and Social Psychology Review, 13,* 62–72. (p. 482)

Coopersmith, S. (1967). *The antecedents of self-esteem.* San Francisco: Freeman. (p. 139)

Copeland, W., Shanahan, L., Miller, S., Costello, E. J., Angold, A., & Maughan, B. (2010). Outcomes of early pubertal timing in young women: A prospective population-based study. *American Journal of Psychiatry, 167,* 1218–1225. (p. 142)

Copen, C. E., Chandra, A., & Febo-Vazquez, I. (2016, January 7). Sexual behavior, sexual attraction, and sexual orientation among adults aged 18–44 in the United States: Data from the 2011–2013 National Survey of Family Growth. Centers for Disease Control and Prevention, *National Health Statistics Reports,* Number 88. (p. 179)

Corballis, M. C. (2002). *From hand to mouth: The origins of language.* Princeton, NJ: Princeton University Press. (p. 317)

Corballis, M. C. (2003). From mouth to hand: Gesture, speech, and the evolution of right-handedness. *Behavioral and Brain Sciences, 26,* 199–260. (p. 317)

Corcoran, D. W. J. (1964). The relation between introversion and salivation. *The American Journal of Psychology, 77,* 298–300. (p. 476)

Coren, S. (1996). *Sleep thieves: An eye-opening exploration into the science and mysteries of sleep.* New York: Free Press. (p. 92, 94)

Corey, D. P., García-Añoveros, J., Holt, J. R., Kwan, K. Y., Lin, S.-Y., Vollrath, M. A., . . . Zhang, D.-S. (2004). TRPA1 is a candidate for the mechanosensitive transduction channel of vertebrate hair cells. *Nature, 432,* 723–730. (p. 218)

Corina, D. P. (1998). The processing of sign language: Evidence from aphasia. In B. Stemmer & H. A. Whittaker (Eds.), *Handbook of neurolinguistics* (pp. 313–329). San Diego, CA: Academic Press. (p. 67)

Corina, D. P., Vaid, J., & Bellugi, U. (1992). The linguistic basis of left hemisphere specialization. *Science, 255,* 1258–1260. (p. 67)

Corkin, S. (2013). *Permanent present tense: The unforgettable life of the amnesic patient.* New York: Basic Books. (p. 284)

Corkin, S., quoted by R. Adelson. (2005, September). Lessons from H. M. *Monitor on Psychology,* p. 59. (p. 284)

Cormier, Z. (2016). Brain scans reveal how LSD affects consciousness. *Nature* (nature.com). (p. 61)

Corneille, O., Huart, J., Becquart, E., & Brédart, S. (2004). When memory shifts toward more typical category exemplars: Accentuation effects in the recollection of ethnically ambiguous faces. *Journal of Personality and Social Psychology, 86,* 236–250. (p. 298)

Cornette, M. M., deRoom-Cassini, T. A., Fosco, G. M., Holloway, R. L., Clark, D. C., & Joiner, T. E. (2009). Application of an interpersonal-psychological model of suicidal behavior to physicians and medical trainees. *Archives of Suicide Research, 13,* 1–14. (p. 500)

Cornier, M.-A. (2011). Is your brain to blame for weight regain? *Physiology & Behavior, 104,* 608–612. (p. 362)

Cornil, Y., & Chandon, P. (2013). From fan to fat? Vicarious losing increases unhealthy eating, but self-affirmation is an effective remedy. *Psychological Science, 24,* 1936–1946. (p. 363)

Coronado-Montoya, S., Levis, A. W., Kwakkenbos, L., Steele, R. J., Turner, E. H., & Thombs, B. D. (2016). Reporting of positive results in randomized controlled trials of mindfulness-based mental health interventions. *PLoS ONE, 11,* 18. (p. 404)

Correa, C., & Louttit, M. (2018, January 24). More than 160 women say Larry Nassar sexually abused them. Here are his accusers in their own words. *The New York Times* (nytimes.com). (p. 429)

Correll, J., Park, B., Judd, C. M., Wittenbrink, B., Sadler, M. S., & Keesee, T. (2007). Across the thin blue line: Police officers and racial bias in the decision to shoot. *Journal of Personality and Social Psychology, 92,* 1006–1023. (p. 436)

Correll, J., Wittenbrink, B., Crawford, M. T., & Sadler, M. S. (2015). Stereotypic vision: How stereotypes disambiguate visual stimuli. *Journal of Personality and Social Psychology, 108,* 219–233. (p. 436)

Corrigan, P. W. (2014). Can there be false hope in recovery? *British Journal of Psychiatry, 205,* 423–424. (p. 555)

Corrigan, P. W., Druss, B. G., & Perlick, D. A. (2014). The impact of mental illness stigma on seeking and participating in mental health care. *Psychological Science in the Public Interest, 15,* 37–70. (p. 499)

Costa, A., Foucart, A., Hayakawa, S., Aparici, M., Apesteguia, J., Heafner, J., & Keysar, B. (2014). Your morals depend on language. *PLoS ONE, 9,* e94842. doi:10.1371/journal.pone.0094842 (p. 319)

Costa, P. T., Jr., & McCrae, R. R. (2011). The five-factor model, five factor theory, and interpersonal psychology. In L. M. Horowitz & S. Strack (Eds.), *Handbook of interpersonal psychology: Theory, research, assessment, and therapeutic interventions* (pp. 91–104). Hoboken, NJ: Wiley. (p. 477)

Costa, P. T., Jr., Terracciano, A., & McCrae, R. R. (2001). Gender differences in personality traits across cultures: Robust and surprising findings. *Journal of Personality and Social Psychology, 81,* 322–331. (p. 377)

Costello, E. J., Compton, S. N., Keeler, G., & Angold, A. (2003). Relationships between poverty and psychopathology: A natural experiment. *Journal of the American Medical Association, 290,* 2023–2029. (pp. 25, 505)

Coughlin, J. F., Mohyde, M., D'Ambrosio, L. A., & Gilbert, J. (2004). *Who drives older driver decisions?* Cambridge, MA: MIT Age Lab. (p. 152)

Couli, J. T., Vidal, F., Nazarian, B., & Macar, F. (2004). Functional anatomy of the attentional modulation of time estimation. *Science, 303,* 1506–1508. (p. B-1)

Coulter, K. C., & Malouff, J. M. (2013). Effects of an intervention designed to enhance romantic relationship excitement: A randomized-control trial. *Couple and Family Psychology: Research and Practice, 2,* 34–44. (p. 451)

Courtney, J. G., Longnecker, M. P., Theorell, T., & de Verdier, M. G. (1993). Stressful life events and the risk of colorectal cancer. *Epidemiology, 4,* 407–414. (p. 390)

Cowan, N. (1988). Evolving conceptions of memory storage, selective attention, and their mutual constraints within the human information-processing system. *Psychological Bulletin, 104,* 163–191. (p. 270)

Cowan, N. (2010). The magical mystery four: How is working memory capacity limited, and why? *Current Directions in Psychological Science, 19,* 51–57. (p. 269)

Cowan, N. (2015). George Miller's magical number of immediate memory in retrospect: Observations on the faltering progression of science. *Psychological Review, 122,* 536–541. (p. 271)

Cowan, N. (2016). Working memory maturation: Can we get at the essence of cognitive growth? *Perspectives on Psychological Science, 11,* 239–264. (p. 269)

Cowart, B. J. (1981). Development of taste perception in humans: Sensitivity and preference throughout the life span. *Psychological Bulletin, 90,* 43–73. (p. 225)

Cowart, B. J. (2005). Taste, our body's gustatory gatekeeper. *Cerebrum, 7,* 7–22. (p. 225)

Cowell, J. M., & Decety, J. (2015). Precursors to morality in development as a complex interplay between neural, socioenvironmental, and behavioral facets. *PNAS, 112,* 12657–12662. (p. 144)

Cox, J. J., Reimann, F., Nicholas, A. K., Thornton, G., Robert, E., Springell, K., . . . Woods, C. G. (2006). An SCN9A channelopathy causes congenital inability to experience pain. *Nature, 444,* 894–898. (p. 223)

Coye, C., Ouattara, K., Zuberbühler, K., & Lemasson, A. (2015). Suffixation influences receivers' behaviour in non-human primates. *Proceedings of the Royal Society B, 282,* 1807. (p. 317)

Coyne, J. C., Ranchor, A. V., & Palmer, S. C. (2010). Meta-analysis of stress-related factors in cancer. *Nature Reviews: Clinical Oncology, 7.* doi:10.1038/ncponc1134-c1 (p. 390)

Coyne, J. C., Stefanek, M., & Palmer, S. C. (2007). Psychotherapy and survival in cancer: The conflict between hope and evidence. *Psychological Bulletin, 133,* 367–394. (p. 391)

Coyne, J. C., & Tennen, H. (2010). Positive psychology in cancer care: Bad science, exaggerated claims, and unproven medicine. *Annals of Behavioral Medicine, 39,* 16–26. (p. 391)

Coyne, J. C., Thombs, B. C., Stefanek, M., & Palmer, S. C. (2009). Time to let go of the illusion that psychotherapy extends the survival of cancer patients: Reply to Kraemer, Kuchler, and Spiegel (2009). *Psychological Bulletin, 135,* 179–182. (p. 391)

Crabbe, J. C. (2002). Genetic contributions to addiction. *Annual Review of Psychology, 53,* 435–462. (p. 110)

Crabtree, S. (2005, January 13). Engagement keeps the doctor away. *Gallup Management Journal* (gmj.gallup.com). (p. B-9)

Crabtree, S. (2011, December 12). *U.S. seniors maintain happiness highs with less social time.* Gallup poll (gallup.com). (p. 158)

Craik, F. I. M., & Tulving, E. (1975). Depth of processing and the retention of words in episodic memory. *Journal of Experimental Psychology: General, 104,* 268–294. (p. 273)

Crandall, C. S. (1988). Social contagion of binge eating. *Journal of Personality and Social Psychology, 55,* 588–598. (p. 532)

Crandall, C. S., & White, M. H., II. (2016, November 17). Trump and the social psychology of prejudice. *Undark.* Retrieved from undark.org/article/trump-social-psychology-prejudice-unleashed (p. 439)

Crawford, M., Chaffin, R., & Fitton, L. (1995). Cognition in social context. Learning and individual differences, special issue: Psychological and psychobiological perspectives on sex differences in cognition: 1. *Theory and Research, 7,* 341–362. (p. 341)

Credé, M., & Kuncel, N. R. (2008). Study habits, skills, and attitudes: The third pillar supporting collegiate academic performance. *Perspectives on Psychological Science, 3,* 425–453. (p. 339)

Creswell, J. D., Bursley, J. K., & Satpute, A. B. (2013). Neural reactivation links unconscious thought to decision making performance. *Social Cognitive and Affective Neuroscience, 8,* 863–869. (p. 305)

Creswell, J. D., Way, B. M., Eisenberger, N. I., & Lieberman, M. D. (2007). Neural correlates of dispositional mindfulness during affect labeling. *Psychosomatic Medicine, 69,* 560–565. (p. 404)

Creswell, K. G., Chung, T., Clark, D., & Martin, C. (2014). Solitary alcohol use in teens is associated with drinking in response to negative affect and predicts alcohol problems in young adulthood. *Clinical Psychological Science, 2,* 602–610. (p. 104)

Crews, F. T., He, J., & Hodge, C. (2007). Adolescent cortical development: A critical period of vulnerability for addiction. *Pharmacology Biochemistry and Behavior, 86,* 189–199. (pp. 103, 142)

Crews, F. T., Mdzinarishvili, A., Kim, D., He, J., & Nixon, K. (2006). Neurogenesis in adolescent brain is potently inhibited by ethanol. *Neuroscience, 137,* 437–445. (p. 103)

Crifasi, C. K., Meyers, J. S., Vernick, J. S., & Webster, D. W. (2015). Effects of changes in permit-to-purchase handgun laws in Connecticut and Missouri on suicide rates. *Preventive Medicine: An International Journal Devoted to Practice and Theory, 79,* 43–49. (p. 501)

Cristea, I. A., Huibers, M. J., David, D., Hollon, S. D., Andersson, G., & Cuijpers, P. (2015). The effects of cognitive behavior therapy for adult depression on dysfunctional thinking: A meta-analysis. *Clinical Psychology Review, 42,* 62–71. (p. 546)

Crivelli, C., Jarillo, S., Russell, J. A., & Fernández-Dols, J. M. (2016a). Reading emotions from faces in two indigenous societies. *Journal of Experimental Psychology: General, 145,* 830–843. (p. 378)

Crivelli, C., Russell, J. A., Jarillo, S., & Fernández-Dols, J. M. (2016b). The fear gasping face as a threat display in a Melanesian society. *PNAS, 113,* 12403–12407. (p. 378)

Crocker, J., & Park, L. E. (2004). The costly pursuit of self-esteem. *Psychological Bulletin, 130,* 392–414. (p. 489)

Crocker, J., Thompson, L. L., McGraw, K. M., & Ingerman, C. (1987). Downward comparison, prejudice, and evaluation of others: Effects of self-esteem and threat. *Journal of Personality and Social Psychology, 52,* 907–916. (p. 439)

Crockett, M. J., Kurth-Nelson, Z., Siegel, J. Z., Dayan, P., & Dolan, R. J. (2014). Harm to others outweighs harm to self in moral decision making. *PNAS, 111,* 17320–17325. (p. 144)

Croft, A., Schmader, T., Block, K., & Baron, A. S. (2014). The second shift reflected in the second generation: Do parents' gender roles at home predict children's aspirations? *Psychological Science, 25,* 1418–1428. (p. 169)

Croft, R. J., Klugman, A., Baldeweg, T., & Gruzelier, J. H. (2001). Electrophysiological evidence of serotonergic impairment in long-term MDMA ("Ecstasy") users. *American Journal of Psychiatry, 158,* 1687–1692. (p. 108)

Crook, T. H., & West, R. L. (1990). Name recall performance across the adult life-span. *British Journal of Psychology, 81,* 335–340. (pp. 153, 154)

Crosier, B. S., Webster, G. D., & Dillon, H. M. (2012). Wired to connect: Evolutionary psychology and social networks. *Review of General Psychology, 16,* 230–239. (p. 448)

Cross-National Collaborative Group. (1992). The changing rate of major depression. *Journal of the American Medical Association, 268,* 3098–3105. (p. 518)

Crouse, K. (2017, September 21). Michael Phelps: A golden shoulder to lean on. *The New York Times* (nytimes.com). (p. 521)

Crowell, J. A., & Waters, E. (1994). Bowlby's theory grown up: The role of attachment in adult love relationships. *Psychological Inquiry, 5,* 1–22. (p. 133)

Croy, I., Bojanowski, V., & Hummel, T. (2013). Men without a sense of smell exhibit a strongly reduced number of sexual relationships, women exhibit reduced partnership security: A reanalysis of previously published data. *Biological Psychology, 92,* 292–294. (p. 225)

Croy, I., Negoias, S., Novakova, L., Landis, B. N., & Hummel, T. (2012). Learning about the functions of the olfactory system from people without a sense of smell. *PLoS ONE 7,* e33365. doi:10.1371/journal.pone.0033365 (p. 225)

Csikszentmihalyi, M. (1990). *Flow: The psychology of optimal experience.* New York: Harper & Row. (p. B-1)

Csikszentmihalyi, M. (1999). If we are so rich, why aren't we happy? *American Psychologist, 54,* 821–827. (p. B-1)

Csikszentmihalyi, M., & Hunter, J. (2003). Happiness in everyday life: The uses of experience sampling. *Journal of Happiness Studies, 4,* 185–199. (p. 147)

Cucchi, A., Ryan, D., Konstantakopoulos, G., Stroumpa, S., Kaçar, A. Ş., Renshaw, S., . . . Kravariti, E. (2016). Lifetime prevalence of non-suicidal self-injury in patients with eating disorders: A systematic review and meta-analysis. *Psychological Medicine, 46,* 1345–1358. (p. 532)

Cuijpers, P. (2017). Four decades of outcome research on psychotherapies for adult depression: An overview of a series of meta-analyses. *Canadian Psychology/Psychologie Canadienne, 58,* 7–19. (p. 552)

Cuijpers, P., Driessen, E., Hollon, S. D., van Oppen, P., Barth, J., & Andersson, G. (2012). The efficacy of non-directive supportive therapy for adult depression: A meta-analysis. *Clinical Psychology Review, 32,* 280–291. (p. 553)

Cuijpers, P., van Straten, A., Schuurmans, J., van Oppen, P., Hollon, S. D., & Andersson, G. (2010). Psychotherapy for chronic major depression and dysthymia: A meta-analysis. *Clinical Psychology Review, 30,* 51–62. (p. 562)

Culbert, K. M., Burt, S. A., McGue, M., Iacono, W. G., & Klump, K. L. (2009). Puberty and the genetic diathesis of disordered eating attitudes and behaviors. *Journal of Abnormal Psychology, 118,* 788–796. (p. 532)

Culbert, K. M., Racine, S. E., & Klump, K. L. (2015). Research review: What we have learned about the causes of eating disorders—a synthesis of sociocultural, psychological, and biological research. *Journal of Child Psychology and Psychiatry, 56,* 1141–1164. (p. 532)

Cummins, R. A. (2006, April 4). *Australian Unity Wellbeing Index: Survey 14.1.* Melbourne, Victoria, Australia: Australian Centre on Quality of Life, Deakin University. (p. 409)

Cunningham, G. B., Ferreira, M., & Fink, J. S. (2009). Reactions to prejudicial statements: The influence of statement content and characteristics of the commenter. *Group Dynamics: Theory, Research, and Practice, 13,* 59–73. (p. 299)

Cunningham, M. R., Roberts, A., Barbee, A. P., Druen, P. B., & Wu, C.-H. (2005). "Their ideas of beauty are, on the whole, the same as ours": Consistency and variability in the cross-cultural perception of female physical attractiveness. *Journal of Personality and Social Psychology, 68,* 261–279. (p. 449)

Cunningham, W. A., Johnson, M. K., Raye, C. L., Gatenby, J. C., Gore, J. C., & Banaji, M. R. (2004). Separable neural components in the processing of Black and White faces. *Psychological Science, 15,* 806–813. (p. 435)

Curci, A., Lanciano, T., Mastandrea, S., & Sartori, G. (2015). Flashbulb memories of the Pope's resignation: Explicit and implicit measure across different religious groups. *Memory, 23,* 529–544. (p. 278)

Currie, T. E., & Little, A. C. (2009). The relative importance of the face and body in judgments of human physical attractiveness. *Evolution and Human Behavior, 30,* 409–416. (p. 449)

Curry, J., Silva, S., Rohde, P., Ginsburg, G., Kratochvil, C., Simons, A., . . . March, J. (2011). Recovery and recurrence following treatment for adolescent major depression. *Archives of General Psychiatry, 68,* 263–269. (p. 517)

Curtis, R. C., & Miller, K. (1986). Believing another likes or dislikes you: Behaviors making the beliefs come true. *Journal of Personality and Social Psychology, 51,* 284–290. (p. 450)

Custers, R., & Aarts, H. (2010). The unconscious will: How the pursuit of goals operates outside of conscious awareness. *Science, 329,* 47–50. (p. 305)

Cyders, M. A., & Smith, G. T. (2008). Emotion-based dispositions to rash action: Positive and negative urgency. *Psychological Bulletin, 134,* 807–828. (p. 368)

Czarna, A. Z., Leifeld, P., Śmieja, M., Dufner, M., & Salovey, P. (2016). Do narcissism and emotional intelligence win us friends? Modeling dynamics of peer popularity using inferential network analysis. *Personality and Social Psychology Bulletin, 42,* 1588–1599. (pp. 326, 489)

Czeisler, C. A., Allan, J. S., Strogatz, S. H., Ronda, J. M., Sanchez, R., Rios, C. D., . . . Kronauer, R. E. (1986). Bright light resets the human circadian pacemaker independent of the timing of the sleep-wake cycle. *Science, 233,* 667–671. (p. 91)

Czeisler, C. A., Duffy, J. F., Shanahan, T. L., Brown, E. N., Mitchell, J. F., Rimmer, D. W., . . . Kronauer, R. E. (1999). Stability, precision, and near-24-hour period of the human circadian pacemaker. *Science, 284,* 2177–2181. (p. 90)

Czeisler, C. A., Kronauer, R. E., Allan, J. S., & Duffy, J. F. (1989). Bright light induction of strong (Type O) resetting of the human circadian pacemaker. *Science, 244,* 1328–1333. (p. 91)

da Cunha-Bang, S., Fisher, P. M., Hjordt, L. V., Perfalk, E., Persson Skibsted, A., Bock, C., . . . Knudsen, G. M. (2017). Violent offenders respond to provocations with high amygdala and striatal reactivity. *Social Cognitive and Affective Neuroscience, 12,* 802–810. (p. 55)

Dai, H., Milkman, K. L., & Riis, J. (2014). The fresh start effect: Temporal landmarks motivate aspirational behavior. *Management Science, 60,* 2563–2582. (p. B-9)

Daley, J. (2011, July/August). What you don't know can kill you. *Discover* (discovermagazine.com). (p. 302)

Daly, M., Delaney, L., Egan, R. F., & Baumeister, R. F. (2015). Childhood self-control and unemployment throughout the life span: Evidence from two British cohort studies. *Psychological Science, 26,* 709–723. (p. 145)

Damasio, A. R. (2003). *Looking for Spinoza: Joy, sorrow, and the feeling brain.* New York: Harcourt. (p. 369)

Damasio, A. R. (2010). *Self comes to mind: Constructing the conscious brain.* New York: Pantheon. (p. 486)

Damian, R. I., & Roberts, B. W. (2015). The associations of birth order with personality and intelligence in a representative sample of U.S. high school students. *Journal of Research in Personality, 58,* 96–105. (p. 478)

Damon, W., Menon, J., & Bronk, K. (2003). The development of purpose during adolescence. *Applied Developmental Science, 7,* 119–128. (p. 147)

Dana, J., Dawes, R., & Peterson, N. (2013). Belief in the unstructured interview: The persistence of an illusion. *Judgment and Decision Making, 8,* 512–520. (p. B-5)

Danelli, L., Cossu, G., Berlingeri, M., Bottini, G., Sberna, M., & Paulesu, E. (2013). Is a lone right hemisphere enough? Neurolinguistic architecture in a case with a very early left hemispherectomy. *Neurocase, 19,* 209–231. (p. 64)

Daniel, T. A., & Katz, J. S. (2017). Primacy and recency effects for taste. *Journal of Experimental Psychology: Learning, Memory, and Cognition.* Advance online publication. http://dx.doi.org/10.1037/xlm0000437 (p. 282)

Danner, D. D., Snowdon, D. A., & Friesen, W. V. (2001). Positive emotions in early life and longevity: Findings from the Nun Study. *Journal of Personality and Social Psychology, 80,* 804–813. (p. 399)

Danso, H., & Esses, V. (2001). Black experimenters and the intellectual test performance of White participants: The tables are turned. *Journal of Experimental Social Psychology, 37,* 158–165. (p. 344)

Danziger, S., & Ward, R. (2010). Language changes implicit associations between ethnic groups and evaluation in bilinguals. *Psychological Science, 21,* 799–800. (p. 319)

Darby, M. M., Yolken, R. H., & Sabunciyan, S. (2016). Consistently altered expression of gene sets in postmortem brains of individuals with major psychiatric disorders. *Translational Psychiatry, 6,* e890. (p. 526)

Darley, J. M. (2009). Morality in the law: The psychological foundations of citizens' desires to punish transgressions. *Annual Review of Law and Social Science, 5,* 1–23. (p. 144)

Darley, J. M., & Alter, A. (2013). Behavioral issues of punishment, retribution, and deterrence. In E. Shafir (Ed.), *The behavioral foundations of public policy* (pp. 181–194). Princeton, NJ: Princeton University Press. (p. 249)

Darley, J. M., & Latané, B. (1968a). Bystander intervention in emergencies: Diffusion of responsibility. *Journal of Personality and Social Psychology, 8,* 377–383. (pp. 453, 454)

Darley, J. M., & Latané, B. (1968b, December). When will people help in a crisis? *Psychology Today,* pp. 54–57, 70–71. (p. 453)

Darrach, B., & Norris, J. (1984, August). An American tragedy. *Life,* pp. 58–74. (p. 530)

Darwin, C. (1859). *On the origin of species by means of natural selection.* London: John Murray. (p. 76)

Darwin, C. (1872). *The expression of the emotions in man and animals.* London: John Murray. (p. 380)

Das, S., Tonelli, M., & Ziedonis, D. (2016). Update on smoking cessation: E-cigarettes, emerging tobacco products trends, and new technology-based interventions. *Current Psychiatry Reports, 18*(5), 51. (p. 105)

Daum, I., & Schugens, M. M. (1996). On the cerebellum and classical conditioning. *Psychological Science, 5,* 58–61. (p. 277)

Davey, G., & Rato, R. (2012). Subjective well-being in China: A review. *Journal of Happiness Studies, 13,* 333–346. (p. 410)

Davey, G. C. L. (1992). Classical conditioning and the acquisition of human fears and phobias: A review and synthesis of the literature. *Advances in Behavior Research and Therapy, 14,* 29–66. (p. 255)

Davey, G. C. L. (1995). Preparedness and phobias: Specific evolved associations or a generalized expectancy bias? *Behavioral and Brain Sciences, 18,* 289–297. (p. 512)

Davidoff, J. (2004). Coloured thinking. *The Psychologist, 17,* 570–572. (p. 319)

Davidson, R. J. (2000). Affective style, psychopathology, and resilience: Brain mechanisms and plasticity. *American Psychologist, 55,* 1196–1209. (p. 374)

Davidson, R. J., & Begley, S. (2012). *The emotional life of your brain: How its unique patterns affect the way you think, feel, and live—and how you can change them.* New York: Hudson Street Press. (p. 369)

Davidson, R. J., Kabat-Zinn, J., Schumacher, J., Rosenkranz, M., Muller, D., Santorelli, S. F., . . . Sheridan, J. F. (2003). Alterations in brain and immune function produced by mindfulness meditation. *Psychosomatic Medicine, 65,* 564–570. (p. 404)

Davidson, R. J., Pizzagalli, D., Nitschke, J. B., & Putnam, K. (2002). Depression: Perspectives from affective neuroscience. *Annual Review of Psychology, 53,* 545–574. (p. 518)

Davidson, R. J., Putnam, K. M., & Larson, C. L. (2000). Dysfunction in the neural circuitry of emotion regulation—a possible prelude to violence. *Science, 289,* 591–594. (p. 442)

Davidson, T. L., & Riley, A. L. (2015). Taste, sickness, and learning. *American Scientist, 103,* 204–211. (p. 255)

Davies, P. (2007). *Cosmic jackpot: Why our universe is just right for life.* Boston: Houghton Mifflin. (p. 77)

Davis, B. E., Moon, R. Y., Sachs, H. C., & Ottolini, M. C. (1998). Effects of sleep position on infant motor development. *Pediatrics, 102,* 1135–1140. (p. 124)

Davis, D. E., Choe, E., Meyers, J., Wade, N., Varias, K., Gifford, A., . . . Worthington, E. L. (2016). Thankful for the little things: A meta-analysis of gratitude interventions. *Journal of Counseling Psychology, 63,* 20–31. (p. 412)

Davis, E. P., Stout, S. A., Molet, J., Vegetabile, B., Glynn, L. M., Sandman, C. A., . . . Baram, T. Z. (2017). Exposure to unpredictable maternal sensory signals influences cognitive development across species. *PNAS, 114,* 10390–10395. (p. 133)

Davis, J. O., & Phelps, J. A. (1995). Twins with schizophrenia: Genes or germs? *Schizophrenia Bulletin, 21,* 13–18. (p. 526)

Davis, J. O., Phelps, J. A., & Bracha, H. S. (1995). Prenatal development of monozygotic twins and concordance for schizophrenia. *Schizophrenia Bulletin, 21,* 357–366. (p. 526)

Davis, J. P., Lander, K., & Jansari, A. (2013). I never forget a face. *The Psychologist, 26,* 726–729. (p. 266)

Davis, K., Christodoulou, J., Seider, S., & Gardner, H. (2011). The theory of multiple intelligences. In R. J. Sternberg & S. B. Kaufman (Eds.), *Cambridge handbook of intelligence*. Cambridge, UK; New York: Cambridge University Press. (p. 324)

Davis, M. (2005). Searching for a drug to extinguish fear. *Cerebrum, 7,* 47–58. (p. 561)

Davison, K. P., Pennebaker, J. W., & Dickerson, S. S. (2000). Who talks? The social psychology of illness support groups. *American Psychologist, 55,* 205–217. (p. 548)

Davison, S. L., & Davis, S. R. (2011). Androgenic hormones and aging—the link with female sexual function. *Hormones and Behavior, 59,* 745–753. (p. 173)

Dawes, R. M. (1980). Social dilemmas. *Annual Review of Psychology, 31,* 169–193. (p. 456)

Dawes, R. M. (1994). *House of cards: Psychology and psychotherapy built on myth.* New York: Free Press. (p. 486)

Dawkins, L., Shahzad, F.-Z., Ahmed, S. S., & Edmonds, C. J. (2011). Expectation of having consumed caffeine can improve performance and moods. *Appetite, 57,* 597–600. (p. 27)

Dawkins, R. (1998). *Unweaving the rainbow: Science, delusion and the appetite for wonder.* Boston: Houghton Mifflin. (p. 77)

Day, F. R., Thompson, D. J., Helgason, H., Chasman, D. I., Finucane, H., Sulem, P., . . . Altmaier, E. (2017). Genomic analyses identify hundreds of variants associated with age at menarche and support a role for puberty timing in cancer risk. *Nature Genetics, 49,* 834–841. (p. 167)

de Boysson-Bardies, B., Halle, P., Sagart, L., & Durand, C. (1989). A cross linguistic investigation of vowel formats in babbling. *Journal of Child Language, 16,* 1–17. (p. 314)

de Bruin, A., Barbara, T., & Della Sala, S. (2015a). Cognitive advantage in bilingualism: An example of publication bias? *Psychological Science, 26,* 99–107. (p. 320)

de Bruin, A., Treccani, B., & Della Sala, S. (2015b). The connection is in the data: We should consider them all. *Psychological Science, 26,* 947–949. (p. 320)

de Chastelaine, M., Mattson, J. T., Wang, T. H., Donley, B. E., & Rugg, M. D. (2016). The neural correlates of recollection and retrieval monitoring: Relationships with age and recollection performance. *NeuroImage, 138,* 164–175. (p. 276)

de Courten-Myers, G. M. (2005, February 4). Personal communication. (p. 59)

De Dreu, C. K. W., Greer, L. L., Handgraaf, M. J. J., Shalvi, S., Van Kleef, G. A., Baas, M., . . . Feith, S. W. W. (2010). The neuropeptide oxytocin regulated parochial altruism in intergroup conflict among humans. *Science, 328,* 1409–1411. (p. 49)

De Dreu, C. K. W., Nijstad, B. A., Baas, M., Wolsink, I., & Roskes, M. (2012). Working memory benefits creative insight, musical improvisation, and original ideation through maintained task-focused attention. *Personality and Social Psychology Bulletin, 38,* 656–669. (p. 271)

de Gee, J., Knapen, T., & Donner, T. H. (2014). Decision-related pupil dilation reflects upcoming choice and individual bias. *PNAS, 111,* E618–E625. (p. 201)

de Gelder, B. (2010, May). Uncanny sight in the blind. *Scientific American,* pp. 60–65. (p. 84)

de Hoogh, A. H. B., den Hartog, D. N., Koopman, P. L., Thierry, H., van den Berg, P. T., van der Weide, J. G., & Wilderom, C. P. M. (2004). Charismatic leadership, environmental dynamism, and performance. *European Journal of Work and Organisational Psychology, 13,* 447–471. (p. B-10)

de la Cruz, L. F., Rydell, M., Runeson, B., D'Onofrio, B. M., Brander, G., Rück, C., . . . Matai-Cols, D. (2017). Suicide in obsessive-compulsive disorder: A population-based study of 36788 Swedish patients. *Molecular Psychiatry, 22,* 1626–1632. (p. 500)

de Lange, M., Debets, L., Ruitenberg, K., & Holland, R. (2012). Making less of a mess: Scent exposure as a tool for behavioral change. *Social Influence, 7,* 90–97. (p. 227)

de Lau, L. M., & Breteler, M. M. (2006). Epidemiology of Parkinson's disease. *The Lancet Neurology, 5,* 525–535.

de la Vega, A., Chang, L. J., Banich, M. T., Wager, T. D., & Yarkoni, T. (2016). Large-scale meta-analysis of human medial frontal cortex reveals tripartite functional organization. *The Journal of Neuroscience, 36,* 6553–6562. (p. 62)

De Neve, J., Christakis, N. A., Fowler, J. H., & Frey, B. S. (2012). Genes, economics, and happiness. *Journal of Neuroscience, Psychology, and Economics, 5,* 193–211. (p. 411)

De Neve, J.-E., Diener, E., Tay, L., & Xuereb, C. (2013). The objective benefits of subjective well-being. In J. F. Helliwell, R. Layard, & J. Sachs (Eds.), *World happiness report 2013.* Volume 2. (pp. 54–79). New York: UN Sustainable Network Development Solutions Network. (pp. 407, B-12)

De Neve, K. M., & Cooper, H. (1998). The happy personality: A meta-analysis of 137 personality traits and subjective well-being. *Psychological Bulletin, 124,* 197–229. (p. 411)

de Waal, F. (2016). *Are we smart enough to know how smart animals are?* New York: Norton. (p. 309)

de Wit, L., Luppino, F., van Straten, A., Penninx, B., Zitman, F., & Cuijpers, P. (2010). Depression and obesity: A meta-analysis of community-based studies. *Psychiatry Research, 178,* 230–235. (p. 365)

De Wolff, M. S., & van IJzendoorn, M. H. (1997). Sensitivity and attachment: A meta-analysis on parental antecedents of infant attachment. *Child Development, 68,* 571–591. (p. 134)

Deal, G. (2011, January 14). Chinese parenting: Thanks, I'll pass. *The Wall Street Journal.* Retrieved from http://blogs.wsj.com/wsjam/2011/01/14/chinese-parenting-thanks-ill-pass/ (p. 149)

Dean, G. (2012, November/December). Phrenology and the grand delusion of experience. *Skeptical Inquirer,* pp. 31–38. (p. 38)

Deary, I. J. (2008). Why do intelligent people live longer? *Nature, 456,* 175–176. (p. 333)

Deary, I. J. (2016, February). Intelligence over time. Quoted in APS Award Address. Association for Psychological Science *Observer,* p. 15. (p. 333)

Deary, I. J., Johnson, W., & Houlihan, L. M. (2009a). Genetic foundations of human intelligence. *Human Genetics, 126,* 215–232. (pp. 336, 338)

Deary, I. J., Pattie, A., & Starr, J. M. (2013). The stability of intelligence from age 11 to age 90 years: The Lothian birth cohort of 1921. *Psychological Science, 24,* 2361–2368. (pp. 332, 333)

Deary, I. J., & Ritchie, S. J. (2016). Processing speed differences between 70- and 83-year-olds matched on childhood IQ. *Intelligence, 55,* 28–33. (p. 333)

Deary, I. J., Thorpe, G., Wilson, V., Starr, J. M., & Whalley, L. J. (2003). Population sex differences in IQ at age 11: The Scottish mental survey 1932. *Intelligence, 31,* 533–541. (p. 340)

Deary, I. J., Whalley, L. J., & Starr, J. M. (2009b). *A lifetime of intelligence: Follow-up studies of the Scottish Mental Surveys of 1932 and 1947.* Washington, DC: American Psychological Association. (p. 332)

Deary, I. J., Whiteman, M. C., Starr, J. M., Whalley, L. J., & Fox, H. C. (2004). The impact of childhood intelligence on later life: Following up the Scottish mental surveys of 1932 and 1947. *Journal of Personality and Social Psychology, 86,* 130–147. (pp. 332, 333)

Deary, I. J., Yang, J., Davies, G., Harris, S. E., Tenesa, A., Liewald, D., . . . Visscher, P. M. (2012). Genetic contributions to stability and change in intelligence from childhood to old age. *Nature, 481,* 212–215. (p. 338)

DeBruine, L. M. (2002). Facial resemblance enhances trust. *Proceedings of the Royal Society of London, 269,* 1307–1312. (p. 447)

DeBruine, L. M. (2004). Facial resemblance increases the attractiveness of same-sex faces more than other-sex faces. *Proceedings of the Royal Society of London B, 271,* 2085–2090. (p. 447)

DeCasper, A. J., Lecanuet, J.-P., Busnel, M.-C., Granier-Deferre, C., & Maugeais, R. (1994). Fetal reactions to recurrent maternal speech. *Infant Behavior and Development, 17,* 159–164. (p. 119)

DeCasper, A. J., & Spence, M. J. (1986). Prenatal maternal speech influences newborns' perception of speech sounds. *Infant Behavior and Development, 9,* 133–150. (p. 119)

Dechêne, A., Stahl, C., Hansen, J., & Wänke, M. (2010). The truth about the truth: A meta-analytic review of the truth effect. *Personality and Social Psychology Review, 14,* 238–257. (pp. 16, 18)

Dechesne, M., Pyszczynski, T., Arndt, J., Ransom, S., Sheldon, K. M., van Knippenberg, A., & Janssen, J. (2003). Literal and symbolic immortality: The effect of evidence of literal immortality on self-esteem striving in response to mortality salience. *Journal of Personality and Social Psychology, 84,* 722–737. (p. 29)

Deci, E. L., Koestner, R., & Ryan, R. M. (1999, November). A meta-analytic review of experiments examining the effects of extrinsic rewards on intrinsic motivation. *Psychological Bulletin, 125,* 627–668. (p. 358)

Deci, E. L., & Ryan, R. M. (2009). Self-determination theory: A consideration of human motivational universals. In P. J. Corr & G. Matthews (Eds.), *The Cambridge handbook of personality psychology.* New York: Cambridge University Press. (p. 353)

Deci, E. L., & Ryan, R. M. (2012). Motivation, personality, and development within embedded social contexts: An overview of self-determination theory. In R. M. Ryan (Ed.), *Oxford handbook of human motivation* (pp. 85–107). Oxford: Oxford University Press. (p. 352)

DeFina, R., & Hannon, L. (2015). The changing relationship between unemployment and suicide. *Suicide and Life-Threatening Behavior, 45,* 217–229. (p. 501)

Dehne, K. L., & Riedner, G. (2005). *Sexually transmitted infections among adolescents: The need for adequate health services.* Geneva, Switzerland: World Health Organization. (p. 175)

DeLamater, J. (2012). Sexual expression in later life: A review and synthesis. *Journal of Sex Research, 49,* 125–141. (p. 151)

DeLamater, J. D., & Sill, M. (2005). Sexual desire in later life. *Journal of Sex Research, 42,* 138–149. (p. 151)

Delaney, H. D., Miller, W. R., & Bisonó, A. M. (2007). Religiosity and spirituality among psychologists: A survey of clinician members of the American Psychological Association. *Professional Psychology: Research and Practice, 38,* 538–546. (p. 556)

Delaunay-El Allam, M., Soussignan, R., Patris, B., Marlier, L., & Schaal, B. (2010). Long-lasting memory for an odor acquired at the mother's breast. *Developmental Science, 13,* 849–863. (p. 121)

Delgado, J. M. R. (1969). *Physical control of the mind: Toward a psychocivilized society.* New York: Harper & Row. (p. 60)

DeLoache, J. S. (1987). Rapid change in the symbolic functioning of very young children. *Science, 238,* 1556–1557. (p. 127)

DeLoache, J. S., Chiong, C., Sherman, K., Islam, N., Vanderborght, M., Troseth, G. L., . . . O'Doherty, K. (2010). Do babies learn from baby media? *Psychological Science, 21,* 1570–1574. (p. 339)

DeLongis, A., Coyne, J. C., Dakof, G., Folkman, S., & Lazarus, R. S. (1982). Relationship of daily hassles, uplifts, and major life events to health status. *Health Psychology, 1,* 119–136. (p. 386)

DeLongis, A., Folkman, S., & Lazarus, R. S. (1988). The impact of daily stress on health and mood: Psychological and social resources as mediators. *Journal of Personality and Social Psychology, 54,* 486–495. (p. 386)

DelPriore, D. J., Schlomer, G. L., & Ellis, B. J. (2017). Impact of fathers on parental monitoring of daughters and their affiliation with sexually promiscuous peers: A genetically and environmentally controlled sibling study. *Developmental Psychology, 53,* 1330–1343. (p. 135)

Dement, W. C. (1978). *Some must watch while some must sleep.* New York: Norton. (p. 87)

Dement, W. C. (1999). *The promise of sleep.* New York: Delacorte Press. (pp. 88, 90, 92, 93)

Dement, W. C., & Wolpert, E. A. (1958). The relation of eye movements, body mobility, and external stimuli to dream content. *Journal of Experimental Psychology, 55,* 543–553. (p. 97)

Demir, E., & Dickson, B. J. (2005). *fruitless* splicing specifies male courtship behavior in *Drosophila. Cell, 121,* 785–794. (p. 181)

Dempster, E., Viana, J., Pidsley, R., & Mill, J. (2013). Epigenetic studies of schizophrenia: Progress, predicaments, and promises for the future. *Schizophrenia Bulletin, 39,* 11–16. (p. 526)

Denissen, J. J. A., Bleidorn, W., Hennecke, M., Luhmann, M., Orth, U., Specht, J., & Zimmermann, J. (2017). Uncovering the power of personality to shape income. *Psychological Science, 29,* 3–13. (p. B-3)

Denissen, J. J. A., Bleidorn, W., Hennecke, M., Luhmann, M., Orth, U., Specht, J., & Zimmermann, J. (2018). Uncovering the power of personality to shape income. *Psychological Science.* Advance online publication. doi:10.1177/0956797617724435 (p. 483)

Dennehy, T. C., & Dasgupta, N. (2017). Female peer mentors early in college increase women's positive academic experiences and retention in engineering. *PNAS, 114,* 5964–5969. (p. 168)

Denny, B. T., Inhoff, M. C., Zerubavel, N., Davachi, L., & Ochsner, K. N. (2015). Getting over it: Long-lasting effects of emotion regulation on amygdala response. *Psychological Science, 26,* 1377–1388. (p. 371)

Denton, K., & Krebs, D. (1990). From the scene to the crime: The effect of alcohol and social context on moral judgment. *Journal of Personality and Social Psychology, 59,* 242–248. (p. 103)

Depla, M. F. I. A., ten Have, M. L., van Balkom, A. J. L. M., & de Graaf, R. (2008). Specific fears and phobias in the general population: Results from the Netherlands Mental Health Survey and Incidence Study (NEMESIS). *Social Psychiatry and Psychiatric Epidemiology, 43,* 200–208. (p. 508)

Dermer, M., Cohen, S. J., Jacobsen, E., & Anderson, E. A. (1979). Evaluative judgments of aspects of life as a function of vicarious exposure to hedonic extremes. *Journal of Personality and Social Psychology, 37,* 247–260. (p. 411)

Desikan, R. S., Cabral, H. J., Hess, C. P., Dillon, W. P., Glastonbury, C. M., Weiner, M. W., & Fischl, B. (2009). Automated MRI measures identify individuals with mild cognitive impairment and Alzheimer's disease. *Brain, 132,* 2048–2057. (p. 266)

DeSteno, D., Petty, R. E., Wegener, D. T., & Rucker, D. D. (2000). Beyond valence in the perception of likelihood: The role of emotion specificity. *Journal of Personality and Social Psychology, 78,* 397–416. (p. 281)

Dettman, S. J., Pinder, D., Briggs, R. J. S., Dowell, R. C., & Leigh, J. R. (2007). Communication development in children who receive the cochlear implant younger than 12 months: Risk versus benefits. *Ear and Hearing, 28*(2, Suppl.), 11S–18S. (p. 218)

Deutsch, J. A. (1972, July). Brain reward: ESP and ecstasy. *Psychology Today,* 46–48. (p. 56)

DeValois, R. L., & DeValois, K. K. (1975). Neural coding of color. In E. C. Carterette & M. P. Friedman (Eds.), *Handbook of perception: Vol. 5. Seeing* (pp. 117–166). New York: Academic Press. (p. 204)

Devilly, G. J. (2003). Eye movement desensitization and reprocessing: A chronology of its development and scientific standing. *Scientific Review of Mental Health Practice, 1,* 113–118. (p. 554)

Dew, M. A., Hoch, C. C., Buysse, D. J., Monk, T. H., Begley, A. E., Houck, P. R., . . . Reynolds, C. F., III. (2003). Healthy older adults' sleep predicts all-cause mortality at 4 to 19 years of follow-up. *Psychosomatic Medicine, 65,* 63–73. (p. 93)

DeWall, C. N., MacDonald, G., Webster, G. D., Masten, C. L., Baumeister, R. F., Powell, C., . . . Eisenberger, N. I. (2010). Acetaminophen reduces social pain: Behavioral and neural evidence. *Psychological Science, 21,* 931–937. (p. 354)

DeWall, C. N., & Pond, R. S., Jr. (2011). Loneliness and smoking: The costs of the desire to reconnect. *Self and Identity, 10,* 375–385. (p. 111)

DeWall, C. N., Pond, R. S., Jr., Campbell, W. K., & Twenge, J. M. (2011). Tuning in to psychological change: Linguistic markers of psychological traits and emotions over time in popular U.S. song lyrics. *Psychology of Aesthetics, Creativity, and the Arts, 5,* 200–207. (p. 136)

DeWall, C. N., Pond, R. S., Jr., Carter, E. C., McCullough, M. E., Lambert, N. M., Fincham, F. D., & Nezlek, J. B. (2014). Explaining the relationship between religiousness and substance use: Self-control matters. *Journal of Personality and Social Psychology, 107,* 339–351. (pp. 112, 406)

Dewar, M., Alber, J., Butler, C., Cowan, N., & Sala, S. D. (2012). Brief wakeful resting boosts new memories over the long term. *Psychological Science, 23,* 955–960. (p. 295)

DeYoung, C. G., Hirsch, J. B., Shane, M. S., Papademetris, X., Rajeevan, N., & Gray, J. R. (2010). Testing predictions from personality neuroscience: Brain structure and the Big Five. *Psychological Science, 21,* 820–828. (p. 478)

Di Tella, R., Haisken-De New, J., & MacCulloch, R. (2010). Happiness adaptation to income and to status in an individual panel. *Journal of Economic Behavior & Organization, 76,* 834–852. (p. 410)

Di Tella, R., & MacCulloch, R. (2010). Happiness adaptation to income beyond "basic needs." In E. Diener, J. Helliwell, & D. Kahneman (Eds.), *International differences in well-being,* pp. 217–247. New York: Oxford University Press. (p. 410)

Diaconis, P. (2002, August 11). Quoted by L. Belkin, The odds of that. *The New York Times* (nytimes.com). (p. 17)

Diaconis, P., & Mosteller, F. (1989). Methods for studying coincidences. *Journal of the American Statistical Association, 84,* 853–861. (p. 17)

Dick, D. M. (2007). Identification of genes influencing a spectrum of externalizing psychopathology. *Current Directions in Psychological Science, 16,* 331–335. (p. 530)

Dickens, W. T., & Flynn, J. R. (2006). Black Americans reduce the racial IQ gap: Evidence from standardization samples. *Psychological Science, 17,* 913–920. (p. 342)

Dickerson, S. S., & Kemeny, M. E. (2004). Acute stressors and cortisol responses: A theoretical integration and synthesis of laboratory research. *Psychological Bulletin, 130,* 355–391. (pp. 386, 396)

Dickson, B. J. (2005, June 3). Quoted in E. Rosenthal, For fruit flies, gene shift tilts sex orientation. *The New York Times* (nytimes.com). (p. 181)

Dickson, N., van Roode, T., Cameron, C., & Paul, C. (2013). Stability and change in same-sex attraction, experience, and identity by sex and age in a New Zealand birth cohort. *Archives of Sexual Behavior, 42,* 753–763. (p. 179)

Diener, E. (2006). Guidelines of national indicators of subjective well-being and ill-being. *Journal of Happiness Studies, 7,* 397–404. (p. 412)

Diener, E. (2013). The remarkable changes in the science of well-being. *Perspectives on Psychological Science, 8,* 663–666. (p. 412)

Diener, E., & Biswas-Diener, R. (2008). *Happiness: Unlocking the mysteries of psychological wealth.* Malden, MA: Blackwell. (p. 410)

Diener, E., Nickerson, C., Lucas, R. E., & Sandvik, E. (2002). Dispositional affect and job outcomes. *Social Indicators Research, 59,* 229–259. (p. 407)

Diener, E., & Oishi, S. (2000). Money and happiness: Income and subjective well-being across nations. In E. Diener & E. M. Suh (Eds.), *Subjective well-being across cultures.* Cambridge, MA: MIT Press. (p. 410)

Diener, E., Oishi, S., & Lucas, R. E. (2003). Personality, culture, and subjective well-being: Emotional and cognitive evaluations of life. *Annual Review of Psychology, 54,* 403–425. (p. 411)

Diener, E., Oishi, S., & Lucas, R. E. (2009). Subjective well-being: The science of happiness and life satisfaction. In S. J. Lopez & C. R. Snyder (Eds.), *The Oxford handbook of positive psychology* (2nd ed., pp. 187–194). New York: Oxford University Press. (p. 412)

Diener, E., Oishi, S., & Lucas, R. E. (2015). National accounts of subjective well-being. *American Psychologist, 70,* 234–242. (p. 412)

Diener, E., Oishi, S., & Park, J. Y. (2014). An incomplete list of eminent psychologists of the modern era. *Archives of Scientific Psychology, 21,* 20–31. (p. 258)

Diener, E., Pressman, S. D., Hunter, J., & Delgadillo-Chase, D. (2017). If, why, and when subjective well-being influences health, and future needed research. *Applied Psychology: Health and Well-Being, 9*(2), 133–167. (p. 392)

Diener, E., & Seligman, M. E. P. (2002). Very happy people. *Psychological Science, 13,* 81–84. (p. 352)

Diener, E., & Tay, L. (2015). Subjective well-being and human welfare around the world as reflected in the Gallup world poll. *International Journal of Psychology, 50,* 135–149. (p. 409)

Diener, E., Tay, L., & Myers, D. G. (2011). The religion paradox: If religion makes people happy, why are so many dropping out? *Journal of Personality and Social Psychology, 101,* 1278–1290. (pp. 23, 411)

Diener, E., Wolsic, B., & Fujita, F. (1995). Physical attractiveness and subjective well-being. *Journal of Personality and Social Psychology, 69,* 120–129. (p. 449)

DiFranza, J. R. (2008, May). Hooked from the first cigarette. *Scientific American,* pp. 82–87. (p. 105)

Dijksterhuis, A., & Aarts, H. (2003). On wildebeests and humans: The preferential detection of negative stimuli. *Psychological Science, 14*, 14–18. (p. 376)

Dijksterhuis, A., & Strick, M. (2016). A case for thinking without consciousness. *Perspectives on Psychological Science, 11*, 117–132. (p. 305)

Dik, B. J., & Duffy, R. D. (2012). *Make your job a calling: How the psychology of vocation can change your life at work.* Conshohocken, PA: Templeton Press. (p. B-1)

Dik, B. J., & Rottinghaus, P. J. (2013). Assessments of interests. In K. F. Geisinger & six others (Eds.). *APA handbook of testing and assessment in psychology, Vol. 2.* Washington, DC: APA. (p. B-3)

DiLalla, D. L., Carey, G., Gottesman, I. I., & Bouchard, T. J., Jr. (1996). Heritability of MMPI personality indicators of psychopathology in twins reared apart. *Journal of Abnormal Psychology, 105*, 491–499. (p. 518)

Dimberg, U., Thunberg, M., & Elmehed, K. (2000). Unconscious facial reactions to emotional facial expressions. *Psychological Science, 11*, 86–89. (pp. 370, 382)

Dimidjian, S., & Hollon, S. D. (2010). How would we know if psychotherapy were harmful? *American Psychologist, 65*, 21–33. (p. 554)

Ding, F., O'Donnell, J., Xu, Q., Kang, N., Goldman, N., & Nedergaard, M. (2016). Changes in the composition of brain interstitial ions control the sleep-wake cycle. *Science, 352*, 550–555. (p. 91)

Dinges, C. W., Varnon, C. A., Cota, L. D., Slykerman, S., & Abramson, C. I. (2017). Studies of learned helplessness in honey bees (*Apis mellifera ligustica*). *Journal of Experimental Psychology: Animal Learning and Cognition, 43*, 147–158. (p. 31)

Dinges, N. G., & Hull, P. (1992). Personality, culture, and international studies. In D. Lieberman (Ed.), *Revealing the world: An interdisciplinary reader for international studies.* Dubuque, IA: Kendall-Hunt. (p. 319)

Dingfelder, S. F. (2010, November). A second chance for the Mexican wolf. *Monitor on Psychology*, pp. 20–21. (pp. 255, 542)

Dion, K. K., & Dion, K. L. (1993). Individualistic and collectivistic perspectives on gender and the cultural context of love and intimacy. *Journal of Social Issues, 49*, 53–69. (p. 491)

Dirix, C. E. H., Nijhuis, J. G., Jongsma, H. W., & Hornstra, G. (2009). Aspects of fetal learning and memory. *Child Development, 80*, 1251–1258. (p. 120)

DiSantis, K. I., Birch, L. L., Davey, A., Serrano, E. L., Zhang, J., Bruton, Y., & Fisher, J. O. (2013). Plate size and children's appetite: Effects of larger dishware on self-served portions and intake. *Pediatrics, 131*, e1451–e1458. (p. 364)

Discover. (1996, May). A fistful of risks, pp. 82–83. (p. 105)

Ditre, J. W., Brandon, T. H., Zale, E. L., & Meagher, M. M. (2011). Pain, nicotine, and smoking: Research findings and mechanistic considerations. *Psychological Bulletin, 137*, 1065–1093. (p. 105)

Ditto, P., Wojcik, S., Chen, E., Grady, R., & Ringel, M. (2015). Political bias is tenacious. *Behavioral and Brain Sciences, 38*. doi:10.1017/S0140525X14001186 (p. 18)

Dixon, J., Durrheim, K., & Tredoux, C. (2007). Intergroup contact and attitudes toward the principle and practice of racial equality. *Psychological Science, 18*, 867–872. (p. 457)

Dobbs, D. (2009). The post-traumatic stress trap. *Scientific American, 300*, 64–69. (p. 510)

Dodge, K. A. (2009). Mechanisms of gene-environment interaction effects in the development of conduct disorder. *Perspectives on Psychological Science, 4*, 408–414. (p. 530)

Dodge, K. A., Bai, Y., Ladd, H. F., & Muschkin, C. G. (2017). Impact of North Carolina's early childhood programs and policies on educational outcomes in elementary school. *Child Development, 88*(3), 996–1014. (p. 339)

Doherty, C., & Kiley, J. (2016, June 22). Key facts about partisanship and political animosity in America. Pew Research (pewresearch.org). (p. 431)

Doherty, E. W., & Doherty, W. J. (1998). Smoke gets in your eyes: Cigarette smoking and divorce in a national sample of American adults. *Families, Systems, and Health, 16*, 393–400. (p. 106)

Dohrenwend, B. P., Levav, I., Shrout, P. E., Schwartz, S., Naveh, G., Link, B. G., Skodol, A., . . . Stueve, A. (1992). Socioeconomic status and psychiatric disorders: The causation-selection issue. *Science, 255*, 946–952. (p. 505)

Dohrenwend, B. P., Pearlin, L., Clayton, P., Hamburg, B., Dohrenwend, B. P., Riley, M., & Rose, R. (1982). Report on stress and life events. In G. R. Elliott & C. Eisdorfer (Eds.), *Stress and human health: Analysis and implications of research* (A study by the Institute of Medicine/National Academy of Sciences). New York: Springer. (p. 385)

DOL. (2015). *Women in labor force.* U.S. Department of Labor. Retrieved from dol.gov/wb/stats/facts_over_time.htm (p. 168)

Dolezal, H. (1982). *Living in a world transformed.* New York: Academic Press. (p. 214)

Dolinoy, D. C., Huang, D., & Jirtle, R. L. (2007). Maternal nutrient supplementation counteracts bisphenol A-induced DNA hypomethylation in early development. *Proceedings of the National Academic of Sciences of the United States of America, 104*, 13056–13061. (p. 74)

Doliński, D., Grzyb, T., Folwarczny, M., Grzybała, P., Krzyszycha, K., Martynowska, K., & Trojanowski, J. (2017). Would you deliver an electric shock in 2015? Obedience in the experimental paradigm developed by Stanley Milgram in the 50 years following the original studies. *Social Psychological and Personality Science, 8*. doi:10.1177/1948550617693060 (p. 426)

Dollfus, S., Lecardeur, L., Morello, R., & Etard, O. (2016). Placebo response in repetitive transcranial magnetic stimulation trials of auditory hallucinations in schizophrenia: A meta-analysis. *Schizophrenia Bulletin, 42*, 301–308. (p. 27)

Domhoff, G. W. (1996). *Finding meaning in dreams: A quantitative approach.* New York: Plenum. (p. 96)

Domhoff, G. W. (2003). *The scientific study of dreams: Neural networks, cognitive development, and content analysis.* Washington, DC: American Psychological Association. (pp. 97, 99)

Domhoff, G. W. (2007). Realistic simulations and bizarreness in dream content: Past findings and suggestions for future research. In D. Barrett & P. McNamara (Eds.), *The new science of dreaming: Content, recall, and personality characteristics* (Vol. 2, pp. 1–27). Westport, CT: Praeger. (p. 96)

Domhoff, G. W. (2010). *The case for a cognitive theory of dreams.* Retrieved from http://www2.ucsc.edu/dreams/Library/domhoff_2010a.html (p. 99)

Domhoff, G. W. (2011). The neural substrate for dreaming: Is it a subsystem of the default network? *Consciousness and Cognition, 20*, 1163–1174. (p. 99)

Domjan, M. (1992). Adult learning and mate choice: Possibilities and experimental evidence. *American Zoologist, 32*, 48–61. (p. 238)

Domjan, M. (1994). Formulation of a behavior system for sexual conditioning. *Psychonomic Bulletin & Review, 1*, 421–428. (p. 238)

Domjan, M. (2005). Pavlovian conditioning: A functional perspective. *Annual Review of Psychology, 56*, 179–206. (p. 238)

Donnellan, M. B., Trzesniewski, K. H., Robins, R. W., Moffitt, T. E., & Caspi, A. (2005). Low self-esteem is related to aggression, antisocial behavior, and delinquency. *Psychological Science, 16*, 328–335. (p. 489)

Donnerstein, E. (1998). *Why do we have those new ratings on television?* Invited address to the National Institute on the Teaching of Psychology. (p. 262)

Donnerstein, E. (2011). The media and aggression: From TV to the internet. In J. Forgas, A. Kruglanski, & K. Williams (Eds.), *The psychology of social conflict and aggression.* New York: Psychology Press. (p. 262)

Dorfman, P., Javidan, M., Hanges, P., Dastmalchian, A., & House, R. (2012). GLOBE: A twenty year journey into the intriguing world of culture and leadership. *Journal of World Business, 47*, 504–518. (p. B-12)

Doss, B. D., Rhoades, G. K., Stanley, S. M., & Markman, H. J. (2009). The effect of the transition to parenthood on relationship quality: An 8-year prospective study. *Journal of Personality and Social Psychology, 96*, 601–619. (p. 157)

Dotan-Eliaz, O., Sommer, K. L., & Rubin, S. (2009). Multilingual groups: Effects of linguistic ostracism on felt rejection and anger, coworker attraction, perceived team potency, and creative performance. *Basic and Applied Social Psychology, 31*, 363–375. (p. 354)

Doty, R. L. (2001). Olfaction. *Annual Review of Psychology, 52*, 423–452. (p. 227)

Douglas, K. S., Guy, L. S., & Hart, S. D. (2009). Psychosis as a risk factor for violence to others: A meta-analysis. *Psychological Bulletin, 135*, 679–706. (p. 502)

Dovidio, J. F., & Gaertner, S. L. (1999). Reducing prejudice: Combating intergroup biases. *Current Directions in Psychological Science, 8*, 101–105. (p. 458)

Dovidio, J. F., ten Vergert, M., Stewart, T. L., Gaertner, S. L., Johnson, J. D., Esses, V. M., . . . Pearson, A. R. (2004). Perspective and prejudice: Antecedents and mediating mechanisms. *Personality and Social Psychology Bulletin, 30*, 1537–1549. (p. 458)

Downing, P. E., Jiang, Y., & Shuman, M. (2001). A cortical area selective for visual processing of the human body. *Science, 293*, 2470–2473. (p. 205)

Downs, E., & Smith, S. L. (2010). Keeping abreast of hypersexuality: A video game character content analysis. *Sex Roles, 62*, 721–733. (p. 177)

Doyle, R. (2005, March). Gay and lesbian census. *Scientific American*, p. 28. (p. 183)

Draganski, B., Gaser, C., Busch, V., Schuierer, G., Bogdahn, U., & May, A. (2004). Neuroplasticity: Changes in grey matter induced by training. *Nature, 427*, 311–312. (p. 39)

Draguns, J. G. (1990). Normal and abnormal behavior in cross-cultural perspective: Specifying the nature of their relationship. *Nebraska Symposium on Motivation 1989, 37*, 235–277. (p. 521)

Drake, B., & Poushter, J. (2016, July 12). In views of diversity, many Europeans are less positive than Americans. Pew Research Center (pewresearch.org). (p. 436)

Drescher, A., & Schultheiss, O. C. (2016). Meta-analytic evidence for higher implicit affiliation and intimacy motivation scores in women, compared to men. *Journal of Research in Personality, 64*, 1–10. (p. 467)

Drew, T., Võ, M. L.-H., & Wolfe, J. M. (2013). The invisible gorilla strikes again: Sustained inattentional blindness in expert observers. *Psychological Science, 24*, 1848–1853. (pp. 82, 83)

Drewelies, J., Wagner, J., Tesch-Römer, C., Heckhausen, J., & Gerstorf, D. (2017). Perceived control across the second half of life: The role of physical health and social integration. *Psychology and Aging, 32*, 76–92. (p. 396)

Driessen, E., Cuijpers, P., de Maat, S. C. M., Abbas, A. A., de Jonghe, F., & Dekker, J. J. M. (2010). The efficacy of short-term psychodynamic psychotherapy for depression: A meta-analysis. *Clinical Psychology Review, 30*, 25–36. (p. 553)

Driessen, E., Hollon, S. D., Bockting, C. L. H., Cuijpers, P., & Turner, E. H. (2015, September 30). Does publican bias inflate the apparent efficacy of psychological treatment for major depressive disorder? A systematic review and meta-analysis of U.S. National Institutes of Health-funded trials. *PLoS ONE 10*, e0137864. (p. 552)

Driessen, E., Van, H. L., Peen, J., Don, F. J., Twisk, J. W. R., Cuijpers, P., & Dekker, J. J. M. (2017). Cognitive-behavioral versus psychodynamic therapy for major depression: Secondary outcomes of a randomized clinical trial. *Journal of Consulting and Clinical Psychology, 85*, 653–663. (p. 553)

Drummond, S. (2010). *Relationship between changes in sleep and memory in older adults.* Presentation at AAAS 2010 Annual Meeting, University of California, San Diego, CA. (p. 92)

Drydakis, N. (2009). Sexual orientation discrimination in the labour market. *Labour Economics, 16*, 364–372. (p. 437)

Drydakis, N. (2015). Sexual orientation discrimination in the United Kingdom's labour market: A field experiment. *Human Relations, 68*, 1769–1796. (p. 437)

Duckworth, A. (2016). *Grit: The power of passion and perseverance.* New York: Scribner. (p. 358)

Duckworth, A. L., Gendler, T. S., & Gross, J. J. (2016). Situational strategies for self-control. *Perspectives on Psychological Science, 11*, 35–55. (p. 359)

Duckworth, A. L., Quinn, P. D., Lynam, D. R., Loeber, R., & Stouthamer-Loeber, M. (2011). Role of test motivation in intelligence testing. *PNAS, 108*, 7716–7720. (p. 339)

Duckworth, A. L., & Seligman, M. E. P. (2005). Discipline outdoes talent: Self-discipline predicts academic performance in adolescents. *Psychological Science, 12*, 939–944. (pp. 357, 398)

Duckworth, A. L., & Seligman, M. E. P. (2006). Self-discipline gives girls the edge: Gender in self-discipline, grades, and achievement tests. *Journal of Educational Psychology, 98*, 198–208. (p. 357)

Duckworth, A. L., Tsukayama, E., & Kirby, T. A. (2013). Is it really self-control? Examining the predictive power of the delay of gratification task. *Personality and Social Psychology Bulletin, 39*, 843–855. (p. 486)

Duclos, S. E., Laird, J. D., Sexter, M., Stern, L., & Van Lighten, O. (1989). Emotion-specific effects of facial expressions and postures on emotional experience. *Journal of Personality and Social Psychology, 57*, 100–108. (p. 381)

Dugan, A. (2015, June 19). *Men, women differ on morals of sex, relationships.* Gallup Poll (gallup.com). (p. 184)

Duggan, J. P., & Booth, D. A. (1986). Obesity, overeating, and rapid gastric emptying in rats with ventromedial hypothalamic lesions. *Science, 231*, 609–611. (p. 362)

Duits, P., Cath, D. C., Lissek, S., Hox, J. J., Hamm, A. O., Engelhard, I. M., . . . Baas, J. M. P. (2015). Updated meta-analysis of classical fear conditioning in the anxiety disorders. *Depression and Anxiety, 32*, 239–253. (p. 510)

Dumont, K. A., Widom, C. S., & Czaja, S. J. (2007). Predictors of resilience in abused and neglected children grown-up: The role of individual and neighborhood characteristics. *Child Abuse & Neglect, 31*, 255–274. (p. 137)

Dunbar, R. I. M., Baron, R., Frangou, A., Pearce, E., van Leeuwin, E. J. C., Stow, J., . . . van Vugt, M. (2011). Social laughter is correlated with an elevated pain threshold. *Proceedings of the Royal Society B, 279*, 1161–1167. (p. 399)

Duncan, L., Yilmaz, Z., Gaspar, H., Walters, R., Goldstein, J., Anttila, V., . . . Bulik, C. M. (2017). Significant locus and metabolic genetic correlations revealed in genome-wide association study of anorexia nervosa. *The American Journal of Psychiatry, 174*, 850–858. (pp. 510, 532)

Dunlop, W. L., & Tracy, J. L. (2013). Sobering stories: Narratives of self-redemption predict behavioral change and improved health among recovering alcoholics. *Journal of Personality and Social Psychology, 104*, 576–590. (p.548)

Dunn, E., & Norton, M. (2013). *Happy money: The science of smarter spending.* New York: Simon & Schuster. (p. 454)

Dunn, E. W., Aknin, L. B., & Norton, M. I. (2008). Spending money on others promotes happiness. *Science, 319*, 1687–1688. (p. 454)

Dunn, E. W., Aknin, L. B., & Norton, M. I. (2014). Pro-social spending and happiness: Using money to benefit others pays off. *Current Directions in Psychological Science, 13*, 347–355. (p. 407)

Dunn, M., & Searle, R. (2010). Effect of manipulated prestige-car ownership on both sex attractiveness ratings. *British Journal of Psychology, 101*, 69–80. (p. 184)

Dunsmoor, J. E., Murty, V. P., Davachi, L., & Phelps, E. A. (2015). Emotional learning selectively and retroactively strengthens memories for related events. *Nature, 520*, 345–348. (p. 278)

Dunson, D. B., Colombo, B., & Baird, D. D. (2002). Changes with age in the level and duration of fertility in the menstrual cycle. *Human Reproduction, 17*, 1399–1403. (p. 151)

Dunster-Page, C., Haddock, G., Wainwright, L., & Berry, K. (2017). The relationship between therapeutic alliance and patient's suicidal thoughts, self-harming behaviours and suicide attempts: A systematic review. *Journal of Affective Disorders, 223*, 165–174. (p. 555)

Dutton, D. G., & Aron, A. P. (1974). Some evidence for heightened sexual attraction under conditions of high anxiety. *Journal of Personality and Social Psychology, 30*, 510–517. (p. 451)

Dutton, D. G., & Aron, A. P. (1989). Romantic attraction and generalized liking for others who are sources of conflict-based arousal. *Canadian Journal of Behavioural Sciences, 21*, 246–257. (p. 451)

Dweck, C. S. (2012a). Implicit theories. In P. A. M. Van Lange, A. Kruglanski, & E. T. Higgins (Eds.), *Handbook of theories of social psychology* (Vol. 2, pp. 43–61). Thousand Oaks, CA: Sage. (p. 339)

Dweck, C. S. (2012b). Mindsets and human nature: Promoting change in the Middle East, the schoolyard, the racial divide, and willpower. *American Psychologist, 67*, 614–622. (p. 339)

Dweck, C. S. (2015, January 1). The secret to raising smart kids. *Scientific American.* Retrieved from scientificamerican.com/article/the-secret-to-raising-smart-kids1/ (p. 339)

Dyrdal, G. M., & Lucas, R. E. (2011). *Reaction and adaptation to the birth of a child: A couple level analysis.* Unpublished manuscript, Michigan State University, East Lansing, MI. (p. 155)

Eagen, K., Stolzenberg, E. B., Bates, A. K., Aragon, M. C. Suchard, M. R., & Rios-Aguilar, C. R. (2016). *The American freshman: National norms 2015.* Los Angeles, Higher Education Research Institute, UCLA. (p. 409)

Eagan, K., Stolzenberg, E. B., Ramirez, J. J., Aragon, M. C., Suchard, M. R., & Hurtado, S. (2014). *The American freshman: National norms fall 2014.* Los Angeles: UCLA Higher Education Research Institute. (p. 355)

Eagleman, D. (2011, September). Secret life of the mind. *Discover,* pp. 50–53. (p. 84)

Eagly, A. H. (2007). Female leadership advantage and disadvantage: Resolving the contradictions. *Psychology of Women Quarterly, 31*, 1–12. (p. B-10)

Eagly, A. H. (2009). The his and hers of prosocial behavior: An examination of the social psychology of gender. *American Psychologist, 64*, 644–658. (p. 185)

Eagly, A. H. (2013, March 20). Hybrid style works, and women are best at it. *The New York Times* (nytimes.com). (p. B-10)

Eagly, A. H., Ashmore, R. D., Makhijani, M. G., & Kennedy, L. C. (1991). What is beautiful is good, but . . .: A meta-analytic review of research on the physical attractiveness stereotype. *Psychological Bulletin, 110*, 109–128. (p. 449)

Eagly, A. H., & Carli, L. (2007). *Through the labyrinth: The truth about how women become leaders.* Cambridge, MA: Harvard University Press. (p. 164)

Eagly, A. H., & Wood, W. (1999). The origins of sex differences in human behavior: Evolved dispositions versus social roles. *American Psychologist, 54*, 408–423. (p. 185)

Eagly, A. H., & Wood, W. (2013). The nature–nurture debates: 25 years of challenges in understanding the psychology of gender. *Perspectives on Psychological Science, 8*, 340–357. (p. 162)

Easterlin, R. A., Morgan, R., Switek, M., & Wang, F. (2012). China's life satisfaction, 1990–2010. *PNAS, 109*, 9670–9671. (p. 410)

Eastman, C. L., Boulos, Z., Terman, M., Campbell, S. S., Dijk, D.-J., & Lewy, A. J. (1995). Light treatment for sleep disorders: Consensus report. VI. Shift work. *Journal of Biological Rhythms, 10*, 157–164. (p. 91)

Eastman, C. L., Young, M. A., Fogg, L. F., Liu, L., & Meaden, P. M. (1998). Bright light treatment of winter depression: A placebo-controlled trial. *Archives of General Psychiatry, 55*, 883–889. (p. 555)

Eastwick, P. W., & Finkel, E. J. (2008a). Speed-dating as a methodological innovation. *The Psychologist, 21*, 402–403. (p. 448)

Eastwick, P. W., & Finkel, E. J. (2008b). Sex differences in mate preferences revisited: Do people know what they initially desire in a romantic partner? *Journal of Personality and Social Psychology, 94*, 245–264. (p. 448)

Eastwick, P. W., Luchies, L. B., Finkel, E. J., & Hunt, L. L. (2014a). The many voices of Darwin's descendants: Reply to Schmitt (2014). *Psychological Bulletin, 140*, 673–681. (p. 449)

Eastwick, P. W., Luchies, L. B., Finkel, E. J., & Hunt, L. L. (2014b). The predictive validity of ideal partner preferences: A review and meta-analysis. *Psychological Bulletin, 140*, 623–665. (p. 449)

Ebbinghaus, H. (1885/1964). *Memory: A contribution to experimental psychology* (H. A. Ruger & C. E. Bussenius, Trans.). New York: Dover. (pp. 272, 286)

Eberhardt, J. L. (2005). Imaging race. *American Psychologist, 60*, 181–190. (p. 435)

Eccles, J. S., Jacobs, J. E., & Harold, R. D. (1990). Gender role stereotypes, expectancy effects, and parents' socialization of gender differences. *Journal of Social Issues, 46*, 183–201. (p. 341)

Eckensberger, L. H. (1994). Moral development and its measurement across cultures. In W. J. Lonner & R. Malpass (Eds.), *Psychology and culture* (pp. 71–78). Boston: Allyn & Bacon. (p. 144)

Eckert, E. D., Heston, L. L., & Bouchard, T. J., Jr. (1981). MZ twins reared apart: Preliminary findings of psychiatric disturbances and traits. In L. Gedda, P. Paris, & W. D. Nance (Eds.), *Twin research: Vol. 3. Pt. B. Intelligence, personality, and development.* New York: Alan Liss. (p. 511)

Eckholm, E. (2010, September 21). Woman on death row runs out of appeals. *The New York Times* (nytimes.com). (p. 331)

Ecklund-Flores, L. (1992, August). *The infant as a model for the teaching of introductory psychology.* Paper presented at the 100th Annual Convention of the American Psychological Association, Washington, DC. (p. 119)

Economist. (2001, December 20). An anthropology of happiness. *The Economist* (economist.com/world/asia). (p. 353)

Eddy, K. T., Tabri, N., Thomas, J. J., Murray, H. B., Keshaviah, A., Hastings, E., . . . Franko, D. L. (2017). Recovery from anorexia nervosa and bulimia nervosa at 22-year follow-up. *Journal of Clinical Psychiatry, 78,* 184–189. (p. 533)

Edelman, B., Luca, M., & Svirsky, D. (2017). Racial discrimination in the sharing economy: Evidence from a field experiment. *American Economic Journal: Applied Economics, 9,* 1–22. (p. 435)

Edwards, A. C., & Kendler, K. S. (2012). A twin study of depression and nicotine dependence: Shared liability or causal relationship? *Journal of Affective Disorders, 142,* 90–97. (p. 106)

Edwards, L. A. (2014). A meta-analysis of imitation abilities in individuals with autism spectrum disorders. *Autism Research, 7,* 363–380. (p. 132)

Edwards, R. R., Campbell, C., Jamison, R. N., & Wiech, K. (2009). The neurobiological underpinnings of coping with pain. *Current Directions in Psychological Science, 18,* 237–241. (p. 223)

Egan, P. J., & Mullin, M. (2012). Turning personal experience into political attitudes: The effects of local weather on Americans' perceptions about global warming. *Journal of Politics, 74,* 796–809. (p. 303)

Egeland, M., Zunszain, P. A., & Pariante, C. M. (2015). Molecular mechanisms in the regulation of adult neurogenesis during stress. *Nature Reviews Neuroscience, 16,* 189–200. (p. 64)

Eibl-Eibesfeldt, I. (1971). *Love and hate: The natural history of behavior patterns.* New York: Holt, Rinehart & Winston. (p. 378)

Eich, E. (1990). Learning during sleep. In R. B. Bootzin, J. F. Kihlstrom, & D. L. Schacter (Eds.), *Sleep and cognition* (pp. 88–108). Washington, DC: American Psychological Association. (p. 97)

Eichstaedt, J. C., Schwartz, H. A., Kern, M. L., Park, G., Labarthe, D. R., Merchant, R. M., ... Seligman, M. E. P. (2015). Psychological language on Twitter predicts county-level heart disease mortality. *Psychological Science, 26,* 159–169. (p. 22)

Ein-Dor, T., Mikulincer, M., Doron, G., & Shaver, P. R. (2010). The attachment paradox: How can so many of us (the insecure ones) have no adaptive advantages? *Perspectives on Psychological Science, 5,* 123–141. (p. 136)

Eippert, F., Finsterbush, J., Bingel, U., & Büchel, C. (2009). Direct evidence for spinal cord involvement in placebo analgesia. *Science, 326,* 404. (p. 223)

Eisenberg, D., Hunt, Speer, & Zivin, K. (2011). Mental health service utilization among college students in the United States. *The Journal of Nervous and Mental Disease, 199,* 301–308. (p. 493)

Eisenberg, N., & Lennon, R. (1983). Sex differences in empathy and related capacities. *Psychological Bulletin, 94,* 100–131. (p. 378)

Eisenberger, N. I., Master, S. L., Inagaki, T. K., Taylor, S. E., Shirinyan, D., Lieberman, M. D., & Naliboff, B. D. (2011). Attachment figures activate a safety signal-related neural region and reduce pain experience. *PNAS, 108,* 11721–11726. (p. 353)

Eisenberger, R., & Aselage, J. (2009). Incremental effects of reward on experienced performance pressure: Positive outcomes for intrinsic interest and creativity. *Journal of Organizational Behavior, 30,* 95–117. (p. 358)

Eklund, A., Nichols, T. E., & Knutsson, H. (2016). Cluster failure: Why fMRI inferences for spatial extent have inflated false-positive rates. *PNAS, 113,* 7900–7905. (p. 20)

Ekman, P. (1994). Strong evidence for universals in facial expressions: A reply to Russell's mistaken critique. *Psychological Bulletin, 115,* 268–287. (p. 378)

Ekman, P. (2016). What scientists who study emotion agree about. *Perspectives on Psychological Science, 11,* 31–34. (pp. 372, 378)

Ekman, P., & Friesen, W. V. (1971). Constants across cultures in the face and emotion. *Journal of Personality and Social Psychology, 17,* 124–129. (p. 379)

Elbogen, E. B., Dennis, P. A., & Johnson, S. C. (2016). Beyond mental illness: Targeting stronger and more direct pathways to violence. *Clinical Psychological Science, 4,* 747–759. (p. 503)

Elfenbein, H. A., & Ambady, N. (2002). On the universality and cultural specificity of emotion recognition: A meta-analysis. *Psychological Bulletin, 128,* 203–235. (p. 378)

Elias, S., Lozano, J., & Bentley, J. (2016). *How executive functioning, anxiety, and technology use impact university students' course performance.* Paper presented at the Western Psychological Association Convention. (p. 355)

Elkind, D. (1970). The origins of religion in the child. *Review of Religious Research, 12,* 35–42. (p. 143)

Elkind, D. (1978). *The child's reality: Three developmental themes.* Hillsdale, NJ: Erlbaum. (p. 143)

Elkins, G., Johnson, A., & Fisher, W. (2012). Cognitive hypnotherapy for pain management. *American Journal of Clinical Hypnosis, 54,* 294–310. (p. 224)

Ellenbogen, J. M., Hu, P. T., Payne, J. D., Titone, D., & Walker, M. P. (2007). Human relational memory requires time and sleep. *PNAS, 104,* 7723–7728. (p. 92)

Ellis, A., & Becker, I. M. (1982). *A guide to personal happiness.* North Hollywood, CA: Wilshire. (p. 242)

Ellis, B. J., Bates, J. E., Dodge, K. A., Fergusson, D. M., John, H. L., Pettit, G. S., & Woodward, L. (2003). Does father absence place daughters at special risk for early sexual activity and teenage pregnancy? *Child Development, 74,* 801–821. (p. 178)

Ellis, B. J., & Boyce, W. T. (2008). Biological sensitivity to context. *Current Directions in Psychological Science, 17,* 183–187. (p. 512)

Ellis, B. J., Schlomer, G. L., Tilley, E. H., & Butler, E. A. (2012). Impact of fathers on risky sexual behavior in daughters: A genetically and environmentally controlled sibling study. *Development and Psychopathology, 24,* 317–332. (p. 167)

Ellis, L., & Ames, M. A. (1987). Neurohormonal functioning and sexual orientation: A theory of homosexuality–heterosexuality. *Psychological Bulletin, 101,* 233–258. (p. 181)

Ellison, K. (2015, November 9). A.D.H.D. rates rise around globe, but sympathy often lags. *The New York Times* (nytimes.com). (p. 498)

Ellison-Wright, I., Glahn, D. C., Laird, A. R., Thelen, S. M., & Bullmore, E. (2008). The anatomy of first-episode and chronic schizophrenia: An anatomical likelihood estimation meta-analysis. *American Journal of Psychiatry, 165,* 1015–1023. (p. 525)

Else-Quest, N. M., Hyde, J. S., & Linn, M. C. (2010). Cross-national patterns of gender differences in mathematics: A meta-analysis. *Psychological Bulletin, 136,* 103–127. (p. 340)

Elzinga, B. M., Ardon, A. M., Heijnis, M. K., De Ruiter, M. B., Van Dyck, R., & Veltman, D. J. (2007). Neural correlates of enhanced working-memory performance in dissociative disorder: A functional MRI study. *Psychological Medicine, 37,* 235–245. (p. 529)

EMDR. (2011, February 18). E-mail correspondence from Robbie Dunton, EMDR Institute (emdr.org). (p. 554)

Emmons, S., Geisler, C., Kaplan, K. J., & Harrow, M. (1997). *Living with schizophrenia.* Muncie, IN: Taylor and Francis (Accelerated Development). (p. 493)

Empson, J. A. C., & Clarke, P. R. F. (1970). Rapid eye movements and remembering. *Nature, 227,* 287–288. (p. 97)

Endendijk, J. J., Beltz, A. M., McHale, S. M., Bryk, K., & Berenbaum, S. A. (2016). Linking prenatal androgens to gender-related attitudes, identity, and activities: Evidence from girls with congenital adrenal hyperplasia. *Archives of Sexual Behavior, 45,* 1807–1815. (p. 166)

Endler, N. S. (1982). *Holiday of darkness: A psychologist's personal journey out of his depression.* New York: Wiley. (pp. 519, 563)

Engen, T. (1987). Remembering odors and their names. *American Scientist, 75,* 497–503. (p. 227)

Engle, R. W. (2002). Working memory capacity as executive attention. *Current Directions in Psychological Science, 11,* 19–23. (p. 269)

English, T., Davis, J., Wei, M., & Gross, J. J. (2017). Homesickness and adjustment across the first year of college: A longitudinal study. *Emotion, 17,* 1–5. (p. 353)

Epley, N., & Dunning, D. (2000). Feeling "holier than thou": Are self-serving assessments produced by errors in self- or social prediction? *Journal of Personality and Social Psychology, 79,* 861–875. (p. 488)

Epley, N., Keysar, B., Van Boven, L., & Gilovich, T. (2004). Perspective taking as egocentric anchoring and adjustment. *Journal of Personality and Social Psychology, 87,* 327–339. (p. 128)

Epley, N., Savitsky, K., & Gilovich, T. (2002). Empathy neglect: Reconciling the spotlight effect and the correspondence bias. *Journal of Personality and Social Psychology, 83,* 300–312. (p. 486)

Epstein, J., Stern, E., & Silbersweig, D. (1998). Mesolimbic activity associated with psychosis in schizophrenia: Symptom-specific PET studies. In J. F. McGinty (Ed.), *Advancing from the ventral striatum to the extended amygdala: Implications for neuropsychiatry and drug use: In honor of Lennart Heimer. Annals of the New York Academy of Sciences, 877,* 562–574. (p. 524)

Epstein, S. (1983a). Aggregation and beyond: Some basic issues on the prediction of behavior. *Journal of Personality, 51,* 360–392. (p. 481)

Epstein, S. (1983b). The stability of behavior across time and situations. In R. Zucker, J. Aronoff, & A. I. Rabin (Eds.), *Personality and the prediction of behavior.* San Diego: Academic Press. (p. 481)

Eranti, S. V., MacCabe, J. H., Bundy, H., & Murray, R. M. (2013). Gender difference in age at onset of schizophrenia: A meta-analysis. *Psychological Medicine, 43,* 155–167. (p. 524)

Erdelyi, M. H. (1985). *Psychoanalysis: Freud's cognitive psychology.* New York: Freeman. (p. 469)

Erdelyi, M. H. (1988). Repression, reconstruction, and defense: History and integration of the psychoanalytic and experimental frameworks. In J. Singer (Ed.), *Repression: Defense mechanism and cognitive style.* Chicago: University of Chicago Press. (p. 469)

Erdelyi, M. H. (2006). The unified theory of repression. *Behavioral and Brain Sciences, 29,* 499–551. (p. 469)

Erel, O., & Burman, B. (1995). Interrelatedness of marital relations and parent–child relations: A meta-analytic review. *Psychological Bulletin, 118,* 108–132. (p. 157)

Erickson, K. I. (2009). Aerobic fitness is associated with hippocampal volume in elderly humans. *Hippocampus, 19,* 1030–1039. (p. 153)

Erickson, K. I., Banducci, S. E., Weinstein, A. M., MacDonald, A. W., III, Ferrell, R. E., Halder, I., . . . Manuck, S. B. (2013). The brain-derived neurotrophic factor Val66Met polymorphism moderates an effect of physical activity on working memory performance. *Psychological Science, 24,* 1770–1779. (p. 153)

Erickson, M. F., & Aird, E. G. (2005). *The motherhood study: Fresh insights on mothers' attitudes and concerns.* New York: The Motherhood Project, Institute for American Values. (p. 157)

Ericsson, K. A. (2001). Attaining excellence through deliberate practice: Insights from the study of expert performance. In M. Ferrari (Ed.), *The pursuit of excellence in education.* Hillsdale, NJ: Erlbaum. (p. 357)

Ericsson, K. A. (2002). Attaining excellence through deliberate practice: Insights from the study of expert performance. In C. Desforges & R. Fox (Eds.), *Teaching and learning: The essential readings* (pp. 4–37). Malden, MA: Blackwell. (p. 325)

Ericsson, K. A. (2006). The influence of experience and deliberate practice on the development of superior expert performance. In K. A. Ericsson, N. Charness, P. J. Feltovich, & R. R. Hoffman (Eds.), *The Cambridge handbook of expertise and expert performance.* Cambridge: Cambridge University Press. (p. 357)

Ericsson, K. A. (2007). Deliberate practice and the modifiability of body and mind: Toward a science of the structure and acquisition of expert and elite performance. *International Journal of Sport Psychology, 38,* 4–34. (p. 357)

Ericsson, K. A., Cheng, X., Pan, Y., Ku, Y., Ge, Y., & Hu, Y. (2017). Memory skills mediating superior memory in a world-class memorist. *Memory, 25,* 1294–1302. (p. 266)

Ericsson, K. A., & Pool, R. (2016). *PEAK: Secrets from the New Science of Expertise.* Boston: Houghton Mifflin. (p. 325)

Ericsson, K. A., Roring, R. W., & Nandagopal, K. (2007). Giftedness and evidence for reproducibly superior performance: An account based on the expert performance framework. *High Ability Studies, 18,* 3–56. (p. 339)

Erikson, E. H. (1963). *Childhood and society.* New York: Norton. (p. 145)

Erikson, E. H. (1983, June). A conversation with Erikson (by E. Hall). *Psychology Today,* pp. 22–30. (p. 137)

Erlich, N., Lipp, O. V., & Slaughter, V. (2013). Of hissing snakes and angry voices: Human infants are differentially responsive to evolutionary fear-relevant sounds. *Developmental Science, 16,* 894–904. (p. 512)

Ermer, E., Cope, L. M., Nyalakanti, P. K., Calhoun, V. D., & Kiehl, K. A. (2012a). Aberrant paralimbic gray matter in criminal psychopathy. *Journal of Abnormal Psychology, 121,* 649–658. (p. 55)

Ermer, E., Kahn, R. E., Salovey, P., & Kiehl, K. A. (2012b). Emotional intelligence in incarcerated men with psychopathic traits. *Journal of Personality and Social Psychology, 103,* 194–204. (p. 530)

Ert, E., Yechiam, E., & Arshavsky, O. (2013). Smokers' decision making: More than mere risk taking. *PLoS ONE, 8*(7), e68064. doi:10.1371/journal.pone.0068064 (p. 145)

Ertmer, D. J., Young, N. M., & Nathani, S. (2007). Profiles of focal development in young cochlear implant recipients. *Journal of Speech, Language, and Hearing Research, 50,* 393–407. (p. 315)

Escasa, M. J., Casey, J. F., & Gray, P. B. (2011). Salivary testosterone levels in men at a U.S. sex club. *Archives of Sexual Behavior, 40,* 921–926. (p. 173)

Escobar-Chaves, S. L., Tortolero, S. R., Markham, C. M., Low, B. J., Eitel, P., & Thickstun, P. (2005). Impact of the media on adolescent sexual attitudes and behaviors. *Pediatrics, 116,* 303–326. (p. 177)

Escobedo, J. R., & Adolphs, R. (2010). Becoming a better person: Temporal remoteness biases autobiographical memories for moral events. *Emotion, 10,* 511–518. (p. 489)

Esposito, G., Yoshida, S., Ohnishi, R., Tsuneoka, Y., Rostagno, M., Yokota, S., . . . Kuroda, K. O. (2013). Infant calming responses during maternal carrying in humans and mice. *Current Biology, 23,* 739–745. (p. 352)

Esser, J. K., & Lindoerfer, J. S. (1989). Groupthink and the space shuttle *Challenger* accident: Toward a quantitative case analysis. *Journal of Behavioral Decision Making, 2,* 167–177. (p. 433)

Esterson, A. (2001). The mythologizing of psychoanalytic history: Deception and self-deception in Freud's accounts of the seduction theory episode. *History of Psychiatry, 12,* 329–352. (p. 468)

Etkin, A., Büchel, C., & Gross, J. J. (2015). The neural bases of emotion regulation. *Nature Reviews Neuroscience, 16,* 693–700. (p. 519)

Etkin, A., & Wager, T. D. (2007). Functional neuroimaging of anxiety: A meta-analysis of emotional processing in PTSD, social anxiety disorder, and specific phobia. *American Journal of Psychiatry, 164,* 1476–1488. (p. 512)

Eurich, T. L., Krause, D. E., Cigularov, K., & Thornton, G. C., III. (2009). Assessment centers: Current practices in the United States. *Journal of Business Psychology, 24,* 387–407. (p. 484)

Euston, D. R., Tatsuno, M., & McNaughton, B. L. (2007). Fast-forward playback of recent memory sequences in prefrontal cortex during sleep. *Science, 318,* 1147–1150. (p. 277)

Evans, C. R., & Dion, K. L. (1991). Group cohesion and performance: A meta-analysis. *Small Group Research, 22,* 175–186. (p. B-10)

Evans, G. W., Palsane, M. N., & Carrere, S. (1987). Type A behavior and occupational stress: A cross-cultural study of blue-collar workers. *Journal of Personality and Social Psychology, 52,* 1002–1007. (p. 391)

Evans, J. St. B. T., & Stanovich, K. E. (2013). Dual-process theories of higher cognition: Advancing the debate. *Perspectives on Psychological Science, 8,* 223–241. (p. 84)

Evenson, K. R., Wen, F., & Herring, A. H. (2016). Associations of accelerometry-assessed and self-reported physical activity and sedentary behavior with all-cause and cardiovascular mortality among U.S. adults. *American Journal of Epidemiology, 184,* 621–632. (p. 401)

Everett, J. A. C., Caviola, L., Kahane, G., Savulescu, J., & Faber, N. S. (2015). Doing good by doing nothing? The role of social norms in explaining default effects in altruistic contexts. *European Journal of Social Psychology, 45,* 230–241. (p. 455)

Evers, A., Muñiz, J., Bartram, D., Boben, D., Egeland, J., Fernández-Hermida, J. R., . . . Urbánek, T. (2012). Testing practices in the 21st century: Developments and European psychologists' opinions. *European Psychologist, 17,* 300–319. (p. 329)

Everson, S. A., Goldberg, D. E., Kaplan, G. A., Cohen, R. D., Pukkala, E., Tuomilehto, J., & Salonen, J. T. (1996). Hopelessness and risk of mortality and incidence of myocardial infarction and cancer. *Psychosomatic Medicine, 58,* 113–121. (p. 399)

Exelmans, L., Custers, K., & Van den Bulck, J. (2015). Violent video games and delinquent behavior in adolescents: A risk factor perspective. *Aggressive Behavior, 41,* 267–279. (p. 445)

Eysenck, H. J. (1952). The effects of psychotherapy: An evaluation. *Journal of Consulting Psychology, 16,* 319–324. (p. 551)

Eysenck, H. J. (1990, April 30). An improvement on personality inventory. *Current Contents: Social and Behavioral Sciences, 22,* 20. (p. 475)

Eysenck, H. J. (1992). Four ways five factors are *not* basic. *Personality and Individual Differences, 13,* 667–673. (p. 475)

Eysenck, H. J., & Grossarth-Maticek, R. (1991). Creative novation behaviour therapy as a prophylactic treatment for cancer and coronary heart disease: Part II—Effects of treatment. *Behaviour Research and Therapy, 29,* 17–31. (p. 403)

Eysenck, H. J., Wakefield, J. A., Jr., & Friedman, A. F. (1983). Diagnosis and clinical assessment: The DSM-III. *Annual Review of Psychology, 34,* 167–193. (p. 497)

Eysenck, S. B. G., & Eysenck, H. J. (1963). The validity of questionnaire and rating assessments of extraversion and neuroticism, and their factorial stability. *British Journal of Psychology, 54,* 51–62. (p. 476)

Fabiano, G. A., Pelham, W. E., Jr., Coles, E. K., Gnagy, E. M., Chronis-Tuscano, A., & O'Connor, B. C. (2008). A meta-analysis of behavioral treatments for attention-deficit/hyperactivity disorder. *Clinical Psychology Review, 29,* 129–140. (p. 498)

Fabiansson, E. C., Denson, T. F., Moulds, M. L., Grisham, J. R., & Schira, M. M. (2012). Don't look back in anger: Neural correlates of reappraisal, analytical rumination, and angry rumination during a recall of an anger-inducing autobiographical memory. *NeuroImage, 59,* 2974–2981. (p. 394)

Fagan, J. F., & Holland, C. R. (2007). Racial equality in intelligence: Predictions from a theory of intelligence as processing. *Intelligence, 35,* 319–334. (p. 344)

Fagan, J. F., & Holland, C. R. (2009). Culture-fair prediction of academic achievement. *Intelligence, 37,* 62–67. (p. 344)

Fagundes, C. P., & Way, B. (2014). Early-life stress and adult inflammation. *Current Directions in Psychological Science, 23,* 277–283. (p. 137)

Faheem, S., Petti, V., & Mellos, G. (2017). Disruptive mood dysregulation disorder and its effect on bipolar disorder. *Annals of Clinical Psychiatry, 29*(1), e1–e8. (p. 516)

Fairbairn, C. E., & Sayette, M. A. (2014). A social-attributional analysis of alcohol response. *Psychological Bulletin, 140,* 1361–1382. (pp. 103, 104)

Fairfield, H. (2012, February 4). Girls lead in science exam, but NOT in the United States. *The New York Times* (nytimes.com). (p. 341)

Fales, M. R., Frederick, D. A., Garcia, J. R., Gildersleeve, K. A., Haselton, M. G., & Fisher, H. E. (2016). Mating markets and bargaining hands: Mate preferences for attractiveness and resources in two national US studies. *Personality and Individual Differences, 88,* 78–87. (p. 184)

Falk, C. F., Heine, S. J., Yuki, M., & Takemura, K. (2009). Why do Westerners self-enhance more than East Asians? *European Journal of Personality, 23,* 183–203. (pp. 17, 488)

Falkner, A. L., Grosenick, L., Davidson, T. J., Deisseroth, K., & Lin, D. (2016). Hypothalamic control of male aggression-seeking behavior. *Nature Neuroscience, 19,* 596–604. (p. 442)

Fan, S. P., Liberman, Z., Keysar, B., & Kinzler, K. D. (2015). The exposure advantage: Early exposure to a multilingual environment promotes effective communication. *Psychological Science, 26,* 1090–1097. (p. 320)

Fang, Z., Spaeth, A. M., Ma, N., Zhu, S., Hu, S., Goel, N., . . . Rao, H. (2015). Altered salience network connectivity predicts macronutrient intake after sleep deprivation. *Scientific Reports, 5,* Article 8215. doi:10.1038/srep08215 (p. 93)

Fanti, K. A., Vanman, E., Henrich, C. C., & Avraamides, M. N. (2009). Desensitization to media violence over a short period of time. *Aggressive Behavior, 35,* 179–187. (p. 263)

Farah, M. J., Rabinowitz, C., Quinn, G. E., & Liu, G. T. (2000). Early commitment of neural substrates for face recognition. *Cognitive Neuropsychology, 17,* 117–124. (p. 64)

Farb, N. A. S., Anderson, A. K., Mayberg, H., Bean, J., McKeon, D., & Segal, Z. V. (2010). Minding one's emotions: Mindfulness training alters the neural expression of sadness. *Emotion, 10,* 25–33. (p. 404)

Farina, A. (1982). The stigma of mental disorders. In A. G. Miller (Ed.), *In the eye of the beholder.* New York: Praeger. (pp. 495, 497)

Farnia, V., Shakeri, J., Tatari, F., Juibari, T. A., Yazdchi, K., Bajoghli, H., . . . Aghaei, A. (2014). Randomized controlled trial of aripiprazole versus risperidone for the treatment of amphetamine-induced psychosis. *The American Journal of Drug and Alcohol Abuse, 40,* 10–15. (p. 524)

Farr, R. H. (2017). Does parental sexual orientation matter? A longitudinal follow-up of adoptive families with school-age children. *Developmental Psychology, 53,* 252–264. (p. 180)

Farrington, D. P. (1991). Antisocial personality from childhood to adulthood. *The Psychologist: Bulletin of the British Psychological Society, 4,* 389–394. (p. 530)

Farsalinos, K. E., Kistler, K. A., Gillman, G., & Voudris, V. (2014). Evaluation of electronic cigarette liquids and aerosol for the presence of selected inhalation toxins. *Nicotine and Tobacco Research, 17,* 168–174. (p. 105)

Farstad, S. M., McGeown, L. M., & von Ranson, K. M. (2016). Eating disorders and personality, 2004–2016: A systematic review and meta-analysis. *Clinical Psychology Review, 46,* 91–105. (p. 532)

Fatemi, S. H., & Folsom, T. D. (2009). The neurodevelopmental hypothesis of schizophrenia, revisited. *Schizophrenia Bulletin, 35,* 528–548. (p. 525)

Fattore, L. (2016). Synthetic cannabinoids—further evidence supporting the relationship between cannabinoids and psychosis. *Biological Psychiatry, 79,* 539–548. (p. 108)

Fazel, S., & Grann, M. (2006). The population impact of severe mental illness on violent crime. *American Journal of Psychiatry, 163,* 1397–1403. (p. 503)

Fazel, S., Langstrom, N., Hjern, A., Grann, M., & Lichtenstein, P. (2009). Schizophrenia, substance abuse, and violent crime. *Journal of the American Medical Association, 301,* 2016–2023. (p. 503)

Fazel, S., Lichtenstein, P., Grann, M., Goodwin, G. M., & Långström, N. (2010). Bipolar disorder and violent crime: New evidence from population-based longitudinal studies and systematic review. *Archives of General Psychiatry, 67,* 931–938. (p. 503)

Fazio, L. K., Brashier, N. M., Payne, B. K., & Marsh, E. J. (2015). Knowledge does not protect against illusory truth. *Journal of Experimental Psychology: General, 144,* 993–1002. (pp. 16, 18)

Fedorenko, E., Scott, T. L., Brunner, P., Coon, W. G., Pritchett, B., Schalk, G., & Kanwisher, N. (2016). Neural correlate of the construction of sentence meaning. *PNAS, 113,* E6256–E6262. (p. 317)

Feeney, D. M. (1987). Human rights and animal welfare. *American Psychologist, 42,* 593–599. (p. 31)

Feigenson, L., Carey, S., & Spelke, E. (2002). Infants' discrimination of number vs. continuous extent. *Cognitive Psychology, 44,* 33–66. (p. 127)

Feinberg, M., Willer, R., Antonenko, O., & John, O. P. (2012). Liberating reason from the passions: Overriding intuitionist moral judgments through emotion reappraisal. *Psychological Science, 23,* 788–795. (p. 145)

Feinberg, M., Willer, R., & Schultz, M. (2014). Gossip and ostracism promote cooperation in groups. *Psychological Science, 25,* 656–664. (p. 352)

Feinberg, T. E., & Mallatt, J. (2016). The nature of primary consciousness: A new synthesis. *Consciousness and Cognition, 43,* 113–127. (p. 80)

Feingold, A. (1992). Good-looking people are not what we think. *Psychological Bulletin, 111,* 304–341. (p. 449)

Feingold, A., & Mazzella, R. (1998). Gender differences in body image are increasing. *Psychological Science, 9,* 190–195. (p. 532)

Feinstein, J. S., Buzza, C., Hurlemann, R., Follmer, R. L., Dahdaleh, N. S., Coryell, W. H., . . . Wemmie, J. A. (2013). Fear and panic in humans with bilateral amygdala damage. *Nature Neuroscience, 16,* 270–272. (p. 55)

Feldman, M. B., & Meyer, I. H. (2010). Comorbidity and age of onset of eating disorders in gay men, lesbians, and bisexuals. *Psychiatry Research, 180,* 126–131. (p. 532)

Feldman, R., Rosenthal, Z., & Eidelman, A. I. (2014). Maternal-preterm skin-to-skin contact enhances child physiologic organization and cognitive control across the first 10 years of life. *Biological Psychiatry, 75,* 56–64. (pp. 123, 397)

Fenigstein, A. (2015). Milgram's shock experiments and the Nazi perpetrators: A contrarian perspective on the role of obedience pressures during the Holocaust. *Theory and Psychology, 25,* 581–598. (p. 427)

Fenn, K. M., & Hambrick, D. Z. (2012). Individual differences in working memory capacity predict sleep-dependent memory consolidation. *Journal of Experimental Psychology: General, 141,* 404–410. (p. 271)

Fenton, W. S., & McGlashan, T. H. (1991). Natural history of schizophrenia subtypes: II. Positive and negative symptoms and long-term course. *Archives of General Psychiatry, 48,* 978–986. (p. 524)

Fenton, W. S., & McGlashan, T. H. (1994). Antecedents, symptom progression, and long-term outcome of the deficit syndrome in schizophrenia. *American Journal of Psychiatry, 151,* 351–356. (p. 524)

Ferguson, C. (2009, June 14). Not every child is secretly a genius. *The Chronicle Review* (chronicle.com). (p. 325)

Ferguson, C. J. (2013a). Spanking, corporal punishment and negative long-term outcomes: A meta-analytic review of longitudinal studies. *Clinical Psychology Review, 33,* 196–208. (p. 249)

Ferguson, C. J. (2013b). Violent video games and the Supreme Court: Lessons for the scientific community in the wake of *Brown v. Entertainment Merchants Association. American Psychologist, 68,* 57–74. (p. 445)

Ferguson, C. J. (2014). Is video game violence bad? *Psychologist, 27,* 324–327. (p. 445)

Ferguson, C. J. (2015). Do angry birds make for angry children? A meta-analysis of video game influences on children's and adolescents' aggression, mental health, prosocial behavior, and academic performance. *Perspectives on Psychological Science, 10,* 646–666. (pp. 445, 466)

Ferguson, C. J., Winegard, B., & Winegard, B. M. (2011). Who is the fairest one of all? How evolution guides peer and media influences on female body dissatisfaction. *Review of General Psychology, 15,* 11–28. (p. 533)

Ferguson, E. D. (1989). Adler's motivational theory: An historical perspective on belonging and the fundamental human striving. *Individual Psychology, 45,* 354–361. (p. 352)

Ferguson, E. D. (2001). Adler and Dreikurs: Cognitive-social dynamic innovators. *Journal of Individual Psychology, 57,* 324–341. (p. 352)

Ferguson, E. D. (2003). Social processes, personal goals, and their intertwining: Their importance in Adlerian theory and practice. *Journal of Individual Psychology, 59,* 136–144. (p. 466)

Ferguson, E. D. (2010). Editor's notes: Adler's innovative contributions regarding the need to belong. *Journal of Individual Psychology, 66,* 1–7. (p. 352)

Ferguson, M. J., & Zayas, V. (2009). Automatic evaluation. *Current Directions in Psychological Science, 18,* 362–366. (pp. 192, 193)

Fergusson, D. M., Boden, J. M., & Horwood, L. J. (2009). Tests of causal links between alcohol abuse or dependence and major depression. *Archives of General Psychiatry, 66,* 260–266. (p. 519)

Fernández-Dols, J.-M., & Ruiz-Belda, M.-A. (1995). Are smiles a sign of happiness? Gold medal winners at the Olympic Games. *Journal of Personality and Social Psychology, 69,* 1113–1119. (p. 379)

Fernandez-Duque, E., Evans, J., Christian, C., & Hodges, S. D. (2015). Superfluous neuroscience information makes explanations of psychological phenomena more appealing. *Journal of Cognitive Neuroscience, 27,* 926–944. (p. 52)

Fernbach, P. M., Rogers, T., Fox, C. R., & Sloman, S. A. (2013). Political extremism is supported by an illusion of understanding. *Psychological Science, 24,* 939–946. (p. 304)

Fernie, G., Peeters, M., Gullo, M. J., Christianson, P., Cole, J. C., Sumnall, H., & Field, M. (2013). Multiple behavioral impulsivity tasks predict prospective alcohol involvement in adolescents. *Addiction, 108,* 1916–1923. (p. 463)

Fernyhough, C. (2008). Getting Vygotskian about theory of mind: Mediation, dialogue, and the development of social understanding. *Developmental Review, 28,* 225–262. (p. 129)

Ferrari, A. J., Charlson, F. J., Norman, R. E., Patten, S. B., Freedman, G., Murray, C. J. L., . . . Whiteford, H. A. (2013). Burden of depressive disorders by country, sex, age, and year: Findings from the Global Burden of Disease Study 2010. *PLOS Medicine, 10,* e1001547. (p. 521)

Ferri, M., Amato, L., & Davoli, M. (2006). Alcoholics Anonymous and other 12-step programmes for alcohol dependence. *Cochrane Database of Systematic Reviews,* Issue 3. Art. No. CD005032. (p. 548)

Ferriman, K., Lubinski, D., & Benbow, C. P. (2009). Work preferences, life values, and personal views of top math/science graduate students and the profoundly gifted: Developmental changes and gender differences during emerging adulthood and parenthood. *Journal of Personality and Social Psychology, 97,* 517–522. (p. 165)

Ferris, C. F. (1996, March). The rage of innocents. *The Sciences*, pp. 22–26. (p. 137)

Festinger, L. (1957). *A theory of cognitive dissonance.* Stanford: Stanford University Press. (p. 420)

Fetvadjiev, V. H., Meiring, D., van de Vijver, F. J., Nel, J. A., Sekaja, L., & Laher, S. (2017). Personality and behavior prediction and consistency across cultures: A multimethod study of blacks and whites in South Africa. *Journal of Personality and Social Psychology.* Advance online publication. doi:10.1037/pspp0000129 (p. 478)

Fichter, M. M., & Quadflieg, N. (2016). Mortality in eating disorders—results of a large prospective clinical longitudinal study. *International Journal of Eating Disorders, 49,* 391–401. (p. 532)

Fiedler, F. E. (1981). Leadership effectiveness. *American Behavioral Scientist, 24,* 619–632. (p. B-10)

Fiedler, F. E. (1987, September). When to lead, when to stand back. *Psychology Today,* pp. 26–27. (p. B-10)

Field, A. P. (2006). Is conditioning a useful framework for understanding the development and treatment of phobias? *Clinical Psychology Review, 26,* 857–875. (p. 510)

Field, T., Diego, M., & Hernandez-Reif, M. (2007). Massage therapy research. *Developmental Review, 27,* 75–89. (p. 123)

Field, T., Hernandez-Reif, M., Feijo, L., & Freedman, J. (2006). Prenatal, perinatal and neonatal stimulation: A survey of neonatal nurseries. *Infant Behavior & Development, 29,* 24–31. (p. 220)

Fielder, R. L., Walsh, J. L., Carey, K. B., & Carey, M. P. (2013). Predictors of sexual hookups: A theory-based, prospective study of first-year college women. *Archives of Sexual Behavior, 42,* 1425–1441. (pp. 26, 177)

Fields, R. D. (2004, April). The other half of the brain. *Scientific American,* pp. 54–61. (p. 40)

Fields, R. D. (2008, March). White matter matters. *Scientific American,* pp. 54–61. (p. 40)

Fields, R. D. (2011, May/June). The hidden brain. *Scientific American,* pp. 53–59. (p. 40)

Fields, R. D. (2013). Neuroscience: Map the other brain. *Nature, 501,* 25–27. (p. 40)

Fincham, F. D., & Bradbury, T. N. (1993). Marital satisfaction, depression, and attributions: A longitudinal analysis. *Journal of Personality and Social Psychology, 64,* 442–452. (p. 417)

Finchilescu, G., & Tredoux, C. (Eds.) (2010). Intergroup relations in post apartheid South Africa: Change, and obstacles to change. *Journal of Social Issues, 66,* 223–236. (p. 457)

Findlay, L. (2017, January 18). *Depression and suicidal ideation among Canadians aged 15 to 24.* Statistics Canada (statcan.gc.ca/pub/82-003-x/2017001/article/14697-eng.htm). (p. 516)

Fine, C. (2010). From scanner to sound bite: Issues in interpreting and reporting sex differences in the brain. *Current Directions in Psychological Science, 19,* 280–283. (p. 52)

Finer, L. B., & Philbin, J. M. (2014). Trends in ages at key reproductive transitions in the United States, 1951–2010. *Women's Health Issues, 24,* e271–279. (p. 149)

Fingelkurts, A. A., & Fingelkurts, A. A. (2009). Is our brain hardwired to produce God, or is our brain hardwired to perceive God? A systematic review on the role of the brain in mediating religious experience. *Cognitive Processes, 10,* 293–326. (p. 63)

Fingerman, K. L., & Charles, S. T. (2010). It takes two to tango: Why older people have the best relationships. *Current Directions in Psychological Science, 19,* 172–176. (p. 158)

Fink, M. (2009). *Electroconvulsive therapy: A guide for professionals and their patients.* New York: Oxford University Press. (p. 563)

Finkel, E. J. (2017). *The all-or-nothing marriage.* New York: Dutton. (p. 156)

Finkel, E. J., DeWall, C. N., Slotter, E. B., McNulty, J. K., Pond, R. S., Jr., & Atkins, D. C. (2012a). Using I3 theory to clarify when dispositional aggressiveness predicts intimate partner violence perpetration. *Journal of Personality and Social Psychology, 102,* 533–549. (p. 448)

Finkel, E. J., & Eastwick, P. W. (2008). Speed-dating. *Current Directions in Psychological Science, 17,* 193–197. (p. 449)

Finkel, E. J., & Eastwick, P. W. (2009). Arbitrary social norms influence sex differences in romantic selectivity. *Psychological Science, 20,* 1290–1295. (p. 448)

Finkel, E. J., Eastwick, P. W., Karney, B. R., Reis, H. T., & Sprecher, S. (2012b, September/October). Dating in a digital world. *Scientific American Mind,* pp. 26–33. (p. 448)

Finkenauer, C., Buyukcan-Tetik, A., Baumeister, R. F., Schoemaker, K., Bartels, M., & Vohs, K. D. (2015). Out of control: Identifying the role of self-control strength in family violence. *Current Directions in Psychological Science, 24,* 261–266. (p. 249)

Finlay, S. W. (2000). Influence of Carl Jung and William James on the origin of alcoholics anonymous. *Review of General Psychology, 4,* 3–12. (p. 548)

Fiore, M. C., Jaén, C. R., Baker, T. B., Bailey, W. C., Benowitz, N. L., Curry, S. J., . . . Wewers, M. E. (2008, May). *Treating tobacco use and dependence: 2008 update.* Rockville, MD: U.S. Department of Health and Human Services, Public Health Service. (p. 106)

Fischer, A., & LaFrance, M. (2015). What drives the smile and the tear: Why women are more emotionally expressive than men. *Emotion Review, 7,* 22–29. (pp. 162, 377)

Fischer, P., & Greitemeyer, T. (2006). Music and aggression: The impact of sexual-aggressive song lyrics on aggression-related thoughts, emotions, and behavior toward the same and the opposite sex. *Personality and Social Psychology Bulletin, 32,* 1165–1176. (p. 444)

Fischer, P., Greitemeyer, T., Kastenmüller, A., Vogrincic, C., & Sauer, A. (2011). The effects of risk-glorifying media exposure on risk-positive cognitions, emotions, and behaviors: A meta-analytic review. *Psychological Bulletin, 137,* 367–390. (p. 444)

Fischer, R., & Boer, D. (2011). What is more important for national well-being: Money or autonomy? A meta-analysis of well-being, burnout, and anxiety across 63 societies. *Journal of Personality and Social Psychology, 101,* 164–184. (p. 409)

Fischhoff, B. (1982). Debiasing. In D. Kahneman, P. Slovic, & A. Tversky (Eds.), *Judgment under uncertainty: Heuristics and biases.* New York: Cambridge University Press. (p. 304)

Fischhoff, B., Slovic, P., & Lichtenstein, S. (1977). Knowing with certainty: The appropriateness of extreme confidence. *Journal of Experimental Psychology: Human Perception and Performance, 3,* 552–564. (p. 303)

Fishbach, A., Dhar, R., & Zhang, Y. (2006). Subgoals as substitutes or complements: The role of goal accessibility. *Journal of Personality and Social Psychology, 91,* 232–242. (p. B-9)

Fisher, G., & Rangel, A. (2014). Symmetry in cold-to-hot and hot-to-cold valuation gaps. *Psychological Science, 25,* 120–127. (p. 361)

Fisher, H. E. (1993, March/April). After all, maybe it's biology. *Psychology Today,* pp. 40–45. (p. 156)

Fisher, H. T. (1984). Little Albert and Little Peter. *Bulletin of the British Psychological Society, 37,* 269. (p. 541)

Fitzgerald, R. J., & Price, H. L. (2015). Eyewitness identification across the life span: A meta-analysis of age differences. *Psychological Bulletin, 141,* 1228–1265. (p. 294)

Flack, W. F. (2006). Peripheral feedback effects of facial expressions, bodily postures, and vocal expressions on emotional feelings. *Cognition and Emotion, 20,* 177–195. (pp. 381, 393)

Flaherty, D. K. (2011). The vaccine-autism connection: A public health crisis caused by unethical medical practices and fraudulent science. *Annals of Pharmacotherapy, 45,* 1302–1304. (p. 131)

Flegal, K. M., Carroll, M. D., Kit, B. K., & Ogden, C. L. (2012). Prevalence of obesity and trends in the distribution of body mass index among US adults, 1999–2010. *JAMA, 307.* (p. 365)

Flegal, K. M., Carroll, M. D., Ogden, C. L., & Curtin, L. R. (2010). Prevalence and trends in obesity among US adults, 1999–2008. *JAMA, 303,* 235–241. (p. 365)

Flegal, K. M., Kruszon-Moran, D., Carroll, M. D., Fryar, C. D., & Ogden, C. L. (2016). Trends in obesity among adults in the United States, 2005 to 2014. *JAMA, 315,* 2284–2291. (p. 365)

Fleischman, D. A., Yang, J., Arfanakis, K., Avanitakis, Z., Leurgans, S. E., Turner, A. D., . . . Buchman, A. S. (2015). Physical activity, motor function, and white matter hyperintensity burden in healthy older adults. *Neurology, 84,* 1294–1300. (p. 153)

Fleming, I., Baum, A., & Weiss, L. (1987). Social density and perceived control as mediator of crowding stress in high-density residential neighborhoods. *Journal of Personality and Social Psychology, 52,* 899–906. (p. 397)

Fleming, J. H., & Scott, B. A. (1991). The costs of confession: The Persian Gulf War POW tapes in historical and theoretical perspective. *Contemporary Social Psychology, 15,* 127–138. (p. 378)

Fletcher, G. J. O., Fitness, J., & Blampied, N. M. (1990). The link between attributions and happiness in close relationships: The roles of depression and explanatory style. *Journal of Social and Clinical Psychology, 9,* 243–255. (p. 417)

Flinker, A., Korzeniewska, A., Shestyuk, A. Y., Franaszczuk, P. J., Dronkers, N. F., Knight, R. T., & Crone, N. E. (2015). Redefining the role of Broca's area in speech. *PNAS, 112,* 2871–2875. (p. 317)

Flora, S. R. (2004). *The power of reinforcement.* Albany, NY: SUNY Press. (p. 250)

Flora, S. R., & Bobby, S. E. (2008, September/October). The bipolar bamboozle. *Skeptical Inquirer,* pp. 41–45. (p. 516)

Flores, A. R., Herman, J. L., Gates, G. J., & Brown, T. N. T. (2016, June). *How many adults identify as transgender in the United States?* Los Angeles: Williams Institute. (p. 171)

Flouri, E., & Buchanan, A. (2004). Early father's and mother's involvement and child's later educational outcomes. *British Journal of Educational Psychology, 74,* 141–153. (p. 135)

Flueckiger, L., Lieb, R., Meyer, A., Witthauer, C., & Mata, J. (2016). The importance of physical activity and sleep for affect on stressful days: Two intensive longitudinal studies. *Emotion, 16,* 488–497. (p. 401)

Flynn, J. R. (2012). *Are we getting smarter? Rising IQ in the twenty-first century.* Cambridge: Cambridge University Press. (p. 342)

Foa, E. B., & Kozak, M. J. (1986). Emotional processing of fear: Exposure to corrective information. *Psychological Bulletin, 99,* 20–35. (p. 541)

Foa, E. B., & McLean, C. P. (2016). The efficacy of exposure therapy for anxiety-related disorders and its underlying mechanisms: The case of OCD and PTSD. *Annual Review of Clinical Psychology, 12,* 1–28. (p. 541)

Foer, J. (2011). *Moonwalking with Einstein: The art and science of remembering everything.* New York: Penguin. (p. 272)

Foley, M. A. (2015). Setting the records straight: Impossible memories and the persistence of their phenomenological qualities. *Review of General Psychology, 19,* 230–248. (p. 291)

Foley, R. T., Whitwell, R. L., & Goodale, M. A. (2015). The two-visual-systems hypothesis and the perspectival features of visual experience. *Consciousness and Cognition, 35,* 225–233. (p. 84)

Fong, C. J., Zaleski, D. J., & Leach, J. K. (2015). The challenge–skill balance and antecedents of flow: A meta-analytic investigation. *Journal of Positive Psychology, 10,* 425–446. (p. B-2)

Fong, K., & Mar, R. A. (2015). What does my avatar say about me? Inferring personality from avatars. *Personality and Social Psychology Bulletin, 41,* 237–249. (p. 481)

Ford, E. S. (2002). Does exercise reduce inflammation? Physical activity and B-reactive protein among U.S. adults. *Epidemiology, 13,* 561–569. (p. 401)

Ford, M. T., Cerasoli, C. P., Higgins, J. A., & Deccesare, A. L. (2011). Relationships between psychological, physical, and behavioural health and work performance: A review and meta-analysis. *Work & Stress, 25,* 185–204. (p. B-8, B-9)

Foree, D. D., & LoLordo, V. M. (1973). Attention in the pigeon: Differential effects of food-getting versus shock-avoidance procedures. *Journal of Comparative and Physiological Psychology, 85,* 551–558. (p. 256)

Forest, A., & Wood, J. (2012). When social networking is not working: Individuals with low self-esteem recognize but do not reap the benefits of self-disclosure on Facebook. *Psychological Science, 23,* 295–302. (p. 486)

Forest, A. L., Kille, D. R, Wood, J. V., & Stehouwer, L. R. (2015). Turbulent times, rocky relationships: Relational consequences of experiencing physical instability. *Psychological Science, 26,* 1261–1271. (p. 229)

Forgas, J. (2017, May 14). Why bad moods are good for you: The surprising benefits of sadness. *The Conversation* (theconversation.com). (p. 514)

Forgas, J. P. (2008). Affect and cognition. *Perspectives on Psychological Science, 3,* 94–101. (p. 407)

Forgas, J. P. (2009, November/December). Think negative! *Australian Science,* pp. 14–17. (p. 514)

Forgas, J. P. (2013). Don't worry, be sad! On the cognitive, motivational, and interpersonal benefits of negative mood. *Current Directions in Psychological Science, 22,* 225–232. (p. 514)

Forgas, J. P., Bower, G. H., & Krantz, S. E. (1984). The influence of mood on perceptions of social interactions. *Journal of Experimental Social Psychology, 20,* 497–513. (p. 281)

Forman, D. R., Aksan, N., & Kochanska, G. (2004). Toddlers' responsive imitation predicts preschool-age conscience. *Psychological Science, 15,* 699–704. (p. 261)

Forsyth, D. R., Lawrence, N. K., Burnette, J. L., & Baumeister, R. F. (2007). Attempting to improve academic performance of struggling college students by bolstering their self-esteem: An intervention that backfired. *Journal of Social and Clinical Psychology, 26,* 447–459. (p. 487)

Foss, D. J., & Hakes, D. T. (1978). *Psycholinguistics: An introduction to the psychology of language.* Englewood Cliffs, NJ: Prentice-Hall. (p. 468)

Foss, D. J., & Pirozzolo, J. W. (2017). Four semesters investigating frequency of testing, the testing effect, and transfer of training. *Journal of Educational Psychology.* Advance online publication. doi:10.1037/edu0000197 (p. 33)

Foster, E., Wildner, H., Tudeau, L., Haueter, S., Ralvenius, W., Jegen, M., . . . Zeilhofer, H. (2015). Targeted ablation, silencing, and activation establish glycinergic dorsal horn neurons as key components of a spinal gate for pain and itch. *Neuron, 85,* 1289–1304.

Foster, J. (2011). Our deadly anorexic pact. *The Daily Mail* (dailymail.co.uk). (p. 532)

Fothergill, E., Guo, J., Howard, L., Kerns, J. C., Knuth, J. D., Brychta, R., . . . Hall, K. D. K. (2016). Persistent metabolic adaptation 6 years after "The Biggest Loser" competition. *Obesity, 24,* 1612–1619. (p. 365)

Foubert, J. D., Brosi, M. W., & Bannon, R. S. (2011). Pornography viewing among fraternity men: Effects on bystander intervention, rape myth acceptance, and behavioral intent to commit sexual assault. *Sexual Addiction & Compulsivity, 18,* 212–231. (p. 176)

Foulkes, D. (1999). *Children's dreaming and the development of consciousness.* Cambridge, MA: Harvard University Press. (p. 99)

Fournier, J. C., DeRubeis, R. J., Hollon, S. D., Dimidjian, S., Amsterdam, J. D., Shelton, R. C., & Fawcett, J. (2010). Antidepressant drug effects and depression severity: A patient-level meta-analysis. *Journal of the American Medical Association, 303,* 47–53. (p. 562)

Fowles, D. C. (1992). Schizophrenia: Diathesis-stress revisited. *Annual Review of Psychology, 43,* 303–336. (p. 524)

Fowles, D. C., & Dindo, L. (2009). Temperament and psychopathy: A dual-pathway model. *Current Directions in Psychological Science, 18,* 179–183. (p. 530)

Fox, A. S., Oler, J. A., Shackman, A. J., Shelton, S. E., Raveendran, M., McKay, D. R., . . . Rogers, J. (2015). Intergenerational neural mediators of early-life anxious temperament. *PNAS, 112,* 9118–9122. (p. 52)

Fox, D. (2010, June). The insanity virus. *Discover,* pp. 58–64. (p. 525)

Fox, K. C. R., Nijeboer, S., Solomonova, E., Domhoff, G. W., & Christoff, K. (2013). Dreaming as mind wandering: Evidence from functional neuroimaging and first-person content reports. *Frontiers in Human Neuroscience, 7,* Article 412. http://dx.doi.org/10.3389/fnhum.2013.00412 (p. 99)

Fox, M. L., Dwyer, D. J., & Ganster, D. C. (1993). Effects of stressful job demands and control on physiological and attitudinal outcomes in a hospital setting. *Academy of Management Journal, 36,* 289–318. (p. 397)

Fox, N. A., Bakermans-Kranenburg, M., Yoo, K. H., Bowman, L. C., Cannon, E. N., Vanderwert, R. E., . . . van IJzendoorn, M. H. (2016). Assessing human mirror activity with EEG mu rhythm: A meta-analysis. *Psychological Bulletin, 142,* 291–313. (p. 260)

Fozard, J. L., & Popkin, S. J. (1978). Optimizing adult development: Ends and means of an applied psychology of aging. *American Psychologist, 33,* 975–989. (p. 152)

Fragaszy, D. M., Eshchar, Y., Visalberghi, E., Resende, B., Laity, K., & Izar, P. (2017). Synchronized practice helps bearded capuchin monkeys learn to extend attention while learning a tradition. *PNAS, 114,* 7798–7805. (p. 259)

Fraley, R. C., Roisman, G. I., Booth-LaForce, C., Owen, M. T., & Holland, A. S. (2013). Interpersonal and genetic origins of adult attachment styles: A longitudinal study from infancy to early adulthood. *Journal of Personality and Social Psychology, 104,* 817–838. (p. 136)

Fraley, R. C., & Tancredy, C. M. (2012). Twin and sibling attachment in a nationally representative sample. *Personality and Social Psychology Bulletin, 38,* 308–316. (p. 135)

Fraley, R. C., Vicary, A. M., Brumbaugh, C. C., & Roisman, G. I. (2011). Patterns of stability in adult attachment: An empirical test of two models of continuity and change. *Journal of Personality and Social Psychology, 101,* 974–992. (p. 136)

Frances, A. J. (2013). *Saving normal: An insider's revolt against out-of-control psychiatric diagnosis, DSM-5, big pharma, and the medicalization of ordinary life.* New York: HarperCollins. (p. 497)

Frances, A. J. (2014, September/October). No child left undiagnosed. *Psychology Today,* pp. 49–50. (p. 497)

Frank, J. D. (1982). Therapeutic components shared by all psychotherapies. In J. H. Harvey & M. M. Parks (Eds.), *The Master Lecture Series: Vol. 1. Psychotherapy research and behavior change.* Washington, DC: American Psychological Association. (pp. 555, 556)

Frankel, A., Strange, D. R., & Schoonover, R. (1983). CRAP: Consumer rated assessment procedure. In G. H. Scherr & R. Liebmann-Smith (Eds.), *The best of The Journal of Irreproducible Results.* New York: Workman. (p. 477)

Frankenburg, W., Dodds, J., Archer, P., Shapiro, H., & Bresnick, B. (1992). The Denver II: A major revision and restandardization of the Denver Developmental Screening Test. *Pediatrics, 89,* 91–97. (p. 124)

Frankl, V. E. (1962). *Man's search for meaning: An introduction to logotherapy.* Boston: Beacon Press. (p. 350)

Franklin, J. C., Ribeiro, J. D., Fox, K. R., Bentley, K. H., Kleiman, E. M., Huang, X., . . . Nock, M. K. (2017). Risk factors for suicidal thoughts and behaviors: A meta-analysis of 50 years of research. *Psychological Bulletin, 143,* 187–232. (p. 501)

Franklin, M., & Foa, E. B. (2011). Treatment of obsessive-compulsive disorder. *Annual Review of Clinical Psychology, 7,* 229–243. (p. 511)

Franz, E. A., Waldie, K. E., & Smith, M. J. (2000). The effect of callosotomy on novel versus familiar bimanual actions: A neural dissociation between controlled and automatic processes? *Psychological Science, 11,* 82–85. (p. 66)

Fraser, M. A., Shaw, M. E., & Cherubin, N. (2015). A systematic review and meta-analysis of longitudinal hippocampal atrophy in healthy human ageing. *NeuroImage, 112,* 364–374. (p. 152)

Frassanito, P., & Pettorini, B. (2008). Pink and blue: The color of gender. *Child's Nervous System, 24,* 881–882. (p. 162)

Frasure-Smith, N., & Lesperance, F. (2005). Depression and coronary heart disease: Complex synergism of mind, body, and environment. *Current Directions in Psychological Science, 14,* 39–43. (p. 392)

Frattaroli, J. (2006). Experimental disclosure and its moderators: A meta-analysis. *Psychological Bulletin, 132,* 823–865. (p. 400)

Frederick, S. (2005). Cognitive reflection and decision making. *Journal of Economic Perspectives, 4,* 25–42. (p. 306)

Fredrickson, B. L. (2013). Positive emotions broaden and build. In E. Ashby Plant & P.G. Devine (Eds.), *Advances on Experimental Social Psychology, 47,* 1–3. Burlington, MA: Academic Press. (p. 407)

Fredrickson, B. L., Grewen, K. M., Coffey, K. A., Algoe, S. B., Firestine, A. M., Arevalo, J. M. G., . . . Cole, S. W. (2013). A functional genomic perspective on human well-being. *PNAS, 110,* 13684–13689. (p. 411)

Freedman, D. H. (2011, February). How to fix the obesity crisis. *Scientific American,* pp. 40–47. (p. 366)

Freedman, D. J., Riesenhuber, M., Poggio, T., & Miller, E. K. (2001). Categorical representation of visual stimuli in the primate prefrontal cortex. *Science, 291,* 312–316. (p. 309)

Freedman, J. L., & Fraser, S. C. (1966). Compliance without pressure: The foot-in-the-door technique. *Journal of Personality and Social Psychology, 4,* 195–202. (p. 419)

Freedman, J. L., & Perlick, D. (1979). Crowding, contagion, and laughter. *Journal of Experimental Social Psychology, 15,* 295–303. (p. 430)

Freedman, R., Lewis, D. A., Michels, R., Pine, D. S., Scultz, S. K., Tamminga, C. A., . . . Yager, J. (2013). The initial field trials of DSM-5: New blooms and old thorns. *American Journal of Psychiatry, 170,* 1–5. (p. 497)

Freeman, D., & Freeman, J. (2013). *The stressed sex: Uncovering the truth about men, women, and mental health.* Oxford: Oxford University Press. (p. 517)

Freeman, E. C., & Twenge, J. M. (2010, January). *Using MySpace increases the endorsement of narcissistic personality traits.* Poster presented at the annual conference of the Society for Personality and Social Psychology, Las Vegas, NV. (p. 356)

Freeman, S., Eddy, S. L., McDonough, M., Smith, M. K., Okoroafor, N., Jordt, H., & Wenderoth, M. P. (2014). Active learning increases student performance in science, engineering, and mathematics. *PNAS, 111,* 8410–8415. (p. 33)

Freeman, W. J. (1991, February). The physiology of perception. *Scientific American,* pp. 78–85. (p. 216)

Frenda, S. J., Patihis, L., Loftus, E. F., Lewis, H. C., & Fenn, K. M. (2014). Sleep deprivation and false memories. *Clinical Psychological Science, 25,* 1674–1681. (p. 295)

Freud, S. (1897, October 15). Letter of Freud to Fliess. In J. M. Masson (Ed.) (1985), *The complete letters of Sigmund Freud to Wilhelm Fleiss, 1887–1904.* Cambridge, MA: Harvard University Press. (p. 464)

Freud, S. (1935: reprinted 1960). *A general introduction to psychoanalysis.* New York: Washington Square Press. (p. 156)

Freyd, J. J., DePrince, A. P., & Gleaves, D. H. (2007). The state of betrayal trauma theory: Reply to McNally—Conceptual issues and future directions. *Memory, 15,* 295–311. (p. 293)

Friedel, J. E., DeHart, W. B., Madden, G. J., & Odum, A. L. (2014). Impulsivity and cigarette smoking: Discounting of monetary and consumable outcomes in current and non-smokers. *Psychopharmacology, 231,* 4517–4526. (p. 463)

Friedman, H. S., & Martin, L. R. (2012). *The longevity project.* New York: Penguin (Plume). (p. 331)

Friedman, M., & Ulmer, D. (1984). *Treating Type A behavior—and your heart.* New York: Knopf. (p. 391, 403)

Friedman, R., & James, J. W. (2008). The myth of the stages of dying, death and grief. *Skeptic, 14*(2), 37–41. (p. 159)

Friedman, R. A. (2012, December 17). In gun debate, a misguided focus on mental illness. *The New York Times* (nytimes.com). (p. 503)

Friedman, R. A. (2017, October 11). Psychiatrists can't stop mass killers. *The New York Times* (nytimes.com). (p. 503)

Friedrich, M., Wilhelhm, I., Born, J., & Friederici, A. D. (2015). Generalization of word meanings during infant sleep. *Nature Communications, 6,* Article 6004. doi:10.1038/ncomms7004 (p. 91)

Friend, T. (2004). *Animal talk: Breaking the codes of animal language.* New York: Free Press. (p. 318)

Friesen, J. P., Campbell, T. H., & Kay, A. C. (2015). The psychological advantage of unfalsifiability: The appeal of untestable religious and political ideologies. *Journal of Personality and Social Psychology, 108,* 515–529. (p. 304)

Frijda, N. H. (1988). The laws of emotion. *American Psychologist, 43,* 349–358. (p. 410)

Frisell, T., Pawitan, Y., Långström, N., & Lichtenstein, P. (2012). Heritability, assortative mating and gender differences in violent crime: Results from a total population sample using twin, adoption, and sibling models. *Behavior Genetics, 42,* 3–18. (pp. 163, 530)

Frith, U., & Frith, C. (2001). The biological basis of social interaction. *Current Directions in Psychological Science, 10,* 151–155. (p. 131)

Fritz, C., Curtin, J., Poitevineau, J., & Tao, F.-C. (2017). Listener evaluations of new and old Italian violins. *PNAS, 114,* 5395–5400. (p. 198)

Fromkin, V., & Rodman, R. (1983). An introduction to language (3rd ed.). New York: Holt, Rinehart & Winston. (p. 314)

Frühauf, S., Gerger, H., Schmidt, H. M., Munder, T., & Barth, J. (2013). Efficacy of psychological interventions for sexual dysfunction: A systematic review and meta-analysis. *Archives of Sexual Behavior, 42,* 915–933. (p. 175)

Fry, A. F., & Hale, S. (1996). Processing speed, working memory, and fluid intelligence: Evidence for a developmental cascade. *Psychological Science, 7,* 237–241. (p. 152)

Fry, D. P. (2012). Life without war. *Science, 336,* 879–884. (p. 458)

Fry, R. (2017, May 5). It's becoming more common for young adults to live at home—and for longer stretches. Pew Research Center (pewresearch.org). (p. 149)

FTC. (2016, January 5). *Lumosity to pay $2 million to settle FTC deceptive advertising charges for its "brain training" program.* Press release. Federal Trade Commission (ftc.gov/news-events/press-releases/2016/01/lumosity-pay-2-million-settle-ftc-deceptive-advertising-charges). (p. 155)

Fu, A., & Markus, H. R. (2014). My mother and me: Why tiger mothers motivate Asian Americans but not European Americans. *Personality and Social Psychology Bulletin, 40,* 739–749. (p. 149)

Fuhrmann, D., Knoll, L. J., & Blakemore, S. J. (2015). Adolescence as a sensitive period of brain development. *Trends in Cognitive Sciences, 19*(10), 558–566. (p. 142)

Fuller, M. J., & Downs, A. C. (1990, June). Spermarche is a salient biological marker in men's development. Poster session presented at the Second Annual Convention of the American Psychological Society, Dallas, TX. (p. 167)

Fuller-Thomson, E., Agbeyaka, S., LaFond, D. M., & Bern-Klug, M. (2016). Flourishing after depression: Factors associated with achieving complete mental health among those with a history of depression. *Psychiatry Research, 242,* 111–120. (p. 517)

Fulmer, C. A., Gelfand, M. J., Kruglanski, A. W., Kim-Prieto, C., Diener, E., Pierro, A., & Higgins, E. T. (2010). On "feeling right" in cultural contexts: How person-culture match affects self-esteem and subjective well-being. *Psychological Science, 21,* 1563–1569. (pp. 411, 483)

Fulmer, I. S., Gerhart, B., & Scott, K. S. (2003). Are the 100 best better? An empirical investigation of the relationship between being a "great place to work" and firm performance. *Personnel Psychology, 56,* 965–993. (p. B-8)

Funder, D. C. (2001). Personality. *Annual Review of Psychology, 52,* 197–221. (p. 478)

Funder, D. C. (2009). Persons, behaviors and situations: An agenda for personality psychology in the postwar era. *Journal of Research in Personality, 43,* 155–162. (p. 483)

Funder, D. C., & Block, J. (1989). The role of ego-control, ego-resiliency, and IQ in delay of gratification in adolescence. *Journal of Personality and Social Psychology, 57,* 1041–1050. (p. 145)

Furnham, A. (1982). Explanations for unemployment in Britain. *European Journal of Social Psychology, 12,* 335–352. (p. 417)

Furnham, A. (2016). Whether you think you can, or you think you can't—you're right. In R. J. Sternberg, S. T. Fiske, & D. J. Foss (Eds.), *Scientists making a difference: One hundred eminent behavioral and brain scientists talk about their most important contributions.* New York: Cambridge University Press. (p. 437)

Furnham, A., & Baguma, P. (1994). Cross-cultural differences in the evaluation of male and female body shapes. *International Journal of Eating Disorders, 15,* 81–89. (p. 365)

Furr, R. M., & Funder, D. C. (1998). A multimodal analysis of personal negativity. *Journal of Personality and Social Psychology, 74,* 1580–1591. (p. 521)

Furukawa, T. A., Levine, S. Z., Tanaka, S., Goldberg, Y., Samara, M., Davis, J. M., . . . Leucht, S. (2015). Initial severity of schizophrenia and efficacy of antipsychotics: Participant-level meta-analysis of 6 placebo-controlled studies. *JAMA Psychiatry, 72,* 14–21. (p. 560)

Furukawa, T. A., Yoshimura, R., Harai, H., Imaizumi, T., Takeuchi, H., Kitamua, T., & Takahashi, K. (2009). How many well vs. unwell days can you expect over 10 years, once you become depressed? *Acta Psychiatrica Scandinavica, 119,* 290–297. (p. 517)

Fuss, J., Steinle, J., Bindila, L., Auer, M. K., Kirchherr, H., Lutz, B., & Gass, P. (2015). A runner's high depends on cannabinoid receptors in mice. *PNAS, 112,* 13105–13108. (p. 43)

Futrell, R., Mahowald, K., & Gibson, E. (2015). Large-scale evidence of dependency length minimization in 37 languages. *PNAS, 112,* 10336–10341. (p. 313)

Gable, S. L., Gonzaga, G. C., & Strachman, A. (2006). Will you be there for me when things go right? Supportive responses to positive event disclosures. *Journal of Personality and Social Psychology, 91,* 904–917. (p. 157)

Gable, S. L., Gosnell, C. L., Maisel, N. C., & Strachman, A. (2012). Safely testing the alarm: Close others' responses to personal positive events. *Journal of Personality and Social Psychology, 103,* 963–981. (p. 399)

Gaddy, M. A., & Ingram, R. E. (2014). A meta-analytic review of mood-congruent implicit memory in depressed mood. *Clinical Psychology Review, 34,* 402–416. (p. 281)

Gaertner, L., Iuzzini, J., & O'Mara, E. M. (2008). When rejection by one fosters aggression against many: Multiple-victim aggression as a consequence of social rejection and perceived groupness. *Journal of Experimental Social Psychology, 44,* 958–970. (p. 355)

Gaissmaier, W., & Gigerenzer, G. (2012). 9/11, Act II: A fine-grained analysis of regional variations in traffic fatalities in the aftermath of the terrorist attacks. *Psychological Science, 23,* 1449–1454. (p. 302)

Gaither, S. E., & Sommers, S. R. (2013). Living with another-race roommate shapes whites' behavior in subsequent diverse settings. *Journal of Experimental Social Psychology, 49,* 272–276. (p. 457)

Galak, J., Leboeuf, R. A., Nelson, L. D., & Simmons, J. P. (2012). Correcting the past: Failures to replicate psi. *Journal of Personality and Social Psychology, 103,* 933–948. (p. 231)

Galambos, N. L. (1992). Parent–adolescent relations. *Current Directions in Psychological Science, 1,* 146–149. (p. 148)

Galanter, E. (1962). Contemporary psychophysics. In R. Brown, E. Galanter, E. H. Hess, & G. Mandler (Eds.), *New directions in psychology* (pp. 87–156). New York: Holt, Rinehart & Winston. (p. 190)

Galanter, M. (2016). *What is Alcoholics Anonymous?* New York: Oxford University Press. (p. 548)

Galati, D., Scherer, K. R., & Ricci-Bitti, P. E. (1997). Voluntary facial expression of emotion: Comparing congenitally blind with normally sighted encoders. *Journal of Personality and Social Psychology, 73,* 1363–1379. (p. 378)

Gale, C. R., Batty, G. D., & Deary, I. J. (2008). Locus of control at age 10 years and health outcomes and behaviors at age 30 years: The 1970 British Cohort Study. *Psychosomatic Medicine, 70,* 397–403. (p. 397)

Galinsky, A. D., Magee, J. C., Inesi, M. E., & Gruenfeld, D. H. (2006). Power and perspectives not taken. *Psychological Science, 17,* 1068–1074. (p. 128)

Galinsky, A. M., & Sonenstein, F. L. (2013). Relationship commitment, perceived equity, and sexual enjoyment among young adults in the United States. *Archives of Sexual Behavior, 42,* 93–104. (p. 186)

Galinsky, E., Aumann, K., & Bond, J. T. (2008). *Times are changing: Gender and generation at work and at home.* Work and Families Institute. Retrieved from familiesandwork.org (p. 488)

Galla, B. M., & Duckworth, A. L. (2015). More than resisting temptation: Beneficial habits mediate the relationship between self-control and positive life outcomes. *Journal of Personality and Social Psychology, 109,* 508–525. (pp. 234, 359)

Gallace, A. (2012). Living with touch. *Psychologist, 25,* 896–899. (p. 83)

Gallace, A., & Spence, C. (2011). To what extent do Gestalt grouping principles influence tactile perception? *Psychological Bulletin, 137,* 538–561. (p. 108)

Gallese, V., Gernsbacher, M. A., Heyes, C., Hickok, G., & Iacoboni, M. (2011). Mirror neuron forum. *Perspectives on Psychological Science, 6,* 369–407. (pp. 132, 259, 260)

Gallo, W. T., Teng, H. M., Falba, T. A., Kasl, S. V., Krumholz, H. M., & Bradley, E. H. (2006). The impact of late career job loss on myocardial infarction and stroke: A 10-year follow up using the health and retirement survey. *Occupational and Environmental Medicine, 63,* 683–687. (p. 392)

Gallup. (2004, August 16). 65% of Americans receive NO praise or recognition in the workplace. E-mail from Tom Rath: bucketbook@gallup.com. (p. B-11)

Gallup. (2017, February 10). Islamophobia: Understanding anti-Muslim sentiment in the West. (p. 438)

Gallup, G. G., Jr., & Frederick, D. A. (2010). The science of sex appeal: An evolutionary perspective. *Review of General Psychology, 14,* 240–250. (p. 449)

Gallup, G. H. (1972). *The Gallup poll: Public opinion 1935–1971* (Vol. 3). New York: Random House. (p. 457)

Gallup, G. H., Jr. (1994, October). Millions finding care and support in small groups. *Emerging Trends,* pp. 2–5. (p. 548)

Gana, K., Broc, G., Saada, Y., Amieva, H., & Quintard, B. (2016). Subjective wellbeing and longevity: Findings from a 22-year cohort study. *Journal of Psychosomatic Research, 85,* 28–34. (p. 392)

Gandhi, A. V., Mosser, E. A., Oikonomou, G., & Prober, D. A. (2015). Melatonin is required for circadian regulation of sleep. *Neuron, 85,* 1193–1199. (p. 90)

Gandhi, T. K., Ganesh, S., & Sinha, P. (2014). Improvement in spatial imagery following sight onset late in childhood. *Psychological Science, 25,* 693–701. (p. 213)

Gandhi, T. K., Singh, A. K., Swami, P., Ganesh, S., & Sinha, P. (2017). Emergence of categorical face perception after extended early-onset blindness. *PNAS, 114,* 6139–6143. (p. 213)

Gangestad, S. W., Thornhill, R., & Garver-Apgar, C. E. (2010). Men's facial masculinity predicts changes in their female partners' sexual interests across the ovulatory cycle, whereas men's intelligence does not. *Evolution and Human Behavior, 31,* 412–424. (p. 449)

Gangwisch, J. E., Babiss, L. A., Malaspina, D., Turner, J. B., Zammit, G. K., & Posner, K. (2010). Earlier parental set bedtimes as a protective factor against depression and suicidal ideation. *Sleep, 33,* 97–106. (p. 93)

Gao, Y., Raine, A., Venables, P. H., Dawson, M. E., & Mednick, S. A. (2010). Association of poor child fear conditioning and adult crime. *American Journal of Psychiatry, 167,* 56–60. (p. 530)

Garcia, J., & Gustavson, A. R. (1997, January). Carl R. Gustavson (1946–1996): Pioneering wildlife psychologist. *APS Observer,* pp. 34–35. (pp. 255, 542)

Garcia, J., & Koelling, R. A. (1966). Relation of cue to consequence in avoidance learning. *Psychonomic Science, 4,* 123–124. (p. 254)

Garcia, J. L., Heckman, J. J., Leaf, D. E., & Prados, M. J. (2016, December). The life-cycle benefits of an influential early childhood program. Working paper 2015-35, Human Capital and Economic Opportunity Global Working Group (hceeconomics.org), University of Chicago. (p. 339)

Garcia, J. R., Reiber, C., Massey, S. G., & Merriwether, A. M. (2012). Sexual hookup culture: A review. *Review of General Psychology, 16,* 161–176. (p. 186)

Garcia, J. R., Reiber, C., Massey, S. G., & Merriwether, A. M. (2013, February). Sexual hook-up culture. *Monitor on Psychology,* pp. 60–66. (pp. 177, 186)

Garcia-Falgueras, A., & Swaab, D. F. (2010). Sexual hormones and the brain: An essential alliance for sexual identity and sexual orientation. *Endocrine Development, 17,* 22–35. (p. 181)

Gardner, H. (1983). *Frames of mind: The theory of multiple intelligences.* New York: Basic Books. (p. 324)

Gardner, H. (1998, March 19). An intelligent way to progress. *The Independent* (London), p. E4. (p. 324)

Gardner, H. (1999a). *Multiple views of multiple intelligence.* New York: Basic Books. (p. 324)

Gardner, H. (1999b, February). Who owns intelligence? *Atlantic Monthly,* pp. 67–76. (p. 327)

Gardner, H. (2006). *The development and education of the mind: The selected works of Howard Gardner.* New York: Routledge/Taylor & Francis. (p. 324)

Gardner, H. (2011). *The theory of multiple intelligences: As psychology, as education, as social science.* Address on the receipt of an honorary degree from José Cela University in Madrid and the Prince of Asturias Prize for Social Science. (p. 324)

Gardner, J., & Oswald, A. J. (2007). Money and mental well-being: A longitudinal study of medium-sized lottery wins. *Journal of Health Economics, 6,* 49–60. (p. 410)

Gardner, R. A., & Gardner, B. I. (1969). Teaching sign language to a chimpanzee. *Science, 165,* 664–672. (p. 317)

Garfield, C. (1986). *Peak performers: The new heroes of American business.* New York: Morrow. (p. 321)

Garon, N., Bryson, S. E., & Smith, I. M. (2008). Executive function in preschoolers: A review using an integrative framework. *Psychological Bulletin, 134,* 31–60. (p. 123)

Garry, M., Loftus, E. F., & Brown, S. W. (1994). Memory: A river runs through it. *Consciousness and Cognition, 3,* 438–451. (p. 469)

Gartrell, N., & Bos, H. (2010). US National Longitudinal Lesbian Family Study: Psychological adjustment of 17-year-old adolescents. *Pediatrics, 126,* 28–36. (p. 180)

Gasiorowska, A., Chaplin, L. N., Zaleskiewicz, T., Wygrab, S., & Vohs, K. D. (2016). Money cues increase agency and decrease prosociality among children: Early signs of market-mode behaviors. *Psychological Science, 27,* 331–344. (p. 281)

Gatchel, R. J., Peng, Y. B., Peters, M. L., Fuchs, P. N., & Turk, D. C. (2007). The biopsychosocial approach to chronic pain: Scientific advances and future directions. *Psychological Bulletin, 133,* 581–624. (pp. 222, 223)

Gates, W. (1998, July 20). Charity begins when I'm ready (interview). *Fortune.* Retrieved from pathfinder.com/fortune/1998/980720/bil7.html (p. 326)

Gavin, K. (2004, November 9). *U-M team reports evidence that smoking affects human brain's natural "feel good" chemical system* [Press release]. Retrieved from http://www.med.umich.edu/ (p. 105)

Gawande, A. (1998, September 21). The pain perplex. *The New Yorker,* pp. 86–94. (p. 223)

Gawin, F. H. (1991). Cocaine addiction: Psychology and neurophysiology. *Science, 251,* 1580–1586. (p. 107)

Gawronski, B., & Quinn, K. (2013). Guilty by mere similarity: Assimilative effects of facial resemblance on automatic evaluation. *Journal of Experimental Social Psychology, 49,* 120–125. (p. 240)

Gazzaniga, M. (2006). *The ethical brain: The science of our moral dilemmas.* New York: HarperPerennial. (p. 66)

Gazzaniga, M. S. (1967, August). The split brain in man. *Scientific American,* pp. 24–29. (p. 65)

Gazzaniga, M. S. (1983). Right hemisphere language following brain bisection: A 20-year perspective. *American Psychologist, 38,* 525–537. (p. 66)

Gazzola, V., Spezio, M. L., Etzel, J. A., Catelli, F., Adolphs, R., & Keysers, C. (2012). Primary somatosensory cortex discriminates affective significance in social touch. *PNAS, 109,* E1657–E1666. (p. 221)

GBD 2015 Obesity Collaborators. (2017). Health effects of overweight and obesity in 195 countries over 25 years. *New England Journal of Medicine, 377,* 13–27. (p. 365)

GBD. (2017). Smoking prevalence and attributable disease burden in 195 countries and territories, 1990–2015: A systematic analysis from the Global Burden of Disease Study 2015. *The Lancet, 389,* 1885–1906. (p. 106)

Ge, X., & Natsuaki, M. N. (2009). In search of explanations for early pubertal timing effects on developmental psychopathology. *Current Directions in Psychological Science, 18,* 327–441. (p. 142)

Ge, Y., Knittel, C. R., MacKenzie, D., & Zoepf, S. (2016, October). Racial and gender discrimination in transportation network companies. NBER Working Paper No. 22776. Retrieved from nber.org/papers/w2276 (p. 435)

Geary, D. C. (2010). Male, female: The evolution of human sex differences (2nd ed.). Washington, DC: American Psychological Association. (p. 165)

Geary, D. C., Salthouse, T. A., Chen, G.-P., & Fan, L. (1996). Are East Asian versus American differences in arithmetical ability a recent phenomenon? *Developmental Psychology, 32,* 254–262. (p. 342)

Geen, R. G., & Quanty, M. B. (1977). The catharsis of aggression: An evaluation of a hypothesis. In L. Berkowitz (Ed.), *Advances in experimental social psychology* (Vol. 10). New York: Academic Press. (p. 393)

Gehring, W. J., Wimke, J., & Nisenson, L. G. (2000). Action monitoring dysfunction in obsessive-compulsive disorder. *Psychological Science, 11,* 1–6. (p. 512)

Geier, A. B., Rozin, P., & Doros, G. (2006). Unit bias: A new heuristic that helps explain the effects of portion size on food intake. *Psychological Science, 17,* 521–525. (p. 364)

Gellis, L. A., Arigo, D., & Elliott, J. C. (2013). Cognitive refocusing treatment for insomnia: A randomized controlled trial in university students. *Behavior Therapy, 44,* 100–110. (p. 95)

Gelman, A. (2009, April 16). Red and blue economies? *FiveThirtyEight.* Retrieved from fivethirtyeight.com/features/red-andblue-economies (p. 18)

Gelman, D. (1989, May 15). Voyages to the unknown. *Newsweek,* pp. 66–69. (p. 379)

Genesee, F., & Gándara, P. (1999). Bilingual education programs: A cross-national perspective. *Journal of Social Issues, 55,* 665–685. (p. 320)

Gentile, D. A. (2009). Pathological video-game use among youth ages 8 to 18: A national study. *Psychological Science, 20,* 594–602. (pp. 102, 445)

Gentile, D. A., & Bushman, B. J. (2012). Reassessing media violence effects using a risk and resilience approach to understanding aggression. *Psychology of Popular Media Culture, 1,* 138–151. (p. 263)

Gentile, D. A., Coyne, S., & Walsh, D. A. (2011). Media violence, physical aggression and relational aggression in school age children: A short-term longitudinal study. *Aggressive Behavior, 37,* 193–206. (p. 263)

Gentner, D. (2016). Language as cognitive tool kit: How language supports relational thought. *American Psychologist, 71,* 650–657. (p. 319)

Gentzkow, M., Shapiro, J. M., & Taddy, M. (2016, July). Measuring polarization in high-dimensional data: Method and application to congressional speech. NBER Working Paper 22423. Retrieved from nber.org/papers/w22423 (p. 431)

Geraerts, E., Bernstein, D. M., Merckelbach, H., Linders, C., Raymaekers, L., & Loftus, E. F. (2008). Lasting false beliefs and their behavioral consequences. *Psychological Science, 19,* 749–753. (p. 290)

Geraerts, E., Schooler, J. W., Merckelbach, H., Jelicic, M., Hauer, B. J. A., & Ambadar, Z. (2007). The reality of recovered memories: Corroborating continuous and discontinuous memories of childhood sexual abuse. *Psychological Science, 18,* 564–568. (p. 293)

Germain, A. (2013). Sleep disturbances as the hallmark of PTSD: Where are we now? *Archives of Journal of Psychiatry, 170,* 372–382. (p. 509)

Gernsbacher, M. A., Dawson, M., & Goldsmith, H. H. (2005). Three reasons not to believe in an autism epidemic. *Current Directions in Psychological Science, 14,* 55–58. (p. 131)

Gershenson, S., Holt, S. B., & Papageorge, N. W. (2016). Who believes in me? The effect of student-teacher demographic match on teacher expectations. *Economics of Education Review, 52,* 209–224. (p. 344)

Gershoff, E. T. (2002). Parental corporal punishment and associated child behaviors and experiences: A meta-analytic and theoretical review. *Psychological Bulletin, 128,* 539–579. (p. 249)

Gershoff, E. T., & Grogan-Kaylor, A. (2016). Spanking and child outcomes: Old controversies and new meta-analyses. *Journal of Family Psychology, 30,* 453–469. (p. 249)

Gershoff, E. T., Grogan-Kaylor, A., Lansford, J. E., Chang, L., Zelli, A., Deater-Deckard, K., & Dodge, K. A. (2010). Parent discipline practices in an international sample: Associations with child behaviors and moderation by perceived normativeness. *Child Development, 81,* 487–502. (p. 249)

Gershon, A., Ram, N., Johnson, S. L., Harvey, A. G., & Zeitzer, J. M. (2016). Daily actigraphy profiles distinguish depressive and interepisode states in bipolar disorder. *Clinical Psychological Science, 4,* 641–650. (p. 514)

Gerst-Emerson, K., & Jayawardhana, J. (2015). Loneliness as a public health issue: The impact of loneliness on health care utilization among older adults. *American Journal of Public Health, 105,* 1013–1019. (p. 353)

Geschwind, N. (1979, September). Specializations of the human brain. *Scientific American, 241,* 180–199. (p. 316)

Geukes, K., Nestler, S., Hutteman, R., Dufner, M., Küfner, A. C., Egloff, B., . . . Back, M. D. (2016). Puffed-up but shaky selves: State self-esteem level and variability in narcissists. *Journal of Personality and Social Psychology.* Advance online publication. doi:10.1037/pspp0000093 (p. 488)

Geurts, D. E., Von Borries, K., Volman, I., Bulten, B. H., Cools, R., & Verkes, R. J. (2016). Neural connectivity during reward expectation dissociates psychopathic criminals from non-criminal individuals with high impulsive/antisocial psychopathic traits. *Social Cognitive and Affective Neuroscience, 11,* 1326–1334. (p. 530)

Giampietro, M., & Cavallera, G. M. (2007). Morning and evening types and creative thinking. *Personality and Individual Differences, 42,* 453–463. (p. 87)

Giancola, P. R., & Corman, M. D. (2007). Alcohol and aggression: A test of the attention-allocation model. *Psychological Science, 18,* 649–655. (p. 442)

Giancola, P. R., Josephs, R. A., Parrott, D. J., & Duke, A. A. (2010). Alcohol myopia revisited: Clarifying aggression and other acts of disinhibition through a distorted lens. *Perspectives on Psychological Science, 5,* 265–278. (p. 104)

Gibbons, F. X. (1986). Social comparison and depression: Company's effect on misery. *Journal of Personality and Social Psychology, 51,* 140–148. (p. 411)

Gibbs, W. W. (1996). Mind readings. *Scientific American, 274,* 34–36. (p. 60)

Gibson, E. J., & Walk, R. D. (1960, April). The "visual cliff." *Scientific American,* pp. 64–71. (p. 208)

Giedd, J. N. (2015, June). The amazing teen brain. *Scientific American,* pp. 33–37. (p. 142)

Giesbrecht, T., Lynn, S. J., Lilienfeld, S. O., & Merckelbach, H. (2008). Cognitive processes in dissociation: An analysis of core theoretical assumptions. *Psychological Bulletin, 134,* 617–647. (p. 528)

Giesbrecht, T., Lynn, S. J., Lilienfeld, S. O., & Merckelbach, H. (2010). Cognitive processes, trauma, and dissociation—Misconceptions and misrepresentations: Reply to Bremmer (2010). *Psychological Bulletin, 136,* 7–11. (p. 528)

Gigerenzer, G. (2004). Dread risk, September 11, and fatal traffic accidents. *Psychological Science, 15,* 286–287. (p. 302)

Gigerenzer, G. (2006). Out of the frying pan into the fire: Behavioral reactions to terrorist attacks. *Risk Analysis, 26,* 347–351. (p. 302)

Gigerenzer, G. (2010). *Rationality for mortals: How people cope with uncertainty.* New York: Oxford University Press. (p. A-1)

Gigerenzer, G. (2015). *Simply rational: Decision making in the real world.* New York: Oxford University Press. (p. 300)

Gilbert, D. T. (2006). *Stumbling on happiness.* New York: Knopf. (pp. 157, 369)

Gilbert, D. T., King, G., Pettigrew, S., & Wilson, T. D. (2016). Comment on "Estimating the reproducibility of psychological science." *Science, 351,* 1037. (p. 20)

Gilbert, D. T., Pinel, E. C., Wilson, T. D., Blumberg, S. J., & Wheatley, T. P. (1998). Immune neglect: A source of durability bias in affective forecasting. *Journal of Personality and Social Psychology, 75,* 617–638. (p. 408)

Gildersleeve, K., Haselton, M., & Fales, M. R. (2014). Do women's mate preferences change across the menstrual cycle? A meta-analytic review. *Psychological Bulletin, 140,* 1205–1259. (p. 173)

Gillen-O'Neel, C., Huynh, V. W., & Fuligni, A. J. (2013). To study or to sleep? The academic costs of extra studying at the expense of sleep. *Child Development, 84,* 133–142. (p. 98)

Gilmore, R. O., & Adolph, K. E. (2017). Video can make behavioural science more reproducible. *Nature Human Behaviour, 1,* s41562–017. (p. 20)

Gilovich, T. (1991). *How we know what isn't so: The fallibility of human reason in everyday life.* New York: Free Press. (p. 18)

Gilovich, T. D. (1996). *The spotlight effect: Exaggerated impressions of the self as a social stimulus.* Unpublished manuscript, Cornell University. (p. 486)

Gilovich, T. D., & Medvec, V. H. (1995). The experience of regret: What, when, and why. *Psychological Review, 102,* 379–395. (p. 158)

Gilovich, T. D., & Savitsky, K. (1999). The spotlight effect and the illusion of transparency: Egocentric assessments of how we are seen by others. *Current Directions in Psychological Science, 8,* 165–168. (p. 486)

Gingerich, O. (1999, February 6). *Is there a role for natural theology today?* Retrieved from http://www.origins.org/real/n9501/natural.html (p. 77)

Gino, G., Wilmuth, C. A., & Brooks, A. W. (2015). Compared to men, women view professional advancement as equally attainable, but less desirable. *PNAS, 112,* 12354–12359. (p. 164)

Giuliano, T. A., Barnes, L. C., Fiala, S. E., & Davis, D. M. (1998). *An empirical investigation of male answer syndrome.* Paper presented at the Southwestern Psychological Association convention. (p. 163)

Gladwell, M. (2000, May 9). The new-boy network: What do job interviews really tell us? *The New Yorker,* pp. 68–86. (p. B-6)

Glasman, L. R., & Albarracín, D. (2006). Forming attitudes that predict future behavior: A meta-analysis of the attitude-behavior relation. *Psychological Bulletin, 132,* 778–822. (p. 418)

Glass, R. M. (2001). Electroconvulsive therapy: Time to bring it out of the shadows. *Journal of the American Medical Association, 285,* 1346–1348. (p. 563)

Glasser, M. F., Coalson, T. S., Robinson, E. C., Hacker, C. D., Harwell, J., Yacoub, E., . . . Van Essen, D. C. (2016). A multi-modal parcellation of human cerebral cortex. *Nature, 536,* 171–178. (p. 53)

Glasser, S. B. (2017, November 13). "They want to know if Trump's crazy." *Politico* (politico.com). (p. 459)

Gleaves, D. H. (1996). The sociocognitive model of dissociative identity disorder: A reexamination of the evidence. *Psychological Bulletin, 120,* 42–59. (p. 529)

Glenn, A. L., & Raine, A. (2014). Neurocriminology: Implications for the punishment, prediction and prevention of criminal behavior. *Nature Reviews Neuroscience, 15,* 54–63. (p. 52)

Glenn, A. L., Raine, A., Yaralian, P. S., & Yang, Y. (2010). Increased volume of the striatum in psychopathic individuals. *Biological Psychiatry, 67*, 52–58. (p. 531)

Gliklich, E., Guo, R., & Bergmark, R. W. (2016). Texting while driving: A study of 1211 US adults with the Distracted Driving Survey. *Preventive Medicine Reports, 4*, 486–489. (p. 82)

Global Burden of Disease Study, 2013 collaborators. (2015). Global, regional, and national incidence, prevalence, and years lived with disability for 301 acute and chronic diseases and injuries in 188 countries, 1990–2013: A systematic analysis for the Global Burden of Disease Study 2013. *The Lancet, 386*, 743–800. (p. 218)

GLSEN. (2012). *The 2011 national school climate survey*. New York: Gay, Lesbian & Straight Education Network (glsen.org). (p. 170)

Glynn, L. M., & Sandman, C. A. (2011). Prenatal origins of neurological development: A critical period for fetus and mothers. *Current Directions in Psychological Science, 20*, 384–389. (p. 120)

Glynn, T. R., Gamarel, K. E., Kahler, C. W., Iwamoto, M., Operario, D., & Nemoto, T. (2017). The role of gender affirmation in psychological well-being among transgender women. *Psychology of Sexual Orientation and Gender Diversity, 3*, 336–344. (p. 171)

Godden, D. R., & Baddeley, A. D. (1975). Context-dependent memory in two natural environments: On land and underwater. *British Journal of Psychology, 66*, 325–331. (p. 281)

Goethals, G. R., & Allison, S. T. (2014). Kings and charisma, Lincoln and leadership: An evolutionary perspective. In G. R. Goethals, S. T. Allison, R. M. Kramer, & D. M. Messick (Eds.), *Conceptions of leadership: Enduring ideas and emerging insights* (pp. 111–124). New York: Palgrave Macmillan. (p. B-10)

Goetz, S. M. M., Tang, L., Thomason, M. E., Diamond, M. P., Hariri, A. R., & Carré, J. (2014). Testosterone rapidly increases neural reactivity to threat in healthy men: A novel two-step pharmacological challenge paradigm. *Biological Psychiatry, 76*, 324–331. (p. 49)

Goff, D. C., Falkai, P., Fleischhacker, W. W., Girgis, R. R., Kahn, R. M., Uchida, H., . . . Lieberman, J. A. (2017). The long-term effects of antipsychotic medication on clinical course in schizophrenia. *The American Journal of Psychiatry, 174*, 840–849. (p. 560)

Goff, D. C., & Simms, C. A. (1993). Has multiple personality disorder remained consistent over time? *Journal of Nervous and Mental Disease, 181*, 595–600. (p. 528)

Golan, O., Ashwin, E., Granader, Y., McClintock, S., Day, K., Leggett, V., & Baron-Cohen, S. (2010). Enhancing emotion recognition in children with autism spectrum conditions: An intervention using animated vehicles with real emotional faces. *Journal of Autism Development and Disorders, 40*, 269–279. (p. 132)

Gold, M., & Yanof, D. S. (1985). Mothers, daughters, and girlfriends. *Journal of Personality and Social Psychology, 49*, 654–659. (p. 148)

Goldberg, J. (2007). *Quivering bundles that let us hear*. Retrieved from hhmi.org/senses/c120.html (p. 218)

Golder, S. A., & Macy, M. W. (2011). Diurnal and seasonal mood vary with work, sleep, and day-length across diverse cultures. *Science, 333*, 1878–1881. (pp. 22, 408)

Goldfried, M. R. (2001). Integrating gay, lesbian, and bisexual issues into mainstream psychology. *American Psychologist, 56*, 977–988. (p. 500)

Goldfried, M. R., Raue, P. J., & Castonguay, L. G. (1998). The therapeutic focus in significant sessions of master therapists: A comparison of cognitive–behavioral and psychodynamic–interpersonal interventions. *Journal of Consulting and Clinical Psychology, 66*, 803–810. (p. 555)

Goldinger, S. D., & Papesh, M. H. (2012). Pupil dilation reflects the creation and retrieval of memories. *Current Directions in Psychological Science, 21*, 90–95. (p. 201)

Goldman, A. L., Pezawas, L., Mattay, V. S., Fischl, B., Verchinski, B. A., Chen, Q., . . . Meyer-Lindenberg, A. (2009). Widespread reductions of cortical thickness in schizophrenia and spectrum disorders and evidence of heritability. *Archives of General Psychiatry, 66*, 467–477. (p. 525)

Goldstein, I., Lue, T. F., Padma-Nathan, H., Rosen, R. C., Steers, W. D., & Wicker, P. A. (1998). Oral sildenafil in the treatment of erectile dysfunction. *New England Journal of Medicine, 338*, 1397–1404. (p. 28)

Goleman, D. (1980, February). 1,528 little geniuses and how they grew. *Psychology Today*, pp. 28–53. (p. 357)

Goleman, D. (2006). *Social intelligence*. New York: Bantam Books. (p. 326)

Golkar, A., Selbing, I., Flygare, O., Öhman, A., & Olsson, A. (2013). Other people as means to a safe end: Vicarious extinction blocks the return of learned fear. *Psychological Science, 24*, 2182–2190. (p. 259)

Gollwitzer, P. M., & Oettingen, G. (2012). Goal pursuit. In P. M. Gollwitzer & G. Oettingen (Eds.), *The Oxford handbook of human motivation*, pp. 208–231. New York: Oxford University Press. (pp. 251, 359)

Gollwitzer, P. M., & Sheeran, P. (2006). Implementation intentions and goal achievement: A meta-analysis of effects and processes. *Advances in Experimental Social Psychology, 38*, 69–119. (p. B-9)

Gómez-Robles, A., Hopkins, W. D., Schapiro, S. J., & Sherwood, C. C. (2015). Relaxed genetic control of cortical organization in humans brains compared with chimpanzees. *PNAS, 112*, 14799–14804. (p. 39)

Gong, H., Liu, Y.-Z., Zhang, Y., Su, W.-J., Lian, Y.-J., Peng, W., & Jiang, C.-L. (2016). Mindfulness meditation for insomnia: A meta-analysis of randomized controlled trials. *Journal of Psychosomatic Research, 89*, 1–6. (p. 404)

Gongola, J., Scurich, N., & Quas, J. A. (2017). Detecting deception in children: A meta-analysis. *Law and Human Behavior, 41*, 44–54. (p. 376)

Gonsalkorale, K., & Williams, K. D. (2006). The KKK would not let me play: Ostracism even by a despised outgroup hurts. *European Journal of Social Psychology, 36*, 1–11. (p. 354)

Goodale, M. A., & Milner, D. A. (2004). *Sight unseen: An exploration of conscious and unconscious vision*. Oxford: Oxford University Press. (p. 84)

Goodall, J. (1986). *The chimpanzees of Gombe: Patterns of behavior*. Cambridge, MA: Harvard University Press. (p. 439)

Goodall, J. (1998). Learning from the chimpanzees: A message humans can understand. *Science, 282*, 2184–2185. (p. 23)

Goode, E. (1999, April 13). If things taste bad, "phantoms" may be at work. *The New York Times* (nytimes.com). (p. 222)

Goodman, G. S. (2006). Children's eyewitness memory: A modern history and contemporary commentary. *Journal of Social Issues, 62*, 811–832. (p. 294)

Goodman, G. S., Ghetti, S., Quas, J. A., Edelstein, R. S., Alexander, K. W., Redlich, A. D., . . . Jones, D. P. H. (2003). A prospective study of memory for child sexual abuse: New findings relevant to the repressed-memory controversy. *Psychological Science, 14*, 113–118. (p. 293)

Goodwin, P. Y., Mosher, W. D., & Chandra, A. (2010, February). *Marriage and cohabitation in the United States: A statistical portrait based on Cycle 6 (2002) of the National Survey of Family Growth* (Vital Health Statistics Series 23, No. 28). Washington, DC: U.S. Department of Health and Human Service, Centers for Disease Control and Prevention, National Center for Health Statistics. (p. 156)

Gopnik, A., Griffiths, T. L., & Lucas, C. G. (2015). When younger learners can be better (or at least more open-minded) than older ones. *Current Directions in Psychological Science, 24*, 87–92. (p. 127)

Gopnik, A., & Meltzoff, A. N. (1986). Relations between semantic and cognitive development in the one-word stage: The specificity hypothesis. *Child Development, 57*, 1040–1053. (p. 320)

Goranson, A., Ritter, R. S., Waytz, A., Norton, M. I., & Gray, K. (2017). Dying is unexpectedly positive. *Psychological Science, 28*, 988–999. (p. 160)

Goranson, R. E. (1978). *The hindsight effect in problem solving*. Unpublished manuscript cited in G. Wood (1984), Research methodology: A decision-making perspective. In A. M. Rogers & C. J. Scheirer (Eds.), *The G. Stanley Hall Lecture Series* (Vol. 4, pp. 193–217). Washington, DC: American Psychological Association. (p. 17)

Gorchoff, S. M., John, O. P., & Helson, R. (2008). Contextualizing change in marital satisfaction during middle age. *Psychological Science, 19*, 1194–1200. (p. 157)

Gordon, A. M., & Chen, S. (2010). When you accept me for me: The relational benefits of intrinsic affirmations from one's relationship partner. *Personality and Social Psychology Bulletin, 36*, 1439–1453. (p. 473)

Gordon, A. M., & Chen, S. (2014). The role of sleep in interpersonal conflict: Do sleepless nights mean worse fights? *Social Psychological and Personality Science, 5*, 168–175. (pp. 93)

Gordon, I., Vander Wyk, B. C., Bennett, R. H., Cordeaux, C., Lucas, M. V., Eilbott, J. A., . . . Pelphrey, K. A. (2013). Oxytocin enhances brain function in children with autism. *PNAS, 110*, 20953–20958. (p. 132)

Gordon, P. (2004). Numerical cognition without words: Evidence from Amazonia. *Science, 306*, 496–499. (p. 319)

Gore-Felton, C., Koopman, C., Thoresen, C., Arnow, B., Bridges, E., & Spiegel, D. (2000). Psychologists' beliefs and clinical characteristics: Judging the veracity of childhood sexual abuse memories. *Professional Psychology: Research and Practice, 31*, 372–377. (p. 293)

Gore, J., & Sadler-Smith, E. (2011). Unpacking intuition: A process and outcome framework. *Review of General Psychology, 15*, 304–316. (p. 305)

Gorka, S. M., Lieberman, L., Shankman, S. A., & Phan, K. L. (2017). Startle potentiation to uncertain threat as a psychophysiological indicator of fear-based psychopathology: An examination across multiple internalizing disorders. *Journal of Abnormal Psychology, 126*, 8. (p. 506)

Gorlick, A. (2010, January 13). Stanford scientists link brain development to chances of recovering vision after blindness. *Stanford Report* (news.stanford.edu). (p. 213)

Gorman, J. (2014, January 6). The brain, in exquisite detail. *The New York Times* (nytimes.com). (p. 53)

Gorrese, A., & Ruggieri, R. (2012). Peer attachment: A meta-analytic review of gender and age differences and associations with parent attachment. *Journal of Youth and Adolescence, 41*, 650–672. (p. 136)

Gosling, S. D. (2008). *Snoop: What your stuff says about you*. New York: Basic Books. (p. 481)

Gosling, S. D., Gladdis, S., & Vazire, S. (2007). *Personality impressions based on Facebook profiles*. Paper presented at the Society for Personality and Social Psychology meeting. (p. 481)

Gosling, S. D., Kwan, V. S. Y., & John, O. P. (2003). A dog's got personality: A cross-species comparative approach to personality judgments in dogs and humans. *Journal of Personality and Social Psychology, 85,* 1161–1169. (p. 477)

Gotink, R. A., Meijboom, R., Vernooij, M. W., Smits, M., & Hunink, M. G. M. (2016). 8-week mindfulness based stress reduction induces brain changes similar to traditional long-term meditation practice—A systematic review. *Brain and Cognition, 108,* 32–41. (p. 404)

Gotlib, I. H., & Hammen, C. L. (1992). *Psychological aspects of depression: Toward a cognitive-interpersonal integration.* New York: Wiley. (p. 521)

Gottesman, I. I. (1991). *Schizophrenia genesis: The origins of madness.* New York: Freeman. (p. 526)

Gottesman, I. I. (2001). Psychopathology through a life span—genetic prism. *American Psychologist, 56,* 867–881. (p. 526)

Gottfredson, L. S. (2002a). Where and why g matters: Not a mystery. *Human Performance, 15,* 25–46. (p. 325)

Gottfredson, L. S. (2002b). g: Highly general and highly practical. In R. J. Sternberg & E. L. Grigorenko (Eds.), *The general factor of intelligence: How general is it?* Mahwah, NJ: Erlbaum. (p. 325)

Gottfredson, L. S. (2003a). Dissecting practical intelligence theory: Its claims and evidence. *Intelligence, 31,* 343–397. (p. 325)

Gottfredson, L. S. (2003b). On Sternberg's "Reply to Gottfredson." *Intelligence, 31,* 415–424. (p. 325)

Gottfried, J. A., O'Doherty, J., & Dolan, R. J. (2003). Encoding predictive reward value in human amygdala and orbitofrontal cortex. *Science, 301,* 1104–1108. (p. 237)

Gottman, J. (1994). *Why marriages succeed or fail: And how you can make yours last.* New York: Simon & Schuster. (p. 157)

Gottman, J. (2007). *Why marriages succeed or fail.* London: Bloomsbury. (p. 452)

Gould, E. (2007). How widespread is adult neurogenesis in mammals? *Nature Neuroscience, 8,* 481–488. (p. 64)

Gould, S. J. (1981). *The mismeasure of man.* New York: Norton. (p. 328)

Gow, A. J., Bastin, M. E., Maniega, S. M., Hernández, M. C. V., Morris, Z., Murray, C., . . . Wardlaw, J. M. (2012). Neuroprotective lifestyles and the aging brain: Activity, atrophy, and white matter integrity. *Neurology, 79,* 1802–1808. (p. 153)

Goyal, M., Singh, S., Sibinga, E. S., Gould, N. F., Rowland-Seymour, A., Sharma, R., . . . Haythornthwaite, J. A. (2014). Meditation programs for psychological stress and well-being: A systematic review and meta-analysis. *JAMA Internal Medicine, 174,* 357–368. (p. 404)

Goyer, J. P., Garcia, J., Purdie-Vaughns, V., Binning, K. R., Cook, J. E., Reeves, S. L., . . . Cohen, G. L. (2017). Self-affirmation facilitates minority middle schoolers' progress along college trajectories. *PNAS, 114*(29), 7594–7599. (p. 344)

Grabe, S., Ward, L. M., & Hyde, J. S. (2008). The role of the media in body image concerns among women: A meta-analysis of experimental and correlational studies. *Psychological Bulletin, 134,* 460–476. (p. 532)

Grabo, A., & van Vugt, M. (2016). Charismatic leadership and the evolution of cooperation. *Evolution and Human Behavior, 37,* 399–406. (p. B-10)

Grady, C. L., McIntosh, A. R., Horwitz, B., Maisog, J. M., Ungeleider, L. G., Mentis, M. J., . . . Haxby, J. V. (1995). Age-related reductions in human recognition memory due to impaired encoding. *Science, 269,* 218–221. (p. 285)

Graf, S., Paolini, S., & Rubin, M. (2014). Negative intergroup contact is more influential, but positive intergroup contact is more common: Assessing contact prominence and contact prevalence in five central European countries. *European Journal of Social Psychology, 44,* 536–547. (p. 457)

Graham, A. M., Fisher, P. A., & Pfeifer, J. H. (2013). What sleeping babies hear: A functional MRI study of interparental conflict and infants' emotion processing. *Psychological Science, 24,* 782–789. (p. 137)

Graham, E. K., Rutsohn, J. P., Turiano, N. A., Bendayan, R., Batterham, P. J., Gerstorf, D., . . . Bastarache, E. D. (2017). Personality predicts mortality risk: An integrative data analysis of 15 international longitudinal studies. *Journal of Research in Personality, 70,* 174–186. (p. 480)

Graham, J., Nosek, B. A., & Haidt, J. (2012, December 12). The moral stereotypes of liberals and conservatives: Exaggeration of differences across the political spectrum. *PLoS ONE 7,* e50092. (p. 435)

Grand, J. A. (2016). Brain drain? An examination of stereotype threat effects during training on knowledge acquisition and organizational effectiveness. *Journal of Applied Psychology.* Advance online publication. doi:10.1037/apl0000171 (p. 344)

Granic, I., Lobel, A., & Engels, R. C. M. E. (2014). The benefits of playing video games. *American Psychologist, 69,* 66–78. (p. 445)

Granqvist, P., Mikulincer, M., & Shaver, P. R. (2010). Religion as attachment: Normative processes and individual differences. *Personality and Social Psychology Review, 14,* 49–59. (p. 136)

Grant, A. M., Gino, F., & Hofmann, D. A. (2011). Reversing the extraverted leadership advantage: The role of employee proactivity. *Academy of Management Journal, 54,* 528–550. (p. 476)

Grant, J. M., Mottet, L. A., Tanis, J., Herman, J. L., Harrison, J., & Keisling, M. (2011). National transgender discrimination survey report on health and health care. National Center for Transgender Equality and National Gay and Lesbian Task Force. (p. 437)

Grant, N., Wardle, J., & Steptoe, A. (2009). The relationship between life satisfaction and health behavior: A cross-cultural analysis of young adults. *International Journal of Behavioral Medicine, 16,* 259–268. (p. 401)

Gray-Little, B., & Burks, N. (1983). Power and satisfaction in marriage: A review and critique. *Psychological Bulletin, 93,* 513–538. (p. 452)

Graybiel, A. M., & Smith, K. S. (2014, June). Good habits, bad habits. *Scientific American, 310,* 38–43. (p. 234)

Green, B. (2002). Listening to leaders: Feedback on 360-degree feedback one year later. *Organizational Development Journal, 20,* 8–16. (p. B-7)

Green, J. D., Sedikides, C., & Gregg, A. P. (2008). Forgotten but not gone: The recall and recognition of self-threatening memories. *Journal of Experimental Social Psychology, 44,* 547–561. (p. 469)

Green, J. T., & Woodruff-Pak, D. S. (2000). Eyeblink classical conditioning: Hippocampal formation is for neutral stimulus associations as cerebellum is for association-response. *Psychological Bulletin, 126,* 138–158. (p. 277)

Green, M. F., & Horan, W. P. (2010). Social cognition in schizophrenia. *Current Directions in Psychological Science, 19,* 243–248. (p. 523)

Greenaway, K. H., Cruwys, T., Haslam, S. A., & Jetten, J. (2016). Social identities promote well-being because they satisfy global psychological needs. *European Journal of Social Psychology, 46,* 294–307. (pp. 352, 438)

Greenaway, K. H., Haslam, S. A., Cruwys, T., Branscombe, N. R., Ysseldyk, R., & Heldreth, C. (2015). From "we" to "me": Group identification enhances perceived personal control with consequences for health and well-being. *Journal of Personality and Social Psychology, 109,* 53–74. (p. 352)

Greenberg, J. (2008). Understanding the vital human quest for self-esteem. *Perspectives on Psychological Science, 3,* 48–55. (p. 486)

Greene, J. (2010). Remarks to an Edge conference: The new science of morality. *The Edge* (edge.org). (p. 145)

Greene, J. D., Sommerville, R. B., Nystrom, L. E., Darley, J. M., & Cohen, J. D. (2001). An fMRI investigation of emotional engagement in moral judgment. *Science, 293,* 2105–2108. (p. 145)

Greenwald, A. G. (1992). *Subliminal semantic activation and subliminal snake oil.* Paper presented to the American Psychological Association Convention, Washington, DC. (p. 193)

Greenwald, A. G., Banaji, M. R., & Nosek, B. A. (2015). Statistically small effects of the implicit association test can have societally large effects. *Journal of Personality and Social Psychology, 108,* 553–561. (p. 435)

Greenwald, A. G., & Pettigrew, T. F. (2014, March). With malice toward none and charity for some: Ingroup favoritism enables discrimination. *American Psychologist, 69,* 645–655. (p. 438)

Greenwald, A. G., Spangenberg, E. R., Pratkanis, A. R., & Eskenazi, J. (1991). Double-blind tests of subliminal self-help audiotapes. *Psychological Science, 2,* 119–122. (p. 193)

Greenwald, G. (2012, March 19). Discussing the motives of the Afghan shooter. *Salon* (salon.com). (p. 456)

Greer, S. G., Goldstein, A. N., & Walker, M. P. (2013). The impact of sleep deprivation on food desire in the human brain. *Nature Communications, 4,* Article 2259. doi:10.1038/ncomms3259 (p. 93)

Gregory, A. M., Rijksdijk, F. V., Lau, J. Y., Dahl, R. E., & Eley, T. C. (2009). The direction of longitudinal associations between sleep problems and depression symptoms: A study of twins aged 8 and 10 years. *Sleep, 32,* 189–199. (pp. 93, 559)

Gregory, R. L. (1978). *Eye and brain: The psychology of seeing* (3rd ed.). New York: McGraw-Hill. (pp. 124, 213)

Gregory, R. L., & Gombrich, E. H. (Eds.). (1973). *Illusion in nature and art.* New York: Charles Scribner's Sons. (p. 197)

Greist, J. H., Jefferson, J. W., & Marks, I. M. (1986). *Anxiety and its treatment: Help is available.* Washington, DC: American Psychiatric Press. (p. 507)

Greitemeyer, T., & Mügge, D. O. (2014). Video games do affect social outcomes: A meta-analytic review of the effects of violent and prosocial video game play. *Personality and Social Psychology Bulletin, 40,* 578–589. (p. 444)

Greyson, B. (2010). Implications of near-death experiences for a postmaterialist psychology. *Review of Religion and Spirituality, 2,* 37–45. (p. 108)

Grèzes, J., & Decety, J. (2001). Function anatomy of execution, mental simulation, observation, and verb generation of actions: A meta-analysis. *Human Brain Mapping, 12,* 1–19. (p. 321)

Griffiths, M. (2001). Sex on the internet: Observations and implications for internet sex addiction. *Journal of Sex Research, 38,* 333–342. (p. 102)

Griggs, R. (2014). Coverage of the Stanford Prison Experiment in introductory psychology textbooks. *Teaching of Psychology, 41,* 195–203. (p. 419)

Grijalva, E., Newman, D. A., Tay, L., Donnellan, M. B., Harms, P. D., Robins, R. W., & Yan, T. (2015). Gender differences in narcissism: A meta-analytic review. *Psychological Bulletin, 141,* 261–310. (p. 488)

Grillon, C., Quispe-Escudero, D., Mathur, A., & Ernst, M. (2015). Mental fatigue impairs emotion regulation. *Emotion, 15,* 383–389. (p. 398)

Grilo, C. M., & Pogue-Geile, M. F. (1991). The nature of environmental influences on weight and obesity: A behavior genetic analysis. *Psychological Bulletin, 110,* 520–537. (p. 365)

Grinker, R. R. (2007). *Unstrange minds: Remapping the world of autism.* New York: Basic Books. (p. 131)

Grobstein, C. (1979, June). External human fertilization. *Scientific American,* pp. 57–67. (p. 119)

Grodin, E. N., & White, T. L. (2015). The neuroanatomical delineation of agentic and affiliative extraversion. *Cognitive, Affective, and Behavioral Neuroscience, 15,* 321–334. (p. 478)

Grønnerød, C., Grønnerød, J. S., & Grøndahl, P. (2015). Psychological treatment of sexual offenders against children: A meta-analytic review of treatment outcome studies. *Trauma, Violence, & Abuse, 16,* 280–290. (p. 170)

Groothuis, T. G. G., & Carere, C. (2005). Avian personalities: Characterization and epigenesis. *Neuroscience and Biobehavioral Reviews, 29,* 137–150. (p. 477)

Gross, A. E., & Crofton, C. (1977). What is good is beautiful. *Sociometry, 40,* 85–90. (p. 450)

Gross, J. J. (2013). Emotion regulation: Taking stock and moving forward. *Emotion, 13,* 359–365. (p. 371)

Grossberg, S. (1995). The attentive brain. *American Scientist, 83,* 438–449. (p. 197)

Grossmann, I., Na, J., Varnum, M. E. W., Park, D. C., Kitayama, S., & Nisbett, R. E. (2010). Reasoning about social conflicts improves into old age. *PNAS, 107,* 7246–7250. (p. 334)

Grossmann, I., & Varnum, M. E. W. (2015). Social structure, infectious diseases, disasters, secularism, and cultural change in America. *Psychological Science, 26,* 311–324. (p. 491)

Groß, J., Blank, H., & Bayen U. J. (2017). Hindsight bias in depression. *Clinical Psychological Science, 5,* 771–788. (p. 520)

Grover, S. & Helliwell, J. F. (2014, December). *How's life at home? New evidence on marriage and the set point for happiness* (NBER Working Paper No. 20794). Retrieved from nber.org/papers/w20794 (p. 353)

Gruber, J. (2011). Can feeling too good be bad? Positive emotion persistence (PEP) in bipolar disorder. *Current Directions in Psychological Science, 20,* 217–221. (p. 515)

Gruber, J., Gilbert, K. E., Youngstrom, E., Kogos Youngstrom, J., Feeny, N. C., & Findling, R. L. (2013). Reward dysregulation and mood symptoms in an adolescent outpatient sample. *Journal of Abnormal Child Psychology, 41,* 1053–1065. (p. 525)

Gruder, C. L. (1977). Choice of comparison persons in evaluating oneself. In J. M. Suls & R. L. Miller (Eds.), *Social comparison processes.* New York: Hemisphere. (p. 410)

Gu, J., Strauss, C., Bond, R., & Cavanagh, K. (2015). How do mindfulness-based cognitive therapy and mindfulness-based stress reduction improve mental health and wellbeing? A systematic review and meta-analysis of mediation studies. *Clinical Psychology Review, 37,* 1–12. (p. 547)

Gu, X., Lohrenz, T., Salas, R., Baldwin, P. R., Soltani, A., Kirk, U., . . . Montague, P. R. (2015). Belief about nicotine selectively modulates value and reward prediction error signals in smokers. *PNAS, 112,* 2539–2544. (p. 101)

Guardino, C. M., Schetter, C. D., Saxbe, D. E., Adam, E. K., Ramey, S. L., & Shalowitz, M. U. (2016). Diurnal salivary cortisol patterns prior to pregnancy predict infant birth weight. *Health Psychology, 35,* 625–633. (p. 385)

Guéguen, N. (2011). Effects of solicitor sex and attractiveness on receptivity to sexual offers: A field study. *Archives of Sexual Behavior, 40,* 915–919. (p. 185)

Guerin, B. (1986). Mere presence effects in humans: A review. *Journal of Personality and Social Psychology, 22,* 38–77. (p. 429)

Guerin, B. (2003). Language use as social strategy: A review and an analytic framework for the social sciences. *Review of General Psychology, 7,* 251–298. (p. 311)

Guertin, C., Pelletier, L. G., Émond, C., & Lalande, G. (2017). Change in physical and psychological health over time in patients with cardiovascular disease: On the benefits of being self-determined, physically active, and eating well. *Motivation and Emotion,* 1–14. (p. 353)

Guiso, L., Monte, F., Sapienza, P., & Zingales, L. (2008). Culture, gender, and math. *Science, 320,* 1164–1165. (p. 341)

Gunderson, E. A., Gripshover, S. J., Romero, C., Dweck, C. S., Goldin-Meadow, S., & Levine, S. C. (2013). Parent praise to 1- to 3-year-olds predicts children's motivational frameworks 5 years later. *Child Development, 84,* 1526–1541. (p. 339)

Gunnery, S. D., & Ruben, M. A. (2016). Perceptions of Duchenne and non-Duchenne smiles: A meta-analysis. *Cognition and Emotion, 30,* 501–515. (p. 376)

Gunter, R. W., & Bodner, G. E. (2008). How eye movements affect unpleasant memories: Support for a working-memory account. *Behaviour Research and Therapy, 46,* 913–931. (p. 554)

Gunter, T. D., Vaughn, M. G., & Philibert, R. A. (2010). Behavioral genetics in antisocial spectrum disorders and psychopathy: A review of the recent literature. *Behavioral Sciences and the Law, 28,* 148–173. (p. 530)

Gunyadin, G., Selcuk, E., & Zayas, V. (2017). Impressions based on a portrait predict, 1-month later, impressions following a live interaction. *Social Psychological and Personality Science, 8,* 36–44. (p. 481)

Guo, J., He, H., Qu, Z., Wang, X., & Liu, C. (2017). Post-traumatic stress disorder and depression among adult survivors 8 years after the 2008 Wenchuan earthquake in China. *Journal of Affective Disorders, 210,* 27–34. (p. 509)

Guo, X., Zhai, J., Liu, Z., Fang, M., Wang, B., Wang, C., . . . Zhao, J. (2010). Effect of antipsychotic medication alone vs combined with psychosocial intervention on outcomes of early-stage schizophrenia. *Archives of General Psychiatry, 67,* 895–904. (p. 560)

Gustavson, C. R., Garcia, J., Hankins, W. G., & Rusiniak, K. W. (1974). Coyote predation control by aversive conditioning. *Science, 184,* 581–583. (p. 255)

Gustavson, C. R., Kelly, D. J., & Sweeney, M. (1976). Prey-lithium aversions I: Coyotes and wolves. *Behavioral Biology, 17,* 61–72. (p. 255)

Gutchess, A. (2014). Plasticity in the aging brain: New directions in cognitive neuroscience. *Science, 346,* 579–582. (pp. 39, 154)

Guttmacher Institute. (1994). *Sex and America's teenagers.* New York: Alan Guttmacher Institute. (pp. 149, 175)

H., Sally. (1979, August). Videotape recording number T–3, Fortunoff Video Archive of Holocaust Testimonies. New Haven, CT: Yale University Library. (p. 469)

Haaker, J., Yi, J., Petrovic, P., & Olsson, A. (2017). Endogenous opioids regulate social threat learning in humans. *Nature Communications, 8,* 15495. (p. 260)

Haapakoski, R., Mathieu, J., Ebmeier, K. P., Alenius, H., & Kivimäki, M. (2015). Cumulative meta-analysis of interleukins 6 and 1ß, tumour necrosis factor a and C-reactive protein in patients with major depressive disorder. *Brain, Behavior, and Immunity, 49,* 206–215. (p. 391)

Haas, A. P., Eliason, M., Mays, V. M., Mathy, R. M., Cochran, S. D., D'Augelli, A. R., . . . Clayton, P. J. (2011). Suicide and suicide risk in lesbian, gay, bisexual, and transgender populations: Review and recommendations. *Journal of Homosexuality, 58,* 10–51. (p. 500)

Habashi, M. M., Graziano, W. G., & Hoover, A. E. (2016). Searching for the prosocial personality: A big five approach to linking personality and prosocial behavior. *Personality and Social Psychology Bulletin, 42,* 1177–1192. (p. 479)

Habel, U., Koch, K., Kellerman, T., Reske, M., Frommann, N., Wolwer, W., . . . Schneider, F. (2010). Training of affect recognition in schizophrenia: Neurobiological correlates. *Social Neuroscience, 5,* 92–104. (p. 558)

Haber, R. N. (1970). How we remember what we see. *Scientific American,* pp. 104–112. (p. 266)

Hadjistavropoulos, T., Craig, K. D., Duck, S. Cano, A., Goubert, L., Jackson, P. L., . . . Fitzgerald, T. D. (2011). A biopsychosocial formulation of pain communication. *Psychological Bulletin, 137,* 910–939. (p. 221)

Haedt-Matt, A. A., & Keel, P. K. (2011). Revisiting the affect regulation model of binge eating: A meta-analysis of studies using ecological momentary assessment. *Psychological Bulletin, 137,* 660–681. (p. 532)

Hafenbrack, A. C., Kinias, Z., & Barsade, S. G. (2014). Debiasing the mind through meditation: Mindfulness and the sunk-cost bias. *Psychological Science, 25,* 369–376. (p. 404)

Hagger, M. S., Chatzisarantis, N. L. D., Alberts, H., Anggono, C. O., Birt, A., Brand, R., . . . Cannon, T. (2016). A multi-lab pre-registered replication of the ego-depletion effect. *Perspectives on Psychological Science, 11,* 546–573. (p. 398)

Hahn, A., Kranz, G., Sladky, R., Kaufmann, U., Ganger, S., Hummer, A., . . . Lanzenberger, R. (2016). Testosterone affects language areas of the adult human brain. *Human Brain Mapping, 37,* 1738–1748. (p. 340)

Haidt, J. (2000). The positive emotion of elevation. *Prevention and Treatment, 3,* article 3. Retrieved from journals.apa.org/prevention/volume3 (p. 144)

Haidt, J. (2002). The moral emotions. In R. J. Davidson, K. Scherer, & H. H. Goldsmith (Eds.), *Handbook of affective sciences.* New York: Oxford University Press. (p. 144)

Haidt, J. (2012). *The righteous mind: Why good people are divided by politics and religion.* New York: Pantheon. (p. 144)

Hajhosseini, B., Stewart, B., Tan, J. C., Busque, S., & Melcher, M. L. (2013). Evaluating deceased donor registries: Identifying predictive factors of donor designation. *American Surgeon, 79,* 235–241. (p. 305)

Hakuta, K., Bialystok, E., & Wiley, E. (2003). Critical evidence: A test of the critical-period hypothesis for second-language acquisition. *Psychological Science, 14,* 31–38. (p. 315)

Halberstadt, J. B., Niedenthal, P. M., & Kushner, J. (1995). Resolution of lexical ambiguity by emotional state. *Psychological Science, 6,* 278–281. (p. 197)

Halberstadt, J., Sherman, S. J., & Sherman, J. W. (2011). Why Barack Obama is Black. *Psychological Science, 22,* 29–33. (p. 440)

Haldeman, D. C. (1994). The practice and ethics of sexual orientation conversion therapy. *Journal of Consulting and Clinical Psychology, 62,* 221–227. (p. 179)

Haldeman, D. C. (2002). Gay rights, patient rights: The implications of sexual orientation conversion therapy. *Professional Psychology: Research and Practice, 33,* 260–264. (p. 179)

Hales, A. H., Kassner, M. P., Williams, K. D., & Graziano, W. G. (2016). Disagreeableness as a cause and consequence of ostracism. *Personality and Social Psychology Review, 42,* 782–797. (p. 354)

Hall, C. S., & Lindzey, G. (1978). *Theories of personality* (2nd ed.). New York: Wiley. (p. 469)

Hall, C. S., Dornhoff, W., Blick, K. A., & Weesner, K. E. (1982). The dreams of college men and women in 1950 and 1980: A comparison of dream contents and sex differences. *Sleep, 5,* 188–194. (p. 96)

Hall, G. (1997). Context aversion, Pavlovian conditioning, and the psychological side effects of chemotherapy. *European Psychologist, 2,* 118–124. (p. 255)

Hall, G. S. (1904). *Adolescence: Its psychology and its relations to physiology, anthropology, sex, crime, religion and education* (Vol. 1). New York: Appleton-Century-Crofts. (p. 141)

Hall, J. A., Gunnery, S. D., & Horgan, T. G. (2016). Gender differences in interpersonal accuracy. In J. A. Hall, M. S. Mast & T. V. West (Eds.), *The social psychology of perceiving others accurately* (pp. 309–327). New York: Cambridge University Press. (p. 377)

Hall, K. M., Knudson, S. T., Wright, J., Charlifue, S. W., Graves, D. E., & Warner, P. (1999). Follow-up study of individuals with high tetraplegia (C1-C4) 14 to 24 years postinjury. *Archives of Physical Medicine and Rehabilitation, 80,* 1507–1513. (p. 408)

Hall, P. A. (2016). Executive-control processes in high-calorie food consumption. *Current Directions in Psychological Science, 25,* 91–98. (p. 365)

Hall, S. S. (2004, May). The good egg. *Discover,* pp. 30–39. (p. 119)

Hall, S., S., Knox, D., & Shapiro, K. (2017). "I have," "I would," "I won't": Hooking up among sexually diverse groups of college students. *Psychology of Sexual Orientation and Gender Diversity, 4,* 233–240. (p. 183)

Hallal, P. C., Andersen, L. B., Bull, F. C., Guthold, R., Haskell, W., & Ekelund, U. (2012). Global physical activity levels: Surveillance progress, pitfalls, and prospects. *The Lancet, 380,* 247–257. (p. 365)

Haller, R., Rummel, C., Henneberg, S., Pollmer, U., & Köster, E. P. (1999). The influence of early experience with vanillin on food preference later in life. *Chemical Senses, 24,* 465–467. (p. 225)

Halmburger, A., Baumert, A., & Schmitt, M. (2015). Anger as driving factor of moral courage in comparison with guilt and global mood: A multimethod approach. *European Journal of Social Psychology, 45,* 39–51. (p. 394)

Halpern, D. (2015). The rise of psychology in policy: The UK's de facto council of psychological science advisers. *Perspectives on Psychological Science, 10,* 768–771. (p. 304)

Halpern, D., Valenzuela, S., & Katz, J. E. (2016). "Selfie-ists" or "Narci-selfiers"?: A cross-lagged panel analysis of selfie taking and narcissism. *Personality and Individual Differences, 97,* 98–101. (p. 483)

Halpern, D. F., Benbow, C. P., Geary, D. C., Gur, R. C., Hyde, J. S., & Gernsbacher, M. A. (2007). The science of sex differences in science and mathematics. *Psychological Science in the Public Interest, 8,* 1–51. (p. 340)

Hambrick, D. Z. (2014, December 2). Brain training doesn't make you smarter. *Scientific American* (scientificamerican.com/article/brain-training-doesn-t-make-you-smarter/). (p. 154)

Hambrick, D. Z., Altmann, E. M., Oswald, F. L., Meinz, E. J., Gobet, F., & Campitelli, G. (2014a). Accounting for expert performance: The devil is in the details. *Intelligence, 45,* 112–114. (p. 357)

Hambrick, D. Z., & Meinz, E. J. (2011). Limits on the predictive power of domain-specific experience and knowledge in skilled performance. *Current Directions in Psychological Science, 20,* 275–279. (p. 357)

Hambrick, D. Z., Oswald, F. L., Altmann, E. M., Meinz, E. J., Gobet, F., & Campitelli, G. (2014b). Deliberate practice: Is that all it takes to become an expert? *Intelligence, 45,* 34–45. (p. 357)

Hamid, A. A., Pettibone, J. R., Mabrouk, O. S., Hetrick, V. L., Schmidt, R., Vander Weele, C. M., . . . Berke, J. D. (2016). Mesolimbic dopamine signals the value of work. *Nature Neuroscience, 19,* 117–126. (pp. 56, 349)

Hamilton, J. L., Stange, J. P., Abramson, L. Y., & Alloy, L. B. (2015). Stress and the development of cognitive vulnerabilities to depression explain sex differences in depressive symptoms during adolescence. *Clinical Psychological Science, 3,* 702–714. (p. 520)

Hammack, P. L. (2005). The life course development of human sexual orientation: An integrative paradigm. *Human Development, 48,* 267–290. (p. 179)

Hammer, E. (2003). How lucky you are to be a psychology major. *Eye on Psi Chi,* 4–5. (p. C-5)

Hammersmith, S. K. (1982, August). *Sexual preference: An empirical study from the Alfred C. Kinsey Institute for Sex Research.* Paper presented at the 90th Annual Convention of the American Psychological Association, Washington, DC. (p. 180)

Hammond, D. C. (2008). Hypnosis as sole anesthesia for major surgeries: Historical and contemporary perspectives. *American Journal of Clinical Hypnosis, 51,* 101–121. (p. 224)

Hampshire, A., Highfield, R. R., Parkin, B. L., & Owen, A. M. (2012). Fractionating human intelligence. *Neuron, 76,* 1225–1237. (p. 324)

Hamza, C. A., Willoughby, T., & Heffer, T. (2015). Impulsivity and nonsuicidal self-injury: A review and meta-analysis. *Clinical Psychology Review, 38,* 13–24. (p. 502)

Han, B., Kott, P. S., Hughes, A., McKeon, R., Blanco, C., & Compton, W. M. (2016). Estimating the rates of deaths by suicide among adults who attempt suicide in the United States. *Journal of Psychiatric Research, 77,* 125–133. (p. 501)

Hanania, R. (2017). The personalities of politicians: A big five survey of American legislators. *Personality and Individual Differences, 108,* 164–167. (p. 479)

Haney, J. L. (2016). Predictors of homonegativity in the United States and the Netherlands using the fifth wave of the World Values Survey. *Journal of Homosexuality, 63,* 1355–1377. (p. 437)

Hänggi, J., Koeneke, S., Bezzola, L., & Jäncke, L. (2010). Structural neuroplasticity in the sensorimotor network of professional female ballet dancers. *Human Brain Mapping, 31,* 1196–1206. (p. 39)

Hankin, B. L., & Abramson, L. Y. (2001). Development of gender differences in depression: An elaborated cognitive vulnerability-transactional stress theory. *Psychological Bulletin, 127,* 773–796. (p. 520)

Hanlon, E. C., Tasali, E., Leproult, R., Stuhr, K. L., Doncheck, E., de Wit, H., . . . Van Cauter, E. (2016). Sleep restriction enhances the daily rhythm of circulating levels of Endocannabinoid 2-Arachidonoylglycerol. *Sleep, 39,* 653–664. (p. 93)

Hannikainen, I., Cabral, G., Machery, E., & Struchiner, N. (2016). A deterministic worldview promotes approval of state paternalism. *Journal of Experimental Social Psychology 70,* 251–259. (p. 397)

Harackiewicz, J. M., Canning, E. A., Tibbetts, Y., Giffen, C. J., Blair, S. S., Rouse, D. I., & Hyde, J. S. (2014). Closing the social class achievement gap for first-generation students in undergraduate biology. *Journal of Educational Psychology, 106,* 375–389. (p. 344)

Harackiewicz, J. M., Canning, E. A., Tibbetts, Y., Priniski, S. J., & Hyde, J. S. (2016). Closing achievement gaps with a utility-value intervention: Disentangling race and social class. *Journal of Personality and Social Psychology, 111,* 745–765. (p. 344)

Harari, G. M., Lane, N. D., Wang, R., Crosier, B. S., Campbell, A. T., & Gosling, S. D. (2016). Using smartphones to collect behavioral data in psychological science: Opportunities, practical considerations, and challenges. *Perspectives on Psychological Science, 11,* 838–854. (p. 22)

Harbaugh, W. T., Mayr, U., & Burghart, D. R. (2007). Neural responses to taxation and voluntary giving reveal motives for charitable donations. *Science, 316,* 1622–1625. (p. 454)

Harber, K. D. (1998). Feedback to minorities: Evidence of a positive bias. *Journal of Personality and Social Psychology, 74,* 622–628. (p. 435)

Harden, K. P. (2012). True love waits? A sibling-comparison study of age at first sexual intercourse and romantic relationships in young adulthood. *Psychological Science, 23,* 1324–1336. (p. 186)

Harden, K. P., & Mendle, J. (2011). Why don't smart teens have sex? A behavioral genetic approach. *Child Development, 82,* 1327–1344. (p. 178)

Hardt, O., Einarsson, E. O., & Nader, K. (2010). A bridge over troubled water: Reconsolidation as a link between cognitive and neuroscientific memory research traditions. *Annual Review of Psychology, 61,* 141–167. (p. 289)

Hare, R. D. (1975). Psychophysiological studies of psychopathy. In D. C. Fowles (Ed.), *Clinical applications of psychophysiology* (pp. 77–105). New York: Columbia University Press. (p. 530)

Harenski, C. L., Harenski, K. A., Shane, M. W., & Kiehl, K. A. (2010). Aberrant neural processing of moral violations in criminal psychopaths. *Journal of Abnormal Psychology, 119,* 863–874. (p. 531)

Harkin, B., Webb, T. L., Chang, B. P. I., Prestwich, A., Conner, M., Kellar, I., . . . Sheeran, P. (2016). Does monitoring goal progress promote goal attainment? A meta-analysis of the experimental evidence. *Psychological Bulletin, 142,* 198–229. (pp. 358, 359, 366, B-9)

Harkins, S. G., & Szymanski, K. (1989). Social loafing and group evaluation. *Journal of Personality and Social Psychology, 56,* 934–941. (p. 430)

Harlow, H. F., Harlow, M. K., & Suomi, S. J. (1971). From thought to therapy: Lessons from a primate laboratory. *American Scientist, 59,* 538–549. (p. 133)

Harmon-Jones, E., Abramson, L. Y., Sigelman, J., Bohlig, A., Hogan, M. E., & Harmon-Jones, C. (2002). Proneness to hypomania/mania symptoms or depression symptoms and asymmetrical frontal cortical responses to an anger-evoking event. *Journal of Personality and Social Psychology, 82,* 610–618. (p. 374)

Harmon-Jones, E., Harmon-Jones, C., & Levy, N. (2015). An action-based model of cognitive-dissonance processes. *Current Directions in Psychological Science, 24*, 184–189. (p. 420)

Harnett, N. G., Shumen, J. R., Wagle, P. A., Wood, K. H., Wheelock, M. D., Baños, J. H., & Knight, D. C. (2016). Neural mechanisms of human temporal fear conditioning. *Neurobiology of Learning and Memory, 136*, 97–104. (p. 240)

Harold, C. M., Oh, I.-S., Holtz, B. C., Han, S., & Giacalone, R. A. (2016). Fit and frustration as drivers of targeted counterproductive work behaviors: A multifoci perspective. *Journal of Applied Psychology, 101*, 1513–1535. (p. B-3)

Harper, C., & McLanahan, S. (2004). Father absence and youth incarceration. *Journal of Research on Adolescence, 14*, 369–397. (p. 443)

Harris, B. (1979). Whatever happened to Little Albert? *American Psychologist, 34*, 151–160. (p. 241)

Harris Interactive. (2010). *2009 eHarmony® marriage metrics study: Methodological notes.* eHarmony. Retrieved from eharmony.com/press-release/31/ (p. 448)

Harris, J. R. (1998). *The nurture assumption: Why children turn out the way they do.* New York: Free Press. (pp. 135, 147)

Harris, J. R. (2002). Beyond the nurture assumption: Testing hypotheses about the child's environment. In J. G. Borkowski, S. L. Ramey, & M. Bristol-Power (Eds.), *Parenting and the child's world: Influences on academic, intellectual, and social-emotional development* (pp. 3–20). Mahwah, NJ: Erlbaum. (p. 147)

Harris, J. R. (2006). *No two are alike: Human nature and human individuality.* New York: Norton. (p. 72)

Harris, J. R. (2009). *The nurture assumption: Why children turn out the way they do, revised and updated.* New York: Free Press. (p. 478)

Harris, M. A., Brett, C. E., Johnson, W., & Deary, I. J. (2016). Personality stability from age 14 to age 77 years. *Psychology and Aging, 31*, 862–874. (p. 118)

Harris, R. J. (1994). The impact of sexually explicit media. In J. Brant & D. Zillmann (Eds.), *Media effects: Advances in theory and research.* Hillsdale, NJ: Erlbaum. (p. 444)

Harrison, G., Hopper, K. I. M., Craig, T., Laska, E., Siegel, C., Wanderling, J., . . . Holmberg, S. K. (2001). Recovery from psychotic illness: A 15-and 25-year international follow-up study. *The British Journal of Psychiatry, 178*, 506–517. (p. 524)

Harrison, L. A., Hurlemann, R., & Adolphs, R. (2015). An enhanced default approach bias following amygdala lesions in humans. *Psychological Science, 26*, 1543–1555. (p. 55)

Harrison, N. A., Johnston, K., Corno, F., Casey, S. J., Friedner, K., Humphreys, K., . . . Kopelman, M. D. (2017). Psychogenic amnesia: Syndromes, outcome, and patterns of retrograde amnesia. *Brain: A Journal of Neurology, 140*, 2498–2510. (p. 527)

Harriston, K. A. (1993, December 24). 1 shakes, 1 snoozes: Both win $45 million. *Washington Post release (in Tacoma News Tribune,* pp. A1, A2). (p. 484)

Harter, J. K., Schmidt, F. L., Asplund, J. W., Killham, E. A., & Agrawal, S. (2010). Causal impact of employee work perceptions on the bottom line of organizations. *Perspectives on Psychological Science, 5*, 378–389. (p. B-9)

Harter, J. K., Schmidt, F. L., & Hayes, T. L. (2002). Business-unit-level relationship between employee satisfaction, employee engagement, and business outcomes: A meta-analysis. *Journal of Applied Psychology, 87*, 268–279. (p. B-8)

Hartl, A. C., Laursen, B., & Cillessen, A. H. (2015). A survival analysis of adolescent friendships: The downside of dissimilarity. *Psychological Science, 26*, 1304–1315. (p. 141)

Hartwig, M., & Bond, C. F., Jr. (2011). Why do lie-catchers fail? A lens model meta-analysis of human lie judgments. *Psychological Bulletin, 137*, 643–659. (p. 376)

Harvey, A. G., & Tang, N. K. Y. (2012). (Mis)perception of sleep in insomnia: A puzzle and a resolution. *Psychological Bulletin, 138*, 77–101. (p. 96)

Harvey, S. B., Øverland, S., Hatch, S. L., Wessely, S., Mykletun, A., & Hotopf, M. (2018). Exercise and the prevention of depression: Results of the HUNT Cohort Study. *American Journal of Psychiatry, 175*, 28–36. (pp. 402, 519)

Harward, S. C., Hedrick, N. G., Hall, C. E., Parra-Bueno, P., Milner, T. A., Pan, E., . . . McNamara, J. O. (2016). Autocrine BDNF–TrkB signalling within a single dendritic spine. *Nature, 538*, 99–103. (p. 279)

Haselton, M. G., & Gildersleeve, K. (2011). Can men detect ovulation? *Current Directions in Psychological Science, 20*, 87–92. (p. 173)

Haselton, M. G., & Gildersleeve, K. (2016). Human ovulation cues. *Current Opinion in Psychology, 7*, 120–125. (p. 173)

Haslam, S. A., & Reicher, S. D. (2007). Beyond the banality of evil: Three dynamics of an interactionist social psychology of tyranny. *Personality and Social Psychology Bulletin, 33*, 615–622. (p. 419)

Haslam, S. A., & Reicher, S. D. (2012). Contesting the "nature" of conformity: What Milgram and Zimbardo's studies really show. *PLoS Biology, 10*, e1001426. (p. 419)

Haslam, S. A., Reicher, S. D., & Birney, M. E. (2014). Nothing by mere authority: Evidence that in an experimental analogue of the Milgram paradigm participants are motivated not by orders but by appeals to science. *Journal of Social Issues, 70*, 473–488. (p. 427)

Haslam, S. A., Reicher, S. D., & Birney, M. E. (2016). Questioning authority: New perspectives on Milgram's "obedience" research and its implications for intergroup relations. *Current Opinion in Psychology, 11*, 6–9. (p. 427)

Hassan, B., & Rahman, Q. (2007). Selective sexual orientation–related differences in object location memory. *Behavioral Neuroscience, 121*, 625–633. (p. 182)

Hassan, J. (2016, October 12). Homophobic attacks in the U.K. have risen 147% since Brexit, report says. *The Washington Post* (washingtonpost.com). (p. 439)

Hassin, R. R. (2013). Yes it can: On the functional abilities of the human unconscious. *Perspectives on Psychological Science, 8*, 195–207. (p. 305)

Hatfield, E. (1988). Passionate and companionate love. In R. J. Sternberg & M. L. Barnes (Eds.), *The psychology of love.* New Haven, CT: Yale University Press. (p. 451)

Hatfield, E. (2016). Love and sex in the marketplace. In R. J. Sternberg, S. T. Fiske, & D. J. Foss (Eds.), *Scientists making a difference: One hundred eminent behavioral and brain scientists talk about their most important contributions.* New York: Cambridge University Press. (p. 448)

Hatfield, E., Mo, Y., & Rapson, R. L. (2015). Love, sex, and marriage across cultures. *Oxford Handbooks Online* (oxfordhandbooks.com). (p. 451)

Hatfield, E., & Sprecher, S. (1986). *Mirror, mirror . . . The importance of looks in everyday life.* Albany: State University of New York Press. (p. 449)

Hathaway, S. R. (1960). *An MMPI Handbook* (Vol. 1, Foreword). Minneapolis: University of Minnesota Press (rev. ed.), 1972. (p. 477)

Hatzenbuehler, M. L. (2011). The social environment and suicide attempts in lesbian, gay, and bisexual youth. *Pediatrics, 127*, 896–903. (p. 500)

Hatzenbuehler, M. L. (2014). Structural stigma and the health of lesbian, gay, and bisexual populations. *Current Directions in Psychological Science, 23*, 127–132. (p. 437)

Hatzigeorgiadis, A., Zourbanos, N., Galanis, E., & Theodorakis, Y. (2011). Self-talk and sports performance: A meta-analysis. *Perspectives on Psychological Science, 6*, 348–356. (p. 546)

Haun, D. B. M., Rekers, Y., & Tomasello, M. (2014). Children conform to the behavior of peers; other great apes stick with what they know. *Psychological Science, 25*, 2160–2167. (p. 144)

Havas, D. A., Glenberg, A. M., Gutowski, K. A., Lucarelli, M. J., & Davidson, R. J. (2010). Cosmetic use of Botulinum Toxin-A affects processing of emotional language. *Psychological Science, 21*, 895–900. (p. 381)

Hawkley, L. C., Hughes, M. E., Waite, L. J., Masi, C. M., Thisted, R. A., & Cacioppo, J. T. (2008). From social structure factors to perceptions of relationship quality and loneliness: The Chicago Health, Aging, and Social Relations Study. *Journal of Gerontology: Series B, 63*, S375–S384. (p. 399)

Haworth, C. M. A., Wright, M. J., Luciano, M., Martin, N. G., de Geus, E. J., van Beijsterveldt, C. E., . . . Plomin, R. (2010). The heritability of general cognitive ability increases linearly from childhood to young adulthood. *Molecular Psychiatry, 15*, 1112–1120. (p. 338)

Haworth, C. M. A., Wright, M. J., Martin, N. W., Martin, N. G., Boomsma, D. I., Bartels, M., . . . Plomin, R. (2009). A twin study of the genetics of high cognitive ability selected from 11,000 twin pairs in six studies from four countries. *Behavior Genetics, 39*, 359–370. (p. 336)

Haxby, J. V. (2001, July 7). Quoted in B. Bower, Faces of perception. Science News, pp. 10–12. See also J. V. Haxby, M. I. Gobbini, M. L. Furey, A. Ishai, J. L. Schouten & P. Pietrini (2001), Distributed and overlapping representations of faces and objects in ventral temporal cortex. *Science, 293*, 2425–2430. (p. 205)

Hayashi, Y., Kashiwagi, M., Yasuda, K., Ando, R., Kanuka, M., Sakai, K., & Itohara, S. (2015). Cells of a common developmental origin regulate REM/non-REM sleep and wakefulness in mice. *Science, 350*, 957–961. (p. 90)

Hays, C., & Carver, L. J. (2014). Follow the liar: The effects of adult lies on children's honesty. *Developmental Science, 17*, 977–983. (p. 262)

Hazan, C., & Shaver, P. R. (1994). Attachment as an organizational framework for research on close relationships. *Psychological Inquiry, 5*, 1–22. (p. 138)

Hazelrigg, M. D., Cooper, H. M., & Borduin, C. M. (1987). Evaluating the effectiveness of family therapies: An integrative review and analysis. *Psychological Bulletin, 101*, 428–442. (p. 547)

HBVA. (2018, accessed February 20). *Honour killings by region, South and Central Asia.* Honour Based Violence Awareness Network. Retrieved from hbv-awareness.com (p. 170)

He, Z., & Jin, Y. (2016). Intrinsic control of axon regeneration. *Neuron, 90*, 437–451. (p. 64)

Headey, B., Muffels, R., & Wagner, G. G. (2010). Long-running German panel survey shows that personal and economic choices, not just genes, matter for happiness. *PNAS, 107*, 17922–17926. (p. 411)

Healy, A. F., Jones, M., Lalchandani, L. A., & Tack, L. A. (2017). Timing of quizzes during learning: Effects on motivation and retention. *Journal of Experimental Psychology: Applied, 23*, 128–137. (p. 246)

Heavey, C. L., & Hurlburt, R. T. (2008). The phenomena of inner experience. *Consciousness and Cognition, 17,* 798–810. (p. 319)

Heberle, A. E., & Carter, A. S. (2015). Cognitive aspects of young children's experience of economic disadvantage. *Psychological Bulletin, 141,* 723–746. (p. 339)

Hedström, P., Liu, K.-Y., & Nordvik, M. K. (2008). Interaction domains and suicides: A population-based panel study of suicides in the Stockholm metropolitan area, 1991–1999. *Social Forces, 2,* 713–740. (p. 501)

Hehman, E., Flake, J. K., & Calanchini, J. (2018). Disproportionate use of lethal force in policing is associated with regional racial biases of residents. *Social Psychological Personality Science,* in press. (p. 426)

Heider, F. (1958). *The psychology of interpersonal relations.* New York: Wiley. (p. 416)

Heiman, J. R. (1975, April). The physiology of erotica: Women's sexual arousal. *Psychology Today,* pp. 90–94. (p. 176)

Hein, G., Morishima, Y., Leiberg, S., Sul, S., & Fehr, E. (2016). The brain's functional network architecture reveals human motives. *Science, 351,* 1074–1078. (p. 455)

Heine, S. J., Proulx, T., & Vohs, K. D. (2006). Meaning maintenance model: On the coherence of human motivations. *Personality and Social Psychology Review, 10,* 88–110. (p. 350)

Hejmadi, A., Davidson, R. J., & Rozin, P. (2000). Exploring Hindu Indian emotion expressions: Evidence for accurate recognition by Americans and Indians. *Psychological Science, 11,* 183–187. (p. 376)

Helfand, D. (2011, January 7). An assault on rationality. *The New York Times* (nytimes.com). (p. 231)

Helleberg, M., Afzal, S., Kronborg, G., Larsen, C. S., Pedersen, G., Pedersen, C., . . . Obel, N. (2013). Mortality attributable to smoking among HIV-1-infected individuals: A nationwide, population-based cohort study. *Clinical Infectious Diseases, 56,* 727–734. (p. 105)

Heller, A. S., Johnstone, T., Schackman, A. J., Light, S. N., Peterson, M. J., Kolden, G. G., . . . Davidson, R. J. (2009). Reduced capacity to sustain positive emotion in major depression reflects diminished maintenance of fronto-striatal brain activation. *PNAS, 106,* 22445–22450. (p. 518)

Heller, S. B. (2014). Summer jobs reduce violence among disadvantaged youth. *Science, 346,* 1219–1222. (p. 145)

Heller, W. (1990, May/June). Of one mind: Second thoughts about the brain's dual nature. *The Sciences,* pp. 38–44. (p. 67)

Helliwell, J., Layard, R., & Sachs, J. (Eds.) (2013). *World happiness report.* New York: The Earth Institute, Columbia University. (pp. 410, 412)

Helliwell, J. F., & Wang, S. (2015). How was the weekend? How the social context underlies weekend effects in happiness and other emotions for U.S. workers. *PLoS ONE, 10,* e0145123. (p. 408)

Helmreich, W. B. (1992). *Against all odds: Holocaust survivors and the successful lives they made in America.* New York: Simon & Schuster. (pp. 137, 469)

Helmreich, W. B. (1994). Personal correspondence. Department of Sociology, City University of New York. (p. 469)

Helms, J. E., Jernigan, M., & Mascher, J. (2005). The meaning of race in psychology and how to change it: A methodological perspective. *American Psychologist, 60,* 27–36. (p. 342)

Helmuth, L. (2001). Boosting brain activity from the outside in. *Science, 292,* 1284–1286. (p. 564)

Helsen, K., Goubert, L., Peters, M. L., & Vlaeyen, J. W. S. (2011). Observational learning and pain-related fear: An experimental study with colored cold pressor tasks. *The Journal of Pain, 12,* 1230–1239. (p. 511)

Hembree, R. (1988). Correlates, causes, effects, and treatment of test anxiety. *Review of Educational Research, 58,* 47–77. (p. 350)

Hemmings, S. M. J., Malan-Müller, S., van den Heuvel, L. L., Demmitt, B. A., Stanislawski, M. A., Smith, D. G., . . . Lowry, C. A. (2017). The microbiome in posttraumatic stress disorder and trauma-exposed controls: An exploratory study. *Psychosomatic Medicine, 79,* 936–946. (p. 514)

Henderlong, J., & Lepper, M. R. (2002). The effects of praise on children's intrinsic motivation: A review and synthesis. *Psychological Bulletin, 128,* 774–795. (p. 358)

Henderson, J. M. (2007). Regarding scenes. *Current Directions in Psychological Science, 16,* 219–222. (p. 194)

Henig, R. M. (2010, August 18). What is it about 20-somethings? *The New York Times Magazine* (nytimes.com). (p. 149)

Henley, N. M. (1989). Molehill or mountain? What we know and don't know about sex bias in language. In M. Crawford & M. Gentry (Eds.), *Gender and thought: Psychological perspectives* (pp. 59–78). New York: Springer-Verlag. (p. 320)

Hennenlotter, A., Dresel, C., Castrop, F., Ceballos Baumann, A., Wohschlager, A., & Haslinger, B. (2008). The link between facial feedback and neural activity within central circuitries of emotion: New insights from Botulinum Toxin-induced denervation of frown muscles. *Cerebral Cortex, 19,* 537–542. (p. 381)

Hennessey, B. A., & Amabile, T. M. (2010). Creativity. *Annual Review of Psychology, 61,* 569–598. (pp. 306, B-11)

Henrich, J., Heine, S. J., & Norenzayan, A. (2010). The weirdest people in the world? *Behavioral and Brain Sciences, 33,* 61–135. (p. 9)

Hensley, C., Browne, J. A., & Trentham, C. E. (2018). Exploring the social and emotional context of childhood animal cruelty and its potential link to adult human violence. *Psychology, Crime & Law, 24*(5). (p. 118)

Hepper, P. (2005). Unravelling our beginnings. *The Psychologist, 18,* 474–477. (p. 119)

Herbenick, D., Reece, M., Schick, V., & Sanders, S. A. (2014). Erect penile length and circumference dimensions of 1,661 sexually active men in the United States. *Journal of Sexual Medicine, 11,* 93–101. (p. 174)

Herbenick, D., Reece, M., Schick, V., Sanders, S. A., Dodge, B., & Fortenberry, J. D. (2010). Sexual behavior in the United States: Results from a national probability sample of men and women ages 14–94. *Journal of Sexual Medicine, 7*(Suppl. 5), 255–265. (p. 178)

Herculano-Houzel, S. (2012). The remarkable, yet not extraordinary, human brain as a scaled-up primate brain and its associated cost. *PNAS, 109*(suppl 1), 10661–10668. (p. 47)

Herholz, S. C., & Zatorre, R. J. (2012). Musical training as a framework for brain plasticity: Behavior, function, and structure. *Neuron, 76,* 486–502. (p. 39)

Herman, C. P., & Polivy, J. (1980). Restrained eating. In A. J. Stunkard (Ed.), *Obesity.* Philadelphia: Saunders. (p. 366)

Herman, C. P., Polivy, J., Pliner, P., & Vartanian, L. R. (2015). Mechanisms underlying the portion-size effect. *Physiology & Behavior, 144,* 129–136. (p. 364)

Herman, C. P., Roth, D. A., & Polivy, J. (2003). Effects of the presence of others on food intake: A normative interpretation. *Psychological Bulletin, 129,* 873–886. (p. 364)

Herman-Giddens, M. E. (2013). The enigmatic pursuit of puberty in girls. *Pediatrics, 132,* 1125–1126. (p. 167)

Herman-Giddens, M. E., Steffes, J., Harris, D., Slora, E., Hussey, M., Dowshen, S. A., . . . Reiter, E. O. (2012). Secondary sexual characteristics in boys: Data from the pediatric research in office settings network. *Pediatrics, 130,* 1058–1068. (p. 166)

Hernandez, A. E., & Li, P. (2007). Age of acquisition: Its neural and computational mechanisms. *Psychological Bulletin, 133,* 638–650. (p. 315)

Hernandez, R., Kershaw, K. N., Siddique, J., Boehm, J. K., Kubzansky, L. D., Diez-Roux, A., . . . Lloyd-Jones, D. M. (2015). Optimism and cardiovascular health: Multi-ethnic study of atherosclerosis (MESA). *Health Behavior and Policy Review, 2,* 62–73. (p. 398)

Herring, D. R., White, K. R., Jabeen, L. N., Hinojos, M., & Terrazas, G. (2013). On the automatic activation of attitudes: A quarter century of evaluative priming research. *Psychological Bulletin, 132,* 1062–1089. (pp. 192, 281)

Herringa, R. J., Phillips, M. L., Fournier, J. C., Kronhaus, D. M., & Germain, A. (2013). Childhood and adult trauma both correlate with dorsal anterior cingulate activation to threat in combat veterans. *Psychological Medicine, 43,* 1533–1542. (p. 512)

Herrmann, E., Call, J., Hernández-Lloreda, M. V., Hare, B., & Tomasello, M. (2007). Humans have evolved specialized skills of social cognition: The cultural intelligence hypothesis. *Science, 317,* 1360–1365. (p. 260)

Herrnstein, R. J., & Loveland, D. H. (1964). Complex visual concept in the pigeon. *Science, 146,* 549–551. (p. 245)

Hershenson, M. (1989). *The moon illusion.* Hillsdale, NJ: Erlbaum. (p. 212)

Hertenstein, M. (2009). *The tell: The little cues that reveal big truths about who we are.* New York: Basic Books. (pp. 118, 392)

Hertenstein, M. J., Hansel, C., Butts, S., Hile, S. (2009). Smile intensity in photographs predicts divorce later in life. *Motivation & Emotion, 33,* 99–105. (p. 118)

Hertenstein, M. J., Keltner, D., App, B., Bulleit, B., & Jaskolka, A. (2006). Touch communicates distinct emotions. *Emotion, 6,* 528–533. (p. 133)

Herz, R. (2007). *The scent of desire: Discovering our enigmatic sense of smell.* New York: Morrow/HarperCollins. (p. 226)

Herz, R. (2012, January 28). You eat that? *The Wall Street Journal* (online.wsj.com). (p. 363)

Herz, R. S. (2001). Ah sweet skunk! Why we like or dislike what we smell. *Cerebrum, 3,* 31–47. (p. 226)

Herz, R. S., Beland, S. L., & Hellerstein, M. (2004). Changing odor hedonic perception through emotional associations in humans. *International Journal of Comparative Psychology, 17,* 315–339. (p. 226)

Hess, E. H. (1956, July). Space perception in the chick. *Scientific American,* pp. 71–80. (p. 213)

Hess, U., & Thibault, P. (2009). Darwin and emotion expression. *American Psychologist, 64,* 120–128. (p. 379)

Hetherington, M. M., Anderson, A. S., Norton, G. N. M., & Newson, L. (2006). Situational effects on meal intake: A comparison of eating alone and eating with others. *Physiology and Behavior, 88,* 498–505. (p. 364)

Hewett, R., & Conway, N. (2015). The undermining effect revisited: The salience of everyday verbal rewards and self-determined motivation. *Journal of Organizational Behavior, 37,* 436–455. (p. 358)

Hickok, G. (2014). *The myth of mirror neurons: The real neuroscience of communication and cognition.* New York: Norton. (pp. 259, 260)

Hickok, G., Bellugi, U., & Klima, E. S. (2001, June). Sign language in the brain. *Scientific American,* pp. 58–65. (p. 67)

Hilgard, E. R. (1986). *Divided consciousness: Multiple controls in human thought and action.* New York: Wiley. (p. 224)

Hilgard, E. R. (1992). Dissociation and theories of hypnosis. In E. Fromm & M. R. Nash (Eds.), *Contemporary hypnosis research.* New York: Guilford. (p. 224)

Hill, A. J. (2007). The psychology of food craving. *Proceedings of the Nutrition Society, 66,* 277–285. (p. 241)

Hill, C. E., & Nakayama, E. Y. (2000). Client-centered therapy: Where has it been and where is it going? A comment on Hathaway. *Journal of Clinical Psychology, 56,* 961–875. (p. 539)

Hills, P. J., Werno, M. A., & Lewis, M. B. (2011). Sad people are more accurate at face recognition than happy people. *Consciousness and Cognition, 20,* 1502–1517. (p. 514)

Hines, M. (2004). *Brain gender.* New York: Oxford University Press. (p. 166)

Hingson, R. W., Heeren, T., & Winter, M. R. (2006). Age at drinking onset and alcohol dependence. *Archives of Pediatrics & Adolescent Medicine, 160,* 739–746. (p. 112)

Hintzman, D. L. (1978). *The psychology of learning and memory.* San Francisco: Freeman. (p. 271)

Hinz, L. D., & Williamson, D. A. (1987). Bulimia and depression: A review of the affective variant hypothesis. *Psychological Bulletin, 102,* 150–158. (p. 532)

Hirsh-Pasek, K., Adamson, L. B., Bakeman, R., Owen, M. T., Golinkoff, R. M., Pace, A., . . . Suma, K. (2015). The contribution of early communication quality to low-income children's language success. *Psychological Science, 26,* 1071–1083. (p. 315)

Hirst, W., & Phelps, E. A. (2016). Flashbulb memories. *Current Directions in Psychological Science, 25,* 36–41. (p. 278)

Hirst, W., Phelps, E. A., Buckner, R. L., Budson, A. E., Cuc, A., Gabrieli, J. D. E., . . . Vaidya, C. J. (2009). Long-term memory for the terrorist attack of September 11: Flashbulb memories, event memories, and the factors that influence their retention. *Journal of Experimental Psychology: General, 138,* 161–176. (p. 278)

Hjelmborg, J. V. B., Fagnani, C., Silventoinen, K., McGue, M., Korkeila, M., Christensen, K., . . . Kaprio, J. (2008). Genetic influences on growth traits of BMI: A longitudinal study of adult twins. *Obesity, 16,* 847–852. (p. 365)

Hjorthøj, C., Stürup, A. E., McGrath, J. J., & Nordentoft, M. (2017). Years of potential life lost and life expectancy in schizophrenia: A systematic review and meta-analysis. *The Lancet Psychiatry, 4,* 295–301. (p. 524)

HMHL. (2002, January). Disaster and trauma. *Harvard Mental Health Letter,* pp. 1–5. (p. 385)

HMHL. (2007, February). Electroconvulsive therapy. *Harvard Mental Health Letter,* Harvard Medical School, pp. 1–4. (p. 563)

Hoang, T. D., Reis, J., Zhu, N., Jacobs, D. R., Jr., Launer, L. J., Whitmer, R. A., . . . Yaffe, K. (2016). Effect of early adult patterns of physical activity and television viewing on midlife cognitive function. *JAMA Psychiatry, 73,* 73–79. (p. 153)

Hobaiter, C., Poisot, T., Zuberbühler, K., Hoppitt, W., & Gruber, T. (2014). Social network analysis shows direct evidence for social transmission of tool use in wild chimpanzees. *PLoS Biology, 16,* e1001960. (p. 310)

Hobbs, W. R., Burke, M., Christakis, N. A., & Fowler, J. H. (2016). Online social integration is association with reduced mortality risk. *PNAS, 113,* 12980–12984. (p. 356)

Hobson, J. A. (1995, September). Quoted in G. H. Colt, The power of dreams. *Life,* pp. 36–49. (p. 97)

Hobson, J. A. (2003). *Dreaming: An introduction to the science of sleep.* New York: Oxford University Press. (p. 98)

Hobson, J. A. (2004). *13 dreams Freud never had: The new mind science.* New York: Pi Press. (p. 98)

Hobson, J. A. (2009). REM sleep and dreaming: Towards a theory of protoconsciousness. *Nature Reviews Neuroscience, 10,* 803–814. (p. 98)

Hochberg, L. R., Serruya, M. D., Friehs, G. M., Mukand, J. A., Saleh, M., Caplan, A. H., . . . Donoghue, J. P. (2006). Neuronal ensemble control of prosthetic devices by a human with tetraplegia. *Nature, 442,* 164–171. (p. 61)

Hochmair, I. (2013, September). *Cochlear implants: The size of the task concerning children born deaf.* Retrieved from www.medel.com/cochlear-implants-facts (p. 218)

Hoebel, B. G., & Teitelbaum, P. (1966). Effects of forcefeeding and starvation on food intake and body weight in a rat with ventromedial hypothalamic lesions. *Journal of Comparative and Physiological Psychology, 61,* 189–193. (p. 362)

Hoeft, F., Watson, C. L., Kesler, S. R., Bettinger, K. E., & Reiss, A. L. (2008). Gender differences in the mesocorticolimbic system during computer game-play. *Journal of Psychiatric Research, 42,* 253–258. (p. 102)

Hoffman, B. M., Babyak, M. A., Craighead, W. E., Sherwood, A., Doraiswamy, P. M., Coons, M. J., & Blumenthal, J. A. (2011). Exercise and pharmacotherapy in patients with major depression: One-year follow-up of the SMILE study. *Psychosomatic Medicine, 73,* 127–133. (p. 402)

Hoffman, D. D. (1998). *Visual intelligence: How we create what we see.* New York: Norton. (p. 206)

Hoffman, H. (2012). Considering the role of conditioning in sexual orientation. *Archives of Sexual Behavior, 41,* 63–71. (p. 238)

Hoffman, H. G. (2004, August). Virtual-reality therapy. *Scientific American,* pp. 58–65. (p. 224)

Hoffman, Y. S. G., Shrira, A., Cohen-Fridel, S., Grossman, E. S., & Bodner, E. (2016). The effect of exposure to missile attacks on posttraumatic stress disorder symptoms as a function of perceived media control and locus of control. *Psychiatry Research, 244,* 51–56. (p. 397)

Hofmann, W., De Houwer, J., Perugini, M., Baeyens, F., & Crombez, G. (2010). Evaluative conditioning in humans: A meta-analysis. *Psychological Bulletin, 136,* 390–421. (p. 404)

Hogan, C. L., Catalino, L. I., Mata, J., & Fredrickson, B. L. (2015). Beyond emotional benefits: Physical activity and sedentary behavior affect psychosocial resources through emotions. *Psychology & Health, 30,* 354–369. (p. 401)

Hogan, R. (1998). Reinventing personality. *Journal of Social and Clinical Psychology, 17,* 1–10. (p. 480)

Hoge, C. W., Terhakopian, A., Castro, C. A., Messer, S. C., & Engel, C. C. (2007). Association of posttraumatic stress disorder with somatic symptoms, health care visits, and absenteeism among Iraq War veterans. *American Journal of Psychiatry, 164,* 150–153. (p. 509)

Hogg, M. A. (1996). Intragroup processes, group structure and social identity. In W. P. Robinson (Ed.), *Social groups and identities: Developing the legacy of Henri Tajfel.* Oxford: Butterworth Heinemann. (p. 438)

Hogg, M. A. (2006). Social identity theory. In P. J. Burke (Ed.), *Contemporary social psychological theories.* Stanford, CA: Stanford University Press. (p. 438)

Hohmann, G. W. (1966). Some effects of spinal cord lesions on experienced emotional feelings. *Psychophysiology, 3,* 143–156. (p. 368)

Hokanson, J. E., & Edelman, R. (1966). Effects of three social responses on vascular processes. *Journal of Personality and Social Psychology, 3,* 442–447. (p. 393)

Holahan, C. K., & Sears, R. R. (1995). *The gifted group in later maturity.* Stanford, CA: Stanford University Press. (p. 331)

Holden, G. W., & Miller, P. C. (1999). Enduring and different: A meta-analysis of the similarity in parents' child rearing. *Psychological Bulletin, 125,* 223–254. (p. 139)

Holland, D., Chang, L., Ernst, T. M., Curran, M., Buchthal, S. D., Alicata, D., . . . Dale, A. M. (2014). Structural growth trajectories and rates of change in the first 3 months of infant brain development. *JAMA Neurology, 71,* 1266–1274. (p. 123)

Holland, J. L. (1996). Exploring careers with a typology: What we have learned and some new directions. *American Psychologist, 51,* 397–406. (p. B-3)

Holle, H., Warne, K., Seth, A. K., Critchley, H. D., & Ward, J. (2012). Neural basis of contagious itch and why some people are more prone to it. *PNAS, 109,* 19816–19821. (p. 422)

Holliday, R. E., & Albon, A. J. (2004). Minimizing misinformation effects in young children with cognitive interview mnemonics. *Applied Cognitive Psychology, 18,* 263–281. (p. 294)

Hollis, K. L. (1997). Contemporary research on Pavlovian conditioning: A "new" functional analysis. *American Psychologist, 52,* 956–965. (p. 238)

Hollon, S. D., DeRubeis, R. J., Fawcett, J., Amsterdam, J. D., Shelton, R. C., Zajecka, J., . . . Gallop, R. (2014). Effect of cognitive therapy with antidepressant medications vs. antidepressants alone on the rate of recovery in major depressive disorder. *JAMA Psychiatry, 71,* 1157–1164. (p. 562)

Holman, E. A., Garfin, D. R., & Silver, R. C. (2014). Media's role in broadcasting acute stress following the Boston marathon bombings. *PNAS, 111,* 93–98. (p. 510)

Holstege, G., Georgiadis, J. R., Paans, A. M. J., Meiners, L. C., van der Graaf, F. H. C. E., & Reinders, A. A. T. S. (2003a). Brain activation during male ejaculation. *Journal of Neuroscience, 23,* 9185–9193. (p. 174)

Holstege, G., Reinders, A. A. T., Paans, A. M. J., Meiners, L. C., Pruim, J., & Georgiadis, J. R. (2003b). *Brain activation during female sexual orgasm* (Annual Conference Abstract Viewer/Itinerary Planner Program No. 727.7). Washington, DC: Society for Neuroscience. (p. 174)

Holt-Lunstad, J., Robles, T. F., & Sbarra, D. A. (2017). Advancing social connection as a public health priority in the United States. *American Psychologist, 72,* 517–530. (p. 399)

Holt-Lunstad, J., Smith, T. B., Baker, M., Harris, T., & Stephenson, D. (2015). Loneliness and social isolation as risk factors for mortality: A meta-analytic review. *Perspectives on Psychological Science, 10,* 227–237. (p. 399)

Holt-Lunstad, J., Smith, T. B., & Layton, J. B. (2010). Social relationships and mortality risk: A meta-analytic review. *PLoS Medicine, 7,* e1000316. (pp. 353, 399)

Holtgraves, T. (2011). Text messaging, personality, and the social context. *Journal of Research in Personality, 45,* 92–99. (p. 479)

Holwerda, T. J., Deeg, D. J., Beekman, A. T., van Tilburg, T. G., Stek, M. L., Jonker, C., & Schoevers, R. A. (2014). Feelings of loneliness, but not social isolation, predict dementia onset: Results from the Amsterdam Study of the Elderly (AMSTEL). *Journal of Neurology, Neurosurgery, and Psychiatry, 85,* 135–142. (p. 353)

Homer, B. D., Solomon, T. M., Moeller, R. W., Mascia, A., DeRaleau, L., & Halkitis, P. N. (2008). Methamphetamine abuse and impairment of social functioning: A review of the underlying neurophysiological causes and behavioral implications. *Psychological Bulletin, 134,* 301–310. (p. 107)

Hoogman, M., Bralten, J., Hibar, D. P., Mennes, M., Zwiers, M. P., Schweren, L. S., . . . de Zeeuw, P. (2017). Subcortical brain volume differences in participants with attention deficit hyperactivity disorder in children and adults: A cross-sectional mega-analysis. *The Lancet Psychiatry, 4,* 310–319. (p. 498)

Hooper, J., & Teresi, D. (1986). *The three-pound universe.* New York: Macmillan. (p. 56)

Hopkins, E. D., & Cantalupo, C. (2008). Theoretical speculations on the evolutionary origins of hemispheric specialization. *Current Directions in Psychological Science, 17,* 233–237. (p. 67)

Hoppenbrouwers, S. S., Bulten, B. H., & Brazil, I. A. (2016). Parsing fear: A reassessment of the evidence for fear deficits in psychopathy. *Psychological Bulletin, 142,* 573–600.(p. 530)

Hopper, L. M., Lambeth, S. P., Schapiro, S. J., & Whiten, A. (2008). Observational learning in chimpanzees and children studied through "ghost" conditions. *Proceedings of the Royal Society, 275,* 835–840. (p. 259)

Horne, J. (2011). The end of sleep: "Sleep debt" versus biological adaptation of human sleep to waking needs. *Biological Psychology, 87,* 1–14. (p. 90)

Horne, Z., Powell, D., Hummel, J. E., & Holyoak, K. J. (2015). Countering antivaccination attitudes. *PNAS, 112,* 10321–10324. (p. 418)

Horowitz, S. S. (2012, November 9). The science and art of listening. *The New York Times* (nytimes.com). (p. 216)

Horta, L., de Mola, C. L., & Victora, C. G. (2015). Breastfeeding and intelligence: Systematic review and meta-analysis. *Acta Paediatrica, 104,* 14–19. (p. 25)

Horvath, J. C., Forte, J. D., & Carter, O. (2015). Quantitative review finds no evidence of cognitive effects in healthy populations from single-session transcranial direct current stimulation (tDCS). *Brain Stimulation, 8,* 535–550. (p. 563)

Horváth, K., Hannon, B., Ujma, P. P., Gombos, F., & Plunkett, K. (2017). Memory in 3-month-old infants benefits from a short nap. *Developmental Science, 21*(1), e12587. (p. 92)

Horwood, L. J., & Fergusson, D. M. (1998). Breastfeeding and later cognitive and academic outcomes. *Pediatrics, 101,* E9. (p. 25)

Hostetter, A. B. (2011). When do gestures communicate? A meta-analysis. *Psychological Bulletin, 137,* 297–315. (p. 317)

Hostinar, C. E., Sullivan, R., & Gunnar, M. R. (2014). Psychobiological mechanisms underlying the social buffering of the hypothalamic-pituitary-adrenocortical axis: A review of animal models and human studies across development. *Psychological Bulletin, 140,* 256–282. (p. 400)

Hou, W.-H., Chiang, P.-T., Hsu, T.-Y., Chiu, S.-Y., & Yen, Y.-C. (2010). Treatment effects of massage therapy in depressed people: A meta-analysis. *Journal of Clinical Psychiatry, 71,* 894–901. (pp. 404, 564)

House, R., Javidan, M., & Dorfman, P. (2001). Project GLOBE: An introduction. *Applied Psychology: An International Review, 50,* 489–505. (p. B-11)

House, R. J., & Singh, J. V. (1987). Organizational behavior: Some new directions for I/O psychology. *Annual Review of Psychology, 38,* 669–718. (p. B-10)

Houser-Marko, L., & Sheldon, K. M. (2008). Eyes on the prize or nose to the grindstone? The effects of level of goal evaluation on mood and motivation. *Personality and Social Psychology Bulletin, 34,* 1556–1569. (p. B-9)

Houts, A. C., Berman, J. S., & Abramson, H. (1994). Effectiveness of psychological and pharmacological treatments for nocturnal enuresis. *Journal of Consulting and Clinical Psychology, 62,* 737–745. (p. 540)

Hovatta, I., Tennant, R. S., Helton, R., Marr, R. A., Singer, O., Redwine, J. M., . . . Barlow, C. (2005). Glyoxalase 1 and glutathione reductase 1 regulate anxiety in mice. *Nature, 438,* 662–666. (p. 511)

Hoyer, G., & Lund, E. (1993). Suicide among women related to number of children in marriage. *Archives of General Psychiatry, 50,* 134–137. (p. 500)

Hsee, C. K., & Ruan, B. (2016). The Pandora effect: The power and peril of curiosity. *Psychological Science, 27,* 659–666. (p. 349)

Hsee, C. K., Yang, A. X., & Wang, L. (2010). Idleness aversion and the need for justifiable busyness. *Psychological Science, 21,* 926–930. (p. B-2)

Hsiang, S. M., Burke, M., & Miguel, E. (2013). Quantifying the influence of climate on human conflict. *Science, 341,* 1212. (p. 443)

Huang, C. (2015). Relation between attributional style and subsequent depressive symptoms: A systematic review and meta-analysis of longitudinal studies. *Cognitive Therapy and Research, 39,* 721–735. (p. 520)

Huang, J., Chaloupka, F. J., & Fong, G. T. (2013). Cigarette graphic warning labels and smoking prevalence in Canada: A critical examination and reformulation of the FDA regulatory impact analysis. *Tobacco Control* (tobaccocontrol.bmj.com/content/early/2013/11/11/tobaccocontrol-2013-051170.full.pdf+html). (p. 303)

Huart, J., Corneille, O., & Becquart, E. (2005). Face-based categorization, context-based categorization, and distortions in the recollection of gender ambiguous faces. *Journal of Experimental Social Psychology, 41,* 598–608. (p. 298)

Hubbard, E. M., Arman, A. C., Ramachandran, V. S., & Boynton, G. M. (2005). Individual differences among grapheme-color synesthetes: Brain-behavior correlations. *Neuron, 45,* 975–985. (p. 229)

Hubel, D. H. (1979, September). The brain. *Scientific American,* pp. 45–53. (p. 194)

Hubel, D. H., & Wiesel, T. N. (1979, September). Brian mechanisms of vision. *Scientific American,* pp. 150–162. (p. 205)

Huber, E., Webster, J. M., Brewer, A. A., MacLeod, D. I. A., Wandell, B. A., Boynton, G. M., . . . Fine, I. (2015). A lack of experience-dependent plasticity after more than a decade of recovered sight. *Psychological Science, 26,* 393–401. (p. 213)

Hucker, S. J., & Bain, J. (1990). Androgenic hormones and sexual assault. In W. L. Marshall, D. R. Laws, & H. E. Barbaree (Eds.), *Handbook of sexual assault: Issues, theories, and treatment of the offender* (pp. 209–229). New York: Plenum Press. (p. 174)

Hudson, J. I., Hiripi, E., Pope, H. G., & Kessler, R. C. (2007). The prevalence and correlates of eating disorders in the National Comorbidity Survey Replication. *Biological Psychiatry, 61,* 348–358. (p. 532)

Hudson, N. W., & Roberts, B. W. (2014). Goals to change personality traits: Concurrent links between personality traits, daily behavior, and goals to change oneself. *Journal of Research in Personality, 53,* 68–83. (p. 476)

Huey, E. D., Krueger, F., & Grafman, J. (2006). Representations in the human prefrontal cortex. *Current Directions in Psychological Science, 15,* 167–171. (p. 62)

Hugenberg, K., & Bodenhausen, G. V. (2003). Facing prejudice: Implicit prejudice and the perception of facial threat. *Psychological Science, 14,* 640–643. (p. 436)

Hugenberg, K., Young, S. G., Bernstein, M. J., & Sacco, D. F. (2010). The categorization–individuation model: An integrative account of the other-race recognition deficit. *Psychological Review, 117,* 1168–1187. (p. 440)

Hughes, J. R. (2010). Craving among long-abstinent smokers: An internet survey. *Nicotine & Tobacco Research, 12,* 459–462. (p. 106)

Hughes, M. L., Geraci, L., & De Forrest, R. L. (2013). Aging 5 years in 5 minutes: The effect of taking a memory test on older adults' subjective age. *Psychological Science, 24,* 2481–2488. (p. 152)

Hulbert, A. (2005, November 20). The prodigy puzzle. *New York Times Magazine* (nytimes.com). (p. 331)

Hull, H. R., Morrow, M. L., Dinger, M. K., Han, J. L., & Fields, D. A. (2007, November 20). Characterization of body weight and composition changes during the sophomore year of college. *BMC Women's Health, 7,* Article 21. Retrieved from http://www.biomedcentral.com/1472-6874/7/21 (p. 93)

Hull, J. G., & Bond, C. F., Jr. (1986). Social and behavioral consequences of alcohol consumption and expectancy: A meta-analysis. *Psychological Bulletin, 99,* 347–360. (p. 104)

Hull, J. M. (1990). *Touching the rock: An experience of blindness.* New York: Vintage Books. (p. 280)

Hull, S. J., Hennessy, M., Bleakley, A., Fishbein, M., & Jordan, A. (2011). Identifying the causal pathways from religiosity to delayed adolescent sexual behavior. *Journal of Sex Research, 48,* 543–553. (p. 178)

Hülsheger, U. R., Anderson, N., & Salgado, J. F. (2009). Team-level predictors of innovation at work: A comprehensive meta-analysis spanning three decades of research. *Journal of Applied Psychology, 94,* 1128–1145. (p. 307)

Human Connectome Project. (2013). The Human Connectome Project (humanconnectome.org). (p. 53)

Hummer, R. A., Rogers, R. G., Nam, C. B., & Ellison, C. G. (1999). Religious involvement and U.S. adult mortality. *Demography, 36,* 273–285. (p. 405)

Humphrey, S. E., Nahrgang, J. D., & Morgeson, F. P. (2007). Integrating motivational, social, and contextual work design features: A meta-analytic summary and theoretical extension of the work design literature. *Journal of Applied Psychology, 92,* 1332–1356. (p. 396)

Humphreys, L. G., & Davey, T. C. (1988). Continuity in intellectual growth from 12 months to 9 years. *Intelligence, 12,* 183–197. (p. 332)

Hunsberger, J. G., Newton, S. S., Bennett, A. H., Duman, C. H., Russell, D. S., Salton, S. R., & Duman, R. S. (2007). Antidepressant actions of the exercise-regulated gene VGF. *Nature Medicine, 13,* 1476–1482. (p. 402)

Hunsley, J., & Bailey, J. M. (1999). The clinical utility of the Rorschach: Unfulfilled promises and an uncertain future. *Psychological Assessment, 11,* 266–277. (p. 468)

Hunsley, J., & Di Giulio, G. (2002). Dodo bird, phoenix, or urban legend? The question of psychotherapy equivalence. *Scientific Review of Mental Health Practice, 1,* 11–22. (p. 553)

Hunt, C., Slade, T., & Andrews, G. (2004). Generalized anxiety disorder and major depressive disorder comorbidity in the National Survey of Mental Health and Well-Being. *Depression and Anxiety, 20,* 23–31. (p. 507)

Hunt, J. M. (1982). Toward equalizing the developmental opportunities of infants and preschool children. *Journal of Social Issues, 38,* 163–191. (p. 338)

Hunt, L. L., Eastwick, P. W., & Finkel, E. J. (2015). Leveling the playing field: Longer acquaintance predicts reduced assortative mating on attractiveness. *Psychological Science, 26,* 1046–1053. (p. 449)

Hunt, M. (1993). *The story of psychology.* New York: Doubleday. (pp. 4, 8, 38, 242, 332)

Hunter, S., & Sundel, M. (Eds.). (1989). *Midlife myths: Issues, findings, and practice implications.* Newbury Park, CA: Sage. (p. 155)

Hurd, Y. L., Michaelides, M., Miller, M. L., & Jutras-Aswad, D. (2013). Trajectory of adolescent cannabis use on addiction vulnerability. *Neuropharmacology, 76,* 416–424. (p. 109)

Hurlburt, R. T., Heavey, C. L., & Kelsey, J. M. (2013). Toward a phenomenology of inner speaking. *Consciousness and Cognition: An International Journal, 22,* 1477–1494. (p. 319)

Hussak, L. J., & Cimpian, A. (2015). An early-emerging explanatory heuristic promotes support for the status quo. *Journal of Personality and Social Psychology, 109,* 739–752. (p. 441)

Hutchinson, R. (2006). *Calum's road.* Edinburgh, Scotland: Burlinn Limited. (p. 358)

Hutchison, K. A., Smith, J. L., & Ferris, A. (2013). Goals can be threatened to extinction using the Stroop task to clarify working memory depletion under stereotype threat. *Social and Personality Psychological Science, 4,* 74–81. (p. 344)

Hutteman, R., Nestler, S., Wagner, J., Egloff, B., & Back, M. D. (2015). Wherever I may roam: Processes of self-esteem development from adolescence to emerging adulthood in the context of international student exchange. *Journal of Personality and Social Psychology, 108,* 767–783. (p. 486)

Hvistendahl, M. (2011). China's population growing slowly, changing fast. *Science, 332,* 650–651. (p. 437)

Hyde, C. L., Nagle, M. W., Tian, C., Chen, X., Paciga, C. A., Wendland, J. R., . . . Winslow, A. R. (2016). Identification of 15 genetic loci associated with risk of major depression in individuals of European descent. *Nature Genetics, 48,* 1031–1036. (p. 518)

Hyde, J. S. (2005). The gender similarities hypothesis. *American Psychologist, 60,* 581–592. (pp. 163, 183)

Hyde, J. S. (2014). Gender similarities and differences. *Annual Review of Psychology, 65,* 373–398. (p. 162)

Hyde, J. S., & Mertz, J. E. (2009). Gender, culture, and mathematics performance. *PNAS, 106,* 8801–8807. (p. 340)

Hymowitz, K., Carroll, J. S., Wilcox, W. B., & Kaye, K. (2013). *Knot yet: The benefits and costs of delayed marriage in America.* Charlottesville: National Marriage Project, University of Virginia. (p. 135)

Iacoboni, M. (2008). *Mirroring people: The new science of how we connect with others.* New York: Farrar, Straus & Giroux. (pp. 259, 260)

Iacoboni, M. (2009). Imitation, empathy, and mirror neurons. *Annual Review of Psychology, 60,* 653–670. (pp. 259, 260)

Ibbotson, P., & Tomasello, M. (2016, November). Language in a new key. *Scientific American,* pp. 71–75. (p. 313)

Ibos, G., & Freedman, D. J. (2014). Dynamic integration of task-relevant visual features in posterior parietal cortex. *Neuron, 83,* 1468–1480. (p. 63)

Idson, L. C., & Mischel, W. (2001). The personality of familiar and significant people: The lay perceiver as a social–cognitive theorist. *Journal of Personality and Social Psychology, 80,* 585–596. (p. 416)

IJzerman, H., & Semin, G. R. (2009). The thermometer of social relations: Mapping social proximity on temperature. *Psychological Science, 20,* 1214–1220. (p. 229)

Ikizer, E. G., & Blanton, H. (2016). Media coverage of "wise" interventions can reduce concern for the disadvantaged. *Journal of Experimental Psychology: Applied, 22,* 135–147. (p. 340)

Ilardi, S. (2016, accessed May 2). *Therapeutic lifestyle change (TLC).* University of Kansas (tlc.ku.edu). (p. 559)

Ilardi, S. S. (2009). *The depression cure: The six-step program to beat depression without drugs.* Cambridge, MA: De Capo Lifelong Books. (pp. 519, 559)

Ilieva, I. P., Hook, C. J., & Farah, M. J. (2015). Prescription stimulants' effects on healthy inhibitory control, working memory, and episodic memory: A meta-analysis. *Journal of Cognitive Neuroscience, 27,* 1069–1089. (p. 105)

Imuta, K., Henry, J. D., Slaughter, V., Selcuk, B., & Ruffman, T. (2016). Theory of mind and prosocial behavior in childhood: A meta-analytic review. *Developmental Psychology, 52,* 1192–1205. (p. 128)

Inagaki, T., & Eisenberger, N. (2013). Shared neural mechanisms underlying social warmth and physical warmth. *Psychological Science, 24,* 2272–2280. (p. 352)

Inbar, Y., Cone, J., & Gilovich, T. (2010). People's intuitions about intuitive insight and intuitive choice. *Journal of Personality and Social Psychology, 99,* 232–247. (p. 305)

Inbar, Y., Pizarro, D., & Bloom, P. (2011). *Disgusting smells cause decreased liking of gay men.* Unpublished manuscript, Tillburg University. (p. 227)

Infurna, F. J., & Luthar, S. S. (2016a). The multidimensional nature of resilience to spousal loss. *Journal of Personality and Social Psychology.* http://dx.doi.org/10.1037/pspp0000095 (pp. 159, 408)

Infurna, F. J., & Luthar, S. S. (2016b). Resilience to major life stressors is not as common as thought. *Perspectives on Psychological Science, 11,* 175–194. (p. 509)

Ingalhalikar, M., Smith, A., Parker, D., Satterthwaite, T. D., Elliott, M. A., Ruparel, K., . . . Verma, R. (2013). Sex differences in the structural connectome of the human brain. *PNAS, 111,* 823–828. (p. 164)

Ingham, A. G., Levinger, G., Graves, J., & Peckham, V. (1974). The Ringelmann effect: Studies of group size and group performance. *Journal of Experimental Social Psychology, 10,* 371–384. (p. 430)

Inglehart, R. (1990). *Culture shift in advanced industrial society.* Princeton, NJ: Princeton University Press. (p. 353)

Ingraham, C. (2016, May 1). Toddlers have shot at least 23 people this year. *The Washington Post* (washingtonpost.com). (p. 302)

Inman, M. L., & Baron, R. S. (1996). Influence of prototypes on perceptions of prejudice. *Journal of Personality and Social Psychology, 70,* 727–739. (p. 299)

Innocence Project. (2015). Eyewitness misidentification. Retrieved from innocenceproject.org/understand/Eyewitness-Misidentification.php (p. 292)

Insel, T., Cuthbert, B., Garvey, M., Heinssen, R., Pine, D. S., Quinn, K., . . . Wang, P. (2010). Research Domain Criteria (RDoC): Toward a new classification framework for research on mental disorders. *American Journal of Psychiatry, 167,* 748–751. (p. 497)

Insel, T. R. (2010). Faulty circuits. *Scientific American, 302,* 44–51. (p. 512)

Insel, T. R., & Cuthbert, B. N. (2015). Brain disorders? Precisely. *Science, 348,* 499–500. (p. 495)

Insel, T. R., & Lieberman, J. A. (2013, May 13). DSM-5 and RDoC: Shared interests. National Institute of Mental Health. [Press release.] Retrieved from nimh.nih.gov/news/science-news/2013/dsm-5-and-rdoc-shared-interests.shtml (p. 497)

International Schizophrenia Consortium. (2009). Common polygenic variation contributes to risk of schizophrenia and bipolar disorder. *Nature, 460,* 748–752. (p. 526)

Inzlicht, M., & Ben-Zeev, T. (2000). A threatening intellectual environment: Why females are susceptible to experiencing problem-solving deficits in the presence of males. *Psychological Science, 11,* 365–371. (p. 344)

Inzlicht, M., & Kang, S. K. (2010). Stereotype threat spillover: How coping with threats to social identity affects aggression, eating, decision making, and attention. *Journal of Personality and Social Psychology, 99,* 467–481. (p. 344)

IPPA. (2017, January 27). Communication from International Positive Psychology Association. (p. 408)

Ipsos. (2010, April 8). *One in five (20%) global citizens believe that alien beings have come down to earth and walk amongst us in our communities disguised as humans.* Retrieved from ipsos.com/en-us/one-five-20-global-citizens-believe-alien-beings-have-come-down-earth-and-walk-amongst-us-our (p. 23)

IPU. (2018). *Women in parliament in 2017: The year in review.* Geneva: Inter-Parliamentary Union (ipu.org). (pp. 164, 169)

Ireland, M. E., & Pennebaker, J. W. (2010). Language style matching in writing: Synchrony in essays, correspondence, and poetry. *Journal of Personality and Social Psychology, 99,* 549–571. (pp. 260, 422)

Ironson, G., Solomon, G. F., Balbin, E. G., O'Cleirigh, C., George, A., Kumar, M., . . . Woods, T. E. (2002). The Ironson-Woods spiritual/religiousness index is associated with long survival, health behaviors, less distress, and low cortisol in people with HIV/AIDS. *Annals of Behavioral Medicine, 24,* 34–48. (p. 406)

Irwin, M. R., Cole, J. C., & Nicassio, P. M. (2006). Comparative meta-analysis of behavioral interventions for insomnia and their efficacy in middle-aged adults and in older adults 55+ years of age. *Health Psychology, 25,* 3–14. (p. 96)

Isaacowitz, D. M. (2012). Mood regulation in real time: Age differences in the role of looking. *Current Directions in Psychological Science, 21,* 237–242. (p. 158)

Ishida, A., Mutoh, T., Ueyama, T., Brando, H., Masubuchi, S., Nakahara, D., . . . Okamura, H. (2005). Light activates the adrenal gland: Timing of gene expression and glucocorticoid release. *Cell Metabolism, 2,* 297–307. (p. 555)

Ishiyama, S., & Brecht, M. (2017). Neural correlates of ticklishness in the rat somatosensory cortex. *Science, 354,* 757–760. (p. 51)

Ising, H. K., Smit, F., Veling, W., Rietdijk, J., Dragt, S., Klaassen, R. M. C., . . . van der Gaag, M. (2015). Cost-effectiveness of preventing first-episode psychosis in ultra-high-risk subjects: Multi-centre randomized controlled trial. *Psychological Medicine, 45,* 1435–1446. (p. 552)

Islam, S. S., & Johnson, C. (2003). Correlates of smoking behavior among Muslim Arab-American adolescents. *Ethnicity & Health, 8,* 319–337. (p. 406)

Iso, H., Simoda, S., & Matsuyama, T. (2007). Environmental change during postnatal development alters behaviour. *Behavioural Brain Research, 179,* 90–98. (p. 64)

Iso-Markku, P., Waller, K., Vuoksimaa, E., Heikkilä, K., Rinne, J., Kaprio, J., & Kujala, U. M. (2016). Midlife physical activity and cognition later in life: A prospective twin study. *Journal of Alzheimer's Disease,* Preprint, 1–15. (p. 153)

Ito, T. A., Miller, N., & Pollock, V. E. (1996). Alcohol and aggression: A meta-analysis on the moderating effects of inhibitory cues, triggering events, and self-focused attention. *Psychological Bulletin, 120,* 60–82. (p. 442)

ITU. (2016, accessed December 26). *ICT facts and figures 2016.* International Telecommunications Union (itu.int/en/ITU-D/Statistics/Documents/facts/ICTFactsFigures2016.pdf). (p. 355)

Ives-Deliperi, V. L., Solms, M., & Meintjes, E. M. (2011). The neural substrates of mindfulness: An fMRI investigation. *Social Neuroscience, 6,* 231–242. (p. 404)

Iyengar, S., & Westwood, S. J. (2015). Fear and loathing across party lines: New evidence on group polarization. *American Journal of Political Science, 59,* 690–707. (p. 18)

Izard, C. E. (1977). *Human emotions.* New York: Plenum Press. (pp. 372, 378)

Izard, C. E. (1994). Innate and universal facial expressions: Evidence from developmental and cross-cultural research. *Psychological Bulletin, 114,* 288–299. (p. 378)

Izawa, S., Matsudaira, K., Miki, K., Arisaka, M., & Tsuchiya, M. (2017). Psychosocial correlates of cortisol levels in fingernails among middle-aged workers. *The International Journal on the Biology of Stress, 20,* 386–389. (p. 391)

Jääskeläinen, E., Juola, P., Hirvonen, N., McGrath, J. J., Saha, S., Isohanni, M., . . . Miettunen, J. (2013). A systematic review and meta-analysis of recovery in schizophrenia. *Schizophrenia Bulletin, 39,* 1296–1306. (pp. 523, 524)

Jablensky, A. (1999). Schizophrenia: Epidemiology. *Current Opinion in Psychiatry, 12,* 19–28. (p. 525)

Jack, R. E., Garrod, O. G. B., Yu, H., Caldara, R., & Schyns, P. G. (2012). Facial expressions of emotion are not culturally universal. *PNAS, 109,* 7241–7244. (p. 378)

Jäckle, S., & Wenzelburger, G. (2015). Religion, religiosity, and the attitudes toward homosexuality—A multilevel analysis of 79 countries. *Journal of Homosexuality, 62,* 207–241. (p. 437)

Jackson, G. (2009). Sexual response in cardiovascular disease. *Journal of Sex Research, 46,* 233–236. (p. 173)

Jackson, J. J., Connolly, J. J., Garrison, S. M., Leveille, M. M., & Connolly, S. L. (2015). Your friends know how long you will live: A 75-year study of peer-rated personality traits. *Psychological Science, 26,* 335–340. (p. 481)

Jackson, J. J., Thoemmes, F., Jonkmann, K., Lüdtke, O., & Trautwein, U. (2012). Military training and personality trait development: Does the military make the man, or does the man make the military? *Psychological Science, 23,* 270–277. (pp. 419, 480)

Jackson, J. M., & Williams, K. D. (1988). *Social loafing: A review and theoretical analysis.* Unpublished manuscript, Fordham University. (p. 430)

Jackson, S. W. (1992). The listening healer in the history of psychological healing. *American Journal Psychiatry, 149,* 1623–1632. (p. 556)

Jacobs, B. L. (1994). Serotonin, motor activity, and depression-related disorders. *American Scientist, 82,* 456–463. (p. 402)

Jacoby, L. L., Bishara, A. J., Hessels, S., & Toth, J. P. (2005). Aging, subjective experience, and cognitive control: Dramatic false remembering by older adults. *Journal of Experimental Psychology: General, 154,* 131–148. (p. 294)

Jacoby, L. L., & Rhodes, M. G. (2006). False remembering in the aged. *Current Directions in Psychological Science, 15,* 49–53. (p. 294)

Jacques, C., & Rossion, B. (2006). The speed of individual face categorization. *Psychological Science, 17,* 485–492. (p. 189)

Jacques-Tiura, A. J., Abbey, A., Parkhill, M. R., & Zawacki, T. (2007). Why do some men misperceive women's sexual intentions more frequently than others do? An application of the confluence model. *Personality and Social Psychology Bulletin, 33,* 1467–1480. (p. 417)

Jaffe, E. (2004, October). Peace in the Middle East may be impossible: Lee D. Ross on naive realism and conflict resolution. *APS Observer,* pp. 9–11. (p. 197)

Jakubovski, E., Varigonda, A. L., Freemantle, N., Taylor, M. J., & Bloch, M. H. (2015). Systematic review and meta-analysis: Dose-response relationship of selective serotonin reuptake inhibitors in major depressive disorder. *American Journal of Psychiatry, 173,* 174–183. (p. 561)

James, K. (1986). Priming and social categorizational factors: Impact on awareness of emergency situations. *Personality and Social Psychology Bulletin, 12,* 462–467. (p. 281)

James, S. E., Herman, J. L., Rankin, S., Keisling, M., Mottet, L., & Anafi, M. (2016). *The report of the 2015 U.S. Transgender Survey.* Washington, DC: National Center for Transgender Equality. (pp. 171, 437)

James, W. (1890). *The principles of psychology* (Vol. 2). New York: Holt. (pp. 6, 221, 283, 295, 368, 380, 420, 485)

Jameson, D. (1985). Opponent-colors theory in light of physiological findings. In D. Ottoson & S. Zeki (Eds.), *Central and peripheral mechanisms of color vision* (pp. 83–102). New York: Macmillan. (p. 211)

Jamieson, J. P. (2010). The home field advantage in athletics: A meta-analysis. *Journal of Applied Social Psychology, 40,* 1819–1848. (p. 429)

Jamieson, J. P., Peters, B. J., Greenwood, E. J., & Altose, A. J. (2016). Reappraising stress arousal improves performance and reduces evaluation anxiety in classroom exam situations. *Social Psychological and Personality Science, 7,* 579–587. (p. 371)

Jamison, K. R. (1993). *Touched with fire: Manic-depressive illness and the artistic temperament.* New York: Free Press. (p. 516)

Jamison, K. R. (1995). *An unquiet mind.* New York: Knopf. (pp. 516, 535, 562)

Janis, I. L. (1982). *Groupthink: Psychological studies of policy decisions and fiascoes.* Boston: Houghton Mifflin. (p. 433)

Janis, I. L. (1986). Problems of international crisis management in the nuclear age. *Journal of Social Issues, 42,* 201–220. (p. 300)

Janoff-Bulman, R., Timko, C., & Carli, L. L. (1985). Cognitive biases in blaming the victim. *Journal of Experimental Social Psychology, 21,* 161–177. (p. 440)

Janssen, S. M. J., Rubin, D. C., & Conway, M. A. (2012). The reminiscence bump in the temporal distribution of the best football players of all time: Pelé, Cruijff or Maradona? *Quarterly Journal of Experimental Psychology, 65,* 165–178. (p. 153)

Jarbo, K., & Verstynen, T. D. (2015). Converging structural and functional connectivity of orbitofrontal, dorsolateral prefrontal, and posterior parietal cortex in the human striatum. *Journal of Neuroscience, 35,* 3865–3878. (p. 53)

Jayakar, R., King, T. Z., Morris, R., & Na, S. (2015). Hippocampal volume and auditory attention on a verbal memory task with adult survivors of pediatric brain tumor. *Neuropsychology, 29,* 303–319. (p. 56)

Jedrychowski, W., Perera, F., Jankowski, J., Butscher, M., Mroz, E., Flak, E., . . . Sowa, A. (2012). Effect of exclusive breastfeeding on the development of children's cognitive function in the Krakow prospective birth cohort study. *European Journal of Pediatrics, 171,* 151–158. (p. 25)

Jeffrey, K., Mahoney, S., Michaelson, J., & Abdallah, S. (2014). Well-being at work: A review of the literature. Retrieved from neweconomics.org/publications/entry/well-being-at-work (p. B-8)

Jenkins, J. G., & Dallenbach, K. M. (1924). Obliviscence during sleep and waking. *American Journal of Psychology, 35,* 605–612. (p. 287)

Jenkins, J. M., & Astington, J. W. (1996). Cognitive factors and family structure associated with theory of mind development in young children. *Developmental Psychology, 32,* 70–78. (p. 128)

Jenkins, S. R. (2017). Not your same old story: New rules for Thematic Apperceptive Techniques (TATs). *Journal of Personality Assessment, 99,* 238–253. (p. 467)

Jensen, J. P., & Bergin, A. E. (1988). Mental health values of professional therapists: A national interdisciplinary survey. *Professional Psychology: Research and Practice, 19,* 290–297. (p. 556)

Jensen, M. P. (2008). The neurophysiology of pain perception and hypnotic analgesia: Implications for clinical practice. *American Journal of Clinical Hypnosis, 51,* 123–147. (p. 224)

Jepson, C., Krantz, D. H., & Nisbett, R. E. (1983). Inductive reasoning: Competence or skill. *The Behavioral and Brain Sciences, 3,* 494–501. (p. A-7)

Jessberger, S., Aimone, J. B., & Gage, F. H. (2008). Neurogenesis. In J. H. Byrne (Ed.), *Learning and memory: A comprehensive reference: Vol. 4. Molecular mechanisms of memory* (pp. 839–858). Oxford: Elsevier. (p. 64)

Jha, P., Ramasundarahettige, C., Landsman, V., Rostron, B., Thun, M. D., Anderson, R. N., . . . Peto, R. (2013). 21st-century hazards of smoking and benefits of cessation in the United States. *New England Journal of Medicine, 368,* 341–350. (p. 105)

Jiang, H., White, M. P., Greicius, M. D., Waelde, L. C., & Spiegel, D. (2016). Brain activity and functional connectivity associated with hypnosis. *Cerebral Cortex.* doi:10.1093/cercor/bhw220 (p. 224)

Jiang, Y., Costello, P., Fang, F., Huang, M., & He, S. (2006). A gender- and sexual orientation-dependent spatial attentional effect of invisible things. *PNAS, 103,* 17048–17052. (p. 192)

Job, V., Dweck, C. S., & Walton, G. M. (2010). Ego depletion—Is it all in your head?: Implicit theories about willpower affect self-regulation. *Psychological Science, 21,* 1686–1693. (pp. 145, 397)

Jobe, T. H., & Harrow, M. (2010). Schizophrenia course, long-term outcome, recovery, and prognosis. *Current Directions in Psychological Science, 19,* 220–225. (p. 523)

Joel, D., Berman, Z., Tavor, I., Wexler, N., Gaber, O., Stein, Y., . . . Assaf, Y. (2015, December). Sex beyond the genitalia: The human brain mosaic. *PNAS, 112,* 15468–15473. (p. 164)

Joel, S., Eastwick, P. W., & Finkel, E. J. (2017). Is romantic desire predictable? Machine learning applied to initial romantic attraction. *Psychological Science, 28,* 1478–1489. (p. 355)

Johnson, D. F. (1997, Winter). Margaret Floy Washburn. *Psychology of Women Newsletter,* pp. 17, 22. (p. 7)

Johnson, D. L., Wiebe, J. S., Gold, S. M., Andreasen, N. C., Hichwa, R. D., Watkins, G. L., & Ponto, L. L. B. (1999). Cerebral blood flow and personality: A positron emission tomography study. *American Journal of Psychiatry, 156,* 252–257. (p. 476)

Johnson, D. P., Rhee, S. H., Friedman, N. P., Corley, R. P., Munn-Chernoff, M., Hewitt, J. K., & Whisman, M. A. (2016). A twin study examining rumination as a transdiagnostic correlate of psychopathology. *Clinical Psychological Science, 4,* 971–987. (p. 520)

Johnson, E. J., & Goldstein, D. (2003). Do defaults save lives? *Science, 302,* 1338–1339. (p. 305)

Johnson, J. A. (2007, June 26). Not so situational. Commentary on the SPSP listserv (spsp-discuss@stolaf.edu). (p. 428)

Johnson, J. G., Cohen, P., Kotler, L., Kasen, S., & Brook, J. S. (2002). Psychiatric disorders associated with risk for the development of eating disorders during adolescence and early adulthood. *Journal of Consulting and Clinical Psychology, 70,* 1119–1128. (p. 532)

Johnson, J. S., & Newport, E. L. (1991). Critical period affects on universal properties of language: The status of subjacency in the acquisition of a second language. *Cognition, 39,* 215–258. (pp. 315, 316)

Johnson, K. (2008, January 29). For many of USA's inmates, crime runs in the family. *USA Today,* pp. 1A, 2A. (p. 163)

Johnson, M. D., & Chen, J. (2015). Blame it on the alcohol: The influence of alcohol consumption during adolescence, the transition to adulthood, and young adulthood on one-time sexual hookups. *Journal of Sex Research, 52,* 570–579. (pp. 103, 177)

Johnson, M. H. (1992). Imprinting and the development of face recognition: From chick to man. *Current Directions in Psychological Science, 1,* 52–55. (p. 134)

Johnson, M. H., & Morton, J. (1991). *Biology and cognitive development: The case of face recognition.* Oxford: Blackwell. (p. 121)

Johnson, R. (2017, August 12). The mystery of S., the man with an impossible memory. *The New Yorker* (newyorker.com). (p. 289)

Johnson, W. (2010). Understanding the genetics of intelligence: Can height help? Can corn oil? *Current Directions in Psychological Science, 19,* 177–182. (p. 337)

Johnson, W., Carothers, A., & Deary, I. J. (2008). Sex differences in variability in general intelligence: A new look at the old question. *Perspectives on Psychological Science, 3,* 518–531. (p. 325)

Johnson, W., Gow, A. J., Corley, J., Starr, J. M., & Deary, I. J. (2010). Location in cognitive and residential space at age 70 reflects a lifelong trait over parental and environmental circumstances: The Lothian Birth Cohort 1936. *Intelligence, 38,* 403–411. (p. 333)

Johnston, L. D., O'Malley, P. M., Bachman, J. G., & Schulenberg, J. E. (2007, May). *Monitoring the Future national results on adolescent drug use: Overview of key findings, 2006.* Bethesda, MD: National Institute on Drug Abuse. (p. 112)

Johnston, L. D., O'Malley, P. M., Miech, R. A., Bachman, J. G., & Schulenberg, J. E. (2018). Monitoring the Future national results on adolescent drug use: Overview of key findings, 2017. Ann Arbor, MI: Institute for Social Research, the University of Michigan. (pp. 106, 107, 110)

Joiner, T. E., Jr. (2006). *Why people die by suicide.* Cambridge, MA: Harvard University Press. (p. 501)

Joiner, T. E., Jr. (2010). *Myths about suicide.* Cambridge, MA: Harvard University Press. (p. 501)

Jokela, M., Elovainio, M., Archana, S.-M., & Kivimäki, M. (2009). IQ, socioeconomic status, and early death: The U.S. National Longitudinal Survey of Youth. *Psychosomatic Medicine, 71,* 322–328. (p. 396)

Jolly, A. (2007). The social origin of mind. *Science, 317,* 1326. (p. 310)

Jones, A. C., & Gosling, S. D. (2005). Temperament and personality in dogs (*Canis familiaris*): A review and evaluation of past research. *Applied Animal Behaviour Science, 95,* 1–53. (p. 477)

Jones, B., Reedy, E. J., & Weinberg, B. A. (2014, January). *Age and scientific genius.* NBER Working Paper Series. Retrieved from nber.org/papers/w19866 (p. 334)

Jones, E. (1957). *Sigmund Freud: Life and Work,* Vol. 3, Pt. 1., Ch. 4. New York: Basic Books. (p. 466)

Jones, J. M. (2012, June 21). Atheists, Muslims see most bias as presidential candidates. Retrieved from gallup.com/poll/155285/atheistsmuslims-bias-presidential-candidates.aspx (p. 437)

Jones, J. M. (2016, November 21). Record-high 77% of Americans perceive nation as divided. Gallup Poll (gallup.com). (p. 431)

Jones, M. C. (1924). A laboratory study of fear: The case of Peter. *Journal of Genetic Psychology, 31,* 308–315. (p. 541)

Jones, S. S. (2007). Imitation in infancy: The development of mimicry. *Psychological Science, 18,* 593–599. (p. 260)

Jones, W. H., Carpenter, B. N., & Quintana, D. (1985). Personality and interpersonal predictors of loneliness in two cultures. *Journal of Personality and Social Psychology, 48,* 1503–1511. (p. 10)

Jordan, A. H., Monin, B., Dweck, C. S., Lovett, B. J., John, O. P., & Gross, J. J. (2011). Misery has more company than people think: Underestimating the prevalence of others' negative emotions. *Personality and Social Psychology Bulletin, 37,* 120–135. (p. 514)

Jordan, G., Deeb, S. S., Bosten, J. M., & Mollon, J. D. (2010). The dimensionality of color vision in carriers of anomalous trichromacy. *Journal of Vision, 10,* ArtID: 12. (p. 204)

Jorm, A. F., Reavley, N. J., & Ross, A. M. (2012). Belief in the dangerousness of people with mental disorders: A review. *Australian and New Zealand Journal of Psychiatry, 46,* 1029–1045. (p. 502)

Jose, A., O'Leary, D., & Moyer, A. (2010). Does premarital cohabitation predict subsequent marital stability and marital quality? A meta-analysis. *Journal of Marriage and Family, 72,* 105–116. (p. 156)

Joseph, J. (2001). Separated twins and the genetics of personality differences: A critique. *American Journal of Psychology, 114,* 1–30. (p. 72)

Joshi, S. H., Espinoza, R. T., Pirnia, T., Shi, J., Wang, Y., Ayers, B., . . . Narr, K. L. (2016). Structural plasticity of the hippocampus and amygdala induced by electroconvulsive therapy in major depression. *Biological Psychiatry, 79,* 282–292. (p. 563)

Jost, J. T., Kay, A. C., & Thorisdottir, H. (Eds.). (2009). *Social and psychological bases of ideology and system justification.* New York: Oxford University Press. (p. 441)

Jovanovic, T., Blanding, N. Q., Norrholm, S. D., Duncan, E., Bradley, B., & Ressler, K. J. (2009). Childhood abuse is associated with increased startle reactivity in adulthood. *Depression and Anxiety, 26,* 1018–1026. (p. 137)

Judge, T. A., Thoresen, C. J., Bono, J. E., & Patton, G. K. (2001). The job satisfaction/job performance relationship: A qualitative and quantitative review. *Psychological Bulletin, 127,* 376–407. (p. B-8)

Jung, R. E., & Haier, R. J. (2013). Creativity and intelligence: Brain networks that link and differentiate the expression of genius. In O. Vartanian, A. S. Bristol, & J. C. Kaufman (Eds.), *Neuroscience of creativity.* Cambridge, MA: MIT Press. (p. 306)

Jung-Beeman, M., Bowden, E. M., Haberman, J., Frymiare, J. L., Arambel-Liu, S., Greenblatt, R., . . . Kounios, J. (2004). Neural activity when people solve verbal problems with insight. *PLoS Biology, 2,* e111. (p. 299)

Just, M. A., Keller, T. A., & Cynkar, J. (2008). A decrease in brain activation associated with driving when listening to someone speak. *Brain Research, 1205,* 70–80. (p. 82)

Kabadayi, C., & Osvath, M. (2017). Ravens parallel great apes in flexible planning for tool-use and bartering. *Science, 357,* 202–203. (p. 309)

Kabat-Zinn, J. (2001). Mindfulness-based interventions in context: Past, present, and future. *Clinical Psychology: Science and Practice, 10,* 144–156. (p. 404)

Kadohisa, M. (2013). Effects of odor on emotion, with implications. *Frontiers in Systems Neuroscience, 7,* 6. (p. 227)

Kagan, J. (1976). Emergent themes in human development. *American Scientist, 64,* 186–196. (p. 136)

Kagan, J. (1984). *The nature of the child.* New York: Basic Books. (p. 133)

Kagan, J. (1995). On attachment. *Harvard Review of Psychiatry, 3,* 104–106. (p. 134)

Kagan, J. (2010). *The temperamental thread: How genes, culture, time, and luck make us who we are.* Washington, DC: Dana Press. (p. 476)

Kagan, J., & Snidman, N. (2004). *The long shadow of temperament.* Cambridge, MA: Belknap Press. (p. 135)

Kahan, D. M. (2015). What is the "science of science communication"? *Journal of Science Communication, 14,* 1–10. (p. 18)

Kahneman, D. (1985, June). Quoted by K. McKean, Decisions, decisions. *Discover,* pp. 22–31. (p. A-6)

Kahneman, D. (1999). Assessments of objective happiness: A bottom-up approach. In D. Kahneman, E. Diener, & N. Schwartz (Eds.), *Understanding well-being: Scientific perspectives on enjoyment and suffering.* New York: Russell Sage Foundation. (p. 223)

Kahneman, D. (2005a, February 10). Are you happy now? *Gallup Management Journal* interview (gmj.gallup.com). (p. 409)

Kahneman, D. (2005b, January 13). What were they thinking? Q&A with Daniel Kahneman. *Gallup Management Journal* (gmj.gallup.com). (p. 301)

Kahneman, D. (2011). *Thinking, fast and slow.* New York: Farrar, Straus and Giroux. (p. 84)

Kahneman, D. (2015, July 18). Quoted by D. Shariatmadari, "Daniel Kahneman: 'What would I eliminate if I had a magic wand? Overconfidence.'" *The Guardian* (theguardian.com). (p. 303)

Kahneman, D., Fredrickson, B. L., Schreiber, C. A., & Redelmeier, D. A. (1993). When more pain is preferred to less: Adding a better end. *Psychological Science, 4,* 401–405. (p. 223)

Kahneman, D., Krueger, A. B., Schkade, D. A., Schwarz, N., & Stone, A. A. (2004). A survey method for characterizing daily life experience: The day reconstruction method. *Science, 306,* 1776–1780. (p. 408)

Kail, R. (1991). Developmental change in speed of processing during childhood and adolescence. *Psychological Bulletin, 109,* 490–501. (p. 152)

Kail, R., & Hall, L. K. (2001). Distinguishing short-term memory from working memory. *Memory & Cognition, 29,* 1–9. (p. 269)

Kaiser, R. H., Andrews-Hanna, J. R., Wager, T. D., & Pizzagalli, D. A. (2015). Large-scale network dysfunction in major depressive disorder: a meta-analysis of resting-state functional connectivity. *JAMA Psychiatry, 72,* 603–611. (p. 519)

Kaiser Family Foundation. (2010, January). *Generation M2: Media in the lives of 8- to 18-year-olds* (by V. J. Rideout, U. G. Foeher, & D. F. Roberts). Menlo Park, CA: Henry J. Kaiser Family Foundation. (p. 356)

Kakinami, L., Barnett, T. A., Séguin, L., & Paradis, G. (2015). Parenting style and obesity risk in children. *Preventive Medicine, 75,* 18–22. (pp. 138, 139)

Kállay, É. (2015). Physical and psychological benefits of written emotional expression: Review of meta-analyses and recommendations. *European Psychologist, 20,* 242–251. (p. 401)

Kamatali, J.-M. (2014, April 4). Following orders in Rwanda. *The New York Times* (nytimes. com). (p. 427)

Kambeitz, J., Kambelitz-Hankovic, L., Cabral, C., Dwyer, D. B., Calhoun, V. C., van den Heuvel, M. P., . . . Malchow, B. (2016). Aberrant functional whole-brain network architecture in patients with schizophrenia: A meta-analysis. *Schizophrenia Bulletin, 42,* Suppl. no. 1, S13–S21. (p. 525)

Kamel, N. S., & Gammack, J. K. (2006). Insomnia in the elderly: Cause, approach, and treatment. *American Journal of Medicine, 119,* 463–469. (p. 89)

Kamenica, E., Naclerio, R., & Malani, A. (2013). Advertisements impact the physiological efficacy of a branded drug. *PNAS, 110,* 12931–12935. (p. 560)

Kamil, A. C., & Cheng, K. (2001). Way-finding and landmarks: The multiple-bearings hypothesis. *Journal of Experimental Biology, 204,* 103–113. (p. 276)

Kaminski, J., Cali, J., & Fischer, J. (2004). Word learning in a domestic dog: Evidence for "fast mapping." *Science, 304,* 1682–1683. (p. 318)

Kampmann, I. L., Emmelkamp, P. M. G., & Morina, N. (2016). Meta-analysis of technology-assisted interventions for social anxiety disorder. *Journal of Anxiety Disorders, 42,* 71–84. (p. 546)

Kandel, D. B., & Raveis, V. H. (1989). Cessation of illicit drug use in young adulthood. *Archives of General Psychiatry, 46,* 109–116. (p. 113)

Kandel, E. (2008, October/November). Quoted in S. Avan, Speaking of memory. *Scientific American Mind,* pp. 16–17. (p. 84)

Kandel, E. (2012, March 5). Interview by Claudia Dreifus: A quest to understand how memory works. *The New York Times* (nytimes.com). (pp. 278, 469)

Kandel, E. (2013, September 6). The new science of mind. *The New York Times* (nytimes. com). (p. 558)

Kandel, E. R., & Schwartz, J. H. (1982). Molecular biology of learning: Modulation of transmitter release. *Science, 218,* 433–443. (p. 278)

Kandler, C., Bleidorn, W., Riemann, R., Angleitner, A., & Spinath, F. M. (2011). The genetic links between the Big Five personality traits and general interest domains. *Personality and Social Psychology Bulletin, 37,* 1633–1643. (p. 71)

Kandler, C., Bleidorn, W., Riemann, R., Angleitner, A., & Spinath, F. M. (2012). Life events as environmental states and genetic traits and the role of personality: A longitudinal twin study. *Behavior Genetics, 42,* 57–72. (p. 74)

Kandler, C., & Riemann, R. (2013). Genetic and environmental sources of individual religiousness: The roles of individual personality traits and perceived environmental religiousness. *Behavior Genetics, 43,* 297–313. (p. 72)

Kandler, C., Riemann, R., & Angleitner, A. (2013). Patterns and sources of continuity and change of energetic and temporal aspects of temperament in adulthood: A longitudinal twin study of self- and peer reports. *Developmental Psychology, 49,* 1739–1753. (p. 135)

Kane, G. D. (2010). Revisiting gay men's body image issues: Exposing the fault lines. *Review of General Psychology, 14,* 311–317. (p. 532)

Kane, J. M., & Mertz, J. E. (2012). Debunking myths about gender and mathematics performance. *Notices of the American Mathematical Society, 59,* 10–21. (p. 341)

Kanwar, A., Malik, S., Prokop, L. J., Sim, L. A., Feldstein, D., Wang, Z., & Murad, M. H. (2013). The association between anxiety disorders and suicidal behaviors: A systematic review and meta-analysis. *Depression and Anxiety, 30,* 917–929. (p. 500)

Kaplan, B. J., Rucklidge, J. J., Romijn, A., & McLeod, K. (2015). The emerging field of nutritional mental health: Inflammation, the microbiome, oxidative stress, and mitochondrial function. *Clinical Psychological Science, 3,* 964–980. (p. 519)

Kaplan, H. I., & Saddock, B. J. (Eds.). (1989). *Comprehensive textbook of psychiatry, V.* Baltimore, MD: Williams and Wilkins. (p. 560)

Kaprio, J., Koskenvuo, M., & Rita, H. (1987). Mortality after bereavement: A prospective study of 95,647 widowed persons. *American Journal of Public Health, 77,* 283–287. (p. 385)

Karacan, I., Aslan, C., & Hirshkowitz, M. (1983). Erectile mechanisms in man. *Science, 220,* 1080–1082. (p. 89)

Karacan, I., Goodenough, D. R., Shapiro, A., & Starker, S. (1966). Erection cycle during sleep in relation to dream anxiety. *Archives of General Psychiatry, 15,* 183–189. (p. 89)

Karasik, L. B., Adolph, K. E., Tamis-LeMonda, C. S., & Bornstein, M. H. (2010). WEIRD walking: Cross-cultural research on motor development. *Behavioral and Brain Sciences, 33,* 95–96. (p. 124)

Karau, S. J., & Williams, K. D. (1993). Social loafing: A meta-analytic review and theoretical integration. *Journal of Personality and Social Psychology, 65,* 681–706. (p. 430)

Karazsia, B. T., Murnen, S. K., & Tylka, T. L. (2017). Is body dissatisfaction changing across time? A cross-temporal meta-analysis. *Psychological Bulletin, 143,* 293–320. (p. 532)

Kark, J. D., Shemi, G., Friedlander, Y., Martin, O., Manor, O., & Blondheim, S. H. (1996). Does religious observance promote health? Mortality in secular vs. religious kibbutzim in Israel. *American Journal of Public Health, 86,* 341–346. (p. 405)

Karlén, J., Ludvigsson, J., Hedmark, M., Faresjö, Å., Theodorsson, E., & Faresjö, T. (2015). Early psychosocial exposures, hair cortisol levels, and disease risk. *Pediatrics, 135,* e1450–e1457. (p. 391)

Karlsgodt, K. H., Sun, D., & Cannon, T. D. (2010). Structural and functional brain abnormalities in schizophrenia. *Current Directions in Psychological Science, 19,* 226–231. (p. 525)

Karni, A., & Sagi, D. (1994). Dependence on REM sleep for overnight improvement of perceptual skills. *Science, 265,* 679–682. (p. 97)

Karpicke, J. D. (2012). Retrieval-based learning: Active retrieval promotes meaningful learning. *Current Directions in Psychological Science, 21,* 157–163. (p. 34)

Karremans, J. C., Frankenhis, W. E., & Arons, S. (2010). Blind men prefer a low waist-to-hip ratio. *Evolution and Human Behavior, 31,* 182–186. (pp. 184, 449)

Kasen, S., Chen, H., Sneed, J., Crawford, T., & Cohen, P. (2006). Social role and birth cohort influences on gender-linked personality traits in women: A 20-year longitudinal analysis. *Journal of Personality and Social Psychology, 91,* 944–958. (p. 165)

Kassin, S. M. (2017). The killing of Kitty Genovese: What else does this case tell us? *Perspectives on Psychological Science, 12,* 374–381. (p. 454)

Katz-Wise, S. L., & Hyde, J. S. (2012). Victimization experiences of lesbian, gay, and bisexual individuals: A meta-analysis. *Journal of Sex Research, 49,* 142–167. (p. 437)

Katz-Wise, S. L., Priess, H. A., & Hyde, J. S. (2010). Gender-role attitudes and behavior across the transition to parenthood. *Developmental Psychology, 46,* 18–28. (p. 165)

Kaufman, J. C., & Baer, J. (2002). I bask in dreams of suicide: Mental illness, poetry, and women. *Review of General Psychology, 6,* 271–286. (p. 516)

Kaufman, J., & Zigler, E. (1987). Do abused children become abusive parents? *American Journal of Orthopsychiatry, 57,* 186–192. (p. 137)

Kaufman, L., & Kaufman, J. H. (2000). Explaining the moon illusion. *PNAS, 97,* 500–505. (p. 212)

Kaufmann, R. K., Mann, M. L., Gopal, S., Liederman, J. A., Howe, P. D., Pretis, F., . . . Gilmore, M. (2017). Spatial heterogeneity of climate change as an experiential basis for skepticism. *PNAS, 114*(1), 67–71. (p. 303)

Kaunitz, L. N., Rowe, E. G., & Tsuchiya, N. (2016). Large capacity of conscious access for incidental memories in natural scenes. *Psychological Science, 27,* 1266–1277. (p. 266)

Kawakami, K., Dunn, E., Karmali, F., & Dovidio, J. F. (2009). Mispredicting affective and behavioral responses to racism. *Science, 323,* 276–278. (p. 436)

Kawamichi, H., Yoshihara, K., Sugawara, S. K., Matsunaga, M., Makita, K., Hamano, Y. H., . . . Sadato, N. (2015). Helping behavior induced by empathic concern attenuates anterior cingulate activation in response to others' distress. *Social Neuroscience, 11,* 109–122. doi:10.1080/17470919.2015.1049709 (p. 454)

Kay, A. C., Baucher, D., Peach, J. M., Laurin, K., Friesen, J., Zanna, M. P., & Spencer, S. J. (2009). Inequality, discrimination, and the power of the status quo: Direct evidence for a motivation to see the way things are as the way they should be. *Journal of Personality and Social Psychology, 97,* 421–434. (p. 441)

Kayser, C. (2007, April/May). Listening with your eyes. *Scientific American Mind,* pp. 24–29. (p. 228)

Kazantzis, N., & Dattilio, F. M. (2010). Definitions of homework, types of homework and ratings of the importance of homework among psychologists with cognitive behavior therapy and psychoanalytic theoretical orientations. *Journal of Clinical Psychology, 66,* 758–773. (p. 546)

Kazantzis, N., Whittington, C., & Dattilio, F. M. (2010). Meta-analysis of homework effects in cognitive and behavioral therapy: A replication and extension. *Clinical Psychology: Science and Practice, 17,* 144–156. (p. 546)

Kazdin, A. E. (2015). Editor's introduction to the special series: Targeted training of cognitive processes for behavioral and emotional disorders. *Clinical Psychological Science, 3,* 38. (p. 544)

Kean, S. (2016, September). The audacious plan to save this man's life by transplanting his head. *The Atlantic* (theatlantic.com). (p. 37)

Kearns, M. C., Ressler, K. J., Zatzick, D., & Rothbaum, B. O. (2012). Early interventions for PTSD: A review. *Depression and Anxiety, 29,* 833–842. (p. 279)

Keesey, R. E., & Corbett, S. W. (1984). Metabolic defense of the body weight set-point. In A. J. Stunkard & E. Stellar (Eds.), *Eating and its disorders.* New York: Raven Press. (p. 363)

Keiser, H. N., Sackett, P. R., Kuncel, N. R., & Brothen, T. (2016). Why women perform better in college than admission scores would predict: Exploring the roles of conscientiousness and course-taking patterns. *Journal of Applied Psychology, 101,* 569–581. (pp. 168, 343)

Keith, S. W., Redden, D. T., Katzmarzyk, P. T., Boggiano, M. M., Hanlon, E. C., Benca, R. M., . . . Allison, D. B. (2006). Putative contributors to the secular increase in obesity: Exploring the roads less traveled. *International Journal of Obesity, 30,* 1585–1594. (p. 365)

Kell, H. J., Lubinski, D., & Benbow, C. P. (2013). Who rises to the top? Early indicators. *Psychological Science, 24,* 648–659. (p. 331)

Keller, C., Hartmann, C., & Siegrist, M. (2016). The association between dispositional self-control and longitudinal changes in eating behaviors, diet quality, and BMI. *Psychology & Health, 31,* 1311–1327. (p. 398)

Kellerman, J., Lewis, J., & Laird, J. D. (1989). Looking and loving: The effects of mutual gaze on feelings of romantic love. *Journal of Research in Personality, 23,* 145–161. (p. 376)

Kelling, S. T., & Halpern, B. P. (1983). Taste flashes: Reaction times, intensity, and quality. *Science, 219,* 412–414. (p. 225)

Kellner, C. H., Knapp, R. G., Petrides, G., Rummans, T. A., Husain, M. M., Rasmussen, K., . . . Fink, M. (2006). Continuation electroconvulsive therapy vs. pharmacotherapy for relapse prevention in major depression: A multisite study from the Consortium for Research in Electroconvulsive Therapy (CORE). *Archives of General Psychiatry, 63,* 1337–1344. (p. 563)

Kelly, A. E. (2000). Helping construct desirable identities: A self-presentational view of psychotherapy. *Psychological Bulletin, 126,* 475–494. (p. 544)

Kelly, D. J., Quinn, P. C., Slater, A. M., Lee, K., Ge, L., & Pascalis, O. (2007). The other-race effect develops during infancy: Evidence of perceptual narrowing. *Psychological Science, 18,* 1084–1089. (p. 447)

Kelly, S. D., Özyürek, A., & Maris, E. (2010). Two sides of the same coin: Speech and gesture mutually interact to enhance comprehension. *Psychological Science, 21,* 260–267. (p. 317)

Kelly, T. A. (1990). The role of values in psychotherapy: A critical review of process and outcome effects. *Clinical Psychology Review, 10,* 171–186. (p. 556)

Kempe, R. S., & Kempe, C. C. (1978). *Child abuse.* Cambridge, MA: Harvard University Press. (p. 137)

Kendall-Tackett, K. A., Williams, L. M., & Finkelhor, D. (1993). Impact of sexual abuse on children: A review and synthesis of recent empirical studies. *Psychological Bulletin, 113,* 164–180. (p. 293)

Kendler, K. S. (1996). Parenting: A genetic-epidemiologic perspective. *The American Journal of Psychiatry, 153,* 11–20. (p. 139)

Kendler, K. S. (1998, January). Major depression and the environment: A psychiatric genetic perspective. *Pharmacopsychiatry, 31*(1), 5–9. (p. 517)

Kendler, K. S., Maes, H. H., Lönn, S. L., Morris, N. A., Lichtenstein, P., Sundquist, J., & Sundquist, K. (2015a). A Swedish national twin study of criminal behavior and its violent, white-collar and property subtypes. *Psychological Medicine, 45,* 2253–2262. (p. 337)

Kendler, K. S., Myers, J., & Zisook, S. (2008). Does bereavement-related major depression differ from major depression associated with other stressful life events? *American Journal of Psychiatry, 165,* 1449–1455. (p. 517)

Kendler, K. S., Neale, M. C., Kessler, R. C., Heath, A. C., & Eaves, L. J. (1994). Parent treatment and the equal environment assumption in twin studies of psychiatric illness. *Psychological Medicine, 24,* 579–590. (p. 71)

Kendler, K. S., Neale, M. C., Thornton, L. M., Aggen, S. H., Gilman, S. E., & Kessler, R. C. (2002). Cannabis use in the last year in a U.S. national sample of twin and sibling pairs. *Psychological Medicine, 32,* 551–554. (p. 110)

Kendler, K. S., Ohlsson, H., Sundquist, J., & Sundquist, K. (2016). Alcohol use disorder and mortality across the lifespan: A longitudinal cohort and co-relative analysis. *JAMA Psychiatry, 73,* 575–581. (p. 103)

Kendler, K. S., Sundquist, K., Ohlsson, H., Palmer, K., Maes, H., Winkleby, M. A., & Sundquist, J. (2012). Genetic and familiar environmental influences on the risk for drug abuse: A Swedish adoption study. *Archives of General Psychiatry, 69,* 690–697. (p. 111)

Kendler, K. S., Turkheimer, E., Ohlsson, H., Sundquist, J., & Sundquist, K. (2015b). Family environment and the malleability of cognitive ability: A Swedish national home-reared and adopted-away cosibling control study. *PNAS, 112,* 4612–4617. (pp. 73, 530)

Kendrick, K. M., & Feng, J. (2011). Neural encoding principles in face perception revealed using non-primate models. In G. Rhodes, A. Calder, M. Johnson, & J. V. Haxby (Eds.), *The Oxford handbook of face perception.* Oxford: Oxford University Press. (p. 266)

Kennard, B. D., Emslie, G. J., Mayes, T. L., Nakonezny, P. A., Jones, J. M., Foxwell, A. A., & King, J. (2014). Sequential treatment of fluoxetine and relapse-prevention CBT to improve outcomes in pediatric depression. *American Journal of Psychiatry, 171,* 1083–1090. (p. 562)

Kennedy, M., Kreppner, J., Knights, N., Kumsta, R., Maughan, B., Golm, D., . . . Sonuga-Barke, E. J. (2016). Early severe institutional deprivation is associated with a persistent variant of adult attention-deficit/hyperactivity disorder: Clinical presentation, developmental continuities and life circumstances in the English and Romanian Adoptees study. *Journal of Child Psychology and Psychiatry, 57,* 1113–1125. (p. 137)

Kenrick, D. T., & Funder, D. C. (1988). Profiting from controversy: Lessons from the person-situation debate. *American Psychologist, 43,* 23–34. (p. 481)

Kenrick, D. T., Griskevicious, V., Neuberg, S. L., & Schaller, M. (2010). Renovating the pyramid of needs: Contemporary extensions build upon ancient foundations. *Perspectives on Psychological Science, 5,* 292–314. (p. 351)

Kenrick, D. T., & Gutierres, S. E. (1980). Contrast effects and judgments of physical attractiveness: When beauty becomes a social problem. *Journal of Personality and Social Psychology, 38,* 131–140. (p. 176)

Kenrick, D. T., Nieuweboer, S., & Buunk, A. P. (2009). Universal mechanisms and cultural diversity: Replacing the blank slate with a coloring book. In M. Schaller, A. Norenzayan, S. Heine, A. Norenzayan, T. Yamagishi, & T. Kameda (Eds.), *Evolution, culture, and the human mind* (pp. 257–271). Mahwah, NJ: Erlbaum. (pp. 123, 184)

Kensinger, E. A. (2007). Negative emotion enhances memory accuracy: Behavioral and neuroimaging evidence. *Current Directions in Psychological Science, 16,* 213–218. (p. 277)

Kenyon, P. (2016, June 29). After Brexit vote, U.K. sees a wave of hate crimes and racist abuse. National Public Radio (npr.org). (p. 439)

Keough, K. A., Zimbardo, P. G., & Boyd, J. N. (1999). Who's smoking, drinking, and using drugs? Time perspective as a predictor of substance use. *Basic and Applied Social Psychology, 2,* 149–164. (p. 463)

Keramati, M., Durand, A., Girardeau, P., Gutkin, B., & Ahmed, S. H. (2017). Cocaine addiction as a homeostatic reinforcement learning disorder. *Psychological Review, 124,* 130–153. (p. 107)

Keresztes, A., Bender, A. R., Bodammer, N. C., Lindenberger, U., Shing, Y. L., & Werkle-Bergner, M. (2017). Hippocampal maturity promotes memory distinctiveness in childhood and adolescence. *PNAS, 114,* 9212–9217. (p. 276)

Kern, M. L., Eichstaedt, J. C., Schwartz, H. A., Dziurzynski, L., Ungar, L. H., Stillwell, D. J., . . . Seligman, M. E. P. (2014). The online social self: An open vocabulary approach to personality. *Assessment, 21,* 158–169. (p. 481)

Kernis, M. H. (2003). Toward a conceptualization of optimal self-esteem. *Psychological Inquiry, 14,* 1–26. (p. 489)

Kerns, J. C., Guo, J., Fothergill, E., Howard, L., Knuth, N. D., Brychta, R., . . . Hall, K. D. (2017). Increased physical activity associated with less weight regain six years after "The Biggest Loser" competition. *Obesity, 25,* 1838–1843. (p. 366)

Kerr, N. L., & Bruun, S. E. (1983). Dispensability of member effort and group motivation losses: Free-rider effects. *Journal of Personality and Social Psychology, 44,* 78–94. (p. 430)

Kessler, M., & Albee, G. (1975). Primary prevention. *Annual Review of Psychology, 26,* 557–591. (p. 566)

Kessler, R. C., Aguilar-Gaxiola, S., Alonso, J., Chatterji, S., Lee, S., Ormel, J., . . . Wang, P. S. (2009). The global burden of mental disorders: An update from the WHO World Mental Health (WMH) Surveys. *Epidemiology and Psychiatric Services, 18,* 23–33. (pp. 503, 504)

Kessler, R. C., Birnbaum, H. G., Shahly, V., Bromet, E., Hwang, I., McLaughlin, K. A., . . . Stein, D. J. (2010). Age differences in the prevalence and co-morbidity of DSM-IV major depressive episodes: Results from the WHO World Mental Health Survey Initiative. *Depression and Anxiety, 27,* 351–364. (pp. 298, 518)

Kessler, R. C., Petukhova, M., Sampson, N. A., Zaslavsky, A. M., & Wittchen, H.-A. (2012). Twelve-month and lifetime morbid risk of anxiety and mood disorders in the United States. *International Journal of Methods in Psychiatric Research, 21,* 169–184. (p. 508)

Kessler, R. C., Soukup, J., Davis, R. B., Foster, D. F., Wilkey, S. A., Van Rompay, M. I., & Eisenberg, D. M. (2001). The use of complementary and alternative therapies to treat anxiety and depression in the United States. *American Journal of Psychiatry, 158,* 289–294. (p. 553)

Keyes, K. M., Maslowsky, J., Hamilton, A., & Schulenberg, J. (2015). The great sleep recession: Changes in sleep duration among U.S. adolescents, 1991–2012. *Pediatrics, 135,* 460–468. (p. 92)

Keynes, M. (1980, December 20/27). Handel's illnesses. *The Lancet,* pp. 1354–1355. (p. 516)

Keys, A., Brozek, J., Henschel, A., Mickelsen, O., & Taylor, H. L. (1950). *The biology of human starvation.* Minneapolis: University of Minnesota Press. (p. 360)

Khanna, S., & Greyson, B. (2014). Daily spiritual experiences before and after near-death experiences. *Psychology of Religion and Spirituality, 6,* 302–309. (p. 108)

Khanna, S., & Greyson, B. (2015). Near-death experiences and posttraumatic growth. *Journal of Nervous and Mental Disease, 203,* 749–755. (p. 108)

Khazanov, G. K., & Ruscio, A. M. (2016). Is low positive emotionality a specific risk factor for depression? A meta-analysis of longitudinal studies. *Psychological Bulletin, 142,* 991–1015. (p. 516)

Khera, M., Bhattacharya, R. K., Blick, G., Kushner, H., Nguyen, D., & Miner, M. M. (2011). Improved sexual function with testosterone replacement therapy in hypogonadal men: Real-world data from the Testim Registry in the United States (TriUS). *Journal of Sexual Medicine, 8,* 3204–3213. (p. 173)

Kiatpongsan, S., & Norton, M. I. (2014). How much (more) should CEOs make? A universal desire for more equal pay. *Perspectives on Psychological Science, 9,* 587–593. (p. 410)

Kiecolt-Glaser, J. K. (2009). Psychoneuroimmunology: Psychology's gateway to the biomedical future. *Perspectives on Psychological Science, 4,* 367–369. (p. 388)

Kiecolt-Glaser, J. K., Loving, T. J., Stowell, J. R., Malarkey, W. B., Lemeshow, S., Dickinson, S. L., & Glaser, R. (2005). Hostile marital interactions, proinflammatory cytokine production, and wound healing. *Archives of General Psychiatry, 62,* 1377–1384. (p. 389)

Kiecolt-Glaser, J. K., Page, G. G., Marucha, P. T., MacCallum, R. C., & Glaser, R. (1998). Psychological influences on surgical recovery: Perspectives from psychoneuroimmunology. *American Psychologist, 53,* 1209–1218. (p. 389)

Kiehl, K. A., & Buckholtz, J. W. (2010). Inside the mind of a psychopath. *Scientific American Mind, 21,* 22–29. (p. 531)

Kiekens, G., Claes, L., Demyttenaere, K., Auerbach, R. P., Green, J. G., Kessler, R. C., . . . Bruffaerts, R. (2016). Lifetime and 12-month nonsuicidal self-injury and academic performance in college freshmen. *Suicide and Life-Threatening Behavior, 46,* 563–576. (p. 502)

Kihlstrom, J. F. (2005). Dissociative disorders. *Annual Review of Clinical Psychology, 1,* 227–253. (p. 529)

Kihlstrom, J. F. (2006). Repression: A unified theory of a will-o'-the-wisp. *Behavioral and Brain Sciences, 29,* 523. (p. 469)

Kilgore, A. (2017, November 9). Aaron Hernandez suffered from most severe CTE ever found in a person his age. *The Washington Post* (washingtonpost.com). (p. 57)

Kille, D. R., Forest, A. L., & Wood, J. V. (2013). Tall, dark, and stable: Embodiment motivates mate selection preferences. *Psychological Science, 24,* 112–114. (p. 229)

Killingsworth, M. A., & Gilbert, D. T. (2010). A wandering mind is an unhappy mind. *Science, 330,* 932. (p. B-2)

Kilpatrick, L. A., Suyenobu, B. Y., Smith, S. R., Bueller, J. A., Goodman, T., Creswell, J. D., . . . Naliboff, B. D. (2011). Impact of mindfulness-based stress reduction training on intrinsic brain activity. *NeuroImage, 56,* 290–298. (p. 404)

Kim, B. S. K., Ng, G. F., & Ahn, A. J. (2005). Effects of client expectation for counseling success, client-counselor worldview match, and client adherence to Asian and European American cultural values on counseling process with Asian Americans. *Journal of Counseling Psychology, 52,* 67–76. (p. 556)

Kim, E. S., Hagan, K. A., Grodstein, F., DeMeo, D. L., De Vivo, I., & Kubzansky, L. D. (2017). Optimism and cause-specific mortality: A prospective cohort study. *American Journal of Epidemiology, 185,* 21–29. (p. 399)

Kim, H., & Markus, H. R. (1999). Deviance or uniqueness, harmony or conformity? A cultural analysis. *Journal of Personality and Social Psychology, 77,* 785–800. (p. 490)

Kim, J., Suh, W., Kim, S., & Gopalan, H. (2012). Coping strategies to manage acculturative stress: Meaningful activity participation, social support, and positive emotion among Korean immigrant adolescents in the USA. *International Journal of Qualitative Studies on Health and Well-Being, 7,* 1–10. (p. 385)

Kim, J. L., & Ward, L. M. (2012). Striving for pleasure without fear: Short-term effects of reading a women's magazine on women's sexual attitudes. *Psychology of Women Quarterly, 36,* 326–336. (p. 177)

Kim, M., Kim, C.-H., Jung, H. H., Kim, S. J., & Chang, J. W. (2018). Treatment of major depressive disorder via magnetic resonance-guided focused ultrasound surgery. *Biological Psychiatry, 83,* e17-e18. (p. 565)

Kim, S. H., Hwang, J. H., Park, H. S., & Kim, S. E. (2008). Resting brain metabolic correlates of neuroticism and extraversion in young men. *NeuroReport, 19,* 883–886. (p. 476)

Kim, S. H., Vincent, L. C., & Goncalo, J. A. (2013). Outside advantage: Can social rejection fuel creative thought? *Journal of Experimental Psychology: General, 142,* 605–611. (p. 307)

Kim, S. Y., Liu, L., & Cao, F. (2017). How does first language (L1) influence second language (L2) reading in the brain? Evidence from Korean-English and Chinese-English bilinguals. *Brain and Language, 171,* 1–13. (p. 317)

Kim, Y. S., Leventhal, B. L., Koh, Y., Fombonne, E., Laska, E., Lim, E., . . . Grinker, R. R. (2011). Prevalence of autism spectrum disorders in a total population sample. *American Journal of Psychiatry, 168,* 904–912. (p. 131)

Kimata, H. (2001). Effect of humor on allergen-induced wheal reactions. *Journal of the American Medical Association, 285,* 737. (p. 399)

Kimble, G. A. (1956). *Principles of general psychology.* New York: Ronald Press. (p. 254)

Kimble, G. A. (1981). *Biological and cognitive constraints on learning.* Washington, DC: American Psychological Association. (p. 254)

Kim-Yeary, K. H., Ounpraseuth, S., Moore, P., Bursac, Z., & Greene, P. (2012). Religion, social capital, and health. *Review of Religious Research, 54,* 331–347. (p. 406)

King, D. W., King, L. A., Park, C. L., Lee, L. O., Pless Kaiser, A., Spiro, A., . . . Keane, T. M. (2015). Positive adjustment among American repatriated prisoners of the Vietnam War: Modeling the long-term effects of captivity. *Clinical Psychological Science, 3,* 861–876. (p. 509)

King, L. A., Heintzelman, S. J., & Ward, S. J. (2016). Beyond the search for meaning: A contemporary science of the experience of meaning in life. *Current Directions in Psychological Science, 25,* 211–216. (p. 350)

King, S., St-Hilaire, A., & Heidkamp, D. (2010). Prenatal factors in schizophrenia. *Current Directions in Psychological Science, 19,* 209–213. (p. 525)

Kinnier, R. T., & Metha, A. T. (1989). Regrets and priorities at three stages of life. *Counseling and Values, 33,* 182–193. (p. 158)

Kinsella, E. L., Ritchie, T. D., & Igou, E. R. (2015). Zeroing in on heroes: A prototype analysis of hero features. *Journal of Personality and Social Psychology, 108,* 114–127. (p. 452)

Kinsey, A. C., Pomeroy, W. B., & Martin, C. E. (1948). *Sexual behavior in the human male.* Bloomington: Indiana University Press. (p. 172)

Kinsey, A. C., Pomeroy, W. B., Martin, C. E., & Gebhard, P. H. (1953). *Sexual behavior in the human female.* Philadelphia: W. B. Saunders. (p. 172)

Kirby, D. (2002). Effective approaches to reducing adolescent unprotected sex, pregnancy, and childbearing. *Journal of Sex Research, 39,* 51–57. (p. 178)

Kirby, T. (2015, September). Ketamine for depression: The highs and lows. *The Lancet Psychiatry, 2,* 783–784. (p. 562)

Kirkpatrick, B., Fenton, W. S., Carpenter, W. T., Jr., & Marder, S. R. (2006). The NIMH-MATRICS consensus statement on negative symptoms. *Schizophrenia Bulletin, 32,* 214–219. (p. 524)

Kirkpatrick, L. (1999). Attachment and religious representations and behavior. In J. Cassidy & P. R. Shaver (Eds.), *Handbook of attachment.* New York: Guilford. (p. 136)

Kirsch, I. (2010). *The emperor's new drugs: Exploding the antidepressant myth.* New York: Basic Books. (p. 27)

Kirsch, I. (2016). The emperor's new drugs: Medication and placebo in the treatment of depression. In *Behind and beyond the brain.* Symposium conducted by the Bial Foundation, March 30–April 2 (www.bial.com/imagem/Programa_e%20_Resumos-Program_and_Abstracts.pdf). (p. 562)

Kirsch, I., Deacon, B. J., Huedo-Medina, T. B., Scoboria, A., Moore, T. J., & Johnson, B. T. (2008). Initial severity and antidepressant benefits: A meta-analysis of data submitted to the Food and Drug Administration. *Public Library of Science Medicine, 5,* e45. (p. 562)

Kirsch, I., Kong, J., Sadler, P., Spaeth, R., Cook, A., Kaptchuk, T. J., & Gollub, R. (2014). Expectancy and conditioning in placebo analgesia: Separate or connected processes? *Psychology of Consciousness; Theory, Research, and Practice, 1,* 51–59. (p. 562)

Kirsch, I., & Sapirstein, G. (1998). Listening to Prozac but hearing placebo: A meta-analysis of antidepressant medication. *Prevention and Treatment, 1,* posted June 26 at (journals.apa.org/prevention/volume1). (p. 562)

Kirsch, I., Wampold, B., & Kelley, J. M. (2016). Controlling for the placebo effect in psychotherapy: Noble quest or tilting at windmills? *Psychology of Consciousness: Theory, Research, and Practice, 3,* 121–131. (p. 562)

Kisley, M. A., Wood, S., & Burrows, C. L. (2007). Looking at the sunny side of life: Age-related change in an event-related potential measure of the negativity bias. *Psychological Science, 18,* 838–843. (p. 158)

Kitahara, C. M., Flint, A. J., de Gonzalez, A. B., Bernstein, L., Brotzman, M., MacInnis, R. J., . . . Hartge, P. (2014, July 8). Association between class III obesity (BMI of 40–59 kg/m2) and mortality: A pooled analysis of 20 prospective studies. *PLoS Medicine.* doi:10.1371/journal.pmed.1001673 (p. 365)

Kitaoka, A. (2016, September 11). Facebook post. Retrieved from facebook.com/ photo.php?fbid=10207806660899237&set=a.2215289656523.118366.1076035621& type=3&theater (p. 202)

Kitayama, S., Chua, H. F., Tompson, S., & Han, S. (2013). Neural mechanisms of dissonance: An fMRI investigation of choice justification. *NeuroImage, 69,* 206–212. (p. 420)

Kitayama, S., Conway, L. G., III, Pietromonaci, P. R., Park, H., & Plaut, V. C. (2010). Ethos of independence across regions in the United States: The production–adoption model of cultural change. *American Psychologist, 65,* 559–574. (p. 491)

Kitayama, S., Ishii, K., Imada, T., Takemura, K., & Ramaswamy, J. (2006). Voluntary settlement and the spirit of independence: Evidence from Japan's "northern frontier." *Journal of Personality and Social Psychology, 91,* 369–384. (p. 490)

Kitayama, S., Park, H., Sevincer, A. T., Karasawa, M., & Uskul, A. K. (2009). A cultural task analysis of implicit independence: Comparing North America, Western Europe, and East Asia. *Journal of Personality and Social Psychology, 97,* 236–255. (pp. 416. 491)

Kitayama, S., Park, J., Boylan, J. M., Miyamoto, Y., Levine, C. S., Markus, H. R., . . . Ryff, C. D. (2015). Expression of anger and ill health in two cultures: An examination of inflammation and cardiovascular risk. *Psychological Science, 26,* 211–220. (p. 392)

Kivimaki, M., Leino-Arjas, P., Luukkonen, R., Rihimaki, H., & Kirjonen, J. (2002). Work stress and risk of cardiovascular mortality: Prospective cohort study of industrial employees. *British Medical Journal, 325,* 857. (p. 396)

Kivipelto, M., & Håkansson, K. (2017, April). A rare success against Alzheimer's. *Scientific American,* pp. 33–37. (p. 153)

Kivlighan, D. M., Goldberg, S. B., Abbas, M., Pace, B. T., Yulish, N. E., Thomas, J. G., . . . Wampold, B. E. (2015). The enduring effects of psychodynamic treatments vis-à-vis alternative treatments: A multilevel longitudinal meta-analysis. *Clinical Psychology Review, 40,* 1–14. (p. 552)

Klahr, A. M., & Burt, S. A. (2014). Elucidating the etiology of individual differences in parenting: A meta-analysis of behavioral genetic research. *Psychological Bulletin, 140,* 544–586. (p. 139)

Klayman, J., & Ha, Y.-W. (1987). Confirmation, disconfirmation, and information in hypothesis testing. *Psychological Review, 94,* 211–228. (p. 300)

Klein, D. N. (2010). Chronic depression: Diagnosis and classification. *Current Directions in Psychological Science, 19,* 96–100. (p. 517)

Klein, D. N., & Kotov, R. (2016). Course of depression in a 10-year prospective study: Evidence for qualitatively distinct subgroups. *Journal of Abnormal Psychology, 125,* 337–348. (p. 517)

Klein, D. N., Schwartz, J. E., Santiago, N. J., Vivian, D., Vocisano, C., Castonguay, L. G., . . . Keller, M. B. (2003). Therapeutic alliance in depression treatment: Controlling for prior change and patient characteristics. *Journal of Consulting and Clinical Psychology, 71,* 997–1006. (p. 555)

Klein, R. A., Ratliff, K. A., Vianello, M., Adams, R. B., Jr., Bahník, Š., Bernstein, M. J., . . . Nosek, B. A. (2014). Investigating variation in replicability: A "many labs" replication project. *Social Psychology, 45,* 142–152. (p. 20)

Kleinke, C. L. (1986). Gaze and eye contact: A research review. *Psychological Bulletin, 1000,* 78–100. (p. 375)

Kleinman, D., & Gollan, T. H. (2016). Speaking two languages for the price of one: Bypassing language control mechanisms via accessibility-driven switches. *Psychological Science, 27,* 700–714. (p. 320)

Kleinmuntz, B., & Szucko, J. J. (1984). A field study of the fallibility of polygraph lie detection. *Nature, 308,* 449–450. (p. 374)

Kleitman, N. (1960, November). Patterns of dreaming. *Scientific American,* pp. 82–88. (p. 87)

Klemm, W. R. (1990). Historical and introductory perspectives on brainstem-mediated behaviors. In W. R. Klemm & R. P. Vertes (Eds.), *Brainstem mechanisms of behavior* (pp. 3–32). New York: Wiley. (p. 54)

Klimstra, T. A., Hale, W. W., III, Raaijmakers, Q. A. W., Branje, S. J. T., & Meeus, W. H. J. (2009). Maturation of personality in adolescence. *Journal of Personality and Social Psychology, 96,* 898–912. (p. 147)

Klimstra, T. A., Kuppens, P., Luyckx, K., Branje, S., Hale, W. W., Oosterwegel, A., . . . Meeus, W. H. J. (2015). Daily dynamics of adolescent mood and identity. *Journal of Research on Adolescence.* Advance online publication. doi:10.1111/jora.12205 (p. 146)

Kline, D., & Schieber, F. (1985). Vision and aging. In J. E. Birren & K. W. Schaie (Eds.), *Handbook of the psychology of aging* (2nd ed., pp. 296–331). New York: Van Nostrand Reinhold. (p. 152)

Kline, N. S. (1974). *From sad to glad.* New York: Ballantine Books. (p. 521)

Klinke, R., Kral, A., Heid, S., Tillein, J., & Hartmann, R. (1999). Recruitment of the auditory cortex in congenitally deaf cats by long-term cochlear electrostimulation. *Science, 285,* 1729–1733. (p. 218)

Kluemper, D. H., McLarty, B. D., Bishop, T. R., & Sen, A. (2015). Interviewee selection test and evaluator assessments of general mental ability, emotional intelligence and extraversion: Relationships with structured behavioral and situational interview performance. *Journal of Business and Psychology, 30,* 543–563. (p. 476)

Klump, K. L., Suisman, J. L., Burt, S. A., McGue, M., & Iacono, W. G. (2009). Genetic and environmental influences on disordered eating: An adoption study. *Journal of Abnormal Psychology, 118,* 797–805. (p. 532)

Knapp, S., & VandeCreek, L. (2000). Recovered memories of childhood abuse: Is there an underlying professional consensus? *Professional Psychology: Research and Practice, 31,* 365–371. (p. 293)

Knickmeyer, E. (2001, August 7). In Africa, big is definitely better. *Seattle Times,* p. A7. (p. 532)

Knight, R. T. (2007). Neural networks debunk phrenology. *Science, 316,* 1578–1579. (p. 63)

Knight, W. (2004, August 2). Animated face helps deaf with phone chat. *NewScientist.com.* (p. 228)

Knoblich, G., & Oellinger, M. (2006, October/November). The Eureka moment. *Scientific American Mind,* pp. 38–43. (p. 299)

Knouse, L. E., Teller, J., & Brooks, M. A. (2017). Meta-analysis of cognitive–behavioral treatments for adult ADHD. *Journal of Consulting and Clinical Psychology, 85,* 737–750. (p. 546)

Knuts, I. J. E., Cosci, F., Esquivel, G., Goossens, L., van Duinen, M., Bareman, M., . . . Schruers, K. R. J. (2010). Cigarette smoking and 35% CO_2 induced panic in panic disorder patients. *Journal of Affective Disorders, 124,* 215–218. (p. 507)

Knutsen, J., Mandell, D. S., & Frye, D. (2015). Children with autism are impaired in the understanding of teaching. *Developmental Science.* doi:10.1111/desc.12368 (p. 131)

Knutsson, A., & Bøggild, H. (2010). Gastrointestinal disorders among shift workers. *Scandinavian Journal of Work, Environment & Health,* 85–95. (p. 90)

Ko, C.-K., Yen, J.-Y., Chen, C.-C., Chen, S.-H., & Yen, C.-F. (2005). Proposed diagnostic criteria of internet addiction for adolescents. *Journal of Nervous and Mental Disease, 193,* 728–733. (p. 102)

Koch, C. (2015, January/February). The face as entryway to the self. *Scientific American Mind,* pp. 26–29. (p. 205)

Koenen, K. C., Moffitt, T. E., Roberts, A. L., Martin, L. T., Kubzansky, L., Harrington, H., . . . Caspi, A. (2009). Childhood IQ and adult mental disorders: A test of the cognitive reserve hypothesis. *American Journal of Psychiatry, 166,* 50–57. (p. 331)

Koenig, H. G., King, D. E., & Carson, V. B. (2012). *Handbook of religion and health* (2nd ed.). New York: Oxford University Press. (p. 404)

Koenig, H. G., & Larson, D. B. (1998). Use of hospital services, religious attendance, and religious affiliation. *Southern Medical Journal, 91,* 925–932. (p. 406)

Koenig, L. B., & Vaillant, G. E. (2009). A prospective study of church attendance and health over the lifespan. *Health Psychology, 28,* 117–124. (p. 406)

Koenigs, M., Young, L., Adolphs, R., Tranel, D., Cushman, F., Hauser, M., & Damasio, A. (2007). Damage to the prefrontal cortex increases utilitarian moral judgements. *Nature, 446,* 908–911. (p. 63)

Kofler, M. J., Raiker, J. S., Sarver, D. E., Wells, E. L., & Soto, E. F. (2016). Is hyperactivity ubiquitous in ADHD or dependent on environmental demands? Evidence from meta-analysis. *Clinical Psychology Review, 46,* 12–24. (p. 498)

Kohlberg, L. (1981). *The philosophy of moral development: Essays on moral development* (Vol. 1). San Francisco: Harper & Row. (p. 143)

Kohlberg, L. (1984). *The psychology of moral development: Essays on moral development* (Vol. 2). San Francisco: Harper & Row. (p. 143)

Kohler, C. G., Walker, J. B., Martin, E. A., Healey, K. M., & Moberg, P. J. (2010). Facial emotion perception in schizophrenia: A meta-analytic review. *Schizophrenia Bulletin, 36,* 1009–1019. (p. 523)

Kohler, I. (1962, May). Experiments with goggles. *Scientific American,* pp. 62–72. (p. 214)

Köhler, W. (1925; reprinted 1957). *The mentality of apes.* London: Pelican. (p. 309)

Kolassa, I.-T., & Elbert, T. (2007). Structural and functional neuroplasticity in relation to traumatic stress. *Current Directions in Psychological Science, 16,* 321–325. (p. 512)

Kolb, B. (1989). Brain development, plasticity, and behavior. *American Psychologist, 44,* 1203–1212. (p. 64)

Kolb, B., & Whishaw, I. Q. (1998). Brain plasticity and behavior. *Annual Review of Psychology, 49,* 43–64. (p. 123)

Kolb, B., & Whishaw, I. Q. (2006). An introduction to brain and behavior (2nd ed.) New York: Worth. (p. 306)

Kolker, K. (2002, December 8). Video violence disturbs some: Others scoff at influence. *The Grand Rapids Press,* pp. A1, A12. (p. 444)

Kolovos, S., van Tulder, M. W., Cuijpers, P., Prigent, A., Chevreul, K., Riper, H., & Bosmans, J. E. (2017). The effect of treatment as usual on major depressive disorder: A meta-analysis. *Journal of Affective Disorders, 210,* 72–81. (p. 552)

Koltko-Rivera, M. E. (2006). Rediscovering the later version of Maslow's hierarchy of needs: Self-transcendence and opportunities for theory, research, and unification. *Review of General Psychology, 10,* 302–317. (p. 350)

Komisaruk, B. R., & Whipple, B. (2011). Non-genital orgasms. *Sexual and Relationship Therapy, 26,* 356–372. (p. 177)

Kondoh, K., Lu, Z., Olson, D. P., Lowell, B. B., & Buck, L. B. (2016). A specific area of olfactory cortex involved in stress hormone responses to predator odours. *Nature, 532,* 103–106. (p. 226)

Konkle, T., Brady, T. F., Alvarez, G. A., & Oliva, A. (2010). Conceptual distinctiveness supports detailed visual long-term memory for real-world objects. *Journal of Experimental Psychology: General, 139,* 558–578. (p. 266)

Kontula, O., & Haavio-Mannila, E. (2009). The impact of aging on human sexual activity and sexual desire. *Journal of Sex Research, 46,* 46–56. (p. 151)

Kornell, N., & Bjork, R. A. (2008). Learning concepts and categories: Is spacing the "enemy of induction"? *Psychological Science, 19,* 585–592. (p. 34)

Kosslyn, S. M. (2005). Reflective thinking and mental imagery: A perspective on the development of posttraumatic stress disorder. *Development and Psychopathology, 17,* 851–863. (p. 510)

Kosslyn, S. M. (2008). The world in the brain. In 2008: What have you changed your mind about? Why? *The Edge* (edge.org). (p. 315)

Kosslyn, S. M., & Koenig, O. (1992). *Wet mind: The new cognitive neuroscience.* New York: Free Press. (p. 47)

Kotchick, B. A., Shaffer, A., & Forehand, R. (2001). Adolescent sexual risk behavior: A multi-system perspective. *Clinical Psychology Review, 21,* 493–519. (p. 177)

Koten, J. W., Jr., Wood, G., Hagoort, P., Goebel, R., Propping, P., Willmes, K., & Boomsma, D. I. (2009). Genetic contribution to variation in cognitive function: An fMRI study in twins. *Science, 323,* 1737–1740. (p. 336)

Kotkin, M., Daviet, C., & Gurin, J. (1996). The *Consumer Reports* mental health survey. *American Psychologist, 51,* 1080–1082. (p. 550)

Kounios, J., & Beeman, M. (2014). The cognitive neuroscience of insight. *Annual Review of Psychology, 65,* 71–93. (p. 299)

Kovelman, I., Shalinsky, M. H., Berens, M. S., & Petitto, L. (2014). Words in the bilingual brain: An fNIRS brain imaging investigation of lexical processing in sign-speech bimodal bilinguals. *Frontiers in Human Neuroscience, 8,* article 606. (p. 317)

Kposowa, A., Hamilton, D., & Wang, K. (2016). Impact of firearm availability and gun regulation on state suicide rates. *Suicide and Life-Threating Behavior, 46,* 678–696. (p. 501)

Kposowa, A. J., & D'Auria, S. (2009). Association of temporal factors and suicides in the United States, 2000–2004. *Social Psychiatry and Psychiatric Epidemiology, 45,* 433–445. (p. 500)

Kraft, C. (1978). A psychophysical approach to air safety: Simulator studies of visual illusions in night approaches. In H. L. Pick, H. W. Leibowitz, J. E. Singer, A. Steinschneider, & H. W. Stevenson (Eds.), *Psychology: From research to practice.* New York: Plenum Press. (p. B-13)

Kraft, T., & Pressman, S. (2012). Grin and bear it: The influence of the manipulated facial expression on the stress response. *Psychological Science, 23,* 137–1378. (p. 381)

Krahé, B., & Berger, A. (2017). Longitudinal pathways of sexual victimization, sexual self-esteem, and depression in women and men. *Psychological Trauma: Theory, Research, Practice, and Policy, 9,* 147–155. (p. 170)

Krakow, B., Germain, A., Warner, T. D., Schrader, R., Koss, M. P., Hollifeld, M., . . . Johnston, L. (2001). The relationship of sleep quality and posttraumatic stress to potential sleep disorders in sexual assault survivors with nightmares, insomnia, and PTSD. *Journal of Traumatic Stress, 14,* 647–665. (p. 170)

Krakow, B., Schrader, R., Tandberg, D., Hollifeld, M., Koss, M. P., Yau, C. L., & Cheng, D. T. (2002). Nightmare frequency in sexual assault survivors with PTSD. *Journal of Anxiety Disorders, 16,* 175–190. (p. 170)

Kramer, A. (2010). Personal communication. (p. 408)

Kramer, A. D. I. (2012). The spread of emotion via Facebook. *Proceedings of the SIGCHI Conference on Human Factors in Computing Systems.* ACM (Association for Computing Machinery), New York, 767–770. (p. 382)

Kramer, A. F., & Erickson, K. I. (2007). Capitalizing on cortical plasticity: Influence of physical activity on cognition and brain function. *Trends in Cognitive Sciences, 11,* 342–348. (p. 401)

Kramer, M. S., Aboud, F., Mironova, E., Vanilovich, I., Platt, R. W., Matush, L., . . . Promotion of Breastfeeding Intervention Trial (PROBIT) Study Group. (2008). Breastfeeding and child cognitive development: New evidence from a large randomized trial. *Archives of General Psychiatry, 65,* 578–584. (p. 27)

Kramer, P. D. (2011, July 9). In defense of antidepressants. *The New York Times* (nytimes.com). (p. 561)

Kranz, F., & Ishai, A. (2006). Face perception is modulated by sexual preference. *Current Biology, 16,* 63–68. (p. 181)

Kranz, G. S., Hahn, A., Kaufmann, U., Küblböck, M., Hummer, A., Ganger, S., . . . Lanzenberger, R. (2014). White matter microstructure in transsexuals and controls investigated by diffusion tensor imaging. *The Journal of Neuroscience, 34,* 15466–15475. (p. 170)

Kraul, C. (2010, October 12). Chief engineer knew it would take a miracle. *The Los Angeles Times* (latimes.com). (p. 230)

Kring, A. M., & Caponigro, J. M. (2010). Emotion in schizophrenia: Where feeling meets thinking. *Current Directions in Psychological Science, 19,* 255–259. (p. 523)

Kring, A. M., & Gordon, A. H. (1998). Sex differences in emotion: Expression, experience, and physiology. *Journal of Personality and Social Psychology, 74,* 686–703. (p. 378)

Kringelbach, M. L., & Berridge, K. C. (2012, August). The joyful mind. *Scientific American,* pp. 40–45. (p. 56)

Krishnan, A., Zhang, R., Yao, V., Theesfeld, C. L., Wong, A. K., Tadych, A., . . . Troyanskaya, O. G. (2016). Genome-wide prediction and functional characterization of the genetic basis of autism spectrum disorder. *Nature Neuroscience.* Advance online publication. doi:10.1038/nn.4353 (p. 131)

Kristof, N. (2017, February 11). Husbands are deadlier than terrorists. *The New York Times* (nytimes.com). (p. 18)

Kristof, N. D. (2004, July 21). Saying no to killers. *The New York Times* (nytimes.com). (p. 453)

Krizan, Z., & Johar, O. (2015). Narcissistic rage revisited. *Journal of Personality and Social Psychology, 108,* 784–801. (p. 488)

Kroes, M. C. W., Tendolkar, I., van Wingen, G. A., van Waarde, J. A., Strange, B. A., & Fernández, G. (2014). An electroconvulsive therapy procedure impairs reconsolidation of episodic memories in humans. *Nature Neuroscience, 17,* 204–206. (p. 289)

Kroll, J. F., Bobb, S. C., & Hoshino, N. (2014). Two languages in mind: Bilingualism as a tool to investigate language, cognition, and the brain. *Current Directions in Psychological Science, 23,* 159–163. (p. 320)

Krosnick, J. A., & Alwin, D. F. (1989). Aging and susceptibility to attitude change. *Journal of Personality and Social Psychology, 57,* 416–425. (p. 118)

Krosnick, J. A., Betz, A. L., Jussim, L. J., & Lynn, A. R. (1992). Subliminal conditioning of attitudes. *Personality and Social Psychology Bulletin, 18,* 152–162. (p. 193)

Kross, E., & Ayduk, O. (2011). Making meaning out of negative experiences by self-distancing. *Current Directions in Psychological Science, 20,* 187–191. (p. 394)

Kross, E., Berman, M., Mischel, W., Smith, E. E., & Wager, T. (2011). Social rejection shares somatosensory representations with physical pain. *PNAS, 108,* 6270–6275. (p. 354)

Kross, E., Bruehlman-Senecal, E., Park, J., Burson, A., Dougherty, A., Shablack, H., . . . Ayduk, O. (2014). Self-talk as a regulatory mechanism: How you do it matters. *Journal of Personality and Social Psychology, 106,* 304–324. (p. 130)

Kruger, J., & Dunning, D. (1999). Unskilled and unaware of it: How difficulties in recognizing one's own incompetence lead to inflated self-assessments. *Journal of Personality and Social Psychology, 77,* 1121–1134. (p. 488)

Kruger, J., Epley, N., Parker, J., & Ng, Z.-W. (2005). Egocentrism over e-mail: Can we communicate as well as we think? *Journal of Personality and Social Psychology, 89,* 925–936. (pp. 128, 377)

Krumhansl, C. L. (2010). Plink: "Thin slices" of music. *Music Perception, 27,* 337–354. (p. 266)

Krupenye, C., Kano, F., Hirata, S., Call, J., & Tomasello, M. (2016). Great apes anticipate that other individuals will act according to false beliefs. *Science, 354,* 110–113. (p. 309)

Krützen, M., Mann, J., Heithaus, M. R., Connor, R. C., Bejder, L., & Sherwin, W. B. (2005). Cultural transmission of tool use in bottlenose dolphins. *PNAS, 102,* 8939–8943. (p. 310)

Kubzansky, L. D., Koenen, K. C., Jones, C., & Eaton, W. W. (2009). A prospective study of posttraumatic stress disorder symptoms and coronary heart disease in women. *Health Psychology, 28,* 125–130. (p. 392)

Kubzansky, L. D., Sparrow, D., Vokanas, P., & Kawachi, I. (2001). Is the glass half empty or half full? A prospective study of optimism and coronary heart disease in the normative aging study. *Psychosomatic Medicine, 63,* 910–916. (p. 392)

Kuehner, C. (2017). Why is depression more common among women than among men? *The Lancet Psychiatry, 4,* 146–158. (p. 517)

Kuhl, P. K., & Meltzoff, A. N. (1982). The bimodal perception of speech in infancy. *Science, 218,* 1138–1141. (p. 314)

Kuhl, P. K., Ramírez, R. R., Bosseler, A., Lin, J. L., & Imada, T. (2014). Infants' brain responses to speech suggest analysis by synthesis. *PNAS, 111,* 11238–11245. (p. 314)

Kühn, S., & Gallinat, J. (2014). Brain structure and functional connectivity associated with pornography consumption. *Journal of the American Medical Association Psychiatry, 71,* 827–834. (p. 176)

Kumar, A., & Gilovich, T. (2013). Talking about what you did and what you have: The differential story utility of experiential and material purchases. *Advances in Consumer Research, 41.* (p. 412)

Kumar, A., & Gilovich, T. (2015). Some "thing" to talk about? Differential story utility from experiential and material purchases. *Personality and Social Psychology Bulletin, 41,* 1320–1331. (p. 412)

Kuncel, N. R., & Hezlett, S. A. (2010). Fact and fiction in cognitive ability testing for admissions and hiring decisions. *Current Directions in Psychological Science, 19,* 339–345. (p. 325)

Kunst-Wilson, W. & Zajonc, R. (*1980*). Affective discrimination of stimuli that cannot be recognized. *Science, 207,* 557–558. (p. 370)

Kupfer, D. J. (2012, June 1). *Dr. Kupfer defends DSM-5. Medscape* (medscape.com). (p. 497)

Kupper, N., & Denollet, J. (2007). Type D personality as a prognostic factor in heart disease: Assessment and mediating mechanisms. *Journal of Personality Assessment, 89,* 265–276. (p. 392)

Kurtycz, L. M. (2015). Choice and control for animals in captivity. *The Psychologist, 28,* 892–893. (p. 31)

Kushlev, K., & Dunn, E. W. (2015). Checking email less frequently reduces stress. *Computers in Human Behavior, 43,* 220–228. (p. 350)

Kushner, M. G., Kim, S. W., Conahue, C., Thuras, P., Adson, D., Kotlyar, M., . . . Foa, E. B. (2007). D-cycloserine augmented exposure therapy for obsessive-compulsive disorder. *Biological Psychiatry, 62,* 835–838. (p. 561)

Kutas, M. (1990). Event-related brain potential (ERP) studies of cognition during sleep: Is it more than a dream? In R. R. Bootzin, J. F. Kihlstrom, & D. Schacter (Eds.), *Sleep and cognition* (pp. 43–57). Washington, DC: American Psychological Association. (p. 86)

Kutcher, E. J., & Bragger, J. D. (2004). Selection interviews of overweight job applicants: Can structure reduce the bias? *Journal of Applied Social Psychology, 34,* 1993–2022. (p. B-6)

Kuttler, A. F., La Greca, A. M., & Prinstein, M. J. (1999). Friendship qualities and social–emotional functioning of adolescents with close, cross-sex friendships. *Journal of Research on Adolescence, 9,* 339–366. (p. 165)

Kuyken, W., Warren, F. C., Taylor, R. S., Whalley, B., Crane, C., Bondolfi, G., . . . Dalgleish, T. (2016). Efficacy of mindfulness-based cognitive therapy in prevention of depressive relapse: An individual patient data meta-analysis from randomized trials. *JAMA Psychiatry, 73,* 565–574. (p. 547)

Kuzawa, C. W., Chugani, H. T., Grossman, L. I., Lipovich, L., Muzik, O., Hof, P. R., . . . Lange, N. (2014). Metabolic costs and evolutionary implications of human brain development. *PNAS, 111,* 13010–13015. (p. 123)

Kvam, S., Kleppe, C. L., Nordhus, I. H., & Hovland, A. (2016). Exercise as a treatment for depression: A meta-analysis. *Journal of Affective Disorders, 202,* 67–86. (p. 402)

Kyaga, S., Landén, M., Boman, M., Hultman, C. M., Långström, N., & Lichtenstein, P. (2013). Mental illness, suicide, and creativity: 40-year prospective total population study. *Journal of Psychiatric Research, 47,* 83–90. (p. 516)

La Londe, K. B., Mahoney, A., Edwards, T. L., Cox, C., Weetjens, B., Durgin, A., & Poling, A. (2015). Training pouched rats to find people. *Journal of Applied Behavior Analysis, 48,* 1–10. (p. 245)

LaCapria, K. (2015, December 17). Kindergarten, stop. Snopes.com. (p. 302)

Laceulle, O. M., Ormel, J., Aggen, S. H., Neale, N. C., & Kendler, K. S. (2011). Genetic and environmental influences on the longitudinal structure of neuroticism: A trait-state approach. *Psychological Science, 24,* 1780–1790. (p. 71)

Lacey, M. (2010, December 11). He found bag of cash, but did the unexpected. *The New York Times* (nytimes.com). (p. 455)

Lachman, M. E. (2004). Development in midlife. *Annual Review of Psychology, 55,* 305–331. (p. 155)

Ladd, G. T. (1887). *Elements of physiological psychology.* New York: Scribner's. (p. 80)

Laeng, B., & Sulutvedt, U. (2014). The eye pupil adjusts to imaginary light. *Psychological Science, 25,* 188–197. (p. 201)

Lafleur, D. L., Pittenger, C., Kelmendi, B., Gardner, T., Wasylink, S., Malison, R. T., . . . Coric, V. (2006). N-acetylcysteine augmentation in serotonin reuptake inhibitor refractory obsessive-compulsive disorder. *Psychopharmacology, 184,* 254–256. (p. 512)

Laird, J. D. (1974). Self-attribution of emotion: The effects of expressive behavior on the quality of emotional experience. *Journal of Personality and Social Psychology, 29,* 475–486. (p. 380)

Laird, J. D. (1984). The real role of facial response in the experience of emotion: A reply to Tourangeau and Ellsworth, and others. *Journal of Personality and Social Psychology, 47,* 909–917. (p. 380)

Laird, J. D., & Lacasse, K. (2014). Bodily influences on emotional feelings: Accumulating evidence and extensions of William James's theory of emotion. *Emotion Review, 6,* 27–34. (p. 380)

Lakin, J. L., Chartrand, T. L., & Arkin, R. M. (2008). I am too just like you: Nonconscious mimicry as an automatic behavioral response to social exclusion. *Psychological Science, 19,* 816–822. (p. 423)

Lally, P., Van Jaarsveld, C. H. M., Potts, H. W. W., & Wardle, J. (2010). How are habits formed: Modelling habit formation in the real world. *European Journal of Social Psychology, 40,* 998–1009. (p. 234)

Lam, C. B., & McBride-Chang, C. A. (2007). Resilience in young adulthood: The moderating influences of gender-related personality traits and coping flexibility. *Sex Roles, 56,* 159–172. (p. 169)

Lam, R. W., Levitt, A. J., Levitan, R. D., Enns, M. W., Morehouse, R., Michalak, E. E., & Tam, E. M. (2006). The Can-SAD study: A randomized controlled trial of the effectiveness of light therapy and fluoxetine in patients with winter seasonal affective disorder. *American Journal of Psychiatry, 163,* 805–812. (p. 555)

Lam, R. W., Levitt, A. J., Levitan, R. D., Michalak, E. E., Cheung, A. H., Morehouse, R., . . . Tam, E. M. (2016). Efficacy of bright light treatment, fluoxetine, and the combination in patients with nonseasonal major depressive disorder: A randomized clinical trial. *JAMA Psychiatry, 73,* 56–63. (p. 555)

Lambert, N. M., DeWall, C. N., Bushman, B. J., Tillman, T. F., Fincham, F. D., Pond, R. S., Jr., & Gwinn, A. M. (2011). *Lashing out in lust: Effect of pornography on nonsexual, physical aggression against relationship partners.* Paper presentation at the Society for Personality and Social Psychology convention. (p. 444)

Lambert, N. M., Negash, S., Stillman, T. F., Olmstead, S. B., & Fincham, F. D. (2012). A love that doesn't last: Pornography consumption and weakened commitment to a romantic partner. *Journal of Social and Clinical Psychology, 31,* 410–438. (p. 176)

Lambert, W. E. (1992). Challenging established views on social issues: The power and limitations of research. *American Psychologist, 47,* 533–542. (p. 320)

Lambert, W. E., Genesee, F., Holobow, N., & Chartrand, L. (1993). Bilingual education for majority English-speaking children. *European Journal of Psychology of Education, 8,* 3–22. (p. 320)

Lambird, K. H., & Mann, T. (2006). When do ego threats lead to self-regulation failure? Negative consequences of defensive high self-esteem. *Personality and Social Psychology Bulletin, 32,* 1177–1187. (p. 489)

Lamm, B., Keller, H., Teiser, J., Gudi, H., Yovsi, R. D., Freitag, C., . . . Vöhringer, I. (2017). Waiting for the second treat: Developing culture-specific modes of self-regulation. *Child Development.* Advance online publication. doi:10.1111/cdev.12847 (p. 145)

Landau, E., Verjee, Z., & Mortensen, A. (2014, February 24). Uganda president: Homosexuals are "disgusting." CNN (cnn.com). (pp. 182, 486)

Landauer, T. (2001, September). Quoted by R. Herbert, You must remember this. *APS Observer,* p. 11. (p. 294)

Landberg, J., & Norström, T. (2011). Alcohol and homicide in Russia and the United States: A comparative analysis. *Journal of Studies on Alcohol and Drugs, 72,* 723–730. (p. 442)

Landry, M. J. (2002). MDMA: A review of epidemiologic data. *Journal of Psychoactive Drugs, 34,* 163–169. (p. 108)

Lane, R. D., Ryan, L., Nadel, L., & Greenberg, L. (2015). Memory reconsolidation, emotional arousal, and the process of change in psychotherapy: New insights from brain science. *Behavioral and Brain Sciences, 38,* e28. (p. 554)

Lange, N., & McDougle, C. J. (2013, October). Help for the child with autism. *Scientific American,* pp. 72–77. (p. 132)

Langer, E. J. (1983). *The psychology of control.* Beverly Hills, CA: Sage. (p. 396)

Langer, E. J., & Abelson, R. P. (1974). A patient by any other name . . .: Clinician group differences in labeling bias. *Journal of Consulting and Clinical Psychology, 42,* 4–9. (p. 499)

Langer, E. J., & Imber, L. (1980). The role of mindlessness in the perception of deviance. *Journal of Personality and Social Psychology, 39,* 360–367. (p. 499)

Langkaas, T. F., Hoffart, A., Øktedalen, T., Ulvenes, P., Hembree, E. A., & Smucker, M. (2017). Exposure to non-fear emotions: A randomized controlled study of exposure-based and rescripting-based imagery in PTSD treatment. *Behavior Research Therapy, 97,* 33–42. (p. 541)

Langlois, J. H., Kalakanis, L., Rubenstein, A. J., Larson, A., Hallam, M., & Smoot, M. (2000). Maxims or myths of beauty? A meta-analytic and theoretical review. *Psychological Bulletin, 126,* 390–423. (p. 449)

Langmeyer, A., Guglhör-Rudan, A., & Tarnai, C. (2012). What do music preferences reveal about personality? A cross-cultural replication using self-ratings and ratings of music samples. *Journal of Individual Differences, 33,* 119–130. (p. 481)

Långström, N. H., Rahman, Q., Carlström, E., & Lichtenstein, P. (2010). Genetic and environmental effects on same-sex sexual behavior: A population study of twins in Sweden. *Archives of Sexual Behavior, 39,* 75–80. (p. 181)

Lankford, A. (2009). Promoting aggression and violence at Abu Ghraib: The U.S. military's transformation of ordinary people into torturers. *Aggression and Violent Behavior, 14,* 388–395. (p. 428)

Larkin, J. E., Brasel, A. M., & Pines, H. A. (2013). Cross-disciplinary applications of I/O psychology concepts: Predicting student retention and employee turnover. *Review of General Psychology, 17,* 82–92. (p. B-12)

Larkin, K., Resko, J. A., Stormshak, F., Stellflug, J. N., & Roselli, C. E. (2002, November). *Neuroanatomical correlates of sex and sexual partner preference in sheep.* Paper presented at the annual meeting of the Society for Neuroscience, Orlando, FL. (p. 181)

Larrick, R. P., Timmerman, T. A., Carton, A. M., & Abrevaya, J. (2011). Temper, temperature, and temptation: Heat-related retaliation in baseball. *Psychological Science, 22,* 423–428. (p. 443)

Larsen, R. J., & Diener, E. (1987). Affect intensity as an individual difference characteristic: A review. *Journal of Research in Personality, 21,* 1–39. (p. 135)

Larson, R. W., & Verma, S. (1999). How children and adolescents spend time across the world: Work, play, and developmental opportunities. *Psychological Bulletin, 125,* 701–736. (p. 342)

Larzelere, R. E. (2000). Child outcomes of non-abusive and customary physical punishment by parents: An updated literature review. *Clinical Child and Family Psychology Review, 3,* 199–221. (p. 249)

Larzelere, R. E., & Kuhn, B. R. (2005). Comparing child outcomes of physical punishment and alternative disciplinary tactics: A meta-analysis. *Clinical Child and Family Psychology Review, 8,* 1–37. (p. 250)

Larzelere, R. E., Kuhn, B. R., & Johnson, B. (2004). The intervention selection bias: An underrecognized confound in intervention research. *Psychological Bulletin, 130,* 289–303. (p. 249)

Lashley, K. S. (1950). In search of the engram. In J. F. Danielli & R. Brown (Eds.), *Symposia of the Society for Experimental Biology: Vol. 4. Physiological mechanisms in animal behaviour* (pp. 454–482). New York: Cambridge University Press. (p. 276)

Lassiter, G. D., & Irvine, A. A. (1986). Video-taped confessions: The impact of camera point of view on judgments of coercion. *Journal of Personality and Social Psychology, 16,* 268–276. (p. 417)

Latané, B. (1981). The psychology of social impact. *American Psychologist, 36,* 343–356. (p. 430)

Latané, B., & Dabbs, J. M., Jr. (1975). Sex, group size and helping in three cities. *Sociometry, 38,* 180–194. (p. 454)

Latzman, R. D., Freeman, H. D., Schapiro, S. J., & Hopkins, W. D. (2015). The contribution of genetics and early rearing experiences to hierarchical personality dimensions in chimpanzees (*Pan troglodytes*). *Journal of Personality and Social Psychology, 109,* 889–900. (p. 477)

Latzman, R. D., Patrick, C. J., Freeman, H. D., Schapiro, S. J., & Hopkins, W. D. (2017). Etiology of triarchic psychopathy dimensions in chimpanzees (*Pan troglodytes*). *Clinical Psychological Science, 5,* 341–354. (p. 530)

Laudenslager, M. L., & Reite, M. L. (1984). Losses and separations: Immunological consequences and health implications. *Review of Personality and Social Psychology, 5,* 285–312. (p. 396)

Laukka, P., Elfenbein, H. A., Thingujam, N. S., Rockstuhl, T., Iraki, F. K., Chui, W., & Althoff, J. (2016). The expression and recognition of emotions in the voice across five nations: A lens model analysis based on acoustic features. *Journal of Personality and Social Psychology, 111,* 686–705. (p. 378)

Laumann, E. O., Gagnon, J. H., Michael, R. T., & Michaels, S. (1994). *The social organization of sexuality: Sexual practices in the United States.* Chicago: University of Chicago Press. (p. 184)

Launay, J. M., Mouillet-Richard, S., Baudry, A., Pietri, M., & Kellermann, O. (2011). Raphe-mediated signals control the hippocampal response to SRI antidepressants via miR-16. *Translational Psychiatry, 1,* e56. (p. 562)

Laws, K. R., & Kokkalis, J. (2007). Ecstasy (MDMA) and memory function: A meta-analytic update. *Human Psychopharmacology: Clinical and Experimental, 22,* 381–388. (p. 108)

Layous, K., & Lyubomirsky, S. (2014). The how, who, what, when, and why of happiness: Mechanisms underlying the success of positive activity interventions. In J. Gruber & J. T. Moskowitz (Eds.), *Positive emotions: Integrating the light and dark sides* (pp. 473–495). New York: Oxford University Press. (p. 411)

Lazaruk, W. (2007). Linguistic, academic, and cognitive benefits of French immersion. *Canadian Modern Language Review, 63,* 605–628. (p. 320)

Lazarus, R. S. (1990). Theory-based stress measurement. *Psychological Inquiry, 1,* 3–13. (p. 386)

Lazarus, R. S. (1991). Progress on a cognitive-motivational-relational theory of emotion. *American Psychologist, 46,* 352–367. (p. 371)

Lazarus, R. S. (1998). *Fifty years of the research and theory of R. S. Lazarus: An analysis of historical and perennial issues.* Mahwah, NJ: Erlbaum. (pp. 371, 384)

Lea, S. E. G. (2000). Towards an ethical use of animals. *The Psychologist, 13,* 556–557. (p. 31)

Leaper, C., & Ayres, M. M. (2007). A meta-analytic review of gender variations in adults' language use: Talkativeness, affiliative speech, and assertive speech. *Personality and Social Psychology Review, 11,* 328–363. (p. 164)

Leary, M. R. (1999). The social and psychological importance of self-esteem. In R. M. Kowalski & M. R. Leary (Eds.), *The social psychology of emotional and behavioral problems.* Washington, DC: APA Books. (p. 486)

Leary, M. R. (2012). Sociometer theory. In L. Van Lange, A. W. Kruglanski, & E. T. Higgins (Eds.), *Handbook of theories of social psychology* (Vol. 2, pp. 141–159). Los Angeles: Sage Publications. (p. 353)

Leary, M. R. (2018). Self-awareness, hypo-egoicism, and psychological well-being. In J. E. Maddux (Ed.), *Subjective well-being and life satisfaction.* New York: Routledge. (p. 520)

Lebedev, A. V., Lövdén, M., Rosenthal, G., Feilding, A., Nutt, D. J., & Carhart-Harris, R. L. (2015). Finding the self by losing the self: Neural correlates of ego-dissolution under psilocybin. *Human Brain Mapping, 36,* 3137–3153. (p. 108)

Leckelt, M., Küfner, A. C. P., Nestler, S., & Back, M. D. (2015). Behavioral processes underlying the decline of narcissists' popularity over time. *Journal of Personality and Social Psychology, 109,* 856–871. (p. 489)

LeDoux, J. (1996). *The emotional brain: The mysterious underpinnings of emotional life.* New York: Simon & Schuster. (p. 277)

LeDoux, J. (2002). *The synaptic self.* London: Macmillan. (p. 370)

LeDoux, J. (2009, July/August). Quoted by K. McGowan, Out of the past. *Discover,* pp. 28–37. (p. 289)

LeDoux, J. (2015). *Anxious: Using the brain to understand and treat fear and anxiety.* New York: Viking. (p. 370)

LeDoux, J. E., & Armony, J. (1999). Can neurobiology tell us anything about human feelings? In D. Kahneman, E. Diener, & N. Schwartz (Eds.), *Well-being: The foundations of hedonic psychology.* New York: Sage. (p. 370)

LeDoux, J. E., & Brown, R. (2017). A higher-order theory of emotional consciousness. *PNAS, 114,* E2016–E2025. (p. 370)

Lee, C. A., Derefinko, K. J., Milich, R., Lynam, D. R., & DeWall, C. N. (2017). Longitudinal and reciprocal relations between delay discounting and crime. *Personality and Individual Differences, 111,* 193–198. (pp. 145, 401)

Lee, C. S., Therriault, D. J., & Linderholm, T. (2012). On the cognitive benefits of cultural experience: Exploring the relationship between studying abroad and creative thinking. *Applied Cognitive Psychology, 26,* 768–778. (p. 307)

Lee, D. S., Kim, E., & Schwartz, N. (2015). Something smells fishy: Olfactory suspicion cues improve performance on the Moses illusion and Wason rule discovery task. *Journal of Experimental Social Psychology, 59,* 47–50. (p. 227)

Lee, G. Y., & Kisilevsky, B. S. (2014). Fetuses respond to father's voice but prefer mother's voice after birth. *Developmental Psychobiology, 56,* 1–11. (p. 119)

Lee, G., Ojha, A., Kang, J.-S., & Lee, M. (2015). Modulation of resource allocation by intelligent individuals in linguistic, mathematical, and visuo-spatial tasks. *International Journal of Psychophysiology, 97,* 14–22. (p. 324)

Lee, L., Frederick, S., & Ariely, D. (2006). Try it, you'll like it: The influence of expectation, consumption, and revelation on preferences for beer. *Psychological Science, 17,* 1054–1058. (p. 196)

Lefaucheur, J.-P., Antal, A., Ayache, S. S., Benninger, D. H., Brunelin, J., Cogiamanian, F., . . . Paulus, W. (2017). Evidence-based guidelines on the therapeutic use of transcranial direct current stimulation (tDCS). *Clinical Neuropsychology, 128,* 56–92. (p. 563)

Lefcourt, H. M. (1982). *Locus of control: Current trends in theory and research.* Hillsdale, NJ: Erlbaum. (p. 397)

Lehman, D. R., Wortman, C. B., & Williams, A. F. (1987). Long-term effects of losing a spouse or child in a motor vehicle crash. *Journal of Personality and Social Psychology, 52,* 218–231. (p. 159)

Leichsenring, F., & Leweke, F. (2017). Social anxiety disorder. *The New England Journal of Medicine, 376,* 2255–2264. (p. 506)

Leichsenring, F., & Rabung, S. (2008). Effectiveness of long-term psychodynamic psychotherapy: A meta-analysis. *JAMA, 300,* 1551–1565. (p. 553)

Leitenberg, H., & Henning, K. (1995). Sexual fantasy. *Psychological Bulletin, 117,* 469–496. (pp. 174, 177)

Lemmer, G., & Wagner, U. (2015). Can we really reduce ethnic prejudice outside the lab? A meta-analysis of direct and indirect contact interventions. *European Journal of Social Psychology, 45,* 152–168. (p. 457)

Lemonick, M. D. (2002, June 3). Lean and hungrier. *Time,* p. 54. (p. 362)

Lenhart, A. (2015a, April 9). *Mobile access shifts social media use and other online activities.* Pew Research Center (pewresearch.org). (p. 165)

Lenhart, A. (2015b, April 9). *Teens, social media & technology overview 2015.* Pew Internet & Research Center (pewinternet.org). (pp. 148, 355)

Lenneberg, E. H. (1967). *Biological foundations of language.* New York: Wiley. (p. 315)

Lennox, B. R., Bert, S., Park, G., Jones, P. B., & Morris, P. G. (1999). Spatial and temporal mapping of neural activity associated with auditory hallucinations. *The Lancet, 353,* 644. (p. 61)

Lenton, A. P., & Francesconi, M. (2010). How humans cognitively manage an abundance of mate options. *Psychological Science, 21,* 528–533. (p. 448)

LePort, A. K. R., Mattfeld, A. T., Dickinson-Anson, H., Fallon, J. H., Stark, C. E. L., Kruggel, F., . . . McGaugh, J. L. (2012). Behavioral and neuroanatomical investigation of highly superior autobiographical memory (HSAM). *Neurobiology of Learning and Memory, 98,* 78–92. (p. 284)

Lepp, A., Barkley, J. E., & Karpinski, A. C. (2014). The relationship between cell phone use, academic performance, anxiety, and satisfaction with life in college students. *Computers in Human Behavior, 31,* 343–350. (p. 356)

Lereya, S. T., Copeland, W. E., Costello, E. J., & Wolke, D. (2015). Adult mental health consequences of peer bullying and maltreatment in childhood: Two cohorts in two countries. *Lancet Psychiatry, 2,* 524–531. (p. 138)

Lesage, A., Lemasson, M., Medina, K., Tsopmo, J., Sebti, N., Potvin, S., & Patry, S. (2016). The prevalence of electroconvulsive therapy use since 1973: A meta-analysis. *Journal of ECT, 32,* 236–242. (p. 563)

Leucht, S., Barnes, T. R. E., Kissling, W., Engel, R. R., Correll, C., & Kane, J. M. (2003). Relapse prevention in schizophrenia with new-generation antipsychotics: A systematic review and exploratory meta-analysis of randomized, controlled trials. *American Journal of Psychiatry, 160,* 1209–1222. (p. 560)

Leucht, S., Leucht, C., Huhn, M., Chaimani, A., Mavridis, D., Helfer, B., . . . Geddes, J. R. (2017). Sixty years of placebo-controlled antipsychotic drug trials in acute schizophrenia: Systematic review, Bayesian meta-analysis, and meta-regression of efficacy predictors. *American Journal of Psychiatry, 174,* 927–942. (p. 5600)

LeVay, S. (1991). A difference in hypothalamic structure between heterosexual and homosexual men. *Science, 253,* 1034–1037. (p. 180)

LeVay, S. (1994, March). Quoted in D. Nimmons, Sex and the brain. *Discover,* pp. 64–71. (p. 180)

LeVay, S. (2011). *Gay, straight, and the reason why: The science of sexual orientation.* New York: Oxford University Press. (pp. 181, 182)

Levenson, R. M., Krupinski, E. A., Navarro, V. M., & Wasserman, E. A. (2015, November 18). Pigeons (*Columba livia*) as trainable observers of pathology and radiology breast cancer images. *PLoS ONE, 10,* e0141357. (p. 245)

Levin, K. H., Shanafelt, T. D., Keran, C. M., Busis, N. A., Foster, L. A., Molano, J. R. V., . . . Cascino, T. L. (2017). Burnout, career satisfaction, and well-being among US neurology residents and fellows in 2016. *Neurology, 89,* 492–501. (p. B-1)

Levin, R., & Nielsen, T. A. (2007). Disturbed dreaming, posttraumatic stress disorder, and affect distress: A review and neurocognitive model. *Psychological Bulletin, 133,* 482–528. (p. 96)

Levin, R., & Nielsen, T. A. (2009). Nightmares, bad dreams, and emotion dysregulation. *Current Directions in Psychological Science, 18,* 84–87. (p. 96)

Levine, J. A., Lanningham-Foster, L. M., McCrady, S. K., Krizan, A. C., Olson, L. R., Kane, P. H., . . . Clark, M. M. (2005). Interindividual variation in posture allocation: Possible role in human obesity. *Science, 307,* 584–586. (p. 365)

Levine, R. (2016). *Stranger in the mirror: The scientific search for self.* Princeton, NJ: Princeton University Press. (pp. 420, 490)

Levine, R., Sato, S., Hashimoto, T., & Verma, J. (1995). Love and marriage in eleven cultures. *Journal of Cross-Cultural Psychology, 26,* 554–571. (p. 451)

Levine, R. V., & Norenzayan, A. (1999). The pace of life in 31 countries. *Journal of Cross-Cultural Psychology, 30,* 178–205. (p. 23)

Levy, D. J., Heissel, J. A., Richeson, J. A., & Adam, E. K. (2016). Psychological and biological responses to race-based social stress as pathways to disparities in educational outcomes. *American Psychologist, 71,* 455–473. (pp. 386, 458)

Levy, P. E. (2003). *Industrial/organizational psychology: Understanding the workplace.* Boston: Houghton Mifflin. (p. B-7)

Lewandowski, G. W., Jr., Aron, A., & Gee, J. (2007). Personality goes a long way: The malleability of opposite-sex physical attractiveness. *Personality Relationships, 14,* 571–585. (p. 450)

Lewinsohn, P. M., Hoberman, H., Teri, L., & Hautziner, M. (1985). An integrative theory of depression. In S. Reiss & R. Bootzin (Eds.), *Theoretical issues in behavior therapy.* Orlando, FL: Academic Press. (p. 516)

Lewinsohn, P. M., Petit, J., Joiner, T. E., Jr., & Seeley, J. R. (2003). The symptomatic expression of major depressive disorder in adolescents and young adults. *Journal of Abnormal Psychology, 112,* 244–252. (p. 516)

Lewinsohn, P. M., Rohde, P., & Seeley, J. R. (1998). Major depressive disorder in older adolescents: Prevalence, risk factors, and clinical implications. *Clinical Psychology Review, 18,* 765–794. (p. 516)

Lewis, C. S. (1960). *Mere Christianity.* New York: Macmillan. (p. 7)

Lewis, C. S. (1967). *Christian reflections.* Grand Rapids, MI: Eerdmans. (p. 285)

Lewis, D. M. G., Al-Shawaf, L., Conroy-Beam, D., Asao, K., & Buss, D. M. (2017). Evolutionary psychology: A how-to guide. *American Psychologist, 72,* 353–373. (p. 186)

Lewis, D. M. G., Russell, E. M., Al-Shawaf, L., & Buss, D. M. (2015). Lumbar curvature: A previously undiscovered standard of attractiveness. *Evolution and Human Behavior, 36,* 345–350. (p. 184)

Lewis, D. O., Pincus, J. H., Bard, B., Richardson, E., Prichep, L. S., Feldman, M., & Yeager, C. (1988). Neuropsychiatric, psychoeducational, and family characteristics of 14 juveniles condemned to death in the United States. *American Journal of Psychiatry, 145,* 584–589. (p. 137)

Lewis, D. O., Yeager, C. A., Swica, Y., Pincus, J. H., & Lewis, M. (1997). Objective documentation of child abuse and dissociation in 12 murderers with dissociative identity disorder. *American Journal of Psychiatry, 154,* 1703–1710. (p. 529)

Li, C.-M., Zhang, X., Hoffman, H. J., Cotch, M. F., Themann, C. L., & Wilson, M. R. (2014). Hearing impairment associated with depression in US adults, National Health and Nutrition Examination Survey 2005–2010. *Otolaryngology—Head & Neck Surgery, 140,* 293–302. (p. 216)

Li, J., Laursen, T. M., Precht, D. H., Olsen, J., & Mortensen, P. B. (2005). Hospitalization for mental illness among parents after the death of a child. *New England Journal of Medicine, 352,* 1190–1196. (p. 159)

Li, L., Abutalebi, J., Emmorey, K., Gong, G., Yan, X., Feng, X., . . . Ding, G. (2017). How bilingualism protects the brain from aging: Insights from bimodal bilinguals. *Human Brain Mapping, 38,* 4109–4124. (p. 320)

Li, N., & DiCarlo, J. J. (2008). Unsupervised natural experience rapidly alters invariant object representation in visual cortex. *Science, 321,* 1502–1506. (p. 212)

Li, N. P., & Kanazawa, S. (2016). Country roads, take me home . . . to my friends: How intelligence, population density, and friendship affect modern happiness. *British Journal of Psychology, 107,* 675–697. (p. 353)

Li, S., Stampfer, M. J., Williams, D. R., & VanderWeele, T. J. (2016). Association of religious service attendance with mortality among women. *JAMA Internal Medicine, 176,* 777–785. (p. 405)

Li, W., Ma, L., Yang, G., & Gan, W.-B. (2017). REM sleep selectively prunes and maintains new synapses in development and learning. *Nature Neuroscience, 20,* 427–437. (p. 91)

Li, Y., Johnson, E. J., & Zaval, L. (2011). Local warming: Daily temperature change influences belief in global warming. *Psychological Science, 22,* 454–459. (p. 303)

Li, Z. H., Jiang, D., Pepler, D., & Craig, W. (2010). Adolescent romantic relationships in China and Canada: A cross-national comparison. *Internal Journal of Behavioral Development, 34,* 113–120. (p. 147)

Liberman, M. C. (2015, August). Hidden hearing loss. *Scientific American,* pp. 49–53. (p. 218)

Libertus, M. E., & Brannon, E. M. (2009). Behavioral and neural basis of number sense in infancy. *Current Directions in Psychological Science, 18,* 346–351. (p. 127)

Licata, A., Taylor, S., Berman, M., & Cranston, J. (1993). Effects of cocaine on human aggression. *Pharmacology Biochemistry and Behavior, 45,* 549–552. (p. 107)

Lichtenstein, E., Zhu, S.-H., & Tedeschi, G. J. (2010). Smoking cessation quitlines: An underrecognized intervention success story. *American Psychologist, 65,* 252–261. (p. 106)

Lick, D. J., Durso, L. E., & Johnson, K. L. (2013). Minority stress and physical health among sexual minorities. *Perspectives on Psychological Science, 8,* 521–548. (p. 386)

Liddle, J. R., Shackelford, T. K., & Weekes-Shackelford, V. W. (2012). Why can't we all just get along? Evolutionary perspectives on violence, homicide, and war. *Review of General Psychology, 16,* 24–36. (p. 163)

Lieberman, M. D., & Eisenberger, N. I. (2015). The dorsal anterior cingulate is selective for pain: Results from large-scale fMRI reverse inference. *PNAS, 112,* 15250–15255. (p. 354)

Lieberman, M. D., Eisenberger, N. L., Crockett, M. J., Tom, S. M., Pfeifer, J. H., & Way, B. M. (2007). Putting feelings into words: Affect labeling disrupts amygdala activity in response to affective stimuli. *Psychological Science, 18,* 421–428. (p. 400)

Lieberman, P. (2013). Synapses, language, and being human. *Science, 342,* 944–945. (p. 318)

Lievens, F., Dilchert, S., & Ones, D. S. (2009). The importance of exercise and dimension factors in assessment centers: Simultaneous examinations of construct-related and criterion-related validity. *Human Performance, 22,* 375–390. (p. 484)

Lifton, R. J. (1961). *Thought reform and the psychology of totalism: A study of "brainwashing" in China.* New York: Norton. (p. 418)

Lilienfeld, S. O. (2009, Winter). Tips for spotting psychological pseudoscience: A student-friendly guide. *Eye of Psi Chi,* pp. 23–26. (p. 230)

Lilienfeld, S. O. (2017). Clinical psychological science: Then and now. *Clinical Psychological Science, 5,* 3–13. (p. 528)

Lilienfeld, S. O., & Arkowitz, H. (2007, December, 2006/January, 2007). Taking a closer look: Can moving your eyes back and forth help to ease anxiety? *Scientific American Mind,* pp. 80–81. (p. 554)

Lilienfeld, S. O., Lynn, S. J., Kirsch, I., Chaves, J. F., Sarbin, T. R., Ganaway, G. K., & Powell, R. A. (1999). Dissociative identity disorder and the sociocognitive model: Recalling the lessons of the past. *Psychological Bulletin, 125,* 507–523. (p. 529)

Lilienfeld, S. O., Marshall, J., Todd, J. T., & Shane, H. C. (2015). The persistence of fad interventions in the face of negative scientific evidence: Facilitated communication for autism as a case example. *Evidence-Based Communication Assessment and Intervention, 8,* 62–101. (pp. 551, 554)

Lilienfeld, S. O., Ritschel, L. A., Lynn, S. J., Cautin, R. L., & Latzman, R. D. (2013). Why many clinical psychologists are resistant to evidence-based practice: Root causes and constructive remedies. *Clinical Psychology Review, 33,* 883–900. (p. 553)

Lilienfeld, S. O., Sauvigné, K. C., Reber, J., Watts, A. L., Hamann, S., Smith, S. F., . . . Tranel, D. (2017). Potential effects of severe bilateral amygdala damage on psychopathic features: A case report. *Personality Disorders: Theory, Research, and Treatment.* Advance online publication. doi:10.1037/per0000230 (p. 530)

Lilienfeld, S. O., Smith, S. F., & Watts, A. L. (2016). Fearless dominance and its implications for psychopathy: Are the right stuff and the wrong stuff flip sides of the same coin? In V. Zeigler-Hill, & D. K. Marcus (Eds.), *The dark side of personality: Science and practice in social, personality, and clinical psychology.* Washington, DC: American Psychological Association, pp. 65–86. (p. 530)

Lilienfeld, S. O., Waldman, I. D., Landfield, K., Watts, A. L., Rubenzer, S., & Fashingbauer, T. R. (2012). Fearless dominance and the U.S. presidency: Implications of psychopathic personality traits for successful and unsuccessful political leadership. *Journal of Personality and Social Psychology, 103,* 489–505. (p. 530)

Lim, D., & DeSteno, D. (2016). Suffering and compassion: The links among adverse life experiences, empathy, compassion, and prosocial behavior. *Emotion, 16,* 175–182. (p. 388)

Lim, J., & Dinges, D. F. (2010). A meta-analysis of the impact of short-term sleep deprivation on cognitive variables. *Psychological Bulletin, 136,* 375–389. (p. 93)

Lima, N., Nascimento, V., Peixoto, J. A. C., Moreira, M. M., Neto, M. L. R., Almeida, J. C., . . . Reis, A. O. A. (2013). Electroconvulsive therapy use in adolescents: A systematic review. *Annals of General Psychiatry, 12,* 17. doi:10.1186/1744-859X-12-17. (p. 563)

Lin, P. (2016). Risky behaviors: Integrating adolescent egocentrism with the theory of planned behavior. *Review of General Psychology, 20,* 392–398. (p. 128)

Lin, X., Chen, W., Wei, F., Ying, M., Wei, W., & Xie, X. (2015). Night-shift work increases morbidity of breast cancer and all-cause mortality: A meta-analysis of 16 prospective cohort studies. *Sleep Medicine, 16,* 1381–1387. (p. 90)

Lin, Z., & Murray, S. O. (2015). More power to the unconscious: Conscious, but not unconscious, exogenous attention requires location variation. *Psychological Science, 26,* 221–230. (p. 305)

Linardon, J., Wade, T. D., de la Piedad Garcia, X., & Brennan, L. (2017). The efficacy of cognitive-behavioral therapy for eating disorders: A systematic review and meta-analysis. *Journal of Consulting and Clinical Psychology, 85,* 1080–1094. (p. 546)

Lind, A., Hall, L., Breidegard, B., Balkenius, C., & Johansson, P. (2014). Speakers' acceptance of real-time speech exchange indicates that we use auditory feedback to specify the meaning of what we say. *Psychological Science, 25,* 1198–1205. (p. 196)

Lindberg, S. M., Hyde, J. S., Linn, M. C., & Petersen, J. L. (2010). New trends in gender and mathematics performance: A meta-analysis. *Psychological Bulletin, 136,* 1125–1135. (p. 340)

Linder, D. (1982). Social trap analogs: The tragedy of the commons in the laboratory. In V. J. Derlega & J. Grzelak (Eds.), *Cooperative and helping behavior: Theories and research.* New York: Academic Press. (p. 456)

Lindner, I., Echterhoff, G., Davidson, P. S. R., & Brand, M. (2010). Observation inflation: Your actions become mine. *Psychological Science, 21,* 1291–1299. (p. 260)

Lindskold, S. (1978). Trust development, the GRIT proposal, and the effects of conciliatory acts on conflict and cooperation. *Psychological Bulletin, 85,* 772–793. (p. 459)

Lindskold, S., & Han, G. (1988). GRIT as a foundation for integrative bargaining. *Personality and Social Psychology Bulletin, 14,* 335–345. (p. 459)

Lindson-Hawley, N., Banting, M., West, R., Michie, S., Shinkins, B., & Aveyard, P. (2016). Gradual versus abrupt smoking cessation: A randomized, controlled noninferiority trial. *Annals of Internal Medicine, 164,* 585–592. (p. 106)

Linehan, M. M., Korslund, K. E., Harned, M. S., Gallop, R. J., Lungu, A., Neacsiu, A. D., . . . Murray-Gregory, A. M. (2015). Dialectical behavior therapy for high suicide risk in individuals with borderline personality disorder: A randomized clinical trial and component analysis. *JAMA Psychiatry, 72,* 475–482. (p. 546)

Lippa, R. A. (2007). The relation between sex drive and sexual attraction to men and women: A cross-national study of heterosexual, bisexual, and homosexual men and women. *Archives of Sexual Behavior, 36,* 209–222. (p. 449)

Lippa, R. A. (2008). Sex differences and sexual orientation differences in personality: Findings from the BBC Internet survey. *Archives of Sexual Behavior, 37,* 173–187. (p. 183)

Lippa, R. A. (2009). Sex differences in sex drive, sociosexuality, and height across 53 nations: Testing evolutionary and social structural theories. *Archives of Sexual Behavior, 38,* 631–651. (p. 183)

Lipsitt, L. P. (2003). Crib death: A biobehavioral phenomenon? *Current Directions in Psychological Science, 12,* 164–170. (p. 124)

Littel, M., Remijn, M., Tinga, A. M., Engelhard, I. M., & van den Hout, M. A. (2017). Stress enhances the memory-degrading effects of eye movements on emotionally neutral memories. *Clinical Psychological Science, 5,* 316–324. (p. 554)

Liu, D., & Baumeister, R. F. (2016). Social networking online and personality of self-worth: A meta-analysis. *Journal of Research in Personality, 64,* 79–89. (p. 356)

Liu, R. T., Cheek, S. M., & Nestor, B. A. (2016). Non-suicidal self-injury and life stress: A systematic meta-analysis and theoretical elaboration. *Clinical Psychology Review, 47,* 1–14. (pp. 92, 502)

Liu, S., Huang, J. L., & Wang, M. (2014). Effectiveness of job search interventions: A meta-analytic review. *Psychological Bulletin, 140,* 1009–1041. (p. B-5)

Liu, Y., Balaraman, Y., Wang, G., Nephew, K. P., & Zhou, F. C. (2009). Alcohol exposure alters DNA methylation profiles in mouse embryos at early neurulation. *Epigenetics, 4,* 500–511. (p. 120)

Livingston, G., & Parker, K. (2011). A tale of two fathers: More are active, but more are absent. Pew Research Center (pewresearch.org). (p. 135)

Livingstone, M., & Hubel, D. (1988). Segregation of form, color, movement, and depth: Anatomy, physiology, and perception. *Science, 240,* 740–749. (p. 206)

Lo, J. C., Chong, P. L., Ganesan, S., Leong, R. L., & Chee, M. W. (2016). Sleep deprivation increases formation of false memory. *Journal of Sleep Research.* Advance online publication. doi:10.1111/jsr.12436 (p. 295)

LoBello, S. G. (2017). The validity of major depression with seasonal pattern: Reply to young. *Clinical Psychological Science, 5,* 755–757. (p. 515)

Locke, K. D., Church, A. T., Mastor, K. A., Curtis, G. J., Sadler, P., McDonald, K., . . . Cabrera, H. F. (2017). Cross-situational self-consistency in nine cultures: The importance of separating influences of social norms and distinctive dispositions. *Personality and Social Psychology Bulletin, 43,* 1033–1049. (p. 481)

Lockwood, L. E., Su, S., & Youssef, N. A. (2015). The role of epigenetics in depression and suicide: A platform for gene-environment interactions. *Psychiatry Research, 228,* 235–242. (p. 512)

Loehlin, J. C. (2012). The differential heritability of personality item clusters. *Behavior Genetics, 42,* 500–507. (p. 71)

Loehlin, J. C. (2016). What can an adoption study tell us about the effect of prenatal environment on a trait. *Behavior Genetics, 46,* 329–333. (p. 338)

Loehlin, J. C., Horn, J. M., & Ernst, J. L. (2007). Genetic and environmental influences on adult life outcomes: Evidence from the Texas Adoption Project. *Behavior Genetics, 37,* 463–476. (p. 73)

Loehlin, J. C., & Nichols, R. C. (1976). *Heredity, environment, and personality.* Austin: University of Texas Press. (p. 71)

Loewenstein, G., Krishnamurti, T., Kopsic, J., & McDonald, D. (2015). Does increased sexual frequency enhance happiness? *Journal of Economic Behavior & Organization, 116,* 206–218. (p. 186)

Loftus, E. F. (2012, July). *Manufacturing memories.* Invited address to the International Congress of Psychology, Cape Town. (p. 289)

Loftus, E. F., & Ketcham, K. (1994). *The myth of repressed memory: False memories and allegations of sexual abuse.* New York: St. Martin's Press. (p. 96)

Loftus, E. F., Levidow, B., & Duensing, S. (1992). Who remembers best? Individual differences in memory for events that occurred in a science museum. *Applied Cognitive Psychology, 6,* 93–107. (p. 290)

Loftus, E. F., & Loftus, G. R. (1980). On the permanence of stored information in the human brain. *American Psychologist, 35,* 409–420. (p. 276)

Loftus, E. F., & Palmer, J. C. (October, 1974). Reconstruction of automobile destruction: An example of the interaction between language and memory. *Journal of Verbal Learning & Verbal Behavior, 13,* 585–589. (p. 290)

Logan, T. K., Walker, R., Cole, J., & Leukefeld, C. (2002). Victimization and substance abuse among women: Contributing factors, interventions, and implications. *Review of General Psychology, 6,* 325–397. (p. 111)

Logue, A. W. (1998a). Laboratory research on self-control: Applications to administration. *Review of General Psychology, 2,* 221–238. (p. 247)

Logue, A. W. (1998b). Self-control. In W. T. O'Donohue (Ed.), *Learning and behavior therapy.* Boston: Allyn & Bacon. (p. 247)

London, P. (1970). The rescuers: Motivational hypotheses about Christians who saved Jews from the Nazis. In J. Macaulay & L. Berkowitz (Eds.), *Altruism and helping behavior.* New York: Academic Press. (p. 261)

Lonergan, M. H., Olivera-Figueroa, L., Pitman, R. K., & Brunet, A. (2013). Propranolol's effects on the consolidation and reconsolidation of long-term emotional memory in healthy participants: A meta-analysis. *Journal of Psychiatry & Neuroscience, 38,* 222–231. (p. 289)

Lonsway, K.A., & Fitzgerald, L.F. (1994). Rape myths: In review. *Psychology of Women Quarterly, 18,* 133–164.

Loomes, R., Hull, L., & Mandy, W. P. L. (2017). What is the male-to-female ratio in autism spectrum disorder? A systematic review and meta-analysis. *Journal of the American Academy of Child & Adolescent Psychiatry, 56,* 466–474. (p. 131)

Lopez, D. J. (2002, January/February). Snaring the fowler: Mark Twain debunks phrenology. *Skeptical Inquirer* (csicop.org). (p. 38)

Lopez-Quintero, C., de los Cobos, P., Hasin, D. S., Okuda, M., Wang, S., Grant, B. F., & Blanco, C. (2011). Probability and predictors of transition from first use to dependence on nicotine, alcohol, cannabis, and cocaine: Results of the national epidemiologic survey on alcohol and related conditions (NESARC). *Drug and Alcohol Dependence, 115,* 120–130. (p. 102)

Loprinzi, P. D., Loenneke, J. P., & Blackburn, E. H. (2015). Movement-based behaviors and leukocyte telomere length among US adults. *Medical Science and Sports Exercise, 47,* 2347–2352. (p. 153)

Lord, C. G., Lepper, M. R., & Preston, E. (1984). Considering the opposite: A corrective strategy for social judgment. *Journal of Personality and Social Psychology, 47,* 1231–1247. (p. 304)

Lord, C. G., Ross, L., & Lepper, M. (1979). Biased assimilation and attitude polarization: The effects of prior theories on subsequently considered evidence. *Journal of Personality and Social Psychology, 37,* 2098–2109. (p. 304)

Lorenz, K. (1937). The companion in the bird's world. *Auk, 54,* 245–273. (p. 134)

Louie, K., & Wilson, M. A. (2001). Temporally structured replay of awake hippocampal ensemble activity during rapid eye movement sleep. *Neuron, 29,* 145–156. (p. 98)

Lourenco, O., & Machado, A. (1996). In defense of Piaget's theory: A reply to 10 common criticisms. *Psychological Review, 103,* 143–164. (p. 130)

Lovaas, O. I. (1987). Behavioral treatment and normal educational and intellectual functioning in young autistic children. *Journal of Consulting and Clinical Psychology, 55,* 3–9. (p. 543)

Low, P. (2012). *The Cambridge declaration on consciousness.* Publicly proclaimed in Cambridge, UK, on July 7, 2012, at the Francis Crick Memorial Conference on Consciousness in Human and Non-Human Animals (fcmconference.org/img/CambridgeDeclarationOnConsciousness. pdf). (p. 309)

Lowry, P. E. (1997). The assessment center process: New directions. *Journal of Social Behavior and Personality, 12,* 53–62. (p. 484)

Lozano, A. M., & Mayberg, H. S. (2015, February). Treating depression at the source. *Scientific American,* pp. 68–73. (p. 564)

Lu, J., Zhong, X., Liu, H., Hao, L., Huang, C. T. L., Sherafat, M. A., . . . Zhang, S. C. (2016). Generation of serotonin neurons from human pluripotent stem cells. *Nature Biotechnology, 34,* 89–94. (p. 64)

Lu, Z.-L., Williamson, S. J., & Kaufman, L. (1992). Behavioral lifetime of human auditory sensory memory predicted by physiological measures. *Science, 258,* 1668–1670. (p. 270)

Lubinski, D. (2009). Cognitive epidemiology: With emphasis on untangling cognitive ability and socioeconomic status. *Intelligence, 37,* 625–633. (p. 331)

Lubinski, D. (2016). From Terman to today: A century of findings on intellectual precocity. *Review of Educational Research, 86,* 900–944. (pp. 331, 332)

Lubinski, D., Benbow, C. P., & Kell, H. J. (2014). Life paths and accomplishments of mathematically precocious males and females four decades later. *Psychological Science, 25,* 2217–2232. (p. 331)

Luby, J. L., Belden, A., Harms, M. P., Tillman, R., & Barch, D. M. (2016). Preschool is a sensitive period for the influence of maternal support on the trajectory of hippocampal development. *PNAS, 113,* 5742–5747. (p. 124)

Lucas, A., Morley, R., Cole, T. J., Lister, G., & Leeson-Payne, C. (1992). Breast milk and subsequent intelligence quotient in children born preterm. *The Lancet, 339,* 261–264. (p. 27)

Lucas, R. E., Clark, A. E., Georgellis, Y., & Diener, E. (2004). Unemployment alters the set point for life satisfaction. *Psychological Science, 15,* 8–13. (p. 411)

Lucas, R. E., & Donnellan, M. B. (2007). How stable is happiness? Using the STARTS model to estimate the stability of life satisfaction. *Journal of Research in Personality, 41,* 1091–1098. (p. 411)

Lucas, R. E., & Donnellan, M. B. (2009). Age differences in personality: Evidence from a nationally representative Australian sample. *Developmental Psychology, 45,* 1353–1363. (p. 118)

Ludwig, A. M. (1995). *The price of greatness: Resolving the creativity and madness controversy.* New York: Guilford Press. (p. 516)

Ludwig, D. S., & Friedman, M. I. (2014). Increasing adiposity: Consequence or cause of overeating? *JAMA, 311,* 2167–2168. (p. 363)

Luethi, M. S., Friese, M., Binder, J., Boesiger, P., Luechinger, R., & Rasch, B. (2016). Motivational incentives lead to a strong increase in lateral prefrontal activity after self-control exertion. *Social Cognitive and Affective Neuroscience, 10,* 1618–1626. (p. 398)

Luhmann, M., & Hawkley, L. C. (2016). Age differences in loneliness from late adolescence to oldest old age. *Developmental Psychology, 52,* 943–959. (p. 158)

Luhmann, M., Hofmann, W., Eid, M., & Lucas, R. E. (2012). Subjective well-being and adaptation to life events: A meta-analysis. *Journal of Personality and Social Psychology, 102,* 592–615. (p. 408)

Lukaszewski, A. W., Simmons, Z. L., Anderson, C., & Roney, J. R. (2016). The role of physical formidability in human social status allocation. *Journal of Personality and Social Psychology, 110,* 385–406. (p. 184)

Lund, T. J., & Dearing, E. (2012). Is growing up affluent risky for adolescents or is the problem growing up in an affluent neighborhood? *Journal of Research on Adolescence, 23,* 274–282. (p. 137)

Lundy, A. C. (1985). The reliability of the Thematic Apperception Test. *Journal of Personality Assessment, 49,* 141–145. (p. 467)

Luppino, F. S., de Wit, L. M., Bouvy, P. F., Stijnen, T., Cuijpers, P., Penninx, W. J. H., & Zitman, F. G. (2010). Overweight, obesity, and depression. *Archives of General Psychiatry, 67,* 220–229. (p. 365)

Luria, A. M. (1968). In L. Solotaroff (Trans.), *The mind of a mnemonist.* New York: Basic Books. (p. 284)

Lustig, C., & Buckner, R. L. (2004). Preserved neural correlates of priming in old age and dementia. *Neuron, 42,* 865–875. (p. 285)

Lutfey, K. E., Link, C. L., Rosen, R. C., Wiegel, M., & McKinlay, J. B. (2009). Prevalence and correlates of sexual activity and function in women: Results from the Boston Area Community Health (BACH) Survey. *Archives of Sexual Behavior, 38,* 514–527. (p. 175)

Lutgendorf, S. K., & Andersen, B. L. (2015). Biobehavioral approaches to cancer progression and survival. *American Psychologist, 70,* 186–197. (p. 390)

Lutgendorf, S. K., Lamkin, D. M., Jennings, N. B., Arevalo, J. M. G., Penedo, F., DeGeest, K., . . . Sood, A. K. (2008). Biobehavioral influences on matrix metalloproteinase expression in ovarian carcinoma. *Clinical Cancer Research, 14,* 6839–6846. (p. 390)

Lutgendorf, S. K., Russell, D., Ullrich, P., Harris, T. B., & Wallace, R. (2004). Religious participation, interleukin-6, and mortality in older adults. *Health Psychology, 23,* 465–475. (p. 406)

Luthar, S. S., Barkin, S. H., & Crossman, E. J. (2013). "I can, therefore I must": Fragility in the upper-middle classes. *Development and Psychopathology, 25,* 1529–1549. (p. 137)

Lutz, P. E., Gross, J. A., Dhir, S. K., Maussion, G., Yang, J., Bramoullé, A., . . . Turecki, G. (2017). Epigenetic regulation of the kappa opioid receptor by child abuse. *Biological Psychiatry.* Advance online publication. doi:10.1016/j.biopsych.2017.07.012 (p. 137)

Luyckx, K., Tildesley, E. A., Soenens, B., Andrews, J. A., Hampson, S. E., Peterson, M., & Duriez, B. (2011). Parenting and trajectories of children's maladaptive behaviors: A 12-year prospective community study. *Journal of Clinical Child and Adolescent Psychology, 40,* 468–478. (p. 139)

Lyall, S. (2005, November 29). What's the buzz? Rowdy teenagers don't want to hear it. *The New York Times* (nytimes.com). (p. 152)

Lykes, V. A., & Kemmelmeier, M. (2014). What predicts loneliness? Cultural difference between individualistic and collectivistic societies in Europe. *Journal of Cross-Cultural Psychology, 45,* 468–490. (p. 10)

Lykken, D. T. (1991). *Science, lies, and controversy: An epitaph for the polygraph.* Invited address upon receipt of the Senior Career Award for Distinguished Contribution to Psychology in the Public Interest, American Psychological Association convention. (p. 374)

Lykken, D. T. (2006). The mechanism of emergenesis. *Genes, Brain & Behavior, 5,* 306–310. (p. 336)

Lynch, G. (2002). Memory enhancement: The search for mechanism-based drugs. *Nature Neuroscience, 5* (suppl.), 1035–1038. (p. 278)

Lynch, G., & Staubli, U. (1991). Possible contributions of long-term potentiation to the encoding and organization of memory. *Brain Research Reviews, 16,* 204–206. (p. 279)

Lynn, M. (1988). The effects of alcohol consumption on restaurant tipping. *Personality and Social Psychology Bulletin, 14,* 87–91. (p. 103)

Lynn, R., Cheng, H., & Wang, M. (2016). Differences in the intelligence of children across thirty-one provinces and municipalities of China and their economic and social correlates. *Intelligence, 58,* 10–13. (p. 342)

Lynn, R., Sakar, C., & Cheng, H. (2015). Regional differences in intelligence, income and other socio-economic variables in Turkey. *Intelligence, 50,* 144–149. (p. 342)

Lynn, R., & Vanhanen, T. (2012). *Intelligence: A unifying construct for the social sciences.* London: Ulster Institute for Social Research. (p. 342)

Lynn, S. J., Laurence, J., & Kirsch, I. (2015). Hypnosis, suggestion, and suggestibility: An integrative model. *American Journal of Clinical Hypnosis, 57,* 314–329. (p. 224)

Lynn, S. J., Lilienfeld, S. O., Merckelbach, H., Giesbrecht, T., McNally, R. J., Loftus, E. F., . . . Malaktaris, A. (2014). The trauma model of dissociation: Inconvenient truths and stubborn fictions. Comment on Dalenberg et al. (2012). *Psychological Bulletin, 140,* 896–910. (p. 528)

Lynn, S. J., Rhue, J. W., & Weekes, J. R. (1990). Hypnotic involuntariness: A social cognitive analysis. *Psychological Review, 97,* 169–184. (p. 224)

Lynne, S. D., Graber, J. A., Nichols, T. R., Brooks-Gunn, J., & Botvin, G. J. (2007). Links between pubertal timing, peer influences, and externalizing behaviors among urban students followed through middle school. *Journal of Adolescent Health, 40,* 181.e7–181.e13. doi:10.1016/j.jadohealth.2006.09.008 (p. 142)

Lyons, A. (2015). Resilience in lesbians and gay men: A review and key findings from a nationwide Australian survey. *International Review of Psychiatry, 27,* 435–443. (p. 179)

Lyons, B. D., Hoffman, B. J., Michel, J. W., & Williams, K. J. (2011). On the predictive efficiency of past performance and physical ability: The case of the National Football League. *Human Performance, 24,* 158–172. (p. 484)

Lyons, D. E., Young, A. G., & Keil, F. C. (2007). The hidden structure of overimitation. *PNAS, 104,* 19751–19756. (p. 260)

Lyons, H. A., Manning, W. D., Longmore, M. A., & Giordano, P. C. (2015). Gender and casual sexual activity from adolescence to emerging adulthood: Social and life course correlates. *Journal of Sex Research, 52,* 543–557. (p. 177)

Lyons, L. (2004, February 3). *Growing up lonely: Examining teen alienation.* Retrieved from gallup.com/poll/10465/growing-lonely-examining-teen-alienation.aspx (p. 146)

Lyons, M. J., Panizzon, M. S., Liu, W., McKenzie, R., Bluestone, N. J., Grant, M. D., . . . Xian, H. (2017). A longitudinal twin study of general cognitive ability over four decades. *Developmental Psychology, 53,* 1170–1177. (p. 330)

Lyubomirsky, S. (2001). Why are some people happier than others? The role of cognitive and motivational processes in well-being. *American Psychologist, 56,* 239–249. (p. 410)

Lyubomirsky, S. (2008). *The how of happiness.* New York: Penguin. (p. 398)

Lyubomirsky, S., Sousa, L., & Dickerhoof, R. (2006). The costs and benefits of writing, talking, and thinking about life's triumphs and defeats. *Journal of Personality and Social Psychology, 90,* 690–708. (p. 401)

Ma, A., Landau, M. J., Narayanan, J., & Kay, A. C. (2017). Thought-control difficulty motivates structure seeking. *Journal of Experimental Psychology: General.* Advance online publication. doi:10.1037/xge0000282 (p. 17)

Ma, D. S., Correll, J., Wittenbrink, B., Bar-Anan, Y., Sriram, N., & Nosek, B. A. (2013). When fatigue turns deadly: The association between fatigue and racial bias in the decision to shoot. *Basic and Applied Social Psychology, 35,* 515–524. (p. 436)

Ma, L. (1997, September). On the origin of Darwin's ills. *Discover,* p. 27. (p. 508)

Maas, J. B. (1999). *Power sleep: The revolutionary program that prepares your mind and body for peak performance.* New York: HarperCollins. (p. 94)

Maas, J. B., & Robbins, R. S. (2010). *Sleep for success: Everything you must know about sleep but are too tired to ask.* Bloomington, IN: Author House. (p. 92)

Maass, A., D'Ettole, C., & Cadinu, M. (2008). Checkmate? The role of gender stereotypes in the ultimate intellectual sport. *European Journal of Social Psychology, 38,* 231–245. (p. 344)

Macan, T. H., & Dipboye, R. L. (1994). The effects of the application on processing of information from the employment interview. *Journal of Applied Social Psychology, 24,* 1291. (p. B-5)

MacCabe, J. H., Lambe, M. P., Cnattingius, S., Torrång, A., Björk, C., Sham, P. C., . . . Hultman, C. M. (2008). Scholastic achievement at age 16 and risk of schizophrenia and other psychoses: A national cohort study. *Psychological Medicine, 38,* 1133–1140. (p. 524)

Maccoby, E. E. (1990). Gender and relationships: A developmental account. *American Psychologist, 45,* 513–520. (p. 164)

Maccoby, E. E. (1998). *The two sexes: Growing up apart, coming together.* Cambridge, MA: Belknap Press. (p. 165)

Maccoby, E. E. (2002). Gender and group process: A developmental perspective. *Current Directions in Psychological Science, 11,* 54–58. (p. 165)

MacCormack, J. K., & Lindquist, K. A. (2016). Bodily contribution to emotion: Schachter's legacy for a psychological constructionist view on emotion. *Emotion Review, 9,* 36–45. (p. 369)

MacDonald, G., & Leary, M. R. (2005). Why does social exclusion hurt? The relationship between social and physical pain. *Psychological Bulletin, 131,* 202–223. (p. 354)

MacDonald, T. K., & Hynie, M. (2008). Ambivalence and unprotected sex: Failure to predict sexual activity and decreased condom use. *Journal of Applied Social Psychology, 38,* 1092–1107. (p. 177)

MacDonald, T. K., Zanna, M. P., & Fong, G. T. (1995). Decision making in altered states: Effects of alcohol on attitudes toward drinking and driving. *Journal of Personality and Social Psychology, 68,* 973–985. (p. 103)

MacFarlane, A. (1978, February). What a baby knows. *Human Nature,* pp. 74–81. (p. 121)

Macfarlane, J. W. (1964). Perspectives on personality consistency and change from the guidance study. *Vita Humana, 7,* 115–126. (p. 141)

Maciejewski, P. K., Maercker, A., Boelen, P. A., & Prigerson, H. G. (2016). "Prolonged grief disorder" and "persistent complex bereavement disorder," but not "complicated grief," are one and the same diagnostic entity: An analysis of data from the Yale Bereavement Study. *World Psychiatry, 15,* 266–275. (p. 497)

MacInnis, C. C., & Hodson, G. (2015). Do American states with more religious or conservative populations search more for sexual content on Google? *Archives of Sexual Behavior, 44,* 137–147. (p. 179)

Mack, A., & Rock, I. (2000). *Inattentional blindness.* Cambridge, MA: MIT Press. (p. 82)

Mackenzie, A. K., & Harris, J. M. (2017). A link between attentional function, effective eye movements, and driving ability. *Journal of Experimental Psychology: Human Perception and Performance, 43,* 381–394. (p. 82)

Mackenzie, J. L., Aggen, S. H., Kirkpatrick, R. M., Kendler, K. S., & Amstadter, A. B. (2015). A longitudinal twin study of insomnia symptoms in adults. *Sleep, 38,* 1423–1430. (p. 90)

MacKenzie, M. J., Nicklas, E., Waldfogel, J., & Brooks-Gunn, J. (2013). Spanking and child development across the first decade of life. *Pediatrics, 132,* e1118–1125. (p. 249)

MacKerron, G., & Mourato, S. (2013). Happiness is greater in natural environments. *Global Environmental Change, 23,* 992–1000. (p. 559)

MacLean, E. L., Hare, B., Nunn, C. L., Addessi, E., Amici, F., Anderson, R. C., . . . Boogert, N. J. (2014). The evolution of self-control. *PNAS, 111,* E2140–E2148. (p. 145)

MacLeod, C., & Clarke, P. J. F. (2015). The attentional bias modification approach to anxiety intervention. *Clinical Psychological Science, 3,* 58–78. (p. 544)

MacLeod, C. M., & Bodner, G. E. (2017). The production effect in memory. *Current Directions in Psychological Science, 26,* 390–395. (p. 295)

Macmillan, M., & Lena, M. L. (2010). Rehabilitating Phineas Gage. *Neuropsychological Rehabilitation, 17,* 1–18. (p. 63)

Macnamara, B. N., Hambrick, D. Z., & Oswald, F. L. (2014). Deliberate practice and performance in music, games, sports, education, and professions: A meta-analysis. *Psychological Science, 25,* 1608–1618. (p. 326) (p. 357)

Macnamara, B. N., Moreau, D., & Hambrick, D. Z. (2016). The relationship between deliberate practice and performance in sports: A meta-analysis. *Perspectives on Psychological Science, 11,* 333–350. (pp. 326, 357)

MacNeilage, P. F., & Davis, B. L. (2000). On the origin of internal structure of word forms. *Science, 288,* 527–531. (p. 314)

MacNeilage, P. F., Rogers, L. J., & Vallortigara, G. (2009). Origins of the left and right brain. *Scientific American, 301,* 60–67. (p. 67)

MacPherson, S. E., Turner, M. S., Bozzali, M., Cipolotti, L., & Shallice, T. (2016). The Doors and People Test: The effect of frontal lobe lesions on recall and recognition memory performance. *Neuropsychology, 30,* 332–337. (p. 62)

Macur, J. (2018, January 24). In Larry Nassar's case, a single voice eventually raised an army. *The New York Times* (nytimes.com). (p. 429)

Madison, G., Mosling, M. A., Verweij, K. J. H., Pedersen, N. L., & Ullen, F. (2016). Common genetic influences on intelligence and auditory simple reaction time in a large Swedish sample. *Intelligence, 59,* 157–162. (p. 336)

Maeda, Y., & Yoon, S. Y. (2013). A meta-analysis on gender differences in mental rotation ability measured by the Purdue spatial visualization tests: Visualization of rotations (PSVT:R). *Educational Psychology Review, 25,* 69–94. (p. 340)

Maes, H. H., Neale, M. C., Ohlsson, H., Zahery, M., Lichtenstein, P., Sundquist, K., . . . Kendler, K. S. (2016). A bivariate genetic analysis of drug abuse ascertained through medical and criminal registries in Swedish twins, siblings and half-siblings. *Behavior Genetics, 46,* 735–741. (p. 111)

Maes, H. H. M., Neale, M. C., & Eaves, L. J. (1997). Genetic and environmental factors in relative body weight and human adiposity. *Behavior Genetics, 27,* 325–351. (p. 365)

Maestripieri, D. (2003). Similarities in affiliation and aggression between cross-fostered rhesus macaque females and their biological mothers. *Developmental Psychobiology, 43,* 321–327. (p. 72)

Maestripieri, D. (2005). Early experience affects the intergenerational transmission of infant abuse in rhesus monkeys. *PNAS, 102,* 9726–9729. (p. 137) .

Magnusson, D. (1990). Personality research—challenges for the future. *European Journal of Personality, 4,* 1–17. (p. 531)

Maguire, E. A., Gadian, D. G., Johnsrude, I. S., Good, C. D., Ashburner, J., Frackowiak, R. S. J., & Frith, C. D. (2000). Navigation-related structural change in the hippocampi of taxi drivers. *PNAS, 97,* 4398–4403. (pp. 39, 124)

Maguire, E. A., Spiers, H. J., Good, C. D., Hartley, T., Frackowiak, R. S. J., & Burgess, N. (2003a). Navigation expertise and the human hippocampus: A structural brain imaging analysis. *Hippocampus, 13,* 250–259. (p. 276)

Maguire, E. A., Valentine, E. R., Wilding, J. M., & Kapur, N. (2003b). Routes to remembering: The brains behind superior memory. *Nature Neuroscience, 6,* 90–95. (p. 272)

Maguire, E. A., Woollett, K., & Spiers, H. J. (2006). London taxi drivers and bus drivers: A structural MRI and neuropsychological analysis. *Hippocampus, 16,* 1091–1101. (p. 39)

Maher, S., Ekstrom, T., & Chen, Y. (2014). Greater perceptual sensitivity to happy facial expression. *Perception, 43,* 1353–1364. (p. 376)

Maia, T. V., & Frank, M. J. (2017). An integrative perspective on the role of dopamine in schizophrenia. *Biological Psychiatry, 81,* 52–66. (p. 524)

Maier, S. F., & Seligman, M. E. P. (2016). Learned helplessness at fifty: Insights from neuroscience. *Psychological Review, 123,* 349–367. (p. 520)

Maier, S. F., Watkins, L. R., & Fleshner, M. (1994). Psychoneuroimmunology: The interface between behavior, brain, and immunity. *American Psychologist, 49,* 1004–1017. (p. 389)

Major, B., Carrington, P. I., & Carnevale, P. J. D. (1984). Physical attractiveness and self-esteem: Attribution for praise from an other-sex evaluator. *Personality and Social Psychology Bulletin, 10,* 43–50. (p. 449)

Major, B., Schmidlin, A. M., & Williams, L. (1990). Gender patterns in social touch: The impact of setting and age. *Journal of Personality and Social Psychology, 58,* 634–643. (p. 164)

Makel, M. C., Kell, H. J., Lubinski, D., Putallaz, M., & Benbow, C. P. (2016). When lightning strikes twice: Profoundly gifted, profoundly accomplished. *Psychological Science, 27,* 1004–1018. (p. 331)

Makel, M. C., Wai, J., Peairs, K., & Putallaz, M. (2016). Sex differences in the right tail of cognitive abilities: An update and cross cultural extension. *Intelligence, 59,* 8–15. (p. 341)

Makin, S. (2015). What really causes autism. *Scientific American, 26,* 56–63. (p. 131)

Maldonado-Molina, M. M., Reingle, J. M., Jennings, W. G., & Prado, G. (2011). Drinking and driving among immigrant and US-born Hispanic young adults: Results from a longitudinal and nationally representative study. *Addictive Behaviors, 36,* 381–388. (p. 503)

Malkiel, B. G. (2016). *A random walk down Wall Street: The time-tested strategy for successful investing* (11th Edition). New York: Norton. (p. 303)

Malle, B. F. (2006). The actor–observer asymmetry in attribution: A (surprising) meta-analysis. *Psychological Bulletin, 132,* 895–919. (p. 417)

Malle, B. F., Knobe, J. M., & Nelson, S. E. (2007). Actor–observer asymmetries in explanations of behavior: New answers to an old question. *Journal of Personality and Social Psychology, 93,* 491–514. (p. 417)

Malmquist, C. P. (1986). Children who witness parental murder: Post-traumatic aspects. *Journal of the American Academy of Child Psychiatry, 25,* 320–325. (p. 469)

Maltby, N., Tolin, D. F., Worhunsky, P., O'Keefe, T. M., & Kiehl, K. A. (2005). Dysfunctional action monitoring hyperactivates frontal-striatal circuits in obsessive-compulsive disorder: An event-related fMRI study. *NeuroImage, 24,* 495–503. (p. 512)

Mampe, B., Friederici, A. D., Christophe, A., & Wermke, K. (2009). Newborns' cry melody is shaped by their native language. *Current Biology, 19,* 1–4. (p. 120)

Maner, J. K., DeWall, C. N, Baumeister, R. F., & Schaller, M. (2007). Does social exclusion motivate interpersonal reconnection? Resolving the "porcupine problem." *Journal of Personality and Social Psychology, 92,* 42–55. (p. 354)

Maner, J. K., Kenrick, D. T., Neuberg, S. L., Becker, D. V., Robertson, T., Hofer, B., . . . Schaller, M. (2005). Functional projection: How fundamental social motives can bias interpersonal perception. *Journal of Personality and Social Psychology, 88,* 63–78. (p. 470)

Mani, A., Mullainathan, S., Shafir, E., & Zhao, J. (2013). Poverty impedes cognitive function. *Science, 341,* 976–980. (p. 339)

Mann, T., Tomiyama, A. J., & Ward, A. (2015). Promoting public health in the context of the "obesity epidemic": False starts and promising new directions. *Perspectives on Psychological Science, 10,* 706–710. (p. 365)

Manning, W., & Cohen, J. A. (2012). Premarital cohabitation and marital dissolution: An examination of recent marriages. *Journal of Marriage and Family 74,* 377–387. (p. 156)

Manson, J. E. (2002). Walking compared with vigorous exercise for the prevention of cardiovascular events in women. *New England Journal of Medicine, 347,* 716–725. (p. 401)

Maquet, P. (2001). The role of sleep in learning and memory. *Science, 294,* 1048–1052. (p. 98)

Maquet, P., Peters, J.-M., Aerts, J., Delfiore, G., Degueldre, C., Luxen, A., & Franck, G. (1996). Functional neuroanatomy of human rapid-eye-movement sleep and dreaming. *Nature, 383,* 163–166. (p. 99)

Mar, R. A., & Oatley, K. (2008). The function of fiction is the abstraction and simulation of social experience. *Perspectives on Psychological Science, 3,* 173–192. (p. 260)

Mar, R. A., Oatley, K., & Peterson, J. B. (2009). Exploring the link between reading fiction and empathy: Ruling out individual differences and examining outcomes. *Communications: The European Journal of Communication, 34,* 407–428. (p. 378)

Marangolo, P., Fiori, V., Sabatini, U., De Pasquale, G., Razzano, C., Caltagirone, C., & Gili, T. (2016). Bilateral transcranial direct current stimulation language treatment enhances functional connectivity in the left hemisphere: Preliminary data from aphasia. *Journal of Cognitive Neuroscience, 28,* 724–738. (p. 317)

Marcus, B., Machilek, F., & Schütz, A. (2006). Personality in cyberspace: Personal web sites as media for personality expressions and impressions. *Journal of Personality and Social Psychology, 90,* 1014–1031. (p. 481)

Margolis, M. L. (2000). Brahms' lullaby revisited: Did the composer have obstructive sleep apnea? *Chest, 118,* 210–213. (p. 95)

Mariani, J., Simonini, M. V., Palejev, D., Tomasini, L., Coppola, G., Szekely, A. M., . . . Vaccarino, F. M. (2012). Modeling human cortical development in vitro using induced pluripotent stem cells. *PNAS, 109,* 12779–12775. (p. 64)

Marinak, B. A., & Gambrell, L. B. (2008). Intrinsic motivation and rewards: What sustains young children's engagement with text? *Literacy Research and Instruction, 47,* 9–26. (p. 358)

Marjonen, H., Sierra, A., Nyman, A., Rogojin, V., Gröhn, O., Linden, A.-M., . . . Kaminen-Ahola, N. (2015). Early maternal alcohol consumption alters hippocampal DNA methylation, gene expression and volume in a mouse model. *PLoS ONE, 10*(5), e0124931. doi:10.1371/journal.pone.0124931 (p. 120)

Markovizky, G., & Samid, Y. (2008). The process of immigrant adjustment: The role of time in determining psychological adjustment. *Journal of Cross-Cultural Psychology, 39,* 782–798. (p. 385)

Marks, A. K., Patton, F., & Coll, C. G. (2011). Being bicultural: A mixed-methods study of adolescents' implicitly and explicitly measured multiethnic identities. *Developmental Psychology, 47,* 270–288. (p. 146)

Markus, G. B. (1986). Stability and change in political attitudes: Observe, recall, and "explain." *Political Behavior, 8,* 21–44. (p. 292)

Markus, H. R., & Kitayama, S. (1991). Culture and the self: Implications for cognition, emotion, and motivation. *Psychological Review, 98,* 224–253. (pp. 319, 393, 556)

Markus, H. R., & Nurius, P. (1986). Possible selves. *American Psychologist, 41,* 954–969. (p. 486)

Marley, J., & Bulia, S. (2001). Crimes against people with mental illness: Types, perpetrators and influencing factors. *Social Work, 46,* 115–124. (p. 503)

Marmot, M. G., Bosma, H., Hemingway, H., Brunner, E., & Stansfeld, S. (1997). Contribution to job control and other risk factors to social variations in coronary heart disease incidents. *The Lancet, 350,* 235–239. (p. 396)

Marsh, A. A., Elfenbein, H. A., & Ambady, N. (2003). Nonverbal "accents": Cultural differences in facial expressions of emotion. *Psychological Science, 14,* 373–376. (p. 378)

Marsh, H. W., & Craven, R. G. (2006). Reciprocal effects of self-concept and performance from a multidimensional perspective: Beyond seductive pleasure and unidimensional perspectives. *Perspectives on Psychological Science, 1,* 133–163. (p. 486)

Marsh, H. W., & Parker, J. W. (1984). Determinants of student self-concept: Is it better to be a relatively large fish in a small pond even if you don't learn to swim as well? *Journal of Personality and Social Psychology, 47,* 213–231. (p. 410)

Marsh, N., Scheele, D., Gerhardt, H., Strang, S., Enax, L., Weber, B., . . . Hurlemann, R. (2017). The neuropeptide oxytocin induces a social altruism bias. *Journal of Neuroscience, 35,* 15696–15701. (p. 49)

Marshall, M. J. (2002). *Why spanking doesn't work.* Springville, UT: Bonneville Books. (p. 249)

Marshall, P. J., & Meltzoff, A. N. (2014). Neural mirroring mechanisms and imitation in human infants. *Philosophical Transactions of the Royal Society: Series B, 369.* doi:10.1098/rstb.2013.0620 (p. 260)

Marteau, T. M. (1989). Framing of information: Its influences upon decisions of doctors and patients. *British Journal of Social Psychology, 28,* 89–94. (p. 305)

Martel, M. M., Levinson, C. A., Langer, J. K., & Nigg, J. T. (2016). A network analysis of developmental change in ADHD symptom structure from preschool to adulthood. *Clinical Psychological Science, 4,* 988–1001. (p. 498)

Martela, F., & Steger, M. F. (2016). The three meanings of meaning in life: Distinguishing coherence, purpose, and significance. *The Journal of Positive Psychology, 11,* 531–545. (p. 350)

Martin, C. K., Anton, S. D., Walden, H., Arnett, C., Greenway, F. L., & Williamson, D. A. (2007). Slower eating rate reduces the food intake of men, but not women: Implications for behavioural weight control. *Behaviour Research and Therapy, 45,* 2349–2359. (p. 366)

Martin, C. L., & Ruble, D. (2004). Children's search for gender cues. *Current Directions in Psychological Science, 13,* 67–70. (p. 169)

Martin, C. L., Ruble, D. N., & Szkrybalo, J. (2002). Cognitive theories of early gender development. *Psychological Bulletin, 128,* 903–933. (p. 169)

Martín, R., Bajo-Grañeras, R., Moratalla, R., Perea, G., & Araque, A. (2015). Circuit-specific signaling in astrocyte-neuron networks in basal ganglia pathways. *Science, 349,* 730–734. (p. 40)

Martin, S. J., Kelly, I. W., & Saklofske, D. H. (1992). Suicide and lunar cycles: A critical review over 28 years. *Psychological Reports, 71,* 787–795. (p. 530)

Martín-María, N., Miret, M., Caballero, F. F., Rico-Uribe, L., Steptoe, A., Chatterji, S., & Ayuso-Mateos, J. (2017). The impact of subjective well-being on mortality: A meta-analysis of longitudinal studies in the general population. *Psychosomatic Medicine, 79,* 565–575. (p. 392)

Martins, Y., Preti, G., Crabtree, C. R., & Wysocki, C. J. (2005). Preference for human body odors is influenced by gender and sexual orientation. *Psychological Science, 16,* 694–701. (p. 181)

Marzoli, D., Custodero, M., Pagliara, A., & Tommasi, L. (2013). Sun-induced frowning fosters aggressive feelings. *Cognition and Emotion, 27,* 1513–1521. (p. 381)

Maslow, A. H. (1970). *Motivation and personality* (2nd ed.). New York: Harper & Row. (pp. 350, 471)

Maslow, A. H. (1971). *The farther reaches of human nature.* New York: Viking Press. (p. 350)

Mason, A. E., Sbarra, D. A., & Mehl, M. R. (2010). Thin-slicing divorce: Thirty seconds of information predict changes in psychological adjustment over 90 days. *Psychological Science, 21,* 1420–1422. (p. 377)

Mason, C., & Kandel, E. R. (1991). Central visual pathways. In E. R. Kandel, J. H. Schwartz, & T. M. Jessell (Eds.), *Principles of neural science* (3rd ed.). New York: Elsevier. (p. 45)

Mason, H. (2003, March 25). *Wake up, sleepy teen.* Retrieved from gallup.com/poll/8059/wake-up-sleepy-teen.aspx (p. 93)

Mason, H. (2005, January 25). *Who dreams, perchance to sleep?* Retrieved from gallup.com/poll/14716/who-dreams-perchance-sleep.aspx (p. 93)

Mason, M. F., & Morris, M. W. (2010). Culture, attribution and automaticity: A social cognitive neuroscience view. *Social Cognitive and Affective Neuroscience, 5,* 292–306. (p. 378)

Mason, R. A., & Just, M. A. (2004). How the brain processes causal inferences in text. *Psychological Science, 15,* 1–7. (p. 67)

Massimini, M., Ferrarelli, F., Huber, R., Esser, S. K., Singh, H., & Tononi, G. (2005). Breakdown of cortical effective connectivity during sleep. *Science, 309,* 2228–2232. (p. 87)

Masten, A. S. (2001). Ordinary magic: Resilience processes in development. *American Psychologist, 56,* 227–238. (p. 137)

Masters, K. S. (2010). The role of religion in therapy: Time for psychologists to have a little faith? *Cognitive and Behavioral Practice, 17,* 393–400. (p. 556)

Masters, K. S., & Hooker, S. A. (2013). Religiousness/spirituality, cardiovascular disease, and cancer: Cultural integration for health research and intervention. *Journal of Consulting and Clinical Psychology, 81,* 206–216. (p. 406)

Masters, W. H., & Johnson, V. E. (1966). *Human sexual response.* Boston: Little, Brown. (p. 174)

Mastroianni, G. R. (2015). Obedience in perspective: Psychology and the Holocaust. *Theory and Psychology, 25,* 657–669. (p. 427)

Mastroianni, G. R., & Reed, G. (2006). Apples, barrels, and Abu Ghraib. *Sociological Focus, 39,* 239–250. (p. 419)

Masuda, T., Ellsworth, P. C., Mesquita, B., Leu, J., Tanida, S., & Van de Veerdonk, E. (2008). Placing the face in context: Cultural differences in the perception of facial emotion. *Journal of Personality and Social Psychology, 94,* 365–381. (p. 379)

Mata, A., Ferreira, M. B., & Sherman, S. J. (2013). The metacognitive advantage of deliberative thinkers: A dual-process perspective on overconfidence. *Journal of Personality and Social Psychology, 105,* 353–373. (p. 306)

Mata, R., Josef, A. K., & Hertwig, R. (2016). Propensity for risk taking across the life span and around the globe. *Psychological Science, 27,* 231–243. (p. 118)

Mataix-Cols, D., Rosario-Campos, M. C., & Leckman, J. F. (2005). A multidimensional model of obsessive-compulsive disorder. *American Journal of Psychiatry, 162,* 228–238. (p. 512)

Mataix-Cols, D., Wooderson, S., Lawrence, N., Brammer, M. J., Speckens, A., & Phillips, M. L. (2004). Distinct neural correlates of washing, checking, and hoarding symptom dimensions in obsessive-compulsive disorder. *Archives of General Psychiatry, 61,* 564–576. (p. 512)

Mather, M. (2016). The affective neuroscience of aging. *Annual Review of Psychology, 67,* 213–238. (p. 158)

Mather, M., Cacioppo, J. T., & Kanwisher, N. (2013). How fMRI can inform cognitive theories. *Perspectives on Psychological Science, 8,* 108–113. (p. 53)

Mather, M., Canli, T., English, T., Whitfield, S., Wais, P., Ochsner, K., . . . Carstensen, L. L. (2004). Amygdala responses to emotionally valenced stimuli in older and younger adults. *Psychological Science, 15,* 259–263. (p. 158)

Mather, M., & Sutherland, M. (2012, February). The selective effects of emotional arousal on memory. *APA Science Brief* (apa.org). (p. 278)

Matson, J. L., & Boisjoli, J. A. (2009). The token economy for children with intellectual disability and/or autism: A review. *Research on Developmental Disabilities, 30,* 240–248. (p. 543)

Matsumoto, D. (1994). *People: Psychology from a cultural perspective.* Pacific Grove, CA: Brooks/Cole. (p. 319)

Matsumoto, D., & Ekman, P. (1989). American-Japanese cultural differences in intensity ratings of facial expressions of emotion. *Motivation and Emotion, 13,* 143–157. (p. 379)

Matsumoto, D., Frank, M. G., & Hwang, H. C. (2015). The role of intergroup emotions on political violence. *Current Directions in Psychological Science, 24,* 369–373. (p. 261)

Matsumoto, D., Willingham, B., & Olide, A. (2009). Sequential dynamics of culturally moderated facial expressions of emotion. *Psychological Science, 20,* 1269–1275. (p. 379)

Mattanah, J. F., Lopez, F. G, & Govern, J. M. (2011). The contributions of parental attachment bonds to college student development and adjustment: A meta-analytic review. *Journal of Counseling Psychology, 58,* 565–596. (p. 136)

Mattheisen, M., Samuels, J. F., Wang, Y., Greenberg, B. D., Fyer, A. J., McCracken, J. T., . . . Riddle, M. A. (2015). Genome-wide association study in obsessive-compulsive disorder: Results from OCGAS. *Molecular Psychiatry, 20,* 337–344. (p. 511)

Matthews, R. N., Domjan, M., Ramsey, M., & Crews, D. (2007). Learning effects on sperm competition and reproductive fitness. *Psychological Science, 18,* 758–762. (p. 238)

Matz, S. C., Kosinski, M., Nave, G., & Stillwell, D. J. (2017). Psychological targeting as an effective approach to digital mass persuasion. *PNAS, 114,* 12714–12719. (p. 479)

Maurer, D., & Maurer, C. (1988). *The world of the newborn.* New York: Basic Books. (p. 121)

Mautz, B., Wong, B., Peters, R., & Jennions, M. (2013). Penis size interacts with body shape and height to influence male attractiveness. *PNAS, 110,* 6925–6693. (p. 184)

Maxmen, A. (2018, January 24). As Cape Town water crisis deepens, scientists prepare for 'Day Zero.' *Nature* (nature.com/articles/d41586-018-01134-x). (p. 456)

Maxwell, S. E., Lau, M. Y., & Howard, G. S. (2015). Is psychology suffering from a replication crisis? What does "failure to replicate" really mean? *American Psychologist, 70,* 487–498. (p. 20)

May, C., & Hasher, L. (1998). Synchrony effects in inhibitory control over thought and action. *Journal of Experimental Psychology: Human Perception and Performance, 24,* 363–380. (p. 86)

May, P. A., Baete, J., Russo, A. J., Elliott, J., Blankenship, J., Kalberg, W. O., . . . Hoyme, H. E. (2014). Prevalence and characteristics of fetal alcohol spectrum disorders. *Pediatrics, 134,* 855–866. (p. 120)

May, R. (1982). The problem of evil: An open letter to Carl Rogers. *Journal of Humanistic Psychology, 22,* 10–21. (p. 473)

Mayberry, R. I., Lock, E., & Kazmi, H. (2002). Linguistic ability and early language exposure. *Nature, 417,* 38. (p. 316)

Mayer, J. D., Caruso, D. R., & Salovey, P. (2016). The ability model of emotional intelligence: Principles and updates. *Emotion Review, 8,* 290–300. (p. 326)

Mayer, J. D., Salovey, P., & Caruso, D. R. (2002). *The Mayer-Salovey-Caruso emotional intelligence test (MSCEIT).* Toronto: Multi-Health Systems. (p. 326)

Mayer, J. D., Salovey, P., & Caruso, D. R. (2012). The validity of the MSCEIT: Additional analyses and evidence. *Emotion Review, 4,* 403–408. (p. 326)

Mazure, C., Keita, G., & Blehar, M. (2002). *Summit on women and depression: Proceedings and recommendations.* Washington, DC: American Psychological Association (apa.org/pi/wpo/women&depression.pdf). (p. 520)

Mazza, S., Gerbier, E., Gustin, M. P., Kasikci, Z., Koenig, O., Toppino, T. C., & Magnin, M. (2016). Relearn faster and retain longer: Along with practice, sleep makes perfect. *Psychological Science, 27,* 1321–1330. (p. 276)

Mazzoni, G., Scoboria, A., & Harvey, L. (2010). Nonbelieved memories. *Psychological Science, 21,* 1334–1340. (p. 291)

Mazzoni, G., & Vannucci, M. (2007). Hindsight bias, the misinformation effect, and false autobiographical memories. *Social Cognition, 25,* 203–220. (p. 292)

McAdams, D. P., & Guo, J. (2015). Narrating the generative life. *Psychological Science, 26,* 475–483. (p. 472)

McAleer, P., Todorov, A., & Belin, P. (2014). How do you say "hello"? Personality impressions from brief novel voices. *PLoS ONE, 9,* 9. (p. 377)

McBurney, D. H. (1996). *How to think like a psychologist: Critical thinking in psychology.* Upper Saddle River, NJ: Prentice-Hall. (p. 62)

McBurney, D. H., & Collings, V. B. (1984). *Introduction to sensation and perception* (2nd ed.). Englewood Cliffs, NJ: Prentice-Hall. (p. 212)

McBurney, D. H., & Gent, J. F. (1979). On the nature of taste qualities. *Psychological Bulletin, 86,* 151–167. (p. 225)

McCabe, K. O., & Fleeson, W. (2016). Are traits useful? Explaining trait manifestations as tools in the pursuit of goals. *Journal of Personality and Social Psychology, 110,* 287–301. (p. 475)

McCain, J. (2017, February 17). Munich speech, reported by *The Guardian* (February 18, 2017), McCain attacks Trump administration and inability to "separate truth from lies." *The Guardian* (theguardian.com). (p. 18)

McCain, J. L., & Campbell, W. K. (2016). Narcissism and social media use: A meta-analytic review. *Psychology of Popular Media Culture.* Advance online publication. doi:10.1037/ppm0000137 (p. 489)

McCann, I. L., & Holmes, D. S. (1984). Influence of aerobic exercise on depression. *Journal of Personality and Social Psychology, 46,* 1142–1147. (p. 402)

McCann, S. J. H. (2017). Higher USA state resident neuroticism is associated with lower state volunteering rates. *Psychological Science, 43,* 1659–1674. (p. 479)

McCann, U. D., Eligulashvili, V., & Ricaurte, G. A. (2000). (±)3,4-Methylenedioxymethamphetamine ("Ecstasy")-induced serotonin neurotoxicity: Clinical studies. *Neuropsychobiology, 42,* 11–16. (p. 108)

McCarthy, J. (2016, August 8). *One in eight U.S. adults say they smoke marijuana.* Gallup Poll (gallup.com). (p. 109)

McCarthy, P. (1986, July). Scent: The tie that binds? *Psychology Today,* pp. 6, 10. (p. 226)

McCauley, C. R. (2002). Psychological issues in understanding terrorism and the response to terrorism. In C. E. Stout (Ed.), *The psychology of terrorism* (Vol. 3). Westport, CT: Praeger/Greenwood. (p. 431)

McCauley, C. R., & Segal, M. E. (1987). Social psychology of terrorist groups. In C. Hendrick (Ed.), *Group processes and intergroup relations.* Beverly Hills, CA: Sage. (p. 431)

McClendon, B. T., & Prentice-Dunn, S. (2001). Reducing skin cancer risk: An intervention based on protection motivation theory. *Journal of Health Psychology, 6,* 321–328. (p. 418)

McClintock, M. K., & Herdt, G. (1996). Rethinking puberty: The development of sexual attraction. *Current Directions in Psychological Science, 5,* 178–183. (p. 166)

McClung, M., & Collins, D. (2007). "Because I know it will!": Placebo effects of an ergogenic aid on athletic performance. *Journal of Sport & Exercise Psychology, 29,* 382–394. (p. 27)

McClure, E. B. (2000). A meta-analytic review of sex differences in facial expression processing and their development in infants, children, and adolescents. *Psychological Bulletin, 126,* 424–453. (p. 377)

McClure, M. J., & Lydon, J. E. (2014). Anxiety doesn't become you: How attachment compromises relational opportunities. *Journal of Personality and Social Psychology, 106,* 89–111. (p. 448)

McConnell, A. R., Brown, C. M., Shoda, T. M., Stayton, L. E., & Martin, C. E. (2011). Friends with benefits: On the positive consequences of pet ownership. *Journal of Personality and Social Psychology, 101,* 1239–1252. (p. 401)

McCrae, R. R., & Costa, P. T., Jr. (1986). Clinical assessment can benefit from recent advances in personality psychology. *American Psychologist, 41,* 1001–1003. (p. 478)

McCrae, R. R., & Costa, P. T., Jr. (1990). *Personality in adulthood.* New York: Guilford Press. (p. 155)

McCrae, R. R., & Costa, P. T., Jr. (1994). The stability of personality: Observations and evaluations. *Current Directions in Psychological Science, 3,* 173–175. (p. 480)

McCrae, R. R., & Costa, P. T., Jr. (2008). The Five-Factor Theory of personality. In O. P. John, R. W., Robins, & L. A. Pervin (Eds.), *Handbook of personality: Theory and research* (3rd ed.). New York: Guilford. (p. 478)

McCrae, R. R., Scally, M., Terraccioani, A., Abecasis, G. R., & Costa, P. T., Jr. (2010). An alternative to the search for single polymorphisms: Toward molecular personality scales for the Five-Factor Model. *Journal of Personality and Social Psychology, 99,* 1014–1024. (p. 478)

McCrae, R. R., Terracciano, A., & 78 members of the Personality Profiles and Cultures Project. (2005). Universal features of personality traits from the observer's perspective: Data from 50 cultures. *Journal of Personality and Social Psychology, 88,* 547–561. (p. 478)

McCrink, K., & Wynn, K. (2004). Large-number addition and subtraction by 9-month-old infants. *Psychological Science, 15,* 776–781. (p. 127)

McCrory, E. J., De Brito, S. A., Sebastian, C. L., Mechelli, A., Bird, G., Kelly, P. A., & Viding, E. (2011). Heightened neural reactivity to threat in child victims of family violence. *Current Biology, 21,* R947–948. (p. 137)

McCullough, M. E., Hoyt, W. T., Larson, D. B., Koenig, H. G., & Thoresen, C. (2000). Religious involvement and mortality: A meta-analytic review. *Health Psychology, 19,* 211–222. (p. 405)

McCullough, M. E., & Laurenceau, J.-P. (2005). Religiousness and the trajectory of self-rated health across adulthood. *Personality and Social Psychology Bulletin, 31,* 560–573. (p. 405)

McCullough, M. E., & Willoughby, B. L. B. (2009). Religion, self-regulation, and self-control: Associations, explanations, and implications. *Psychological Bulletin, 135,* 69–93. (p. 406)

McDaniel, M. A., Bugg, J. M., Liu, Y., & Brick, J. (2015). When does the test-study-test sequence optimize learning and retention? *Journal of Experimental Psychology: Applied, 21,* 370–382. (pp. 14, 35, 49, 58, 68, 78, 85, 100, 114, 122, 140, 150, 160, 171, 187, 198, 214, 232, 242, 253, 264, 274, 282, 295, 310, 322, 334, 345, 359, 366, 375, 382, 394, 413, 433, 446, 460, 473, 492, 505, 513, 522, 534, 549, 557, 568, A-8, B-14)

McDaniel, M. A., Howard, D. C., & Einstein, G. O. (2009). The read-recite-review study strategy: Effective and portable. *Psychological Science, 20,* 516–522. (pp. 14, 33, 35, 49, 58, 68, 78, 85, 100, 114, 122, 140, 150, 160, 171, 187, 198, 214, 232, 242, 253, 264, 274, 282, 295, 310, 322, 334, 345, 359, 366, 375, 382, 394, 413, 433, 446, 460, 473, 492, 505, 513, 522, 534, 549, 557, 568, A-8, B-14)

McDermott, R., Tingley, D., Cowden, J., Frazzetto, G., & Johnson, D. D. P. (2009). Monoamine oxidase A gene (MAOA) predicts behavioral aggression following provocation. *PNAS, 106,* 2118–2123. (p. 441)

McDonald, P. (2012). Workplace sexual harassment 30 years on: A review of the literature. *International Journal of Management Reviews, 14,* 1–17. (p. 169)

McDuff, D., Kodra, E., el Kallouby, R., & LaFrance, M. (2017). A large-scale analysis of sex differences in facial expressions. *PLoS ONE, 12*(4), e0173942. (p. 377)

McEvoy, S. P., Stevenson, M. R., McCartt, A. T., Woodward, M., Hawroth, C., Palamara, P., & Ceracelli, R. (2005). Role of mobile phones in motor vehicle crashes resulting in hospital attendance: A case-crossover study. *British Medical Journal, 331,* 428. http://dx.doi.org/10.1136/bmj.38537.397512.55 (p. 82)

McEvoy, S. P., Stevenson, M. R., & Woodward, M. (2007). The contribution of passengers versus mobile phone use to motor vehicle crashes resulting in hospital attendance by the driver. *Accident Analysis and Prevention, 39,* 1170–1176. (p. 82)

McFarland, C., & Ross, M. (1987). The relation between current impressions and memories of self and dating partners. *Psychological Bulletin, 13,* 228–238. (p. 292)

McFarland, S., & Carnahan, T. (2009). A situation's first powers are attracting volunteers and selecting participants: A reply to Haney and Zimbardo (2009). *Personality and Social Psychology Bulletin, 35,* 815–818. (p. 419)

McGaugh, J. L. (1994). Quoted by B. Bower, Stress hormones hike emotional memories. *Science News, 146,* 262. (p. 278)

McGaugh, J. L. (2003). *Memory and emotion: The making of lasting memories.* New York: Columbia University Press. (p. 278)

McGaugh, J. L. (2015). Consolidating memories. *Annual Review of Psychology, 66,* 1–24. (p. 277)

McGaugh, J. L., & LePort, A. (2014). Remembrance of all things past. *Scientific American, 310,* 40–45. (p. 284)

McGhee, P. E. (June, 1976). Children's appreciation of humor: A test of the cognitive congruency principle. *Child Development, 47,* 420–426. (p. 128)

McGowan, P. O., Sasaki, A., D'Alessio, A. C., Dymov, S., Labonté, B., Szyl, M., . . . Meaney, M. J. (2009). Epigenetic regulation of the glucocorticoid receptor in human brain associates with childhood abuse. *Nature Neuroscience, 12,* 342–348. (p. 512)

McGrath, J. J., & Welham, J. L. (1999). Season of birth and schizophrenia: A systematic review and meta-analysis of data from the Southern hemisphere. *Schizophrenia Research, 35,* 237–242. (p. 525)

McGrath, J. J., Welham, J., & Pemberton, M. (1995). Month of birth, hemisphere of birth and schizophrenia. *British Journal of Psychiatry, 167,* 783–785. (p. 525)

McGue, M. (2010). The end of behavioral genetics? *Behavioral Genetics, 40,* 284–296. (p. 75)

McGue, M., & Bouchard, T. J., Jr. (1998). Genetic and environmental influences on human behavioral differences. *Annual Review of Neuroscience, 21,* 1–24. (p. 72)

McGue, M., Bouchard, T. J., Jr., Iacono, W. G., & Lykken, D. T. (1993). Behavioral genetics of cognitive ability: A life-span perspective. In R. Plomin & G. E. McClearn (Eds.), *Nature, nurture and psychology.* Washington, DC: American Psychological Association. (pp. 337, 338)

McGurk, H., & MacDonald, J. (1976). Hearing lips and seeing voices. *Nature, 264,* 746–748. (p. 228)

McHugh, P. R. (1995). Resolved: Multiple personality disorder is an individually and socially created artifact. *Journal of the American Academy of Child and Adolescent Psychiatry, 34,* 957–959. (p. 528)

McKay, J. (2000). Building self-esteem in children. In M. McKay & P. Fanning (Eds.), *Self-esteem.* New York: New Harbinger/St. Martins. (p. 486)

McKellar, J., Stewart, E., & Humphreys, K. (2003). Alcoholics Anonymous involvement and positive alcohol-related outcomes: Cause, consequence, or just a correlate? A prospective 2-year study of 2,319 alcohol-dependent men. *Journal of Consulting and Clinical Psychology, 71,* 302–308. (p. 548)

McKenna, K. Y. A., Green, A. S., & Gleason, M. E. J. (2002). What's the big attraction? Relationship formation on the internet. *Journal of Social Issues, 58,* 9–31. (p. 448)

McKinnon, M. C., Palombo, D. J., Nazarov, A., Kumar, N., Khuu, W., & Levine, B. (2015). Threat of death and autobiographical memory: A study of passengers from flight AT236. *Clinical Psychological Science, 3,* 487–502. (p. 289)

McKone, E., Kanwisher, N., & Duchaine, B. C. (2007). Can generic expertise explain special processing for faces? *Trends in Cognitive Sciences, 11,* 8–15. (p. 205)

McLaughlin, K. A., Sheridan, M. A., Tibu, F., Fox, N. A., Zeanah, C. H., & Nelson, C. A. (2015). Causal effects of the early caregiving environment on development of stress response systems in children. *PNAS, 112,* 5637–5642. (p. 137)

McLaughlin, M. (2010, October 2). J. K. Rowling: Depression, the "terrible place that allowed me to come back stronger." *The Scotsman* (scotsman.com). (p. 516)

McLean, C. P., & Anderson, E. R. (2009). Brave men and timid women? A review of the gender differences in fear and anxiety. *Clinical Psychology Review, 29,* 496–505. (p. 507)

McMurray, B. (2007). Defusing the childhood vocabulary explosion. *Science, 317,* 631. (p. 313)

McNally, R. J. (2003). *Remembering trauma.* Cambridge, MA: Harvard University Press. (pp. 293, 510)

McNally, R. J. (2007). Betrayal trauma theory: A critical appraisal. *Memory, 15,* 280–294. (p. 293)

McNally, R. J. (2012). Are we winning the war against posttraumatic stress disorder? *Science, 336,* 872–874. (pp. 88, 510)

McNally, R. J., & Geraerts, E. (2009). A new solution to the recovered memory debate. *Perspectives on Psychological Science, 4,* 126–134. (p. 293)

McNeil, B. J., Pauker, S. G., & Tversky, A. (1988). On the framing of medical decisions. In D. E. Bell, H. Raiffa, & A. Tversky (Eds.), *Decision making: Descriptive, normative, and prescriptive interactions* (pp. 562–568). New York: Cambridge University Press. (p. 305)

McNulty, J. K., Olson, M. A., Meltzer, A. L., & Shaffer, M. J. (2013). Though they may be unaware, newlyweds implicitly know whether their marriage will be satisfying. *Science, 342,* 1119–1120. (p. 305)

Meador, B. D., & Rogers, C. R. (1984). Person-centered therapy. In R. J. Corsini (Ed.), *Current psychotherapies* (3rd ed.). Itasca, IL: Peacock. (p. 539)

Medda, P., Toni, C., Mariani, M. G., De Simone, L., Mauri, M., & Perugi, G. (2015). Electroconvulsive therapy in 197 patients with a severe, drug-resistant bipolar mixed state: Treatment outcome and predictors of response. *The Journal of Clinical Psychiatry, 76,* 1168–1173. (p. 563)

Mednick, S. A., Huttunen, M. O., & Machon, R. A. (1994). Prenatal influenza infections and adult schizophrenia. *Schizophrenia Bulletin, 20,* 263–267. (p. 525)

Medvec, V. H., Madey, S. F., & Gilovich, T. (1995). When less is more: Counterfactual thinking and satisfaction among Olympic medalists. *Journal of Personality and Social Psychology, 69,* 603–610. (p. 489)

Mehl, M., Gosling, S. D., & Pennebaker, J. W. (2006). Personality in its natural habitat: Manifestations and implicit folk theories of personality in daily life. *Journal of Personality and Social Psychology, 90,* 862–877. (p. 481)

Mehl, M. R., Vazire, S., Holleran, S. E., & Clark, C. S. (2010). Eavesdropping on happiness: Well-being is related to having less small talk and more substantive conversations. *Psychological Science, 21,* 539–541. (p. 412)

Mehlum, L., Ramberg, M., Tørmoen, A. J., Haga, E., Diep, L. M., Stanley, B. H., . . . Grøholt, B. (2016). Dialectical behavior therapy compared with enhanced usual care for adolescents with repeated suicidal and self-harming behavior: Outcomes over a one-year follow-up. *Journal of the American Academy of Child & Adolescent Psychiatry, 55,* 295–300. (p. 546)

Mehta, D., Klengel, T., Conneely, K. N., Smith, A. K., Altmann, A., Pace, T. W., . . . Binder, E. B. (2013). Childhood maltreatment is associated with distinct genomic and epigenetic profiles in posttraumatic stress disorder. *PNAS, 110,* 8302–8307. (p. 512)

Mehta, M. R. (2007). Cortico-hippocampal interaction during up-down states and memory consolidation. *Nature Neuroscience, 10,* 13–15. (p. 277)

Meichenbaum, D. (1977). *Cognitive-behavior modification: An integrative approach.* New York: Plenum Press. (p. 545)

Meichenbaum, D. (1985). *Stress inoculation training.* New York: Pergamon. (p. 545)

Mejia, Z. (2017, November 17). What billionaire Amazon founder Jeff Bezos did at 30 to avoid living with regret. CNBC. Retrieved from cnbc.com/2017/11/17/what-amazons-jeff-bezos-did-at-30-to-avoid-living-with-regret.html (p. 476)

Melby-Lervåg, M., Redick, T. S., & Hulme, C. (2016). Working memory training does not improve performance on measures of intelligence or other measures of "far transfer": Evidence from a meta-analytic review. *Perspectives on Psychological Science, 11,* 512–534. (p. 154)

Melioli, T., Bauer, S., Franko, D. L., Moessner, M., Ozer, F., Chabrol, H., & Rodgers, R. F. (2016). Reducing eating disorder symptoms and risk factors using the internet: A meta-analytic review. *International Journal of Eating Disorders, 49,* 19–31. (p. 533)

Mellers, B., Stone, E., Atanasov, P., Rohrbaugh, N., Metz, S. E., Ungar, L., . . . Tetlock, P. (2015). The psychology of intelligence analysis: Drivers of prediction accuracy in world politics. *Journal of Experimental Psychology: Applied, 21,* 1–14. (p. 303)

Meltzoff, A. N. (1988). Infant imitation after a 1-week delay: Long-term memory for novel acts and multiple stimuli. *Developmental Psychology, 24,* 470–476. (p. 260)

Meltzoff, A. N., Kuhl, P. K., Movellan, J., & Sejnowski, T. J. (2009). Foundations for a new science of learning. *Science, 325,* 284–288. (pp. 260, 314)

Meltzoff, A. N., & Moore, M. K. (1989). Imitation in newborn infants: Exploring the range of gestures imitated and the underlying mechanisms. *Developmental Psychology, 25,* 954–962. (p. 260)

Meltzoff, A. N., & Moore, M. K. (1997). Explaining facial imitation: A theoretical model. *Early Development and Parenting, 6,* 179–192. (p. 260)

Melvill, H. (1855). Partaking in other men's sins. Sermon at St. Margaret's Church, Lothbury, England. No. 2,365 in the "Penny Pulpit" series. Reprinted in *The golden lecture: Forty-five sermons delivered at St. Margaret's Church, Lothbury.* London: James Paul. (p. 415)

Melzack, R. (1992, April). Quoted in Phantom limbs. *Scientific American,* pp. 120–126. (p. 222)

Melzack, R. (1998, February). Quoted in Phantom limbs. *Discover,* p. 20. (p. 222)

Melzack, R. (2005). Evolution of the neuromatrix theory of pain. *Pain Practice, 5,* 85–94. (p. 222)

Melzack, R., & Katz, J. (2013). Pain. *Wiley Interdisciplinary Reviews: Cognitive Science, 4,* 1–15. (p. 222)

Melzack, R., & Wall, P. D. (1965). Pain mechanisms: A new theory. *Science, 150,* 971–979. (p. 222)

Melzack, R., & Wall, P. D. (1983). *The challenge of pain.* New York: Basic Books. (p. 222)

Mendelson, J. L., Gates, J. A., & Lerner, M. D. (2016). Friendship in school-age boys with autism spectrum disorders: A meta-analytic summary and developmental, process-based model. *Psychological Bulletin, 142,* 601–622. (p. 131)

Mendes, E. (2010, June 2). *U.S. exercise levels up, but demographic differences remain.* Gallup poll (gallup.com). (p. 402)

Mendes, E., & McGeeney, K. (2012, July 9). Women's health trails men's most in former Soviet Union. Gallup (gallup.com). (p. 517)

Mendle, J., Turkheimer, E., & Emery, R. E. (2007). Detrimental psychological outcomes associated with early pubertal timing in adolescent girls. *Developmental Review, 27,* 151–171. (p. 142)

Mendolia, M., & Kleck, R. E. (1993). Effects of talking about a stressful event on arousal: Does what we talk about make a difference? *Journal of Personality and Social Psychology, 64,* 283–292. (p. 400)

Merari, A. (2002). *Explaining suicidal terrorism: Theories versus empirical evidence.* Invited address to the American Psychological Association. (p. 431)

Mercer, T. (2015). Wakeful rest alleviates interference-based forgetting. *Memory, 23,* 127–137. (p. 287)

Meriac, J. P., Hoffman, B. J., Woehr, D. J., & Fleisher, M. S. (2008). Further evidence for the validity of assessment center dimensions: A meta-analysis of the incremental criterion-related validity of dimension ratings. *Journal of Applied Psychology, 93,* 1042–1052. (p. 484)

Merikangas, K. R., Jin, R., He, J. P., Kessler, R. C., Lee, S., Sampson, N. A., . . . Zarkov, Z. (2011). Prevalence and correlates of bipolar spectrum disorder in the world mental health survey initiative. *Archives of General Psychiatry, 68,* 241–251. (p. 516)

Merskey, H. (1992). The manufacture of personalities: The production of multiple personality disorder. *British Journal of Psychiatry, 160,* 327–340.(p. 528)

Merzenich, M. (2007). Quoted in the Posit Science Brain Fitness Program. Retrieved from positscience.com/ (p. 154)

Mesman, J., van Ijzendoorn, M., Behrens, K., Carbonell, O. A., Cárcamo, R., Cohen-Paraira, I., . . . Kondo-Ikemura, K. (2015). Is the ideal mother a sensitive mother? Beliefs about early childhood parenting in mothers across the globe. *International Journal of Behavioral Development, 40,* 385–397. (p. 133)

Mesoudi, A. (2009). How cultural evolutionary theory can inform social psychology and vice versa. *Psychological Review, 116,* 929–952. (p. 422)

Messerli, F. H. (2012). Chocolate consumption, cognitive function, and Nobel laureates. *The New England Journal of Medicine, 367,* 1562–1564. (p. 23)

Messias, E., Eaton, W. W., & Grooms, A. N. (2011). Economic grand rounds: Income inequality and depression prevalence across the United States: An ecological study. *Psychiatric Services, 62,* 710–712. (p. 443)

Meston, C. M., & Buss, D. M. (2007). Why humans have sex. *Archives of Sexual Behavior, 36,* 477–507. (p. 176)

Metcalfe, J. (1986). Premonitions of insight predict impending error. *Journal of Experimental Psychology: Learning, Memory, and Cognition, 12,* 623–634. (p. 299)

Metcalfe, J. (1998). Cognitive optimism: Self-deception or memory-based processing heuristics. *Personality and Social Psychology Review, 2,* 100–110. (p. 303)

Metzler, D. (2011, Spring). Vocabulary growth in adult cross-fostered chimpanzees. *Friends of Washoe, 32,* 11–13. (p. 317)

Meyer, A., Proudfit, G. H., Bufferd, S. J., Kujawa, A. J., Laptook, R. S., Torpey, D. C., & Klein, D. N. (2015). Self-reported and observed punitive parenting prospectively predicts increased error-related brain activity in six-year-old children. *Journal of Abnormal Child Psychology, 43,* 821–829. (p. 139)

Meyer-Bahlburg, H. F. L. (1995). Psychoneuroendocrinology and sexual pleasure: The aspect of sexual orientation. In P. R. Abramson & S. D. Pinkerton (Eds.), *Sexual nature/sexual culture* (pp. 135–153). Chicago: University of Chicago Press. (p. 181)

Meyerhoff, J., & Rohan, K. J. (2016). Treatment expectations for cognitive-behavioral therapy and light therapy for seasonal affective disorder: Change across treatment and relation to outcome. *Journal of Consulting and Clinical Psychology, 84,* 898–906. (p. 555)

Mez, J., Daneshvar, D. H., Kiernan, P. T., Abdolmohammadi, B., Alvarez, V. E., Huber, B. R., . . . Cormier, K. A. (2017). Clinicopathological evaluation of chronic traumatic encephalopathy in players of American football. *Journal of the American Medical Association, 318,* 360–370. (p. 57)

Miao, C., Humphrey, R. H., & Qian, S. (2016). Leader emotional intelligence and subordinate job satisfaction: A meta-analysis of main, mediator, and moderator effects. *Personality and Individual Differences, 102,* 13–24. (p. 326)

Michael, R. B., Garry, M., & Kirsch, I. (2012). Suggestion, cognition, and behavior. *Current Directions in Psychological Science, 21,* 151–156. (p. 27)

Michaels, J. W., Bloomel, J. M., Brocato, R. M., Linkous, R. A., & Rowe, J. S. (1982). Social facilitation and inhibition in a natural setting. *Replications in Social Psychology, 2,* 21–24. (p. 429)

Michalka, S. W., Kong, L., Rosen, M. L., Shinn-Cunningham, B., & Somers, D. C. (2015). Short-term memory for space and time flexibly recruit complementary sensory-biased frontal lobe attention networks. *Neuron, 87,* 882–892. (p. 276)

Middlebrooks, J. C., & Green, D. M. (1991). Sound localization by human listeners. *Annual Review of Psychology, 42,* 135–159. (p. 220)

Miech, R. A., Johnston, L. D., O'Malley, P. M., Bachman, J. G., & Schulenberg, J. E. (2016). *Monitoring the Future national survey results on drug use, 1975–2015: Volume I, Secondary school students.* Ann Arbor: Institute for Social Research, The University of Michigan. (p. 110)

Miers, R. (2009, Spring). Calum's road. *Scottish Life,* pp. 36–39, 75. (p. 358)

Mihura, J. L., Meyer, G. J., Bombel, G., & Dumitrascu, N. (2015). Standards, accuracy, and questions of bias in Rorschach meta-analyses: Reply to Wood, Garb, Nezworski, Lilienfeld, and Duke (2015). *Psychological Bulletin, 141,* 250–260. (p. 468)

Mihura, J. L., Meyer, G. J., Dumitrascu, N., & Bombel, G. (2013). The validity of individual Rorschach variables: Systematic reviews and meta-analyses of the comprehensive system. *Psychological Bulletin, 139,* 548–605. (p. 468)

Mikulincer, M., & Shaver, P. R. (2001). Attachment theory and intergroup bias: Evidence that priming the secure base schema attenuates negative reactions to out-groups. *Journal of Personality and Social Psychology, 81,* 97–115. (p. 439)

Milan, R. J., Jr., & Kilmann, P. R. (1987). Interpersonal factors in premarital contraception. *Journal of Sex Research, 23,* 289–321. (p. 187)

Miles, D. R., & Carey, G. (1997). Genetic and environmental architecture of human aggression. *Journal of Personality and Social Psychology, 72,* 207–217. (p. 441)

Milgram, S. (1963). Behavioral study of obedience. *Journal of Abnormal and Social Psychology, 67,* 371–378. (p. 425)

Milgram, S. (1974). *Obedience to authority.* New York: Harper & Row. (pp. 425, 426, 428)

Miller, B. G., Kors, S., & Macfie, J. (2017). No differences? Meta-analytic comparisons of psychological adjustment in children of gay fathers and heterosexual parents. *Psychology of Sexual Orientation and Gender Diversity, 4,* 14–22. (p. 180)

Miller, C. H., Hamilton, J. P., Sacchet, M. D., & Gotlib, I. H. (2015). Meta-analysis of functional neuroimaging of major depressive disorder in youth. *JAMA Psychiatry, 72,* 1045–1053. (p. 519)

Miller, G. (2004). Axel, Buck share award for deciphering how the nose knows. *Science, 306,* 207. (p. 226)

Miller, G. (2008). Tackling alcoholism with drugs. *Science, 320,* 168–170. (p. 111)

Miller, G. (2012). Drone wars: Are remotely piloted aircraft changing the nature of war? *Science, 336,* 842–843. (pp. 276, 427)

Miller, G. A. (1956). The magical number seven, plus or minus two: Some limits on our capacity for processing information. *Psychological Review, 63,* 81–97. (p. 271)

Miller, G. E., & Blackwell, E. (2006). Turning up the heat: Inflammation as a mechanism linking chronic stress, depression, and heart disease. *Current Directions in Psychological Science, 15,* 269–272. (p. 392)

Miller, J. F., Neufang, M., Solway, A., Brandt, A., Trippel, M., Mader, I., . . . Schulze-Bonhage, A. (2013). Neural activity in human hippocampal formation reveals the spatial context of retrieved memories. *Science, 342,* 1111–1114. (p. 276)

Miller, J. G., & Bersoff, D. M. (1995). Development in the context of everyday family relationships: Culture, interpersonal morality and adaptation. In M. Killen & D. Hart (Eds.), *Morality in everyday life: A developmental perspective* (pp. 259–282). New York: Cambridge University Press. (p. 144)

Miller, L. K. (1999). The savant syndrome: Intellectual impairment and exceptional skill. *Psychological Bulletin, 125,* 31–46. (p. 325)

Miller, M., Azrael, D., & Hemenway, D. (2002). Household firearm ownership levels and suicide across U.S. regions and states, 1988–1997. *Epidemiology, 13,* 517–524. (p. 501)

Miller, M., Swanson, S. A., & Azrael, D. (2016). Are we missing something pertinent? A bias analysis of unmeasured confounding in the firearm-suicide literature. *Epidemiologic Reviews, 38,* 62–69. (p. 501)

Miller, N. E. (1985, February). Rx: Biofeedback. *Psychology Today,* pp. 54–59. (p. 403)

Miller, P. (2012, January). A thing or two about twins. *National Geographic,* pp. 38–65. (p. 71)

Miller, P. J. O., Aoki, K., Rendell, L. E., & Amano, M. (2008). Stereotypical resting behavior of the sperm whale. *Current Biology, 18,* R21–R23. (p. 87)

Milner, A. D., & Goodale, M. A. (2008). Two visual systems reviewed. *Neuropsychologia, 46,* 774–785. (p. 84)

Milojev, P., & Sibley, C. G. (2017). Normative personality trait development in adulthood: A 6-year cohort-sequential growth model. *Journal of Personality and Social Psychology, 112,* 510–526. (p. 478)

Milrod, B., Chambless, D. L., Gallop, R., Busch, F. N., Schwalberg, M., McCarthy, K. S., . . . Barber, J. P. (2015, June 9). Psychotherapies for panic disorder: A tale of two sites. *Journal of Clinical Psychiatry, 77,* 927–935. (p. 546)

Mineka, S. (1985). The frightful complexity of the origins of fears. In F. R. Brush & J. B. Overmier (Eds.), *Affect, conditioning and cognition: Essays on the determinants of behavior.* Hillsdale, NJ: Erlbaum. (p. 511)

Mineka, S. (2002). Animal models of clinical psychology. In N. Smelser & P. Baltes (Eds.), *International encyclopedia of the social and behavioral sciences.* Oxford: Elsevier Science. (p. 511)

Mineka, S., & Oehlberg, K. (2008). The relevance of recent developments in classical conditioning to understanding the etiology and maintenance of anxiety disorders. *Acta Psychologica, 127,* 567–580. (p. 510)

Mineka, S., & Zinbarg, R. (1996). Conditioning and ethological models of anxiety disorders: Stress-in-dynamic-context anxiety models. In D. Hope (Ed.), *Perspectives on anxiety, panic, and fear* (Nebraska Symposium on Motivation). Lincoln: University of Nebraska Press. (pp. 512, 567)

Minsky, M. (1986). *The society of mind.* New York: Simon & Schuster. (p. 81)

Mischel, W. (1968). *Personality and assessment.* New York: Wiley. (p. 481)

Mischel, W. (1981). Current issues and challenges in personality. In L. T. Benjamin, Jr. (Ed.), *The G. Stanley Hall Lecture Series* (Vol. 1). Washington, DC: American Psychological Association. (p. 484)

Mischel, W. (2014). *The marshmallow test: Mastering self-control.* Boston: Little, Brown. (pp. 145, 247)

Mischkowski, D., Kross, E., & Bushman, B. (2012). Flies on the wall are less aggressive: Self-distancing "in the heat of the moment" reduces aggressive thoughts, angry feelings and aggressive behavior. *Journal of Experimental Social Psychology, 48,* 1187–1191. (p. 394)

Miserandino, M. (1991). Memory and the seven dwarfs. *Teaching of Psychology, 18,* 169–171. (p. 267)

Mishkin, M. (1982). A memory system in the monkey. *Philosophical Transactions of the Royal Society of London: Biological Sciences, 298,* 83–95. (p. 277)

Mishkin, M., Suzuki, W. A., Gadian, D. G., & Vargha-Khadem, F. (1997). Hierarchical organization of cognitive memory. *Philosophical Transactions of the Royal Society of London: Biological Sciences, 352,* 1461–1467. (p. 277)

Mishra, A., & Mishra, H. (2010). Border bias: The belief that state borders can protect against disasters. *Psychological Science, 21,* 1582–1586. (p. 320)

Mita, T. H., Dermer, M., & Knight, J. (1977). Reversed facial images and the mere-exposure hypothesis. *Journal of Personality and Social Psychology, 35,* 597–601. (p. 447)

Mitani, J. C., Watts, D. P., & Amsler, S. J. (2010). Lethal intergroup aggression leads to territorial expansion in wild chimpanzees. *Current Biology, 20,* R507–R509. (p. 310)

Mitchell, G. (2012). Revisiting truth or triviality: The external validity of research in the psychological laboratory. *Perspectives on Psychological Science, 7,* 109–117. (p. 30)

Mitchell, J. P. (2009). Social psychology as a natural kind. *Cell, 13,* 246–251. (p. 486)

Mitte, K. (2008). Memory bias for threatening information in anxiety and anxiety disorders: A meta-analytic review. *Psychological Bulletin, 134,* 886–911. (p. 506)

Miu, A. S., & Yeager, D. S. (2015). Preventing symptoms of depression by teaching adolescents that people can change: Effects of a brief incremental theory of personality intervention at 9-month follow-up. *Clinical Psychological Science, 3,* 726–743. (p. 566)

Mobbs, D., Yu, R., Meyer, M., Passamonti, L., Seymour, B., Calder, A. J., . . . Dalgeish, T. (2009). A key role for similarity in vicarious reward. *Science, 324,* 900. (p. 259)

Moffitt, T. E., Arsenault, L., Belsky, D., Dickson, N., Hancox, R. J., Harrington, H., . . . Caspi, A. (2011). A gradient of childhood self-control predicts health, wealth, and public safety. *PNAS, 108,* 2693–2698. (p. 398)

Moffitt, T. E., Caspi, A., Harrington, H., & Milne, B. J. (2002). Males on the life-course-persistent and adolescence-limited antisocial pathways: Follow-up at age 26 years. *Development and Psychopathology, 14,* 179–207. (p. 118)

Moffitt, T. E., Harrington, H., Caspi, A., Kim-Cohen, J., Goldberg, D., Gregory, A. M., & Poulton, R. (2007). Depression and generalized anxiety disorder: Cumulative and sequential comorbidity in a birth cohort followed prospectively to age 32 years. *Archives of General Psychiatry, 64,* 651–660. (p. 507)

Moffitt, T. E., Poulton, R., & Caspi, A. (2013). Lifelong impact of early self-control. *American Scientist, 101,* 352–359. (p. 118)

Moghaddam, F. M. (2005). The staircase to terrorism: A psychological exploration. *American Psychologist, 60,* 161–169. (p. 431)

Molenberghs, P., Ogilivie, C., Louis, W. R., Decety, J., Bagnall, J., & Bain, P. G. (2015). The neural correlates of justified and unjustified killing: An fMRI study. *Social Cognitive and Affective Neuroscience, 10,* 1397–1404. (p. 63)

Möller-Levet, C. S., Archer, S. N., Bucca, G., Laing, E. E., Slak, A., Kabiljo, R., . . . Dijk, D.-J. (2013). Effects of insufficient sleep on circadian rhythmicity and expression amplitude of the human blood transcriptome. *PNAS, 110,* E1132–E1141. (p. 93)

Mommersteeg, P. M. C., Schoemaker, R. G., Naudé, P. J., Eisel, U. L., Garrelds, I. M., Schalkwijk, C. G., . . . Denollet, J. (2016). Depression and markers of inflammation as predictors of all-cause mortality in heart failure. *Brain, Behavior, and Immunity, 57,* 144–150. (p. 392)

Mondloch, C. J., Lewis, T. L., Budreau, D. R., Maurer, D., Dannemiller, J. L., Stephens, B. R., & Kleiner-Gathercoal, K. A. (1999). Face perception during early infancy. *Psychological Science, 10,* 419–422. (p. 121)

Money, J. (1987). Sin, sickness, or status? Homosexual gender identity and psychoneuroendocrinology. *American Psychologist, 42,* 384–399. (pp. 179, 181)

Money, J., Berlin, F. S., Falck, A., & Stein, M. (1983). *Antiandrogenic and counseling treatment of sex offenders.* Baltimore: Johns Hopkins University School of Medicine, Department of Psychiatry and Behavioral Sciences. (p. 174)

Monroe, S. M., & Reid, M. W. (2009). Life stress and major depression. *Current Directions in Psychological Science, 18,* 68–72. (p. 517)

Monroe, S. M., & Simons, A. D. (1991). Diathesis-stress theories in the context of life stress research: Implications for the depressive disorders. *Psychological Bulletin, 110,* 406–425. (p. 496)

Montagne, A., Barnes, S. R., Sweeney, M. D., Halliday, M. R., Sagare, A. P., Zhao, Z., . . . Zlokovic, B. V. (2015). Blood-brain barrier breakdown in the aging human hippocampus. *Neuron, 85,* 296–302. (p. 152)

Montoya, R. M., & Horton, R. S. (2013). A meta-analytic investigation of the processes underlying the similarity-attraction effect. *Journal of Social and Personal Relationships, 30,* 64–94. (p. 450)

Montoya, R. M., & Horton, R. S. (2014). A two-dimensional model for the study of interpersonal attraction. *Personality and Social Psychology Review, 18,* 59–86. (p. 450)

Montoya, R. M., Horton, R. S., Vevea, J. L., Citkowicz, M., & Lauber, E. A. (2017). A re-examination of the mere exposure effect: The influence of repeated exposure on recognition, familiarity, and liking. *Psychological Bulletin, 143,* 459–498. (p. 447)

Mook, D. G. (1983). In defense of external invalidity. *American Psychologist, 38,* 379–387. (p. 30)

Moon, C., Lagercrantz, H., & Kuhl, P. K. (2013). Language experienced in utero affects vowel perception after birth: A two-country study. *Acta Paediatrica, 102,* 156–160. (p. 119)

Moorcroft, W. H. (2003). *Understanding sleep and dreaming.* New York: Kluwer Academic/Plenum Press. (pp. 87, 99)

Moore, D. W. (2004, December 17). Sweet dreams go with a good night's sleep. *Gallup News Service* (gallup.com). (p. 90)

Moore, D. W. (2005, June 16). Three in four Americans believe in paranormal. *Gallup News Service* (gallup.com). (p. 229)

Moore, S. C., Lee, I., Weiderpass, E., Campbell, P. T., Sampson, J. N., Kitahara, C. M., . . . Patel, A. V. (2016). Association of leisure-time physical activity with risk of 26 types of cancer in 1.44 million adults. *JAMA Internal Medicine, 176,* 816–825. (p. 103)

Moore, S. C., Patel, A. V., Matthews, C. E., Berrington de Gonzalez, A., Park, Y., Katki, H. A., . . . Lee, I.-M. (2012). Leisure time physical activity of moderate to vigorous intensity and mortality: A large pooled cohort analysis. *PLoS Medicine, 9,* e1001335. (p. 401)

Moos, R. H., & Moos, B. S. (2005). Sixteen-year changes and stable remission among treated and untreated individuals with alcohol use disorders. *Drug and Alcohol Dependence, 80,* 337–347. (p. 548)

Moos, R. H., & Moos, B. S. (2006). Participation in treatment and Alcoholics Anonymous: A 16-year follow-up of initially untreated individuals. *Journal of Clinical Psychology, 62,* 735–750. (p. 548)

Mor, N., & Winquist, J. (2002). Self-focused attention and negative affect: A meta-analysis. *Psychological Bulletin, 128,* 638–662. (p. 520)

More, H. L., Hutchinson, J. R., Collins, D. F., Weber, D. J., Aung, S. K. H., & Donelan, J. M. (2010). Scaling of sensorimotor control in terrestrial mammals. *Proceedings of the Royal Society: Series B, 277,* 3563–3568. (p. 40)

Moreira, M. T., Smith, L. A., & Foxcroft, D. (2009). Social norms interventions to reduce alcohol misuse in university or college students. *Cochrane Database of Systematic Reviews 2009,* Issue 3, Article CD006748. doi:10.1002/14651858.CD006748.pub2 (p. 112)

Moreland, R. L., & Zajonc, R. B. (1982). Exposure effects in person perception: Familiarity, similarity, and attraction. *Journal of Experimental Social Psychology, 18,* 395–415. (p. 447)

Morelli, G. A., Rogoff, B., Oppenheim, D., & Goldsmith, D. (1992). Cultural variation in infants' sleeping arrangements: Questions of independence. *Developmental Psychology, 26,* 604–613. (p. 139)

Moreno, C., Laje, G., Blanco, C., Jiang, H., Schmidt, A. B., & Olfson, M. (2007). National trends in the outpatient diagnosis and treatment of bipolar disorder in youth. *Archives of General Psychiatry, 64,* 1032–1039. (p. 516)

Morey, R. A., Inan, S., Mitchell, T. V., Perkins, D. O., Lieberman, J. A., & Belger, A. (2005). Imaging frontostriatal function in ultra-high-risk, early, and chronic schizophrenia during executive processing. *Archives of General Psychiatry, 62,* 254–262. (p. 524)

Morgan, A. B., & Lilienfeld, S. O. (2000). A meta-analytic review of the relation between antisocial behavior and neuropsychological measures of executive function. *Clinical Psychology Review, 20,* 113–136. (p. 531)

Morgenthaler, T. I., Hashmi, S., Croft, J. B., Dort, L., Heald, J. L., & Mullington, J. (2016). High school start times and the impact on high school students: What we know, and what we hope to learn. *Journal of Clinical Sleep Medicine, 12,* 1681–1689. (p. 93)

Mori, K., & Mori, H. (2009). Another test of the passive facial feedback hypothesis: When you face smiles, you feel happy. *Perceptual and Motor Skills, 109,* 1–3. (p. 381)

Morin, R. (2014, July 2). Facebook's experiment causes a lot of fuss for little result. Pew Research Center (pewresearch.org). (p. A-8)

Moriuchi, J. M., Klin, A., & Jones, W. (2017). Mechanisms of diminished attention to eyes in autism. *American Journal of Psychiatry, 174,* 26–35. (p. 131)

Morris, G., Baker-Ward, L., & Bauer, P. J. (2010). What remains of that day: The survival of children's autobiographical memories across time. *Applied Cognitive Psychology, 24,* 527–544. (p. 124)

Morris, M. (2015, September 18). Damaging labels do transgender people a disservice. *Edmonton Journal* (edmontonjournal.com). (p. 171)

Morrison, A. R. (2003, July). The brain on night shift. *Cerebrum,* pp. 23–36. (p. 89)

Morrison, M., Tay, L., & Diener, E. (2014). *Subjective well-being across the lifespan worldwide.* Paper presented at the Society for Personality and Social Psychology convention, Austin, Texas. (p. 158)

Mortensen, P. B. (1999). Effects of family history and place and season of birth on the risk of schizophrenia. *New England Journal of Medicine, 340,* 603–608. (p. 525)

Moruzzi, G., & Magoun, H. W. (1949). Brain stem reticular formation and activation of the EEG. *Electroencephalography and Clinical Neurophysiology, 1,* 455–473. (p. 54)

Moscovici, S. (1985). Social influence and conformity. In G. Lindzey & E. Aronson (Eds.), *The handbook of social psychology* (3rd ed.). Hillsdale, N.J.: Erlbaum. (p. 428)

Moses, E. B., & Barlow, D. H. (2006). A new unified treatment approach for emotional disorders based on emotion science. *Current Directions in Psychological Science, 15,* 146–150. (p. 546)

Mosher, C. E., & Danoff-Burg, S. (2008). Agentic and communal personality traits: Relations to disordered eating behavior, body shape concern, and depressive symptoms. *Eating Behaviors, 9,* 497–500. (p. 169)

Mosher, W. D., Chandra, A., & Jones, J. (2005, September 15). *Sexual behavior and selected health measures: Men and women 15–44 years of age, United States, 2002* (Advance Data from Vital and Health Statistics No. 362). Hyattsville, MD: National Center for Health Statistics. (p. 179)

Mosing, M. A., Zietsch, B. P., Shekar, S. N., Wright, M. J., & Martin, N. G. (2009). Genetic and environmental influences on optimism and its relationship to mental and self-rated health: A study of aging twins. *Behavior Genetics, 39,* 597–604. (p. 399)

Mosnier, I., Bebear, J.-P., Marx, M., Fraysse, B., Truy, E., Lina-Granade, G., . . . Sterkers, O. (2015). Improvement of cognitive function after cochlear implantation in elderly patients. *JAMA Otolaryngology—Head & Neck Surgery, 141,* 442–450. (p. 218)

Moss, A. C., & Albery, I. P. (2009). A dual-process model of the alcohol–behavior link for social drinking. *Psychological Bulletin, 135,* 516–530. (p. 104)

Moss, A. J., Allen, K. F., Giovino, G. A., & Mills, S. L. (1992, December 2). Recent trends in adolescent smoking, smoking-update correlates, and expectations about the future. *Advance Data No. 221* (from Vital and Health Statistics of the Centers for Disease Control and Prevention). (p. 112)

Motivala, S. J., & Irwin, M. R. (2007). Sleep and immunity: Cytokine pathways linking sleep and health outcomes. *Current Directions in Psychological Science, 16,* 21–25. (p. 93)

Moulin, S., Waldfogel, J., & Washbrook, E. (2014). Baby bonds: Parenting, attachment, and a secure base for children. *Sutton Trust,* 1–42. (p. 134)

Moxley, J. H., Ericsson, K. A., Charness, N., & Krampe, R. T. (2012). The role of intuition and deliberative thinking in experts' superior tactical decision-making. *Cognition, 124,* 72–78. (p. 306)

Moyer, K. E. (1983). The physiology of motivation: Aggression as a model. In C. J. Scheier & A. M. Rogers (Eds.), *The G. Stanley Hall Lecture Series* (Vol. 3, pp. 123–139). Washington, DC: American Psychological Association. (p. 441)

Mrkva, K. (2017). Giving, fast and slow: Reflection increases costly (but not uncostly) charitable giving. *Journal of Behavioral Decision Making.* Advance online publication. doi:10.1002/bdm.2023. (p. 81)

Mroczek, D. K., & Kolarz, D. M. (1998). The effect of age on positive and negative affect: A developmental perspective on happiness. *Journal of Personality and Social Psychology, 75,* 1333–1349. (p. 155)

Mueller, P. A., & Oppenheimer, D. M. (2014). The pen is mightier than the keyboard: Advantages of longhand over laptop note-taking. *Psychological Science, 25,* 1159–1168. (pp. 34, 295)

Muhlnickel, W. (1998). Reorganization of auditory cortex in tinnitus. *PNAS, 95,* 10340–10343. (p. 61)

Mulcahy, N. J., & Call, J. (2006). Apes save tools for future use. *Science, 312,* 1038–1040. (p. 309)

Muldoon, S., Taylor, S. C., & Norma, C. (2016). The survivor master narrative in sexual assault. *Violence Against Women, 22,* 565–587. (p. 170)

Muller, J. E., Mittleman, M. A., Maclure, M., Sherwood, J. B., & Tofler, G. H. (1996). Triggering myocardial infarction by sexual activity. *Journal of the American Medical Association, 275,* 1405–1409. (p. 174)

Muller, J. E., & Verrier, R. L. (1996). Triggering of sudden death—Lessons from an earthquake. *New England Journal of Medicine, 334,* 461. (pp. 173, 385)

Mullin, C. R., & Linz, D. (1995). Desensitization and resensitization to violence against women: Effects of exposure to sexually violent films on judgments of domestic violence victims. *Journal of Personality and Social Psychology, 69,* 449–459. (p. 263)

Mulrow, C. D. (1999, March). Treatment of depression—newer pharmacotherapies, summary. *Evidence Report/Technology Assessment, 7.* Agency for Health Care Policy and Research, Rockville, MD. Retrieved from ahrq.gov/clinic/deprsumm.htm (p. 561)

Murayama, K., Pekrun, R., Lichtenfeld, S., & vom Hofe, R. (2013). Predicting long-term growth in students' mathematics achievement: The unique contributions of motivation and cognitive strategies. *Child Development, 84,* 1475–1490. (p. 339)

Murdik, L., Breska, A., Lamy, D., & Deouell, L. Y. (2011). Integration without awareness: Expanding the limits of unconscious processing. *Psychological Science, 22,* 764–770. (p. 81)

Murphy, K. R., & Cleveland, J. N. (1995). *Understanding performance appraisal: Social, organizational, and goal-based perspectives.* Thousand Oaks, CA: Sage. (p. B-7)

Murphy, S. T., Monahan, J. L., & Zajonc, R. B. (1995). Additivity of nonconscious affect: Combined effects of priming and exposure. *Journal of Personality and Social Psychology, 69,* 589–602. (p. 370)

Murray, H. (1938). *Explorations in personality.* New York: Oxford University Press. (p. 357)

Murray, H. A. (1933). The effect of fear upon estimates of the maliciousness of other personalities. *Journal of Social Psychology, 4,* 310–329. (p. 467)

Murray, H. A., & Wheeler, D. R. (1937). A note on the possible clairvoyance of dreams. *Journal of Psychology, 3,* 309–313. (pp. 21, 230)

Murray, R., Jones, P., O'Callaghan, E., Takei, N., & Sham, P. (1992). Genes, viruses, and neurodevelopmental schizophrenia. *Journal of Psychiatric Research, 26,* 225–235. (p. 525)

Murray, S. L., Bellavia, G. M., Rose, P., & Griffin, D. W. (2003). Once hurt, twice hurtful: How perceived regard regulates daily marital interactions. *Journal of Personality and Social Psychology, 84,* 126–147. (p. 198)

Murty, V. P., Calabro, F., & Luna, B. (2016). The role of experience in adolescent cognitive development: Integration of executive, memory, and mesolimbic systems. *Neuroscience & Biobehavioral Reviews.* Advance online publication. doi:10.1016/j.neubiorev.2016.07.034 (p. 124)

Musick, M. A., Herzog, A. R., & House, J. S. (1999). Volunteering and mortality among older adults: Findings from a national sample. *Journals of Gerontology, 54B,* 173–180. (p. 406)

Muusses, L. D., Kerkhof, P., & Finkenauer, C. (2015). Internet pornography and relationship quality: A longitudinal study of within and between partner effects of adjustment, sexual satisfaction and sexually explicit internet material among newly-weds. *Computers in Human Behavior, 45,* 77–84. (p. 25)

Mydans, S. (2002, May 17). In Pakistan, rape victims are the 'criminals.' *The New York Times.* Retrieved from nytimes.com/2002/05/17/world/in-pakistan-rape-victims-are-the-criminals.html (p. 440)

Myers, D. G. (1992). *The pursuit of happiness.* New York: William Morrow. (p. xx)

Myers, D. G. (1993). *The pursuit of happiness.* New York: Harper. (pp. xx, 411)

Myers, D. G. (2000). *The American paradox: Spiritual hunger in an age of plenty.* New Haven, CT: Yale University Press. (p. 411)

Myers, D. G. (2010). *Social psychology* (10th ed.). New York: McGraw-Hill. (p. 487)

Myers, D. G., & Bishop, G. D. (1970). Discussion effects on racial attitudes. *Science, 169,* 78–779. (p. 431)

Myers, D. G., & Diener, E. (1995). Who is happy? *Psychological Science, 6,* 10–19. (p. 411)

Myers, D. G., & Diener, E. (1996, May). The pursuit of happiness. *Scientific American* (scientificamerican.com/article/the-pursuit-of-happiness/). (p. 411)

Myers, D. G., & Scanzoni, L. D. (2005). *What God has joined together?* San Francisco: Harper. (pp. 157, 179)

Myers, T. A., & Crowther, J. H. (2009). Social comparison as a predictor of body dissatisfaction: A meta-analytic review. *Journal of Abnormal Psychology, 118,* 683–698. (p. 532)

Myre, G. (2000, April 27). McCain still can't forgive guards at "Hanoi Hilton." *The Washington Post.* Retrieved from washingtonpost.com/wp-dyn/content/article/2008/08/13/AR2008081302644.html (p. 567)

Nagourney, A. (2002, September 25). For remarks on Iraq, Gore gets praise and scorn. *The New York Times* (nytimes.com). (p. 418)

Nagourney, A., Sanger, D. E., & Barr, J. (2018, January 13). Hawaii panics after alert about incoming missile is sent in error. *The New York Times* (nytimes.com). (p. 47)

Napolitan, D. A., & Goethals, G. R. (1979). The attribution of friendliness. *Journal of Experimental Social Psychology, 15,* 105–113. (p. 416)

NAS. (2011). *Statistics: How many people have autism spectrum disorders.* National Autistic Society (autism.org.uk). (p. 131)

Nasie, M., Diamond, A. H., & Bar-Tal, D. (2016). Young children in intractable conflicts: The Israeli case. *Personality and Social Psychology Review, 20,* 365–392. (p. 458)

Nathan, D. (2011). *Sybil exposed: The extraordinary story behind the famous multiple personality case.* Simon and Schuster. (p. 528)

Nathanson, L., Rivers, S. E., Flynn, L. M., & Brackett, M. A. (2016). Creating emotionally intelligent schools with RULER. *Emotion Review, 8,* 1–6. (p. 326)

National Academies of Sciences, Engineering, and Medicine. (2017). *The health effects of cannabis and cannabinoids: The current state of evidence and recommendations for research.* Washington, DC: National Academies Press. (p. 109)

National Academy of Sciences. (2001). *Exploring the biological contributions to human health: Does sex matter?* Washington, DC: National Academy Press. (p. 168)

National Academy of Sciences. (2002). *The polygraph and lie detection.* Washington, DC: National Academies Press. (p. 374)

National Center for Health Statistics. (1990). *Health, United States, 1989.* Washington, DC: U.S. Department of Health and Human Services. (p. 152)

National Research Council. (1990). *Human factors research needs for an aging population.* Washington, DC: National Academy Press. (p. 153)

National Safety Council. (2017). *Injury Facts®, 2017 Edition,* pp. 156–157. Itasca, IL: National Safety Council. (p. 302)

Naumann, L. P., Vazire, S., Rentfrow, P. J., & Gosling, S. D. (2009). Personality judgments based on physical appearance. *Personality and Social Psychology Bulletin, 35,* 1661–1671. (p. 481)

Nausheen, B., Carr, N. J., Peveler, R. C., Moss-Morris, R., Verrill, C., Robbins, E., . . . Gidron, Y. (2010). Relationship between loneliness and proangiogenic cytokines in newly diagnosed tumors of colon and rectum. *Psychosomatic Medicine, 72,* 912–916. (p. 390)

NCASA. (2007). *Wasting the best and the brightest: Substance abuse at America's colleges and universities.* New York: National Center on Addiction and Drug Abuse, Columbia University. (p. 112)

NCD Risk Factor Collaboration. (2016). Trends in adult body-mass index in 200 countries from 1975 to 2014: A pooled analysis of 1698 population-based measurement studies with 19.2 million participants. *The Lancet, 387,* 1377–1396. (p. 365)

Neal, D. T., Wood, W., & Drolet, A. (2013). How do people adhere to goals when willpower is low? The profits (and pitfalls) of strong habits. *Journal of Personality and Social Psychology, 104,* 959–975. (p. 234)

Nedeltcheva, A. V., Kilkus, J. M., Imperial, J., Schoeller, D. A., & Penev, P. D. (2010). Insufficient sleep undermines dietary efforts to reduce adiposity. *Annals of Internal Medicine, 153,* 435–441. (p. 365)

NEEF. (2015). Fact sheet: Children's health and nature. National Environmental Education Foundation. Retrieved from neefusa.org/resource/children%E2%80%99s-health-and-nature-fact-sheet (p. 559)

Neese, R. M. (1991, November/December). What good is feeling bad? The evolutionary benefits of psychic pain. *The Sciences,* pp. 30–37. (pp. 221, 255)

Neimeyer, R. A., & Currier, J. M. (2009). Grief therapy: Evidence of efficacy and emerging directions. *Current Directions in Psychological Science, 18,* 352–356. (p. 160)

Neisser, U. (1979). The control of information pickup in selective looking. In A. D. Pick (Ed.), *Perception and its development: A tribute to Eleanor J. Gibson* (pp. 209–219). Hillsdale, NJ: Erlbaum. (pp. 82, 83)

Neisser, U., Boodoo, G., Bouchard, T. J., Jr., Boykin, A. W., Brody, N., Ceci, S. J., . . . Urbina, S. (1996). Intelligence: Knowns and unknowns. *American Psychologist, 51,* 77–101. (p. 343)

Neisser, U., Winograd, E., & Weldon, M. S. (1991). Remembering the earthquake: "What I experienced" vs. "How I heard the news." Paper presented to the Psychonomic Society convention. (p. 278)

Neitz, J., Carroll, J., & Neitz, M. (2001). Color vision: Almost reason enough for having eyes. *Optics & Photonics News, 12,* 26–33. (p. 204)

Neitz, J., Geist, T., & Jacobs, G. H. (1989). Color vision in the dog. *Visual Neuroscience, 3,* 119–125. (p. 204)

Nelson, C. A., III, Fox, N. A., & Zeanah, C. H., Jr. (2013). Anguish of the abandoned child. *Scientific American, 308,* 62–67. (p. 157)

Nelson, C. A., III, Fox, N. A., & Zeanah, C. H., Jr. (2014). *Romania's abandoned children.* Cambridge, MA: Harvard University Press. (pp. 137, 338)

Nelson, C. A., III, Furtado, E. Z., Fox, N. A., & Zeanah, C. H., Jr. (2009). The deprived human brain. *American Scientist, 97,* 222–229. (p. 338)

Nelson, J., Klumparendt, A., Doebler, P., & Ehring, T. (2017). Childhood maltreatment and characteristics of adult depression: A meta-analysis. *The British Journal of Psychiatry, 210,* 96–104. (p. 517)

Nelson, M. D., Saykin, A. J., Flashman, L. A., & Riordan, H. J. (1998). Hippocampal volume reduction in schizophrenia as assessed by magnetic resonance imaging. *Archives of General Psychiatry, 55,* 433–440. (p. 525)

Nelson, S. K., Kushlev, K., English, T., Dunn, E. W., & Lyubomirsky, S. (2013). In defense of parenthood: Children are associated with more joy than misery. *Psychological Science, 24,* 3–10. (pp. 157, 338)

Nemeth, C. J., & Ormiston, M. (2007). Creative idea generation: Harmony versus stimulation. *European Journal of Social Psychology, 37,* 524–535. (p. 433)

Nemmi, F., Nymberg, C., Helander, E., & Klingberg, T. (2016). Grit is associated with structure of nucleus accumbens and gains in cognitive training. *Journal of Cognitive Neuroscience, 28,* 1688–1699. (p. 358)

Nes, R. B., Czajkowski, N., & Tambs, K. (2010). Family matters: Happiness in nuclear families and twins. *Behavior Genetics, 40,* 577–590. (p. 411)

Ness, E. (2016, January/February). FDA OKs sex drug for women. *Discover,* p. 45. (p. 28)

Nestadt, G., & Samuels, J. (1997). Epidemiology and genetics of obsessive-compulsive disorder. *International Review of Psychiatry, 9,* 61–71. (p. 509)

Nestler, E. J. (2011). Hidden switches in the mind. *Scientific American, 305,* 76–83. (p. 519)

Nestoriuc, Y., Rief, W., & Martin, A. (2008). Meta-analysis of biofeedback for tension-type headache: Efficacy, specificity, and treatment moderators. *Journal of Consulting and Clinical Psychology, 76,* 379–396. (p. 403)

Nettle, D., Andrews, C., & Bateson, M. (2017). Food insecurity as a driver of obesity in humans: The insurance hypothesis. *Behavioral and Brain Sciences, 40,* e105. (p. 365)

Neubauer, D. N. (1999). Sleep problems in the elderly. *American Family Physician, 59,* 2551–2558. (p. 89)

Neumann, R., & Strack, F. (2000). "Mood contagion": The automatic transfer of mood between persons. *Journal of Personality and Social Psychology, 79,* 211–223. (pp. 382, 422)

Newcomb, M. D., & Harlow, L. L. (1986). Life events and substance use among adolescents: Mediating effects of perceived loss of control and meaninglessness in life. *Journal of Personality and Social Psychology, 51,* 564–577. (p. 111)

Newell, B. R. (2015). "Wait! Just let me not think about that for a minute": What role do implicit processes play in higher-level cognition? *Current Directions in Psychological Science, 24,* 65–70. (p. 306)

Newport, C., Wallis, G., Reshitnyk, Y., & Siebeck, U. E. (2016). Discrimination of human faces by archerfish (*Toxotes chatareus*). *Scientific Reports, 6,* 27523. (p. 266)

Newport, E. L. (1990). Maturational constraints on language learning. *Cognitive Science, 14,* 11–28. (p. 316)

Newport, F. (1999, accessed April 28, 2016). Americans today much more accepting of a woman, black, Catholic, or Jew as president. Gallup Poll (gallup.com). (p. 437)

Newport, F. (2001, February). Americans see women as emotional and affectionate, men as more aggressive. *The Gallup Poll Monthly,* pp. 34–38. (p. 377)

Newport, F. (2012, December 19). *To stop shootings, Americans focus on police, mental health.* Gallup (gallup.com). (p. 502)

Newport, F. (2013a, July 25). In U.S. 87% approve of Black-White marriage, vs. 4% in 1958. *Gallup Poll* (gallup.com). (p. 436)

Newport, F. (2013b, July 31). *Former smokers say best way to quit is just to stop "cold turkey."* Gallup Poll (gallup.com). (pp. 102, 106)

Newport, F. (2014, June 2). *In U.S., 42% believe creationist view of human origins.* Gallup. Gallup Poll (gallup.com). (p. 77)

Newport, F. (2015, July 9). *Most U.S. smartphone owners check phone at least hourly.* Gallup Poll (gallup.com). (p. 355)

Newport, F., Argrawal, S., & Witters, D. (2010, December 23). *Very religious Americans lead healthier lives.* Gallup poll (gallup.com). (p. 406)

Newport, F., & Pelham, B. (2009, December 14). *Don't worry, be 80: Worry and stress decline with age.* Gallup Poll (gallup.com). (p. 385)

Newport, F., & Wilke, J. (2013, August 2). *Most in U.S. want marriage, but its importance has dropped.* Gallup Poll (gallup.com). (p. 156)

Newton, E. L. (1991). The rocky road from actions to intentions. *Dissertation Abstracts International, 51,* 4105. (p. B-13)

Newton, I. (1704). *Opticks: Or, a treatise of the reflexions, refractions, inflexions and colours of light.* London: Royal Society. (p. 203)

Ng, J. Y. Y., Ntoumanis, N., Thøgersen-Ntoumani, C., Deci, E. L., Ryan, R. M., Duda, J. L., & Williams, G. C. (2012). Self-determination theory applied to health contexts: A meta-analysis. *Perspectives on Psychological Science, 7,* 325–340. (p. 396)

Ng, S. H. (1990). Androcentric coding of man and his in memory by language users. *Journal of Experimental Social Psychology, 26,* 455–464. (p. 320)

Ng, T. W. H., & Feldman, D. C. (2009). How broadly does education contribute to job performance. *Personnel Psychology, 62,* 89–134. (p. B-6)

Ng, T. W. H., Sorensen, K. L., & Yim, F. H. K. (2009). Does the job satisfaction–job performance relationship vary across cultures? *Journal of Cross-Cultural Psychology, 40,* 761–796. (p. B-8)

Ng, W. W. H., Sorensen, K. L., & Eby, L. T. (2006). Locus of control at work: A meta-analysis. *Journal of Organizational Behavior, 27,* 1057–1087. (p. 397)

Nguyen, H.-H. D., & Ryan, A. M. (2008). Does stereotype threat affect test performance of minorities and women? A meta-analysis of experimental evidence. *Journal of Applied Psychology, 93,* 1314–1334. (p. 344)

NHTSA. (2000). *Traffic safety facts 1999: Older population.* Washington, DC: National Highway Traffic Safety Administration (ntl.bts.gov). (p. 152)

Nicholson, I. (2011). "Torture at Yale": Experimental subjects, laboratory torment and the "rehabilitation" of Milgram's "Obedience to Authority." *Theory and Psychology, 21,* 737–761. (p. 427)

Nickell, J. (Ed.). (1994). *Psychic sleuths: ESP and sensational cases.* Buffalo, NY: Prometheus Books. (p. 230)

Nickell, J. (2005, July/August). The case of the psychic detectives. *Skeptical Inquirer.* Retrieved from skeptically.org/skepticism/id10.html (p. 230)

Nickerson, R. S. (1999). How we know—and sometimes misjudge—what others know: Imputing one's own knowledge to others. *Psychological Bulletin, 125,* 737–759. (p. B-13)

Nickerson, R. S. (2002). The production and perception of randomness. *Psychological Review, 109,* 330–357. (p. 17)

Nickerson, R. S. (2005). Bertrand's chord, Buffon's needles, and the concept of randomness. *Thinking & Reasoning, 11,* 67–96. (p. 17)

Nicolas, S., & Levine, Z. (2012). Beyond intelligence testing: Remembering Alfred Binet after a century. *European Psychologist, 17,* 320–325. (p. 328)

Nicolaus, L. K., Cassel, J. F., Carlson, R. B., & Gustavson, C. R. (1983). Taste-aversion conditioning of crows to control predation on eggs. *Science, 220,* 212–214. (p. 255)

NIDA. (2002). *NIDA Research Report Series: Methamphetamine abuse and addiction* (NIH Publication No. 02-4210). Bethesda, MD: National Institute on Drug Abuse. (p. 107)

NIDA. (2005, May). *DrugFacts: Methamphetamine.* Bethesda, MD: National Institute on Drug Abuse. (p. 107)

Nielsen, K. M., Faergeman, O., Larsen, M. L., & Foldspang, A. (2006). Danish singles have a twofold risk of acute coronary syndrome: Data from a cohort of 138,290 persons. *Journal of Epidemiology and Community Health, 60,* 721–728. (p. 400)

Nielsen, M., & Tomaselli, K. (2010). Overimitation in Kalahari Bushman children and the origins of human cultural cognition. *Psychological Science, 21,* 729–736. (p. 260)

Nietzsche, F. (1889/1990). *Twilight of the idols and the Anti-Christ: Or how to philosophize with a hammer* (R. J. Hollindale, translator). New York: Penguin Classics. (p. 509)

Nieuwenstein, M. R., Wierenga, T., Morey, R. D., Wicherts, J. M., Blom, T. N., Wagenmakers, E., & van Rijn, H. (2015). On making the right choice: A meta-analysis and large-scale replication attempt of the unconscious thought advantage. *Judgment and Decision Making, 10,* 1–17. (p. 306)

NIH. (2001, July 20). *Workshop summary: Scientific evidence on condom effectiveness for sexually transmitted disease (STD) prevention.* Bethesda, MD: National Institute of Allergy and Infectious Diseases, National Institutes of Health. (p. 175)

NIH. (2010). *Teacher's guide: Information about sleep.* National Institutes of Health (nih.gov). (p. 92)

NIH. (2013, January 24). *Prenatal inflammation linked to autism risk.* National Institutes of Health (nih.gov). (p. 131)

NIH. (2015, December). *College drinking.* Bethesda, MD: National Institute of Alcohol Abuse and Alcoholism, National Institutes of Health. (p. 103)

NIH. (2016). *NIH Senior Health.* National Institutes of Health. Retrieved from nihseniorhealth.gov/parkinsonsdisease/whatcausesparkinsonsdisease/01.html (p. 44)

Nikles, M., Stiefel, F., & Bourquin, C. (2017). What medical students dream of: A standardized and data-driven approach. *Dreaming.* Advance online publication. doi:10.1037/drm0000057 (p. 96)

Nikolas, M. A., & Burt, A. (2010). Genetic and environmental influences on ADHD symptom dimensions of inattention and hyperactivity: A meta-analysis. *Journal of Abnormal Psychology, 119,* 1–17. (p. 498)

Nikolova, H., & Lamberton, C. (2016). Men and the middle: Gender differences in dyadic compromise effects. *Journal of Consumer Research.* Advance online publication. doi:10.1093/jcr/ucw035 (p. 154)

Niles, A. N., Craske, M. G., Lieberman, M. D., & Hur, C. (2015). Affect labeling enhances exposure effectiveness for public speaking anxiety. *Behavior Research and Therapy, 68,* 27–36. (p. 400)

NIMH. (2015). *Any mental illness (AMI) among U.S. adults.* National Institute of Mental Health (nimh.nih.gov/health/statistics/prevalence/any-mental-illness-ami-among-us-adults.shtml). (p. 504)

NIMH. (2017, accessed February 27). *Research Domain Criteria (RDoC)*. National Institute of Mental Health (nimh.nih.gov/research-priorities/rdoc). (p. 497)

Ninio, J., & Stevens, K. A. (2000) Variations on the Hermann grid: An extinction illusion. *Perception, 29*, 1209–1217. (p. 202)

Nir, Y., & Tononi, G. (2010). Dreaming and the brain: From phenomenology to neurophysiology. *Trends in Cognitive Sciences, 14*, 88–100. (p. 99)

Nisbett, R. (2015). *Mindware: Tools for smart thinking*. New York: Farrar, Straus and Giroux. (p. A-7)

Nisbett, R. E. (1987). Lay personality theory: Its nature, origin, and utility. In N. E. Grunberg, R. E. Nisbett et al. (Eds.), *A distinctive approach to psychological research: The influence of Stanley Schachter*. Hillsdale, NJ: Erlbaum. (p. B-5)

Nisbett, R. E. (2003). The geography of thought: How Asians and Westerners think differently . . . and why. New York: Free Press. (p. 416)

Nisbett, R. E. (2009). *Intelligence and how to get it: Why schools and culture count*. New York: Norton. (p. 342)

Nisbett, R. E., Aronson, J., Blair, C., Dickens, W., Flynn, J., Halpern, D. F., & Turkheimer, E. (2012). Intelligence: New findings and theoretical developments. *American Psychologist, 67*, 130–159. (pp. 337, 341, 342)

Nisbett, R. E., & Cohen, D. (1996). *Culture of honor: The psychology of violence in the South*. Boulder, CO: Westview Press. (p. 443)

Nisbett, R. E., & Ross, L. (1980). *Human inference: Strategies and shortcomings of social judgment*. Englewood Cliffs, NJ: Prentice-Hall. (p. 301)

Nizzi, M. C., Demertzi, A., Gosseries, O., Bruno, M. A., Jouen, F., & Laureys, S. (2012). From armchair to wheelchair: How patients with a locked-in syndrome integrate bodily changes in experienced identity. *Consciousness and Cognition, 21*, 431–437. (p. 409)

Nock, M. (2016, May 6). Five myths about suicide. *The Washington Post* (washingtonpost.com). (p. 500)

Nock, M. K. (2010). Self-injury. *Annual Review of Clinical Psychology, 6*, 339–363. (p. 502)

Nock, M. K., Borges, G., Bromet, E. J., Alonso, J., Angermeyer, M., Beautrais, A., . . . Williams, D. (2008). Cross-national prevalence and risk factors for suicidal ideation, plans, and attempts. *British Journal of Psychiatry, 192*, 98–105. (p. 501)

Nock, M. K., & Kessler, R. C. (2006). Prevalence of and risk factors for suicide attempts versus suicide gestures: Analysis of the National Comorbidity Survey. *Journal of Abnormal Psychology, 115*, 616–623. (p. 502)

Noel, J. G., Forsyth, D. R., & Kelley, K. N. (1987). Improving the performance of failing students by overcoming their self-serving attributional biases. *Basic and Applied Social Psychology, 8*, 151–162. (p. 398)

Noice, H., & Noice, T. (2006). What studies of actors and acting can tell us about memory and cognitive functioning. *Current Directions in Psychological Science, 15*, 14–18. (p. 274)

Nolen-Hoeksema, S. (2001). Gender differences in depression. *Current Directions in Psychological Science, 10*, 173–176. (p. 520)

Nolen-Hoeksema, S. (2003). *Women who think too much: How to break free of overthinking and reclaim your life*. New York: Holt. (p. 520)

Nolen-Hoeksema, S., & Larson, J. (1999). *Coping with loss*. Mahwah, NJ: Erlbaum. (p. 159)

Nook, E. C., Ong, D. C., Morelli, S. A., Mitchell, J. P., & Zaki, J. (2016). Prosocial conformity: Prosocial norms generalize across behavior and empathy. *Personality and Social Psychology Bulletin, 42*, 1045–1062. (p. 425)

Nørby, S. (2015). Why forget? On the adaptive value of memory loss. *Perspectives on Psychological Science, 10*, 551–578. (p. 283)

NORC. (2016a). National Opinion Research Center (University of Chicago) General Social Survey data, 1972 through 2014, accessed via sda.berkeley.edu. (p. 353)

NORC. (2016b). *New insights into Americans' perceptions and misperceptions of obesity treatments, and the struggles many face*. Chicago: National Opinion Research Center and the American Society for Metabolic and Bariatric Surgery (norc.org). (p. 365)

Nordgren, L. F., McDonnell, M.-H. M., & Loewenstein, G. (2011). What constitutes torture? Psychological impediments to an objective evaluation of enhanced interrogation tactics. *Psychological Science, 22*, 689–694. (p. 198)

Nordgren, L. F., van der Pligt, J., & van Harreveld, F. (2006). Visceral drives in retrospect: Explanations about the inaccessible past. *Psychological Science, 17*, 635–640. (p. 361)

Nordgren, L. F., van der Pligt, J., & van Harreveld, F. (2007). Evaluating Eve: Visceral states influence the evaluation of impulsive behavior. *Journal of Personality and Social Psychology, 93*, 75–84. (p. 361)

Norko, M. A., Freeman, D., Phillips, J., Hunter, W., Lewis, R., & Viswanathan, R. (2017). Can religion protect against suicide? *Journal of Nervous and Mental Disease, 205*, 9–14. (p. 500)

Norman, D. A. (2001). *The perils of home theater*. Retrieved from jnd.org/dn.mss/ProblemsOfHomeTheater.html (p. B-12)

Norman, E. (2010). "The unconscious" in current psychology. *European Psychologist, 15*, 193–201. (p. 469)

Norris, A. L., Marcus, D. K., & Green, B. A. (2015). Homosexuality as a discrete class. *Psychological Science, 26*, 1843–1853. (p. 179)

North, A. (2016, November 8). A wave of harassment after Trump's victory. *The New York Times* (nytimes.com). (p. 439)

Norton, K. L., Olds, T. S., Olive, S., & Dank, S. (1996). Ken and Barbie at life size. *Sex Roles, 34*, 287–294. (p. 533)

Nosek, B. A., Alter, G., Banks, G. C., Borsboom, D., Bowman, S. D., Breckler, S. J., . . . Yarkoni, T. (2015). Promoting an open research culture: Author guidelines for journals could help to promote transparency, openness, and reproducibility. *Science, 348*, 1422–1425. (p. 20)

Nowakowski, M. E., McCabe, R., Rowa, K., Pellizzari, J., Surette, M., Moayyedi, P., & Anglin, R. (2016). The gut microbiome: Potential innovations for the understanding and treatment of psychopathology. *Canadian Psychology/Psychologie Canadienne, 57*, 67–75. (p. 514)

NSC. (2010). Transportation mode comparisons. In *Injury facts 2010 edition*. National Safety Council (nsc.org). (p. 82)

NSF. (2001, October 24). *Public bounces back after Sept. 11 attacks, national study shows*. National Science Foundation. Retrieved from nsf.gov/od/lpa/news/press/ol/pr0185.htm (p. 385)

NSF. (2006, August 16). *The ABCs of back-to-school sleep schedules: The consequences of insufficient sleep* [Press release]. National Sleep Foundation (sleepfoundation.org). (p. 93)

NSF. (2013). *2013 International Bedroom Poll: Summary of findings*. National Sleep Foundation (sleepfoundation.org). (p. 90)

NSF. (2016, accessed November 29). *Sleepwalking*. National Sleep Foundation (sleepfoundation.org). (p. 95)

Nugent, N. R., Goldberg, A., & Uddin, M. (2016). Topical review: The emerging field of epigenetics: Informing models of pediatric trauma and physical health. *Journal of Pediatric Psychology, 41*, 55–64. (p. 74)

Nurmikko, A. V., Donoghue, J. P., Hochberg, L. R., Patterson, W. R., Song, Y.-K., Bull, C. W., . . . Aceros, J. (2010). Listening to brain microcircuits for interfacing with external world—Progress in wireless implantable microelectronic neuroengineering devices. *Proceedings of the IEEE, 98*, 375–388. (p. 61)

Nussinovitch, U., & Shoenfeld, Y. (2012). The role of gender and organ specific autoimmunity. *Autoimmunity Reviews, 11*, A377–A385. (p. 389)

Nuttin, J. M., Jr. (1987). Affective consequences of mere ownership: The name letter effect in twelve European languages. *European Journal of Social Psychology, 17*, 381–402. (p. 447)

Nye, C. D., Su, R., Rounds, J., & Drasgow, F. (2012). Vocational interests and performance: A quantitative summary of over 60 years of research. *Perspectives on Psychological Science, 7*, 384–403. (p. B-3)

O'Brien, E., & Ellsworth, P. C. (2012). Saving the last for best: A positivity bias for end experiences. *Psychological Science, 23*, 163–165. (p. 223)

O'Brien, F., Bible, J., Liu, D., & Simons-Morton, B. (2017). Do young drivers become safer after being involved in a collision? *Psychological Science, 28*(4), 407–413. (p. 239)

O'Brien, L., Albert, D., Chein, J., & Steinberg, L. (2011). Adolescents prefer more immediate rewards when in the presence of their peers. *Journal of Research on Adolescence, 21*, 747–753. (p. 148)

O'Connor, P., & Brown, G. W. (1984). Supportive relationships: Fact or fancy? *Journal of Social and Personal Relationships, 1*, 159–175. (p. 556)

O'Donnell, L., Stueve, A., O'Donnell, C., Duran, R., San Doval, A., Wilson, R. F., . . . Pleck, J. H. (2002). Long-term reduction in sexual initiation and sexual activity among urban middle schoolers in the reach for health service learning program. *Journal of Adolescent Health, 31*, 93–100. (p. 178)

O'Donovan, A., Neylan, T. C., Metzler, T., & Cohen, B. E. (2012). Lifetime exposure to traumatic psychological stress is associated with elevated inflammation in the heart and soul study. *Brain, Behavior, and Immunity, 26*, 642–649. (p. 391)

O'Hara, R. E., Gibbons, F. X., Gerrard, M., Li, Z., & Sargent, J. D. (2012). Greater exposure to sexual content in popular movies predicts earlier sexual debut and increased sexual risk taking. *Psychological Science, 23*, 984–993. (p. 177)

O'Leary, T., Williams, A. H., Franci, A., & Marder, E. (2014). Cell types, network homeostasis, and pathological compensation from a biologically plausible ion channel expression model. *Neuron, 82*, 809–821. (p. 39)

O'Neill, M. J. (1993). *The relationship between privacy, control, and stress responses in office workers*. Paper presented to the Human Factors and Ergonomics Society convention. (p. 396)

O'Sullivan, M., Frank, M. G., Hurley, C. M., & Tiwana, J. (2009). Police lie detection accuracy: The effect of lie scenario. *Law and Human Behavior, 33*, 530–538. (p. 376)

Oakley, D. A., & Halligan, P. W. (2013). Hypnotic suggestion: Opportunities for cognitive neuroscience. *Nature Reviews Neuroscience, 14*, 565–576. (p. 224)

Obama, B. (2017, January 10). President Obama's farewell address. *The New York Times* (nytimes.com). (p. 18)

Oberman, L. M., & Ramachandran, V. S. (2007). The simulating social mind: The role of the mirror neuron system and simulation in the social and communicative deficits of autism spectrum disorders. *Psychological Bulletin, 133,* 310–327. (p. 132)

Ochsner, K. N., Ray, R. R., Hughes, B., McRae, K., Cooper, J. C., Weber, J., . . . Gross, J. J. (2009). Bottom-up and top-down processes in emotion generation: Common and distinct neural mechanisms. *Psychological Science, 20,* 1322–1331. (p. 370)

Odgers, C. L., Caspi, A., Nagin, D. S., Piquero, A. R., Slutske, W. S., Milne, B. J., . . . Moffitt, T. E. (2008). Is it important to prevent early exposure to drugs and alcohol among adolescents? *Psychological Science, 19,* 1037–1044. (p. 112)

Oelschläger, M., Pfannmöller, J., Langer, I., & Lotze, M. (2014). Using of the middle finger shapes reorganization of the primary somatosensory cortex in patients with index finger. *Restorative Neurology and Neuroscience, 32,* 507–515. (p. 64)

Oettingen, G., & Mayer, D. (2002). The motivating function of thinking about the future: Expectations versus fantasies. *Journal of Personality and Social Psychology, 83,* 1198–1212. (p. 399)

Offer, D., Ostrov, E., Howard, K. I., & Atkinson, R. (1988). *The teenage world: Adolescents' self-image in ten countries.* New York: Plenum Press. (p. 148)

Ogden, J. (2012, January 16). HM, the man with no memory. *Psychology Today* (psychologytoday.com). (p. 284)

Ogihara, Y., Fujita, H., Tominaga, H., Ishigaki, S., Kashimoto, T., Takahashi, A., . . . Uchida, Y. (2015). Are common names becoming less common? The rise in uniqueness and individualism in Japan. *Frontiers in Psychology, 6,* article 1490. (p. 491)

Ogunnaike, O., Dunham, Y., & Banaji, M. R. (2010). The language of implicit preferences. *Journal of Experimental Social Psychology, 46,* 999–1003. (p. 319)

Ohgami, H., Terao, T., Shiotsuki, I., Ishii, N., & Iwata, N. (2009). Lithium levels in drinking water and risk of suicide. *British Journal of Psychiatry, 194,* 464–465. (p. 562)

Ohi, K., Shimada, T., Nitta, Y., Kihara, H., Okubo, H., Uehara, T., & Kawasaki, Y. (2016). The five-factor model personality traits in schizophrenia: A meta-analysis. *Psychiatry Research, 240,* 34–41. (p. 478)

Öhman, A. (2009). Of snakes and faces: An evolutionary perspective on the psychology of fear. *Scandinavian Journal of Psychology, 50,* 543–552. (p. 512)

Oishi, S., & Diener, E. (2014). Can and should happiness be a policy goal? *Policy Insights from Behavioral and Brain Sciences, 1,* 195–203. (p. 350)

Oishi, S., Diener, E. F., Lucas, R. E., & Suh, E. M. (1999). Cross-cultural variations in predictors of life satisfaction: Perspectives from needs and values. *Personality and Social Psychology Bulletin, 25,* 980–990. (p. 351)

Oishi, S., & Kesebir, S. (2015). Income inequality explains why economic growth does not always translate to an increase in happiness. *Psychological Science, 26,* 1630–1638. (p. 410)

Oishi, S., Kesebir, S., & Diener, E. (2011). Income inequality and happiness. *Psychological Science, 22,* 1095–1100. (p. 443)

Oishi, S., Kesebir, S., Miao, F., Talhelm, T., Endo, U., Uchida, Y., . . . Norasakkunkit, V. (2013). Residential mobility increases motivation to expand social network. But why? *Journal of Experimental Social Psychology, 49,* 217–223. (p. 353)

Oishi, S., Schiller, J., & Blair, E. G. (2013). Felt understanding and misunderstanding affect the perception of pain, slant, and distance. *Social Psychological and Personality Science, 4,* 259–266. (p. 197)

Oishi, S., & Schimmack, U. (2010a). Culture and well-being: A new inquiry into the psychological wealth of nations. *Perspectives in Psychological Science, 5,* 463–471. (p. 412)

Oishi, S., & Schimmack, U. (2010b). Residential mobility, well-being, and mortality. *Journal of Personality and Social Psychology, 98,* 980–994. (p. 353)

Okada, K., & Samreth, S. (2013). A study on the socio-economic determinants of suicide: Evidence from 13 European OECD countries. *Journal of Behavioral Economics, 45,* 78–85. (p. 500)

Okbay, A., Beauchamp, J. P., Fontana, M. A., Lee, J. J., Pers, T. H., Rietveld, C. A., . . . Oskarsson, S. (2016). Genome-wide association study identifies 74 loci associated with educational attainment. *Nature, 533,* 539–542. (p. 70)

Okimoto, T. G., & Brescoll, V. L. (2010). The price of power: Power seeking and backlash against female politicians. *Personality and Social Psychology Bulletin, 36,* 923–936. (p. 164)

Okuyama, T., Kitamura, T., Roy, D. S., Itohara, S., & Tonegawa, S. (2016). Ventral CA1 neurons store social memory. *Science, 353,* 1536–1541. (p. 276)

Olatunji, B. O., & Wolitzky-Taylor, K. B. (2009). Anxiety sensitivity and the anxiety disorders: A meta-analytic review and synthesis. *Psychological Bulletin, 135,* 974–999. (p. 507)

Olds, J. (1975). Mapping the mind onto the brain. In F. G. Worden, J. P. Swazey, & G. Adelman (Eds.), *The neurosciences: Paths of discovery* (pp. 375–400). Cambridge, MA: MIT Press. (p. 56)

Olds, J., & Milner, P. (1954). Positive reinforcement produced by electrical stimulation of the septal area and other regions of rat brain. *Journal of Comparative and Physiological Psychology, 47,* 419–427. (p. 56)

Olff, M., Langeland, W., Draijer, N., & Gersons, B. P. R. (2007). Gender differences in posttraumatic stress disorder. *Psychological Bulletin, 135,* 183–204. (p. 510)

Olfson, M., Gerhard, T., Huang, C., Crystal, S., & Stroup, T. S. (2015). Premature mortality among adults with schizophrenia in the United States. *JAMA Psychiatry, 72,* 1172–1181. (p. 518)

Olfson, M., & Marcus, S. C. (2009). National patterns in antidepressant medication treatment. *Archives of General Psychiatry, 66,* 848–856. (p. 562)

Oliner, S. P., & Oliner, P. M. (1988). *The altruistic personality: Rescuers of Jews in Nazi Europe.* New York: Free Press. (p. 261)

Olivé, I., Templemann, C., Berthoz, A., & Heinze, H.-J. (2015). Increased functional connectivity between superior colliculus and brain regions implicated in bodily self-consciousness during the rubber band illusion. *Human Brain Mapping, 36,* 717–730. (p. 81)

Olivola, C. Y., & Todorov, A. (2010). Elected in 100 milliseconds: Appearance-based trait inferences and voting. *Journal of Nonverbal Behavior, 54,* 83–110. (p. 376)

Olshansky, S. J. (2011). Aging of U.S. Presidents. *Journal of the American Medical Association, 306,* 2328–2329. (p. 396)

Olson, K. R., Key, A. C., & Eaton, N. R. (2015). Gender cognition in transgender children. *Psychological Science, 26,* 467–474. (pp. 85, 170)

Olson, R. L., Hanowski, R. J., Hickman, J. S., & Bocanegra, J. (2009, September). *Driver distraction in commercial vehicle operations.* Washington, DC: U.S. Department of Transportation, Federal Motor Carrier Safety Administration. (p. 82)

Olsson, A., Nearing, K. I., & Phelps, E. A. (2007). Learning fears by observing others: The neural systems of social fear transmission. *Social Cognitive and Affective Neuroscience, 2,* 3–11. (p. 511)

Oman, D., Kurata, J. H., Strawbridge, W. J., & Cohen, R. D. (2002). Religious attendance and cause of death over 31 years. *International Journal of Psychiatry in Medicine, 32,* 69–89. (p. 405)

ONS. (2015, September 23). *Personal well-being in the UK, 2014/2015.* Office for National Statistics (ons.gov.uk/). (p. 412)

Ooi, J., Dodd, H. F., Stuijfzand, B. G., Walsh, J., & Broeren, S. (2016). Do you think I should be scared? The effect of peer discussion on children's fears. *Behaviour Research and Therapy, 87,* 23–33. (p. 547)

Open Science Collaboration. (2015). Estimating the reproducibility of psychological science. *Science, 349,* 943. (p. 20)

Open Science Collaboration. (2017). Maximizing the reproducibility of your research. In S. O. Lilienfeld & I. D. Waldman (Eds.), *Psychological science under scrutiny: Recent challenges and proposed solutions.* New York: Wiley. (p. 20)

Opp, M. R., & Krueger, J. M. (2015). Sleep and immunity: A growing field with clinical impact. *Brain, Behavior, and Immunity, 47,* 1–3. (p. 93)

Oquendo, M. A., Galfalvy, H. C., Currier, D., Grunebaum, M. F., Sher, L., Sullivan, G. M., . . . Mann, J. J. (2011). Treatment of suicide attempters with bipolar disorder: A randomized clinical trial comparing lithium and valproate in the prevention of suicidal behavior. *The American Journal of Psychiatry, 168,* 1050–1056. (p. 562)

Orehek, E., & Human, L. J. (2017). Self-expression on social media: Do tweets present accurate and positive portraits of impulsivity, self-esteem, and attachment style? *Personality and Social Psychology Bulletin, 43,* 60–70. (p. 481)

Oren, D. A., & Terman, M. (1998). Tweaking the human circadian clock with light. *Science, 279,* 333–334. (p. 90)

Orth, U., & Robins, R. W. (2014). The development of self-esteem. *Current Directions in Psychological Science, 23,* 381–387. (p. 486)

Orth, U., Robins, R. W., Meier, L. L., & Conger, R. D. (2016). Refining the vulnerability model of low self-esteem and depression: Disentangling the effects of genuine self-esteem and narcissism. *Journal of Personality and Social Psychology, 110,* 133–149. (pp. 514, 519)

Orth, U., Robins, R. W., Trzesniewski, K. H., Maes, J., & Schmitt, M. (2009). Low self-esteem is a risk factor for depressive symptoms from young adulthood to old age. *Journal of Abnormal Psychology, 118,* 472–478. (p. 517)

Osborne, L. (1999, October 27). A linguistic big bang. *The New York Times Magazine* (nytimes.com). (p. 313)

Osgood, C. E. (1962). *An alternative to war or surrender.* Urbana: University of Illinois Press. (p. 459)

Osgood, C. E. (1980). GRIT: A strategy for survival in mankind's nuclear age? Paper presented at the Pugwash Conference on New Directions in Disarmament. (p. 459)

Oskarsson, A. T., Van Voven, L., McClelland, G. H., & Hastie, R. (2009). What's next? Judging sequences of binary events. *Psychological Bulletin, 135,* 262–285. (p. 17)

OSS Assessment Staff. (1948). *The assessment of men.* New York: Rinehart. (p. 484)

Ossher, L., Flegal, K. E., & Lustig, C. (2012). Everyday memory errors in older adults. *Aging, Neuropsychology, and Cognition, 20,* 220–242. (p. 154)

Ossola, A. (2014). This woman sees 100 times more colors than the average person. *Popular Science.* Retrieved from popsci.com/article/science/woman-sees-100-times-more-colors-average-person (p. 204)

Öst, L. -G., Havnen, A., Hansen, B., & Kvale, G. (2015). Cognitive behavioral treatments of obsessive–compulsive disorder. A systematic review and meta-analysis of studies published 1993–2014. *Clinical Psychology Review, 40,* 156–169. (p. 546)

Öst, L. -G., & Hugdahl, K. (1981). Acquisition of phobias and anxiety response patterns in clinical patients. *Behaviour Research and Therapy, 16,* 439–447. (p. 510)

Österman, K., Björkqvist, K., & Wahlbeck, K. (2014). Twenty-eight years after the complete ban on the physical punishment of children in Finland: Trends and psychosocial concomitants. *Aggressive Behavior, 40,* 568–581. (p. 249)

Ostfeld, A. M., Kasl, S. V., D'Atri, D. A., & Fitzgerald, E. F. (1987). *Stress, crowding, and blood pressure in prison.* Hillsdale, NJ: Erlbaum. (p. 397)

Osvath, M., & Karvonen, E. (2012). Spontaneous innovation for future deception in a male chimpanzee. *PLoS ONE, 7,* e36782. (p. 309)

Oswald, F. L., Mitchell, G., Blanton, H., Jaccard, J., & Tetlock, P. E. (2013). Predicting ethnic and racial discrimination: A meta-analysis of IAT criterion studies. *Journal of Personality and Social Psychology, 105,* 171–192. (p. 435)

Oswald, F. L., Mitchell, G., Blanton, H., Jaccard, J., & Tetlock, P. E. (2015). Using the IAT to predict ethnic and racial discrimination: Small effect sizes of unknown societal significance. *Journal of Personality and Social Psychology, 108,* 562–571. (p. 435)

Otgaar, H., & Baker, A. (2018). When lying changes memory for the truth. *Memory, 1,* 2–14. (p. 290)

Ott, B. (2007, June 14). Investors, take note: Engagement boosts earnings. *Gallup Management Journal* (gmj.gallup.com). (p. B-9)

Ott, C. H., Lueger, R. J., Kelber, S. T., & Prigerson, H. G. (2007). Spousal bereavement in older adults: Common, resilient, and chronic grief with defining characteristics. *Journal of Nervous and Mental Disease, 195,* 332–341. (p. 159)

Ouellette, J. A., & Wood, W. (1998). Habit and intention in everyday life: The multiple processes by which past behavior predicts future behavior. *Psychological Bulletin, 124,* 54–74. (p. B-6)

Overall, N. C., Fletcher, G. J. O., Simpson, J. A., & Fillo, J. (2015). Attachment insecurity, biased perceptions of romantic partners' negative emotions, and hostile relationship behavior. *Journal of Personality and Social Psychology, 108,* 730–749. (p. 136)

Owen, A. M. (2014). Disorders of consciousness: Diagnostic accuracy of brain imaging in the vegetative state. *Nature Review: Neurology, 10,* 370–371. (p. 81)

Owen, A. M., Coleman, M. R., Boly, M., Davis, M. H., Laureys, S., & Pickard, J. D. (2006). Detecting awareness in the vegetative state. *Science, 313,* 1402. (p. 81)

Owen, R. (1814). First essay in *New view of society or the formation of character.* Quoted in *The story of New Lamark.* New Lamark Mills, Lamark, Scotland: New Lamark Conservation Trust, 1993. (p. B-8)

Oxfam. (2005, March 26). *Three months on: New figures show tsunami may have killed up to four times as many women as men.* [Oxfam press release] (oxfam.org.uk). (p. 168)

Özçaliskan, S., Lucero, C., & Goldin-Meadow, S. (2016). Is *seeing gesture* necessary to *gesture* like a native speaker? *Psychological Science, 27,* 737–747. (p. 317)

Ozer, E. J., Best, S. R., Lipsey, T. L., & Weiss, D. S. (2003). Predictors of posttraumatic stress disorder and symptoms in adults: A meta-analysis. *Psychological Bulletin, 1,* 52–73. (p. 509)

Ozer, E. J., & Weiss, D. S. (2004). Who develops posttraumatic stress disorder? *Current Directions in Psychological Science, 13,* 169–172. (p. 510)

Özgen, E. (2004). Language, learning, and color perception. *Current Directions in Psychological Science, 13,* 95–98. (p. 320)

Pace-Schott, E. F., Germain, A., & Milad, M. R. (2015). Effects of sleep on memory for conditioned fear and fear extinction. *Psychological Bulletin, 141,* 835–857. (p. 91)

Pace-Schott, E. P., & Spencer, R. M. C. (2011). Age-related changes in the cognitive function of sleep. *Progress in Brain Research, 191,* 75–89. (p. 92)

Padgett, V. R. (1989). *Predicting organizational violence: An application of 11 powerful principles of obedience.* Paper presented to the American Psychological Association convention. (p. 427)

Page, S. E. (2007). The difference: How the power of diversity creates better groups, firms, schools, and societies. Princeton, NJ: Princeton University Press. (p. 433)

Palejwala, M. H., & Fine, J. G. (2015). Gender differences in latent cognitive abilities in children aged 2 to 7. *Intelligence, 48,* 96–108. (p. 340)

Palladino, J. J., & Carducci, B. J. (1983). *"Things that go bump in the night": Students' knowledge of sleep and dreams.* Paper presented at the meeting of the Southeastern Psychological Association. (p. 86)

Pallier, C., Colomé, A., & Sebastián-Gallés, N. (2001). The influence of native-language phonology on lexical access: Exemplar-based versus abstract lexical entries. *Psychological Science, 12,* 445–448. (p. 314)

Palmer, D. C. (1989). A behavioral interpretation of memory. In L. J. Hayes (Ed.), *Dialogues on verbal behavior: The first international institute on verbal relations* (pp. 261–279). Reno, NV: Context Press. (p. 281)

Palmer, S., Schreiber, C., & Box, C. (1991). *Remembering the earthquake: "Flashbulb" memory for experienced vs. reported events.* Paper presented to the Psychonomic Society convention. (p. 278)

Palomar-García, M. Á., Bueichekú, E., Ávila, C., Sanjuán, A., Strijkers, K., Ventura-Campos, N., & Costa, A. (2015). Do bilinguals show neural differences with monolinguals when processing their native language? *Brain and Language, 142,* 36–44. (p. 320)

Palombo, D. J., McKinnon, M. C., McIntosh, A. R., Anderson, A. K., Todd, R. M., & Levine, B. (2015). The neural correlates of memory for a life-threatening event: An fMRI study of passengers from Flight AT236. *Clinical Psychological Science.* https://doi.org/10.1177/2167702615589308. (p. 52)

Pan, S. C., Pashler, H., Potter, Z. E., & Rickard, T. C. (2015). Testing enhances learning across a range of episodic memory abilities. *Journal of Memory and Language, 83,* 53–61. (p. 272)

Pandey, J., Sinha, Y., Prakash, A., & Tripathi, R. C. (1982). Right-left political ideologies and attribution of the causes of poverty. *European Journal of Social Psychology, 12,* 327–331. (p. 417)

Pänkäläinen, M., Kerola, T., Kampman, O., Kauppi, M., & Hintikka, J. (2016). Pessimism and risk of death from coronary heart disease among middle-aged and older Finns: An eleven-year follow-up study. *BMC Public Health, 16,* 1124. (p. 392)

Panksepp, J. (2007). Neurologizing the psychology of affects: How appraisal-based constructivism and basic emotion theory can coexist. *Perspectives on Psychological Science, 2,* 281–295. (p. 374)

Pantev, C., Oostenveld, R., Engelien, A., Ross, B., Roberts, L. R., & Hoke, M. (1998). Increased auditory cortical representation in musicians. *Nature, 392,* 811–814. (p. 39)

Paolini, S., Harwood, J., Rubin, M., Husnu, S., Joyce, N., & Hewstone, M. (2014). Positive and extensive intergroup contact in the past buffers against the disproportionate impact of negative contact in the present. *European Journal of Social Psychology, 44,* 548–562. (p. 457)

Pardini, D. A., Raine, A., Erickson, K., & Loeber, R. (2014). Lower amygdala volume in men is associated with childhood aggression, early psychopathic traits, and future violence. *Biological Psychiatry, 75,* 73–80. (p. 530)

Park, C. L. (2007). Religiousness/spirituality and health: A meaning systems perspective. *Journal of Behavioral Medicine, 30,* 319–328. (p. 406)

Park, D. C., & McDonough, I. M. (2013). The dynamic aging mind: Revelations from functional neuroimaging research. *Perspectives on Psychological Science, 8,* 62–67. (p. 153)

Park, G., Lubinski, D., & Benbow, C. P. (2008). Ability differences among people who have commensurate degrees matter for scientific creativity. *Psychological Science, 19,* 957–961. (p. 306)

Park, G., Schwartz, H. A., Eichstaedt, J. C., Kern, M. L., Kosinski, M., Stillwell, D. J., . . . Seligman, M. E. P. (2015). Automatic personality assessment through social media language. *Journal of Personality and Social Psychology, 108,* 934–952. (p. 481)

Park, G., Yaden, D. R., Schwartz, H. A., Kern, M. L., Eichstaedt, J. C., Kosinski, M., . . . Seligman, M. E. P. (2016). Women are warmer but no less assertive than men: Gender and language on Facebook. *PLoS ONE.* doi:10.1371/journal.pone.0155885 (p. 165)

Parker, C. P., Baltes, B. B., Young, S. A., Huff, J. W., Altmann, R. A., LaCost, H. A., & Roberts, J. E. (2003). Relationships between psychological climate perceptions and work outcomes: A meta-analytic review. *Journal of Organizational Behavior, 24,* 389–416. (p. B-8)

Parker, E. S., Cahill, L., & McGaugh, J. L. (2006). A case of unusual autobiographical remembering. *Neurocase, 12,* 35–49. (p. 284)

Parker, K., & Wang, W. (2013. March 14). *Modern parenthood: Roles of moms and dads converge as they balance work and family.* Retrieved from pewsocialtrends.org/2013/03/14/modern-parenthood-roles-of-moms-and-dads-converge-as-they-balance-work-and-family/ (pp. 164, 187)

Parkes, A., Wight, D., Hunt, K., Henderson, M., & Sargent, J. (2013). Are sexual media exposure, parental restrictions on media use and co-viewing TV and DVDs with parents and friends associated with teenagers' early sexual behaviour? *Journal of Adolescence, 36,* 1121–1133. (p. 177)

Parkinson's Foundation. (2018). Statistics. Parkinson's Foundation. Retrieved from http://parkinson.org/Understanding-Parkinsons/Causes-and-Statistics/Statistics (p. 44)

Parnia, S., Spearpoint, K., de Vos, G., Fenwick, P., Goldberg, D., Yang, J., . . . Wood, M. (2014). AWARE—AWAreness during REsuscitation—A prospective study. *Resuscitation, 85,* 1799–1805. (p. 108)

Parsaik, A. K., Mascarenhas, S. S., Hashmi, A., Prokop, L. J., John, V., Okusaga, O., & Singh, B. (2016). Role of botulinum toxin in depression. *Journal of Psychiatric Practice, 22,* 99–110. (p. 381)

Parsons, T. D., & Rizzo, A. A. (2008). Affective outcomes of virtual reality exposure therapy for anxiety and specific phobias: A meta-analysis. *Journal of Behavior Therapy and Experimental Psychiatry, 39,* 250–261. (p. 541)

Partanen, E., Kujala, T., Näätänen, R., Liitola, A., Sambeth, A., & Huotilainen, M. (2013). Learning-induced neural plasticity of speech processing before birth. *PNAS, 110,* 15145–15150. (p. 119)

Parthasarathy, S., Vasquez, M. M., Halonen, M., Bootzin, R., Quan, S. F., Martinez, F. D., & Guerra, S. (2015). Persistent insomnia is associated with mortality risk. *American Journal of Medicine, 128,* 268–275. (p. 93)

Paşca, A. M., Sloan, S. A., Clarke, L. E., Tian, Y., Makinson, C. D., Huber, N., . . . Smith, S. J. (2015). Functional cortical neurons and astrocytes from human pluripotent stem cells in 3D culture. *Nature Methods, 12,* 671–678. (p. 64)

Pascoe, E. A., & Richman, L. S. (2009). Perceived discrimination and health: A meta-analytic review. *Psychological Bulletin, 135,* 531–554. (p. 386)

Passell, P. (1993, March 9). Like a new drug, social programs are put to the test. *The New York Times,* pp. C1, C10. (p. 28)

Patihis, L. (2016). Individual differences and correlates of highly superior autobiographical memory. *Memory, 24,* 961–978. (p. 284)

Patihis, L., Frenda, S. J., LePort, A. K., Petersen, N., Nichols, R. M., Stark, C. E., . . . Loftus, E. F. (2013). False memories in highly superior autobiographical memory individuals. *PNAS, 110,* 20947–20952. (p. 289)

Patihis, L., Ho, L. Y., Tingen, I. W., Lilienfeld, S. O., & Loftus, E. F. (2014a). Are the "memory wars" over? A scientist-practitioner gap in beliefs about repressed memory. *Psychological Science, 25,* 519–530. (pp. 288, 293)

Patihis, L., Lilienfeld, S. O., Ho, L. Y., & Loftus, E. F. (2014b). Unconscious repressed memory is scientifically questionable. *Psychological Science, 25,* 1967–1968. (p. 288)

Patterson, F. (1978, October). Conversations with a gorilla. *National Geographic,* pp. 438–465. (p. 317)

Patterson, G. R., Chamberlain, P., & Reid, J. B. (1982). A comparative evaluation of parent training procedures. *Behavior Therapy, 13,* 638–650. (p. 250)

Patterson, M., Warr, P., & West, M. (2004). Organizational climate and company productivity: The role of employee affect and employee level. *Journal of Occupational and Organizational Psychology, 77,* 193–216. (p. B-8)

Pauker, K., Weisbuch, M., Ambady, N., Sommers, S. R., Adams, R. B., Jr., & Ivcevic, Z. (2009). Not so Black and White: Memory for ambiguous group members. *Journal of Personality and Social Psychology, 96,* 795–810. (p. 342)

Paulesu, E., Demonet, J.-F., Fazio, F., McCrory, E., Chanoine, V., Brunswick, N., . . . Frith, U. (2001). Dyslexia: Cultural diversity and biological unity. *Science, 291,* 2165–2167. (p. 10)

Pauletti, R. E., Menon, M., Cooper, P. J., Aults, C. D., & Perry, D. G. (2017). Psychological androgyny and children's mental health: A new look with new measures. *Sex Roles, 76,* 705–718. (p. 169)

Pauly, K., Finkelmeyer, A., Schneider, F., & Habel, U. (2013). The neural correlates of positive self-evaluation and self-related memory. *Social Cognitive and Affective Neuroscience, 8,* 878–886. (p. 486)

Paunesku, D., Walton, G. M., Romero, C., Smith, E. N., Yeager, D. S., & Dweck, C. S. (2015). Mind-set interventions are a scalable treatment for academic underachievement. *Psychological Science, 26,* 784–793. (p. 339)

Paus, T., Zijdenbos, A., Worsley, K., Collins, D. L., Blumenthal, J., Giedd, J. N., . . . Evans, A. C. (1999). Structural maturation of neural pathways in children and adolescents: In vivo study. *Science, 283,* 1908–1911. (p. 123)

Pavlenko, A. (2014). *The bilingual mind and what it tells us about language and thought.* New York: Cambridge University Press. (p. 319)

Pavlov, I. (1927). *Conditioned reflexes: An investigation of the physiological activity of the cerebral cortex.* Oxford: Oxford University Press. (pp. 236, 240)

Payne, B. K. (2006). Weapon bias: Split-second decisions and unintended stereotyping. *Current Directions in Psychological Science, 15,* 287–291. (p. 436)

Payne, B. K., & Corrigan, E. (2007). Emotional constraints on intentional forgetting. *Journal of Experimental Social Psychology, 43,* 780–786. (p. 288)

Payne, B. K., Krosnick, J. A., Pasek, J., Lelkes, Y., Akhtar, O., & Tompson, T. (2010). Implicit and explicit prejudice in the 2008 American presidential election. *Journal of Experimental Social Psychology, 46,* 367–374. (p. 436)

Pearce, M. J., Koenig, H. G., Robins, C. J., Nelson, B., Shaw, S. F., Cohen, H. J., & King, M. B. (2015). Religiously integrated cognitive behavioral therapy: A new method of treatment for major depression in patients with chronic medical illness. *Psychotherapy, 52,* 56–66. (p. 556)

Peck, E. (2015, April 29). Harvard Business School launches new effort to attract women. *Huffington Post* (huffingtonpost.com). (p. 164)

Peckham, A. D., McHugh, R. K., & Otto, M. W. (2010). A meta-analysis of the magnitude of biased attention in depression. *Depression and Anxiety, 27,* 1135–1142. (p. 516)

Pedersen, A., Zachariae, R., & Bovbjerg, D. H. (2010). Influence of psychological stress on upper respiratory infection—A meta-analysis of prospective studies. *Psychosomatic Medicine, 72,* 823–832. (p. 390)

Peigneux, P., Laureys, S., Fuchs, S., Collette, F., Perrin, F., Reggers, J., . . . Maquet, P. (2004). Are spatial memories strengthened in the human hippocampus during slow wave sleep? *Neuron, 44,* 535–545. (p. 277)

Pelham, B., & Crabtree, S. (2008, October 8). *Worldwide, highly religious more likely to help others.* Gallup Poll (gallup.com). (p. 455)

Pelham, B. W. (1993). On the highly positive thoughts of the highly depressed. In R. F. Baumeister (Ed.), *Self-esteem: The puzzle of low self-regard.* New York: Plenum. (p. 487)

Pelham, B. W. (2009, October 22). About one in six Americans report history of depression. *Gallup* (gallup.com). (p. 517)

Pelham, W. E., Jr., Fabiano, G. A., Waxmonsky, J. G., Greiner, A. R., Gnagy, E. M., Pelham, W. E., . . . Murphy, S. A. (2016). Treatment sequencing for childhood ADHD: A multiple-randomization study of adaptive medication and behavioral interventions. *Journal of Clinical Child and Adolescent Psychology, 45,* 396–415. (p. 498)

Pennebaker, J. (1990). *Opening up: The healing power of confiding in others.* New York: William Morrow. (pp. 401, 469)

Pennebaker, J. W. (1985). Traumatic experience and psychosomatic disease: Exploring the roles of behavioral inhibition, obsession, and confiding. *Canadian Psychology, 26,* 82–95. (p. 400)

Pennebaker, J. W. (2011). *The secret life of pronouns: What our words say about us.* New York: Bloomsbury Press. (p. 481)

Pennebaker, J. W., Barger, S. D., & Tiebout, J. (1989). Disclosure of traumas and health among Holocaust survivors. *Psychosomatic Medicine, 51,* 577–589. (p. 400)

Pennebaker, J. W., Gosling, S. D., & Ferrell, J. D. (2013). Daily online testing in large classes: Boosting college performance while reducing achievement gaps. *PLoS ONE, 8,* e79774. (p. 273)

Pennebaker, J. W., & O'Heeron, R. C. (1984). Confiding in others and illness rate among spouses of suicide and accidental death victims. *Journal of Abnormal Psychology, 93,* 473–476. (p. 400)

Pennisi, E. (2016). The power of personality. *Science, 352,* 644–647. (p. 477)

Peplau, L. A., & Fingerhut, A. W. (2007). The close relationships of lesbians and gay men. *Annual Review of Psychology, 58,* 405–424. (pp. 157, 183)

Pepperberg, I. M. (2009). *Alex & me: How a scientist and a parrot discovered a hidden world of animal intelligence—and formed a deep bond in the process.* New York: Harper. (p. 309)

Pepperberg, I. M. (2012). Further evidence for addition and numerical competence by a grey parrot (Psittacus erithacus). *Animal Cognition, 15,* 711–717. (p. 309)

Pepperberg, I. M. (2013). Abstract concepts: Data from a grey parrot. *Behavioural Processes, 93,* 82–90. (p. 309)

Pereg, D., Gow, R., Mosseri, M., Lishner, M., Rieder, M., Van Uum, S., & Koren, G. (2011). Hair cortisol and the risk for acute myocardial infarction in adult men. *Stress, 14,* 73–81. (p. 391)

Pereira, A. C., Huddleston, D. E., Brickman, A. M., Sosunov, A. A., Hen, R., McKhann, G. M., . . . Small, S. A. (2007). An *in vivo* correlate of exercise-induced neurogenesis in the adult dentate gyrus. *PNAS, 104,* 5638–5643. (pp. 64, 153)

Pereira, G. M., & Osburn, H. G. (2007). Effects of participation in decision making on performance and employee attitudes: A quality circles meta-analysis. *Journal of Business Psychology, 22,* 145–153. (p. B-10)

Pergamin-Hight, L., Bakermans-Kranenburg, M. J., van IJzendoorn, M. H., & Bar-Haim, Y. (2012). Variations in the promoter region of the serotonin transporter gene and biased attention for emotional information: A meta-analysis. *Biological Psychiatry, 71,* 373–379. (p. 512)

Pergamin-Hight, L., Naim, R., Bakermans-Kranenburg, M. J., van IJzendoorn, M. H., & Bar-Haim, Y. (2015). Content specificity of attention bias to threat in anxiety disorders: A meta-analysis. *Clinical Psychology Review, 35,* 10–18. (p. 507)

Perilloux, H. K., Webster, G. D., & Gaulin, S. J. (2010). Signals of genetic quality and maternal investment capacity: The dynamic effects of fluctuating asymmetry and waist-to-hip ratio on men's ratings of women's attractiveness. *Social Psychology and Personality Science, 1,* 34–42. (pp. 184, 449)

Perkins, A., & Fitzgerald, J. A. (1997). Sexual orientation in domestic rams: Some biological and social correlates. In L. Ellis & L. Ebertz (Eds.), *Sexual orientation: Toward biological understanding* (p. 107–128). Westport, CT: Praeger. (p. 180)

Perkins, A. M., Inchley-Mort, S. L., Pickering, A. D., Corr, P. J., & Burgess, A. P. (2012). A facial expression for anxiety. *Journal of Personality and Social Psychology, 102,* 910–924. (p. 375)

Perrachione, T. K., Del Tufo, S. N., & Gabrieli, J. D. E. (2011). Human voice recognition depends on language ability. *Science, 333,* 595. (p. 317)

Perrett, D. I., Harries, M., Mistlin, A. J., & Chitty, A. J. (1990). Three stages in the classification of body movements by visual neurons. In H. Barlow, C. Blakemore, & M. Weston-Smith (Eds.), *Images and understanding* (pp. 94–108). Cambridge, England: Cambridge University Press. (p. 205)

Perrett, D. I., Hietanen, J. K., Oram, M. W., & Benson, P. J. (1992). Organization and functions of cells responsive to faces in the temporal cortex. *Philosophical Transactions of the Royal Society of London: Series B, 335,* 23–30. (p. 205)

Perrett, D. I., May, K. A., & Yoshikawa, S. (1994). Facial shape and judgments of female attractiveness. *Nature, 368,* 239–242. (p. 205)

Perry, G. (2013). Behind the shock machine: The untold story of the notorious Milgram psychology experiments. New York: New Press. (p. 427)

Perry, G. (2018). *The lost boys: Inside Muzafer Sherif's Robbers Cave experiment.* Melbourne/London: Scribe. (p. 458)

Person, C., Tracy, M., & Galea, S. (2006). Risk factors for depression after a disaster. *Journal of Nervous and Mental Disease, 194,* 659–666. (p. 567)

Pert, C. B. (1986). Quoted in J. Hooper & D. Teresi, *The three-pound universe.* New York: Macmillan. (p. 56)

Pert, C. B., & Snyder, S. H. (1973). Opiate receptor: Demonstration in nervous tissue. *Science, 179,* 1011–1014. (p. 43)

Perugini, E. M., Kirsch, I., Allen, S. T., Coldwell, E., Meredith, J., Montgomery, G. H., & Sheehan, J. (1998). Surreptitious observation of responses to hypnotically suggested hallucinations: A test of the compliance hypothesis. *International Journal of Clinical and Experimental Hypnosis, 46,* 191–203. (p. 224)

Peschel, E. R., & Peschel, R. E. (1987). Medical insights into the castrati in opera. *American Scientist, 75,* 578–583. (p. 173)

Pescosolido, B. A., Martin, J. K., Long, J. S., Medina, T. R., Phelan, J. C., & Link, B. G. (2010). "A disease like any other"? A decade of change in public reactions to schizophrenia, depression, and alcohol dependence. *American Journal of Psychiatry, 167,* 1321–1330. (p. 527)

Pesko, M. F. (2014). Stress and smoking: Associations with terrorism and causal impact. *Contemporary Economic Policy, 32,* 351–371. (p. 105)

Peter, C. J., Fischer, L. K., Kundakovic, M., Garg, P., Jakovcevski, M., Dincer, A., . . . Akbarian, S. (2016). DNA methylation signatures of early childhood malnutrition associated with impairments in attention and cognition. *Biological Psychiatry, 80,* 765–774. (p. 74)

Peter, J., & Valkenburg, P. M. (2016). Adolescents and pornography: A review of 20 years of research. *Journal of Sex Research, 53,* 509–531. (p. 444)

Peters, K., & Kashima, Y. (2015). A multimodal theory of affect diffusion. *Psychological Bulletin, 141,* 966–992. (p. 382)

Peters, M., Rhodes, G., & Simmons, L. W. (2007). Contributions of the face and body to overall attractiveness. *Animal Behaviour, 73,* 937–942. (p. 449)

Peters, T. J., & Waterman, R. H., Jr. (1982). *In search of excellence: Lessons from America's best-run companies.* New York: Harper & Row. (p. 251)

Petersen, J. L., & Hyde, J. S. (2010). A meta-analytic review of research on gender differences in sexuality, 1993–2007. *Psychological Bulletin, 136,* 21–38. (p. 183)

Petersen, J. L., & Hyde, J. S. (2011). Gender differences in sexual attitudes and behaviors: A review of meta-analytic results and large datasets. *Journal of Sex Research, 48,* 149–165. (p. 173)

Peterson, C., & Barrett, L. C. (1987). Explanatory style and academic performance among university freshmen. *Journal of Personality and Social Psychology, 53,* 603–607. (p. 398)

Peterson, C., Peterson, J., & Skevington, S. (1986). Heated argument and adolescent development. *Journal of Social and Personal Relationships, 3,* 229–240. (p. 143)

Peterson, L. R., & Peterson, M. J. (1959). Short-term retention of individual verbal items. *Journal of Experimental Psychology, 58,* 193–198. (p. 271)

Petitto, L. A., & Marentette, P. F. (1991). Babbling in the manual mode: Evidence for the ontogeny of language. *Science, 251,* 1493–1496. (p. 314)

Pettegrew, J. W., Keshavan, M. S., & Minshew, N. J. (1993). 31P nuclear magnetic resonance spectroscopy: Neurodevelopment and schizophrenia. *Schizophrenia Bulletin, 19,* 35–53. (p. 524)

Petticrew, M., Bell, R., & Hunter, D. (2002). Influence of psychological coping on survival and recurrence in people with cancer: Systematic review. *British Medical Journal, 325,* 1066. (p. 390)

Petticrew, M., Fraser, J. M., & Regan, M. F. (1999). Adverse life events and risk of breast cancer: A meta-analysis. *British Journal of Health Psychology, 4,* 1–17. (p. 390)

Pettigrew, T. F., & Tropp, L. R. (2011). *When groups meet: The dynamics of intergroup contact.* New York: Psychology Press. (p. 457)

Pew. (2006). Remembering 9/11. Pew Research Center (pewresearch.org). (p. 278)

Pew. (2007, July 18). Modern marriage: "I like hugs. I like kisses. But what I really love is help with the dishes." Pew Research Center (pewresearch.org). (p. 452)

Pew. (2009, November 4). *Social isolation and new technology: How the internet and mobile phones impact Americans' social networks.* Pew Research Center (pewresearch.org). (p. 356)

Pew. (2010, July 1). *Gender equality universally embraced, but inequalities acknowledged: Men's lives often seen as better.* Pew Research Center (pewglobal.org). (p. 169)

Pew. (2011, December 15). *17% and 61%—Texting, talking on the phone and driving.* Pew Research Center (pewresearch.org). (p. 82)

Pew. (2013a, June 4). *The global divide on homosexuality.* Pew Research Center, Global Attitudes Project (pewglobal.org). (p. 178)

Pew. (2013b, June 13). *A survey of LGBT Americans.* Pew Research Center (SDT_LGBT-Americans_06-2013.pdf). (p. 437)

Pew. (2014a, January 27). Climate change: Key data points from Pew Research. Pew Research Center (pewresearch.org). (p. 303)

Pew. (2014b). *Global views of morality.* Pew Research Center, Global Attitudes Project (pewglobal.org). (pp. 177, 437)

Pew. (2015, November 4). *Raising kids and running a household: How working parents share the load.* Pew Research Center (pewsocialtrends.org). (p. 154)

Pew. (2016, September 28). *Where the public stands on religious liberty vs. nondiscrimination.* Pew Forum (pewforum.org). (p. 457)

Pew. (2017). Internet/broadband technology fact sheet. Pew Research Center. Retrieved from pewinternet.org/fact-sheet/internet-broadband/ (p. 334)

Pfaff, L. A., Boatwright, K. J., Potthoff, A. L., Finan, C., Ulrey, L. A., & Huber, D. M. (2013). Perceptions of women and men leaders following 360-degree feedback evaluations. *Performance Improvement Quarterly, 26,* 35–56. (p. B-10)

Pfundmair, M., Zwarg, C., Paulus, M., & Rimpel, A. (2017). Oxytocin promotes attention to social cues regardless of group membership. *Hormones and Behavior, 90,* 136–140. (p. 49)

Phelps, J. A., Davis J. O., & Schartz, K. M. (1997). Nature, nurture, and twin research strategies. *Current Directions in Psychological Science, 6,* 117–120. (p. 526)

Philbeck, J. W., & Witt, J. K. (2015). Action-specific influences on perception and postperceptual processes: Present controversies and future directions. *Psychological Bulletin, 141,* 1120–1144. (p. 197)

Philip Morris. (2003). Philip Morris USA youth smoking prevention. Teenage attitudes and behavior study, 2002. In *Raising kids who don't smoke,* Vol. 1(2). (p. 112)

Phillips, A. C., Batty, G. D., Gale, C. R., Deary, I. J., Osborn, D., MacIntyre, K., & Carroll, D. (2009). Generalized anxiety disorder, major depressive disorder, and their comorbidity as predictors of all-cause and cardiovascular mortality: The Vietnam Experience Study. *Psychosomatic Medicine, 71,* 395–403. (p. 399)

Phillips, A. L. (2011). A walk in the woods. *American Scientist, 69,* 301–302. (p. 559)

Phillips, D. P. (1985). Natural experiments on the effects of mass media violence on fatal aggression: Strengths and weaknesses of a new approach. In L. Berkowitz (Ed.), *Advances in experimental social psychology* (Vol. 19, pp. 207–250). Orlando, FL: Academic Press. (p. 423)

Phillips, D. P., Carstensen, L. L., & Paight, D. J. (1989). Effects of mass media news stories on suicide, with new evidence on the role of story content. In C. R. Pfeffer (Ed.), *Suicide among youth: Perspectives on risk and prevention* (pp. 101–116). Washington, DC: American Psychiatric Press. (p. 423)

Phillips, J. L. (1969). *Origins of intellect: Piaget's theory.* San Francisco: Freeman. (p. 128)

Phillips, W. J., Fletcher, J. M., Marks, A. D. G., & Hine, D. W. (2016). Thinking styles and decision making: A meta-analysis. *Psychological Bulletin, 142,* 260–290. (p. 306)

Piaget, J. (1930). *The child's conception of physical causality.* London: Routledge & Kegan Paul. (p. 125)

Piaget, J. (1932). *The moral judgment of the child* (M. Gabain, Trans.). New York: Harcourt, Brace & World. (p. 143)

Piazza, J. R., Charles, S. T., Silwinski, M. J., Mogle, J., & Almeida, D. M. (2013). Affective reactivity to daily stressors and long-term risk of reporting a chronic health condition. *Annals of Behavioral Medicine, 45,* 110–120. (p. 386)

Picardi, A., Fagnani, C., Nisticò, L., & Stazi, M. A. (2011). A twin study of attachment style in young adults. *Journal of Personality, 79,* 965–992. (p. 134)

Picchioni, M. M., & Murray, R. M. (2007). Schizophrenia. *British Medical Journal, 335,* 91–95. (p. 524)

Picci, G., Gotts, S. J., & Scherf, K. S. (2016). A theoretical rut: Revisiting and critically evaluating the generalized under/over-connectivity hypothesis of autism. *Developmental Science, 19,* 524–549. (p. 131)

Picci, G., & Scherf, K. S. (2016). From caregivers to peers: Puberty shapes human face perception. *Psychological Science, 27,* 1461–1473. (p. 147)

Piekarski, D. J., Routman, D. M., Schoomer, E. E., Driscoll, J. R., Park, J. H., Butler, M. P., & Zucker, I. (2009). Infrequent low dose testosterone treatment maintains male sexual behavior in Syrian hamsters. *Hormones and Behavior, 55,* 182–189. (p. 173)

Pierce, L. J., Klein, D., Chen, J., Delcenserie, A., & Genesee, F. (2014). Mapping the unconscious maintenance of a lost first language. *PNAS, 111,* 17314–17319. (p. 125)

Pietschnig, J., & Voracek, M. (2015). One century of global IQ gains: A formal meta-analysis of the Flynn effect (1909–2013). *Perspectives on Psychological Science, 10,* 282–306. (p. 342)

Piliavin, J. A. (2003). Doing well by doing good: Benefits for the benefactor. In C.L.M. Keyes & J. Haidt (Eds.), *Flourishing: Positive psychology and the life well-lived* (pp. 227–247). Washington, DC: American Psychological Association. (p. 145)

Pillemer, D. B. (1998). *Momentous events, vivid memories.* Cambridge, MA: Harvard University Press. (p. 153)

Pillemer, D. B., Ivcevic, Z., Gooze, R. A., & Collins, K. A. (2007). Self-esteem memories: Feeling good about achievement success, feeling bad about relationship distress. *Personality and Social Psychology Bulletin, 33,* 1292–1305. (p. 354)

Pilley, J. W. (2013). *Chaser: Unlocking the genius of the dog who knows a thousand words.* Boston: Houghton Mifflin. (p. 318)

Pinker, S. (1990, September-October). Quoted by J. de Cuevas, "No, she held them loosely." *Harvard Magazine,* pp. 60–67. (p. 312)

Pinker, S. (1995). The language instinct. *The General Psychologist, 31,* 63–65. (p. 318)

Pinker, S. (1998). Words and rules. *Lingua, 106,* 219–242. (p. 311)

Pinker, S. (2005, April 22). The science of gender and science: A conversation with Elizabeth Spelke. Harvard University. *The Edge* (edge.org). (p. 340)

Pinker, S. (2008). *The sexual paradox: Men, women, and the real gender gap.* New York: Scribner. (p. 164)

Pinker, S. (2010, June 10). Mind over mass media. *The New York Times,* A31. (p. 357)

Pinker, S. (2011, September 27). A history of violence. *The Edge* (edge.org). (p. 445)

Pinker, S. (2014). *The village effect: Why face-to-face contact matters.* Toronto: Random House Canada. (p. 356)

Pinker, S. (2015, June 8). The trauma of residential schools is passed down through the generations. *The Globe and Mail* (globeandmail.com). (p. 75)

Pinkham, A. E., Griffin, M., Baron, R., Sasson, N. J., & Gur, R. C. (2010). The face in the crowd effect: Anger superiority when using real faces and multiple identities. *Emotion, 10,* 141–146. (p. 376)

Pinquart, M. (2015). Associations of parenting styles and dimensions with academic achievement in children and adolescents: A meta-analysis. *Educational Psychology Review,* 1–19. doi:10.1007/s10648-015-9338-y (p. 139)

Pipe, M.-E., Lamb, M. E., Orbach, Y., & Esplin, P. W. (2004). Recent research on children's testimony about experienced and witnessed events. *Developmental Review, 24,* 440–468. (p. 294)

Pipher, M. (2002). *The middle of everywhere: The world's refugees come to our town.* New York: Harcourt Brace. (pp. 353, 385)

Pitcher, D., Walsh, V., Yovel, G., & Duchaine, B. (2007). TMS evidence for the involvement of the right occipital face area in early face processing. *Current Biology, 17,* 1568–1573. (p. 205)

Pitman, R. K., & Delahanty, D. L. (2005). Conceptually driven pharmacologic approaches to acute trauma. *CNS Spectrums, 10,* 99–106. (p. 279)

Pitman, R. K., Sanders, K. M., Zusman, R. M., Healy, A. R., Cheema, F., Lasko, N. B., . . . Orr, S. P. (2002). Pilot study of secondary prevention of posttraumatic stress disorder with propranolol. *Biological Psychiatry, 51,* 189–192. (p. 279)

Pittinsky, T. L., & Diamante, N. (2015). Global bystander nonintervention. *Peace and Conflict: Journal of Peace Psychology, 21,* 226–247. (p. 453)

Place, S. S., Todd, P. M., Penke, L., & Asendorph, J. B. (2009). The ability to judge the romantic interest of others. *Psychological Science, 20,* 22–26. (p. 376)

Plant, E. A., & Peruche, B. M. (2005). The consequences of race for police officers' responses to criminal suspects. *Psychological Science, 16,* 180–183. (p. 436)

Plassmann, H., O'Doherty, J., Shiv, B., & Rangel, A. (2008). Marketing actions can modulate neural representations of experienced pleasantness. *PNAS, 105,* 1050–1054. (p. 225)

Platek, S. M., & Singh, D. (2010) Optimal waist-to-hip ratios in women activate neural reward centers in men. *PLoS ONE, 5,* e9042. doi:10.1371/journal.pone.0009042. (p. 449)

Pliner, P. (1982). The effects of mere exposure on liking for edible substances. *Appetite: Journal for Intake Research, 3,* 283–290. (p. 364)

Pliner, P., Pelchat, M., & Grabski, M. (1993). Reduction of neophobia in humans by exposure to novel foods. *Appetite, 20,* 111–123. (p. 364)

Plomin, R. (1999). Genetics and general cognitive ability. *Nature, 402,* C25–C29. (p. 323)

Plomin, R. (2011). Why are children in the same family so different? Nonshared environment three decades later. *International Journal of Epidemiology, 40,* 582–592. (pp. 72, 149)

Plomin, R., & Bergeman, C. S. (1991). The nature of nurture: Genetic influence on "environmental" measures. *Behavioral and Brain Sciences, 14,* 373–427. (p. 74)

Plomin, R., & Daniels, D. (1987). Why are children in the same family so different from one another? *Behavioral and Brain Sciences, 10,* 1–60. (p. 149)

Plomin, R., & DeFries, J. C. (1998). The genetics of cognitive abilities and disabilities. *Scientific American, 278,* 62–69. (p. 338)

Plomin, R., DeFries, J. C., Knopik, V. S., & Neiderhiser, J. M. (2016). Top 10 replicated findings from behavioral genetics. *Perspectives on Psychological Science, 11,* 3–23. (pp. 70, 336)

Plomin, R., DeFries, J. C., McClearn, G. E., & Rutter, M. (1997). *Behavioral genetics.* New York: Freeman. (pp. 365, 526)

Plomin, R., McClearn, G. E., Pedersen, N. L., Nesselroade, J. R., & Bergeman, C. S. (1988). Genetic influence on childhood family environment perceived retrospectively from the last half of the life span. *Developmental Psychology, 24,* 37–45. (p. 74)

Plomin, R., & McGuffin, P. (2003). Psychopathology in the postgenomic era. *Annual Review of Psychology, 54,* 205–228. (p. 518)

Plomin, R., Reiss, D., Hetherington, E. M., & Howe, G. W. (January, 1994). Nature and nurture: Genetic contributions to measures of the family environment. *Developmental Psychology, 30,* 32–43. (p. 74)

Plotkin, H. (1994). *Darwin machines and the nature of knowledge.* Cambridge, MA: Harvard University Press. (p. 518)

Plous, S., & Herzog, H. A. (2000). Poll shows researchers favor lab animal protection. *Science, 290,* 711. (p. 31)

Pluess, M., & Belsky, J. (2013). Vantage sensitivity: Individual differences in response to positive experiences. *Psychological Bulletin, 139,* 901–916. (p. 512)

Poelmans, G., Pauls, D. L., Buitelaar, J. K., & Franke, B. (2011). Integrated genomewide association study findings: Identification of a neurodevelopmental network for attention deficit hyperactivity disorder. *American Journal of Psychiatry, 168,* 365–377. (p. 498)

Polanin, J. R., Espelage, D. L., & Pigott, T. D. (2012). A meta-analysis of school-based bully prevention programs' effects on bystander intervention behavior. *School Psychology Review, 41,* 47–65. (p. 13)

Polderman, T. J. C., Benyamin, B., de Leeuw, C. A., Sullivan, P. F., van Bochoven, A., Visscher, P. M., & Posthuma, D. (2015). Meta-analysis of the heritability of human traits based on fifty years of twin studies. *Nature Genetics, 47,* 702–709. (pp. 70, 511, 518)

Poldrack, R. A., Halchenko, Y. O., & Hanson, S. J. (2009). Decoding the large-scale structure of brain function by classifying mental states across individuals. *Psychological Science, 20,* 1364–1372. (p. 52)

Polivy, J., Herman, C. P., & Coelho, J. S. (2008). Caloric restriction in the presence of attractive food cues: External cues, eating, and weight. *Physiology and Behavior, 94,* 729–733. (p. 364)

Pollak, S., Cicchetti, D., & Klorman, R. (1998). Stress, memory, and emotion: Developmental considerations from the study of child maltreatment. *Developmental Psychopathology, 10,* 811–828. (p. 240)

Pollak, S. D., & Kistler, D. J. (2002). Early experience is associated with the development of categorical representations for facial expressions of emotion. *PNAS, 99,* 9072–9076. (p. 376)

Pollak, S. D., & Tolley-Schell, S. A. (2003). Selective attention to facial emotion in physically abused children. *Journal of Abnormal Psychology, 112,* 323–328. (p. 376)

Pollard, R. (1992). *100 years in psychology and deafness: A centennial retrospective.* Invited address to the American Psychological Association convention, Washington, DC. (p. 317)

Pollatsek, A., Romoser, M. R. E., & Fisher, D. L. (2012). Identifying and remediating failures of selective attention in older drivers. *Current Directions in Psychological Science, 21,* 3–7. (p. 152)

Pollick, A. S., & de Waal, F. B. M. (2007). Ape gestures and language evolution. *PNAS, 104,* 8184–8189. (p. 317)

Poole, D. A., & Lindsay, D. S. (1995). Interviewing preschoolers: Effects of nonsuggestive techniques, parental coaching and leading questions on reports of nonexperienced events. *Journal of Experimental Child Psychology, 60,* 129–154. (p. 291)

Poole, D. A., & Lindsay, D. S. (2001). Children's eyewitness reports after exposure to misinformation from parents. *Journal of Experimental Psychology: Applied, 7,* 27–50. (p. 291)

Pope, D., & Simonsohn, U. (2011). Round numbers as goals: Evidence from baseball, SAT takers, and the lab. *Psychological Science, 22,* 71–79. (p. A-1)

Pope Francis. (2015). *Encyclical Letter Laudato Si' of the Holy Father Francis on care for our common home (official English-language text of encyclical).* Retrieved from w2.vatican.va (pp. 77, 418)

Poropat, A. E. (2014). Other-rated personality and academic performance: Evidence and implications. *Learning and Individual Differences, 34,* 24–32. (p. 342)

Porter, D., & Neuringer, A. (1984). Music discriminations by pigeons. *Journal of Experimental Psychology: Animal Behavior Processes, 10,* 138–148. (p. 245)

Porter, S., & Peace, K. A. (2007). The scars of memory: A prospective, longitudinal investigation of the consistency of traumatic and positive emotional memories in adulthood. *Psychological Science, 18,* 435–441. (p. 293)

Poulton, R., Moffitt, T. E., & Silva, P. A. (2015). The Dunedin multidisciplinary health and development study: Overview of the first 40 years, with an eye to the future. *Social Psychiatry and Psychiatric Epidemiology, 50,* 679–693. (p. 398)

Poundstone, W. (2014). *How to predict the unpredictable. The art of outsmarting almost everyone.* London: OneWorld. (p. 17)

Poushter, J. (2016, February 22). *Smartphone ownership and internet usage continues to climb in emerging economies.* Pew Research Center (pewglobal.org). (p. 355)

Powell, R., Digdon, N. A., Harris, B., & Smithson, C. (2014). Correcting the record on Watson, Rayner and Little Albert: Albert Barger as "Psychology's Lost Boy." *American Psychologist, 69,* 600–611. (p. 241)

Powell, R. A., & Boer, D. P. (1994). Did Freud mislead patients to confabulate memories of abuse? *Psychological Reports, 74,* 1283–1298. (p. 468)

Powell, R. A., & Schmaltz, R. M. (2017, July). Did Little Albert actually acquire a conditioned fear of animals? What the film evidence tells us. Paper presented at the Vancouver International Conference on the Teaching of Psychology. (p. 241)

Power, R. A., Steinberg, S., Bjornsdottir, G., Rietveld, C. A., Abdellaoui, A., Nivard, M. M., . . . Stefansson, K. (2015). Polygenic risk scores for schizophrenia and bipolar disorder predict creativity. *Nature Neuroscience, 18,* 953–955. (p. 515)

Power, R. A., Tansey, K. E., Buttenschøn, H. N., Cohen-Woods, S., Bigdeli, T., Hall, L. S., . . . Teumer, A. (2017). Genome-wide association for major depression through age at onset stratification: Major depressive disorder working group of the psychiatric genomics consortium. *Biological Psychiatry, 81,* 325–335. (p. 518)

PPP. (2016, December 9). Trump remains unpopular; voters prefer Obama on SCOTUS pick. Public Policy Polling. Retrieved from http://www.publicpolicypolling.com/wp-content/uploads/2017/09/PPP_Release_National_120916.pdf (p. 18)

Prather, A. A., Janicki-Deverts, D., Hall, M. H., & Cohen, S. (2015). Behaviorally assessed sleep and susceptibility to the common cold. *Sleep, 38,* 1353–1359. (p. 93)

Pratt, L. A., Brody, D. J., & Gu, Q. (2017, August). Antidepressant use among persons aged 12 and over: United States, 2011–2014. *NCHS Data Brief, 283,* 1–8. (p. 520)

Preckel, F., Lipnevich, A., Boehme, K., Branderner, L., Georgi, K., Könen, T., . . . Roberts, R. (2013). Morningness–eveningness and educational outcomes: The lark has an advantage over the owl at high school. *British Journal of Educational Psychology, 83,* 114–134. (p. 87)

Premack, D. G., & Woodruff, G. (1978). Does the chimpanzee have a theory of mind? *Behavioral and Brain Sciences, 1,* 515–526. (p. 128)

Prentice, D. A., & Miller, D. T. (1993). Pluralistic ignorance and alcohol use on campus: Some consequences of misperceiving the social norm. *Journal of Personality and Social Psychology, 64,* 243–256. (p. 112)

Primack, B. A., Shensa, A., Escobar-Viera, C. G., Barrett, E. L., Sidani, J. E., Colditz, J. B., & James, A. E. (2016). Use of multiple social media platforms and symptoms of depression and anxiety: A nationally-representative study among U.S. young adults. *Computers in Human Behavior, 69,* 1–9. (p. 356)

Profet, M. (1992). Pregnancy sickness as adaptation: A deterrent to maternal ingestion of teratogens. In J. H. Barkow, L. Cosmides, & J. Tooby (Eds.), *The adapted mind: Evolutionary psychology and the generation of culture* (pp. 327–366). New York: Oxford University Press. (p. 76)

Proffitt, D. R. (2006a). Distance perception. *Current Directions in Psychological Research, 15,* 131–135. (p. 197)

Proffitt, D. R. (2006b). Embodied perception and the economy of action. *Perspectives on Psychological Science, 1,* 110–122. (p. 197)

Project Match Research Group. (1997). Matching alcoholism treatments to client heterogeneity: Project MATCH posttreatment drinking outcomes. *Journal of Studies on Alcohol, 58,* 7–29. (p. 548)

Pronin, E. (2013). When the mind races: Effects of thought speed on feeling and action. *Current Directions in Psychological Science, 22,* 283–288. (p. 515)

Pronin, E., & Ross, L. (2006). Temporal differences in trait self-ascription: When the self is seen as another. *Journal of Personality and Social Psychology, 90,* 197–209. (p. 417)

Propper, R. E., Stickgold, R., Keeley, R., & Christman, S. D. (2007). Is television traumatic? Dreams, stress, and media exposure in the aftermath of September 11, 2001. *Psychological Science, 18,* 334–340. (p. 96)

Prot, S., Gentile, D. A., Anderson, C. A., Suzuki, K., Horiuchi, Y., Jelic, M., . . . Lam, B. C. P. (2014). Long-term relations among prosocial-media use, empathy, and prosocial behavior. *Psychological Science, 25,* 358–368. (pp. 261, 444)

Protzko, J., Aronson, J., & Blair, C. (2013). How to make a young child smarter: Evidence from the database of raising intelligence. *Perspectives on Psychological Science, 8,* 25–40. (p. 339)

Provine, R. R. (2001). *Laughter: A scientific investigation.* New York: Penguin. (p. 23)

Provine, R. R. (2012). *Curious behavior: Yawning, laughing, hiccupping, and beyond.* Cambridge, MA: Harvard University Press. (pp. 22, 422)

Provine, R. R., Krosnowski, K. A., & Brocato, N. W. (2009). Tearing: Breakthrough in human emotional signaling. *Evolutionary Psychology, 7,* 52–56. (p. 380)

Pryor, J. H., Hurtado, S., DeAngelo, L., Blake, L. P., & Tran, S. (2011). *The American freshman: National norms fall 2010.* Los Angeles: UCLA Higher Education Research Institute. (p. 165)

Pryor, J. H., Hurtado, S., Saenz, V. B., Korn, J. S., Santos, J. L., & Korn, W. S. (2006). *The American freshman: National norms for Fall 2006.* Los Angeles: UCLA Higher Education Research Institute. (p. 520)

Pryor, J. H., Hurtado, S., Saenz, V. B., Lindholm, J. A., Korn, W. S., & Mahoney, K. M. (2005). *The American freshman: National norms for Fall 2005.* Los Angeles: UCLA Higher Education Research Institute. (p. 184)

Pryor, J. H., Hurtado, S., Sharkness, J., & Korn, W. S. (2007). *The American freshman: National norms for fall 2007.* Los Angeles: UCLA Higher Education Research Institute. (p. 165)

Psaltopoulou, T., Sergentanis, T. N., Panagiotakos, D. B., Sergentanis, I. N., Kosti, R., & Scarmeas, N. (2013). Mediterranean diet, stroke, cognitive impairment, and depression: A meta-analysis. *Annals of Neurology, 74,* 580–591. (p. 519)

Psychologist. (2003). Who's the greatest? *The Psychologist, 16,* 170–175. (p. 130)

PTC. (2007, January 10). Dying to entertain: Violence on prime time broadcast TV, 1998 to 2006. Parents Television Council (parentstv.org). (p. 262)

Puhl, R. M., Latner, J. D., O'Brien, K., Luedicke, J., Forhan, M., & Danielsdottir, S. (2015). Cross-national perspectives about weigh-based bullying in youth: Nature, extent and remedies. *Pediatric Obesity, 11,* 241–250. (p. 365)

Punamäki, R. L., & Joustie, M. (1998). The role of culture, violence, and personal factors affecting dream content. *Journal of Cross-Cultural Psychology, 29,* 320–342. (p. 96)

Putnam, F. W. (1991). Recent research on multiple personality disorder. *Psychiatric Clinics of North America, 14,* 489–502. (p. 528)

Putnam, R. (2000). *Bowling alone.* New York: Simon and Schuster. (p. 422)

Puttonen, S., Kivimäki, M., Elovainio, M., Pulkki-Råback, L., Hintsanen, M., Vahtera, J., . . . Keltikangas-Järvinen, L. (2009). Shift work in young adults and carotid artery intima–media thickness: The Cardiovascular Risk in Young Finns study. *Atherosclerosis, 205,* 608–613. (p. 90)

Pyszczynski, T. A., Motyl, M., Vail, K. E., III, Hirschberger, G., Arndt, J., & Kesebir, P. (2012). Drawing attention to global climate change decreases support for war. *Peace and Conflict: Journal of Peace Psychology, 18,* 354–368. (p. 458)

Pyszczynski, T. A., Rothschild, Z., & Abdollahi, A. (2008). Terrorism, violence, and hope for peace: A terror management perspective. *Current Directions in Psychological Science, 17,* 318–322. (p. 439)

Pyszczynski, T. A., Solomon, S., & Greenberg, J. (2002). *In the wake of 9/11: The psychology of terror.* Washington, DC: American Psychological Association. (p. 439)

Qaseem, A., Kansagara, D., Forciea, M. A., Cooke, M., & Denberg, T. D., for the Clinical Guidelines Committee of the American College of Physicians. (2016). Management of chronic insomnia disorder in adults: A clinical practice guideline from the American College of Physicians. *Annals of Internal Medicine, 165,* 125–133. (p. 553)

Qin, H.-F., & Piao, T.-J. (2011). Dispositional optimism and life satisfaction of Chinese and Japanese college students: Examining the mediating effects of affects and coping efficacy. *Chinese Journal of Clinical Psychology, 19,* 259–261. (p. 399)

Qiu, L., Lin, H., Ramsay, J., & Yang, F. (2012). You are what you tweet: Personality expression and perception on Twitter. *Journal of Research in Personality, 46,* 710–718. (p. 481)

Quaedflieg, C. W. E. M., & Schwabe, L. (2017). Memory dynamics under stress. *Memory.* Advance online publication. http://dx.doi.org/10.1080/09658211.2017.1338299 (p. 288)

Quasha, S. (1980). *Albert Einstein: An intimate portrait.* New York: Forest. (p. 332)

Quinn, P. C., Bhatt, R. S., Brush, D., Grimes, A., & Sharpnack, H. (2002). Development of form similarity as a Gestalt grouping principle in infancy. *Psychological Science, 13,* 320–328. (p. 208)

Quiroga, R. Q., Fried, I., & Koch, C. (2013, February). Brain cells for grandmother. *Scientific American,* pp. 30–35. (p. 206)

Quoidbach, J., Dunn, E. W., Hansenne, M., & Bustin, G. (2015). The price of abundance: How a wealth of experiences impoverishes savoring. *Personality and Social Psychology Bulletin, 41,* 393–404. (p. 409)

Quoidbach, J., Dunn, E. W., Petrides, K. V., & Mikolajczak, M. (2010). Money giveth, money taketh away: The dual effect of wealth on happiness. *Psychological Science, 21,* 759–763. (p. 409)

Rabbitt, P. (2006). Tales of the unexpected: 25 years of cognitive gerontology. *The Psychologist, 19,* 674–676. (p. 154)

Raby, K. L., Cicchetti, D., Carlson, E. A., Cutuli, J. J., Englund, M. M., & Egeland, B. (2012). Genetic and care-giving-based contributions to infant attachment: Unique associations with distress reactivity and attachment security. *Psychological Science, 23,* 1016–1023. (p. 134)

Raby, K. L., Roisman, G. I., Fraley, R. C., & Simpson, J. A. (2014). The enduring predictive significance of early maternal sensitivity: Social and academic competence through age 32 years. *Child Development, 86*, 695–708. (p. 136)

Racsmány, M., Conway, M. A., & Demeter, G. (2010). Consolidation of episodic memories during sleep: Long-term effects of retrieval practice. *Psychological Science, 21*, 80–85. (p. 91)

Radford, B. (2010, March 5). Missing persons and abductions reveal psychics' failures. Retrieved from seeker.com/missing-persons-and-abductions-reveal-psychics-failures-1765030268.html (p. 230)

Radford, B. (2013, May 8). Psychic claimed Amanda Berry was dead. Retrieved from seeker.com/psychic-claimed-amanda-berry-was-dead-1767492815.html (p. 230)

Radua, J., Schmidt, A., Borgwardt, S., Heinz, A., Schlagenhauf, F., McGuire, P., & Fusar-Poli, P. (2015). Ventral striatal activation during reward processing in psychosis: A neurofunctional meta-analysis. *JAMA Psychiatry, 72*, 1243–1251.

Rahl, H. A., Lindsay, E. K., Pacilio, L. E., Brown, K. W., & Creswell, J. D. (2016). Brief mindfulness meditation training reduces mind wandering: The critical role of acceptance. *Emotion.* Advance online publication. dx.doi.org/10.1037/emo0000250 (p. 404)

Rahman, Q. (2015, July 24). "Gay genes": Science is on the right track, we're born this way. Let's deal with it. *The Guardian* (theguardian.com). (p. 181)

Rahman, Q., & Koerting, J. (2008). Sexual orientation-related differences in allocentric spatial memory tasks. *Hippocampus, 18*, 55–63. (p. 182)

Rahman, Q., & Wilson, G. D. (2003). Born gay? The psychobiology of human sexual orientation. *Personality and Individual Differences, 34*, 1337–1382. (p. 181)

Rahman, Q., Wilson, G. D., & Abrahams, S. (2004). Biosocial factors, sexual orientation and neurocognitive functioning. *Psychoneuroendocrinology, 29*, 867–881. (pp. 182, 183)

Raichle, M. (2010, March). The brain's dark energy. *Scientific American*, pp. 44–49. (p. 85)

Raila, H., Scholl, B. J., & Gruber, J. (2015). Seeing the world through rose-colored glasses: People who are happy and satisfied with life preferentially attend to positive stimuli. *Emotion, 15*, 449–462. (p. 407)

Raine, A. (1999). Murderous minds: Can we see the mark of Cain? *Cerebrum: The Dana Forum on Brain Science 1*(1), 15–29. (p. 531)

Raine, A. (2005). The interaction of biological and social measures in the explanation of antisocial and violent behavior. In D. M. Stoff & E. J. Susman (Eds.) *Developmental psychobiology of aggression*. New York: Cambridge University Press. (p. 531)

Raine, A. (2013). *The anatomy of violence: The biological roots of crime*. New York: Pantheon. (p. 442)

Raine, A., Lencz, T., Bihrle, S., LaCasse, L., & Colletti, P. (2000). Reduced prefrontal gray matter volume and reduced autonomic activity in antisocial personality disorder. *Archives of General Psychiatry, 57*, 119–127. (p. 531)

Rainie, L., Purcell, K., Goulet, L. S., & Hampton, K. H. (2011, June 16). *Social networking sites and our lives*. Pew Research Center (pewresearch.org). (p. 356)

Rainville, P., Duncan, G. H., Price, D. D., Carrier, B., & Bushnell, M. C. (1997). Pain affect encoded in human anterior cingulate but not somatosensory cortex. *Science, 277*, 968–971. (p. 224)

Raison, C. L., Klein, H. M., & Steckler, M. (1999). The moon and madness reconsidered. *Journal of Affective Disorders, 53*, 99–106. (p. 530)

Rajendran, G., & Mitchell, P. (2007). Cognitive theories of autism. *Developmental Review, 27*, 224–260. (p. 131)

Raji, C. A., Merrill, D. A., Eyre, H., Mallam, S., Torosyan, N., Erickson, K.I. . . . Kuller, L. H. (2016). Longitudinal relationships between caloric expenditure and gray matter in the cardiovascular health study. *Journal of Alzheimer's Disease, 52*, 719–729. (p. 153)

Ramachandran, V. S., & Blakeslee, S. (1998). *Phantoms in the brain: Probing the mysteries of the human mind*. New York: Morrow. (pp. 64, 222)

Ramírez-Esparza, N., Gosling, S. D., Benet-Martínez, V., Potter, J. P., & Pennebaker, J. W. (2006). Do bilinguals have two personalities? A special case of cultural frame switching. *Journal of Research in Personality, 40*, 99–120. (p. 319)

Ramos, M. R., Cassidy, C., Reicher, S., & Haslam, S. A. (2012). A longitudinal investigation of the rejection-identification hypothesis. *British Journal of Social Psychology, 51*, 642–660. (p. 458)

Randall, D. K. (2012, September 22). Rethinking sleep. *The New York Times* (nytimes.com). (p. 90)

Randi, J. (1999, February 4). 2000 club mailing list e-mail letter. (p. 231)

Randler, C. (2008). Morningness–eveningness and satisfaction with life. *Social Indicators Research, 86*, 297–302. (p. 87)

Randler, C. (2009). Proactive people are morning people. *Journal of Applied Social Psychology, 39*, 2787–2797. (p. 87)

Rapoport, J. L. (1989). The biology of obsessions and compulsions. *Scientific American, 260*, 83–89. (pp. 509, 512)

Räsänen, S., Pakaslahti, A., Syvalahti, E., Jones, P. B., & Isohanni, M. (2000). Sex differences in schizophrenia: A review. *Nordic Journal of Psychiatry, 54*, 37–45. (p. 524)

Rasmussen, H. N., Scheier, M. F., & Greenhouse, J. B. (2009). Optimism and physical health: A meta-analytic review. *Annals of Behavioral Medicine, 37*, 239–256. (p. 398)

Rasmussen, K. (2016). Entitled vengeance: A meta-analysis relating narcissism to provoked aggression. *Aggressive Behavior.* Advance online publication. doi:10.1002/ab.21632 (p. 488)

Ratcliff, K. S. (2013). The power of poverty: Individual agency and structural constraints. In K. M. Fitzpatrick (Ed.), *Poverty and health: A crisis among America's most vulnerable* (vol. 1), pp. 5–30. Santa Barbara, CA: Praeger. (p. 410)

Rath, T., & Harter, J. K. (2010, August 19). Your friends and your social well-being: Close friendships are vital to health, happiness, and even workplace productivity. *Gallup Management Journal* (gmj.gallup.com). (p. B-11)

Rathbone, C. J., Salgado, S., Akan, M., Havelka, J., & Berntsen, D. (2016). Imagining the future: A cross-cultural perspective on possible selves. *Consciousness and Cognition, 42*, 113–124. (p. 486)

Rattan, A., Savani, K., Naidu, N. V. R., & Dweck, C. S. (2012). Can everyone become highly intelligent? Cultural differences in and societal consequences of beliefs about the universal potential for intelligence. *Journal of Personality and Social Psychology, 103*, 787–803. (p. 340)

Ravizza, S. M., Uitvlught, M. G., & Fenn, K. M. (2017). Logged in and zoned out. *Psychological Science, 28*, 171–180. (p. 295)

Ray, J., & Kafka, S. (2014, May 6). *Life in college matters for life after college*. Gallup (gallup.com/poll). (p. B-12)

Ray, O., & Ksir, C. (1990). Drugs, society, and human behavior (5th ed.). St. Louis: Times Mirror/Mosby. (p. 107)

Raynor, H. A., & Epstein, L. H. (2001). Dietary variety, energy regulation, and obesity. *Psychological Bulletin, 127*, 325–341. (p. 363)

Reason, J. (1987). The Chernobyl errors. *Bulletin of the British Psychological Society, 40*, 201–206. (p. 433)

Reason, J., & Mycielska, K. (1982). *Absent-minded? The psychology of mental lapses and everyday errors*. Englewood Cliffs, NJ: Prentice-Hall. (p. 196)

Rebar, A. L., Stanton, R., Geard, D., Short, C., Duncan, M. J., & Vandelanotte, C. (2015). A meta-meta-analysis of the effect of physical activity on depression and anxiety in non-clinical adult populations. *Health Psychology Review, 9*, 366–378. (p. 401)

Rechenberg, K. (2016). Nutritional interventions in clinical depression. *Clinical Psychological Science, 4*(1), 144–162. (p. 519)

Redden, J. P., Mann, T., Vickers, Z., Mykerezi, E., Reicks, M., & Elsbernd, E. (2015). Serving first in isolation increases vegetable intake among elementary schoolchildren. *PLoS ONE, 10*, e0121283. (p. 364)

Reebs, A., Yuval, K., & Bernstein, A. (2017). Remembering and responding to distressing autobiographical memories: Exploring risk and intervention targets for posttraumatic stress in traumatized refugees. *Clinical Psychological Science, 5*, 789–797. (p. 509)

Reed, D. (2011, January). Quoted in P. Miller, A thing or two about twins. *National Geographic*, pp. 39–65. (p. 74)

Reed, P. (2000). Serial position effects in recognition memory for odors. *Journal of Experimental Psychology: Learning, Memory, and Cognition, 26*, 411–422. (p. 282)

Rees, M. (1999). *Just six numbers: The deep forces that shape the universe*. New York: Basic Books. (p. 77)

Reeves, A., McKee, M., & Stuckler, D. (2014). Economic suicides in the Great Recession in Europe and North America. *British Journal of Psychiatry, 205*, 246–247. (p. 501)

Regan, P. C., & Atkins, L. (2007). Sex differences and similarities in frequency and intensity of sexual desire. *Social Behavior and Personality, 34*, 95–102. (p. 183)

Reichenberg, A., Cederlöf, M., McMillan, A., Trzaskowski, M., Kapara, O., Fruchter, E., . . . Plomin, R. (2016). Discontinuity in the genetic and environmental causes of the intellectual disability spectrum. *PNAS, 113*, 1098–1103. (p. 331)

Reichenberg, A., & Harvey, P. D. (2007). Neuropsychological impairments in schizophrenia: Integration of performance-based and brain imaging findings. *Psychological Bulletin, 133*, 833–858. (p. 523)

Reichert, R. A., Robb, M. B., Fender, J. G., & Wartella, E. (2010). Word learning from baby videos. *Archives of Pediatrics & Adolescent Medicine, 164*, 432–437. (p. 339)

Reicher, S., & Haslam, S. A. (2006). Rethinking the psychology of tyranny: The BBC prison study. *British Journal of Social Psychology, 45*, 1–40. (p. 419)

Reichow, B. (2012). Overview of meta-analyses on early intensive behavioral intervention for young children with autism spectrum disorders. *Journal of Autism and Developmental Disorders, 42*, 512–520. (p. 543)

Reid, V. M., Dunn, K., Young, R. J., Amu, J., Donovan, T., & Reissland, N. (2017). The human fetus preferentially engages with face-like visual stimuli. *Current Biology, 27*, 1825–1828. (p. 121)

Reifman, A. S., Larrick, R. P., & Fein, S. (1991). Temper and temperature on the diamond: The heat-aggression relationship in major league baseball. *Personality and Social Psychology Bulletin, 17,* 580–585. (p. 443)

Reimann, F., Cox, J. J., Belfer, I., Diatchenko, L., Zaykin, D. V., McHale, D. P., . . . Woods, C. G. (2010). Pain perception is altered by a nucleotide polymorphism in SCN9A. *PNAS, 107,* 5148–5153. (pp. 222, 223)

Reimão, R. N., & Lefévre, A. B. (1980). Prevalence of sleep-talking in childhood. *Brain and Development, 2,* 353–357. (p. 95)

Reiner, W. G., & Gearhart, J. P. (2004). Discordant sexual identity in some genetic males with cloacal exstrophy assigned to female sex at birth. *New England Journal of Medicine, 350,* 333–341. (p. 167)

Reinhart, R. J. (2017, June 20). Terrorism fears drive more in US to avoid crowds. Gallup poll (gallup.com). (p. 301)

Reis, H. T., & Aron, A. (2008). Love: What is it, why does it matter, and how does it operate? *Perspectives on Psychological Science, 3,* 80–86. (p. 451)

Reis, H. T., Smith, S. M., Carmichael, C. L., Caprariello, P. A., Tsa, F.-F., Rodrigues, A., & Maniaci, M. R. (2010). Are you happy for me? How sharing positive events with others provides personal and interpersonal benefits. *Journal of Personality and Social Psychology, 99,* 311–329. (p. 352)

Reis, M., Ramiro, L., Camacho, I., Tomé, G., Brito, C., & Gaspar de Matos, G. (2017). Does having a pet make a difference? Highlights from the HBSC Portuguese study. *European Journal of Developmental Psychology.* (p. 401)

Reis, S. M. (2001). Toward a theory of creativity in diverse creative women. In M. Bloom & T. Gullotta (Eds.), *Promoting creativity across the life span* (pp. 231–275). Washington, DC: CWLA Press. (p. 306)

Reisenzein, R. (1983). The Schachter theory of emotion: Two decades later. *Psychological Bulletin, 94,* 239–264. (p. 369)

Reiser, M. (1982). *Police psychology.* Los Angeles: LEHI. (p. 230)

Reitz, A. K., Motti-Stefanidi, F., & Asendorpf, J. B. (2016). Me, us, and them: Testing sociometer theory in a socially diverse real-life context. *Journal of Personality and Social Psychology, 110,* 908–920. (p. 486)

Reitzle, M. (2006). The connections between adulthood transitions and the self-perception of being adult in the changing contexts of East and West Germany. *European Psychologist, 11,* 25–38. (p. 149)

Reivich, K., Gillham, J. E., Chaplin, T. M., & Seligman, M. E. P. (2013). *From helplessness to optimism: The role of resilience in treating and preventing depression in youth.* New York: Springer Science & Business Media. (p. 545)

Rekker, R., Keijsers, L., Branje, S., & Meeus, W. (2015). Political attitudes in adolescence and emerging adulthood: Developmental changes in mean level, polarization, rank-order stability, and correlates. *Journal of Adolescence, 41,* 136–147. (p. 118)

Remick, A. K., Polivy, J., & Pliner, P. (2009). Internal and external moderators of the effect of variety on food intake. *Psychological Bulletin, 135,* 434–451. (p. 364)

Remington, A., Swettenham, J., Campbell, R., & Coleman, M. (2009). Selective attention and perceptual load in autism spectrum disorder. *Psychological Science, 20,* 1388–1393. (p. 131)

Remley, A. (1988, October). From obedience to independence. *Psychology Today,* pp. 56–59. (p. 138)

Ren, D., Wesselmann, E., & Williams, K. D. (2016). Evidence for another response to ostracism: Solitude seeking. *Social Psychological and Personality Science, 7(3),* 204–212. (p. 476)

Renner, M. J., & Renner, C. H. (1993). Expert and novice intuitive judgments about animal behavior. *Bulletin of the Psychonomic Society, 31,* 551–552. (p. 123)

Renninger, K. A., & Granott, N. (2005). The process of scaffolding in learning and development. *New Ideas in Psychology, 23,* 111–114. (p. 129)

Rentfrow, P. J., & Gosling, S. D. (2003). The do re mi's of everyday life: The structure and personality correlates of music preferences. *Journal of Personality and Social Psychology, 84,* 1236–1256. (p. 481)

Rentfrow, P. J., & Gosling, S. D. (2006). Message in a ballad: The role of music preferences in interpersonal perception. *Psychological Science, 17,* 236–242. (p. 481)

Repacholi, B. M., Meltzoff, A. N., Toub, T. S., & Ruba, A. L. (2016). Infants' generalizations about other people's emotions: Foundations for trait-like attributions. *Developmental Psychology, 52,* 364. (p. 128)

Rescorla, R. A., & Wagner, A. R. (1972). A theory of Pavlovian conditioning: Variations in the effectiveness of reinforcement and nonreinforcement. In A. H. Black & W. F. Perokasy (Eds.), *Classical conditioning II: Current theory.* New York: Appleton-Century-Crofts. (p. 256)

Resnick, M. D., Bearman, P. S., Blum, R. W., Bauman, K. E., Harris, K. M., Jones, J., . . . Udry, J. R. (1997). Protecting adolescents from harm: Findings from the National Longitudinal Study on Adolescent Health. *Journal of the American Medical Association, 278,* 823–832. (pp. 26, 83, 148)

Resnick, S. M. (1992). Positron emission tomography in psychiatric illness. *Current Directions in Psychological Science, 1,* 92–98. (p. 524)

Reuters. (2000, July 5). *Many teens regret decision to have sex (National Campaign to Prevent Teen Pregnancy survey).* Retrieved from washingtonpost.com (p. 177)

Reuters. (2015, November 25). *Most important problem facing the U.S. today.* Reuters Polling. Retrieved from polling.reuters.com/#!poll/SC8/type/smallest/dates/20150901-20151125/collapsed/true/spotlight/1 (p. 301)

Reyna, V. F., Chick, C. F., Corbin, J. C., & Hsia, A. N. (2014). Developmental reversals in risky decision making: Intelligence agents show larger decision biases than college students. *Psychological Science, 25,* 76–84. (p. 305)

Reyna, V. F., & Farley, F. (2006). Risk and rationality in adolescent decision making: Implications for theory, practice, and public policy. *Psychological Science in the Public Interest, 7,* 1–44. (p. 142)

Reynolds, G. (2009, November 18). Phys ed: Why exercise makes you less anxious. *The New York Times blog.* Retrieved from well.blogs.nytimes.com (p. 402)

Rhodes, E. (2017, August). Back to academia . . . and elephants. *The Psychologist,* pp. 12–13. (p. 240)

Rhodes, M. G., & Anastasi, J. S. (2012). The own-age bias in face recognition: A meta-analytic and theoretical review. *Psychological Bulletin, 138,* 146–174. (p. 439)

Riccelli, R., Toschi, N., Nigro, S., Terracciano, A., & Passamonti, L. (2017). Surface-based morphometry reveals the neuroanatomical basis of the five-factor model of personality. *Social Cognitive and Affective Neuroscience, 12,* 671–684. (p. 478)

Ricciardelli, L. A., & McCabe, M. P. (2004). A biopsychosocial model of disordered eating and the pursuit of muscularity in adolescent boys. *Psychological Bulletin, 130,* 179–205. (p. 532)

Rice, M. E., & Grusec, J. E. (1975). Saying and doing: Effects on observer performance. *Journal of Personality and Social Psychology, 32,* 584–593. (p. 262)

Richardson, J. T. E., & Zucco, G. M. (1989). Cognition and olfaction: A review. *Psychological Bulletin, 105,* 352–360. (p. 227)

Richardson, M., Abraham, C., & Bond, R. (2012). Psychological correlates of university students' academic performance: A systematic review and meta-analysis. *Psychological Bulletin, 138,* 353–387. (p. 339)

Richeson, J. A., & Shelton, J. N. (2007). Negotiating interracial interactions. *Current Directions in Psychological Science, 16,* 316–320. (p. 457)

Rickard, I. J., Frankenhuis, W. E., & Nettle, D. (2014). Why are childhood family factors associated with timing of maturation? A role for internal prediction. *Perspectives on Psychological Science, 9,* 3–15. (p. 167)

Rieff, P. (1979). *Freud: The mind of a moralist* (3rd ed.). Chicago: University of Chicago Press. (p. 469)

Rieger, G., Savin-Williams, R., Chivers, M. L., & Bailey, J. M. (2016). Sexual arousal and masculinity-femininity of women. *Journal of Personality and Social Psychology, 111,* 265–283. (p. 182)

Riemer, H., Shavitt, S., Koo, M., & Markus, H. R. (2014). Preferences don't have to be personal: Expanding attitude theorizing with a cross-cultural perspective. *Psychological Review, 121,* 619–648. (p. 416)

Rietveld, C. A., Conley, D., Eriksson, N., Esko, T., Medland, S. E., Vinkhuyzen, A. A. E., . . . Koellinger, P. D. (2014). Replicability and robustness of genome-wide-association studies for behavioral traits. *Psychological Science, 25,* 1975–1986. (p. 336)

Rietveld, C. A., Medland, S. E., Derringer, J., Yang, J., Esko, T., Martin, N. W., . . . Koellinger, P. D. (2013). GWAS of 126,559 individuals identifies genetic variants associated with educational attainment. *Science, 340,* 1467–1471. (p. 336)

Rigoni, J. B., & Asplund, J. (2016a, July 7). *Strengths-based development: The business results.* The Gallup Organization (gallup.com). (p. B-12)

Rigoni, J. B., & Asplund, J. (2016b, July 12). *Global study: ROI for strengths-based development.* The Gallup Organization (gallup.com). (p. B-12)

Riley, L. D., & Bowen, C. (2005). The sandwich generation: Challenges and coping strategies of multigenerational families. *The Family Journal, 13,* 52–58. (p. 155)

Rimfeld, K., Kovas, Y., Dale, P. S., & Plomin, R. (2016). True grit and genetics: Predicting academic achievement from personality. *Journal of Personality and Social Psychology, 111,* 780–789. (p. 358)

Rindermann, H., & Ceci, S. J. (2009). Educational policy and country outcomes in international cognitive competence studies. *Perspectives on Psychological Science, 4,* 551–577. (p. 342)

Riordan, M. (2013, March 19). *Tobacco warning labels: Evidence of effectiveness.* Washington, DC: The Campaign for Tobacco-Free Kids (tobaccofreekids.org). (p. 303)

Ripke, S., Wray, N. R., Lewis, C. M., Hamilton, S. P., Weissman, M. M., Breen, G., . . . Heath, A. C. (2013). A mega-analysis of genome-wide association studies for major depressive disorder. *Molecular Psychiatry, 18,* 497–511. (p. 518)

Ritchie, S. J., Dickie, D. A., Cox, S. R., Hernandez, M. del C. V., Corley, J., Royle, N. A., . . . Deary, I. J. (2015). Brain volumetric changes and cognitive ageing during the eighth decade of life. *Human Brain Mapping, 36,* 4910–4925. (p. 152)

Ritchie, S. J., Wiseman, R., & French, C. C. (2012). Failing the future: Three unsuccessful attempts to replicate Bem's "retroactive facilitation of recall" effect. *PLoS ONE, 7,* e33r23 (plosone.org). (p. 231)

Ritter, S. M., Damian, R. I., Simonton, D. K., van Baaren, R. B., Strick, M., Derks, J., & Dijksterhuis, A. (2012). Diversifying experiences enhance cognitive flexibility. *Journal of Experimental Social Psychology, 48,* 961–964. (p. 307)

Rizzolatti, G., Fadiga, L., Fogassi, L., & Gallese, V. (2002). From mirror neurons to imitation: Facts and speculations. In A. N. Meltzoff & W. Prinz (Eds.), *The imitative mind: Development, evolution, and brain bases.* Cambridge, England: Cambridge University Press. (p. 259)

Rizzolatti, G., Fogassi, L., & Gallese, V. (2006, November). Mirrors in the mind. *Scientific American, 295,* 54–61. (p. 259)

Roberson, D., Davidoff, J., Davies, I. R. L., & Shapiro, L. R. (2004). The development of color categories in two languages: A longitudinal study. *Journal of Experimental Psychology: General, 133,* 554–571. (p. 319)

Roberson, D., Davies, I. R. L., Corbett, G. G., & Vandervyver, M. (2005). Free-sorting of colors across cultures: Are there universal grounds for grouping? *Journal of Cognition and Culture, 5,* 349–386. (p. 319)

Roberti, J. W., Storch, E. A., & Bravata, E. A. (2004). Sensation seeking, exposure to psychosocial stressors, and body modifications in a college population. *Personality and Individual Differences, 37,* 1167–1177. (p. 349)

Roberts, A. L., Glymour, M. M., & Koenen, K. C. (2013). Does maltreatment in childhood affect sexual orientation in adulthood? *Archives of Sexual Behavior, 42,* 161–171. (pp. 118, 180)

Roberts, B. W., & DelVecchio, W. F. (2000). The rank-order consistency of personality traits from childhood to old age: A quantitative review of longitudinal studies. *Psychological Bulletin, 126,* 3–25. (p. 480)

Roberts, B. W., Kuncel, N. R., Shiner, R., Caspi, A., & Goldberg, L. R. (2007). The power of personality: The comparative validity of personality traits, socioeconomic status, and cognitive ability for predicting important life outcomes. *Perspectives on Psychological Science, 2,* 313–345. (p. 480)

Roberts, B. W., Luo, J., Briley, D. A., Chow, P. I., Su, R., & Hill, P. L. (2017). A systematic review of personality trait change through intervention. *Psychological Bulletin, 143,* 117–141. (p. 552)

Roberts, L. (1988). Beyond Noah's ark: What do we need to know? *Science, 242,* 1247. (p. 397)

Roberts, T.-A. (1991). Determinants of gender differences in responsiveness to others' evaluations. *Dissertation Abstracts International, 51*(08–B). (p. 164)

Robertson, K. F., Smeets, S., Lubinski, D., & Benbow, C. P. (2010). Beyond the threshold hypothesis: Even among the gifted and top math/science graduate students, cognitive abilities, vocational interests, and lifestyle preferences matter for career choice, performance, and persistence. *Current Directions in Psychological Science, 19,* 346–351. (p. 306)

Robins, L. N., Davis, D. H., & Goodwin, D. W. (1974). Drug use by U.S. Army enlisted men in Vietnam: A follow-up on their return home. *American Journal of Epidemiology, 99,* 235–249. (p. 113)

Robins, L., & Regier, D. (Eds.). (1991). *Psychiatric disorders in America.* New York: Free Press. (p. 505)

Robinson, F. P. (1970). *Effective study.* New York: Harper & Row. (p. 33)

Robinson, J. P., & Martin, S. (2008). What do happy people do? *Social Indicators Research, 89,* 565–571. (p. B-2)

Robinson, J. P., & Martin, S. (2009). Changes in American daily life: 1965–2005. *Social Indicators Research, 93,* 47–56. (p. 262)

Robinson, O. J., Cools, R., Carlisi, C. O., & Drevets, W. C. (2012). Ventral striatum response during reward and punishment reversal learning in unmedicated major depressive disorder. *American Journal of Psychiatry, 169,* 152–159. (p. 518)

Robinson, T. E., & Berridge, K. C. (2003). Addiction. *Annual Review of Psychology, 54,* 25–53. (p. 102)

Robinson, T. N., Borzekowski, D. L. G., Matheson, D. M., & Kraemer, H. C. (2007). Effects of fast food branding on young children's taste preferences. *Archives of Pediatric and Adolescent Medicine, 161,* 792–797. (p. 196)

Robinson, V. M. (1983). Humor and health. In P. E. McGhee & J. H. Goldstein (Eds.), *Handbook of humor research: Vol. II. Applied studies.* New York: Springer-Verlag. (p. 399)

Robles, T. F. (2015). Marital quality and health: Implications for marriage in the 21st century. *Current Directions in Psychological Science, 23,* 427–432. (p. 400)

Rochat, F. (1993). *How did they resist authority? Protecting refugees in Le Chambon during World War II.* Paper presented at the American Psychological Association convention. (p. 428)

Rock, I., & Palmer, S. (1990, December). The legacy of Gestalt psychology. *Scientific American,* pp. 84–90. (p. 208)

Rodin, J. (1986). Aging and health: Effects of the sense of control. *Science, 233,* 1271–1276. (pp. 396, 397)

Roediger, H. L. (1980). Memory metaphors in cognitive psychology. *Memory & Cognition, 8,* 231–246. (p. 268)

Roediger, H. L., III. (2013). Applying cognitive psychology to education: Translational educational science. *Psychological Science in the Public Interest, 14,* 1–3. (pp. 272, 273)

Roediger, H. L., III., & DeSoto, K. A. (2016). Was Alexander Hamilton president? *Psychological Science, 27,* 644–650. (p. 290)

Roediger, H. L., III, & Finn, B. (2010, March/April). The pluses of getting it wrong. *Scientific American Mind,* pp. 39–41. (p. 33)

Roediger, H. L., III, & Geraci, L. (2007). Aging and the misinformation effect: A neuropsychological analysis. *Journal of Experimental Psychology, 33,* 321–334. (p. 294)

Roediger, H. L., III, & Karpicke, J. D. (2006). Test-enhanced learning: Taking memory tests improves long-term retention. *Psychological Science, 17,* 249–255. (pp. 33, 272)

Roediger, H. L., III, & McDaniel, M. A. (2007). Illusory recollection in older adults: Testing Mark Twain's conjecture. In M. Garry H. Hayne (Ed.), *Do justice and let the sky fall: Elizabeth F. Loftus and her contributions to science, law, and academic freedom.* Mahwah, NJ: Erlbaum. (p. 294)

Roediger, H. L., III, & McDermott, K. B. (1995). Creating false memories: Remembering words not presented in lists. *Journal of Experimental Psychology: Learning, Memory, and Cognition, 21,* 803–814. (p. 292)

Roediger, H. L., III, Meade, M. L., & Bergman, E. T. (2001). Social contagion of memory. *Psychonomic Bulletin & Review, 8,* 365–371. (p. 292)

Roediger, H. L., III, Wheeler, M. A., & Rajaram, S. (1993). Remembering, knowing, and reconstructing the past. In D. L. Medin (Ed.), *The psychology of learning and motivation: Advances in research and theory* (Vol. 30). Orlando, FL: Academic Press. (p. 292)

Roehling, P. V., Roehling, M. V., & Moen, P. (2001). The relationship between work-life policies and practices and employee loyalty: A life course perspective. *Journal of Family and Economic Issues, 22,* 141–170. (p. B-11)

Roelofs, T. (2010, September 22). Somali refugee takes oath of U.S. citizenship year after his brother. *The Grand Rapids Press* (mlive.com). (p. B-8)

Roenneberg, T., Kuehnle, T., Pramstaller, P. P., Ricken, J., Havel, M., Guth, A., & Merrow, M. (2004). A marker for the end of adolescence. *Current Biology, 14,* R1038–R1039. (p. 87)

Roepke, A. M. (2015). Psychosocial interventions and posttraumatic growth: A meta-analysis. *Journal of Consulting and Clinical Psychology, 83,* 129. (p. 567)

Roepke, A. M., & Seligman, M. E. P. (2015). Doors opening: A mechanism for growth after adversity. *Journal of Positive Psychology, 10,* 107–115. (p. 567)

Roese, N. J., & Summerville, A. (2005). What we regret most . . . and why. *Personality and Social Psychology Bulletin, 31,* 1273–1285. (p. 158)

Roese, N. J., & Vohs, K. D. (2012). Hindsight bias. *Perspectives on Psychological Science, 7,* 411–426. (p. 16)

Roesser, R. (1998). *What you should know about hearing conservation.* Retrieved from betterhearing.org/ (p. 218)

Rogers, C. R. (1961). *On becoming a person: A therapist's view of psychotherapy.* Boston: Houghton Mifflin. (pp. 472, 539)

Rogers, C. R. (1980). *A way of being.* Boston: Houghton Mifflin. (pp. 471, 472, 539)

Rogers, C. R. (1985, February). Quoted by M. L. Wallach & L. Wallach, How psychology sanctions the cult of the self. *Washington Monthly,* pp. 46–56. (p. 473)

Rogers, T., & Feller, A. (2016). Discouraged by peer excellence: Exposure to exemplary peer performance causes quitting. *Psychological Science, 27,* 365–374. (p. 410)

Rogers, T., & Milkman, K. L. (2016). Reminders through association. *Psychological Science, 27,* 973–986. (p. 280)

Rohan, K. J., Mahon, J. N., Evans, M., Ho, S., Meyerhoff, J., Postolache, T. T., & Vacek, P. M. (2015). Randomized trial of cognitive-behavioral therapy versus light therapy for seasonal affective disorder: Acute outcomes. *The American Journal of Psychiatry, 172,* 862–869. (p. 555)

Rohan, K. J., Roecklein, K. A., Lindsey, K. T., Johnson, L. G., Lippy, R. D., Lacy, T. J., & Barton, F. B. (2007). A randomized controlled trial of cognitive-behavioral therapy, light therapy, and their combination for seasonal affective disorder. *Journal of Consulting and Clinical Psychology, 75,* 489–500. (p. 555)

Rohner, R. P., & Veneziano, R. A. (2001). The importance of father love: History and contemporary evidence. *Review of General Psychology, 5,* 382–405. (p. 135)

Rohrer, J. M., Egloff, B., Kosinski, M., Stillwell, D., & Schmukle, S. C. (2018). In your eyes only? Discrepancies and agreement between self- and other-reports of personality from age 14 to 29. *Journal of Personality and Social Psychology,* in press. (p. 478)

Rohrer, J. M., Egloff, B., & Schmukle, S. C. (2015). Examining the effects of birth order on personality. *PNAS, 112,* 14224–14229. (pp. 478, A-8)

Roiser, J. P., Cook, L. J., Cooper, J. D., Rubinsztein, D. C., & Sahakian, B. J. (2005). Association of a functional polymorphism in the serotonin transporter gene with abnormal emotional processing in Ecstasy users. *American Journal of Psychiatry, 162,* 609–612. (p. 108)

Rokach, A., Orzeck, T., Moya, M., & Expósito, F. (2002). Causes of loneliness in North America and Spain. *European Psychologist, 7,* 70–79. (p. 10)

Romano, A., Balliet, D., Yamagishi, T., & Liu, J. H. (2017). Parochial trust and cooperation across 17 societies. *PNAS, 114,* 12702–12707. (p. 438)

Romelsjö, A., Danielsson, A., Wennberg, P., & Hibell, B. (2014). Cannabis use and drug related problems among adolescents in 27 European countries: The utility of the prevention paradox. *Nordic Studies on Alcohol and Drugs, 31,* 359–369. (p. 112)

Romens, S. E., McDonald, J., Svaren, J., & Pollak, S. D. (2015). Associations between early life stress and gene methylation in children. *Child Development, 86,* 303–309. (p. 137)

Ronald, A., & Hoekstra, R. A. (2011). Autism spectrum disorders and autistic traits: A decade of new twin studies. *American Journal of Medical Genetics Part B, 156,* 255–274. (p. 70)

Ronay, R., & von Hippel, W. (2010). The presence of an attractive woman elevates testosterone and physical risk taking in young men. *Social Psychology and Personality Science, 1,* 57–64. (p. 173)

Root, T. L., Thornton, L. M., Lindroos, A. K., Stunkard, A. J., Lichtenstein, P., Pedersen, N. L., . . . Bulik, C. M. (2010). Shared and unique genetic and environmental influences on binge eating and night eating: A Swedish twin study. *Eating Behaviors, 11,* 92–98. (p. 532)

Roper, K. R. (2016, July 19). Public Facebook post. Retrieved from facebook.com/kate.riffleroper/posts/1746348308987959 (p. 301)

Roper, S. D., & Chaudhari, N. (2017). Taste buds: Cells, signals, and synapses. *Nature Reviews Neuroscience, 18,* 485–497. (p. 225)

Roque, L., Verissimo, M., Oliveira, T. F., & Oliveira, R. F. (2012). Attachment security and HPA axis reactivity to positive and challenging emotional situations in child–mother dyads in naturalistic settings. *Developmental Psychobiology, 54,* 401–411. (p. 135)

Rosch, E. (1978). Principles of categorization. In E. Rosch & B. L. Lloyd (Eds.), *Cognition and categorization.* Hillsdale, NJ: Erlbaum. (p. 298)

Rose, A. J., & Rudolph, K. D. (2006). A review of sex differences in peer relationship processes: Potential trade-offs for the emotional and behavioral development of girls and boys. *Psychological Bulletin, 132,* 98–131. (p. 163)

Rose, H., & Rose, S. (2016). *Can neuroscience change our minds?* Cambridge, UK: Polity. (p. 52)

Rose, J. S., Chassin, L., Presson, C. C., & Sherman, S. J. (1999). Peer influences on adolescent cigarette smoking: A prospective sibling analysis. *Merrill-Palmer Quarterly, 45,* 62–84. (pp. 112, 147)

Rose, R. J., Viken, R. J., Dick, D. M., Bates, J. E., Pulkkinen, L., & Kaprio, J. (2003). It *does* take a village: Nonfamiliar environments and children's behavior. *Psychological Science, 14,* 273–277. (p. 147)

Roselli, C. E., Larkin, K., Schrunk, J. M., & Stormshak, F. (2004). Sexual partner preference, hypothalamic morphology and aromatase in rams. *Physiology and Behavior, 83,* 233–245. (p. 181)

Roselli, C. E., Resko, J. A., & Stormshak, F. (2002). Hormonal influences on sexual partner preference in rams. *Archives of Sexual Behavior, 31,* 43–49. (p. 181)

Rosenbaum, M. (1986). The repulsion hypothesis: On the nondevelopment of relationships. *Journal of Personality and Social Psychology, 51,* 1156–1166. (p. 450)

Rosenberg, E. L., Zanesco, A. P., King, B. G., Aichele, S. R., Jacobs, R. L., Bridwell, D. A., . . . Saron, C. D. (2015). Intensive meditation training influences emotional responses to suffering. *Emotion, 15,* 775–790. (p. 404)

Rosenberg, N. A., Pritchard, J. K., Weber, J. L., Cann, H. M., Kidd, K. K., Zhivotosky, L. A., & Feldman, M. W. (2002). Genetic structure of human populations. *Science, 298,* 2381–2385. (p. 342)

Rosenberg, T. (2010, November 1). The opt-out solution. *The New York Times.* Retrieved from http://opinionator.blogs.nytimes.com/2010/11/01/the-opt-out-solution/ (p. 304)

Rosenblum, L. D. (2013, January). A confederacy of senses. *Scientific American,* pp. 73–78. (p. 228)

Rosenfeld, M. J. (2013, August 26). Personal communication. (p. 156)

Rosenfeld, M. J. (2014). Couple longevity in the era of same-sex marriage in the United States. *Journal of Marriage and Family, 76,* 905–911. (p. 156)

Rosenfeld, M. J., & Thomas, R. J. (2012). Searching for a mate: The rise of the internet as a social intermediary. *American Sociological Review, 77,* 523–547. (pp. 156, 448)

Rosenhan, D. L. (1973). On being sane in insane places. *Science, 179,* 250–258. (p. 497)

Rosenkranz, M. A., Davidson, R. J., Maccoon, D. G., Sheridan, J. F., Kalin, N. H., & Lutz, A. (2013). A comparison of mindfulness-based stress reduction and an active control in modulation of neurogenic inflammation. *Brain, Behavior, and Immunity, 27,* 174–184. (p. 404)

Rosenquist, P. B., McCall, W. V., & Youssef, N. (2016). Charting the course of electroconvulsive therapy: Where have we been and where are we headed? *Psychiatric Annals, 46,* 647–651. (p. 563)

Rosenthal, E. (2009, November 2). When texting kills, Britain offers path of prison. *The New York Times* (nytimes.com). (p. 82)

Rosenthal, R., Hall, J. A., Archer, D., DiMatteo, M. R., & Rogers, P. L. (1979). The PONS test: Measuring sensitivity to nonverbal cues. In S. Weitz (Ed.), *Nonverbal communication* (2nd ed.). New York: Oxford University Press. (p. 376)

Rosenzweig, M. R., Krech, D., Bennett, E. L., & Diamond, M. C. (1962). Effects of environmental complexity and training on brain chemistry and anatomy: A replication and extension. *Journal of Comparative and Physiological Psychology, 55,* 429–437. (p. 123)

Roseth, C. J., Johnson, D. W., & Johnson, R. T. (2008). Promoting early adolescents' achievement and peer relationships: The effects of cooperative, competitive, and individualistic goal structures. *Psychological Bulletin, 134,* 223–246. (p. 458)

Ross, J. (2006, December). Sleep on a problem . . . it works like a dream. *The Psychologist, 19,* 738–740. (p. 92)

Ross, L. (1977). The intuitive psychologist and his shortcomings: Distortions in the attribution process. In L. Berkowitz (Ed.) *Advances in experimental social psychology* (Vol. 10). New York: Academic Press. (p. 416)

Ross, M., McFarland, C., & Fletcher, G. J. O. (1981). The effect of attitude on the recall of personal histories. *Journal of Personality and Social Psychology, 40,* 627–634. (p. 288)

Ross, M., Xun, W. Q. E., & Wilson, A. E. (2002). Language and the bicultural self. *Personality and Social Psychology Bulletin, 28,* 1040–1050. (p. 319)

Rossi, P. J. (1968). Adaptation and negative aftereffect to lateral optical displacement in newly hatched chicks. *Science, 160,* 430–432. (p. 213)

Rossion, B., & Boremanse, A. (2011). Robust sensitivity to facial identity in the right human occipito-temporal cortex as revealed by steady-state visual-evoked potentials. *Journal of Vision, 11*(2), Article 16. doi:10.1167/11.2.16 (p. 189)

Rotge, J.-Y., Lemogne, C., Hinfray, S., Huguet, P., Grynszpan, O., Tartour, E., . . . Fossati, P. (2015). A meta-analysis of the anterior cingulate contribution to social pain. *Social Cognitive and Affective Neuroscience, 10,* 19–27. (p. 354)

Roth, B., Becker, N., Romeyke, S., Schäfer, S., Domnick, F., & Spinath, F. M. (2015). Intelligence and school grades: A meta-analysis. *Intelligence, 53,* 118–137. (p. 330)

Roth, B., Hahn, E., & Spinath, F. M. (2016). Income inequality, life satisfaction, and economic worries. *Social Psychological and Personality Science.* Advance online publication. doi:10.1177/1948550616664955 (p. 410)

Roth, T., Roehrs, T., Zwyghuizen-Doorenbos, A., Stpeanski, E., & Witting, R. (1988). Sleep and memory. In I. Hindmarch & H. Ott (Eds.), *Benzodiazepine receptor ligands, memory and information processing* (pp. 140–145). Berlin, Germany: Springer-Verlag. (p. 97)

Rothbart, M., Fulero, S., Jensen, C., Howard, J., & Birrell, P. (1978). From individual to group impressions: Availability heuristics in stereotype formation. *Journal of Experimental Social Psychology, 14,* 237–255. (p. 440)

Rothbaum, F., & Tsang, B. Y.-P. (1998). Lovesongs in the United States and China: On the nature of romantic love. *Journal of Cross-Cultural Psychology, 29,* 306–319. (p. 491)

Rotheneichner, P., Lange, S., O'Sullivan, A., Marschallinger, J., Zaunmair, P., Geretsegger, C., . . . Couillard-Despres, S. (2014). Hippocampal neurogenesis and antidepressive therapy: Shocking relations. *Neural Plasticity, 2014,* 723915. (p. 563)

Rothman, A. J., & Salovey, P. (1997). Shaping perceptions to motivate healthy behavior: The role of message framing. *Psychological Bulletin, 121,* 3–19. (p. 305)

Rottensteiner, M., Leskinen, T., Niskanen, E., Aaltonen, S., Mutikainen, S., Wikgren, J., . . . Kujala, U. M. (2015). Physical activity, fitness, glucose homeostasis, and brain morphology in twins. *Medicine and Science in Sports and Exercise, 47,* 509–518. (p. 153)

Rotton, J., & Kelly, I. W. (1985). Much ado about the full moon: A meta-analysis of lunar-lunacy research. *Psychological Bulletin, 97,* 286–306. (p. 530)

Rounds, J., & Su, R. (2014). The nature and power of interests. *Current Directions in Psychological Science, 23,* 98–103. (p. B-3)

Rovee-Collier, C. (1989). The joy of kicking: Memories, motives, and mobiles. In P. R. Solomon, G. R. Goethals, C. M. Kelley, & B. R. Stephens (Eds.), *Memory: Interdisciplinary approaches* (pp. 151–179). New York: Springer-Verlag. (p. 125)

Rovee-Collier, C. (1993). The capacity for long-term memory in infancy. *Current Directions in Psychological Science, 2,* 130–135. (p. 281)

Rovee-Collier, C. (1997). Dissociations in infant memory: Rethinking the development of implicit and explicit memory. *Psychological Review, 104,* 467–498. (p. 125)

Rovee-Collier, C. (1999). The development of infant memory. *Current Directions in Psychological Science, 8,* 80–85. (p. 125)

Rowe, D. C. (1990). As the twig is bent? The myth of child-rearing influences on personality development. *Journal of Counseling and Development, 68,* 606–611. (p. 72)

Rowe, D. C., Almeida, D. M., & Jacobson, K. C. (1999). School context and genetic influences on aggression in adolescence. *Psychological Science, 10,* 277–280. (p. 441)

Roy, J., & Forest, G. (2017). Greater circadian disadvantage during evening games for the National Basketball Association (NBA), National Hockey League (NHL) and National Football League (NFL) teams travelling westward. *Journal of Sleep Research*. Advance online publication. doi:10.1111/jsr.12565 (p. 91)

Rozin, P., Dow, S., Mosovitch, M., & Rajaram, S. (1998). What causes humans to begin and end a meal? A role for memory for what has been eaten, as evidenced by a study of multiple meal eating in amnesic patients. *Psychological Science, 9*, 392–396. (p. 363)

Rozin, P., Haddad, B., Nemeroff, C., & Slovic, P. (2015). Psychological aspects of the rejection of recycled water: Contamination, purification and disgust. *Judgment and Decision Making, 10*, 50–63. (p. 240)

Rozin, P., Millman, L., & Nemeroff, C. (1986). Operation of the laws of sympathetic magic in disgust and other domains. *Journal of Personality and Social Psychology, 50*, 703–712. (p. 240)

Ruau, D., Liu, L. Y., Clark, J. D., Angst, M. S., & Butte, A. J. (2012). Sex differences in reported pain across 11,000 patients captured in electronic medical records. *Journal of Pain, 13*, 228–234. (p. 222)

Ruback, R. B., Carr, T. S., & Hopper, C. H. (1986). Perceived control in prison: Its relation to reported crowding, stress, and symptoms. *Journal of Applied Social Psychology, 16*, 375–386. (p. 396)

Rubenstein, J. S., Meyer, D. E., & Evans, J. E. (2001). Executive control of cognitive processes in task switching. *Journal of Experimental Psychology: Human Perception and Performance, 27*, 763–797. (p. 82)

Rubenstein, L. M., Freed, R. D., Shapero, B. G., Fauber, R. L., & Alloy, L. B. (2016, June). Cognitive attributions in depression: Bridging the gap between research and clinical practice. *Journal of Psychotherapy Integration, 26*, 103–115. (p. 420)

Ruberton, P. M., Gladstone, J., & Lyubomirsky, S. (2016). How your bank balance buys happiness. *Emotion, 16*, 575–580. (p. 409)

Rubin, D. C., Rahhal, T. A., & Poon, L. W. (1998). Things learned in early adulthood are remembered best. *Memory and Cognition, 26*, 3–19. (p. 153)

Rubin, J. Z., Pruitt, D. G., & Kim, S. H. (1994). *Social conflict: Escalation, stalemate, and settlement.* New York: McGraw-Hill. (p. 459)

Rubin, L. B. (1985). *Just friends: The role of friendship in our lives.* New York: Harper & Row. (p. 165)

Rubin, Z. (1970). Measurement of romantic love. *Journal of Personality and Social Psychology, 16*, 265–273. (p. 375)

Rubinstein, G. (2016). Modesty doesn't become me: Narcissism and the Big Five among male and female candidates for the *Big Brother* TV show. *Journal of Individual Differences, 37*, 223–230. (p. 489)

Rubio-Fernández, P., & Geurts, B. (2013). How to pass the false-belief task before your fourth birthday. *Psychological Science, 24*, 27–33. (p. 128)

Ruchlis, H. (1990). *Clear thinking: A practical introduction.* Buffalo, NY: Prometheus Books. (p. 299)

Rueckert, L., Doan, T., & Branch, B. (2010). *Emotion and relationship effects on gender differences in empathy.* Presented at the annual meeting of the Association for Psychological Science, Boston, MA. (p. 378)

Rueger, S. Y., Malecki, C. K., Pyun, Y., Aycock, C., & Coyle, S. (2016). A meta-analytic review of the association between perceived social support and depression in childhood and adolescence. *Psychological Bulletin, 142*, 1017–1067. (p. 399)

Ruffin, C. L. (1993). Stress and health—little hassles vs. major life events. *Australian Psychologist, 28*, 201–208. (p. 386)

Rule, B. G., & Ferguson, T. J. (1986). The effects of media violence on attitudes, emotions, and cognitions. *Journal of Social Issues, 42*, 29–50. (p. 263)

Rumbaugh, D. M. (1977). *Language learning by a chimpanzee: The Lana project.* New York: Academic Press. (p. 317)

Rumbaugh, D. M., & Washburn, D. A. (2003). *Intelligence of apes and other rational beings.* New Haven, CT: Yale University Press. (p. 318)

Runeson, B., Haglund, A., Lichtenstein, P., & Tidemalm, C. (2016). Suicide risk after nonfatal self-harm: A national cohort study, 2000–2008. *Journal of Clinical Psychiatry, 77*, 240–256. (p. 502)

Ruotsalainen, H., Kyngäs, H., Tammelin, T., & Kääriäinen, M. (2015). Systematic review of physical activity and exercise interventions on body mass indices, subsequent physical activity and psychological symptoms in overweight and obese adolescents. *Journal of Advanced Nursing, 71*, 2461–2477. (p. 366)

Rushton, J. P. (1975). Generosity in children: Immediate and long-term effects of modeling, preaching, and moral judgment. *Journal of Personality and Social Psychology, 31*, 459–466. (p. 262)

Russell, B. (1930/1985). *The conquest of happiness.* London: Unwin Paperbacks. (p. 410)

Ruthsatz, J., & Urbach, J. B. (2012). Child prodigy: A novel cognitive profile places elevated general intelligence, exceptional working memory and attention to detail at the root of prodigiousness. *Intelligence, 40*, 419–426. (p. 357)

Rutledge, R. B., Skandali, N., Dayan, P., & Dolan, R. J. (2014). A computational and neural model of momentary subjective well-being. *PNAS, 111*, 12252–12257. (p. 410)

Rutz, C., Klump, B. C., Komarczyk, L., Leighton, R., Kramer, R., Wischnewski, S., . . . Masuda, B. M. (2016). Discovery of species-wide tool use in the Hawaiian crow. *Nature, 537*, 403–407. (p. 309)

Ryan, B. (2016, March 8). *Women's life ratings get better with full-time jobs.* Gallup World Poll (gallup.com). (p. 165)

Ryan, P. (2015, December 15). Quoted by Editorial Board of *The New York Times.* Don't blame mental illness for gun violence. *The New York Times* (nytimes.com). (p. 502)

Ryan, R. (1999, February 2). Quoted by Alfie Kohn, In pursuit of affluence, at a high price. *The New York Times* (nytimes.com). (p. 410)

Ryan, R. M., & Deci, E. L. (2000). Self-determination theory and the facilitation of intrinsic motivation, social development, and well-being. *American Psychologist, 55*, 68–78. (p. 352)

Ryan, R. M., & Deci, E. L. (2004). Avoiding death or engaging life as accounts of meaning and culture: Comment on Pyszczynski et al. (2004). *Psychological Bulletin, 130*, 473–477. (p. 489)

Rydell, R. J., Rydell, M. T., & Boucher, K. L. (2010). The effect of negative performance stereotypes on learning. *Journal of Personality and Social Psychology, 99*, 883–896. (p. 344)

Ryder, J. G., & Holtzheimer, P. E. (2016). Deep brain stimulation for depression: An update. *Current Behavioral Neuroscience Reports, 3*, 102–108. (p. 564)

Saad, L. (2002, November 21). *Most smokers wish they could quit.* Retrieved from gallup.com/poll/7270/most-smokers-wish-they-could-quit.aspx (p. 106)

Saad, L. (2015, July 13). Nearly half of smartphone users can't imagine life without it. Gallup (gallup.com). (p. 355)

Sabbagh, M. A., Xu, F., Carlson, S. M., Moses, L. J., & Lee, K. (2006). The development of executive functioning and theory of mind: A comparison of Chinese and U.S. preschoolers. *Psychological Science, 17*, 74–81. (p. 128)

Sabesan, R., Schmidt, B. P., Tuten, W. S., & Roorda, A. (2016). The elementary representation of spatial and color vision in the human retina. *Science Advances, 2*, e1600797. (p. 202)

Sachdev, P., & Sachdev, J. (1997). Sixty years of psychosurgery: Its present status and its future. *Australian and New Zealand Journal of Psychiatry, 31*, 457–464. (p. 565)

Sackett, P. R., & Walmsley, P. T. (2014). Which personality attributes are most important in the workplace? *Perspectives on Psychological Science, 9*, 538–551. (p. 479)

Sacks, O. (1985). *The man who mistook his wife for a hat.* New York: Summit Books. (pp. 227, 284)

Sadato, N., Pascual-Leone, A., Grafman, J., Ibanez, V., Deiber, M.-P., Dold, G., & Hallett, M. (1996). Activation of the primary visual cortex by Braille reading in blind subjects. *Nature, 380*, 526–528. (p. 64)

Sadler, M. S., Correll, J., Park, B., & Judd, C. M. (2012b). The world is not Black and White: Racial bias in the decision to shoot in a multiethnic context. *Journal of Social Issues, 68*, 286–313. (p. 436)

Sadler, M. S., Meagor, E. L., & Kaye, M. E. (2012a). Stereotypes of mental disorders differ in competence and warmth. *Social Science and Medicine, 74*, 915–922. (p. 497)

Sagan, C. (1977). *The dragons of Eden: Speculations on the evolution of human intelligence.* New York: Ballantine. (p. 190)

Sagan, C. (1987, February 1). The fine art of baloney detection. *Parade.* (p. 231)

Saint Louis, C. (2017, February 2). Pregnant women turn to marijuana, perhaps harming infants. *The New York Times* (nyti.ms/2k6F9wc). (p. 120)

Saks, E. (2007, August 27). A memoir of schizophrenia. *Time* (time.com). (p. 560)

Salas-Wright, C. P., Vaughn, M. G., Hodge, D. R., & Perron, B. E. (2012). Religiosity profiles of American youth in relation to substance use, violence, and delinquency. *Journal of Youth and Adolescence, 41*, 1560–1575. (p. 112)

Salchegger, S. (2016). Selective school systems and academic self-concept: How explicit and implicit school-level tracking relate to the big-fish–little-pond effect across cultures. *Journal of Educational Psychology, 108*, 405–423. (p. 410)

Salehi, I., Hosseini, S. M., Haghighi, M., Jahangard, L., Bajoghli, H., Gerber, M., . . . Brand, S. (2016). Electroconvulsive therapy (ECT) and aerobic exercise training (AET) increased plasma BDNF and ameliorated depressive symptoms in patients suffering from major depressive disorder. *Journal of Psychiatric Research, 76*, 1–8. (p. 563)

Salgado, J. F., & Moscoso, S. (2002). Comprehensive meta-analysis of the construct validity of the employment interview. *European Journal of Work and Organizational Psychology, 11*, 299–326. (p. 476)

Salk, R. H., Hyde, J. S., & Abramson, L. Y. (2017). Gender differences in depression in representative national samples: Meta-analyses of diagnoses and symptoms. *Psychological Bulletin, 143*, 783–822. (p. 517)

Salmon, P. (2001). Effects of physical exercise on anxiety, depression, and sensitivity to stress: A unifying theory. *Clinical Psychology Review, 21*, 33–61. (pp. 402, 559)

Salovey, P. (1990, January/February). Interview. *American Scientist*, pp. 25–29. (p. 407)

Salthouse, T. A. (2009). When does age-related cognitive decline begin? *Neurobiology of Aging, 30,* 507–514. (p. 333)

Salthouse, T. A. (2010). Selective review of cognitive aging. *Journal of the International Neuropsychological Society, 16,* 754–760. (pp. 332, 334)

Salthouse, T. A. (2013). Within-cohort age-related differences in cognitive functioning. *Psychological Science, 24,* 123–130. (p. 333)

Salthouse, T. A. (2014). Why are there different age relations in cross-sectional and longitudinal comparisons of cognitive functioning? *Current Directions in Psychological Science, 23,* 252–256. (p. 332)

Salthouse, T. A., & Mandell, A. R. (2013). Do age-related increases in tip-of-the-tongue experiences signify episodic memory impairments? *Psychological Science, 24,* 2489–2497. (p. 287)

Samson, D. R., Crittenden, A. N., Mabulla, I. A., Mabulla, A. Z. P., & Nunn, C. L. (2017). Chronotype variation drives night-time sentinel-like behaviour in hunter-gatherers. *Processing of the Royal Society B, 284*(1858), 20170967. doi:10.5061/dryad.jd651/2 (p. 86)

Sanacora, G., Frye, M. A., McDonald, W., Mathew, S. J., Turner, M. S., Schatzberg, A. F., . . . Nemeroff, C. B. (2017). A consensus statement on the use of ketamine in the treatment of mood disorders. *JAMA Psychiatry, 74,* 399–405. (p. 562)

Sánchez-Álvarez, N., Extremera, N., & Fernández-Berrocal, P. (2016). The relation between emotional intelligence and subjective well-being: A meta-analytic investigation. *Journal of Positive Psychology, 11,* 276–285. (p. 326)

Sánchez-Villegas, A., Henríquez-Sánchez, P., Ruiz-Canela, M., Lahortiga, F., Molero, P., Toledo, E., & Martínez-González, M. A. (2015). A longitudinal analysis of diet quality scores and the risk of incident depression in the SUN Project. *BMC Medicine, 13,* 1. ([p. 559)

Sanders, A. R., Martin, E. R., Beecham, G. W., Guo, S., Dawood, K., Rieger, G., . . . Bailey, J. M. (2015). Genome-wide scan demonstrates significant linkage for male sexual orientation. *Psychological Medicine, 45,* 1379–1388. (p. 181)

Sandler, W., Meir, I., Padden, C., & Aronoff, M. (2005). The emergence of grammar: Systematic structure in a new language. *PNAS, 102,* 2261–2265. (p. 313)

Sandoval, M., Leclerc, J. A., & Gómez, R. L. (2017). Words to sleep on: Naps facilitate verb generalization in habitually and nonhabitually napping preschoolers. *Child Development, 88*(5), 1615–1626. (p. 92)

Sandstrom, A. (2015, December 2). *Religious groups' policies on transgender members vary widely.* Pew Research Center (pewresearch.org). (p. 171)

Santos, H. C., Varnum, M. E. W., & Grossmann, I. (2017). Global increases in individualism. *Psychological Science, 28,* 1228–1239. (p. 491)

Sanz, C., Blicher, A., Dalke, K., Gratton-Fabri, L., McClure-Richards, T., & Fouts, R. (1998, Winter-Spring). Enrichment object use: Five chimpanzees' use of temporary and semi-permanent enrichment objects. *Friends of Washoe, 19,* 9–14. (p. 317)

Sanz, C., Morgan, D., & Gulick, S. (2004). New insights into chimpanzees, tools, and termites from the Congo Basin. *American Naturalist, 164,* 567–581. (p. 310)

Sapadin, L. A. (1988). Friendship and gender: Perspectives of professional men and women. *Journal of Social and Personal Relationships, 5,* 387–403. (p. 165)

Saphire-Bernstein, S., Way, B. M., Kim, H. S, Sherman, D. K., & Taylor, S. E. (2011). Oxytocin receptor gene (OXTR) is related to psychological resources. *PNAS, 108,* 15118–15122. (p. 394)

Sapolsky, R. (2005). The influence of social hierarchy on primate health. *Science, 308,* 648–652. (pp. 396, 397)

Sapolsky, R. (2010, November 14). This is your brain on metaphors. *The New York Times* (nytimes.com). (p. 373)

Sapolsky, R. (2015, September 3). Caitlyn Jenner and our cognitive dissonance. *Nautilus.* Retrieved from nautil.us/issue/28/2050/caitlyn-jenner-and-our-cognitive-dissonance (p. 171)

Sarro, E. C., Wilson, D. A., & Sullivan, R. M. (2014). Maternal regulation of infant brain state. *Current Biology, 24,* 1664–1669. (p. 123)

Satel, S., & Lilienfeld, S. G. (2013). *Brainwashed: The seductive appeal of mindless neuroscience.* New York: Basic Books. (p. 52)

Sato, K. (1987). Distribution of the cost of maintaining common resources. *Journal of Experimental Social Psychology, 23,* 19–31. (p. 456)

Saulny, S. (2006, June 21). A legacy of the storm: Depression and suicide. *The New York Times* (nytimes.com). (p. 385)

Saurat, M., Agbakou, M., Attigui, P., Golmard, J., & Arnulf, I. (2011). Walking dreams in congenital and acquired paraplegia. *Consciousness and Cognition, 20,* 1425–1432. (p. 97)

Savage-Rumbaugh, E. S., Murphy, J., Sevcik, R. A., Brakke, K. E., Williams, S. L., & Rumbaugh, D. M., with commentary by Bates, E. (1993). Language comprehension in ape and child. *Monographs of the Society for Research in Child Development, 58,* 1–254. (p. 318)

Savage-Rumbaugh, E. S., Rumbaugh, D., & Fields, W. M. (2009). Empirical Kanzi: The ape language controversy revisited. *Skeptic, 15,* 25–33. (p. 318)

Savani, K., & Rattan, A. (2012). A choice mind-set increases the acceptance and maintenance of wealth inequality. *Psychological Science, 23,* 796–804. (p. 417)

Savelieva, K., Pulkki-Råback, L., Jokela, M., Kubzansky, L. D., Elovainio, M., Mikkilä, V., . . . Keltikangas-Järvinen, L. (2016). Intergenerational transmission of socioeconomic position and ideal cardiovascular health: 32-year follow-up study. *Health Psychology.* Advance online publication. doi:10.1037/hea0000441 (p. 397)

Savic, I., Berglund, H., & Lindstrom, P. (2005). Brain response to putative pheromones in homosexual men. *PNAS, 102,* 7356–7361. (p. 181)

Savin-Williams, R., Joyner, K., & Rieger, G. (2012). Prevalence and stability of self-reported sexual orientation identity during young adulthood. *Archives of Sexual Behavior, 41,* 103–110. (p. 178)

Savitsky, K., Epley, N., & Gilovich, T. D. (2001). Do others judge us as harshly as we think? Overestimating the impact of our failures, shortcomings, and mishaps. *Journal of Personality and Social Psychology, 81,* 44–56. (p. 486)

Savitsky, K., & Gilovich, T. D. (2003). The illusion of transparency and the alleviation of speech anxiety. *Journal of Experimental Social Psychology, 39,* 618–625. (p. 486)

Savoy, C., & Beitel, P. (1996). Mental imagery for basketball. *International Journal of Sport Psychology, 27,* 454–462. (p. 321)

Sawyer, A. C. P., Miller-Lewis, L. R., Searle, A. K., & Sawyer, M. G. (2015). Is greater improvement in early self-regulation associated with fewer behavioral problems later in childhood? *Developmental Psychology, 51,* 1740–1755. (p. 145)

Sawyer, M. G., Arney, F. M., Baghurst, P. A., Clark, J. J., Graetz, B. W., Kosky, R. J., . . . Zubrick, S. R. (2000). *The mental health of young people in Australia.* Canberra: Mental Health and Special Programs Branch, Commonwealth Department of Health and Aged Care. (p. 518)

Sayer, L. C. (2016). Trends in women's and men's time use, 1965–2012: Back to the future? In S. M. McHale, V. King, J. Van Hook, and A. Booth (Eds.), *Gender and couple relationships.* Cham, Switzerland: Springer International. (p. 187)

Sayette, M. A., Loewenstein, G., Griffin, K. M., & Black, J. J. (2008). Exploring the cold-to-hot empathy gap in smokers. *Psychological Science, 19,* 926–932. (p. 105)

Sayette, M. A., Reichle, E. D., & Schooler, J. W. (2009). Lost in the sauce: The effects of alcohol on mind wandering. *Psychological Science, 20,* 747–752. (p. 104)

Sayette, M. A., Schooler, J. W., & Reichle, E. D. (2010). Out for a smoke: The impact of cigarette craving on zoning out during reading. *Psychological Science, 21,* 26–30. (p. 105)

Sbarra, D. A., Hasselmo, K., & Bourassa, K. J. (2015). Divorce and health: Beyond individual differences. *Current Directions in Psychological Science, 24,* 109–113. (p. 385)

Scaini, S., Belotti, R., Ogliari, A., & Battaglia, M. (2016). A comprehensive meta-analysis of cognitive-behavioral interventions for social anxiety disorder in children and adolescents. *Journal of Anxiety Disorders, 42,* 105–112. (p. 553)

Scarborough, E., & Furumoto, L. (1987). *Untold lives: The first generation of American women psychologists.* New York: Columbia University Press. (p. 6)

Scarf, D., Boy, K., Reinert, A. U., Devine, J., Güntürkün, O., & Colombo, M. (2016). Orthographic processing in pigeons (*Columba livia*). *PNAS, 113,* 11272–11276. (p. 317)

Scarr, S. (1984, May). What's a parent to do? A conversation with E. Hall. *Psychology Today,* pp. 58–63. (p. 339)

Scarr, S. (1989). Protecting general intelligence: Constructs and consequences for interventions. In R. J. Linn (Ed.), *Intelligence: Measurement, theory, and public policy.* Champaign: University of Illinois Press. (p. 325)

Scarr, S. (1990). Back cover comments on J. Dunn & R. Plomin, *Separate lives: Why siblings are so different.* New York: Basic Books. (p. 74)

Scarr, S. (1993, May/June). Quoted in Nature's thumbprint: So long, superparents. *Psychology Today,* p. 16. (p. 149)

Schab, F. R. (1991). Odor memory: Taking stock. *Psychological Bulletin, 109,* 242–251. (p. 227)

Schachter, S., & Singer, J. E. (1962). Cognitive, social and physiological determinants of emotional state. *Psychological Review, 69,* 379–399. (p. 369)

Schacter, D. L. (1992). Understanding implicit memory: A cognitive neuroscience approach. *American Psychologist, 47,* 559–569. (p. 285)

Schacter, D. L. (1996). *Searching for memory: The brain, the mind, and the past.* New York: Basic Books. (pp. 276, 285, 469)

Schafer, G. (2005). Infants can learn decontextualized words before their first birthday. *Child Development, 76,* 87–96. (p. 314)

Schaffer, A., Isometsä, E. T., Tondo, L., Moreno, D., Turecki, G., Reis, C., . . . Ha, K. (2015). International society for bipolar disorders task force on suicide: Meta-analyses and meta-regression of correlates of suicide attempts and suicide deaths in bipolar disorder. *Bipolar Disorders, 17,* 1–16. (p. 516)

Schaie, K. W., & Geiwitz, J. (1982). *Adult development and aging.* Boston: Little, Brown. (p. 332)

Schalock, R. L., Borthwick-Duffy, S., Bradley, V. J., Buntinx, W. H. E., Coulter, D. L., & Craig, E. M. (2010). *Intellectual disability: Definition, classification, and systems of supports* (11th ed.). Washington, DC: American Association on Intellectual and Developmental Disabilities. (p. 331)

Schein, E. H. (1956). The Chinese indoctrination program for prisoners of war: A study of attempted brainwashing. *Psychiatry, 19*, 149–172. (p. 419)

Schetter, C. D., Schafer, P., Lanzi, R. G., Clark-Kauffman, E., Raju., T. N. K., & Hillemeier, M. M. (2013). Shedding light on the mechanisms underlying health disparities through community participatory methods: The stress pathway. *Perspectives on Psychological Science, 8*, 613–633. (p. 386)

Schiavi, R. C., & Schreiner-Engel, P. (1988). Nocturnal penile tumescence in healthy aging men. *Journal of Gerontology: Medical Sciences, 43*, M146–M150. (p. 89)

Schick, V., Herbenick, D., Reece, M., Sanders, S. A., Dodge, B., Middlestadt, S. E., & Fortenberry, J. D. (2010). Sexual behaviors, condom use, and sexual health of Americans over 50: Implications for sexual health promotion for older adults. *Journal of Sexual Medicine, 7*(Suppl. 5), 315–329. (p. 151)

Schiffenbauer, A., & Schiavo, R. S. (1976). Physical distance and attraction: An intensification effect. *Journal of Experimental Social Psychology, 12*, 274–282. (p. 430)

Schilt, T., de Win, M. M. L, Koeter, M., Jager, G., Korf, D. J., van den Brink, W., & Schmand, B. (2007). Cognition in novice Ecstasy users with minimal exposure to other drugs. *Archives of General Psychiatry, 64*, 728–736. (p. 108)

Schimel, J., Arndt, J., Pyszczynski, T., & Greenberg, J. (2001). Being accepted for who we are: Evidence that social validation of the intrinsic self reduces general defensiveness. *Journal of Personality and Social Psychology, 80*, 35–52. (p. 473)

Schink, T., Kreutz, G., Busch, V., Pigeot, I., & Ahrens, W. (2014). Incidence and relative risk of hearing disorders in professional musicians. *Occupational and Environmental Medicine, 71*, 472–476. (p. 218)

Schizophrenia Working Group of the Psychiatric Genomics Consortium. (2014). Biological insights from 108 schizophrenia-associated genetic loci. *Nature, 511*, 421–427. (p. 526)

Schlaug, G., Jancke, L., Huang, Y., & Steinmetz, H. (1995). In vivo evidence of structural brain asymmetry in musicians. *Science, 267*, 699–701. (p. 52)

Schlomer, G. L., Del Giudice, M., & Ellis, B. J. (2011). Parent–offspring conflict theory: An evolutionary framework for understanding conflict within human families. *Psychological Review, 118*, 496–521. (p. 148)

Schmidt, F. L., & Hunter, J. E. (1998). The validity and utility of selection methods in personnel psychology: Practical and theoretical implications of 85 years of research findings. *Psychological Bulletin, 124*, 262–274. (pp. 484, B-6)

Schmidt, M. F. H., & Tomasello, M. (2012). Young children enforce social norms. *Current Directions in Psychological Science, 21*, 232–236. (p. 144)

Schmitt, D. P. (2003). Universal sex differences in the desire for sexual variety: tests from 52 nations, 6 continents, and 13 islands. *Journal of Personality and Social Psychology, 85*, 85–104. (p. 183)

Schmitt, D. P. (2007). Sexual strategies across sexual orientations: How personality traits and culture relate to sociosexuality among gays, lesbians, bisexuals, and heterosexuals. *Journal of Psychology and Human Sexuality, 18*, 183–214. (p. 183)

Schmitt, D. P., & Allik, J. (2005). Simultaneous administration of the Rosenberg Self-Esteem Scale in 53 nations: Exploring the universal and culture-specific features of global self-esteem. *Journal of Personality and Social Psychology, 89*, 623–642. (p. 488)

Schmitt, D. P., Allik, J., McCrae, R. R., & Benet-Martínez, V., Reips, U.-D. (2007). The geographic distribution of Big Five personality traits: Patterns and profiles of human self-description across 56 nations. *Journal of Cross-Cultural Psychology, 38*, 173–212. (p. 478)

Schmitt, D. P., & Fuller, R. C. (2015). On the varieties of sexual experience: Cross-cultural links between religiosity and human mating strategies. *Psychology of Religion and Spirituality, 7*, 314–326. (p. 178)

Schmitt, D. P., Jonason, P. K., Byerley, G. J., Flores, S. D., Illbeck, B. E., O'Leary, K. N., & Qudrat, A. (2012). A reexamination of sex differences in sexuality: New studies reveal old truths. *Current Directions in Psychological Science, 21*, 135–139. (p. 177)

Schmitt, D. P., & Pilcher, J. J. (2004). Evaluating evidence of psychological adaptation: How do we know one when we see one? *Psychological Science, 15*, 643–649. (p. 76)

Schmitt, E. (2017, September 27). Navy returns to compasses and pencils to help avoid collisions at sea. *The New York Times* (nytimes.com). (p. 93)

Schnall, E., Wassertheil-Smoller, S., Swencionis, C., Zemon, V., Tinker, L., O'Sullivan., M. J., . . . Goodwin, M. (2010). The relationship between religion and cardiovascular outcomes and all-cause mortality in the women's health initiative observational study. *Psychology and Health, 25*, 249–263. (p. 405)

Schnall, S., Haidt, J., Clore, G. L., & Jordan, A. (2008). Disgust as embodied moral judgment. *Personality and Social Psychology Bulletin, 34*, 1096–1109. (p. 227)

Schneider, M., and Preckel, F. (2017, March 23). Variables associated with achievement in higher education: A systematic review. *Psychological Bulletin.* (p. xxiv)

Schneider, W. J., & McGrew, K. S. (2012). The Cattell-Horn-Carroll model of intelligence In In Flanagan D. P., Harrison P. L. (Eds.), *Contemporary intellectual assessment: Theories, tests, and issues* (3rd ed.). New York: Guilford Press. (p. 324)

Schneier, B. (2007, May 17). Virginia Tech lesson: Rare risks breed irrational responses. *Wired* (wired.com). (p. 302)

Schoen, R., & Canudas-Romo, V. (2006). Timing effects on divorce: 20th century experience in the United States. *Journal of Marriage and Family, 68*, 749–758.

Schoeneman, T. J. (1994). Individualism. In V. S. Ramachandran (Ed.), *Encyclopedia of human behavior* (Vol. 2, pp. 631–643). San Diego: Academic Press. (p. 491)

Schofield, J. W. (1986). Black-White contact in desegregated schools. In M. Hewstone & R. Brown (Eds.), *Contact and conflict in intergroup encounters*. Oxford: Basil Blackwell. (p. 457)

Scholtz, S., Miras, A. D., Chhina, N., Prechtl, C. G., Sleeth, M. L., Daud, N. M., . . . Vincent, R. P. (2013). Obese patients after gastric bypass surgery have lower brain-hedonic responses to food than after gastric banding. *Gut, 63*, 891–902. (p. 362)

Schonfield, D., & Robertson, B. A. (1966). Memory storage and aging. *Canadian Journal of Psychology, 20*, 228–236. (p. 154)

Schooler, J. W., Gerhard, D., & Loftus, E. F. (1986). Qualities of the unreal. *Journal of Experimental Psychology: Learning, Memory, and Cognition, 12*, 171–181. (p. 292)

Schorr, E. A., Fox, N. A., van Wassenhove, V., & Knudsen, E. I. (2005). Auditory–visual fusion in speech perception in children with cochlear implants. *PNAS, 102*, 18748–18750. (p. 218)

Schrauzer, G. N., & Shrestha, K. P. (1990). Lithium in drinking water and the incidences of crimes, suicides, and arrests related to drug addictions. *Biological Trace Element Research, 25*, 105–113. (p. 562)

Schrauzer, G. N., & Shrestha, K. P. (2010). Lithium in drinking water. *British Journal of Psychiatry, 196*, 159.

Schreiber, F. R. (1973). *Sybil.* Chicago: Regnery. (p. 528)

Schroeder, J., Caruso, E. M., & Epley, N. (2016). Many hands make overlooked work: Over-claiming of responsibility increases with group size. *Journal of Experimental Psychology: Applied, 22*, 238–246. (p. 430)

Schroeder, J., & Epley, N. (2015). The sound of intellect: Speech reveals a thoughtful mind, increasing a job candidate's appeal. *Psychological Science, 26*, 877–891. (p. 216)

Schroeder, J., & Epley, N. (2016). Mistaking minds and machines: How speech affects dehumanization and anthropomorphism. *Journal of Experimental Psychology: General, 145*, 1427–1437. (p. 216)

Schuch, F. B., Vancampfort, D., Richards, J., Rosenbaum, S., Ward, P. B., & Stubbs, B. (2016a). Exercise as a treatment for depression: A meta-analysis adjusting for publication bias. *Journal of Psychiatric Research, 77*, 42–51. (p. 402)

Schuch, F. B., Vancampfort, D., Rosenbaum, S., Richards, J., Ward, P. B., & Stubbs, B. (2016b). Exercise improves physical and psychological quality of life in people with depression: A meta-analysis including the evaluation of control group response. *Psychiatry Research, 241*, 47–54. (pp. 558, 559)

Schultheiss, O. C., & Pang, J. S. (2007). Measuring implicit motives. In R. W. Robins, R. C. Fraley, & R. F. Krueger (Eds.), *Handbook of research methods in personality psychology* (pp. 322–345). New York: Guilford Press. (p. 467)

Schultheiss, O., Wiemers, U., & Wolf, O. (2014). Implicit need for achievement predicts attenuated cortisol responses to difficult tasks. *Journal of Research in Personality, 48*, 84–92. (p. 467)

Schuman, H., & Scott, J. (1989). Generations and collective memories. *American Sociological Review, 54*, 359–381. (p. 153)

Schumann, K., & Ross, M. (2010). Why women apologize more than men: Gender differences in thresholds for perceiving offensive behavior. *Psychological Science, 21*, 1649–1655. (p. 164)

Schutte, N. S., Malouff, J. M., Thorsteinsson, E. B., Bhullar, N., & Rooke, S. E. (2007). A meta-analytic investigation of the relationship between emotional intelligence and health. *Personality and Individual Differences, 42*, 921–933. (p. 326)

Schutte, N. S., Palanisamy, S. K. A., & McFarlane, J. R. (2016). The relationship between positive characteristics and longer telomeres. *Psychology & Health, 31*, 1466–1480. (p. 326)

Schuyler, A. C., Kintzle, S., Lucas, C. L., Moore, H., & Castro, C. A. (2017). Military sexual assault (MSA) among veterans in Southern California: Associations with physical health, psychological health, and risk behaviors. *Traumatology, 23*, 223–234. (p. 170)

Schwartz, B. (1984). *Psychology of learning and behavior* (2nd ed.). New York: Norton. (pp. 241, 510)

Schwartz, H. A., Eichstaedt, J. C., Kern, M. L., Dziurzynski, L., Ramones, S. M., Agrawal, M., . . . Ungar, L. H. (2013). Personality, gender, and age in the language of social media: The open-vocabulary approach. *PLoS ONE, 8*(9), e73791. doi:10.1371/journal.pone.0073791 (pp. 162, 165)

Schwartz, J. M., Stoessel, P. W., Baxter, L. R., Jr., Martin, K. M., & Phelps, M. E. (1996). Systematic changes in cerebral glucose metabolic rate after successful behavior modification treatment of obsessive-compulsive disorder. *Archives of General Psychiatry, 53*, 109–113. (pp. 546, 558)

Schwartz, P. J. (2011). Season of birth in schizophrenia: A maternal-fetal chronobiological hypothesis. *Medical Hypotheses, 76*, 785–793. (p. 525)

Schwartz, S. (2012). Dreams, emotions and brain plasticity. In *Aquém e além do cérebro* [Behind and beyond the brain]. Bial: Fundação Bial Institution of Public Utility. (p. 98)

Schwartz, S. H., & Rubel-Lifschitz, T. (2009). Cross-national variation in the size of sex differences in values: Effects of gender equality. *Journal of Personality and Social Psychology, 97*, 171–185. (p. 164)

Schwartz, S. J., Lilienfeld, S. O., Meca, A., & Sauvigné, K. C. (2016). The role of neuroscience within psychology: A call for inclusiveness over exclusiveness. *American Psychologist, 71*, 52–70. (p. 52)

Schwartz, S. J., Unger, J. B., Zamboanga, B. L., & Szapocznik, J. (2010). Rethinking the concept of acculturation: Implications for theory and research. *American Psychologist, 65*, 237–251. (p. 503)

Schwartzman-Morris, J., & Putterman, C. (2012). Gender differences in the pathogenesis and outcome of lupus and of lupus nephritis. *Clinical and Developmental Immunology*, 604892. (p. 389)

Schwarz, A. (2012, June 9). Risky rise of the good-grade pill. *The New York Times* (nytimes.com). (p. 498)

Schwarz, A., & Cohen, S. (2013, March 31). A.D.H.D. seen in 11% of U.S. children as diagnoses rise. *The New York Times* (nytimes.com). (p. 498)

Schwarz, N., Strack, F., Kommer, D., & Wagner, D. (1987). Soccer, rooms, and the quality of your life: Mood effects on judgments of satisfaction with life in general and with specific domains. *European Journal of Social Psychology, 17*, 69–79. (p. 281)

Sclafani, A. (1995). How food preferences are learned: Laboratory animal models. *PNAS, 54*, 419–427. (p. 364)

Scoboria, A., Wade, K. A., Lindsay, D. S., Azad, T., Strange, D., Ost, J., & Hyman, I. E. (2017). A mega-analysis of memory reports from eight peer-reviewed false memory implantation studies. *Memory, 25*, 146–163. (p. 290)

Scopelliti, I., Loewenstein, G., & Vosgerau, J. (2015). You call it "self-exuberance"; I call it "bragging": Miscalibrated predictions of emotional responses to self-promotion. *Psychological Science, 26*, 903–914. (p. 483)

Scott, D. J., Stohler, C. S., Egnatuk, C. M., Wang, H., Koeppe, R. A., & Zubieta, J.-K. (2007). Individual differences in reward responding explain placebo-induced expectations and effects. *Neuron, 55*, 325–336. (p. 223)

Scott, K. M., Wells, J. E., Angermeyer, M., Brugha, T. S., Bromet, E., Demyttenaere, K., . . . Kessler, R. C. (2010). Gender and the relationship between marital status and first onset of mood, anxiety and substance use disorders. *Psychological Medicine, 40*, 1495–1505. (p. 156)

Scott-Sheldon, L. A. J., Carey, K. B., Elliott, J. C., Garey, L., & Carey, M. P. (2014). Efficacy of alcohol interventions for first-year college students: A meta-analytic review of randomized controlled trials. *Journal of Consulting and Clinical Psychology, 82*, 177–188. (p. 104)

Scullin, M. K., & Bliwise, D. L. (2015). Sleep, cognition, and normal aging: Integrating a half century of multidisciplinary research. *Perspectives on Psychological Science, 10*, 97–137. (p. 93)

Scullin, M. K., & McDaniel, M. A. (2010). Remembering to execute a goal: Sleep on it! *Psychological Science, 21*, 1028–1035. (p. 288)

Sdorow, L. M. (2005). The people behind psychology. In B. Perlman, L. McCann, & W. Buskist (Eds.), *Voices of experience: Memorable talks from the National Institute on the Teaching of Psychology*. Washington, DC: American Psychological Society. (p. 468)

Seal, K. H., Bertenthal, D., Miner, C. R., Sen, S., & Marmar, C. (2007). Bringing the war back home: Mental health disorders among 103,788 U.S. veterans returning from Iraq and Afghanistan seen at Department of Veterans Affairs facilities. *Archives of Internal Medicine, 167*, 467–482. (p. 509)

Sedley, W., Gander, P. E., Kumar, S., Oya, H., Kovach, C. K., Nourski, K. V., . . . Griffiths, T. D. (2015). Intracranial mapping of a cortical tinnitus system using residual inhibition. *Current Biology, 25*, 1208–1214. (p. 222)

Sedlmeier, P., Eberth, J., Schwarz, M., Zimmermann, D., Haarig, F., Jaeger, S., & Kunze, S. (2012). The psychological effects of meditation: A meta-analysis. *Psychological Bulletin, 138*, 1139–1171. (p. 404)

Seehagen, S., Konrad, C., Herbert, J. S., & Schneider, S. (2015). Timely sleep facilitates declarative memory consolidation in infants. *PNAS, 112*, 1625–1629. (p. 92)

Seeman, P., Guan, H.-C., & Van Tol, H. H. M. (1993). Dopamine D4 receptors elevated in schizophrenia. *Nature, 365*, 441–445. (p. 524)

Seery, M. D. (2011). Resilience: A silver lining to experiencing adverse life events. *Current Directions in Psychological Science, 20*, 390–394. (pp. 137, 385)

Segal, N. L. (2005). *Indivisible by two: Lives of extraordinary twins.* Cambridge: Harvard University Press. (p. 73)

Segal, N. L. (2013). Personality similarity in unrelated look-alike pairs: Addressing a twin study challenge. *Personality and Individual Differences, 54*, 23–28. (p. 71)

Segal, N. L., Graham, J. L., & Ettinger, U. (2013). Unrelated look-alikes: Replicated study of personality similarity and qualitative findings on social relatedness. *Personality and Individual Differences, 55*, 169–174. (p. 71)

Segal, N. L., McGuire, S. A., & Stohs, J. H. (2012). What virtual twins reveal about general intelligence and other behaviors. *Personality and Individual Differences, 53*, 405–410. (p. 337)

Segall, M. H., Dasen, P. R., Berry, J. W., & Poortinga, Y. H. (1990). *Human behavior in global perspective: An introduction to cross-cultural psychology.* New York: Pergamon Press. (pp. 130, 168)

Sege, R., Nykiel-Bub, L., & Selk, S. (2015). Sex differences in institutional support for junior biomedical researchers. *Journal of American Medical Association, 314*, 1175–1177. (p. 168)

Segerstrom, S. C. (2007). Stress, energy, and immunity. *Current Directions in Psychological Science, 16*, 326–330. (p. 384)

Segerstrom, S. C., Taylor, S. E., Kemeny, M. E., & Fahey, J. L. (1998). Optimism is associated with mood, coping, and immune change in response to stress. *Journal of Personality and Social Psychology, 74*, 1646–1655. (p. 398)

Seibert, S. E., Wang, G., & Courtright, S. H. (2011). Antecedents and consequences of psychological and team empowerment in organizations: A meta-analytic review. *Journal of Applied Psychology, 96*, 981–1003. (pp. B-9, B-11)

Sejnowski, T. (2016, January 20). Quoted in "Memory capacity of brain is 10 times more than previously thought." *KurzweilAI Accelerating Intelligence News* (kurzweilai.net). (p. 275)

Self, C. E. (1994). *Moral culture and victimization in residence halls.* Unpublished master's thesis, Bowling Green State University, Bowling Green, OH. (p. 112)

Seli, P., Risko, E. F., Smilek, D., & Schacter, D. L. (2016). Mind-wandering with and without intention. *Trends in Cognitive Sciences, 20*, 605–617. (p. 104)

Seligman, M. (2016). How positive psychology happened and where it is going. In R. J. Sternberg, S. T. Fiske & D. J. Foss (Eds.), *Scientists making a difference: One hundred eminent behavioral and brain scientists talk about their most important contributions.* New York: Cambridge University Press, pp. 478–480. (p. 408)

Seligman, M. E. P. (1975). *Helplessness: On depression, development and death.* San Francisco: Freeman. (p. 396)

Seligman, M. E. P. (1991). *Learned optimism: How to change your mind and your life.* New York: Knopf. (pp. 80, 520, 521)

Seligman, M. E. P. (1994). *What you can change and what you can't.* New York: Knopf. (p. 486)

Seligman, M. E. P. (1995). The effectiveness of psychotherapy: The *Consumer Reports* study. *American Psychologist, 50*, 965–974. (pp. 521, 550, 552)

Seligman, M. E. P. (2002). *Authentic happiness: Using the new positive psychology to realize your potential for lasting fulfillment.* New York: Free Press. (pp. 10, 408, 486)

Seligman, M. E. P. (2011). *Flourish: A visionary new understanding of happiness and well-being.* New York: Free Press. (p. 10)

Seligman, M. E. P. (2012, May 8). Quoted in A. C. Brooks, America and the value of "earned success." *The Wall Street Journal* (wsj.com). (p. 487)

Seligman, M. E. P., Ernst, R. M., Gillham, J., Reivich, K., & Linkins, M. (2009). Positive education: Positive psychology and classroom interventions. *Oxford Review of Education, 35*, 293–311. (p. 545)

Seligman, M. E. P., & Maier, S. F. (1967). Failure to escape traumatic shock. *Journal of Experimental Psychology, 74*, 1–9. (p. 396)

Seligman, M. E. P., Steen, T. A., Park, N., & Peterson, C. (2005). Positive psychology progress: Empirical validation of interventions. *American Psychologist, 60*, 410–421. (pp. 10, 408)

Seligman, M. E. P., & Yellen, A. (1987). What is a dream? *Behavior Research and Therapy, 25*, 1–24. (p. 87)

Selimbeyoglu, A., & Parvizi, J. (2010). Electrical stimulation of the human brain: Perceptual and behavioral phenomena reported in the old and new literature. *Frontiers in Human Neuroscience, 4*, 1–11. (p. 51)

Sellers, H. (2010). *You don't look like anyone I know.* New York: Riverhead Books. (p. 189)

Selye, H. (1936). A syndrome produced by diverse nocuous agents. *Nature, 138*, 32. (p. 386)

Selye, H. (1976). *The stress of life.* New York: McGraw-Hill. (p. 386)

Selzam, S., Krapohl, E., von Stumm, S., O'Reilly, P. F., Rimfeld, K., Kovas, Y., . . . Plomin, R. (2016). Predicting educational achievement from DNA. *Molecular Psychiatry, 22*, 267–272. (p. 337)

Senghas, A., & Coppola, M. (2001). Children creating language: How Nicaraguan Sign Language acquired a spatial grammar. *Psychological Science, 12*, 323–328. (p. 313)

Sengupta, S. (2001, October 10). Sept. 11 attack narrows the racial divide. *The New York Times* (nytimes.com). (p. 458)

Senju, A., Southgate, V., White, S., & Frith, U. (2009). Mindblind eyes: An absence of spontaneous theory of mind in Asperger syndrome. *Science, 325,* 883–885. (p. 131)

Sergeant, S., & Mongrain, M. (2014). An online optimism intervention reduces depression in pessimistic individuals. *Journal of Consulting and Clinical Psychology, 82,* 263–274. (p. 399)

Service, R. F. (1994). Will a new type of drug make memory-making easier? *Science, 266,* 218–219. (p. 279)

Sest, N., & March, E. (2017). Constructing the cyber-troll: Psychopathy, sadism, and empathy. *Personality and Individual Differences, 119,* 69–72. (p. 430)

Sexton, C. E., Betts, J. F., Demnitz, N., Dawes, H., Ebmeier, K. P., & Johansen-Berg, H. (2016). A systematic review of MRI studies examining the relationship between physical fitness and activity and the white matter of the ageing brain. *NeuroImage, 131,* 81–90. (p. 64)

Shackman, A. J., Tromp, D. P., Stockbridge, M. D., Kaplan, C. M., Tillman, R. M., & Fox, A. S. (2016). Dispositional negativity: An integrative psychological and neurobiological perspective. *Psychological Bulletin, 142,* 1275–1314. (p. 478)

Shadish, W. R., & Baldwin, S. A. (2005). Effects of behavioral marital therapy: A meta-analysis of randomized controlled trials. *Journal of Consulting and Clinical Psychology, 73,* 6–14. (p. 553)

Shadish, W. R., Montgomery, L. M., Wilson, P., Wilson, M. R., Bright, I., & Okwumabua, T. (1993). Effects of family and marital psychotherapies: A meta-analysis. *Journal of Consulting and Clinical Psychology, 61,* 992–1002. (p. 547)

Shaffer, R. (2013, September–October). The psychic: Years later, Sylvia Browne's accuracy remains dismal. *Skeptical Inquirer,* pp. 30–35. (p. 230)

Shafir, E. (Ed.). (2013). *The behavioral foundations of public policy.* Princeton, NJ: Princeton University Press. (p. 4)

Shafir, E., & LeBoeuf, R. A. (2002). Rationality. *Annual Review of Psychology, 53,* 491–517. (p. 305)

Shaki, S. (2013). What's in a kiss? Spatial experience shapes directional bias during kissing. *Journal of Nonverbal Behavior, 37,* 43–50. (p. 10)

Shallcross, A. J., Ford, B. Q., Floerke, V. A., & Mauss, I. B. (2013). Getting better with age: The relationship between age, acceptance, and negative affect. *Journal of Personality and Social Psychology, 104,* 734–749. (p. 158)

Shamir, B., House, R. J., & Arthur, M. B. (1993). The motivational effects of charismatic leadership: A self-concept based theory. *Organizational Science, 4,* 577–594. (p. B-10)

Shanahan, L., McHale, S. M., Osgood, D. W., & Crouter, A. C. (2007). Conflict frequency with mothers and fathers from middle childhood to late adolescence: Within- and between-families comparisons. *Developmental Psychology, 43,* 539–550. (p. 147)

Shane, S. (2015, June 24). Homegrown extremists tied to deadlier toll than jihadis in U.S. since 9/11. *The New York Times* (nytimes.com). (p. 438)

Shankar, S. (2016, June 1). Is the spelling bee success of Indian-Americans a legacy of British colonialism? *The Conversation* (theconversation.com). (p. 340)

Shannon, B. J., Raichle, M. E., Snyder, A. Z., Fair, D. A., Mills, K. L., Zhanga, D., . . . Kiehl, K. A. (2011). Premotor functional connectivity predicts impulsivity in juvenile offenders. *PNAS, 108,* 11241–11245. (p. 142)

Shapin, S. (2013, October 15). The man who forgot everything. *The New Yorker* (newyorker.com). (p. 285)

Shapiro, D. (1999). *Psychotherapy of neurotic character.* New York: Basic Books. (p. 538)

Shapiro, F. (1989). Efficacy of the eye movement desensitization procedure in the treatment of traumatic memories. *Journal of Traumatic Stress, 2,* 199–223. (p. 554)

Shapiro, F. (1999). Eye movement desensitization and reprocessing (EMDR) and the anxiety disorders: Clinical and research implications of an integrated psychotherapy treatment. *Journal of Anxiety Disorders, 13,* 35–67. (p. 554)

Shapiro, F. (Ed.). (2002). *EMDR as an integrative psychotherapy approach: Experts of diverse orientations explore the paradigm prism.* Washington, DC: APA Books. (p. 554)

Shapiro, F. (2007). EMDR and case conceptualization from an adaptive information processing perspective. In F. Shapiro, F. W. Kaslow, & L. Maxfield (Eds.), *Handbook of EMDR and family therapy processes.* Hoboken, NJ: Wiley. (p. 554)

Shapiro, F. (2012, March 2). The evidence on E.M.D.R. *The New York Times* (nytimes.com). (p. 554)

Shapiro, K. A., Moo, L. R., & Caramazza, A. (2006). Cortical signatures of noun and verb production. *Proceedings of the National Academic of Sciences, 103,* 1644–1649. (p. 317)

Shappell, S., Detweiler, C., Holcomb, K., Hackworth, C., Boquet, A., & Wiegmann, D. A. (2007). Human error and commercial aviation accidents: An analysis using the human factors analysis and classification system. *Human Factors, 49,* 227–242. (p. B-13)

Shargorodsky, J., Curhan, S. G., Curhan, G. C., & Eavey, R. (2010). Changes of prevalence of hearing loss in US adolescents. *JAMA, 304,* 772–778. (p. 218)

Shariff, A. F., Greene, J. D., Karremans, J. C., Luguri, J. B., Clark, C. J., Schooler, J. W., . . . Vohs, K. D. (2014). Free will and punishment: A mechanistic view of human nature reduces retribution. *Psychological Science, 25,* 1563–1570. (p. 29)

Sharma, A. R., McGue, M. K., & Benson, P. L. (1998). The psychological adjustment of United States adopted adolescents and their nonadopted siblings. *Child Development, 69,* 791–802. (p. 73)

Shattuck, P. T. (2006). The contribution of diagnostic substitution to the growing administrative prevalence of autism in US special education. *Pediatrics, 117,* 1028–1037. (p. 131)

Shaver, P. R., Morgan, H. J., & Wu, S. (1996). Is love a basic emotion? *Personal Relationships, 3,* 81–96. (p. 372)

Shaw, B. A., Liang, J., & Krause, N. (2010). Age and race differences in the trajectories of self-esteem. *Psychology and Aging, 25,* 84–94. (p. 118)

Shaw, J., & Porter, S. (2015). Constructing rich false memories of committing crime. *Psychological Science, 26,* 291–301. (p. 290)

Shedler, J. (2009, March 23). *That was then, this is now: Psychoanalytic psychotherapy for the rest of us.* Unpublished manuscript, Department of Psychiatry, University of Colorado Health Sciences Center, Aurora, CO. (p. 538)

Shedler, J. (2010a, November/December). Getting to know me. *Scientific American Mind,* pp. 53–57. (p. 538)

Shedler, J. (2010b). The efficacy of psychodynamic psychotherapy. *American Psychologist, 65,* 98–109. (p. 553)

Sheeber, L. B., Feil, E. G., Seeley, J. R., Leve, C., Gau, J. M., Davis, B., . . . Allan, S. (2017). Mom-net: Evaluation of an internet-facilitated cognitive behavioral intervention for low-income depressed mothers. *Journal of Consulting and Clinical Psychology, 85,* 355–366. (p. 546)

Sheehan, S. (1982). *Is there no place on earth for me?* Boston: Houghton Mifflin. (p. 523)

Sheikh, S., & Janoff-Bulman, R. (2013). Paradoxical consequences of prohibitions. *Journal of Personality and Social Psychology, 105,* 301–315. (p. 250)

Sheldon, K. M., Elliot, A. J., Kim, Y., & Kasser, T. (2001). What is satisfying about satisfying events? Testing 10 candidate psychological needs. *Journal of Personality and Social Psychology, 80,* 325–339. (p. 352)

Sheldon, K. M., & Lyubomirsky, S. (2012). The challenge of staying happier: Testing the hedonic adaptation prevention model. *Personality and Social Psychology Bulletin, 38,* 670–680. (p. 412)

Sheltzer, J. M., & Smith, J. C. (2014). Elite male faculty in the life sciences employ fewer females. *PNAS, 111,* 10107–10112. (p. 168)

Shen, L., Fishbach, A., & Hsee, C. K. (2015, February). The motivating-uncertainty effect: Uncertainty increases resource investment in the process of reward pursuit. *Journal of Consumer Research, 41,* 1301–1315. (p. 349)

Shen, W., Yuan, Y., Liu, C., & Luo, J. (2017). The roles of the temporal lobe in creative insight: An integrated review. *Thinking & Reasoning, 23,* 321–375. (p. 306)

Shenton, M. E. (1992). Abnormalities of the left temporal lobe and thought disorder in schizophrenia: A quantitative magnetic resonance imaging study. *New England Journal of Medicine, 327,* 604–612. (p. 525)

Shepard, R. N. (1990). *Mind sights: Original visual illusions, ambiguities, and other anomalies.* New York: Freeman. (p. 32)

Shepherd, C. (1997, April). News of the weird. *Funny Times,* p. 15. (p. 71)

Shergill, S. S., Bays, P. M., Frith, C. D., & Wolpert, D. M. (2003). Two eyes for an eye: The neuroscience of force escalation. *Science, 301,* 187. (p. 456)

Sherif, M. (1966). *In common predicament: Social psychology of intergroup conflict and cooperation.* Boston: Houghton Mifflin. (p. 457)

Sherif, M., Radhakrishnan, R., D'Souza, D. C., & Ranganathan, M. (2016). Human laboratory studies on cannabinoids and psychosis. *Biological Psychiatry, 79,* 526–538. (p. 108)

Sherman, G. D., Lee, J. J., Cuddy, A. J. C., Renshon, J., Oveis, C., Gross, J. J., & Lerner, J. S. (2012). Leadership is associated with lower levels of stress. *PNAS, 109,* 17903–17907. (p. 397)

Sherman, L. E., Payton, A. A., Hernandez, L. M., Greenfield, P. M., & Dapretto, M. (2016). The power of the like in adolescence: Effects of peer influence on neural and behavioral responses to social media. *Psychological Science, 27,* 1027–1035. (pp. 148, 355)

Sherman, P. W., & Flaxman, S. M. (2001). Protecting ourselves from food. *American Scientist, 89,* 142–151. (p. 364)

Sherman, R. A., Rauthmann, J. F., Brown, N. A., Serfass, D. S., & Jones, A. B. (2015). The independent effects of personality and situations on real-time expressions of behavior and emotion. *Journal of Personality and Social Psychology, 109,* 872–888. (p. 481)

Sherry, D., & Vaccarino, A. L. (1989). Hippocampus and memory for food caches in black-capped chickadees. *Behavioral Neuroscience, 103,* 308–318. (p. 276)

Shettleworth, S. J. (1973). Food reinforcement and the organization of behavior in golden hamsters. In R. A. Hinde & J. Stevenson-Hinde (Eds.), *Constraints on learning.* London: Academic Press. (p. 256)

Shettleworth, S. J. (1993). Where is the comparison in comparative cognition? Alternative research programs. *Psychological Science, 4,* 179–184. (p. 276)

Shiell, M. M., Champoux, F., & Zatorre, R. (2014). Enhancement of visual motion detection thresholds in early deaf people. *PLOS ONE, 9*(2), e90498. doi:10.1371/journal.pone.0090498 (p. 64)

Shifren, J. L., Monz, B. U., Russo, P. A., Segreti, A., & Johannes, C. B. (2008). Sexual problems and distress in United States women: Prevalence and correlates. *Obstetrics & Gynecology, 112,* 970–978. (p. 175)

Shilsky, J. D., Hartman, T. J., Kris-Etherton, P. M., Rogers, C. J., Sharkey, N. A., & Nickols-Richardson, S. M. (2012). Partial sleep deprivation and energy balance in adults: An emerging issue for consideration by dietetics practitioners. *Journal of the Academy of Nutrition and Dietetics, 112,* 1785–1797. (p. 93)

Shiromani, P. J., Horvath, T., Redline, S., & Van Cauter E. (Eds.) (2012). *Sleep loss and obesity: Intersecting epidemics.* New York: Springer Science. (p. 93)

Shockley, K. M., Ispas, D., Rossi, M. E., & Levine, E. L. (2012). A meta-analytic investigation of the relationship between state affect, discrete emotions, and job performance. *Human Performance, 25,* 377–411. (pp. B-8, B-9)

Shor, E., Roelfs, D. J., Bugyi, P., & Schwartz, J. E. (2012). Meta-analysis of marital dissolution and mortality: Reevaluating the intersection of gender and age. *Social Science & Medicine, 75,* 46–59. (pp. 353, 400)

Shor, E., Roelfs, D. J., & Yogev, T. (2013). The strength of family ties: A meta-analysis and meta-regression of self-reported social support and mortality. *Social Networks, 35,* 626–638. (p. 399)

Shors, T. J. (2014). The adult brain makes new neurons, and effortful learning keeps them alive. *Current Directions in Psychological Science, 23,* 311–318. (p. 39)

Short, M., Gradisar, M., Wright, H., Dewald, J., Wolfson, A., & Carskadon, M. (2013). A cross-cultural comparison of sleep duration between U.S. and Australian adolescents: The effect of school start time, parent-set bedtimes, and extra-curricular load. *Health Education Behavior, 40,* 323–330. (p. 90)

Short, S. J., Lubach, G. R., Karasin, A. I., Olsen, C. W., Styner, M., Knickmeyer, R. C., . . . Coe, C. L. (2010). Maternal influenza infection during pregnancy impacts postnatal brain development in the rhesus monkey. *Biological Psychiatry, 67,* 965–973. (p. 525)

Shrestha, A., Nohr, E. A., Bech, B. H., Ramlau-Hansen, C. H., & Olsen, J. (2011). Smoking and alcohol during pregnancy and age of menarche in daughters. *Human Reproduction, 26,* 259–265. (p. 167)

Shuffler, M. L., Burke, C. S., Kramer, W. S., & Salas, E. (2013). Leading teams: Past, present, and future perspectives. In M. G. Rumsey (Ed.), *The Oxford handbook of leadership.* New York: Oxford University Press. (p. B-10)

Shuffler, M. L., DiazGranados, D., & Salas, E. (2011). There's a science for that: Team development interventions in organizations. *Current Directions in Psychological Science, 20,* 365–372. (p. B-10)

Shuwairi, S. M., & Johnson, S. P. (2013). Oculomotor exploration of impossible figures in early infancy. *Infancy, 18,* 221–232. (p. 127)

Sicarli, F., Baird, B., Perogamvros, L., Bernardi, G., LaRocque, J. J., Riedner, B., . . . Tononi, G. (2017). The neural correlates of dreaming. *Nature Neuroscience, 20,* 872–878. (p. 90)

Siegel, J. M. (1982, October). Quoted in J. Hooper, Mind tripping. *Omni,* pp. 72–82, 159–160. (p. 108)

Siegel, J. M. (2009). Sleep viewed as a state of adaptive inactivity. *Nature Reviews Neuroscience, 10,* 747–753. (p. 91)

Siegel, J. M. (2012). Suppression of sleep for mating. *Science, 337,* 1610–1611. (p. 91)

Siegel, R. K. (1977, October). Hallucinations. *Scientific American,* pp. 132–140. (p. 108)

Siegel, R. K. (1980). The psychology of life after death. *American Psychologist, 35,* 911–931. (p. 108)

Siegel, R. K. (1984, March 15). Personal communication. (p. 108)

Siegel, R. K. (1990). *Intoxication: Life in pursuit of artificial paradise.* New York: Pocket Books. (pp. 109, 400)

Siegel, S. (2005). Drug tolerance, drug addiction, and drug anticipation. *Current Directions in Psychological Science, 14,* 296–300. (p. 241)

Silber, M. H., Ancoli-Israel, S., Bonnet, M. H., Chokroverty, S., Grigg-Damberger, M. M., Hirshkowitz, M., . . . Iber, C. (2007). The visual scoring of sleep in adults. *Journal of Clinical Sleep Medicine, 3,* 121–131. (p. 87)

Silbersweig, D. A., Stern, E., Frith, C., Cahill, C., Holmes, A., Grootoonk, S., . . . Frackowiak, R. S. J. (1995). A functional neuroanatomy of hallucinations in schizophrenia. *Nature, 378,* 176–179. (p. 524)

Silva, C. E., & Kirsch, I. (1992). Interpretive sets, expectancy, fantasy proneness, and dissociation as predictors of hypnotic response. *Journal of Personality and Social Psychology, 63,* 847–856. (p. 224)

Silva, K., Bessa, J., & de Sousa, L. (2012). Auditory contagious yawning in domestic dogs (*Canis familiaris*): First evidence for social modulation. *Animal Cognition, 15,* 721–724. (p. 422)

Silver, M., & Geller, D. (1978). On the irrelevance of evil: The organization and individual action. *Journal of Social Issues, 34,* 125–136. (p. 428)

Silver, N. (2012). *The signal and the noise: Why so many predictions fail—but some don't.* New York: Penguin. (p. 151)

Silver, R. C., Holman, E. A., Anderson, J. P., Poulin, M., McIntosh, D. N., & Gil-Rivas, V. (2013). Mental- and physical-health effects of acute exposure to media images of the September 11, 2001 attacks and Iraq War. *Psychological Science, 24,* 1623–1634. (p. 385)

Silver, R. C., Holman, E. A., McIntosh, D. N., Poulin, M., & Gil-Rivas, V. (2002). Nationwide longitudinal study of psychological responses to September 11. *Journal of the American Medical Association, 288,* 1235–1244. (p. 385)

Silverman, K., Evans, S. M., Strain, E. C., & Griffiths, R. R. (1992). Withdrawal syndrome after the double-blind cessation of caffeine consumption. *New England Journal of Medicine, 327,* 1109–1114. (p. 105)

Silverman, L. (2015, April 12). Ranulph Fiennes: Marathon des Sables was hell on Earth. *The Telegraph.* Retrieved from http://www.telegraph.co.uk/goodlife/11529641/Ranulph-Fiennes-Marathon-des-Sables-was-hell-on-Earth.html (p. 383)

Silverstein, B. H., Snodgrass, M., Shevrin, H., & Kushwaha, R. (2015). P3b, consciousness, and complex unconscious processing. *Cortex, 73,* 216–227. (p. 81)

Silwa, J., & Frehwald, W. A. (2017). A dedicated network for social interaction processing in the primate brain. *Science, 356,* 745–749. (p. 62)

Simek, T. C., & O'Brien, R. M. (1981). *Total golf: A behavioral approach to lowering your score and getting more out of your game.* Huntington, NY: B-MOD Associates. (p. 251)

Simek, T. C., & O'Brien, R. M. (1988). A chaining-mastery, discrimination training program to teach Little Leaguers to hit a baseball. *Human Performance, 1,* 73–84. (p. 251)

Simon, H. A., & Chase, W. G. (1973). Skill in chess. *American Scientist, 61,* 394–403. (p. 325)

Simon, V., Czobor, P., Bálint, S., Mésáros, A., & Bitter, I. (2009). Prevalence and correlates of adult attention-deficit hyperactivity disorder: Meta-analysis. *British Journal of Psychiatry, 194,* 204–211. (p. 498)

Simons, D. J., Boot, W. R., Charness, N., Gathercole, S. E., Chabris, C. F., Hambrick, D. Z., & Stine-Morrow, E. A. L. (2016). Do "brain-training" programs work? *Psychological Science in the Public Interest, 17,* 103–186. (p. 154)

Simons, D. J., & Chabris, C. F. (1999). Gorillas in our midst: Sustained inattentional blindness for dynamic events. *Perception, 28,* 1059–1074. (p. 82)

Simons, D. J., & Chabris, C. F. (2011). What people believe about how memory works: A representative survey of the U.S. population. *PLoS ONE, 6,* e22757. (p. 289)

Simons, D. J., & Levin, D. T. (1998). Failure to detect changes to people during a real-world interaction. *Psychonomic Bulletin & Review, 5,* 644–649. (p. 83)

Simonsohn, U., & Gino, F. (2013). Daily horizons: Evidence of narrow bracketing in judgment from 10 years of M.B.A. admissions interviews. *Psychological Science, 24,* 219–224. (p. B-6)

Simonton, D. K. (1988). Age and outstanding achievement: What do we know after a century of research? *Psychological Bulletin, 104,* 251–267. (p. 334)

Simonton, D. K. (1990). Creativity in the later years: Optimistic prospects for achievement. *The Gerontologist, 30,* 626–631. (p. 334)

Simonton, D. K. (1992). The social context of career success and course for 2,026 scientists and inventors. *Personality and Social Psychology Bulletin, 18,* 452–463. (p. 307)

Simonton, D. K. (2000). Methodological and theoretical orientation and the long-term disciplinary impact of 54 eminent psychologists. *Review of General Psychology, 4,* 13–24. (p. 263)

Simonton, D. K. (2012a). Teaching creativity: Current findings, trends, and controversies in the psychology of creativity. *Teaching of Psychology, 39,* 217–222. (p. 307)

Simonton, D. K. (2012b, November–December). The science of genius. *Scientific American Mind,* pp. 35–41. (p. 307)

Simpson, A., & Rios, K. (2016). How do U.S. Christians and atheists stereotype one another's moral values? *International Journal for the Psychology of Religion, 26,* 320–336. (p. 435)

Sin, N. L., Graham-Engeland, J. E., Ong, A. D., & Almeida, D. M. (2015). Affective reactivity to daily stressors is associated with elevated inflammation. *Health Psychology, 34,* 154–1165. (p. 386)

Sinclair, R. C., Hoffman, C., Mark, M. M., Martin, L. L., & Pickering, T. L. (1994). Construct accessibility and the misattribution of arousal: Schachter and Singer revisited. *Psychological Science, 5,* 15–18. (p. 369)

Singer, J. L. (1981). Clinical intervention: New developments in methods and evaluation. In L. T. Benjamin, Jr. (Ed.), *The G. Stanley Hall Lecture Series* (Vol. 1). Washington, DC: American Psychological Association. (p. 553)

Singer, T., Seymour, B., O'Doherty, J., Kaube, H., Dolan, R. J., & Frith, C. (2004). Empathy for pain involves the affective but not sensory components of pain. *Science, 303,* 1157–1162. (pp. 223, 260)

Singh, D. (1993). Adaptive significance of female physical attractiveness: Role of waist-to-hip ratio. *Journal of Personality and Social Psychology, 65,* 293–307. (p. 185)

Singh, D., & Randall, P. K. (2007). Beauty is in the eye of the plastic surgeon: Waist–hip ratio (WHR) and women's attractiveness. *Personality and Individual Differences, 43,* 329–340. (p. 185)

Singh, S. (1997). *Fermat's enigma: The epic quest to solve the world's greatest mathematical problem.* New York: Bantam Books. (p. 306)

Singh, S., & Riber, K. A. (1997, November). Fermat's last stand. *Scientific American,* pp. 68–73. (p. 307)

Sio, U. N., Monahan, P., & Ormerod, T. (2013). Sleep on it, but only if it is difficult: Effects of sleep on problem solving. *Memory and Cognition, 41,* 159–166. (p. 92)

Sireteanu, R. (1999). Switching on the infant brain. *Science, 286,* 59–61. (p. 218)

Sit, D. K., McGowan, J., Wiltrout, C., Diler, R. S., Dills, J., Luther, J., . . . Terman, M. (2018). Adjunctive bright light therapy for bipolar depression: A randomized double-blind placebo-controlled trial. *American Journal of Psychiatry, 175*(2), 131–139. (p. 555)

Sixtus, E., Fischer, M. H., & Lindemann, O. (2017). Finger posing primes number comprehension. *Cognitive Processing, 18,* 237–248. (p. 229)

Skeem, J., Kennealy, P., Monahan, J., Peterson, J., & Appelbaum, P. (2016). Psychosis uncommonly and inconsistently precedes violence among high-risk individuals. *Clinical Psychological Science, 4,* 40–49. (p. 502)

Skeem, J. L., & Cooke, D. J. (2010). Is criminal behavior a central component of psychopathy? Conceptual directions for resolving the debate. *Psychological Assessment, 22,* 433–445. (p. 530)

Skinner, B. F. (1953). *Science and human behavior.* New York: Macmillan. (p. 247)

Skinner, B. F. (1956). A case history in scientific method. *American Psychologist, 11,* 221–233. (p. 248)

Skinner, B. F. (1961, November). Teaching machines. *Scientific American, 205,* 90–112. (pp. 247, 248)

Skinner, B. F. (1966). *The behavior of organisms: An experimental analysis.* New York: Appleton-Century-Crofs. (Original work published 1938.) (p. 250)

Skinner, B. F. (1983, September). Origins of a behaviorist. *Psychology Today,* pp. 22–33. (p. 250)

Skinner, B. F. (1989). Teaching machines. *Science, 243,* 1535. (p. 251)

Sklar, L. S., & Anisman, H. (1981). Stress and cancer. *Psychological Bulletin, 89,* 369–406. (p. 390)

Skoog, G., & Skoog, I. (1999). A 40-year follow-up of patients with obsessive-compulsive disorder. *Archives of General Psychiatry, 56,* 121–127. (p. 509)

Skov, R. B., & Sherman, S. J. (1986). Information-gathering processes: Diagnosticity, hypothesis-confirmatory strategies, and perceived hypothesis confirmation. *Journal of Experimental Social Psychology, 22,* 93–121. (pp. 300, B-6)

Slagt, M., Dubas, J. S., Deković, M., & van Aken, M. A. (2016). Differences in sensitivity to parenting depending on child temperament: A meta-analysis. *Psychological Bulletin, 142,* 1068–1110. (p. 135)

Slatcher, R. B., Selcuk, E., & Ong, A. (2015). Perceived partner responsiveness predicts diurnal cortisol profiles 10 years later. *Psychological Science, 26,* 972–982. (p. 400)

Slaughter, V., Imuta, K., Peterson, C. C., & Henry, J. D. (2015). Meta-analysis of theory of mind and peer popularity in the preschool and early school years. *Child Development, 86,* 1159–1174. (p. 128)

Sloan, R. P. (2005). *Field analysis of the literature on religion, spirituality, and health.* Columbia University. Retrieved from metanexus.net/tarp (p. 405)

Sloan, R. P., & Bagiella, E. (2002). Claims about religious involvement and health outcomes. *Annals of Behavioral Medicine, 24,* 14–21. (p. 405)

Sloan, R. P., Bagiella, E., & Powell, T. (1999). Religion, spirituality, and medicine. *The Lancet, 353,* 664–667. (p. 405)

Sloan, R. P., Bagiella, E., VandeCreek, L., & Poulos, P. (2000). Should physicians prescribe religious activities? *New England Journal of Medicine, 342,* 1913–1917. (p. 405)

Slopen, N., Glynn, R. J., Buring, J., & Albert, M. A. (2010, November 23). Job strain, job insecurity, and incident cardiovascular disease in the Women's Health Study. *Circulation, 122*(21, Suppl.), Abstract A18520. (p. 392)

Slovic, P. (2007). "If I look at the mass I will never act": Psychic numbing and genocide. *Judgment and Decision Making, 2,* 79–95. (p. 303)

Slovic, P., Västfjälla, D., Erlandsson, A., & Gregory, R. (2017). Iconic photographs and the ebb and flow of empathic response to humanitarian disasters. *PNAS, 114,* 640–644. (p. 303)

Slutske, W. S., Moffitt, T. E., Poulton, R., & Caspi, A. (2012). Undercontrolled temperament at age 3 predicts disordered gambling at age 32: A longitudinal study of a complete birth cohort. *Psychological Science, 23,* 510–516. (p. 118)

Smalarz, L., & Wells, G. L. (2015). Contamination of eyewitness self-reports and the mistaken identification problem. *Current Directions in Psychological Science, 24,* 120–124. (p. 292)

Small, M. F. (1997). Making connections. *American Scientist, 85,* 502–504. (p. 140)

Smedley, A., & Smedley, B. D. (2005). Race as biology is fiction, racism as a social problem is real: Anthropological and historical perspectives on the social construction of race. *American Psychologist, 60,* 16–26. (p. 342)

Smelser, N. J., & Mitchell, F. (Eds.). (2002). *Terrorism: Perspectives from the behavioral and social sciences.* Washington, DC: National Research Council, National Academies Press. (p. 440)

Smith, A. (1776). An inquiry into the nature and causes of the wealth of nations. London: W. Strahan and T. Cadell. (p. 456)

Smith, A. (1983). Personal correspondence. (p. 524)

Smith, A. M., Floerke, V. A., & Thomas, A. K. (2016). Retrieval practice protects memory against acute stress. *Science, 354,* 1046–1048. (p. 272)

Smith, A. R., Dodd, D. R., Forrest, L. N., Witte, T. K., Bodell, L., Ribeiro, J. D., . . . Bartlett, M. (2016). Does the interpersonal-psychological theory of suicide provide a useful framework for understanding suicide risk among eating disorder patients? A test of the validity of the IPTS. *International Journal of Eating Disorders, 49,* 1082–1086. (p. 532)

Smith, B. C. (2011, January 16). The senses and the multi-sensory. *World Question Center* (edge.org). (p. 228)

Smith, C. (2006, January 7). Nearly 100, LSD's father ponders his "problem child." *The New York Times* (nytimes.com). (p. 108)

Smith, G. E. (2016). Healthy cognitive aging and dementia prevention. *American Psychologist, 71,* 268–275. (pp. 153, 448)

Smith, J. A., & Rhodes, J. E. (2014). Being depleted and being shaken: An interpretative phenomenological analysis of the experiential features of a first episode of depression. *Psychology and Psychotherapy: Theory, Research and Practice, 88,* 197–209. (p. 516)

Smith, J. C., Nielson, K. A., Woodard, J. L., Seidenberg, M., Durgerian, S., Hazlett, K. E., . . . Rao, S. M. (2014, April 23). Physical activity reduces hippocampal atrophy in elders at genetic risk for Alzheimer's disease. *Frontiers in Aging Neuroscience, 6,* 61. (p. 153)

Smith, M. B. (1978). Psychology and values. *Journal of Social Issues, 34,* 181–199. (p. 473)

Smith, M. L., & Glass, G. V. (1977). Meta-analysis of psychotherapy outcome studies. *American Psychologist, 32,* 752–760. (p. 552)

Smith, M. L., Glass, G. V., & Miller, R. L. (1980). *The benefits of psychotherapy.* Baltimore: Johns Hopkins Press. (pp. 551, 552)

Smith, M. M., Sherry, S. B., Chen, S., Saklofske, D. H., Mushquash, C., Flett, G. L., & Hewitt, P. L. (2018). The perniciousness of perfectionism: A meta-analytic review of the perfectionism-suicide relationship. *Journal of Personality, 86*(3), 522–542. (p. 500)

Smith, P. B., & Tayeb, M. (1989). Organizational structure and processes. In M. Bond (Ed.), *The cross-cultural challenge to social psychology.* Newbury Park, CA: Sage. (p. B-11)

Smith, S. F., Lilienfeld, S. O., Coffey, K., & Dabbs, J. M. (2013). Are psychopaths and heroes twigs off the same branch? Evidence from college, community, and presidential samples. *Journal of Research in Personality, 47,* 634–646. (p. 530)

Smith, S. J., Axelton, A. M., & Saucier, D. A. (2009). The effects of contact on sexual prejudice: A meta-analysis. *Sex Roles, 61,* 178–191. (p. 457)

Smith, S. L., Pieper, K., & Choueiti, M. (2017, February). Inclusion in the director's chair? Gender, race, & age of film directors across 1,000 films from 2007–2016. Media, Diversity, & Social Change Initiative, University of Southern California Annenberg School for Communications and Journalism. (p. 437)

Smith, S. M., Nichols, T. E., Vidaurre, D., Winkler, A. M., Behrens, T. E., Glasser, M. F., . . . Miller, K. L. (2015). A positive-negative mode of population covariation links brain connectivity, demographics, and behavior. *Nature Neuroscience, 18,* 1565–1567. (p. 53)

Smith, T. W., & Baucom, B. R. W. (2017). Intimate relationships, individual adjustment, and coronary heart disease: Implications of overlapping associations in psychosocial risk. *American Psychologist, 72,* 578–589. (p. 400)

Smith, T. W., Marsden, P. V., & Hout, M. (2017). *General social surveys, 1972–2016 cumulative file* (ICPSR31521-v1). Chicago: National Opinion Research Center. Ann Arbor, MI: Inter-university Consortium for Political and Social Research. doi:10.3886/ICPSR31521.v1 (p. 249)

Smits, I. A. M., Dolan, C. V., Vorst, H. C. M., Wicherts, J. M., & Timmerman, M. E. (2011). Cohort differences in big five personality traits over a period of 25 years. *Journal of Personality and Social Psychology, 100,* 1124–1138. (p. 401)

Smolak, L., & Murnen, S. K. (2002). A meta-analytic examination of the relationship between child sexual abuse and eating disorders. *International Journal of Eating Disorders, 31,* 136–150.(p. 532)

Snedeker, J., Geren, J., & Shafto, C. L. (2007). Starting over: International adoption as a natural experiment in language development. *Psychological Science, 18,* 79–86. (p. 315)

Sniekers, S., Stringer, S., Watanabe, K., Jansen, P. R., Coleman, J. R. I., Krapohl, E., . . . Posthuma, D. (2017). Genome-wide association meta-analysis of 78,308 individuals identifies new loci and genes influencing human intelligence. *Nature Genetics, 49,* 1107–1112. (p. 337)

Snipes, D. J., Calton, J. M., Green, B. A., Perrin, P. B., & Benotsch, E. G. (2017). Rape and posttraumatic stress disorder (PTSD): Examining the mediating role of explicit sex-power beliefs for men versus women. *Journal of Interpersonal Violence, 32,* 2453–2470. (p. 170)

Snippe, E., Simons, C. J., Hartmann, J. A., Menne-Lothmann, C., Kramer, I., Booij, S. H., . . . Wichers, M. (2016). Change in daily life behaviors and depression: Within-person and between-person associations. *Health Psychology, 35,* 433–441. (p. 402)

Snodgrass, S. E., Higgins, J. G., & Todisco, L. (1986). *The effects of walking behavior on mood.* Paper presented at the American Psychological Association convention. (p. 393)

Snyder, F., & Scott, J. (1972). The psychophysiology of sleep. In N. S. Greenfield & R. A. Sterbach (Eds.), *Handbook of psychophysiology* (pp. 645–708). New York: Holt, Rinehart & Winston. (p. 98)

Snyder, S. H. (1984). Neurosciences: An integrative discipline. *Science, 225,* 1255–1257. (p. 497)

Snyder, S. H. (1986). *Drugs and the brain.* New York: Scientific American Library. (p. 562)

Soderstrom, N. C., Kerr, T. K., & Bjork, R. A. (2016). The critical importance of retrieval—and spacing—for learning. *Psychological Science, 27,* 223–230. (p. 272)

Solomon, B. C., & Jackson, J. J. (2014). The long reach of one's spouse: Spouses' personality influences occupational success. *Psychological Science, 25,* 2189–2198. (p. B-8)

Solomon, D. A., Keitner, G. I., Miller, I. W., Shea, M. T., & Keller, M. B. (1995). Course of illness and maintenance treatments for patients with bipolar disorder. *Journal of Clinical Psychiatry, 56,* 5–13. (p. 562)

Solomon, Z., Greene, T., Ein-Dor, T., Zerach, G., Benyamini, Y., & Ohry, A. (2014). The long-term implications of war captivity for mortality and health. *Journal of Behavioral Medicine, 37,* 849–859. (p. 388)

Solomon, Z., Tsur, N., Levin, Y., Uziel, O., Lahav, M., & Ohry, A. (2017). The implications of war captivity and long-term psychopathology trajectories for telomere length. *Psychoneuroendocrinology, 81,* 122–128. (p. 388)

Somerville, L. H., Jones, R. M., Ruberry, E. J., Dyke, J. P., Glover, G., & Casey, B. J. (2013). The medial prefrontal cortex and the emergence of self-conscious emotion in adolescence. *Psychological Science, 24,* 1554–1562. (p. 142)

Song, S. (2006, March 27). Mind over medicine. *Time,* p. 47. (p. 224)

Sontag, S. (1978). *Illness as metaphor.* New York: Farrar, Straus, & Giroux. (p. 390)

Sood, A. K., Armaiz-Pena, G. N., Halder, J., Nick, A. M., Stone, R. L., Hu, W., . . . Lutgendorf, S. K. (2010). Adrenergic modulation of focal adhesion kinase protects human ovarian cancer cells from anoikis. *Journal of Clinical Investigation, 120,* 1515–1523. (p. 390)

Soto, C. J., & John, O. P. (2017). The next big five inventory (BFI-2): Developing and assessing a hierarchical model with 15 facets to enhance bandwidth, fidelity, and predictive power. *Journal of Personality and Social Psychology, 113,* 117–143. (p. 477)

Soussignan, R. (2001). Duchenne smile, emotional experience, and autonomic reactivity: A test of the facial feedback hypothesis. *Emotion, 2,* 52–74. (p. 381)

South, S. C., Krueger, R. F., Johnson, W., & Iacono, W. G. (2008). Adolescent personality moderates genetic and environmental influences on relationships with parents. *Journal of Personality and Social Psychology, 94,* 899–912. (p. 139)

Sowell, T. (1991, May/June). Cultural diversity: A world view. *American Enterprise,* pp. 44–55. (p. 459)

Spanos, N. P. (1986). Hypnosis, nonvolitional responding, and multiple personality: A social psychological perspective. *Progress in Experimental Personality Research, 14,* 1–62. (p. 528)

Spanos, N. P. (1994). Multiple identity enactments and multiple personality disorder: A sociocognitive perspective. *Psychological Bulletin, 116,* 143–165. (p. 528)

Spanos, N. P. (1996). *Multiple identities and false memories: A sociocognitive perspective.* Washington, DC: American Psychological Association Books. (p. 528)

Spanos, N. P., & Coe, W. C. (1992). A social-psychological approach to hypnosis. In E. Fromm & M. R. Nash (Eds.), *Contemporary hypnosis research* (pp. 102–130). New York: Guilford Press. (p. 224)

Sparks, S., Cunningham, S. J., & Kritikos, A. (2016). Culture modulates implicit ownership-induced self-bias in memory. *Cognition, 153,* 89–98. (p. 274)

Sparrow, B., Liu, J., & Wegner, D. M. (2011). Google effects on memory: Cognitive consequences of having information at our fingertips. *Science, 333,* 776–778. (p. 269)

Spaulding, S. (2013). Mirror neurons and social cognition. *Mind and Language, 28,* 233–257. (p. 260)

Spearman, C. (1904). "General intelligence," objectively determined and measured. *American Journal of Psychology, 15,* 201–292. (p. 323)

Spector, T. (2012). *Identically different: Why you can change your genes.* London: Weidenfeld & Nicolson. (p. 74)

Speer, N. K., Reynolds, J. R., Swallow, K. M., & Zacks, J. M. (2009). Reading stories activates neural representations of visual and motor experiences. *Psychological Science, 20,* 989–999. (pp. 260, 317)

Spelke, E. S., Bernier, E. P., & Skerry, A. E. (2013). Core social cognition. In M. R. Banaji & S. A. Gelman (Eds.), *Navigating the social world: What infants, children, and other species can teach us* (pp. 11–16). New York: Oxford University Press. (p. 127)

Spencer, K. M., Nestor, P. G., Perlmutter, R., Niznikiewicz, M. A., Klump, M. C., Frumin, M., . . . McCarley, R. W. (2004). Neural synchrony indexes disordered perception and cognition in schizophrenia. *PNAS, 101,* 17288–17293. (p. 524)

Spencer, S. J., Logel, C., & Davies, P. G. (2016). Stereotype threat. *Annual Review of Psychology, 67,* 415–437. (p. 344)

Spencer, S. J., Steele, C. M., & Quinn, D. M. (1997). *Stereotype threat and women's math performance.* Unpublished manuscript, Hope College. (p. 344)

Sperling, G. (1960). The information available in brief visual presentations. *Psychological Monographs, 74* (Whole No. 498). (p. 270)

Sperry, R. W. (1964). *Problems outstanding in the evolution of brain function.* The James Arthur Lecture, delivered at the American Museum of Natural History, New York, NY. Cited in R. Ornstein (1977), *The psychology of consciousness* (2nd ed.). New York: Harcourt Brace Jovanovich. (p. 66)

Sperry, R. W. (1985). Changed concepts of brain and consciousness: Some value implications. *Zygon, 20,* 41–57. (p. 206)

Spiegel, A. (2015, January 8). Dark thoughts. From "Invisibilia," National Public Radio (npr.org). (p. 544)

Spiegel, D. (2007). The mind prepared: Hypnosis in surgery. *Journal of the National Cancer Institute, 99,* 1280–1281. (p. 224)

Spiegel, D. (2008, January 31). *Coming apart: Trauma and the fragmentation of the self.* Dana Foundation (dana.org). (p. 529)

Spielberger, C., & London, P. (1982). Rage boomerangs. *American Health, 1,* 52–56. (p. 392)

Sprecher, S., Treger, S., & Sakaluk, J. K. (2013). Premarital sexual standards and sociosexuality: Gender, ethnicity, and cohort differences. *Archives of Sexual Behavior, 42,* 1395–1405. (p. 183)

Spring, B., Pingitore, R., Bourgeois, M., Kessler, K. H., & Bruckner, E. (1992). *The effects and non-effects of skipping breakfast: Results of three studies.* Paper presented at the American Psychological Association convention. (p. 366)

Sproesser, G., Schupp, H. T., & Renner, B. (2014). The bright side of stress-induced eating: Eating more when stressed but less when pleased. *Psychological Science, 25,* 58–65. (pp. 354, 363)

Squire, L. R., & Zola-Morgan, S. (1991, September 20). The medial temporal lobe memory system. *Science, 253,* 1380–1386. (p. 277)

Srivastava, S., McGonigal, K. M., Richards, J. M., Butler, E. A., & Gross, J. J. (2006). Optimism in close relationships: How seeing things in a positive light makes them so. *Journal of Personality and Social Psychology, 91,* 143–153. (p. 399)

St-Onge, M.-P., McReynolds, A., Trivedi, Z. B., Roberts, A. L., Sy, M., & Hirsch, J. (2012). Sleep restriction leads to increased activation of brain regions sensitive to food stimuli. *American Journal of Clinical Nutrition, 95,* 818–824. (p. 93)

St. Clair, D., Xu, M., Wang, P., Yu, Y., Fang, Y., Zhang, F., . . . He, L. (2005). Rates of adult schizophrenia following prenatal exposure to the Chinese famine of 1959–1961. *Journal of the American Medical Association, 294,* 557–562. (p. 525)

Stacey, D., Bilbao, A., Maroteaux, M., Jia, T., Easton, A. E., Longueville, S., . . . the IMAGEN Consortium. (2012). *RASGRF2* regulates alcohol-induced reinforcement by influencing mesolimbic dopamine neuron activity and dopamine release. *PNAS, 109,* 21128–21133. (p. 111)

Stafford, T., & Dewar, M. (2014). Tracing the trajectory of skill learning with a very large sample of online game players. *Psychological Science, 25,* 511–518. (p. 272)

Stager, C. L., & Werker, J. F. (1997). Infants listen for more phonetic detail in speech perception than in word-learning tasks. *Nature, 388,* 381–382. (p. 314)

Stahl, A. E., & Feigenson, L. (2015). Observing the unexpected enhances infants' learning and exploration. *Science, 348,* 91–94. (p. 127)

Stanley, D., Phelps, E., & Banaji, M. (2008). The neural basis of implicit attitudes. *Current Directions in Psychological Science, 17,* 164–170. (p. 435)

Stanley, S., & Rhoades, G. (2016a, July 19). Testing a relationship is probably the worst reason to cohabit. *Family Studies* (family-studies.org). (p. 156)

Stanley, S., & Rhoades, G. (2016b, July/August). The perils of sowing your wild oats. *Psychology Today*, pp. 40–42. (p. 156)

Stanley, S. M., Rhoades, G. K., Amato, P. R., Markman, H. J., & Johnson, C. A. (2010). The timing of cohabitation and engagement: Impact on first and second marriages. *Journal of Marriage and Family*, 72, 906–918. (p. 156)

Stanovich, K. (1996). *How to think straight about psychology*. New York: HarperCollins. (p. 462)

Stanovich, K. E., & West, R. F. (2014a). The assessment of rational thinking: IQ ≠ RQ. *Teaching of Psychology*, 41, 265–271. (p. 345)

Stanovich, K. E., & West, R. F. (2014b). What intelligence tests miss. *Psychologist*, 27, 80–83. (p. 345)

Stanovich, K. E., West, R. F., & Toplak, M. E. (2013). My side bias, rational thinking, and intelligence. *Current Directions in Psychological Science*, 22, 259–264. (pp. 305, 345)

Starcke, K., & Brand, M. (2016). Effects of stress on decisions under uncertainty: A meta-analysis. *Psychological Bulletin*, 142, 909–933. (p. 385)

Stark, R. (2003a). For the glory of God: How monotheism led to reformations, science, witch-hunts, and the end of slavery. Princeton, NJ: Princeton University Press. (p. 3)

Stark, R. (2003b, October-November). False conflict: Christianity is not only compatible with science—it created it. *American Enterprise*, pp. 27–33. (p. 3)

Starzynski, L. L., Ullman, S. E., & Vasquez, A. L. (2017). Sexual assault survivors' experiences with mental health professionals: A qualitative study. *Women & Therapy*, 40, 228–246. (p. 170)

Statista. (2017). *Reported violent crime in the United States from 1990 to 2015*. Retrieved from statista.com/statistics/191219/reported-violent-crime-rate-in-the-usa-since-1990 (p. 18)

Statistics Canada. (1999, September). *Statistical report on the health of Canadians*. Prepared by the Federal, Provincial and Territorial Advisory Committee on Population Health for the Meeting of Ministers of Health, Charlottetown, P. E. I. (p. 385)

Statistics Canada. (2011). *Marital status: Overview, 2011*. Table 2: Divorces and crude divorce rates, Canada, provinces and territories, 1981 to 2008. Retrieved from statcan.gc.ca/pub/91-209-x/2013001/article/11788/tbl/tbl2-eng.htm (p. 156)

Statistics Canada. (2013). Table A.5.1. Second language immersion program enrolments in public elementary and secondary schools, Canada, provinces and territories, 2005/2006 to 2009/2010. Retrieved from statcan.gc.ca/pub/81-595-m/2011095/tbl/tbla.5.1-eng.htm (p. 320)

Staub, E. (1989). *The roots of evil: The psychological and cultural sources of genocide*. New York: Cambridge University Press. (p. 419)

Stavrinos, D., Pope, C. N., Shen, J., & Schwebel, D. C. (2017). Distracted walking, bicycling, and driving: Systematic review and meta-analysis of mobile technology and youth crash risk. *Child Development*. Advance online publication. doi:10.1111/cdev.12827 (p. 82)

Steel, P., Schmidt, J., & Schultz, J. (2008). Refining the relationship between personality and subject well-being. *Psychological Bulletin*, 134, 138–161. (p. 411)

Steele, C. M. (1990, May). A conversation with Claude Steele. *APS Observer*, pp. 11–17. (p. 342)

Steele, C. M. (1995, August 31). Black students live down to expectations. *The New York Times* (nytimes.com). (p. 344)

Steele, C. M. (2010). *Whistling Vivaldi: And other clues to how stereotypes affect us*. New York: Norton. (p. 344)

Steele, C. M., & Josephs, R. A. (1990). Alcohol myopia: Its prized and dangerous effects. *American Psychologist*, 45, 921–933. (p. 104)

Steele, C. M., Spencer, S. J., & Aronson, J. (2002). Contending with group image: The psychology of stereotype and social identity threat. *Advances in Experimental Social Psychology*, 34, 379–440. (p. 344)

Steinberg, L. (1987, September). Bound to bicker. *Psychology Today*, pp. 36–39. (p. 148)

Steinberg, L. (2001). We know some things: Parent–adolescent relationships in retrospect and prospect. *Journal of Research on Adolescence*, 11, 1–19. (p. 138)

Steinberg, L. (2007). Risk taking in adolescence: New perspectives from brain and behavioral science. *Current Directions in Psychological Science*, 16, 55–59. (p. 142)

Steinberg, L. (2010, March). Analyzing adolescence (Interview by Sara Martin). *Monitor on Psychology*, pp. 26–29. (p. 142)

Steinberg, L. (2012, Spring). Should the science of adolescent brain development inform public policy? *Issues in Science and Technology*, pp. 67–78. (p. 142)

Steinberg, L. (2013). The influence of neuroscience on U.S. Supreme Court decisions involving adolescents' criminal culpability. *Nature Reviews Neuroscience*, 14, 513–518. (p. 142)

Steinberg, L. (2015). How to improve the health of American adolescents. *Perspectives on Psychological Science*, 10, 711–715. (p. 178)

Steinberg, L., Cauffman, E., Woolard, J., Graham, S., & Banich, M. (2009). Are adolescents less mature than adults? Minors' access to abortion, the juvenile death penalty, and the alleged APA "flip-flop." *American Psychologist*, 64, 583–594. (p. 142)

Steinberg, L., Lamborn, S. D., Darling, N., Mounts, N. S., & Dornbusch, S. M. (1994). Overtime changes in adjustment and competence among adolescents from authoritative, authoritarian, indulgent, and neglectful families. *Child Development*, 65, 754–770. (p. 139)

Steinberg, L., & Morris, A. S. (2001). Adolescent development. *Annual Review of Psychology*, 52, 83–110. (p. 147)

Steinberg, L., & Scott, E. S. (2003). Less guilty by reason of adolescence: Developmental immaturity, diminished responsibility, and the juvenile death penalty. *American Psychologist*, 58, 1009–1018. (p. 142)

Steinberg, N. (1993, February). Astonishing love stories (from an earlier United Press International report). *Games*, p. 47. (p. 447)

Steiner, J. L., Murphy, E. A., McClellan, J. L., Carmichael, M. D., & Davis, J. M. (2011). Exercise training increases mitochondrial biogenesis in the brain. *Journal of Applied Physiology*, 111, 1066–1071. (p. 153)

Steinert, C., Munder, T., Rabung, S., Hoyer, J., & Leichsenring, F. (2017). Psychodynamic therapy: As efficacious as other empirically supported treatments? A meta-analysis testing equivalence of outcomes. *American Journal of Psychiatry*, 174, 943–953. (p. 553)

Stellar, J. E., John-Henderson, N., Anderson, C. L., Gordon, A. M., McNeil, G. D., & Keltner, D. (2015). Positive affect and markers of inflammation: Discrete positive emotions predict lower levels of inflammatory cytokines. *Emotion*, 15, 129–133. (p. 407)

Stender, J., Gosseries, O., Bruno, M.-A., Charland-Verville, V., Vanhaudenhuyse, A., Demertzi, A., . . . Laurey, S. (2014). Diagnostic precision of PET imaging and functional MRI in disorders of consciousness: A clinical validation study. *The Lancet*, 384, 514–522. (p. 81)

Stephens-Davidowitz, S. (2013, December 7). How many American men are gay? *The New York Times* (nytimes.com). (p. 179)

Stephens-Davidowitz, S. (2014). The effects of racial animus on a black candidate: Evidence using Google search data. *Journal of Public Economics*, 118, 26–40. (pp. 436, 437)

Stephens-Davidowitz, S. (2017). *Everybody lies: Big data, new data, and what the internet can tell us about who we really are*. New York: Dey St. (Morrow). (pp. 22, 97, 468)

Steptoe, A., Chida, Y., Hamer, M., & Wardle, J. (2010). Author reply: Meta-analysis of stress-related factors in cancer. *Nature Reviews: Clinical Oncology*, 7. doi:10.1038/ncponc1134-c2 (p. 390)

Steptoe, A., & Wardle, J. (2011). Positive affect measured using ecological momentary assessment and survival in older men and woman. *PNAS*, 108, 18244–18248. (p. 392)

Steptoe, A., & Wardle, J. (2017). Life skills, wealth, health, and wellbeing later in life. *PNAS*, 114, 4354–4359. (p. 357)

Stern, M., & Karraker, K. H. (1989). Sex stereotyping of infants: A review of gender labeling studies. *Sex Roles*, 20, 501–522. (p. 196)

Sternberg, E. M. (2009). *Healing spaces: The science of place and well-being*. Cambridge, MA: Harvard University Press. (p. 389)

Sternberg, R. J. (1985). *Beyond IQ: A triarchic theory of human intelligence*. New York: Cambridge University Press. (p. 325)

Sternberg, R. J. (1988). Applying cognitive theory to the testing and teaching of intelligence. *Applied Cognitive Psychology*, 2, 231–255. (p. 306)

Sternberg, R. J. (2003). Our research program validating the triarchic theory of successful intelligence: Reply to Gottfredson. *Intelligence*, 31, 399–413. (p. 306)

Sternberg, R. J. (2006). The Rainbow Project: Enhance the SAT through assessments of analytical, practical, and creative skills. *Intelligence*, 34, 321–350. (p. 307)

Sternberg, R. J. (2011). The theory of successful intelligence. In R. J. Sternberg & S. B. Kaufman (Eds.), *The Cambridge handbook of intelligence*. New York: Cambridge University Press. (p. 325)

Sternberg, R. J., & Grajek, S. (1984). The nature of love. *Journal of Personality and Social Psychology*, 47, 312–329. (p. 452)

Sternberg, R. J., & Kaufman, J. C. (1998). Human abilities. *Annual Review of Psychology*, 49, 479–502. (p. 323)

Sternberg, R. J., & Lubart, T. I. (1991). An investment theory of creativity and its development. *Human Development*, 34, 1–31. (p. 306)

Sternberg, R. J., & Lubart, T. I. (1992). Buy low and sell high: An investment approach to creativity. *Psychological Science*, 1, 1–5. (p. 306)

Sterzing, P. R., Shattuck, P. T., Narendorf, S. C., Wagner, M., & Cooper, B. P. (2012). Bullying involvement and autism spectrum disorders: Prevalence and correlates of bullying involvement among adolescents with an autism spectrum disorder. *Archives of Pediatric and Adolescent Medicine*, 166, 1058–1064. (p. 131)

Stetter, F., & Kupper, S. (2002). Autogenic training: A meta-analysis of clinical outcome studies. *Applied Psychophysiology and Biofeedback*, 27, 45–98. (p. 403)

Stevenson, H. W. (1992). Learning from Asian schools. *Scientific American*, 267, 70–76. (p. 342)

Stevenson, R. J. (2014). Flavor binding: Its nature and cause. *Psychological Bulletin, 140,* 487–510. (p. 228)

Stice, E. (2002). Risk and maintenance factors for eating pathology: A meta-analytic review. *Psychological Bulletin, 128,* 825–848. (p. 532)

Stice, E., Ng, J., & Shaw, H. (2010). Risk factors and prodromal eating pathology. *Journal of Child Psychology and Psychiatry, 51,* 518–525. (p. 532)

Stice, E., Spangler, D., & Agras, W. S. (2001). Exposure to media-portrayed thin-ideal images adversely affects vulnerable girls: A longitudinal experiment. *Journal of Social and Clinical Psychology, 20,* 270–288. (p. 533)

Stickgold, R. (2000, March 7). Quoted in S. Blakeslee, For better learning, researchers endorse "sleep on it" adage. *The New York Times,* p. F2. (p. 98)

Stickgold, R. (2012). Sleep, memory and dreams: Putting it all together. In *Aquém e além do cérebro* [Behind and beyond the brain]. Bial: Fundação Bial Institution of Public Utility. (p. 97)

Stillman, T. F., Baumeister, R. F., Vohs, K. D., Lambert, N. M., Fincham, F. D., & Brewer, L. E. (2010). Personal philosophy and personnel achievement: Belief in free will predicts better job performance. *Social Psychological and Personality Science, 1,* 43–50. (p. 397)

Stillman, T. F., Lambet, N. M., Fincham, F. D., & Baumeister, R. F. (2011). Meaning as magnetic force: Evidence that meaning in life promotes interpersonal appeal. *Social Psychological and Personality Science, 2,* 13–20. (p. 566)

Stinson, D. A., Logel, C., Zanna, M. P., Holmes, J. G., Cameron, J. J., Wood, J. V., & Spencer, S. J. (2008). The cost of lower self-esteem: Testing a self- and social-bonds model of health. *Journal of Personality and Social Psychology, 94,* 412–428. (p. 401)

Stith, S. M., Rosen, K. H., Middleton, K. A., Busch, A. L., Lunderberg, K., & Carlton, R. P. (2000). The intergenerational transmission of spouse abuse: A meta-analysis. *Journal of Marriage and the Family, 62,* 640–654. (p. 262)

Stockton, M. C., & Murnen, S. K. (1992, June). *Gender and sexual arousal in response to sexual stimuli: A meta-analytic review.* Paper presented at the Fourth Annual Convention of the American Psychological Society, San Diego, CA. (p. 176)

Stoll, G., Rieger, S., Lüdtke, O., Nagengast, B., Trautwein, U., & Roberts, B. W. (2017). Vocational interests assessed at the end of high school predict life outcomes assessed 10 years later over and above IQ and big five personality traits. *Journal of Personality and Social Psychology, 113,* 167–184. (p. B-3)

Stone, A. A., & Neale, J. M. (1984). Effects of severe daily events on mood. *Journal of Personality and Social Psychology, 46,* 137–144. (p. 408)

Stone, A. A., Schwartz, J. E., Broderick, J. E., & Deaton, A. (2010). A snapshot of the age distribution of psychological well-being in the United States. *PNAS, 107,* 9985–9990. (p. 158)

Stone, A. A., Schwartz, J. E., Broderick, J. E., & Shiffman, S. S. (2005). Variability of momentary pain predicts recall of weekly pain: A consequences of the peak (or salience) memory heuristic. *Personality and Social Psychology Bulletin, 31,* 1340–1346. (p. 223)

Stone, G. (2006, February 17). Homeless man discovered to be lawyer with amnesia. *ABC News* (abcnews.go.com). (p. 527)

Stop Street Harrassment. (2018). *The facts behind the #metoo movement: A national study on sexual harassment and assault.* Reston, Virginia. (p. 170)

Storbeck, J., Robinson, M. D., & McCourt, M. E. (2006). Semantic processing precedes affect retrieval: The neurological case for cognitive primary in visual processing. *Review of General Psychology, 10,* 41–55. (p. 371)

Storm, B. C., & Jobe, T. A. (2012). Retrieval-induced forgetting predicts failure to recall negative autobiographical memories. *Psychological Science, 23,* 1356–1363. (p. 278)

Storm, L., Tressoldi, P. E., & Di Risio, L. (2010a). Meta-analysis of free-response studies, 1992–2008: Assessing the noise reduction model in parapsychology. *Psychological Bulletin, 136,* 471–485. (p. 230)

Storm, L., Tressoldi, P. E., & Di Risio, L. (2010b). A meta-analysis with nothing to hide: Reply to Hyman (2010). *Psychological Bulletin, 136,* 491–494. (p. 230)

Storms, M. D. (1973). Videotape and the attribution process: Reversing actors' and observers' points of view. *Journal of Personality and Social Psychology, 27,* 165–175. (p. 417)

Storms, M. D. (1983). *Development of sexual orientation.* Washington, DC: Office of Social and Ethical Responsibility, American Psychological Association. (p. 180)

Storms, M. D., & Thomas, G. C. (1977). Reactions to physical closeness. *Journal of Personality and Social Psychology, 35,* 412–418. (p. 430)

Stothart, C., Mitchum, A., & Yehnert, C. (2015). The attentional cost of receiving a cell phone notification. *Journal of Experimental Psychology: Human Perception and Performance, 41,* 893–897. (p. 195)

Stowell, J. R., Oldham, T., & Bennett, D. (2010). Using student response systems ("clickers") to combat conformity and shyness. *Teaching of Psychology, 37,* 135–140. (p. 424)

Strack, F. (2016). Reflection on the smiling preregistered replication report. *Perspectives on Psychological Science, 11,* 929–930. (p. 381)

Strain, J. F., Womack, K. B., Didenbani, N., Spence, J. S., Conover, H., Hart, J., Jr., . . . Cullum, C. M. (2015). Imaging correlates of memory and concussion history in retired National Football League athletes. *JAMA Neurology, 72,* 773–780. (p. 56)

Strand, L. B., Mukamal, K. J., Halasz, J., Vatten, L. J., & Janszky, I. (2016). Short-term public health impact of the July 22, 2011, terrorist attacks in Norway: A nationwide register-based study. *Psychosomatic Medicine, 78,* 525–531. (p. 385)

Strang, S., Utikal, V., Fischbacher, U., Weber, B., & Falk, A. (2014). Neural correlates of receiving an apology and active forgiveness: An fMRI study. *PLoS ONE, 9,* e87654. (p. 394)

Strange, D., Hayne, H., & Garry, M. (2008). A photo, a suggestion, a false memory. *Applied Cognitive Psychology, 22,* 587–603. (p. 291)

Strasburger, V. C., Jordan, A. B., & Donnerstein, E. (2010). Health effects of media on children and adolescents. *Pediatrics, 125,* 756–767. (p. 262)

Stratton, G. M. (1896). Some preliminary experiments on vision without inversion of the retinal image. *Psychological Review, 3,* 611–617. (p. 214)

Straub, R. O., Seidenberg, M. S., Bever, T. G., & Terrace, H. S. (1979). Serial learning in the pigeon. *Journal of the Experimental Analysis of Behavior, 32,* 137–148. (p. 318)

Straus, M. A., & Gelles, R. J. (1980). *Behind closed doors: Violence in the American family.* New York: Anchor/Doubleday. (p. 249)

Straus, M. A., Sugarman, D. B., & Giles-Sims, J. (1997). Spanking by parents and subsequent antisocial behavior of children. *Archives of Pediatric Adolescent Medicine, 151,* 761–767. (p. 249)

Strawbridge, W. J. (1999). *Mortality and religious involvement: A review and critique of the results, the methods, and the measures.* Paper presented at a Harvard University conference on religion and health, sponsored by the National Institute for Health Research and the John Templeton Foundation. (p. 405)

Strawbridge, W. J., Cohen, R. D., & Shema, S. J. (1997). Frequent attendance at religious services and mortality over 28 years. *American Journal of Public Health, 87,* 957–961. (p. 405)

Strick, M., Dijksterhuis, A., Bos, M. W., Sjoerdsma, A., & van Baaren, R. B. (2011). A meta-analysis on unconscious thought effects. *Social Cognition, 29,* 738–762. (p. 305)

Strick, M., Dijksterhuis, A., & van Baaren, R. B. (2010). Unconscious-thought effects take place off-line, not on-line. *Psychological Science, 21,* 484–488. (p. 305)

Stroebe, M., Finenauer, C., Wijngaards-de Meij, L., Schut, H., van den Bout, J., & Stroebe, W. (2013). Partner-oriented self-regulation among bereaved parents: The costs of holding in grief for the partner's sake. *Psychological Science, 24,* 395–402. (p. 159)

Stroebe, W. (2012). The truth about Triplett (1898), but nobody seems to care. *Perspectives on Psychological Science, 7,* 54–57. (p. 429)

Stroebe, W. (2013). Firearm possession and violent death: A critical review. *Aggression and Violent Behavior, 18,* 709–721. (p. 441)

Stroebe, W., Schut, H., & Stroebe, M. S. (2005). Grief work, disclosure and counseling: Do they help the bereaved? *Clinical Psychology Review, 25,* 395–414. (p. 160)

Stroud, L. R., Panadonatos, G. D., Rodriguez, D., McCallum, M., Salisbury, A. L., Phipps, M. G., . . . Marsit, C. J. (2014). Maternal smoking during pregnancy and infant stress response: Test of a prenatal programming hypothesis. *Psychoneuroendocrinology, 48,* 29–40. (p. 120)

Strully, K. W. (2009). Job loss and health in the U.S. labor market. *Demography, 46,* 221–246. (p. 385)

Stuart, G. J., & Spruston, N. (2015). Dendritic integration: 60 years of progress. *Nature Neuroscience, 18,* 1713–1721. (p. 39)

Stubbs, B., Vancampfort, D., Rosenbaum, S., Firth, J., Cosco, T., Veronese, N., . . . Schuch, F. B. (2017). An examination of the anxiolytic effects of exercise for people with anxiety and stress-related disorders: A meta-analysis. *Psychiatry Research, 249,* 102–108. (p. 402)

Studte, S., Bridger, E., & Mecklinger, A. (2017). Sleep spindles during a nap correlate with post sleep memory performance for highly rewarded word-pairs. *Brain and Language, 167,* 28–35. (p. 88)

Štulhofer, A., Šoh, D., Jelaska, N., Baćak, V., & Landripet, I. (2011). Religiosity and sexual risk behavior among Croatian college students, 1998–2008. *Journal of Sex Research, 48,* 360–371. (p. 178)

Stutzer, A., & Frey, B. S. (2006). Does marriage make people happy, or do happy people get married? *Journal of Socio-Economics, 35,* 326–347. (p. 407)

Subrahmanyam, K., & Greenfield, P. (2008). Online communication and adolescent relationships. *The Future of Children, 18,* 119–146. (p. 148)

Suddath, R. L., Christison, G. W., Torrey, E. F., Casanova, M. F., & Weinberger, D. R. (1990). Anatomical abnormalities in the brains of monozygotic twins discordant for schizophrenia. *New England Journal of Medicine, 322,* 789–794. (p. 527)

Sue, S., Zane, N., Hall, G. C. N., & Berger, L. K. (2009). The case for cultural competency in psychotherapeutic interventions. *Annual Review of Psychology, 60,* 525–548. (p. 556)

Suedfeld, P., & Mocellin, J. S. P. (1987). The "sensed presence" in unusual environments. *Environment and Behavior, 19,* 33–52. (p. 108)

Sugaya, L., Hasin, D. S., Olfson, M., Lin, K.-H., Grant, B. F., & Blanco, C. (2012). Child physical abuse and adult mental health: A national study. *Journal of Traumatic Stress, 25,* 384–392. (p. 138)

Suglia, S. F., Kara, S., & Robinson, W. R. (2014). Sleep duration and obesity among adolescents transitioning to adulthood: Do results differ by sex? *The Journal of Pediatrics, 165,* 750–754. (p. 93)

Sulik, M. J., Blair, C., Mills-Koonce, R., Berry, D., Greenberg, M., & Family Life Project Investigators. (2015). Early parenting and the development of externalizing behavior problems: Longitudinal mediation through children's executive function. *Child Development, 86,* 1588–1603. (p. 139)

Sullivan, K. T., Pasch, L. A., Johnson, M. D., & Bradbury, T. N. (2010). Social support, problem solving, and the longitudinal course of newlywed marriage. *Journal of Personality and Social Psychology, 98,* 631–644. (p. 452)

Sullivan, P. F., Neale, M. C., & Kendler, K. S. (2000). Genetic epidemiology of major depression: Review and meta-analysis. *American Journal of Psychiatry, 157,* 1552–1562. (p. 518)

Suls, J. M., & Tesch, F. (1978). Students' preferences for information about their test performance: A social comparison study. *Journal of Experimental Social Psychology, 8,* 189–197. (p. 410)

Summers, M. (1996, December 9). Mister Clean. *People Weekly,* pp. 139–142. (p. 493)

Sun, G. J., Zhou, Y., Ito, S., Bonaguidi, M. A., Stein-O'Brien, G., Kawasaki, N. K., . . . Song, H. (2015). Latent tri-lineage potential of adult hippocampal neural stem cells revealed by Nf1 inactivation. *Nature Neuroscience, 18,* 1722–1724. (p. 64)

Sundstrom, E., De Meuse, K. P., & Futrell, D. (1990). Work teams: Applications and effectiveness. *American Psychologist, 45,* 120–133. (p. B-11)

Sung, S., Simpson, J. A., Griskevicius, V., Sally, I., Kuo, C., Schlomer, G. L., & Belsky, J. (2016). Secure infant-mother attachment buffers the effect of early-life stress on age of menarche. *Psychological Science, 27,* 667–674. (p. 167)

Sunstein, C. R., Bobadilla-Suarez, S., Lazzaro, S. C., & Sharot, T. (2016). How people update beliefs about climate change: Good news and bad news. Social Science Research Network (ssrn.com). (p. 304)

Suomi, S. J. (1986). Anxiety-like disorders in young nonhuman primates. In R. Gettleman (Ed.), *Anxiety disorders of childhood.* New York: Guilford Press. (p. 511)

Suomi, S. J., Collins, M. L., Harlow, H. F., & Ruppenthal, G. C. (1976). Effects of maternal and peer separations on young monkeys. *Journal of Child Psychology and Psychiatry, 17,* 101–112. (p. 220)

Suppes, P. (1982). Quoted in R. H. Ennis, Children's ability to handle Piaget's propositional logic: A conceptual critique. In S. Modgil & C. Modgil (Eds.), *Jean Piaget: Consensus and controversy* (pp. 101–130). New York: Praeger. (p. 129)

Surgeon General. (1986). *The Surgeon General's workshop on pornography and public health,* June 22–24. Report prepared by E. P. Mulvey & J. L. Haugaard and released by Office of the Surgeon General on August 4, 1986. (p. 444)

Surgeon General. (2012). *Preventing tobacco use among youth and young adults: A report of the Surgeon General.* Rockville, MD: Department of Health and Human Services, Office of the Surgeon General. (p. 112)

Surgeon General's Office. (1999). *Mental health: A report of the surgeon general.* Rockville, MD: U.S. Department of Health and Human Services. (p. 503)

Susser, E. S., Neugenbauer, R., Hoek, H. W., Brown, A. S., Lin, S., Labovitz, D., & Gorman, J. M. (1996). Schizophrenia after prenatal famine. *Archives of General Psychiatry, 53*(1), 25–31. (p. 525)

Sutcliffe, J. S. (2008). Insights into the pathogenesis of autism. *Science, 321,* 208–209. (p. 131)

Sutin, A. R., Ferrucci, L., Zonderman, A. B., & Terracciano, A. (2011). Personality and obesity across the adult life span. *Journal of Personality and Social Psychology, 101,* 579–592. (p. 480)

Swami, V. (2015). Cultural influences on body size ideals: Unpacking the impact of Westernization and modernization. *European Psychologist, 20,* 44–51. (p. 365)

Swami, V., Frederick, D. A., Aavik, T., Alcalay, L., Allik, J., Anderson, D., . . . Zivcic-Becirevic, I. (2010). The attractive female body weight and female body dissatisfaction in 26 countries across 10 world regions: Results of the International Body Project I. *Personality and Social Psychology Bulletin, 36,* 309–325. (p. 532)

Swann, W. B., Jr., Chang-Schneider, C., & McClarty, K. L. (2007). Do people's self-views matter? Self-concept and self-esteem in everyday life. *American Psychologist, 62,* 84–94. (p. 486)

Swart, H., Hewstone, M., Christ, O., & Voci, A. (2011). Affective mediators of intergroup contact: A three-wave longitudinal study in South Africa. *Journal of Personality and Social Psychology, 101,* 1221–1238. (p. 457)

Swartz, J. R., Hariri, A. R., & Williamson, D. E. (2016). An epigenetic mechanism links socioeconomic status to changes in depression-related brain function in high-risk adolescents. *Molecular Psychiatry, 22,* 209–214. (p. 74)

Swift, A. (2013, October 28). *Personal safety top reason Americans own guns today.* Gallup (gallup.com). (p. 441)

Swift, A. (2016, November 9). Americans' perception of US crime problem are steady. *Gallup.* Retrieved from gallup.com/poll/197318/americans-perceptions-crime-problem-steady.aspx (p. 18)

Symbaluk, D. G., Heth, C. D., Cameron, J., & Pierce, W. D. (1997). Social modeling, monetary incentives, and pain endurance: The role of self-efficacy and pain perception. *Personality and Social Psychology Bulletin, 23,* 258–269. (p. 223)

Symond, M. B., Harris, A. W. F., Gordon, E., & Williams, L. M. (2005). "Gamma synchrony" in first-episode schizophrenia: A disorder of temporal connectivity? *American Journal of Psychiatry, 162,* 459–465. (p. 524)

Symons, C. S., & Johnson, B. T. (1997). The self-reference effect in memory: A meta-analysis. *Psychological Bulletin, 121,* 371–394. (p. 274)

Szkodny, L. E., Newman, M. G., & Goldfried, M. R. (2014). Clinical experiences in conducting empirically supported treatments for generalized anxiety disorder. *Behavior Therapy, 45,* 7–20. (p. 546)

Tackett, J. L., Herzhoff, K., Kushner, S. C., & Rule, N. (2016). Thin slices of child personality: Perceptual, situational, and behavioral contributions. *Journal of Personality and Social Psychology, 110,* 150–166. (p. 481)

Tadmor, C. T., Galinsky, A. D., & Maddux, W. W. (2012). Getting the most out of living abroad: Biculturalism and integrative complexity as key drivers of creative and professional success. *Journal of Personality and Social Psychology, 103,* 520–542. (p. 307)

Taha, F. A. (1972). A comparative study of how sighted and blind perceive the manifest content of dreams. *National Review of Social Sciences, 9*(3), 28. (p. 97)

Taheri, S. (2004, December 20). Does the lack of sleep make you fat? *University of Bristol Research News* (bristol.ac.uk). (p. 365)

Taheri, S., Lin, L., Austin, D., Young, T., & Mignot, E. (2004). Short sleep duration is associated with reduced leptin, elevated ghrelin, and increased body mass index. *PLoS Medicine, 1,* e62. (p. 365)

Tajfel, H. (Ed.). (1982). *Social identity and intergroup relations.* New York: Cambridge University Press. (p. 438)

Takizawa, R., Maughan, B., & Arseneault, L. (2014). Adult health outcomes of childhood bullying victimization: Evidence from a five-decade longitudinal British birth cohort. *American Journal of Psychiatry, 171,* 777–784. (p. 148)

Talarico, J. M., & Moore, K. M. (2012). Memories of "the rivalry": Differences in how fans of the winning and losing teams remember the same game. *Applied Cognitive Psychology, 26,* 746–756. (p. 278)

Talbot, M. (1999, October). The Rorschach chronicles. *The New York Times* (nytimes.com). (p. 466)

Talhelm, T., Zhang, X., Oishi, S., Shimin, C., Duan, D., Lan, X., & Kitayama, S. (2014). Large-scale psychological differences within China explained by rice versus wheat agriculture. *Science, 344,* 603–608. (p. 490)

Tamres, L. K., Janicki, D., & Helgeson, V. S. (2002). Sex differences in coping behavior: A meta-analytic review and an examination of relative coping. *Personality and Social Psychology Review, 6,* 2–30. (p. 165)

Tanaka, T., Yamamoto, T., & Haruno, M. (2017). Brain response patterns to economic inequity predict present and future depression indices. *Nature Human Behavior, 1,* 748–756. (p. 410)

Tang, S.-H., & Hall, V. C. (1995). The overjustification effect: A meta-analysis. *Applied Cognitive Psychology, 9,* 365–404. (p. 358)

Tang, Y. Y., Ma, Y., Wang, J., Fan, Y., Feng, S., Lu, Q., . . . Posner, M. I. (2007). Short-term meditation training improves attention and self-regulation. *PNAS, 104,* 17152–17156. (p. 404)

Tannen, D. (1990). *You just don't understand: Women and men in conversation.* New York: Morrow. (p. 163)

Tannen, D. (2001). *You just don't understand: Women and men in conversation.* New York: HarperCollins. (p. 10)

Tanner, J. M. (1978). *Fetus into man: Physical growth from conception to maturity.* Cambridge, MA: Harvard University Press. (p. 165)

Tardif, T., Fletcher, P., Liang, W., Zhang, Z., Kaciroti, N., & Marchman, V. A. (2008). Baby's first 10 words. *Developmental Psychology, 44,* 929–938. (p. 314)

Tarrant, M., Branscombe, N. R., Warner, R. H., & Weston, D. (2012). Social identity and perceptions of torture: It's moral when we do it. *Journal of Experimental Social Psychology, 48,* 513–518. (p. 456)

Tasbihsazan, R., Nettelbeck, T., & Kirby, N. (2003). Predictive validity of the Fagan test of infant intelligence. *British Journal of Developmental Psychology, 21,* 585–597. (p. 332)

Tatlow, D. K. (2016, June 11). Doctor's plan for full-body transplants raises doubts even in daring China. *The New York Times* (nytimes.com). (p. 37)

Taubes, G. (2001). The soft science of dietary fat. *Science, 291,* 2536–2545. (p. 366)

Taubes, G. (2002, July 7). What if it's all been a big fat lie? *The New York Times* (nytimes.com). (p. 366)

Tausch, N., Hewstone, M., Kenworthy, J. B., Psaltis, C., Schmid, K., Popan, J. R., . . . Hughes, J. (2010). Secondary transfer effects of intergroup contact: Alternative accounts and underlying processes. *Journal of Personality and Social Psychology, 99,* 282–302. (p. 457)

Tavernier, R., & Willoughby, T. (2014). Bidirectional associations between sleep (quality and duration) and psychosocial functioning across the university years. *Developmental Psychology, 50,* 674–682. (p. 93)

Tavernise, S. (2013, February 13). To reduce suicide rates, new focus turns to guns. *The New York Times* (nytimes.com). (p. 501)

Tavernise, S. (2016, February 29). "Female Viagra" only modestly increases sexual satisfaction, study finds. *The New York Times* (nytimes.com). (p. 28)

Tavris, C. (1982, November). Anger defused. *Psychology Today,* pp. 25–35. (p. 393)

Tavris, C., & Aronson, E. (2007). *Mistakes were made (but not by me).* Orlando, FL: Harcourt. (p. 288)

Tay, L., & Diener, E. (2011). Needs and subjective well-being around the world. *Journal of Personality and Social Psychology, 101,* 354–365. (p. 351)

Taylor-Covill, G. A., & Eves, F. F. (2016). Carrying a biological "backpack": Quasi-experimental effects of weight status and body fat change on perceived steepness. *Journal of Experimental Psychology: Human Perception and Performance, 42,* 331–338. (p. 197)

Taylor, C. (2017). Creativity and mood disorder: A systematic review and meta-analysis. *Perspectives on Psychological Science, 12,* 1040-1076. (p. 515)

Taylor, C. A., Manganello, J. A., Lee, S. J., & Rice, J. C. (2010). Mothers' spanking of 3-year-old children and subsequent risk of children's aggressive behavior. *Pediatrics, 125,* 1057–1065. (p. 250)

Taylor, K., & Rohrer, D. (2010). The effects of interleaved practice. *Applied Cognitive Psychology, 24,* 837–848. (p. 34)

Taylor, L. E., Swerdfeger, A. L., & Eslick, G. D. (2014). Vaccines are not associated with autism: An evidence-based meta-analysis of case-control and cohort studies. *Vaccine, 32,* 3623–3629. (p. 131)

Taylor, P. (2014). *The next America: Boomers, millennials, and the looming generational showdown.* New York: Public Affairs. (p. 135)

Taylor, P. J., Gooding, P., Wood, A. M., & Tarrier, N. (2011). The role of defeat and entrapment in depression, anxiety, and suicide. *Psychological Bulletin, 137,* 391–420. (p. 501)

Taylor, P. J., Russ-Eft, D. F., & Chan, D. W. L. (2005). A meta-analytic review of behavior modeling training. *Journal of Applied Psychology, 90,* 692–709. (p. 261)

Taylor, S. (2013). Molecular genetics of obsessive-compulsive disorder: A comprehensive meta-analysis of genetic association studies. *Molecular Psychiatry, 18,* 799–805. (p. 511)

Taylor, S., Kuch, K., Koch, W. J., Crockett, D. J., & Passey, G. (1998). The structure of posttraumatic stress symptoms. *Journal of Abnormal Psychology, 107,* 154–160. (p. 321)

Taylor, S. E. (2002). *The tending instinct: How nurturing is essential to who we are and how we live.* New York: Times Books. (p. 165)

Taylor, S. E. (2006). Tend and befriend: Biobehavioral bases of affiliation under stress. *Current Directions in Psychological Science, 15,* 273–277. (p. 388)

Taylor, S. E., Cousino, L. K., Lewis, B. P., Gruenewald, T. L., Gurung, R. A. R., & Updegraff, J. A. (2000). Biobehavioral responses to stress in females: Tend-and-befriend, not fight-or-flight. *Psychological Review, 107,* 411–430. (p. 388)

Taylor, S. F., Bhati, M. T., Dubin, M. J., Hawkins, J. M., Lisanby, S. H., Morales, O., . . . Watcharotone, K. (2017). A naturalistic, multi-site study of repetitive transcranial magnetic stimulation therapy for depression. *Journal of Affective Disorders, 208,* 284–290. (p. 564)

Taylor, S. P., & Chermack, S. T. (1993). Alcohol, drugs and human physical aggression. *Journal of Studies on Alcohol, Supplement 11,* 78–88. (p. 442)

Taylor, V. J., & Walton, G. M. (2011). Stereotype threat undermines academic learning. *Personality and Social Psychology Bulletin, 37,* 1055–1067. (p. 344)

Tedeschi, R. G., & Calhoun, L. G. (2004). Posttraumatic growth: Conceptual foundations and empirical evidence. *Psychological Inquiry, 15,* 1–18. (p. 567)

Teghtsoonian, R. (1971). On the exponents in Stevens' law and the constant in Ekman's law. *Psychological Review, 78,* 71–80. (p. 193)

Teicher, M. H., & Samson, J. A. (2016). Annual research review: Enduring neurobiological effects of childhood abuse and neglect. *Journal of Child Psychology and Psychiatry, 57,* 241–266. (p. 137)

Teller. (2009, April 20). Quoted by J. Lehrer, Magic and the brain: Teller reveals the neuroscience of illusion. *Wired Magazine* (wired.com). (p. 83)

Telzer, E. H., Flannery, J., Shapiro, M., Humphreys, K. L., Goff, B., Gabard-Durman, L., . . . Tottenham, N. (2013). Early experience shapes amygdala sensitivity to race: An international adoption design. *The Journal of Neuroscience, 33,* 13484–13488. (p. 439)

ten Brinke, L., Liu, C. C., Keltner, D., & Srivastava, S. B. (2016a). Virtues, vices, and political influence in the U.S. Senate. *Psychological Science, 27,* 85–93. (p. B-11)

ten Brinke, L., Vohs, K. D., & Carney. D. (2016b). Can ordinary people detect deception after all? *Trends in Cognitive Sciences, 20,* 579–588. (p. 376)

Tenenbaum, H. R., & Leaper, C. (2002). Are parents' gender schemas related to their children's gender-related cognitions? A meta-analysis. *Developmental Psychology, 38,* 615–630. (p. 169)

Tenopyr, M. L. (1997). Improving the workplace: Industrial/organizational psychology as a career. In R. J. Sternberg (Ed.), *Career paths in psychology: Where your degree can take you.* Washington, DC: American Psychological Association. (p. B-5)

Tepper, S. J. (2000). Fiction reading in America: Explaining the gender gap. *Poetics, 27,* 255–275. (p. 378)

Terada, S., Sakurai, Y., Nakahara, H., & Fujisawa, S. (2017). Temporal and rate coding for discrete event sequences in the hippocampus. *Neuron, 94,* 1248–1262. (p. 276)

Terao, T., Ohgami, H., Shlotsuki, I., Ishil, N., & Iwata, N. (2010). Author's reply. *British Journal of Psychiatry, 196,* 160. (p. 562)

Terrace, H. S. (1979, November). How Nim Chimpsky changed my mind. *Psychology Today,* pp. 65–76. (p. 318)

Terre, L., & Stoddart, R. (2000). Cutting edge specialties for graduate study in psychology. *Eye on Psi Chi, 23,* 26. (p. C-1)

Terrell, J., Kofink, A., Middleton, J., Rainear, C., Murphy-Hill, E., Parnin, C., & Stallings, J. (2017). Gender differences and bias in open source: Pull request acceptance of women versus men. *PeerJ Computer Science, 3,* e111. (p. 168)

Tesser, A., Forehand, R., Brody, G., & Long, N. (1989). Conflict: The role of calm and angry parent-child discussion in adolescent development. *Journal of Social and Clinical Psychology, 8,* 317–330. (p. 147)

Testa, R. J., Michaels, M. S., Bliss, W., Rogers, M. L., Balsam, K. F., & Joiner, T. (2017). Suicidal ideation in transgender people: Gender minority stress and interpersonal factors. *Journal of Abnormal Psychology, 126,* 125–136. (p. 500)

Tetlock, P. E. (1988). Monitoring the integrative complexity of American and Soviet policy rhetoric: What can be learned? *Journal of Social Issues, 44,* 101–131. (p. 459)

Tetlock, P. E. (1998). Close-call counterfactuals and belief-system defenses: I was not almost wrong but I was almost right. *Journal of Personality and Social Psychology, 75,* 639–652. (p. 17)

Tetlock, P. E. (2005). *Expert political judgement: How good is it? How can we know?* Princeton, NJ: Princeton University Press. (p. 17)

Tetlock, P. E., & Gardner, D. (2016). *Superforecasting: The art and science of prediction.* New York: Broadway Books. (p. 17)

Thaler, L., Arnott, S. R., & Goodale, M. A. (2011). Neural correlates of natural human echolocation in early and late blind echolocation experts. *PLoS ONE, 6,* e20162. (p. 39)

Thaler, L., Milne, J. L., Arnott, S. R., Kish, D., & Goodale, M. A. (2014). Neural correlates of motion processing through echolocation, source hearing, and vision in blind echolocation experts and sighted echolocation novices. *Journal of Neurophysiology, 111,* 112–127. (p. 39)

Thaler, R. H. (2015, May 8). Unless you are Spock, irrelevant things matter in economic behavior. *The New York Times* (nytimes.com). (p. 469)

Thaler, R. H., & Sunstein, C. R. (2008). *Nudge: Improving decisions about health, wealth, and happiness.* New Haven, CT: Yale University Press. (p. 304)

Thatcher, R. W., Walker, R. A., & Giudice, S. (1987). Human cerebral hemispheres develop at different rates and ages. *Science, 236,* 1110–1113. (pp. 117, 123)

Thayer, R. E. (1987). Energy, tiredness, and tension effects of a sugar snack versus moderate exercise. *Journal of Personality and Social Psychology, 52,* 119–125. (p. 402)

Thayer, R. E. (1993). Mood and behavior (smoking and sugar snacking) following moderate exercise: A partial test of self-regulation theory. *Personality and Individual Differences, 14,* 97–104. (p. 402)

The Guardian. (2014, August 12). Maryam Mirzakhani: "The more I spent time on maths, the more excited I got." *The Guardian* (theguardian.com). (p. 341)

Théoret, H., Halligan, H., Kobayashi, M., Fregni, F., Tager-Flusberg, H., & Pascual-Leone, A. (2005). Impaired motor facilitation during action observation in individuals with autism spectrum disorder. *Current Biology, 15,* R84–R85. (p. 132)

Thernstrom, M. (2006, May 14). My pain, my brain. *The New York Times* (nytimes.com). (p. 223)

Thibodeau, R., Jorgensen, R. S., & Kim, S. (2006). Depression, anxiety, and resting frontal EEG asymmetry: A meta-analytic review. *Journal of Abnormal Psychology, 115,* 715–729. (p. 52)

Thiel, A., Hadedank, B., Herholz, K., Kessler, J., Winhuisen, L., Haupt, W. F., & Heiss, W.-D. (2006). From the left to the right: How the brain compensates progressive loss of language function. *Brain and Language, 98,* 57–65. (p. 64)

Thomas, A., & Chess, S. (1986). The New York Longitudinal Study: From infancy to early adult life. In R. Plomin & J. Dunn (Eds.), *The study of temperament: Changes, continuities, and challenges* (pp. 39–52). Hillsdale, NJ: Erlbaum. (p. 118)

Thomas, L. (1992). *The fragile species.* New York: Scribner's. (pp. 77, 551)

Thompson, G. (2010). The $1 million dollar challenge. *Skeptic Magazine, 15,* 8–9. (p. 231)

Thompson, J. K., Jarvie, G. J., Lahey, B. B., & Cureton, K. J. (1982). Exercise and obesity: Etiology, physiology, and intervention. *Psychological Bulletin, 91,* 55–79. (p. 366)

Thompson, P. M., Cannon, T. D., Narr, K. L., van Erp, T., Poutanen, V.-P., Huttunen, M., . . . Toga, A. W. (2001). Genetic influences on brain structure. *Nature Neuroscience, 4,* 1253–1258. (p. 336)

Thompson, P. M., Giedd, J. N., Woods, R. P., MacDonald, D., Evans, A. C., & Toga, A. W. (2000). Growth patterns in the developing brain detected by using continuum mechanical tensor maps. *Nature, 404,* 190–193. (p. 123)

Thompson, R., Emmorey, K., & Gollan, T. H. (2005). "Tip of the fingers" experiences by Deaf signers. *Psychological Science, 16,* 856–860. (p. 287)

Thompson-Schill, S. L., Ramscar, M., & Chrysikou, E. G. (2009). Cognition without control: When a little frontal lobe goes a long way. *Current Directions in Psychological Science, 18,* 259–263. (p. 123)

Thomson, K. S., & Oppenheimer, D. M. (2016). Investigating an alternate form of the cognitive reflection test. *Judgment and Decision Making, 11,* 99–113. (p. 306)

Thorndike, E. L. (1898). Animal intelligence: An experimental study of the associative processes in animals. *Psychological Review Monograph Supplement, 2,* 4–160. (p. 244)

Thorne, J., with Larry Rothstein. (1993). *You are not alone: Words of experience and hope for the journey through depression.* New York: HarperPerennial. (p. 493)

Thornicroft, G., Chatterji, S., Evans-Lacko, S., Gruber, M., Sampson, N., Aguilar-Gaxiola, S., . . . Bruffaerts, R. (2017). Undertreatment of people with major depressive disorder in 21 countries. *British Journal of Psychiatry, 210,* 119–124. (p. 514)

Thornton, B., & Moore, S. (1993). Physical attractiveness contrast effect: Implications for self-esteem and evaluations of the social self. *Personality and Social Psychology Bulletin, 19,* 474–480. (p. 449)

Thorpe, W. H. (1974). *Animal nature and human nature.* London: Metheun. (p. 318)

Tibbetts, Y., Harackiewicz, J. M., Canning, E. A., Boston, J. S., Priniski, S. J., & Hyde, J. S. (2016). Affirming independence: Exploring mechanisms underlying a values affirmation intervention for first-generation students. *Journal of Personality and Social Psychology, 110,* 635–659. (p. 344)

Tick, B., Bolton, P., Happé, F., Rutter, M., & Rijsdijk, F. (2015). Heritability of autism spectrum disorders: A meta-analysis of twin studies. *Journal of Child Psychology and Psychiatry, 57,* 585–595. (p. 131)

Tickle, J. J., Hull, J. G., Sargent, J. D., Dalton, M. A., & Heatherton, T. F. (2006). A structural equation model of social influences and exposure to media smoking on adolescent smoking. *Basic and Applied Social Psychology, 28,* 117–129. (p. 111)

Tiedens, L. Z. (2001). Anger and advancement versus sadness and subjugation: The effect of negative emotion expressions on social status conferral. *Journal of Personality and Social Psychology, 80,* 86–94. (p. 394)

Tielbeek, J. J., Johansson, A., Polderman, T. J., Rautiainen, M. R., Jansen, P., Taylor, M., . . . Viding, E. (2017). Genome-wide association studies of a broad spectrum of antisocial behavior. *JAMA Psychiatry, 74,* 1242–1250. (p. 530)

Tigbe, W. W., Granat, M. H., Sattar, N., & Lean, M. E. J. (2017). Time spent in sedentary posture is associated with waist circumference and cardiovascular risk. *International Journal of Obesity, 41,* 689–696. (p. 401)

Tiggemann, M., & Miller, J. (2010). The internet and adolescent girls' weight satisfaction and drive for thinness. *Sex Roles, 63,* 79–90. (p. 532)

Tiihonen, J., Lönnqvist, J., Wahlbeck, K., Klaukka, T., Niskanen, L., Tanskanen, A., & Haukka, J. (2009). 11-year follow-up of mortality in patients with schizophrenia: A population-based cohort study (FIN11 study). *The Lancet, 374,* 260–267. (p. 560)

Tiihonen, J., Rautiainen, M. R., Ollila, H. M., Repo-Tiihonen, E., Virkkunen, M., Palotie, A., . . . Paunio, T. (2015). Genetic background of extreme violent behavior. *Molecular Psychiatry, 20,* 786–792. (p. 441)

Time/CNN Survey. (1994, December 19). Vox pop: Happy holidays, *Time.* (p. 514)

Timmerman, T. A. (2007). "It was a thought pitch": Personal, situational, and target influences on hit-by-pitch events across time. *Journal of Applied Psychology, 92,* 876–884. (p. 443)

Tinbergen, N. (1951). *The study of instinct.* Oxford: Clarendon. (p. 348)

Tirrell, M. E. (1990). Personal communication. (p. 239)

Tobin, D. D., Menon, M., Menon, M., Spatta, B. C., Hodges, E. V. E., & Perry, D. G. (2010). The intrapsychics of gender: A model of self-socialization. *Psychological Review, 117,* 601–622. (p. 169)

Todd, R. M., MacDonald, M. J., Sedge, P., Robertson, A., Jetly, R., Taylor, M. J., & Pang, E. W. (2015). Soldiers with posttraumatic stress disorder see a world full of threat: Magnetoencephalography reveals enhanced tuning to combat-related cues. *Biological Psychiatry, 78,* 821–829. (p. 52)

Todes, D. P. (2014). *Ivan Pavlov: A Russian life in science.* New York: Oxford University Press. (p. 236)

Toews, P. (2004, December 30). *Dirk Willems: A heart undivided.* Mennonite Brethren Historical Commission (mbhistory.org/profiles/dirk.en.html). (p. 415)

Tolin, D. F. (2010). Is cognitive-behavioral therapy more effective than other therapies? A meta-analytic review. *Clinical Psychology Review, 30,* 710–720. (p. 553)

Tolman, E. C., & Honzik, C. H. (1930). Introduction and removal of reward, and maze performance in rats. *University of California Publications in Psychology, 4,* 257–275. (p. 257)

Toma, C., & Hancock, J. (2013). Self-affirmation underlies Facebook use. *Personality and Social Psychology Bulletin, 369,* 321–331. (p. 487)

Tomaka, J., Blascovich, J., & Kelsey, R. M. (1992). Effects of self-deception, social desirability, and repressive coping on psychophysiological reactivity to stress. *Personality and Social Psychology Bulletin, 18,* 616–624. (p. 487)

Toni, N., Buchs, P.-A., Nikonenko, I., Bron, C. R., & Muller, D. (1999). LTP promotes formation of multiple spine synapses between a single axon terminal and a dendrite. *Nature, 402,* 421–442. (p. 279)

Topolinski, S., & Reber, R. (2010). Gaining insight into the "aha" experience. *Current Directions in Psychological Science, 19,* 401–405. (p. 299)

Torrey, E. F. (1986). *Witchdoctors and psychiatrists.* New York: Harper & Row. (p. 556)

Torrey, E. F., & Miller, J. (2002). *The invisible plague: The rise of mental illness from 1750 to the present.* New Brunswick, NJ: Rutgers University Press. (p. 525)

Torrey, E. F., Miller, J., Rawlings, R., & Yolken, R. H. (1997). Seasonality of births in schizophrenia and bipolar disorder: A review of the literature. *Schizophrenia Research, 28,* 1–38. (p. 525)

Totterdell, P., Kellett, S., Briner, R. B., & Teuchmann, K. (1998). Evidence of mood linkage in work groups. *Journal of Personality and Social Psychology, 74,* 1504–1515. (p. 423)

Towers, S., Gomez-Lievano, A., Khan, M., Mubayi, A., & Castillo-Chavez, C. (2015) Contagion in mass killings and school shootings. *PLoS ONE 10,* e0117259. (p. 421)

Tracy, J. L., Cheng, J. T., Robins, R. W., & Trzesniewski, K. H. (2009). Authentic and hubristic pride: The affective core of self-esteem and narcissism. *Self and Identity, 8,* 196–213. (p. 489)

Tracy, J. L., & Robins, R. W. (2004). Show your pride: Evidence for a discrete emotion expression. *Psychological Science, 15,* 194–197. (p. 372)

Tracy, J. L., Shariff, A. F., Zhao, W., & Henrich, J. (2013). Cross-cultural evidence that the nonverbal expression of pride is an automatic status signal. *Journal of Experimental Psychology: General, 142,* 163–180. (p. 375)

Traffanstedt, M. K., Mehta, S., & LoBello, S. G. (2016). Major depression with seasonal variation: Is it a valid construct? *Clinical Psychological Science, 4,* 825–834. (p. 515)

Trahan, L. H., Stuebing, K. K., Fletcher, J. M., & Hiscock, M. (2014). The Flynn effect: A meta-analysis. *Psychological Bulletin, 140,* 1332–1360. (p. 342)

Trautwein, U., Lüdtke, O., Köller, O., & Baumert, J. (2006). Self-esteem, academic self-concept, and achievement: How the learning environment moderates the dynamics of self-concept. *Journal of Personality and Social Psychology, 90,* 334–349. (p. 486)

Treanor, M., Brown, L. A., Rissman, J., & Craske, M. G. (2017). Can memories of traumatic experiences or addiction be erased or modified? A critical review of research on the disruption of memory reconsolidation and its applications. *Perspectives on Psychological Science, 12,* 290–305. (p. 289)

Treffert, D. A. (2010). *Islands of genius: The beautiful mind of the autistic, acquired, and sudden savant.* Philadelphia: Jessica Kinsley. (p. 324)

Treffert, D. A., & Christensen, D. D. (2005). Inside the mind of a savant. *Scientific American, 293,* 108–113. (p. 325)

Treisman, A. (1987). Properties, parts, and objects. In K. R. Boff, L. Kaufman, & J. P. Thomas (Eds.), *Handbook of perception and human performance* (pp. 159–198). New York: Wiley. (p. 208)

Tremblay, P., & Dick, A. S. (2016). Broca and Wernicke are dead, or moving past the classic model of language neurobiology. *Brain and Language, 162,* 60–71. (p. 317)

Tremblay, R. E., Pihl, R. O., Vitaro, F., & Dobkin, P. L. (1994). Predicting early onset of male antisocial behavior from preschool behavior. *Archives of General Psychiatry, 51,* 732–739. (p. 530)

Triandis, H. C. (1994). *Culture and social behavior.* New York: McGraw-Hill. (pp. 443, 491)

Trickett, E. (2009). Community psychology: Individuals and interventions in community context. *Annual Review of Psychology, 60,* 395–419. (p. 13)

Trillin, C. (2006, March 27). Alice off the page. *The New Yorker,* p. 44. (p. 472)

Triplett, N. (1898). The dynamogenic factors in pacemaking and competition. *American Journal of Psychology, 9,* 507–533. (p. 429)

Trotter, J. (2014). The power of positive coaching. *Sports Illustrated* (mmqb.si.com). (p. B-9)

Trumbo, M. C., Leiting, K. A., McDaniel, M. A., & Hodge, G. K. (2016). Effects of reinforcement on test-enhanced learning in a large, diverse introductory college psychology course. *Journal of Experimental Psychology: Applied, 22,* 148–160. (pp. 33, 272)

Trump, D. J. (2017, August 8). Tweet from @realDonaldTrump. (p. 104)

Trut, L. N. (1999). Early canid domestication: The farm-fox experiment. *American Scientist, 87,* 160–169. (p. 75)

Tsai, J. L., Ang, J. Y. Z., Blevins, E., Goernandt, J., Fung, H. H., Jiang, D., . . . Haddouk, L. (2016). Leaders' smiles reflect cultural differences in ideal affect. *Emotion, 16,* 183–195. (p. 379)

Tsai, J. L., & Chentsova-Dutton, Y. (2003). Variation among European Americans in emotional facial expression. *Journal of Cross-Cultural Psychology, 34,* 650–657. (p. 380)

Tsai, J. L., Knutson, B., & Fung, H. H. (2006). Cultural variation in affect valuation. *Journal of Personality and Social Psychology, 90,* 288–307. (p. 379)

Tsai, J. L., Miao, F. F., Seppala, E., Fung, H. H., & Yeung, D. Y. (2007). Influence and adjustment goals: Sources of cultural differences in ideal affect. *Journal of Personality and Social Psychology, 92,* 1102–1117. (p. 379)

Tsang, Y. C. (1938). Hunger motivation in gastrectomized rats. *Journal of Comparative Psychology, 26,* 1–17. (p. 361)

Tsvetkova, M., & Macy, M. W. (2014). The social contagion of generosity. *PLoS ONE, 9,* e87275. (p. 455)

Tuber, D. S., Miller, D. D., Caris, K. A., Halter, R., Linden, F., & Hennessy, M. B. (1999). Dogs in animal shelters: Problems, suggestions, and needed expertise. *Psychological Science, 10,* 379–386. (p. 31)

Tucker-Drob, E. (2012). Preschools reduce early academic-achievement gaps: A longitudinal twin approach. *Psychological Science, 23,* 310–319. (p. 339)

Tucker-Drob, E. M., & Bates, T. C. (2016). Large cross-national differences in gene x socioeconomic status interaction on intelligence. *Psychological Science, 27,* 138–149. (p. 339)

Tucker-Drob, E., & Briley, D. A. (2014). Continuity of genetic and environmental influences on cognition across the life span: A meta-analysis of longitudinal twin and adoption studies. *Psychological Bulletin, 140,* 949–979. (p. 332)

Tuerk, P. W. (2005). Research in the high-stakes era: Achievement, resources, and No Child Left Behind. *Psychological Science, 16,* 419–425. (p. 339)

Tuk, M. A., Zhang, K., & Sweldens, S. (2015). The propagation of self-control: Self-control in one domain simultaneously improves self-control in other domains. *Journal of Experimental Psychology: General, 144,* 639–654. (p. 398)

Tullett, A. M., Kay, A. C., & Inzlicht, M. (2015). Randomness increases self-reported anxiety and neurophysiological correlates of performance monitoring. *Social Cognitive and Affective Neuroscience, 10,* 628–635. (p. 17)

Tully, T. (2003). Reply: The myth of a myth. *Current Biology, 13,* R426. (p. 237)

Turner, J. C. (1987). Rediscovering the social group: A self-categorization theory. New York: Basil Blackwell. (p. 438)

Turner, J. C. (2007). Self-categorization theory. In R. Baumeister & K. Vohs (Eds.), *Encyclopedia of social psychology.* Thousand Oaks, CA: Sage. (p. 438)

Turner, N., Barling, J., & Zacharatos, A. (2002). Positive psychology at work. In C. R. Snyder & S. J. Lopez (Eds.), *The handbook of positive psychology.* New York: Oxford University Press. (p. B-10)

Turner, W. A., & Casey, L. M. (2014). Outcomes associated with virtual reality in psychological interventions: Where are we now? *Clinical Psychology Review, 34,* 634–644. (p. 541)

Turpin, A. (2005, April 3). The science of psi. *FT Weekend,* pp. W1, W2. (p. 230)

Tversky, A. (1985, June). Quoted in K. McKean, Decisions, decisions. *Discover,* pp. 22–31. (p. 301)

Tversky, A., & Kahneman, D. (1974). Judgment under uncertainty: Heuristics and biases. *Science, 185,* 1124–1131. (p. 300)

Twenge, J. M. (2006). *Generation me.* New York: Free Press. (p. 488)

Twenge, J. M., Abebe, E. M., & Campbell, W. K. (2010a). Fitting in or standing out: Trends in American parents' choices for children's names, 1880–2007. *Social Psychology and Personality Science, 1,* 19–25. (pp. 490, 491)

Twenge, J. M., Baumeister, R. F., Tice, D. M., & Stucke, T. S. (2001). If you can't join them, beat them: Effects of social exclusion on aggressive behavior. *Journal of Personality and Social Psychology, 81,* 1058–1069. (p. 355)

Twenge, J. M., & Campbell, W. K. (2008). Increases in positive self-views among high school students: Birth-cohort changes in anticipated performance, self-satisfaction, self-liking, and self-competence. *Psychological Science, 19,* 1082–1086. (p. 472)

Twenge, J. M., Dawson, L., & Campbell, W. K. (2016a). Still standing out: Children's names in the United States during the Great Recession and correlations with economic indicators. *Journal of Applied Social Psychology, 46,* 663–670. (pp. 490, 491)

Twenge, J. M., & Foster, J. D. (2010). Birth cohort increases in narcissistic personality traits among American college students, 1982–2009. *Social Psychological and Personality Science, 1,* 99–106. (p. 488)

Twenge, J. M., Gentile, B., DeWall, C. N., Ma, D., Lacefield, K., & Schurtz, D. R. (2010b). Birth cohort increases in psychopathology among young Americans, 1938–2007: A cross-temporal meta-analysis of the MMPI. *Clinical Psychology Review, 30,* 145–154. (pp. 177, 397)

Twenge, J. M., Joiner, T. E., Rogers, M. L., & Martin, G. N. (2018). Increases in depressive symptoms, suicide-related outcomes, and suicide rates among U.S. adolescents after 2010 and links to increased new media screen time. *Clinical Psychological Science, 6*(1), 3–17. (p. 500)

Twenge, J. M., Sherman, R. A., & Wells, B. E. (2016b). Sexual inactivity during young adulthood is more common among US millennials and iGen: Age, period, and cohort effects on having no sexual partners after age 18. *Archives of Sexual Behavior, 6,* 1–8. (p. 177)

Twenge, J. M., Sherman, R. A., & Wells, B. E. (2017). Declines in sexual frequency among American adults, 1989–2014. *Archives of Sexual Behavior, 46,* 2389–2401. (p. 23)

Twenge, J. M., Zhang, L., & Im, C. (2004). It's beyond my control: A cross-temporal meta-analysis of increasing externality in locus of control, 1960–2002. *Personality and Social Psychology Review, 8,* 308–319. (p. 397)

Twiss, C., Tabb, S., & Crosby, F. (1989). Affirmative action and aggregate data: The importance of patterns in the perception of discrimination. In F. Blanchard & F. Crosby (Eds.), *Affirmative action: Social psychological perspectives.* New York: Springer-Verlag. (p. A-5)

U.S. Department of Justice. (2018, accessed February 20). Sexual assault. United States Department of Justice. Retrieved from justice.gov (p. 170)

U.S. Equal Employment Opportunity Commission. (2018, accessed February 20). *Sexual harassment.* Equal Employment Opportunity Commission (eeoc.gov). (p. 170)

U.S. Senate Intelligence Committee. (2004, July 9). *Report of the Select Committee on Intelligence on the U.S. intelligence community's prewar intelligence assessments on Iraq.* Washington, DC: Author. (p. 433)

Uchida, Y., & Kitayama, S. (2009). Happiness and unhappiness in East and West: Themes and variations. *Emotion, 9,* 441–456. (p. 411)

Uchino, B. N., Cacioppo, J. T., & Kiecolt-Glaser, J. K. (1996). The relationship between social support and physiological processes: A review with emphasis on underlying mechanisms and implications for health. *Psychological Bulletin, 119,* 488–531. (p. 400)

Uchino, B. N., & Way, B. M. (2017). Integrative pathways linking close family ties to health: A neurochemical perspective. *American Psychologist, 72,* 590–600. (p. 400)

Udry, J. R. (2000). Biological limits of gender construction. *American Sociological Review, 65,* 443–457. (p. 166)

Uga, V., Lemut, M. C., Zampi, C., Zilli, I., & Salzarulo, P. (2006). Music in dreams. *Consciousness and Cognition, 15,* 351–357. (p. 96)

Ullén, F., Hambrick, D. Z., & Mosing, M. A. (2016). Rethinking expertise: A multifactorial gene–environment interaction model of expert performance. *Psychological Bulletin, 142,* 427–446. (p. 357)

UN. (2011, November 17). Discriminatory laws and practices and acts of violence against individuals based on their sexual orientation and gender identity. Report of the United Nations High Commissioner for Human Rights. (p. 437)

UN. (2015a). *Human development report 2015.* New York: United Nations Development Programme. (p. 169)

UN. (2015b). *The world's women: Trends and statistics.* United Nations Statistics Division. (p. 437)

UNAIDS. (2013). *Global report: UNAIDS report on the global AIDS epidemic 2013.* Joint United Nations Programme on HIV/AIDS (unaids.org). (p. 175)

Underwood, E. (2013). Short-circuiting depression. *Science, 342,* 548–551. (p. 564)

Underwood, E. (2016). Cadaver study challenges brain stimulation methods. *Science, 352,* 397. (p. 563)

Underwood, E. (2017). Brain implant trials spur ethical discussions. *Science, 358,* 710. (p. 564)

Ungar, L. (2014). Quiz: How long will you live? *Time Magazine.* Retrieved from http://time.com/3485579/when-will-i-die-life-expectancy-calculator/?xid=time_socialflow_twitter&utm_campaign=time&utm_source=twitter.com&utm_medium=social (p. 353)

Ungerleider, S. (2005). *Mental training for peak performance, revised & updated edition.* New York: Rodale. (p. 321)

Urbain, C., De Tiège, X., De Beeck, M. O., Bourguignon, M., Wens, V., Verheulpen, D., . . . Peigneux, P. (2016). Sleep in children triggers rapid reorganization of memory-related brain processes. *NeuroImage, 134,* 213–222. (p. 91)

Urry, H. L., & Gross, J. J. (2010). Emotion regulation in older age. *Current Directions in Psychological Science, 19,* 352–357. (p. 158)

Urry, H. L., Nitschke, J. B., Dolski, I., Jackson, D. C., Dalton, K. M., Mueller, C. J., . . . Davidson, R. J. (2004). Making a life worth living: Neural correlates of well-being. *Psychological Science, 15,* 367–372. (p. 374)

Vaillant, G. (2013, May). What makes us happy, revisited? *The Atlantic* (theatlantic.com/magazine/archive/2013/05/thanks-mom/309287/). (p. 355)

Vaillant, G. E. (1977). *Adaptation to life.* New York: Little, Brown. (p. 292)

Vaillant, G. E. (2002). *Aging well: Surprising guideposts to a happier life from the landmark Harvard study of adult development.* Boston: Little, Brown. (p. 400)

Valenstein, E. S. (1986). *Great and desperate cures: The rise and decline of psychosurgery.* New York: Basic Books. (p. 565)

Valentine, S. E., Bankoff, S. M., Poulin, R. M., Reidler, E. B., & Pantalone, D. W. (2015). The use of dialectical behavior therapy skills training as standalone treatment: A systematic review of the treatment outcome literature. *Journal of Clinical Psychology, 71,* 1–20. (p. 546)

Valkenburg, P. M., & Peter, J. (2009). Social consequences of the internet for adolescents: A decade of research. *Current Directions in Psychological Science, 18,* 1–5. (pp. 148, 356)

van Anders, S. M. (2012). Testosterone and sexual desire in healthy women and men. *Archives of Sexual Behavior, 41,* 1471–1484. (p. 173)

Van Bavel, J. J., Mende-Siedlecki, P., Brady, W. J., & Reinero, D. A. (2016). Contextual sensitivity in scientific reproducibility. *PNAS, 23,* 6454–6459. (p. 20)

Van Bockstaele, B., Verschuere, B., Tibboel, H., De Houwer, J., Crombez, G., & Koster, E. H. W. (2014). A review of current evidence for the causal impact of attentional bias on fear and anxiety. *Psychological Bulletin, 140,* 682–721. (p. 511)

Van Dam, N. T., van Vugt, M. K., Vago, D. R., Schmalzl, L., Saron, C. D., Olendzki, A., . . . Meyer, D. E. (2018). Mind the hype: A critical evaluation and prescriptive agenda for research on mindfulness and meditation. *Perspectives on Psychological Science, 13,* 36–61. (p. 404)

van de Bongardt, D., Reitz, E., Sandfort, T., & Deković, M. (2015). A meta-analysis of the relations between three types of peer norms and adolescent sexual behavior. *Personality and Social Psychology Review, 19,* 203–234. (p. 177)

van de Waal, E., Borgeaud, C., & Whiten, A. (2013). Potent social learning and conformity shape a wild primate's foraging decisions. *Science, 340,* 483–485. (p. 259)

Van den Akker, A. L., Asscher, J., & Prinzie, P. (2014). Mean-level personality development across childhood and adolescence: A temporary defiance of the maturity principle and bidirectional associations with parenting. *Journal of Personality and Social Psychology, 107,* 736–750. (p. 118)

van den Berg, S. M., de Moor, M. H., Verweij, K. J., Krueger, R. F., Luciano, M., Vasquez, A. A., . . . Gordon, S. D. (2016). Meta-analysis of genome-wide association studies for extraversion: Findings from the genetics of personality consortium. *Behavior Genetics, 46,* 170–182. (p. 478)

van den Bos, K., & Spruijt, N. (2002). Appropriateness of decisions as a moderator of the psychology of voice. *European Journal of Social Psychology, 32,* 57–72. (p. B-11)

Van den Bulck, J., Çetin, Y., Terzi, Ö., & Bushman, B. J. (2016). Violence, sex, and dreams: Violent and sexual media content infiltrate our dreams at night. *Dreaming, 26,* 271–279. (p. 97)

Van den Bussche, E., Van Den Noortgate, W., & Reynvoet, B. (2009). Mechanisms of masked priming: A meta-analysis. *Psychological Bulletin, 135,* 452–477. (p. 192)

van der Lee, R., & Ellemers, N. (2015). Gender contributes to personal research funding success in The Netherlands. *PNAS, 112,* 12349–12353. (p. 164)

van der Linden, S. L., Leiserowitz, A. A., Feinberg, G. D., & Maibach, E. W. (2015). The scientific consensus on climate change as a gateway belief: Experimental evidence. *PLoS ONE 10,* e0118489. (p. 418)

van Dijk, W. W., Van Koningsbruggen, G. M., Ouwerkerk, J. W., & Wesseling, Y. M. (2011). Self-esteem, self-affirmation, and schadenfreude. *Emotion, 11,* 1445–1449. (p. 487)

van Emmerik, A. A. P., Reijntjes, A., & Kamphuis, J. H. (2013). Writing therapy for posttraumatic stress: A meta-analysis. *Psychotherapy and Psychosomatics, 82,* 82–88. (p. 401)

van Engen, M. L., & Willemsen, T. M. (2004). Sex and leadership styles: A meta-analysis of research published in the 1990s. *Psychological Reports, 94,* 3–18. (p. 164)

van Geel, M., Goemans, A., & Vedder, P. (2015). A meta-analysis on the relation between peer victimization and adolescent non-suicidal self-injury. *Psychiatry Research, 230,* 364–368. (p. 502)

van Haren, N. E., Schnack, H. G., Koevoets, M. G., Cahn, W., Pol, H. E. H., & Kahn, R. S. (2016). Trajectories of subcortical volume change in schizophrenia: A 5-year follow-up. *Schizophrenia Research, 173,* 140–145. (p. 525)

Van Haren, N. M., Rijsdijk, F., Schnack, H. G., Picchioni, M. M., Toulopoulou, T., Weisbrod, M., . . . Kahn, R. S. (2012). The genetic and environmental determinants of the association between brain abnormalities and schizophrenia: The schizophrenia twins and relatives consortium. *Biological Psychiatry, 71,* 915–921. (p. 525)

van Hemert, D. A., Poortinga, Y. H., & van de Vijver, F. J. R. (2007). Emotion and culture: A meta-analysis. *Cognition and Emotion, 21,* 913–943. (p. 379)

van Honk, J., Schutter, D. J., Bos, P. A., Kruijt, A.-W., Lentje, E. G., & Baron-Cohen, S. (2011). Testosterone administration impairs cognitive empathy in women depending on second-to-fourth digit ratio. *PNAS, 108,* 3448–3452. (p. 131)

Van Horn, J., Irimia, A., Torgerson, C., Chambers, M., Kikinis, R., & Toga, A. (2012). Mapping connectivity damage in the case of Phineas Gage. *PLOS ONE, 7*(5), e37454. doi:10.1371/journal.pone.0037454 (p. 63)

van IJzendoorn, M. H., Fearon, P., & Bakermans-Kranenburg, M. (2017). Attachment—public and scientific. *The Psychologist, 30,* 6-9. (p. 137)

van IJzendoorn, M. H., & Juffer, F. (2006). The Emanual Miller Memorial Lecture 2006: Adoption as intervention. Meta-analytic evidence for massive catch-up and plasticity in physical, socio-emotional, and cognitive development. *Journal of Child Psychology and Psychiatry, 47,* 1228–1245. (p. 73)

van Ijzendoorn, M. H., Juffer, F., & Poelhuis, C. W. K. (2005). Adoption and cognitive development: A meta-analytic comparison of adopted and nonadopted children's IQ and school performance. *Psychological Bulletin, 131,* 301–316. (p. 73)

van IJzendoorn, M. H., & Kroonenberg, P. M. (1988). Cross-cultural patterns of attachment: A meta-analysis of the strange situation. *Child Development, 59,* 147–156. (p. 134)

van IJzendoorn, M. H., Luijk, M. P. C. M., & Juffer, F. (2008). IQ of children growing up in children's homes: A meta-analysis on IQ delays in orphanages. *Merrill-Palmer Quarterly, 54,* 341–366. (pp. 137, 338)

Van Kesteren, P. J. M., Asscheman, H., Megens, J. A. J., & Gooren, L. J. G. (1997). Mortality and morbidity in transsexual subjects treated with cross-sex hormones. *Clinical Endocrinology, 47,* 337–342. (p. 171)

Van Leeuwen, M. S. (1978). A cross-cultural examination of psychological differentiation in males and females. *International Journal of Psychology, 13,* 87–122. (p. 168)

van Praag, H. (2009). Exercise and the brain: Something to chew on. *Trends in Neuroscience, 32,* 283–290. (p. 402)

Van Tongeren, D. R., DeWall, C. N., Green, J. D., Cairo, A. H., Davis, D. E., & Hook, J. N. (2018). Self-regulation facilitates meaning in life. *Review of General Psychology.* Advance online publication. http://dx.doi.org/10.1037/gpr0000121 (p. 350)

Van Yperen, N. W., & Buunk, B. P. (1990). A longitudinal study of equity and satisfaction in intimate relationships. *European Journal of Social Psychology, 20,* 287–309. (p. 452)

Van Zeijl, J., Mesman, J., van IJzendoorn, M. H., Bakermans-Kranenburg, M. J., Juffer, F., Stolk, M. N., . . . Alink, L. R. A. (2006). Attachment-based intervention for enhancing sensitive discipline in mothers of 1- to 3-year-old children at risk for externalizing behavior problems: A randomized controlled trial. *Journal of Consulting and Clinical Psychology, 74,* 994–1005. (p. 135)

van Zuiden, M., Geuze, E., Willemen, H. L., Vermetten, E., Maas, M., Amarouchi, K., . . . Heijnen, C. J. (2012). Glucocorticoid receptor pathway components predict posttraumatic stress disorder symptom development: A prospective study. *Biological Psychiatry, 71,* 309–316. (p. 137)

Vance, E. B., & Wagner, N. N. (1976). Written descriptions of orgasm: A study of sex differences. *Archives of Sexual Behavior, 5,* 87–98. (p. 174)

vanDellen, M. R., Campbell, W. K., Hoyle, R. H., & Bradfield, E. K. (2011). Compensating, resisting, and breaking: A meta-analytic examination of reactions to self-esteem threat. *Personality and Social Psychological Review, 15,* 51–74. (p. 487)

VanderLaan, D. P., Forrester, D. L., Petterson, L. J., & Vasey, P. L. (2012). Offspring production among the extended relatives of Samoan men and Fa'afafi ne. *PloS ONE, 7,* e36088. (p. 181)

VanderLaan, D. P., & Vasey, P. L. (2011). Male sexual orientation in Independent Samoa: Evidence for fraternal birth order and maternal fecundity effects. *Archives of Sexual Behavior, 40,* 495–503. (p. 181)

VanderWeele, T. J., Li, S., & Kawachi, I. (2017). Religious service attendance and suicide rates—reply. *JAMA Psychiatry, 74,* 197–198. (p. 500)

VanderWeele, T. J., Li, S., Tsai, A. C., & Kawachi, I. (2016). Association between religious service attendance and lower suicide rates among U.S. women. *Journal of American Medication Association Psychiatry, 73,* 845–851. (p. 500)

Vanhalst, J., Soenens, B., Luyckx, K., Van Petegem, S., Weeks, M. S., & Asher, S. R. (2015). Why do the lonely stay lonely? Chronically lonely adolescents' attributions and emotions in situations of social inclusion and exclusion. *Journal of Personality and Social Psychology, 109,* 932–948. (p. 354)

Vardi, N. (2017, January 17). Inside the Obama stock market's 235% return. *Forbes* (forbes.com). (p. 18)

Varnum, M. E. W., Grossmann, I., Kitayama, S., & Nisbett, R. E. (2010). The origin of cultural differences in cognition: The social orientation hypothesis. *Current Directions in Psychological Science, 19,* 9–13. (p. 491)

Vaughn, K. B., & Lanzetta, J. T. (1981). The effect of modification of expressive displays on vicarious emotional arousal. *Journal of Experimental Social Psychology, 17,* 16–30. (p. 381)

Vazsonyi, A., Ksinan, A., Mikuška, J., & Jiskrova, G. (2015). The Big Five and adolescent adjustment: An empirical test across six cultures. *Personality and Individual Differences, 83,* 234–244. (p. 478)

Vecera, S. P., Vogel, E. K., & Woodman, G. F. (2002). Lower region: A new cue for figure-ground assignment. *Journal of Experimental Psychology: General, 13,* 194–205. (p. 210)

Veenhoven, R. (2014, accessed March 17). World database of happiness. Retrieved from worlddatabaseofhappiness.eur.nl (p. 411)

Veenhoven, R. (2015). Informed pursuit of happiness: What we should know, do know and can get to know. *Journal of Happiness Studies, 16,* 1035–1071. (p. 411)

Vekassy, L. (1977). Dreams of the blind. *Magyar Pszichologiai Szemle, 34,* 478–491. (p. 97)

Verbeek, M. E. M., Drent, P. J., & Wiepkema, P. R. (1994). Consistent individual differences in early exploratory behaviour of male great tits. *Animal Behaviour, 48,* 1113–1121. (p. 477)

Verduyn, P., Ybarra, O., Résibois, M., Jonides, J., & Kross, E. (2017). Do social network sites enhance or undermine subjective well-being? A critical review. *Social Issues and Policy Review, 11,* 274–302. (p. 355)

Verhaeghen, P., & Salthouse, T. A. (1997). Meta-analyses of age–cognition relations in adulthood: Estimates of linear and nonlinear age effects and structural models. *Psychological Bulletin, 122,* 231–249. (p. 152)

Vermetten, E., Schmahl, C., Lindner, S., Loewenstein, R. J., & Bremner, J. D. (2006). Hippocampal and amygdalar volumes in dissociative identity disorder. *American Journal of Psychiatry, 163,* 630–636. (p. 528)

Verschuere, B., & Meijer, E. H. (2014). What's on your mind? Recent advances in memory detection using the concealed information test. *European Psychologist, 19,* 162–171. (p. 374)

Vezzali, L., Stathi, S., Giovannini, D., Capozza, D., & Trifiletti, E. (2015). The greatest magic of Harry Potter: Reducing prejudice. *Journal of Applied Social Psychology, 45,* 105–121. (p. 260)

Victora, C. G., Horta, B. L., de Mola, C. L., Quevedo, L., Pinheiro, R. T., Gigante, D. P., . . . Barros, F. C. (2015). Association between breastfeeding and intelligence, educational attainment, and income at 30 years of age: A prospective birth cohort study from Brazil. *Lancet Global Health, 3,* e199–205 (thelancet.com/lancetgh). (p. 25)

Vieselmeyer, J., Holguin, J., & Mezulis, A. (2017). The role of resilience and gratitude in posttraumatic stress and growth following a campus shooting. *Psychological Trauma: Theory, Research, Practice, and Policy, 9,* 62–69. (p. 408)

Vigerland, S., Lenhard, F., Bonnert, M., Lalouni, M., Hedman, E., Ahlen, J., . . . Ljótsson, B. (2016). Internet-delivered cognitive behavior therapy for children and adolescents: A systematic review and meta-analysis. *Clinical Psychology Review, 50,* 1–10. (p. 546)

Vigliocco, G., & Hartsuiker, R. J. (2002). The interplay of meaning, sound, and syntax in sentence production. *Psychological Bulletin, 128,* 442–472. (p. 312)

Vining, E. P. G., Freeman, J. M., Pillas, D. J., Uematsu, S., Carson, B. S., Brandt, J., . . . Zukerberg, A. (1997). Why would you remove half a brain? The outcome of 58 children after hemispherectomy—The Johns Hopkins Experience: 1968 to 1996. *Pediatrics, 100,* 163–171. (p. 64)

Visich, P. S., & Fletcher, E. (2009). Myocardial infarction. In J. K. Ehrman, P. M., Gordon, P. S. Visich, & S. J. Keleyian (Eds.). *Clinical exercise physiology,* 2nd ed. Champaign, IL: Human Kinetics. (p. 401)

Visser, B. A., Ashton, M. C., & Vernon, P. A. (2006). Beyond g: Putting multiple intelligences theory to the test. *Intelligence, 34,* 487–502. (p. 327)

Vita, A. J., Terry, R. B., Hubert, H. B., & Fries, J. F. (1998). Aging, health risks, and cumulative disability. *New England Journal of Medicine, 338,* 1035–1041. (p. 106)

Vitello, P. (2012, August 1). George A. Miller. A pioneer in cognitive psychology, is dead at 92. *The New York Times* (nytimes.com). (p. 271)

Vitiello, M. V. (2009). Recent advances in understanding sleep and sleep disturbances in older adults: Growing older does not mean sleeping poorly. *Current Directions in Psychological Science, 18,* 316–320. (p. 96)

Vitória, P. D., Salgueiro, M. F., Silva, S. A., & De Vries, H. (2009). The impact of social influence on adolescent intention to smoke: Combining types and referents of influence. *British Journal of Health Psychology, 14,* 681–699. (p. 112)

Vliegenthart, J., Noppe, G., van Rossum, E. F. C., Koper, J. W., Raat, H., & van den Akker, E. L. T. (2016). Socioeconomic status in children is associated with hair cortisol levels as a biological measure of chronic stress. *Psychoneuroendocrinology, 65,* 9–14. (p. 391)

Vocks, S., Tuschen-Caffier, B., Pietrowsky, R., Rustenbach, S. J., Kersting, A., & Herpertz, S. (2010). Meta-analysis of the effectiveness of psychological and pharmacological treatments for binge eating disorder. *International Journal of Eating Disorders, 43,* 205–217. (p. 533)

Vogel, G. (2010). Long-fought compromise reached on European animal rules. *Science, 329,* 1588–1589. (p. 31)

Vogel, N., Schilling, O. K., Wahl, H.-W., Beekman, A. T. F., & Penninx, B. W. J. H. (2013). Time-to-death-related change in positive and negative affect among older adults approaching the end of life. *Psychology and Aging, 28,* 128–141. (p. 155)

Vohs, K. D., Baumeister, R. F., & Schmeichel, B. J. (2012). Motivation, personal beliefs, and limited resources all contribute to self-control. *Journal of Experimental Social Psychology, 48,* 943–947. (p. 398)

Vohs, K. D., Mead, N. L., & Goode, M. R. (2006). The psychological consequences of money. *Science, 314,* 1154–1156. (p. 281)

Volkow, N. D., Swanson, J. M., Evins, A. E., DeLisi, L. E., Meier, M. H., Gonzalez, R., . . . Baler, R. (2016). Effects of cannabis use on human behavior, including cognition, motivation, and psychosis: a review. *JAMA Psychiatry, 73,* 292–297. (p. 109)

Volkow, N. D., Wang, G. J., Kollins, S. H., Wigal, T. L., Newcorn, J. H., Telang, F., . . . Swanson, J. M. (2009). Evaluating dopamine reward pathway in ADHD: Clinical implications. *Journal of the American Medical Association, 302,* 1084–1091. (p. 498)

von Békésy, G. (1957, August). The ear. *Scientific American,* pp. 66–78. (p. 219)

von Hippel, W. (2007). Aging, executive functioning, and social control. *Current Directions in Psychological Science, 16,* 240–244. (p. 153)

von Hippel, W. (2015, July 17). Do people become more prejudiced as they grow older? *BBC News Magazine* (bbc.com/news/magazine-33523313). (p. 153)

von Hippel, W., & Trivers, R. (2011). The evolution and psychology of self-deception. *Behavioral and Brain Sciences, 34,* 1–56. (p. 487)

von Senden, M. (1932). *The perception of space and shape in the congenitally blind before and after operation.* Glencoe, IL: Free Press. (p. 213)

von Stumm, S., Hell, B., & Chamorro-Premuzic, T. (2011). The hungry mind: Intellectual curiosity is the third pillar of academic performance. *Perspectives on Psychological Science, 6,* 574–588. (p. 340)

von Stumm, S., & Plomin, R. (2015). Breastfeeding and IQ growth from toddlerhood through adolescence. *PLoS ONE, 10,* e0138676. (p. 25)

Vonk, J., Jett, S. E., & Mosteller, K. W. (2012). Concept formation in American black bears, *Ursus americanus. Animal Behaviour, 84,* 953–964. (p. 309)

Vorona, R. D., Szklo-Coxe, M., Wu, A., Dubik, M., Zhao, Y., & Ware, J. C. (2011). Dissimilar teen crash rates in two neighboring Southeastern Virginia cities with different high school start times. *Journal of Clinical Sleep Medicine, 7,* 145–151. (p. 94)

Vosoughi, S., Roy, D., & Aral, S. (2018). The spread of true and false news online. *Science, 359,* 1146–1151. (p. 18)

Voss, U., Tuin, I., Schermelleh-Engel, K., & Hobson, A. (2011). Waking and dreaming: Related but structurally independent. Dream reports of congenitally paraplegic and deaf-mute persons. *Consciousness and Cognition, 20,* 673–687. (p. 97)

Voyer, D., & Voyer, S. D. (2014). Gender differences in scholastic achievement: A meta-analysis. *Psychological Bulletin, 140,* 1174–1204. (p. 340)

VPC. (2015, June). *Firearm justifiable homicides and non-fatal self-defense gun use: An analysis of Federal Bureau of Investigation and National Crime Victimization Survey Data.* Washington, DC: Violence Policy Center (vpc.org). (p. 501)

VPC. (2016, January 4). States with weak gun laws and higher gun ownership lead nation in gun deaths, new data for 2014 confirms. Violence Policy Center (vpc.org). (p. 441)

Vrij, A., & Fisher, R. P. (2016). Which lie detection tools are ready for use in the criminal justice system? *Journal of Applied Research in Memory and Cognition, 5,* 302–307. (p. 374)

Vukasović, T., & Bratko, D. (2015). Heritability of personality: A meta-analysis of behavior genetic studies. *Psychological Bulletin, 141,* 769–785. (p. 478)

Vyse, S. (2016, March/April). Guns: Feeling safe ≠ being safe. *Skeptical Inquirer,* pp. 27–30. (p. 501)

Waber, R. L., Shiv, B., Carmon, Z. & Ariely, D. (2008). Commercial features of placebo and therapeutic efficacy. *Journal of the American Medical Association, 299,* 1016–1017. (p. 27)

Wacker, J., Chavanon, M.-L., & Stemmler, G. (2006). Investigating the dopaminergic basis of extraversion in humans: A multilevel approach. *Journal of Personality and Social Psychology, 91,* 177–187. (p. 476)

Wade, K. A., Garry, M., Read, J. D., & Lindsay, D. S. (2002). A picture is worth a thousand lies: Using false photographs to create false childhood memories. *Psychonomic Bulletin & Review, 9,* 597–603. (p. 291)

Wadley, J., & Lee, J. (2016, September 23). Compared with Europe, American teens have high rates of illicit drug use. Michigan News (University of Michigan). (p. 110)

Wagar, B. M., & Cohen, D. (2003). Culture, memory, and the self: An analysis of the personal and collective self in long-term memory. *Journal of Experimental Social Psychology, 39,* 458–475. (p. 274)

Wagemans, J., Elder, J. H., Kubovy, M., Palmer, S. E., Peterson, M. A., Singh, M., & von der Heydt, R. (2012a). A century of Gestalt psychology in visual perception: I. Perceptual grouping and figure–ground organization. *Psychological Bulletin, 138,* 1172–1217. (p. 207)

Wagemans, J., Feldman, J., Gepshtein, S., Kimchi, R., Pomerantz, J. R, van der Helm, P., & van Leeuwen, C. (2012b). A century of Gestalt psychology in visual perception: II. Conceptual and theoretical foundations. *Psychological Bulletin, 138,* 1218–1252. (p. 207)

Wagenmakers, E.-J. (2014, June 25). *Bem is back: A skeptic's review of a meta-analysis on psi.* Retrieved from centerforopenscience.github.io/osc/2014/06/25/a-skeptics-review (p. 231)

Wagenmakers E.-J., Beek T., Dijkhoff L., Gronau Q. F., Acosta A., Adams R. B., Jr., . . . Zwaan R. A. (2016). Registered replication report: Strack, Martin, & Stepper (1988). *Perspectives on Psychological Science, 11,* 917–928. (p. 381)

Wagenmakers, E.-J., Wetzels, R., Borsboom, D., & van der Maas, H. (2011). Why psychologists must change the way they analyze their data: The case of psi. *Journal of Personality and Social Psychology, 100,* 1–12. (p. 231)

Wager, R. D., & Atlas, L. Y. (2013). How is pain influenced by cognition? Neuroimaging weighs in. *Perspectives on Psychological Science, 8,* 91–97. (p. 223)

Wagner, D., Becker, B., Koester, P., Gouzoulis-Mayfrank, E., & Daumann, J. (2012). A prospective study of learning, memory, and executive function in new MDMA users. *Addiction, 108,* 136–145. (p. 108)

Wagner, J., Gerstorf, D., Hoppmann, C., & Luszcz, M. A. (2013). The nature and correlates of self-esteem trajectories in late life. *Journal of Personality and Social Psychology, 105,* 139–153. (p. 158)

Wagner, J., Ram, N., Smith, J., & Gerstorf, D. (2016). Personality trait development at the end of life: Antecedents and correlates of mean-level trajectories. *Journal of Personality and Social Psychology, 111,* 411–429. (p. 158)

Wagner, K., & Dobkins, K. R. (2011). Synaesthetic associations decrease during infancy. *Psychological Science, 22,* 1067–1072. (p. 229)

Wagstaff, G. (1982). Attitudes to rape: The "just world" strikes again? *Bulletin of the British Psychological Society, 13,* 275–283. (p. 417)

Wakefield, J. C., Schmitz, M. F., First, M. B., & Horwitz, A. V. (2007). Extending the bereavement exclusion for major depression to other losses: Evidence from the National Comorbidity Survey. *Archives of General Psychiatry, 64,* 433–440. (p. 517)

Wakefield, J. C., & Spitzer, R. L. (2002). Lowered estimates—but of what? *Archives of General Psychiatry, 59,* 129–130. (p. 510)

Walfisch, A., Sermer, C., Cressman, A., & Koren, G. (2014). Breast milk and cognitive development—the role of confounders: A systematic review. *BMJ Open, 3,* e003259. (p. 25)

Walker, E., Shapiro, D., Esterberg, M., & Trotman, H. (2010). Neurodevelopment and schizophrenia: Broadening the focus. *Current Directions in Psychological Science, 19,* 204–208. (pp. 525, 526)

Walker, M. P., & van der Helm, E. (2009). Overnight therapy? The role of sleep in emotional brain processing. *Psychological Bulletin, 135,* 731–748. (pp. 93, 559)

Walker, W. R., Skowronski, J. J., & Thompson, C. P. (2003). Life is pleasant—and memory helps to keep it that way! *Review of General Psychology, 7,* 203–210. (p. 158)

Wall, P. D. (2000). *Pain: The science of suffering.* New York: Columbia University Press. (p. 222)

Wallace, D. S., Paulson, R. M., Lord, C. G., & Bond, C. F., Jr. (2005). Which behaviors do attitudes predict? Meta-analyzing the effects of social pressure and perceived difficulty. *Review of General Psychology, 9,* 214–227. (p. 418)

Wallach, M. A., & Wallach, L. (1983). *Psychology's sanction for selfishness: The error of egoism in theory and therapy.* New York: Freeman. (p. 473)

Walsh, J. L., Fielder, R. L., Carey, K. B., & Carey, M. P. (2013). Female college students' media use and academic outcomes: Results from a longitudinal cohort study. *Emerging Adulthood, 1,* 219–232. (p. 356)

Walsh, R. (2011). Lifestyle and mental health. *American Psychologist, 66,* 579–592. (pp. 558, 559)

Walster (Hatfield), E., Aronson, V., Abrahams, D., & Rottman, L. (1966). Importance of physical attractiveness in dating behavior. *Journal of Personality and Social Psychology, 4,* 508–516. (p. 448)

Walton, G. M., & Spencer S. J. (2009). Latent ability: Grades and test scores systematically underestimate the intellectual ability of negatively stereotyped students. *Psychological Science, 20,* 1132–1139. (p. 344)

Wampold, B. E. (2001). *The great psychotherapy debate: Models, methods, and findings.* Mahwah, NJ: Erlbaum. (p. 555)

Wampold, B. E. (2007). Psychotherapy: The humanistic (and effective) treatment. *American Psychologist, 62,* 857–873. (p. 555)

Wampold, B. E., Flückiger, C., Del Re, A. C., Yulish, N. E., Frost, N. D., Pace, B. T., . . . Hilsenroth, M. J. (2017). In pursuit of truth: A critical examination of meta-analyses of cognitive behavior therapy. *Psychotherapy Research, 27,* 14–32. (p. 552)

Wang, F., DesMeules, M., Luo, W., Dai, S., Lagace, C. & Morrison, H. (2011). Leisure-time physical activity and marital status in relation to depression between men and women: A prospective study. *Health Psychology, 30,* 204–211. (p. 402, 435)

Wang, J., Häusermann, M., Wydler, H., Mohler-Kuo, M., & Weiss, M. G. (2012). Suicidality and sexual orientation among men in Switzerland: Findings from 3 probability surveys. *Journal of Psychiatric Research, 46,* 980–986. (p. 179)

Wang, J., He, L., Liping, J., Tian, J., & Benson, V. (2015a). The "positive effect" is present in older Chinese adults: Evidence from an eye tracking study. *PLoS ONE, 10,* e0121372. doi:10.1371/journal.pone.0121372 (pp. 158, 385)

Wang, J., Plöderl, M., Häusermann, M., & Weiss, M. G. (2015b). Understanding suicide attempts among gay men from their self-perceived causes. *Journal of Nervous and Mental Disease, 203,* 499–506. (p. 179)

Wang, J., Rao, Y., & Houser, D. E. (2017a). An experimental analysis of acquired impulse control among adult humans intolerant to alcohol. *PNAS, 114,* 1299–1304. (p. 398)

Wang, J., Wei, Q., Bai, T., Zhou, X., Sun, H., Becker, B., . . . Kendrick, K. (2017b). Electroconvulsive therapy selectively enhanced feedforward connectivity from fusiform face area to amygdala in major depressive disorder. *Social Cognitive and Affective Neuroscience 2,* 1983–1992. (p. 563)

Wang, J. X., Rogers, L. M., Gross, E. Z., Ryals, A. J., Dokucu, M. E., Brandstatt, K. L., . . . Voss, J. L. (2014). Targeted enhancement of cortical-hippocampal brain networks and associative memory. *Science, 345,* 1054–1057. (p. 276)

Wang, S. (2014, March 29). How to think about the risk of autism. *The New York Times* (nytimes.com). (p. 131)

Wang, S.-H., Baillargeon, R., & Brueckner, L. (2004). Young infants' reasoning about hidden objects: Evidence from violation-of-expectation tasks with test trials only. *Cognition, 93,* 167–198. (p. 126)

Wang, Y., Highhouse, S., Lake, C. J., Petersen, N. L., & Rada, T. B. (2017). Meta-analytic investigations of the relation between intuition and analysis. *Journal of Behavioral Decision Making, 30,* 15–25. (pp. 84, 145)

Wang, Z., Lukowski, S. L., Hart, S. A., Lyons, I. M., Thompson, L. A., Kovas, Y., . . . Petrill, S. A. (2015). Is math anxiety always bad for math learning? The role of math motivation. *Psychological Science, 26,* 1863–1876. (p. 350)

Ward, A., & Mann, T. (2000). Don't mind if I do: Disinhibited eating under cognitive load. *Journal of Personality and Social Psychology, 78,* 753–763. (p. 366)

Ward, B. W., Dahlhamer, J. M., Galinsky, A. M., & Joestl, S. S. (2014, July 15). *Sexual orientation and health among U.S. adults: National Health Interview Survey, 2013* (National Health Statistics Reports No. 77). Retrieved from cdc.gov/nchs/data/nhsr/nhsr077.pdf (p. 178)

Ward, C. (1994). Culture and altered states of consciousness. In W. J. Lonner & R. Malpass (Eds.), *Psychology and culture* (pp. 59–64). Boston: Allyn & Bacon. (p. 101)

Ward, J. (2003). State of the art synaesthesia. *The Psychologist, 16,* 196–199. (p. 229)

Ward, K. D., Klesges, R. C., & Halpern, M. T. (1997). Predictors of smoking cessation and state-of-the-art smoking interventions. *Journal of Social Issues, 53,* 129–145. (p. 106)

Wardle, J., Cooke, L. J., Gibson, L., Sapochnik, M., Sheiham, A., & Lawson, M. (2003). Increasing children's acceptance of vegetables: A randomized trial of parent-led exposure. *Appetite, 40,* 155–162. (p. 225)

Wargo, E. (2007, December). Understanding the have-knots. *APS Observer,* pp. 18–21. (p. 403)

Washburn, M. F. (1908). *The animal mind: A textbook of comparative psychology.* New York: The Macmillan Company. (pp. 6, 309)

Washington Post. (2017). Fatal force. Retrieved from washingtonpost.com/graphics/national/police-shootings-2016/?tid=a_inl and washingtonpost.com/graphics/national/police-shootings/ (p. 436)

Wason, P. C. (1960). On the failure to eliminate hypotheses in a conceptual task. *Quarterly Journal of Experimental Psychology, 12,* 129–140. (p. 300)

Wason, P. C. (1981). The importance of cognitive illusions. *The Behavioral and Brain Sciences, 4,* 356. (p. 300)

Wasserman, E. A. (1993). Comparative cognition: Toward a general understanding of cognition in behavior. *Psychological Science, 4,* 156–161. (p. 245)

Wasserman, E. A. (1995). The conceptual abilities of pigeons. *American Scientist, 83,* 246–255. (p. 309)

Wastell, C. A. (2002). Exposure to trauma: The long-term effects of suppressing emotional reactions. *Journal of Nervous and Mental Disorders, 190,* 839–845. (p. 401)

Waterman, A. S. (1988). Identity status theory and Erikson's theory: Commonalities and differences. *Developmental Review, 8,* 185–208. (p. 147)

Watkins, E. R. (2008). Constructive and unconstructive repetitive thought. *Psychological Bulletin, 134,* 163–206. (p. 514)

Watkins, J. G. (1984). The Bianchi (L. A. Hillside Strangler) case: Sociopath or multiple personality? *International Journal of Clinical and Experimental Hypnosis, 32,* 67–101. (p. 528)

Watson, D. (2000). *Mood and temperament.* New York: Guilford Press. (pp. 402, 408, 500)

Watson, J. B. (1913). Psychology as the behaviorist views it. *Psychological Review, 20,* 158–177. (pp. 80, 236, 241)

Watson, J. B. (1924). The unverbalized in human behavior. *Psychological Review, 31,* 339–347. (p. 241)

Watson, J. B., & Rayner, R. (1920). Conditioned emotional reactions. *Journal of Experimental Psychology, 3,* 1–14. (p. 241)

Watson, R. I., Jr. (1973). Investigation into deindividuation using a cross-cultural survey technique. *Journal of Personality and Social Psychology, 25*, 342–345. (p. 430)

Watts, T. W., Dundan, G. J., & Quan, H. (2018, May). Revisiting the marshmallow test: A conceptual replication investigating links between early delay of gratification and later outcomes. *Psychological Science*, 1–19. (p. 145)

Way, B. M., Creswell, J. D., Eisenberger, N. I., & Lieberman, M. D. (2010). Dispositional mindfulness and depressive symptomatology: Correlations with limbic and self-referential neural activity during rest. *Emotion, 10*, 12–24. (p. 404)

Wayment, H. A., & Peplau, L. A. (1995). Social support and well-being among lesbian and heterosexual women: A structural modeling approach. *Personality and Social Psychology Bulletin, 21*, 1189–1199. (p. 157)

Waytz, A., Young, L. L., & Ginges, J. (2014). Motive attribution asymmetry for love vs. hate drives intractable conflict. *PNAS, 111*, 15687–15692. (p. 456)

Weber, A., Fernald, A., & Diop, Y. (2017). When cultural norms discourage talking to babies: Effectiveness of a parenting program in rural Senegal. *Child Development, 88*, 1513–1526. (p. 140)

Webster, G. D., DeWall, C. N., Pond, R. S., Jr., Deckman, T., Jonason, P. K., Le, B. M., . . . Bator, R. J. (2014). The Brief Aggression Questionnaire: Psychometric and behavioral evidence for an efficient measure of trait aggression. *Aggressive Behavior, 40*, 120–139. (p. 29)

Wechsler, D. (1972). "Hold" and "Don't Hold" tests. In S. M. Chown (Ed.), *Human aging*. New York: Penguin. (p. 332)

Wegner, D. M., & Ward, A. F. (2013). How Google is changing your brain. *Scientific American, 309*, 58–61. (p. 269)

Wei, W., Lu, H., Zhao, H., Chen, C., Dong, Q., & Zhou, X. (2012). Gender differences in children's arithmetic performance are accounted for by gender differences in language abilities. *Psychological Science, 23*, 320–330. (p. 137)

Weidman, A. C., Tracy, J. L., & Elliot, A. J. (2016). The benefits of following your pride: Authentic pride promotes achievement. *Journal of Personality, 84*, 607–622. (p. 489)

Weingarden, H., & Renshaw, K. D. (2012). Early and late perceived pubertal timing as risk factors for anxiety disorders in adult women. *Journal of Psychiatric Research, 46*, 1524–1529. (p. 142)

Weingarten, G. (2002, March 10). Below the beltway. *The Washington Post*, p. WO3. (p. B-1)

Weinstein, N. D., Ryan, W. S., DeHaan, C. R., Przbylski, A. K., Legate, N., & Ryan, R. M. (2012). Parental autonomy support and discrepancies between implicit and explicit sexual identities: Dynamics of self-acceptance and defense. *Journal of Personality and Social Psychology, 102*, 815–832. (p. 470)

Weir, K. (2013, May). Captive audience. *Monitor on Psychology*, pp. 44–49. (p. 31)

Weisbuch, M., Ivcevic, Z., & Ambady, N. (2009). On being liked on the web and in the "real world": Consistency in first impressions across personal webpages and spontaneous behavior. *Journal of Experimental Social Psychology, 45*, 573–576. (p. 481)

Weiser, E. B. (2015). #Me: Narcissism and its facets as predictors of selfie-posting frequency. *Personality and Individual Differences, 86*, 477–481. (p. 356)

Weiskrantz, L. (2009). *Blindsight: A case study spanning 35 years and new developments*. Oxford: Oxford University Press. (p. 84)

Weiskrantz, L. (2010). Looking back: Blindsight in hindsight. *The Psychologist, 23*, 356–358. (p. 84)

Weiss, A., & King, J. E. (2015). Great ape origins of personality maturation and sex differences: A study of orangutans and chimpanzees. *Journal of Personality and Social Psychology, 108*, 648–664. (p. 478)

Weiss, A., Wilson, M. L., Collins, D. A., Mhungu, D., Kamenya, S., Foerster, S., & Pusey, A. E. (2017). Personality in the chimpanzees of Gombe National Park. *Nature: Scientific Data, 4*, #170146. (p. 477)

Weissman, M. M., Wickramaratne, P., Gameroff, M. J., Warner, V., Pilowsky, D., Kohad, R. G., . . . Talati, A. (2016). Offspring of depressed parents: 30 years later. *American Journal of Psychiatry, 173*, 1024–1032. (p. 518)

Weisz, J. R., Kuppens, S., Ng, M. Y., Eckshtain, D., Ugueto, A. M., Vaughn-Coaxum, R., . . . Weersing, V. R. (2017). What five decades of research tells us about the effects of youth psychological therapy: A multilevel meta-analysis and implications for science and practice. *American Psychologist, 72*, 79–117. (p. 552)

Welborn, B. L., Gunter, B. C., Vesich, I. S., & Lieberman, M. D. (2017). Neural correlates of the false consensus effect: Evidence for motivated projection and regulatory restraint. *Journal of Cognitive Neuroscience, 29*, 708–717. (p. 470)

Welch, J. M., Lu, J., Rodriquiz, R. M., Trotta, N. C., Peca, J., Ding, J.-D., . . . Feng, G. (2007). Cortico-striatal synaptic defects and OCD-like behaviours in *Sapap3*-mutant mice. *Nature, 448*, 894–900. (p. 512)

Welch, W. W. (2005, February 28). Trauma of Iraq war haunting thousands returning home. *USA Today* (usatoday.com). (p. 509)

Welker, K. M., Baker, L., Padilla, A., Holmes, H., Aron, A., & Slatcher, R. B. (2014). Effects of self-disclosure and responsiveness between couples on passionate love within couples. *Personal Relationships, 21*, 692–708. (p. 452)

Weller, S. C., & Davis-Beaty, K. (2002). Condom effectiveness in reducing heterosexual HIV transmission. *Cochrane Database of Systematic Reviews*, Issue 1, Article CD003255. doi:10.1002/14651858.CD003255 (p. 175)

Wells, D. L. (2009). The effects of animals on human health and well-being. *Journal of Social Issues, 65*, 523–543. (p. 401)

Wells, G. L. (1981). Lay analyses of causal forces on behavior. In J. Harvey (Ed.), *Cognition, social behavior and the environment*. Hillsdale, NJ: Erlbaum. (p. 234)

Wenze, S. J., Gunthert, K. C., & German, R. E. (2012). Biases in affective forecasting and recall in individuals with depression and anxiety symptoms. *Personality and Social Psychology Bulletin, 38*, 895–906. (p. 519)

Werner, L., Geisler, J., & Randler, C. (2015). Morningness as a personality predictor of punctuality. *Current Psychology, 34*, 130–139. (p. 87)

Westen, D. (1996). *Is Freud really dead? Teaching psychodynamic theory to introductory psychology*. Presentation to the Annual Institute on the Teaching of Psychology, St. Petersburg Beach, FL. (p. 467)

Westen, D. (1998). The scientific legacy of Sigmund Freud: Toward a psychodynamically informed psychological science. *Psychological Bulletin, 124*, 333–371. (p. 468)

Westen, D. (2007). *The political brain: The role of emotion in deciding the fate of the nation*. New York: PublicAffairs. (p. 371)

Westen, D., & Morrison, K. (2001). A multidimensional meta-analysis of treatments for depression, panic, and generalized anxiety disorder: An empirical examination of the status of empirically supported therapies. *Journal of Consulting and Clinical Psychology, 69*, 875–899. (p. 553)

Wetherell, J. L., Petkus, A. J., White, K. S., Nguyen, H., Kornblith, S., Andreescu, C., . . . Lenze, E. J. (2013). Antidepressant medication augmented with cognitive-behavioral therapy for generalized anxiety disorder in older adults. *American Journal of Psychiatry, 170*, 782–789. (p. 561)

Whalen, P. J., Shin, L. M., McInerney, S. C., Fisher, H., Wright, C. I., & Rauch, S. L. (2001). A functional MRI study of human amygdala responses to facial expressions of fear versus anger. *Emotion, 1*, 70–83. (p. 87)

Whelan, R., Conrod, P. J., Poline, J.-B., Lourdusamy, A., Banaschewski, T., Barker, G. J., . . . Garavan, H. (2012). Adolescent impulsivity phenotypes characterized by distinct brain networks. *Nature Neuroscience, 15*, 920–925. (p. 142)

Whisman, M. A., Johnson, D. P., & Rhee, S. H. (2014). A behavior genetic analysis of pleasant events, depressive symptoms, and their covariation. *Clinical Psychological Science, 2*, 535–544. (p. 515)

Whitaker, K. J., Vértes, P. E., Romero-Garcia, R., Váša, F., Moutoussis, M., Prabhu, G., . . . Tait, R. (2016). Adolescence is associated with genomically patterned consolidation of the hubs of the human brain connectome. *PNAS, 113*, 9105–9110. (p. 142)

White, H. R., Brick, J., & Hansell, S. (1993). A longitudinal investigation of alcohol use and aggression in adolescence. *Journal of Studies on Alcohol, Supplement 11*, 62–77. (p. 442)

White, L., & Edwards, J. (1990). Emptying the nest and parental well-being: An analysis of national panel data. *American Sociological Review, 55*, 235–242. (p. 157)

White, R. A. (1998). Intuition, heart knowledge, and parapsychology. *Journal of the American Society for Psychical Research, 92*, 158–171. (p. 231)

White, R. E., Kross, E., & Duckworth, A. L. (2015). Spontaneous self-distancing and adaptive self-reflection across adolescence. *Child Development, 86*, 1272–1281. (p. 394)

Whitehurst, L. N., Cellini, N., McDevitt, E. A., Duggan, K. A., & Mednick, S. C. (2016). Autonomic activity during sleep predicts memory consolidation in humans. *PNAS, 113*, 7272–7277. (pp. 92, 277)

Whitelock, C. F., Lamb, M. E., & Rentfrow, P. J. (2013). Overcoming trauma: Psychological and demographic characteristics of child sexual abuse survivors in adulthood. *Clinical Psychological Science, 1*, 351–362. (p. 138)

Whiten, A., & Boesch, C. (2001, January). Cultures of chimpanzees. *Scientific American*, pp. 60–67. (p. 310)

Whiten, A., & Byrne, R. W. (1988). Tactical deception in primates. *Behavioral and Brain Sciences, 11*, 233–244. (p. 22)

Whiten, A., Spiteri, A., Horner, V., Bonnie, K. E., Lambeth, S. P., Schapiro, S. J., & de Waal, F. B. M. (2007). Transmission of multiple traditions within and between chimpanzee groups. *Current Biology, 17*, 1038–1043. (p. 259)

Whiting, B. B., & Edwards, C. P. (1988). *Children of different worlds: The formation of social behavior*. Cambridge, MA: Harvard University Press. (p. 139)

Whitley, B. E., Jr. (1999). Right-wing authoritarianism, social dominance orientation, and prejudice. *Journal of Personality and Social Psychology, 77*, 126–134. (p. 438)

Whitlock, J. R., Heynen, A. L., Shuler, M. G., & Bear, M. F. (2006). Learning induces long-term potentiation in the hippocampus. *Science, 313*, 1093–1097. (p. 278)

WHO. (2000). *Effectiveness of male latex condoms in protecting against pregnancy and sexually transmitted infections.* World Health Organization (who.int). (p. 175)

WHO. (2003). *The male latex condom: Specification and guidelines for condom procurement.* Department of Reproductive Health and Research, Family and Community Health, World Health Organization. Retrieved from who.int/iris/bitstream/10665/42873/1/9241591277.pdf (p. 175)

WHO. (2004a). *Prevention of mental disorders: Effective interventions and policy options. Summary report.* Geneva: World Health Organization, Department of Mental Health and Substance Abuse. (pp. 495, 504)

WHO. (2004b). *Promoting mental health: Concepts, emerging evidence, practice. Summary report.* Geneva: World Health Organization, Department of Mental Health and Substance Abuse. (p. 504)

WHO. (2008). *Mental health (nearly 1 million annual suicide deaths).* Geneva: World Health Organization. Retrieved from who.int/mental_health/en (p. 500)

WHO. (2011). Country reports and charts available. Geneva: World Health Organization. Retrieved from int/mental_health/prevention/suicide/country_reports/en/index.html (p. 500)

WHO. (2012). *WHO global estimates on prevalence of hearing loss: Mortality and burden of diseases and prevention of blindness and deafness.* World Health Organization (who.int/pbd/deafness/WHO_GE_HL.pdf). (p. 105)

WHO. (2013, November). *Sexually transmitted infections (STIs)* (Fact Sheet No. 110). World Health Organization. Retrieved from who.int/mediacentre/factsheets/fs110/en/ (p. 175)

WHO. (2014a, accessed September 20). Chain-free initiative. Geneva: World Health Organization. Retrieved from emro.who.int/mental-health/chain-free-initiative (p. 495)

WHO. (2014b). *Global status report on alcohol and health 2014.* World Health Organization (who.int/substance_abuse/publications/global_alcohol_report/msb_gsr_2014_1.pdf). (p. 102)

WHO. (2014c, October). *Mental disorders.* World Health Organization. Retrieved from who.int/mediacentre/factsheets/fs396/en/ (p. 500)

WHO. (2016a). Global status on road safety 2015. World Health Organization (who.int/violence_injury_prevention/road_safety_status/2015/en/). (p. B-13)

WHO. (2016b, November). *Violence against women. Intimate partner and sexual violence against women.* Fact Sheet. World Health Organization (who.int/mediacentre/factsheets/fs239/en/). (p. 437)

WHO. (2017b). *The determinants of health.* World Health Organization. Retrieved from http://www.who.int/hia/evidence/doh/en/ (p. 353)

WHO. (2017c). *Mental disorders.* World Health Organization. Retrieved from who.int/mediacentre/factsheets/fs396/en (pp. 493, 516, 524)

WHO. (2017a). *Depression.* World Health Organization. Retrieved from who.int/mediacentre/factsheets/fs369/en (p. 514)

Whooley, M. A., de Jonge, P., Vittinghoff, E., Otte, C., Noos, R., Carney, R. M., . . . Browner, W. S. (2008). Depressive symptoms, health behaviors, and risk of cardiovascular events in patients with coronary heart disease. *JAMA, 300,* 2379–2388. (p. 392)

Whorf, B. L. (1956). Science and linguistics. In J. B. Carroll (Ed.), *Language, thought, and reality: Selected writings of Benjamin Lee Whorf.* Cambridge, MA: MIT Press. (p. 319)

Wicherts, J. M., Dolan, C. V., Carlson, J. S., & van der Maas, H. L. J. (2010). Raven's test performance of sub-Saharan Africans: Mean level, psychometric properties, and the Flynn effect. *Learning and Individual Differences, 20,* 135–151. (p. 342)

Wickelgren, I. (2009, September/October). I do not feel your pain. *Scientific American Mind,* pp. 51–57. (pp. 222, 227)

Wickelgren, W. A. (1977). *Learning and memory.* Englewood Cliffs, NJ: Prentice-Hall. (p. 274)

Widiger, T. A., Gore, W. L., Crego, C., Rojas, S. L., & Oltmanns, J. R. (2016). Five-factor model and personality disorder. In T. A. Widiger (Ed.), *The Oxford handbook of the five factor model of personality.* New York: Oxford University Press. (p. 478)

Wiens, A. N., & Menustik, C. E. (1983). Treatment outcome and patient characteristics in an aversion therapy program for alcoholism. *American Psychologist, 38,* 1089–1096. (p. 542)

Wierson, M., & Forehand, R. (1994). Parent behavioral training for child noncompliance: Rationale, concepts, and effectiveness. *Current Directions in Psychological Science, 3,* 146–149. (p. 251)

Wierzbicki, M. (1993). Psychological adjustment of adoptees: A meta-analysis. *Journal of Clinical Child Psychology, 22,* 447–454. (p. 73)

Wiesel, T. N. (1982). Postnatal development of the visual cortex and the influence of environment. *Nature, 299,* 583–591. (pp. 124, 213)

Wiesner, W. H., & Cronshaw, S. P. (1988). A meta-analytic investigation of the impact of interview format and degree of structure on the validity of the employment interview. *Journal of Occupational Psychology, 61,* 275–290. (p. B-6)

Wigdor, A. K., & Garner, W. R. (1982). *Ability testing: Uses, consequences, and controversies.* Washington, DC: National Academy Press. (p. 343)

Wilcox, W. B., & DeRose, L. (2017, March 27). In Europe, cohabitation is stable . . . right? Brookings Institution (www.brookings.edu). (p. 136)

Wilcox, W. B., & Marquardt, E. (2011, December). *When baby makes three: How parenthood makes life meaningful and how marriage makes parenthood bearable.* Charlottesville, VA: National Marriage Project, University of Virginia. (p. 135)

Wilder, D. A. (1981). Perceiving persons as a group: Categorization and intergroup relations. In D. L. Hamilton (Ed.), *Cognitive processes in stereotyping and intergroup behavior.* Hillsdale, NJ: Erlbaum. (p. 438)

Wiley, J., & Jarosz, A. F. (2012). Working memory capacity, attentional focus, and problem solving. *Current Directions in Psychological Science, 21,* 258–262. (p. 271)

Wilford, J. N. (1999, February 9). New findings help balance the cosmological books. *The New York Times* (nytimes.com). (p. 77)

Wilkinson, R., & Pickett, K. (2009). The *spirit level: Why greater equality makes societies stronger.* London: Bloomsbury Press. (pp. 410, 443)

Wilkowski, B. M., Robinson, M. D., & Troop-Gordon, W. (2011). How does cognitive control reduce anger and aggression? The role of conflict monitoring and forgiveness processes. *Journal of Personality and Social Psychology, 98,* 830–840. (p. 442)

Willett, L. L., Halvorsen, A. J., McDonald, F. S., Chaudhry, S. I., & Arora, V. M. (2015). Gender differences in salary of internal medicine residency directors: A national survey. *The American Journal of Medicine, 128,* 659–665. (p. 164)

Williams, C. L., & Berry, J. W. (1991). Primary prevention of acculturative stress among refugees. *American Psychologist, 46,* 632–641. (p. 385)

Williams, E. F., Dunning, D., & Kruger, J. (2013). The hobgoblin of consistency: Algorithmic judgment strategies underlie inflated self-assessments of performance. *Journal of Personality and Social Psychology, 104,* 976–994. (p. 488)

Williams, J. E., & Best, D. L. (1990). *Measuring sex stereotypes: A multination study.* Newbury Park, CA: Sage. (pp. 163, 164)

Williams, K. D. (2007). Ostracism. *Annual Review of Psychology, 58,* 425–452. (pp. 354, 355)

Williams, K. D. (2009). Ostracism: A temporal need-threat model. *Advances in Experimental Social Psychology, 41,* 275–313. (p. 354)

Williams, K. D., & Sommer, K. L. (1997). Social ostracism by coworkers: Does rejection lead to loafing or compensation? *Personality and Social Psychology Bulletin, 23,* 693–706. (p. 424)

Williams, L. A., & Bartlett, M. Y. (2015). Warm thanks: Gratitude expression facilitates social affiliation in new relationships via perceived warmth. *Emotion, 15,* 1–5. (p. 352)

Williams, L. A., & DeSteno, D. (2009). Adaptive social emotion or seventh sin? *Psychological Science, 20,* 284–288. (p. 489)

Williams, L. E., & Bargh, J. A. (2008). Experiencing physical warmth promotes interpersonal warmth. *Science, 322,* 606–607. (p. 229)

Williams, N. M., Zaharieva, I., Martin, A., Langley, K., Mantripragada, K., Fossdal, R., . . . Thapar, A. (2010). Rare chromosomal deletions and duplications in attention-deficit hyperactivity disorder: A genome-wide analysis. *The Lancet, 376,* 1401–1408. (p. 498)

Williams, S. L. (1987, August). *Self-efficacy and mastery-oriented treatment for severe phobias.* Paper presented at the 95th Annual Convention of the American Psychological Association, New York, NY. (p. 541)

Williams, T. (2015, March 17). Missouri executes killer who had brain injury. *The New York Times* (nytimes.com). (p. 63)

Williams, W. W., & Ceci, S. J. (2015). National hiring experiments reveal 2:1 faculty preference for women on STEM tenure track. *PNAS, 112,* 5360–5365. (p. 168)

Willingham, D. T. (2010, Summer). Have technology and multitasking rewired how students learn? *American Educator, 34,* 23–28, 42. (pp. 271, 357)

Willis, J., & Todorov, A. (2006). First impressions: Making up your mind after a 100-ms. exposure to a face. *Psychological Science, 17,* 592–598. (pp. 371, 376)

Willmuth, M. E. (1987). Sexuality after spinal cord injury: A critical review. *Clinical Psychology Review, 7,* 389–412. (p. 177)

Willoughby, B. J., Carroll, J. S., & Busby, D. M. (2014). Differing relationship outcomes when sex happens before, on, or after first dates. *Journal of Sex Research, 51,* 52–61. (p. 26)

Willoughby, T., Heffer, T., & Hamza, C. A. (2015). The link between nonsuicidal self-injury and acquired capability for suicide: A longitudinal study. *Journal of Abnormal Psychology, 124,* 1110–1115. (p. 502)

Wilson, A. E., & Ross, M. (2001). From chump to champ: People's appraisals of their earlier and present selves. *Journal of Personality and Social Psychology, 80,* 572–584. (p. 489)

Wilson, B., Smith, K., & Petkov, C. I. (2015). Mixed-complexity artificial grammar learning in humans and macaque monkeys: Evaluating learning strategies. *European Journal of Neuroscience, 41,* 568–578. (p. 318)

Wilson, R. E., Gosling, S. D., & Graham, L. T. (2012). A review of Facebook research in the social sciences. *Perspectives on Psychological Science, 7,* 203–220. (p. 148)

Wilson, R. S. (1979). Analysis of longitudinal twin data: Basic model and applications to physical growth measures. *Acta Geneticae Medicae et Gemellologiae, 28,* 93–105. (p. 124)

Wilson, R. S., Arnold, S. E., Schneider, J. A., Tang, Y., & Bennett, D. A. (2007). The relationship between cerebral Alzheimer's disease pathology and odour identification in old age. *Journal of Neurology, Neurosurgery, and Psychiatry, 78,* 30–35. (p. 155)

Wilson, R. S., & Matheny, A. P., Jr. (1986). Behavior genetics research in infant temperament: The Louisville Twin Study. In R. Plomin & J. Dunn (Eds.), *The study of temperament: Changes, continuities, and challenges* (pp. 81–97). Hillsdale, NJ: Erlbaum. (p. 135)

Wilson, T. D. (2002). *Strangers to ourselves: Discovering the adaptive unconscious.* Cambridge, MA: Harvard University Press. (p. 81)

Wilson, T. D., Reinhard, D. A., Westgate, E. C., Gilbert, D. T., Ellerbeck, N., Hahn, C., . . . Shaked, A. (2014). Just think: The challenges of the disengaged mind. *Science, 345,* 75–77. (p. 349)

Wilson, W. A., & Kuhn, C. M. (2005, April). How addiction hijacks our reward system. *Cerebrum,* pp. 53–66. (p. 111)

Wimber, M., Alink, A., Charest, I., Kriegeskorte, N., & Anderson, M. C. (2015). Retrieval induces adaptive forgetting of competing memories via cortical pattern suppression. *Nature Neuroscience, 18,* 582–589. (p. 287)

Wimmer, R. D., Schmitt, L. I., Davidson, T. J., Nakajima, M., Deisseroth, K., & Halassa, M. M. (2015). Thalamic control of sensory selection in divided attention. *Nature, 526,* 705–709. (p. 54)

Windholz, G. (1989, April-June). The discovery of the principles of reinforcement, extinction, generalization, and differentiation of conditional reflexes in Pavlov's laboratories. *Pavlovian Journal of Biological Science, 26,* 64–74. (p. 239)

Windholz, G. (1997). Ivan P. Pavlov: An overview of his life and psychological work. *American Psychologist, 52,* 941–946. (p. 238)

Winer, E. S., & Salem, T. (2016). Reward devaluation: Dot-probe meta-analytic evidence of avoidance of positive information in depressed persons. *Psychological Bulletin, 142,* 18–78. (p. 516)

Winkler, A., Dòrsing, B., Rief, W., Shen, Y., & Glombiewski, J. A. (2013). Treatment of internet addiction: A meta-analysis. *Clinical Psychology Review, 33,* 317–329. (p. 102)

Winner, E. (2000). The origins and ends of giftedness. *American Psychologist, 55,* 159–169. (p. 332)

Winsler, A., Deutsch, A., Vorona, R. D., Payne, P. A., & Szklo-Coxe, M. (2015). Sleepless in Fairfax: The difference one more hour of sleep can make for teen hopelessness, suicidal ideation, and substance use. *Journal of Youth and Adolescence, 44,* 362–378. (p. 93)

Winter, W. C., Hammond, W. R., Green, N. H., Zhang, Z., & Bilwise, D. L. (2009). Measuring circadian advantage in Major League Baseball: A 10-year retrospective study. *International Journal of Sports Physiology and Performance, 4,* 394–401. (p. 91)

Wirth, J. H., Sacco, D. F., Hugenberg, K., & Williams, K. D. (2010). Eye gaze as relational evaluation: Averted eye gaze leads to feelings of ostracism and relational devaluation. *Personality and Social Psychology Bulletin, 36,* 869–882. (p. 354)

Wiseman, R., & Greening, E. (2002). The Mind Machine: A mass participation experiment into the possible existence of extra-sensory perception. *British Journal of Psychology, 93,* 487–499. (p. 231)

Witt, J. K., & Brockmole, J. R. (2012). Action alters object identification: Wielding a gun increases the bias to see guns. *Journal of Experimental Psychology: Human Perception and Performance, 38,* 1159–1167. (p. 197)

Witt, J. K., Linkenauger, S. A., & Proffitt, D. R. (2012). Get me out of this slump! Visual illusions improve sports performance. *Psychological Science, 23,* 397–399. (p. 197)

Witt, J. K., & Proffitt, D. R. (2005). See the ball, hit the ball: Apparent ball size is correlated with batting average. *Psychological Science, 16,* 937–938. (p. 197)

Wittek, C. T., Finserås, T. R., Pallesen, S., Mentzoni, R. A., Hanss, D., Griffiths, M. D., & Molde, H. (2016). Prevalence and predictors of video game addiction: A study based on a national representative sample of gamers. *International Journal of Mental Health and Addiction, 14,* 672-686. (p. 102)

Witter, D. P., & Ward, H. E. (2016). Overview of the current use of deep brain stimulation in psychiatric disorders. *Psychiatric Annals, 46,* 631–636. (p. 564)

Witters, D. (2014, October 20). *U.S. adults with children at home have greater joy, stress.* Gallup (gallup.com/poll/178631/adults-childrenhome-greaterjoy-stress.aspx). (p. 157)

Witters, D., & Wood, J. (2015, January 14). *Heart attacks and depression closely linked.* Gallup (gallup.com). (p. 392)

Wittgenstein, L. (1922). *Tractatus logico-philosophicus* (C. K. Ogden, Trans.). New York: Harcourt, Brace. (p. 77)

Witvliet, C. V. O., & Vrana, S. R. (1995). Psychophysiological responses as indices of affective dimensions. *Psychophysiology, 32,* 436–443. (p. 374)

Wixted, J. T., & Ebbesen, E. B. (1991). On the form of forgetting. *Psychological Science, 2,* 409–415. (p. 286)

WKYT. (2017). Kentucky fans set crowd roar world record. Retrieved from wkyt.com/content/news/Kentucky-fans-set-crowd-roar-world-record-412059133.html (p. 217)

Wölfer, R., & Hewstone, M. (2015, August). Intra-versus intersex aggression. Testing theories of sex differences using aggression networks. *Psychological Science, 26,* 1285–1294. (p. 163)

Wolfinger, N. H. (2015). *Want to avoid divorce? Wait to get married, but not too long.* Institute for Family Studies (family-studies.org/want-to-avoid-divorce-wait-toget-married-but-not-too-long/). (p. 156)

Wolfson, A. R., & Carskadon, M. A. (1998). Sleep schedules and daytime functioning in adolescents. *Child Development, 69,* 875–887. (p. 98)

Wolke, D., Copeland, W. E., Angold, A., & Costello, E. J. (2013). Impact of bullying in childhood on adult health, wealth, crime, and social outcomes. *Psychological Science, 24,* 1958–1970. (p. 138)

Wolpe, J. (1958). *Psychotherapy by reciprocal inhibition.* Stanford, CA: Stanford University Press. (p. 541)

Wolpe, J., & Plaud, J. J. (1997). Pavlov's contributions to behavior therapy: The obvious and the not so obvious. *American Psychologist, 52,* 966–972. (p. 541)

Wonderlich, S. A., Joiner, T. E., Jr., Keel, P. K., Williamson, D. A., & Crosby, R. D. (2007). Eating disorder diagnoses: Empirical approaches to classification. *American Psychologist, 62,* 167–180. (p. 532)

Wondra, J. D., & Ellsworth, P. C. (2015). An appraisal theory of empathy and other vicarious emotional experiences. *Psychological Review, 122,* 411–428. (p. 378)

Wong, D. F., Wagner, H. N., Tune, L. E., Dannals, R. F., Pearlson, G. D., Links, J. M., . . . Gjedde, A. (1986). Positron emission tomography reveals elevated D_2 dopamine receptors in drug-naive schizophrenics. *Science, 234,* 1588–1593. (p. 524)

Wong, M. M., & Csikszentmihalyi, M. (1991). Affiliation motivation and daily experience: Some issues on gender differences. *Journal of Personality and Social Psychology, 60,* 154–164. (p. 164)

Wood, D., Bruner, J., & Ross, G. (1976). The role of tutoring in problem solving. *Journal of Child Psychology and Child Psychiatry, 17,* 89–100. (p. 129)

Wood, E., Ricketts, T., & Perry, G. (2018). EMDR as a treatment for long-term depression: A feasibility study. *Psychology and Psychotherapy,* in press. (p. 554)

Wood, J. M. (2003, May 19). Quoted in R. Mestel, Rorschach tested: Blot out the famous method? Some experts say it has no place in psychiatry. *The Los Angeles Times.* Retrieved from articles.latimes.com/2003/may/19/health/he-rorschach19 (p. 468)

Wood, J. M., Bootzin, R. R., Kihlstrom, J. F., & Schacter, D. L. (1992). Implicit and explicit memory for verbal information presented during sleep. *Psychological Science, 3,* 236–239. (p. 288)

Wood, J. M., Garb, H. N., Nezworski, M. T., Lilienfeld, S. O., & Duke, M. C. (2015). A second look at the validity of widely used Rorschach indices: Comment on Mihura, Meyer, Dumitrascu, and Bombel (2013). *Psychological Bulletin, 141,* 236–249. (p. 468)

Wood, J. M., Nezworski, M. T., Garb, H. N., & Lilienfeld, S. O. (2006). The controversy over the Exner Comprehensive System and the Society for Personality Assessment's white paper on the Rorschach. *Independent Practitioner, 26.* (p. 468)

Wood, J. V., Saltzberg, J. A., & Goldsamt, L. A. (1990a). Does affect induce self-focused attention? *Journal of Personality and Social Psychology, 58,* 899–908. (p. 520)

Wood, J. V., Saltzberg, J. A., Neale, J. M., Stone, A. A., & Rachmiel, T. B. (1990b). Self-focused attention, coping responses, and distressed mood in everyday life. *Journal of Personality and Social Psychology, 58,* 1027–1036. (p. 520)

Wood, W. (1987). Meta-analytic review of sex differences in group performance. *Psychological Bulletin, 102,* 53–71. (p. 164)

Wood, W., & Eagly, A. H. (2002). A cross-cultural analysis of the behavior of women and men: Implications for the origins of sex differences. *Psychological Bulletin, 128,* 699–727. (p. 163)

Wood, W., & Eagly, A. H. (2007). Social structural origins of sex differences in human mating. In S. W. Gagestad & J. A. Simpson (Eds.), *The evolution of mind: Fundamental questions and controversies* (pp. 383–390). New York: Guilford Press. (p. 163)

Wood, W., Kressel, L., Joshi, P. D., & Louie, B. (2014a). Meta-analysis of menstrual cycle effects on women's mate preferences. *Emotion Review, 6,* 229–249. (p. 173)

Wood, W., Labrecque, J. S., Lin, P.-T., & Rúnger, D. (2014b). Habits in dual process models. In J. Sherman, B. Gawronski, & Y. Trope (Eds.), *Dual process theories of the social mind.* New York: Guilford Press. (p. 234)

Wood, W., Lundgren, S., Ouellette, J. A., Busceme, S., & Blackstone, T. (1994). Minority influence: A meta-analytic review of social influence processes. *Psychological Bulletin, 115,* 323–345. (p. 428)

Woolcock, N. (2004, September 3). Driver thought everyone else was on wrong side. *The Times,* p. 22. (p. 425)

Woolett, K., & Maguire, E. A. (2011). Acquiring "the knowledge" of London's layout drives structural brain changes. *Current Biology, 21,* 2109–2114. (p. 276)

Woolley, A. W., Chabris, C. F., Pentland, A., Hasmi, N., & Malone, T. W. (2010). Evidence for a collective intelligence factor in the performance of human groups. *Science, 330,* 686–688. (p. B-10)

Woolley, K., & Fishbach, A. (2017). Immediate rewards predict adherence to long-term goals. *Personality and Social Psychology Bulletin, 43,* 151–162. (pp. 252, 359)

World Federation for Mental Health. (2005). ADHD: The hope behind the hype. World Federation for Mental Health (wfmh.org). (p. 498)

Worldwatch Institute (2017). Meat production continues to rise. Retrieved July 24, 2017, from worldwatch.org/node/5443 (p. 31)

Worobey, J., & Blajda, V. M. (1989). Temperament ratings at 2 weeks, 2 months, and 1 year: Differential stability of activity and emotionality. *Developmental Psychology, 25,* 257–263. (p. 135)

Wortman, C. B., & Silver, R. C. (1989). The myths of coping with loss. *Journal of Consulting and Clinical Psychology, 57,* 349–357. (p. 159)

Wren, C. S. (1999, April 8). Drug survey of children finds middle school a pivotal time. *The New York Times* (nytimes.com). (p. 112)

Wright, J. (2006, March 16). *Boomers in the bedroom: Sexual attitudes and behaviours in the boomer generation.* Retrieved from ipsos-na.com/news-polls/pressrelease.aspx?id=3011 (p. 151)

Wright, P., Takei, N., Rifkin, L., & Murray, R. M. (1995). Maternal influenza, obstetric complications, and schizophrenia. *American Journal of Psychiatry, 152,* 1714–1720. (p. 525)

Wright, P. H. (1989). Gender differences in adults' same- and cross-gender friendships. In R. G. Adams & R. Blieszner (Eds.), *Older adult friendships: Structure and process.* Newbury Park, CA: Sage. (p. 163)

Wrzesniewski, A., & Dutton, J. E. (2001). Crafting a job: Revisioning employees as active crafters of their work. *Academy of Management Review.* (p. B-1)

Wrzesniewski, A., Schwartz, B., Cong, X., Kane, M., Omar, A., & Kolditz, T. (2014). Multiple types of motives don't multiply the motivation of West Point cadets. *PNAS, 111,* 10990–10995. (p. 358)

Wu, H. Y., Kung, F. Y., Chen, H. C., & Kim, Y. H. (2016). Academic success of "Tiger Cubs": Self-control (not IQ) predicts academic growth and explains girls' edge in Taiwan. *Social Psychological and Personality Science.* Advanced online publication. doi:10.1177/1948550616675667 (p. 398)

Wu, S., Wu, F., Ding, Y., Hou, J., Bi, J., & Zhang, Z. (2017). Advanced parental age and autism risk in children: A systematic review and meta-analysis. *Acta Psychiatrica Scandinavica, 135,* 29–41. (p. 131)

Wu, X., Zhang, Z., Zhao, F., Wang, W., Li, Y., Bi, L., . . . Sun, Y. (2016). Prevalence of internet addiction and its association with social support and other related factors among adolescents in china. *Journal of Adolescence, 52,* 103–111. (p. 102)

Wucherpfennig, F., Rubel, J. A., Hofmann, S. G., & Lutz, W. (2017). Processes of change after a sudden gain and relation to treatment outcome—Evidence for an upward spiral. *Journal of Consulting and Clinical Psychology, 85,* 1199–1210. (p. 552)

Wulsin, L. R., Vaillant, G. E., & Wells, V. E. (1999). A systematic review of the mortality of depression. *Psychosomatic Medicine, 61,* 6–17. (p. 392)

Wyatt, J. K., & Bootzin, R. R. (1994). Cognitive processing and sleep: Implications for enhancing job performance. *Human Performance, 7,* 119–139. (pp. 97, 288)

Wynn, K. (1992). Addition and subtraction by human infants. *Nature, 358,* 749–759. (p. 127)

Wynn, K. (2000). Findings of addition and subtraction in infants are robust and consistent: Reply to Wakeley, Rivera, and Langer. *Child Development, 71,* 1535–1536. (p. 127)

Wynn, K. (2008). Some innate foundations of social and moral cognition. In K. Wynn (Ed.), *The innate mind: Vol. 3. Foundations and the future* (pp. 330–347). New York: Oxford University Press.

Wynne, C. D. L. (2004). *Do animals think?* Princeton, NJ: Princeton University Press. (p. 318)

Wynne, C. D. L. (2008). Aping language: A skeptical analysis of the evidence for nonhuman primate language. *Skeptic, 13,* 10–13. (pp. 127, 318)

Wysocki, C. J., & Gilbert, A. N. (1989). National Geographic Smell Survey: Effects of age are heterogeneous. *Annals of the New York Academy of Sciences, 561,* 12–28. (p. 227)

Xie, L., Kang, H., Xu, Q., Chen, M. J., Liao, Y., Thiyagarajan, M., . . . Nedergaard, M. (2013). Sleep drives metabolite clearance from the adult brain. *Science, 342,* 373–377. (p. 91)

Xu, J., Murphy, S. L., Kochanek, K. D., & Bastian B. A. (2016, February 16). Deaths: Final data for 2013. *National Vital Statistics Report, 64*(2). Centers for Disease Control and Prevention (cdc.gov). (p. 302)

Xu, J., & Potenza, M. N. (2012). White matter integrity and five-factor personality measures in healthy adults. *NeuroImage, 59,* 800–807. (p. 478)

Xu, Y., & Corkin, S. (2001). H.M. revisits the Tower of Hanoi puzzle. *Neuropsychology, 15,* 69–79. (p. 285)

Yamaguchi, M., Masuchi, A., Nakanishi, D., Suga, S., Konishi, N., Yu, Y. Y., & Ohtsubo, Y. (2015). Experiential purchases and prosocial spending promote happiness by enhancing social relationships. *The Journal of Positive Psychology,* 1–9. (p. 407)

Yang, G., Lai, G. S. W., Cichon, J., Ma, L., Li, W., & Gan, W.-B. (2014). Sleep promotes branch-specific formation of dendritic spines after learning. *Science, 344,* 1173–1178. (p. 91)

Yang, J., & Hofmann, J. (2015). Action observation and imitation in autism spectrum disorders: an ALE meta-analysis of fMRI studies. *Brain Imaging and Behavior,* 1–10. (p. 132)

Yang, Y., Cao, S., Shields, G. S., Teng, Z., & Liu, Y. (2017). The relationships between rumination and core executive functions: A meta-analysis. *Depression and Anxiety, 34,* 37–50. (p. 520)

Yang, Y., & Raine, A. (2009). Prefrontal structural and functional brain imaging findings in antisocial, violent, and psychopathic individuals: A meta-analysis. *Psychiatry Research: Neuroimaging, 174,* 81–88. (p. 63)

Yang, Y. C., Boen, C., Gerken, K., Li, T., Schorpp, K., & Harris, K. M. (2016). Social relationships and physiological determinants of longevity across the human life span. *PNAS, 113,* 578–583. (p. 353)

Yankelovich Partners. (1995, May/June). Growing old. *American Enterprise,* p. 108. (p. 151)

Yarnell, P. R., & Lynch, S. (1970, April 25). Retrograde memory immediately after concussion. *The Lancet,* pp. 863–865. (p. 279)

Yates, A. (1989). Current perspectives on the eating disorders: I. History, psychological and biological aspects. *Journal of the American Academy of Child and Adolescent Psychiatry, 28,* 813–828. (p. 532)

Yates, A. (1990). Current perspectives on the eating disorders: II. Treatment, outcome, and research directions. *Journal of the American Academy of Child and Adolescent Psychiatry, 29,* 1–9. (p. 532)

Ybarra, O. (1999). Misanthropic person memory when the need to self-enhance is absent. *Personality and Social Psychology Bulletin, 25,* 261–269. (p. 487)

Yeager, D. S., Johnson, R., Spitzer, B. J., Trzesniewski, K. H., Powers, J., & Dweck, C. S. (2014). The far-reaching effects of believing people can change: Implicit theories of personality shape stress, health, and achievement during adolescence. *Journal of Personality and Social Psychology, 106,* 867–884. (p. 339)

Yeager, D. S., Lee, H. Y., & Jamieson, J. P. (2016a). How to improve adolescent stress responses: Insights from integrating implicit theories of personality and biopsychosocial models. *Psychological Science, 27,* 1078–1091. (p. 339)

Yeager, D. S., Miu, A. S., Powers, J., & Dweck, C. S. (2013). Implicit theories of personality and attributions of hostile intent: A meta-analysis, an experiment, and a longitudinal intervention. *Child Development, 84,* 1651–1667. (p. 339)

Yeager, D. S., Walton, G. M., Brady, S. T., Akcinar, E. N., Paunesku, D., Keane, L., . . . Gomez, E. M. (2016b). Teaching a lay theory before college narrows achievement gaps at scale. *PNAS, 113,* E3341–E3348. (p. 344)

Yehuda, R., Daskalakis, N. P., Bierer, L. M., Bader, H. N., Klengel, T., Holsboer, F., & Binder, E. B. (2016). Holocaust exposure induced intergenerational effects on FKBP5 methylation. *Biological Psychiatry, 80,* 372–380. (p. 74)

Yerkes, R. M., & Dodson, J. D. (1908). The relation of strength of stimulus to rapidity of habit-formation. *Journal of Comparative Neurology and Psychology, 18,* 459–482. (p. 350)

Yiend, J., Parnes, C., Shepherd, K., Roche, M.-K., & Cooper, M. J. (2014). Negative self-beliefs in eating disorders: A cognitive-bias-modification study. *Clinical Psychological Science, 2,* 756–766. (p. 532)

YOU. (2009, September 10). Wow, look at Caster now! *YOU* (you.co.za/). (p. 168)

You, J., Lin, M., & Leung, F. (2015). A longitudinal moderated mediation model of nonsuicidal self-injury among adolescents. *Journal of Abnormal Child Psychology, 43,* 381–390. (p. 502)

Young, C., & Lim, C. (2014). Time as a network good: Evidence from unemployment and the standard workweek. *Sociological Science, 1,* 10–27. (p. 408)

Young, S. G., Hugenberg, K., Bernstein, M. J., & Sacco, D. F. (2012). Perception and motivation in face recognition: A critical review of theories of the cross-race effect. *Personality and Social Psychology Review, 16,* 116–142. (p. 440)

Young, S. M., & Pinsky, D. (2006). Narcissism and celebrity. *Journal of Personality, 40,* 463–471. (p. 489)

Youngentob, S. L., & Glendinning, J. I. (2009). Fetal ethanol exposure increases ethanol intake by making it smell and taste better. *PNAS, 106,* 5359. (p. 120)

Youngentob, S. L., Kent, P. F., Sheehe, P. R., Molina, J. C., Spear, N. E., & Youngentob, L. M. (2007). Experience-induced fetal plasticity: The effect of gestational ethanol exposure on the behavioral and neurophysiologic olfactory response to ethanol odor in early postnatal and adult rats. *Behavioral Neuroscience, 121,* 1293–1305. (p. 120)

Younger, J., Aron, A., Parke, S., Chatterjee, N., & Mackey, S. (2010) Viewing pictures of a romantic partner reduces experimental pain: Involvement of neural reward systems. *PLoS ONE, 5,* e13309. (p. 353)

Yount, K. M., James-Hawkins, L., Cheong, Y. F., & Naved, R. T. (2017). Men's perpetration of partner violence in Bangladesh: Community gender norms and violence in childhood. *Psychology of Men & Masculinity.* Advance online publication. http://dx.doi.org/10.1037/men0000069 (p. 163)

Youyou, W., Kosinski, M., & Stillwell, D. (2015). Computer-based personality judgments are more accurate than those made by humans. *PNAS, 112,* 1036–1040. (p. 479)

Yuen, R. K., Merico, D., Cao, H., Pellecchia, G., Alipanahi, B., Thiruvahindrapuram, B., . . . Wu, X. (2016). Genome-wide characteristics of de novo mutations in autism. *NPJ Genomic Medicine, 1.* (p. 131)

Yuki, M., Maddux, W. W., & Masuda. T. (2007). Are the windows to the soul the same in the East and West? Cultural differences in using the eyes and mouth as cues to recognize emotions in Japan and the United States. *Journal of Experimental Social Psychology, 43*, 303–311. (p. 379)

Yuval, K., Zvielli, A., & Bernstein, A. (2017). Attentional bias dynamics and posttraumatic stress in survivors of violent conflict and atrocities: New directions in clinical psychological science of refugee mental health. *Clinical Psychological Science, 5*, 64–73. (p. 509)

Zagorsky, J. L. (2007). Do you have to be smart to be rich? The impact of IQ on wealth, income and financial distress. *Intelligence, 35*, 489–501. (p. 326)

Zahrt, O. H., & Crum, A. J. (2017). Perceived physical activity and mortality: Evidence from three nationally representative U.S. samples. *Health Psychology, 36*, 1017–1025. (p. 401)

Zainulbhai, H. (2016, March 8). Strong global support for gender equality, especially among women. Pew Research Center (pewresearch.org). (p. 437)

Zajonc, R. B. (1965). Social facilitation. *Science, 149*, 269–274. (p. 429)

Zajonc, R. B. (1980). Feeling and thinking: Preferences need no inferences. *American Psychologist, 35*, 151–175. (p. 370)

Zajonc, R. B. (1984a). On the primacy of affect. *American Psychologist, 39*, 117–123. (p. 370)

Zajonc, R. B. (1984b, July 22). Quoted by D. Goleman, Rethinking IQ tests and their value. *The New York Times*, p. D22. (p. 328)

Zajonc, R. B. (2001). Mere exposure: A gateway to the subliminal. *Current Directions in Psychological Science, 10*, 224–228. (p. 447)

Zajonc, R. B., & Markus, G. B. (1975). Birth order and intellectual development. *Psychological Review, 82*, 74–88. (p. A-8)

Zakaria, F. (2017). How big data can reveal your political views. CNN interview with researcher Michal Kosinski. Retrieved from cnn.com/videos/tv/2017/03/05/exp-gps-michal-kosinski-big-data-election-trump.cnn (p. 479)

Zanarini, M. C., Williams, A. A., Lewis, R. E., Reich, R. B., Vera, S. C., Marino, M. F., . . . Frankenburg, R. F. (1997). Reported pathological childhood experiences associated with the development of borderline personality disorder. *American Journal of Psychiatry, 154*, 1101–1106. (p. 170)

Zannas, A. S., Provençal, N., & Binder, E. B. (2015). Epigenetics of posttraumatic stress disorder: current evidence, challenges, and future directions. *Biological Psychiatry, 78*, 327–335. (p. 512)

Zaslavsky, O., Palgi, Y., Rillamas-Sun, E., LaCroix, A. Z., Schnall, E., Woods, N. F., . . . Shrira, A. (2015). Dispositional optimism and terminal decline in global quality of life. *Developmental Psychology, 51*, 856–863. (p. 399)

Zauberman, G., & Lynch, J. G., Jr. (2005). Resource slack and propensity to discount delayed investments of time versus money. *Journal of Experimental Psychology: General, 134*, 23–37. (p. 303)

Zaval, L., Keenan, E. A., Johnson, E. J., & Weber, E. U. (2014). How warm days increase belief in global warming. *Nature Climate Change, 4*, 143–147. (p. 303)

Zeelenberg, R., Wagenmakers, E.-J., & Rotteveel, M. (2006). The impact of emotion on perception. *Psychological Science, 17*, 287–291. (p. 370)

Zeidner, M. (1990). Perceptions of ethnic group modal intelligence: Reflections of cultural stereotypes or intelligence test scores? *Journal of Cross-Cultural Psychology, 21*, 214–231. (p. 342)

Zeineh, M. M., Engel, S. A., Thompson, P. M., & Bookheimer, S. Y. (2003). Dynamics of the hippocampus during encoding and retrieval of face-name pairs. *Science, 299*, 577–580. (p. 276)

Zelenski, J. M., & Nisbet, E. K. (2014). Happiness and feeling connected: The distinct role of nature relatedness. *Environmental Behavior, 46*, 3–23. (p. 357)

Zell, E., & Alicke, M. D. (2010). The local dominance effect in self-evaluation: Evidence and explanations. *Personality and Social Psychology Review, 14*, 368–384. (p. 410)

Zell, E., Krizan, Z., & Teeter, S. R. (2015). Evaluating gender similarities and differences using metasynthesis. *American Psychologist, 70*, 10–20. (p. 162)

Zentner, M., & Eagly, A. H. (2015). A sociocultural framework for understanding partner preferences of women and men: Integration of concepts and evidence. *European Journal of Social Psychology, 26*, 328–373. (p. 168)

Zhang, J., Fang, L., Yow-Wu, B. W., & Wieczorek, W. F. (2013). Depression, anxiety, and suicidal ideation among Chinese Americans: A study of immigration-related factors. *The Journal of Nervous and Mental Disease, 201*, 17–22. (p. 517)

Zhang, W., Jiao, B., Zhou, M., Zhou, T., & Shen, L. (2016). Modeling Alzheimer's disease with induced pluripotent stem cells: Current challenges and future concerns. *Stem Cells International, 2016*, 7828049. (p. 64)

Zhong, C.-B., Dijksterhuis, A., & Galinsky, A. D. (2008). The merits of unconscious thought in creativity. *Psychological Science, 19*, 912–918. (p. 307)

Zhu, W. X., Lu, L., & Hesketh, T. (2009). China's excess males, sex selective abortion, and one child policy: Analysis of data from 2005 national intercensus survey. *British Medical Journal (BMJ), 338*, b1211. (p. 437)

Zhuo, C., Tao, R., Jiang, R., Lin, X., & Shao, M. (2017). Cancer mortality in patients with schizophrenia: Systematic review and meta-analysis. *The British Journal of Psychiatry, 211*, 7–13. (p. 524)

Zilbergeld, B. (1983). *The shrinking of America: Myths of psychological change.* Boston: Little, Brown. (p. 551)

Zill, N., & Wilcox, W. B. (2017, June 8). What happens at home doesn't stay there: It goes to school. Institute for Family Studies (ifstudies.org). (p. 136)

Zillmann, D. (1989). Effects of prolonged consumption of pornography. In D. Zillmann & J. Bryant (Eds.), *Pornography: Research advances and policy considerations* (pp. 127–157). Hillsdale, NJ: Erlbaum. (p. 176)

Zillmann, D., & Bryant, J. (1984). Effects of massive exposure to pornography. In N. Malamuth & E. Donnerstein (Eds.), *Pornography and sexual aggression.* Orlando, FL: Academic Press. (p. 444)

Zimbardo, P., Wilson, G., & Coulombe, N. (2016). How porn is messing with your manhood. *Skeptic.* Retrieved from skeptic.com/reading_room/how-porn-is-messing-with-your-manhood (p. 176)

Zimbardo, P. G. (1970). The human choice: Individuation, reason, and order versus deindividuation, impulse, and chaos. In W. J. Arnold & D. Levine (Eds.), *Nebraska Symposium on Motivation, 1969.* Lincoln, NE: University of Nebraska Press. (p. 430)

Zimbardo, P. G. (1972, April). Pathology of imprisonment. *Transaction/Society*, pp. 4–8. (p. 419)

Zimbardo, P. G. (2001, September 16). *Fighting terrorism by understanding man's capacity for evil.* Op-ed essay distributed by spsp-discuss@stolaf.edu. (p. 439)

Zimbardo, P. G. (2004, May 25). Journalist interview re: Abu Ghraib prison abuses: Eleven answers to eleven questions. Unpublished manuscript, Stanford University.

Zimbardo, P. G. (2007, September). Person x situation x system dynamics. *The Observer* (Association for Psychological Science), p. 43. (p. 419)

Zinzow, H. M., Amstadter, A. B., McCauley, J. L., Ruggiero, K. J., Resnick, H. S., & Kilpatrick, D. G. (2011). Self-rated health in relation to rape and mental health disorders in a national sample of college women. *Journal of American College Health, 59*, 588–594. (p. 170)

Zogby, J. (2006, March). *Survey of teens and adults about the use of personal electronic devices and head phones.* Utica, NY: Zogby International. (p. 218)

Zoma, M., & Gielen, U. P. (2015). How many psychologists are there in the world? *International Psychology Bulletin, 19*, 47–50. (p. 8)

Zou, L. Q., van Hartevelt, T. J., Kringelbach, M. L., Cheung, E. F., & Chan, R. C. (2016). The neural mechanism of hedonic processing and judgment of pleasant odors: An activation likelihood estimation meta-analysis. *Neuropsychology, 30*, 970–979. (p. 226)

Zubieta, J.-K., Bueller, J. A., Jackson, L. R., Scott, D. J., Xu, Y., Koeppe, R. A., . . . Stohler, C. S. (2005). Placebo effects mediated by endogenous opioid activity on μ-opioid receptors. *Journal of Neuroscience, 25*, 7754–7762. (p. 223)

Zubieta, J.-K., Heitzeg, M. M., Smith, Y. R., Bueller, J. A., Xu, K., Xu, Y., . . . Goldman, D. (2003). COMT val158met genotype affects μ-opioid neurotransmitter responses to a pain stressor. *Science, 299*, 1240–1243. (p. 223)

Zucco, G. M. (2003). Anomalies in cognition: Olfactory memory. *European Psychologist, 8*, 77–86. (p. 227)

Zucker, G. S., & Weiner, B. (1993). Conservatism and perceptions of poverty: An attributional analysis. *Journal of Applied Social Psychology, 23*, 925–943. (p. 417)

Zuckerberg, M. (2012, February 1). Letter to potential investors. Quoted by S. Sengupta & C. C. Miller, "Social mission" vision meets Wall Street. *The New York Times* (nytimes.com). (p. 352)

Zuckerman, M. (1979). *Sensation seeking: Beyond the optimal level of arousal.* Hillsdale, NJ: Erlbaum. (p. 349)

Zuckerman, M. (1999). *Vulnerability to psychopathology: A biosocial model.* Washington, DC: American Psychological Association. (p. 496)

Zuckerman, M. (2009). Sensation seeking. In M. Zuckerman (Ed.), *Handbook of individual differences in social behavior.* New York: Guilford Press. (p. 349)

Zuckerman, M., Li, C., & Hall, J. A. (2016). When men and women differ in self-esteem and when they don't: A meta-analysis. *Journal of Research in Personality, 64*, 34–51. (p. 147)

Zunick, P. V., Fazio, R. H., & Vasey, M. W. (2015). Directed abstraction: Encouraging broad, personal generalizations following a success experience. *Journal of Personality and Social Psychology, 109*, 1–19. (p. 545)

Zuzanek, J. (2013). Does being well-off make us happier? Problems of measurement. *Journal of Happiness Studies, 14*, 795–815. (p. 410)

Zvolensky, M. J., & Bernstein, A. (2005). Cigarette smoking and panic psychopathology. *Current Directions in Psychological Science, 14*, 301–305. (p. 507)

Zvolensky, M. J., Bakhshaie, J., Sheffer, C., Perez, A., & Goodwin, R. D. (2015). Major depressive disorder and smoking relapse among adults in the United States: A 10-year, prospective investigation. *Psychiatry Research, 226*, 73–77. (p. 105)

Name Index

Subject Index